November 4–8, 2013
Berlin, Germany

Association for
Computing Machinery

Advancing Computing as a Science & Profession

CCS'13 VOL 2 of 2

The Proceedings of the 2013 ACM SIGSAC Conference on Computer and Communications Security

Sponsored by:

ACM SIGSAC

Supported by:

HGS, Army Research Office, BOSCH, SAP, NSF, Indiana University, CISCO, Intel, Google, Fraunhofer SIT, Heise Security, Microsoft Research, NXP, Kobil, Sirrix AG, Certgate, and IBM Research

Association for
Computing Machinery

Advancing Computing as a Science & Profession

The Association for Computing Machinery
2 Penn Plaza, Suite 701
New York, New York 10121-0701

Notice to Past Authors of ACM-Published Articles
ACM intends to create a complete electronic archive of all articles and/or other material previously published by ACM. If you have written a work that has been previously published by ACM in any journal or conference proceedings prior to 1978, or any SIG Newsletter at any time, and you do NOT want this work to appear in the ACM Digital Library, please inform permissions@acm.org, stating the title of the work, the author(s), and where and when published.

ISBN: 978-1-4503-2477-9 (Digital)

ISBN: 978-1-4503-2689-6 (Print)

Additional copies may be ordered prepaid from:

ACM Order Department
PO Box 30777
New York, NY 10087-0777, USA

Phone: 1-800-342-6626 (USA and Canada)
+1-212-626-0500 (Global)
Fax: +1-212-944-1318
E-mail: acmhelp@acm.org
Hours of Operation: 8:30 am – 4:30 pm ET

Printed in the USA

CCS 2013 General Chair's Welcome

Information and communications security has become a fundamental element in our highly and globally computerized life. To tackle current and future security and privacy challenges adequately and globally, we need not only to advance research but also to bring together, from all over the world, researchers, developers and academics, as well as professionals from government agencies, research labs and corporate sectors.

The ACM Conference on Computer and Communications Security (CCS) is a leading forum, providing a highly suitable environment to conduct intellectual discussions and to exchange ideas. CCS is, in fact, the flagship annual conference of the Special Interest Group on Security, Audit and Control (SIGSAC) of the Association of Computing Machinery (ACM) and the oldest ACM conference in this field. Its reputation continues to grow and is reflected in its highly selective and prestigious technical program.

From 2002-2012, the number of paper submissions increased from about 150 to about 430. This year (2013), after more than a decade, CCS has moved to Europe/Germany. With 530 submissions we have witnessed the highest submission record in the history of CCS. Further, on the sponsorship side, CCS 2013 received over $125,000 funding support from various high-profile sources: The Army Research Office (ARO), The National Science Foundation (NSF), Bosch, Horst Görtz Stiftung (HGS), Fraunhofer SIT, SAP, Certgate, Google, Heise Security, Intel, Microsoft Research, NXP Semiconductors, IBM Research, Kobil and Sirrix AG. The Organizing Committee of CCS 2013 has put together an outstanding program that includes 105 papers (a new record), several keynote as well as invited speakers from academia, industry and government, 9 specialized pre- and post-conference workshops, 3 tutorials, 39 posters and demos, and one social event.

Given the above submission records causing an increased conference scale, organizing and setting up the program of CCS 2013 required a highly dedicated, committed and professional organizing committee, a strong technical program committee, and sponsoring decision makers who appreciate the high standards and impact of this flagship conference.

We are most grateful to the authors of the submitted papers (both to the main conference and to the workshops). We thank the technical program committee members and the program chairs as well as the external reviewers, who enabled a high quality review process. We thank the CCS 2013 Organizing Committee for selecting the workshops and tutorials on timely topics and cutting-edge technologies, and for the website design and maintenance, publications, publicity, local arrangements and registrations. Special acknowledgements go to the CCS Steering Committee, particularly to Prof. Elisa Bertino who strongly supported us with her advice. We thank the staff of the ACM for assisting us throughout the organization and publication process, the Center for Advanced Security Research Darmstadt (CASED) and the Fraunhofer SIT for providing their infrastructure and public relations. Last but not least, we would like to express our gratitude to our generous sponsors.

We wish you a pleasant stay in Berlin, a productive and highly utilized conference, and an exciting week at CCS 2013!

Ahmad-Reza Sadeghi
CCS 2013 General Chair
Technische Universität Darmstadt, Germany

CCS 2013 Program Chairs' Welcome

We are pleased to present to you the proceedings of the 2013 ACM Conference on Computer and Communications Security (CCS 2013), held in Berlin, Germany, November 4-8, 2013.

This year we received 530 submissions from 38 countries. This represents a record on at least two counts: it is both the largest number of submissions received by a computer security conference and the largest year-over-year submission increase (over 25%) to date. Remarkably, nearly half of the authors have professional affiliations in countries outside North America, with most in Europe and Asia-Pacific regions. A Program Committee comprising 82 experts from 16 countries as well as 310 external reviewers evaluated these submissions in the customary double-blind manner. At the end of the review process, 105 papers were selected for inclusion in the program, representing an acceptance rate of about 20%.

The review process was organized into three phases. After a first review phase, the authors of each paper were sent at least two preliminary reviews and were given an opportunity to respond to the comments received. During the second phase, reviews were updated as necessary, and in some cases additional reviews were solicited. At the end of the second phase, 403 papers received at least 3 reviews, 120 received 4, and 7 received 5. The third phase included discussion of papers that remained under consideration at that stage, and after intensive debate, the final acceptance decisions were made.

As is typically the case with very competitive conferences, many of the papers that could not be included in the program contained interesting ideas. Some also included new research results worth reporting to the security community. For these reasons, we encouraged the authors of these papers to consider submitting their work to the specialized workshops associated with CCS, as appropriate. Other works that could not be accepted for the program, will surely see the light of day in other leading venues after suitable improvement. We hope that all authors benefitted from the feedback received from the CCS reviewers and that the review process has helped them improve their papers.

We are very grateful to the members of the Program Committee for their hard work, professionalism, and responsiveness under very tight deadlines. On average, each individual reviewed 21 papers, and nearly a third of the members volunteered to help shepherd accepted papers towards improved presentations. Most engaged in lively discussions on both submissions and author responses, and updated their reviews to reflect valuable insights derived from those discussions. We are also indebted to the external reviewers whose focused expertise added substantial value to the feedback for authors. Moreover, we want to thank the CCS 2013 conference committee: the general chair, workshop co-chairs, tutorial co-chair, and other chairs and organizers, as well as the steering committee, for numerous discussions on how to produce an exceptional program and for their hard work on the production of these proceedings.

Lastly, we thank all authors for submitting their work to CCS 2013 and to all attendees for their participation in technical discussion and debate. We hope that you find the program stimulating and enjoyable, and that your contributions will help further computer and communication security.

Virgil Gligor
ACM CCS '13 Program Chair
Carnegie Mellon University, USA

Moti Yung
ACM CCS '13 Program Chair
Google, USA

Table of Contents

Session 3-C: Protocol Analysis & Synthesis

Keynote Talk 1

Session 4-A: Network Security

Session 4-B: Critical Infrastructures

Session 4-C: Attribute-based Encryption

Session 5-A: Programming Securely

Session 5-B: Secure Multiparty Computation

Session 5-C: Formal Methods

Session 6-A: Mobile Security Issues

Session 6-B: Randomness

Session 6-C: Hardware Security

Session 8-C: Be Aware & Beware

Keynote Talk 2

Session 9-A: Crypto Tools

Session 9-B: Audit & Code Randomization

Session 9-C: Mobile Privacy

Session 10-A: Graphics, Vision & Security

Session 10-B: Authentication

Session 10-C: Privacy Issues

Session 11-A: Web and Code Security

Session 11-B: Crypto Symbolic Analysis

Session 11-C: Security/Cryptographic Utilities

Demonstration Presentations

Poster Presentations

Workshop Summaries

Tutorial Overviews

ACM CCS 2013 – Organization

General Chair: Ahmad-Reza Sadeghi *(TU Darmstadt, CASED, Intel ICRI-SC, Germany)*

Program Chairs: Virgil Gligor *(Carnegie Mellon University, USA)*
Moti Yung *(Columbia University, USA)*

Workshop Co-Chairs: Stefan Katzenbeisser *(TU Darmstadt, CASED, Intel ICRI-SC, Germany)*
Christopher Kruegel *(University of California at Santa Barbara, USA)*

Tutorial Co-Chairs: Thorsten Holz *(Ruhr-Universität Bochum, Germany)*
Gregory Neven *(IBM Research, Zurich Research Laboratory, Switzerland)*

Poster/Demo Chairs: Fabian Monrose *(University of North Carolina at Chapel Hill, USA)*
Thomas Schneider *(TU Darmstadt, EC SPRIDE, Germany)*
Carmela Troncoso *(Gradiant, Spain)*

Publicity Co-Chairs: Thomas Gross *(University of Newcastle upon Tyne, UK)*
Matthias Hollick *(TU Darmstadt, Germany)*
Jun Li *(University of Oregon, USA)*
Ivan Martinovic *(University of Oxford, UK)*
Matthew Smith *(Leibnitz Universität Hannover, Germany)*

Event Management: Wiebke Kronz *(TU Darmstadt, CASED, Intel ICRI-SC, Germany)*
Anette Mittenhuber *(TU Darmstadt, CASED, Germany)*

Public Relations: Oliver Küch *(Fraunhofer SIT, CASED, Germany)*

Website: Lucas Davi *(TU Darmstadt, CASED, Intel ICRI-SC, Germany)*

Local Organization: Stephan Heuser *(TU Darmstadt, CASED, Intel ICRI-SC, Germany)*
Christian Wachsmann, *(TU Darmstadt, CASED, Intel ICRI-SC, Germany)*
Christoph Busold *(TU Darmstadt, CASED, Intel ICRI-SC, Germany)*
Alexandra Dmitrienko *(Fraunhofer SIT, Germany)*
Sven Wohlgemuth *(TU Darmstadt, CASED, Germany)*
Mihai Bucicoiu *(TU Darmstadt, CASED, Intel ICRI-SC, Germany)*

Steering Committee: Elisa Bertino *(Purdue University, USA)*
George Danezis *(Microsoft Research Cambridge, UK)*
Trent Jaeger *(Pennsylvania State University, USA)*
Carl Landwehr *(University of Maryland, USA)*
John Mitchell *(Stanford University, USA)*
Giovanni Vigna *(University of California at Santa Barbara, USA)*
Marianne Winslet *(University of California at Urbana Champaign, USA)*

Program Committee: Gail-Joon Ahn *(Institute of North Carolina at Charlotte, USA)*
Bill Arbaugh *(University of Maryland, USA)*
Mikhail Atallah *(Purdue University, USA)*
Giuseppe Ateniese *(University of Rome, Italy)*
David Basin *(ETH Zurich, Swizerland)*
Lujo Bauer *(Carnegie Mellon University, USA)*
Konstantin Beznosov *(University of British Columbia, Canada)*
Matt Bishop *(University of California at Davis, USA)*
David Brumley *(Carnegie Mellon University, USA)*
Kevin Butler *(University of Oregon, USA)*
Jan Camenisch *(IBM Research, Zurich Research Laboratory, Swizerland)*
Srdjan Capkun *(ETH Zurich, Swizerland)*
Alvaro Cardenas *(University of Texas at Dallas, USA)*
Liqun Chen *(Hewlett-Packard Laboratories, UK)*
Stephen Chong *(Harvard University, USA)*
Nicolas Christin *(Carnegie Mellon University, USA)*
Veronique Cortier *(CNRS, Loria, France)*
Weidong Cui *(Microsoft Research, USA)*
Reza Curtmola *(New Jersey Institute of Technology, USA)*
Anupam Datta *(Carnegie Mellon University, USA)*
Roberto Di Pietro *(Università di Roma Tre, Italy)*
Wenliang Du *(Syracuse University,USA)*
David Evans *(University of Virginia, USA)*
Peter Gutmann *(University of Auckland, New Zealand)*
J. Alex Halderman *(University of Michigan, USA)*
Cormac Herley *(Microsoft Research, USA)*
Thorsten Holz *(Ruhr-Universität Bochum, Germany)*
Nicholas Hopper *(University of Minnesota, USA)*
Yih-Chun Hu *(University of Illinois at Urbana Champaign, USA)*
Sotiris Ioannidis *(FORTH-ICS, Greece)*
Trent Jaeger *(Pennsylvania State University, USA)*
Sushil Jajodia *(George Mason University, USA)*
Rob Johnson *(Stony Brook University, USA)*
Ari Juels *(RSA Laboratories, USA)*
Apu Kapadia *(Indiana University, USA)*
Jonathan Katz *(University of Maryland, USA)*
Stefan Katzenbeisser *(TU Darmstadt, CASED, Intel ICRI-SC, Germany)*
Angelos Keromytis *(Columbia University, USA)*
Florian Kerschbaum *(SAP Research, Germany)*
Yongdae Kim *(KAIST, Korea)*
Engin Kirda *(Northeastern University, USA)*
Farinaz Koushanfar *(Rice University, USA)*
Wenke Lee *(Georgia Institute of Technology, USA)*
Brian N. Levine *(UMass Amherst, USA)*
Yingjiu Li *(Singapore Management University, Singapore)*

Program Committee (continued):

Z. Morley Mao *(Columbia University, USA)*
Jonathan McCune *(Google, USA)*
Catherine Meadows *(Naval Research Laboratory, USA)*
Refik Molva *(EURECOM, France)*
Fabian Monrose *(University of North Carolina at Chapel Hill, USA)*
Andrew Myers *(Cornell University, USA)*
David Naccache *(Ecole Normale Supérieure, France)*
Cristina Nita-Rotaru *(Purdue University, USA)*
Alina Oprea *(RSA Security, USA)*
Panos Papadimitratos *(KTH Stockholm, Sweden)*
Bryan Parno *(Microsoft Research, USA)*
Benny Pinkas *(Bar-Ilan University, Israel)*
Mike Reiter *(University of North Carolina at Chapel Hill, USA)*
Volker Roth *(Freie Universität Berlin, Germany)*
Ravi Sandhu *(University of Texas at San Antonio, USA)*
Vyas Sekar *(Stony Brook University, USA)*
Simha Sethumadhavan *(Columbia University, USA)*
Shiuhpyng Shieh *(National Chiao Tung University, Taiwan)*
Clay Shields *(Georgetown University, USA)*
Radu Sion *(Stony Brook University, USA)*
Sean Smith *(Dartmouth College, USA)*
Sal Stolfo *(Columbia University, USA)*
Patrick Tague *(Carnegie Mellon University, USA)*
Roberto Tamassia *(Brown University, USA)*
George Theodorakopoulos *(Cardiff University, UK)*
Wade Trappe *(Rutgers University, USA)*
Patrick Traynor *(Georgia Institute of Technology, USA)*
Carmela Troncoso *(Gradiant, Spain)*
Vijay Varadharajan *(Macquarie University, Australia)*
Michael Waidner *(Fraunhofer SIT, Germany)*
Jesse Walker *(Intel, USA)*
Bogdan Warinschi *(University of Bristol, UK)*
Brent Waters *(University of Texas at Austin, USA)*
Robert Watson *(Cambridge University, UK)*
Nicholas Weaver *(ICSI, USA)*
Dongyan Xu *(Purdue University, USA)*

Poster/Demo Program Committee:

Juan Caballero *(IMDEA Madrid, Spain)*
Emiliano De Cristofaro *(PARC, USA)*
William Enck *(North Carolina State University, USA)*
Damon McCoy *(George Mason University, USA)*
Prateek Mittal *(University of California at Berkeley, USA)*
Thomas Ristenpart *(University of Wisconsin, USA)*
Julie Thorpe *(University of Ontario Institute of Technology, Canada)*
Ingrid Verbauwhede *(KU Leuven, Belgium)*

Additional Reviewers:

Amit Ahlawat
Massimiliano Albanese
Mohammed Almeshekah
Chaitrali Amrutkar
Elli Androulaki
Spyros Antonatos
Owen Arden
George Argyros
Aslan Askarov
Elias Athanasopoulos
Man Ho Au
Thanassis Avgerinos
Adam Aviv
Monir Azraoui
Basim Baig
Sumeet Bajaj
Ero Balsa
Davide Balzarotti
Boaz Barak
Adam Bates
Andrew Baumann
Alessandra De Benedictis
Emery Berger
David Bernhard
Sebastian Biedermann
Marina Blanton
Jeremiah Blocki
Nathaniel Boggs
Joseph Bonneau
Yazan Boshmaf
Kevin Bowers
Dan Brown
Christina Brzuska
Xiang Cai
Henry Carter
Sang Kil Cha
Rohit Chadha
Sambuddho Chakravarty
Sang-Yoon Chang
Peter Chapman
Chong-Kuan Chen
Pokai Chen
Vincent Cheval
Jerry Chiang
Michael Cheng Yi Cho
Hyunwoo Choi
Jaeyoung Choi
Kai-Min Chung
Michael Clarkson
Robert Cochran
Alessandro Colantonio
Cas Cremers
Emiliano De Cristofaro
Özgür Dagdelen
George Danezis
Mohammad Torabi Dashti
Lucas Davi
Zhui Deng
Alexandra Dmitrienko
Yevgeniy Dodis
Adam Doupe
Maria Dubovitskaya
Manuel Egele
Kaoutar Elkhiyaoui
William Enck
Robert Enderlein
Santiago Escobar
Antonio Faonio
Dario Fiore
Aurélien Francillon
Mario Frank
Sara Foresti
David Galindo
Deepak Garg
Paolo Gasti
Robert Gawlik
Xinyang Ge
John Geddes
Marco Ghiglieri
Ian Goldberg
Samantha Gottlieb
Robert Griffin
Oren Halvani
Kevin Hamlen
Kristiyan Haralambiev
Eiji Hayashi
Carmit Hazay
Nadia Heninger
Ryan Henry
Victor Heorhiadi
Michael Herrmann
Martin Hirt
Johannes Hoffmann
Owen Hofmann
Peter Honeyman
Byeongdo Hong
Hyunwook Hong
Endadul Hoque
Chia-Wei Hsu
Hongxin Hu
Yan Huang
Markus Huber
Sungjae Hwang
Qatrunnada Ismail
Malika Izabachene
Asim Jamshed
Kangkook Jee
Limin Jia
Xing Jin
Yiming Jing
Andrew Johnson
Lukas Kalabis
Seny Kamara
Nikos Karapanos
Nikolaos Karvelas
Michael Kasper
James Kelley
Vasileios P Kemerlis
Peter Kieseberg
Dongkwan Kim
Eunsoo Kim
Hongil Kim
Yu Seung Kim
Markulf Kohlweiss
Saranga Komanduri
Joonho Kong
Divyan Konidala
Georgios Kontaxis
Kari Kostiainen

Steve Kremer
Stephan Krenn
Christopher Kruegel
Marc Kuehrer
Anil KurmusChinawat Isradisaikul
Divya Kurthakoti
Cheolhyun Kwak
Minhee Kwon
Alptekin Küpçü
Tanja Lange
Adam Langley
Meixing Le
Hyojeong Lee
Youjin Lee
Anja Lehmann
Iraklis Leontiadis
Chaz Lever
Bing-Han Li
Ninghui Li
Peng Li
Shuai Li
Alana Libonati
Jed Liu
Giovanni Livraga
Andreas Lochbihler
Flavio Lombardi
Long Lu
Giuseppe Antonio Di Luna
Tongbo Luo
Tom Magrino
Ahmad Mahmoody
Ken Mai
Claudio Marforio
Matthew Maurer
Michelle Mazurek
Breno De Medeiros
Carlos Medrano
Byungho Min
Kazuhiro Minami
Bruno Conchina Montalto
Benjamin Mood
Scott Moore
Collin Mulliner
Arslan Munir
Divya Muthukumaran
Ryan Riley
Thomas Ristenpart
Shishir Nagaraja
Gregory Neven
Andrew Newell
Rishab Nithyanand
Adam O'Neill
Olga Ohrimenko
Melek Önen
Simon Oya
Omkant Pandey
Antonis Papadogiannakis
Charalampos Papamanthou
Vasilis Pappas
Ravi Pappu
Chunsung Park
Kenneth Paterson
Kenny Paterson
Sameer Patil
Arpita Patra
Mathias Payer
Marcus Peinado
Andreas Peter
Theofilos Petsios
Patrick Longa Pierola
Jérémy Planul
Joe Pletcher
Iasonas Polakis
Michalis Polychronakis
Marios Pomonis
Miodrag Potkonjak
Franz-Stefan Preiss
Pasquale Puzio
Sasa Radomirovic
Carla Rafols
Himanshu Raj
Kim Ramchen
Paul Ratazzi
Sasa Rdomirovic
Joel Reardon
Brad Reaves
Alexandre Rebert
Tazchy Reinman
Junghwan Rhee
Alfredo Rial
Ben Riva
Jean-Marc Robert
Masoud Rostami
Yves Roudier
Yannis Rouselakis
Arnab Roy
Carlos Rubio
Sandra Rueda
Malek Ben Salem
Brendan Saltaformaggio
Ralf Sasse
Guillaume Scerri
Thomas Schneider
Sebastian Schrittwieser
Max Schuchard
Steffen Schulz
Matthias Schunter
Edward Schwartz
Elaine Shi
Dongwan Shin
Hocheol Shin
Reza Shokri
Matteo Signorini
Hervais Simo
Dimitrios Simos
Arunesh Sinha
Karsten Sohr
Yingbo Song
Ebrahim Songhori
Claudio Soriente
Kyle Soska
Angelo Spognardi
Christoph Sprenger
Dannie Stanley
Emil Stefanov
Martin Stopczynski
William Sumner
Kun Sun
Yuqiong Sun
Gelareh Taban
Nirupama Talele
Rob Templeman
Stefano Tessaro
Abhradeep Guha Thakurta
Nikos Triandopoulos

Mahesh Tripunitara
Jonathan Trostle
Michael Carl Tschantz
Uday Tupakula
Mathieu Turuani
Yavgeniy Vahlis
Giorgos Vasiliadis
Amit Vasudevan
Daniele Venturi
Nino Vincenzo Verde
Giovanni Vigna
Hayawardh Vijayakumar
Antonio Villani
Sabrina De Capitani Di Vimercati
Jonathan Voris
Adam Waksman
Robert Walls
Chi-Wei Wang
Chiawei Wang
Lingyu Wang
Shumiao Wang
Yang Wang
Zhan Wang
Gaven J Watson
Lei Wei
Zachary Weinberg
Cyrille Wiedling
Peter Williams
Maverick Woo
Eric Wustrow
Qiang Yan
Dejun Yang
York Yannikos
Ting-Fang Yen
Yung Yi
Jun Yuan
Angeliki Zavou
Danfeng Zhang
Yinqian Zhang
Yizhou Zhang
Zhi-Kai Zhang
Hang Zhao
Ziming Zhao
Lan Zhou
Zhibin Zhou
Sebastian Zimmeck

CCS 2013 Sponsor & Supporters

Sponsor:

Supporters:

Supporters (continued):

Polyglots: Crossing Origins by Crossing Formats

Jonas Magazinius
Chalmers University of Technology
Gothenburg, Sweden
jonas.magazinius@chalmers.se

Billy K. Rios
Cylance, Inc.
Irvine, CA, USA

Andrei Sabelfeld
Chalmers University of Technology
Gothenburg, Sweden
andrei@chalmers.se

ABSTRACT

In a heterogeneous system like the web, information is exchanged between components in versatile formats. A new breed of attacks is on the rise that exploit the mismatch between the expected and provided content. This paper focuses on the root cause of a large class of attacks: *polyglots*. A polyglot is a program that is valid in multiple programming languages. Polyglots allow multiple interpretation of the content, providing a new space of attack vectors. We characterize what constitutes a dangerous format in the web setting and identify particularly dangerous formats, with PDF as the prime example. We demonstrate that polyglot-based attacks on the web open up for insecure communication across Internet origins. The paper presents novel attack vectors that infiltrate the trusted origin by *syntax injection* across multiple languages and by *content smuggling* of malicious payload that appears formatted as benign content. The attacks lead to both *cross-domain leakage* and *cross-site request forgery*. We perform a systematic study of PDF-based injection and content smuggling attacks. We evaluate the current practice in client/server content filtering and PDF readers for polyglot-based attacks, and report on vulnerabilities in the top 100 Alexa web sites. We identify five web sites to be vulnerable to syntax injection attacks. Further, we have found two major enterprise cloud storage services to be susceptible to content smuggling attacks. Our recommendations for protective measures on server side, in browsers, and in content interpreters (in particular, PDF readers) show how to mitigate the attacks.

Categories and Subject Descriptors

K.6.5 [**Security and Protection**]: Unauthorized access

Keywords

Web Security; Polyglot; Injection; Cross-domain

CCS'13, November 4–8, 2013, Berlin, Germany.

http://dx.doi.org/10.1145/2508859.2516685.

1. INTRODUCTION

Web application security is concerned with protecting information as it is manipulated by web applications. This is an important area because "attacks against web applications constitute more than 60% of the total attack attempts observed on the Internet" [11].

Internet origins at stake.

The different trust domains correspond to different Internet origins. A major goal for web application security is preventing undesired communication across origins. With the goal of separating information from the different origins, today's browsers enforce the *same-origin policy* (SOP). SOP only allows access between two documents if they share the origin. In addition, a document can only directly communicate with the server from which it originates.

Classical cross-domain attacks.

There are several classes of cross-domain attacks that circumvent SOP. The OWASP top 10 list [10] places both *injection* and *cross-site scripting* (XSS) attacks among the three top security risks for web applications. A classical XSS attack injects a malicious script in the context of a trusted origin. This opens up opportunities for leaking sensitive information that users might have in the context of the trusted origin such as cookies, personal information, and session tokens.

XSS attacks are relatively well understood by researchers and developers [17]. Known defenses include various flavors of *sanitization* on server side and the *content security policy* [12] (CSP) on client side. Sanitization is often performed by the server to filter possibly malicious input data before it is used in the generated web pages. Content security policy puts requirement on the structure of the document and the origins of the scripts that are included by web pages.

Crossing origins by crossing formats.

This paper focuses on a new breed of attacks and its root cause: *polyglots*. A polyglot is a program that is valid in multiple programming languages. In a heterogeneous system like the web, information is exchanged between components in versatile formats. This gives rise to attacks that exploit the mismatch between the expected and provided content. Polyglots allow multiple interpretation of the content, providing a new space of attack vectors. An attacker can use a malicious polyglot to infiltrate a vulnerable origin. Once infiltrated, the polyglot is embedded from within the attacker's web site, such that the browser is coerced to interpret the polyglot in an unexpected context, e.g., a plug-in. According to the SOP, content loaded in a plug-in is considered to belong to the origin from which the content was requested. Thus, the polyglot is allowed to communicate with the vulnerable origin. A victim, authenticated in the vulnerable origin, who visits the attacker's web site will trigger the malicious polyglot. This allows the polyglot to abuse the credentials of the victim in its communication with the vulnerable service. The scenario is explained in detail in Section 2.3, where we present novel attack vectors that are based on (i) *syntax injection* that operate across multiple languages and on (ii) *content smuggling* that supply malicious payload that appears formatted as benign content. The attacks lead to both *cross-domain leakage* and *cross-site request forgery*.

The existing defense mechanisms fall short to prevent these attacks from achieving cross-domain communication. On the server side, sanitization is specific to the target language of the web application. Sanitizing unexpected formats is typically not considered. On the client side, CSP has no effect unless the content is interpreted as HTML. This opens up opportunities for attacks that are based on other formats.

The first steps in exploiting formats in the context of the web have been taken by researchers. Two noteworthy examples are GIFAR [4] and cross-origin CSS attacks [7] (Section 6 discusses further related work). GIFAR is based on polyglots that combine the GIF and JAR (Java archive) formats. The former is used as benign and the latter as malicious to bypass SOP. Cross-origin CSS attacks inject fragments of CSS code into an existing web page to extract information from the existing web page.

Generalizing polyglot attacks.

The paper is the first to present a generalized description of polyglot attacks. We identify the necessary ingredients for polyglot attacks. We characterize what constitutes a dangerous format in the web setting and identify particularly dangerous formats, with PDF as the prime example. We demonstrate that polyglot-based attacks on the web open up for insecure communication across Internet origins.

PDF polyglots.

Having identified PDF as a particularly dangerous format, we perform a novel in-depth study of PDF-based injection and content smuggling attacks. Our findings expose new attack vectors, which we demonstrate both conceptually and by proof-of-concept web pages.

Evaluation and mitigation.

We evaluate the current practice in client/server content filtering and PDF readers for polyglot-based attacks, and report on vulnerabilities in the top 100 Alexa web sites. Unfortunately, several major web sites do not protect against polyglot attacks. Five out of the top 100 Alexa web sites are vulnerable to syntax injection attacks. In addition, we have found two major enterprise cloud storage services to be susceptible to content smuggling attacks. Our recommendations for protective measures on server side, in browsers, and in content interpreters (such as PDF readers) show how to mitigate the attacks.

Overview.

The paper is organized as follows. Section 2 explains the concept of crossing origins by crossing formats, identifies necessary ingredients, and provides attack scenarios. Section 3 focuses on the PDF format and describes concrete vulnerabilities and attacks. Section 4 evaluates the current practice in client/server content filtering and PDF readers and report on vulnerabilities in the top 100 Alexa web sites. Section 5 suggests mitigation for servers, clients, and PDF readers. Section 6 discusses the related work. Section 7 concludes and outlines future work.

2. CROSSING ORIGINS AND FORMATS

This section describes how formats can be crossed and how that can be abused to cross origins by circumventing the same-origin policy. We describe cross-origin information leaks, generalize the problem of crossing formats to *polyglots*, and present the characteristics of a malicious polyglot. From that we derive two attack vectors and show how previous work on the subject relate to these vectors.

2.1 Crossing origins

By crossing origins we mean being able to request and access content across domains, which is normally restricted under the same-origin policy. Recall that SOP only allows two documents accessing each others' content and resources if they share the origin. Similarly, a document can only directly communicate with the server from which it originates. This is not to be confused with *cross-origin resource sharing* (CORS) [16], which is an intentional relaxation of SOP.

While there are exceptions to this policy, e.g., images, scripts, and style sheets are allowed to be included as resources across origins, access to these resources is restricted to prevent information leaks. As an example, the including document is prevented from accessing the image data of images loaded across origins.

Not all elements are as carefully restricted from information leaks as images. Scripts loaded across origins become part of the document and inherit the origin of the including document, which allows the script to communicate with the server from which the *document* originates. Such scripts are also able to interact with the document, e.g. by adding nodes, which in turn require new content to be requested. Since these requests are not restricted by the SOP, this creates a side channel that permits cross-origin information leakage. At the same time, the including document is prevented from inspecting the source of the script and can only observe the public side-effects that the script produce as it is executed.

Other examples of problematic elements include the *object* and *embed* tags. These tags allow inclusion of resources that may require a plug-in to run. The plug-in is selected based on the MIME-type of the content, but because the server delivering the content might not be able to determine its format, the tags allow a developer to set the type attribute to guide the browser in which plug-in to run. When the type attribute is used, the corresponding plug-in is run regardless of the MIME-type provided by the server. In the event that the provided MIME-type do not match that for which the plug-in is designed, e.g., *text/html* for a PDF plug-in, it is up to the plug-in to respond to the content it is served. Known methods of handling MIME-types, such as content-sniffing, are effective in this situation, but they have to be employed by each and every plug-in. Most plug-ins will disregard the MIME-type of the content and attempt to parse it. As with images, the content handled by the plug-in is executed in the origin it was served from. This implies that the containing page is restricted from directly accessing the content handled by the plug-in, and that the content can communicate freely with the origin it was loaded from. However, a number of plug-ins provide an API for interaction between the plug-in and the document. The browsers are forced to rely on the plug-ins to employ correct security measures. Section 4 shows that even state-of-the-art plug-ins fail to properly do so, emphasizing the importance of the issue.

2.2 Crossing formats

A polyglot is perhaps most commonly known as a person who speaks several languages. However, the term is widely used in several scientific fields. In computer science, a *polyglot* is a program that is valid in multiple programming languages. In this paper we use a broader definition of a programming language, not limited to code meant for compilation to machine code or scripting languages, but extended to any format that requires interpretation before rendering.

A polyglot is composed by combining syntax from two different formats A and B. It leverages various syntactic language constructs that are either common between the formats; or constructs that are language specific but carrying different meaning in each language. To maintain validity across languages, one must ensure that constructs specific to A are not interpreted in the format of B, and vice versa. This is often accomplished by hiding the language specific constructs, in segments interpreted as comments or plain text of the other format.

Certain languages are particularly suitable for creating polyglots. These languages either have a lot of constructs in common with other languages, such as the C language, or are error tolerant in that the parser ignores that which it cannot interpret, such as HTML. The latter allows for ample opportunity to hide any code specific to format A, as long as there is no overlap with the syntax of format B.

A malicious polyglot of two formats, A and B, where A is benign in nature and B contains a malicious payload, is composed as $A||B$. he benign format, A, is a widely accepted format with limited capabilities, but with the opportunity of hiding arbitrary data, e.g. an image with comment fields. The malicious format, B, has additional capabilities, e.g., execute scripts or send requests. This kind of polyglot can be used for malicious purposes when there is a difference between the assumed run-time context, and the actual context it is executed in. In the assumed context $A||B$ is interpreted as the benign format, A. In the actual context, however, $A||B$ is coerced to be interpreted as the malicious format, B, containing the payload.

Even if a verification process exists, it will verify that the content is valid in the assumed context. Due to the nature of the polyglot, the content is verified as valid and benign, but subsequently, in the actual context, the malicious content is executed.

Coercing content to be interpreted as a different type can be accommodated in the context of the web. If the content is loaded using an *img* tag it will be interpreted as an image, if a *script* tag is used it will be interpreted as a script. Certain tags, e.g., the *object* tag and *embed* tag, even let the developer decide which type to interpret the content as. To prevent abuse, the browsers employ content-type sniffing for certain content-types, a practice which has historically led to security issues, as illustrated below.

Barth et al. [3] define *chameleon* documents as a benign file type crossbred with malicious HTML content. The attack targets the content-sniffing algorithm used in the browser and the document is crafted in such a way that the browser will detect the content type as HTML. The paper proceeds to describe how an attacker can create a chameleon document, that is valid PostScript, but will be identified as HTML. This issue allows exploitation when there is a mismatch between a web site's content validation filter and the browser's content-sniffing algorithm.

In literature we find, apart from chameleons, other names for similar, related concepts. Brandis [4] refer to *GIFAR* attacks, based on one of the early instances of attacks based on GIF images that are also valid JAR files. Sundareswaran et al. [14, 13] discuss GIFAR-related attacks as a form of *content repurposing* attack. In this paper the term content smuggling is used as it best represents how a polyglot can infiltrate an origin.

While these articles document known instances of polyglot attacks, the attack method has not been generalized until this paper. Under our generalization, previous work corresponds to instances. For example, we show that GIFAR attacks describe a form of content smuggling, Section 2.3.2, and cross-origin CSS attacks [7] describe a form of syntax injection attacks, Section 2.3.1. The added value of our paper is a generalized view on polyglot attacks and focus on new instances of polyglots that involve the PDF format.

Two attacker-centric components require special attention; the infiltration of an origin, i.e. the attack vector, and the exploitation of an infiltrated origin, i.e. the payload.

2.3 Attack vectors

The general pattern of a polyglot attack is described in the following scenario, illustrated in Figure 1. The target of the attack is the web site *vulnerable.com*. It has been infiltrated by an attacker to serve a malicious polyglot within its sensitive origin (1). The content is served by *vulnerable.com* as the benign format, e.g., an image, harmless to users of the web site. The victim in this scenario is an authenticated user of *vulnerable.com*. At some point, while still authenticated to *vulnerable.com*, the unsuspecting victim visits the attackers web site *attacker.com* (2). Upon visiting *attacker.com*, the web site uses a plug-in to embed the polyglot from *vulnerable.com* as the malicious format (3). This is achieved by setting the type attribute to the MIME-type of the corresponding plug-in, which will override the MIME-type supplied by *vulnerable.com*. When loaded in the plug-in the malicious polyglot is executed in the *vulnerable.com* origin (4), as described in Section 2.1. The impact depends on the payload and the capabilities of the malicious format.

This paper describes two vectors for infiltrating an origin, either via syntax injection, or content smuggling. In the case of syntax injection, existing content is manipulated to become a polyglot, whereas with content smuggling, a polyglot is used to evade content filters. The vectors are described below with more detailed scenarios.

2.3.1 Syntax injection

In a cross-site scripting attack user input is used to compose an HTML document. Fragments of HTML syntax in

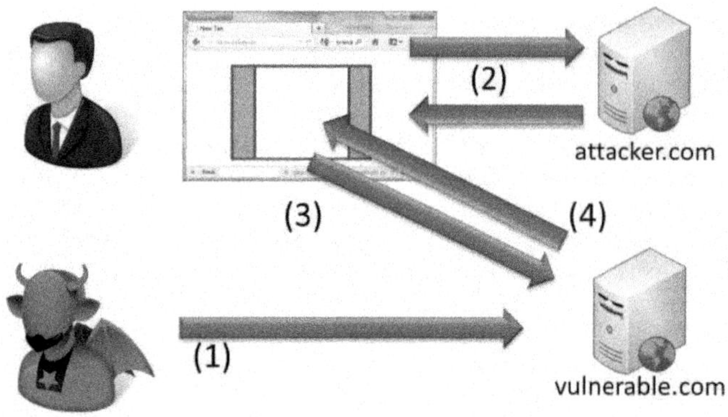

Figure 1: Overview of the scenario

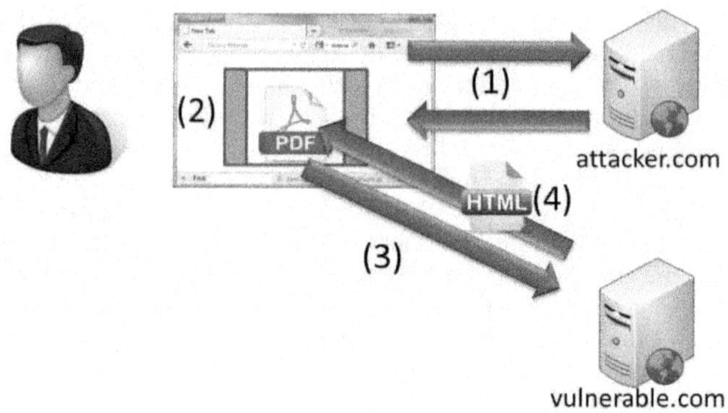

Figure 2: Syntax injection scenario

the input alters the semantic of the document to execute attacker supplied script code. Similarly, in a syntax injection attack the vulnerable target will compose an HTML document from attacker controlled input containing syntax of a foreign format. The resulting document is a polyglot which is benign when viewed as the HTML, but malicious when viewed as the injected format. While the web site serves the content as HTML, it is in the hands of the attacker to decide how it is interpreted when embedded in the attackers web page. Examples of such services include social networks, search engines, i.e., nearly any dynamic web site driven by user interaction. The targeted service is assumed to employ server-side cross-site scripting sanitization. For the attack to be successful, the input must bypass this sanitization. The sanitization filter will remove or encode problematic characters in the input related to HTML-syntax. The injected format will pose as a new context, unknown to the filter. Chances are that the injected format will pass the filter unnoticed.

Previous work documents an instance of a polyglot attack based on syntax injection, though not phrased in those terms. Huang et al. [7] describe a cross-origin *cascading style-sheet* (CSS) attack. This attack injects fragments of CSS syntax in a HTML document, thereby making it a HTML/CSS polyglot. The error-tolerant parsing of style sheets allow the polyglot to parsed as valid CSS. The capabilities of CSS provide trivial cross-origin leakage. The paper proposes a defense technique which has been adopted by all major browsers, which implies that the attacks outlined in their paper are now ineffective. Instead, Section 3 will show practical attacks based on other formats.

Scenario.

The scenario, illustrated in Figure 2, describes how the attack proceeds from the infiltration of the origin to the compromise of the victim. Again, the victim is an authenticated user of *vulnerable.com* that unsuspectingly visits the attackers malicious web site, *attacker.com* (1). The *attacker.com* web site uses a plug-in to embed a web page with vulnerable input parameters from *vulnerable.com* (2). In the parameters of the request the attacker injects the syntax of the malicious format (3). The response from *vulnerable.com* is a polyglot served as the benign content type (4), but the attacker's page coerces the content to be interpreted as the malicious content type by the plug-in. The malicious payload is executed in the origin of *vulnerable.com* and can leverage the credentials of the victim to further exploit the vulnerability.

2.3.2 Content smuggling

The vulnerable target of a content smuggling attack, lets users upload files that are subsequently served under the origin of the service. Examples of such potentially vulnerable services are cloud storage services, image databases, social networks, conference management systems or job broker services. Such a service accepts a limited set of benign file-formats, and the files are run through a filter to verify that they belong to this set, e.g. images or documents, before being served to the end user. The filter will verify the file under the assumption that it conforms strictly to one format. By submitting a polyglot to such a service, an attacker can evade the filter as the polyglot does conform to the benign format. If the polyglot is publicly accessible, it can be embedded in the attackers page. Since the attacker is in control over which format the polyglot is interpreted as, it is embedded as the malicious format and thereby the service is vulnerable to a content smuggling attack.

The GIFAR attack is a polyglot attack based on content smuggling. In this attack a benign GIF-image and a malicious JAR-file is combined to create a GIF/JAR polyglot. By submitting the combined GIFAR to a service, the attacker can execute a Java applet under the origin of the targeted service. The Java runtime has been updated to prevent this kind of abuse. Instead, Section 3 will show practical attacks based on other formats.

Scenario.

The content smuggling scenario proceeds as illustrated in Figure 3. Similarly to the previous scenarios, the victim is an authenticated user of a targeted vulnerable web site, *vulnerable.com.* To give more context to the scenario, *vulnerable.com* can be a cloud storage service. The target is infiltrated by the attacker (1), who uploads a polyglot to the web site. The polyglot is verified to be benign under the assumption that it belongs an allowed file type. While still authenticated to *vulnerable.com*, the victim visits the attackers web site, *attacker.com* (2). The *attacker.com* site embeds the polyglot from *vulnerable.com* (3), which is served as the benign type, but coerced to be interpreted as the malicious content type by the plug-in (4). The malicious format of the

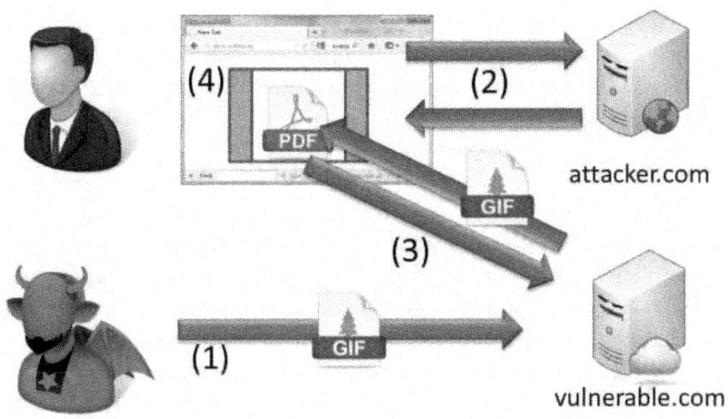

Figure 3: Content smuggling scenario

embedded polyglot is activated and a possible payload is to extract all the files stored in the victims account.

2.4 Payloads

The consequences of exploiting an infiltrated origin depend on the capabilities of the format used. These consequences span from abusing the credentials of the victim to forge requests to the vulnerable web site, to extracting sensitive information about the victim that is stored on the vulnerable web site.

Cross-site request forgery.

If the format has the capability of issuing requests, in particular POST requests within the boundaries of the SOP, that includes the victims credentials,then the attacker can mount a *cross-site request forgery* (CSRF) attack. Web sites protect against these attacks by generating a token with each response that has to be included in the subsequent request. However, if the format also have the capability of reading the response of the issued request, it can extract the token and thereby circumvent the CSRF protection.

Cross-origin information leakage.

Additionally, if the format allows communication with the origin of the attacker, then the attacker can extract sensitive user information and leak it across origins. If the format is not restricted by the SOP, it can communicate directly with the attackers server. Otherwise, if the format can interact with the document that embeds the polyglot, the communication could be tunneled through this channel.

3. VULNERABILITIES AND ATTACKS

In this section we give concrete examples of the attacks described in Section 2, using the PDF format as the running example. We begin by detailing how the design decision made in the PDF-standard make it highly suitable for creating malicious polyglots. Throughout this section Adobe Reader is the assumed target. A comparison between readers can be found in Section 4.

The reader is invited to visit the test page [1] for practical demonstration of the attacks from this section. These attacks show that the vulnerabilities we focus on are exploitable in practice.

Listing 1: Sample PDF file

```
%PDF-1.4
1 0 obj
<< /Type /Catalog
   /Outlines 2 0 R
   /Pages 3 0 R
>>
endobj
2 0 obj
<< /Type Outlines
   /Count 0
>>
endobj
3 0 obj
<< /Type /Pages
   /Kids [4 0 R]
   /Count 1
>>
endobj
4 0 obj
<< /Type /Page
   /Parent 3 0 R
   /MediaBox [0 0 612 792]
   /Contents 5 0 R
   /Resources << /ProcSet 6 0 R >>
>>
endobj
5 0 obj << /Length 35 >>
stream
   ...Page-marking operators...
endstream
endobj
6 0 obj
   [/PDF]
endobj
xref
0 7
0000000000 65535 f
0000000009 00000 n
0000000074 00000 n
0000000120 00000 n
0000000179 00000 n
0000000300 00000 n
0000000384 00000 n
trailer
<< /Size 7
   /Root 1 0 R
>>
startxref
408
%%EOF
```

3.1 Portable Document Format

The *Portable Document Format* (PDF) is a widely used document format capable of displaying text, rendering graphics, scripting, animation and other dynamic content. It is a container format in the sense that it allows embedding of files and resources.

According to the PDF specification [8] a PDF file is composed of a header, several objects, a cross-reference section and a trailer. Listing 1 shows a sample of how a PDF file is structured and its elements. Supposedly, it is also a minimal PDF file according to the specification.

3.1.1 Header

The header consists of the string "%PDF-" followed by a version number. The version is denoted by a major and a minor version number of the form "*M.m*". Because the version can be specified elsewhere, the version number is not required to be part of the header.

3.1.2 Objects

Objects can be direct or indirect, the difference being that an indirect object has labels which are used for referring to the object from another object. Object labels are numbered and begin with the string "*N n* obj", where "N" is the object number and "n" is the revision number. Similarly object references are of the form "*N n* R". The label is optionally ended with the keyword "endobj".

There are eight basic types of basic objects; booleans, integers, strings, names, arrays, dictionaries, streams and the null object. For the intents and purposes of this article, we will focus on the string, dictionary, name and stream objects.

String objects.

There are two types of strings; literal and hexadecimal. Literal strings are enclosed by the "(" and ")" characters. Any character can occur in a literal string, even parentheses if they are balanced, e.g. a matching closing parenthesis for every opened parenthesis. In hexadecimal strings each character is represented by its corresponding hexadecimal value, enclosed by the "<" and ">" characters.

Dictionary objects.

Dictionary objects are a name-value map delimited by the "<<" and ">>" tokens. The names are name objects and the values are objects of any type. Name objects begin with the "/" character, followed by a string of non-whitespace characters. Each dictionary has a type, either specified by the "/Type" name or inferred from the context in which it occurs. The type declares which kind of element the dictionary is describing, e.g. a page or an annotation. Dictionaries form the structure of the document by connecting objects through references, e.g. relating a page to its contents. A special type of dictionary describes *actions*. Actions are triggered when a certain event occur, such as a file is opened or a page is displayed, and the action dictionary specify how it is handled. Actions can be used to, among other things, go to a specific page, play a sound, execute JavaScript or launch a command.

Stream objects.

A stream is an unlimited sequence of bytes. A stream object is indirect and consists of a dictionary, describing the stream, and the associated stream delimited by the "stream" and "endstream" keywords. According to the specification, the stream dictionary shall contain a *Length* name to specify the length of the stream. In practice this can be omitted as long as the delimiting keywords are in place. PDF supports encoding of streams, in which case the dictionary describe which filters are required to decode the stream.

3.1.3 Cross-reference

The cross-reference section is a record of the location of indirect objects within a file. The location is specified as the byte offset from the beginning of the file. The cross-reference section is opened with the "xref" keyword, followed by one record for each indirect object. The cross-reference section will be reconstructed if missing and can therefore be omitted.

3.1.4 Trailer

The trailer is composed of a trailer dictionary, a pointer to the cross-reference section and an end-of-file marker. The trailer dictionary is introduced by the "trailer" keyword. *Root* is in practice the only mandatory name in the trailer dictionary, referencing the root of the document structure. The "startxref" keyword is followed by the number of bytes from the beginning of the file to the first cross-reference section. As with the cross-reference section, it can be omitted. The string "%%EOF" marks the end-of-file, but can be omitted.

3.2 PDF-based polyglots

Several design choices in the PDF specification make the format particularly suitable for making polyglots. One such design choice is the error tolerant parser. This is in part motivated by another design choice namely PDF being a container format. This implies that a PDF file can, by design, contain foreign syntax that could interfere with the syntax of the file. Another motivation is that PDF files are designed to be both forward- and backward-compatible. Readers implementing an older version of the specification do not recognize new features and behave as if they were not present in the file. The implementation notes of the specification describes some exceptions to the requirements of the specification, such as the header can occur anywhere within the first 1024 bytes of the file. This flexibility gives plenty of room for combining with syntax of another format. The specification declares many components to be required in a PDF file, but as can be seen in Section 3.1, in practice several components can be omitted [15]. The code in Listing 2 shows the minimal syntax required for a malformed, but valid PDF file.

Listing 2: Minimal PDF file

```
%PDF-
trailer <</Root<</Pages<<>>>>>>
```

Furthermore the PDF format is of particular interest to us because of its many capabilities. Some examples include executing JavaScript, launching commands, and issuing HTTP requests. The HTTP requests are restricted to the origin of the PDF file, and will include any cookies associated with that origin. Adobe Reader also includes a Flash runtime to play embedded Flash files on systems that do not have the Flash runtime installed.

When a PDF document is embedded in a web page, the corresponding plug-in is executed to render the content. Recall from Section 2.1 that the plug-in is selected based on the MIME-type, either supplied by the server or in the type attribute with preference for the later. Also recall that the browser rely on the plug-in to handle the situation when the MIME-type supplied by the server is inconsistent with the MIME-type of the plug-in. In the case of the Adobe Reader plug-in, it disregards the MIME-type supplied by the server and will attempt to interpret any content as PDF. Listing 3 shows how arbitrary content can be rendered as PDF format.

Listing 3: HTML for embedding PDF content

```
<embed type="application/pdf"
src="vulnerable.com/?input=%PDF...">
```

In recent versions of Adobe Reader certain measures have been taken to prevent creating PDF-based polyglots. In accordance with our recommendations, Adobe Reader has made the parsing more strict by attempting to match the first bytes of the file against a set of known signatures. If a match is found, the parser will abort loading of the document. However, this does not fully defend against PDF-based polyglot attacks. The problem of this approach is that there are a number of file formats that lack a reliable signature, e.g., HTML. Also, for this approach to be reliable, the signature must match the signature enforced by other interpreters of the format. A notable counterexample is the signature used for the JPG format. While the signature is correct according to the specification of the format, several JPG interpreters will allow slightly malformed signatures. Such a malformed signature will bypass the check in Adobe Reader and still be rendered correctly in a viewer. This opens up for PDF-based polyglot attacks.

3.3 PDF attacks

As explained in Section 2.3 there are two vectors for polyglot attacks; *syntax injection* and *content smuggling*. PDF is a suitable format for both vectors as it is both a text based format with error tolerant parsing, and has widespread acceptance as a document format, often preferred over other document formats.

3.3.1 Syntax injection

As the scenario details in Section 2.3.1, the attacker in a syntax injection attack manipulates a vulnerable service to include PDF syntax in existing content, e.g. HTML-documents. The PDF syntax is typically injected through user input used by the vulnerable service in the composition of documents. An example of a suitable fragment to inject is shown in Listing 4. The resulting content is subsequently embedded in the attackers page as PDF, as exemplified in Listing 3. As mentioned in Section 3.2, the embedded PDF can issue requests to the origin it came from, carrying the cookies associated with that origin. These requests allow for the extraction of sensitive user data that can either be communicated back to the attacker, or be leveraged in further attacks.

Thus far, exploitation of vulnerable services have been discussed, excluding the specific conditions under which a service is vulnerable. In order to exploit the vulnerability, the injected syntax must pass through any existing filters unchanged or at least with its semantics preserved. If user input in an HTML-document is not sanitized, any syntax would be unchanged and the service is vulnerable to less sophisticated attacks, e.g. cross-site scripting, therefore sanitized user input is of greater concern. Based on the PDF samples in Listings 2 and 4, we can derive the set of tokens required to build a PDF. Assuming that alpha-numeric characters pass through a sanitization filter unmodified, the set of tokens is $\{\%, <<, >>, /\}$. As can be noted, there is a small but significant overlap with the tokens of HTML, which implies that many web sites protected against cross-site scripting attacks are also protected against PDF-based polyglot attacks. One of the problems of filtering input for inclusion in a web page are the many contexts in which the input can be included. A problem made even more complex by the diversity of languages the page contains. Language incompatibilities force context dependent filtering, where the same input is treated differently based on the context in which it is included. In certain contexts angle brackets are often left untouched by filters.

HTML comments.

No HTML enclosed in comments, "<–" and "–>", will be rendered, and therefore filters consider this context safe. To prevent input from escaping the comment by injecting an end comment token, certain filters remove any occurrences of "–>", but leave the rest of the input untouched. HTML comments are meaningless to PDF, and the result is a valid HTML/PDF polyglot.

JavaScript strings.

In an in-line JavaScript context, user input is often included in the shape of a JavaScript string, delimited by single or double quotes. In this context only a few characters require encoding, as they can break the string context. Naturally, any single or double quotes need escaping, as well as any carriage return or line feed characters. In the spirit of making minimal changes to the input, certain web sites only escape these characters. This is sufficient to prevent cross-site scripting attacks, but fail to protect against PDF-based polyglot attacks.

Note that not only in-line JavaScript falls short in this regard. JavaScript object notation (JSON) is used in modern web sites as a data transport. This is particularly common in web sites that provide an API to interact with the offered services. JSON encoded information suffer the same problem as in-line JavaScript, thereby extending the attack surface further.

3.3.2 Content smuggling

Due to the nature of the PDF, it can without much effort be combined with just about any other format. This provides ample opportunity to create malicious polyglots where PDF is either the benign or the malicious format. Consequently, this significantly expands the attack surface, making it important to take measures to protect against these attacks.

PDF as the benign format.

Services like job brokers commonly let the user upload a CV in the form of a PDF-file. Before such PDF-files are published to recruiters, they are verified to not contain any malicious payload. Such a verification only extends to the PDF format itself. An attacker can produce a PDF that is valid and benign, but also a polyglot hiding another malicious format, such as Flash. As described in the content smuggling scenario in Section 2.3.2, the uploaded PDF file is then embedded on the attacker's web site, but now as the malicious format. Using social engineering, the attacker can persuade the victim to visit the web site.

Creating a PDF/Flash polyglot is no major challenge. A proof-of-concept can easily be created by storing the PDF source code as a static string variable in the malicious Flash source code. When compiling Flash, the output is compressed by default to save space, thereby obfuscating the PDF source code. However, tools exist that decompress the Flash files, which restores the plain PDF code.

PDF as the malicious format.

In the content smuggling scenario in Section 2.3.2, the attacker uploads the PDF polyglot to a vulnerable content hosting service. A server-side verification process will base its verification on the benign formats it expects to receive. The polyglot is designed to verify correctly as the benign format, and the verification is likely to miss the malicious PDF components, as it is unaware of the alternate interpretation of the content.

Given the extensive capabilities of the PDF format, exploiting a content smuggling vulnerability with a PDF-based polyglot attack, can be done without much effort. To prevent the attack, the verification process have to actively search for and remove PDF specific syntax. The impact of exploitation depends on the payload used in the attack.

3.4 PDF payloads

As discussed in Section 2.4, there are two approaches to exploiting these vulnerabilities; cross-site request forgery, and cross-origin information leakage. Both of these require extracting information from the vulnerable service, which is something that can be achieved using the capabilities of the PDF format.

In order to extract information and leak across origins, a communication channel is established. PDF documents provide multiple ways of generating HTTP requests; many of which allow cross-origin communication, but are, out of security concerns, only one-way in the sense that the PDF document will never see the result. Therefore, the focus is directed towards two methods that allow bidirectional communication; XML external entities, and embedded Flash. Since the document will retain the origin from which it was served, all requests issued from the document will include any cookies associated with the target origin.

XML External Entities.

The PDF JavaScript API includes a method to parse XML documents, called XMLData.parse. The XML document being processed may in turn rely on external entities, required for the parsing of the document, which the XML parser will request. The request is bound to the origin of the document, and the response is included in the XML document. The source code of the XML document reflects this response and can be retrieved at a later point, resulting in a bidirectional communication channel. As the response is included in the XML, the result has to be well-formed XML. This puts a restriction on the content that can be requested using this method. Considering that HTML pages are rarely well-formed this method may be too restricted in practice.

Listing 4 contains an example PDF document that uses XML external entities. The one-way method *getURL* is used to communicate the information back to the attacker. Given the compact size of the example, it is useful for the syntax injection scenario in Section 2.3.1, which require injection of small syntax fragments.

As of version 10.1.5, in accordance with our recommendations, XML external entities has been removed. Thereby the risks of leakage of sensitive information is significantly reduced.

Embedded Flash.

By embedding a Flash file in the PDF document the capabilities of the format can be extended even further. The Flash runtime supports bidirectional communication in accordance with SOP. The embedded Flash inherits the origin of the PDF document, thus it can request and read any document from the originating server. Unlike the XML method, there are no restrictions on what content can be requested, thus making it the most versatile of the available communication methods. The only drawback using this approach is the significant increase in terms of file size. Even the compact Flash code in Listing 5 will result in a 6 kB Flash file. This suggests that this method might be better suited for the content smuggling scenario in Section 2.3.2, rather than the syntax injection scenario.

Cross-origin communication in Flash adheres to the same-origin policy. However, this is not a restriction, since Flash also supports cross-origin communication via cross-origin resource sharing. Using CORS, a web server can relax the SOP to allow access to specified content. An attacker can set an allow-all cross-origin policy, such as in Listing 6, that open up for two way communication.

Listing 4: PDF using XML for communication

```
%PDF-
1 0 obj<<>>stream
xml = '<!DOCTYPE foo[<!ENTITY x ' +
  'SYSTEM "'+URL+'">]><foo>&x;</foo>';
var doc = XMLData.parse(xml);
getURL('attacker.com/?secret='+
  doc.saveXML())
endstream
trailer<</Root
   <</Pages<<>>
      /OpenAction
      <</S/JavaScript/JS 1 0 R>>
   >>
>>
```

Listing 5: Flash code for communication

```
package {
  import flash.net.*;
  import flash.display.Sprite;
  public class Secret extends Sprite {
    var u:String;
    var r:URLRequest;
    var l:URLLoader;
    public function Secret() {
      u = 'vulnerable.com/secret';
      r = new URLRequest(u);
      l = new URLLoader(r);

      l.addEventListener('complete',
        function():void {
          u = 'attacker.com/?' + r.data;
          r = new URLRequest(u);
          l = new URLLoader(r);
        });
}}}
```

Listing 6: Allow-all crossdomain.xml

```
<cross-domain-policy>
  <allow-access-from domain="*" />
</cross-domain-policy>
```

4. EVALUATION

This section details the evaluation performed to investigate the prevalence of the vulnerabilities from Section 3. The evaluation covers various instances of affected components, such as browsers and PDF interpreters, content sanitization filter, and a study of the Alexa top 100 web sites.

4.1 Instances

To better understand how this problem presents itself, a comparison of browser and reader instances is presented. We compare all major browsers and two of the most common readers.

4.1.1 Readers

Section 3 focuses on the Adobe PDF Reader as the attack surface, due to its standing as the most commonly used reader. To give a comparison, the Google Chrome built-in PDF reader was selected as it is the default reader to users of the browser.

As mentioned in Section 2, the browser rely on the reader plug-in to implement correct security measures, in order to prevent cross-domain leakage. Unlike Adobe Reader, the Chrome browser built-in PDF reader refuses to render content that was served with an inappropriate MIME-type if the content is delivered across origins. This effectively prevents the attacks in Section 3. If the Chrome browser is configured to use the Adobe Reader plug-in, it will behave the same as in other browsers and the content will be interpreted as PDF.

4.1.2 Browsers

The behavior of cross-domain embedding of PDF resources is studied in the major browsers, i.e., Firefox, Safari, Opera, Google Chrome and Internet Explorer. The study shows that all major browsers are susceptible to the attacks outlined in Section 3, with some minor differences detailed below and summarized in Table 1. In Table 1, "Yes" for the columns "object" and "embed" indicates that the corresponding tag can be used to embed a PDF document, and for the column "Adobe is default" it indicates that Adobe Reader is commonly the default PDF reader.

Firefox, Safari and Opera.

The browsers, Firefox, Safari and Opera, are all susceptible to the attacks outlined as per Section 3, without any restrictions or modifications.

Google Chrome.

Google's browser, Chrome, has built-in support for displaying PDF documents. The built-in PDF reader is used by default by the browser, unless it has been explicitly disabled by the user. Certain complex PDF documents can not be handled by the built-in reader. The built-in reader will then prompt the user to open the document in Adobe Reader. As previously noted in Section 4.1.1, the built-in reader is not vulnerable to attacks. Hence, Chrome is only susceptible when the Adobe Reader plug-in is used to render the document.

Internet Explorer.

Microsoft's browser, Internet Explorer, is susceptible to the attacks. However, it seems to only support embedding of PDF documents using the *embed* tag. This is not a major obstacle in exploiting the vulnerability, as the *embed* and *object* tags are interchangeable in this respect.

	object	embed	Adobe is default
Firefox	Yes	Yes	Yes
Chrome	Yes	Yes	No
Safari	Yes	Yes	Yes
Opera	Yes	Yes	Yes
Internet Explorer	No	Yes	Yes

Table 1: Comparison of browsers

4.2 Alexa top 100

We have conducted two studies to evaluate the prevalence of the problem on popular sites, covering the Alexa top 100 web sites. Because of their dominance on the web, these web sites are also the most exposed to security threats. The first study covers PDF-based polyglot attacks using syntax injection as the infiltration method; the second covers content smuggling. We refrain from mentioning names of individual web sites to prevent exploitation before the issues have been properly dealt with. We are in contact with the maintainers of the web sites to help mitigate the vulnerabilities.

Syntax injection.

The study is based on supplying the web sites with the benign minimal PDF in Listing 2, and examining the corresponding responses to this input. The sample contains the essential keywords and tokens required to perform a syntax injection based polyglot attack. If these tokens pass through unaltered, the web site is considered vulnerable. The process has been conducted manually and only input parameters on publicly accessible pages, those that do not require authentication, were tested. Considering that most inputs are available only to authenticated users, the results suggests that more web sites are likely vulnerable in input that do require authentication.

The conclusion is that nine web sites out of the hundred apply insufficient content filtering with respect to the PDF format. Out of the nine found to be vulnerable; five were susceptible to PDF based polyglot attacks, and four applied insufficient content filtering, but the input was reflected in a way that prevented exploitation, e.g. the header appeared after 1024 bytes.

Three of the five vulnerable web sites could also be determined to be vulnerable to traditional XSS attacks in the same input parameters. The remaining two web sites found susceptible only to polyglot attacks and not XSS attacks are of particular interest since they employ proper measures to protect against XSS attacks, and yet fall short in defeating this new breed of attacks.

1. The first web site reflected user input in an inline JavaScript context, inside a string. To prevent cross-site scripting in this context, the following measures were taken: the JavaScript string delimiters and the backslash character were properly escaped, and the string "</script>" was removed. These measures are sufficient to protect against XSS attacks, but do not prevent an attacker from injecting valid PDF syntax.
2. The second web site reflected the user input in an HTML-comment context. The only measure taken

to prevent XSS attacks in this context was removing any occurrence of the character sequence "->". Again, while successfully preventing XSS attacks, this measure is ineffective in preventing an attacker from injecting PDF syntax.

Content smuggling.

Further, a smaller study was conducted, not covering the full Alexa top 100, but targeting popular cloud storage services. This study is based on polyglot content being uploaded to the service and subsequently analyzed to determine which origin it was served under. We have found two major enterprise cloud storage services to be susceptible to attacks. Both services make an effort to follow current best practices, see Section 5.2.1, but fail to cover certain scenarios for content upload.

The first service serves almost all uploaded content from a sandboxed origin; the exception being the user's avatar image that are served under the sensitive origin. An attacker could upload a specially crafted avatar image that, when embedded as PDF on the attackers web site, can access and modify the contents of the victim's cloud storage.

The second service lets the user publish a public link to an HTML representation of the content. The content is served under the sensitive origin and is therefore carefully processed to prevent generation of malicious HTML, but fails to take other formats into account. A specially crafted file will result in the generation of valid PDF syntax that, when embedded as PDF on the attackers web site, can access and modify the contents of the victim's cloud storage.

We are currently advising both service providers to help mitigate these vulnerabilities.

5. MITIGATION

This section gives advice on various mitigation approaches available for each of the affected components, both server-side and client-side. We provide one general mitigation approach that covers a significant segment of the potential attack vectors, and provide specific mitigation suggestions for affected components.

Although some of the mitigation suggestions below are already in place (e.g., the Chrome builtin PDF reader), the state of the art is far from being satisfactory. As our paper demonstrates, the polyglot attacks are a real threat. It is the paper's main value to bring attention to polyglot attacks and the importance of mitigation against them.

5.1 General approach

It should be noted that preventing polyglots, and thereby polyglot attacks, in the general case is a complex task, as one would need to take all potentially malicious formats in to account. Mitigating instances of polyglot attacks based on particular formats are significantly more straightforward. Our approach is not attempting to prevent polyglots as such, but provide details about the context in which the content will be interpreted, such that an informed decision can be made on whether rendering the content constitutes a security risk or not.

The relation between web server and the browser is central in a web environment, but there is no common agreement on the type of content communicated between server and client. As mentioned in Section 2.1, in each response the web server sends a header representing its view on the type of content delivered, however, the browser is free to ignore the provided type and can even be instructed to do so. Often the browser knows precisely the context in which the content will be rendered and the types suitable for these contexts. As an example, when content is loaded in an *object* tag with a type attribute, as is the case throughout the paper, the browser already has exact knowledge as to which types the requested content can be interpreted as in this context. A natural defense technique is to send the expected types along with the request. The web server then compares the expected types to the assumed type and react accordingly, e.g., if the assumed type is HTML and the expected type is PDF, an error can be sent back to the client. On the client side, the browser verifies the type in the response matches any of the expected types, possibly alerting the user if there is a mismatch. This mutual agreement between client and server can help mitigate both syntax injection and content smuggling. Furthermore, this approach can be implemented in the web server itself, as opposed to a web application, since the web server makes the final decision on the supplied content-type.

The expected type is useful also to a web application that performs content filtering on the fly. At the point when the content is being requested, it only requires verification against the expected type.

There are limitations to this technique; If a context has multiple possible types, e.g., an *img* tag, a polyglot between two of the types can evade detection. The specific cases where this situation occurs in an exploitable way are rare, and further work can help in determining and mitigating such vulnerabilities.

5.2 Specific approaches

Apart from the general approach described above, there are mitigation approaches that are specific to each of the components involved. These are recommended to be used until general approaches for mitigating polyglot attacks are widely adopted.

5.2.1 Server-side mitigation

As a content provider on the Internet today there are precautions that one can take to mitigate this class of vulnerabilities. Which precautions to take depend on the kind of services provided. The mitigation recommendations for syntax injection apply to all services that generate content based on user input, and the content smuggling recommendations apply to services that serve user-supplied files.

Syntax injection.

Preventing syntax injection on the server-side poses severe challenges. Even server-side filtering of HTML syntax to prevent cross-side scripting attacks has proved difficult due to the many contexts in which JavaScript can be introduced. Filtering all potentially harmful tokens from all formats in which a document may be interpreted is hardly possible.

To prevent attacks based on a specific format, e.g., a PDF-based syntax injection attack, the task is simpler. As discussed in Section 3.3.1, the token-set identified in Section 3.3.1, are essential to create valid PDF syntax. Filtering user input to remove or encode these characters effectively mitigates the vulnerability. Luckily, because of the significant overlap with the token-set of HTML, many of the contexts where user input can occur are already being protected. Special attention is required in contexts are not traditionally filtered for HTML tokens, e.g. JSON.

Content smuggling.

The current best-practice recommendation on hosting user-supplied content is to serve the content from a sandboxed origin that is completely separate, as per SOP, and isolated from the sensitive services. These best-practices, provided by Google [18], successfully prevents content smuggling attacks as the restrictions of the SOP prevents the content from accessing any sensitive resources in the origin of the web service.

These recommendations come with a caveat to be taken into consideration. Some user supplied content is only meant to be accessible to certain authenticated users, e.g. photos that are only shared with friends. In that case, the service needs to transfer the credentials required to authenticate the user from the sensitive origin to the sandboxed origin, without actually revealing the credentials used in the sensitive origin. Revealing the credentials, e.g. using the same cookies on both origins, defeats the purpose of the sandbox origin entirely. Currently there is no uniform solution to this problem. Some common solutions are encountered: using the hashed credentials of the sensitive origin; or generating public, but obscured, links that are later shared manually.

5.2.2 Browser

Traditionally, browser vendors have allowed the browser to override the MIME-type provided by the server for compatibility reasons. This is a compromise to deal with the situation that the server is confused as to what kind of content it is serving. This compromise has repeatedly shown to lead to security issues. The affected browser vendors can help mitigate this problem by limiting the ways content can be coerced to be interpreted as a particular format.

In the case of PDF-based polyglots, and other polyglots that require a plugin, the browser can intervene when there is a mismatch between the content-type provided by the server and the type attribute of the *object* tag. The vulnerability can be mitigated by acknowledging that there is a potential security issue in interpreting the supplied content in the requested format and alerting the user to this threat.

An intuitive approach would be to for the browsers to employ similar content-sniffing for content rendered in plug-ins, as is already done with content native to the browser. However, this intuition fails to take into account that the very reason for using plug-ins is that the format is unknown to the browser. One may argue that the browser is as confused as the originating server as to the actual format of the content, and that the issue would be best resolved by the corresponding plug-in.

5.2.3 Interpreter / Plugin

As a general rule of thumb, the interpreter must at the very least alert the user if the served content-type differs from the expected. A preferred alternative is to not attempt to interpret the content at all. This holds true especially when the served content-type is well known and radically different from that which the interpreter is designed for.

As for the PDF file format, the underlying design decisions have led to the current parsing being very relaxed. As discussed in Section 3.2 the PDF format is a container format; designed to embed syntax from other files. Even when parsing strictly according to the specification, it is a simple task to create a PDF-based polyglot. Making the parsing more strict and enforcing many of the specified requirements will make it harder to create polyglots, reducing the attack surface. In accordance with this recommendation, Adobe has taken the first steps to prevent PDF-based polyglots. Recent versions of the reader compares the first bytes of the document against a set of known file signatures. While this is a step in the right direction, this kind of black listing has its drawbacks. The difficulty is that a number of file formats that lack a reliable signatures, e.g., HTML.

A different approach is restricting capabilities of the format, sticking to the essential features. The more capable the format is, the more likely it is to introduce security flaws. In the latest version of their reader Adobe has made progress also in this respect by restricting the possibilities for bidirectional communication.

6. RELATED WORK

Recall that the added value of our paper is a generalized account of polyglot attacks and focus on new instances of polyglots that involve the PDF format. We briefly report on related instances of polyglot attacks.

Backes et al. [2] explore the power of the PostScript language. PostScript allows executable content and access to sensitive information from the environment such as the user id. This work demonstrates how to compromise reviewer anonymity in a peer-reviewing process by maliciously crafting a PostScript document.

As discussed in Section 2, GIFAR [4] is based on polyglots that combine the GIF and JAR (Java archive) formats. The former is used as benign and the latter as malicious to bypass SOP. The Java virtual machine vendors have since then mitigated these attacks by patching the virtual machine to be more conservative on the format of the executed files.

PDFAR [5] polyglots combine the PDF and JAR formats, where PDF serves as benign and JAR serves as malicious. Such a polyglot is possible due to the liberty of the requirements on the headers of PDF files. Mitigation against GIFAR attacks in the Java virtual machine effectively applies to PDFAR attacks.

Nagra [9] demonstrates GIF/JavaScript polyglots by the same file being interpreted as a script and as an image and informally discuses possible security implications.

Barth et al. [3] investigate the security implications of content sniffing by browsers. They present content-sniffing XSS attacks by crossbreeding HTML with other formats like PostScript. They show attacks on real systems like HotCRP, where an uploaded document in the PostScript format is interpreted as malicious HTML by the browser. They also propose a content-sniffing algorithm that helps defending against this class of attacks while maintaining compatibility.

Sundareswaran and Squicciarini [14, 13] discuss image repurposing for GIFAR attacks. They present the AntiGifar tool for client-side protection. AntiGifar models the benign behavior of a user by a control-flow graph and detects possible anomalies when the interactions of the user and browser with the web site deviate from the control-flow model.

As mentioned in Section 2, Huang et al. [7] study an HTML/CSS attack. This attack injects fragments of CSS syntax in a HTML document, thereby making it a HTML/CSS polyglot. The error-tolerant parsing of style sheets allow the polyglot to parsed as valid CSS. The capabilities of CSS provide trivial cross-origin leakage. As discussed earlier, the paper's defense technique has been adopted by all major browsers, which implies that the attacks outlined in their paper are now ineffective.

Wolf's OMG WTF PDF presentation [15] is one of the inspirations for our work. The presentation explores the liberty of the PDF format. In addition, it highlights that PDF interpreters often disregard the specification demands. This is particularly relevant as it allows crossbreeding PDF with such formats as ZIP and EXE.

Heiderich et al. [6] explore the Scalable Vector Graphics (SVG) format. They discover attacks that allow SVG files, embedded via the *img* tag, to run arbitrary JavaScript. One of the attack vectors involves an SVG/HTML polyglot that behaves differently depending on the context in which it is accessed. When included in the *img* tag, the file is interpreted as SVG, whereas when it is accessed directly it is interpreted as malicious HTML.

7. CONCLUSIONS

We have put a spotlight on a new breed of attacks that smuggle malicious payload formatted as benign content. We have identified polyglots as the root cause for this class of attacks. In a systematic study, we have characterized the necessary ingredients for polyglot-based attacks on the web and arrive at the PDF format to be particularly dangerous.

Our empirical studies in the web setting confirm vulnerabilities in the current content filters both in the server side and in browsers, as well as in the PDF interpreters. These vulnerabilities open up for insecure communication across Internet origins and allow attacking web sites from the top 100 Alexa list.

To mitigate the attacks, we suggest general measures against polyglot-based attacks. These measures are a combination of protection on the server side, in browsers, and in content interpreters such as PDF readers.

The affected vendors have been made aware of the vulnerabilities. These vendors include Adobe (notified instantly after discovering the security implications of polyglot PDFs) and the major browser vendors. We have also contacted the vulnerable web sites from the top 100 Alexa list. Following responsible disclosure, we refrain from providing the names of the vulnerable web sites.

Future work includes identification of further formats vulnerable to polyglot-based attacks. Versatile media content formats such as the Windows Media Video format are of particular concern because of their potential for executing scripts.

Further investigation of the PDF format might lead to enhanced possibilities to bypass content filters by alternative character sets.

Acknowledgments

This work was funded by the European Community under the ProSecuToR and WebSand projects and the Swedish research agencies SSF and VR.

8. REFERENCES

[1] Demo page for crossing origins by crossing formats. `http://internot.noads.biz`, August 2013.

[2] M. Backes, M. Durmuth, and D. Unruh. Information flow in the peer-reviewing process. In *Proc. IEEE Symp. on Security and Privacy*, pages 187–191, May 2007.

[3] A. Barth, J. Caballero, and D. Song. Secure content sniffing for web browsers, or how to stop papers from reviewing themselves. In *Proc. IEEE Symp. on Security and Privacy*, pages 360–371, May 2009.

[4] R. Brandis. Exploring Below the Surface of the GIFAR Iceberg. An EWA Australia Information Security Whitepaper. Electronic Warfare Associates-Australia, February 2009.

[5] N. Dhanjani, B. Hardin, and B. Rios. *Hacking: The Next Generation*. O'Reilly Media, August 2009.

[6] M. Heiderich, T. Frosch, M. Jensen, and T. Holz. Crouching tiger - hidden payload: security risks of scalable vectors graphics. In *ACM Conference on Computer and Communications Security*, pages 239–250, October 2011.

[7] L.-S. Huang, Z. Weinberg, C. Evans, and C. Jackson. Protecting browsers from cross-origin css attacks. In *ACM Conference on Computer and Communications Security*, pages 619–629, October 2010.

[8] Adobe Systems Incorporated. ISO 32000-1:2008 Document management - Portable document format, 2008.

[9] J. Nagra. GIF/Javascript Polyglots. `http://www.thinkfu.com/blog/gifjavascript-polyglots`, February 2009.

[10] Open Web Application Security Project (OWASP). OWASP Top 10 2013. `https://www.owasp.org/index.php/Top_10_2013`, 2013.

[11] SANS (SysAdmin, Audit, Network, Security) Institute. The top cyber security risks. `http://www.sans.org`, September 2009.

[12] B. Sterne and A. Barth. Content Security Policy 1.0 (W3C Candidate Recommendation). `http://www.w3.org/TR/CSP`, November 2012.

[13] S. Sundareswaran and A. Squicciarini. DeCore: Detecting Content Repurposing Attacks on Clients' Systems. In *Proc. International Conference on Security and Privacy in Communication Networks (SecureComm)*, pages 199–216. Springer-Verlag, September 2010.

[14] S. Sundareswaran and A. Squicciarini. Image repurposing for gifar-based attacks. In *Collaboration, Electronic messaging, Anti-Abuse and Spam Conference*, July 2010.

[15] J. Wolf. OMG WTF PDF. Presentation at the Chaos Computer Congress, December 2010.

[16] World Wide Web Consortium. Cross-Origin Resource Sharing. `http://www.w3.org/TR/2012/WD-cors-20120403/`, April 2012.

[17] XSSed Team. XSS Attacks Information. `http://www.xssed.com`, 2012.

[18] M. Zalewski. Content hosting for the modern web. `http://googleonlinesecurity.blogspot.se/2012/08/content-hosting-for-modern-web.html`, August 2012.

ViceROI: Catching Click-Spam in Search Ad Networks

Vacha Dave*
UC San Diego
vacha@cs.ucsd.edu

Saikat Guha
Microsoft Research India
saikat@microsoft.com

Yin Zhang
Univ. of Texas at Austin
yzhang@cs.utexas.edu

ABSTRACT

Click-spam in online advertising, where unethical publishers use malware or trick users into clicking ads, siphons off hundreds of millions of advertiser dollars meant to support free websites and apps. Ad networks today, sadly, rely primarily on security through obscurity to defend against click-spam. In this paper, we present Viceroi, a principled approach to catching click-spam in search ad networks. It is designed based on the intuition that click-spam is a profit-making business that needs to deliver higher return on investment (ROI) for click-spammers than other (ethical) business models to offset the risk of getting caught. Viceroi operates at the ad network where it has visibility into all ad clicks. Working with a large real-world ad network, we find that the simple-yet-general Viceroi approach catches over six very different classes of click-spam attacks (e.g., malware-driven, search-hijacking, arbitrage) without any tuning knobs.

Categories and Subject Descriptors

K.6.5 [**Management of Computing and Information Systems**]: Security and Protection—*Advertising Fraud*

Keywords

Click-Spam, Click-Fraud, Invalid Clicks, Traffic Quality

1. INTRODUCTION

Background and motivation. Click-spam in online advertising, where unethical publishers[1] trick users into clicking ads or use malware to click on ads, hurts the online economy by siphoning off millions of advertiser dollars meant to support free websites and apps [27]. Reputed ad networks[2] attempt to filter click-spam to increase advertisers' confidence in their network [29]. Click-spam, however, is an arms-race and attacks have evolved to avoid detection [4].

Ad networks today filter click-spam *reactively* and in an *ad-hoc* manner — when a specific attack is detected (often by the impacted advertiser), the ad networks creates a filter tuned to the detected attack [29]. For example, if an advertiser complains getting thousands of clicks from a single IP address none of which convert into paying customers, the ad network may start filtering all clicks from that specific IP address (or that /24 subnet). Reactive filtering harms advertisers since attacks may go undetected for months; in one case it was estimated that click-spammers siphoned off at least $14 million over 4 years before being taken down [5]. Furthermore, ad-hoc point-solutions are quickly circumvented by attackers, e.g., avoiding the IP blacklist by using a distributed botnet, potentially adding months before the attack is rediscovered by a more savvy advertiser. A controlled measurement study conducted in 2012 found that major ad networks still missed ongoing click-spam attacks that accounted for an estimated 10–25% of clicks in the study [4].

Ad networks recognize their point-solutions to be weak and rely primarily on *security through obscurity* for protection — they fiercely guard their filtering techniques in fear that "unethical [parties] will immediately take advantage of this information to conduct more sophisticated fraudulent activities undetectable by [the ad network]'s methods" [29]. The evolution of click-spam malware, however, demonstrates the futility of relying primarily on security through obscurity. The TDL4 botnet for instance, which is estimated to have siphoned millions, avoids threshold based filters by performing only one click per IP address per day (but doing so from millions of bots), avoids browser signature based filters by plugging into real browsers, and avoids user behavior based filters by gating malware actions on user actions [4].

Approach and contributions. We had three goals in designing Viceroi: 1) *proactively* filter click-spam attacks, 2) in a way that even after we *publicly disclose* our approach it is hard (but perhaps not impossible) for click-spammers to circumvent, and 3) *simple and performant* enough that it can be deployed at Internet scales. Briefly, Viceroi meets these three goals as follows (Section 4 presents design details).

First, proactive filtering requires a very *general* approach that makes no assumptions about the specific attack mechanism. Thus as the click-spammer evolves the attack mechanisms over time, the basic filtering approach remains unaffected. A test of whether an approach is general enough in practice is to see the diversity of attacks the approach can

*Work done while at Microsoft Research India
[1]Publishers are websites, apps, or games that show ads in exchange for a fraction of the revenue generated by ad clicks.
[2]Ad networks aggregate ads from advertisers and broker them to publishers, e.g., Google AdSense, Bing Ads, Baidu.

CCS'13, November 4–8, 2013, Berlin, Germany.

http://dx.doi.org/10.1145/2508859.2516688.

detect without any tuning parameters. Viceroi detected six very different classes of ongoing click-spam attacks — including malware-driven, search-hijacking, arbitrage, conversion-fraud, ad-injection, and parked-domains — without any tuning knobs. Section 6 presents detailed case-studies.

Second, publicly disclosing the Viceroi approach without weakening it (i.e., rejecting the flawed ad networks' practice of security primarily through obscurity) requires us to focus on *invariants* — something the click-spammer cannot easily change without undermining his business model. Viceroi is designed around a simple invariant that we identified — that a click-spam attack must have higher return-on-investment (ROI) for the click-spammer than a ethical publisher to offset the risk of getting caught. Viceroi, in essence, flags publishers with anomalously high ROI. While publisher ROI is hard to estimate, in practice we found per-user revenue a close proxy. To avoid detection by Viceroi, click-spammers must reduce their per-user revenue to that of an ethical publisher. At which point, without the economic incentive to offset the risk of getting caught (by approaches complementing Viceroi), the net effect is a disincentive to commit click-spam.

Finally, to operate at Internet scales, Viceroi must deal with massive volumes of noisy ad network data efficiently and with low false-positives. Viceroi has very good performance on ROC and precision-recall curves (around 90% typically). Furthermore, in simulated attacks, Viceroi has withstood attacks against adversaries several times more powerful than the ones known today.

We believe Viceroi meets all three goals as evidenced by a large ad network deploying several aspects of our approach.

2. TERMINOLOGY

At it's simplest, online search advertising has three players; *advertisers* who want to advertise a product or service, *publishers* that run websites (search engines, news sites, blog sites), mobile apps and games that display the ads, and *ad networks* (like Google AdSense, Bing Ads, Baidu, and Yahoo) that connect advertisers with the publishers. There are two kinds of publishers: publishers owned and operated (O&O) by the ad network, e.g., google.com shows ads from Google's ad network, and syndicated publishers not controlled by the ad network, e.g., ask.com is a syndicated publisher for Google ads.

Cost-per-click (CPC) or Pay-per-click (PPC) is the dominant charging model for search ads — advertisers pay the ad network only when their ad is clicked. Ad networks typically pay syndicated publishers 70% of the revenue generated by ad clicks on their site. While there are other charging models (e.g., pay per impression, pay per action) we focus solely on pay-per-click search ads in this paper since they dominate online ad revenues and are growing [24].

Click-Spam is a click the advertiser pays for where the user did not intend to visit the advertiser's page. It includes clicks through dedicated click-spam malware, accidental clicks, clicks where the user was confused or tricked into clicking, cases where the user clearly intended to go somewhere else (e.g., a navigational query for YouTube in a search engine) which is hijacked into an ad click for something unrelated to the query, and so on.

Syndicated publishers, because of the strong financial motive, have been known to fraudulently generate clicks to inflate their paychecks [5]. Note that O&O publishers are

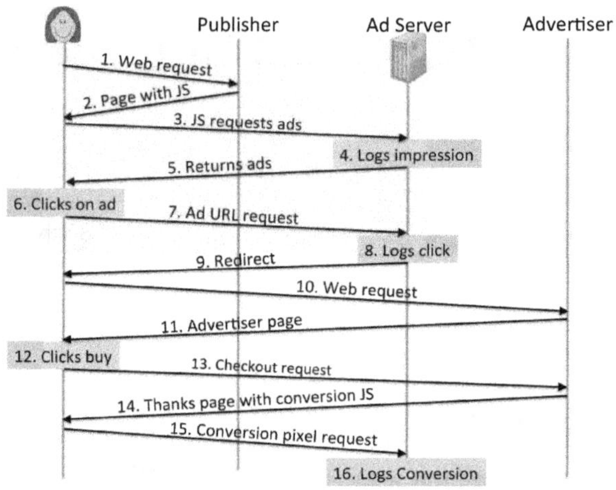

Figure 1: Anatomy of an ad click

unlikely to knowingly generate click-spam since the ad network defrauding its own customers (the advertisers) would generate massive negative PR resulting in advertisers taking their business elsewhere.

Ad networks focused on their long-term reputation (if they are caught being *complicit* in syndicate generated click-spam) are driven to filter click-spam and offer discounts to advertisers to reduce the impact of click-spam.

Anatomy of a ad click. Figure 1 shows the anatomy of a click. Ad networks provide publishers a library with which to fetch ads. This may be JavaScript the publisher can embed into their website or app, or may be server-side code (e.g., PHP or Java). As shown in step 3, the JavaScript code (running in the user's browser) or PHP/Java code (running in the publisher's webserver — not shown) contacts the ad network's server to fetch a set of ads that it populates the website/app with. The code identifies the publisher when contacting the ad network's server, which logs the request. This is called an *ad impression* (step 4). Each ad returned (step 5) contains a unique identifier that is used for tracking clicks on that ad.

If the user clicks the ad (step 6), the user's browser (or app) makes an HTTP request to the ad network with the unique identifier for that ad impression (step 7), which logs the *ad click* (step 8). The log record contains the unique identifier, which is used to lookup the ad advertiser that will be charged (and how much), the publisher that will be paid, the user that originally fetched the ad (for fraud detection), and so on. *Every single ad click is logged by the ad network.*

The HTTP response to the above request redirects the browser to the advertiser's webpage (typically using HTTP 302 response code; steps 9–11). The ad network cannot, in general, track the user's activity on the advertiser site. An advertiser can choose to embed JavaScript code provided by the ad network into certain pages (e.g., payment confirmation page, mailing list subscription page). When (if) the user visits the marked pages (step 14), the JavaScript informs the ad network that the user has performed some action deemed desirable by the advertiser (step 15). This is called an *ad conversion.* The ad network uses cookies to link conversion events back to the unique identifier of the ad impression and ad click (step 16); the conversion event may take place hours or days after the original ad click.

The ad network uses the conversion signal (or lack thereof) to provide bulk discounts to the advertiser as per the *smart-pricing* algorithm [6,8]. The intuition behind smart-pricing is that if a publisher sends traffic that doesn't lead to desirable actions (like buying, email signups), then the traffic is not useful to the advertiser. The smart-pricing algorithm computes a penalty score for syndicated publishers. The lesser the traffic converts for that publisher, the higher the publisher's penalty score, and the more the discount offered to all advertisers for clicks on their ads when shown on that publisher's site, and thus the less the money paid out to that publisher.

3. RELATED WORK

Ad networks and click-spam. Little is known about how ad networks fight click-spam. Commissioned as part of a lawsuit settlement between advertisers and Google, Tuzhilin in [29] reports on his external audit of Google's click-spam filtering system as of July 2006. The system passively analyzes every ad click from log data. It contains several filters each tuned to catching a very specific attack signature. Viceroi can be implemented as such a filter in an ad network.

Characterizing Click-spam. There have been several studies that characterize the nature of click-spam, elaborating on specific attacks [1,2,20,21] after they have been detected. Viceroi differs from these as it flags malicious publishers, regardless of the attack vectors. There has also been some work on traffic quality provided by purchased traffic [28,32]. A broader measurement study finds that the current generation of click-spam is generated with a wide variety of bot and non-bot mechanisms where users are tricked into clicking on ads [4]. The study [4] uses bluff ads [10], which is an active measurement technique. Viceroi on the other hand is purely passive.

Click-spam detection. Research in click-spam detection has focused almost exclusively on (early generation) bots. Sbotminer [31] detects search engine bots by looking for anomalies in query distribution. Others, such as Sleuth [19] and detectives [18] detect unusual collusion among users' associated with diverse publishers (that may be indicative of bot behavior). PremiumClicks [13], Bluff ads [10] and User-Driven Access Control [25] aim to authenticate user presence (as opposed to automated bots) to mitigate click-spam. Viceroi is a more general approach that proactively targets all forms of click-spam including non-bot mechanisms (like arbitrage, and search-hijacking) as well as sophisticated bots.

Spam and Click-spam. A lot of work has been done to understand the spam ecosystem. [14,17]. While both spam and click-spam are Internet abuses used for profiteering, the economics of spam and click-spam are different. Click-spam through search hijacking requires the spammer to pay 18¢ per install [3] (i.e., $180K for 1M installs in 2011), and nets a fraction of the per-click revenue (typically less than $1) per-user per-day. In contrast email spam costs almost nothing to send to 1M users ($20 to rent [23]), and nets $30 per victim [17] per-campaign. Spam needs a real product being peddled and a market for the same, while click-spam does not. The low-margin many-users nature of click-spam makes the economics fundamentally different from the high-margin few-victims nature of traditional spam.

4. VICEROI DESIGN

We begin first with the insight behind Viceroi, followed by the detailed design.

4.1 Insight

As mentioned, our goal is to design a click-spam filtering approach that does not rely on security through obscurity, and cannot easily be circumvented by click-spammers. Past approaches have looked for anomalies in ad impressions, clicks, conversions, browser signatures, timing analysis, user behavior, etc. Unfortunately, none of these are tamper-proof — malware that has complete control of a computer can fake any of these with ease.

Profit. For click-spam to be economically viable, the click-spammer must turn a profit, i.e., the revenue he collects from each click must (on average) cover his costs for generating that click.

Generally speaking, there is a fixed cost and an incremental cost (per-click) for the click-spammer. Click-spammers renting botnets to generate clicks must pay the botmaster. Click-spammers using cheap human labor to generate clicks (in click-farms) must pay the workers. Click-spammers using arbitrage to generate clicks (described later) must pay for cheap ads on a second ad network to acquire users. Click-spammers laundering clicks from adult sites must pay the adult website to acquire clicks [11]. When the click-spammer has control over the user or user's computer (e.g., click-farm or botnet), the fixed cost for getting that control is high (typically, in the tens of cents [15,22]) but there is little if any incremental cost since the click-spammer can generate as many clicks as needed. When the click-spammer buys individual clicks (e.g., arbitrage, click laundering), there is a per-click incremental-cost (typically, on the order of 1¢ [9]) and little if any fixed costs.

Revenues are incremental, i.e., the click-spammer makes money for each ad click (there is no fixed component). The click-spammer turns a profit if his fixed costs (amortized over all clicks) plus his incremental costs per-click are (on average) lower than his incremental per-click revenue.

Risk. For click-spam to be economically *desirable*, the click-spammer must turn a higher profit than an ethical publisher to offset the risk of the click-spammer getting caught. Since click-spammers can be legally penalized [5], if he were not making higher profits than an ethical publisher, then it would be strictly safer for the click-spammer to make the same profit ethically and not run the risk of legal actions. Potential for higher profits gives an click-spammer the incentive for taking higher risk.

Insight: A click-spammer has higher ROI than ethical publishers. In a sense, this higher ROI justifies the higher risk the click-spammer must carry, regardless of the specific mechanism the click-spammer is using to commit click-spam.

4.2 Intuition

As discussed above, there are only four variables that control the click-spammer's profits: (i) fixed and (ii) incremental costs of generating the click, (iii) the number of clicks the fixed-cost is amortized over, and the (iv) incremental revenue per-click. Of these the click-spammer cannot control his fixed- or incremental- costs since they are set by the underground market for purchasing bots, cheap labor, and clicks. To command higher profits than ethical pub-

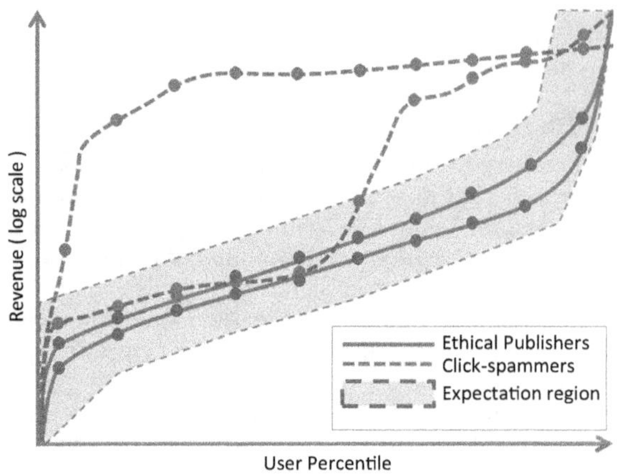

Figure 2: Intuition behind Viceroi. Idealized illustration (for clarity) based on actual ad network log data.

lishers the click-spammer has exactly two options. First, to increase the number of clicks his fixed-costs are amortized over. And second, to increase his incremental revenue by clicking on more lucrative ads. More clicks as well as clicks on more expensive ads (per-user) results in more revenue (per-user) as compared to ethical publishers.

In its simplest form, Viceroi could look for higher than expected revenue per user for a given publisher. Putting this into practice complicates matters slightly.

The first complication arises from the diversity in revenue per user for ethical publishers — there is no single number that can serve as our baseline. Furthermore, the vast difference between publisher sizes (ranging from individual blog sites to multi-billion dollar companies) massively skews the data. Surprisingly, we found from data collected at a large ad network, that the revenue per user for a diverse set of manually-verified ethical publishers (including a search engine, several blog sites, a content portal, an e-commerce website, and a job listings site) all fall within a narrow range on a log scale, while that for many well-known click-spammers lies well outside this range. Viceroi thus uses an expected *log-revenue range* per user (learned dynamically from labeled data) as its baseline for ethical publishers.

The second complication arises from click-spammers using a mix of ethical and unethical ways of generating clicks to disguise their operation. For instance, a click-spammer may acquire some organic traffic and supplement it with bot traffic, in effect lowering his overall revenue per user. To account for this, instead of using a single number, Viceroi compares the *distribution* or revenue per user against a baseline distribution. As illustrated in Figure 2, the expected log-revenue range is expressed as a band around the baseline distribution. The figure is an idealized illustration (for clarity) based on actual log data. In the figure, the solid green lines represent ethical publishers and the shaded region represents the band around this baseline. The verified ethical publishers, we found, agree not only on the log-revenue range, their distributions are fully contained within the band as well. While many click-spammers fall outside the band either entirely or in parts. An ad network can choose to either discount clicks outside the band, or all clicks from a given publisher.

4.3 Detailed Design

Viceroi has two components: i) an offline part that analyzes (past) click logs over multiple timescales to identify click-spammers and regions in their revenue per user distribution that are anomalous, and ii) an online part that identifies whether a given click would fall in the anomalous region (thus allowing that click to be discounted at billing time).

Inputs. Viceroi requires ad click logs that contain the publisher, user, and revenue for each click. In practice we have found good results for as little as two weeks of past click logs. Viceroi also requires a small diverse set of publishers (around 10) to be identified as ethical publishers, which are used to determine the baseline.

Algorithm. Viceroi performs the following steps in order.

1. For each publisher-user pair, Viceroi computes the log of the sum of ad click revenues generated by the given user on the publisher's site.

2. For each publisher, Viceroi sorts the per-user log-revenue sums and retains a vector of N quantile values. Recall that quantile values are sampled at regular intervals from the probability distribution function (PDF) of a random variable. In our evaluation we found $N = 100$ to offer good performance before diminishing returns kicks in.

3. For the baseline, Viceroi computes the point-wise average of the quantile vectors for the given set of ethical publishers.

4. Finally, for each publisher Viceroi computes the point-wise difference between the publisher's quantile vector and the baseline quantile vector. The publishers click-spam score is simply the L1 norm of the difference vector (i.e., sum of the N point-wise differences).

   Given a threshold τ (which characterizes the width of the band around the baseline), if the click-spam score is higher than $N\tau$ the publisher is flagged, and all quantile points where the point-wise difference exceeds τ is recorded for use in the online component.

5. In the online component, whenever an ad is clicked, Viceroi checks if the publisher is flagged and the user clicking the ad falls in the flagged quantile region. If so, the click is discounted.

Automatic Parameter Tuning (τ). To automatically learn the optimal value for τ, the ad network configures a target false-positive rate (e.g., 0.5%) and provides some labeled data that contain both positive and negative click-spam cases. The labeled data may be a combination of manual investigations conducted by the ad network, high-confidence output from existing ad network filters, other sources of ground-truth e.g., Bluff ads [10], etc. Viceroi then performs a parameter sweep for different values of τ and picks the one that maximizes the number of clicks flagged given the hard constraint on false-positives.

5. DEPLOYMENT AND EVALUATION

We partnered with a major ad network to deploy and evaluate our approach. The ad network serves ads to many publishers that cater to both general and niche audiences. The

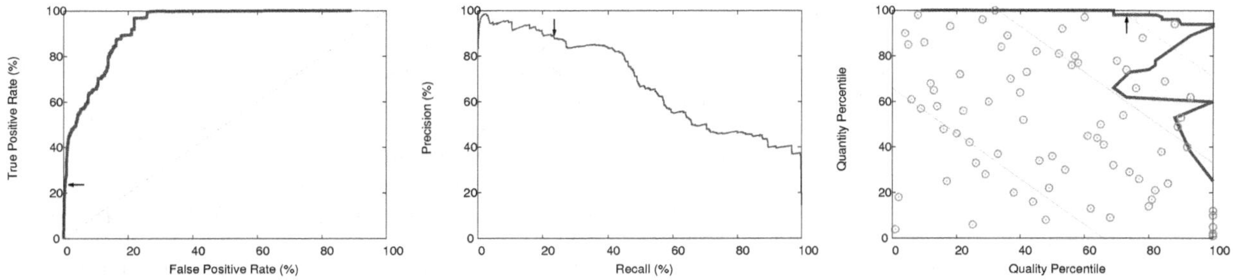

(a) ROC Curve (b) Precision-Recall Curve (c) Ranking Curve

Figure 3: Performance characteristics of Viceroi, viewed through different lenses, as we perform a sweep over threshold values. Arrow marks the threshold picked by out auto-tuning algorithm given a maximum acceptable false-positive rate of 0.5%.

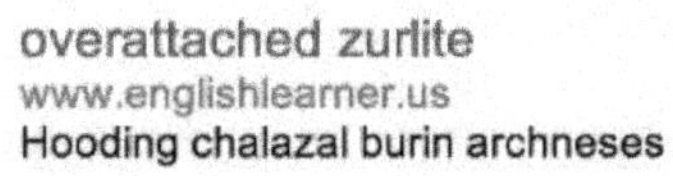

Figure 4: Bluff ad that we ran to augment the ad network's ground-truth heuristic with active measurements.

ad network has two tiers of publishers: premium publishers (bound by contracts and SLAs), and self-serve publishers where anyone can sign-up.

Data. We use the premium publishers as our set of ethical publishers to establish Viceroi's baseline. Viceroi analyzed logs containing millions of ad click records covering a three week period in January 2013. Each ad click record contains the publisher, user, revenue, and whether the ad network's internal ground-truth heuristic considered it click-spam. Overall, the raw dataset covers thousands of unique publishers and millions of unique users.

We augmented the ad network's internal ground-truth heuristic using Bluff ads [10]. Bluff ads are ads with nonsense content (e.g., Figure 4). Few, if any, users are expected to intentionally click on bluff ads. And since bluff ads haven't been adopted yet by any major ad network, click-spam attacks have not yet evolved to avoid them [4]. We ran bluff ads after we found Viceroi flagging many publishers that the ad network's ground-truth heuristic did not flag. After manual investigation (with some help from the ad network), we determined the flagged publishers were indeed engaging in click-spam, and we went about acquiring ground-truth through Bluff ads to fill gaps in the ad network's labeling. Overall our bluff ads had over 4.3M impressions and attracted 7K clicks from 5.6K unique IP addresses and 5.8K unique referring domains.

Lastly, we use internal ad network metrics on the performance of nearly hundred existing filters along two axis: quality and quantity. The lower the false positive score, the higher the quality. And the more clicks flagged, the higher the quantity. We use this to benchmark Viceroi against the industry's state-of-the-art.

Parameters. The only parameter in our approach is the maximum acceptable false positive rate (used for automatically tuning the threshold τ). We perform a full parameter sweep in our evaluation. The ad network indicated it is comfortable with a false-positive rate around 0.5%, i.e., the network is willing to not charge for 0.5% of valid clicks, in effect giving advertisers a 0.5% discount across the board as long as Viceroi demonstrates significantly higher true-positive rates.

Evaluation Metrics. We evaluate our approach against standard metrics for evaluating binary classifiers — true positive rate, false positive rate, precision, and recall. A true positive (TP) is when both Viceroi and ground-truth flags a publisher as click-spam; a true negative (TN) is similarly when both flag it as not click-spam. A false positive (FP) is when Viceroi flags a publisher as click-spam while the ground-truth does not, and vice-versa for false negative (FN). We take the conservative approach and count all misclassifications against Viceroi even though we are aware that the ground-truth data is not perfect.

We additionally rank Viceroi's performance against existing ad network filters.

Evaluation. Figure 3 shows the performance characteristics of our approach through various lenses. Each graph conducts a parameter sweep on the threshold value τ. The arrow in each plot marks the optimal value for τ as selected by our auto-tuning approach given a maximum acceptable false-positive rate of 0.5%.

Figure 3(a) plots the ROC curve for Viceroi as the threshold parameter is varied. Each point represents some threshold value given a target false positive rate[3] (on x-axis); the y-value is the true positive rate[4] at that threshold. The diagonal line represents the ROC curve for a completely random classifier. The ideal operating point is the upper-left corner. As is evident from the figure, Viceroi performs quite well — at 0.5% false positive rate, it achieves 23.6% true positive rate.

Figure 3(b) plots Viceroi's Precision-Recall curve as the threshold parameter is varied. Recall (same as true-positive rate) tracks what fraction of click-spam we catch. Precision[5] tracks the fraction of true positives in everything we catch, i.e., the more false positives we admit for a given recall, the lower the precision. The ideal operating point is anywhere close to the top edge[6]. Our highest precision on the dataset is 98.6% at a recall of 2.5%. At the operating point chosen by our tuning algorithm we have a precision of 88.3% and a recall of 23.6%.

[3]False positive rate $(FPR) = \frac{FP}{FP+TN}$

[4]Recall = True positive rate $(TPR) = \frac{TP}{TP+FN}$

[5]Precision = $\frac{TP}{TP+FP}$

[6]Note Viceroi complements existing ad network filters. A false-negative for Viceroi, while sub-optimal, is acceptable because another filter can still flag it.

Figure 3(c) ranks Viceroi against the existing ad network filters. The x-value of any point is its quality percentile, i.e., the fraction of ad network filters with a higher false positive rate than that approach. The y-value is similarly the quantity percentile, i.e., the fraction of filters catching fewer clicks than that approach. The isolated points plot the ranking of the ad network filters, and the line plots Viceroi's ranking as we vary the threshold. The solid gray diagonal lines divide the plot into three regions: points in the upper-right region are high performance filters that achieve either high quality percentile and reasonable quantity percentile, or vice versa. The middle region has moderate performance filters that achieve reasonable quality and quantity percentiles. And the lower-right region has the remaining low performance filters. The ideal operating point is the top-right corner, but there is no approach that simultaneously has the best rank along both the quality and quantity axis. The filter with the highest quality score has quantity percentile of 12, while the filter with the highest quantity score has a quality percentile of 32.

For most threshold values Viceroi operates in the high performance region of Figure 3(c). At the operating point chosen by our auto-tuning algorithm, Viceroi has a quality percentile of 73 and a quantity percentile of 98. There is only one existing ad network filter in our dataset that performs better than Viceroi (i.e., to the right of the dotted diagonal line passing through the arrow). The filter targets a very specific click-spam attack signature in traffic originating from a particular IP address range.

Overall we find that Viceroi has very good Precision-Recall and ROC characteristics, and at the operating point picked by our auto-tuning algorithm ranks among the best existing ad network filters while being far more general.

6. CASE-STUDIES

Viceroi flagged about several hundred publishers out of the tens of thousands provided. Working with the ad network we manually investigated around hundred websites associated with the publishers we flagged. Based on manual investigations Viceroi appears to have caught at least *six (very) different classes* of click-spam (one of which the ad network had previously not seen an example of), and caught at least three different publishers in *each class*. So far we have manually investigated less than a tenth of the websites Viceroi flagged. We did not encounter any obvious false positives out of the publishers we investigated, though there are several where we do not fully understand their modus operandi yet.

6.1 Conversion-Spam Enhanced Click-Spam

What: Conversion-spam is a technique used by click-spammers to increase the potency of their click-spam attacks as we describe below. Recall from Section 2 that ad conversion events are logged when a user performs some desirable action on the advertiser's site, and smart-pricing penalizes publishers that result in poor conversion rates. Conversion-spam takes advantage of the fact that smart-pricing, which reduces the click-spammer's revenue, relies on the absence of conversion signals, which simply are HTTP requests initiated from the user's browser (Figure 1) that malware can manipulate.

Conversion-spam. This sets the stage for conversion-spam as predicted in [29]. A click-spammer who sends clicks, but not conversions (i.e. buyers), eventually gets smart-priced. If such a click-spammer were to somehow trigger conversion-signals on the advertiser's site, the ad network would be led to believe that the traffic is of good quality and not activate the smart-pricing discount, thus resulting in higher profits for the click-spammer.

Viceroi flagged several websites either confirmed or are highly likely to be engaging in conversion-spam (based on the evidence we present below). In fact, Viceroi found three distinct approaches to committing conversion-spam among the websites we investigated[7]. Two of these approaches had previously not been seen operating in the wild. We have presented our investigation results to multiple ad networks.

Why high ROI: Conversion-spam disproportionately increases the ROI of any given click-spam approach. This is because the fraudulent conversion-signals deactivate the publisher smart-pricing discount for not just the advertiser that suffered from conversion-spam, but rather *for all* advertisers whose ads show up on the publisher's website. Thus, a small amount of conversion-spam can cause a significant boost in ROI for the click-spammer. The ingenuity of the conversion-spam approaches below simply underscores our insight that click-spammer's will maximize their profits in any way they can.

Some that we catch: Proving conversion-spam is hard because ad networks receive essentially a single-bit conversion-signal from the advertiser with absolutely no visibility into what that bit means (i.e., newsletter sign-up or actual sale). Advertisers typically do not have systems sophisticated enough to catch conversion-spam in real-time.

We use a novel technique for attracting conversion-spam. Building upon the Bluff ads approach by Haddadi et al. [10], we design what we call Bluff forms. *Bluff forms* are forms on pages with nonsense content, that ask the user for nonsense information. These forms are set as the landing page for a Bluff ad which is known to concentrate click-spam traffic. Figure 5 shows a screenshot of our bluff form — it asks the user for nonsensical information: mobile pen number, computer eigen name, and eyelid email on a page titled Computer Repair via Mobile English that users reach after clicking the overattached zurlite ad (Figure 4) — in other words, complete nonsense. *734 users submitted our bluff form in 26 days.*

We heavily instrumented our bluff form using JavaScript to gather user activity telemetry and logged all HTTP traffic to the server that hosted the bluff form. We then manually investigated the publishers that sent us these users. We identified three distinct classes of conversion-spam. Viceroi flagged publishers associated with the domains we received bluff form submissions from.

Type 1: Mostly-Automated (malware driven). We received 315 and 107 bluff form submissions from traffic coming from Reeturn.com and AffectSearch.com respectively. Later, in Section 6.4 we find both these publishers use the ZeroAccess malware for click-spam; the ZeroAccess malware family is known to embed a browser control that allows the malware to run JavaScript. The time spent on the bluff form by both sets of traffic is uniformly distributed between exactly 60s–160s; it perfectly fits the line $60 + 100x$ between $x = [0, 1]$ (with correlation coefficient $r = 0.98$ for AffectSearch.com and $r = 0.99$ for Reeturn.com), i.e., the malware waits exactly $60 + \text{random}(100)$ seconds. After this delay the form is

[7]We also detected a fourth approach that we are currently in the process of compiling conclusive evidence about.

Figure 5: Bluff form we used to catch conversion-spam.

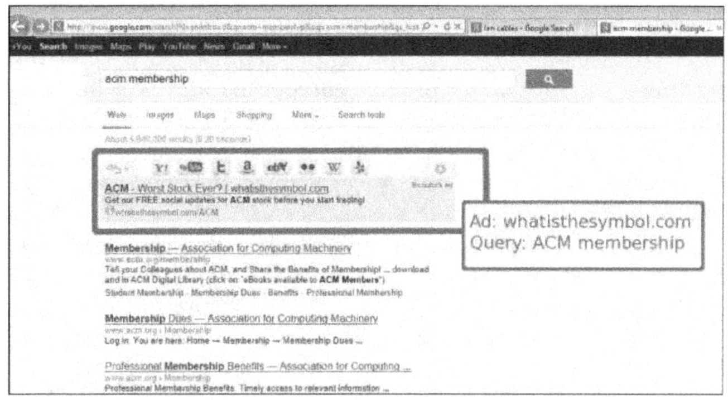

Figure 6: Buzzdock injecting ads into a search result page. The original search results are pushed down and an (irrelevant) ad occupies prime on-screen real-estate even when the search engine chose to not show any ads for the query.

submitted without entering any input. We infected a honeypot with a ZeroAccess binary we found online and observed the bot funneling clicks on ads on both AffectSearch.com and Reeturn.com.

Type 2: Semi-automated (potentially, click farm). We received 10 bluff form submissions from a family of parked domain websites like JJBargains.com. Looking among the domains associated with this publisher that Viceroi flagged, we noticed that only a small set of users appear (repeatedly) to be clicking on ads shown by this publisher, and these users do not appear to click ads for any other publishers in the dataset. Interestingly, some (but not all) users present a malformed user-agent string. All users filled out neatly formatted phone numbers for mobile pen number and a neatly capitalized Caucasian female first names for computer eigen name; in contrast, most other non-empty submissions on the bluff form (which we assume were curious users) filled in a random assortment of characters. Given the small number of users, clicking ads on a single publisher, filling forms in a standardized but human-like manner, and presenting malformed user-agent strings, we suspect this publisher is using a click-farm with custom software that assists human clickers in performing click-spam and conversion-spam.

Type 3: Massively crowd-sourced. We flagged some domains associated with an unnamed publisher. We did not receive Bluff form submissions from this publisher; the ad network informed us that they had terminated their relationship with the unnamed publisher before we conducted our Bluff form experiment. The publisher is a large online gambling site that offers users free virtual chips if they click on ads and "fill any forms" on the landing page.

Remedy. Bluff forms are relatively easy to avoid (once click-spammers wise up to them) and thus are of use only in the short-term and at small scales to smoke out some instances of conversion-spam. The fundamental problem stoking conversion-spam, however, is its connection to smart-pricing that creates an economic incentive for conversion-spam. We believe the best way to root out conversion-spam is for the smart-pricing algorithm to consider only conversion signals that require the user to actually make a non-trivial purchase on the advertiser site (similar to the proposal in [13]) since it would create an economic burden for the click-spammer. Coordinating such a scheme across advertisers is, however, likely to be challenging.

6.2 Ad Injection

What: Normally the publisher website controls where, how many, and what ads are shown on that website by inserting iframes or using JavaScript. An ad injector is a party unaffiliated with the publisher website that modifies the website as seen by the user by either inserting ads where there were none, or by replacing the ads added by the publisher with ads the ad injector wants to instead show. These modifications can be done from within the user's browser (if the ad injector is a browser plugin), or can be done through in-network elements that perform deep-packet-inspection. To the ad network, an ad injector appears as simply another publisher. Any clicks on ads injected by the ad injector are accounted towards the ad injector's payout, and the legitimate publisher whose website was modified makes no money from the ad click. Phorm and NebuAd (now defunct) were two for-profit companies that created in-network ad injection middleboxes, deployed by some ISPs, that injected ads into websites belonging to non-profit organizations [12]. While these in-network ad injectors lost the battle (due to the ISPs suffering a PR backlash), the battle seems to now have moved into the users' browsers.

Why click-spam: By showing ads on a publisher site where a user expects some other content he is highly likely to click, ad injectors confuse users (and advertisers end up paying for it). Consider, for instance, a user searching for acm membership with the expectation that either the first search result or the first ad result (chosen by his preferred search engine) will take him to his intended destination. Because of the ad injector Buzzdock, he is presented the search-results page in Figure 6 instead where prime on-screen real-estate — the position of the first search result — now shows an entirely irrelevant ad (even when the original search engine chose to not show any ads for this query). If the user clicks the first blue link, perhaps reflexively, the advertiser must pay for a spam click. Other sites where we've found Buzzdock injecting ads include Amazon and eBay search results (where the ads are formatted to match the site content, but take users away from the site after the users intentionally searched on the shopping site), as well as in search results on Yelp, YouTube, Wikipedia and other high-traffic sites.

Why high ROI: Ad injectors have an anomalously high ROI per user because for the traffic acquisition cost of installing a single browser plugin (25¢ per install [15]) they can inject ads into prime on-screen real-estate *across the entire web*, and collect money from all clicks intentional or not.

Some that we catch: Viceroi flagged traffic from the following ad injectors:

Buzzdock. Browser plugin typically bundled with freeware or adware software found online (e.g., PDF readers); installed by default with the host software[8]; and not removed when the host software is uninstalled. Ads are formatted to match the look-and-feel of the site into which ads are injected. *Wajam and B00kmarks* are two others that follow identical business model as Buzzdock.

Remedy. In the short-term, ad networks for whom these ad injectors are publishers can filter their clicks (and cut off their revenue) if the ad injectors are in violation of ad network policy. For ad networks where ad injectors are compliant with policy, PR pressure or advertiser outrage may help convince these ad networks to change policy (as happened with ISPs and in-network ad injection). In the long-term, legal precedent may create a strong disincentive for business models that deprive legitimate publishers of advertising revenue. Towards this end Facebook is currently litigating against Sambreel Holdings, the company behind Buzzdock and PageRage, the latter being an ad injector that injected ads into the Facebook site.

6.3 Search Hijacking

What: Search hijacking refers to some party unexpectedly redirecting the user's search queries away from their preferred search engine to a page full of ads formatted to look like search results. The search hijacker earns revenue from each ad click. The hijacking may be performed through in-network elements (e.g., ISP DNS servers), in-browser elements (e.g., plugins and toolbars), or deceiving or confusing the user into changing their browser search settings.

Why click-spam: Search hijacking hijacks search queries regardless of whether the search query is navigational (i.e., queries for a specific site, e.g., youtube), informational (i.e., broad queries with multiple potential intents, e.g., bay area), or transactional (i.e., queries with commercial intent, e.g., san francisco hotel). Navigational and informational queries (estimated to be 75% [26] of search queries) are hard to monetize. Advertisers rely on the search engine to *not show* their ads for such queries, and reputed search engine use the opportunity to present a more pleasing user experience by not showing ads for these queries. Search hijackers, on the other hand, bombard the user with ads for these queries and make advertisers pay for the resulting clicks. That said, this is a gray-area since the user (presumably) read the ad before deciding to click on it (or so search hijackers argue).

In practice, search hijackers make the situation significantly less gray by explicitly increasing the likelihood that the user will unintentionally click on ads. Not only are the ads typically shown on a white background mimicking organic search results (while the convention is to use shaded backgrounds for ads), accidental clicks *anywhere in vast areas of white-space* (see Figure 7) result in an ad click.

[8]Ad injectors typically argue that users consented to installing it, however, an overwhelming fraction of users with ad injectors are either entirely unaware of them or unaware of what they do. [7]

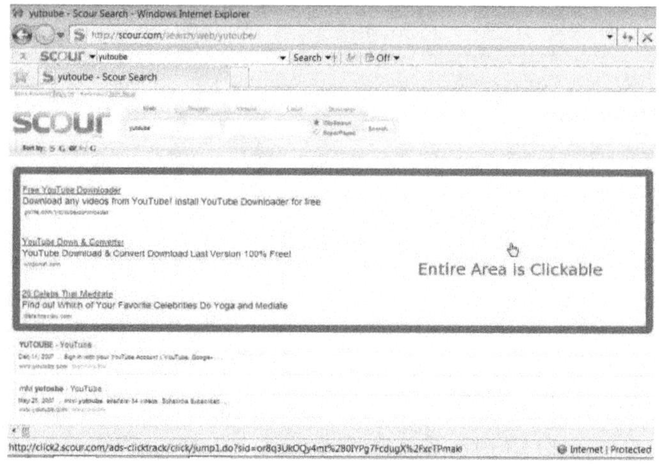

Figure 7: Search hijacking by the Scour toolbar. Ads (indistinguishable from search results) are shown for queries including navigational and informational queries. Accidental clicks on white-space results in an ad click. For query yutoube, the first link (an ad) goes to a spyware download.

Why high ROI: Search hijackers get as much traffic as a legitimate search engine would, but where a legitimate search engine have far more organic search clicks than ad clicks, search hijackers extract predominantly ad clicks from that traffic. Thus for the cost of acquiring a single user, search hijackers reap orders of magnitude more ad clicks than a legitimate search engine.

Some that we catch: Viceroi flagged traffic from three different classes of search hijacking, and multiple publishers in each class:

Type 1: In-network hijacking (of DNS NX records). Viceroi flagged traffic from at least two large US ISPs (RoadRunner by Time Warner Cable, and Cox Communication) where the DNS servers operated by the ISPs appear to hijack DNS NX responses (i.e., for non-existent domain names) and redirects the browser to a search hijack page with the non-existent domain as the search query. These queries are, by definition, navigational queries. The results page is full of (irrelevant) ads even when the query is an obvious typo for a specific site.

Type 2: In-browser hijacking (via toolbars). Viceroi flagged traffic from a number of toolbars that hijack search queries entered in the browser's search box or address bar. These include SmartAddressbar, BenefitBar, CertifiedToolbar, SearchNut and many others. They are installed stealthily (bundled with freeware) and hard to remove. The hijacked search results could easily be mistaken for a Google search results page at first glance, with upwards of ten ads and few, if any, actual search results.

SearchNut is unique in that it combines the DNS NX behavior above with in-browser hijacking. If the domain does not exist, the toolbar intercepts the NX (in the browser) and redirects the browser to a page laden with ads.

Type 3: Default search hijacking. Viceroi flagged traffic from some sites that present a popup, which if the user clicks, sets the site as the default search engine for the user. This includes Scour, Efacts, and ClickShield. These sites also offer to change the user's homepage to their search engines.

Remedy. Legitimate competition in web search is good. However, these "search engines" appear to exist for the sole purpose of showing ads and not for innovating in web search (indeed some don't even show organic results). Any action a large search ad network might take against them would likely be construed an act of stifling competition. Advertisers (the parties hurt most by having their ads be shown for navigational and informational queries) are in a better position to fix the problem. One approach may be for advertisers to demand the ability to opt-out from having their ads being shown by search hijackers.

6.4 Malware, Arbitrage, and Parked Domains

Lastly, Viceroi caught three additional classes of click-spam driven by malware, arbitrage, and parked domains. These three classes of click-spam were previously mentioned in [4] where the authors used ad-hoc techniques to find an example of each. Viceroi not only detected these three classes in a general manner, it flagged traffic from at least three separate instances of each of these three classes.

Malware. It is well-known that some click-spammers use infected hosts to click on ads on their site. These click-spammers have a high ROI because botnets are practically a commodity. The authors discuss the super stealthy TDL4 botnet in [4]. We flagged traffic coming not only from a TDL4 botnet, but also from a second botnet called ZeroAccess. We infected a VM with a ZeroAccess malware binary and found it to be far more aggressive than TDL4 in that ZeroAccess performed many clicks a day as compared to TDL4's stealthy one-click-per-day. ZeroAccess very deliberately striped its clicks across a large number of big and small ad network, and across many publisher websites. We suspect where TDL4 achieves stealthiness in the time domain, ZeroAccess does the same by spreading the load. ZeroAccess, which is newer than TDL4, apparently reuses many TDL4 components [30].

Viceroi flagged clicks from many of the publisher websites that we noticed our ZeroAccess bot clicking on. This includes, as mentioned, AffectSearch and Reeturn which have a 36.11% overlap in users (strongly suggesting that they use the same botnet). Recall that Viceroi is based purely on ROI distributions and is entirely oblivious to user overlap; this overlap thus represents additional validation that Viceroi is effective. Other websites that Viceroi flagged that have high overlap with AffectSearch include BuscarLatam[9] and FreeSearchBuddy (78.87% and 40% overlap respectively).

Observe that botnets are becoming a commodity service as we find large "service providers" catering to a broad customer base. This is bound to drive (bot) traffic acquisition cost down still further, increasing click-spammer profits. In the next section we simulate some straw-man scenarios involving massive botnets and whether our approach can still catch them.

Arbitrage. Some click-spammers acquire (cheap) traffic by running ads for low popularity keywords on one ad network, and then showing clicking users (more expensive) ads from a different ad network [4]. These click-spammers manage a high ROI by buying low-cost traffic and selling high-payout ads. Ad networks penalize publisher websites that show too many ads on the landing page. This penalty is manifested as a higher cost-per-click for the advertiser

[9]A Spanish language search engine that initially frustrated our investigation attempts due to the language-barrier.

Figure 8: Arbitrage by starprices.co.uk. Original page has no ads. User sees ads in prime screen real estate when coming in from ads, along with attractive green buttons.

(in this case, higher traffic acquisition cost for the click-spammer). The click-spammers get around this penalty by cloaking their landing page — when the ad network's crawler or review teams visit the page the click-spammer shows a page without ads, but when a user clicks their ads the page now show (almost exclusively) just ads. Viceroi flagged clicks from the starprices.co.uk family of websites (Figure 8), and savingcentral.co.uk family of websites, which we confirmed to be arbitrage.

Parked Domains. Lastly, parked domain hosting services have high ROI because they have minimal traffic acquisition costs — domains are registered by someone else before they are parked with the provider, the domains receive traffic from users mis-typing (or clicking on links elsewhere on the web to now-defunct domains), and the provider can serve dynamically generated ad laden pages for an arbitrary number of domains from a single server. Viceroi flagged clicks coming from a large number of parked domains hosted on Sedo (also called out by [4]), Skenzo, and Parked.com.

7. DISCUSSION

While Viceroi catches a diverse range of existing attacks, a natural next question is how click-spam may evolve. Given the insight in Section 4 that click-spammers must have higher ROI than ethical publishers, the core Viceroi approach (of comparing publisher revenue per user distributions against a benchmark set of ethical publishers) we believe will still be sound, but the finer details like the sensitivity to the (at-present auto-tuned) τ threshold may increase as click-spammers accept lower revenues so they can play within the margins.

Sybil Publishers. To avoid detection by Viceroi, one way to reduce (apparent) revenue per user is for a publisher to appear as multiple publishers (Sybils) each making a fraction of the original revenue. Indeed such attempts have been reported [4]. If the Sybils share the same bank-account to receive ad network payments, they can be trivially recombined. Acquiring multiple bank-accounts to receive payments is a high-overhead (and high-risk) task [16].

Sybil Users. Another way to reduce (apparent) revenue per user is for the click-spammer to make each user he controls appear as multiple users. Note that this approach does not apply to click-spam mechanisms where the click-spammer does not have the ability to run arbitrary code

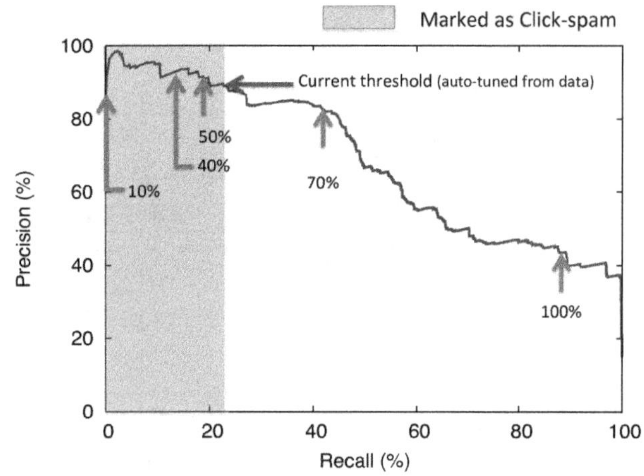

Figure 9: Impact of a click-spammer ethically acquiring traffic. Viceroi catches the click-spammer as long as more than half the traffic is click-spam.

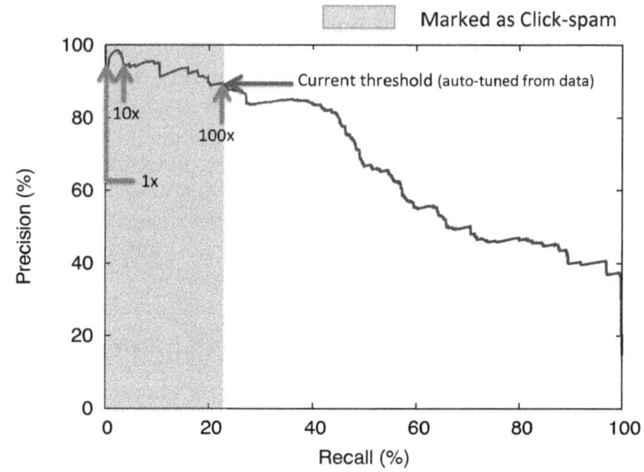

Figure 10: Impact of click-spammer growing botnet size. Viceroi continues to catch the click-spammer up to two orders of magnitude increase in botnet size.

from the user's device (e.g., arbitrage, parked domains, and in-network search hijacking). Even when the click-spammer can run arbitrary code, whether he can successfully inflate the user count depends on how the ad network counts users. Certain user identifiers like IP addresses are hard to fake[10].

Collusion. One way to play within the margins is for the click-spammer to collude with an ethical publisher. The idea is for the click-spammer to add ethically-acquired cover traffic to avoid detection. We simulate such an arrangement by pairing a click-spammer from our dataset with a randomly chosen ethical publisher from the dataset with roughly the same number of users. We perform a parameter sweep where the click-spammer replaces $x\%$ of his users with users acquires from the (now no-longer) ethical publisher with x ranging from 0% to 100%. At $x = 0$ the simulated publisher is identical to the original click-spammer and Viceroi flags it. At $x = 100$ the simulated publisher is identical to the original ethical publisher, and Viceroi doesn't flag it. We are interesting in learning at what point the transition occurs.

Figure 9 shows the position of the simulated publisher relative to the auto-tuned value of τ — positions to the left of τ are flagged by Viceroi as click-spam, and positions to the right of τ are not. We find that as the simulated publisher gradually adds more ethically acquired users, his position drifts closer to the τ threshold, falling right on the boundary when the simulated publisher has a roughly 50-50 split between ethical clicks and click-spam. As the fraction of ethical clicks starts dominating, Viceroi stops flagging the publisher.

We believe this behavior is desirable for the ad network since it creates a positive incentive for click-spammers to reform their ways. Where a click-spammer would make no revenue from click-spam if he were to operate in the shaded region, if he were to grow his users in line with how an ethical publisher acquires users, he would exit the shaded region and start making money (ethically). Over time the threshold may be moved farther to the right to further incent good behavior.

Brute Force. Another way to play within the margins is for the click-spammer to dramatically increase the size of the botnet while making the bots click less. This has the overall effect of increasing fixed-costs while holding revenue constant, in essence decreasing the revenue per user, which is necessary for the click-spammer to exit the shaded region in Figure 2 to avoid getting flagged. To determine how much larger a botnet the click-spammer needs, we simulate botnets up to 2 orders of magnitude larger than click-spammers flagged by Viceroi. We are interested in learning how much head-room is present in Viceroi's current choice of threshold τ.

Figure 10 shows the position of the simulated click-spammer relative to the auto-tuned value of τ. The click-spammer's current botnet size (labeled as 1x) is comfortably in the region flagged by Viceroi. As we increase it by an order of magnitude, the simulated click-spammer moves closer to the τ thresholds. With two orders of magnitude larger a botnet, the click-spammer is on the borderline. Beyond this Viceroi's current choice of τ does not flag the spammer. Note that in the process the click-spammer's fixed-costs increases commensurately by two orders of magnitude while holding revenue constant; i.e., the click-spammer's profits drop up to by 99% in the process. We cannot answer, however, whether click-spam through botnets will remain economically viable even after a two orders of magnitude drop in profits. Nevertheless, we believe that the learned threshold τ has sufficient head-room when dealing with significantly larger botnets than today.

8. SUMMARY

In this paper we present Viceroi, a general approach to catching click-spam. It is designed around the invariant that click-spam is a business (for click-spammers) that needs to deliver high ROI to offset the risk of getting caught. We evaluate our approach on a large real-world ad-network dataset and find six different classes of click-spam linked to conversion fraud, ad injection, search hijacking, malware, arbitrage, and parked domains. We additionally find evidence

[10]Note IP spoofing is not an option since all communication between the user device and the ad network goes over HTTP, which requires the user device to be able to receive and respond to inbound TCP packets from the ad network.

of many sub-classes of these types including automated and semi-automated conversion fraud, hijacking through DNS interception, and find multiple publishers benefiting from each of these models. The Viceroi approach flags click-spam through all these mechanisms without any tuning knobs, has good performance on ROC and precision-recall curves, and is resilient against click-spammers using larger botnets over time. Furthermore, our approach is ranked among the best existing filters deployed by the ad-network today while being far more general. We additionally present the novel bluff form technique for catching conversion fraud.

Acknowledgements

We'd like to thank the anonymous reviewers and our shepherd, Vyas Sekar for their comments. We'd also like to acknowledge Geoff Voelker for his feedback on the paper. The paper is much improved because of their inputs and suggestions. Additionally, we are greatly indebted to Jigar Mody, Dennis Minium, Shiva Nagabhushanswamy, Tommy Blizard and Nikola Livic, without whose help and inputs, this work would not have been possible.

9. REFERENCES

[1] ALRWAIS, S. A., GERBER, A., DUNN, C. W., SPATSCHECK, O., GUPTA, M., AND OSTERWEIL, E. Dissecting Ghost Clicks: Ad Fraud Via Misdirected Human Clicks. In *Proceedings of the 28th Annual Computer Security Applications Conference (ACSAC)* (Orlando, FL, 2012), pp. 21–30.

[2] BLIZARD, T., AND LIVIC, N. Click-fraud monetizing malware: A survey and case study. In *Proceedings of the 7th International Conference on Malicious and Unwanted Software (MALWARE)* (Fajardo, PR, Oct. 2012), pp. 67–72.

[3] CABALLERO, J., GRIER, C., KREIBICH, C., AND PAXSON, V. Measuring Pay-per-Install: The Commoditization of Malware Distribution. In *Proceedings of the 20th USENIX Security Symposium* (San Francisco, CA, Aug. 2011).

[4] DAVE, V., GUHA, S., AND ZHANG, Y. Measuring and Fingerprinting Click-Spam in Ad Networks. In *Proceedings of the Annual Conference of the ACM Special Interest Group on Data Communication (SIGCOMM)* (Helsinki, Finland, Aug. 2012), pp. 175–186.

[5] FBI. Operation Ghost Click: International Cyber Ring That Infected Millions of Computers Dismantled. *Federal Bureau of Investigation Press Releases* (Sept. 2011). http://1.usa.gov/12c8Vhr.

[6] GOOGLE INC. About smart pricing. *AdWords Help* (Apr. 2013). http://bit.ly/XObpxY.

[7] GOOGLE INC. buzzdock. *Google Search* (May 2013). http://bit.ly/17MoGPq.

[8] GOOGLE INC. How Google uses conversion data. *AdWords Help* (Mar. 2013). http://bit.ly/YJHUnF.

[9] GOOGLE INC. Payment Options and Minimum Payment Amounts. *Google AdWords* (May 2013). http://bit.ly/XZhRmH.

[10] HADDADI, H. Fighting Online Click-Fraud Using Bluff Ads. *Computer Communication Review (CCR) 40*, 2 (Apr. 2010), 21–25.

[11] IPEIROTIS, P. Uncovering an advertising fraud scheme. Or "the Internet is for porn". *Blog: A Computer Scientist in a Business School* (Mar. 2011). http://bit.ly/LqYyTs.

[12] JESDANUN, A. Ad Targeting Based on ISP Tracking Now in Doubt. *Associated Press* (Sept. 2008).

[13] JUELS, A., STAMM, S., AND JAKOBSSON, M. Combating Click Fraud via Premium Clicks. In *Proceedings of the 16th USENIX Security Symposium* (Boston, MA, Aug. 2007), pp. 1–10.

[14] KANICH, C., KREIBICH, C., LEVCHENKO, K., ENRIGHT, B., VOELKER, G. M., PAXSON, V., AND SAVAGE, S. Spamalytics: An Empirical Analysis of Spam Marketing Conversion. In *Proceedings of the 15th ACM Conference on Computer and Communications Security (CCS)* (Alexandria, VA, Oct. 2008), pp. 3–14.

[15] LATTIN, P. Cost Per Download or Cost Per Install Marketing. *Performance Marketing Insider* (Sept. 2011). http://bit.ly/Xdq85I.

[16] LEVCHENKO, K., PITSILLIDIS, A., CHACHRA, N., ENRIGHT, B., FÉLEGYHÁZI, M., GRIER, C., HALVORSON, T., KANICH, C., KREIBICH, C., LIU, H., MCCOY, D., WEAVER, N., PAXSON, V., VOELKER, G. M., AND SAVAGE, S. Click Trajectories: End-to-End Analysis of the Spam Value Chain. In *Proceedings of the 32nd IEEE Symposium on Security and Privacy (Oakland)* (Oakland, CA, May 2011), pp. 431–446.

[17] MCCOY, D., PITSILLIDIS, A., JORDAN, G., WEAVER, N., KREIBICH, C., KREBS, B., VOELKER, G. M., SAVAGE, S., AND LEVCHENKO, K. PharmaLeaks: Understanding the Business of Online Pharmaceutical Affiliate Programs. In *Proceedings of the 21st USENIX Security Symposium* (Bellevue, WA, Aug. 2012).

[18] METWALLY, A., AGRAWAL, D., AND EL ABBADI, A. DETECTIVES: DETEcting Coalition hiT Inflation attacks In adVertIsing nEtworks Streams. In *Proceedings of the 16th International World Wide Web Conference (WWW)* (Banff, Canada, May 2007), pp. 241–250.

[19] METWALLY, A., EMEKÇI, F., AGRAWAL, D., AND EL ABBADI, A. SLEUTH: Single-pubLisher attack dEtection Using correlaTion Hunting. *Proceedings of the VLDB Endowment (PVLDB) 1*, 2 (Aug. 2008), 1217–1228.

[20] MILLER, B., PEARCE, P., GRIER, C., KREIBICH, C., AND PAXSON, V. What's Clicking What? Techniques and Innovations of Today's Clickbots. In *Proceedings of the Conference on Detection of Intrusions and Malware & Vulnerability Assessment (DIMVA)* (Amsterdam, Netherlands, July 2011), pp. 164–183.

[21] MOORE, T., LEONTIADIS, N., AND CHRISTIN, N. Fashion Crimes: Trending-Term Exploitation on the Web. In *Proceedings of the 18th ACM Conference on Computer and Communications Security (CCS)* (Chicago, IL, Oct. 2011), pp. 455–466.

[22] OLLMANN, G. Want to rent an 80-120k DDoS Botnet? *Blog: Damballa* (Aug. 2009). http://bit.ly/W9Hh2x.

[23] PANDALABS. Panda Labs Security Report. *Panda Security Press Center* (Apr. 2011). http://bit.ly/150bmHw.

[24] PARKER, P. IAB & PwC: Search Still Tops Online Ad Revenues, And Share Grew In 2011. *Blog: Search Engine Land* (Apr. 2012). http://selnd.com/12WlgoH.

[25] ROESNER, F., KOHNO, T., MOSHCHUK, A., PARNO, B., WANG, H. J., AND COWAN, C. User-Driven Access Control: Rethinking Permission Granting in Modern Operating Systems. In *Proceedings of the 33rd IEEE Symposium on Security and Privacy (Oakland)* (San Francisco, CA, May 2012), pp. 224–238.

[26] ROSE, D. E., AND LEVINSON, D. Understanding User Goals in Web Search. In *Proceedings of the 13th International World Wide Web Conference (WWW)* (New York, NY, May 2004), pp. 13–19.

[27] SINCLAIR, L. Click fraud rampant in online ads, says Bing. *The Australian* (May 2011). http://bit.ly/LqYval.

[28] SPRINGBORN, K., AND BARFORD, P. Impression Fraud in Online Advertising via Pay-Per-View Networks. In *Proceedings of the 22nd USENIX Security Symposium* (Washington, DC, Aug. 2013).

[29] TUZHILIN, A. The Lane's Gift v. Google Report. *Google Official Blog* (July 2006). http://bit.ly/13ABxSZ.

[30] WYKE, J. Sophos Technical Paper: ZeroAccess Botnet – Mining and Fraud for Massive Financial Gain. *Sophos Labs* (Sept. 2012). http://bit.ly/12ftRai.

[31] YU, F., XIE, Y., AND KE, Q. SBotMiner: large scale search bot detection. In *Proceedings of the ACM International Conference on Web Search and Data Mining (WSDM)* (New York City, NY, Feb. 2010), pp. 421–430.

[32] ZHANG, Q., RISTENPART, T., SAVAGE, S., AND VOELKER, G. M. Got Traffic? An Evaluation of Click Traffic Providers. In *Proceedings of Joint WICOW/AIRWeb Workshop on Web Quality* (Hyderabad, India, Mar. 2011), pp. 19–26.

mXSS Attacks: Attacking well-secured Web-Applications by using innerHTML Mutations

Mario Heiderich
Horst Goertz Institute for IT Security
Ruhr-University Bochum, Germany
mario.heiderich@rub.de

Jörg Schwenk
Horst Goertz Institute for IT Security
Ruhr-University Bochum, Germany
joerg.schwenk@rub.de

Tilman Frosch
Horst Goertz Institute for IT Security
Ruhr-University Bochum, Germany
tilman.frosch@rub.de

Jonas Magazinius
Chalmers University of Technology, Sweden
jonas.magazinius@chalmers.se

Edward Z. Yang
Stanford University, USA
ezyang@stanford.edu

ABSTRACT

Back in 2007, Hasegawa discovered a novel Cross-Site Scripting (XSS) vector based on the mistreatment of the backtick character in a single browser implementation. This initially looked like an implementation error that could easily be fixed. Instead, as this paper shows, it was the first example of a new class of XSS vectors, the class of *mutation-based XSS (mXSS)* vectors, which may occur in `innerHTML` and related properties. mXSS affects all three major browser families: IE, Firefox, and Chrome.

We were able to place stored mXSS vectors in high-profile applications like Yahoo! Mail, Rediff Mail, OpenExchange, Zimbra, Roundcube, and several commercial products. mXSS vectors bypassed widely deployed server-side XSS protection techniques (like HTML Purifier, kses, htmlLawed, Blueprint and Google Caja), client-side filters (XSS Auditor, IE XSS Filter), Web Application Firewall (WAF) systems, as well as Intrusion Detection and Intrusion Prevention Systems (IDS/IPS). We describe a scenario in which seemingly immune entities are being rendered prone to an attack based on the behavior of an involved party, in our case the browser. Moreover, it proves very difficult to mitigate these attacks: In browser implementations, mXSS is closely related to performance enhancements applied to the HTML code before rendering; in server side filters, strict filter rules would break many web applications since the mXSS vectors presented in this paper are harmless when sent to the browser.

This paper introduces and discusses a set of seven different subclasses of mXSS attacks, among which only one was previously known. The work evaluates the attack surface, showcases examples of vulnerable high-profile applications, and provides a set of practicable and low-overhead solutions to defend against these kinds of attacks.

CCS'13, November 4–8, 2013, Berlin, Germany.

http://dx.doi.org/10.1145/2508859.2516723.

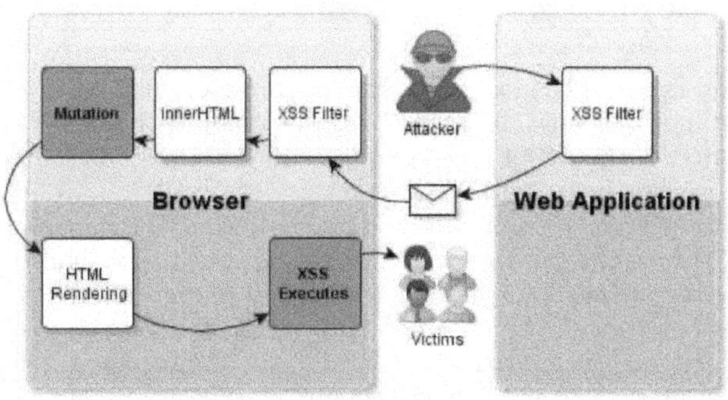

Figure 1: Information flow in an mXSS attack.

Categories and Subject Descriptors

K.6.5 [**Security and Protection**]: Unauthorized access

General Terms

Security

Keywords

Cross-Site-Scripting (XSS); Web Security; Browser Security; InnerHTML; mutation-based XSS (mXSS)

1. INTRODUCTION

Mutation-based Cross-Site-Scripting (mXSS).

Server- and client-side XSS filters share the assumption that their HTML output and the browser-rendered HTML content are mostly identical. In this paper, we show how this premise is *false* for important classes of web applications that use the `innerHTML` property to process user-contributed content. Instead, this very content is *mutated* by the browser, such that a harmless string that passes nearly all of the deployed XSS filters is subsequently transformed into an active XSS attack vector by the browser layout engine itself.

The information flow of an mXSS attack is shown in Figure 1: The attacker carefully prepares an HTML or XML formatted string and injects it into a web application. This string will be filtered or even rewritten in a server-side XSS

Description	Section
Backtick Characters breaking Attribute Delimiter Syntax	3.1
XML Namespaces in Unknown Elements causing Structural Mutation	3.2
Backslashes in CSS Escapes causing String-Boundary Violation	3.3
Misfit Characters in Entity Representation breaking CSS Strings	3.4
CSS Escapes in Property Names violating entire HTML Structure	3.5
Entity-Mutation in non-HTML Documents	3.6
Entity-Mutation in non-HTML context of HTML documents	3.7

Table 1: Overview on the mXSS vectors discussed in this paper

filter, and will then be passed to the browser. If the browser contains a client-side XSS filter, the string will be checked again. At this point, the string is still harmless and cannot be used to execute an XSS attack.

However, as soon as this string is inserted into the brower's DOM by using the `innerHTML` property, the browser will *mutate* the string. This mutation is highly unpredictable since it is not part of the specified `innerHTML` handling, but is a proprietary optimization of HTML code implemented differently in each of the major browser families. The mutated string now contains a valid XSS vector, and the attack will be executed on rendering of the new DOM element. Both server- and client side filters were unable to detect this attack because the string scanned in these filters did not contain any executable code.

Mutation-based XSS (mXSS) makes an impact on all three major browser families (IE, Firefox, Chrome). Table 1 gives an overview on the mXSS subclasses discovered so far, and points to their detailed description. A web application is vulnerable if it inserts user-contributed input with the help of `innerHTML` or related properties into the DOM of the browser. It is difficult to statistically evaluate the number of websites affected by the seven attack vectors covered in this paper, since automated testing fails to reliably detect all these attack prerequisites: If `innerHTML` is only used to insert trusted code from the web application itself into the DOM, it is not vulnerable. However, it can be stated that amongst the 10.000 most popular web pages, roughly one third uses the `innerHTML` property, and about 65% use JavaScript libraries like jQuery [7], who abet mXSS attacks by using the *innerHTML* property instead of the corresponding DOM methods.

However, it is possible to single out a large class of vulnerable applications (Webmailers) and name high-profile state-of-the-art XSS protection techniques that can be circumvented with mXSS. Thus the alarm we want to raise with this paper is that an important class of web applications is affected, and that nealy all XSS mitigation techniques fail.

Webmail Clients.

Webmail constitutes a class of web applications particularly affected by mutation-based XSS: nearly all of them (including e.g. Microsoft Hotmail, Yahoo! Mail, Rediff Mail, OpenExchange, Roundcube and other tools and providers) were vulnerable to the vectors described in this paper. These applications use the `innerHTML` property to display user-generated HTML email content. Before doing so, the content is thoroughly filtered by server-side anti-XSS libraries in recognition of the dangers of a stored XSS attack. The vectors described in this paper will pass through the filter because the HTML string contained in the email body does not form a valid XSS vector – but would require only a single *innerHTML* access to be turned into an attack by the browser itself.

Here the attacker may submit the attack vector within the HTML-formatted body of an email. Most webmail clients do not use *innerHTML* to display this email in the browser, but a simple click on the "Reply" button may trigger the attack: to attach the contents of the mail body to the reply being edited in the webmail client, mostly *innerHTML* access is used.

HTML Sanitizers.

We analysed a large variety of HTML sanitizers such as HTML Purifier, htmLawed, OWASP AntiSamy, jSoup, kses and various commercial providers. At the time of testing, all of them were (and many of them still are) vulnerable against mXSS attacks. Although some of the authors reacted with solutions, the major effort was to alert the browser vendors and trigger fixes for the *innerHTML*-transformations. In fact, several of our bug reports have led to subsequent changes in browser behavior. To protect users, we have decided to anonymise names of several formerly affected browsers and applications used as examples in our work.

This paper makes the following contributions:

1. We identify an undocumented but long-existing threat against web applications, which enables an attacker to conduct XSS attacks, even if strong server- and client-side filters are applied. This novel class of attack vectors utilize performance-enhancement peculiarities present in all major browsers, which *mutate* a given HTML string before it is rendered. We propose the term *mXSS* (for Mutation-based XSS) to describe this class of attacks to disambiguate and distinguish them from classic, reflected, persistent and DOM-based XSS attacks.

2. We discuss client- and server-side mitigation mechanisms. In particular, we propose and evaluate an in-browser protection script, entirely composed in JavaScript, which is practical, feasible and has low-overhead. With this script, a web application developer can implement a fix against mXSS attacks without relying on server-side changes or browser updates. The script overwrites the getter methods of the DOM properties we identified as vulnerable and changes the HTML handling into an XML-based processing, thereby effectively mitigating the attacks and stopping the mutation effects[1].

3. We evaluated this attack in three ways: first, we analyzed the attack surface for mXSS and give a rough estimate the number of vulnerable applications on the

[1]In result, one can purposefully choose XML-based processing for security-critical sites and HTML-based processing for performance-critical sites.

Internet; second, we conducted a field study testing commonly used web applications such as Yahoo! Mail and other high profile websites, determining whether they could be subjected to mXSS attacks; third, we have examined common XSS filter software such as AntiSamy, HTML Purifier, Google Caja and Blueprint for mXSS vulnerabilities, subsequently reporting our findings back to the appropriate tool's author(s).

2. PROBLEM DESCRIPTION

In the following sections, we describe the attack vectors which arise from the use of the *innerHTML* property in websites. We will outline the history of findings and recount a realistic attack scenario. The problems we identify leave websites vulnerable against the novel kind of mXSS attacks, even if the utilized filter software fully protects against the dangers of the classic Cross-Site Scripting.

2.1 The innerHTML Property

Originally introduced to browsers by Microsoft with Internet Explorer 4, the property quickly gained popularity among web developers and was adopted by other browsers, despite being non-standard. The use of *innerHTML* and *outerHTML* is supported by each and every one of the commonly used browsers in the present landscape. Consequently, the W3C started a specification draft to unify *innerHTML* rendering behaviors across browser implementations [20].

An HTML element's *innerHTML* property deals with creating HTML content from arbitrarily formatted strings on write access on the one hand, and with serializing HTML DOM nodes into strings on read access on the other. Both directions are relevant in scope of our paper – the read access is necessary to trigger the mutation while the write access will attach the transformed malicious content to the DOM. The W3C working draft document, which is far from completion, describes this process as generation of an ordered set of nodes from a string valued attribute. Due to being attached to a certain *context node*, if this attribute is evaluated, all children of the context node are replaced by the (ordered) node-set generated from the string.

To use *innerHTML*, the DOM interface of `element` is enhanced with an `innerHTML` attribute/property. Setting of this attribute can occur via the *element*.`innerHTML`=*value* syntax, and in this case the attribute will be evaluated immediately. A typical usage example of `innerHTML` is shown in Listing 1: when the HTML document is first rendered, the `<p>` element contains the `"First text"` text node. When the anchor element is clicked, the content of the `<p>` element is replaced by the `"New <b>second</b> text."` HTML formatted string.

Listing 1: Example on `innerHTML` usage

```
<script type="text/javascript">
  var new = "New <b>second<\/b> text.";
  function Change () {
    document.all.myPar.innerHTML = new;
  }
</script>
<p id="myPar">First text.</p>
<a href="javascript:Change()">
  Change text above!
</a>
```

`outerHTML` displays similar behavior with single exception: unlike in the `innerHTML` case, the whole context (not only the *content* of the context node) will be replaced here. The *innerHTML*-access *changes the utilized markup though* for several reasons and in differing ways depending on the user agent. The following code listings show some (non security-related) examples of these performance optimizations:

Listing 2: Examples for internal HTML mutations to save CPU cycles

```
<!-- User Input -->
<s class="">hello&#x20;<b>goodbye</b>

<!-- Browser-transformed Output -->
<S>hello <B>goodbye</B></S>
```

The browser – in this case Internet Explorer 8 – mutates the input string in multiple ways before sending it to the layout engine: the empty *class* is removed, the tag names are set to upper-case, the markup is sanitized and the HTML entities are resolved. These transformations happen in several scenarios:

1. Access to the *innerHTML* or *outerHTML* properties of the affected or parent HTML element nodes;
2. Copy (and subsequent paste) interaction with the HTML data containing the affected nodes;
3. HTML editor access via the *contenteditable* attribute, the *designMode* property or other DOM method calls like *document.execCommand()*;
4. Rendering the document in a print preview container or similar intermediate views. Browsers tend to use the *outerHTML* property of the HTML container or the innerHTML.

For the sake of brevity, we will use the term *innerHTML*-access to refer to some or all of the items from the above list.

2.2 Problem History and Early Findings

In 2006, a non-security related bug report was filed by a user, noting an apparent flaw in the print preview system for HTML documents rendered by a popular web browser. Hasegawa's 2007 analysis [11] of this bug report showed that once the *innerHTML* property of an element's container node in an HTML tree was accessed, the attributes delimited by backticks or containing values starting with backticks were replaced with regular ASCII quote delimiters: the content had *mutated*. Often the regular quotes disappeared, leaving the backtick characters unquoted and therefore vulnerable to injections. As Hasegawa states, an attacker can craft input operational for bypassing XSS detection systems because of its benign nature, yet having a future possibility of getting transformed by the browser into a code that executes arbitrary JavaScript code. An example vector is being discussed in Section 3.1. This behavior constitutes a fundamental basis for our research on the attacks and mitigations documented in this paper.

2.3 Mutation-based Cross-Site Scripting

Certain websites permit their users to submit inactive HTML aimed at visual and structural improvement of the content they wish to present. Typical examples are web-mailers (visualization of HTML-mail content provided by the *sender* of the e-mail) or collaborative editing of complex HTML-based documents (HTML content provided by all editors).

To protect these applications and their users from XSS attacks, website owners tend to call server-side HTML filters like e.g. the HTML Purifier, mentioned in Section 5.1, for assistance. These HTML filters are highly skilled and configurable tool-kits, capable of catching potentially harmful HTML and removing it from benign content. While it has become almost impossible to bypass those filters with regular HTML/Javascript strings, the mXSS problem has yet to be tackled by most libraries. The core issue is as follows: the HTML markup an attacker uses to initiate an mXSS attack is considered harmless and contains no active elements or potentially malicious attributes – the attack vector examples shown in Section 3 demonstrate that.

Only the browser will transform the markup internally (each browser family in a different manner), thereby unfolding the embedded attack vector and executing the malicious code. As previously mentioned, such attacks can be labeled mXSS – XSS attacks that are only successful because the attack vector is *mutated* by the browser, a result of behavioral mishaps introduced by the internal HTML processing of the user agents.

3. EXPLOITS

The following sections describe a set of *innerHTML*-based attacks we discovered during our research on DOM mutation and string transformation. We present the code purposefully appearing as sane and inactive markup before the transformation occurs, while it then becomes an active XSS vector executing the example method `xss()` after that said transformation. This way server- and client-side XSS filters are being elegantly bypassed.

The code shown in Listing 3 provides one basic example of how to activate (Step 2 in the chain of events described in Section 4) each and any of the subsequently following exploits – it simply concatenates an empty string to an existing *innerHTML* property. The exploits can further be triggered by the DOM operations mentioned in Section 2.2. Any *innerHTML*-access mentioned in the following sections signifies a reference to a general usage of the DOM operations framed by this work.

Listing 3: Code-snippet – illustrating the minimal amount of DOM-transaction necessary to cause and trigger mXSS attacks

```
<script>
window.onload = function(){
  document.body.innerHTML += '';
}
</script>
```

We created a test-suite to analyze the *innerHTML* transformations in a systematic way; this tool was later published on a related website dedicated to HTML and HTML5 security implications [2]. The important *innerHTML*-transformations are highlighted in the code examples to follow.

3.1 Backtick Characters breaking Attribute Delimiter Syntax

This DOM string-mutation and the resulting attack technique was first publicly documented in 2007, in connection with the original print-preview bug described in Section 2.2. Meanwhile, the attack can only be used in legacy browsers as their modern counterparts have deployed effective fixes against this problem. Nevertheless, the majority of tested web applications and XSS filter frameworks remain vulnerable against this kind of attack – albeit measurable existence of a legacy browser user-base. The code shown in Listing 4 demonstrates the initial attack vector and the resulting transformation performed by the browser engine during the processing of the *innerHTML* property.

Listing 4: innerHTML-access to an element with backtick attribute values causes JavaScript execution

```
<!-- Attacker Input -->
<img src="test.jpg" alt="``onload=xss()" />

<!-- Browser Output -->
<IMG alt=``onload=xss() src="test.jpg">
```

3.2 XML Namespaces in Unknown Elements causing Structural Mutation

A browser that does not yet support the HTML5 standard is likely to interpret elements such as *article*, *aside*, *menu* and others as *unknown elements*. A developer can decide how an unknown element is to be treated by the browser: A common way to pass these instructions is to use the *xmlns* attribute, thus providing information on which XML namespace the element is supposed to reside on. Once the *xmlns* attribute is being filled with data, the visual effects often do not change when compared to none or empty namespace declarations. However, once the *innerHTML* property of one of the element's container nodes is being accessed, a very unusual behavior can be observed. The browser prefixes the unknown but namespaced element with the XML namespace that in itself contains unquoted input from the *xmlns* attribute. The code shown in Listing 5 demonstrates this case.

Listing 5: innerHTML-access to an unknown element causes mutation and unsolicited JavaScript execution

```
<!-- Attacker Input -->
<article xmlns="urn:img src=x
    onerror=xss()//">123

<!-- Browser Output -->
<img src=x onerror=xss()//:article xmlns="urn:img
    src=x onerror=xss()//">123</img src=x
    onerror=xss()//:article>
```

The result of this structural mutation and the pseudo-namespace allowing white-space is an injection point. It is

[2]innerHTML Test-Suite, `http://html5sec.org/innerhtml`, 2012

through this point that an attacker can simply abuse the fact that an attribute value is being rendered despite its malformed nature, consequently smuggling arbitrary HTML into the DOM and executing JavaScript. This problem was reported and fixed in the modern browsers. A similar issue was discovered and published by Silin [3].

3.3 Backslashes in CSS Escapes causing String-Boundary Violation

To properly escape syntactically relevant characters in CSS property values, the CSS1 and CSS2 specifications propose CSS escapes. These cover the Unicode range and allow to, for instance, use the single-quote character without risk. This is possible even inside a CSS string that is delimited by single quotes. Per specification, the correct usage for CSS escapes inside CSS string values would be: `property: 'v\61 lue'`. The escape sequence is representing the *a* character, based on its position in the ASCII table of characters. Unicode values can be represented by escaping sequences such as *\20AC* for the € glyph, to give one example.

Several modern browsers nevertheless break the security promises indicated by the correct and standards-driven usage of CSS escapes. In particular, it takes place for the *innerHTML* property of a parent element being accessed. We observed a behavior that converted escapes to their canonical representation. The sequence `property: 'val\27ue'` would result in the *innerHTML* representation `PROPERTY: 'val'ue'`. An attacker can abuse this behavior by injecting arbitrary CSS code hidden inside a properly quoted and escaped CSS string. This way HTML filters checking for valid code that observes the standards can be bypassed, as depicted in Listing 6.

Listing 6: innerHTML-access to an element using CSS escapes in CSS strings causes JavaScript execution

```
<!-- Attacker Input -->
<p style="font-family:'ar\27\3bx\3a
    expression\28xss\28\29\29\3bial'"></p>

<!-- Browser Output -->
<P style="FONT-FAMILY: 'ar
    ';x:expression(xss());ial'"></P>
```

Unlike the backtick-based attacks described in Section 3.1, this technique allows recursive mutation. This means that, for example, a double-escaped or double-encoded character will be double-decoded in case that *innerHTML*-access occurs twice. More specifically, the `\5c 5c` escape sequence will be broken down to the `\5c` sequence after first *innerHTML*-access, and consequently decoded to the \ character after the second *innerHTML*-access.

During our attack surface's evaluation, we discovered that some of the tested HTML filters could be bypassed with the use of `&#amp;x5c 5c 5c 5c` or alike sequences. Due to the backslashes' presence allowed in CSS property values, the HTML entity representation combined with the recursive decoding feature had to be employed for code execution and attack payload delivery.

[3]Silin, A., *XSS using "xmlns" attribute in custom tag when copying innerHTML*, `http://html5sec.org/?xmlns#97`, Dec. 2011

The attacks that become possible through this technique range from overlay attacks injecting otherwise unsolicited CSS properties (such as positioning instructions and negative margins), to arbitrary JavaScript execution, font injections (as described by Heiderich et al. [14]), and the DHTML behavior injections for levering XSS and ActiveX-based attacks.

3.4 Misf t Characters in Entity Representation breaking CSS Strings

Combining aforementioned exploit with enabling CSS-escape decoding behavior results in yet another interesting effect observable in several browsers. That is, when both CSS escape and the canonical representation for the double-quote character inside a CSS string are used, the render engine converts them into a single quote, regardless of those two characters seeming unrelated. This means that the `\22`, `"`, `"` and `"` character sequences will be converted to the ' character upon *innerHTML*-access. Based on the fact that both characters have syntactic relevance in CSS, the severity of the problems arising from this behavior is grand. The code example displayed in Listing 7 shows a mutation-based XSS attack example. To sum up and underline once again, it is based on fully valid and inactive HTML and CSS markup that will unfold to active code once the *innerHTML*-access is involved.

Listing 7: innerHTML-access to an element using CSS strings containing misfit HTML entities causes JavaScript execution

```
<!-- Attacker Input -->
<p style="font-family:'ar&quot;;x=
    expression(xss())/*ial'"></p>

<!-- Browser Output -->
<P style="FONT-FAMILY: 'ar';x=expression(
    xss())/*ial'"></P>
```

We can only speculate about the reasons for this surprising behavior. One potential explanation is that in case when the *innerHTML* transformation might lead the `\22`, `"`, `"` and `"` sequences to be converted into the actual double-quote character ("), then – given that the attribute itself is being delimited with double-quotes – an improper handling could not only break the CSS string but even disrupt the syntactic validity of the surrounding HTML. An attacker could abuse that to terminate the attribute with a CSS escape or HTML entity, and, afterwards, inject crimson HTML to cause an XSS attack.

Our tests showed that it is not possible to break the HTML *m*arkup syntax with CSS escapes once used in a CSS string or any other CSS property value. The mutation effects only allow CSS strings to be terminated illegitimately and lead to an introduction of new CSS property-value pairs. Depending on the browser, this may very well lead to an XSS exploit executing arbitrary JavaScript code. Supporting this theory, the attack technique shown in Section 3.5 considers markup integrity but omits CSS string sanity considerations within the transformation algorithm of HTML entities and CSS escapes.

3.5 CSS Escapes in Property Names violating entire HTML Structure

As mentioned in Section 3.4, an attacker cannot abuse mutation-based attacks to break the markup structure of the document containing the style attribute hosting the CSS escapes and entities. Thus far, the CSS escapes and entities were used exclusively in CSS property values and not in the property names. Applying the formerly discussed techniques to CSS property names instead of values forces some browsers into a completely different behavior, as demonstrated in Listing 8.

Listing 8: innerHTML-access to an element with invalid CSS property names causes JavaScript execution

```
<!-- Attacker Input -->
<img style="font-fa\22on-
    load\3dxss\28\29\20mily:'arial'" src="test
    .jpg" />

<!-- Browser Output -->
<IMG style="font-fa"onload=xss() mily:
    'arial'" src="test.jpg">
```

Creating a successful exploit, which is capable of executing arbitrary JavaScript, requires an attacker to first terminate the style attribute by using a CSS escape. Therefore, the injected code would trigger the exploit code while it still follows the CSS syntax rules. Otherwise, the browser would simply remove the property-value pair deemed invalid. This syntax constraint renders several characters useless for creating exploits. White-space characters, colon, equals, curly brackets and the semi colon are among them. To bypass the restriction, the attacker simply needs to escape those characters as well. We illustrate this in Listing 8. By escaping the entire attack payload, the adversary can abuse the mutation feature and deliver arbitrary CSS-escaped HTML code.

Note that the attack only works with the double-quote representation inside double-quoted attributes. Once a website uses single-quotes to delimit attributes, the technique can be no longer applied. The *innerHTML*-access will convert single quotes to double quotes. Then again, the \22 escape sequence can be used to break and terminate the attribute value. The code displayed in Listing 9 showcases this yet again surprising effect.

Listing 9: Example for automatic quote conversion on innerHTML-access

```
<!-- Example Attacker Input -->
<p style='fo\27\22o:bar'>

<!-- Example Browser Output -->
<P style="fo'"o: bar"></P>
```

3.6 Entity-Mutation in non-HTML Documents

Once a document is being rendered in XHTML/XML mode, different rules apply to the handling of character entities, non-wellformed content including unquoted attributes, unclosed tags and elements, invalid elements nesting and other aspects of document structure. A web-server can instruct a browser to render a document in XHTML/XML by setting a matching MIME type via Content-Type HTTP headers; in particular the MIME *text/xhtml*, *text/xml*, *application/xhtml+xml* and *application/xml* types can be employed for this task (more exotic MIME types like *image/svg +xml* and *application/vnd.wap.xhtml+xml* can also be used).

These specific and MIME-type dependent parser behaviors cause several browsers to show anomalies when, for instance, CSS strings in style elements are exercised in combination with (X)HTML entities. Several of these behaviors can be used in the context of mutation-based XSS attacks, as the code example in Listing 10 shows.

Listing 10: innerHTML-access to an element with encoded XHTML in CSS string values causes JavaScript execution

```
<!-- Attacker Input -->
<style>*{font-family:'ar&lt;img
    src=&quot;test.jpg&quot;
    onload=&quot;xss()&quot;/&gt;ial'}</style>

<!-- Browser Output -->
<style>*{font-family:'ar<img src="test.jpg"
    onload="xss()"/>ial'}</style>
```

Here-above, the browser automatically decodes the HTML entities hidden in the CSS string specifying the font family. By doing so, the parser must assume that the CSS string contains actual HTML. While in *text/html* neither a mutation nor any form or parser confusion leading to script execution would occur, in *text/xhtml* and various related MIME type rendering modes, a CSS style element is supposed to be capable of containing other markup elements. Thus, without leaving the context of the style element, the parser decides to equally consider the decoded *img* element hidden in the CSS string, evaluate it and thereby execute the JavaScript connected to the successful activation of the event handler. This problem is unique to the WebKit browser family, although similar issues were spotted in other browser engines. Beware that despite a very small distribution of sites using MIME types such as *text/xhtml*, *text/xml*, *application/x-html+xml* and *application/ xml* (0.0075% in the Alexa Top 1 Million website list), an attacker might abuse MIME sniffing, frame inheritance and other techniques to force a website into the necessary rendering mode, purposefully acting towards a successful exploit execution. The topic of security issues arising from MIME-sniffing has been covered by by Barth et al., Gebre et al. and others [2,3,8].

3.7 Entity-Mutation in non-HTML context of HTML documents

In-line SVG support provided in older browsers could lead to XSS attacks originating in HTML entities that were embedded inside style and similar elements, which are by default evaluated in their canonic form upon the occurrence of *innerHTML*-access. This problem has been reported and mitigated by the affected browser vendors and is listed here to further support our argument. The code example in Listing 11 showcases anatomy of this attack. This vulnerability was present in a popular open-source user agent and has been since fixed successfully, following a bug report.

Listing 11: Misusing HTML entities in inline-SVG CSS-string properties to execute arbitrary JavaScript

```
<!-- Attacker Input -->
<p><svg><style>*{font-family:'
    &lt&sol;style&gt;&ltimg/src=x&Tab;
    onerror=xss()&sol;&sol;'}</style></svg></p
    >

<!-- Browser Output -->
<p><svg><style>*{font-family:'
    </style></svg><img src="x" onerror="xss()"
    />'}</p>
```

3.8 Summary

In order to initiate the mutation, all of the exploits shown here require a single access to the *innerHTML* property of a surrounding container, while except for the attack vector discussed in Section 3.1, all other attacks can be upgraded to allow recursive mutation – making double-, triple- and further multiply-encoded escapes and entities useful in the attack scenario, immediately when multiple *innerHTML*-access to the same element takes place. The attacks were successfully tested against a large range of publicly available web applications and XSS filters – see Section 4.

4. ATTACK SURFACE

The attacks outlined in this paper target the client-side web application components, e.g. JavaScript code, that use the *innerHTML* property to perform dynamic updates to the content of the page. Rich text editors, web email clients, dynamic content management systems and components that pre-load resources constitute the examples of such features. In this section we detail the conditions under which a web application is vulnerable. Additionally, we attempt to estimate the prevalence of these conditions in web pages at present.

The basic conditions for a mutation event to occur are the serialization and deserialization of data. As mentioned in Section 2, mutation in the serialization of the DOM-tree occurs when the *innerHTML* property of a DOM-node is accessed. Subsequently, when the mutated content is parsed back into a DOM-tree, e.g. when assigned to *innerHTML* or written to the document using `document.write`, the mutation is activated.

The instances in Listing 12 are far from being the exclusive methods for a mutation event to occur, but they exemplify vulnerable code patterns. In order for an attacker to exploit such a mutation event, it must take place on the attacker-supplied data. This condition makes it difficult to statistically estimate the number of vulnerable websites, however, the attack surface can be examined through an evaluation of the number of websites using such vulnerable code patterns.

Listing 12: Code snippets – vulnerable code patterns

```
// Native JavaScript / DOM code
a.innerHTML = b.innerHTML;
a.innerHTML += 'additional content';
a.insertAdjacentHTML('beforebegin', b.
    innerHTML);
document.write(a.innerHTML);

// Library code
$(element).html('additional content');
```

4.1 InnerHTML Usage

Since an automated search for *innerHTML* does not determine the exploitability of its usage, it can only serve as an indication for the severity of the problem. To evaluate the prevalence of *innerHTML* usage on the web, we conducted a study of the Alexa top 10,000 most popular web sites. A large fraction of approximately one third of these web sites utilized vulnerable code patterns, like the ones in Listing 12, in their code for updating page content. Major websites like Google, Amazon, EBay and Microsoft could be identified among these. Again, this does not suggest that these web sites can be exploited. We found an overall of 74.5% of the Alexa Top 1000 websites to be using *innerHTML*-assignments. While the usage of *innerHTML* is very common, the circumstances under which it is vulnerable to exploitation are in fact hard to quantify. Note though that almost all applications applied with an editable HTML area are prone to being vulnerable.

Additionally, there are some notable examples of potentially vulnerable code patterns identifiable in multiple and commonly used JavaScript libraries, e.g. jQuery [7] and SWFObject [27]. Indeed, more than 65% of the top 10,000 most popular websites do employ one of these popular libraries (with 48,87% using jQuery), the code of which could be used to trigger actual attacks. Further studies have to be made as to whether or not web applications reliant on any of these libraries are affected, as it largely depends on how the libraries are used. In certain cases, a very specific set of actions needs to be performed if the vulnerable section of the code is to be reached. Regardless, library's inclusion always puts a given website at risk of attacks.

Ultimately, we queried the Google Code Search Engine (GCSE) as well as the Github search tool to determine which libraries and public source files make use of potentially dangerous code patterns. The search query yielded an overall 184,000 positive samples using the GCSE and 1,196,000 positive samples using the Github search tool. While this does not provide us with an absolute number of vulnerable websites, it shows how widely the usage of *innerHTML* is distributed; any of these libraries using vulnerable code patterns in combination with user-generated content is likely to be vulnerable to mXSS attacks.

4.2 Web-Mailers

A class of web applications particularly vulnerable to m-XSS attacks are classic web-mailers – applications that facilitates receiving, reading and managing HTML mails in a browser. In this example, the fact that HTML Rich-Text Editors (RTE) are usually involved, forms the basis for the use of the *innerHTML* property, which is being triggered with almost any interaction with the mail content. This includes composing, replying, spell-checking and other common features of applications of this kind. A special case of attack vector is sending an mXSS string within the body of an HTML-formatted mail. We analyzed commonly used web-mail applications and spotted mXSS vulnerabilities in almost every single one of them, including e.g. Microsoft Hotmail, Yahoo! Mail, Rediff Mail, OpenExchange, Roundcube, and many other products – some of which cannot yet be named for the sake of user protection. The discovery was quickly followed with bug reports sent to the respective vendors, which were acknowledged.

4.3 Server-Side XSS Filters

The class of mXSS attacks poses a major challenge for server-side XSS filters. To completely mitigate these attacks, they would have to *simulate* the mutation effects of the three major browser families in hopes of determining whether a given string may be an mXSS vector. At the same time, they should not filter benign content, in order not to break the web application. The fixes applied to HTML sanitizers, as mentioned in the introduction, are new rules for *known* mutation effects. It can be seen as a challenging task to develop new filtering paradigms that may discover even unknown attack vectors.

5. MITIGATION TECHNIQUES

The following sections will describe a set of mitigation techniques that can be applied by website owners, developers, or even users to protect against the cause and impact of mutation XSS attacks. We provide details on two approaches. The first one is based on a server-side filter, whereas the other focuses on client-side protection and employs an interception method in critical DOM properties access management.

5.1 Server-side mitigation

Avoiding outputting server content otherwise incorrectly converted by the browsers is the most direct mitigation strategy. In specific terms, the flawed content should be replaced with semantically equivalent content which is converted properly. Let us underline that the belief stating that "well-formed HTML is unambiguous" is false: only a browser-dependent subset of well-formed HTML will be preserved across *innerHTML*-access and -transactions.

A comprehensible and uncomplicated policy is to simply disallow any of the special characters for which browsers are known to have trouble with when it comes to a proper conversion. For many HTML attributes and CSS properties this is not a problem, since their set of allowed values already excludes these particular special characters. Unfortunately, in case of free-form content, such a policy may be too stringent. For HTML attributes, we can easily refine our directive by observing that ambiguity only occurs when the browser omits quotes from its serialized representation. Insertion of quotes can be guaranteed by, for example, appending a trailing whitespace to text, a change unlikely to modify the semantics of the original text. Indeed, the W3C specification states that user agents may ignore surrounding whitespace in attributes. A more aggressive transformation would only insert a space when the attribute was to be serialized without quotes, yet contained a backtick. It should be noted that backtick remains the only character which causes Internet Explorer to mis-parse the resulting HTML.

For CSS, refining our policy is more difficult. Due to the improper conversion of escape sequences, we cannot allow any CSS special characters in general, even in their escaped form. For URLs in particular, parentheses and single quotes are valid characters in a URL, but are simultaneously considered special characters in CSS. Fortunately, most major web servers are ready to accept percent encoded versions of these characters as equivalent, so it is sufficient to utilize the common percent-escaping for these characters in URLs instead.

We have implemented these mitigation strategies in HTML Purifier, a popular HTML filtering library [32]; as HTML Purifier does not implement any anomaly detection, the filter was fully vulnerable to these attacks. These fixes were reminiscent of similar security bugs that were tackled in 2010 [31] and subsequent releases in 2011 and 2012. In that case, the set of unambiguous encodings was smaller than that suggested by the specification, so a very delicate fix had to be crafted in result, both fixing the bug and still allowing the same level of expressiveness. Since browser behavior varies to a great degree, a server-side mitigation of this style is solely practical for the handling of a subset of HTML, which would normally be allowed for high-risk user-submitted content. Furthermore, this strategy cannot protect against dynamically generated content, a limitation which will be addressed in the next section. Note that problems such as the backtick-mutation still affect the HTML Purifier as well as Blueprint and Google Caja; they have only just been addressed successfully by the OWASP Java HTML Sanitizer Project [4].

5.2 Client-side mitigation

Browsers implementing ECMA Script 5 and higher offer an interface for another client-side fix. The approach makes use of the developer-granted possibility to overwrite the handlers of *innerHTML* and *outerHTML*-access to intercept the performance optimization and, consequently, the markup mutation process as well. Instead of permitting a browser to employ its own proprietary HTML optimization routines, we utilize the internal XML processor a browser provides via DOM. The technique describing the wrapping and sanitation process has been labeled *TrueHTML*.

The TrueHTML relies on the *XMLSerializer* DOM object provided by all of the user agents tested. The *XMLSerializer* can be used to perform several operations on XML documents and strings. Interestingly, `XMLSerializer.serialize ToString()` will accept an arbitrary DOM structure or node collection and transform it into an XML string. We decided to replace the *innerHTML*-getters with an interceptor to process the accessed contents as if they were actual XML. This has the following benefits:

1. The resulting string output is free from all mutations described and documented in Section 3. The attack surface can therefore be mitigated by a simple replacement of the browsers' *innerHTML*-access logic with our own code. The code has been made available to a selected group of security researches in the field, who have been tasked with ensuring its robustness and reliability.

2. The *XMLSerializer* object is a browser component. Therefore, the performance impact is low compared to other methods of pre-processing or filtering *innerHTML*-data before or after mutations take place. We elaborate on the specifics of the performance impact in the 6 Section.

3. The solution is transparent and does not require additional developer effort, coming down to a single Java-

[4]OWASP Wiki, `https://www.owasp.org/index.php/OWASP_Java_HTML_Sanitizer_Project`, Feb. 2013

Script implementation. No existing JavaScript or DOM code needs to be modified, the script hooks silently into the necessary property accessors and replaces the insecure browser code. At present, the script works on all modern browsers tested (Internet Explorer, Firefox, Opera and Chrome) and can be extended to work on Internet Explorer 6 or earlier versions.

4. The *XMLSerializer* object post-validates potentially invalid code and thereby provides yet another level of sanitation. That means that even insecure or non-well-formed user-input can be filtered and kept free from mutation XSS and similar attack vectors.

5. The TrueHTML approach is generic, transparent and website-agnostic. This means that a user can utilize this script as a core for a protective browser extension, or apply the user-script to globally protect herself against cause and impact of mutation XSS attacks.

6. EVALUATION

This section is dedicated to description of settings and dataset used for evaluating the performance penalty introduced by TrueHTML. We focus on assessing the client-side mitigation approach. While HTMLPurifier has been changed to reflect determination for mitigating this class of attacks, the new features are limited to adding items on the internal list of disallowed character combinations. This does not measurably increase the overhead introduced by HTMLPurifier. Performance takes a central stage as a focus of our query, as the transfer overhead introduced by TrueHTML is exceptionally low. The *http archive*[5] has analysed a set of more than 290,000 URLs and over the course of this project it has been determined that the average transfer size of a single web page is more than 1,200 kilobyte, 52kB of which are taken up by HTML content and 214kB by JavaScript. The prototype of TrueHTML is implemented in only 820 byte of code, which we consider to be a negligible transfer overhead.

6.1 Evaluation Environment

To assess the overhead introduced by TrueHTML in a realistic scenario, we conducted an evaluation based on the Alexa top 10,000 most popular web sites. We crawled these sites with a recursion depth of one. As pointed out in Section 4, approximately one third of these sites make use of innerHTML. In a next step we determine the performance impact of TrueHTML in a web browser by accessing 5,000 URLs randomly chosen from this set. Additionally, we assess the performance of TrueHTML in typical useage scenarios, like displaying an e-mail in a web mailer or accessing popular websites, as well as, investigate the relation between page load time overhead and page size in a controlled environment.

To demonstrate the versatility of the client-side mitigation approach, we used different hardware platforms for the different parts of the evaluation. The Alexa traffic ranking data on virtual machines constituted the grounds for performing this evaluation. Each instance was assigned one core of an Intel Xeon X5650 CPU running at 2.67GHz and had access to 2 GB RAM. The instances ran Ubuntu 12.04 Desktop and Mozilla Firefox 14.0.1. As an example for a mid-range system, we used a laptop with an Intel Core2Duo CPU at 1.86GHz and 2GB RAM, running Ubuntu 12.04 Desktop and Mozilla Firefox 16.0.2, so that to assess the performance in typical usage scenarios.

The evaluation environment is completed by a proxy server to inject TrueHTML into the HTML context of the visited pages.Once a website has been successfully loaded in the browser, we log the URL and the user-perceived page loading time using the Navigation Timing API defined by the W3C Web Performance Working Group [29]. We measure this time as the difference between the time when the `onload` event is fired and the time immediately after the user agent finishes prompting to unload the previous document, as per the `performance.timing.navigationStart` method.

6.2 Evaluation Results

Using the virtual machines we first determine the user-perceived page loading time of the unaltered pages. In a second run we use the proxy server to inject TrueHTML and measure the page loading time again. We calculate the overhead as the increase of page loading time in percentage ratios of the loading time the page needed without TrueHTML. The minimum overhead introduced by TrueHTML is 0.01% while the maximum is 99.94%. On average, TrueHTML introduces an overhead of 30.62%. The median result is 25.73%, the 90th percentile of the overhead is 68.37%. However, the significance of these results is limited as we are unable to control for network-induced delay. In order to eliminate these effects, we conducted the following experiments locally.

Using the laptop, we determined how the user experience is affected by TrueHTML in typical scenarios, e.g. browsing popular webpages. We therefore assigned `document.body.innerHTML` of an otherwise empty DOM to the content of a typical email body of a multipart message (consisting of both the content types text/plain and text/html), the scraped content of the landing pages of `google.com`, `yahoo.com`, `baidu.com`, `duckduckgo.com`, `youtube.com`, and the scraped content of a map display on Google Maps, as well as of a Facebook profile and a Twitter timeline. Each generated page was accessed three times and the load times logged per criteria described earlier on. The data were generated locally, thus the results do not contain network-induced delays. Table 2 shows the average values.

The results of the previous test show that the user-perceived page load time is not only dependent on the size of the content, but also reliant on the structure and type of the markup. While the data show that in no case the user experience is negatively affected in the typical use cases, this kind of evaluation does not offer a generic insight into how TrueHTML performance overhead relates to content size and the amount of markup elements. To evaluate this in a controlled environment, we generate a single `<p></p>` markup fragment that contains 1kB of text. Again, we assigned `document.body.innerHTML` of an otherwise empty DOM this markup element between one and one hundred times, creating pages containing one element with 1kB text content, scaling up to pages containing one thousand with 1000kB of text content. As before, the data was generated locally. We compare page load times with and without TrueHTML as described above. While the load time increases slightly with size and the amount of markup elements, it can be seen from

[5] `http://www.httparchive.org/`, Nov. 2012

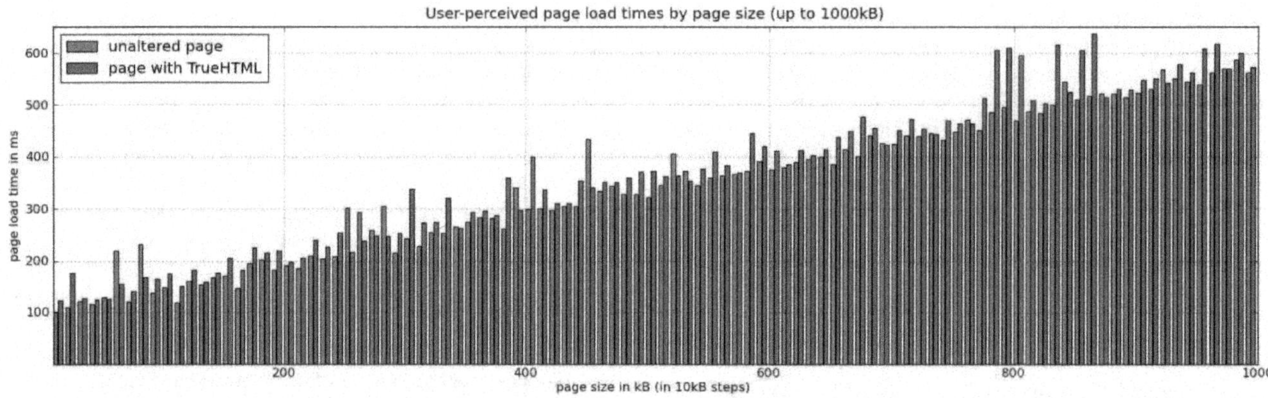

Figure 2: Page load time plotted against page size/#markup elements

Figure 2 that the performance penalty introduced through TrueHTML does not raise significantly.

Content	Size	w/o TH	w/ TH
DuckDuckGo	8.2 kB	336 ms	361 ms
Email Body	8.5 kB	316 ms	349 ms
Baidu.com	11 kB	336 ms	466 ms
Facebook profile	58 kB	539 ms	520 ms
Google	111 kB	533 ms	577 ms
Youtube	174 kB	1216 ms	1346 ms
Twitter timeline	190 kB	1133 ms	1164 ms
Yahoo	244 kB	893 ms	937 ms
Google Maps	299 kB	756 ms	782 ms

Table 2: User-perceived page load times ordered by content size with and without TrueHTML (TH)

7. RELATED WORK

XSS. First reported back in the year 2000 [6], Cross-Site Scripting (XSS) attacks gained recognition and attention from a larger audience with the Samy MySpace worm in 2005 [17]. Several types of XSS attacks have been described thus far.

Reflected XSS, which typically present a user with an HTML document accessed with maliciously manipulated parameters (GET, HTTP header, cookies). These parameters are sent to the server for application logic processing and the document is then rendered along with the injected content.

Stored XSS, which is injected into web pages through user-contributed content stored on the server. Without proper processing on the server-side, scripts will be executed for any user that visits a web page with this content.

DOM XSS, or *XSS of the third kind*, which was first described by Klein [18]. It may be approached as a type of reflected XSS attack where the processing is done by a JavaScript library within the browser rather than on the server. If the malicious script is placed in the hash part of the URL, it is not even sent to the server, meaning that server-side protection techniques fail in that instance.

Server-side mitigation techniques range from simple character encoding or replacement, to a full rewriting of the HTML code. The advent of DOM XSS was one of the main reasons for introducing XSS filters on the client-side. The IE8 XSS Filter was the first fully integrated solution [25], timely followed by the Chrome XSS Auditor in 2009 [4]. For Firefox, client-side XSS filtering is implemented through the NoScript extension[6]. XSS attack mitigation has been covered in a wide range of publications [5, 8, 9, 16, 26, 35]. Noncespaces [10] use randomized XML namespace prefixes as a XSS mitigation technique, which would make detection of injected content reliable. DSI [23] tries to achieve the same goal based on a classification of HTML content into trusted and untrusted content on the server side, subsequently changing browser parsing behavior to take this distinction into account. Blueprint [21] generates a model of the user input on the server-side and transfers this model, together with the user-contributed content, to the browser; browser behavior is modified by injecting a Javascript library to process the model along with the input. While the method to implement Blueprint in current browsers is remarkably similar to our mitigation approach, it seems hard to exclude the mXSS string from the model as it looks like legitimate content. mXSS attacks are likely to bypass all three of those defensive techniques given that the browser itself is instrumented to create the attack payload from originally benign-looking markup.

Mutation-based Attacks. Weinberger et al. [30] give an example where innerHTML is used to execute a DOM-based XSS; this is a different kind of attack than those described in this paper, because no mutations are imposed on the content, and the content did not pass the server-side filter. Comparable XSS attacks based on changes to the HTML markup have been initially described for client-side XSS filters. Vela Nava et al. [24] and Bates et al. [4] have shown that the IE8 XSS Filter could once be used to "weaponize" harmless strings and turn them into valid XSS attack vectors by applying a mutation carried out by the regular expressions used by the XSS Filter, thus circumventing server-side protection. Zalewski covers concatenation problems based on NUL strings in *innerHTML* assignments in the *Browser Security Handbook* [33] and later dedicates a section to backtick mutation in his book "The Tangled Web" [34].

[6]mXSS is mostly not in scope for these, thus remains undetected

Other mutation-based attacks have been reported by Barth et al. [1] and Heiderich [13]. Here, mutation may occur *after* client-side filtering (WebKit corrected a self-closing script tag before rendering, thus activating the XSS vector) or *during* XSS filtering (XSS Auditor strips the `code` attribute value from an applet tag, thus activating a second malicious code source). Hooimeijer et al. describe dangers associated with sanitization of content [15] and claim that they were able, for each of a large number of XSS vectors, to produce a string that would result in that valid XSS vector *after* sanitization. The vulnerabilities described by Kolbitsch et al. may form the basis for an extremely targeted attack by web malware [19]. Those authors state that attack vectors may be prepared for taking into account the mutation behavior of different browser engines. Further, our work can be seen as another justification of the statement from Louw et al. [22]: "The main obstacle a web application must overcome when implementing XSS defenses is the divide between its understanding of the web content represented by an HTML sequence and the understanding web browsers will have of the same".

We show that there is yet another data processing layer in the browser, which managed to remain unknown to the web application up till now. Note that our tests showed that Blueprint would have to be modified to be able to handle prevention of mXSS attacks. The current status of standardization can be retrieved from [20]. Aside from the aforementioned "print preview problem" referenced in Section 2.2, another early report on XSS vulnerabilities connected to *innerHTML* was filed in 2010 for WebKit browsers by Vela Nava [28]. Further contributions to this problem scope have been submitted by Silin, Hasegawa and others, being subsequently documented on the HTML5 Security Cheatsheet [12].

8. CONCLUSION

The paper describes a novel attack technique based on a problematic and mostly undocumented browser behavior that has been in existence for more than ten years – initially introduced with Internet Explorer 4 and adopted by other browser vendors afterwards. It identifies the attacks enabled by this behavior and delivers an easily implementable solution and protection for web application developers and site-owners. The discussed browser behavior results in a widely usable technique for conducting XSS attacks against applications otherwise immune to HTML and JavaScript injections. These internal browser features transparently convert benign markup, so that it becomes an XSS attack vector once certain DOM properties – such as *innerHTML* and *outerHTML* – are being accessed or other DOM operations are being performed. As we label this kind of attack Mutation-based XSS (mXSS), we dedicate this paper to thoroughly introducing and discussing this very attack. Subsequently, we analyze the attack surface and propose an action plan for mitigating the dangers via several measurements and strategies for web applications, browsers and users. We also supply research-derived evaluations of the feasibility and practicability of the proposed mitigation techniques.

The insight gained from this publication indicates the prevalence of risks and threats caused by the multilayer approach that the web is being designed with. Defensive tools and libraries must gain awareness of the additional processing layers that browsers possess. While server- as well as client-side XSS filters have become highly skilled protection tools to cover and mitigate various attack scenarios, mXSS attacks pose a problem that has yet to be overcome by the majority of the existing implementations. A string mutation occurring during the communication between the single layers of the communication stack from browser to web application and back is highly problematic. Given its place and time of occurrence, it cannot be predicted without detailed case analysis.

9. REFERENCES

[1] A. Barth. Bug 29278: XSSAuditor bypasses from sla.ckers.org. https://bugs.webkit.org/show_bug.cgi?id=29278.

[2] A. Barth, J. Caballero, and D. Song. Secure content sniffing for web browsers, or how to stop papers from reviewing themselves. In *Security and Privacy, 2009 30th IEEE Symposium on*, pages 360–371. IEEE, 2009.

[3] A. Barua, H. Shahriar, and M. Zulkernine. Server side detection of content sniffing attacks. In *Software Reliability Engineering (ISSRE), 2011 IEEE 22nd International Symposium on*, pages 20–29. IEEE, 2011.

[4] D. Bates, A. Barth, and C. Jackson. Regular expressions considered harmful in client-side XSS filters. In *Proceedings of the 19th international conference on World wide web*, WWW '10, pages 91–100, 2010.

[5] P. Bisht and V. N. Venkatakrishnan. XSS-GUARD: Precise Dynamic Prevention of Cross-Site Scripting Attacks. In *Conference on Detection of Intrusions and Malware & Vulnerability Assessment*, 2008.

[6] CERT.org. CERT Advisory CA-2000-02 Malicious HTML Tags Embedded in Client Web Requests. http://www.cert.org/advisories/CA-2000-02.html, 2012.

[7] T. j. Foundation. jQuery: The Write Less, Do More, JavaScript Library. http://jquery.com/, Nov. 2012.

[8] M. Gebre, K. Lhee, and M. Hong. A robust defense against content-sniffing xss attacks. In *Digital Content, Multimedia Technology and its Applications (IDC), 2010 6th International Conference on*, pages 315–320. IEEE, 2010.

[9] B. Gourdin, C. Soman, H. Bojinov, and E. Bursztein. Toward secure embedded web interfaces. In *Proceedings of the Usenix Security Symposium*, 2011.

[10] M. V. Gundy and H. Chen. Noncespaces: Using randomization to defeat Cross-Site Scripting attacks. *Computers & Security*, 31(4):612–628, 2012.

[11] Y. Hasegawa, Mar. 2007.

[12] M. Heiderich. HTML5 Security Cheatsheet. http://html5sec.org/.

[13] M. Heiderich. *Towards Elimination of XSS Attacks with a Trusted and Capability Controlled DOM.* PhD thesis, Ruhr-University Bochum, 2012.

[14] M. Heiderich, M. Niemietz, F. Schuster, T. Holz, and J. Schwenk. Scriptless attacks–stealing the pie without touching the sill. In *ACM Conference on Computer and Communications Security (CCS)*, 2012.

[15] P. Hooimeijer, B. Livshits, D. Molnar, P. Saxena, and M. Veanes. Fast and precise sanitizer analysis with bek. In *Proceedings of the 20th USENIX conference on Security*, SEC'11, pages 1–1, Berkeley, CA, USA, 2011. USENIX Association.

[16] M. Johns. *Code Injection Vulnerabilities in Web Applications - Exemplified at Cross-site Scripting.* PhD thesis, University of Passau, Passau, July 2009.

[17] S. Kamkar. *Technical explanation of The MySpace Worm.*

[18] A. Klein. DOM Based Cross Site Scripting or XSS of the Third Kind. *Web Application Security Consortium*, 2005.

[19] C. Kolbitsch, B. Livshits, B. Zorn, and C. Seifert. Rozzle: De-Cloaking Internet Malware. In *Proc. IEEE Symposium on Security & Privacy*, 2012.

[20] T. Leithead. Dom parsing and serialization (w3c editor's draft 07 november 2012). http://dvcs.w3.org/hg/innerhtml/raw-file/tip/index.html.

[21] M. T. Louw and V. N. Venkatakrishnan. Blueprint: Robust Prevention of Cross-site Scripting Attacks for Existing Browsers. In *Proceedings of the 2009 30th IEEE Symposium on Security and Privacy*, SP '09, pages 331–346, Washington, DC, USA, 2009. IEEE Computer Society.

[22] M. T. Louw and V. N. Venkatakrishnan. Blueprint: Robust Prevention of Cross-site Scripting Attacks for Existing Browsers. Proc. IEEE Symposium on Security & Privacy, 2009.

[23] Y. Nadji, P. Saxena, and D. Song. Document Structure Integrity: A Robust Basis for Cross-site Scripting Defense. In *NDSS*. The Internet Society, 2009.

[24] E. V. Nava and D. Lindsay. Abusing Internet Explorer 8's XSS Filters. http://p42.us/ie8xss/Abusing_IE8s_XSS_Filters.pdf.

[25] D. Ross. IE8 XSS Filter design philosophy in-depth. http://blogs.msdn.com/b/dross/archive/2008/07/03/ie8-xss-filter-design-philosophy-in-depth.aspx, Apr. 2008.

[26] P. Saxena, D. Molnar, and B. Livshits. SCRIPTGARD: Automatic context-sensitive sanitization for large-scale legacy web applications. In *Proceedings of the 18th ACM conference on Computer and communications security*, pages 601–614. ACM, 2011.

[27] B. van der Sluis. swfobject - SWFObject is an easy-to-use and standards-friendly method to embed Flash content, which utilizes one small JavaScript file. http://code.google.com/p/swfobject/.

[28] E. Vela. Issue 43902: innerHTML decompilation issues in textarea. http://code.google.com/p/chromium/issues/detail?id=43902.

[29] W3C. Navigation Timing. http://www.w3.org/TR/2012/PR-navigation-timing-20120726/, July 2012.

[30] J. Weinberger, P. Saxena, D. Akhawe, M. Finifter, E. C. R. Shin, and D. Song. A systematic analysis of xss sanitization in web application frameworks. In *ESORICS*, 2011.

[31] E. Z. Yang. HTML Purifier CSS quoting full disclosure. http://htmlpurifier.org/, Sept. 2010.

[32] E. Z. Yang. HTML Purifier. http://htmlpurifier.org/, Mar. 2011.

[33] M. Zalewski. Browser Security Handbook. http://code.google.com/p/browsersec/wiki/Main, July 2010.

[34] M. Zalewski. *The Tangled Web: A Guide to Securing Modern Web Applications.* No Starch Press, 2011.

[35] G. Zuchlinski. The Anatomy of Cross Site Scripting. *Hitchhiker's World*, 8, Nov. 2003.

When Private Set Intersection Meets Big Data: An Efficient and Scalable Protocol

Changyu Dong
Dept. of Computer and Information Sciences
University of Strathclyde
Glasgow, UK
changyu.dong@strath.ac.uk

Liqun Chen
Hewlett-Packard Laboratories
Bristol, UK
liqun.chen@hp.com

Zikai Wen
Dept. of Computer and Information Sciences
University of Strathclyde
Glasgow, UK
wjb12186@uni.strath.ac.uk

ABSTRACT

Large scale data processing brings new challenges to the design of privacy-preserving protocols: how to meet the increasing requirements of speed and throughput of modern applications, and how to scale up smoothly when data being protected is big. Efficiency and scalability become critical criteria for privacy preserving protocols in the age of Big Data. In this paper, we present a new Private Set Intersection (PSI) protocol that is extremely efficient and highly scalable compared with existing protocols. The protocol is based on a novel approach that we call *oblivious Bloom intersection*. It has linear complexity and relies mostly on efficient symmetric key operations. It has high scalability due to the fact that most operations can be parallelized easily. The protocol has two versions: a basic protocol and an enhanced protocol, the security of the two variants is analyzed and proved in the semi-honest model and the malicious model respectively. A prototype of the basic protocol has been built. We report the result of performance evaluation and compare it against the two previously fastest PSI protocols. Our protocol is orders of magnitude faster than these two protocols. To compute the intersection of two million-element sets, our protocol needs only 41 seconds (80-bit security) and 339 seconds (256-bit security) on moderate hardware in parallel mode.

Categories and Subject Descriptors

D.4.6 [**OPERATING SYSTEMS**]: Security and Protection—*Cryptographic controls*

Keywords

Private Set Intersection; Bloom Filters

1. INTRODUCTION

In many countries, protecting data privacy is no longer optional but a legal obligation. Legislation includes various US privacy laws (HIPAA, COPPA, GLB, FRC, etc.), European Union Data Protection Directive, and more specific national privacy regulations. It is a challenging task for organizations because they have to protect data in use and transmission. To this end, many security solutions have been proposed to enable privacy-preserving data processing. The amount of data to be processed and protected becomes increasingly large. For example, geneticists need to search 3 billion base pairs in personal genome to find genetic disorders that might cause diabetes or cancers, epidemiologists need to link multiple medical databases that contain millions of patients' records to identify risk factors for diseases, and online retailers want to correlate petabytes of their transaction records with customers' social network activities, hoping to increase customer satisfaction. Any privacy-preserving data processing service is not cost free and this has brought us new challenges: how to meet the increasing requirements of speed and throughput of modern applications, and how to scale up smoothly when data being protected is big? With the prevalence of large scale data processing, efficiency and scalability become critical criteria for designing a privacy-preserving protocol in the age of "Big Data".

The subject of study in this paper is the Private Set Intersection (PSI) problem. Namely, two parties, a client and a server, want to jointly compute the intersection of their private input sets in a manner that at the end the client learns the intersection and the server learns nothing. The PSI problem has been extensively studied for two reasons, firstly set intersection is a foundational primitive and secondly it has many practical applications. For example, PSI has been proposed as a building block in applications such as privacy preserving data mining [4], human genome research [6], homeland security [16], Botnet detection [33], social networks [32], location sharing [35] and cheater detection in online games [11]. Many PSI protocols have been proposed, e.g. [21, 30, 23, 13, 24, 27, 12, 16, 15, 28, 5, 25]. PSI protocols are often criticized as being impractical because the performance becomes unacceptable when the input size or the security parameter becomes large, and it is difficult to improve the performance by just adding hardware proportionally.

The criticism is not unfounded. Currently two protocols claim to be the fastest PSI protocol: the RSA-OPRF-based protocol by De Cristofaro et al [16, 17] and the garbled circuit protocol by Huang et al [25]. Both protocols have a highly optimized implementation. We obtained the source code from the authors of these two protocols and tested the performance. To compute the intersection of two 1,048,576-element (2^{20}) sets, De Cristofaro's protocol needs 10.6 minutes at 80-bit security, but requires a much longer time at 256-bit security. We estimate the time to be approximately 131 hours from tests with smaller sets. The tests with million-element sets on Huang's protocol were unsuccessful because the Java Virtual Machine ran out of memory on the client computer that has 16 GB RAM. From tests with smaller sets, we estimate that Huang's protocol requires 27 hours and 51 hours respectively to compute the intersection at 80-bit and 256-bit security. Clearly to use PSI in real world applications, we need more practical protocols.

Contributions We present a new PSI protocol that is much more

CCS'13, November 4–8, 2013, Berlin, Germany.

http://dx.doi.org/10.1145/2508859.2516701.

efficient than all the already existing PSI protocols. The protocol is designed based on a novel two-party computation approach, which makes use of a new variant of Bloom filters that we call *garbled Bloom filters*, and we refer the new approach as *oblivious Bloom intersection*. The ideas of garbled Bloom filters and oblivious Bloom intersection are general and have their own interests.

Our PSI protocol has two versions: a basic protocol, security of which can be proved in the semi-honest model, and an enhanced protocol, security of which can be proved in the malicious model. The basic protocol has linear complexity (with a small constant factor) and relies mostly on symmetric key operations. It is fast even with large input sets, and when the security parameter increases, the performance degrades gracefully. Test results show it is orders of magnitude faster than the previous best protocols. The enhanced protocol is an extension of the basic protocol, that only increases the cost by a factor proportional to the security parameter.

Apart from efficiency, another big advantage of the protocol is scalability: the computational, memory and communication complexities are all linear in the size of the input sets. More attractively, most operations in the protocol can be performed in the SPMD (single program, multiple data) fashion, which means little effort is required to separate the computation into a number of parallel tasks. Therefore it can fully take the advantage of parallel processing capacity provided by current multi-core CPUs, GPGPUs (General-purpose graphics processing unit) and cloud computing. As a result, the protocol is particularly suitable for Big Data oriented applications that have to process data in a parallelized and/or distributed way.

We have implemented a proof of concept prototype of the basic protocol. To compute the intersection of two million-element sets, it needs only 41 seconds (80-bit) and 5.65 minutes (256-bit) on two moderate computers in parallel mode.

Organization The paper is organized as follows: in section 2, we review the related work, in section 3 we introduce the notation and building blocks; in section 4, we present the garbled Bloom filter data structure, the semi-honest protocol, analyze the security and provide a simulation-based proof; in section 5 we show how to extend the basic protocol to achieve security against malicious adversaries; in section 6 we show a prototype of the basic protocol and the performance evaluation result; in section 7, we conclude the paper.

2. RELATED WORK

The concept and first protocol of Private Set Intersection were introduced by Freedman et al in [21]. Their protocol is based on oblivious polynomial evaluation. Along this line, Kissner and Song [30] proposed protocols in multiparty settings, Dachman-Soled et al [13], and Hazay and Nissim [24] proposed protocols which are more efficient in the presence of malicious adversaries. Hazey and Lindell [23] proposed another approach for PSI which is based on oblivious pseudorandom function (OPRF) evaluation. This approach is further improved by Jarecki and Liu [27, 28] and De Cristofaro et al [16, 15]. There are also a number of variants of PSI protocols, which aim to achieve more features than the original PSI concept. Camenisch and Zaverucha [12] proposed a PSI protocol which requires the input sets to be signed and certified by a trusted party, Ateniese et al [5] proposed a PSI protocol that also hides the size of the client's input set. Among the above protocols, the most efficient protocol is the protocol by De Cristofaro et al [16, 15]. It has linear complexity and requires $O(n)$ public key operations, where n is the size of the set. The performance of this protocol is affected significantly by n and the security parameter. Recently, Huang et al [25] presented a semi-honest PSI protocol based on garble circuits. This protocol requires $O(nlogn)$ symmetric key operations and a small number of public key operations. The authors demonstrated that in certain cases this protocol is significantly more efficient than the previous PSI protocols. At low security settings, De Cristofaro's protocol [16] is the fastest but at high security settings, Huang's protocol [25] is more efficient.

Recently a few PSI protocols based on Bloom filters were proposed. In [31], the parties AND their Bloom filters by a secure multiplication protocol and each party obtains an intersection Bloom filter. They then query the resulting Bloom filter to obtain the intersection. However the protocol is not secure because the intersection Bloom filter leaks information about other party's sets. In [29], Bloom filters are used in conjunction with the Goldwasser Micali homomorphic encryption.The semi-honest version of the protocol requires kn hash operations and $(k\log_2 e + kl + k + 2l)n$ modular multiplications, where k and l are parameters controlling false positive and e is the base of natural logarithms. Our basic protocol requires $2(k+k\log_2 e)n$ hash operations and a few hundred public key operations (independent to n). The total number of operations in our basic protocol is much less than the protocol in [29]. Given that a modular multiplication is faster than a public key operation but slower than a hash operation, for large input sets (i.e. a large value of n), the PSI scheme in [29] would be slower than our basic protocol. The protocol also has a higher communication overhead than ours, as each bit in the Bloom filter and the encrypted elements has to be expanded to a group element. The version secure in the malicious model requires a trusted party to certify the client's set, thus is hard to compare fairly with our enhanced protocol.

3. PRELIMINARIES

3.1 Notation

A function $\mu(\cdot)$ is *negligible in* n, or just *negligible*, if for every positive polynomial $p(\cdot)$ and any sufficiently large n it holds that $\mu(n) \leq 1/p(n)$. A *probability ensemble* indexed by I is a sequence of random variables indexed by a countable index set I. Namely, $X = \{X_i\}_{i \in I}$ where each X_i is a random variable. Two distribution ensembles $X = \{X_n\}_{n\in\mathbb{N}}$ and $Y = \{Y_n\}_{n\in\mathbb{N}}$ are *computationally indistinguishable*, denoted by $X \stackrel{c}{\equiv} Y$ if for every probabilistic polynomial-time (PPT) algorithm D, there exists a negligible function $\mu(\cdot)$ such that for every $n \in \mathbb{N}$,

$$|Pr[D(X_n, 1^n) - 1] - Pr[D(Y_n, 1^n) = 1]| \leq \mu(n)$$

For a set X, we denote by $x \stackrel{r}{\leftarrow} X$ the process of choosing an element x of X uniformly at random.

3.2 Bloom Filters

A Bloom filter [9] is a compact data structure for probabilistic set membership testing. A Bloom filter is an array of m bits that can represent a set S of at most n elements. A Bloom filter comes with a set of k independent uniform hash functions $H = \{h_0, ..., h_{k-1}\}$ such that each h_i maps elements to index numbers over the range $[0, m-1]$ uniformly. In the rest of the paper, we use (m, n, k, H)-Bloom filter to denote a Bloom filter parameterized by (m, n, k, H), use BF_S to denote a Bloom filter that encodes the set S, and use $BF_S[i]$ to denote the bit at index i in BF_S.

Initially, all bits in the array are set to 0. To insert an element $x \in S$ into the filter, the element is hashed using the k hash functions to get k index numbers. The bits at all these indexes in the bit array are set to 1, i.e. set $BF_S[h_i(x)] = 1$ for $0 \leq i \leq k-1$. To check if an item y is in S, y is hashed by the k hash functions, and all locations y hashes to are checked. If any of the bits at the locations is 0 , y is not in S, otherwise y is *probably* in S.

Because the hash functions are deterministic, if y is encoded in the filter then in the query phase every $BF_S[h_i(y)]$ must be 1, so a Bloom filter never yields a false negative. However, a false positive is possible, i.e. it is possible that y is not in the set S, but all $BF_S[h_i(y)]$ are set to 1. The probability that a particular bit in the Bloom filter is set to 1 is $p = 1 - (1 - 1/m)^{kn}$, and according to [10], the upper bound of the false positive probability is:

$$\epsilon = p^k \times (1 + O(\frac{k}{p}\sqrt{\frac{\ln m - k \ln p}{m}})) \quad (1)$$

which is negligible in k.

In practice we often need to build a Bloom filter with a capped false positive probability, i.e. it represents any set of at most n elements from a universe in a manner that allows false positive probability to be at most ε. The efficiency of such a Bloom filter depends on the parameters m and k. It turns out the lower bound of m in this case is $m \geq n \log_2 e \cdot \log_2 1/\varepsilon$, where e is the base of natural logarithms. The optimal number of hash functions is $k = (m/n) \cdot \ln 2$ and if m is also optimal then the optimal k is $\log_2 1/\varepsilon$. In the rest of the paper, we always assume optimal k and m unless otherwise stated.

A standard Bloom filter trick is that if we have two (m, n, k, H)-Bloom filters that each encodes a set S_1 and S_2, we can obtain another (m, n, k, H)-Bloom filter $BF_{S_1 \cap S_2}$ by bit-wisely ANDing BF_{S_1} and BF_{S_2}. The resulting Bloom filter has no false negative, which means the query result of any element $y \in S_1 \cap S_2$ against $BF_{S_1 \cap S_2}$ is always true. The false positive probability of the resulting Bloom filter is no higher than either of the constituent Bloom filter [37]. Note that due to collisions, it is possible that the jth bit is set in BF_{S_1} by an element in $S_1 - S_1 \cap S_2$ and jth bit is set in BF_{S_2} by an element in $S_2 - S_1 \cap S_2$. Therefore the resulting Bloom filter usually contains more 1 bits than the Bloom filter built from scratch using $S_1 \cap S_2$.

3.3 Secret Sharing

Secret sharing is a fundamental cryptographic primitive. It allows a dealer to split a secret s into n shares such that the secret s can be recovered efficiently with any subset of t or more shares. With any subset of less than t shares, the secret is unrecoverable and the shares give no information about the secret. Such a system is called a (t, n)-secret sharing scheme. An example of such a scheme is Shamir's secret sharing scheme [40].

When $t = n$, an efficient and widely used secret sharing scheme can be obtained by simple $\oplus$ (XOR) operations [39]. The scheme works by generating $n - 1$ random bit strings $r_1, ..., r_{n-1}$ of the same length as the secret s, and computing $r_n = r_1 \oplus, ..., \oplus r_{n-1} \oplus s$. Each r_i is a share of the secret. It is easy to see that s can be recovered by computing $r_1 \oplus, ..., \oplus r_n$ and any subset of less than n shares reveals no information about the secret.

3.4 Oblivious Transfer

Oblivious transfer [38, 20] allows a sender to send part of its input to a receiver in a manner that protects both parties. Namely, the sender does not know which part the receiver receives and the receiver does not learn any information about the other part of the sender's input. Generally, an oblivious transfer protocol can be denoted as OT_l^m. The notation means the sender holds m pairs l-bit strings $(x_{j,0}, x_{j,1})$ $(0 \leq j \leq m-1)$, while the receiver holds an m-bit selection string $r = (r_0, ..., r_{m-1})$. At the end of the protocol execution, the receiver outputs x_{j,r_j} for $0 \leq j \leq m-1$.

Oblivious transfer protocols are costly and often become the efficiency bottleneck in protocol design. However it has been shown by Beaver that it is possible to obtain a large number oblivious transfers given only a small number of actual oblivious transfer calls [7]. In this direction, efficient *OT extensions* were proposed in [26]. The extensions rely on the Random Oracle Model [8] (or the existence of correlation robust hash functions) and can reduce OT_l^m to $\text{OT}_\lambda^\lambda$ where λ is a security parameter. The latter can be further reduced to λ invocations of OT_λ^1. In our implementation, we use the above OT extension scheme to reduce the actual cost of an OT_λ^m invocation to λ calls to the Naor-Pinkas OT protocol [34]. For the detail of the reduction, please consult [26].

3.5 The Semi-honest Model

We prove the security of the basic protocol in the presence of *static semi-honest* adversaries. In the model, the adversary controls one of the two parties and follows the protocol specification exactly. However, it may try to learn more information about the other party's input. The definitions and model are according to [22].

A two-party protocol π computes a function that maps a pair of inputs to a pair of outputs $f : \{0,1\}^* \times \{0,1\}^* \rightarrow \{0,1\}^* \times \{0,1\}^*$, where $f = (f_1, f_2)$. For every pair of inputs $x, y \in \{0,1\}^*$, the output-pair is a random variable $(f_1(x,y), f_2(x,y))$. The first party obtains $f_1(x,y)$ and the second party obtains $f_2(x,y)$. The function can be asymmetric such that only one party gets the result. It is captured as $f(x,y) \stackrel{def}{=} (f_1(x,y), \Lambda)$, where Λ denotes the empty string.

In the semi-honest model, a protocol π is secure if whatever can be computed by a party in the protocol can be obtained from its input and output only. This is formalized by the simulation paradigm. We require a party's *view* in a protocol execution to be simulatable given only its input and output. The view of the party i during an execution of π on (x,y) is denoted by $\mathsf{view}_i^\pi(x,y)$ and equals $(w, r^i, m_1^i, ..., m_t^i)$ where $w \in (x,y)$ is the input of i, r^i is the outcome of i's internal random coin tosses and m_j^i represents the jth message that it received.

DEFINITION 1. *Let $f = (f_1, f_2)$ be a deterministic function. We say that the protocol π securely computes f in the presence of static semi-honest adversaries if there exists probabilistic polynomial-time algorithms S_1 and S_2 such that*

$$\{S_1(x, f_1(x,y))\}_{x,y} \stackrel{c}{\equiv} \{\mathsf{view}_1^\pi(x,y)\}_{x,y}$$

$$\{S_2(y, f_2(x,y))\}_{x,y} \stackrel{c}{\equiv} \{\mathsf{view}_2^\pi(x,y)\}_{x,y}$$

4. THE BASIC PROTOCOL

In this section we present the basic protocol that is secure in the semi-honest model. Conceptually the protocol is very simple: the client computes a Bloom filter that encodes its set C and the server computes a garbled Bloom filter (see below) that encodes its set S. Then they run an oblivious transfer protocol so that the client obtains a garbled Bloom filter that represents the intersection and the server learns nothing. Then the client queries the intersection garbled Bloom filter and obtains the intersection.

4.1 Garbled Bloom Filters

We introduce a new variant of Bloom filters called garbled Bloom filters (GBF). A garbled Bloom filter is the garbled version of a standard Bloom filter. From a high level point of view, there is no difference between a garbled Bloom filter and a Bloom filter: it encodes a set of at most n elements in an array of length m, it supports membership query with no false negative and negligible false positive. To add an element, the element is mapped by k independent uniform hash functions into k index numbers and the corresponding array locations are set. To query an element, the element is mapped by the same k hash functions into k index numbers and the corresponding array locations are checked.

From a low level point of view, a garbled Bloom filter is backed by a different data structure. Namely, instead of using an array of bits, a garbled Bloom filter uses an array of λ-bit strings, where λ is a security parameter. In the rest of the paper, we use (m, n, k, H, λ)-garbled Bloom filter to denote a garbled Bloom filter parameterized by (m, n, k, H, λ), we denote a garbled Bloom filter encoding a set S by GBF_S and denote the λ-bit string at index i by $GBF_S[i]$.

To add an element $x \in S$ to a garbled Bloom filter, we split the element into k λ-bit shares using the the XOR-based secret sharing scheme as described in section 3.3. The element is also mapped into k index numbers and we store one share in each location $h_i(x)$. Note this is a very loose description, the actual process is more complicated. To query an element y, we collect all bit strings at $h_i(y)$ and XOR them together. If the result is y then y is in S, otherwise y is not in S. The correctness is obvious: if $y \in S$, the XOR operation will recover y from its k shares which are retrievable from the garbled Bloom filter by their indexes. If $y \notin S$, then the probability of the XOR result is the same as y is negligible in λ. The algorithm to encode a set into a garbled Bloom filter and the algorithm to query an element are given in Algorithm 1 and 2.

Algorithm 1: $BuildGBF(S, n, m, k, H, \lambda)$

```
   input : A set S, n, m, k, λ, H = {h_0, ...h_{k-1}}
   output: An (m, n, k, H, λ)-garbled Bloom filter GBF_S
1  GBF_S= new m-element array of bit strings;
2  for i = 0 to m − 1 do
3      GBF_S[i]=NULL;  // NULL is the special symbol that means "no value"
4  end
5  for each x ∈ S do
6      emptySlot = −1, finalShare= x;
7      for i=0 to k-1 do
8          j = h_i(x);            // get an index by hashing the element
9          if GBF_S[j]==NULL then
10             if emptySlot ==−1 then
11                 emptySlot=j;       // reserve this location for finalShare
12             else
13                 GBF_S[j] ←r {0,1}^λ;    // generate a new share
14                 finalShare=finalShare⊕GBF_S[j];
15             end
16         else
17             finalShare=finalShare⊕GBF_S[j]; // reuse a share
18         end
19     end
20     GBF_S[emptySlot]=finalShare;       // store the last share
21 end
22 for i = 0 to m − 1 do
23     if GBF_S[i]==NULL then
24         GBF_S[i] ←r {0,1}^λ;
25     end
26 end
```

In Algorithm 1, we first create an empty garbled Bloom filter and initialize each location to NULL (line 1-4). To add $x \in S$, we split x into k shares on the fly and store the shares in $GBF_S[h_i(x)]$ (line 5-21). Note that in this process, some location $j = h_i(x)$ may have been occupied by a previously added element. In this case we reuse the existing share stored at $GBF_S[j]$ (line 16-18). For example, in Figure 1 we first add x_1 to GBF_S and split it into 3 shares s_1^1, s_1^2, s_1^3. Then when we add x_2, $GBF_S[4]$ has already been occupied by s_1^2. So we reuse the string s_1^2 as a share of x_2,

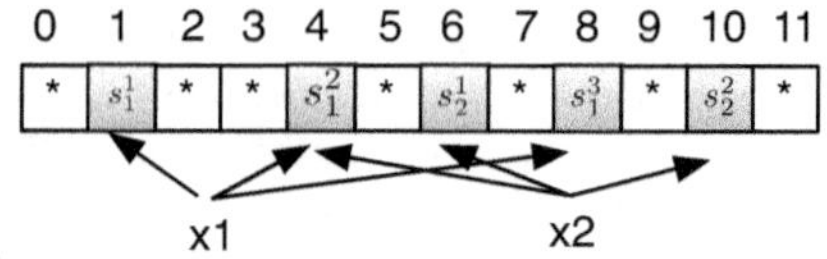

Figure 1: Add elements into a garbled Bloom filter

i.e. $x_2 = s_1^2 \oplus s_2^1 \oplus s_2^2$. This is because if we replace s_1^2 with another string, x_1 will not be recoverable in the query phase. Reusing shares will not cause security problems as far as the protocol concerns, we will show in Theorem 3 that the probability of getting all shares of an element that is not in the intersection in our protocol is negligible. After adding all elements in S, we generate and store random λ-bit strings at all locations that are still NULL (line 22-26). Algorithm 1 will succeed with an overwhelming probability, as stated in Theorem 1. When m and k are optimal, the success probability in Theorem 1 is approximately $1 - 2^{-k}$.

Algorithm 2: $QueryGBF(GBF_S, x, k, H)$

```
input : A gabled Bloom filter GBF_S, an element x, k,
        H = {h_0, ...h_{k-1}}
output: True if x ∈ S, False otherwise
recovered = {0}^λ;
for i = 0 to k − 1 do
    j = h_i(x);
    recovered = recovered ⊕ GBF_S[j];
end
if recovered == x then
    return True;
else
    return False;
end
```

THEOREM 1. *Algorithm 1 will succeed with a probability at least* $1 - p'^k \times (1 + O(\frac{k}{p'}\sqrt{\frac{\ln m - k \ln p'}{m}}))$ *where* $p' = 1 - (1 - 1/m)^{k(n-1)}$.

PROOF. Algorithm 1 fails when *emptySlot* remains -1 after the inner loop (line 20). This happens when adding an element to the GBF, all locations the element hashes to have been occupied by previously added elements. Because in this case, at most $n - 1$ elements have been added to the GBF, the probability of a particular position is occupied is at most $p' = 1 - (1 - 1/m)^{k(n-1)}$. The probability of all k locations have been occupied can be obtained in the same way as the false positive probability of an (m, n, k, H)-BF, which is at most $p'^k \times (1 + O(\frac{k}{p'}\sqrt{\frac{\ln m - k \ln p'}{m}}))$. The success probability is then 1 minus the probability of failure. □

In a garbled Bloom filter, each location is a λ-bit string that is either a share of certain elements or a random string. Analogously, a share in a gabled Bloom filter is equivalent to a "1" bit in a Bloom filter, and a random string is equivalent to a "0" bit. Same as the Bloom filters, there is no false negative when using a GBF because all shares of an encoded element are guaranteed to be retrievable and the XOR-based secret sharing scheme always produces the original element when all shares are available. When using a GBF, we need to consider and differentiate the following two probabilities:

- The collision probability of a GBF is the probability when y is not in S, but it hashes to the same set of index numbers as some $x \in S$. A collision does not cause false positive: the *recovered* string (Algorithm 2) is x but not y so the query result is still false. However it reveals x. The collision probability is negligible in k. Loosely, we can use the upper bound of the false positive probability of a Bloom filter as the upper bound of the collision probability of a garbled Bloom filter. Note that collisions do not affect the security of our protocol, but may be a concern if a GBF is used in other protocols.

- The false positive probability of GBF_S is the probability when y is not in S but the *recovered* string equals y coincidentally. This probability is at most $2^{-\lambda}$.

More formally, we have the following theorem:

THEOREM 2. *Let GBF_S be an (m, n, k, H, λ)-garbled Bloom filter, (i) $\forall y \notin S, x \in S : Pr[(\bigoplus_{i=0}^{k-1} GBF_S[h_i(y)]) = x] \leq \epsilon$, where ϵ is the maximum false positive probability in equation (1). (ii) $\forall y \notin S : Pr[(\bigoplus_{i=0}^{k-1} GBF_S[h_i(y)]) = y] \leq 2^{-\lambda}$.*

PROOF. We start from the collision probability. Let BF_S be the (m, n, k, H)-Bloom filter that encodes the same set S as GBF_S. Now for any $y \notin S$, we query y against both GBF_S and BF_S. Whenever the GBF query results in a collision, the Bloom filter query must return a false positive. This is because by definition, y hashes to the same set of index numbers as some $x \in S$, so all locations are set to 1 in BF_S by x, therefore the Bloom filter query returns true, but $y \notin S$ so this is a false positive. Since a GBF collision implies a Bloom filter false positive, the collision probability is bounded by the false positive probability of the Bloom filter.

Let's consider the false positive probability of a GBF. A false positive occurs when y is not in S but the *recovered* string equals y. The *recovered* string is $GBF_S[h_0(y)] \oplus \ldots \oplus GBF_S[h_{k-1}(y)]$. Each constitution string $GBF_S[h_i(y)]$ is either a share of certain elements or a random string. When $y \notin S$, there are three cases:

Case 1: All constitution strings are shares of the same element in S. We denote the probability of this case as p_1. In this case for sure $recovered \neq y$ because $y \notin S$.

Case 2: The constitution strings are shares of several elements in S. We denote the probability of this case as p_2. In this case we can divide the constitution strings into several groups of size at most $k-1$, each group contains the shares of a particular element. From the security of the XOR-based secret sharing scheme, the XOR result of each group should be a uniformly random string. Therefore the $recovered$ string is a uniformly random string.

Case 3: At least one of the constitution strings is a random string. The probability of this case as $p_3 = 1 - p_1 - p_2$. In this case the $recovered$ string is also a uniformly random string.

In all three cases, a false positive occurs if $recovered = y$. In case 1, the false positive probability is 0. In the other two cases, the false positive probability is $2^{-\lambda}$. Let B denote the event that a false positive occurs, and let a_1, a_2, a_3 denote the events that case 1, case 2, case 3 occurs respectively, by the law of total probability, the false positive probability is:

$$\begin{aligned} Pr[B] &= Pr[a_1]Pr[B|a_1] + Pr[a_2]Pr[B|a_2] + Pr[a_3]Pr[B|a_3] \\ &= 0 \cdot p_1 + 2^{-\lambda} \cdot p_2 + 2^{-\lambda} \cdot p_3 \\ &= 2^{-\lambda}(1 - p_1) \leq 2^{-\lambda} \end{aligned}$$

□

In summary, with proper parameters, a garbled Bloom filter exhibits similar properties when encoding set membership: no false negative and negligible false positive.

4.2 Produce an Intersection GBF

In this section we show how to produce an intersection garbled Bloom filter from an (m, n, k, H, λ)-garbled Bloom filter and an (m, n, k, H)-Bloom filter. The idea is quite similar to creating an intersection Bloom filter by ANDing two Bloom filters.

Let's say we have an (m, n, k, H)-Bloom filter BF_C that encodes a set C and an (m, n, k, H, λ)-garbled Bloom filter GBF_S that encodes a set S. We use Algorithm 3 to build the intersection garbled Bloom filter $GBF_{C \cap S}$.

Algorithm 3: $GBFIntersection(GBF_S, BF_C, m)$

```
input : An (m, n, k, H, λ)-garbled Bloom filter GBF_S, an
        (m, n, k, H)-Bloom filter BF_C, m
output: An (m, n, k, H, λ)-garbled Bloom filter GBF_{C∩S}
GBF_{C∩S} = new m-element array of bit strings;
for i = 0 to m − 1 do
    if BF_C[i] == 1 then
        GBF_{C∩S}[i] = GBF_S[i];
    else
        GBF_{C∩S}[i] ←r {0,1}^λ;
    end
end
```

The intuition of the algorithm is this: if an element x is in $C \cap S$, then for every position i it hashes to, $BF_C[i]$ must be a 1 bit and $GBF_S[i]$ must be a share of x. Therefore by running the algorithm, all shares of x are copied to the new garbled Bloom filter. That is, all elements in $C \cap S$ are preserved in the new garbled Bloom filter. On the other hand, if x is not in $C \cap S$, then with a high probability, at least one share will not be copied. Or in other words, elements not in $C \cap S$ are eliminated from the new garbled Bloom filter. Thus the new garbled Bloom filter is indeed a garbled Bloom filter that encodes the intersection. Formally, we have the following theorem:

THEOREM 3. *Let $GBF_{C \cap S}$ be an (m, n, k, H, λ)-garbled Bloom filter produced in Algorithm 3. For $0 \leq i \leq k-1$, let a_i be the event that $GBF_{C \cap S}[h_i(x)]$ equals the ith share of x, we have (i) $\forall x \in C \cap S$: $Pr[a_0 \wedge \ldots \wedge a_{k-1}] = 1$, (ii) $\forall x \notin C \cap S$: $Pr[a_0 \wedge \ldots \wedge a_{k-1}]$ is negligible in k.*

PROOF. The first part: we can see from the algorithm that for any element $x \in C \cap S$, all the shares will be copied from GBF_S to $GBF_{C \cap S}$ because the corresponding locations in BF_C are all set to 1.

The second part: Firstly, $GBF_{C \cap S}$ does not encode any element $x \notin S$ because GBF_S contains no share of any element $x \notin S$. Secondly, for any element $x \in S - C \cap S$, the probability of all its shares are copied from GBF_S to $GBF_{C \cap S}$ is ϵ, where ϵ is the upper bound of the false positive probability of an (m, n, k, H)-BF. This is because if all shares of x are copied to $GBF_{C \cap S}$ then it means all locations that x hashes to in BF_C are set to 1. However $x \notin C \cap S$ and consequently $x \notin C$, then it implies a false positive when we query x against BF_C and the probability is ϵ. □

From security point of view, a more interesting property of the intersection GBF is that it is indistinguishable from a GBF built from scratch that encodes $C \cap S$.

THEOREM 4. *Given sets C, S and their intersection $C \cap S$, let $GBF_{C \cap S}$ be an (m, n, k, H, λ)-garbled Bloom filter produced by Algorithm 3 from GBF_S and BF_C, let $GBF'_{C \cap S}$ be another (m, n, k, H, λ)-garbled Bloom filter produced by Algorithm 1 using $C \cap S$, we have $GBF_{C \cap S} \stackrel{c}{\equiv} GBF'_{C \cap S}$.*

PROOF. Given $GBF_{C \cap S}$, we modify it to get $GBF''_{C \cap S}$. We scan $GBF_{C \cap S}$ from the beginning to the end and for each location i, we modify $GBF_{C \cap S}[i]$ using the following procedure:

1. If $GBF_{C\cap S}[i]$ is a share of an element in $C \cap S$, then do nothing.
2. Else if $GBF_{C\cap S}[i]$ is a random string, do nothing.
3. Else if $GBF_{C\cap S}[i]$ is a share of an element in $S - C \cap S$, replace it with a uniformly random λ-bit string.

The result is $GBF''_{C\cap S}$. Every $GBF_{C\cap S}[i]$ must fall into one of these three cases, so there is no unhandled case.

Now we argue that the distribution of $GBF''_{C\cap S}$ is identical to $GBF'_{C\cap S}$. To see that, let's compare each location in $GBF''_{C\cap S}$ and $GBF'_{C\cap S}$. From Algorithm 1 and the above procedure, we can see that $GBF''_{C\cap S}$ and $GBF'_{C\cap S}$ contain only shares of elements in $C \cap S$ and random strings. Because $GBF''_{C\cap S}$ and $GBF'_{C\cap S}$ use the same set of hash functions, for each $0 \le i \le m-1$, $GBF''_{C\cap S}[i]$ is a share of an element in $C \cap S$ iff $GBF'_{C\cap S}[i]$ is a share of the same element; $GBF''_{C\cap S}[i]$ is a random string iff $GBF'_{C\cap S}[i]$ is a random string. The distribution of a share depends only on the element and the random strings are uniformly distributed. So the distribution of every location in $GBF''_{C\cap S}$ and $GBF'_{C\cap S}$ are identical therefore the distributions of $GBF''_{C\cap S}$ and $GBF'_{C\cap S}$ are identical.

Then we argue that the distribution of $GBF''_{C\cap S}$ is identical to $GBF_{C\cap S}$ except for a negligible probability η.

Case 1, $GBF_{C\cap S}$ encodes at least one elements in $S - C \cap S$. In this case the distribution of $GBF''_{C\cap S}$ differs from the distribution of $GBF_{C\cap S}$. From Theorem 3, the probability of each element in $S - C \cap S$ being encoded in $GBF_{C\cap S}$ is ϵ. Since there are $d = |S| - |C \cap S|$ elements in $S - C \cap S$, the probability of at least one element is falsely contained in $GBF_{C\cap S}$ is:

$$\eta = \sum_{i=1}^{d} \binom{d}{i} \cdot \epsilon^i = \sum_{i=1}^{d} \frac{d(d-1)...(d-i+1)}{i(i-1)...1} \cdot \epsilon^i \le \sum_{i=1}^{d} (d\epsilon)^i \le 2d\epsilon$$

As we can see η is negligible if ϵ is negligible.

Case 2: $GBF_{C\cap S}$ encodes only elements from $C \cap S$. In this case, each element in $S - C\cap S$ may leave up to $k-1$ shares in $GBF_{C\cap S}$. The only difference between $GBF_{C\cap S}$ and $GBF''_{C\cap S}$ is that in $GBF''_{C\cap S}$, all "residue" shares of elements in $S - C \cap S$ are replaced by random strings. From the security of the XOR-based secret sharing scheme, the residue shares should be uniformly random (otherwise they leak information about the elements). Thus the procedure does not change the distribution when modifying $GBF_{C\cap S}$ into $GBF''_{C\cap S}$. So the distributions of $GBF_{C\cap S}$ and $GBF''_{C\cap S}$ are identical. The probability of this case is at least $1-\eta$.

Since $GBF''_{C\cap S} \equiv GBF'_{C\cap S}$ always holds and $GBF_{C\cap S} \equiv GBF''_{C\cap S}$ holds in case 2, we can conclude that $Pr[GBF_{C\cap S} \equiv GBF'_{C\cap S}] \ge 1 - \eta$ thus

$|Pr[D(GBF_{C\cap S}) = 1] - Pr[D(GBF'_{C\cap S}) = 1]| \le \eta$ □

Theorem 4 shows that the probability of $GBF_{C\cap S}$ and $GBF'_{C\cap S}$ are distinguishable is η. In our implementation we set $k = \lambda$ so ϵ is about $2^{-\lambda}$, then a question may arise whether this is appropriate: since η is bounded by $2d\epsilon$, will the security be weakened? For example if $\lambda = 80$ and $d = 2^{20}$, will the security be weakened to about 60-bit rather then desired 80-bit? The answer is no. Loosely speaking, a bigger d means that an adversary can distinguish $GBF_{C\cap S}$ and $GBF'_{C\cap S}$ with a smaller number of attempts, but in each attempt the amount of computation required to distinguish the two also increases. Therefore the total amount of work needed to distinguish the two remains unchanged. We demonstrate it through the following game: an adversary can query an oracle with two sets S and C of its choice. The oracle randomly chooses $b \xleftarrow{r} \{0,1\}$, if $b = 1$, it returns $GBF_{C\cap S}$, if $b = 0$, it returns

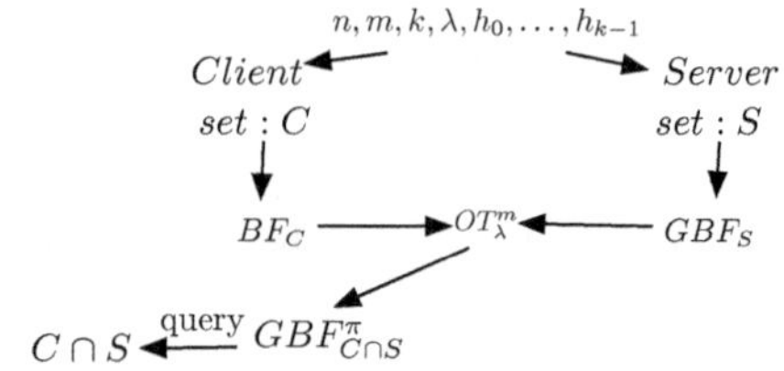

Figure 2: The basic PSI protocol $\pi_\cap$

$GBF'_{C\cap S}$.The adversary can repeatedly query the oracle. At the end of the game, it challenges the oracle and outputs b'. It wins the game if $b' = b$. The advantage is $|Pr[b' = b] - \frac{1}{2}|$. As we show in Theorem 5, the advantage depends only on ϵ, not η.

THEOREM 5. *For an adversary runs in time t, the adversary's advantage in the above game is no more than* $O(t) \cdot \epsilon$.

PROOF. In each oracle query, the adversary has a probability of η to distinguish $GBF_{C\cap S}$ and $GBF'_{C\cap S}$. Therefore if it makes q oracle queries, the advantage will be $q \cdot \eta$. The number of oracle queries the adversary can make is t/t_d, where t_d is the time needed to check whether the GBF encodes an element that is not in the intersection. As there is no way other than querying the GBF to decide, the best the adversary can do is to query all elements in $S - C\cap S$ against the GBF. Therefore $t_d = |S - C\cap S| \cdot t_g = d \cdot t_g$, where t_g is the time of a GBF query. Therefore the advantage of the adversary is: $q \cdot \eta = \frac{t}{t_d} \cdot \eta \le \frac{t}{d \cdot t_g} \cdot 2d\epsilon = O(t) \cdot \epsilon$. □

4.3 Oblivious Bloom Intersection

The idea of the basic protocol is shown in Figure 2. That is, to run Algorithm 3 by two parties using oblivious transfer. Thus we call it oblivious Bloom intersection. The protocol runs as follows:

1. The server's private input is S, and the client's private input is C. The auxiliary inputs include the security parameter λ, the maximum set size n, the optimal Bloom filter parameters m, k and $H = \{h_0, ..., h_{k-1}\}$. The parameter k is set to be the same as the security parameter λ.
2. The client generates an (m, n, k, H)-BF that encodes its private set C, the server generates an (m, n, k, H, λ)-GBF that encodes its private set S. The client uses its Bloom filter as the selection string and acts as the receiver in an OT^m_λ protocol. The server acts as the sender in the OT protocol to send m pair of λ-bit strings $(x_{i,0}, x_{i,1})$ where $x_{i,0}$ is a uniformly random string and $x_{i,1}$ is $GBF_S[i]$. For $0 \le i \le m-1$, if $BF_C[i]$ is 0, then the client receives a random string, if $BF_C[i]$ is 1 it receives $GBF_S[i]$. The result is $GBF^\pi_{C\cap S}$.
3. The client computes the intersection by querying all elements in its set against $GBF^\pi_{C\cap S}$.

At the end of step 2, the client receives a new garbled Bloom filter $GBF^\pi_{C\cap S}$. The OT protocol does exactly what we want to achieve in Algorithm 3.

THEOREM 6. *Given an* (m, n, k, H, λ)*-Garbled Bloom filter* GBF_S *and an* (m, n, k, H)*-Bloom filter* BF_C*. the garbled Bloom filter* $GBF^\pi_{C\cap S}$ *is equivalent to a garbled Bloom filter* $GBF_{C\cap S}$ *that is built by Algorithm 3 using* GBF_S *and* BF_C *.*

PROOF. Let's run the algorithm and protocol simultaneously and use the same random coins for the random strings that are to be placed in $GBF^\pi_{C\cap S}$ and $GBF_{C\cap S}$. From the description of the algorithm and the protocol, we can see that for $0 \le i \le m-1$,

	PK ops	SK ops	Memory	Comm.
Huang's	$O(\lambda)$	$O(n \log n)$	$O(n \log n)$	$O(n \log n)$
De Cristofaro's	$O(n)$	$O(n)$	$O(n)$	$O(n)$
The Basic Protocol	$O(\lambda)$	$O(n)$	$O(n)$	$O(n)$

Table 1: Asymptotic Costs Comparison: n is size of the input sets, λ is the security parameter, PK (SK) ops means public (symmetric) key operations.

if $BF_C[i] = 1$, then $GBF^{\pi}_{C\cap S}[i] = GBF_{C\cap S}[i] = GBF_S[i]$; if $BF_C[i] = 0$, then $GBF^{\pi}_{C\cap S}[i] = GBF_{C\cap S}[i] = r_i$ where r_i is a uniformly random strings. Therefore the two garbled Bloom filters are equivalent. □

Informally, the correctness of the protocol follows from Theorem 3 and 6. The protocol produces a garbled Bloom filter that encodes $C \cap S$, then by querying it the client can obtain the correct intersection except for a negligible probability. To see why the protocol is secure, notice that the only messages being sent in the protocol are the messages in the OT protocol. The client's privacy is protected because the server learns no information about BF_C in the OT execution. The server's privacy is protected because the client receives only $GBF^{\pi}_{C\cap S}$ from the server and it contains only information about elements in $C \cap S$.

The reader may have noticed that the OT protocol can also be used to AND two Bloom filters in a similar way and create an intersection Bloom filter $BF_{C\cap S}$ on the client side. Then do we really need the garbled Bloom filter? Can the server just encode its set into a Bloom filter and run the protocol? The quick answer is we do need the garbled Bloom filter. $BF_{C\cap S}$ leaks information about the server's set because it contains more 1 bits than the Bloom filter built from scratch using $C \cap S$. The expected number of additional 1 bits is $\frac{(t_S - t_\cap)(t_C - t_\cap)}{m - t_\cap}$, where $t_S, t_C, t_\cap$ are the number of 1 bits in BF_S, BF_C and the the Bloom filter built from scratch using $C \cap S$ respectively [37]. The additional knowledge the client gets is the additional 1 bits in $BF_{C\cap S}$.

The protocol makes a single call to OT^m_λ, so the efficiency depends largely on the efficiency of the underlying OT protocol. If we use the semi-honest OT extension protocol from [26] and the Naor-Pinkas OT [34], then:

Computational complexity: To build BF_C or GBF_S, each party needs $k \cdot n$ hash operations. Then the server needs λ public key operations and the client need 2λ public key operations for the Naor-Pinkas OT, and both parties need $m = kn \log_2 e \approx 1.44kn$ hash operations for the OT extension.

Memory complexity: The client needs to keep a copy of the Bloom filter and a copy of the intersection Garbled Bloom filter which in total need at most $(\lambda + 1)m$ bits. This can be optimized to $(\lambda/2 + 1)m$ bits because the client can throw away the string received when $BF_C[i] = 0$ and leave $GBF^{\pi}_{C\cap S}[i] = NULL$. The server needs to store the garbled Bloom filter that is $\lambda \cdot m$ bits.

Communication complexity: The main data sent in the protocol is a bit matrix required by the OT extension and the strings sent by the server in the OT extension. In total $2\lambda \cdot m$ bits. All other communication costs are much less significant and can be ignored.

A quick asymptotic costs comparison of Huang's, De Cristofaro's and our basic protocol is shown in Table 1.

4.4 Security Analysis

Now we sketch the security proof of the basic protocol. The basic protocol is secure in the semi-honest model. The main theorem is stated below:

THEOREM 7. *Let C, S be two sets from a predefined universe, $f_\cap$ be the set intersection function defined as:*

$$f_\cap(C, S) = (f_C(C, S), f_S(C, S)) = (C \cap S, \Lambda).$$

Assuming the underlying OT^m_λ protocol is secure, then the basic PSI protocol $\pi_\cap$ in Section 4.3 securely computes $f_\cap$ in the presence of semi-honest adversaries.

PROOF. (sketch) If the OT^m_λ is secure then the simulators for the sender and receiver are guaranteed to exist, we can use them as subroutines when constructing our simulators.

Server's view We start from the case in which the server is corrupted. We construct a simulator Sim_S that receives the server's private input and output and generates the view of the server in the protocol. Given S, the simulator Sim_S uniformly chooses its random coins r^s and generates the garbled Bloom filter GBF_S that encodes its set S. Then Sim_S invokes the simulator of the OT sender Sim^{OT}_{snd} that is guaranteed to exist. Sim_S obtains Sim^{OT}_{snd}'s view for the OT protocol. Finally Sim_S outputs the simulated view: $(S, r^s, \mathsf{Sim}^{OT}_{snd}(GBF_S, \Lambda))$. We then need to show that the view is indistinguishable from a view in an execution of $\pi_\cap$. A view of the real protocol execution contains the input S, the random coins and the messages in the OT protocol. In the simulated view, the input set S is the same as in the view of a real execution, the outcome of internal random coins r^s is uniformly random thus the distribution is the same as in a real execution. As the OT protocol is secure, then the distribution of the view produced by $\mathsf{Sim}^{OT}_{snd}(GBF_S, \Lambda)$ should be indistinguishable from the view in a real execution of the OT protocol. Thus we conclude the simulated view is indistinguishable from a real view.

Client's view We construct a simulator Sim_C that is given the client's private input C and the output $C \cap S$. Sim_C chooses its random coins r^c. It then generates the Bloom filter BF_C to encode its set and the garbled Bloom filter $GBF_{C\cap S}$ from scratch using Algorithm 1. It then invokes the simulator of the OT receiver Sim^{OT}_{rec} with BF_C and $GBF_{C\cap S}$. Sim_C obtains the view for the OT protocol. Finally Sim_C outputs the simulated view: $(C, r^c, GBF_{C\cap S}, \mathsf{Sim}^{OT}_{rec}(BF_C, GBF_{C\cap S}))$. The view of a real protocol execution contains the input set C, the random coins, the garbled Bloom filter $GBF^{\pi}_{C\cap S}$, and the messages in the OT protocol. In the simulated view, the input set C and r^c should be indistinguishable from the counter parts in the real view. The garbled Bloom filter $GBF_{C\cap S}$ is indistinguishable from $GBF^{\pi}_{C\cap S}$ as we have shown in Theorem 4 and 6. The rest parts in the views are the simulated OT messages and the OT messages in the real execution. As the OT protocol is secure, then they should be indistinguishable. Thus we conclude the simulated view is indistinguishable from a real view.

Combine the above, we conclude that:

$$\{\mathsf{Sim}_S(S, f_S(C,S)\}_{C,S} \stackrel{c}{\equiv} \{\mathsf{view}^{\pi}_S(C,S)\}_{C,S}$$

$$\{\mathsf{Sim}_C(C, f_C(C,S))\}_{C,S} \stackrel{c}{\equiv} \{\mathsf{view}^{\pi}_C(C,S)\}_{C,S}$$

and finish our proof. □

5. THE ENHANCED PROTOCOL

In this section, we present a fully secure PSI protocol whose security holds in the presence of malicious parties. The protocol is shown in Figure 3. The security model and proof can be found in the full version [19].

In the basic protocol, the interaction between the two parties is essentially an oblivious transfer. At the first glance, it seems that we can easily obtain a fully secure protocol by replacing the semi-honest OT protocol with one that is secure against malicious parties. However, this is not enough. A fully secure OT protocol can prevent malicious behaviors such as changing input during the protocol execution but it cannot prevent a malicious client from mounting a full universe attack.

Server's input: Set S
Client's input: Set C
Auxiliary input: the security parameter λ , parameters for BF and GBF $n, k = \lambda, m = 2kn, H = \{h_0, \ldots, h_{k-1}\}$, a secure block cipher E.

1. The client generates a Bloom filter BF_C. The client then generates m λ-bit random strings, say $r_0, \ldots r_{m-1}$. The client sends the random strings to the server.
2. The server generates the garbled Bloom filter GBF_S. The server generates a random key sk for the block cipher E. For $0 \leq i \leq m-1$, the server computes $c_i = E(sk, r_i||GBF_S[i])$. The server also uses a $(m/2, m)$-secret sharing scheme to split sk into m shares $(t_0, \ldots, t_{m-1})$.
3. The server and the client engage in an OT protocol that is secure against malicious parties. The client uses BF_C as the selection string and the server uses as input two sets of strings c_i and t_i $(0 \leq i \leq m-1)$. As a result of the protocol, if $BF_C[i] = 1$, the client receives c_i; if $BF_C[i] = 0$,the client receives t_i.
4. The client recovers sk from the shares it received in the OT. The client creates a garbled Bloom filter $GBF_{C\cap S}$ of size m as follows. For $0 \leq i \leq m-1$ if $BF_C[i] = 0$ then $GBF_{C\cap S}[i] \xleftarrow{r} \{0,1\}^\lambda$; if $BF_C[i] = 1$, the client decrypts c_i and gets $d_i = E^{-1}(sk, c_i)$, checks whether the first λ-bit equals r_i that is sent in step 1. If yes then skip the first λ bits in d_i and copy the second λ bits to $GBF_{C\cap S}[i]$. Otherwise output $\perp$ and terminate. Finally, the client queries $GBF_{C\cap S}$ with its own set C and outputs $C \cap S$.

Figure 3: The Enhanced PSI protocol

In a full universe attack, a malicious client encodes the full universe of all possible elements in its Bloom filter and uses it in the PSI protocol to learn the server's entire set. A Bloom filter can easily represent the full universe by setting all the bits to 1. This is a special feature of Bloom filters and it causes a problem when we try to construct a simulator for the client in the malicious model. Namely, when the adversary uses the all-one Bloom filter, the simulator needs to enumerate all elements in the universe and send them to the trusted party in the ideal process. Without making any assumptions, the universe is potentially too large and a polynomial time algorithm may fail to enumerate all elements.

To prevent the full universe attack, we add a step to make sure that the client's Bloom filter is not all-one. More specifically, the server uses a symmetric key block cipher to encrypt strings in its garbled Bloom filter before transferring them to the client. It forces the client to behave honestly by splitting the key into m shares using a $(m/2, m)$-secret sharing scheme. The client uses the bit array in its Bloom filter as the selection string to receive the intersection garbled Bloom filter and the shares of the key. If the bit in the selection string is 0, the client receives a share of the key; if the bit is 1, the client receives an encrypted string in GBF_S. The intuition is that if the client cheats by using an all-one Bloom filter, it will not be able to gather enough shares to recover the key, and thus will not be able to decrypt the encrypted garbled Bloom filter. In the protocol we set $m = 2kn$ in order to make sure that the client's Bloom filter has at least $m/2$ 0 bits to receive enough shares to recover the key. Since the client has at most n elements and each element needs to be hashed k times, then the number of 1 bits in BF_C will never exceed $kn = m/2$, consequently the number of 0 bits will always be at least $m/2$. Although in this setting m is not optimal, the overhead is acceptable given the optimal number of m is about $1.44kn$.

The added step will not affect the client's privacy, but may affect the correctness of the protocol if a malicious server sends wrong shares of the key or uses a different key to encrypt its garbled Bloom filter. The client cannot detect it because the key is random and the strings in the garbled Bloom filter look random. To prevent this malicious behavior, we also require the client to send m λ-bit random strings $(r_0, \ldots, r_{m-1})$ to the server before the OT. For each $GBF_S[i]$, the server encrypts $r_i||GBF_S[i]$ ($||$ means concatenation) and sends the ciphertext in the OT. After the transfer, the client can recover the key and decrypt the received ciphertexts. If the server is honest, then the client can correctly decrypt using the key it recovered and r_i should present in the decrypted message. For each garbled Bloom filter string the client received, the probability of the server getting away with cheating is $2^{-\lambda}$.

	Ours	De Cristofaro's	Huang's
80	SHA-1, NIST P-192 curve	RSA 1024, SHA-1	1024-bit p, 160-bit q, SHA-1
128	SHA-1 (filter), SHA-256 (OT), NIST P-256 curve	RSA 3072, SHA-1	3072-bit p, 256-bit q, SHA-1
192	SHA-1 (filter), SHA-384 (OT), NIST P-384 curve	RSA 7680, SHA-1	7680-bit p, 384-bit q, SHA-256
256	SHA-1 (filter), SHA-512 (OT), NIST P-521 curve	RSA 15360, SHA-1	15360-bit p, 512-bit q, SHA-256

Table 2: Security parameters and settings

Efficiency In [26] a fully secure version of the OT extension protocol is given. It uses the cut-and-choose approach to ensure a malicious party can cheat with at most $2^{-\Omega(\lambda)}$ probability. The major overhead of the fully secure protocol is introduced by the non-optimal m and cut-and-choose, which increase the communication and computation complexity of the semi-honest one by a factor of 1.4λ. Overhead introduced by other parts of our protocol is small. The additional computational overhead in our protocol includes: the server needs to perform m encryptions and to use the threshold secret sharing scheme to split the key, the client needs to perform $m/2$ decryptions, to recover the key. The additional communication overhead in our protocol includes: $m \cdot \lambda$ bits for sending the random strings of in step 1.

6. IMPLEMENTATION AND EVALUATION

6.1 Implementation

We have implemented a prototype of the basic protocol in C. The source code (and its Java port) is released online[1]. It uses OpenSSL (1.0.1e) for the cryptographic operations. We currently use keyed SHA-1 to build/query Bloom filters and garbled Bloom filters[2]. Namely each $h_i(x)$ is instantiated as $sha1(s_i||x)$ mod m, where s_i is a unique salt. We implement the semi-honest OT extension protocol [26] on top of the Naor-Pinkas OT protocol [34].

[1] http://personal.cis.strath.ac.uk/changyu.dong/PSI/PSI.html

[2] Cryptographically strong hash functions are not necessary here. Later we will change to more efficient hash functions e.g. MurmurHash [2] that has been used by Apache Hadoop and Cassandra in their Bloom filter implementation.

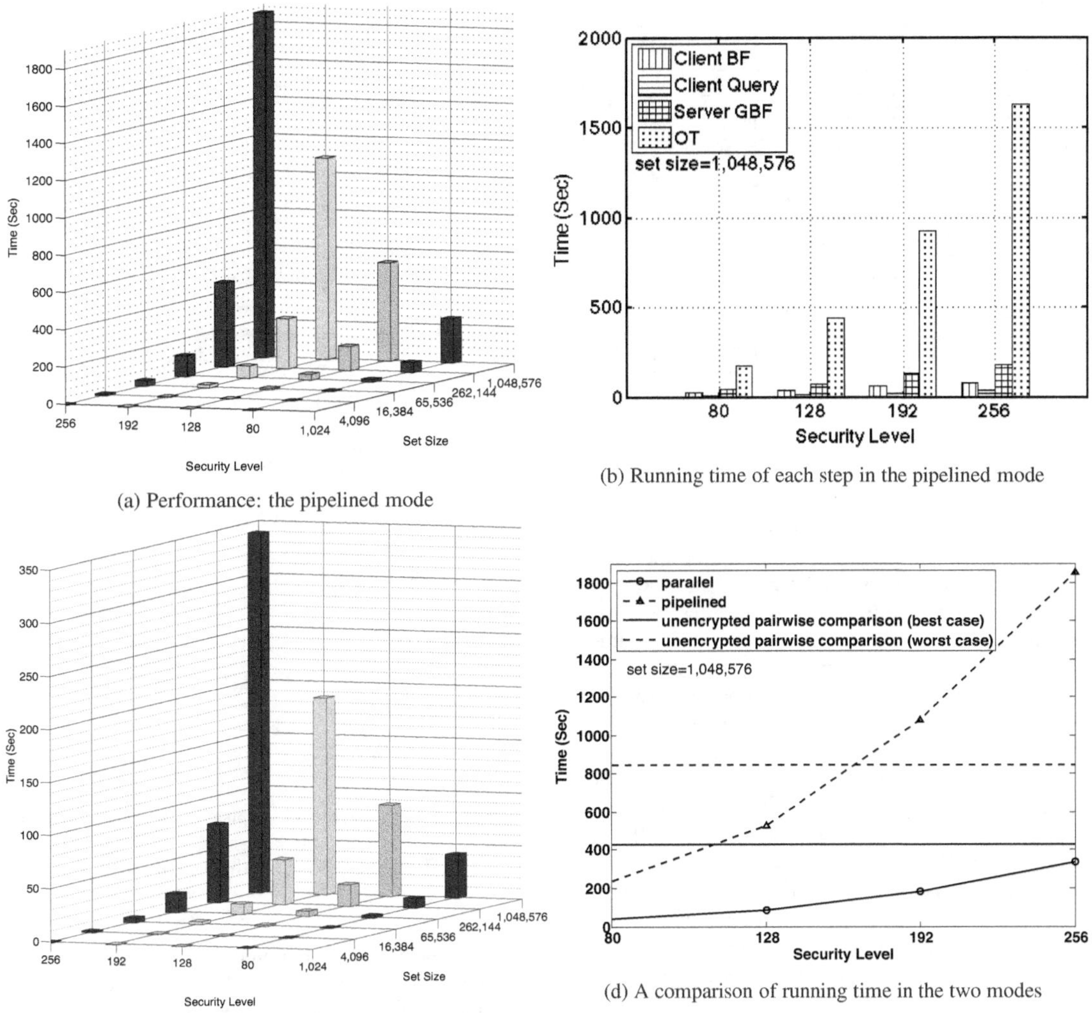

(a) Performance: the pipelined mode

(b) Running time of each step in the pipelined mode

(c) Performance: the parallel mode

(d) A comparison of running time in the two modes

Figure 4: Performance of our basic protocol

The hash functions in the OT extension protocol are instantiated depending on the security parameters. When hash values need to be truncated, the truncation follows the steps specified by the NIST [14]. We use the NIST elliptic curve groups over $\mathbb{F}_p$ [36] for the public key operations required by the Naor-Pinkas OT protocol. We use elliptic curve groups because they are much faster than integer groups at high security levels.

The C prototype has two executables, one for the client and one for the server. The client and server communicate through TCP. The prototype can work in two modes: pipelined and parallel. In the pipelined mode, on each side, the computation is done in a single thread, an additional thread transmits data in parallel when possible. Parallel data transmission enables the server or the client to start working immediately without waiting for the other party to complete its computation. The parallel mode extends the pipeline mode by utilizing all CPU cores and distributing tasks on all cores evenly. Our test result shows that the parallel mode can improve the performance significantly on multicore systems. This is due to the fact that the computation in our protocol is dominated by independent hashing. Namely, on each side, n independent set elements each needs to be hashed k times to build the Bloom filter or the garbled Bloom filter, also hashing of m matrix rows are needed in the OT extension protocol. As the data to be hashed is independent, this is a perfect SPMD (single program multiple data) scenario. The program detects the number of cores available, decides the number of threads, evenly allocates a portion of data to each thread, and then launch the threads to execute the tasks in parallel. The hash values are then consumed by main threads that run the protocol. This approach requires only minimal changes to the program structure. For example, only one line (line 8) needs to be changed in Algorithm 1. Namely instead of hashing the element, the algorithm reads from an array a precomputed index number.

6.2 Performance Evaluation

In this section we show the performance evaluation results of our prototype. All experiments were conducted on two Mac computers. The server is a Mac Pro with 2 Intel E5645 6-core 2.4GHz CPUs, 32 GB RAM and runs Mac OS X 10.8. The client is a Macbook Pro laptop with an Intel 2720QM quad-core 2.2 GHz CPU, 16 GB RAM and runs Mac OS X 10.7. The two computers are connected by 1000M Ethernet. The security settings of the experiments in this and the next section are summarized in Table 2. In all experiments we set BF/GBF parameter $k = \lambda$ so the false positive probability of a BF is at most $2^{-\lambda}$, we set m to be the optimal value $kn \log_2 e$. For example, at 80-bit security $k = \lambda = 80$, and when $n = 2^{20}$, $m = 120795960$. We use randomly generated `int` sets in the ex-

Set size / protocol	80-bit Security					
	2^{10}	2^{12}	2^{14}	2^{16}	2^{18}	2^{20}
Huang's(Java)	19	65	331	2049	22853	98468†
Our pipelined (Java)	0.693	2.34	7.02	31.5	110.6	426
Our parallel (Java)	0.195	0.431	1.42	6.31	25	91
De Cristofaro's (C)	0.590	2.41	9.84	41.3	159	641
Our pipelined (C)	0.275	0.863	3.37	13.9	54.0	237
Our parallel (C)	0.075	0.207	0.642	2.49	9.49	40.9
	256-bit Security					
Huang's (Java)	32	157	733	4647	43156	185570†
Our pipelined (Java)	8.2	20.3	68.44	313.4	1298	5421
Our parallel (Java)	1.5	3.2	10.5	54	215	1132
De Cristofaro's (C)	462	1850	7419	29654	118286	473144†
Our pipelined (C)	4.09	8.94	29.8	113	453	1852
Our parallel (C)	0.741	1.53	4.68	17.8	74.2	339

All time shown in the table are in seconds. † – estimated running time

Table 3: Performance comparison

periments. We measure the total running time of the protocol. The measurement starts from the client sending the request and ends immediately after the client outputting the intersection. The time includes all operations such as building the Bloom filter, building the garbled Bloom filter, the full OT extension protocol (including the underlying Naor-Pinkas OT), data transmission, and the client-side query for obtaining the intersection. We do not, however, include the time for initialization tasks, e.g. to generate random sets, to interpret the command line arguments, and to setup sockets.

We first show the performance of the prototype working in the pipelined mode. In the pipelined mode, all computation on each side is done in a single thread. We vary the set size (n) from 2^{10} to 2^{20} and security parameters (λ and k) from 80 to 256. The result is shown in Figure 4a. We can see the running time increases almost linearly in the set size at each security level. And for each increase in security parameter, the running time increases only by a factor of approximately 2. We also measured the time for each individual step of the protocol. In the experiments, we fix the set size (2^{20}) and vary only security levels. The result is shown in Figure 4b. We can see the protocol running time is dominated by the OT execution. This suggests that with a more efficient OT protocol, the total running time can be further reduced.

Then we show the performance of the parallel mode. In the parallel mode, we use multiple threads for computation. The result is shown in Figure 4c. The total running time in the parallel mode is much less than in the pipelined mode. At 80-bit security, million elements set intersection can be done in 41 seconds. In the highest security setting, the same computation can be done in 339 seconds – that is less than 6 minutes. A comparison of the performance in the two modes is shown in Figure 4d. The client has 4 cores and the server has 12 cores, and we can see that the parallel mode is about 5 times faster than the pipelined mode. This shows that our protocol can fully take the advantage of the multicore architecture. We believe the ability to easily scale up to multiple cores is a clear advantage of our protocol and makes the protocol suitable for large scale private data processing.

The performance of our protocol can even beat some inefficient plain algorithms in some settings. For example, Figure 4d shows the time needed for a single threaded C program to compute the intersection of two unencrypted random sets ($n = 2^{20}$) by pairwisely comparing the elements. It needs 429 seconds in the best case when $C = S$, and needs 844 seconds in the worst case when $C \cap S = \emptyset$.

6.3 Performance Comparison

We compared the performance of our basic protocol against two

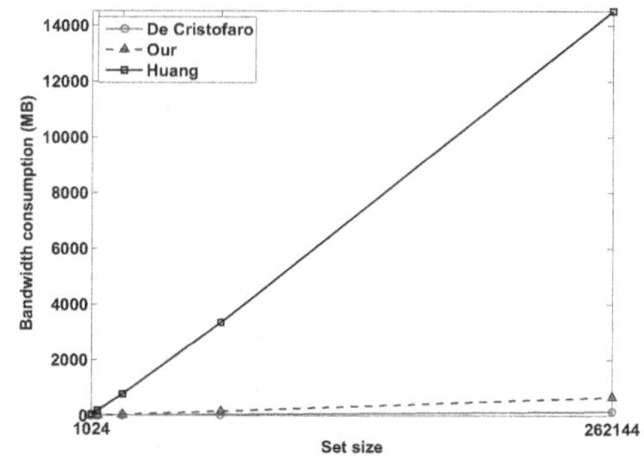

(a) Bandwidth Consumption: 80-bit security

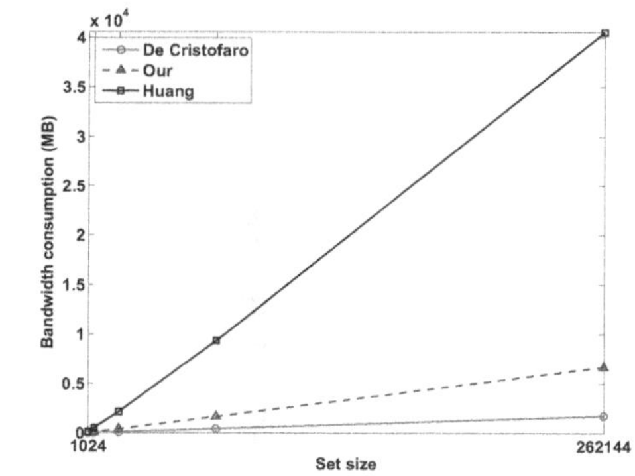

(b) Bandwidth Consumption: 256-bit security

Figure 5: Bandwidth Consumption Comparison

other semi-honest PSI protocols. The protocols we compared to are De Cristofaro's RSA-OPRF protocol (implemented in C) and Huang's Sort-Compare-Shuffle with Waksman Network protocol (implemented in Java). They are previously the fastest PSI protocols and the code has been optimized by the authors. We test the two protocols on the same hardware and OSes that we use for testing ours. De Cristofaro's C implementation is compiled with OpenSSL 1.0.1e and GMP 5.1.1 using gcc. The RSA public exponent is 3 in all tests. We run Huang's Java code using Java 1.7.0_12. The element bit length in Huang's protocol is set to 32. As it is unfair to compare the performance of Huang's Java code with our C code, we ported our C code to Java and measured the performance.

We measured the total running time of the protocols. De Cristofaro's code outputs running time so we use the output directly[3]. Huang's code has no such output, and we measure the running time of the $execution()$ function in the $Program$ class.

The comparison in Table 3 shows that in all settings, both modes of our protocol are faster than the other two protocols. Both De Cristofaro's implementation and Huang's implementation pipeline the protocol execution, which is exactly what we do in the pipelined mode. Therefore the performance of these three can be compared directly[4]. The performance of De Cristofaro's protocol is close to ours at 80-bit security and is faster than Huang's. But when the se-

[3]We exclude the running time of the last step in the protocol. In this step the client searches the hash values received in the protocol to find the intersection. This step is excluded because it uses an inefficient pairwise comparison and the authors plan to replace it with a hashtable search.

[4]De Cristofaro's code uses two threads on each side for computation. But this does not affect the comparison result.

curity parameter increases to 256-bit, it becomes much slower than our protocol and Huang's. This is because De Cristofaro's protocol is based mainly on public key operations, while ours and Huang's protocols rely on mostly symmetric key operations. Put aside differences caused by languages and implementation, our protocol is faster than Huang's because it requires the same number of public key operations but significantly less symmetric key operations. For example, at 80-bit security with 2^{20} input size, our protocol requires 0.4 billion symmetric key operations, while Huang's requires 8.5 billion (1.7 billion non-free gates, each requires 4 symmetric key operations to build and another 1 to evaluate).

We skip the test with the biggest input size (2^{20}) on De Cristofaro's protocol at 256-bit security because it would take too long. The running time of De Cristofaro's protocol is linear in the input size, our estimation is that it would need 131 hours to finish. This estimation is based on the result of test with 2^{18}-element sets at the same security level. The JVM on the client computer ran out of memory (16 GB) when we testing Huang's protocol with 2^{20}-element sets at 80-bit security. The test was repeated twice and both times we got the same error. We could not finish the test but base on the test result of input size 2^{18}, we estimate the test would need 27 hours. This estimation is somehow far from the time reported by the authors, that is 6 hours. However the test had been running for more than 24 hours before the JVM threw the error. Therefore we believe the estimation is reasonable. We observed excessive paging activities during the test on the client computer because the JVM occupied all free memory (14 GB). This may account for the difference between our estimation and the authors' measurement. Because at 256-bit security Huang's protocol requires even more memory, we skip the test with 2^{20} input size and estimate the running time to be 51 hours from test result of input size 2^{18}.

We also measured bandwidth consumption of the protocols. As we couldn't finish the tests with the other protocols using 2^{20} input size, the largest input size we used in the experiment was 2^{18}. The results are shown in Figure 5. As we can see, the bandwidth consumption of De Cristofaro's and our protocol is almost linear. Our protocol consumes more bandwidth than De Cristofaro's protocol but less than Huang's protocol.

6.4 Further Parallelization

GPGPUs For many personal computers, a readily available massive parallel computing device is the graphic cards. Modern GPUs have hundreds of processing cores and can provide ample computation cycles and high memory bandwidth to massively parallel applications. The computation in our protocol can be easily parallelized and therefore is an ideal application for GPU acceleration. We have started implementing the protocol on top of OpenCL [3]. A test on our GPU version of SHA-1 shows that on an ATI Radeon HD 5770 graphic card, it only takes 37.5 milliseconds to perform 1 million hash operations. This is about 5 times faster than a single 2.4 GHz CPU core.

Extremely Big Data Set & Cloud Computing In practice, to process extremely big data set, we have to distribute the task on multiple computers. New computing paradigms such as cloud computing make it possible to execute such distributed tasks "on demand". Our protocol can be easily deployed on cloud platforms. Here we show how to do it with the semi-honest protocol. The fully secure protocol case is similar. From a high level point of view, the client and the server throw their elements into bins using an hash function. Each side has b bins and each bin contains about $\lceil \frac{n}{b} \rceil$ elements. Then they build Bloom filters and garbled Bloom filters for each bin. The parameter k is still determined by the desired false positive probability, the parameter m is determined by k and

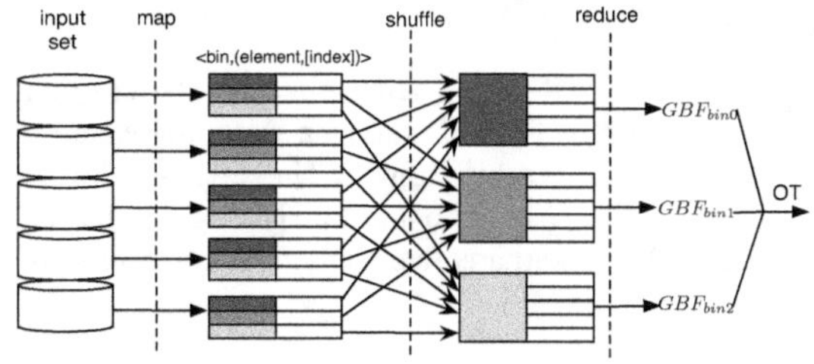

Figure 6: MapReduce on the server side

the bin size. The filters are associated with the bin number. Then for each $0 \leq i < b$, the server uses OT to transfer the garbled Bloom filter for bin i to the client, who uses its Bloom filter for bin i as the selection string. The client then queries all elements in its bin i against the received garbled Bloom filter and adds any positive elements into the result set. In the end, the client has the intersection. Conceptually, this splits a big set into b smaller sets that each can be handled by a single node. It is correct because the two parties use the same hash function so an element thrown by the server into bin i will also be threw by the client into bin i. The idea can be implemented using the MapReduce programming model [18] easily. For example, figure 6 depicts the MapReduce procedure of the first step on the server side with 3 bins: the map function takes a portion of the input set and maps an element into a key-value pair such that the key is the bin number and the value is a tuple consists of the element and k index numbers. The MapReduce framework shuffles and groups together the values returned by the map function that have the same key. The reduce function generates a garbled Bloom filter of a certain bin and outputs it for OT. We are currently experimenting with Hadoop [1] to implement the protocol in MapReduce.

7. CONCLUSION AND FUTURE WORK

In this paper we presented a highly efficient and scalable PSI protocol based on oblivious Bloom intersection. The protocol depends mostly on efficient symmetric key operations and the operations can be parallelized easily. We presented two variants of the protocol: the basic one is secure in the semi-honest model and the enhanced one is secure in the malicious model. The performance evaluation and comparison results show that our protocol is orders of magnitude faster than the previously fastest protocols. The results also show that our protocol can fully utilize the parallel processing capability provided by the multicore architecture. The efficiency and scalability make our protocol suitable for large scale privacy preserving data processing.

As discussed in Section 6.4, we are in the process of prototyping the protocol on GPGPUs and MapReduce. The preliminary results of this work is encouraging. We hope more parallelization options could enable more applications in various computing environments.

In the field of cryptographic protocols, we have seen many examples that a new protocol improves performance of previous work by using a better algorithm. It is different in this work: the performance gain comes mainly from a better data structure. We would like to continue our research along this line. Namely we will investigate, adapt and design better data structures, so that they can be used in the design of more efficient cryptographic protocols.

Acknowledgements

Changyu Dong is supported by a science faculty starter grant from the University of Strathclyde. Zikai Wen is supported by an undergraduate research internship from the University of Strathclyde. We thank Emiliano De Cristofaro and Yan Huang for sharing their PSI source code. We also thank the anonymous reviewers for their helpful comments.

8. REFERENCES

[1] Hadoop. http://hadoop.apache.org/.

[2] Murmurhash. https://code.google.com/p/smhasher/.

[3] Opencl. http://www.khronos.org/opencl/.

[4] C. C. Aggarwal and P. S. Yu, editors. *Privacy-Preserving Data Mining - Models and Algorithms*, volume 34 of *Advances in Database Systems*. Springer, 2008.

[5] G. Ateniese, E. De Cristofaro, and G. Tsudik. (If) size matters: Size-hiding private set intersection. In *Public Key Cryptography*, pages 156–173, 2011.

[6] P. Baldi, R. Baronio, E. De Cristofaro, P. Gasti, and G. Tsudik. Countering gattaca: efficient and secure testing of fully-sequenced human genomes. In *ACM Conference on Computer and Communications Security*, pages 691–702, 2011.

[7] D. Beaver. Correlated pseudorandomness and the complexity of private computations. In *STOC*, pages 479–488, 1996.

[8] M. Bellare and P. Rogaway. Random oracles are practical: A paradigm for designing efficient protocols. In *ACM Conference on Computer and Communications Security*, pages 62–73, 1993.

[9] B. H. Bloom. Space/time trade-offs in hash coding with allowable errors. *Commun. ACM*, 13(7):422–426, 1970.

[10] P. Bose, H. Guo, E. Kranakis, A. Maheshwari, P. Morin, J. Morrison, M. H. M. Smid, and Y. Tang. On the false-positive rate of bloom filters. *Inf. Process. Lett.*, 108(4):210–213, 2008.

[11] E. Bursztein, M. Hamburg, J. Lagarenne, and D. Boneh. Openconflict: Preventing real time map hacks in online games. In *IEEE Symposium on Security and Privacy*, pages 506–520, 2011.

[12] J. Camenisch and G. M. Zaverucha. Private intersection of certified sets. In *Financial Cryptography*, pages 108–127, 2009.

[13] D. Dachman-Soled, T. Malkin, M. Raykova, and M. Yung. Efficient robust private set intersection. In *ACNS*, pages 125–142, 2009.

[14] Q. Dang. SP 800-107 (rev. 1). recommendation for applications using approved hash algorithms. Technical report, Gaithersburg, MD, United States, 2012.

[15] E. De Cristofaro, J. Kim, and G. Tsudik. Linear-complexity private set intersection protocols secure in malicious model. In *ASIACRYPT*, pages 213–231, 2010.

[16] E. De Cristofaro and G. Tsudik. Practical private set intersection protocols with linear complexity. In *Financial Cryptography*, pages 143–159, 2010.

[17] E. De Cristofaro and G. Tsudik. Experimenting with fast private set intersection. In *TRUST*, pages 55–73, 2012.

[18] J. Dean and S. Ghemawat. Mapreduce: Simplified data processing on large clusters. In *OSDI*, pages 137–150, 2004.

[19] C. Dong, L. Chen, and Z. Wen. When private set intersection meets big data: An efficient and scalable protocol. Cryptology ePrint Archive, Report 2013/515, 2013.

[20] S. Even, O. Goldreich, and A. Lempel. A randomized protocol for signing contracts. *Commun. ACM*, 28(6):637–647, 1985.

[21] M. J. Freedman, K. Nissim, and B. Pinkas. Efficient private matching and set intersection. In *EUROCRYPT*, pages 1–19, 2004.

[22] O. Goldreich. *The Foundations of Cryptography - Volume 2, Basic Applications*. Cambridge University Press, 2004.

[23] C. Hazay and Y. Lindell. Efficient protocols for set intersection and pattern matching with security against malicious and covert adversaries. In *TCC*, pages 155–175, 2008.

[24] C. Hazay and K. Nissim. Efficient set operations in the presence of malicious adversaries. In *Public Key Cryptography*, pages 312–331, 2010.

[25] Y. Huang, D. Evans, and J. Katz. Private set intersection: Are garbled circuits better than custom protocols? In *NDSS*, 2012.

[26] Y. Ishai, J. Kilian, K. Nissim, and E. Petrank. Extending oblivious transfers efficiently. In *CRYPTO*, pages 145–161, 2003.

[27] S. Jarecki and X. Liu. Efficient oblivious pseudorandom function with applications to adaptive OT and secure computation of set intersection. In *TCC*, pages 577–594, 2009.

[28] S. Jarecki and X. Liu. Fast secure computation of set intersection. In *SCN*, pages 418–435, 2010.

[29] F. Kerschbaum. Outsourced private set intersection using homomorphic encryption. In *ASIACCS*, pages 85–86, 2012.

[30] L. Kissner and D. X. Song. Privacy-preserving set operations. In *CRYPTO*, pages 241–257, 2005.

[31] D. Many, M. Burkhart, and X. Dimitropoulos. Fast private set operations with sepia. Technical Report 345, Mar 2012.

[32] G. Mezzour, A. Perrig, V. D. Gligor, and P. Papadimitratos. Privacy-preserving relationship path discovery in social networks. In *CANS*, pages 189–208, 2009.

[33] S. Nagaraja, P. Mittal, C.-Y. Hong, M. Caesar, and N. Borisov. Botgrep: Finding P2P bots with structured graph analysis. In *USENIX Security Symposium*, pages 95–110, 2010.

[34] M. Naor and B. Pinkas. Efficient oblivious transfer protocols. In *SODA*, pages 448–457, 2001.

[35] A. Narayanan, N. Thiagarajan, M. Lakhani, M. Hamburg, and D. Boneh. Location privacy via private proximity testing. In *NDSS*, 2011.

[36] NIST. Recommended elliptic curves for federal government use, 1999.

[37] O. Papapetrou, W. Siberski, and W. Nejdl. Cardinality estimation and dynamic length adaptation for bloom filters. *Distributed and Parallel Databases*, 28(2-3):119–156, 2010.

[38] M. O. Rabin. How to exchange secrets by oblivious transfer. *Technical Report TR-81, Harvard Aiken Computation Laboratory*, 1981.

[39] B. Schneier. *Applied cryptography - protocols, algorithms, and source code in C (2. ed.)*. Wiley, 1996.

[40] A. Shamir. How to share a secret. *Commun. ACM*, 22(11):612–613, 1979.

Privacy-Preserving Matrix Factorization

Valeria Nikolaenko
Stanford University
valerini@cs.stanford.edu

Stratis Ioannidis
Technicolor
stratis.ioannidis@technicolor.com

Udi Weinsberg
Technicolor
udi.weinsberg@technicolor.com

Marc Joye
Technicolor
marc.joye@technicolor.com

Nina Taft
Technicolor
nina.taft@technicolor.com

Dan Boneh
Stanford University
dabo@cs.stanford.edu

ABSTRACT

Recommender systems typically require users to reveal their ratings to a recommender service, which subsequently uses them to provide relevant recommendations. Revealing ratings has been shown to make users susceptible to a broad set of inference attacks, allowing the recommender to learn private user attributes, such as gender, age, *etc.* In this work, we show that a recommender can profile items without ever learning the ratings users provide, or even which items they have rated. We show this by designing a system that performs matrix factorization, a popular method used in a variety of modern recommendation systems, through a cryptographic technique known as garbled circuits. Our design uses oblivious sorting networks in a novel way to leverage sparsity in the data. This yields an efficient implementation, whose running time is $\Theta(M \log^2 M)$ in the number of ratings M. Crucially, our design is also highly parallelizable, giving a linear speedup with the number of available processors. We further fully implement our system, and demonstrate that even on commodity hardware with 16 cores, our privacy-preserving implementation can factorize a matrix with 10K ratings within a few hours.

Categories and Subject Descriptors

K.4.1 [**Computers and Society**]: Public Policy Issues—*privacy*; H.2.8 [**Database Management**]: Database Applications—*data mining, algorithms, design, performance*; G.1.6 [**Numerical Analysis**]: Optimization—*gradient methods*

Keywords

Garbled circuits; matrix factorization; multi-party computation; privacy; recommender systems

1. INTRODUCTION

A great deal of research and commercial activity in the last decade has led to the wide-spread use of recommendation systems. Such systems offer users personalized recommendations for many kinds of items, such as movies, TV shows, music, books, hotels, restaurants, and more. To receive useful recommendations, users supply substantial personal information about their preferences, trusting that the recommender will manage this data appropriately.

Nevertheless, earlier studies [49, 37, 47, 1, 46] have identified multiple ways in which recommenders can abuse such information or expose the user to privacy threats. Recommenders are often motivated to resell data for a profit [6], but also use it to extract information beyond what is intentionally revealed by the user. For example, even records of user preferences typically not perceived as sensitive, such as movie ratings or a person's TV viewing history, can be used to infer a user's political affiliation, gender, *etc.*, [61]. The private information that can be inferred from the data in a recommendation system is constantly evolving as new data mining and inference methods are developed, for either malicious or benign purposes. In the extreme, records of user preferences can be used to even *uniquely identify a user*: Naranyan and Shmatikov strikingly demonstrated this by de-anonymizing the Neflix dataset [49]. As such, even if the recommender is not malicious, an unintentional leakage of such data makes users susceptible to linkage attacks [46]. Because we cannot always foresee future inference threats, accidental information leakage, or insider threats (purposeful leakage), it is appealing to consider how one might build a recommendation system in which users do not reveal their personal data in the clear.

In this work, we study a widely used collaborative filtering technique known as matrix factorization [31, 5], that was instrumental in winning the Netflix prize competition [35], and is a core component in many real world recommendation systems. It is not a priori clear whether matrix factorization can be performed in a privacy-preserving way; there are several challenges associated with this task. First, to address the privacy concerns raised above, matrix factorization should be performed without *the recommender ever learning the users' ratings, or even which items they have rated.* This requirement is key: earlier studies [61] show that even knowing which movie a user has rated can be used to infer, *e.g.*, her gender. Second, such a privacy-preserving algorithm ought to be *efficient*, and scale gracefully (*e.g.*, linearly) with the number of ratings submitted by users. The privacy requirements imply that our matrix factorization algorithm ought to be *data-oblivious*: its execution ought to not depend on the user input. Moreover, the operations performed by matrix factorization are non-linear; thus, it is not a-priori clear how to implement matrix factorization efficiently under both

CCS'13, November 4–8, 2013, Berlin, Germany.

http://dx.doi.org/10.1145/2508859.2516751.

of these constraints. Finally, in a practical, real-world scenario, users have limited communication and computation resources, and should not be expected to remain online after they have supplied their data. We thus seek a "send-and-forget" type solution, operating in the presence of users that move back and forth between being online and offline from the recommendation service.

We make the following contributions.

- We design a protocol that meets all of the above goals for privacy, efficiency and practicality. Our protocol is hybrid, combining partially homomorphic encryption with Yao's garbled circuits.
- We propose and use in our design a novel data-oblivious algorithm for matrix factorization. Implemented as a garbled circuit, it yields complexity $O(M \log^2 M)$, where M the number of submitted ratings. This is within a $\log^2 M$ factor of matrix factorization complexity in the clear. We achieve this by using Batcher sorting networks, allowing us to leverage sparsity in submitted ratings.
- Crucially, using sorting networks as a core component of our design allows us to take full advantage of the parallelization that such sorting networks enable. We incorporate this and several other optimizations in our design, illustrating that garbled circuits for matrix factorization can be brought into the realm of practicality.
- Finally, we implement our entire system using the FastGC framework [24] and evaluate it with real-world datasets. We modified the FastGC framework in two important ways, by enabling parallelized garbling and computation across multiple processors, and by reducing the memory footprint by partitioning the circuit in layers. Further additional optimizations, including reusing sorting results, and implementing operations via free XOR gates [34], allow us to run matrix factorization over 10^4 ratings within a few hours. Given that recommender systems execute matrix factorization on, *e.g.*, a weekly basis, this is acceptable for most real-life applications.

To the best of our knowledge, we are the first to enable matrix factorization over encrypted data. Although sorting networks have been used before for simple computations, our work is the first to apply sorting networks to leverage matrix sparsity, especially in a numerical task as complex as matrix factorization. Overcoming scalability and performance challenges, our solution is close to practicality for modern day recommendation services.

The remainder of this paper is organized as follows. Section 2 outlines the problem of privacy-preserving matrix factorization. Our solution is presented in Section 3. We discuss extensions in Section 4 and our implementation and experimental results in Sections 5 and 6, respectively.

2. PROBLEM STATEMENT

2.1 Matrix Factorization

In the standard "collaborative filtering" setting [35], n users rate a subset of m possible items (*e.g.*, movies). For $[n] := \{1, \dots, n\}$ the set of users, and $[m] := \{1, \dots, m\}$ the set of items, we denote by $\mathcal{M} \subseteq [n] \times [m]$ the user/item pairs for which a rating has been generated, and by $M = |\mathcal{M}|$ the total number of ratings. Finally, for $(i,j) \in \mathcal{M}$, we denote by $r_{ij} \in \mathbb{R}$ the rating generated by user i for item j.

In a practical setting, both n and m are large numbers, typically ranging between 10^4–10^6. In addition, the ratings provided are *sparse*, that is, $M = \Theta(n+m)$, which is much smaller than the total number of potential ratings $n \cdot m$. This is consistent with typical user behavior, as each user may rate only a relatively small number of items (not depending on m, the "catalogue" size).

Given the ratings in $\mathcal{M}$, a recommender system wishes to predict the ratings for user/item pairs in $[n] \times [m] \setminus \mathcal{M}$. Matrix factorization performs this task by fitting a bi-linear model on the existing ratings. In particular, for some small dimension $d \in \mathbb{N}$, it is assumed that there exist vectors $u_i \in \mathbb{R}^d$, $i \in [n]$, and $v_j \in \mathbb{R}^d$, $j \in [m]$, such that

$$r_{ij} = \langle u_i, v_i \rangle + \varepsilon_{ij}$$

where ε_{ij} are i.i.d. Gaussian random variables. The vectors u_i and v_j are called the *user* and *item* profiles, respectively. We will use the notation $U = [u_i^T]_{i \in [n]} \in \mathbb{R}^{n \times d}$ for the $n \times d$ matrix whose i-th row comprises the profile of user i, and $V = [v_j^T]_{i \in [m]} \in \mathbb{R}^{m \times d}$ for the $m \times d$ matrix whose j-th row comprises the profile of item j.

Given the ratings $\{r_{ij} : (i,j) \in \mathcal{M}\}$, the recommender typically computes the profiles U and V by performing the following *regularized least squares minimization:*[1]

$$\min_{U,V} \frac{1}{M} \sum_{(i,j)\in\mathcal{M}} (r_{ij} - \langle u_i, v_j \rangle)^2 + \lambda \sum_{i\in[n]} \|u_i\|_2^2 + \mu \sum_{j\in[m]} \|v_j\|_2^2 \quad (1)$$

for some positive $\lambda, \mu > 0$. The computation of U, V through (1) is a computationally intensive task even in the clear, and is typically performed by recommenders in "batch-mode", *e.g.*, once a week, using ratings collected thus far. These profiles are subsequently used to predict ratings through:

$$\hat{r}_{ij} = \langle u_i, v_j \rangle, \quad i \in [n], j \in [m] \ . \quad (2)$$

The regularized mean square error in (1) is not a convex function; several methods for performing this minimization have been proposed in literature [35, 31, 5]. We focus on gradient descent [35], a popular method used in practice, which we review below. Denoting by $F(U,V)$ the regularized mean square error in (1), gradient descent operates by iteratively adapting the profiles U and V through the adaptation rule

$$\begin{aligned} u_i(t) &= u_i(t-1) - \gamma \nabla_{u_i} F(U(t-1), V(t-1)), \\ v_i(t) &= v_i(t-1) - \gamma \nabla_{v_i} F(U(t-1), V(t-1)), \end{aligned} \quad (3)$$

where $\gamma > 0$ a small gain factor and

$$\begin{aligned} \nabla_{u_i} F(U,V) &= -2\textstyle\sum_{j:(i,j)\in\mathcal{M}} v_j (r_{ij} - \langle u_i, v_j \rangle) + 2\lambda u_i, \\ \nabla_{v_j} F(U,V) &= -2\textstyle\sum_{i:(i,j)\in\mathcal{M}} u_i (r_{ij} - \langle u_i, v_j \rangle) + 2\mu v_i, \end{aligned} \quad (4)$$

where $U(0)$ and $V(0)$ consist of uniformly random norm 1 rows (*i.e.*, profiles are selected u.a.r. from the norm 1 ball).

2.2 Setting

Figure 1 depicts the actors in our privacy-preserving matrix factorization system. Each user $i \in [n]$ wants to keep her ratings $\{r_{ij} : (i,j) \in \mathcal{M}\}$ private. The recommender system (RecSys), performs the privacy-preserving matrix factorization, while a *crypto-service provider* (CSP), enables this private computation.

[1] Assuming Gaussian priors on the profiles U and V, the minimization (1) corresponds to maximum likelihood estimation of U and V.

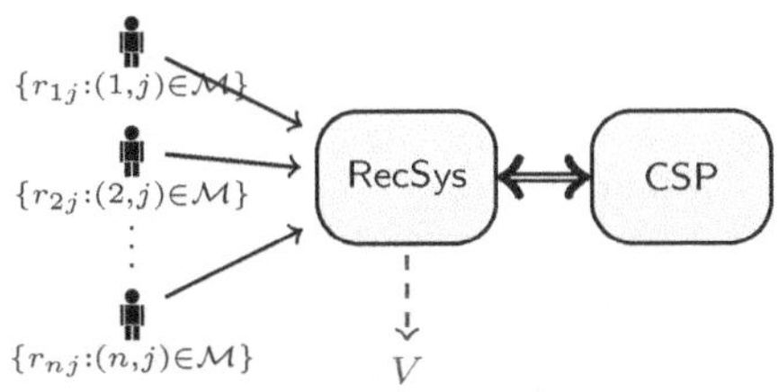

Figure 1: The parties in our first protocol design. The recommender system learns nothing about users' ratings, other than the model V.

Our objective is to design a protocol that allows the RecSys to execute matrix factorization while *neither the RecSys nor the CSP learn anything other than the item profiles,*[2] *i.e.*, V (the sole output of RecSys in Fig. 1). In particular, neither should learn a user's ratings, or even which items she has actually rated. Clearly, a protocol that allows the recommender to learn *both* user *and* item profiles reveals too much: in such a design, the recommender can trivially infer a user's ratings from the inner product (2). As such, our focus is on designing a privacy-preserving protocol in which the recommender learns only the item profiles.

There is a utility in learning the item profiles alone. First, the embedding of items in $\mathbb{R}^d$ through matrix factorization allows the recommender to infer (and encode) similarity: items whose profiles have small Euclidean distance are items that are rated similarly by users. As such, the task of learning the item profiles is of interest to the recommender beyond the actual task of recommendations. Second, having obtained the item profiles, there is a way the recommender can use them to provide relevant recommendations without any additional data revelation by users: the recommender can send V to a user (or release it publicly); knowing her ratings, i can infer her (private) profile u_i by solving (1) w.r.t. u_i through ridge regression [15]. Having u_i and V, she can subsequently predict all ratings through (2).

Both of these scenarios presume that neither the recommender nor the users object to the public release of V. However, in Section 4.1 we show that there is also a way to easily extend our design so that *users learn their predicted ratings* while *the recommender learns nothing, not even* V. For the sake of simplicity, as well as on account of the utility of such a protocol to the recommender, our main focus is on allowing the recommender to learn the item profiles. This design is also the most technically challenging; we treat the second case as an extension to this basic design.

We note that, in general, both output of the profile V or the rating predictions for a user may reveal something about other users' ratings. In pathological cases where there are, *e.g.*, only two users, both revelations may let the users discover each other's ratings. We do not address such cases; when the privacy implications of the revelation of item profiles or individual ratings are not tolerable, techniques such as adding noise can be used, as discussed in Section 7.

Threat Model. Our security guarantees will hold under the *honest but curious* threat model [17]. In other words, the RecSys and CSP follow the protocols we propose as prescribed; however, these interested parties may elect to analyze protocol transcripts, even off-line, in order to infer some additional information. We further assume that the recommender and CSP do not collude; the case of a malicious RecSys is discussed in Section 4.

[2] Technically, our algorithm also leaks the number of items rated by each user, though this can be easily rectified through a simple protocol modification.

3. LEARNING THE ITEM PROFILES

In this section, we present a solution allowing the recommender system to learn only the item profiles V. Our approach is based on Yao's garbled circuits. In short, in a basic architecture, the CSP prepares a garbled circuit that implements matrix factorization, and provides it to the RecSys. Oblivious transfer is used to obtain the garbled inputs from users without revealing them to either the CSP or the RecSys. Our design augments this basic architecture to enable users to be offline during the computation phase, as well as to submit their ratings only once.

We begin by discussing how Yao's protocol for secure multi-party computation applies, and then focus on the challenges that arise in implementing matrix factorization as a circuit. Our solution yields a circuit with a complexity within a polylogarithmic factor of matrix factorization performed in the clear by using *sorting networks*; an additional advantage of this implementation is that the garbling and the execution of our circuit is highly parallelizable.

3.1 A Privacy-Preserving Protocol for Matrix Factorization

Yao's Garbled Circuits. Yao's garbled circuit method, outlined in Appendix A, can be applied to our setting in a manner similar to the privacy-preserving auction and ridge regression settings studied in [48] and [50], respectively. In brief, assume for now that there exists a circuit that implements matrix factorization: this circuit receives as input user's ratings, supplied as tuples of the form

$$(i, j, r_{ij}) \text{ with } (i, j) \in \mathcal{M}\,,$$

where r_{ij} represents the rating r_{ij} of user i on item j, and outputs the item profiles V. Given M, the CSP garbles this circuit and sends it to the RecSys. In turn, through proxy oblivious transfer [48] between the users, the RecSys and the CSP, the RecSys receives the circuit inputs and evaluates V.

As garbled circuits can only be used once, any future computation on the same ratings would require the users to resubmit their data through proxy oblivious transfer. For this reason, we adopt a hybrid approach, combining public-key encryption with garbled circuits, as in [57, 50]. Applied to our setting, in a hybrid approach the CSP advertises a public key. Each user i encrypts her respective inputs (j, r_{ij}) and submits them to the RecSys. Whenever the RecSys wishes to perform matrix factorization over M accumulated ratings, it reports M to the CSP. The CSP provides the RecSys with a garbled circuit that (a) decrypts the inputs and then (b) performs matrix factorization; (Yao's complete protocol can be found in Appendix A). Nikolaenko *et al.* [50] avoid decryption within the circuit by using masks and homomorphic encryption; we adapt this idea to matrix factorization, departing however from [50] by only requiring a *partially* homomorphic encryption scheme.

We note that our protocol, and the ones outlined above, leak beyond V also the number of ratings generated by each user. This can easily be remedied, *e.g.*, by pre-setting the maximum number of ratings the user may provide and

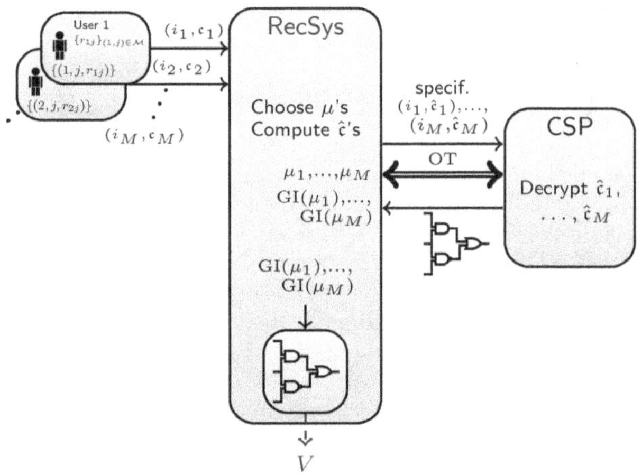

Figure 2: Protocol overview: Learning item profiles V through a garbled circuit. Each user submits encrypted item-rating pairs to the RecSys. The RecSys masks these pairs and forwards them to the CSP. The CSP decrypts them, and embeds them in a garbled circuit sent to the RecSys. The garbled values of the masks (denoted by GI) are obtained by the RecSys through oblivious transfer.

padding submitted ratings with "null" entries; for simplicity, we describe the protocol without this padding operation.

Detailed Description. We use public key encryption as follows. Each user i encrypts her respective inputs (j, r_{ij}) under the CSP's public key, $\mathsf{pk}_{\mathsf{csp}}$, with a semantically secure encryption algorithm $\mathcal{E}_{\mathsf{pk}}$, and, for each item j she rated, submits a pair $(i, \mathfrak{c})$ with $\mathfrak{c} = \mathcal{E}_{\mathsf{pk}_{\mathsf{csp}}}(j, r_{ij})$ to the RecSys, where M ratings are submitted in total. A user that submitted her ratings can go off-line.

We require that the CSP's public-key encryption algorithm is *partially* homomorphic: a constant can be applied to an encrypted message without the knowledge of the corresponding decryption key. Clearly, an additively homomorphic scheme such as Paillier [52] or Regev [56] can be used to add a constant, but hash-ElGamal (see, *e.g.*, [7, § 3.1]), which is only partially homomorphic, suffices and can be implemented more efficiently in this case; we review this implementation in Appendix B.

Upon receiving M ratings from users—recalling that the encryption is partially homomorphic—the RecSys obscures them with random masks $\hat{\mathfrak{c}} = \mathfrak{c} \oplus \mu$, and sends them to the CSP together with the complete specifications needed to build a garbled circuit. In particular, the RecSys specifies the dimension of the user and item profiles (*i.e.*, parameter d), the total number of ratings (*i.e.*, parameter M), the total number of users and items (*i.e.*, n and m), as well as the number of bits used to represent the integer and fractional parts of a real number in the garbled circuit.

Upon receiving the encryptions, the CSP decrypts them and gets the masked values: $(i, (j, r_{ij}) \oplus \mu)$. Then, using the matrix factorization circuit as a blueprint, the CSP prepares a Yao's garbled circuit that

(a) takes as input the garbled values corresponding to the masks—this is denoted by $\mathrm{GI}(\mu)$ on Figure 2;
(b) removes the mask μ to recover the corresponding tuple (i, j, r_{ij});
(c) performs matrix factorization; and
(d) outputs the item profiles V.

The CSP subsequently makes the garbled circuit available to the RecSys. Then, it engages in an oblivious transfer protocol with the RecSys so that the RecSys obtains garbled values of the masks: $\mathrm{GI}(\mu)$. Finally, the RecSys evaluates the circuit, whose final (ungarbled) output comprises the requested profiles V.

We note that, in contrast to the solution presented in Appendix A, the circuit recovers (i, j, r_{ij}) by simply removing the mask through the XOR operation, rather than using decryption. Most importantly, as discussed in Section 5, XOR operations can be performed very efficiently in a garbled circuit implementation [34].

To complete the above protocol, we need to provide a circuit that implements matrix factorization. Before we discuss our design, we first describe a naïve solution below.

3.2 A Naïve Design

The gradient descent operations outlined in Eqs. (3)–(4) involve additions, subtractions and multiplications of real numbers. These operations can be efficiently implemented in a circuit [50]. The K iterations of gradient descent (3) correspond to K circuit "layers", each computing the new values of U and V from values in the preceding layer. The final output of the circuit are the item profiles V outputted the last layer, while the user profiles are discarded.

Observe that the time complexity of computing each iteration of gradient descent is $\Theta(M)$, when operations are performed in the clear, *e.g.*, in the RAM model: each gradient computation (4) involves adding $2M$ terms, and profile updates (3) can be performed in $\Theta(n+m) = \Theta(M)$ time.

The main challenge in implementing gradient descent as a circuit lies in doing so efficiently. To illustrate this, consider the following naïve implementation:

1. For each pair $(i, j) \in [n] \times [m]$, generate a circuit that computes from input the indicators $\delta_{ij} = \mathbb{1}_{(i,j)\in\mathcal{M}}$, which is 1 if i rated j and 0 otherwise.
2. At each iteration, using the outputs of these circuits, compute each item and user gradient as a summation over m and n products, respectively, where:

$$\nabla_{u_i} F(U, V) = -2 \textstyle\sum_{j\in[m]} \delta_{ij} \cdot v_j (r_{ij} - \langle u_i, v_j \rangle) + 2\lambda u_i,$$
$$\nabla_{v_j} F(U, V) = -2 \textstyle\sum_{i\in[n]} \delta_{ij} \cdot u_i (r_{ij} - \langle u_i, v_j \rangle) + 2\mu v_j.$$

Unfortunately, this implementation is inefficient: every iteration of the gradient descent algorithm has a circuit complexity of $\Theta(nm)$. When $M \ll nm$, as is usually the case in practice, the above circuit is drastically less efficient than gradient descent in the clear; in fact, the quadratic cost $\Theta(nm)$ is prohibitive for most datasets.

3.3 A Simple Counting Circuit

The inefficiency of the naïve implementation arises from the inability to identify which users rate an item and which items are rated by a user at the time of the circuit design, mitigating the ability to leverage the inherent sparsity in the data. The question that thus naturally arises is how to perform such a matching efficiently within a circuit.

We illustrate our main idea for performing this matching through a simple counting circuit. Let $c_j = |\{i : (i, j) \in \mathcal{M}\}|$

be the number of ratings item $j \in [m]$ received. Suppose that we wish to design a circuit that takes as input the set $\mathcal{M}$ and outputs the counts $\{c_j\}_{j\in[m]}$. This task's complexity in the RAM model is $\Theta(m+M)$, as all c_j can be computed simultaneously by a single pass over $\mathcal{M}$. In contrast, a naïve circuit implementation using "indicators", as in the previous section, yields a circuit complexity $\Theta(nm)$. Nevertheless, we show it is possible to construct a circuit that returns $\{c_j\}_{j\in[m]}$ in $\Theta\big((m+M)\log^2(m+M)\big)$ steps using a *sorting network* (see Appendix C).

We first describe the algorithm that performs this operation, and then discuss how we implement it as a circuit.

1. Given $\mathcal{M}$ as input, construct an array $\mathbf{S}$ of $m+M$ tuples. First, for each $j \in [m]$, create a tuple of the form $(j, \perp, 0)$, where the "null" symbol $\perp$ is a placeholder. Second, for each $(i, j) \in \mathcal{M}$, create a tuple of the form $(j, 1, 1)$, yielding:
$$\mathbf{S} = \begin{pmatrix} 1 & 2 & \dots & m & j_1 & j_2 & \dots & j_M \\ \perp & \perp & \dots & \perp & 1 & 1 & \dots & 1 \\ 0 & 0 & \dots & 0 & 1 & 1 & \dots & 1 \end{pmatrix}.$$
Intuitively, the first m tuples will serve as "counters", storing the number of ratings per item. The remaining M tuples contain the "input" to be counted. The third element in each tuple serves as a binary flag, separating counters from input.
2. Sort the tuples in increasing order w.r.t. the item ids, *i.e.*, the 1st element in each tuple. If two ids are equal, break ties by comparing tuple flags, *i.e.*, the 3rd elements in each tuple. Hence, after sorting, each "counter" tuple is succeeded by "input" tuples with the same id:
$$\mathbf{S} = \begin{pmatrix} 1 & 1 & \dots 1 & \dots & m & m & \dots & m \\ \perp & 1 & \dots 1 & \dots & \perp & 1 & \dots & 1 \\ 0 & 1 & \dots 1 & \dots & 0 & 1 & \dots & 1 \end{pmatrix}.$$
3. Starting from the right-most tuple, move from right to left, adding the values of the second entries in each tuple; if a counter tuple (*i.e.*, a zero flag) is reached, store the computed value at the $\perp$ entry, and restart the counting. More formally, denote by $s_{\ell,k}$ the ℓ-th element of the k-th tuple. This "right-to-left" pass amounts to the following assignments:
$$s_{2,k} \leftarrow s_{3,k} + s_{3,k+1} \cdot s_{2,k+1}\,, \qquad (5)$$
for k ranging from $M+m-1$ down to 1.
4. Sort the array again in increasing order, this time w.r.t. the flags $s_{3,k}$. The resulting array's first m tuples contain the counters, which are released as output.

The above algorithm can be readily implemented as a circuit that takes as input $\mathcal{M}$ and outputs (j, c_j) for every item $j \in [m]$. Step 1 can be implemented as a circuit with input the tuples $(i, j) \in \mathcal{M}$ and output the initial array S, using $\Theta(m+M)$ gates. The sorting operations can be performed using, *e.g.*, Batcher's sorting network (*cf.* Appendix C) which takes as input the initial array and outputs the sorted array, requiring $\Theta((m+M)\log^2(m+M))$ gates. Finally, the right-to-left pass can be implemented as a circuit that performs (5) on each tuple, also with $\Theta(m+M)$ gates. Crucially, the pass is data-oblivious: (5) discriminates "counter" from "input" tuples through flags $s_{3,k}$ and $s_{3,k+1}$, but the same operation is performed on all k.

3.4 Our Efficient Design

Algorithm 1 Matrix Factorization Circuit

Input: Tuples (i, j, r_{ij})
Output: V

1: Initialize matrix $\mathbf{S}$
2: **Sort** tuples with respect to rows 1 and 3
3: **Copy** user profiles (left pass): for $k=2\dots M+n$
$$s_{\mathbf{5},k} \leftarrow s_{3,k} \cdot s_{\mathbf{5},k-1} + (1 - s_{3,k}) \cdot s_{\mathbf{5},k}$$
4: **Sort** tuples with respect to rows 2 and 3
5: **Copy** item profiles (left pass): for $k=2\dots M+m$
$$s_{\mathbf{6},k} \leftarrow s_{3,k} \cdot s_{\mathbf{6},k-1} + (1 - s_{3,k}) \cdot s_{\mathbf{6},k}$$
6: Compute the gradient contributions: $\forall k < M+m$
$$\begin{bmatrix} s_{\mathbf{5},k} \\ s_{\mathbf{6},k} \end{bmatrix} \leftarrow \begin{bmatrix} s_{3,k} \cdot 2\gamma s_{\mathbf{6},k}(s_{4,k} - \langle s_{\mathbf{5},k}, s_{\mathbf{6},k}\rangle) + (1 - s_{3,k}) \cdot s_{\mathbf{5},k} \\ s_{3,k} \cdot 2\gamma s_{\mathbf{5},k}(s_{4,k} - \langle s_{\mathbf{5},k}, s_{\mathbf{6},k}\rangle) + (1 - s_{3,k}) \cdot s_{\mathbf{6},k} \end{bmatrix}$$
7: **Update** item profiles (right pass): for $k=M+m-1\dots1$
$$s_{\mathbf{6},k} \leftarrow s_{\mathbf{6},k} + s_{3,k+1} \cdot s_{\mathbf{6},k+1} + (1 - s_{3,k}) \cdot 2\gamma\mu s_{\mathbf{6},k}$$
8: **Sort** tuples with respect to rows 1 and 3
9: **Update** user profiles (right pass): for $k=M+n-1\dots1$
$$s_{\mathbf{5},k} \leftarrow s_{\mathbf{5},k} + s_{3,k+1} \cdot s_{\mathbf{5},k+1} + (1 - s_{3,k}) \cdot 2\gamma\lambda s_{\mathbf{5},k}$$
10: **If** # of iterations is less than K, **goto** 3
11: **Sort** tuples with respect to rows 3 and 2
12: **Output** item profiles $s_{\mathbf{6},k}$, $k = 1, \dots, m$

Motivated by the above approach, we design a circuit for matrix factorization based on sorting, whose complexity is $\Theta((n+m+M)\log^2(n+m+M))$, *i.e.*, within a polylogarithmic factor of the implementation in the clear. The circuit operations are described in Algorithm 1. In summary, as in the simple counting example above, both the input data (the tuples (i, j, r_{ij})) and placeholders for both user and item profiles are stored together in an array. Through appropriate sorting operations, user or item profiles can be placed close to the input with which they share an identifier; linear passes through the data allow the computation of gradients, as well as updates of the profiles.

We again first describe the algorithm in detail and then discuss its implementation as a circuit. As before, the null symbol $\perp$ indicates a placeholder; when sorting, it is treated as $+\infty$, *i.e.*, larger than any other number.

Initialization. The algorithm receives as input the sets $L_i = \{(j, r_{ij}) : (i, j) \in \mathcal{M}\}$, and constructs an $n+m+M$ array of tuples $\mathbf{S}$. The first n and m tuples of $\mathbf{S}$ serve as placeholders for the user and item profiles, respectively, while the remaining M tuples store the inputs L_i. More specifically, for each user $i \in [n]$, the algorithm constructs a tuple $(i, \perp, 0, \perp, u_i, \perp)$, where $u_i \in \mathbb{R}^d$ is the initial profile of user i, selected at random from the unit ball. For each item $j \in [m]$, the algorithm constructs the tuple $(\perp, j, 0, \perp, \perp, v_j)$, where $v_j \in \mathbb{R}^d$ is the initial profile of item j, also selected at random from the unit ball. Finally, for each pair $(i, j) \in \mathcal{M}$, the corresponding tuple $(i, j, 1, r_{ij}, \perp, \perp)$, where r_{ij} is i's rating to j. The resulting array is shown in Figure 3(a).

$$\begin{pmatrix} 1: & 1 & \cdots & n & \perp & \cdots & \perp & i_1 & \cdots & i_M \\ 2: & \perp & \cdots & \perp & 1 & \cdots & m & j_1 & \cdots & j_M \\ 3: & 0 & \cdots & 0 & 0 & \cdots & 0 & 1 & \cdots & 1 \\ 4: & \perp & \cdots & \perp & \perp & \cdots & \perp & r_{i_1 j_1} & \cdots & r_{i_M j_M} \\ \mathbf{5}: & u_1 & \cdots & u_n & \perp & \cdots & \perp & \perp & \cdots & \perp \\ \mathbf{6}: & \perp & \cdots & \perp & v_1 & \cdots & v_m & \perp & \cdots & \perp \end{pmatrix}$$

(a) Initial state

$$\begin{pmatrix} 1: & 1 & 1\cdots 1 & \cdots & n & n\cdots n & \perp & \cdots & \perp \\ 2: & \perp & j_1\cdots j_{k_1} & \cdots & \perp & j_1 \cdots j_{k_n} & 1 & \cdots & m \\ 3: & 0 & 1\cdots 1 & \cdots & 0 & 1\cdots 1 & 0 & \cdots & 0 \\ 4: & \perp & r_{1j_1}\cdots r_{1j_{k_1}} & \cdots & \perp & r_{nj_1}\cdots r_{nj_{k_n}} & \perp & \cdots & \perp \\ \mathbf{5}: & u_1 & \perp\cdots\perp & \cdots & u_n & \perp\cdots\perp & \perp & \cdots & \perp \\ \mathbf{6}: & \perp & \perp\cdots\perp & \cdots & \perp & \perp\cdots\perp & v_1 & \cdots & v_m \end{pmatrix}$$

(b) After sorting w.r.t. user ids

Figure 3: Data structure S used by Alg. 1. Fig. (a) indicates the initial state, and (b) shows the result after sorting w.r.t. the user ids, breaking ties through flags, as in Line 2 of Alg. 1. Bold rows 5, 6 correspond to d-dimensional (rather than scalar) values. Note that a left pass as in line 3 of Alg. 1 will copy user profiles to their immediately adjacent tuples.

We again denote by $s_{\ell,k}$ the ℓ-th element of the k-th tuple. Intuitively, these elements serve the following roles:

- $s_{1,k}$: user identifiers in $[n]$
- $s_{2,k}$: item identifiers in $[m]$
- $s_{3,k}$: a binary flag indicating if the tuple is a "profile" or "input" tuple
- $s_{4,k}$: ratings in "input" tuples
- $s_{\mathbf{5},k}$: user profiles in $\mathbb{R}^d$
- $s_{\mathbf{6},k}$: item profiles in $\mathbb{R}^d$

Gradient Descent. In brief, gradient descent iterations comprise of the following three steps:

1. **Copy profiles.** At each iteration, the profiles u_i, v_j of each user i and each item j are copied to the corresponding elements $s_{\mathbf{5},k}$ and $s_{\mathbf{6},k}$ of each "input" tuple in which i and j appear. This is implemented in Lines 2 to 5 of Algorithm 1. To copy, *e.g.*, the user profiles, **S** is sorted using the user id (*i.e.*, $s_{1,k}$) as a primary index and the flag (*i.e.*, $s_{3,k}$) as a secondary index. An example of such a sorting applied to the initial state of **S** can be found in Figure 3(b). Subsequently, the user ids are copied by traversing the array from left to right (a "left" pass), as described formally in Line 3. This copies $s_{\mathbf{5},k}$ from each "profile" tuple to its adjacent "input" tuples; item profiles are copied similarly.
2. **Compute gradient contributions.** After profiles are copied, each "input" tuple corresponding to, *e.g.*, (i, j) stores the rating r_{ij} (in $s_{4,k}$) as well as the profiles u_i and v_j (in $s_{\mathbf{5},k}$ and $s_{\mathbf{6},k}$, respectively), as computed in the last iteration. From these, the following are computed:

$$v_j(r_{ij} - \langle u_i, v_j\rangle), \text{ and } u_i(r_{ij} - \langle u_i, v_j\rangle),$$

which amount to the "contribution" of the tuple in the gradients w.r.t. u_i and v_j, as given by (4). These replace the $s_{\mathbf{5},k}$ and $s_{\mathbf{6},k}$ elements of the tuple, as indicated by Line 6. Through appropriate use of flags, this operation affects "input" tuples, leaving "profile" tuples unchanged.
3. **Update profiles.** Finally, the user and item profiles are updated, as shown in Lines 7 to 9. Through appropriate sorting, "profile" tuples are made again adjacent to the "input" tuples with which they share ids. The updated profiles are computed through a right-to-left traversing of the array (a "right pass"). This operation adds the contributions of the gradients as it traverses "input" tuples. Upon encountering a "profile" tuple, the summed gradient contributions are added to the profile, scaled appropriately. After passing a profile, the summation of gradient contributions restarts from zero, through appropriate use of the flags $s_{3,k}, s_{3,k+1}$.

The above operations are repeated K times, the number of desirable iterations of gradient descent.

Output. Finally, at the termination of the last iteration, the array is sorted w.r.t. the flags (*i.e.*, $s_{3,k}$) as a primary index, and the item ids (*i.e.*, $s_{2,k}$) as a secondary index. This brings all item profile tuples in the first m positions in the array, from which the item profiles can be extracted.

Each of the above operations is data-oblivious, and can be implemented as a circuit. Copying and updating profiles requires $\Theta(n+m+M)$ gates, so the overall complexity is determined by sorting, which yields a $\Theta((n+m+M)\log^2(n+m+M))$ cost when using Batcher's circuit. As we will see in Section 6, sorting and the gradient computation in Line 6 are the most computationally intensive operations; fortunately, both are highly paralellizable. In addition, sorting can be further optimized by reusing previously computed comparisons at each iteration. We discuss these and other optimizations in Section 5.3.

4. EXTENSIONS

4.1 Privacy-Preserving Recommendations

We now extend our design to a system that enables a user to learn her predicted ratings r_{ij}, for all $j \in [m]$, as given by (2). However, *neither the RecSys nor the CSP learn anything about the users* beyond how many ratings they generated; in particular, neither learns V. Again, these guarantees hold under the *honest-but-curious* threat model.

To implement this functionality, at the beginning of the protocol, each user i chooses a random mask ϑ_i (this mask will be used to hide user's i profile u_i), encrypts it under the CSP's public key using any semantically secure encryption scheme $\mathcal{E}$ and sends it to the RecSys. We denote by $\mathfrak{t}_i = \mathcal{E}_{\mathsf{pk}_{\mathsf{csp}}}(\vartheta_i)$ the encrypted value.

The protocol then proceeds as described in Section 3 but with the following modifications. Initially, the RecSys forwards to the CSP the encrypted masks $\mathfrak{t}_i$ ($i \in [n]$), which are then decrypted by the CSP. Hence the CSP knows the plain value of the masks ϑ_i ($i \in [n]$). Likewise, on its side, the CSP chooses random masks ϱ_j for $j \in [m]$ (mask ϱ_j will be used to hide item profile v_j). The circuit built by the CSP again performs matrix factorization, as described in Section 3; however, rather than outputting $V = (v_j^T)_{j\in[m]}$, the circuit now outputs the item profiles masked with ϱ_j *and* the user profiles masked with ϑ_i:

$$\hat{v}_j = v_j + \varrho_j \quad \text{and} \quad \hat{u}_i = u_i + \vartheta_i$$

for $j \in [m]$ and $i \in [n]$. At the end of the protocol, the RecSys sends the respective $\hat{u}_i$ to each user i, who can then recover her profile u_i by removing the mask: $u_i = \hat{u}_i - \vartheta_i$.

The above execution, which is as computationally intensive as learning V in Section 3, can be performed as frequently as matrix factorization in real-life systems, *e.g.*, once a week.

In between such computations, whenever a user i wishes to get recommendations, she encrypts her profile under her own public key pk_i with an additively homomorphic encryption scheme $\mathfrak{E}_{\mathsf{pk}_i}$ (like Paillier's cryptosystem [52])[3] and sends the resulting value $\mathfrak{E}_{\mathsf{pk}_i}(u_i)$ to the RecSys. The RecSys forwards $\mathfrak{E}_{\mathsf{pk}_i}(u_i)$ to the CSP and also computes, for $j \in [m]$, $\mathfrak{E}_{\mathsf{pk}_i}(\langle u_i, \hat{v}_j \rangle)$. The CSP in turn computes for $j \in [m]$, $\mathfrak{E}_{\mathsf{pk}_i}(\langle u_i, \varrho_j \rangle)$, and returns this value to the RecSys. The RecSys subtracts $\mathfrak{E}_{\mathsf{pk}_i}(\langle u_i, \varrho_j \rangle)$ from $\mathfrak{E}_{\mathsf{pk}_i}(\langle u_i, \hat{v}_j \rangle) = \mathfrak{E}_{\mathsf{pk}_i}(\langle u_i, v_j + \varrho_j \rangle)$ to obtain the encryption of the predicted ratings $\hat{r}_{ij} = \mathfrak{E}_{\mathsf{pk}_i}(\langle u_i, v_j \rangle)$ for all items $j \in [m]$ and sends them to the user i. The user uses her private decryption key to obtain in the clear the predictions $r_{i1}, \ldots, r_{im}$.

4.2 Malicious RecSys

Our basic protocol, as described in Section 3, operates under the honest-but-curious model. However, a malicious RecSys can alter, duplicate or drop user ratings as a means to have the output model leak information about individual ratings. For example, the RecSys can provide inputs to the circuit from only a single user and feed dummy ratings for the remaining ones. It would then learn from the output model the set of items that were rated by this victim user: the RecSys simply observes which of the learned item profiles has a non-unit norm. This would clearly violate user privacy.

In order to prevent the RecSys from misbehaving, we need the CSP to build a circuit that, beyond outputting V, also verifies that the input to the circuit contains *all* user ratings, that the ratings were not changed, and that no dummy ratings were input. To do so we require users to obtain one-time MAC keys (one key per rating) from the CSP which they then use to sign their ratings. The CSP builds a circuit that verifies these MACs, making sure that the ratings were not altered, and that the exact number of ratings submitted by each user are provided as input to the circuit.

Our approach is to have each user first communicate with the CSP, reporting the number of ratings that she will send to the RecSys. The CSP in return sends the user a set of one-time MAC keys for each rating tuple, which the user uses for signing each tuple (j, r_{ij}). The garbled circuit the CSP builds verifies each input tuple with a specific MAC key, requiring the RecSys to provide the exact inputs as reported by the users to the CSP, sorted w.r.t. i and j. Any deviation from this order or the introduction of dummy ratings will result in a verification failure. Assume that the output of the verification circuit for each signed tuple is a bit that is set to 1 if the verification succeeds and 0 otherwise. The verification bits of all input tuples are fed into an AND gate, so that if at least one verification fails, the output of the AND gate is 0. If the outputs of this AND gate is 0 then the circuit sets its overall output to 0. This way, if at least one verification failed the circuit simply outputs 0. We chose to use fast one-time MACs based on pairwise independent hash functions so that the number of gates needed to verify these MACs is relatively small.

[3]Specifically, it is required that the encryptions of two messages $\mathfrak{E}_{\mathsf{pk}}(m_1)$ and $\mathfrak{E}_{\mathsf{pk}}(m_2)$ satisfy $\mathfrak{E}_{\mathsf{pk}}(m_1) \star \mathfrak{E}_{\mathsf{pk}}(m_2) = \mathfrak{E}_{\mathsf{pk}}(m_1 + m_2)$ for some binary operator $\star$. To ease notation, we use multiplication for $\star$ as is the case for Paillier encryption.

5. IMPLEMENTATION

We implemented our system to assess its practicality. Our garbled circuit construction was based on FastGC, a publicly available garbled circuit framework [24].

5.1 FastGC

FastGC [24] is a Java-based open-source framework, which enables circuit definition using elementary XOR, OR and AND gates. Once circuits are constructed, FastGC handles garbling, oblivious transfer and garbled circuit evaluation.

FastGC incorporates several known optimizations that aim to improve its memory foot-print and garbling and execution times. These optimizations include so-called "free" XOR gates [34], in which XOR evaluation is decryption-free and thereby of negligible cost, and garbled-row reduction for non-XOR gates [53], which reduces communication by 25%. FastGC also provides an "addition of 3 bits" circuit [33], enabling additions with 4 "free" XOR gates and one AND gate. OT extensions [27] are also implemented: these significantly increase the number of transfers made during OT, reducing communication overhead and lowering execution time.

Finally, FastGC enables the garbling and evaluation to take place concurrently on two separate machines. The CSP processes gates into garbled tables and transmits them to the RecSys in the order defined by circuit structure. Once a gate was evaluated its corresponding table is immediately discarded, which brings memory consumption caused by the garbled circuit to a constant.

5.2 Extensions to the Framework

Before garbling and executing the circuit, FastGC represents *the entire ungarbled circuit* in memory as a set of Java objects. These objects incur a significant memory overhead relative to the memory footprint of the ungarbled circuit, as only a subset of the gates is garbled and/or executed at any point in time. Moreover, although FastGC performs garbling in parallel to the execution process as described above, both operations occur in a sequential fashion: gates are processed one at a time, once their inputs are ready. Clearly, this implementation is not amenable to parallelization.

We modified the framework to address these issues, reducing the memory footprint of FastGC but also enabling paralellized garbling and computation across multiple processors. In particular, we introduced the ability to partition a circuit horizontally into sequential "layers", each one comprising a set of vertical "slices" that can be executed in parallel. A layer is created in memory only when all its inputs are ready. Once it is garbled and evaluated, the entire layer is removed from memory, and the following layer can be constructed, thus limiting the memory footprint to the size of the largest layer. The execution of a layer uses a scheduler that assigns its slices to threads, which run in parallel. Although we implemented parallelization on a single machine with multiple cores, our implementation can be extended to run across different machines in a straightforward manner since no shared state between slices is assumed.

Finally, to implement the numerical operations outlined in Algorithm 1, we extended FastGC to support addition and multiplications over the reals with fixed-point number representation, as well as sorting. For sorting, we used Batcher's sorting network [3]. Fixed-point representation introduces a tradeoff between the accuracy loss resulting from truncation and the size of circuit, which we explore in Section 6.

5.3 Optimizing Algorithm 1

We optimize the implementation of Algorithm 1 in multiple ways. In particular, we (a) reduce the cost of sorting by reusing comparisons computed in the beginning of the circuit's execution, (b) reduce the size of array S, (c) optimize swap operations by using XORs, and (d) parallelize computations. We describe these optimizations in detail below.

Comparison Reuse. As described in Appendix C, the basic building block of a sorting network is a compare-and-swap circuit, that compares two items and swaps them if necessary, so that the output pair is ordered. Observe that the sorting operations (Lines 4 and 8) of Algorithm 1 perform identical comparisons between tuples at each of the K gradient descent iterations, using exactly the same inputs per iteration. In fact, each sorting permutes the tuples in array S in exactly the same manner, at each iteration.

We exploit this property by performing the comparison operations for each of these sortings *only once*. In particular, we perform sortings of tuples of the form $(i, j, \mathit{flag}, \mathit{rating})$ in the beginning of our computation (without the payload of user or item profiles), *e.g.*, w.r.t. i and the flag first, j and the flag, and back to i and the flag. Subsequently, we reuse the outputs of the comparison circuits in each of these sortings as input to the swap circuits used during gradient descent. As a result, the "sorting" network applied at each iteration does not perform any comparisons, but simply permutes tuples (*i.e.*, it is a "permutation" network).

Row Reduction. Precomputing all comparisons allows us to also drastically reduce the size of tuples in S. To begin with, observe that the rows corresponding to user or item ids are only used in Algorithm 1 as input to comparisons during sorting. Flags and ratings are used during copy and update phases, but their relative positions are identical at each iteration. Moreover, these positions are produced as outputs when sorting the tuples $(i, j, \mathit{flag}, \mathit{rating})$ at the beginning of our computation. As such, "permutation" operations performed at each iteration need only be applied to user and item profiles; all other rows are removed from S.

One more trick reduces the cost of permutations by an additional factor of 2. We fix one set of profiles, *e.g.*, users, and permute only item profiles. Then, item profiles rotate between two states, each one reachable from the other through permutation: one in which they are aligned with user profiles and partial gradients are computed, and one in which item profiles are updated and copied.

XOR Optimization. Given that XOR operations can be executed for "free", we optimize comparison, swap, update and copying operations by using XORs wherever possible. For comparisons, we reduce the use of AND and OR gates using a technique by Kolesnikov *et al.* [33]. Swap operations are implemented as follows: for $b \leftarrow x > y$ the comparison bit between tuples x and y (which, by the above optimizations, is pre-computed at the beginning of circuit execution), a swap is performed as:

$$x' \leftarrow [b \wedge (x \oplus y)] \oplus x, \text{ and } y' \leftarrow x' \oplus (x \oplus y)$$

Finally, copy operations are also optimized to use XOR's. Observe that the copy operation takes two elements x and y and a flag s and outputs a new element y' which is equals y if $s = 0$ and x, otherwise. This is performed as follows:

$$x' \leftarrow y \oplus [s \wedge (x \oplus y)]$$

Parallelization. As discussed in Section 3.4, sorting and gradient computations constitute the bulk of the computation in our circuit (copying and updating contribute no more than 3% of the execution time and 0.4% of the non-XOR gates); we parallelize these operations through our extension of FastGC. Gradient computations are clearly parallelizable; sorting networks are also highly parallelizable (parallelization is the main motivation behind their development). Moreover, since many of the parallel slices in each sort are identical, we reused the same FastGC objects defining the circuit slices with different inputs, significantly reducing the need to repeatedly create and destroy objects in memory.

6. EXPERIMENTS

We now assess the performance of our implementation. We use two commodity servers, 1.9GHz 16-cores 128GB RAM each, one acting as the RecSys and the other as the CSP. We use both real and synthetic datasets. For the real dataset we use MovieLens, a movie rating dataset that is commonly used for recommender systems research, that consists of 943 users that submit 100K ratings to 1682 movies.

We use the following evaluation metrics. Our solution introduces inaccuracies due to our use of fixed-point representation of real numbers. Thus, our goal here is to understand the relative error of our approach compared to a system that operates in the clear with floating point representation. Let $E(U, V)$ denote the squared error for a given user's profile U and items profiles V, $E(U, V) = \sum_{(i,j)\in\mathcal{M}}(r_{ij} - u_i^T v_j)^2$; we define the *relative error* as

$$|E(U^*, V^*) - E(U, V)|/E(U, V)$$

where U^* and V^* are computed using our solution and U and V are computed using gradient descent executed in the clear over floating point arithmetic, *i.e.*, with minimal precision loss. Our *time* metric captures the execution time needed to garble and evaluate the circuit. We note that we exclude the encryption and decryption times performed by the users and the CSP, since these are short in duration compared to the circuit processing time. The *communication* metric is defined by the number of bytes that are transmitted between the CSP and RecSys; it captures the size of the circuit, namely the number of non-XOR gates, but unlike the time metric, communication is not affected by parallelization.

The relative error of our solution using the complete MovieLens dataset is shown in Figure 4. We study the relative error over a range of parameters, varying the number of bits allocated to the fractional part of the fixed point representation and the number of iterations of gradient descent. Overall we see that for more than 20 bits, the relative errors are very low. When the number of bits is small, the gradient descent method may converge to a different local minimum of (1) than the one reached in the clear. Beyond 20 bits allocated for the fractional part, our solution converges to the same local minimum, and errors decrease exponentially with additional bits. The relative error increases with the number of iterations because the errors introduced by the fixed point representations accumulate across the iterations, however this increase is very small. We note that this should not be confused with the regularized least square error (1), which actually decreases when using more iterations.

In the following experiments we used synthetic data with 100 users, 100 items, a dimension of 10 for the user and item profiles, 20 bits for the fractional part of the fixed-point

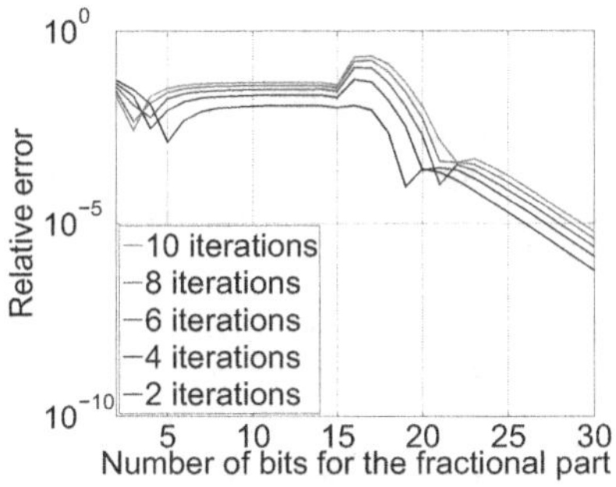

Figure 4: Relative errors due to fixed point representation

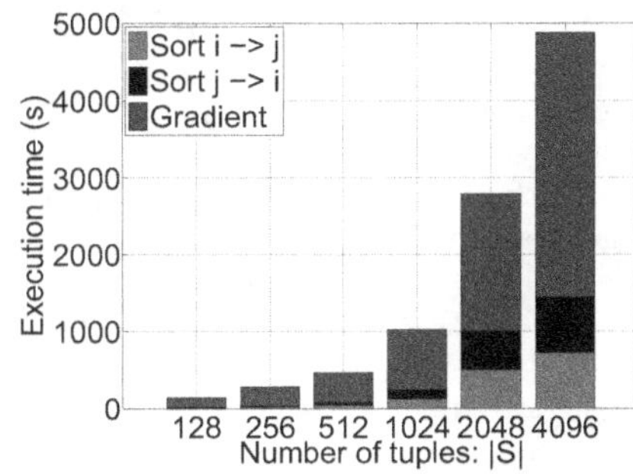

Figure 5: Execution time per iteration w.r.t. no. of tuples

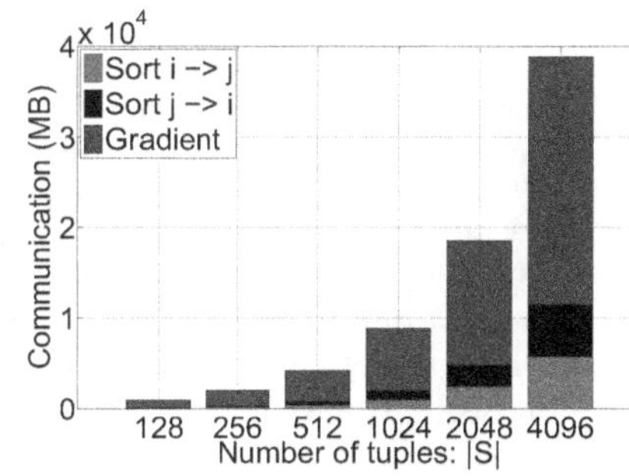

Figure 6: Communication cost per iteration w.r.t. no. of tuples

representation (36 bits overall). We measure the time and communication it takes to perform (garble and evaluate) a single iteration of gradient descent. Clearly with T iterations execution and communication grow by a factor T.

Figure 5 shows the increase in time per iteration as we increase the number of ratings in the dataset (the logarithmic x-axis corresponds to the number of tuples in $\mathbf{S}$ that grows with $\mathcal{M}$ since n and m are fixed). The plot also illustrates the proportion of time spent in various sections of our algorithm. We note that, in all executions, the time spent on update and copy phases, which are more difficult to parallelize, never exceeded 3%, and thus is omitted from the plots as it is not visible.

The plot confirms that the growth is almost linear with the number of ratings, $\Theta(M \log^2 M)$. Furthermore, we observe that more than 2/3 of the execution time is spent on gradient computations (mainly due to vector multiplication operations), while the remaining 1/3 is due to sorting operations. As both operations are highly parallelizable, this illustrates that the execution time can be significantly reduced through parallelization.

Similarly, Figure 6 plots the amount of bytes communicated between the CSP and RecSys for garbling and evaluating a single iteration. The plot shows the same properties as the execution time, namely that the size scales almost linearly with the number of ratings and that the majority of the circuit is devoted to gradient computations. In all implementations, copy and update operations did not contribute more that 0.1% of the gates in the circuit.

As an example for the time and communication performance for a real dataset, we limited our MovieLens dataset to the 40 most popular movies. This corresponds to 14683 ratings generated by 940 users. One iteration of gradient descent with parameters set to achieve error of 10^{-4} took 2.9hr. These experiments were performed on a machine with 16 cores; real-life systems use much more powerful hardware (*e.g.*, hundreds of Amazon EC2 servers). Moreover, operations are highly parallelizable. As such, with access to industry-level equipment this timing can be brought to the realm of practicality, especially given that recommender systems run matrix factorization on, *e.g.*, a weekly basis.

7. RELATED WORK

Secure multiparty computation (MPC) was initially proposed by Yao [62, 63]. There are presently many frameworks that implement Yao garbled circuits [45, 23, 24, 44, 53, 25, 36]. A different approach to general purpose MPC is based on secret-sharing schemes and another is based on fully-homomorphic encryption (FHE). Secret-sharing schemes have been proposed for a variety of linear algebra operations, such as solving a linear system [51], linear regression [29, 30, 21], and auctions [10]. Secret-sharing requires at least three non-colluding online authorities that equally share the workload of the computation, and communicate over multiple rounds; the computation is secure as long as no two of them collude. Garbled circuits assumes only *two* non-colluding authorities and far less communication which is better suited to the scenario where the RecSys is a cloud service and the CSP is implemented in a trusted hardware component. Non-linear computation through fully homomorphic encryption [16] may be used to reduce the workload on the CSP compared to garbled circuits, but current FHE schemes [39, 20] for simpler algebraic computations are not as efficient as garbled circuit approaches [50].

Centralized garbled-circuit computation of a function over a large number of individual inputs was introduced by Naor *et al.* in the context of auctions [48]. Our approach is closest to the privacy-preserving regression computation in [50], though implementing matrix factorization efficiently as a circuit introduces challenges not present in regression. Beyond [50], hybrid approaches combining garbled circuits with other methods (such as HE or secret-sharing) have been used for, *e.g.*, face and fingerprints recognition [57, 26], and learning a decision tree [41]; such discrete function evaluations differ considerably from matrix factorization.

Irrespective of the cryptographic primitive used, the main challenge in building an efficient algorithm for secure multiparty computation is in implementing the algorithm in a *data-oblivious* fashion, *i.e.*, so that the execution path does not depend on the input. In general, any RAM program executable in bounded time T can be converted to a $O(T^3)$ Turing machine [8], and any bounded T-time TM can be converted to a circuit of size $O(T \log T)$ [54], which is data-oblivious. This results in a $O(T^3 \log T)$ complexity, which is prohibitive in most applications. A survey of algorithms for which efficient data-oblivious implementations are unknown can be found in [11]: matrix factorization broadly falls into the category of Data Mining summarization problems.

Sorting networks were originally developed to enable sorting parallelization as well as an efficient hardware implementation. Several recent works exploit the data-obliviousness of sorting networks for cryptographic purposes which, in turn, has lead to renewed interest in oblivious sorting protocols beyond sorting networks (*e.g.*, [18, 22]). There are many recent data-oblivious algorithms using sorting as a building block, including compaction and selection [60, 19], the computation of a convex hull and all-nearest neighbors [13], as well as weighted set intersection [28]; the simple counting protocol in Section 3.3 is a variation upon these schemes. Nevertheless, these operations are much simpler than matrix factorization; to the best of our knowledge, we are the first to apply oblivious sorting on such a numerical task.

Privacy in recommender systems has been studied under several contexts, including the use of trusted hardware [1] as well as the susceptibility of a system to shilling attacks (*i.e.*, the injection of false ratings to manipulate the recommendation outcome) [38, 47]. An approach orthogonal to ours that introduces privacy in recommender systems is differential privacy [12, 46]. By adding noise, differential privacy guarantees that the distribution of the system's output is insensitive to any individual's record, preventing the inference of any single user's data from the output. However, differential privacy does not protect data from the recommender system itself. Crucially, differential privacy can be combined with secure computation [58], in our case by incorporating noise addition within the garbled circuit factorizing the input matrix. Differential privacy can thus be used to enhance the privacy properties of our protocol, ensuring not only that the data remains private during computation, but also the final result does not expose individual user data.

8. CONCLUSIONS AND FUTURE WORK

We presented a protocol for matrix factorization on user ratings that remain encrypted at all times. This critical building block allows a recommender to learn item profiles without learns *anything* about users' ratings, providing users protection from inference threats and accidental information leakage. Our hybrid approach combines partially homomorphic encryption and Yao's garbled circuits. To the best of our knowledge, we are the first to apply oblivious sorting to a numerical task as complex as matrix factorization. Through this key idea, that also enables us to highly parallelize our implementation, we overcome scalability and performance needs, and bring matrix factorization on encrypted data into the realm of practicality.

There are several future directions for this work. First, we hope to deploy our system over a cloud compute service (*e.g.*, using Hadoop on Amazon EC2), which will enable an increase in the range of datasets that we can process. A second direction is to investigate the application of our approach to other equally intensive machine learning tasks, especially ones that exhibit an underlying bipartite structure in computations; we could thus leverage sorting networks again to achieve performance scalability.

A third direction is to extend our protocol to work under different security models, *e.g.*, a malicious CSP. A malicious CSP can create an incorrect circuit, which can be handled with standard techniques for verifying garbled circuits [43, 40]. Moreover, it can feed the wrong inputs to the circuit, *e.g.*, maliciously altered masked values as described in Section 3.1. The latter attack reveals no additional information to the CSP, but it may corrupt the result of the computation. Therefore additional techniques should be designed to ensure that either the CSP provided the correct inputs to the circuit or that the output of the recommendation circuit closely approximates the ratings provided by users.

Acknowledgments. The last author is supported by NSF.

9. REFERENCES

[1] E. Aïmeur, G. Brassard, J. M. Fernandez, and F. S. M. Onana. ALAMBIC: A privacy-preserving recommender system for electronic commerce. *Int. J. Inf. Sec.*, 7(5), 2008.

[2] M. Ajtai, J. Komlós, and E. Szemerédi. An $O(n \log n)$ sorting network. In *STOC*, 1983.

[3] K. E. Batcher. Sorting networks and their applications. In *Proc. AFIPS Spring Joint Computer Conference*, 1968.

[4] M. Bellare and S. Micali. Non-interactive oblivious transfer and applications. In *CRYPTO*, 1990.

[5] E. J. Candès and B. Recht. Exact matrix completion via convex optimization. *Foundations of Computational Mathematics*, 9(6), 2009.

[6] J. F. Canny. Collaborative filtering with privacy. In *IEEE S&P*, 2002.

[7] B. Chevallier-Mames, P. Paillier, and D. Pointcheval. Encoding-free ElGamal encryption without random oracles. In *PKC*, 2006.

[8] S. A. Cook and R. A. Reckhow. Time bounded random access machines. *J. Computer and System Sciences*, 1973.

[9] T. H. Cormen, C. E. Leiserson, R. L. Rivest, and C. Stein. *Introduction to Algorithms*. MIT Press, 2nd edition, 2001.

[10] I. Damgård and T. Toft. Trading sugar beet quotas - secure multiparty computation in practice. *ERCIM News*, 2008.

[11] W. Du and M. J. Atallah. Secure multi-party computation problems and their applications: A review and open problems. In *New Security Paradigms Workshop*, 2001.

[12] C. Dwork. Differential privacy. In *ICALP*, 2006.

[13] D. Eppstein, M. T. Goodrich, and R. Tamassia. Privacy-preserving data-oblivious geometric algorithms for geographic data. In *18th SIGSPATIAL*, 2010.

[14] S. Even, O. Goldreich, and A. Lempel. A randomized protocol for signing contracts. *Commun. ACM*, 28(6), 1985.

[15] J. Friedman, T. Hastie, and R. Tibshirani. *The Elements of Statistical Learning: Data Mining, Inference and Prediction*. Springer, 2nd edition, 2009.

[16] C. Gentry. Fully homomorphic encryption using ideal lattices. In *STOC*, 2009.

[17] S. Goldwasser and M. Bellare. *Lecture Notes on Cryptography*. MIT, 2001.

[18] M. T. Goodrich. Randomized shellsort: A simple oblivious sorting algorithm. In *SODA*, 2010.

[19] M. T. Goodrich. Data-oblivious external-memory algorithms for the compaction, selection, and sorting of outsourced data. In *SPAA*, 2011.

[20] T. Graepel, K. Lauter, and M. Naehrig. ML confidential: Machine learning on encrypted data. Cryptology ePrint Archive, Report 2012/323, 2012.

[21] R. Hall, S. E. Fienberg, and Y. Nardi. Secure multiple linear regression based on homomorphic encryption. *J. Official Statistics*, 2011.

[22] K. Hamada, R. Kikuchi, D. Ikarashi, K. Chida, and K. Takahashi. Practically efficient multi-party sorting protocols from comparison sort algorithms. In *ICISC*, 2013.

[23] W. Henecka, S. Kögl, A.-R. Sadeghi, T. Schneider, and I. Wehrenberg. TASTY: Tool for automating secure two-party computations. In *CCS*, 2010.

[24] Y. Huang, D. Evans, J. Katz, and L. Malka. Faster secure two-party computation using garbled circuits. In *USENIX Security*, 2011.

[25] Y. Huang, J. Katz, and D. Evans. Quid-pro-quo-tocols: Strengthening semi-honest protocols with dual execution. In *IEEE S&P*, 2012.

[26] Y. Huang, L. Malka, D. Evans, and J. Katz. Efficient privacy-preserving biometric identification. In *NDSS*, 2011.

[27] Y. Ishai, J. Kilian, K. Nissim, and E. Petrank. Extending oblivious transfers efficiently. In *CRYPTO*, 2003.

[28] K. V. Jónsson, G. Kreitz, and M. Uddin. Secure multi-party sorting and applications. Cryptology ePrint Archive, Report 2011/122, 2011.

[29] A. F. Karr, W. J. Fulp, F. Vera, S. S. Young, X. Lin, and J. P. Reiter. Secure, privacy-preserving analysis of distributed databases. *Technometrics*, 2007.
[30] A. F. Karr, X. Lin, A. P. Sanil, and J. P. Reiter. Privacy-preserving analysis of vertically partitioned data using secure matrix products. *J. Official Statistics*, 2009.
[31] R. H. Keshavan, A. Montanari, and S. Oh. Learning low rank matrices from $O(n)$ entries. In *Allerton*, 2008.
[32] D. E. Knuth. *The Art Of Computer Programming — Volume 3 / Sorting and Searching.* Addison-Wesley, 2nd edition, 1998.
[33] V. Kolesnikov, A.-R. Sadeghi, and T. Schneider. Improved garbled circuit building blocks and applications to auctions and computing minima. In *CANS*, 2009.
[34] V. Kolesnikov and T. Schneider. Improved garbled circuit: Free XOR gates and applications. In *ICALP*, 2008.
[35] Y. Koren, R. M. Bell, and C. Volinsky. Matrix factorization techniques for recommender systems. *IEEE Computer*, 2009.
[36] B. Kreuter, A. Shelat, and C.-H. Shen. Billion-gate secure computation with malicious adversaries. In *USENIX Security*, 2012.
[37] S. K. Lam, D. Frankowski, and J. Riedl. Do you trust your recommendations? An exploration of security and privacy issues in recommender systems. In *ETRICS 2006*, 2006.
[38] S. K. Lam and J. Riedl. Shilling recommender systems for fun and profit. In *WWW*, 2004.
[39] K. Lauter, M. Naehrig, and V. Vaikuntanathan. Can homomorphic encryption be practical? In *CCSW*, 2011.
[40] Y. Lindell. Fast cut-and-choose based protocols for malicious and covert adversaries. *IACR Cryptology ePrint Archive*, 2013.
[41] Y. Lindell and B. Pinkas. Privacy preserving data mining. *J. Cryptology*, 2002.
[42] Y. Lindell and B. Pinkas. A proof of security of Yao's protocol for two-party computation. *J. Cryptology*, 2009.
[43] Y. Lindell and B. Pinkas. Secure two-party computation via cut-and-choose oblivious transfer. *J. Cryptology*, 2012.
[44] Y. Lindell, B. Pinkas, and N. P. Smart. Implementing two-party computation efficiently with security against malicious adversaries. In *SCN*, 2008.
[45] D. Malkhi, N. Nisan, B. Pinkas, and Y. Sella. Fairplay – Secure two-party computation system. In *USENIX Security*, 2004.
[46] F. McSherry and I. Mironov. Differentially private recommender systems: Building privacy into the Netflix prize contenders. In *KDD*, 2009.
[47] B. Mobasher, R. Burke, R. Bhaumik, and C. Williams. Toward trustworthy recommender systems: An analysis of attack models and algorithm robustness. *ACM Trans. Internet Techn.*, 7(4), 2007.
[48] M. Naor, B. Pinkas, and R. Sumner. Privacy preserving auctions and mechanism design. In *1st ACM Conference on Electronic Commerce*, 1999.
[49] A. Narayanan and V. Shmatikov. Robust de-anonymization of large sparse datasets. In *IEEE S&P*, 2008.
[50] V. Nikolaenko, U. Weinsberg, S. Ioannidis, M. Joye, D. Boneh, and N. Taft. Privacy-preserving ridge regression on hundreds of millions of records. In *IEEE S&P*, 2013.
[51] K. Nissim and E. Weinreb. Communication efficient secure linear algebra. In *TCC*, 2006.
[52] P. Paillier. Public-key cryptosystems based on composite degree residuosity classes. In *EUROCRYPT*, 1999.
[53] B. Pinkas, T. Schneider, N. P. Smart, and S. C. Williams. Secure two-party computation is practical. In *ASIACRYPT*, 2009.
[54] N. Pippenger and M. J. Fischer. Relations among complexity measures. *J. ACM*, 26(2), 1979.
[55] M. O. Rabin. How to exchange secrets by oblivious transfer. Technical Report TR-81, Aiken Computation Laboratory, Harvard University, 1981.
[56] O. Regev. On lattices, learning with errors, random linear codes, and cryptography. *J. ACM*, 56(6), 2009.
[57] A.-R. Sadeghi, T. Schneider, and I. Wehrenberg. Efficient privacy-preserving face recognition. In *ICISC*, 2009.
[58] E. Shi, T.-H. H. Chan, E. G. Rieffel, R. Chow, and D. Song. Privacy-preserving aggregation of time-series data. In *NDSS*, 2011.
[59] Y. Tsiounis and M. Yung. On the security of ElGamal based encryption. In *PKC*, 1998.
[60] G. Wang, T. Luo, M. T. Goodrich, W. Du, and Z. Zhu. Bureaucratic protocols for secure two-party sorting, selection, and permuting. In *CCS*, 2010.
[61] U. Weinsberg, S. Bhagat, S. Ioannidis, and N. Taft. BlurMe: Inferring and obfuscating user gender based on ratings. In *RecSys*, 2012.
[62] A. C.-C. Yao. Protocols for secure computations. In *FOCS*, 1982.
[63] A. C.-C. Yao. How to generate and exchange secrets. In *FOCS*, 1986.

APPENDIX

A. YAO'S GARBLED CIRCUITS

Yao's protocol (a.k.a. *garbled circuits*) [63] (see also [42]) is a generic method for secure multi-party computation. In a variant thereof (adapted from [48, 50]), the protocol is run between a set of n input owners, where a_i denotes the private input of user i, $1 \leq i \leq n$, an evaluator, that wishes to evaluate $f(a_1, \ldots, a_n)$, and a third party, the crypto-service provider or CSP in short. At the end of the protocol, the evaluator learns the value of $f(a_1, a_2, \ldots, a_n)$ but no party learns more than what is revealed from this output value. The protocol requires the function f can be expressed as a Boolean circuit, *e.g.* as a graph of OR, AND, NOT and XOR gates, and that the evaluator and the CSP do not collude.

Oblivious Transfer. *Oblivious transfer* (OT) [55, 14] is an important building block of Yao's protocol. OT is two-party protocol between a chooser and a sender. The sender has two ℓ-bit strings σ_0 and σ_1. The chooser selects a bit b and *exactly* obtains from the sender the string σ_b, *without the sender learning the value of* b. In addition, the chooser *learns nothing about* σ_{1-b} (beyond its length).

Oblivious transfer protocols can be constructed from many cryptographic assumptions. We describe below a protocol based on the Decision Diffie-Hellman assumption [4].

Let $\mathbb{G} = \langle g \rangle$ be a cyclic group of order q in which the decisional Diffie-Hellman (DDH) assumption holds. Let also Ω be an encoding map from $\{0,1\}^\ell$ onto $\mathbb{G}$. Finally, let $c \in \mathbb{G}$ whose discrete logarithm is unknown. The chooser chooses $x \in_R \mathbb{Z}_q$ and computes $y_b = g^x$ and $y_{1-b} = c/g^x$. She sends y_0 to the sender. The sender represents σ_0 and σ_1 as elements in $\mathbb{G}$: $\omega_0 = \Omega(\sigma_0)$ and $\omega_1 = \Omega(\sigma_1)$. She chooses $r_0, r_1 \in_R \mathbb{Z}_q$, recovers $y_1 = c/y_0$, and computes $C_0 = (g^{r_0}, \omega_0\, {y_0}^{r_0})$ and $C_1 = (g^{r_1}, \omega_1\, {y_1}^{r_1})$. The sender sends C_0, C_1 to the chooser. Upon receiving C_0, C_1, the chooser computes ω_b as $\omega_b\, {y_b}^{r_b}/(g^{r_b})^x$ using secret value x and obtains $\sigma_b = \Omega^{-1}(\omega_b)$.

Circuit Garbling. The key idea behind Yao's protocol resides in the circuit encoding. To each wire w_i of the circuit, the CSP associates two random cryptographic keys, $K^0_{w_i}$ and $K^1_{w_i}$, that respectively correspond to the bit-values $b_i = 0$ and $b_i = 1$. Next, for each binary gate g (*e.g.*, an OR-gate) with input wires (w_i, w_j) and output wire w_k, the CSP computes the four ciphertexts

$$\mathrm{Enc}_{(K_{w_i}^{b_i},K_{w_j}^{b_j})}(K_{w_k}^{g(b_i,b_j)}) \quad \text{for } b_i, b_j \in \{0,1\} \ . \qquad (6)$$

The set of these four *randomly ordered* ciphertexts defines the garbled gate. See [45] for an efficient implementation. For example, as illustrated on Fig. 7, given the pair of keys $(K_{w_i}^0, K_{w_j}^1)$ it is possible to recover the key $K_{w_k}^1$ by decrypting $\mathrm{Enc}_{(K_{w_i}^0,K_{w_j}^1)}(K_{w_k}^1)$. However, the other key, namely $K_{w_k}^0$, cannot be recovered. More generally, it is worth noting that the knowledge of $(K_{w_i}^{b_i}, K_{w_j}^{b_j})$ yields only the value of $K_{w_k}^{g(b_i,b_j)}$ and that no other output values can be recovered for the corresponding gate.

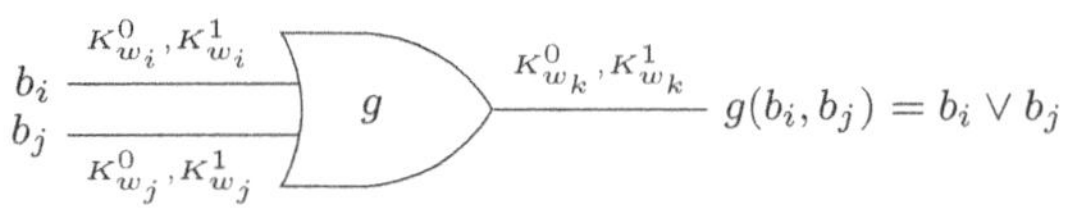

b_i	b_j	$g(b_i,b_j)$	Garbled value
0	0	0	$\mathrm{Enc}_{(K_{w_i}^0,K_{w_j}^0)}(K_{w_k}^0)$
0	1	1	$\mathrm{Enc}_{(K_{w_i}^0,K_{w_j}^1)}(K_{w_k}^1)$
1	0	1	$\mathrm{Enc}_{(K_{w_i}^1,K_{w_j}^0)}(K_{w_k}^1)$
1	1	1	$\mathrm{Enc}_{(K_{w_i}^1,K_{w_j}^1)}(K_{w_k}^1)$

Figure 7: Example of a garbled OR-gate.

Circuit Evaluation. We are now ready to present the complete protocol for evaluating f. The CSP generates a private and public key, and makes the latter available to the users. Each user i encrypts her private input a_i under the CSP's public key to get $\mathfrak{c}_i$, and sends $\mathfrak{c}_i$ to the evaluator. Upon receiving all encrypted inputs, the evaluator contacts the CSP to build a garbled circuit performing the steps of (a) decrypting the encrypted input values, using the CSP's private key and (b) evaluating function f.

The CSP provides the evaluator with the garbled gates of this circuit, each comprising a random permutation of the ciphertexts (6), as well as the graph representing how these connect. It also provides the correspondence between the garbled value and the real bit-value for the circuit-output wires (the outcome of the computation): if w_k is an circuit-output wire, the pairs $(K_{w_k}^0, 0)$ and $(K_{w_k}^1, 1)$ are given to the evaluator. To transfer the garbled values of the input wires, the CSP engages in an oblivious transfer with the evaluator, so that evaluator obliviously obtains the garbled-circuit input values corresponding to the $\mathfrak{c}_i$'s; this ensures that the CSP does not learn the user inputs and that the evaluator can only compute the function on these inputs alone. Having the garbled inputs, the evaluator can "evaluate" each gate sequentially, by decrypring gate and obtaining the keys necessary to decrypt the output of the gates it connects to.

B. HASH-ELGAMAL ENCRYPTION

Let $\mathbb{G} = \langle g \rangle$ be a cyclic group of order q and $H : \mathbb{G} \to \{0,1\}^\ell$ be a cryptographic hash function. The public key is $\mathsf{pk} = (g, y)$ where $y = g^x$ for some random $x \in \mathbb{Z}_q$, and the private key is $\mathsf{sk} = x$. A message $m \in \{0,1\}^\ell$ is encrypted using

$$\mathcal{E}_{\mathsf{pk}} : \{0,1\}^\ell \to \mathbb{G} \times \{0,1\}^\ell, m \mapsto \mathfrak{c} = (g^\rho, m \oplus H(y^\rho))$$

for some random $\rho \in \mathbb{Z}_q$. Letting $\mathfrak{c} = (\mathfrak{c}^{(1)}, \mathfrak{c}^{(2)})$, it is worth remarking that one can publicly mask the ciphertext $\mathfrak{c}$ with any chosen random mask $\mu \in \{0,1\}^\ell$ as

$$\hat{\mathfrak{c}} = (\mathfrak{c}^{(1)}, \mathfrak{c}^{(2)} \oplus \mu) \ .$$

Decrypting $\hat{\mathfrak{c}} = (\hat{\mathfrak{c}}^{(1)}, \hat{\mathfrak{c}}^{(2)})$ then yields the masked message $\hat{m} = m \oplus \mu$. Indeed, we have

$$\begin{aligned} \hat{\mathfrak{c}}^{(2)} \oplus H\big((\hat{\mathfrak{c}}^{(1)})^x\big) &= (\mathfrak{c}^{(2)} \oplus \mu) \oplus H\big((g^\rho)^x\big) \\ &= \big((m \oplus H(y^\rho)) \oplus \mu\big) \oplus H(y^\rho) \\ &= m \oplus \mu \ . \end{aligned}$$

The scheme can be shown to be semantically secure in the random oracle model, under the Decision Diffie-Hellman assumption [59].

C. SORTING NETWORKS

Sorting networks [9, 32] are circuits that sort an input sequence $(a_1, a_2, \ldots, a_n)$ into a monotonically increasing sequence $(a_1', a_2', \ldots, a_n')$. They are constructed by wiring together *compare-and-swap* circuits, their main building block. A *compare-and-swap* circuit is a binary operator taking on input a pair (a_1, a_2), and returning the sorted pair (a_1', a_2') where $a_1' = \min(a_1, a_2)$ and $a_2' = \max(a_1, a_2)$. For graphical convenience, a comparator is usually represented as a vertical line, as illustrated in Figure 8(a). Note that elements are swapped if and only if the first element is larger than the second one. Figure 8(b) shows a sorting network example.

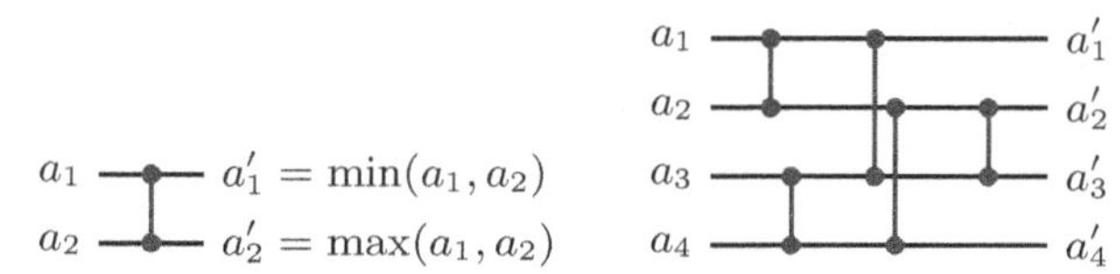

(a) Compare-and-Swap circuit (b) Sorting network

Figure 8: Networks of compare-and-swap elements.

Sorting networks were specifically designed to admit an efficient hardware implementation, but also to be highly parallelizable. The efficiency of the sorting network can be measured by its size (the total number of comparisons) or depth (the maximum number of stages, where each stage comprises comparisons that can be executed in parallel). The depth of the network reflects the parallel running time of the sorting.

For example, in Figure 8(b) the comparisons (a_1, a_2) and (a_3, a_4) can be executed in parallel; so can comparisons (a_1, a_3) and (a_2, a_4). As such, the depth of this network is 3, which is the maximum number of compare-and-swaps along each "line". The network can be computed in 3 timesteps with 2 processors or in 5 timesteps with just one processor.

The best known (and asymptotically optimal) sorting network is the AKS network [2] that achieves size $O(n \log n)$ and depth $O(\log n)$. Being an important theoretical discovery, the AKS network has no pratical application because of a large constant. Efficient networks that are often used in practice achieve depth $O(\log^2 n)$ and size $O(n \log^2 n)$. These include Batcher, odd-even merge sort, bitonic sort, and Shell sort networks [32]. In the presence of p processors, the running time of these networks is $O(n(\log^2 n/p)$. Empirical studies indicate that, in practice, Batcher has better average performance than most widely used algorithms [60].

PICCO: A General-Purpose Compiler for Private Distributed Computation

Yihua Zhang, Aaron Steele, and Marina Blanton
Department of Computer Science and Engineering
University of Notre Dame, Notre Dame, IN, USA
{yzhang16,asteele2,mblanton}@nd.edu

ABSTRACT

Secure computation on private data has been an active area of research for many years and has received a renewed interest with the emergence of cloud computing. In recent years, substantial progress has been made with respect to the efficiency of the available techniques and several implementations have appeared. The available tools, however, lacked a convenient mechanism for implementing a *general-purpose* program in a secure computation framework suitable for execution in not fully trusted environments. This work fulfills this gap and describes a system, called PICCO, for converting a program written in an extension of C into its distributed secure implementation and running it in a distributed environment. The C extension preserves all current features of the programming language and allows variables to be marked as private and be used in general-purpose computation. Secure distributed implementation of compiled programs is based on linear secret sharing, achieving efficiency and information-theoretical security. Our experiments also indicate that many programs can be evaluated very efficiently on private data using PICCO.

Categories and Subject Descriptors

K.6 [**Management of Computing and Information Systems**]: Security and Protection; C.2.4 [**Computer-Communication Networks**]: Distributed Systems—*distributed applications*

Keywords

Secure multi-party computation; secure computation outsourcing; general-purpose computation; compiler; source-to-source translator; linear secret sharing; parallel execution

1. INTRODUCTION

This work is motivated by the broad goal of developing techniques suitable for secure and general data processing and outsourcing. The desire to compute on sensitive data without having to reveal more information about the data than necessary has led to several decades of research in the area of secure multi-party computation (SMC). Today, cloud computing serves as a major motivation for the development of secure data processing techniques suitable for use in outsourced environments. This is because security and privacy considerations are often cited as one of the top impediments to harnessing the benefits of cloud computing to the fullest extent.

Despite the sheer volume of research literature on privacy-preserving computation and newly appearing secure outsourcing techniques, most of the available techniques focus on a rather narrow domain, namely, integer-based arithmetic. Little or no attention has been paid to other types of computation, as well as to data structures and algorithms suitable for secure data processing in not fully trusted environments. With the recent progress in the performance of basic secure computation techniques and the shift toward cloud computing, we believe that it is the prime time to enable privacy-preserving execution of any functionality or program, or *general-purpose* secure data processing.

Toward this goal, this work introduces PICCO (Private dIstributed Computation COmpiler) — a system for translating a general-purpose program for computing with private data into its secure implementation and executing the program in a distributed environment. The main component of PICCO is a source-to-source compiler that translates a program written in an extension of the C programming language with provisions for annotating private data to its secure distributed implementation in C. The resulting program can consequently be compiled by the native compiler and securely run by a number of computational nodes in the cloud or similar environment. Besides the compiler, PICCO includes programs that aid secure execution of user programs in a distributed environment by preprocessing private inputs and recovering outputs at the end of the computation.

Our desire to build as general of a tool as possible is supported by two important aspects of this work:

- We make a distinction between the participant(s) who hold private inputs, participant(s) who receive the output, and computational parties who conduct the computation. This allows the framework to be used in many contexts including privacy-preserving collaborative computation with multiple participants and secure computation outsourcing by one or multiple clients.
- The goal of this work is to support as wide of a range of functionalities as possible, i.e., as long as the functionality is known at the run-time, it can be securely evaluated in our framework. Toward this goal, we supplement the functionality of C with a number of private data types and operations on them, and incorporate them in standard types of constructions used in C. For example, unlike other compilers, PICCO has support for floating point arithmetic on private data.

We hope that our system will aid accessibility and wider adoption of general-purpose secure computation and outsourcing.

CCS'13, November 4–8, 2013, Berlin, Germany.

ACM 978-1-4503-2477-9/13/11 ...$15.00.
http:///dx.doi.org/10.1145/2508859.2516752.

Performance is a key factor for secure computation. For that reason, PICCO utilizes lightweight information-theoretically secure techniques based on secret sharing to build secure distributed implementations of user programs. The resulting implementations promise to be particularly efficient and suitable for large-scale applications, as evidenced by our experiments.

The remainder of this work describes the design and implementation of our system as well as reports on the performance of a number of programs compiled and executed using PICCO.

2. RELATED WORK

There are a number of existing tools and compilers for secure two- and multi-party computation, which are relevant in the context of this work. They include Fairplay [35], FairplayMP [8], Sharemind [10], VIFF [19], SEPIA [14], TASTY [28], and a secure two-party compiler for (a subset of) ANSI C [29]. While many of them were designed to support a rather general types of computation (normally on integers) and some have attractive properties, due to efficiency and flexibility goals that we target to achieve we choose to build our own compiler instead of directly extending one of the existing tools. In particular, the features that we find crucial are: (i) support for multi-party computation, (ii) support for a variable number of participants (including separation between computational, input, and output parties), (iii) the use of standard linear secret sharing techniques, (iv) applicability of techniques for malicious adversaries, (v) support for arithmetic of desired precision, and (vi) efficiency. None of the above mentioned tools simultaneously achieve the desired properties (or can be modified to achieve them at a relatively small cost).

In more detail, Fairplay [35] was the first compiler for secure two-party computation based on evaluation of garbled Boolean circuits. It allows a user to specify a function to be securely evaluated in a high-level language SFDL, compile it, and run the corresponding protocol. The circuit optimization part of compilation is known to have large memory requirements [9]. FairplayMP [8] extends Fairplay with multi-party functionality. It uses several interactive operations on secret-shared values for the evaluation of each Boolean gate, resulting in a performance disadvantage compared to multi-party solutions that directly build on a linear secret sharing scheme. TASTY [28] is a recent tool that combines two-party garbled circuit evaluation with computation based on homomorphic encryption. The desired functionality is specified in a custom language TASTYL, which is a subset of python. Another recent two-party compiler [37] was developed with the goal of extensibility, which would permit different techniques to be used in a single protocol. The most recent two-party compiler [29] allows a program written in ANSI C to be compiled into a garbled circuit. The current limitations of it include no coverage of real numbers, pointers, or variable-length numeric data types.

Sharemind [10] is the most developed and efficient tool to date with a built-in support of integer arithmetic, arrays, and matrices. It has a number of operations written in the assembly language, which results in an efficient implementation. A C-like language SecreC was developed for specifying the desired computation [31]. Unfortunately, Sharemind uses non-standard secret-sharing techniques with three parties, which do not automatically extend to other numbers of computational parties. In addition, the use of non-standard arithmetic makes many existing techniques inapplicable, including techniques for security against malicious adversaries. Sharemind also supports only integers of fixed 32-bit length.

SEPIA [14] is a library for secure distributed processing of network data based on linear secret sharing techniques. It has an explicit separation between computational parties and the parties who contribute inputs and obtain outputs. It was developed for the purposes of privacy-preserving intrusion detection and has features inherent to this application which limit its applicability to a wider range of collaborative computation.

Tool/compiler	No. parties	Basic technique	Varying precision	Non-int arithmetic	Type of parallelism
Fairplay	2	GC	√		N/A
C compiler [29]	2	GC		√	N/A
TASTY	2	GC & HE	√		N/A
FairplayMP	≥ 3	GC & SS	√		N/A
Sharemind	3	additive SS		√	arrays
VIFF	≥ 3	linear SS	√		each interactive op
This work	≥ 3	linear SS	√	√	loops, arrays, and user-specified

Table 1: Summary of related work.

VIFF [19] is a compiler based on standard multi-party linear secret sharing techniques. It was designed to be suitable, and has support, for security in presence of malicious parties and uses specially designed for this purpose asynchronous techniques. VIFF tries to parallelize as many operations as possible, with each interactive operation implemented as a callback. This means that all operations are scheduled when a protocol starts, but each operation is executed when its inputs become available. Unfortunately, the choice of the programming language in which it is implemented and the way parallelism is handled (with a heavy-weight thread per elementary operation) makes it unnecessarily slow in practice.

Lastly, the compiler described in [32] is complementary to our work, and if computational parties coincide with output parties, it can be used to optimize performance of user-specified programs.

The features of the available compilers and tools are summarized in Table 1. Parallel execution optimizations are not applicable to some tools where the computation can always be realized in a constant number of rounds. In the table, GC stands for garbled circuits, HE for homomorphic encryption, and SS for secret sharing.

3. FRAMEWORK

In this work, we utilize a threshold linear secret sharing scheme for representation of and secure computation over private values. We choose to concentrate on this setting due to its flexibility and speed. Throughout this work, we thus use the multi-party setting in which $n > 2$ parties securely evaluate a function on private inputs and output the result to the recipients of the computation. We divide all participants into three groups: The input parties distribute their inputs in the form of shares to the computational parties prior to the computation. The computational parties carry out the computation on secret-shared data. Upon completion of the computation, they communicate their shares of the result to the output parties, who reconstruct the values and learn the result. Note that there are no constraints on how these three groups are formed, and a single entity can be involved in a protocol taking on one or more of the above roles. This formulation of secure computation is flexible enough to naturally fit several broad categories of collaborative and individual computing needs. In particular, a number of parties with a private input each can engage in secure function evaluation themselves and learn the result (or their respective results). Alternatively, they can choose a subset of them, a number of outside parties, or a combination of the above to carry out the computation, while each input owner distributes her private data to the parties who carry out the computation. Another very important scenario consists of a single entity outsourcing its computation to a number of computational nodes. In this case, the data owner will be the only input and output party. Finally, the setup also allows two parties with private inputs to seek help of one or more additional servers and proceed with secure evaluation of their function using multi-party techniques.

We refer to computational parties as $P_1, \ldots, P_n$ and assume that they are connected by secure authenticated channels with each other. Each input and output party also establishes secure channels with P_1 through P_n. With a (n, t)-secret sharing scheme, any private value is secret-shared among n parties such that any $t + 1$ shares can be used to reconstruct the secret, while t or fewer parties cannot learn any information about the shared value, i.e., it is perfectly protected in information-theoretic sense. Therefore, the value of n and t should be chosen such that an adversary is unable to corrupt more than t computational parties (for instance, data owners can acquire nodes located at different cloud service providers).

In a linear secret sharing scheme, a linear combination of secret-shared values can be performed by each computational party locally, without any interaction, but multiplication of secret-shared values requires communication between all of them. In particular, we utilize Shamir secret sharing scheme [38], in which a secret value s is represented by a random polynomial of degree t with the free coefficient set to s. Each share of s corresponds to the evaluation of the polynomial on a unique non-zero point. All operations are performed in a field $\mathbb{F}$ (normally $\mathbb{Z}_p$ for a small prime p larger than any value that needs to be represented). Then given $t + 1$ or more shares, the parties can reconstruct the polynomial using Lagrange interpolation and learn s. Possession of t or fewer shares, however, information-theoretically reveals no information about s. With this representation, any linear combination of secret-shared values is computed locally by each party using its shares, while multiplication involves multiplying shares locally then applying interactive re-sharing and interpolation operations to reduce the degree of the resulting polynomial from $2t$ to t. This places a restriction on the value of t and we require that $t < n/2$. Multiplication is used as the basic building block that requires interaction. More generally, a multivariate polynomial of degree k can be evaluated by the computational parties using a single interaction when $kt < n$. In our case, by assuming $t < n/2$ the parties can compute multiplication or evaluate any multivariate polynomial of degree 2 using a single interaction. We implement multiplication as given in [26], where each party transmits $n-1$ messages resulting in $O(n^2)$ overall communication. More advanced techniques (such as [22]) allow for linear communication complexity per multiplication and can be employed to optimize communication.

A number of operations that we utilize for arithmetic use pseudo-random secret sharing (PRSS) [18], which allows the computational parties to agree on shares of a random value without communication. We refer the reader to [18] for additional details.

Throughout this work we assume that the participants are semi-honest (also known as honest-but-curious or passive), in that they perform the computation as prescribed, but might attempt to learn additional information from the messages that they receive. Security in presence of semi-honest adversaries is commonly defined by assuming ideal functionality, in which the computation is performed by a trusted third party, and showing that the real execution of a protocol does not reveal any additional information about private data than in the ideal model. In our setting security means that the combined view of any coalition of t or less computational parties can be simulated without access to the private data. We anticipate that PICCO will often be used in the setting when the computational parties do not contribute any input and do not receive any output (i.e., the case of secure computation outsourcing).

We use existing efficient protocols for computation on integer and floating point values that have previously been shown secure in our security model. Furthermore, by the composition theorem [15], these building blocks can be combined together to achieve security of the overall computation. Because we do not introduce any new cryptographic protocols but rather build an automated tool for their composition, we omit formal security definitions.

Performance of secure computation protocols is of a paramount importance for their practical use, and in our framework performance of a protocol is normally measured in terms of two parameters: (i) the number of interactive operations (multiplications, distributing shares of a secret, or opening a secret-shared value) necessary to perform the computation and (ii) the number of sequential interactions, i.e., rounds. Our goal is to minimize both of those parameters and in particular bring the round complexity as close as possible to the optimal complexity that can be achieved in a custom solution with the fastest available building blocks.

One interesting component of this work to be explored is the use of parallelism in the compiled functionalities. Our goal is to avoid too restrictive and too general use of parallelism found in prior work and instead incorporate enough flexibility that will provide fast runtime of compiled programs. That is, in frameworks similar to ours, Sharemind [10] provides parallelism only at the level of arrays, where multiple instances of an operation applied to each cell of the array are performed in a batch. This is insufficient for reducing the round complexity of many types of computation to a practical level. In VIFF [19], on the other hand, each interactive operation is allocated its own thread and is scheduled at the program initiation, but is executed when its inputs become available. Managing a large number of threads (many of which are not necessary) slows down the execution. We propose to provide parallelism which is still restrictive, but general enough for efficient execution.

We build on the knowledge of distributed systems compilers such as OMPi [23] to achieve efficiency in compilation and execution.

4. COMPILER DESIGN

4.1 Overview

We choose to implement our compiler as a source-to-source translator. It is designed to take a program written in an extension of C, where data to be protected are marked as private, and transform it into a C program that implements SMC. The transformed program can then be compiled by each computational party using a native compiler into an executable code. The C language was chosen due to its popularity and, more importantly, performance reasons. By translating a user program into the source code of its secure implementation and using a native compiler to produce binary code, we can ensure that our compiler can be used on any platform and we are able to take advantage of optimizations available in native compilers. Figure 1(a) shows the compilation process of a user-specified program. Besides the user program itself, our compiler takes as its input a configuration file which contains parameters associated with the setup of secure computation that do not change with each program. These parameters include the specification of the secret sharing scheme (the values n and t and optional modulus or its size in bits), and the number of input and output parties. The compiler determines the optimal modulus size for secret sharing based on the program content. After the user translates her program into C code corresponding to its secure implementation, the user supplies the transformed program to each computational party. Each computational party locally compiles the code and is ready to start the execution upon the receipt of the input data.

When the user would like to initiate secure computation, the user produces shares of the input data and sends each share to the respective computational party. The execution process is shown in

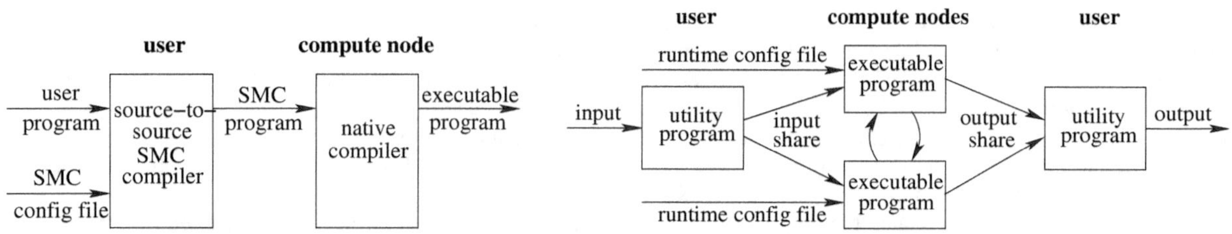

(a) Compilation (b) Execution

Figure 1: Compilation and execution of secure computation using PICCO.

Figure 1(b), where small utility programs are used for producing shares of the input and assembling the output from the produced shares. The runtime configuration file specifies information about the runtime setup and in particular contains IP addresses of computational parties and their public keys for the purpose of establishing secure channels. Once the user transmits shares of her input variables to the computational parties, the parties can start the computation. During the execution, the computational parties read shares of input data from user transmission and produce shares of output data. Upon computation completion, each computation party transmits shares of output variables to the user, who reconstructs the values using the utility program. This means that the client inputs data during an offline stage and is not an active participant of the computation. The compiled program is instructed to read input variables from user transmission according to the variable types.

The figure illustrates the case when a single user is the only input provider and output receiver. When, however, the computation is performed on behalf of a number of parties, they must jointly perform source-to-source translation of their target computation and separately supply shares of their respective inputs to the computational parties. In that case, each input variable in the program is annotated with the id of the input party supplying it and each output variable with the id of the party receiving it. This means that during the computation the compiled program will read an input variable from the transmission of the corresponding input party and write shares of an output variable to the file destined to the output party as specified in the program.

4.2 Specification of user programs

A program that specifies a functionality for secure collaborative computation or outsourcing is written in an extension of C. We extend C with support for private data types and operations on them. Public variables are handled without protection and our source-to-source compiler does not modify computation on them. For that reason, in the description that follows we treat private values and the interaction between private and public values.

Private and public variable qualifiers. A programmer can declare a variable to be either public or private using standard data types. To ensure that no information is accidentally leaked about a private variable, a variable will default to a private data type. For example, declarations `private int x` and `int x` will both create a private variable `x` of integer type.

Private data types. Because the length of the representation of numeric data types has a large influence on performance of secure computation, we allow lengths of private variables to be configurable, with set default values to aid usability. That is, the programmer can specify the length of numeric data types in bits and use the default value when the bitlength is not set. For example, if private integers are declared to be of type `int<20>`, we can set the field size to be of the minimum value necessary for computing with 20-bit integers. Support for custom-length data types is one of the features that distinguishes this work from some other compilers and SMC implementations such as [10] and [29].

For integer arithmetic, users can define private variables to be of type `char`, `short`, `int`, `long`, `long long`, and custom x-bit `int<`x`>`. The bitlength of standard data types is set according to the platform on which the program is being translated into secure implementation, but both standard-size and custom-size data types are implemented as integers with their bitlength recorded in the translated code.

To realize private floating point arithmetic, we use representation (and corresponding operations) from [7]. In particular, each floating point number is represented as a 4-tuple $\langle v, p, s, z \rangle$, where v is an ℓ-bit significand, p is a k-bit exponent, and s and z are sign and zero bits, respectively. The user can specify standard types `float`, `double`, and `long double` as well as custom-length `float<`x,y`>` with x-bit significand and y-bit exponent.

Operations on private data types. We provide support for many operations on private integer and floating point numbers. In particular, we implement integer addition +, subtraction −, multiplication `*`, division `/`, left and right shifts « and », bitwise XOR `^`, AND `&` and OR `|`, comparisons and equality tests. We also support floating point addition, subtraction, multiplication, division, and comparisons. The set of supported operations can be easily extended with additional operations and conversions between selected data types.

With the current implementation, users can perform operations on strings using arrays of one-byte integers `char`, but in the future we plan to provide built-in functions for string manipulation.

Built-in I/O functions. The programmer can specify variables that should be read from the input using special function `smcinput`. The function takes two arguments: the name of the variable to read and the id of the input party from whom the variable (or shares of the variable) come. For example, specifying `smcinput(x,1)` for private integer `x` will instruct the compiled program to read shares of an integer number from the transmission of input party 1. For private floating point numbers, shares of four elements of the floating point representation will be read. Because the input parties supply their data offline, `smcinput` is used for both private and public variables which during execution are read from the transmitted file of the appropriate input party.

Similarly, `smcoutput` is used to specify output variables and the output party who is to learn each of them. That is, including `smcoutput(x,1)` for private `x` will instruct the compiled program to output shares of `x` into a file which at the end of the computation is sent to output party 1. Both `smcinput` and `smcoutput` can be called anywhere in the program.

Conditional statements and loop constructs. All conditions in conditional statements can be private, which will allow if-statements to be evaluated obliviously. The only exception is that in loops the termination condition must either be public or be evaluated privately, after which its result is revealed to the parties carrying out the computation. In other words, the function being evaluated must be known at the run time. To the best of our knowledge, private conditions are not supported in most secure computation tools and in particular are not available in any SMC software based on secret sharing (i.e., Sharemind or VIFF).

Support for concurrent execution. One of the most important design decisions that determines performance of compiled secure protocols is how parallelism is achieved. Because latency of interactive operations dominates performance of multi-party protocols in this setting, recent literature concentrated on techniques that lower round complexity of operations. For that reason, it is important to be able to execute several interactive operations in parallel.

A number of existing tools that adopt the same or similar frameworks have a variable degree of support for parallel execution of operations. For example, Sharemind executes all instances of an operation defined for each element of a (one- or two-dimensional) array in a batch. SEPIA runs a number of operations in a batch in each time slot (called round in [14]) using an application-specific implementation of parallelism. VIFF provides the most flexible way of parallel execution, in which an interactive operation is initiated as soon as its inputs are available. Experience with VIFF, however, shows that the cost of managing a large number of threads (many of which are often unnecessary) slows down protocol execution [25].

We believe that to achieve efficient execution of a broad range of functionalities, the available options for parallelizing the execution should not be either too narrow or unnecessarily too flexible. That is, the parallelism offered by Sharemind and SEPIA will allow for efficient execution of many functionalities, but can be very limiting for other applications and operations. The callback mechanism of VIFF, on the other hand, results in large overheads which can often be avoided. For these reasons, we support parallel execution of parts of a program in the ways defined next. Our goal is to provide enough flexibility to achieve very efficient performance for a broad range of programs while avoiding unnecessary slowdown due to managing threads for every elementary operation.

1. We support parallel execution of loop iterations, which generalizes Sharemind's and SEPIA's batch processing of identical operations. Because many programs require sequential execution of loop iterations, we leave it to the programmer to decide whether parallel or sequential execution should take place. The distinction is made using different syntax in the code. The conventional syntax, e.g., `for (statement; condition; statement) {statement; ...}` is used for sequential execution, and modified syntax, e.g., `for (statement; condition; statement) [statement; ...]` is used to execute all iterations of the loop in parallel.
2. For the programs in which execution of different code in parallel is possible and desirable (and parallel execution cannot be specified using a loop construct), we will offer a mechanism to specify the code that should be executed in parallel. We will use similar syntax with code enclosed in `[]` brackets for these purposes. For example, construction `[statement1;] [statement2;]` indicates that the two statements can be executed concurrently.

The use of loops with concurrent execution of loop iterations dictates the rule that the conditions affecting the number of loop iterations (i.e., the loop terminating conditions) are not allowed to be modified within the loop iterations. This is due to the obvious fact that the loop iterations must be scheduled without executing their contents and thus the number of loop iterations should be known or computable without executing instructions contained in the loop iterations. This implies that only for-loops can be specified to use simultaneous execution of loop iterations.

Array operations. As an additional mechanism for improving performance of distributed computation, we provide the ability for the programmer to specify operations on private vectors (arrays). For example, the user can specify expression `A*B` on private arrays `A` and `B` of the same size, which will lead to element-wise multiplication of `A` and `B`, i.e., multiplication of each element of `A` to the corresponding element of `B`. Besides the operations on private data types listed above, we support the inner product computation on two vectors using syntax `A@B`, which can be particularly efficiently implemented. Also, the I/O functions `smcinput` and `smcoutput` can be used with array variables to input/output a block of values at a time, using the third argument to specify the number of elements. For example, `smcinput(A,1,100)` reads 100 values into array `A` from the data of party 1.

We also provide a way of using portions of multi-dimensional arrays in (one-dimensional) array operations. This is performed by specifying the index in each dimension except the last one. For example, if matrix `A` is declared to be a two-dimensional array, notation `A[`i`]` will refer to the ith row of `A` (or elements `A[`i`][`j`]` for all j). This can, for instance, lead to an efficient implementation of matrix multiplications and other operations.

Enforcement of secure data flow. To ensure that no information about private values is leaked during program execution, we place certain restrictions on the data flow that involves both private and public data. In particular, statements that assign an expression that contains private values to a public variable are not allowed. This includes the case when the expression consists of function evaluation with a private return data type. The opposite, however, is true: a private variable can be assigned a public value, which is subsequently converted to shares.

In circumstances when the user intentionally wants to reveal certain information about a private value, we provide a built-in function `smcopen` that reveals the content of a private variable. For example, if the computation requires that the sign of private `x` is to be publicly revealed, the user can write

```
if (x >= 0) a = 1;
b = smcopen(a);
```

with private `a` and public `b`. This provides a mechanism for intentional declassification of information about private values and ensures that information is not accidentally leaked in an incorrectly written assignment.

Another restriction is related to enforcing secure data flow when conditional statements with a private condition are used. In particular, assignments to public variables within the scope of such statements are not allowed. This is due to the fact that by observing the value of a public variable after executing a conditional statement with a private condition, the result of the condition evaluation can be learned, which leaks information about private values. The same applies to functions called from the inside of a conditional statement with a private condition: the function must have no public side effects. This in particular means that the function is not allowed to modify global or shared public variables or public arguments passed by reference. This can be generalized to any instructions or computation with observable action, e.g., jump statements, which may leak information about the private condition.

Limitations and future work. Our current implementation does not provide support for pointers in user programs besides the use of arrays (note that the size of allocated memory for an array can depend on prior computation). This limitation is also present in all other tools and compilers including ANSI C-based [29]. As our goal is to build as a general-purpose tool as possible, adding support for pointers is our most immediate goal for future work.

Another future work direction consists of adding resilience to malicious behavior. A number of existing techniques can be directly applied to our framework, e.g., asynchronous implementation in [19]. As part of future work we plan to evaluate performance of compiled programs in malicious security model.

4.3 Processing of user programs

When our compiler receives a user-specified program, it parses it and builds an abstract syntax tree (AST), which is consequently used to produce a modified program that implements secure distributed computation. To create a grammar for our extension of C, we build on existing source-to-source translators that parse C code. In particular, we build on an open-source OpenMP compiler OMPi [23]. We use flex [3] and bison [1] for defining tokens, specifying the context-free grammar, and building the AST.

Besides the AST, during parsing the compiler also builds and maintains a symbol table of defined variables and functions together with their types. Once the input program is parsed, the compiler performs transformations on the AST if necessary and outputs a modified program. All computation on public values is left unchanged, while all operations that use private values will be transformed into secure computation using GMP library [5] for large-precision arithmetic.[1]

Program transformations. The first transformation that the compiler performs on the input program is that of locating the main function within the user's code and renaming it into function called `old_main`. The main function of the transformed program contains necessary declarations for secure distributed computation and consequently calls the user's original main `old_main`.

Each private variable in the original user's program is transformed into one or more GMP large-precision variables of type `mpz_t` for storing its share, and all operations on private variables are rewritten to execute on GMP variables using the corresponding SMC algorithms. For example, declaration of a private integer variable `x` will result in declaring `x` of type `mpz_t` and initializing it using a call to `mpz_init()`. A private floating point variable is transformed into a structure that contains four variables of type `mpz_t`.

Now, because each operation on private variables needs to be modified to reflect operating on secret shares and call the corresponding secure distributed operations, evaluation of expressions on private variables introduces temporary variables in the modified program. For example, expression `x+y*z` on private integer `x`, `y`, and `z` will be transformed into statements `mpz_mul(tmp,y,z);` `mpz_add(tmp,x,tmp);` based on the precedence order of operators in the grammar. Our compiler is optimized to use the minimal number of temporary variables that ensure correct execution of the original program.

Another transformation that we perform is changing arguments of functions with private return values. Due to the implementation specifics of the `mpz_t` data type, functions cannot return variables of type `mpz_t`. For that reason, we change the arguments of all user-declared functions with private return values to include an extra argument passed by the reference which corresponds to the return value of the function and the return type is set to void. This does not restrict the way functions can be specified by the programmer and is transparent to the users.

[1]We note that the choice of a large number arithmetic library is not detrimental to the operation of the compiler.

Variable initialization. If a private variable is initialized to a constant (e.g., as in `int a=5`), the implementation needs to convert the constant to its shares. To achieve this, we create instructions for the computational parties in the transformed program to generate random shares of 0 (using a pseudo-random sharing of zero PRZS from [18]) and add the constant to each share. This will result in properly distributed shares of the constant, but it means that the value of the constant will be known to the computational parties. We choose to treat these private initialization constants as public because it complies with the intuition that the program's source code should not be treated as private. Furthermore, in many circumstances the constants to which private variables are initialized are indeed public, which simplifies their processing. For example, if a private variable is used in a computation of summation of private values, the fact that it is initialized to 0 does not need to be protected. In the event that a private variable needs to be initialized to a private constant, it should be input using a call to `smcinput`.

Handling of program input and output. Recall that input and output parties are not active participants in the computation. Thus, when a variable is specified to be read from the input using the `smcinput` function, its value will come from one of the input parties prior to the computation. Similarly, the content of every variable used in a call to `smcoutput` is stored by the computational parties until the end of the computation. At that point all values recorded for output party i will be transmitted to that party by all computational nodes. Because `smcinput` and `smcoutput` functions are the only available mechanism for I/O operations, we use the same interface for both public and private variables.

When a call to `smcinput` or `smcoutput` with arguments var and i is observed in the user program, the compiler looks up the type of variable var in the symbol table that stores all declared variables. The compiler than replaces a call to `smcinput` in the transformed program with instructions for reading data of the appropriate type from the input of party i and placing it in variable var. Similarly, a call to `smcoutput` is replaced with instructions for writing the content of var according to its type to the output destined to output party i. The type of variable var determines how many fields are used to represent the variable and their lengths. For example, a private floating point variable is represented by four random field $\mathbb{F}$ elements (secret shares), while a public integer is represented by a single value of its declared size.

Because a user program might be processed using multi-threaded implementation, the compiler instructs the transformed program to read the input of all parties into a data structure (that also maintains variable names) before the computation starts. The data structure allows each thread to access the variables it reads or writes from the memory without having to implement I/O synchronization.

Implementation of numeric operations. Numeric operations on private values constitute a significant portion of our implementation of secure distributed computation, and we briefly describe how these operations are implemented. Integer addition, subtraction, and multiplication are basic building blocks for computation on secret shares. Integer division is implemented according to [7], right shift « x is implemented as multiplication by 2^x, and left shift is implemented using truncation as in [16]. Integer bitwise operations are implemented using bit decomposition according to [17] followed by the corresponding bitwise computation using arithmetic operations. That is, for each bit i of operands $a = a_1 \ldots a_\ell$ and $b = b_1 \ldots b_\ell$, XOR is implemented as $a_i \oplus b_i = a_i + b_i - 2a_ib_i$, AND is implemented as $a_i \wedge b_i = a_ib_i$, and OR is implemented as $a_i \vee b_i = a_i + b_i - a_ib_i$. Comparisons and equality tests are implemented according to [16]. All operations can be used on both signed and unsigned integers. The complexities of division, bit decomposition, comparisons, and equality tests are linear in the bitlength of the operands, and the complexity of truncation is linear in the number of bits being truncated. All floating point operations (addition, subtractions, multiplication, and division) are implemented according to [7].

Implementation of array variables. To be able to support direct operations on arrays of private data types using the traditional syntax (e.g., infix notation for binary operators), the compiler must know the size of the arrays. While the size of an array generally cannot be determined in C due to the use of pointers, in our C extension arrays of private elements are created through a controlled interface. This allows us to internally represent private arrays after program parsing as a structure consisting of a field that stores the size of the array and a field with the array elements themselves. The size is then used to rewrite operations on private arrays into secure distributed computation, where all elements of the array are processed together. For example, multiplying two private arrays of size n will lead to executing n element-wise multiplications in one round of computation. This means that all operations are processed using the round complexity of only one operation, but in some cases even greater computational savings are possible. For example, inner product computation can be realized using only a single interactive operation regardless of the size of the arrays. Recall that our setting allows us to evaluate any multivariate polynomial of degree 2 using a single interaction between the computational parties which results in a particularly efficient inner product protocol.

Note that, while our current implementation does not support pointers besides arrays, using a structure to represent a private array can be made compatible with implementations with full support for pointers. In particular, we can make a pointer to a private array to point to the second field of the structure that stores array elements to achieve data compatibility.

Memory access at private locations. When the user-specified code contains access to an element of an array at a private location, we protect the location information by touching all elements of the array.[2] Private indexing is implemented as a multiplexer, where we first privately bit-decompose the index and then evaluate the multiplexer according to its Boolean formula. AND gates (multiplications) are computed for each element of the array in parallel, after which the result is locally added together by each computational node. NOT operation of bit b is implemented as $1-b$. The result of this operation is always private regardless of the type of the data stored in the array.

Handling of private data types in assignments. To ensure that information about private values is not accidentally leaked, the compiler checks all assignment statements and produces a terminal error if a private expression is being assigned to a public variable. This is enforced using the AST, in which each node is marked as public or private and private status propagates from a child to its parent. Then a node that corresponds to assignment is not permitted to be composed of a public variable and private expression.

This check covers the cases when the expression contains function calls and the return type of at least one function used in the expression is known to be private. If, however, a function call is used, but its return type is not known (i.e., function declaration cannot be found), the compiler displays a warning of a potential violation of secure data flow (i.e., unknown data type and a potential information leakage). The goal of these checks is to help the programmer avoid unintentional information leakage without restricting the functionality. Public variables can be assigned values based on private data through `smcopen` calls.

If, on the other hand, a private variable is assigned a public expression, the compiler rewrites the code to convert the result of the expression evaluation to secret shares and then assign the resulting private value to the variable.

Handling of conditional statements. As mentioned earlier, if-statements with private conditions are not allowed to contain observable public actions in their body to prevent information leakage about private conditions. To enforce this constraint, the compiler analyzes all statements in the body of the conditional statement (recursively parsing all constructions) to detect violations and produce a terminal error is a violation is found. Similarly, the compiler extracts the list of functions called from the body of a conditional statement with a private condition. For each such function, if its content is known, the compiler analyzes its body for public side effects (such as changes to public global or shared variables) and produces a terminal error if such side effects are present. If, however, the content of the function is not known, the compiler produces a warning indicating a possible information leakage. Note that private side effects in functions called from the body of an if-statement with a private condition are permitted.

If no terminal errors have been found, the compiler proceeds with transforming the if-statements with private conditions. As the first step, the compiler determines all variables, the values of which are modified within the body of the if-statement (by searching through the list of statements for assignment operations), and their values are preserved in temporary variables. Next, the body is evaluated as if the condition was true and the condition of the if-statement is also privately evaluated. Now all variables affected by the instructions in the body of the if-statement are updated as if the condition holds and we need to roll back to their original values if the condition does not hold. To accomplish this, we update each affected variable v by setting its value to $c \cdot v + (1-c)v_{orig}$, where c is a private bit corresponding to the result of evaluating the condition and v_{orig} is the original value of v prior to executing the body of the if-statement.

If the if-statement contains the else clause, we repeat the process for all variables modified within the body of the else clause with two important differences: the private condition no longer needs to be evaluated, and each variable v affected by the body of the else clause is updated to $(1-c)v + c \cdot v_{orig}$ after executing all instructions in the else clause. This approach allows us to support arbitrary constructions while using the minimal amount of resources.

The above approach allows us to evaluate private conditional statements that modify ordinary variables efficiently, but can lead to suboptimal memory use when the variables are arrays. In particular, if the body of an if-statement modifies a single element of the array (or a small number of them), storing the original content of the entire array may result in substantial amount of extra memory. For example, in constructions of the type

```
for (i=0; i<n; i++)
  if (a[i]<0) a[i]=-a[i];
```

with private array `a`, there is no need to make a copy of the entire array `a` for each conditional statement. Similarly, if a function receives an index into a global array as its parameter and conditionally modified the element at that index, storing a copy of the array is wasteful. To mitigate the problem, we make special provisions for array handling. In particular, if an element of an array is modified within the body of a conditional statement with private condition and that assignment is not surrounded by a loop, the element of the array is treated as an ordinary variable, i.e., only a copy

[2]For large-sized arrays or databases, alternative techniques such as oblivious RAM [27] or the approach from [33] are likely to result in faster performance and their use will be investigated as part of this project.

of the element is made, not a copy of the array. If, on the other hand, the assignment is within the scope of a loop that affects the element's index within the array, that assignment will correspond to modifications to a number of array elements. In that case, we create a single temporary variable and in each loop iteration store the current value of the array element to be modified prior to executing the assignment operation. This will ensure that the optimal amount of memory is used by the program. For example, if the original program contains code

```
if (t>0)
  for (i=0; i<n; i+=5)
    a[i]=a[i]+1;
```

with private `t` and `a`, it will be transformed into:

```
mpz_t cond1;
mpz_t tmp1;
smc_gt(t,0,cond1);
for (i=0; i<n; i+=5) {
  tmp1=a[i];
  a[i]=a[i]+1;
  a[i]=cond1*a[i]+(1-cond1)*tmp1;
}
```

where the above code is a simplification of the actual code produced and `smc_gt` corresponds to secure distributed implementation of the greater than operation that stores the result of comparing its first two arguments into the third argument.

Handling of parallel constructs. Recall that we support two ways for the programmer to specify that portions of the code can be processed concurrently: (1) parallel loop iterations and (2) arbitrary parts of code that can be processed simultaneously. While both constructions use similar syntax, their implementations differ. In particular, a number of identical operations from different loop iterations can be efficiently processed in a batch (using the same number of rounds as that of a single loop iteration), with the overall load partitioned among the available cores via threads. In the second case, however, the only available mechanism for parallelizing the computation is by executing the portions of the code that can be concurrently processed in different threads. Threads can also be used within a single operation (not visible to the programmer) to provide the fastest execution of that operation.

In what follows, we first describe how we handle batch execution used for parallel loop constructs only, and then address the use of threads, which are used for concurrent execution of both loop iterations and arbitrary code.

Batch execution. When the compiler observes a loop construction with parallel iterations indicated using square brackets, it transforms the instructions contained in loop iterations using batch execution. As the first step, the transformed program will need to determine the number of loop iterations that should be scheduled for batch execution. For that reason, the compiler places loop specification code (without the loop's body) in the transformed program, so that the number of loop iterations can be computed at run time. In the case when loops with parallel iterations are nested in the user program, all iterations can still be processed using a single batch.

A loop construction, all iterations of which can be executed simultaneously, must be written in such a way that its iterations update independent memory locations. This can be achieved using arrays and similar data structures. Each iteration, therefore, can consist of statements that operate on array indices computed using arbitrary expressions. For example, a program can contain:

```
for (i=1; i<n; i*=3) [
  a[i]=b[i*i]*c[i+2];
  c[i-1]=b[i+1]*k;
]
```

where `a`, `b`, and `c` are arrays consisting of private elements and `k` is a private value. Our compiler handles this by creating code in the transformed program that allocates an integer array for storing array indices used in each expression or assignment. This array contains indices for each array operand and the array being updated (when applicable). By doing this, we can pass only necessary array elements used in the operation to its batch execution. This process is repeated for all operations within the statement. When a batch operation is executed, the transformed program uses the computed index array together with the start address of each array operand and the array being updated to perform computation. For example, batch execution of the first statement in the loop above will pass the address of arrays `a`, `b`, and `c` together with index array consisting of indices i for all i specified in the loop, indices $i \cdot i$, and indices $i+2$ to the multiplication operation. Execution of the second statement does not use array indices associated with the second operand.

When the body of a loop with parallel execution contains a private condition, the transformed program needs to store a copy of the variables being modified, evaluate the private condition in a batch, and compute the value of each variable v as $c \cdot v + (1-c)v_{orig}$, where c is the result of condition evaluation. Unlike regular loops, where we could store the original value of array elements one at a time right before the modification, the use of batch operations requires that we store all necessary data before the operation.

Thread management. To ensure that the number of threads is limited and the overhead associated with their management does not become overwhelming, a transformed program that uses concurrent execution is written to maintain a thread pool with provisions to maximize CPU utilization and avoid deadlocks (when a task assigned to a thread is blocked waiting on a child task and the child task is unable to acquire a thread). For loops with parallelizable iterations, we divide all iterations in batches of a predefined size, and place the next batch in a queue to be picked up by an available thread. This will ensure that the context switching overhead is very low relative to the overall computation time even for loops with a very large number of iterations. Given a specific setup, the optimal number of threads in the thread pool and the optimal batch size can be determined experimentally.

Our thread management mechanism is similar to that used in OMPi [23] and is realized as follows. Each user program starts by running in a single thread, and we refer to the code that can be scheduled to run in a separate thread as a task. Each task maintains a data structure (called task node) that stores information about its environment including local (i.e., visible only to the running thread) and shared (i.e., shared by all running threads) variables necessary for its execution. Furthermore, each thread from the thread pool manages a queue data structure (called task queue) that stores task nodes corresponding to the tasks whose execution is pending. The queue structure maintained by each thread has a fixed upper bound, which means that it can store only a certain number of tasks to execute. When a new task is being created, the thread that creates it will normally store it in its task queue, although there is a mechanism to indicate that the task execution must start immediately. When the task queue is full, but a new task is received, the thread will suspend the task it was running (which spawned the new task), and execute the newly received task to its completion. This ensures that no tasks are ever lost due to queue overflow. Lastly, to minimize the overall idle time for threads, the compiler applies the work-stealing strategy [24], which allows an idle thread to execute a task from another thread's queue.

The thread management mechanism on which we build did not require a thread to communicate with other nodes and thus had no provisions for a thread to retrieve only its own communication off the network. For that reason, if execution of a compiled program uses multiple threads, at the point of execution where multiple threads are created, we also create a manager thread that handles incoming communication in behalf of all other threads. In particular, the manager thread listens to the sockets corresponding to all peer nodes with which the current node communicates and reads the data once it becomes available. After retrieving the data from a specific socket for a specific thread (each transmission is now marked with thread id), the manager thread signals the receiving thread that it now has data available. This ensures that each thread correctly receives data destined to it. Sending the data, on the other hand, is handled by each thread as before, after securing a lock for mutual exclusion on the socket that the thread wants to use.

To the best of our knowledge, no implementation other than VIFF supports multi-threaded execution and this topic has not been sufficiently treated in the SMC literature.

Modulus computation. The programmer can specify the size of the modulus or the modulus itself[3] to be used for secure computation. If that information is not provided, the compiler computes the minimum modulus size necessary for correct and secure operation. The size is computed based on the bitlength of the declared variables and operations on them. The algorithm proceeds by computing the maximum bitlength of all declared variables and maximum bitlength necessary for carrying out the specified operations. For example, for integer data types, the algorithm computes the maximum of all declared bitlengths ℓ_i, $\max(\ell_1, \ell_2) + \kappa$ for each comparison operation on arguments of bitlengths ℓ_1 and ℓ_2, where κ is the statistical security parameter, $\ell_1 + \kappa$ for each right shift operation on an argument of bitlength ℓ_1, and $2\max(\ell_1, \ell_2) + \kappa + 1$ for each division on arguments of bitlengths ℓ_1 and ℓ_2.

Once the modulus size is determined, our compiler chooses the modulus of the appropriate size and includes it in the transformed user program. The compiler also outputs the modulus to a runtime configuration file for use with other components of the system.

4.4 Supplemental programs

While our source-to-source translator is the main component of PICCO, the system also contains two utility programs for private input preprocessing and private output assembly as shown in Figure 1(b). Here we briefly describe their functionality.

As mentioned earlier, each input and output variable is marked with the id of the input party supplying or receiving it, and the computational parties receive data from each input party prior to the computation start. To aid the input parties with creating their input transmissions, we instruct the compiler to produce a supplemental configuration file (not shown in Figure 1) in addition to the transformed user program itself. The configuration file contains the modulus necessary for share manipulation and a list of input and output variables (in the order of appearance of `smcinput` and `smcoutput` function calls) annotated with their input/output type, data type, and the id of the responsible input or output party.

At runtime, every input party will provide this configuration file to the input utility program. The program will prompt the user for the id and will ask to input data marked with that user's id in the configuration file. Data entry can be done either manually or from a file. The utility program consequently converts private inputs into their shares while leaving public inputs unchanged and produces n output files. The input party communicates the ith produced file to computational party P_i.

[3]When the user chooses the modulus for secure computation, the modulus has to be some prime $p > n$ for the computation to be carried in the field $\mathbb{Z}_p$ or be equal to 256 to indicate that the computation is in the field GF(2^8).

The output utility program has a similar functionality: Upon receipt of output transmissions from at least $t + 1$ computational parties, an output party will input the supplemental configuration file together with the user id into the program. The output utility program consequently reconstructs user data according to the data types and outputs the result to the user.

5. PERFORMANCE EVALUATION

In this section we provide experimental results using PICCO. Following [29], we create a number of user programs of various functionalities, compile and run them in the distributed setting, and measure their performance. To fully evaluate the effect of parallel execution (using array operations, batching, and threads), for each tested functionality we provide its basic version as well as optimized version that uses concurrent execution features of PICCO. The types of computations tested as part of this work include:

1. A mix of arithmetic operations consisting of 90% additions and 10% multiplications with 10 input and 5 output variables. The basic functionality sequentially executes all operations, while the optimized version uses batch operations.
2. Multiplication of two matrices. The basic and optimized user programs are given in Figures 2 and 3, respectively. For compactness of presentation, we assume that the second matrix is given as the transpose of the matrix to be multiplied. Computing the transpose uses only local memory operations and does not increase the overall runtime.
3. Mergesort computation that outputs the median of the sorted array. The programs are given in Figures 4 and 5.
4. Computation of the Hamming distance between two binary vectors. The programs are given in Figures 6 and 7.
5. Evaluation of one block of AES on a private 128-bit message using private 128-bit key.
6. Computation of the edit distance between two strings of equal size via dynamic programming. The cost of insertion, deletion, and substitution is fixed and set to 1.
7. Matching of two fingerprints consisting of an equal number of minutiae. Each minutia point consists of x and y coordinates in a two-dimensional space, as well as its orientation.

The source code of the last three programs is omitted, but will be reported in the full version. Instead, we give a brief description. For compactness of presentation of other programs, we use array operations with input/output functions even in unoptimized programs, which introduces only a marginal improvement on the runtime of basic programs. All of the programs included in the experiments use integer arithmetic, which facilitates comparison of their performance with the same functionalities produced using other tools. Performance of our implementation of floating point operations, however, can be found in [7], including performance of executing multiple instances of an operation in a batch.

The results of the experiments for $n = 3$ computational parties are given in Table 2. We consider this value of n to be commonly used in practice. Because the number of computational parties is independent of the number of input owners and output recipients, in cases of both single client computation outsourcing and secure collaborative computation it is possible to find three independent computational parties which are unlikely to collude with each other. The programs our compiler produces are written in C/C++ using the GMP [5] library for large number arithmetic, the Boost libraries [2] for communication, and OpenSSL [6] for securing the computation. Our LAN experiments were conducted using 2.4 GHz 6-core machines running Red Hat Linux and connected through 1 Gb/s Ethernet. Our WAN experiments used machines from the GENI infrastructure [4], where two of the machines were

Experiment	Modulus p length (bits)	Basic functionality LAN (ms)	Basic functionality WAN (ms)	Optimized functionality LAN (ms)	Optimized functionality WAN (ms)	Sharemind LAN (ms)	Sharemind WAN (ms)	Two-party compiler [29] LAN (ms)	Two-party compiler [29] WAN (ms)
100 arithmetic operations	33	1.40	315	**0.18**	**31.6**	71	203	1,198	1,831
1000 arithmetic operations	33	13.4	3,149	**0.60**	**32.3**	82	249	3,429	5,823
3000 arithmetic operations	33	42.7	9,444	**1.60**	**34.5**	127	325	10,774	11,979
5×5 matrix multiplication	33	17.7	3,936	**0.27**	**31.6**	132	264	3,419	5,244
8×8 matrix multiplication	33	67.8	16,126	**0.45**	**32.1**	168	376	18,853	21,843
20×20 matrix multiplication	33	1,062	251,913	**2.41**	**35.7**	1,715	2,961	N/A	N/A
Median, mergesort, 32 elements	81	703.7	98,678	**256.7**	6,288	7,115	22,208	4,450	**5,906**
Median, mergesort, 64 elements	81	1,970	276,277	**649.6**	**12,080**	15,145	47,636	N/A	N/A
Median mergesort, 256 elements	81	13,458	1,894,420	**3,689**	**47,654**	66,023	203,044	N/A	N/A
Median mergesort, 1024 elements	81	86,765	–	**20,579**	**170,872**	317,692	869,582	N/A	N/A
Hamming distance, 160 bits	9	21.2	5,038	**0.17**	**31.1**	72	188	793	816
Hamming distance, 320 bits	10	42.3	10,092	**0.22**	**31.3**	102	203	850	1,238
Hamming distance, 800 bits	11	105.8	25,205	**0.35**	**31.5**	117	254	933	989
Hamming distance, 1600 bits	12	212.7	50,816	**0.57**	**31.8**	132	284	1,037	1,265
AES, 128-bit key and block	8	319.1	75,874	**35.1**	**3,179**	652 [34]	N/A	N/A	N/A
Edit distance, 100 elements	57	48,431	9,479,330	**4,258**	**116,632**	69,980	214,286	N/A	N/A
Edit distance, 200 elements	57	201,077	–	**16,038**	**432,456**	196,198	498,831	N/A	N/A
Fingerprint matching, 20 minutiae	66	3,256	541,656	**830**	**74,704**	24,273	75,820	N/A	N/A
Fingerprint matching, 40 minutiae	66	13,053	2,140,630	**2,761**	172,455	55,088	**172,266**	N/A	N/A

Table 2: Performance of representative programs using PICCO.

```
public int main() {
   public int i, j, k, S;
   smcinput(S, 1, 1);
   int A[S][S], B[S][S], C[S][S];
   smcinput(A, 1, S*S);
   smcinput(B, 1, S*S);

   for (i = 0; i < S; i++)
     for (j = 0; j < S; j++)
       C[i][j] = 0;

   for (i = 0; i < S; i++)
     for (j = 0; j < S; j++)
       for (k = 0; k < S; k++)
         C[i][j] += A[i][k]*B[k][j];

   smcoutput(C, 1, S*S);
   return 0;
}
```

Figure 2: Basic matrix multiplication program.

```
public int main() {
   public int i, j, S;
   smcinput(S, 1, 1);
   int A[S][S], B[S][S], C[S][S];

   smcinput(A, 1, S*S);
   //assume B is given as transpose of original B
   smcinput(B, 1, S*S);

   for (i = 0; i < S; i++) [
     for (j = 0; j < S; j++) [
        C[i][j] = A[i] @ B[j];
     ]
   ]
   smcoutput(C, 1, S*S);
   return 0;
}
```

Figure 3: Matrix multiplication program that uses concurrent computation.

located on the same LAN and one at a different location. All machines were running Fedora 15 with either 4 cores using 3.0 GHz or 8 cores using 2.4 GHz. The pairwise round-trip times between the machines were 0.2 msec, 63 msec, and 63 msec. Each experiment was run 5 times and the mean time over the runs and computational parties is reported in the table. We omit unoptimized experiments with excessive runtime. Also, batch execution in the optimized functionalities does not use threads as the number of operations in batch execution is not sufficiently large to exceed the threshold and be divided into threads.

As can be seen from Table 2, the running time of unoptimized programs for arithmetic operations, matrix multiplication, and Hamming distance grows linearly with the number of multiplications that they use. That is, performing multiplication of 5×5 matrices, computing 125-element Hamming distance, and performing 1250 arithmetic operations takes very similar amount of time for both LAN and WAN experiments. For these functionalities, combining multiple interactive operations into a single batch results in tremendous performance improvement. That is, using a loop with concurrent iterations in arithmetic operations program and using vector operations in the remaining functionalities, the round complexity of all of these programs reduces to 1. For programs and batches of small size (e.g., 10 multiplications in 100 arithmetic operations program), the overall time can hardly be distinguished from the time that a single operation takes. For computation of larger size, however, although round complexity does not change, both increased computation and communication contribute to the overall time. Consider, for example, optimized matrix multiplication results. In the LAN experiments, almost all of the overhead for 20×20 matrix multiplication (8,000 multiplications, but only 400 interactive operations) is due to computation. In the WAN experiments, however, most of the time is still contributed by communication (sending and receiving shares for one batch operation). The execution times for matrix multiplication can be compared to that of the Hamming distance, where the optimized functionality always invokes one multiplication operation regardless of the problem size. The Hamming distance results tell us how the computational effort increases as the problem size increases and communication remains the same.

To summarize, for these types of functionalities, the use of concurrent loop iterations and vector operations brings the round com-

```
public int K=32;
private int A[K];

void mergesort(public int l, public int r) {
   public int i, j, k, m, size;
   size = r - l + 1;
   int tmp;

   if (r > l) {
      m = (r + l)/2;
      mergesort(l, m);
      mergesort(m + 1, r);

      for (i = size >> 1; i > 0; i = i >> 1)
         for (j = 0; j < size; j += 2*i)
            for (k = j; k < j + i; k++)
               if (A[k+l] > A[k+i+l]) {
                  tmp = A[k+l];
                  A[k+l] = A[k+i+l];
                  A[k+i+l] = tmp;
               }
   }
}

public int main() {
   public int i, median = K/2;
   smcinput(A, 1, K);
   mergesort(0, K-1);
   smcoutput(A[median], 1);
   return 0;
}
```

Figure 4: Basic mergesort median program.

```
void mergesort(public int l, public int r) {
   public int i, j, k, m, size;
   size = r - l + 1;
   int tmp[size];

   if (r > l) {
      m = (r + l)/2;
      [ mergesort(l, m); ]
      [ mergesort(m + 1, r); ]

      for (i = size >> 1; i > 0; i = i >> 1)
        for (j = 0; j < size; j += 2*i) [
          for (k = j; k < j + i; k++) [
            tmp[k] = A[k+l];
            if (A[k+l] > A[k+i+l]) {
               A[k+l] = A[k+i+l];
               A[k+i+l] = tmp[k];
            }
          ]
        ]
   }
}
```

Figure 5: Mergesort median program that uses concurrent computation (the difference from basic program).

```
public int main() {
   public int i, M;
   smcinput(M, 1, 1);
   private int<1> A[M], B[M];
   private int<10> dist = 0;

   smcinput(A, 1, M);
   smcinput(B, 1, M);
   for (i = 0; i < M; i++)
     dist += A[i] ^ B[i];

   smcoutput(dist, 1);
   return 0;
}
```

Figure 6: Basic Hamming distance program.

plexity to the minimal single round and thus the performance is bounded by a one-way communication delay from below. In our experiments, the performance was improved by 2–3 orders of magnitude depending on the problem size and the savings will continue to increase for larger computational problems. The use of threads additionally improves the running time for problems of large size by a small factor that depends on the number of cores.

Mergesort computation is dominated by $O(m \log^2 m)$ comparisons for a set of size m and this growth is reflected in the runtimes of the unoptimized (sequential) functionality. The use of concurrent loop iterations greatly decreases the time that the merge step takes, but for this functionality the use of threads to concurrently sort the first half and the second half of the set also improves the performance. The round complexity of mergesort is $O(\log^2 m)$ comparisons, but we do not achieve it because the number of threads is limited to the number of cores. (Likewise, our Sharemind program written in a similar way does not achieve optimal round complexity.)

For the AES implementation, the best performance can be achieved when the computation is in GF(2^8) and thus the user needs to specify this field as a configuration parameter. Then the user secret-shares each byte of the key and message with the computational nodes. Recall that each round of AES consists of AddRoundKey, SubBytes, ShiftRows, and MixColumns algorithms and the most complex part of round key computation is the same as SubBytes. When using arithmetic in GF(2^8), all operations other than S-box computation in SubBytes and round key computation are linear and thus are performed non-interactively. Instead of following the traditional implementations of the S-box as a table lookup, we write the user program to compute the transformation directly, where the computation of the inverse and bit decomposition is implemented as suggested in [20]. One round of key expansion and one round of block cipher are computed simultaneously, where all bytes of the block are processed in parallel.

We obtain that the compiled program performs the key expansion and one block of AES encryption in only 35 msec, which is clearly very competitive even compared to custom implementations that do not use a compiler. In particular, in recent years several publications optimize evaluation of AES in the context of secure multi-party computation. The results range from circuit minimization techniques [12, 13] to concrete realizations in the two-party and multi-party settings. In the two-party setting, [36], [28], and [30] report 7 sec, 3.3 sec, and (without key expansion) 0.2 sec evaluation time, respectively, for AES using custom (as opposed to compiler-generated) circuits. In the multi-party setting, the results are available for 3 computational parties on a LAN. [20] reports 2 sec in a setting similar to ours, the fastest recent results in the Sharemind framework [34] are 652 msec, and, most notably, [33] reports 9 msec without key expansion using an implementation with 2 concurrent threads (and 14.3 msec using a single thread) based on a new lookup-table protocol of high efficiency. The last approach can be integrated into our compiler for achieving high-performance table lookups for AES and other purposes. Also, [21] reports runtime on the order of minutes (offline and online work without key expansion) in two stronger security models (while all other results cited above are in the semi-honest model).

The edit distance program uses dynamic programming to fill in the cells of a $(m + 1) \times (m + 1)$ grid, where m is the length of

```
public int main() {
   public int i, M;
   smcinput(M, 1, 1);
   private int<1> A[M], B[M];
   private int<10> dist;

   smcinput(A, 1, M);
   smcinput(B, 1, M);
   dist = A @ B;
   dist = -2*dist;
   for (i = 0; i < M; i++) {
      dist += A[i] + B[i];
   }
   smcoutput(dist, 1);
   return 0;
}
```

Figure 7: Hamming distance program that uses concurrent computation.

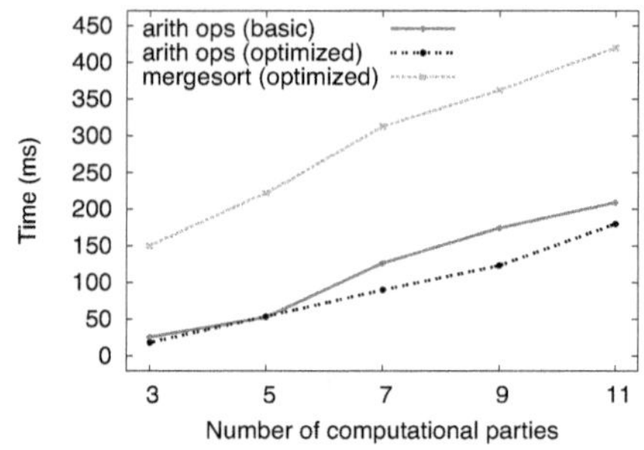

Figure 8: Performance of selected programs with a varying number of computational parties on a LAN.

the input strings. Each cell at position (i, j) is computed as the minimum of three distances computed from the distances at cells $(i-1, j)$, $(i, j-1)$, $(i-1, j-1)$ and the result of comparison of the characters at positions i and j. The optimized version of the program processes all cells on a diagonal in parallel, resulting in $2m-3$ rounds that compute the minimum function.

Lastly, the fingerprint program compares one minutia of fingerprint A to all minutiae of fingerprint B, and among those that matched (i.e., within close Euclidean distance and small angle) chooses the one with the closest distance. The chosen minutia in fingerprint B is marked as no longer available. The process is repeated with all other minutiae of fingerprint A, where all minutiae marked as no longer available are ignored in finding a matching. The output of the algorithm is the number of minutiae marked as having a mate in the other fingerprint. The optimized version of this program runs all distance and orientation comparisons for a minutia in fingerprint A in parallel. It then also computes the minimum and its location using a tree with $\log m$ rounds of comparisons for m-minutia fingerprints. Note that the computation cannot reveal if a minutia in B already has a mate or not close enough to a minutia in A, and thus for each minutia in A we have to treat all minutiae in B in the same way.

For comparison, we also provide performance of secure two-party computation compiler from [29] and Sharemind [10]. The former is a general-purpose compiler for ANSI C for the two-party setting and it is informative to compare performance of programs produced using the compiler. In Table 2 we list runtimes for similar programs when available as reported in [29]. The latter is a framework that allows a program written in language called SecreC to be compiled into secure distributed implementation for 3 computational parties. The tool is constantly evolving and well optimized, while the language currently has a few limitations such as no support for if-statements with a private condition[4]. We chose Sharemind for its speed, as other general secure multi-party computation tools and compilers such as FairplayMP and VIFF result in slower performance. We run Sharemind experiments in the same setups as our LAN and WAN experiments.

From Table 2, it is clear that despite using more computational parties and highly interactive techniques, the performance of programs compiled using PICCO compares very favorably to those compiled using the two-party approach of [29]. In particular, the largest difference we observe is by more than 3 orders of magnitude for some LAN experiments. Performance of the programs executed through Sharemind is also slower than with PICCO, especially for simple programs on a LAN. In our Sharemind experiments we were unable to match the performance reported in [11], despite extensive use of the available (batch) optimization mechanisms. Furthermore, we experience a large 4-fold reduction in execution time of arithmetic operations programs by replacing operations of the form $a = a + a$ with operations of the form $b = a + a$, where a and b are vectors. This could be in part due to excessive logging (which we were unable to disable) and is not the expected behavior. The execution of interactive multiplication operations is more costly and execution of local addition operations should take a small fraction of the overall time, regardless of how addition operations are handled in the user program. We conclude that Sharemind was optimized for massively-parallel computation with low amortized cost per operation, but not general-purpose computation where sequential execution is common. Furthermore, Sharemind is likely to outperform PICCO when a large number of homogeneous operations are to be run in parallel, but we expect our tool to result in lower execution time for general-purpose functionalities.

To investigate the impact of varying the number of computational parties on the performance, we conducted additional experiments. The programs that we chose are unoptimized 1000 arithmetic operations, optimized 1000 arithmetic operations, and 32-element mergesort, which provide insights into the performance of plain multiplications, batch multiplications, and combination of batch and multi-threaded implementation, respectively. To perform multiplication, each computational party transmits $n-1$ messages and performs Lagrange interpolation that in the most general form involves quadratic (in the number of parties) computation. On a LAN, this computation contributes a substantial portion of the overall time and [25] reports that the growth in multiplication time can be best described by function $f(n) = 0.009n^2 + 0.006n + 0.799$. We, however, observe that in the semi-honest setting all parties send their data as prescribed and the set of available shares is known. This means that Lagrange coefficients used during interpolation can be precomputed, resulting in linear computation time. Furthermore, we reconstruct only the free coefficient of the polynomial that encodes the secret as opposed to the entire polynomial. This gives us that the work a computational party performs for a single interactive operation is linear in n, but the total volume of communication placed on the network is quadratic in n. Our LAN results (using a new set of machines) are given in Figure 8, where optimized arithmetic operations' time is scaled up by a factor of 20. We can observe linear or slightly higher than linear growth in n.

[4]SecreC allows for comparisons and other basic predicates to be evaluated on private values outside of if-statements. This has similar expressiveness to using if-statements with arbitrary conditions over private variables, but results in degradation of usability, as the programmer has to expand and rewrite all if-statements by hand.

6. CONCLUSIONS

The goal of this is work is to enable secure execution of general-purpose programs in not fully trusted environments. Toward this goal, we introduce PICCO — a suite of programs for compiling a user program written in an extension of C with variables that need be protected marked as private, into its secure distributed implementation, and running it in a distributed setting. Our implementation uses techniques based on secret sharing with several optimizations to improve the runtime. This results in efficient secure execution suitable for sizeable computations in a variety of settings.

Acknowledgments

We are grateful to Ethan Blanton for valuable suggestions on the design of the compiler, Dan Bogdanov for the help with Sharemind experiments, and anonymous reviewers for their valuable feedback. This work was supported in part by grants CNS-1319090 and CNS-1223699 from the National Science Foundation and FA9550-13-1-0066 from the Air Force Office of Scientific Research. Any opinions, findings, and conclusions or recommendations expressed in this publication are those of the authors and do not necessarily reflect the views of the funding agencies. We also acknowledge the NSF-sponsored Global Environment for Network Innovations (GENI) test bed, which allowed us to run WAN experiments.

7. REFERENCES

[1] Bison – GNU parser generator. http://www.gnu.org/software/bison.

[2] Boost C++ libraries. http://www.boost.org.

[3] flex: The Fast Lexical Analyzer. http://flex.sourceforge.net.

[4] GENI: Global environment for network innovations. http://www.geni.net.

[5] GMP – The GNU Multiple Precision Arithmetic Library. http://gmplib.org.

[6] OpenSSL: The open source toolkit for SSL/TLS. http://www.openssl.org.

[7] M. Aliasgari, M. Blanton, Y. Zhang, and A. Steele. Secure computation on floating point numbers. In *NDSS*, 2013.

[8] A. Ben-David, N. Nisan, and B. Pinkas. FairplayMP: A system for secure multi-party computation. In *CCS*, 2008.

[9] M. Blanton. Empirical evaluation of secure two-party computation models. Technical Report TR 2005-58, CERIAS, Purdue University, 2005.

[10] D. Bogdanov, S. Laur, and J. Willemson. Sharemind: A framework for fast privacy-preserving computations. In *ESORICS*, pages 192–206, 2008.

[11] D. Bogdanov, M. Niitsoo, T. Toft, and J. Willemson. High-performance secure multi-party computation for data mining applications. *IJIS*, 11(6):403–418, 2012.

[12] J. Boyar and R. Peralta. A new combinational logic minimization technique with applications to cryptology. In *Symposium on Experimental Algorithms*, 2010.

[13] J. Boyar and R. Peralta. A small depth-16 circuit for the AES S-box. In *Information Security and Privacy Research*, pages 287–298, 2012.

[14] M. Burkhart, M. Strasser, D. Many, and X. Dimitropoulos. SEPIA: Privacy-preserving aggregation of multi-domain network events and statistics. In *USENIX Security Symposium*, pages 223–240, 2010.

[15] R. Canetti. Security and composition of multiparty cryptographic protocols. *Journal of Cryptology*, 13(1):143–202, 2000.

[16] O. Catrina and S. de Hoogh. Improved primitives for secure multiparty integer computation. In *Security and Cryptography for Networks (SCN)*, pages 182–199, 2010.

[17] O. Catrina and A. Saxena. Secure computation with fixed-point numbers. In *FC*, pages 35–50, 2010.

[18] R. Cramer, I. Damgård, and Y. Ishai. Share conversion, pseudorandom secret-sharing and applications to secure computation. In *TCC*, pages 342–362, 2005.

[19] I. Damgård, M. Geisler, and M. Krøigård. Asynchronous multiparty computation: Theory and implementation. In *PKC*, pages 160–179, 2009.

[20] I. Damgård and M. Keller. Secure multiparty AES. In *FC*, pages 367–374, 2010.

[21] I. Damgård, M. Keller, E. Larraia, C. Miles, and N. Smart. Implementing AES via an actively/covertly secure dishonest-majority MPC protocol. IACR Cryptology ePrint Archive Report 2012/262, 2012.

[22] I. Damgård and J. Nielsen. Scalable and unconditionally secure multiparty computation. In *CRYPTO*, 2007.

[23] V. Dimakopoulos, E. Leontiadis, and G. Tzoumas. A portable C compiler for OpenMP V.2.0. In *European Workshop on OpenMP (EWOMP)*, pages 5–11, 2003.

[24] M. Frigo, C. Leiserson, and K. Randall. The implementation of the Cilk-5 multithreaded language. In *PLDI*, pages 212–223, 1998.

[25] M. Geisler. *Cryptographic protocols: Theory and implementation*. PhD thesis, Aarhus University, 2010.

[26] R. Gennaro, M. Rabin, and T. Rabin. Simplified VSS and fast-track multiparty computations with applications to threshold cryptography. In *PODC*, pages 101–111, 1998.

[27] O. Goldreich. Towards a theory of software protection and simulation by oblivious RAMs. In *STOC*, 1987.

[28] W. Henecka, S. Kogl, A.-R. Sadeghi, T. Schneider, and I. Wehrenberg. TASTY: Tool for Automating Secure Two-partY computations. In *CCS*, pages 451–462, 2010.

[29] A. Holzer, M. Franz, S. Katzenbeisser, and H. Veith. Secure two-party computations in ANSI C. In *CCS*, 2012.

[30] Y. Huang, D. Evans, J. Katz, and L. Malka. Faster secure two-party computation using garbled circuits. In *USENIX Security Symposium*, 2011.

[31] R. Jagomägis. SecreC: A privacy-aware programming language with applications in data mining. Master's thesis, University of Tartu, 2010.

[32] F. Kerschbaum. Automatically optimizing secure computation. In *CCS*, pages 703–714, 2011.

[33] J. Launchbury, I. Diatchki, T. DuBuisson, and A. Adams-Moran. Efficient lookup-table protocol in secure multiparty computation. In *ICFP*, pages 189–200, 2012.

[34] S. Laur, R. Talviste, and J. Willemson. From oblivious AES to efficient and secure database join in the multiparty setting. In *ACNS*, pages 84–101, 2013.

[35] D. Malkhi, N. Nisan, B. Pinkas, and Y. Sella. Fairplay – a secure two-party computation system. In *USENIX Security Symposium*, pages 287–302, 2004.

[36] B. Pinkas, T. Schneider, N. Smart, and S. Williams. Secure two-party computation is practical. In *ASIACRYPT*, 2009.

[37] A. Schroepfer, F. Kerschbaum, and G. Mueller. L1 – An intermediate language for mixed-protocol secure computation. In *COMPSAC*, pages 298–307, 2011.

[38] A. Shamir. How to share a secret. *Communications of the ACM*, 22(11):612–613, 1979.

Düppel: Retrofitting Commodity Operating Systems to Mitigate Cache Side Channels in the Cloud

Yinqian Zhang
Department of Computer Science
University of North Carolina at Chapel Hill
Chapel Hill, NC, USA
yinqian@cs.unc.edu

Michael K. Reiter
Department of Computer Science
University of North Carolina at Chapel Hill
Chapel Hill, NC, USA
reiter@cs.unc.edu

ABSTRACT

This paper presents the design, implementation and evaluation of a system called Düppel that enables a tenant virtual machine to defend itself from cache-based side-channel attacks in public clouds. Düppel includes defenses for time-shared caches such as per-core L1 and L2 caches. Experiments in the lab and on public clouds show that Düppel effectively obfuscates timing signals available to an attacker VM via these caches and incurs modest performance overheads (at most 7% and usually much less) in the common case of no side-channel attacks. Moreover, Düppel requires no changes to hypervisors or support from cloud operators.

Categories and Subject Descriptors

D.4.6 [**OPERATING SYSTEMS**]: Security and Protection—*Information flow controls*

General Terms

Security

Keywords

Side-channel attack; cross-VM side channel; cache-based side channel

1. INTRODUCTION

The threat of side-channel attacks in multi-tenant public clouds is becoming a realistic security concern [29, 38]. In such attacks as demonstrated to date, shared CPU caches enable virtual machines (VM) administered by competing organizations to exfiltrate sensitive information from each other. This has recently been shown to be possible despite considerable interference and background "noise" from the hypervisor and other activities on the machine [38].

Most approaches to address these attacks have focused on altering the cloud platform in some way (see Sec. 2). However, to our knowledge, these defenses have not gained traction in existing public clouds. Rather, a typical tenant of a public cloud concerned about these attacks is left with little choice but to try to *defend itself*. One approach is to construct its software to resist side channels (e.g., [21, 18, 11]), but these techniques can result in significant slowdown. A second approach is to run its VMs on an isolated machine (possibly verifying this isolation using side channels itself [37]), though existing cloud providers that offer this service charge more for it.

In this paper we explore a third possibility, namely a method by which a tenant can construct its VMs to automatically inject additional noise into the timings that an attacker might observe from caches. Since these timings are the most common side-channels by which an attacker infers sensitive information about a victim VM, injecting noise into them will generally make the attacker's job more difficult. Our implementation of this idea, called Düppel[1], modifies only the guest OS kernel and is general enough to protect arbitrary types of user-space applications. Düppel can be configured to protect the user-space application, any dynamically linked libraries it uses, or both. Düppel does not need support from hypervisors or cloud providers. To our knowledge, our scheme is the first work that provides tenant VM OS layer mitigation of cross-VM side channels.

Unlike the noise overcome by previous attacks, the noise injected by Düppel is designed specifically to confound attacks mounted via timing the per-core L1 cache (or per-core L2 cache, if present) on the platform. Düppel does so by repeatedly cleaning the L1 cache alongside the execution of its tenant workload, at a pace that it adjusts based upon the possibility with which timings reflecting the workload execution could actually have been observed from another VM. We also discuss extensions of Düppel to defeat timing attacks via other time-shared resources such as the branch prediction cache, should attacks via this cache [4, 3, 14] someday be adapted to a virtualized setting. We emphasize, however, that even with just addressing the L1 cache, Düppel already interferes with all known cryptographic side-channel attacks that have been demonstrated in a virtualized SMP environment. (See Sec. 8 for further discussion on this point.)

Overhead of Düppel is modest. In tests on Amazon EC2, we show that file download latencies and server throughput over a TLS-protected connection from an Apache web server suffer by at most 4% when Düppel is configured to

[1]Düppel takes its name from a radar countermeasure developed by the German Luftwaffe during World War II, in which aircraft disperse clouds of tiny pieces of material to interfere with radar.

CCS'13, November 4–8, 2013, Berlin, Germany.
Copyright 2013 ACM 978-1-4503-2477-9/13/11 ...$15.00.
http://dx.doi.org/10.1145/2508859.2516741.

protect the OpenSSL library. We also demonstrate using the PARSEC benchmarks and other programs that computational workloads suffer by up to 7% when the applications are protected by Düppel. We believe that these overheads are acceptable given the substantial challenge involved in defending against cache-based side-channels with no help from the underlying hardware or hypervisor.

The rest of this paper is organized as follows. We discuss related work in Sec. 2. We present necessary background in Sec. 3 and then present the design of Düppel in Sec. 4 and Sec. 5. We describe our implementation in Sec. 6 and its evaluation in Sec. 7. We discuss possible extensions and limitations in Sec. 8 and conclude in Sec. 9.

2. RELATED WORK

Side-channel attacks on CPU microarchitectures for extracting cryptographic keys from a victim entity have been studied in different contexts. The particular form of these attacks with which we are concerned are *access-driven attacks*, in which the attacker runs a program on the system that is performing the cryptographic operation of interest. The attacker program monitors usage of a shared hardware component to learn information about the key, e.g., the data cache [27, 25, 24, 31, 13], instruction cache [1, 2, 38], floating-point multiplier [5], or branch-prediction cache [4, 3]. Our work specifically aims at defending against access-driven cache-based side-channel attacks in the cloud, an example of which was recently demonstrated by Zhang et al. [38].

Countermeasures to cache side-channel attacks can be applied to various layers in a computer system. In mitigating cross-VM side channels, prior works can roughly be classified into one of the following categories, based on the layer in which the countermeasure is implemented.

Hardware-layer approaches. The first category includes proposals of new cache designs by applying the idea of resource partitioning (e.g., [26, 33, 34, 12]) or access randomization (e.g., [34, 35, 16]) to mitigate timing channels in CPU caches on the hardware layer. Other works have proposed approaches to eliminate fine-grained timing sources in hardware designs [20]. Compared to implementations in other layers, hardware methods usually have lower performance overhead. However, adoption of new hardware techniques is a complex process, which may involve considerations of side effects (e.g., power consumption) and economic feasibility. Therefore, it might take years before these techniques are merged into production and finally used in clouds.

Hypervisor-layer approaches. Countermeasures in the second category intend to mitigate cache timing side channels by adapting the hypervisor. One direction along this line is to hide nuances in the program execution time, either by providing a fuzzy timer [32] or by forcing all executions to be deterministic [6]. However these approaches will exclude many applications that rely on a fine-grained timer from running in the cloud. A conceptually similar but more comprehensive solution is provided by Li et al. [19], in which all sources of timing channels a VM can observe are identified and categorized; they are mitigated either by aggregating timing events among multiple VM replicas, or by making them deterministic functions of other channels. Another direction is to partition the shared resources in the hypervisor [28, 30, 17]. In particular, Raj et al. [28] statically partition the last level cache (LLC) into several regions and allow VMs to make use of different regions by partitioning physical memory pages accordingly. Kim et al. [17] improved the performance by dynamically partitioning the LLCs and extended the protection to L1 cache as well.

OS-layer approaches Previous OS-layer approaches were mostly proposed to defend against cross-process side-channel attacks, e.g., [27, 31, 13]. To our knowledge, our approach is the first to modify the OS layer to mitigate cross-VM side channels.

Application-level approaches. The last approach is to construct side-channel resistant software implementations. For example, the program counter security model [21, 11] eliminates key-dependent control flows by transforming the software source code. Other efforts focus on side-channel free cryptographic implementations (e.g., [18]). These approaches incur significant overheads in some cases (e.g., Coppens et al. [11] indicate up to 24×).

3. BACKGROUND

3.1 CPU Caching Architectures

Modern CPU microarchitectures extensively make use of hardware caches to speed up expensive operations. The hardware caches on an x86 platform may include data caches, instruction caches, translation lookaside buffers (TLB), trace caches, branch target buffers (BTB) in the branch prediction unit, etc. These caches are similar in their functionalities. The most commonly known caches are data and instruction caches sitting between the processor cores and the main memory, establishing a storage hierarchy in which each level stores the interim data for the next level storage system for quick reference. Most contemporary multi-core processors are equipped with separate L1 data and instruction caches for each core, plus one (or two) unified LLC for the whole CPU package. In some Intel CPUs, a unified L2 cache exists per core, mediating data exchange between L1 caches and the LLC. Modern cache sizes range from several kilobytes (KB) to several gigabytes (GB). They are usually organized as a sequence of blocks denoted *cache lines* with fixed size. Caches are usually *set-associative*. A w-way set-associative cache is partitioned into m sets, each with w lines of size b. If the size of the cache is denoted by c, we have $m = c/(w \times b)$.

3.2 Cache-based Side-Channel Attacks

A technique commonly used in cache-based access-driven side-channel attacks is the PRIME-PROBE protocol. Although in previous works, the attacker and victim in this protocol would typically be OS processes, we describe the protocol here with the attacker and defender being virtual machines, to illustrate the threats relevant to the cloud.

In a PRIME-PROBE protocol, as introduced by Osvik et al. [25], a VCPU (a virtual CPU belonging to a VM) U of the attacker's VM spies on a victim's VCPU V by measuring the cache load in a given cache in the following manner:

PRIME: U fills one or more cache sets.

IDLE: U waits for a prespecified PRIME-PROBE *interval* while the cache is utilized by V.

PROBE: U times the duration to refill the same cache sets with the same data to measure V's cache activity on those sets.

Cache activity induced by V during the interval between U's PRIME and PROBE will evict U's data from the cache sets and replace them with V's. This will result in a noticeably higher timing measurement in U's PROBE phase than if there had been little activity from V. Of course, PROBing also accomplishes PRIMing the cache sets (i.e., evicting all data other than U's), and so repeatedly PROBing, with one PRIME-PROBE interval between each PROBE, eliminates the need to separately conduct a PRIME step.

A CPU cache, in regard to side-channel attacks, is either time-shared by the attacker and victim, or simultaneously shared by the two entities. An example of a time-shared cache is the L1 cache in an SMT-disabled[2] processor, in which the cache is dedicated to a single CPU core and can only be shared by two threads running on the same core in turns. It has been shown in previous research that SMT facilitates CPU-based side channel attacks because two threads can simultaneously use CPU resources [27, 31, 1, 2, 4]. As most cloud infrastructures disable SMT for performance or security purposes (see Sec. 8.2), per-core caches in these environments are time-shared, and so Düppel focuses on defending against side channels in this case.

4. GOALS

The anticipated attack scenario is in public IaaS clouds, where the attacker has full control of a VM co-located with the Düppel-protected VM and is capable of exploiting per-core caches as side channels to exfiltrate sensitive information. We assume the underlying CPU is based on x86 architecture and is *not* equipped with SMT. Such hardware configurations dominate modern public clouds. The two VMs in question may time-share the same CPU core, thus time-sharing the L1 instruction cache, L1 data cache, the unified L2 cache (if any), BTBs, TLBs and other caching architectures in a CPU core. We further assume the attacker can obtain a copy of the software stack running in the Düppel-protected system and so can experiment with it to learn the cache behavior that it induces. The cloud provider controls the hypervisor, which operates as is—it neither facilitates the side-channel attacks nor does anything to thwart such threats.

In light of this threat model, we have the following goals for Düppel:

GOAL 1. *Düppel should mitigate side-channel attacks via time-shared caches.*

The implementation of Düppel that we develop here addresses side channels using the L1 (or, if any, L2) per-core caches, which are time-shared caches. The principles for addressing side channels in these caches should apply to addressing them in other time-shared caches, as well.

GOAL 2. *Düppel should not require any hypervisor modification.*

An important design principle of Düppel is to permit its adoption by cloud tenants on modern cloud infrastructures without any additional support from the cloud providers.

GOAL 3. *Düppel should not require modifying applications or libraries.*

Though many secrets that might be targeted in side-channel attacks are handled in applications and third-party linked libraries, the sheer number and diversity of applications and libraries makes modifying all of them an unattractive proposition. Instead, a goal for Düppel is to protect such secrets without modifications to these components. We therefore adopted the guest OS kernel as the (sole) location in which to implement our techniques.

GOAL 4. *Düppel should induce little performance overhead.*

To be used in practice, Düppel must impose little performance burden on the system. This may require Düppel to operate in different modes during its lifecycle.

5. CLEANSING TIME-SHARED CACHES

Because attacks on time-shared caches must involve cache PROBing via CPU preemption, the intuition behind Düppel is that a guest VM (and the OS that runs on it) can protect its own execution against side-channel attacks by adding noise to these caches very frequently so that side-channel readings by the attacker are confounded by noise added between PRIMEs and PROBEs.

5.1 Basic Design

Düppel employs periodic cache cleansing to mitigate side channels in time-shared caches, e.g., L1 data/instruction caches and unified, per-core L2 caches, if any. The principles for addressing these caches could be used to address branch predication caches, as well. The basic idea is illustrated in Fig. 1. As described in Sec. 3.2, PRIME-PROBE protocols on time-shared caches work as illustrated in Fig. 1(a): the attacker periodically preempts the victim's VCPU by gaming the hypervisor scheduler and then PROBEs the cache, which takes some time due to cache/memory access latency. After the attacker relinquishes the physical CPU, the victim VCPU is scheduled for a short period until the attacker preempts it again.

Periodic cache cleansing, as illustrated in Fig. 1(b), works by cleansing the time-shared cache (ideally) between the attacker's PROBEs. Specifically, cleansing involves Düppel itself PRIMing the cache in random order until all of the entries have been evicted. The cache cleansing process is accomplished by an kernel thread that is periodically invoked by Düppel.

Key to the success of this technique is a fine-grained resolution timer in the guest OS kernel that can be periodically triggered to execute cache cleansing. There are several possible timers that might be utilized for this purpose:

- **Hardware Timers** On x86 platforms, the hardware timers include the programmable interval timer (PIT), the local advanced programmable interrupt controller timer (Local APIC), the high precision event timer (HPET), and the advanced configuration and power interface (ACPI) power management timer. Performance monitoring units (PMU) can also be regarded as a type of hardware timer, since they can be set to trigger upon hardware events that occur with predictable rates. In modern IaaS clouds, e.g., Amazon EC2 and Rackspace, most guest VMs run on paravirtualized Xen platforms. However, in such settings, none of the above hardware timers can be set to trigger by a guest VM.

[2]"SMT" is Simultaneous Multi-Threading, or HyperThreading in Intel's terminology.

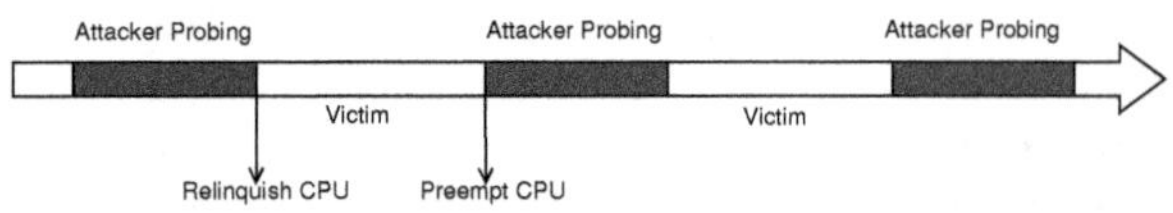

(a) Attackers exploits time-shared caches by preempting victim VCPUs.

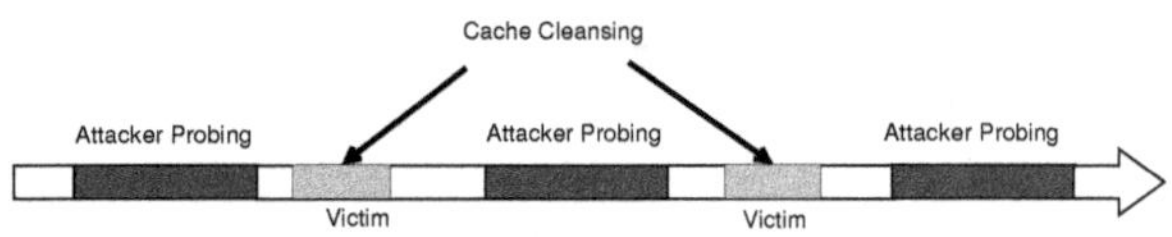

(b) Periodic time-shared cache cleansing.

Figure 1: Attack and defense on time-shared caches

- **Software Timers** A software timer may be as complex as a Linux high-resolution timer (hrtimer) or as simple as a piece of code that busy loops and periodically invokes the execution of the timer handling code using interrupts. These interrupts can include network I/O interrupts and inter-processor interrupts (IPI), the latter of which was used by Zhang et al. [38]. In paravirtualized VMs, although IPIs are also virtualized (as are I/O interrupts), they offer more stable and shorter interrupt delays. The delay of an IPI timer can be as low as $3\mu s$, while that of the hrtimer is usually higher than 15 to $20\mu s$.

The timers used in Düppel are hrtimers and software timers generated by IPIs. Periodic cache cleansing activities can operate in two modes: *sentinel* mode and *battle* mode. The sentinel mode is used when frequent cache cleansing is not critical, and thus the interval between two cleansings can be longer—as long as Düppel can detect abnormal activities and switch to battle mode quickly. The hrtimers are employed in sentinel mode because it induces lower performance overhead (conforming to GOAL 4). The much more rapid IPI timers are used in the battle mode, where intervals between cache cleansings are required to be as short as possible and the performance overhead is less of a concern when under active side-channel attacks.

5.2 Optimizations

We discuss in this section a few design optimizations that reduce the performance impact of Düppel.

5.2.1 Limiting the Protection Scope

Düppel's periodic cleansing of the L1 cache impacts the performance of the victim's application. As such, ideally Düppel would be triggered only when necessary. Fortunately, we can limit the scope of protection by allowing the users of Düppel to define specific operations as sensitive so that cache cleansing is triggered only when sensitive operations run. For instance, in a TLS-protected web server, cryptographic routines in the OpenSSL library might be considered sensitive operations. The goal is to automatically enable Düppel when needed and disable Düppel when sensitive operations finish.

Düppel implements this mechanism by exploiting CPU page-level execution protections. Düppel first marks the memory pages that contain the instructions of the sensitive operations as non-executable. Thus every time these instructions are executed, page faults trigger Düppel. Then Düppel can disable the execution protection to prevent further page faults and start the cache cleansing timer to trigger cleansing each of the time-shared caches N times (Sec. 5.1). At the end of the N-th cleansing, the execution protection is re-enabled.

If N is very small, unfinished sensitive operations will trigger the page fault again to initiate another N timer interrupts, and the overhead of frequently changing page-level protections can be huge. If N is too big, Düppel will keep running after the sensitive operation ends. In our design, Düppel dynamically adjusts N with the following algorithms: N changes value in the range of $[N_{min}, N_{max}]$, each time by adding Δ. Δ may vary in the range of $[\Delta_{min}, \Delta_{max}]$ and $[-\Delta_{max}, -\Delta_{min}]$. If the page fault takes place right after (i.e., no more than a threshold of L cycles) re-enabling execution protection, Δ doubles if it was positive or becomes Δ_{min} otherwise; if the page fault happens later than L, Δ doubles in the negative direction or becomes $-\Delta_{min}$.

Alternative Approaches. Instead of exploiting page execution protection, another way to dynamically enable and disable Düppel is to modify the user level application. For example, to protect dynamically linked libraries, the most convenient way is to modify the procedure linkage table entries of the relevant processes so that every library call related to the protected library function will first go through a wrapper function. Similarly it is possible to use preloaded libraries to overwrite (to provide a wrapper for) the library routines. In order to protect sensitive operations in the executables, one either needs to instrument the functions in the executables or insert breakpoints and use `ptrace` to intercept `SIGTRAP` signals sent to the protected process. These approaches, however, violate GOAL 3 and so are not adopted by Düppel.

5.2.2 Skipping Unnecessary Cache Cleansings

We further optimize Düppel to skip unnecessary cache cleansings. Before cleansing the L1 cache (and any other time-shared caches), Düppel first determines if the VCPU it is running on has been preempted since it last ran on the VCPU. If preemption took place, it then determines if the process interrupted by the current timer interrupt is related to the sensitive operations to be protected. If both answers are yes, Düppel will cleanse the cache; otherwise, it skips the cache cleansing step.

A paravirtualized Xen guest VM can detect VCPU preemption by exploiting shared data structures between the guest and the hypervisor. In particular, Xen uses a shared memory page that contains a value of the timestamp counter to help the guest VM keep track of the system time. The counter value is updated at every hypervisor context switch if it is different from the version stored in the hypervisor, which is only changed every one second. At the end of each cache cleansing, Düppel modifies the shared counter value by one, which compared to the 64-bit counter value is rather small. (Greater changes may confuse the guest OS.) The next context switch will force a change of the counter value, and therefore will be detected by Düppel. One caveat is that the guest can voluntarily relinquish the VCPU, as well, which occurs when the VCPU is idle or at certain points during VCPU setup. Düppel instruments the code locations at which the guest VM kernel issues hypercalls to relinquish the VCPU, to help distinguish voluntary context switches and VCPU preemptions.

6. IMPLEMENTATION

We implemented Düppel as a kernel component (1.4K lines of C code) in paravirtualized Linux that runs on Xen guest virtual machines. Specifically, our prototype implementation modifies Linux kernel v2.6.32. It operates on both Xen 4.0 hypervisors in our lab setting and Xen 3.0 hypervisors (as reported) in Amazon Web Services.

Architecture. We provided an entry in the `/proc` file system which allows user-space tools to input user specified parameters to Düppel. These parameters include names of the protected applications and libraries. (It is currently possible to protect a subset or all of the libraries in one or multiple processes.) Our implementation extends the memory region management component of the Linux kernel to monitor the creation, deletion and splitting of the memory regions related to the protected applications and libraries. A list of pointers to these memory regions is maintained by Düppel. This list is adjusted dynamically by Düppel with the creation and termination of the protected processes. Read-Copy-Update (RCU) synchronization mechanisms are used to guarantee exclusive modifications and wait-free reads to this data structure with very low overhead. All memory pages belonging to the memory regions maintained in the list are disallowed to be executed by modifying the corresponding page table entries. This can be enforced by modifying the default page protection flags of the memory regions, which will be propagated to all newly mapped memory pages due to on-demand paging [9]. Although the same memory pages can also be mapped to other processes in the system, they can be executed normally since they have separate page tables.

We also instrumented the page fault handler so that every page fault goes through an additional check: faults caused by user-space execute accesses to pages that are already in memory are passed to Düppel to further examine if the faults take place in the protected memory regions. As such page faults are otherwise rare, the performance overhead caused by modifications to the critical page fault handling procedure is minimal.

Workflow of Düppel. The main logic of Düppel works as follows: Düppel traps the page faults caused by executing the protected memory regions, and it then enables the page execution for all pages belonging to the list of memory regions. Then it initiates the periodic cache cleansing. After N cleansings have been performed, Düppel stops and enables page-execution protection in the page tables, indicating the end of a protection epoch.

Additionally, a counter recording the times a VCPU is preempted is maintained by Düppel to determine in which mode it should operate cache cleansing, i.e., sentinel mode or battle mode (Sec. 5.1). If the counter is greater than a threshold—empirically determined as 10 in our evaluation (see Sec. 7)—Düppel enters the battle mode; otherwise it runs in sentinel mode. The counter is updated as an exponential moving average (or EMA) of the number of VCPU preemptions in the current and previous time epochs, with $\lambda = 0.5$ where λ is a constant that determines the depth of memory of the EMA [15] . Each time epoch is roughly 1ms (rounded down to a number of CPU cycles that is a power of 2 for efficiency). Even if the attacker is aware of Düppel's parameters and refrains from preempting the victim (and so PROBing) less than 10 times per ms to cause Düppel to stay in sentinel mode, the L1 caches will nevertheless be cleansed at least 50 times per millisecond.

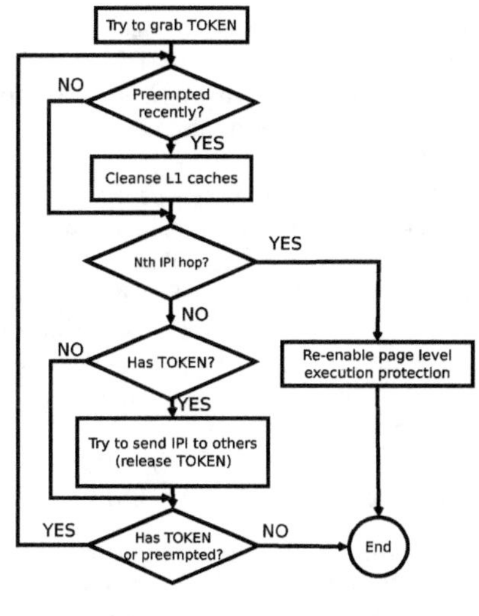

Figure 2: A token-based IPI synchronization algorithm.

Cache cleansing modes and operations. When operated in sentinel mode, Düppel induces periodic timer interrupts and then tries to detect preemption (see Sec. 5.2.2) on all VCPUs. Once a preemption on a VCPU is detected, it sends an IPI to launch the next timer on that VCPU. As more preemptions are detected, Düppel enters battle mode, in which it will send IPIs to all the other cores that are available to process the IPI interrupts. The reason for sending IPIs to all such VCPUs (vs. only one) is to avoid cases where the VCPU being sent an IPI is not running (e.g., is preempted or out of credit to run), thereby causing the cache-cleansing interrupts to pause.

We implemented a token-based VCPU synchronization algorithm in Düppel (shown in Fig. 2) to avoid race conditions. An atomic variable serves as the token and one or more VCPUs simultaneously in the IPI context will try an *atomic exchange* to grab the token. So, only one VCPU will get it. After the cache cleansing job is done (or skipped), the VCPU with the token will try to send IPIs to all other VCPUs that have finished the last-round cache cleansing to pass along the token. As such, releasing tokens may not always be successful. Failure in passing the token or detection of another VCPU preemption at this point will force it to go over the cache cleaning cycle again. If the preemption counter goes below the threshold value, Düppel jumps back to sentinel mode.

7. EVALUATION

7.1 Security Evaluation

In this section, we report the results of our security evaluation of Düppel in a lab environment. Our lab testbed was equipped with a single-socket quad-core Intel Core 2 Q9650 processor with an operating frequency of 3.0GHz. It had two levels of caches: both L1 data and instruction caches were

8-way set-associative and 32KB in size; two 24-way 6MB unified L2 caches, each served two CPU cores. All caches had 64-byte cache lines. We ran a Xen 4.0 hypervisor on the hardware; Dom0, the management domain in Xen, was given a single VCPU.

To evaluate Düppel under attack, i.e., when it operates with the presence of a side-channel attacker, we assigned two VCPUs to the VM that ran Düppel, and two VCPUs to a co-resident attacker VM. We facilitated the attack by pinning the VCPUs to the physical cores so that one attacker VCPU and one Düppel VCPU shared the same L1 caches. Düppel was configured to cleanse both the L1 data cache and the L1 instruction cache.

7.1.1 *Attacking a "Dummy" Victim*

Victim. The "dummy" victim application in these experiments had two "dummy" functions composed of "nop" instructions. The instructions in each of them were mapped to different regions in the L1 instruction cache, occupying all cache lines in several cache sets. The victim application executed in a loop, alternating between these two functions. As such, the victim had distinguishable access patterns in the L1 instruction cache—all cache sets associated with the two functions were thoroughly evicted while other cache sets were almost entirely untouched.

Attacker. We leveraged the side-channel attack code of Zhang et al. [38], which exploits IPIs to periodically preempt the victim VCPU and PRIME-PROBE the L1 instruction cache to collect timing results from each cache set. The two VCPUs in the attacker's VM have different roles: the *IPI VCPU* keeps looping and periodically sends IPIs to the *attacker VCPU*. The *attacker VCPU* is otherwise idle and only executes cache PROBing functions when triggered by receiving IPIs. The interval between two consecutive IPIs sent to the *attacker VCPU* is determined by the attacker, and is varied in our experiments as a tuned parameter. Each cache PROBing takes about 42000 CPU cycles (roughly 14μs), and one hypervisor context switch takes about 600 cycles. The IPI intervals, therefore, are the desired PRIME-PROBE intervals plus the time required for PROBing and context switches. Longer IPI intervals will give more chances to the victim to run, but multiple functions may run in the same PRIME-PROBE interval, leaving the cache too noisy to interpret. Shorter IPI intervals may cause more than one IPI to be delivered at the same time, making the PRIME-PROBE protocol fail. The range for the attacker's IPI interval that we evaluated was from 50000 CPU cycles to 90000 cycles.

Effectiveness of cache cleansing. Our first attempt in evaluating the effectiveness of Düppel's cache cleansing was to measure the fraction of cache lines *not* evicted by Düppel prior to the attacker PROBing the cache. Information leaks can happen either when Düppel is not run between the attacker's PRIME and PROBE, or when Düppel is run but it does not have enough time to cleanse the entire cache before being preempted by the attacker. The results of our tests are shown in Fig. 3(a). From the graph, we can see that when the attacker chooses a long IPI interval (>70000 cycles) or a short IPI interval (<65000 cycles), the potential information leak is minimal.

When the attacker's IPI interval is short (<65000 cycles), contention may result in IPIs issued by Düppel being significantly delayed or even "starved" by the attacker. However, recall that Düppel is designed to repeatedly cleanse the cache if it detects preemption; so even with less frequent IPI interrupts, Düppel will still consume most of the CPU time in cache cleansing to make sure the victim secret is not leaked through side channels. With longer IPI intervals (>70000 cycles), the IPIs issued by Düppel will be delivered on time and Düppel is able to finish the cache cleansing without being preempted, thus allowing the victim to run normally while being protected. However, when the IPI interval is between 65000 and 70000 cycles, Düppel only gets to cleanse a fraction of the cache before being preempted. This is the worst-case scenario for Düppel's protection scheme. Fig. 3(b) also helps illustrate this phenomenon. The y-axis in this figure is the fraction of attacker's PRIME-PROBE trials in which the victim application ran at all.

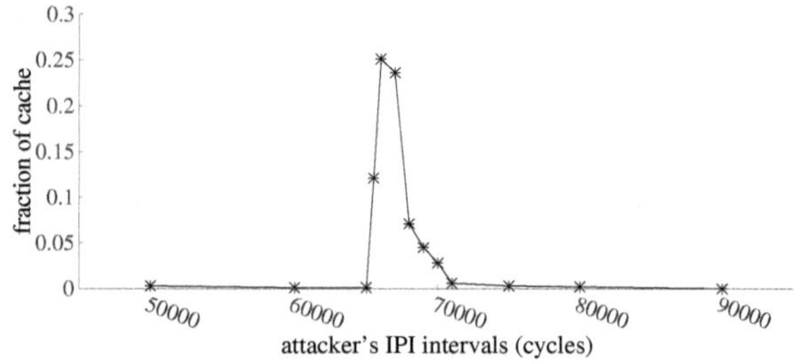

(a) Average fraction of cache potentially occupied by victim application data upon preemption

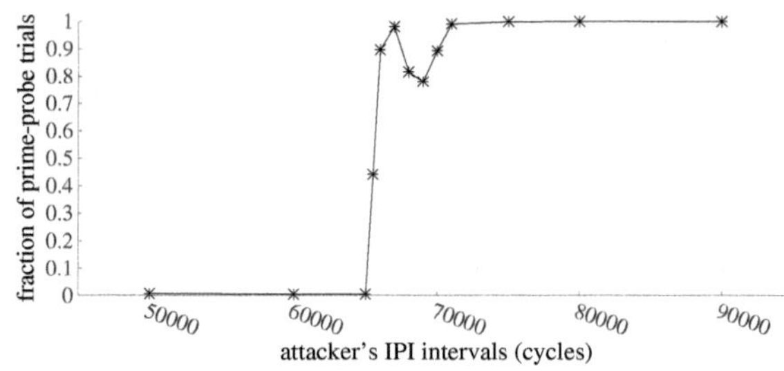

(b) IPI intervals during which the victim application executed at all

Figure 3: Cache cleansing effectiveness under different attacker IPI intervals.

In the worst case, when the attacker's IPI interval is 66000 CPU cycles, about 25% of the cache lines are not evicted by Düppel but might contain victim application data. This provides the opportunity for some information leakage to the attacker, but the risk is far less than in the absence of Düppel. Fig. 4 shows the attacker's cache readings from the PRIME-PROBE trials in this case. Each column in the heatmap represents the cache set indicated on the x-axis; the y-axis is the index of PRIME-PROBE readings. In Fig. 4(a) we can see that without Düppel, the attacker can easily observe the cache pattern (the alternating cache usage on the left) of the victim application. In contrast, even with 25% of the cache lines possibly containing victim application data not evicted by Düppel, as shown in Fig. 4(b), the victim's cache patterns are substantially obfuscated.

More quantitatively, in this worst-case scenario we measured the difference, for each cache set, of the average PROBE results (averaged over 100000 PRIME-PROBE trials) for that cache set when one dummy function ran versus the aver-

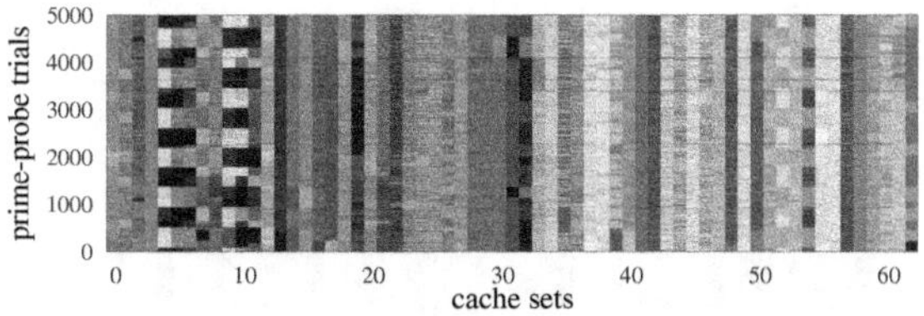

(a) w/o Düppel

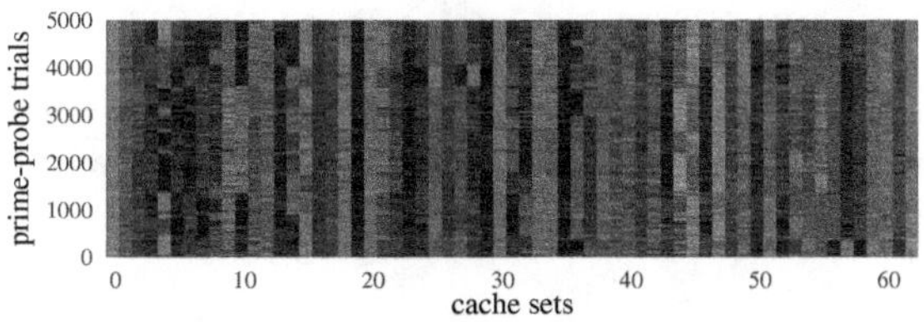

(b) w/ Düppel

Figure 4: Attacker's view of L1 instruction cache timings. The x-axis represents the cache sets; the y-axis represents the attacker's prime-probe trials. The darker the cell in the heatmap, the longer it takes the attacker to probe the cache.

age for that cache set when the other dummy function did. Without Düppel enabled, this difference-per-cache-set, averaged over all cache sets, was 32.7 cycles with a standard deviation of 13.2 cycles. However, cache sets to which one or the other dummy function mapped clearly divulged which dummy function had executed, exhibiting a difference-per-cache-set up to 190 CPU cycles — almost 12 standard deviations above the mean. (By comparison, the maximum difference-per-cache-set among cache sets not associated with either dummy function was only 22 cycles.) With Düppel enabled, the difference-per-cache-set, averaged over all cache sets, was 3.3 cycles with a standard deviation of 2.1 cycles. Among those cache sets to which either dummy function mapped, the maximum difference-per-cache-set dropped to 8 cycles, which is less than three standard deviations above the mean and, moreover, even less than the maximum difference-per-cache-set among cache sets not associated with either dummy function (which stayed basically unchanged from the Düppel-disabled case). In this respect, Düppel brought the timings of the cache sets occupied by the dummy functions largely "in line" with the timings of other cache sets.

7.1.2 Case Study: Square and Multiply

As a case study, we examined the victim application attacked by Zhang et al. [38], namely the modular exponentiation implementation in the **`libgcrypt`** v.1.5.0 cryptographic library, which uses a textbook square-and-multiply algorithm. In this attack, the goal of the attacker was to extract a secret exponent used in this routine by PROBing the L1 instruction cache to infer the sequence of squares and multiplies executed. Here we focus on the accuracy of the first stage of the Zhang et al. attack, which involves classification of PRIME-PROBE timing vectors using a three-class support vector machine (SVM) — one class for "square", one for "multiply", and one for "other". While subsequent stages of the attack pipeline can filter out a small rate of misclassifications, a reasonably accuracy of the SVM classifications is necessary for the attack to work.

Op	Classification: Square	Multiply	Other
Square	1740 (0.84)	43 (0.02)	298 (0.14)
Multiply	14 (0.01)	2213 (0.94)	123 (0.05)
Other	272 (0.05)	225 (0.04)	5072 (0.91)

(a) w/o Düppel

Op	Classification: Square	Multiply	Other
Square	26 (0.01)	699 (0.39)	1055 (0.59)
Multiply	26 (0.01)	938 (0.48)	987 (0.51)
Other	86 (0.01)	3367 (0.54)	2816 (0.45)

(b) w/ Düppel

Figure 5: Confusion matrix of SVM classification in tests in Sec. 7.1.2.

Training the SVM was performed using the same approach as taken in the Zhang et al. work. In particular, to collect data for training, the "victim" repeatedly performed modular exponentiations, while informing the data collector via shared memory when it begins or ends a square or multiply. In this way, the data collector could associate its PROBE results of the L1 instruction cache with the ground-truth operation that was being performed when the PROBE was performed. Like Zhang et al. [38] we used a linear kernel in the SVM classifier. In each experiment, the SVM was trained with the labeled 90000 PRIME-PROBE results and then tested on an additional 10000 PRIME-PROBE results.

Fig. 5 shows the confusion matrix that resulted from an experiment in which both training and testing were conducted with Düppel disabled (Fig. 5(a)) and one in which both training and testing were conducted with Düppel enabled (Fig. 5(b)). With Düppel disabled, the SVM classifies the testing PROBE results with accuracy over 90%, which is well enough in our experience to enable the subsequent stages of the Zhang et al. attack. When Düppel is enabled, however, the SVM classification fails badly with an accuracy of only about 38%. In our experience, continuing the Zhang et al. attack from this point would be extremely difficult. This is, of course, not a proof that no exploitable side-channel still exists, and it is conceivable that a persistent and adaptive attacker could still make progress; however, we believe that Düppel should substantially increase the complexity of doing so.

7.2 Performance Evaluation

We conducted the performance evaluation of Düppel primarily in a public cloud environment, Amazon Web Services. The specification of processors in the Amazon EC2 cloud environment was not of our own choice. But through `cpuid` instructions, we determined that the platform was equipped with two 2.4GHz Intel Xeon E5645 processors, each of which had six cores per package with hyper-threading supported but disabled. Its L1 data caches were 32KB, 8-way set-associative; L1 instruction caches were also 32KB but with only 4 ways. One 8-way unified L2 cache was dedicated to each core, with 256KB capacity. Additionally, it had one 12MB 16-way L3 cache per CPU package. All caches had 64-byte cache lines. The shared info pages [10, Ch. 3] reported the Xen version to be `xen-3.0-x86_64`. The number

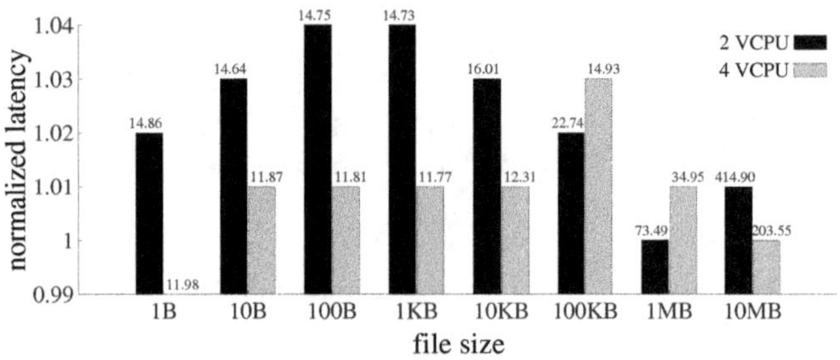

Figure 6: Düppel's overheads for file download latency with different file sizes. Labels on top of the bars represent the baseline latency (without Düppel) in ms.

of Dom0 VCPUs was unknown. As in the lab settings, we implemented Düppel in Linux kernel v2.6.32 in the cloud. Düppel was configured to protect the L1 caches and the unified L2 cache.

7.2.1 *Securing TLS Libraries*

In the following experiments we evaluate the performance overhead of Düppel when protecting `apache2` processes and the OpenSSL library (`libcrypto.so`) to which they were linked. We are particularly interested in preventing side channel attacks against the cryptographic operations provided by `libcrypto.so` during the Transport Layer Security (TLS) protocol used in `https` connections. We ran an apache 2.2.24 web server with `libcrypto.so` version 1.0.0. We ran the web server in one VM in the EC2 cloud and ran the client in another VM in the same availability zone in order to minimize network latency.

File download latency Fig. 6 shows results of an experiment to test the impact of Düppel on file download latency. We ran `apache bench` on the client and requested static pages with varying file sizes. The results reported are average values of 10000 requests for each file size. These experiments show that the impact of Düppel on file download latency was less than 4% in the worst case.

File download throughput Fig. 7 shows the file download throughput degradation induced by Düppel in our web server experiments. In these experiments, we used another web server performance measurement tool, `httperf` [22], to produce the largest rate of requests for a 177-byte file (the default `index.html` file installed with `apache2`) for which the server could keep up. In order to saturate a server with 2 VCPUs, the requests were sent from 2 clients running `httperf` from distinct machines in the same availability zone in AWS; for the 4-VCPU server, 4 clients were employed in the test. Only one request was issued per connection and the SSL sessions were not reused. The timeout value for which `httperf` waited for the server's response was set to 1s. We confirmed by running the `top` utility that at its saturation point the server was CPU-bound; the throughput and server CPU usage both reached their limits simultaneously. Thus the throughput degradation was actually caused by Düppel rather than other factors. As this figure illustrates, the maximum throughput of the 2-VCPU server dropped from 267.1 replies per second to 258 replies per second, yielding a degradation of 3.4%. In the 4-VCPU case, the server's maximum throughput dropped only 1.4%, decaying from 545.3

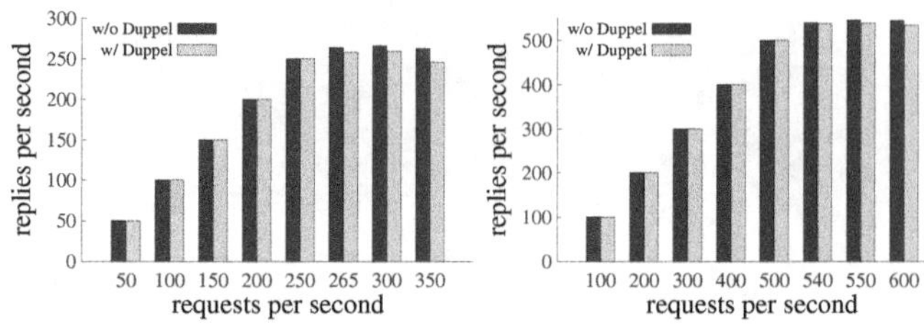

(a) 2-VCPU server (b) 4-VCPU server

Figure 7: File download rate in replies per second with different requests per second, with and without Düppel.

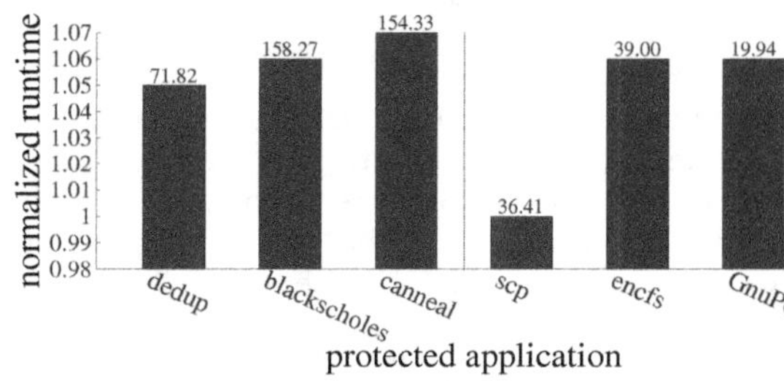

Figure 8: Runtime overhead of Düppel for different applications. Labels on top of the bars represent the baseline runtime (without Düppel) in seconds.

replies per second to 537.7 replies per second. In all cases, the throughput overheads induced by Düppel were modest.

Local experiments We repeated the above file download latency and throughput experiments in a more controlled environment in our lab. In these tests, the clients and server were connected through a 1Gb/s LAN. The qualitative results shown in Fig. 6 and Fig. 7 persisted in our local tests, e.g., with an induced latency degradation by Düppel of at most 3% and a throughput degradation of at most 2.1%.

7.2.2 *Securing Other Applications*

We also evaluated Düppel in protecting other applications. We first picked three applications, `blackscholes`, `canneal` and `dedup`, from the PARSEC benchmarks [7, 8] to simulate different types of applications. `blackscholes` simulates financial analysis and, in particular, calculates the prices of a portfolio of options using Black Scholes partial differential equations. `canneal` uses cache-aware simulated annealing to design chips that minimize routing costs. `dedup` is short for "deduplication," which is a compression approach that combines global and local compression in order to obtain a high compression ratio. We selected these benchmark applications to represent CPU-bound applications with different amounts of memory and cache usage. The inputs to these benchmarks were `native` (see [8]) and the number of threads was the same as the number of VCPUs in the VM. We specified the entire executables to be sensitive, and so Düppel was always enabled while the programs were running.

In addition, we selected three applications that involve cryptographic operations, which are more likely to be of interest to attackers: `GnuPG`, `encfs`, and `scp`. `GnuPG` is part of the GNU project and implements the OpenPGP stan-

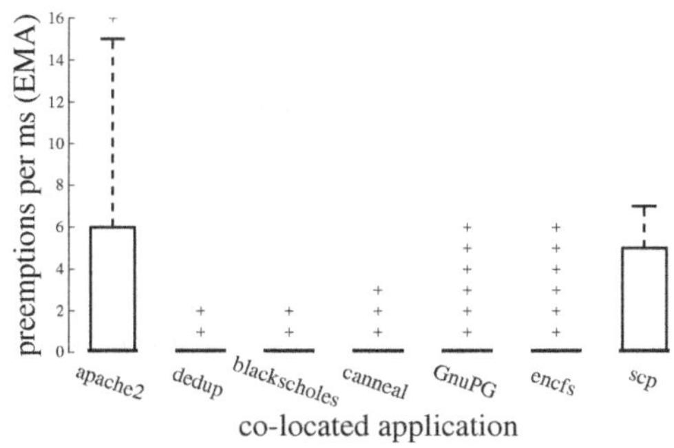

Figure 9: Victim VCPU preemptions per ms (exponential moving average) induced by co-located application in lab.

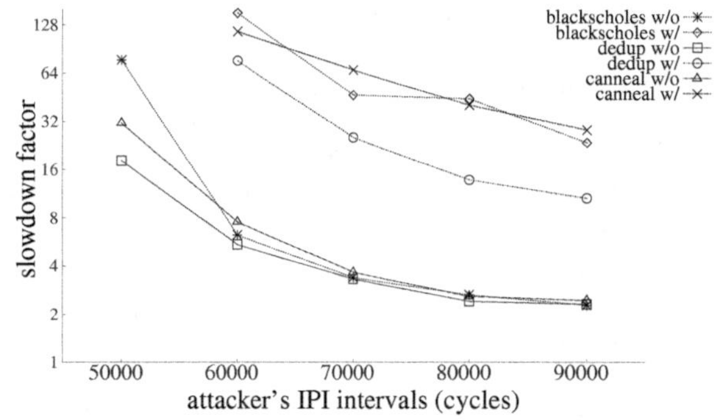

Figure 10: Performance overhead (averaged over five runs) when under prime-probe attacks on L1 instruction caches, w/ and w/o Düppel.

dard. We evaluated the time for it to decrypt a 1GB file encrypted using ElGamal encryption, with Düppel specified to protect `libgcrypt.so`. `encfs` is an encrypted filesystem in userspace. By encrypting a 1GB file, we evaluated the runtime of its file-encryption procedure with Düppel protecting its `libcrypto.so` library. `scp` is a network data transfer protocol built on top of secure shell (`ssh`). We transferred a 1GB file using `scp` to evaluate the latency overhead due to Düppel, again configured to protect `libcrypto.so`. All experiments above were run 10 times (except for `dedup` which was run 30 times due to large variance) on a 2-VCPU server in the AWS cloud. The average runtime degradations are shown in Fig. 8. As can be seen there, Düppel induced less than 7% performance overhead in all cases.

7.2.3 Sentinel/Battle Mode Switching

As described in Sec. 5.1 and Sec. 6, a switch from sentinel mode to battle mode occurs whenever the moving average of the number of VCPU preemptions per millisecond exceeds an empirically determined, fixed threshold of 10 in our prototype. We developed a set of experiments to examine if this threshold will trigger spurious mode switches when co-located with regular, benign applications. In particular, we employed techniques similar to that described in Sec. 5.2.2 to detect VCPU preemptions. Instead of trying to detect a VCPU preemption during each timer interrupt, we tested VCPU preemptions in a loop so that every preemption was captured. We first ran experiments in our local testbed in which an application running on another VM (with only one VCPU) was pinned to share a core with the VM in which we counted preemptions. As such, the number of VCPU preemptions caused by the benchmark application on the shared CPU core was counted. Fig. 9 illustrates the boxplot of the number of VCPU preemptions per millisecond (exponential moving average), where each box shows the first, second and third quartiles, each whisker extends to cover points within 1.5× the interquartile range, and outliers are marked with plus signs ("+"). As shown, these benchmark applications rarely caused the exponential moving average of VCPU preemptions to exceed the threshold of 10; e.g., the `apache2` web server induced a false alarm rate of 3% and all other benchmarks induced no false alarms. It is worth noting that in this test the `apache2` web server had been saturated already.

We also ran experiments in the Amazon EC2 cloud, specifically on four distinct instance types ("m1 medium", "m1 large", "m1 xlarge" and "c1 large") in each of three different availability zones in the US East region ("us-east-1a", "us-east-1c" and "us-east-1d"). The experiments were conducted from 8:00am Aug 10, 2013 to 8:00am Aug 11, 2013. Since we had no knowledge of the applications co-located with our VMs in the cloud, we assumed that the co-resident VMs and their applications were "benign" in terms of side channels. In these tests, the *maximum* false alarm rate witnessed on any of these machines was 8.22×10^{-6}.

7.2.4 Performance Overhead When Being Attacked

Cache-based side-channel attacks, especially on the L1 cache, are essentially also performance degradation attacks. Moreover, Düppel will further degrade the whole system's performance when being attacked. In Fig. 10 we show the results of our lab evaluation of the runtime overhead on `blackscholes`, `canneal` and `dedup` benchmarks under side-channel attacks on the L1 instruction caches, with and without Düppel. The victim was pinned to run only on the core being attacked for these tests. As can be seen in the figure, the attacker alone degraded the victim's performance by up to two orders of magnitude, and Düppel only compounded that cost. Suffering such a denial-of-service may be preferable to succumbing to side-channel attacks. Moreover, since VCPUs are usually not pinned in real clouds, the duration of such a denial-of-service can be expected to be short.

8. DISCUSSION

8.1 Extensions of Düppel

Extension to other cache side channels. In principle, Düppel can defend against side-channel attacks on other types of time-shared caches, as well. For instance, the BTB and TLB can be cleansed together with L1 caches. However, BTB attacks were only demonstrated in non-virtualized systems, while cross-VM attacks on TLBs are unlikely because TLBs are flushed on context switch.

Extension to other clouds. Düppel can be implemented in the guest OS for cloud platforms other than Amazon, as well, as long as the virtualization substrate supports paravirtualized Xen guests and customized OS kernels. We expect Düppel to also work on Rackspace and GoGrid, for example.

Extension to kernel routines. Düppel can be extended to protect sensitive operations in the guest OS kernel, as well. The difficulty, however, is that the Linux kernel is monolithic, and so the code and data memory sections of kernel routines are not cleanly separated from the rest of the kernel. Düppel will have to look for all memory pages that contain kernel routines and mark them as non-executable.

8.2 Limitations

SMT-enabled cloud platforms. When SMT is enabled on processors, some time-shared caches can become simultaneously shared caches (e.g., L1 caches). Düppel may not be effective in this case. However, from our previous experience [38], as well as prior documented evidence [27, 25], SMT-enabled CPUs are more vulnerable to side-channel attacks. Moreover, as clouds often charge by CPU computing units, with SMT-enabled cores the estimated computing units per VM would become unreliable if more than one VCPU shared the same CPU core at the same time. Therefore, we anticipate that cloud providers will not enable SMT in production clouds for both security and accounting considerations.

The simultaneously shared caches. A simultaneously shared cache, e.g., the last level cache, might also be targeted by side-channel attacks. Again, Düppel does not address this possibility. Compared with time-shared caches, PROBing simultaneously shared caches can be done without VCPU preemption and with frequencies limited only by the cache and memory access latencies and the sizes of the caches utilized. Although fine-grained cache observations are possible in such situations, the challenges that attackers face to extract sensitive information may be prohibitive. The first challenge stems from the fact that most LLCs are physically indexed. As such, attackers must have prior knowledge of the physical addresses of the memory regions of the victim application [23], which is usually allocated dynamically and may vary each time it is run. Second, exploiting last level caches when the victim and attacker run on different cores can be sensitive to cache coherence properties. For example, PROBing on an LLC in an exclusive caching hierarchy (as compared with inclusive caches) will not invalidate contents in the lower-level caches of another core. As such, the victim's activity may be hidden in lower level caches and never leaked to the last level cache at all. Moreover, to our knowledge, last level caches in the processors used in cloud platforms usually serve more than two cores; in this case, side-channel observations are subject to more background noise from cores that are not running the victim application. We believe for these reasons, side-channel attacks in simultaneously shared caches in virtualized SMP environments have been limited so far to extracting only coarse information [29] or have needed to leverage additional hypervisor features (e.g., sharing memory pages between the victim and attacker VMs [36]).

9. CONCLUSION

In this paper, we presented Düppel, a system to mitigate cache side channels in public clouds by retrofitting commodity operating systems. Düppel cleanses time-shared caches (e.g., per-core L1 and L2 caches) to confound side channels through them. We detailed our implementation of Düppel in Linux for paravirtualized Xen, demonstrated the security effectiveness of our prototype in tests on lab machines, and evaluated the performance impact of our prototype on a public cloud. To our knowledge, Düppel is the first general and efficient technique to enable tenants to defend themselves from cache-based side-channel attacks in public clouds, without help from the hypervisor or cloud operator.

9.1 Acknowledgements

We thank Dr. Weidong Cui and the anonymous reviewers for suggestions that led to improvements to this paper. This work was supported in part by NSF grants 0910483 and 1330599, the Science of Security Lablet at North Carolina State University, a gift from VMWare and Google PhD Fellowship to Yinqian Zhang.

10. REFERENCES

[1] O. Aciiçmez. Yet another microarchitectural attack: Exploiting I-cache. In *Proceedings of the 2007 ACM Workshop on Computer Security Architecture*, pages 11–18, 2007.

[2] O. Aciiçmez, B. B. Brumley, and P. Grabher. New results on instruction cache attacks. In *Proceedings of the 12th International Conference on Cryptographic Hardware and Embedded Systems*, pages 110–124, 2010.

[3] O. Aciiçmez, S. Gueron, and J.-P. Seifert. New branch prediction vulnerabilities in openSSL and necessary software countermeasures. In *Proceedings of the 11th IMA International Conference on Cryptography and Coding*, pages 185–203, 2007.

[4] O. Aciiçmez, C. K. Koç, and J.-P. Seifert. On the power of simple branch prediction analysis. In *Proceedings of the 2nd ACM Symposium on Information, Computer and Communications Security*, pages 312–320, 2007.

[5] O. Aciicmez and J.-P. Seifert. Cheap hardware parallelism implies cheap security. In *Proceedings of the Workshop on Fault Diagnosis and Tolerance in Cryptography*, pages 80–91, 2007.

[6] A. Aviram, S. Hu, B. Ford, and R. Gummadi. Determinating timing channels in compute clouds. In *Proceedings of the 2010 ACM Cloud Computing Security Workshop*, pages 103–108, 2010.

[7] C. Bienia, S. Kumar, J. P. Singh, and K. Li. The PARSEC benchmark suite: Characterization and architectural implications. In *Proceedings of the 17th International Conference on Parallel Architectures and Compilation Techniques*, Oct. 2008.

[8] C. Bienia and K. Li. PARSEC 2.0: A new benchmark suite for chip-multiprocessors. In *Proceedings of the 5th Workshop on Modeling, Benchmarking and Simulation*, June 2009.

[9] D. Bovet and M. Cesati. *Understanding The Linux Kernel.* Oreilly & Associates, 2005.

[10] D. Chisnall. *The Definitive Guide to the Xen Hypervisor (Prentice Hall Open Source Software Development Series).* Prentice Hall PTR, Nov. 2007.

[11] B. Coppens, I. Verbauwhede, K. D. Bosschere, and B. D. Sutter. Practical mitigations for timing-based side-channel attacks on modern x86 processors. In *Proceedings of the 30th IEEE Symposium on Security and Privacy*, pages 45–60, 2009.

[12] L. Domnitser, A. Jaleel, J. Loew, N. Abu-Ghazaleh, and D. Ponomarev. Non-monopolizable caches: Low-complexity mitigation of cache side channel attacks. *ACM Transactions on Architecture and Code Optimization*, 8(4), Jan. 2012.

[13] D. Gullasch, E. Bangerter, and S. Krenn. Cache games – bringing access-based cache attacks on AES to practice. In *Proceedings of the 2011 IEEE Symposium on Security and Privacy*, pages 490–505, 2011.

[14] R. Hund, C. Willems, and T. Holz. Practical timing side channel attacks against kernel space ASLR. In *Proceedings of the 2013 IEEE Symposium on Security and Privacy*, May 2013.

[15] J. S. Hunter. The exponentially weighted moving average. *Journal of Quality Technology*, 18:203–210, 1986.

[16] G. Keramidas, A. Antonopoulos, D. Serpanos, and S. Kaxiras. Non deterministic caches: a simple and effective defense against side channel attacks. *Design Automation for Embedded Systems*, 12:221–230, 2008.

[17] T. Kim, M. Peinado, and G. Mainar-Ruiz. STEALTHMEM: System-level protection against cache-based side channel attacks in the cloud. In *Proceedings of the 21st USENIX Conference on Security Symposium*, 2012.

[18] R. Könighofer. A fast and cache-timing resistant implementation of the AES. In *Topics in Cryptology – CT-RSA 2008*, volume 4964 of *Lecture Notes in Computer Science*, pages 187–202, 2008.

[19] P. Li, D. Gao, and M. K. Reiter. Mitigating access-driven timing channels in clouds using StopWatch. In *Proceedings of the 43rd IEEE/IFIP International Conference on Dependable Systems and Networks*, June 2013.

[20] R. Martin, J. Demme, and S. Sethumadhavan. TimeWarp: Rethinking timekeeping and performance monitoring mechanisms to mitigate side-channel attacks. In *Proceedings of the 39th International Symposium on Computer Architecture*, pages 118–129, 2012.

[21] D. Molnar, M. Piotrowski, D. Schultz, and D. Wagner. The program counter security model: Automatic detection and removal of control-flow side channel attacks. In *Proceedings of the 8th International Conference on Information Security and Cryptology*, pages 156–168, 2006.

[22] D. Mosberger and T. Jin. httperf – a tool for measuring web server performance. *ACM SIGMETRICS Performance Evaluation Review*, 26(3):31–37, Dec. 1998.

[23] K. Mowery, S. Keelveedhi, and H. Shacham. Are AES x86 cache timing attacks still feasible? In *Proceedings of the 2012 ACM Cloud Computing Security Workshop*, CCSW '12, pages 19–24, New York, NY, USA, 2012. ACM.

[24] M. Neve and J.-P. Seifert. Advances on access-driven cache attacks on AES. In *Proceedings of the 13th International Conference on Selected Areas in Cryptography*, pages 147–162, 2007.

[25] D. A. Osvik, A. Shamir, and E. Tromer. Cache attacks and countermeasures: the case of AES. In *Topics in Cryptology – CT-RSA 2006*, volume 3860 of *Lecture Notes in Computer Science*, pages 1–20, 2006.

[26] D. Page. Partitioned cache architecture as a side-channel defense mechanism. `http://eprint.iacr.org/2005/280`, 2005.

[27] C. Percival. Cache missing for fun and profit. In *Proceedings of BSDCon 2005*, 2005.

[28] H. Raj, R. Nathuji, A. Singh, and P. England. Resource management for isolation enhanced cloud services. In *Proceedings of the 2009 ACM Cloud Computing Security Workshop*, pages 77–84, 2009.

[29] T. Ristenpart, E. Tromer, H. Shacham, and S. Savage. Hey, you, get off of my cloud: Exploring information leakage in third-party compute clouds. In *Proceedings of the 16th ACM Conference on Computer and Communications Security*, pages 199–212, 2009.

[30] J. Shi, X. Song, H. Chen, and B. Zang. Limiting cache-based side-channel in multi-tenant cloud using dynamic page coloring. In *Proceedings of the 2011 IEEE/IFIP 41st International Conference on Dependable Systems and Networks Workshops*, pages 194–199, 2011.

[31] E. Tromer, D. A. Osvik, and A. Shamir. Efficient cache attacks on AES, and countermeasures. *Journal of Cryptology*, 23(2):37–71, Jan. 2010.

[32] B. C. Vattikonda, S. Das, and H. Shacham. Eliminating fine grained timers in Xen. In *Proceedings of the 3rd ACM Cloud Computing Security Workshop*, pages 41–46, 2011.

[33] Z. Wang and R. B. Lee. Covert and side channels due to processor architecture. In *Proceedings of the 22nd Computer Security Applications Conference*, pages 473–482, 2006.

[34] Z. Wang and R. B. Lee. New cache designs for thwarting software cache-based side channel attacks. In *Proceedings of the 34th International Symposium on Computer Architecture*, pages 494–505, 2007.

[35] Z. Wang and R. B. Lee. A novel cache architecture with enhanced performance and security. In *Proceedings of the 41st IEEE/ACM International Symposium on Microarchitecture*, pages 83–93, 2008.

[36] Y. Yarom and K. Falkner. Flush+Reload: a high resolution, low noise, L3 cache side-channel attack. `http://eprint.iacr.org/2013/448`, 2013.

[37] Y. Zhang, A. Juels, A. Oprea, and M. K. Reiter. HomeAlone: Co-residency detection in the cloud via side-channel analysis. In *Proceedings of the 2011 IEEE Symposium on Security and Privacy*, pages 313–328, May 2011.

[38] Y. Zhang, A. Juels, M. K. Reiter, and T. Ristenpart. Cross-VM side channels and their use to extract private keys. In *Proceedings of the 2012 ACM Conference on Computer and Communications Security*, pages 305–316, 2012.

Tappan Zee (North) Bridge: Mining Memory Accesses for Introspection

Brendan Dolan-Gavitt
Georgia Tech
brendan@cc.gatech.edu

Tim Leek
MIT Lincoln Laboratory
tleek@ll.mit.edu

Josh Hodosh
MIT Lincoln Laboratory
josh.hodosh@ll.mit.edu

Wenke Lee
Georgia Tech
wenke@cc.gatech.edu

ABSTRACT

The ability to introspect into the behavior of software at runtime is crucial for many security-related tasks, such as virtual machine-based intrusion detection and low-artifact malware analysis. Although some progress has been made in this task by automatically creating programs that can passively retrieve kernel-level information, two key challenges remain. First, it is currently difficult to extract useful information from user-level applications, such as web browsers. Second, discovering points within the OS and applications to hook for *active monitoring* is still an entirely manual process. In this paper we propose a set of techniques to mine the memory accesses made by an operating system and its applications to locate useful places to deploy active monitoring, which we call *tap points*. We demonstrate the efficacy of our techniques by finding tap points for useful introspection tasks such as finding SSL keys and monitoring web browser activity on five different operating systems (Windows 7, Linux, FreeBSD, Minix and Haiku) and two processor architectures (ARM and x86).[1]

Categories and Subject Descriptors

D.4.6 [**Operating Systems**]: Security and Protection

General Terms

Design, Security

Keywords

Introspection; active monitoring; reverse engineering

[1]This work is sponsored by the Assistant Secretary of Defense for Research & Engineering under Air Force Contract #FA8721-05-C-0002. Opinions, interpretations, conclusions and recommendations are those of the author and are not necessarily endorsed by the United States Government.

CCS'13, November 4–8, 2013, Berlin, Germany.

ACM 978-1-4503-2477-9/13/11 ...$15.00.
http://dx.doi.org/10.1145/2508859.2516697 .

1. INTRODUCTION

Many security applications have a need to inspect the internal workings of software. Host-based intrusion detection systems, malware analyses, and digital forensics all depend to some degree on being able to obtain information about software that is by design undocumented and hidden from public view. Thus, to operate correctly, security software is typically built on *reverse engineering*, the art and practice of elucidating the undocumented principles on which software is built.

Unfortunately, reverse engineering is expensive, time consuming, and requires a high degree of expertise. The problem is exacerbated by the fact that, to protect against tampering, security applications are often hosted in environments separated from the target being inspected, such as a separate virtual machine. Because of this, their visibility into the target is often limited to low-level features such as memory and CPU state, and any higher-level information must be reconstructed based on reverse engineered knowledge.

This problem, which we will refer to as the *introspection problem*, has been approached by a number of recent research efforts such as Virtuoso [11] and VMST [12]. Existing systems, however, have a number of limitations. First, they focus on retrieving kernel-level information. However, a great deal of security-relevant information exists only at user-level, such as URLs being visited by the browser, instant messages and emails sent by desktop clients, and system and application log messages. Second, they require that the desired information be accessible through some public interface (a public API in the case of Virtuoso, and a userland program or kernel module in the case of VMST). This means that some security-relevant information may be inaccessible to such tools. Finally, Payne et al. [25] argue that many security applications need some form of *active monitoring*; that is, they need to be notified when certain system events occur. Current solutions to the introspection problem provide no way of locating places in the system where it would be useful to interpose.

In this paper, we attempt to address the limitations of past solutions by examining a rich source of information about system and application activity: memory accesses observed at runtime. Our key insight is that a memory accesses made at different points in a program can be treated as streams of related information. For example, when visiting a URL, a web browser must write to memory the URL that is being visited, and it will generally do so at the same point in the program. By intercepting memory accesses made at this program point we can observe all URLs visited. These program points, which we call *tap points*, provide a natural place to interpose to extract security-relevant information, and could be integrated into an active monitoring system such as Lares [25].

There are several challenges that must be overcome to make use of tap points. The first is the sheer amount of data that must be sifted through. In ten minutes' worth of execution on a Windows 7 system, for example, we observed a total of 18.9 *million* unique tap points which read and wrote a total of 32.8 gigabytes of data. To overcome this challenge, we make use of techniques from information retrieval and machine learning, described in Section 4, to quickly zero in on the tap points that read or write information relevant to introspection.

Second, simply setting up an environment in which one can observe every memory access made by the whole system (OS and applications) poses a challenge. Whole-system emulators such as QEMU [4] provide the necessary basis for such instrumentation, but intercepting and analyzing every memory access online is not practical: the resulting system is so slow that network connections time out and the guest OS may think that programs have become unresponsive. To solve this problem, we add *record and replay* to QEMU, which allows executions to be recorded with low overhead. Our heavyweight analyses are then run on the replayed execution to analyze every memory access made *without* perturbing the system under inspection. We describe our system, Tappan Zee Bridge (TZB),[2] in detail in Section 5.

Finally, previous systems have required significant effort to support new architectures. This problem has become more pressing in recent years, as ARM-based devices such as smartphones have exploded in popularity. Because TZB looks at memory accesses, rather than inspecting binary code, it naturally supports a wide variety of architectures with minimal effort. To demonstrate this, our evaluation includes the ARM architecture in addition to x86, and the techniques we describe easily generalize to other architectures.

The remainder of this paper is structured as follows. Section 2 precisely defines what a tap point is. We then explore that definition and its impact on the scope of our work and the assumptions it rests on in Section 3. Section 4 describes techniques for finding tap points of interest. We then discuss our system, Tappan Zee Bridge (TZB), which implements these techniques, as well as PANDA (Platform for Architecture-Neutral Dynamic Analysis), a new dynamic analysis platform on which TZB is built, in Section 5. We evaluate TZB in Section 6, and show that it is capable of finding tap points useful for introspection in a wide variety of applications, operating systems, and architectures. Finally, we describe the limitations of our approach in Section 7, related work in this area in Section 8, and offer concluding remarks in Section 9.[3]

[2]So named because the northbridge on Intel architectures traditionally carried data between the CPU and RAM.

[3]All software described in this paper (i.e. PANDA and TZB) is open source and can be downloaded at `http://github.com/moyix/panda/`.

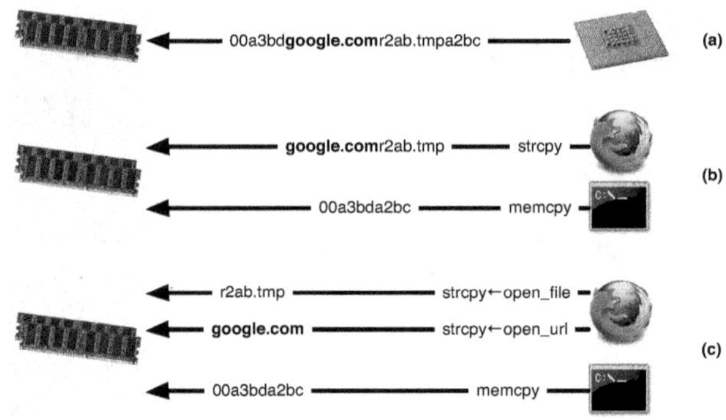

Figure 1: Three different ways of defining a tap point: (a) as a single stream of information from the CPU to RAM ; (b) split up according to program and location within program ; (c) split up according to program, location within program, and calling context.

2. DEFINING TAP POINTS

At the heart of our approach is an abstraction on top of memory accesses made by the CPU, the *tap point*. A tap point is a point in a system at which we wish to capture a series of memory accesses for introspection purposes; however, the exact definition of "a point in a system" will make a great deal of difference in how effective our approach can be.

A naive approach to defining tap points would be to simply group memory accesses by the program counter that made them (e.g., EIP/RIP on x86 and R15 on ARM). This approach fails in two common cases: first, memory accesses made by bulk copy functions, such as `memcpy` and `strcpy`, would all be grouped together, which would commingle data from different parts of the program into the same tap point. In addition, looking only at the program counter would conflate accesses from different programs.

Instead, we define tap points as the triple

$$(caller, program\_counter, address\_space)$$

Including the caller and the address space (the `CR3` register on x86, and the `CP15 c2` register on ARM) separates out memory accesses into streams that should, in general contain the same type of data.[4] Figure 1 shows the effect of choosing various definitions of a tap point when looking for the place where the browser writes the URL entered by the user ("google.com"). At the coarsest granularity (a), one can simply look at all writes from the CPU to RAM; however, the desired information is buried among reams of irrelevant data. Separating out tap points by program and program counter (b) is better, but still combines uses of `strcpy` that contain different information — in this case, a filename and a URL. By including the calling context (c), we can finally obtain a tap point that contains just the desired information.

[4]Making use of tap points defined this way in the real world is slightly more difficult, since a program's address space will differ and its code may be relocated by ASLR. These complications can be overcome with a minor amount of engineering, however.

It is possible that some tap points may require deeper information about the calling context (for example, if an application has its own wrapper around `memcpy`), but in practice we have found that just one level of calling context is usually sufficient. In addition, because TZB uses a whole-system emulator that can watch every call and return, we can obtain the call stack to an arbitrary depth for any tap point. This makes it easy to add extra context for a given tap point, if it is found that doing so separates out the desired information. Examples of tap points that require more than one level of callstack information are given in Sections 6.1.2 and 6.1.3.

Conversely, one might wonder whether this definition of a tap point may split up data that should logically be kept together. To mitigate this problem case, we introduce the idea of *correlated tap points*: we can run a pass over the recorded execution that notices when two tap points write to adjacent locations in memory in a short period of time (currently 5 memory accesses). The idea is that these tap points may be more usefully considered jointly; for example, a single data structure may have its fields set by successive writes. These writes would come from different program counters, and hence would be split into different tap points, but it may be more useful to examine the data structure as a whole. By noticing this correlation we can analyze the data from the combined tap point.

3. SCOPE AND ASSUMPTIONS

The goal of Tappan Zee Bridge is to find points at which to interpose for active monitoring. More precisely, our goal is to speed the current entirely manual process by which applications or operating systems are reverse engineered in order to locate tap points for active monitoring. It should be noted that we do not aim to surpass those manual efforts. We have no automatic way, for instance, of knowing for certain if a tap point will fail to output crucial data or, alternately, spew out superfluous information under some future conditions. This is a separate problem to which we see no ready solution. Static analysis of candidate tap points or extensive testing are good stop-gaps, but nothing short of fully understanding enormous binary code bases can really give complete assurance that a tap point won't miss or cause false alarms in the future.

In this section, we explore how our definition of a tap point and our focus on active monitoring shape the scope of our work.

First and most obviously, our focus on memory accesses necessarily limits our scope to information that is read from or written to RAM at some point. Although this is quite broad, there are notable exceptions. For example, TRESOR [24] performs AES encryption without storing the key or encryption states in RAM by making clever use of the x86 debug registers and the AES-NI instruction set. Aside from such special cases, however, this assumption is not particularly limiting.

Second, our goal of finding tap points suitable for active monitoring motivates a design that treats memory accesses at tap points as sources of *streaming* data. Our algorithms, therefore, typically work in a streaming fashion as the system executes, remembering only a fixed amount of state for each tap point. Although this is a natural fit for active monitoring, where events should be reported as soon as possible,

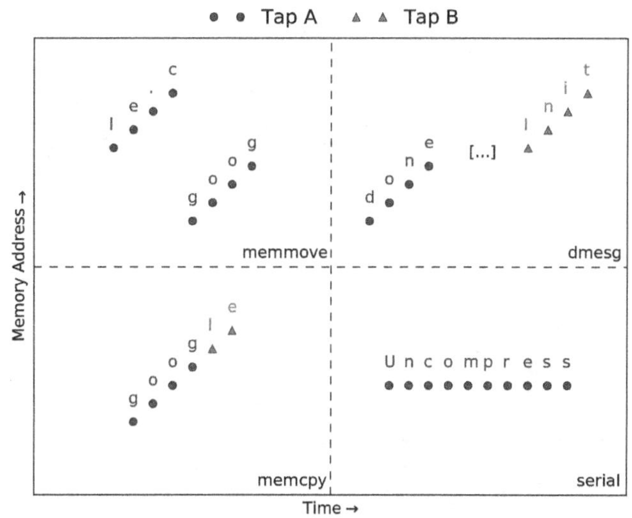

Figure 2: Patterns of memory access that we might wish to monitor using TZB.

it makes handling data whose *spatial* order in memory differs from its *temporal* order as it is accessed more difficult.

Third, the *encoding* of the data sought must be to some extent guessable. For example, to search for a string, one must know what encodings are likely to be used by the system to represent strings. In general this is not a severe limitation, but it does come up; we discuss one such case in Section 6.2.2.

Finally, the use of calling context in the definition of a tap point raises the question of how much context is necessary or useful. Our current system uses only the most recent caller, but we have seen both situations where this is not enough and where it is too much. Overall, however, one level of calling context has proved to be a reasonable choice for a wide variety of introspection tasks.

To better illustrate the boundaries of our technique, consider Figure 2, which plots the address of data written by different tap points over time for four patterns of memory access. In the bottom two quadrants, we have cases that are challenging, but currently well-supported by TZB. In the bottom-left, a standard `memcpy` implementation on x86 makes a copy in 4-byte chunks using `rep movsd`, and then does a two-byte `movsw` to get the remainder of the string. Because the access occurs across two different instructions, TZB sees two different tap points. Our tap point correlation mechanism correctly deduces that the accesses are related, however, because they operate on adjacent ranges in a short span of time.

The case shown in the bottom right quadrant would be tricky if we looked only at memory access spatially and not temporally. Here, a utility function writes data out to a serial port by making one-byte writes to a memory-mapped I/O address.[5] Because TZB sees these memory writes in temporal order, ignoring the address, the data is seen normally and the analyses we describe all operate correctly.

[5]Although not reported in this paper, this case is one we actually encountered while experimenting with an embedded firmware.

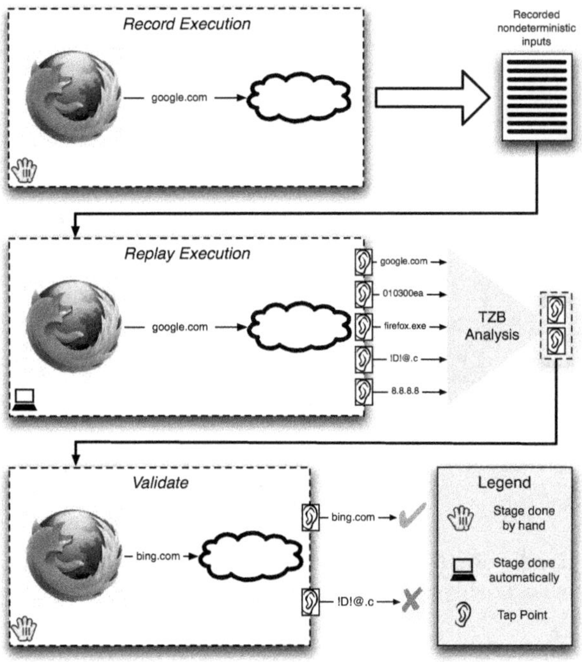

Figure 3: The workflow for using TZB to locate points at which to interpose for active monitoring.

The upper quadrants show cases that are currently not handled by TZB. In the upper left, `memmove` copies a buffer in reverse order when the source and destination overlap. Thus, when viewed in temporal order, a copy of a string like "12345678" would be seen by TZB as "56781234". This case is unlikely to be handled by TZB without a significant redesign, as its view of memory accesses is inherently streaming.

Finally, the upper right, which represents the case of `dmesg` on Linux, is an example of the "dilemma of context". Although the function, `do_syslog`, that writes log data to memory is called from multiple places (creating multiple tap points), it writes to the same contiguous buffer. Unlike the `memcpy` case, a significant amount of time may pass before the next function calls `do_syslog`, and so our tap correlation, which only considers memory accesses within a fixed time window, will not notice that the tap points ought to be grouped together. We believe that this case could be overcome with additional engineering work, but this is left to future work.

4. SEARCH STRATEGIES

To find useful *tap points* in a system—places from which to extract data for introspection—using Tappan Zee Bridge, one begins by creating a recording that captures the desired OS or application behavior. For example, if the end goal is to be notified each time a user loads a new URL in Firefox, one would create a recording of Firefox visiting several URLs. This recording is made by emulating the OS and application inside of the dynamic analysis platform PANDA (described in more detail in Section 5.1), which can capture and record all sources of non-determinism with low overhead, allowing for later deterministic replay. Next, one can run one or more analyses that seek out the desired information among all memory accesses seen during the execution. Analyses in TZB take the form of PANDA plugins that are called on each memory access made during a replayed execution and, at the end, write out a report on the tap points analyzed. Finally, the tap points found should be validated to ensure that they do, in fact, provide the desired information. Such assurance can be gained either by examining the data in the tap point in new executions, or by examining the code around the tap point. This workflow is illustrated in Figure 3.

In this section, we describe three different ways of finding tap points grouped according to a standard epistemic classification scheme [26]: searching for "known knowns"—tap points where the content of the desired data is known; searching for "known unknowns"—tap points where the kind of data sought is known, but its precise format is not; and finally "unknown unknowns"—tap points where the type and format of the data sought are not known, and we are instead simply trying to find "interesting" tap points.

4.1 Known Knowns

The simplest case is finding data that one knows is likely to be read or written by a tap point, and where the encoding of the data is easily guessed. For example, to find a tap point that can be used to notify the hypervisor whenever a URL is entered in a browser, one can visit a known sequence of URLs, and then monitor all tap points, searching for specific byte sequences that make up those URLs. The same holds for other data whose representation when written to memory is predictable: filenames, window titles, registry key names, and so on. For this kind of data, simple string searching is usually sufficient to zero in on the few tap points that handle the data of interest, and in our experience it is one of the most effective techniques for finding useful tap points.

4.2 Known Unknowns

A second tap point application involves finding tap points for things about which we have limited knowledge. We can easily assemble corpora of exemplars to represent a semantic class: English prose, kernel messages, or mail headers. These examples need not come from tap points but can easily be collected directly from interacting with the operating system itself. From such a corpus, we can readily build a statistical model, with which we can build a distance measure for scoring and ranking tap points by how close their contents are to the model.

In addition to such statistical methods, we can also search using an oracle. This is the case, for example, with tap points that write encryption keys. Although the exact key may not be known in advance, we can check whether a given byte string is a valid decryption key by trying to decrypt our sample data.

4.3 Unknown Unknowns

The final strategy for finding useful tap points is also the least focused. If there is no specific introspection quantity sought, one might instead wish to find interesting tap points, for some suitable definition of "interesting." To support this scenario, TZB offers a form of unsupervised learning—clustering—to group together tap points that handle similar data. The idea is that one can then examine exemplars from each cluster, rather than being forced to look through a large number of tap points. Thus, our use of clustering functions as a form of *data triage*.

5. IMPLEMENTATION

In this section, we describe both the dynamic analysis platform employed to build TZB, but also TZB-specific algorithmic and data-structure solutions.

5.1 PANDA

TZB makes extensive use of the Platform for Architecture-Neutral Dynamic Analysis (PANDA), which was developed by the authors in collaboration with Northeastern University.

PANDA is based upon version 1.0.1 of the QEMU machine emulator [4]. QEMU is an excellent and common choice for whole-system dynamic analysis for two main reasons. First, performance is good (about 5x slowdown over native). Second, every basic block of guest code is disassembled by the host in order to emulate, which means that there are opportunities to interpose analyses at the basic block or even instruction level, if desired. QEMU lowers instructions to an intermediate language (IL) in order to employ a single back-end code generator, the Tiny Code Generator (TCG). This IL means dynamic analyses can potentially be written once and re-used for all 14 architectures supported by QEMU. Further, this version of QEMU is capable of booting and running modern operating systems such as Windows 7 (earlier versions of QEMU such as 0.9.1 cannot).

There are three main aspects to PANDA that make it very convenient for building dynamic analyses. First, PANDA provides a plug-in architecture that readily permits writing guest analyses in C and C++. Plug-in code is executed from a number of standard callback locations: before and after basic blocks, memory read and writes, etc. This is not unlike the schemes employed in other whole-system dynamic analysis platforms such as BitBlaze [29] and S2E [7]. In addition, plugins can export functionality that can then be used in other plugins, allowing complex behavior to be built up from simple components. From a software engineering perspective, PANDA's plugin architecture allows the various analyses supported by TZB to be cleanly separated from the main emulator, which makes for a much more comprehensible and maintainable codebase.

The second aspect of PANDA that makes it an excellent dynamic analysis platform is nondeterministic record and replay (RR). In our formulation of RR, we begin a recording by invoking QEMU's built-in snapshot capability. Subsequently, we record all inputs to the CPU, including `ins`, interrupts, and DMA. Recording imposes a small overhead (10-20%) but not enough to perturb execution. During replay, we revert to a snapshot and proceed to pull CPU inputs from a log when required. Unlike many other RR schemes, we do not record and replay device inputs, which means we cannot "go live" at any point during replay. But we can perform repeated replays of an entire operating system under arbitrary instrumentation load without worrying about this perturbing application or operating system operation. This capability is vital to TZB: without record and replay, the heavyweight analyses we perform would make the system unusably slow.

The final aspect of PANDA worth mentioning is its integration of LLVM. QEMU lowers basic blocks of guest code to its own IL, which PANDA can, additionally, re-render as basic blocks of LLVM code via a module extracted from S2E. We omit further discussion of this capability as it is not used by TZB.

5.2 Callstack Monitoring

As explained in Section 2, tap points need information about the calling context. Keeping track of this information requires some knowledge about the CPU architecture on which the OS is running, and so we decided to encapsulate this task into a single plugin. TZB's other analyses can then query the current call stack to arbitrary depth by invoking `get_callers` and not worry about the details described in this section.

To track call stack information, the `callstack` plugin examines each basic block as it is translated, looking for an (architecture-specific) call instruction (currently, we look for `call` on x86 and `bl` and `mov lr, pc` on ARM). If the block includes a call instruction, then we push the return address onto a shadow stack after each time that block executes.

Detecting the return from a function does not require any architecture-specific code. Before the execution of every basic block, we check whether the address we are about to execute is at the top of the stack; if so, we pop it. We only need to check the starting address of the basic block, because by definition a return terminates a basic block, so the return address will always fall at the beginning of a block.

We note that these techniques may fail if traditional call-return semantics are violated. For example, if a program emulated calls and returns by manually pushing the return address and using a direct jump, it would not be detected as a call. However, for non-malicious compiler-generated code, we have found that the algorithm described here works well.

5.3 Fixed String Searching

Searching for fixed strings is one of the most effective tools for finding useful tap points. Because we have to sift through many gigabytes of data that pass through tap points during any given execution, it is vital that string search be efficient in both time and space.

To satisfy these constraints, we developed `stringsearch`, a plugin which requires only one byte of memory per search string and per tap point. This one-byte counter tracks, for a given tap point, how many bytes of the search string have been matched by the data seen at the tap point so far. Whenever a byte is read from or written to memory, we can check what the next byte in the search string is using this position, and compare it to the byte passing through the tap point. If it matches, the counter is incremented; if it does not match, the counter is reset to zero. When the counter equals the length of the search string, we know that the search string has passed through the tap point, and we report a match. Note that because the counter is only one byte, our matcher only supports strings up to 256 bytes long; this cap could be easily raised to 65,536 bytes by using a two-byte counter, at the cost of doubling the memory requirements. Thus far, 256-byte strings have been more than sufficient.

This effectively implements a very simple deterministic finite automaton (DFA) matcher. Indeed, we believe that it should be possible to efficiently implement a streaming basic regular expression matcher that requires only an amount of memory logarithmic in the number of states needed to represent the expression. We leave this generalization to future work, however.

5.4 Statistical Search and Clustering

Collecting bigram statistics on data that passes through each tap point is an efficient way to enable "fuzzy" search based on some training examples, as well as enabling clustering. To implement this we collect bigram statistics for all tap points seen in execution, as well as for the exemplar; the data seen at each tap point is thus represented as a sparse vector with 65,536 elements (one for each possible pair of bytes).

To search, we can then sort the tap points seen by taking the distance (according to some metric) from the exemplar. For our metric, we have chosen to use Jensen-Shannon divergence [18], which is a smoothed and symmetrized version of the classic Kullback-Leibler divergence [16] (also known as information gain). We also examined the Euclidean and cosine distance metrics, but found their performance to be consistently worse. Jensen-Shannon divergence between two probability distributions P and Q is defined as:

$$JSD(P,Q) = H\left(\frac{P+Q}{2}\right) - \frac{H(P)+H(Q)}{2}$$

where H is Shannon entropy.

Bigram collection is done by maintaining, for each tap point, two pieces of information: (1) the last byte that passed through the tap point, so that we can see bigrams that span a single memory access; (2) a histogram of all byte pairs seen at the tap point. The latter of these must be maintained sparsely: because our bigrams are based on bytes, a dense histogram would require 65,536 integers' worth of storage per tap point. Given that most of the executions examined in this paper contain upwards of 500,000 tap points, this would require more than 120GB of memory, which is clearly infeasible (and wasteful, since most of those entries would be zero).

Instead, we store the histogram sparsely, using a C++ Standard Template Library `std::map<uint16_t,int>`. This keeps memory usage down without sacrificing any accuracy, but it does introduce some extra complexity when processing the resulting histograms, as our search software must support sparse vectors rather than simple arrays. Because of this additional complexity, we opted to implement the search and clustering algorithms ourselves, after some initial prototyping using SciPy's `sklearn` toolkit.

Our clustering is based on the venerable k-means algorithm [31], but using the Jensen-Shannon divergence described in the previous section. As in the statistical search case, we use bigram statistics for our feature vectors. Initialization uses the KMeans++ algorithm [2], which helps guarantee that the initial cluster centers are widely separated. We evaluate the performance of this clustering compared to an expert labeling in Section 6.3.

Our statistical search tool is implemented in 246 lines of C++, and computes the Jensen-Shannon divergence between a training histogram (dense) and a set of sparse histograms. Our K-Means clustering tool is 481 lines of C++ code, and outputs a clustering of the sparse histograms using Jensen-Shannon divergence as a distance metric.[6] Both tools are multithreaded, which greatly speeds up the computation.

5.5 Finding SSL/TLS Keys

We have also implemented a PANDA plugin called `keyfind`, which locates tap points that write SSL/TLS master secrets. The SSL/TLS master secret is a 48-byte string from which an SSL/TLS-encrypted session's keys are derived; thus, if a tap point that writes the master key can be found, encrypted network traffic can be decrypted and analyzed.

The plugin operates on a recording in which a program initiates an encrypted connection to some server and an encrypted packet sent by the client (captured using, e.g., `tcpdump`). The `keyfind` uses each 48 bytes accessed at each tap point as a trial decryption key for a sample packet sent by the client. If the decrypted packet's Message Authentication Code (MAC) verifies that the packet was decrypted correctly then we can conclude that the tap point can be used to decrypt SSL/TLS connections made by the program under inspection. In Section 6.2.1 we show how this technique can be used to spy on connections made by the Sykipot malware, without performing a (potentially detectable) man in the middle attack.

6. EVALUATION

In this section, we evaluate the efficacy of our various tap point search strategies, described in Section 4, at finding tap points useful for introspection. Our experiments are motivated by real-world introspection applications, and so for each experiment we describe a typical application for the tap points found. Each experiment was also generally performed on a variety of different operating sytems, applications, and architectures in order to evaluate TZB's ability to handle a diverse range of introspection targets.

For the sake of readability, we have attempted to use symbolic names for addresses wherever possible in the following results. It is hoped that these will be more meaningful to the reader than the raw addresses, but we emphasize that debug information is in no way required for TZB to work.

6.1 Known Knowns

6.1.1 URL Access

Monitoring visited URLs is likely to be useful for host-based intrusion detection and prevention systems. For example, an IDS may wish to verify that outgoing requests were initiated by a human rather than malware on the users's machine, or match URLs visited against a blacklist of malicious sites. This poses a challenge for existing introspection solutions, as URL load notification is not generally exposed by a public API, and the data resides in a user application (the browser).

To find URL tap points, we created training executions by visiting a set of three URLs (Google, Facebook, and Bing) in the following operating systems and browsers: Epiphany on Debian squeeze (armel and amd64); Firefox 16.0.2, Opera 12.10, and Internet Explorer 8.0.7601.17514 on Windows 7 SP1 (x86); and WebPositive r580 on Haiku (x86). We used the `stringsearch` plugin to search for the ASCII and UTF-16 representations of the three URLs, and then validated

[6]The use of this distance metric is justified theoretically because Jensen-Shannon distance is a Bregman divergence [3] and empirically because our clustering typically converges after around 30 iterations.

Browser	Caller	PC
Deb Epiphany (arm)	`WebCore::KURL::KURL+0x30`	`WebCore::KURL::init+0x70`
Deb Epiphany (amd64)	`webkit_frame_load_uri+0xc3`	`WebCore::KURL::init+0x368`
Win7 IE8 (x86)	`ieframe!CAddressEditBox::_Execute+0xaa`	`ieframe!StringCchCopyW+0x50`
Win7 Firefox (x86)	`xul!nsAutoString::nsAutoString+0x1a`	`xul!nsAString_internal::Assign+0x1d`
Win7 Chrome (x86)	`msftedit!CTxtEdit::OnTxChar+0x105`	`msftedit!CTxtSelection::PutChar+0xb8`
Win7 Opera (x86)	`Opera.dll+0x2cf6c6`	`Opera.dll+0x142783`
Haiku WebPositive (x86)	`BWebPage::LoadURL+0x3a`	`BMessage::AddString+0x26`

Table 1: Tap points found that write the URL typed into the browser by the user.

each tap point found to ensure that it wrote only the desired data. The results can be seen in Table 1.

6.1.2 TLS/SSL Master Secrets

Monitoring SSL/TLS-encrypted traffic is a classic problem for intrusion detection systems. Currently, hypervisor- or network- based IDSes that wish to analyze encrypted traffic must perform a man-in-the-middle attack on the connection, presenting a false server certificate to the client. Not only does this require the client to cooperate by trusting certificates signed by the intrusion detection system, it also takes control of the certificate verification process out of the hands of the client—a dangerous step, given that many existing SSL/TLS interception proxies have a history of certificate trust vulnerabilities [15].

Instead of a man-in-the-middle attack, we can instead use TZB to find a tap point that reads or writes the SSL/TLS master secret for each encrypted connection, giving us a "man-on-the-inside". Because this secret must be generated for each SSL/TLS connection, if we can find such a tap point, it can then be provided to the IDS to decrypt and, if necessary, modify the content of the SSL stream.

To find the location of these tap points, we ran a modified copy of OpenSSL's `s_server` utility that prints out the SSL/TLS master key any time a connection is made. We then recorded executions in which we visited the server with each of our tested SSL clients, and noted the SSL/TLS master secret. Finally, we used `stringsearch` to search for a tap point that wrote the master key, and verified that the tap wrote exactly one master key per connection. For this test, we used: OpenSSL s_client 0.9.8 on Debian squeeze (armel), OpenSSL s_client 0.9.8 and Epiphany 2.30.6 on Debian squeeze (amd64), and Firefox 16.0.2, Google Chrome 23.0.1271.64, Opera 12.10, and Internet Explorer 8.0.7601 on Windows 7 SP1 (x86). The results are shown in Table 2.

There is one particular point of interest to observe in these results. In the case of Epiphany on Debian, we found that one level of callstack information was *not* sufficient—with only the immediate caller, the tap point contains more data than just the SSL/TLS master secret. This is because the version of Epiphany uses SSLv3 to make connections, and the pseudo-random function (PRF) used in SSLv3 has the form

$$MD5(SHA1(\ldots))$$

The other implementations instead use TLSv1.0, where the PRF has the form

$$MD5(\ldots) \oplus SHA1(\ldots)$$

This final XOR operation is done from a unique program point, so the tap point that results from it contains only TLS master keys. This points to a potential complication of using tap points for introspection: it is not always clear in advance how many levels of call stack information will be required.

We were successful in locating tap points for all SSL/TLS clients tested. We note that uncovering similar information using traditional techniques would have required significant expertise and reverse engineering of both open source and proprietary software.

6.1.3 File Access

Monitoring file accesses is a requirement for many host-based security applications, including on-access anti-virus scanners. Thus, locating a tap point at which system-wide file accesses can be observed is of considerable importance. However, because previous approaches to the introspection problem [11, 12] passively retrieve information from the guest and are not event-driven, they cannot be used in this scenario.

To find such a tap point, we created recordings in which we opened files in various operating systems. Specifically, in each OS we created 100 files, each named after ten successive digits of π. The operating systems chosen for this test were: Debian squeeze (amd64), Debian squeeze (armel), Windows 7 SP1 32-bit, FreeBSD 9.0, and Haiku R1 Alpha 3 (all on x86). We then searched for tap points that wrote strings matching the ASCII and UTF-16 encodings of the filenames using the `stringsearch` analysis plugin. The UTF-16 encodings were included because it was known that Windows 7 uses UTF-16 for strings pervasively, allowing us to surmise that on Windows URLs would likely be UTF-16 encoded. Finally, we looked at the tap points found by `stringsearch`, and validated them by hand.

The results are shown in Table 3. For most of the operating systems we had no difficulty finding a tap point that contained the name of each file as it was accessed. The one exception was Windows 7, where the most promising tap point not only wrote file results, but also a number of unrelated objects such as registry key names. As in the SSL case, the root cause of this was insufficient calling context: in Windows several different things fall under the umbrella of a "named object", and these were all being captured at this tap point. We found that four levels of calling context were sufficient to restrict the tap point to just file accesses; the "deepest" caller was `IopCreateFile` (which, despite its name, is used for both opening existing files and creating new ones).

6.2 Known Unknowns

6.2.1 SSL Malware

The need to snoop on SSL-encrypted connections arises in malware analysis as well. Two features distinguish this case from that of intercepting the traffic of benign SSL clients presented in the previous section. First, the ability to de-

Client	Caller	PC	Process
Deb OpenSSL (arm)	`tls1_generate_master_secret+0x9c`	`tls1_PRF+0x90`	openssl
Deb OpenSSL (amd64)	`ssl3_send_client_key_exchange+0x437`	`tls1_generate_master_secret+0x108`	openssl
Deb Epiphany (arm)	`md_write+0x74`	`md5_write+0x68`	epiphany
Deb Epiphany (amd64)	`md_write+0x60`	`md5_write+0x49`	epiphany
Haiku WebPositive (x86)	`tls1_generate_master_secret+0x65`	`tls1_PRF+0x14b`	WebPositive
Win7 Chrome (x86)	`chrome!NSC_DeriveKey+0x1241`	`chrome!TLS_PRF+0xa0`	chrome.exe
Win7 IE8 (x86)	`ncrypt!Tls1ComputeMasterKey@32+0x57`	`ncrypt!PRF@40`	lsass.exe
Win7 Firefox (x86)	`softokn3!NSC_DeriveKey+0xe85`	`freebl3!TLS_PRF+0xbb`	firefox.exe
Win7 Opera (x86)	`Opera.dll+0x2eb06e`	`Opera.dll+0x50251`	opera.exe

Table 2: Tap points found that write the SSL/TLS master secret for each SSL/TLS connection.

Target	Caller	PC
Debian (amd64)	`getname+0x13e`	`strncpy_from_user+0x52`
Debian (arm)	`getname+0x88`	`__strncpy_from_user+0x10`
Haiku (x86)	`EntryCache::Lookup+0x27`	`hash_hash_string+0x1b`
FreeBSD (x86)	`namei+0xd1`	`copyinstr+0x38`
Windows 7 (x86)	`ObpCaptureObjectName+0xcb`	`memcpy+0x33`

Table 3: Tap points found for file access on different operating systems.

crypt the traffic without a man in the middle is even more important: in contrast to benign clients, we cannot assume that malware will accept certificates signed by our certificate authority. Second, we cannot rely on having access to the server's master secret, as the server is under the attacker's control. This means that our previous strategy of using a simple string search for the master secret will not work here.

Instead, we located the tap point in the SSL-enabled malware using our `keyfind` plugin, which performs trial decryption on a packet sent by the malware using each possible 48-byte sequence written to memory as a key and verifies whether the Message Authentication Code is valid. Although this is much slower than a string match, it is the only available option, since the key is not known in advance.

To test the plugin, we obtained a copy of a version of the Sykipot trojan released around October 31st, 2012 [13] (MD5: `34a1010846c0502f490f17b66fb05a12`). We then created a recording in which we executed the malware; simultaneously, we captured network traffic using `tcpdump`. We noted that the malware made several encrypted connections to `https://www.hi-techsolutions.org/`, and provided one of the encrypted packets from these connections as input to the `keyfind` plugin. The plugin found the same tap point as the Windows 7 IE8 experiment described earlier, indicating that both the malware and IE8 likely use the same underlying system mechanism to make SSL connections. The key found was able to decrypt the connections contained in the packet dump.[7]

6.2.2 *Finding* `dmesg`

System logs are an invaluable resource, both for security and system administration. In an introspection-based security system, for example, one might want to find a tap point that contains the system's logs so that they can be stored securely outside the guest virtual machine. However, because the format of system logs is particular to each OS, we need some mechanism that can find tap points that write data that "looks like" a log based on an exemplar. The statistical search described in Section 4.2 is a good fit for this task: by training on the output of `dmesg` on one OS, we can find `dmesg`-like tap points on other systems.

To locate these system log tap points, we first created a training exemplar by running the `dmesg` command on a Debian sid (amd64) host and computing the bigram probabilities for the output. We then created recordings in which we booted five operating systems (Debian squeeze (armel), Debian squeeze (amd64), Minix R3-2.0 (i386), FreeBSD 9.0-RELEASE (i386), and Haiku R1 Alpha 3 (i386)), and computed the same bigram statistics. We then sorted the tap points seen in each operating system boot according to their Jensen-Shannon distance from the training distribution, and manually examined data written by the tap point for each of the top 30 results in each operating system. Table 4 shows, for each operating system tested, the tap point that we determined to be the system log, and its rank in the search results.

We can see that in all cases the correct result is in the top 10. There are two additional features of Table 4 that bear mentioning. First, the reader will note that the two Debian systems have a caller of "N/A". This is because the memory writes that make up `dmesg` are done in `do_syslog`, which is called from multiple functions. In these cases, including the caller splits up information that is semantically the same. We detected this case by noticing that several of the top-ranked results in the Linux experiments had the same program counter, and that they appeared to contain different sections of the same log. Second, the tap point found for Haiku was also incomplete—some lines were truncated. By using our tap point correlation plugin, we determined that we were missing a second tap point that was correlated with the main one; the two together formed the write portions of a `memcpy` of the log messages. Once this second tap point was included, we could see all the log messages produced by Haiku.

We also attempted to find an analogous log message tap point on Windows 7, but were not successful. This is a result of the way Windows logging works: rather than logging string-based messages, applications and system services create a manifest declaring possible log events, and then refer to them by a generated numeric code. Human-readable messages are not stored, and instead are generated when the user views the log. This means that there is no tap point

[7]The malware also has a second layer of encryption, which is custom and not based on SSL; we did not attempt to decrypt this second layer.

OS	Caller	PC	Kernel?	Rank
FreeBSD (x86)	`msglogstr+0x28`	`msgbuf_addstr+0x19a`	Yes	1
Haiku (x86)	`ring_buffer_peek+0x59`	`memcpy_generic+0x14`	Yes	1
Debian (arm)	N/A	`do_syslog+0x18c`	Yes	4
Debian (amd64)	N/A	`do_syslog+0x163`	Yes	4
Minix (x86)	`0x190005ee`	`0x190009d4`	No	8
Windows 7 (x86)	Not Found	Not Found	?	?

Table 4: Tap points that write the system log (dmesg) on several UNIX-like operating systems. All tap points were located in the kernel, except for Minix, which is a microkernel. We were unable to find a tap point analogous to dmesg in Windows.

that will contain log messages of the type used in our **dmesg** training, and the methods described in this paper are largely inapplicable unless a training example for the binary format can be found. However, because the event log query API is public [23], existing tools such as Virtuoso [11] might be a better fit for this use case.

Anecdotally, the ability to uncover a tap point that writes the kernel logs has also been useful for diagnosing problems when adding support for new platforms to QEMU. For an unrelated research task, we attempted to boot the Raspberry Pi [1] kernel inside QEMU, but found that it hung without displaying any output early on in the boot process. By locating the **dmesg** tap point, we discovered that the last log message printed was "Calibrating delay loop..."; based on this we determined that the guest was hung waiting for a timer interrupt that was not yet implemented in QEMU.

6.3 Unknown Unknowns: Clustering

To test the effectiveness of clustering tap points based on bigram statistics and Jensen-Shannon distance, we carried out an experiment that compared the clusters generated algorithmically to a set of labels generated by two of the co-authors manually examining the data. We created six recordings representing different workloads on two operating systems (Windows 7 and FreeBSD 9.0). From FreeBSD, we took recordings of boot, shutdown, running applications (**ps**, **cat**, **ls**, **top**, and **vi**), and a one-minute recording of the system sitting idle, for a total of four recordings. On Windows we created two recordings: running applications (**cmd.exe**, **dir**, the Task Manager, Notepad), and one minute of the system sitting idle.[8]

Next, we sampled a subset of the tap points found in each recording. Given that the vast majority of tap points do not write interesting information, we opted not to sample uniformly from the all tap points found. Instead, we performed an initial k-means clustering with $k = 100$, and then picked out tap points at various distances from each cluster center. We chose the tap point at σ standard deviations from the center, for $\sigma \in \{0, 0.5, 0.75, 1.0, 1.25, 1.5, 1.75, 2.0\}$ for a total of 2,926 samples[9]. Finally, we dumped the data from each of the sampled tap points, blinded them by assigning each a unique id, and then provided the data files to our two labelers. Each labeler independently assigned labels to each of the samples using the labels described in Table 5, and the two labelers then worked together to reconcile their labels.

Finally, we ran a k-means clustering with $k = 10$; 10 was chosen because it was a round number reasonably close to the number of labels our human evaluators gave to the data. We then used the Adjusted Rand Index [14] to score the quality of our clustering relative to our hand-labeled examples. The Adjusted Rand Index for a clustering ranges from -1 to 1; clusterings which are independent of the hand labeling will receive a score that is negative or close to zero. As can be seen in Table 6, our clustering did not match up very well on the hand-labeled samples. Note, however, that labeling criteria were selected without knowledge of the sizes of categories or whether or not the distance metric would effectively discriminate, so it is perhaps unsurprising that the correspondence is poor.

There is some hope, however. Regardless of the apparently poor clustering performance with respect to hand-labeling, we decided to determine if the clusters from our 100-mean clustering of FreeBSD's boot process contained new and interesting data and if finding that data would be facilitated by them. First, we determined to which of the clusters data from the FreeBSD's **dmesg** and filename tap points (found in Sections 6.2.2 and 6.1.3) was assigned. We were heartened to learn that these two text-like tap points had been sent to the same cluster. We proceeded to explore this cluster of approximately 5000 tap points, and found that, indeed, the vast majority of the tap points contained readable text of some sort. Further, in the course of about thirty minutes of spelunking around this cluster, we found not only kernel messages and filenames but a stone soup of shell scripts, process listings kernel configuration, GraphViz data, and so on. A selection of these tap point contents is provided in Appendix 9. We did not exhaustively examine this cluster, but plan to do so soon, as it appears to contain much of interest for active monitoring. If clustering has focused us on one out of 100 clusters, this is potentially a big savings.

6.4 Accuracy

Leaving aside the clustering results for the moment, the analyses implemented in TZB are extremely effective at helping to identify interposition points for active monitoring. In the evaluations based on string searching, we found that the number of tap points we had to look at manually was at most 262 (URLs under IE8) and in the best case we only had to examine two tap points (for SSL keys under Firefox, Opera, Haiku, and OpenSSL on ARM). The number of tap points that need to be examined is related to how widely the data is propagated in the system and how common the string be-

[8]Although we would have preferred to include Windows boot and shutdown recordings, at the time our replay system had a bug (now fixed) that prevented these recordings from being replayed.

[9]The alert reader will note that this is smaller than the 4,800 samples one would expect from taking 8 samples from 100 clusters in each of 6 recordings. This is because some clusters did not have very high variance, and so in many cases there were fewer than 8 samples at the required distance from the center.

Abbrv.	Description	Count
bp	binary pattern	2318
rd	repeated dword	400
mz	mostly zero	141
rq	repeated quadword	19
fnu	filenames unicode	8
woa	words ascii	8
wou	words unicode	7
inu	integers unicode	6
bu	binary uniform	5
ura	URLs ascii	5
rs	repeated short	4
fna	filenames ascii	2
rb	repeated byte	2
vr	very redundant	1

Table 5: Labels given to the sampled tap points by human evaluators, along with the number of times each occurred.

Recording	ARI
FreeBSD Apps	0.018
FreeBSD Boot	0.048
FreeBSD Idle	0.021
FreeBSD Shutdown	0.074
Win7 Apps	0.029
Win7 Idle	-0.003

Table 6: Quality of clustering as measured by the Adjusted Rand Index, which ranges from -1 to 1, with 1 being a clustering that perfectly matches the hand-labeled examples.

ing searched for is; thus, it is natural that URLs visited in the browser would appear in many tap points, whereas the SSL/TLS master key would not. Qualitatively speaking, we found that once the candidate tap points had been selected by `stringsearch` for a given execution, it took at most an hour to find one that sufficed for the task at hand.

For the `dmesg` evaluation, we also examined the quality of the results found for each operating system using the standard "Precision at 10" metric, which is just the number of results found in the top 10 that were actually relevant to the query. In this case, this is simply the fraction of results in the top 10 that appeared to contain the system log (even if it was incomplete). Based on this metric, the precision of our retrieval was between 20% (on Minix) and 100% (on Haiku). This means that if one looked at all of the top 10 entries, it is guaranteed that one would find the correct tap point.

7. LIMITATIONS AND FUTURE WORK

Although TZB is currently very useful for finding interception points for *active monitoring*, it is not currently usable in every scenario where introspection is needed. Because the interception points are triggered by executing code, they are only usable in *online* analysis. However, the need for introspection also arises in *post-mortem* analysis, specifically in forensic memory analysis. Whereas previous solutions such as Virtuoso [11] were able to operate equally well on memory images or live virtual machines, TZB is only applicable to the live case. In future work, we hope to combine Virtuoso-like techniques with TZB to produce offline programs that can locate in memory the buffers on which TZB's tap points operate.

Another limitation of TZB is its reliance on callstack information to locate interposition points. In current systems, keeping track of an arbitrary number of callers for each process is prohibitively expensive; although stack walking is faster (since it only needs to be invoked when the monitored code is executed), it is insecure, unreliable, and not available on every architecture. We hope to examine how existing solutions such as compiler modifications [32, 8] or dynamic binary translation [27] can be used to efficiently maintain the shadow stack information needed for TZB. We also note that Intel's Haswell architecture, which as of this writing has just been released, has hardware support for keeping track of calls and returns [33]; this would provide an excellent base on which to build a low-overhead security system based on TZB tap points.

Code generated at runtime (i.e., JIT or injected code) may make re-identification of a discovered tap point difficult or even impossible. Given the rise of languages that depend on JIT runtimes, better solutions are needed for this scenario, and the problem of how to make use of tap points in JIT code should be explored further.

Finally, as seen in Section 6.3, the clustering results are promising, but not yet fully developed. We hope to gain a better understanding of the data found in tap points and seek out better features and models for clustering in future work.

8. RELATED WORK

Although, to our knowledge, there is no existing work on mining the contents of memory accesses for introspection, we drew inspiration from a variety of sources. These can be roughly grouped into three categories: work on automating virtual machine introspection, research on automated reverse engineering, and efforts that examine memory access patterns, typically through visualization. In this section, we describe in more detail previous work in these three areas.

Virtual machine introspection has been targeted for automation by several recent research efforts because of the *semantic gap problem*: security applications running outside the guest virtual machine need to reconstruct high-level information from low-level data sources, but doing so requires knowledge of internal data structures and algorithms that is costly to acquire and maintain. To address this problem, researchers have sought ways of bridging this gap automatically. Virtuoso [11] uses dynamic traces of in-guest programs to extract out-of-guest tools that compute the same information. However, because it is based on dynamic analysis, incomplete training may cause the generated programs to malfunction. Two related approaches attempt to address this limitation: *process out-grafting* [30] moves monitored processes to the security VM while redirecting their system calls to the guest VM, allowing tools in the security VM to directly examine the process, while VMST [12] selectively redirects the memory accesses of tools like `ps` and `netstat` from the security VM so that their results are obtained from the guest VM. TZB extends these approaches by finding points in applications and the OS at which to perform active monitoring.

Based on the observation that memory accesses in dynamic execution can reveal the structure of data in memory, several papers have proposed methods for automatically deducing the structure of protocols [6, 19, 9], file formats [10, 20], and in-memory data structures [17, 28, 21]. One particular insight we have drawn from this body of work is the idea that the point in a program at which a piece of data is accessed, along with its calling context, can be used as a proxy for determining the type of the data. TZB leverages this insight to separate out memory accesses into streams of related data.

Finally, there has been some research on examining memory accesses made by a single program or a whole system, typically using visualization. Burzstein et al. [5] found that by visualizing the memory of online strategy games, they could identify the region of memory used to decide how much of the in-game map was visible to the player, which greatly reduces the work required to create a "map hack" and allow the player to see the entire map at once. Outside the academic world, the ICU64 visual debugger [22] allows users to visualize and modify the entire memory of a Commodore 64 system, enabling a variety of cheats and enhancements to C64 games. Although TZB does not use visualization, it shares with this previous work the understanding that memory accesses can be a rich source of information about a running program.

9. CONCLUSION

In this paper we have presented TZB, a system that automatically locates candidate memory accesses for active monitoring of applications or operating systems. This is a task that previously required extensive reverse engineering by domain experts. We have successfully used TZB to identify a broad range of tap points, including ones to dynamically extract SSL keys, URLs typed into browsers, and the names of files being opened. TZB is built atop the QEMU-based PANDA platform as a set of plug-ins and its operation is operating system and architecture agnostic, affording it impressive scope for application. This is a powerful technique that has already transformed how the authors perform RE tasks. By reframing a difficult RE task as a principled search through streaming data provided by dynamic analysis, TZB allows manual effort to be refocused on more critical and less automatable tasks like validation.

Acknowledgments

This material is based upon work supported in part by the National Science Foundation under grants no. CNS-1017265 and no. CNS-0831300, and the Office of Naval Research under grant no. N000140911042. Any opinions, findings, and conclusions or recommendations expressed in this material are those of the authors and do not necessarily reflect the views of the National Science Foundation or the Office of Naval Research.

10. REFERENCES

[1] Raspberry Pi: An ARM GNU/Linux box for $25. `http://www.raspberrypi.org/`.

[2] D. Arthur and S. Vassilvitskii. k-means++: the advantages of careful seeding. In *Proceedings of the ACM-SIAM symposium on Discrete algorithms*, 2007.

[3] A. Banerjee, S. Merugu, I. S. Dhillon, and J. Ghosh. Clustering with Bregman divergences. *J. Mach. Learn. Res.*, 6, Dec. 2005.

[4] F. Bellard. QEMU, a fast and portable dynamic translator. In *USENIX Annual Technical Conference*, 2005.

[5] E. Bursztein, M. Hamburg, J. Lagarenne, and D. Boneh. OpenConflict: Preventing real time map hacks in online games. In *Proceedings of the IEEE Symposium on Security and Privacy*, 2011.

[6] J. Caballero, H. Yin, Z. Liang, and D. Song. Polyglot: automatic extraction of protocol message format using dynamic binary analysis. In *Proceedings of the ACM conference on Computer and communications security*, 2007.

[7] V. Chipounov, V. Kuznetsov, and G. Candea. S2E: A platform for in-vivo multi-path analysis of software systems. *ACM SIGARCH Computer Architecture News*, 39(1), 2011.

[8] T. Chiueh and F. Hsu. RAD: a compile-time solution to buffer overflow attacks. In *International Conference on Distributed Computing Systems*, 2001.

[9] W. Cui, J. Kannan, and H. J. Wang. Discoverer: automatic protocol reverse engineering from network traces. In *Proceedings of the USENIX Security Symposium*, 2007.

[10] W. Cui, M. Peinado, K. Chen, H. J. Wang, and L. Irun-Briz. Tupni: automatic reverse engineering of input formats. In *Proceedings of the 15th ACM conference on Computer and communications security*, 2008.

[11] B. Dolan-Gavitt, T. Leek, M. Zhivich, J. Giffin, and W. Lee. Virtuoso: Narrowing the semantic gap in virtual machine introspection. In *Proceedings of the IEEE Symposium on Security and Privacy*, May 2011.

[12] Y. Fu and Z. Lin. Space traveling across VM: Automatically bridging the semantic-gap in virtual machine introspection via online kernel data redirection. In *Proceedings of the IEEE Symposium on Security and Privacy*, May 2012.

[13] K. Gilbert. Hurricane sandy serves as lure to deliver Sykipot. `http://securityblog.verizonbusiness.com/2012/10/31/hurricane-sandy-serves-as-lure-to-deliver-sykipot/`.

[14] L. Hubert and P. Arabie. Comparing partitions. *Journal of Classification*, 2(1), 1985.

[15] J. Jarmoc. SSL/TLS interception proxies and transitive trust. In *Black Hat Europe*, March 2012.

[16] S. Kullback and R. A. Leibler. On information and sufficiency. *Annals of Mathematical Statistics*, 22, 1951.

[17] J. Lee, T. Avgerinos, and D. Brumley. TIE: Principled reverse engineering of types in binary programs. In *Network and Distributed System Security Symposium*, 2011.

[18] J. Lin. Divergence measures based on the Shannon entropy. *IEEE Trans. Inf. Theor.*, 37(1), Sept. 2006.

[19] Z. Lin, X. Jiang, D. Xu, and X. Zhang. Automatic protocol format reverse engineering through context-aware monitored execution. In *Network and Distributed Systems Symposium*, 2008.

[20] Z. Lin and X. Zhang. Deriving input syntactic structure from execution. In *Proceedings of the ACM SIGSOFT International Symposium on Foundations of software engineering*, 2008.

[21] Z. Lin, X. Zhang, and D. Xu. Automatic reverse engineering of data structures from binary execution.

In *Network and Distributed System Security Symposium*, 2010.

[22] mathfigure. ICU64: Real-time hacking of a C64 emulator.

[23] Microsoft Corporation. EvtQuery function. `http://msdn.microsoft.com/en-us/library/windows/desktop/aa385466(v=vs.85).aspx`.

[24] T. Müller, F. C. Freiling, and A. Dewald. TRESOR runs encryption securely outside RAM. In *Proceedings of the 20th USENIX conference on Security*, 2011.

[25] B. D. Payne, M. Carbone, M. Sharif, and W. Lee. Lares: An architecture for secure active monitoring using virtualization. In *IEEE Symposium on Security and Privacy*, 2008.

[26] D. Rumsfeld. DoD news briefing - Secretary Rumsfeld and Gen. Myers. February 2002.

[27] S. Sinnadurai, Q. Zhao, and W. Wong. Transparent runtime shadow stack: Protection against malicious return address modifications. `http://citeseerx.ist.psu.edu/viewdoc/summary?doi=10.1.1.120.5702`, 2008.

[28] A. Slowinska, T. Stancescu, and H. Bos. Howard: A dynamic excavator for reverse engineering data structures. In *Network and Distributed Systems Symposium*, 2011.

[29] D. Song, D. Brumley, H. Yin, J. Caballero, I. Jager, M. G. Kang, Z. Liang, J. Newsome, P. Poosankam, and P. Saxena. BitBlaze: A new approach to computer security via binary analysis. In *Information systems security*. 2008.

[30] D. Srinivasan, Z. Wang, X. Jiang, and D. Xu. Process out-grafting: an efficient "out-of-vm" approach for fine-grained process execution monitoring. In *Proceedings of the ACM conference on Computer and communications security*, 2011.

[31] H. Steinhaus. Sur la division des corp materiels en parties. *Bull. Acad. Polon. Sci*, 1, 1956.

[32] Vendicator. Stack shield: A "stack smashing" technique protection tool for Linux. `http://www.angelfire.com/sk/stackshield/`.

[33] Z. Yan. perf, x86: Haswell LBR call stack support. `http://lwn.net/Articles/535152/`.

APPENDIX

A. SAMPLE TAP POINT CONTENTS

Here, we reproduce a selection of tap points from the same cluster as dmesg and filename tap points.

```
/etc/rc.d/ipfw/etc/rc.d/NETWORKING/etc/rc.d/netwait/etc/rc
.d/mountcritremote/etc/rc.d/devfs/etc/rc.d/ipmon/etc/rc.d/
mdconfig2/etc/rc.d/newsyslog

r=/sNsnWs/fuiebu/ r=ceremdsecd_t_co_artpachg=tSooadSebaabf
/faa_N_=_peOfA=fA=feTr=tul.n=_eo/.b_Yt_vtectvifat=a=-sd_Ee
Ofu=u_Oy:nF:tRseeeeEfciOtmdtuinlrlrrlpp/nppfpcepinl=l=.llN
lNlgllpl_.4l_l_2/l_l_22lileldlylo- 21laltlat=rrrsbgrskgni/

russian|Russian Users Accounts:  :charset=KOI8-R:         :
lang=ru_RU.KOI8-R:      :       :passwd_format=md5:     :co
pyright=/etc/COPYRIGHT:       :welcome=/etc/motd:     :sete
nv=MAIL=/var/mail/$,BLOCKSIZE=K,FTP_PASSIVE_MODE=YES:

nss_compat.so.1dhclientShared object ''nss_compat.so.1'' n
```

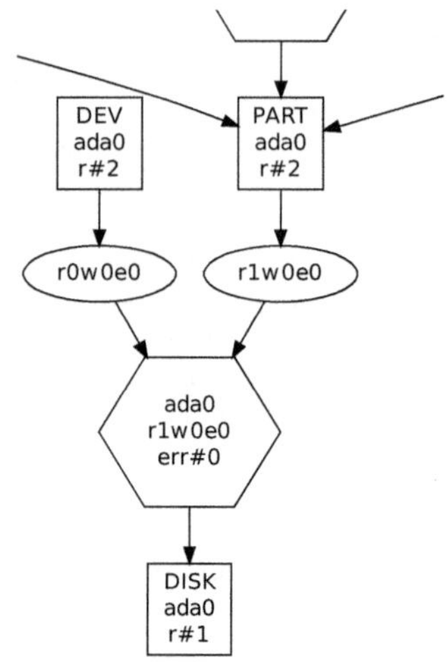

Figure 4: Detail from rendering of Graphviz file captured from a FreeBSD boot tap point, apparently depicting disk geometry

```
ot found, required by ''dhclient''nss_nis.so.1dhclientShar
ed object ''nss_nis.so.1'' not found, required by ''dhclie
nt''nss_files.so.1dhclientShared object ''nss_files.so.1''

digraph geom {
z0xc1d8de00 [shape=box,label=''PART\nada0\nr#2''];
z0xc1f4f640 [label=''r1w0e0''];
z0xc1f4f640 -> z0xc1e9eb00;

/sbin/in/bin/sh/bin/stt/sbin/sysctl/bin/ps/sbin/sysctl/sbi
n/rcorde/bin/cat/sbin/md/sbin/sysctl/sbin/sysctl/bin/ken/s
bin/dumpon/bin/ln/bin/ps/sbin/sysctl/sbin/sysctl/sbin/sysc
tl/sbin/sysctl/bin/ps/bin/dd/sbin/sysctl/bin/dat/bin/df/sb

/boot/kernel/kernel00000000-0000-0000-0000-000000000000000
00000-0000-0000-0000-000000000000000000000-0000-0000-0000-0
00000000000993c915d-3e9f-11e2-a557-525400123456993c915d-3e
9f-11e2-a557-525400123456/boot/kernel/kernel/boot/kernel/k
...
modulesoptions       CONFIG_AUTOGENERATED
ident   GENERIC
machine i386
cpu     I686_CPU
cpu     I586_CPU
cpu     I486_CPU

<mesh>
  <class id=''0xc10362c0''>
    <name>FD</name>
  </class>
  <class id=''0xc1009a80''>

#!/bin/sh
#
# $FreeBSD: release/9.0.0/etc/rc.d/newsyslog 197947 2009-1
0-10 22:17:03Z dougb $
...
set_rcvar()
{
        case $# in
        0)
                echo ${name}_enable
                ;;
        1)
```

Towards Reducing the Attack Surface of Software Backdoors

Felix Schuster and Thorsten Holz
Horst Görtz Institute for IT-Security
Ruhr-University Bochum, Germany
{firstname.lastname}@rub.de

ABSTRACT

Backdoors in software systems probably exist since the very first access control mechanisms were implemented and they are a well-known security problem. Despite a wave of public discoveries of such backdoors over the last few years, this threat has only rarely been tackled so far.

In this paper, we present an approach to reduce the attack surface for this kind of attacks and we strive for an automated identification and elimination of backdoors in binary applications. We limit our focus on the examination of server applications within a client-server model. At the core, we apply variations of the *delta debugging* technique and introduce several novel heuristics for the identification of those regions in binary application that backdoors are typically installed in (i.e., authentication and command processing functions). We demonstrate the practical feasibility of our approach on several real-world backdoors found in modified versions of the popular software tools *ProFTPD* and *OpenSSH*. Furthermore, we evaluate our implementation not only on common instruction set architectures such as x86/x64, but also on commercial off-the-shelf embedded devices powered by a MIPS32 processor.

Categories and Subject Descriptors

K.6.5 [**Security and Protection**]: Unauthorized access

General Terms

Security

Keywords

Software Backdoors; Dynamic Analysis; Binary Analysis

1. INTRODUCTION

In today's computing environment, we typically rely on software components that are not implemented by ourselves,

CCS'13, November 4–8, 2013, Berlin, Germany.

ACM 978-1-4503-2477-9/13/11 ...$15.00.
http://dx.doi.org/10.1145/2508859.2516716.

but from a (potentially untrusted) third party, e.g., a commercial provider or an open source project. This is a common practice and natural consequence of the complexity of modern computer systems. Of course, executing unknown code has several security implications; among others it involves the question whether the executable has some undocumented, unwanted, or hidden functionality [35]. Purposefully (or even unintentionally) the program could for example have an undocumented account that is only available upon specific conditions [2], or offer another kind of remote access to an adversary [3–5]. In the best case, such code does not cause any harm at all, but it is a challenging problem to determine if an unknown piece of (binary) code contains a backdoor. From an attacker's perspective, especially server applications are an interesting target for the deployment of backdoors: such applications are typically remotely reachable and an attacker can abuse them to obtain access to a system that can afterwards be used as a stepping stone to attack further machines within a network. Hence, our focus within this paper lies on network services since we view them as some of the most relevant attack targets.

Towards Prevention of (Software) Backdoors.

While lots of work on implementing and detecting backdoors in hardware has been published recently (e.g., [6, 21, 24, 36]), the area of software backdoors has not received much attention. Previous work in that area has mainly addressed authentication routines. For example, Dai et al. introduced an approach to eliminate backdoors from *response-computable authentication* routines, i.e., the typical challenge-response based authentication [12]. Their idea is to reduce the attack surface by eliminating potential triggers for a backdoor. However, an attacker could still add a backdoor by adding additional command handlers or installing mechanisms that entirely bypass the authentication process in a server application on certain triggers.

To address the problem, the idea of *privilege separation* can be used to split an application into different trust domains (e.g., [9, 30]). Nevertheless, an attacker with broad access to an application's source code can still install backdoors within sufficiently privileged components and thus a certain attack surface remains. The problem is further complicated in cases where we do not have access to source code, but need to perform our analysis on the binary level only.

Automated Identification of Sensitive Components.

In this paper, we address the problem of software backdoors in server applications and introduce an automated way to detect and to disable certain types of backdoors in a given binary program. Our approach consists of three phases:

In the first phase, we identify the specific regions in a given binary that are especially prone to attacks, i.e., the authentication routines and code related to command dispatching and command handling functionality. By closely monitoring the server application while it processes inputs automatically generated according to a protocol specification and analyzing the resulting traces, we can spot these parts in a precise and automated way. We leverage the idea of *delta debugging/differential analysis* [16,40] and introduce an algorithm to identify the relevant regions of a given binary application.

In the second phase, once the initial components of interest are identified, we use this knowledge to determine suspicious components in an application, e.g., hidden command handlers or edges not taken in the control flow graph (CFG) of an authentication routine. To this end, we introduce several heuristics that enable us to determine which code regions are suspicious. Furthermore, we aggregate information that can serve as a starting point for further automated (or manual) investigations.

In an optional third phase, the results from the previous phases can be used to modify or instrument the server application in an automated way such that program parts identified as suspicious are monitored or disabled at runtime. As a side effect, this feature can be used as a flexible way to enable dynamic reconfiguration of server applications for which no source code is available.

Results.

We have implemented our approach to detect and to disable software backdoors in server applications in a tool called WEASEL. For the recording of traces and other runtime analyses, WEASEL employs `gdb`, the standard debugger for the GNU software system. `gdb` is available for a large number of operating systems and hardware architectures and WEASEL currently contains adapter code for x86, x64 and MIPS-32 processor architectures running Linux operating systems, enabling the analysis of a wide range of platforms.

We have successfully tested WEASEL with seven different server applications on different platforms including a widespread corporate VoIP telephone and a popular consumer router. In all cases, we were able to precisely and automatically identify the key program parts involved in the authentication process or the dispatching and handling of commands. We were able to detect known real-world backdoors contained in certain versions of ProFTPD and OpenSSH [2, 15]. Furthermore, as a case study, graduate students from our group have implemented eleven different kinds of backdoors for ProFTPD. Our tool can be used to detect or disable the majority of these artificial backdoors as well. This demonstrates the practical feasibility of the approach to reduce the attack surface for software backdoors.

To demonstrate a potential mitigation approach, WEASEL is also capable of transforming a given binary application to reduce the set of available commands. This is implemented by precisely identifying the command dispatcher functions leveraging automated data structure identification methods [25,31]. Once we have found the specific data structures, we modify them such that certain commands are inaccessible.

In summary, this paper makes the following contributions:

- We introduce an automated way to identify critical parts in server applications that are typically prone to backdoors. We show how this information can be used a) to detect backdoors and hidden functionality and b) to reduce the attack surface for backdoors in legacy binary software.
- We implemented our techniques in a tool called WEASEL for x86, x64 and MIPS32 systems running different versions of Linux. The code is freely available at `https://github.com/flxflx/weasel`.
- We show how several real-world backdoors for ProFTPD and OpenSSH can be successfully discovered using our techniques. Furthermore, we evaluated our techniques with other examples of binary programs on different platforms, including COTS embedded devices.

2. RELATED WORK

Backdoors in computer systems are a well-known security problem. Over the last few years, the security community has mainly focused on backdoors in integrated circuits and ways to detect or implement such hardware backdoors [6,19, 21,24,33,34,36]. Furthermore, several backdoors in different components of a computer such as network cards [32] or directly in the CPU [14] were proposed. Our approach is orthogonal to such work since we focus on the detection of backdoors on the binary level, an area that has received almost no attention so far.

Wysopal et al. [37] presented a pattern-based, static analysis approach to identify backdoors in software. The main limitation is that patterns need to be specified in advance, which implies that potential backdoors need to be known before the analysis can be carried out. Nevertheless, the results delivered by our tool could be used to improve the accuracy of such a static analysis approach: for example, a static ASCII string should be more likely to represent a static password when it is referenced in or close to a function identified to be involved in the authentication process of an application.

Geneiatakis et al. [18] recently proposed a similar (although not backdoor-related) technique to ours to identify *authentication-points* in server applications using Intel's *Pin* tool [26]. Our approach can be applied to a broader range of platforms and environments and is fully automated. In fact, our implementation only requires a remote `gdb` instance to connect to and automatically collects all required traces on function and basic block level, while invoking the corresponding server application repeatedly without requiring any supervision. By only relying on `gdb`, we are able to analyze software on COTS embedded devices such as routers or VoIP telephones without special effort. We think that this is especially useful in the context of backdoors given the often high criticality of such devices and the rather large amount of corresponding backdoors publicly reported lately [3–5]. Furthermore, we consider *implicit edges* in the CFG of a function induced by conditional instructions as described in Section 4, a problem not addressed in prior work.

A basic insight for backdoor detection is that some kind of trigger needs to be present such that an attacker can activate the backdoor. As a result, work on automated identification or silencing of triggers is also related to our work. Brumley et al. [10] demonstrated how trigger-based behavior in malware can be identified and Dai et al. introduced an approach to eliminate backdoors from *response-computable authentication* routines, i.e., the typical challenge-response based authentication [12]. While such approaches reduce the attack surface, an attacker can still implement a backdoor and bypass the approach (e.g., by adding additional command handlers or completely bypassing the authentication process). Our approach complements such approaches and helps to reduce the attack surface even further.

Somewhat related to our approach is the idea of *privilege separation*, i.e., the process of splitting an application into different trust domains [9, 11, 22, 28, 30, 39]. Note that such approaches do not completely mitigate the risk of backdoors since an attacker can still install backdoors within sufficiently privileged components. The backdoors for SSH servers analyzed in Section 5 demonstrate that this is indeed a problem in practice.

3. APPROACH

We now provide a high-level overview of our approach before presenting implementation details in the next section.

3.1 Attacker Model for Software Backdoors

There are many different mechanisms an attacker can use to bypass implemented security mechanisms. To narrow down the scope of the discussions, we first define the term *backdoor* in the context of this paper to illustrate the capabilities of an attacker:

Definition: *A backdoor is a hidden, undocumented, and unwanted program or a program modification/manipulation that on certain triggers bypasses security mechanisms or performs unwanted/undocumented malicious actions.*

The definition should be seen as an intuitive and tangible description of what a backdoor is. Note that a backdoor can be either *intentional* or *unintentional*, depending on whether it was created on purpose or as a dangerous side-effect of some other "harmless" activity (e.g., debugging access with elevated privileges that is not disabled in the release version of a product). Naturally, there are unlimited ways how an attacker can implement a backdoor in a given software system: an adversary can for example purposely introduce buffer overflow vulnerabilities or flawed cryptographic modules, both of which complicate the analysis significantly. In general, the problem of detecting software backdoors is undecidable and thus we strive for an automated way to at least reduce the attack surface and detect certain cases of backdoors in practice.

For the remainder of this paper, we focus on the following classes of backdoors as part of our attacker model:

- flawed authentication routines
- hidden commands and services

In fact, most of the recently publicly disclosed backdoors fall into these two classes [2–5, 15, 20, 27] and thus we think that this constraint for the problem space is reasonable.

Running Example.

As our running example, we illustrate a backdoor that attackers added to the ProFTPD server. This example highlights the challenges we face and explains some of the issues we have to deal with. Note that the example is in C code, while we perform our analysis on the binary level.

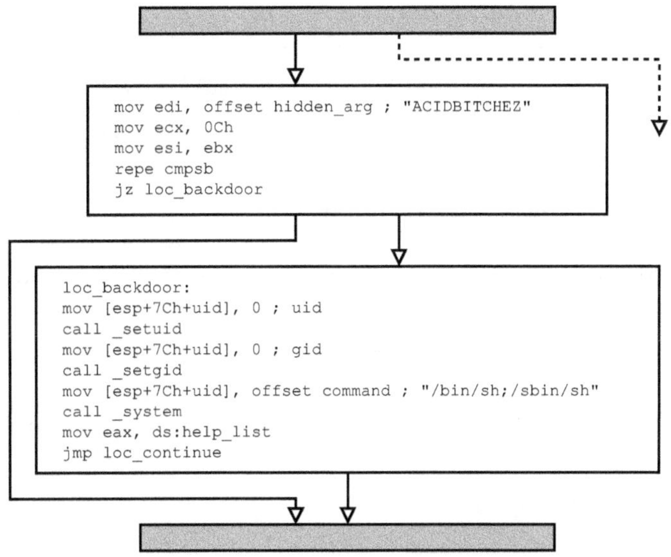

Figure 1: The two additional basic blocks in the flow graph of the function *pr_help_add_response()* in ProFTPD implementing the `ACIDBITCHEZ` backdoor

At the end of November 2010, the distribution server of the ProFTPD project was compromised and a snippet of code was added to one of the source files of ProFTPD 1.3.3c [2]. In essence, a function responsible for the processing of the standard FTP command HELP was modified in such a way that passing the argument **`ACIDBITCHEZ`** would result in immediate privileged access to the corresponding system (a *root shell*) for an unauthenticated user. The actual malicious code introduced by the attacker is shown in Listing 1. The backdoor was (likely manually) detected about three days later and then eliminated by removing the changes.

Listing 1: Backdoor in ProFTPD server

```
if (strcmp(target,"ACIDBITCHEZ") == 0)
{
  setuid(0);
  setgid(0);
  system("/bin/sh;/sbin/sh");
}
```

The central goal of our approach is to automatically identify such harmful extensions. The scope of our approach is limited to binary code, mainly since we often do not have access to source code.

Malicious additions to binary software can often be reliably detected by static analysis techniques [16] when at least one supposedly benign version of the software is available. Typically the deployment of a simple backdoor introduces a handful of additional basic blocks to the CFG of a function that handles external inputs. Figure 1 depicts the malicious addition to the CFG of the function **`pr_help_add_response()`** in ProFTPD that constitutes the backdoor of our running example. In such a case, binary software comparison approaches [16, 17] are likely capable to detect these suspicious code regions. Unfortunately, in practice we typically do not have access to such a version that can reliably be trusted for most software systems. This is why our approach does not rely on the existence of such a version. Instead, we examine the behavior of a single version of binary software at runtime and apply techniques that extend the idea of Zeller's *delta debugging* approach [40] on binary level as explained in the following.

3.2 Analysis Approach

We argue that there are four parts of a server application that are generically prone to the two backdoor classes in our focus. These parts are:

- authentication validation code
- specific authentication validation result handling code (e.g., code that terminates a session in case of invalid credentials)
- command parsing code
- specific command handling code

To identify these parts in a given server application, we record runtime traces for multiple different inputs and compare them. The intuition behind this approach is the following: consider for example the authentication mechanism of a server application such as ProFTPD. By definition, the purpose of each authentication mechanism is to decide whether or not a third party sufficiently proved its identity to qualify for legitimate elevation of privilege. The process is similar in case of command dispatching: different operations are performed for different commands and arguments. In order to behave differently for different inputs, a server application in general needs at one point during runtime to leave the common execution path and follow an exclusive execution path accordingly[1]. By comparing control flow traces for various inputs, it is possible to determine *common* execution paths and those that are *exclusive* to a certain group of inputs. In the next step, it is often possible to determine *deciders* and *handlers* on function or on basic block level. In the case of the authentication process, *deciders* perform the actual authentication validation, while *handlers* process the validation result. In the case of the command dispatching process, *deciders* parse and dispatch commands, while *handlers* implement the commands' specific functionality.

In general, the following possibilities exist for a server application to implement exclusive execution paths for different inputs:

C1 through exclusive function invocations

C2 through exclusive paths inside commonly invoked functions (i.e., exclusive basic blocks)

C3 without exclusive program parts, but through an exclusive execution order of common functions and basic blocks

In our empirical studies of different server applications we found that the two cases C1 and C2 are by far the most common in practice. Case C3 is not entirely unlikely to be encountered, though: consider for example a server application implementing the available commands in an internal scripting language. Runtime traces both on function and on basic block level for different inputs of such a server application would differ, but possibly not contain any exclusive program parts.

Cases C1 and C2 will receive the most attention for the rest of this work. An intuitive and straightforward approach for the identification of *handlers* and *deciders* in these cases is the following: Given two traces T_0 and T_1 for different inputs (e.g., valid password and invalid password), *handlers* can be identified by determining the set of exclusive functions/basic blocks for each of the two traces: $S_{T_0,ex} = S_{T_0} \setminus S_{T_1}$ and $S_{T_1,ex} = S_{T_1} \setminus S_{T_0}$. In turn, the corresponding *deciders* are necessarily in $S_{common} = S_{T_0} \cap S_{T_1}$ and are likely parents of exclusive functions/basic blocks in $S_{ex} = S_{T_0,ex} \cup S_{T_1,ex}$.

Built upon this basic idea for the identification of *deciders* and *handlers*, we have developed the algorithm A-WEASEL which is described in the following.

3.2.1 The A-WEASEL Algorithm

The A-WEASEL algorithm is an integral part of our approach. It is described in detail in Appendix A and we provide a high-level overview now. The algorithm starts working on function level traces only since they can be collected on virtually any platform where `gdb` (but possibly no instrumentation solution like Pin) is available in a straightforward and efficient way. Basic block level traces are collected as needed.

Given a set of traces of a server application on function level for different *protocol runs* (e.g., traces for different FTP commands), we recursively compute a combined *decision tree* composed of *deciders* and top-level *handlers* as depicted in Figure 2. Handlers are initially identified by simply determining the set $S_{T,ex} = S_T \setminus S_{common}$ of exclusive functions for each trace and can be shared between multiple traces. For each identified decider (or handler shared between multiple traces) on function level, traces on basic block level are recorded dynamically for all corresponding protocol runs[2]. Given these basic block traces, we compute the *internal decision tree* of the respective function. For example in Figure 2 the internal decision tree of the decider function **z** is generated from corresponding basic block level traces for protocol runs 1 and 2. A-WEASEL is recursively invoked with the applying set of function level sub-traces for each identified decider function.

A-WEASEL reliably determines the decision tree for a given set of traces, though it is only applicable for the aforementioned server application implementation case C1 or a combination of cases C1 and C2. This is due to the algorithm depending on the identification of exclusive handlers: if there are no functions that are exclusive to a certain subset of all traces, no handlers can be identified (and as a consequence, no deciders as well). In order to cope with server applications that are implemented strictly according to cases C2 and C3 as well and to improve overall results, we implemented a set of additional algorithms in WEASEL that are outlined in the following.

[1]One could probably draw scenarios where the different features of a server application are entirely implemented by differences in the data flow only and not in the control flow. Due to the lack of real-world relevance of such scenarios, they are not considered further here.

[2]We record basic block level traces of functions in a call stack sensitive manner. This way we can ensure that only the certain invocations of interest of a function are examined on basic block level.

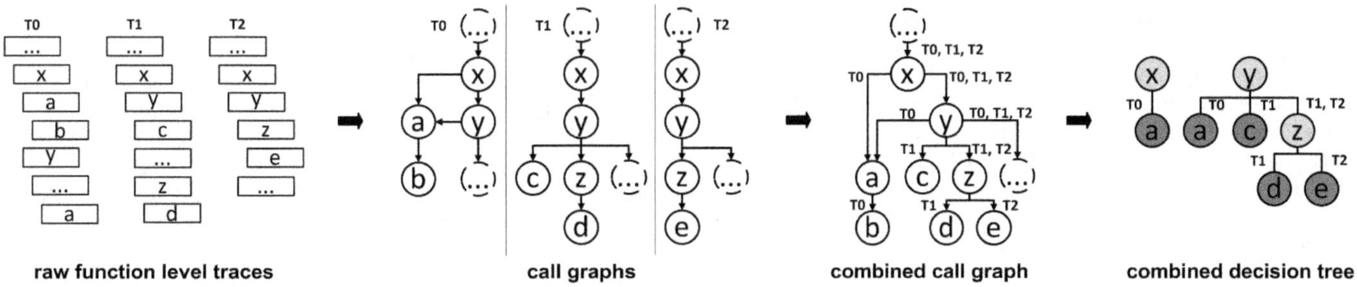

Figure 2: Schematic derivation of the *decision tree* (right) from the examplary function level traces $T1$, $T2$ and $T3$ (left). The functions a, b, c, d, e and z are not contained in all traces and are thus *exclusive* to certain traces. The functions x, y and z are *deciders*, while a, c, d and e are top-level *handlers*.

Differential Return Value Comparison.

A major drawback of A-WEASEL is that it fails to identify *decider* and *handler* functions when decisions made at runtime only manifest in differences in the execution flow on basic block level. To cope with this problem, WEASEL records exactly two traces for each protocol run. Functions with different return values in both traces are added to the set of functions to ignore. This way, irrelevant functions in our context such as `malloc()` or `time()` are filtered out. Functions with the same return value in both traces, but different return values between different protocol runs, are treated as handlers by A-WEASEL. By applying this technique, A-WEASEL for example correctly identifies the function `sys_auth_passwd()` as decider in the authentication process of OpenSSH (see Section 5.1.1), which it would have not otherwise. Though there are numerous ways a function can signal its outcome to its caller, the described technique only takes immediate return values of functions into account.

Scoring Heuristics.

WEASEL contains a set of simple heuristic scoring algorithms that aim at identifying *deciders* and estimating their importance by comparing the structure of the call graphs of a given set of traces. The algorithms are used to rank the importance of *deciders* identified by A-WEASEL. Besides, they can partly serve as a fall back when server applications are encountered that do not implement exclusive functionality through exclusive function invocations (cases C2 and C3 as discussed above). All algorithms have in common that they require a *reference trace* which the other traces are compared to. When examining the authentication process, the trace for valid credentials serves as reference trace, while in the case of the command dispatching process a specially recorded trace for a knowingly invalid command serves this purpose.

For instance, one algorithm attempts to remove loops from all traces, determines the longest common subsequence of calls between all traces and the reference trace and assigns scores to functions according to their positions in the common sub-sequences (scores increase towards the end as those functions are believed to be more likely to be responsible for the decision to split execution paths). An even simpler algorithm assigns scores to deciders linear to the amount of exclusive children. The scores assigned to functions by the different algorithms are summed up.

3.3 Application of Analysis Results

Once the *deciders* as well as the *handlers* are known for the authentication or the command dispatching process of a server application, further analysis can be conducted. The goal is to identify possible backdoors and to enable the hardening of legacy binary applications.

3.3.1 Discovering Suspicious Program Paths

When the functions or basic blocks handling a successful authentication or a certain command are known, we can apply existing methods of static and dynamic binary analysis for the detection of backdoors. A straightforward approach which we apply here is the static enumeration and comparison of all syscalls and external library calls reachable in the static call graph from identified handlers (we utilize the third party tool *IDA Pro* for this). For example, even invocations of `socket()` or `send()` should be considered suspicious when they are only referenced from one of multiple handlers. In the case of our running example, the installed backdoor in the HELP command can be identified this way (see Section 5.2 for a detailed discussion). Moreover, identified deciders and handlers can be used as starting points for more complicated analysis techniques such as *symbolic execution* [23]. Starting symbolic execution at the entry-point of identified handler code should in many cases – and especially for complex software such as ProFTPD – deliver better and more cost-effective results than approaches examining an entire application. In order to be able to apply techniques of symbolic execution, one of course always needs to declare certain memory as symbolic. Identifying memory regions that are worthwhile to declare as symbolic poses a challenge when examining single functions. To tackle this problem, we have implemented an analysis module for WEASEL that compares the arguments of identified deciders in different traces and heuristically searches for differences (see Section 4.2.2). In the case of a typical password validation function it is then for example possible to determine that certain arguments are pointers to memory regions with varying contents (e.g., username and password). In the next step, these memory regions could be marked as symbolic when analyzing the respective function with symbolic execution techniques.

3.3.2 Disabling Functionality

One can very well think of scenarios where it is desirable to disable certain functionality of a legacy server application. For example it might be known that certain commands are vulnerable to attacks. Instead of shutting the whole service down or applying error-prone filtering on the network level, our approach allows for the disabling of single commands by means of binary instrumentation or binary rewriting. In the case of our running example, effective protection can already be achieved by simply writing an illegal instruction at the start of the handler for the HELP command, causing the respective fork of the server to crash and exit when the command is issued.

Backdoors in the authentication process, like for example hardcoded credentials, often manifest in additional edges and nodes in the CFG of one of the involved decider functions. These additional edges and nodes are usually not contained in any recorded basic block trace for legitimate input. We call such edges "cold". For complex software, cold edges and nodes are only a rather weak indication for the presence of a backdoor, as there are usually many benign basic blocks that are only visited under rare conditions. Nevertheless, knowledge of cold edges in decider functions of the authentication process can be used to increase the protection level of applications: techniques for binary instrumentation or rewriting can for example be used to log access to edges identified as *cold* during runtime over a longer period. In case an edge is taken for the first time, an alert can be triggered and the incident can be investigated. In practice, we suggest the utilization of a training phase during which additional benign paths are discovered and successively enabled before the final rewriting/instrumenting takes place. Entirely disabling cold edges in decider functions might severely weaken the security of an application, e.g., the protection against password brute-forcing could be rendered non-functional. In the following, we use the term of "cutting an edge" in order to refer to the monitoring or disabling of an edge.

Another application of our approach is the identification and elimination of undocumented commands. Command deciders of server applications of classes C1 or C2 dispatch recognized commands either through conditional and static (e.g., JZ OFFSET) or dynamic (e.g., CALL EAX) branches to their designated handlers. The latter is the case for our running example: when a command is recognized in ProFTPD, a *C* structure describing it is loaded from a static table. Each such structure contains a pointer to the handler function for the corresponding command, which is called by the decider/dispatcher through a CALL EAX instruction. For server applications built in a similar way, two interesting measures become possible on top of our basic approach:

- Once several command handlers are known, a likely location and size of the table(s) holding the command-describing structures in memory can be determined. In the next step, it is possible to identify all available commands and unwanted commands can easily be eliminated using techniques of binary instrumentation or rewriting.
- Once the point of execution is known where the control flow is dynamically transferred to a command handler, techniques of binary instrumentation or rewriting can be used to prevent the execution of unknown or unwanted command handlers.

We have developed a module for our analysis framework that heuristically checks for tables containing command descriptors given a set of pointers to command handlers (see Section 4.2).

3.3.3 Enforcing Authentication

When deciders and handlers of the authentication process of an application can be linked to certain authentication levels, it becomes possible to determine the authentication level of an active session by examining the execution flow of the corresponding thread at runtime. Combined with the knowledge of whereabouts of command handlers, fine-grained access control or defense mechanisms such as *shadow authentication* [13] can be realized. In our running example, it would be possible to limit the availability of the HELP command to those threads that were observed successfully authenticating before.

4. IMPLEMENTATION

The core of the analysis framework WEASEL is our library PYGDB. It is written for Python 2.7 and implements a client for the *GDB Remote Serial Protocol* [1] and thus needs to be connected to a remote `gdbserver` instance. PYGDB supports all basic debugging tasks from setting breakpoints to following forks. Currently our software supports environments running Linux on x86, x64, or MIPS32 platforms.

The tracing engine is built on top of PYGDB and supports tracing on function as well as on basic block level. As PYGDB is designed to not include comprehensive disassemblers for its supported platforms, basic blocks are initially identified by stepping single instructions.

The tracer is aware of *implicit edges* in the CFG induced by conditional instructions and records *virtual basic blocks* accordingly. To understand the need for this consider the x86 conditional move instruction `CMOVZ`: data is only moved from the source to the destination operand in case the *zero-flag* is set (e.g., as the result of a compare operation). Compilers use such instructions to efficiently translate simple *if-then* constructs. Taking this into account can be crucial for successfully detecting and disabling backdoors (see Sections 5.1.1 and 5.2).

4.1 Protocol Player

In order to fully automate the analysis process, we developed a system for the specification and playback of protocols. Similar to existing work in the realm of fuzz testing of software [7,8], we describe protocols in a block-based manner according to their specifications. The blocks describing a protocol are ordered in *levels* and are grouped by *strings* and *privilege levels*. Our description of the FTP protocol according to RFC 959 [29] for example possesses nine levels, the strings CMDARG0, CMDARG1 and CMDARG2 and the privilege levels NOAUTH, ANONYMOUS and AUTH.

Before traces of a certain server application are recorded, the corresponding *protocol description* is compiled to a set of specific *protocol scripts*. Compiled scripts are solely built of the atoms PUSH_DATA, SEND, RECV and WAIT, and the virtual atoms START_RECORDING and STOP_RECORDING. The last two are automatically inserted by the *protocol compiler* before and after the atoms of interest. When the *protocol processor* encounters one of them while playing the protocol, it activates/deactivates the tracer. We thus ensure that as little noise as possible is recorded. In order to be able to describe interactive elements in protocols (such as for example the PING/PONG messages in the IRC protocol), each atom can dynamically yield new atoms in reaction to the state of the protocol run.

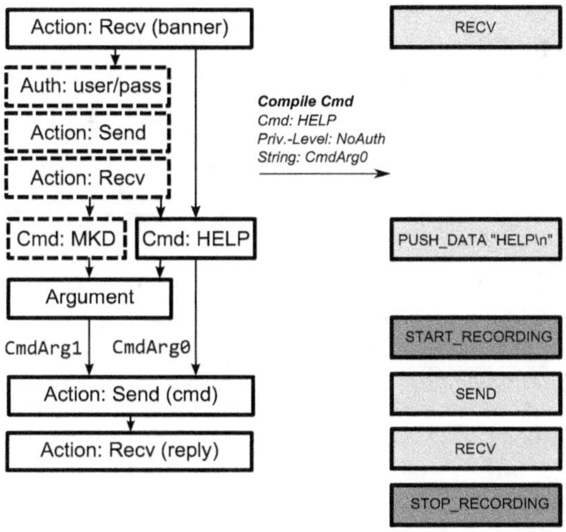

Figure 3: Scheme of the description of the FTP protocol (two commands) and the correspond compiled script of the command HELP. Blocks not available for privilege level NoAuth are dashed. Atoms are gray. Virtual atoms are dark-gray.

Figure 3 schematically shows the description of two commands of the FTP protocol: the command HELP accepts none or one argument. Accordingly, it belongs to the strings CmdArg0 and CmdArg1. As the command is available in any session – unauthenticated as well as authenticated – it belongs to all three privilege levels. In contrast, the command MKD belongs to the privilege levels Anonymous and Authenticated, and solely the string CmdArg1 as it expects one argument and is only available in authenticated sessions.

4.2 Analysis Modules

We implemented two analysis modules that work on the results delivered by the A-WEASEL analysis algorithms described in Section 3.

4.2.1 Function Pointer Table Identifier

Many server applications written in C/C++ store command descriptors including pointers to *handler* functions in central data structures such as arrays. We have implemented an analysis module that scans the memory of a server application at runtime for pointers to previously identified handler functions. When the distance in memory between several identified pointers to handler functions is of equal size, we assume that a table of command descriptors was found (compare [25, 31]). In the next step, we attempt to heuristically determine the beginning and end of the respective table. Once such a table is identified it is possible to check for pointers to unknown command handlers and thus identify undocumented commands.

4.2.2 Differential Function Arguments Identifier

There are several scenarios in which it might be desirable to identify those arguments of a *decider* function that are protocol run specific (see Section 3.3.1). A simple example is a password validation function that expects (among other not session specific arguments) pointers to both the username and the password entered by a user. We implemented an analysis module that – given the list of decider functions of a server application – tries to heuristically identify such arguments. The module replays the different protocol runs and examines the stack at the entrance to the given decider functions in a differential manner. The module thus only works for calling conventions passing arguments on the stack. The module distinguishes between *data* and *pointers* and tries to identify pointers by dereferencing values in memory and checks if the resulting address resides in the same type of memory for each protocol run. Thereby, the module differentiates between the following types of memory: stack, heap, and binary image. If a value in memory is found to be pointing to the same type of accessible memory for each protocol run, it is assumed that it is in fact a pointer. Otherwise it is assumed to be plain data. In this case, the data is compared between all protocol runs. In case of any difference, the argument is marked as protocol run specific. The analysis module follows alleged pointers up to a certain level of depth. This way it is possible to identify protocol run specific arguments passed inside of nested data structures.

5. EVALUATION

To demonstrate the practical feasibility of our approach, we evaluated our analysis framework Weasel with several open and closed source server applications for different protocols and platforms. The results are briefly summarized in Table 1. All applications were tested in a standard configuration. For the sake of simplicity, Weasel was limited to only consider traces of login attempts for the following cases: Valid username/valid password (*valid-pw*) and valid username/invalid password (*invalid-pw*). In its default configuration, Weasel also considers the third case of an invalid username. This can for example be useful for the detection of backdoors triggering on certain usernames. The amount of function call events in a single trace ranged from 3 (BusyBox Telnetd authentication) to 12,335 (ProFTPD command dispatching). Due to space constraints, we discuss the test results of only three server applications in more detail in the following. For the other four applications, the test results were satisfactory to the extent that Weasel correctly identified handlers and deciders of both the authentication and the command dispatching process with little to no noise.

5.1 Detailed Analysis of SSH Servers

Due to their practical relevance, we first focus on software backdoors for SSH server implementations. The description of our SSH protocol is limited to the *SSH Authentication Protocol* (SSH-AUTH) according to RFC 4252 [38]. Other aspects of the SSH protocol, such as the transport layer, are not considered for our purposes. RFC 4252 specifies the following authentication methods for SSH-AUTH: *password*, *publickey*, *hostbased*, and *none*. The corresponding protocol specification in Weasel treats these four methods as commands.

5.1.1 OpenSSH (x64)

For OpenSSH we chose a version that was recently reported by an antivirus vendor to have been found in the wild containing the following backdoors [15]:

Table 1: **Overview of evaluation results for various server applications. The *decision tree* column describes the calculated command dispatching and authentication decision trees in the form <*number of decider functions*>/<*number of handler functions*>.**

Server	Platform	Protocol	Dec. Tree (Cmd, Auth)	Remarks
BusyBox Telnetd	MIPS32 (D-Link DIR-300)	Telnet	1/0, 0/0	Does not support Telnet commands (IAC).
Dropbear SSH	MIPS32 (Siemens Open-Stage 40)	SSH-AUTH	3/9, 1/2	See Section 5.1.2
OpenSSH	x64	SSH-AUTH	2/2, 4/7 (monitor proc.) 2/3, 3/3 (slave proc.)	See Section 5.1.1
ProFTPD	MIPS32, x86, x64	FTP	6/60, 5/37 (x64)	See Section 5.2
Pure-FTPd	x64	FTP	2/29, 1/11	Results similar to unmodified ProFTPD
NcFTPD (closed source)	x86, x64	FTP	4/40, 2/11 (x64)	Results similar to unmodified ProFTPD
Dancer-IRCD	x64	IRC	2/28, 2/12	Command handler table automatically identified.

X1 On startup, the server sends the hostname and port on which it is listening to remote web hosts presumingly controlled by the attackers.

X2 A master password enables logins under arbitrary accounts without knowledge of the actual corresponding passwords (*password* and *keyboard-interactive* authentication).

X3 A master public key enables logins under arbitrary accounts with knowledge of the corresponding private key (*publickey* authentication).

X4 Credentials used in any successful login attempts are sent to the remote web hosts (*password* and *keyboard-interactive* authentication).

As no source code is publicly available for this malicious version of OpenSSH, we had to limit our evaluation to the x64 platform. Due to the privilege separating architecture of OpenSSH [30], WEASEL automatically generates decision trees for two processes: a privileged process called *monitor* and an unprivileged process called *slave*.

Authentication.

Backdoor X4 can be easily spotted from the decision tree of the monitor process for the SSH *password* authentication as depicted in Figure 4. The decision tree only contains the decider functions located at virtual addresses `40B440h` (`auth_password()`), `420E20h` (`mm_answer_authpassword()`), `412EB0h` (`auth_log()`), and `40B390h` (`sys_auth_passwd()`) in the binary file[3]. The scoring algorithms of WEASEL rank the decider `auth_password()` as most important. It leads to five exclusive handlers for *valid-pw* that are all called from the same handler basic block and implement backdoor X4. Of these exclusive handlers, the one at addresses `43BF50h` can automatically be identified as highly suspicious, as it (among others) statically calls the functions `socket()`, `connect()` and `write()`. Manual analysis reveals that this handler function attempts to send data to remote web hosts. Correspondingly, the handler function at address `43BAF0h` implements URL encoding of strings.

The basic block level decision tree of `auth_password()` contains 13 deciders and two exclusive handlers for the *valid-pw* protocol run (see Figure 4). While one of the handlers contains backdoor X4 as described above, the other handler is a legitimate virtual basic block induced by the conditional assembly instruction `SETNZ DL`, which sets the return value of the function according to the validity of the password. Of the 13 deciders in the basic block level decision tree, eleven are cold. Most importantly, these cold edges are related to the optional PAM authentication[4], password expiration handling and backdoor X2 (*master password*). The attacker implemented this backdoor by adding a short piece of code at the beginning of `auth_password()`: each password to check is compared to a predefined one. In case of a match, the function returns, falsely indicating a successful authentication to its caller. The backdoor is automatically rendered inoperative by *cutting* (see Section 3.3.2) the cold edges in `auth_password()`. As WEASEL's protocol description of SSH-AUTH does not cover the *publickey* authentication method, we cannot find the backdoor X3. Note that this is only a limitation of the current protocol description as the implementations of backdoor X3 and backdoor X2 are very similar on assembler level. WEASEL cannot be used to identify backdoor X1 (*notification of remote web hosts on startup*), because it is designed to only examine the authentication and command dispatching processes of server applications.

The decision tree of the slave process is not depicted. It consists of three deciders, two handlers for *invalid-pw* and a single handler for *valid-pw*. As static analysis hints at nothing suspicious in these functions, the slave process is not further discussed here.

Command Dispatching.

As for the authentication, command dispatching in OpenSSH stretches over a monitor and a slave process. For the slave process, WEASEL identifies only the function at `414960h` (`input_userauth_request()`) as decider. Also, the deci-

[3]The actual malicious binary file does not contain debugging symbols and thus names of function cannot be obtained directly. For reasons of clearness, the names of functions of interest for this paper were manually resolved by comparing assembly code and OpenSSH source code.

[4]Code path related to PAM were not taken during testing, as PAM was not enabled in our employed default configuration.

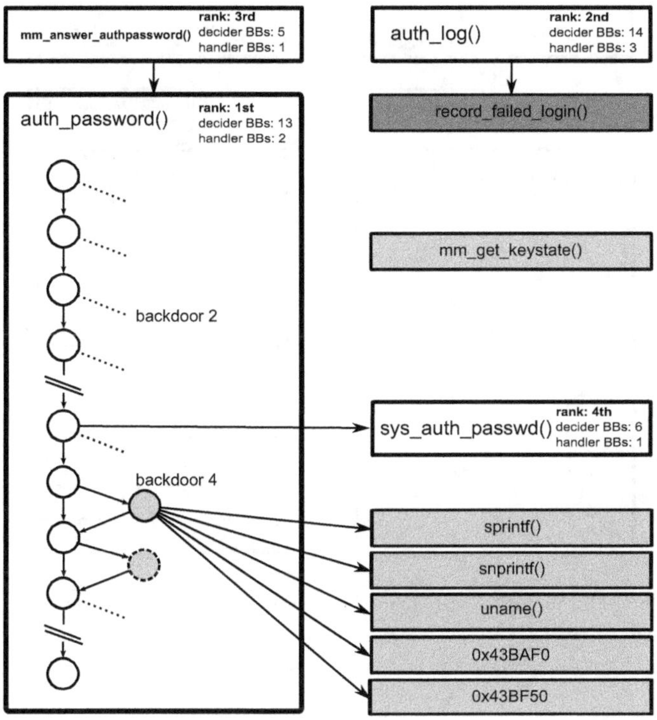

Figure 4: Decision tree for the password authentication in the monitor process of the malicious version of OpenSSH. Functions are rectangles, basic blocks are circles. Deciders are white, handlers for *valid-pw* are gray, handlers for *invalid-pw* are dark-gray. Cold edges are dotted.

sion tree of the slave process only contains exclusive handler functions for the protocol runs of the commands *password*, *publickey* and *none*: `41BF00h` (`userauth_passwd()`), `41CA50h`(`userauth_pubkey()`) and `41BE20h` (`userauth_none()`), respectively. These results suggests that the *host-based* authentication method is disabled – a circumstance that can be verified by manual analysis. Based on this results, WEASEL's analysis module that heuristically scans for function pointer tables as described in Section 4.2 automatically and unambiguously identifies the correct address and size of the command descriptor table in the `.data` section of the binary file, spanning from virtual address `674678h` to `6746f8h`. The table, which is defined in the OpenSSH source code under the identifier `authmethods`, contains simple structures of three members (*name*, *handler function*, *enabled flag*) describing all available authentication methods of the server. Interestingly, the analysis module identifies two handler functions not contained in any of the collected traces: `41BD40h`(`userauth_kbdint()`) and `41B9F0h` (`userauth_hostbased()`). While the latter belongs to the disabled authentication method *hostbased*, the former belongs to the well-known authentication method *keyboard-interactive* which is not described in RFC 4252 (and suffers as well from backdoors X2 and X4). This demonstrates the ability of WEASEL to identify handlers for unknown commands. The decision tree of the monitor process contains only the monitor-side handler function for the *password* authentication method. We do not discuss it further due to space restrictions.

5.1.2 Dropbear SSH (MIPS32)

We examined a binary-only version of Dropbear SSH server shipped as part of the firmware of the Siemens VoIP desk telephone *OpenStage 40*. Function and basic block traces were recorded remotely on the embedded hardware. We were able to automatically and unambiguously identify important deciders and handlers in both the authentication and the command dispatching process of the SSH server.

Authentication.

The rather small decision tree computed from the *valid-pw* and *invalid-pw* protocol runs is depicted in Figure 5.

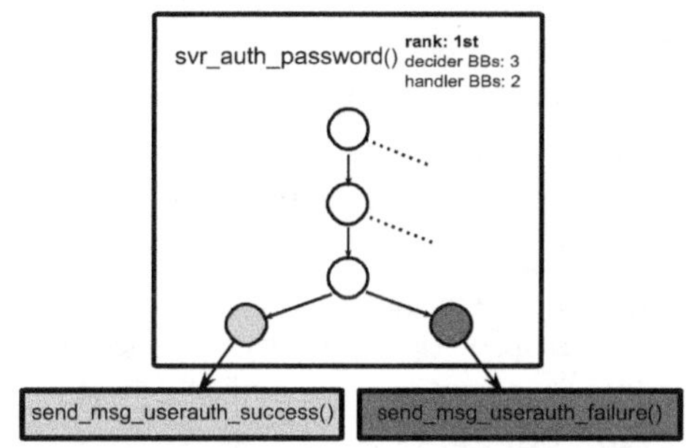

Figure 5: Decision tree of the authentication process of Dropbear SSH.

The only identified decider `svr_auth_password()` evaluates the correctness of a password by a simple string comparison and, depending on the outcome, subsequently calls one of the two identified handlers. No suspicious external functions are reachable from either handler.

Command Dispatching.

The decision tree computed from the protocol runs corresponding to the four authentication methods of the SSH-AUTH protocol contains three deciders, with `recv_msg_userauth_request()` ranking first. From this decider, the only exclusive handlers `svr_auth_password()` and `svr_auth_pubkey()` are called, which belong to the *password* and the *publickey* authentication method, respectively. The application does not contain exclusive handlers for the other authentication methods. As Dropbear SSH in general does not dispatch commands via function pointer tables, WEASEL does in this case correctly not recognize any function pointer tables of interest. The two identified exclusive handler functions were not found to lead to any suspicious calls.

5.2 ProFTPD (x86, x64, MIPS32)

Graduate students from our group not related to this project were asked to implement an arbitrary set of backdoors for ProFTPD in addition to the real-world backdoor of our running example. We have chosen ProFTPD since it is a complex program (e.g., FTP is a non-trivial protocol, it contains different software modules, and there were real-world attacks against this program) but still has a manageable code base. Altogether, eleven different backdoors were developed in a not supervised manner.

Seven out of these eleven backdoors interfere with the authentication or command dispatching process of ProFTPD and can thus theoretically be identified using WEASEL. The other four backdoors implement malicious functionality like a covert out-of-band interactive shell that cannot be found by applying the described detection approach. We thus evaluate WEASEL on the following set of backdoors containing the seven artificial backdoors and our running example:

- Y1 *Acidbitchez*: our real-world running example.
- Y2 *Happy hour*: at a certain time of day all passwords are accepted by the server.
- Y3 *Blessed one*: for a certain client IP address all passwords are accepted.
- Y4 *File access*: hidden commands for unauthorized file access bypassing the authentication process.
- Y5 *Credentials stealing 1*: validated credentials are stored and made available via a hidden command.
- Y6 *Credentials stealing 2*: validated credentials are sent via DNS requests to a remote server.
- Y7 *Self-modifying authentication*: in case of a certain process ID, the central authentication function is rewritten on startup of the application to accept arbitrary passwords.
- Y8 *Authentication module*: a malicious auth. module.

We analyzed a version of ProFTPD containing this backdoors on WEASEL's supported platforms x86, x64 and MIPS-32. Since the high-level results were identical for all platforms, we discuss them together (concrete numbers apply at least to the x64 version). We demonstrate that it is possible to reliably detect or to disable backdoors Y1–Y6, substantiating our approach to reduce the attack surface.

We cannot cope with backdoors Y7 and Y8: Backdoor Y7 can only be detected when during testing by chance a case is encountered where the authentication function is actually being overwritten (i.e., the backdoor triggers on a certain process ID). Backdoor Y8 can not be identified as WEASEL currently does not evaluate dynamically loaded modules.

Authentication.

The decision tree computed from the *valid-pw* and *invalid-pw* protocol runs is depicted in Figure 6. On the function level, four deciders are identified, with **auth_pass()** with 78 deciders on basic block level, 25 handler functions for *valid-pw* and the 1st scoring rank being clearly dominant. Though, three of the eleven backdoors are located in the decider function **pr_auth_authenticate()**, which only leads to a single handler function (**do_back()**) for *valid-pw*. This handler function belongs to backdoor Y6 and stores credentials once they are successfully validated. The function can automatically be identified as highly suspicious, as it (among other activities) statically calls the standard functions **mmap()**, **shm_open()**, **socket()**, and **sendto()**. Two of the nine cold decider basic blocks in **pr_auth_authenticate()** lead to the implementations of backdoors Y2 and Y3, respectively. Thus cutting cold edges in the identified deciders would effectively render these backdoors non-functional.

In the x86 version of our modified ProFTPD server the code implementing the "happy hour" backdoor (Y2) in **pr_auth_authenticate()** uses the conditional instruction **CMOVZ** to manipulate the outcome of the function. This underlines the need to consider *implicit edges* when examining a function's CFG since we would otherwise overlook this case.

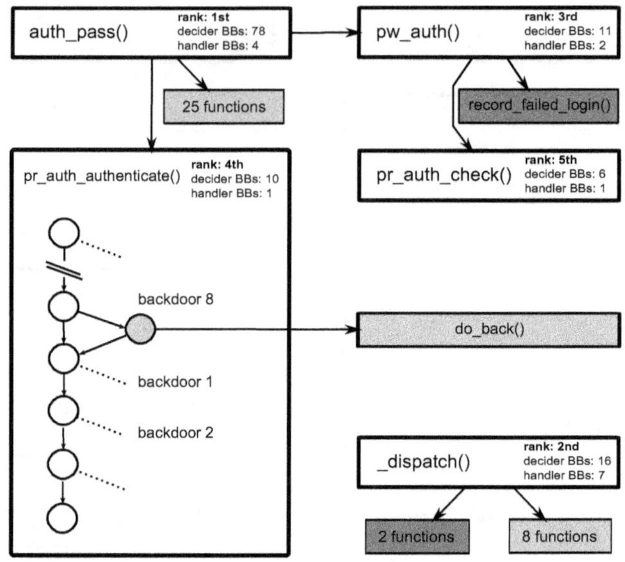

Figure 6: Decision tree of the authentication process of ProFTPD.

Command Dispatching.

WEASEL's protocol description of FTP was modelled according to RFC 959 [29] and contains 34 commands (e.g., **HELP** and **MKD**). The function level decision tree consists of six deciders (of which **pr_cmd_dispatch_phase()** ranks 1st) and 60 handlers. Out of those handlers, 43 are exclusive to a single protocol run. By manual analysis it can be verified that these exclusive handlers indeed implement each of the 34 commands. For the majority of commands there exists exactly one exclusive handler. Subsequently, it is easily possible to automatically identify the backdoor of our running example (Y1): among the external functions reachable from **HELP** command's only exclusive handler **core_help()** in the static CFG are the aforementioned in this context highly suspicious ones **setegid()**, **seteuid()** and **system()**. Accordingly, the corresponding **HELP** command can be identified as suspicious and further defensive measures can be applied.

WEASEL automatically and correctly identifies the addresses and sizes of exactly five function pointer tables in the address space of the respective ProFTPD process: **core_cmdtab**, **xfer_cmdtab**, **auth_cmdtab**, **ls_cmdtab**, and **delay_cmdtab**. The first one is the largest and contains 35 entries describing the core set of the commands supported by ProFTPD. Eight entries in **core_cmdtab** contain function pointers that are not contained in any of the recorded traces. By examining the respective entries in the table in the binary program, they can already be identified to be corresponding to the following commands: **EPRT**, **EPSV**, **MDTM**, **SIZE**, **DOWNLOAD**, **UPLOAD**, **GSM** and **RSLV**. While the first four are known benign FTP commands that are simply not defined in RFC 959, the last four belong to the backdoors Y4, Y5 and Y6. The other four identified function pointer tables also partly contain pointers to functions that were not encountered during testing. These functions correspond either to known commands (e.g., **xfer_log_stor()**) or the benign FTP command **PROT**, which is not defined in RFC 959 as well.

6. CONCLUSIONS

In this paper, we presented an approach towards the automatic detection and disabling of certain types of backdoors in server applications by carefully examining runtime traces for different protocol runs. Our implementation of the approach in the form of a tool called WEASEL automatically captures these traces by repeatedly invoking a server application under test according to a formal, block-based specification of the respective protocol. As WEASEL only relies on `gdbserver` for the recording of traces, it is widely applicable to a variety of platforms and we discussed several empirical analysis results that demonstrate how WEASEL can be used to precisely detect relevant code parts and data structures within a given binary application.

7. ACKNOWLEDGMENTS

We thank Andreas Maaß and Martin Steegmanns for implementing the discussed artificial backdoors, Moritz Contag for assisting with the development of our tool, and the anonymous reviewers for helpful comments. This work has been supported by the German Federal Ministry of Education and Research (BMBF) under support code 16BP12302; EUREKA-Project SASER.

8. REFERENCES

[1] GDB Remote Serial Protocol. `http://sourceware.org/gdb/onlinedocs/gdb/Remote-Protocol.html`.

[2] ProFTPD Backdoor Unauthorized Access Vulnerability, 2010. `http://www.securityfocus.com/bid/45150`.

[3] Backdoor Found In Arcadyan-based Wi-Fi Routers, 2012. `http://it.slashdot.org/story/12/04/26/1411229/backdoor-found-in-arcadyan-based-wi-fi-routers`.

[4] RuggedCom - Backdoor Accounts in my SCADA network? You don't say..., 2012. `http://seclists.org/fulldisclosure/2012/Apr/277`.

[5] Samsung printers contain hidden, hard-coded management account, 2012. `http://www.zdnet.com/samsung-printers-contain-hidden-hard-coded-management-account-7000007928/`.

[6] D. Agrawal, S. Baktir, D. Karakoyunlu, P. Rohatgi, and B. Sunar. Trojan Detection using IC Fingerprinting. In *IEEE Symposium on Security and Privacy*, 2007.

[7] D. Aitel. An Introduction to SPIKE, the Fuzzer Creation Kit. `www.blackhat.com/presentations/bh-usa-02/bh-us-02-aitel-spike.ppt`, 2002. Presented at Black Hat US.

[8] P. Amini and A. Portnoy. Fuzzing Sucks! Introducing Sulley Fuzzing Framework. `pentest.cryptocity.net/files/fuzzing/sulley/introducing_sulley.pdf`, 2007. Presented at Black Hat US.

[9] A. Bittau, P. Marchenko, M. Handley, and B. Karp. Wedge: Splitting Applications into Reduced-privilege Compartments. In *USENIX Symposium on Networked Systems Design and Implementation*, 2008.

[10] D. Brumley, C. Hartwig, Z. Liang, J. Newsome, D. X. Song, and H. Yin. Automatically identifying trigger-based behavior in malware. In W. Lee, C. Wang, and D. Dagon, editors, *Botnet Detection*, volume 36 of *Advances in Information Security*, pages 65–88. Springer, 2008.

[11] D. Brumley and D. Song. Privtrans: automatically partitioning programs for privilege separation. In *USENIX Security Symposium*, 2004.

[12] S. Dai, T. Wei, C. Zhang, T. Wang, Y. Ding, Z. Liang, and W. Zou. A framework to eliminate backdoors from response-computable authentication. In *IEEE Symposium on Security and Privacy*, 2012.

[13] M. Dalton, C. Kozyrakis, and N. Zeldovich. Nemesis: preventing authentication & access control vulnerabilities in web applications. In *USENIX Security Symposium*, 2009.

[14] L. Duflot. CPU Bugs, CPU Backdoors and Consequences on Security. In *European Symposium on Research in Computer Security (ESORICS)*, 2008.

[15] S. Duquette. Linux/SSHDoor.A Backdoored SSH daemon that steals passwords, jan 2013. `http://www.welivesecurity.com/2013/01/24/linux-sshdoor-a-backdoored-ssh-daemon-that-steals-passwords/`.

[16] H. Flake. Structural comparison of executable objects. In *Conference on Detection of Intrusions and Malware & Vulnerability Assessment (DIMVA)*, 2004.

[17] D. Gao, M. K. Reiter, and D. Song. Binhunt: Automatically finding semantic differences in binary programs. In *Information and Communications Security*, pages 238–255. Springer, 2008.

[18] D. Geneiatakis, G. Portokalidis, V. P. Kemerlis, and A. D. Keromytis. Adaptive defenses for commodity software through virtual application partitioning. In *ACM Conference on Computer and Communications Security (CCS)*, 2012.

[19] Y. L. Gwon, H. T. Kung, and D. Vlah. DISTROY: detecting integrated circuit Trojans with compressive measurements. In *USENIX Workshop on Hot Topics in Security*, 2011.

[20] J. S. Havrilla. Borland/Inprise Interbase SQL database server contains backdoor superuser account with known password, 2001. `http://www.kb.cert.org/vuls/id/247371`.

[21] M. Hicks, M. Finnicum, S. T. King, M. M. K. Martin, and J. M. Smith. Overcoming an untrusted computing base: Detecting and removing malicious hardware automatically. In *IEEE Symposium on Security and Privacy*, 2010.

[22] D. Kilpatrick. Privman: A library for partitioning applications. In *USENIX Annual Technical Conference, FREENIX Track*, 2003.

[23] J. C. King. Symbolic execution and program testing. *Communications of the ACM*, 19(7):385–394, 1976.

[24] S. T. King, J. Tucek, A. Cozzie, C. Grier, W. Jiang, and Y. Zhou. Designing and implementing malicious hardware. In *USENIX Workshop on Large-Scale Exploits and Emergent Threats (LEET)*, 2008.

[25] J. Lee, T. Avgerinos, and D. Brumley. Tie: Principled reverse engineering of types in binary programs. In *Symposium on Network and Distributed System Security (NDSS)*, 2011.

[26] C.-K. Luk, R. Cohn, R. Muth, H. Patil, A. Klauser, G. Lowney, S. Wallace, V. J. Reddi, and K. Hazelwood. Pin: building customized program analysis tools with dynamic instrumentation. In *ACM SIGPLAN Conference on Programming Language Design and Implementation (PLDI)*, 2005.

[27] H. D. Moore. Shiny Old VxWorks Vulnerabilities, 2010. `https://community.rapid7.com/community/metasploit/blog/2010/08/02/shiny-old-vxworks-vulnerabilities`.

[28] D. G. Murray and S. Hand. Privilege separation made easy: trusting small libraries not big processes. In *European Workshop on System Security (EuroSec)*, 2008.

[29] J. Postel and J. Reynolds. File Transfer Protocol. RFC 959 (INTERNET STANDARD), Oct. 1985. Updated by RFCs 2228, 2640, 2773, 3659, 5797.

[30] N. Provos, M. Friedl, and P. Honeyman. Preventing privilege escalation. In *USENIX Security Symposium*, 2003.

[31] A. Slowinska, T. Stancescu, and H. Bos. Howard: A dynamic excavator for reverse engineering data structures. In *Symposium on Network and Distributed System Security (NDSS)*, 2011.

[32] S. Sparks, S. Embleton, and C. C. Zou. A chipset level network backdoor: bypassing host-based firewall & ids. In *ACM Symposium on Information, Computer and Communications Security (ASIACCS)*, 2009.

[33] C. Sturton, M. Hicks, D. Wagner, and S. T. King. Defeating UCI: Building Stealthy and Malicious Hardware. In *IEEE Symposium on Security and Privacy*, 2011.

[34] M. Tehranipoor and F. Koushanfar. A Survey of Hardware Trojan Taxonomy and Detection. *IEEE Design & Test of Computers*, 27(1), 2010.

[35] K. Thompson. Reflections on trusting trust. *Commun. ACM*, 27(8), Aug. 1984.

[36] A. Waksman and S. Sethumadhavan. Silencing hardware backdoors. In *IEEE Symposium on Security and Privacy*, 2011.

[37] C. Wysopal, C. Eng, and T. Shields. Static detection of application backdoors - detecting both malicious software behavior and malicious indicators from the static analysis of executable code. *Datenschutz und Datensicherheit*, 34(3):149–155, 2010.

[38] T. Ylonen and C. Lonvick. The Secure Shell (SSH) Authentication Protocol. RFC 4252 (Proposed Standard), Jan. 2006.

[39] S. Zdancewic, L. Zheng, N. Nystrom, and A. C. Myers. Secure program partitioning. *ACM Trans. Comput. Syst.*, 20(3):283–328, Aug. 2002.

[40] A. Zeller. Isolating cause-effect chains from computer programs. In *ACM SIGSOFT Symposium on Foundations of Software Engineering*, 2002.

Appendix A. A-WEASEL ALGORITHM

Given a set of n traces on function level the A-WEASEL algorithm recursively performs the following steps:

1 Determine the set of functions present in all n traces:

$$S_{common,funcs} = S_{T_0,funcs} \cap S_{T_1,funcs} \cap \ldots \cap S_{T_{n-1},funcs}$$

2 For each trace, determine the set of exclusive functions:

$$S_{T_i,ex,funcs} = S_{T_i,funcs} \setminus S_{common,funcs}$$

3 For each exclusive function in each set $S_{T_i,ex,funcs}$, determine the minimum number of call stack levels needed to distinguish between all of its invocations in the call graph (CG) of T_i. We denote the minimum call stack needed for distinction the *signature call stack* of an invocation. A new set $S_{T_i,ex,funcs,callstack}$ containing all invocations with different signature call stacks of all functions in $S_{T_i,ex,funcs}$ is created:

$$S_{T_i,ex,funcs,callstack} = \delta(S_{T_i,ex,funcs})$$

4 For each set $S_{T_i,ex,funcs,callstack}$, remove those invocations of exclusive functions from the set that are *dominated* by other exclusive functions in the call graph of the corresponding trace T_i:

$$S_{T_i,ex,funcs,top} = \varphi(S_{T_i,ex,funcs,callstack})$$

Thus only top-level invocations of exclusive functions of T_i are contained in the set.

5 Group all remaining invocations in all sets $S_{T_i,ex,funcs,top}$ according to their signature call stacks. Invocations with compatible signature call stacks are grouped together. Two signature call stacks are compatible if both are equal or are equal up to the end of one of the two call stack. Note how each group only corresponds to one specific exclusive function and can at most contain one specific invocation from each trace.

6 The immediate parent function in the common call stack of a group's exclusive function is necessarily in set $S_{common,funcs}$ and is added as *decider* to the *decision tree*. Note that several groups can also share a common decider function. In case a group consists of only a single invocation from a single trace, the corresponding exclusive function is added as *handler* to the decision tree. Recursion ends in this case.

7 For each group, dynamically trace the corresponding *decider* function for the group's common signature call stack for all applicable protocol runs on basic block level. From the recorded basic block traces, the internal *decision tree* of the decider function for the signature call stack is generated by a similar but simpler algorithm.

8 For each group recursively execute A-WEASEL. For each invocation belonging to the group, a self-contained and minimal sub-trace T_i' is cut from the original trace T_i that starts with the corresponding signature call stack. A-WEASEL is executed on the set of all such sub-traces corresponding to the group. I.e., A-WEASEL is executed on the sub-CGs of the *decider* identified for the group for all applying traces.

9 In case a *decider* function is found to be a leaf in the resulting decision tree and does not exhibit any control flow differences on basic block level for applicable protocol runs, it is transformed into a common *handler* function.

Verifiable Delegation of Computation on Outsourced Data

Michael Backes
Saarland University, MPI-SWS
Saarbrücken, Germany

Dario Fiore
MPI-SWS
Saarbrücken, Germany

Raphael M. Reischuk
Saarland University
Saarbrücken, Germany

ABSTRACT

We address the problem in which a client stores a large amount of data with an untrusted server in such a way that, at any moment, the client can ask the server to compute a function on some portion of its outsourced data. In this scenario, the client must be able to efficiently verify the correctness of the result despite no longer knowing the inputs of the delegated computation, it must be able to keep adding elements to its remote storage, and it does not have to fix in advance (i.e., at data outsourcing time) the functions that it will delegate. Even more ambitiously, clients should be able to verify in time independent of the input-size – a very appealing property for computations over huge amounts of data.

In this work we propose novel cryptographic techniques that solve the above problem for the class of computations of quadratic polynomials over a large number of variables. This class covers a wide range of significant arithmetic computations – notably, many important statistics. To confirm the efficiency of our solution, we show encouraging performance results, e.g., correctness proofs have size below 1 kB and are verifiable by clients in less than 10 milliseconds.

Categories and Subject Descriptors

K.6.5 [**Management of Computing and Information Systems**]: Security and Protection

Keywords

Verifiable Delegation of Computation; CloudComputing; Secure Data Outsourcing; Homomorphic MACs; Amortized Closed-Form Efficient PRF

1. INTRODUCTION

Given the emergence of cloud computing (an infrastructure where clients or businesses lease computing and storage resources from powerful service providers), it is of critical importance to provide integrity guarantees for outsourced data management. Consider for example the following scenario. A client has a collection of a large (potentially unbounded) amount of data $D = D_1, D_2, D_3, \ldots$, for instance, environmental data such as air pollution levels at fixed time intervals (e.g., every hour), and it may wish to compute statistics on such data. If the client's memory is not large enough to store the entire data, the client might consider relying on a cloud service and storing the data on a remote server $\mathcal{S}$. Other significant examples of this scenario include arbitrary files at remote storage systems, as well as endless data streams such as financial data (e.g., price fixing data from the stock markets, financial figures and revenues of companies), experimental data (e.g., genetic data, laboratory measurements), and further environmental data (e.g., surface weather observations). In this scenario, we hence have a client who incrementally sends D to a server $\mathcal{S}$, the server stores D, and at certain points in time the client asks $\mathcal{S}$ to compute a function on (a portion of) the currently outsourced data. We stress that the data D and its size cannot be fixed in advance as the client may need to add additional data to the outsourced storage. Analogously, the client might not know in advance what functions it will apply on the outsourced data (e.g., it may wish to compute several statistics).

However, if the server is *untrusted* (i.e., it is malicious or becomes prey to an external attack), how can the client verify that the results provided by the server are correct? This question naturally leads to two important requirements: (1) *security*, meaning that the server should be able to "prove" the correctness of the delegated computation for some function f; and (2) *efficiency*, meaning that the client should be able to check the proof by requiring significantly fewer resources than those that are needed to compute f (including both computation and communication). Furthermore, if we consider computations over very large sets of inputs (e.g., statistics on huge data sets), we want to be more ambitious and envision the achievement of (3) *input-independent efficiency*, meaning that verifying the correctness of a computation $f(D_1, \ldots, D_n)$ requires time *independent* of n. Moreover, two further requirements are crucial in this setting: (4) *unbounded storage*, meaning that the size of the outsourced data should not be fixed a-priori, i.e., clients should be able to outsource any (possibly growing) amount of data; and (5) *function-independence*, meaning that a client should be able to outsource its data without having to know in advance the functions that it will delegate later.

CCS'13, November 4–8, 2013, Berlin, Germany.

ACM 978-1-4503-2477-9/13/11 ...$15.00.
http://dx.doi.org/10.1145/2508859.2516681.

RELATION WITH VERIFIABLE COMPUTATION. The problem of securely and efficiently outsourcing the computation of a function f to a remote server has been the subject of many works in the so-called field of *verifiable computation.* Most of these works achieve the goals of security (1) and efficiency (2), but they inevitably fail in achieving requirements (3)–(5). Roughly speaking, the issue is that most existing work requires the client to know (i.e., to store a local copy of) the input D for the verification of the delegated function (e.g., in SNARG-based approaches [10, 25] and in signatures of correct computation [40]), or, otherwise, to send D to the server *all at once* (rather than sending it over time) and to keep a small local state which would *not* allow to append additional data at a later time (e.g., in [44, 22]). Perhaps more critically, many of the existing solutions in this area require the delegator to run in time proportional to the input size n of the delegated function, e.g., in time $\mathsf{poly}(n)$. In the various existing protocols, these limitations arise for different reasons (see Section 1.1 for a more detailed discussion). However, even if verification in these works is more efficient than running f, we think that, for computations over huge data sets, a $\mathsf{poly}(n)$ overhead is still unacceptably high.

The only approach that comes close to achieving requirements (1)–(5) is the work by Chung et al. on memory delegation [20]. The authors propose a scheme based on techniques from [29] which exploit the power of the PCP theorem [6]. With this scheme, a client can delegate a broad class of computations over its outsourced memory fulfilling the requirements from above (except for verification efficiency, which requires time $\log n$, instead of constant time). While providing a satisfying solution in theory, this approach suffers from the usual impracticality issues of general-purpose PCP techniques and hence does not lead to truly practical solutions to the problem.

Our Contribution. In this work, we address the problem of verifiable delegation of computations on (growing) outsourced data. Our main contribution is the first *practical* protocol that achieves all five of the requirements stated before. Namely, a client can (continuously) store a large amount of data $D = D_1, D_2, D_3 \dots$ with the server, and then, at certain points in time, it can request the computation of a function f on (a portion of) the outsourced data, e.g., $v = f(D_{i_1}, \dots, D_{i_n})$. Using our protocol, the server sends to the client a short piece of information vouching for the correctness of v. The protocol achieves input-independent efficiency in the amortized model: after a single precomputation with cost $|f|$, the client can verify *every* subsequent evaluation of f in *constant* time, i.e., regardless of the input size n. Moreover, fulfilling properties (4)–(5), we have that data outsourcing and function delegation are completely *decoupled*, i.e., the client can *continuously* add elements to the remote storage, and the delegated functions do *not* have to be fixed a priori. This means that the cost of outsourcing the data can be, in fact, excluded from the delegation; think for instance of incrementally outsourcing a large data stream during an entire year, and then computing statistics on the data at the end of the year.

Our solution works for computations over integers in the ring $\mathbb{Z}_p$ (where p is a large prime of roughly 2λ bits, for a security parameter λ), and supports the evaluation of arithmetic circuits of degree up to 2. This restricted class of computations is enough to capture a wide range of significant arithmetic computations, such as meaningful statistics, including counting, summation, (weighted) average, arithmetic mean, standard deviation, variance, covariance, weighted variance with constant weights, quadratic mean (aka root-mean square – RMS), mean squared error (MSE), the Pearson product-moment correlation coefficient, the coefficient of determination (R^2), and the least squares fit of a data set $\{(x_i, v_i)\}_{i=1}^n$ (in the case when the x_i are universal constants, e.g., days of the year)[1].

Our key technical contribution is the introduction of *homomorphic MACs with efficient verification.* This cryptographic primitive extends homomorphic message authenticators [27] by adding a crucial efficiency property for the verification algorithm. We propose a first realization of homomorphic MACs with efficient verification (see Section 1.2 for an overview of our techniques), and we prove its security under the Decision Linear assumption [11]. Using the above construction we build an efficient protocol that can be implemented using bilinear pairings.

To demonstrate the practicality of our solution, we evaluate the concrete operations that have to be performed by the client and the server, as well as the bandwidth overhead introduced by the protocol for transferring the proofs. If we consider 80 bits of security and an implementation of symmetric pairings [35] on a standard desktop machine, we observe the following costs (see Table 2 for the 128-bit case): For outsourcing a data item D_i, the client needs to perform a single modular exponentiation in 0.24ms. This operation yields a very short authentication tag of size 0.08kB, which is sent to the server along with D_i. For the verification of a computation result v, the client receives a proof σ_v of size 0.21kB from the server, and can check this proof by computing one pairing and one multi-exponentiation in 1.06ms.

As we mentioned before, we achieve input-independent efficiency in an amortized sense. So, the above verification costs are obtained after the precomputation of some concise information ω_f related to the delegated function f. Precomputing ω_f takes the same time as computing f (with almost no additional overhead!), it does not require knowledge of the input data, and ω_f can be re-used an unbounded number of times to verify several evaluations of f on many different outsourced data sets. To generate the proof σ_v related to the evaluation of a function f, the server has to run f with an additional, yet constant, overhead – derived from replacing additions in f with a group operation, and replacing multiplications with a pairing. Although our solution can still not capture general-purpose computations, the above performance evaluation shows that for our case of interest we achieve results that are encouraging for a practical deployment of this protocol.

1.1 Related Work

MEMORY DELEGATION. The work of Chung et al. [20] on memory delegation and streaming delegation is the closest one to the model considered in our work. In memory delegation the client uploads his memory to the server (in an offline phase), and it can later ask the server to update the outsourced memory and to compute a function f on its entire memory (in an online phase). In streaming delegation the memory can be updated only by appending elements. The main advantages of the work of Chung et al. over our results are that: (i) the client can change values in the outsourced memory, (ii) they provide solutions for more expressive computations (i.e., a 4-round protocol for arbitrary poly-time programs). However, their solutions also suffer some disad-

[1]The least squares fit for this case can indeed be computed using a linear function [13].

vantages. First, they require the client to be stateful (in our solution the client keeps only a *fixed* secret key). Second, in streaming delegation, the size N of the stream has to be a-priori bounded. Such a bound also affects the client's memory since it requires a local storage size of approximately $\log N$ at the client, meaning that N cannot be chosen arbitrarily long, and thus the stream cannot be endless. Also, in their solutions, the client still runs in time $\mathsf{polylog}(n)$ in the online phase, where n is the size of the entire memory.

AUTHENTICATED DATA STRUCTURES. A line of research which addresses a problem closely related to the one considered in this paper is the existing work on *authenticated data structures* [39, 50]. This area considers a setting in which clients want to securely delegate certain operations on data structures that are stored at untrusted remote servers. Existing work addresses both static settings and dynamic settings (where data structures can be updated), and it mostly focuses on specific data structure operations, such as range search queries over databases [31, 36], authenticated dictionaries [21, 41, 30], and set operations over a dynamic collection of sets [42]. However, none of the works in this area considers the secure outsourcing of arbitrary or arithmetic computations (e.g., statistics) over remotely stored data.

MULTI-FUNCTION VERIFIABLE COMPUTATION. The notion of *multi-function verifiable computation* proposed by Parno, Raykova, and Vaikuntanathan [44] is close to our model, in that a client can delegate the computation of many functions $f_1, f_2, \ldots$ on the same input D, while being able to efficiently verify the results. Even though multi-function verifiable computation does not require the client to fix the function f before outsourcing the data, this model still falls short of our requirements. The main problem is that in multi-function verifiable computation, the client has to store some information τ_D for every input D on which it will ask to compute a function $f_i(D)$. Furthermore, there is no possibility of updating τ_D without locally storing the previous data. This essentially means that the data D has to be sent all at once, thus ruling out all applications in the growing data scenario.

HOMOMORPHIC SIGNATURES AND MACS. The problem of realizing homomorphic message authentication schemes in both the symmetric setting (MACs) and in the asymmetric setting (signatures) has been considered by many prior works. Homomorphic signatures were first proposed by Johnson et al. [32]. However, since then, most works focus solely on *linear functions*, mainly because of the important application to network coding [12]. Several efficient schemes for linear functions have been proposed both in the random oracle model [12, 26, 14, 16] and in the standard model [1, 3, 17, 18, 23, 4, 5]. Three more recent works consider the case of larger classes of functions [13, 27, 15]. Boneh and Freeman [13] proposed a realization of homomorphic signatures for bounded constant degree polynomials. Gennaro and Wichs [27] introduced homomorphic MACs and gave a construction for arbitrary computations which is proven secure in a weaker model where the adversary cannot ask verification queries. Catalano and Fiore [15] proposed realizations of homomorphic MACs that, despite capturing a restricted class of computations (i.e., arithmetic circuits with polynomially-bounded degree), support verification queries and are more efficient than previous works.

However, virtually all of the above works suffer the problem of having a verification algorithm which runs in time proportional to the function. Gennaro and Wichs [27] discuss the possibility of verifying a MAC in time better than executing the function, and propose some general solutions for their scheme which are based on fully homomorphic encryption and SNARGs [37]. However, neither the proposed solutions nor the suggested techniques yield schemes that achieve input-independent efficiency, and they do not seem to lead to practically efficient solutions, at least not as practical as required in this work.

SUCCINCT NON-INTERACTIVE ARGUMENTS OF KNOWLEDGE (SNARKS). A solution for realizing fully homomorphic signatures would be to use succinct non-interactive arguments of knowledge (SNARKs) [10]. For a given NP statement, this primitive allows for producing a succinct argument for proving knowledge of the corresponding witness. The main advantage of SNARKs is the succinctness of the argument (i.e., its size is independent of the size of both the NP statement and its witness), which can thus be verified efficiently. However, SNARKs are not as practically efficient as we might wish, and require either the random oracle model [37] or non standard, non-falsifiable, assumptions [28].

VERIFIABLE COMPUTATION. As we mentioned earlier, the problem considered by our work and addressed via homomorphic authenticators is related to the notion of verifiable computation for which there exits a vast literature, ranging from works for arbitrary computations [33, 37, 29, 24, 19, 2, 44, 25, 43] to works for specific classes of computations [9, 22, 40, 16]. In verifiable computation, a client wants to delegate a computationally heavy task to a remote server while being able to verify the result in a very efficient way. As we mentioned before, most of these works suffer several limitations that do not make them appropriate for the model considered in this paper. For example, many existing solutions require the delegator to run in time proportional to the input size of the delegated function. This limitation arises for different reasons. For instance, in the definition proposed by Gennaro, Gentry, and Parno [24] (and later adopted in several works, e.g., [19, 9, 44, 22]), to delegate the computation of $f(D)$, the client has to compute an encoding $\tau_{D,f}$ of D, which *depends* on the function f. However, if we want to choose f after outsourcing D, the computation of $\tau_{D,f}$ is no longer possible. Alternatively, one could keep the entire input D locally and then compute $\tau_{D,f}$ from D and f, which would yield a running time proportional to the input size. In other work (e.g., [33, 37, 29]) the efficiency requirement for a client is to run in time $\mathsf{poly}(n, \log T)$, when delegating a function f that runs in time T and takes inputs of size n.

Furthermore, as observed by Gennaro and Wichs [27], even if it is possible to reinterpret some of the results on verifiable computation in the setting of homomorphic message authenticators, the resulting solutions are still not appropriate. In particular, they might require a client to send the data all at once and would not allow for composition of several authenticated computations. We refer the reader to [27] for a thorough discussion about this.

Another interesting line of work in this area recently proposed efficient systems for verifiable computation [47, 46, 45, 51]. The proposed solutions also work in a model where the client needs to know the input of the computation, and it also has to engage in an interactive protocol with the server in order to verify the results. In contrast, our work considers a completely non-interactive setting in which the proof is transferred from the server to the client in a single round of communication. In the past there have been proposals of practical solutions, but of limited provable security: e.g., solutions based on audit (e.g., [38, 8]) or secure co-processors (e.g., [49, 52]) which prove the computation as correct, under the assumption that the adversary cannot tamper with the processor. Compared to these results, our work relies only on standard cryptographic assumptions, and does not require any trusted hardware.

1.2 A High-Level Overview of Our Techniques

To obtain our solution we build on the notion of *homomorphic message authenticators* proposed by Gennaro and Wichs [27], a primitive which can be considered the secret-key equivalent of homomorphic signatures [13]. The basic idea of homomorphic MACs is that a user can use a secret key to generate a set of tags $\sigma_1, \ldots, \sigma_n$ authenticating values $D_1, \ldots, D_n$ respectively. Then, *anyone* can homomorphically execute a function f over $(\sigma_1, \ldots, \sigma_n)$ to generate a *short* tag σ that authenticates D as the output of $f(D_1, \ldots, D_n)$. At first glance, homomorphic MACs seem to perfectly fit the problem of verifiable computations on (growing) outsourced data. However, a closer look at this primitive reveals that this idea lacks the very important property of efficient verification. As discussed in Section 1.1, the issue is that in all existing constructions the verification algorithm of homomorphic MACs runs in time proportional to the description of the function. Our key contribution is therefore to solve this efficiency issue by proposing a definition and a *first* practical realization of *homomorphic MACs with efficient verification.*

The starting point for the design of our construction is the homomorphic MAC scheme of Catalano and Fiore [15]: to authenticate a value $m \in \mathbb{Z}_p$, one "encodes" m into a degree-1 polynomial $y \in \mathbb{Z}_p[x]$ such that $y(0) = m$ and $y(\alpha) = \mathsf{F}_K(\mathsf{L})$. Here $\alpha \in \mathbb{Z}_p$ is a secret value randomly chosen by the client, and $\mathsf{F}_K(\cdot)$ is a pseudorandom function that is used to "randomize" a label L. One can think of a label as arbitrary information (e.g., a string) chosen by the client to describe the meaning of the authenticated value m (e.g., "air pollution on 2013/08/14 at 9:06:12"). Given a set of n authentication polynomials $y_1, \ldots, y_n$, the server creates a new MAC y which authenticates (i.e., it proves) that m is the result of $f(m_1, \ldots, m_n)$, e.g., f could be the variance of pollution levels at all time instants within a specific day/year etc. More specifically, the basic idea in [15] is to compute y by homomorphically executing the function f on the corresponding authentication polynomials, i.e., $y = f(y_1, \ldots, y_n)$. By the design of the y_i, this computation satisfies $y(0) = f(m_1, \ldots, m_n)$ and also $y(\alpha) = f(\mathsf{F}_K(\mathsf{L}_1), \ldots, \mathsf{F}_K(\mathsf{L}_n))$. Hence, the client can test whether a value m' (proposed by the server) is indeed the result of a computation $f(m_1, \ldots, m_n)$ by checking whether the MAC y provided by the server verifies the two conditions: (i) $y(0) = m'$ and (ii) $y(\alpha) = f(\mathsf{F}_K(\mathsf{L}_1), \ldots, \mathsf{F}_K(\mathsf{L}_n))$.

However, the Catalano-Fiore homomorphic MAC cannot be adopted in our setting: verifying a MAC for a function f requires the client to compute $W = f(\mathsf{F}_K(\mathsf{L}_1), \ldots, \mathsf{F}_K(\mathsf{L}_n))$ to perform check (ii), but this clearly takes the same time T as that for computing f — exactly what we want to avoid! One may then hope that once this value W is computed, it could be re-used, e.g., to verify other computations involving f. Unfortunately, this would require the re-use of labels, which is not possible at all: it is forbidden by the security definition used in [15]. More critically, the security of the Catalano-Fiore MAC completely breaks down in the presence of label re-use!

In our work, we solve this critical issue with two main ideas. Very informally, we first elaborate a model that allows us to partially, but *safely*, re-use labels. Then, we introduce the construction of a pseudorandom function which allows us to precompute a piece of label-independent information ω_f, such that ω_f can be re-used to compute W very efficiently (when the labels L_i are known).

To allow for a meaningful re-use of labels, we split labels in two dimensions, thus elaborating a model of *multi-labels.* A multi-label L consists of two components (Δ, τ) where Δ is the *data set identifier* and τ is the *input identifier.* A data set identifier could for instance be "air pollution on 2013/08/14"; and an input identifier could be used to identify a time, e.g., 9:06:12 am. For the example of the stock market data, the values could be the stock market prices for a company C at different times T. Then, the data set identifier could be the name of C while the input identifier could be the date and time T of the stock market price. The data set identifier is essentially a way of grouping together homogeneous data (e.g., data of the same population over which one wants to compute significant statistics) in such a way that one can compute within a data set Δ.

While a multi-label $\mathsf{L} = (\Delta, \tau)$ can still *not* be re-used to authenticate different messages, this model does allow us to assign the *same* input identifiers τ to as many messages as we need, as long as such messages lie in different data sets. In any case, a re-use of a complete multi-label for authentication purposes would not make much sense, as multi-labels are used by clients to "remember" and categorize the outsourced data. This transition from labels to multi-labels is natural: think again of the air pollution levels for a specific day. The input identifiers capture the hours of a day. Hence, the input identifiers might be re-used for other days, but the combination of date and time would never be re-used.

The use of multi-labels, however, does not in itself solve the issue of the inefficient verification algorithm: in this case one still has to compute $W = f(\mathsf{F}_K(\Delta, \tau_1), \ldots, \mathsf{F}_K(\Delta, \tau_n))$. Our key technical tool for achieving efficient verification is the introduction of a pseudorandom function F with a new property that we call *amortized closed-form efficiency*: if one precomputes some information ω_f related to a program f with input identifiers $\tau_1, \ldots, \tau_n$, but *independent* of the data set Δ, then it is possible to use ω_f to compute W, for *any* data set Δ, very efficiently, e.g., in constant time. Amortized closed-form efficiency essentially extends the closed-form efficiency of Benabbas et al. [9] to the setting in which the *same* function f is evaluated on *many pseudorandom* inputs.[2]

If we consider the example mentioned before, then one can precompute the verification information ω_f for the function "variance of the air pollution levels at all time instants within a day" (without knowing the actual data), and then use such

[2]We notice that the amortized extension was necessary in our case: while previous works [9, 22] used the PRF to obtain a shorter description of the function f (e.g., by defining the coefficients of a polynomial in a pseudorandom way), this is not possible in our case where the description of f remains arbitrary.

ω_f for verifying the computation of this statistic on *any* specific day (i.e., the data set) in constant time.

We propose an efficient instantiation of amortized closed-form efficient PRFs whose security is based on standard PRFs and on the Decision Linear assumption [11], thereby achieving amortized closed-form efficiency in constant time, i.e., independent of the input size n. Our PRF maps pairs of binary strings (Δ, τ) to pseudorandom values in a group $\mathbb{G}$ of prime order p. For this technical reason, we changed the Catalano-Fiore MAC (which works with a PRF mapping to $\mathbb{Z}_p$) so as to encode the MACs y into elements of $\mathbb{G}$, and we used pairings to "simulate" the ring behavior over $\mathbb{Z}_p$ for all those computations that require at most one multiplication, i.e., arithmetic circuits of degree bounded by 2.

1.3 Organization of the Paper

The paper is organized as follows. In Section 2 we review notation and basic definitions. In Section 3 we introduce the notions of multi-labeled programs and the definition of homomorphic message authenticators with efficient verification for multi-labeled programs. Next, Section 4 contains the description of two technical tools that will be important for the design of our new construction of homomorphic MACs: algorithms for the homomorphic evaluation of arithmetic circuits, and pseudorandom functions with amortized closed-form efficiency. Finally, in Section 5, we give our construction of homomorphic MACs with efficient verification, we discuss its efficiency, and we prove its security.

Due to space constraints, some detailed descriptions and proofs appear in an extended version of this work [7].

2. PRELIMINARIES

We will denote with $\lambda \in \mathbb{N}$ a security parameter. We say that a function ϵ is *negligible* if it vanishes faster than the inverse of any polynomial. If S is a set, $x \leftarrow_{\mathcal{R}} S$ denotes the process of selecting x uniformly at random in S. If $\mathcal{A}$ is a probabilistic algorithm, $x \leftarrow_{\mathcal{R}} \mathcal{A}(\cdot)$ denotes the process of running $\mathcal{A}$ on some input and assigning its output to x.

Algebraic Tools. Let $\mathcal{G}(1^\lambda)$ be an algorithm that on input the security parameter 1^λ, outputs the description of bilinear groups $\mathsf{bgpp} = (p, \mathbb{G}, \mathbb{G}_T, e, g)$ where $\mathbb{G}$ and $\mathbb{G}_T$ are groups of the same prime order $p > 2^\lambda$, $g \in \mathbb{G}$ is a generator and $e : \mathbb{G} \times \mathbb{G} \to \mathbb{G}_T$ is an efficiently computable bilinear map. We call such an algorithm $\mathcal{G}$ a *bilinear group generator.*

Arithmetic Circuits. Informally, an arithmetic circuit takes input variables $X = \{\tau_1 \dots \tau_n\}$ over a field $\mathbb{F}$ on its incoming wires, and computes over these inputs using addition and multiplication gates. For lack of space, we refer the interested reader to [48] for a useful survey on this subject. Here we only review some definitions useful for our work. Arithmetic circuits evaluate polynomials in the following way. Addition (resp. multiplication) gates compute the polynomial obtained by the sum (resp. product) of the two polynomials on their incoming wires. The output of the circuit is the value returned by its last gate. The *degree of a gate* is defined as the total degree of the polynomial computed by that gate. The *degree* $\deg(f)$ of a circuit f is the maximal degree of all its gates. In this paper, we restrict our interest to families of circuits $\{f_\lambda\}$ over $\mathbb{F}$ with $\deg(f_\lambda) \leq 2$.

3. HOMOMORPHIC MACS WITH EFFICIENT VERIFICATION

Homomorphic message authenticators were first defined by Gennaro and Wichs [27]. Their definition was tailored to the model of labeled programs defined therein. Roughly speaking, a labeled program is a function f (e.g., a circuit) which takes in n variable inputs such that each of these variables is assigned a label τ (e.g., a binary string). One may think of such labeling of variables as a way to give useful names to the variables of a program. Using this model, homomorphic message authenticators were defined in [27] in such a way that a message m is authenticated with respect to a label τ. Binding m with τ essentially means that the value m can be assigned to those input variables of a labeled program f whose label is τ. This, however, imposes a limitation: a label *cannot* be re-used for multiple messages, i.e., one cannot authenticate two different messages m, m' with respect to the same label τ. This limitation makes perfect sense if one considers labeling of the data as a way to uniquely "categorize" the data, which is useful, for instance, in cases where a user outsources her data to a remote server and does not keep a local copy of the data. However, for the purpose of labeling programs, the re-use limitation also requires changing the labeling of the variable inputs of f whenever f is executed on a different set of inputs.

In other words, labels are useful to identify both concrete data items and variable inputs of programs. The current definition of homomorphic MACs, however, focuses more on a labeling mechanism for data items, instead of capturing the notion of identifying the program inputs. In the next section, we bridge this gap by introducing so-called *multi-labels* that aim to capture both useful properties of labels: program variable labeling and data labeling. Thereafter, we give a definition of homomorphic MACs for multi-labeled programs.

3.1 Multi-Labeled Programs

We elaborate a variation of labeled programs that we call *multi-labeled programs.* The basic idea behind our model is to introduce the notion of a *multi-label* L, which consists of two parts: a *data set identifier* Δ and an *input identifier* τ. Input identifiers, in isolation, are used to label the variable inputs of a function f, whereas the combination of both, i.e., the full multi-label $\mathsf{L} = (\Delta, \tau)$, is used to uniquely identify a specific data item. Precisely, binding a value m with multi-label (Δ, τ) means that m can be assigned to those input variables with input identifier τ. The pair (Δ, τ) is necessary to uniquely identify m. While one can still not re-use a pair (Δ, τ) for authentication purposes, one can re-use the input identifier τ, instead.

For the sake of illustration, consider the multi-labeled approach as a separation of data items into two independent dimensions. One might think of a database table, e.g., storing air pollution levels, where some function $f : \mathcal{M}^n \to \mathcal{M}$ is evaluated over n columns (labeled $\tau_1, \dots, \tau_n$). Each such column could represent a point in time, e.g., 7:05, 07:10, etc. This computation is performed for each row (labeled Δ_i) of the table. Each such row could represent a different day, e.g., 2013/08/14, 2013/08/15, etc. We hence evaluate $f_{\Delta_i}(\tau_1, \dots, \tau_n)$ for each row i, hence for each day.

LABELED PROGRAMS. First, we review the notion of labeled programs introduced by Gennaro and Wichs [27]. While this notion was given for the case of Boolean circuits $f : \{0,1\}^n \rightarrow \{0,1\}$, here we generalize it to the case of any function f defined over an appropriate set $\mathcal{M}$. A *labeled program* $\mathcal{P}$ is defined by a tuple $(f, \tau_1, \ldots, \tau_n)$ where $f : \mathcal{M}^n \rightarrow \mathcal{M}$ is a function on n variables, and each $\tau_i \in \{0,1\}^*$ is the label of the i-th variable input of f. Labeled programs allow for composition as follows. Given labeled programs $\mathcal{P}_1, \ldots, \mathcal{P}_t$ and given a function $g : \mathcal{M}^t \rightarrow \mathcal{M}$, the *composed program* $\mathcal{P}^*$ corresponds to evaluating g on the outputs of $\mathcal{P}_1, \ldots, \mathcal{P}_t$. The composed program is compactly denoted as $\mathcal{P}^* = g(\mathcal{P}_1, \ldots, \mathcal{P}_t)$. The labeled inputs of $\mathcal{P}^*$ are all distinct labeled inputs of $\mathcal{P}_1, \ldots, \mathcal{P}_t$, i.e., all inputs with the same label are grouped together in a single input of the new program. If $f_{id} : \mathcal{M} \rightarrow \mathcal{M}$ is the canonical identity function and $\tau \in \{0,1\}^*$ is a label, then $\mathcal{I}_\tau = (f_{id}, \tau)$ denotes the *identity program* for input label τ. Notice that any program $\mathcal{P} = (f, \tau_1, \ldots, \tau_n)$ can be expressed as the composition of n identity programs $\mathcal{P} = f(\mathcal{I}_{\tau_1}, \ldots, \mathcal{I}_{\tau_n})$.

MULTI-LABELED PROGRAMS. Intuitively, multi-labeled programs are an extension of labeled programs in which a labeled program $\mathcal{P}$ is augmented with a data set identifier Δ. Formally, we define a *multi-labeled program* $\mathcal{P}_\Delta$ as a pair $(\mathcal{P}, \Delta)$ where $\mathcal{P} = (f, \tau_1, \ldots, \tau_n)$ is a labeled program (as defined above) and $\Delta \in \{0,1\}^*$ is a binary string called the *data set identifier*. Multi-labeled programs allow for composition within the same data set in the most natural way, i.e., given multi-labeled programs $(\mathcal{P}_1, \Delta), \ldots, (\mathcal{P}_t, \Delta)$ having the same data set identifier Δ, and given a function $g : \mathcal{M}^t \rightarrow \mathcal{M}$, the *composed multi-labeled program* $\mathcal{P}^*_\Delta$ is the pair $(\mathcal{P}^*, \Delta)$ where $\mathcal{P}^*$ is the composed program $g(\mathcal{P}_1, \ldots, \mathcal{P}_t)$, and Δ is the data set identifier shared by all the $\mathcal{P}_i$. If $f_{id} : \mathcal{M} \rightarrow \mathcal{M}$ is the canonical identity function and $\mathsf{L} = (\Delta, \tau) \in (\{0,1\}^*)^2$ is a multi-label, then $\mathcal{I}_\mathsf{L} = (f_{id}, \mathsf{L})$ denotes the *identity multi-labeled program* for data set Δ and input label τ. As for labeled programs, any multi-labeled program $\mathcal{P}_\Delta = ((f, \tau_1, \ldots, \tau_n), \Delta)$ can also be expressed as the composition of n identity multi-labeled programs: $\mathcal{P}_\Delta = f(\mathcal{I}_{\mathsf{L}_1}, \ldots, \mathcal{I}_{\mathsf{L}_n})$ where $\mathsf{L}_i = (\Delta, \tau_i)$.

It is worth noting that, in the notation of [27], a multi-labeled program $\mathcal{P}_\Delta = ((f, \tau_1, \ldots, \tau_n), \Delta)$ is essentially a labeled program $(f, \mathsf{L}_1, \ldots, \mathsf{L}_n)$ where each string L_i is a multi-label (Δ, τ_i). The main difference here is the (explicit) notion of labeled data sets that we use in order to group together several inputs, similarly to the definition used for homomorphic signatures [13, 23]. This explicit splitting will turn out to be crucial in order to achieve the desired property of efficient verification.

3.2 Hom. MACs for Multi-Labeled Programs

We review the notion of homomorphic message authenticators [27, 15]. We have adapted the definition to our model of multi-labeled programs as defined in the previous section.

DEFINITION 1. *A* homomorphic message authenticator scheme $\mathsf{HomMAC\text{-}ML}$ for multi-label programs *is a tuple of algorithms* $(\mathsf{KeyGen}, \mathsf{Auth}, \mathsf{Ver}, \mathsf{Eval})$ *satisfying four properties:* authentication correctness, evaluation correctness, succinctness, *and* security. *More precisely:*

$\mathsf{KeyGen}(1^\lambda)$: *given the security parameter λ, the key generation algorithm outputs a secret key* sk *and a public evaluation key* ek.

$\mathsf{Auth}(\mathsf{sk}, \mathsf{L}, m)$: *given the secret key* sk*, a multi-label $\mathsf{L} = (\Delta, \tau)$ and a message $m \in \mathcal{M}$, it outputs a tag σ.*

$\mathsf{Ver}(\mathsf{sk}, \mathcal{P}_\Delta, m, \sigma)$: *given the secret key* sk*, a multi-labeled program $\mathcal{P}_\Delta = ((f, \tau_1, \ldots, \tau_n), \Delta)$, a message $m \in \mathcal{M}$, and a tag σ, the verification algorithm outputs 0 (reject) or 1 (accept).*

$\mathsf{Eval}(\mathsf{ek}, f, \vec{\sigma})$: *on input the evaluation key* ek*, a circuit $f : \mathcal{M}^n \rightarrow \mathcal{M}$ and a vector of tags $\vec{\sigma} = (\sigma_1, \ldots, \sigma_n)$, the evaluation algorithm outputs a new tag σ.*

AUTHENTICATION CORRECTNESS. Informally speaking, a homomorphic MAC has authentication correctness if any tag σ generated by the algorithm $\mathsf{Auth}(\mathsf{sk}, \mathsf{L}, m)$ authenticates m with respect to the identity program $\mathcal{I}_\mathsf{L}$. More formally, we say that a scheme $\mathsf{HomMAC\text{-}ML}$ satisfies authentication correctness if for any message $m \in \mathcal{M}$, all keys $(\mathsf{sk}, \mathsf{ek}) \leftarrow_\mathcal{R} \mathsf{KeyGen}(1^\lambda)$, any multi-label $\mathsf{L} = (\Delta, \tau) \in (\{0,1\}^*)^2$, and any tag $\sigma \leftarrow_\mathcal{R} \mathsf{Auth}(\mathsf{sk}, \mathsf{L}, m)$, we have that $\mathsf{Ver}(\mathsf{sk}, \mathcal{I}_\mathsf{L}, m, \sigma) = 1$ holds with probability 1.

EVALUATION CORRECTNESS. This property aims at capturing that if the evaluation algorithm is run on a vector of tags $\vec{\sigma} = (\sigma_1, \ldots, \sigma_n)$ such that each σ_i authenticates some message m_i as the output of a multi-labeled program $(\mathcal{P}_i, \Delta)$, then the tag σ produced by Eval must authenticate $f(m_1, \ldots, m_n)$ as the output of the composed program $(f(\mathcal{P}_1, \ldots, \mathcal{P}_n), \Delta)$. More formally, let us fix a pair of keys $(\mathsf{sk}, \mathsf{ek}) \leftarrow_\mathcal{R} \mathsf{KeyGen}(1^\lambda)$, a function $g : \mathcal{M}^t \rightarrow \mathcal{M}$ and any set of message/program/tag triples $\{(m_i, \mathcal{P}_{\Delta,i}, \sigma_i)\}_{i=1}^t$ such that all multi-labeled programs $\mathcal{P}_{\Delta,i} = (\mathcal{P}_i, \Delta)$ (i.e., share the same data set identifier Δ) and $\mathsf{Ver}(\mathsf{sk}, \mathcal{P}_{\Delta,i}, m_i, \sigma_i) = 1$. If $m^* = g(m_1, \ldots, m_t)$, $\mathcal{P}^* = g(\mathcal{P}_1, \ldots, \mathcal{P}_t)$, and $\sigma^* = \mathsf{Eval}(\mathsf{ek}, g, (\sigma_1, \ldots, \sigma_t))$, then $\mathsf{Ver}(\mathsf{sk}, \mathcal{P}^*_\Delta, m^*, \sigma^*) = 1$ holds with probability 1.

SUCCINCTNESS. The size of a tag is bounded by some fixed polynomial in the security parameter, which is independent of the number n of inputs taken by the evaluated circuit.

SECURITY. A homomorphic MAC has to satisfy the following notion of unforgeability. Let $\mathsf{HomMAC\text{-}ML}$ be a homomorphic MAC scheme as defined above and let $\mathcal{A}$ be an adversary. $\mathsf{HomMAC\text{-}ML}$ is said to be unforgeable if for every PPT adv. $\mathcal{A}$, we have $\Pr[\mathsf{HomUF\text{-}CMA}_{\mathcal{A},\mathsf{HomMAC\text{-}ML}}(\lambda) = 1] \leq \epsilon(\lambda)$ where $\epsilon(\lambda)$ is a negligible function. The experiment $\mathsf{HomUF\text{-}CMA}_{\mathcal{A},\mathsf{HomMAC\text{-}ML}}(\lambda)$ is the one defined below.

Setup The challenger generates $(\mathsf{sk}, \mathsf{ek}) \leftarrow_\mathcal{R} \mathsf{KeyGen}(1^\lambda)$ and gives ek to $\mathcal{A}$.

Authentication queries The adversary can adaptively ask for tags on multi-labels and messages of its choice. Given a query (L, m) where $\mathsf{L} = (\Delta, \tau)$, the challenger proceeds as follows: If (L, m) is the first query with data set identifier Δ, then the challenger initializes an empty list $T_\Delta = \emptyset$ for data set identifier Δ. If T_Δ does not contain a tuple $(\tau, \cdot)$ (i.e., the multi-label (Δ, τ) was never queried), the challenger computes $\sigma \leftarrow_\mathcal{R} \mathsf{Auth}(\mathsf{sk}, \mathsf{L}, m)$, returns σ to $\mathcal{A}$ and updates the list $T_\Delta \leftarrow T_\Delta \cup (\tau, m)$. If $(\tau, m) \in T_\Delta$ (i.e., the query was previously made), then the challenger replies with the same tag generated before. If T_Δ contains a tuple (τ, m') for some message $m' \neq m$, then the challenger ignores the query.

Verification queries The adversary has access to a verification oracle as follows: Given a query $(\mathcal{P}_\Delta, m, \sigma)$ from $\mathcal{A}$, the challenger replies with the output of $\mathsf{Ver}(\mathsf{sk}, \mathcal{P}_\Delta, m, \sigma)$.

Forgery The adversary terminates the experiment by returning a forgery $(\mathcal{P}^*_{\Delta^*}, m^*, \sigma^*)$ for some $\mathcal{P}^*_{\Delta^*} = (\mathcal{P}^*, \Delta^*)$

and $\mathcal{P}^* = (f^*, \tau_1^*, \ldots, \tau_n^*)$. Notice that, equivalently, $\mathcal{A}$ can implicitly return such a tuple as a verification query $(\mathcal{P}^*_{\Delta^*}, m^*, \sigma^*)$ during the experiment.

Before describing the outcome of this experiment, we review the notion of well-defined programs with respect to a list T_Δ [15]. A labeled program $\mathcal{P}^* = (f^*, \tau_1^*, \ldots, \tau_n^*)$ is *well-defined with respect to* T_{Δ^*} if either one of the following two cases holds:

- there exist messages $m_1, \ldots, m_n$ such that the list T_{Δ^*} contains all tuples $(\tau_1^*, m_1), \ldots, (\tau_n^*, m_n)$. Intuitively, this means that the entire input space of f for data set Δ^* has been authenticated.
- there exist indices $i \in \{1, \ldots, n\}$ such that $(\tau_i^*, \cdot) \notin T_{\Delta^*}$ (i.e., $\mathcal{A}$ never asked authentication queries with multi-label (Δ^*, τ_i^*)), and the function $f^*(\{m_j\}_{(\tau_j, m_j) \in T_{\Delta^*}} \cup \{\tilde{m}_j\}_{(\tau_j, \cdot) \notin T_{\Delta^*}})$ outputs the same value for all possible choices of $\tilde{m}_j \in \mathcal{M}$. Intuitively, this case means that the unauthenticated inputs never contribute to the computation of f.

To define the output of the experiment HomUF−CMA, we say it outputs 1 if and only if $\mathsf{Ver}(\mathsf{sk}, \mathcal{P}^*_{\Delta^*}, m^*, \sigma^*) = 1$ and one of the following conditions holds:

- *Type 1 Forgery:* no list T_{Δ^*} was created during the game, i.e., no message m has been authenticated with respect to a data set identifier Δ^* during the experiment.
- *Type 2 Forgery:* $\mathcal{P}^*$ is well-defined w.r.t. T_{Δ^*} and $m^* \neq f^*(\{m_j\}_{(\tau_j, m_j) \in T_{\Delta^*}})$, i.e., m^* is not the correct output of the labeled program $\mathcal{P}^*$ when executed on previously authenticated messages $(m_1, \ldots, m_n)$.
- *Type 3 Forgery:* $\mathcal{P}^*$ is not well-defined w.r.t. T_{Δ^*}.

Our definition is obtained by extending the one by Catalano and Fiore [15] to our model of multi-labeled programs. The resulting definition is very close to the one proposed by Freeman for homomorphic signatures [23], with the exception that we allow for arbitrary labels, and we do not impose any a-priori fixed bound on the number of elements in a data set.

In the most general case where f can be any function, it might not be possible to efficiently (i.e., in polynomial time) check whether a program $\mathcal{P}$ is well-defined w.r.t. a list T. However, for more specific classes of computations, this is not an issue. For example, Freeman showed that this is not a problem for linear functions [23]. In the following proposition (whose proof appears in the full version), we show a similar result for the classes of computations considered in our work, i.e., arithmetic circuits defined over the finite field $\mathbb{Z}_p$ where p is a prime of roughly λ bits, and whose degree d is bounded by a polynomial. In particular, we show that any adversary who wins by producing a Type 3 forgery can be converted into one who outputs a Type 2 forgery.

PROPOSITION 1. *Let $\lambda \in \mathbb{N}$ be the security parameter, let $p > 2^\lambda$ be a prime number, and let $\{f_\lambda\}$ be a family of arithmetic circuits over $\mathbb{Z}_p$ whose degree is bounded by some polynomial $d = poly(\lambda)$. If for any adversary $\mathcal{B}$ producing a Type 2 forgery we have that* $\Pr[\mathsf{HomUF{-}CMA}_{\mathcal{B},\mathsf{HomMAC\text{-}ML}}(\lambda) = 1] \leq \epsilon$, *then for any adversary $\mathcal{A}$ producing a Type 3 forgery it holds* $\Pr[\mathsf{HomUF{-}CMA}_{\mathcal{A},\mathsf{HomMAC\text{-}ML}}(\lambda) = 1] \leq \epsilon + d/p$.

3.3 Homomorphic MACs with Efficient Verification for Multi-Labeled Programs

In this section we introduce a new property for homomorphic MACs that we call *efficient verification*. Informally, a homomorphic MAC satisfies efficient verification if it is possible to verify a tag σ against a multi-labeled program $\mathcal{P}_\Delta = (\mathcal{P}, \Delta)$ in less time than that required to compute $\mathcal{P}$. We define this efficiency property in an amortized sense, so that the verification is more efficient when the same program $\mathcal{P}$ is executed on different data sets. The formal definition follows.

DEFINITION 2. *Let* HomMAC-ML = (KeyGen, Auth, Ver, Eval) *be a homomorphic MAC scheme for multi-labeled programs as defined in the previous section.* HomMAC-ML *satisfies efficient verification if there exist two additional algorithms* (VerPrep, EffVer) *as follows:*

$\mathsf{VerPrep}(\mathsf{sk}, \mathcal{P})$: *on input the secret key* sk *and a labeled program $\mathcal{P} = (f, \tau_1, \ldots, \tau_n)$, this algorithm generates a concise verification key $\mathsf{VK}_\mathcal{P}$. We stress that this verification key does* not *depend on any data set identifier Δ.*

$\mathsf{EffVer}(\mathsf{sk}, \mathsf{VK}_\mathcal{P}, \Delta, m, \sigma)$: *given the secret key* sk*, a verification key $\mathsf{VK}_\mathcal{P}$, a data set identifier Δ, a message $m \in \mathcal{M}$ and a tag σ, the efficient verification algorithm outputs 0 (reject) or 1 (accept).*

The above algorithms are required to satisfy the following two properties:

CORRECTNESS. *Let* $(\mathsf{sk}, \mathsf{ek}) \leftarrow_\mathcal{R} \mathsf{KeyGen}(1^\lambda)$ *be honestly generated keys, and $(\mathcal{P}_\Delta, m, \sigma)$ be any program/message/tag tuple with $\mathcal{P}_\Delta = (\mathcal{P}, \Delta)$ such that $\mathsf{Ver}(\mathsf{sk}, \mathcal{P}_\Delta, m, \sigma) = 1$. Then, for every $\mathsf{VK}_\mathcal{P} \leftarrow_\mathcal{R} \mathsf{VerPrep}(\mathsf{sk}, \mathcal{P})$, we have* $\Pr[\mathsf{EffVer}(\mathsf{sk}, \mathsf{VK}_\mathcal{P}, \Delta, m, \sigma) = 1] = 1$.

AMORTIZED EFFICIENCY. *Let $\mathcal{P}_\Delta = (\mathcal{P}, \Delta)$ be a program, let $(m_1, \ldots, m_n) \in \mathcal{M}^n$ be any vector of inputs, and let $t(n)$ be the time required to compute $\mathcal{P}(m_1, \ldots, m_n)$. If $\mathsf{VK}_\mathcal{P} \leftarrow \mathsf{VerPrep}(\mathsf{sk}, \mathcal{P})$, then the time required for $\mathsf{EffVer}(\mathsf{sk}, \mathsf{VK}_\mathcal{P}, \Delta, m, \sigma)$ is $O(1)$, i.e., independent of n.*

Notice that in our efficiency requirement, we do not include the time needed to compute $\mathsf{VK}_\mathcal{P}$. The reason is, since $\mathsf{VK}_\mathcal{P}$ is independent of Δ, the same $\mathsf{VK}_\mathcal{P}$ can be re-used in many verifications involving the same labeled program $\mathcal{P}$ but many different Δ. In this sense, the cost of computing $\mathsf{VK}_\mathcal{P}$ is *amortized* over many verifications of the same function on different data sets.

Application to Verifiable Computation on Outsourced Data. A homomorphic MAC scheme with efficient verification can be easily used to obtain a protocol for verifiable delegation of computations on outsourced data, satisfying the requirements (1)–(5) mentioned in Section 1. Below, we sketch such a protocol between a client $\mathcal{C}$ and a server $\mathcal{S}$:

Setup: $\mathcal{C}$ generates the keys $(\mathsf{sk}, \mathsf{ek}) \leftarrow_\mathcal{R} \mathsf{KeyGen}(1^\lambda)$ for a homomorphic MAC, sends ek to $\mathcal{S}$ and stores sk.

Data Outsourcing: to outsource a value m, $\mathcal{C}$ first authenticates m wrt. some multi-label L, i.e., $\sigma \leftarrow_\mathcal{R} \mathsf{Auth}(\mathsf{sk}, \mathsf{L}, m)$, and then sends (m, L, σ) to the server. It is easy to see that this phase satisfies the requirements of unbounded storage (4) and function independence (5).

Client's Preparation: assume that $\mathcal{C}$ needs to evaluate a labeled program $\mathcal{P} = (f, \tau_1, \ldots, \tau_n)$ on some of its outsourced data sets. In this preparation phase (offline), the client computes and stores $\mathsf{VK}_\mathcal{P} \leftarrow_\mathcal{R} \mathsf{VerPrep}(\mathsf{sk}, \mathcal{P})$ (independently of any Δ).

Delegation: when the client wants to compute $\mathcal{P}$ on a data set Δ (online), it simply sends $(\mathcal{P}, \Delta)$ to the server.[3]

Computation: to compute $(\mathcal{P}, \Delta)$, where $\mathcal{P} = (f, \tau_1, \ldots, \tau_n)$, the server first looks for the corresponding data $(m_1, \ldots, m_n)$ and tags $(\sigma_1, \ldots, \sigma_n)$ according to the labeling previously sent by $\mathcal{C}$. Next, $\mathcal{S}$ computes $m = f(m_1, \ldots, m_n)$ and $\sigma \leftarrow \mathsf{Eval}(\mathsf{ek}, f, \sigma_1, \ldots, \sigma_n)$, and sends (m, σ) to $\mathcal{C}$.

Verification: given the result (m, σ) sent by $\mathcal{S}$, the client checks that m is the correct output of the multi-labeled program $(\mathcal{P}, \Delta)$ by running $\mathsf{EffVer}(\mathsf{sk}, \mathsf{VK}_\mathcal{P}, \Delta, m, \sigma)$. By the amortized efficiency property of the homomorphic MAC, we obtain that $\mathcal{C}$ achieves amortized input-independent efficiency (3) – and thus also efficiency (2) – in verifying the delegated computations.

Finally, from the unforgeability of the homomorphic MAC, it is straightforward to see that the server cannot induce the client to accept incorrect results (1).

4. UTILITIES

This section provides some technical tools that will be useful to obtain our construction of homomorphic MACs with efficient verification.

4.1 Hom. Evaluation of Arithmetic Circuits

In the next two sections, we describe algorithms for the homomorphic evaluation of an arithmetic circuit $f : \mathcal{M}^n \to \mathcal{M}$ over values defined in some appropriate set $\mathcal{J} \neq \mathcal{M}$.

Homomorphic Evaluation over Polynomials. As a first example, we consider the case in which $\mathcal{J}$ is a ring of polynomials. More formally, let $\mathcal{J}_{\mathsf{poly}} = \mathbb{Z}_p[x_1, \ldots, x_m]$ be the ring of polynomials in variables $x_1, \ldots, x_m$ over $\mathbb{Z}_p$. For every fixed tuple $\vec{a} = (a_1, \ldots, a_m) \in \mathbb{Z}_p^m$, let $\phi_{\vec{a}} : \mathcal{J}_{\mathsf{poly}} \to \mathbb{Z}_p$ be the function defined by $\phi_{\vec{a}}(y) = y(a_1, \ldots, a_m)$ for any $y \in \mathcal{J}_{\mathsf{poly}}$. By the substitution property of polynomials, $\phi_{\vec{a}}$ is a homomorphism from $\mathcal{J}_{\mathsf{poly}} = \mathbb{Z}_p[x_1, \ldots, x_m]$ to $\mathbb{Z}_p$, i.e., $\forall y_1, y_2 \in \mathcal{J}_{\mathsf{poly}}$ it holds: $\phi_{\vec{a}}(y_1 + y_2) = \phi_{\vec{a}}(y_1) + \phi_{\vec{a}}(y_2)$ and $\phi_{\vec{a}}(y_1 \cdot y_2) = \phi_{\vec{a}}(y_1) \cdot \phi_{\vec{a}}(y_2)$. By simple induction, we then observe that for a given arithmetic circuit $f : \mathbb{Z}_p^n \to \mathbb{Z}_p$, there exists another circuit $\hat{f} : \mathcal{J}_{\mathsf{poly}}^n \to \mathcal{J}_{\mathsf{poly}}$ such that $\forall y_1, \ldots, y_n \in \mathcal{J}_{\mathsf{poly}}$: $\phi_{\vec{a}}(\hat{f}(y_1, \ldots, y_n)) = f(\phi_{\vec{a}}(y_1), \ldots, \phi_{\vec{a}}(y_n))$. The circuit $\hat{f}$ is basically the same as f, except that operations in $\mathbb{Z}_p$ are replaced by the corresponding operations in $\mathbb{Z}_p[x_1, \ldots, x_m]$. We formally write the computation of $\hat{f}$ as the algorithm $\mathsf{PolyEval}(m, f, y_1, \ldots, y_n)$, for which the following property holds: for any homomorphism $\phi_{\vec{a}}$ defined by $\vec{a} = (a_1, \ldots, a_m) \in \mathbb{Z}_p^m$, and for any circuit f and any values $y_1, \ldots, y_n \in \mathcal{J}_{\mathsf{poly}}$:

$$\phi_{\vec{a}}(\mathsf{PolyEval}(m, f, y_1, \ldots, y_n)) = f(\phi_{\vec{a}}(y_1), \ldots, \phi_{\vec{a}}(y_n))$$

We remark that in our work we will use $\mathsf{PolyEval}$ only for f of degree 2, and with $m = 1$ and $m = 2$.

[3]While in general the description of $\mathcal{P}$ may be large, here we assume the case in which $\mathcal{P}$ has a succinct description, e.g., "daily variance of the air pollution levels at every 5 minutes". Hence, the cost of communicating $\mathcal{P}$ can, in fact, be ignored.

Homomorphic Evaluation over Bilinear Groups. As a second example, we show how to homomorphically evaluate arithmetic circuits, of degree at most 2, over prime order groups with bilinear maps. Let $\mathsf{bgpp} = (p, \mathbb{G}, \mathbb{G}_T, e, g)$ be the description of bilinear groups where $\mathbb{G}$ has prime order p. If we fix a generator $g \in \mathbb{G}$, then $\mathbb{G}$ and the additive group $(\mathbb{Z}_p, +)$ are isomorphic by considering the isomorphism $\phi_g(x) = g^x$ for every $x \in \mathbb{Z}_p$. Similarly, by the property of the pairing function e, we also have that $\mathbb{G}_T$ and the additive group $(\mathbb{Z}_p, +)$ are isomorphic by considering $\phi_{g_T}(x) = e(g, g)^x$. Since ϕ_g and ϕ_{g_T} are isomorphisms there also exist the corresponding inverses $\phi_g^{-1} : \mathbb{G} \to \mathbb{Z}_p$ and $\phi_{g_T}^{-1} : \mathbb{G}_T \to \mathbb{Z}_p$, even though these are not known to be efficiently computable.

For every arithmetic circuit $f : \mathbb{Z}_p^n \to \mathbb{Z}_p$ of degree at most 2, we define $\mathsf{GroupEval}(f, X_1, \ldots, X_n)$ to be the algorithm which homomorphically evaluates f with inputs in $\mathbb{G}$ and output in $\mathbb{G}_T$ in such a way that, for every tuple $(X_1, \ldots, X_n) \in \mathbb{G}^n$, and every such circuit f, we have that

$$\mathsf{GroupEval}(f, X_1, \ldots, X_n) = e(g, g)^{f(x_1, \ldots, x_n)} \quad (1)$$

holds, where $x_i = \phi_g^{-1}(X_i), \forall i = 1, \ldots, n$.

Given a circuit f of degree at most 2, and given an n-tuple of values $(X_1, \ldots, X_n) \in \mathbb{G}^n$, $\mathsf{GroupEval}$ intuitively proceeds as follows. It computes additions by using the group operation in $\mathbb{G}$ or in $\mathbb{G}_T$. To compute multiplications, it uses the pairing function, e.g., $R = e(R_1, R_2)$, thus "lifting" the result to the group $\mathbb{G}_T$. By our assumption on the degree of f, one can see that multiplication is well defined. A more formal description of $\mathsf{GroupEval}$ and a proof that it satisfies Equation (1) are given in the full version.

4.2 Pseudorandom Functions with Amortized Closed-Form Efficiency

Here we introduce one of most important technical tools for our construction, that is the notion of pseudorandom functions with *amortized closed-form efficiency*. This primitive is an extension of closed-form efficient PRFs proposed by Benabbas et al. [9], and later refined by Fiore and Gennaro [22]. As we will show in Section 5, this new notion of PRFs will be crucial for achieving the property of efficient verification in our homomorphic MAC realization.

In a nutshell, closed-form efficient PRFs [9] are defined like standard PRFs with the additional requirement of satisfying the following efficiency property. Assume there exists a computation $\mathsf{Comp}(R_1, \ldots, R_n, \vec{z})$ which takes random inputs $R_1, \ldots, R_n$ and arbitrary inputs $\vec{z}$, and runs in time $t(n, |\vec{z}|)$. Also, think of the case in which each R_i is generated as $\mathsf{F}_K(\mathsf{L}_i)$. Then the PRF F is said to satisfy closed-form efficiency for $(\mathsf{Comp}, \vec{\mathsf{L}})$ if, by knowing the seed K, one can compute $\mathsf{Comp}(\mathsf{F}_K(\mathsf{L}_1), \ldots, \mathsf{F}_K(\mathsf{L}_n), \vec{z})$ in time strictly less than t. Here, the key observation is that in the pseudorandom case all the R_i values have a shorter "closed-form" representation (as function of K), and this might also allow for a shorter closed-form representation of the computation.

Starting from the above considerations, we introduce a new property for PRFs that we call *amortized closed-form efficiency*. Our basic idea is to address computations $\mathsf{Comp}(R_1, \ldots, R_n, \vec{z})$ of the above form, but then consider the case in which all values R_i are generated as $\mathsf{F}_K(\Delta, \tau_i)$. Basically, we interpret the PRF inputs L_i as pairs of values (Δ, τ_i), all sharing the same Δ component. Then, we informally say that F satisfies amortized closed-form efficiency if it is possible to compute ℓ computations $\{\mathsf{Comp}(\mathsf{F}_K(\Delta_j,\tau_1),\ldots,\mathsf{F}_K(\Delta_j,\tau_n),\vec{z})\}_{j=1}^{\ell}$ in time strictly less than $\ell\cdot t$. More detailed definitions follow.

A PRF consists of two algorithms (KG,F) such that (1) the key generation KG takes as input the security parameter 1^λ and outputs a secret key K and some public parameters pp that specify domain $\mathcal{X}$ and range $\mathcal{R}$ of the function, and (2) the function $\mathsf{F}_K(x)$ takes input $x\in\mathcal{X}$ and uses the secret key K to compute a value $R\in\mathcal{R}$. As usual, a PRF must satisfy the pseudorandomness property. Namely, we say that (KG,F) is *secure* if for every PPT adversary $\mathcal{A}$ we have that:

$$|\Pr[\mathcal{A}^{\mathsf{F}_K(\cdot)}(1^\lambda,\mathsf{pp})=1]-\Pr[\mathcal{A}^{\Phi(\cdot)}(1^\lambda,\mathsf{pp})=1]|\le\epsilon(\lambda)$$

where $\epsilon(\lambda)$ is negligible, $(K,\mathsf{pp})\leftarrow_{\mathcal{R}}\mathsf{KG}(1^\lambda)$, and $\Phi:\mathcal{X}\to\mathcal{R}$ is a random function.

For any PRF (KG,F) we define *amortized closed-form efficiency* as follows.

DEFINITION 3 (AMORTIZED CLOSED-FORM EFFICIENCY). *Consider a computation* Comp *that takes as input n random values $R_1,\ldots,R_n\in\mathcal{R}$ and a vector of m arbitrary values $\vec{z}=(z_1,\ldots,z_m)$, and assume that the computation of* $\mathsf{Comp}(R_1,\ldots,R_n,z_1,\ldots,z_m)$ *requires time $t(n,m)$.*

Let $\vec{\mathsf{L}}=(\mathsf{L}_1,\ldots,\mathsf{L}_n)$ be arbitrary values in the domain $\mathcal{X}$ of F such that each can be interpreted as $\mathsf{L}_i=(\Delta,\tau_i)$. We say that a PRF (KG,F) satisfies amortized closed-form efficiency *for $(\mathsf{Comp},\vec{\mathsf{L}})$ if there exist algorithms $\mathsf{CFEval}^{\mathsf{off}}_{\mathsf{Comp},\vec{\tau}}$ and $\mathsf{CFEval}^{\mathsf{on}}_{\mathsf{Comp},\Delta}$ such that:*

1. *Given $\omega\leftarrow\mathsf{CFEval}^{\mathsf{off}}_{\mathsf{Comp},\vec{\tau}}(K,\vec{z})$, we have $\mathsf{CFEval}^{\mathsf{on}}_{\mathsf{Comp},\Delta}(K,\omega)=\mathsf{Comp}(\mathsf{F}_K(\Delta,\tau_1),\ldots,\mathsf{F}_K(\Delta,\tau_n),z_1,\ldots,z_m)$*
2. *the running time of $\mathsf{CFEval}^{\mathsf{on}}_{\mathsf{Comp},\Delta}(K,\omega)$ is $o(t)$.*

We remark two important facts on our definition. First, the computation of $\omega\leftarrow\mathsf{CFEval}^{\mathsf{off}}_{\mathsf{Comp},\vec{\tau}}(K,\vec{z})$ does *not* depend on Δ, which means that the same value ω can be re-used in $\mathsf{CFEval}^{\mathsf{on}}_{\mathsf{Comp},\Delta}(K,\omega)$ to compute $\mathsf{Comp}(\mathsf{F}_K(\Delta,\tau_1),\ldots,\mathsf{F}_K(\Delta,\tau_n),\vec{z})$ for many different Δ. Second, the efficiency property puts a restriction only on the running time of $\mathsf{CFEval}^{\mathsf{on}}$. This is related to the previous remark, and it captures the idea of achieving efficiency in an *amortized* sense when considering many evaluations of $\mathsf{Comp}(\mathsf{F}_K(\Delta,\tau_1),\ldots,\mathsf{F}_K(\Delta,\tau_n),\vec{z})$, each with a different data set identifier Δ. More concretely, this means that one can precompute ω once, and then use it to run $\mathsf{CFEval}^{\mathsf{on}}$ as many times as he needs, almost for free.

It is worth noting that the structure of Comp may enforce some constraints on the range $\mathcal{R}$ of the PRF, and that due to the pseudorandomness property, the output distribution of $\mathsf{CFEval}^{\mathsf{on}}_{\mathsf{Comp},\Delta}(K,\mathsf{CFEval}^{\mathsf{off}}_{\mathsf{Comp},\vec{\tau}}(K,\vec{z}))$ (over the random choice of K) is computationally indistinguishable from the output distribution of $\mathsf{Comp}(R_1,\ldots,R_n,\vec{z})$ (over the random choices of the $R_i\in\mathcal{R}$).

4.3 A PRF with Amortized Closed-Form Efficiency for GroupEval

We propose an efficient construction of a pseudorandom function which satisfies amortized closed-form efficiency for the algorithm $\mathsf{GroupEval}$, given in Section 4.1.

Our PRF construction uses two generic pseudorandom functions which map binary strings to integers in $\mathbb{Z}_p$ (where p is a sufficiently large prime number), together with a weak PRF whose security relies on the Decision Linear assumption, first introduced by Boneh, Boyen, and Shacham [11].

OUR PSEUDORANDOM FUNCTION. Here we describe our PRF with amortized closed-form efficiency:

$\mathsf{KG}(1^\lambda)$. Let $\mathsf{bgpp}=(p,\mathbb{G},\mathbb{G}_T,e,g)$ be a bilinear group description. The key generation chooses two seeds K_1,K_2 for a family of PRFs $\mathsf{F}'_{K_{1,2}}:\{0,1\}^*\to\mathbb{Z}_p^2$. Finally, it outputs $K=(\mathsf{bgpp},K_1,K_2)$ and $\mathsf{pp}=\mathsf{bgpp}$. The parameters define a function F with domain $\mathcal{X}=\{0,1\}^*\times\{0,1\}^*$ and range $\mathbb{G}$, as described below.

$\mathsf{F}_K(x)$. Let $x=(\Delta,\tau)\in\mathcal{X}$ be the input value. To compute the corresponding output $R\in\mathbb{G}$, the algorithm generates values $(u,v)\leftarrow\mathsf{F}'_{K_1}(\tau)$ and $(a,b)\leftarrow\mathsf{F}'_{K_2}(\Delta)$, and then outputs $R=g^{ua+vb}$.

We first show that the above function is pseudorandom, and then we will show that it admits amortized closed-form efficiency for $\mathsf{GroupEval}$.

THEOREM 1. *If F' is a pseudorandom function and the Decision Linear assumption holds for $\mathcal{G}$, then the function (KG,F) described above is a pseudorandom function.*

For lack of space, the proof of Theorem 1 appears only in the full version of this work. Here we notice that the pseudorandomness essentially follows from the security of the PRF F', and the fact that $R=g^{ua+vb}=U^aV^b=f_{a,b}(U,V)$ is a weak pseudorandom function under the Decision Linear assumption. To prove the weak pseudorandomness of $f_{a,b}(\cdot,\cdot)$ we use the random self-reducibility property of the Decision Linear problem, shown in Lemma 7 in [34].

AMORTIZED CLOSED-FORM EFFICIENCY. Here we show that the pseudorandom function described before satisfies amortized closed-form efficiency for $(\mathsf{GroupEval},\vec{\mathsf{L}})$.

$\mathsf{CFEval}^{\mathsf{off}}_{\mathsf{GroupEval},\vec{\tau}}(K,f)$. Let $K=(\mathsf{bgpp},K_1,K_2)$ be a secret key as generated by $\mathsf{KG}(1^\lambda)$. For $i=1$ to n, compute $(u_i,v_i)\leftarrow\mathsf{F}'_{K_1}(\tau_i)$, and set $\vec{\rho}_i=(0,u_i,v_i)$: $\vec{\rho}_i$ are essentially the coefficients of a degree 1 polynomial $\rho_i(z_1,z_2)$ in two (unknown) variables z_1,z_2.

Next, run $\vec{\rho}\leftarrow\mathsf{PolyEval}(2,f,\rho_1,\ldots,\rho_n)$ to compute the coefficients $\vec{\rho}$ of a polynomial $\rho(z_1,z_2)$ such that $\forall z_1,z_2\in\mathbb{Z}_p$ it holds $\rho(z_1,z_2)=f(\rho_1(z_1,z_2),\ldots,\rho_n(z_1,z_2))$.

Finally, output $\omega_f=\vec{\rho}$.

$\mathsf{CFEval}^{\mathsf{on}}_{\mathsf{GroupEval},\Delta}(K,\omega_f)$. Let $K=(\mathsf{bgpp},K_1,K_2)$ be a secret key and let $\omega_f=\vec{\rho}$ be as computed by the previous algorithm. The online evaluation algorithm first generates $(a,b)\leftarrow\mathsf{F}'_{K_2}(\Delta)$, and then it uses the coefficients $\vec{\rho}$ to compute $w=\rho(a,b)$, and it finally outputs $W=e(g,g)^w$.

We observe that the complexity of the online algorithm depends on the size of $\vec{\rho}$, hence on the number of coefficients of a two-variate polynomial whose degree is the same as the degree of f. In general, for f of degree d, this would be $|\vec{\rho}|=\binom{d+2}{d}$. Considering our specific case of $\mathsf{GroupEval}$ which evaluates arithmetic circuits of degree at most 2, and by observing that the degree-0 coefficient is always 0, we obtain a vector $\vec{\rho}$ which can be represented with 5 elements of $\mathbb{Z}_p$. Moreover, we observe the interesting fact that, due to the bound $deg(f)\le 2$ and due to having only $m=2$ variables, the computation of $\vec{\rho}$ using $\mathsf{PolyEval}(2,f,\rho_1,\ldots,\rho_n)$ can be done at roughly the same cost of running f.

It is not hard to check that the above algorithms satisfy the properties of correctness and amortized efficiency given in Definition 3. In particular, correctness follows from the the correctness properties of PolyEval and GroupEval. A formal proof of this property appears in the full version.

5. HOMOMORPHIC MACS WITH EFFICIENT VERIFICATION

In this section, we describe our construction of homomorphic MACs with efficient verification for multi-labeled programs as introduced in Section 3.3. In particular, the following theorem summarizes the main result of this work which is obtained by combining the EVH−MAC construction (see below) and our concrete instantiation of the PRF with amortized closed-form efficiency based on the Decision Linear assumption (Section 4.3).

THEOREM 2. *If the Decision Linear assumption holds, then* EVH−MAC *is a secure homomorphic message authenticator which supports evaluations of any arithmetic circuit f of degree at most* 2*, and achieves efficient verification, i.e.,* EVH−MAC *has amortized efficiency in which the offline verification* VerPrep *takes time* $O(|f|)$*, and the online verification* EffVer *takes time* $O(1)$.

Our construction works for circuits whose additive gates do not get inputs labeled by constants. As mentioned in [15], this can be done without loss of generality as one can use an equivalent circuit with a special variable/label for the constant 1 and publish the MAC of 1. Our scheme EVH−MAC is defined as follows:

KeyGen(1^λ). Run $\mathsf{bgpp} \leftarrow_{\mathcal{R}} \mathcal{G}(1^\lambda)$ to generate the description of bilinear groups. Let $\mathsf{bgpp} = (p, \mathbb{G}, \mathbb{G}_T, e, g)$ as defined above. Let the message space $\mathcal{M}$ be $\mathbb{Z}_p$. Choose a random value $\alpha \leftarrow_{\mathcal{R}} \mathbb{Z}_p$, and run $(K, \mathsf{pp}) \leftarrow_{\mathcal{R}} \mathsf{KG}(1^\lambda)$ to obtain the seed K of a pseudorandom function $\mathsf{F}_K : \{0,1\}^* \times \{0,1\}^* \to \mathbb{G}$. Output the secret key $\mathsf{sk} = (\mathsf{bgpp}, \mathsf{pp}, K, \alpha)$, and the evaluation key $\mathsf{ek} = (\mathsf{bgpp}, \mathsf{pp})$.

Auth$(\mathsf{sk}, \mathsf{L}, m)$. To authenticate a message $m \in \mathbb{Z}_p$ with multi-label $\mathsf{L} = (\Delta, \tau)$ where $\Delta \in \{0,1\}^\lambda$ is the identifier of a data set and $\tau \in \{0,1\}^\lambda$ is an input identifier, proceed as follows. First, compute $R \leftarrow \mathsf{F}_K(\Delta, \tau)$ and then compute values $(y_0, Y_1) \in \mathbb{Z}_p \times \mathbb{G}$ by setting: $y_0 = m$ and $Y_1 = (R \cdot g^{-m})^{1/\alpha}$. Finally, output the tag $\sigma = (y_0, Y_1)$.

If we let $y_1 \in \mathbb{Z}_p$ be the (unique) value such that $Y_1 = g^{y_1}$, then (y_0, y_1) are basically the coefficients of a degree-1 polynomial $y(x)$ that evaluates to m on the point 0 (i.e., $y(0) = m$) and it evaluates to $r = \phi_g^{-1}(R)$ on a hidden random point α (i.e., $y(\alpha) = r$).

Eval$(\mathsf{ek}, f, \vec{\sigma})$. The homomorphic evaluation algorithm takes as input the evaluation key $\mathsf{ek} = (\mathsf{bgpp}, \mathsf{pp})$, an arithmetic circuit $f : \mathbb{Z}_p^n \to \mathbb{Z}_p$, and a vector $\vec{\sigma}$ of tags $(\sigma_1, \ldots, \sigma_n)$.

Eval proceeds gate-by-gate as follows. At every gate f_g, given two tags σ_1, σ_2 (or a tag σ_1 and a constant $c \in \mathbb{Z}_p$), it runs the algorithm $\sigma \leftarrow \mathsf{GateEval}(\mathsf{ek}, f_g, \sigma_1, \sigma_2)$ described below that returns a new tag σ, which is in turn passed on as input to the next gate in the circuit. When the computation reaches the last gate of the circuit f, Eval outputs the tag vector σ obtained by running GateEval on such last gate. To complete the description of Eval we thus describe the subroutine GateEval:

GateEval$(\mathsf{ek}, f_g, \sigma^{(1)}, \sigma^{(2)})$. Let $\sigma^{(i)} = (y_0^{(i)}, Y_1^{(i)}, \hat{Y}_2^{(i)}) \in \mathbb{Z}_p \times \mathbb{G} \times \mathbb{G}_T$ for $i = 1, 2$ (see below for the special case when one of the two inputs is a constant $c \in \mathbb{Z}_p$). For ease of description, whenever $\hat{Y}_2^{(i)}$ is not defined, we assume $\hat{Y}_2^{(i)} = 1 \in \mathbb{G}_T$. The goal is to compute $(y_0, Y_1, \hat{Y}_2)$ as follows. For an **addition** with gate f_+, compute $y_0 = {y_0}^{(1)} + {y_0}^{(2)}$, $Y_1 = Y_1^{(1)} \cdot Y_1^{(2)}$, and $\hat{Y}_2 = \hat{Y}_2^{(1)} \cdot \hat{Y}_2^{(2)}$. For a **multiplication** with gate $f_\times$ compute $y_0 = {y_0}^{(1)} \cdot {y_0}^{(2)}$, $Y_1 = (Y_1^{(1)})^{y_0^{(2)}} \cdot (Y_1^{(2)})^{y_0^{(1)}}$, and $\hat{Y}_2 = e(Y_1^{(1)}, Y_1^{(2)})$. Because of our assumption that $deg(f) \leq 2$, we can assume that $\sigma^{(i)} = (y_0^{(i)}, Y_1^{(i)}) \in \mathbb{Z}_p \times \mathbb{G}$ for both $i = 1, 2$. For a **multiplication with a constant**, where one of the two inputs, say σ_2, is a constant $c \in \mathbb{Z}_p$, compute $y_0 = c \cdot {y_0}^{(1)}$, $Y_1 = (Y_1^{(1)})^c$, and $\hat{Y}_2 = (Y_2^{(1)})^c$. Return $\sigma = (y_0, Y_1, \hat{Y}_2)$.

Ver$(\mathsf{sk}, \mathcal{P}_\Delta, m, \sigma)$. Let $\mathsf{sk} = (\mathsf{bgpp}, \mathsf{pp}, K, \alpha)$ be a secret key. Let $\mathcal{P}_\Delta = (\mathcal{P}, \Delta)$ be a multi-labeled program for $\mathcal{P} = (f, \tau_1, \ldots, \tau_n)$ and data set Δ. Let $m \in \mathbb{Z}_p$ be the result to be verified, and let $\sigma = (y_0, Y_1, \hat{Y}_2)$ be a tag. The verification proceeds as follows. For $i = 1$ to n, compute $R_i \leftarrow \mathsf{F}_K(\Delta, \tau_i)$. Then run $W \leftarrow \mathsf{GroupEval}(f, R_1, \ldots, R_n) \in \mathbb{G}_T$, as described in Section 4.1. Finally, check the following equations:

$$m = y_0 \tag{2}$$

$$W = e(g,g)^{y_0} \cdot e(Y_1, g)^\alpha \cdot (\hat{Y}_2)^{\alpha^2} \tag{3}$$

If both checks are satisfied, then output 1, and 0 otherwise.

Finally, to complete the description of EVH−MAC we give the algorithms for efficient verification:

VerPrep$(\mathsf{sk}, \mathcal{P})$. Let $\mathcal{P} = (f, \vec{\tau})$ be a labeled program where $f \in \mathbb{Z}_p^n \to \mathbb{Z}_p$ is an arithmetic circuit and $\vec{\tau} = (\tau_1, \ldots, \tau_n)$ is a vector of input identifiers for f. The algorithm computes concise verification information $\mathsf{VK}_\mathcal{P} = \omega$ where ω is obtained by using the offline closed-form efficient algorithm of F for GroupEval, i.e., $\omega \leftarrow \mathsf{CFEval}^{\mathsf{off}}_{\mathsf{GroupEval}, \vec{\tau}}(K, f)$.

EffVer$(\mathsf{sk}, \mathsf{VK}_\mathcal{P}, \Delta, m, \sigma)$. Let $\mathsf{sk} = (\mathsf{bgpp}, \mathsf{pp}, K, \alpha)$ be a secret key. Let $\mathsf{VK}_\mathcal{P} = \omega$ be the concise verification information for $\mathcal{P}$. Let $m \in \mathbb{Z}_p$ be the result to be verified and let $\sigma = (y_0, Y_1, \hat{Y}_2)$ be a tag. The online verification proceeds as follows. First, it runs the online closed-form efficient algorithm of F for GroupEval, in order to compute $W \leftarrow \mathsf{CFEval}^{\mathsf{on}}_{\mathsf{GroupEval}, \Delta}(K, \omega)$. Finally, it runs the same checks (2) and (3) as in standard verification. If both checks are satisfied, then output 1. Otherwise output 0.

Efficiency Analysis. We discuss the concrete efficiency of our scheme when implemented with specific security parameters of 80 and 128 bits. In particular, we consider the bandwidth costs for sending the MACs over the network, and the computational timings of the various algorithms at both the client and the server. The timings are obtained by evaluating the most significant operations performed by our algorithms, namely modular exponentiations and pairing computations. For our evaluation, we consider an implementation of Type-A (symmetric) pairings using the PBC library [35], on an 2.5 GHz Intel Core i5 workstation running Mac OS X 10.8.3. The timings of all basic operations needed by our scheme are summarized in Table 1. In addition, we note that by using 80 (resp. 128) bits of security, an element of $\mathbb{Z}_p$ can be represented with 160 (resp. 256) bits, an element of $\mathbb{G}$ with 512 (resp. 1536) bits, and an element of $\mathbb{G}_T$ with 1024 (resp. 3072) bits. Most clients' costs are

Operation	Time (ms)	
	80-bits	128-bits
Pairing	1.23	12
* Pairing	0.62	6.34
Exp. in $\mathbb{G}$	1.83	9.55
* Exp. in $\mathbb{G}$	0.24	1.34
Exp. in $\mathbb{G}_T$	0.22	1.15
* Exp. in $\mathbb{G}_T$	0.05	0.26
Multiexp(2). in $\mathbb{G}$	2.53	13.34
Multiexp(3). in $\mathbb{G}_T$	0.44	2.45

* Costs obtained using precomputation.

Table 1: Summary of costs per operation (in ms).

Operations at the client side	Time (ms)		Size of tags (kB)	
	80 bits	128 bits	80 bits	128 bits
Data Outsourcing	0.24	1.34	0.08	0.22
Verif. w/o prep.	1.06	8.79	0.21	0.59

Table 2: Clients' costs to outsource and to verify.

summarized in Table 2. Below we illustrate how they are obtained, and we give more details on the remaining costs.

To obtain the bandwidth costs, we observe that the MAC σ created by the client, i.e., as generated by Auth, consists of two elements $(y_0, Y_1) \in \mathbb{Z}_p \times \mathbb{G}$, whereas the MAC returned by Eval may include the additional element $\hat{Y}_2 \in \mathbb{G}_T$.

Next, let us consider the computational performances of the algorithms of EVH−MAC. To authenticate a data item, the client runs Auth, whose cost basically boils down to that of computing Y_1. The latter requires one PRF evaluation to generate R (which amounts to one exponentiation in $\mathbb{G}$), plus two other exponentiations, one for m, and one for α^{-1}. However, with a more careful look at our PRF construction, we observe that this operation can be optimized by computing directly $Y_1 = g^{(ua+vb-m)/\alpha}$, a *single* exponentiation in $\mathbb{G}$ (with precomputation on the fixed basis g). For verification, the client has to first prepare the re-usable verification information $\mathsf{VK}_{\mathcal{P}}$ using VerPrep. The cost of this algorithm depends on the computation of $\omega \leftarrow \mathsf{CFEval}^{\mathsf{off}}_{\mathsf{GroupEval},\mathcal{F}}(K, f)$, which is essentially the same as computing the function f (no exponentiations, pairings or group operations are needed). Such value $\mathsf{VK}_{\mathcal{P}}$ is stored by the client (its size amounts to at most 5 elements of $\mathbb{Z}_p$), and it can be re-used over and over when running $\mathcal{P}$ on different data sets, thus amortizing the cost of its computation. To verify a MAC using EffVer in the online phase, the client needs to compute only one pairing (with precomputation on the fixed g), i.e., $e(Y_1, g)$, and one multi-exponentiation with three bases[4], for $e(g,g)^{y_0-w}e(Y_1,g)^{\alpha}(\hat{Y}_2)^{\alpha^2}$. To conclude our analysis, we consider the cost required to the server for generating the correctness proofs, i.e., to run Eval. As one can notice, Eval evaluates the circuit f with an additional, constant, overhead which derives from replacing every addition of f with the group operation (in either $\mathbb{G}$ or $\mathbb{G}_T$), and every multiplication with one multi-exponentiation in $\mathbb{G}$ plus one pairing.

Correctness and Security. For lack of space, we formally prove correctness and security properties of our construction only in the full version of this work. Below we provide the reader with some intuitive ideas.

Roughly speaking, correctness is based on the following facts: (i) our MACs "encode" polynomials $y(x)$ satisfying $y(0) = m$ and $y(\alpha) = r_{(\Delta,\tau)}$; (ii) by the property of GroupEval, the verification can recompute $w = f(r_{(\Delta,\tau_1)}, \ldots, r_{(\Delta,\tau_n)})$ "in the exponent"; (iii) Eval essentially evaluates PolyEval "in the exponent", thus preserving the property on $y(\alpha)$, i.e., $y(\alpha) = w$. Correctness of EffVer instead follows from the correctness of the amortized closed-form efficiency for GroupEval (see Section 4.3).

The security of EVH−MAC is shown via the following theorem whose proof is contained in the long version [7].

THEOREM 3. *Let λ be the security parameter,* F *be a pseudorandom function with security ϵ_{F}, and $\mathcal{G}$ be a bilinear group generator. Then, any PPT adversary $\mathcal{A}$ making Q verification queries has probability at most $\epsilon = 2\cdot\epsilon_{\mathsf{F}} + \frac{8Q}{p-2(Q-1)}$ of breaking the security of* EVH−MAC.

[4]Here we observed that the explicit computation of $W = e(g,g)^w$ in $\mathsf{CFEval}^{\mathsf{on}}$ can be avoided by directly considering $e(g,g)^{y_0-w}$.

6. REFERENCES

[1] S. Agrawal and D. Boneh. Homomorphic MACs: MAC-based integrity for network coding. In *ACNS*, 2009.

[2] B. Applebaum, Y. Ishai, and E. Kushilevitz. From secrecy to soundness: Efficient verification via secure computation. In *ICALP 2010, Part I*, 2010.

[3] N. Attrapadung and B. Libert. Homomorphic network coding signatures in the standard model. In *PKC*, 2011.

[4] N. Attrapadung, B. Libert, and T. Peters. Computing on authenticated data: New privacy definitions and constructions. In *ASIACRYPT*, 2012.

[5] N. Attrapadung, B. Libert, and T. Peters. Efficient completely context-hiding quotable and linearly homomorphic signatures. In *PKC*, 2013.

[6] L. Babai. Trading group theory for randomness. In *STOC*, 1985.

[7] M. Backes, D. Fiore, and R. M. Reischuk. Verifiable delegation of computation on outsourced data. Cryptology ePrint Archive, Report 2013/469, 2013. `http://eprint.iacr.org/`.

[8] M. Belenkiy, M. Chase, C. C. Erway, J. Jannotti, A. Küpçü, and A. Lysyanskaya. Incentivizing outsourced computation. In *NetEcon*, 2008.

[9] S. Benabbas, R. Gennaro, and Y. Vahlis. Verifiable delegation of computation over large datasets. In *CRYPTO*, 2011.

[10] N. Bitansky, R. Canetti, A. Chiesa, and E. Tromer. From extractable collision resistance to succinct non-interactive arguments of knowledge, and back again. In *ITCS*, 2012.

[11] D. Boneh, X. Boyen, and H. Shacham. Short group signatures. In *CRYPTO*, 2004.

[12] D. Boneh, D. Freeman, J. Katz, and B. Waters. Signing a linear subspace: Signature schemes for network coding. In *PKC*, 2009.

[13] D. Boneh and D. M. Freeman. Homomorphic signatures for polynomial functions. In *EUROCRYPT*, 2011.

[14] D. Boneh and D. M. Freeman. Linearly homomorphic signatures over binary fields and new tools for lattice-based signatures. In *PKC*, 2011.

[15] D. Catalano and D. Fiore. Practical homomorphic MACs for arithmetic circuits. In *EUROCRYPT*, 2013.

[16] D. Catalano, D. Fiore, R. Gennaro, and K. Vamvourellis. Algebraic (trapdoor) one way functions and their applications. In *TCC*, 2013.

[17] D. Catalano, D. Fiore, and B. Warinschi. Adaptive pseudo-free groups and applications. In *EUROCRYPT*, 2011.

[18] D. Catalano, D. Fiore, and B. Warinschi. Efficient network coding signatures in the standard model. In *PKC*, 2012.

[19] K.-M. Chung, Y. Kalai, and S. P. Vadhan. Improved delegation of computation using fully homomorphic encryption. In *CRYPTO*, 2010.

[20] K.-M. Chung, Y. T. Kalai, F.-H. Liu, and R. Raz. Memory delegation. In *CRYPTO*, 2011.

[21] G. Di Battista and B. Palazzi. Authenticated relational tables and authenticated skip lists. In *DBSec*, 2007.

[22] D. Fiore and R. Gennaro. Publicly verifiable delegation of large polynomials and matrix computations, with applications. In *CCS*, 2012.

[23] D. M. Freeman. Improved security for linearly homomorphic signatures: A generic framework. In *PKC*, 2012.

[24] R. Gennaro, C. Gentry, and B. Parno. Non-interactive verifiable computing: Outsourcing computation to untrusted workers. In *CRYPTO*, 2010.

[25] R. Gennaro, C. Gentry, B. Parno, and M. Raykova. Quadratic span programs and succinct NIZKs without PCPs. In *EUROCRYPT*, 2013.

[26] R. Gennaro, J. Katz, H. Krawczyk, and T. Rabin. Secure network coding over the integers. In *PKC*, 2010.

[27] R. Gennaro and D. Wichs. Fully homomorphic message authenticators. Cryptology ePrint Archive, Report 2012/290, 2012. `http://eprint.iacr.org/`.

[28] C. Gentry and D. Wichs. Separating succinct non-interactive arguments from all falsifiable assumptions. In *STOC*, 2011.

[29] S. Goldwasser, Y. T. Kalai, and G. N. Rothblum. Delegating computation: interactive proofs for muggles. In *STOC*, 2008.

[30] M. T. Goodrich, R. Tamassia, and J. Hasic. An efficient dynamic and distributed cryptographic accumulator. In *ISC*, 2002.

[31] M. T. Goodrich, R. Tamassia, N. Triandopoulos, and R. Cohen. Authenticated data structures for graph and geometric searching. In *CT-RSA*, 2003.

[32] R. Johnson, D. Molnar, D. X. Song, and D. Wagner. Homomorphic signature schemes. In *CT-RSA*, 2002.

[33] J. Kilian. A note on efficient zero-knowledge proofs and arguments. In *STOC*, 1992.

[34] A. B. Lewko and B. Waters. Efficient pseudorandom functions from the decisional linear assumption and weaker variants. In *CCS*, 2009.

[35] B. Lynn. PBC: The pairing-based crypto library.

[36] C. Martel, G. Nuckolls, P. Devanbu, M. Gertz, A. Kwong, and S. G. Stubblebine. A general model for authenticated data structures. *Algorithmica*, 39(1):21–41, 2004.

[37] S. Micali. CS proofs. In *35th FOCS*, 1994.

[38] F. Monrose, P. Wyckoff, and A. D. Rubin. Distributed execution with remote audit. In *NDSS*, 1999.

[39] M. Naor and K. Nissim. Certificate revocation and certificate update. In *USENIX Security*, 1998.

[40] C. Papamanthou, E. Shi, and R. Tamassia. Signatures of correct computation. In *TCC*, 2013.

[41] C. Papamanthou and R. Tamassia. Time and space efficient algorithms for two-party authenticated data structures. In *ICICS*, 2007.

[42] C. Papamanthou, R. Tamassia, and N. Triandopoulos. Optimal verification of operations on dynamic sets. In *CRYPTO*, 2011.

[43] B. Parno, J. Howell, C. Gentry, and M. Raykova. Pinocchio: Nearly practical verifiable computation. In *IEEE Symposium on Security and Privacy*, 2013.

[44] B. Parno, M. Raykova, and V. Vaikuntanathan. How to delegate and verify in public: Verifiable computation from attribute-based encryption. In *TCC*, 2012.

[45] S. Setty, B. Braun, V. Vu, A. Blumberg, B. Parno, and M. Walfish. Resolving the conflict between generality and plausibility in verified computation. EuroSys 2013.

[46] S. Setty, R. McPherson, A. Blumberg, and M. Walfish. Making argument systems for outsourced computation practical (sometimes). In *NDSS*, 2012.

[47] S. Setty, V. Vu, N. Panpalia, B. Braun, A. Blumberg, and M. Walfish. Taking proof-based verified computation a few steps closer to practicality. In *USENIX Security Symposium*, 2012.

[48] A. Shpilka and A. Yehudayoff. Arithmetic circuits: A survey of recent results and open questions. *Foundations and Trends in TCS*, 2010.

[49] S. W. Smith and S. Weingart. Building a high-performance, programmable secure coprocessor. *Computer Networks*, 1999.

[50] R. Tamassia. Authenticated data structures. In G. Battista and U. Zwick, editors, *Algorithms - ESA*. Springer, 2003.

[51] V. Vu, S. Setty, A. Blumberg, and M. Walfish. A hybrid architecture for interactive verifiable computation. In *IEEE Security and Privacy*, 2013.

[52] B. Yee. *Using Secure Coprocessors*. PhD thesis, Carnegie Mellon University, 1994.

Outsourced Symmetric Private Information Retrieval

Stanislaw Jarecki
U. California Irvine
stasio@ics.uci.edu

Charanjit Jutla
IBM Research
csjutla@us.ibm.com

Hugo Krawczyk
IBM Research
hugo@ee.technion.ac.il

Marcel Rosu
U. California Irvine
marcelrosu@gmail.com

Michael Steiner
IBM Research
msteiner@us.ibm.com

ABSTRACT

In the setting of searchable symmetric encryption (SSE), a data owner $\mathcal{D}$ outsources a database (or document/file collection) to a remote server $\mathcal{E}$ in encrypted form such that $\mathcal{D}$ can later search the collection at $\mathcal{E}$ while hiding information about the database and queries from $\mathcal{E}$. Leakage to $\mathcal{E}$ is to be confined to well-defined forms of data-access and query patterns while preventing disclosure of explicit data and query plaintext values. Recently, Cash et al. presented a protocol, OXT, which can run arbitrary boolean queries in the SSE setting and which is remarkably efficient even for very large databases.

In this paper we investigate a richer setting in which the data owner $\mathcal{D}$ outsources its data to a server $\mathcal{E}$ but $\mathcal{D}$ is now interested to allow clients (third parties) to search the database such that clients learn the information $\mathcal{D}$ authorizes them to learn but nothing else while $\mathcal{E}$ still does not learn about the data or queried values as in the basic SSE setting. Furthermore, motivated by a wide range of applications, we extend this model and requirements to a setting where, similarly to private information retrieval, the client's queried values need to be hidden also from the data owner $\mathcal{D}$ even though the latter still needs to authorize the query. Finally, we consider the scenario in which authorization can be enforced by the data owner $\mathcal{D}$ without $\mathcal{D}$ learning the policy, a setting that arises in court-issued search warrants.

We extend the OXT protocol of Cash et al. to support arbitrary boolean queries in all of the above models while withstanding adversarial non-colluding servers ($\mathcal{D}$ and $\mathcal{E}$) and arbitrarily malicious clients, and while preserving the remarkable performance of the protocol.

CCS'13, November 4–8, 2013, Berlin, Germany.

http://dx.doi.org/10.1145/2508859.2516730.

1. INTRODUCTION

Consider a database DB composed of collection of documents or records and an application that needs to search DB based on the keywords contained in these records. For example, DB can be a medical relational database with records indexed by a set of attributes (e.g., name, zipcode, medical condition, etc.), an email repository indexed by English words and/or envelope information (date, sender, receivers, etc.), a collection of webpages indexed by text and metadata, etc. A search query consists of a boolean expression on keywords that returns all documents whose associated keywords satisfy that expression. In this paper we are concerned with applications where the database is outsourced to an external server $\mathcal{E}$ and search is performed at $\mathcal{E}$ *privately.* That is, $\mathcal{E}$ stores an encrypted version of the original database DB (plus some metadata) and answers encrypted queries from clients such that the client obtains the documents matching his query without $\mathcal{E}$ learning plaintext information about the data and queries.

The most basic setting of private data outsourcing as described above is where the owner of the data itself, $\mathcal{D}$, is the party performing the search at $\mathcal{E}$. In this setting, $\mathcal{D}$ initially processes DB into an encrypted database EDB and sends it to $\mathcal{E}$. $\mathcal{D}$ only keeps a set of cryptographic keys that allows her to later run encrypted searches on $\mathcal{E}$ and decrypt the matching documents returned by $\mathcal{E}$. This setting is known as *searchable symmetric encryption (SSE)* and has been studied extensively [29, 15, 16, 10, 13, 11, 24]. While most of the research has focused on single-keyword searches (i.e., return all documents containing a given keyword), recently Cash et al. [9] provided the first SSE solution, the OXT protocol, that can support in a practical and private way arbitrary boolean queries on sets of keywords and in very large DBs. The leakage to $\mathcal{E}$, which is formally specified and proven in [9], is in the form of data-access and query patterns, never as direct exposure of plaintext data or searched values.

In this work we are concerned with richer outsourcing scenarios where multiple third parties (clients) access the data at $\mathcal{E}$ but only through queries authorized by the data owner $\mathcal{D}$. For example, consider a hospital outsourcing an (encrypted) database to an external service $\mathcal{E}$ such that clients (doctors, administrators, insurance companies, etc.) can search the database but only via queries authorized according to the hospital's policy and without these clients learning information on non-matching documents. As before, $\mathcal{E}$ should learn as little as possible about data and queries.

In this multi-client scenario (to which we refer as *MC-SSE*), $\mathcal{D}$ provides search tokens to clients based on their queries and according to a given authorization policy. Security considers multiple clients acting maliciously and possibly colluding with each other (trying to gain information beyond what they are authorized for) and a semi-trusted server $\mathcal{E}$ which acts as "honest-but-curious" but does not collude with clients. Extending SSE solutions to the multi-client scenario is straightforward when (a) search tokens are fully determined by the query and (b) the SSE protocol does not return false positives (returning false positives, i.e. documents that do not match a query, is allowed in SSE since the recipient in that case is the owner of the data but not in the multi-client setting where clients are not allowed to learn data they were not authorized for). In such cases, $\mathcal{D}$ would receive the client's query, generate the corresponding SSE search tokens as if $\mathcal{D}$ herself was searching the database, and provide the tokens to the client together with a signature that $\mathcal{E}$ can check before processing the search. However, for enabling general boolean queries, the SSE OXT protocol of [9] requires a number of tokens that is not known a-priori (it depends on the searched data, not only on the query) and therefore the above immediate adaptation does not work.

Our first contribution is in extending the OXT protocol from [9] to the MC-SSE setting while preserving its full boolean-query capabilities and performance. In this extension, $\mathcal{D}$ provides the client $\mathcal{C}$ with a set of query-specific trapdoors which the client can then transform into search tokens as required by OXT. The set of trapdoors given to $\mathcal{C}$ is fully determined by the query and independent of the searched data. An additional subtle technical challenge posed by OXT is how to allow $\mathcal{E}$ to verify that the search tokens presented by $\mathcal{C}$ are authorized by $\mathcal{D}$. The simple solution is for $\mathcal{D}$ to sign the trapdoors, however in OXT these trapdoors need to be hidden from $\mathcal{E}$ (otherwise $\mathcal{E}$ can learn information about unauthorized searches) so a simple signature on them cannot be verified by $\mathcal{E}$. Our solution uses a *homomorphic signature* by $\mathcal{D}$ on the trapdoors that $\mathcal{C}$ can then transform homomorphically into signatures on the search tokens. We show that forging the tokens or their signatures is infeasible even by fully malicious clients.

The resulting MC-OXT protocol preserves the full functional properties of OXT, namely support for arbitrary boolean queries, the same level of privacy (i.e., same leakage profile) with respect to $\mathcal{E}$, and the same remarkable performance. Privacy with respect to clients is near-optimal (see Section 3.1 for why such leakage may be inevitable) with leakage confined only to information on the number of documents matching one of the query terms (typically, the least-frequent term).

Next, we extend the MC-OXT protocol to an even more challenging setting we call Outsourced Symmetric Private Information Retrieval (OSPIR), where on top of the MC-SSE requirements, one asks that *client queries be hidden from $\mathcal{D}$* - similarly to the Private Information Retrieval (PIR) primitive. This requirement arises in important outsourcing scenarios. In the medical database example mentioned above, the hospital authorizes doctors or other parties to search the medical database according to certain policy; however, in some cases the actual query values are to be kept secret from the hospital itself (due to privacy, liability and regulatory requirements). Only the minimal information for determining the compliance of a query to the policy should be disclosed to the hospital. For example, the policy may indicate that only conjunctions with a minimal number of terms are allowed or that the query needs to include at least three of a set of attributes, etc. In such a case, there is no need for the hospital to learn the particular values being searched (such as a specific last name or medical condition). In other cases, as in outsourced patent or financial information search, the provider $\mathcal{D}$ may want to enforce that a client $\mathcal{C}$ pays for the type of query it is interested in but $\mathcal{C}$ wants to keep his query hidden from both $\mathcal{D}$ and $\mathcal{E}$. Applications to intelligence scenarios are discussed in [18] (see also [32]).

Thus, we relax the query privacy requirement with respect to $\mathcal{D}$ to allow for minimal information needed for $\mathcal{D}$ to determine policy compliance. Specifically, we consider the case where keywords are formed by pairs of attribute-values. For example, in a relational database, attributes are defined by the database columns (e.g., SSN, name, citizenship, etc.), while in an email repository attributes can refer to envelope information such as sender and receivers or to the message body (in which case the values are, say, English words). In this case, a policy defines the class of boolean expressions allowed for a given client and the attributes that may be used as inputs into these expressions. In order to enforce the policy, $\mathcal{D}$ learns the boolean expression and attributes but nothing about the searched values. For policies defined via classes of attributes (e.g. allowing any attribute from the set of attributes {name, city, zipcode}) leakage to $\mathcal{D}$ can be further reduced by revealing the class and not the specific attributes in the query.

Our most advanced result is extending the OXT protocol to the above OSPIR setting. The resultant protocol, OSPIR-OXT, adds some crucial new ingredients to OXT: It uses *oblivious PRFs (OPRF)* for hiding the query values from $\mathcal{D}$, uses attribute-specific keys for enforcing policy compliance, and uses homomorphic signatures (or the more general abstraction of *shared OPRFs*) for query verification by $\mathcal{E}$. A further extension of the protocol accommodates an external policy manager, e.g., a judge in a warrant-based search, who checks policy compliance and allows server $\mathcal{D}$ to enforce the policy without learning the attributes being searched.

Performance-wise our extensions to OXT preserve the protocol's performance in both pre-processing (creating EDB) and search phases. $\mathsf{OSPIR\text{-}OXT}$ adds to the computational cost by adding a few exponentiations but these are generally inexpensive relative to the I/O cost (especially thanks to common-base exponentiation optimizations). The protocols we provide for MC-SSE and OSPIR models support encrypted search over database containing tens of billions record-keyword pairs, for example a full snapshot of English Wikipedia or a 10-TByte, 100M-record US-census database (see Sections 4.3 and 4.4).

We achieve provable security against adaptive adversarial honest-but-curious server $\mathcal{E}$, against arbitrarily malicious (but non-colluding[1] with $\mathcal{E}$) server $\mathcal{D}$, and against arbitrarily malicious clients. Our security models extend the SSE model [13, 11, 9] to the more complex settings of MC-SSE and OSPIR. In all cases security is defined in the real-vs-ideal model and is parametrized by a specified leakage function $\mathcal{L}(\mathsf{DB}, \mathbf{q})$. A protocol is said to be secure with leakage profile $\mathcal{L}(\mathsf{DB}, \mathbf{q})$ against adversary $\mathcal{A}$ if the actions of $\mathcal{A}$ on adversarially-chosen input DB and queries set $\mathbf{q}$ can be simulated with access to the leakage information $\mathcal{L}(\mathsf{DB}, \mathbf{q})$ only

[1] See Section 5.1.

(and not to DB or **q**). This allows modeling and bounding partial leakage allowed by SSE protocols. It means that even an adversary that has full information about a database, or even chooses it, does not learn anything from the protocol execution other than what can be derived solely from the defined leakage profile.

Related work: Searchable symmetric encryption (SSE) has been extensively studied [29, 15, 16, 10, 13, 11, 24] (see [13, 11] for more on related work). Most SSE research focused on single-keyword search, and after several solutions with complexity linear in the database size, Curtmola et al. [13] present the first solution for single-keyword search whose complexity is linear in the number of matching documents. They also improve on previous security models, in particular by providing an adaptive security definition and a solution in this model.

Extending single-keyword SSE to search by conjunctions of keywords was considered in [16, 7, 2], but all these schemes had $O(|\mathsf{DB}|)$ search complexity. The first SSE which can handle very large DBs and supports conjunctive queries is the OXT protocol discussed above, given by Cash et al. [9]. The MC-SSE and OSPIR schemes we present are based on this protocol and they preserve its performance and privacy characteristics.

Extension of the two-party client-server model of SSE to the multi-client setting was considered by Curtmola et al, [13], but their model disallowed per-query interaction between the data owner and the client, leading to a relatively inefficient implementation based on broadcast encryption. Multi-client SSE setting which allows such interaction was considered by Chase and Kamara [11] as SSE with "controlled disclosure", and by Kamara and Lauter [23], as "virtual private storage", but both considered only single-keyword queries and did not support query privacy from the data owner. De Cristofaro et al. [12] extended multi-client SSE to the OSPIR setting, which supports query privacy, but only for the case of single-keyword queries. In recent independent work, Pappas et al. [27] provide support for boolean queries in a setting similar to our OSPIR setting (but with honest-but-curious clients).

SSE schemes which support efficient updates of the encrypted database appeared in [30, 24] for single-keyword SSE. The OXT SSE scheme of [9] which supports arbitrary boolean queries, has been extended to the dynamic case in [8], and the same techniques apply to the MC-SSE and OSPIR schemes presented in this paper.

Recently Islam et al. [19] showed that frequency analysis revealed by access control patterns in SSE schemes can be used to predict single-keyword queries. Such attacks, although harder to stage, are possible for conjunctive queries as well, but the general masking and padding countermeasures suggested in [19] are applicable to the MC-OXT and OSPIR-OXT protocols.

In other directions, SSE was extended to the *public key* setting, allowing any party to encrypt into the database, first for single-keyword search [5, 31, 1, 3, 6, 28], and later for conjunctive queries as well [6], but all these PKSE schemes have $O(|\mathsf{DB}|)$ search complexity. Universally composable SSE was introduced by [25], also with $O(|\mathsf{DB}|)$ search complexity.

Multi-client SSE and OSPIR models are related to the work on multi-client ORAM, e.g. see the recent work of Huang and Goldberg [17], which aims for stronger privacy protection of client's queries from server $\mathcal{E}$, but multi-client ORAM supports DB lookups by (single) indexes instead of (boolean formulas on) keywords, and they can currently support much smaller DB sizes.

Paper organization. We first present our protocols for the case of conjunctive queries: in Section 2 we recall the basic OXT protocol [9], suitably reformulated for our generalizations, in Section 3 we address the multi-client SSE model, and in Section 4 we handle the OSPIR model. In Section 4.2 we explain how to extend support for general boolean queries. Our security models and claims are presented concisely in Section 5 — a complete treatment is deferred to the full version [20]. While the main implementation details and performance analysis is deferred to a companion paper [8], we provide some information on computational cost and performance measurements from our implementation in Section 4.3 and 4.4, respectively.

2. SSE AND THE OXT PROTOCOL

We first recall the SSE OXT protocol from [9] that forms the basis for our solution to searchable encryption in the more advanced MC and OSPIR models.

SSE protocols and formal setting [9]**.** Let λ be a security parameter. A database $\mathsf{DB} = (\mathsf{ind}_i, \mathsf{W}_i)_{i=1}^d$ is a list of identifier and keyword-set pairs, where $\mathsf{ind}_i \in \{0,1\}^\lambda$ is a document identifier and $\mathsf{W}_i \subseteq \{0,1\}^*$ is a list of keywords in that document. We set W to $\bigcup_{i=1}^d \mathsf{W}_i$. A *query* $\psi(\bar{w})$ is specified by a tuple of keywords $\bar{w} \in \mathsf{W}^*$ and a boolean formula ψ on $\bar{w}$. We write $\mathsf{DB}(\psi(\bar{w}))$ for the set of identifiers of documents that "satisfy" $\psi(\bar{w})$. Formally, this means that $\mathsf{ind}_i \in \mathsf{DB}(\psi(\bar{w}))$ iff the formula $\psi(\bar{w})$ evaluates to true when we replace each keyword w_j with true or false depending on if $w_j \in \mathsf{W}_i$ or not (in particular $\mathsf{DB}(w) = \{\mathsf{ind}_i \text{ s.t. } w \in \mathsf{W}_i\}$). Below we let d denote the number of records in DB, $m = |\mathsf{W}|$, and $N = \sum_{w \in \mathsf{W}} |\mathsf{DB}(w)|$.

A *searchable symmetric encryption (SSE) scheme* Π consists of an algorithm EDBSetup and a protocol Search fitting the following syntax. EDBSetup takes as input a database DB and a list of document decryption keys RDK, and outputs a secret key K along with an encrypted database EDB. The search protocol proceeds between a *client* $\mathcal{C}$ and *server* $\mathcal{E}$, where $\mathcal{C}$ takes as input the secret key K and a query $\psi(\bar{w})$ and $\mathcal{E}$ takes as input EDB. At the end of the protocol $\mathcal{C}$ outputs a set of (ind, rdk) pairs while $\mathcal{E}$ has no output. We say that an SSE scheme is *correct* if for all DB, RDK and all queries $\psi(\bar{w})$, for $(K, \mathsf{EDB}) \leftarrow \mathsf{EDBSetup}(\mathsf{DB}, \mathsf{RDK})$, after running Search with client input $(K, \phi(\bar{w}))$ and server input EDB, the client outputs $\mathsf{DB}(\phi(\bar{w}))$ and $\mathsf{RDK}[\mathsf{DB}(\phi(\bar{w}))]$ where $\mathsf{RDK}[S]$ denotes $\{\mathsf{RDK}[\mathsf{ind}] \mid \mathsf{ind} \in S\}$. Correctness can be statistical (allowing a negligible probability of error) or computational (ensured only against computationally bounded attackers - see [9]).

Note (conjunctive vs. Boolean queries). Throughout the paper we present our protocols for the case of conjunctive queries where a query consists of n keywords $\bar{w} = (w_1, \ldots, w_n)$ and it returns all documents containing all these keywords. The adaptation to the case of boolean queries is described in Section 4.2.

Note (the array RDK*).* Our SSE syntax, and the OXT description in Figure 1, includes as input to EDBSetup an array RDK that contains, for each document in DB, a key rdk used to encrypt that document. When a client retrieves the index ind of a document matching its query, it also retrieves the *record-decrypting key* rdk needed to decrypt that record. This mechanism is not strictly needed in the SSE setting (where rdk could be derived from ind using a PRF with a secret key known to $\mathcal{C}$) and it is not part of the original OXT in [9], but it is needed in the more advanced models considered later. This extension does not change the functionality and security properties of OXT as analyzed in [9]).

Note (retrieval of matching encrypted records). Our formalism defines the output of the SSE protocol as the set of ind identifiers pointing to the encrypted records matching the query, together with the associated record decryption key. For the sake of generality, we do not model the processing and retrieval of encrypted records. This allows us to decouple the storage and processing of document payloads (which can be done in a variety of ways, with varying types of leakage) from the storage and processing of the metadata, which is the focus of our protocols.

SSE Security. The SSE setting considers security w.r.t. an adversarial server $\mathcal{E}$, hence security is parametrized via a leakage function capturing information learned by $\mathcal{E}$ from the interaction with $\mathcal{C}$. See Section 5.

2.1 The OXT Protocol

The OXT protocol [9] is presented in Figure 1; see [9] for full design rationale and analysis. Here we provide a high level description as needed for the extensions to this protocol we introduce in the following sections.

The basis of OXT is the following simple search algorithm over *unencrypted* databases. The algorithm uses two types of data structures. First, for every keyword w there is an inverted index (a list) I_w pointing to the indices ind of all documents that contain w. Then, for every document ind there is a list L_{ind} of all keywords contained in document ind. To search for a conjunction $\bar{w} = (w_1, \ldots, w_n)$, the client chooses the estimated least frequent keyword [2] in $\bar{w}$, say w_1, and checks for each $\mathsf{ind} \in I_{w_1}$ whether $w_i \in L_{\mathsf{ind}}$, $i = 2, \ldots, n$. If this holds for all $2 \le i \le n$ then ind is added to the result set. As a performance optimization, instead of maintaining a list L_{ind} for each ind, one can fix a hash function f and keep a data structure representing the set $X = \{f(w, \mathsf{ind}) : w \in \mathsf{W}, \mathsf{ind} \in \mathsf{DB}(w)\}$. Thus, the check $w \in L_{\mathsf{ind}}$ can be replaced with the check $f(w, \mathsf{ind}) \in X$. Protocol OXT adapts this algorithm to the encrypted setting as follows (we start with the description of a simplified version, corresponding to protocol BXT in [9], and then move to the more specific details of OXT).

For each keyword $w \in \mathsf{W}$ an inverted index (corresponding to I_w above), referred to as $\mathsf{TSet}(w)$, is built pointing to all the ind values of documents in $\mathsf{DB}(w)$. Each $\mathsf{TSet}(w)$ is identified by a string called $\mathsf{stag}(w)$ and ind values in $\mathsf{TSet}(w)$ are encrypted under a secret key K_e. Both $\mathsf{stag}(w)$ and K_e are computed as a PRF applied to w with secret keys known to $\mathcal{C}$ only. In addition, a data structure called XSet is built as an "encrypted equivalent" of the above set X as follows. First, for each $w \in \mathsf{W}$, a value $\mathsf{xtrap}(w) = F(K_X, w)$ is computed where K_X is a secret PRF key then for each $\mathsf{ind} \in \mathsf{DB}(w)$ a value $\mathsf{xtag} = f(\mathsf{xtrap}(w), \mathsf{ind})$ is added to XSet where f is an unpredictable function of its inputs (e.g., f can be a PRF used with $\mathsf{xtrap}(w)$ as the key and ind as input). The output EDB from the EDBSetup phase includes $\mathsf{TSet} = \{\mathsf{TSet}(w)\}_{w \in \mathsf{W}}$ and the set XSet. In the Search protocol for a conjunction $(w_1, \ldots, w_n)$, the client $\mathcal{C}$ chooses the conjunction's s-term (i.e., the estimated least frequent keyword in the conjunction, which we assume to be w_1), computes $\mathsf{stag}(w_1)$ and K_e using $\mathcal{C}$'s secret keys and computes $\mathsf{xtrap}_i = F(K_X, w_i)$ for each $i = 2, \ldots, n$. It then sends $(K_e, \mathsf{stag}, \mathsf{xtrap}_2, \ldots, \mathsf{xtrap}_n)$ to the server $\mathcal{E}$. $\mathcal{E}$ uses stag to retrieve $\mathsf{TSet}(w_1)$, uses K_e to decrypt the ind values in $\mathsf{TSet}(w_1)$, and sends back to $\mathcal{C}$ those ind for which $f(\mathsf{xtrap}_i, \mathsf{ind}) \in \mathsf{XSet}$ for all $i = 2, \ldots, n$.

The OXT protocol from Figure 1 follows the above logic but instantiates it in a way that minimizes leakage to $\mathcal{E}$. Rather than assuming a specific implementation of TSet, [9] abstracts this data structure through an API that we adopt here. Specifically, the abstract TSetSetup operation receives a collection $\mathbf{T}$ of lists $\mathbf{t}(w)$ for each $w \in \mathsf{W}$ and builds the TSet data structure out of these lists; it returns TSet and a key K_T. Then, $\mathsf{TSetRetrieve}(\mathsf{TSet}, \mathsf{stag}(w))$ instantiates the retrieval of a $\mathsf{TSet}(w)$ via its handle $\mathsf{stag}(w)$ which is computed by a function $\mathsf{TSetGetTag}(K_T, w)$ (typically a PRF). The elements in the $\mathbf{t}(w)$ lists are called *tuples* and their contents are defined by the OXT protocol. A TSet implementation provides two crucial security properties [9]: *privacy* in that the TSet datastructure does not reveal anything about the tuple lits in $\mathbf{T}$ except their summary length $\sum_w |\mathbf{T}[w]|$; and *correctness* in that (except for negligible probability) $\mathsf{TSetRetrieve}(\mathsf{TSet}, \mathsf{stag})$ returns $\mathbf{T}[w]$ for $\mathsf{stag} = \mathsf{TSetGetTag}(K_T, w)$, and it returns an empty set for all other stag values.

Next, we note that using the protocol described above leads to significant leakage in that the xtrap value allows $\mathcal{E}$ to check whether $\mathsf{xtag} = f(\mathsf{xtrap}, \mathsf{ind}) \in \mathsf{XSet}$ for each value ind ever seen by $\mathcal{E}$, revealing correlation statistics between each s-term and each x-term ever queried by $\mathcal{C}$. This motivates the main mechanism in OXT, i.e. the instantiation of the function f via a two-party computation in which $\mathcal{E}$ inputs an encrypted value ind, $\mathcal{C}$ inputs xtrap and the ind-decryption key, and $\mathcal{E}$ gets the value of $\mathsf{xtag} = f(\mathsf{xtrap}, \mathsf{ind})$ without learning either the xtrap or ind values themselves. For this OXT uses a blinded DH computation over a group G (with generator g of prime order p). However, to avoid the need for interaction between $\mathcal{E}$ and $\mathcal{C}$ in the Search phase, the *blinding factors are pre-computed and stored as part of the tuples in the* TSet *lists.* Specifically, indexes ind are replaced in the computation of f with dedicated per-record values $\mathsf{xind} \in Z_p^*$ (computed as $F_p(K_I, \mathsf{ind})$ where F_p is a PRF with range Z_p^*), $\mathsf{xtrap}(w)$'s are implemented as $g^{F_p(K_X, w)}$ (K_I and K_X are secret keys kept by $\mathcal{C}$), and xtag is re-defined as $(\mathsf{xtrap}(w))^{\mathsf{xind}}$. The blinding factor in the underlying two-party computation is pre-computed during EDBSetup and stored in the TSet. Namely, each tuple corresponding to a keyword w and document index ind contains a blinded value $y_c = \mathsf{xind} \cdot z_c^{-1}$ for $\mathsf{xind} = F_p(F_I, \mathsf{ind})$ where z_c is an element in Z_p^* derived (via a PRF) from w and a tuple counter c (this counter, incremented for each tuple in the tuple list associated with w, ensures independence of each blinding value z_c).

During search, the server $\mathcal{E}$ needs to compute the xtag values $g^{F_p(K_X, w_i) \cdot \mathsf{xind}}$ for each xind in $\mathsf{TSet}(w_1)$ and then test these for membership in XSet. To enable this the client sends, for the c-th tuple in $\mathbf{t}$, an n-long array $\mathsf{xtoken}[c]$ de-

[2]The estimated least frequent keyword is called the conjunction's *s-term*; the other terms in a conjunction are called *x-terms*.

EDBSetup(DB, RDK)

Key Generation. $\mathcal{D}$ picks key K_S for PRF F_τ and keys K_T, K_X, K_I for PRF F_p. F_τ and F_p are PRF's which output strings in respectively $\{0,1\}^\tau$ and Z_p^*, and τ is a security parameter.

- Initialize XSet to an empty set, and initialize $\mathbf{T}$ to an empty array indexed by keywords from W.
- For each $w \in \mathsf{W}$, build the tuple list $\mathbf{t}$ and insert elements into set XSet as follows:
  - Initialize $\mathbf{t}$ to be an empty list.
  - Set $\mathsf{strap} \leftarrow F_\tau(K_S, w)$ and $(K_z, K_e) \leftarrow (F_\tau(\mathsf{strap}, 1), F_\tau(\mathsf{strap}, 2))$.
  - Initialize $c \leftarrow 0$; then for all ind in $\mathsf{DB}(w)$ in random order:
    * Set $\mathsf{rdk} \leftarrow \mathsf{RDK}(\mathsf{ind})$, $\mathsf{e} \leftarrow \mathsf{Enc}(K_e, (\mathsf{ind}|\mathsf{rdk}))$, $\mathsf{xind} \leftarrow F_p(K_I, \mathsf{ind})$.
    * Set $c \leftarrow c + 1$, $z_c \leftarrow F_p(K_z, c)$, $y \leftarrow \mathsf{xind} \cdot z_c^{-1}$. Append (e, y) to $\mathbf{t}$.
    * Set $\mathsf{xtag} \leftarrow g^{F_p(K_X, w) \cdot \mathsf{xind}}$ and add xtag to XSet.
  - $\mathbf{T}[w] \leftarrow \mathbf{t}$.
- Create $(\mathsf{TSet}, K_T) \leftarrow \mathsf{TSetSetup}(\mathbf{T})$, and output key $K = (K_S, K_X, K_T, K_I)$ and $\mathsf{EDB} = (\mathsf{TSet}, \mathsf{XSet})$.

Search protocol

Client $\mathcal{C}$ on input K defined as above and a conjunctive query $\bar{w} = (w_1, \ldots, w_n)$:

- Sets $\mathsf{stag} \leftarrow \mathsf{TSetGetTag}(K_T, w_1)$; $\mathsf{strap} \leftarrow F_\tau(K_S, w_1)$, $(K_z, K_e) \leftarrow (F_\tau(\mathsf{strap}, 1), F_\tau(\mathsf{strap}, 2))$.
- Sends to the server $\mathcal{E}$ the message $(\mathsf{stag}, \mathsf{xtoken}[1], \mathsf{xtoken}[2], \ldots)$ where $\mathsf{xtoken}[\cdot]$ are defined as:
  - For $c = 1, 2, \ldots$, until $\mathcal{E}$ sends stop:
    * Set $z_c \leftarrow F_p(K_z, c)$ and set $\mathsf{xtoken}[c, i] \leftarrow g^{F_p(K_X, w_i) \cdot z_c}$ for $i = 2, \ldots, n$.
    * Set $\mathsf{xtoken}[c] \leftarrow (\mathsf{xtoken}[c, 2], \ldots, \mathsf{xtoken}[c, n])$.

Server $\mathcal{E}$ on input $\mathsf{EDB} = (\mathsf{TSet}, \mathsf{XSet})$ responds as follows:

- Retrieve $\mathbf{t} \leftarrow \mathsf{TSetRetrieve}(\mathsf{TSet}, \mathsf{stag})$ from TSet.
- For $c = 1, \ldots, |\mathbf{t}|$ do:
  - Retrieve (e, y) from the c-th tuple in $\mathbf{t}$
  - If $\forall i = 2, \ldots, n : \mathsf{xtoken}[c, i]^y \in \mathsf{XSet}$ then send e to client $\mathcal{C}$.
- When last tuple in $\mathbf{t}$ is reached, sends stop to $\mathcal{C}$ and halt.

For each received e client $\mathcal{C}$ computes $(\mathsf{ind}|\mathsf{rdk}) \leftarrow \mathsf{Dec}(K_e, \mathsf{e})$ and outputs $(\mathsf{ind}, \mathsf{rdk})$.

Figure 1: OXT: OBLIVIOUS CROSS-TAGS SSE SCHEME

fined by $\mathsf{xtoken}[c, i] := g^{F_p(K_X, w_i) \cdot z_c}$, $i = 1, \ldots, n$, where z_c is the precomputed blinding derived by $\mathcal{C}$ from w (via a PRF) and the tuple counter c. $\mathcal{E}$ then performs the T-set search to get the results for w_1, and for each c it filters the c-th result by testing if $\mathsf{xtoken}[c, i]^{y_c} \in \mathsf{XSet}$ for all $i = 2, \ldots, n$. This protocol is correct because $\mathsf{xtoken}[c, i]^{y_c} = g^{F_p(K_X, w_i) \cdot z_c \cdot \mathsf{xind} \cdot z_c^{-1}} = g^{F_p(K_X, w_i) \cdot \mathsf{xind}}$, meaning that the server correctly recomputes the pseudorandom values in the XSet. Putting these ideas together results in the OXT protocol of Figure 1. Note that $\mathcal{C}$ sends the xtoken arrays (each holding several values of the form $g^{F_p(K_X, w_i) \cdot z_c}$) until instructed to stop by $\mathcal{E}$. There is no other communication from server to client (alternatively, server can send the number of elements in $\mathsf{TSet}(w)$ to the client who will respond with such number of xtoken arrays).

Note. The OXT protocol in Figure 1 derives keys K_e, K_z slightly differently than in the OXT description of [9]. The modified key derivation is closer to what we need for MC-OXT and OSPIR-OXT protocols presented in the following sections, without affecting the functionality or security of OXT.

3. MULTI-CLIENT SSE

We present an extension of the OXT protocol for the *multi-client SSE (MC-SSE)* setting described in the introduction and in more detail below. The extension preserves the functionality of OXT, supporting any boolean query, and superb performance, while securely serving multiple clients, all of which can behave maliciously.

Multi-Client SSE Setting. In MC-SSE there is the owner $\mathcal{D}$ of the plaintext database DB, an external server $\mathcal{E}$ that holds the encrypted database EDB, and clients that receive tokens from $\mathcal{D}$ in order to perform search queries at $\mathcal{E}$. In other words, $\mathcal{D}$ is outsourcing her search service to a third party but requires clients to first obtain search tokens from her. Her goal is to ensure service to clients via $\mathcal{E}$ while leaking as little as possible information to $\mathcal{E}$ about the plaintext data and queries, and preventing clients from running any other DB queries than those for which $\mathcal{D}$ issued them a token. This is a natural outsourcing setting of increasing value in cloud-based platforms, and it was described by Chase and Kamara [11] as an *SSE with controlled disclosure.*

Formally, the MC-SSE setting changes the syntax of an SSE scheme by including an additional algorithm GenToken which on input the secret key K, generated by the data owner $\mathcal{D}$ in the EDBSetup procedure, and a boolean query $\psi(\bar{w})$, submitted by client $\mathcal{C}$, generates a search-enabling value token. Then, procedure Search is executed by server $\mathcal{E}$ on input EDB, but instead of the client $\mathcal{C}$ running on input K and query $\psi(\bar{w})$ (as in SSE), $\mathcal{C}$ runs on input consisting only of the search token token. Correctness is defined similarly to the SSE case, namely, assuring (except for negligible error probability) that $\mathcal{C}$'s output sets $\mathsf{DB}(\psi(\bar{w}))$ and $\mathsf{RDK}[\mathsf{DB}(\psi(\bar{w}))]$. Security is treated in Section 5.

3.1 The MC-OXT Protocol

We describe the changes to OXT from Figure 1 needed to support boolean queries in the MC-SSE setting. As before, the protocol is described for conjunctions with the adaptation to boolean queries described in Section 4.2.

$\mathsf{EDBSetup}(\mathsf{DB}, \mathsf{RDK})$. This pre-processing phase is identical to the one in OXT except for the addition of a key K_M shared between $\mathcal{D}$ and $\mathcal{E}$. The output from this phase is $K = (K_S, K_X, K_T, K_M)$ kept by $\mathcal{D}$ and $\mathsf{EDB} = (K_M, \mathsf{TSet}, \mathsf{XSet})$ stored at $\mathcal{E}$.

$\mathsf{GenToken}(K, \bar{w})$. This is the new MC-specific phase in which $\mathcal{D}$, using key K, authorizes $\mathcal{C}$ for a conjunction $\bar{w} = w_1, \ldots, w_n$ and provides $\mathcal{C}$ with the necessary tokens to enable the search at $\mathcal{E}$. We assume w_1 to be the s-term (and chosen by $\mathcal{D}$ who has knowledge of term frequencies). Specifically, $\mathcal{D}$ performs the following operations. She sets $\mathsf{stag} \leftarrow \mathsf{TSetGetTag}(K_T, w_1)$ and $\mathsf{strap} \leftarrow F_\tau(K_S, w_1)$, same as $\mathcal{C}$ does in OXT. Then, for $i = 2, ..., n$, she picks $\rho_i \leftarrow Z_p^*$ and sets $\mathsf{bxtrap}_i \leftarrow g^{F_p(K_X, w_i) \cdot \rho_i}$. Finally, she sets $\mathsf{env} \leftarrow \mathsf{AuthEnc}(K_M, (\mathsf{stag}, \rho_2, ..., \rho_n))$ and outputs $\mathsf{token} = (\mathsf{env}, \mathsf{strap}, \mathsf{bxtrap}_2, \ldots, \mathsf{bxtrap}_n)$ (which $\mathcal{C}$ uses in the search phase).

To see how this enables search as in OXT, first note that with $\mathsf{xtrap}_i = g^{F_p(K_X, w_i)}$, $i = 2, \ldots, n$, the client can produce the values $g^{F_p(K_X, w_i) \cdot z_c}$ needed in the Search phase of OXT. Hence, $\mathcal{D}$ could just provide the xtrap_i values to $\mathcal{C}$. However, $\mathcal{D}$ needs to be able to sign (or MAC) these values so that $\mathcal{E}$ can check that $\mathcal{C}$ is authorized to this query and, e.g., did not truncate a conjunction or mix parts from different queries. Signing the plain xtrap values does not work since these values must not be seen by $\mathcal{E}$ (it would allow $\mathcal{E}$ to learn information from unauthorized searches). The solution is to provide $\mathcal{C}$ with a *homomorphic signature* that $\mathcal{C}$ can convert into individual signatures for all tokens sent to $\mathcal{E}$. This is accomplished as follows: $\mathcal{D}$ picks one-time blinding factors $\rho_2, \ldots, \rho_n$ and provides $\mathcal{C}$ with *blinded* (or MAC'ed) xtrap values $\mathsf{bxtrap}_i = \mathsf{xtrap}_i^{\rho_i}$ for $j = 2, \ldots, n$, while providing the blinding factors $(\rho_2, \ldots, \rho_n)$ to $\mathcal{E}$ in an encrypted and authenticated envelope env. To produce $g^{F_p(K_X, w_i) \cdot z_c}$ during Search, $\mathcal{C}$ will compute $\mathsf{bxtrap}_i^{z_c}$ and $\mathcal{E}$ will raise this value to $1/\rho_i$. Security relies on the fact that if $\mathcal{C}$ provides $\mathcal{E}$ with values other than those given by $\mathcal{D}$, then when raised to $1/\rho_i$ by $\mathcal{E}$ (where ρ_i is random and unknown to $\mathcal{C}$) the resulting values will not correspond to elements of XSet except with negligible probability.

Search *Protocol.* The Search protocol reflects the above changes: On $\mathsf{token} = (\mathsf{env}, \mathsf{strap}, \mathsf{bxtrap}_2, ..., \mathsf{bxtrap}_n)$, $\mathcal{C}$ computes (K_z, K_e) from strap as in OXT. Then, it sends to $\mathcal{E}$ the value env as well as the sequence $\mathsf{bxtoken}[1], \mathsf{bxtoken}[2], \ldots$ which contains the same values as $\mathsf{xtoken}[1], \mathsf{xtoken}[2], \ldots$ in OXT up to the blinding exponents ρ_i. Specifically, the values $\mathsf{bxtoken}[c, i]$, for $i = 2, \ldots, n$, are computed by $\mathcal{C}$ as $(\mathsf{bxtrap}_i)^{z_c}$. On the receiving side, $\mathcal{E}$ verifies the authenticity of env and decrypts it to find stag, which it uses to retrieve $\mathsf{TSet}(w_1)$, and $\rho_2, \ldots, \rho_n$. The only change from OXT is that the operation $\mathsf{xtoken}[c, i]^y$ is replaced with $\mathsf{bxtoken}[c, i]^{y/\rho_i}$.

Note *(masking the size of* $\mathsf{TSet}(w_1)$*).* MC-OXT leaks to $\mathcal{C}$ the size of $\mathsf{TSet}(w_1) = \mathsf{DB}(w_1)$ given by the number of bxtoken vectors requested by $\mathcal{E}$. Note that the exact size of this set can easily be masked by $\mathcal{E}$ requesting more bxtoken values from $\mathcal{C}$ than needed. We observe that some form of leakage on the frequency of the least frequent term in the conjunction appears to be inherent even for plaintext search algorithms. Indeed, it is likely (though there seem to be no proven lower bounds) that running time will be noticeably different for conjunctions with all terms being infrequent from the case that all terms are very frequent, except if short searches are artificially padded to full database size (or if conjunctions are pre-computed). Two considerations in masking the size of $\mathsf{TSet}(w_1)$ are that (i) the masked size should be chosen as a step function of $|\mathsf{TSet}(w_1)|$ (and not, say, a fixed linear function); (ii) During search, $\mathcal{E}$ should return to $\mathcal{C}$ all results matching a query only after $\mathcal{E}$ received all the bxtoken vectors from $\mathcal{C}$; indeed, sending the results as soon as they are found to match the query would leak information on $|\mathsf{TSet}(w)|$ to $\mathcal{C}$ (since no ind's will be returned after $\mathcal{C}$ sends $|\mathsf{TSet}(w)|$ tokens). In the full version [20] we show a strategy applied by $\mathcal{D}$ during EDBSetup to allow $\mathcal{E}$ to send results as soon as they are found while avoiding the above leakage.

4. OUTSOURCED SYMMETRIC PIR

The OSPIR (for Outsourced Symmetric PIR) setting augments the MC-SSE setting with an additional requirement: The database owner $\mathcal{D}$ should learn as little as possible about queries performed by clients while still being able to verify the compliance of these queries to her policy. Here we extend MC-OXT to this setting by augmenting the token generation component GenToken to support "blinding" by the client of query requests sent to $\mathcal{D}$, and adding a mechanism for $\mathcal{D}$ to enforce policy-compliance of the query when only having access to their blinded versions. OSPIR-OXT supports *attribute-based policies* where $\mathcal{D}$ learns information about query attributes but nothing about values (e.g., $\mathcal{D}$ may learn that a query includes a last-name, a zipcode and two words from a text field but nothing about the actual queried keywords). The security model adds $\mathcal{D}$ as a new adversarial entity trying to learn $\mathcal{C}$'s hidden query values. Refer to the introduction for more discussion about the OSPIR setting and attribute-based policies.

OSPIR SSE Syntax. An OSPIR-SSE scheme replaces the GenToken procedure which in MC-SSE is executed by the data owner $\mathcal{D}$ on the cleartext client's query $\bar{w}$, with a two-party protocol between $\mathcal{C}$ and $\mathcal{D}$ that allows $\mathcal{C}$ to compute a search-enabling token without $\mathcal{D}$ learning $\bar{w}$. In addition, $\mathcal{D}$ should be able to enforce an attribute-based query-authorization policy on these queries. For this, we assume that keyword set W is partitioned into m *attributes*, and let $I(w)$ denote the attribute of keyword w.[3] An attribute-based policy is represented by a set of attribute-sequences

[3] We assume that the string representing w has its attribute encoded into it, i.e. $w = (i, val)$ for $i = I(w)$, so that Ryan as a first name is distinguished from Ryan as a last name.

P s.t. a conjunctive query $\bar{w} = (w_1, ..., w_n)$ is *allowed by policy* P if and only if the sequence of attributes $\mathsf{av}(\bar{w}) = (I(w_1), ..., I(w_n))$ corresponding to this query is an element in set P. Using this notation, the goal of the GenToken protocol is to let $\mathcal{C}$ compute token corresponding to its query $\bar{w}$ only if $\mathsf{av}(\bar{w}) \in \mathsf{P}$. Reflecting these goals, an OSPIR-SSE scheme is a tuple $\Sigma = (\mathsf{EDBSetup}, \mathsf{GenToken}, \mathsf{Search})$ where EDBSetup is an algorithm run by $\mathcal{D}$ on inputs (DB, RDK) with outputs (EDB, K), GenToken is a protocol run by $\mathcal{C}$ on input $\bar{w}$ and by $\mathcal{D}$ on input (P, K), with $\mathcal{C}$ outputting token or $\perp$ and $\mathcal{D}$ outputting av, and Search is a protocol run by $\mathcal{C}$ on input token and by $\mathcal{E}$ on input EDB, with $\mathcal{C}$ outputting a set of ind's matching his query and the corresponding set of rdk's.

4.1 The OSPIR-OXT Protocol

The OSPIR-OXT protocol addresses the above OSPIR setting by enhancing MC-OXT with query-hiding techniques that allow $\mathcal{D}$ to authorize queries without learning the queried values. Most changes with respect to MC-OXT are in the GenToken protocol. EDBSetup remains mostly unchanged except for the implementation of the PRFs, and Search is essentially unmodified.

We introduce the two main tools used in the design of GenToken. First, instead of the use of regular PRFs for stag and xtag computations in OXT and MC-OXT, the OSPIR-OXT protocol uses an an "oblivious PRF" (OPRF) computation between $\mathcal{C}$ and $\mathcal{D}$. A PRF $F(K, w)$ is called oblivious [26] if there is a two-party protocol in which $\mathcal{C}$ inputs w, $\mathcal{D}$ inputs K, $\mathcal{C}$ learns the value of $F(K, w)$ and $\mathcal{D}$ learns nothing. A simple example is the Hashed DH OPRF which we use in our implementation of the OSPIR-OXT protocol, defined as $F(K, x) = H(x)^K$ where H is a hash function onto $G \setminus \{1\}$ where G is a group of prime order p, and K is chosen at random in Z_p^*. In this case, the OPRF protocol consists of $\mathcal{C}$ sending $a = H(x)^r$ for random r in Z_p^*, $\mathcal{D}$ sending back $b = a^K$ and $\mathcal{C}$ computing $H(x)^K$ as $b^{1/r}$. The second tool used in GenToken is needed to enforce an *attribute-based policy* and guarantee that only queries on authorized attributes can generate valid tokens for search at $\mathcal{E}$. To enforce such policies we have $\mathcal{D}$ use a different key for each possible attribute; for example, when a stag (or xtag) is requested for attribute 'zipcode' the key that $\mathcal{D}$ inputs into the OPRF computation is different than the key used for attribute 'name' or attribute 'text'. The point is that if $\mathcal{C}$ claims to be querying zipcode but actually enters the keyword "Michael" into the OPRF computation, the output for $\mathcal{C}$ will be the tag $F(K_{zip}$, "Michael"), where K_{zip} is a zipcode-specific key, which will match no tag stored at $\mathcal{E}$.

To obtain OSPIR-OXT we combine the above two tools with an authorization mechanism similar to the one used in MC-OXT via a homomorphic signature (using the ρ_i exponents) for binding together the n tokens corresponding to an n-term conjunctive query in a way that $\mathcal{E}$ can verify. We describe the changes to MC-OXT (defined via Figure 1 and the modifications in Section 3) required by OSPIR-OXT. We first replace the PRF F_p used in computing xtrap and xtag values with a PRF F_G which maps w directly onto the group G generated by g, i.e. we set xtrap as $F_G(K_X, w)$ instead of $g^{F_p(K_X,w)}$, hence xtag = (xtrap)^{xind} will now be computed as $F_G(K_X, w)^{\mathsf{xind}}$ instead of $g^{F_p(K_X,w)\cdot \mathsf{xind}}$. We similarly replace the PRF F_τ used in computing the strap value with the PRF F_G, i.e. we set strap as $F_G(K_S, w)$ instead of $F_\tau(K_S, w)$. (Since we use strap as a key to F_τ in deriving (K_z, K_e), we assume that a PRF F_τ key can be extracted from a random group element.)

We also make a specific assumption on the implementation of the function TSetGetTag used to derive stag(w) value, i.e., the handle pointing to the set TSet(w) which is computed as TSetGetTag(K_T, w). First, we assume that TSetGetTag is implemented using PRF F_G. Second, to enable enforcement of attribute-based policies we assume that the key K_T in TSetGetTag is formed by an array of F_G keys $K_T = (K_T[1], ..., K_T[m])$, where $K_T[i]$ is the key to be used only for keywords with attribute $I(w) = i$. For notational convenience we define a PRF F_G^m s.t. $F_G^m(K_T, w) = F_G(K_T[I(w)], w)$, and we set stag($w$) = TSetGetTag($K_T, w$) to $F_G^m(K_T, w)$. Since we explicitly handle the keys used in the TSetGetTag implementation we also need to modify the TSet API: We will initialize TSet as TSet $\leftarrow$ TSetSetup$'(\mathbf{T})$, where $\mathbf{T}$ indexes the tuple lists $\mathbf{t}(w)$ not by the keywords w but by the corresponding stag(w) values. (This API change does not affect existing TSet implementations [9] because they internally use stag(w) = TSetGetTag(K_T, w) to store the $\mathbf{t}(w)$ list.) The PRF we use in the computation of xtag's will be similarly attribute-partitioned. Namely, K_X is also an array of m independent F_G keys $K_X = (K_X[1], \ldots, K_X[m])$, the xtrap value for keyword w is defined as $F_G^m(K_X, w)$, and the xtag corresponding to keyword w and index xind is set to $(F_G^m(K_X, w))^{\mathsf{xind}}$.

In OSPIR-OXT, there are two two-party protocols involved in the computation of F_G. In the first case, the protocol implements an OPRF computation in which $\mathcal{C}$ enters an input w, $\mathcal{D}$ enters a key K_S, and the output is $F_G(K_S, w)$ for $\mathcal{C}$ and $\perp$ for $\mathcal{D}$. In the second case, F_G^m is computed via a protocol, that we call a *shared OPRF* (S-OPRF), in which $\mathcal{C}$ inputs w and $i = I(w)$, and $\mathcal{D}$ enters a key K and additional input $\rho \in Z_p^*$; the output learned by $\mathcal{D}$ is i, and the output learned by $\mathcal{C}$ is $(F_G^m(K, x))^\rho = (F_G(K[i], x))^\rho$. Note that the pair of outputs $((F_G^m(K, x))^\rho, \rho)$ can be seen as a secret sharing of $F_G^m(K, x)$, hence the name shared-OPRF. OSPIR-OXT uses the OPRF protocol to let $\mathcal{C}$ learn the strap value corresponding to the w_1 s-term, i.e. strap = $F_G(K_S, w_1)$, without $\mathcal{D}$ learning w_1. The S-OPRF protocol is used to let $\mathcal{C}$ compute a *blinded stag* bstag = $[F_G^m(K_T, w_1)]^{\rho_1}$ and the *blinded xtraps* $\mathsf{bxtrap}_i = [F_G^m(K_I, w_i)]^{\rho_i}$, for $i = 2, ..., n$. The functionality of the blinding ρ_i is the same as in the case of MC-OXT, namely, as a form of homomorphic signature binding and authorizing stag and xtrap's that $\mathcal{E}$ can verify. As in MC-OXT, $\mathcal{E}$ will receive the corresponding (de)blinding factors $\rho_1, \ldots, \rho_n$ in the authenticated envelope env.

To simplify the description of OSPIR-OXT, we assume that both OPRF and S-OPRF protocols take a single round of interaction between $\mathcal{C}$ and $\mathcal{D}$, as is indeed the case for several efficient OPRF's of interest [14, 21], including the Hashed Diffie-Hellman OPRF [22] used in our implementation below. We denote $\mathcal{C}$'s initial computation in the OPRF protocol as $(a, r) \leftarrow \mathsf{OPRF}.\mathcal{C}_1(x)$ (a is the value sent to $\mathcal{D}$ and r is randomness used by $\mathcal{C}$), $\mathcal{D}$'s response computation as $b \leftarrow \mathsf{OPRF}.\mathcal{D}(K, a)$, and $\mathcal{C}$'s local computation of the final output as $\mathsf{OPRF}.\mathcal{C}_2(b, r)$. We use the corresponding notation in the case of S-OPRF, except that S-OPRF.$\mathcal{D}$ takes as an input a triple (K, i, a) where i is an attribute and outputs a pair (b, ρ). See below for a simple implementation of these procedures for the case of the Hashed Diffie-Hellman OPRF.

GenToken protocol

- Client $\mathcal{C}$, on input $\bar{w} = (w_1, ..., w_n)$ where w_1 is chosen as s-term:
  - Compute $(a_s, r_s) \leftarrow \mathsf{OPRF}.\mathcal{C}_1(w_1)$, and $(a_i, r_i) \leftarrow \mathsf{S\text{-}OPRF}.\mathcal{C}_1(w_i)$ for each $i = 1, ..., n$.
  - Send $(a_s, a_1, ..., a_n)$ and $\mathsf{av} = (I(w_1), ..., I(w_n))$ to $\mathcal{D}$.
- Data owner $\mathcal{D}$, on input policy P and master key $K = (K_S, K_X, K_T, K_I, K_P, K_M)$:
  - Abort if av is not in policy set P. Otherwise set av as $\mathcal{D}$'s local output.
  - Compute $b_s \leftarrow \mathsf{OPRF}.\mathcal{D}(K_S, a_s)$.
  - Compute $(b_1, \rho_1) \leftarrow \mathsf{S\text{-}OPRF}.\mathcal{D}(K_T, I_1, a_1)$, and $(b_i, \rho_i) \leftarrow \mathsf{S\text{-}OPRF}.\mathcal{D}(K_X, I_i, a_i)$ for $i = 2, .., n$.
  - Set $\mathsf{env} \leftarrow \mathsf{AuthEnc}(K_M, (\rho_1, \rho_2, ..., \rho_n))$ and send $(\mathsf{env}, b_s, b_1, ..., b_n)$ to $\mathcal{C}$.
- $\mathcal{C}$ outputs $\mathsf{token} = (\mathsf{env}, \mathsf{strap}, \mathsf{bstag}, \mathsf{bxtrap}_2, ..., \mathsf{bxtrap}_n)$ where $\mathsf{strap} \leftarrow \mathsf{OPRF}.\mathcal{C}_2(b_s, r_s)$, $\mathsf{bstag} \leftarrow \mathsf{S\text{-}OPRF}.\mathcal{C}_2(b_1, r_1)$, and $\mathsf{bxtrap}_i \leftarrow \mathsf{S\text{-}OPRF}.\mathcal{C}_2(b_i, r_i)$ for $i = 2, ..., n$.

Figure 2: TOKEN GENERATION IN OSPIR-OXT

OSPIR-OXT **Specification.** With the above ingredients and notation we specify OSPIR-OXT on the basis of MC-OXT via the following changes.

Keys. Select key K_S for F_G; K_T and K_X for F_G^m; K_I for F_p; and K_M for the authenticated encryption scheme.

EDBSetup. Follow the EDBSetup procedure of MC-OXT except for computing $\mathsf{strap} \leftarrow F_G(K_S, w)$ and $\mathsf{xtag} \leftarrow (F_G^m(K_X, w))^{\mathsf{xind}}$, and for implementing the TSetGetTag procedure as $\mathsf{TSetGetTag}(K_T, w) = F_G^m(K_T, w)$, which means that we compute $\mathsf{stag}(w) \leftarrow F_G^m(K_T, w)$; index $\mathbf{t}(w)$ in $\mathbf{T}$ by $\mathsf{stag}(w)$ instead of by w itself; and generate TSet using the modified API procedure $\mathsf{TSetSetup}'(\mathbf{T})$.

GenToken protocol. This is the main change with respect to OSPIR-OXT; it follows the above mechanisms and is presented in Figure 2.

Search protocol. Same as MC-OXT except that stag is not included under env but rather it is provided to $\mathcal{E}$ by $\mathcal{C}$ as bstag from which $\mathcal{E}$ computes $\mathsf{stag} \leftarrow (\mathsf{bstag})^{1/\rho_1}$.

Instantiation via Hashed Diffie-Hellman OPRF. Our implementation and analysis of OSPIR-OXT assumes the use of Hashed DH OPRF mentioned above, namely, $F_G(K, x) = (H(x))^K$. The instantiations of OPRF and S-OPRF protocols in this case are as follows. $\mathsf{OPRF}.\mathcal{C}_1(x)$ and $\mathsf{S\text{-}OPRF}.\mathcal{C}_1(x)$ both pick random r in Z_p^*, set $a \leftarrow (H(x))^r$, and output (a, r). Procedure $\mathsf{OPRF}.\mathcal{D}(K, a)$, where $K \in Z_p^*$ is a key for PRF F_G, outputs $b \leftarrow a^K$. Procedure $\mathsf{S\text{-}OPRF}.\mathcal{D}(K, i, a)$, where $i \in \{1, ..., m\}$ and $K = (K[1], \ldots, K[m]) \in (Z_p^*)^m$ is a key for PRF F_G^m, picks random ρ in Z_p^*, computes $b \leftarrow a^{K[i]\cdot\rho}$, and outputs (b, ρ). Procedures $\mathsf{OPRF}.\mathcal{C}_1(b, r)$ and $\mathsf{S\text{-}OPRF}.\mathcal{C}_1(b, r)$ both output $b^{1/r}$. Note that if parties follow the protocol, $\mathcal{C}$'s final output is equal to $(H(x))^K = F_G(K, x)$ in the OPRF protocol, while in the S-OPRF protocol it is equal to $(H(x))^{K[i]\cdot\rho}$, which is equal to $(F_G^m(K, x))^\rho$ if $i = I(x)$. These OPRF and S-OPRF protocols emulate their corresponding ideal functionalities in ROM under so-called One-More Gap Diffie-Hellman assumption [22], see Section 5.

Figure 3 shows the OSPIR-OXT scheme instantiated with the above Hashed DH OPRF. It helps to visualize the entire protocol and it reflects our actual implementation. In Figure 3 we denote keys K_T and K_X of PRF F_G^m by vectors of exponents in Z_p^*, respectively $(k_1, \ldots, k_m)$ and $(e_1, \ldots, e_m)$, where m is the number of attributes. Also, because of the specific OPRF instantiation we equate a_s to a_1 in $\mathcal{C}$'s message of the GenToken protocol, instead of computing these two blinded versions of keyword w_1 separately, as in Figure 2.

4.2 Supporting Boolean Queries

For simplicity we presented our protocols for the case of conjunctions. The protocols can be readily adapted to search boolean queries in "searchable normal form (SNF)", i.e., of the form "$w_1 \wedge \phi(w_2, \ldots, w_m)$" (intended to return any document that matches keyword w_1 and in addition satisfies the formula ϕ on the remaining keywords). In this case, OXT and its derivatives change only in the way $\mathcal{E}$ determines which tuples match a query (i.e., which values e it sends back to $\mathcal{C}$). Specifically, in OXT the c-th tuple matches if and only if $\mathsf{xtoken}[c, i]^{y/\rho_i} \in \mathsf{XSet}$ for all $2 \leq i \leq n$. Instead, for boolean queries as above, $\mathcal{E}$ will have a set of boolean variables $v_2, \ldots, v_n$ and will set v_i to the truth value of the predicate $\mathsf{xtoken}[c, i]^{y/\rho_i} \in \mathsf{XSet}$. A tuple is matching if and only if the result of evaluating ϕ on these values returns true. The complexity of boolean search is same as for conjunctions, i.e., proportional to $|\mathsf{DB}(w_1)|$, and leakage to $\mathcal{E}$ is the same as for a conjunctive query on the same set of keywords except that $\mathcal{E}$ also learns the expression ϕ being evaluated. See [9] for details and support of other forms of boolean queries.

In the OSPIR-SSE setting, supporting boolean queries requires policies that are defined in terms of such queries. Specifically, a policy will determine a set of allowed pairs (ψ, I) where ψ is a symbolic boolean expression and I a sequence of attributes, one per each variable in ψ. Thus, leakage to $\mathcal{D}$ will include I (as in the case of conjunctions) plus the symbolic expression being evaluated.

4.3 Computational Cost

Here we provide an operations count for OSPIR-OXT when instantiated with the DH-based OPRF noting its (mild) overhead over the original OXT protocol from [9]. The computational cost of OSPIR-OXT is easy to quantify by inspecting Figure 3 in Page .

The cost of pre-processing (EDBSetup) is dominated by operations related to the group G, mainly exponentiations: For every $w \in \mathsf{W}$:

1. One hashing operation, $H(w)$, of keyword w into an element of the group G.
2. Two exponentiations: $\mathsf{strap}(w) = (H(w))^{K_S}$ and $\mathsf{stag}(w) = (H(w))^{k_i}$.
3. For every ind in $\mathsf{DB}(w)$: One exponentiation $H(w)^{e_i \cdot \mathsf{xind}}$ for computing an XSet element.

The first two items are specific to OSPIR-OXT while the third is from the original OXT protocol, except that here the base for exponentiation is changed from the generator g in OXT to the value $H(w)$. Hence the overhead introduced by OSPIR-OXT is given by the first two items and the variable base. Importantly, the overhead for the first two items is only linear in $|\mathsf{W}|$, typically much smaller than the number of exponentiations in OXT (item 3), namely one per pair (w, ind) for $\mathsf{ind} \in \mathsf{DB}(w)$. As for the latter exponentiations, while the bases are variable, each $H(w)$ is typically used with a very large number of exponentiations (as the number of documents containing w) hence allowing for significant same-base optimizations. The hashing of w into the group G (item 1) is modeled as a random oracle, hence it rules out algebraic implementations such as $g^{h(w)}$. For the elliptic curves groups we use, H is realized by sampling a field element e and a bit b from a PRNG seeded with w until (e, b) is the compressed representation of a valid group element. Depending on the particular nature of a curve, the generic square root algorithms required in solving the Weierstrass equation, though, can be extremely inefficient: Our original implementation for the chosen NIST 224p curve using OpenSSL's standard algorithms was more than an order of magnitude slower than a normal exponentiation and considerably more when common-base optimization is used. By implementing our own algorithm inspired by [4] and optimizing it for this particular field, we could reduce the cost down to the order of an exponentiation. Once all these optimizations are in place, the performance of OSPIR-OXT is remarkable as shown in Section 4.4 and, in much more details, in a companion paper [8].

The dominating cost of GenToken is just $2n + 1$ exponentiations for the client and $n + 1$ for $\mathcal{D}$.

Finally, the cost of query processing between $\mathcal{C}$ and $\mathcal{E}$ (Search) on a n-term SNF expression is as follows:

1. $\mathcal{C}$ computes $n - 1$ exponentiations for each tuple in $\mathsf{TSet}(w_1)$
2. $\mathcal{E}$ performs *up to* $n-1$ exponentiations for each element in $\mathsf{TSet}(w_1)$.

Note that $\mathcal{C}$ can apply same-base optimization to the exponentiations since each term in the SNF expression has its own fixed base. On the other hand, $\mathcal{E}$ cannot use same-base optimizations. However, note that as soon as one of the values $\mathsf{xtoken}[c, i]^{y/\rho_i}$ for a conjunction is found not to be in XSet, the other terms for this conjunction do not have to be evaluated (hence avoiding the need for these exponentiations). Similarly, for general Boolean expressions, early termination can be exploited to reduce costly computation. This highlights an important optimization for query processing (especially for queries with large $\mathsf{TSet}(w_1)$ sets): Besides choosing the s-term as a term with high-entropy to keep $\mathsf{TSet}(w_1)$ small, also choose the evaluation order of x-terms of an SNF expression such that it maximizes the probability of early termination and, hence, reduces the number of (expected) exponentiations executed by $\mathcal{E}$, e.g., for conjunctions order the x-terms in descending order of entropy (equivalently, ascending order of frequency).

Note (frequency ordering). In the OSPIR setting the client may not know the frequency of terms in the database and $\mathcal{D}$ will not know the query values to choose such terms optimally. Thus, the exact mechanism for determining the above ordering will depend on the specific setting. In our implementation we decide on ordering based on typical entropy of attributes; e.g., assuming last names have more entropy than names, and names more entropy than addresses, etc. (note that an attribute-based ordering is more privacy-preserving for the client than a value-based one).

4.4 Implementation and performance

The practicality of the proposed schemes was validated by experiments on DBs which included e.g. English-language Wikipedia (13,284,801 records / 2,732,311,945 indexed tuples), and a synthetic US census database (100 million records / 22,525,274,592 index tuples, resulting in EDB with 1.7 TB TSet and 0.4 TB XSet). To illustrate search efficiency, in the census DB case we executed complex queries like

SELECT ID WHERE FNAME='CHARLIE' AND SEX='FEMALE' AND NOT (STATE='NY' OR STATE='MA' OR STATE='PA' OR STATE='NJ)

in about 4 seconds on an IBM Blade dual Intel 4-core Xeon processor and storage provided by a (low-end) 6.2TB RAID-5 storage system. Preprocessing of such large DBs (TSet and XSet creation) has been feasible by, among other things, optimization of common-base exponentiations, achieving aggregated (parallel) rate of about 500,000 exp.'s/sec. for the NIST 224p elliptic curve.

See [8] for details on implementation and performance as well as for the extension of OXT and OSPIR-OXT to support dynamic databases (where documents can be added, deleted and modified).

5. SECURITY

We analyze security of the OSPIR-SSE scheme. We focus on the OSPIR case as it is the more comprehensive setting and it contains MC-SSE as a special case. The SSE-OXT protocol is analyzed in the SSE setting in [9].

5.1 Security and Correctness Def nitions

SSE security definitions where the only adversarial entity is server $\mathcal{E}$ are provided in prior work. Here we follow the definitions from [9] - which in turn follow [11, 13] - and extend them to the MC setting by considering multiple malicious clients and to the OSPIR setting by adding also the data owner $\mathcal{D}$ as an adversarial entity. All security definitions follow the ideal/real model framework of secure computation and are parametrized by a *leakage function* $\mathcal{L}$ bounding the information leaked to an adversarial party in addition to the intended output for that party. Specifically, we ask that whatever an adversary can do by running the real protocol on data and queries *chosen by the adversary*, a simulator can do solely on the basis of the leakage function.

Correctness. We say that an OSPIR-SSE scheme Σ = (EDBSetup, GenToken, Search) is *computationally correct* if for every efficient algorithm A, there is a negligible probability that the following experiment outputs 0. On inputs (DB, RDK) and $\bar{w}^{(1)}, \ldots, \bar{w}^{(m)}$ provided by A, execute (K, EDB) $\leftarrow$ EDBSetup(DB, RDK); and for $i = 1, 2, \ldots$, execute protocol GenToken on $\mathcal{C}$'s input $\bar{w}^{(i)}$ and $\mathcal{D}$'s inputs (P, K), denote $\mathcal{C}$'s output as $\mathsf{token}^{(i)}$, execute protocol Search between $\mathcal{C}$ on input $\mathsf{token}^{(i)}$ and $\mathcal{E}$ on input EDB and denote $\mathcal{C}$'s outputs as a pair ($\mathsf{indSet}^{(i)}, \mathsf{rdkSet}^{(i)}$). Output 1 if for each i we have that $\mathsf{indSet}^{(i)} = \mathsf{DB}(\bar{w}^{(i)})$ and $\mathsf{rdkSet}^{(i)} = \mathsf{RDK}[\mathsf{DB}(\bar{w}^{(i)})]$. Otherwise output 0.

Security against adversarial server $\mathcal{E}$. Security against adversarial (honest-but-curious) $\mathcal{E}$ has been the focus of prior SSE work. Adapting the definition of $\mathcal{L}$-semantic security against adaptive attacks (by the server $\mathcal{E}$) from [9] to our setting is straightforward and is omitted here.

Security against adversarial clients. The definition captures the information leaked to a malicious client in addition to the intended output DB($\bar{w}$) and the corresponding record-decrypting keys RDK[DB($\bar{w}$)]. The definition compares the real execution to an emulation of an interaction with algorithm $\mathsf{I\text{-}SSE}_{\mathcal{L}}$, which models an ideal functionality of the OSPIR-SSE scheme instantiated with the leakage function $\mathcal{L}$. The interactive algorithm $\mathsf{I\text{-}SSE}_{\mathcal{L}}$, running on local input (DB, RDK, P), answers queries $\bar{w} \in \mathsf{W}^*$ by checking if $\mathsf{av}(\bar{w}) \in \mathsf{P}$. If the check verifies, then it replies to this $\bar{w}$ with a triple (DB($\bar{w}$), RDK[DB($\bar{w}$)], $\mathcal{L}$(DB, $\bar{w}$)), and if $\mathsf{av}(\bar{w}) \notin \mathsf{P}$ then it sends back a rejection symbol $\perp$.

DEFINITION 1. *Let* Π = (EDBSetup, GenToken, Search) *be an OSPIR-SSE scheme. Given algorithms* $\mathcal{L}$, A, *and* $S = (S_0, S_1, S_2)$ *we define experiments (algorithms)* $\mathbf{Real}^{\Pi}_A(\lambda)$ *and* $\mathbf{Ideal}^{\Pi}_{A,S}(\lambda)$ *as follows:*

$\mathbf{Real}^{\Pi}_A(\lambda)$**:** $A(1^\lambda)$ *chooses* (DB, RDK, P), *and the experiment runs* (K, EDB) $\leftarrow$ EDBSetup(DB, RDK). *Adversary A can then adaptively invoke instances of the protocol* GenToken *and* Search, *interacting with party $\mathcal{D}$ running on input K and* P *in the first case and with party $\mathcal{E}$ running on input* EDB *in the second case. Note that A can behave arbitrarily in all these protocol instances. Let q be the number of* GenToken *instances and let* av_i *be $\mathcal{D}$'s local output in the i-th instance. If at any point A halts and outputs a bit b, the game outputs* $(b, \mathsf{av}_1, \ldots, \mathsf{av}_q)$.

$\mathbf{Ideal}^{\Pi}_{A,S}(\lambda)$**:** $A(1^\lambda)$ *chooses* (DB, RDK, P) *as above, while the experiment initializes* $S = (S_0, S_1, S_2)$ *by running* $\mathsf{st} \leftarrow S_0(1^\lambda)$. *Subsequently, each time A invokes an instance of protocol* GenToken, *it interacts with the experiment running* $S_1(\mathsf{st}, \mathsf{P})$, *whereas if A invokes an instance of protocol* Search, *it interacts with the experiment running* $S_2(\mathsf{st})$. *Both S_1 and S_2 algorithms are allowed to update the global simulator's state* st *while interacting with A. Both can issue queries $\bar{w}$ to* $\mathsf{I\text{-}SSE}_{\mathcal{L}}$(DB, RDK, P). *Let q be the number of these queries and let* $\mathsf{av}_i = I(\bar{w}_i)$, *where $\bar{w}_i$ is the i-th query. As above, if at any point A halts and outputs a bit b, the game outputs* $(b, \mathsf{av}_1, \ldots, \mathsf{av}_q)$.

We call Π $\mathcal{L}$-*semantically-secure against malicious clients if for any efficient algorithm A there is an efficient algorithm S s.t. the statistical difference between tuples* $(b, \mathsf{av}_1, \ldots, \mathsf{av}_q)$ *output by experiments* $\mathbf{Real}^{\Pi}_A$ *and* $\mathbf{Ideal}^{\Pi}_{A,S}$ *is a negligible function of the security parameter* λ.

Security against adversarial data owner. Security against a data-owner $\mathcal{D}$ models privacy of the client's queries $\bar{w}$ against malicious $\mathcal{D}$, given an adaptive choice of the client's queries. Similarly to the case of security against either the client $\mathcal{C}$ or the EDB-storing server $\mathcal{E}$, this security definition also allows for leakage of some information $\mathcal{L}(\bar{w})$ regarding the query $\bar{w}$ to $\mathcal{D}$.

DEFINITION 2. *Let* Π = (EDBSetup, GenToken, Search) *be an OSPIR-SSE scheme. Given algorithms* $\mathcal{L}$, A, *and* S *we define experiments (algorithms)* $\mathbf{Real}^{\Pi}_A(\lambda)$ *and* $\mathbf{Ideal}^{\Pi}_{A,S}(\lambda)$ *as follows:*

$\mathbf{Real}^{\Pi}_A(\lambda)$**:** *Adversary* $A(1^\lambda)$ *can adaptively invoke any number of* GenToken *instances by specifying a query $\bar{w}$ and interacting with party $\mathcal{C}$ running the* GenToken *protocol on input $\bar{w}$. At any point A can halt and output a bit, which the game uses as its own output.*

$\mathbf{Ideal}^{\Pi}_{A,S}(\lambda)$**:** *Adversary* $A(1^\lambda)$ *can adaptively invoke any number of* GenToken *instances as above, but for any query $\bar{w}$ which A specifies, it interacts with S running on input $\mathcal{L}(\bar{w})$. As above if A halts and output a bit, the game uses this bit as its own output.*

We call Π $\mathcal{L}$-semantically-secure against malicious data owner *if for any efficient alg. A there is an efficient alg. S s.t.* $\Pr[\mathbf{Real}^{\Pi}_A(\lambda){=}1] - \Pr[\mathbf{Ideal}^{\Pi}_{A,S}(\lambda){=}1] \leq \mathrm{neg}(\lambda)$.

Note (non-collusion between $\mathcal{D}$ and $\mathcal{E}$). We stress that even though the data owner $\mathcal{D}$ can be arbitrarily malicious, we assume that $\mathcal{D}$ and $\mathcal{E}$ do not collude. Indeed, client's security in the OSPIR-OXT scheme we propose is not maintained against such collusion. Moreover, providing query-privacy from $\mathcal{D}$ under collusion with $\mathcal{E}$ would have the (impractical) cost of a single-server symmetric PIR protocol. The hospital example mentioned in the introduction, is a case where such non-collusion requirement makes sense. Indeed, it is the hospital interest not to learn the queries: It helps avoiding liability and complying with regulations as well as withstanding potential insider attacks. Similarly, for a service providing private access to a database (e.g. to a patent repository) preserving client privacy is part of its very business model. See also [18].

5.2 Security of OSPIR-OXT

Correctness of OSPIR-OXT. We first argue that protocol OSPIR-OXT is correct.

THEOREM 3. *The OSPIR-SSE scheme* OSPIR-OXT *instantiated with the Hashed Diffie-Hellman OPRF is computationally correct assuming that the DDH assumption holds, that the T-set implementation is computationally correct, that F_p is a secure PRF, and assuming the Random Oracle Model for hash function H.*

Since T-set implementation is computationally correct, any correctness errors can only come from collisions in PRF functions, including function F_{K_X,K_I} effectively used in computing xtag values, defined as $F_{K_X,K_I}(w, \mathsf{ind}) = (F^m_G(K_X, w))^{F_p(K_I, \mathsf{ind})}$. But assuming the PRF property of F_p, and the PRF property of F^m_G, which holds under DDH in ROM, function F_{K_X,K_I} is a PRF too, and so collision probability is negligible, resulting in negligible error probability over the execution of the OSPIR-OXT correctness experiment.

Security of OSPIR-OXT. Using the security notions explained above we describe the security properties of the OSPIR-SSE scheme OSPIR-OXT instantiated with the Hashed Diffie-Hellman OPRF, as shown in Figure 3. We first state the OM-GDH security assumption required for the security of the OPRF and S-OPRF sub-protocols of this OSPIR-OXT instantiation.

One-More Gap Diffie-Hellman (OM-GDH). Let $G = G_\lambda$ be a prime order cyclic group of order $p = p(\lambda)$ generated by g. We say that the *One-More Gap Diffie-Hellman (OM-GDH) assumption* holds in G if $\mathbf{Adv}^{\text{ddh}}_{G,A}(\lambda)$ is negligible for all efficient adversaries A, where $\mathbf{Adv}^{\text{ddh}}_{G,A}(\lambda)$ is defined as the probability that A wins the following game: (1) The game chooses random t in Z_p^* and two random elements h_1, h_2 in G; (2) A, on input h_1, h_2, specifies a single query a to the Diffie-Hellman oracle, which on input a returns $b \leftarrow a^t$; (3) A can make any number of queries to a *Decisional Diffie-Hellman* oracle $\mathsf{DDH}_t(\cdot,\cdot)$, which on input (h, v) returns 1 if $v = h^t$ and 0 otherwise; (4) Finally A outputs two values v_1, v_2, and we say that A *wins* the game if $v_1 = (h_1)^t$ and $v_2 = (h_2)^t$.

Security against adversarial server $\mathcal{E}$. The OSPIR-SSE scheme OSPIR-OXT is $\mathcal{L}_{\text{oxt}}$-semantically-secure against adaptive server $\mathcal{E}$ under the same assumptions and for the same leakage function $\mathcal{L}_{\text{oxt}}$ as the underlying SSE scheme OXT of [9]. This is because the specific PRF's used by OSPIR-OXT in EDB construction are instantiations of general PRF's considered in OXT, and because $\mathcal{E}$'s view of the Search protocol in the OSPIR-OXT scheme can be generated from $\mathcal{E}$'s view of Search in the OXT scheme. Specifically, each ρ_i in env is random in Z_p^*, and bstag and each bxtoken$[c,i]$ value in Figure 3 can be computed by exponentiating values stag and xtoken$[c,i]$ in Figure 1 to, respectively, ρ_1 and ρ_i.

Security against adversarial client $\mathcal{C}$. Let $\mathsf{Mask}(|\mathsf{DB}(w_1)|)$ denote an upper bound on $|\mathsf{DB}(w_1)|$ used by $\mathcal{E}$ to mask the size of $\mathsf{TSet}(w_1)$ when responding to $\mathcal{C}$'s queries as described at the end of Section 3.

THEOREM 4. *Let $\mathcal{L}$ be a defined as $\mathcal{L}(\mathsf{DB}, \bar{w}) = \mathsf{Mask}(|\mathsf{DB}(w_1)|)$ for $\bar{w} = (w_1, ..., w_n)$. OSPIR-SSE scheme* OSPIR-OXT *instantiated with the Hashed Diffie-Hellman OPRF is $\mathcal{L}$-semantically-secure against malicious clients assuming that the One-More Gap Diffie-Hellman assumption holds in G, that F_p is a secure PRF, that the T-set implementation is (computationally) correct, that* (AuthEnc, AuthDec) *is an IND-CPA and Strongly-UF-CMA authenticated encryption scheme, and assuming the Random Oracle Model for hash function H.*

PROOF. See full version [20]. □

Security against adversarial data owner $\mathcal{D}$. In our OSPIR-SSE scheme a malicious $\mathcal{D}$ learns nothing about clients' query $\bar{w} = (w_1, \ldots, w_n)$ except for the vector of attributes $\mathsf{av}(\bar{w}) = (I(w_1), \ldots, I(w_n))$.

THEOREM 5. *Let $\mathcal{L}$ be a leakage function defined as $\mathcal{L}(\bar{w}) = \mathsf{av}(\bar{w})$. OSPIR-SSE scheme* OSPIR-OXT *instantiated with the Hashed Diffie-Hellman OPRF is $\mathcal{L}$-semantically-secure against malicious data owner.*

PROOF. See full version [20]. □

Note that the $\mathcal{D}$'s view of the GenToken protocol in the OSPIR-OXT scheme consists of the attribute vector $\mathsf{av}(\bar{w})$ and the values $a_s, a_1, ..., a_n$. In the Hashed DH OPRF instantiation of this scheme in Figure 3, these values are formed as $a_j \leftarrow H(w_j)^{r_j}$ for random r_j's in Z_p^* (additionally, a_s is set to a_1). Since G is of prime order, every element in $G \backslash \{1\}$ is a generator, and thus each a_j is uniform in G. Thus $\mathcal{D}$'s view of the GenToken protocol can be trivially simulated from $\mathcal{L}(\bar{w}) = \mathsf{av}(\bar{w})$.

5.3 Extensions: Reducing Leakage to $\mathcal{D}$

In the full version [20] we show how to adapt OSPIR-OXT to a setting where a third party, called a policy manager, authorizes queries while $\mathcal{D}$ can enforce them without learning the policy, the boolean expression or the queried attributes; only the number of such attributes is learned by $\mathcal{D}$. This setting is precisely what is needed to implement searches authorized by a warrant while keeping the searched information hidden from all parties except the authorized searcher.

In addition, OSPIR-OXT can be extended (even without introducing a policy manager) so that the leakage about queried attributes to $\mathcal{D}$ is further limited to the minimum needed to make policy decisions (e.g., $\mathcal{D}$ may not need to know the exact attributes in a query but only the attribute classes they belong to).

Acknowledgment

Supported by the Intelligence Advanced Research Projects Activity (IARPA) via Department of Interior National Business Center (DoI / NBC) contract number D11PC20201. The U.S. Government is authorized to reproduce and distribute reprints for Governmental purposes notwithstanding any copyright annotation thereon. Disclaimer: The views and conclusions contained herein are those of the authors and should not be interpreted as necessarily representing the official policies or endorsements, either expressed or implied, of IARPA, DoI/NBC, or the U.S. Government.

6. REFERENCES

[1] M. Abdalla, M. Bellare, D. Catalano, E. Kiltz, T. Kohno, T. Lange, J. Malone-Lee, G. Neven, P. Paillier, and H. Shi. Searchable encryption revisited: Consistency properties, relation to anonymous IBE, and extensions. In V. Shoup, editor, *CRYPTO 2005*, volume 3621 of *LNCS*, pages 205–222. Springer, Aug. 2005.

[2] L. Ballard, S. Kamara, and F. Monrose. Achieving efficient conjunctive keyword searches over encrypted data. In S. Qing, W. Mao, J. López, and G. Wang, editors, *ICICS 05*, volume 3783 of *LNCS*, pages 414–426. Springer, Dec. 2005.

[3] M. Bellare, A. Boldyreva, and A. O'Neill. Deterministic and efficiently searchable encryption. In A. Menezes, editor, *CRYPTO 2007*, volume 4622 of *LNCS*, pages 535–552. Springer, Aug. 2007.

[4] D. J. Bernstein. Faster square roots in annoying finite fields. `http://cr.yp.to/papers/sqroot.pdf`, 2001.

[5] D. Boneh, G. Di Crescenzo, R. Ostrovsky, and G. Persiano. Public key encryption with keyword search. In C. Cachin and J. Camenisch, editors, *EUROCRYPT 2004*, volume 3027 of *LNCS*, pages 506–522. Springer, May 2004.

[6] D. Boneh and B. Waters. Conjunctive, subset, and range queries on encrypted data. In S. P. Vadhan,

editor, *TCC 2007*, volume 4392 of *LNCS*, pages 535–554. Springer, Feb. 2007.

[7] J. W. Byun, D. H. Lee, and J. Lim. Efficient conjunctive keyword search on encrypted data storage system. In *EuroPKI*, pages 184–196, 2006.

[8] D. Cash, J. Jaeger, S. Jarecki, C. Jutla, H. Krawczyk, M.-C. Roşu, and M. Steiner. Dynamic Searchable Encryption in Very Large Databases: Data Structures and Implementation. Manuscript, 2013.

[9] D. Cash, S. Jarecki, C. Jutla, H. Krawczyk, M. Rosu, and M. Steiner. Highly-scalable searchable symmetric encryption with support for boolean queries. Crypto'2013. Cryptology ePrint Archive, Report 2013/169, Mar. 2013. http://eprint.iacr.org/2013/169.

[10] Y.-C. Chang and M. Mitzenmacher. Privacy preserving keyword searches on remote encrypted data. In J. Ioannidis, A. Keromytis, and M. Yung, editors, *ACNS 05*, volume 3531 of *LNCS*, pages 442–455. Springer, June 2005.

[11] M. Chase and S. Kamara. Structured encryption and controlled disclosure. In *ASIACRYPT 2010*, LNCS, pages 577–594. Springer, Dec. 2010.

[12] E. D. Cristofaro, Y. Lu, and G. Tsudik. Efficient techniques for privacy-preserving sharing of sensitive information. In J. M. McCune, B. Balacheff, A. Perrig, A.-R. Sadeghi, A. Sasse, and Y. Beres, editors, *TRUST*, volume 6740 of *Lecture Notes in Computer Science*, pages 239–253. Springer, 2011.

[13] R. Curtmola, J. A. Garay, S. Kamara, and R. Ostrovsky. Searchable symmetric encryption: improved definitions and efficient constructions. In A. Juels, R. N. Wright, and S. Vimercati, editors, *ACM CCS 06*, pages 79–88. ACM Press, Oct. / Nov. 2006.

[14] M. J. Freedman, Y. Ishai, B. Pinkas, and O. Reingold. Keyword search and oblivious pseudorandom functions. In J. Kilian, editor, *TCC 2005*, volume 3378 of *LNCS*, pages 303–324. Springer, Feb. 2005.

[15] E.-J. Goh. Secure indexes. Cryptology ePrint Archive, Report 2003/216, 2003. http://eprint.iacr.org/.

[16] P. Golle, J. Staddon, and B. R. Waters. Secure conjunctive keyword search over encrypted data. In M. Jakobsson, M. Yung, and J. Zhou, editors, *ACNS 04*, volume 3089 of *LNCS*, pages 31–45. Springer, June 2004.

[17] Y. Huang and I. Goldberg. Outsourced private information retrieval with pricing and access control. Technical Report 2013-11, Centre for Applied Cryptographic Research (CACR), University of Waterloo, Feb. 2013.

[18] IARPA. Security and Privacy Assurance Research (SPAR) Program - BAA, 2011. http://www.iarpa.gov/solicitations_spar.html/.

[19] M. Islam, M. Kuzu, and M. Kantarcioglu. Access pattern disclosure on searchable encryption: Ramification, attack and mitigation. In *Proceedings of the Symposium on Network and Distributed Systems Security (NDSS 2012)*, San Diego, CA, Feb. 2012. Internet Society.

[20] S. Jarecki, C. Jutla, H. Krawczyk, M. C. Rosu, and M. Steiner. Outsourced symmetric private information retrieval. http://eprint.iacr.org/2013/.

[21] S. Jarecki and X. Liu. Efficient oblivious pseudorandom function with applications to adaptive OT and secure computation of set intersection. In O. Reingold, editor, *TCC 2009*, volume 5444 of *LNCS*, pages 577–594. Springer, Mar. 2009.

[22] S. Jarecki and X. Liu. Fast secure computation of set intersection. In *SCN 10*, LNCS, pages 418–435. Springer, 2010.

[23] S. Kamara and K. Lauter. Cryptographic cloud storage. In *Financial Cryptography Workshops*, pages 136–149, 2010.

[24] S. Kamara, C. Papamanthou, and T. Roeder. Dynamic searchable symmetric encryption. In *Proc. of CCS'2012*, 2012.

[25] K. Kurosawa and Y. Ohtaki. UC-secure searchable symmetric encryption. In *Financial Cryptography*, page 285, 2012.

[26] M. Naor and O. Reingold. Number-theoretic constructions of efficient pseudo-random functions. In *38th FOCS*, pages 458–467. IEEE Computer Society Press, Oct. 1997.

[27] V. Pappas, B. Vo, F. Krell, S. G. Choi, V. Kolesnikov, A. Keromytis, and T. Malkin. Blind Seer: A Scalable Private DBMS. Manuscript, 2013.

[28] E. Shi, J. Bethencourt, H. T.-H. Chan, D. X. Song, and A. Perrig. Multi-dimensional range query over encrypted data. In *2007 IEEE Symposium on Security and Privacy*, pages 350–364. IEEE Computer Society Press, May 2007.

[29] D. X. Song, D. Wagner, and A. Perrig. Practical techniques for searches on encrypted data. In *2000 IEEE Symposium on Security and Privacy*, pages 44–55. IEEE Computer Society Press, May 2000.

[30] P. van Liesdonk, S. Sedhi, J. Doumen, P. H. Hartel, and W. Jonker. Computationally efficient searchable symmetric encryption. In *Proc. Workshop on Secure Data Management (SDM)*, pages 87–100, 2010.

[31] B. R. Waters, D. Balfanz, G. Durfee, and D. K. Smetters. Building an encrypted and searchable audit log. In *NDSS 2004*. The Internet Society, Feb. 2004.

[32] WSJ. U.S. Terrorism Agency to Tap a Vast Database of Citizens. Wall Street Journal 12/13/12. http://alturl.com/ot72x.

Group operations. G is a cyclic group of prime order p generated by an element g. H is a hash function with range in $G \setminus \{1\}$.

EDBSetup(DB, RDK)

Key Generation. $\mathcal{D}$ picks key K_S and two vectors of elements $K_T = (k_1, \ldots, k_m)$ and $K_X = (e_1, \ldots, e_m)$ at random in Z_p^* (m = number of attributes); key K_I for PRF F_p; and key K_M for a symmetric authenticated encryption AuthEnc. F_p and F_τ are PRF's which outputs strings in respectively Z_p^* and $\{0,1\}^\tau$, and τ is a security parameter.

- Initialize XSet to an empty set, and initialize **T** to an empty array indexed by group elements in G.
- For each $w = (i, val) \in \mathsf{W}$, build the tuple list **t** and add elements to set XSet as follows:
  - Initialize **t** to an empty list.
  - Set $\mathsf{strap} \leftarrow (H(w))^{K_S}$, $\mathsf{stag} \leftarrow (H(w))^{k_i}$ $[= F_G^m(K_T, w)]$, $(K_z, K_e) \leftarrow (F_\tau(\mathsf{strap}, 1), F_\tau(\mathsf{strap}, 2))$.
  - Initialize $c \leftarrow 0$; then for all ind in $\mathsf{DB}(w)$ in random order:
    - * Set $\mathsf{rdk} \leftarrow \mathsf{RDK}(\mathsf{ind})$, $\mathsf{e} \leftarrow \mathsf{Enc}(K_e, (\mathsf{ind}|\mathsf{rdk}))$, $\mathsf{xind} \leftarrow F_p(K_I, \mathsf{ind})$.
    - * Set $c \leftarrow c+1$, $z_c \leftarrow F_p(K_z, c)$, $y \leftarrow \mathsf{xind} \cdot z_c^{-1}$. Append (e, y) to **t**.
    - * Set $\mathsf{xtag} \leftarrow H(w)^{e_i \cdot \mathsf{xind}}$ $[= (F_G^m(K_X, w))^{\mathsf{xind}}]$ and add xtag to XSet.
  - $\mathbf{T}[\mathsf{stag}] \leftarrow \mathbf{t}$.
- Create $\mathsf{TSet} \leftarrow \mathsf{TSetSetup}'(\mathbf{T})$, and output key $K = (K_S, K_X, K_T, K_I, K_M)$ and $\mathsf{EDB} = (\mathsf{TSet}, \mathsf{XSet}, K_M)$.

GenToken protocol

Client $\mathcal{C}$ on input a conjunctive query $\bar{w} = (w_1, ..., w_n)$, where w_1 is chosen as s-term, proceeds as follows:

- Pick $r_1, ..., r_n \xleftarrow{\$} Z_p^*$ and set $a_j \leftarrow (H(w_j))^{r_j}$ for $j = 1, \ldots, n$.
- Send to $\mathcal{D}$ the blinded queries $a_1, \ldots, a_n$ and the attribute sequence $\mathsf{av} = (I(w_1), \ldots, I(w_n))$.

Data owner $\mathcal{D}$ on input policy P and key K proceeds as follows:

- Abort if $\mathsf{av} \notin P$. Otherwise set av as a local output. Pick $\rho_1, \ldots, \rho_n \xleftarrow{\$} Z_p^*$.
- Set $\mathsf{strap}' \leftarrow (a_1)^s$, $\mathsf{bstag}' \leftarrow (a_1)^{k_{i_1} \cdot \rho_1}$ $[= (a_1)^{K_T[i_1] \cdot \rho_1}]$, and $\mathsf{bxtrap}'_j \leftarrow (a_j)^{e_{i_j} \cdot \rho_j}$ $[= (a_j)^{K_X[i_j] \cdot \rho_j}]$ for $j = 2, \ldots, n$.
- Reply to $\mathcal{C}$ with $(\mathsf{strap}', \mathsf{bstag}', \mathsf{bxtrap}'_2, \ldots, \mathsf{bxtrap}'_n)$ and $\mathsf{env} = \mathsf{AuthEnc}_{K_M}(\rho_1, \ldots, \rho_n)$.

$\mathcal{C}$ sets:

- $\mathsf{strap} \leftarrow (\mathsf{strap}')^{r_1^{-1}}$; $\mathsf{bstag} \leftarrow (\mathsf{bstag}')^{r_1^{-1}}$; $\mathsf{bxtrap}_j \leftarrow (\mathsf{bxtrap}'_j)^{r_j^{-1}}$ $(\forall_{j=2,\ldots,n})$;
- $\mathsf{token} \leftarrow (\mathsf{env}, \mathsf{strap}, \mathsf{bstag}, \mathsf{bxtrap}_2, \ldots, \mathsf{bxtrap}_n)$.

Search protocol

Client $\mathcal{C}$ on input token proceeds as follows:

- Set $(K_z, K_e) \leftarrow F(_\tau(\mathsf{strap}, 1), F(\mathsf{strap}, 2))$, and send to $\mathcal{E}$ the message $(\mathsf{env}, \mathsf{bstag}, \mathsf{bxtoken}[1], \mathsf{bxtoken}[2], \ldots)$ defined as follows:
  - For $c = 1, 2, \ldots$, until $\mathcal{E}$ sends stop:
    - * Set $z_c \leftarrow F_p(K_z, c)$ and set $\mathsf{bxtoken}[c, i] \leftarrow (\mathsf{bxtrap}_i)^{z_c}$ for $i = 2, \ldots, n$.
    - * Set $\mathsf{bxtoken}[c] \leftarrow (\mathsf{bxtoken}[c, 2], \ldots, \mathsf{bxtoken}[c, n])$.

Server $\mathcal{E}$ on input $\mathsf{EDB} = (\mathsf{TSet}, \mathsf{XSet}, K_M)$ responds as follows:

- Upon receiving env, bstag from $\mathcal{C}$, decrypt/verify env; if verification fails return "no results" and stop.
- Set $\mathsf{stag} \leftarrow (\mathsf{bstag})^{1/\rho_1}$ and retrieve $\mathbf{t} \leftarrow \mathsf{TSetRetrieve}(\mathsf{TSet}, \mathsf{stag})$ from TSet.
- For $c = 1, \ldots, |\mathbf{t}|$ do:
  - Receive $\mathsf{bxtoken}[c]$ from $\mathcal{C}$ and retrieve value (e, y) from the c-th tuple in **t**.
  - Check if $\mathsf{bxtoken}[c, i]^{y/\rho_i} \in \mathsf{XSet}$ for all $i = 2, \ldots, n$. If so, send e to $\mathcal{C}$ (else nothing is returned for this tuple).
  - When last tuple in **t** is reached, send stop to $\mathcal{C}$ and halt.

For each received e client $\mathcal{C}$ computes $(\mathsf{ind}|\mathsf{rdk}) \leftarrow \mathsf{Dec}(K_e, \mathsf{e})$ and outputs $(\mathsf{ind}, \mathsf{rdk})$.

Figure 3: OSPIR-OXT INSTANTIATED FOR CONJUNTIONS WITH THE HASHED DIFFIE-HELLMAN OPRF

Membership Privacy: A Unifying Framework For Privacy Definitions

Ninghui Li, Wahbeh Qardaji, Dong Su, Yi Wu, Weining Yang
Department of Computer Science and CERIAS, Purdue University
{ninghui,wqardaji,su17,wu510,yang469}@cs.purdue.edu

ABSTRACT

We introduce a novel privacy framework that we call Membership Privacy. The framework includes positive membership privacy, which prevents the adversary from significantly increasing its ability to conclude that an entity is in the input dataset, and negative membership privacy, which prevents leaking of non-membership. These notions are parameterized by a family of distributions that captures the adversary's prior knowledge. The power and flexibility of the proposed framework lies in the ability to choose different distribution families to instantiate membership privacy. Many privacy notions in the literature are equivalent to membership privacy with interesting distribution families, including differential privacy, differential identifiability, and differential privacy under sampling. Casting these notions into the framework leads to deeper understanding of the strengthes and weaknesses of these notions, as well as their relationships to each other. The framework also provides a principled approach to developing new privacy notions under which better utility can be achieved than what is possible under differential privacy.

Categories and Subject Descriptors

K.4.1 [**COMPUTERS AND SOCIETY**]: Privacy

Keywords

Differential Privacy; Privacy Notions; Membership Privacy

1. INTRODUCTION

The spate of privacy related incidents [30, 3, 27, 17] has spurred a long line of research in privacy notions for data publishing and analysis [30, 29, 24, 21]. A privacy notion that is increasingly gaining acceptance is differential privacy [7, 10]. Informally, differential privacy requires any individual entity in a dataset to have only a limited impact on the output. More specifically, differential privacy requires that any two neighboring input datasets will induce output distributions that are close in the sense that the probabilities of each possible output differ by a bounded multiplicative factor. There are two major flavors of differential privacy, depending on the condition under which two datasets are considered to be neighbors. In [19], these were referred to as unbounded and bounded differential privacy. In *Unbounded Differential Privacy (UDP)*, T and T' are neighbors if T can be obtained from T' by adding or removing an entity. In *Bounded Differential Privacy (BDP)*, T and T' are neighbors if T can be obtained from T' by replacing one entity in T' with another entity.

Because privacy is a social notion with many facets, there is a long tradition in the research community to examine the various technical formulations of privacy in order to understand their strengthes and weaknesses. Several researchers have questioned whether differential privacy provides sufficient protection, and how to choose the ϵ parameter. In [19], Kifer and Machanavajjhala argued that it is incorrect to claim that differential privacy is robust to arbitrary background knowledge. In [5], Cormode argued that differential privacy does not prevent inferential disclosure. That is, from differentially private output, it is possible to infer potentially sensitive information about an individual with non-trivial accuracy. In [20], Lee and Clifton argued that while the parameter ϵ in ϵ-DP limits how much one individual can affect the output, it does not limit how much information is revealed about an individual; and this does not match legal definition of privacy, which requires protection of individually identifiable data. Lee and Clifton proposed the notion of differential identifiability. At the same time, it has been recognized that differential privacy may be too restrictive in some settings, and there are several efforts that aim at relaxing it, including differential privacy under sampling [22] and crowd blending privacy [15].

This paper is motivated by these lines of work. Our aim is to gain a deeper understanding of privacy both as a social concept and in terms of technical formulations. We begin by analyzing the recent privacy incidents. Our analysis concludes that what society often views as a privacy breach is the ability of an adversary to either re-identify or assert the membership of an individual in a supposedly "anonymized" dataset. Hence, a privacy measure needs to protect everyone in the anonymized dataset against membership disclosure. Such a privacy definition, however, is incomplete without specifying the adversary's prior knowledge about what might be in the dataset. The need to consider this background knowledge is indeed apparent from recent privacy breaches [3, 27].

We combine these two requirements and introduce a novel privacy framework that we call Membership Privacy. This framework comprises of two notions: Positive Membership Privacy (PMP), which prevents an adversary from significantly improving its confidence that an entity is in the input dataset; and Negative Membership Privacy (NMP), which prevents an adversary from significantly improving its confidence that an entity is not in the dataset. These notions are parameterized by two parameters $\mathbb{D}$ and γ. The

CCS'13, November 4–8, 2013, Berlin, Germany.

ACM 978-1-4503-2477-9/13/11 ...$15.00.
http://dx.doi.org/10.1145/2508859.2516686 .

Distribution Family	Description of Distributions in the Family	Equivalent Privacy Notion
$\mathbb{D}_U$	Includes all distributions over $2^{\mathcal{U}}$; all other families are sub-families of this.	Privacy with no Utility
$\mathbb{D}_I$	Includes all mutually independent (MI) distributions	Unbounded Differential Privacy [8]
$\mathbb{D}_I^2$	Sub-family of $\mathbb{D}_I$. Includes MI distributions that have only two datasets with non-zero probability, i.e., distributions in which $\Pr[T \cup \{t\}] = p$ and $\Pr[T] = 1 - p$.	Unbounded Differential Privacy
$\mathbb{D}_F^\beta$	Sub-family of $\mathbb{D}_I$. Includes MI distributions such that all entities have probability in $\{0, \beta\}$, i.e., all entities that may appear have a fixed probability.	Differential Privacy Under Sampling [22]
$\mathbb{D}_B$	Includes distributions that are the conditional distributions of some MI distribution conditioned upon that all datasets with non-zero probability have the same size.	Bounded Differential Privacy [10]
$\mathbb{D}_B^2$	Sub-family of $\mathbb{D}_B$. Includes distributions where $\Pr[T \cup \{t_1\}] = p$ and $\Pr[T \cup \{t_2\}] = 1 - p$	Bounded Differential Privacy
$\mathbb{D}_C^m$	Sub-family of $\mathbb{D}_B$. Includes all distributions in which $\Pr[\{T \cup \{t_1\}] = \Pr[T \cup \{t_2\}] = \Pr[T \cup \{t_m\}] = \frac{1}{m}$ and $T \cup \{t_1, \cdots, t_m\} = \mathcal{U}$	Differential Identifiability [20]
$\mathbb{D}_N$	Sub-family of $\mathbb{D}_F^{0.5}$. Include the single uniform distribution over all subsets of $\mathcal{U}$, i.e., all entities have probability 0.5.	New Privacy Notion

Table 1: Distributions for which membership privacy is considered in this paper, and their equivalent privacy notions in the literature.

first parameter captures an adversary's prior knowledge. In particular, $\mathbb{D}$ is a set of probability distributions. Each element $\mathcal{D} \in \mathbb{D}$ is a probability distribution over all possible datasets, and encodes one possible state of prior knowledge of the adversary. $\mathbb{D}$ as a set captures all states of prior knowledge against which membership privacy is guaranteed. The second parameter γ is a number that is greater than or equal to 1; it limits the increase in confidence of accurate membership assertion.

The power of the membership privacy framework is demonstrated by the fact that many privacy notions in the literature are equivalent to membership privacy with interesting distribution families. These notions and their corresponding distribution families are given in Table 1. For example, Unbounded Differential Privacy (UDP) is equivalent to membership privacy in $\mathbb{D}_I$, the family of all mutually independent (MI) distributions. Similarly, Bounded Differential Privacy (BDP) is equivalent to membership privacy under $\mathbb{D}_B$, the family that includes those obtained by conditioning a MI distribution such that all datasets with non-zero probability have the same size. Differential identifiability [20] and Differential Privacy under Sampling [22] are also instantiations of membership privacy.

Identifying the family under which a privacy notion guarantees membership privacy provides deeper understanding of the power and limitation of the privacy notion. For example, this framework enables us to show that under what condition differential identifiability is equivalent to BDP and under what condition that it is strictly weaker. We stress that almost all privacy notions make some assumptions about the adversary's background knowledge. For example, differential privacy's main assumption is independence, as also pointed out in [19]. The only membership privacy notion without any assumption is the one under $\mathbb{D}_U$, the family that includes all distributions. We show that this essentially requires giving up all utility. This is another formulation of the "no free lunch" result in [19, 8, 12].

As all practical privacy notion requires some assumptions on the allowed distributions, it makes sense to analyze whether the assumption made in a notion is appropriate for a given setting, and choose a privacy that is neither too strong nor too weak, in order to maximize utility. Our membership privacy framework enables such analysis. One could develop privacy notions that are stronger than differential privacy (satisfying membership privacy for beyond $\mathbb{D}_I$), as well as ones that are weaker (satisfying membership privacy for a sub-family of $\mathbb{D}_I$).

It has often been recognized that differential privacy can be too strong to satisfy in some settings, and there are some efforts aiming at relaxing it. Our membership privacy framework provides a principled way to conduct this. For example, one weaker privacy notion that may be useful for some applications is membership privacy under $\mathbb{D}_N$, which includes the single uniform distribution over all possible datasets. As a demonstration that this notion enables higher utility, we show that under this notion it is possible to compute the max value of a set with high accuracy, which is difficult to do under differential privacy.

The rest of the paper is organized as follows. In Section 2, we analyze privacy incidents and motivate membership privacy. We then introduce the membership privacy framework in Section 3, show how differential privacy fits in the framework in Section 4, and consider several other instantiations of the framework in Section 5. Finally, we discuss related work in Section 6 and conclude in Section 7.

2. WHAT IS PRIVACY?

Similar to other contexts in security and privacy, the concept of privacy is easier to define by identifying what are privacy breaches. Privacy can then be simply defined by requiring that no privacy breach occurs. As privacy is a social concept, any formalization of privacy violation must be based on what the society perceives as privacy breaches. In this section, we examine several well-publicized privacy incidents in data publishing in recent years, and identify the common features of what the society considered to be privacy breaches. We show that the disclosures in these incidents all fall into a general class that we call positive membership disclosures. In such an disclosure, when given the published dataset, an adversary can find an entity t and assert with high confidence that t's data is in the original dataset.

2.1 Privacy Incidents

An early and well publicized privacy incident is from the supposedly anonymized medical visit data made available by the Group Insurance Commission (GIC) [30]. While the obvious personal identifiers are removed, the published data included zip code, date of birth, and gender, which are sufficient to uniquely identify a significant fraction of the population. Sweeney [30] showed that by correlating this data with the publicly available Voter Registration

List for Cambridge Massachusetts, medical visits about many individuals can be easily identified, including those of William Weld, a former governor of Massachusetts. We note that even without access to the public voter registration list, the same privacy breaches can occur. Many individuals' birthdate, gender and zip code are public information. This is especially the case with the advent of social media, including Facebook, where users share seemingly innocuous personal information to the public.

Another well-known privacy incident came from publishing web search logs. In 2006, AOL released three months of search logs involving 650,000 users. The only privacy protection technique used is replacing user ids with random numbers. This proved to be a failure. Two New York Time journalists [3] were able to re-identify Thelma Arnold, a 62 year old women living in Lilburn, Ga. from the published search logs. Ms. Arnold's search log includes her last name and location names near where she lived. The reporters were able to cross-reference this information with phonebook entries. After the New York Time article is published, the data was immediately retracted by AOL. Later a class action lawsuit was filed against AOL. This scandal led to the resignation of AOL's CTO and the dismissal of two employees.

In 2009, Netflix released a dataset containing the movie rating data from 500,000 users as part of a one-million dollar challenge to the data mining research community for developing effective algorithms for predicting users' movie preferences based on their viewing history and ratings. While the data was anonymized in order to protect users' privacy, Narayanan and Schmatikov [27] showed that an adversary who has some knowledge about a subscriber's movie viewing experience can easily identify the subscriber's record if it is present in the dataset. For example, [27] shows that, from the profiles of 50 IMDB users, at least 2 of them also appear in the Netflix dataset.

Another privacy incident targeted the Genome-Wide Association Studies (GWAS). These studies normally compare the DNA of two groups of participants: people with the disease (cases) and similar people without (controls). Each person's DNA mutations (single-nucleotide polymorphisms, or SNPs) at indicative locations are read, and the data is then analyzed. Traditionally, researchers publish aggregate frequencies of SNPs for participants in the two groups. In 2008, Homer et al. [17] proposed attacks that could tell with high confidence whether an individual is in the case group, assuming that the individual's DNA is known. The attack works even if the group includes hundreds of individuals. Because of the privacy concerns from such attacks, a number of institutions, including the US National Institute of Health (NIH) and the Wellcome Trust in London all decided to restrict access to data from GWAS. Such attacks need access to the victim's DNA data and publicly available genomic database to establish the likely SNP frequencies in the general population.

2.2 Lessons from Privacy Incidents

From these incidents, we learn the following lessons.

Re-identification matters. In the GIC, AOL, and Netflix incidents, one is able to correctly identify *one individual*'s record from supposedly anonymous data. This fact alone is sufficient for the society to agree that privacy is breached. It does not matter whether an adversary has learnt additional sensitive information about the individual.

Positive assertion of membership matters. In the GWAS example, only aggregate information is published and there is no individual record for re-identification to occur. However, so long as the adversary can positively assert that one individual's data is in the input dataset based on the output, this is considered a privacy breach.

Must protect everyone. In several attacks, only a single individual is re-identified; however, that is sufficient to cause widespread privacy concerns and serious consequences (e.g., the AOL case). This suggests that privacy protection must apply to *every individual*. A method that on average offers good protection, but may compromise some individual's privacy is not acceptable.

No separation of Quasi-Identifier and Sensitive Attributes. Much of database privacy research assumes the division of all attributes into quasi-identifiers (QIDs) and sensitive attributes (SA), where the adversary is assumed to know the QIDs, but not SAs. This separation, however, is very hard to obtain in practice. No such separation exists in the cases of AOL, Netflix, or GWAS. Even though only some attributes are used in the GIC incident, it is difficult to assume that they are the only QIDs. Other attributes in the GIC data includes visit date, diagnosis, etc. There may well exist an adversary who knows this information about some individuals, and if with this knowledge these individuals' record can be re-identified, it is still a serious privacy breach. The same difficulty is true for publishing any kind of census, medical, or transactional data. When publishing anonymized microdata, one has to defend against all kinds of adversaries, some know one set of attributes, and others know a different set. An attribute about one individual may be known by some adversaries, and unknown (and thus should be considered sensitive) for other adversaries. In summary, one should assume that for every individual, there may exist an adversary who knows *all attributes* of that individual.

2.3 Positive Membership Disclosure

The discussions above suggest that a privacy breach is a positive assertion of membership for some entity t all attributes of which may be known by the adversary. We note that re-identification, i.e., pointing to some feature of the output dataset and concluding that this feature reflects that t is in the input dataset, implies an assertion of positive membership. Therefore, any reidentification attack will also result in a positive membership assertion. After all, if one cannot be sure that an entity t is in the input dataset, one cannot be sure that a particular feature in the dataset is attributable to t.

> **Privacy breach = Positive Membership Disclosure:** Given an input dataset T, we say that the output $O = \mathcal{A}(T)$ is subject to positive membership disclosure, when there exists a entity t such that an adversary can assert: the fact that O is output indicates that it is highly likely that t is in the input dataset T.

Note that whether positive membership disclosure occurs or not is not just a property of the output $O = \mathcal{A}(T)$. In order to say that O indicates t is in the input dataset, one must consider the behavior of the algorithm $\mathcal{A}$ on datasets that do not include t.

Some authors have considered privacy breaches as attribute disclosures, i.e., the ability to infer one's sensitive attributes from the data publishing. In [5], it has been shown that while satisfying differential privacy, one could still build reasonably accurate classifier to learn sensitive attribute values of some entity. We argue that attribute disclosure is problematic as a privacy notion. As shown by Dwork and others [8], attribute disclosure may occur even if an entity's data is not included in the input dataset. For example, suppose that one conducts a study and collects data from individuals in a particular population group, e.g., of a certain age and ethnicity group, and these individuals are willing to share their data. Further suppose publishing this dataset enables one to learn new attribute information about this group, e.g., they have a much higher probability of have some disease than the general population. This new attribute information, however, applies to any individual in this population group, even the ones that do not contribute data, and enables the learning of new sensitive attribute information about the individual. We believe that calling such an attribute disclosure a privacy violation is incorrect. Under this interpretation of privacy, an individual could claim privacy violation if there is any data about anyone with some common feature (e.g., is of the same gender) as the individual.

3. THE MEMBERSHIP PRIVACY FRAMEWORK

In this section, we introduce our framework for formalizing membership privacy. More specifically, we introduce the notion of Positive Membership Privacy (PMP), which prevents Positive Membership Disclosure. To enable establishing a clear connection with differential privacy, we also introduce Negative Membership Privacy (NMP), which prevents an adversary from increasing significantly the confidence that a particular entity's data does not occur in the dataset.

3.1 Notations

We assume that there is a universe $\mathcal{U}$ of entities, and each dataset is generated by choosing a set $T \subseteq \mathcal{U}$ of entities to be included in the dataset. That is, there is a deterministic procedure G such that every dataset is given by $G(T)$ for some $T \subseteq \mathcal{U}$. Below, we often abuse the terminology and call T the dataset.

Each entity $t \in \mathcal{U}$ corresponds to a physical entity that exists in the physical world and needs privacy protection. For example, in many scenarios, a physical entity corresponds to an individual, i.e., a human being.

When we are working with relational datasets, typically an entity corresponds to one tuple. However, it is possible that in some scenarios one would need to have an entity corresponding to a set of tuples. For example, in a database of medical insurance information for employees and their family members, it may be necessary to treat an employee's family as an entity. When we deal with non-relational datasets such as social network data, one may want to choose a social network account as an entity so that when the account is not included, the dataset should not include any information related to the account.

The adversary may have prior beliefs about what the dataset is; this is captured by a distribution $\mathcal{D}$ over $2^{\mathcal{U}}$, the powerset of $\mathcal{U}$. A distribution $\mathcal{D}$ assigns a probability to each possible subset of $\mathcal{U}$. From the adversary's point of view, the dataset is a random variable drawn according to the distribution $\mathcal{D}$. We use $\mathbf{T}$ to denote this random variable.

When publishing a dataset, often one is unable to fix one particular distribution $\mathcal{D}$. One needs to defend against multiple adversaries that may have very different beliefs. Even if one is concerned with a single adversary, it is often impossible to know exactly what the adversary believes. Therefore, we need to consider a family of possible distributions. This is modeled by $\mathbb{D}$, which is a set of distributions. That is, each $\mathcal{D} \in \mathbb{D}$ is a distribution over $2^{\mathcal{U}}$. The family $\mathbb{D}$ specifies what kind of background knowledge regarding the underlying dataset we allow the adversary to have. For perfect privacy, one would desire $\mathbb{D}$ to include all possible distributions over $2^{\mathcal{U}}$. However, as we show later, achieving such perfect privacy would require not publishing any meaningful information of the underlying dataset.

3.2 Positive Membership Privacy

While the notion of membership privacy has been alluded to in several papers, e.g., [19, 20], it has not been formalized to deal with the possibility of different kinds of background knowledge for the adversary. We now provide such a formalization.

DEFINITION 3.1. ***[Positive Membership Privacy ((𝔻, γ)-PMP)]:*** *We say that a mechanism $\mathcal{A}$ provides γ-positive membership privacy under a family $\mathbb{D}$ of distributions over $2^{\mathcal{U}}$, i.e., $((\mathbb{D},\gamma)$-PMP), where $\gamma \geq 1$, if and only if for any $S \subseteq \mathsf{range}(\mathcal{A})$, any distribution $\mathcal{D} \in \mathbb{D}$, and any entity $t \in \mathcal{U}$, we have*

$$\Pr_{\mathcal{D},\mathcal{A}}[t \in \mathbf{T} \mid \mathcal{A}(\mathbf{T}) \in S] \leq \gamma \Pr_{\mathcal{D}}[t \in \mathbf{T}] \tag{1}$$

$$\text{and } \Pr_{\mathcal{D},\mathcal{A}}[t \notin \mathbf{T} \mid \mathcal{A}(\mathbf{T}) \in S] \geq \frac{\Pr_{\mathcal{D}}[t \notin \mathbf{T}]}{\gamma} \tag{2}$$

where $\mathbf{T}$ is a random variable drawn according to the distribution $\mathcal{D}$.

With a slight abuse of notation, we use S to denote the event $\mathcal{A}(\mathbf{T}) \in S$, t to denote the event that $t \in \mathbf{T}$ and $\neg\, t$ to denote the event that $t \notin \mathbf{T}$. Equation (1) can then be written as $\frac{\Pr_{\mathcal{D},\mathcal{A}}[t|S]}{\Pr_{\mathcal{D}}[t]} \leq \gamma$, where $\Pr_{\mathcal{D}}[t]$ denotes the prior belief that entity t is in an input dataset sampled from the distribution $\mathcal{D}$, and $\Pr_{\mathcal{D},\mathcal{A}}[t|S]$ denotes the posterior belief that t is in the input dataset after observing that the event S has happened for the output of $\mathcal{A}$. When $\mathcal{D}$ and $\mathcal{A}$ are obvious from the context, we drop them from the subscript and write $\Pr[t]$ and $\Pr[t|S]$. Equation (1) requires that $\Pr[t|S]$ can increase at most by a factor of γ over the prior belief $\Pr[t]$.

Equation (1) by itself, however, may not offer sufficient protection when the prior belief $\Pr[t]$ is already quite large. For example, setting $\gamma = 1.2$ might seem a reasonable strong privacy protection. However, if $\Pr[t] = 0.85$, then Equation (1) will bound the posterior belief $\Pr[t|S]$ to be less than $0.85 * 1.2 = 1.02$. This allows an adversary to be 100% certain that t is in the input dataset after observing the output, which is arguably undesirable.

Equation (2), which can be written as $\frac{\Pr[\neg\, t|S]}{\Pr[\neg\, t]} \geq \frac{1}{\gamma}$, provides a more effective upper-bound for the posterior belief $\Pr[t|S]$ when the prior is large. In the above example, $\Pr[\neg\, t|S]$ is lower-bounded by $(1-0.85)/1.2 = 0.125$, i.e., $\Pr[t|S]$ can increase from 0.85 to at most 0.875. Equations (1) and (2) together are equivalent to:

$$\begin{aligned}\Pr[t|S] &\leq \min\left(\gamma \Pr[t], 1 - \frac{\Pr[\neg\, t]}{\gamma}\right) \\ &= \min\left(\gamma \Pr[t], \frac{\gamma - 1 + \Pr[t]}{\gamma}\right).\end{aligned} \tag{3}$$

For example, suppose $\gamma = 2$, then PMP requires that $\Pr[t|S] \leq \min\left(2\Pr[t], \frac{1+\Pr[t]}{2}\right)$. In the rest of the paper, we often use Equation (3) as the formulation of the PMP condition.

3.3 Satisfying PMP

In the rest of this section, we establish a relationship between PMP's bounding of $\Pr[t|S]$ in Equations (1) and (2) to a condition bounding $\frac{\Pr[S|\,t]}{\Pr[S|\neg\, t]}$, which is more directly controlled by choosing an appropriate mechanism. This is also key to establish the relationship of PMP with differential privacy. To start, note that by the Bayes' theorem, we have

$$\Pr[t|S] = \frac{\Pr[S|\,t]\Pr[t]}{\Pr[S|\,t]\Pr[t] + \Pr[S|\neg t]\Pr[\neg\, t]}. \tag{4}$$

LEMMA 3.2. *For any mechanism $\mathcal{A}$, distribution $\mathcal{D}$, and $\gamma \geq 1$, if for any entity t s.t. $0 < \Pr[t] < 1$ and any output event S, $\mathcal{A}$ satisfies $\Pr[S|t] \leq \gamma \cdot \Pr[S|\neg t]$, then $\mathcal{A}$ provides $(\{\mathcal{D}\}, \gamma)$-PMP.*

PROOF. For any t, if $\Pr[t] = 0$ or $\Pr[t] = 1$, then for any S, $\Pr[t|S] = \Pr[t]$, trivially satisfying Equation (3). If $0 < \Pr[t] < 1$, for any S, from Equation (4), we have

$$\Pr[t|S] = \Pr[t] \cdot \frac{\Pr[S|t]}{\Pr[t]\Pr[S|t]+(1-\Pr[t])\Pr[S|\neg t]}$$

Note that the denumerator above is a weighted average of $\Pr[S|t]$ and $\Pr[S|\neg t]$. Since $\Pr[S|t] \leq \gamma \Pr[S|t]$ because $\gamma \geq 1$, and $\Pr[S|t] \leq \gamma \Pr[S|\neg t]$ from the given condition, it must be that

$$\Pr[S|t] \leq \gamma(\Pr[t]\Pr[S|t] + (1-\Pr[t])\Pr[S|\neg t]).$$

And thus $\Pr[t|S] \leq \gamma \Pr[t]$. Similarly, we have

$$\Pr[\neg t|S] = \Pr[\neg t]\frac{\Pr[S|\neg t]}{\Pr[S|t]\Pr[t]+\Pr[S|\neg t](1-\Pr[t])} \geq \Pr[\neg t]\frac{1}{\gamma}$$

The last step above is because $\Pr[S|\neg t] \geq \frac{\Pr[S|t]}{\gamma}$ (from given condition) and $\Pr[S|\neg t] \geq \frac{\Pr[S|\neg t]}{\gamma}$ (from $\gamma \geq 1$). □

Note that the above relationship is one-directional. Bounding $\frac{\Pr[S|t]}{\Pr[S|\neg t]} \leq \gamma$ under a distribution $\mathcal{D}$ is sufficient but not necessary for satisfying PMP. Below we show that an equivalence exists between the two when one aims at satisfying PMP for all distributions in a family that has the property that we call downward scalable, which essentially means that within the family, one could scale down the probability $\Pr[t]$ to an arbitrarily small value. We first need to define what we call a t-scaled distribution.

DEFINITION 3.3 (t-SCALED DISTRIBUTION). *Given a distribution $\mathcal{D}$, we say that $\mathcal{D}'$ is t-scaled from $\mathcal{D}$ if there exist two constants c_1 and c_2 such that*

$$\forall T \subseteq \mathcal{U} \quad \Pr_{\mathcal{D}'}[T] = \begin{cases} c_1 \Pr_{\mathcal{D}}[T] & \text{when } t \in T, \\ c_2 \Pr_{\mathcal{D}}[T] & \text{when } t \notin T \end{cases}$$

The following property is the reason why we introduce the notion of t-scaled distribution.

LEMMA 3.4. *If $\mathcal{D}'$ is t-scaled from $\mathcal{D}$, then for any mechanism $\mathcal{A}$ and any output event S, we have $\Pr_{\mathcal{D}',\mathcal{A}}[S|\,t] = \Pr_{\mathcal{D},\mathcal{A}}[S|\,t]$ and $\Pr_{\mathcal{D}',\mathcal{A}}[S|\neg\,t] = \Pr_{\mathcal{D},\mathcal{A}}[S|\neg\,t]$.*

PROOF. Let c_1 and c_2 be the scaling parameter. We have

$$\begin{aligned}
\Pr_{\mathcal{D}',\mathcal{A}}[S|\,t] &= \frac{\sum_{T:t\in T}\Pr_{\mathcal{D}'}[T]\Pr_{\mathcal{A}}[S|\,T]}{\sum_{T:t\in T}\Pr_{\mathcal{D}'}[T]} \\
&= \frac{\sum_{T:t\in T} c_1\Pr_{\mathcal{D}}[T]\Pr_{\mathcal{A}}[S|\,T]}{\sum_{T:t\in T} c_1\Pr_{\mathcal{D}}[T]} = \Pr_{\mathcal{D},\mathcal{A}}[S|\,t] \\
\Pr_{\mathcal{D}',\mathcal{A}}[S|\neg\,t] &= \frac{\sum_{T:t\notin T}\Pr_{\mathcal{D}'}[T]\Pr_{\mathcal{A}}[S|\,T]}{\sum_{T:t\in T}\Pr_{\mathcal{D}'}[T]} \\
&= \frac{\sum_{T:t\notin T} c_2\Pr_{\mathcal{D}}[T]\Pr_{\mathcal{A}}[S|\,T]}{\sum_{T:t\notin T} c_2\Pr_{\mathcal{D}}[T]} = \Pr_{\mathcal{D},\mathcal{A}}[S|\,t]
\end{aligned}$$

□

DEFINITION 3.5 (DOWNWARD SCALABLE FAMILIES). *We say that that a family $\mathbb{D}$ is downward scalable if and only if for any distribution $\mathcal{D} \in \mathbb{D}$, any entity t such that $0 < \Pr_{\mathcal{D}}[t] < 1$, and any $p > 0$, $\mathbb{D}$ also contains a distribution $\mathcal{D}'$ that is t-scaled from $\mathcal{D}$ such that $\Pr_{\mathcal{D}'}[t] < p$.*

The following theorem is helpful for establishing equivalence of other privacy notions with PMP.

THEOREM 3.6. *Given a mechanism $\mathcal{A}$, γ, and a downward scalable family $\mathbb{D}$, $\mathcal{A}$ satisfies $(\mathbb{D},\gamma)$-PMP if and only if for any $\mathcal{D} \in \mathbb{D}$, any entity t s.t. $0 < \Pr[t] < 1$, and any S, we have $\Pr[S|t] \leq \gamma \cdot \Pr[S|\neg\,t]$.*

PROOF. The "if" direction is implied by Lemma 3.2. For the "only if" direction, assume, for the sake of contradiction, that $\mathcal{A}$ provides $(\mathbb{D},\gamma)$-PMP yet does not satisfy the condition, then there exists a distribution $\mathcal{D} \in \mathbb{D}$ and entity t such that $0 < \Pr_{\mathcal{D}}[t] < 1$ and $\Pr_{\mathcal{D},\mathcal{A}}[S|t] > \gamma \cdot \Pr_{\mathcal{D},\mathcal{A}}[S|\neg\,t]$. There are two cases.

Case one: $\Pr_{\mathcal{D},\mathcal{A}}[S|t] > 0$ and $\Pr_{\mathcal{D},\mathcal{A}}[S|\neg\,t] = 0$. Let $p = \frac{1}{\gamma}$. Because $\mathbb{D}$ is downward scalable, it must contain a $\mathcal{D}'$ which is t-scaled from $\mathcal{D}$ such that $\Pr_{\mathcal{D}'}[t] = p' < p = \frac{1}{\gamma}$. Because $\mathcal{D}'$ is t-scaled from $\mathcal{D}$, we have $\Pr_{\mathcal{D}',\mathcal{A}}[S|\neg\,t] = \Pr_{\mathcal{D},\mathcal{A}}[S|\neg\,t] = 0$, and thus $\Pr_{\mathcal{D}',\mathcal{A}}[t|S] = 1$ (if $\neg\,t$ cannot result in S, observing S means t must be true). Therefore, $\Pr_{\mathcal{D}',\mathcal{A}}[t|S] = 1 = \gamma p > \gamma p' = \gamma \Pr_{\mathcal{D}'}[t]$, which contradicts the fact that $\mathcal{A}$ satisfies $(\mathbb{D},\gamma)$-PMP.

Case two: $\Pr_{\mathcal{D},\mathcal{A}}[S|t] = \alpha \Pr_{\mathcal{D},\mathcal{A}}[S|\neg t]$, where $\alpha > \gamma \geq 1$. Because $\mathbb{D}$ is downward scalable, it must contains a $\mathcal{D}'$ which is t-scaled from $\mathcal{D}$ such that $\Pr_{\mathcal{D}'}[t] = p' < p$ for an arbitrarily small p, and that $\Pr_{\mathcal{D}',\mathcal{A}}[S|\,t] = \alpha \Pr_{\mathcal{D}',\mathcal{A}}[S|\neg\,t]$, and thus under $\mathcal{D}'$ We have:

$$\begin{aligned}
\frac{\Pr[t|S]}{\Pr[t]} &= \frac{\Pr[S|\,t]}{p'\Pr[S|\,t]+(1-p')\Pr[S|\neg t]} \\
&= \frac{\alpha\Pr[S|\neg\,t]}{p'\alpha\Pr[S|\neg\,t]+(1-p')\Pr[S|\neg\,t]} \\
&= \frac{\alpha}{\alpha p'+1-p'}
\end{aligned}$$

Note that the above can be made arbitrarily close to α by forcing p' to be arbitrarily small, as $\alpha > \gamma$, one could choose a small p' (forcing $p' < \frac{\alpha-\gamma}{\gamma(\alpha-1)}$ suffices) to make the above $> \gamma$, contradicts the fact that $\mathcal{A}$ satisfies $(\mathbb{D},\gamma)$-PMP. □

3.4 Infeasibility of PMP under Arbitrary Distributions

PMP is parameterized by $\mathbb{D}$. Given two families of distributions $\mathbb{D}_1$ and $\mathbb{D}_2$ such that $\mathbb{D}_1 \subseteq \mathbb{D}_2$, if $\mathcal{A}$ provides $(\mathbb{D}_2,\gamma)$-PMP, then $\mathcal{A}$ also provides $(\mathbb{D}_1,\gamma)$-PMP. Therefore, to provide the maximum level of privacy, it is desirable to provide $(\mathbb{D},\gamma)$-PMP for as large a family $\mathbb{D}$ as possible. We use $\mathbb{D}_U$ to denote the largest family of distributions, namely the set of all distributions over $2^{\mathcal{U}}$. Unfortunately, achieving PMP under $\mathbb{D}_U$ requires $\mathcal{A}$ to provide almost no utility, as $\mathcal{A}$ must provide very similar output distributions on any pair of dataset T_1 and T_2, even if when $T_1 = \emptyset$ and $T_2 = \mathcal{U}$

PROPOSITION 3.7. *If an algorithm $\mathcal{A}$ provides $(\mathbb{D}_{\mathcal{U}},\gamma)$-PMP, then for any datasets (T_1,T_2) such that $T_1 \setminus T_2 \neq \emptyset$, and any $S \subseteq \mathsf{range}(\mathcal{A})$, it must be*

$$\Pr[\mathcal{A}(T_1) \in S] \leq \gamma \Pr[\mathcal{A}(T_2) \in S] \tag{5}$$

PROOF. If $\mathcal{A}$ provides $(\mathbb{D}_{\mathcal{U}},\gamma)$-PMP, then it must provide γ-PMP for the family that consists of all distributions of the form $\{\langle T_1 : p\rangle, \langle T_2 : 1-p\rangle\}$. Clearly, this family is downward scalable. Let t be any tuple in $T_1 \setminus T_2$, from Theorem 3.6, $\mathcal{A}$ must satisfy $\forall S$, $\Pr[S|\,t] \leq \gamma \Pr[S|\neg t]$. Note that $\Pr[S|\,t] = \Pr[S|\,T_1]$ and $\Pr[S|\neg\,t] = \Pr[S|\,T_2]$; thus (5) holds. □

Proposition 3.7 requires $\mathcal{A}$'s output on any pair of datasets to be close. For example, when $T_1 = \mathcal{U}$ and $T_2 = \emptyset$, and $\mathcal{A}$ is supposed to answer a simple counting query. For any result that $\mathcal{A}(\mathcal{U})$ may return with probability p, $\mathcal{A}(\emptyset)$ must also return it with probability at least $\frac{p}{\gamma}$. This destroys the utility of publishing $\mathcal{A}(T)$, since one could compute $\mathcal{A}(\emptyset)$, and the distribution of $\mathcal{A}(T)$ for any T would be similar. Therefore, we must be content with choosing some subfamilies of $\mathbb{D}_U$ for PMP.

3.5 Negative Membership Privacy

Note that satisfying PMP will upper-bound $\Pr[t|S]$; however, PMP does not lower-bound $\Pr[t|S]$. That is, it is permitted that after observing an output, one concludes with high confidence that an entity is not in the input dataset. While we believe that for the vast majority of cases, satisfying PMP is sufficient for privacy protection, it is possible that in some unusual situations one desires protection against inference of non-membership as well as inference of membership.

DEFINITION 3.8. ***[Negative Membership Privacy** $((\mathbb{D},\gamma)$**-NMP)]:** We say that a mechanism $\mathcal{A}$ provides γ-negative membership privacy under a distribution family $\mathbb{D}$ ($(\mathbb{D},\gamma)$-NMP), if and only if for any $S \subseteq \mathsf{range}(\mathcal{A})$, any $\mathcal{D} \in \mathbb{D}$, and any tuple $t \in \mathcal{U}$, we have both $\Pr[\neg t|S] \le \gamma \cdot \Pr[\neg t]$ and $\Pr[t|S] \ge \frac{\Pr[t]}{\gamma}$, which are equivalent to*

$$\Pr[\neg\, t|S] \le \min\left(\gamma \Pr[\neg t], \frac{\gamma - 1 + \Pr[\neg t]}{\gamma}\right), \tag{6}$$

and to

$$\Pr[t|S] \ge \max\left(\gamma \Pr[t] - \gamma + 1, \frac{\Pr[t]}{\gamma}\right) \tag{7}$$

The properties of NMP are analogous to PMP.

DEFINITION 3.9 (UPWARD SCALABLE FAMILIES). *We say that that a family $\mathbb{D}$ is upward scalable if and only if for any distribution $\mathcal{D} \in \mathbb{D}$, any entity t such that $0 < \Pr_{\mathcal{D}}[t] < 1$, and any probability $\Pr_{\mathcal{D}}[t] < p < 1$, $\mathbb{D}$ also contains a distribution $\mathcal{D}'$ that is t-scaled from $\mathcal{D}$ such that $\Pr_{\mathcal{D}'}[t] > p$.*

THEOREM 3.10. *For any mechanism $\mathcal{A}$, γ, and any upward scalable family $\mathbb{D}$, $\mathcal{A}$ satisfies $(\mathbb{D},\gamma)$-NMP if and only if for any $\mathcal{D} \in \mathbb{D}$, any entity t, any entity t s.t. $0 < \Pr[t] < 1$, and any S, we have $\Pr[S|\neg t] \le \gamma \cdot \Pr[S|t]$.*

The proof for Theorem 3.10 is analogous of the proof for Theorem 3.6, and is omitted here.

3.6 Privacy Axioms

In [18], it is suggested that all privacy notions should satisfy the two axioms: the Privacy Axiom of Choice and the Axiom of Transformation Invariance. The following two theorems show that $(\mathbb{D},\gamma)$-PMP satisfy both axioms.

THEOREM 3.11. *Given two mechanisms $\mathcal{A}_1$ and $\mathcal{A}_2$ that both satisfy $(\mathbb{D},\gamma)$-PMP, for any $p \in [0,1]$, let $\mathcal{A}_p$ be the mechanism that outputs $\mathcal{A}_1$ with probability p and $\mathcal{A}_2$ with probability $1-p$, then $\mathcal{A}_p$ satisfies $(\mathbb{D},\gamma)$-PMP.*

Proof is Appendix A.1

THEOREM 3.12. *Given $\mathcal{A}_1$ that satisfies $(\mathbb{D},\gamma)$-PMP, and any algorithm $\mathcal{A}_2$, $\mathcal{A}(\cdot) = \mathcal{A}_2(\mathcal{A}_1(\cdot))$ satisfies $(\mathbb{D},\gamma)$-PMP.*

Proof is Appendix A.2. The same results hold for NMP; we omit explicitly stating them here.

4. DIFFERENTIAL PRIVACY AS MEMBERSHIP PRIVACY

Informally, differential privacy requires that the output of a data analysis mechanism is not overly affected by any single tuple in the input dataset.

DEFINITION 4.1 (ϵ-DIFFERENTIAL PRIVACY [8, 10]). *A mechanism $\mathcal{A}$ gives ϵ-differential privacy if for any pair of neighboring datasets T and T', and any $S \subseteq Range(\mathcal{A})$,*

$$\Pr[\mathcal{A}(T) \in S] \le e^{\epsilon} \cdot \Pr[\mathcal{A}(T') \in S].$$

There are two major flavors of differential privacy, depending on the condition under which two datasets are considered to be neighbors. In [19], these were referred to as unbounded and bounded differential privacy. In *Unbounded Differential Privacy (UDP)*, T and T' are neighbors if T can be obtained from T' by adding or removing an entity. In *Bounded Differential Privacy (BDP)*, T and T' are neighbors if T can be obtained from T' by replacing one entity in T' with another entity.

In UDP, closeness in output distributions is required only between two datasets that contain the same number of entities. Therefore, one could output the accurate total number of entities in a dataset without affecting BDP at all. Thus, there exist algorithms that satisfy ϵ-BDP for $\epsilon = 0$ and yet do not satisfy ϵ'-UDP for any value of ϵ'. On the other hand, any algorithm that satisfies ϵ-UDP must also satisfy 2ϵ-BDP, since replacing one entity can be achieved by removing an entity and then adding another.

In the rest of this section, we show that these two differential privacy notions are instantiations of the membership privacy framework, by choosing particular families of distributions. This relationship enables a clear understanding of the power and limitations of differential privacy.

4.1 Unbounded Differential Privacy

We first establish the relation between UDP and membership privacy. We decompose the UDP condition into the conjunction of the following two conditions.

DEFINITION 4.2 (POSITIVE AND NEGATIVE UDP). *A mechanism $\mathcal{A}$ gives ϵ-positive unbounded differential privacy if and only if for any dataset T, any entity t, and any $S \subseteq Range(\mathcal{A})$,*

$$\Pr[\mathcal{A}(T \cup \{t\}) \in S] \le e^{\epsilon} \cdot \Pr[\mathcal{A}(T) \in S]. \tag{8}$$

A mechanism $\mathcal{A}$ gives ϵ-negative unbounded differential privacy if and only if for any dataset T, any entity t, and any $S \subseteq Range(\mathcal{A})$,

$$\Pr[\mathcal{A}(T) \in S] \le e^{\epsilon} \cdot \Pr[\mathcal{A}(T \cup \{t\}) \in S]. \tag{9}$$

As it turns out, UDP corresponds to membership privacy under the family of *mutually independent* distributions.

DISTRIBUTION FAMILY 4.3. ***$\mathbb{D}_I$: Mutually Independent (MI) Distributions.** We say that a distribution is mutually independent if and only if it can be characterized by assigning a probability p_t to each tuple t such that the probability of any dataset T is given by*

$$\Pr[T] = \prod_{t \in T} p_t \prod_{t \notin T} (1 - p_t)$$

$\mathbb{D}_I$ includes all such mutually independent distributions over $\mathcal{U}$.

We note that $\mathbb{D}_I$ includes distributions in which the probabilities for different entities differ. In particular, $\mathbb{D}_I$ includes distributions where some entities have probability 1 and some other entities have probability 0. We also observe that in a mutually independent distribution, we have

$$\Pr[T \cup \{t\}] = \Pr[T] q_t, \text{ where } q_t = \frac{p_t}{1 - p_t} \tag{10}$$

We note that the definition for positive UDP essentially means that $\frac{\Pr[S|t]}{\Pr[S|\neg t]} \le e^{\epsilon}$ for all prior distributions such that each distribution has just two possible datasets: $D \cup \{t\}$ and D. We use $\mathbb{D}_I^2$ to denote the family that includes all such distributions.

DISTRIBUTION FAMILY 4.4. ***$\mathbb{D}_I^2$: 1-out-2 MI Distributions.** $\mathbb{D}_I^2$ includes every MI distribution for which there are only two* *datasets with nonzero probability. In other words, there exists t such that $0 < \Pr[t] < 1$, and furthermore, for any $t' \neq t$, either $\Pr[t'] = 1$ or $\Pr[t'] = 0$. In such a distribution, only two datasets are possible: $T \cup \{t\}$ and T, where $T = \{t \in \mathcal{U} \mid \Pr[t] = 1\}$.*

Clearly, $\mathbb{D}_I^2$ is a subset of $\mathbb{D}_I$. Also, $\mathbb{D}_I^2$ is both upward and downward scalable. Combining the observation that positive UDP is equivalent to $\frac{\Pr[S|t]}{\Pr[S|\neg t]} \leq e^\epsilon$ for $\mathbb{D}_I^2$ with Theorem 3.6, it follows that ϵ-positive UDP is equivalent to $(\mathbb{D}_I^2, e^\epsilon)$-PMP.

The elegance and power of differential privacy lies in the fact that while positive UDP directly achieves PMP only for $\mathbb{D}_I^2$, it turns that this is sufficient for achieving PMP for the larger family $\mathbb{D}_I$, as shown by the following theorem.

THEOREM 4.5. *A mechanism $\mathcal{A}$ satisfies ϵ-positive UDP if and only if it provides $(\mathbb{D}_I, e^\epsilon)$-PMP.*

PROOF. The "if" direction is trivial since $\mathbb{D}_I$ is a superset of $\mathbb{D}_I^2$, and ϵ-positive UDP is equivalent to $(\mathbb{D}_I^2, e^\epsilon)$-PMP.

For the "only if" direction. If $\mathcal{A}$ satisfies ϵ-positive UDP, then given any distribution $\mathcal{D} \in \mathbb{D}_I$, for any entity t, we want to show that $\frac{\Pr[S|t]}{\Pr[S|\neg t]} \leq e^\epsilon$. Satisfying positive UDP gives us $\frac{\Pr[S|T \cup \{t\}]}{\Pr[S|T]} \leq e^\epsilon$ for any individual dataset T. Let T_i range over $2^{\mathcal{U}-\{t\}}$, i.e., T_i ranges over all datasets without t, then $T_i \cup \{t\}$ ranges over all datasets that contain the tuple t. We have

$$\begin{aligned}
\frac{\Pr[S|t]}{\Pr[S|\neg t]} &= \frac{\left(\sum_{T_i} \Pr[T_i \cup \{t\}] \Pr[S|T_i \cup \{t\}]\right) / \sum_{T_i} \Pr[T_i \cup \{t\}]}{\left(\sum_{T_i} \Pr[T_i] \Pr[S|T_i]\right) / \sum_{T_i} \Pr[T_i]} \\
&= \frac{\left(\sum_{T_i} \Pr[T_i] \cdot q_t \Pr[S|T_i \cup \{t\}]\right) / \sum_{T_i} \Pr[T_i] \cdot q_t}{\left(\sum_{T_i} \Pr[T_i] \Pr[S|T_i]\right) / \sum_{T_i} \Pr[T_i]} \\
&= \frac{\sum_{T_i} \Pr[T_i] \Pr[S|T_i \cup \{t\}]}{\sum_{T_i} \Pr[T_i] \Pr[S|T_i]} \\
&\leq \frac{\sum_{T_i} \Pr[T_i] \Pr[S|T_i] e^\epsilon}{\sum_{T_i} \Pr[T_i] \Pr[S|T_i]} = e^\epsilon
\end{aligned}$$

The second equality above uses the fact that $\mathcal{D}$ is mutually independent and therefore $\Pr[T_i \cup \{t\}] = \Pr[T_i] q_t$ (Equation 10). The $\leq$ above uses the positive UDP condition. □

A natural question is whether ϵ-positive UDP would satisfy PMP for distributions that are not mutually independent. The following observations hints that in a sense the family of all mutually-independent distributions is the limit for which UDP guarantees PMP. This corroborates the analysis that differential privacy's protection is limited to the case where all entities are mutually independent [19].

Consider the following distribution $\mathcal{D}_{NI}^k$, in which all entities except for $t_1, t_2, \cdots, t_k$ are independent from any other sets of entities but $t_1, t_2, \cdots, t_k$ are totally correlated, i.e., either all of them or none of them are included. It is easy to see that satisfying ϵ-positive UDP satisfies $(\mathcal{D}_{NI}^k, e^{k\epsilon})$-PMP; however, there exist mechanisms that satisfy ϵ-positive UDP, yet does not satisfy γ-PMP for any $\gamma < e^{k\epsilon}$.

Consider the mechanism that outputs the number of $t_1, t_2, \cdots, t_k$ in the dataset by adding to it random noise drawn from the Laplace distribution $\mathsf{Lap}\left(\frac{1}{\epsilon}\right)$, where $\Pr[\mathsf{Lap}(\beta) = x] = \frac{1}{2\beta} e^{-|x|/\beta}$. This satisfies ϵ-positive UDP. Now consider the event $S = k$, we have $\frac{\Pr[S|t_1]}{\Pr[S|\neg t_1]} = \frac{1}{e^{k\epsilon}}$. Therefore, $\frac{\Pr[S|t_1]}{\Pr[t_1]} = \frac{1}{p + (1-p)\frac{1}{e^{k\epsilon}}}$, which can get arbitrarily close to $e^{k\epsilon}$ by choosing very small p. Thus, for any $\gamma < e^{k\epsilon}$, we can choose p so that $\frac{\Pr[S|t_1]}{\Pr[t_1]} > \gamma$, violating γ-PMP.

Similar to Theorem 4.5, we can show that ϵ-negative UDP is equivalent to $(\mathbb{D}_I, e^\epsilon)$-NMP. We omit the proof here.

4.2 Bounded Differential Privacy

We now consider how BDP relates to membership privacy. We first note that unlike the unbounded version of differential privacy, BDP has a symmetry to it and cannot be decomposed into a positive condition and a negative condition.

Because BDP only requires closeness in output distributions among datasets of the same size, we must limit to distributions where all datasets that have non-zero probabilities have the same number of entities. We introduce the following two families.

DISTRIBUTION FAMILY 4.6. $\mathbb{D}_B$: ***Bounded Mutually Independent (BMI) Distributions.*** *We say a distribution is a BMI distribution if it is the conditional distribution of a mutually independent distribution given that all datasets with non-zero probability has the same size. $\mathbb{D}_B$ includes all such BMI distributions.*

DISTRIBUTION FAMILY 4.7. $\mathbb{D}_B^2$: ***1-out-of-2 BMI Distributions.*** *We say a BMI distribution is a 1-out-of-2 BMI distribution if each distribution has exactly two datasets with nonzero probability. That is, all except for two entities have probability of either 1 or 0, and it is required that the size of the sampled dataset is $1 + |\{t| \Pr[t] = 1\}|$.*

By Definition, ϵ-BDP is equivalent to satisfying $\frac{\Pr[S|t]}{\Pr[S|\neg t]} \leq e^\epsilon$ for distributions in $\mathbb{D}_B^2$. Thus, ϵ-BDP is equivalent to $(\mathbb{D}_B^2, e^\epsilon)$-PMP (from Theorem 3.6). The following theorem shows that ϵ-BDP achieves PMP for all distributions in $\mathbb{D}_B$.

THEOREM 4.8. *A mechanism $\mathcal{A}$ satisfies ϵ-BDP if and only if it provides $(\mathbb{D}_B, e^\epsilon)$-PMP.*

PROOF. The "if" direction follows straightforwardly from the fact that ϵ-BDP is equivalent to $\mathbb{D}_B^2$ and that $\mathbb{D}_B^2 \subset \mathbb{D}_B$.

For the "only if" direction, similar to the proof of the unbounded case, we would show that for any t, we have $\frac{\Pr[S|t]}{\Pr[S|\neg t]} \leq e^\epsilon$ assuming that we have $(\mathbb{D}_B, e^\epsilon)$-PMP.

Let T_2 range over all datasets such that $|T_2| = k - 1 \wedge t \notin T_2$, and T_1 ranges over all datasets such that $|T_1| = k \wedge t \notin T_1$. We have

$$\begin{aligned}
\frac{\Pr[S|t]}{\Pr[S|\neg t]} &= \frac{\left(\sum_{T_2} \Pr[T_2 \cup \{t\}] \Pr[S|T_2 \cup \{t\}]\right) / \Pr[t]}{\left(\sum_{T_1} \Pr[T_1] \Pr[S|T_1]\right) / \Pr[\neg t]} \\
&= \frac{\left(\sum_{T_2} \Pr[T_2 \cup \{t\} | t] \Pr[S|T_2 \cup \{t\}]\right)}{\left(\sum_{T_1} \Pr[T_1 | \neg t] \Pr[S|T_1]\right)}
\end{aligned}$$

The main idea of the remaining proof is to construct a joint distribution $P_{k,k-1}$ defined on all pairs of (T_1, T_2) such that $T_2 \subseteq T_1$ (so that $T_2 \cup \{t\}$ is a neighbor of T_1) while the margin distribution of $P_{k,k-1}$ on T_1, T_2 is $\Pr(T_1|\neg t)$ and $\Pr(T_2 \cup \{t\}|t)$. The existence of such a joint distribution when we do not have size constraints on T_1, T_2 is trivial as we can simply take $T_1 = T_2$ and this is also essentially how we prove the unbounded case. The proof for the existence of such a distribution for the bounded privacy case is technically more challenging as we need to show the existence of a such distribution when T_1 is sampled from all sets of size $k - 1$ that does not contain t and T_2 is sampled from all sets of size k that does not contains t. Formally, we prove the following lemma:

LEMMA 4.9. *For any k-bouneded mutually independent distribution P_k defined on n entities, there exists a distribution $P_{k,k-1}$ defined on pair (T_1, T_2) satisfying that $|T_1| = k, |T_2| = k - 1, T_2 \subset T_1 \subseteq [n], t \notin T_1$. The margin probability of $P_{k,k-1}$ on T_1 is $\Pr(T_1|\neg t)$ and on T_2 is $\Pr(T_2 \cup \{t\}|t)$.*

Assuming the correctness of Lemma 4.9 and by the margin property of $P_{k,k-1}$, we know that

$$\frac{\Pr[S|t]}{\Pr[S|\neg t]} = \frac{\sum_{(T_1,T_2)} \Pr_{P_{k,k-1}}[T_1,T_2] \cdot \Pr[S|T_2 \cup \{t\}]}{\sum_{(T_1,T_2)} \Pr_{P_{k,k-1}}[T_1,T_2] \cdot \Pr[S|T_1]} \quad (11)$$

Notice that $T_2 \cup \{t\}$ and T_1 are adjacent to each other according to the definition of bounded differential privacy, and therefore $\frac{\Pr[S|T_2 \cup \{t\}]}{\Pr[S|T_1]} \leq e^{\epsilon}$. This directly implies that (11) $\leq e^{\epsilon}$. □

The complete proof of Lemma 4.9 is quite involved. We first show that the existence of the distribution $P_{k,k-1}$ is equivalent to the existence of a perfect solution in certain network flow problem; then we use a generalization of Hall's marriage theorem (see [14]) to show the existence of such a perfect solution in the network. The full proof appears in Appendix A.3.

5. OTHER INSTANTIATIONS

The membership privacy framework enables one to design and choose privacy notions suitable for particular situations by choosing appropriate families of distributions. We have shown that choosing $\mathbb{D}_U$, the family that includes all possible distributions, results in a privacy notion that is likely too strong. We have also shown that UDP corresponds to choosing $\mathbb{D}_I$, the family that includes all mutually independent distributions, and that BDP corresponds to choosing $\mathbb{D}_I^B$, that family that includes all bounded mutually independent distributions.

In this section, we explore membership privacy under three other families of distributions. The first one is $\mathbb{D}_N$, the family that includes the single uniform distribution over all possible subsets of $\mathcal{U}$. The second one corresponds to differential identifiability [20], and the third one corresponds to differential privacy under sampling [22].

5.1 PMP Under the Uniform Distribution

The flexibility offered by PMP enables data publishers to have more choices in trading off privacy versus utility. Here we show that it is possible to satisfy PMP under a more restrictive family of distributions while providing a much better utility than it is known to be possible under differential privacy. We consider PMP under the following family.

DISTRIBUTION FAMILY 5.1. ***$\mathbb{D}_N$: Non-informative Distribution** $\mathbb{D}_N$ includes a single distribution $\mathcal{D}_N$, the uniform distribution such that each subset of $\mathcal{U}$ has the same probability $\frac{1}{2^{|\mathcal{U}|}}$.*

Note that $\mathbb{D}_N$, which contains a single distribution, should not be confused with $\mathbb{D}_U$, which contains an infinite number of distributions. Under $\mathcal{D}_N$, we have $\Pr[t] = \frac{1}{2}$ for every entity t. PMP under $\mathbb{D}_N$ means that one assumes an uninformed adversary that has no prior knowledge about the possible dataset, which may be reasonable for some data publishing scenarios. We note that mechanisms that satisfy syntactic privacy notions such as k-anonymity generally does not satisfy $(\mathbb{D}_N, \gamma)$-PMP, because from anonymized dataset one can tell membership with high confidence even assuming the uninformed prior. We now show that it is possible to satisfy $\mathbb{D}_N$ while providing significantly more utility than satisfying differential privacy. As an example, we consider the universe $\mathcal{U}$ to be one where each entity has a single numerical attribute, e.g., income. And our goal is to publish the maximum income value in $T \subset \mathcal{U}$. Naturally the global range of the income attribute is very large, while the max value of most datasets is likely to be much smaller than the global max.

It is very difficult to compute max while satisfying differential privacy. The global sensitivity of the max function is very high. By changing one entity, the max may change all the way from the lowest possible value to the highest possible value. Therefore, whether one applies the Laplacian mechanism or the exponential mechanism, the amount of noise one has to add would dominate the result.

When one aims at satisfying $(\mathbb{D}_N, \gamma)$-PMP, however, it is possible to output the max of a set with very high accuracy. For simplicity of explnanation, let us sort all entities in $\mathcal{U}$ based on their income value, and use the index to refer to these entities. That is, 1 denote the entity with smallest income value, and $n = |\mathcal{U}|$ denotes the entity with the largest income value, and we use c_i to denote the income of element i.

DEFINITION 5.2 (k-MAX MECHANISM). *The k-Max mechanism, parameterized by an integer $k \geq 2$, works as follows. Given a dataset T, let j be the largest element in T, the mechanism gives a value picked at uniform random from the following set:*

$$C = \begin{cases} \{c_j, c_{j+1}, \cdots, c_{j+k-1}\} & \text{when } j+k-1 \leq n, \\ \{c_{n-k+1}, c_{n-k+2}, \cdots, c_n\} & \text{otherwise} \end{cases}$$

We note that this mechanism is highly accurate when k is not large. It outputs the value of an element whose rank in the *universe* is within distance k of the true max of the dataset. For example, suppose that the elements in the universe have values that are the first 10000 prime numbers (up to 104729), on a dataset that has four entities with values $\{2, 5, 113, 9851\}$, the mechanism 3-Max outputs one of 9851, 9857, 9859 each with probability $\frac{1}{3}$, which is remarkably close to the true max. The intuition that this satisfies PMP is that no matter which of the three value is outputted, the posterior probability that the entity with value 9851 (or any other entity) is in the input is not significantly higher than the prior probability of $\frac{1}{2}$; it is at most $\frac{7}{12}$ according to the following proposition.

PROPOSITION 5.3. *The k-Max mechanism satisfies $(\mathbb{D}_N, \gamma)$-PMP for $\gamma = \frac{2^k-1}{2^k-2}$.*

PROOF. Because for any i, we have $\Pr[i] = \frac{1}{2}$, we need to show that for each i, j, $\Pr[i|c_j] \leq \min(\frac{\gamma}{2}, \frac{\gamma-0.5}{\gamma})$.

Consider $\Pr[i|c_j]$, when c_j is the output, we know that the true max element in the input must be with distance k of j. Let M_j denote the set of entities that are possible true max when c_j is output, and $s_j = |M_j|$ denote the number of elements in M_j, and m_j denote the max in M_j. When $j \leq n-k$, then $M_j = \{j-k+1, \cdots, j\}$ includes exactly k elements. When $j > n-k$, then all elements in $\{j-k+1, \cdots, j\}$ are still in M_j, but M_j may include elements with rank $> j$. (For example, when $k=2$ and c_{n-1} is output, both n and $n-2$ may be the true max.) In any case, we always have $s_j \geq k$.

When c_j is output, we know that at least one element in M_j must appear, and no element with index $> m_j$ can appear. The event under which that c_j is output can be divided into $2^{s_j}-1$ equal-probability events, each corresponding to the selection of one subset of M_j to be included in T ($\emptyset$ is not allowed). For each event, the probability that c_j is output is exactly $\frac{1}{k}$. Each i in M_j is included in 2^{s_j-1} of the events, and not included in $2^{s_j-1}-1$ of them.

We have $\Pr[i|c_j] = 0$ when $i > m_j$, and $\Pr[i|c_j] = \frac{1}{2}$ when $i \leq j-k$. When $j-k < i \leq m_j$, we have $\Pr[i|c_j] = \frac{2^{s_j-1}}{2^{s_j}-1}$ because when c_j is output, there are $2^{s_j}-1$ equally likely possibilities, and i appears in 2^{s_j-1} of these possibilities.

Therefore, we want $\frac{2^{(s_j-1)}}{2^{s_j}-1} \leq \min(\frac{\gamma}{2}, \frac{\gamma-0.5}{\gamma})$. Because $s_j \geq k$, the above holds when $\frac{2^{(k-1)}}{2^k-1} \leq \min(\frac{\gamma}{2}, \frac{\gamma-0.5}{\gamma})$, solving which gets $\gamma \geq \max\left(\frac{2^k}{2^k-1}, \frac{2^k-1}{2^k-2}\right) = \frac{2^k-1}{2^k-2}$. □

This means that one obtains $(\mathbb{D}_N, \frac{3}{2})$-PMP for $k=2$, $(\mathbb{D}_N, \frac{7}{6})$-PMP for $k=3$, and $(\mathbb{D}_N, \frac{15}{14})$-PMP for $k=4$.

This example demonstrates that when one is willing to accept a privacy notion weaker than differential privacy, then one can obtain dramatic improvement in utility for some queries. k-Max is just a preliminary example. Many other data analysis tasks may become significantly more accurate under this weaker privacy notion. We also note that the accuracy of k-Max is also due in part to satisfying only PMP and not NMP. k-Max does not satisfy $(\mathbb{D}_N, \gamma)$-NMP for any γ, as observing output c_j can reduce the posterior probability of some large entities to 0.

We emphasize that we are not arguing that $(\mathbb{D}_N, \gamma)$-PMP is a suitable privacy notion for all situations. Indeed even differential privacy is not; as it is unsuitable when one cannot make the independence assumption. We believe that a range of privacy notions is needed in practice. We also stress than $(\mathbb{D}_N, \gamma)$-PMP is by no means the only meaningful relaxation of differential privacy in the membership privacy framework; and it is interesting future work to explore other family of distributions which would induce useful privacy notions.

5.2 Differential Identifiability

In [20], Lee and Clifton argued that there are no clear guidelines on how to set ϵ for ϵ-differential privacy, because ϵ limits how much one individual can affect the resulting output, not how much information is revealed about an individual; and this does not match legal definitions of privacy, which require protection of *individually identifiable data* [1, 2]. From analysis of US HIPAA safe harbor rule [2], it is concluded that the goal of the privacy policy is met if one limits the estimate of the probability that an individual is in the data to approximately 1.5%. Lee and Clifton thus propose the following notion.

DEFINITION 5.4. *(ρ-differential identifiability (DI) [20]) A mechanism $\mathcal{A}$ is said to satisfy ρ-DI if for any dataset T, any entity $t \in T$, let $T' = T \setminus \{t\}$, for any output event S*

$$\Pr[t \in \mathbf{T} | \mathcal{A}(\mathbf{T}) \in S, T'] \leq \rho,$$

where $\mathbf{T}$ is a random variable drawn from the following distribution: each dataset $T' \cup \{t'\}$, where $t' \in \mathcal{U} \setminus T'$ is equally likely.

The notion of ρ-DI aims at limiting the posterior probability that the tuple t is in the input dataset after observing the output event S. To be able to compute the posterior probability, one has to assume some prior beliefs the adversary may have. The notion of ρ-DI specifies the allowed distributions to be from the following families.

DISTRIBUTION FAMILY 5.5. *$\mathbb{D}_C^m$: **1-out-of-m equal-probability choice BMI Distributions.** $\mathbb{D}_C^m$, where $m \geq 2$ is a positive integer, includes every distributions that is fully specified by fixing a set $T \subset \mathcal{U}$ such that $|\mathcal{U} \setminus T| = m$. To sample a dataset from the distribution, one includes T plus one additional entity sampled uniformly at random from $\mathcal{U} \setminus T$. In other words, in each distribution only one entity is uncertain, and this entity is assumed to be drawn uniform from m possible entities.*

$\mathbb{D}_C^m$ is a sub-family of $\mathbb{D}_B$, the family of BMI distributions, as it allows only BMI distributions that satisfy three further conditions. First, the sampled dataset must have size $1 + |\{t \mid p_t = 1\}|$. Second, there must exist m entities with probability between 0 and 1. Third, all these m entities must have the same probability.

To determine whether a non-trivial mechanism $\mathcal{A}$ satisfies ρ-DI or not, one has to also specify the value m; thus it is more appropriate to say (ρ, m)-DI, which requires that for any distribution in $\mathbb{D}_C^m$ and any output event S, we have $\Pr[t|S] \leq \rho$. Note that (ρ, m)-DI makes sense only when $\rho > \frac{1}{m}$.

THEOREM 5.6. *(ρ, m)-DI is equivalent to $(\mathbb{D}_C^m, \gamma)$-PMP for $\gamma = \rho m$ for $\gamma = \max\left(\rho m, \frac{m-1}{m(1-\rho)}\right)$.*

PROOF. (ρ, m)-DI means that for any distribution in $\mathbb{D}_C^m$ and any entity with prior probability $\frac{1}{m}$, the posterior is at most ρ, i.e. $\Pr[t|S] \leq \rho$.

$(\mathbb{D}_C^m, \gamma)$-PMP means that for any distribution in $\mathbb{D}_C^m$, $\Pr[t|S] \leq \min\left(\gamma \Pr[t], \frac{\gamma - 1 + \Pr[t]}{\gamma}\right) = \min\left(\frac{\gamma}{m}, 1 - \frac{m-1}{m\gamma}\right)$.

We only need to prove that $\rho = \min\left(\frac{\gamma}{m}, 1 - \frac{m-1}{m\gamma}\right)$. There are two cases.

Case one: we have $\rho m \leq \frac{m-1}{m(1-\rho)}$, and thus $\gamma = \frac{m-1}{m(1-\rho)}$, and $\min\left(\frac{\gamma}{m}, 1 - \frac{m-1}{m\gamma}\right) = \min\left(\frac{m-1}{m^2(1-\rho)}, \rho\right) = \rho$ because $\rho \leq \frac{m-1}{m^2(1-\rho)}$ from the case condition.

Case two: we have $\rho m > \frac{m-1}{m(1-\rho)}$, and thus $\gamma = \rho m$, and $\min\left(\frac{\gamma}{m}, 1 - \frac{m-1}{m\gamma}\right) = \min\left(\rho, 1 - \frac{(m-1)/m}{\rho m}\right) = \rho$ because from the case condition, we have $1 - \frac{(m-1)/m}{\rho m} > 1 - \frac{(m-1)/m}{\frac{m-1}{m(1-\rho)}} = \rho$. □

The following theorem show an interesting relationship between DI and BDP.

THEOREM 5.7. *When $\rho > \frac{1}{2}$, $(\rho, 2)$-DI is equivalent to ϵ-BDP for $\epsilon = \ln\left(\frac{\rho}{1-\rho}\right)$. However, when $m > 2$ and $\rho > \frac{1}{m-1}$, it is possible to satisfy (ρ, m)-DI while violating ϵ-BDP for any ϵ.*

PROOF. When $m = 2$, $(\rho, 2)$-DI requires that on all dataset pairs T_1 and T_2 that have the same number of entities and differ in only one entity, when T_1 and T_2 are equally likely, we have $\Pr[T_1|S] \leq \rho$, i.e., $\Pr[T_1|S] = \frac{\Pr[S|T_1]}{\Pr[S|T_1] + \Pr[S|T_2]} \leq \rho$; this holds if and only if $\Pr[S|T_1] \leq \frac{\rho}{1-\rho} \Pr[S|T_2]$; hence the equivalence with $\ln\left(\frac{\rho}{1-\rho}\right)$-BDP.

When $m > 2$ and $\rho > \frac{1}{m-1}$, consider the following case, the universe consists of m entities $t_1 \cdots t_m$, the mechanism $\mathcal{A}$, on input dataset T outputs a value chosen at uniform random from $\{1, \cdots, m\}$, except for the case $T = \{t_1\}$, when it outputs a value chosen at uniform random from $\{2, \cdots, m\}$.

This trivially satisfies the DI condition for any input dataset containing more than one entities, since the output is always uniform. When one consider datasets containing exactly one entity, it satisfies the DI condition too. First consider the case 1 is the output. We have $\Pr[t_1|1] = 0 < \rho$, and when $i \neq 1$, we have $\Pr[t_i|1] = \frac{1}{m-1} < \rho$, because each of $\{t_2\}, \cdots, \{t_m\}$ is equally likely. Then consider the case when $j \neq 1$ as the output, we have $\Pr[t_1|j] = \frac{1/(m-1)}{1/(m-1) + (m-1)/m} = \frac{m}{m^2 - m + 1} < \frac{m}{m^2 - m} = \frac{1}{m-1} < \rho$ and when $i \neq 1$, $\Pr[t_i|j] < \frac{1}{m-1} < \rho$.

However, this mechanism violates ϵ-BDP for any ϵ because $\Pr[1|\{t_2\}] = \frac{1}{m} > e^\epsilon \Pr[1|\{t_1\}] = 0$ for any ϵ. □

5.3 Differential Privacy Under Sampling

In [22], Li et al. proposed a relaxation to differential privacy that exploits the adversary's uncertainty about the dataset. While the original definition of differential privacy assumes that the adversary has precise knowledge of all the tuples in the dataset, Li et al. argue that this, in fact, might be too strong for some data publishing scenarios. Instead, it is reasonable to relax the assumption to that the adversary knows all attributes of a tuple t (but not whether t is in the dataset), and in addition statistical information about the rest of the dataset D. The privacy notion should prevent such an adversary from substantially distinguishing between D and $D \cup \{t\}$ based on the output. This intuition is formalized using the following definition.

DEFINITION 5.8 ((β,ϵ)-DPS [22]). *An algorithm $\mathcal{A}$ gives (β,ϵ)-DPS if and only if the algorithm $\mathcal{A}_\beta$ gives ϵ-UDP, where $\mathcal{A}_\beta$ denotes the algorithm to first sample each tuple with probability β, and then apply $\mathcal{A}$ to the sampled dataset.*

Similar to our analysis of differential privacy, we focus on positive DPS. It turns out that (β,ϵ)-DPS is equivalent to PMP for the following family.

DISTRIBUTION FAMILY 5.9. $\mathbb{D}_F^\beta$: ***Fixed-probability Mutually Independent Distributions.*** *This is a sub-family of $\mathbb{D}_I$. It includes all mutually independent distributions such that $\forall_t \Pr[t] \in \{0,\beta\}$. In other words, all entities that may appear have the same probability.*

THEOREM 5.10. *A randomized mechanism satisfies (β,ϵ)-Positive DPS if and only if it satisfies $(\mathbb{D}_F^\beta,\gamma)$-PMP for $\gamma = \max\left(e^\epsilon, \frac{e^\epsilon-1+\beta}{\beta e^\epsilon}\right)$.*

Proof is given in Appendix A.4.

6. RELATED WORK

A number of syntactic privacy definitions have proposed over the years; the most prominent ones include k-anonymity [30, 29], l-diversity [24] and t-closeness [21]. Their weaknesses have been often identified. See, e.g., Dwork [9] for a survey. Instead, Dwork argues that we should consider privacy protection problems in a more rigorous and formal way. This is the motivation of the research of differential privacy. The notion of differential privacy was developed in a series of works [6, 13, 4, 11, 8], and several methods of satisfying have been developed [8, 11, 26, 28].

In [5], Cormode argued that differential privacy does not prevent inferential disclosure. It is shown that, from differentially private output, it is possible to infer potentially sensitive information about an individual with non-trivial accuracy. In Section 2.3, we argued that it may be inappropriate to use prevention of attribute disclosure as the privacy objective. In this paper, we formalize membership disclosure, and show that it closely matches the social and legal definitions of privacy. Lee and Clifton [20] proposed the notion of ρ-differential identifiability, which captures membership disclosure under specific adversarial background knowledge. This notion is a special case of membership privacy, and we analyze it in Section 5.2. Li et al. [22] relax an adversary's background knowledge by sampling the dataset prior to applying the privacy mechanism. We analyze differential privacy under sampling and its relation to our privacy notion in Section 5.3.

In [19], Kifer and Machanavajjhala argued that it is not possible to provide privacy and utility without making assumptions about how the data are generated. Our modeling of the attacker's background knowledge in terms of a family of distributions complies with their finding. Kifer et al. also questioned whether the differential privacy guarantees when data points are correlated. Our analysis suggests that differential privacy only guarantees membership protection under distributions where data points are mutually independent.

Kifer and Lin [18] proposed the privacy axioms of choice and the axiom of transformation, which we show that membership privacy satisfy. They also introduce a generalization of differential privacy, called generic differential privacy, which follows the syntactic structure of differential privacy, but allows more flexible definition of neighboring datasets and the condition between that $\Pr[S|D]$ and $\Pr[S|D']$ should satisfy. A similar approach is taken by Machanavajjhala et al. [23], which introduced a framework called ϵ-privacy, which limits the impact the inclusion of one entity can have on the adversary's belief about the individual's attribute value. Gehrke et al. [16] introduced zero-knowledge based definition of privacy, which defines a mechanism to be private if its output can be simulated by a simulator with access to some aggregate function of the data, but without direct access to the data. One needs to choose appropriate aggregate function to instantiate the privacy notion. Gehrke et al. [15] then introduced crowd-blending privacy, which combines safe k-anonymization and differential privacy. We also generalize differential privacy; however, our approach differs in that we formalize membership privacy, which is justified from analysis of privacy incidents, and in that our notion is parameterized by families of dataset distributions.

In an attempt to make differential privacy more amenable to more sensitive queries, several relaxations have been developed, including (ϵ,δ)-differential privacy [6, 13, 4, 11]. Machanavajjhala et al. [25] introduced a variant of (ϵ,δ)-differential privacy called (ϵ,δ)-probabilistic differential privacy. Roughly, all these relaxations use δ to bound the probability that ϵ-DP is violated. Our privacy framework does not yet deal with this relaxation of allowing a δ of error probability. It is interesting future work to investigate how they can be accommodated by extending membership privacy to allow such an error probability.

7. CONCLUSIONS

Through analysis of the recent privacy incidents, we have concluded that what society often views as a privacy breach is the ability of an adversary to either re-identify or assert the membership of any individual in a supposedly "anonymized" dataset. Thus we introduce the membership privacy framework. We have demonstrated that differential privacy and several other related privacy notions are instantiations of the framework.

Identifying the family under which a privacy notion guarantees membership privacy provides deeper understanding of the power and limitation of the privacy notion. In particular, they identify the assumptions that are made by the privacy notion. As all practical privacy notion requires some assumptions on the allowed distributions, it makes sense to analyze whether the assumption made in a notion is appropriate for a given setting, and choose a privacy that is neither too strong nor too weak, in order to maximize utility. Our framework enables the development of new privacy notions. We believe that the membership privacy framework opens doors for future research at developing new privacy notions, understanding and comparing privacy notions, and designing mechanisms for satisfying different privacy notions.

Acknowledgement. This paper is based upon work supported by the United States National Science Foundation under Grant No. 1116991, and by the United States AFOSR.

8. REFERENCES

[1] Directive 95/46/ec of the European Parliament and of the council of 24 october 1995 on the protection of individuals with regard to the processing of personal data and on the free movement of such data. *Official Journal L*, 281(23/11):0031–0050, 1995.

[2] Standard for privacy of individually identifiable health information. *Federal Register*, 67(157):53 181–53 273, Aug 2002. http://www.hhs.gov/ocr/privacy/hipaa/administrative/privacyrule/index.html.

[3] M. Barbaro and J. Tom Zeller. A face is exposed for aol searcher no. 4417749. New York Times, Aug 2006.

[4] A. Blum, C. Dwork, F. McSherry, and K. Nissim. Practical privacy: the SuLQ framework. In *PODS*, pages 128–138, 2005.

[5] G. Cormode. Personal privacy vs population privacy: learning to attack anonymization. In *KDD*, pages 1253–1261, 2011.

[6] I. Dinur and K. Nissim. Revealing information while preserving privacy. In *PODS*.

[7] C. Dwork. Differential privacy. In *in ICALP*, pages 1–12. Springer, 2006.

[8] C. Dwork. Differential privacy. In *ICALP*, pages 1–12, 2006.

[9] C. Dwork. An ad omnia approach to defining and achieving private data analysis. In *PinKDD '07*, pages 1–13, Berlin, Heidelberg, 2008. Springer-Verlag.

[10] C. Dwork, F. Mcsherry, K. Nissim, and A. Smith. Calibrating noise to sensitivity in private data analysis. In *In Proceedings of the 3rd Theory of Cryptography Conference*, pages 265–284. Springer, 2006.

[11] C. Dwork, F. McSherry, K. Nissim, and A. Smith. Calibrating noise to sensitivity in private data analysis. In *TCC*, pages 265–284, 2006.

[12] C. Dwork and M. Naor. On the difficulties of disclosure prevention in statistical databases or the case for differential privacy. *Journal of Privacy and Confidentiality*, 2(1):8, 2010.

[13] C. Dwork and K. Nissim. Privacy-preserving datamining on vertically partitioned databases. In *CRYPTO*, pages 528–544. Springer, 2004.

[14] D. Gale. A theorem on flows in networks. *Pacific Journal of Mathematics*, 7(2):1073–1082, 1957.

[15] J. Gehrke, M. Hay, E. Lui, and R. Pass. Crowd-blending privacy. In *CRYPTO*, pages 479–496, 2012.

[16] J. Gehrke, E. Lui, and R. Pass. Towards privacy for social networks: a zero-knowledge based definition of privacy. In *TCC*, pages 432–449, Berlin, Heidelberg, 2011. Springer-Verlag.

[17] N. Homer, S. Szelinger, M. Redman, D. Duggan, W. Tembe, J. Muehling, J. V. Pearson, D. A. Stephan, S. F. Nelson, and D. W. Craig. Resolving individuals contributing trace amounts of DNA to highly complex mixtures using high-density SNP genotyping microarrays. *PLoS Genet*, 4(8):e1000167+, 08 2008.

[18] D. Kifer and B.-R. Lin. Towards an axiomatization of statistical privacy and utility. In *PODS*, PODS '10, pages 147–158, New York, NY, USA, 2010. ACM.

[19] D. Kifer and A. Machanavajjhala. No free lunch in data privacy. In *SIGMOD*, pages 193–204, 2011.

[20] J. Lee and C. Clifton. Differential identifiability. In *KDD*, pages 1041–1049, 2012.

[21] N. Li, T. Li, and S. Venkatasubramanian. t-closeness: Privacy beyond k-anonymity and l-diversity. In *ICDE*, pages 106–115, 2007.

[22] N. Li, W. Qardaji, and D. Su. On sampling, anonymization, and differential privacy or, k-anonymization meets differential privacy. In *ASIACCS*, pages 32–33, 2012.

[23] A. Machanavajjhala, J. Gehrke, and M. Götz. Data publishing against realistic adversaries. *Proc. VLDB Endow.*, 2(1):790–801, Aug. 2009.

[24] A. Machanavajjhala, J. Gehrke, D. Kifer, and M. Venkitasubramaniam. ℓ-diversity: Privacy beyond k-anonymity. In *ICDE*, page 24, 2006.

[25] A. Machanavajjhala, D. Kifer, J. M. Abowd, J. Gehrke, and L. Vilhuber. Privacy: Theory meets practice on the map. In *ICDE*, pages 277–286, 2008.

[26] F. McSherry and K. Talwar. Mechanism design via differential privacy. In *FOCS*, pages 94–103, 2007.

[27] A. Narayanan and V. Shmatikov. Robust de-anonymization of large sparse datasets. In *S&P*, pages 111–125, 2008.

[28] K. Nissim, S. Raskhodnikova, and A. Smith. Smooth sensitivity and sampling in private data analysis. In *STOC*, pages 75–84, 2007.

[29] P. Samarati. Protecting respondents' identities in microdata release. *IEEE Trans. on Knowl. and Data Eng.*, 13:1010–1027, November 2001.

[30] L. Sweeney. k-anonymity: A model for protecting privacy. *Int. J. Uncertain. Fuzziness Knowl.-Based Syst.*, 10(5):557–570, 2002.

APPENDIX

A. PROOFS

A.1 Proof of Theorem 3.11

PROOF. For any $S \subseteq \text{Range}(\mathcal{A})$,

$$\Pr[t|\mathcal{A} \in S] = p\Pr[t \mid \mathcal{A}_1(T) \in S] + (1-p)\Pr[t|\mathcal{A}_2(T) \in S] \le p \cdot \gamma \Pr[t] + (1-p)\gamma \Pr[t] = \gamma \Pr[t]$$

By a similar argument, we know that

$$\Pr[\neg t|\mathcal{A} \in S] \ge \frac{\Pr[\neg t]}{\gamma}$$

and therefore $\mathcal{A}$ also satisfies $(\mathbb{D}, \gamma)$-PMP.

It is easy to see that above proof can be generalized to the case that the mechanism $\mathcal{A}$ is the combination of more than two mechanisms; i.e., we have a set of k mechanisms and $\mathcal{A}$ is set to be $\mathcal{A}_i$ with some probability p_i for any $p_1, p_2, \dots, p_k \ge 0$ such that $\sum_{i=1}^{k} p_i = 1$. In fact, this can be generalized to the case where the number of methods is infinite. □

A.2 Proof of Theorem 3.12

PROOF. Let us first prove for the case that $\mathcal{A}_2$ is a deterministic mechanism. For any $S \subseteq Range(A_2)$, we define $S' = \{s|A_2(s) \in S, s \in Range(\mathcal{A}_1)\}$.

We know then

$$\Pr[t|\mathcal{A}_2(\mathcal{A}_1(T)) \in S|] = \Pr[t|\mathcal{A}_1(T)) \in S'] \le \gamma \Pr[t]$$

and

$$\Pr[\neg t|\mathcal{A}_2(\mathcal{A}_1(T)) \in S|] = \Pr[\neg t|\mathcal{A}_1(T)) \in S'] \ge \frac{\Pr[\neg t]}{\gamma}$$

As for a randomized mechanism $\mathcal{A}_2$, it can be viewed as combinations of a set of deterministic mechanisms. Suppose it is a combination of $\mathcal{A}_2^1, \mathcal{A}_2^2 \dots, \mathcal{A}_2^k$ with probability p_i to choose $\mathcal{A}_2^i$. We know then $\mathcal{A}_2(\mathcal{A}_1(\cdot))$ is set to be $\mathcal{A}_2^i(\mathcal{A}_1(\cdot))$ with probability

p_i. Clearly, each $\mathcal{A}_2^i(A_1(\cdot))$ satisfies $(\mathbb{D},\gamma)$-PMP as $\mathcal{A}_2^i$ is a deterministic mechanism. Also by the proof of Theorem 3.11, we know that $\mathcal{A}_2^i(A_1(\cdot))$ also satisfies $(\mathbb{D},\gamma)$-PMP. □

A.3 Proof of Lemma 4.9

PROOF OF LEMMA 4.9. Suppose we have a mutually independent distribution with probability $p_1, p_2, \dots, p_n$ on each entity $t \in [n]$. Let P_k be its k-bounded distribution. For any particular T of size k, it is easy to see that

$$\Pr_{P_k}[T] \propto \prod_{t\in T} p_t \prod_{t\notin T}(1-p_t).$$

If we divide $\prod_{t\in T} p_t \prod_{t\notin T}(1-p_t)$ by $\prod_{t\in[n]}(1-p_t)$ (which is a constant independent of T), we get that $\Pr_{P_k}[T] \propto \prod_{t\in T}\frac{p_t}{1-p_t}$. Let us denote $\prod_{t\in T}\frac{p_t}{1-p_t}$ as $p(T)$. We know then

$$\Pr_{P_k}[T] = \frac{p(T)}{\sum_{T\subseteq[n],|T|=k} p(T)}.$$

In addition, under distribution P_k, for any $t \in [n]$ and T_1 that contains t,

$$\Pr[T_1|t] = \frac{p(T_1)}{\sum_{t\in T,|T|=k} p(T)} = \frac{p(T_1\backslash\{t\})}{\sum_{t\notin T,|T|=k-1} p(T)} \quad (12)$$

and for any $t \notin T_2$,

$$\Pr[T_2|\neg t] = \frac{p(T_2)}{\sum_{t\notin T,|T|=k} p(T)}. \quad (13)$$

The existence of $P_{k,k-1}$ is equivalent to whether there exists a good solution for the following network flow problem on a bipartite graph $G(U,V,E)$. Here each vertex in U is corresponding to some set T_2 such that $|T_2| = k$ and $t \notin T_2$ and each vertex in V is corresponding to some set $|T_1| = k-1$ and $t \notin T_1$. There is an edge between (T_1,T_2) if $T_2 \subset T_1$. There is $\Pr[T_2|\neg t]$ amount of goods on each node T_2 and the capacity for each node T_1 in V is $\Pr[T_1 \cup \{t\}|t]$. We can only ship goods along the edges and the question is whether there exists a "perfect flow" so that we can ship all the goods from the U side to the V side without violating the capacity constraints on the V side. This problem is equivalent to the existence of $P_{k,k-1}$ as essentially $\Pr(T_1,T_2)$ is corresponding to the amount of goods we want to ship from T_2 to T_1.

A necessary condition for the existence of the perfect flow is that: for any $W \subseteq U$ and let the neighbor of W in G to be $N(W)$, we have that

$$\sum_{T_2\in W} \Pr[T_2|\neg t] \ge \sum_{T_1\in N(W)} \Pr[T_1\cup\{t\}|t]; \quad (14)$$

By [14] (which is a generalization of Hall's marriage theorem), (14) is also a sufficient condition for the existence of the perfect flow. To prove (14), if we denote $q_i = \frac{p_i}{1-p_i}$ and use (12),(13), it is equivalent to show that

$$\frac{\sum_{T_2\in W}\prod_{i\in T_2} q_i}{\sum_{|T|=k,t\notin T}\prod_{i\in T} q_i} \le \frac{\sum_{T_1\in N(W)}\prod_{i\in T_1} q_i}{\sum_{|T|=k-1,t\notin T}\prod_{i\in T} q_i}$$

or equivalently

$$\left(\sum_{T_2\in W}\prod_{i\in T_2} q_i\right)\cdot\left(\sum_{|T|=k-1,t\notin T}\prod_{i\in T} q_i\right) \le \left(\sum_{T_1\in N(W)}\prod_{i\in T_1} q_i\right)\cdot\left(\sum_{|T|=k,t\notin T}\prod_{i\in T} q_i\right)$$

If we expand the left hand side and also the right hand side of the above expression, we would get the sum of many terms of the form $q(S) = \prod_S q_i$ for S being a multiset such that $t \notin S$ and $|S| = 2k-1$. We know that the number of times $q(S)$ appear on the left hand side is equal to the number of different $T_2 \in W$ so that $T_2 \subseteq S$ and $S\backslash T_2$ has distinct elements. Let us call such T_2 "good" for S. The number of times $q(S)$ appear in the right is equal to the number of different T_1 in $N(W)$ so that $S\backslash T_1$ has distinct elements. Let us also call such T_1 "good" for S. Suppose U_2 contains all the T_2 good for S in W and U_1 contains all the T_1 good for S in $N(W)$. It remains to prove the following claim.

LEMMA A.1. *For any W and S (which defines U_1, U_2), we have that $|U_1| \ge |U_2|$.*

We would prove this by induction on k (or equivalently the size of $|S| = 2k-1$). It is easy to check when k=1, above claim holds. Suppose that $|U_2| \le |U_1|$ holds for any $k < k_0$. When $k = k_0$, first let us consider the case that the elements in S are all distinct. We construct a graph $G(U_1,U_2,E)$ where the edge is added between any $T_1 \in U_1$ and $T_2 \in U_2$ such that $T_1 \subset T_2$.

For any T_2, we know that $T_2\backslash\{e\}$ for any $e \in T_2$ must be in U_1. Therefore, any T_2 in U_2 has exactly k neighbours. On the other hand, for any $T_1 \in U_1$, any its neighbor in U_2 must be of the form $T_1 \cup \{e\}$ for some e in $S\backslash T_1$ and there are at most $|S| - |T_1| = k$ of such e. If we count the number of edges from U_2 side, there are $k \cdot U_2$ such edges. And if we count the number of edges from U_1 side, there are at most $k \cdot |U_1|$ edges. Therefore, $|U_1| \ge |U_2|$.

When some element e in S are not distinct, it must be the case that it can appear in both T_1 and $S\backslash T_1$ (and also T_2 and $S\backslash T_2$). This also means that e appear exactly twice in S. Then essentially we reduce it to the case when $W' = \{T\backslash\{e\}|e \in T \in W\}$and $S' = S\backslash\{e\}$ and $k' = k_0 - 1$ and therefore holds by induction. □

A.4 Proof of Theorem 5.10

PROOF. Let $\Lambda_\beta(T)$ denote the process of sampling tuples from T with probability β. Then, by definition, $\mathcal{A}$ satisfies (β,ϵ)-Positive DPS means for each T, t, and S, we have $\frac{\Pr[A(\Lambda_\beta(T\cup\{t\}))\in S]}{\Pr[A(\Lambda_\beta(T))\in S]} \le e^\epsilon$, which is equivalent to

$$\begin{aligned}\frac{\Pr[A(\Lambda_\beta(T\cup\{t\}))\in S]}{\Pr[A(\Lambda_\beta(T))\in S]} &= \frac{(1-\beta)\Pr[A(\Lambda_\beta(T))\in S]+\beta\Pr[A(\Lambda_\beta(T)\cup\{t\})\in S]}{\Pr[A(\Lambda_\beta(T))\in S]}\\ &= 1-\beta+\beta\frac{\Pr[A(\Lambda_\beta(T)\cup\{t\})\in S]}{\Pr[A(\Lambda_\beta(T))\in S]} \le e^\epsilon\end{aligned}$$

Hence, (β,ϵ)-Positive DPS is equivalent to $\forall T\forall t\forall S$

$$\frac{\Pr_{\mathcal{D}}[S|t]}{\Pr_{\mathcal{D}}[S|\neg t]} = \frac{\Pr[A(\Lambda_\beta(T)\cup\{t\})\in S]}{\Pr[A(\Lambda_\beta(T))\in S]} \le \frac{e^\epsilon-1+\beta}{\beta}$$

where $\mathcal{D}$ such that all entities in $T\cup\{t\}$ have probability β, and all other entities have probability 0; clearly $\mathcal{D} \in \mathbb{D}_F^\beta$. In fact, there is a one-to-one correspondence between a pair of T and t in DPS definition, and such a distribution in $\mathbb{D}_F^\beta$ and a tuple t such that $\Pr[t] = \beta$.

By definition, that $\mathcal{A}$ satisfies $(\mathbb{D}_F^\beta,\gamma)$-PMP means that for each $\mathcal{D} \in \mathbb{D}_F^\beta$, and S, we have $\Pr[t|S] \le \min(\gamma\beta, 1-\frac{1-\beta}{\gamma})$. As $\Pr[t|S] = \frac{\Pr[S|t]\beta}{\Pr[S|t]\beta+\Pr[S|\neg t](1-\beta)} = \frac{1}{1+\frac{1-\beta}{\beta}\frac{\Pr[S|\neg t]}{\Pr[S|t]}}$.

We only need to show that by selecting $\gamma = \max\left(e^\epsilon, \frac{e^\epsilon-1+\beta}{\beta e^\epsilon}\right)$, the two conditions $\frac{\Pr_{\mathcal{D}}[S|t]}{\Pr_{\mathcal{D}}[S|\neg t]} \le \frac{e^\epsilon-1+\beta}{\beta}$ and $\frac{1}{1+\frac{1-\beta}{\beta}\frac{\Pr[S|\neg t]}{\Pr[S|t]}} \le \min(\gamma\beta, 1-\frac{1-\beta}{\gamma})$ become equivalent. Note that $\frac{\Pr_{\mathcal{D}}[S|t]}{\Pr_{\mathcal{D}}[S|\neg t]} \le \frac{e^\epsilon-1+\beta}{\beta}$ if and only if $\frac{1}{1+\frac{1-\beta}{\beta}\frac{\Pr[S|\neg t]}{\Pr[S|t]}} \le \frac{e^\epsilon-1+\beta}{e^\epsilon}$.

Case one, when $e^\epsilon \ge \frac{e^\epsilon-1+\beta}{\beta e^\epsilon}$, we have $\beta e^\epsilon e^\epsilon \ge e^\epsilon - 1 + \beta$, $\gamma = e^\epsilon$ and $\min(\gamma\beta, 1-\frac{1-\beta}{\gamma}) = \min(\beta e^\epsilon, \frac{e^\epsilon-1+\beta}{e^\epsilon}) = \frac{e^\epsilon-1+\beta}{e^\epsilon}$. Case two, when $e^\epsilon < \frac{e^\epsilon-1+\beta}{\beta e^\epsilon}$, is similar. □

Geo-Indistinguishability: Differential Privacy for Location-Based Systems

Miguel E. Andrés
École Polytechnique
mandres@lix.polytechnique.fr

Nicolás E. Bordenabe
INRIA and École Polytechnique
nbordenabe@lix.polytechnique.fr

Konstantinos Chatzikokolakis
CNRS and École Polytechnique
kostas@lix.polytechnique.fr

Catuscia Palamidessi
INRIA and École Polytechnique
catuscia@lix.polytechnique.fr

ABSTRACT

The growing popularity of location-based systems, allowing unknown/untrusted servers to easily collect huge amounts of information regarding users' location, has recently started raising serious privacy concerns. In this paper we introduce geo-indistinguishability, a formal notion of privacy for location-based systems that protects the user's exact location, while allowing approximate information – typically needed to obtain a certain desired service – to be released.

This privacy definition formalizes the intuitive notion of protecting the user's location within a radius r with a level of privacy that depends on r, and corresponds to a generalized version of the well-known concept of *differential privacy*. Furthermore, we present a mechanism for achieving geo-indistinguishability by adding controlled random noise to the user's location.

We describe how to use our mechanism to enhance LBS applications with geo-indistinguishability guarantees without compromising the quality of the application results. Finally, we compare state-of-the-art mechanisms from the literature with ours. It turns out that, among all mechanisms independent of the prior, our mechanism offers the best privacy guarantees.

Categories and Subject Descriptors

C.2.0 [**Computer–Communication Networks**]: General—*Security and protection*; K.4.1 [**Computers and Society**]: Public Policy Issues—*Privacy*

Keywords

Location-based services; Location privacy; Location obfuscation; Differential privacy; Planar Laplace distribution

1. INTRODUCTION

In recent years, the increasing availability of location information about individuals has led to a growing use of systems that record and process location data, generally referred to as "location-based systems". Such systems include (a) Location Based Services (LBSs), in which a user obtains, typically in real-time, a service related to his current location, and (b) location-data mining algorithms, used to determine points of interest and traffic patterns.

The use of LBSs, in particular, has been significantly increased by the growing popularity of mobile devices equipped with GPS chips, in combination with the increasing availability of wireless data connections. A resent study in the US shows that in 2012, 46% of the adult population of the country owns a smartphone and, furthermore, that 74% of those owners use LBSs [1]. Examples of LBSs include mapping applications (e.g., Google Maps), Points of Interest (POI) retrieval (e.g., AroundMe), coupon/discount providers (e.g., GroupOn), GPS navigation (e.g., TomTom), and location-aware social networks (e.g., Foursquare).

While location-based systems have demonstrated to provide enormous benefits to individuals and society, the growing exposure of users' location information raises important privacy issues. First of all, location information itself may be considered as sensitive. Furthermore, it can be easily linked to a variety of other information that an individual usually wishes to protect: by collecting and processing accurate location data on a regular basis, it is possible to infer an individual's home or work location, sexual preferences, political views, religious inclinations, etc. In its extreme form, monitoring and control of an individual's location has been even described as a form of slavery [12].

Several notions of privacy for location-based systems have been proposed in the literature. In Section 2 we give an overview of such notions, and we discuss their shortcomings in relation to our motivating LBS application. Aiming at addressing these shortcomings, we propose a *formal privacy definition* for LBSs, as well as a randomized technique that allows a user to disclose *enough location information* to obtain the desired service, while satisfying the aforementioned privacy notion. Our proposal is based on a generalization of *differential privacy* [14] developed in [8]. Like differential privacy, our notion and technique abstract from the side information of the adversary, such as any prior probabilistic knowledge about the user's actual location.

As a running example, we consider a user located in Paris who wishes to query an LBS provider for nearby restaurants in a private way, i.e., by disclosing some approximate information z instead of his exact location x. A crucial question is: what kind of privacy guarantee can the user expect in this scenario? To formalize this notion, we consider the level of privacy *within a radius*. We say that the user enjoys *ℓ-privacy within* r if, any two locations at distance at most r produce observations with "similar" distributions, where the "level of similarity" depends on ℓ. The idea is that ℓ rep-

CCS'13, November 4–8, 2013, Berlin, Germany.

ACM 978-1-4503-2477-9/13/11 ...$15.00.
http://dx.doi.org/10.1145/2508859.2516735.

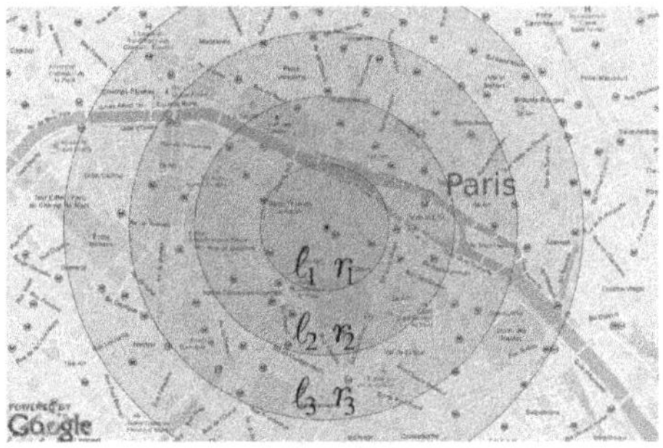

Figure 1: Geo-indistinguishability: privacy varying with r.

resents the user's *level* of privacy for that radius: the smaller ℓ is, the higher is the privacy.

In order to allow the LBS to provide a useful service, we require that the (inverse of the) level of privacy ℓ depend on the radius r. In particular, we require that it is proportional to r, which brings us to our definition of *geo-indistinguishability*:

> A mechanism satisfies ϵ-geo-indistinguishability iff for any radius $r > 0$, the user enjoys ϵr-privacy within r.

This definition implies that the user is protected within any radius r, but with a level $\ell = \epsilon r$ that increases with the distance. Within a short radius, for instance $r = 1$ km, ℓ is small, guaranteeing that the provider cannot infer the user's location within, say, the 7th arrondissement of Paris. Farther away from the user, for instance for $r = 1000$ km, ℓ becomes large, allowing the LBS provider to infer that with high probability the user is located in Paris instead of, say, London. Figure 1 illustrates the idea of privacy levels decreasing with the radius.

We develop a mechanism to achieve geo-indistinguishability by perturbating the user's location x. The inspiration comes from one of the most popular approaches for differential privacy, namely the Laplacian noise. We adopt a specific planar version of the Laplace distribution, allowing to draw points in a *geo-indistinguishable* way; moreover, we are able to do so efficiently, via a transformation to polar coordinates. However, as standard (digital) applications require a finite representation of locations, it is necessary to add a discretization step. Such operation jeopardizes the privacy guarantees, for reasons similar to the rounding effects of finite-precision operations [29]. We show how to preserve geo-indistinguishability, at the price of a degradation of the privacy level, and how to adjust the privacy parameters in order to obtain a desired level of privacy.

We then describe how to use our mechanism to enhance LBS applications with geo-indistinguishability guarantees. Our proposal results in highly configurable LBS applications, both in terms of privacy and accuracy (a notion of utility/quality-of-service for LBS applications providing privacy via location perturbation techniques). Enhanced LBS applications require extra bandwidth consumption in order to provide both privacy and accuracy guarantees, thus we study how the different configurations affect the bandwidth overhead using the Google Places API [2] as reference to measure bandwidth consumption. Our experiments showed that the bandwidth overhead necessary to enhance LBS applications with very high levels of privacy and accuracy is not-prohibitive and, in most cases, negligible for modern applications.

Finally, we compare our mechanism with other ones in the literature, using the privacy metric proposed in [36]. It turns our that our mechanism offers the best privacy guarantees, for the same utility, among all those which do not depend on the prior knowledge of the adversary. The advantages of the independence from the prior are obvious: first, the mechanism is designed once and for all (i.e. it does not need to be recomputed every time the adversary changes, it works also in simultaneous presence of different adversaries, etc.). Second, and even more important, it is applicable also when we do not know the prior.

Contribution.

This paper contributes to the state-of-the-art as follows:

- We show that our generalized notion of differential privacy [8], instantiated with the Euclidean metric, can be naturally applied to location privacy, and we discuss the privacy guarantees that this definition provides. (Location privacy was only briefly mentioned in [8] as a possible application.)
- We also extend it to location traces, using the d_∞ metric, and show how privacy degrades when traces become longer.
- We propose a mechanism to efficiently draw noise from a planar Laplace distribution, which is not trivial. Laplacians on general metric spaces were briefly discussed in [8], but no efficient method to draw from them was given. Furthermore, we cope with the crucial problems of discretization and truncation, which have been shown to pose significant threats to mechanism implementations [29].
- We describe how to use our mechanism to enhance LBS applications with geo-indistinguishability guarantees.
- We compare our mechanism to a state-of-the-art mechanism from the literature [36] as well as a simple cloaking mechanism, obtaining favorable results.

Road Map.

In Section 2 we discuss notions of location privacy from the literature and point out their weaknesses and strengths. In Section 3 we formalize the notion of geo-indistinguishability in three equivalent ways. We then proceed to describe a mechanism that provides geo-indistinguishability in Section 4. In Section 5 we show how to enhance LBS applications with geo-indistinguishability guarantees. In Section 6 we compare the privacy guarantees of our methods with those of two other methods from the literature. Section 7 discusses related work and Section 8 concludes.

The interested reader can find the proofs in the report version of this paper [4], which is available online.

2. EXISTING NOTIONS OF PRIVACY

In this section, we examine various notions of location privacy from the literature, as well as techniques to achieve them. We consider the motivating example from the introduction, of a user in Paris wishing to find nearby restaurants with good reviews. To achieve this goal, he uses a handheld device (e.g.. a smartphone) to query a public LBS provider. However, the user expects his location to be kept private: informally speaking, the information sent to the provider should not allow him to accurately infer the user's location. Our goal is to provide a *formal* notion of privacy that adequately captures the user's expected privacy. From the point of view of the employed mechanism, we require a technique that can be performed in real-time by a handheld device, without the need of any trusted anonymization party.

Expected Distance Error.

Expectation of distance error [35, 36, 23] is a natural way to quantify the privacy offered by a location-obfuscation mechanism. Intuitively, it reflects the degree of accuracy by which an adversary can guess the real location of the user by observing the obfuscated location, and using the side-information available to him.

There are several works relying on this notion. In [23], a perturbation mechanism is used to confuse the attacker by crossing paths of individual users, rendering the task of tracking individual paths challenging. In [36], an optimal location-obfuscation mechanism (i.e., achieving maximum level of privacy for the user) is obtained by solving a linear program in which the contraints are determined by the quality of service and by the user's profile.

It is worth noting that this privacy notion and the obfuscation mechanisms based on it are explicitly defined in terms of the adversary's side information. In contrast, our notion of geo-indistinguishability abstracts from the attacker's prior knowledge, and is therefore suitable for scenarios where the prior is unknown, or the same mechanism must be used for multiple users. A detailed comparison with the mechanism of [36] is provided in Section 6.

k-anonymity.

The notion of k-anonymity is the most widely used definition of privacy for location-based systems in the literature. Many systems in this category [21, 19, 30] aim at protecting the user's *identity*, requiring that the attacker cannot infer which user is executing the query, among a set of k different users. Such systems are outside the scope of our problem, since we are interested in protecting the user's *location*.

On the other hand, k-anonymity has also been used to protect the user's location (sometimes called l-diversity in this context), requiring that it is indistinguishable among a set of k points (often required to share some semantic property). One way to achieve this is through the use of *dummy locations* [25, 33]. This technique involves generating $k - 1$ properly selected dummy points, and performing k queries to the service provider, using the real and dummy locations. Another method for achieving k-anonymity is through *cloaking* [6, 13, 38]. This involves creating a cloaking region that includes k points sharing some property of interest, and then querying the service provider for this cloaking region.

Even when side knowledge does not explicitly appear in the definition of k-anonymity, a system cannot be proven to satisfy this notion unless assumptions are made about the attacker's side information. For example, dummy locations are only useful if they look equally likely to be the real location from the point of view of the attacker. Any side information that allows to rule out any of those points, as having low probability of being the real location, would immediately violate the definition.

Counter-measures are often employed to avoid this issue: for instance, [25] takes into account concepts such as ubiquity, congestion and uniformity for generating dummy points, in an effort to make them look realistic. Similarly, [38] takes into account the user's side information to construct a cloaking region. Such counter-measures have their own drawbacks: first, they complicate the employed techniques, also requiring additional data to be taken into account (for instance, precise information about the environment or the location of nearby users), making their application in real-time by a handheld device challenging. Moreover, the attacker's actual side information might simply be inconsistent with the assumptions being made.

As a result, notions that abstract from the attacker's side information, such as differential privacy, have been growing in popularity in recent years, compared to k-anonymity-based approaches.

Differential Privacy.

Differential Privacy [14] is a notion of privacy from the area of statistical databases. Its goal is to protect an individual's data while publishing aggregate information about the database. Differential privacy requires that modifying a single user's data should have a negligible effect on the query outcome. More precisely, it requires that the probability that a query returns a value v when applied to a database D, compared to the probability to report the same value when applied to an *adjacent* database D' – meaning that D, D' differ in the value of a single individual – should be within a bound of e^ϵ. A typical way to achieve this notion is to add controlled random noise to the query output, for example drawn from a Laplace distribution. An advantage of this notion is that a mechanism can be shown to be differentially private independently from any side information that the attacker might possess.

Differential privacy has also been used in the context of location privacy. In [28], it is shown that a synthetic data generation technique can be used to publish statistical information about commuting patterns in a differentially private way. In [22], a quadtree spatial decomposition technique is used to ensure differential privacy in a database with location pattern mining capabilities.

As shown in the aforementioned works, differential privacy can be successfully applied in cases where *aggregate* information about several users is published. On the other hand, the nature of this notion makes it poorly suitable for applications in which only a single individual is involved, such as our motivating scenario. The secret in this case is the location of a single user. Thus, differential privacy would require that any change in that location should have negligible effect on the published output, making it impossible to communicate any useful information to the service provider.

To overcome this issue, Dewri [11] proposes a mix of differential privacy and k-anonymity, by fixing an anonymity set of k locations and requiring that the probability to report the same obfuscated location z from any of these k locations should be similar (up to e^ϵ). This property is achieved by adding Laplace noise to each Cartesian coordinate independently. There are however two problems with this definition: first, the choice of the anonymity set crucially affects the resulting privacy; outside this set no privacy is guaranteed at all. Second, the property itself is rather weak; reporting the geometric median (or any deterministic function) of the k locations would satisfy the same definition, although the privacy guarantee would be substantially lower than using Laplace noise.

Nevertheless, Dewri's intuition of using Laplace noise[1] for location privacy is valid, and [11] provides extensive experimental analysis supporting this claim. Our notion of geo-indistinguishability provides the formal background for justifying the use of Laplace noise, while avoiding the need to fix an anonymity set by using the generalized variant of differential privacy from [8].

Other location-privacy metrics.

[10] proposes a location cloaking mechanism, and focuses on the evaluation of Location-based Range Queries. The degree of privacy is measured by the size of the cloak (also called *uncertainty region*), and by the coverage of sensitive regions, which is the ratio between the area of the cloak and the area of the regions inside the cloak that the user considers to be sensitive. In order to deal with the side-information that the attacker may have, ad-hoc solutions are proposed, like patching cloaks to enlarge the uncertainty region or

[1]The planar Laplace distribution that we use in our work, however, is different from the distribution obtained by adding Laplace noise to each Cartesian coordinate, and has better differential privacy properties (c.f. Section 4.1).

delaying requests. Both solutions may cause a degradation in the quality of service.

In [5], the real location of the user is assumed to have some level of inaccuracy, due to the specific sensing technology or to the environmental conditions. Different obfuscation techniques are then used to increase this inaccuracy in order to achieve a certain level of privacy. This level of privacy is defined as the ratio between the accuracy before and after the application of the obfuscation techniques.

Similar to the case of k-anonymity, both privacy metrics mentioned above make implicit assumptions about the adversary's side information. This may imply a violation of the privacy definition in a scenario where the adversary has some knowledge about the user's real location.

Transformation-based approaches.

A number of approaches for location privacy are radically different from the ones mentioned so far. Instead of cloaking the user's location, they aim at making it completely invisible to the service provider. This is achieved by transforming all data to a different space, usually employing cryptographic techniques, so that they can be mapped back to spatial information only by the user [24, 20]. The data stored in the provider, as well as the location send by the user are encrypted. Then, using techniques from *private information retrieval*, the provider can return information about the encrypted location, without ever discovering which actual location it corresponds to.

A drawback of these techniques is that they are computationally demanding, making it difficult to implement them in a handheld device. Moreover, they require the provider's data to be encrypted, making it impossible to use existing providers, such as Google Maps, which have access to the real data.

3. GEO-INDISTINGUISHABILITY

In this section we formalize our notion of geo-indistinguishability. As already discussed in the introduction, the main idea behind this notion is that, for any radius $r > 0$, the user enjoys ϵr-privacy within r, i.e. the level of privacy is proportional to the radius. Note that the parameter ϵ corresponds to the level of privacy at one unit of distance. For the user, a simple way to specify his privacy requirements is by a tuple (ℓ, r), where r is the radius he is mostly concerned with and ℓ is the privacy level he wishes *for that radius*. In this case, it is sufficient to require ϵ-geo-indistinguishability for $\epsilon = \ell/r$; this will ensure a level of privacy ℓ within r, and a proportionally selected level for all other radii.

So far we kept the discussion on an informal level by avoiding to explicitly define what ℓ-privacy within r means. In the remaining of this section we give a formal definition, as well as two characterizations which clarify the privacy guarantees provided by geo-indistinguishability.

Probabilistic model.

We first introduce a simple model used in the rest of the paper. We start with a set $\mathcal{X}$ of *points of interest*, typically the user's possible locations. Moreover, let $\mathcal{Z}$ be a set of possible *reported values*, which in general can be arbitrary, allowing to report obfuscated locations, cloaking regions, sets of locations, etc. However, to simplify the discussion, we sometimes consider $\mathcal{Z}$ to also contain spatial points, assuming an operational scenario of a user located at $x \in \mathcal{X}$ and communicating to the attacker a randomly selected location $z \in \mathcal{Z}$ (e.g. an obfuscated point).

Probabilities come into place in two ways. First, the attacker might have side information about the user's location, knowing, for example, that he is likely to be visiting the Eiffel Tower, while unlikely to be swimming in the Seine river. The attacker's side information can be modeled by a *prior* distribution π on $\mathcal{X}$, where $\pi(x)$ is the probability assigned to the location x.

Second, the selection of a reported value in $\mathcal{Z}$ is itself probabilistic; for instance, z can be obtained by adding random noise to the actual location x (a technique used in Section 4). A *mechanism* K is a probabilistic function for selecting a reported value; i.e. K is a function assigning to each location $x \in \mathcal{X}$ a probability distribution on $\mathcal{Z}$, where $K(x)(Z)$ is the probability that the reported point belongs to the set $Z \subseteq \mathcal{Z}$, when the user's location is x.[2] Starting from π and using Bayes' rule, each observation $Z \subseteq \mathcal{Z}$ of a mechanism K induces a *posterior* distribution $\sigma = \mathbf{Bayes}(\pi, K, Z)$ on $\mathcal{X}$, defined as $\sigma(x) = \frac{K(x)(Z)\pi(x)}{\sum_{x'} K(x')(Z)\pi(x')}$.

We define the *multiplicative distance* between two distributions σ_1, σ_2 on some set $\mathcal{S}$ as $d_\mathcal{P}(\sigma_1, \sigma_2) = \sup_{S \subseteq \mathcal{S}} |\ln \frac{\sigma_1(S)}{\sigma_2(S)}|$, with the convention that $|\ln \frac{\sigma_1(S)}{\sigma_2(S)}| = 0$ if both $\sigma_1(S), \sigma_2(S)$ are zero and ∞ if only one of them is zero.

3.1 Definition

We are now ready to state our definition of geo-indistinguishability. Intuitively, a privacy requirement is a constraint on the distributions $K(x), K(x')$ produced by two different points x, x'. Let $d(\cdot,\cdot)$ denote the Euclidean metric. Enjoying ℓ-privacy within r means that for any x, x' s.t. $d(x, x') \leq r$, the distance $d_\mathcal{P}(K(x), K(x'))$ between the corresponding distributions should be at most l. Then, requiring ϵr-privacy for all radii r, forces the two distributions to be similar for locations close to each other, while relaxing the constraint for those far away from each other, allowing a service provider to distinguish points in Paris from those in London.

DEFINITION 3.1 (GEO-INDISTINGUISHABILITY). *A mechanism K satisfies ϵ-geo-indistinguishability iff for all x, x':*

$$d_\mathcal{P}(K(x), K(x')) \leq \epsilon d(x, x')$$

Equivalently, the definition can be formulated as $K(x)(Z) \leq e^{\epsilon d(x,x')} K(x')(Z)$ for all $x, x' \in \mathcal{X}, Z \subseteq \mathcal{Z}$. Note that for all points x' within a radius r from x, the definition forces the corresponding distributions to be at most ϵr distant.

The above definition is very similar to the one of differential privacy, which requires $d_\mathcal{P}(K(x), K(x')) \leq \epsilon d_h(x, x')$, where d_h is the Hamming distance between databases x, x', i.e. the number of individuals in which they differ. In fact, geo-indistinguishability is an instance of a generalized variant of differential privacy, using an arbitrary metric between secrets. This generalized formulation has been known for some time: for instance, [31] uses it to perform a compositional analysis of standard differential privacy for functional programs, while [16] uses metrics between individuals to define "fairness" in classification. On the other hand, the usefulness of using different metrics to achieve different privacy goals and the semantics of the privacy definition obtained by different metrics have only recently started to be studied [8]. This paper focuses on location-based systems and is, to our knowledge, the first work considering privacy under the Euclidean metric, which is a natural choice for spatial data.

Note that in our scenario, using the Hamming metric of standard differential privacy – which aims at completely protecting the

[2] For simplicity we assume distributions on $\mathcal{X}$ to be discrete, but allow those on $\mathcal{Z}$ to be continuous (c.f. Section 4). All sets to which probability is assigned are implicitly assumed to be measurable.

value of an individual – would be too strong, since the only information is the location of a single individual. Nevertheless, we are not interested in completely hiding the user's location, since some approximate information needs to be revealed in order to obtain the required service. Hence, using a privacy level that depends on the Euclidean distance between locations is a natural choice.

A note on the unit of measurement.

It is worth noting that, since ϵ corresponds to the privacy level for one unit of distance, it is affected by the unit in which distances are measured. For instance, assume that $\epsilon = 0.1$ and distances are measured in meters. The level of privacy for points one kilometer away is 1000ϵ, hence changing the unit to kilometers requires to set $\epsilon = 100$ in order for the definition to remain unaffected. In other words, if r is a physical quantity expressed in some unit of measurement, then ϵ has to be expressed in the inverse unit.

3.2 Characterizations

In this section we state two characterizations of geo-indistinguishability, obtained from the corresponding results of [8] (for general metrics), which provide intuitive interpretations of the privacy guarantees offered by geo-indistinguishability.

Adversary's conclusions under hiding.

The first characterization uses the concept of a *hiding function* $\phi : \mathcal{X} \rightarrow \mathcal{X}$. The idea is that ϕ can be applied to the user's actual location before the mechanism K, so that the latter has only access to a hidden version $\phi(x)$, instead of the real location x. A mechanism K with hiding applied is simply the composition $K \circ \phi$. Intuitively, a location remains private if, regardless of his side knowledge (captured by his prior distribution), an adversary draws the same conclusions (captured by his posterior distribution), regardless of whether hiding has been applied or not. However, if ϕ replaces locations in Paris with those in London, then clearly the adversary's conclusions will be greatly affected. Hence, we require that the effect on the conclusions depends on the maximum distance $d(\phi) = \sup_{x \in \mathcal{X}} d(x, \phi(x))$ between the real and hidden location.

THEOREM 3.1. *A mechanism K satisfies ϵ-geo-indistinguishability iff for all $\phi : \mathcal{X} \rightarrow \mathcal{X}$, all priors π on $\mathcal{X}$, and all $Z \subseteq \mathcal{Z}$:*

$$d_{\mathcal{P}}(\sigma_1, \sigma_2) \leq 2\epsilon d(\phi) \quad \textit{where} \quad \begin{aligned} \sigma_1 &= \mathbf{Bayes}(\pi, K, Z) \\ \sigma_2 &= \mathbf{Bayes}(\pi, K \circ \phi, Z) \end{aligned}$$

Note that this is a natural adaptation of a well-known interpretation of standard differential privacy, stating that the attacker's conclusions are similar, regardless of his side knowledge, and regardless of whether an individual's real value has been used in the query or not. This corresponds to a hiding function ϕ removing the value of an individual.

Note also that the above characterization compares two *posterior* distributions. Both σ_1, σ_2 can be substantially different than the initial knowledge π, which means that an adversary does learn some information about the user's location.

Knowledge of an informed attacker.

A different approach is to measure how much the adversary learns about the user's location, by comparing his prior and posterior distributions. However, since some information is allowed to be revealed by design, these distributions can be far apart. Still, we can consider an *informed* adversary who already knows that the user is located within a set $N \subseteq \mathcal{X}$. Let $d(N) = \sup_{x,x' \in N} d(x, x')$ be the maximum distance between points in x. Intuitively, the user's location remains private if, regardless of his prior knowledge within N, the knowledge obtained by such an informed adversary should be limited by a factor depending on $d(N)$. This means that if $d(N)$ is small, i.e. the adversary already knows the location with some accuracy, then the information that he obtains is also small, meaning that he cannot improve his accuracy. Denoting by $\pi_{|N}$ the distribution obtained from π by restricting to N (i.e. $\pi_{|N}(x) = \pi(x|N)$), we obtain the following characterization:

THEOREM 3.2. *A mechanism K satisfies ϵ-geo-indistinguishability iff for all $N \subseteq \mathcal{X}$, all priors π on $\mathcal{X}$, and all $Z \subseteq \mathcal{Z}$:*

$$d_{\mathcal{P}}(\pi_{|N}, \sigma_{|N}) \leq \epsilon d(N) \quad \textit{where} \quad \sigma = \mathbf{Bayes}(\pi, K, Z)$$

Note that this is a natural adaptation of a well-known interpretation of standard differential privacy, stating that in informed adversary who already knows all values except individual's i, gains no extra knowledge from the reported answer, regardless of side knowledge about i's value [17].

Abstracting from side information.

A major difference of geo-indistinguishability, compared to similar approaches from the literature, is that it abstracts from the side information available to the adversary, i.e. from the prior distribution. This is a subtle issue, and often a source of confusion, thus we would like to clarify what "abstracting from the prior" means. The goal of a privacy definition is to restrict the information *leakage* caused by the observation. Note that the lack of leakage does not mean that the user's location cannot be inferred (it could be inferred by the prior alone), but instead that the adversary's knowledge does not increase *due to the observation.*

However, in the context of LBSs, no privacy definition can ensure a small leakage under any prior, and at the same time allow reasonable utility. Consider, for instance, an attacker who knows that the user is located at some airport, but not which one. The attacker's prior knowledge is very limited, still any useful LBS query should reveal at least the user's city, from which the exact location (i.e. the city's airport) can be inferred. Clearly, due to the side information, the leakage caused by the observation is high.

So, since we cannot eliminate leakage under any prior, how can we give a reasonable privacy definition without restricting to a particular one? First, we give a formulation (Definition 3.1) which does not involve the prior at all, allowing to verify it without knowing the prior. At the same time, we give two characterizations which explicitly quantify over all priors, shedding light on how the prior affects the privacy guarantees.

Finally, we should point out that differential privacy abstracts from the prior in exactly the same way. Contrary to what is sometimes believed, the user's value is *not protected* under any prior information. Recalling the well-known example from [14], if the adversary knows that Terry Gross is two inches shorter than the average Lithuanian woman, then he can accurately infer the height, even if the average is release in a differentially private way (in fact no useful mechanism can prevent this leakage). Differential privacy does ensure that her risk is the same whether she participates in the database or not, but this might me misleading: it does not imply the lack of leakage, only that it will happen anyway, whether she participates or not!

3.3 Protecting location sets

So far, we have assumed that the user has a single location that he wishes to communicate to a service provider in a private way (typically his current location). In practice, however, it is common for a user to have multiple points of interest, for instance a set of past locations or a set of locations he frequently visits. In this case, the user might wish to communicate to the provider some information that depends on all points; this could be either the whole set of points itself, or some aggregate information, for instance their centroid. As in the case of a single location, privacy is still a requirement; the provider is allowed to obtain only approximate information about the locations, their exact value should be kept private. In this section, we discuss how ϵ-geo-indistinguishability extends to the case where the secret is a tuple of points $\mathbf{x} = (x_1, \ldots, x_n)$.

Similarly to the case of a single point, the notion of distance is crucial for our definition. We define the distance between two tuples of points $\mathbf{x} = (x_1, \ldots, x_n), \mathbf{x}' = (x'_1, \ldots, x'_n)$ as:

$$d_\infty(\mathbf{x}, \mathbf{x}') = \max_i d(x_i, x'_i)$$

Intuitively, the choice of metric follows the idea of reasoning within a radius r: when $d_\infty(\mathbf{x}, \mathbf{x}') \leq r$, it means that all x_i, x'_i are within distance r from each other. All definitions and results of this section can be then directly applied to the case of multiple points, by using d_∞ as the underlying metric. Enjoying ℓ-privacy within a radius r means that two tuples at most r away from each other, should produce distributions at most ϵr apart.

Reporting the whole set.

A natural question then to ask is how we can obfuscate a tuple of points, by independently applying an existing mechanism K_0 to each individual point, and report the obfuscated tuple. Starting from a tuple $\mathbf{x} = (x_1, \ldots, x_n)$, we independently apply K_0 to each x_i obtaining a reported point z_i, and then report the tuple $\mathbf{z} = (z_1, \ldots, z_n)$. Thus, the probability that the combined mechanism K reports $\mathbf{z}$, starting from $\mathbf{x}$, is the product of the probabilities to obtain each point z_i, starting from the corresponding point x_i, i.e. $K(\mathbf{x})(\mathbf{z}) = \prod_i K_0(x_i)(z_i)$.

The next question is what level of privacy does K satisfy. For simplicity, consider a tuple of only two points (x_1, x_2), and assume that K_0 satisfies ϵ-geo-indistinguishability. At first look, one might expect the combined mechanism K to also satisfy ϵ-geo-indistinguishability, however this is not the case. The problem is that the two points might be *correlated*, thus an observation about x_1 will reveal information about x_2 and vice versa. Consider, for instance, the extreme case in which $x_1 = x_2$. Having two observations about the same point reduces the level of privacy, thus we cannot expect the combined mechanism to provide the same level of privacy.

Still, if K_0 satisfies ϵ-geo-indistinguishability, then K can be shown to satisfy $n\epsilon$-geo-indistinguishability, i.e. a level of privacy that scales linearly with n. Due to this scalability issue, the technique of independently applying a mechanism to each point is only useful when the number of points is small. Still, this is sufficient for some applications, such as the case study of Section 5. Note, however, that this technique is by no means the best we can hope for: similarly to standard differential privacy [7, 32], better results could be achieved by adding noise to the whole tuple $\mathbf{x}$, instead of each individual point. We believe that using such techniques we can achieve geo-indistinguishability for a large number of locations with reasonable noise, leading to practical mechanisms for highly mobile applications. We have already started exploring this direction of future work.

Reporting an aggregate location.

Another interesting case is when we need to report some aggregate information obtained by $\mathbf{x}$, for instance the centroid of the tuple. In general we might need to report the result of a query $f : \mathcal{X}^n \to \mathcal{X}$. Similarly to the case of standard differential privacy, we can compute the real answer $f(\mathbf{x})$ and the add noise by applying a mechanism K to it. If f is Δ-sensitive wrt d, d_∞, meaning that $d(f(\mathbf{x}), f(\mathbf{x}')) \leq \Delta d_\infty(\mathbf{x}, \mathbf{x}')$ for all $\mathbf{x}, \mathbf{x}'$, and K satisfies geo-indistinguishability, then the composed mechanism $K \circ f$ can be shown to satisfy $\Delta\epsilon$-geo-indistinguishability.

Note that when dealing with aggregate data, standard differential privacy becomes a viable option. However, one needs to also examine the loss of utility caused by the added noise. This highly depends on the application: differential privacy is suitable for publishing aggregate queries with *low sensitivity*, meaning that changes in a single individual have a relatively small effect on the outcome. On the other hand, location information often has high sensitivity. A trivial example is the case where we want to publish the complete tuple of points. But sensitivity can be high even for aggregate information: consider the case of publishing the centroid of 5 users located anywhere in the world. Modifying a single user can hugely affect their centroid, thus achieving differential privacy would require so much noise that the result would be useless. For geo-indistinguishability, on the other hand, one needs to consider the distance between points when computing the sensitivity. In the case of the centroid, a small (in terms of distance) change in the tuple has a small effect on the result, thus geo-indistinguishability can be achieved with much less noise.

4. A MECHANISM TO ACHIEVE GEO-INDISTINGUISHABILITY

In this section we present a method to generate noise so to satisfy geo-indistinguishability. We model the location domain as a discrete[3] Cartesian plane with the standard notion of Euclidean distance. This model can be considered a good approximation of the Earth surface when the area of interest is not too large.

(a) First, we define a mechanism to achieve geo-indistinguishability in the ideal case of the continuous plane.

(b) Then, we discretized the mechanism by remapping each point generated according to (a) to the closest point in the discrete domain.

(c) Finally, we truncate the mechanism, so to report only points within the limits of the area of interest.

4.1 A mechanism for the continuous plane

Following the above plan, we start by defining a mechanism for geo-indistinguishability on the continuous plane. The idea is that whenever the actual location is $x_0 \in \mathbb{R}^2$, we report, instead, a point $x \in \mathbb{R}^2$ generated randomly according to the noise function. The latter needs to be such that the probabilities of reporting a point in a certain (infinitesimal) area around x, when the actual locations are x_0 and x'_0 respectively, differs at most by a multiplicative factor $e^{-\epsilon\, d(x_0, x'_0)}$.

We can achieve this property by requiring that the probability of generating a point in the area around x decreases exponentially with the distance from the actual location x_0. In a linear space this is exactly the behavior of the Laplace distribution, whose probability density function (pdf) is ${\epsilon}/{2}\, e^{-\epsilon\, |x-\mu|}$. This distribution has been used in the literature to add noise to query results on statistical databases, with μ set to be the actual answer, and it can be shown to satisfy ϵ-differential privacy [15].

There are two possible definitions of Laplace distribution on higher dimensions (multivariate Laplacians). The first one, investigated

[3] For applications with digital interface the domain of interest is discrete, since the representation of the coordinates of the points is necessarily finite.

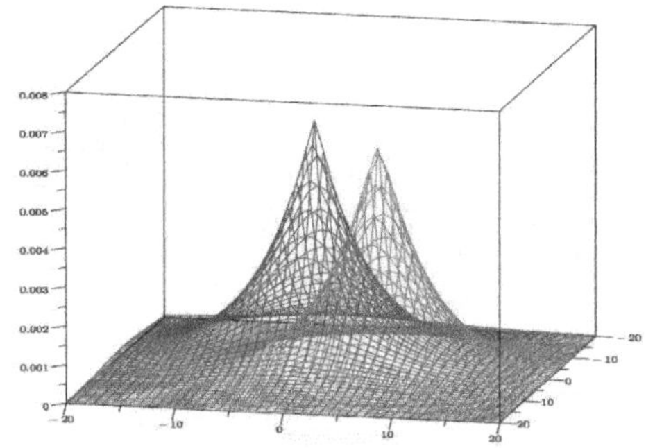

Figure 2: The pdf of two planar Laplacians, centered at $(-2, -4)$ and at $(5, 3)$ respectively, with $\epsilon = 1/5$.

in [27], and used also in [17], is obtained from the standard Laplacian by replacing $|x - \mu|$ with $d(x, \mu)$. The second way consists in generating each Cartesian coordinate independently, according to a linear Laplacian. For reasons that will become clear in the next paragraph, we adopt the first approach.

The probability density function.

Given the parameter $\epsilon \in \mathbb{R}^+$, and the actual location $x_0 \in \mathbb{R}^2$, the pdf of our noise mechanism, on any other point $x \in \mathbb{R}^2$, is:

$$D_\epsilon(x_0)(x) = \frac{\epsilon^2}{2\,\pi}\, e^{-\epsilon\, d(x_0, x)} \tag{1}$$

where ${\epsilon^2}/{2\,\pi}$ is a normalization factor. We call this function *planar Laplacian centered at* x_0. The corresponding distribution is illustrated in Figure 2. It is possible to show that (i) the projection of a planar Laplacian on any vertical plane passing by the center gives a (scaled) linear Laplacian, and (ii) the corresponding mechanism satisfies ϵ-geo-indistinguishability. These two properties would not be satisfied by the second approach to the multivariate Laplacian.

Drawing a random point.

We illustrate now how to draw a random point from the pdf defined in (1). First of all, we note that the pdf of the planar Laplacian depends only on the distance from x_0. It will be convenient, therefore, to switch to a system of polar coordinates with origin in x_0. A point x will be represented as a point (r, θ), where r is the distance of x from x_0, and θ is the angle that the line $x\,x_0$ forms with respect to the horizontal axis of the Cartesian system. Following the standard transformation formula, the pdf of the *polar Laplacian* centered at the origin (x_0) is:

$$D_\epsilon(r, \theta) = \frac{\epsilon^2}{2\,\pi}\, r\, e^{-\epsilon\, r} \tag{2}$$

We note now that the polar Laplacian defined above enjoys a property that is very convenient for drawing in an efficient way: *the two random variables that represent the radius and the angle are independent.* Namely, the pdf can be expressed as the product of the two marginals. In fact, let us denote these two random variables by R (the radius) and Θ (the angle). The two marginals are:

$$\begin{aligned} D_{\epsilon,R}(r) &= \textstyle\int_0^{2\pi} D_\epsilon(r, \theta)\, d\theta \;=\; \epsilon^2\, r\, e^{-\epsilon\, r} \\ D_{\epsilon,\Theta}(\theta) &= \textstyle\int_0^{\infty} D_\epsilon(r, \theta)\, dr \;=\; \frac{1}{2\,\pi} \end{aligned}$$

Hence we have $D_\epsilon(r, \theta) = D_{\epsilon,R}(r)\; D_{\epsilon,\Theta}(\theta)$. Note that $D_{\epsilon,R}(r)$ corresponds to the pdf of the *gamma distribution* with shape 2 and scale $1/\epsilon$.

Drawing a point (r, θ) from the polar Laplacian
1. draw θ uniformly in $[0, 2\pi)$
2. draw p uniformly in $[0, 1)$ and set $r = C_\epsilon^{-1}(p)$

Figure 3: Method to generate Laplacian noise.

Thanks to the fact that R and Θ are independent, in order to draw a point (r, θ) from $D_\epsilon(r, \theta)$ it is sufficient to draw separately r and θ from $D_{\epsilon,R}(r)$ and $D_{\epsilon,\Theta}(\theta)$ respectively.

Since $D_{\epsilon,\Theta}(\theta)$ is constant, drawing θ is easy: it is sufficient to generate θ as a random number in the interval $[0, 2\pi)$ with uniform distribution.

We now show how to draw r. Following standard lines, we consider the cumulative distribution function (cdf) $C_\epsilon(r)$:

$$C_\epsilon(r) \;=\; \int_0^r D_{\epsilon,R}(\rho) d\rho \;=\; 1 - (1 + \epsilon\, r)\, e^{-\epsilon\, r}$$

Intuitively, $C_\epsilon(r)$ represents the probability that the radius of the random point falls between 0 and r. Finally, we generate a random number p with uniform probability in the interval $[0, 1)$, and we set $r = C_\epsilon^{-1}(p)$. Note that

$$C_\epsilon^{-1}(p) = -\tfrac{1}{\epsilon}\left(W_{-1}\left(\tfrac{p-1}{e}\right) + 1\right)$$

where W_{-1} is the Lambert W function (the -1 branch), which can be computed efficiently and is implemented in several numerical libraries (MATLAB, Maple, GSL, ...).

4.2 Discretization

We discuss now how to approximate the Laplace mechanism on a grid $\mathcal{G}$ of discrete Cartesian coordinates. Let us recall the points (a) and (b) of the plan, in light of the development so far: Given the actual location x_0, report the point x in $\mathcal{G}$ obtained as follows:

(a) first, draw a point (r, θ) following the method in Figure 3,

(b) then, remap (r, θ) to the closest point x on $\mathcal{G}$.

We will denote by $K_\epsilon : \mathcal{G} \to \mathcal{P}(\mathcal{G})$ the above mechanism. In summary, $K_\epsilon(x_0)(x)$ represents the probability of reporting the point x when the actual point is x_0.

It is not obvious that the discretization preserves geo-indistinguishability, due to the following problem: In principle, each point x in $\mathcal{G}$ should gather the probability of the set of points for which x is the closest point in $\mathcal{G}$, namely

$$R(x) = \{y \in \mathbb{R}^2 \mid \forall x' \in \mathcal{G}.\; d(y, x') \leq d(y, x')\}$$

However, due to the finite precision of the machine, the noise generated according to (a) is already discretized in accordance with the polar system. Let $\mathcal{W}$ denote the discrete set of points actually generated in (a). Each of those points (r, θ) is drawn with the probability of the area between r, $r + \delta_r$, θ and $\theta + \delta_\theta$, where δ_r and δ_θ denote the precision of the machine in representing the radius and the angle respectively. Hence, step (b) generates a point x in $\mathcal{G}$ with the probability of the set $R_{\mathcal{W}}(x) = R(x) \cap \mathcal{W}$. This introduces some irregularity in the mechanism, because the region associated to $R_{\mathcal{W}}(x)$ has a different shape and area depending on the position of x relatively to x_0. The situation is illustrated in Figure 4 with $R_0 = R_{\mathcal{W}}(x_0)$ and $R_1 = R_{\mathcal{W}}(x_1)$.

Geo-indistinguishability of the discretized mechanism.

We now analyze the privacy guarantees provided by our discretized mechanism. We show that the discretization preserves

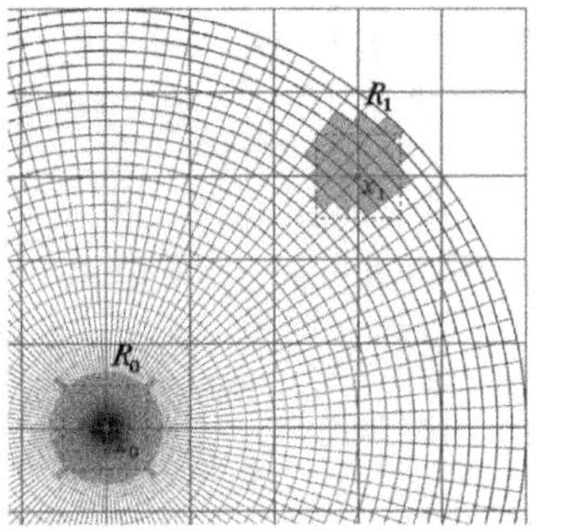

Figure 4: Remapping the points in polar coordinates to points in the grid.

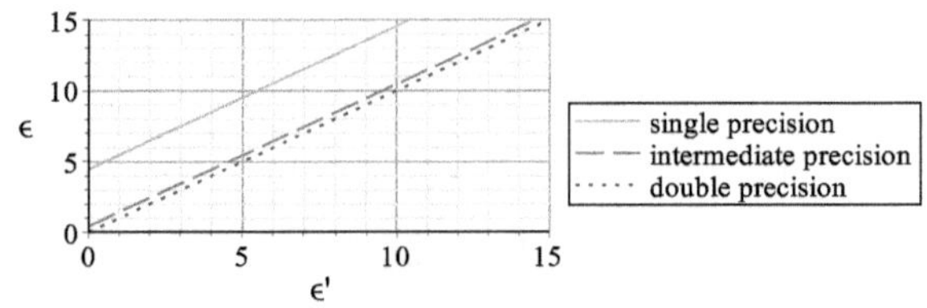

Figure 5: The relation between ϵ and ϵ' for $r_{\max} = 10^2$ km.

Input: x — point to sanitize
ϵ — privacy parameter
$u, v, \delta_\theta, \delta_r$ — precision parameters
$\mathcal{A}$ — acceptable locations
Output: Sanitized version z of input x

1. $\epsilon' \leftarrow \max \epsilon'$ satisfying Thm 4.1 for $r_{\max} = \text{diam}(\mathcal{A})$
2. draw θ unif. in $[0, 2\pi)$ — draw angle
3. draw p unif. in $[0, 1)$, set $r \leftarrow C_{\epsilon'}^{-1}(p)$ — draw radius
4. $z \leftarrow x + \langle r\cos(\theta), r\sin(\theta)\rangle$ — to cartesian, add vectors
5. $z \leftarrow \text{closest}(z, \mathcal{A})$ — truncation
6. **return** z

Figure 6: The Planar Laplace mechanism PL_ϵ

geo-indistinguishability, at the price of a degradation of the privacy parameter ϵ.

For the sake of generality we do not require the step units along the two dimensions of $\mathcal{G}$ to be equal. We will call them *grid units*, and will denote by u and v the smaller and the larger unit, respectively. We recall that δ_θ and δ_r denote the precision of the machine in representing θ and r, respectively. We assume that $\delta_r \leq r_{\max}\delta_\theta$. The following theorem states the geo-indistinguishability guarantees provided by our mechanism: $K_{\epsilon'}$ satisfies ϵ-geo-indistinguishability, within a range $r_{\max}$, provided that ϵ' is chosen in a suitable way that depends on ϵ, on the length of the step units of $\mathcal{G}$, and on the precision of the machine.

THEOREM 4.1. *Assume $r_{\max} < {}^{u}/_{\delta_\theta}$, and let $q = {}^{u}/_{r_{\max}\delta_\theta}$. Let $\epsilon, \epsilon' \in \mathbb{R}^+$ such that*

$$\epsilon' + \frac{1}{u}\ln\frac{q + 2e^{\epsilon' u}}{q - 2e^{\epsilon' u}} \leq \epsilon$$

Then $K_{\epsilon'}$ provides ϵ-geo-indistinguishability within the range of $r_{\max}$. Namely, if $d(x_0, x), d(x_0', x) \leq r_{\max}$ then:

$$K_{\epsilon'}(x_0)(x) \leq e^{\epsilon\, d(x_0, x_0')} K_{\epsilon'}(x_0')(x).$$

The difference between ϵ' and ϵ represents the additional noise needed to compensate the effect of discretization. Note that $r_{\max}$, which determines the area in which ϵ-geo-indistinguishability is guaranteed, must be chosen in such a way that $q > 2e^{\epsilon' u}$. Furthermore there is a trade-off between ϵ' and $r_{\max}$: If we want ϵ' to be close to ϵ then we need q to be large. Depending on the precision, this may or may not imply a serious limit on $r_{\max}$. Vice versa, if we want $r_{\max}$ to be large then, depending on the precision, ϵ' may need to be significantly smaller than ϵ, and furthermore we may have a constraint on the minimum possible value for ϵ, which means that we may not have the possibility of achieving an arbitrary level of geo-indistinguishability.

Figure 5 shows how the additional noise varies depending on the precision of the machine. In this figure, $r_{\max}$ is set to be 10^2 km, and we consider the cases of double precision (16 significant digits, i.e., $\delta_\theta = 10^{-16}$), single precision (7 significant digits), and an intermediate precision of 9 significant digits. Note that with double precision the additional noise is negligible.

Note that in Theorem 4.1 the restriction about $r_{\max}$ is crucial. Namely, ϵ-geo-indistinguishability does not hold for arbitrary distances for any finite ϵ. Intuitively, this is because the step units of $\mathcal{W}$ (see Figure 4) become larger with the distance r from x_0. The step units of $\mathcal{G}$, on the other hand, remain the same. When the steps in $\mathcal{W}$ become larger than those of $\mathcal{G}$, some x's have an empty $R_{\mathcal{W}}(x)$. Therefore when x is far away from x_0 its probability may or may not be 0, depending on the position of x_0 in $\mathcal{G}$, which means that geo-indistinguishability cannot be satisfied.

4.3 Truncation

The Laplace mechanisms described in the previous sections have the potential to generate points everywhere in the plane, which causes several issues: first, digital applications have finite memory, hence these mechanisms are not implementable. Second, the discretized mechanism of Section 4.2 satisfies geo-indistinguishability only within a certain range, not on the full plane. Finally, in practical applications we are anyway interested in locations within a finite region (the earth itself is finite), hence it is desirable that the reported location lies within that region. For the above reasons, we propose a truncated variant of the discretized mechanism which generates points only within a specified region and fully satisfies geo-indistinguishability. The full mechanism (with discretization and truncation) is referred to as "Planar Laplace mechanism" and denoted by PL_ϵ.

We assume a finite set $\mathcal{A} \subset \mathbb{R}^2$ of admissible locations, with diameter $\text{diam}(\mathcal{A})$ (maximum distance between points in $\mathcal{A}$). This set is *fixed*, i.e. it does not depend on the actual location x_0. Our truncated mechanism $PL_\epsilon : \mathcal{A} \rightarrow \mathcal{P}(\mathcal{A} \cap \mathcal{G})$ works like the discretized Laplacian of the previous section, with the difference that the point generated in step (a) is remapped to the closest point in $\mathcal{A} \cap \mathcal{G}$. The complete mechanism is shown in Figure 6; note that step 1 assumes that $\text{diam}(\mathcal{A}) < {}^{u}/_{\delta_\theta}$, otherwise no such ϵ' exists.

THEOREM 4.2. *PL_ϵ satisfies ϵ-geo-indistinguishability.*

5. ENHANCING LBSs WITH PRIVACY

In this section we present a case study of our privacy mechanism in the context of LBSs. We assume a simple client-server architecture where users communicate via a trusted mobile application (the client – typically installed in a smart-phone) with an unknown/untrusted LBS provider (the server – typically running on the cloud). Hence, in contrast to other solutions proposed in the literature, our approach does not rely on trusted third-party servers.

In the following we distinguish between *mildly-location-sensitive* and *highly-location-sensitive* LBS applications. The former cate-

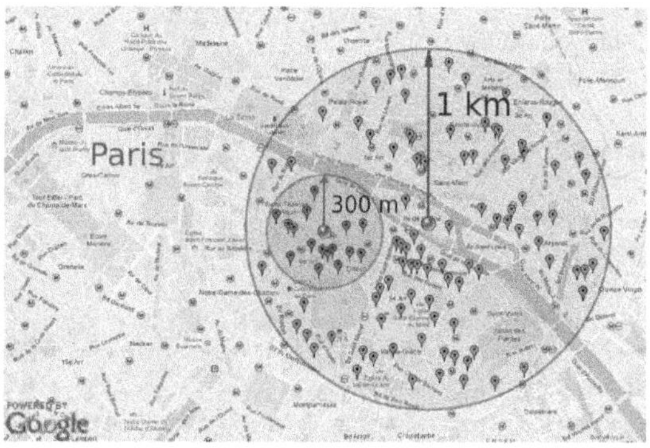

Figure 7: AOI and AOR of 300 m and 1 km radius respectively.

gory corresponds to LBS applications offering a service that does not heavily rely on the precision of the location information provided by the user. Examples of such applications are weather forecast applications and LBS applications for retrieval of certain kind of POI (like gas stations). Enhancing this kind of LBSs with geo-indistinguishability is relatively straightforward as it only requires to obfuscate the user's location using the Planar Laplace mechanism (Figure 6).

Our running example lies within the second category: For the user sitting at Café Les Deux Magots, information about restaurants nearby Champs Élysées is considerably less valuable than information about restaurants around his location. Enhancing highly-location-sensitive LBSs with privacy guarantees is more challenging. Our approach consists on implementing the following three steps:

1. Implement the Planar Laplace mechanism (Figure 6) on the client application in order to report to the LBS server the user's obfuscated location z rather than his real location x.

2. Due to the fact that the information retrieved from the server is about POI nearby z, the area of POI information retrieval should be increased. In this way, if the user wishes to obtain information about POI within, say, 300 m of x, the client application should request information about POI within, say, 1 km of z. Figure 7 illustrates this situation. We will refer to the blue circle as *area of interest* (AOI) and to the grey circle as *area of retrieval* (AOR).

3. Finally, the client application should filter the retrieved POI information (depicted by the pins within the area of retrieval in Figure 7) in order to provide to the user with the desired information (depicted by pins within the user's area of interest in Figure 7).

Ideally, the AOI should always be fully contained in the AOR. Unfortunately, due to the probabilistic nature of our perturbation mechanism, this condition cannot be guaranteed (note that the AOR is centered on a randomly generated location that can be arbitrarily distant from the real location). It is also worth noting that the client application cannot dynamically adjust the radius of the AOR in order to ensure that it always contains the AOI as this approach would completely jeopardize the privacy guarantees: on the one hand, the size of the AOR would leak information about the user's real location and, on the other hand, the LBS provider would know with certainty that the user is located within the retrieval area. Thus, in order to provide geo-indistinguishability, the AOR has to be defined *independently* from the randomly generated location.

Since we cannot guarantee that the AOI is fully contained in the AOR, we introduce the notion of *accuracy*, which measures the probability of such event. In the following, we will refer to an LBS application in abstract terms, as characterized by a location perturbation mechanism K and a fixed AOR radius. We use rad_R and rad_I to denote the radius of the AOR and the AOI, respectively, and $\mathcal{B}(x, r)$ to denote the circle with center x and radius r.

5.1 On the accuracy of LBSs

Intuitively, an LBS application is (c, rad_I)-accurate if the probability of the AOI to be fully contained in the AOR is bounded from below by a *confidence factor* c. Formally:

DEFINITION 5.1 (LBS APPLICATION ACCURACY). *An LBS application* (K, rad_R) *is* (c, rad_I)*-accurate iff for all locations* x *we have that* $\mathcal{B}(x, rad_I)$ *is fully contained in* $\mathcal{B}(K(x), rad_R)$ *with probability at least* c*.*

Given a privacy parameter ϵ and accuracy parameters (c, rad_I), our goal is to obtain an LBS application (K, rad_R) satisfying both ϵ-geo-indistinguishability and (c, rad_I)-accuracy. As a perturbation mechanism, we use the Planar Laplace PL_ϵ (Figure 6), which satisfies ϵ-geo-indistinguishability. As for rad_R, we aim at finding the minimum value validating the accuracy condition. Finding such minimum value is crucial to minimize the bandwidth overhead inherent to our proposal. In the following we will investigate how to achieve this goal by *statically* defining rad_R as a function of the mechanism and the accuracy parameters c and rad_I.

For our purpose, it will be convenient to use the notion of (α, δ)-usefulness, which was introduced in [7]. A location perturbation mechanism K is (α, δ)*-useful* if for every location x the reported location $z = K(x)$ satisfies $d(x, z) \leq \alpha$ with probability at least δ. In the case of the Planar Laplace, it is easy to see that, by definition, the α and δ values which express its usefulness are related by C_ϵ [4], the cdf of the Gamma distribution:

OBSERVATION 5.1. *For any* $\alpha > 0$*,* PL_ϵ *is* (α, δ)*-useful if* $\alpha \leq C_\epsilon^{-1}(\delta)$.

Figure 8 illustrates the (α, δ)-usefulness of PL_ϵ for $r = 0.2$ (as in our running example) and various values of ℓ (recall that $\ell = \epsilon r$). It follows from the figure that a mechanism providing the privacy guarantees specified in our running example (ϵ-geo-indistinguishability, with $\ell = \ln(4)$ and $r = 0.2$) generates an approximate location z falling within 1 km of the user's location x with probability 0.992, falling within 690 meters with probability 0.95, falling within 560 meters with probability 0.9, and falling within 390 meters with probability 0.75.

We now have all the necessary ingredients to determine the desired rad_R: By definition of usefulness, if PL_ϵ is (α, δ)-useful then the LBS application (PL_ϵ, rad_R) is (δ, rad_I)-accurate if $\alpha \leq rad_R - rad_I$. The converse also holds if δ is maximal. By Observation 5.1, we then have:

PROPOSITION 5.2. *The LBS application* (PL_ϵ, rad_R) *is* (c, rad_I)*-accurate if* $rad_R \geq rad_I + C_\epsilon^{-1}(c)$.

Therefore, it is sufficient to set $rad_R = rad_I + C_\epsilon^{-1}(c)$.

Coming back to our running example ($\epsilon = \ln(4)/0.2$ and $rad_I = 0.3$), taking a confidence factor c of, say, 0.95, leads to a $(0.69, 0.95)$-useful mechanism (because $C_\epsilon^{-1}(c) = 0.69$). Thus, $(PL_\epsilon, 0.99)$ is both $\ln(4)/0.2$-geo-indistinguishable and $(0.95, 0.3)$-accurate.

[4]For simplicity we assume that $\epsilon' = \epsilon$ (see Figure 6), since their difference is negligible under double precision.

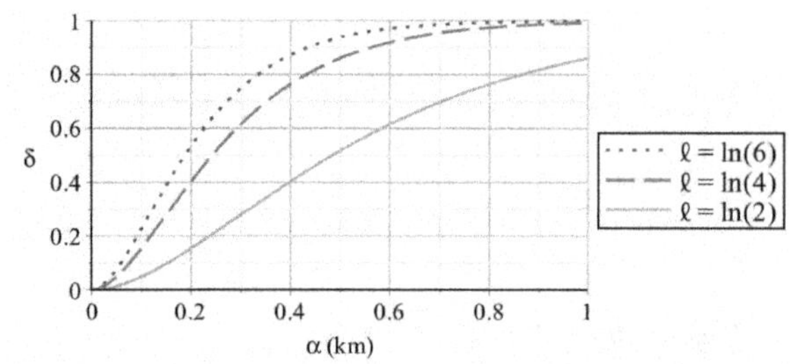

Figure 8: (α, δ)**-usefulness for** $r = 0.2$ **and various values of** ℓ**.**

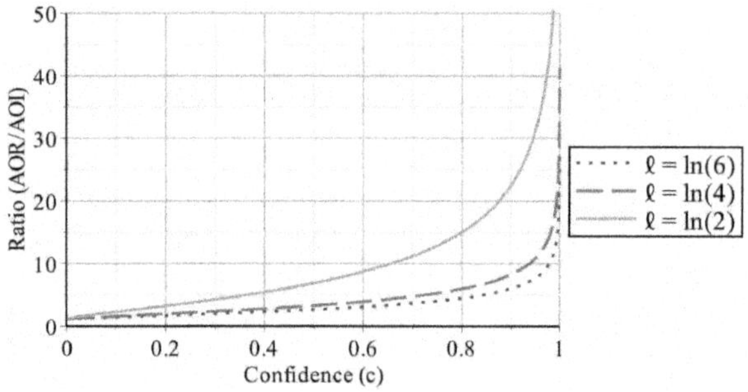

Figure 9: AOR vs AOI ratio for various levels of privacy and accuracy (using fixed $r = 0.2$ **and** $rad_I = 0.3$**).**

5.2 Bandwidth overhead analysis

As expressed by Proposition 5.2, in order to implement an LBS application enhanced with geo-indistinguishability and accuracy it suffices to use the Planar Laplace mechanism and retrieve POIs for an enlarged radius rad_R. For each query made from a location x, the application needs to (i) obtain $z = PL_\epsilon(x)$, (ii) retrieve POIs for AOR $= \mathcal{B}(z, rad_R)$, and (iii) filter the results from AOR to AOI (as explained in step 3 above). Such implementation is straightforward and computationally efficient for modern smart-phone devices. In addition, it provides great flexibility to application developer and/or users to specify their desired/allowed level of privacy and accuracy. This, however, comes at a cost: bandwidth overhead.

In the following we turn our attention to investigating the bandwidth overhead yielded by our approach. We will do so in two steps: first we investigate how the AOR size increases for different privacy and LBS-specific parameters, and then we investigate how such increase translates into bandwidth overhead.

Figure 9 depicts the overhead of the AOR versus the AOI (represented as their ratio) when varying the level of confidence (c) and privacy (ℓ) and for fixed values $rad_I = 0.3$ and $r = 0.2$. The overhead increases slowly for levels of confidence up to 0.95 (regardless of the level of privacy) and increases sharply thereafter, yielding to a worst case scenario of a about 50 times increase for the combination of highest privacy ($\ell = \log(2)$) and highest confidence ($c = 0.99$).

In order to understand how the AOR increase translates into bandwidth overhead, we now investigate the density (in km^2) and size (in KB) of POIs by means of the Google Places API [2]. This API allows to retrieve POIs' information for a specific `location`, `radius` around the location, and POI's `type` (among many other optional parameters). For instance, the HTTPS request:

```
https://maps.googleapis.com/maps/api/place/nearby
search/json?location=48.85412,2.33316 &
radius=300 & types=restaurant & key=myKey
```

Restaurants in Paris		Accuracy $rad_I = 0.3$ $c = 0.9$	$c = 0.95$	$c = 0.99$
Privacy r=0.2	ℓ=log(6)	162 KB	216 KB	359 KB
	ℓ=log(4)	235 KB	318 KB	539 KB
	ℓ=log(2)	698 KB	974 KB	1.7 MB

Restaurants in Buenos Aires		Accuracy $rad_I = 0.3$ $c = 0.9$	$c = 0.95$	$c = 0.99$
Privacy r=0.2	ℓ=log(6)	26 KB	34 KB	54 KB
	ℓ=log(4)	38 KB	51 KB	86 KB
	ℓ=log(2)	112 KB	156 KB	279 KB

Table 1: Bandwidth overhead for restaurants in Paris and in Buenos Aires for various levels of privacy and accuracy.

returns information (in JSON format) including location, address, name, rating, and opening times for all restaurants up to 300 meters from the location (48.85412, 2.33316) – which corresponds to the coordinates of Café Les Deux Magots in Paris.

We have used the APIs `nearbysearch` and `radarsearch` to calculate the average number of POIs per km^2 and the average size of POIs' information (in KB) respectively. We have considered two queries: restaurants in Paris, and restaurants in Buenos Aires. Our results show that there is an average of 137 restaurants per km^2 in Paris and 22 in Buenos Aires, while the average size per POI is 0.84 KB.

Combining this information with the AOR overhead depicted in Figure 9, we can derive the average bandwidth overhead for each query and various combinations of privacy and accuracy levels. For example, using the parameter combination of our running example (privacy level $\epsilon = \log(4)/0.2$, and accuracy level $c = 0.95, rad_I = 0.3$) we have a 10.7 ratio for an average of 38 ($\simeq (137/1000^2) \times (300^2 \times \pi)$) restaurants in the AOI. Thus the estimated bandwidth overhead is $39 \times (10.7 - 1) \times 0.84$KB $\simeq 318$ KB.

Table 1 shows the bandwidth overhead for restaurants in Paris and Buenos Aires for the various combinations of privacy and accuracy levels. Looking at the worst case scenario, from a bandwidth overhead perspective, our combination of highest levels of privacy and accuracy (taking $\ell = \log(2)$ and $c = 0.99$) with the query for restaurants in Paris (which yields to a large number of POIs – significantly larger than average) results in a significant bandwidth overhead (up to 1.7MB). Such overhead reduces sharply when decreasing the level of privacy (e.g., from 1.7 MB to 557 KB when using $\ell = \log(4)$ instead of $\ell = \log(2)$). For more standard queries yielding a lower number of POIs, in contrast, even the combination of highest privacy and accuracy levels results in a relatively insignificant bandwidth overhead.

Concluding our bandwidth overhead analysis, we believe that the overhead necessary to enhance an LBS application with geo-indistinguishability guarantees is not prohibitive even for scenarios resulting in high bandwidth overhead (i.e., when combining very high privacy and accuracy levels with queries yielding a large number of POIs). Note that 1.7MB is comparable to 35 seconds of Youtube streaming or 80 seconds of standard Facebook usage [3]. Nevertheless, for cases in which minimizing bandwidth consumption is paramount, we believe that trading bandwidth consumption for privacy (e.g., using $\ell = \log(4)$ or even $\ell = \log(6)$) is an acceptable solution.

5.3 Further challenges: using an LBS multiple times

As discussed in Section 3.3, geo-indistinguishability can be naturally extended to multiple locations. In short, the idea of being *ℓ-private within r* remains the same but for all locations simultaneously. In this way the locations, say, x_1, x_2 of a user employing the LBS twice remain indistinguishable from all pair of locations at (point-wise) distance at most r (i.e., from all pairs x'_1, x'_2 such that $d(x_1, x'_1) \leq r$ and $d(x_2, x'_2) \leq r$).

A simple way of obtaining geo-indistinguishability guarantees when performing multiple queries is to employ our technique for protecting single locations to *independently* generate approximate locations for each of the user's locations. In this way, a user performing n queries via a mechanism providing ϵ-geo-indistinguishability enjoys $n\epsilon$-geo-indistinguishability (see Section 3.3).

This solution might be satisfactory when the number of queries to perform remains fairly low, but in other cases impractical, due to the privacy degradation. It is worth noting that the canonical technique for achieving standard differential privacy (based on adding noise according to the Laplace distribution) suffers of the same privacy degradation problem (ϵ increases linearly on the number of queries). Several articles in the literature focus on this problem (see [32] for instance). We believe that the principles and techniques used to deal with this problem for standard differential privacy could be adapted to our scenario (either directly or motivationally).

6. COMPARISON WITH OTHER METHODS

In this section we compare the performance of our mechanism with that of other ones proposed in the literature. Of course it is not interesting to make a comparison in terms of geo-indistinguishability, since other mechanisms usually do not satisfy this property. We consider, instead, the (rather natural) Bayesian notion of privacy proposed in [36], and the trade-off with respect to the *quality of service* measured according to [36], and also with respect to the notion of accuracy illustrated in the previous section.

The mechanisms that we compare with ours are:

1. The obfuscation mechanism presented in [36]. This mechanism works on discrete locations, called *regions*, and, like ours, it reports a location (region) selected randomly according to a probability distribution that depends on the user's location. The distributions are generated automatically by a tool which is designed to provide optimal privacy for a given quality of service and a given adversary (i.e., a given prior, representing the side knowledge of the adversary). It is important to note that in presence of a different adversary the optimality is not guaranteed. This dependency on the prior is a key difference with respect to our approach, which abstracts from the adversary's side information.

2. A simple cloaking mechanism. In this approach, the area of interest is assumed to be partitioned in *zones*, whose size depends on the level of privacy we want yo achieve. The mechanism then reports the zone in which the exact location is situated. This method satisfies k-anonymity where k is the number of locations within each zone.

In both cases we need to divide the area of interest into a finite number of regions, representing the possible locations. We consider for simplicity a grid, and, more precisely, a 9×9 grid consisting of 81 square regions of 100 m of side length. In addition, for the cloaking method, we overlay a grid of $3 \times 3 = 9$ zones. Figure 10 illustrates the setting: the regions are the small squares with black borders. In the cloaking method, the zones are the larger squares with blue borders. For instance, any point situated in one of the regions $1, 2, 3, 10, 11, 12, 19, 20$ or 21, would be reported as zone 1. We assume that each zone is represented by the central region. Hence, in the above example, the reported region would be 11.

Privacy and Quality of Service.

As already stated, we will use the metrics for privacy and for the quality of service proposed in [36].

The first metric is called *Location Privacy* (LP) in [36]. The idea is to measure it in terms of the *expected estimation error* of a "rational" Bayesian adversary. The adversary is assumed to have some side knowledge, expressed in terms of a probability distribution on the regions, which represents the *a priori* probability that the user's location is situated in that region. The adversary tries to make the best use of such prior information, and combines it with the information provided by the mechanism (the reported region), so to guess a location (remapped region) which is as close as possible to the one where the user really is. More precisely, the goal is to infer a region that, in average, minimizes the distance from the user's exact location.

Formally, LP is defined as:

$$LP = \sum_{r, r', \hat{r} \in R} \pi(r) K(r)(r') h(\hat{r}|r') d(\hat{r}, r)$$

where R is the set of all regions, π is the prior distribution over the regions, $K(r)(r')$ gives the probability that the real region r is reported by the mechanism as r', $h(\hat{r}|r')$ represents the probability that the reported region r' is remapped into $\hat{r}$, in the optimal remapping h, and d is the distance between regions. "Optimal" here means that h is chosen so to minimize the above expression, which, we recall, represents the expected distance between the user's exact location and the location guessed by the adversary.

As for the quality of service, the idea in [36] is to quantify its opposite, the *Service Quality Loss* (*SQL*), in terms of the expected distance between the reported location and the user's exact location. In other words, the service provider is supposed to offer a quality proportional to the accuracy of the location that he receives. Unlike the adversary, he is not expected to have any prior knowledge and he is not expected to guess a location different from the reported one. Formally:

$$SQL = \sum_{r, r' \in R} \pi(r) K(r)(r') d(r', r)$$

where π, $K(r)(r')$ and d are as above.

It is worth noting that for the optimal mechanism in [36] *SQL* and LP coincide (when the mechanism is used in presence of the same adversary for which it has been designed), i.e. the adversary does not need to make any remapping.

Comparing the LP for a given SQL.

In order to compare the three mechanisms, we set the parameters of each mechanism in such a way that the *SQL* is the same for all of them, and we compare their *LP*. As already noted, for the optimal mechanism in [36] *SQL* and *LP* coincide, i.e. the optimal remapping is the identity, when the mechanism is used in presence of the same adversary for which it has been designed. It turns out that, when the adversary's prior is the uniform one, *SQL* and *LP* coincide also for our mechanism and for the cloaking one.

We note that for the cloaking mechanism the *SQL* is fixed and it is 107.03 m. In our experiments we fix the value of *SQL* to be

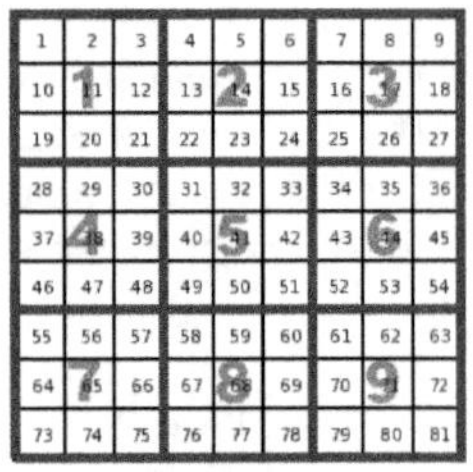

Figure 10: The division of the map into regions and zones.

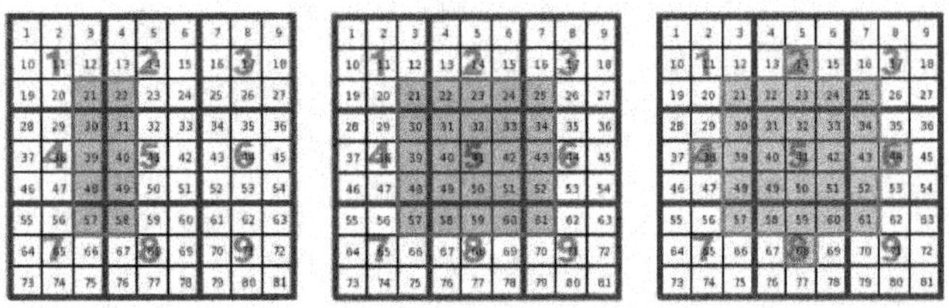

(a) (b) (c)

Figure 11: Priors considered for the experiments.

that one for all the mechanisms. We find that in order to obtain such *SQL* for our mechanism we need to set $\epsilon = 0.0162$ (the difference with ϵ' in this case is negligible). The mechanism of [36] is generated by using the tool explained in the same paper.

Figure 11 illustrates the priors that we consider here: in each case, the probability distribution is accumulated in the regions in the purple area, and distributed uniformly over them. Note that it is not interesting to consider the uniform distribution over the whole map, since, as explained before, on that prior all the mechanisms under consideration give the same result.

Figure 12 illustrates the results we obtain in terms of *LP*, where (a), (b) and (c) correspond to the priors in Figure 11. The optimal mechanism is considered in two instances: the one designed exactly for the prior for which it is used ("optimal-rp", where "rp" stands for real prior), and the one designed for the uniform distribution on all the map ("optimal-unif", which is not necessarily optimal for the priors considered here). As we can see, the Planar Laplace mechanism offers the best *LP* among the mechanisms which do not depend on the prior, or, as in the case of optimal-unif, are designed with a fixed prior. When the prior has a more circular symmetry the performance approaches the one of optimal-rp (the optimal mechanism).

Comparing the LP for a given accuracy.

The *SQL* metric defined above is a reasonable metric, but it does not cover all natural notions of quality of service. In particular, in the case of LBSs, an important criterion to take into account is the additional bandwidth usage. Therefore, we make now a comparison using the notion of accuracy, which, as explained in previous section, provides a good criterion to evaluate the performance in terms of bandwidth. Unfortunately we cannot compare our mechanism to the one of [36] under this criterion, because the construction of the latter is tied to the *SQL*. Hence, we only compare our mechanism with the cloaking one.

We recall that an LBS application (K, rad_R) is (c, rad_I)-accurate if for every location x the probability that the area of interest (AOI) is fully contained in the area of retrieval (AOR) is at least c. We need to fix rad_I (the radius of the AOI), rad_R (the radius of the

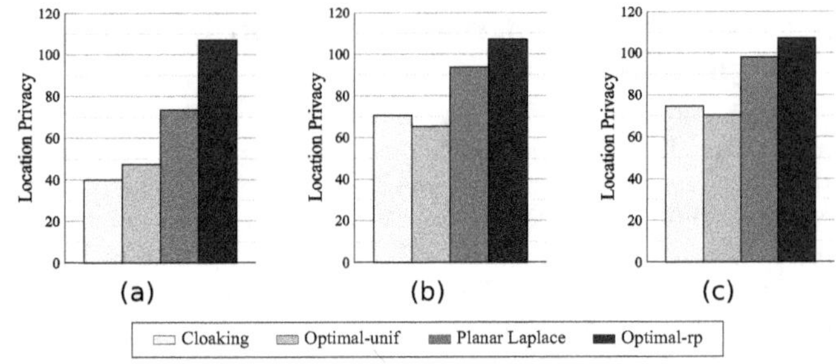

Figure 12: Location Privacy for $SQL = 107.03$ m.

AOR), and c so that the condition of accuracy is satisfied for both methods, and then compute the respective *LP* measures. Let us fix $rad_I = 200$ m, and let us choose a large confidence factor, say, $c = 0.99$. As for rad_R, it will be determined by the cloaking method.

Since the cloaking mechanism is deterministic, in order for the condition to be satisfied the AOR for a given location x must extend around the zone of x by at least rad_I, In fact, x could be in the border of the zone. Given that the cloaking method reports the center of the zone, and that the distance between the center and the border (which is equal to the distance between the center and any of the corners) is $\sqrt{2} \cdot 150$ m, we derive that rad_R must be at least $(200 + \sqrt{2} \cdot 150)$ m. Note that in the case of this method the accuracy is independent from the value of c. It only depends on the difference between rad_R and rad_I, which in turns depends on the length s of the side of the region: if the difference is at least $\sqrt{2} \cdot s/2$, then the condition is satisfied (for every possible x) with probability 1. Otherwise, there will be some x for which the condition is not satisfied (i.e., it is satisfied with probability 0).

In the case of our method, on the other hand, the accuracy condition depends on c and on ϵ. More precisely, as we have seen in previous section, the condition is satisfied if and only if $C_\epsilon^{-1}(c) \leq rad_R - rad_I$. Therefore, for fixed c, the maximum ϵ only depends on the difference between rad_R and rad_I and is determined by the equation $C_\epsilon^{-1}(c) = rad_R - rad_I$. For the above values of rad_I, rad_R, and c, it turns out that $\epsilon = 0.016$.

We can now compare the *LP* of the two mechanisms with respect to the three priors above. Figure 13 illustrates the results. As we can see, our mechanism outperforms the cloaking mechanism in all the three cases.

For different values of rad_I the situation does not change: as explained above, the cloaking method always forces rad_R to be larger than rad_I by (at least) $\sqrt{2} \cdot 150$ m, and ϵ only depends on this value. For smaller values of c, on the contrary, the situation changes, and becomes more favorable for our method. In fact, as argued above, the situation remains the same for the cloacking method (since its accuracy does not depend on c), while ϵ decreases (and consequently LP increases) as c decreases. In fact, for a fixed $r = rad_R - rad_I$, we have $\epsilon = C_r^{-1}(c)$. This follows from $r = C_\epsilon^{-1}(c)$ and from the fact that r and ϵ, in the expression that defines $C_\epsilon(r)$, are interchangeable.

7. RELATED WORK

Much of the related work has been already discussed in Section 2, here we only mention the works that were not reported there. There are excellent works and surveys [37, 26, 34] that summarize the different threats, methods, and guarantees in the context of location privacy.

LISA [9] provides location privacy by preventing an attacker from relating any particular point of interest (POI) to the user's lo-

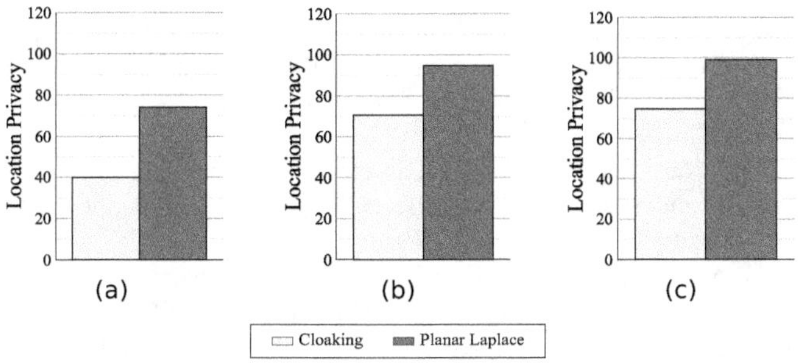

Figure 13: Location Privacy for $rad_R = (\sqrt{2} \cdot 150 + 200)$ m and $c = 0.99$.

cation. That way, the attacker cannot infer which POI the user will visit next. The privacy metric used in this work is *m-unobservability*. The method achieves m-unobservability if, with high probability, the attacker cannot relate the estimated location to at least m different POIs in the proximity.

SpaceTwist [39] reports a fake location (called the "anchor") and queries the geolocation system server incrementally for the nearest neighbors of this fake location until the k-nearest neighbors of the real location are obtained.

In a recent paper [29] it has been shown that, due to finite precision and rounding effects of floating-point operations, the standard implementations of the Laplacian mechanism result in an irregular distribution which causes the loss of the property of differential privacy. In [18] the study has been extended to the planar Laplacian, and to any kind of finite-precision semantics. The same paper proposes a solutions for the truncated version of the planar laplacian, based on a snapping meccanism, which maintains the level of privacy at the cost of introducing an additional amount of noise.

8. CONCLUSION AND FUTURE WORK

In this paper we have presented a framework for achieving privacy in location-based applications, taking into account the desired level of protection as well as the side-information that the attacker might have. The core of our proposal is a new notion of privacy, that we call geo-indistinguishability, and a method, based on a bivariate version of the Laplace function, to perturbate the actual location. We have put a strong emphasis in the formal treatment of the privacy guarantees, both in giving a rigorous definition of geo-indistinguishability, and in providing a mathematical proof that our method satisfies such property. We also have shown how geo-indistinguishability relates to the popular notion of differential privacy. Finally, we have illustrated the applicability of our method on a POI-retrieval service, and we have compared it with other mechanisms in the literature, showing that it outperforms those which do not depend on the prior.

In the future we aim at extending our method to cope with more complex applications, possibly involving the sanitization of several (potentially related) locations. One important aspect to consider when generating noise on several data is the fact that their correlation may degrade the level of protection. We aim at devising techniques to control the possible loss of privacy and to allow the composability of our method.

9. ACKNOWLEDGEMENTS

This work was partially supported by the European Union 7th FP under the grant agreement no. 295261 (MEALS), by the projects ANR-11-IS02-0002 LOCALI and ANR-12-IS02-001 PACE, and by the INRIA Large Scale Initiative CAPPRIS. The work of Miguel E. Andrés was supported by a QUALCOMM grant. The work of Nicolás E. Bordenabe was partially funded by the French Defense Procurement Agency (DGA) by a PhD grant.

10. REFERENCES

[1] Pew Internet & American Life Project. http://pewinternet.org/Reports/2012/Location-based-services.aspx.

[2] Google Places API. https://developers.google.com/places/documentation/.

[3] Vodafone Mobile data usage Stats. http://www.vodafone.ie/internet-broadband/internet-on-your-mobile/usage/.

[4] M. Andrés, N. Bordenabe, K. Chatzikokolakis, and C. Palamidessi. Geo-indistinguishability: Differential privacy for location-based systems. Technical report, 2012. http://arxiv.org/abs/1212.1984.

[5] C. A. Ardagna, M. Cremonini, E. Damiani, S. D. C. di Vimercati, and P. Samarati. Location privacy protection through obfuscation-based techniques. In *Proc. of DAS*, volume 4602 of *LNCS*, pages 47–60. Springer, 2007.

[6] B. Bamba, L. Liu, P. Pesti, and T. Wang. Supporting anonymous location queries in mobile environments with privacygrid. In *Proc. of WWW*, pages 237–246. ACM, 2008.

[7] A. Blum, K. Ligett, and A. Roth. A learning theory approach to non-interactive database privacy. In *Proc. of STOC*, pages 609–618. ACM, 2008.

[8] K. Chatzikokolakis, E. Andrés, Miguel, E. Bordenabe, Nicolás, and C. Palamidessi. Broadening the scope of Differential Privacy using metrics. In *Proc. of PETS*, volume 7981 of *LNCS*, pages 82–102. Springer, 2013.

[9] Z. Chen. *Energy-efficient Information Collection and Dissemination in Wireless Sensor Networks.* PhD thesis, University of Michigan, 2009.

[10] R. Cheng, Y. Zhang, E. Bertino, and S. Prabhakar. Preserving user location privacy in mobile data management infrastructures. In *Proc. of PET*, volume 4258 of *LNCS*, pages 393–412. Springer, 2006.

[11] R. Dewri. Local differential perturbations: Location privacy under approximate knowledge attackers. *IEEE Trans. on Mobile Computing*, 99(PrePrints):1, 2012.

[12] J. E. Dobson and P. F. Fisher. Geoslavery. *Technology and Society Magazine, IEEE*, 22(1):47–52, 2003.

[13] M. Duckham and L. Kulik. A formal model of obfuscation and negotiation for location privacy. In *Proc. of PERVASIVE*, volume 3468 of *LNCS*, pages 152–170. Springer, 2005.

[14] C. Dwork. Differential privacy. In *Proc. of ICALP*, volume 4052 of *LNCS*, pages 1–12. Springer, 2006.

[15] C. Dwork. A firm foundation for private data analysis. *Communications of the ACM*, 54(1):86–96, 2011.

[16] C. Dwork, M. Hardt, T. Pitassi, O. Reingold, and R. S. Zemel. Fairness through awareness. In *Proc. of ITCS*, pages 214–226. ACM, 2012.

[17] C. Dwork, F. Mcsherry, K. Nissim, and A. Smith. Calibrating noise to sensitivity in private data analysis. In *Proc. of TCC*, volume 3876 of *LNCS*, pages 265–284. Springer, 2006.

[18] I. Gazeau, D. Miller, and C. Palamidessi. Preserving differential privacy under finite-precision semantics. In *Proc. of QAPL*, volume 117 of *EPTCS*, pages 1–18. OPA, 2013.

[19] B. Gedik and L. Liu. Location privacy in mobile systems: A personalized anonymization model. In *Proc. of ICDCS*, pages 620–629. IEEE, 2005.

[20] G. Ghinita, P. Kalnis, A. Khoshgozaran, C. Shahabi, and K.-L. Tan. Private queries in location based services: anonymizers are not necessary. In *Proc. of SIGMOD*, pages 121–132. ACM, 2008.

[21] M. Gruteser and D. Grunwald. Anonymous usage of location-based services through spatial and temporal cloaking. In *Proc. of MobiSys*. USENIX, 2003.

[22] S.-S. Ho and S. Ruan. Differential privacy for location pattern mining. In *Proc. of SPRINGL*, pages 17–24. ACM, 2011.

[23] B. Hoh and M. Gruteser. Protecting location privacy through path confusion. In *Proc. of SecureComm*, pages 194–205. IEEE, 2005.

[24] A. Khoshgozaran and C. Shahabi. Blind evaluation of nearest neighbor queries using space transformation to preserve location privacy. In *Proc. of SSTD*, volume 4605 of *LNCS*, pages 239–257. Springer, 2007.

[25] H. Kido, Y. Yanagisawa, and T. Satoh. Protection of location privacy using dummies for location-based services. In *Proc. of ICDE Workshops*, page 1248, 2005.

[26] J. Krumm. A survey of computational location privacy. *Personal and Ubiquitous Computing*, 13(6):391–399, 2009.

[27] K. Lange and J. S. Sinsheimer. Normal/independent distributions and their applications in robust regression. *J. of Comp. and Graphical Statistics*, 2(2):175–198, 1993.

[28] A. Machanavajjhala, D. Kifer, J. M. Abowd, J. Gehrke, and L. Vilhuber. Privacy: Theory meets practice on the map. In *Proc. of ICDE*, pages 277–286. IEEE, 2008.

[29] I. Mironov. On significance of the least significant bits for differential privacy. In *Proc. of CCS*, pages 650–661. ACM, 2012.

[30] M. F. Mokbel, C.-Y. Chow, and W. G. Aref. The new casper: Query processing for location services without compromising privacy. In *Proc. of VLDB*, pages 763–774. ACM, 2006.

[31] J. Reed and B. C. Pierce. Distance makes the types grow stronger: a calculus for differential privacy. In *Proc. of ICFP*, pages 157–168. ACM, 2010.

[32] A. Roth and T. Roughgarden. Interactive privacy via the median mechanism. In *Proc. of STOC*, pages 765–774, 2010.

[33] P. Shankar, V. Ganapathy, and L. Iftode. Privately querying location-based services with sybilquery. In *Proc. of UbiComp*, pages 31–40. ACM, 2009.

[34] K. G. Shin, X. Ju, Z. Chen, and X. Hu. Privacy protection for users of location-based services. *IEEE Wireless Commun*, 19(2):30–39, 2012.

[35] R. Shokri, G. Theodorakopoulos, J.-Y. L. Boudec, and J.-P. Hubaux. Quantifying location privacy. In *Proc. of S&P*, pages 247–262. IEEE, 2011.

[36] R. Shokri, G. Theodorakopoulos, C. Troncoso, J.-P. Hubaux, and J.-Y. L. Boudec. Protecting location privacy: optimal strategy against localization attacks. In *Proc. of CCS*, pages 617–627. ACM, 2012.

[37] M. Terrovitis. Privacy preservation in the dissemination of location data. *SIGKDD Explorations*, 13(1):6–18, 2011.

[38] M. Xue, P. Kalnis, and H. Pung. Location diversity: Enhanced privacy protection in location based services. In *Proc. of LoCA*, volume 5561 of *LNCS*, pages 70–87. Springer, 2009.

[39] M. L. Yiu, C. S. Jensen, X. Huang, and H. Lu. Spacetwist: Managing the trade-offs among location privacy, query performance, and query accuracy in mobile services. In *Proc. of ICDE*, pages 366–375. IEEE, 2008.

Control-Alt-Hack: The Design and Evaluation of a Card Game for Computer Security Awareness and Education

Tamara Denning[†], Adam Lerner[†], Adam Shostack*, and Tadayoshi Kohno[†]

[†]Computer Science & Engineering
University of Washington
Seattle, WA, USA
{tdenning, lerner, yoshi}@cs.washington.edu

*adam@homeport.org

ABSTRACT

We scoped, designed, produced, and evaluated the effectiveness of a recreational tabletop card game created to raise awareness of—and alter perceptions regarding—computer security. We discuss our process, the challenges that arose, and the decisions we made to address those challenges. As of May 2013, we have shipped approximately 800 free copies to 150 educators. We analyze and report on feedback from 22 of these educators about their experiences using *Control-Alt-Hack* with over 450 students in classroom and non-classroom contexts. The responses from the 14 educators who reported on their use of the game in a classroom context variously indicated that: their students' awareness of computer security as a complex and interesting field was increased (11/14); they would use the game again in their classroom (10/14); and they would recommend the game to others (13/14). Of note, 2 of the 14 classroom educators reported that they would not have otherwise covered the material. Additionally, we present results from user studies with 11 individuals and find that their responses indicate that 8 of the 11 had an increased awareness of computer security or a changed perception; furthermore, all of our intended goals are touched upon in their responses.

Categories and Subject Descriptors

K.3.2 [**COMPUTERS AND EDUCATION**]: Computer and Information Science Education

Keywords

Card game; computer science education; computer security and privacy; computer security education; game; outreach; privacy; security; security awareness; security education; security outreach; tabletop security; tabletop games.

1. INTRODUCTION

We believe that there is vast benefit to be offered from raising people's awareness of computer security. Exposing many different kinds of individuals to ideas that make them think about computer security—however briefly—could potentially benefit the status of computer security as whole:

Current and Future Users. The more people prioritize security, the more they might express it with their purchasing power, and the more willing they might be to engage in security and privacy behaviors that require time or effort.

Current and Future Developers. The more developers prioritize security, the more willing they might be to take action. This might mean taking security training, refreshing their knowledge of best security practices, taking more care with their code, or simply thinking to reach out to their institution's security team.

Current and Future Management. If management prioritizes security, they might dedicate more resources to developing and maintaining secure products and systems, or reward security-promoting behaviors via the institution's incentive structure.

Future Technologists. We encourage as many people as possible to consider computer security and computer science as a profession, in order to increase the strength of the field as a whole.

There are many avenues to increase people's awareness of security: publicity campaigns, integration into popular culture, and education and training are just a few. In our work, our desire to create an artifact that exposes people to thinking about security and that facilitates ad hoc, social interactions led us to design *Control-Alt-Hack®: White Hat Hacking for Fun and Profit*: a recreational, tabletop card game about computer security. As of May 2013, approximately 800 requested copies of Control-Alt-Hack have been shipped to 150 educators.

We sent these educators surveys, and 22 educators representing over 450 students submitted feedback about their experiences using Control-Alt-Hack inside and outside of the classroom. Analysis of the evaluation data has indicated that we have had some success meeting our design goals. Of the educators who reported using the game in their classrooms: 11 out of 14 indicated in their responses that the game played a role in increasing their students' awareness of computer security; 11 out of 14 indicated that the game was engaging or filled a social role in the classroom; 13 out of 14 indicated that they would suggest the game to others; and 10 out of 14 said that they would use the game in their class again. In terms of reaching new audiences, 2 of the classroom educators reported that they would not have otherwise covered the security material in Control-Alt-Hack. Furthermore, in a user study we conducted with 11 participants, 8 of the 11 provided evidence that they were thinking in new ways about computer security after playing the game.

In this paper, we:

- Describe and explore the manner in which unconventional tools, and specifically a physical game, can reach new audiences—or be used in new contexts—in order to raise overall awareness or alter perceptions about security;

CCS'13, November 4–8, 2013, Berlin, Germany.

ACM 978-1-4503-2477-9/13/11…$15.00.
http://dx.doi.org/10.1145/2508859.2516753

Figure 1. A photo of the game box and contents.
Photo Credit: Juliet Fiss. © University of Washington

- Explicate and critique our design process, the constraints that arose throughout its course, and the tradeoffs that we made to further our project goals;
- Present our analysis evaluating the success of our tool in reaching its desired audience and achieving its intended goals;
- Based on our knowledge and our evaluation, discuss the contexts in which the game is less suitable, and our takeaway lessons regarding how this reflects the design tradeoffs that we made to meet our goals;
- Contribute to the knowledge foundation for those interested in creating tools that utilize unconventional methods or reach new audiences, in order to ultimately improve the state of computer security as a whole.

2. PROJECT GOALS

2.1 Goals

Awareness Goals. As motivated by Section 1, our primary goal is to increase people's awareness of computer security needs and challenges, so that they can be more informed technology builders and consumers. This includes:

(1) Increasing understanding of the importance of computer security, and the potential risks with inadequate security safeguards.

(2) Conveying the breadth of technologies for which computer security is relevant, including not only conventional computing platforms like laptops and Web servers, but also emerging platforms like pervasive technologies and cyber-physical systems.

(3) Improving understanding of the diversity of potential threats that security designers must consider and the creativity of attackers.

Perception Goals (Secondary Goal). We additionally seek to show that the information technology community and its professions are open to people of diverse backgrounds. Providing even fictional role-models could help encourage interest in computer science and computer security. More specifically, we aim:

(1) To work against negative, dissuasive, or niche stereotypes about people in these fields, and to allow players to identify with one or more of the characters in order to envision themselves in the field.

(2) To highlight the variety of professional and personal opportunities available to people with these skills.

Exposure Goal. We seek to have as wide an impact with our Awareness and Perception Goals as possible—the more people that play this game, the more opportunities our game has to increase awareness or change perception.

2.2 Why a Game?

We believe that games are well positioned to address our specific project goals. If designed well, we argue that games can be an appropriate tool for seeding a large audience of people with a modest amount of security information. Briefly:

- Games can be fun, which gets people engaged.
- Games can give you permission to explore ideas and ask questions.
- Games are intended to have intrinsic entertainment value, which gets people to pick them up and use them on their own time.

Given the subject matter, it may seem natural to have created a computer game, rather than a physical tabletop game. Both formats have their merits and their limitations, and in creating our tool we chose to explore the problem space via a physical game. Part of our reasoning in doing so was to take advantage of some of the following factors:

- Physical games may appeal to people who do not enjoy computer games.
- Aside from requiring a surface on which to play, physical games generally do not require extensive setup or have resource dependencies.
- Having a game lying around in a physical space provides the opportunity to read through some of the cards, even if the game is not being actively played.

While the following properties are not exclusive to physical games:

- Physical games can create social environments, which can foster interaction and discussion of ideas encountered.
- Because physical games can create interaction between players, they are suitable for use in social gatherings.

2.3 Target Audience

No game strongly appeals to everyone. While we sought to make our game as broadly appealing as possible to raise security awareness within a very large audience, it is most practical to target a specific demographic.

Primary Education Audience. Our primary target audience is people with an affinity for computer science and engineering but without requiring significant computer security education, training, or experience. We target in particular those who are early in their careers, including computer science and engineering undergraduate students, high school students, and recent graduates. For example, a high school student in AP Computer Science might play this game, as might a recent hire in software development, test, or management. This goal means that our primary target audience is technically inclined and consists of roughly 15- to 30-year-olds.

Secondary Education Audiences: High school and undergraduate students in the Science, Technology, Engineering,

Figure 2. The character art from the portrait side of 12 of the game's 16 Hacker cards. © University of Washington

and Math (STEM) disciplines; software developers; gamers; and the broader public.

Security Community: As a vector for increased dissemination.

3. GAME DESIGN

In this section we give a brief, high-level tour of our game development process.

3.1 Choosing Game Mechanics

A game's "mechanics" includes all numeric and logical elements of the game that contribute to game play; for example, a game's mechanics might consist of its rules, the number and type of game decks, and the numbers or gameplay actions on those cards. It can be challenging to design mechanics that lead to well-balanced games. Variables include: the number of players; the time it takes to learn the rules; the time it takes to play; replay value; cooperative versus competitive paradigms; the ability to rebound from a losing streak; and the variety of winning strategies. The story, flavor text, and art rest on top of the mechanics.

We initially explored creating game mechanics from scratch. However, since we are computer security researchers and not experts in game mechanics, we chose to license a system from a pre-existing game and then create all new game content. This approach allowed us to forgo playtesting the mechanics—a necessary, time-consuming step to ensure game balance and enjoyment. We did do playtesting to review our game content, which we discuss in Section 3.2.

We explored the rules and mechanics of a number of games available for sale in gaming stores for a game that would support our desired design goals. For example, we wanted a game where a player took on the role of a character, so that they could identify with someone in the computer security field (Perception Goals); we immediately gravitated towards games whose characters featured a variety of skills, in order to highlight the somewhat eclectic specializations that can help improve—or break—a system's security. We also wanted a game that would naturally support a variety of textually-heavy scenarios or encounters.

We licensed the *Ninja Burger* mechanic from Steve Jackson Games [28], best known for their *Munchkin* card game and the *GURPS* roleplaying system. Ninja Burger met our above criteria, and we transformed the game into *Control-Alt-Hack: White Hat Hacking for Fun and Profit*. Instead of delivering burgers in fun scenarios in the quest to become the next branch manager, our players tackle a range of technically-themed scenarios with the goal of becoming the next company CEO.

3.2 Feedback Process

We solicited feedback on iterations of the Control-Alt-Hack card deck to gather suggestions to improve the game and assess its ability to meet our goals. These formative evaluations took the form of playtest sessions or "show and tell" sessions, and were conducted with a variety of parties, including: undergraduates in an introductory computer science course (n=10); undergraduates involved in a computer security competition (n=5); graduate students affiliated with a computer security lab (n=8); graduate students (unaffiliated with a security lab) who have an interest in gaming (n=2); computer science professors (n=2); a computer science lecturer (n=1); a former high school teacher of computer science, now an undergraduate lecturer (n=1); outreach officers (n=3); and assorted non-experts (n=14). In response to this evaluation feedback, we: changed specific card text, modified art, and added new cards to help keep track of gameplay decisions.

3.3 Brief Overview of Control-Alt-Hack

The following is the premise of the game:

> *You and your fellow players work for Hackers, Inc.: a small, elite computer security company of ethical (a.k.a., white hat) hackers who perform security audits and provide consultation services. Their motto? "You Pay Us to Hack You."*
>
> *Your job is centered around Missions—tasks that require you to apply your hacker skills (and a bit of luck) in order to succeed. Use your Social Engineering and Network Ninja skills to break the region's power grid, or apply a bit of Hardware Hacking and Software Wizardry to convert your*

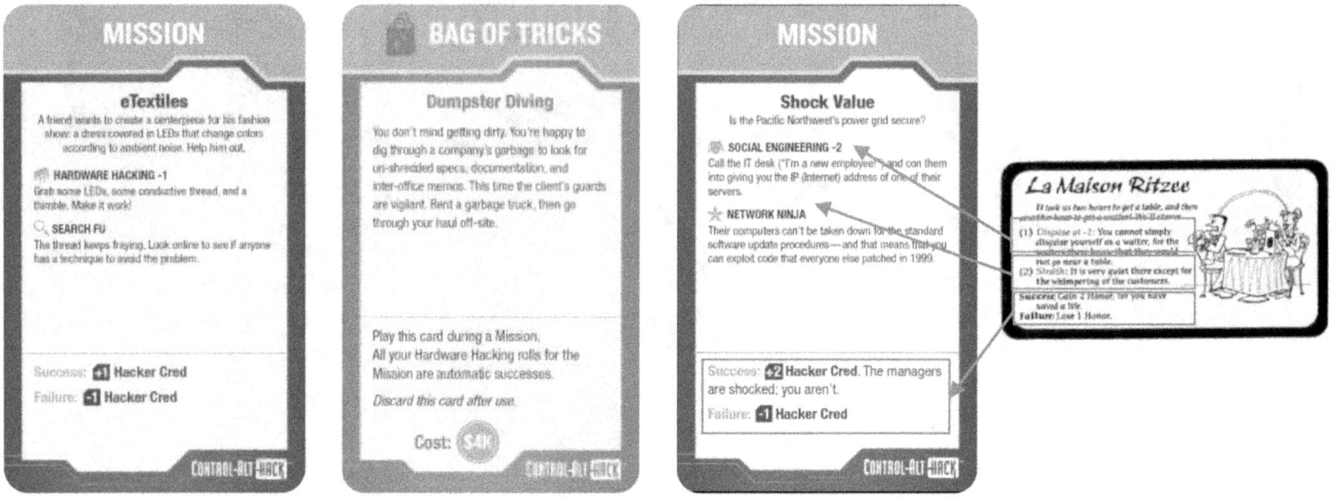

Figure 3. From left to right: (a) a Mission demonstrating the usage of technical skills for artistic purposes (Perception Goal (2)); (b) a Bag of Tricks card illustrating a particular attack threat (Awareness Goal (3)); and (c) a Mission describing a social engineering attack on an SCADA system (Awareness Goals (2) & (3)), along with the mappings to the original Ninja Burger card. © University of Washington

robotic vacuum cleaner into an interactive pet toy...no two jobs are the same. So pick up the dice, and get hacking!

Figure 1 shows the game box and contents. Figures 2 and 3 show some of the game art and card contents.

Each turn each player attempts a single Mission, so players get to see a number of Missions throughout the course of the game. By incorporating a large number of technologies and security threats into the Mission narratives, we communicate a variety of security ideas throughout the course of the game.

3.4 Juggling Design Constraints

Our game creation process was driven by goals and constraints, some occasionally in direct conflict; seeking optimal solutions (or pleasing compromises) took significant effort and iteration.

3.4.1 Text

In creating the cards' textual content, we balanced a number of goals and restrictions: (1) Including Technical Content; (2) Mapping Game Mechanics; (3) Offering Comprehensibility; (4) Maintaining Brevity; and (5) Incorporating Humor.

Including Technical Content. We began by creating a list of the content we wanted to cover in order to address our Awareness Goals and convey the range and depth of computer security issues: we brainstormed lists of technologies, attacks, defenses, attacker types, and the range of human assets that can be impacted by system breaches. Table 7 in the Appendix (Section A.1) gives some sample card titles and topics, along with examples of specific research that inspired their inclusion. We sought topics that would be relevant and interesting to players through personal (e.g., social networks), educational (e.g., browser cookies), or professional experience (e.g., patching) or through the news and media (e.g., credit card theft). During the Feedback Process (Section 3.2), we solicited feedback on the selection and technical accuracy of the content which we portrayed.

Most of the game relates to computer security: of the 56 Mission cards, 44 deal directly with security topics, 6 with technological activities (as in Figure 3a), and the remaining 6 deal with related topics like puzzles, the role of computer security in history, or the value of professional networking. For content balance and enjoyability, we intentionally did not want all of the cards to focus on computer security topics.

Mapping Game Mechanics. The characters, their skills, and the Missions—which require the use of various combinations of those skills—in Control-Alt-Hack are isomorphic to those in Ninja Burger in order to preserve game balance. Significant iteration and exploration was required to create reasonably realistic and fun story justifications for the combinations of skills required for all 56 Missions. See the Mission "Shock Value" in Figure 3(c) for an example where it was necessary to invent an attack requiring Social Engineering and Network Ninja skills, along with a mapping from the original Ninja Burger card. Similar effort was required to create content for the game's 72 Entropy cards and 16 Hacker cards.

Offering Comprehensibility. Given our target audience (Section 2.3), our goal of creating enthusiasm for computer security and computer science (Perception Goals), and our desire to reach a broad audience (Exposure Goal), we needed to make our text understandable to those without extensive security experience—without sacrificing technical integrity. We attempted to always make the meaning of terms implicitly clear, explicitly clear, or irrelevant to understanding the overall gist of the card. For example, "Shock Value" in Figure 3(c) parenthetically defines an IP address as an Internet address, and "Dumpster Diving" in Figure 3(b) defines dumpster diving within the text of the card.

Observe how this latter card also incorporates additional learning content: the card helps illustrate that defensive measures (guards, in this case) are not always effective, and that the creativity of attackers can be surprising (such as renting a garbage truck, which many people may not have thought possible).

Incorporating Humor. We incorporated humor into the game in order to make it more enjoyable. The humor primarily (but not exclusively) took the form of: (1) puns; (2) popular culture references; or (3) sexual innuendo, although we attempted to keep the innuendo tasteful and respectful, and we evaluated the cards with stakeholder groups prior to finalizing them (Section 3.2). For example, "Shock Value" in Figure 4(c) has puns, and "eTextiles" in Figure 3(a) has a popular culture reference in its Hardware Hacking task.

Responding Participant	Course	Class Size	Student Level	Prior Security Experience	Would have covered [the security material in Control-Alt-Hack] otherwise?	Time Taken	Supplementary assignment involving Control-Alt-Hack
E1-classroom	Information Software Technology	30	HS	No / Some Informal	Yes	60 min	No
E4-classroom	Unknown	12	UG	No / Some Informal	Yes	50 min	Yes
E6-classroom	Computer Science	75	HS	Some Informal	No	75 min	No
E7-classroom	Cyber-Security and Information Assurance	56	UG	No / Some Informal	Yes	120 min	Yes
E8-classroom	Computer and Network Security	10	UG, G	Some Informal / Prior Educational	Yes	120 min	No
E9-classroom	Computers and Information Technology	60	HS	Prior Educational	No	75 min	No
E10-classroom	Game Design	65	HS	No / Some Informal	Yes	90 min	Yes
E12-classroom	Computer Security	22	UG	Prior Educational	No*	80 min	Yes
E13-classroom	IT Security	8	UG	Prior Educational	Yes	45 min	No
E14-classroom	Information Security	15	UG	Some Informal / Prior Educational	Yes	120 min	No
E16-classroom	Intro CS Web Design	35	HS	No	Yes	40 min	No
E17-classroom	Cyber Security	2	HS	Prior Educational	Yes	30 min	No
E18-classroom	Fundamentals of Information Security	30	UG	No / Some Informal / Prior Educational / Prior Professional	Yes	75 min	Yes
E19-classroom	Computer and Network Security	27	UG	No / Some Informal	Yes	60 min	No

Table 1. Classroom-based educator activity contexts. The shaded cells represent cases of interest, some of which are discussed in Sections 6.4 and A.4. HS = high school; UG = undergraduate; G = graduate.

*We believe this response to be an error or a misinterpretation of the question's meaning.

3.4.2 Visuals

We directed illustration and graphic design as part of the game's content creation process. We purposefully allocated a non-trivial portion of our resources to these visuals for two reasons: (a) to make it easier for players to identify with and project themselves onto Hacker characters (Perception Goals); and (b) to make the game visually appealing, hopefully attracting players (Exposure Goal) and implicitly showing that a focus on technology does not preclude placing importance on aesthetics (Perception Goals).

In creating Hacker portraits, we addressed the Perception and Exposure Goals by balancing the characters' genders and ethnicities and by showing them engaging in a variety of hobbies. Figure 2 shows the character art from the portrait side of 12 of the 16 Hacker cards.

Table 2. Non-classroom-based educator activity contexts

	Context	Time Taken
E2-ACM	Extra-curricular activity with undergrads in the ACM	150 min
E3-vetting	University instructors vetting the game	150 min
E5-no-play*	Instructor vetting the game with adult friends*	N/A*
E11-checkout	Provided as a checkout for students to play with friend and family	150 min
E15-vetting	Instructor vetting with graduate students, faculty, and staff	60 min
E20-vetting-didn't-read**	Instructor vetting**	N/A**
E21-lunch	Departmental staff lunch	60 min
E22-vetting	Instructor vetting	90 min

*After reading the rules, they did not understand how to play, so they stopped.

**The instructor chose not to read cards or play due to the list of PG-14 cards supplied on the web site.

4. DISTRIBUTION, EXPOSURE, AND PRELIMINARY IMPACT

In order to reach a diverse set of audiences (Exposure Goal), we chose to make Control-Alt-Hack available via two different avenues:

(1) Available for free to educators who submit a request via http://www.controlalthack.com. As of July 2013, the supply of games allocated to educators has been nearly depleted.

(2) Available for sale on Amazon.com via RGB Hats, LLC, which was founded by two of the co-authors and which licensed the game from the University of Washington. This distribution method also allows production of the game to be self-sustaining.

From when the game was made available in November through March, we shipped approximately 800 copies of the game to 150 different educators who requested copies. Approximately 50 copies were also handed out at the SIGCSE 2013 poster session. Together, these educators served as the recruitment pool for our summative evaluation of the game (Section 6). Additionally, over

	Positive Functions		Critiques				
	Social / Engagement	Awareness	Takes a long time to learn	Takes a long time to play	Not enough fun	Not enough educational value	Has inappropriate content
E1-classroom	X	X	X	X			
E4-classroom	X	X					
E6-classroom	X		X				
E7-classroom	X	X					
E8-classroom	X	X				X	
E9-classroom	X	X	X				
E10-classroom	X	X					
E12-classroom		X		X		X	
E13-classroom	X		X			X	
E14-classroom	X	X	X	X			
E16-classroom		X	X				
E17-classroom						X	
E18-classroom	X	X	X				
E19-classroom	X	X					

Table 3. Classroom-based educator survey analysis results.

300 copies have been distributed at a variety of NSF-sponsored job fairs, competitions, and similar events.

We were invited to present a talk on the game at a large web company's internal security training conference, and an optional play session was held at the conclusion of the hands-on training.

5. EVALUATION METHOD

In this paper we present evaluations of Control-Alt-Hack via two methods:

- **Primary:** Feedback surveys from educators who requested copies of the game; and
- **Secondary:** User studies performed with the game.

Both methods were approved by the University of Washington's Human Subjects Institutional Review Board.

5.1 Educator Feedback Surveys

We distributed online feedback surveys via email to the 150 instructors who received educator copies prior to May 2013. Section A.2 in the Appendix shows the questions asked on the educator survey. 22 educators submitted responses to the surveys.

Coding. Two researchers analyzed the survey responses independently and formed preliminary opinions about the categories that emerged from the data. The researchers then compared the categories and formed a cohesive coding scheme via consensus. The primary coder recoded the educator surveys according to this coding scheme. (Complying with our institution's conflict management plan, one of the researchers has no financial interest in RGB Hats, LLC.) In the evaluation, we used the survey in its entirety as the unit of analysis, rather than individual responses; that is to say, if part of an educator's response received the code "Awareness," it did not matter which question on the survey elicited the relevant response, and it did not matter how many times the survey was coded for "Awareness."

The primary coder and the secondary coder had 93% agreement across all educator surveys (N=22) and codes (N=7); there were 11 cases where the primary and the reliability coder disagreed. All cases are provided in the Appendix (Section A.3), along with contextual quotes. Except for one case in which the reliability coder misread the data and coded an error, the primary coder's results—the results reported in the paper—always represent the stricter of the two viewpoints. That is, we report the upper bound on our interpretation of the critiques to the game and the lower bound on the game's role in engagement and awareness.

The primary and secondary coders independently labeled educator activities as classroom-based or non-classroom-based activities; they had 100% agreement. Tables 1 and 2 list information about classroom- and non-classroom-based activities, respectively.

5.2 User Studies

We posted recruitment ads inviting participants to join us for a games study session on: an institution-wide electronic bulletin board; and in the local Craigslist gigs listings. We held two game study sessions: one with 7 people (M=3, F=4) divided into two gameplay groups; and one with 4 people in one gameplay group (M=1, F=3). The participants covered a range of ages (mean=31, min=18, max=50, median=29). 5 of the participants could be categorized as "hobbyist" gamers, and 6 had casual or little gaming experience. Each session lasted approximately 2 hours. Participants were compensated $20 for their time. Following consent paperwork, participants filled out a short pre-gameplay survey. After this participants were shown a 15-minute video introducing them to gameplay; we used a video for consistency between sessions. Participants played for 40-60 minutes, then filled out a short post-gameplay questionnaire.

Coding. Two researchers independently analyzed the survey responses for themes and categories. (Complying with our institution's conflict management plan, one of the researchers has no financial interest in RGB Hats, LLC.) The researchers discussed and came to a consensus regarding the data of interest in the survey responses. The data in question is presented as direct quotations, and the goal mappings were decided via consensus coding.

6. EDUCATOR SURVEY RESULTS

The 22 educators who responded to the survey used the game with over 450 students at the high school, undergraduate, and graduate levels in computer science, computer security, and game design courses. These courses were primarily, although not exclusively, based in the United States. The educator survey results are the primary evaluation of Control-Alt-Hack in this study.

As previously mentioned, the educator survey responses fell into one of two categories: feedback about an activity using Control-Alt-Hack that took place in a classroom, or feedback about an activity using Control-Alt-Hack that took place outside of a classroom. Many of the reported non-classroom activities were from educators who were vetting the game for classroom use, and subsequently decided not to use the game; the other non-classroom activities were an ACM gathering, a lunch activity, and offering the game to students to check out and take home. Table 1 provides additional information on the classroom activities (N=14), and Table 2 provides additional information on the non-classroom activities (N=8).

6.1 Positive Functions

Appreciation of the game expressed in educator surveys generally described the game as fulfilling one of two functions: being fun or serving a social function (Social/Engagement); or increasing students' awareness of computer security or computer science issues (Awareness).

Social/Engagement (Classroom: 11/14; Non-Classroom: 2/8). "Social/Engagement" was marked when the educator was deemed to be indicating that usage of the game was fun, engaging, and/or contributed to serve a social function, such as an icebreaker or a breather before a test. The following quotes are two examples:

- **E7-classroom (56 undergraduates, Cyber-Security and Information Awareness):** *"It worked as a way to break the ice and get students from diverse majors get to know [sic] each other and get thinking about the topics of the course."*
- **E19-classroom (27 undergraduates, Computer and Network Security):** *"I just wanted to reiterate how great my students thought the game was! The students begged me to leave the game in the student lounge so they could continue to play, and from what I hear it's made a trip or two out to our weekly majors night at the pub."*

Awareness (Classroom: 11/14; Non-Classroom: 1/8). "Awareness" was marked when the educator was deemed to be indicating that usage of the game served to increase students' awareness of security in some fashion, such as: increasing exposure to domain terminology; raising awareness of career opportunities; stimulating discussion; or stimulating critical thinking. The following quotes are two examples:

- **E9-classroom (60 high school students, Computers and Information Technology):** *"The game did not necessarily teach security methods, but it did a great job of teaching vocabulary and literacy."…"It increased awareness of my program, and it got more students interested in computer science."*
- **E19-classroom (27 undergraduates, Computer and Network Security):** *"They really got into it and there was a lot of strategizing"…"They were mainly focused on causing pain to their classmates, but as I wandered around the room I heard some great discussions about the tradeoffs of choosing various hackers' skill sets, what various missions meant, etc."*

Table 3 shows the Positive Functions results from the classroom-based educator responses, and Table 4 shows the results from the non-classroom-based educator responses.

Overall, in the classroom contexts, 11 of the 14 educators indicated that the game served a Social/Engagement role, and a different set of 11 educators indicated that the game served to increase Awareness. For the educators who did not provide responses that indicated that the game raised awareness, two were courses about computer security; these educators also indicated that the game did not have enough educational content (Section 6.2). This suggests that although our design goals were aligned with the intentions of educators not already teaching a computer security course, the goals were not well aligned with some educators' intentions in using the game in security-focused courses.

In the non-classroom contexts, 2 of the educators' responses indicated that the game filled a Social/Engagement role (E2-ACM, E15-vetting), and 1 of the educators indicated that the

	Positive Functions		Critiques				
	Social / Engagement	Awareness	Takes a long time to learn	Takes a long time to play	Not enough fun	Not enough educational value	Has inappropriate content
E2-ACM	X	X				X	
E3-vetting					X	X	
E5-no-play*			X				
E11-checkout						X	
E15-vetting	X		X			X	
E20-vetting-didn't-read**							X
E21-lunch			X				
E22-vetting					X	X	

Table 4. Non-classroom-based educator survey analysis results.

*Educator did not play the game due to not understanding the rules.

**The educator did not read the cards, but responded based on the list of PG-14 cards listed on the website.

game helped increase Awareness (E2-ACM). The relative lack of educators reporting positive game functions in non-classroom activities could be a result of the fact that many of the responses in the non-classroom context were from educators who played the game (or not, in 2 cases) out of the classroom in order to vet it for its suitability for use in the classroom. In many of those cases, the educator decided not to use Control-Alt-Hack in the classroom (Section 6.3 and Table 5), so it is not surprising that they do not comment that the game serves positive functions.

6.1.1 Discussion

Overall, we find that the feedback on the game—in the classrooms in which it was used—shows promising indications that it performs multiple positive functions.

Awareness. In most of the surveys, educators' comments indicated that the game helped raise students' awareness of issues related to computer security. Raising individuals' awareness of the risks, challenges, technologies, and professions involved in computer security was a large part of our purpose in creating the game (Goals, Section 2.1).

Social/Engagement. Again in most of the surveys, educators' comments indicated that the game served a Social/Engagement role in the classroom. This is promising for two reasons: first, it is somewhat correlated with "fun," which can increase engagement or encourage people outside of the classroom to pick up the game. Second, some of the educators used the game specifically because they had need of a non-traditional educational activity; Section 6.4 explores the cases where the educators used the game, but would not have otherwise covered comparable security material. The apparent success of the game's Social/Engagement function, as represented in the evaluation, suggests that the produced game is aligned with our Exposure Goal.

6.2 Critiques and Tradeoffs

The critiques of the game contained in educators' responses were analyzed as falling into one or more of five somewhat self-explanatory statements: (1) Takes a long time to learn; (2) Takes a long time to play; (3) Not enough fun; (4) Not enough educational value; and (5) Has inappropriate content. We discuss the critiques at some length because many of them directly reflect the design tradeoffs that we selected to meet our intended goals.

Takes a long time to learn. Examples:

- **E5-no-play:** *"Honestly, after reading over the rules, we didn't understand how to play it, and we gave up. So sorry!"*
- **E15-vetting:** *"The game itself is too complex to easily teach and use for the first time."*

Following the shipment of the game to educators, we have created a new video that walks viewers through game setup and gameplay in a shorter, clearer format (a video of an hour-long conference talk was previously available which contained an explanation of how to play), which we will publish online; the new video is 10 minutes long. Some of the learning curve is due to the complexity of the game mechanics that we chose (Section 3.1); however, we accepted a level of complexity as a good tradeoff for increased replay value and the in-game opportunities to strategize.

Takes a long time to play. Examples:

- **E14-classroom (15 undergraduates, Information Security):** *"Shorten the game and eliminate some components."*
- **E12-classroom (22 undergraduates, Computer Security):** *"Students reported that they enjoyed the game, but that the hour twenty was pushing the limit."*

Gameplay duration can vary depending upon the number of players, players' familiarity with the rules, and the emergent characteristics of a particular game instance. Potentially long gameplay can make the game unwieldy for the classroom setting; however, the gameplay duration can be an asset in other social settings. Many educators indicated positive results even when playing a version of the game truncated to fit into a class period.

Not enough fun. One example (the only other instance an example of coder disagreement, and is given in the Appendix):

- **E3-vetting:** *"The feedback from the instructors trying the game is that it didn't seem very enjoyable to play or strategic. It may be that more experience will change this, but the first impression was not positive."*

While the players in the above example (adult instructors) are not our primary target audience, there is no guarantee that the instructors' students would have found the game fun. We do not have sufficient data to confidently predict who will or will not enjoy the game; nevertheless, observation and anecdotes suggest at the very least that if the audience is familiar with and enjoys the style of game on which Control-Alt-Hack is based, then it is relatively likely that they will find the game fun.

Not enough educational value. Examples:

- **E11-checkout:** *"The game could use more specificity around computer activity. My students were hoping for a higher level of rigor."*
- **E17-classroom:** *"Since we approached the game expecting to be tested on our knowledge of vulnerabilities and penetration techniques, we were dissatisfied in that manner, but we enjoyed the overall concept."*

We intentionally chose a lower level of technical depth in the design phase in order to further the Exposure Goal and be comprehensible to a wider portion of our target audience; in the case of these classrooms that decision was not well aligned with instructors' intentions. We recognize that the game is not a good fit for students with a more advanced security background who are hoping to learn new material; this would only be accomplished if the game were paired with a supplementary activity, as some educators chose to do (see Section A.4 in Appendix).

Has inappropriate content. There is only one instance of this critique appearing in the data:

- **E20-vetting-didn't-read:** *"I didn't have time to vet the game for appropriateness and, from what I did read on the above site, I felt that the cards significantly contributed to a learning environment hostile to women."*

We do not wish to create an environment hostile to women, and kept gender issues at the forefront of our minds during game development. We took care to make references gender-neutral or gender-balanced: for example, the CEO is a woman, half of the Hacker cards are female, and with one exception, all innuendo is gender-neutral (a Mission card about cell phone security has the title "That's What She Said"). We recognize that innuendo can make an environment more hostile to women, particularly if the environment already has uncomfortable overtones; however, during the design phase we gathered feedback on the appropriateness of our content from multiple parties, including a former (female) teacher of high school computer science and 3 (female) outreach officers (Section 3.2), and incorporated it into the game. For example, we redid the style of dress of one of the female Hackers in response to their comments. The materials we distribute to educators included a list of PG-14 cards which can be reviewed for content and/or removed from the deck.

6.2.1 Discussion

Table 3 presents the classroom-based educator experiences coded for the goals and critiques; Table 4 presents the same for the non-classroom-based educator experiences.

The most prominent critique was that the game takes a long time to learn (classroom: 4/14, non-classroom: 3/8). From observation and anecdotes, individuals who are familiar with this style of game find it fairly quick to pick up. For example, E13-classroom gave this quote: "*The students with some game experience found it obvious and intuitive. They would say "this is easy."*" Additionally, we suggest that educators could make the start of gameplay smoother by pre-designating individuals to learn the rules and play together ahead of time, so that those individuals can then seed gameplay groups during the activity.

The second most prominent critique was that the game did not have enough educational value (classroom: 4/14, non-classroom: 5/8). As previously mentioned, many of the non-classroom educators reported on the experience wherein they vetted the game, and chose not to use it in their classroom. Control-Alt-Hack may not be suitable for all educational contexts, but its educational value can be increased by pairing it with or using it to bootstrap a level-appropriate supplementary activity, as done by 5 of the classroom educators.

The third most common critique—and the only other critique expressed by educators who used the game in the classroom—was that the game took too long to play. Control-Alt-Hack may not be suitable for all class formats and in all contexts; however, from observation and anecdotes we tentatively find that having more than 4 players in a game significantly extends the duration of gameplay; we therefore suggest staying below 5 players in a game. Responses indicate that there is some value in playing a short game, even if players do not have time to finish; educators who provided as little as 40 minutes of time to play (E16-classroom) reported some positive results. Additionally, gameplay is somewhat modular, with logical periodic stopping points; if players are already familiar with gameplay, then individual rounds are of manageable lengths.

Table 5. Classroom-use and non-classroom-use responses as to whether or not educator would use the game again, and whether or not the educator would suggest the game to others.

Group	Educator	Would Use Again	Would Suggest to Others
Classroom	E1-classroom	Yes	Yes
	E4-classroom	Yes	Yes
	E6-classroom	No	Yes
	E7-classroom	Yes	Yes
	E8-classroom	No*	Yes
	E9-classroom	Yes	Yes
	E10-classroom	Yes	Yes
	E12-classroom	No**	Yes
	E13-classroom	Yes	Yes
	E14-classroom	Yes	Yes
	E16-classroom	Yes	Yes
	E17-classroom	No	No
	E18-classroom	Yes	Yes
	E19-classroom	Yes	Yes
Non-Classroom	E2-ACM	Yes	Yes
	E3-vetting	No	No
	E5-no-play	No	No
	E11-checkout	Yes	Yes
	E15-vetting	No	No
	E20-vetting-didn't-read	No	No
	E21-lunch	Yes***	Yes***
	E22-vetting	No	No

*Might instead use with high school students or interns.

**Not in class because of time constraints. Maybe as an out-of-class exercise.

***Yes, but only with additional material, and dependent upon going over it a few more times to understand how to incorporate.

6.3 "Would Use Again"

To serve as an overall assessment of the game's usefulness, we asked educators the following questions on the surveys:

> *Would you use Control-Alt-Hack again in your classroom? Why or why not?*
>
> *Would you suggest Control-Alt-Hack to others? Why or why not?*

Educators' responses are given in Table 5. Overall, the results are promising. 13 of the 14 educators who used the game in their classrooms reported that they would suggest the game to others, and 10 of them reported that they would use Control-Alt-Hack again. E8-classroom responded that they would not use the game with those who already had some familiarity with the subject, but might with high school students or interns, and E12-classroom clarified that they would not use the game again in class due to time constraints, but might as an out-of-class exercise; for both of these educators, this suggests that they still find merit in the game, even if it is not an appropriate match for their instructional needs. E17-classroom indicated elsewhere in responses that the game did not contain sufficient educational content (Table 3), so we surmise that is why they will not use the game again or recommend it to others. As mentioned in the previous section, the educational level of our game was an intentional decision related to our Primary Audience and Exposure Goals (Section 2).

For the non-classroom experiences with the game, 5 of the educators were playing the game with other instructors, friends, graduate students, or staff to vet its use, and did not subsequently report on using the game in their classrooms. The remaining 3 educators would use the game again and would suggest it to others (E2-ACM, E11-checkout, and E21-lunch). E21-lunch clarified that they might use the game again and recommend it to others, but only with supplementary educational material and after further consideration. These three scenarios—an extracurricular club, a checkout, and a staff lunch—are highly aligned with the social, ad hoc interaction model supported by choosing to create a recreational game.

6.4 Reaching New Audiences

Interestingly, 2 of the 14 educators who used Control-Alt-Hack in their classrooms reported that they would not have covered similar security material in any other format. An additional educator gave this response, but was teaching a computer security course (E12-classroom), so this response may have been in error or a misinterpretation of our intention when posing the question (*If you had not used Control-Alt-Hack, would you still have covered the material?*); it is also possible that the educator intended to convey that they would not have covered topics included in the game such as physical security or cyber-physical security. We are conservative and count this response as an error. If the educators in the remaining contexts would not have covered

	Participant quote	Goal Mappings
A	"Slightly. I was aware that active testing and debugging are needed to improve security + add to innovation, but the reminder was helpful. The game led me to think about some aspects of modern life I don't usually consider."	Awareness #2: Breadth of Technologies
B	"I have to be honest and say that I've never heard of a "white hat" hacker before. I've always associated hackers with a negative term. Computer security consists of a lot more tasks than I had at first thought it had. Computer security applies to a lot of areas, like cars and phone apps, which I hadn't thought of."†	Awareness #2: Breadth of Technologies
C	---	
D	---	
E	"Not much. There was stuff such as not leaving laptops or usb drives out where others can get at them that I had known about but never gave much thought to before."	Awareness #3: Creativity of Adversaries
F	"Little bit w/ thinking of different scenarios like the small level computer hacking. In general I think of bigger hacking crimes when I think of hacking."	Awareness #1: Importance/Impact of Security* Awareness #2: Breadth of Technologies*
G	"No except that hacking might be fun – to use the knowledge to help solve a problem."	Perception #2: Professional Opportunities*
L	---	
M	"Yes. I didn't give much thought to it before or how many different ways it could be approached."	Awareness #3: Creativity of Adversaries*
N	"No, except that its [sic] very complicated."	Awareness #3: Creativity of Adversaries*
O	"Certainly lightens the mood for my outlook on C.S. and sheds some light for understanding reality of tasks involved."	Perception #1: Counter-Stereotype Awareness #3: Creativity of Adversaries*

†This was actually in response to the question: *Now that you've performed the activity, what do you think of when you think of computer security? (This may or may not have changed.)*

*These goals are only potentially implicated in the response. We invite the reader to perform personal interpretations.

Table 6. User responses and mappings to our design goals. Participants with no quotes did not provide evidence indicating that their awareness or perception of computer security changed. Project goals are fully articulated in Section 2.1.

comparable security material, however, then these classrooms represent instances where the game can serve to increase security awareness, presumably precisely because of its non-traditional format:

- E6-classroom: 75 high school students in a Computer Science course with some prior informal security experience.
- E9-classroom: 60 high school students in a Computers and Information Technology course with prior educational security experience.

This exposure of individuals in our Primary Audience (Section 2.3) to more security content than they might otherwise have been exposed is an indication of success.

7. USER STUDY RESULTS

With the educator surveys—the primary evaluation method of Control-Alt-Hack in this study—we gained the valuable perspectives of informed and expert individuals, as well as secondhand access to a large population of students. We also, however, wished to more directly study individuals' experiences with the game, and therefore performed a supplementary user study. We primarily simulated the experience of individuals of varying backgrounds picking up and playing the game in a non-classroom-setting. Section 5.2 provides background on the participants.

In performing the user study, we received participant responses that indicated that—at least in the short term—we are increasing or reinforcing participants' awareness and/or improving their perception of computer security and computer science, as per our Awareness and Perception Goals articulated in Section 2.1.

Table 6 presents participant quotes in response to the prompt on the post-gameplay questionnaire:

> *After performing the activity, some people say that their perception of computer security has changed, while others don't feel that it has changed much at all. Would you say that your perception of computer security has changed? If so, how?*

8 of the 11 participants provided responses which gave some indication that their awareness of computer security issues increased or their perceptions about the field were changed. Interestingly, even though some of these participants responded that their perception of computer security had not changed (2 out of the 8), they proceeded to elaborate and provide qualitative evidence that they were engaged with one of our learning goals. For the remaining 3 participants, none of their responses suggested that their awareness had increased or that their perceptions had changed. Some participants (3/11) supplied critiques on the game; however, the sentiments in those critiques are covered by the educators' critiques (Section 6.2), and we do not discuss them further here.

There is a range of participant responses present even in our small sample size. The Goal Mappings column provides a loose mapping from the participant's response to our project goals; the process is subjective, and we invite readers to interpret different mappings from participant responses to project goals.

The project goals are fully articulated in Section 2.1, but they might be paraphrased and shortened as follows:

- Awareness Goal #1: Importance/Impact of Security;
- Awareness Goal #2: Breadth of Technologies;
- Awareness Goal #3: Creativity of Adversaries;
- Perception Goal #1: Counter-Stereotype; and
- Perception Goal #2: Professional Opportunities.

All of the goals appear at least once in Table 6, suggesting that we have had some success in crafting the game to touch upon the issues in question.

8. REFLECTIONS

We take this opportunity to discuss some of our reflections from going through the process of creating, distributing, and evaluating a computer security-themed tabletop card game for the purpose of promoting computer security awareness and education.

Physical Games in Security Education. There is a long history of using games in education (Section 9), and our work further attests to the benefits and value of using a game—and in our case, a physical game—in educational settings. Such games do not always match the needs of the relevant educators, but when they do match, they can provide valuable catalysts for engaging students and achieving certain learning objectives—in our case, our Awareness and Perception goals.

Game Mechanics Tradeoffs. Our main observations concern the selection of game mechanics. Overall, working with pre-existing mechanics was a positive experience, especially given our lack of expertise in the area. We wish to re-emphasize, however, the fact that mechanics directly dictate or heavily influence gameplay properties, including: how long it takes to learn to play a game; how long games take to play; the replay value of a game; and the ability to form diverse strategies. Additionally, we were particularly interested in how much textual content could be inserted into the game. These variables, which ultimately contribute to an (unclearly defined) function that dictates gameplay enjoyment, are somewhat interdependent. For example, the replay value of a game is somewhat dictated by how much the game facilitates strategizing; a game's available strategies, in turn, have some relationship with the complexity of the game's rules, which directly affects the amount of time that it takes to learn a game, and partially affects the amount of time that it takes to play a game.

While these gameplay properties do not have clean-cut direct or inverse relationships, they nonetheless impact one another. When choosing or creating gameplay mechanics, sometimes tradeoffs will be necessary. It is critical to prioritize these properties in order to attempt to achieve an optimal fit.

Communication and Representation. One of our takeaways from the educator surveys was the relative importance of communicating to educators the exact nature of the game that we were distributing. While we did distribute cover letters with shipped games, they were insufficiently precise regarding the nature of the game. We never intended to design a game to teach penetration testing methods. Educators have a number of responsibilities, and may be too busy to fully vet a game before its use; it is therefore critical to provide as much information as possible regarding the nature of a game and its intended usage scenarios.

Graphic Design and Illustration. While we did not attempt to directly measure the contribution of the aesthetics of the game to achieving our goals, we do not wish to suggest its irrelevance by eliminating it from the discussion. From observation, we can comment that the graphic design, illustration, and production quality of the game seem to have a large effect at least on its initial reception. Perhaps the most poignant repeated comment that we have received upon presenting the game to others is, "It's like a real game!" The difference between these individuals' apparent expectations and their reaction to Control-Alt-Hack is an implicit commentary on their expectations regarding "educational games." Further study could help place the relevance of game aesthetics in the context of overall success.

9. RELATED WORK

We separate our discussion of related work into work on commercial games and games created more as research endeavors.

9.1 Commercial Games

Previous commercial tabletop card games dealing with computer security include games such as Fantasy Flight Games' *Android: Netrunner*, published in 2012, and Steve Jackson Game's *Hacker*, published in 1992 (now out of print). We believe that our contribution is distinct in several ways. First, we take many opportunities to ground our card contents in a variety of current technologies and actual attack threats (see Section A.1 and Table 7 in Appendix). While this means that Control-Alt-Hack is at risk of becoming outdated, this also means that it is particularly topical. Second, while these games undoubtedly helped—and continue to help—attract people to computer science and computer security, they portray hacking—and hackers—in the style of a particular niche (although compelling) subculture. We chose, primarily via graphic design and illustration choices, to embrace a more non-traditional hacker "tone" in the hopes of connecting with a slightly different audience. Third, since we created our card game specifically with awareness goals in mind, we are also contributing an evaluation of our game in education contexts.

9.2 Games in Research

Gondree et al. [11] gives an overview of some of the benefits of using casual games to impart modest security information; they reference Klopfer et al.'s [14] five freedoms essential to play, and reinterpret those freedoms as mapping to the adversarial, exploratory aspects of computer security.

[d0x3d!] is a tabletop board game designed to casually introduce a wide audience to some of the terminology and adversarial thinking that is involved in network security [8]. *Exploit!* is a card game that is primarily intended for entertainment for the security audience, not education [5]. *Elevation of Privilege* [18, 27], *Protection Poker* [33], and *OWASP Cornucopia* [20] are meant to help train and augment threat modeling and risk assessment in software development.

CyberCIEGE [4] and CyberProtect [30] are electronic games that have players act as network administrators who must utilize limited resources to manage overall network risk.

There are a variety of Capture-the-Flag competitions (e.g., [6, 21]), which are competitive and engaging ways to promote or simulate offensive security. There are also some defensive competitions, such as the Collegiate Cyber Defense Competition [19].

Educational research communities have looked at a variety of aspects of using games in education: for example, making educational games adapt to skill level [1], using game development as a vehicle for programming assignments [24], using games to teach specific topics such as computer ethics [2], or using games to teach how to detect phishing emails [25]. We stress, however, that educational games are used to teach a variety of topics beyond computer science or computer security, such as mathematical fractions (e.g., [3]) or algebra (e.g., [31]).

In the context of security education research, but not in the context of games, there have been numerous explorations of methods for helping students learn the technical skills necessary to protect computer systems against attackers (e.g., [17, 32]).

10. CONCLUSION

In this paper we presented the design and evaluation of Control-Alt-Hack, a card game for increasing computer security awareness. Our goal was to generate awareness of security issues and improve the accuracy of people's perception of computer security as a discipline and career choice. Critically, we traded some technical complexity in the topics discussed in exchange for increased engagement: put another way, we set out to create a game that players could find inherently fun, from which they might learn incidentally in the course of enjoying the gameplay.

Our evaluation of the game, primarily derived from the experiences of 22 educators representing over 450 students, suggests that we accomplished our goals. Educators who used the game in their classrooms overwhelmingly indicated that they would suggest the game to others, while the majority reported both that they would use the game again and that students enjoyed the game and experienced increased security awareness. 2 educators teaching non-security computer science courses would not have taught the material without the game. A supplementary evaluation with 11 users suggested that even among a small number of participants, their reactions are aligned with a number of our goals in creating the game.

We view these results as a strong signal suggesting that our game represents an effective model for disseminating ideas and encouraging interest in computer security. We hope that our process for selecting mechanics, designing content, and evaluating our effectiveness is informative to those wishing to undertake similar endeavors, and we hope that further research will explore the usage of educational or awareness-raising games to engage and inspire.

11. ACKNOWLEDGMENTS

This work was supported in part by Intel Labs, an Intel PhD Fellowship, the ACM Special Interest Group on Computer Science Education, and the US National Science Foundation (NSF) under awards CNS-0846065 and CNS-1247216. Any opinions, findings, and conclusions or recommendations expressed in this article are the authors' and don't necessarily reflect the views of the funding agencies.

Tamara Denning and Tadayoshi Kohno are founders and equity owners of RGB Hats, LLC, a private, for-profit company which has licensed the subject technology from the University of Washington. This research is subject to the conditions of a financial conflict of interest management plan established by the University of Washington.

We thank everyone who playtested, provided feedback, or otherwise helped improve the game. We thank those who graciously lent us their names and biographic details: Deborah Alterman, Mike Clarke, Alexei Czeskis, Karla Danson, Iva Dermendjieva, Miro Enev, Roxana Geambasu, Sidhant Gupta, Dan Halperin, Melody Kadenko, Karl Koscher, Gabe Maganis, Cynthia Matuszek, Temitope Oluwafemi, Franzi Roesner. We thank Steve Jackson for licensing his game and providing feedback, and Deborah Alterman and Mike Clarke at the University of Washington's Center for Commercialization for helping obtain the license. We also thank and acknowledge the following people: Gravity Creative (Graphic Design), Rob Kelly (Character Illustrations), Web Design / Development (Thomas Winegarden), Juliet Fiss (Product Photos), and Tina Wegner (Production Manager).

12. REFERENCES

[1] E. Andersen. Optimizing Adaptivity in Educational Games. Foundations of Digital Games, 2012.

[2] B. Brinkman. The Heart of a Whistle-blower: A Corporate Decision-Making Game for Computer Ethics Classes. SIGCSE Technical Symposium, 2009.

[3] Center for Game Science. Refraction. http://centerforgamescience.org/portfolio/refraction/.

[4] The Center for Information Systems Security Studies and Research, Naval Postgraduate School. CyberCIEGE. http://cisr.nps.edu/cyberciege/.

[5] Core Impact. Exploit! http://www.coresecurity.com.

[6] DEF CON. DEF CON Capture the Flag. https://www.defcon.org/html/links/dc-ctf.html.

[7] T. Denning, C. Matuszek, K. Koscher, J. R. Smith, and T. Kohno. A Spotlight on Security and Privacy Risks with Future Household Robots: Attacks and Lessons. Ubicomp, 2009.

[8] [d0x3d!]. http://www.d0x3d.com.

[9] S. Drimer and S. J. Murdoch. Keep Your Enemies Close: Distance Bounding Against Smartcard Relay Attacks. USENIX Security, 2007.

[10] A. J. Feldman, J. A. Halderman, and E. W. Felten. Security Analysis of the Diebold AccuVote-TS Voting Machine. Electronic Voting Technology Workshop, 2007.

[11] M. Gondree, Z. N.J. Peterson, and T. Denning. Security through Play. *IEEE Security & Privacy*, 11(3), 2013.

[12] G. Gu, J. Zhang, and W. Lee. BotSniffer: Detecting Botnet Command and Control Channels in Network Traffic. Network and Distributed System Security Symposium (NDSS), 2008.

[13] M. Hicks, M. Finnicum, S.T. King, M. Martin, J.M. Smith. Overcoming an Untrusted Computing Base: Detecting and Removing Malicious Hardware Automatically. IEEE Symposium on Security and Privacy, 2010.

[14] E. Klopfer, S. Osterweil, and K. Salen, Moving Learning Games Forward: Obstacles, Opportunities, and Openness. The Education Arcade, 2009.

[15] K. Koscher, A. Czeskis, F. Roesner, S. Patel, T. Kohno, S. Checkoway, D. McCoy, B. Kantor, D. Anderson, H. Shacham, and S. Savage. Experimental Security Analysis of a Modern Automobile. IEEE Symposium on Security and Privacy, 2010.

[16] C. Li, A. Raghunathan, N.K. Jha. Hijacking an Insulin Pump: Security Attacks and Defenses for a Diabetes Therapy System. Healthcom, 2011.

[17] P. Mateti. A Laboratory-Based Course on Internet Security. SIGCSE Technical Symposium, 2009.

[18] Microsoft. Elevation of Privilege. http://www.microsoft.com/security/sdl/adopt/eop.aspx.

[19] National Collegiate Cyber Defense Competition. http://www.nationalccdc.org/.

[20] OWASP. OWASP Cornucopia Ecommerce Website Edition. https://www.owasp.org/index.php/OWASP_Cornucopia.

[21] PlaidCTF. http://play.plaidctf.com.

[22] A. Rabkin. Personal Knowledge Questions for Fallback Authentication: Security Questions in the Era of Facebook. Symposium On Usable Privacy and Security (SOUPS), 2008.

[23] F. Roesner, T. Kohno, and D. Wetherall. Detecting and Defending Against Third-Party Tracking on the Web. USENIX Symposium on Networked Systems Design and Implementation (NDSI), 2012.

[24] K. Seaborn, M. S. El-Nasr, D. Milam, and D. Yung. Programming, PWNed: Using Digital Game Development to Enhance Learners' Competency and Self-Efficacy in a High School Computing Science Course. SIGCSE Technical Symposium, 2012.

[25] S. Sheng, B. Magnien, P. Kumaraguru, A. Acquisti, L.F. Cranor, J.Hong, and E. Nunge. Anti-Phishing Phil: The Design and Evaluation of a Game That Teaches People Not to Fall for Phish. Symposium on Usable Privacy and Security (SOUPS), 2007.

[26] B. Shimanovsky, J. Feng, and M. Potkonjak. Hiding Data in DNA. Information Hiding, 2002.

[27] A. Shostack. Elevation of Privilege: Drawing Developers into Threat Modeling. Microsoft Technical Paper, 2012.

[28] Steve Jackson Games. http://www.sjgames.com.

[29] L. Sweeney. Weaving Technology and Policy Together to Maintain Confidentiality. *Journal of Law, Medicine & Ethics*, 25(2-3), 1997.

[30] US Department of Defense. CyberProtect. http://iase.disa.mil/eta/cyber-protect/launchpage.htm.

[31] WeWantToKnow. DragonBox. http://www.dragonboxapp.com/.

[32] G. White and G. Nordstrom. Security Across the Curriculum: Using Computer Security to Teach Computer Science Principles. National Information Systems Security Conference, 1996.

[33] L. Williams, A. Meneely, and G. Shipley. Protection Poker: The New Software Security "Game." *IEEE Security & Privacy*, 8(3), 2010.

[34] E. Wustrow, S. Wolchok, I. Goldberg, and J. A. Halderman Telex: Anticensorship in the Network Infrastructure. USENIX Security, 2011.

A. APPENDIX

A.1 Card Topics and Research Papers

Table 7 gives some examples of Mission cards that were inspired by research results. These examples list one relevant research project per Mission; we acknowledge that other examples exist and that this is not a comprehensive list.

A.2 Educator Survey Contents

The questions asked in the online survey distributed to educators are given below:

1. How did you use Control-Alt-Hack®? Please describe the activity.
2. How long did the activity take?
3. Were there any written or oral components that students turned in or presented as part of the activity? If so, please describe.
4. Did you present or assign any supplementary materials? If so, please describe.
5. What, if anything, worked well with the activity?
6. What, if anything, would you do differently if you were to do the activity again?
7. How would you describe students' level of enjoyment and/or engagement with the activity?
8. How would you describe students' level of learning with the activity? On what particular topics was their learning focused?
9. Why did you choose to use Control-Alt-Hack® in your classroom?
10. Would you use Control-Alt-Hack® again in your classroom?
11. Why or why not?
12. Would you suggest Control-Alt-Hack® to others?
13. Why or why not?
14. If you had not used Control-Alt-Hack®, would you still have covered the material?
15. Did you cover the material using another (additional) method?
16. If applicable: What additional method did you use to cover the material?
17. If applicable: How would you compare these two methods (Control-Alt-Hack® and the additional method) of covering the material? What are the pros of each? What are the cons?
18. If applicable: If you had not used Control-Alt-Hack®, what alternative method would you have used to cover the material?
19. If applicable: How would you compare these two methods (Control-Alt-Hack® and the alternative method) of covering the material? What are the pros of each? What are the cons?

Card Title	Card Topic	Example Inspirational Research
[CENSORED]	Working on steganographic anti-censorship software	[34]
A Healthy Dose of Security	Consulting to improve the security of an insulin pump	[16]
A Rash Decision	Cross-correlating data sources to de-anonymize medical records	[29]
Cookie-Blocked	Writing a web browser extension to circumvent tracking cookies	[23]
Crash Test Dummy	Hacking an automobile	[15]
E. coli Cryptography	Implementing cryptography via synthetic biology	[26]
Hay Baby, Hay Baby, Hay	Demonstrating that a dating site has insecure password recovery questions	[22]
Here's Looking at You, Kid	Analyzing the security of a WiFi-enabled, webcam-equipped toy robot	[7]
I'd Tap That	Pen testing the security of a contactless payment system	[9]
Mr. Botneto	Measuring a botnet's growth, then reverse engineering the C&C algorithm	[12]
One Hacker, Won Vote	Pen testing an electronic voting machine	[10]
Trojan Protection	Looking for backdoors in the outsourced production of hardware	[13]

Table 7. Example Mission card titles, topics, and example research that inspired them.

20. What is the subject of your class?
21. What is the class format (e.g., MWF 50-min 10-week course, 2-hour training seminar, etc.)?
22. How many students participated in the activity?
23. What is the level of the students in your class?
24. What is the (approximate) level of student experience with computer science and/or computer security?
25. Is there anything else that you would like to add that we have not addressed?

A.3 Educator Survey Coding Disagreements

We include all 11 cases where the primary coder's and the secondary coder's coding results did not agree. The examples are given below, along with the quotes from the survey which were primarily responsible for the distinction between the coding results.

As mentioned in Section 5.1, except for one case in which the secondary coder misread the data and coded an error (Case 6), the primary coder's results—the results reported in the paper—always represent the stricter of the two viewpoints. That is, in the Results Section we report the upper bound on our interpretation of the critiques to the game and the lower bound on the game's role in engagement and awareness.

A.3.1 Positive Role

Below we provide information on the cases where the primary and reliability coder disagreed when coding the positive role(s) that the game performed. In all cases, the reliability coder coded the game as playing the role, while the primary coder did not. Quotes that led the reliability coder to code the game as "Social / Engagement" or "Awareness" are given below.

Social / Engagement:

- Case 1 (E11-checkout). *"It was a 7/10. the students enjoyed it but the word did not spread around and ignite students."*
- Case 2 (E12-classroom). *"Students reported that they enjoyed the game, but that the hour twenty was pushing the limit."*
- Case 3 (E16-classroom). *"The kids were all engaged with the game and playing it through." "Would rate it 8/10."*
- Case 4 (E22-vetting). *"They seemed engaged, although not so much that I would expect they would play it for fun."*

Awareness:

- Case 5 (E21-lunch). *"Brought up some terminology that staff and IT had not heard before. "pwned" :-)"*

A.3.2 Critiques and Tradeoffs

Below we provide information on the cases where the primary and reliability coder disagreed when coding critiques made to the game. In all cases except one (Case 6, coded in error), the primary coder coded the educator as offering that critique, while the reliability coder did not. Quotes that led primary coder to code the critique are given below.

Takes a long time to learn:

- Case 6 (E10-classroom): The disagreement was due to the reliability coder misreading the response. The reference to the presentation and the gameplay taking too long together was a reference to instructor's syllabus content, not the video introducing the game's rules.

Takes a long time to play:

- Case 7 (E1-classroom): [*Q: What, if anything, would you do differently if you were to do the activity again?*] *"have more play time during the topic"*

Not enough fun:

- Case 8 (E22-vetting): *"They seemed engaged, though not so much that I would expect them to play it for fun"*

Not enough educational value:

- Case 9 (E2-ACM): *"Learning was not so much learned throughout the game, but it did pose interesting questions that the students were curious about"*
- Case 10 (E3-vetting): *"I worry the card game will seem like a card game"*
- Case 11 (E12-classroom): *"Most students reported a low level of learning, the topics that were reported positively were presenting the students with real world context for what they were learning"*

A.4 Control-Alt-Hack-themed Assignments

5 of the 14 educators who used Control-Alt-Hack in the classroom reported using a custom assignment in concert with the game, as described below:

E4-classroom (12 undergraduate students with little or no prior security experience): Students were asked to identify at least three tasks from Mission cards that seemed interesting. A follow-up exercise may be to have them research real-life situations where the theme of one of the tasks is involved.

E7-classrooom (56 undergraduate students in a Cyber-Security and Information Assurance course, with little or no prior security experience): Students were asked to take a scenario from a card and craft a research paper inspired by the scenario.

E10-classroom (65 high school students in a Game Design course with little or no security background): Students were required to answer essay questions about the game and how it is put together. Optional questions asked about the game's relation to the IT industry and hacker culture.

E12-classroom (22 undergraduates in a Computer Security Course with prior educational security experience): Students wrote one to two paragraphs discussing the activity.

E18-classroom (30 undergraduate students in a Fundamentals of Information Security course with a variety of security backgrounds). Two questions were asked before the game: (1) *What does information security mean to you?*; and (2) *What skills are required in white-hat hacking?* Two questions were asked after the game: (1) *Did your answers to the previous questions change as a result of the game—and if so, how?*; and (2) *As a result of the game, did you discover any threats you hadn't considered—and if so, what?*

While some of the above assignments are similar to activities we propose on our web site (http://www.controlalthack.com), some of the assignments are original and demonstrate an interesting integration of the game into existing course plans and practices.

Security Analysis of a Widely Deployed Locking System

Michael Weiner
Technische Universität München
m.weiner@tum.de

Maurice Massar
Technische Universität Kaiserslautern
massar@unix-ag.uni-kl.de

Erik Tews
Technische Universität Darmstadt
erik@datenzone.de

Dennis Giese
Technische Universität Darmstadt
dennis.giese@stud.tu-darmstadt.de

Wolfgang Wieser
Ludwig-Maximilians-Universität München
wolfgang.wieser@physik.uni-muenchen.de

ABSTRACT

Electronic locking systems are rather new products in the physical access control market. In contrast to mechanical locking systems, they provide several convenient features such as more flexible access rights management, the possibility to revoke physical keys and the claim that electronic keys cannot be cloned as easily as their mechanical counterparts. While for some electronic locks, mechanical flaws have been found [1], only a few publications analyzed the cryptographic security of electronic locking systems [2, 3]. In this paper, we analyzed the electronic security of an electronic locking system which is still widely deployed in the field.

We reverse-engineered the radio protocol and cryptographic primitives used in the system. While we consider the system concepts to be well-designed, we discovered some implementation flaws that allow the extraction of a system-wide master secret with a brute force attack or by performing a Differential Power Analysis attack [4] to any electronic key. In addition, we discovered a weakness in the Random Number Generator that allows opening a door without breaking cryptography under certain circumstances. We suggest administrative and technical countermeasures against all proposed attacks.

Finally, we give an examination of electronic lock security standards and recommend changes to one widely used standard that can help to improve the security of newly developed products.

CCS'13, November 4–8, 2013, Berlin, Germany.

ACM 978-1-4503-2477-9/13/11 ...$15.00.
http://dx.doi.org/10.1145/2508859.2516733.

Categories and Subject Descriptors

C.2.0 [**Computer-Communication Networks**]: General—*Security and protection (e.g., firewalls)*; C.2.1 [**Network Architecture and Design**]: Wireless communication

Keywords

Cryptography; DES; Embedded Security; Physical Security; Side-Channel Attack; Power Analysis; PRNG; Locking System.

1. INTRODUCTION

Locks might be the most frequently used symbol icon when it comes to explaining IT security and cryptography. While mechanical locks have evolved for more than two millenniums, digital access control systems have only been increasing their market share in the last decades. Such systems allow greater flexibility when it comes to managing access control for a large number of users for a facility and easy revocation of lost keys. They also provide the user with the advantage that only one single token is needed for accessing many different locks.

Furthermore, electronic locking system manufacturers claim that it is difficult to copy or clone keys, or – in other words – forge the authenticity of key owners. In general, the authenticity of a person or object can be ensured by the means of knowledge, ownership or inherent properties [5]. In the case of almost all mechanical locks, the ownership of a key can be tracked down to the knowledge of its shape that can be observed and cloned easily. Some attacks even focus on reconstructing mechanical keys from newspaper or television images [6]. This is not possible for electronic access tokens such as smartcards or electronic transponders: even though they are supposed to contain secret keys, cryptographic algorithms and protocols shall ensure their secrecy.

However, the exact functionality of electronic locks is often undocumented in contrast to mechanical locks with public technical principles. This violates Kerckhoff's principle [7] and makes it difficult for third parties to independently evaluate the security of electronic locking systems. In the past, several widely deployed electronic security systems with a lack of public documentation were found out to be vulnerable against mathematical or side-channel attacks [2, 8, 9].

While NXP (Mifare Classic) and Legic (Prime) have improved the security of their new products after a public analysis of their products [8, 9], we could not find much information about SimonsVoss, one of the leading companies for for electronic locking systems in Europe. Their products include electronic locks, the corresponding access tokens, as well as equipment that is used to run and integrate the system into the existing infrastructure of a company. Reference customers include banks, hospitals, transportation companies, power plants, food and water supply companies, courts, prisons and military installations.

Currently, there are two product lines from SimonsVoss on the market. *System 3060 Generation 1 (G1)* has been available since 1997 [10] and is discouraged for new installations and replaced by their new main product line, *System 3060 Generation 2 (G2)* introduced in 2007 [11]. However, G1 is still sold for existing G1 setups. G1 and G2 differ in the communication protocol and the use of cryptographic primitives, but G2 locks and transponders have the same outer appearance as their G1 counterparts sold as of 2007 [10].

The cryptographic security of Generation 2 has recently been analyzed by Strobel et al. [3]. The researchers reverse-engineered the cryptographic primitives and found out that the random number generator in their locks allowed the derivation of transponder secrets, which can be used to create a valid transponder without having physical access to it. According to the manufacturer, this vulnerability no longer exists in newly deployed locks and a patch is available for existing installations.

In this paper, we present our analysis of the SimonsVoss System 3060 *Generation 1 (G1)* electronic access control system. In Section 2, we outline the general structure of the system and the wireless protocol. Section 3 describes a low-cost method to reverse engineer the system and the used cryptographic methods. A discussion of possible attack vectors can be found in Section 4. We outline multiple realistic attack scenarios that all allow an attacker to open a lock without the consent of the operator with a justifiable effort. Of course we also present countermeasures against the attack in Section 5. In Section 6, we recap our attack scenarios and match them with recognized standards for electronic locks.

2. SYSTEM CONCEPT

This section gives an overview of the SimonsVoss System 3060 G1 by describing the devices involved as well as their identifiers. Furthermore, the communication between the devices is outlined and the important secrets are explained.

2.1 Devices

The analyzed locking system consists of at least three types of devices.

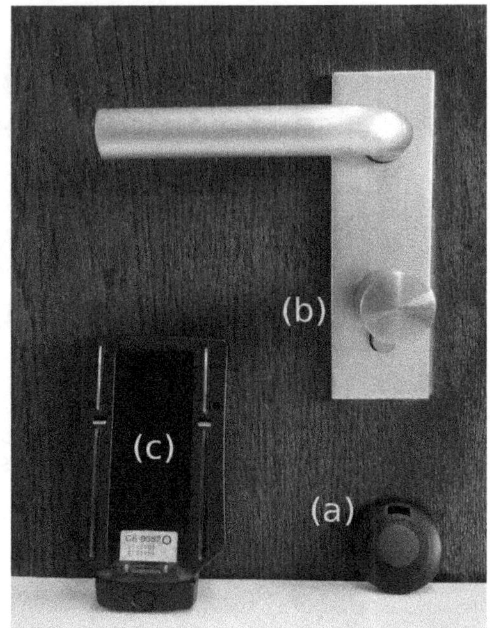

Figure 1: Transponder (a), Lock (b) and Configuration Device (c)

2.1.1 Transponder (TR)

The physical keys of the system are called transponders. They have one button that initiates a data transfer to a lock or configuration device when pushed. Transponders can be programmed for up to three locking systems. They do not have globally unique serial numbers that would be visible during regular operation. Transponders will be abbreviated TR.

2.1.2 Lock (LK)

Mechanical locks as well as electrical relays are unlocked or activated by an authorized transponder. In the following, cylinders, relays and other devices against which a transponder authenticates itself will be called lock (LK).

2.1.3 Configuration Device (CD)

Configuration devices (CD) are used to program locks and transponders.

Figure 1 shows a transponder and a PalmCD configuration device next to a mounted lock. The PalmCD is discontinued and has been replaced by a product named SmartCD, but it is compatible with G1 installations.

In addition to those three types of devices, additional components like a central user account database and communication links to emergency and alarm systems might be added to the system.

2.2 Identifiers

2.2.1 Overview

The Transponder ID (`TID`) is a 13 bit number identifying transponders within a locking system. Its scope is constrained to the locking system. Locks are identified by their 14 bit Lock ID (`LID`), which only needs to be unique within the locking system. Finally, the Locking System ID (`SID`) identifies a locking system. Its length is not specified, but we assume it to be 14 bits. Even though the SID can be freely configured in some cases, the ID should be globally unique. During our radio protocol analyses, we figured out that all of these IDs are 16 bit values on the radio layer. The additional bits are used as parity values and flag bits we did not analyze any further.

2.2.2 *Special TIDs*

There exist special TIDs that are used for configuration and other purposes. One of these TIDs serves the purpose of opening all locks of one locking system in emergency situations, i.e. *all* locks consider this TID as authorized independently of the access control configuration. While the original configuration software does not allow programming transponders with this ID, we found out that a custom program communicating with an original Configuration Device can program this "emergency opening" TID, or, in other words, create a master transponder authorized for all locks of a particular locking system.

2.3 Communication

2.3.1 *Purpose*

From an abstract point of view, communication between TR, LK and CD serves three main purposes.

- Programming LK or reading out log files
- Programming TR
- Authenticating TR against LK

In this paper, we will focus on the last type of communication as the attacks are only based on the last mentioned type.

2.3.2 *Modulation and Encoding*

The components communicate over a 25 kHz radio signal. The bits are encoded using Differential Manchester Encoding, the encoded symbols are modulated using a simple On-Off-Keying scheme.

The low carrier frequency of the signal allows recording with an ordinary laptop computer with a sound card and a coil connected to the microphone input of the card. Also, this equipment can be used to transmit custom commands with a coil connected to the speaker output. Please note that there exist sound cards using hardware low-pass filters. Such cards cannot be used for our analyses.

2.3.3 *TR authentication*

Unlocking a cylinder implies running a challenge-response protocol with a 32 bit challenge C and a 40 bit response R in which the transponder authenticates itself to the lock. Figure 2 depicts an authentication of TR against LK. One arrow represents one message consisting of preamble, payload and an 8 bit odd parity value.

The status flags of the transponder include a timezone that can be used to grant time-dependent access rights. We did not analyze the lock status flags any further.

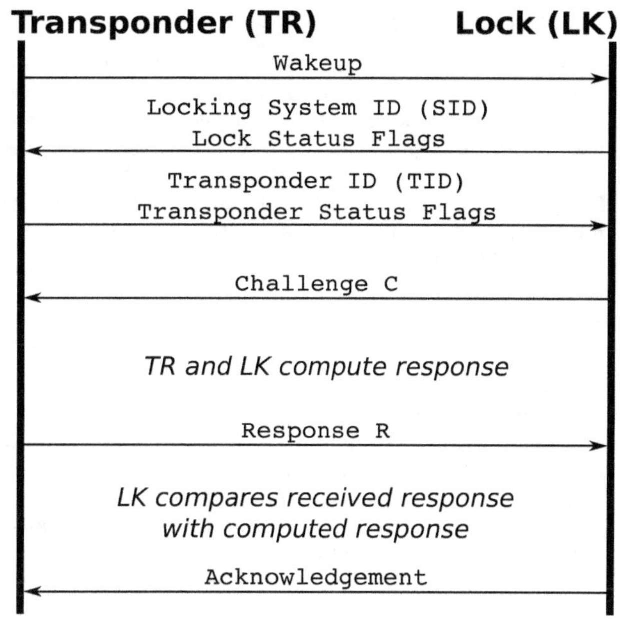

Figure 2: Transponder Authentication Protocol

2.4 Secrets

2.4.1 *System Secret*

All components of one locking system share one common locking system key [12]. Anyone knowing this key can, for example,

- program new transponders with the correct system key and a TID of choice. These transponders can be used to impersonate every user in the system.
- re-configure locks, add new authorizations or remove existing authorizations and extract logfiles.
- program a master key for the system that will open any lock regardless of the current configuration of that lock.

2.4.2 *Superordinate Keys*

There also exist superordinate keys that aim at increasing the convenience of large-scale configurations. The system concept allows special transponders that are authorized for more than three locking systems that a transponder can regularly manage. Such transponders could be used, for example, by firefighers or cleaning staff. Conceptually, this is implemented by reserving three different TIDs to each of which one distinct "superordinate key" is assigned. When these TIDs, which are referred to as "red", "green" and "blue" in the documentation [12], authenticate against a lock, the corresponding superordinate key serves as a replacement for the system secret during the response calculation. Superordinate keys cannot be used for programming locks.

3. REVERSE-ENGINEERING

During the radio protocol analysis, we could not see any kind of simple pattern in the response messages. To successfully attack this challenge response authentication scheme, we had to reverse engineer the cryptographic algorithms that were used to generate the responses to the challenges.

By a prior observation of different challenge-response pairs with different `TID`s and `SID`s we knew that the `TID` (16 bit), challenge `C` (32 bit) and a 56 bit key k were used as an input to the challenge computation, while the `SID` was not.

We assumed that the scheme is based on DES [13] for two reasons:

- Configuring different locking systems with identical configuration, but different passwords, leads to 64 differing bits in the communication between PC software and CD, excluding additional checksums. Out of those 64 bits, every eighth bit could be identified as a parity bit. This pattern is used in DES to reduce the effective key length from 64 to 56 bits. This key is a global system secret and used for all locks and transponders in the system.
- A Simple Power Analysis (SPA) [4] revealed 16 repeating sequences in an averaged power trace. The assumption seems reasonable that each sequence corresponds to one of the 16 DES rounds. A trace of the response computation is depicted in Figure 3. The magnetic field intensity was measured close to the power pin of the microcontroller of the transponder to serve as an indicator of its current consumption.

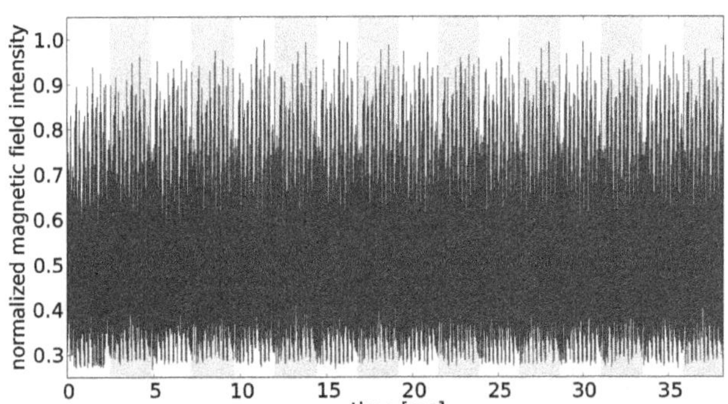

Figure 3: Trace of the supposed DES computation

However, an unknown function $\mathrm{f_{in}}$ is used at the input to prepare a 64 bit plaintext using `TID` and challenge `C`, and another unknown function $\mathrm{f_{out}}$ extracts the 40 bit response `R` from the 64 bit ciphertext:

$$\mathtt{R} = \mathrm{f_{out}}(\mathrm{DES}(\mathrm{f_{in}}(\mathtt{TID}, \mathtt{C}), k))$$

To reverse engineer these algorithms we had a number of choices: Previous successful attacks [14, 15] used invasive methods against the chip that involve opening the package. The program code can then be extracted by microprobing the ROM data bus. Alternatively, one may read out the ROM directly using microprobing or clear the memory protection bits using UV light or a laser/focused ion beam.

As those approaches are rather difficult to execute, we decided to start with an easier approach: a blind power glitching attack. Using glitching, one may skip one or more instructions executed on the chip or cause an incorrect or partial execution of these instructions. The output of such an incorrect execution of the program flow might reveal details of the algorithm executed on the chip. In contrast to many other power glitching attacks that use an FPGA, all we required for a successful attack was an AVR microcontroller generating the glitches and controlling the I/O pins of the PIC microcontroller under attack. For this purpose, we de-soldered the microcontroller from a transponder and placed it into a custom setup as shown in Figure 4.

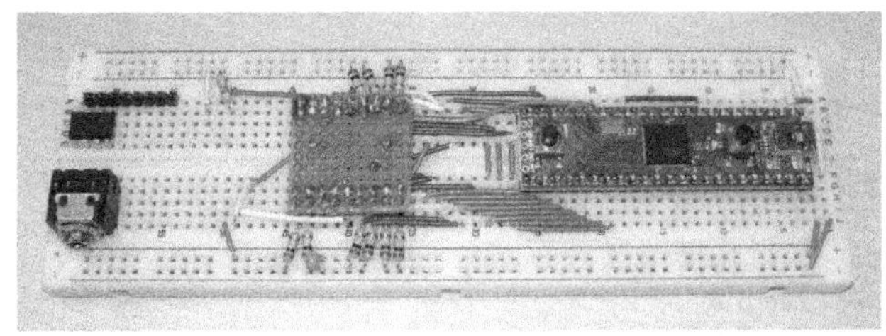

Figure 4: Power glitching setup

This attack was aimed at revealing the unknown functions f_{in} and f_{out}, verifying if DES is really used during the response computation, as well as finding possible modifications of the DES standard.

We assumed that a conditional branch instruction is used to jump from the end of one supposed DES round back to its beginning unless 16 rounds have already been executed. Our intention was locating this instruction and causing the power glitch to skip this instruction, such that only one round is executed instead of 16. As we did not know the exact position of the conditional branch instruction to attack, we iterated over all clock cycles during the response computation and observed the execution time until the controller started to transmit the response. We found out that when glitching a certain clock cycle, the controller began transmitting the response after roughly 1/16 of the expected number of clock cycles.

As the next step, we needed to reconstruct the dependency between input and output bits. For this reason, we observed the glitched response r of a randomly chosen challenge `C`, as well as the response r' of a challenge $\mathtt{C}' = \mathtt{C} \oplus 2^i$ where one bit of `C` was inverted. We repeated this procedure for all bit positions i and for a large number of challenges C. This procedure was repeated for all other possible inputs to the response computation, such as the `SID`, `TID` and the timezone.

The corresponding response pairs r and r' differed in 1, 4, 5, 8 or 9 bits, depending on the position i of the flipped input bit. A deeper analysis revealed that this corresponds to a single round of DES. A single bit difference corresponds to the left side of the Feistel network, and a 4 to 9 bit difference corresponds to the right side of the Feistel network where the bit was used as input to one or two S-Boxes.

Analyzing these outputs, we were able to derive the unknown mappings $\mathrm{f_{in}}$ and $\mathrm{f_{out}}$ that generate a DES plaintext and extract the response `R`. We have decided not to publish these mappings because they are not required to understand the rest of this paper, but would make it easier to reproduce our results to actually cause damage by attacking a G1 locking system for non-academic purposes.

4. ATTACKS

After having reverse engineered the authentication scheme, we were able to discover multiple practical attacks against the system.

4.1 PRNG

After we had implemented our first radio sniffer and gained a basic understanding of the radio protocol, we were able to record the challenges sent by the lock to the transponder.

4.1.1 Introduction

Subsequent challenges we observed from regular authentication runs appeared to be subsequent states of a 32 bit Linear Feedback Shift Register (LFSR) being clocked twice between two challenges; only the seven least significant bits of a challenge could not be expressed as a linear function of the previous challenge.

To analyze the behavior of the PRNG more deeply, we implemented a transponder emulator that continuously requested challenges but aborted each authentication run after receiving the challenge. In contrast to our first observations, challenges obtained in this way seemed to be states of an LFSR that only is clocked once – not twice – between each challenge. Furthermore, we observed that now, *all* bits could be expressed as a linear function of the previous challenge. The following list of subsequent challenges in binary representation shows the simplicity of the scheme.

```
00000111100100001101101100110011
10000011110010000110110110011001
01000001111001000011011011001100
10100000111100100001101101100110
01010000011110010000110110110011
10101000001111001000011011011001
01010100000111100100001101101100
10101010000011110010000110110110
11010101000001111001000011011011
11101010100000111100100001101101
```

The next challenge sent by the lock was just the previous challenge with all bits rotated by one, and one bit updated with a new value. This single bit is generated by an LFSR in Fibonacci configuration with the characteristic polynomial $x^{32}+x^{31}+x^{29}+x^{28}+x+1$. A block diagram of this LFSR is shown in Figure 5.

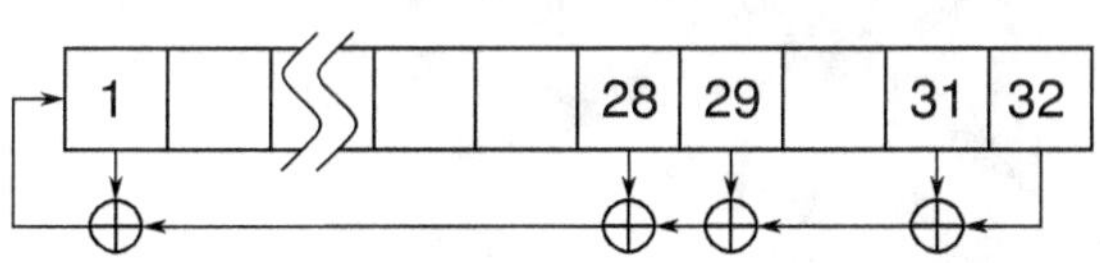

Figure 5: Block diagram of LFSR

Surprisingly, the feedback polynomial is not irreducible, and can be written as $(x^{31}+x^{28}+1)(x+1)$. We observed that it generates two non-trivial cycles of length $2^{31}-1$.

Regular updates of the LFSR can be modeled as XORing its seven least significant bits with a random value and then clocking it twice. However, 1205 non-linear updates we analyzed never left the initial LFSR cycle, so we assume that at latest after $2^{31}-1$ challenges, a challenge is repeated in all cases.

A flow chart depicting our simplified model of the behavior of locks during transponder authentication is shown in the Appendix in Figure 9.

4.1.2 Attacks on the PRNG

The weak PRNG can be used to attack the lock in various scenarios. We call the first attack a *return then unlock* attack. Imagine a system where people are allowed to borrow transponders for a limited time. For example, housekeeping might be allowed to borrow a transponder during the day to clean up an office. Afterwards the transponder is returned.

Due to the PRNG design, an attacker can predict the next challenge after having executed an aborted protocol run with the lock. The attacker, who is in temporary possession of a transponder, can use this transponder to generate a valid response for the predicted challenge. An attacker may borrow such a transponder, execute an aborted protocol run with a door he would like to unlock later, and then return the transponder. Later, he returns to the door and opens it with the previously generated response. Having already returned the transponder for this door gives him plausible deniability. Instead, the person who was in possession of the transponder when the door was unlocked will be suspected of having opened the door.

If the lock was opened once, the attacker cannot predict seven of the 32 challenge bits, if the lock was opened twice, he is missing nine bits, and so on. In the general case, the attacker needs to collect 2^{2n+5} challenges to be prepared for n regular openings ($1 \leq n \leq 13$) before he wants to open the door using his predicted challenges and the appropriate responses.

The attack can be extended to a more general attack. If a protocol run has been interrupted, the PRNG state is simply updated by clocking the LFSR. This means that all possible states of the LFSR cycle have an order that is determined by the feedback polynomial. Assume that an adversary has control over a transponder for a longer time such as, for example, a weekend. He can query the transponder with 2^k challenges, which all have the same distance in the LFSR state order (2^{31-k}). In average, we were able to get a response every 1.5 seconds, so that 2^{17} challenge-response pairs can be gathered in less than 55 hours. The attacker can now return the transponder.

If the attacker would like to open a specific lock, he runs one protocol run with the door to obtain the current PRNG state. He will be less than 2^{14} challenges in LFSR order away from a challenge he already knows the response for. He now needs to execute 2^{13} linear updates of the PRNG of the lock in average, until the lock chooses a challenge he knows the response for and can open the lock. If a single update takes him 3 seconds, he can open the door in less than 7 hours in average.

In general, the creation of a lookup-table of 2^k entries will take $1.5 \cdot 2^k$ seconds assuming that capturing one challenge-response pair requires roughly 1.5 seconds. The average time to open the lock is $1.5 \cdot 2^{31-k-1}$ seconds. While this attack is quite simple and does not require many computing resources, the consumed time is still considerable.

4.2 Brute-Force

One of the simplest approaches to attack the system is a brute-force search for the correct key. As only 40 bits of the DES output are used for the response, the key cannot be determined uniquely using a single challenge-response pair, so at least two pairs are required. An adversary can use the first challenge-response pair to determine all DES keys that generate that response from the challenge, giving the adversary 2^{16} key candidates in average. These candidates are then tested against a second challenge-response pair. With a probability close to 1, only one of the 2^{16} keys will also generate the correct response for the second challenge.

The effort for the first state is roughly equivalent to a full DES brute force attack, while the second stage, i.e. testing 2^{16} keys, only requires negligible resources. Doing a full DES brute force attack is affordable for almost any adversary today. For example, CloudCracker [16] runs an FPGA cluster that can search the entire DES key space in 24 hours. This service is currently offered for a price of 100 US$.

While the cost of such an attack is quite low, it still requires either involving a third party, or buying expensive equipment to perform the attack on site.

4.3 Differential Power Analysis

Differential Power Analysis (DPA) [4] is an attack aimed at revealing the secret key of cryptographic operations that targets the hardware on which a cryptographic algorithm is running. For attacking a device, an adversary needs to perform multiple cryptographic operations using the same key, but different input data. For each operation, he records a *power trace* containing the amplitude of a *leakage source* over time. Assuming that different data values processed by a device lead to a different power consumption, the adversary can chose the current consumption of a device as the leakage source; another possible leakage source is the electro-magnetic radiation [17].

The adversary can then create hypotheses about *intermediate values* of the cryptographic operation that depend on a known value (usually the plain- or ciphertext of an encryption run) and a small portion of the unknown secret key. These hypotheses can be tested using mathematical methods that combine them with the power traces. The best fitting hypothesis eventually reveals a small portion of the key. This process can be repeated for all intermediates values that depend on varying input data such that in the best case, the full key can be recovered.

When a transponder authenticates against a lock, both lock and transponder perform the modified DES algorithm as described in Section 3 with the same key and plaintext. While it is known that unprotected devices performing DES encryption can be attacked using a DPA attack, our scenario does not allow a complete standard attack because some bits of the plaintext are constant and cannot be altered. In this section, we have adapted to those restrictions and show that a DPA in combination with an exhaustive search of the remaining key space can be applied to transponders in a very short time.

From a technical perspective, it is advisable to perform a DPA attack on locks: The adversary can freely chose a different `TID` for each trace. Attacking a transponder implies that the `TID` is constant for all traces, such that out of the 64 bit plaintext, 32 bits remain constant while only the 32 bit challenge generates differences.

Attacking transponders is more attractive to an adversary from a practical perspective, as they can usually be carried away and placed into a measurement setup without attracting any attention. Therefore, we chose to implement a DPA attack on a regular transponder programmed with a `TID` and the 56 bit system key.

We designed our measurement setup to allow real-world attacks. The following design rules allow attacking programmed transponders and avoid the necessity of physical modifications to it. Using those rules, it is possible to create a measurement setup of which the application to a specific transponder cannot be detected by regular visual inspection of the transponder circuit board (e.g. there are no ripped up wires on the transponder PCB).

- We used the electro-magnetic radiation as a leakage source [17].
- We emulated pushing the transponder button by the use of available test pads on the circuit board.
- We used the one of the TX outputs of the microcontroller as a trigger signal for the oscilloscope to time-synchronize traces.
- While in most DPA setups, the device under test is provided with an external clock that is synchronized to the sampling clock of the oscilloscope, we captured the transponder clock for each trace and achieved synchronization by the means of post-processing in software.

We conducted a proof-of-concept implementation of the measurement setup. An electro-magnetic probe at the power supply pins of the MCU was used to capture the radiation. A sophisticated adversary can use a bed-of-nails, which has been known from PCB production tests for decades [18], for the required electrical connections to minimize the trace he leaves; our proof-of-concept implementation is satisfied by using soldered wires. The measurement setup is depicted in Figure 6.

Figure 6: Proof-of-concept DPA setup of transponder

We decided to start with a standard Correlation Power Analysis (CPA) [19] on DES using the S-Box outputs of the first round as intermediate values. As a power model, we used the Hamming Weight of the intermediates.

Using a transponder as a target device leads to the fact that 32 of the 64 bits are constant, and only the 32 bit challenge provides variation of the inputs. Two of the eight DES S-Boxes are completely fed by the challenge. We refer to them as S_A and S_B. For two other S-Boxes that we name S_C and S_D, five of the six input bits are fed by the challenge, while one bit is constant.

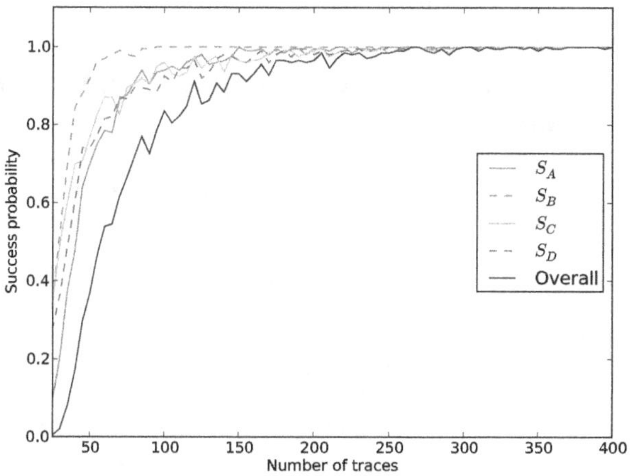

Figure 7: Success probability over number of traces

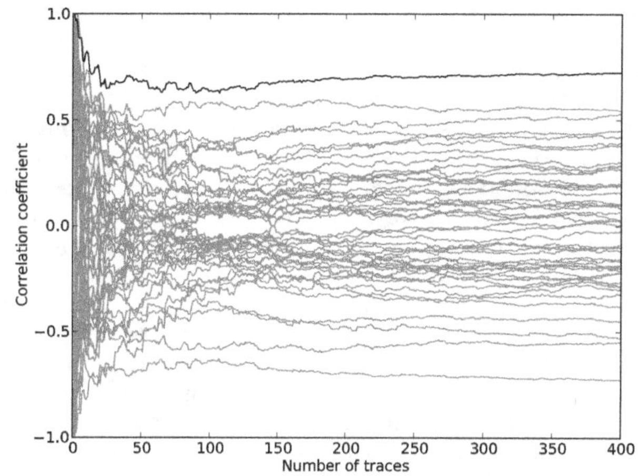

Figure 8: Correlation of S_D subkey candidates over traces

Figure 7 shows the success probability over the number of traces. It was created using 3367 traces in total. The success probability was determined by observing the relative occurrence of cases in which the correct subkey candidate position is above a certain threshold, as described below. Each point on each of the four S-Box curves was created by randomly selecting the appropriate number of traces and observing the relative occurrence over 200 runs.

We found out that the subkeys feeding S_A and S_B can be found out after roughly 100 to 150 traces. For those S-Boxes, the success probability is defined as the probability that the correct subkey has the highest absolute value of correlation coefficient for all possible subkeys. Revealing the subkeys of both S_A and S_B reduces the key space by 12 bits.

For S_C and S_D, we discovered that due to the fact of one input bit being constant, there exist *subkey pairs* for which 20 or more out of the 32 possible combinations (5 challenge bits) have the same hamming weight. We observed that in the correlation result it can occur that several distinct subkey candidates lead to correlation values that are very close to each other. We observed that for S_C pairs of two subkey candidates have similar correlation results, where for S_D, there exist pairs of four subkey candidates with this property. Figure 8 shows the correlation over traces for S_D and depicts that phenomenon.

In a worst-case scenario, the CPA on S_C provides 5 bits of information, while attacking S_D only gives 4 bits of information. Correspondingly, in Figure 7, we assume an attack successful if the correct subkey is within the topmost two candidates for S_C and if the correct subkey is within the topmost four candidates for S_D.

According to Figure 7, the overall success probability of recovering 21 bits exceeds 99 % after 300 traces. Our measurement setup requires less than 1.5 seconds to capture one trace, so the attack can be successful with a 99 % probability after 7.5 minutes.

The number of required traces for a successful attack appears surprisingly low to us. A possible explanation for this is the microcontroller itself: The PIC18LC58B only consists of the CPU core. Apart from the GPIO pins, it does not have any peripheral components that would introduce additional noise; the controller is not even equipped with a brown-out detection or interrupt controller.

As a complete CPA result, 21 bits can be revealed in the worst-case scenario. This implies that only 35 bits of the DES keyspace are remaining. That can be used for an exhaustive search of the remaining key space in a very short time: Our test system, a laptop computer with a Intel Core i5-2450M processor running at 2.5 GHz, could search a 32 bit key subspace in 1m58s using a bit-sliced implementation of DES [20]. As a consequence, searching the whole remaining 35 bit key space requires less than 16 minutes on a laptop computer.

5. COUNTERMEASURES

We have shown different ways how the system can be attacked in practice and outlined the attack procedure. We would like to suggest countermeasures that can be deployed for new and existing systems.

5.1 Administrative Options

An attacker's knowledge about a system key gives him access to all locks that are programmed with this key while transponders normally can be programmed for three locking systems, i.e. three different `SID`s with three different keys. Locking system administrators can split large locking systems up into different smaller locking systems. This should be done in accordance with the "need to know" principle, such that each transponder shall only know keys to these areas for which it is intended. In an industry building, this can be, for example,

- one distinct `SID`/key for all external doors
- one distinct `SID`/key for each department
- one distinct `SID`/key for doors to administrative or infrastructural rooms such as server rooms or central heating rooms

With this configuration, an attacker does not get full access to a complete building when a transponder is compromised. For example, if an attacker steals a regular employee transponder that is authorized for office doors within his department, the attacker cannot enter other departments or unlock external doors. Service staff can, for example, use superordinate keys as described in Section 2.4.2 to get access to more than three locking systems.

This countermeasure is easily implementable without any hardware or software modification. It requires reprogramming transponders and locks once, which is often done in a regular manner anyway. However, the availability of only three locking system slots can make the separation of one big locking system difficult.

The security can be further improved by frequently updating the keys of locking systems in critical locations, such as for external doors or server rooms. This requires a secure update procedure for both locks and transponders. Employees with access to security critical locations can for example, be required to regularly show up in person in order to get a key update. For the updates of locks, it must be ensured that the transmission of key updates is not intercepted.

5.2 Key Derivation

One of the major design problems of this system is the existence of a common system secret that is known to every transponder and every lock in the system. Extraction of this secret by an attacker compromises the entire locking system. As an improvement, one should keep the value of a single device as little as possible and thereby restrict the damage the compromise of a single device can cause.

Starting from a theoretical point of view, using signatures and asymmetric cryptography sounds like a good solution. A central, well protected CA could issue digital certificates to all transponders and locks and also permissions could be embedded in this certificates. These devices could then use those certificates and their private keys for authentication and authorization. However the hardware used in those devices is not capable of executing current asymmetric algorithms with secure key sizes providing a reasonable response time and battery usage.

We would therefore like to introduce the idea of deriving the transponder key from a common system key, which is known to all locks in the system. Using a one way key derivation function, and taking the system key and the transponder ID as input, a transponder key is derived and stored on the transponder. The transponder does not need to know the system key. When a transponder communicates with a lock, the transponder transmits his ID first, and then the lock can also determine the transponder key. If a transponder should ever be lost and all keys are extracted, the attacker can only use those keys to obtain the permissions of this specific transponder, but not of other transponders in the system. Because such a key derivation function can be built using only building blocks from symmetric cryptography, this approach would only need a small amount of additional hardware resources.

SimonsVoss System 3060 Generation 2 (G2) already implements a key derivation scheme that provides each transponder with an individual key, such that only the locks need to know the system-wide key [3].

Also, sufficient key lengths should be chosen for such a system. We currently see 80 bits of symmetric key length as the absolute minimum, but suggest to use 128 bit keys to have security for the foreseeable future. The system we examined was designed almost two decades ago, and a new system should be based on security parameters that can be expected to be secure for at least 20 years and have a reasonable security margin.

5.3 Differential Power Analysis - Hiding and Masking

Hiding and Masking are the two state-of-the art concepts to reduce the leakage that can be exploited by a DPA attack [4, 21]. Hiding aims at reducing the amplitude of the leaking signal while the goal of masking is to make the leaking signal appear as random as possible. Masking can implemented in software at the cost of significantly increasing the memory consumption and execution time.

The PIC16LC58B on the transponder only has 73 bytes of RAM [22]. While we do not know the exact RAM usage while the response is computed, it seems very likely that implementing a masking scheme on that controller would exceed the RAM availability. However, in contrast to the more than 15 year old PIC16LC58B, state-of-the art microcontrollers – or, better – smart card controllers are equipped with enough resources for implementing a masking scheme. Furthermore, the execution time of a masked DES implementation must not exceed the time between transmission of the challenge and expected time of response reception (around 60 ms).

5.4 PRNG Improvement

In Section 4.1 we developed an attack against the random number generator in the locks that is used to generate challenges to transponders. The problem of the current LFSR design is its simplicity, and the low complexity for the attacker to predict PRNG outputs.

Designing and implementing a secure PRNG under the given constraints is a difficult task. We could not find one single solution that offers a high level of security but also retains compatibility and minimizes the effort required to deploy our proposal. Therefore, we split our proposals into three categories.

- **Long-term** modifications require modification of hardware and revising the system concept, while achieving a high level of security.
- **Medium-term** changes are satisfied with software updates of locks and the configuration device.
- **Short-term** improvements shall be implementable by only updating the firmware of the locks.

Considering long-term modifications, it is advisable to use a hardware-based True Random Number Generator, as found on Smart Card and security controllers, instead of – or at least in combination with – a software-based PRNG. An alternative to embedded TRNG circuits can be RF or supply voltage noise. As such components use physical randomness instead of computations, predictions of random numbers are avoided. Furthermore, it is advisable to significantly increase the size of the challenges to render the creation of look-up tables infeasible in practice. We suggest a minimum challenge size of 64 bits.

As a medium-term improvement, we suggest to introduce the ability to update the seed of the PRNG in a secure manner. As an example, the Configuration Devices can be used to provide additional randomness to the locks during programming cycles. In addition, the short-term proposals shall be included.

As for short-term improvements, all possible sources of randomness shall be considered:

- initial seed, supplied by the manufacturer
- timestamps of successful authentications (configuration devices and transponders)
- *hidden parts of previous challenge/response pairs* (not recommended for security reasons)

Note that it is advisable to avoid deriving PRNG seeds from system secrets. This may give an adversary the opportunity to collect information about the secret.

DES is already available due to the authentication scheme and can be used to actually generate challenges depending on an internal state as well as the entropy sources as mentioned above.

As an example, a random number could be generated using $rand = \text{DES}(\text{key} = mseed \oplus tval, \text{plaintext} = ctr)$, where $mseed$ is a lock-individual random seed programmed by the manufacturer, $tval$ denotes the least significant bits of the timestamps of the previous n successful authentications, and ctr is a counter.

5.5 Protected Hardware

The used microcontroller was susceptible to power glitching and a classic Differential Power Analysis attack. Modern microcontrollers usually have a Brown Out Detection circuitry that makes glitching attacks more difficult. Some controllers also provide hardware support for cryptographic algorithms [23]. However, those protection mechanisms usually are implemented in a low-cost manner and can often be broken without a high effort [24].

In contrast to microcontrollers, the resistance of Smart Card or Secure Access Module (SAM) chips against these and other attacks is a major design goal and such controllers are usually much harder to break than off-the-shelf microcontrollers in terms of equipment and knowledge required as well as attack time. As locking systems are security products par excellence, it seems reasonable for them to use modern security controllers.

Surprisingly, we do not know any widely spread battery-powered locking systems that use smart card or SAM controllers, or deploy any other countermeasures against hardware attacks.

6. PRACTICAL RELEVANCE

Besides the theoretical results we showed in the paper, we would like to discuss the practical relevance and importance of our findings in this section.

The security of mechanical locks has been examined for more than a century and requirements for mechanical locks have been standardized. A very common standard for the security of mechanical locks is VdS 2156-1 [25] which defines multiple levels of security for mechanical locks. A lock has to resist against an attacker who uses lockpicking tools for at least 3 or 6 minutes, depending on the required security level. In addition to that, high security locks must use keys, that cannot be cloned easily.

All attacks we presented need a total attack time of more than 6 minutes. Also the transponders have a protection against unauthorized cloning which however can be defeated using the brute force attack or the side channel attack in Section 4. According to our understanding, this would not prevent a high security certification according to VdS 2156-1.

However, there are important differences between the attacks we presented, and typical attacks on mechanical locks:

- To attack a mechanical lock, one usually needs to be with the lock during the attack, and this can be easily noticed by other people near the lock. Also it could leave non removable traces on the lock itself. Our proposed attacks might remain unnoticed.
- Our total attack time when cloning a transponder or escalating privileges is longer than 6 minutes, while the time spent with a lock is even less than 3 minutes. However, this is more a key cloning attack than an attack on the lock itself.
- While picking locks or cloning mechanical keys usually requires some human skills to operate the equipment properly, the attacks we presented can be heavily automatized and afterwards be done by persons with no or little training in picking locks.

For electronic systems, there exists the additional standard VdS 2156-2 [26] with more specific requirements. The standard describes *intelligent attacks*, and a lock needs to withstand such an attack for 10 to 90 minutes, depending on the security level. The standard also describes requirements for wireless access tokens:

- The transmission of the "opening code" must be *encrypted*. However, no keylength or other details of the used encryption scheme are specified.
- The "code" may only be transmitted upon an explicit action, and third parties may not read out the transponder or determine usable information.

It is our understanding that [26] only aims at outsider attacks where an adversary is not in possession of a transponder knowing the system secret of a lock being attacked. Therefore, we assume that our publication does not affect the compliance of the SimonsVoss System 3060 G1 locking system to this standard. While a compliance with [25, 26] may be helpful from an insurance and liability perspective, we strongly believe that especially [26] is not sufficient for ensuring state-of-the-art security of electronic locks. In particular, we see the following weaknesses in this standard:

- While the transmission shall be "encrypted", no requirements are given with respect to the cryptographic primitives to be used. We suggest requiring accepted and strong cryptographic algorithms with a sufficiently large key space, as well as a proper design of the cryptographic protocols.
- While the protection against "intelligent attacks" is required, that term is not properly defined. In our notion, this could mean anything from brute-force attacks over the exploitation of weaknesses in the cryptographic algorithms and protocols up to side-channel or fault attacks. The range of intelligent attacks is very broad and reducing this whole spectrum to one term

makes the comparison between different products difficult. We suggest properly defining requirements for distinct attack types.

- The notion of attack time in the area of electronic locks is ambiguous. For mechanical attacks, it is usually clear that attack time refers to the time the attacker must be physically close to the lock. We propose to clearly distinguish between *access token availability time* in which the transponder or other access token must be in the possession of the attacker, the *lock availability time* in which the attacker must be physically close to the clock and the *computation time* in which neither access token nor lock needs to be accessible by the attacker.

In addition to those suggestions, we strongly recommend to define testing procedures in order to allow independent compliance verification.

In its current version, the VdS standards do not motivate the locking system industry to enforce state-of-the-art electronic security in their products.

The German Federal Office for Information Security (BSI, Bundesamt für Sicherheit in der Informationstechnik) fills this gap by issuing more detailed technical guidelines about the security of electronic identification and access control systems. These guidelines are primarily important for governmental organizations, but also may be helpful for security aware institutions that need to select appropriate products.

TR-03126-5 [27] gives a detailed analysis of RFID systems for the generic use case of "employee identification". It describes the system architecture and components of RFID systems, gives examples of more concrete use cases, discusses security requirements and points out possible attack vectors and countermeasures. TL-03405 [28] defines security requirements and test criteria concretely for electronic locking systems, and TL-03424 [29] defines the requirements for electronic keys in particular.

The requirements defined by [27, 28, 29] are comprehensive and go down to a detailed technical level, for example, by defining the cryptographic algorithms to be used. Examples of such requirements are

- 3-DES, AES or cryptographic algorithms with a comparable security level shall be used to protect transmissions.
- Secret keys shall be stored in a secure manner, for example by using Secure Authentication Modules (SAM).
- A system and its devices shall be certified at least to Common Criteria EAL 3 [30].
- The secret keys of replaced or lost components shall be declared invalid unless it is ensured that the keys cannot be read out.

To conclude our standards review, relying on the VdS certifications may lead to a false sense of security on the customer side in spite of the fact that many locking systems, besides SimonsVoss, are potentially vulnerable. We believe that the requirements from the BSI standards are a good approach towards designing secure locking systems, and that products designed or even certified to the current BSI guidelines may provide higher security. However, there do not exist many BSI-certified products, we even have not found any major locking system manufacturer advertising protection against particular hardware attacks, such as side-channel attacks.

From an attacker's point of view, our Brute Force and Power Analysis attacks have the advantage to mechanical attacks that they can hardly be discovered: The only trace the attacker potentially leaves is an entry in the access log of the lock, however logging is a feature which is only available in more expensive model variants of locks. If logging is enabled, the attacker can download the access log and select a `TID` to impersonate that causes the least suspicion. This cannot only disguise the intrusion, but also lead to a false accusation of non-involved persons in the case that suspicious activities are discovered. While this type of attack seems too elaborate for small-time criminals, we believe that it is a realistic threat with respect to large-scale attacks such as espionage, intelligence operations or organized crime.

7. CONCLUSION

In this paper, we have reverse engineered and analyzed the SimonsVoss System 3060 Generation 1 electronic locking system, and we determined the level of difficulty for a successful attack. SimonsVoss products are used to protect sensitive infrastructures. We found an attack against the PRNG in our analyzed G1 locks, and we showed that the G1 system concept uses one master secret that is known to all devices of a particular locking system. We explained that this secret can be extracted by eavesdropping on transponder authentication runs followed by a brute-force attack, or by conducting a Differential Power Analysis attack against a transponder. We proposed countermeasures against all discussed attacks.

We also examined security standards for electronic locks and found out that the VdS standards might not be sufficient to enforce a high level of security. It is our impression that this gap may lead the locking system industry in a wrong direction; we would not be surprised about other products from other manufacturers that show electronic vulnerabilities as well.

What we did not evaluate in this paper is the surrounding environment that also protects critical installations besides the locks. Attacking a lock is just one out of many ways to gain access to a building or room. Other methods may be attacks on the door or windows of the room itself, without attacking the lock directly. Stealing a valid transponder or bribing/blackmailing/impersonating somebody who has access to the room could also be a successful attack strategy. We still think that most attackers aiming at breaking into a SimonsVoss System 3060 G1-secured facility will choose another way than using a cryptographic attack against the door lock – a system is only as secure as the weakest link in the chain.

Acknowledgements

This work was partly funded by the German Federal Ministry of Education and Research (BMBF) in the project SIBASE through grant number 01S13020A and within the project EC SPRIDE and also by the Hessian LOEWE excellence initiative within CASED. We would also like to thank Jan Morawek, starbug and krikkit from the Chaos Computer Club in Germany for their ideas and support.

8. REFERENCES

[1] M. W. Tobias, M. Fiddler, and T. Bluzmanis, "Invisible Access - Opening New Doors to Insecurity," DEFCON 17, 2009, http://defcon.org/images/defcon-17/dc-17-presentations/defcon-17-marc_weber_tobias-matt_fiddler-invisible_access.pdf, accessed on 26.07.2013.

[2] M. Kasper, T. Kasper, A. Moradi, and C. Paar, "Breaking keeloq in a flash: On extracting keys at lightning speed," in *Progress in Cryptology – AFRICACRYPT 2009*, ser. Lecture Notes in Computer Science, B. Preneel, Ed. Springer Berlin Heidelberg, 2009, vol. 5580, pp. 403–420. [Online]. Available: http://dx.doi.org/10.1007/978-3-642-02384-2_25

[3] D. Strobel, B. Driessen, T. Kasper, G. Leander, D. Oswald, F. Schellenberg, and C. Paar, "Fuming acid and cryptanalysis: Handy tools for overcoming a digital locking and access control system," in *Advances in Cryptology – CRYPTO 2013*, ser. Lecture Notes in Computer Science, R. Canetti and J. Garay, Eds. Springer Berlin Heidelberg, 2013, vol. 8042, pp. 147–164. [Online]. Available: http://dx.doi.org/10.1007/978-3-642-40041-4_9

[4] P. Kocher, J. Jaffe, and B. Jun, "Differential power analysis," in *Advances in Cryptology — CRYPTO' 99*, ser. Lecture Notes in Computer Science, M. Wiener, Ed. Springer Berlin Heidelberg, 1999, vol. 1666, pp. 388–397. [Online]. Available: http://dx.doi.org/10.1007/3-540-48405-1_25

[5] S. Spitz, M. Pramateftakis, and J. Swoboda, *Kryptographie und IT-Sicherheit.* Wiesbaden, Germany: Vieweg + Teubner Verlag / Springer Fachmedien, 2011.

[6] J. Weyers, "Showing your keys on TV: What could possibly go wrong?" 2013, https://program.ohm2013.org/event/49.html, accessed on 16.08.2013.

[7] A. Kerckhoffs, "La cryptographie militaire," *Journal des sciences militaires*, 1883.

[8] F. Garcia, G. Koning Gans, R. Muijrers, P. Rossum, R. Verdult, R. Schreur, and B. Jacobs, "Dismantling mifare classic," in *Computer Security - ESORICS 2008*, ser. Lecture Notes in Computer Science, S. Jajodia and J. Lopez, Eds. Springer Berlin Heidelberg, 2008, vol. 5283, pp. 97–114. [Online]. Available: http://dx.doi.org/10.1007/978-3-540-88313-5_7

[9] H. Plötz and K. Nohl, "Peeling away layers of an rfid security system," in *Financial Cryptography and Data Security*, ser. Lecture Notes in Computer Science, G. Danezis, Ed. Springer Berlin Heidelberg, 2012, vol. 7035, pp. 205–219. [Online]. Available: http://dx.doi.org/10.1007/978-3-642-27576-0_17

[10] "SimonsVoss Technologies AG: Historie," http://www.simons-voss.de/Historie.32.0.html, accessed on 24.07.2013.

[11] "SECURITY 2006 Messe News," 2006, http://web.archive.org/web/20061211054124/http://www.simons-voss.de/fileadmin/media/home/Internet_Flyer_deutsch.pdf, accessed on 26.08.2013.

[12] "Handbuch LSM - Benutzer," Tech. Rep., Jul 2010, http://www.simons-voss.de/fileadmin/php/fileadmin/downloads/ger/lsm/HB_LSM_30_Benutzer_V1.0_D.pdf, accessed on 26.07.2013.

[13] N. F. PUB, "46-3. data encryption standard," *Federal Information Processing Standards, National Bureau of Standards, US Department of Commerce*, 1977.

[14] bunnie, "Hacking the PIC 18F1320," 2007, http://www.bunniestudios.com/blog/?page_id=40, accessed on 26.07.2013.

[15] "Unmarked Die Revisions :: Part I," 2007, http://www.flylogic.net/blog/?p=9, accessed on 26.07.2013.

[16] "CloudCracker - Dictionaries," https://www.cloudcracker.com/dictionaries.html, accessed on 13.08.2013.

[17] K. Gandolfi, C. Mourtel, and F. Olivier, "Electromagnetic analysis: Concrete results," in *Cryptographic Hardware and Embedded Systems — CHES 2001*, ser. Lecture Notes in Computer Science, Koç, ÇetinK. and Naccache, David and Paar, Christof, Ed. Springer Berlin Heidelberg, 2001, vol. 2162, pp. 251–261. [Online]. Available: http://dx.doi.org/10.1007/3-540-44709-1_21

[18] J. H. Stewart, "Future testing of large LSI circuit cards," in *Semiconductor Test Symposium.* IEEE, 1977, pp. 6–15.

[19] E. Brier, C. Clavier, and F. Olivier, "Correlation power analysis with a leakage model," in *Cryptographic Hardware and Embedded Systems - CHES 2004*, ser. Lecture Notes in Computer Science, M. Joye and J.-J. Quisquater, Eds. Springer Berlin Heidelberg, 2004, vol. 3156, pp. 16–29. [Online]. Available: http://dx.doi.org/10.1007/978-3-540-28632-5_2

[20] Matthew Kwan, "Bitslice DES," http://www.darkside.com.au/bitslice/, accessed on 12.08.2013.

[21] S. Mangard, E. Oswald, and T. Popp, *Power Analysis Attacks: Revealing the Secrets of Smart Cards (Advances in Information Security).* Secaucus, NJ, USA: Springer-Verlag New York, Inc., 2007.

[22] "PIC16C5X Data Sheet," Microchip Technology Inc., Tech. Rep., 2002, http://ww1.microchip.com/downloads/en/devicedoc/30453d.pdf, accsessed on 26.07.2013.

[23] "PIC16C5X Data Sheet," Microchip Technology Inc., Tech. Rep., 2002, http://ww1.microchip.com/downloads/en/devicedoc/30453d.pdf, accessed on 12.08.2013.

[24] I. Kizhvatov, "Side channel analysis of avr xmega crypto engine," in *Proceedings of the 4th Workshop on Embedded Systems Security*, ser. WESS '09. New York, NY, USA: ACM, 2009, pp. 8:1–8:7. [Online]. Available: http://doi.acm.org/10.1145/1631716.1631724

[25] "VdS-Richtlinien für mechanische Sicherungseinrichtungen - Schließzylinder mit Einzelsperrschließung," VdS, Tech. Rep., 2012.

[26] "VdS-Richtlinien für mechanische Sicherungseinrichtungen - Schließzylinder mit Einzelsperrschließung - Teil 2: Elektronische Schließzylinder," VdS, Tech. Rep., 2012.

[27] "BSI TR-03126-5, Technische Richtlinie für den sicheren RFID-Einsatz (TR RFID), Einsatzgebiet

elektronischer Mitarbeiterausweis," Bundesamt für Sicherheit in der Informationstechnik, Tech. Rep., 2010.

[28] "BSI TL-03405, Anforderungen und Prüfbedingungen für elektronische Schließzylinder und Schließsysteme," Bundesamt für Sicherheit in der Informationstechnik, Tech. Rep., 2010.

[29] "BSI TL-03424, Ergänzung zu BSI TL elektronische Schließsysteme, Zutrittskontrollanlagen; Anforderungen für elektronische Schlüssel," Bundesamt für Sicherheit in der Informationstechnik, Tech. Rep., 2011.

[30] "Common Criteria for Information Technology Security Evaluation, Part 3: Security assurance components," Tech. Rep., 2012, https://www.niap-ccevs.org/Documents_and_Guidance/cc_docs.cfm, accessed on 25.08.2013.

APPENDIX

Additional Figures

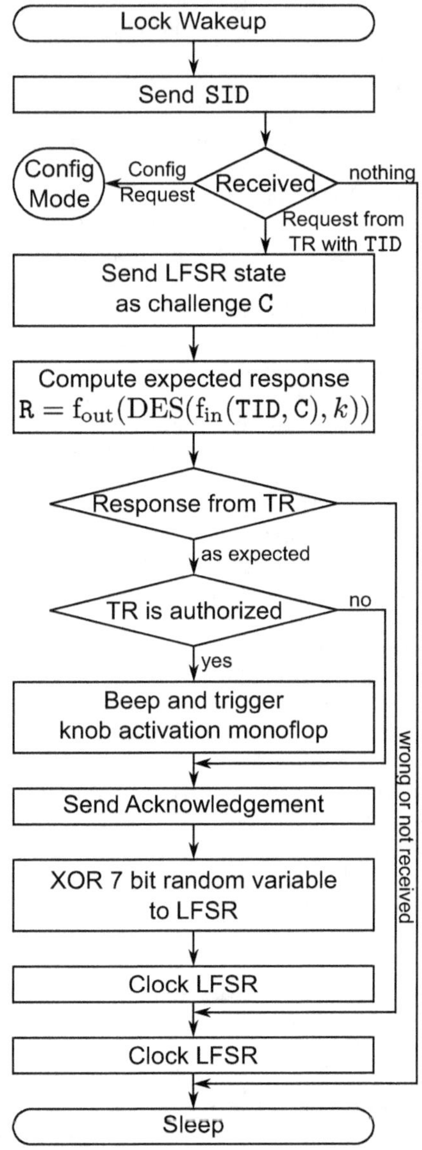

Figure 9: LK behavior during TR authentication

The Cyber Arms Race

Mikko Hypponen
F-Secure, Finland
mikko.hypponen@f-secure.com

ABSTRACT

When Internet became commonplace in the mid-1990s, the decision makers ignored it. They did not see it as important or in any way relevant to them. As a direct result, global freedom flourished in the unrestricted online world. Suddenly people all over the world had in their reach something truly and really global. And suddenly, people were not just consuming content; they were creating content for others.

But eventually politicians and leaders realized just how important the Internet is. And they realized how useful the Internet was for other purposes — especially for the purposes of doing surveillance on citizens.

The two arguably most important inventions of our generation — the Internet and the mobile phones — changed the world. However, they both turned out to be perfect tools for the surveillance state. And in a surveillance state, everybody is assumed guilty.

Internet surveillance became front page material when Edward Snowden started leaking information on PRISM, Xkeyscore and other NSA programs in the summer of 2013.

But do not get me wrong. I do understand the need for doing both monitoring and surveillance. If somebody is suspected for running a drug ring, planning a school shooting, or participating in a terror organization, he should be monitored with a relevant court order.

However, that is not what PRISM is about. PRISM is not about monitoring suspicious people. PRISM is about monitoring everyone. It is about monitoring people that are known to be innocent. And it is about building dossiers on everyone, eventually going back decades. Such dossiers based on our Internet activity will build a thorough picture of us. And if the powers-that-be ever need to find a way to twist your hand, they would certainly find something suspicious or embarrassing on everyone, if they have enough of their internet history recorded.

United States intelligence agencies have a full legal right to monitor foreigners. Which does not sound too bad — until you realize that most of us are foreigners to the Americans. In fact, 96% of the people on the planet turn out to be such "foreigners." And when these people use US-based services, they are legally under surveillance. When the PRISM leaks started, US intelligence tried to calm the rest of the world by explaining that there is no need to worry and that these programs were just about fighting terrorists. But then further leaks proved that the United States was using their tools to monitor the European Commission and the United Nations as well. It is difficult for them to argue that they would be trying to find terrorists in the European Union headquarters.

Another argument we have heard from the US intelligence apparatus is that everyone else is doing internet surveillance too. And indeed, most countries do have intelligence agencies, and most of them do monitor what other countries are doing. However, United States has an unfair advantage. Almost all of the common internet services, search engines, webmails, web browsers and mobile operating systems come from the USA. Put in another way: How many Spanish politicians and decision makers use American services? Answer: All of them. And how many American politicians and decision makers use Spanish services? Answer: None of them. All this should make it obvious that we foreigners should not use US based services. They have proven to us that they are not trustworthy. Why would we voluntarily hand our data to a foreign intelligence agency?

But in practice, it is very hard to avoid using services like Google, Facebook, LinkedIn, Dropbox, Amazon, Skydrive, iCloud, Android, Windows, iOS and so on. This is a clear example on the failure of Europe, Asia and Africa to compete with the USA on Internet services. And when the rest of the world does produce a global hit, like Skype or Nokia, it typically ends up acquired by an American company, bringing it under US control.

But if you are not doing anything wrong, why worry about this? Or, if you are worrying about this, what do you have to hide? My answer to his question is that I have nothing to hide but I have nothing in particular that I would want to share with an intelligence agency either. In particular, I have nothing to share with a foreign intelligence agency. If we really need a big brother, I would rather have a domestic big brother than a foreign big brother.

People have asked me if they really should worry about PRISM. I have told them that they should not be worried — they should be outraged instead. We should not just accept such blanket and wholesale surveillance from one country onto the rest of the world.

CCS'13, November 4–8, 2013, Berlin, Germany.

ACM 978-1-4503-2477-9/13/11 ...$15.00.
http://dx.doi.org/10.1145/2508859.2516756 .

Advancements in computing power and data storage have made wholesale surveillance possible. But they have also made leaking possible. That is how Edward Snowden could steal three laptops which contained so much information that printed on paper it would be a long row of trucks full of paper. Leaking has become so easy, it will keep organizations worrying about getting caught over any wrongdoing. We might wish this would force organizations to avoid unethical practices. While governments are watching over us, they know were watching over them.

Categories and Subject Descriptors

K.4.2 [**Social Issues**]: Abuse and crime involving computers

Keywords

privacy; surveillance; monitoring

Short Bio

Mikko Hypponen is the Chief Research Officer of F-Secure in Finland. He has been working in the area of computer security for over 20 years and has fought the biggest virus outbreaks in the net, including Loveletter, Conficker and Stuxnet. His TED Talk on computer security has been translated to over 35 languages. His columns have been published in the New York Times, Wired, CNN and BBC. Mr. Hypponen sits in the advisory boards of the ISF and the Lifeboat foundation

How to Keep a Secret: Leakage Deterring Public-key Cryptosystems

Aggelos Kiayias
National and Kapodistrian University of Athens
Dept. of Informatics and Telecommunications
aggelos@di.uoa.gr

Qiang Tang
National and Kapodistrian University of Athens
& University of Connecticut
qiang@cse.uconn.edu

ABSTRACT

How is it possible to prevent the sharing of cryptographic functions? This question appears to be fundamentally hard to address since in this setting the owner of the key *is* the adversary: she wishes to share a program or device that (potentially only partly) implements her main cryptographic functionality. Given that she possesses the cryptographic key, it is impossible for her to be *prevented* from writing code or building a device that uses that key. She may though be *deterred* from doing so. We introduce *leakage-deterring* public-key cryptosystems to address this problem. Such primitives have the feature of enabling the embedding of owner-specific *private data* into the owner's public-key so that given access to *any* (even partially functional) implementation of the primitive, the recovery of the data can be facilitated. We formalize the notion of leakage-deterring in the context of encryption, signature, and identification and we provide efficient generic constructions that facilitate the recoverability of the hidden data while retaining privacy as long as no sharing takes place.

Categories and Subject Descriptors

K.6 [**Management of Computing and Information Systems**]: Security and Protection; E.3 [**Data Encryption**]: Public key Cryptosystems

Keywords

Public-key Cryptography, Self-enforcement, Key Management, Leakage-deterring

1. INTRODUCTION

Consider any organization that maintains a PKI supporting various cryptographic functions including public-key encryption, signatures and identification. How is it possible to prevent individuals from sharing their cryptographic functions? Certified PKI members, out of convenience or even malice, can delegate their private keys to each other (or even to outsiders), thus violating accountability and organizational policy. Even worse, delegation can be partial: for instance, a public-key encryption user can share (or, in fact, even sell) an implementation that only decrypts messages of a certain form (e.g., only e-mails from a specific source). Seemingly, very little can be done to prevent this as the adversary in this case is the owner of the cryptographic key: inevitably practice has shown that no matter how much one protects a cryptographic implementation, a determined attacker can always reverse engineer it.

The above scenario puts forth the central problem our work aims to solve: how is it possible to prevent the sharing of cryptographic functions? The main challenge here is that the owner of the key is adversarial: she wishes to share a program or hardware device that (potentially only partly) implements her main cryptographic functionality. Given that she possesses the cryptographic key (either in software or hardware), it is impossible for her to be prevented from delegating it. However, as we highlight, there can be ways for her to be *deterred* from doing so. A straightforward deterrence mechanism would be to identify and penalize the sharing behavior. However, the enforcement of a penalty mechanism is contingent to detecting the act of sharing — something that limits the effectiveness of penalties: a cautious adversary can keep itself "below the radar" and thus remain penalty-free. To address this we put forth and explore a more proactive approach.

A cryptographic scheme will be called *leakage-deterring* if the release of any implementation of the cryptographic function (e.g, decryption, signing), leads to the recovery of some private information (that the owner prefers to keep hidden) by anyone that possesses the implementation. Leakage deterrence is thus achieved in the sense that sharing the cryptographic function in any form incurs the penalty of revealing the private information (while non-sharing maintains its privacy).

Note that a leakage-deterring primitive should retain its original functionality (e.g., encryption, signing, identification) but it will also offer two additional operations: first, it is possible to embed private data into the public-key of the primitive in a way that they are (at least) semantically secure. The embedding operation is facilitated through an interaction with an authority that vouches for the integrity of the private data and is akin to a PKI certification of the owner's public-key. In this fashion, the primitive's public-

CCS'13, November 4–8, 2013, Berlin, Germany.

http://dx.doi.org/10.1145/2508859.2516691 .

key becomes "enhanced" and is a carrier of private information itself (i.e., a ciphertext) — otherwise the intended functionality of the primitive should remain unchanged. The second operation that is offered by a leakage-deterring primitive comes into play when the owner of the secret key produces an implementation of the main operation in the form of a "box" and shares it with other entities (in software or hardware). Given such a box, any entity that receives it can utilize a public recovering algorithm that will interact with the box and produce the private data that are embedded into the owner's enhanced public-key.

In a nutshell, designing a leakage-deterring scheme requires the transformation of the public-key of the primitive into a (one-time) ciphertext that can be decrypted by *any* working implementation of the cryptographic functionality. The main challenge comes precisely from this latter requirement: any working implementation of the cryptographic functionality should be usable as a decryption key that unlocks the private data embedded into the public-key, even if the adversarial implementor takes into account the recoverability algorithm and the enhanced public-key that carries the private data when implementing the functionality.

To appreciate the complexity of the problem, consider a naive attempt to produce a leakage-deterring public-key encryption (PKE): the authority certifies as the enhanced public key the pair (pk, ψ) where $\psi = \mathbf{Enc}(pk, s)$ and s is the private data related to the owner. Recoverability can be attempted by feeding ψ into a decryption box. It is apparent that this construction can be defeated by an adversarial implementation of decryption that given input c, it decrypts it only in the case $c \neq \psi$ (or even $\mathbf{Dec}(c) \neq s$). The constructions we seek should facilitate recoverability even if the adversarial box implementor releases implementations that work for *arbitrary* input distributions of her choice.

The applications of leakage-deterring cryptographic primitives are in any context where the intentional leakage of a cryptographic functionality should be deterred or restricted in some fashion or in a context where the leakage of an implementation should enable the computation of a value that is otherwise hidden. In the most simple scenario, the enhanced public-key contains some piece of information that the owner prefers to keep secret (e.g., her credit-card number or similar piece of private information as suggested by Dwork, Lotspiech and Naor [9] that introduced the concept of *self-enforcement* – in a related but different context – see below). It follows that the system setup "self-enforces" the owner to keep the cryptographic functionality to herself. Depending on the deployment environment, different types of secret-information can be used. We describe more application scenarios of leakage deterring cryptographic primitives in section 5.

Our Contributions. We introduce, formalize and implement leakage-deterring cryptographic primitives for public-key encryption, digital signatures, and identification schemes. The main technical contributions we provide are three different techniques for constructing leakage-deterring cryptographic primitives. Our techniques enable the secure embedding of private information into the public key of the primitive in a way that is recoverable given any (even partially) working implementation. Our first method, applies to encryption that is partially homomorphic; given a box that works only for some adversarially chosen distributions we show how to exploit the homomorphic property to appropriately manipulate a target ciphertext and make it decryptable by the adversarial decryption box. Our second method, which can rely on any encryption scheme, hides the key that unlocks the private information into an exponentially large key space that is encoded in the public-keys. By using appropriate redundancy in the public key space we enable the tracing of the vector of keys that identify the private information, out of any (even partially working) implementation. Achieving recoverability while maintaining small ciphertext size in this setting requires an involved recoverability algorithm which is one of the highlights of our contributions. Finally, our third method applies to signature and identification schemes. It uses the fact that working implementations of suitably chosen such primitives can be used to build "knowledge extractors." These are algorithms that reveal information about the secret-key of the underlying primitives which we use to hide the private information.

Our first construction for public-key encryption requires a standard homomorphic property and achieves constant size ciphertexts while offering recoverability for any (non-trivial) adversarial distribution. The second construction is generic and the size of ciphertexts is a parameter that increases as the min-entropy of the allowed adversarial distributions becomes smaller. We analyze our constructions in the IND-CPA setting and then present a generic transformation to obtain IND-CCA2 security.[1] It is evident that there is a trade-off between privacy and recoverability. For encryption schemes, we aim at maximizing the recoverability while privacy can only be achieved if no decryption query is allowed. For the case of signatures, we present a construction that maintains the privacy of the embedded information even if the adversary has arbitrary access to the signing functionality (which is most desirable since digital signatures are typically publicly available). We still manage to enable recoverability by exploiting the random oracle model and non-black-box access to the implementation. Security properties of our identification schemes are shown in the standard model. To attain privacy in the standard model we utilize strong extractors for random variables with high conditional unpredictability.

Related work. The most relevant work to ours is [9] that introduced self-enforcement as a way of avoiding illegal content redistribution in a multi-user setting. Self-enforcement was argued in that paper by ensuring (under certain assumptions) that an owner has only two options when implementing a decoder: either using her private key (that includes private personal information), or encoding a derived key that is of size proportional to the data to be decrypted. In our terminology, this means that the schemes of [9] exhibit a leakage-deterrence/program-length tradeoff and hence are not leakage-deterring *per se*. Furthermore, recoverability in [9] is only "white-box" as opposed to the

[1]It may come as a surprise that recoverability and IND-CCA2 can actually coexist. Attaining IND-CCA2 intuitively means that a decryption oracle basically leaks no useful information about manipulated ciphertexts. Thus, the recovering algorithm can seemingly do nothing useful with access to a decryption implementation beyond decrypting valid ciphertexts, which if related to the enhanced public-key can be rejected. Still, the paradox can be resolved, if one observes that the decryption oracle should be useless only with respect to breaking the security of regular ciphertexts and not the security of the data that are somehow embedded into the enhanced public-key.

black-box nature that our constructions achieve. In another related line of work [5, 27, 4, 21] it was discussed how to deter a user from transferring her credentials (or the secret key directly) to others in the context of identification systems. The techniques from these works – by nature – were restricted to only identification schemes and digital signatures. The primitive of circular encryption introduced in [4] might look promising at first sight to achieve leakage-deterrence in the public-key encryption setting as well, however, no recovery algorithm which works for all partial implementations is immediately apparent. Indeed, recall that the technically most challenging aspect of leakage-deterring cryptosystems is in the design of black-box recoverability and for this, techniques other than circular encryption are needed. Interestingly, our embedding techniques eventually obviate the need for circular encryption altogether as they can hide the owner private data in an information-theoretic sense and hence the secret-key can be safely embedded into the public-key without jeopardizing the security of the scheme. Furthermore, for the case of identification and signature schemes, the idea of taking advantage of the knowledge extractor for preventing the transfer of identification tokens has been utilized before [5, 27, 4, 21] (in the sense that sharing a token implies sharing the key). In our construction we go beyond this, by showing that the secret key can be of sufficient (pseudo)entropy so that it can hide arbitrary information (and not merely itself). In fact we show that no additional intractability assumptions are necessary for achieving leakage-deterring signature and identification schemes. Other forms of leakage deterring techniques were considered in various settings, e.g., limited delegation [13], data collection [14], e-payments [31] or designated verifier signatures in [26, 32] in the form of *non-delegatability* (which is a weaker notion than our leakage-deterring concept).

Another related notion, introduced in [28], dealt with the problem *copyrighting* a public-key decryption function: a single public-key decryption functionality should be implemented in many distinct ways so that if an implementation is derived from some of them, then it is possible to discover the index of at least one of the implementations that was used. This notion was further investigated in [23] and was related to traitor tracing schemes [6]. In the context of public-key encryption, the objective of copyrighting a function or of a traitor tracing scheme is orthogonal to ours. While in both cases we deal with adversarial implementations of cryptographic functionalities (hence the similarities in terminology), the adversarial goal is different: in the case of traitor tracing, the adversary has many different implementations of the same functionality and tries to produce a new one that is hard to trace back to the ones she is given. In an attack against a leakage-deterring scheme on the other hand the adversary possesses an implementation of a cryptographic functionality and tries to modify it in a way that it cannot be used to extract some information that is hidden in the primitive's public-key. Combining the two functionalities in one is an interesting question and we leave it as open problem (a step towards this general direction but in a much weaker model than ours was suggested in the work of [24] but the leakage-deterring aspect (in our terminology) was found to be insecure in [22]).

Accountable authority identity based encryption (AIBE) [15, 16, 25, 30] considers the problem of judging whether an implementation of decryption belongs to the owner or the PKG (in the context of IBE). In this setting, both the owner and the PKG may be the potential adversary who try to implicate the other. Hence, some property similar to our recoverability is needed. In any case, the single bit decisional output required by AIBE is much weaker than our recoverability requirement in leakage-deterring public-key encryption (even in the IBE setting) where by interacting with a decryption box, one should recover the whole private data embedded in the enhanced public-key.

Finally we should point out that the notion of leakage deterrence is different from the notion of leakage-resilience (see e.g., [20, 10]). Our notion aims at constructing schemes with the property that *intensional* leakage of the cryptographic functionality implies the revelation of some private owner information (hence they are "leakage-deterring"), while the leakage-resilience notion aims at ensuring that the unintentional leakage (as in the case of side channel attacks) provides no useful information to an adversary.

2. DEFINITIONS AND SECURITY MODEL

2.1 Leakage-deterring Cryptosystems

A leakage-deterring cryptographic primitive includes two additional algorithms on top of the regular algorithms the primitive normally possess: **EnKey**$(\cdot)$, which embeds some (private) owner related information into the public key, and **Rec**$(\cdot)$ which recovers the private information from the public key by interacting with any non-trivial implementation (or "box") which can be executed by anyone. While the concept of a leakage-deterring cryptographic primitive can be defined in abstract terms for a wide class of primitives we find it more instructive to present it for three main cryptographic primitives individually; we focus on encryption; definitions of leakage-deterring signatures and identification are similar and we defer them for the full version. With these examples at hand, it is relatively straightforward to derive leakage-deterring definitions for other cryptographic primitives following the same general structure (see also remarks below).

Leakage-deterring Public Key Encryption:

- **KeyGen**(1^λ): On input security parameter λ, this algorithm returns a key pair (pk, sk).
- **EnKey**(O, A): This is a protocol between two parties O (owner) and A (authority), with inputs (pk, sk, s) and (pk, s) respectively that has the objective to embed the private owner's data s into his public-key; the protocol terminates with the owner O obtaining an enhanced key pair (epk, esk) while A obtains simply the enhanced epk.
- **Enc**(epk, m): On input a message m and the user's enhanced public key epk, this algorithm returns a ciphertext c.
- **Dec**(esk, c): On input a ciphertext c and enhanced secret key esk, this algorithm returns m or $\perp$ (fail).
- **Rec**$^{B,\mathcal{D}}(epk, \delta)$:[2] Using access to a decryption box B and a plaintext distribution $\mathcal{D}$ (which is supposedly the

[2]Having access to $\mathcal{D}$ is necessary; to see that, consider the following simple example: the box processes the input only if the message encrypted is of the form $sc||m$ for some secret string sc; otherwise it outputs $\perp$. It follows that without

one that B is suited for and is correct with probability δ), as well as input the enhanced public key *epk* for a certain user, this algorithm outputs s or $\perp$ (fail).

Remarks. One can think of **EnKey** as an extension of a public-key certification operation by an authority. The owner may still utilize (pk, sk) for the primitive's operation (as in a PKI one may still use an uncertified key) but *epk* is the key designated for public use.

The definitions for other primitives are similar and we present them in the full version. They share the same basic structure in terms of the syntax of the recovering algorithm but there is some variability across primitives with respect to when this algorithm is supposed to operate. We tackle this question in the following section. Furthermore, we note that in the **Rec** algorithm, one may distinguish several ways that the algorithm may have access to the main functionality box (which is assumed to be resettable, i.e., it does not maintain state from one query to the next). Specifically, beyond black-box access we will also consider a certain type of non-black-box access.

2.2 Correctness and Security Modeling

In this section we introduce the main security requirements for leakage-deterring cryptographic primitives. In general any leakage-deterring primitive should offer *privacy* for the owner (as long as no implementation of the primitive is leaked) and *recoverability*, i.e., that the recovering algorithm will be able to produce the private data of the owner as long as it has access to a *non-trivial* implementation of the cryptographic primitive. Finally, it is important that the introduction of the additional functionality does not disturb the standard cryptographic properties of the primitive. We examine these properties below.

Privacy (of Owner's Data): For an honest owner who does not leak any non-trivial box, the privacy of its data bound in the enhanced public key should be protected. To define the property formally we introduce the following game between a challenger and an adversary $\mathcal{A}$.

- The challenger runs $\mathbf{KeyGen}(\cdot)$ and sends to the adversary $\mathcal{A}$ the public key *pk*.
- The adversary $\mathcal{A}$ chooses two private strings s_0, s_1 and sends them to the challenger.
- The challenger chooses b and simulates $\mathbf{EnKey}(\cdot)$ on s_b and *pk*, *sk*; it sends *epk* to the adversary.
- $\mathcal{A}$ returns his guess b' about b.

If there is no efficient adversary $\mathcal{A}$ that can correctly guess b with non-negligible advantage, i.e., for all PPT $\mathcal{A}$, $|\Pr[b' = b] - \frac{1}{2}| \leq \epsilon$ where ϵ is a negligible function, we say the leakage-deterring cryptographic scheme achieves privacy (in the sense of indistinguishability). Furthermore, in the above game, we may allow the adversary to observe the cryptographic functionality on a certain input distribution. If the above definition holds even in the case that the adversary has access to an oracle $\mathcal{O}(esk, \cdot)$ (that is dependent on the enhanced secret-key of the owner, e.g., decryption oracle or signing oracle w.r.t. some plaintext distribution $\mathcal{D}$) we will say that the scheme achieves privacy with respect to the secret-key oracle $\mathcal{O}(esk, \cdot)$. Note that for privacy we consider both owner and authority honest. It is possible to extend the model to the case of a dishonest authority but this goes beyond our current scope.

Recoverability (of Owner's Data): If a dishonest owner releases a functional box B, anyone having access to B should be able to recover the owner's private data from the enhanced public key *epk*. Formally, consider the following game between a challenger and an adversary $\mathcal{A}$:

- The adversary $\mathcal{A}$ on input 1^λ generates a key pair (sk, pk) and submits it together with the owner private data s to the challenger.
- The challenger acting as the authority runs **EnKey** with the adversary (playing the role of the owner) to produce the enhanced key pair (epk, esk).
- $\mathcal{A}$ outputs an implementation B and a distribution $\mathcal{D}$.
- The challenger outputs the value $s' = \mathbf{Rec}^{B,\mathcal{D}}(epk, \delta)$.

For a given δ, we will say that the leakage-deterring cryptographic primitive satisfies black-box recoverability with respect to the class of input distributions $\mathscr{D}$, if for any efficient adversary $\mathcal{A}$ the following event in the game above happens with negligible probability.

$$(B \text{ is } \delta\text{-correct w.r.t. } \mathcal{D}) \wedge (\mathcal{D} \in \mathscr{D}) \wedge (s' \neq s)$$

The predicate "B is δ-correct w.r.t. $\mathcal{D}$" takes a different form depending on the cryptographic primitive and is intended to capture the fact that the box produced by the adversary should have some minimum utility parameterized by δ.

Consider the case of a PKE scheme $(\mathbf{KeyGen}, \mathbf{Enc}, \mathbf{Dec})$. The predicate for δ-correctness w.r.t. $\mathcal{D}$ in this case is as follows: $\Pr[B(\mathbf{Enc}(epk, m)) = m] \geq \delta$, s.t. $m \leftarrow \mathcal{D}$ where the random variables $epk, \mathcal{D}, B$ are defined as in the game. It is worth noting that the largest class of distributions $\mathscr{D}$ we can hope recoverability to work for is one that includes those distributions whose *predicting probability*[3] is by a non-negligible amount smaller than δ; otherwise, one can implement a decryption box by always returning the most probable sample from $\mathcal{D}$. In a similar vein, we define correctness for digital signatures and identification in the full version.

We will also consider a form of the above definition where a non-black-box technique is used for recovering the owner's private data. In this case we can think of the **Rec** algorithm as a family of algorithms parameterized by the box algorithm B (as opposed to being a single algorithm with black-box access to B).

We next compare privacy and recoverability and observe a natural trade-off between the two properties. *Privacy* w.r.t. a secret-key oracle $\mathcal{O}(esk, \cdot)$ for a distribution $\mathcal{D}$ (i.e., when adversarial access to the cryptographic primitive is allowed for input distribution $\mathcal{D}$) can not be achieved if the leakage-deterring cryptographic primitive satisfies black-box *recoverability* w.r.t. $\mathscr{D}$, in case $\mathcal{D} \in \mathscr{D}$. This easily follows from the fact that the privacy adversary can simulate the **Rec** algorithm with the help of the secret key oracle.

Correctness Properties. Leakage-deterring cryptographic primitives should satisfy correctness in the usual sense (albeit correctness should be expressed with respect to the enhanced

knowledge of $\mathcal{D}$, the box is useless. This counterexample applies to the other leakage-deterring primitives.

[3]Denoted by $p(\mathcal{D})$ is equal to $2^{-\mathbf{H}_\infty(\mathcal{D})}$, where $\mathbf{H}_\infty(\mathcal{D}) = -\log \max_x \Pr[x \in \mathcal{D}]$ is the min-entropy of $\mathcal{D}$.

public and secret-keys). The extension of the definitions is straightforward and we defer them for the full version.

Security Properties. We next consider how the individual security properties for leakage-deterring primitives should be amended. In general, the original security property (e.g., IND-CPA or unforgeability) should be retained with respect to the enhanced public and secret-keys even in the presence of a corrupted authority running the **EnKey** protocol.

IND-CPA/CCA Security (leakage-deterring public-key encryption with dishonest authority): Consider the following game between the adversary and the challenger:

- The challenger runs **KeyGen**$(\cdot)$ to get (pk, sk) and returns pk to the adversary $\mathcal{A}$.
- The adversary $\mathcal{A}$ selects s and playing the role of the authority runs **EnKey**$(\cdot)$ with the challenger on input pk, s.
- The adversary $\mathcal{A}$ chooses two messages m_0, m_1, and sends them to the challenger.
- The challenger randomly picks a bit $b \in \{0,1\}$, and gives $\mathcal{A}$ the encryption of m_b under epk.
- Finally, $\mathcal{A}$ returns a guess b' about b.

Suppose there is no efficient adversary $\mathcal{A}$ that can output a correct guess about b with non-negligible advantage, i.e, $|Pr[b' = b] - \frac{1}{2}| \leq \epsilon$, where ϵ is a negligible function. In this case, we say that the leakage-deterring encryption is IND-CPA-secure (with dishonest authority).

If we allow the adversary to ask decryption queries at anytime before outputting the guess (it can be both before and after receiving the challenge ciphertext, with the only restriction being that the challenge ciphertext cannot be queried), then we refer to this as IND-CCA2 security.

We can also consider the security definition with an honest authority, in which case both **KeyGen**, **EnKey** are executed by the challenger. The definitions of unforgeability for the case of digital signatures and impersonation resistance for identification schemes are in the same vein and are deferred for the full version.

3. LEAKAGE-DETERRING PUBLIC KEY ENCRYPTION

In this section, we present constructions of leakage-deterring public key encryption schemes. We start with a construction from any *additive* homomorphic encryption to demonstrate our first technique for implementing recoverability, then, we show a generic construction of IND-CPA secure leakage-deterring PKE from any IND-CPA secure encryption along with an improvement that achieves constant size ciphertexts. In section 3.3, we provide a general way to achieve IND-CCA2 security for all leakage-deterring encryption schemes.

3.1 IND-CPA-secure Leakage-deterring PKE from Homomorphic Encryption

Recall the trivial solution presented in the introduction (encrypting the owner's private data with its public-key). It does not work because an adversarial decryption box is able to test whether the queries fed by the recovering algorithm match the ciphertext stored in epk. A seeming fix is to query via rerandomizing the ciphertext contained in the enhanced public key. However, given that the private data are known to the attacker, the adversarial box can check for them and still refuse to cooperate. So in some sense to go around the problem one has to re-randomize the plaintext as well! (so that after re-randomization, the plaintexts should be distributed according to $\mathcal{D}$ but in a way that is still somehow useful for decrypting the private data). We provide a solution along these lines in this section.

Informally, an encryption algorithm $E(\cdot)$ has a homomorphic property if $E(m_1 + m_2) = E(m_1) \cdot E(m_2)$ for some operations $(+, \cdot)$ over plaintexts and ciphertexts respectively. For instance, we can submit a ciphertext $c^* \cdot E(r)$ to the decryption box B, and retrieve the message in c^* from the answer by subtracting r. This method would be effective for our purpose only if B satisfies correctness w.r.t. to random distributions over the whole message space. However we would like a solution that works *even* for adversarially chosen distributions that are unknown at the time of the generation of epk. The recovering technique we introduce below achieves this goal.

First assume that we have an underlying encryption E : (**KeyGen**, **Enc**, **Dec**) that is an IND-CPA secure PKE with a homomorphic property. Specifically, we assume that for any message m and any a, b from the message space, $\mathbf{Enc}(m)^a \cdot \mathbf{Enc}(b)$ is identically distributed to $\mathbf{Enc}(am + b)$. We call the following construction Scheme-I.

- **KeyGen**(1^λ): Run the **KeyGen** algorithm of E, return (pk, sk).
- **EnKey**(O, A): This is a protocol between O and A with input (pk, sk, s) and (pk, s) respectively. A randomly chooses $n = |s|$ messages $\omega_i, i = 1, \ldots, n$ according to the uniform distribution over $\{0,1\}$. Then A calculates $s_i' = \omega_i \oplus s_i$, $\{c_i = E(pk, \omega_i)\}, s' = s_1' \ldots s_n'$. The protocol terminates with O obtaining the enhanced key pair (epk, esk) where $epk = (pk, \{c_i\}, s')$, and $esk = sk$, while A gets only the enhanced public key epk.
- **Enc**(epk, m): This algorithm runs the encryption algorithm **Enc**, returning $c = \mathbf{Enc}(pk, m)$.
- **Dec**(esk, c): This algorithm runs the decryption algorithm **Dec**, returning $m = \mathbf{Dec}(sk, c)$.
- **Rec**$^{B,\mathcal{D}}(epk, \delta)$: With access to a decryption box B and a distribution $\mathcal{D}$, over which B works with δ-correctness, the objective of this algorithm is to transform the ciphertexts $c_1, \ldots, c_n$ found in the epk to ciphertexts that look *inconspicuous* from the point of view of the box B. For each ciphertext c_i the algorithm will operate as follows. First it will calculate a sufficiently long sequence of pairs (x, y) (the exact length N of the sequence depends on the parameters of B and $\mathcal{D}$ and will be determined in our security analysis). For each pair, the algorithm first independently samples two plaintexts m_0, m_1 according to $\mathcal{D}$. Then it calculates x, y by solving the following linear system:

$$\begin{cases} 0 \cdot x + y = m_0 \\ 1 \cdot x + y = m_1 \end{cases}$$

Let $(x_l, y_l)_{l=1,\ldots,N}$ be the pairs produced by running the above procedure N times and $m_{0,l}, m_{1,l}$ be the pair of plaintexts used as constant terms of the linear system for the l-th sample. Having calculated those, the algorithm computes $c'_{i,l} = c_i^{x_l} \cdot E(pk, y_l)$ for $l = 1, \ldots, N$, and feeds B with those ciphertexts (observe that their corresponding plaintexts follow the distribution $\mathcal{D}$). Let $a_1, \ldots, a_N$, be the answers of the box B where $a_l = \perp$ if the box does not provide an answer for the l-th ciphertext. Now consider the modified answer sequence defined as follows:

$$a_l^* = \begin{cases} (a_l - y_l)/x_l & a_l \in \{m_{0,l}, m_{1,l})\} \wedge x_l \neq 0 \\ \perp & \text{otherwise} \end{cases}$$

Note that $a_l^* \in \{0, 1, \perp\}$. If the majority symbol among the non-$\perp$ symbols of $\langle a_1^*, \ldots, a_N^* \rangle$ is defined, the recovering algorithm calculates it as v_i and proposes it as the decryption of c_i (otherwise the algorithm fails). This procedure is repeated for all ciphertexts $c_1, \ldots, c_n$ thus forming $v = v_1 \ldots v_n$. Finally, the recovering algorithm proposes as the private data of the owner the string $s' \oplus v$ where s' is parsed from the epk.

Security Analysis: We will analyze correctness and three security properties, i.e, *security, privacy, recoverability*. First observe that correctness is trivial, according to the correctness of the underlying encryption scheme E while IND-CPA security is also relatively obvious since the extra information exposed due to our extension are some independent values $(\omega_1 \ldots \omega_n, s)$. Now regarding the privacy property, we can see that the **EnKey** algorithm in Scheme-I is a KEM/DEM mechanism [7], using a KEM which encrypts each bit of the key with a secure encryption. Given $\{c_i\}$, the adversary is not able to predict the bit ω_i with a sufficient bias, thus every ω_i is random conditioned on the adversary's view. This proves privacy (assuming no secret-key oracle $\mathcal{O}(esk, \cdot)$ is given). Regarding recoverability we can prove it w.r.t. essentially any distribution $\mathcal{D}$. The **Rec** algorithm produces a sequence of ciphertexts with plaintexts following $\mathcal{D}$ whose correct decryption reveals the bits ω_i by a majority argument. As long as the correctness of the box B is non-negligibly larger than the predicting probability of $\mathcal{D}$ (which is a necessary characteristic of "box usefulness") the recovering algorithm will produce the ω_i values with overwhelming certainty since it can do a perfect simulation of ciphertexts with $\mathcal{D}$ distributed plaintexts. The complete proofs of all those facts can be found in the full version (available by the authors). Among others, there we establish that $N = O(\alpha^{-2} \log^6 \lambda)$ is sufficient where α represents the gap between the prediction probability of $\mathcal{D}$ and δ.

3.2 Generic IND-CPA Leakage-deterring PKE with Honest Authority

In this section, we show that leakage-deterring PKE can be based on *any* secure PKE (even without a homomorphic property). We will only consider IND-CPA security with honest authority in this section and we will show how to go beyond this and achieve security against dishonest authorities (and actually IND-CCA2) in the next section.

Linear-Size Construction. To make the exposition more accessible we present first a less efficient construction (with linear size ciphertexts in the length of hidden information); then we show our main generic construction which is constant size. Consider a semantically secure public key encryption E. The main idea of the construction is as follows. For each bit of private data there is a pair of public keys, and the owner has only one of the secret keys. The ambiguity of which secret key the owner has offers the opportunity for the recovering algorithm to work. We call this construction Scheme-II, details are as follows:

- **KeyGen**(1^λ): This algorithm generates $n = |s|$ key pairs $(pk_1, sk_1), \ldots, (pk_n, sk_n)$.
- **EnKey**(O, A): (O, A) inputs $(pk_1, \ldots, pk_n, s, sk_1, \ldots, sk_n)$, and $(pk_1, \ldots, pk_n, s)$ respectively, where $s \in \{0,1\}^n$. A randomly generates $r \in \{0,1\}^n$ which we call indicating string, and n new random public keys $pk'_1, \ldots, pk'_n$. The enhanced public key epk is n pairs of public keys $(pk_1^0, pk_1^1), \ldots, (pk_n^0, pk_n^1)$, together with $s' = r \oplus s$, where for $i = 1, \ldots, n$, $pk_i^{r_i} = pk_i, pk_i^{1-r_i} = pk'_i$, and the enhanced secret key is $esk = (sk, r)$, where $sk = (sk_1, \ldots, sk_n)$.
- **Enc**(epk, m):This algorithm picks $m_1, \ldots, m_{n-1}$ randomly, and computes $m_n = m - \sum_{i=1}^{n-1} m_i$ (wlog we assume that additive secret-sharing works over the plaintext space). It outputs the ciphertext $c = [(c_1^0, c_1^1), \ldots, (c_n^0, c_n^1)]$, where $c_i^0 = \mathbf{Enc}(pk_i^0, m_i), c_i^1 = \mathbf{Enc}(pk_i^1, m_i)$.
- **Dec**(esk, c): To decrypt ciphertext c, this algorithm chooses from c the ciphertexts corresponding to the indicating string r, and returns $m = \sum_{i=1}^n \mathbf{Dec}(sk_i, c_i^{r_i})$.
- **Rec**$^{B,\mathcal{D}}(epk, \delta)$: With access to a decryption box B and a plaintext distribution $\mathcal{D}$ for which the box supposedly works with δ-correctness, the algorithm recovers each bit s_i of s by repeating the following procedure N times (the exact value of N will be specified in the analysis):

  It first samples m, m' independently, according to $\mathcal{D}$, randomly chooses $m_1, \ldots, m_{i-1}, m_{i+1}, \ldots, m_n$, and computes $m_i^0 = m - \sum_{j \neq i} m_j$, and $m_i^1 = m' - \sum_{j \neq i} m_j$.

  Then it feeds B with $[(c_1^0, c_1^1), \ldots, (c_n^0, c_n^1)]$, where for all $j \neq i$, c_j^0, c_j^1 encrypts the same message m_j while $c_i^0 = \mathbf{Enc}(pk_i^0, m_i^0), c_i^1 = \mathbf{Enc}(pk_i^1, m_i^1)$.

  The algorithm records a 0, if the response from the box is m, 1 if the response is m', and $\perp$ in any other case including the case $m = m'$. For each i, the algorithm will propose r_i to be the majority of the recorded non-$\perp$ values (the algorithm fails if majority is not well-defined).

  The above procedure is repeated for all $i \in \{1, \ldots, n\}$ to form a string r, and finally, the algorithm outputs $s = s' \oplus r$, where s' is parsed from epk.

Security Analysis. We now analyze the security properties of Scheme-II. Let us call an encryption using a single pair of keys as a "unit building block". It is not hard to see that IND-CPA security of the unit building block implies the IND-CPA of scheme-II (assuming authority is honest and taking into account the security of additive secret-sharing). Regarding privacy, observe that s is perfectly hidden within epk as a one-time pad ciphertext. Finally, regarding recoverability w.r.t any distribution $\mathcal{D}$, the recovering algorithm can attempt to query different encrypted messages in any single unit location. Due to the secret-sharing, any box (even partly successful) has to include a key for each coordinate. Due to these facts, the recovering algorithm can detect which secret key does the owner possess at each location something that leads to the calculation of the indicating string and hence the recovery of the private data. A detailed analysis can be found in the full version (available by the authors) where we show that a value for N as in scheme-I is sufficient.

Main Generic Construction. In the previous construction, the sender splits the message into n pieces. This makes the ciphertext size (number of ciphertext units) linear in the length of the owner's private data. We now improve the generic construction to achieve a ciphertext size $O(\log \frac{1}{\delta})$ by using an error correcting code to create the indicating string, where δ is a specified minimum decryption probability required by adversarial implementations and is a parameter of the construction. We call this construction Scheme-III.

- **KeyGen**(1^λ): Same as in Scheme II.
- **EnKey**(O, A): (O, A) have inputs $(pk_1, \ldots, pk_m, s, sk)$, and $(pk_1, \ldots, pk_m, s)$ respectively where $s \in \{0,1\}^n$; the parameter m is selected based on n according to an ECC (e.g., the one of [17]) that corrects up to $\frac{m}{5}$ errors. A randomly generates $\tilde{r} \in \{0,1\}^n$, computes the indicating string $r = ECC(\tilde{r})$. Also, A selects m random public keys $pk'_1, \ldots, pk'_m$. The protocol terminates with O obtaining (epk, esk) and A obtaining epk, where epk is $(pk_1^0, pk_1^1), \ldots, (pk_m^0, pk_m^1)$, together with $s' = \tilde{r} \oplus s$, and for $i = 1, \ldots, m$, $pk_i^{r_i} = pk_i, pk_i^{1-r_i} = pk'_i$, and $esk = (sk, r)$.
- **Enc**(epk, m): To encrypt a message m, the algorithm first chooses a random subset $S \subseteq \{1, \ldots, m\}$ with size $t = 5 \ln \frac{4}{\delta}$; we denote the i-th element of S by S_i. Then it randomly picks $m_1, \ldots, m_{t-1}$, and computes $m_t = m - \sum_{i=1}^{t-1} m_i$. The ciphertext $c = [S, (c_1^0, c_1^1), \ldots, (c_t^0, c_t^1)]$, where $c_i^b = \mathbf{Enc}(pk_{S_i}^b, m_i)$ for $b \in \{0,1\}$.
- **Dec**(esk, c): To decrypt ciphertext c, this algorithm chooses from c the ciphertexts corresponding to the indicating string r projected on S, and returns $m = \sum_{i=1}^t \mathbf{Dec}(sk_{S_i}, c_i^{r_{S_i}})$.
- **Rec**$^{B,\mathcal{D}}(epk, \delta)$: With access to a decryption box B and a plaintext distribution $\mathcal{D}$, the algorithm recovers each bit s_i of s by repeating the following procedure N times (the exact number will be specified in the analysis):

  It first randomly selects a subset $S \subseteq \{1, \ldots, m\}$ with size t.

  If $i \in S$, and i is the k-th element of S, the algorithm randomly chooses m, m' independently according to $\mathcal{D}$ as well as random values $m_1, \ldots, m_{k-1}, m_{k+1}, \ldots, m_t$. Then, it computes $m_k^0 = m - \sum_{j \neq k} m_j$, and $m_k^1 = m' - \sum_{j \neq i} m_j$. It feeds B with $[S, (c_1^0, c_1^1), \ldots, (c_t^0, c_t^1)]$ where, for all $j \neq k$, the pair c_j^0, c_j^1 encrypts the same message m_j using pk_i^0, pk_i^1 respectively, while $c_k^b = \mathbf{Enc}(pk_i^b, m_k^b)$ for $b \in \{0,1\}$.

  If $i \notin S$, the algorithm proceeds by performing a regular encryption of a plaintext from $\mathcal{D}$.

  If $i \in S$ and the response of the decryption box is m, the algorithm records 0; if $i \in S$ and the response is m', this algorithm records a 1; Otherwise (in any other case including $i \notin S$ or $m = m'$), it records $\perp$.

  For each i the majority of the non-$\perp$ recorded values is proposed as the value of r_i. If no majority is defined, a random bit is produced as r_i.

  The above procedure is repeated for all $i \in \{1, \ldots, m\}$, and a string r is formed. The decoding algorithm of ECC is now executed on r to obtain $\tilde{r}$. The algorithm terminates by returning $s = s' \oplus \tilde{r}$, where s' is parsed from epk.

Security Analysis: The IND-CPA and privacy properties are essentially the same as in scheme II. We only discuss recoverability which is significantly more complex. The intuition is that because of the error correcting code, the **Rec** algorithm would work as long as a linear fraction of bits of r can be recovered. As we will prove in the appendix, suppose that q is the number of positions among the m for which our recoverability procedure fails. We will show that the probability of correct decryption will become roughly smaller than $e^{-tq/m} = \delta^{5q/m}$. From this we derive that any decryption box operating with probability at least δ (as postulated) can make our algorithm fail in at most $m/5$ of the m secret keys which is sufficient for correct decoding. The full analysis is presented in the appendix B.

3.3 Generic CCA2 Secure Construction with Dishonest Authority

In this section, we introduce a simple general method to construct an IND-CCA2 secure leakage-deterring encryption with dishonest authority from a leakage-deterring PKE which is IND-CPA secure with honest authority, and an IND-CCA2 secure standard PKE. The main idea is to compose these two encryptions to form a nested encryption with the outer layer encryption being the IND-CCA2 secure one. *Recoverability* could be maintained because the **Rec** algorithm can run the **Rec** algorithm of the inner leakage-deterring encryption to collect queries, and encrypt them using the outer layer public key to form its own recovering queries.

Construction: Suppose E_1 is an IND-CPA secure leakage-deterring PKE (with an honest authority), and E_2 is an IND-CCA2 secure PKE. We call the following construction Scheme-IV.

- **KeyGen**(1^λ): This algorithm executes the **KeyGen** algorithm of both E_1, E_2, and returns $\{(pk_i, sk_i)\}_{i=1,2}$.
- **EnKey**(O, A): This is a protocol between O, A with inputs (pk_i, sk_i, s) and (pk_i, s) respectively; it proceeds by executing the **EnKey** protocol of E_1 to get (epk_1, esk_1) first, and this protocol terminates with O obtaining enhanced key pair (epk, esk), and A obtaining epk only, where $(epk, esk) = ((epk_1, pk_2), (esk_1, sk_2))$.
- **Enc**(epk, m): To encrypt a message m, this algorithm runs the encryption algorithms of both of E_1, E_2, and returns the ciphertext as $c = \mathbf{Enc}(pk_2, \mathbf{Enc}(epk_1, m))$
- **Dec**(esk, c): To decrypt a ciphertext c, this algorithm runs the decryption algorithms of both E_1, E_2 and returns $m = \mathbf{Dec}(esk_1, \mathbf{Dec}(sk_2, c))$.
- **Rec**$^{B,\mathcal{D}}(epk, \delta)$: With access to a decryption box B and a plaintext distribution $\mathcal{D}$, this algorithm calls the **Rec** algorithm R_1 of E_1. For each query c of R_1, this algorithm feeds B with $\mathbf{Enc}(pk_2, c)$. It then passes the responses of the box to R_1 and returns whatever R_1 returns.

Security Analysis: *Correctness* is obvious, and *Privacy* and *Recoverability* are not influenced by the extra outer layer encryption. To see IND-CCA2 security with dishonest authority, first, even if the authority has part of the secret key for the inner layer enhanced public key epk_1, any message will be protected using the outer layer encryption E_2; further, CCA security also easily follows from the CCA security of E_2: the simulator can answer decryption oracle queries by asking the E_2 challenger to decrypt the outer layer, and decrypt the inner ciphertext locally using esk_1. Details can be found in the full version.

We remark that the generic method above can be also applied to the identity based setting; in that case, we can use the one-time signature paradigm to achieve CCA2 security. We omit further details.

4. LEAKAGE-DETERRING SIGNATURE & IDENTIFICATION

In this section, we design leakage-deterring signatures and identification schemes. The main idea is that we treat any functional box as an unforgeability or impersonation adversary, and then take advantage of "witness extractability" used in the security arguments of the underlying primitive to extract the secret-key which will unlock the private data; in this case we have non-black-box recoverability. We stress that our constructions do not employ any additional intractability assumptions than the underlying primitives.

4.1 Leakage-deterring Signature In the Random Oracle Model

We construct a leakage-deterring signature scheme based on a class of Σ-protocol-based signature schemes as in [29]. The security proofs of these signatures rely on the fact that if the adversary can forge one signature, then he could also forge another correlated signature for the same message with the same random tape but a different random oracle. Using these two forgeries that are correlated, one can extract the secret key of the owner.

Our construction of leakage-deterring signature is based on two independent digital signatures instances $\mathbf{Sig}_0$ and $\mathbf{Sig}_1$ that are unforgeable under adaptively chosen message attacks. Further, $\mathbf{Sig}_1$ is required to be unforgeable in the random oracle(RO) model following [29]; specifically, the signature has the form of $(m, \sigma_1, h, \sigma_2)$ as in [29], and satisfies $h = H(m, \sigma_1)$, and σ_2 only depends on m, σ_1, h, where H is a RO. We call the following construction Scheme-V.

- $\mathbf{KeyGen}(1^\lambda)$: This algorithm executes the **KeyGen** algorithm of $\mathbf{Sig}_0$, and returns the key pair (pk_0, sk_0).

- $\mathbf{EnKey}(O, A)$: This protocol is executed between O, A with inputs (pk_0, sk_0, s), and (pk_0, s) respectively. A runs **KeyGen** algorithm of $\mathbf{Sig}_1$ to generate a key pair (pk_1, sk_1). The protocol terminates with O obtaining (epk, esk), and A obtaining epk, where $epk = (pk_0, pk_1, H(sk_1) \oplus s)$, and $esk = (sk_0, sk_1)$.

- $\mathbf{Sign}(esk, m)$: On input a message m, this algorithm returns the signature $\sigma = (\sigma_0, \sigma_1)$, where it holds $\sigma_0 = \mathbf{Sign}_0(sk_0, m)$, and $\sigma_1 = \mathbf{Sign}_1(sk_1, m) = (\sigma_1^1, h_1, \sigma_1^2)$.

- $\mathbf{Verify}(epk, m, \sigma)$: On input a message-signature pair (m, σ) and enhanced public key $epk = (pk, pk')$, this algorithm returns 1 if both of the two signatures are valid, 0 otherwise.

- $\mathbf{Rec}^{\mathcal{D}}(epk, B, \delta)$: The recovering algorithm follows the security proof argument of [29]: Whenever the box B asks a random oracle query (suppose total number of such queries is bounded by q), the algorithm selects a uniform response from the range of the random oracle and feeds it to the box; it also maintains a table of all these queries. The recovering algorithm samples a message m according to $\mathcal{D}$ and simulates the box B on m. When the box outputs a valid signature σ_0, σ_1, where $\sigma_1 = (\sigma_1^1, h_1, \sigma_1^2)$, algorithm checks the table and identifies the index i of the first query from B on (m, σ_1^1). Then, it rewinds B to the state prior to the i-th query, and continues the simulation picking new random query responses.

  The above procedure is repeated until the box outputs another valid signature (σ_0', σ_1') on the same message m, where $\sigma_1' = (\sigma_1^1, h_1', \sigma_2')$, and also the index i that (m, σ_1^1) was queried is the same for both σ_1 and σ_1'. Refer to the appendix for a more formal explanation of knowledge extraction.

  Now the algorithm can extract the second secret key sk_1 from $(m, \sigma_1^1, h_1, \sigma_1^2), (m, \sigma_1^1, h, \sigma_2')$ using the Σ protocol properties of the scheme that define $\mathbf{Sig}_1$. The recovery of s follows immediately.

Security Analysis: We now analyze the three properties. It is easy to see that unforgeability against adaptively chosen message attacks can be derived from the property of $\mathbf{Sig}_0$ as any forgery will imply also a forgery of $\mathbf{Sig}_0$. Note that signing queries are easy to simulate because the simulator has the secret key for $\mathbf{Sig}_1$, and can ask signing queries to the challenger for $\mathbf{Sig}_0$. *Privacy* w.r.t. a secret-key oracle for any distribution can be achieved because any successful privacy attacker will have to eventually query sk_1 to the random oracle hence violating the unforgeability of $\mathbf{Sig}_1$. Note that *recoverability* cannot violate *privacy* w.r.t. an arbitrary secret key oracle, since it is achieved now via a non-black-box technique. It uses the fact that rewinding the signing box and controlling the random coins in an execution, one can always find a pair of signatures that reveal the secret key, something that yields the private data. Details of the analysis are in the full version.

4.2 Leakage-deterring Identification

We will construct a leakage-deterring identification scheme by using a similar approach as in the signature case. However here we will show our construction secure in the *standard model*, and thus we need a novel method to embed the owner private data into the enhanced public key. In fact we will need no additional assumption beyond the one employed for the underlying scheme.

Our construction of a leakage-deterring identification scheme is based on the class of identification schemes which are derived from zero-knowledge proofs of knowledge protocols that can be parallely composed. We utilize the fact that given access to the code of any box that implements the identification functionality, one can rewind the box and implement the knowledge extractor assured to exist due to the soundness property of the zero-knowledge proof. We call the following construction Scheme-VI and is based on a parameter t that we specify below.

- **KeyGen**(1^λ): This algorithm executes the **KeyGen** algorithm of the underlying identification scheme, and returns the key pair (pk, sk).
- **EnKey**(O, A): This is a protocol executed between O, A with inputs (pk, sk, s), and (pk, s) respectively. A runs **KeyGen** algorithm to generate t new key pairs $(pk_1, sk_1), \ldots, (pk_t, sk_t)$, and further, A calculates $s' = r \oplus s$, where $r = Ext(sk_1 || \ldots || sk_t, \rho)$ and Ext is a strong randomness extractor (see below for implementation remarks) while ρ is the random seed. The protocol terminates with O obtaining (epk, esk), and A obtaining epk, where $epk = (pk, pk_1, \ldots, pk_t, s', \rho)$, and $esk = (sk, sk_1, \ldots, sk_t)$.
- **Identify**(P, V): This protocol is executed between P, V with inputs (epk, esk), and epk respectively. The protocol is the parallel composition of the $t+1$ underlying identification schemes. The protocol terminates with V outputting 1 if he accepts the proof of knowledge of all secret keys, and 0 otherwise.
- **Rec**(epk, B): The algorithm given B, runs the knowledge extractor algorithm for the parallel composition of the t schemes until all the secret keys of $\{sk_1, \ldots, sk_t\}$ are recovered. Then it applies the randomness extractor on ρ and returns $s = s' \oplus Ext(sk_1 || \ldots || sk_t, \rho)$

Security Analysis: We now analyze the security properties. *Recoverability* is essentially the same as the *recoverability* of Scheme-V. *Impersonation resistance* is also similar to the *unforgeability* property of Scheme-IV; this property mainly relies on the fact that nothing related to the original secret key of the owner sk is added to the epk, therefore the security of identification using the original (pk, sk) can be reduced to the impersonation resistance of Scheme-V. Regarding *privacy*, according to impersonation resistance, after seeing a polynomial number of transcripts of interaction between P, V, there is still unpredicatability on the secret key, (otherwise, one can impersonate by eavesdropping) then applying the strong extractor one can get pure randomness out of the secret-keys, and thus the owner data is hidden computationally. Details are given in the full version.
Remark1: The strong randomness extractor Ext should work on any source with sufficient conditional unpredictability along the lines of [19]. For instance, we can use the extractor derived from the Goldreich-Levin hard-core predicate [12]. Intuitively, one can think of the view (protocol transcripts adaptively queried) of the adversary as the output of a one way function on input $\{sk_i\}$. Using this, [12] implies an extractor of $\log \lambda$ bits per instance and thus t should be as long as $|s|/\log \lambda$.
Remark2: If one is willing to allow additional intractability assumptions, a more compact construction for leakage-deterring signature (in the RO model) and leakage-deterring identification is also possible[4]. The construction would utilize two key pairs $(pk_0, sk_0), (pk_1, sk_1)$ and the secret information will be embedded as $E(pk_1, s)$, thus only sk_1 will be used by the recoverability algorithm. Observe now that privacy will rely on the security of the encryption scheme (and thus may require assumptions going beyond the underlying identification scheme). Furthermore reusing the same key for signing and decrypting may not always be secure and some specialized systems would need to be employed, for instance cf. [18].

[4]We thank an anonymous reviewer for pointing this out.

Scheme	Ciphertext/Signature Size	Enc/Sign Time
I	1	1
III	$O(\log \frac{1}{\delta})$	$O(\log \frac{1}{\delta})$
V	2	2

Table 1: Efficiency of main leakage-deterring (LD) schemes, the size and time denote the ratio of the LD-scheme to the underlying primitive.

5. LEAKAGE-DETERRING CRYPTOSYSTEMS IN PRACTICE

In this section we first summarize the efficiency of our main constructions of leakage-deterring public key primitives in Table 5. Then we explore in more detail practical scenarios where leakage-deterring cryptosystems can be used to provide novel solutions to security problems related to sharing and transferring cryptographic functions.

Let us start with a more detailed motivating scenario: consider a user that maintains all her e-mail encrypted on a mailserver. The user is approached by someone wishing to buy all e-mails sent by the e-mail address x@y in the past, present and future. Using a regular encryption, the user may release to the attacker an implementation of her decryption function that works only if the plaintext is an e-mail sent by x@y (and rejects all other input). If the user does not care about the secrecy of the e-mails from x@y, she has no strong reason to be deterred from releasing the implementation (all her other messages can still be relatively safe assuming the implementation is sufficiently obfuscated or delivered in hardware). Using our encryption however, she is deterred: if she releases the above implementation (even in the form of a hardware token) an adverse action is guaranteed to take place (via the recoverability algorithm): her private information will be revealed. Obviously, a determined secret-key owner can always decrypt and release the plaintexts corresponding to those e-mails individually. But this has to be done one by one, at a potentially high cost. In this scenario, leakage-deterring public-key encryption ensures there is no way to optimize this operation: if one wants to provide access to his decryption he has to do it on a "per-case" basis. Within a PKI this enforces secret-key owners to practice more responsible secret-key management.

Recall privacy w.r.t. to secret key oracles (that would be the CCA flavor of our privacy property) and recoverability can not be achieved simultaneously in the general case: the two properties are mutually exclusive. Thus, one needs to choose a proper trade-off if he wants to implement leakage-deterring public key schemes. Regarding PKE, our objective in this work is to maximize the scope of recoverability: it should work for all (even partially functional) implementations; this makes our primitive most useful from a self-enforcement perspective and necessitates the restrictions we have made in terms of the privacy property. If the user wishes the private information to remain hidden, she should provide no access to her secret-key. In the case of signature/identification schemes the situation is more tricky since by nature of the functionality, the user is expected to release signatures/identification transcripts publicly (which in some cases they may even be adaptively selected). Thus, we must compromise and weaken our recoverability property in some way. We resolved this by adopting a non-black-box recoverability algorithm. As expected, if the implementation becomes "obfuscated" then recoverability would be infeasible. We believe the trade-offs we utilized are natural for the primitives studied, but of course different tradeoffs can be possible between privacy and recoverability, and we leave them as future work.

Depending on different application scenarios, we can embed various types of private owner information to deter the leakage of a cryptographic functionality:

Self-enforcement. In the context of self-enforcement the owner of the cryptographic functionality has embedded into her enhanced public-key some private information that she normally prefers to keep secret. This can be e.g., her credit-card number or similar piece of private information as suggested by Dwork, Lotspiech and Naor [9] that introduced self-enforcement (in a different context - see related work in the introduction). In this way, when using our leakage-deterring primitives, if the owner releases any implementation of the cryptographic functionality, any recipient of the implementation will become privy to the hidden information. This property "self-enforces" the owner to keep the functionality to herself and solves the problem of how to deter the sharing of software or hardware devices that implement cryptographic functionalities.

All-or-nothing sharing of cryptographic functions. In this scenario, the owner is obliged to embed the secret key of the cryptographic primitive itself into the enhanced public-key (in practice this can be done e.g., by a trusted key generator algorithm which will be running the embedding algorithm that is executed by the authority in our model). Using our techniques this means that any working implementation of the cryptographic functionality would leak the whole secret-key. In this sense, the cryptographic functionality becomes "unobfuscatable", any program that partially implements it, say for some types of inputs, can be transformed to a program that implements it perfectly. Leakage-deterring primitives used in this way suggest a type of *all-or-nothing* property for cryptographic keys: owners of a cryptographic functionality cannot partially share it, they either have to keep it to themselves or share it fully. In practice, one can expect that this is also a type of self-enforcing mechanism: either all information about the cryptographic key will be leaked or none.

Anonymity revocation from implementations. In this setting, the owner of the cryptographic functionality operates it under a pseudonym (i.e., the enhanced public-key is certified but without openly identifying the owner). However, the embedded information is ensured by the authority to be either the owner's real identity or an identity credential that the owner prefers to hide. In this setting, using our methodology, if any working implementation of the functionality is confiscated, it will be possible to use the recovering algorithm to reveal the hidden identity credential. This in turn, ensures some level of accountability: the owner remains pseudonymous as long as he does not share the cryptographic functionality but can be identified in case any (even partially working) implementation is leaked.

6. CONCLUSIONS AND OPEN PROBLEMS

We introduced the notion of leakage-deterring cryptosystems. Our schemes have the property that whenever an owner releases an (even partially) "functional" box for others to use instead of herself, anyone who has access to the box can recover some private information that is embedded into the public-key of the owner. We defined the security properties of these primitives and we provided several constructions for public key encryption, signatures, and identification.

Since this is the first step in the formal investigation of such primitives, several interesting open questions remain. A natural question is how to combine the notion with traitor tracing and other multi-user oriented cryptosystems. Another direction is with respect to CCA2 security: our construction can potentially be optimized for efficiency and avoid the nesting of two encryptions. A third direction is to see to what extent it is feasible to construct leakage-deterring signatures and identification with black-box recoverability in the standard model or more generally explore the tradeoff between recoverability and privacy. Last but not least, it would be desirable to see how the trust to the authority can be reduced (and e.g., obviate the need for the authority to know the secret information).

Acknowledgements.

This work was supported by European Research Council Project CODAMODA. The first author was also partially supported by Marie Curie project RECUP.

7. REFERENCES

[1] M. Bellare and O. Goldreich. On defining proofs of knowledge. In *CRYPTO*, pages 390–420, 1992.

[2] M. Bellare and G. Neven. Multi-signatures in the plain public-key model and a general forking lemma. In *ACM CCS*, pages 390–399, 2006.

[3] M. Bellare and P. Rogaway. Random oracles are practical: A paradigm for designing efficient protocols. In *ACM CCS*, pages 62–73, 1993.

[4] J. Camenisch and A. Lysyanskaya. An efficient system for non-transferable anonymous credentials with optional anonymity revocation. In *EUROCRYPT*, pages 93–118, 2001.

[5] R. Canetti, M. Charikar, S. R. Sridhar Rajagopalan, A. Sahai, and A. Tomkins. Non-transferrable anonymous credentials. US Patent 7,222,362., 2008.

[6] B. Chor, A. Fiat, and M. Naor. Tracing traitors. In *CRYPTO*, pages 257–270, 1994.

[7] R. Cramer and V. Shoup. Design and analysis of practical public-key encryption schemes secure against adaptive chosen ciphertext attack. *SIAM J. Comput.*, 33(1):167–226, 2004.

[8] I. Damgard. On σ- protocols. In *http://www.daimi.au.dk/ ivan/Sigma.pdf*, 2010.

[9] C. Dwork, J. B. Lotspiech, and M. Naor. Digital signets: Self-enforcing protection of digital information (preliminary version). In *STOC*, pages 489–498, 1996.

[10] S. Dziembowski and K. Pietrzak. Leakage-resilient cryptography. In *FOCS*, pages 293–302, 2008.

[11] A. Fiat and A. Shamir. How to prove yourself: Practical solutions to identification and signature problems. In *CRYPTO*, pages 186–194, 1986.

[12] O. Goldreich and L. A. Levin. A hard-core predicate for all one-way functions. In *STOC*, pages 25–32, 1989.

[13] O. Goldreich, B. Pfitzmann, and R. L. Rivest. Self-delegation with controlled propagation-or-what if you lose your laptop. In *CRYPTO*, pages 153–168, 1998.

[14] P. Golle, F. McSherry, and I. Mironov. Data collection with self-enforcing privacy. In *ACM CCS*, pages 69–78, 2006.

[15] V. Goyal. Reducing trust in the pkg in identity based cryptosystems. In *CRYPTO*, pages 430–447, 2007.

[16] V. Goyal, S. Lu, A. Sahai, and B. Waters. Black-box accountable authority identity-based encryption. In *ACM CCS*, pages 427–436, 2008.

[17] V. Guruswami and P. Indyk. Expander-based constructions of efficiently decodable codes. In *FOCS*, pages 658–667, 2001.

[18] S. Haber and B. Pinkas. Securely combining public-key cryptosystems. In *ACM CCS*, pages 215–224, 2001.

[19] C.-Y. Hsiao, C.-J. Lu, and L. Reyzin. Conditional computational entropy, or toward separating pseudoentropy from compressibility. In *EUROCRYPT*, pages 169–186, 2007.

[20] Y. Ishai, A. Sahai, and D. Wagner. Private circuits: Securing hardware against probing attacks. In *CRYPTO*, pages 463–481, 2003.

[21] M. Jakobsson, A. Juels, and P. Q. Nguyen. Proprietary certificates. In *CT-RSA*, pages 164–181, 2002.

[22] A. Kiayias and M. Yung. Breaking and repairing asymmetric public-key traitor tracing. In *Digital Rights Management Workshop*, pages 32–50, 2002.

[23] A. Kiayias and M. Yung. Traitor tracing with constant transmission rate. In *EUROCRYPT*, pages 450–465, 2002.

[24] H. Komaki, Y. Watanabe, G. Hanaoka, and H. Imai. Efficient asymmetric self-enforcement scheme with public traceability. In *Public Key Cryptography*, pages 225–239, 2001.

[25] B. Libert and D. Vergnaud. Towards black-box accountable authority ibe with short ciphertexts and private keys. In *Public Key Cryptography*, pages 235–255, 2009.

[26] H. Lipmaa, G. Wang, and F. Bao. Designated verifier signature schemes: Attacks, new security notions and a new construction. In *ICALP*, pages 459–471, 2005.

[27] A. Lysyanskaya, R. L. Rivest, A. Sahai, and S. Wolf. Pseudonym systems. In *International Workshop on Selected Areas in Cryptography*, SAC '99, pages 184–199, 2000.

[28] D. Naccache, A. Shamir, and J. P. Stern. How to copyright a function? In *Public Key Cryptography*, pages 188–196, 1999.

[29] D. Pointcheval and J. Stern. Security arguments for digital signatures and blind signatures. *J. Cryptology*, 13(3):361–396, 2000.

[30] A. Sahai and H. Seyalioglu. Fully secure accountable-authority identity-based encryption. In *Public Key Cryptography*, pages 296–316, 2011.

[31] T. Sander and A. Ta-Shma. Auditable, anonymous electronic cash extended abstract. In *CRYPTO*, pages 555–572, 1999.

[32] S. F. Shahandashti and R. Safavi-Naini. Construction of universal designated-verifier signatures and identity-based signatures from standard signatures. In *Public Key Cryptography*, pages 121–140, 2008.

APPENDIX

Due to the page limit, we only put some preliminaries and the most involved security analysis for scheme-III here, while all other related contents (omitted definitions, security proofs, and identity based constructions) are in the full version.

A. PRELIMINARIES

We recall some known primitives and results which we utilized in our constructions or security analysis.

Proof of Knowledge: [1] A proof of knowledge protocol is one that a prover convinces the verifier he knows a witness to a publicly known polynomial-time predicate. This is a protocol between two parties P, V where P proves a statement $x \in L$ for a language L's instance x with its witness w from a witness set denoted by $W(x)$. The protocol has two properties:

- Completeness: Honest prover always convinces the verifier: $\Pr[V(P(x,w)) = 1 \wedge w \in W(x)] = 1$.
- Soundness: There exist an efficient "knowledge extractor" who interacts with prover, and outputs the witness with probability close to the success probability that P convinces V. Formally, $\Pr[\mathbf{Ext}^P(x) \in W(x)] \geq \Pr[V(P(x)) = 1] - \epsilon$, where ϵ is negligible.

Σ-Protocol: [8] One frequently used type of proof of knowledge protocol is the class of Σ-protocol, which have a three move structure (a, e, z), starting with the prover sending a 'commit' message a, then the verifier sending a 'challenge' message e, and finally the prover answering with a 'response' message z. Using the Fiat-Shamir transformation [11], one can construct a signature scheme based on such protocol in the random oracle model [3]. Security of such signature schemes is comprehensively studied in [29], and it mainly relies on the existence of a knowledge extractor algorithm (which is implied by the soundness of the protocol).

General Forking Lemma: [2] The general forking lemma states that that if an adversary, on inputs drawn from some distribution, produces an output, then the adversary will produce another correlated output with different inputs from same distribution and same random tape. Rigorously, let $\mathcal{A}$ be a probabilistic algorithm, with inputs $(x, r_1, \ldots, r_q; \rho)$ that outputs a pair (J, σ), where ρ refers to the random tape of $\mathcal{A}$ (that is, the random coins $\mathcal{A}$ will make). Suppose further that x is sampled from some distribution X, and R is a set of size $|R|$ and r_i is sampled uniformly from R. Let acc be the probability for $J \geq 1$. We can then define a "forking algorithm" as follows,

- on input x: pick a random tape ρ for $\mathcal{A}$.
- $r_1, \ldots, r_q \xleftarrow{r} R$, $(J, \sigma) \leftarrow \mathcal{A}(x, r_1, \ldots, r_q; \rho)$
- If $J = 0$, return $(0, \epsilon, \epsilon)$.
- $r'_J, \ldots, r'_q \xleftarrow{r} R$
- $(J', \sigma') \leftarrow \mathcal{A}(x, r_1, \ldots, r_{J-1}, r'_J, \ldots, r'_q; \rho)$
- If $J' = J$ and $r_J \neq r'_J$ then return $(1, \sigma, \sigma')$, otherwise, return $(0, \varepsilon, \varepsilon)$.

Let frk be the probability that $\mathcal{A}$ outputs (b, σ, σ'), and $b = 1$, then $\text{frk} \geq acc(\frac{acc}{q} - \frac{1}{|R|})$.

B. ANALYSIS FOR SCHEME-III

THEOREM 1. *Scheme-III parameterized by any $\delta > 0$, achieves IND-CPA (with honest authority), privacy (without secret-key oracle), and black-box recoverability w.r.t. the class of distributions $\mathscr{D}_\delta = \{\mathcal{D} \mid \mathbf{H}_\infty(\mathcal{D}) \geq \log|s| + \log\frac{1}{\delta} - c\}$, where c is a constant (depending on the ECC) and $|s|$ the length of the private information.*

PROOF. The most involved part of the proof is related to recoverability, so we mainly analyze this property. It is not difficult to see that the way we sample m_0, m_1 in the **Rec** algorithm, every query is an encryption of a message independently sampled from $\mathcal{D}$ (the only exception is that $\mathcal{D}$ almost always outputs only one message but in this case, any box becomes "trivial"). Thus, the recovering query is identically distributed as normal decryption queries and B would have δ-correctness for a random recovering query!

The main challenge in the proof of the theorem is the fact that the box B might behave differently depending on i and thus force us to err in a number of locations i. We will prove that we can bound this number and hence our error-correction layer will be sufficient for recovering the hidden information in the *epk*. Let $\delta_i = \Pr[B \text{ decrypts correctly} \mid i \in S]$. We divide the indices $i \in \{1, \ldots, m\}$ in two sets, Bad and Good, we define $i \in \mathsf{Good}$ if and only if $\delta_i \geq \kappa + \alpha_0 = \delta_0$, where $\kappa = p(\mathcal{D}) = 2^{-\mathbf{H}_\infty(\mathcal{D})}$ denoting the predicting probability and $\alpha_0 = (\delta - \kappa)/m^2$. We will later estimate the number of repetition for each i, denoted by N, such that, if $i \in \mathsf{Good}$ the recoverability will return the proper bit in the i-th coordinate with overwhelming probability. In order to upper bound the size of Bad consider the following. Let D be the event of correct decryption. We have that,

$$\begin{aligned}\Pr[\mathsf{D}] &= \Pr[\mathsf{D} \mid S \cap \mathsf{Bad} = \emptyset] \cdot \Pr[S \cap \mathsf{Bad} = \emptyset] \\ &+ \Pr[\mathsf{D} \mid S \cap \mathsf{Bad} \neq \emptyset] \cdot \Pr[S \cap \mathsf{Bad} \neq \emptyset],\end{aligned}$$

Regarding $\Pr[S \cap \mathsf{Bad} = \emptyset]$ observe that if $k = |\mathsf{Bad}|$, this probability is bounded by $p(k,t) = C^t_{m-k}/C^t_m = \prod_{i=0}^{t-1}(1 - \frac{k}{m-i}) \leq (1 - \frac{k}{m})^t$. From inequality $e^x \geq 1 + x$, we can get $p(k,t) \leq e^{-kt/m}$. Regarding $\Pr[\mathsf{D} \mid S \cap \mathsf{Bad} \neq \emptyset]$ note that it is bounded by $\sum_{i \in \mathsf{Bad}} \delta_i \leq m(\kappa + \alpha_0)$ (This bound follows directly from the fact that $\Pr[F \mid \cup_{i=1}^n A_i] \leq \sum_{i=1}^n \Pr[F|A_i]$, for any event F, A_i). We now derive the following,

$$\delta \leq \Pr[\mathsf{D}] \leq e^{-tk/m} + m(\kappa + \alpha_0),$$

from which we obtain the upper bound $k \leq \frac{m}{t} \cdot \ln(\delta - m(\kappa + \alpha_0))^{-1}$. Now observe that due to the condition for the min-entropy, we derive a bound on $\kappa \leq 2^c\delta/|s| = c'\delta/|s|$, for some constant c'. From the choice of α_0, we can prove that $\delta - m(\kappa + \alpha_0) \geq \delta/4$ as long as c is selected appropriately (taking into account the error-correcting rate which is constant). We plug this condition and the fact that $t = 5\ln(4\delta^{-1})$ into the above bound for k, we conclude that $k \leq m\ln(4\delta^{-1})/5\ln(4\delta^{-1}) = m/5$.

Now we analyze the number of repetitions needed for an $i \in \mathsf{Good}$(in terms of an asymptotic function of the security parameter λ) to guarantee we are almost certain that s will be returned in the **Rec** algorithm.

First, an experiment is useful only if $m_0 \neq m_1$, otherwise, we will always record a $\perp$ for this query. The probability of having one useful experiment after sampling N_0 pairs of (m_0, m_1) will be $1 - \mathbf{Col}(\mathcal{D})^{N_0}$, where $\mathbf{Col}(\mathcal{D})$ is the collusion probability of distribution $\mathcal{D}$ which denotes the probability of sampling a same element from two independent trials. Observe that $\mathbf{Col}(\mathcal{D}) < 1 - \gamma$, for some non-negligible γ, if $\mathcal{D}$ is not trivial which has probability almost 1 over one element. If we repeat $N_0 = 2\log^2\lambda$ times sampling, we will get a useful experiment with probability almost 1.

Second, randomly selecting S will not always contain i to be a "useful query" for recovering i. But sampling S randomly instead of always containing some i aims at producing the recovering queries indistinguishable from normal ciphertext. Suppose now the target of the recovering algorithm is the i-th bit, in one selection, the probability $\Pr[i \in S]$ is $C^{t-1}_{m-1}/C^t_m = t/m$. From the lower tail of Chernoff bound, the probability of selecting N_1 times without hitting i once is smaller than $e^{-(\frac{N_1 t}{2m} - 1)}$. After randomly sample $4m/t$ times, one will be sure that one of the subsets will contain i, and one useful query is created.

Further, In one useful query which contains the target location i, only two answers (m_0, m_1) would be considered possibly correct, all other answers could be simply ignored (denoted by $\perp$). The probability of getting at least one correct answer after repeating N_2 times useful experiments is $1 - (1 - (\kappa + \alpha_0))^{N_2}$, if $N_2 = O(\log^2\lambda)$, this probability is almost 1(with negligibly small difference).

Next, in one useful query, the probability of returning an incorrect but non-$\perp$ answer is at most κ, since this happens only when the box returns m_b while the correct answer is m_{1-b}, for $b = 0, 1$ (recall these two messages are independently sampled from $\mathcal{D}$). Now we focus on non-$\perp$ answers only, the probability of an incorrect answer appearing among the non-$\perp$ answers is at most $q = \frac{\kappa}{2\kappa + \alpha_0}$ (This can be argued as follows: suppose $\kappa = p + \eta$,where p is the probability of returning an incorrect but non-$\perp$ answer in one query and $\eta \geq 0$; then, the probability of obtaining an incorrect (but non-$\perp$) answer among all non-$\perp$ answers is at most $\frac{p}{\delta_0 + p} \leq \frac{p+\eta}{\delta_0 + p + \eta} = q$). Suppose X is the random variable that denotes the number of appearances of incorrect (but non-$\perp$) answers after collecting N_3 non-$\perp$ answers, and μ denotes the expectation of X which is no bigger than $N_3 q$. The probability that correct answers do not constitute the majority is $\Pr[X \geq \frac{N_3}{2}]$. Using the upper tail of the Chernoff bound:$\Pr[X > (1 + \beta)\mu)] \leq e^{\frac{-\beta^2\mu}{3}}$, we can verify that this probability is bounded by $\exp(-N_3\alpha_0^2/(24p(\mathcal{D})^2 + 6p(\mathcal{D})\alpha_0))$. So if we collect more than $N_3 = O(\alpha_0^{-2}\log^2\lambda)$ non-$\perp$ symbols, the majority will be occupied by the correct answers with probability almost 1, and hence we can recover the bit.

Combining these procedures, in total, if the recovering procedure repeats $N_0 \times N_1 \times N_2 \times N_3 = O(\alpha_0^{-2} m \log^6\lambda) = O(\alpha^{-2}\lambda^5\log^6\lambda)$ times (given that the length of the codeword $m = O(\lambda)$, and $\alpha = \delta - p(\mathcal{D})$), one can recover r_i correctly with overwhelming probability as long as $i \in \mathsf{Good}$. Since the number of errors in recovering r is bounded by k, and the ECC is able to correct up to $\frac{m}{5}$ errors, and $\frac{m}{5} \geq k$, thus $\tilde{r}$ will be recovered correctly with overwhelming probability and hence also s. (note that if we can reset the box across experiments the ciphertexts for which $i \notin S$ can be just omitted, saving a factor of N_1). □

Remark: In this construction, the ciphertext size is parameterized by the correctness δ which is influenced by the min-entropy of the distribution the box works on. Essentially, if the min-entropy is getting smaller, then ciphertext size increases.

Zero-Knowledge Using Garbled Circuits

or How To Prove Non-Algebraic Statements Efficiently*

Marek Jawurek
SAP, Karlsruhe
Germany
marek@jawurek.net

Florian Kerschbaum
SAP, Karlsruhe
Germany
florian.kerschbaum@sap.com

Claudio Orlandi
Aarhus University
Denmark
orlandi@cs.au.dk

ABSTRACT

Zero-knowledge protocols are one of the fundamental concepts in modern cryptography and have countless applications. However, after more than 30 years from their introduction, there are only very few languages (essentially those with a group structure) for which we can construct zero-knowledge protocols that are efficient enough to be used in practice.

In this paper we address the problem of how to construct efficient zero-knowledge protocols for generic languages and we propose a protocol based on Yao's garbled circuit technique.

The motivation for our work is that in many cryptographic applications it is useful to be able to prove efficiently statements of the form e.g., "I know x s.t. $y = \text{SHA-256}(x)$" for a common input y (or other "unstructured" languages), but no efficient protocols for this task are currently known.

It is clear that zero-knowledge is a subset of secure two-party computation (i.e., any protocol for generic secure computation can be used to do zero-knowledge). The main contribution of this paper is to construct an efficient protocol for the special case of secure two-party computation where only one party has input (like in the zero-knowledge case). The protocol achieves active security and is essentially only twice as slow as the passive secure version of Yao's garbled circuit protocol. This is a great improvement with respect to the *cut-n-choose* technique to make Yao's protocol actively secure, where the complexity grows linearly with the security parameter.

Categories and Subject Descriptors

D.4.6 [**Operating Systems**]: Security and Protection—*Cryptographic controls*; C.2.4 [**Computer-Communication Networks**]: Distributed Systems—*distributed applications*

Keywords

Zero-Knowledge Proof; Garbled Circuits; Efficiency

1. INTRODUCTION

Zero-knowledge (ZK) protocols have countless applications in cryptography and therefore efficiency is of paramount importance. Consequently, a huge effort has been put into designing efficient ZK protocols for *specific tasks*. In particular there are very efficient protocols for languages with some algebraic structure. There are, for instance, efficient protocols for proving knowledge and relations of discrete logarithms [Sch89, CDS94], for proving that RSA public keys are well formed [CM99], for statements in post-quantum cryptography [BD10, JKPT12, MV03], for bilinear equations [GS12, GSW10], for shuffles [BG12, KMW12] and frameworks for modular design of zero-knowledge protocols [CKS11].

However, *generic constructions* for ZK protocols use Karp reductions to NP-complete languages and are therefore too impractical to be used in practice. In particular, so far there has been no practical solution to problems that do not exhibit an algebraic structure. Examples for protocols that could be used in many cryptographic applications are e.g., the problem of efficiently proving statements of the form "I know x s.t. $y = \text{SHA-256}(x)$" or "I know k s.t. $y_1 = \text{AES}_k(y_2)$" (the common input is y in the first example and (y_1, y_2) in the second)[1].

In this work we provide a *generic* and *efficient* solution for proving any such statements in zero-knowledge, by constructing a protocol based on Yao's garbled circuits technique. The complexity of our protocol is proportional to the size of the circuit of the NP verification function. To support the validity of our efficiency claim, we present also a *proof-of-concept* implementation of our protocol. The performance measurements of our prototypical implementation show the viability of our protocol for realistic problems.

1.1 Zero-Knowledge and 2PC

Zero-knowledge proofs were introduced more than 30 years ago by Goldwasser, Micali and Rackoff [GMR85]. A zero-knowledge argument (ZK) is an interactive protocol that allows a prover P to persuade a verifier V of the validity of some NP statement y by using the knowledge of a witness w. Informally, an honest prover should be able to

*A full version of this paper is available at [JKO13].

[1]Note that in both cases the prover is not only showing that the instance belongs to the language (both languages are trivial), but moreover that the prover *knows* a valid witness for this. So these proofs are meaningful as we believe that it is hard to compute such a witness.

CCS'13, November 4–8, 2013, Berlin, Germany.

ACM 978-1-4503-2477-9/13/11 ...$15.00.
http://dx.doi.org/10.1145/2508859.2516662 .

convince an honest verifier of the validity of the statements (*completeness*). Moreover, a zero-knowledge protocol should give guarantees against corrupted parties: Even a malicious prover cannot persuade an honest verifier of a false statement (*soundness*) and even a malicious verifier does not learn anything from the execution of the protocol, except for the validity of the statement itself, hence the name "zero-knowledge".

Approximately at the same time, Yao [Yao82] introduced the problem of two-party secure computation (2PC) and showed how to solve it using the famous "garbled circuits" construction. In 2PC the parties hold secret inputs x_1 and x_2 respectively and want to jointly compute some function $z = f(x_1, x_2)$ while keeping their inputs secret.

Observe that ZK is a proper subset of 2PC: ZK is an instance of 2PC where there is an asymmetry between the parties and only P holds an input w (the witness for the NP statement) and where the function $f_y(w)$ outputs `accept` iff w is a valid witness for y (note that y here is not a secret, and therefore is not considered as an input but as part of the circuit description).

However, with few notable exception (see the related work in Section 1.6), the techniques used to implement efficient zero-knowledge protocols and the techniques used to implement efficient secure computation are very different from each other.

1.2 ZK with 2PC techniques

From a very high-level point of view, our construction works as follows: V and P run the standard (passive-secure) Yao protocol, where V acts as the circuit constructor and P acts as the circuit evaluator. After the evaluation P sends V the output key (this step can be seen as a *conditional disclosure of secret* [GIKM98, AIR01]). The security of Yao's protocol implies that a computationally bounded P cannot guess the output key corresponding to the output value `accept` unless he has a valid witness for y.

This first, partial solution works in the case of a semi-honest verifier and it is described in Section 3. However, this protocol is not zero-knowledge against a malicious V, who can mount all the well-known active attacks against Yao's protocol (garbling a function different than the one he is supposed to, selective failure attack during the input phase [KS06] etc.).

1.3 Actively secure ZK

To make our protocol actively secure one can use off-the-shelf solutions for two-party computation with active security, like the *cut-n-choose* technique. In *cut-n-choose*, the circuit constructor sends multiple copies of the circuit to the circuit evaluator, who chooses a random subset of the circuits. Then the circuit constructor "opens" the chosen garbled circuits so that the other party can verify that they garble the correct function, and then they evaluate the remaining unopened garbled circuits. However even with the most recent versions of *cut-n-choose* (e.g. [FJN+13, Lin13, HKE13]), the complexity of the resulting protocol still grows with the statistical security parameter and this represents a big drawback in practice.

Our approach for active security is different and takes advantage of the difference between ZK and 2PC. In the case of ZK the verifier V (i.e., the circuit constructor), has no secrets. Therefore, after the protocol is completed, V can "open" the circuit and let P verify that it computes the right function. This allows to achieve *active security* by using only a single garbled circuit.

1.4 Protocol idea

In a nutshell our actively secure protocol works as follows: P and V run the OTs, where P uses as inputs the bits of his witness, and V inputs the keys for the input layer of the garbled circuit. Then V sends the garbled circuit (if the employed OT has two rounds, the garbled circuit can be sent with the second message of the OT). Now the prover can evaluate the circuit and retrieve the output key Z corresponding to the circuit output being "accept" or "reject". However, the prover does not reveal this key just yet. It rather commits to it and waits with revealing the actual value until after the verifier "opens" the garbled circuit and the prover can check the honesty of the verifier. Note that we need the OT protocol to have "committing" properties, as it is important for the prover to verify that the keys revealed in this stage are consistent with the ones used previously in the OT phase.

1.5 Applications

Private-key cryptographic primitives (such as block ciphers and hash functions) are orders of magnitude faster than their public-key counterparts: this is mostly due to the fact that the algebraic structure of many number-theoretic assumptions allows for more efficient attacks than those for symmetric primitives. Therefore to achieve the same level of security, the parameters used in public key cryptography are much bigger than the ones used in symmetric key cryptography.

However this extra algebraic structure allows for the construction of naturally efficient protocols and advanced functionalities. For example, AES encryption is much faster than RSA encryption. However, if one wants to be able to prove that the encrypted message has a particular structure (for instance, in escrow applications) one needs to take into account the efficiency of the zero-knowledge protocol as well, and therefore public-key primitives are sometimes favoured over symmetric key primitives because the public key schemes are compatible with the most efficient zero-knowledge protocols. The results of this paper change the state of things and allow for proving statements about cryptographic protocols with no algebraic structure in an practically efficient way.

As a motivating real life example, consider the following event: In 2010 Julian Assange released a "thermonuclear file insurance" i.e., a 1.4GB file allegedly consisting of an AES encryption of highly sensitive information. This encrypted data has been released as a countermeasure to protect WikiLeaks from being shut down by the U.S. government. The file had been extensively distributed using peer-to-peer application, and therefore simply releasing the encryption key would allow a great number of people to have access to this secret information. Note that it is important that the secret key is short, and can therefore be released in a very short time and with a wide variety of means, if one wants to.

It is natural to wonder whether this is just an empty threat (i.e., the file just contains random data) or whether the encrypted file really contains sensitive information. To show that the file actually contains sensitive information, one could imagine a randomized check in which the verifier

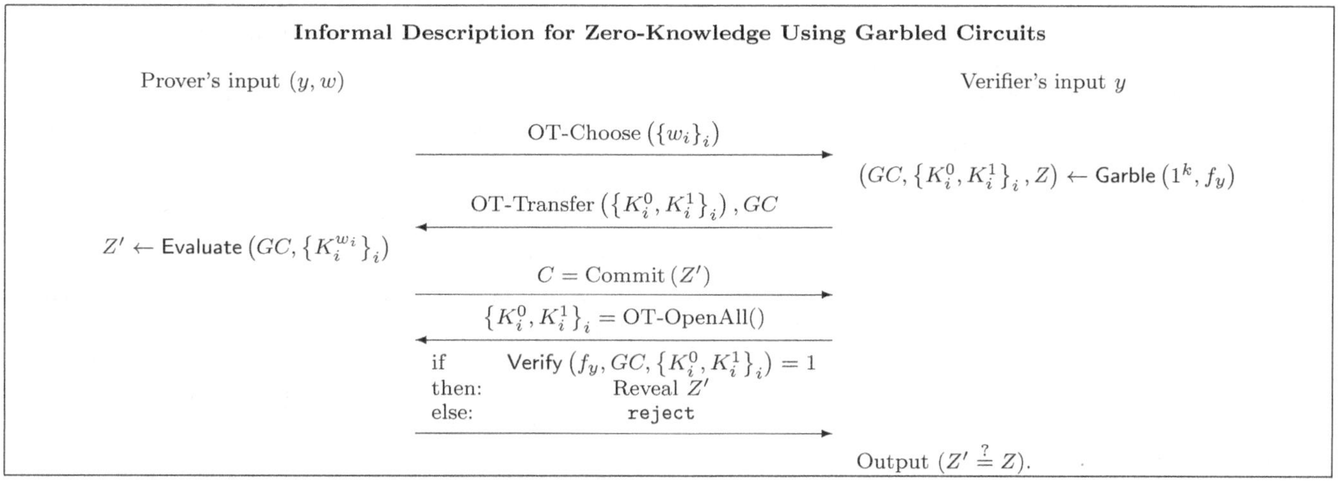

Figure 1: An informal description of our zero-knowledge protocol.

asks to see the decryption of a random, but small portion of the file. To do this without releasing the decryption key a zero-knowledge protocol that "works well" with AES is required.

Finally, consider the Fiat-Shamir [FS86] heuristic for NIZK or signatures, widely used in practice due to its extreme efficiency. In many application it is desirable to prove that "I know a proof of x" or "I have a signature on m" without revealing the proof/signature. Doing so requires an efficient way to prove non-algebraic statement about the hash-functions used to instantiate the random oracle in the Fiat-Shamir construction.

1.6 Related Work

As discussed before, although zero-knowledge and secure computation are clearly related, few works have been exploiting MPC techniques in zero-knowledge protocols. Some few notable exceptions are listed here. Ishai, Kushilevitz, Ostrovsky and Sahai [IKOS07] use MPC protocols for honest majority to achieve efficient zero-knowledge protocols; their idea is to have the prover simulate "in its head" n parties running an MPC protocol for the verification function and commit to their internal states. Then the verifier gets to pick a subset of the parties and checks that their state is consistent with an accepting verification. Intuitively, given that the MPC protocol is secure against a minority of passively-corrupted players, the proof is zero-knowledge. This allows to construct zero-knowledge protocols with very good asymptotic complexity. However, as the authors goal is to optimize for asymptotic complexity, IKOS use tools that are rather cumbersome in practice (see the full version for a detailed comparison.). Designing a "practically efficient" protocol in the IKOS framework is an interesting open problem.

Gennaro, Gentry and Parno [GGP10] combine garbled circuits with fully-homomorphic encryption to obtain a verifiable computation protocol but due to the use of fully-homomorphic encryption this protocol is far from being practical. Bitansky and Paneth [BP12] also use Yao garbled circuits in order to achieve zero-knowledge protocols, however their constructions fall short of the goal and they only achieve *witness hiding* and *weak zero-knowledge* (two strictly weaker properties than zero-knowledge). Moreover, their construction uses point obfuscation as a tool, and therefore their security reduction makes non black-box use of the adversary and requires non-standard cryptographic assumptions. This is inherent, as their goal is to build 3-round protocols and it is known that black-box 3-round zero-knowledge is impossible under standard assumptions [GK96]. By relaxing the requirement on round-complexity we achieve full zero-knowledge using only standard assumptions and a black-box security reduction.

A number of papers investigate the feasibility (e.g., [GOS06a, GOS06b]) and the efficiency (e.g., [Gro10, Lip12, GGPR13]) of *non-interactive* zero-knowledge proofs for SAT. On the positive side, those protocols are non-interactive. On the negative side, all these protocols require expensive public key operations (exponentiations and pairings) for each gate in the circuit, and therefore our protocol is more efficient in practice, as it can be seen from the timings reported in [PHGR13]. It is a very interesting open problem to construct a protocol that is non-interactive and only uses cheap (symmetric) cryptographic primitives at the same time.

1.7 Structure

The remainder of this paper is structured as follows: Section 2 introduces and defines preliminaries for the presentation of our protocol. Section 3 then presents our protocol for an honest verifier as a warm-up. Then, in Section 4, we build upon that and present our actively secure protocol for a malicious verifier. Finally, in Section 5 we describe a prototype implementation and the results of our experiments regarding its performance.

2. PRELIMINARIES

Let $[n] = \{1, \dots, n\}$. If S is a set $x \in_R S$ denotes a uniformly random element sampled from S. We call a function $\epsilon : \mathbb{N} \rightarrow \mathbb{R}^+$ negligible if for every polynomial p and big enough n, $\epsilon(n) < 1/p(n)$.

Let $L \subset \{0,1\}^*$ be a language in NP and M_L be the language verification function i.e., for all $y \in L$ there exist a string w of length polynomial in the size of y s.t. $M_L(y, w) =$ `accept` and for all $y \notin L, w \in \{0,1\}^*$ then $M_L(y, w) =$ `reject`.

2.1 Defining Security

We use the standard security notion for static, active (malicious) adversaries defined as indistinguishability between the real world (where the adversary interacts with a honest party) and the ideal world (where the adversary interacts with a simulator with access to the ideal functionality), see [Can00, Can01, Gol04]. We will write our proofs in an hybrid model where real world parties have oracle access to a given functionality, while in the ideal world the simulator "controls" this functionality. We use the standard commitment functionality and slight augmentation of the oblivious transfer (OT) functionality.

All our simulators are straight-line and the protocols achieve UC-security [Can01] when instantiated with UC secure oblivious transfers, for instance [PVW08, DNO08].

For the sake of simplicity, we neglect some details from our ideal functionalities, such as the fact that all the communication can be deleted and delayed by the adversary. This has no impact on our proofs as we only prove static security.

2.2 Zero-Knowledge: The Ideal Functionality

We define the task of zero-knowledge with an ideal functionality, as in [Can01]. This is a convenient way of defining all the properties we want from a zero-knowledge protocol (including the *proof-of-knowledge* property) in a compact way.

The ideal functionality $\mathcal{F}^R_{\text{ZK}}$

- $\mathcal{F}^R_{\text{ZK}}$ is parametrized by a binary relation R.
- On input $(\texttt{prove}, sid, x, w)$ from P and $(\texttt{verify}, sid, x')$ from V, if $x = x'$ and $R(x,w) = 1$ output $(\texttt{verified}, x)$ to V.

Figure 2: The ideal functionality $\mathcal{F}^R_{\text{ZK}}$ for Zero-Knowledge

The ideal functionality $\mathcal{F}_{\text{COT}}$

Choose: On input $(\texttt{choose}, id, b)$ from the receiver, with $b \in \{0,1\}$, if no messages of the form $(\texttt{choose}, id, \cdot)$ is present in memory, store $(\texttt{choose}, id, b)$ and send $(\texttt{chosen}, id)$ to the sender.

Transfer: On input $(\texttt{transfer}, id, tid, m_0, m_1)$ from the sender, with $m_0, m_1 \in \{0,1\}^k$, if no messages of the form $(\texttt{transfer}, id, tid, \cdot, \cdot)$ is present in memory and a message of the form $(\texttt{choose}, id, b)$ is stored, send $(\texttt{transferred}, id, tid, m_b)$ to the receiver.

Open-all: On input $(\texttt{open-all})$ from the sender, reveal all messages $(\texttt{transfer}, id, m_0, m_1)$ to the receiver. Then the functionality halts and does not reply to any further command.

Figure 3: The ideal functionality $\mathcal{F}_{\text{COT}}$ for OT with Sender Verifiability

2.3 A Weak Flavor of Committing Oblivious Transfer

One of the ingredients in our construction is a flavor of oblivious transfer, defined in Figure 3. Similar primitives appeared in literature under the name of *verifiable OT* [Cré89], *committed OT* [CvdGT95], *authenticated OT* [NNOB12] just to name a few. The main difference here is that we only need to have commitments to the sender's input, and not the receiver, like in the notion of *committing OT* [KS06]. In fact, our flavor of OT is even weaker than *committing OT*, as we do not need to have individual commitments to the messages. The only extra property we need is that after all the OTs have been performed, the sender can reveal all its input messages to the receiver and cannot lie about them. This can in general be achieved by letting the sender commit to a seed in the beginning of the protocol, and then run any secure OT protocol using the output of a pseudorandom generator on the seed as its random tape. Then the open-all phase can be implemented by simply letting the sender reveal the seed and all the messages.

In Appendix A we show how some "natural" (and efficient) OT protocols already satisfy this extra property and securely implement the $\mathcal{F}_{\text{COT}}$ functionality.

The ideal functionality $\mathcal{F}_{\text{COM}}$

Commit: On input $(\texttt{commit}, id, m)$ from the sender, with $m \in \{0,1\}^*$, if no messages of the form $(\texttt{commit}, id, \cdot)$ is present in memory, store $(\texttt{commit}, id, m)$ and send $(\texttt{committed}, id, |m|)$ to the receiver.

Reveal: On input $(\texttt{reveal}, id)$ from the sender, if a message of the form $(\texttt{commit}, id, m)$ is present in memory send $(\texttt{reveal}, id, m)$ to the receiver.

Figure 4: The ideal functionality $\mathcal{F}_{\text{COM}}$ for commitment

2.4 Commitment

We describe the protocol in an hybrid model where parties have access to the $\mathcal{F}_{\text{COM}}$ functionality. The $\mathcal{F}_{\text{COM}}$ functionality can be implemented in a black-box way given the $\mathcal{F}_{\text{COT}}$ functionality[2], or it is also possible to implement directly UC commitment in an efficient way using e.g., the protocol in [Lin11]). The (standard) commitment functionality is presented for completeness in Figure 4.

2.5 Garbling Scheme Requirements

We follow and extend the definition of garbled circuits by Bellare et al. [BHR12b]. A *verifiable* projective garbling scheme is defined by a tuple $\mathcal{G} = (\mathsf{Gb}, \mathsf{En}, \mathsf{De}, \mathsf{Ev}, \mathsf{ev}, \mathsf{Ve})$[3] such that:

- The garbled circuit generation function Gb is a randomized algorithm that on input a security parameter 1^k and the description of a Boolean function $f : \{0,1\}^n \to \{0,1\}$, with $n = \text{poly}(k)$ and $|f| = \text{poly}(k)$ outputs a triple of strings (GC, e, d).

- The algorithm ev allows to evaluate the function described by f i.e., $\mathsf{ev}(f, x) = f(x)$.

- The encoding function En is a deterministic function that uses e to map an input x to a *garbled input* X. In this paper we will only be concerned with *projective* schemes where $e = (\{K_i^0, K_i^1\}_{i\in[n]})$ and the garbled

[2]The committer inputs her message at the choice bit in the OT, while the verifier inputs two random strings as the messages of the OT. To decommit, the received random message is revealed. To break the binding property one would have to guess the message that was *not* chose in the OT, thus breaking the security of the OT protocol.

[3]A *standard* garbling scheme as defined by Bellare et al. does not contain the Ve procedure.

input X is simply $\{K_i^{x_i}\}_{i\in[n]}$, and therefore we will not further use the En function in the paper.

- The evaluation function Ev is a deterministic function that evaluates a garbled circuit GC on an encoded input X and produces an encoded output Z'.
- The decoding function De, using the string d, decodes the encoded output Z' into a plaintext output z. In this paper we are only interested in whether $z = 1$ (i.e., the NP relation accepts), therefore we let $d = Z'$ and $\mathsf{De}(d, Z)$ outputs $z = 1$ if $Z' \stackrel{?}{=} Z$ or $z = 0$ otherwise (we will drop the De notation from now on).
- In addition to the standard algorithms, a *verifiable* garbled scheme has an extra procedure Ve that, on input garbled circuit GC, a description of a Boolean function $f : \{0,1\}^n \to \{0,1\}$ and the input encoding information $e = \{K_i^0, K_i^1\}_{i\in[n]}$ outputs `accept` or `reject`.

The correctness and security definitions that we are going to provide are very similar to those given by Bellare et al., but they are relaxed to be as loose as they can while being sufficient for our goal. The hope is that our relaxed definitions can be achieved by simpler or more efficient garbling schemes that do not achieve the definitions given by Bellare et al.

DEFINITION 1 (CORRECTNESS). *Let $\mathcal{G}$ be a verifiable projective garbling scheme described as above. We say that $\mathcal{G}$ enjoys* correctness *if for all $n = \text{poly}(k), f : \{0,1\}^n \to \{0,1\}$ and all $x \in \{0,1\}^n$ s.t. $f(x) = 1$ the following probability*

$$\Pr\left(\begin{array}{l}\mathsf{Ev}(GC, \{K_i^{x_i}\}_{i\in[n]}) \neq Z : \\ (GC, \{K_i^0, K_i^1\}_i, Z) \leftarrow \mathsf{Gb}(1^k, f)\end{array}\right)$$

is negligible in k.

Intuitively, Definition 1 says that it is possible to recover the secret Z by evaluating a honestly generated circuit with input keys corresponding to a value x such that $f(x) = 1$. This is clearly implied by the standard correctness requirement that asks for correctness on all possible values of x.

DEFINITION 2 (SOUNDNESS). *Let $\mathcal{G}$ be a garbling scheme described as above. We say that $\mathcal{G}$ enjoys* authenticity *if for all $n = \text{poly}(k), f : \{0,1\}^n \to \{0,1\}$ and all pairs $x \in \{0,1\}^n$ s.t. $f(x) = 0$ and for all PPT $\mathcal{A}$, the following probability:*

$$\Pr\left(\begin{array}{l}\mathcal{A}(f, x, GC, \{K_i^{x_i}\}_{i\in[n]}) = Z : \\ (GC, \{K_i^0, K_i^1\}_i, Z) \leftarrow \mathsf{Gb}(1^k, f)\end{array}\right)$$

is negligible in k.

Intuitively, Definition 2 (which is a more succinct way of describing the "authenticity" property of Bellare et al., when restricted to our setting) says that no malicious evaluator can extract the secret Z unless she has access to input keys corresponding to a value x such that $f(x) = 1$.

DEFINITION 3 (VERIFIABILITY). *Let $\mathcal{G}$ be a garbling scheme described as above. We say that $\mathcal{G}$ enjoys* verifiability *if for all $n = \text{poly}(k), f : \{0,1\}^n \to \{0,1\}$ and all $x, y \in \{0,1\}^n$ with $x \neq y$ and $f(x) = f(y) = 1$ and for all PPT $\mathcal{A}$ the probability:*

$$\Pr\left(\begin{array}{l}\mathsf{Ev}(GC, \{K_i^{x_i}\}_{i\in[n]}) \neq \\ \mathsf{Ev}(GC, \{K_i^{y_i}\}_{i\in[n]}) : \\ \quad \mathsf{Ve}(f, GC, \{K_i^0, K_i^1\}_{i\in[n]}) = \mathtt{accept} \\ \quad (GC, \{K_i^0, K_i^1\}_{i\in[n]}) \leftarrow \mathcal{A}(1^k, f)\end{array}\right)$$

is negligible in k.

In addition, we require the existence of a expected polynomial time algorithm Ext *s.t., for all x satisfying $f(x) = 1$ the probability:*

$$\Pr\left(\begin{array}{l}\mathrm{Ext}(GC, \{K_i^0, K_i^1\}_{i\in[n]}) \neq \\ \mathsf{Ev}(GC, \{K_i^{x_i}\}_{i\in[n]}) : \\ \quad \mathsf{Ve}(f, GC, \{K_i^0, K_i^1\}_{i\in[n]}) = \mathtt{accept} \\ \quad (GC, \{K_i^0, K_i^1\}_{i\in[n]}) \leftarrow \mathcal{A}(1^k, f)\end{array}\right)$$

is negligible in k.

Intuitively, Definition 3 says that even a malicious constructor cannot create circuits that are successfully verifiable (i.e., make Ve output `accept`) and at the same time can output different values as a function of the evaluator's input x, as long as $f(x) = 1$. Jumping ahead, this is going to guarantee that the verifier cannot distinguish between different witnesses used by the prover.

Moreover, we require that the input of the testing function is enough to extract the secret in polynomial time. Note that this is trivial when it is easy to find an x s.t., $f(x) = 1$ but non-trivial otherwise. Jumping ahead, this extra guarantee will enable our simulator to extract the secret Z from the input of the malicious verifier to the oblivious transfer protocol, and it is therefore crucial to prove the zero-knowledge protocol. Intuitively, this is because this requirement ensures that the verifier already knows the (unique) secret Z when he sends the garbled circuit to the prover, and therefore the verifier is not learning any information when he receives back the secret Z as the output of the circuit evaluation by the prover (given that the check passes).

It is natural at this point to ask if there exist garbling schemes satisfying this definition. In Appendix B we discuss the most efficient Yao garbling schemes and argue how they satisfy all these properties under reasonable assumptions. Correctness follows from the correctness of Yao's construction. Intuitively soundness follows from the privacy of Yao's protocol (the output keys are encrypted using a secure encryption scheme under the input keys). The last requirement is satisfied by any garbling scheme good enough to be used in a *cut-n-choose* context. Note that the extraction requirement is very natural in Yao's scheme because, having access to all input keys, one can "fully decrypt" every garbled gate iteratively and get access to the key corresponding to the output bit 1 even without computing an input x such that $f(x) = 1$.

3. WARM-UP: HONEST VERIFIER ZERO-KNOWLEDGE

It is trivial to construct zero-knowledge proofs when the prover is semi-honest. However, it is in some cases interesting to consider a relaxation of zero-knowledge in which the verifier is semi-honest i.e., where the verifier follows the protocol correctly but then tries to extract additional information about the prover's witness from the transcript of the protocol. This notion can be found in the literature under the name of *honest-verifier zero-knowledge* or HVZK.

In this section we start by presenting an efficient protocol for this scenario. Note however, that our protocols are private coin zero-knowledge protocols and therefore standard transformations from HVZK to full ZK cannot be used[4].

[4]In a public-coin zero-knowledge protocol, the verifier does not have any private randomness and is limited to sam-

Constructing HVZK protocols using garbled circuits is relatively easy, and the main idea is as follows: the verifier, acting as the circuit constructor, constructs a Yao circuit that evaluates the function f_y. This function outputs 1 if $R(y, w) = 1$ otherwise it outputs 0. Then the parties run $n = |w|$ OTs, where V acting as the sender inputs the keys corresponding to the input wires and P inputs the bits of its witness $(w_1, \ldots, w_n)$. Now V sends the garbled circuit to P,[5] who evaluates and sends V the output of the evaluation of the garbled circuit. The formal description of the protocol is provided in Figure 5. Note that the algorithm Ve is not needed in this case. Note also that if the OT protocol has a two move form, then the whole protocol has only 3 moves (first *choose* from P to V, then *transfer* and GC from V to P and finally S' from P to V).

The protocol π_{HVZK}.

Let $\mathcal{G} = (\mathsf{Gb}, \mathsf{Ev})$ be a garbling scheme. Let L be an NP language with $|w| < n = \text{poly}(|y|)$ and $f_y : \{0,1\}^n \rightarrow \{0,1\}$ be the verification function that outputs 1 if w is a valid witness for y.
Both parties have input y and a security parameter 1^k. In addition, the prover P has input $w = (w_1, \ldots, w_n)$.

1. For all $i \in [n]$, P sends $(\texttt{choose}, i, w_i)$ to $\mathcal{F}_{\text{OT}}$;
2. $\mathcal{F}_{\text{OT}}$ sends V messages $(\texttt{chosen}, i)$ (for all $i \in [n]$);
3. V runs $(GC, \{K_i^1, K_i^0\}_{i\in[n]}, Z) \leftarrow \mathsf{Gb}(1^k, f_y)$;
4. For all $i \in [n]$, V sends to $\mathcal{F}_{\text{OT}}$ the input $(\texttt{transfer}, i, K_0^i, K_1^i)$;
5. $\mathcal{F}_{\text{OT}}$ sends P messages $(\texttt{transferred}, i, K_i')$ (for all $i \in [n]$);
6. V sends GC to P;
7. P runs $Z' \leftarrow \mathsf{Ev}(GC, \{K_i'\}_{i\in[n]})$ and sends Z' to V;
8. V outputs $\texttt{accept}$ iff $Z = Z'$;

Figure 5: The protocol for honest-verifier zero-knowledge in the $\mathcal{F}_{\text{OT}}$-hybrid model

THEOREM 1. *Let $\mathcal{G}$ be a garbling scheme satisfying Definition 1 and 2. Then protocol π_{HVZK} in Figure 5 securely implements the zero knowledge functionality $\mathcal{F}_{\text{ZK}}^R$ in the presence of an actively corrupted P or a passively corrupted V in the $\mathcal{F}_{\text{OT}}$-hybrid model.*

PROOF. When playing against a corrupted P^*: the simulator S extracts P^*'s input $w^* = (w_1^*, \ldots, w_n^*)$ from the first step by simulating the $\mathcal{F}_{\text{OT}}$ functionality and the simulator continues the protocol like an honest verifier with the only exception that at the end, it outputs $\texttt{accept}$ iff w^* is a valid witness for y. We argue that the view of P^* in the real world and in a simulated execution are computationally close as follows: up to the last step the view of P^* is distributed identically in the two settings (the simulator acts as an honest verifier except for its final output), and due to Definition 2 the probability that the corrupted P^* manages to make the real verifier output $\texttt{accept}$ when he does not input a valid witness in the OT phase is negligible.

The simulator can produce the view of a passively corrupted V^* by simulating the messages of the $\mathcal{F}_{\text{OT}}$ functionality in Step 2. In Step 7, the simulator chooses sets Z' to be Z, the output of Gb (instead of the output of Ev). Due to Definition 1 the two values are equal except with negligible probability. □

pling random challenges and sending them to the prover. In this case it is possible to transform an HVZK into a ZK by letting the verifier commits to his challenges ahead of time and/or by sampling them using a coin flip protocol. In addition, public coin ZK protocols can be turned into non-interactive zero-knowledge protocols (NIZK) using the Fiat-Shamir heuristic. This is not possible for our construction, as here the messages sent by the verifier are not simply its random choices.

[5]Note that this is the proper order of things. If the circuit is sent before the OTs then the garbling scheme needs to be secure against adaptive attacks at the price of reduced efficiency, see [BHR12a].

4. ZERO-KNOWLEDGE FROM GARBLED CIRCUITS

In this section we describe our final protocol, that achieves full zero-knowledge also in the presence of a malicious verifier. An intuitive explanation of the protocol has been provided in the introduction, and therefore we proceed to formally describe the protocol in Figure 6 and prove its security. Note that the steps $1-6$ are the same as in the protocol π_{HVZK}.

The protocol π_{ZK}.

Let $\mathcal{G} = (\mathsf{Gb}, \mathsf{Ev}, \mathsf{Ve})$ be a garbling scheme. Let L be an NP language with $|w| < n = \text{poly}(|y|)$ and $f_y : \{0,1\}^n \rightarrow \{0,1\}$ be the verification function that outputs 1 if w is a valid witness for y.
Both parties have input y and a security parameter 1^k. In addition, the prover P has input $w = (w_1, \ldots, w_n)$.

1. For all $i \in [n]$, P sends $(\texttt{choose}, i, w_i)$ to $\mathcal{F}_{\text{COT}}$;
2. $\mathcal{F}_{\text{COT}}$ sends V messages $(\texttt{chosen}, i)$ (for all $i \in [n]$);
3. V runs $(GC, \{K_i^1, K_i^0\}_{i\in[n]}, Z) \leftarrow \mathsf{Gb}(1^k, f_y)$;
4. For all $i \in [n]$, V sends to $\mathcal{F}_{\text{COT}}$ the input $(\texttt{transfer}, i, K_0^i, K_1^i)$;
5. $\mathcal{F}_{\text{COT}}$ sends P messages $(\texttt{transferred}, i, K_i')$ (for all $i \in [n]$);
6. V sends GC to P;
7. P runs $Z' \leftarrow \mathsf{Ev}(GC, \{K_i'\}_{i\in[n]})$; In case the function Ev aborts, set Z' to $\perp$;
8. P send $(\texttt{commit}, 1, Z')$ to $\mathcal{F}_{\text{COM}}$ and $\mathcal{F}_{\text{COM}}$ outputs $(\texttt{committed}, 1, |Z'|)$ to V;
9. V sends the message $(\texttt{open-all})$ to the $\mathcal{F}_{\text{COT}}$ functionality;
10. $\mathcal{F}_{\text{COT}}$ sends P, for all $i \in [n]$, the values $(\texttt{transfer}, i, K_0^i, K_1^i)$;
11. P runs $\mathsf{Ve}(GC, \{K_i^0, K_0^1\}_{i\in[n]})$, if the output is not $\texttt{accept}$, P terminates the protocol. Otherwise, if Ve outputs $\texttt{accept}$, P sends $(\texttt{reveal}, 1)$ to $\mathcal{F}_{\text{COM}}$;
12. When V receives $(\texttt{reveal}, 1, Z')$ from $\mathcal{F}_{\text{COM}}$, V outputs $\texttt{accept}$ if $Z' \stackrel{?}{=} Z$;

Figure 6: The protocol for honest-verifier zero-knowledge in the $(\mathcal{F}_{\text{COT}}, \mathcal{F}_{\text{COM}})$-hybrid model

THEOREM 2. *Let $\mathcal{G}$ be a garbling scheme satisfying Definition 1, 2 and 3. Then protocol π_{ZK} in Figure 5 securely implements the zero knowledge functionality $\mathcal{F}_{\text{ZK}}^R$ in the pres-*

ence of actively corrupted parties in the $(\mathcal{F}_{\text{COT}}, \mathcal{F}_{\text{COM}})$*-hybrid model.*

PROOF. When playing against a corrupted P^*: the simulator S extracts P^*'s input $w^* = (w_1^*, \ldots, w_n^*)$ from the first step by simulating the $\mathcal{F}_{\text{COT}}$ functionality and the simulator continues the protocol like an honest verifier with the only exception that at the end, it outputs `accept` iff w^* is a valid witness for y. We argue that the view of P^* in the real world and in a simulated execution are computationally close as follows: up to the last step the view of P^* is distributed identically in the two settings (the simulator acts as an honest verifier except for its final output): as discussed, the simulator only outputs `accept` when P^* uses a valid witness in the OT phase, while a real verifier will accept if the value received from the prover in step 11 is a valid opening of the commitment and Z is consistent with the secret hidden in the garbled circuit. But this can only happen with negligible probability if w is s.t. $f(w) = 1$: for the sake of contradiction, assume that P^* can use w s.t. $f(w) = 0$ in the OT phase and yet input $Z' = Z$ to the ideal commitment functionality in Step 8, then P^* can be used in a straightforward way to break the soundness property of the garbled circuit as defined in Definition 2.[6]

When playing against a corrupted V^*: The simulator sends messages $(\texttt{chosen}, i)$ to V^* and extracts V^*'s input $\{(K^*)_i^0, (K^*)_i^1\}_{i\in[n]}$ from step 4 by simulating the $\mathcal{F}_{\text{COT}}$ functionality. It then receives GC in step 6, sends the `committed` message to V^*, and waits to receive the message (`open-all`) from V^*. Finally in step 12, the simulator sends

$$Z' \leftarrow \text{Ext}(GC, \{(K^*)_i^0, (K^*)_i^1\}_{i\in[n]})$$

to V^* if $\mathsf{Ve}(GC, \{(K^*)_i^0, (K^*)_i^1\}_{i\in[n]})$ accepts or $Z' = \perp$ otherwise.

Note that the simulator sends the `committed` message even if it already knows that the Ve is going to fail. We argue that this simulated view of a malicious verifier is indistinguishable from the view of the interaction with a real prover: note that if the verifier "cheats" (i.e., sends keys and circuit that make Ve reject) then the simulator always commits to the value $\perp$ in step 8 while an honest prover might commit to a different value (i.e., the output of the evaluation function on the garbled circuit with a specific set of input keys). As we are using an ideal commitment scheme, this does not change the distribution of the view of the adversary: in this case in fact (both in the simulated view and in the real world) the protocol ends at step 10, and the verifier does not get to see the committed value. In the other case i.e., when the verifier behaves honestly and the simulator commits to the secret value Z, then the view of the adversary in the real world and in the simulated execution is computationally close: this is guaranteed by Definition 3 that states that the output of the circuit is unique and therefore independent from the actual witness used – therefore the value committed by the simulator and the value committed by an honest prover are the same except with negligible probability. □

[6]This is where we need to use the fact that the commitment is "extractable", as it guarantees that the adversary P^* computed the value Z using only the set of keys received from the OT phase and not the extra information received during the `openall` phase.

5. EXPERIMENTAL RESULTS

To show that our protocol π_{ZK} can be used in practice we implemented it and measured its performance. We stress that the goal of this section is not to show the best possible implementation of our protocol, but to show that the overhead to get active security on top of passive security when using garbled circuits for the case of zero-knowledge (as opposed to general 2PC) is very limited.

5.1 Choosing the Building Blocks

We chose only publicly available tools to implement our protocol, instead of creating an ad-hoc implementation from scratch. While this negatively affects our performance, it allows anyone interested in verifying our results to do so with only minimal effort.

5.1.1 Garbled Circuits

For the implementation of Gb and Ev we chose FastGC [HEKM11]. FastGC implements the evaluation of garbled circuits with state-of-the-art techniques like free-XOR [KS08] or pipelining [HEKM11]. Furthermore we employed GCParser [EMZ12] that parses circuit descriptions in an intermediate language for use with FastGC. This allows us to use the circuits available at [ST12] with little additional manipulation.

5.1.2 Commitment Scheme

The commitment scheme used by the prover in step 8 can be implemented as $\text{Com}(m, r) = \text{SHA-256}(m||r)$. This is an UC commitment scheme in the random oracle model: the use of the random oracle model seems necessary here, as we know that UC commitments are impossible to realize in the plain model and we do not wish to use impractical setup assumptions like the common reference string.

Note however that one has to be very careful and implement the commitment scheme in such a way that the commitment scheme is "non-malleable" with respect to the garbling scheme: this means that seeing the garbled circuit GC, the input keys and the opening in step 9 should not help a corrupted prover create and correctly open a commitment C for the secret Z. To see why this is necessary, consider an (artificial) garbling scheme that includes a commitment C to Z in the description of the garbled circuit GC. Now a malicious prover can simply send back to V this commitment C, wait for V to perform `open-all` in step 9. At this point he can open the commitment and make V accept, completely breaking the *soundness* of the protocol. To avoid this, one needs to use "different random oracles" for the commitment and for the circuit generator – in practice one could e.g., use different prefixes for the two different functions or use completely different functions e.g., AES to garble the circuit and SHA in the commitment.

5.1.3 Oblivious Transfer

We implemented Naor-Pinkas [NPS99] OT (NPOT) using the SCAPI library [EFLL12]. As SCAPI's backend driver we chose the MIRACL Crypto SDK[7] and used the group of points of the Koblitz 224 curve. We tested the use of OT-extension, but due to the low number of input bits in our applications (the witness size), we found that using OT-extension produced worse results than simply using one OT per input bit.

[7]`https://certivox.com/solutions/miracl-crypto-sdk/`

5.2 Experiments

We have measured performance in four experiments:

HVZK AES: P proves knowledge of private k so that $c = \text{AES}_k(x)$ for public plaintext x and public ciphertext c using protocol π_{HVZK}. AES key expansion for k is performed in the circuit. The bit lengths of the circuit's inputs are: $|k|_2 = |c|_2 = |x|_2 = 128$. This is essentially a passive secure evaluation of AES, and therefore gives us a "base case" to measure the performance of our protocol.

ZK AES: As HVZK AES but this time we run the complete π_{ZK} protocol.

MD5: P proves knowledge of private x so that $h = \text{MD5}(x)$ for public hash h using π_{ZK}. The circuit only performs one invocation of the MD5 compression function, x is padded outside the circuit. The bit lengths of the circuit's inputs are: $|x|_2 = 512, |h|_2 = 128$.

SHA-256: P proves knowledge of private x so that $h = \text{SHA-256}(x)$ for public hash h using π_{ZK}. The circuit only performs one invocation of the SHA-256 compression function, x is padded outside the circuit. The bit lengths of the circuit's inputs are: $|x|_2 = 512, |h|_2 = 256$

5.3 Implementation details

In all experiments both parties, prover and verifier, were executed on the same "Intel(R) Core(TM) i7-2600 CPU 3.40GHz" and 16GBytes of RAM and averaged over 100 runs. However, prover and verifier had their own JVM and communicated over (local) network sockets.[8]

5.4 Performance measurements

In Figure 1 we present our results. The individually measured operations are characterized next[9]:

Circuit Parsing (1): P and V both independently parse the GC's description in the intermediate language. Furthermore this also includes some initializations. Clearly the time for parsing can be amortized over multiple executions or could be precomputed once and for all.

Oblivious Transfers: P and V run NPOT with the witness and the keys corresponding the input wires as inputs.

Circuit Generation/Evaluation: P and V evaluate the GC using the pipelining technique: Both traverse the circuit in parallel and V creates and sends a garbled table (GTT) whenever he and P encounter a gate. P decrypts the respective entry in the GTT. FastGC's use of the free-XOR technique only requires GTT for AND and OR gates. Finally, P commits to the GC's output.

Circuit Parsing (2): During the circuit verification, the prover parses the circuit again. This is just an implementation issue due to the "black-box" use of FastGC but could clearly be optimized away.

Circuit verification: V sends P the seed it used for the random creation of wire labels of the circuit and the OT. Furthermore, it also sends its inputs to the circuit to P. P starts evaluating it in the role of V. P compares the output it creates (the GTTs) to the GTTs it received from V previously. P accepts if both are equal for the entire GC. In this case it opens the commitment and V verifies the opening.

5.4.1 *Discussion of results*

Our experiments show that thanks to our protocol we can prove complex non-algebraic statements in only a few seconds.

We believe that our main contribution can be seen by comparing the timings of HVZK AES and ZK AES. Our protocol achieves active security on top of passive security with a slowdown of less than 20% with respect to the passive secure version, much better than the factor 2 we would have predicted.

The absolute value of $1.7s$ for AES ZK shows the competitiveness of our approach versus the standard techniques for active secure two-party computation: the best solution based on Yao on standard hardware [SS11][10] reports a time of $192s$ for one AES evaluation. The GMW-based active secure protocol in [NNOB12] requires $64s$ per AES instance (the timings go down to $2.5s$ but only when running many instances in parallel).

We conjecture that all our timings could be reduced by a significant factor if we were willing to sacrifice generality for performance: to see why, compare the timings for HVZK AES with the timings for passive secure 2PC of AES reported in [HEKM11], performing almost the same task[11]: they have a timing of $0.2s$ versus our $1.4s$. We believe that the main reason for this (apart from running the code on different hardware)[12] is that the AES circuit is hard-coded in their Java program and thus they do not perform circuit parsing at runtime – this generates also less overhead during evaluation. Therefore we believe that an ad-hoc implementation of our protocol for a specific circuit could run much faster than our prototype.

Acknowledgement.

We thank Yan Huang for his support with FastGC and his OT implementation, Stefan Tillich for his support with their circuits, Yael Ejgenberg for support for the SCAPI framework and Omkant Pandey for noticing an issue in a previous version of this paper. The third author is supported by The Danish Council for Independent Research (DFF) Grant 11-116416/FTP.

[8] As shown in the table, the communication complexity of the protocol is just a few hundreds kilobytes, so moving the protocol to a LAN should not change the timings significantly.

[9] Note that those operations are quite different from the idealized version of π_{ZK}. The reason for this is that in the "idealized" protocol V generates the whole circuit and then sends it to P. This generates a lot of idle time for the parties, while to get more efficiency it is useful to have both parties work in parallel.

[10] [KSS12] reports better timings, but they run their experiments on machines with more than 60000 cores.

[11] Their implementation performs the AES key expansion at the prover side – this is not a problem when the prover is semi-honest but cannot be done in our case.

[12] They also instantiate the NPOT in the multiplicative group of $\mathbb{Z}_p$ with $p = 1024$ while we use the Koblitz 224 curve which is considered more secure.

Operation	AES Decrypt HVZK Prover	Verifier	AES Decrypt ZK Prover	Verifier	MD5 ZK Prover	Verifier	SHA256 ZK Prover	Verifier
Circuit Parsing (1)	239 ± 3	243 ± 4	239 ± 3	247 ± 3	336 ± 5	343 ± 3	565 ± 6	585 ± 9
Oblivious Transfers	731 ± 4	766 ± 5	736 ± 4	772 ± 5	2078 ± 7	2115 ± 7	2081 ± 7	2118 ± 8
Circuit Generation/Evaluation	335 ± 3	298 ± 3	332 ± 3	296 ± 3	605 ± 8	602 ± 8	1701 ± 7	1700 ± 7
Circuit Parsing (2)			91 ± 1		82 ± 1		240 ± 1	
Circuit Verification			163 ± 1		410 ± 2		1059 ± 15	
Total time	1404 ± 6		1667 ± 6		3617 ± 11		5761 ± 20	
Data transferred	256256 ± 0		262022 ± 2		1069647 ± 3		3052635 ± 4	
P's input bits	128				512		512	
#Gates	6927				29211		91080	

Table 1: Execution times and confidence intervals in milliseconds with confidence level 99%, averaged over 100 runs, rounded to ms. #Gates is the sum of AND and OR gates. The *total* runtime is the time (in ms) between the establishment of the network connection and the point where V accepts/rejects. *Data transferred* is the number of bytes exchanged between P and V. *P's inputs* indicates the number of input bits for which OTs have to be executed. *#Gates* is the number of non-free gates in the circuits.

6. REFERENCES

[AIR01] William Aiello, Yuval Ishai, and Omer Reingold. Priced oblivious transfer: How to sell digital goods. In Birgit Pfitzmann, editor, *EUROCRYPT*, volume 2045 of *Lecture Notes in Computer Science*, pages 119–135. Springer, 2001.

[BD10] Rikke Bendlin and Ivan Damgård. Threshold decryption and zero-knowledge proofs for lattice-based cryptosystems. In *TCC*, pages 201–218, 2010.

[BG12] Stephanie Bayer and Jens Groth. Efficient zero-knowledge argument for correctness of a shuffle. In *EUROCRYPT*, pages 263–280, 2012.

[BHKR13] Mihir Bellare, Viet Tung Hoang, Sriram Keelveedhi, and Phillip Rogaway. Efficient garbling from a fixed-key blockcipher. In *IEEE Symposium on Security and Privacy*, pages 478–492, 2013.

[BHR12a] Mihir Bellare, Viet Tung Hoang, and Phillip Rogaway. Adaptively secure garbling with applications to one-time programs and secure outsourcing. In *ASIACRYPT*, pages 134–153, 2012.

[BHR12b] Mihir Bellare, Viet Tung Hoang, and Phillip Rogaway. Foundations of garbled circuits. In *ACM Conference on Computer and Communications Security*, pages 784–796, 2012.

[BP12] Nir Bitansky and Omer Paneth. Point obfuscation and 3-round zero-knowledge. In *TCC*, pages 190–208, 2012.

[Can00] Ran Canetti. Security and composition of multiparty cryptographic protocols. *J. Cryptology*, 13(1):143–202, 2000.

[Can01] Ran Canetti. Universally composable security: A new paradigm for cryptographic protocols. FOCS, 2001. Updated version at `http://eprint.iacr.org/2000/067`.

[CDS94] Ronald Cramer, Ivan Damgård, and Berry Schoenmakers. Proofs of partial knowledge and simplified design of witness hiding protocols. In *CRYPTO*, pages 174–187, 1994.

[CKKZ12] Seung Geol Choi, Jonathan Katz, Ranjit Kumaresan, and Hong-Sheng Zhou. On the security of the "free-XOR" technique. In *TCC*, pages 39–53, 2012.

[CKS11] Jan Camenisch, Stephan Krenn, and Victor Shoup. A framework for practical universally composable zero-knowledge protocols. In *ASIACRYPT*, pages 449–467, 2011.

[CM99] Jan Camenisch and Markus Michels. Proving in zero-knowledge that a number is the product of two safe primes. In *EUROCRYPT*, pages 107–122, 1999.

[Cré89] Claude Crépeau. Verifiable disclosure of secrets and applications (abstract). In *EUROCRYPT*, pages 150–154, 1989.

[CvdGT95] Claude Crépeau, Jeroen van de Graaf, and Alain Tapp. Committed oblivious transfer and private multi-party computation. In *CRYPTO*, pages 110–123, 1995.

[DNO08] Ivan Damgård, Jesper Buus Nielsen, and Claudio Orlandi. Essentially optimal universally composable oblivious transfer. In *ICISC*, pages 318–335, 2008.

[EFLL12] Yael Ejgenberg, Moriya Farbstein, Meital Levy, and Yehuda Lindell. Scapi: The secure computation application programming interface. Cryptology ePrint Archive, Report 2012/629, 2012. `http://crypto.biu.ac.il/scapi`.

[EMZ12] David Evans, William Melicher, and Samee Zahur. *Interpreter for Garbled Circuits Intermediate Language*, 2012. `http://mightbeevil.org/gcparser/`.

[FJN+13] Tore Kasper Frederiksen, Thomas Pelle Jakobsen, Jesper Buus Nielsen, Peter Sebastian Nordholt, and Claudio Orlandi. Minilego: Efficient secure two-party computation from general assumptions. In *EUROCRYPT*, 2013.

[FS86] Amos Fiat and Adi Shamir. How to prove yourself: Practical solutions to identification and signature problems. In *CRYPTO*, pages 186–194, 1986.

[GGP10] Rosario Gennaro, Craig Gentry, and Bryan Parno. Non-interactive verifiable computing: Outsourcing computation to untrusted workers. In *CRYPTO*, pages 465–482, 2010.

[GGPR13] Rosario Gennaro, Craig Gentry, Bryan Parno, and Mariana Raykova. Quadratic span programs and succinct nizks without pcps. In *EUROCRYPT*, pages 626–645, 2013.

[GIKM98] Yael Gertner, Yuval Ishai, Eyal Kushilevitz, and Tal Malkin. Protecting data privacy in private information retrieval schemes. In Jeffrey Scott Vitter, editor, *STOC*, pages 151–160. ACM, 1998.

[GK96] Oded Goldreich and Hugo Krawczyk. On the composition of zero-knowledge proof systems. *SIAM J. Comput.*, 25(1):169–192, 1996.

[GMR85] Shafi Goldwasser, Silvio Micali, and Charles Rackoff. The knowledge complexity of interactive proof-systems (extended abstract). In Robert Sedgewick, editor, *STOC*, pages 291–304. ACM, 1985.

[Gol04] Oded Goldreich. *Foundations of Cryptography Volume 2, Basic Applications.* Cambridge University Press, 2004.

[GOS06a] Jens Groth, Rafail Ostrovsky, and Amit Sahai. Non-interactive zaps and new techniques for nizk. In *CRYPTO*, pages 97–111, 2006.

[GOS06b] Jens Groth, Rafail Ostrovsky, and Amit Sahai. Perfect non-interactive zero knowledge for np. In *EUROCRYPT*, pages 339–358, 2006.

[Gro10] Jens Groth. Short pairing-based non-interactive zero-knowledge arguments. In *ASIACRYPT*, pages 321–340, 2010.

[GS12] Jens Groth and Amit Sahai. Efficient noninteractive proof systems for bilinear groups. *SIAM J. Comput.*, 41(5):1193–1232, 2012.

[GSW10] Essam Ghadafi, Nigel P. Smart, and Bogdan Warinschi. Groth-sahai proofs revisited. In *Public Key Cryptography*, pages 177–192, 2010.

[HEKM11] Yan Huang, David Evans, Jonathan Katz, and Lior Malka. Faster secure two-party computation using garbled circuits. In *USENIX Security Symposium*, 2011.

[HKE13] Yan Huang, Jonathan Katz, and Dave Evans. Efficient secure two-party computation using symmetric cut-and-choose. In *CRYPTO*, 2013.

[IKOS07] Yuval Ishai, Eyal Kushilevitz, Rafail Ostrovsky, and Amit Sahai. Zero-knowledge from secure multiparty computation. In David S. Johnson and Uriel Feige, editors, *STOC*, pages 21–30. ACM, 2007.

[JKO13] Marek Jawurek, Florian Kerschbaum, and Claudio Orlandi. Zero-knowledge using garbled circuits: How to prove non-algebraic statements efficiently. Cryptology ePrint Archive, Report 2013/073, 2013. `http://eprint.iacr.org/`.

[JKPT12] Abhishek Jain, Stephan Krenn, Krzysztof Pietrzak, and Aris Tentes. Commitments and efficient zero-knowledge proofs from learning parity with noise. In *ASIACRYPT*, pages 663–680, 2012.

[KMW12] Shahram Khazaei, Tal Moran, and Douglas Wikström. A mix-net from any cca2 secure cryptosystem. In *ASIACRYPT*, pages 607–625, 2012.

[KS06] Mehmet S. Kiraz and Berry Schoenmakers. A protocol issue for the malicious case of yao's garbled circuit construction. In *In Proceedings of 27th Symposium on Information Theory in the Benelux*, pages 283–290, 2006.

[KS08] Vladimir Kolesnikov and Thomas Schneider. Improved garbled circuit: Free XOR gates and applications. In *ICALP (2)*, pages 486–498, 2008.

[KSS12] Benjamin Kreuter, Abhi Shelat, and Chih-Hao Shen. Towards billion-gate secure computation with malicious adversaries. *IACR Cryptology ePrint Archive*, 2012:179, 2012.

[Lin11] Yehuda Lindell. Highly-efficient universally-composable commitments based on the ddh assumption. In *EUROCRYPT*, pages 446–466, 2011.

[Lin13] Yehuda Lindell. Fast cut-and-choose based protocols for malicious and covert adversaries. In *CRYPTO*, 2013.

[Lip12] Helger Lipmaa. Progression-free sets and sublinear pairing-based non-interactive zero-knowledge arguments. In *TCC*, pages 169–189, 2012.

[MV03] Daniele Micciancio and Salil P. Vadhan. Statistical zero-knowledge proofs with efficient provers: Lattice problems and more. In *CRYPTO*, pages 282–298, 2003.

[NNOB12] Jesper Buus Nielsen, Peter Sebastian Nordholt, Claudio Orlandi, and Sai Sheshank Burra. A new approach to practical active-secure two-party computation. In *CRYPTO*, pages 681–700, 2012.

[NPS99] Moni Naor, Benny Pinkas, and Reuban Sumner. Privacy preserving auctions and mechanism design. In *ACM Conference on Electronic Commerce*, pages 129–139, 1999.

[PHGR13] Bryan Parno, Jon Howell, Craig Gentry, and Mariana Raykova. Pinocchio: Nearly practical verifiable computation. In *IEEE Symposium on Security and Privacy*, pages 238–252, 2013.

[PVW08] Chris Peikert, Vinod Vaikuntanathan, and Brent Waters. A framework for efficient and composable oblivious transfer. In *CRYPTO*, pages 554–571, 2008.

[Sch89] Claus-Peter Schnorr. Efficient identification and signatures for smart cards. In *CRYPTO*, pages 239–252, 1989.

[SS11] Abhi Shelat and Chih-Hao Shen. Two-output secure computation with malicious adversaries. In *EUROCRYPT*, pages 386–405, 2011.

[ST12] Nigel Smart and Stefan Tillich. Circuits of basic functions suitable for mpc and fhe, 2012.

http://www.cs.bris.ac.uk/Research/CryptographySecurity/MPC/.

[Yao82] Andrew Chi-Chih Yao. Protocols for secure computations (extended abstract). In *FOCS*, pages 160–164. IEEE Computer Society, 1982.

APPENDIX

A. PROTOCOLS FOR $\mathcal{F}_{\mathrm{COT}}$

In this section we discuss the relationship between the $\mathcal{F}_{\mathrm{OT}}$ functionality and the $\mathcal{F}_{\mathrm{COT}}$ functionality. While it is clear that the $\mathcal{F}_{\mathrm{OT}}$ functionality cannot be used in a black box way to run $\mathcal{F}_{\mathrm{COT}}$, we argue that any protocol based on computational assumptions can be used to implement $\mathcal{F}_{\mathrm{COT}}$. (Oblivious transfer can be instantiated using non-computational assumptions, such as noisy channels, quantum cryptography etc. We do not expect these kind of protocols to work in our context.) This can be done by letting the sender commit to a random seed s at the beginning of the protocol and then use the output of a pseudorandom generator $PRG(s)$ as its random tape in the protocol. Then during the `open-all` phase the sender reveals the seed and the messages and the receiver can check that the messages are consistent.

In order to make the paper self-contained, we describe here two efficient OT protocols that can be used to instantiate our construction, and discuss how those protocols already commit the sender to his choice of messages.

A.1 OT with UC-Security

We consider the UC-secure OT protocol proposed in [PVW08], instantiated using discrete logarithm. The reason for this choice is that the PVW OT appears to be the most efficient protocol for UC-OT in the literature. Let $(\mathbb{G}, q, g)$ be the description of a group of prime order q generated by g where the decisional Diffie-Hellman assumption is believed to hold.

CRS: The parties have access to a random string:

$$(g_0, h_0, g_1, h_1) \in \mathbb{G}^4$$

Choose: R chooses a random $\alpha \in_R \mathbb{Z}_q$, computes

$$g = (g_b)^\alpha, h = (h_b)^\alpha$$

and sends (g, h) to S;

Transfer: The sender operates in the following way:

1. S chooses random $r_0, s_0, r_1, s_1 \in_R \mathbb{Z}_q^4$ and computes

$$u_0 = g_0^{r_0} h_0^{s_0}, v_0 = g^{r_0} h^{s_0}$$

$$u_1 = g_1^{r_1} h_1^{s_1}, v_1 = g^{r_1} h^{s_1}$$

2. S sends R the values (u_0, w_0) where $w_0 = v_0 \cdot m_0$, and (u_1, w_1) where $w_1 = v_1 \cdot m_1$;

Retrieve: R outputs: $m_b = w_b \cdot (u_b)^{-\alpha}$

In [PVW08] the authors prove that this protocol securely implement the $\mathcal{F}_{\mathrm{OT}}$ functionality in the CRS-hybrid model. We can easily augment this protocol with the following procedure:

Open-All: S sends R the randomness r_0, r_1, s_0, s_1. R checks that

$$u_0 = g_0^{r_0} h_0^{s_0} \text{ and } u_1 = g_1^{r_1} h_1^{s_1}$$

and aborts if not. Otherwise, compute

$$v_0 = g^{r_0} h^{s_0} \text{ and } v_1 = g^{r_1} h^{s_1}$$

and output

$$m_0 = w_0 \cdot v_0^{-1} \text{ and } m_1 = w_1 \cdot v_1^{-1}$$

The sender cannot lie about the messages without breaking the discrete logarithm assumption: the values u_0, u_1 can be seen as Pedersen commitments, and if the adversary can find two different openings then the adversary can be used to find the discrete logarithms of h_i in base g_i for some $i \in \{0, 1\}$.

A.2 Naor-Pinkas OT

A problem with PVW OT is that it requires a common-reference string. Naor and Pinkas [NPS99] proposed a very efficient OT protocol in the plain model. It does not satisfy full-simulatabilty as PVW, but it is appears a good choice in practice as it uses fewer exponentiations and does not require a common reference string. The protocol proceeds as follows:

Setup: The sender chooses a random $d \in_R \mathbb{G}$ and sends it to the receiver.;

Choose: The receiver chooses a random $\alpha \in_R \mathbb{Z}_q$, computes $h_b = g^\alpha$ and $h_{1-b} = d \cdot (h_b)^{-1}$, and sends h_0 to the sender.

Transfer The sender computes $h_1 = d \cdot (h_0)^{-1}$, and sends

$$(c_0, c_1, c_2) = (h_0^r \cdot m_0, h_1^r \cdot m_1, g^r)$$

to the receiver.

Retrieve: R outputs: $m_b = c_b \cdot (c_2)^{-\alpha}$

This protocol can be augmented in the following way:

Open-All: The sender reveals r to the receiver, who checks that $c_2 = g^r$ and in this case outputs

$$m_0 = c_0 \cdot (h_0)^{-r} \text{ and } m_1 = c_1 \cdot (h_1)^{-r}$$

In this case the transfer message is a perfectly binding commitment to m_0, m_1, therefore no adversary can send inconsistent values.

We remark that if we use this OT protocol in our construction the simulator cannot extract the witness (i.e., the choice bits) of the prover/receiver, and in order to argue that the protocol π_{ZK} is also a proof-of-knowledge we need to rely on some extra assumption on the garbling scheme or by rewriting the proof in the random oracle model.

A.2.1 Saving on Communication Complexity

In both protocols the "Open-All" procedure simply consists of having the sender reveal all of its internal coins to the receiver. In practice one could have the sender producing his random tape by stretching a short seed with a pseudorandom generator. Then the receiver can regenerate the random tape on his side and perform the same computation as described above. This helps saving in communication complexity.

B. WHICH GARBLING SCHEME CAN BE USED?

The protocol described in Section 4 is compatible with every garbling schemes that can be used in standard cut-n-choose protocols. In particular, it is possible to use very optimized garbling schemes. To make the paper self-contained, we describe in this section such a garbling scheme that combines the state of the art optimizations for Yao Gates i.e., free XOR [KS08], permutation bits [NPS99], garbled row-reduction [NPS99].

This means that to garble a gate 4 evaluations of encryption are needed, and a garbled gate consists of only 3 ciphertexts (therefore saving on communication complexity). The evaluation of the gate consists of a single decryption.

How to garble gates.

For the sake of exposition we will only describe how to garble NAND gates – as those are complete for Boolean circuits. It is straightforward to see how to garble other non-linear gates (remember that XOR-gates will be "for free").

Free-XOR: When generating the circuit, the circuit constructor chooses a random $\Delta \in \{0,1\}^k$ and then, for each wire in the circuit, it will choose the key K_0 corresponding to the bit 0 at random in $\{0,1\}^k$ and set $K_1 = K_0 \oplus \Delta$ for each wire in the circuit.

This allows to evaluate XOR gates for free: let $L_0, L_1 \in \{0,1\}^k$ be the keys associated to the left input wire and R_0, R_1 corresponding to the right input wire and O_0, O_1 the keys associated to the output wire. Remember that $L_0 \oplus L_1 = R_0 \oplus R_1 = O_0 \oplus O_1 = \Delta$. Then, if the circuit constructor sets $O_0 = L_0 \oplus R_0$ it is easy to see that the circuit evaluator can use two keys L_a, R_b (without knowing a, b) to compute $O_{a\oplus b}$ as follows:

$$\begin{aligned} L_a \oplus R_b &= L_0 \oplus a \cdot \Delta \oplus R_0 \oplus b \cdot \Delta \\ &= (L_0 \oplus R_0) \oplus (a \oplus b) \cdot \Delta \\ &= O_{a\oplus b} \end{aligned}$$

Encryption scheme: Let L, R be the input keys for a gate with identifier id and O the output key. We define some key derivation function KDF and encrypt the output key under the input keys as follows:

$$C = \mathsf{KDF}(L, R, id) \oplus O$$

In our implementation we use the same KDF as FastGC i.e., we hash the input keys and the id using SHA-1.

In [BHKR13], is suggested to use a different KDF based on the assumption that AES with a random (constant) key behaves like a random permutation. This can lead to efficiency improvements, especially when using new CPUs where AES encryption is implemented directly as a machine instruction.

Note that, as with every other free-XOR based construction, we need to assume that the KDF satisfies some kind of related key-attack security [CKKZ12].

Point-and-permute: We call the least significant bit of every key the permutation bit and write $p_K = lsb(K)$ and we assume that $lsb(\Delta) = 1$. (This is not a problem as in our application the prover will learn all input keys (and therefore Δ) and can therefore check it during Ve.)

Then, for each gate in the circuit Gb samples random $L, R \in \{0,1\}^k$ and computes:

1. Define
$$\rho^0 = p_L \wedge p_R \qquad \rho^1 = p_L \wedge \overline{p_R}$$
$$\rho^2 = \overline{p_L} \wedge p_R \qquad \rho^3 = \overline{p_L} \wedge \overline{p_R}$$
2. Compute $O_0 = \mathsf{KDF}(L_{p_L}, R_{p_R}, id) \oplus \rho^0\Delta$;
3. Compute:
$$\alpha_1 = O_{\rho^1} \oplus \mathsf{KDF}(L_{p_L}, R_{\overline{p_R}}, id)$$
$$\alpha_2 = O_{\rho^2} \oplus \mathsf{KDF}(L_{\overline{p_L}}, R_{p_R}, id)$$
$$\alpha_3 = O_{\rho^3} \oplus \mathsf{KDF}(L_{\overline{p_L}}, R_{\overline{p_R}}, id)$$
4. Output $(id, \alpha_1, \alpha_2, \alpha_3)$

Evaluation: The function Ev on input $(id, \alpha_1, \alpha_2, \alpha_3)$, L', R' does:

1. Define $\alpha_0 = 0^k$.
2. Compute $p_{L'} = lsb(L')$ and $p_{R'} = lsb(R')$ and let $j = 2p_{L'} + p_{R'}$.
3. Compute $O' = \alpha_j \oplus \mathsf{KDF}(L', R', id)$;

Remember that the requirement for correctness is: Let $(gg, O_0) \leftarrow \mathsf{Gb}(id, L_0, R_0, \Delta)$, then for all $a, b \in \{0,1\}$

$$\mathsf{Ev}(gg, L_a, R_b) = O_{a\wedge b}$$

except with negligible probability over the choices of L_0, R_0, Δ and the random coins of Gb and Ev.

This is the case because, let $L' = L_a, R' = R_b$, then $lsb(L') = a \oplus p_L$ and $lsb(R') = b \oplus p_R$. Then by construction $\rho^j = a \wedge b$ and

$$\alpha_j = O_{\rho^j} \oplus \mathsf{KDF}(L_a, R_b, id)$$

and therefore

$$O' = O_{\rho^j} = O_{(p_L \oplus a)\wedge(p_R \oplus b)} \ .$$

Elligator: Elliptic-curve points indistinguishable from uniform random strings

Daniel J. Bernstein[1,4]
djb@cr.yp.to

Mike Hamburg[2]
mhamburg@cryptography.com

Anna Krasnova[3]
anna@mechanical-mind.org

Tanja Lange[4]
tanja@hyperelliptic.org

[1]Department of Computer Science, University of Illinois at Chicago, USA
[2]Cryptography Research, a division of Rambus, USA
[3]Privacy & Identity lab, Institute for Computing and Information Sciences, Radboud University Nijmegen, The Netherlands
[4]Department of Mathematics and Computer Science, Technische Universiteit Eindhoven, The Netherlands

ABSTRACT

Censorship-circumvention tools are in an arms race against censors. The censors study all traffic passing into and out of their controlled sphere, and try to disable censorship-circumvention tools without completely shutting down the Internet. Tools aim to shape their traffic patterns to match unblocked programs, so that simple traffic profiling cannot identify the tools within a reasonable number of traces; the censors respond by deploying firewalls with increasingly sophisticated deep-packet inspection.

Cryptography hides patterns in user data but does not evade censorship if the censor can recognize patterns in the cryptography itself. In particular, elliptic-curve cryptography often transmits points on known elliptic curves, and those points are easily distinguishable from uniform random strings of bits.

This paper introduces high-security high-speed elliptic-curve systems in which elliptic-curve points are encoded so as to be indistinguishable from uniform random strings. At a lower level, this paper introduces a new bijection between strings and about half of all curve points; this bijection is applicable to every odd-characteristic elliptic curve with a point of order 2, except for curves of j-invariant 1728. This paper also presents guidelines to construct, and two examples of, secure curves suitable for these encodings.

Categories and Subject Descriptors

E.3 [**Data encryption**]: Public key cryptosystems

Keywords

Censorship circumvention; elliptic curves; injective maps

1. INTRODUCTION

Elliptic-curve cryptography (ECC) is arguably the most important tool in modern public-key cryptography. It provides public-key encryption, signatures, non-interactive key exchange, and many higher-level security features. It offers an attractive combination of high security, high speed, and (often critical for deployment) small space consumption.

However, for applications in censorship circumvention, ECC has a security problem. ECC protocols naturally send elliptic-curve points in the clear as long-term public keys, ephemeral public keys, ciphertext prefixes, challenges, etc. These points, even in compressed form, are obvious: they are easy to distinguish from uniform random strings.

There have been some ad-hoc workarounds for this problem, notably for ElGamal ciphertext prefixes, using a curve-or-twist technique introduced by Möller (see below). But each new ECC-based protocol faces the same problem. Protocol designers unaware of the issue continue building protocols that are trivially visible to attackers. Designers requiring keys and ciphertexts to be indistinguishable from uniform are forced to modify those protocols, hoping that the modifications do not compromise other forms of security.

The main goal of this paper is to eliminate this problem. The solution presented here works for a wide range of elliptic-curve protocols, essentially every protocol in which the transmitted curve points are generated at random. There is no longer any need for, e.g., ad-hoc handling of ciphertext prefixes; this paper's technique works for all of the types of elliptic-curve points mentioned above.

1.1 Distinguishers

We use the standard NIST P-256 elliptic curve as an example to illustrate the difficulties. A public key on the NIST P-256 elliptic curve is a pair (x, y) of integers satisfying the equation $y^2 = x^3 - 3x + b$ modulo the prime $2^{256} - 2^{224} + 2^{192} + 2^{96} - 1$, where b is a standard constant. There are at least three obvious ways for an attacker to distinguish this public key from a uniform random string:

- Least severe: Normally x and y are represented as integers between 0 and $2^{256} - 2^{224} + 2^{192} + 2^{96} - 2$ inclusive, encoded as 256-bit strings. If the attacker sees a 256-bit string representing an integer larger than $2^{256} - 2^{224} + 2^{192} + 2^{96} - 2$ then the attacker knows that the string is not a valid value of x or of y. If the attacker sees a user sending a series of (e.g.) 2^{35} 256-bit strings, and the largest string is close to $2^{256} - 2^{224}$, then the attacker is reasonably confident that the user is sending curve points. See Section 2.6 for details.

  One can dismiss this attack as being too slow to be of interest, but we prefer more robust cryptographic

Public domain. This work was supported by the National Science Foundation under grant 1018836, by the Netherlands Organisation for Scientific Research (NWO) under grants 639.073.005 and 040.09.003, by the National Science Council of Taiwan under NSC 101-2915-I-001-019, by the European Commission under Contract ICT-2007-216676 ECRYPT II, and by SIDN.nl (http://www.sidn.nl/). Part of this work was done while Bernstein, Krasnova, and Lange visited Academia Sinica; they wish to thank Bo-Yin Yang for his hospitality. Permanent ID of this document: 711e2f8601805e06e5fbb3c5953dd5d1. Date: 2013.08.28.
CCS'13, November 4–8, 2013, Berlin, Germany.
ACM 978-1-4503-2477-9/13/11. http://dx.doi.org/10.1145/2508859.2516734.

primitives that maintain security with heavy use. The user can cover all integers between 0 and $2^{256}-1$ by randomizing the representations of small integers x and y, but this adds very little security: the attacker easily collects statistics showing that some integers appear half as often as others.

A secure solution is to randomly represent x and y as integers between 0 and, e.g., $2^{320}-1$. Another secure solution, with smaller keys, is to switch to an elliptic curve using a prime much closer to a power of 2, such as NIST P-224 (prime $2^{224}-2^{96}+1$, lower security level) or Bernstein's Curve25519 from [6] (prime $2^{255}-19$).

- More severe: The attacker simply checks the curve equation. If a 512-bit string has the form (x, y) where $y^2 = x^3 - 3x + b$ modulo this prime then the attacker is confident that the user is sending a public key.

  Many ECC systems save space by compressing y to one (random-looking) bit: the sign in $\pm\sqrt{x^3-3x+b}$. Some ECC systems save space by eliminating y entirely. The cost for the legitimate user of computing a square root is almost always outweighed by the benefit of reducing keys to half size. Both of these mechanisms have the side effect of stopping this attack.

- Most severe: The attacker checks whether $x^3 - 3x + b$ is a square modulo this prime. This has chance 1/2 of occurring for a uniform random string, but if it occurs repeatedly then the attacker is reasonably confident that the user is sending public keys.

The third attack is difficult to stop. Our solution requires a quite drastic change in how curve points are represented as strings; this representation is the main topic of this paper.

Our solution is not limited to public keys: it also protects other randomly generated elliptic-curve points, such as the points appearing in ciphertexts in elliptic-curve versions of the ElGamal encryption system and points appearing in signature systems. See Section 2.

1.2 Previous work

Several years ago, in [40], Möller proposed a variant of the ElGamal encryption system that provides indistinguishability for ciphertexts as follows:

- Alice's public key is a pair $(aP, a'P')$ where a and a' are secret integers, P is a standard base point on an elliptic curve $E(\mathbf{F}_{2^n})$ over some binary field $\mathbf{F}_{2^n}$, and P' is a standard base point on a nontrivial quadratic twist $E'(\mathbf{F}_{2^n})$ of the same curve.
- To encrypt a message m using public key $(aP, a'P')$, Bob chooses a random integer b, chooses randomly between aP and $a'P'$, sends the x-coordinate of bP or bP' respectively, hashes $b(aP)$ or $b(a'P')$ respectively to obtain a secret key, and sends an encryption of m using this secret key.
- Alice recovers bP or bP' from the x-coordinate. Alice multiplies bP or bP' by a or a' to obtain abP or $a'bP'$, hashes it to obtain the same secret key, and decrypts the message. Möller requires Alice to perform tests to decide whether the input is on E or on E' and to recover the whole point bP or bP'. We comment that the "Montgomery ladder" handles both cases together if a' is chosen as a. (For Montgomery-ladder background see [41], [16], and, for the binary case, [39].) This eliminates the need for such tests and offers efficient curve arithmetic.

The idea in Möller's proposal is that each element of $\mathbf{F}_{2^n}$ is a valid x-coordinate on E or its twist. The x-coordinate sent here can therefore be any element of $\mathbf{F}_{2^n}$, and in fact the distribution of the x-coordinates is indistinguishable from the uniform distribution of n-bit strings. Möller slightly adjusts the choices so that the distribution is exactly uniform.

Young and Yung present in [49] a modified version of Möller's twist idea to achieve DDH security in the standard model. In their version Alice's public key consists of M points on each curve; Bob picks one of the curves and computes shared secrets with all M points on that curve. The shared key of length M is derived taking just one bit per DH shared secret.

Our approach encodes points on a *single* curve as strings indistinguishable from uniform random strings. This has several obvious advantages over Möller's system. We obtain indistinguishability not just for ciphertexts but also for public keys. Möller's system has double-length public keys, while our public keys have minimal length. Möller's approach is limited to ElGamal encryption, while our approach handles a much wider range of ECC systems; see Section 2. Möller needs cryptographic security not just for E but also for E'; in our system twist security is not required, although we still suggest it as a desirable feature (see Section 4). Since our proposal does not need to work with twists, achieving solutions in the standard model can be done simply using the standard methods.

1.3 Application context

Möller's curve-or-twist approach is used in StegoTorus [47]. StegoTorus is an extension to Tor [19] for censorship circumvention. It makes Tor traffic resemble Skype, general HTTPS traffic, etc. and relies on secure communication with a StegoTorus server. Establishing a link with this server requires deriving temporary key material using the public key of the server. This key material is used to encrypt communication of a subsequent ephemeral DH key exchange. StegoTorus uses Möller's example parameters over $\mathbf{F}_{2^{163}}$.

For comparison, typical ECC protocols carry out a DH key exchange in the clear; see, e.g., the ntor example below. StegoTorus needs to encrypt its key exchange because the points sent in the key exchange are easily distinguishable from uniform random data. This encryption adds the outer Möller layer, doubling the space used for the initial communication. This also slows down the client, slows down the server, doubles the size of server public keys (one point on the curve, one point on the twist), and requires implementations to handle computations on two curves.

We eliminate all of these issues by solving the underlying problem, namely the point distinguishability. The points that we send in a DH key exchange are indistinguishable from uniform random strings. See Sections 2, 3, and 5.

Telex [48] is another censorship-circumvention tool. Telex messages pose as regular TLS messages to random uncensored sites; the only difference is that the nonce field contains a cryptographic value instead of a random value. The public key of the Telex server is a pair of points (aP, aP'), with P on an elliptic curve $E(\mathbf{F}_q)$ and P' on a nontrivial quadratic twist. Telex servers use deep-packet inspection on all traffic passing through them and identify Telex messages by checking whether the nonce field interpreted as $\alpha||\beta$ satisfies the following conditions. Interpret α as the x-coordinate of a point R on E or E' and compute aR on the appropriate curve. Identify the message as a Telex message if β matches a salted hash of aR, and route it according to some other, encrypted information.

The use of curves in Telex follows Möller's proposal except for the choice of finite field and the choice of equal secrets. The proposed parameters have $q = 2^{168} - 2^8 - 1$ so that the distribution of values in $\mathbf{F}_q$ is indistinguishable from that of length-168 strings. The attempted decryption performs a complete point recovery from x and uses standard Weierstrass-curve arithmetic to compute the scalar multiplications. We comment again that the "Montgomery ladder" is more efficient, handling both cases together. We also comment that the system could use somewhat larger finite fields, gaining security, without reducing the 56-bit hash size and without going beyond the standard TLS 224-bit nonce size: servers would allow only points R with a fixed number of implicit trailing zeros, and clients would repeatedly generate points until meeting that condition.

This paper's solution to the point-distinguishability problem would not save bandwidth for Telex connections but would still simplify implementations, removing any need to handle the twist, and would reduce public keys to half size, potentially a useful feature for small clients keeping track of many different Telex servers.

As a third protocol we consider ntor [30], a handshake protocol proposed for Tor achieving anonymity and one-way authentication with forward secrecy. This protocol assumes that Tor relays have public keys on an elliptic curve. The following is a simplified version of the ntor protocol, skipping certificates and saved session states, but presenting all parts relevant to the choice of curve group and representation. To extend a Tor circuit to a relay with public key $B = bP$ a client picks a random value x, computes $X = xP$, and sends X to the server. The server picks a random y, computes $Y = yP$, computes two secret keys as $k'||k = H(yX, bX, B, X, Y)$ for some hash function H, computes $t_B = \text{MAC}_{k'}(B, X, Y)$ (an authenticator under key k'), and sends $Y||t_B$ to the client. The client computes $\bar{k}'||\bar{k} = H(xY, xB, B, X, Y)$ and verifies that $t_B = \text{MAC}_{\bar{k}'}(B, X, Y)$. If the verification is successful, the client is convinced that it is communicating with the correct server: nobody other than the client and the relay could compute $xB = bX$. Both sides can use $k = \bar{k}$ for transmitting encrypted messages.

Tor currently uses SSL links to superencrypt its traffic. However, one can easily imagine ntor being steganographically encoded inside a cover channel, with the goal of circumventing censorship, on top of the original goals of anonymity, one-way authentication, and forward secrecy. This raises the question of how the curve points can be hidden. Using a pair of points xP, xP' in place of X does not work: it is even easier to distinguish from uniform than a single point. Möller's curve-or-twist approach, using a pair of points in place of the server's long-term key B, also does not work: the client is free to pick X on the curve or the twist, but the server is then forced to pick Y on the same curve as X, and this is something visible to a censor.

Our solution applies straightforwardly to this protocol. It does not need twists; it ensures that the encodings of points on a single curve are uniformly distributed. More generally, our solution can be used to encode as many points as desired during one session or across sessions.

Our solution is also useful for several earlier applications: password-authenticated key exchange [13], ID-based encryption [12], pseudorandom-number generation [35, 36], and kleptography [49]. Note that [49] includes a treatment of covert channels and steganography, predating both StegoTorus and Telex.

1.4 Mapping strings to elliptic-curve points

Shallue and van de Woestijne at ANTS 2006 [45] gave a positive answer to the following question in pure algorithmic number theory: there is, provably, a (very easy) *probabilistic* polynomial-time algorithm that, given any elliptic curve E over any sufficiently large finite field $\mathbf{F}_q$, constructs a nonzero element of the group $E(\mathbf{F}_q)$; is there, provably, a *deterministic* polynomial-time algorithm for the same task? Shallue and van de Woestijne did more than construct a single point: they built a function $\phi : \mathbf{F}_q \to E(\mathbf{F}_q)$ such that each element of $E(\mathbf{F}_q)$ has at most C preimages, for a particular constant C; and they built a deterministic polynomial-time algorithm that computes $\phi(t)$ given q, E, and t. Trying $C+1$ elements of $\mathbf{F}_q$ produces a nonzero element of $E(\mathbf{F}_q)$.

Some cryptographic protocols rely on hashing strings to curve points. For example, in the Boneh–Franklin identity-based encryption scheme [12], public keys are points on pairing-friendly curves, and a user with identity i has public key $H(i)$. Boneh and Franklin constructed a suitable function H for certain supersingular curves. Icart at Crypto 2009 [32] pointed out that the Shallue–van de Woestijne function ϕ produced suitable functions H for any elliptic curve, allowing the Boneh–Franklin system to be adapted to much more efficient non-supersingular (but still pairing-friendly) curves. Icart and subsequent authors explored various replacements ϕ for the Shallue–van de Woestijne function; see [32], [15], [26], [25], [20], [27], [23], and [21].

The reader should be wondering why one cannot simply define $\phi(t)$ by trying consecutive field elements x starting from t (for example, trying $x = t$, $x = t+1$, $x = t+2$, etc. in the prime-field case) until finding a curve point (x, y). The answer for Shallue and van de Woestijne is that this is not *proven* to take polynomial time. On the other hand, there is overwhelming evidence for the conjecture that this takes polynomial time, and in cryptography there is no harm in making such a conjecture; cryptography is built on a foundation of conjectures that are much easier to question, such as the conjecture that there is no fast ECDL algorithm. This simple function from $\mathbf{F}_q$ to $E(\mathbf{F}_q)$ is exactly what is used in many papers on identity-based cryptography.

The real objection to this algorithm is that it does not take *constant* time. In many applications the time leaks secret information. One can compute the same function for almost all inputs in constant time by choosing an upper bound C on the number of consecutive field elements required with very high probability, say $C = 100$, and then always testing exactly C values of x; but testing C times for squares turns out to be a performance bottleneck.

It should be obvious that any of the functions ϕ mentioned above allows a public key $\phi(t) \in E(\mathbf{F}_q)$ to be represented as an element $t \in \mathbf{F}_q$, using a computation of $Q \mapsto \{t : \phi(t) = Q\}$ to encode a point and a computation of $t \mapsto \phi(t)$ to decode a point. However, this approach raises several important performance issues for key generation:

- The usual key-generation method produces a uniform random curve point by scalar multiplication, but there is no reason to think that this curve point can be expressed in the form $\phi(t)$. If it cannot then the user must try again, generating a new key.
- Even worse, to generate a *uniform* distribution of elements $t \in \mathbf{F}_q$ the user must generate a uniform random curve point Q, compute the number $k = \#\{t : \phi(t) = Q\}$ of preimages of the point, restart with probability $1 - k/C$, and finally select a uniform random preimage of the point. (This is what statisticians call "rejection sampling"; more advanced sampling methods are inapplicable since there is no way to generate a uniform random curve point with a specified value of k.) The average number of points generated is then $C\#E(\mathbf{F}_q)/q \approx C$. Applications that need real-time guarantees must budget for even more than C.
- Each of these C points takes time for not just a computation of Q but also a computation of $\{t : \phi(t) = Q\}$. This is the main bottleneck if ϕ is slow to invert.

In many protocols, ephemeral ECC keys are generated for every protocol run, and these computations can easily dominate the overall protocol performance. Of course, even in protocols where key generation is rare, each use of t incurs the cost of computing $\phi(t)$.

We propose two ways to minimize these performance problems: Elligator 1 and Elligator 2. Elligator 1 takes an encoding function ϕ that is implicit in the very recent paper [23] by Fouque, Joux, and Tibouchi. This function, in the cases we consider, maps $\{0, 1, 2, 3, \ldots, (q-1)/2\}$ *injectively* to $E(\mathbf{F}_q)$; see Theorem 4. Since the number of points on E over $\mathbf{F}_q$ is about q we have to try only about 2 points on average before finding a point of the form $\phi(t)$, and we do not need to randomize the preimage t. Not every elliptic curve is suitable for this function, but the curve requirements for Elligator 1 are compatible with state-of-the-art criteria for curve security and curve performance.

Fouque, Joux, and Tibouchi suggested that injectivity would be useful for a naive form of ElGamal encryption in which a message m is encoded injectively as an elliptic-curve point and then simply added to abP. We highlight the new anti-censorship application, namely encoding *points* as *strings* rather than encoding strings as points; we drastically simplify the definition of this function, while accelerating its forward and inverse computation; and we introduce a high-security high-speed elliptic curve that supports the function. See Section 4 for the curve, Section 3 for the function, and Section 2 for the cryptographic applications.

Elligator 2 introduces a new injective map ψ to elliptic curves. Elligator 2 has similar performance characteristics to Elligator 1. The main advantage of Elligator 2 is that it applies to more curves: in fact, every odd-characteristic elliptic curve that has a point of order 2, except for curves of j-invariant 1728. See Section 5 for this new map.

2. ELLIPTIC-CURVE PROTOCOLS

This section presents various elliptic-curve protocols in which public keys, ciphertexts, etc. are indistinguishable from uniform random strings. These protocols include all of the fundamental ECC constructions: static and ephemeral key exchange, encryption, and signatures.

The prerequisite for all of these protocols is an injective map ι from a set of strings $S \subseteq \{0,1\}^b$ to an elliptic-curve group $E(\mathbf{F}_q)$. We require $\#S$ to be very close to 2^b, so that a uniform random element of S is indistinguishable from a uniform random b-bit string; see Section 2.6. We have two different methods to construct ι and S, as mentioned above; see Sections 3 and 5.

The idea, as explained in Section 1, is for each string $\tau \in S$ to represent the curve point $\iota(\tau)$, i.e., for the point $\iota(\tau)$ to be encoded as the string τ. A uniform random element of $\iota(S)$, encoded in this way, is indistinguishable from a uniform random b-bit string. We do not require $\iota(S)$ to be all of $E(\mathbf{F}_q)$; our protocols compensate for this by repeatedly generating curve points until finding elements of $\iota(S)$. For our constructions $\#\iota(S)$ is about $(1/2)\#E(\mathbf{F}_q)$, requiring only about 2 repetitions on average, as mentioned in Section 1.

Our primary objective in this section is to illustrate how easily ι can be used to systematically hide elliptic-curve points in a wide range of protocols. We do not mean to suggest that all of these protocols are being used in contexts where they need to be hidden from censors; but there is no obvious dividing line between protocols that would be useful for those contexts and protocols that would not.

Consider, for example, static ECDH public keys. A static public key might be distributed openly, as part of a cryptographic software package, in which case it does not add any new risk of censorship; changing the encoding of the public key does nothing to hide the package from a censor. On the other hand, if a client already has all necessary cryptographic software, and a server broadcasts a series of static public keys by encoding those keys inside otherwise innocent web pages or other cover traffic, then indistinguishability from uniform is exactly the tool needed to defend those public keys against a censor with an accurate model of the cover traffic. A censored Tor client should be able to see frequent updates of public keys for Tor bridges, for example; see [1] for a detailed discussion of the speed at which various governments detect and suppress access to Tor bridges.

2.1 Notation and domain parameters

To simplify the protocol statements we assume that the elliptic-curve group $E(\mathbf{F}_q)$ is cyclic: specifically, that it is generated by a standard base point P of order n. In the case that n is not prime (for example, n is 4 times a prime in Section 4) we do *not* restrict points to a prime-order subgroup: any proper subgroup is trivially distinguishable from the full group. For non-cyclic groups the protocols would have to be modified to handle multiple generators.

Let H denote a hash function, and let $||$ denote concatenation of strings. Symmetric authenticated encryption of a message M using a secret key k is denoted as $c = \mathrm{Enc}_k(m)$, decryption as $m = \mathrm{Dec}_k(c)$. A standard security requirement for symmetric encryption is that the ciphertexts are indistinguishable from uniform (see, e.g., [3]); one can, for example, safely use AES in counter mode. For authentication there is a split in the literature between authenticators aiming at the "PRF" property, which guarantees indistinguishability, and authenticators aiming merely at the "MAC" property, which guarantees unforgeability but does not guarantee indistinguishability; we require the PRF property. See [44] for a unified security notion for authenticated encryption that guarantees indistinguishability from uniform random bit strings.

2.2 Long-term Diffie–Hellman keys

Each user U sets up a public key:

1. U generates a random integer u.
2. U computes $P_U = uP$. If $P_U \notin \iota(S)$ then U repeats from step 1.
3. U publishes $\iota^{-1}(P_U) = \tau_U$ and keeps u secret.

The encoding τ_U of the public key is a string which can be broadcast; it is indistinguishable from a random string.

Without further communication users Alice and Bob can compute a shared secret from their public strings τ_A and τ_B. Alice can compute this key as follows and then use it to authenticate and encrypt a message to Bob:

1. Alice computes $\iota(\tau_B) = P_B$.
2. Alice computes $k = H(u_A P_B)$.

Upon receiving an encrypted message from Alice, Bob can likewise compute the same shared secret and then decrypt the message and verify the authenticator:

1. Bob computes $\iota(\tau_A) = P_A$.
2. Bob computes $k = H(u_B P_A)$.

2.3 ElGamal encryption

Assume u_B and $P_B = u_B P$ is a static key pair of Bob and that Bob has published $\tau_B = \iota^{-1}(P_B)$. Alice wants to send Bob a message M. To encrypt the message she performs the following steps:

1. She generates a random integer r.
2. She computes the point $R = rP$. If $R \notin \iota(S)$ she repeats from step 1.
3. She computes $\iota^{-1}(R) = \tau_R$.
4. She computes $P_B = \iota(\tau_B)$.
5. She computes the shared key value $k = H(rP_B)$.
6. She encrypts message m using key k: $c = \text{Enc}_k(m)$.
7. She sends the tuple (τ_R, c) as an encryption of m.

To decrypt the received message, Bob:

1. computes $\iota(\tau_R) = R$,
2. computes the same shared key value: $k = H(u_B R)$, and
3. decrypts the message: $m = \text{Dec}_k(c)$.

ElGamal encryption also appears in [23] as an application of an injective map between strings and curve points, but our application is completely different from the application in [23]. There is a critical difference in the underlying encryption methods: we use symmetric cryptography to encrypt the message m using a key derived from rP_B, whereas [23] adds rP_B to a curve point M that represents m. This is exactly where [23] uses an injective map, namely to encode the string m as a curve point M. Note, however, that this also (1) prevents [23] from encrypting long messages and (2) allows malleability, in violation of the basic security standards for public-key encryption. We instead use the standard "KEM/DEM" structure to provide secure public-key encryption, and as a consequence do not need to encode strings as curve points. We use an injective map for a completely different reason: we encode curve points as strings, preventing those points from being recognized by censors.

2.4 Short-term Diffie–Hellman keys

In this protocol, Alice and Bob agree on a shared secret without using long-term keys. This protocol is important as a way to provide forward secrecy. Of course, this provides no authentication, but authentication can be added as a subsequent layer.

1. Alice and Bob generate short-term keys as follows:
   (a) Generate a random integer r.
   (b) Compute point $R = rP$. If $R \notin \iota(S)$ repeat from step 1a.
2. Alice sends $\mu_A = \iota^{-1}(R_A)$ to Bob; Bob sends $\mu_B = \iota^{-1}(R_B)$ to Alice.
3. Alice decodes $R_B = \iota(\mu_B)$; Bob decodes $R_A = \iota(\mu_A)$.
4. Alice computes the shared key value $k = H(r_A R_B)$; Bob computes the same k as $H(r_B R_A)$.

2.5 Schnorr signatures

Assume that u_B and $P_B = u_B P$ are respectively private and public keys of Bob, where $P_B \in \iota(S)$ and Bob has published $\tau_B = \iota^{-1}(P_B)$. To sign a message m, Bob performs the following steps:

1. Choose a random integer r.
2. Compute $R = rP$. If $R \notin \iota(S)$, repeat from step 1.
3. Compute $\tau = \iota^{-1}(R)$.
4. Compute $h = H(\tau || \tau_B || m)$.
5. Compute $s = r + hu_B \pmod{n}$.
6. The signature is the tuple $\psi = (\tau, s)$.

The integer s must be encoded so as to be indistinguishable from uniform; see Section 2.6.

To verify the signature (τ, s), Alice performs the following steps:

1. Compute $P_B = \iota(\tau_B)$.
2. Compute $R = \iota(\tau)$.
3. Compute $h = H(\tau || \tau_B || m)$.
4. Compare $R + hP_B$ and sP. If they are equal, accept. Otherwise, reject.

Schnorr's original signature system actually sent (h, s). We follow "EdDSA" from [8] in sending an encoding of (R, s); security is the same, since one can reconstruct (h, s) from (R, s) and vice versa. The advantage of (R, s) is that it allows batching, making signature verification about twice as fast, as explained in [8]. Our use of ι makes this signature indistinguishable from a uniform random string.

We also follow EdDSA in including the public key τ_B in the hash. Robert Ransom has pointed out that if the public key is omitted from the hash then an attacker who does not know it can calculate it by first computing h and then computing $(sP - R)/h$, and as a consequence can see that two signatures come from the same public key. Ransom has also suggested a different way of hiding signatures from someone who does not know τ_B: namely, encrypting the signatures with a secret-key cipher keyed by a hash of τ_B. Of course, indistinguishability is unachievable against an attacker who *does* know τ_B: the attacker can simply verify the signature.

We encode R as τ both for transmission and for input to H. We could safely switch to a different encoding for input to H. In particular, we could use the same encoding used in EdDSA. This would make our signatures compatible with EdDSA signatures: anyone could convert an EdDSA signature into a signature of our form and vice versa.

2.6 Detecting differences from uniform

These protocols transmit uniform random elements of S. Usually S is not the set of *all* b-bit strings, so uniform random elements of S are not exactly uniform random b-bit strings. This is not a security problem if $\#S$ is very close to 2^b; we now analyze quantitatively what "very close" means.

Consider a channel that normally sends k independent uniform random b-bit strings. A user modifies the channel to instead transmit k independent uniform random elements of S. The censor's goal is to take action against the modified channel without taking action against the original channel.

The obvious strategy for the censor is to take action if and only if all of the b-bit strings are elements of S. This has no false negatives, but it produces a false positive whenever k independent uniform random b-bit strings happen to all be elements of S. If $\#S = 2^b - \delta$ then a false positive occurs with probability $(\#S/2^b)^k = (1 - \delta/2^b)^k \approx \exp(-k\delta/2^b)$. This strategy maximizes the difference in action probability between the original and modified channels; hence S^k is indistinguishable from $(\{0,1\}^b)^k$ when $k\delta/2^b$ is small.

Consider, for example, the NIST P-256 set $S = \{0, 1, 2, \ldots, 2^{256} - 2^{224} + 2^{192} + 2^{96} - 2\}$, with $b = 256$. Here $\delta \approx 2^{224}$. If the censor sees $k = 2^{35}$ sessions then $k\delta/2^b \approx 8$ so the censor will take action for the original channel with probability only about $\exp(-8) \approx 0.000335$. This may be an acceptable level of collateral damage.

As a second example illustrating the importance of the ratio $k\delta/2^b$, consider a set S of size $2^{256} - \delta$ where $\delta \le 2^{160}$. This time a censor seeing $k \le 2^{64}$ sessions has $k\delta/2^b \le 2^{-32}$ so the probability is larger than 0.99999999; i.e., the censor will take action against practically every channel.

The encodings that we consider for elements of $E(\mathbf{F}_q)$ typically have $\#S = (q+1)/2$. In each of our recommended examples, $\#S$ is between $2^b - 2^{b/2}$ and 2^b, so $k\delta/2^b \le k/2^{b/2}$. The probability difference is therefore negligible until k, the number of strings transmitted, grows to a noticeable fraction of $2^{b/2}$. This cannot be a concern when $E(\mathbf{F}_q)$ is chosen to resist standard discrete-logarithm attacks: those attacks take time only about $2^{b/2}$.

We also encode integers modulo $n = \#E(\mathbf{F}_q)$ as strings in Section 2.5. By Hasse's theorem, n is within $2\sqrt{q}$ of $q+1$, so if q is very close to 2^{b+1} then n is also forced to be very close to 2^{b+1}. Note that taking q slightly below 2^{b+1} does not force n to be below 2^{b+1}; for $n > 2^{b+1}$ we still use a $(b+1)$-bit encoding, restarting the protocol in Section 2.5 in the extremely unlikely case that an integer is 2^{b+1} or larger.

2.7 Active attacks

Censors can try replacing random-looking strings by other strings (possibly strings outside S) to see whether this has any visible effect. Presumably this replacement will *disrupt* communication, but protocol designers and implementors must take care to ensure that this replacement does not allow the censor to *detect* communication.

We briefly point out an attack against the password-authenticated key-exchange protocol of [13]; this attack is not in the censorship context, but it illustrates both the value of avoiding twists and the difficulty of protecting against active attacks. In the protocol of [13], Alice sends an encryption (using a shared password as a secret key) of either a point on a curve or a point on the twist of the curve; indistinguishability is important here for the ciphertext to avoid leaking information. Bob sends back two points, one on the curve and one on the twist; information is carried by the point on the same curve used by Alice, while the other point is random. Our attack is to actively rerandomize one of the two points sent by Bob. If this point is on the same curve then Alice aborts; if this point is not on the same curve then Alice does not notice and communication continues. This information leak allows the attacker to exclude half of all possible passwords, and repeating the attack allows the attacker to quickly find the right password.

3. ELLIGATOR 1: THE INJECTIVE MAP

Section 2 needs an injective map ι from a large set S of strings to $E(\mathbf{F}_q)$. Elligator 1 is one choice of ι; Elligator 2, introduced in Section 5, is another choice of ι. This section presents the mathematical details of Elligator 1: the construction of ι, how to compute ι, how to test whether a curve point is in the image of ι, and how to invert ι on curve points in the image. To help the reader visualize the mathematical structure of ι we include a picture as Figure 1.

We impose certain requirements on q and E for Elligator 1: we consider only primes q; we require q to be congruent to 3 modulo 4; we require E to be a complete Edwards curve; and we impose an extra algebraic requirement ($c = 2/s^2$ in Theorem 1) that allows only half of all complete Edwards curves. Approximately 1/16 of all isomorphism classes of elliptic curves over all finite fields satisfy these requirements. (Asymptotically 100% of all finite fields, ordered by size, are prime fields; 50% of those primes are congruent to 3 modulo 4; 25% of elliptic curves over those fields are complete Edwards curves; 50% of those satisfy the extra algebraic requirement.) See Section 4 for specific choices of q and E.

The heart of ι is a function $\phi : \mathbf{F}_q \to E(\mathbf{F}_q)$ defined in Theorem 1 and Definition 2. This function satisfies $\phi(t) = \phi(-t)$ for each $t \in \mathbf{F}_q$ but has no other collisions (see Theorem 3), so its restriction to $\{0, 1, 2, \ldots, (q-1)/2\}$ is injective. Theorem 4 simply defines S as $\{0, 1, 2, \ldots, (q-1)/2\}$ represented in little-endian form as b-bit strings, where $b = \lfloor \log_2 q \rfloor$, and defines ι as the corresponding representation of ϕ. For indistinguishability we add the requirement that $(q+1)/2$ be extremely close to 2^b.

As mentioned in Section 1, this function ϕ was introduced by Fouque, Joux, and Tibouchi in [23]. Our main contributions in this section are a much more concise definition of ϕ; much more direct proofs of the relevant properties of ϕ; a simple method to invert ϕ; and a simple test for whether a curve point is in the image of ϕ.

The function $-\phi$ has the same useful properties as ϕ. Our choice of sign is not the same as the choice in [23]: in the notation below, the ratio is $\chi(c)$, i.e., $\chi(2)$. This choice of sign slightly simplifies our formulas for the forward and inverse maps, although it is not the main simplification compared to [23]. We also comment that $\phi(t) = -\phi(1/t)$ for $t \ne 0$.

Computing ι in a sensible way is almost as fast as traditional point decompression, not a serious bottleneck compared to scalar multiplication. Inverting ι is slightly slower, but testing whether a curve point is in the image of ι is very fast. See Section 3.5 for further performance analysis.

3.1 Squares, square roots, and χ

Fix a prime power $q \equiv 3 \pmod 4$. In defining ι we consider only primes q for simplicity (so that $0, 1, 2, \ldots, (q-1)/2$ are distinct field elements) but our ϕ theorems also apply to prime powers.

Define $\chi : \mathbf{F}_q \to \mathbf{F}_q$ by $\chi(a) = a^{(q-1)/2}$. If a is a non-zero square then $\chi(a) = 1$; if a is a non-square then $\chi(a) = -1$; if $a = 0$ then $\chi(a) = 0$. Note that $(q-1)/2$ is odd since $q \equiv 3 \pmod 4$, so $\chi(-1) = -1$, so -1 is not a square. More

Figure 1: The structure of our encoding function ι^{-1}, a bijection from a large subset of $E(\mathbf{F}_q)$ to a large set S of b-bit strings. The elliptic curve E is required to be a complete Edwards curve, shown on the left together with a sample element $P = (x, y)$ of $E(\mathbf{F}_q)$. A sample b-bit output is shown on the right. See Theorems 1, 3, and 4 and Definition 2 for further details regarding the function in the middle.

generally, $\chi(\chi(a)) = \chi(a)$. There are several easy ways to manipulate χ arguments: for example, $\chi(ab) = \chi(a)\chi(b)$, $\chi(1/a) = \chi(a) = 1/\chi(a)$ if $a \neq 0$, and $\chi(a^2) = 1$ if $a \neq 0$.

If a is a square then $a^{(q+1)/4}$ is a square root of a: its square is $a^{(q+1)/2} = \chi(a)a = a$. More precisely, $a^{(q+1)/4}$ is the **principal** square root of a: the unique square root that is a square. Any square root b of a satisfies $b = \chi(b)a^{(q+1)/4}$.

The function χ is called a **quadratic character**. See [38] for further background on finite fields.

3.2 The map

THEOREM 1. *Let q be a prime power congruent to 3 modulo 4. Let s be a nonzero element of $\mathbf{F}_q$ with $(s^2-2)(s^2+2) \neq 0$. Define $c = 2/s^2$. Then $c(c-1)(c+1) \neq 0$.*

Define $r = c + 1/c$ and $d = -(c+1)^2/(c-1)^2$. Then $r \neq 0$, and d is not a square.

The following elements of $\mathbf{F}_q$ are defined for each $t \in \mathbf{F}_q \setminus \{\pm 1\}$:

$$u = (1-t)/(1+t),$$
$$v = u^5 + (r^2-2)u^3 + u,$$
$$X = \chi(v)u,$$
$$Y = (\chi(v)v)^{(q+1)/4}\chi(v)\chi(u^2 + 1/c^2),$$
$$x = (c-1)sX(1+X)/Y,$$
$$y = (rX - (1+X)^2)/(rX + (1+X)^2).$$

Furthermore $x^2 + y^2 = 1 + dx^2y^2$; $uvXYx(y+1) \neq 0$; and $Y^2 = X^5 + (r^2-2)X^3 + X$.

PROOF. $\mathbf{c(c-1)(c+1) \neq 0}$**:** By definition $c = 2/s^2$ so $c \neq 0$. By hypothesis $s^2 \neq 2$ and $s^2 \neq -2$ so $c \neq 1$ and $c \neq -1$.

$\boldsymbol{r \neq 0}$**:** If $r = 0$ then $c = -1/c$ so $c^2 = -1$, contradiction.

***d* is not a square:** Otherwise $-1 = d(c-1)^2/(c+1)^2$ is a square, contradiction.

***u* is defined and $\boldsymbol{u \neq 0}$:** By hypothesis $1 + t \neq 0$ and $1 - t \neq 0$.

$\boldsymbol{v \neq 0}$**:** $r^2 - 2 = c^2 + 1/c^2$ so $v = u(u^2+c^2)(u^2+1/c^2)$. If $v = 0$ then there are three possibilities: $u = 0$, contradiction; or $u^2+c^2 = 0$ so $-1 = (u/c)^2$, contradiction; or $u^2+1/c^2 = 0$ so $-1 = (uc)^2$, contradiction.

$\boldsymbol{XY \neq 0}$**, so *x* is defined:** As above $u^2 + 1/c^2 \neq 0$ so all factors in X and Y are nonzero.

$\boldsymbol{1 + X \neq 0}$**, so** $\boldsymbol{x \neq 0}$**:** If $X = -1$ then $u = -\chi(v)$ so $v = -\chi(v)(1 + r^2 - 2 + 1) = -\chi(v)r^2$ so $\chi(v) = -\chi(v)$, contradiction.

$\boldsymbol{(X, Y)}$ **satisfies** $\boldsymbol{Y^2 = X^5 + (r^2-2)X^3 + X}$**:** $X = \chi(v)u$ so $X^5 + (r^2-2)X^3 + X = \chi(v)(u^5 + (r^2-2)u^3 + u) = \chi(v)v$. Also $\chi(v)v$ is a square so $(\chi(v)v)^{(q+1)/2} = \chi(v)v$ so $Y^2 = \chi(v)v$.

$\boldsymbol{rX + (1+X)^2 \neq 0}$**, so *y* is defined:** If $rX = -(1+X)^2$ then $(r^2+4r)X^2 = X^4 - 2X^2 + 1$ so

$$Y^2 = X(X^4 + (r^2-2)X^2 + 1) = X^3(2r^2 + 4r)$$
$$= rX \cdot X^2(2r+4) = -(1+X)^2X^2(s + 2/s)^2$$

so -1 is a square, contradiction.

$\boldsymbol{y + 1 \neq 0}$**:** If $y = -1$ then $(rX - (1+X)^2)/(rX + (1+X)^2) = -1$ so $rX - (1+X)^2 = -(rX + (1+X)^2)$ so $rX = 0$, contradiction.

$\boldsymbol{x^2 + y^2 = 1 + dx^2y^2}$**:** First $(c-1)^2s^2 = (c-1)^2(2/c) = 2(r-2)$ so

$$Y^2(1-x^2) = Y^2 - (c-1)^2s^2X^2(1+X)^2$$
$$= X^5 + (r^2-2)X^3 + X - 2(r-2)X^2(1+X)^2$$
$$= X(rX - (1+X)^2)^2.$$

Similarly $-d = (c + 2 + 1/c)/(c - 2 + 1/c) = (r+2)/(r-2)$ so $-d(c-1)^2s^2 = 2(r+2)$ so

$$Y^2(1 - dx^2) = Y^2 - d(c-1)^2s^2X^2(1+X)^2$$
$$= X^5 + (r^2-2)X^3 + X + 2(r+2)X^2(1+X)^2$$
$$= X(rX + (1+X)^2)^2.$$

Note that $Y^2(1-dx^2) \neq 0$, and divide: $(1-x^2)/(1-dx^2) = (rX - (1+X)^2)^2/(rX + (1+X)^2)^2 = y^2$; i.e., $x^2 + y^2 = 1 + dx^2y^2$. □

DEFINITION 2. *In the situation of Theorem 1, the* **decoding function** *for the complete Edwards curve $E : x^2 + y^2 = 1 + dx^2y^2$ is the function $\phi : \mathbf{F}_q \to E(\mathbf{F}_q)$ defined as follows: $\phi(\pm 1) = (0, 1)$; if $t \notin \{\pm 1\}$ then $\phi(t) = (x, y)$.*

3.3 Inverting the map

THEOREM 3. *In the situation of Definition 2:*

1. *If $t \in \mathbf{F}_q$ then the set of preimages of $\phi(t)$ under ϕ is $\{t, -t\}$.*
2. *$\phi(\mathbf{F}_q)$ is the set of $(x, y) \in E(\mathbf{F}_q)$ such that*
   - *$y + 1 \neq 0$;*
   - *$(1+\eta r)^2 - 1$ is a square, where $\eta = \dfrac{y-1}{2(y+1)}$; and*
   - *if $\eta r = -2$ then $x = 2s(c-1)\chi(c)/r$.*
3. *If $(x, y) \in \phi(\mathbf{F}_q)$ then the following elements $\bar{X}, z, \bar{u}, \bar{t}$ of $\mathbf{F}_q$ are defined and $\phi(\bar{t}) = (x, y)$:*

$$\bar{X} = -(1+\eta r) + ((1+\eta r)^2 - 1)^{(q+1)/4},$$
$$z = \chi((c-1)s\bar{X}(1+\bar{X})x(\bar{X}^2 + 1/c^2)),$$
$$\bar{u} = z\bar{X},$$
$$\bar{t} = (1-\bar{u})/(1+\bar{u}).$$

PROOF. Statement 1 of the theorem has two parts: a forward statement $\phi(t) = \phi(-t)$, and a reverse statement that there are no other preimages. Statement 2 also has two parts: a forward statement that any $(x, y) \in \phi(\mathbf{F}_q)$ satisfies certain conditions, and a reverse statement that any element of $E(\mathbf{F}_q)$ satisfying those conditions is in $\phi(\mathbf{F}_q)$. We organize the proof as (A) forward 1; (B) 3, forward 2, and reverse 1; (C) reverse 2.

A. Fix $t \in \mathbf{F}_q$. We now show that $\phi(t) = \phi(-t)$. This is the forward part of statement 1 in the theorem.

If $t \in \{\pm 1\}$ then $\phi(t) = (0,1) = \phi(-t)$ by definition. Assume from now on that $t \notin \{\pm 1\}$.

Define u, v, X, Y, x, y from t as in Theorem 1. Then $\phi(t) = (x, y)$ by definition.

Put $t' = -t$, and define u', v', X', Y', x', y' the same way from t'. Then $\phi(t') = (x', y')$. The proof strategy is to compare successively u' to u, v' to v, etc., concluding that $x' = x$ and $y' = y$.

$\boldsymbol{u'} = (1-t')/(1+t') = (1+t)/(1-t) = 1/u$.

$\boldsymbol{v'} = u'^5 + (r^2-2)u'^3 + u' = \frac{1}{u^5} + (r^2-2)\frac{1}{u^3} + \frac{1}{u}$, so $v'u^6 = u + (r^2-2)u^3 + u^5 = v$; i.e., $v' = v/u^6$. Note that $\chi(v') = \chi(v)$ since $\chi(u^6) = 1$.

$\boldsymbol{X'} = \chi(v')u' = \chi(v)/u = 1/(\chi(v)u) = 1/X$ since $\chi(v) = 1/\chi(v)$.

$$\boldsymbol{y'} = \frac{rX' - (1+X')^2}{rX' + (1+X')^2} = \frac{r\frac{1}{X} - (1+\frac{1}{X})^2}{r\frac{1}{X} + (1+\frac{1}{X})^2} = \frac{rX - (X+1)^2}{rX + (X+1)^2} = y.$$

$\boldsymbol{Y'} = (\chi(v')v')^{(q+1)/4}\chi(v')\chi(u'^2 + 1/c^2)$. This takes the most work; the first and third factors each need careful analyses. The second factor is easy: $\chi(v') = \chi(v)$ as above.

First factor: $\chi(v')v' = \chi(v)v/u^6$. Note that the product $\chi(u)u^3$ is a square and is therefore the principal square root of u^6; i.e., $(u^6)^{(q+1)/4} = \chi(u)u^3$. Hence $(\chi(v')v')^{(q+1)/4} = (\chi(v)v/u^6)^{(q+1)/4} = (\chi(v)v)^{(q+1)/4}\chi(u)/u^3$.

Third factor: Recall that $v = u(u^2 + c^2)(u^2 + 1/c^2)$ and that $\chi(a) = \chi(ab^2)$ for any $b \neq 0$. Thus

$$\begin{aligned}\chi(u'^2 + 1/c^2) &= \chi\big(c^2u^4(u'^2 + 1/c^2)(u^2 + 1/c^2)^2\big)\\ &= \chi\big(u^2(c^2 + u^2)(u^2 + 1/c^2)^2\big)\\ &= \chi\big(uv(u^2 + 1/c^2)\big).\end{aligned}$$

Now multiply to obtain $Y' = Y\chi(u)\chi(uv)/u^3 = Y/(\chi(v)u)^3 = Y/X^3$. Finally

$$\begin{aligned}\boldsymbol{x'} &= (c-1)sX'(1+X')/Y' = (c-1)s\frac{1}{X}\left(1+\frac{1}{X}\right)\Big/\frac{Y}{X^3}\\ &= (c-1)sX(1+X)/Y = x.\end{aligned}$$

Hence $\phi(-t) = (x', y') = (x, y) = \phi(t)$ as claimed.

B. Fix $t \in \mathbf{F}_q$, and define $(x, y) = \phi(t)$. We show that $\bar{X}, z, \bar{u}, \bar{t}$ in the theorem are defined and that $\bar{t} \in \{t, -t\}$, so $\phi(\bar{t}) = (x, y)$; this is statement 3 in the theorem. We also show the forward part of statement 2: namely, $y + 1 \neq 0$; $(1+\eta r)^2 - 1$ is a square, where $\eta = (y-1)/(2(y+1))$; and if $\eta r = -2$ then $x = 2s(c-1)\chi(c)/r$. We also show the reverse part of statement 1: there are no preimages of $\phi(t)$ other than t and $-t$.

The definition of ϕ has two cases: if $t \in \{1, -1\}$ then $(x, y) = (0, 1)$; if $t \notin \{1, -1\}$ then u, v, X, Y, x, y are defined in Theorem 1. Note that in the second case $x \neq 0$ by Theorem 1, so in particular t is not a preimage of $(0, 1)$.

In the first case $y + 1 = 2 \neq 0$; $\eta = 0$; $(1+\eta r)^2 - 1 = 0$ is a square; $\bar{X} = -1$; $z = 0$; $\bar{u} = 0$; and $\bar{t} = 1 \in \{t, -t\}$. As noted above, 1 and -1 are the only preimages of $(0, 1)$.

What remains is the second case. Here $y + 1 \neq 0$ by Theorem 1. The equation $y = (rX - (1+X)^2)/(rX + (1+X)^2)$ implies $X^2 + (2 + r(y-1)/(y+1))X + 1 = 0$, i.e., $X^2 + 2(1+\eta r)X + 1 = 0$. Note that this forces the discriminant $4(1+\eta r)^2 - 4$ to be a square; i.e., $(1+\eta r)^2 - 1$ is a square. Divide by X to see that $X + 1/X = -2(1+\eta r)$.

If $\eta r = -2$ then $(X-1)^2 = 0$ so $X = 1$ so $u \in \{\pm 1\}$; the case $u = -1$ forces $1 - t = -(1+t)$, contradiction, so $u = 1$ and $t = 0$; so $v = r^2$, so $Y = (r^2)^{(q+1)/4}\chi(1 + 1/c^2) = \chi(r)r\chi(r/c) = r\chi(c)$, so $x = 2(c-1)s\chi(c)/r$ as claimed; also note for future reference that $y = (r-4)/(r+4)$, i.e., $\phi(0) = (2(c-1)s\chi(c)/r, (r-4)/(r+4))$.

Define $t' = -t$, and define u', v', X', Y', x', y' as in Part A of this proof. Then $X' = 1/X$, so $X + X' = -2(1+\eta r)$.

By construction $1 + \eta r + \bar{X}$ is a square root of $(1+\eta r)^2 - 1$; i.e., $\bar{X}^2 + 2(1+\eta r)\bar{X} + 1 = 0$. Now $(\bar{X} - X)(\bar{X} - X') = \bar{X}^2 - (X + X')\bar{X} + XX' = \bar{X}^2 + 2(1+\eta r)\bar{X} + 1 = 0$ so $\bar{X} = X$ or $\bar{X} = X'$. This forces $\bar{u} = u$ or $\bar{u} = u'$, since the definition of z turns out to match $\chi(v)$ and $\chi(v')$:

- If $\bar{X} = X$ then $(c-1)s\bar{X}(1+\bar{X}) = xY$ so $z = \chi\big(x^2Y(X^2 + 1/c^2)\big) = \chi(Y)\chi(X^2 + 1/c^2)$. Note that $(\chi(v)v)^{(q+1)/4}$ is a square and $\chi(u^2 + 1/c^2) = \chi(X^2 + 1/c^2)$, so $\chi(Y) = \chi(v)\chi(X^2 + 1/c^2)$, so $z = \chi(v)$, so $\bar{u} = \chi(v)X = u$, so $\bar{t} = t$.
- If $\bar{X} = X'$ then similarly $z = \chi(v')$, $\bar{u} = u'$, and $\bar{t} = t' = -t$.

To summarize, $\bar{t} \in \{t, -t\}$, so $\phi(\bar{t}) = (x, y)$.

The same logic also shows that there are no preimages p of (x, y) except for t and $-t$. Indeed, if $(x, y) = \phi(p)$ then substituting p for t in the same proof shows that $\bar{t} \in \{p, -p\}$, so $p \in \{\bar{t}, -\bar{t}\} = \{t, -t\}$.

C. Fix $(x, y) \in E(\mathbf{F}_q)$. Assume that $y + 1 \neq 0$; that $(1+\eta r)^2 - 1$ is a square, where $\eta = (y-1)/(2(y+1))$; and that if $\eta r = -2$ then $x = 2s(c-1)\chi(c)/r$. We now show that $(x, y) \in \phi(\mathbf{F}_q)$. This is the reverse part of statement 2 of the theorem.

If $x = 0$ then $(x, y) = (0, \pm 1)$ from the curve equation; but $y + 1 \neq 0$, so $(x, y) = (0, 1) = \phi(1) \in \phi(\mathbf{F}_q)$ as claimed. Assume from now on that $x \neq 0$.

If $y = 1$ then $x = 0$ from the curve equation, contradiction. Hence $y \neq 1$; i.e., $\eta \neq 0$.

Define $X = -(1+\eta r) + ((1+\eta r)^2 - 1)^{(q+1)/4}$. As above $1 + \eta r + X$ is a square root of $(1+\eta r)^2 - 1$, so $X^2 + 2(1+\eta r)X + 1 = 0$. This quadratic equation has several consequences. First, $X \neq 0$. Second, $rX + (1+X)^2 \neq 0$: otherwise subtract to see that $(1 - 2\eta)rX = 0$, so $1 = 2\eta$, so $y - 1 = y + 1$, contradiction. Third, $X \neq -1$: otherwise $\eta = 0$, contradiction. Fourth, $y = (rX - (1+X)^2)/(rX + (1+X)^2)$.

If $X = 1$ then $y = (r-4)/(r+4)$; also $\eta r = -2$ so by assumption $x = 2s(c-1)\chi(c)/r$ so $(x, y) = \phi(0) \in \phi(\mathbf{F}_q)$. Assume from now on that $X \neq 1$.

Observe that

$$\begin{aligned}&(rX + (1+X)^2)^2(1 - y^2)\\ &\quad - (rX + (1+X)^2)^2 - (rX - (1+X)^2)^2\\ &\quad = 4rX(1+X)^2.\end{aligned}$$

Recall that $-d = (r+2)/(r-2)$ and similarly observe that

$$\begin{aligned}&(rX + (1+X)^2)^2(1 - dy^2)\\ &\quad = (rX + (1+X)^2)^2 + \frac{r+2}{r-2}(rX - (1+X)^2)^2\\ &\quad = (2r/(r-2))(X^4 + (r^2-2)X^2 + 1).\end{aligned}$$

Note that $1 - dy^2 \neq 0$ since d is not a square. Divide:

$$x^2 = \frac{1 - y^2}{1 - dy^2} = \frac{2(r-2)X^2(1+X)^2}{X^5 + (r^2-2)X^3 + X}.$$

Define $Y = (c-1)sX(1+X)/x$. Then

$$\begin{aligned}Y^2 &= (c-1)^2s^2X^2(1+X)^2/x^2\\ &= 2(r-2)X^2(1+X)^2/x^2\\ &= X^5 + (r^2-2)X^3 + X.\end{aligned}$$

Define $z = \chi\big(Y(X^2 + 1/c^2)\big)$. Both Y and $X^2 + 1/c^2$ are nonzero, so $z \in \{\pm 1\}$.

Define $u = zX$. Then $u \in \{\pm X\}$. Note that $u \neq -1$, since $X \notin \{\pm 1\}$.

Define $v = u^5 + (r^2 - 2)u^3 + u$. Then $v = z(X^5 + (r^2-2)X^3 + X) = zY^2$, so $\chi(v) = \chi(z) = z$. Hence $X = \chi(v)u$ and $Y^2 = \chi(v)v$. Furthermore $\chi(v) = z = \chi(Y(X^2 + 1/c^2)) = \chi(Y(u^2+1/c^2))$, so $\chi(Y) = \chi(v)\chi(u^2+1/c^2)$, so $Y = (\chi(v)v)^{(q+1)/4}\chi(v)\chi(u^2+1/c^2)$.

Finally define $t = (1-u)/(1+u)$. Then $t \notin \{\pm 1\}$ and $u = (1-t)/(1+t)$. The formulas for u, v, X, Y, x, y in Theorem 1 are all satisfied, so $(x, y) = \phi(t) \in \phi(\mathbf{F}_q)$ as claimed. □

3.4 Encoding as strings

THEOREM 4. *In the situation of Definition 2, assume that q is prime, and define $b = \lfloor \log_2 q \rfloor$. Define $\sigma : \{0,1\}^b \to \mathbf{F}_q$ by $\sigma(\tau_0, \tau_1, \ldots, \tau_{b-1}) = \sum_i \tau_i 2^i$. Define $S = \sigma^{-1}(\{0, 1, 2, \ldots, (q-1)/2\})$. Define $\iota : S \to E(\mathbf{F}_q)$ as follows: $\iota(\tau) = \phi(\sigma(\tau))$. Then $\#S = (q+1)/2$; ι is an injective map from S to $E(\mathbf{F}_q)$; and $\iota(S) = \phi(\mathbf{F}_q)$.*

PROOF. First $2^b \leq q$ so the integers $0, 1, \ldots, 2^b - 1$ are distinct in $\mathbf{F}_q$; hence σ is injective. Furthermore $2^b > q/2$ so $\{0, 1, \ldots, (q-1)/2\}$ is a subset of $\{0, 1, \ldots, 2^b - 1\}$; hence each of $0, 1, \ldots, (q-1)/2$ has a preimage under σ, and S has exactly $(q+1)/2$ elements.

If $\iota(\tau) = \iota(\tau')$ then $\phi(\sigma(\tau)) = \phi(\sigma(\tau'))$, so $\sigma(\tau) = \pm\sigma(\tau')$ by Theorem 3; but $\sigma(\tau)$ and $\sigma(\tau')$ are both in $\{0, 1, \ldots, (q-1)/2\}$, so $\sigma(\tau) = \sigma(\tau')$, so $\tau = \tau'$. Hence ι is injective.

Each element of $\iota(S)$ has the form $\phi(\sigma(\tau))$ and is therefore in $\phi(\mathbf{F}_q)$. Conversely, if $P \in \phi(\mathbf{F}_q)$ then $P = \phi(t)$ for some $t \in \mathbf{F}_q$, so also $P = \phi(-t)$ by Theorem 3. At least one of $t, -t$ is in $\{0, 1, \ldots, (q-1)/2\}$, i.e., in $\sigma(S)$, so P is in $\phi(\sigma(S)) = \iota(S)$. □

3.5 Performance analysis

The definitions of u, v, X, Y, x, y in Theorem 1 involve divisions by $1 + t$, c, Y, and $rX + (1 + X)^2$. The reciprocal of c is trivially precomputed, and the other divisions are easily replaced by a few multiplications: one simply stores field elements as fractions, i.e., works in projective coordinates. There are several easy ways to reduce the number of multiplications: for example, factor $u^5 + (r^2 - 2)u^3 + u$ as $u(u^2 + c^2)(u^2 + 1/c^2)$, and reuse $u^2 + 1/c^2$ in computing Y.

The main bottlenecks are then the following exponentiations: computing $\chi(v)$ (used repeatedly); computing $\chi(u^2 + 1/c^2)$; computing $(\chi(v)v)^{(q+1)/4}$, the principal square root of $\chi(v)v$; and computing a final division if the output (x, y) is needed in affine coordinates instead of projective coordinates. The only essential exponentiation is for the square-root computation: the χ computations and division can use Euclid's algorithm (blinded to protect against timing attacks) rather than exponentiation.

Similar comments apply to inverting ϕ (or ι). There is one essential exponentiation, the square-root computation to obtain $\bar{X}$ in Theorem 3. There are also two exponentiations that can be replaced by Euclidean computations: one χ computation to obtain z, and one division to obtain the final output $\bar{t}$. Fractions eliminate the initial division by $2(y+1)$, but fractions cannot be used for $\bar{t}$, since the goal is to obtain the unique string representing $\bar{t}$.

It is easier to test, given $(x, y) \in \mathbf{F}_q \times \mathbf{F}_q$, whether $(x, y) \in \phi(\mathbf{F}_q)$ (i.e., whether $(x, y) \in \iota(S)$) without inverting ϕ. One first checks $x^2 + y^2 = 1 + dx^2y^2$ to verify $(x, y) \in E(\mathbf{F}_q)$, if this is not already known. Then, by Theorem 3, $(x, y) \in \phi(\mathbf{F}_q)$ if and only if the following three conditions are satisfied:

- $y + 1 \neq 0$;
- $(1 + \eta r)^2 - 1$ is a square, where $\eta = (y-1)/(2(y+1))$; i.e., $r(y-1)(r(y-1) + 4(y+1))$ is a square;
- if $\eta r = -2$ (equivalently, if $r(y-1) = -4(y+1)$) then $x = 2s(c-1)\chi(c)/r$.

This requires a few multiplications and one χ computation.

4. CONSTRUCTION OF A SUITABLE ELLIPTIC CURVE FOR ELLIGATOR 1

This section introduces a new high-security high-speed elliptic curve, called Curve1174, that supports the injective map presented in Section 3. In particular, this section specifies Curve1174; presents the criteria that we used to construct Curve1174; and analyzes the extent to which various previous curves meet the same criteria.

Curve1174 illustrates state-of-the-art criteria for choosing elliptic curves. It is compatible with Elligator 1, and is also compatible with the new map Elligator 2 introduced in the next section. It is even more concisely expressible than the existing Curve25519 curve.

We do not mean to suggest that users of Curve25519 are required to switch to Curve1174 to take advantage of this paper. Curve25519 is fully compatible with Elligator 2.

4.1 The curve

Curve1174 is the Edwards curve $x^2 + y^2 = 1 - 1174x^2y^2$ over the field $\mathbf{F}_q$, where q is the prime number $2^{251} - 9$. The coefficient -1174 is a non-square in $\mathbf{F}_q$, so Curve1174 is a complete Edwards curve by [9, Theorem 3.3]: the sum of any two points (x_1, y_1) and (x_2, y_2) in Curve1174$(\mathbf{F}_q)$ is

$$\left(\frac{x_1y_2 + y_1x_2}{1 - 1174x_1x_2y_1y_2}, \frac{y_1y_2 - x_1x_2}{1 + 1174x_1x_2y_1y_2}\right),$$

with no divisions by 0 and no exceptional cases. The neutral element of the curve is $(0, 1)$.

To see that we have the desired injective map, note that q is congruent to 3 modulo 4; define s as the element

1806494121122717992522804053500797229648438766985538871240722010849934886421

of $\mathbf{F}_q$ (split onto two lines here for readability); define $c = 2/s^2$; and define $d = -(c+1)^2/(c-1)^2$. Then $d = -1174$. The Edwards curve in Theorem 1 and Definition 2, for this choice of (q, s), is exactly Curve1174.

Curve1174 is birationally equivalent to the Montgomery curve $(4/1175)V^2 = U^3 + (4/1175 - 2)U^2 + U$ by [9, Theorem 3.2]. The leading coefficient $4/1175$ is a non-square in $\mathbf{F}_q$, so $V^2 = U^3 + (4/1175 - 2)U^2 + U$ is a nontrivial quadratic twist of this curve. The Sage computer-algebra system [46] counts points on this curve in under 10 seconds on a laptop using the following script:

```
q=2^251-9
E=EllipticCurve(GF(q),[0,4/1175-2,0,1,0])
print E.trace_of_frobenius()
# output -45330879683285730139092453152713398836
```

The number of points on the twist is thus $q + 1 + t$, and the number of points on Curve1174 is $q + 1 - t$, where $t = 45330879683285730139092453152713398836$. These integers

$q+1+t, q+1-t$ have the form $4p_0, 4p_1$ respectively, where p_0 and p_1 are primes close to 2^{249}. Generic methods to compute a discrete logarithm on Curve1174 or its twist take approximately $\sqrt{\pi 2^{247}} \approx 2^{124.3}$ group operations on average.

The point $(U, V) = (4, 192257776421116702304087124422 0551478340301270840905838377461328496334409 6)$ on the Montgomery curve $(4/1175)V^2 = U^3 + (4/1175 - 2)U^2 + U$ has order $4p_1$. The corresponding point on Curve1174 is $(x, y) = (4/V, 3/5)$.

Curve1174 and its twist do not have any structure allowing fast pairings or other special approaches to computing discrete logarithms. The primes p_0 and p_1 do not equal the field characteristic q. The order of q modulo p_0 is not small: it is $(p_0 - 1)/2$. The order of q modulo p_1 is not small: it is $p_1 - 1$. The endomorphism ring of Curve1174 has a large discriminant: up to squares this discriminant equals $t^2 - 4q$, which is divisible once by the prime 16156741511402499233387034925579 9, so the discriminant must be a multiple of this prime.

4.2 Design criteria

We consider only prime fields. Bernstein, citing subfield attacks from [28] and [18], wrote in [6] that prime fields "have the virtue of minimizing the number of security concerns for elliptic-curve cryptography"; see [22] and [43] for recent developments of the attack strategy from [18]. Similarly, the Brainpool standard [14] and NSA's Suite B standards [37] require prime fields. There is general agreement that prime fields are the safe, conservative choice for ECC. Prime fields also perform very well across a wide range of processors; the current ECC speed records on high-end Intel processors take advantage of special Intel support for binary fields (see [42]), but most CPUs do not have any comparable support.

We consider only primes q congruent to 3 modulo 4. This is required for the injective map ϕ. These primes also have the well-known benefit of allowing very simple square-root computations; most other primes allow square-root computations at similar *speed* but with more complicated methods.

We consider only complete Edwards curves, i.e., curves $x^2 + y^2 = 1 + dx^2y^2$ where d is not a square. This is required for the injective map. About 25% of all elliptic curves over $\mathbf{F}_q$ are expressible as complete Edwards curves, as mentioned in [9, Abstract] and experimentally verified in [7, Section 4]. Complete Edwards curves also have the advantages of being extremely fast and of allowing a single addition formula with no exceptions. Complete Edwards curves are also expressible as Montgomery curves supporting very fast and uniform Montgomery-ladder computations.

To protect against generic discrete-logarithm algorithms we impose the standard requirement of a large prime dividing the number of curve points. This forces q to be even larger, where the gap accounts for the cofactor: the number of curve points divided by this prime. To minimize the performance problems of a large q we consider only Edwards curves with minimal cofactor, namely 4. The number of curve points is 4 times a prime for slightly below 1% of all choices of d, for the size of q that we consider below.

We also impose the requirement of "twist security": a large prime dividing the number of points on the quadratic twist of the curve. This prevents "twist attacks" against protocols that use the "Montgomery ladder" without checking that incoming points are on the curve; this defense was proposed by Bernstein in [5, page 23] and [4]. For $q \equiv 3 \pmod 4$ roughly 1/10000 of all choices of d have the number of points on the curve and the number of points on the twist each being 4 times a prime.

We require d to have the form $-(c+1)^2/(c-1)^2$ with $c = 2/s^2$. This is required for the injective map, and covers about half of all non-squares d for $q \equiv 3 \pmod 4$.

For standard performance reasons we take q very close to, but not above, a power of 2. The primes $q \equiv 3 \pmod 4$ within 32 of 2^e for $200 \le e \le 300$ are $2^{206} - 5$, $2^{212} - 29$, $2^{226} - 5$, $2^{243} - 9$, $2^{251} - 9$, and $2^{285} - 9$. Note that these fields ensure that σ^{-1} covers nearly all of $\{0, 1, \ldots, 2^b - 1\}$ giving a very close to uniform distribution of the encoding function. We focus on the last two of these primes as providing quantitatively safe security levels, and choose $2^{251} - 9$ as being obviously faster.

Some curve operations involve multiplications by d. To speed up these multiplications we take the smallest possible d in absolute value, subject to the other requirements. The choice $d = -1174$ for $q = 2^{251} - 9$ is smaller than expected.

4.3 Previous curves over prime fields

There is a long history of specific elliptic curves being designed to meet various security and performance criteria. For example, almost fifteen years ago the IEEE P1363 standard [33, Sections A.9–A.12]

- specified curves $y^2 = x^3 - 3x + b$ to "provide the fastest arithmetic on elliptic curves";
- imposed various further conditions upon these curves, with the security goal of making discrete logarithms difficult to compute; and
- specified a procedure to generate "verifiably pseudo-random" curves meeting these conditions.

NIST's standard curves P-192, P-224, P-256, P-384, and P-521 were generated as follows: five particular prime fields were chosen with the goal of maximizing performance; the IEEE P1363 procedure was used to generate one curve over each of those fields.

Subsequent research developed new security and performance criteria for curves over prime fields: twist security, Montgomery compatibility, Edwards compatibility, and completeness. The NIST curves, unsurprisingly, flunk these criteria: choosing cofactor 1 for $y^2 = x^3 - 3x + b$ is incompatible with both Montgomery and Edwards, and one cannot expect twist security if it is not demanded in advance. Newer curves meet all of these criteria: for example, Curve25519 was explicitly designed for twist security and Montgomery compatibility, and was shown in [9] to also be expressible as a complete Edwards curve.

These extra criteria do not improve discrete-logarithm security, but they do improve real-world security. They allow the *simplest* implementations to be *correct* implementations, whereas for other curves the simplest implementations that seem to work actually have hidden flaws that compromise security. See, e.g., [11, Section 4.1], [34], and [24].

We are imposing a new security condition to support censorship circumvention: namely, an efficient way to encode a large fraction of all curve points as strings indistinguishable from uniform random strings. The generality of Elligator 1 makes it easy to imagine how this security condition could be accidentally met by previously generated curves:

- The advantages of complete Edwards curves have been well known for five years.
- The advantages of Montgomery curves have been well known for even longer. A random Montgomery curve has a good chance of being expressible as a complete Edwards curve; see [7, Section 4].
- All complete Edwards curves over $\mathbf{F}_q$ for $q \equiv 3 \pmod 4$ meet the new security condition. Half of these curves are within the streamlined case expressed by Theorem 1.

Given the amount of speed optimization of Curve25519 (see [6], [29], [17], [8], and [10]) and the wide deployment of Curve25519 in several applications (see, e.g., [2]) one of our initial goals for this paper was to show that Curve25519 meets this security condition. However, Elligator 1 is clearly limited to $q \equiv 3 \pmod 4$, while Curve25519 is defined over $\mathbf{F}_q$ with $q \equiv 1 \pmod 4$. We provide two different solutions for this problem: Elligator 2 (see Section 5) and Curve1174.

We would expect serious implementations of Curve1174 to be competitive in speed with Curve25519. Curve1174 has some small advantages: for example, $2^{251} - 9$ is closer to a power of 2 than $2^{255}-19$ is; 1174 is considerably smaller than 486662; and square roots modulo $2^{251} - 9$ are slightly easier than square roots modulo $2^{255} - 19$. On the other hand, Curve25519 also has a small advantage: it is expressible in "-1-twisted Edwards form", allowing the speedup explained in [31]. Obviously applications already using Curve25519 should not switch away from it, but for new applications it is not clear which curve is better.

5. ELLIGATOR 2: HANDLING GENERIC CURVES WITH A POINT OF ORDER 2

This section introduces a new injective map ψ to any elliptic curve of the form $y^2 = x^3+Ax^2+Bx$ with $AB(A^2-4B) \neq 0$ over any odd finite field, i.e., any finite field of odd characteristic. We emphasize that the characteristic is not required to be 3 modulo 4. This curve shape includes all Montgomery curves $y^2 = x^3+Ax^2+x$ except $y^2 = x^3+x$, and in particular it includes Curve25519.

Any curve of this form has a point $(0,0)$ of order 2. Conversely, over any odd finite field, almost every elliptic curve having a point of order 2 can be written in this form. Indeed, an elliptic curve over an odd finite field can always be written as $y^2 = u^3+a_2u^2+a_4u+a_6$; a point of order 2 on this curve must have the form $(r,0)$ where $r^3+a_2r^2+a_4r+a_6 = 0$; substituting $u = x+r$ produces the curve $y^2 = x^3 + Ax^2 + Bx$ where $A = a_2 + 3r$ and $B = a_4 + 2a_2r + 3r^2$. This curve must have $B(A^2 - 4B) \neq 0$ since it is elliptic. The only exceptional case is $A = 0$, i.e., curves whose j-invariant equals 1728; this section assumes $A \neq 0$.

5.1 Squares

Fix an odd prime power q. As in Section 3.1 we define $\chi : \mathbf{F}_q \to \mathbf{F}_q$ by $\chi(a) = a^{(q-1)/2}$, and we have $\chi(a)$ equal to 1, -1, or 0 when a is, respectively, a non-zero square, a non-square, or zero.

The definition of Elligator 2 is parametrized by a **square-root function** for $\mathbf{F}_q$: a function $\sqrt{\ } : \mathbf{F}_q^2 \to \mathbf{F}_q$ such that $\sqrt{a^2} \in \{a, -a\}$ for each $a \in \mathbf{F}_q$, where $\mathbf{F}_q^2$ means $\{a^2 : a \in \mathbf{F}_q\}$. Note that a square-root function $\sqrt{\ }$ is completely described by its image $\sqrt{\mathbf{F}_q^2}$.

For $q \equiv 3 \pmod 4$ one can take the principal square root as a square-root function, i.e., take $\sqrt{\mathbf{F}_q^2} = \mathbf{F}_q^2$, as in Section 3.1; but the concept of principal square roots does not generalize to $q \equiv 1 \pmod 4$. For any odd prime q one can take $\sqrt{\mathbf{F}_q^2} = \{0, 1, \ldots, (q-1)/2\}$. Other choices sometimes have computational benefits.

The definition of Elligator 2 is also parametrized by a non-square $u \in \mathbf{F}_q$. If $q \equiv 3 \pmod 4$ then one can take $u = -1$. If $q \equiv 5 \pmod 8$ then one can take $u = 2$. Finding a non-square is an easy computation in general since about half of the elements of $\mathbf{F}_q$ are non-squares. For efficiency it is desirable to choose u to be small, or otherwise to choose u to speed up multiplications by u.

5.2 The map

THEOREM 5. *Let q be an odd prime power. Let A, B be elements of $\mathbf{F}_q$ such that $AB(A^2 - 4B) \neq 0$. Let u be a non-square in $\mathbf{F}_q$. Let $\sqrt{\ }$ be a square-root function for $\mathbf{F}_q$. Define R as the set*

$$\{r \in \mathbf{F}_q : 1 + ur^2 \neq 0,\ A^2ur^2 \neq B(1 + ur^2)^2\}.$$

The following elements of $\mathbf{F}_q$ are defined for each nonzero $r \in R$:

$$v = -A/(1 + ur^2),$$
$$\epsilon = \chi(v^3 + Av^2 + Bv),$$
$$x = \epsilon v - (1 - \epsilon)A/2,$$
$$y = -\epsilon\sqrt{x^3 + Ax^2 + Bx}.$$

Furthermore $v\epsilon xy \neq 0$ and $y^2 = x^3 + Ax^2 + Bx$.

If $q \equiv 1 \pmod 4$ and $A^2 - 4B$ is a non-square in $\mathbf{F}_q$ then $R = \mathbf{F}_q$.

PROOF. **v is defined and $v \neq 0$:** By hypothesis $A \neq 0$ and $1 + ur^2 \neq 0$.

$v^3+Av^2+Bv \neq 0$ and $\epsilon \neq 0$: Note that $v+vur^2 = -A$ so $v^2 + Av = v(v+A) = v(-vur^2)$. If $v^2 + Av + B = 0$ then $v^2ur^2 = B$ so, using the definition of v, $A^2ur^2 = B(1+ur^2)^2$, contradicting the definition of R. Hence $v^2 + Av + B \neq 0$, so $v^3 + Av^2 + Bv \neq 0$, so $\epsilon \neq 0$.

$x^3 + Ax^2 + Bx$ is a nonzero square and $x \neq 0$: There are two cases. First case: $\epsilon = 1$, i.e., $v^3 + Av^2 + Bv$ is a nonzero square. Then $x = v$ so $x^3 + Ax^2 + Bx$ is a nonzero square; and $x \neq 0$ since $v \neq 0$.

Second case: $\epsilon = -1$, i.e., $v^3 + Av^2 + Bv$ is a non-square. Then $x = -v - A = vur^2$. All factors v, u, r^2 here are nonzero so $x \neq 0$; note also that $\chi(x) = \chi(v)\chi(u) = -\chi(v)$. Furthermore $x(x + A) = (-v - A)(-v) = v(v + A)$ so $x^2 + Ax + B = v^2 + Av + B$ so $\chi(x^3 + Ax^2 + Bx) = -\chi(v^3 + Av^2 + Bv) = -\epsilon = 1$ so $x^3 + Ax^2 + Bx$ is a nonzero square.

y is defined, $y^2 = x^3 + Ax^2 + Bx$, and $y \neq 0$: $x^3 + Ax^2 + Bx$ is a nonzero square so $\sqrt{x^3 + Ax^2 + Bx}$ is defined; all factors in $y = -\epsilon\sqrt{x^3 + Ax^2 + Bx}$ are nonzero, and $y^2 = x^3 + Ax^2 + Bx$.

If $q \equiv 1 \pmod 4$ and $A^2 - 4B$ is a non-square then $R = \mathbf{F}_q$: Fix $r \in \mathbf{F}_q$, and write $s = ur^2$. Then $\chi(s) \in \{0, -1\}$ while $\chi(\pm 1) = 1$ so $s \neq \pm 1$. In particular $1 + ur^2 \neq 0$.

Suppose that $A^2s = B(1 + s)^2$. Subtract $4Bs$ to obtain $(A^2-4B)s = B(1-s)^2$. Multiply to obtain $(A^2-4B)A^2s^2 = B^2(1 + s)^2(1 - s)^2$. By hypothesis $\chi(A^2 - 4B) = -1$ so $\chi((A^2 - 4B)A^2s^2) \in \{-1, 0\}$, while all of $B, 1 + s, 1 - s$ are nonzero so $\chi(B^2(1 + s)^2(1 - s)^2) = 1$, contradiction. Consequently $A^2ur^2 \neq B(1 + ur^2)^2$. □

DEFINITION 6. *In the situation of Theorem 5, the* **decoding function** *for the Weierstrass curve* $E : y^2 = x^3 + Ax^2 + Bx$ *is the function* $\psi : R \to E(\mathbf{F}_q)$ *defined as follows:* $\psi(0) = (0,0)$*; if* $r \neq 0$ *then* $\psi(r) = (x,y)$*.*

With more work one can extend the definition of ψ to cover elements of $\mathbf{F}_q$ outside R. For example, if $A^2 - 4B$ is a square then one can map any square roots in $\mathbf{F}_q$ of $(A^2-2B\pm A\sqrt{A^2-4B})/(2uB)$ to $((-A\pm\sqrt{A^2-4B})/2, 0)$. However, our main interest is in the case $R = \mathbf{F}_q$, and then this extra work is unnecessary.

5.3 Inverting the map

THEOREM 7. *In the situation of Definition 6:*

1. *If* $r \in R$ *then the set of preimages of* $\psi(r)$ *under* ψ *is* $\{r, -r\}$*.*
2. $\psi(R)$ *is the set of* $(x,y) \in E(\mathbf{F}_q)$ *such that*
   - $x \neq -A$*,*
   - *if* $y = 0$ *then* $x = 0$*, and*
   - $-ux(x+A)$ *is a square in* $\mathbf{F}_q$*.*
3. *If* $(x,y) \in \psi(R)$ *then the following element* $\bar{r}$ *of* R *is defined and* $\psi(\bar{r}) = (x,y)$*:*

$$\bar{r} = \begin{cases} \sqrt{-x/((x+A)u)} & \text{if } y \in \sqrt{\mathbf{F}_q^2}; \\ \sqrt{-(x+A)/(ux)} & \text{if } y \notin \sqrt{\mathbf{F}_q^2}. \end{cases}$$

PROOF. **1.** If $r = 0$ then $r = -r$ so $\psi(r) = \psi(-r)$. If $r \neq 0$ then Theorem 5 defines $\psi(r)$ purely in terms of r^2 so $\psi(r) = \psi(-r)$.

Conversely, assume that $\psi(r) = \psi(r')$; our goal is to show that $r' \in \{r, -r\}$. If $r = 0$ then $\psi(r) = (0,0)$, and otherwise $\psi(r)$ has nonzero coordinates by Theorem 5; hence $r = 0$ if and only if $r' = 0$. The only remaining case is that $r \neq 0$ and $r' \neq 0$.

Define v', ϵ', x', y' from r' as in Theorem 5. Then $(x',y') = \psi(r') = \psi(r) = (x,y)$. Furthermore $y = -\epsilon\sqrt{x^3+Ax^2+Bx}$ and $y' = -\epsilon'\sqrt{(x')^3+A(x')^2+B(x')}$ so $\epsilon' = \epsilon$ since $\sqrt{\ }$ is a function. Next $x = \epsilon v-(1-\epsilon)A/2$ and $x' = \epsilon' v' - (1-\epsilon')A/2$ so $v' = v$. Finally $1+ur^2 = 1+u(r')^2$ so $r' \in \{r, -r\}$ as claimed.

2. Fix $r \in R$, and write $(x,y) = \psi(r)$. If $r = 0$ then $(x,y) = (0,0)$ so $x = 0$; $x \neq -A$; and $-ux(x+A) = 0$ is a square. If $r \neq 0$ then (x,y) is defined in Theorem 5, and there are two cases. The first case is that $\epsilon = 1$; then $x = v \neq -A$ since $ur^2 \neq 0$. The second case is that $\epsilon = -1$; then $x = -v - A \neq -A$ since $v \neq 0$. In both cases $y \neq 0$ by Theorem 5, and $-ux(x+A) = -uv(v+A) = -uv(-vur^2) = u^2v^2r^2$, which is a square.

Conversely, assume that $(x,y) \in E(\mathbf{F}_q)$, that $x \neq -A$, then if $y = 0$ then $x = 0$, and that $-ux(x+A)$ is a square. Our goal is to show that $(x,y) \in \psi(R)$. We will in fact show more: $(x,y) = \psi(\bar{r})$ where $\bar{r}$ is defined as in the third part of the theorem statement.

If $y = 0$ then $x = 0$ by assumption. Furthermore $y = \sqrt{0} \in \sqrt{\mathbf{F}_q^2}$ and $-x/((x+A)u) = 0$ so $\bar{r}$ is defined as 0. Hence $(x,y) = (0,0) = \psi(0) = \psi(\bar{r})$ as claimed.

Assume from now on that $y \neq 0$. The curve equation then implies that $x \neq 0$. Now $(x+A)u$ and ux are both nonzero, and both $-x/((x+A)u)$ and $-(x+A)/(ux)$ are squares, so $\bar{r}$ is defined and nonzero. We will see below that $1+u\bar{r}^2 \neq 0$ and $A^2u\bar{r}^2 \neq B(1+u\bar{r}^2)^2$, so $\bar{r} \in R$. Define $\bar{v}, \bar{\epsilon}, \bar{x}, \bar{y}$ as in Theorem 5.

If $y \in \sqrt{\mathbf{F}_q^2}$ then $\bar{r}^2 = -x/((x+A)u)$ so $1+u\bar{r}^2 = A/(x+A)$ so $\bar{v} = -x - A$ so $\chi(\bar{v}) = \chi(-x-A) = \chi(ux) = -\chi(x)$. Next $\bar{v}^2 + A\bar{v} + B = x^2 + Ax + B$ so $\bar{\epsilon} = \chi(\bar{v}^3 + A\bar{v}^2 + B\bar{v}) = -\chi(x^3+Ax^2+Bx) = -1$. Consequently $\bar{x} = -\bar{v} - A = x$ and $\bar{y} = -\bar{\epsilon}\sqrt{x^3+Ax^2+Bx} = \sqrt{x^3+Ax^2+Bx} = y$.

The remaining case is that $y \notin \sqrt{\mathbf{F}_q^2}$, i.e., $y = -\sqrt{x^3+Ax^2+Bx}$. Then $\bar{r}^2 = -(x+A)/(ux)$ so $1+u\bar{r}^2 = -A/x$ so $\bar{v} = x$. Now $\bar{v}^3+A\bar{v}^2+B\bar{v} = x^3+Ax^2+Bx$ so $\bar{\epsilon} = 1$. Consequently $\bar{x} = \bar{v} = x$ and $\bar{y} = -\bar{\epsilon}\sqrt{x^3+Ax^2+Bx} = -\sqrt{x^3+Ax^2+Bx} = y$.

In both cases we have $\bar{v}^2 + A\bar{v} + B = x^2 + Ax + B \neq 0$ so $A^2u\bar{r}^2 \neq B(1+u\bar{r}^2)^2$.

3. Fix $(x,y) \in \psi(R)$. We showed above that $x \neq -A$; that if $y = 0$ then $x = 0$; and that $-ux(x+A)$ is a square. We also showed that under these conditions $\bar{r}$ is defined and $\psi(\bar{r}) = (x,y)$. □

5.4 Encoding as strings

THEOREM 8. *In the situation of Definition 6, assume that* q *is prime, that* $q \equiv 1 \pmod 4$*, and that* $A^2 - 4B$ *is not a square in* $\mathbf{F}_q$*. Define* $b = \lfloor \log_2 q \rfloor$*. Define* $\sigma : \{0,1\}^b \to \mathbf{F}_q$ *by* $\sigma(\rho_0, \rho_1, \ldots, \rho_{b-1}) = \sum_i \rho_i 2^i$*. Define* $S = \sigma^{-1}(\{0,1,2,\ldots,(q-1)/2\})$*. Define* $\iota : S \to E(\mathbf{F}_q)$ *as follows:* $\iota(\rho) = \psi(\sigma(\rho))$*. Then* $\#S = (q+1)/2$*;* ι *is an injective map from* S *to* $E(\mathbf{F}_q)$*; and* $\iota(S) = \psi(\mathbf{F}_q)$*.*

PROOF. Note that $R = \mathbf{F}_q$ by Theorem 5; i.e., ψ is defined on all of $\mathbf{F}_q$. The rest of the proof is identical to the proof of Theorem 4 with ϕ replaced by ψ, τ replaced by ρ, Theorem 1 replaced by Theorem 5, and Theorem 3 replaced by Theorem 7. □

5.5 Application of ψ to Curve25519

Curve25519 is the curve $y^2 = x^3 + Ax^2 + Bx$ over $\mathbf{F}_q$ with $q = 2^{255} - 19$, $A = 486662$, and $B = 1$. Here $q \equiv 1 \pmod 4$ and $A^2 - 4B$ is a non-square in $\mathbf{F}_q$, so $R = \mathbf{F}_q$.

We take $u = 2$. We copy from [8] the following standard efficiently computable square-root function for $\mathbf{F}_q$. Given a square $a \in \mathbf{F}_q$ compute $b = a^{(q+3)/8}$; note that $q \equiv 5 \pmod 8$, so $(q+3)/8$ is an integer. Then $b^4 = a^2$, i.e., $b^2 \in \{a, -a\}$. Define $\sqrt{a}$ as $|b|$ if $b^2 = a$ and as $|b\sqrt{-1}|$ otherwise. Here $|b|$ means b if $b \in \{0,1,\ldots,(q-1)/2\}$, otherwise $-b$.

Computing ι takes 1 square-root computation, 1 inversion, 1 computation of χ, and a few multiplications. Note that the inversion and the square-root computation can be combined into one exponentiation, as in [8]. The computation of χ can also be combined into the square-root computation as follows. First compute a power of $v^3 + Av^2 + Bv$ as above, obtaining a square root of $v^3 + Av^2 + Bv$ if $v^3 + Av^2 + Bv$ is a square. If the square of this power turns out to match $v^3 + Av^2 + Bv$ then $\epsilon = 1$ and $x = v$. Otherwise $\epsilon = -1$, $x = vur^2$, and $x^3+Ax^2+Bx = ur^2(v^3+Av^2+Bv)$; multiply the previous power by r and by a precomputed power of u to obtain a square root of $x^3 + Ax^2 + Bx$.

Similar comments apply to computing the inverse map. Checking for $P \in \iota(S)$ takes 1 squaring and a computation of χ to obtain $\chi((x+A/2)^2 - A^2/4) = \chi(x(x+A))$.

This map and its inverse seem simplest to describe in Weierstrass coordinates, but maps to and from Edwards form, and other curve shapes, are also easily obtained.

6. REFERENCES

[1] APPELBAUM, J., AND DINGLEDINE, R. How governments have tried to block Tor, 2011. http://ftp.ccc.de/congress/28C3/mp4-h264-HQ/28c3-4800-en-how_governments_have_tried_to_block_tor_h264.mp4.

[2] APPLE. iOS security, 2012. http://images.apple.com/iphone/business/docs/iOS_Security_Oct12.pdf.

[3] BELLARE, M., DESAI, A., JOKIPII, E., AND ROGAWAY, P. A concrete security treatment of symmetric encryption. In *FOCS* (1997), IEEE Computer Society, pp. 394–403.

[4] BERNSTEIN, D. J. Current consensus on ECC, 2001. https://groups.google.com/forum/message/raw?msg=sci.crypt/mu_paShEU3w/m491pYxHbtAJ.

[5] BERNSTEIN, D. J. A software implementation of NIST P-224, 2001. http://cr.yp.to/talks.html#2001.10.29.

[6] BERNSTEIN, D. J. Curve25519: New Diffie-Hellman speed records. In *Public Key Cryptography* (2006), M. Yung, Y. Dodis, A. Kiayias, and T. Malkin, Eds., vol. 3958 of *LNCS*, Springer, pp. 207–228.

[7] BERNSTEIN, D. J., BIRKNER, P., JOYE, M., LANGE, T., AND PETERS, C. Twisted Edwards curves. In *AFRICACRYPT* (2008), S. Vaudenay, Ed., vol. 5023 of *LNCS*, Springer, pp. 389–405.

[8] BERNSTEIN, D. J., DUIF, N., LANGE, T., SCHWABE, P., AND YANG, B.-Y. High-speed high-security signatures. *J. Cryptographic Engineering 2*, 2 (2012), 77–89.

[9] BERNSTEIN, D. J., AND LANGE, T. Faster addition and doubling on elliptic curves. In *ASIACRYPT* (2007), K. Kurosawa, Ed., vol. 4833 of *LNCS*, Springer, pp. 29–50.

[10] BERNSTEIN, D. J., AND SCHWABE, P. NEON crypto. In *CHES* (2012), E. Prouff and P. Schaumont, Eds., vol. 7428 of *LNCS*, Springer, pp. 320–339.

[11] BIEHL, I., MEYER, B., AND MÜLLER, V. Differential fault attacks on elliptic curve cryptosystems. In *CRYPTO* (2000), M. Bellare, Ed., vol. 1880 of *LNCS*, Springer, pp. 131–146.

[12] BONEH, D., AND FRANKLIN, M. K. Identity-based encryption from the Weil pairing. In *CRYPTO* (2001), J. Kilian, Ed., vol. 2139 of *LNCS*, Springer, pp. 213–229.

[13] BOYD, C., MONTAGUE, P., AND NGUYEN, K. Q. Elliptic curve based password authenticated key exchange protocols. In *ACISP* (2001), V. Varadharajan and Y. Mu, Eds., vol. 2119 of *LNCS*, Springer, pp. 487–501.

[14] BRAINPOOL. ECC Brainpool standard curves and curve generation, v. 1.0, 2005. http://www.ecc-brainpool.org/download/Domain-parameters.pdf.

[15] BRIER, E., CORON, J.-S., ICART, T., MADORE, D., RANDRIAM, H., AND TIBOUCHI, M. Efficient indifferentiable hashing into ordinary elliptic curves. In *CRYPTO* (2010), T. Rabin, Ed., vol. 6223 of *LNCS*, Springer, pp. 237–254.

[16] BRIER, E., AND JOYE, M. Weierstraß elliptic curves and side-channel attacks. In *Public Key Cryptography* (2002), D. Naccache and P. Paillier, Eds., vol. 2274 of *LNCS*, Springer, pp. 335–345.

[17] COSTIGAN, N., AND SCHWABE, P. Fast elliptic-curve cryptography on the Cell Broadband Engine. In *AFRICACRYPT* (2009), B. Preneel, Ed., vol. 5580 of *LNCS*, Springer, pp. 368–385.

[18] DIEM, C. The GHS attack in odd characteristic. *J. Ramanujan Mathematical Society 18* (2003), 1–32.

[19] DINGLEDINE, R., MATHEWSON, N., AND SYVERSON, P. F. Tor: The second-generation onion router. In *USENIX Security Symposium* (2004), USENIX, pp. 303–320.

[20] FARASHAHI, R. R. Hashing into Hessian curves. In *AFRICACRYPT* (2011), A. Nitaj and D. Pointcheval, Eds., vol. 6737 of *LNCS*, Springer, pp. 278–289.

[21] FARASHAHI, R. R., FOUQUE, P.-A., SHPARLINSKI, I., TIBOUCHI, M., AND VOLOCH, J. F. Indifferentiable deterministic hashing to elliptic and hyperelliptic curves. *Math. Comput. 82*, 281 (2013).

[22] FAUGÈRE, J.-C., PERRET, L., PETIT, C., AND RENAULT, G. Improving the complexity of index calculus algorithms in elliptic curves over binary fields. In *EUROCRYPT* (2012), D. Pointcheval and T. Johansson, Eds., vol. 7237 of *LNCS*, Springer, pp. 27–44.

[23] FOUQUE, P.-A., JOUX, A., AND TIBOUCHI, M. Injective encodings to elliptic curves. In *ACISP* (2013), C. Boyd and L. Simpson, Eds., vol. 7959 of *LNCS*, Springer, pp. 203–218.

[24] FOUQUE, P.-A., LERCIER, R., RÉAL, D., AND VALETTE, F. Fault attack on elliptic curve Montgomery ladder implementation. In *FDTC* (2008), L. Breveglieri, S. Gueron, I. Koren, D. Naccache, and J.-P. Seifert, Eds., IEEE Computer Society, pp. 92–98.

[25] FOUQUE, P.-A., AND TIBOUCHI, M. Deterministic encoding and hashing to odd hyperelliptic curves. In *Pairing* (2010), M. Joye, A. Miyaji, and A. Otsuka, Eds., vol. 6487 of *LNCS*, Springer, pp. 265–277.

[26] FOUQUE, P.-A., AND TIBOUCHI, M. Estimating the size of the image of deterministic hash functions to elliptic curves. In *LATINCRYPT* (2010), M. Abdalla and P. S. L. M. Barreto, Eds., vol. 6212 of *LNCS*, Springer, pp. 81–91.

[27] FOUQUE, P.-A., AND TIBOUCHI, M. Indifferentiable hashing to Barreto-Naehrig curves. In *LATINCRYPT* (2012), A. Hevia and G. Neven, Eds., vol. 7533 of *LNCS*, Springer, pp. 1–17.

[28] FREY, G. How to disguise an elliptic curve (Weil descent), 1998. http://www.cacr.math.uwaterloo.ca/conferences/1998/ecc98/slides.html.

[29] GAUDRY, P., AND THOMÉ, E. The mpFq library and implementing curve-based key exchanges. In *SPEED: software performance enhancement for encryption and decryption* (2007), pp. 49–64.

[30] GOLDBERG, I., STEBILA, D., AND USTAOGLU, B. Anonymity and one-way authentication in key exchange protocols. *Des. Codes Cryptography 67*, 2 (2013), 245–269.

[31] HISIL, H., WONG, K. K.-H., CARTER, G., AND DAWSON, E. Twisted Edwards curves revisited. In *ASIACRYPT* (2008), J. Pieprzyk, Ed., vol. 5350 of *LNCS*, Springer, pp. 326–343.

[32] ICART, T. How to hash into elliptic curves. In *CRYPTO* (2009), S. Halevi, Ed., vol. 5677 of *LNCS*, Springer, pp. 303–316.

[33] INSTITUTE OF ELECTRICAL AND ELECTRONICS ENGINEERS. *P1363 Draft Standard Specifications for Public Key Cryptography*. IEEE, 1999.

[34] IZU, T., AND TAKAGI, T. Exceptional procedure attack on elliptic curve cryptosystems. In *Public Key Cryptography* (2003), Y. Desmedt, Ed., vol. 2567 of *LNCS*, Springer, pp. 224–239.

[35] KALISKI JR., B. S. A pseudo-random bit generator based on elliptic logarithms. In *CRYPTO* (1986), A. M. Odlyzko, Ed., vol. 263 of *LNCS*, Springer, pp. 84–103.

[36] KALISKI JR., B. S. *Elliptic Curves and Cryptography: A Pseudorandom Bit Generator and Other Tools*. PhD thesis, MIT, 1988. MIT/LCS/TR-411.

[37] LAW, L. E., AND SOLINAS, J. A. Suite B cryptographic suites for IPsec, 2011. https://tools.ietf.org/html/rfc6379.

[38] LIDL, R., AND NIEDERREITER, H. *Finite Fields*. Encyclopedia of Mathematics and its Applications. Cambridge University Press, 1997.

[39] LÓPEZ, J., AND DAHAB, R. Fast multiplication on elliptic curves over $GF(2^m)$ without precomputation. In *CHES* (1999), Ç. K. Koç and C. Paar, Eds., vol. 1717 of *LNCS*, Springer, pp. 316–327.

[40] MÖLLER, B. A public-key encryption scheme with pseudo-random ciphertexts. In *Computer Security—ESORICS 2004*, P. Samarati, P. Ryan, D. Gollmann, and R. Molva, Eds., vol. 3193 of *LNCS*. Springer Berlin Heidelberg, 2004, pp. 335–351.

[41] MONTGOMERY, P. L. Speeding the Pollard and elliptic curve methods of factorization. *Math. Comp. 48*, 177 (1987), 243–264.

[42] OLIVEIRA, T., LÓPEZ, J., ARANHA, D. F., AND RODRÍGUEZ-HENRÍQUEZ, F. Lambda coordinates for binary elliptic curves. In *CHES* (2013), G. Bertoni and J.-S. Coron, Eds., vol. 8086 of *LNCS*, Springer, pp. 311–330.

[43] PETIT, C., AND QUISQUATER, J.-J. On polynomial systems arising from a Weil descent. In *ASIACRYPT* (2012), X. Wang and K. Sako, Eds., vol. 7658 of *LNCS*, Springer, pp. 451–466.

[44] ROGAWAY, P., AND SHRIMPTON, T. A provable-security treatment of the key-wrap problem. In *EUROCRYPT* (2006), S. Vaudenay, Ed., vol. 4004 of *LNCS*, Springer, pp. 373–390.

[45] SHALLUE, A., AND VAN DE WOESTIJNE, C. Construction of rational points on elliptic curves over finite fields. In *ANTS* (2006), F. Hess, S. Pauli, and M. E. Pohst, Eds., vol. 4076 of *LNCS*, Springer, pp. 510–524.

[46] STEIN, W., ET AL. *Sage Mathematics Software (Version 2.9)*. The Sage Development Team, 2013. http://www.sagemath.org.

[47] WEINBERG, Z., WANG, J., YEGNESWARAN, V., BRIESEMEISTER, L., CHEUNG, S., WANG, F., AND BONEH, D. StegoTorus: a camouflage proxy for the Tor anonymity system. In *ACM Conference on Computer and Communications Security* (2012), T. Yu, G. Danezis, and V. D. Gligor, Eds., ACM, pp. 109–120.

[48] WUSTROW, E., WOLCHOK, S., GOLDBERG, I., AND HALDERMAN, J. A. Telex: Anticensorship in the network infrastructure. In *USENIX Security Symposium* (2011), USENIX Association.

[49] YOUNG, A. L., AND YUNG, M. Kleptography from standard assumptions and applications. In *SCN* (2010), J. A. Garay and R. D. Prisco, Eds., vol. 6280 of *LNCS*, Springer, pp. 271–290.

ASIST: Architectural Support for Instruction Set Randomization

Antonis Papadogiannakis, Laertis Loutsis, Vassilis Papaefstathiou, Sotiris Ioannidis
Institute of Computer Science, Foundation for Research and Technology – Hellas
{papadog, laertis, papaef, sotiris}@ics.forth.gr

ABSTRACT

Code injection attacks continue to pose a threat to today's computing systems, as they exploit software vulnerabilities to inject and execute arbitrary, malicious code. Instruction Set Randomization (ISR) is able to protect a system against remote machine code injection attacks by randomizing the instruction set of each process. This way, the attacker will inject invalid code that will fail to execute on the randomized processor. However, all the existing implementations of ISR are based on emulators and binary instrumentation tools that (i) incur a significant runtime performance overhead, (ii) limit the ease of deployment of ISR, (iii) cannot protect the underlying operating system kernel, and (iv) are vulnerable to evasion attempts trying to bypass ISR protection.

To address these issues we propose ASIST: an architecture with hardware and operating system support for ISR. We present the design and implementation of ASIST by modifying and mapping a SPARC processor onto an FPGA board and running our modified Linux kernel to support the new features. The operating system loads the randomization key of each running process into a newly defined register, and the modified processor decodes the process's instructions with this key before execution. Moreover, ASIST protects the system against attacks that exploit kernel vulnerabilities to run arbitrary code with elevated privileges, by using a separate randomization key for the operating system. We show that ASIST transparently protects all applications and the operating system kernel from machine code injection attacks with less than 1.5% runtime overhead, while only requiring 0.7% additional hardware.

Categories and Subject Descriptors

D.4.6 [**Operating Systems**]: Security and Protection—*Invasive software*; C.0 [**General**]: Hardware/software interfaces; System architectures

Keywords

Instruction Set Randomization; Code Injection Attacks; Architectural Support; Hardware Support; Security; Performance

CCS'13, November 4–8, 2013, Berlin, Germany.
Copyright 2013 ACM 978-1-4503-2477-9/13/11 ...$15.00.
http://dx.doi.org/10.1145/2508859.2516670.

1. INTRODUCTION

Code injection attacks exploit software vulnerabilities to inject and execute arbitrary malicious code, allowing the attacker to obtain full access to the vulnerable system. There are several ways to achieve arbitrary code execution through the exploitation of a software vulnerability. The vast majority of code injection attacks exploit vulnerabilities that allow the diversion of control flow to the injected malicious code. Arbitrary code execution is also possible through the modification of non-control-data [17]. The most commonly exploited vulnerabilities for code injection attacks are buffer overflows [2]. Despite considerable research efforts [20, 21, 23, 25, 50], buffer overflow vulnerabilities remain a major security threat [18]. Other vulnerabilities that allow the corruption of critical data are format-string errors [19] and integer overflows [51].

Remotely exploitable vulnerabilities are continuously being discovered in popular network applications [7,8] and operating system kernels [3, 4, 6, 16]. Thus, code injection attacks remain one of the most common security threats [2], exposing significant challenges to current security systems. For instance, the massive outbreak of the Conficker worm in 2009 infected more than 10 million machines worldwide [40]. Like most of the Internet worms, Conficker was based on a typical code injection attack that exploited a vulnerability in Windows RPC [5]. Along with the continuous discovery of new remotely exploitable vulnerabilities and zero-day attacks, the increasing complexity and sophisticated evasive methods of attack techniques [24, 37] has significantly reduced the effectiveness of attack detection systems.

Instruction Set Randomization (ISR) [9, 10, 13, 29, 31, 41] has been proposed to defend against *any* type of code injection attack. ISR randomizes the instruction set of a processor so that an attacker is not able to know the processor's "language" to inject meaningful code. Therefore, any injected code will fail to accomplish the desirable malicious behavior, probably resulting in invalid instructions. To prevent successful machine code injections, ISR techniques encrypt the instructions of a possibly vulnerable program with a program-specific key. This key actually defines the valid instruction set for this program. The processor decrypts at runtime every instruction of the respective process with the same key. Only the correctly encrypted instructions will lead to the intended code execution after decryption. Any injected code that is not encrypted with the correct key will result in irrelevant or invalid instructions.

Existing ISR implementations use binary transformation tools to encrypt the programs. For runtime decryption they use emulators [13,31], or dynamic binary instrumentation tools [9,10,29,41]. However, they have several limitations: (i) They incur a significant runtime performance overhead due to the software emulator or instrumentation tool. This overhead is prohibitive for a wide adoption of such techniques. (ii) Deployment is limited by the necessity of several tools, like emulators, and manual encryption of the programs that are protected with ISR. (iii) They are vulnerable to code injection attacks into the underlying emulator or instrumentation tools. More importantly, they do not protect against attacks targeting kernel vulnerabilities [3, 4, 6, 16], which are becoming an increasingly attractive target for attackers. (iv) Most ISR implementations are vulnerable to evasion attacks aiming to guess the encryption key and bypass ISR protection [48, 53].

To address these issues we propose ASIST: a hardware/software scheme to support ISR on top of an unmodified ISA. Hardware extensions to enhance security have been proposed in the past [23, 28, 44, 50]. We advocate that hardware support for ISR is essential to guard against code injection attacks, at both user- and kernel-level, without incurring significant performance penalty at runtime.

ASIST uses distinct per-process keys and another key for the operating system kernel's code. To support runtime decryption at the CPU, we propose the use of two new registers in the ASIST-enabled processor: the *oskey* and *usrkey* registers, which contain the kernel's key and the user-level key of the running process. These registers are memory mapped and they are only accessible by the operating system via privileged instructions. Our implementation for the SPARC architecture maps these registers into a new Address Space Identifier (ASI). The operating system is responsible for reading or generating the key of each program at load time, and associating it with the respective process. It is also responsible for storing at the *usrkey* register the key of the next process scheduled for execution at a context switch. Whenever a trap to kernel is called, the CPU enters into supervisor mode and the value of the *oskey* register is used to decrypt instructions. When the CPU is not in supervisor mode, it decrypts each instruction using the *usrkey* register.

We explore two possible choices for implementing the decryption unit at the instruction fetch pipeline stage of the modified processor. We also implement two different encryption algorithms, (i) XOR and (ii) Transposition, and use different key sizes. Additionally, we compare two alternative techniques for encrypting the executable code: (i) statically, by adding a new section in ELF that contains the key and encrypting all code sections with this key using a binary transformation tool, and (ii) dynamically, by generating a random key at load time and encrypting with this key at the page fault handler all the memory mapped pages that contain code. The dynamic encryption approach can support dynamically linked shared libraries, whereas static encryption requires statically linked binaries. We discuss and evaluate the advantages of each approach in terms of security and performance. Our modified processor can also encrypt the return address at each function call and decrypt it before returning to caller. This way, ASIST protects the system from return-oriented programming (ROP) attacks [14, 45], but not from jump-oriented programming (JOP) attacks [12].

To demonstrate the feasibility of our approach we present the prototype implementation of ASIST by modifying the Leon3 SPARC V8 processor [1], a 32-bit open-source synthesizable processor [26]. We also modified the Linux kernel 3.8 to support the implemented hardware features for ISR and evaluate our prototype. Our experimental evaluation results show that ASIST is able to prevent code injection attacks practically without any performance overhead, while adding less than 1% of additional hardware to support ISR with our design. Our results also indicate that the proposed dynamic code encryption at the page fault handler does not impose any significant overhead, due to the low page fault rate for pages with executable code. This outcome makes our dynamic encryption approach very appealing, as it is able to *transparently* encrypt any executable program, it generates a different random key at each execution, and it supports shared libraries with negligible overhead.

The main contributions of this work are:

- We propose ASIST: the first hardware-based support for ISR to prevent machine code injections without any performance overhead. We demonstrate the feasibility of hardware-based support for ISR by presenting the design, implementation, and experimental evaluation of ASIST.
- We introduce a dynamic code encryption technique that transparently encrypts pages with executable code at the page fault handler, using a randomly generated key for each execution. We show that this technique supports shared libraries and does not impose significant overhead to the system.
- We explore different choices for the decryption unit in hardware, we compare static and dynamic encryption, as well as different encryption algorithms and key sizes in order to improve the resistance of ISR against evasion attempts.
- We show that a hardware-based ISR implementation, like ASIST, is able to protect the system against attacks that exploit OS kernel vulnerabilities.
- We evaluated our prototype implementation with hardware-enabled ISR and we showed that it is able to prevent code injection attacks with negligible overhead.

2. INSTRUCTION SET RANDOMIZATION

In this section we describe our threat model, give some background on ISR, and discuss the main limitations of existing implementations that emphasize the need for hardware support.

2.1 Threat Model

Remote and local machine code injection attacks. The threat model we address in this work is the remote or local exploitation of any software vulnerability that allows the diversion of the control flow to execute arbitrary, malicious code. We address vulnerabilities in the stack, heap, or BSS, e.g., any buffer overflow that overwrites the return address, a function pointer, or any control data. We focus on protecting the potentially vulnerable systems against *any* type of machine code injection attacks.

Kernel vulnerabilities. Remotely exploitable vulnerabilities on the operating system kernel [3, 4, 6, 16] are becoming an increasingly attractive target for attackers. Our threat model includes code injection attacks based on kernel vulnerabilities. We propose an architecture that is capable of protecting the operating system kernel as well. We also address attacks that use a kernel vulnerability to run user-level code with elevated kernel privileges [32].

Return-to-libc and ROP attacks. Instead of injecting new code into a vulnerable program, an attacker can execute existing code upon changing the control flow of a vulnerable system: re-direct the execution to existing library functions, attacks typically known as *return-to-libc* attacks [35], or use existing instruction sequences ending with a *ret* instruction (called *gadgets*) to implement the attack, a technique known as *return-oriented programming* (ROP) [14, 45]. Although ISR protects a system against any type of code injection attacks, its threat model does not address return-to-libc and ROP attacks. Existing implementations of ISR follow this threat model. However, due to the rise of such attacks, we aim to protect systems from them using the same hardware.

Key guessing attacks. Existing ISR implementations are vulnerable to key guessing or key stealing attacks [48, 53]. This way, sophisticated attackers may be able to bypass the ISR protection mechanism, by guessing the key and then injecting and executing code that is correctly encoded with this key. In this work, we aim to design and implement ISR in a way that it will be very difficult for attackers to guess or infer the code randomization key.

ISR Implementation	Runtime Overhead	Shared Libraries	Self-modifying Code	Hardware Support	Encryption	Dynamic Encryption	Kernel Protection	ROP Prevention
Bochs emulator [31]	High	No	No	No	XOR with 32-bit key	No	No	No
Valgrind tool [9, 10]	High	Yes	API	No	XOR with random key	Yes	No	No
Strata SDT [29]	Medium	No	No	No	AES with 128-bit key	No	No	No
EMUrand emulator [13]	Medium	No	No	No	XOR with 32-bit key	No	No	No
Pin tool [41]	Medium	Yes	Partially	No	XOR with 16-bit key	No	No	No
ASIST	Zero	Yes	API	Yes	XOR with 32-bit–128-bit key, Transposition with 160-bit key	Yes	Yes	Yes

Table 1: *Comparison of ASIST with existing ISR implementations.* ASIST provides a hardware-based implementation of ISR without runtime overhead, it supports the necessary features of current systems and protects against kernel vulnerabilities.

2.2 Defense with ISR

ISR protects a system against any native code injection attacks. To accomplish this, ISR uses per-process randomized instruction sets. This way, the attacker cannot inject any meaningful code into the memory of the vulnerable program. The injected code will not perform the intended malicious behavior and will probably crash after just a few instructions [9]. To apply the ISR idea, existing implementations first encrypt the binary code of each program with the program's secret key before it is loaded for execution. The program's key defines the mapping of the encrypted instructions to the real instructions supported by the CPU. Then, at runtime, the randomized processor decrypts every instruction with the proper program's key before execution. Injected instruction sequences that have not been correctly encrypted will result in irrelevant or invalid instructions after the obligatory decryption. On the other hand, correctly encrypted code will be decrypted and executed normally.

2.3 Limitations of Existing Implementations

Existing ISR Implementations use binary transformation tools, such as `objcopy`, to encrypt the code of user-level programs that will be protected. For runtime decryption they use emulators [33] or dynamic binary instrumentation tools [34,36,42]. In Table 1 we list and compare all the existing ISR implementations.

Kc et al. [31] implemented ISR by modifying the `Bochs` emulator [33] using XOR with a 32-bit key in their prototype. The use of an emulator results in significant slowdown, up to 290 times slower execution on CPU intensive applications. Barrantes et al. [9,10] use `Valgrind` [36] to decrypt applications' code, which is encrypted with XOR and a random key equal to the program's length. This prototype supports shared libraries by copying each randomized library per process, and offers an API for self-modifying code. However, the performance overhead with Valgrind is also very high, up to 2.9 times slower than native execution. Hu et al. [29] implemented ISR with a software dynamic translation tool [42] using AES encryption with 128-bit key size. Dynamic translation results in lower but still significant performance overhead, that is close to 17% on average and as high as 250%. To reduce runtime overhead, Boyd et al. [13] proposed a selective ISR that limits the emulated and randomized execution only to code sections that are more likely to contain a vulnerability. Portokalidis and Keromytis [41] implemented ISR with shared libraries support using Pin [34]. The runtime overhead ranges from 10% to 75% for popular applications, while it has four-times slower execution when memory protection is applied to Pin's code.

The main limitations of the existing ISR implementations are:

1. *High runtime performance overhead.* All the existing implementations of ISR have a considerable runtime overhead, which becomes significantly higher for CPU-intensive applications. This is because all the proposed systems use extra software to emulate or translate the instructions before they are executed, which results to more instructions and increased execution times. We argue that the most efficient approach is a hardware-based implementation of ISR.
2. *Deployment difficulties.* The need for several tools, such as emulators and binary instrumentation tools, as well as the need for manual encryption and the partial support for shared libraries limit the ease of deployment of ISR. On the other hand, we aim to build a system that will transparently protect any program without modifications.
3. *Cannot protect kernel vulnerabilities.* None of the existing ISR prototype implementations is able to defend against attacks exploiting kernel vulnerabilities [3,4,6,16,32]. Such attacks are getting increasingly popular and allow attackers to run code with kernel privileges. Although Pin has been extended with PinOS to instrument kernel's code as well [15], it has not been used to implement ISR support for the kernel. Even in this case, the code of PinOS would not be protected, while the use of a virtual machine in PinOS would impose a significant performance overhead.
4. *Cannot prevent ROP attacks.* ISR cannot protect a vulnerable program against ROP attacks [14,45], which use existing code to harm the system. This is because ISR was proposed to prevent code injection attacks, not code-reuse attacks. However, due to the rise of such attacks recently, we would like to easily extend an ISR system to provide defenses against ROP attacks.
5. *Evasion attacks by guessing the encryption key.* Many of the proposed ISR implementations are vulnerable to evasion attacks that try to guess the encryption key and inject valid code into the vulnerable system [48,53]. Sovarel et al. [48] demonstrate the feasibility of an incremental attack that uses partial key guessing to reduce the number of tries needed to find the key. Also, attackers may be able to steal or infer the encryption key when memory secrecy breaks [53].

To put our work into context, we compare ASIST with other ISR implementations in Table 1. ASIST is the only ISR implementation with hardware support, resulting in negligible runtime overhead for any type of applications. ASIST also supports a new dynamic code encryption approach that allows the transparent encryption of any application with shared libraries. To defend against attempts to guess or steal the encryption key, ASIST (i) stores the encryption key in a hardware register accessible only by the kernel through privileged instructions, and avoids storing the key in process's memory, (ii) generates a new random key at each execution of the same program when dynamic encryption is used, (iii) supports large key sizes up to 128-bit, and (iv) besides XOR and transposition (already implemented), it supports more secure encryption algorithms in case of memory disclosure. Moreover, ASIST prevents the execution of injected code at the kernel by using separate keys for user-level programs and kernel's code. Finally, ASIST is able to prevent ROP attacks using return address encryption.

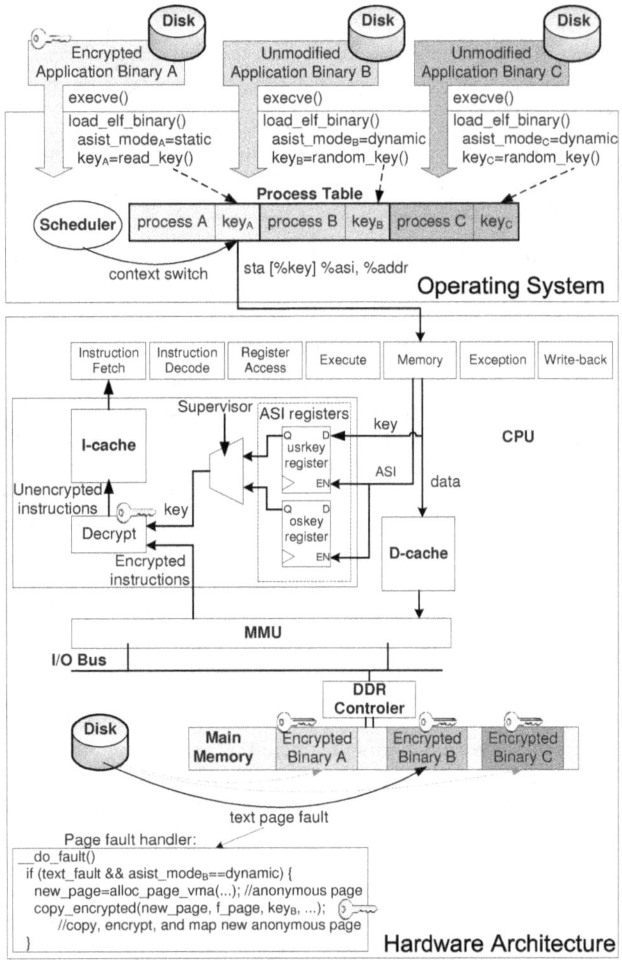

Figure 1: *ASIST architecture.* The operating system reads the key from the ELF binary (static encryption) or randomly generates a new key (dynamic encryption), saves the key in the process table, and stores the key of the running process in the *usrkey* register. The processor decrypts each instruction with *usrkey* or *oskey* register, according to the *supervisor* bit.

3. ASIST ARCHITECTURE

Our architecture spans hardware, operating system and user space (see Figure 1), to support hardware-assisted ISR. ASIST supports two alternative ways of code encryption: static and dynamic. In static encryption, the key is pre-defined and exists within the executable file, while all code sections are already encrypted with this key. In case of dynamic encryption, the executable file is unmodified and the key is decided randomly by the respective loader of the operating system at the beginning of each execution. The code sections are encrypted dynamically at runtime whenever a code page is requested from file system and before this page gets mapped to the process's virtual address space.

The processor has been extended with two new registers: *usrkey* and *oskey*, which store the keys of the running user-level process and operating system kernel's code respectively. The operating system keeps the key of each process in a respective field in the process table, and stores the key of the next process that is scheduled for execution in the *usrkey* register using the *sta* privileged SPARC instruction. Moreover, the processor is modified to decrypt each instruction before the instruction fetch cycle, using one of the above two registers as a key, according to the supervisor bit.

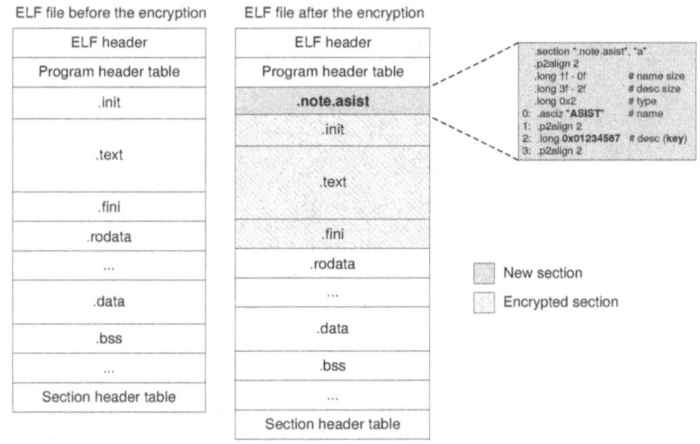

Figure 2: *The ELF format of a statically encrypted executable file.* The key is stored in a new note section inside the ELF file, and all the code sections are encrypted with this key.

3.1 Encryption

We support two possible options for encrypting an executable program: static and dynamic encryption. In static encryption, the program is encrypted before each execution with a pre-defined key. In dynamic encryption, a key is randomly generated at the binary loader, and all code pages are encrypted with this key at the page fault handler before they are mapped to the process's address space.

The main advantage of static code encryption is that it has no runtime overhead. However, this approach has several drawbacks. First, the same key is used for each execution, which makes it susceptible to brute force attacks trying to guess this key. Second, each executable file needs to be encrypted before running. Third, static encryption does not support shared libraries; all programs must be statically linked with all necessary libraries. In contrast, dynamic encryption has a number of advantages: it generates a random key at each execution so it cannot be easily guessed, it encrypts all executables transparently without the need to run an encryption program, and it is able to support shared libraries. The drawback of dynamic encryption is a potential runtime overhead to encrypt a code page when it is loaded to memory at a code page fault. In Section 5 we show that due to the low number of code page faults, dynamic encryption is very efficient.

3.1.1 Static Binary Encryption

To statically encrypt an ELF executable we extended `objcopy` with a new flag (`--encrypt-code`). The encryption key can be provided by the user, else it is randomly chosen by the tool. Figure 2 shows the modifications of a statically encrypted ELF executable file. We add a new note section (`.note.asist`) inside the encrypted ELF file that contains the program's encryption key. We also changed the ELF binary loader in the Linux kernel to read the note section from the ELF, get the key, and store it in a new field (`key`) of the current process. In this mode of operation we set a new field per process (`asist_mode`) to static. The key is stored in the process table and is used by the kernel to update the *usrkey* hardware register each time this process is scheduled for execution.

Our static encryption tool also finds and encrypts all the code sections in ELF. Therefore, all needed libraries must be statically linked, to be properly encrypted. Moreover, it is important to completely separate code from data into different sections by the linker. This is because the encryption of any data, which are not decrypted by the modified processor, will probably disrupt the program execution. Fortunately, many linkers are configured this way. Similarly, compiler optimizations like *jump tables*, which are used to perform faster switch statements with indirect jumps, should be also moved to a separate, non-code section.

To address the issue of using the same key at all executions, which may facilitate a key guessing attack, one approach could be to re-encrypt the binary after a process crash. Another approach could be to encrypt the original binary at the user-level part of `execve()`, by randomly generating a new key and copying the binary into an encrypted one. However, we do not recommend this approach due to the extra time needed to copy and encrypt the entire binary at load time, especially for large binaries that are also statically linked with large libraries. Encrypting the entire binary is probably an unnecessary overhead, as many parts of the code that will be encrypted are unlikely to be actually executed.

3.1.2 Dynamic Code Encryption

We now introduce a new technique to dynamically encrypt a program's code before it is loaded into the process's memory. This approach is based on the fact that every page with executable code will be loaded from disk (or buffer cache) to the process's address space the first time it is accessed by the program through a page fault. Thus, we decided to perform the code encryption at this point. This way, ASIST encrypts only the code pages that are actually used by the program at each execution.

First, the ELF binary loader is modified to randomly generate a new key, which is stored into the process table. It also sets the `asist_mode` field of the current process to dynamic. The code encryption is performed by the page fault handler at a text page fault, i.e., on a page containing executable code, if the process that is responsible for the page fault uses dynamic encryption according to `asist_mode`. Then, a new anonymous page is allocated, and the code page fetched from disk (or buffer cache) is encrypted and copied on this page using the process's encryption key. The new page is finally mapped to the process's address space.

We allocate an anonymous page, i.e., a page that is not backed by a file, and copy the encrypted code on this page, so that the changes will not be stored at the original binary file. Although processes running the same code could share the respective code pages in physical memory, we have a separate copy of each page with executable code for each process, as they have different keys. This may result in a small memory overhead, but it is necessary in order to use a different key per process and achieve better isolation. In practice, the memory allocated for code accounts only for a small fraction of the total memory. Note that we can still benefit from buffer cache, as we copy the cached page.

We also modified the `fork()` system call to randomly generate a new key for the child process. When the modified `fork()` copies the parent process's page table, it omits copying its last layer so that the child's code pages will not be mapped with pages encrypted with the parent's key. To operate correctly, the dynamic encryption approach requires a separation of code and data per each page. For this, we modify the linker to align the ELF headers, data, and code sections to a new page, by adding the proper padding.

3.1.3 Shared Libraries

Our dynamic code encryption technique supports the use of shared libraries without extra effort. The code of a shared library is encrypted with each process's key on the respective page fault when loading a page to process's address space, as we explained above. In this way we have a separate copy of each shared library's page for each process. This is necessary in order to use a different key per process, which offers better protection and isolation.

3.1.4 Self-Modifying Code

The design we presented does not support randomized programs with self-modifying code or runtime code generation, i.e., programs that modify their code or generate and execute new code. To support such programs, we added a new system call in Linux kernel: `asist_encrypt(char *buf, int size)`. This system call encrypts the code that exists in the memory region starting from `buf` with `size` bytes length, using the current process's key that is stored in process table. However, the `buf` buffer may be vulnerable to a code injection attack, e.g., due to a buffer overflow vulnerability in the program that may lead to the injection of malicious code into `buf`. Then, this code will be correctly encrypted using `asist_encrypt()` and will be successfully executed. Like previous work supporting ISR with self-modifying code [9], we believe that programs should carefully use the `asist_encrypt()` system call to avoid malicious code injection in `buf`.

3.1.5 Encryption Algorithms and Key Size

The simplest, and probably the fastest, encryption algorithm is to XOR each bit of the code with the respective bit of the key. Since code is much larger than a typical key, the bits of the key are reused. To accelerate encryption we XOR code and key as words, instead of bits. However, XOR was found to be susceptible to key guessing and key extraction attacks [48, 53]. In our prototype we implemented XOR encryption with key size that can range from 32-bit to 128-bit, to reduce the probability of a successful guess. The key size should be a multiple of 32-bit to support XOR between 32-bit words. We also implemented *transposition*, which is a stronger encryption algorithm than XOR. In transposition we shuffle the bits of a 32-bit word using an 160-bit key. For each bit of the encrypted word we choose one of the 32 bits of the original word based on the respective bits of the key. We use the `asist_mode` flag to define the encryption algorithm, key size, and encryption method.

3.1.6 Tolerance to Key Guessing Attacks

To evade ISR protection, an attacker can try to guess the encryption key and inject code encrypted with this key. The probability of a successful guess with XOR encryption is $1/2^{key\ size}$, e.g., $1/2^{32}$ for 32-bit key and $1/2^{128}$ for 128-bit key. In case of transposition, the probability of a successful guess is 1/32!, which is much lower than the respective probability with XOR. In case of a single guess, all the above probabilities seem good enough to protect a system. However, if the same key is used consistently, e.g., in case of static encryption, a brute force attack can be used to eventually guess the correct key. Sovarel et al. [48] present an incremental attack that reduces the number of tries needed to find the encryption key by observing system's behavior. ASIST can address such attacks with dynamic encryption, as a new key is generated before each execution. Barrantes et al. [9] show that code injections in systems protected with ISR result in the execution of at most five instructions before causing an exception. Therefore, with dynamic encryption, the probability of success of a brute force or incremental attack remains $1/2^{key\ size}$ with XOR or 1/32! with transposition.

3.2 Hardware Support

Figure 3 outlines ASIST's hardware architecture for ISR support when using XOR with a 32-bit key. We added two new registers to store the encryption keys: *usrkey* and *oskey*. These registers are memory mapped using a new Address Space Identifier (ASI), and are accessible only by the operating system through two privileged SPARC instructions: *sta* (store word to alternate space) and *lda* (load word from alternate space). The operating system sets the *usrkey* register using *sta* with the key of the user-level process that

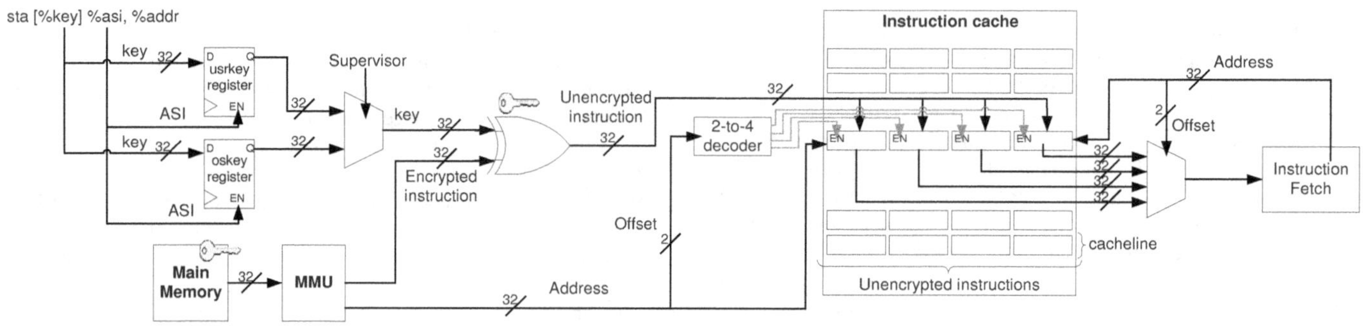

Figure 3: *ASIST hardware support for runtime instruction decryption.* We see the modified ASIST processor that decrypts every instruction with XOR and 32-bit key before the instruction cache. The key of the user-level running process is stored in *usrkey* register, and operating system's key is stored in *oskey* register. The supervisor bit defines which of these two keys will be used.

is scheduled for execution before each context switch. In case of a 32-bit key, a single *sta* instruction can store the entire key. For larger keys, more than one *sta* instructions may be needed.

The ASIST processor chooses between *usrkey* and *oskey* for decrypting instructions based on the value of the *Supervisor* bit. The Supervisor bit is 0 when the processor executes user-level code, so the *usrkey* is used for decryption, and it is 1 when the processor executes kernel's code (supervisor mode), so the *oskey* is selected. When a trap instruction is executed (*ta* instruction in SPARC), control is transferred from user to kernel and the Supervisor bit changes from 0 to 1; interrupts are treated similarly. Thus, the next instructions will be decrypted with *oskey*. Control is transferred back to user from kernel with the *return from trap* instruction (*rett* in SPARC). Then the Supervisor bit becomes 0 and the *usrkey* is used. The context switch is performed when the operating system runs, and *oskey* is used for decryption. Then the proper key of the process that will run immediately after *rett* is stored at *usrkey*.

The decryption unit is placed before the instruction fetch cycle, when instructions are moved from memory to the instruction cache. We should note that decryption fits in the processor's pipeline and *no* extra cycle is spent on it. Therefore, we expect no runtime overhead from the hardware decryption part. We expect a slight increase on the cost and on the power consumption due to the extra hardware we used. Also, ASIST's hardware architecture is backwards compatible with programs and operating system kernels that are not encrypted. We set the default value of the key registers to zero, which has no effect on the decryption.

3.2.1 Placement of the Decryption Unit

We decided to place the decryption unit as early as possible in the modified processor to avoid adding any performance overhead or spend an extra cycle, and to avoid breaking any runtime optimizations made by the processor. There are two possible choices for placing the decryption unit: before and after the instruction cache. Figure 4 presents the two options. When the decryption unit is after the instruction cache, the instructions are stored encrypted and the decryption takes place at each fetch cycle. Therefore, it is on the critical path of the processor and may add a delay for more complex decryption algorithms. Also, as the decryption circuit is utilized at each fetch cycle, it may result in increased power consumption. However, this approach protects the system from a possible code injection in the instruction cache.

On the other hand, when the decryption unit is located before the instruction cache, it is accessed only on instruction cache misses. This leads to reduced power consumption for decryption, as the instructions that are executed many times, e.g., in loops, are found decrypted in the instruction cache. Also, an increased delay for more complex encryption at this point will not have significant impact to the overall performance of the processor. In this case, instructions are stored unencrypted into the instruction cache, which could be vulnerable to code injections in the instruction cache. However, to the best of our knowledge, it is not possible to inject code in the instruction cache without passing from the path we have modified to decrypt each instruction. For this reason, we selected to place the decryption unit before the instruction cache.

3.2.2 Decryption Algorithms and Key Size

Figure 5 shows the implementation of XOR decryption with 128-bit key. Since each encrypted instruction in our architecture is a 32-bit word, we need to select the proper 32-bit part of the 128-bit key, the same part that was used in the encryption of this instruction. Thus, we use the two last bits of the instruction's address to select the correct 32-bit part of the 128-bit key using a multiplexer, and finally decrypt the instruction. The same approach is used for XOR decryption with other key sizes, multiple of 32 bits.

The implementation of decryption with transposition, as shown in Figure 6, requires significantly more hardware. This is because it needs 32 multiplexers, one per bit of the decrypted instruction. Each multiplexer has 32 input lines with all the 32 bits of the encrypted instruction, to choose the proper bit. It also has 5 select lines that define the selection of the input bit at each position. The select lines of each multiplexer are part of the 160-bit key. Besides the additional hardware, the runtime operation of transposition is equally fast with XOR, as it does not spend an extra cycle and does not impose any delay to the processor. To dynamically select the decryption algorithm and key size, we have added another memory mapped register: *asist_mode*.

3.2.3 Return Address Encryption

To transparently protect a system against return-to-libc and ROP attacks [14, 45], we extended our hardware design to provide protection of the return address integrity without any runtime overhead. To this end, we slightly modified the ASIST processor to encrypt the return address in each function call using the process's key, and decrypt it just before returning to the caller. This is similar to the XOR random canary defense [21], which uses `mprotect()` to hide the canary table from attackers. On the other hand, we take advantage of the two hardware key registers, which are not accessible by an attacker, to hide the encryption key. Also, our hardware implementation does not impose any performance overhead.

In the SPARC V8 architecture, function calls are performed with the *call* synthetic instruction, which is equal to *jmpl func_addr,%o7*.

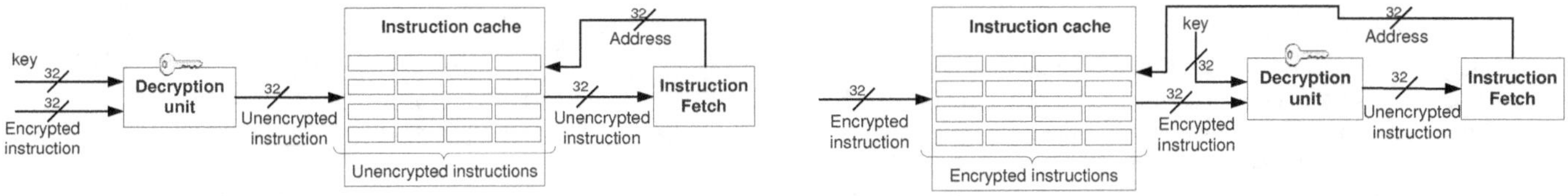

(a) Decryption before the instruction cache

(b) Decryption after the instruction cache

Figure 4: ***Alternative choices for the placement of the decryption unit in the ASIST-enabled processor.***

Hence, *call* writes the contents of the program counter (PC), i.e., the return address, into the *o7* register, and then transfers the control to the function's address *func_addr*. To return from a function, the *ret* synthetic instruction is used, which is equal to *jmpl %i7+8,%g0* when returning from a normal subroutine (*i7* register in the callee is the same with *o7* register in the caller) and *jmpl %o7+8,%g0* when returning from a leaf subroutine.

To encrypt the return address on each function call, we just XOR the value of the PC with the *usrkey* register when a *call* or *jmpl* instruction is executed and the value of the PC is stored into the *o7* register. The return address, i.e., the *i7* register in the callee, is decrypted with *usrkey* when a *jmpl* instruction uses the *i7* register (or *o7* in case of leaf subroutine) to change the control flow (*ret* instrunction). Thus, the modified processor will return to the *(%i7 XOR usrkey)+8* address.

This way, the return address remains always encrypted, e.g., when it is pushed onto the stack (window overflow), and it is always decrypted by the *jmpl* instruction when returning. Hence, any modification of the return address, e.g., though a stack-based buffer overflow or fake stack by changing the stack base pointer, or any *ret* instructions executed by a ROP exploit without the proper *call*, will lead to an unpredictable return address upon decryption, as the *usrkey* is unknown to the attacker.

Note that *jmpl* is also used for indirect jumps, not only for function calls and return, so our modified *jmpl* decrypts the given address only when the *i7* (or *o7*) register is used. This is a usual convention for function calls in SPARC and it should be obeyed, i.e., the *i7* and *o7* registers should not be used for any indirect jumps besides returning from function calls. Also, the calling conventions should be strictly obeyed: return address cannot be changed in any legal way before returning, and *ret* instructions without a preceding *call* instruction cannot be called without a system crash. As the calling conventions are not always strictly obeyed in several legacy applications and libraries, the use of return address encryption may not be always possible. Therefore, although ASIST offers this hardware feature, it may or may not be enabled by the software. We use one bit of the *asist_mode* register to define whether the return address encryption will be enabled or not.

3.3 Operating System Support

We now describe the new functionality we added in the operating system to support the ASIST hardware features for ISR in order to protect the system from attacks against possibly vulnerable user-level processes and kernel's vulnerabilities.

3.3.1 Kernel Modifications

In our prototype we modified the Linux kernel, and we ported our changes to 2.6.21 and 3.8 kernel versions. First, we added two new fields in the process table records (`task_struct` in Linux kernel): the process's *key* and the *asist_mode*. We initialize the process's key to zero and asist_mode to dynamic, so each unencrypted program will be dynamically encrypted.

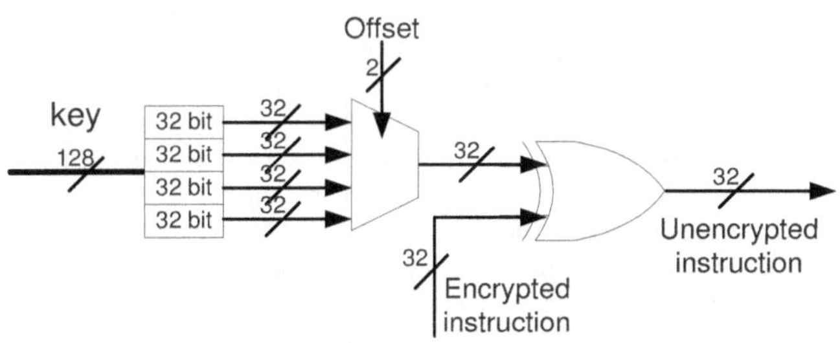

Figure 5: ***Decryption using XOR with 128-bit key.*** **Based on the last two bits of the instruction's address (offset) we select the respective 32-bit part of the 128-bit key for decryption.**

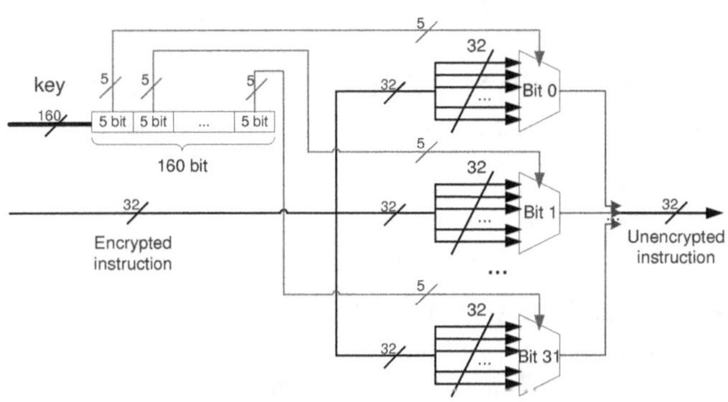

Figure 6: ***Decryption using transposition with 160-bit key.*** **The implementation of transposition requires significantly more hardware, because it needs 32 multiplexers with all the 32 bits of the encrypted instruction as input lines in each one.**

We changed the binary ELF loader to read the key of the executable ELF file, in case it is statically encrypted, or generate a random key, in case of dynamic encryption, after calling the `execve()` system call. Then, the loader stores the process's key to the respective process table record. We also changed the scheduler to store the key of the next process that is scheduled to run in the *usrkey* register before *each* context switch. For this, we added an *sta* instruction before the context switch to store a 32-bit key. For larger keys, the number of *sta* instructions depends on key size.

To implement dynamic encryption and shared library support we modified the page fault handler. For each page fault, we first check whether it is related to code (text page fault) and whether the process that caused the page fault uses dynamic code encryption. If so, we allocate a new anonymous page that is not backed by any file. Upon the reception of the requested page from disk (or buffer cache), we encrypt its data with process's key and copy it at the same step into the newly allocated page. Then, the new page is mapped into the process's address space. Eventually, this page will contain the code that will be accessed by the process.

3.3.2 *Kernel Encryption*

To encrypt kernel's code we used the same approach with static binary encryption. We modified an uncompressed kernel image by (i) adding a new note section that contains the kernel's encryption key, and (ii) identifying and encrypting all code sections. We had to carefully separate code from data into different sections while building the kernel image. The *oskey* register saves the key of kernel's encrypted code. We modified the bootloader to read and then store the kernel's key into the *oskey* register with an *sta* instruction, just before the control is transfered from bootloader to kernel. Since *oskey* is initialized with zero, which has no effect in XOR decryption that is also default, the unencrypted code of the bootloader can be successfully executed in the randomized processor.

We decided to statically encrypt the kernel's code so as to not add any delay to the boot process. Due to this, the key is decided once when the kernel image is built and encrypted, and it cannot change without re-encryption. Another option would be to encrypt the kernel's code while booting, using a new key that is randomly generated at this point. This option could add a further delay to the boot process. However, most systems typically use a compressed kernel image that is decompressed while booting. Thus, we can encrypt the kernel's code during the kernel loading stage when the image is decompressed into memory. The routine that decompresses and loads the kernel to memory must first generate a random key and then encrypt the kernel's code along with decompression.

4. ASIST PROTOTYPE IMPLEMENTATION

In this section we describe the ASIST prototype implementation, we present the results of the hardware synthesis using an FPGA board, in terms of additional hardware needed compared to the unmodified processor, and finally we discuss how the proposed system can be easily ported to other architectures and systems.

4.1 Hardware Implementation

We modified Leon3 SPARC V8 processor [1], a 32-bit open-source synthesizable processor [26], to implement the security features of ASIST for hardware-based ISR support, as we described in Section 3.2. All hardware modifications required fewer than 100 lines of VHDL code. Leon3 uses a single-issue, 7-stage pipeline. Our implementation has 8 register windows, an 16 KB 2-way set associative instruction cache, and a 16 KB 4-way set associative data cache. We synthesized and mapped the modified ASIST processors on a Xilinx XUPV5 ML509 FPGA board [54]. The FPGA has 256 MB DDR2 SDRAM memory and the design operates at 80 MHz clock frequency. It also has several peripherals including an 100Mb Ethernet interface.

4.2 Additional Hardware

Table 2 shows the results of the synthesis for three different hardware implementations of ASIST, using XOR decryption with 32-bit and 128-bit keys, and decryption with transposition using 160-bit key. We compare them with the unmodified Leon3 processor as a baseline to measure the additional hardware used by ASIST to implement ISR functionality in each case. We see that ASIST with XOR encryption and 32-bit key adds less than 1% of additional hardware, both in terms of additional flip flops (0.73%) and lookup tables (0.61%). When a larger key of 128 bits is used for encryption, we observe a slight increase in the number of flip flops (2.81%) due to the larger registers needed to store the two 128-bit keys. The implementation of transposition results in significantly more hardware used, both for flip flops (6.62% increase) and lookup tables (6.87% increase). This is due to the larger circuit used for the hardware implementation of transposition, which consists of 32 multiplexers with 32 input lines each, as we showed in Section 3.2.2.

Synthesized Processor	Flip Flops	LUTs
Vanilla Leon3	9,227	16,986
XOR with 32-bit key	9,294 (0.73% increase)	17,090 (0.61% increase)
XOR with 128-bit key	9,486 (2.81% increase)	17,116 (0.77% increase)
Transposition with 160-bit key	9,838 (6.62% increase)	18,153 (6.87% increase)

Table 2: *Additional hardware used by ASIST.* We see that ASIST adds just 0.6%–0.7% more hardware with XOR decryption using a 32-bit key, while it adds significantly more hardware (6.6%–6.9%) when using transposition.

4.3 Kernel and Software Modifications

The resulting system is a full-featured SPARC workstation using a Linux operating system. We modified the Linux kernel as we described in Section 3.3. We ported our Linux kernel modifications in 2.6.21 and 3.8.0 kernel versions. We built a cross compilation tool chain with `gcc` version 4.7.2 and `uClibc` version 0.9.33.2 to cross compile the Linux kernel, libraries, and user-level applications. Thus, all programs running in our system (both vanilla and ASIST), including vulnerable programs and benchmarks, were cross compiled with this tool chain on another PC. We slightly modified linker scripts to separate code and data for both static and dynamic code encryption, and align headers, code, and data into separate pages in case of dynamic encryption. To implement static encryption, we extended `objcopy` with the `--encrypt-code` flag. The key can be provided by the user or randomly chosen.

4.4 Portability to Other Systems

Our approach is easily portable to other architectures and operating systems. Regarding ASIST's hardware extensions, implementing new registers that are accessible by the operating system is quite easy in most architectures, including x86. Encrypting the return address at each function call and decrypting it before returning depends on the calling convention at each architecture. For instance, in x86 it can be implemented by slightly modifying *call* and *ret* instructions. In our current design, we have implemented the runtime instruction decryption for RISC architectures that use fixed-length instructions. Thus, porting the decryption functionality in other RISC systems will be straight-forward. On the other hand, CISC architectures such as x86 support variable-length instructions. However, our approach can also be implemented in such architectures with minor modifications. Since instructions reside in memory before they are executed, we can simply encrypt them without the need of precise disassembly, e.g., in blocks of 32-bits, depending on the key size. In architectures with variable-length instructions this encryption will not be aligned at each instruction, but this is not an issue. The memory blocks will be decrypted accordingly by the modified processor before execution. For instance, a memory block can be decrypted based on the byte offset of its respective memory address. Also, since we have placed the decryption unit before the instruction cache, decryption is performed at each *word* that is stored in cache, rather than at each instruction.

We have implemented our prototype by modifying the Linux kernel. However, the same modifications can be made in other operating systems as well, as we change generic kernel modules such as the binary loader, the process scheduler and context switch, and the page fault handler. These modules exist in all modern operating systems and they can be changed respectively to support the hardware features offered by a randomized processor.

CVE Reference	Vulnerability Description	Access Vector	Location	Vulnerable Program
CVE-2010-1451	Linux kernel before 2.6.33 does not properly implement a non-executable stack on SPARC platform	Local	Stack	Custom
CVE-2013-0722	Buffer overflow due to incorrect user-supplied input validation	Remote	Stack	Ettercap 0.7.5.1 and earlier
CVE-2012-5611	Buffer overflow that allows remote authenticated users to execute arbitrary code via a long argument to the GRANT FILE command	Remote	Stack	Oracle MySQL 5.1.65 and MariaDB 5.3.10
CVE-2002-1549	Buffer overflow that allows to execute arbitrary code via a long HTTP GET request	Remote	Stack	Light HTTPd (lhttpd) 0.1
CVE-2002-1337	Buffer overflow that allows to execute arbitrary code via certain formatted address fields	Remote	BSS	Sendmail 5.79 to 8.12.7
CVE-2002-1496	Buffer overflow that allows to execute arbitrary code via a negative value in the Content-Length HTTP header	Remote	Heap	Null HTTPd Server 0.5.0 and earlier
CVE-2010-4258	Linux kernel allows to bypass access_ok() and overwrite arbitrary kernel memory locations by NULL pointer dereference to gain privileges	Local	Kernel	Linux kernel before 2.6.36.2
CVE-2009-3234	Buffer overflow that allows to execute arbitrary user-level code via a "big size data" to the perf_counter_open() system call	Local	Kernel stack	Linux kernel 2.6.31-rc1
CVE-2005-2490	Buffer overflow that allows to execute arbitrary code by calling sendmsg() and modifying the message contents in another thread	Local	Stack	Linux kernel before 2.6.13.1

Table 3: *Representative subset of code injection attacks tested with ASIST.* We see that ASIST is able to successfully prevent code injection attacks targeting vulnerable user-level programs as well as kernel vulnerabilities.

5. EXPERIMENTAL EVALUATION

We mapped our prototype onto an FPGA running two versions of the Linux kernel, 2.6.21 and 3.8, as described in Section 4. We used the Ethernet adapter of the FPGA and configured the system with networking and a static IP address. This allows for remote exploitation attempts for our security evaluation, and for evaluating the performance of a Web server. As the available memory on the FPGA is only 256 MB, and there is no local disk in the system, we used NFS to mount a partition of a local PC that contains all the cross compiled programs needed for the evaluation. To avoid measuring NFS delays in our evaluation, we copied each executable program in the local RAM file system before its execution.

We evaluated the ASIST prototype that uses XOR encryption with a 32-bit key, comparing static and dynamic encryption implementations with an unmodified system (vanilla processor and unmodified operating system). We observed that using a larger key or transposition instead of XOR for encrypting instructions has the same effectiveness on preventing code injection attacks and the same efficiency in terms of performance. We did not use the return address encryption in our security and performance evaluation.

5.1 Security Evaluation

To demonstrate the effectiveness of ASIST at preventing code injection attacks exploiting user- or kernel-level vulnerabilities, we tested a representative sample of attacks shown in Table 3. The first six attacks target buffer overflow vulnerabilities on user-level programs, while the last three attacks target a NULL pointer dereference and two buffer overflow vulnerabilities of the Linux kernel.

First, we ran a vanilla 2.6.21 kernel, which does not properly implement a non-executable stack on SPARC. We built a custom program with a typical stack-based buffer overflow vulnerability, and we used a large command-line argument to inject SPARC executable code into the program's stack, which was successfully executed by overwriting the return address. We then used an ASIST modified kernel without enabling the return address encryption, and we ran a statically encrypted version of the vulnerable program with the same argument. In this case, the program was terminated with an illegal instruction exception, as the unencrypted injected code could not be executed. Similarly, we ran an unencrypted version of the vulnerable program and relied on the page fault handler for dynamic code encryption. Again, the injected code caused an illegal instruction exception due to the ISR.

We performed similar tests with all the other vulnerable programs: Ettercap, which is a packet capture tool, MariaDB database, Light HTTPd and Null HTTPd webservers, and sendmail. These programs were cross compiled with our toolchain and encrypted with our extended `objcopy` tool. In all cases our remotely injected shellcode was executed successfully only on the vanilla system, while ASIST always prevented the execution of the injected code and resulted in illegal instruction exception.

We also tested attacks exploiting three kernel vulnerabilities with and without ASIST. We cross compiled, modified and encrypted three different kernel versions for each one: 2.6.21, 2.6.31-rc1 and 2.6.11. When running the vanilla kernel on the unmodified processor, the kernel exploits resulted in the successful execution of the provided user-level code with kernel privileges. On the other hand, the encrypted kernels with ASIST resulted in kernel panic for all the exploits, avoiding a system compromise with kernel privileges.

5.2 Performance Evaluation

To evaluate ASIST's performance we compare (i) vanilla Leon3 with unmodified Linux kernel (Vanilla), (ii) ASIST with static encryption (ASIST-Static), and (iii) ASIST with dynamic code encryption (ASIST-Dynamic), when running the SPEC CPU2006 benchmark suite and two real world applications.

5.2.1 Benchmarks

We ran all the integer benchmarks from the SPEC CPU2006 suite (CINT2006) [49], which includes several CPU-intensive applications. Figure 7 shows the slowdown of each benchmark when using ASIST with static and dynamic encryption, compared to the vanilla system. We see that both ASIST implementations impose less than 1.5% slowdown in all benchmarks. For most benchmarks, ASIST exhibits almost the same execution times as with the unmodified system. This is due to the hardware-based instruction decryption, which does not add any observable delay. Moreover, the modified kernel performs minor extra tasks: it reads the key from the executable file (for static encryption) or it randomly generates a new key (for dynamic encryption) only once per each execution, while it adds just one extra instruction before each context switch. We notice a slight deviation from the vanilla execution time only for three of the benchmarks: `gcc`, `sjeng`, and `h264ref`. For these benchmarks, we observe a slight slowdown of 1%–1.2% in static and 1%–1.5% in dynamic encryption. This deviation is probably due to the different linking configurations (statically linked versus dynamically linked shared libraries).

One might expect that the dynamic encryption approach would experience a considerable performance overhead due to the extra memory copy and extra work needed to encrypt code pages at each text page fault. However, our results in Figure 7 indicate that

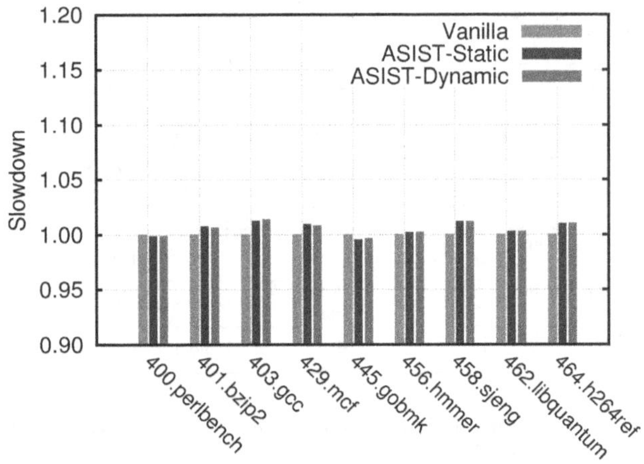

Figure 7: ***Runtime overhead using the SPEC CPU2006 benchmark suite.*** **We see that both ASIST implementations have negligible runtime overhead compared to the vanilla system.**

Benchmark	Data page faults per second	Text page faults per second
400.perlbench	38.4964	1.97215
401.bzip2	44.3605	0.193831
403.gcc	60.3235	3.93358
429.mcf	51.7769	0.0497679
445.gobmk	25.4735	0.905984
456.hmmer	0.0546246	0.0223249
458.sjeng	71.9751	0.0676988
462.libquantum	5.18675	0.0486765
464.h264ref	3.19614	0.0333707

Table 4: ***Data and text page faults per second when running the SPEC CPU2006 benchmark suite.*** **All benchmarks have very few text page faults per second, which explains the negligible overhead of the dynamic encryption approach.**

dynamic encryption performs equally well with static encryption. Thus, our proposed approach to dynamically encrypt program code at the page fault handler, instead of statically encrypt the code before program's execution, does not seem to add any extra overhead.

To better understand the performance of this approach, we instrumented the Linux kernel to measure the data and text page faults of each process that uses the dynamic encryption mode. Table 4 shows the data and text page faults per second for each benchmark. We see that all benchmarks have a very low rate of text page faults, and most of them experience significantly less than one text page fault per second. Moreover, we observe that the vast majority of page faults are for data pages, while only a small percentage of the total page faults are related to code. Therefore, we notice a negligible overhead with dynamic code encryption at the page fault handler for two main reasons: (i) as we see in Table 4, text page faults are very rare, and (ii) the overhead of the extra memory copy and page encryption is significantly less that the page fault's overhead for fetching the requested page from disk. Note that in our setup we use a RAM file system instead of an actual disk, so a production system may experience an even lower overhead.

The very low page fault rate for pages that contain executable code makes the dynamic encryption a very appealing approach, as it imposes practically zero runtime overhead, and at the same time it supports shared libraries and transparently generates a new key at each program execution.

5.2.2 Real-world Applications

We evaluated ASIST with two real-world applications. First, we ran the `lighttpd` Web server in a vanilla system and in the two versions of ASIST. We used another machine located in the local network to repeatedly download 14 files of different sizes, ranging from 1 KB to 8 MB, and we measured the average download time for each file. Figure 8 shows the slowdown of the download time as a function of the file size for each system. We see that ASIST does not impose any considerable delay, as the download time remains within 1% of the vanilla system for all files. We also notice that both static and dynamic encryption implementations perform almost equally good. We measured the page faults caused by `lighttpd`: 261 data page faults per second, and just 0.013 text page fault per second. Thus, the dynamic encryption did not add any runtime overhead to the server. Moreover, we observed that most of the text page faults occur during the first few milliseconds of the `lighttpd` execution, when the code is loaded into memory, and then practically no text page fault occurs.

In our last benchmark we ran an `sqlite3` database in the vanilla and in the two ASIST setups. To evaluate the performance of `sqlite3` we used the C/C++ SQLite interface to implement a simple benchmark that reads a large tab-separated file and updates a table's entries with the respective values. Figure 9 shows the slowdown when inserting data into the database using this benchmark as a function of the number of insertions. ASIST imposes less than 1% slowdown on the database's operation for both static and dynamic approaches, even on small datasets that do not provide ASIST with enough time to amortize the encryption overhead.

6. RELATED WORK

Instruction Set Randomization. ISR was initially introduced as a generic defense against code injections by Kc et al. [31] and Barrantes et al. [9, 10]. To demonstrate the feasibility of ISR, they proposed implementations with `bochs` [33] and `Valgrind` [36] respectively. Hu et al. [29] implemented ISR with Strata SDT tool [42] using AES as a stronger encryption for instruction randomization. Boyd et al. [13] propose a selective ISR to reduce the runtime overhead. Portokalidis and Keromytis [41] implemented ISR using Pin [34] with moderate overhead and shared libraries support. In Section 2.3 we described in more detail all the existing software-based ISR implementations and we compared them with ASIST. ASIST addresses most of the limitations of the existing ISR approaches owing to its simple and efficient hardware support.

Defenses against code injection attacks. Modern hardware platforms support non-executable data protection, such as the No eXecute (NX) bit [38]. NX bit prevents stack or heap data from being executed, so it is capable to protect against code inject attacks without performance degradation. However, its effectiveness depends on its proper use by software. For instance, an application may not set the NX bit on all data segments due to backwards compatibility constraints, self-modifying code, or bad programming practices. We believe that ASIST can be used complementary to NX bit to serve as an additional layer of security, e.g., in case that NX bit may not be applicable or can be bypassed. For instance, many ROP exploits use the code of `mprotect()` to make executable pages with injected code, bypassing the NX bit protection. This way, they can execute arbitrary code to implement the attack without the need of more specific gadgets, which may not be easy to find, e.g., due to the use of Address Space Layout Randomization (ASLR). In contrast, these exploits cannot execute any injected code in a system using ASIST, as this code will not be correctly encrypted. Thus, ASIST with ASLR provides a stronger defense.

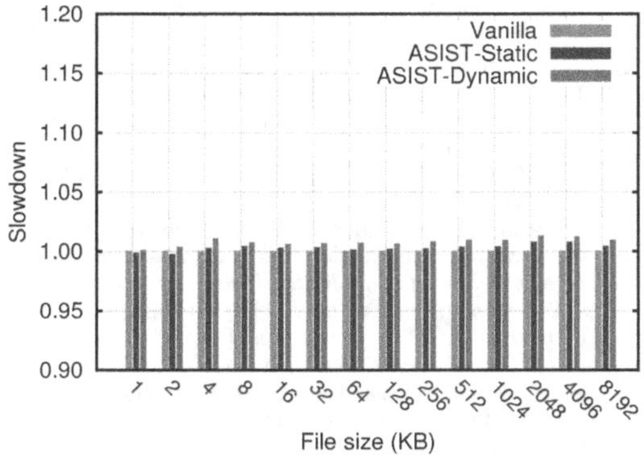

Figure 8: ***Slowdown when downloading different files from a lighttpd Web server as a function of the file size.*** **We see that ASIST adds less than 1% delay for all file sizes.**

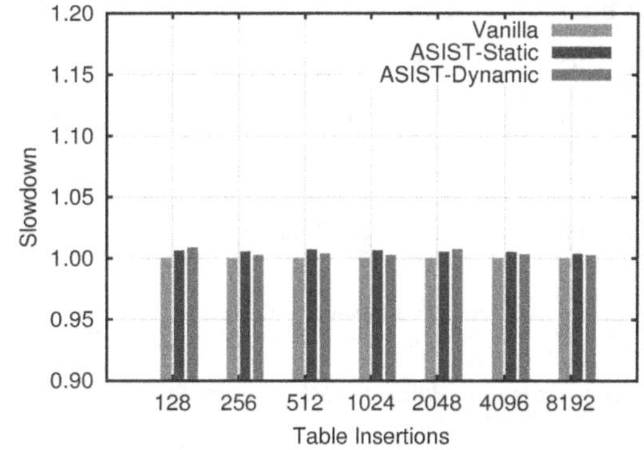

Figure 9: ***Slowdown when inserting data into sqlite3 as a function of the number of insertions.*** **We see that ASIST experiences less than 1% slowdown even for very small datasets.**

A recent attack demonstrated by Snow et al. [47] is also able to bypass NX bit and ASLR protection using ROP. First, it exploits a memory disclosure to map process's memory layout, and then it uses a disassembler to dynamically discover gadgets that can be used for the ROP attack. ASIST with ASLR, however, is able to prevent this attack: even if memory with executable code leaks to the attacker, the instructions will be encrypted with a randomly-generated key. This way, attacker will not be able to disassemble the code and find useful gadgets. ASIST ensures that key does not reside in process's memory, while stronger encryption algorithms (like AES) can also fit in our design to avoid inferring the key.

SecVisor [43] protects the kernel from code injection attacks using a hypervisor to prevent unauthorized code execution. While SecVisor focuses on kernel's code integrity, ASIST prevents the execution of unauthorized code in both user- and kernel-level.

Defenses against buffer overflow attacks. StackGuard [21] uses canaries to protect the stack, while PointGuard [20] encrypts all pointers while they reside in memory and decrypts them before they are loaded into a register. Both techniques are implemented with compiler extensions, so they require program recompilation. In contrast, BinArmor [46] protects existing binaries from buffer overflows without access to source code, by discovering the data structures and then rewriting the binary.

Other randomization-based defenses. Address Space Layout Randomization (ASLR) [39] randomizes the memory layout of a process at runtime or at compile time to protect against code-reuse attacks. Giuffrida et al. [27] propose an approach with address space randomization to protect the operating system kernel. Bhatkar et al. [11] present randomization techniques for the addresses of the stack, heap, dynamic libraries, routines and static data in an executable. Wartell et al. [52] randomize the instruction addresses at each execution to address code-reuse attacks. Jiang et al. [30] prevent code injections by randomizing the system call numbers.

Hardware support for security. There are numerous research efforts aiming to provide hardware support for security without sacrificing performance. Dalton et al. [22, 23] propose a hardware-based architecture for dynamic information flow tracking, by extending a SPARC V8 processor with four tag bits per each register and memory word, as well as with tag propagation and runtime checks to defend against buffer overflows and high-level attacks. Greathouse et al. [28] present a design for accelerating dynamic analysis techniques with hardware support for unlimited watchpoints. These efforts significantly reduce the performance cost for dynamic information flow analysis, which has a very high overhead in software-based implementations. Frantzen and Shuey [25] implement a hardware-assisted technique for the SPARC architecture to protect the return address. Tuck et al. [50] propose hardware encryption to protect function pointers from buffer overflow attacks with improved performance, extending the computationally expensive software-based pointer encryption used by pointguard [20]. Our approach is similar to these works: we also propose hardware support for another existing technique that prevents the execution of any code that is not authorized to run in the system.

7. CONCLUSIONS

We have presented the design, implementation and evaluation of ASIST: a hardware-assisted architecture for ISR support. ASIST is designed to offer (i) improved performance, without runtime overhead, (ii) improved security, by protecting the operating system and resisting key guessing attempts, and (iii) transparent operation, with shared libraries support and no need for any program modifications. Our experimental evaluation shows that ASIST does not impose any significant overhead (less than 1.5%), while it is able to prevent code injection attacks that exploit user-level and kernel-level vulnerabilities. We have also proposed a new approach for dynamic code encryption at the page fault handler when code is first loaded into process's memory. This approach transparently encrypts unmodified binaries that may use shared libraries with a new key at each execution, offering protection against incremental key guessing attacks. Our results indicate that dynamic code encryption is efficient, without adding any overhead, due to the low text page fault rate. Our work shows that ASIST can address most of the limitations of existing software-based ISR implementations while adding less than 0.7% additional hardware to a SPARC processor. We believe that ASIST can be easily ported to other architectures to strengthen existing defenses against code injection attacks.

Acknowledgments

We thank the anonymous reviewers for their valuable feedback. We also thank the Computer Architecture and VLSI Systems Lab of FORTH-ICS for providing access to FPGAs and design tools. The project was co-financed by the European Regional Development Fund (ERDF) and national funds, under the Operational Programme "Competitiveness & Entrepreneurship" (OPCE II), Measure "COOPERATION" (Action I). This work was also supported in part by the European Union's Prevention of and Fight against Crime Programme "Illegal Use of Internet" - ISEC 2010 Action Grants, grant ref. HOME/2010/ISEC/AG/INT-002, and by the FP7 projects NECOMA and SysSec, funded by the European Commission under Grant Agreements No. 608533 and No. 257007.

8. REFERENCES

[1] The SPARC Architecture Manual, Version 8. www.sparc.com/standards/V8.pdf.

[2] USA National Vulnerability Database. http://web.nvd.nist.gov/view/vuln/statistics.

[3] Linux Kernel Remote Buffer Overflow Vulnerabilities. http://secwatch.org/advisories/1013445/, 2006.

[4] OpenBSD IPv6 mbuf Remote Kernel Buffer Overflow. http://www.securityfocus.com/archive/1/462728/30/0/threaded, 2007.

[5] Microsoft Security Bulletin MS08-067 – Critical. http://www.microsoft.com/technet/security/Bulletin/MS08-067.mspx, 2008.

[6] Microsoft Windows TCP/IP IGMP MLD Remote Buffer Overflow Vulnerability. http://www.securityfocus.com/bid/27100, 2008.

[7] Microsoft security advisory (975191): Vulnerabilities in the ftp service in internet information services. http://www.microsoft.com/technet/security/advisory/975191.mspx, 2009.

[8] Microsoft security advisory (975497): Vulnerabilities in smb could allow remote code execution. http://www.microsoft.com/technet/security/advisory/975497.mspx, 2009.

[9] E. G. Barrantes, D. H. Ackley, S. Forrest, and D. Stefanović. Randomized Instruction Set Emulation. *ACM Transactions on Information and System Security*, 8(1), 2005.

[10] E. G. Barrantes, D. H. Ackley, T. S. Palmer, D. Stefanovic, and D. D. Zovi. Randomized Instruction Set Emulation to Disrupt Binary Code Injection Attacks. In *ACM Conference on Computer and Communications Security (CCS)*, 2003.

[11] S. Bhatkar, D. C. DuVarney, and R. Sekar. Address Obfuscation: an Efficient Approach to Combat a Board Range of Memory Error Exploits. In *USENIX Security Symposium*, 2003.

[12] T. Bletsch, X. Jiang, V. W. Freeh, and Z. Liang. Jump-Oriented Programming: A New Class of Code-Reuse Attack. In *ACM Symposium on Information, Computer and Communications Security (ASIACCS)*, 2011.

[13] S. W. Boyd, G. S. Kc, M. E. Locasto, A. D. Keromytis, and V. Prevelakis. On the General Applicability of Instruction-Set Randomization. *IEEE Transactions on Dependable Secure Computing*, 7(3), 2010.

[14] E. Buchanan, R. Roemer, H. Shacham, and S. Savage. When Good Instructions Go Bad: Generalizing Return-Oriented Programming to RISC. In *ACM Conference on Computer and Communications Security (CCS)*, 2008.

[15] P. P. Bungale and C.-K. Luk. PinOS: A Programmable Framework for Whole-System Dynamic Instrumentation. In *ACM SIGPLAN/SIGOPS Conference on Virtual Execution Environments (VEE)*, 2007.

[16] H. Chen, Y. Mao, X. Wang, D. Zhou, N. Zeldovich, and M. F. Kaashoek. Linux Kernel Vulnerabilities: State-of-the-Art Defenses and Open Problems. In *Asia-Pacific Workshop on Systems (APSys)*, 2011.

[17] S. Chen, J. Xu, E. C. Sezer, P. Gauriar, and R. K. Iyer. Non-Control-Data Attacks Are Realistic Threats. In *USENIX Security Symposium*, 2005.

[18] S. Christey and A. Martin. Vulnerability Type Distributions in CVE. http://cve.mitre.org/docs/vuln-trends/vuln-trends.pdf, 2007.

[19] C. Cowan, M. Barringer, S. Beattie, G. Kroah-Hartman, M. Frantzen, and J. Lokier. FormatGuard: Automatic Protection From printf Format String Vulnerabilities. In *USENIX Security Symposium*, 2001.

[20] C. Cowan, S. Beattie, J. Johansen, and P. Wagle. PointguardTM: Protecting Pointers from Buffer Overflow Vulnerabilities. In *USENIX Security Symposium*, 2003.

[21] C. Cowan, C. Pu, D. Maier, H. Hintony, J. Walpole, P. Bakke, S. Beattie, A. Grier, P. Wagle, and Q. Zhang. StackGuard: Automatic Adaptive Detection and Prevention of Buffer-Overflow Attacks. In *USENIX Security Symposium*, 1998.

[22] M. Dalton, H. Kannan, and C. Kozyrakis. Raksha: A Flexible Information flow Architecture for Software Security. In *ACM/IEEE International Symposium on Computer Architecture (ISCA)*, 2007.

[23] M. Dalton, H. Kannan, and C. Kozyrakis. Real-World Buffer Overflow Protection for Userspace & Kernelspace. In *USENIX Security Symposium*, 2008.

[24] D. Danchev. Managed polymorphic script obfuscation services. http://ddanchev.blogspot.com/2009/08/managed-polymorphic-script-obfuscation.html, 2009.

[25] M. Frantzen and M. Shuey. StackGhost: Hardware Facilitated Stack Protection. In *USENIX Security Symposium*, 2001.

[26] Gaisler Research. Leon3 synthesizable processor. http://www.gaisler.com.

[27] C. Giuffrida, A. Kuijsten, and A. S. Tanenbaum. Enhanced Operating System Security Through Efficient and Fine-grained Address Space Randomization. In *USENIX Security Symposium*, 2012.

[28] J. L. Greathouse, H. Xin, Y. Luo, and T. Austin. A Case for Unlimited Watchpoints. In *ACM Intrnational Conference on Architectural Support for Programming Languages and Operating Systems (ASPLOS)*, 2012.

[29] W. Hu, J. Hiser, D. Williams, A. Filipi, J. W. Davidson, D. Evans, J. C. Knight, A. Nguyen-Tuong, and J. Rowanhill. Secure and Practical Defense Against Code-Injection Attacks using Software Dynamic Translation. In *ACM SIGPLAN/SIGOPS Conference on Virtual Execution Environments (VEE)*, 2006.

[30] X. Jiang, H. J. Wangz, D. Xu, and Y.-M. Wang. RandSys: Thwarting Code Injection Attacks with System Service Interface Randomization. In *IEEE International Symposium on Reliable Distributed Systems (SRDS)*, 2007.

[31] G. S. Kc, A. D. Keromytis, and V. Prevelakis. Countering Code-Injection Attacks With Instruction-Set Randomization. In *ACM Conference on Computer and Communications Security (CCS)*, 2003.

[32] V. P. Kemerlis, G. Portokalidis, and A. D. Keromytis. kGuard: Lightweight Kernel Protection Against Return-to-User Attacks. In *USENIX Security Symposium*, 2012.

[33] K. P. Lawton. Bochs: A Portable PC Emulator for Unix/X. *Linux Journal*, 1996.

[34] C.-K. Luk, R. Cohn, R. Muth, H. Patil, A. Klauser, G. Lowney, S. Wallace, V. J. Reddi, and K. Hazelwood. Pin: Building Customized Program Analysis Tools with Dynamic Instrumentation. In *ACM SIGPLAN Conference on Programming Language Design and Implementation (PLDI)*, 2005.

[35] Nergal. The Advanced return-into-lib(c) Exploits: PaX Case Study. *Phrack*, 11(58), 2001.

[36] N. Nethercote and J. Seward. Valgrind: A Framework for heavyweight Dynamic Binary Instrumentation. In *ACM SIGPLAN Conference on Programming Language Design and Implementation (PLDI)*, 2007.

[37] J. Oberheide, M. Bailey, and F. Jahanian. PolyPack: An Automated Online Packing Service for Optimal Antivirus Evasion. In *USENIX Workshop on Offensive Technologies (WOOT)*, 2009.

[38] L. D. Paulson. New Chips Stop Buffer Overflow Attacks. *IEEE Computer*, 37(10), 2004.

[39] PaX Tream. Homepage of PaX. http://pax.grsecurity.net/.

[40] P. Porras, H. Saidi, and V. Yegneswaran. Conficker C analysis. *SRI International*, 2009.

[41] G. Portokalidis and A. D. Keromytis. Fast and Practical Instruction-Set Randomization for Commodity Systems. In *Annual Computer Security Applications Conference (ACSAC)*, 2010.

[42] K. Scott, N. Kumar, S. Velusamy, B. Childers, J. W. Davidson, and M. L. Soffa. Retargetable and Reconfigurable Software Dynamic Translation. In *International Symposium on Code Generation and Optimization: Feedback-Directed and Runtime Optimization (CGO)*, 2003.

[43] A. Seshadri, M. Luk, N. Qu, and A. Perrig. SecVisor: A Tiny Hypervisor to Provide Lifetime Kernel Code Integrity for Commodity OSes. In *ACM Symposium on Operating Systems Principles (SOSP)*, 2007.

[44] S. Sethumadhavan, S. J. Stolfo, A. Keromytis, J. Yang, and D. August. The SPARCHS Project: Hardware Support for Software Security. In *SysSec Workshop*, 2011.

[45] H. Shacham. The Geometry of Innocent Flesh on the Bone: Return-into-libc without Function Calls (on the x86). In *ACM Conference on Computer and Communications Security (CCS)*, 2007.

[46] A. Slowinska, T. Stancescu, and H. Bos. Body Armor for Binaries: Preventing Buffer Overflows Without Recompilation. In *USENIX Annual Technical Conference (ATC)*, 2012.

[47] K. Z. Snow, L. Davi, A. Dmitrienko, C. Liebchen, F. Monrose, and A.-R. Sadeghi. Just-In-Time Code Reuse: On the Effectiveness of Fine-Grained Address Space Layout Randomization. In *IEEE Symposium on Security and Privacy*, 2013.

[48] A. N. Sovarel, D. Evans, and N. Paul. Where's the FEEB? the Effectiveness of Instruction Set Randomization. In *USENIX Security Symposium*, 2005.

[49] Standard Performance Evaluation Corporation (SPEC). SPEC CINT2006 Benchmarks. http://www.spec.org/cpu2006/CINT2006.

[50] N. Tuck, B. Calder, and G. Varghese. Hardware and Binary Modification Support for Code Pointer Protection From Buffer Overflow. In *IEEE/ACM International Symposium on Microarchitecture (MICRO)*, 2004.

[51] X. Wang, H. Chen, Z. Jia, N. Zeldovich, and M. F. Kaashoek. Improving Integer Security for Systems with KINT. In *USENIX Symposium on Operating System Design and Implementation (OSDI)*, 2012.

[52] R. Wartell, V. Mohan, K. W. Hamlen, and Z. Lin. Binary Stirring: Self-randomizing Instruction Addresses of Legacy x86 Binary Code. In *ACM Conference on Computer and Communications Security (CCS)*, 2012.

[53] Y. Weiss and E. G. Barrantes. Known/Chosen Key Attacks against Software Instruction Set Randomization. In *Annual Computer Security Applications Conference (ACSAC)*, 2006.

[54] Xilinx. Xilinx University Program XUPV5-LX110T Development System. http://www.xilinx.com/support/documentation/boards_and_kits/ug347.pdf, 2011.

librando: Transparent Code Randomization for Just-in-Time Compilers

Andrei Homescu
University of California, Irvine
Irvine, CA, USA

Stefan Brunthaler
University of California, Irvine
Irvine, CA, USA

Per Larsen
University of California, Irvine
Irvine, CA, USA

Michael Franz
University of California, Irvine
Irvine, CA, USA

ABSTRACT

Just-in-time compilers (JITs) are here to stay. Unfortunately, they also provide new capabilities to cyber attackers, namely the ability to supply input programs (in languages such as JavaScript) that will then be compiled to executable code. Once this code is placed and marked as executable, it can then be leveraged by the attacker.

Randomization techniques such as constant blinding raise the cost to the attacker, but they significantly add to the burden of implementing a JIT. There are a great many JITs in use today, but not even all of the most commonly used ones randomize their outputs.

We present librando, the first comprehensive technique to harden JIT compilers in a completely generic manner by randomizing their output transparently ex post facto. We implement this approach as a system-wide service that can simultaneously harden multiple running JITs. It hooks into the memory protections of the target OS and randomizes newly generated code on the fly when marked as executable.

In order to provide "black box" JIT hardening, librando needs to be extremely conservative. For example, it completely preserves the contents of the calling stack, presenting each JIT with the illusion that it is executing its own generated code. Yet in spite of the heavy lifting that librando performs behind the scenes, the performance impact is surprisingly low. For Java (HotSpot), we measured slowdowns by a factor of $1.15\times$, and for compute-intensive JavaScript (V8) benchmarks, a slowdown of $3.5\times$. For many applications, this overhead is low enough to be practical for general use today.

Categories and Subject Descriptors

D.3.4 [**Programming Languages**]: Processors—*Compilers, Code generation*; D.4.6 [**Operating Systems**]: Security and Protection

General Terms

Languages, Security, Performance

CCS'13, November 4–8, 2013, Berlin, Germany.

ACM 978-1-4503-2477-9/13/11 ...$15.00.
http://dx.doi.org/10.1145/2508859.2516675.

Keywords

JIT compilers, diversification, security, JIT spraying, code reuse attacks, return-oriented programming, binary rewriting, randomization

1. MOTIVATION

Our computing infrastructure depends on high performance delivered by just-in-time (JIT) compilers to a large degree. Efficiently executing JavaScript is a prerequisite for complex Web 2.0 applications. Similarly, Java's success rests on performance delivered by efficient dynamic code generation. From the early beginnings, JIT compilers had to focus on producing code quickly. Usually, they achieve this by optimizing the common case and forgoing time-intensive optimizations altogether. As a result, this leads to highly predictable code generation, which attackers exploit for malicious purposes. This is evidenced by the rising threats of *JIT spraying* [2] and similar attacks on sandboxes in JITs. The former is particularly interesting: JIT spraying relies on JIT compilers emitting constants present in input source code directly into binary code. Due to variable length encoding, attackers can encode and subsequently divert control flow to arbitrary malicious code arranged this way.

This attack vector is innate and specific to JIT compilers. From a security perspective, the state-of-the-art in the field is to address JIT spraying by encrypting and decrypting constants. This addresses the code injection part of JIT spraying, but attackers can fall back on code-reuse techniques. Specifically, return-oriented programming [26] for JIT compiled code is problematic. Instead of finding gadgets in statically generated code (as they would do an a generic return-oriented programming attack), an attacker uses the JIT compiler to create new binary code containing the necessary gadgets by supplying specially crafted source code. The ubiquity of JIT compilers amplifies this security risk to such a degree that JITs become a liability.

Recent work [9, 14, 11, 10, 22, 29] addresses code-reuse attacks by attacking its foundation: the software monoculture. By diversifying the binary code, attackers cannot construct reliable attack code, because the binary code layout differs for each end-user. Consequently, diversity increases the costs for attackers, ultimately rendering them too costly. Unfortunately, existing approaches to artificial software diversity do not protect dynamically emitted code from a just-in-time compiler. We address this challenge by describing the first fully automatic technique to diversify existing JIT compilers in a black-box fashion. Similar to the successful frontend-backend separation in traditional compilers, our proposed black-box approach has the advantage over a white-box solution—where developers would manually add diversification directly to JIT compiler source code—of not requiring duplicated work for every existing JIT compiler. Besides the obvious savings in implementation time, the black-box approach allows for faster time-to-market for patches, without having to rely on vendors to supply patches to known vulnerabilities. Another benefit is the added security for legacy JIT compilers available only in binary form, where extra defenses cannot be added by changing the source code.

Summing up, we make the following contributions:

- We present librando, the first automated software diversity solution for hardening existing JIT compilers in a black box fashion. Our solution implements two popular defensive techniques: NOP insertion and constant blinding.
- We describe two optimizations (the *Return Address Map* and optional white box diversification—taking advantage of compiler cooperation) to improve the performance of librando.
- We demonstrate applicability of black box diversification on two pervasive industrial-strength JIT compilers: Oracle's HotSpot (used in the Java Virtual Machine) and Google's V8 (used in the Chrome web browser). We then report the results of our analysis of librando performance. We show that we successfully protect:

  HotSpot (a JIT compiler for Java—a statically-typed language) with an overhead of 15%.

  V8 (a JIT compiler for JavaScript—a dynamically-typed language) with a slowdown of 3.5×.

2. BACKGROUND

A JIT compiler transforms a program written in a high-level language (HLL), generating native code at program run-time. The compiler emits native code into a code cache, after parsing and optimizing HLL source code. The compiler itself is written in another programming language, which we call the host language. JIT compilers also contain a language runtime, which is a library of functions that are written in the host language and provide or manage access to system resources. Some examples of such resources are files, networks, operating system threads and complex data structures (maps, trees). When compiling a HLL program, the JIT compiler emits native calls into the runtime whenever the program uses these resources. Figure 1 shows a high-level structure of a JIT compiler and its interactions with the generated code. After emitting all or part of the native code (usually enough code to start execution of the program), the compiler branches to the entry point of the HLL program. The generated code continues execution, calling into other generated functions or the language runtime. The HLL program continues until termination, making repeated calls into the runtime whenever needed.

From a security point of view, JIT compilers have one characteristic that is important in our context: predictability. As JIT compilers usually optimize code for performance, there are only a few optimal translations of HLL code to native code, and a JIT compiler emits one of these. When presented with the same HLL code many times repeatedly, a compiler will emit the same native code; attackers can use this characteristic to their advantage. This is not a problem specific to JIT compilers, but compilers in general; however, predictability of JIT compilers has not been fully explored.

JIT spraying [2] is one recent attack that relies on predictability of JIT compilers. This attack is a form of code injection targeted at dynamically generated code. In its original form, it relies on

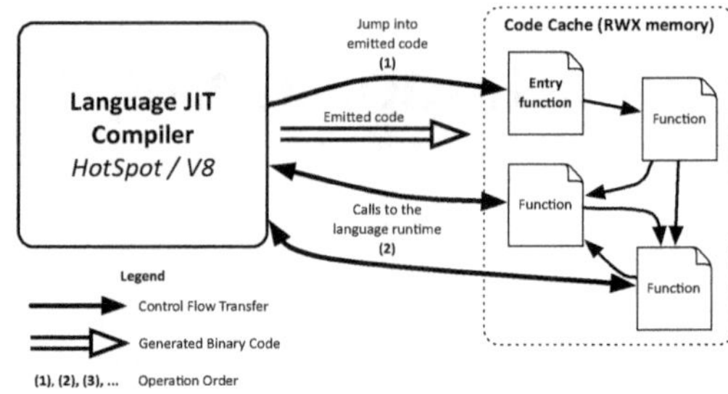

Figure 1: High-level structure of a JIT compiler.

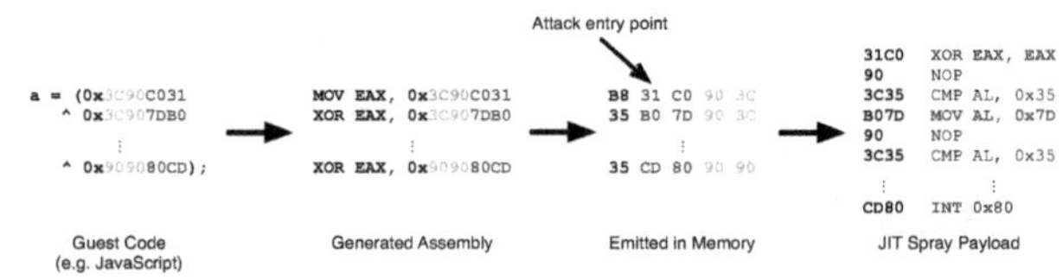

Figure 2: JIT spraying example. The 32-bit constants from HLL code (shown in light and dark grey) appear inside native code, in little-endian form.

one unintended behavior of many JIT compilers: HLL program constants reach native code unmodified, therefore becoming part of the executable code. The attacker injects short sequences (32-bit constants in the original paper), and later jumps to the injected sequence through a separate attack vector. Figure 2 shows an example of code injected using constants. For the attack to work, the attacker must also predict the remaining bytes inserted between the controlled sequences, and use those bytes as part of the payload; this is often possible in practice, due to the predictability of the compiler. This allows the attacker to execute arbitrary native code, even when running on a compiler that runs the generated code in a sandbox (with restricted access to memory, for example).

For many years, most arbitrary code execution attacks used the same method of gaining control of the program: code injection attacks. To prevent these, most operating systems now forbid the same page to be both writable and executable at the same time. Sidestepping this measure, a new class of attacks against applications surfaced and gained popularity: code reuse attacks. Instead of adding new executable code to an application, code reuse attacks locate reusable code sequences inside the application, then thread these sequences into a program written by the attacker. Shacham described one of the first versions of this attack, called Return-Oriented Programming (ROP) [26]; he named the code sequences *gadgets*. A gadget is simply a valid sequence of binary code that the attacker can execute successfully (the gadget decodes correctly and does not contain invalid instructions); a gadget can start anywhere inside the generated code (including in the middle of a proper instruction) and spans one or more of the original instructions emitted by the compiler. ROP uses only gadgets that end in a `RET` instruction (encoded by the `C3` byte on x86); the attacker places addresses of gadgets on the stack on consecutive stack slots, so that each gadget proceeds to the next one using a return. Later work [3] extends this idea to other indirect branch instructions.

This attack is even more potent in the presence of a JIT compiler, as an attacker that controls HLL code can emit an arbitrary amount of native code containing gadgets (by emitting as much HLL code as needed to generate all the gadgets for the attack); Figure 3 illustrates

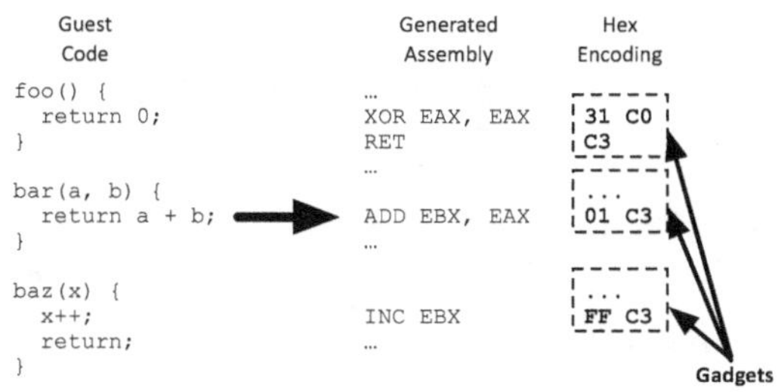

Figure 3: Code reuse example. The compiler transforms HLL code into native code containing ROP gadgets. The C3 byte encodes the RET instruction at the end of a gadget.

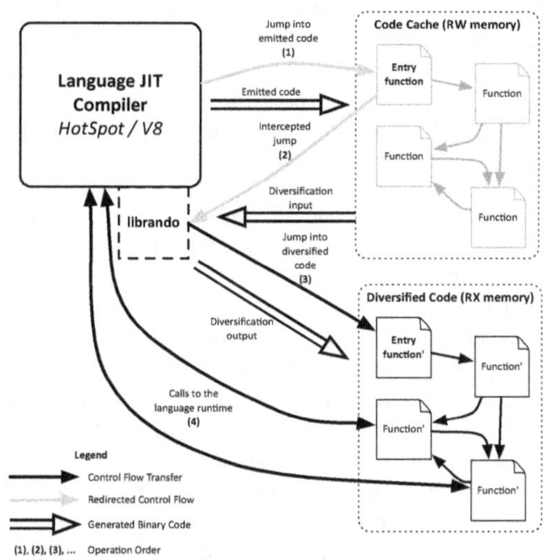

Figure 4: A JIT compiler with librando attached, with the control flow graph of the dynamically generated program. Greyed out edges represent branches that are redirected or never taken after diversification.

how HLL code sequences become gadgets. For example, this can be a problem for web browsers that include a JavaScript compiler, as many web pages include JavaScript code from unreliable (or hostile) sources. Another problem is that current anti-ROP defenses [16, 20, 22, 10, 14, 11] target ahead-of-time compilers or binary rewriters, but do not offer protection to dynamically generated code.

3. DESIGN

The librando library diversifies code generated by a JIT compiler. It reads all code emitted by the compiler, dissassembles the code, randomizes it, and then writes the randomized output to memory. Figure 4 shows the structure of dynamically generated code, as a function call graph.

The library diversifies dynamically-generated code under one of the following models (illustrated in Figure 5):

Black box diversification with no assistance from the compiler (the compiler is a black box and the library has no knowledge of compiler internals). The library attaches to the compiler and intercepts all branches into and out of dynamically-generated code, without requiring any changes to compiler internals.

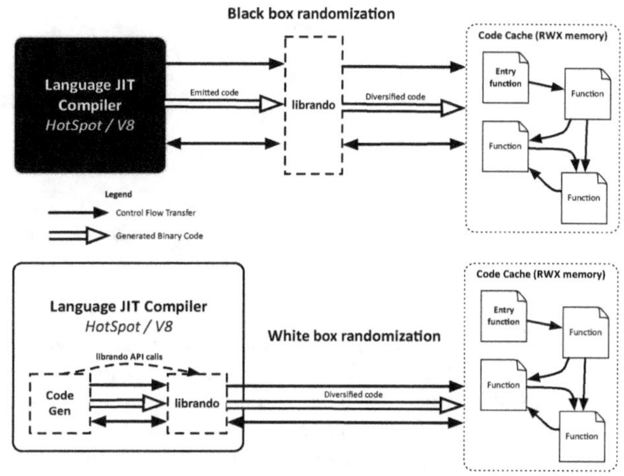

Figure 5: Black and white box diversification architecture.

White box diversification with some assistance from the compiler (the library has some knowledge of compiler internals). The code emitter notifies librando through an API when it starts running undiversified code. The library provides the diversified code addresses to the compiler, and the compiler executes diversified code directly. We change all compiler branches into emitted code to use the addresses returned by librando. This approach is intended as a middle ground between the previous model and a manual implementation of randomization for each compiler, and it requires that compiler source code is available.

As the first security measure, librando prevents execution of all code generated dynamically by the compiler. Instead, the library disassembles the code into a control flow graph, diversifies every basic block in this graph, and then writes the diversified blocks to a separate executable area. All branches (including function calls and returns) to the original undiversified code are redirected to the diversified code (Figure 6 shows an example of a diversified block). While the undiversified code remains available and writable, the compiler or HLL program cannot execute it anymore. The library intercepts all memory allocation functions (the mmap function family on Linux) that return executable memory, then removes the executable flag on all intercepted allocation requests. The library also keeps an internal list of all memory allocated by these requests, and uses this list to distinguish between accesses to undiversified code and all other memory accesses.

In the black box diversification model, the library transparently intercepts all branches to protected blocks. To do this, we protect all undiversified code pages against execution, then catch all attempts to execute these protected pages. The library installs a handler for the segmentation fault signal (SIGSEGV in Linux), which is raised whenever a processor instruction attempts to access memory it does not have permission for. Whenever the processor attempts to execute a non-executable page, it triggers a page fault in the MMU. The operating system handles this fault and calls our SIGSEGV signal handler. The library then redirects execution to diversified code.

While static disassembly of binary code accurately is impossible in the general case [6] (due to the need to distinguish code from data), dynamic disassembly is much simpler for one reason: we only

Undiversified

```
@0xB4EC52C0E0   CMP RAX, QWORD PTR [R13 - 40]
@0xB4EC52C0E4   JNE 0xB4EC52C0F6
@0xB4EC52C0EA   MOV RAX, 0x23E0A7104161
@0xB4EC52C0F4   JMP 0xB4EC52C100
```

Diversified

```
@0x0x7F8E7C952BCA   CMP RAX, QWORD PTR [R13 - 40]
                    NOP [90]
@0x0x7F8E7C952BCF   JNE 0x7F8E7C952BE3
@0x0x7F8E7C952BD5   MOV RAX, 0x23E0A7104161
                    NOP [66 90]
@0x0x7F8E7C952BE1   JMP 0x7F8E7C95339A
```

Figure 6: Block contents and diversification example.

disassemble bytes that we are certain represent code. Our use of signals guarantees this: the signal handler is always called when the JIT compiler executes an undiversified instruction at some address, so the bytes at that address (and the entire block starting at that address) are guaranteed to be code. The same is true for all blocks in the control flow graph containing that instruction, since we follow direct branches to find more code.

We make a few simplifying assumptions about the emitted code that reduced our implementation effort significantly:

No stack pointer reuse On the x86 architecture, the stack pointer register (RSP) is available as a general-purpose register. The x86 64-bit ABI reserves this register for its intended purpose, as stack register. However, compilers only need to follow the ABI when calling into external libraries and system code; they can ignore its guidelines inside emitted code. Code emitted by a JIT compiler might use another register to keep track of the HLL stack, and re-use RSP for another purpose. Generally, JIT compilers do not do this in practice, so we assume that this register always points to the top of a valid native stack. This allows both code emitted by the compiler and by librando to use several stack manipulation instructions, such as PUSH, CALL and RET.

No self-modifying code While it is possible for a JIT compiler to emit code that modifies itself, this is usually not the case. We assume that only the compiler can modify code. Once emitted code starts executing, it remains unchanged. This assumption simplifies our implementation, as we only have to detect code changes originating in the compiler itself; therefore, we can safely discard old versions of modified code, without the risk of having to continue execution inside discarded code.

Calls paired with returns Compilers often use the CALL x86 instruction for calls and RET for the corresponding returns, but not always. The former pushes the return address on the native stack and branches to a function, while the latter pops the return address and branches to it. There are equivalent instruction sequences with the same behavior which a compiler can use instead, perhaps to push/pop the return address to another stack. However, there is a performance penalty from using these sequences, as modern processors use an internal return address stack to improve branch prediction for CALL/RET pairs, and only for those pairs. A compiler optimized for performance always uses this combination for function calls, simplifying our implementation as well. Consequently, librando only needs to analyze and rewrite these instructions when redirecting function calls.

Our technique diversifies code by relocating emitted code blocks, rewriting the code, and inserting instructions. To preserve HLL program semantics, a diversification library must be transparent to both the compiler and the compiled program. We identified several pieces of program state which librando must preserve when rewriting code (related work [4, 17, 25] identifies a superset of these for general-purpose dynamic binary rewriters):

Processor register contents including the flags register. The library inserts instructions that hold intermediate values in registers. Also, some inserted instructions (like ADD and XOR) modify the processor flags register. The library attempts to only add instructions that do not change any registers or flags; where this is not possible, it temporarily saves the register(s) to the stack, performs the computation, then restores the register(s).

Native stack contents Some JIT compilers use the native stack for HLL code, while others switch to a separate stack when branching to HLL code. To support the former, the library must preserve all contents of the native stack inside diversified code. This must be true not only during execution of dynamically generated code, but also during calls into the runtime, as the runtime itself may read or write to the native stack. For example, the V8 runtime walks the native stack during garbage collection to find all pointers to data and code. Changing any such pointer or any other data on the stack leads to program errors and crashes. Therefore, native stack contents must be identical when running with and without librando. This includes return addresses; when a diversified function calls another diversified function, the former must push the undiversified address on the stack. Figure 7 illustrates this transformation. The original call pushes the address of the next instruction on the stack, then jumps to the called function. We replace it with a PUSH/JMP pair that pushes the undiversified return address. There is one exception to this restriction: we consider any memory past the top of the stack (below RSP) to be unused, so we use it to save registers.

Undiversified code instructions JIT compilers frequently emit code with temporary placeholders, then later replace them with other instructions. The compiler usually uses fixed instruction sequences for these placeholders, so it first checks their contents before patching. In other cases, certain instruction sequences are used to flag properties of emitted code. The library cannot modify any of the original, undiversified code in-place, as it cannot distinguish between regular code and these placeholders. Even if the compiler never reads back the former, it may read back and validate the contents of the latter, then crash or execute incorrectly. The library is required to preserve the undiversified code at all times, as originally emitted by the compiler.

POSIX signals Some JIT compilers (such as HotSpot) intercept POSIX signals and install their own handlers. We intercept the SIGSEGV signal to catch execution and write attempts on undiversified code, but pass all other signals (including SIGSEGV we do not handle) back to the JIT compiler.

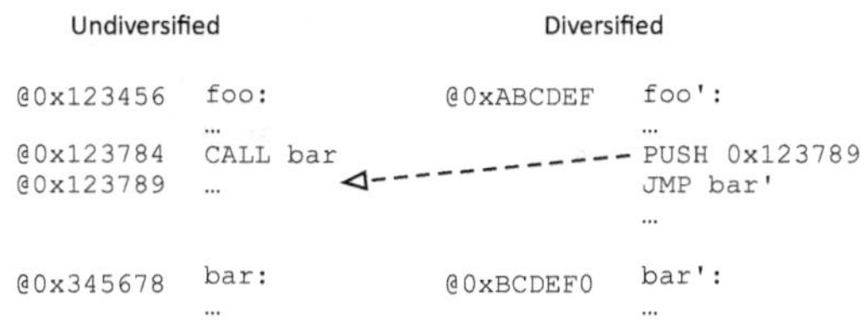

Figure 7: Rewriting the `CALL` instruction.

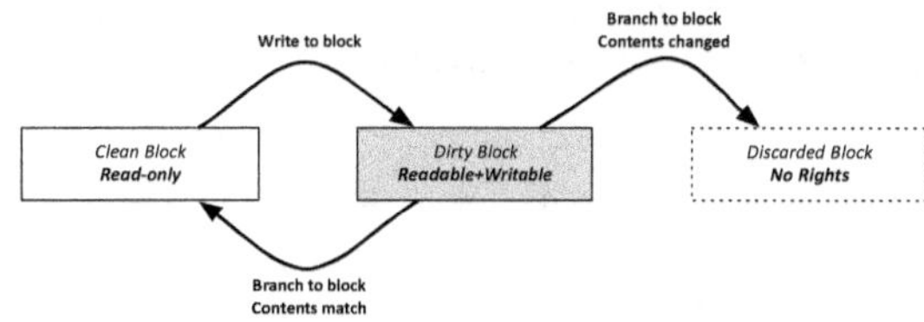

Figure 8: Per-block finite state machine that handles block changes.

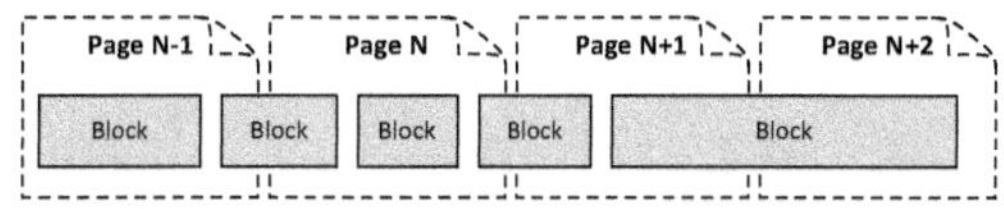

Figure 9: Blocks spanning several memory pages and crossing page boundaries.

3.1 Code Relocation

In our control flow graph, a block is a maximal continuous run of instructions, so that the block ends in an unconditional branch instruction, but contains no such instruction inside. We also break blocks at function calls (the `CALL` instruction) and returns, but not at conditional branches; a basic block can have one or more conditional branches inside. However, we use one heuristic to split blocks: whenever a block contains a number of consecutive zeroes over a given threshold, we break the block after a small number of those zeroes. This is needed because compilers sometimes emit code only partially (or lazily), initializing the remainder with zeroes. The compiler emits the rest of the code at a later moment, after some event triggers generation of the missing code. We implemented this heuristic to support the V8 compiler, which uses lazy code generation.

Many JIT compilers perform garbage collection on generated code, discarding unused code and reusing that space for new code. The compiler will write and later execute this new code in place of the old version. This happens frequently in the modern JIT compilers we investigated. We detect such changes, discard the diversified versions of old blocks, then read the new blocks and integrate them into the existing control flow graph. To detect all changes to a block, librando marks it read-only after diversification using the `mprotect` function on Linux. If the compiler writes to the block later, the library allows the write to succeed, but marks the block as dirty.

The `mprotect` function has one significant restriction: it can only change access rights on zones aligned to hardware pages; on x86, a page is 4096 bytes by default. There are several issues to consider when using `mprotect` to protect a block. First, a single page may contain more than one block. Second, a block may be spread across several consecutive pages. Third, for each page, one or two blocks might cross its boundaries, one at each end. Figure 9 shows examples of all three cases. Instead of marking a block as read-only, librando actually marks all pages containing that block as read-only. However, those pages may contain other blocks that the compiler might never modify.

After librando marks a page as read-only, the operating system starts notifying the library of all writes to read-only pages. We also use POSIX signals to receive these notifications. The operating system calls the `SIGSEGV` signal handler each time a processor instruction tries to write to a protected page, as long as the page is protected. However, this occurs before the actual instruction writes the data; we have to either emulate the instruction itself (while keeping the page read-only), or make the page writable and allow the original instruction to execute. As emulating x86 instructions correctly requires significant development effort, we choose the latter solution. However, once we allow writes to a page, there is no way to catch each write to that page separately; the processor will allow all writes to succeed without generating a page fault. At this point, the only information available to librando is that at least one byte in that page may have been modified, but nothing more. Therefore, we mark all blocks contained in a writable page as dirty. The next time librando intercepts a branch to undiversified code, it checks all dirty blocks to verify that the VM has actually modified their contents. The library only discards and re-diversifies changed blocks, keeping unchanged blocks as they are. Figure 8 shows this process per block, in the form of a finite state machine.

To check whether a block has been modified, the library compares the new contents of the block against its original contents. However, this requires that two copies of each block be stored: the original and current code. To save memory space, we do not store both copies in memory; instead, each block stores a hash code of its original contents. Every time librando checks if a block has been modified, it hashes the current contents of the block and compares the hash code to the one stored in the block. If the hash codes match, librando assumes that the block has not been changed; otherwise, it discards the block. While there is a very small possibility of collision (where the contents of a block change, but the hash remains the same), we performed all our experiments and benchmarks successfully with this optimization. A librando user has the option of disabling hashing and verifying the entire contents of blocks, which guarantees correctness.

The user attaches librando to a JIT compiler in one of several ways: either by linking it (statically or dynamically) to the compiler, or through the `LD_PRELOAD` environment variable on Linux. The latter mechanism preloads a library into a process at program start-up time, allowing the library to override some of the program's symbols. We used the latter approach in our evaluation, but the former is preferred in an actual deployment for increased security.

3.2 Diversification

The main security benefits from librando come from rewriting the generated code. We propose two rewriting techniques that harden the generated code against attacks.

NOP Insertion. Code reuse attacks rely on the code having predictable location (address) and contents. We implement one fine-grained instruction-level code layout randomization technique: *NOP insertion*. To randomize code layout, we randomly insert NOP instructions (instructions without effects) into the diversified blocks, between the existing instructions. This technique has been used successfully in other work to change instruction or block align-

```
Data: Input block B. Probability p of NOP insertion.
Result: Block B with NOPs inserted.
begin
    for each instruction i ∈ B do
        Pick a random real number in [0.0, 1.0]
        v ← random()
        if v < p then
            i → insert(randomNOP())
        end
    end
end
```

Algorithm 1: NOP insertion algorithm.

ment to improve performance [12], security [18, 31, 14, 11], or provide contention mitigation [28]. NOP insertion pushes each proper instruction forward by a random offset (the total length of all preceding inserted NOPs), making the location of each instruction more difficult to predict. Since the total length of NOPs accumulates as more instructions are added, uncertainty of code addresses increases as more code is generated. This technique makes it difficult for an attacker to predict not only addresses of known code, but also distances between known locations. The attacker might try to learn the address of some known code object, and access all other code relatively to this address. This requires that the attacker know relative locations of code in advance; NOP insertion makes this much less likely, since NOPs displace instructions randomly.

We implemented the algorithm (shown in Algorithm 1) as a single linear-time pass over the instructions in each block. After each proper instruction, the algorithm decides whether to insert a NOP or not by coin toss. In our tests, we set the probability of NOP insertion to $p = 0.5$, but this can be adjusted for better performance or more security. If the algorithm inserts a NOP, the next step picks a NOP randomly from a set of candidates. We used the smallest three NOP instructions from the set of canonical NOPs recommended by the Intel architecture manual [13]: `90`, `66 90`, and `0F 1F 00`.

Constant Blinding. We previously described JIT spraying as an example of a code injection attack against JIT compilers. In general, these attacks rely on the compiler emitting native code that contains some binary sequence from the source-program as-is. In the particular case of JIT spraying, this sequence is a set of 32-bit constants emitted as immediate operands to x86 instructions. Recently, JavaScript compilers have started to implement their own defensive measures particular to this attack [24]. There are two ways that a HLL program value winds up in the executable code region: the compiler stores the value either close to the code (without executing it as code), or as an immediate instruction operand. In the former case, NOP insertion shifts the location of the value by a random offset, making its location hard to guess. For the latter case, there is one simple solution based on obfuscation: emit each immediate operand in an encrypted form, then decrypt its value at run-time using a few extra instructions. We pick a random value (a *cookie*) for every operand, blind the operand using the cookie, emit the original instruction with the blinded immediate, then emit the decryption code. While other implementations use an XOR operation for encryption, we do not use it since it alters the arithmetic flags, so librando would have to save them. Fortunately, the processor provides an addition in struction that leaves the flags intact: `LEA`. Therefore, we blind the original value by subtracting the cookie from it, then add an immediate-operand `LEA` to add the cookie back. Figure 10 shows an example of this transformation.

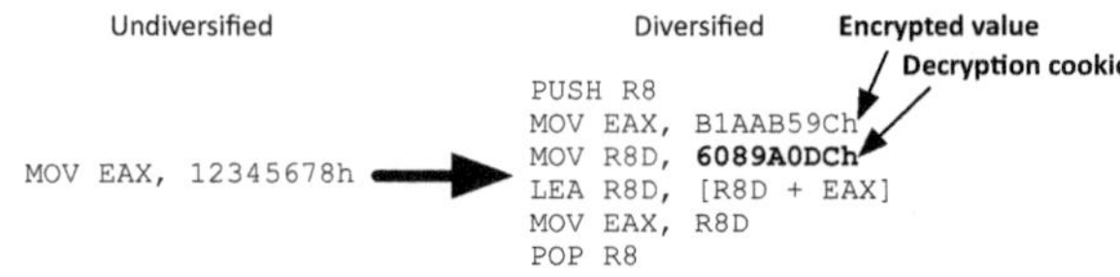

Figure 10: Example of blinding the immediate operand of an instruction. `12345678h` is replaced with `B1AAB59Ch`+`6089A0DCh` (modulo 2^{32}).

Operation	Form	Opcode
MOV	MOV EAX, imm32	B8
	MOV ECX, imm32	B9
	...	
	MOV EDI, imm32	BF
	MOV reg, imm32	C7
PUSH	PUSH imm32	68
IMUL	IMUL reg, reg, imm32	69
TEST	TEST EAX, imm32	A9
	TEST reg, imm32	F7
Arithmetic	op reg, imm32	81
	ADD EAX, imm32	05
	OR EAX, imm32	0D
	ADC EAX, imm32	15
	...	
	CMP EAX, imm32	3D

Table 1: x86 instructions with 32-bit immediate operands. The arithmetic class contains `ADD`, `ADC`, `SUB`, `SBB`, `AND`, `OR`, `XOR` and `CMP`.

The x86 architecture supports 8-, 16-, 32- and 64-bit immediate values for many instructions. We encountered only the latter two types in most code we analyzed, so we implemented only these sizes; the others can be trivially added. Table 1 shows all x86 instructions that accept a 32-bit immediate. There is only a single instruction that accepts a 64-bit immediate (the `REX.W + B8` encoding of `MOV`). Everytime librando encounters one of these instructions, it transforms the instruction to the equivalent encrypted sequence. Each instruction from Table 1 was sufficiently different from the others, so we implemented different blinding code manually for each type of instruction.

3.3 Optimizations

Intercepting branches to all generated code and rewriting their contents has a cost in program performance, as our evaluation will show. We propose several optimizations to our approach to reduce this cost as much as possible.

The Return Address Map. One of the restrictions of our design was transparency of the native stack. Even when executing diversified code, the native stack must have the same contents as it would have under undiversified code. We meet this requirement through one change: we rewrite call instructions to push undiversified return addresses on the stack, as shown in Figure 7. However, this has one significant drawback: the later `RET` matching the replaced call pops the undiversified address and branches to it. Since this address is now non-executable, this generates a page fault and a call to our signal handler. As the `SIGSEGV` handler is called after the processor interrupts the execution of another instruction, the operating system saves a lot of processor state before calling the handler; this makes signal handlers very slow. For this reason, `RET` instructions in diversified code are also expensive.

Undiversified → Diversified

```
RET   ──►   # Load return address into RDI
            MOV RDI, DWORD PTR [RSP]
            CALL RAM_lookup
            # If lookup did not return a diversified address
            # then keep the original
            CMP RAX, RDI
            JE return
            # otherwise, replace the undiversified return address
            MOV DWORD PTR [RSP], RAX

            return:
            RET
```

Figure 11: Rewriting the `RET` instruction to use the *Return Address Map*.

To improve performance, we prevent the `SIGSEGV` signal from being triggered. We rewrite return instructions, adding code to handle the case when the return address is in undiversified code that also has a corresponding diversified address. In as few instructions as possible, the diversified `RET` instruction now looks for the return address in a data structure that maps undiversified to diversified addresses (we call this data structure the *Return Address Map*). If an entry is found, execution continues in diversified code; otherwise, the original address is used as-is. Figure 11 shows how this optimization rewrites the `RET` instruction.

We store the address mapping in a hash map. We require a data structure that supports three operations: lookup, insertion and removal. The library adds the addresses of a block to the map whenever it diversifies the block, then removes the addresses when it discards the block. One significant factor in the choice of data structure is that lookups are far more frequent than the other operations (every `RET` performs a lookup), so the data structure implementation must perform the former as efficiently as possible. We use a cuckoo hash map for this goal [21], as it provides both fast constant-time lookups (we implemented a lookup function in 28 lines of assembly code) and good memory utilization.

As returns are essentially just indirect branches (a pop followed by a branch to the popped value), we also use this data structure to optimize all other indirect branches. We extend the map to all basic block addresses (not just return addresses), then prepend hash map lookups to all branches with unknown targets (where the target is not a direct address, but one loaded from a register or memory).

White Box Diversification. With the *Return Address Map* handling all diversified-to-diversified-code indirect branches, and the rewriting of all direct branches to target diversified code, the signal handler only intercepts branches entering or exiting the diversified code (mainly the compiler and the language runtime). Some HLL programs make many calls to the runtime (either explicitly as function calls, or implicitly through language features or inline caches), so the overhead from the signal handler remains significant. This overhead is difficult to reduce without making changes to the compiler itself, so the next step in optimization is **white box diversification**. Under this model, librando provides an interface to the compiler, which the latter uses to notify the former of branches to generated code, with the goal of avoiding the signal handler. JIT compilers frequently have one or a few centralized places in their source code that all jumps to generated code pass through; by manually inserting calls to librando in these few places, we can significantly reduce the overhead of compiler-to-undiversified-code jumps. For example, we identified a single function in V8 (called `FUNCTION_CAST`) that returns the memory address of a JavaScript function; by inserting a single line that calls librando from `FUNCTION_CAST`, we completely intercepted all indirect jumps and function calls from V8 to generated code.

In many cases, functions in the language runtime are implemented in a host language such as C; generated code calls these functions directly (using the `CALL` instruction), and control flow returns from the runtime to generated code not through explicit branches, but through function returns. A host language compiler (gcc, for example) generates these returns automatically, so we cannot manually insert calls to librando for all of them. Also, programs written in a higher-level language usually do not have direct access to the native stack, so they cannot change the return address through host language code. For this reason, we implemented a compiler-level extension for LLVM that adds a new function attribute–`rando_hash_return`. The compiler adds calls to librando at the return sites of all functions marked with this attribute; whenever such a function returns, librando checks whether the function returns to undiversified code or not. As there is no automatic analysis that can determine whether a runtime function is called from the runtime or not, the librando user has to find all functions that can be called from generated code and manually add this flag to all of them[1].

Table 2 shows the two operations that librando provides to the compiler. Using only this small API, most (if not all) invocations of the signal handler disappear.

4. EVALUATION

We implemented librando as a dynamic library for Linux and loaded it into compilers using the `LD_PRELOAD` mechanism. We evaluated the performance impact of librando on two JIT compilers: V8 (the JavaScript compiler included in the Google Chrome browser) and HotSpot (the Java client compiler from Oracle). We ran all benchmarks on a 2.2GHz Intel Xeon E5-2660 system with 32 GiB of memory, running Ubuntu Linux with kernel version 3.2.0.

First, we benchmarked V8 using the benchmark suite included with the compiler. These benchmarks stress different parts of the compiler (integer operation optimizations, floating points optimizations, inline caches, regular expression implementation) differently, and the overhead of librando varies accordingly. We sought to determine the performance impact of control flow rewriting (without diversification), our proposed optimizations, as well as the diversification techniques. We first tested librando under the black box model without optimizations or randomizations, and gradually added them one by one in the following order: the `Return Address Map` (RAM), NOP insertion, then constant blinding. We then implemented white box randomization by manually changing V8 to interact with librando (we changed 70 lines of code in total), then ran all the benchmarks again to measure the effects of this interaction.

Figure 12 shows the results of our tests. The benchmark suite reported both a per-test score, as well as the geometric mean of all benchmarks (the `Total` column). The overall impact of librando on the V8 benchmark suite is around 3.5x, with all optimizations and randomizations enabled; without randomizations, this overhead is approximately 2.7x. This overhead is not uniform across all benchmarks; `NavierStokes`, for example, shows an overhead between 1.2× and 1.4×. The fastest benchmarks (as well as the second best-performing one, `Crypto`) have a similar structure where the impact of our approach is small: nested loops of primitive numeric operations, where the types of variables are mostly static (either integers or numbers). Most of the time spent in these benchmarks

[1]Most such functions in V8 are defined using a macro called `RUNTIME_FUNCTION`, so we easily added the flag by searching for all uses of this macro.

Function	Description
`rando_redirect(addr)`	Diversifies (if needed) the code starting at `addr` and returns the diversified address
`rando_hash_return()`	Checks the return address of the current function and replaces it with the diversified equivalent

Table 2: Application Programming Interface provided by librando.

is in a highly-optimized loop that does not branch or call outside the loop. The V8 compiler emits very well optimized code once for such structures, then executes it for a substantial amount of time. Primitive operations are implemented directly as native instructions, so they contain very few calls to the runtime.

Second, we benchmarked the HotSpot client compiler for Java, using the Computer Language Shootout Game benchmarks [8]. Figure 13 shows the per-benchmark slowdown factor for each benchmark, as well as the geometric mean over all four tests. Note that the overall slowdown is smaller for HotSpot; the main cause for this is that Java is a statically-typed object-oriented language, where the data types of values are known ahead-of-time. While Java object instances can have different types at runtime (based on the program class hierarchy), primitive values have fixed types and primitive operations can be emitted very efficiently on the first attempt. HotSpot needs to collect substantially less type information than V8, as so much is already available, so it requires a lot less time to fully optimize a program. In our Java benchmarks, we see the same behavior we saw in the `NavierStokes` test for V8. We see an average slowdown of about 1.08× (a procentual slowdown of 8%) for rewriting and around 1.15× (15%) with full diversification. However, as the impact of rewriting is now much smaller, we start to notice a significant impact from NOP insertion. Since so much of the benchmarks's execution time is now spent in a very small loop (a few instructions in length), every extra instruction starts to count. On `fannkuchredux`, NOP insertion at $p_{\mathrm{NOP}} = 0.5$ almost triples the overhead (from 15% to almost 40%).

In addition to these tests, we also ran the same benchmarks on V8 and HotSpot without the *Return Address Map* optimization. V8 showed an average slowdown factor of 50× (with a maximum of 232× for `EarleyBoyer`), much higher than the 2.7× slowdown for the optimized version. The impact on HotSpot is less severe (about 1.6× slowdown without `RAM` as opposed to 1.08× with it), but still substantial. The `Return Address Map` optimization is crucial to librando performance. However, we leave further enhancements to our choice and implementation of data structure (cuckoo hash with hand-implemented lookup) to future work, as some of our experiments showed that there is still room for some improvements. We ran the Language Shootout benchmark `binarytreesredux` (a recursive binary tree implementation in Java that makes extensive use of function calls) on HotSpot and observed a slowdown of approximately 70x, even with the `RAM` optimization enabled. Further profiling of both this benchmark and all V8 benchmarks showed that around 25% of time spent inside librando takes place inside the `RAM` lookup function, even with our optimized implementation (28 assembly instructions in total).

Overall, the performance impact depends greatly on the structure and goal of the HLL program, but also on features of the HLL. As we have shown, a statically-typed but just-in-time-compiled language has much lower diversification overhead than a dynamically-typed program. Another factor to account for is the ratio of time spent in generated code versus time spent in the compiler or runtime. This technique has higher overhead when new code is generated with high frequency (as is the case with dynamically-typed languages), and on other transitions from generated code to the outside. However, synthetic CPU-bound benchmarks are not completely representative of the average workload of a JIT compiler; these benchmarks perform very little input/output operations, and the time spent in the few such operations is small. In contrast, real-world code interacts much more with the rest of the system, and also makes much more use of external libraries. When the execution time of a program is dominated by input and output, or by calls to libraries, the overhead should be much smaller. Our results show an upper-bound for this overhead. This upper-bound is also not necessarily significant in a real-world application; for example, we linked the Chrome browser to librando and used it to visit various web pages, some only containing static content and some using JavaScript heavily. We observed no noticeable degradation in browsing experience.

5. RANDOMIZATION DISCUSSION

We designed librando as a framework for intercepting and securing dynamically-generated code. While the library only supports two randomization techniques at present, the design allows for more to be easily added. Based on our experience implementing the current randomizations, we believe new ones could be added without much effort. Examples of possible randomizations include (related work [9, 14, 22, 29] also discusses and implements some of these for statically-generated code diversification):

mmap Address Randomization On current operating systems, ASLR guarantees that addresses returned by mapping functions (`mmap` and similar) are randomized. However, this required that ASLR is supported and enabled on the system. In many cases, it is possible for the program (or librando) to ask for a mapping at a specific address, instead of letting the operating system pick the address. By asking for a randomized address, librando can add address randomization even on systems where ASLR is not enabled (some systems also allow for ASLR to be disabled on a per-program basis, so librando could be used only on those programs).

Basic Block Reordering Our diversifier can emit basic blocks in any order (although some orders have better performance than others, due to spatial locality). While we currently impose no order on the blocks, the implementation can be extended to explicitly reorder blocks randomly. This randomization would be complementary to address randomization and NOP insertion; the former randomizes the location of the entire executable region of code, basic block reordering would reorder blocks inside the region and NOP insertion would randomize instructions inside each block. The techniques would operate at different levels of granularity to provide even more randomization of the location of an instruction.

Equivalent Instruction Substitution The x86 instruction set has several possible encodings for some of the most used instructions. Randomly replacing some of these encodings with equivalent ones changes the code without changing its behavior. In other cases, it is possible to change one or more instruction with an equivalent sequence of other instructions, while also maintaining behavior. Making such changes has a similar effect on security as NOP insertion.

Register Re-allocation Register operands are encoded inside one or more bytes of an x86 instruction. By randomizing the

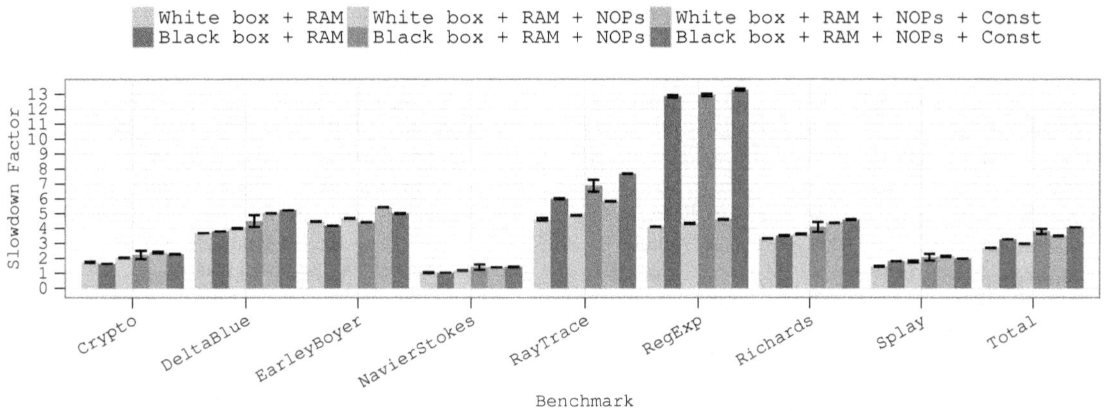

Figure 12: V8 benchmark results.

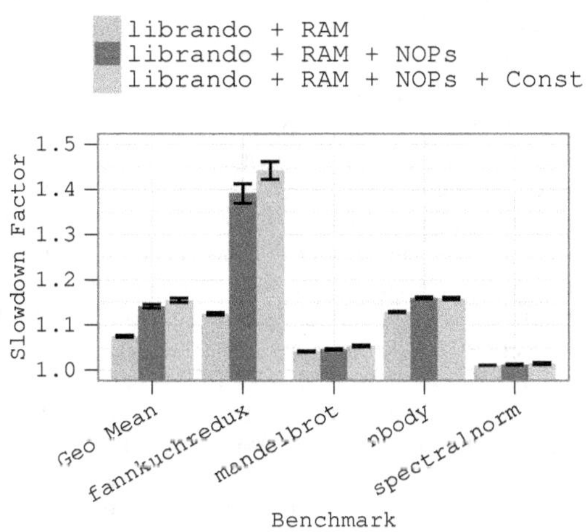

Figure 13: HotSpot benchmark results.

registers allocated to program values, librando can randomize instruction encoding further. However, this requires a dataflow analysis stage to identify the unique values stored in physical registers and their live ranges.

Instruction Reordering As an alternative (or complement) to inserting NOPs, we could reorder the instructions of each basic block. However, this requires that all dataflow dependencies are preserved; an instruction that generates a value cannot be moved after instructions that use the value. This requires running an algorithm to determine all data dependencies.

6. RELATED WORK

6.1 JIT Compiler Protection

One way of improving JIT compiler security is manually adding security checks and diversity by modifying the compiler. JITDefender [5] hinders JIT spraying attacks by marking all HLL code pages as non-executable; the compiler changes these pages to executable on entry to the generated code, and changes them back on return to the compiler or runtime. This effectively prevents an attacker from redirecting any other branch (other than the intended ones) to dynamically generated code. INSeRT [30] adds code randomization (concretely, it randomizes the operand of every emitted instruction) through a white box approach, requiring manual changes to the native code emitter inside the compiler. Both approaches successfully hinder most JIT spraying and code reuse attacks against HLL code, but require changes to the compiler; they are not feasible when source code is not available, or the modified code cannot be deployed. On the other hand, librando can harden a compiler without requiring any cooperation from the compiler itself.

A similar line of research investigates JIT code generation from inside a sandbox (where control flow is restricted, and code must follow certain restrictions). Native Client [31] is a sandboxed execution environment which adds static checks to native code that enforces restrictions on branch targets (such as 16-byte alignment for all targets). The original implementation of the system did not allow dynamic code generation at all, but later work [1] added this feature. The JIT extensions adds an API to the sandbox that a JIT compiler uses to generate new code; before executing that code, the sandbox verifies that the new code respects all restrictions imposed by Native Client, and therefore cannot break out of the sandbox. Another of their contributions was an in-depth analysis on the different types of NOPs to insert, which they use to enforce basic block alignment; here, we use NOPs for randomization. This is, in some ways, similar to our white box diversification approach: librando can be viewed as the sandbox that the JIT compiler runs inside.

6.2 Software Diversity

Cohen [6] first introduced the idea of raising the costs to the attacker by randomization, and presented several possible ways of doing this: equivalent instruction substitution, instruction reordering, extra jump or call insertions and many others. Forrest et al. [7] later described one of the first practical implementations of these ideas, randomizing the layout of the program stack and global variables. They demonstrate that software diversity increases security (preventing stack-based attacks) with a small performance overhead.

Address space layout randomization (ASLR) is an operating system-level randomization technique that places parts of the program at random addresses. While this is not possible for the entire program (executable code is typically compiled as position-dependent code that must be loaded at fixed addresses), it is active for some significant areas like the stack and memory obtained from `mmap`. This technique is enabled on all major operating systems (Windows, Linux, Mac OS) and has significant security benefits. However, it is not a sufficient security measure against code reuse attacks, since only the base address of a region is randomized. If the attacker somehow determines that base address, they gain access to the rest of the code as well, as the contents remain the same and in the same positions. Researchers have shown that ASLR has very low entropy on 32-bit systems [27] (taking just a few minutes to find the base address by brute force), so ASLR by itself does not provide strong security. It may be possible to find the randomized base address even on 64-bit systems through means other than brute force (for example, through some other information leak in the application).

A more fine-grained defense against code reuse attacks is code randomization. Recent years have seen a resurgence of this approach; related work randomizes code layout at the compiler level [9, 14, 11], virtual machine level [10] or through static binary rewriting [22, 29]. These implementations use various randomization techniques to diversify code: instruction and basic block reordering, register re-allocation, instruction substitution and NOP insertion (we discuss these techniques in Section 5). Much progress has been made in this area in a short while, showing that diversification has a positive impact on software security with negligible impact on performance. However, these defenses only diversify code available to the compiler or rewriter; even virtual machine-based solutions [10] rely on some rewriting of the main program binary itself. To our knowledge, no existing code layout randomization implementation handles dynamically generated code.

6.3 Binary Rewriting

There is significant research into dynamic rewriting of program code at run-time. DynamoRIO [4], PIN [17], Valgrind [19], and Strata [25] all intercept and rewrite program code at run-time, for purposes such as instrumentation, profiling, identifying program errors and increasing security The transparency restrictions in their designs are very similar to the restrictions we described for librando. However, one difference that sets librando apart from other rewriters is the limited scope of code rewriting: librando only intercepts and rewrites dynamically generated code, whereas all other rewriters handle all of the application code. For static program code, we envision that a compiler-level diversification solution is used on statically generated code; librando is only meant to diversify code which ahead-of-time diversification solution cannot protect. Our approach allows the JIT compiler and language runtime to run natively, only intercepting dynamically generated code; all other solutions would intercept and rewrite everything, starting with the first instruction in the JIT compiler. Another difference is that dynamic rewriters are designed as frameworks that allow arbitrary changes to the intercepted code, which increases their complexity significantly, whereas the magnitude of our changes to the code is very small and security-focused (adding NOPs and rewriting instruction operands). For example, Valgrind disassembles executed code and converts it to an intermediate representation (IR), which all code transformations operate on. After all transformations are done, Valgrind converts this IR back to x86 code; this two-way translation is not needed by librando.

Existing dynamic binary rewriters have been used for security. Program Shepherding [15] (implemented using DynamoRIO) and libdetox [23] add security checks before branches, function calls and system calls by intercepting and rewriting program blocks. These checks only allow branches to allowed code addresses, determined algorithmically or from a given list. This effectively defends against code reuse attacks (and more), albeit using a different approach from diversification. Our proposed solution has similar goals, but different methods: we randomize code layout, restricting whatever knowledge the attacker possesses of program code. While deterministic techniques are successful at hardening applications, they are also vulnerable in one regard: if an attacker finds a flaw in such a technique, they are able to attack all hardened targets using this flaw. Randomization, on the other hand, does not assume safety of the defense itself; instead, the goal is to restrict any successful attack to only a small subset of possible targets.

7. CONCLUSIONS

Traditional code injection attacks are becomming increasingly hard. This prompted the evolution of attacks targeted at JITs: JIT spraying and code reuse attacks. We describe librando, a binary rewriting library that hardens JIT compilers, and generally any software that generates new code at run-time, against these attacks. Our library supports randomization of code from a JIT compiler without requiring any internal changes to the compiler. This approach is portable to any existing or new compiler, providing increased security while saving man-months or -years of development effort; instead of having to redo the effort of implementing security measures on every JIT, developers may opt to use our library to secure their compiler. The library can also be used as an interim measure, providing security at a temporary performance penalty until security measures are implemented more efficiently in the compiler itself. In cases where compiler source code is not available, or where recompilation and reinstallation are not feasible, this penalty is preferable to the loss in security. If compiler source code is available, compiler developers can improve diversification performance through white box diversification, by adding calls from the compiler to librando. We also presented an optimization with substantial impact on performance: the *Return Address Map*. We successfully tested our work on two industrial-strength JIT compilers, both widely used at present. Our evaluation showed that the impact of diversification depends greatly on the workload; librando provides great security benefits at low performance cost (around 15%) for statically-typed languages (where it can be enabled at all times), and at a larger cost (a 3-4× slowdown) for dynamically-typed languages.

We have extended the reach of automated software diversity to also encompass code generated by a JIT compiler. While we are sure that we have not seen the last of JIT specific attacks, librando gives defenders a quick and comprehensive response.

8. ACKNOWLEDGMENTS

We thank the anonymous reviewers for their insightful comments and suggestions.

This material is based upon work partially supported by the Defense Advanced Research Projects Agency (DARPA) under contracts D11PC20024 and N660001-1-2-4014, by the National Science Foundation (NSF) under grant No. CCF-1117162, and by a gift from Google. Any opinions, findings, and conclusions or recommendations expressed in this material are those of the authors and do not necessarily reflect the views of the Defense Advanced Research Projects Agency (DARPA), its Contracting Agents, the National Science Foundation, or any other agency of the U.S. Government.

9. REFERENCES

[1] J. Ansel, P. Marchenko, U. Erlingsson, E. Taylor, B. Chen, D. L. Schuff, D. Sehr, C. L. Biffle, and B. Yee.

Language-independent sandboxing of just-in-time compilation and self-modifying code. In *Proceedings of the 32nd ACM SIGPLAN Conference on Programming Language Design and Implementation*, pages 355–366, 2011.

[2] D. Blazakis. Interpreter exploitation. In *Proceedings of the 4th USENIX Workshop on Offensive technologies*, WOOT'10, 2010.

[3] T. Bletsch, X. Jiang, V. Freeh, and Z. Liang. Jump-oriented programming: a new class of code-reuse attack. In *Proceedings of the 6th ACM Symposium on Information, Computer and Communications Security*, ASIACCS '11, pages 30–40, 2011.

[4] D. Bruening, T. Garnett, and S. Amarasinghe. An infrastructure for adaptive dynamic optimization. In *Proceedings of the 2003 International Symposium on Code Generation and Optimisation*, CGO '03, 2003.

[5] P. Chen, Y. Fang, B. Mao, and L. Xie. JITDefender: A defense against JIT spraying attacks. In *Proceedings of the 26th IFIP TC 11 International Information Security Conference*, SEC '11, pages 142–153, 2011.

[6] F. Cohen. Operating system protection through program evolution. *Computers and Security*, 12(6):565–584, Oct. 1993.

[7] S. Forrest, A. Somayaji, and D. Ackley. Building diverse computer systems. In *Proceedings of the 6th Workshop on Hot Topics in Operating Systems*, HotOS '97, pages 67–72, 1997.

[8] B. Fulgham. The computer language benchmarks game. `http://shootout.alioth.debian.org/`, 2012.

[9] C. Giuffrida, A. Kuijsten, and A. S. Tanenbaum. Enhanced operating system security through efficient and fine-grained address space randomization. In *Proceedings of the 21st USENIX Security Symposium*, pages 475–490, 2012.

[10] J. Hiser, A. Nguyen-Tuong, M. Co, M. Hall, and J. W. Davidson. ILR: Where'd my gadgets go? In *Proceedings of the 33rd IEEE Symposium on Security and Privacy*, S&P '12, pages 571–585, 2012.

[11] A. Homescu, S. Neisius, P. Larsen, S. Brunthaler, and M. Franz. Profile-guided automated software diversity. In *Proceedings of the 2013 International Symposium on Code Generation and Optimization*, CGO '13, 2013.

[12] R. Hundt, E. Raman, M. Thuresson, and N. Vachharajani. Mao – an extensible micro-architectural optimizer. In *Proceedings of the 9th IEEE/ACM International Symposium on Code Generation and Optimization*, CGO '11, pages 1–10, 2011.

[13] Intel Corporation. *Intel 64 and IA-32 Architectures Software Developer's Manual*, August 2012.

[14] T. Jackson, B. Salamat, A. Homescu, K. Manivannan, G. Wagner, A. Gal, S. Brunthaler, C. Wimmer, and M. Franz. Compiler-generated software diversity. In S. Jajodia, A. K. Ghosh, V. Swarup, C. Wang, and X. S. Wang, editors, *Moving Target Defense*, volume 54 of *Advances in Information Security*, pages 77–98. Springer New York, 2011.

[15] V. Kiriansky, D. Bruening, and S. Amarasinghe. Secure execution via program shepherding. In *Proceedings of the 11th USENIX Security Symposium*, pages 191–206, 2002.

[16] J. Li, Z. Wang, X. Jiang, M. Grace, and S. Bahram. Defeating return-oriented rootkits with "return-less" kernels. In *Proceedings of the 5th European Conference on Computer Systems*, EuroSys '10, pages 195–208, 2010.

[17] C.-K. Luk, R. Cohn, R. Muth, H. Patil, A. Klauser, G. Lowney, S. Wallace, V. J. Reddi, and K. Hazelwood. Pin: building customized program analysis tools with dynamic instrumentation. In *Proceedings of the ACM SIGPLAN 2005 Conference on Programming Language Design and Implementation*, PLDI '05, pages 190–200, 2005.

[18] S. McCamant and G. Morrisett. Evaluating SFI for a CISC architecture. In *Proceedings of the 15th USENIX Security Symposium*, pages 209–224, 2006.

[19] N. Nethercote and J. Seward. Valgrind: A program supervision framework. *Electronic Notes in Theoretical Computer Science*, 2003.

[20] K. Onarlioglu, L. Bilge, A. Lanzi, D. Balzarotti, and E. Kirda. G-Free: Defeating return-oriented programming through gadget-less binaries. In *Proceedings of the 26th Annual Computer Security Applications Conference*, ACSAC '10, pages 49–58, 2010.

[21] R. Pagh and F. F. Rodler. Cuckoo hashing. *Journal of Algorithms*, 51(2):122–144, 2004.

[22] V. Pappas, M. Polychronakis, and A. D. Keromytis. Smashing the gadgets: Hindering return-oriented programming using in-place code randomization. In *Proceedings of the 33rd IEEE Symposium on Security and Privacy*, S&P '12, pages 601–615, 2012.

[23] M. Payer and T. R. Gross. Fine-grained user-space security through virtualization. In *Proceedings of the 2011 ACM SIGPLAN/SIGOPS International Conference on Virtual Execution Environments*, VEE '11, pages 157–168, 2011.

[24] C. Rohlf and Y. Ivnitskiy. Attacking clientside JIT compilers. In *Black Hat USA*, 2011.

[25] K. Scott, N. Kumar, S. Velusamy, B. R. Childers, J. W. Davidson, and M. L. Soffa. Retargetable and reconfigurable software dynamic translation. In *Proceedings of the 2003 International Symposium on Code Generation and Optimisation*, CGO '03, 2003.

[26] H. Shacham. The geometry of innocent flesh on the bone: Return-into-libc without function calls (on the x86). In *Proceedings of the 14th ACM Conference on Computer and Communications Security*, CCS '07, pages 552–561, 2007.

[27] H. Shacham, M. Page, B. Pfaff, E. Goh, N. Modadugu, and D. Boneh. On the effectiveness of address-space randomization. In *Proceedings of the 11th ACM Conference on Computer and Communications Security*, CCS '04, pages 298–307, 2004.

[28] L. Tang, J. Mars, and M. L. Soffa. Compiling for niceness: mitigating contention for QoS in warehouse scale computers. In *Proceedings of the 10th IEEE/ACM International Symposium on Code Generation and Optimization*, CGO '12, pages 1–12, 2012.

[29] R. Wartell, V. Mohan, K. W. Hamlen, and Z. Lin. Binary stirring: Self-randomizing instruction addresses of legacy x86 binary code. In *Proceedings of the 19th ACM Conference on Computer and Communications Security*, CCS '12, pages 157–168, 2012.

[30] T. Wei, T. Wang, L. Duan, and J. Luo. INSeRT: Protect dynamic code generation against spraying. In *Proceedings of the 2011 International Conference on Information Science and Technology*, ICIST '11, pages 323–328, 2011.

[31] B. Yee, D. Sehr, G. Dardyk, J. B. Chen, R. Muth, T. Ormandy, S. Okasaka, N. Narula, and N. Fullagar. Native client: A sandbox for portable, untrusted x86 native code. In *Proceedings of the 30th IEEE Symposium on Security and Privacy*, S&P '09, pages 79–93, 2009.

LogGC: Garbage Collecting Audit Log

Kyu Hyung Lee, Xiangyu Zhang, and Dongyan Xu
Department of Computer Science and CERIAS, Purdue University
West Lafayette, IN, 47907, USA
kyuhlee@purdue.edu, xyzhang@cs.purdue.edu, dxu@cs.purdue.edu

ABSTRACT

System-level audit logs capture the interactions between applications and the runtime environment. They are highly valuable for forensic analysis that aims to identify the root cause of an attack, which may occur long ago, or to determine the ramifications of an attack for recovery from it. A key challenge of audit log-based forensics in practice is the sheer size of the log files generated, which could grow at a rate of Gigabytes per day. In this paper, we propose LogGC, an audit logging system with garbage collection (GC) capability. We identify and overcome the unique challenges of garbage collection in the context of computer forensic analysis, which makes LogGC different from traditional memory GC techniques. We also develop techniques that instrument user applications at a small number of selected places to emit additional system events so that we can substantially reduce the false dependences between system events to improve GC effectiveness. Our results show that LogGC can reduce audit log size by 14 times for regular user systems and 37 times for server systems, without affecting the accuracy of forensic analysis.

Categories and Subject Descriptors

K.6.5 [**Management of Computing and Information Systems**]: Security and Protection—*Unauthorized access (e.g., hacking, phreaking) ; Invasive software(e.g., viruses, worms, Trojan horses)*; D.4.2 [**Operating System**]: Storage Management—*Garbage Collection*

Keywords

Attack Provenance; Audit Log; Garbage Collection; Reverse Engineering

1. INTRODUCTION

System-level audit logs record the interactions between applications and the underlying operating system (OS), such as file opens, reads and writes; socket reads and write; and process creations and terminations. Each of these is recorded as an event in the audit log, consisting of process/user/group id involved in the event, as well as the type and parameters of the event. In attack forensics, audit logs are critical to the construction of causal graphs. A causal graph shows the causality relations between system-level objects (e.g., files and sockets) and subjects (e.g., processes), *including those that existed in the past*. For instance, a process p_1 is causally dependent on another process p_2 if p_2 spawns p_1; a process p is causally dependent on a file f if p reads f; and a file f is dependent on p if f is created or modified by p. Causal graphs can be used to track the root cause of an attack. Upon observing a suspicious symptom (e.g., a zombie process) in the system, the administrator can use the casual graph to determine what had initially led to the presence of this process, which could be that a careless user viewed a phishing email, clicked an embedded URL, visited a malicious web site, triggered a driver-by download which compromised the system. Note that the initial attack may have happened days or even weeks before the symptom is observed. Hence the audit log and the derived causal graph are needed to disclose the attack path. Furthermore, the causal graph will disclose the damages or contaminations caused by the attack.

Recent work has focused on generating accurate, complete causal graphs from audit logs. Traditional causal graphs [13, 16] may suffer from imprecision caused by dependence explosion, where an event is unnecessarily dependent on too many other events and the corresponding causal graph is excessively large for human inspection. BEEP [20] involves program instrumentation to reduce the granularity of subjects from processes to "units" for fewer false-positive dependences. Other efforts propose using timestamps [12] or file offsets [23] to capture dependences more accurately.

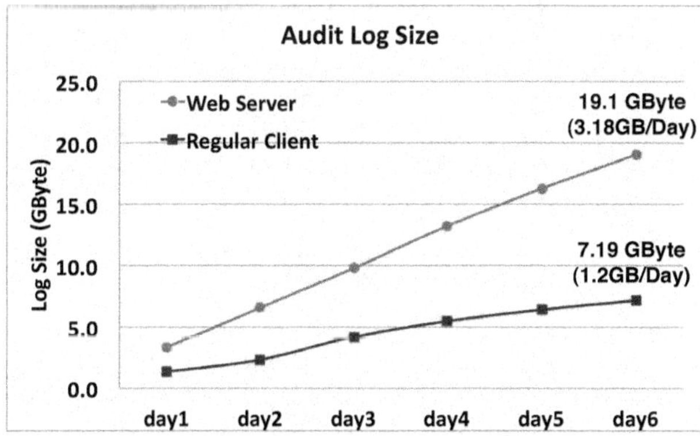

Figure 1: Audit log growth.

However, a major hindrance of audit log-based attack forensics in practice is the sheer size of audit logs. According to [16], even compressed audit logs grow at the rate of 1.2GB/day. Our own ear-

CCS'13, November 4–8, 2013, Berlin, Germany.

http://dx.doi.org/10.1145/2508859.2516731 .

lier work [20] shows an audit log growth rate of 800MB/day. Fig. 1 shows how audit log size grows over time in moderately loaded server and client machines, respectively in our experiments. We can see that the audit logs grow at an average rate of 3.18GB/day (server) and 1.2GB/day (client), incurring excessive space and processing overhead. Unfortunately, the reduction of audit log volume has not received sufficient research attention.

To fundamentally reduce audit log volume, we make a key observation: Many event entries in an audit log can be removed without affecting future forensic analysis. Such entries are about operations on system objects (e.g., files, sockets) that *neither influence nor are influenced by other processes or system objects*. We call such objects *unreachable objects*. We monitored a lab machine for a period of six days and observed that each day more than 94% of the objects accessed were destroyed (or terminated) and over 80% of those destroyed objects had very short lifetime, usually exclusively within a single process. These objects are likely to be unreachable, which suggests room for log reduction.

The log reduction problem we address shares some conceptual similarity to garbage collection (GC) in heap memory management. We hence call our solution LogGC . However, the two problems are technically different as memory GC is an instantaneous problem, namely, it focuses on removing unreachable heap memory objects in a *snapshot* of the memory. In contrast, we are trying to remove redundancy in audit logs that record *history* over a long period of time. We also face challenges that are caused by the unique requirements of forensic analysis and the coarse object granularity in audit logging.

The main contributions of LogGC are the following.

- We develop a basic GC algorithm that works directly on audit logs, each of which is a flat sequence of events. The algorithm can be invoked at any moment during system execution, taking the current audit log and generating a new and reduced audit log (Section 2).

- An important requirement in forensic analysis is to understand attack ramifications, which entails supporting *forward* causal analysis. The basic GC algorithm, which is an adaptation of a classic reachability-based memory GC algorithm, is incapable of supporting forward analysis. We hence propose a new extension to the algorithm (Section 3).

- To improve GC effectiveness, we leverage our previous technique BEEP [20] to partition a process to multiple *execution units*. We also propose a new technique to partition a data file into *logical data units*, by instrumenting user applications at a small set of code locations to emit additional system events. As such, better precision can be achieved and many more unreachable events can be exposed and garbage-collected (Section 4).

- We propose to leverage applications' own log files to further remove event entries in audit logs (Section 5).

- We conduct extensive evaluation of LogGC on a pool of real-world applications. Our results show that LogGC can garbage-collect 92.89% of the original audit logs for client systems and 97.35% for server systems. Furthermore, through a number of case studies, we show that the reduced logs are equally effective in forensic analysis.

Assumptions and Limitations of LogGC First, we trust the OS as LogGC collects, stores, and reduces audit logs at the kernel level. Hence, a kernel-level attack could disable LogGC and tamper with the audit log. However, LogGC can be implemented at the hypervisor level to mitigate such risks.

Second, we assume that, when LogGC initially starts, all user programs and files in the system are "clean". Attacks against these programs and files will hence be logged by LogGC . If LogGC begins with a compromised program, the program could disrupt LogGC by generating bogus system-level events. Note that while a program that gets compromised when LogGC is active may perform the same attack, the attack will be captured by LogGC . Our first two assumptions are standard for many existing system-level auditing techniques [12, 15, 16, 17, 20, 23].

Third, LogGC instruments user programs to partition executions and data files. While applicable to most application *binaries*, for some applications (e.g., `mysql`), our current file partitioning technique requires the user to inspect the application's *source code* using a profiler and select the instrumentation points from a small number of options provided by the profiler. The manual efforts are minor – only 15 statements were selected and instrumented for `mysql`. More importantly, this is a one-time effort. The user also needs to provide a small set of training inputs for LogGC to determine the instrumentation points. However, the instrumentation points are not sensitive to the inputs.

Finally, while LogGC can preprocess a large pool of commonly used applications, users may install new applications. If a user installs a new long running application (e.g. servers or UI programs), he/she may need to instrument the application for identification of execution units. If the user installs an application that induces a large number of dependences through files (i.e., by writing to a file and reading it later), such as a database application, he/she may also need to instrument the application for partitioning a file into data units. In the worst case where a newly installed application is not instrumented, LogGC can still garbage collect logs from the existing applications without affecting the un-reduced log entries generated from the new application.

2. BASIC DESIGN

Redundancy abounds in audit logs. Many applications create and operate on temporary files during execution. Such files are destroyed after the applications terminate. As a result, no future system behavior will be affected by these files. Keeping their provenance is hence unnecessary. An application may only read files or receive information from remote hosts, and send the contents to display without saving them. After the application terminates, its provenance is of no interest for future forensic analysis.

In this section, we present a basic algorithm that garbage-collects redundant entries in an audit log. It is analogous to garbage collection in memory management. We define *root objects* as the live processes and files at the time LogGC is invoked. We then traverse backward in the audit log. If any root object is directly or transitively dependent on a logged event, the event is marked reachable. In the end, all unreachable log entries are removed from the audit log. Different from classic GC, our algorithm will operate on the log file, which is a linear sequence of events, instead of a reference graph of memory cells. Moreover, the dependences between event entries are often not explicit. For example, assume a process receives a packet and saves it to a file. This leads to two event entries, one is a socket read and the other is a file write. It is not easy to infer the dependence between the two events from the audit log. A conservative approximation made by many existing audit logging techniques (also called provenance tracing) [12, 15, 16, 17, 20, 23] is to assume that an event is dependent on all the preceding input events for the same process.

Event type	Events
Input	file read; socket read
Output	file write (excluding `stdout`); socket write; process spawn; chmod; chown; link; truncate; create
Dead-end	write to `stdout`; file deletion*; process kill*

* denotes destruction events.

Table 1: Classification of event types

Before explaining the algorithm, we first classify logged events into three categories (Table 1) as the algorithm will behave differently based on type of events.

- An *input* event is one that receives data from input devices.
- An *output* event is one that creates influence on some other system object and such influence will persist beyond the completion of this event.
- A *dead-end* event is one that has effect only on objects directly involved in the event and the effect will *not* create dependences in subsequent execution of the system. For example, writes to `stdout` will not influence any system object.

Algorithm 1 Basic Audit Log Garbage Collection Algorithm

Input:	L - the audit log F - the current live files.	P - the current live processes.
Output:	L' - the new audit log.	
Definition	*ReachableProc* - the set of reachable processes. *ReachableObj* - reachable system objects (e.g. files).	

```
1: L' ← nil
2: ReachableProc ← P
3: ReachableObj ← F
4: for each event e ∈ L in reverse order do
5:     if e is an output event involving an object in ReachableObj then
6:         L' ← e · L'
7:         ReachableProc ← ReachableProc ∪ the process of e
8:     else if e is an input event involving a process in ReachableProc then
9:         L' ← e · L'
10:        ReachableObj ← ReachableObj ∪ the objects operated by e
```

The basic algorithm is Algorithm 1. It takes the audit log, and the current set of live processes and live files as input, and produces a reduced audit log. It leverages two data structures *ReachableProc* and *ReachableObj* to maintain the set of reachable processes and system objects, respectively. We say a process, either alive or terminated, is reachable if a live process or file is directly or transitively dependent on it. Reachable system objects are similarly defined.

The algorithm first initializes *ReachableProc* with the set of live processes and *ReachableObj* with the set of live files. It then starts traversing the events in L in the reverse order. If an output event e in the log operates on a reachable object (line 5), the event becomes reachable and gets inserted to the output log L'. In the mean time, the process involved in the event is set to reachable. According to lines 8, 9, and 10, all the preceding input events in the process become reachable too. Note that setting the process reachable only affects the events preceding e, all the events that happen after e are not reachable even though they involve the same reachable process.

The algorithm is presented with a high level of abstraction. At the implementation level, LogGC also handles reuse of file ids and socket ids, and supports various system objects beyond files and sockets.

Example. Consider the example in Fig. 2. The live file and process are shown on the right bottom of the figure. The algorithm traverses backward. Log entries 8, 7, 6 are garbage-collected as they do not operate on any reachable objects or involve a reachable process.

(1) Proc_A spawn(O)	Proc_C	O - output type
(2) Proc_A write(O)	File1	I - input type
(3) Proc_A read(I)	File2	D - dead-end Type
(4) Proc_B read(I)	File1	
(5) Proc_B write(O)	File2	
(6) Proc_B read(I)	File1	
(7) Proc_B delete(D)	File1	Live processes: Proc_C
(8) Proc_B read(I)	Socket	Live files : File2

Figure 2: An example of the basic GC algorithm. An event entry consists of the process id, the event name (event type), and the system object being operated on.

Entry 5 is an output event with live file `File2` so it is inserted to the output log file. In the mean time, `Proc_B` becomes reachable. Hence, all the input events with `Proc_B` preceding entry 5 become reachable including the read of `File1` in entry 4. As a result, `File1` becomes a reachable object, which leads to entry 2 being inserted to the new log. Entry 1 is the creation of a live process and hence retained. It is worth mentioning that although entry 3 involves a reachable object `File2`, it is not an output event and hence garbage-collected.

Despite its simplicity, such a basic design is insufficient in practice. We will discuss how we handle various challenges in the following sections.

3. SUPPORTING FORWARD ANALYSIS

The basic design enables inspection of the history of any live object, which is a backward analysis. An equally important usage of audit logs is to facilitate understanding of attack ramifications, namely identification of damages that have been inflicted during an attack. We call this a *forward analysis* as it inspects the audit log in a forward fashion to look for ramifications of an event (e.g., the root attack event).

Fig. 3 (a) shows a causal graph generated from the audit log of the following hypothetical attack, with the numbers representing the corresponding events in the graph: (1) The user visited a malicious web site at "`x.x.x.x:80`"; `Firefox` is exploited such that (2) it spawns a backdoor process and (3) downloads a malicious dynamic library file `x.so`. (4) Later, the user launches the `ls` command in `bash`. (5) The `ls` process makes use of the malicious `x.so`. As a result, (6) while the process emits to the screen as usual, it also (7) removes an important file `.permission` and (8) the malicious library file `x.so`.

Assume that the user later notices the backdoor process, which is the only trail left by the attack (without analyzing the audit log). By performing backward analysis on the audit log, he can backtrack to the earlier visit to the malicious web site. However, to identify the damages caused by the attack, he also needs to perform forward analysis starting from the site visit event (1). As such, the past existence of the malicious library `x.so` and its removal of the important file and the library itself can be disclosed.

However, the basic design presented in Section 2 is insufficient for forward analysis because it garbage-collects all dead-end events since they will not affect any live system object in the future. However, *some dead-end events (e.g. file removal and process termination) become important when performing forward analysis.*

Revisiting the example in Fig. 3 (a), at the time of GC, only `bash` and the backdoor processes are alive. Files `x.so` and `.permission` have been removed from the file system. After applying Algorithm 1, only events 1 and 2 are left. While this is sufficient to disclose the causality of the backdoor, it loses information about the malicious library and the damages it caused. Note that `stdout`

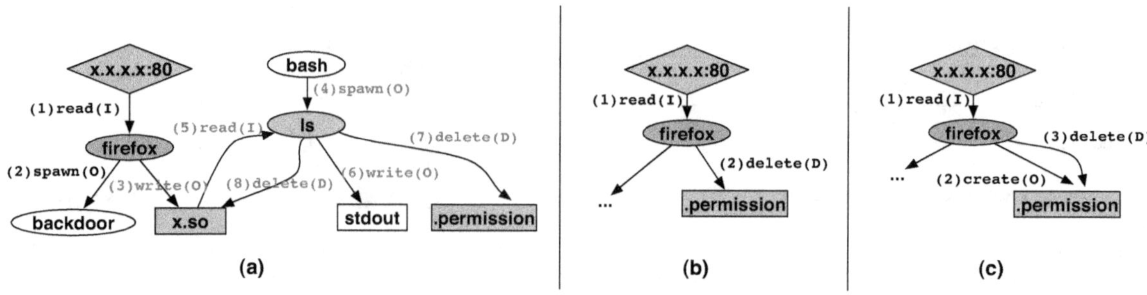

Figure 3: Causal graph examples. Ovals, diamonds and boxes represent processes, sockets and files, respectively. Edges denote events, annotated with numbers representing their order in the audit log, event names and types (i.e., *I* for input, *O* for output, and *D* for dead-end). The shaded shapes represent those no longer live at the GC time. Events in light blue denote those garbage-collected following Algorithm 1.

is a special file such that the "output-to-stdout" event at step (6) is considered a dead-end event (Table 1) and hence garbage-collected.

We cannot simply keep all dead-end events. Intuitively, keeping a dead-end event means that it may be of importance for forensic analysis. As such, events that may have led to the event must also be important. In other words, we cannot garbage-collect the input events preceding the dead-end event. Consider the example in Fig. 3 (b). It shows another hypothetical scenario in which (1) `firefox` visited a malicious web site and was exploited and (2) the infected `firefox` removed an important file `.permission` as part of the malicious payload. Suppose `firefox` has been terminated when GC is performed. If we keep the dead-end event 2, we need to keep the preceding input event 1 in order to understand its cause. However, if we were to keep all dead-end events and their preceding input events, garbage collection would not be effective at all.

One observation is that we do not need to consider all kinds of dead-end events as not all of them are of interest to forensic analysis. In particular, only those that cause destructive effects on the system are of interest, such as file removal and process termination. We call these events *destruction events*, such as the ones annotated with '*' in Table 1.

Log	Accessed Files	Deleted Files	
		Total	Temp Files
User1	14,909	11,981 (80.36%)	10,118 (84.45%)
User2	2,373	1,211 (51.03%)	1,197 (98.92%)
User3	2,991	2,046 (68.41%)	1,985 (97.02%)
User4	7,611	4,902 (64.41%)	2,610 (53.24%)
User5	2,988	1,416 (47.39%)	1,401 (98.94%)
Total	30,872	21,556 (69.82%)	17,311 (80.31%)

Table 2: Number of deleted files and temporary files

Unfortunately, considering destruction events only is still too expensive as many programs generate and delete a large number of files in their life time. Note that since a file deletion is a destruction event, it prevents us from garbage-collecting all the preceding input events. Fig. 3 (c) shows a typical execution pattern in `firefox`: it involves creating and removing a large number of files. These files are used to save/cache pages temporarily. They will be deleted when `firefox` is closed. In this scenario, if we retain all file deletions, there would not be many events that can be garbage-collected.

In Table 2, we have collected and analyzed five different audit logs from machines of different users with different settings (detailed settings in Section 6). Each log corresponds to one day's execution. The table shows the number of accessed files in each execution (column two) and the number of files that are deleted (column three). Observe that most of the accessed files are deleted. If we retain such deletions, the saving from garbage collection would be small.

Fortunately, another observation comes to the rescue: Most of the deleted files are temporary files. *A temporary file is defined as a file whose entire life time belongs exclusively to a single process.* In other words, a temporary file is only accessed (created/read/written/deleted) by a single process. Besides web browsers, document viewer applications and compilers also use temporary files very often. As shown in the fourth column, 80.31% deleted files are temporary files. Such deletions have little forensic value and hence can be garbage-collected, which will transitively provide other garbage collection opportunities.

Hence, our final solution that supports forward attack analysis is as follows. *Upon a dead-end event, we check if it is a destruction event. If not, it will be garbage-collected. Otherwise, we will further determine if it is a file deletion event. If so, it will be retained and its process is set reachable, except when it is a temporary file deletion, which will be garbage-collected.* We perform a forward preprocessing to identify all temporary files before each GC procedure. When we retain a destruction event, we do not set the object being destroyed reachable, because the content of the object is not important but rather the deletion action itself is. As such, the preceding outputs to the object are still eligible for garbage collection.

One possible concern is that the attacker may exploit an application in such a way that the compromised application downloads a malicious library file, executes it and finally removes it. Since all these events occur within the same process, according to our policy, we consider the malicious library a temporary file and may garbage-collect its history. In this case, if the malicious library has ever affected or changed the system, such as changing other files or sending packets, its events will be marked as reachable by our traversal algorithm and thus retained. Otherwise, the event will never appear in any causal graph even though it is the deletion of a malicious library file. Therefore, it is safe to remove the event.

4. PROVENANCE TRACING WITH FINER GRANULARITY

In the basic design, attack provenance tracing is conducted at the system level, meaning that audit log entries are events captured by the OS. This is also the default setting of the Linux audit system. However, we observe that system-level tracing is overly coarse-grained, which substantially limits the effectiveness of audit log GC. In particular, the following two problems are dominant.

First, since we cannot afford tracing instruction level dependences in practice, we have to conservatively assume that an event is dependent on all preceding *input* events involving the same pro-

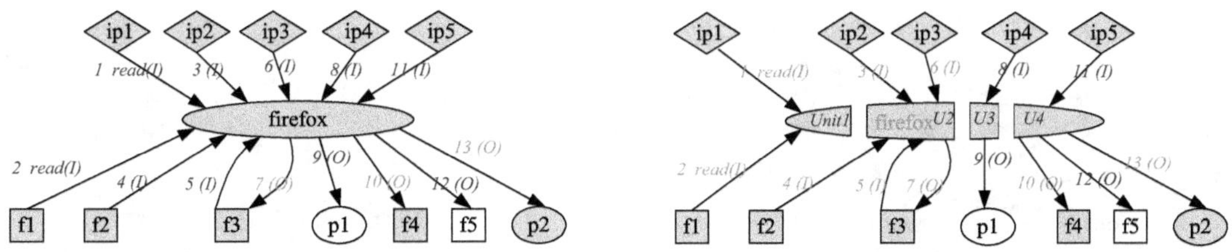

(a) before partition **(b) after partition**

Figure 4: Partitioning a process execution into units. Event names may be omitted if inferable from context.

cess. Consequently, during garbage collection, if an event of a process becomes reachable, meaning that it may directly/transitively affect live processes or objects, the process becomes reachable, making all the preceding input events of the process reachable. It further implies that the objects operated in those events will also become reachable. This is particularly problematic for long running processes.

Consider a sample execution of `firefox` in Fig. 4. It accessed a number of URLs with different IP addresses, read and wrote a number of files, and spawned two processes. At the time of garbage collection, the process has terminated and many of the files accessed are also removed. The child process `p1` and file `f5` are still alive. Following the basic GC algorithm, live file `f5` makes `firefox` process reachable when the backward traversal reaches event 12, preventing garbage-collection of any input event before that. Consequently, only events 7, 10, and 13 are removed. In practice, audit logs are dominated by event entries from long running processes that may run for hours or even days.

Second, treating a file as a single object such that any read of the file is considered dependent on all preceding writes is too coarse-grained for some applications, especially those that need to repeatedly read/write to a file. For example, `mysql` creates an index file and a data file for each table. Upon receiving a query, `mysql` usually first reads the index file to find the location of a tuple (in the data file) given the tuple id. Then it reads the tuple from the data file and sends it back to the user. The index and data files need to be frequently updated. They also stay alive as long as the table is alive. According to our basic GC strategy, none of the reads/writes to these files can be garbage-collected.

Fig. 5 (a) shows three SQL queries executed by three `mysql` processes. In the first update query, `mysql` first reads the index file, which stores ids and locations of tuples in a B-Tree as shown in the figure. The corresponding table is shown in the data file. In this case, `mysql` first reads the root node in the index file which is the requested node (id=3) and finds the location of the tuple (event 1). Then it updates both the index file and the data file. In the second select query, `mysql` first reads the root node from the index file (event 4), which does not satisfy the `where` clause. It then further reads the child node in the index file (event 5), which satisfies the clause. Then `mysql` reads the data file to get the tuple (event 6) and returns it (event 7). In the third delete query, `mysql` reads individual tuples from the data file (events 8 and 10) and then checks them against the `where` condition. If the condition is satisfied, tuple deletion is performed by updating the index file (events 9 and 11).

According to Algorithm 1, since both the data and index files are alive, none of the writes to them can be garbage-collected, making the preceding reads non-garbage-collectable. Consequently, none of the events can be removed. Note that a simple idea that uses file offsets [23] to detect more precise dependences does not work here because `mysql` tends to read many input tuples to memory to process a query, but only a (possibly small) subset of them are used in computing the result tuples (e.g., the delete query in the previous example).

We have conducted an experiment in which we applied the basic GC algorithm to audit logs of `firefox` and `mysql`. Our results show that only 0.07% and 0.0004% of them can be garbage-collected, respectively. And the log entries from `mysql` can be as large as 90.68% of the overall audit log in a server system.

4.1 Dividing Process into Execution Units

To overcome the first problem discussed earlier in this section (i.e., treating a process as a single subject), we adopt our earlier solution called BEEP [20] by dividing a process into execution units. The basic idea is that the execution of a long running program is dominated by event handling loops. According to our study of over 100 applications [20], event handling loops are present in most of those applications and each loop iteration can be considered as a logical execution unit that handles an individual external request. Hence, instead of considering an event dependent on all preceding input events in the life time of an entire process, BEEP considers that it is only dependent on the preceding input events in the *same unit*.

Consider the example in Fig. 4 (b). The execution of `firefox` in (a) is divided into four units corresponding to four event handling loop iterations, each accessing an individual URL. As such, events 1-6 can be garbage-collected. This is because the reachable output events 12 and 9 only cause the input events in their units (i.e., `u4` and `u3`) to be marked as reachable. Note that the history of live objects, i.e., process `p1` and file `f5`, is correctly preserved.

We adapt the binary profiling technique in BEEP to identify event handling loops in a binary program. Loop entries and exits are instrumented to emit special system events that serve as unit delimiters. We also identify workflows between units that may introduce cross-unit dependences. Details can be found in [20]. Since these are not our contribution, details are elided.

4.2 Dividing File into Data Units

To address the second problem (i.e., treating a file as a single object), we propose to divide a file into data units such that dependences can be defined with respect to the smaller data units.

Consider the example in Fig. 5 (b). The data file is divided into units with each unit being a tuple. Furthermore, since index files are completely internal to `mysql`, reads and writes on them are of no forensic interest and hence removed. We are now able to garbage-collect all events except 6 and 7. Observe that with the finer granularity, we can claim that tuple 3 is not reachable hence event 3 can be garbage-collected.

However, dividing files into data units is highly challenging. One may have to have knowledge about the internal structure of a file. Also, one has to identify all operations on data units. When an

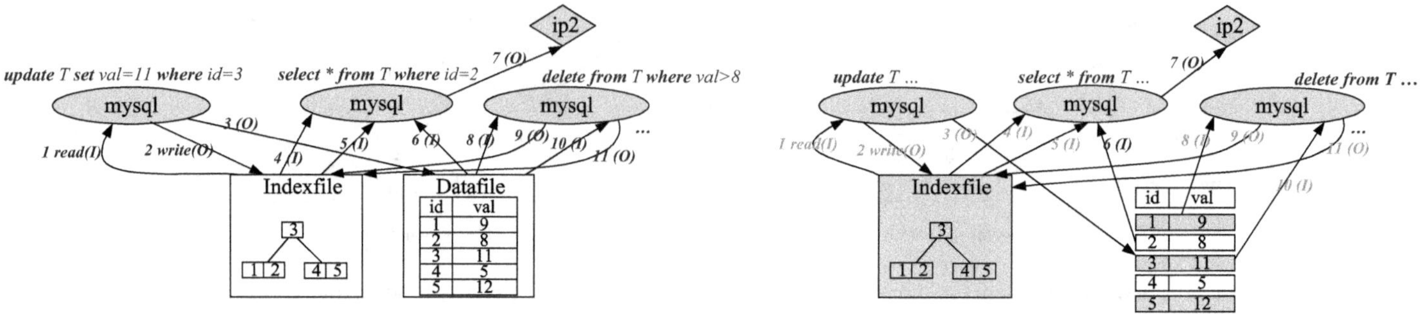

(a) before partition **(b) after partition**

Figure 5: Partitioning data files into units improves garbage collection.

operation is performed, the specific units being operated on need to be figured out. For instance, `mysql` has 1.2M lines of code. It is prohibitively difficult for a non-`mysql` developer to identify such information manually. Instruction-level tracing may determine data provenance precisely down to the byte level. However, it is too expensive to be useful for production systems.

Solution Overview. Our solution is to leverage a *profiler* to identify and instrument a small number of places in the application program such that special system events will be emitted by our instrumentation to disclose the provenance of data units. Take `mysql` as an example, given a query, the result tuples are computed from some input tuples that may come from multiple tables. We identify the code locations that *exclusively* access those input tuples used in computing the result tuples and instrument the code to emit the ids of the input tuples to the audit log. When an output tuple is written to disk, we also emit a write event tagged with its tuple id. Since all such events occur within the execution unit handling a single query, by following the default strategy that considers an output event (i.e., tuple write) as dependent on all preceding input events (i.e., input tuple reads), we can correctly determine the tuple-level dependences and allow more garbage collection.

Consider the example in Fig. 6 (a). It shows a piece of pseudo-code[1] that models the procedure that `mysql` handles the query on top of the figure, which performs a join query between tables `t1` and `t2` and writes the result table to `t3`. `Mysql` first loads all the tuples of `t1` and stores them to the cache. It then loads individual tuples of `t2` and compares their value fields with those in the cache. If there is a matching pair, the corresponding data fields are extracted (lines 12-14) and used to compose the result tuple. Finally, the result tuple is written at line 18.

With our solution, we will identify and instrument lines 12 and 13 for input tuples. Particularly, we will add a special system call after line 12 to emit the tuple id of `t1` and another one after line 13 to emit the tuple id of `t2`. According to the semantics of the code snippet, since lines 12 and 13 are within the true branch of the comparison at line 11, the tuples represented by the two lines must be the input tuples used to compute the output tuple. The result tuple composition at line 17 is also instrumented to emit the output tuple id. As such, we can associate the output tuple with the corresponding input tuples via the default audit log analysis.

In the following, we explain our techniques to identify those instrumentation points. Our discussion will be mainly focused on `mysql` as it is the core database engine for many web service applications.

[1]The real code is too complex to present and explain with limited space.

Definitions: $Pv[\&x]$ - the provenance of a variable x, which is a set of input tuple ids.
pc: op $(y_1, ..., y_n)$ - an instruction at pc that has op as the opcode and y_1,..., y_n the operand variables.
$S[pc]$ - aggregated provenance set for the instruction at pc.

Instruction	Action
id=readRecord("t",&*buf*,&*s*...)	for (i=0 to s-1) $Pv[buf+i]$={ id}
pc: x=op $(y_1,...,y_n)$	$Pv[\&x]= Pv[\&y_1] \cup ... \cup Pv[\&y_n]$ $S[pc]=S[pc] \cup Pv[\&x]$

Table 3: Instruction-level provenance profiler

Algorithm 2 Identifying instrumentation points for input tuples

```
execute mysql on a given query with the provenance profiler
Let "pc: writeRecord(...,out_buf,s...)" be the instruction emitting the output tuple
pv←Pv[out_buf]∪...∪Pv[out_buf+s−1]
R←{}
for each executed instruction i do
    l ← the program counter of i
    if S[l]⊂ pv and all tuples in S[l] belong to one table then
        R← R∪{l}
return the minimum subset(s) of R whose provenance covers pv
```

Detecting Output Tuple Writes. The first profiling technique is to identify instrumentation points that disclose writes of output tuples. For each query category (i.e. select, join, aggregation, update, and insert), we have a small set of training runs (2 5). If we observe a write to data file, we manually identify the tuple id in the output buffer and leverage a data dependence tracking technique to back-track to the earliest point that defines the tuple id value. For example, if a tuple id is generated using a counter "`id=counter++`" at line 1, and then copied at lines 2, 3, and 4, which is the final tuple write, we backtrack to line 1. Essentially, we identify the root of the data dependence chain to the tuple id such that all instruction instances along the chain have the same id value.

Detecting Dependent Input Tuples. The second profiling technique is to identify instrumentation points that can disclose the input tuples that are used to compute individual output tuples. The basic idea is to leverage an *instruction level* provenance tracing technique that can precisely compute the set of ids of the input tuples that are directly or transitively used to compute a value at any program point. As such, given an output tuple, we can precisely know its input tuple provenance. Then we inspect the set of executed instructions to determine a minimal subset such that the union of their provenance sets is precisely the provenance of the output tuple. In other words, each of the instructions in the sub-

insert into t3 (**select** t1.id, t2.id, t2.val **from** t1, t2 **where** t1.val = t2.val);

```
   /*read all t1 tuples and store them into cache */
1  while (...) {
2      id1=readRecord ("t1", &buf1, &s1, ...);
3      store_cache(<"t1", buf1, s1>);
4  }
5  /*read each t2 tuple and check against the cached t1
6    tuples. If any pair matches, a new tuple is composed
7    and inserted to t3*/
8  while (...) {
9    id2=readRecord("t2", &buf2, &s2, ...);
10   for (each record <"t1", buf1, s1> in cache)
11       if (getField(buf1, "t1.val")==getField(buf2,"t2.val") {
12           v1=getField(buf1, "t1.id");
13           v2=getField(buf2, "t2.id");
14           v3=getField(buf2, "t2.val");
15           buf3=newTuple();
16           insertField(buf3, id3++);
17           insertField(buf3, v1); ...; insertField(buf3, v3);
18           writeRecord("t3", buf3, ...);
         }
   }
```

(a) Code

t1

id	val
1	9
2	4

t2

id	val
5	9
6	26

	Trace	Pv[]	S[]
2_1	id1=readRecord ("t1",&buf1, ...);	Pv[$a1$...($a1$+7)]={1}	S[2]={1}
	...		
2_2	id1=readRecord ("t1",&buf1,...);	Pv[$a2$...($a2$+7)]={2}	S[2]={1,2}
	...		
9_1	id2=readRecord ("t2",&buf2,...);	Pv[$b1$...($b1$+7)]={5}	S[9]={5}
	...		
11_1	if (true)		
12_1	v1=getField(buf1, "t1.id");	Pv[&v1]=Pv[$a1$]={1}	S[12]={1}
13_1	v2=getField(buf2, "t2.id");	Pv[&v2]=Pv[$b1$]={5}	S[13]={5}
14_1	v3=getField(buf2, "t2.val");	Pv[&v3]=Pv[$b1$+4]={5}	S[14]={5}
16_1	insertField(buf3, id3++);		
17_1	insertField(buf3, v1-v3);	Pv[($c1$+4)...($c1$+11)]={1,5}	S[17]={1,5}
18_1	writeRecord("t3",buf3,...);		
	...		
9_2	id2=readRecord ("t2",&buf2,...);	Pv[$b2$...($b2$+7)]={6}	S[9]={5,6}

(b) Execution with the Profiler

Figure 6: Using profiling to determine instrumentation points. The code snippet models how `mysql` handles the query on top. Function `readRecord("table_name",&buf, &s)` reads a tuple from data file, returns it in `buf` that is allocated inside the function, the size is set in `s` and the tuple id is the return value; `store_cache()` stores a tuple to cache; `getField()` gets a tuple field from a buffer given the field label; `insertField()` inserts a field to a buffer; `writeRecord()` writes a tuple (buffer) to a given table. Symbols $a1$, $a2$, $b1$, $b2$, and $c1$ in (b) denote the different buffer address values. The subscripts in statement labels denote instances. Each data field is 4 byte long.

set has processed (part of) the dependent input tuples. We hence can instrument these instructions to emit the ids of the tuples that they process. Note that instruction-level tracing is *only used for profiling*.

The semantic rules of the instruction-level provenance tracer are presented in Table 3, which specifies the action the tracer takes upon an instruction. Function `readRecord()` loads a tuple from data file. The result tuple is stored in `buf` with size `s`. The function returns the tuple id. When an invocation of the function is encountered, it is considered a source of input provenance. Therefore, the corresponding action is to set the provenance of each individual byte in `buf`, which stores the data fields of the tuple, to the input tuple id. This function is an abstraction of four functions in `mysql`, namely, `_mi_read_static_record()`, `_mi_read_rnd_static_record()`, `_mi_read_dynamic_record()`, and `_mi_read_rnd_dynamic_record()`.

The last row shows the rule for assignments. We normalize the right-hand-side to an operation on a set of operands. The provenance of the left-hand-side is computed as the union of the operand provenance sets. We also compute the aggregated provenance set of the instruction, which is essentially the union of provenance sets of all the executed instances of the instruction.

Algorithm 2 shows how to identify the instrumentation points, leveraging the instruction-level tracer. It first executes `mysql` with a given query. Lines 2 and 3 compute the provenance of the output, stored in *pv*. Set *R* denotes the candidate instrumentation points, which are denoted by program counters. In lines 5-8, the algorithm traverses all the executed instructions and determines the candidate instructions. The candidacy requires that the aggregated provenance of an instruction must be a subset of the output provenance. Otherwise, it must be an instruction that does not exclusively process dependent input tuples, such as line 2 in Fig. 6 (a), which processes all input tuples. Furthermore, the instruction should exclusively process input tuples from the same table. Otherwise, it is an instruction that aggregates information from multiple tables. It is usually impossible to acquire the original tuple ids at such an instruction. For example, line 17 in Fig. 6 (a) has exactly the output provenance. However, since it is just a composition of fields from input tuples, it is in general difficult to extract input tuple ids from the composed result. With the candidate set, at line 6, the algorithm identifies the minimal set of instructions that can cover the output provenance. It may return multiple such sets.

Fig. 6 (b) shows a sample profiling run. The input tables are shown on top. One can see that there will be just one result tuple, whose provenance is tuple 1 from `t1` and tuple 1 from `t2`. The figure shows part of the execution trace. The *Pv* and *S* sets are also shown for each executed statement. The program first loads tuples from `t1`, which leads to the provenance sets of the buffer to be set to {1} and {2} in the two respective instances of instruction 2. Then, the program reads `t2` and compares tuples. Since the first tuple of `t2` matches the first tuple of `t1`, lines 12-14 are executed to extract data from input tuples. Hence, their provenance includes the corresponding input tuple id. At the end, the aggregated provenance of line 2 is {1,2}, line 9 is {5,6}, line 12 is {1}, and lines 13 and 14 are {5}. Since the output provenance is {1,5}, the minimal cover set could be lines 12 and 13 or 12 and 14, which are the places reported by the algorithm.

Even though our discussion is driven by a specific query, the algorithm is generic. We apply it to a training set of various types of queries. Since the profiler can only give hints about the instrumentation points, we assume that human users will inspect the source code to eventually determine the instrumentation points from the reported ones. In practice, the human efforts are small and they are one-time efforts. We instrumented a total of 15 places in *mysql* after inspecting about 40 places suggested by the profiler. The instrumentation supports typical select, join, aggregation, update, insert and sub-queries with nesting level of 2. We have validated that it can correctly identify tuple-level dependences in the standard database workloads from RUBiS [5] and SysBench [1].

Discussion. In this work, we do not consider *control dependences* between tuples. For example, in the following query:

select * **from** t1 **where** t1.val > (**select** avg(val) **from** t1);

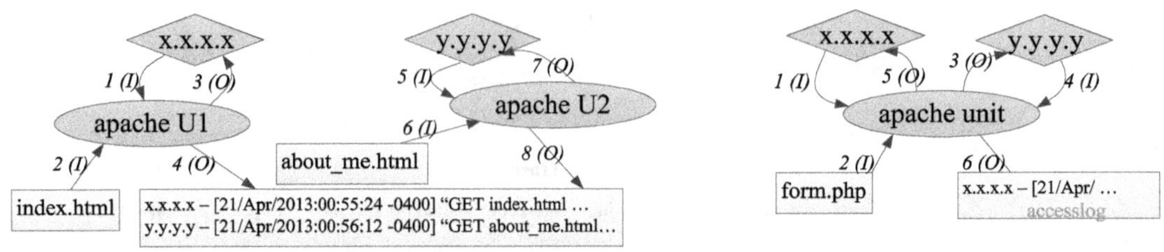

(a) Leveraging Apache AccessLog

(b) Apache Log Alone is Insufficient

Figure 7: Apache application log examples.

Our instrumentation will emit the ids of tuples whose values are greater than the average. However, all tuples in `t1` are correlated to the output tuples as they are used to compute the average, which is used in the `where` condition. It is analogous to the traditional concept of program control dependence. In this work, we deem such precise tuple control dependences of limited forensic value. Note that even though SQL injection attacks are often achieved by manipulating `where` conditions, knowing the tuples that are used in malicious `where` clauses are unlikely useful as they often serve only as a true condition enabling other malicious actions, which will be captured by LogGC .

If a query generates multiple output tuples, the output tuples will belong to the same execution unit. However, we cannot simply consider a tuple output event as dependent on all the preceding tuple input events in the same unit. Instead, we leverage the fact that output tuples are computed one after another. Hence a tuple output event is only dependent on those preceding tuple input events that are in between this output event and the immediate preceding output event.

Finally, since instrumentation points for data units are produced by the profiler and validated manually by the user, it is possible that they be incomplete and unsound (i.e., inducing false tuple dependences). Also, the profiler takes regular use cases provided by the user to determine the instrumentation points. Our experience does show that our techniques are sufficiently effective. Section 6.3 shows that LogGC with data units effectively reduces log size without affecting forensic analysis of realistic attack scenarios. The results show that the reduced logs (7 times smaller than the original ones) are equally or even more effective in forensic analysis that involves databases. In the future, we plan to develop more automated techniques to statically determine instrumentation points.

5. LEVERAGING APPLICATION LOGS

We observe that many long running applications have the following two characteristics: (1) They have their own log files that record some execution status (we call them the application logs to distinguish from audit logs); (2) They often send data to remote users through socket writes. For instance, `apache` records every remote request it receives and the status of fulfilling the request. It also sends the requested (html) file back to the remote client through socket writes. On one hand, the two characteristics make garbage collection difficult, because both application log file writes and socket writes are output events. According to our earlier discussion, any preceding input events within the same unit may have dependence with those output events hence they cannot be garbage-collected. On the other hand, the two properties also provide an opportunity to prune more events in the audit log if they are already present in the application logs.

Fig. 7 (a) shows two execution units of `apache` that handle requests for `index.html` and `about_me.html`, respectively. They both have the following event pattern: socket read to receive the request; file read to load the file; socket write to send the file; and file write to the application log to record the history. This is also the dominant event pattern for `apache`. Both socket write and file write prevent garbage-collecting any other events. According to our experience, such server programs can generate as much as 71.4% of audit log events.

To address this problem, we propose to leverage the application logs themselves. More specifically, we observe that the aforementioned event pattern (as shown in Fig. 7 (a)) forms a small isolated causal graph independent of the other events in the audit log. It simply receives the request and returns the file. It does not affect other objects in the system except the application log. Furthermore, all events in the graph can be inferred from the application log. In Fig. 7(a), all the four events can be inferred from the application log and hence removed from the audit log.

One important criterion for replacing audit log events with application log events is that the events are self-contained. They do not have dependence with any past event or induce any dependence with future events. For example, if `about_me.html` in Fig. 7 (a) has been modified in the past by some user request, which is recorded in the audit log, events in the second unit will not be garbage-collected. In case of a malicious modification, this will allow us to back-track to the malicious change and determine its ramifications. Furthermore, if a unit produces side effects on the system, such as writing to a file or writing to a database (e.g., via socket `y.y.y.y` to the `mysql` server in Fig. 7.(b)), its events will not be garbage collected.

We apply this strategy to server programs (e.g., web server and ftp server) and user applications that generate their own logs, with the exception of `mysql` because we rely on the tuple-level events to perform garbage collection.

6. EVALUATION

We have implemented a LogGC prototype composed of training, profiling, instrumentation, log analysis and garbage collection components. The training and profiling components are implemented on PIN [21], instrumentation is through a binary rewriting tool PEBIL [19]. The log analysis and garbage collection components are implemented in C++.

Table 4 shows a list of sample applications we have installed and preprocessed for our evaluation. For each application, we have trained and instrumented it to support process and file partitioning. Columns 3 and 4 indicate applications that make use of temporary files and have application logs, respectively. Recall that we garbage-collect temporary file deletions, which enables removing other dependent events. The last column indicates if an application needs to be instrumented for data unit partition. Currently, we only instrument `mysql` to achieve more log reduction.

	Logs	Total	Basic GC		Execution Unit		Temp file		Application Logs		Data Unit	
		# logs	# logs	(%)	# logs	(%)	# logs	(%)	# logs	(%)	# logs	(%)
One day execution	User1	1,159,680	745,424	64.28%	667,104	57.52%	308,144	26.57%	172,688	14.89%	-	-
	User2	985,185	984,261	99.91%	685,233	69.55%	602,715	61.18%	197,718	20.01%	108,172	10.98%
	User3	1,329,854	1,246,804	93.75%	618,572	46.51%	134,859	10.14%	83,595	6.29%	-	-
	User4	1,921,038	1,920,363	99.96%	247,409	12.88%	228,428	11.89%	61,100	3.18%	-	-
	User5	973,789	592,521	60.85%	300,824	30.89%	238,577	24.5%	1,403	0.14%	-	-
	Average	1,273,909	1,097,875	86.18%	503,828	39.55%	302,545	23.75%	108,470	8.51%	90,668	7.11%
Web server benchmark	Rubis1	8,676,521	8,676,260	100.00%	8,467,229	97.59%	8,355,045	96.29%	7,886,531	90.90%	259,139	2.99%
	Rubis2	8,433,427	8,433,345	100.00%	8,433,142	100.00%	8,323,800	98.70%	7,812,483	92.64%	166,968	1.98%
	Rubis3	8,352,924	8,352,842	100.00%	8,352,630	100.00%	8,243,034	98.68%	7,731,299	92.56%	206,786	2.48%
	Rubis4	8,900,179	8,897,798	99.97%	8,126,108	91.30%	8,011,739	90.02%	7,508,254	84.36%	326,705	3.67%
	Rubis5	7,933,792	7,933,710	100.00%	7,933,501	100.00%	7,829,530	98.69%	7,209,876	90.88%	161,523	2.04%
	Average	8,459,368	8,458,791	99.99%	8,262,522	97.67%	8,152,629	96.37%	7,629,688	90.19%	224,224	2.65%
Applications	Firefox	3,260,948	3,258,628	99.93%	1,518,640	46.57%	999,160	30.64%	371,336	11.39%	-	-
	MC	16,020	15,940	99.50%	2,380	14.86%	1,685	10.52%	5	0.03%	-	-
	Mplayer	452,400	452,338	99.99%	252,296	55.77%	0	0.00%	0	0%	-	-
	Pidgin	47,018	47,018	100%	9,475	20.15%	8,605	18.30%	231	0.49%	-	-
	Pine	91,215	91,215	100%	44,982	49.31%	41,769	45.79%	970	1.06%	-	-
	Proftpd	51,906	51,404	99.03%	20,044	38.62%	20,044	38.62%	3,156	6.08%	-	-
	Sendmail	7,321	7,176	98.02%	6,376	87.09%	4,560	62.29%	684	9.34%	-	-
	Sshd	148,885	148,885	100%	148,885	100%	148,885	100%	72	0.05%	-	-
	Vim	98,791	98,791	100%	98,142	99.34%	4,213	4.26%	4,191	4.24%	-	-
	W3m	128,569	127,330	99.04%	127,302	99.01%	80,934	62.95%	32,914	25.60%	-	-
	Wget	80112	80112	100%	40,344	50.36%	40,344	50.36%	40,344	50.36%	-	-
	Xpdf	76,015	76,015	100%	27,401	36.05%	0	0%	0	0%	-	-
	Yafc	477	477	100%	477	100%	477	100%	477	100%	-	-
	Audacious	216,428	216,427	100%	9,031	4.17%	867	0.4%	867	0.4%	-	-
	Bash	1,325	111	8.38%	109	8.23%	109	8.23%	109	8.23%	-	-
	Apache	3,951,923	3,951,523	99.99%	3,951,130	99.98%	3,951,130	99.98%	490,023	12.40%	-	-
	Mysqld	38,344,585	38,344,430	100%	37,363,478	97.44%	37,363,395	97.44%	36,865,575	96.14%	631,115	1.65%

Table 5: Number of log entries after garbage collection.

	Applications	Temp	Log	Data unit
Servers	Sshd-5.9	N	Y	N
	Sendmail-8.12.11	N	N	N
	Proftpd-1.3.4	N	Y	N
	Apache-2.2.21	N	Y	N
	Cherokee-1.2.1	N	Y	N
	Squid-3.2.6	Y	Y	N
	Gmediaserver-0.13.0	N	Y	N
	MySQL-5.1.66	Y	Y	Y
UI Programs	Wget-1.13	N	N	N
	W3m-0.5.2	Y	Y	N
	Pine-4.64	N	N	N
	MidnightCommand-4.6.1	Y	Y	N
	Vim-7.3	Y	Y	N
	Bash-4.2	N	Y	N
	Firefox-11	Y	Y	N
	Yafc-1.1.1	N	N	N
	Pidgin-2.10.6	Y	Y	N
	Xpdf-3.03	Y	N	N
	Mplayer-1.1	Y	N	N
	Audacious-2.5.4	Y	N	N

Table 4: Application description

6.1 Effectiveness

Regular User Systems. In the first experiment, we collect audit logs from machines of five different users (with the same system image). Each log is collected from one day's execution. The users have different usage patterns. User1 is a software developer who used `Vim` editor and compilers a lot. He also downloaded and installed several tools during the one-day experiment. User2 ran a web server and a public ftp server. User3 mostly used `Firefox` for web surfing and `Xpdf` to view PDF files. He also used the `Pidgin` chat client to communicate with friends. User4 watched a set of movies using `Mplayer` and also used `Audacious` to listen to music. User5 used the system in the console mode. He used text-based applications such as `W3m` for the Web and `pine` for emails.

We ran LogGC at the end of the one-day execution. The results are presented in Table 5. The third column shows the total number of log entries in each original audit log. Columns 4 and 5 present the reduced log size (and percentage) when we perform the basic GC algorithm (Section 2), except that we do not garbage collect any dead-end event, in order to support forward analysis (Section 3). The results in the first 5 rows show that the basic algorithm is not very effective. It can reduce 35%/40% for the logs of User1/User5 because they ran short-running applications hence false dependences, which would unnecessarily prevent garbage collection, are less likely.

Columns 6 and 7 show log reduction when we use execution partitioning for long running applications on top of the basic algorithm. In the first five rows, we can remove an average of 60.45% of the audit logs. In columns 8 and 9, we additionally garbage-collect temporary file deletions, which also enables collecting the events that they depend on (Section 3). LogGC reduces an average of 76.25% of the original log entries. In columns 10 and 11, we remove the redundant entries captured in application logs (Section 5). The results show that LogGC reduces 91.49% of the original logs. The last two columns show log reduction when we use data unit partitioning (Section 4.1). Only User2 used `mysql` as the backend for his web server. LogGC can reduce half of the remaining entries for User2. Finally, the average size of the remaining logs (of the five users) is only 7.11% of the original size, indicating an order of magnitude of reduction.

Server Systems. In the next experiment, we focus on evaluating LogGC on server system logs. We use RUBiS [5] which is an auction service similar to eBay. We setup the auction site using the default configuration with `apache` as frontend and `mysql` as backend. In our setup, both `apache` and `mySQL` are located in the same machine. After initialization, we have 9 tables in the database which contain 33,721 items for sale in 20 categories. This database is acquired from [5]. Then we use the client emulator that acts as users (buyers or sellers) of the bidding system. The client emulator uses 27 pre-defined transitions such as user registration, item registration, item browsing by category, bidding, buying and leaving comments during execution. We use all 5 different setups for client emulation provided by RUBiS. Each execution emulates 240 users performing 60,000 to 70,000 transitions and lasts 20 to 30 minutes. We acquire the audit log of the bidding server after each execution and apply LogGC .

The "Web server benchmark" rows in Table 5 show the results. We can observe that most GC strategies are not as effective as on user systems. With "execution partitioning", "temp file" and "application log" strategies, we can reduce only 10% of the logs (columns 10 and 11) even though both `apache` and `mysql` have independent execution units, temporary files, and application logs. This is because the executions heavily access the index and data files in the database such that most execution units become reachable through file-level dependences. Columns 12 and 13 show the reduced log size with data unit partitioning. Only 2.65% of the log entries need to be preserved on average, corresponding to a 37-time reduction.

Per Application Results. We also present the results for individual applications. They are aggregated from the aforementioned user system executions and server executions. We observe that the events from some applications can be completely garbage-collected such as `Mplayer` and `Xpdf`. `Mplayer` is a video player and it interacts with the screen and the sound card. But its execution does not affect system execution in the future. Similarly, `Xpdf` only displays PDF files on the screen. On the other hand, we cannot garbage collect any events from `Yafc`, an ftp client, because the user downloaded files using `Yafc` and kept all the files in the system. Similar explanation applies to `W3m` and `Wget`.

6.2 Performance

Table 6 shows the performance of LogGC. The experiments were performed on an Intel Core i7-3770 CPU with 4GB memory running Linux 2.6.35. The execution time of LogGC is mainly divided to two parts: the log parsing time and the GC time. The table shows that LogGC is reasonably efficient. It processes 3GB of logs in about 2 minutes, with parsing time being the dominant factor. Table 7 shows the runtime overhead incurred by data unit instrumentation, using two popular benchmarks: RUBiS and SysBench. The results show that the runtime overhead is very low.

Log	Parsing time (s)	GC time (s)
User1	35.97	3.76
User2	22.09	2.65
User3	26.71	2.82
User4	47.47	4.52
User5	23.65	3.17
Rubis1	104.88	10.62
Rubis2	101.21	9.45
Rubis3	101.09	9.48
Rubis4	102.89	10.13
Rubis5	98.21	9.16

Table 6: Garbage collection performance.

Benchmarks	Response time (ms)		Overhead (%)
	Without Instrumentation	With Instrumentation	
RUBiS	4,769.6	4,825.6	1.17%
SysBench	44.68	45.58	2.04%

Table 7: Runtime overhead for data unit instrumentation.

6.3 Attack Investigation

In this section, we show that the reduced audit logs are equally informative in forensic analysis through a number of case studies. We adopt eight attack scenarios previously used to evaluate related approaches [12, 20]. For each attack scenario, we generate the causal graphs from both the original log and the reduced logs, starting from an attack symptom event (for backward analysis) or the root attack event (for forward analysis). Then we compare the two graphs to verify if they contain all causal relations pertinent to the attack and further, if they carry any unrelated ones. To avoid having over-sized graphs, the original logs are generated with execution partitioning (i.e., BEEP) [20]. In other words, we are comparing graphs from LogGC with graphs by BEEP (only).

Scenarios	# of audit log entries		Back-ward	For-ward
	Total	After GC		
1. Trojan attack [20]	356,798	9,614 (2.69%)	Match	Match
2. Attack ramification [20]	690,231	50,271 (7.30%)	Match	Match
3. Information theft [20]	572,712	178,213 (31.12%)	-	Match
4. Illegal storage [12]	212,321	59,236 (27.90%)	Match	Match
5. Content destruction [12]	328,297	37,282 (11.36%)	Match	-
6. Unhappy student [12]	572,385	45,821 (8.01%)	Match	Match
7. Compromised database [12]	102,415	4,657 (4.55%)	Match	Better
8. Weak password [12]	182,346	43,214 (23.70%)	Better	Better

Table 8: Attack scenarios ("Match" means identical causal graphs with and without LogGC; "Better" means a smaller and precise graph with LogGC.)

Table 8 summarizes the results. The second and third columns show the number of audit log entries in the original and reduced logs, respectively. The last two columns show the results of causal graph comparison in both backward and forward analysis. The results show that all causal graphs by LogGC capture the minimal and precise attack paths and the right set of attack ramifications; whereas the graphs from the original logs either are identical to their counterparts or contain extra (and unrelated) causal relations.

In the **first** scenario ("trojan attack"), the victim received a phishing email that contained a malicious URL. The user clicked it and `firefox` visited the malicious page. The user downloaded a backdoor trojan and executed it. The administrator later detected the backdoor program and started forensic analysis. In the **second** scenario, the attacker exploited a vulnerability of `Proftpd` to acquire a root shell and installed a backdoor. Then he modified *.bash_history* to remove the footprint. The user later noticed the backdoor process. The causal graphs (from both the original and the reduced logs) precisely capture that the attacker modified `.bash_history`. The **third** scenario involves information theft. An insider used `vim` to open three classified files and two other html files. He copied some classified information from *secret_1* to *secret.html* and also modified *index.html*. Then an external attacker connected to the web server and read *secret.html*. LogGC does not garbage collect the `httpd` units that sent the modified html files and thus the reduced log contains the event that sent *secret.html* to the attacker. The forward casual graphs from the secret files clearly tracks down the attack, including the attacker's IP through which he retrieved the secret information. In the **fourth** scenario, the attacker launched a `pwck` local escalation exploit to get a root shell and then modified */etc/passwd* and */etc/shadow* to create an account. Then the attacker created directories and downloaded illegal files, including a trojaned `ls` to hide the illegal files. A victim user used the trojaned `ls` and created two files in his home directory. Later, the attacker logged into the system using the created account and downloaded more illegal files. The administrator later detected the trojaned `ls` and started forensic analysis. There are two forward causal graphs in this case. The first one starting from the trojaned `ls` identifies the victim user and the files generated, which may be compromised. The second one from */etc/passwd* is larger because it includes all `ssh` login activities. The attacker's login and download activities are captured but events from normal users are

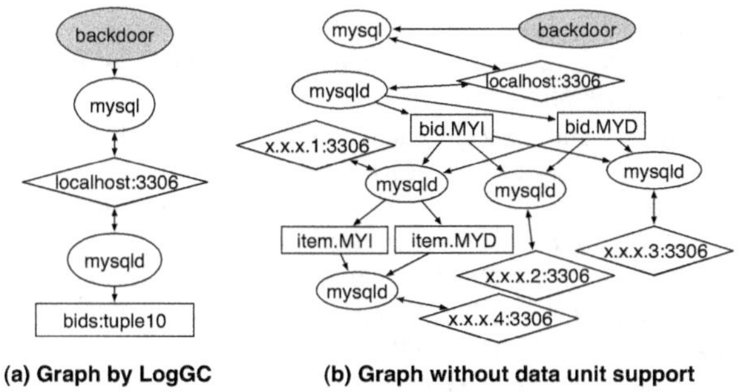

Figure 8: Causal graph comparison for attack scenario 7.

also included. In the **fifth** scenario ("content destruction"), the attacker exploited a `sendmail` vulnerability to get a root shell and he deleted files from other users' directories. The victim detected some of his files were missing and restored them from backup storage. In the **sixth** scenario, the attacker launched a remote attack on the ftp server and modified some file permissions to globally writable. Two other malicious users modified a victim's files and copied them into their own directories. The victim later detected that his files were globally writable.

In the next two scenarios, *mysql* played an important role on the attack paths. LogGC hence produces better causal graphs than those derived from the original logs. In the **seventh** scenario, the attacker launched a remote attack on the Samba daemon to get a root shell and created a backdoor. The attacker logged in later through the backdoor and issued SQL queries to remove some transaction from the local database. Later the user accessed the database and detected problems. We performed backward analysis from the backdoor. The causal graphs from both the reduced log and the original log are identical. However, data units prove to be very effective for forward analysis such that we can precisely pinpoint tuples affected by the attacker. In contrast, the graph from the original log indicates that the entire table may be affected by the attacker. In Fig. 8, we compare the forward causal graphs for this case with and without data unit support. The graph by LogGC (with data unit support) precisely detects the tuple modified by the attacker, whereas the graph without data unit support indicates that the entire *bid* table was affected and it also shows three other users who accessed table *bid* even though they did not access the modified tuple. The user from `x.x.x.1` modified a tuple in table *item* after he read *bid* hence table `item` is considered affected. After that, another user from `x.x.x.4` accessed table *item* and thus is also included in the graph. As a result, the graph by LogGC contains 5 nodes which precisely capture the attack ramifications, whereas the graph without data unit support has 16 nodes including 10 unrelated objects and users.

In the last scenario, the administrator used `photo-gallery` to upload digital pictures and created an account with a weak password for the user. Before the user changed the password, the attacker grabbed the password using dictionary attack. The attacker logged into the gallery program, uploaded some pictures, and viewed the user's album. The user later detected the attacker's pictures. The graphs by LogGC are precise in revealing the attack: The backward graph includes 47 nodes and the forward graph contains 61 nodes. Both are verified to carry the precise set of forensic information items related to this attack. In contrast, the backward graph from the original log contains 326 nodes and the forward graph has 517 nodes. Most of them are introduced by false database dependences.

7. RELATED WORK

Classic Garbage Collection. There is a large body of work on garbage collecting in-memory objects [4, 9, 10, 14]. The nature of our problem has some similarity to classic garbage collection. However we cannot simply use classic GC for provenance log reduction for the following reasons. First, we have to operate on audit logs with a flat structure instead of on memory reference graphs in classic GC. Second, classic GC only needs to identify object reachability in one direction; but we have to consider both forward and backward directions to cater for attack forensic needs. Third, classic GC can make use of very precise byte level reference information to determine reachability; whereas we only have the coarse-grain system level dependences in audit logs. As shown in our experiments, a basic reachability-based GC algorithm can hardly work on audit logs.

System-level Provenance. In recent years, significant progress has been made on tracking system-level dependences for attack forensics using audit logs [3, 8, 11, 13, 16, 17, 18, 20, 22, 23, 24]. These techniques use audit logs to identify root cause of an attack and perform forward tracking to reveal the attack's impacts. LogGC complements these techniques by garbage collecting audit logs to substantially reduce their size without affecting forensic analysis accuracy. In particular, while we leverage the execution partitioning technique in BEEP [20], LogGC and BEEP differ in that: (1) LogGC focuses on garbage-collecting audit logs whereas BEEP does not; (2) BEEP cannot handle dependences with database engines, which are critical to reducing server audit logs and generating precise causal graphs.

System-level replay techniques have been proposed to roll back a victim system after an attack [6, 12, 15]. They record system-wide execution events so that the whole system can be replayed from a checkpoint. LogGC may potentially complement these techniques by garbage-collecting unnecessary events from execution logs without affecting replay fidelity.

Database Provenance. There exists a line of research in providing fine-grain data lineage for database systems. Trio [2] and SubZero [25] introduce new features to manage fine-grain lineage along with data. They track provenance by transforming/reversing queries. As such, they need to know the queries before hand, without instrumenting the database engine.

Log Compression. Some existing techniques involve compressing provenance logs via a web graph compression technique [26] or detecting common sub-trees and then compressing them [7]. As log compression techniques, they are orthogonal to LogGC . We envision future integration of LogGC and these techniques.

8. CONCLUSION

We present LogGC, a GC-enabled audit logging system towards practical computer attack forensics. Audit log garbage collection poses new challenges beyond traditional memory GC techniques. It should support both forward and backward forensic analysis whereas traditional memory GC only needs to support one direction of correlation. Moreover, the granularity of existing audit logging approach is insufficient, especially for long running programs and database servers. We propose a technique that partitions a database file into data units so that dependences can be captured at tuple level. Together with our earlier solution of partitioning a process into execution units, LogGC greatly reduces false dependences that prevent effective GC. LogGC entails instrumenting user programs only at a few locations, incurring low overhead (< 2.04%). Without any compression, LogGC can reduce audit log size by a factor of 14 for user systems and 37 for server systems. The reduced audit logs preserve all necessary information for full forensic analysis.

9. ACKNOWLEDGMENT

We would like to thank the anonymous reviewers and our shepherd, Wenliang Du, for their insightful comments. This research has been supported in part by DARPA under Contract 12011593 and by NSF under awards 0917007 and 0845870. Any opinions, findings, and conclusions in this paper are those of the authors only and do not necessarily reflect the views of DARPA and NSF.

10. REFERENCES

[1] http://sysbench.sourceforge.net.

[2] P. Agrawal, O. Benjelloun, A. D. Sarma, C. Hayworth, S. Nabar, T. Sugihara, and J. Widom. Trio: a system for data, uncertainty, and lineage. In *Proceedings of the 32nd international conference on Very large data bases*, VLDB 2006.

[3] P. Ammann, S. Jajodia, and P. Liu. Recovery from malicious transactions. *IEEE Transaction on Knowledge and Data Engineering*, September, 2002.

[4] A. W. Appel. Simple generational garbage collection and fast allocation. *Software Practice and Experience*, 1989.

[5] E. Cecchet, J. Marguerite, and W. Zwaenepoel. Performance and scalability of ejb applications. In *Proceedings of the 17th ACM SIGPLAN conference on Object-oriented programming, systems, languages, and applications*, OOPSLA 2002.

[6] R. Chandra, T. Kim, M. Shah, N. Narula, and N. Zeldovich. Intrusion recovery for database-backed web applications. In *Proceedings of the 23th ACM Symposium on Operating Systems Principles*, SOSP 2011.

[7] A. P. Chapman, H. V. Jagadish, and P. Ramanan. Efficient provenance storage. In *Proceedings of the ACM SIGMOD international conference on Management of data*, SIGMOD 2008.

[8] J. Chow, B. Pfaff, T. Garfinkel, K. Christopher, and M. Rosenblum. Understanding data lifetime via whole system simulation. In *Proceedings of the 13th conference on USENIX Security Symposium*, SSYM 2004.

[9] L. P. Deutsch and D. G. Bobrow. An efficient, incremental, automatic garbage collector. *Communications of the ACM*, 1976.

[10] E. W. Dijkstra, L. Lamport, A. J. Martin, C. S. Scholten, and E. F. M. Steffens. On-the-fly garbage collection: an exercise in cooperation. *Communications of the ACM*, 1978.

[11] A. Goel, W.-c. Feng, W.-c. Feng, and D. Maier. Automatic high-performance reconstruction and recovery. *Computer Networks*, April, 2007.

[12] A. Goel, K. Po, K. Farhadi, Z. Li, and E. de Lara. The taser intrusion recovery system. In *Proceedings of the 22th ACM symposium on Operating systems principles*, SOSP 2005.

[13] X. Jiang, A. Walters, D. Xu, E. H. Spafford, F. Buchholz, and Y.-M. Wang. Provenance-aware tracing of worm break-in and contaminations: A process coloring approach. In *Proceedings of the 26th IEEE International Conference on Distributed Computing Systems*, ICDCS 2006.

[14] R. Jones and R. Lins. *Garbage collection: algorithms for automatic dynamic memory management*. John Wiley & Sons, Inc., 1996.

[15] T. Kim, X. Wang, N. Zeldovich, and M. F. Kaashoek. Intrusion recovery using selective re-execution. In *Proceedings of the 9th USENIX conference on Operating systems design and implementation*, OSDI 2010.

[16] S. T. King and P. M. Chen. Backtracking intrusions. In *Proceedings of the 19th ACM symposium on Operating systems principles*, SOSP 2003.

[17] S. T. King, Z. M. Mao, D. G. Lucchetti, and P. M. Chen. Enriching intrusion alerts through multi-host causality. In *Proceedings of the 13th Annual Network and Distributed System Security Symposium*, NDSS 2005.

[18] S. Krishnan, K. Z. Snow, and F. Monrose. Trail of bytes: efficient support for forensic analysis. In *Proceedings of the 17th ACM conference on Computer and communications security*, CCS 2010.

[19] M. Laurenzano, M. Tikir, L. Carrington, and A. Snavely. Pebil: Efficient static binary instrumentation for linux. In *Proceedings of the IEEE International Symposium on Performance Analysis of Systems and Software*, ISPASS 2010.

[20] K. H. Lee, X. Zhang, and D. Xu. High accuracy attack provenance via binary-based execution partition. In *Proceedings of the 20th Annual Network and Distributed System Security Symposium*, NDSS 2013.

[21] C. Luk, R. Cohn, R. Muth, H. Patil, A. Klauser, G. Lowney, S. Wallace, V. Reddi, and K. Hazelwood. Pin: building customized program analysis tools with dynamic instrumentation. In *Proceedings of the ACM SIGPLAN conference on Programming language design and implementation*, PLDI 2005.

[22] J. Newsome and D. X. Song. Dynamic taint analysis for automatic detection, analysis, and signature generation of exploits on commodity software. In *Proceedings of the 13th Annual Network and Distributed System Security Symposium*, NDSS 2005.

[23] S. Sitaraman and S. Venkatesan. Forensic analysis of file system intrusions using improved backtracking. In *Proceedings of the 3rd IEEE International Workshop on Information Assurance*, IWIA 2005.

[24] D. Tariq, M. Ali, and A. Gehani. Towards automated collection of application-level data provenance. In *Proceedings of the 4th USENIX conference on Theory and Practice of Provenance*, TaPP 2012.

[25] E. Wu, S. Madden, and M. Stonebraker. Subzero: a fine-grained lineage system for scientific databases. In *Proceedings of the 29th IEEE international conference on Data Engineering*, ICDE 2013.

[26] Y. Xie, D. Feng, Z. Tan, L. Chen, K.-K. Muniswamy-Reddy, Y. Li, and D. D. Long. A hybrid approach for efficient provenance storage. In *Proceedings of the 21st ACM international conference on Information and knowledge management*, CIKM 2012.

Identity, Location, Disease and More: Inferring Your Secrets from Android Public Resources

Xiaoyong Zhou[1], Soteris Demetriou[2], Dongjing He[2], Muhammad Naveed[2], Xiaorui Pan[1], XiaoFeng Wang[1], Carl A. Gunter[2], Klara Nahrstedt[2]
[1]School of Informatics and Computing, Indiana University, Bloomington, IN USA
[2]Department of Computer Science, University of Illinois, Urbana-Champaign, IL USA
{zhou, xiaopan, xw7}@indiana.edu,
{sdemetr2, dhe6, naveed2, cgunter, klara}@illinois.edu

ABSTRACT

The design of Android is based on a set of unprotected shared resources, including those inherited from Linux (e.g., Linux public directories). However, the dramatic development in Android applications (*app* for short) makes available a large amount of public background information (e.g., social networks, public online services), which can potentially turn such originally harmless resource sharing into serious privacy breaches. In this paper, we report our work on this important yet understudied problem. We discovered three unexpected channels of information leaks on Android: per-app data-usage statistics, ARP information, and speaker status (on or off). By monitoring these channels, an app without *any* permission may acquire sensitive information such as smartphone user's identity, the disease condition she is interested in, her geo-locations and her driving route, from top-of-the-line Android apps. Furthermore, we show that using existing and new techniques, this zero-permission app can both determine when its target (a particular application) is running and send out collected data stealthily to a remote adversary. These findings call into question the soundness of the design assumptions on shared resources, and demand effective solutions. To this end, we present a mitigation mechanism for achieving a delicate balance between utility and privacy of such resources.

Categories and Subject Descriptors

D.4.6 [**OPERATING SYSTEMS**]: Security and Protection—*Security kernels*; K.4.1 [**COMPUTERS AND SOCIETY**]: Public Policy Issues—*Privacy*

Keywords

Mobile Security, Privacy, Information Leaks

1. INTRODUCTION

Compared with the phenomenal progress in smartphone technologies, the ways smartphones are being used today are even more stunning. Increasingly, they become primary devices not only for the traditional phone calling, but for email checking, messaging, mapping/navigation, entertainment, social networking and even for activities as important as healthcare and investment management. This abrupt development challenges the limits of smartphone designers' imagination, and naturally calls into question whether the original security designs of smartphone systems, like Android, are ready for those highly diverse, fast-evolving applications. Indeed, recent years have seen waves of Android-based malware [3, 7] that exploit different vulnerabilities within this new computing platform, highlighting the security and privacy threats it is facing.

Android's security protection has been under scrutiny for years. A few weaknesses of the system, such as permission re-delegation [21] and capability leaks [27], are revealed by researchers. Particularly, a recent blog [16] from Leviathan Security Group describes the malicious activities that could be performed by an app without any permissions, including reading from SD card, accessing a list of installed apps, getting some device and system information (GSM and SIM vendor ID, the Android ID and kernel version) and pinging through a Linux Shell. Most of the problems reported here are either implementation weaknesses or design ambiguities that lead developers to inadvertent exposures. Examples include SD card read and unauthorized ping, which have all been fixed. The rest turn out to be less of a concern, as they are almost impossible to exploit in practice (GSM/SIM/Android ID, which leads to nothing more than mobile country code and mobile network code).

Actually, the design of Android takes security seriously. It is built upon a sandbox and permission model, in which each app is isolated from others by Linux user-based protection and required to explicitly ask for permissions to access the resources outside its sandbox before it can be installed on a phone. Compared with what are provided by conventional desktop-oriented OSes, even Linux on which Android is built, this security design looks pretty solid.

Information leaks from public resources. In our research, we are asking a different question: *assuming that Android's security design has been faithfully implemented and apps are well protected by their developers, what can a malicious app still learn about the user's private information without any permissions at all?* For such a zero-permission app, all it can access are a set of seemingly harmless resources shared across users (i.e. apps), which are made publicly available by Android and its underlying Linux, for the purpose of facilitating coordination among apps and simplifying access control. However, the rapidly-evolving designs and functionalities of emerging apps, particularly their rich and diverse background information (e.g., social network, public online services, etc.), begin to invalidate such design assumptions, turning thought-to-be innocuous data into serious information leaks.

For example, consider the list of apps installed on an Android phone, which can be obtained by calling the pubic API `PackageManager.getInstalledApplications()` or looking at

CCS'13, November 4–8, 2013, Berlin, Germany.
Copyright 2013 ACM 978-1-4503-2477-9/13/11 ...$15.00.
http://dx.doi.org/10.1145/2508859.2516661 .

User IDs (UID) within a Linux Shell. Such an app list is not considered sensitive by Google and UIDs are never thought to be confidential on Linux. However, for some healthcare apps (e.g., diabetes app) and life-style apps (e.g., gay social network like Hornet), simply knowing their names can lead to a grave infringement on their users' privacy. As another example, network data usage of an app is deliberately published by Android through its Linux public directory, aiming to help a smartphone user keep track of the app's mobile data consumption. However, we found in our research that this piece of apparently harmless and also useful data can actually be used to fingerprint a user's certain online activity, such as tweeting. This knowledge, combined with the background information that comes with the Twitter app (i.e., public tweets), can be used to infer the user's true identity, using an inference technique we developed (Section 3.2).

Our study. An in-depth understanding of such information leaks from Android public resources is critical, as it reveals the gap between the fundamental limitations of Android security design and the diversity in the ways the system is utilized by app developers. This understanding will be invaluable for the future development of securer mobile OSes that support the evolving utility. However, a study on the problem has never been done before. In this paper, we report our first step on this crucial yet understudied direction.

Our study inspects public resources disclosed at both the Android and its Linux layers and analyzes the impact such exposures can have on the private information maintained by a set of popular apps, in the presence of the rich background information they bring in. This research leads to a series of stunning discoveries on what can actually be inferred from those public resources by leveraging such auxiliary information. Specifically, by monitoring the network-data usage statistics of high-profile Android apps, such as Twitter, WebMD (app by a leading healthcare information provider [1]) and Yahoo! Finance (one of the most widely-used stock apps), one can find out a smartphone user's true identity, disease conditions and stocks one is interested in, without any permissions at all. Looking at the public trace of Address Resolution Protocol (ARP) stored under a public Linux directory, a zero-permission adversary can locate the user with good accuracy. Even the status of a smartphone's speaker (on or off), which can be conveniently identified through a public Android API, `AudioManager.isMusicActive`, turns out to be a serious information leak. We show that when a GPS navigator is being used, from the audio-on/off status, an inference technique we built can figure out the place the smartphone user goes and her driving route. A video demo of these attacks is posted online [12].

All such information leaks are found to be strongly related to the fallacies of design assumptions instead of mere implementation bugs. Every piece of information here is actually meant to be disclosed by Android and most of such data has been extensively used by legitimate Android apps: for example, hundreds of data usage monitors are already out there [5], relying on the usage statistics to keep track of a user's mobile data consumption. Therefore, fixing these information leaks must be done carefully to avoid undermining the basic functions of these existing apps and to strike a balance between system utility and data protection. To this end, we have designed a preliminary mitigation approach that controls the way data usage information is released, which helps to better understand how to achieve such a delicate trade-off.

Contributions. We summarize the contributions of the paper as follows:

• *Understanding of information leaks from Android public resources.* Different from prior research that mainly focuses on implementation flaws within Android, our study contributes to a better understanding of an understudied yet fundamental weakness in Android design: the information leaks from the resources that are not originally considered to be confidential and therefore made available for improving system usability. This has been achieved through a suite of new inference techniques designed to demonstrate that highly-sensitive user data can be recovered from the public resources, in the presence of rich background information provided by popular apps and online resources.

• *First step toward mitigating this new threat.* We have developed a new mitigation approach, aiming to preserve the utility of such public data to the legitimate parties while controlling the way that an adversary can use it to derive user secrets.

Roadmap. The rest of the paper is organized as follows: Section 2 analyzes the privacy risks of Android public resources and the adversary model; Section 3, 4 and 5 elaborate the new side channels we discovered and the techniques we use to infer confidential information from them; Section 6 describes our mitigation approach; Section 7 compares our work with prior related research and Section 8 concludes the paper.

2. THREATS TO PUBLIC RESOURCES

2.1 Leaks from Public Resources

Android is an operating system built on top of Linux. Its security model is based upon Linux's kernel level protection (process separation, file system access control). Specifically, each Android app is assigned with a unique user ID and runs as that user. Sensitive resources are usually mapped to special Linux groups such as inet, gps, etc. This approach, called *application sandboxing*, enables the Linux kernel to separate an app from other running apps. Within a sandbox, an app can invoke Android APIs to access system resources. The APIs that operate on sensitive resources, including camera, location, network, etc., are protected by permissions. An app needs to explicitly request (using AndroidManifest.xml) from the device's user such permissions during its installation so as to get assigned to the Linux groups of the resources under protection, before it can utilize such resources.

Public resources on Android. Like any operating system, Android provides a set of shared resources that underprivileged users (apps without any permission) can access. This is necessary for making the system easy to use for both app developers and end users. Following is a rough classification of the resources available to those zero-permission apps:

• *Linux layer: public directories.* Linux historically makes available a large amount of resources considered harmless to normal users, to help them coordinate their activities. A prominent example is the process information displayed by the `ps` command (invoked through `Runtime.getRuntime.exec`), which includes each running process's user ID, Process ID (PID), memory and CPU consumption and other statistics.

Most of such resources are provided through two virtual filesystems, the proc filesystem (procfs) and the sys filesystem (sysfs). The procfs contains public statistics about a process's use of memory, CPU, network resources and other data. Under the sysfs directories, one can find device/driver information, network environment data (`/sys/class/net/`) and more. Android inherits such public resources from Linux and enhances the system with new ones (e.g. `/proc/uid_stat`). For example, the network traffic statistics (`/proc/uid_stat/tcp_snd` and `/proc/uid_stat/tcp_rcv`) are extensively utilized [5] to keep track of individual apps' mobile data consumption.

• *Android layer: Android public APIs*. In addition to the public resources provided by Linux, Android further offers public APIs to enable apps to get access to public data and interact with each other. An example is `AudioManager.requestAudioFocus`, which coordinates apps' use of the audio resource (e.g, muting the music when a phone call comes in).

Privacy risks. All such public resources are considered to be harmless and their releases are part of the design which is important to the system's normal operations. Examples include the coordinations among users through `ps` and among the apps using audio resources through `AudioManager.requestAudioFocus`. However, those old design assumptions on the public resources are becoming increasingly irrelevant in front of the fast-evolving ways to use smartphones. We found that the following design/use gaps are swiftly widening:

• *Gap between Linux design and smartphone use*. Linux comes with the legacy of its original designs for workstations and servers. Some of its information disclosure, which could be harmless in these stationary environments, could become a critical issue for mobile phones. For example, Linux makes the MAC address of the wireless access points (WAP) available under its procfs. This does not seem to be a big issue for a workstation or even a laptop back a few years ago. For a smartphone, however, knowledge about such information will lead to disclosure of a phone user's location, particularly with the recent development that databases have been built for fingerprinting geo-locations with WAPs' MAC addresses (called *Basic Service Set Identification, or BSSID*).

• *Gap between the assumptions on Android public resources and evolving app design, functionalities and background information*. Even more challenging is the dramatic evolution of Android apps. For example, an app is often dedicated to a specific website. Therefore, the adversary no longer needs to infer the website a user visits, as it can be easily found out by looking at which app is running (through `ps` for example). Most importantly, today's apps often come with a plethora of background information like tweets, public posts and public web services such as Google Maps. As a result, even very thin information about the app's behavior (e.g., posting a message), as exposed by the public resources, could be linked to such public knowledge to recover sensitive user data.

Information leaks. In our research, we carefully analyzed the ways that public resources are utilized by the OS and popular apps on Android, together with the public online information related to their operations. Our study discovered three confirmed new sources of information leaks:

• *App network-data usage* (Section 3). We found that the data usage statistics disclosed by the procfs can be used to precisely fingerprint an app's behavior and even infer its input data, by leveraging online resources such as tweets published by Twitter. To demonstrate the seriousness of the information leakage from those usage data, we develop a suite of inference techniques that can reveal a phone user's identity from the network-data consumption of Twitter app, the disease conditions she is interested in from that of WebMD app and the stock she is looking at from Yahoo! Finance app.

• *Public ARP information* (Section 4). We discovered that the public ARP data released by Android (under its Linux public directory) contains the BSSID of the WAP a phone is connected to, and demonstrate how to practically utilize such information to locate a phone user through BSSID databases.

• *Audio status API* (Section 5). We show that the public audio status information (speaker on/off) collected from a GPS navigator can be used to fingerprint a driving route. We further present an inference technique that uses Google Maps and the status information to practically identify her driving route on the map.

We built a zero-permission app that stealthily collects information for these attacks. A video demo is posted online [12].

2.2 Zero-Permission Adversary

Adversary model. The adversary considered in our research runs a zero-permission app on the victim's smartphone. Such an app needs to operate in a stealthy way to visually conceal its presence from the user and also minimize its impact on a smartphone's performance. On the other hand, the adversary has the resources to analyze the data gathered by the app using publicly available background information, for example, through crawling the public information released by social networks, searching Google Maps, etc. Such activities can be performed by ordinary Internet users.

What the adversary can do. In addition to collecting and analyzing the information gathered from the victim's device, a zero-permission malicious app needs a set of capabilities to pose a credible privacy threat. Particularly, it needs to send data across the Internet without the INTERNET permission. Also, it should stay aware of the system's *situation*, i.e., which apps are currently running. This enables the malicious app to keep a low profile, start data collection only when its target app is being executed. Here we show how these capabilities can be obtained by the app without any permission.

• *Networking*. Leviathan's blog describes a zero-permission technique to smuggle out data across the Internet [16]. The idea is to let the sender app use the `URI ACTION_VIEW` Intent to open a browser and sneak the payload it wants to deliver to the parameters of an HTTP `GET` from the receiver website. We re-implemented this technique in our research and further made it stealthy. Leviathan's approach does not work when the screen is off because the browser is `paused` when the screen is off. We improved this method to smuggle data right before the screen is off or the screen is being unlocked. Specifically, our app continuously monitors `/lcd_power` (`/sys/class/lcd/panel/lcd_power` on Galaxy Nexus), an LCD status indicator released under the sysfs. Note that this indicator can be located under other directory on other devices, for example, `sys/class/backlight/s6e8aa0` on Nexus Prime. When the indicator becomes zero, the phone screen dims out, which allows our app to send out data through the browser without being noticed by the user. After the data transmission is done, our app can redirect the browser to Google and also set the phone to its home screen to cover this operation.

• *Situation awareness*. Our zero permission app defines a list of target applications such as stock, health, location applications and monitors their activities. It first checks whether those packages are installed on the victim's system (`getInstalledApplications()`) and then periodically calls `ps` to get a list of active apps and their PIDs. Once a target is found to be active, our app will start a thread that closely monitors the `/proc/uid_stats/[uid]` and the `/proc/[pid]/` of the target.

3. GETTING YOUR IDENTITY, HEALTH AND INVESTMENT INFORMATION

In this section, we report our study on information leaks from public data usage statics.

3.1 Usage Monitoring and Analysis

Mobile-data usage statistics. Mobile data usages of Android are made public under `/proc/uid_stat/` (per app) and

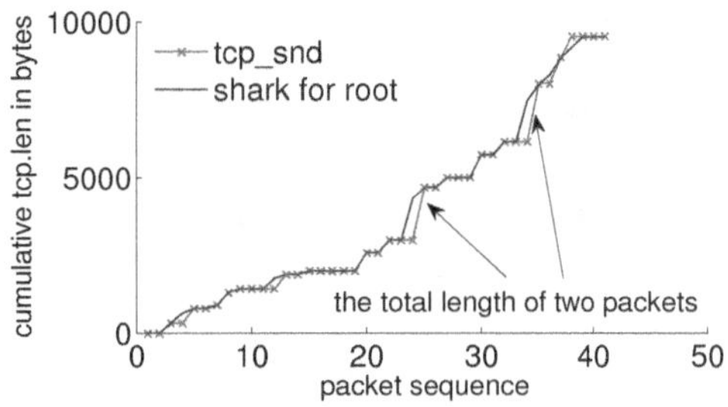

Figure 1: Monitor tool precision

Table 1: Performance overhead of the monitor tool: there the baseline is measured by AnTuTu [8]

	Total	CPU	GPU	RAM	I/O
Baseline	3776	777	1816	588	595
Monitor Tool	3554	774	1606	589	585
Overhead	5.8%	0.3%	11.6%	-0.1%	1.7%

/sys/class/net/[interface] /statistics/ (per interface). The former is newly introduced by Android to keep track of individual apps. These directories can be read by *any* app directly or through TrafficStats, a public API class. Of particular interest here are two files /proc/uid_stat/[uid]/tcp_rcv and /proc/uid_stat/[uid]/tcp_snd, which record the total numbers of bytes received and sent by a specific app respectively. We found that these two statistics are actually aggregated from TCP packet payloads: for every TCP packet received or sent by an app, Android adds the length of its payload onto the corresponding statistics. These statistics are extensively used for mobile data consumption monitoring [5]. However, our research shows that their updates can also be leveraged to fingerprint an app's network operations, such as sending HTTP POST or GET messages.

Stealthy and realtime monitoring. To catch the updates of those statistics in real time, we built a data-usage monitor that continuously reads from tcp_rcv and tcp_snd of a target app to record increments in their values. Such an increment is essentially the length of the payload delivered by a single or multiple TCP packets the app receives and sends, depending on how fast the monitor samples from those statistics. Our current implementation has a sampling rate of 10 times per second. This is found to be sufficient for picking up individual packets most of the time, as illustrated in Figure 1, in which we compare the packet payloads observed by Shark for Root (a network traffic sniffer for 3G and WiFi), when the user is using Yahoo! Finance, with the cumulative outbound data usage detected by our usage monitor.

From the figure we can see that most of the time, our monitor can separate different packets from each other. However, there are situations in which only the cumulative length of multiple packets is identified (see the markers in the figure). This requires an analysis that can tolerate such non-determinism, which we discuss later.

In terms of performance, our monitor has a very small memory footprint, only 28 MB, even below that of the default Android keyboard app. When it is running at its peak speed, it takes about 7% of a core's cycles on a Google Nexus S phone. Since all the new phones released today are armed with multi-core CPUs, the monitor's operations will not have noticeable impacts on the performance of the app running in the foreground as demonstrated by a test described in Table 1 measured using AnTuTu [8] with a sampling rate of 10Hz for network usage and 50Hz for audio logging (Section 5). To make this data collection stealthier, we adopted a strategy that samples intensively only when the target app is being executed, which is identified through ps (Section 2.2).

Analysis methodology. The monitor cannot always produce deterministic outcomes: when sampling the same packet sequence twice, it may observe two different sequences of increments from the usage statistics. To obtain a reliable traffic fingerprint of a target app's activity we designed a methodology to bridge the gap between the real sequence and what the monitor sees.

Our approach first uses Shark for Root to analyze a target app's behavior (e.g., click on a button) offline - i.e in a controlled context - and generate a payload-sequence signature for the behavior. Once our monitor collects a sequence of usage increments from the app's runtime on the victim's Android phone, we compare this usage sequence with the signature as follows. Consider a signature $(\cdots, s_i, s_{i+1}, \cdots, s_{i+n}, \cdots)$, where $s_{i,\cdots,i+n}$ are the payload lengths of the TCP packets with the same direction (inbound/outbound), and a sequence $(\cdots, m_j, \cdots)$, where m_j is an increment on a usage statistic (tcp_rcv or tcp_snd) of the direction of s_i, as observed by our monitor. Suppose that all the elements before m_j match the elements in the signature (those prior to s_i). We say that m_j also matches the signature elements if either $m_j = s_i$ or $m_j = s_i + \cdots + s_{i+k}$ with $1 < k \leq n$. The whole sequence is considered to *match* the signature if all of its elements match the signature elements.

For example, consider that the signature for requesting the information about a disease condition *ABSCESS* by WebMD is $(458, 478, 492 \rightarrow)$, where "$\rightarrow$" indicates outbound traffic. Usage sequences matching the signature can be $(458, 478, 492 \rightarrow)$, $(936, 492 \rightarrow)$ or $(1428 \rightarrow)$.

The payload-sequence signature can vary across different mobile devices, due to the difference in the User-Agent field on the HTTP packets produced by these devices. This information can be acquired by a zero-permission app through the android.os.Build API, which we elaborate in Appendix A.

3.2 Identity Inference

A person's identity, such as name, email address, etc., is always considered to be highly sensitive [35, 19, 15, 29] and should not be released to an untrusted party. For a smartphone user, unauthorized disclosure of her identity can immediately reveal a lot of private information about her (e.g., disease, sex orientation, etc.) simply from the apps on her phone. Here we show how one's identity can be easily inferred using the shared resources and rich background information from Twitter.

Twitter is one of the most popular social networks with about 500 million users worldwide. It is common for Twitter users to use their mobile phones to tweet extensively and from diverse locations. Many Twitter users disclose there identity information which includes their real names, cities and sometimes homepage or blog URL and even pictures. Such information can be used to discover one's accounts on other social networks, revealing even more information about the victim according to prior research [26]. We also performed a small range survey on the identity information directly disclosed from public Twitter accounts to help us better understand what kind of information users disclose and at which extend. By manually analyzing randomly selected 3908 accounts (obvious bot accounts excluded), we discovered that 78.63% of them apparently have users' first and last names there, 32.31% set the users' locations, 20.60% include bio descriptions and 12.71% provide URLs. This indicates that the attack we describe below poses a realistic threat to Android users' identity.

The idea. In our attack, a zero-permission app monitors the mobile-data usage count tcp_snd of the Twitter 3.6.0 app when it is running. When the user send tweets to the Twitter server, the app detects this event and send its timestamp to the malicious server stealthily. This gives us a vector of timestamps for the user's tweets, which we then use to search the tweet history through public Twitter APIs for the account whose activities are consistent with the vector: that is, the account's owner posts her tweets at the moments recorded by these timestamps. Given a few of timestamps, we can uniquely identify that user. An extension of this idea could also be applied to other public social media and their apps, and leverage other information as vector elements for this identity inference: for example, the malicious app could be designed to figure out not only the timing of a blogging activity, but also the number of characters typed into the blog through monitoring the CPU usage of the keyboard app, which can then be correlated to a published post.

To make this idea work, we need to address a few technical challenges. Particularly, searching across all 340 million tweets daily is impossible. Our solution is using less protected data, the coarse location (e.g, city) of the person who tweets, to narrow down the search range (see Section 4).

Fingerprinting tweeting event. To fingerprint the tweeting event from the Twitter app, we use the aforementioned methodology to first analyze the app *offline* to generate a signature for the event. This signature is then compared with the data usage increments our zero-permission app collects *online* from the victim's phone to identify the moment she tweets.

Specifically, during the offline analysis, we observed the following TCP payload sequence produced by the Twitter app: $(420|150, 314, 580\text{–}720)$. The first element here is the payload length of a TLS Client Hello. This message normally has 420 bytes but can become 150 when the parameters of a recent TLS session are reused. What follow are a 314-byte payload for Client Key Exchange and then that of an encrypted HTTP request, either a `GET` (download tweets) or a `POST` (tweet). The encrypted `GET` has a relatively stable payload size, between 541 and 544 bytes. When the user tweets, the encrypted `POST` ranges from 580 to 720 bytes, due to the tweet's 140-character limit. So, the length sequence can be used as a signature to determine when a tweet is sent.

As discussed before, what we want to do here is to use the signature to find out the timestamp when the user tweets. The problem here is that our usage monitor running on the victim's phone does not see those packets and can only observe the increments in the data-usage statistics. Our offline analysis shows that the payload for Client Hello can be reliably detected by the monitor. However, the time interval between the Key-Exchange message and `POST` turns out to be so short that it can easily fall through the cracks. Therefore, we have to resort to the aforementioned analysis methodology (Section 3.1) to compare the data-usage sequence collected by our app with the payload signature: a tweet is considered to be sent when the increment sequence is either $(420|150, 314, 580\text{–}720)$ or $(420|150, 894\text{–}1034)$.

Identity discovery. From the tweeting events detected, we obtain a sequence of timestamps $T = [t_1, t_2, \cdots, t_n]$ that describe when the phone user tweets. This sequence is then used to find out the user's Twitter ID from the public index of tweets. Such an index can be accessed through the Twitter Search API [4]: one can call the API to search the tweets from a certain geo-location within 6 to 8 days. Each query returns 1500 most recent tweets or those published in the prior days (1500 per day). An unauthorized user can query 150 times every hour.

To collect relevant tweets, we need to get the phone's geo-location, which is specified by a triplet (latitude, longitude, radius) in the twitter search API. Here all we need is a *coarse location* (at city level) to set these parameters. Android has permissions to control the access to both coarse and fine locations of a phone. However, we found that the user's fine location could be inferred once she connects her phone to a Wi-Fi hotspot (see Section 4). Getting her coarse location in this case is much easier: our zero-permission app can invoke the mobile browser to visit a malicious website, which can then search her IP in public IP-to-location databases [11] to find her city. This allows us to set the query parameters using Google Maps. Note that smartphone users tend to use Wi-Fi whenever possible to conserve their mobile data (see Section 4), which gives our app chances to get their coarse locations. Please note that we do not require the user to geo-tag each tweet. The twitter search results include the tweets in a area as long as the user specified her geo-location in her profile.

As discussed before, our app can only sneak out the timestamps it collects from the Twitter app when the phone screen dims out. This could happen minutes away from the moment a user tweets. For each timestamp $t_i \in T$, we use the twitter API to search for the set of users u_i who tweet in that area in $t_i \pm 60s$ (due to the time skew between mobile phone and the twitter server). The target user is in the set $U = \cap u_i$. When U contains only one twitter ID, the user is identified. For a small city, oftentimes 1500 tweets returned by a query are more than enough to cover the delay including both the $t_i \pm 60s$ period and the duration between the tweet event and the moment the screen dims out. For a big city with a large population of Twitter users, however, we need to continuously query the Twitter server to dump the tweets to a local database, so when our app report a timestamp, we can search it in the database to find those who tweet at that moment.

Table 2: City information and Twitter identity exploitation

Location	Population	City size	Time interval covered (radius)	# of timestamps
Urbana	41,518	11.58 mi^2	243 min (3 mi)	3
Bloomington	81,381	19.9 mi^2	87 min (3 mi)	5
Chicago	2,707,120	234 mi^2	141 sec (3 mi)	9

Attack evaluation. We evaluated the effectiveness of this attack at three cities, Urbana, Bloomington and Chicago. Table 2 describes these cities' information.

We first studied the lengths of the time intervals the 1500 tweets returned by a Twitter query can cover in these individual cities. To this end, we examined the difference between the first and the last timestamps on 1500 tweets downloaded from the Twitter server through a single API call, and present the results in Table 2. As we can see here, for small towns with populations below 100 thousand, all the tweets within one hour and a half can be retrieved through a single query, which is sufficient for our attack: it is conceivable that the victim's phone screen will dim out within that period after she tweets, allowing the malicious app to send out the timestamp through the browser. However, for Chicago, the query outcome only covers 2 minutes of tweets. Therefore, we need to continuously dump tweets from the Twitter server to a local database to make the attack work.

In the experiment, we ran a script that repeatedly called the Twitter Search API, at a rate of 135 queries per hour. All the results without duplicates were stored in a local SQL database. Then, we posted tweets through the Twitter app on a smartphone, under the surveillance of the zero-permission app. After obvious robot Twitter accounts were eliminated from the query results, our Twitter ID were recovered by merely 3 timestamps at Urbana, 5 timestamps at Bloomington and 9 timestamps in Chicago, which is aligned with the city size and population.

3.3 Health and Investment

In this section, we show that the data-usage statistics our zero-permission app collects also leak out apps' sensitive inputs, e.g.,

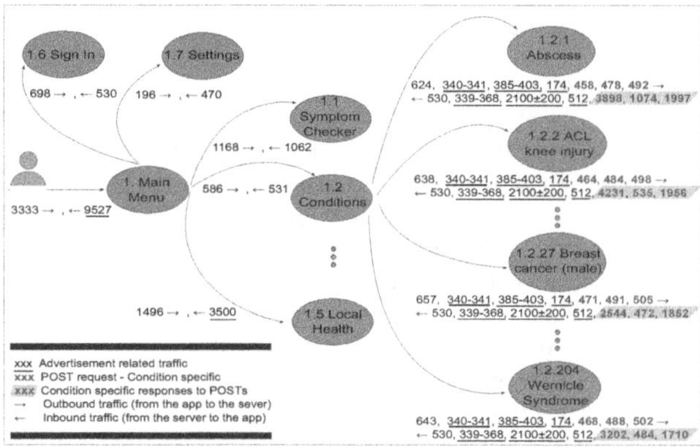

Figure 2: WebMD Finite State Machine

disease conditions a user selects on WebMD mobile [6]. This has been achieved by fingerprinting her actions with data-usage sequences they produce. The same attack technique also works on Yahoo! Finance, which is elaborated in Appendix B.

WebMD mobile. WebMD mobile is an extremely popular Android health and fitness app, which has been installed $1 \sim 5$ million times in the past 30 days [6]. To use the app, one first clicks to select 1 out of 6 sections, such as "Symptom Checker", "Conditions" and others. In our research, we analyzed the data under the "Conditions" section, which includes a list of disease conditions (e.g., Asthma, Diabetes, etc.). Each condition, once clicked on, leads to a new screen that displays the overview of the disease, its symptoms and related articles. All such information is provided through a simple, fixed user interface running on the phone, while the data there is downloaded from the web. We found that the changes of network usage statistics during this process can be reliably linked to the user's selections on the interface, revealing the disease she is interested in.

Our attack. Again, we first analyzed the app offline (i.e. in a controlled context) using Shark for Root, and built a detailed finite state machine (FSM) for it based on the payload lengths of TCP packets sent and received when the app moves from one screen (a state of the FSM) to another. The FSM is illustrated in Figure 2. Specifically, the user's selection of a section is characterized by a sequence of bytes, which is completely different from those of other sections. Each disease under the "Conditions" section is also associated with a distinctive payload sequence.

In particular, every time a user clicks on a condition she is interested in, the app produces 4 `GET` requests (with 3 `GET`s for ads); and then 3 `POST` requests to acquire the content for that condition. Among them, all ad-related requests and responses have predictable payload lengths (e.g., 174 bytes for `GET ads/dcfc.gif`) and can therefore be easily identified. The rest of the traffic (1 GET request, 3 `POST` requests and their responses) is characterized by distinctive payload lengths that can be used to fingerprint individual disease conditions. Just based on the POST requests, we can already classify all 204 conditions into 32 categories. The response payload sizes further help us uniquely identify all 204 conditions.

In a real attack, however, our zero-permission app cannot see the traffic. The usage increments it collects could come from the combination of two packets. This issue was addressed in our research using the technique described in Section 3.1, which compares an observed increment to the cumulative length of multiple packets.

Attack evaluation. We ran our malware on a Google Nexus S 4G phone while using WebMD mobile. The usage data collected and delivered by our app was further compared to the traffic signatures we built offline. We found that the increment sequences matched well with the signatures in all 204 cases, in which we unequivocally identified the disease conditions being visited.

4. FINDING WHERE YOU ARE

The precise location of a smartphone user is widely considered to be private and should not be leaked out without the user's explicit consent. Android guards such information with a permission `ACCESS_FINE_LOCATION`. The information is further protected from the websites that attempt to get it through a mobile browser (using `navigator.geolocation.getCurrentPosition`), which is designed to ask for user's permission when this happens. In this section, we show that despite all such protections, our zero-permission app can still access location-related data, which enables accurate identification of the user's whereabout, whenever her phone connects to a Wi-Fi hotspot.

As discussed before, Wi-Fi has been extensively utilized by smartphone users to save their mobile data. In particular, many users' phones are in an auto-connect mode. Therefore, the threat posed by our attack is very realistic. In the presence of a Wi-Fi connection, we show in Section 3.2 that a phone's coarse location can be obtained through the gateway's IP address. Here, we elaborate how to retrieve its fine location using the link layer information Android discloses.

4.1 Location Inference

We found that the BSSID of a Wi-Fi hotspot and signal levels perceived by the phone are disclosed by Android through procfs. Such information is location-sensitive because hotspots' BSSIDs have been extensively collected by companies (e.g., Google, Skyhook, Navizon, etc.) for location-based services in the absence of GPS. However, their databases are proprietary, not open to the public. In this section, we show how we address this challenge and come up with an end-to-end attack.

BSSID-based geo-location. In proc files `/proc/net/arp` and `/proc/net/wireless`, Android documents the parameters of Address Resolution Protocol (ARP) it uses to talk to a network gateway (a hotspot in the case of Wi-Fi connections) and other wireless activities. Of particular interest to us is the BSSID (in the arp file), which is essentially the gateway's MAC address, and wireless signal levels (in the wireless file). Both files are accessible to a zero-permission app. The app we implemented periodically reads from procfs once every a few seconds to detect the existence of the files, which indicates the presence of a Wi-Fi connection.

The arp file is inherited from Linux, on which its content is considered to be harmless: an internal gateway's MAC address does not seem to give away much sensitive user information. For smartphone, however, such an assumption no longer holds. More and more companies like Google, Skyhook and Navizon are aggressively collecting the BSSIDs of public Wi-Fi hotspots to find out where the user is, so as to provide location-based services (e.g., restaurant recommendations) when GPS signals are weak or even not available. Such information has been gathered in different ways. Some companies like Skyhook wireless and Google have literally driven through different cities and mapped all the BSSID's they detected to their corresponding GPS locations. Others like Navizon distribute an app with both GPS and wireless permissions. Such an app continuously gleans the coordinates of a phone's geo-locations together with the BSSIDs it sees there, and uploads such information to a server that maintains a BSSID location database.

All such databases are proprietary, not open to the public. Actually we talked to Skyhook in an attempt to purchase a license for querying their database with the BSSID collected by our zero-permission app. They were not willing to do that due to their

Table 3: Geo-location with a Single BSSID

Location	Total BSSIDs Collected	Working BSSIDs	Error
Home	5	4	0ft
Hospital1	74	2	59ft
Hospital2	57	4	528ft
Subway	6	4	3ft
Starbucks	43	3	6ft
Train/Bus Station	14	10	0ft
Church	82	3	150ft
Bookstore	34	2	289ft

concerns that our analysis could impact people's perceptions about the privacy implications of BSSID collection.

Exploiting commercial location services. Many commercial apps that offer location-based service need a permission ACCESS_WIFI_STATE, so they can collect the BSSIDs of all the surrounding hotspots for geo-locating their users. In our case, however, our zero-permission app can only get a *single* BSSID, the one for the hotspot the phone is currently in connection with. We need to understand whether this is still enough for finding out the user's location. Since we cannot directly use those proprietary databases, we have to leverage these existing apps to get the location. The idea is to understand the protocol these apps run with their servers to generate the right query that can give us the expected response.

Specifically, we utilized the Navizon app to develop such an indirect query mechanism. Like Google and Skyhook, Navizon also has a BSSID database with a wide coverage [2], particularly in US. In our research, we reverse-engineered the app's protocol by using a proxy, and found that there is no authentication in the protocol and its request is a list of BSSIDs and signal levels encoded in Base64. Based upon such information, we built a "querier" server that uses the information our app sneaks out to construct a valid Navizon request for querying its database for the location of the target phone.

4.2 Attack Evaluation

Data collection. To understand the seriousness of this information leak, we ran our zero-permission app to collect BSSID data from the Wi-Fi connections made at places in Urbana and Chicago, including home, hospital, church, bookstore, train/bus station and others. The results are illustrated in Table 3.

Results. Our app easily detected the presence of Wi-Fi connections and stealthily sent out the BSSIDs associated with these connections. Running our query mechanism, we successfully identified all these locations from Navizon. On the other hand, we found that not every hotspot can be used for this purpose: after all, the Navizon database is still far from complete. Table 3 describes the numbers of the hotspots good for geo-locations at different spots and their accuracy.

5. KNOWING WHERE YOU GO

As discussed before, information leaks happen not only on the Linux layer of Android but also on its API level. In this section, we report our study of an audio public API that gives away one's driving route.

5.1 Driving Route Inference

Speaker usage information. Android offers a set of public APIs that any apps, including those without any permissions, can call. An example is AudioManager.isMusicActive, through which an app can find out whether any sound is being played by the phone. This API is used to coordinate apps' access to the speaker. This

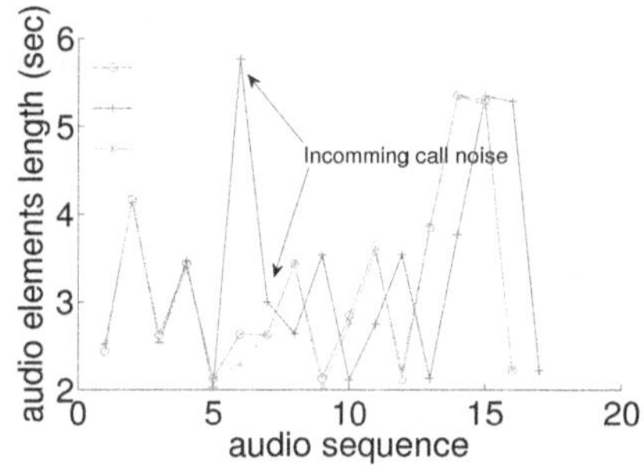

Figure 3: Audio elements similarity when driving on the same route

seemingly harmless capability, however, turns out to reveal sensitive information in the presence of the powerful Google Maps API.

Consider a GPS navigation app one uses when she is driving. Such an app typically gives turn-by-turn voice guidance. During this process, a zero-permission app that continuously invokes the isMusicActive API can observe when the voice is being played and when it is off. In this way, it can get a sequence of *speech lengths* for voice direction *elements*, such as "turn left onto the Broadway avenue", which are typically individual sentences. The content of such directions is boilerplate but still diverse, depending on the names of street/avenues, and one driving route typically contains many such direction elements. These features make the length sequence a high dimensional vector that can be used to fingerprint a driving route, as discovered in our research.

Audio status logger. To collect such speech-length sequences, we implemented an audio-state logger into our zero-permission app. Similar to the data-usage monitor, this component is invoked only when the target app is found to be running (Section 3.1). In this case, we are looking for the process com.google.android.apps.maps, Google's navigation app. Once the process is discovered, our app runs the logger to continuously call isMusicActive, with a sampling rate of 50 per second. Whenever a change to the speaker status is detected, it records the new status and the timestamp of this event. At the end of the navigation, the app sneaks out this sequence (see Section 2.2), which is then used to reconstruct individual elements in the speech-length sequence through looking for the timestamp of an "on" speaker state with its preceding state being "off", and the timing for its subsequent state change that goes the other way around.

Route fingerprinting simulator. Using the audio-status logger, we recorded the speech length sequences when we drove from home to office three times at Bloomington. Figure 3 shows the comparisons among those sequences. Here we consider that two speech-length elements match if their difference is below 0.05 second, which is the error margin of the speaker status sampling. As we can see from the figure, those sequences all match well, except a spike caused by an incoming call in one trip.

To understand whether such sequences are sufficiently differentiable for fingerprinting a route, we further built an app that simulates the navigation process during driving. The app queries the Google Maps API [9] to get a route between a pair of addresses, which is in the form of a polyline, that is, a list of nodes (positions with GPS coordinates) and line segments between the consecutive nodes. Specifically, we turn on the "*allow mock gps*" option of an Android phone. This replaces the physical GPS with a simulator, which replays the gps coordinates of the route to Google Navigator and records the voice guidance along the route to measure the lengths of its speech elements.

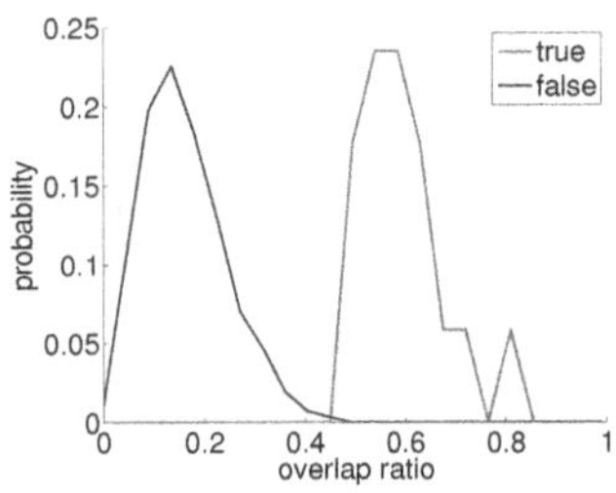

Figure 4: Audio length sequence distinguishability

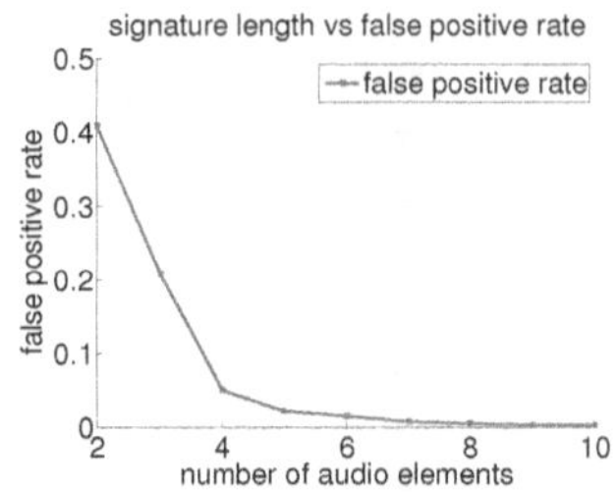

Figure 5: False positive rate vs number of audio elements

In our research, we randomly chose 1000 *test routes* in Bloomington with the similar driving time and number of elements as those of the routes for 10 real drives to get their speechlength sequences using our simulator. These sequences were compared with the length sequences recorded from the real routes, as illustrated in Figure 4. Here we use a variant of Jaccard index, called *overlap ratio*, to measure the similarity of two length sequences in a normalized way: given sequences s and s' and their longest common subsequence $\bar{s}$, their overlap ratio is defined as $R(s, s') = \frac{|\bar{s}|}{|s|+|s'|-|\bar{s}|}$. Figure 4 shows the distribution of the ratios between the sequences in real and test sets (which are associated with *different* routes) together with the distribution of the ratios between the speech-length sequences of real drives and the simulated drives on the same routes. As we can see here, for two different routes, their speech-length sequences are very different (mean: 0.1827, standard deviation: 0.0817), while two identical routes always have highly similar length sequences (mean: 0.6146, standard deviation: 0.0876). Based on these two distributions, we set a threshold of 0.5 for determining when two sequences "match": that is, they are considered to be related to the same route.

Figure 4 shows that speech-length sequences can effectively fingerprint their driving routes. A caveat here is that such a sequence should not be too short. Figure 5 illustrates what happens when comparing short sequences extracted from real driving routes with those of the same lengths randomly sampled from the 1000 test sequences. We can see here that false positives (i.e., matches between the sequences from different routes) begin to show up when sequence lengths go below 9.

5.2 Attack Methodology

Given a speech-length sequence, we want to identify its route on the map. To this end, we developed a suite of techniques for the following attacks: (1) fingerprinting a few "Points of interest" (PoI) the user might go, such as hospitals, airport and others, to find out whether the user indeed goes there and when she goes; (2) collecting a large number of possible routes the user might use (based on some background information) and searching these routes for the target speech-length sequence.

Location fingerprinting. To fingerprint a PoI, we first find a set of start addresses surrounding it from Google Maps and then run our driving-simulation app from these addresses to the target. This gives us a set of speech-length sequences for the driving routes to the PoI, which we treat as a signature for the location. To ensure that such a signature is unlikely to have false positives, the start addresses are selected in a way that their routes to the PoI have at least 10 speech elements (Figure 5).

For each speech length sequence received from our zero permission app, our approach extracts a substring at the end of the sequence according to the lengths of a target PoI's signature sequences. On such a substring are the last steps of the route our app observes, which are used to compare with the signature. If the substring matches any signature sequences (i.e., with an overlap ratio above the threshold), we get strong evidence that the smartphone user has been to the fingerprinted location.

Scalable sequence matching. More challenging here is to locate a user's driving route on the map. For this purpose, we need some background knowledge to roughly determine the area that covers the route. As discussed before (Section 3.2 and 4), we can geo-locate the user's home and other places she frequently visits when her phone is set to auto connect. At the very least, finding the city one is currently in can be easily done in the presence of Wi-Fi connection. Therefore, in our research, we assume that we know the user's start location or a place on her route and the rough area (e.g., city) she goes. Note that simply knowing one's start and destination cities can be enough for getting such information: driving between two cities typically goes through a common route segment, whose speech-length sequence can be used to locate the entrance point of the destination city (e.g., a highway exit) on the length sequence recorded during the victim's driving. Furthermore, since we can calculate from the timestamps on the sequence the driving time between the known location and the destination, the possible areas of the target can be roughly determined.

However, even under these constraints, collecting speech-length sequences in a large scale is still difficult: our driving simulator takes 2 to 5 minutes to complete a 10-mile route in Bloomington (necessary for getting all the speech elements on the route), which is much faster than a real drive, but still too slow to handle thousands (or more) of possible routes we need to inspect. Here we show how to make such a large-scale search possible.

Given a known point on the route and a target area, we developed a crawler using Google API to download the routes from the point to the residential addresses in the target area [10]. Each route here comes with a set of driving directions (e.g. *html_instructions*) in text and an estimated driving time. Such text directions are roughly a subset of the audio directions used by Google Navigator for the same route, with some standard road name abbreviations ("Rd", "Dr", etc.).

For each route with text directions, our approach replaces their abbreviations with the full names [13], calls the Google text-to-speech (TTS) engine to synthesize the audio for each sentence, and then measures the length of each audio element. This produces a sequence of speech lengths, which we call a *TTS sequence*. Comparing a TTS sequence with its corresponding speech-length sequence from a real drive (the *real sequence*), the former is typically a subset of the latter. An example is illustrated in Table 4. Based on this observation, we come up with a method to search a large number of TTS sequences, as follows.

We first extract all the subsequences on a real sequence under the constraint that two neighboring elements on a subsequence must be within a distance of 3 on the original sequence: that is, on the real sequence, there must be no more than 2 elements sitting in between these two elements. These subsequences are used to search TTS sequences for those with substrings that match them. The example in Table 4 shows a TTS sequence that matches a subsequence on the real sequence. As a result of the search, we get a list of TTS sequences ranked in a descending order according to each sequence's overlap ratio with the real sequence calculated with the longest subsequence (under the above constraint) shared between them. We then pick up top TTS sequences, run our simulator on their source and destination addresses to generate their full speech-length sequences, and compare them with the real sequence to find its route.

Table 4: Comparison between a Navigation Sequence and a Text Direction/TTS Sequence

Google Navigator	Real Length	Google Direction API	Synthesis Audio Length
Turn left onto south xxx street, then turn right onto west xxx road	4.21	N/A	N/A
Turn right onto west xxx road	2.05	Turn right onto west xxx Road	2.15
Continue onto west xxx Road for a mile	2.53	N/A	N/A
In one thousand feet, turn right onto xxxxx ** north	4.07	N/A	N/A
Turn right onto xxxxx ** north	2.74	Turn right onto xxxxx ** north	2.72

Table 5: Route Identification Result. The third column is the highest overlap ratio of a wrong route within the top 10 TTS sequences. FP indicates false positive. All FP routes (actually similar routes) are marked out in Figure 6.

Route No.	result(ratio)	Top ratio of a wrong route	Notes(error)
1	found (0.813)	0.579 (FP)	similar route (0.2mi)
2	found (1.0)	0.846 (FP)	similar route (0.5mi)
3	found (0.615)	0.462	
4	missed	0.412	
5	missed	0.32	
6	found (0.846)	0.667 (FP)	similar route (0.3mi)
7	found (0.714)	0.415	
8	found (0.5)	0.345	
9	found (0.588)	0.261	
10	found (0.6)	0.292	

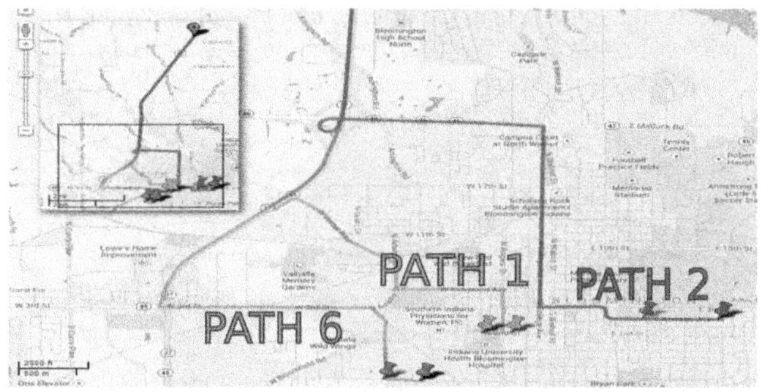

Figure 6: Three FP Routes and Their Corresponding TP Routes. Each FP/TP pair has most of their routes overlapped.

5.3 Attack Evaluation

Location determination. We fingerprinted two PoIs in Bloomington, i.e Bloomington Hospital and Indianapolis International Airport (IND) using our driving simulator. For the hospital, 19 routes with at least 10 audio elements on their speech-length sequences were selected from Google Maps, which cover all the paths to the place. The airport has only 4 paths to get in and get out, each having at least 10 audio elements. We first evaluated the false positives of these signatures with 200 routes with similar lengths, and did not observe any false match. Then we compared the signatures with 4 real driving sequences collected by our zero-permission app from the trips to these PoIs (2 for each PoI), they all matched the right routes in the signatures.

Driving-route identification. We further tried to locate 10 speech-length sequences our zero-permission app collected from real drives from a highway exit to 10 random locations in Bloomington. To this end, we randomly selected 1000 residential addresses from each of the 5 ZIP code areas in the town using the local family website [10] and called the Google Direction API to get the routes from the highway exit (which was supposed to be known) to these 5000 addresses, together with the Google driving routes for the 10 real sequences. Then, the TTS sequences of those 5010 routes were compared with the 10 real-drive speech length sequences collected by our malicious app. For each real sequence, 10 TTS sequences with the highest overlap ratios as described in Section 5.2 were picked out for a validation that involves simulating drives on these TTS sequences' routes, measuring their speech-length sequences and comparing them with the length sequences of the real drives. In the end, we identified 11 routes using the 0.5 threshold for the overlap ratio (see Table 5). Among them, 8 are true positives, the real routes we drove.

Also, the 3 false positives are actually the routes that come very close to the routes of 3 real-drive sequences (see Figure 6), with two within 0.3 miles of the real targets and one within 0.5 miles. Note that in all these cases, the real routes were also found and ranked higher than those false positives. This actually indicates that our approach works very well: even when the real-drive routes were not among the routes we randomly sampled on the map (from the highway exit to 5000 random addresses), the approach could still identify those very close to the real routes, thereby locating the smartphone user to the neighborhood of the places she went.

6. MITIGATION AND DISCUSSION

Given the various public resources on Android, the information leaks we found are very likely to be just a tip of the iceberg. Finding an effective solution to this problem is especially challenging with rich background information of users or apps gratuitously available on the web. To mitigate such threats, we first take a closer look at the attacks discovered in our research. The ARP data has not been extensively utilized by apps and can therefore be kept away from unauthorized parties by changing the related file's access privilege to `system`. A simple solution to control the audio channel can be to restrict the access to its related APIs, such as `isMusicActive`, only to system processes whenever sensitive apps (e.g. navigation related) are running in the foreground. The most challenging facet of such a mitigation venture is to address the availability mechanism of the data usage statistics, which have already been used by hundreds of apps to help Android users keep track of their mobile data consumption. Merely removing them from the list of public resources is not an option. In this section, we report our approach on mitigating the threat deriving from the statistics availability, while maintaining their utility.

6.1 Mitigation Strategies

To suppress information leaks from the statistics available through `tcp_rcv` and `tcp_snd`, we can release less accurate information. Here we analyze a few strategies designed for this purpose.

Round up and round down. One strategy is to reduce the accuracy of the available information by rounding up or down the actual number of bytes sent or received by an app to a multiple of a given integer before disclosing that value to the querying process. This approach is reminiscent of a predominant defense strategy against traffic analysis, namely packet padding [20, 36]. The difference between that and our approach is that we can not only round up but also round down to a target number and also work on accumulated payload lengths rather than the size of an individual packet. This enables us to control the information leaks at a low cost, in terms of impact on data utility.

Specifically, let d be the content of a data usage counter (`tcp_rcv` or `tcp_snd`) and α an integer given to our enforcement framework implemented on Android (Section 6.2). When the counter is queried by an app, our approach first finds a number k such that

$k\alpha \leq d \leq (k+1)\alpha$ and reports $k\alpha$ to the app when $d-k\alpha < 0.5\alpha$ and $(k+1)\alpha$ otherwise.

Aggregation. A limitation of the simple rounding strategy results from the fact that it still gives away the payload size of each packet, even though the information is perturbed. As a result, it cannot hide packets with exceedingly large payloads. To address this issue, we can accumulate the data usage information of multiple queries, for example, conditions on WebMD the user looks at, and only release the cumulative result when a time interval expires. This can be done, for example, by updating an app's data usage to the querying app once every week, which prevents the adversary from observing individual packets.

6.2 Enforcement Framework

To enforce the aforementioned policies, we designed and implemented a preliminary framework, which is elaborated below.

Permission Design. A naive idea would be adding yet another permission to Android's already complex permission system and have any data monitoring app requesting this permission in AndroidManifest.xml. However, prior research shows that the users do not pay too much attention to the permission list when installing apps, and the developers tend to declare more permissions than needed [25]. On the other hand, the traffic usage data generated by some applications (e.g banking applications) is exceptionally sensitive, at a degree that the app developer might not want to divulge them even to the legitimate data monitoring apps. To address this problem, our solution is to let an app specify special "permissions" to Android, which defines how its network usage statistics should be released. Such permissions, which are essentially a security policy, was built into the Android permission system in our research. Using the usage counters as an example, our framework supports four policies: *NO_ACCESS*, *ROUNDING*, *AGGREGATION* and *NO_PROTECTION*. These policies determine whether to release an app's usage data to a querying app, how to release this information and when to do that. They are enforced at a `UsageService`, a policy enforcement mechanism we added to Android, by holding back the answer, adding noise to it (as described in Section 6.1) or periodically updating the information.

Enforcement mechanism. Under our framework, public resources on the Linux layer, such as the data usage counters, are set to be accessible only by system or root users. Specifically, for the `/proc/uid_stat/` resources, we modified the `create_stat` file in `drivers/mis/uid_stat.c` of the Android Linux kernel and changed the mode of `entry` to disable direct access to the proc entries by any app. With direct access turned off, the app will have to call the APIs exposed in `TrafficStats.java` and `NetworkStats.java` such as `getUidTxBytes()` to gain access to that information. In our research, we modified these APIs so that whenever they are invoked by a query app that requests a target app's statistics, they pass the parameters such as the target's `uid` through IPC to the `UsageService`, which checks how the target app (`uid`) wants to release its data before responding to the query app with the data (which can be perturbed according to the target's policy). In our implementation, we deliberately kept the API interface unchanged so existing data monitor apps can still run.

Defense Evaluation. To understand the effectiveness our technique, we first evaluated the round up and round down scheme using the WebMD app. Figure 7 illustrates the results: with α increasing from 16 to 1024, the corresponding number of conditions that can be uniquely identified drops from 201 to 1. In other words, except a peculiar condition *DEMENTIA IN HEAD INJURY* whose total reply

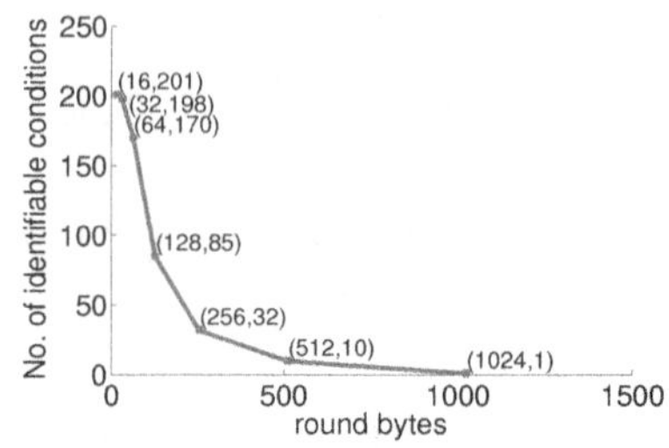

Figure 7: Effectiveness of round up and round down

payload has 13513 bytes with its condition overview of 11106 bytes (a huge deviation from the average case), all other conditions can no longer be determined from the usage statistics when the counter value is rounded to a multiple of 1024 bytes. Note that the error incurred by this rounding strategy is no more than 512 bytes, which is low, considering the fact that the total data usage of the app can be several megabytes. Therefore its impact on the utility of data consumption monitoring apps is very small (below 0.05%).

We further measured the delay caused by the modified APIs and the new `UsageService` on a Galaxy Nexus, which comes from permission checking and IPC, to evaluate the overhead incurred by the enforcement mechanism we implemented. On average, this mechanism brought in a 22.4ms delay, which is negligible.

Limitations of our Defence. We found that it is challenging to come up with a bullet proof defense against all those information leaks for the following reasons. a) Shared resources are present all over the Linux's file system from `/proc/[pid]/`, `/proc/uid_stat/[uid]`, network protocols like `/proc/net/arp` or `/proc/net/wireless` and even some Android OS APIs. b) Public resources are different across different devices. Some of this information is leaked by third party drivers like the LCD backlit status which is mounted in different places in the `/sys` file system on different phones. c) Traffic usage is also application related. For the round up and round down defense strategy to be applied successfully, the OS must be provided with the traffic patterns of the apps it has to protect before calculating an appropriate round size capable of both securing them from malicious apps and introducing sufficiently small noise to the data legitimate traffic monitoring apps collect. A more systematic study is needed here to better understand the problem.

7. RELATED WORK

Information leaks have been studied for decades and new discoveries continue to be made in recent years [33, 39, 37]. Among them, most related to our work is the work on the information leaks from procfs, which includes using the ESP/EIP data to infer keystrokes [38] and leveraging memory usages to fingerprint visited websites [31]. However, it is less clear whether those attacks pose a credible threat to Android, due to the high non-determinism of its memory allocation [31] and the challenges in keystroke analysis [38]. In comparison, our work shows that the usage statistics under procfs can be practically exploited to infer an Android user's sensitive information. The attack technique used here is related to prior work on traffic analysis [20]. However, those approaches assume the presence of an adversary who sees encrypted packets. Also, their analysis techniques cannot be directly applied to smartphone. Our attack is based upon a different adversary model, in which an app uses public resources to infer the content of the data received by a target app on the same device. For this purpose, we need to build different inference techniques based on the unique features of mobile computing, particularly the rich background information (i.e., social network, BSSID databases and Google Maps) that comes with the target app and the mobile OS.

Information leaks have been discovered on smartphone by both academia and the hacker community [21, 27, 16]. Most of known problems are caused by implementation errors, either in Android or within mobile apps. By comparison, the privacy risks come from shared resources in the presence of emerging background information have not been extensively studied on mobile devices. Up to our knowledge, all prior research on this subject focuses on the privacy implications of motion sensors or microphones [34, 17, 32, 18, 28]. What has never been done before is a systematic investigation on what can be inferred from the public resources exposed by both Linux and Android layers.

New techniques for better protecting user privacy on Android also continue to pop up [22, 23, 27, 30, 14, 24, 21]. Different from such research, our work focuses on the new privacy risks emerging from the fast-evolving smartphone apps, which could render innocuous public resources related to sensitive user information.

8. CONCLUSION

In this paper, we report our study on information leaks from Android public resources. The study reveals that highly sensitive data of a smartphone user, such as her identity, interested disease conditions, geo-location, driving route and more can actually be reliably inferred from such resources by analyzing popular apps. Our findings call into question the design assumption made by Android developers on public resources and demand new effort to address such privacy risks. To this end, we further present a preliminary design for mitigating the threats to selected public resources, while still maintaining their utility.

9. ACKNOWLEDGMENTS

The authors at Indiana University are supported in part by National Science Foundation CNS-1017782 and CNS-1117106. We also acknowledge the grant HHS-90TR0003/01 from the Office of the National Coordinator for Health Information Technology at the Department of Health and Human Services (HHS). The views in this paper represent opinions of the authors only.

10. REFERENCES

[1] ReadWrite A Tech Blog. http://readwrite.com/2011/05/10/doctor_in_your_pocket_webmd_comes_to_android. Accessed: 13/02/2013.

[2] Wifi coverage map. http://www.navizon.com/navizon_coverage_wifi.htm. Accessed: 13/02/2013.

[3] Fbi issues android smartphone malware warning. http://www.forbes.com/sites/billsinger/2012/10/15/fbi-issues-android-smartphone-malware-warning/, 2012.

[4] Get search, twitter api. https://dev.twitter.com/docs/api/1/get/search, 2012.

[5] Google play. https://play.google.com/store/search?q=traffic+monitor&c=apps, 2012.

[6] Google play: Webmd for android. http://www.webmd.com/webmdapp, 2012.

[7] Smart phone malware: The six worst offenders. http://www.nbcnews.com/technology/technolog/smart-phone-malware-six-worst-offenders-125248, 2012.

[8] Antutu benchmark. https://play.google.com/store/apps/details?id=com.antutu.ABenchMark, 2013.

[9] The google directions api. https://developers.google.com/maps/documentation/directions/, 2013.

[10] Locate family. http://www.locatefamily.com/, 2013.

[11] Lookup ip address location. http://whatismyipaddress.com/ip-lookup, 2013.

[12] Online demo. https://sites.google.com/site/sidedroid/, 2013.

[13] Standard address abbreviations. http://www.kutztown.edu/admin/adminserv/mailfile/guide/abbrev.html, 2013.

[14] A. R. Beresford, A. Rice, N. Skehin, and R. Sohan. Mockdroid: trading privacy for application functionality on smartphones. In *Proceedings of the 12th Workshop on Mobile Computing Systems and Applications*, HotMobile '11, pages 49–54, New York, NY, USA, 2011. ACM.

[15] H. Berghel. Identity theft, social security numbers, and the web. *Commun. ACM*, 43(2):17–21, Feb. 2000.

[16] P. Brodley and leviathan Security Group. Zero Permission Android Applications. http://leviathansecurity.com/blog/archives/17-Zero-Permission-Android-Applications.html. Accessed: 13/02/2013.

[17] L. Cai and H. Chen. Touchlogger: inferring keystrokes on touch screen from smartphone motion. In *Proceedings of the 6th USENIX conference on Hot topics in security*, HotSec'11, pages 9–9, Berkeley, CA, USA, 2011. USENIX Association.

[18] L. Cai and H. Chen. On the practicality of motion based keystroke inference attack. In *Proceedings of the 5th international conference on Trust and Trustworthy Computing*, TRUST'12, pages 273–290, Berlin, Heidelberg, 2012. Springer-Verlag.

[19] J. Camenisch, a. shelat, D. Sommer, S. Fischer-Hübner, M. Hansen, H. Krasemann, G. Lacoste, R. Leenes, and J. Tseng. Privacy and identity management for everyone. In *Proceedings of the 2005 workshop on Digital identity management*, DIM '05, pages 20–27, New York, NY, USA, 2005. ACM.

[20] S. Chen, R. Wang, X. Wang, and K. Zhang. Side-channel leaks in web applications: A reality today, a challenge tomorrow. In *Security and Privacy (SP), 2010 IEEE Symposium on*, pages 191 –206, may 2010.

[21] M. Dietz, S. Shekhar, Y. Pisetsky, A. Shu, and D. S. Wallach. Quire: Lightweight provenance for smart phone operating systems. In *20th USENIX Security Symposium*, San Francisco, CA, Aug. 2011.

[22] W. Enck, P. Gilbert, B.-G. Chun, L. P. Cox, J. Jung, P. McDaniel, and A. N. Sheth. Taintdroid: an information-flow tracking system for realtime privacy monitoring on smartphones. In *Proceedings of the 9th USENIX conference on Operating systems design and implementation*, OSDI'10, pages 1–6, Berkeley, CA, USA, 2010. USENIX Association.

[23] W. Enck, D. Octeau, P. McDaniel, and S. Chaudhuri. A study of android application security. In *Proceedings of the 20th USENIX conference on Security*, SEC'11, pages 21–21, Berkeley, CA, USA, 2011. USENIX Association.

[24] W. Enck, M. Ongtang, and P. McDaniel. On lightweight mobile phone application certification. In *Proceedings of the 16th ACM CCS*, CCS '09, pages 235–245, New York, NY, USA, 2009. ACM.

[25] A. P. Felt, E. Chin, S. Hanna, D. Song, and D. Wagner. Android permissions demystified. In *Proceedings of the 18th ACM conference on Computer and communications security*, CCS '11, pages 627–638, New York, NY, USA, 2011. ACM.

[26] T. Govani and H. Pashley. Student awareness of the privacy implications when using facebook. *unpublished paper presented at the "Privacy Poster Fair" at the Carnegie Mellon University School of Library and Information Science*, 9, 2005.

[27] M. Grace, Y. Zhou, Z. Wang, and X. Jiang. Systematic detection of capability leaks in stock Android smartphones. In *Proceedings of the 19th Network and Distributed System Security Symposium (NDSS)*, Feb. 2012.

[28] J. Han, E. Owusu, T.-L. Nguyen, A. Perrig, and J. Zhang. Accomplice: Location inference using accelerometers on smartphones. In *Proceedings of the 4th International Conference on Communication Systems and Networks*, Bangalore, India, 2012.

[29] S. B. Hoar. Identity Theft: The Crime of the New Millennium. *Oregon Law Review*, 80:1423–1448, 2001.

[30] P. Hornyack, S. Han, J. Jung, S. Schechter, and D. Wetherall. These aren't the droids you're looking for: retrofitting android to protect data from imperious applications. In *Proceedings of the 18th ACM CCS*, CCS '11, pages 639–652, New York, NY, USA, 2011. ACM.

[31] S. Jana and V. Shmatikov. Memento: Learning secrets from process footprints. In *Proceedings of the 2012 IEEE Symposium on Security and Privacy*, SP '12, pages 143–157, Washington, DC, USA, 2012. IEEE Computer Society.

[32] E. Owusu, J. Han, S. Das, A. Perrig, and J. Zhang. Accessory: password inference using accelerometers on smartphones. In *Proceedings of the 12th Workshop on Mobile Computing Systems Applications*, HotMobile '12, pages 9:1–9:6, New York, NY, USA, 2012. ACM.

[33] T. Ristenpart, E. Tromer, H. Shacham, and S. Savage. Hey, you, get off of my cloud: exploring information leakage in third-party compute clouds. In *Proceedings of the 16th ACM CCS*, pages 199–212, New York, NY, USA, 2009. ACM.

[34] R. Schlegel, K. Zhang, X. yong Zhou, M. Intwala, A. Kapadia, and X. Wang. Soundcomber: A stealthy and context-aware sound trojan for smartphones. In *NDSS*. The Internet Society, 2011.

[35] D. J. Solove. Identity Theft, Privacy, and the Architecture of Vulnerability. *Hastings Law Journal*, 54:1227 – 1276, 2002-2003.

[36] Q. Sun, D. R. Simon, Y.-M. Wang, W. Russell, V. N. Padmanabhan, and L. Qiu. Statistical identification of encrypted web browsing traffic. In *IEEE Symposium on Security and Privacy*. Society Press, 2002.

[37] C. V. Wright, L. Ballard, S. E. Coull, F. Monrose, and G. M. Masson. Uncovering spoken phrases in encrypted voice over ip conversations. *ACM Trans. Inf. Syst. Secur.*, 13(4):35:1–35:30, Dec. 2010.

[38] K. Zhang and X. Wang. Peeping tom in the neighborhood: keystroke eavesdropping on multi-user systems. *analysis*, 20:23, 2010.

[39] Y. Zhang, A. Juels, M. K. Reiter, and T. Ristenpart. Cross-vm side channels and their use to extract private keys. In *Proceedings of the 2012 ACM conference on Computer and communications security*, CCS '12, pages 305–316, New York, NY, USA, 2012. ACM.

APPENDIX

A. USER-AGENT CONSTRUCTION

Many mobile apps use HTTP for data exchange and the traffic generated during this process always involves a User-Agent field. User-Agent is related to the phone's type, brand and Android OS version. For example, the User-Agent of the Yahoo! Finance app on a Nexus S phone is `User-Agent: YahooMobile/1.0 (finance; 1.1.8.1187014079); (Linux; U; Android 4.1.1; sojus Build/JELLY_BEAN);`. Given that the format of this field is known, all we need here is a set of parameters (type, brand, OS version etc.) for building up the field, which is important for estimating the length of the field and the payload that carries the field. Such information can be easily obtained by our app, without any permission, from `android.os.Build` and `System.getProperty("http agent")`.

B. PERSONAL INVESTMENT INFERENCE

Knowing your personal investment. A person's investment information is private and highly sensitive. Here we demonstrate how an adversary can infer her financial interest from the network data usage of Yahoo! Finance, a popular finance app on Google Play with nearly one million users. We discover that Yahoo! Finance discloses a unique network data signature when the user is adding or clicking on a stock.

Stock search autocomplete. Similar to all aforementioned attacks, here we consider that a zero-permission app running in the background collects network data usage related to Yahoo! Finance and sends it to a remote attacker when the device's screen dims out. Searching for a stock in Yahoo! Finance generates a unique network data signature, which can be attributed to its network-based autocomplete feature (i.e., suggestion list) that returns suggested stocks according to the user's input. Consider for example the case when a user looks for Google's stock (GOOG). In response to each letter she enters, the Yahoo! Finance app continuously updates a list of possible autocomplete options from the Internet, which is characterized by a sequence of unique payload lengths. For example, typing "G" in the search box produces 281 bytes outgoing and 1361 to 2631 bytes incoming traffic. We found that each time the user enters an additional character, the outbound HTTP `GET` packet increases by one byte. In its HTTP response, a set of stocks related to the letters the user types will be returned, whose packet size depends on the user's input and is unique for each character combination.

Stock news signature. From the dynamics of mobile data usage produced by the suggestion lists, we can identify a set of candidate stocks. To narrow it down, we further studied the signature when a stock code is clicked upon. We found that when this happens, two types of HTTP `GET` requests will be generated, one for a chart and the other for related news. The HTTP response for news has more salient features, which can be used to build a signature. Whenever a user clicks on a stock, Yahoo! Finance will refresh the news associated with that stock, which increases the `tcp_rcv` count. This count is then used to compare with the payload sizes of the HTTP packets for downloading stock news from Yahoo! so as to identify the stock chosen by the user. Also note that since the size of the HTTP `GET` for the news is stable, 352 bytes, our app can always determine when a news request is sent.

Attack evaluation. In our study, we ran our zero-permission app to monitor the Yahoo! Finance app on a Nexus S 4G smartphone. From the data-usage statistics collected while the suggestion list was being used to add 10 random stocks onto the stock watch list, we managed to narrow down the candidate list to 85 possible stocks that matched the data-usage features of these 10 stocks. Further analyzing the increment sequence when the user clicked on a particular stock code, which downloaded related news to the phone, we were able to uniquely identify each of the ten stocks the user selected among the 85 candidates.

Preventing Accidental Data Disclosure in Modern Operating Systems

Adwait Nadkarni
North Carolina State University
Raleigh, North Carolina, USA
anadkarni@ncsu.edu

William Enck
North Carolina State University
Raleigh, North Carolina, USA
enck@cs.ncsu.edu

ABSTRACT

Modern OSes such as Android, iOS, and Windows 8 have changed the way consumers interact with computing devices. Tasks are often completed by stringing together a collection of purpose-specific user applications (e.g., a barcode reader, a social networking app, a document viewer). As users direct this workflow between applications, it is difficult to predict the consequence of each step. Poor selection may result in accidental information disclosure when the target application unknowingly uses cloud services. This paper presents Aquifer as a policy framework and system for preventing accidental information disclosure in modern operating systems. In Aquifer, application developers define secrecy restrictions that protect the entire user interface workflow defining the user task. In doing so, Aquifer provides protection beyond simple permission checks and allows applications to retain control of data even after it is shared.

Categories and Subject Descriptors

D.4.6 [**Operating Systems**]: Security and Protection—*access controls, information flow controls*

Keywords

OS security; access control; information flow control

1. INTRODUCTION

Operating system security architectures are currently undergoing a fundamental change. Modern OSes [32, 42], such as Android, iOS, and Windows 8, take the suggestion of decades of security research [45, 22, 35, 14] and run each application as a unique security principal. While having finer-grained security principals prevents many obvious attacks, complete sandboxing [19] is inadequate.

Applications share data with one another, perhaps more so now than in the past. Consider the Android platform where applications are designed to work together to perform a larger, user-defined task. For example, a shopping app might: 1) invoke a barcode scanner app that uses the camera to read the UPC from an item, 2) look up that item on the Web, and then 3) use a social networking app to share the item and best deal with friends. This modularity strikes a balance between simple UNIX tools (e.g., `sed`, `grep`) and monolithic GUI applications (e.g., MS Office).

CCS'13, November 4–8, 2013, Berlin, Germany.

ACM 978-1-4503-2477-9/13/11 ...$15.00.
http://dx.doi.org/10.1145/2508859.2516677.

A key challenge for modern OS security is controlling this user-directed workflow between apps and preventing accidental information disclosure. For example, a photo of a whiteboard containing meeting notes might be inadvertently uploaded to a social networking site, or a confidential document might be inadvertently stored on a cloud server when viewed. Accidental disclosure is growing concern for consumer privacy, and has been a large concern for companies and organizations attempting to comply with the many data security compliance standards, e.g., HIPAA [39], GLBA [38], PCI DSS [30], and IRS 1075 [40].

Preventing accidental disclosure is not as simple as restricting the set of applications an application with sensitive data can interact with (e.g., Saint [29]). A trusted application receiving data might share that data with another application that has unexpected disclosure. Hence, in a collaborative application environment, we must address the accidental disclosure problem as one of information flow. Specifically, we identify the *data intermediary problem* as a growing concern for modern OSes. The data intermediary problem is a subtype of secure information flow vulnerability that results when user choices dictate data flows between user-facing apps and apps lose control of the data.

In this paper, we present Aquifer as a policy framework and system to mitigate accidental information disclosure in modern operating systems. Aquifer is specifically designed to protect large, application-specific, user data objects such as office documents, voice or written notes, and images. In Aquifer, developers of applications that originate data objects specify secrecy restrictions based on the runtime context and the purpose of the app. This policy restricts all apps participating in a user interface workflow that Aquifer dynamically constructs as the user navigates different applications. Aquifer enforces two types of secrecy restrictions: *export restrictions* ensure only specific apps can export the data off the host, and *required restrictions* ensure that specific apps are involved in workflows when exporting controlled data objects read from persistent storage. This policy is specified using a decentralized information flow control (DIFC) motivated language that allows many data owners on a workflow to participate in secrecy restrictions. In effect, Aquifer allows applications to gain control of shared sensitive data, thereby addressing the data intermediary problem for these large data objects.

This paper makes the following contributions:

- *We identify the data intermediary problem as a growing concern for modern operating systems.* While the data intermediary problem is present in traditional commodity OSes, the lack of application separation did not expose it as a concern.
- *We propose the Aquifer policy framework for addressing accidental disclosures that result from the data intermediary problem in modern OSes.* Aquifer allows app developers to contribute DIFC-based secrecy restrictions to protect application-specific data objects. We formally define the policy logic and prove its safety.
- *We provide a proof-of-concept implementation of Aquifer and integrate it with Android.* We demonstrate how Aquifer can be practically realized within an existing platform, and provide three case studies by modifying popular open source applications.

The remainder of this paper proceeds as follows. Section 2 provides a use case and problem definition. Section 3 overviews our approach. Section 4 formally defines the Aquifer policy logic. Section 5 describes the Aquifer system design. Section 6 details the implementation. Section 7 evaluates Aquifer's policy compatibility and performance. Section 8 discusses limitations. Section 9 overviews related work. Section 10 concludes.

2. MOTIVATION AND PROBLEM

Modern operating systems such as Android, iOS, and Windows 8 present a new programming abstraction for software developers. Instead of placing all functionality into a single window with multiple dialog boxes, the application's user interface is separated into multiple screens where each screen handles a specific task. To complete a task, the user navigates through a series of screens. These screens may be in the same or different applications. For example, Android applications use intents addressed to action strings (see Section 2.4) to help the OS find the best application for a task. Similarly, Windows 8 provides "share charms" to help users complete tasks with different applications. Finally, iOS provides limited sharing and navigation between applications using URL protocol handlers.

In each of these OSes, applications are treated as separate security principles, although the specific security mechanisms differ. Android separates applications as different UNIX user IDs, and Windows 8 uses SUIDs. In contrast, iOS runs all applications as the `mobile` user with a generic sandbox policy. However, digital signatures are used to identify applications, and permission state (e.g., location access) is saved per-application.

Throughout the remainder of the paper, we frequently use Android to simplify discussion and provide concrete examples. Our choice of Android is motivated by several factors. Most importantly, Android provides the most flexible sharing model between applications. As the following discussion will make clear, sharing data between applications underlies the security problem. Android is also open source, used by hundreds of millions of consumers, and well described in security literature. We believe that other modern OSes

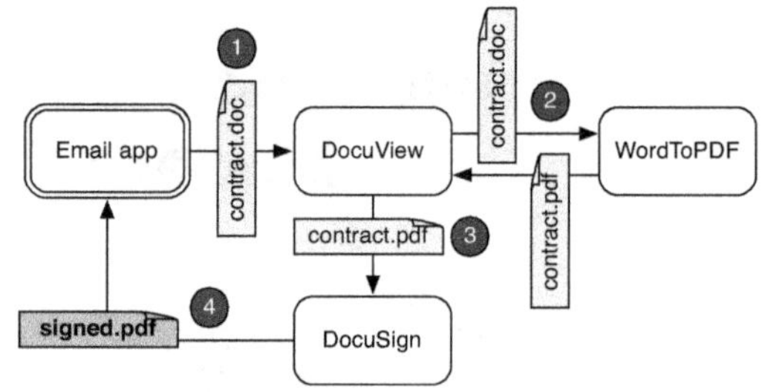

Figure 1: Document signing use case with four apps. A confidential contract received via Email is 1) read in a viewer, 2) converted to PDF, 3) embedded with a written signature, and 4) Emailed back to the sender.

that provide clear sharing abstractions (e.g., share charms in Windows 8) can benefit from our policy abstractions and design; however the implementation details will differ.

2.1 Use Case: Signing a Document

The following example provides a simple use case of how a user Alice might physically sign a document using several applications in a modern OS. Note that this is just one of many potential ways Alice can execute this task.

Alice receives a confidential contract in her business *Email* app. She needs to sign and return the contract, but does not have access to a printer or a scanner. Therefore, Alice uses the *DocuSign* app on her smartphone to digitally attach a written copy of her signature. The task begins by Alice accessing the message containing `contract.doc` in the *Email* app. Alice reads `contract.doc` by sharing it with the *DocuView* app. After reading `contract.doc`, Alice wishes to sign it with *DocuSign*; however, *DocuSign* only operates on PDF files. Therefore, Alice shares `contract.doc` with the *WordToPDF* app to create `contract.pdf`, which returns the PDF to *DocuView*. Alice then shares `contract.pdf` with *DocuSign*, which embeds a copy of her written signature, creating `signed.pdf`. The file is then shared with the *Email* app to return the signed contract via Email. This task workflow is depicted in Figure 1.

2.2 Problem Definition

The document signing use case provides an example of how a user might combine several applications to accomplish a task. In the example, the business *Email* app received a confidential contract. Based on the email headers, *Email* knows `contract.doc` should not be exported off of the host by any application except itself. However, Alice needs to modify `contract.doc` in ways that *Email* does not support. One of the valuable features of modern OSes is the large collection of third-party applications that act as modules to perform specific tasks. While these apps provide valuable functionality, they also present a security risk: once *Email* shares `contract.doc` with another app, it loses control of it, which may result in accidental disclosures that violate compliance regulations (e.g., HIPAA [39], GLBA [38], PCI DSS [30], and IRS 1075 [40]). For example, the *WordToPDF* application might perform the PDF conversion on a cloud server, or *DocuView* might synchronize viewed documents with cloud storage. Similarly, `signed.pdf` containing the user's written signature should only be used when the user intends. The user may be unaware (or not think of) the sometimes subtle implications of selecting which apps to use.

The preceding example demonstrates the *data intermediary problem.* This problem occurs whenever the user directs an application to share sensitive data with another application that may not be trusted with that data. From the *Email* app's perspective, all of the other applications are *data intermediaries* in performing the user's task of signing `contract.doc`. We have created a specific term for this subproblem to differentiate it from secure information flow problems that result from background processing. The data intermediary problem is specific to information flows that result from user choices in selecting applications to process data. Furthermore, the problem is most apparent in modern OSes, because they 1) distinguish applications as security principals, and 2) provide modular applications to perform larger user tasks. We note that the data intermediary problem has always been present in operating systems; however, it made little sense to discuss when all user applications ran with the user's ambient authority.

For the purposes of this paper, we focus on the data intermediary problem with respect to accidental data disclosure that results from user selection. We leave the much harder threat model of a malicious application as the motivation for future work. However, we note that the primitives described in this paper can form the basis of a system to defend against this stronger adversary.

2.3 Threat Model

While our work is motivated by data security compliance regulations, we do not focus on the specific compliance rules themselves. Instead, we seek to address the broader challenge of creating mechanisms that help prevent the accidental disclosure portion of the data intermediary problem. We are specifically concerned with preventing the accidental export of large, application-specific, user data. There are potentially many data owners with different secrecy requirements. Therefore, an application may be both a data owner and a data intermediary, depending on the policy perspective, and each data owner's secrecy requirements must be met, even if doing so prevents data from being used.

Accidental data disclosure may occur in various ways. The user may share data with the wrong application (e.g., sharing a photo of whiteboard meeting notes via a social networking app). Such data export may not comply with the owner's policy, but may still occur through the user's interaction. Poorly programmed applications may also unknowingly leak private data to the cloud. For example, a document editor might backup documents to the cloud, and an app might send data as part of targeted advertisements.

The work in this paper does not seek to prevent malicious data disclosure. That is, we do not address side channels or collusion between applications. We also do not consider malicious daemons that operate outside our confinement. Finally, we are specifically concerned with data on the host and do not address exposure of data from cloud services once it is allowed to leave the host.

2.4 Background: Android

Android runs a Linux kernel, but defines its own application runtime environment. The Java-based middleware API forces developers to design their applications within a component framework. Android defines four component types: *activity*, *service*, *content provider*, and *broadcast receiver*. Activity components define the application's user interface. Each UI screen is defined by a different activity component. The other components types run in the background and are started by the Android middleware as needed. These component types provide daemon-like functionality. Service components are general purpose daemons; content provider components act as database daemons, and broadcast receiver components listen for messages.

Android's *binder* framework provides process control and IPC between components. Applications generally do not interact with binder directly. Instead, they use *intent messages*, which start activity and service components, and send messages to broadcast receiver components. The key attribute of intent messages is their ability to be sent to implicit addresses. For this, Android uses *action strings*, such as `ACTION_VIEW` and `ACTION_SEND`. Applications define *intent filters* to register to receive messages addressed to specific action strings. The Android framework then automatically determines potential intent message destinations (i.e. resolves the intent), presenting the user with a list of targets if a single destination must be chosen from a set.

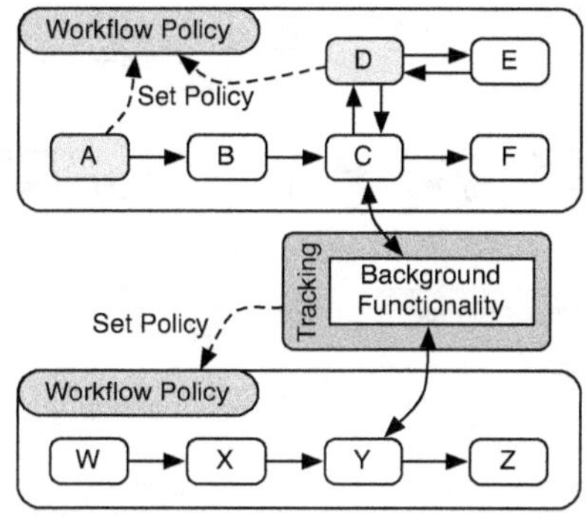

Figure 2: Aquifer policy abstraction

3. OVERVIEW

Aquifer is designed around the concept of a *user interface workflow.* As previously discussed, an emergent property of modern OS applications is that they are relatively simple, purpose or service specific, and often combined with other apps to perform a larger task. When the user performs a task, the execution transitions between UI screens. The next UI screen can be in the same or different application. Aquifer tracks the specific instances of the UI screens used to perform the user's task and abstracts them as a UI workflow.

Security policy is applied to the UI workflow abstraction, as shown in Figure 2. We choose the UI workflow abstraction to define security policy, because it approximates the task at hand. All operations performed as part of this task will have similar security requirements. Frequently, the task will be centered around a single data object and its derivative objects, as demonstrated in the document signing use case.

Note that UI workflows are not necessarily linear. They are dynamically defined as the user navigates functionality on the host. This includes branches to perform subtasks. For example, a user interacting with a shopping application may navigate to a barcode scanner to retrieve the UPC code of a product via a camera. When this branch returns, the user continues the task. As shown in Figure 2, Aquifer

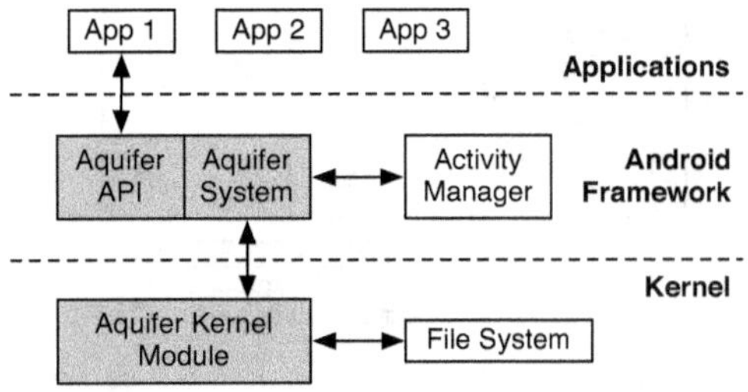

Figure 3: Aquifer architecture for Android

allows applications on the branch to contribute to secrecy restrictions (e.g., UI screen D).

Figure 3 depicts the Aquifer architecture for Android. Aquifer provides an API for applications to manage policy. This policy is enforced by the Aquifer System, which places hooks into Android's Activity Manager service. Finally, Aquifer has a small kernel component to monitor file communication.

Aquifer is built around the following principles:

Decentralized policy specification: Modern OSes increasingly contain application-specific data. Therefore OS providers cannot practically define security policy. Instead, Aquifer uses the multiple-owner policy semantics of decentralized information flow control (DIFC) [27]. Since each application is a potential stakeholder on data, DIFC provides a well-founded notion of data ownership and an articulation in each context of what each principal is trusted to do with that data.

Developers & Users define policy: The developers of applications that own data can frequently identify security sensitive data. Aquifer then infers user intention from the UI workflow. While this reduces the burden on the user, it does not entirely eliminate it. Sometimes the application must distinguish between confidential and public data. This context can frequently be acquired via preliminary labeling, which ranges by application. For example, the Email app in our use case could determine secrecy requirements from an Email header set by the sender. Applications such as note apps (e.g., Evernote) already have semantic tags on data (e.g., business, personal) that can be leveraged. User data labeling has been shown to be useful for specifying policy [23]. In other cases (e.g., DocuSign), the policy specification is inherent to the functionality of the app.

Compatibility with legacy applications: Aquifer focuses protection on large, application-specific, data objects. Applications frequently process these data objects locally. This allows Aquifer to be compatible with most legacy applications and only requires modifications of applications that must specify policy (i.e., data owners). If no secrecy restrictions are specified, Aquifer uses a default-allow policy.

Minimizing policy violations: Policy violations confuse users by either prompting the user to make security decisions, or breaking functionality. Aquifer helps minimize policy violations by allowing applications to influence the functionality available to users. For example, Android uses "action strings" (e.g., `ACTION_SEND`, `ACTION_VIEW`, `ACTION_EDIT`) that help the OS find an appropriate consumer for shared data. When Android finds multiple possible recipients, the user is presented a list of targets from which to choose. Similar functionality is provided by Windows 8's share charm. If the user chooses a target application that attempts to export data, and the UI workflow export restriction denies the app to use the network, a security exception will result. Often, this will break the functionality of the app, resulting in a poor user experience. Therefore, to prevent such scenarios from even occurring, Aquifer allows a data owner to specify a UI workflow filter that limits the potential targets.

Compatibility with background functionality: UI screens may communicate with daemons (e.g., service and content provider components in Android). If interaction with a daemon passes sensitive data between two UI workflows, e.g., between screens C and Y in Figure 2, Aquifer must propagate the policy restrictions to the receiving workflow. However, Aquifer cannot simply propagate the workflow security policy to the daemon process, as this would cause the daemon and subsequent UI workflows to be restricted by all previous UI workflow policies. Ultimately this would result in an unusable system. Therefore, Aquifer requires a more precise method of tracking information within daemons. For this, Aquifer could leverage systems such as TaintDroid [13] and CleanOS [37]. However, the primary focus of this paper is the ability to specify and enforce security policies with respect to the UI workflow. Therefore, for our prototype implementation, we use a lighter weight heuristic based on tracking file descriptors used by daemons (see Section 5.3).

4. AQUIFER POLICY

A key challenge of Aquifer is defining the appropriate policy semantics for addressing the data intermediary problem in modern OSes. We first motivate the security policy types supported by Aquifer and then formally define the logic.

4.1 Policy Types

The primary concern of Aquifer is accidental export of high-value, application-specific user data. Therefore, our secrecy restrictions are defined with respect to export control. Export restrictions allow any functionality *on* the host, but prevent leakage to remote parties that are not mediated by the framework. As mentioned in Section 3, Aquifer uses a default-allow policy to ensure compatibility with legacy applications processing unconstrained data objects. However, the policy becomes default-deny if restrictions are present.

Based on a manual survey of Android applications, we identified the need for the following secrecy restrictions.

Export Restrictions: The most basic type of secrecy restriction is a whitelist of applications that are allowed to send data off the device. Frequently, the whitelist contains only the application that specifies the export restriction. For example, in the document signing use case in Section 2, the *Email* app wishes to ensure that only it can send `contract.doc` and derivative files off the host. We allow an application to specify a list to support suites of applications or lists of known trusted applications.

Required Restrictions: The second type of secrecy restriction is motivated by copies of files left on persistent storage. Required restrictions ensure that cached copies of files cannot be later exported without the knowledge of the data owner. In our document signing use case, *DocuSign* may wish to protect the handwritten signature of Alice by ensuring that a file containing the signature can only be sent off the device when *DocuSign* participates in the workflow. Since *DocuSign* is the trusted authority for handwritten signature data, it trusts itself to ensure user approval for using a workflow that involves sending a signed document off the host. Required restrictions are particularly useful for applications that provide a UI for the user to choose and return a specific file. Finally, while it is likely that applications will only specify a single required restriction, Aquifer allows a list. We currently require all applications on the list to be present on the workflow. In the future, we will explore the usefulness of "k of" policies.

Filters: A direct consequence of enforcement of export restrictions is access control violations, and Aquifer attempts to reduce these violations through workflow filters. Aquifer allows applications to define these UI workflow filters specifically to enhance usability. In the case of Android, filters limit the results of intent resolution shown to the user. Similar filters can be constructed for Windows 8's share charm.

4.2 Policy Logic

Aquifer formalizes the export, required, and filter policy types into a logic. Our logic is motivated by the decentralized label model (DLM) [27]. We chose DLM over other DIFC logics [41, 47, 48, 25, 24, 36] due to its clear owner semantics in the policy label. We extend DLM by replacing the set of readers with a tuple containing our export, required, and filter restrictions. Note that Aquifer uses DIFC to control data export and not interaction between apps.

Aquifer uses applications as security principals. We chose applications over UI screens, because the fine granularity of UI screens would be cumbersome to specify and manage. Developers defining security policy do not necessarily know the UI screens in other applications.

The UI workflow policy itself is a collection of owner policies, where each owner is an application. The owner policy contains an export list, a required list, and a workflow filter:

Definition 1 (Export list)**.** An export list E is a set of applications that may access the network while participating in the UI workflow.

Definition 2 (Required list)**.** A required list R is a set of applications that all must have been present on the UI workflow at sometime in the past for any application on the UI workflow to access the network.

Definition 3 (Workflow filter)**.** A workflow filter F is a set of tuples $\{(s_1, T_1), \ldots, (s_n, T_n)\}$, each containing an action string s_i and a set of targets T_i. If the normal resolution of an intent message sent to action string s_i is a set of apps N, then the resulting allowed target applications is $N \cap T_i$.

To simplify discussion, we define functions for retrieving the action string and set of targets from a workflow filter. For a filter F, $actions(F)$ returns the set of all action strings in F. Similarly, for a filter F and an action string s, $targets(F, s)$ returns the set of target applications for action string s. Note that for the following logic to be correct, we assume that there does not exist an s such that $targets(F, s) = \emptyset$. If this occurs, Aquifer simply removes s from $actions(F)$, implying there are no restrictions for s (default allow).

Having defined export lists, workflow filters, and required lists, we can now define a workflow label.

Definition 4 (Workflow label)**.** A workflow label L is an expression $L = \{O_1 : (E_1, R_1, F_1); \ldots; O_n : (E_n, R_n, F_n)\}$, where O_i is an owner (application) and E_i, R_i, and F_i are an export list, required list, and workflow filter, respectively, specified by O_i.

A label L contains a set of owners denoted $owners(L)$, which is the set of all owners that have specified a restriction for the UI workflow (i.e., $O_1, \ldots, O_n$ in Definition 4). To modify L (i.e., add, remove, or change), an owner O_i must contain the active UI screen and can only modify its portion of L (i.e., O_1 cannot change E_2, R_2, or F_2).

We define functions for retrieving the parts of an owner's policy from a label L. Care is needed to account for Aquifer's default allow policy when no restrictions are specified by an owner. Let the set of all applications be $\mathcal{A}$, and the set of all possible action strings be $\mathcal{S}$. For each owner O_i, $exports(L, O_i)$ returns E_i, unless $O_i \notin owners(L)$ or $E_i = \emptyset$, in which case $exports(L, O_i)$ returns $\mathcal{A}$. Semantically, this means O_i does not have any export restrictions. Similarly, for each owner O_i, $filters(L, O_i)$ returns F_i, unless $O_i \notin owners(L)$ or $F_i = \emptyset$, in which case it returns $\{(s, \mathcal{A}) | \forall s \in \mathcal{S}\}$. In contrast, for each owner O_i, $requires(L, O_i)$ returns R_i regardless if O_i exists or if R_i is specified.

A useful concept is the *effective* policy. That is, given a label L with multiple owners, what policy should be enforced. We define the effective export list, required list, and workflow filter as follows.

Definition 5 (Effective export list)**.** For a workflow label L, the effective export list $E_e = \bigcap exports(L, O), \forall O \in owners(L)$.

Definition 6 (Effective required list)**.** For a workflow label L, the effective required list $R_e = \bigcup requires(L, O), \forall O \in owners(L)$.

Definition 7 (Effective workflow filter)**.** For a workflow label L, the effective workflow filter F_e is the set of tuples containing action string and corresponding target application set created by taking the union of all action strings and the intersection of the targets for those action strings. More precisely, $F_e = \{(s_i, T_i) \mid s_i \in \bigcup actions(F) \text{ and } T_i = \bigcap targets(F, s_i), \forall F \in filters(L, O), \forall O \in owners(L)\}$.

There are various scenarios in which Aquifer must combine two workflow labels, e.g., propagating a workflow label from a file, or through a daemon. When this occurs, we join the two labels L_1 and L_2 to create a new label that is the least restrictive label that maintains all of the restrictions specified by L_1 and L_2 [27].

Definition 8 (Label join $\sqcup$)**.** For workflow labels L_1 and L_2, the join $L = L_1 \sqcup L_2$ is a new label ensuring the following for all owners O:

$$\begin{aligned} owners(L) &= owners(L_1) \cup owners(L_2) \\ exports(L, O) &= exports(L_1, O) \cap exports(L_2, O) \\ requires(L, O) &= requires(L_1, O) \cup requires(L_2, O) \\ filters(L, O) &= \{(s_i, T_i) | s_i \in actions(F_1) \cup actions(F_2), \\ &\quad T_i = targets(s_i, F_1) \cap targets(s_i, F_2), \\ &\quad \text{where } F_1 = filters(L_1, O), \\ &\quad F_2 = filters(L_2, O)\} \end{aligned}$$

Similar to the definition of an effective workflow filter, the last rule ensures that the workflow filter for the new label L contains the union of action strings in L_1 and L_2, and the intersection of the target applications for each of those action strings. Finally, we note that when the above conditions results in the universal set for one of the restriction lists, our implementation removes the list to indicate default allow.

5. AQUIFER SYSTEM DESIGN

The Aquifer system enforces the Aquifer policy logic within a modern operating system. While we try to keep our description general, we frequently provide concrete examples using the Android platform.

5.1 Managing UI Workflows

As described in Section 3, Aquifer defines and enforces policy with respect to a UI workflow. A UI workflow is a graph that tracks the history of UI screens that comprise the user's task. This section discusses how Aquifer identifies and manages the workflow.

Identifying the Workflow: As the user navigates to new a new UI screen (e.g., Android activity component instance), Aquifer adds the screen to the workflow. Aquifer does not need to store the exact workflow graph to enforce the workflow label policy. Aquifer needs to keep track of: 1) W_V, a list of applications the workflow has visited (for effective required list R_e), and 2) W_R, a list of metadata for currently "running" UI screens (for effective export list E_e). The metadata required for W_R is dependent on the specific Aquifer implementation and the information required to enforce the policy. For this discussion, we assume it contains at least the app name and process identifier.

Ideally, we would like to start each UI screen in a separate process. This allows Aquifer to easily enforce the workflow policy by turning network access on and off for the process. If the same process is used in two simultaneous UI workflows with labels L_1 and L_2, Aquifer must assign both workflows the label $L_1 \sqcup L_2$ in order to preserve the restrictions on both workflows. This can lead to overly restrictive policy.

At first, separate processes for UI screens seemed straightforward for our Android implementation of Aquifer. Android is designed to allow components to transparently interoperate with components in different processes. Therefore, conceptually we could modify the Android framework to start each activity component instance in a separate process. However, we ran into two problems. First, activity components are simply Java objects that extend the *Activity* class and sometimes share global variables with the rest of the application. In such cases, starting the activity component in a new process causes the application to crash when an uninitialized value of a global object is retrieved. Second, in the cases when activity components could be run in a separate process, Android did not provide an easy mechanism to start multiple processes if multiple instances of that activity component are needed.

To account for these limitations, we made the following compromise. When starting an activity component, Aquifer checks if the process for that component already exists. If not, a new process is started, and there is no problem. If a process does exist, Aquifer determines if it is part of the current UI workflow. If so, the activity is started in this process. If not, Aquifer terminates the process. If applications are developed following Android's recommended conventions, an activity should save its state to persistent storage when Android calls the *onStop()* callback, indicating the activity is no longer visible. Aquifer then starts a new process for the activity for this UI workflow.

This approach is less desirable than poly-instantiation (suggested above), because if applications do not save their state, data loss may result. An undesirable user experience may also result if an activity component in the middle of a UI task is terminated, or if activities call each other in a loop. One way developers can reduce the impact of Aquifer's need to terminate processes is to develop their applications such that each activity starts in a separate process. This can be easily done using annotations in the app's manifest file.

Policy Administration: Only the active (i.e., currently displayed) UI screen can modify the UI workflow policy. Aquifer exports a policy management API to applications that includes the ability to query, set, and remove the export list, required list, and workflow filter for that application. We note that a UI screen can only retrieve and modify the policy for the application that contains it. This keeps an application from reading the policies set by other applications, but it does not prevent it from learning the effective policy, which can be queried by testing network access.

Removing Unrelated Policy: In developing Aquifer for Android, we identified an opportunity to remove unnecessary restrictions from the UI workflow label L. Activity components can be started in two ways: *startActivity()* and *startActivityForResult()*. The former method never returns a value, whereas the latter does. Aquifer leverages this artifact by pruning the workflow label as follows. When UI workflow branch returns, Aquifer determines if the activity component was started for a result. If not, Aquifer checks if owner policy can be removed. An owner policy for application O can be removed from L if and only if: 1) no UI screen of app O exists in the set of running UI screens W_R, and 2) no past UI screen (e.g., activity component instance) of app O returned a value. To ensure the latter condition, we modified W_V to include an extra bit of information indicating whether or not a UI screen for the application was started for a result. Note that this heuristic is conservative and may not remove an owner policy if a value was returned on a branch that later does not return a value. Once W_R is empty, Aquifer terminates the workflow.

5.2 Enforcing Policy

The Aquifer UI workflow policy restricts which applications can send data to the network. The workflow label contains a list of owners and corresponding export lists, required lists, and workflow filters that are used to calculate the effective export list E_e, effective required list R_e, and effective workflow filter F_e.

Aquifer enforces E_e and R_e by controlling the network access of the process containing the UI screen. Since applications are security principals, it does not matter if each UI screen runs in its own process, or all UI screens for an application run in the same process. For each process p corresponding to application $app(p)$, Aquifer enables network access if and only if:

$$(E_e = \emptyset \vee app(p) \in E_e) \wedge (\forall r \in R_e, r \in W_V)$$

Simply put, this equation implements default allow only if E_e is empty and all r in R_e are satisfied. Otherwise, the application corresponding to p must be listed in E_e.

Aquifer must re-evaluate the network access control for each process on a UI workflow whenever: *a*) an application on the UI workflow modifies its policy, or *b*) a new UI screen is added to the workflow. The latter condition is only necessary when the application for the added UI screen completes the restriction requirement for satisfying R_e.

Finally, as described in Definition 3, Aquifer enforces workflow filters by reducing the list of applications shown to the user on transitions between UI screens.

5.3 Tracking Background Functionality

Aquifer is designed to enforce security policy on user facing software. However, UI screens sometimes use background functionality such as daemons and file storage. When this occurs, Aquifer must carefully propagate policy labels between UI workflows.

UI Screen Accessing a Daemon: Daemons may be accessed by multiple workflows. Simply joining labels whenever a UI screen accesses a daemon will quickly result in all workflows having the same overly restrictive label. To avoid this, Aquifer uses intelligent tracking in daemons.

One method of intelligent tracking is to incorporate fine-grained tracking (e.g., TaintDroid [13] and CleanOS [37]). Unfortunately, existing systems would require substantial retrofitting to enforce Aquifer policy. TaintDroid can only track 32 distinct identifiers. CleanOS extends TaintDroid to store identifiers in the taint tag bitvector; however, this storage cannot be used directly for Aquifer workflow labels. Furthermore, the source code for CleanOS was not available at the time of writing. Since the focus of this paper is the UI workflow security semantics, and not building another fine-grained data tracking framework, we reduced the scope of our tracking to OS-visible objects allowing coarse kernel mediation (i.e., files).

By restricting Aquifer to tracking files, we only need to track open file descriptors sent between UI screens and daemons. Android applications can pass file descriptors through binder. This commonly occurs with content provider components. Consider an activity component in application A that wants to read an image file that is owned by application B. App B can use a content provider component to share the image file with other applications without the image file being world readable. To do this, app B allows app A to query its content provider for a content URI, or passes the content URI directly to app A (e.g., `content://app_b/img/42`). App A can then open a *FileInputStream* for app B's content provider using this URI. Behind the scenes, app B's process will open the image file and pass the open file descriptor to app A using binder. App A can then read from the image file as if it opened the file itself.

Aquifer for Android implicitly tracks file descriptors in daemons by leveraging Linux's `file_permission` LSM hook. This hook is invoked whenever an inode is read or written, as opposed to the commonly used `inode_permission` hook, which is invoked when the file is opened. `file_permission` provides Aquifer the file and the process performing the read or write, regardless of how the process obtained the file descriptor. Using `file_permission` also avoids ambiguous read-write file open masks, as well as properly propagating labels when the workflow label changes between file open and file write. However, these advantages come at the cost of degraded performance that results from retrieving the file's label for each read and write operation.

UI Screen Accessing a File: By using `file_permission`, Aquifer leverages the Linux kernel's tracking of file descriptors. Hence, even when a file is written through a daemon, Aquifer sees the UI screen accessing the file directly. When a process in a UI workflow reads or writes a file, Aquifer propagates the workflow label to and from the file in a standard way. Let the workflow have label L_W and the file have label L_F. If the UI screen writes to a file, the file's label is updated to $L_W \sqcup L_F$. If the UI screen reads from a file, the UI workflow label becomes $L_W \sqcup L_F$.

To accomplish these updates, Aquifer relies on a kernel module and the userspace Aquifer Service. When a file is read or written, a kernel hook extracts L_F from the file (e.g., from its xattr) and notifies the Aquifer Service via an upcall, sending L_F and the access mode. The Aquifer Service updates L_W (if necessary) and returns a new L_F (if necessary). The kernel module then stores the new L_F with the file (e.g., in its xattr) if necessary.

Finally, propagating labels to persistent storage using file granularity means that Aquifer cannot handle sub-file data items such as database records. This limitation is currently in place for implementation and performance reasons.

6. IMPLEMENTATION

We implemented Aquifer for Android v4.0.3 (ICS) and the Linux Kernel v3.0.8 (omap). Aquifer adds approximately 2,200 lines of code in the Android Framework, and approximately 1,000 lines in the kernel. The source code is available at `http://research.csc.ncsu.edu/security/aquifer`.

The core userspace implementation is the *Aquifer Service*, a new system service responsible for maintaining the workflow abstraction and policy language calculus. The Aquifer Service is invoked by hooks placed in Android's ActivityManager service. These hooks inform Aquifer when system state changes affect the UI workflow state. The hooks are also used to filter intent resolution before presenting results to the user. The Aquifer Service also exposes an API to applications to safely add and modify their owner policies.

Aquifer uses a Linux security module (LSM) to mediate file access and a file descriptor transfer between processes. We use the `file_permission` LSM hook to only propagate the label if the data is read or written. The file policy is stored in extended attributes (xattrs), and the Aquifer LSM forwards file events and file policy to the Aquifer Service via a netlink socket. We also ensure that the SDcard is also formatted to support xattrs.

The final component of our implementation is the *Aquifer device* driver, which provides a channel for the userspace Aquifer Service to communicate with the Aquifer LSM. The Aquifer Service uses this interface to manipulate the network access privilege of a process. The Aquifer Service also sets up the netlink socket with the LSM via this interface to receive events about file accesses.

7. EVALUATION

We now evaluate Aquifer by accessing the need and appropriateness of its protection, proving the safety of label joins, and measuring the performance overhead. We also provide three case studies to demonstrate Aquifer in practice.

7.1 Application Survey

To understand the need for Aquifer and addressing the data intermediary problem, we performed a manual survey of Android applications.

Survey Setup: We selected the top 50 free Android applications from 10 categories in the Google Play Store (500

Table 1: Application Survey Results

Characteristic	Number of Apps
Data sources	85 (17%)
Data intermediaries	140 (28%)
Value from Export Policy	70 (14%)
Value from Regulate Policy	78 (15.6%)

apps total). We chose categories based on use of privacy-sensitive application-specific data or the ability to use such data. For example, we omitted game-related categories, news and magazines, etc. We selected the following categories: Business, Communication, Media and Video, Music and Audio, Photography, Personalization, Productivity, Shopping, Social, and Tools.

Our application survey began by reading the market description of the application. For example, we identified if it creates or acquires data from the cloud. If we could identify a potential need for Aquifer, we studied the application manifest and manually ran the application as needed. Specifically, we looked at the types of interaction an application uses, e.g., complete isolation, data sharing in workflows, storing data in shared storage, as well as the type of data that was shared, i.e., we ignored data with no security or privacy value. Finally, we created a list of workflows that each app can be a part of to gain insight into how Aquifer's policies could enhance application security.

Results: Table 1 provides the statistics from our study. We found a number of data sources that produced and shared data. Apps that did not produce any data, but processed data from other apps, were classified as intermediaries. We identified a larger number of intermediaries, which suggests more applications provide data services than produce data. This motivates the need to address the data intermediary problem. We also categorized applications based on the usefulness of Aquifer's export and required restriction policies. These results motivate the appropriateness of Aquifer policy.

The application study also identified many interesting use cases. For example, some applications facilitate business meetings by sharing of files during meetings. Aquifer can be used to help protect confidential business files against inadvertent exposure. We also identified many free applications that provide value-add capabilities, e.g., image transformation. There are reasons why users may wish to edit photographs on the phone. The user may wish to ensure the intermediary does not export copies, particularly if the user is a professional photographer.

7.2 Security Evaluation

Aquifer specifically seeks to protect application-specific data that cannot be enforced by system security policy. The security and privacy sensitivity of application-specific data is often only known to the developer and the user. We seek to reduce the onus on the user by having developers specify security policy. We note that app developers already participate in policy by specifying which permissions an app uses, and assigning permissions to restrict app interfaces.

Aquifer allows app developers to specify host export restrictions on data used by a UI workflow. The policy for a UI workflow is maintained in a workflow label L (Definition 4). When information from one UI workflow is propagated to another UI workflow via files, Aquifer merges the two workflow labels using the join ($\sqcup$) operator (Definition 8). Section 4 claimed the join operation ensures the resulting label is at least as restrictive as both the original labels.

Table 2: Microbenchmark Results

Benchmark	Android	Aquifer	Overhead
App load	188.49±5.36 ms	192.07±6.30 ms	1.9%
App filter	194.12±7.91 ms	195.22±7.52 ms	0.55%
Net access	108.60±6.48 ms	109.64±6.31 ms	0.53%
Policy change	-	1.98±1.27 ms	-
File Read (1MB)	4.76±0.09 ms	5.23±0.22 ms	9.87%
File Write (1MB)	23.89±0.45 ms	25.44±0.86 ms	6.49%

We formally prove the safety of the join operation and hence of the Aquifer policy language. We do this in two parts. First, we define an *effective* restriction relation that ensures the evaluated policy is more restrictive. Then, we define an *owner* restriction relation that ensures that all of an owner's restrictions are maintained. This is important, because while L_2 may be effectively more restrictive than L_1, an owner's restrictions may be changed at a later time by another owner such that L_2 is no longer more restrictive than L_1. With these two definitions, we can define an overall restriction relation that is needed to prove the safety of Aquifer. The formal proof is provided in Appendix A.

7.3 Performance Evaluation

To understand the performance overhead of Aquifer, we performed several microbenchmarks. The experiments were performed on a Samsung Galaxy Nexus (maguro) running Android v4.0.3 and Aquifer built on the same version. We performed each experiment at least 50 times. Average results with 95% confidence intervals are shown in Table 2.

App load time: Aquifer initializes its UI workflow structures when the first application is loaded. This consists of creating a new label and data structures for W_V and W_R to maintain the workflow state. We compared the time to start the first application of a UI workflow in Aquifer to a baseline application load time in Android. The average overhead is 3.58 ms, which is negligible.

App filtering: Aquifer filters the potential target applications when Android uses an implicit intent to start an activity component. We measured the time between sending an intent message and the resolution of the final list of applications presented to the user. Aquifer only causes a negligible delay of 1.1 ms.

Network access check: Aquifer places a hook in the kernel that is called every time a process attempts to access the network. For this experiment, we created an application with an activity component that attempts to access the network repeatedly. Since Android already performs a similar check to enforce its `INTERNET` permission, Aquifer's additional checks have negligible impact.

Workflow policy change: An application with an active activity can modify the UI workflow policy label, which requires recalculation of the effective policy and reassignment of network privileges to all workflow participants. This policy re-evaluation only takes 1.98 ms.

Label propagation on read and write: Each file read operation requires Aquifer to retrieve the file's label from its xattr and *join* it to the workflow's label. Each file write operation requires Aquifer to retrieve the file's label, modify it, and store the new label. For this experiment, we measured the overhead of reading and writing a 1MB file

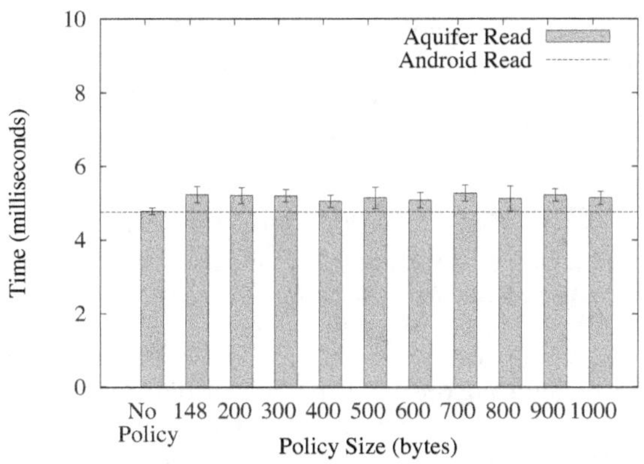

(a) File Read

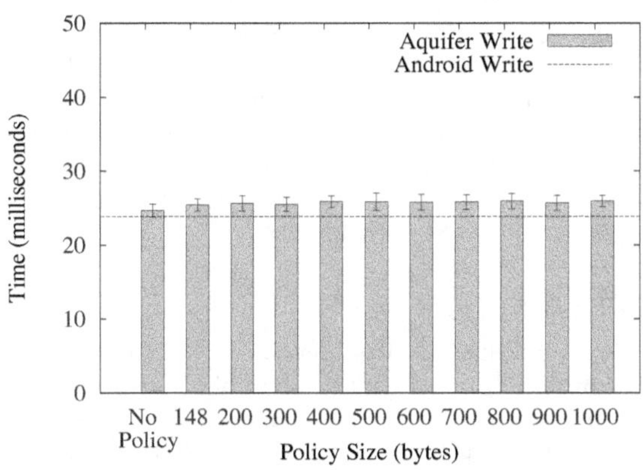

(b) File Write

Figure 4: Aquifer File Label Propagation Time. Error bars indicate 95% confidence intervals

with a small workflow policy. We performed each read and write 50 times, flushing after each write, and sleeping 500 ms between consecutive measurements. Table 2 shows an overhead of 6.49% for writes and 9.87% for reads. Note that while Aquifer writes are more complex than reads, the read overhead is greater, because the read time is significantly less than the write time. Furthermore, a production version of Aquifer could cache policies in memory to avoid unnecessary xattr operations.

To further investigate the read and write overhead, we performed a more detailed study of the time required. We repeated the previous experiment, but used a range of workflow label sizes and complexities. We started with a simple single owner label containing an owner policy of 148 bytes and increased gradually to a fairly complex label containing multiple owners and occupying 1KB. Figure 4 shows the time required for Aquifer to perform the read and write label propagation based on the policy size. The horizontal line shows the time to perform the read and write in Android without Aquifer modifications. There are four contributors to this overhead: 1) context switches when transporting labels from kernel space to user space and vice versa; 2) performing the xattr operations, 3) marshalling and unmarshalling the policy to and from the binary form; and 4) copying the data itself.

Figure 4 shows a relatively constant overhead, indicating that the setup cost of context switches and xattr operations overwhelms the cost of marshalling data and copying data between buffers. Finally, the overhead for reading and writ-

```
AquiferList exportList = new AquiferList();
exportList.add(this.getPackageName());

AquiferFilter filter = new AquiferFilter();
filter.addTarget(android.intent.ACTION_SEND, this.
 getPackageName());

AquiferPolicy policy = new AquiferPolicy();
policy.setExportList(exportList);
policy.setFilter(filter);

IAquiferService aquifer = IAquiferService.Stub.
 asInterface(ServiceManager.getService("Aquifer"));
aquifer.addPolicy(policy);
```

Listing 1: Aquifer policy modifications to K-9E Mail

ing empty labels is negligible, as we avoid propagating empty labels.

7.4 Case Studies

To demonstrate how Aquifer works in practice, we performed three case studies involving open source Android applications such as K-9 Mail, OI File Manager, and PDFView.

7.4.1 Case Study 1 (Confidential PDF)

K-9 Mail is an open source fork of the original Email client in the Android Open Source Project (AOSP). We modified K-9 Mail to create K-9E Mail, an enterprise email client for use by the employees of a fictional enterprise. We also used the open source PDFView application, which we modified to emulate an intermediary that backs up the files accessed by the user to the user's account in the cloud.

Our modifications of PDFView include 1) sending the PDF file to a network server, and 2) saving a version of a PDF file, and then on a later invocation of PDFView, opening the saved file and sending it to the network. PDFView does not go out of its way to collect data, rather data is collected only as a consequence of using it.

K-9E Mail allows the user to view attachments in other applications. For our case study, we use an Email with the file `contract.pdf` attached. When the user selects to view `contract.pdf`, K-9E Mail creates an intent message with the implicit address `ACTION_VIEW` and the datatype set to `application/pdf`. When K-9E Mail uses this intent to start an activity, Android displays a chooser allowing the user to select the viewer. In our case study, this chooser contains the default DocumentViewer app and our modified PDFView app. We verified that the PDF could be viewed by both DocumentViewer and PDFView while running in the Aquifer enhanced Android framework, without any modification to either app. When we viewed `contract.pdf`, PDFView successfully exported the PDF as designed.

We then modified K-9E Mail to be Aquifer-aware. For the case study, we included logic to identify a PDF as *confidential* if the filename contains strings such as "contract," "confidential," "secret," etc. Note that we used this classification scheme purely for demonstration purposes. A production version of an Aquifer-aware Email client could be much more intelligent (e.g., scan the subject and body for keywords, use predefined X-Headers, etc.). The Email client should also provide the user visual clues that the attachment is treated as confidential, and potentially a method to declassify an attachment in the event of false labeling.

Our second modification was to set the owner policy for the UI workflow before a *confidential* attachment is viewed.

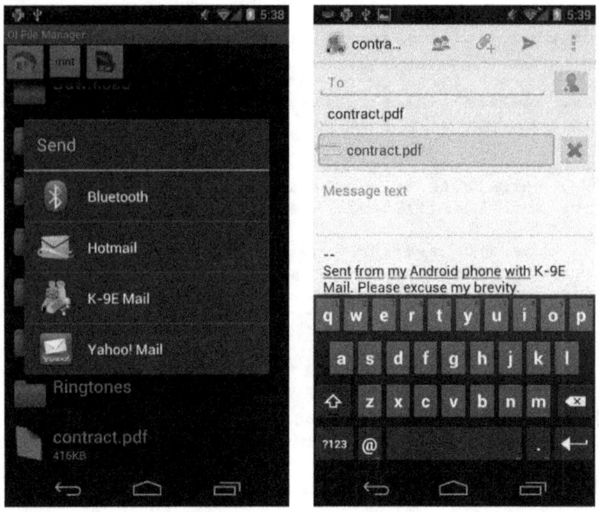

(a) Without Filter Policy (b) With Filter Policy

Figure 5: Aquifer Workflow Filter, a) Without policy and b) With Policy that allows only K-9E Mail

We used the following owner policy.

$$E = \{\texttt{K9EMail}\}$$
$$R = \{\}$$
$$F = \{(\texttt{ACTION\_SEND}, \{\texttt{K9EMail}\})\}$$

This policy ensures that only K-9E Mail can export the data, and if any application in the UI workflow uses the `ACTION_SEND` action string to start an activity, only K-9E Mail will be displayed, filtering out other options (e.g., YahooMail, HotMail), as shown in Figure 5. Adding this policy to K-9 Mail required very few changes, as shown in Listing 1.

We then re-performed our previous experiment. This time, when PDFView attempted to send `contract.pdf`, it could not reach the network. Furthermore, when PDFView saved a copy of `contract.pdf`, the workflow label was copied with it. When we later invoked PDFView as part of an unrestricted UI workflow, it read `contract.pdf` (due to our changes) and the workflow was successfully labeled, again keeping PDFView from exporting the document.

7.4.2 Case Study 2 (Choosers)

The previous case study shows how K-9E Mail can share data while ensuring that only it can export the data off the device. In this case study, we demonstrate how K-9E Mail can allow a larger set of applications to export the data only if the user's consent is provided.

For this case study, K-9E Mail trusts all other applications to send confidential documents off the host, but only if the user selects the file as part of a workflow. This policy is valuable to prevent accidental backup to cloud storage by other applications the user might have installed. This policy goal is accomplished using a trusted chooser application and a *require* restriction. For example, if K-9E Mail trusts the OI File Manager, the following policy can protect documents saved to the SDcard from accidental disclosure.

$$E = \{\texttt{ALL}\}$$
$$R = \{\texttt{OI File Manager}\}$$
$$F = \{\}$$

Using this policy, Aquifer allows the original K-9 Mail app to send the saved attached document when both, 1) starting the OI File Manager from K-9 Mail to choose an attachment, and 2) starting OI File Manager first and sharing the document with K-9 Mail.

7.4.3 Case Study 3 (Document Viewers)

Our final case study evaluates whether or not Aquifer policies are compatible with popular data intermediaries. We downloaded 25 of the most popular free document and image viewers and editors. Each was shared a file that has an Aquifer policy that prevents the intermediary from opening network connections. For the 25 applications, we encountered 0 application crashes due to access control failures. We found that seven of the applications (e.g., KingSoft Office, Olive office) contain advertisement libraries that immediately make network connections, before displaying the document. However, when Aquifer denies these network connections, the applications handle the denied connection without error and without usability impact (except for the absence of the ad). This use case supports our hypothesis that many data intermediary applications are built with modularity in mind and have limited dependencies on the Internet.

8. DISCUSSION

Aquifer policy specification may lead to usability failures if application developers do not predict all of the ways in which the user might construct a UI workflow. One potential case is when regulate restrictions can conflict with filters. Regulate restrictions require an app to participate on a workflow. However, if that app is not included in a workflow filter, the user may never be able to navigate through it. This example demonstrates a need for developers to coordinate on Aquifer policy at some level.

Another type of unexpected usability failure due to Aquifer policy results when a user clicks on a hyperlink in a protected document. If the Web browser is not in the export list, it will fail to navigate to the URL when launched from the workflow containing the document. Technically, the URL was part of the document and should not be exported. However, a policy may wish to include a trusted Web browser in the export list to ensure hyperlink functionality.

Finally, as discussed in our first case study, there are various situations when the app developer may need to indicate to the user that data is classified in order to avoid user confusion that may lead to access control violations. Such situations must be addressed on an application-specific basis.

9. RELATED WORK

Modern OSes, such as Android, iOS, and Windows 8, take the suggestion of decades of security research [45, 22, 35, 14] and run each application as a unique security principal. In these systems, security policy is defined with respect to permissions, which are granted to apps and restrict access to APIs and other applications. Research has criticized Android's permission framework for being both too coarse grained [3, 16] and too confusing for users [17]. Researchers have built enhanced security frameworks around Android permissions [15, 29, 7, 28, 6], some of which ease policy specification, while others make it more complicated.

Ultimately, permissions lack transitive semantics, which make them insufficient to express the security goals of modern OSes, as demonstrated by Android permission privilege escalation attacks [9, 20]. IPC Inspection [18] adds transitivity by reducing app permissions at runtime, similar to Biba low watermark [5]. Unfortunately, this requires apps to request extra permissions to operate, resulting in permission bloat. In contrast, Quire [11] adds IPC provenance records to help developers prevent confused deputy attacks. From the secrecy perspective, TaintDroid [13] and AppFence [21] use dynamic taint analysis to determine when privacy sensitive values such as location and phone identifiers are sent to the network. However, they lack the necessary policy semantics to address the data intermediary problem.

Traditionally, OS protection systems provide transitive protection semantics using information flow control (IFC) [10, 4, 5]. IFC labels subjects and objects, and uses a lattice to define a relation between the labels. Original IFC systems (e.g., MLS [4]) use a central definition of security labels, which does not meet the needs of software that defines new types of information (i.e., apps in modern operating systems). Myers and Liskov [27] defined a decentralized label model (DLM) that has formed the policy model for several decentralized information flow control (DIFC) operating systems (e.g., Asbestos [41], HiStar [47], Flume [25, 24], Laminar [33], and Fabric [26, 2]). DIFC allows applications to define their own label types.

Aquifer's policy is based on DIFC semantics, but it is optimized for the specific needs of the data intermediary problem. Traditional DIFC regulates interaction between processes and access to data objects. In modern OSes like Android, apps are frequently purpose specific and complex tasks are performed in user-driven workflows. Strict restrictions on communication and data sharing among applications would disrupt these workflows and limit the user to using only specific applications. Therefore, we relax DIFC constraints to enable greater inter-app data sharing, providing applications with a mechanism to control exfiltration of their data off the device instead.

Previous systems have controlled accidental data disclosure. Compartmented Mode Workstations (CMW) [8] assign and propagate sensitivity labels to data objects and processes (e.g. a screenshot has the label of the highest secrecy level of the data windows captured in it). A user action that leads to a flow from a high secrecy to a low secrecy level is met with a dialog box, confirming if the action was intended. Trusted Window Systems [31, 34] prevent accidental cut-and-paste actions by the user from a high-secrecy document to a low-secrecy document altogether.

Other factors leading to accidental data exposure, such as missing access control checks and poor programming have also motivated research. Resin [46] allows the programmer to configure application level data assertions to prevent accidental information leaks in Web applications. Resin is designed to help programmers detect vulnerabilities and bugs in their own applications, but does not provide Aquifer-like information flow guarantees in a multi-application environment. Liquid Machines [44] provides enterprise support for policy compliant remote content access using encryption. The use of encryption may restrict the user from using third party applications.

Finally, we are not the first to consider the challenges of modern operating systems. The ServiceOS project at Microsoft Research, which includes MashupOS [42] and Gazelle [43], considers similar problems, but focuses on Web browsers. Also under this umbrella project is Access Control Gadgets (ACG) [32], which uses trusted UI widgets to infer user intentions when accessing sensors (e.g., camera, microphone). ACGs are a generalization of the much earlier concept of a "powerbox," which is a trusted dialog box originally used by CapDesk [12] and DarpaBrowser [1] to grant a process access to a file based on the user's natural file selection process. Along these lines, Aquifer infers data access based on the UI workflow as the user performs a task.

10. CONCLUSION

Modern operating systems have changed both the way users use software and the underlying security architecture. These two changes make accidental data disclosures easier. To address this problem, we presented the Aquifer security framework that assigns host export restrictions on all data accessed as part of a UI workflow. Our key insight was that when applications in modern operating systems share data, it is part of a larger workflow to perform a user task. Each application on the UI workflow is a potential data owner, and therefore can contribute to the security restrictions. The restrictions are retained with data as it is written to storage and propagated to future UI workflows that read it. In doing so, we enable applications to sensibly retain control of their data after it has been shared as part of the user's tasks.

Acknowledgements

This work was supported in part by an NSA Science of Security Lablet grant at North Carolina State University and NSF grants CNS-1222680 and CNS-1253346. Any opinions, findings, and conclusions or recommendations expressed in this material are those of the authors and do not necessarily reflect the views of the funding agencies. We would also like to thank Patrick McDaniel, Patrick Traynor, Kevin Butler, Tsung-Hsuan Ho, Ashwin Shashidharan, Vasant Tendulkar, and the anonymous reviewers for their valuable feedback during the writing of this paper.

11. REFERENCES

[1] A Capability Based Client: The DarpaBrowser. http://www.combex.com/papers/darpa-report/html/.

[2] O. Arden, M. D. George, J. Liu, K. Vikram, A. Askarov, and A. C. Myers. Sharing Mobile Code Securely With Information Flow Control. In *Proceedings of the IEEE Symposium on Security and Privacy*, 2012.

[3] D. Barrera, H. G. Kayacik, P. C. van Oorshot, and A. Somayaji. A Methodology for Empirical Analysis of Permission-Based Security Models and its Application to Android. In *Proceedings of the ACM Conference on Computer and Communications Security*, Oct. 2010.

[4] D. E. Bell and L. J. LaPadula. Secure Computer Systems: Mathematical Foundations. Technical Report MTR-2547, Vol. 1, MITRE Corp., Bedford, MA, 1973.

[5] K. J. Biba. Integrity considerations for secure computer systems. Technical Report MTR-3153, MITRE, Apr. 1977.

[6] S. Bugiel, L. Davi, A. Dmitrienko, T. Fischer, A.-R. Sadeghi, and B. Shastry. Toward Taming Privilege-Escalation Attacks on Android. In *Proceedings of Network and Distributed System Security Symposium*, 2012.

[7] M. Conti, V. T. N. Nguyen, and B. Crispo. CRePE: Context-Related Policy Enforcement for Android. In *Proceedings Information Security Conference*, 2010.

[8] P. T. Cummings, D. A. Fullam, M. J. Goldstein, M. J. Gosselin, J. Picciotto, J. P. Woodward, and J. Wynn. Compartimented Mode Workstation: Results Through

Prototyping. In *In the IEEE Symposium on Security and Privacy*. IEEE, 1987.

[9] L. Davi, A. Dmitrienko, A.-R. Sadeghi, and M. Winandy. Privilege Escalation Attacks on Android. In *Proceedings of the 13th Information Security Conference (ISC)*, Oct. 2010.

[10] D. E. Denning. A Lattice Model of Secure Information Flow. *Comm. of the ACM*, 19(5):236–243, May 1976.

[11] M. Dietz, S. Shekhar, Y. Pisetsky, A. Shu, and D. S. Wallach. Quire: Lightweight Provenance for Smart Phone Operating Systems. In *Proceedings of the 20th USENIX Security Symposium*, August 2011.

[12] E and CapDesk. http://www.combex.com/tech/edesk.html.

[13] W. Enck, P. Gilbert, B.-G. Chun, L. P. Cox, J. Jung, P. McDaniel, and A. N. Sheth. TaintDroid: An Information-Flow Tracking System for Realtime Privacy Monitoring on Smartphones. In *Proceedings of the 9th USENIX Symposium on Operating Systems Design and Implementation (OSDI)*, Oct. 2010.

[14] W. Enck, P. McDaniel, and T. Jaeger. PinUP: Pinning User Files to Known Applications. In *Proceedings of Annual Computer Security Applications Conference*, 2008.

[15] W. Enck, M. Ongtang, and P. McDaniel. On Lightweight Mobile Phone Application Certification. In *Proceedings of the 16th ACM Conference on Computer and Communications Security (CCS)*, Nov. 2009.

[16] A. P. Felt, K. Greenwood, and D. Wagner. The Effectiveness of Application Permissions. In *Proceedings of the USENIX Conference on Web Application Development (WebApps)*, 2011.

[17] A. P. Felt, E. Ha, S. Egelman, A. Haney, E. Chin, and D. Wagner. Android Permissions: User Attention, Comprehension and Behavior. In *Proceedings of the Symposium on Usable Privacy and Security*, 2012.

[18] A. P. Felt, H. J. Wang, A. Moshchuk, S. Hanna, and E. Chin. Permission Re-Delegation: Attacks and Defenses. In *Proceedings of USENIX Security Symposium*, 2011.

[19] I. Goldberg, D. Wagner, R. Thomas, and E. Brewer. A Secure Environment for Untrusted Helper Applications: Confining the Wily Hacker. In *Proceedings of the USENIX Security Symposium*, 1996.

[20] M. Grace, Y. Zhou, Z. Wang, and X. Jiang. Systematic Detection of Capability Leaks in Stock Android Smartphones. In *Proceedings of the Network and Distributed System Security Symposium*, Feb. 2012.

[21] P. Hornyack, S. Han, J. Jung, S. Schechter, and D. Wetherall. These Aren't the Droids You're Looking For: Retrofitting Android to Protect Data from Imperious Applications. In *Proceedings of the ACM Conference on Computer and Communications Security (CCS)*, 2011.

[22] S. Ioannidis, S. Bellovin, and J. Smith. Sub-Operating Systems: A New Approach to Application Security. In *Proceedings of ACM SIGOPS European workshop*, 2002.

[23] P. F. Klemperer, Y. Liang, M. L. Mazurek, M. Sleeper, B. Ur, L. Baur, L. F. Cranor, N. Gupta, and M. K. Reiter. Tag, You Can See It! Using Tags for Access Control in Photo Sharing. In *Proceedings of the ACM SIGCHI Conference on Human Factors in Computing Systems (CHI)*, 2012.

[24] M. Krohn and E. Tromer. Noninterference for a Practical DIFC-Based Operating System. In *Proceedings of the IEEE Symposium on Security and Privacy*, 2009.

[25] M. Krohn, A. Yip, M. Brodsky, N. Cliffer, M. F. Kaashoek, E. Kohler, and R. Morris. Information Flow Control for Standard OS Abstractions. In *Proceedings of ACM Symposium on Operating Systems Principles*, 2007.

[26] J. Liu, M. D. George, K. Vikram, X. Qi, L. Waye, and A. C. Myers. Fabric: A Platform for Secure Distributed Computation and Storage. In *Proceedings of the ACM Symposium on Operating Systems Principles (SOSP)*, 2009.

[27] A. C. Myers and B. Liskov. A Decentralized Model for Information Flow Control. In *Proceedings of the ACM Symposium on Operating Systems Principles*, 1997.

[28] M. Nauman, S. Khan, and X. Zhang. Apex: Extending Android Permission Model and Enforcement with User-defined Runtime Constraints. In *Proceedings of ASIACCS*, 2010.

[29] M. Ongtang, S. McLaughlin, W. Enck, and P. McDaniel. Semantically Rich Application-Centric Security in Android. In *Proceedings of the 25th Annual Computer Security Applications Conference*, 2009.

[30] Payment Card Industry (PCI). Data Security Standard: Requirements and Security Assessment Procedures, Version 2.0, Oct. 2010. Available at https://www.pcisecuritystandards.org/security_standards/documents.php.

[31] J. Picciotto. Towards trusted cut and paste in the X Window System. In *Proceedings of the Seventh Annual Computer Security Applications Conference*. IEEE, 1991.

[32] F. Roesner, T. Kohno, A. Moshchuk, B. Parno, H. J. Wang, and C. Cowan. User-Driven Access Control: Rethinking Permission Granting in Modern Operating Systems. In *Proceedings of the IEEE Symposium on Security and Privacy*, 2012.

[33] I. Roy, D. E. Porter, M. D. Bond, K. S. McKinley, and E. Witchel. Laminar: Practical Fine-Grained Decentralized Information Flow Control. In *Proc. of the Conference on Programming Language Design and Implementation*, 2009.

[34] J. S. Shapiro, J. Vanderburgh, E. Northup, and D. Chizmadia. Design of the EROS trusted window system. In *Proceedings of the USENIX Security Symposium*, 2004.

[35] P. Snowberger and D. Thain. Sub-Identities: Towards Operating System Support for Distributed System Security. Technical Report 2005-18, University of Notre Dame, Department of Computer Science and Engineering, 2005.

[36] D. Stefan, A. Russo, D. Mazieres, and J. C. Mitchell. Disjunctive Category Labels. In *Proc. of NordSec*, 2011.

[37] Y. Tang, P. Ames, S. Bhamidipati, A. Bijlani, R. Geambasu, and N. Sarda. CleanOS: Limiting Mobile Data Exposiure with Idle Eviction. In *Proceedings of the USENIX Symposium on Operating Systems Design and Implementation (OSDI)*, 2012.

[38] US Congress. Gramm-Leach-Bliley Act, Finiancial Privacy Rule. 15 USC §6801-§6809, Nov. 1999. Available at http://www.law.cornell.edu/uscode/usc_sup_01_15_10_94_20_I.html.

[39] US Congress. Health Insurance Portability and Accountability Act of 1996, Privacy Rule. 45 CFR 164, Aug. 2002. Available at http://www.access.gpo.gov/nara/cfr/waisidx_07/45cfr164_07.html

[40] US Internal Revenue Service (IRS). Publication 1075: Safeguards for Protecting Federal Tax Returns and Return Information, 2010. Available at http://www.irs.gov/pub/irs-pdf/p1075.pdf.

[41] S. Vandebogart, P. Efstathopoulos, E. Kohler, M. Krohn, C. Frey, D. Ziegler, F. Kaashoek, R. Morris, and D. Mazières. Labels and Event Processes in the Asbestos Operating System. *ACM Transactions on Computer Systems (TOCS)*, 25(4), December 2007.

[42] H. J. Wang, X. Fan, J. Howell, and C. Jackson. Protection and Communication Abstractions for Web Browsers in MashupOS. In *Proceedings of the ACM Symposium on Operating Systems Principles (SOSP)*, 2007.

[43] H. J. Wang, C. Grier, A. Moshchuk, S. T. King, P. Choudhury, and H. Venter. The Multi-Principle OS Construction of the Gazelle Web Browser. In *Proceedings of the USENIX Security Symposium*, 2009.

[44] B. Week. Company Overview of Liquid Machines, Inc. http://investing.businessweek.com/research/stocks/private/snapshot.asp?privcapId=3079632.

[45] D. Wichers, D. Cook, R. Olsson, J. Crossley, P. Kerchen, K. Levitt, and R. Lo. PACL's: An Access Control List Approach to Anti-viral Security. In *Proceedings of the 13th National Computer Security Conference*, 1990.

[46] A. Yip, X. Wang, N. Zeldovich, and M. F. Kaashoek. Improving application security with data flow assertions. In *Proceedings of the ACM SIGOPS 22nd symposium on Operating systems principles*, 2009.

[47] N. Zeldovich, S. Boyd-Wickizer, E. Kohler, and D. Mazières. Making Information Flow Explicit in HiStar. In *Proceedings of the 7th symposium on Operating Systems Design and Implementation (OSDI)*, pages 263–278, 2006.

[48] N. Zeldovich, S. Boyd-Wickizer, and D. Mazieres. Securing Distributed Systems with Information Flow Control. In *Proceedings of the USENIX Symposium on Networked Systems Design and Implementation*, 2008.

APPENDIX

A. AQUIFER POLICY SAFETY PROOF

We now prove the safety of the join operation in the Aquifer policy logic. Before proving the join operation ensures policy restriction, we must define a restriction relation. We do this in two parts. First, we define an *effective* restriction relation that ensures the evaluated policy is more restrictive. Then, we define an *owner* restriction relation that ensures that all of an owner's restrictions are maintained. This is important, because while L_2 may be effectively more restrictive than L_1, an individual owner's restrictions may be changed at a later time by another owner such that L_2 is no longer more restrictive than L_1. With these two definitions, we can define an overall restriction relation that is needed to prove the safety of Aquifer.

Definition 9 (Effective restriction relation $\sqsubseteq_e$). Let L_1 and L_2 be workflow labels with effective export lists, required lists, and workflow filters E_{1e}, E_{2e}, R_{1e}, R_{2e}, F_{1e}, and F_{2e}, respectively. L_2 is effectively more restrictive than L_1, denoted $L_1 \sqsubseteq_e L_2$, if and only if:

$$\begin{gathered} E_{1e} \supseteq E_{2e} \\ R_{1e} \subseteq R_{2e} \\ actions(F_{1e}) \subseteq actions(F_{2e}) \\ \forall s \in actions(F_{1e}), targets(F_{1e}, s) \supseteq targets(F_{2e}, s) \end{gathered}$$

Conceptually, Definition 9 ensures that (1) L_2 has less exporters than L_1, (2) L_2 has more required apps on the workflow than L_1, and (3) any workflow filters in L_1 are enforced by L_2 with targets that are more restrictive (less than) those in L_1.

Definition 10 (Owner restriction relation $\sqsubseteq_O$). Let L_1 and L_2 be workflow labels, O be the owner for which the relation is evaluated, $F_1 = filters(L_1, O)$, and $F_2 = filters(L_2, O)$. L_2 is more restrictive than L_1 for owner O, denoted $L_1 \sqsubseteq_O L_2$, if and only if:

$$\begin{gathered} exports(L_1, O) \supseteq exports(L_2, O) \\ requires(L_1, O) \subseteq requires(L_2, O) \\ actions(F_1) \subseteq actions(F_2) \\ \forall s \in actions(F_1), targets(F_1, s) \supseteq targets(F_2, s) \end{gathered}$$

Conceptually, Definition 10 ensures the same properties as Definition 9, but with respect to owner O.

Definition 11 (Restriction relation $\sqsubseteq$). Let L_1 and L_2 be workflow labels. L_2 is more restrictive than L_1, denoted $L_1 \sqsubseteq L_2$, if and only if $L_1 \sqsubseteq_e L_2$ *and* $\forall O \in owners(L_1), L_1 \sqsubseteq_O L_2$.

We now prove the safety of the Aquifer policy language.

Theorem 1. *The Aquifer policy language is safe.*

Proof. We prove the safety of the Aquifer policy language by construction. Let L_1 and L_2 be workflow labels. Workflow policy propagation creates a new label $L_1 \sqcup L_2$. We must show that $L_1 \sqsubseteq L_1 \sqcup L_2$ and $L_2 \sqsubseteq L_1 \sqcup L_2$.

Based on Definition 11, $L_1 \sqsubseteq L_1 \sqcup L_2$ iff (a) for all $O \in owners(L_1), L_1 \sqsubseteq_O L_1 \sqcup L_2$ and (b) $L_1 \sqsubseteq_e L_1 \sqcup L_2$.

Condition (a) is satisfies Definition 10 by expanding $L_1 \sqcup L_2$ using Definition 8, as follows. For all owners $O \in owners(L_1)$, let $F_1 = filters(L_1, O)$ and $F_2 = filters(L_2, O)$, then

$$\begin{gathered} exports(L_1, O) \supseteq exports(L_1, O) \cap exports(L_2, O) \\ requires(L_1, O) \subseteq requires(L_1, O) \cup requires(L_2, O) \\ actions(F_1) \subseteq actions(F_1) \cup actions(F_2) \end{gathered}$$

$$\begin{aligned} \forall s \in actions(F_1), & targets(F_1, s) \\ & \supseteq targets(F_1, s) \cap targets(F_2, s) \end{aligned}$$

Condition (b) is satisfies Definition 9 by expanding $L_1 \sqcup L_2$ using Definition 8 and applying Definitions 5-6 to determine the effective policy.

Export list: for L_1, $E_{1e} = \bigcap exports(L_1, O)$ for all $O \in owners(L_1)$. For $L_1 \sqcup L_2$, $E_{12e} = \bigcap(exports(L_1, O) \cap exports(L_2, O))$ for all $O \in (owners(L_1) \cup owners(L_2))$. To satisfy Definition 9, we must show $E_{1e} \supseteq E_{12e}$. If an export list exists for an owner O_i in L_2 but not L_1, $exports(L_1, O)$ will return the set of all applications (see Section 4) and the intermediate stage will be $exports(L_2, O)$. However, if this contains an application that was not in E_{1e} it will be removed in the outer intersection. Therefore, $E_{1e} \supseteq E_{12e}$.

Required list: for L_1, $R_{1e} = \bigcup requires(L_1, O)$ for all $O \in owners(L_1)$. For $L_1 \sqcup L_2$, $R_{12e} = \bigcup(requires(L_1, O) \cup requires(L_2, O))$ for all $O \in (owners(L_1) \cup owners(L_2))$. Clearly, $R_{1e} \subseteq R_{1e2}$, which satisfies Definition 9.

Workflow Filters: for L_1,

$$\begin{aligned} F_{1e} = & \{(s, T) \mid s \in \bigcup actions(F) \text{ and } T = \bigcap targets(F, s), \\ & \forall F \in filters(L_1, O), \forall O \in owners(L_1)\} \end{aligned}$$

For $L_1 \sqcup L_2$,

$$\begin{aligned} F_{12e} = & \{(s, T) \mid s \in \bigcup(actions(F_1) \cup actions(F_2)) \\ & \text{and } T = \bigcap(targets(F_1, s) \cap targets(F_2, s)), \\ & \forall F_1 \in filters(L_1, O), \forall F_2 \in filters(L_2, O), \\ & \forall O \in (owners(L_1) \cup owners(L_2))\} \end{aligned}$$

Definition 9 first requires showing that $actions(F_{1e}) \subseteq actions(F_{12e})$. This is true, because F_{12e} contains all of the action strings in the filters for both L_1 and L_2. Second, we must show that $\forall s \in actions(F_{1e}), targets(F_{1e}) \subseteq targets(F_{12e})$. This is ensured by the intersection of targets when generating F_{12e}. This completes the conditions needed to satisfy Definition 9, as well as Definition 11 for $L_1 \sqsubseteq L_1 \sqcup L_2$. The proof that $L_2 \sqsubseteq L_1 \sqcup L_2$ follows similarly and is not shown for brevity. □

AppIntent: Analyzing Sensitive Data Transmission in Android for Privacy Leakage Detection

Zhemin Yang
Fudan University
yangzhemin@fudan.edu.cn

Min Yang
Fudan University
m_yang@fudan.edu.cn

Yuan Zhang
Fudan University
yuanxzhang@fudan.edu.cn

Guofei Gu
Texas A&M University
guofei@cse.tamu.edu

Peng Ning
NC State University
pning@ncsu.edu

X. Sean Wang
Fudan University
xywangcs@fudan.edu.cn

Abstract

Android phones often carry personal information, attracting malicious developers to embed code in Android applications to steal sensitive data. With known techniques in the literature, one may easily determine if sensitive data is being transmitted out of an Android phone. However, transmission of sensitive data in itself does not necessarily indicate privacy leakage; a better indicator may be whether the transmission is by user intention or not. When transmission is not intended by the user, it is more likely a privacy leakage. The problem is how to determine if transmission is *user intended*. As a first solution in this space, we present a new analysis framework called AppIntent. For each data transmission, AppIntent can efficiently provide a sequence of GUI manipulations corresponding to the sequence of events that lead to the data transmission, thus helping an analyst to determine if the data transmission is user intended or not. The basic idea is to use symbolic execution to generate the aforementioned event sequence, but straightforward symbolic execution proves to be too time-consuming to be practical. A major innovation in AppIntent is to leverage the unique Android execution model to reduce the search space without sacrificing code coverage. We also present an evaluation of AppIntent with a set of 750 malicious apps, as well as 1,000 top free apps from Google Play. The results show that AppIntent can effectively help separate the apps that truly leak user privacy from those that do not.

Categories and Subject Descriptors

D.4.6 [**Operating Systems**]: Security and Protection; D.2.5 [**Software Engineering**]: Testing and Debugging—*Symbolic execution*

Keywords

Android security; privacy leakage detection; symbolic execution

CCS'13, November 4–8, 2013, Berlin, Germany.

http://dx.doi.org/10.1145/2508859.2516676 .

1. INTRODUCTION

With the growing popularity of Android, millions of applications (or *apps* for short) are available to users from a variety of Internet sites (called *app markets*). While users enjoy the rich features of the apps, their sensitive personal data, such as phone numbers, current locations, and contact information, may be stealthily collected and misused by the ill-intended developers of some apps. A recent study has showed that Android apps frequently transmit private data to unknown destinations without user consent [46]. To protect users, there is a great need for strong analysis tools that Android app markets can use to identify and remove malicious apps.

State-of-the-art approaches of privacy leakage detection on smartphones focus on detecting sensitive data transmission, i.e., whether personal data leaves the device [21, 22, 26, 30, 40, 29]. However, in this era of mobile apps with cloud computing, what constitutes a privacy leakage by mobile apps is a subject that needs reconsideration. Many benign apps provide services from the cloud to end users. These apps normally need to collect sensitive data such as location, contact, to send out to the cloud. Malicious apps that steal user data may also exhibit the same behavior, namely transmitting private information to the cloud (or via other means). Therefore, transmission of sensitive data by itself may not indicate true privacy leakage; a better indicator should be whether the transmission is *user intended or not.*

- *User-intended data transmission.* To use the function provided by an app, a user often tolerates his/her private data being sent out via some communication channels. For example, when using SMS management apps [3], a user can forward an SMS message to a third party, by several button clicking on the touchscreen. As another example, when using a location-based service [7], a user usually knows his/her location is sent out to get interesting contents tailored to the location. Since this kind of functional use of sensitive data is consistent with user intention, we should not treat this kind of transmission as a privacy leakage.
- *Unintended data transmission.* The irregular transmission of sensitive data performed by an app, which is unknown to users and irrelevant to the function user enjoys, is defined as unintended data transmission, or privacy leakage. In most cases, users are unaware of this kind of transmission because the malicious apps always do that in a stealthy manner.

The above shows that whether sensitive data transmission is a privacy leakage or not actually depends on whether the transmission is user intended or not. Unfortunately, due to the complex nature of user intention and different/unpredictable settings of different apps, it is almost impossible to have an automated method to determine user intentions. Alternatively, it is more practical to design an automated tool to provide a human analyst with the context information in which the data transmission occurs. Intuitively presented context information will make the task of the human analyst easier in determining if the transmission is user intended. This motivates our work on the *AppIntent* framework. Given sensitive data transmission, AppIntent derives the input data and user interaction inputs that lead to the transmission. The context information of the transmission shown to the analyst is in the form of a sequence of UI manipulations (i.e., GUI screens along with the highlighted GUI controls that indicate the supposed user operations) that is captured from a controlled execution of the app with the derived input data and user interaction. By looking at the displayed UI manipulations, a human analyst can then make a judgement.

Symbolic execution is an effective technique to extract feasible inputs that can trigger specific behaviors of a program such as particular transmission of sensitive data. The key idea of symbolic execution is to systematically explore feasible paths of the program under analysis by reducing the search space from an infinite number of possible data inputs to a finite number of data scopes (represented by symbolic inputs). However, existing symbolic execution techniques mainly focus on non-interactive programs [10, 16, 28, 39]. Dealing with events triggered by user actions in GUI apps is challenging because the possibly large number of combinations of input events can severely worsen the path explosion problem during symbolic execution. However, in AppIntent, user interactions cannot be abstracted away from apps for symbolic execution because user interaction is an essential part to judge whether the transmission is intended by the user or not.

To deal with the path explosion problem, we have developed a new symbolic execution technique called *event-space constraint guided symbolic execution* for Android apps. We first apply static analysis to the target app to identify the possible execution paths leading to the sensitive data transmission under analysis (such as sending SMS). We then use these paths as the basis to generate our event-space constraints, which represent all the possible event sequences for the given execution paths by considering the call graph and the Android execution model. Our guided symbolic execution then considers only the paths that satisfy the event-space constraints. Our experiments show that these constraints restrict the search space very effectively since the number of execution paths to be explored during the guided symbolic execution is usually small.

To evaluate the effectiveness of *AppIntent*, we perform an extensive experimental evaluation using real-world apps including 750 malicious apps reported in [46] and 1,000 top free apps from Google Play, to detect whether they transmit user's private data and to distinguish whether the transmission is user intended or not. In our experimental results, 252 apps have sensitive data transmission, among which 224 apps contain user *unintended* transmission while other 28 apps contain only *user-intended* data transmission.

The contribution of this paper is fourfold. First, we note that sensitive data transmission does not always indicate privacy leakage; rather, user-intended data transmission should be discriminated from user-unintended. Second, we develop an event-space constraint guided symbolic execution technique, which effectively reduces the event search space in symbolic execution for Android apps. As a result, event inputs as well as data inputs related to each propagation path of data transmission can be effectively extracted. Third, we develop a dynamic program analysis platform to execute the app driven by the discovered event and data inputs, so that we can display the sequence of UI manipulations, emulating the entire process leading to the data transmission. Finally, we evaluate our approach by using 750 reported malicious apps, as well as 1,000 top free apps from Google Play. Some interesting findings are also provided together with the evaluation results.

The rest of this paper is organized as follows. Section 2 introduces the challenge of symbolic execution for Android, and Section 3 gives an overview of the AppIntent framework. Section 4 presents the details of event-space constraint guided symbolic execution. The dynamic analysis platform of AppIntent is depicted in Section 5. Section 6 presents the evaluation of AppIntent using real-world Android apps. Section 7 discusses the related work, and Section 8 concludes this paper and points out some future research directions.

2. BACKGROUND: SYMBOLIC EXECUTION FOR ANDROID APPS

Symbolic execution is a program analysis technique that has been used in a wide range of applications such as test case generation [14, 17, 27, 28, 34, 39], fuzz testing [35], and security flaws detection [13, 15, 20, 26, 31, 42]. It is a traversal process, which explores a search space during the analysis process. The general idea of symbolic execution is to limit the search space because its execution time and practicability depend on this scope. For those non-interactive programs, symbolic execution can efficiently explore the search space of data inputs through a well-defined classification of these inputs. However, symbolic execution faces unresolved challenges when it is applied to GUI apps.

GUI apps, which are widely used in computers and handheld devices, are driven by not only data inputs, but also event inputs. Users can interact with apps by triggering runtime events such as clicking a certain button. Event inputs, which introduce highly variable program behaviors and hard to be classified into input scopes, greatly increase the search space of GUI apps. To the best of our knowledge, there are no efficient solutions to this problem, and most of the existing symbolic execution approaches for GUI apps sacrifice code coverage for performance by applying random scheduling strategy [38], exhaustively searching possibilities (to an upper bound of event sequences) [25], or assuming that event handlers will not cooperate with each other [24]. Recently, Contest [9] reduces the symbolic execution time of smartphone apps to 5%-36% of the original running time by utilizing profiling results, but the cost of this analysis is still too high.

When modeling the space of runtime event inputs, the most important characteristic of the space is the possible orders of events. In most cases, the behavior of a GUI app can be represented by the events triggered by the user along with the order of these events.

2.1 Android Basis

Similar to Java GUI apps, Android apps are usually driven by runtime events and callbacks. The non-determinism introduced by arbitrarily and distinctively triggered events increases the complexity when exploring the search space and severely challenges the symbolic execution of GUI apps. The search space of events is decided by Android programming and execution model, which needs a careful consideration in analysis.

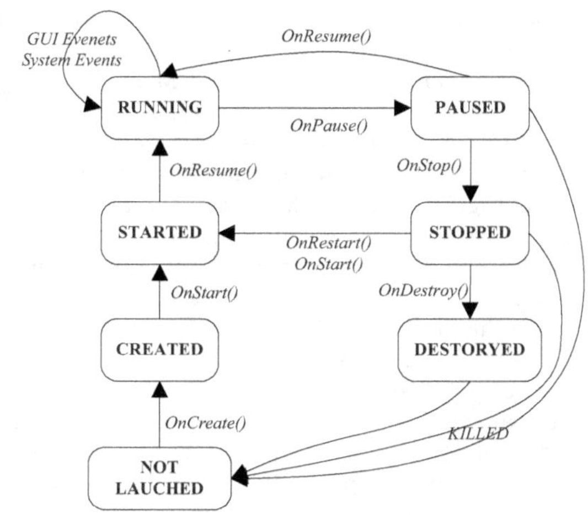

Figure 1: Android application model. This figure depicts the lifecycle of Android activities. The lifecycle of other components are similar.

There are two major kinds of events in Android: callbacks to manipulate the state transition of an app, and listeners to handle system events and user interactions with GUI components:

Android Events: Callbacks of Lifecycle States. Unlike in the common Java world, Android app does not have a unique program entry such as main(). Instead, it is composed of one or more components which work together to fulfill the functionality. The major type of components in Android is activity. An activity represents a single screen with a user interface. The other components, e.g., services, content providers, and BroadcastReceivers, are background tasks that perform long-running operations or respond to other threads. For each component, app developers override callback functions, which are commonly used to maintain its lifecycle, as depicted in Figure 1. These callbacks are expected to be automatically invoked by Android application manager. Therefore, symbolic execution faces a severe challenge because of the non-deterministic and unbounded triggering order of callbacks. For example, a possible execution could be *(OnStart ⇒ OnPause ⇒ OnResume ⇒ OnPause ⇒ OnResume ⇒...)*. It will further worsen the already notorious search space explosion problem of traditional symbolic execution. Actually, symbolic execution may never finish because the search space is infinite. We propose a guided symbolic execution mechanism which can effectively solve this problem with static analysis.

Android Events: GUI Events and System Events. An app running on Android is commonly GUI based, and its execution is typically driven by events from the specific GUI controls (represented as a *View* object) that the user interacts with. An app contains a collection of nested interfaces, called event listeners. These listeners capture user interactions with the app GUI. When respective interactions occurs on the GUI controls, for example, if a button is clicked by a user, the pre-defined event handlers are triggered correspondingly. System events are handled in the same way. Like callbacks, runtime events are also non-deterministic. They can be triggered in any order and at any time, thus exhaustively executing all possible sequences of events is a task that will never end. Fortunately, events in an Android app are commonly invoked when the state of the app is *RUNNING*. In this state, the main thread is hung to wait for incoming events. Thus, the event triggering behavior commonly depends on the order, not the exact triggering time.

3. GOAL AND OVERALL ARCHITECTURE

AppIntent is not an automated method to detect unintended data transmission, which is probably a mission impossible. Instead, as a first step in this space, AppIntent is designed to be an automated tool to present to a human analyst the sequence of UI manipulations that corresponds to the sequence of events that leads to the sensitive data transmission, thereby facilitating the discrimination of whether sensitive data transmission is user intended or not.

Our Goal. To achieve our vision, we have the following three goals:

- Produce the critical app inputs that lead to sensitive data transmission. Specific to Android GUI apps, inputs are always composed of: a) Data inputs which contain text inputs from outside; b) Event inputs from user interactions through GUI interface and from system through IPC. In addition, we need to track down the root-cause that gives rise to the transmission and filter out the massive set of irrelevant inputs.
- Guarantee a good code coverage. To find all feasible paths, we need to thoroughly traverse diverse program paths that may lead to a leakage, and at the same time, we want to ensure low false positive as well as low false negative rate during this analysis. In addition, to enable large-scale validation tasks, we do not want too much overhead.
- Provide an easy-to-understand tool for human analysts to ascertain under what circumstance the sensitive data transmission happens. Using the produced app inputs, we need to conduct the execution of an app according to each feasible path. We want to exercise the app's functionality automatically, which can emulate users' operations, and by observing the UI manipulation and prompting, we can then easily judge whether the data transmission is essential for a user-intended functionality.

Overall Architecture. Figure 2 depicts the overall architecture of AppIntent, which analyzes a target app in two steps:

- *Event-space Constraint Guided Symbolic Execution.* The first step is to generate critical inputs incurring sensitive data transmission. We adopt static taint analysis to preprocess and extract all possible data transmission paths as well as possible events related to each path, which helps to construct an event-space con-

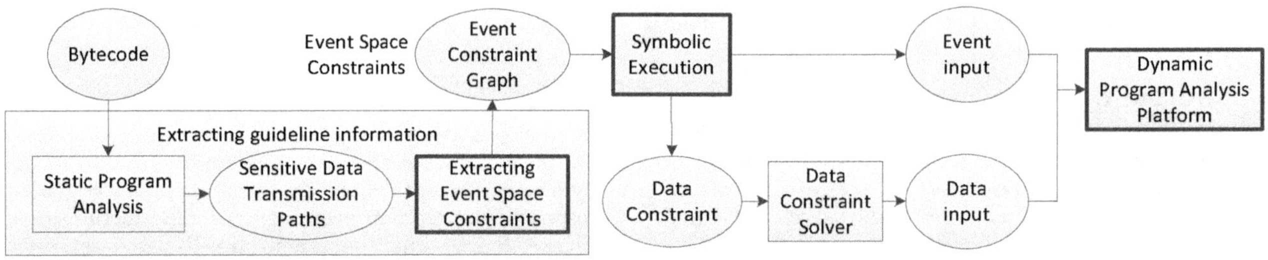

Figure 2: Overall Architecture of AppIntent

straint graph. Subsequently the graph is used in the guided symbolic execution to extract critical inputs. Meanwhile, code coverage is guaranteed due to the nature of symbolic technique. The detail is introduced in Section 4.

- *Dynamic Program Analysis Platform.* Inputs generated in the first step is not intuitive enough though they precisely tell under what conditions transmission would happen. Using these inputs, we adopt Android `InstrumentationTestRunner` [1] to automate the app execution step by step, which reflects users' interactions in UI manipulations, and the sensitive data propagation is also tailored to the related UI for a better understanding. We believe it can effectively visualize the root cause of the transmission so that we can intuitively judge whether the transmission is user intended or not.

4. EVENT-SPACE CONSTRAINT GUIDED SYMBOLIC EXECUTION

In this section, we present our event-space constraint guided symbolic execution technique for Android apps. We show how to reduce the search space considerably and finish the symbolic execution in an acceptable amount of time without sacrificing the code coverage.

We begin with an intuitive example, and then present an overview of this stage, followed by a detailed description of how to construct the event-space constraint graph using static analysis. Finally we describe how the graph facilitates guided symbolic execution.

4.1 A Concrete Example

Here we use an app, *Anzhuoduanxin* [3], to demonstrate how our event-space constraint guided symbolic execution works. The app has a program path containing the transmission of an SMS message when a user forwards a new incoming message. For easy understanding, as depicted in Figure 3, we simplify the data propagation to a path involving only one BroadcastReceiver, *PushReceiver*, and two activities, *MessagePopup* and *ComposeMessageActivity*. The new message is handled in the *onReceive()* method of *PushReceiver* that starts up the activity *MessagePopup*, and the message is displayed in the foreground on which a user can click the FORWARD button to invoke the *forward()* method that starts up the activity *ComposeMessageActivity*. On the next user interface, the user can click the SEND button to invoke the *sendMessage()* method to have the message forwarded.

In our symbolic execution, we first use static taint analysis to identify all possible transmission paths, and then we extract instructions of sensitive data propagation with the context information along each path. In our example, we get the path: $\{OnReceive$, i1$\} \Rightarrow \{startNewMessagesQuery$, i2$\} \Rightarrow \{forward$, i3$\} \Rightarrow \{forward$, i4$\} \Rightarrow \{sendMessage$, i5$\} \Rightarrow \{sendMessage$, i6$\}$. Then we construct an event-space constraint graph according to the information gathered in static analysis. As Figure 4 shows, those massive irrelevant events to this path have been filtered out, and only 18 events related to this path, including lifecycle callbacks, GUI events, and system events, are kept. We connect these events with edges according to the lifecycle state transition and the call graph. This event-space constraint graph is used as a guideline for symbolic execution to find sequenced events that possibly incur the transmission. Since our goal is to find the root cause and disclose the context of the user actions, we only need to find the shortest paths that cover the sensitive data transmission instructions respectively. As Figure 5 shows, for the given transmission, we get only two chains of events in sequence, which will be verified during symbolic execution, with a very small overhead. On our dynamic program analysis platform, the feasible chain is used to emulate a user's operations step by step automatically, which demonstrates which functionality is executed when sensitive data transmission happens. In this case, we can easily determine that this is indeed user-intended data transmission.

4.2 Overview of Event-space Constraint Guided Symbolic Execution

As stated earlier, the major challenge symbolic execution faces is the problem of space explosion, which is dramatically worsened by the Android GUI interaction and execution model. A complete app-wide symbolic execution is not scalable due to the large number of possible events. Actually, to achieve sensitive data transmission, usually only a small portion of events will be triggered in sequence, along with sequenced instructions that propagate the data. This motivates us that if we are provided with a set of instructions that possibly incur the transmission, we only need to consider and extract the events that may trigger at least one instruction of the set, as well as the possible prerequisites of these events. In this way, the event search scope can be greatly limited to those related events instead of massive irrelevant events while code coverage is guaranteed. We construct an event-space constraint graph aided by static analysis, and it facilitates symbolic execution in finding possible sequences of events that are used to reproduce the transmission.

In the following, we first give a definition of this special graph, and then explain how to obtain this graph by static program analysis.

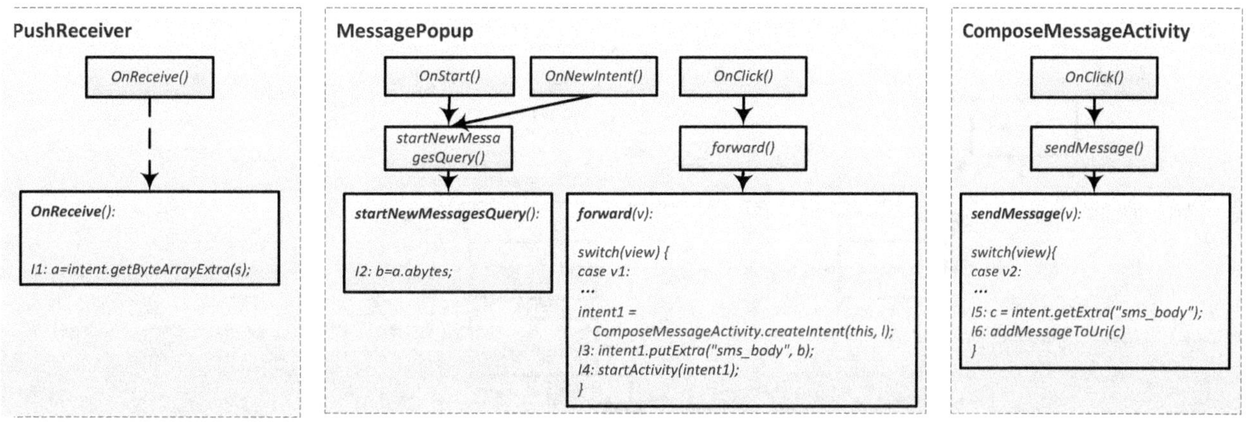

Figure 3: A simplified SMS forwarding case.

4.3 Construction of the Event-space Constraint Graph

As depicted in Figure 4, the event-space constraint graph is a directed graph, with each node in the graph representing a lifecycle callback, a GUI event, or a system event. There are two kinds of nodes:

- A thick-line node represents an event of which the event handler method contains at least one instruction of a given data propagation path. We call this kind of events *critical events*.
- A thin-line node represents an event which is a prerequisite for a critical event, and it does not contain any instructions of the given path. Such an event could be either a lifecycle callback of the activity that contains this critical event, or an event belonging to any prerequisite component that eventually starts up the activity that contains this critical event. We call this kind of events *essential events*.

A directed edge in the graph represents the order of precedence for two adjacent nodes. Edges can be calculated according to the lifecycle state transition and the call graph together.

Basically, for the graph, we ensure:

- All critical events should be included.
- All lifecycle callbacks of an activity that contains a critical event should be included.
- Any event belonging to a prerequisite component that eventually starts up an activity containing a critical event should be included, as well as its lifecycle callbacks.
- No edge violates the predefined order of the lifecycle state transition or the sequence of the call graph.

4.3.1 Extracting Critical Events

To build the the event-space constraint graph, first of all, we need to extract all critical events according to the given data transmission path. For each instruction in the path, we backward traverse the call graph to find all events that might trigger it. As shown in Figure 3, backward traversing the call graph from instruction 2 (i2), we can get two critical events, *OnStart()* and *OnNewIntent()*. We may introduce some false positives due to the limitation of static analysis techniques, but symbolic execution can eliminate these false positives later. In this phase, we finally obtain sequenced critical events, <*PushReceiver, onReceive*>, <*MessagePopup, OnStart|OnNewIntent*>, <*MessagePopup, OnClick*>, and <*ComposeMessageActivity, OnClick*>.

An activity may have different views to lay out various user controls (e.g. buttons), on which a user interacts with the app, and user interactions of various views are usually handled by the same handler method. The above critical events that we have extracted are from only the call graph and does not have the information about views except the handler methods. It poses a difficulty for the later guided symbolic execution. To solve this issue, we build a program dependency graph, extract branch conditions for view parameters from the graph, and annotate the critical events with these conditions as the context information. As depicted in Figure 3, the extracted branch condition for i3 and i4 is `view==v1`. After that, if we find that a critical event involves different views, we divide this event into several thick-line nodes, with respect to each view. Other GUI events are handled in a similar way.

4.3.2 Extracting Essential Events

So far, we get all the critical events that contain the instructions of the given transmission path, but they are just the critical interior nodes to symbolically execute the path. According to the Android runtime execution model, we also need to collect the essential events that are the prerequisites to the critical nodes, in order to behave well during symbolic execution. For example, an execution can not directly invoke *OnResume()* before the app is activated by invoking *OnCreate()* and *OnStart()* in sequence. Actually, an app strictly follows the state transition order of the app lifecycle, as illustrated in Figure 1. For each critical event of a component, we first supplement those missing lifecycle callbacks with directed edges according to the origin order. And then, aided by the call graph, we supplement all prerequisite components that eventually start up the activity which contains a critical event, as well as edges produced according the call graph. Meanwhile, the corresponding lifecycle callbacks of these prerequisite components are added in. In Android, inter-component communications are implemented through *Intents*. Thus, if a component receives an intent from another one, we treat the sender of the intent as the prerequisite of the receiver component, and add a directed edge to represent their order. Especially, if an intent is used

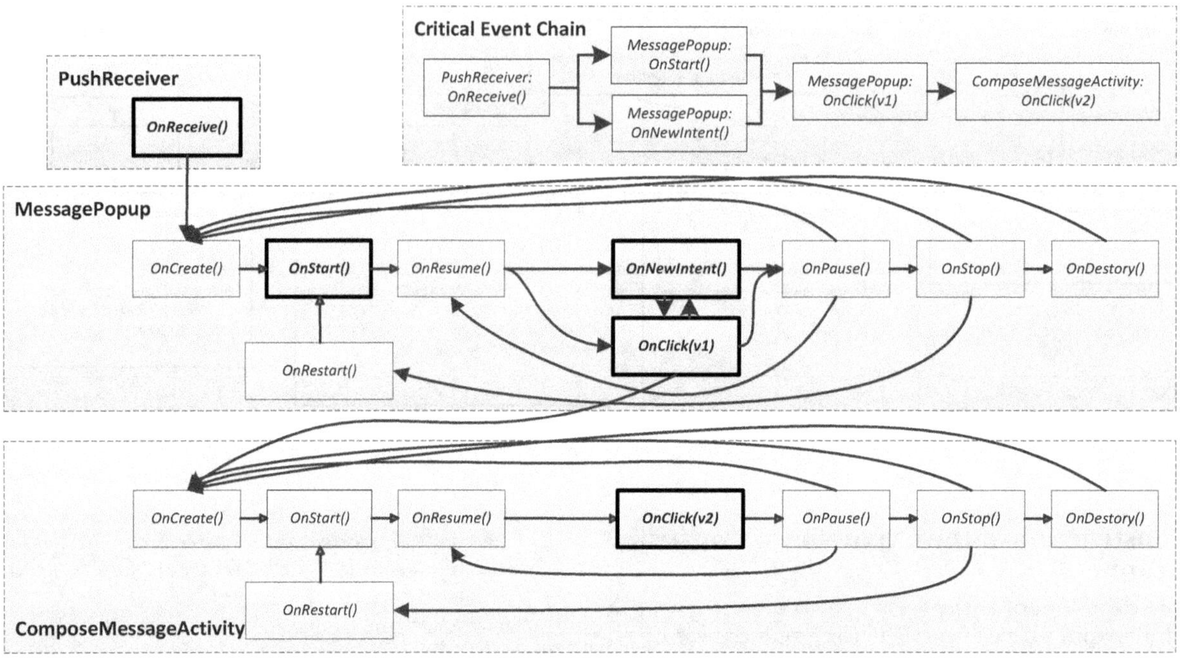

Figure 4: The extracted event-space constraint graph of the given example.

to start a new activity or service, the *onCreate()* callback of created component is marked as the receiver of the intent. In the current version of AppIntent, we only track intents that eventually start a new activity or service, as well as broadcast messages that are properly handled by a *BroadcastReceiver*, because they are officially documented by Google [2] and most of the apps use these two approaches to send intents. The intents with undocumented usage (which we envision could be handled in a similar way) are left to future work. The supplemental process will not end until there is no any prerequisite components found.

Upon finishing the above steps, we finish constructing the event-space constraint graph. As noted earlier in this section, for a given transmission path, all related events, including the critical and the essential events, have been extracted. The subsequent symbolic execution only needs to traverse this graph for sequenced events that possibly trigger the transmission and verifies whether it is a valid path. Since massive irrelevant events have been filtered out, the search scope is greatly reduced while the code coverage is guaranteed well.

4.4 Guided Symbolic Execution

We now explain how to traverse the above constructed graph to derive all possible sequenced events as the guideline to symbolic execution. The process of guided symbolic execution is depicted in Algorithm 1, in which P represents the events that are triggered before the last traversed critical event, and C represents the data constraints that should be fulfilled to reach the current execution point. If C is empty, then none of the data inputs can result in the target execution, i.e., the path can never be covered in any program execution.

Algorithm 1 works as follows. Our symbolic execution traverses the event-space constraint graph using the thick-line nodes as step stones. Each time when we proceed from a

$G \leftarrow$ Event-space Constraint Graph
$CEC \leftarrow$ Critical Events Chain of G
$C \leftarrow \emptyset$, $P \leftarrow \emptyset$
$StartPoint \leftarrow$ App Entrance of the Main Activity
Procedure `TraverseGraph`(ce)
  forall the ne : $< ce, ne > \in CEC$ **do**
    $mp \leftarrow$ FindMinimalPath(ce, ne, G)
    $C \leftarrow$ SymbolicExecute_Forward(C, mp)
    $P \leftarrow P \oplus mp$
    if $\forall$ e : $< ne, e > \notin CEC$ **then**
      Output: C as Data Constraint, P as Event Inputs
      exit()
    end
    else if C != $\emptyset$ **then**
      TraverseGraph(ne)
    end
    $C \leftarrow$ SymbolicExecute_Rollback(C, mp)
    $P \leftarrow P - mp$
  end
end
`TraverseGraph` ($StartPoint$)
Output: No feasible inputs found

Algorithm 1: Event-space Constraint Guided Symbolic Execution thick-line node, possible successors of this critical event are extracted from the event-space constraint graph. Since any of the successors can be the next critical event, we randomly pick an event first and calculate a feasible path from the current critical event to the chosen successor. Since only the essential prerequisites are needed, we extract the minimal path (using the Dijistra's algorithm) as a chain of events, which are sequentially triggered in the symbolic execution. If the event chain is revealed to be not available to any inputs ($C == \emptyset$), or all possible successors in critical event chains are already explored ($\forall\, e : < ne, e > \notin CEC$), we rollback the symbolic execution and try to trigger other feasible critical events.

Using Figure 4 as an example, guided by the event-space constraint graph, our symbolic execution explores a much smaller event space, as illustrated in Figure 5, and reports the following event chain as event inputs: { <*PushReceiver, OnReceive*>, <*MessagePopup, OnCreate*>, <*MessagePopup, OnStart*>, <*MessagePopup, OnResume*>, <*MessagePopup, OnClick*(v1)>, <*ComposeMessageActivity, OnCreate*>, < *ComposeMessageActivity, OnStart*>, < *ComposeMessageActivity, OnResume*>, < *ComposeMessageActivity, OnClick*(v2)> }. In addition, by using a modified version of `choco` data constraint solver [6], we generate corresponding data inputs according to the data constraints calculated in the symbolic execution.

5. DYNAMIC ANALYSIS PLATFORM

By using our event-space constraint guided symbolic execution, we can extract app inputs to trigger a given sensitive data transmission path. Although these inputs provide all the preconditions of target data transmission, they might not be intuitive enough for human to understand. To display these preconditions in an easy-to-understand manner, we set up a dynamic analysis platform to present which functionality is used when the transmission happens. With the help of Android `InstrumentationTestRunner` [1], a driven execution can be conducted for each sensitive data transmission path. AppIntent automatically generates a test case based on the inputs gathered before, and attaches it to the app by repackaging the original Android apk. Then, by running the test case though the Android activity manager, a controlled execution with the following features are presented:

- *Automatically trigger Event Inputs.* Events in the event chain are automatically triggered by performing corresponding operations. For example, to trigger a clicking event, a `performClick` operation is applied to the corresponding view, and we call the `setTestProviderLocation` method for a location change event. AppIntent currently does not support runtime events like phone call events because Android `InstrumentationTestRunner` does not support them. Since in most cases, view context of each event is already attached to the event chain, we can use the attached context directly for GUI events. On the other hand, if there is no view constraint, we randomly pick a view from the manifest file as the context of event. In addition, between each two GUI events, we generate a short delay so that analysts have time to observe the GUI display of each step.
- *Automatically provide Data Inputs.* Most of the data inputs generated by symbolic execution are text inputs to GUI elements, and we directly set the corresponding text field with the expected value. Some app inputs are messages from system or other apps, so we can attach these inputs to corresponding event messages. Besides, some apps trigger specific behavior based on the wall time of the Android system. For example, some malicious behavior happens only if a certain amount of time passed in the current execution. We explicitly generate sleep operations if data constraint relies on the current system time. In the current version of AppIntent, we do not support network inputs because we generate test cases through Android `InstrumentationTestRunner` [1], which cannot intercept and modify network inputs. This could be improved by hooking the network interfaces in the Android framework, which is our future work.
- *Highlight activated views of GUI events.* Activated view of each GUI event provides essential context, which represents a GUI element on the screen, for each user interaction. For example, if a clicking event is triggered, we need to know what element on the user interface is clicked by user. Thus, AppIntent highlights GUI element by setting its background color to red, as depicted in Figure 7(a) and Figure 7(b). For GUI elements whose view cannot be obtained by Android `InstrumentationTestRunner`, e.g., the list items, we highlight these elements by triggering some dialog box to display the view information.
- *Highlight sensitive data read and transmission.* To figure out whether the functionality of the app requires sensitive data transmission, our controlled execution needs to reveal when the data loading and transmission happen during the presented event chain. We highlight these two execution points by raising a notification dialog box, as depicted in Figure 7(c) and Figure 7(d).

6. EVALUATION

In the implementation of AppIntent, we first leverage DED [23] to decompile Android DEX files into Java bytecode. We implement our event-space constraint graph extraction on top of soot [8] and the guided symbolic execution engine on top of JavaPathfinder [10]. We implement the controlled execution and dynamic analysis platform on top of `InstrumentationTestRunner` [1]. In this section, we present our evaluation results on the effectiveness and accuracy of AppIntent. In our evaluation, the event-space constraint guided symbolic execution uses an Intel Xeon machine with 2 eight-core 2.0Ghz CPUs and 32 GB physical memory, which runs Debian Linux with kernel version 2.6.32. The controlled execution of AppIntent is run on Android 2.3.

6.1 Evaluation Methodology

In order to evaluate the effectiveness of AppIntent and its key techniques, we need to answer the following two questions: (i) When producing app inputs leading to some sensitive data transmission, to what extent does event-space constraint guided symbolic execution reduce the search space while guaranteeing the code coverage? (ii) Using the controlled execution based on app inputs, how effective is AppIntent to distinguish unintended data transmission with user-intended one?

In the following, we evaluate the execution time of symbolic execution with or without our technique to answer the first question and use two sets of real-world Android apps

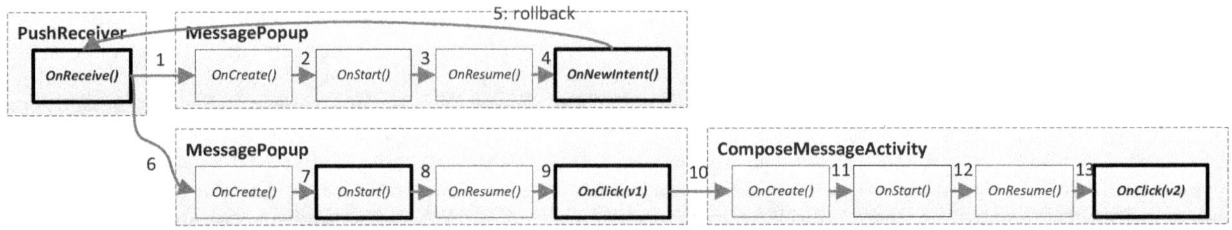

Figure 5: Event chains explored in symbolic execution by traversing the graph in Figure 4

to answer the second one. Besides, we provide some findings about sensitive data transmission patterns which are revealed by the result of AppIntent.

6.2 Effectiveness of Event-space Constraint Guided Symbolic Execution

To illustrate the effect of event-space constraint guided symbolic execution, we choose 3 famous apps from Google Play as samples. Among them, Maps is the Google map, Youlu is an SMS management app, and WeChat (a.k.a. Weixin) is a popular chatting tool. As presented in Table 1, without the help of event-space constraint graph, symbolic execution cannot finish in 5 days when we explore only 20 triggered events for the target app. This clearly demonstrates that exhaustively exploring event space is not scalable and practical. On the other hand, symbolic execution cannot cover the critical events in *WeChat* in this configuration, and failed to cover critical events in two cases(*Youlu* and *WeChat*) if we lower the threshold to 10 events. This means that naively limiting the search space can damage the effectiveness of symbolic execution. However, guided by event-space constraint graph, normally less than two hours are needed to explore the limited exploration space, and extract app inputs corresponding to the sensitive data transmission, without sacrificing the code coverage. Thus, it is clear that compared to existing approaches, guided symbolic execution proposed in this paper can greatly increase the exploration effectiveness.

Case	Origin (10 events) (hours)	Origin (20 events) (hours)	AppIntent (hours)
Maps	5.43	>120	0.40
Youlu	0.97	>120	0.13
WeChat	21.56	>120	1.33

Table 1: Running time of symbolic execution. Column 2 and 3 represent the running time when symbolic execution explores ten or twenty triggered events without the help of our event-space constraint guided symbolic execution. Column 4 shows the execution time of AppIntent.

6.3 Effectiveness on Analyzing Sensitive Data Transmission

In this experiment, two sets of real-world Android apps are selected to evaluate the effectiveness of AppIntent. The first set contains 750 malware apps from [46], which are known to perform malicious activities such as information leakage, money stealing, and privilege escalation. The second set contains 1,000 top free Android apps downloaded from Google Play. To compare with state-of-the-art privacy leakage approaches, we evaluate the same test datasets with TaintDroid [22] driven by MonkeyRunner. The results are depicted in Table 2. To verify the result of AppIntent, we perform manual analysis, in which we not only check whether apps reported by AppIntent transmit sensitive data, but also verify whether apps eliminated by AppIntent do not contain sensitive transmission.

As from the table, static taint analysis (the first step of AppIntent) detects 582 (442+140) cases of possible sensitive data transmission from two datasets. We find that 164 cases are false positives, which are eliminated by the next step of AppIntent, guided symbolic execution. With a manual analysis of the code of these programs, we find that most false positives in static analysis are caused by the insufficient context information and dead code, such as debugging code wrapped by *if(debug)* branches. There are another 44 cases from static analysis that failed to pass our symbolic execution. A further investigation shows that DED is unable to transform 42 cases from dex format to Java classfile, and the other two cases contain native code that currently cannot be handled by AppIntent. To check whether the app inputs generated by symbolic execution trigger sensitive data transmission, we applied manual analysis on the result of symbolic execution, and found that all cases transmit sensitive data defined in this paper.

With the app inputs extracted in symbolic execution, AppIntent successfully generates controlled executions for 358 (288+70) apps, among which, 245 (219+26) have been identified as unintended data transmission. We notice that the top free apps still have user unintended leakages, among which most apps are SNS (Social Networking Service) apps or apps that have embedded advertising modules. The leakage of SMS and contacts are all found in SNS apps. On the other side, malware may also contain both user intended and non-intended transmission, because malicious data leakage can hide behind some normal data transmission to bypass the state-of-the-art security validations. For example, we found that an application acts like an SNS app in disguise, but in the background, it stealthily transmits user contacts without user consent. It is worth noting that the current version of AppIntent failed to execute test cases of 43 apps because they are driven by network input, which is not supported by `InstrumentationTestRunner`. This could be further supported by instrumenting control code in Android framework.

As a comparison, TaintDroid can only detect 165 (125+40) cases as possible privacy leakage, most of which are leakage of device IDs. This is much less than AppIntent. Furthermore, the result of TaintDroid is hard to verify because it does not contain corresponding app inputs. Through our manual investigation, among these cases, 151 cases are also

Source	Malicious Apps: AppIntent (Static/ Symbolic/ Controlled Execution)	Malicious Apps: Unintended/ Intended Data Transmission	Malicious Apps: Local Logging	Malicious Apps: TaintDroid	Google Play Apps: AppIntent (Static/ Symbolic/ Controlled Execution)	Google Play Apps: Unintended/ Intended Data Transmission	Google Play Apps: Local Logging	Google Play Apps: TaintDroid
Device ID	389/256/ 246	198/0	73	101	98/43/43	24/0	19	37
Phone Info	53/50/50	50/0	1	0	0/0/0	0/0	0	19
Location	76/68/67	46/4	18	11	36/15/15	0/13	2	5
Contacts	13/13/13	1/10	2	0	10/10/10	1/9	1	3
SMS	27/27/17	16/3	0	0	9/8/8	1/7	0	0
Total	442/304/288	219/17	74	125	140/70/70	26/29	22	40

Table 2: Sensitive data transmission apps detected. The first part depicts the results of the chosen malware, and the second part are results of apps from Google Play. For each dataset, the first column represents the type of sensitive data transmitted, while Column 2 depicts the reported data transmission cases after each phase of AppIntent. Column 3 presents the number of data transmission of each kind. Column 4 depicts the number of sensitive data written to the local logging system. Column 5 lists the number of possible leakage cases detected by TaintDroid.

covered by AppIntent while 14 cases not. We manually checked the code of ten apps reported by TaintDroid but not reported in AppIntent, and found that nine of them do not actually leak privacy information. The remaining four cases either failed in DED, or contain native code that is not covered by AppIntent. In the 151 cases that are reported by both AppIntent and TaintDroid, 20 cases are actually classified as user-intended data transmission by AppIntent, which means they are not true privacy leakage. Since TaintDoird does not provide corresponding app input to trigger the sensitive data transmission, it cannot distinguish user-intended data transmission from unintended one.

In addition, we also have several interesting findings:

Finding 1: Data transmission of device IDs and phone numbers are very common but typically not noticed by most smartphone users. Among the detected unintended data transmission in the two selected datasets, most cases are transmission of device IDs or phone numbers. We also notice that almost all data transmission cases of device IDs and phone numbers do not inform users the operation. We believe that it occurs because Android apps use such information as the unique user identifier when connected to their own server.

Finding 2: Lots of apps write sensitive data into local logging system. Among the tested datasets, 96 (74+22) apps log sensitive data into local logging system, which is bad practice and may lead to indirect privacy leakage. Additionally, we find that not only device IDs and phone numbers are written to Android logs, but also locations and user contacts are temporally stored in several cases. These logged data can be leveraged by malicious apps that steal Android log instead of transmitting sensitive data directly. Since privacy leakage detection approaches do not cover leakage of local logging, such apps could bypass existing detection tools.

6.4 Analysis Time

Our static analysis phase costs 96 hours to analyze all 1,750 apps, among which 70 hours are used in static taint analysis. The analysis time can be further reduced by distributing the analysis workload to multiple machines. Since each application costs about 3.3 minutes on average, the analysis time is almost negligible to the Android market operators.

Our symbolic execution costs 5 to 134 minutes to verify a certain path reported by static analysis, depending on the search space and the complexity of the app. Verifying different paths can also be processed in parallel because exploring the possible search space of each sensitive data transmission path does not depend on information of other paths. As an offline analysis tool, such a validation time is also acceptable to the marketplaces that have enough computing power.

6.5 Case Studies

We now present two case studies from our evaluation: one represents user-intended data transmission (*Anzhuoduanxin*) and the other represents unintended transmission (*Tapsnake*). Video demonstrations of AppIntent for both cases are available at [4, 5].

Anzhuoduanxin [3] is an SMS management app that provides a set of SMS-related functions such as creating new messages or forwarding a cached message to another user. With the help of our event-space constraint guided symbolic execution, AppIntent generates two feasible app inputs that trigger sensitive SMS data transmission: Figure 6(a) depicts one of the feasible inputs, and a simplified version of the other is depicted in Figure 5. Without loss of generality, we choose the first one to illustrate here.

Our dynamic analysis platform accepts this input and creates an execution as demonstrated in the video [4]. In this case, the controlled execution first selects a record among the list which represents all conversation records stored in this phone. Then, by choosing a message and clicking a button that presents "forward" in Chinese (Figure 7(a)), the app user can forward this message to someone else. This message can be sent to anyone by typing a named receiver and clicking a button titled "send"(Figure 7(b) and Figure 7(c)). This execution is commonly used for forwarding a stored message to a friend of the app user, thus it should not be classified as malicious/unintended behavior.

Tapsnake is a malicious app that stealthily transmits user locations to a predefined third party receiver. Depicted in Figure 6(b), the app input generated by AppIntent shows that two components are activated when the location information is transmitted to a third-party user in Tapsnake: the

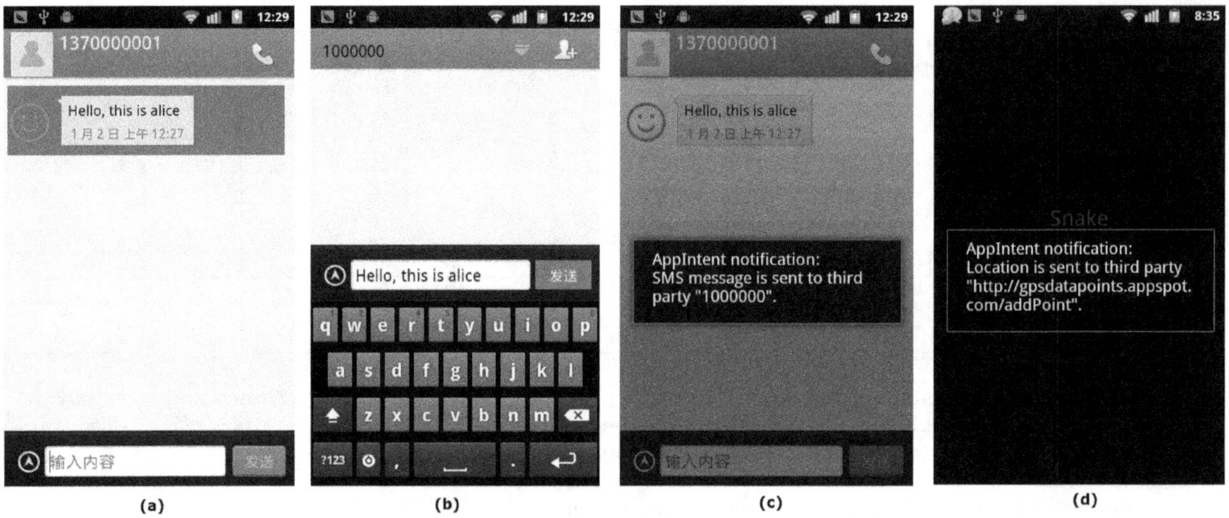

Figure 7: Screen shots of case studies.

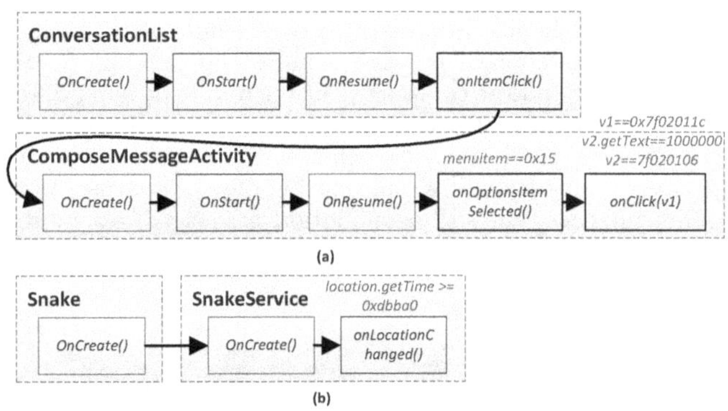

Figure 6: Feasible app inputs for sensitive data transmission in case studies.

main activity of this app, and an embedded Service which registers an event listener for location change event. Based on this input, the corresponding execution, demonstrated in the video [5], waits until the current time is greater than 0xdbba0 (which represents 15 minutes from the beginning of the wall time) Then, the location information is sent after a location change event is performed (Figure 7(d)). Since the original application is a simple "snake" video game, and its functionality does not depend on the location information, thus this behavior is unintended.

6.6 Usability of AppIntent

To evaluate how useful the information provided by AppIntent is, we randomly selected 100 cases reported, and used them to evaluate the user experience. Since AppIntent mainly focuses on providing enough information for discriminating user-intended data transmission from unintended one at app markets, we invited three Android experts in our usability study. During the evaluation, we first introduced AppIntent to them with less than 15 minutes, and let them get familiar with the given cases. Then, we ran the driven executions generated by AppIntent in our Samsung Nexus S mobile phone and showed them to all three participants. After that, participants were asked to fill a sheet in which each case should be classified as "user-intended" or "unintended". We find that they can make their decision in less than one minute after the driven execution finishes, which shows that AppIntent greatly speeds up the process in validating Android apps.

The results from these three users are unambiguously the same as our judgement in 98 cases. However, there are some different opinions in two cases, which are both data transmission of IMEI. Two out of three expects classified them into user-intended because they think these apps need the IMEI number to fulfill their functionality, while we classified them as unintended data transmission because there is no direct relation between the data transmission and the user experience. This evaluation shows that AppIntent is still a great assistance tool with high usability in practice. And it certainly also has some room to be improved in the future.

7. RELATED WORK

AppIntent seems to be the first to systematically study a method to separate user-intended Android data transmission from unintended ones. All other existing Android privacy leakage detection approaches only detect sensitive data transmission. Static Taint Analysis [21, 40] focuses on identifying the possible privacy leakage path with the help of reachability analysis and program slicing. However, these approaches commonly introduce a lot of false positives and cannot separate user-intended operations from unintended ones because of lacking user intention and context information. On the other side, Dynamic Taint Tracking techniques [22, 41] track the sensitive data at runtime by instrumenting profiling code to the original app code. They cannot be applied to automatically detect privacy leakages in marketplaces because they report leakage only if such dangerous propagation happens to occur in the execution. While not implemented, Vision [26] argues that user granting of sensitive data usage can be represented by End-user license agreements(EULA) and explicit notification during the execution. Similarly, BLADE [32] detects web drive-by download malware by recognizing whether it has user consent or not. However, mobile apps commonly do not provide EULA or notification even if the data transmission is user-intended (e.g. SMS forwarding). Pegasus [18] detects malicious behaviors that can be characterized by the temporal order in which an application uses APIs and permissions, and similar to this paper, it focuses on detecting malicious app behaviors that are inconsistent with the GUI events. Nevertheless, privacy leakages cannot be modeled as app usage of permissions or APIs, thus many privacy leakages cannot be detected by such approach. Besides, Pegasus verifies program behaviors based on application-specific properties, which are difficult to specify without the knowledge of application code. Recently, VetDroid [44] enhances Dynamic Taint Tracking by generating specifications for sensitive operations. However, the specification mainly focuses on the application logic but does not pay attention to the trigger condition of each operation.

AppIntent needs to extract app inputs to distinguish user-intended data transmission from unintended one. SmartDroid [45] proposes a hybrid static and dynamic analysis method to reveal UI-based event trigger conditions based on sensitive Android APIs. However, in order to generate a reproducible driven execution, we need both event inputs and data inputs. In this sense, AppIntent provides a more complete and systematic approach. Besides, instead of Android APIs, we need finer-grained analysis of app behaviors to detect privacy leakages. AppIntent proposes a symbolic execution approach for Android GUI apps to extract inputs. The search space explosion of symbolic execution is a well-known issue. Earlier guided symbolic executions direct the exploration with static analysis result [11, 33, 36, 37] or profiled program behavior[14, 19, 43]. All these approaches focus on the explosion caused by the data input space, and cannot reduce the search space of runtime events in Android. On the other hand, there is little work on limiting the event space. In order to limit the search space, Ganov, et.al [25] set an upper bound to the number of event sequences generated, Kudzu [38] used a random generated event order, and Ganov, et.al [24] proposed to generate test cases by symbolically executing each event handler separately. Although these features can limit the exploration of event space, they greatly sacrifice the code coverage. Contest [9] seeks to prune redundant event sequences by checking *subsumption conditions*, and can reduce the running time of symbolic execution to 5%-36% of the original execution time. However, the event space is still large after the pruning and the path explosion problem still exists. To the best of our knowledge, all existing approaches either trade accuracy for performance or suffering poor scalability. In this paper, by using the result of static analysis as the guideline, event-space constraint guided symbolic execution explores event space efficiently without sacrificing the accuracy.

8. CONCLUSION AND FUTURE WORK

This paper addresses one of the major challenges faced by smartphone markets - how to detect privacy leakage in Android apps. Unlike previous approaches that simply consider the transmission of private data as privacy leakage, we argue that such transmission may not indicate a true privacy leakage, instead, a better indicator should be whether the transmission is user intended or not. We present AppIntent, a new app validation framework to help human analysts determine if data transmission is intended by the user. With the help of event-space constraint guided symbolic execution technique proposed in this paper, the search space of symbolic execution is effectively bounded so that AppIntent can extract app inputs that represent user interactions in an acceptable amount of time. With the help of the dynamic analysis platform, AppIntent can also intuitively display the context information of the sensitive data transmission.

Our current techniques have the following limitations, which are also our future work. First, native code is currently not supported by AppIntent. Thus, privacy leakages in native code cannot be captured. Second, since the Android `InstrumentationTestRunner` [1] does not support instrumentation of network input, our dynamic analysis platform cannot simulate network inputs generated by symbolic execution. This could be solved by instrumenting code in Android network interface. Finally, AppIntent fails to analyze some apps because the DEX decompilation tool, DED [23], failed to decompile these apps. We plan to use Dexpler [12], which can directly parse DEX files, in soot, so that the decompilation from DEX to Java bytecode is not needed.

Acknowledgments

We thank the anonymous reviewers for their insightful comments, and ChenHao Qu for his assistance in experiments. This work is funded by China National Natural Science Foundation under grants numbered 61103078 and 61300027, grants from the Science and Technology Commission of Shanghai Municipality numbered 11DZ2281500, 11511504404, 135-11504402 and 13JC1400800, a research grant from a joint program between China Ministry of Education and Intel numbered MOE-INTEL201202, Fundamental Research Funds for the Central Universities in China and Shanghai Leading Academic Discipline Project numbered B114. This work is partially supported by the National Science Foundation under Grant no. CNS-0954096.

9. REFERENCES

[1] Android instrumentationtestrunner. http://developer.android.com/reference/android/test/InstrumentationTestRunner.html.

[2] Android intent. http://developer.android.com-/reference/android/content/Intent.html.

[3] anzhuoduanxin. http://dx.91.com/.

[4] Appintent demo: Anzhuoduanxin. http://www.youtube.com/watch?v=RRqWQk4ztmI.

[5] Appintent demo: Tapsnake. http://www.youtube.com/watch?v=L4IvXzpYqzw.

[6] Choco data constraint solver. http://www.emn.fr/z-info/choco-solver/.

[7] Google map. http://www.google.com/mobile/maps/.

[8] soot analysis framework. http://www.sable.mcgill.ca/soot/.

[9] S. Anand, M. Naik, H. Yang, and M. J. Harrold. Automated concolic testing of smartphone apps. In *Proc. FSE*, 2012.

[10] S. Anand, C. S. Pasareanu, and W. Visser. Jpf-se: A symbolic execution extension to java pathfinder. In *TACAS 2007*, pages 134–138, 2007.

[11] D. Babic, L. Martignoni, S. McCamant, and D. Song. Statically-directed dynamic automated test generation. In *Proc. ISSTA*, pages 12–22, 2011.

[12] A. Bartel, J. Klein, Y. Le Traon, and M. Monperrus. Dexpler: converting android dalvik bytecode to jimple for static analysis with soot. In *Proc. SOAP*, 2012.

[13] P. Bisht, T. Hinrichs, N. Skrupsky, and V. N. Venkatakrishnan. Waptec: whitebox analysis of web applications for parameter tampering exploit construction. In *CCS*, pages 575–586, 2011.

[14] P. Boonstoppel, C. Cadar, and D. R. Engler. Rwset: Attacking path explosion in constraint-based test generation. In *TACAS*, 2008.

[15] D. Brumley, J. Newsome, D. Song, H. Wang, and S. Jha. Towards automatic generation of vulnerability signatures. In *IEEE Symposium on Security and Privacy*, 2006.

[16] C. Cadar, D. Dunbar, and D. R. Engler. Klee: Unassisted and automatic generation of high-coverage tests for complex systems programs. In *OSDI*, pages 209–224, 2008.

[17] C. Cadar, V. Ganesh, P. M. Pawlowski, D. L. Dill, and D. R. Engler. Exe: automatically generating inputs of death. In *CCS*, pages 322–335, 2006.

[18] K. Z. Chen, N. Johnson, V. D'Silva, S. Dai, K. MacNamara, T. Magrino, E. X. Wu, M. Rinard, and D. Song. Contextual policy enforcement in android applications with permission event graphs. In *Proc. NDSS*, 2013.

[19] C. Y. Cho, D. Babic, P. Poosankam, K. Z. Chen, D. Song, and E. X. Wu. Mace: Model-inference-assisted concolic exploration for protocol and vulnerability discovery. In *USENIX Security*, 2011.

[20] M. Costa, M. Castro, L. Zhou, L. Zhang, and M. Peinado. Bouncer: securing software by blocking bad input. In *SOSP*, pages 117–130, 2007.

[21] M. Egele, C. Kruegel, E. Kirda, and G. Vigna. Pios: Detecting privacy leaks in ios applications. In *NDSS*, 2011.

[22] W. Enck, P. Gilbert, B.-G. Chun, L. P. Cox, J. Jung, P. McDaniel, and A. N. Sheth. Taintdroid: an information-flow tracking system for realtime privacy monitoring on smartphones. In *OSDI*, pages 1–6, 2010.

[23] W. Enck, D. Octeau, P. McDaniel, and S. Chaudhuri. A Study of Android Application Security. In *USENIX Security*, 2011.

[24] S. R. Ganov, C. Killmar, S. Khurshid, and D. E. Perry. Test generation for graphical user interfaces based on symbolic execution. In *AST*, pages 33–40, 2008.

[25] S. R. Ganov, C. Killmar, S. Khurshid, and D. E. Perry. Event listener analysis and symbolic execution for testing gui applications. In *ICFEM*, 2009.

[26] P. Gilbert, B.-G. Chun, L. P. Cox, and J. Jung. Vision: automated security validation of mobile apps at app markets. In *Proc. MCS)*, 2011.

[27] P. Godefroid. Compositional dynamic test generation. In *POPL*, pages 47–54, 2007.

[28] P. Godefroid, N. Klarlund, and K. Sen. Dart: directed automated random testing. In *PLDI*, pages 213–223, 2005.

[29] M. C. Grace, W. Zhou, X. Jiang, and A.-R. Sadeghi. Unsafe exposure analysis of mobile in-app advertisements. In *WiSec*, 2012.

[30] P. Hornyack, S. Han, J. Jung, S. Schechter, and D. Wetherall. These aren't the droids you're looking for: retrofitting android to protect data from imperious applications. In *CCS*, pages 639–652, 2011.

[31] A. Kieyzun, P. J. Guo, K. Jayaraman, and M. D. Ernst. Automatic creation of sql injection and cross-site scripting attacks. In *ICSE*, pages 199–209, 2009.

[32] L. Lu, V. Yegneswaran, P. Porras, and W. Lee. Blade: an attack-agnostic approach for preventing drive-by malware infections. In *Proc. CCS*, pages 440–450, 2010.

[33] K.-K. Ma, K. Y. Phang, J. S. Foster, and M. Hicks. Directed symbolic execution. In *Proc. SAS*, 2011.

[34] D. Molnar, X. C. Li, and D. A. Wagner. Dynamic test generation to find integer bugs in x86 binary linux programs. In *USENIX Security*, pages 67–82, 2009.

[35] G. Patrice, Y. L. Michael, and A. M. David. Automated whitebox fuzz testing. In *NDSS*, 2008.

[36] N. Rungta, E. G. Mercer, and W. Visser. Efficient testing of concurrent programs with abstraction-guided symbolic execution. In *Proc. SPIN*, 2009.

[37] R. Santelices and M. J. Harrold. Exploiting program dependencies for scalable multiple-path symbolic execution. In *Proc. ISSTA*, 2010.

[38] P. Saxena, D. Akhawe, S. Hanna, F. Mao, S. McCamant, and D. Song. A symbolic execution framework for javascript. *Security and Privacy, IEEE Symposium on*, 0:513–528, 2010.

[39] K. Sen, D. Marinov, and G. Agha. Cute: a concolic unit testing engine for c. In *ESEC/SIGSOFT FSE*, pages 263–272, 2005.

[40] O. Tripp, M. Pistoia, S. J. Fink, M. Sridharan, and O. Weisman. Taj: effective taint analysis of web applications. In *PLDI*, pages 87–97, 2009.

[41] N. Vachharajani, M. J. Bridges, J. Chang, R. Rangan, G. Ottoni, J. A. Blome, G. A. Reis, M. Vachharajani, and D. I. August. Rifle: An architectural framework for user-centric information-flow security. In *MICRO*, pages 243–254, 2004.

[42] T. Wang, T. Wei, Z. Lin, and W. Zou. Intscope: Automatically detecting integer overflow vulnerability in x86 binary using symbolic execution. In *NDSS*, 2009.

[43] T. Xie, N. Tillmann, P. de Halleux, and W. Schulte. Fitness-guided path exploration in dynamic symbolic execution. In *Proc. DSN*, 2009.

[44] Y. Zhang, M. Yang, B. Xu, Z. Yang, G. Gu, P. Ning, X. Wang, and B. Zang. Vetting undesirable behaviors in android apps with permission use analysis. In *CCS*, 2013.

[45] C. Zheng, S. Zhu, S. Dai, G. Gu, X. Gong, and W. Zou. Smartdroid: An automatic system for revealing ui-based trigger conditions in android applications. In *Proc. SPSM*, October 2012.

[46] Y. Zhou and X. Jiang. Dissecting android malware: Characterization and evolution. In *IEEE Symposium on Security and Privacy*, 2012.

Cross-origin pixel stealing: Timing attacks using CSS filters

Robert Kotcher, Yutong Pei, Pranjal Jumde*
Carnegie Mellon University
{rkotcher, ypei, pjumde}@andrew.cmu.edu

Collin Jackson
Carnegie Mellon University
collin.jackson@sv.cmu.edu

ABSTRACT

Timing attacks rely on systems taking varying amounts of time to process different input values. This is usually the result of either conditional branching in code or differences in input size. Using CSS default filters, we have discovered a variety of timing attacks that work in multiple browsers and devices. The first attack exploits differences in time taken to render various DOM trees. This knowledge can be used to determine boolean values such as whether or not a user has an account with a particular website. Second, we introduce pixel stealing. Pixel stealing attacks can be used to sniff user history and read text tokens.

Categories and Subject Descriptors

K.4.4 [**Computers and Society**]: Electronic Commerce Security; K.4.1 [**Computers and Society**]: Public Policy Issues - Privacy

General Terms

Security, Experimentation

Keywords

CSS-Filters, CSS-Shaders, OpenGL ES, Timing Attacks, Privacy

1. INTRODUCTION

In this section we discuss CSS filters and describe how web content is rendered in browsers. Finally we introduce other timing attacks to provide a basis for our own work.

1.1 CSS filter specification

Cascading Style Sheets, CSS, is a declarative styling language that applies and prioritizes styling rules to elements of a web document (also known as Document Object Model elements or "DOM elements"). Some of the latest members of the CSS feature family, filter effects, are descendants of the W3C SVG specification[11] that allow developers to apply personalized style to arbitrary web content. Filters are, as of recently, GPU accelerated [12, 22] giving developers a robust new way to stylize arbitrary DOM elements through simple CSS attributes. While filters are not implemented in all browsers, support does exist in WebKit browsers including Safari, and mobile browsers such as iOS Safari, Blackberry, and Chrome for Android. Google Chrome is based on Blink which is a fork of WebKit in the area of graphics [9, 11].

*These author contributed equally to this paper

CCS'13, November 4–8, 2013, Berlin, Germany.
ACM 978-1-4503-2477-9/13/11.
http://dx.doi.org/10.1145/2508859.2516712

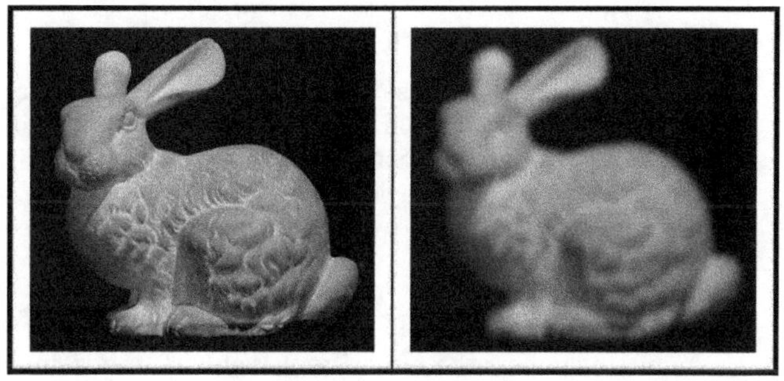

Figure 1: Image of the Stanford bunny with a CSS blur filter

There are three types of CSS filters. The first, built-in filters, are canned effects that are parameterized and can be specified directly as an attribute-value pair in a CSS class. Figure 1 shows the Stanford bunny with a blur filter applied to the right panel.

The second type, SVG filters, are similar effects that can be applied to SVG content.

The final type, CSS shaders, was proposed by Adobe to the W3C FX task force[18] in October, 2011 as a complement to CSS filters. Shaders are now referred to as CSS custom filter effects. The CSS custom filter effects allow web developers to write OpenGL ES shader programs that operate on arbitrary web content. Content is applied either through separate text files specified with a url or directly through HTML5 tags[18]. The proposed feature is now a part of the CSS Filter Effect draft[1], and prototype implementation has started and is available in developer builds. Because custom filters are experimental, they must first be enabled by entering chrome://flags in the URL bar.

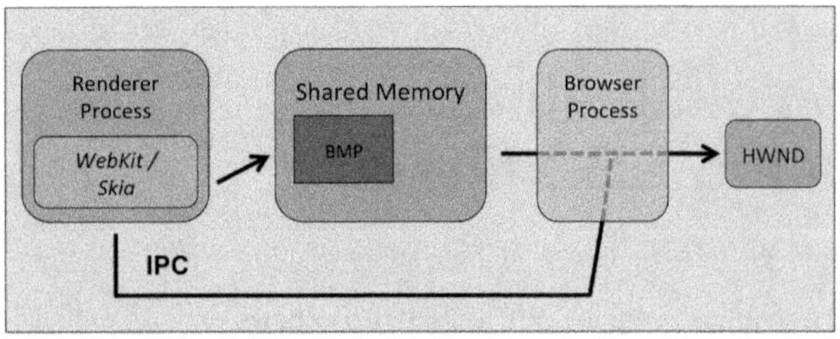

Figure 2: CPU rendering path in WebKit

1.2 Rendering DOM content

DOM content is transformed to a rasterized image in several steps. We summarize CPU and GPU rendering in WebKit in this section. Since the root cause of our timing attack is not clear, we provide this section as a possible starting point for further research. Information in this section was consolidated from the Chromium Design Documents [5, 15].

As of this paper, the majority of WebKit's rendering algorithms are performed on a single process [15] which it shares with the sandboxed web application. Figure 2 shows how content is rendered using the CPU.

DOM elements are stored internally as nodes of a tree structure whose root is the Document node for all instances. Each node of a corresponding tree structure of RenderObjects defines the physical layout of a unique DOM element. Sets of RenderObjects are mapped to elements of a RenderLayer tree. While DOM nodes model document data, the RenderObjects and RenderLayers provide hierarchical views that ultimately talk to the GraphicsContext, a wrapper for Google's Skia Graphics engine [6, 15, 20]. A distinct RenderLayer can be created for a RenderObject if any of the following are true:

- It is the root element for the page
- It has explicit CSS properties (relative, absolute, or transform)
- It is transparent
- It has an overflow, mask or reflection
- It has a CSS filter
- It corresponds to a canvas or video element

We found that WebKit reads a RenderLayer tree structure from root to leaves, using an algorithm similar to Painter's Algorithm; i.e. WebKit traverses the entire tree of RenderElements in order to resolve pixel depth[15] and create a bitmap by painting elements from furthest away to nearest. This approach to depth resolution is inefficient [7, 16] and in this paper we describe a timing attack on user privacy that is possible because of this. Only after the RenderLayers have finished providing pixels to a buffer in shared memory can a separate browser process take over rendering to the correct tab[15] or iframe element.

The GPU can be used to render content more quickly. While a description of GPU rendering mechanisms is out of the scope of this paper, its important to know that additional structures are built for GPU rendering and may also account for timing differences.

1.3 Timing attacks

Timing attacks work when a system takes different amounts of time to process different inputs [4, 10, 14, 19]. Vulnerabilities tend to occur as a result of inherent behavior, not "buggy code". Scenarios allowing for successful timing attacks have been found in performance optimized code [2, 14] browser caching [4, 10], DNS caching [10], CBC encryption, and RAM cache hits [14]. By timing these properties, an attacker can gain insight into a large amount of information.

Timing attacks are usually regarded as an invasion of a user's privacy [4, 10]. Exposing Private Information by Timing Web Applications [4] by Bortz et al defines two families of web timing attacks:

A *Direct timing attack* can be used to determine boolean values such as a user's login status or content data size such as the relative size of a shopping cart [4]. A direct timing attack is carried out by the attacker's browser against a victim web server.

In contrast to direct timing attacks, *cross-site timing* attacks rely on a user to visit, and remain on, a malicious page while a cross-site exchange is made. Our proposals are all cross-site timing attacks.

2. RELEVANT SECURITY TOPICS

New features usually arrive with their own set of security considerations, and CSS filters are no exception. Much work has already gone into safe integration of CSS filters into web browsers. We first present a threat model for our timing attacks. Then we discuss security in CSS custom filters, browsers, and browser policies.

2.1 Threat model

The threat model for our timing attacks is a web attacker who operates a malicious domain. The attacker is either able to provide content that keeps a user engaged on a webpage for an extended period of time, or is able to open another window in front of the window being attacked.

2.2 Security in CSS custom filters

Our attempts to look for new timing channels in browser rendering engines stemmed from an interesting attack proposal by Adam Barth [2], who showed that simply removing access to sensitive information in custom filters is not enough to protect web pages from malicious filter developers. He suggested that a fragment shader could contain code similar to the following:

Listing 1: Abstract timing attack on color

```
if (pixelColor != 0x000) {
    for (int i = 0; i < MAX_INT; i++) {;}
}
```

As a result we can determine whether or not pixelColor is black by observing the amount of time taken for the shader to output a final pixel value. There are many ways an attacker could use this approach to steal an unsettling amount of sensitive information.

W3C has now recommended that shaders restrict all direct access to rendered content [19]. Some researchers suspected that custom shaders are still vulnerable. They did not have a proof-of-concept to support their claim[2].

2.3 Security in Browsers

While we were able to get our attack to work in several browsers, Chromium was the one we spent the most time with. This section is about security in browsers, but focuses on Chromium's implementation specifically. The two concepts in this section are relevant to our work and include flow of fragment data and multi-process browser architecture.

1. **Flow of fragment data.** One security feature that makes GPU-accelerated graphics rendering difficult to measure is a one-directional flow of fragment data. The application's control over hardware-accelerated rendering is revoked as soon as commands and data are passed to the *command buffer*. There is no mechanism that can be used to retrieve GPU output.

2. **Multi-process architecture.** This is another important feature is Chromium's multi-process model. By separating the browser kernel from rendering engine instances, Chromium wants to prevent the attacker from installing persistent malware/keyloggers and stealing local files [3, 5, 15]. These measures are effective at what they are designed to do. They are unable, however, to hide timing differences in the rendering engine. If anything, isolation of the rendering engine makes timing differences more noticeable.

2.4 Security in Web Policies

It turns out that CSS filters are indifferent as to whether or not the actual rendered content is cross-origin[18], and we believe that browser policies regarding filters should only be part of a larger effort to contain cross-origin information. CSS filters still violate Same-Origin Policy (SOP) because they access cross-origin content when X-Frame-Options are not used. As a result, setting X-Frame-Options to Deny is the only way to ensure timing attacks will fail to work on a framed web page.

3. OUR PROPOSED TIMING ATTACKS

In this section we demonstrate how cross-site timing attacks may be used to invade a user's privacy and to steal sensitive data. First we explain our approach to collecting timing data. Second we show how timing data can be used to determine a user's login status on arbitrary websites. Finally we present pixel stealing and how it can be used to sniff user history and steal cross-origin text tokens.

3.1 Collecting data using requestAnimationFrame

We found that the entire rendering process can be timed through *requestAnimationFrame*[8], which allows a web page to provide a callback for the browser to call when an animation frame is available for painting. The function *requestAnimationFrame* is implemented in Gecko and WebKit, and the code below demonstrates how it can be used to measure the average framerate of a browser window.

Listing 2: Measuring Framerate with javascript

```
FramerateFinder = function() {
  var tFrames = 0,
      avgFramerate = 0,
      startTime;

  var updateAvgFramerate = function() {
    var elapsed = timer.now() - startTime;
    avgFramerate = tFrames / elapsed;
    avgFramerate = avgFramerate * 1000;
  }

  var step = function() {
    tFrames += 1;
    requestAnimationFrame(step);
  }

  var start = function() {
    startTime = timer.now();
    step();
  }
}
```

The function *start* begins a series of calls to *step*, which increases the total frame count by one and passes itself to *requestAnimationFrame*. The total frame count is incremented each frame, and the current average framerate can be calculated with *updateAvgFramerate* at any time.

3.2 Determining a user's login status

The simplest attack we implemented is to detect a user's login status. While simple, it is important to protect against attacks such as this because they can reveal a significant amount of insight about a user's online behavior. For instance we could use this data to quickly determine which web users are T-Mobile customers.

For many websites, a user with an authentication cookie will be directed to a personalized home page, while other users are sent to a 'catch-all' home page. Normally, a login page has a different DOM structure than that of a user's homepage. If a CSS filter is applied to documents with different tree structures, we found the corresponding frame rates to be different since WebKit always traverses the entire RenderObject tree when building a RenderLayer tree. Assume example.com/home is the user's homepage and example.com/login is the login page.

An attacker could determine whether or not a user has authentication cookies for a website in the following way:

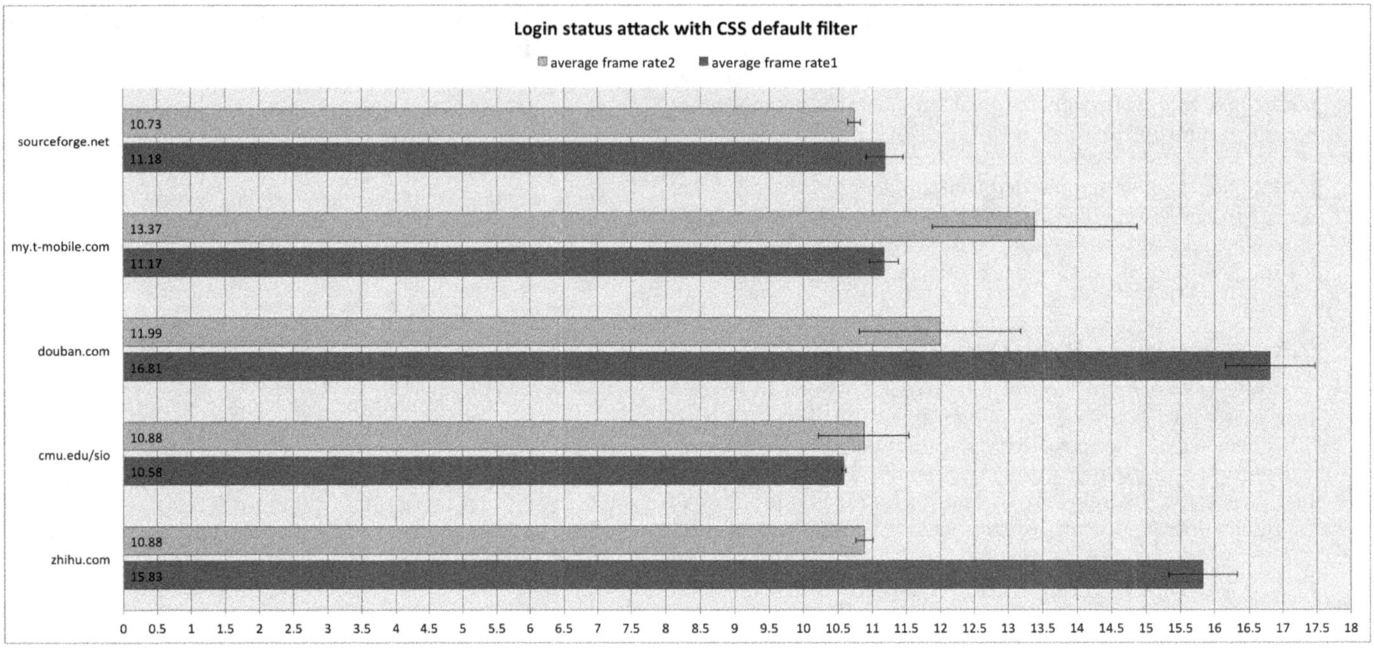

Figure 3: We performed the login attack on five high-traffic websites. (hardware: 2012 MacbookPro Retina with Intel Core i7 3720QM / Nvidia GT650M; browser: Google Chrome).

1. **Malicious reference page created.** The attacker copies the example.com login page and all referenced content from the victim's web server at example.com/login.html to a location on his server as a "reference page", and the attacker saves it to www.attacker.com/reference .html.
2. **Dummy page is created.** The attacker creates a dummy page with <iframe id="attack-iframe" src="example.com">. This page resides at www.attacker.com/ attack.html. The victim must browse to this page for the attack to occur.
3. **Victim is engaged.** A victim using a vulnerable browser visits www.attacker.com/attack.html, and is engaged for a short period of time.
4. **Shaders are applied.** A CSS built-in filter is rapidly re-applied to the iframe, causing the framed page to rerender without refreshing. Example code for this step is in Listing 3.
5. **Victim's data is collected.** After some time, the average framerate is determined.
6. **Reference page is timed.** The iframe loads the reference page on the attacker's server, located at www.attacker.com/reference.html, and the same process is repeated for the new page. Data must be collected from both pages since timing between devices may differ.
7. **Data is analyzed.** The total frame counts for both pages are returned to the attacker's server to be compared.

Listing 3: Toggle filter

```
<style>
  .filter{
    -webkit-filter: blur(10px);
    -moz-filter: blur(10px);
  }
</style>

<script>
  function alternate(){
    $("#attack-iframe")
      .toggleClass("filter");
  }
  setInterval(alternate, time);
</script>
```

We found that this attack also works in Firefox by using an *svg-image-blur* effect instead of *webkit-filter*, since Firefox allows a user to apply SVG filters to DOM elements. As with most web timing attacks, timing data is an approximation of the true runtime of a process. Our attack is less noisy than typical web application timing attack[4] though, since there is no network latency or packet-loss involved.

The results in Figure 3 show how the relative size of a page can be determined with CSS default filters. Notice that the page when the user is logged in produces a different average framerate than the homepage when the user is not logged in because their DOM trees are different.

3.3 Pixel Stealing with CSS filters

Next we describe a general technique that we have discovered can be used to read a field of arbitrary pixels from the user's browser window. We fill the screen with a single color and examine the way in which the browser window's average framerate changes by reading it with *requestAnimationFrame*.

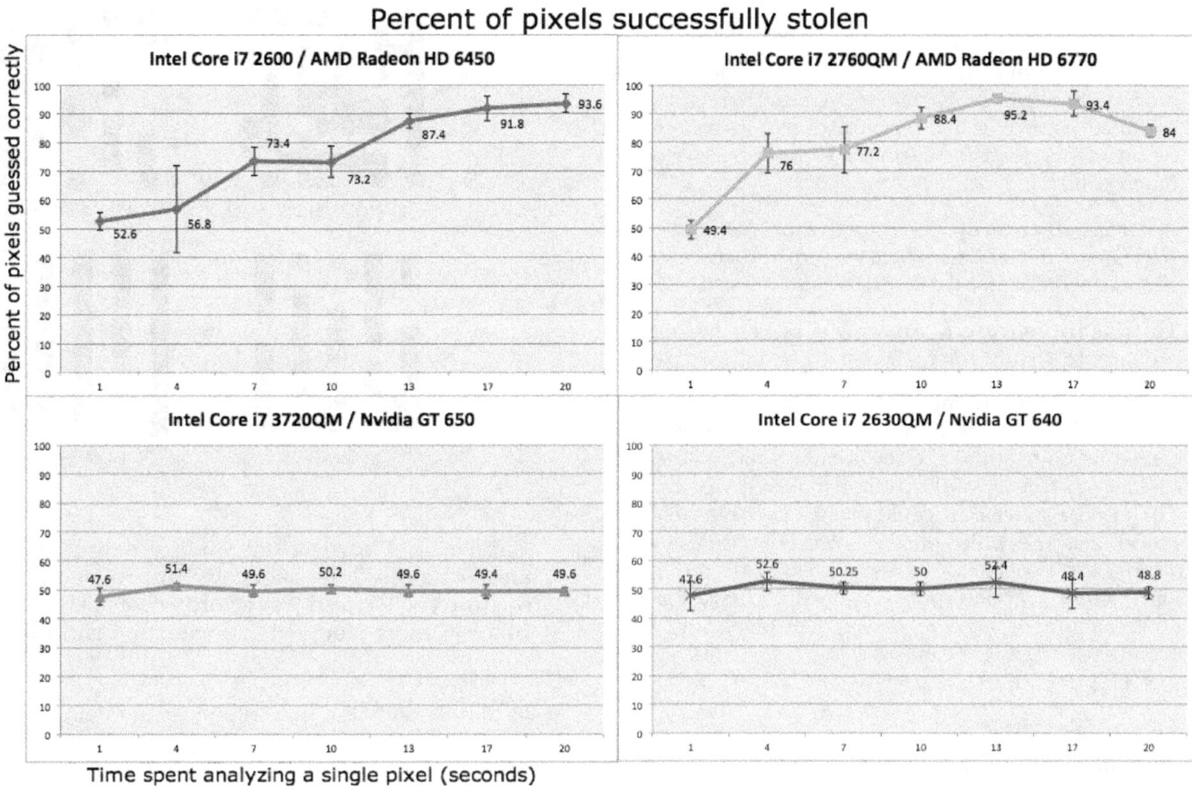

Figure 4: Using the same test that produced the bitmaps shown in Figure 5, we determined how accuracy differed across different devices.

3.3.1 Focusing on a Single Pixel without anti-aliasing

We found that enlarging the pixel to the size of the user's screen exaggerated timing differences. This section describes our technique.

Listing 4: Enlarging a single pixel

```
#malicious-iframe {
    overflow: hidden;
    width: 1px;
    height: 1px;
    margin-top: 0px;
    margin-left: 0px;
}

#pixel-container {
    top: calc(50% - 1px);
    left: calc(50% - 1px);
    width: 1px;
    height: 1px;
}

#pixel-container-container {
    width: 999px;
    height: 999px;
    -webkit-filter: custom(url(enlarge.vs)
        mix(url(enlarge.fs)), 4 4);
}
```

To enlarge a pixel to the size of the screen without anti-aliasing, we first apply the style rules for #malicious-iframe to a borderless iframe. The iframe contains the webpage under attack. By setting margin-left and margin-top to values less than or equal to zero, different offsets onto the victim page can be achieved.

Next we position the iframe inside a div of class #pixel-container. This div is centered inside its parent element, #pixel-container-container. This class defines a CSS filter that scales the pixel-sized iframe to a much bigger size. The width and height are odd-valued to ensure that the single-pixel iframe will be in the center.

3.3.2 Pixel Stealing

We use the above mechanism to traverse a bitmap of pixels by setting margin-top and margin-left in the malicious iframe. Our attack performs arbitrary transformations on the scaled pixel, determines the average framerate during the transformations, and interprets the the resulting value for each pixel. A pixel stealing attack occurs in the following way:

1. **Expand a single pixel.** The attacker builds a mechanism that can expand a pixel to the size of the user agent's screen.
2. **Victim page is framed.** The attacker frames a website that has neglected to use X-Frame-Options.
3. **Vicitm visits malicious page.** A victim user visits the attacker's malicious web page, and is tricked into

remaining on the page for the duration of the attack.

4. **Page is traversed.** In an attack, a malicious website may want to traverse each pixel in a target region of the intended website or in a target region of its source code. An arbitrary transformation is repeatedly performed on each pixel.

5. **Average framerate is captured.** *RequestAnimationFrame* determines the average framerate on the browser window for each target pixel.

6. **Data is interpreted.** An array of pixel measurements are sent to the attacker's server to be interpreted.

Collecting and interpreting pixel data turned out to be an interesting problem by itself, and we tried several methods that helped us understand the set of values returned by the attack. The most successful attempt involved writing code with a JQueryUI slider that could change the threshold that separated black and white pixels, however writing a script to interpret the pixel data for us proved to be more than sufficient. The script interpreted values by deciding what thresholds should be used to distinguish black and white pixel framerates. Using a canvas element we could visually examine the pixel values.

3.3.3 Our Results

We initially tested our pixel stealing idea by running black and white pixels through shaders with arbitrary transformation matrices. Our intuition was if there existed two colors that could create distinct timing channels, black and white would be the most likely candidates. Our intuition turned out to be correct.

A proof-of-concept attack involved recreating a 10 × 10 bitmap of black and white pixels to determine the timing consistencies of a user's device. A higher percent of correctly-guessed pixels implies a more vulnerable user agent. Results from this initial test indicated that stealing cross-origin pixels could be achieved with high enough accuracy to make pixel stealing attacks practical. We conducted tests that measured each pixel's color for 4, 12, and 20 seconds, and the results are shown in Figure 5. Compare our results with the actual bitmap in (d).

In this test, we counted the number of pixels that were guessed correctly out of 100. If our attack was returning random values, we would expect about 50 pixels to be correct regardless of time spent per pixel. The chance that exactly half of the pixels are guessed correctly is 50%. The chance that more than 60% of a bitmap's pixels are chosen correctly on any given test is just 6%. Figure 4 shows accuracy for various devices. Half of the setups we tried were vulnerable.

3.3.4 Possible Attack Scenarios in Practice

Once a bitmap of pixel colors can be determined over https, attack possibilities are endless. The most interesting attack we implemented involves stealing tokens of cross-origin text. We were able to read a fake token that we retrieved across origins. This token was stolen from a machine with an AMD Radeon HD 6770 and Intel Core i7:

We also used our pixel stealing attack to implement history sniffing. Until recently, a user's history could be determined

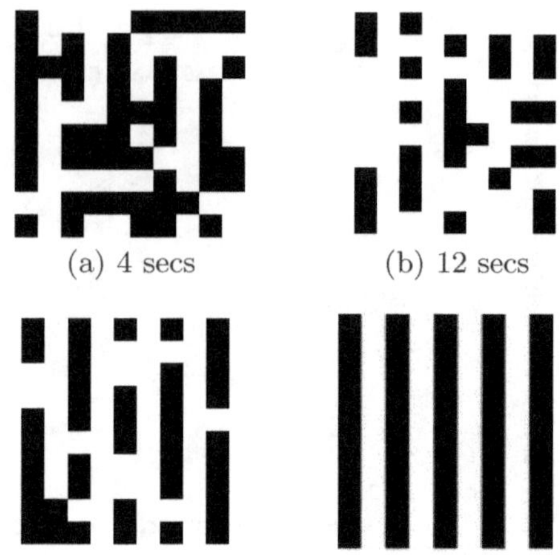

(a) 4 secs (b) 12 secs (c) 20 secs (d) original

Figure 5: The original pixel stealing tests (a), (b), and (c) show how accuracy improves as the amount of time (4, 12, and 20 seconds respectively) spent per pixel is increased. (d) shows the original bitmap.

by simply adding a link to a page and determining its color by calling *getComputedStyle()*[13] since visited links have different colors than non-visited links. Browsers will now lie [21] if this function is called on a link.

The following attack can be used to determine whether or not a user has visited a particular website:

1. **Victim visits malicious page.** The malicious page initializes with a block of ascii text (say, ascii value 219) that hrefs to a website that is known to not exist.

2. **Link is expanded.** A pixel from the link is expanded to the size of the user's screen.

3. **Data is collected.** The malicious web page allows a sufficient amount of time to pass while measuring the page framerate using *requestAnimationFrame*.

4. **Process is repeated.** Steps 2-4 are repeated two more times. The first is for this page, which will return results for a URL that we know the user has visited. The second is for a URL we are curious about.

5. **Data is analyzed.** We can determine if the user visited the victim URL by comparing it with the framerate of our two test URLs.

By using the pixel stealing technique described above, it is possible to determine whether or not a user has visited a website by analyzing a single pixel.

3.3.5 Complications and Solutions

We have found that the best results can be obtained when the input pixel field is restricted to black and white only. We combined several filter effects to achieve a close estimate of a black and white transform. We ended up using the following filter combination:

(a) Original Text

(b) Text after applying filters

(c) Stolen Text

Figure 6: (a) shows the original bitmap of anti-aliased pixels in Google Chrome for a text token. We applied filters to approximate a black and white version of the token, shown in (b). Finally, (c) shows the cross-origin token of text that we stole with our timing attack.

Listing 5: Filter effects to achieve a close estimate of a black and white transform

```
.black-and-white {
-webkit-filter: saturate(0%)
                grayscale(100%)
                brightness(69%)
                contrast(100%);
}
```

Notice in Figure 7 that without the use of these filter effects, non-black pixels are usually interpreted as white. This sample of cross-origin HTML text is easily recognized as the letter "h" in Figure 7, but without default filters, many letters with curves such as "S" and "R" were nearly impossible to read.

A final challenge we faced with this attack was finding a reasonable amount of time to spend on each pixel. It is important that all pixels are read before the user closes his or her browser window. To get a better understanding of the accuracy achieved as a result of various amounts of time spent per pixel on several graphics cards, see Figure 4. While history sniffing or stealing small text tokens is possible in practice, stealing medium-sized images or large tokens may not be.

Under what conditions do the attacks fail? We determined that running shaders in background tabs produces undesirable performance, and will cause an attack to fail. Running the attack in a background window will have the same performance results and an attack in the foreground. Running the attack on a div or iframe element whose opacity equals *0.0* will not work, but covering it with another DOM does work.

4. CONCLUSIONS AND FUTURE WORK

In this paper we show that timing attacks using CSS filters can reveal sensitive information such as text tokens. Our work uses both default and custom filters to exploit timing channels in rendering engines of various browsers. A paper that cites the original version of this paper shows that the timing attacks can also be performed with SVG filters [17].

An easy solution would be to simply place shaders and filters under the restrictions of the Same-Origin Policy, but this would entirely defeat the purpose of these features. This would also likely be covering up a larger problem that is present across multiple browsers. Creating awareness in the security community seems like the best way to proceed.

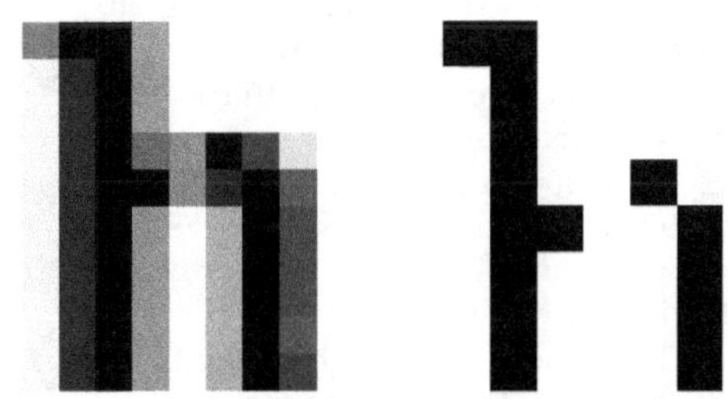

Figure 7: Attempts to read text without converting to black and white made letter curvature difficult to capture.

5. ACKNOWLEDGEMENTS

We would like to thank Eric Chen and Lin-Shung Huang for their guidance and support to our research.

6. REFERENCES

[1] Adobe. Css shaders. http://www.adobe.com/devnet/html5/articles/css-shaders.html.

[2] A. Barth. Adam barth's proposal. http://www.schemehostport.com/2011/12/timing-attacks-on-css-shaders.html.

[3] A. Barth, C. Jackson, C. Reis, and T. Team. The security architecture of the chromium browser, 2008.

[4] A. Bortz and D. Boneh. Exposing private information by timing web applications. In *Proceedings of the 16th international conference on World Wide Web*, pages 621–628. ACM, 2007.

[5] Chromium. Gpu command buffer. http://www.chromium.org/developers/design-documents/gpu-command-buffer.

[6] Chromium. Graphics and skia. http://www.chromium.org/developers/design-documents/graphics-and-skia.

[7] CMU. Spatial data structures. http://www.cs.cmu.edu/afs/cs/academic/class/15462-f12/www/lec_slides/lec13.pdf.

[8] R. Crawfis. Mozilla window.requestanimationframe. https://developer.mozilla.org/en-US/docs/DOM/window.requestAnimationFrame.

[9] A. Deveria. Can i use css filter effects? http://caniuse.com/css-filters.

[10] E. W. Felten and M. A. Schneider. Timing attacks on web privacy. In *Proceedings of the 7th ACM conference on Computer and communications security*, pages 25–32. ACM, 2000.

[11] HTML5Rocks. Catch-all for html5 rocks website. http://updates.html5rocks.com.

[12] R. Hudea, R. Cabanier, and V. Hardy. enriching the web with css filters.

[13] C. Jackson, A. Bortz, D. Boneh, and J. C. Mitchell. Protecting browser state from web privacy attacks. In *Proceedings of the 15th international conference on World Wide Web*, pages 737–744. ACM, 2006.

[14] P. C. Kocher. Timing attacks on implementations of diffie-hellman, rsa, dss, and other systems. In *Advances in Cryptology—CRYPTO'96*, pages 104–113. Springer, 1996.

[15] V. Kokkevis. Gpu accelerated compositing in chrome. http://www.chromium.org/developers/design-documents/gpu-accelerated-compositing-in-chrome.

[16] I. LiTH. Painter's algorithm. http://www.computer-graphics.se/TSBK07-files/PDF12/6b.pdf.

[17] P. Stone. Pixel perfect timing attacks with html5. http://www.contextis.com/files/Browser_Timing_Attacks.pdf.

[18] W3. Css shader proposal. https://dvcs.w3.org/hg/FXTF/raw-file/tip/custom/index.html.

[19] W3. Shader security. http://www.w3.org/Graphics/fx/wiki/CSS_Shaders_Security.

[20] Webkit. Accelerated rendering and compositing. http://trac.webkit.org/wiki/Accelerated%20rendering%20and%20compositing.

[21] Z. Weinberg, E. Y. Chen, P. R. Jayaraman, and C. Jackson. I still know what you visited last summer: Leaking browsing history via user interaction and side channel attacks. In *Security and Privacy (SP), 2011 IEEE Symposium on*, pages 147–161. IEEE, 2011.

[22] S. White. Accelerated css filters landed in chromium. http://blog.chromium.org/2012/06/accelerated-css-filters-landed-in.html.

Seeing Double: Reconstructing Obscured Typed Input from Repeated Compromising Reflections

Yi Xu, Jared Heinly, Andrew M. White, Fabian Monrose and Jan-Michael Frahm
Department of Computer Science, University of North Carolina at Chapel Hill
Chapel Hill, North Carolina, USA
{yix,jheinly,amw,fabian,jmf}@cs.unc.edu

ABSTRACT

Of late, threats enabled by the ubiquitous use of mobile devices have drawn much interest from the research community. However, prior threats all suffer from a similar, and profound, weakness — namely the requirement that the adversary is either within visual range of the victim (e.g., to ensure that the pop-out events in reflections in the victim's sunglasses can be discerned) or is close enough to the target to avoid the use of expensive telescopes. In this paper, we broaden the scope of the attacks by relaxing these requirements and show that breaches of privacy are possible even when the adversary is around a corner. The approach we take overcomes challenges posed by low image resolution by extending computer vision methods to operate on small, high-noise, images. Moreover, our work is applicable to all types of keyboards because of a novel application of fingertip motion analysis for key-press detection. In doing so, we are also able to exploit reflections in the eyeball of the user or even repeated reflections (i.e., a reflection of a reflection of the mobile device in the eyeball of the user). Our empirical results show that we can perform these attacks with high accuracy, and can do so in scenarios that aptly demonstrate the realism of this threat.

Categories and Subject Descriptors: K.4.1 [Computers and Society]: Privacy

General Terms: Human Factors, Security

Keywords: Compromising Emanations; Mobile Devices

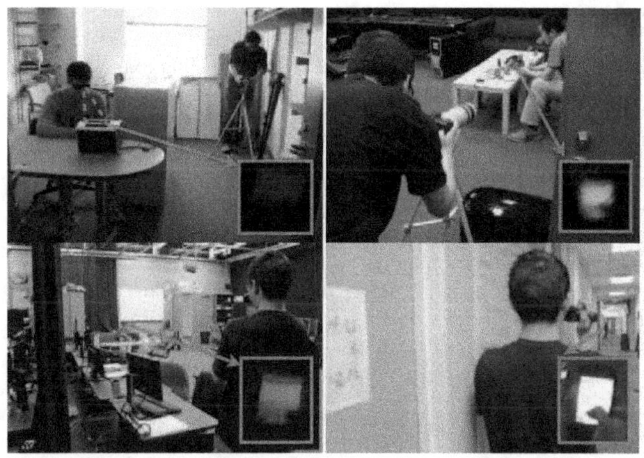

Figure 1: Some example threat scenarios that we investigated. Top left: Through reflection from sunglasses and toaster; Top right: Through reflection from eyeball and mirror; Bottom left: Through reflection from sunglasses; Bottom Right: Direct long-distance view. Note: As with the remaining figures in this work, this image is best viewed in color.

1. INTRODUCTION

Gone are the days when mobile phones were used exclusively for voice communication. Today, as these handheld devices have become more sophisticated, they are routinely used for a myriad of everyday activities that include checking email, text messaging, performing financial transactions, and finding directions to a location of interest. Inevitably, as our day-to-day reliance on these devices increases, the sensitive information (e.g., passwords) input on these devices becomes increasingly valuable to prying eyes.

While the academic community has long acknowledged that the ubiquity of these devices provides new opportunities for privacy abuse (as users communicate private data in ways more vulnerable to eavesdropping than ever before), the severity of the threat posed by advancements in computer vision techniques is only now being well understood [3, 34]. As a case in point, both Raguram et al. [34] and Maggi et al. [29] recently showed that modern touch-screen smartphones may offer a greater privacy threat than their traditional counterparts. The increased risk comes from the fact that many touch-screen smartphones utilize virtual keyboards that overcome the perceived lack of tactile feedback by providing users with visual confirmation (a key "pop-out" effect) as a key is pressed. These effects, however, provide strong visual cues that can be exploited by an attacker to help identify the keys tapped on the victim's device.

The techniques used to leverage the so-called compromising reflections in these prior works have raised our collective awareness of the realism of these threats. However, they all suffer from a similar, and profound, weakness — namely the requirement that the adversary is either within visual range of the victim (e.g., to ensure that the pop-out events in reflections in the victim's sunglasses can be discerned [34]) or is close enough to the target to avoid the use of expensive telescopes [3].

In this paper, we push the limits of these attacks by exploiting even more fundamental, and harder to conceal, observable events. That is, unlike prior work, we do not rely on the attacker's ability to capture detail (e.g., a key pop-out event) on the screen, but instead target a common factor in user interaction with mobile devices: the

CCS'13, November 4-8, 2013, Berlin, Germany.
ACM 978-1-4503-2477-9/13/11.
http://dx.doi.org/10.1145/2508859.2516709 .

relationship between a user's fingers and the keyboard. By tracking the positions of a user's fingers as they move across the virtual keyboard, we can successfully reconstruct the typed input. In particular, we show that even using inexpensive consumer devices (e.g., small hand-held camcorders), we can successfully perform a reconstruction attack as long as both the device's orientation and the user's fingers are detectable.

Tracking fingers, rather than recognizing displayed images, broadens the class of vulnerable devices to include those without any pop-out effect, such as Apple's iPad. Moreover, our approach is capable of operating at significant distances from the victim (e.g., up to 50 meters away with a camcorder). Perhaps most importantly, our approach operates effectively even for *repeated reflections*, i.e., *reflections of reflections* in nearby objects. This feat allows us to reconstruct typed input from the image of a mobile phone's screen on a user's eyeball as reflected through a nearby mirror (see Figure 1), extending the privacy threat to include situations where the adversary is located *around a corner* from the user.

Our approach operates despite low resolution images (a natural consequence of increasing the distance between target and camera) and high noise levels (due to reduced light levels in reflections of objects as compared to the originals). To overcome these challenges and achieve our goals, we extend a large body of work on object detection and tracking in the area of computer vision. Specifically, we extend existing finger tracking mechanisms to consider spatial context in order to reliably locate fingertips in the images. In addition, we propose a novel method for identifying fingertip trajectories based on robust estimation.

2. RELATED WORK

Techniques for undermining a user's privacy via several forms of compromising emanations have a rich and storied history (e.g., [1–3, 6, 7, 12, 16, 21, 29, 33, 41, 43, 49]). Probably the earliest of these ideas is embodied in the work of van Eck [41] and Highland [16] on compromising signals from electromagnetic radiation. That work was later extended by Kuhn and Kuhn [21], wherein it was argued that a telescope could be used to spy on reflections of a computer screen from afar. Intuitively, the light emitted from the display was modeled as a function of time and space, and then analyzed using signal processing methods. Naturally, the captured light is a disturbed signal of the light emitted by the screen, where disturbances include atmospheric effects, dispersion, attenuation, or lens distortion of the capture device. Regardless of these disturbances, Kuhn and Kuhn [21] show that by utilizing an expensive telescope with a wide aperture, they were able to reconstruct text on a 32×24 cm display from 60 m away.

More recently, Backes et al. [2, 3] overcame the requirement of direct line-of-sight. The key innovation was to exploit reflections to vary the path of light between the target screen and the observer, and showed it was possible to leverage the reflection off a human eyeball (reading a very large 36 pt text font from a distance of 10 m). However, the approach still used a high-powered telescope inheriting the drawbacks of high cost along with limited versatility and ability to go undetected. In addition, the setting of Backes et al. did not have to consider motion (of either the victim's device or the adversary), and also was not concerned with the daunting task of automatically reconstructing text from typed input.

The use of less expensive and more practical equipment was introduced by Raguram et al. [34]. Unlike the approach we present, that method relies on detecting the presence of key pop-outs in virtual keyboards. While that approach worked well for direct line-of-sight attacks, reconstructions involving a single reflection (in this case, off the victim's sunglasses) did not perform as well [34]. A related approach that also relied on the ability to detect pop-outs was proposed by Maggi et al. [29]. However, the approach of Maggi et al. is sensitive to movement of the device and camera and suffers in the presence of occlusions (including the fingers of the device's user). Neither approach could handle reconstructions of low resolution images of reflections of reflections in nearby objects.

Within the computer vision and human computer interaction communities, work on finger tracking for gesture recognition [8, 32], virtual input systems [40, 48], virtual object manipulation [25, 26], and hand writing recognition [19, 46] all share similarities to our application of finger motion analysis. Probably the most germane of these is the work of Iturbe et al. [18] which uses finger movement to control a virtual input system in which a user's finger is modeled as a straight line and its movement is used to determine the button being pointed to by the user. Unfortunately, their approach quickly fails for small mobile devices where the fingers need to bend in order to reach the keys. Similarly, Jin et al. [19] utilized finger input for character writing recognition. In their approach, the user's finger is isolated using a background modeling technique. Next, the path taken by the finger is tracked as the user writes individual letters, effectively recognizing the letter through the trajectory of the finger. Sadly, the approach of Jin et al. [19] can not be directly applied to mobile devices as users do not spell words by forming one character at a time, but instead interact with a keyboard via a series of touch events.

Lastly, Kerdvibulvech and Saito [20] apply a novel technique for tracking the fingers while a user plays a guitar. Instead of trying to uniquely identify each individual finger, the authors use a neural network classifier to recognize known patterns corresponding to different chord formations. While promising, their approach is also not applicable in our setting, as the way users type on mobile devices can differ significantly for the same user (e.g., switching between typing with one, two, or several fingers), and even more among different users, making the learning strategy less practical. Nevertheless, as we show later, we found that by combining many of the strengths of prior works alongside our own enhancements, we are able to achieve a solution that surpasses previous attempts in terms of its practically, range, and robustness.

3. BACKGROUND

Before introducing our approach, we provide pertinent background information that is helpful in understanding the set of challenges that impact how well an adversary can observe reflected objects in a scene.

Obviously, the size of the object in the captured images is of critical importance and naturally depends on the size of the object itself. Another factor is the focal length of the camera. Loosely speaking, the size of the object in the image for direct line-of-sight can be computed as:

$$Size_{Direct} = \underbrace{\frac{Sensor\,Resolution}{Sensor\,Size}}_{\text{pixel scale}} \cdot \underbrace{\frac{Object\,Size}{\frac{Target\,Distance}{Focal\,Length} - 1}}_{\text{size on sensor}} \quad (1)$$

Intuitively, the observed size is dependent on the physical size of the projection of the object on the sensor and the characteristics of the camera sensor, namely the size and number of pixels (picture elements). The size of the object on the sensor (its projection) is controlled by the focal length, the distance to the object, and the object size. Focal length can be viewed as the amount of magnification of the image, where longer focal lengths (zoom lenses) provide higher magnifications. Thus, by using a lens with a longer focal length, an adversary can gain a better view of the target. The final size of the image of the device in pixels (given the image's size on the sensor) then depends on the ratio between how many pixels are on the image sensor (*SensorResolution*) and the physical size of that sensor (*SensorSize*). At the same focal length, for example, the size of the object in pixels tends to decrease with full frame sensors found in high-end digital SLRs compared to cheaper digital camcorders with smaller sensors but the same video resolution.

In addition to the physical object size, the size of the object on the image sensor also depends on the presence and shape of any reflecting surfaces between the observer and the object. For instance, if the reflecting object is convex (e.g., a pair of sunglasses or the human eyeball), the size of the observed object will be much smaller than if observed with direct line-of-sight. When an object is viewed via a reflection, the final observed size can be computed as:

$$Size_{Reflection} = Size_{Direct} * \frac{1}{\frac{2\,Distance\,from\,Surface}{Curvature\,Radius}+1} \quad (2)$$

Thus, the curvature of the reflecting surface is an important factor in the observed size. The more curved the reflecting surface is, the more the light will be bent. For convex surfaces, the bending of the light will result in a smaller observed object size. Lastly, the distance between the reflecting surface and the target object itself (*Distance from Surface*) naturally affects the observed object size.

Takeaway. One way to acquire a larger observed size is to simply reduce the distance to the target object. However, from an adversarial point of view, it is desirable to be as far away as possible from the victim. Hence, a better solution would be to use a lens with a long focal length. For similar reasons, cameras with higher pixel density in their sensors are preferred. Finally, the curvature of any reflecting surface must be taken into account. For example, the human eyeball has a typical curvature of about 8 mm [2]. Hence, when people look at an object 25 cm away, the reflection in their eyeball will be about 60 times smaller than with direct line-of-sight.

Impact of Diffraction. The quality of the acquired image is significantly influenced by the wave properties of the light. When light comes near the edge of the lens, not all light rays traveling from the object pass directly through the lens to the image sensor. Instead, a fraction of the light diffuses and travels in every direction, leading to a blurring of the image. This phenomenon is called diffraction and cannot be eliminated. It presents a physical boundary for the effective resolution of the object in the captured image (commonly referred to as the *Rayleigh Criterion* [2]).

The maximum effective size of the observed object (*Max Size*) can be approximated as:

$$Max\,Size = \frac{Aperture/Wavelength}{1.22\ Target\,Distance} * \frac{Object\,Size}{\frac{2Distance\,from\,Surface}{Curvature\,Radius}+1} \quad (3)$$

Notice that the actual amount of diffraction is impacted by the wavelength of the light (*Wavelength*). While the adversary has no control over this factor, we include it here for completeness (along with the well-known constant scale factor of $1/1.22$ for circular apertures [37]). However, the adversary can select a lens with an appropriate aperture (i.e., opening of the lens), which lets the desired amount of unobstructed light pass through the lens.

Takeaway. The larger the aperture of the lens, the smaller the amount of diffraction. It is for precisely this reason that prior work (e.g., [2, 3, 21]) resorted to the use of telescopes. However, lenses with large apertures are typically very expensive, costing well over \$1,000 per square cm [2], and are difficult to conceal.

Impact of Noise. A very significant factor that affects the quality of the acquired image of the target object is imaging noise. Noise is a random variation in a pixel's intensity, causing the image to appear speckled. As noted by Nakamura [30], there can be several types of background noise in the captured image, each with a constant noise level. To avoid visual impact on the image quality by the noise, the exposure time is typically chosen so that the overall amount of light overwhelms the background noise making it hardly noticeable. However, for video capture, the exposure is naturally limited to the time of a frame, which for darker scenes makes the background noise become more noticeable. The resulting noise causes significant challenges in identifying fine detail.

Typically, cameras with large sensors are more resistant to noise, as their pixels are usually larger and can capture more photons of light. For that reason, the larger sensors provided in digital SLR cameras (as opposed to cellphones or point-and-shoot cameras) are desirable for photography even though they provide a smaller number of pixels on the object.

Taken as a whole, the aforementioned factors present challenges that *severely* limit the use of existing techniques (e.g., [2, 3, 34, 35]) when considering reconstruction of typed input from repeated reflections. For instance, the recently used technique of identifying salient feature points [34, 35] within the image in order to facilitate alignment will fail because the poor image resolution does not provide the required details for the salient feature points. The approach suggested by [29] faces similar challenges. Additionally, the low image quality (e.g., as acquired from a reflection in the eyeball) prevents the detection of fine detail. Therefore, the key pop-out events exploited by previous work will no longer be distinguishable.

4. AUTOMATED TRANSCRIPTION

Our proposed method successfully transcribes the text typed on a keyboard by exploiting video of the user typing (either directly or through up to two reflections from nearby objects). In practice, we must overcome all of the aforementioned challenges of image resolution, diffraction, and noise. To do so, we devise techniques that are resistant to low resolution, blurring, and noise. Figure 2 shows a high-level depiction of our approach.

We take as input a recording of the target device while the user types on its keyboard. First, we roughly estimate the location of the device in the image (Stage ❶). Next, the image of the device is aligned to a known reference template of the device's keyboard layout (Stage ❷). Then, the fingertips are identified in the video and the locations of the fingertips over the video frames are combined into trajectories (Stage ❸). These trajectories are then analyzed to identify the pressed keys (Stage ❹). From these pressed keys we then reconstruct the typed text (Stage ❺). Finally, as an optional post-processing step, we apply a language model in order to improve the readability of the final text (Stage ❻). Aside from some initial input in Stage ❶ to identify the first frame containing the target device, the entire process is fully automated. In what follows, we discuss each step in turn.

Stage ❶: Tracking

With a recording in hand, we first identify the device (phone, iPad, etc.) in the video so that we can focus our remaining analyses on only the relevant parts of the image. Depending on the number of reflections and the distance between the victim and the observer, the device is often only seen in a small region of each video frame (refer to Figure 3 for an example of reflection in an eyeball).

In order to identify the device's location in every frame, we utilize a tracking framework based on AdaBoost [15]. The basic idea is as follows. First, the user selects the region of the first video

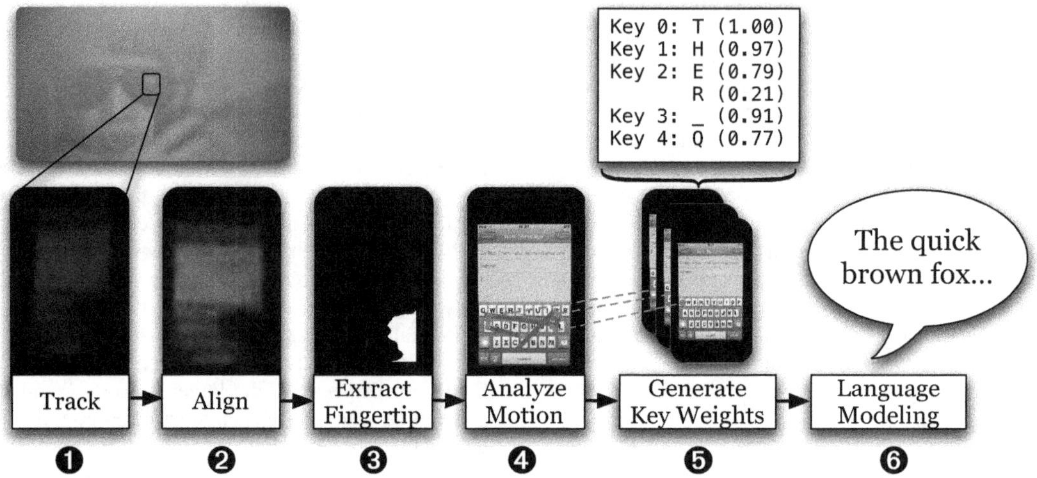

Figure 2: Overall design depicting the stages of our approach. First we track the motion of the mobile device (Stage ❶). Then the mobile device is aligned to a template (Stage ❷). In the stabilized image the finger is extracted (Stage ❸) and its fingertip trajectory is computed (Stage ❹). From the trajectories the likely pressed keys are identified (Stage ❺). As an optional step, we apply a language model to improve the quality of the reconstructed text (Stage ❻).

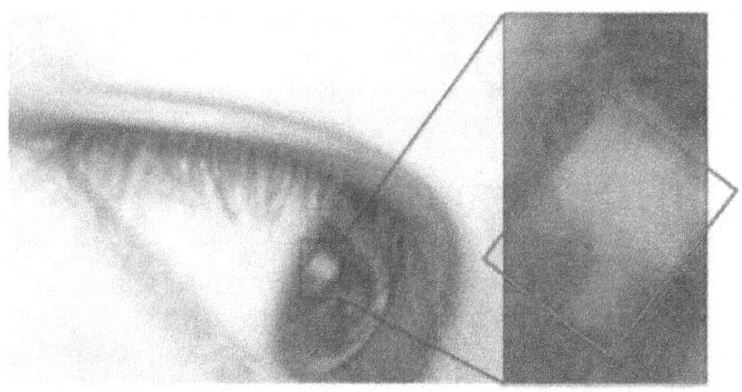

Figure 3: The captured image showing a reflection (of the victim's screen) as observed in the eyeball.

frame (corresponding to the device) that should be localized. Given this initial position, AdaBoost learns the appearance of the target object, and then automatically determines its location in all succeeding video frames. Since AdaBoost tracking works relatively well even in the presence of noise, we can successfully track small or even partially occluded objects in the image. The latter is important because the device is usually occluded by the fingers as the victim types on the keyboard.

That said, despite its robustness to noise, a straightforward application of AdaBoost tracking frequently fails in our setting. This is because tracking relies on the target device maintaining a similar appearance between frames, which is not necessarily the case with the noisy images we must process. In order to mitigate this problem, we average each video frame with the temporally preceding and trailing frame in the sequence. In this manner, each image is the combination of three consecutive frames, which reduces noise as random variation will be smoothed.[1] Although averaging could cause motion blur if there is significant scene motion between the frames, we found that in practice this is not a significant issue because of the high frame rate (30 frames per second) and the small motion of both the device and the user between frames.

Stage ❷: Alignment

Stage ❶ acquired the rough position of the device in each frame. The task in Stage ❷ is to determine the exact location of each key in the video frame (so that later stages can identify the keys which were most likely pressed). In general, the device will have varying orientation, scale, and image position in the video. In order to determine a mapping between the image in the video and a reference keyboard layout of the device (lifted, for example, from a manual), we must estimate the transformation that will align the device in the video to a reference image of the device's layout.

Prior work [29, 34] faced a similar challenge, and used salient points in the image as visual features to determine the transformation. In our setting, however, those visually distinct salient feature points are no longer visible. Thus we must overcome this challenge in a different manner. The approach we take is to utilize a line detection technique that provides a more robust set of features to achieve the same goal.

Preliminary Alignment: As an initial step, we first reduce the noise present in the images by employing anisotropic filtering [45]. This technique (detailed in Appendix A) can be used to intelligently preserve line structure in the image (otherwise often lost in normal noise reduction techniques), while simultaneously suppressing noise in the remaining parts of the image.

To determine the correct orientation of the device, we transform the video image so that all of the device's lines become either horizontal or vertical. This is accomplished by detecting edges within the image [11], and then using the lines to vote for the device's orientation using a Hough transform. The Hough transform is a voting scheme, where each detected line in the image votes for all possible orientations of the device that conform with the line's own orientation. For robustness, our voting scheme exploits the fact that lines of the same orientation will have a common vanishing point; hence each line is voting for its corresponding vanishing point (see Appendix B). Then, the vertical and horizontal vanishing points

[1]Gaussian noise is reduced by a factor of $\sqrt{3}$.

with the most votes represent the dominant vertical and horizontal line directions in the image. With this information at hand, we can successfully transform the device to its proper orientation.

Note, however, that even with the correct orientation, the image is still not aligned with the reference keyboard layout (i.e., the template) as the size and position may still differ. To handle this, we once again turn to a Hough transformation to vote on the translation and scale for aligning the image to the reference image of the device. The voting process relies on correspondences between the detected lines in the current frame and the lines in the template. A descriptor is built for each line in the current frame and the reference image, representing the appearance of each line's surroundings. The lines then vote for possible translation and scaling settings, and their votes are weighted by the similarity of the lines' descriptors. This voting results in a translation and scale in each of the x and y directions. Although the scale should be equal in both directions, we allow different scales (allowing affine transformation) to overcome small artifacts of slightly misaligned rotations. Appendix C details the computed transformation.

Refinement: A result of the Hough transform above is that the voting space will be quantized, leading to small residual misalignments. To provide an alignment that is stable across multiple frames and is as precise as possible we include a final refinement step (termed dense alignment [4, 38]). As opposed to relying on only lines, this step considers all pixels in the image to compute the final alignment. We employ a non-linear optimization in the parameters of the alignment (rotation, scale, translation) using the sum of squared differences between the overlapping pixels of the current and the first frame as an error metric for the residual misalignment. The final alignments are more stable and accurate (to sub-pixel precision) and are thus better suited for further analysis. An example alignment is shown in Figure 4.

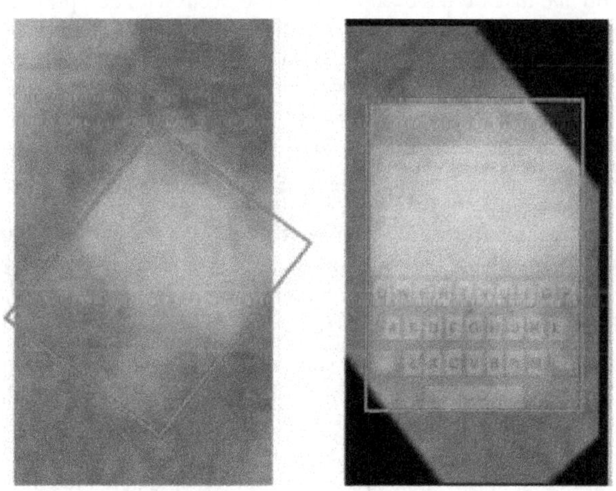

Figure 4: Cropped image (left) and alignment result (right) from Stage ❷ (overlaid with a reference device layout).

Stage ❸: Fingertip Extraction

At this point, the images are now aligned to the reference layout, and we are now primarily concerned with identifying the fingers as they interact with the device.

Similar to Jin et al. [19] and Nguyen et al. [31], we leverage Gaussian modeling of the appearance of the fingers as well as the appearance of the device. Intuitively, at this point, we consider the keyboard area in our input image as consisting primarily of two main colors: a lighter color corresponding to the bright screen, and a darker color corresponding to the user's fingers. Gaussian modeling allows us to represent their respective appearance by two different Gaussian distributions. The idea is to assign each pixel in the keyboard area of the image to either one of the two distributions based on whichever has the highest likelihood for the pixel under consideration. To learn the different distributions, we analyze the pixel colors of the first $n = 50$ frames.

In essence, by assigning each pixel to one of the two Gaussian distributions we convert the input image into a binary image (e.g., the right image in Figure 5). This strategy effectively segments the fingers and the device's screen and allows us to isolate the position and orientation of the fingers. To isolate the position, we simply model the user's finger as an ellipse, and then attempt to fit an ellipse to the boundary of the segmentation. In practice, this means that we must identify points of high curvature along the boundary of the finger's segmentation and then apply an ellipse-fitting regression function to determine the best fit (see Figure 5).

To identify the location of the tip of the finger, we assume that the fingertip corresponds to one of the four apexes of the ellipse. In practice, only three of the four apexes are reasonable fingertip locations because the finger only covers the keyboard from the left, right, or bottom. To determine which of the three cases is present, we consider the intersection of the ellipse with the device's boundary and select the appropriate apex. Specifically, if the ellipse intersects with the left and bottom edges of the device, then we assume that the finger is moving into view from the left; if the ellipse intersects with the right and bottom, it moves in from the right, and if the ellipse only intersects with the bottom, then it is moves into view from the bottom. Notice that by repeating the above process several times (and ignoring already identified fingers) we can detect multiple fingers on the screen and locate the fingertip for each.

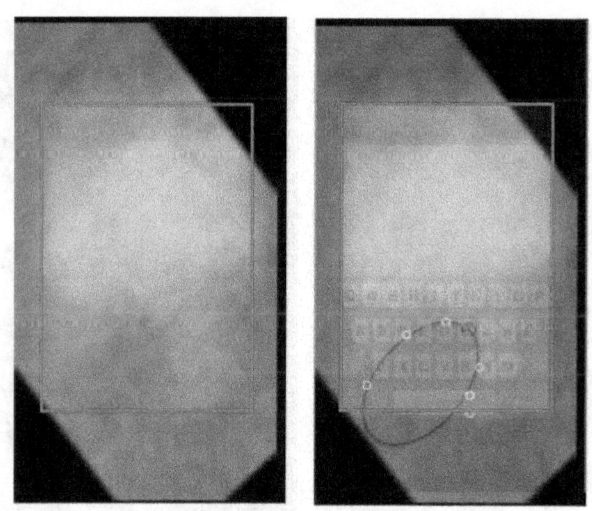

Figure 5: Input aligned image (left) and finger region extraction (right). Shown in the right image is the ellipse fitting (blue ellipse), segmentation (cyan), points with high curvature (yellow), detected fingertip (red circle), and an overlaid reference device layout.

Stage ❹: Fingertip Motion Analysis

We now turn our attention to how we identify the relative position of the fingers when keys are pressed. We take advantage of the insight that when one presses a key, the finger typically hovers at a certain position or suddenly changes direction in order to move to the next key. That observation allows us to use the location of the fingertip to identify when a key is pressed. To infer the series of likely keys pressed as the victim types, we combine the locations of the fingertips extracted in Stage ❸ into trajectories for each fingertip. The trajectory of a fingertip represents its path through time, and by analyzing this path, we can deduce when a key was pressed.

To accomplish this, we propose a robust method that represents the fingertip trajectories as a curve in 3D space (where the dimensions are the u, v location in the image, corresponding to the x-y plane, and the video frame number). When a fingertip stops moving, the location in the x-y plane will cease to change, but the frame number will still increase. Hence a stopped fingertip describes a line segment in the frame number direction that is perpendicular to the x-y plane and originates at the stopping position u, v.

To find these stopping positions or the direction changes, we approximate the entire 3D curve as a set of line segments. In order to identify the individual line segments, we use a robust model fitting technique called RANSAC [13]. Loosely speaking, the RANSAC algorithm will find a consistent model (a 3D line in this case) in the presence of noisy data even with a small number of correct data points complying with the model. Every time we run RANSAC, we model a part of the 3D curve as a line segment. Next, we remove the previously modeled part of the curve, and focus on the remaining portions. By running RANSAC repeatedly, and removing the modeled parts, we obtain a set of 3D line segments that approximate the original fingertip trajectory.

Given the set of line segments, stopping positions (u, v) are determined by line segments that are nearly perpendicular to the x-y plane. Likewise, sudden changes in direction are detected by finding two adjacent lines with a large change of direction between them. Figure 6 shows an example trajectory and the inferred line segment approximation.

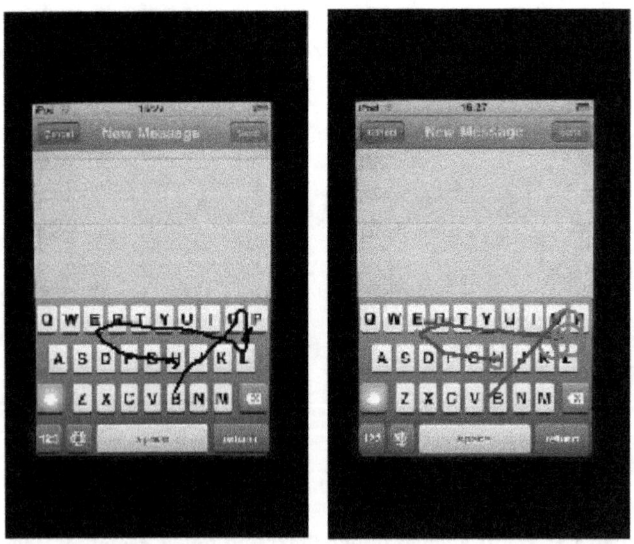

Figure 6: Fingertip trajectory (left) and line modeling (right). The red circles indicate stopping positions for the word "hello", where the size of the circle corresponds to uncertainty in the stopping position.

Stage ❺: Inferring the Keys Pressed

Given the stopping positions inferred in Stage ❹, we now move on to determining what keys were likely pressed. This task is somewhat complicated by the fact that users rarely make contact with the surface of the device with the precise tip of their finger(s). Moreover, when a user types, her fingers will not necessarily be at the same place each time they hit a particular key. Therefore, to determine which key was most likely pressed, we apply image recognition techniques to identify different positions of the user's finger with respect to the keyboard when pressing a key.

To learn the appearance of different key presses, we manually labeled 87 videos, recording the time and position of each key that was pressed. For each key on the keyboard, we collect a sample of its surrounding area as a pixel patch that is 60×100 pixels (matching the aspect ratio of a typical keyboard key). When the key under consideration is pressed, we identify the patch as a positive training sample for that key, and also use it as a negative training sample for all of the other keys on the keyboard. For each of these patches, we extract dense SIFT descriptors [42] and use these to train an AdaBoost classifier. In the end, we have a classifier for each key, where the sole purpose of the classifier is to determine whether or not its associated key has been pressed given an example pixel patch as input.

With this set of classifiers, we then analyze the key-press events detected in Stage ❹. Our analyses show that each event typically lasts anywhere from 10 to 20 frames, and during this time the finger stays at a relatively fixed location. We collect three adjacent frames from the middle of the duration, and extract from each a 60 by 100 pixel patch (corresponding in size to the training patch above) centered at the detected fingertip location. These patches are then fed into each of the nearby classifiers, with each classifier outputting its confidence of a key-press as a value in a range of $[0, 1]$ (with 1 being high confidence). By averaging the confidence scores of each classifier (one for each key) from the three chosen frames, we create a set of possible key-presses and their associated confidence levels. If the maximum confidence in the set falls below a predefined threshold ($\delta = 0.5$), we assume the key-press was invalid and discard the event. For a valid event with key-press confidence above δ, we record all the possible keys and their scores. By repeating this process for each key-press event, the final output of this stage is a sequence of key-press sets, where each set has a list of keys and their associated confidence values.

Note also that we do not explicitly detect presses of the "space" button, but instead treat longer pauses between key-press events as the space character. Likewise, shorter pauses are identified as the gaps between different letters in a word. Similar ideas for detecting spaces were utilized by Raguram et al. [34] and Balzarotti et al. [5].

Stage ❻: Language Model

As an optional post-processing step, we can feed the candidate keys and associated confidence values from the previous stage into a language model in order to achieve more accurate and readable results.

Similar to Raguram et al. [34], we view the language modeling task as a *noisy channel decoding* problem and adapt techniques from the speech recognition community to perform this inference (a process known as *maximum likelihood decoding*). In particular, we employ a *cascade* of models, each of which represents a stage in the process of transforming a sequence of candidate character sets with associated confidence values into words and phrases. Each model in the cascade is represented as a *weighted finite state transducer (WFST)*, i.e., a finite state machine with an output tape in addition to the input tape, which maps sequences in one representation to sequences in another. For instance, speech recognition systems often include a component (known as the *lexicon*) which maps sequences of *phones*, the distinct sounds which comprise speech, to (valid) words. A sequence of such component models can then be used to model more complex mappings, such as that from an acoustic signal to a sequence of words and phrases, by *composition* of the WFST representations of the component models. With a lexicon as the first component, taking as input a sequence of phones, a second component (often an n-gram language model) maps the resulting sequence of words to likely phrases. The composition of these two models, itself a WFST, maps sequences of phones to likely phrases.

One advantage of the uniform representation of these components as WFSTs is that the *decoding* or inference step (i.e., finding the most likely phrase corresponding to the input sequence of sounds) can be performed on the composition of the component models rather than proceeding sequentially through component models. In other words, traditional speech recognition cascades were effectively Markov chains: the output of each component depended only on the output of the previous component. Often, the resource-intensive nature of the speech recognition task forced the pruning of unlikely sequences, e.g., phones after the application of a component model. Thus a sequence of phones which might be considered unlikely (but not impossible) in the absence of a language model might be pruned in the early stages of such a speech recognition system. A WFST cascade, on the other hand, can be represented as a single WFST, which allows for inference from all components simultaneously and mitigates many problems resulting from pruning.

In our case, the input for the language modeling stage is a sequence of key-press events with character labels and associated confidence values, including marked spaces. We then employ a composite WFST model to smooth over any potential errors in the earlier stages by modifying the output words and phrases to more closely match natural English language. We first apply an edit distance model $\mathscr{E}$ for error correction. Conceptually, the edit distance model produces, for each input string, a set of similar strings each weighted by (keyboard) edit distance from the input string. We then employ a dictionary model $\mathscr{D}$, which prunes those strings which do not result in dictionary words, and an n-gram language model $\mathscr{L}$, which promotes sequences of words that appear more frequently in English and demotes those which appear rarely. Then the cascade model can be represented as $\mathscr{C} = \mathscr{E} \circ \mathscr{D} \circ \mathscr{L}$. To find the most likely sequence of words corresponding to an input sequence of character sets (as output by the previous stage), the input is first represented as a finite state acceptor $\mathscr{I}$. Then the shortest path through the WFST $\mathscr{I} \circ \mathscr{C}$ gives the most likely series of English words given the input sequence of predicted character sets.

Our n-gram language model $\mathscr{L}$ is a unigram model trained on the Brown corpus [14]. The dictionary model $\mathscr{D}$ is based on the 'medium' word list from the Spell Checker Oriented Word Lists[2] with roman numerals, unusual abbreviations, and proper nouns removed. For the keyboard edit distance, we define the distance between two keys as the normalized product of the difference in rows (on a 'vertical' axis through Q and Z) plus one and the difference in keys (on a 'horizontal' axis through A and L) plus one. For instance, the (unnormalized) distance between A and B is $(1+1)*(4+1) = 10$, since A and B are a single row apart vertically and four keys apart horizontally. We offset by one in each case to avoid zero values if the keys are in the same row or column.

5. EVALUATION

Recall that one of the key motivating scenarios driving our design is the ability to reconstruct the typed input from repeated reflections. From an adversarial point of view, we are also interested in understanding the realism of the threat posed by an adversary performing such an attack from as far as possible, yet relying on inexpensive equipment. In what follows, we provide an analysis of our results under these conditions.

[2]wordlist.sourceforge.net

Device Name	Focal Length	Aperture	Sensor Size	Resolution
Canon 60D DSLR, 400mm Lens	400mm	F/5.6	22.3 × 14.9mm	5184 × 3456
Canon VIXIA HG21 Camcorder	57mm	F/3.0	4.84 × 3.42mm	1920 × 1080

Table 1: Specifications of the cameras used in our evaluation.

For the case of multiple reflections, we make use of a Canon 60D digital SLR ($700) with 400mm Lens ($1340). For experiments with direct line-of-sight and a single reflection, we use a Canon VIXIA HG21 Camcorder ($1000). These devices are considerably smaller than the telescopes used previously [2, 3, 21] and are also more affordable. The specifications are listed in Table 1.

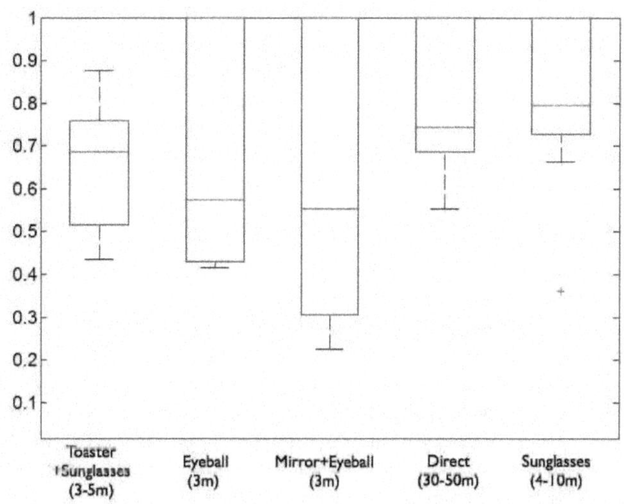

Figure 7: METEOR scores for our approach, broken down by scenario.

For our lab-based evaluation, five different subjects took part in our experiments. To explore different typing conditions, we asked the subjects to perform 3 different styles of typing: typing a specific sentence, providing a quick response to a question (e.g., as one might do when text messaging), and typing a password of their choosing. The chosen sentences are from "The Art of the War" and the questions from SMS messages collected by NUS [9]. In all, we collected 73 responses containing 584 total words. In addition, we collected 15 passwords (each consisting of 5 to 8 lower-case characters).

To gauge our performance, we evaluate the reconstruction results for sentences and passwords using separate metrics. The reason is obvious: the use of a natural language model can easily improve the result of the former, while for passwords a better measure is to examine how many guesses are required to recover the password given our initial hypothesis.

For evaluating the quality of our reconstructed text, we use the METEOR metric proposed by Lavie and Denkowski [24]. Essentially, METEOR scores machine translation hypotheses (i.e., our guesses) by aligning them to one or more reference translations.

Scenario	Distance	Reference Sentence	Reconstructed Results	METEOR Score
Toaster+Sunglasses[C1]	3m	when your round is a short one you take a walk	when your round is a short one he take a walk	0.88
	3m	when it is a long one you take a cab	when a is a long is you the a can	0.43
Mirror+Eyeball[C1]	3m	when it is a long one	when it is a long one	1.00
	3m	i am busy tonight	i at be tonight	0.33
Sunglasses[C2]	4m	if you know your enemy and you know yourself you need not fear the results of a hundred battles	if you know your enemy and you know yourself you need not fear the results of a hundred battles	1.00
	10m	if you know neither the enemy nor yourself you will succumb in every battle	if you his neither the enemy for yourself to will succumb in every battle	0.71
Direct view[C2]	30m	when your round is a short one you take a walk	when your round is a short one you take a walk	1.00
	50m	i plan to stay at home	i men to stay at home	0.74

Table 2: Example reconstructions. [C1]: Using Canon 60D DSLR($700) with 400mm Lens($1340). [C2]: Using Canon VIXIA HG21 Camcorder($1000).

It estimates human perception of the readability of the sentence in terms of the adequacy and fluency of the translation. METEOR assigns scores on a scale from 0.0 to 1.0, with 1.0 indicating a perfect translation. As a guide for interpreting METEOR scores, Lavie [23] suggests that scores of 0.5 or higher indicate understandable translations, while scores of 0.7 or higher indicate good or fluent translations. Examples from our experiments are shown in Table 2.

5.1 Results

The aggregate results of our approach, including confidence intervals, are illustrated in Figure 7. Notice that in every circumstance, our reconstruction results in an average METEOR score above 0.5, indicating an understandable level. Additionally, we reconstructed 23% (17/73) of the sentences perfectly, and 92% (67/73) of all the sentences have a METEOR score above 0.5. All of the captured videos were within the automatic focus and exposure limits of the cameras, leading to no unusable videos which might occur in more challenging environments. We remind the reader that these results are already obtained in situations where previous efforts [29, 34, 35] fail, either due to an increased distance from the target or an additional reflection. These results, as well as the individual examples in Table 2, indicate that our attack is quite stable to changes in the distance to the target and the number and type of reflecting surfaces.

Closer look: Double Reflections

In order to evaluate the performance of double-reflection attacks we conducted the following experiments. First, we position a user with sunglasses at a desk with a nearby toaster. The user then types on an iPhone 4, and an attacker observes the typed input from a concealed location around a corner of 60 to 90 degrees by leveraging the two reflections. For the second setup, the user is once again at a desk, but instead of relying on the reflection from sunglasses, we use the reflection from the user's own eye. To enable this attack, we utilized a small mirror instead of the toaster. The use of the mirror does not influence the image quality but provides the additional ability to attack around the corner. The results without the mirror are similar (Figure 7). These scenarios are illustrated in Figure 8.

The use of multiple reflections naturally limits the information we can acquire from the target. With the double reflection, the main limitation of the system is the contrast between the user's fingers and the device's screen. After two reflections, the device's screen

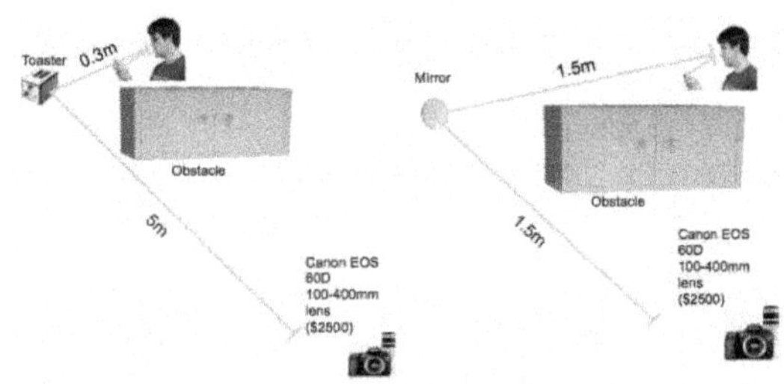

Figure 8: Left: the cellphone image reflects from the user's sunglasses, off the toaster's surface, and is then captured by the camera. Right: the cellphone image reflects from user's eyeball, off the mirror, and then is captured by the camera.

can barely be recognized by a human (see Figure 9). The contrast between the device screen and the background is so low that it is much harder to extract the device screen and finger regions. Yet we are still able to achieve results with an understandable level (0.65). In Figure 10, we illustrate the effect that contrast has on the final result. Reflections significantly reduce the contrast of the image. The RMS contrast (standard deviation of the pixel intensities) takes values in the range $[0.0, 0.5]$, where 0.0 corresponds to an image with uniform color and 0.5 corresponds to a checkerboard pattern of black and white squares. The RMS contrast in our experiments drops from around 0.35 in direct view to 0.03 with two reflections. This leads to difficulties in finger region extraction and therefore lower METEOR scores.

In the reflection off the eyeball (Figure 11), the finger and keyboard are even more difficult to discern. The image is both small and significantly blurred. Backes et al. [2] discuss the theoretical boundary that a telescope with a 62 cm aperture from a distance of 2 m would be required in order to obtain a full resolution image from the reflection of an eyeball. In our setting (i.e., a lens with a 7.1 cm aperture from a distance of 3 m), we achieve understandable reconstruction results with less than $1/10^{th}$ of the full resolution. The main problem with the reflection from the eyeball is the blurring caused by diffraction and noise, as discussed in Section 3, as well as partial occlusion by the eyelashes.

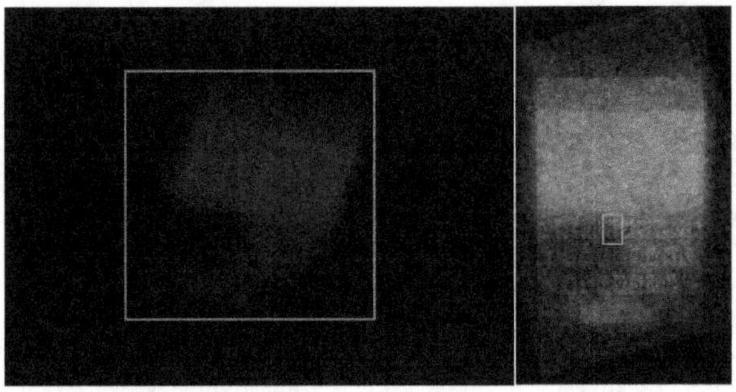

Figure 9: Example double-reflection from sunglasses and a toaster. Left: Captured image; Right: (correctly) identified keypress (T, with confidence 0.55). The brightness of the detected image (right) is adjusted for viewing convenience and has been overlaid with a reference device layout.

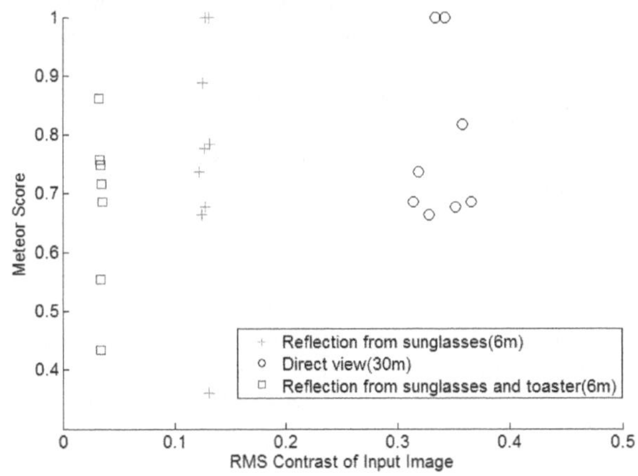

Figure 10: Plot of captured RMS contrast versus METEOR score for the three different scenarios (direct, single-reflection, and repeated reflections).

Closer look: Single Reflection and Direct Sight

Compared with the prior state of the art, our attack can be executed from a much farther distance, as illustrated in Figure 12. For example, using the same equipment (Canon VIXIA HG21 Camcorder), the approach of Raguram et al. [35] can only run a direct attack at 24 m and a single-reflection attack at 4 m, while our work increased the distance to be 50 m and 10 m respectively (see Figure 7) while maintaining comparable results.

Devices without Pop-ups

As a final experiment to demonstrate that our design is applicable to a broad range of devices, we include a preliminary study on a device (a first generation iPad) with a virtual keyboard but no pop-out events. In this case, the iPad was placed at a distance of 4 meters from a pair of sunglasses which were in turn situated 4 meters from our camera. As the iPad's screen is considerably larger than the iPhone 4, it is perhaps not surprising that we are able to perfectly reconstruct all 8 sentences tested.

5.1.1 Password Guessing

We also apply our approach to the reconstruction of passwords. While passwords typically chosen by users may follow certain distributions that make them easier to guess, we assume that passwords are chosen with sufficient randomness to mitigate any language modeling, and therefore exclude the optional Stage ❻ from this portion of the analysis. We instead examine the classification results from Stage ❺ directly. One advantage of our approach is that the output of Stage ❺ is a sequence of sets of candidate keys with associated confidence values. We therefore have a natural ordering with which we can prioritize our password guessing strategy.

We implement this ordering with a best-first search, where the 'best' candidate password is the string which maximizes the product of the confidence values for the individual keypresses. We can calculate this product for each child of a given candidate password, where a child is identical to the candidate except that a single character has been replaced with the next most likely character for that position. Beginning with the most likely candidate, i.e., that for which the individual confidence values are maximized, we check if the candidate matches the password for which we are looking. If not, we add each child of the candidate to a priority queue, ordered by the product of the confidence values. Once the children of one

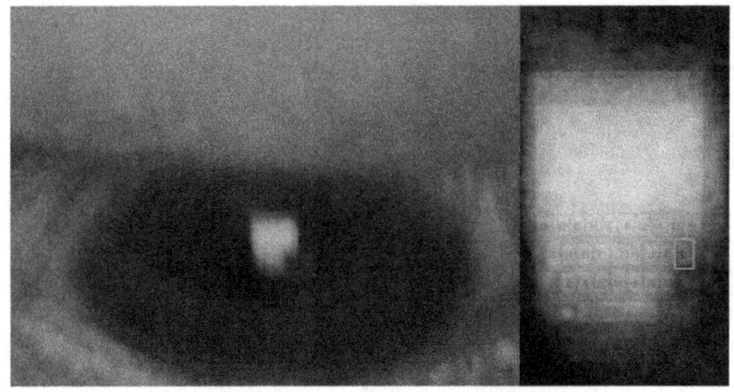

Figure 11: Example double-reflection from an eyeball and mirror. Left: Captured image; Right: candidate keys (I with confidence 0.10, L with confidence 0.07, and the correct key O with confidence 1.00). The right image has been overlaid with a reference device layout.

Figure 12: Example single reflection from 10m. Left: Single reflection from 10m (correctly predicting I with confidence 1.0). Right: Direct view from 50m (correctly predicting T with confidence 1.0). Both images have been overlaid with a reference device layout.

Scenario	Distance	Reference (Typed)	Top Guess	Number of Guesses
Direct Sight	30m	bjtam	bjtam	1
		mstys	matya	47
		dlxmzd	elxmad	64
		zywmxq	atahxq	5967
	50m	wabjta	ewbjta	3
		tatsta	tatata	10
		wdlxmzd	wdiebae	277
Eyeball and Mirror	3m	jrairbf	jfairbf	3
		hvgcjyx	hvccnyx	620
		bgditv	cgcitv	3
Sunglasses and Toaster	3m	sjyfh	sjyfn	2
		aluhe	aauce	14
		kydhwria	kydhwria	1
		jyerpsk	jynraak	21
	5m	hdyeri	hdierx	6

Table 3: Expected number of guesses required to identify user passwords given a ranking, by decreasing confidence, of candidates.

Stage Name	Time Spent (sec/frame)	Percentage
Stage 1: Tracking	0.228	8.4%
Stage 2: Alignment	1.054	38.9%
Stage 3: Finger Extraction	1.042	38.4%
Stage 4: Fingertip Analysis	0.123	4.5%
Stage 5: Key Weight Generation	0.256	9.4%
Stage 6: Language Model	0.007	0.2%
Total	2.708	100.0%

Table 4: Runtime performance of our approach.

candidate are added, the candidate is discarded, the highest priority candidate is drawn from the queue, and the process begins anew.

Letters outside of the candidate set are assigned a weight of 10^{-6}, which is significantly smaller than the weights of any observed keypresses. This accounts for cases where the actual key is not contained within the predicted set. We break ties randomly, i.e., we report the average-case estimates when multiple candidates have the same value for the product of the confidence values.

Table 3 shows our password guessing results. Of the 15 passwords used, 6 were reconstructed in 3 or fewer guesses, 12 in less than 100 guesses, and all 15 in less than 6000 guesses. Random guessing of passwords would result in almost 6 million guesses for 5-letter passwords and almost 155 million guesses for 6-letter passwords, in expectation. Accordingly, our approach results in a speedup of four orders of magnitude. That said, we remind the reader that the passwords used were those chosen by our test subjects. Unfortunately, our test subjects chose passwords which were between 5 and 8 characters long and consisted of only lower-case letters. However, since the mobile devices in which we are interested simply overlay the lower-case keyboard with an upper-case, numeric, or symbolic keyboard as necessary, extending our analysis to cover these cases would not be difficult.

5.1.2 *Runtime Performance*

The overall performance is 0.37 frames per second, the composition of which is shown in Table 4. The current version of our approach is mainly implemented in MATLAB; only the tracking scheme in Stage ❶ is optimized with C++ and the use of a GPU. As such, re-implementation of the remainder of our approach in C++ and/or on the GPU would likely result in a significant speedup.

6. MITIGATIONS

Our attack invalidates a significant portion of prior defences (e.g., like eliminating key pop-up events (Raguram et al.)). Perhaps the most natural mitigation is to apply a privacy screen/film to the device. This will limit the amount of light emitted, making reconstruction of reflected images (with inherently reduced brightness) extremely difficult. Moreover, it will significantly limit the possibility of direct sight attacks by narrowing the angle of screen observation. However, many materials are diffuse reflectors (reflection in all directions), which may lift the restriction on viewing angle imposed by privacy films by allowing an adversary to exploit the reflection rather than a direct view of the screen.

More esoteric mitigations that are focused on hindering the recovery of sensitive input (e.g., passwords) call for the application of gaze-based passwords [22, 44], shoulder-surfing resistant graphical password schemes (e.g., [17, 36]), and randomized keyboards [39, 47]. Gaze-based password systems, for example, take into consideration the focus of the user's eyes on the screen as the source of input, greatly reducing the ability of an adversary without an unobstructed view of the user's eyes and orientation with respect to the screen [22, 44]. Likewise, randomized keyboards permute on-screen keyboard layouts as the user enters her password [39, 47], effectively thwarting shoulder-surfing attacks during such times.

Clearly, these proposals would hamper the ability to reconstruct entered passwords using approaches similar to ours; in particular, attacking either the graphical password schemes or the randomized keyboard schemes would require the ability to discern detail on the screen of the device. That said, all of these proposals are limited to password entry, and as such, only offer a partial solution to this challenge of limiting recovery of typed input exposed via compromising reflections. Moreover, the real-world usability of these proposals remains unclear.

7. CONCLUSIONS

In this paper, we provide a technique for accurately reconstructing the text typed on a mobile device, with a broader range of credible threats that underscore the realism of the attack. Specifically, we show that it is possible to perform such attacks in a number of challenging scenarios: on devices with any type of virtual or physical keyboard, without direct line-of-sight, and at distances farther away from the victim than previously thought possible. Our attack can even directly use reflections on the eye-ball, which was not possible before due to the noise and physical boundaries of the optics in prior work. Our empirical analysis, which covers a number of scenarios (including direct line-of-sight, single reflections, and repeated reflections) as well as a range of distances (3 m - 50 m), demonstrates the success of our approach and underscores the significance of this privacy threat.

8. ACKNOWLEDGEMENTS

We are thankful to the anonymous reviewers for their insightful comments. This work is supported by a grant from the National Science Foundation, under award number 1148895.

References

[1] D. Asonov and R. Agrawal. Keyboard acoustic emanations. In *Proceedings of the IEEE Symposium on Security and Privacy*, 2004.

[2] M. Backes, M. Durmuth, and D. Unruh. Compromising reflections-or-how to read LCD monitors around the corner. In *Proceedings of the IEEE Symposium on Security and Privacy*, 2008.

[3] M. Backes, T. Chen, M. Dürmuth, H. Lensch, and M. Welk. Tempest in a teapot: Compromising reflections revisited. In *Proceedings of the IEEE Symposium on Security and Privacy*, 2009.

[4] S. Baker and I. Matthews. Lucas-Kanade 20 years on. *International Journal of Computer Vision*, 56(3):221–255, 2004.

[5] D. Balzarotti, M. Cova, and G. Vigna. ClearShot: Eavesdropping on keyboard input from video. In *Proceedings of the IEEE Symposium on Security and Privacy*, 2008.

[6] L. Cai and H. Chen. Touchlogger: inferring keystrokes on touch screen from smartphone motion. In *USENIX Workshop on Hot Topics in Security (HotSec)*, 2011.

[7] L. Cai and H. Chen. On the practicality of motion based keystroke inference attack. *Trust and Trustworthy Computing*, pages 273–290, 2012.

[8] A. Chaudhary, J. Raheja, and S. Raheja. A vision based geometrical method to find fingers positions in real time hand gesture recognition. *Journal of Software*, 7(4): 861–869, 2012.

[9] T. Chen and M.-Y. Kan. Creating a live, public short message service corpus: The NUS SMS corpus. *Language Resources and Evaluation*, 2011.

[10] R. Collins and R. Weiss. Vanishing point calculation as a statistical inference on the unit sphere. In *Proceedings of the Third International Conference on Computer Vision*, 1990.

[11] R. O. Duda and P. E. Hart. Use of the Hough transformation to detect lines and curves in pictures. *Communications of the ACM*, 15(1):11–15, 1972.

[12] F. Elibol, U. Sarac, and I. Erer. Realistic eavesdropping attacks on computer displays with low-cost and mobile receiver system. In *Proceedings of the 20th European Signal Processing Conference*, 2012.

[13] M. Fischler and R. Bolles. Random sample consensus: a paradigm for model fitting with applications to image analysis and automated cartography. *Communications of the ACM*, 24(6):381–395, 1981.

[14] W. N. Francis and H. Kucera. Brown corpus manual. Technical report, Dept. of Linguistics, Brown University, 1979.

[15] H. Grabner, M. Grabner, and H. Bischof. Real-time tracking via on-line boosting. In *Proceedings of the British Machine Vision Conference*, volume 1, pages 47–56, 2006.

[16] H. J. Highland. Electromagnetic radiation revisited. *Computer Security*, 5:85–93, June 1986.

[17] B. Hoanca and K. J. Mock. Password entry scheme resistant to eavesdropping. In *Security and Management*, 2008.

[18] X. Iturbe, A. Altuna, A. Ruiz de Olano, and I. Martinez. VHDL described finger tracking system for real-time human-machine interaction. In *International Conference on Signals and Electronic Systems*, 2008.

[19] L. Jin, D. Yang, L. Zhen, and J. Huang. A novel vision-based finger-writing character recognition system. *Journal of Circuits, Systems, and Computers*, 16(03):421–436, 2007.

[20] C. Kerdvibulvech and H. Saito. Vision-based detection of guitar players' fingertips without markers. In *Computer Graphics, Imaging and Visualisation*, 2007.

[21] M. Kuhn and C. Kuhn. Compromising emanations: eavesdropping risks of computer displays. Technical report, University of Cambridge, 2003.

[22] M. Kumar, T. Garfinkel, D. Boneh, and T. Winograd. Reducing shoulder-surfing by using gaze-based password entry. In *Symposium on Usable Privacy and Security*, 2007.

[23] A. Lavie. Evaluating the output of machine translation systems. *AMTA Tutorial*, 2010.

[24] A. Lavie and M. J. Denkowski. The METEOR metric for automatic evaluation of machine translation. *Machine Translation*, 23(2-3):105–115, 2009.

[25] B. Lee and J. Chun. Manipulation of virtual objects in marker-less AR system by fingertip tracking and hand gesture recognition. In *Proceedings of the 2nd International Conference on Interaction Sciences*, 2009.

[26] T. Lee and T. Hollerer. Handy AR: Markerless inspection of augmented reality objects using fingertip tracking. In *IEEE International Symposium on Wearable Computers*, 2007.

[27] E. Lutton, H. Maitre, and J. Lopez-Krahe. Contribution to the determination of vanishing points using Hough transform. *Transactions on Pattern Analysis and Machine Intelligence*, 16(4):430–438, 1994.

[28] M. Magee and J. Aggarwal. Determining vanishing points from perspective images. *Computer Vision, Graphics, and Image Processing*, 26(2):256–267, 1984.

[29] F. Maggi, A. Volpatto, S. Gasparini, G. Boracchi, and S. Zanero. A fast eavesdropping attack against touchscreens. In *Information Assurance and Security (IAS)*. IEEE, 2011.

[30] J. Nakamura. *Image sensors and signal processing for digital still cameras*. CRC, 2005.

[31] D. Nguyen, T. Pham, and J. Jeon. Fingertip detection with morphology and geometric calculation. In *IEEE/RSJ International Conference on Intelligent Robots and Systems*, 2009.

[32] K. Oka, Y. Sato, and H. Koike. Real-time fingertip tracking and gesture recognition. *Computer Graphics and Applications*, 22(6):64–71, 2002.

[33] E. Owusu, J. Han, S. Das, A. Perrig, and J. Zhang. Accessory: password inference using accelerometers on smartphones. In *Proceedings of the Twelfth Workshop on Mobile Computing Systems & Applications*. ACM, 2012.

[34] R. Raguram, A. White, D. Goswami, F. Monrose, and J. Frahm. iSpy: automatic reconstruction of typed input from compromising reflections. In *Proceedings of the ACM Conference on Computer and Communications Security*, 2011.

[35] R. Raguram, A. M. White, Y. Xu, J.-M. Frahm, P. Georgel, and F. Monrose. On the privacy risks of virtual keyboards: automatic reconstruction of typed input from compromising reflections. *IEEE Transactions on Dependable and Secure Computing*, 2013.

[36] L. Sobrado and J.-C. Birget. Graphical passwords. *The Rutgers Scholar*, 4, 2002.

[37] E. Stelzer. Contrast, resolution, pixelation, dynamic range and signal-to-noise ratio: fundamental limits to resolution in fluorescence light microscopy. *Journal of Microscopy*, 189 (1):15–24, 1998.

[38] R. Szeliski. Image alignment and stitching: A tutorial. *Foundations and Trends in Computer Graphics and Vision*, 2006.

[39] D. S. Tan, P. Keyani, and M. Czerwinski. Spy-resistant keyboard: More secure password entry on public touch screen displays. In *Proceedings of the 17th Australia Conference on Computer-Human Interaction*, 2005.

[40] N. Ukita and M. Kidode. Wearable virtual tablet: fingertip drawing on a portable plane-object using an active-infrared camera. In *Proceedings of the International Conference on Intelligent User Interfaces*. ACM, 2004.

[41] W. van Eck. Electromagnetic radiation from video display units: an eavesdropping risk? *Computer Security*, 4: 269–286, December 1985.

[42] A. Vedaldi and B. Fulkerson. VLFeat: An open and portable library of computer vision algorithms. In *Proceedings of the International Conference on Multimedia*, 2010.

[43] M. Vuagnoux and S. Pasini. Compromising electromagnetic emanations of wired and wireless keyboards. In *Proceedings of the* 18th *USENIX Security Symposium*, 2009.

[44] J. Weaver, K. J. Mock, and B. Hoanca. Gaze-based password authentication through automatic clustering of gaze points. In *IEEE International Conference on Systems, Man and Cybernetics*, 2011.

[45] J. Weickert. *Anisotropic diffusion in image processing*, volume 1. Teubner Stuttgart, 1998.

[46] D. Yang, L. Jin, and J. Yin. An effective robust fingertip detection method for finger writing character recognition system. In *Proceedings of the International Conference on Machine Learning and Cybernetics*, 2005.

[47] Y. Zhang, P. Xia, J. Luo, Z. Ling, B. Liu, and X. Fu. Fingerprint attack against touch-enabled devices. In *Security and Privacy in Smartphones and Mobile Devices*, SPSM '12, 2012.

[48] Z. Zhang. Vision-based interaction with fingers and papers. In *Proceedings International Symposium on the CREST Digital Archiving Project*, 2003.

[49] L. Zhuang, F. Zhou, and J. Tygar. Keyboard acoustic emanations revisited. In *Proceedings of the 12th ACM Conference on Computer and Communications Security*, 2005.

APPENDIX

A. ANISOTROPIC DIFFUSION

Our alignment to the reference layout (Section 4) is based on image edges. Hence we opt for anisotropic diffusion, which is a noise suppression algorithm that maintains edges in the image. Our anisotropic diffusion is in the spirit of the method proposed by Weickert [45], which was designed to preserve all detected edges in the image. In our work however, we only preserve images edges that are along the dominant directions of the boundaries of the mobile device. This not only reduces noise but also effectively suppresses spurious lines, as for example, caused by reflections on the screen. The diffusion process is described by:

$$u' = \begin{cases} \partial_t u = div((1-c(\phi)(1-D(J_\rho(\nabla u_\sigma))))\nabla u) \\ c(\theta) = K_\Sigma(\phi - Dir_1) + K_\Sigma(\phi - Dir_2) \\ D(J_\rho(\nabla u_\sigma)) = U^T \begin{pmatrix} 1/(1+\lambda_1) & 0 \\ 0 & 1 \end{pmatrix} U \end{cases} \quad (4)$$

where u is the pixel value of the original image, u' is the new pixel value, and ϕ is the angle of the eigenvector of the biggest eigenvalue λ_1 of J_ρ (the Jacobian matrix of the image at pixel u). The matrix U is the unitary matrix consisting of the eigenvectors of J_ρ. K_Σ is a Gaussian kernel with parameter Σ, and Dir_1, Dir_2 are the pre-calculated dominant directions. The resulting filter output has the following properties:

1) If the edge is strongly deviating from the main direction (i.e. has a large angle to the dominant direction), it will be blurred since Equation (4) converges to $\partial_t u = div(\nabla u)$.

2) Edges along the dominant directions will be enhanced along the edge since $D(J_\rho(\nabla u_\sigma))$ becomes very small. This means the edge will not be blurred and will maintain its high contrast.

3) In addition, the areas alongside the edges in the dominant directions will be smoothed in the direction parallel to the edge to suppress the noise since in this direction we also have $\partial_t u = div(\nabla u)$.

In summary this will ensure an effective noise suppression while maintaining edges in the dominant directions, which are then used to align the device image to the reference layout.

B. VANISHING POINTS

Vanishing points are points in the 2D projected image where lines that are parallel converge. There is a large body of work on estimating vanishing points. Most of the methods are based on premarked points and mainly aim to solve problems when there is significant skew in the directions of the lines, such as [28]. However, these methods fail in our application because the vanishing points are so far away that the data matrix becomes singular. Alternative methods are based on transformations such as the Hough transform [27] and Sphere representation [10].

Due to its ability to detect multiple vanishing points at once we chose to use a Hough transform to calculate the vanishing points. The Hough transform is a voting scheme in the parameter space where every pixel along a line segment votes for all compatible parameterizations of its line. The detected lines are then chosen as the local maxima in the voting space. We use the angular representation $xcos\theta + ysin\theta = \rho$ of line segments for the voting, which avoids the singularity of vertical lines in the slope and bias parameterization of lines. The Hough transformation then provides the θ_i, ρ_i of all lines l_i in the image. These lines are then used to compute the vanishing point $v = (x, y)$ through solving:

$$\begin{pmatrix} x \\ y \end{pmatrix} = \begin{pmatrix} \rho \frac{d\theta}{d\rho} \cos\theta - \sin\theta \\ \rho \frac{d\rho}{d\theta} \sin\theta + \cos\theta \end{pmatrix} * \frac{1}{d\theta/d\rho} \quad (5)$$

for each of the lines. To combine the information from all lines along each of the major directions we use regression to compute $d\theta/d\rho$ and θ. This is then used in solving for the vanishing points (x, y) with Equation (5), which results in the horizontal vanishing point v_x and the vertical vanishing point v_y. Assuming v_x, v_y are normalized to satisfy $\|v_x\| = \|v_y\| = 1$ the camera rotation matrix R is given by

$$R = \begin{pmatrix} v_x \\ v_y \\ v_x \times v_y \end{pmatrix}$$

Applying the inverse rotation ensures the device screen plane and the coordinate systems x-y-plane are parallel, effectively removing any rotation-related distortion from the image.

C. TRANSLATION ALIGNMENT

The transformation of a given image to the template can be viewed as rotation of the camera followed by translation and zoom. Our method uses the Hough transformation to extract the camera's rotation, translation, and scale as explained in Section 4. Here, we introduce how to compute the resulting transformation given estimated parameters.

The vanishing points reveal the rotation information. For instance, all the horizontal lines on the device correspond to a vanishing point (x, y) on the image plane, which is calculated as described above. The direction of these lines can be calculated as the direction from the center of the camera to the pixel (x, y). For a pinhole camera, this 3D direction *Direction* can be represented as: $(x - c_x, y - c_y, f)^T$ with (c_x, c_y) being the coordinate of the center of the image and f representing the focal length of the camera normalized by the physical size of the pixels. These are intrinsic parameters modeling the imaging parameters of the camera sensor and lens.

With the vanishing points, we acquire the two dominant directions of the edges of the device as $Direction_h = (x_h, y_h, z_h)$ and $Direction_v = (x_v, y_v, z_v)$. The edges of the device can be transformed to become horizontal and vertical with following equation:

$$\begin{pmatrix} x' \\ y' \end{pmatrix} = \frac{\begin{pmatrix} \frac{x-c_x}{f} x_h + \frac{y-c_y}{f} y_h + z_h \\ \frac{x-c_x}{f} x_v + \frac{y-c_y}{f} y_v + z_v \end{pmatrix} * f}{\det \begin{pmatrix} x_h & y_h & z_h \\ x_v & y_v & z_v \\ \frac{x-c_x}{f} & \frac{y-c_y}{f} & 1 \end{pmatrix}} + \begin{pmatrix} c_x \\ c_y \end{pmatrix}$$

Here, point (x, y) in the image is transformed to (x', y'). This equation virtually rotates the camera in the 3D space so that the coordinate systems x-y-plane is parallel with the device's boundary. As discussed in Section 4, the translation parameters are calculated using a Hough transform using the weighted line voting. Considering the parameters acquired by the line matching (translations t_x, t_y and scaling s_x, s_y in x-direction and y-direction respectively), the transformation performing translation and scale alignment is given as: $(x'', y'')^T = (s_x x' + t_x, s_y y' + t_y)^T$. This maps the previous transformation result (x', y') to the point (x'', y''). In this way, we successfully transform the device screen's image into the template's coordinate system.

The Robustness of Hollow CAPTCHAs

Haichang Gao, Wei Wang, Jiao Qi,
Xuqin Wang, Xiyang Liu
Institute of Software Engineering
Xidian University, Xi'an, Shaanxi
710071, P.R.China
hchgao@xidian.edu.cn

Jeff Yan
School of Computing Science
Newcastle University, UK
Jeff.Yan@ncl.ac.uk

ABSTRACT

CAPTCHA is now a standard security technology for differentiating between computers and humans, and the most widely deployed schemes are text-based. While many text schemes have been broken, hollow CAPTCHAs have emerged as one of the latest designs, and they have been deployed by major companies such as Yahoo!, Tencent, Sina, China Mobile and Baidu. A main feature of such schemes is to use contour lines to form connected hollow characters with the aim of improving security and usability simultaneously, as it is hard for standard techniques to segment and recognize such connected characters, which are however easy to human eyes. In this paper, we provide the first analysis of hollow CAPTCHAs' robustness. We show that with a simple but novel attack, we can successfully break a whole family of hollow CAPTCHAs, including those deployed by all the major companies. While our attack casts serious doubt on the viability of current designs, we offer lessons and guidelines for designing better hollow CAPTCHAs.

Categories and Subject Descriptors

K.6.5 [**Management of Computing and Information Systems**]: Security and Protection—*authentication, unauthorized access*

General Terms

Security, Human Factors.

Keywords

CAPTCHA; Convolutional Neural Network; Graph search; Security

1. INTRODUCTION

Since its invention, CAPTCHA has been widely deployed for defending against undesirable and malicious bot programs on the Internet [20]. The most widely used CAPTCHAs are text-based schemes [24], which typically require users to solve a text recognition task.

A good CAPTCHA should be friendly for humans to solve but hard for computers. It turns out that this balance between security and usability is hard to achieve. So far, many text CAPTCHAs have been broken, including those deployed by major companies such as Microsoft, Yahoo! and Google [8, 23]. However, as predicted in [23], CAPTCHAs are going through the same process of evolutionary development, just like cryptography and digital watermarking, with an iterative process in which successful attacks lead to the development of a next generation of systems.

In the last couple of years, Hollow CAPTCHAs have emerged as one of the latest text-based designs. They have been deployed by major websites such as Yahoo!, Baidu, Sina, Tencent and the online payment system (CmPay) of China Mobile, each serving tens of millions users on a daily basis. A main feature of such hollow CAPTCHAs is to use contour lines to form connected characters (see Figure 1) with the aim of improving security and usability simultaneously, as it is hard for state-of-the-art character recognition programs to segment and recognize such connected characters, which are however easy to human eyes.

(a) Yahoo! (b) Tencent (c) Sina (d) CmPay (e) Baidu

Figure 1: Hollow CAPTCHAs.

Given the high profiles of the companies that have deployed hollow CAPTCHAs, it is of practical relevance to examine the robustness of such hollow schemes, i.e. their resistance to automated attacks, which is an important se-

CCS'13, November 04 - 08, 2013, Berlin, Germany.
Copyright 2013 ACM 978-1-4503-2477-9/13/11 ...$15.00.
http://dx.doi.org/10.1145/2508859.2516732 .

curity property. On the other hand, as Hollow CAPTCHAs represent a new type of text scheme, it is also of academic interest to study their design and security. To our best knowledge, no such studies are available in the literature.

In this paper, we provide the first analysis of the robustness of hollow CAPTCHAs. We show that with a novel and generic attack, we can successfully break a whole family of hollow CAPTCHAs. The success rates of our attack on Yahoo!, Tencent, Sina, CmPay and Baidu schemes are 36%, 89%, 59%, 66% and 51%, respectively. It takes just seconds for our attack to break each of the schemes on a standard desktop computer. Therefore, our attack imposes a realistic threat, which might be misused by adversaries.

As a variety of design features are used in the hollow schemes, we also pinpoint which features contribute to security, and which do not. Our analysis provides a set of guidelines for designing hollow CAPTCHAs, and a method from comparing security of different schemes. We also discuss how to design better hollow CAPTCHAs.

This paper is organized as follows. Section 2 discusses related work. Section 3 provides an overview of five representative hollow CAPTCHAs. Section 4 gives an overview of our attack, and Section 5 describes the attack in details. Section 6 shows our attack results. Section 7 discusses lessons we have learnt, and how to design better hollow CAPTCHAs. Section 8 concludes the paper.

2. RELATED WORK

Moni Naor [15] first discussed the notion of Automated Turing Tests, but did not providing a formal definition or concrete designs. The first practical Automated Turing Test was developed by Alta Vista [12] to prevent bots from automatically registering web pages. This system was effective for a while but then was defeated by common OCR (Optical Character Recognition) technology.

In 2003, Mori and Malik [13] used sophisticated object recognition algorithms to break Gimpy (which used clutter interference) and EZ-Gimpy (which used texture backgrounds), achieving a success rate of 33% and 92%. Moy et al [14] developed distortion estimation techniques to attack EZ-Gimpy with a success rate of 99% and four-letter Gimpy-r with a success rate of 78%. In 2005, Chellapilla et al [19] successfully broke a range of CAPTCHAs with a success rate ranging from 4.89% to 66.2%. Early attack efforts also include the PWNtcha project [3].

In 2006, Yan and El Ahmad [22] broke most visual schemes provided at Captchaservice.org, a publicly available web service for CAPTCHA generation, with a success rate of nearly 100% by simply counting the number of pixels of each segmented character, although these schemes were all resistant to the best OCR software on the market. New character segmentation techniques for attacking a number of text-based CAPTCHAs were developed by Yan and El Ahmad [23] in 2008, including the earlier mechanisms designed and deployed by Microsoft, Yahoo! and Google, and these have achieved a segmentation success rate of 92% against Microsoft CAPTCHA. In 2010, Yan's team broke the text-based CAPTCHAs that depend partially on the Gestalt Perception principle by merging black and shared white components to form individual characters [9].

In 2011, Bursztein et al. showed that 13 CAPTCHAs on popular websites were vulnerable to automated attacks [7], but they achieved zero success on harder schemes such as reCAPTCHA and Google's own scheme. In the same year, Yan's team published an effective attack on both of these schemes [8]. The CAPTCHA using moving-images in NuCaptcha which provided users with sloshing characters was analyzed by Xu et al in 2012 [21]. Table 1 lists some text CAPTCHAs that were successfully attacked.

We note that hollow CAPTCHAs have never been discussed in the literature prior to our current paper, and that they are distinct from other text-based CAPTCHAs discussed to date.

3. HOLLOW CAPTCHAS: POPULAR REAL WORLD SCHEMES

We choose to study 5 CAPTCHAs listed in Figure 1, which we consider represent the state of the art of hollow CAPTCHA designs, for two main reasons.

First, these schemes have been deployed by popular real world websites, and have an impact on hundreds of millions of users. For example, Yahoo!, Baidu, Sina and Tencent are all among the largest websites in the world; CmPay [2] is the online payment system of China Mobile, which enjoys a 70% share of the domestic mobile service market in China and has nearly 700 million users. Yahoo! use their hollow CAPTCHA in services such as their email system and password helper [6]. Sina use their scheme for services such as Weibo [4], the most popular micro blog platform in China with about 500 million users (also a Chinese equivalent to Twitter). The Baidu scheme is used for their account registration and maintenance [1]. With 600+ million users, Baidu is the largest search engine in China and one of the largest social network platforms. The Tencent scheme is used in their security center service [5].

Second, these schemes represent a range of different designs, with a variety of design features. For example, some schemes use interference arcs (e.g. CmPay and Baidu); others do not (e.g. Yahoo!, Tencent and Sina). Yahoo! uses character strings of a varied length, while others all use a fixed string length. Some schemes (e.g. Yahoo!) intentionally introduce a significant variation in the thickness of hollow portions across characters, and even in a single character; others do not vary this thickness much and it is more or less uniform.

A common feature is that all characters are presented as hollow objects. In general, hollow schemes appear to be a clever idea. First proposed by Google, Crowding Characters Together (CCT) has been widely adopted. This standard security mechanism for text CAPTCHAs improves security but has usability issues. For example, when characters are crowded together too much, confusing character pairs will appear and it is hard for people to recognize them [24]. However, hollow schemes allow characters connected or overlapped with each other, but maintain a reasonable usability. In a sense, this approach can be regarded as a clever variant of the CCT segmentation-resistant mechanism.

Since there are only (or mainly) randomly-generated contours in each CAPTCHA, it becomes difficult to detect each character's features using standard technologies. Common character recognition methods, such as template matching and other feature-based algorithms, that are effective in recognizing solid characters, are inapplicable to hollow characters. Moreover, characters' contour lines may connect or overlap with each other to prevent segmentation. When

Table 1: CAPTCHAs which have been attacked successfully

Origin	Samples	Success rate	Comments
Captchaservice.org [22]		92%	Weaknesses: constant pixel count of the same character, non-textured background, constant colors, no perturbation, only capital characters used
Clubic [3]	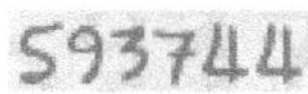	100%	Weaknesses: constant font, no rotation, no deformation, aligned glyph, constant background, weak color variation, weak perturbation
Slashdot [3]	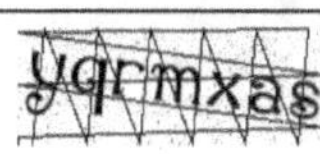	89%	Weaknesses: constant font, no deformation, constant colors, weak perturbation, weak color variation
Microsoft [23]		60%	Weaknesses: easy to tell random arcs from valid characters by examining characteristics, easy to locate connected characters by 'even cut'
Google [8]		62%	Weaknesses: non-textured background, constant colors, no perturbation
NuCaptcha [21]		36.3%	Weaknesses: weak overlapping, constant color of 'codewords', short length of 'codewords', constant font
Megaupload [9]		78.3%	Weaknesses: shared components are white, non-textured background,constant font, short and fixed length, no perturbation

there are interference arcs, contour lines will be cut through or otherwise interrupted. Presumably, this will make it even harder for computers to recognize hollow characters.

We also note that two main segmentation-resistant mechanisms, namely CCT and interference arcs, have never been used simultaneously in a single CAPTCHA design before. However, some hollow CAPTCHAs apply the two mechanisms together, without introducing serious usability concerns in our experience.

4. OUR ATTACK: AN OVERVIEW

The key insight behind our attack is the following. We can manage to extract from hollow CAPTCHAs character strokes or components, and convert them to solid ones. This is not straightforward, as some contour lines are broken; we need to automatically repair them first. Furthermore, standard methods like Color Filling Segmentation (CFS, introduced in [23]) will pick up not just character strokes or components, but also those that do not belong to any character and which we call noise components. Therefore, it is essential to differentiate between legitimate character strokes and noise components automatically.

On the other hand, character strokes extracted this way are not linked with each other. Instead, they are scattered around. We implement a convolutional neural network (CNN) [11, 16, 18] as our recognition engine. CNN provides partial invariance to translation, rotation, scale and deformation. It extracts successively larger features in a hierarchical set of layers. Besides, as a stable and fast classifier, CNN has been successfully applied to character recognition; it takes only milliseconds to classify a character image.

Next, just like piecing together a jigsaw puzzle, we use our CNN recognition engine to try different combinations of adjacent strokes. With a graph search algorithm that we have designed, we can find the most likely combination as the right result with a good success rate.

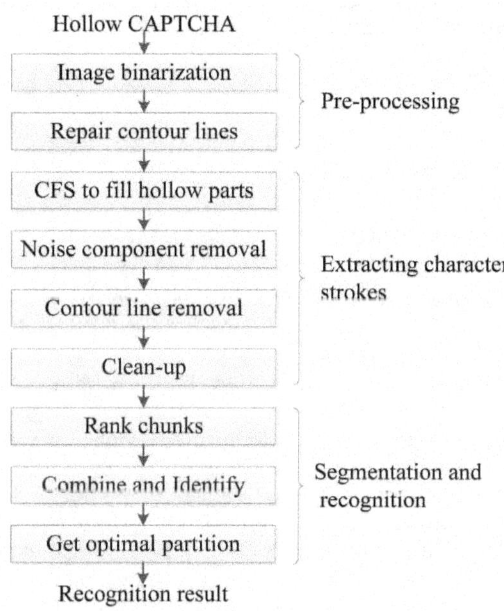

Figure 2: The pipeline of our attack.

The high-level flow of our attack, shown in Figure 2, includes three main sequential steps: 1) pre-processing prepares each challenge image with standard techniques; 2) extracting character strokes; 3) segmentation and recognition with the CNN engine assisted graph search.

5. OUR ATTACK: TECHNICAL DETAILS

We choose Yahoo! and CmPay as examples to explain key techniques in our general attack. Note that these techniques are generically applicable to all the schemes, as evi-

(a) (b)

Figure 3: Binarized images. (a)Yahoo!, (b)CmPay.

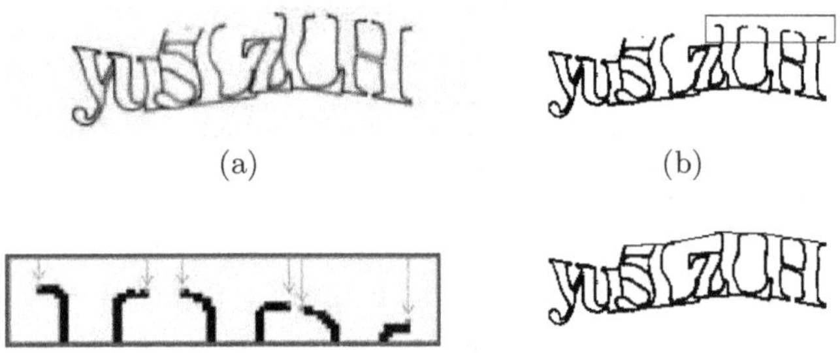

(a) (b) (c) (d)

Figure 4: Repair contour lines. (a)The original image, (b)A blue rectangle indicates some identified break points, (c)The amplified blue rectangle where break points are highlighted in red, (d)The image with breakpoints connected.

denced later by our implementation and evaluation (details see Section 6).

5.1 Pre-processing

Image binarization. This is to covert a color or grayscale image into black-and-white one. We use the standard Otsu's threshold method [17]. Figure 3 shows the binarized images.

In the cases of CmPay and Baidu, binarization does not just convert an image into black-and-white, but also removes thin interference arcs whose colors differ significantly from both hollow characters and thick arcs.

Repair contour lines. Some challenges use hollow characters whose contour lines are broken (e.g. Figure 4 (a)), for which CFS will fail filling the hollow parts. In the case of CmPay, binarization created broken contours, too (see Figure 3 (b)). In order to make CFS work, these broken contour lines must be repaired. We use Lee's algorithm [10] to automatically detect and then repair broken contours. This algorithm was initially designed for solving maze routing problems.

First, we identify break points in contour lines. Similar to the maze solving problem, a contour is regarded as the corridor, and break points as dead-ends in the maze. We use Lee's algorithm to traverse the contour line, and mark the dead-end pixel of each path in red (e.g. Figure 4 (c)). Then, we examine the relative positions of each pair of break points, and draw a one-pixel-thick line to connect those pairs that look valid (see Figure 4 (d)).

Incorrect connections may be created e.g. Figures 4(d) and 5, but our attack can cope with them, as explained later.

Figure 5: Contour repair: another example

(a) (b)

Figure 6: Images after CFS: (a)Yahoo!, (b)CmPay

5.2 Extracting Character Strokes

Fill hollow parts with CFS. This uses a flooding algorithm to detect connected non-black pixel blocks. It will pick up both character components and noise ones, if they have closed contours. We use a distinct color to fill, and thus identify, each component. After this step, the background color in an image is set to lightgray, but contour lines and other solid parts such as thick interference arcs remain in black. Figure 6 shows the images after CFS.

Noise component removal. As illustrated in Figure 7, there are at least three types of undesirable components (or chunks) which we consider as noise: 1) the closed part within a character, 2) those formed by two connected characters, and 3) those formed by wrong connections introduced by the contour repair algorithm.

We first define parameters θ and δ for each color component: $\theta = C_g/C$ and $\delta = C/S$, where C_g denotes the number of edge pixels that have a lightgray neighbor, C denotes the total number of edge pixels in this component, and S denotes the total number of pixels in this component.

With properly chosen threshold values a and b, we have the following: if $\theta < a$ for a component, it is a noise component of the first two types; if $\delta < b$, it is a noise component of the third type. We determine the values a and b via a learning algorithm that analyzes a small sample set of data.

In schemes like CmPay, an additional type of noise components was introduced by thick interference arcs. However, they are easy to remove by detecting such arcs' existence.

We have tested our noise component removal on all the 5 hollow schemes, and it works on all of them. Components surviving our noise removal are considered to belong to character bodies, and are thus preserved (see Figure 8).

Contour line removal. Removing contour lines is straightforward for CmPay, but requires more subtle techniques for the Yahoo! scheme. We have implemented both the straightforward and the more subtle approaches. Which ap-

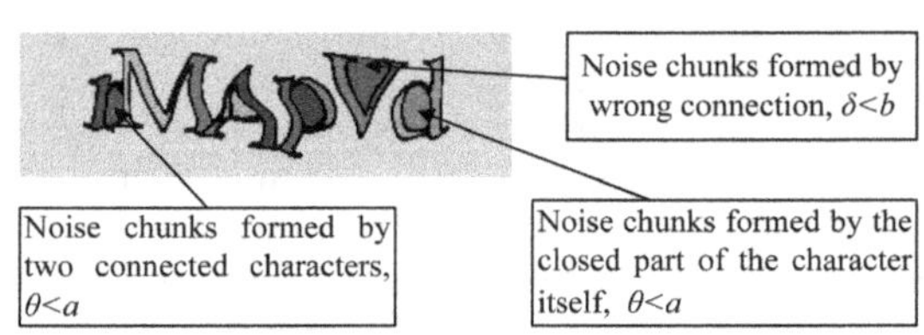

Figure 7: Three types of noise components.

(a) (b)

Figure 8: After removing noise components. (a)Yahoo!, (b)CmPay.

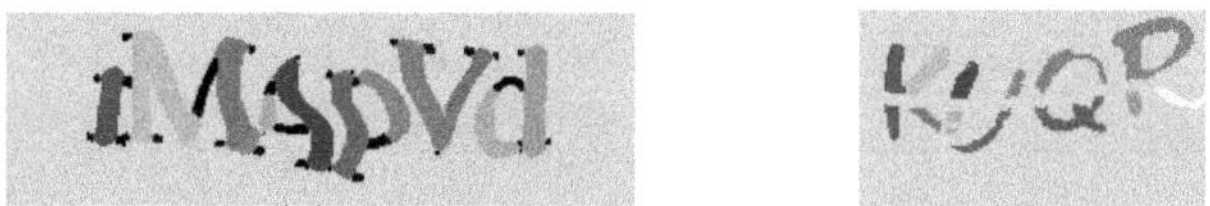

(a) (b)

Figure 9: After contour line removal. (a)Yahoo!, (b)CmPay.

proach is needed for handling a particular Cpatcha scheme can be automatically determined.

After removing the noise components in the CmPay scheme, black pixels are the interference arcs and contour lines, and all character strokes are in non-black colors. So it is straightforward to remove both contour lines and the interference arcs by switching all black pixels to the background color.

In the Yahoo! scheme, after removing noise components, black pixels in an image are character contours, incorrect connecting lines introduced by our contour repair algorithm, or a character stroke. We need to remove the first two types of black pixels, but keep the third. The second type is always of one-pixel thickness, and easy to remove first. Then we perform an image dilation on each stroke filled with a non-black color. The stroke is dilated to cover its surrounding contour line. That is, the dilation algorithm switches the contour line to the color of the stroke body to merge them. After this step, all remaining large blocks of black pixels have to be character strokes. Figure 9 shows images after contour removal.

Clean-up. Tiny pixel blocks might be created by contour line removal. In clean-up, they are either removed directly or merged with adjacent larger strokes via an automated algorithm. Figure 10 shows the resulting images. After this step, what remain in an image are all character strokes or components.

5.3 Segmentation and Recognition

The next step is to find how to form strokes into individual characters and recognize what the characters are. Now the problem is similar to a jigsaw puzzle in that each stroke is a piece of a master design. However, there is no fixed pattern for us to exploit for finding the right combination. The number of strokes is always larger than the number of characters to be formed, and the latter is a variable in schemes

(a) (b)

Figure 10: After clean-up. (a)Yahoo!, (b)CmPay.

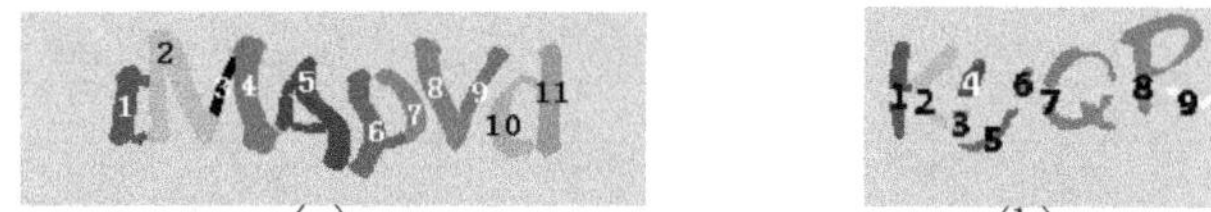

(a) (b)

Figure 11: What remains are all character strokes, rank ordered. (a)Yahoo!, (b)CmPay.

such as Yahoo!; so there can be many possible combinations. Our approach is to combine adjacent strokes into possible characters and determine the most likely result.

First, all strokes in an image are numbered in an incremental order from the upper left to lower right (Figure 11).

Then we try to combine strokes or components following the incremental rank order. An $n \times n$ table is built for each image, where n is the total number of strokes in the image. A cell at the intersection of row i and column k in the table indicates whether it is feasible to combine strokes i, $i+1$, ..., k altogether to form a single component.

If such a combination is infeasible, the cell (i, k) will be set to NULL. This occurs in one of the following three scenarios: (1) when its row index i is larger than its column index k (we try combinations only in a monotonic order); (2) when the width of the combination is greater than the largest possible character width, which is empirically established with a simple analysis of the sample set of data; (3) when the width of the combination is less than the smallest possible character width, which is also empirically established with a simple analysis of the sample set.

If it is feasible to combine strokes i, $i+1$, ..., k to form a single component, we let the CNN decide which character this component is likely to be, and the cell (i, k) stores the neural network's recognition result, along with a confidence level the CNN feels about this result. This feasibility condition is met in all situations except the above three.

In our implementation, an image input to the CNN is normalized to the size of 28 × 28; the output confidence level is calculated after layer-by-layer forward propagation. Since the activation function used is a scaled version of the hyperbolic tangent [11], scaling causes the confidence level to vary between -1.7159 and 1.7159. The larger a confidence value is, the more likely the recognition result is correct.

Tables 2 and 3 show a $n \times n$ table for the Yahoo! sample and the CmPay sample, respectively. For example, in table 2, the cell (1, 1) indicates that the CNN recognize this single stroke as 'r' with a confidence level of .479; the cell (1, 3) indicates that the combination of strokes 1, 2 and 3 is recognized as 'M' with a confidence level of .432. Each empty cell (i, k) indicates that a combination of strokes i, $i+1$, ..., k is infeasible for one reason or another.

A $n \times n$ table gives all plausible stroke combinations for an image. Our task now is to use information in the table to find the most likely way of forming characters, i.e., finding the best segmentation or partition.

Each $n \times n$ table is actually equivalent to a directed and weighted graph. Figure 12 gives such graphs that are equivalent to Tables 2 and 3, respectively. In each graph, the nodes are numbered from 1 to $n+1$, and nodes 1, 2, ... n represent the corresponding strokes, respectively. An arc $< i, j >$ (i.e. a directed edge linking vertexes i and j) indicates that the combination of strokes from i to $j-1$ is feasible, and

Table 2: The $n \times n$ table generated by CNN for the Yahoo! sample in Figure 11.

	1	2	3	4	5	6	7	8	9	10	11
1	*r/0.479*	A/-0.157	M/0.432								
2		A/-0.027	M/-0.358	*M/1.025*							
3				T/0.01	W/-0.43						
4				L/0.255	W/0.216						
5					*A/0.482*	V/-0.2	V/-0.242				
6						V/0.238	*p/1.087*	A/-0.384			
7							y/-0.151	w/-0.462	V/-0.127		
8								V/0.358	*V/1.11*	H/-0.088	w/0.238
9									r/-0.035	6/-0.519	M/-0.255
10										c/0.554	*d/1.075*
11											

Table 3: The $n \times n$ table generated by CNN for the CmPay sample in Figure 11

	1	2	3	4	5	6	7	8	9
1		*K/0.935*	K/0.781	H/-0.229					
2		K/0.647	4/0.493	4/-0.445					
3					6/0.593	*U/0.692*			
4					6/0.06	U/0.688			
5					J/0.093	U/-0.332			
6									
7							*Q/1.102*		
8								R/0.229	*R/1.057*
9									S/1

the associated weight gives both the recognition result of this combination and the confidence level calculated by the neural network for this result. That is, the number of arcs in a graph equals to the number of non-empty cells in its corresponding table.

Now, our task of finding the best segmentation and thus the most likely recognition result is equivalent to the following graph search problem:

- Find a path that starts from node 1 and ends at node $n+1$, and in which each node is traversed only once, and a node always has a larger index number than all its predecessor(s).

- The path's length (i.e. the number of edges on the path) is exactly the same as the number of characters that are supposed to be in a CAPTCHA image.

  Note: the rationales are the following: *all* the strokes in an image will be used to form individual characters, but each stroke will be used only once and no stroke is shared in adjacent characters.

- The sum of confidence levels along the path is the largest possible in the graph.

We use a depth-first-search (DFS) algorithm to select the optimal partition which has the highest confidence sum. It is simple for our algorithm to cope with schemes like Yahoo!, where a varied string length is used.

For convenience, we utilize the $n \times n$ tables to implement the graph search algorithm. The search always starts from the first row in table, and progresses from the smallest index number to the largest in an incremental order.

The pseudo code below sketches the recognition process. $S_{i,j}$ denotes the resulting character which the CNN recognizes as the component combined from strokes $i, i+1, ..., j$; $a_{i,j}$ is the confidence level calculated by the CNN for this result; *step* represents the number of characters that has been recognized; *sum* represents the confidence value sum of strokes 1 to j, and S represents the recognition result of combined strokes numbered from 1 to j.

As generated by our attack program, tables 4 and 5 show all likely partitions and for each partition, its sum of confidence levels. The italicized items highlighted in red in each table indicate the optimal partition that has the highest sum of confidence levels and that matches a legitimate length of CAPTCHA strings. In both cases, 'rMApVd' and 'KUQR' are correct recognition results.

We note that simply choosing the cells with a relatively large confidence level does not work (well). The reason is that this greedy strategy skips many possible combinations, and thus the recognition success will be low. In comparison, our algorithm performs a thorough search of each graph, and will not miss any possible results. In Table 2, the confidence levels in the cells (1, 1) and (5, 5), both of which are on the optimal path, are actually smaller than that in the cell (10, 10), which is however not on the optimal path.

The sum value p of the selected partition is described as follows: $p = max\,(a_{1,i} + a_{i+1,j} + \cdots + a_{m+1,k} + a_{k+1,n})$, where $0 < i < j < m < k < n$, and we assume that the optimal partition consists of strokes numbered from 1 to i, then strokes i+1 to j, ..., m+1 to k, and finally strokes k+1 to n. The number of polynomial terms in the equation equals the string length in the CAPTCHA.

Table 4: Every likely result and its confidence sum for the Yahoo! Sample in Figure 11

Result	Confidence	Result	Confidence	Result	Confidence	Result	Confidence	Result	Confidence
rATAVyVM	1.135	rATAVyVd	3.216	rATAVyw	1.27	rATAVwrd	1.76	rATAVwM	0.465
rATAVVd	2.131	rATApVrd	3.431	rATApVM	2.136	rATApVd	4.218	rATApw	2.271
rATAArd	1.6	rATAAM	0.305	rATVyVrd	1.508	rATVyVM	0.213	rATVyVd	2.295
rATVyw	0.348	rATVwrd	0.838	rATVwM	-0.456	rATVVd	1.209	rATVVrd	1.618
rATVVM	0.323	rATVVd	2.405	rAVVyVrd	1.506	rAVVyVM	0.211	rAVVyVd	2.293
rAVVyw	0.346	rAVVwrd	0.836	rAVVwM	-0.458	rAVVVd	1.207	rAVpVrd	2.507
rAVpVM	1.212	rAVpVd	3.294	rAVArd	0.676	rMLAVyVM	1.056	rMLAVyVd	3.138
rMLAVyw	1.191	rMLAVwrd	1.681	rMLAVwM	0.386	rMLAVVd	2.052	rMLApVrd	3.352
rMLApVM	2.057	rMLApVd	4.139	rMLApw	2.192	rMLAArd	1.521	rMLAAM	0.226
rMLVyVrd	1.43	rMLVyVM	0.135	rMLVyVd	2.217	rMLVyw	0.27	rMLVwrd	0.76
rMLVwM	-0.534	rMLVVd	1.131	rMLVVrd	1.54	rMLVVM	0.245	rMLVVd	2.327
rMwVyVrd	1.349	rMwVyVM	0.053	rMwVyVd	2.135	rMwVyw	0.188	rMwVwrd	0.679
rMwVwM	-0.616	rMwVVd	1.05	rMwpVrd	2.35	rMwpVM	1.055	rMwpVd	3.136
rMwArd	0.519	rMAVyVrd	3.472	rMAVyVM	2.177	rMAVyVd	4.259	rMAVyw	2.312
rMAVwrd	2.802	rMAVwM	1.507	rMAVVd	3.173	rMApVrd	4.473	rMApVM	3.178
rMApVd	***5.26***	rMAArd	2.642	rMVyVrd	2.551	rMVyVM	1.255	rMVyVd	3.337
rMVwrd	1.881	rMVVrd	2.661	ATAVyVrd	1.821	ATAVyVM	0.526	ATAVyVd	2.608
ATAVyw	0.661	ATAVwrd	1.151	ATAVwM	-0.143	ATAVVd	1.522	ATApVrd	2.822
ATApVM	1.527	ATApVd	3.609	ATAArd	0.991	ATVyVrd	0.9	ATVyVM	-0.394
ATVyVd	1.686	ATVwrd	0.23	ATVVrd	1.01	AVVyVrd	0.897	AVVyVM	-0.397
AVVyVd	1.684	AVVwrd	0.227	AVpVrd	1.899	MLAVyVrd	2.663	MLAVyVM	1.367
MLAVyVd	3.449	MLAVyw	1.502	MLAVwrd	1.993	MLAVwM	0.698	MLAVVd	2.364
MLApVrd	3.664	MLApVM	2.369	MLApVd	4.45	MLAArd	1.833	MLVyVrd	1.741
MLVyVM	0.446	MLVyVd	2.528	MLVwrd	1.071	MLVVrd	1.851	MwVyVrd	1.66
MwVyVM	0.365	MwVyVd	2.447	MwVwrd	0.99	MwpVrd	2.661		

Table 5: Every likely result and its confidence sum for the CmPay sample in Figure 11

Result	Confidence	Result	Confidence	Result	Confidence
KUQR	***3.786***	KUQR	3.632	HUQR	1.598

```
DepthFirstSearch()
i ← 1
step ← 0
p ← 0
sum ← 0
R ← NIL
S ← NIL
Traverse(i, step, sum, S)
print R
```

```
Traverse(i, step, sum, S)
for j ← i to n
if a_{i,j} ≠ NULL
   then sum ← sum + a_{i,j}
        S ← strcat(S, S_{i,j})
        step ← step + 1
   else continue
        if step ∈ CAPTCHA length and p < sum
           then p ← sum
                R ← S
                if step ≤ max CAPTCHA length
                   then Traverse(j + 1, step, sum, S)
```

Table 6: The success rate and speed of our attack

Scheme	Success on sample set	Success on test set (T)	Avg time per challenge (R)	Avg time per success (T/R)
Yahoo!	56%	36%	5.30 seconds	14.72 seconds
Tencent	93%	89%	1.23 seconds	1.38 seconds
Sina	63%	59%	1.77 seconds	3.00 seconds
CmPay	73%	66%	4.25 seconds	6.43 seconds
Baidu	57%	51%	3.87 seconds	7.58 seconds

6. EVALUATIONS

We have implemented our attack and tested it on all the 5 hollow schemes. We present our evaluations as follows.

Data Collection. For each of the 5 schemes, we collected from the corresponding website 1000 random CAPTCHAs as a sample set, and another 500 as a test set. For schemes like Yahoo!, Tencent and CmPay, the data were collected in August 2012; for schemes such as Sina and Baidu, the data were collected in April 2013.

Training Neural Network. The template library for training our convolutional neural network was prepared manually. We extracted 4244 characters from Yahoo! samples, 3754 characters from Tencent samples, 2680 characters from Sina samples, 3670 characters from CmPay samples, and 2940 characters from Baidu samples, to train the CNN.

Success Rate. We follow a common practice to evaluate our attack's success. For the Yahoo! scheme, we achieved a success rate of 56% on the sample set. That is, 56% of the challenges were entirely guessed correctly. Then we ran our attack on the test set, about which our program had

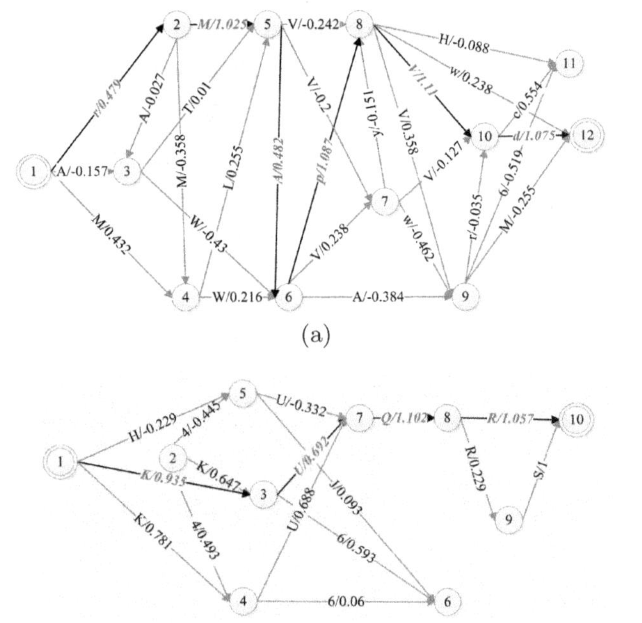

Figure 12: The equivalent graphs of Tables 2 and 3.

no prior knowledge about any particular sample within; we achieved a success rate of 36%.

Similarly, we ran our attack on all other schemes. The success rates are listed in Table 6. For the Tencent scheme, we achieved 93% success on the sample set and 89% on the test set. For Sina, we achieved 63% success on the sample set and 59% on the test set. For CmPay, our success was 73% on the sample set and 66% on the test set. For Baidu, our success was 57% on the sample set and 51% on the test set.

A commonly accepted goal for CAPTCHA robustness is to prevent automated attacks from achieving a success rate of higher than 0.01% [23]. Bursztein et al [7] considered this goal too ambitious, and they suggested that a CAPTCHA scheme is broken when the attacker achieves an accuracy rate of at least 1%. According to either criterion, all the five hollow schemes are successfully and terribly broken by our attack.

In reality, an attacker could achieve a success rate even higher than reported here, as he could simply skip a challenge if the confidence level for recognizing it is not large enough. Instead, he could keep requesting new challenges, and only when he is confident enough with a recognition result, he submits the answer to the CAPTCHA.

Attack Speed. We implemented our attack in C#, and tested it on a desktop computer with a 2.53 GHz Intel Core 2 CPU and 4 GB RAM. The attack was run ten times on each data set, and the average speed was recorded. Table 6 summarizes the speed of our attack on each scheme. On average, it takes only seconds to attack a CAPTCHA in any of these schemes. Besides, We also estimate an average time for successfully breaking a CAPTCHA in each scheme: on average, it takes 3 – 15 seconds. Clearly, our attack is efficient and poses a realistic threat to all the hollow schemes.

Other Classifiers. We also tested other classifiers such as Support Vector Machine, Back-Propagation Neural Network and template matching. The CNN engine has achieved the best overall performance for both attack speed and success rate.

Our DFS algorithm is not optimal. We did not optimize this algorithm for a simple reason: we measured the time consumption for each step in our attack. It turns out that 'contour line removal' and 'clean-up' take about 58% of the time of the whole attack, but 'segmentation and recognition' takes only about 13%.

7. DISCUSSIONS

7.1 Novelty

To our best knowledge, this is the first security analysis on the state of the art of hollow CAPTCHAs. We used some standard techniques in pre-processing, and also used CFS, which has been a standard method for analyzing text CAPTCHA robustness since its introduction in [23]. However, the key component of our attack, the graph search algorithm based segmentation and recognition, is absolutely novel. Overall, the combination of these and other techniques has led to a novel attack.

State of the art attacks on the CCT based CAPTCHAs, such as [7] and [8], do not work on the hollow CAPTCHAs studied in this paper.

Among all the related work we have discussed earlier, the attack reported in [9] on a MegaUpload CAPTCHA is the only one that has a slight similarity to our attack. However, that attack was designed for a single CAPTCHA; it is ad hoc and not applicable to attacking hollow CAPTCHAs. Moreover, that attack focused on segmentation, and did not involve character recognition at all.

7.2 Generic Value

Our attack is applicable to a variety of hollow CAPTCHAs. It works on schemes with thin contours (e.g. Yahoo!) and on schemes with thick contours (e.g. Tencent); on schemes with interference arcs (e.g CmPay) and on schemes without such arcs (e.g. Yahoo!); on schemes with a fixed length (e.g. Sina) and on schemes with a varied length (e.g. Yahoo!). Table 7 summarizes the main features of these schemes. As they represent different designs, each with distinctive features, our attack is of some generic value.

7.3 Lessons

Our attack helps to identify which design features contribute to a hollow CAPTCHA's security, and which do not. Design features that *do* help security include the following.

Overlapped or connected characters are still the most crucial security feature, as by design it provides (some) segmentation resistance. It significantly contributes to the security of all the 5 schemes.

String length matters. This was first observed in [23] and then confirmed in [7]. First, it is good to use a relatively large length. The more characters used in a CAPTCHA image, the more components remain after preprocessing, and the larger the solution space will be. This will decrease an attack's success and speed. The more characters used, the harder for brute-force guessing, too. Second, it is good to use a varied length, which does not give away useful information to aid attackers. Attackers have to try multiple

Table 7: Main features of five hollow CAPTCHAs

Scheme	Interference Arcs	Broken Contour Line	Contour Line Thickness	Hollow Styles	String Length	Character Overlap	Alphabet Size
Yahoo!	No	Sometimes	Uniform	Varied	Varied (6-8)	Yes	28
Tencent	No	No	Varied	Uniform	Fixed (4)	Yes	25
Sina	No	No	Varied	Uniform	Fixed (4)	Yes	28
CmPay	Yes	After binarization	Varied	Uniform	Fixed (4)	Yes	30
Baidu	Yes	No	Varied	Uniform	Fixed (4)	Yes	51

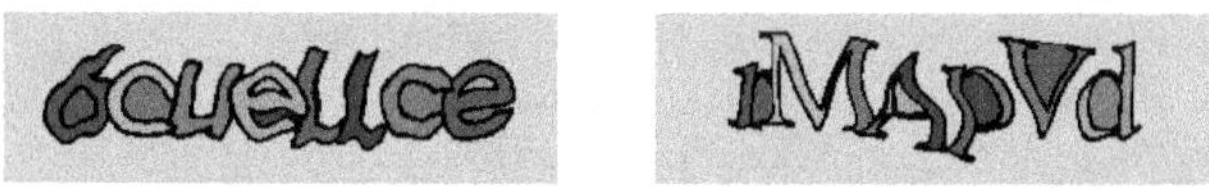

(a) (b)

Figure 13: Yahoo!'s hollow styles: (a)thick strokes vs. (b)thin strokes (both after CFS).

possible lengths, which increases the search space for our graph algorithm, and could decrease its success and speed.

Broken contours considerably increase the difficulty level of designing and implementing an effective attack. In particular, they disable the otherwise powerful CFS. Broken contours introduced by design or after binarization are both good for security, but the former wins our recommendation as it is probably easier to control by a CAPTCHA generator.

Thick interference arcs cut across characters, not just dividing characters to fragments but also introducing noise components. This considerably increases the difficulty level of designing and implementing an effective attack.

Hollow styles. Varying thickness of hollow portions is an important style feature that contributes to security. Some hollow portions in the Yahoo! scheme were so thin that their contour lines were squashed together, which prevents the portions from being picked up by CFS. This not only increases the number of strokes in an image, but also makes it a challenge to cope with those squashed strokes.

In the Yahoo! scheme, another variation in hollow styles is heavily used. Namely, two font types are used, creating two styles: one we call the 'thick strokes', and the other the 'thin strokes' (see Figure 13). Until now, what is explicitly discussed in this paper is the 'thin strokes'. In the 'thick strokes', character strokes can be completely picked up by CFS, leading to not just fewer components than in the 'thin strokes', but also a simplified treatment by the follow-up attack procedures. That is, 'thick strokes' is a weaker design than 'thin strokes' in terms of security. Note that our attack is applicable to both types, and our program automatically handles both the types.

Having multiple designs and deploying them alternately in a random order is good for security, as first suggested in [26] and then confirmed in [7]. However, randomly alternating two hollow styles in the Yahoo! scheme is probably only marginally useful for improving security, as the alternatives are not equally strong.

Varying width of individual characters is a design feature that is somehow related to hollow styles but beyond that. It contributes to security for the following reasons. The larger the width difference between the thinnest character and the fattest one, the larger a search space faces our graph search algorithm, and the more likely it will give inaccurate results.

Design features that *do not* help security include:

Complete contours, which help CFS to pick up character strokes.

Contour thickness. Thinning [25] contour lines to a uniform thickness is useful for our attack, but not essential. Therefore, we do not consider variations in contour thickness contributes much to security.

Thin interference arcs, which are easily removed by binarization.

Fixed string length, which gives away useful information to aid segmentation.

Short string length, which reduces an attack's search space and increase its chance of success.

This set of 'Does' and 'Don'ts' constitutes a set of design guidelines for the security of hollow CAPTCHAs. It also provides a method for comparing different designs, as well as explaining and pinpointing why one scheme is better than the other in terms of security.

For example, although broken, the Yahoo! scheme is apparently the best among all the 5 schemes, and the following features contribute to its unique strength: 1) Using a relatively large string length, and the length is not fixed. 2) Variations in hollow portions' thickness. 3) Variations in the width of individual characters width.

The second best is Baidu. Its unique strength lies in its large alphabet set, which have 58 characters including digits and upper- and lower-case letters. This is the largest alphabet set among the five schemes. It significantly increases the solution space for individual characters, and makes it harder for the CNN engine to accurately recognize the characters. In particular, with a limited number of training data, it is unsurprising that the CNN engine will decrease our attack's success. On the other hand, interference arcs marginally contribute to the security of this scheme, too.

To the contrary, Tencent is the worst design, as it made the worst choices for almost all security features.

7.4 Towards Better Designs

Although broken, the Yahoo! scheme has some good security features. It is unwise to throw away its current design and start from scratch. Instead, we explore how to evolve this scheme into a better design. Plausible options include the following.

Increasing the alphabet size, which is currently among the smallest across the 5 schemes. This is a simple but effective solution, and with little negative impact on usability (if confusing characters are excluded from the alphabet).

Using broken contours more often. In its current design, not all of the Yahoo! challenges contain broken contours. It is useful to make challenges with broken contours occur more often, since this will likely decrease our attack's success rate and increase the time it takes to succeed.

More fundamentally, introducing more broken points in each challenge will likely significantly increase security. Breaking contour lines badly or at least creating a large number of broken points at random locations will make it hard to repair the contours. If the repair algorithm does not work, attackers will be unable to rely on the otherwise effective CFS method to extract character strokes any more.

Introducing thick interference arcs to cut through characters so that when adjacent strokes are combined for tests, combined characters contain either extra strokes or lack essential parts. This will confuse the CNN engine, leading to incorrect recognition results. Also, cutting-through arcs can be used to create a large number of components in an image. The more components the CNN engine has to try to combine, the lower the attack's success rate and speed.

Increasing the length of each CAPTCHA string helps, too, for the same reason as above.

Increasing the variation in character widths. The larger the gap between the smallest and largest width of individual characters in an image, the larger a solution set our graph search algorithm is required to go through. This might significantly slow down our attack.

Some of these measures (such as increasing the string length) only have a linear effect on the search space, but methods such as 'using broken contours more often' theoretically would be much more effective in thwarting attacks.

We note that careful studies are needed to establish how well these advised measures will work, and more importantly, some measures may decrease recognition success for humans. It is important to strike the right balance between security and usability. It remains an open problem what design will be eventually both secure and usable, and whether this design is mission impossible. Nonetheless, our discussions offer practical suggestions for improving hollow CAPTCHA designs.

8. SUMMARY AND CONCLUSION

We have shown that hollow CAPTCHAs, a new type of text scheme, have serious security problems. With a simple attack, we have broken the hollow schemes deployed by Yahoo!, Tencent, Sina, CmPay and Baidu with a success rate of 36%, 89%, 59%, 66%, and 51%, respectively. As these schemes are different from each other, and each with distinctive design features, our work casts serious doubt on the current generation of hollow CAPTCHAs.

Hollow CAPTCHA is a clever idea in that it improves usability while keeping characters connected or touching each other, but this idea has unexpected security consequences. A key issue in text CAPTCHA design is to find a segmentation-resistant mechanism that is secure and user-friendly simultaneously. The hollow CAPTCHA approach does not achieve this goal yet.

By comparing representative designs of popular hollow CAPTCHAs, we have identified good design features for better security. We have also discussed how to create next generation of better designs. However, it remains an open problem how to design CAPTCHAs that are both secure and usable, and this is our ongoing work. Overall, our work contributes to advancing the current collective understanding of CAPTCHA design.

9. ACKNOWLEDGEMENTS

We thank Lindsay Marshall, Feng Hao and anonymous reviewers for helpful comments. Xidian authors are supported by the National Natural Science Foundation of China (60903198) and the Fundamental Research Funds for the Central Universities.

10. REFERENCES

[1] Baidu. `https://passport.baidu.com/reg`.

[2] China mobile. `https://cmpay.10086.cn/`.

[3] Pwntcha - captcha decoder web site. `http://sam.zoy.org/pwntcha/`.

[4] Sina weibo. `http://weibo.com/signup/signup.php`.

[5] Tencent security center. `http://aq.qq.com/cn2/findpsw/findpsw_index`.

[6] Yahoo! password helper. `https://edit.yahoo.com/forgot?stage=fe100&src=&intl=us&done=http://www.yahoo.com&partner=reg`.

[7] Elie Bursztein, Matthieu Martin, and John Mitchell. Text-based captcha strengths and weaknesses. In *Proceedings of the 18th ACM conference on Computer and communications security*, pages 125–138. ACM, 2011.

[8] Ahmad S El Ahmad, Jeff Yan, and Mohamad Tayara. *The Robustness of Google CAPTCHAs.* Computing Science Technical Report CS-TR-1278, Newcastle University, UK, 2011.

[9] Ahmad Salah El Ahmad, Jeff Yan, and Lindsay Marshall. The robustness of a new captcha. In *Proceedings of the Third European Workshop on System Security*, pages 36–41. ACM, 2010.

[10] Jeffrey H Hoel. Some variations of lee's algorithm. *Computers, IEEE Transactions on*, 100(1):19–24, 1976.

[11] Yann LeCun, Léon Bottou, Yoshua Bengio, and Patrick Haffner. Gradient-based learning applied to document recognition. *Proceedings of the IEEE*, 86(11):2278–2324, 1998.

[12] Mark D Lillibridge, Martin Abadi, Krishna Bharat, and Andrei Z Broder. Method for selectively restricting access to computer systems, February 27 2001. US Patent 6,195,698.

[13] Greg Mori and Jitendra Malik. Recognizing objects in adversarial clutter: Breaking a visual captcha. In *Computer Vision and Pattern Recognition, 2003. Proceedings. 2003 IEEE Computer Society Conference on*, volume 1, pages I–134. IEEE, 2003.

[14] Gabriel Moy, Nathan Jones, Curt Harkless, and Randall Potter. Distortion estimation techniques in solving visual captchas. In *Computer Vision and Pattern Recognition, 2004. CVPR 2004. Proceedings of the 2004 IEEE Computer Society Conference on*, volume 2, pages II–23. IEEE, 2004.

[15] Moni Naor. Verification of a human in the loop or identification via the turing test. *Unpublished draft from http://www. wisdom. weizmann. ac. il/~ naor/PAPERS/human abs. html*, 1996.

[16] M. O'Neill. Cnn. `http://www.codeproject.com/Articles/16650/Neural-Network-for-Recognition-of-Handwritten-Digi`.

[17] Nobuyuki Otsu. A threshold selection method from gray-level histograms. *Automatica*, 11(285-296):23–27, 1975.

[18] Patrice Simard, David Steinkraus, and John C Platt. Best practices for convolutional neural networks applied to visual document analysis. In *ICDAR*, volume 3, pages 958–962, 2003.

[19] PY Simard. Using machine learning to break visual human interaction proofs (hips. *Advances in neural information processing systems*, 17:265–272, 2005.

[20] Luis Von Ahn, Manuel Blum, and John Langford. Telling humans and computers apart automatically. *Communications of the ACM*, 47(2):56–60, 2004.

[21] Y Xu, G Reynaga, S Chiasson, JF Frahm, F Monrose, and PC Van Oorschot. Security and usability challenges of moving-object captchas: decoding codewords in motion. In *21st USENIX Security Symposium*, 2012.

[22] Jeff Yan and Ahmad Salah El Ahmad. Breaking visual captchas with naive pattern recognition algorithms. In *Computer Security Applications Conference, 2007. ACSAC 2007. Twenty-Third Annual*, pages 279–291. IEEE, 2007.

[23] Jeff Yan and Ahmad Salah El Ahmad. A low-cost attack on a microsoft captcha. In *Proceedings of the 15th ACM conference on Computer and communications security*, pages 543–554. ACM, 2008.

[24] Jeff Yan and Ahmad Salah El Ahmad. Usability of captchas or usability issues in captcha design. In *Proceedings of the 4th symposium on Usable privacy and security*, pages 44–52. ACM, 2008.

[25] TY Zhang and Ching Y. Suen. A fast parallel algorithm for thinning digital patterns. *Communications of the ACM*, 27(3):236–239, 1984.

[26] Bin B Zhu, Jeff Yan, Qiujie Li, Chao Yang, Jia Liu, Ning Xu, Meng Yi, and Kaiwei Cai. Attacks and design of image recognition captchas. In *Proceedings of the 17th ACM conference on Computer and communications security*, pages 187–200. ACM, 2010.

Anonymous Credentials Light

Foteini Baldimtsi
Brown University
foteini@cs.brown.edu

Anna Lysyanskaya
Brown University
anna@cs.brown.edu

ABSTRACT

We define and propose an efficient and provably secure construction of blind signatures with attributes. Prior notions of blind signatures did not yield themselves to the construction of anonymous credential systems, not even if we drop the unlinkability requirement of anonymous credentials. Our new notion in contrast is a convenient building block for anonymous credential systems. The construction we propose is efficient: it requires just a few exponentiations in a prime-order group in which the decisional Diffie-Hellman problem is hard. Thus, for the first time, we give a provably secure construction of anonymous credentials that can work in the elliptic group setting without bilinear pairings and is based on the DDH assumption. In contrast, prior provably secure constructions were based on the RSA group or on groups with pairings, which made them prohibitively inefficient for mobile devices, RFIDs and smartcards. The only prior efficient construction that could work in such elliptic curve groups, due to Brands, does not have a proof of security.

Categories and Subject Descriptors

D.4.6 [**Security and Protection**]: [Cryptographic controls, Authentication]

Keywords

Anonymous credentials; attributes; blind signatures; lightweight devices; private identity management.

1. INTRODUCTION

Anonymous credentials, envisioned by David Chaum [17], and first fully realized by Camenisch and Lysyanskaya [13], have proved to be a centrally important building block in privacy-minded identity management systems currently under development [43, 35, 16]. They allow users to prove possession of credentials without revealing any other information about themselves; when such a proof is carried out, it cannot be linked to previous uses of the same credential, or to any other identifying information about the user. Additionally, they give the users the ability to privately obtain credentials. The reason that they have become so popular is that they strictly adhere to data minimization principles [30]: no electronic transaction should require its participants to needlessly reveal private information. These principles are at the core of European privacy standards [37, 36] and also the National Strategy for Trusted Identities in Cyberspace (NSTIC) published by the U.S. government [41].

Efficiency considerations are important when deploying these algorithms in practice. While on a PC, the Camenisch-Lysyanskaya credentials [13] and follow-up work [5, 10, 11, 14] take only a fraction of a second of CPU time, in mobile devices, smartcards and RFID cards, they are not yet as practical as we may wish for certain applications. The issue is that all existing anonymous credential systems use either the RSA group, or groups that admit bilinear pairings, and the security parameter choice needed to provide security under the required assumptions in these groups makes these systems too expensive for smartcards and mobile devices (i.e. original CL credentials require an RSA group with bitlength 2048 or a pairing with 128 bits of security). Bichsel et. al. [6] show an efficient implementation of CL credentials on a standard Java card, where they achieve an execution time for an RSA exponentiation for a base of 1984 bits and an exponent of 1024 bits of 1.3 seconds by using the hardware accelerator for RSA of the chosen card. As a result, more than 16 seconds are required in order to show one credential which is not practical for most applications. Moreover, hardware implementations have high development cost (compared to software) and are not easy to update.

From the efficiency point of view, therefore, the UProve credential system [35] (based on Brands' work [8, 9], acquired and implemented by Microsoft) seems attractive. UProve does not allow unlinkable reuse of credentials: in order to unlinkably use a credential again, a user must get it reissued. Yet, these "linkable" credentials can serve as the basis for e-cash, where a user is not supposed to use a coin more than once, anyway. The UProve credential issuing protocol, as well as the algorithm for verifying a credential, are practical enough for the more advanced end of RFID technology, since they can work in any group where the discrete logarithm problem is hard (thus can be based on ECC), and require just a few exponentiations in this group. Software implementations of ECC multiplication are much faster than the equivalent RSA exponentiation [27] (hardware accelerators could also speed up both ECC and RSA implementa-

CCS'13, November 04–08 2013, Berlin, Germany.
Copyright 2013 ACM 978-1-4503-2477-9/13/11 ...$15.00.
http://http://dx.doi.org/10.1145/2508859.2516687.

tions by an order of magnitude or more; today there exist RFID chips that perform ECC multiplication in 0.4 seconds [44]).

So perhaps one could use these "linkable" anonymous credentials and just have them reissued as many times as needed. However, UProve is not provably secure! No proof of security has been given under any reasonable assumption; and in fact, recently, Baldimtsi and Lysyanskaya [4] showed that all known approaches for proving security in the random oracle model will fail for the Brands blind signature scheme on which UProve is based, under essentially any assumption.

One might ask what happens if, instead of the Brands blind signature, one tries to construct linkable anonymous credentials from a provably secure blind signature scheme. Unfortunately, blind signatures as traditionally defined [40, 39, 29, 1] do not give any consideration to users' attributes. In a blind signature, a user is free to choose whichever message he wants signed. In a credential scheme, a user should be able to get his particular attribute set signed by the signer. The signers can verify that what they are signing is the correct attribute set, even though they cannot see exactly what they are signing. For example, a signer might want to sign a user's secret key, his age, and his citizenship information, and wants to be able to verify that this is indeed what she is signing. Attributes are, in fact, essential: without them, it is impossible to tie a credential to a particular user's identity, and so users would be able to just pool each others' credentials as desired, instead of tying them to a particular secret key. Moreover, giving the user the ability to choose any message means that the content of the signed messages has not been vetted by the signer at all.

Thus, a better question is: how do we extend the notion of a blind signature so that it can efficiently accommodate anonymous credentials — if not full anonymous credentials a-la Camenisch and Lysyanskaya, then at least linkable lightweight anonymous credentials a-la Brands?

Blind Signature with Attributes. In this paper, for the first time, we define *blind signatures with attributes.* In such a blind signature scheme, the signer and the user both get as input a cryptographic commitment C to the user's attributes; this way, the user can prove that the commitment contains the correct attributes via a separate zero-knowledge proof. As output, the user obtains another, unlinkable, commitment $\tilde{C}$ to the same attributes, and a signature on this commitment and a message of the user's choice. *Blindness* ensures that, even upon seeing two signatures obtained this way on commitments of his own choice, the signer cannot link a signature to its issuing. *Unforgeability* ensures that a user cannot produce more signatures than he was issued, and also that the multiset of openings to the input commitments is the same as the multiset of openings to the output commitments.

From Blind Signatures with Attributes to Anonymous Credentials. It is easy to see that this is the right building block for linkable anonymous credentials: a user with a particular set of attributes can form a commitment C to these attributes, prove in zero-knowledge that he has committed to the correct attributes, and then obtain a credential by running a blind signature with attributes on input this commitment. He can then prove that he has a credential with the desired attributes by revealing his signature and the output commitment $\tilde{C}$, and proving in zero knowledge that $\tilde{C}$ corresponds to the needed attributes.

For example, suppose that we allow users to obtain and anonymously show age credentials. Then Alice will form a commitment C to her secret key sk and her age age, prove to the signer, who serves as an identity validator, that she has committed to sk that corresponds to her pk and to the correct age, and run a blind signature with attributes protocol to obtain a fresh commitment $\tilde{C}$ on the same sk and age, and a signature σ. Then, when she needs to prove her age, she can reveal $(\tilde{C}, \sigma)$ and prove that the age inside commitment $\tilde{C}$ allows her entry to some age-restricted resource, for example a video store that requires viewers to be over 13. If she wants to do it again, she needs to run the blind signature with attributes protocol with the signer again. She can further anonymously obtain credentials that are connected to her identity: let's say that the video store wants to give her a credential for a free movie; she can obtain it by running a blind signature with attributes with the video store. She will form her input commitment C' by committing to the same sk and age as in $\tilde{C}$ and proving to the video store that she did so (by proving equality of committed values); once she runs the protocol with the video store, she receives an output $(\tilde{C}', \sigma)$, which is a credential from the video store (and not from the original signer) on her (sk, age) — even though the video store never saw the public key at all. More interestingly, we can require the free movie to be a single-use credential, by additional clever use of attributes (see Section 4), so that Alice can be traced if she tries to get two free movies using the same single-use credential more than once. Thus we see that blind signatures with attributes are the right building block for linkable anonymous credentials.

Construction. In addition to the definition, we solve the open problem of constructing anonymous credentials based on the DDH assumption. We give a lightweight construction of blind signatures with attributes; because of the connection to single use anonymous credentials we call our construction "anonymous credentials light" (ACL). In the random-oracle model, our construction is unlinkable under the decisional Diffie-Hellman assumption, and unforgeable under the discrete-logarithm assumption for sequential composition (we leave extending it to concurrent self-composition as an open problem). Our construction is inspired by the Abe blind signature [1] in which, unlike other provably secure blind signatures [7, 12, 34, 40, 22], blinding still preserves some structural elements into which attributes can be embedded. Unfortunately Abe's construction, as it was first presented, had a faulty proof of security as it was later found by Abe and Ohkubo [33]. The original proof was in the RO model for concurrent composition but it turned out to only be valid for an adversary with overwhelming success probability so they ended up presenting a new proof in the generic model. In the other hand, we manage to proof our scheme in the RO model by limiting our attention to sequential composition only. Moreover, our analysis indicates that Abe's scheme may be provable under DDH in the RO model for sequential composition.

Related Work and Comparisons. Let's now take a closer look in our ACL construction and compare it with other well known blind signature and credential schemes. For our comparisons we focus on the efficiency of signing (which is analogous to the credential issuing), the cost of

	Brands [8]		Abe [1]		ACL Scheme		CL credentials [13] Rsa		CL credentials [13] Pairings	
Efficiency	S^1	U^2	S	U	S	U	S	U	S	U
Signing[3]	2	12	6	12	7	13	10	8	15	14p
Verification	7	0	11	1	11	1	NC[4]		5+6p	9+6p
Sign. size	6 elem.		9 elem.		9 elem.		$\sim 0^5$		$\sim 0^5$	
Blindness	✓		✓		✓		✓		✓	
Prov. Unforg.	✗		GM[6]		✓		✓		✓	
Attributes	✓		✗		✓		✓		✓	

[1] Signer, [2] User, [3] In number of exponentiations
[4] Non-comparable, [5] It can be used multiple times
[6] Generic group model

Table 1: Comparison of anonymous credentials

verification of the signature/credential, the size of the signature/credential, the security of the schemes i.e. blindness and unforgeability and whether the schemes support attributes which is obviously not going to be the case for a "traditional" blind signature scheme.

The ACL construction consists of three phases: registration, preparation and validation. Registration is the most expensive phase, but it need not be repeated for the same user/signer pair should the user need his credential reissued (as long as his attribute set is the same). Preparation and validation require the signer to perform 7 exponentiations, while the user performs 13; verification requires 8 exponentiations. These numbers are essentially the same as Abe's blind signature; Brands' blind signature at the heart of UProve requires essentially the same number of exponentiations for signature issue, and 4 exponentiations fewer for verification. Thus, we get comparable efficiency to the most efficient examples of protocols that either lack essential features (such as previously provable secure blind signatures) or provable security (such as UProve). We also compare ourselves to the Camenisch-Lysyanskaya [13] which is significantly less efficient during issuing due to the use of pairings or RSA group but is a multi-use credential, thus we denote the signature/credential size to be close to zero since it can be used multiple times. See Table 1 for the comparisons.

A related work is due to Guajardo et al. [25] where they proposed "encrypted anonymous credentials". The idea is that an issuer can certify encrypted attributes in such a way that none of the involved parties, including the user, can learn the value of the attributes. This is an interesting application but cannot be used as a building block so it is incomparable to our work. Moreover, their construction [25] is based on Brands scheme which as mentioned above cannot be proven one-more unforgeable [4].

Recommended parameter setting. For 128 bit security we recommend using a group of 576 bits[1]. In order to achieve an equivalent security level with CL credentials keys of 3072 bits would be required.

Implementation. In an independent work [28] we have implemented the ACL scheme using an NFC enabled smartphone: the BlackBerry Bold 9900. The implementation has been tailored for payments in transportation systems where our ACL construction is being used as an e-cash scheme (which, as we mentioned above, is a direct application of "single-use" credentials). Our implementation is mostly a proof of concept and we used a 160 bit elliptic curve group. Briefly, the signing/issuing takes a total of 300 milliseconds including terminal, communication and smartphone execution time, while spending (i.e. verification of the signature) takes about 380 milliseconds when 2 attributes are revealed which would be less if no attributes were revealed.

[1]Please refer to the proof of Theorem 4 for a justification of this number.

2. PRELIMINARIES

2.1 Basic Assumptions

The following two standard cryptographic assumptions are useful in the paper.

Definition 1. (*Discrete Logarithm Assumption*) Let k be the security parameter. Let G_k be a set of groups such that G_k is a group of order q (k-bit prime) and generator g. Then, for every polynomial time algorithm $\mathcal{A}$ it holds that:

$$Pr[h \leftarrow G; x \leftarrow A(h) : x = \log_g h] \leq \nu(k)$$

where $\nu(k)$ is a negligible function.

Definition 2. (*Decisional Diffie-Hellman Assumption*) Let DH be an instance generator that, on input the security parameter 1^k outputs (G, q, g, A, B, C) where G is a cyclic group of order q (k-bit prime) with generator g, and, for randomly chosen $a, b \in \mathbb{Z}_q$, $A = g^a$, $B = g^b$ and $C = g^{ab}$. Let $Rand$ be an instance generator that, on input 1^k outputs (G, q, g, A, B, C) where G,q,g,A and B are as above, while $C = g^c$ for a random $c \in \mathbb{Z}_q$. We assume that DH and $Rand$ are computationally indistinguishable.

2.2 Witness Relations and Interactive Proofs

A witness relation for a language $L \in \mathcal{NP}$ is defined as:

Definition 3. (*Witness relation* [23]) A witness relation for a language $L \in \mathcal{NP}$ is a binary relation R_L that is polynomially bounded (i.e., $(h, x) \in R_L$ implies $|x| \leq \text{poly}(|h|)$), is polynomial-time-recognizable and characterizes L by

$$L = \{h : \exists x \text{ s.t. } (h, x) \in R_L\}.$$

For $h \in L$, any x satisfying $(h, x) \in R_L$ is called a *witness* (for the membership $h \in L$). By $R_L(h)$ we denote the set of witnesses for the membership $h \in L$; that is, $R_L(h) = \{x : (h, x) \in R_L\}$.

Definition 4. (*Interactive Proof System [24]*) An interactive proof system with soundness error $s \in [0, 1]$ for a language L with witness relation R_L is a pair of algorithms (P, V) where v is probabilistic polynomial time and the following properties hold:

1. Completeness. For every $h \in L$ and every $x \in R_L(h)$,
$$Pr[\langle P(x), V\rangle(h) = 1] = 1.$$
2. s-Soundness. For every $h \notin L$, every $z \in \{0, 1\}^*$ and every interactive algorithm P^*
$$Pr[\langle P^*(z), V\rangle(h) = 0] \geq 1 - s.$$

A useful property in the above setting would be if the verifier V wouldn't learn anything useful from P about the witness x besides the fact that P knows x. This property is called *zero knowledge*. If soundness error s is negligible, then this interactive proof system has *strong soundness*.

Definition 5. (*Honest Verifiable Zero Knowledge (HVZK)*) An interactive proof system (P, V) for a language L is said to be *honest verifiable zero knowledge* if there exists a probabilistic polynomial time algorithm S (the Simulator) such that for all $h \in L$:

$$\text{view}_V[\langle P, V\rangle](h) \approx S(h),$$

where view_V is the view of the honest verifier V of the interaction between V and P on input h.

2.3 Σ-Protocols

Σ-protocols are a class of interactive proofs where the Prover and the Verifier (P, V) have a common input h and P proves in zero-knowledge that he knows a value x such that $(h, x) \in R_L$. Their main characteristic is that they have exactly 3 rounds of the following type: (1) P sends a message a to V, (2) V responds with a random challenge c chosen from a domain of size $\Theta(k)$ and (3) P resents a reply r. V decides whether to accept or not given the information he has seen: (h, a, c, r). Formally:

Definition 6. (*Σ-Protocol*) A protocol $\mathcal{P}$ is said to be a Σ-protocol for a relation R_L if:

- $\mathcal{P}$ is of the above three rounds form, and if (P, V) follow the protocol, the verifier always accepts.
- From any h and any pair of accepting conversations on input h, (a, c, r), (a, c', r') where $c \neq c'$, one can efficiently compute x such that $(h, x) \in R_L$ (special soundness).
- There exists a polynomial-time simulator S, which on input h and a random c outputs an accepting conversation of the form (a, c, r), with the same probability distribution as conversations between the honest P, V on input h (special honest-verifier zero-knowledge).

An example of a Σ-protocol is the Schnorr Identification scheme [42]. Let G be a group of prime order q with generator g, and let $\mathbb{Z}_q$ denote the field of integers modulo q. Schnorr's identification scheme works as follows:

Prover$(q, g, h = g^x)$		Verifier(q, g, h)
$y \leftarrow \mathbb{Z}_q$, $a = g^y$	$\xrightarrow{a}$	
	$\xleftarrow{c}$	$c \leftarrow \mathbb{Z}_q$
$r = y + cx \bmod q$	$\xrightarrow{r}$	$g^r \stackrel{?}{=} ah^c$

Σ-protocols are an essential building block for blind signatures and anonymous credentials. For example Brands' [8] and Abe's [1] schemes are based on a Σ-protocol, while CL anonymous credentials [13] uses ZK proofs which are based on Σ-protocols.

2.4 Fiat-Shamir Heuristic

Fiat and Shamir [21] proposed a method to transform any three-round interactive proof system with negligible soundness error, such as Σ-protocols, into a digital signature using a hash function, modeled as a random oracle.

To transform a three-round proof system into a signature scheme, one could, instead of a random c, compute $c = H(a, m)$, where H is a hash function. Then, the Fiat-Shamir transformation uses c to create a signature $\sigma(m) = (a, r)$. Famous digital signatures that have been constructed from Σ-protocols using the Fiat-Shamir heuristic include Schnorr's [42] and GQ signatures [26] and they have been proven secure in the RO model [39].

2.5 OR-proof

Let $\mathcal{P}$ be a Σ-protocol for a relation R_L, (h_0, h_1) be a common input to (P, V) and P knows a x such that $h_b, x \in R_L$ for $b \in \{0, 1\}$. An OR-proof protocol $\mathcal{P}_{OR}$ is a Σ-protocol for proving that either $(h_0, x) \in R_L$ or $(h_1, x) \in R_L$ [20][2].

The main idea of an OR-proof is that P will complete two Σ protocols Σ_0, Σ_1, one for h_0 and one for h_1 in such a way that the verifier will not be able to tell for which of the two P knows the corresponding witness. For h_b the prover can actually follow the real Σ protocol while for h_{1-b} he will have to use a simulator M to create his answers. A $\mathcal{P}_{OR}$ protocol works as follows:

1. P computes the first message of Σ_b, a_b, using (h_b, x) as input. P randomly chooses c_{1-b} and runs the simulator M on input (h_{1-b}, c_{1-b}) and receives $(a_{1-b}, c_{1-b}, r_{1-b})$ as an output. Then, P sends a_0, a_1 to V.
2. V chooses a random string e and sends it to P.
3. P sets $c_b = e \oplus c_{b-1}$ and computes the answer r_b to challenge c_b using h_b, a_b, c_b, x as input. He sends c_0, c_1, r_0, r_1 to V.
4. V checks that $e = c_0 \oplus c_1$ and that both (a_0, c_0, r_0) and (a_1, c_1, r_1) are accepting conversations.

Let $R_{OR} = \{((h_0, h_1), x) | (h_0, x) \in R_L \text{ or } (h_1, x) \in R_L\}$. Then:

THEOREM 1 ([20]). *The $\mathcal{P}_{OR}$ protocol is a Σ-protocol for R_{OR}. Moreover, for any verifier V^*, the probability distribution of conversations between P and V^*, where x is such that $(h_b, x) \in R_L$, is independent of b.*

2.6 Generalized Pedersen Commitment

A non-interactive commitment takes as input a message (or set of messages) m and randomness R and outputs a value that, on the one hand, reveals no information about the message but, on the other hand, it is hard to find a (m', R') such that $Commit(m; R) = Commit(m', R')$ but $m \neq m'$ (see [31] for a standard definition and treatment). The Pedersen commitment is a commitment scheme based on the discrete logarithm assumption [38]. Here we give a generalized version that allows a commitment to a set of messages $(L_1, \ldots, L_n)$. The scheme is defined as follows:

1. *Setup*: On input the security parameter 1^k and the maximum number of messages n, pick a group G of prime order $q = \Theta(2^k)$ with generators $h, h_1, \ldots, h_n$.
2. $Commit(L_1, \ldots, L_n; R) = h^R \prod_{i=1}^{n} h_i^{L_i}$; and $L_i \in \mathbb{Z}_q$.

The Pedersen commitment scheme (constructed from a corresponding Σ-protocol) is information theoretically hiding and computationally binding. It is also important that there are efficient zero-knowledge proof protocols for proving that a commitment C is to a particular set of values; or to a set of values that satisfy a rich class of relations [8, 15, 19].

2.7 Combined Commitment Scheme

Let $Commit_1$ be a commitment scheme that takes as input its parameters $params_1$, n messages $(L_1, \ldots, L_n)$ to which we will refer to as *attributes* from now on and randomness R_1

[2]This is based on a more general result due to Cramer et. al. [18] where they present a protocol in which the prover demonstrates knowledge of the solution to some subset of n problem instances out of a collection of subsets.

and outputs a commitment C_1. Let $Commit_2$ be a commitment scheme that takes as input its parameters $params_2$, an attribute L_0 and randomness R_2 and outputs a commitment C_2. Suppose that another commitment scheme, *Commit*, is a *combination* of these two commitments; i.e., on input C_1 and C_2 it produces a commitment C to the combined attributes $(L_0, L_1, \ldots, L_n)$ with combined randomness $R = R_1 + R_2$.

For example, this can be instantiated by a generalized Pedersen commitment scheme: the parameters for the combined scheme are generators $(h, h_0, \ldots, h_n)$, $Commit_1(L_1, \ldots, L_n; R_1) = (\prod_{i=1}^{n} h_i^{L_i})h^{R_1}$, $Commit_2(L_0; R_2) = h_0^{L_0}h^{R_2}$, and a combined commitment can be obtained either by multiplying together the two component commitments, or by computing it from scratch as $Commit(L_0, L_1, \ldots, L_n; R) = (\prod_{i=0}^{n} h_i^{L_i})h^R$.

2.8 Blinded Pedersen Commitment Scheme

Here, we note that the Pedersen commitment scheme can be further extended. Let $(h, h_1, \ldots, h_n)$ be the parameters of the Pedersen commitment. Consider an additional parameter $z \in G$, where $z \neq 1$. Let $C = Commit(L_1, \ldots, L_n; R)$. Then the values (z^γ, C^γ) can also be viewed as a commitment to the same $(L_1, \ldots, L_n)$ with randomness (R, γ). Let us define a new commitment scheme, which we will call the *blinded* Pedersen commitment scheme: $Commit^B(L_1, \ldots, L_n; R, \gamma) = (z^\gamma, Commit(L_1, \ldots, L_n; R)^\gamma)$, where *Commit* is the Pedersen commitment. It is easy to see that this commitment is unconditionally hiding, same as Pedersen. It is also easy to see that it is binding: given (z^γ, C^γ), γ is uniquely defined, and therefore so is C, which is binding. Finally, using well-known Σ-protocols, it is easy to see that the same set of relations that can be proven about values inside a Pedersen commitment can be proven about values inside a blinded Pedersen commitment.

3. DEFINITION OF SECURE BLIND SIGNATURES WITH ATTRIBUTES

In this section, for the first time, we define what a blind signature scheme with attributes is and its security properties. For definitions of standard (without attributes) blind signatures please refer to [29].

Definition 7. (Blind signatures with attributes)
Let $Commit(x; r)$ be a non-interactive commitment scheme whose parameters *params* are generated by a trusted party *TP* and let n be the maximum number of messages the scheme can support. A blind signature scheme with n attributes, for this commitment scheme, consists of three algorithms: *KeyGen*, *BlindSign*, *Verify* where *BlindSign* is a protocol between the Signer(S) and the User(U).

- $KeyGen(1^k, params)$: is a probabilistic polynomial time key generation algorithm. It takes as input the security parameter k and the public parameters of the commitment scheme and outputs (pk, sk) where pk is the signer's public key and sk is his secret key.
- *BlindSign*: is an interactive, probabilistic polynomial time protocol between S and U. The common input is the Signer's public key pk, the parameters of the commitment scheme *params* and $C = Commit(L_1, \ldots, L_n; R)$ where $(L_1, \ldots, L_n)$ is the set of attributes and R is some randomness. The Signer's private input is sk and User's private input is $(L_1, \ldots, L_n, R)$ and the message, m, that he wishes to have signed. The User's output in the protocol is a pair $(\tilde{R}, \sigma)$, where $\sigma = \sigma(m, \tilde{C})$ is the Signer's signature on $(m, \tilde{C})$, and $\tilde{C} = Commit(L_1, \ldots, L_n; \tilde{R})$; the Signer's output is "completed".
- $Verify(PK, m, \tilde{C}, \sigma)$: is the signature verification algorithm; i.e. a deterministic polynomial time algorithm that gets as input the public key, the message, a commitment to the attributes and the blind signature on the message and attributes and checks the validity of the signature σ. If it is valid the algorithm outputs "1", otherwise outputs "0".

A blind signature scheme with attributes is secure if it is both blind and unforgeable. Blindness is defined in a similar way as in blind signature schemes without attributes: the Signer is unable to view the messages and the attributes he signs (protection for the User). A malicious Signer, $\mathcal{A}$, cannot link a $(m, \tilde{C}, \sigma)$ tuple to any particular execution of the protocol, even if $\mathcal{A}$ chooses $m, L_1, \ldots, L_n$.

Definition 8. (Blindness for blind signatures with attributes) Let $\mathcal{A}$ be a malicious Signer and $b \in \{0, 1\}$ be a randomly chosen bit which is kept secret from $\mathcal{A}$. $\mathcal{A}$ will try to guess the value b by performing the following steps:

1. $(pk, sk) \leftarrow KeyGen(1^k)$
2. $\{m_0, m_1, \overrightarrow{L_0}, \overrightarrow{L_1}, R_0, R_1\} \leftarrow \mathcal{A}(1^k, pk, sk)$ (i.e. $\mathcal{A}$ produces two messages $\{m_0, m_1\}$, polynomial in 1^k, and two attribute vectors $\overrightarrow{L_0}, \overrightarrow{L_1}$ with the corresponding randomness).
3. $\mathcal{A}(1^k, pk, sk, m_0, m_1, \overrightarrow{L_0}, \overrightarrow{L_1}, R_0, R_1)$ engages in two parallel (and arbitrarily interleaved as desired by $\mathcal{A}$) interactive protocols, the first with $U(pk, \{m_b, \overrightarrow{L_0}, R_0\})$ and the second with $U(pk, \{m_{1-b}, \overrightarrow{L_1}, R_1\})$.
4. $\mathcal{A}$ only gets signatures and the corresponding blinded commitments for the instances that didn't fail; for the ones that failed $\mathcal{A}$ gets nothing. If neither of the User instances failed, then $\mathcal{A}$ gets two signatures and the corresponding blinded commitments: $\sigma(m_0, \tilde{C}_b), \tilde{C}_b$ and $\sigma(m_1, \tilde{C}_{1-b}), \tilde{C}_{1-b}$. Otherwise, $\mathcal{A}$ outputs $\perp$.
5. $\mathcal{A}$ outputs a bit b'.

Then the probability, taken over the choice of b, over coin-flips of the key-generation algorithm, the coin-flips of $\mathcal{A}$, and (private) coin-flips of both users (from step 3), that $b' = b$ is at most $\frac{1}{2} + \nu(k)$, where $\nu(k)$ is a negligible function.

We give the definition of one-more unforgeability for the sequential composition case.

Definition 9. (Sequential one-more $(\ell, \ell+1)$ unforgeability for blind signatures with attributes) (KeyGen, BlindSign, Verify) is a one-more unforgeable blind signature scheme with respect to *Commit* if $\forall$ probabilistic polynomial time adversaries $\mathcal{A}$, the probability that $\mathcal{A}$ wins in the following game is negligible:

1. $(pk, sk) \leftarrow KeyGen(1^k)$
2. $\mathcal{A}(pk, params)$ engages in polynomially many (in k) adaptive, sequential interactive protocols with polynomially many copies of the signer, where $\mathcal{A}$ decides in

an adaptive fashion when to stop. For every execution, $\mathcal{A}$ forms a commitment C_i and picks a message m_i and invokes $S(pk, sk, C_i)$. Let ℓ be the number of executions, where the Signer output "completed" in the end of the protocol.

3. $\mathcal{A}$ outputs a collection $\{(\tilde{C}_1, m_1, \sigma_1), \ldots, (\tilde{C}_j, m_j, \sigma_j)\}$ where $(\tilde{C}_i, m_i, \sigma_i)$ for $1 \leq i \leq j$ are all accepted by $Verify(pk, \tilde{C}_i, m_i, \sigma_i)$, and all $(\tilde{C}_i, m_i)$'s are distinct.

We say that $\mathcal{A}$ wins the game if either:

1. $j > \ell$ (i.e. $\mathcal{A}$ outputs more $(\tilde{C}, m, \sigma)$ tuples than he received).
2. $\mathcal{A}$ opens the sets of commitments $\{C_i\}$ and $\{\tilde{C}_i\}$ and the resulting multisets do not match.

4. FROM BLIND SIGNATURES WITH ATTRIBUTES TO SINGLE-USE CREDENTIALS

Single-use anonymous credentials ensure that a credential cannot be used more than once: if used more than once, the user's identity can be discovered, and the user can be penalized. This is a generalization of off-line electronic cash [17], in that such a credential can also contain attributes, while e-cash does not necessarily have any connection to a user's identity. Here we construct single-use anonymous credentials from blind signatures with attributes using standard techniques [17, 8, 11].

Recall our definition of combined commitment schemes $(Commit_1, Commit_2, Commit)$ from Section 2.7. Consider the following construction of a single-use credential with n attributes from a blind signature scheme with $n + 1$ attributes. The common inputs to the User and Signer are the Signer's public key for verifying signatures, and a commitment C_1 to the User's attributes $(L_1, \ldots, L_n)$[3]. We assume that the attribute L_1 contains the user's identity, so that learning that attribute will allow one to trace the user. The Signer's private input is its signing key, while the User's private input is the message m that the user wants signed (m will serve as the serial number for this credential, so the user needs to have chosen it at random during the signing protocol) and the opening to C_1, $(L_1, \ldots, L_n; R_1)$. The commitment C_1 corresponds to this user's identity and never changes; each time this user obtains a signature, they input the same C_1.

First, the User forms a commitment $C_2 = Commit_2(L_0; R_2)$ for random (L_0, R_2); this commitment is specific to this credential, and the value L_0 will be used in the double-spending equation, below. Next, the user submits C_2 to the signer and provides a zero-knowledge proof of knowledge of its opening.

Next, the User and the Signer carry out the blind signature protocol relative to the combined commitment scheme $Commit$, whereby the User's output is a fresh commitment $\tilde{C}$ to the values $(L_0, \ldots, L_n)$ and randomness $\tilde{R}$, and the signature σ on $(m, \tilde{C})$.

To use this credential to a verifier V, the User reveals $(m, \tilde{C}, \sigma)$, obtains from V a challenge c, and reveals the double-spending equation $cL_1 + L_0$ (the multiplication and addition is in whatever ring the committed values belong to) and whatever other attributes are needed for the transaction; the User then provides a zero-knowledge proof that these values were revealed correctly, relative to commitment $\tilde{C}$.

[3]We assume that there exists an external procedure to validate the user's identity.

To trace a user who spent a single-use credential twice, it is sufficient to examine two double-spending equations for the same credential. If double spending occurred, then the attribute L_1, which encodes the User's identity, will be revealed.

The following theorem is stated informally because we omitted a formal definition of single-use anonymous credentials.

THEOREM 2. *(Informal) Let KeyGen, BlindSign, Verify be a blind signature scheme with $n + 1$ attributes, associated with the commitment scheme Commit which is a combination of $Commit_1$ and $Commit_2$ as explained above. Then the above construction is a single-use credential scheme with n attributes.*

5. OUR CONSTRUCTION: ACL

Let's now describe our proposed construction of a blind signature scheme with attributes, called "Anonymous Credentials Light" (ACL). ACL is based on Abe's blind signature scheme [1] which has been modified appropriately so that it will also allow the users to encode attributes in the signatures they get in a provably secure way. Abe's scheme is a witness indistinguishable variant of the Schnorr signature scheme where the Signer owns a *real public key* $y = g^x$ and a *tag public key* $z = g^w$. The idea is that the signature can be issued only with the real secret key x but no one can distinguish which of the two (real or tag) secret keys was used (remember the OR-proof technique presented above).

Although the modification seems straightforward, proving the security of the resulting scheme turns out to be challenging as we will see later in the next section.

5.1 Setup

Let G be a group of prime order q and g be a generator of this group. Let $\mathcal{H} : \{0,1\}^* \rightarrow \mathbb{Z}_q$ be a hash function. We assume the existence of a trusted party, TP, which chooses G, g and outputs $params = (q, G, g, h, h_0, \ldots, h_n)$ where $h, h_0, \ldots, h_n \in G$ and n is the maximum number of attributes a User can possibly have. We will use $(h_0, \ldots, h_n)$ as parameters of the combined Pedersen commitment scheme $Commit$.

The Signer picks his secret key $x \in_R \mathbb{Z}_q$ and computes his *real public key* to be $y = g^x \bmod q$. The TP given (G, q, g, h, y) outputs z which is the *tag public key* of the Signer (this can also be done using a hash function $H_z : \{0,1\}^* \rightarrow G$ that acts as a random oracle). The public key of the Signer is (G, q, g, h, y, z), and the private key is x. We will use $(z, h_0, \ldots, h_n)$ as parameters for the blinded Pedersen commitment scheme $Commit^B$.

5.2 Signature/ Credential Issuing

The signature issuing protocol will be described in three phases: registration, preparation and validation. The registration phase actually only needs to happen once for each user/set of attributes and also, preparation and validation phases can happen simultaneously (we choose to present them separately in order to describe the construction in a more modular way).

The signature issuing protocol is basically a $\mathcal{P}_{OR}$-protocol for proving knowledge of one of the following:

- y-side: proof of knowledge x of $y = g^x$
- z-side: proof of knowledge (w_1, w_2) of $z_1 = g^{w_1}$, $z_2 = h^{w_2}$ (where z_1, z_2 are the so called "one-time" tag keys created by the signer using input from the user).

Notice that the z-side witness in not known to the Signer, so the z-side proof will be done by simulation following the OR-proof technique paradigm described in Appendix 2.5.

5.2.1 *Registration*

The User's input includes the system parameters *params*, the signer's real public key y, the message m to be signed and $(L_1, \ldots, L_n; R)$ where $L_1, \ldots, L_n$ is a set of attributes and R is some randomness. The Signer also gets as input the system parameters *params*, a commitment $C = Commit(L_1, \ldots, L_n; R)$ and his secret key x. During registration the User and the Signer carry out a standard interactive zero-knowledge proof of knowledge protocol where the User creates a proof π_1 to convince the Signer that he knows an opening of the commitment C.

5.2.2 *Preparation*

The Signer prepares z_1 and z_2 (the z-side proof). He first picks $rnd \in \mathbb{Z}_q$ and creates the "one-time" tag keys: $z_1 = Cg^{rnd}$ and $z_2 = z/z_1$. The Signer sends rnd to the User in order to convince him that $\log_g z_1$ is not known to him. The User first checks that $rnd \neq 0$ and then computes himself $z_1 = Cg^{rnd}$ and then picks $\gamma \in \mathbb{Z}_q^*$ and blinds z, z_1, z_2 into $\zeta = z^\gamma$, $\zeta_1 = z_1^\gamma, \zeta_2 = \zeta/\zeta_1$ so that $\log_z z_1 = \log_\zeta \zeta_1$ holds.

Finally, the User picks $\tau \in \mathbb{Z}_q$ and computes $\eta = z^\tau$ (this will serve as an element of an additional Schnorr signature that proves knowledge of γ such that $\zeta = z^\gamma$).

5.2.3 *Validation*

In this phase two Σ protocols are going to take place and combined according to the OR-proof. By (a, c, r) we are going to denote the transcript of Σ_y and by (a', c', r') we will denote the transcript of Σ_z. The Signer will compute Σ_z himself and Σ_y in interaction with the user.

1. The Signer begins by creating a for Σ_y by picking a random $u \in \mathbb{Z}_q$ and computing $a = g^u$. Then, for Σ_z, following the OR-proof he picks random $c' \in \mathbb{Z}_q$ and $r' = \{r'_1, r'_2 \in \mathbb{Z}_q\}$. and sets $a'_1 = g^{r'_1} z_1^{c'}$ and $a'_2 = h^{r'_2} z_2^{c'}$. Finally he sends to the User $a, a' = \{a'_1, a'_2\}$.
2. The User checks whether $a, a'_1, a'_2 \in G$ and then picks blinding factors $t_1, t_2, t_3, t_4, t_5 \in_R \mathbb{Z}_q$ and blinds a into $\alpha = ag^{t_1} y^{t_2}$ and a'_1, a'_2 into $\alpha'_1 = {a'_1}^\gamma g^{t_3} \zeta_1^{t_4}$ and $\alpha'_2 = {a'_2}^\gamma h^{t_5} \zeta_2^{t_4}$. We denote $\alpha' = \{\alpha'_1, \alpha'_2\}$. Then, computes $\varepsilon = \mathcal{H}(\zeta, \zeta_1, \alpha, \alpha', \eta, m)$ where m is the message to be signed. The User sends to the Signer $e = (\varepsilon - t_2 - t_4) \bmod q$.
3. The Signer, according to the OR-proof technique, computes $c = e - c' \bmod q$ and $r = u - cx \bmod q$. Then, sends (c, r, c', r') to the User.
4. Finally, the User "unblinds" the received values and gets: $\rho = r + t_1 \bmod q$, $\omega = c + t_2 \bmod q$, $\rho'_1 = \gamma r'_1 + t_3 \bmod q$, $\rho'_2 = \gamma r'_2 + t_5 \bmod q$, $\omega' = c' + t_4 \bmod q$, $\mu = \tau - \omega'\gamma \bmod q$.

Signer$(params, x, C)$		User$(params, y, m, (L_1, \ldots, L_n; R))$
Registration		$C = h_0^R h_1^{L_1} h_2^{L_2} \ldots h_n^{L_n}$ π_1
	$\xleftrightarrow{\pi_1}$	
Preparation $rnd \in_R \mathbb{Z}_q$ $z_1 = Cg^{rnd}$ $z_2 = z/z_1$		
	$\xrightarrow{rnd}$	check if $rnd \neq 0$ $z_1 = Cg^{rnd}$ $\gamma \in_R \mathbb{Z}_q^*$ $\zeta = z^\gamma$ $\zeta_1 = z_1^\gamma$ $\zeta_2 = \zeta/\zeta_1$ $\tau \in_R \mathbb{Z}_q$ $\eta = z^\tau$
Validation $u, r'_1, r'_2, c' \in_R \mathbb{Z}_q$ $a = g^u$ y-side $a'_1 = g^{r'_1} z_1^{c'}$ $a'_2 = h^{r'_2} z_2^{c'}$ z-side		
	$\xrightarrow{a, a' = \{a'_1, a'_2\}}$	check if $a, a'_1, a'_2 \in G$ $t_1, t_2, t_3, t_4, t_5 \in_R \mathbb{Z}_q$ $\alpha = ag^{t_1} y^{t_2}$ y-side $\alpha'_1 = {a'_1}^\gamma g^{t_3} \zeta_1^{t_4}$ $\alpha'_2 = {a'_2}^\gamma h^{t_5} \zeta_2^{t_4}$ z-side $\varepsilon = \mathcal{H}_2(\zeta, \zeta_1, \alpha, \alpha'_1, \alpha'_2, \eta, m)$ $e = (\varepsilon - t_2 - t_4) \bmod q$
	$\xleftarrow{e}$	
$c = e - c' \bmod q$ $r = u - cx \bmod q$		
	$\xrightarrow{c, r, c', r' = \{r'_1, r'_2\}}$	$\rho = r + t_1 \bmod q$ $\omega = c + t_2 \bmod q$ $\rho'_1 = \gamma r'_1 + t_3 \bmod q$ $\rho'_2 = \gamma r'_2 + t_5 \bmod q$ $\omega' = c' + t_4 \bmod q$ $\mu = \tau - \omega'\gamma \bmod q$

Table 2: Proposed ACL construction

A signature is a 8-tuple $\sigma = (m, (\zeta, \zeta_1, \rho, \omega, \rho' = \{\rho'_1, \rho'_2\}, \omega', \mu))$ where ζ_1 encodes the attributes of the User $((\zeta, \zeta_1)$ corresponds to $\tilde{C}$, which is a blinded Pedersen commitment to $(L_1, \ldots, L_n)$ with randomness $(R, \gamma))$.

In Table 2 we describe all the phases of our construction.

5.2.4 *Verification*

A signature tuple (m, ζ_1, σ) (where ζ_1 corresponds to $\tilde{C}$) verifies if $\zeta \neq 1$ and

$$\omega + \omega' = \mathcal{H}(\zeta, \zeta_1, g^\rho y^\omega, g^{\rho'_1} \zeta_1^{\omega'}, h^{\rho'_2} \zeta_2^{\omega'}, z^\mu \zeta^{\omega'}, m) \bmod q.$$

5.3 Discussion

As briefly mentioned in the description of our construction there are certain "tricks" we can do to improve its efficiency. First of all notice that the *Registration* phase only needs to happen once for each User and a corresponding set of attributes. The Signer stores the attribute commitment C together with some identification information asked from the User (e.g. passport, ID). Then, it is sufficient if every time in the beginning of the *Signature Issuing* protocol the User identifies himself to the Signer in order to prove ownership of his account. Moreover, notice that *Preparation* and *Validation* phases can be combined and executed simultaneously. As a result, the whole signing protocol consists of three rounds.

Let's now discuss the differences between our ACL construction and the blind signature protocol described by Abe [1]. The basic advantage of ACL is that allows for the encoding of users' attributes in the signatures they receive from the Signer. In order for this to happen we need the *Registration* phase during which the User commits to his set of attributes. Those attributes are then encoded in the signature in ζ_1. The crucial difference from Abe's approach is that z_1 can no longer be computed as the result of some hash function given a random input *rnd*. In ACL, z_1 needs to include the attribute commitment C so $z_1 = Cg^{rnd}$ (we need the g^{rnd} factor so that two different signature issuings with the same user cannot be linked to each other). This is the step where the blinded signature inherits some structure from the values the signer can see in the signing step, and allows the encoding of attributes. The fact that z_1 is not the result of a hash function $\mathcal{H}'$ makes our security analysis different from Abe's. We can no longer define $\mathcal{H}'$ so that it will return the output we need, instead we will have to make use of ZK extractors. Unfortunately, we cannot take advantage of Abe's analysis because it only applied to special types of adversaries [33]. Of independent interest, our analysis indicates that, for sequential composition, Abe's blind signature may still be provably secure under DDH in the RO model. The formal analysis follows in the next section.

6. PROOF OF SECURITY

The correctness of the scheme is straightforward, see our full version [3].

THEOREM 3 (BLINDNESS). *The proposed scheme satisfies blindness under the Decisional Diffie-Hellman assumption in the random oracle model.*

PROOF. We wish to show that, when interacting with a challenger as described in the definition of blindness, the adversary cannot guess which signature is which (i.e. the adversary should not be able to tell which signature corresponds to each instance and each attribute set). We distinguish between two types of signatures that a challenger might output: a signature $\sigma = (m, (\zeta, \zeta_1, \rho, \omega, \rho_1', \rho_2', \omega', \mu))$ is *correct* for a particular interaction with the signer if there exists a value γ such that $\zeta = z^\gamma$ and $\zeta_1 = z_1^\gamma$ where z_1 is the value corresponding to this interaction with the signer, and the signature verifies. A signature is *fake* if no such γ exists. Note that it is easy for a challenger to generate both kinds of signatures: a correct signature can simply be output by correctly following the user's side of the protocol. With control of the random oracle, a fake signature is computed as follows: first, the challenger picks ζ and ζ_1 at random from G, and let $\zeta_2 = \zeta/\zeta_1$. Next, it picks random $\rho, \omega, \rho_1', \rho_2', \omega', \mu$ from $\mathbb{Z}_q$ and sets the random oracle such that $\omega + \omega' = \mathcal{H}(\zeta, \zeta_1, g^\rho y^\omega, g^{\rho_1'}\zeta_1^{\omega'}, h^{\rho_2'}\zeta_2^{\omega'}, z^\mu \zeta^{\omega'}, m)$, which ensures that the fake signature verifies.

We will prove the theorem by a hybrid argument. Consider the following three games in which the adversarial signer engages in two signature issuing instances with a challenger who outputs two signatures:

1. `Real`: The challenger outputs two correct signatures, σ_1, σ_2, in random order by honestly following the protocol. A correct signature is one that is honestly generated by interacting with the signer. Thus, in a correct signature the user blinds z, z_1 by the same γ so that $\log_z(z_1) = \log_\zeta(\zeta_1)$.
2. `Hybrid`: The challenger's output consists of a randomly picked correct signature and a fake signature, in random order. In a fake signature the challenger doesn't use the same random γ to blind z and z_1 so that $\log_z(z_1) \neq \log_\zeta(\zeta_1)$ except for negligible probability. Above, we explained how a fake signature can be generated, assuming that the challenger controls the random oracle.
3. `Fake`: The challenger outputs two fake signatures.

Now, what we need to prove is that `Real`≈`Hybrid` and `Hybrid`≈`Fake`. Then, it holds that `Real` ≈ `Fake` which proves the blindness of the ACL scheme since the view of the adversary is indistinguishable no matter if he receives two correct or two fake signatures.

Case 1: `Real`≈`Hybrid`
Suppose that there exists a poly-time adversary $\mathcal{A}$ who is successful in distinguishing between `Real` and `Hybrid` with probability $1/2 + \epsilon$, where the advantage ϵ is not negligible. We then show that there exists a poly-time algorithm $\mathcal{B}$ that solves the DDH problem with non-negligible advantage.

The reduction $\mathcal{B}$ gets as input an instance (g, A, B, D) where (g, A, B, D) is a DDH instance. $\mathcal{B}$ first fixes $z = A$ and then sets $h_0 = g^{e_0}$, and $h_1, \dots, h_n$ to $A^{e_0}, \dots, A^{e_n}$ for randomly chosen $e_i \in \mathbb{Z}_q$. $\mathcal{B}$ sends the parameters to $\mathcal{A}$. The adversary $\mathcal{A}$ creates his public key y and sends y to $\mathcal{B}$ along with messages m_0, m_1, commitments C_0, C_1 and openings $(\overrightarrow{L_0}, \overrightarrow{L_1})$ which are two attributes vectors of size n. $\mathcal{A}$ and $\mathcal{B}$ engage in two interleaving registration and signature issuing instances. During the registration phase we have: $C_{(j)} = A^{k_1^{(j)}}$, $(k_1^{(j)} = e_0 R + e_1 L_{j,1} + \dots + e_n L_{j,n})$ honestly created, for $j \in \{0, 1\}$. Note that the value $k_1^{(j)}$ is known to the reduction $\mathcal{B}$.

Then, during the two signature issuing instances, $\mathcal{A}$ computes $z_1^{(j)} = A^{k_1^{(j)}} g^{rnd^{(j)}}$ where $rnd^{(j)}$ was sent to $\mathcal{B}$. $\mathcal{B}$ responds with random $e^{(j)}$ and then computes two signatures σ_1, σ_2 in the following way:

$\mathcal{B}$ flips two random coins: $coin, b \in \{0, 1\}$. Then, lets σ_{2-coin} be the correct signature on $(m_0, \tilde{C}_b)$ (where $\tilde{C}$ is denoted as ζ_1 in our scheme) for the corresponding instance, and σ_{coin+1} be a signature on $(m_1, \tilde{C}_{1-b})$ generated from the input to $\mathcal{B}$, as follows: set $\zeta^{(j)} = D$ and $\zeta_1^{(j)} = D^{k_1^{(j)}} B^{rnd^{(j)}}$; let $\zeta_2^{(j)} = \zeta^{(j)}/\zeta_1^{(j)}$, randomly choose $\rho, \omega, \rho_1', \rho_2', \omega', \mu$, and then define $\mathcal{H}$ so that the signature verifies.

After receiving the signatures, $\mathcal{A}$ outputs `Real` or `Hybrid`. If $\mathcal{A}$ outputs `Real` then $\mathcal{B}$ outputs "DH" or $\mathcal{B}$ outputs "random" otherwise.

Let us analyze the success of $\mathcal{B}$ in distinguishing Diffie-Hellman tuples from random tuples. If the input (g, A, B, D) is a DH tuple, then: $\zeta^{(j)} = D = g^{ab} = A^b = z^b$ and $\zeta_1^{(j)} = D^{k_1^{(j)}} B^{rnd^{(j)}} = g^{abk_1^{(j)}} g^{brnd^{(j)}} = (g^{ak_1^{(j)}} g^{rnd^{(j)}})^b = (A^{k_1^{(j)}} g^{rnd^{(j)}})^b = z_1^b$ so, the signature σ_{coin+1} is distributed identically to a correct signature, and this is precisely the `Real` game. Similarly, if the input is not a DH tuple then it is the `Hybrid` game. Therefore, $\mathcal{B}$ will be correct exactly when $\mathcal{A}$ is and will distinguish a DH tuple with probability $1/2 + \epsilon$, which contradicts to the DDH assumption.

Case 2: `Hybrid`≈`Fake`
Similarly, we build a reduction $\mathcal{B}$ which given an adversary $\mathcal{A}$, who distinguishes between `Hybrid` and `Fake` with probability $1/2 + \epsilon$, solves the DDH problem.

Working in a similar way we did before, $\mathcal{B}$ will now create a fake signature and one using the input tuple. If $\mathcal{A}$ outputs

Hybrid then $\mathcal{B}$ will output "DH" or "not DH" otherwise. If the input is a DH instance then the output will correspond to the Hybrid game and to the Fake otherwise. So, $\mathcal{B}$ will be successful whenever $\mathcal{A}$ is and will break the DDH assumption with non-negligible advantage ϵ which is a contradiction.

Finally, since Real$\approx$Hybrid and Hybrid$\approx$Fake it follows that Real$\approx$Fake. □

THEOREM 4 (ONE-MORE UNFORGEABILITY). *The signature issuing protocol is $(\ell, \ell+1)-$unforgeable for polynomially bounded ℓ if the discrete logarithm problem is intractable and $\mathcal{H}$ is a random oracle.*

Outline of the proof We first discuss the witness indistinguishability of the protocol (Lemma 1), which allows us to to simulate the Signer with either y-side or z-side witness(es) to extract the witness of the other side. Then, in Lemma 2 we prove that in order for the User to get a valid signature, he has to blind (z, z_1) into (ζ, ζ_1) only in such a way that $\log_z \zeta = \log_{z_1} \zeta_1$. In Lemma 3 we prove that is infeasible to create a valid signature without engaging in the issuing protocol with the legitimate Signer. From Lemmas 2 and 3 we see that if a User engages in the signature issuing protocol ℓ times and outputs $\ell+1$ signatures, then, there exist at least two valid signatures linked to a particular run of the issuing protocol. Finally, it needs to be proven that a forger who manages to produce two signatures from a single protocol run can be used to solve the discrete logarithm problem.

We will denote the i-th execution of the issuing protocol by run_i. Recall that a transcript of run_i of the issuing protocol contains values $(z_{1,i}, z_{2,i})$; by the z-side witness of run_i we denote $(w_{1,i}, w_{2,i})$ such that $z_{1,i} = g^{w_{1,i}}$ and $z_{2,i} = h^{w_{2,i}}$.

Consider an alternative signing algorithm that, instead of using the y-side witness in the issuing protocol, uses the z-side witness. Let $params = (q, G, h, z, \{h_j\})$ be the public parameters, and y be the public key of the Signer. Suppose that the registration and the preparation phases of the signing protocol for run_i resulted in the signer and the user setting up the values $z_{1,i} = g^{w_{1,i}}$, $z_{2,i} = h^{w_{2,i}}$. The alternative signing algorithm takes as input the public parameters $params$, the public key y, the preparation phase output (z_1, z_2) and the values $(w_{1,i}, w_{2,i})$ instead of the secret key x, and works as follows:

1. Generate $c_i, r_i \in_U \mathbb{Z}_q$ and set $a_i := g^{r_i} y^{c_i}$.
2. Compute $a'_{1,i} := g^{u_{1,i}}$ and $a'_{2,i} := h^{u_{2,i}}$ with $u_{1,i}, u_{2,i} \in_U \mathbb{Z}_q$.
3. Sends $a_i, a'_{1,i}, a'_{2,i}$ to the user.
4. Given e_i from user, compute $c'_i := e_i - c_i \bmod q$, $r'_{1,i} := u_{1,i} - c'_i w_{1,i} \bmod q$ and $r'_{2,i} := u_{2,i} - c'_i w_{2,i} \bmod q$.
5. Send $r_i, c_i, r'_{1,i}, r'_{2,i}, c'_i$ to the user.

Definition 10. The signing protocol that was described above is called *the z-side signer.*

LEMMA 1. *The signer's output is perfectly indistinguishable from the output of a z-side signer.*

PROOF. Follows from the result of Cramer [18]. □

Note that, in order to run the z-side signer, it is necessary to somehow get the corresponding witness. We will see later that, with black-box access to an adversarial user in the registration phase, a reduction can use standard Σ-protocol extraction techniques in order to learn the representations of C; if the reduction is, in addition, given the discrete logarithms of all the public parameters to the base g, it will be able to compute the z-side witness, and so, inside a reduction, the z-side signer can be invoked.

LEMMA 2. *(Restrictive Blinding) Let $\mathcal{A}$ be a User that engages in the signature issuing protocol ℓ times, and outputs a valid signature $\sigma = (m, (\zeta, \zeta_1, \rho, \omega, \rho'_1, \rho'_2, \omega', \mu))$. Let run_i denote the i-th execution of the protocol and $z_{1,i}$ denote z_1 used by the signer $\mathcal{S}$ in run_i. For polynomially bounded ℓ and for all polynomial-time $\mathcal{A}$, the probability that $\log_z \zeta \neq \log_{z_{1,i}} \zeta_1$ holds for all i, is negligible if the discrete logarithm problem is intractable and $\mathcal{H}$ is a random oracle.*

PROOF. Let $\mathcal{A}$ have at most q_h accesses to $\mathcal{H}$ and ask at most ℓ signatures to $\mathcal{B}$. Let $\sigma = (m, (\zeta, \zeta_1, \rho, \omega, \rho'_1, \rho'_2, \omega', \mu))$ be a signature that $\mathcal{A}$ outputs and satisfies $\log_z \zeta \neq \log_{z_{1,i}} \zeta_1$ for all i with probability ϵ_0 which is not negligible in n (q_h and ℓ are bounded by a polynomial in the security parameter n). We randomly fix an index $I \in \{1, \ldots, \ell\}$ and regard $\mathcal{A}$ as successful only if the RO query for the resulting signature was during the I-th run. (If the resulting signature does not correspond to any query, then $\mathcal{A}$ is successful only with negligible probability due to the randomness of $\mathcal{H}$.) Let $(\mathbf{G}; \mathbf{q}; \mathbf{g}; \mathbf{Y})$ be an instance of the DL problem.

Reduction Algorithm: $\mathcal{B}$ first sets $(p, q, g) := (\mathbf{p}, \mathbf{q}, \mathbf{g})$. Then, it flips a coin $\chi \in_U \{0, 1\}$ to either select $y := \mathbf{Y}$ (case $\chi = 0$), or $h := \mathbf{Y}$ (case $\chi = 1$) and also guesses a random index $I \in \{1, \ldots, \ell\}$.

Case $y = \mathbf{Y}$: (extracting y-side witness)

1. *Key Generation*: $\mathcal{B}$ selects $k, k', \{k_j\} \in_U \mathbb{Z}_q$, for $0 \leq j \leq n$, and sets $h := g^k$ and $h_j := g^{k_j}$, $z = g^{k'}$. As a result of setting the parameters this way, $\mathcal{B}$ will always be able to compute z-side witnesses, as long as $\mathcal{B}$ can successfully extract the user's attributes and randomness in the registration phase.
2. *Registration:* $\mathcal{B}$ extracts values $(L_1, \ldots, L_n, R)$ using a knowledge extractor for proof π_1 (since we only worry about sequential composition the extractor may rewind) and defines $K = k_0 R + \sum_{ij1}^{n} k_j L_j$ (so that $C = g^K$).
3. *Preparation:* $\mathcal{B}$ selects $w_{1,i} \in \mathbb{Z}_q$ and sets $rnd = w_{1,i} - K$. Then, computes $w_{2,i} = (k' - w_{1,i})/k \bmod q$ (so we have $z_{1,i} = g^{w_{1,i}}, z_{2,i} = h^{w_{2,i}}$). $\mathcal{B}$ sends rnd to $\mathcal{A}$.
4. *Validation:* $\mathcal{B}$ runs $\mathcal{A}$ using the z-side signer described above. At the end of each run_i the z-side signer sends: $r_i, c_i, r'_{1,i}, r'_{2,i}, c'_i$ to $\mathcal{A}$. $\mathcal{B}$ simulates $\mathcal{H}$ by returning $\varepsilon \in_U \mathbb{Z}_q$ to the random oracle queries issued by $\mathcal{A}$. $\mathcal{A}$ outputs a signature $\sigma = (\zeta, \zeta_1, \rho, \omega, \rho'_1, \rho'_2, \omega', \mu)$, that corresponds to some ε.
5. If the RO query for the resulting signature σ happened in run_I then move to the next step, otherwise the reduction fails.
6. *Rewinding*: Reset and restart $\mathcal{A}$ with the same setting. For run_I and after, $\mathcal{B}$ simulates $\mathcal{H}$ with $\tilde{\varepsilon} \in_U \mathbb{Z}_q$. $\mathcal{A}$ outputs a signature, say $\tilde{\sigma} = (\zeta, \zeta_1, \tilde{\rho}, \tilde{\omega}, \tilde{\rho'_1}, \tilde{\rho'_2}, \tilde{\omega'}, \tilde{\mu})$. If $\omega \neq \tilde{\omega}$, $\mathcal{B}$ outputs $x := (\rho - \tilde{\rho})/(\tilde{\omega} - \omega) \bmod q$. The simulation fails, otherwise.

Case $h = \mathbf{Y}$: (extracting z-side witness)

1. *Key generation*: $\mathcal{B}$ selects $x, \{k_j\} \in_U \mathbb{Z}_q$ and sets $y := g^x$ and $h_j := g^{k_j}$. It also selects $w_1, w_2 \in_U \mathbb{Z}_q$ and sets $z := g^{w_1} h^{w_2}$.

2. *Signature Issuing*: $\mathcal{B}$ runs $\mathcal{A}$ simulating the signer as follows.

   (a) For $i \neq I$, $\mathcal{B}$ follows the protocol with y-side witness, x.

   (b) For $i = I$, $\mathcal{B}$ engages in the issuing protocol using the z-side witness (w_1, w_2) as follows.

      i. *Registration:* Extract values $(L_1, \ldots, L_n; R)$ using a ZK extractor and define $K = k_0 R + \sum_{i=1}^{n} k_i L_i$ (so that $C = g^K$).

      ii. *Preparation:* Set $rnd = w_1 - K$ (so we have $z_{1,I} = g^{w_1}, z_{2,I} = h^{w_2}$). $\mathcal{B}$ sends rnd to $\mathcal{A}$.

      iii. *Validation:* $\mathcal{B}$ runs $\mathcal{A}$ using the z-side signer and at the end of run_I sends $(r_I, c_I, r'_{1I}, r'_{2I}, c'_I)$ to $\mathcal{A}$.

   $\mathcal{B}$ simulates $\mathcal{H}$ by returning $\varepsilon \in_U \mathbb{Z}_q$ to the RO queries made by $\mathcal{A}$.

3. $\mathcal{A}$ outputs a signature, say $\sigma = (\zeta, \zeta_1, \rho, \omega, \rho'_1, \rho'_2, \omega', \mu)$, that corresponds to some ε. If the RO query for the forged signature didn't happen in run_I then fail, else move to the next step.
4. *Rewinding*: Rewind and restart $\mathcal{A}^*$ with the same setting. For run_I and forward, $\mathcal{B}$ simulates $\mathcal{H}$ by returning $\tilde{\varepsilon} \in_U \mathbb{Z}_q$.
5. $\mathcal{A}$ outputs a signature, say $\tilde{\sigma} = (\zeta, \zeta_1, \tilde{\rho}, \tilde{\omega}, \tilde{\rho'_1}, \tilde{\rho'_2}, \tilde{\omega'}, \tilde{\mu})$, that corresponds to some $\tilde{\varepsilon}$. If $\omega' \neq \tilde{\omega'}$, $\mathcal{B}$ computes $w'_1 = (\rho'_1 - \tilde{\rho'}_1)/(\mu - \tilde{\mu}) \bmod q$, $w'_2 = (\rho'_2 - \tilde{\rho'_2})/(\mu - \tilde{\mu}) \bmod q$, and outputs $w = (w_1 - w'_1)/(w'_2 - w_2) \bmod q$ (where $w = \log_g h$). Simulation fails otherwise.

Evaluation of success probability The reduction is successful when it gets $\omega \neq \tilde{\omega}$ for $\chi = 0$ or when it gets $\omega' \neq \tilde{\omega}'$ for $\chi = 1$. What we need to argue about is that, independently of the choice of χ, the above will happen with non negligible probability. Note that we construct the reduction by giving different responses after the Ith run (for a randomly chosen $I \in \{1, \ldots, \ell\}$) when rewinding and we let the reduction fail if the forgery didn't happen in run_I.

Let us now fix the adversary's view and his RO tape. Once everything is fixed, we notice that $\mathcal{A}$'s forgery, is uniquely determined by c' and ε. We now consider two cases: (1) $\omega' = \omega$ with non negligible probability even if ε and c' change (after rewinding). In this case $\omega' = \tilde{\omega'}$ and thus $\omega \neq \tilde{\omega}$: $\omega + \omega' = \varepsilon \neq \tilde{\varepsilon} = \tilde{\omega} + \tilde{\omega'}$, so the y-side witness can be extracted. (2) $\omega' \neq \omega$ with non negligible probability if ε and c' change. So, when we run the adversary again with access to z-side witness and with different $\tilde{\varepsilon}$ we get two signatures from him where $\omega = \tilde{\omega}$ and thus $\omega' \neq \tilde{\omega'}$ and thus we can extract the z-side witness. Since we fail if the forgery didn't happen in run_I we do not need to consider what happens when we run $\mathcal{A}$ with y-side witness for $\chi = 1$ and $i \neq I$.

What is left to show is that for $\chi = 1$, the z-side witness, (w'_1, w'_2), extracted is not the one that B already knows. Remember that the reduction in the beginning, selects $w_1, w_2 \in_U \mathbb{Z}_q$ and sets $z := g^{w_1} h^{w_2}$ and in run_I sets rnd so that $z_{1,I} = g^{w_1}, z_{2,I} = h^{w_2}$. The signature that $\mathcal{A}$ produces contains proofs that $\zeta = z^{\gamma}, \zeta_1 = g^{w'_1}$ and $\zeta_2 = h^{w'_2}$, so $w'_1 = \gamma w_1$ and $w'_2 = \gamma w_2$ and we can extract those w'_1, w'_2 by rewinding. For the forgery that $\mathcal{A}$ outputs it holds $\log_z \zeta \neq \log_{z_{1,I}} \zeta_1$ (by definition of Lemma 2) which guarantees that we will obtain two different representations of z. □

LEMMA 3. *Any poly-time adversary $\mathcal{A}$ outputs a valid signature without interacting with the Signer only with negligible probability if the discrete logarithm problem is intractable and $\mathcal{H}$ is a random oracle.*

PROOF. *(sketch)* In order to prove this we are going to use the *oracle replay attack* suggested by Pointcheval and Stern to prove unforgeability of blind signatures [40]. Similar to the proof of Lemma 2 we randomly fix an index $I \in \{1, \ldots, \ell\}$ and regard $\mathcal{A}$ as successful only if the RO query for the resulting signature was during the I-th run. Accordingly, it is equivalent to assuming an adversary, we will call it $\mathcal{A}^*$, that asks $\mathcal{H}$ only once and succeeds with probability $\epsilon_1 \geq \epsilon_0/q_h$. Given this modified $\mathcal{A}^*$ we construct the reduction $\mathcal{B}$ that solves the discrete logarithm problem by simulating the interaction. Given $\mathbf{Y} \in G$, we construct a reduction $\mathcal{B}$ that finds $\log_g \mathbf{Y}$ in $\mathbb{Z}_q$. During *key generation*, $\mathcal{B}$ first selects $\omega, \xi, \{k_i\}$ randomly and sets $y = \mathbf{Y}, h = g^w, h_i = g^{k_i} z = \mathbf{Y} g^{\xi}$. ($\mathcal{B}$ does not need to simulate the signer, so it can put $\mathbf{Y}$ in both y and z.) Then, $\mathcal{B}$ invokes $\mathcal{A}^*$ twice with the same initial settings and different ε and $\tilde{\varepsilon}$ as answers of $\mathcal{H}$. The resulting signatures are $\sigma = (\zeta, \zeta_1, \rho, \omega, \rho'_1, \rho'_2, \omega', \mu)$ and $\tilde{\sigma} = (\zeta, \zeta_1, \tilde{\rho}, \tilde{\omega}, \tilde{\rho'_1}, \tilde{\rho'_2}, \tilde{\omega'}, \tilde{\mu})$. Since $\omega + \omega' = \varepsilon \neq \tilde{\varepsilon} = \tilde{\omega} + \tilde{\omega'}$, at least one of $\omega \neq \tilde{\omega}$ or $\omega' \neq \tilde{\omega'}$ happens.

In the case that $\omega \neq \tilde{\omega}$, $\mathcal{B}$ computes $\log_g \mathbf{Y} = (\rho - \tilde{\rho})/(\tilde{\omega} - \omega) \bmod q$. For the case $\omega' \neq \tilde{\omega'}$, $\mathcal{B}$ computes $\gamma = \log_z \zeta = (\mu - \tilde{\mu})/(\omega' - \tilde{\omega'}) \bmod q$, $w_1 = \log_g \zeta_1 = (\rho'_1 - \tilde{\rho'_1})/(\omega' - \tilde{\omega'}) \bmod q$, $w_2 = \log_g \zeta_2 = (\rho'_2 - \tilde{\rho'_2})/(\omega' - \tilde{\omega'}) \bmod q$, and $\log_g \mathbf{Y} = \log_g z - \xi = (w_1 + w_2/w)/\gamma - \xi \bmod q$. □

PROOF. *(Theorem 4).* Suppose that there exists adversary $\mathcal{A}$ that outputs $\ell + 1$ valid signatures with probability ϵ not negligible after interacting with the Signer at most ℓ times. The case $\ell = 0$ has been ruled out by Lemma 3. We consider $\ell \geq 1$.

By Lemmas 2 and 3, among the $\ell+1$ signatures, there exist at least two signature-message pairs which contain (ζ, ζ_1) and $(\bar{\zeta}, \bar{\zeta_1})$ such that $\log_\zeta \zeta_1 = \log_{\bar{\zeta}} \bar{\zeta_1} = \log_z z_{1I}$ holds for z_{1I} used in run_I for some I in $\{1, \ldots, \ell\}$. Now, there exist two queries to $\mathcal{H}$ that correspond to those signatures. In a similar way as in the proof of Lemma 2, we guess the indices of these queries and regard $\mathcal{A}$ as being successful only when the guess is correct. We consider an equivalent adversary $\mathcal{A}^*$ that asks $\mathcal{H}$ only twice and succeeds with probability $\epsilon^* = \epsilon/\binom{q_h}{2}$ in producing two signatures in the expected relation.

We construct a reduction $\mathcal{B}$ that, given $(\mathbf{p}, \mathbf{q}, \mathbf{g}, \mathbf{Y})$, solves $\log_g \mathbf{Y}$ in $\mathbb{Z}_q$ by using $\mathcal{A}^*$.

Reduction Algorithm: $\mathcal{B}$ sets $(p, q, g) := (\mathbf{p}, \mathbf{q}, \mathbf{g})$. It then flips a coin, $\chi \in_U \{0, 1\}$, to select either $y := \mathbf{Y}$ (case $\chi = 0$), or $y := g^x$ with randomly chosen x (case $\chi = 1$).

1. *Setup:* If $\chi = 0$, set up and use the z-side signer. Set $h, h_0, \ldots, h_n$ such that their discrete logarithm base g is known. Else, set up the y-side signer by letting $y = g^x$ for a randomly chosen x; set up $h, h_0, \ldots, h_n$ such that their discrete logarithm base Y is known.
2. *Registration:* If $\chi = 0$, extract $(R, L_0, \ldots, L_n)$. Else follow the protocol.
3. *Preparation:* Follow the protocol.
4. *Validation:* If $\chi = 0$, use the z-side signer, else follow the protocol.

5. *Responding to the RO queries:* $\mathcal{B}$ simulates $\mathcal{H}$ by returning random values, say ε_1 and ε_2, to the two RO queries.
6. *Rewinding:* When $\mathcal{A}^*$ outputs two signatures $(\sigma^{(1)} = (\zeta^{(1)}, \zeta_1^{(1)}, \rho^{(1)}, \omega^{(1)}, \rho_1'^{(1)}, \rho_2'^{(1)}, \omega'^{(1)}, \mu^{(1)}))$ and $(\sigma^{(2)} = (\zeta^{(2)}, \zeta_1^{(2)}, \rho^{(2)}, \omega^{(2)}, \rho_1'^{(2)}, \rho_2'^{(2)}, \omega'^{(2)}, \mu^{(2)}))$ corresponding to ε_1 and ε_2, $\mathcal{B}$ resets the adversary and this time responds to the two RO queries with $\tilde{\varepsilon}_1$ and $\tilde{\varepsilon}_2$.
7. *Interacting with $\mathcal{A}^*$ after rewinding* is the same as before, according to the value of χ.
8. *Extracting:* When $\mathcal{A}^*$ again outputs two signatures $(\tilde{\sigma}^{(1)} = (\zeta^{(1)}, \zeta_1^{(1)}, \tilde{\rho}^{(1)}, \tilde{\omega}^{(1)}, \tilde{\rho'}_1^{(1)}, \tilde{\rho'}_2^{(1)}, \tilde{\omega'}^{(1)}, \tilde{\mu}^{(1)})$ and $(\tilde{\sigma}^{(2)} = (\zeta^{(2)}, \zeta_1^{(2)}, \tilde{\rho}^{(2)}, \tilde{\omega}^{(2)}, \tilde{\rho'}_1^{(2)}, \tilde{\rho'}_2^{(2)}, \tilde{\omega'}^{(2)}, \tilde{\mu}^{(2)})$ corresponding to $\tilde{\varepsilon}_1$ and $\tilde{\varepsilon}_2$, do: if $\chi = 0$ and $\omega^{(1)} \neq \tilde{\omega}^{(1)}$ or $\omega^{(2)} \neq \tilde{\omega}^{(2)}$, then extract the y-side witness as described in the proof of Lemma 2; else if $\chi = 1$ and $\omega'^{(1)} \neq \tilde{\omega'}^{(1)}$ or $\omega'^{(2)} \neq \tilde{\omega'}^{(2)}$, then extract the z-side witness as described in Lemma 2.

Evaluation of success probability. Here we need to show that $\mathcal{B}$ will extract the witness that it doesn't already know with non-negligible probability (otherwise, χ is revealed). Consider all the q^2 possible $(\varepsilon_1, \varepsilon_2)$ pairs that can be given as responses to $\mathcal{A}^*$'s two RO queries. Let *succ* be the set of pairs $(\varepsilon_1, \varepsilon_2)$ for which $\mathcal{A}^*$ succeeds: $succ = \{(\varepsilon_1, \varepsilon_2) | \mathcal{A}$ breaks the seq. one-more unforgeability$\}$. What we want to show is that for a random pair $(\varepsilon_1, \varepsilon_2) \in succ$ there exists $(\tilde{\varepsilon_1}, \tilde{\varepsilon_2}) \in succ$ such that $\mathcal{A}^*$ produces the same e with non-negligible probability in the run where the first RO query happened. Notice that the transcript (i.e. the messages exchanged between the Signer and $\mathcal{A}^*$) of these two runs has to be the same. We call such a pair $(\tilde{\varepsilon_1}, \tilde{\varepsilon_2})$ *good* for $(\varepsilon_1, \varepsilon_2)$.

Consider $\mathcal{A}^*$ is run twice: once with $(\varepsilon_1, \varepsilon_2)$ and once with $(\tilde{\varepsilon_1}, \tilde{\varepsilon_2})$, both times producing two message-signature pairs corresponding to z_{1I}. Taken together, $(\varepsilon_1, \varepsilon_2)$, $(\tilde{\varepsilon_1}, \tilde{\varepsilon_2})$, the transcript of the runs and the four message-signature pairs allow the reduction to compute either a y side or a z side witness. However, we need to argue that, with non-negligible probability, this will be a witness the reduction doesn't already know. Since the transcripts are identical, the joint distribution of the two views ($\mathcal{A}^*$'s view in the first run and its view, after the rewinding, in the second run) is independent of χ.

First, note that there are only q possible e's but q^2 possible $(\tilde{\varepsilon_1}, \tilde{\varepsilon_2})$, and so there can only be a negligible fraction of $(\varepsilon_1, \varepsilon_2)$ for which no *good* $(\tilde{\varepsilon_1}, \tilde{\varepsilon_2})$ exists. Suppose that $(\tilde{\varepsilon_1}, \tilde{\varepsilon_2})$ is *good* for $(\varepsilon_1, \varepsilon_2)$ but $(\varepsilon_1^*, \varepsilon_2^*)$ is not; moreover, the reduction that gives $(\varepsilon_1, \varepsilon_2)$ before rewinding, and $(\varepsilon_1^*, \varepsilon_2^*)$ after rewinding, can only compute the witness it already knows (i.e. if $\chi = 0$, it can compute the z-side witness, and for $\chi = 1$ the y-side). Then for the same choice of χ, the reduction would be computing the witness it does *not* already know if, instead, it used $(\tilde{\varepsilon_1}, \tilde{\varepsilon_2})$ and $(\varepsilon_1^*, \varepsilon_2^*)$. For example, if $\chi = 0$ we would have $\omega \neq \tilde{\omega}$ and $\omega = \tilde{\omega^*}$ respectively, which implies that $\tilde{\omega} \neq \tilde{\omega^*}$ and thus by choosing $(\varepsilon_1, \varepsilon_2)$ and $(\varepsilon_1^*, \varepsilon_2^*)$ the y side witness could be extracted. Since it is just as likely to pick $(\varepsilon_1, \varepsilon_2)$ or $(\tilde{\varepsilon_1}, \tilde{\varepsilon_2})$ for the values before rewinding, it is just as likely to succeed as to fail, independently of χ (this analysis was first given by Abe and Okamoto [2]).

Finally, the only thing left to prove is that an adversary cannot open the sets of commitments $\{C^{(i)}\}$ and $\{\zeta^{(i)}, \zeta_1^{(i)}\}$ to two different multisets. Note that $\zeta^{(i)}$ uniquely determines $\gamma^{(i)}$, and by Lemma 2, it follows that for every i, there exists some $z_1^{(i')}$ such that $\zeta_1^{(i)} = (z_1^{(i')})^{\gamma^{(i)}}$. Thus, an alternative opening of the commitment $\{\zeta^{(i)}, \zeta_1^{(i)}\}$ gives rise to an alternative representation of $z_1^{(i')}$ in bases $h, h_1, \ldots, h_n, g$. In turn, by standard techniques, this breaks the discrete logarithm assumption. (The reduction will just honestly emulate the signer, and embed the DL instance into the parameters $h, h_1, \ldots, h_n, g$.) $\square$

Setting parameters. Note that our reduction is not tight: an adversary $\mathcal{A}$ whose success probability is ϵ gives rise to the reduction $\mathcal{B}$ with the same runtime but success probability $\epsilon / \binom{q_h}{2} \approx \epsilon / q_h^2$. This, in other words means that if $\mathcal{A}$ takes time t to break unforgeability with probability ϵ, then our reduction, $\mathcal{B}$, in order to break the discrete logarithm assumption with the same success probability would need time $t \cdot q_h^2$. So, if $\mathcal{A}$ breaks unforgeability faster than in time 2^k, then $\mathcal{B}$ breaks DL in time faster than $2^k \cdot q_h^2 = 2^{k+2\log q_h}$. Thus, we need to set the parameters to be sufficiently large so that is reasonable to assume that the reduction would take time $2^{k+2\log q_h}$ to break DL directly.

As suggested by NIST [32] in order to tolerate an adversary whose computational power is 2^k, one needs an elliptic curve group of size 2^{2k} which for our reduction should be $2^{2(k+2\log q_h)}$. Now, let's be very conservative and assume that $q_h = 2^{80}$, thus the factor $\binom{q_h}{2}$ we lose is of 160-bits. Thus, if we want to achieve 128-bit security we would need an elliptic curve group where the bit size of an element is $2(128 + 2 \cdot 80) = 576$-bits. Note that the equivalent security level for RSA requires 3072-bit keys.

7. ACKNOWLEDGMENTS

We thank the anonymous reviewers for their helpful comments and suggestions. We also thank our collaborators at the Pay-As-You-Go project for discussions on the use of anonymous credential systems in lightweight devices and especially Gesine Hinterwälder. This work was supported by NSF grants 0964379 and 1012060.

8. REFERENCES

[1] M. Abe. A secure three-move blind signature scheme for polynomially many signatures. In *EUROCRYPT'01*, pages 136–151, 2001.

[2] M. Abe and T. Okamoto. Provably secure partially blind signatures. In *CRYPTO'00*, pages 271–286. Springer-Verlag, 2000.

[3] F. Baldimtsi and A. Lysyanskaya. Anonymous credentials light. Cryptology ePrint Archive, Report 2012/298, 2012.

[4] F. Baldimtsi and A. Lysyanskaya. On the security of one-witness blind signature schemes. Cryptology ePrint Archive, Report 2012/197, 2012.

[5] M. Belenkiy, M. Chase, M. Kohlweiss, and A. Lysyanskaya. Compact e-cash and simulatable vrfs revisited. In *Pairing '09*, pages 114–131, 2009.

[6] P. Bichsel, J. Camenisch, T. Groß, and V. Shoup. Anonymous credentials on a standard java card. CCS '09, pages 600–610. ACM, 2009.

[7] A. Boldyreva. Threshold signatures, multisignatures and blind signatures based on the

gap-diffie-hellman-group signature scheme. PKC '03, pages 31–46, London, UK, UK, 2003. Springer-Verlag.

[8] S. Brands. Untraceable off-line cash in wallets with observers. In *CRYPTO'93*, pages 302–318, 1993.

[9] S. A. Brands. Rethinking public key infrastructures and digital certificates: Building in privacy. MIT Press, Cambridge-London, August 2000.

[10] J. Camenisch and T. Groß. Efficient attributes for anonymous credentials. In *Proceedings of the 15th ACM conference on Computer and communications security*, CCS '08, 2008.

[11] J. Camenisch, S. Hohenberger, and A. Lysyanskaya. Compact e-cash. In *EUROCRYPT '05, volume 3494 of LNCS*, pages 302–321. Springer-Verlag, 2005.

[12] J. Camenisch, M. Koprowski, and B. Warinschi. Efficient blind signatures without random oracles. SCN'04, pages 134–148, 2005.

[13] J. Camenisch and A. Lysyanskaya. An efficient system for non-transferable anonymous credentials with optional anonymity revocation. EUROCRYPT '01, pages 93–118, London, UK, 2001. Springer-Verlag.

[14] J. Camenisch and A. Lysyanskaya. Signature schemes and anonymous credentials from bilinear maps. In *CRYPTO'04, LNCS 3152*, pages 56 – 72, 2004.

[15] J. Camenisch and M. Michels. Proving in zero-knowledge that a number is the product of two safe primes. EUROCRYPT'99. Springer-Verlag, 1999.

[16] J. Camenisch, F.-H. Simone, and K. Rannenberg. Privacy and identity management for life. In *ISBN 978-3-642-20316-9*. Springer, 2012.

[17] D. Chaum. Blind signatures for untraceable payment. In *Crypto'82*, pages 199–203, 1982.

[18] R. Cramer, I. Damgård, and B. Schoenmakers. Proofs of partial knowledge and simplified design of witness hiding protocols. In *CRYPTO '94*, pages 174–187. Springer-Verlag, 1994.

[19] I. Damgård. Commitment schemes and zero-knowledge protocols. In *Lectures on Data Security, Modern Cryptology in Theory and Practice, Summer School, Aarhus, Denmark, July 1998*. Springer-Verlag, 1999.

[20] I. Damgård. On σ- protocols. In *Course Notes, http://www.daimi.au.dk/~ivan/Sigma.ps*, 2002.

[21] A. Fiat and A. Shamir. How to prove yourself: Practical solutions to identification and signature problems. In *CRYPTO '86*, pages 186–194. Springer-Verlag, 1986.

[22] S. Garg, V. Rao, A. Sahai, D. Schröder, and D. Unruh. Round optimal blind signatures. In *CRYPTO'11*, pages 630–648, 2011.

[23] O. Goldreich. *Foundations of Cryptography, vol. 1: Basic Tools*. Cambridge University Press, 2001.

[24] S. Goldwasser, S. Micali, and C. Rackoff. The knowledge complexity of interactive proof systems. *SIAM J. Comput.*, 18:186–208, February 1989.

[25] J. Guajardo, B. Mennink, and B. Schoenmakers. Anonymous credential schemes with encrypted attributes. In *Cryptology and Network Security*, pages 314–333. Springer, 2010.

[26] L. C. Guillou and J.-J. Quisquater. A practical zero-knowledge protocol fitted to security microprocessor minimizing both transmission and memory. In *EUROCRYPT '88*, pages 123–128, 1988.

[27] N. Gura, A. Patel, A. Wander, H. Eberle, and S. C. Shantz. Comparing elliptic curve cryptography and rsa on 8-bit cpus. In *CHES'04*, pages 119–132, 2004.

[28] G. Hinterwälder, C. T. Zenger, F. Baldimtsi, A. Lysyanskaya, C. Paar, and W. P. Burleson. Efficient e-cash in practice: NFC-based payments for public transportation systems. In *Privacy Enhancing Technologies - PETS'13*, pages 40–59, 2013.

[29] A. Juels, M. Luby, and R. Ostrovsky. Security of blind digital signatures (extended abstract). In *CRYPTO'97*, pages 150–164. Springer-Verlag, 1997.

[30] M. Langheinrich. Privacy by design - principles of privacy - aware ubiquitous systems. In *Ubicomp 2001: Ubiquitous Computing*, volume 2201, pages 273–291. Springer Berlin, Heidelberg, 2001.

[31] A. J. Menezes, P. C. V. Oorschot, and S. A. Vanstone. Handbook of applied cryptography, 1997.

[32] NIST. The case for elliptic curve cryptography, 2009. `http://www.nsa.gov/business/programs/elliptic_curve.shtml`.

[33] M. Ohkubo and M. Abe. Security of three-move blind signature schemes reconsidered. In *SCIS'03, Symposium on Cryptography and Information Security*, 2003.

[34] T. Okamoto. Efficient blind and partially blind signatures without random oracles. In *TCC'06*, volume 3876 of *Lecture Notes in Computer Science*, pages 80–99. Springer, 2006.

[35] C. Paquin. U-prove cryptographic specification v1.1. In *Microsoft Technical Report, http://connect.microsoft.com/site1188*, February 2011.

[36] E. Parliament and C. of the European Union. Regulation (ec) 45/2001. In *Official Journal of the European Union*, 2001.

[37] E. Parliament and C. of the European Union. Directive 2009/136/ec. In *Official Journal of the European Union*, 2009.

[38] T. P. Pedersen. Non-interactive and information-theoretic secure verifiable secret sharing. CRYPTO '91. Springer-Verlag.

[39] D. Pointcheval and J. Stern. Security arguments for digital signatures and blind signatures. In *Journal Of Cryptology*, volume 13, pages 361–396, 2000.

[40] D. Pointcheval and J. Stern. Provably secure blind signature schemes. In *Asiacrypt '96, LNCS 1163*, pages 252–265. Springer-Verlag, Feb 2011.

[41] H. A. Schmidt. National strategy for trusted identities in cyberspace. In *Cyberwar Resources Guide, Item 163, http://www.projectcyw-d.org/resources/items/show/163*, 2010.

[42] C. P. Schnorr. Efficient identification and signatures for smart cards. CRYPTO '89, pages 239–252, 1989.

[43] I. S. Team. Specification of the identity mixer cryptographic library, version 2.3.0. In *IBM Research Report*, 2010.

[44] G. J. R. B. Zhang, H. and K. Fu. Moo: A batteryless computational rfid and sensing platform. In *Tech. Rep. UM-CS-2011-020, UMass Amherst Department of Computer Science*, 2011.

Heart-to-Heart (H2H): Authentication for Implanted Medical Devices

Masoud Rostami
Rice University
Houston, TX
masoud@rice.edu

Ari Juels
RSA Laboratories
Cambridge, MA
ari.juels@rsa.com

Farinaz Koushanfar
Rice University
Houston, TX
farinaz@rice.edu

ABSTRACT

We present Heart-to-Heart (H2H), a system to authenticate external medical device controllers and programmers to Implantable Medical Devices (IMDs). IMDs, which include pacemakers and cardiac defibrillators, are therapeutic medical devices partially or wholly embedded in the human body. They often have built-in radio communication to facilitate non-invasive reprogramming and data readout. Many IMDs, though, lack well designed authentication protocols, exposing patients to over-the-air attack and physical harm.

H2H makes use of ECG (heartbeat data) as an authentication mechanism, ensuring access only by a medical instrument in physical contact with an IMD-bearing patient. Based on statistical analysis of real-world data, we propose and analyze new techniques for extracting time-varying randomness from ECG signals for use in H2H. We introduce a novel cryptographic device pairing protocol that uses this randomness to protect against attacks by active adversaries, while meeting the practical challenges of lightweight implementation and noise tolerance in ECG readings. Finally, we describe an end-to-end implementation in an ARM-Cortex M-3 microcontroller that demonstrates the practicality of H2H in current IMD hardware.

Previous schemes have had goals much like those of H2H, but with serious limitations making them unfit for deployment—such as naïvely designed cryptographic pairing protocols (some of them recently broken). In addition to its novel analysis and use of ECG entropy, H2H is the first physiologically-based IMD device pairing protocol with a rigorous adversarial model and protocol analysis.

Categories and Subject Descriptors

J.3 [**Computer Applications**]: Life and Medical Sciences - Medical information systems; C.3 [**Computer Systems Organization**]: Special-Purpose and Application-Based System, Real-time and embedded systems

General Terms

Security, Design

CCS'13, November 4–8, 2013, Berlin, Germany.

http://dx.doi.org/10.1145/2508859.2516658.

Keywords

Implantable Medical Devices; IMD Security; Security Protocols

1. INTRODUCTION

Implantable Medical Devices (IMDs) apply continuous monitoring and automatic therapies to the treatment of chronic medical disorders. Implanted either partially or fully in patients' bodies, IMDs are often sophisticated devices containing batteries, embedded CPUs, radios, sensors, and actuators. As clinical trials validate IMDs' efficacy [22] and as IMDs treat a broadening range of disorders, their use is growing. For instance, in the United States, over 100,000 patients a year receive implantable cardioverter defibrillators (ICDs) [19], which detect dangerous heart rhythms and administer electric shocks to restore normal activity. Other IMDs include pacemakers, neurostimulators, and implantable drug pumps.

Powered IMDs generally contain radios for communication with external devices called *commercial device programmers* that can reprogram IMDs and extract patient data from them. Such wireless communication permits safe, non-invasive access to IMDs. But it also brings the security risks of embedded control into the human body. Seminal work by Halperin et al. [20], for example, exposes design flaws in a common ICD that enable attackers to seize unauthorized control wirelessly, and potentially harm victims.

Our work here addresses the tension between two critical requirements for IMDs. On the one hand, IMDs must offer reasonably permissive access-control policies when life-threatening medical events occur. Emergency responders may need to reprogram IMDs or extract patient data from them, and shouldn't incur fatal treatment delays by contacting care providers for device-specific keys or passwords. On the other hand, overly loose access-control policies expose IMDs to unauthorized wireless access, such as those illustrated by the Halperin et al. attack, that can physically harm patients or expose their medical data [20].

1.1 Heart-to-Heart (H2H)

Our solution is a system called *Heart-to-Heart* (H2H). H2H implements a simple access-control policy for IMDs that we call "touch to access": A medical instrument (e.g., commercial device programmer), which we call generically a *Programmer*, obtains access to a patient's IMD if and only if it has significant physical contact with the patient's body. An important facet of touch-to-access is *forward security*. Authentication to the IMD lapses once the instrument loses physical contact with the patient.

Touch-to-access offers a practical and effective balance between the competing access requirements of permissiveness in emergencies and resistance to attacks. The policy is also common sense: Physical access to a patient means the ability to harm or cure.

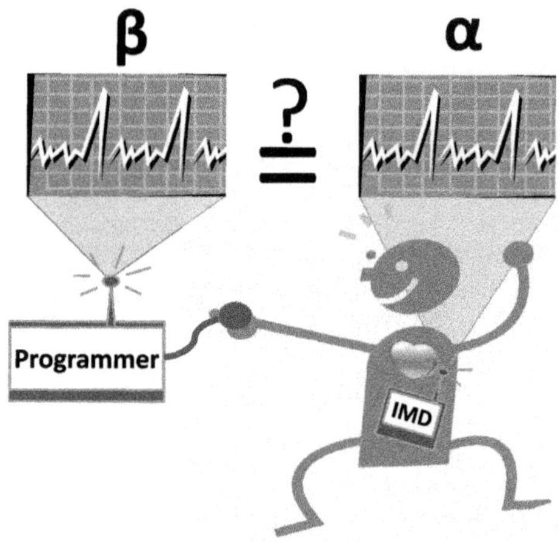

Figure 1: Basic H2H operation. The Programmer and IMD take individual ECG readings, respectively β and α. If $\beta \approx \alpha$, then the IMD grants access to the Programmer.

H2H enforces a touch-to-access policy using a time-varying biometric, often called a *physiological value* (PV). When a Programmer seeks access to an IMD, it initiates an authentication session. The IMD takes a reading α of the PV; at the same time, the Programmer takes its own reading β. If β is "nearly equal" to α, then the Programmer obtains access to the IMD. ("Near equality," as we explain later, is needed because PV readings are noisy.)

The H2H architecture can in principle rely on any PV, but we focus here specifically on use of the waveform produced by the heart, known as an ECG (electrocardiogram). Thus H2H is well suited for authentication to cardiac IMDs such as ICDs and pacemakers, today the largest class of powered IMDs. In principle, though, H2H can work with *any* IMD equipped to measure ECG anywhere in the body, not just cardiac devices. As we show, suitably processed ECG samples effectively constitute a low-bandwidth stream of random bits well suited to forward-secure authentication.

Briefly, then, in H2H a Programmer and IMD take independent, time-synchronous ECG readings. The IMD compares the two results to enforce a touch-to-access policy on wireless access by the Programmer. Figure 1 depicts the basic operation of H2H.

1.2 Challenges and contributions

Several previous schemes have sought to perform ECG-based pairing with IMDs like H2H, but have had serious shortcomings. Most notably, previous schemes have relied on cryptographic pairing protocols without rigorous adversarial modeling or security analysis. As a result, two of the most recent of them [23,48] were shown in a 2013 paper [39] to have serious cryptographic flaws.

Thus designing a practical system such as H2H with rigorous security assurances has effectively remained an open problem, one that raises several technical challenges.

The first challenge is demonstrating that ECG is a suitable PV for authentication. H2H derives a *key source* from the patient's ECG signal, a sequence of key bits that authenticate a Programmer to an IMD. Secure touch-to-access authentication requires that the key source be *truly random*, ideally that constituent bits have high entropy and are statistically independent from one another and over time. The key source is then hard for an attacker to guess without physical access to the patient and also ensures forward-security, i.e., that old key source bits don't reveal future ones.

Previous work has explored the statistical properties of ECG waveforms for key generation, but not the important impact of read error rates on authentication false positive and false negative rates. We present experiments on real patient ECG data showing that it's possible (with errors) to extract roughly four truly random and statistically uncorrelated bits from the ECG wave corresponding to a single heartbeat. Collection over a 15-second interval suffices for strong Programmer authentication (a false acceptance rate of about 2.7×10^{-9} and false rejection rate of 10^{-4}).

We also introduce an optimal scheme in H2H for testing PV validity, i.e., testing $\alpha \approx \beta$. Our scheme relies on the Neyman-Pearson Lemma, rather than naïvely on Hamming distance, as in previous work.

Good statistical properties, however, don't ensure that ECG can enforce the touch-to-access policy in H2H. Recently developed systems can read cardiac rhythms *remotely* via videocamera, and even accurately measure a patient's pulse. (Skin color changes subtly with cardiac rhythms.) In Section 3.3, we very briefly report our implementation and test results for the best known of these systems [35] and show that it doesn't reveal statistically significant information about the ECG key source used by H2H.

Given a good key source, a *cryptographic pairing protocol* is needed between the Programmer and IMD. Two features of H2H make cryptographic pairing a challenge. First, when the Programmer and IMD synchronously sample the key source, their respective readings β and α are *noisy*: Often $\beta \approx \alpha$, but exact equality $\beta = \alpha$ isn't obtained. Cryptographic tools such as password-authenticated key agreement (e.g., [5]) require exact equality, while error-tolerant ones, e.g., [14,24], sacrifice entropy needlessly in our setting here.

Second, the IMD has tight *computational and power constraints*. Microcontrollers in common use for IMDs today can perform only lightweight cryptography. As IMDs are long-lived devices (with an average lifetime today of five to seven years [15]), and battery replacement requires surgical intervention, power conservation is essential. H2H can protect new IMDs as well as legacy in-vivo IMDs with upgradable firmware, as long as the H2H implementation meets the IMD's limited memory and computational resources.

We present a new pairing protocol that exploits the fact that key source bits are statistically uncorrelated, and thus that we can treat α and β as one-time authentication values. We demonstrate its security in a strong adversarial model that includes man-in-the-middle attacks, such as the jam-and-replay attacks feasible in a wireless environment.

Our H2H pairing protocol requires only a low-exponent RSA encryption (tens of modular multiplications) and a few AES invocations and hash computations by the IMD. We demonstrate a full implementation of H2H on an ARM Cortex-M3 processor.

In summary then, our contributions are:

- *Statistical characterization of ECG for authentication:* Using real-world ECG measurements [30], we experimentally quantify the extractable entropy in ECG signals. (We demonstrate use of the Neyman-Pearson Lemma to achieve optimal use of this randomness.)
- *Cryptographic pairing protocol:* We present a novel, lightweight, noise-tolerant cryptographic scheme for Programmer-to-IMD pairing in H2H. We formalize an adversarial model and outline proofs of security.
- *Implementation:* We describe a full implementation of H2H in an ARM Cortex-M3 processor, reporting resource requirements such as code size and power consumption, and demonstrating the feasibility of H2H for use in contemporary IMDs.

Organization

We introduce our statistical model for ECG waveforms and operational, trust, and adversarial models for H2H in Section 2. A detailed statistical analysis of real-world ECG waveforms and our proposed entropy extraction techniques follows in Section 3. We specify the cryptographic device-pairing protocol for H2H in Section 4. We describe an implementation of H2H in Section 5. We review related work in Section 6, and conclude in Section 7 with a discussion of future work. Appendix A outlines a security analysis of the H2H device-pairing protocol; detailed modeling and analysis is deferred for the full version of this paper.

2. MODELING

Before diving into details on H2H, some basics on ECG and our associated statistical model are in order, as well as discussion of our operational, trust, and adversarial models.

2.1 ECG model

Figure 2 is a schematic depiction of the ECG waveform of a healthy patient. The so-called R-peak is the most prominent feature of the ECG waveform; it corresponds to the "beat" in a heartbeat. The time between two consecutive R-peaks, or the heartbeat duration, is commonly referred as the inter-pulse interval (IPI). As the figure shows, a typical ECG cycle includes other physiologically significant, named features: The P-wave, which occurs before the R-peak, the QRS complex, which includes sharp valleys before and after the R-peak, denoted by Q and S respectively, and the T-wave, following the S valley.

The heart rhythm is governed by the parasympathetic nervous system, in which many non-linearly interacting processes give the IPI its well-studied chaotic nature [7,31]. The ECG waveform, and parasympathetic network more generally, are influenced by both long-term trends such as circadian rhythm and short-term temperature and respiratory changes. Thus ECG waves simultaneously exhibit both long term patterns and short-term chaotic behavior.

The ECG signal is well modeled as a stochastic process. The existence of long-term patterns renders the process non-stationary, meaning that the parameters of its underlying distribution, e.g., mean and variance, fluctuate over time. We introduce transforms for H2H, however, that eliminate long-term variations, creating a residual signal that is well-approximated by a wide-sense stationary stochastic process, i.e., one whose first and second moments don't change over time. Previous work observed a strongly random element in IPI time series values [7], motivating later use of IPIs as a natural source of randomness [9].

Like H2H, previous systems also exploited the natural *synchronization* property of IPIs. Slight shifts in the time interval over which IPIs are derived don't impact IPI values, which are computed relative to R-peaks, not absolute time.

Entropy and security: We show that it is possible to extract four *high-grade* random bits per IPI from our processed ECG source, i.e., bits that have maximal entropy and are fully uncorrelated. We use this entropy measure to characterize the security of H2H formally using our main theorem, Theorem 1. An important new aspect of our work is quantification and use of the different error rates incurred by individual high-grade random bits via the Neyman-Pearson Lemma. This simple approach marks a notable advance over earlier work, which assigned the same significance to all random bits. Our improvement enables authentication with the optimal, i.e., minimum possible, false positive rate for a given false negative constraint.

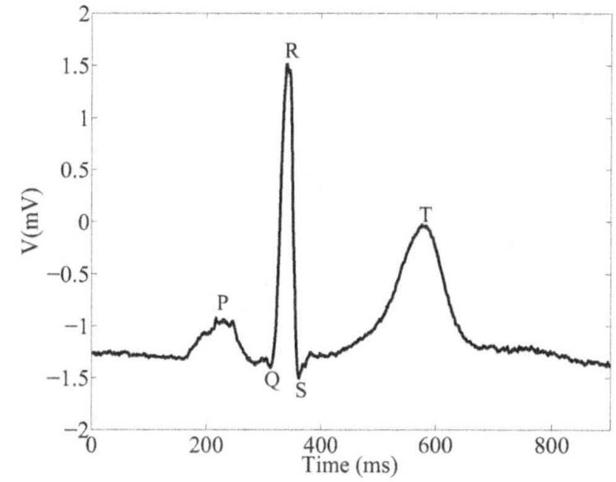

Figure 2: A typical ECG waveform from lead V2 which is recorded from chest. R-peak is the most prominent feature.

2.2 Operational and trust models

We envision use of H2H primarily for *emergency* authentication, when medical personnel, e.g., emergency medical technicians (EMTs), need access to a patient's IMD, but have no pre-established keys or trust relationship. Rapid and reliable access to the IMD is important. Thus H2H harvests PV randomness efficiently to achieve quick authentication.

We assume no public-key infrastructure (PKI) for certification of trustworthy programmers. The challenges of key revocation, tamperproofing of programmers to prevent key compromise, etc., are substantial. Similarly, we assume it's impractical for medical personnel to contact an authority on the fly for access credentials, as this approach would require an infrastructure of broad (indeed, worldwide) and robust trust relationships. Thus H2H relies exclusively on the touch-to-access policy for authentication.

The ECG waveform goes flat when an acute heart attack occurs. Similarly, in some late-stage terminal diseases, the parasympathetic network collapses and as a result, the ECG waveform loses most of its entropy. The hugely distorted ECG waveform resulting from such conditions is readily identifiable. In such cases, H2H is designed to enter a promiscuous mode in which any Programmer may access the IMD: For these acute events, the risks of medical failure greatly outweigh those of malicious attack. Additionally, these extreme medical conditions occur rarely.

In non-emergency situations, for instance, when a patient is receiving routine medical care, it may be practical for medical personnel to retrieve device-specific keys. But in unusual situations, e.g., patients traveling abroad, lost keys, and so forth, H2H is additionally useful as a secondary or backup authentication mechanism.

2.3 Adversarial model

We design H2H for a strong adversarial model that assumes the presence of an attacker during a Programmer-to-IMD authentication session. This adversary is active. It has complete network control, i.e., can drop (jam), modify, replay, and forge messages at will. (The adversary can't compromise the Programmer or IMD, which would render protection of the IMD impossible.) While the presence of an adversary during a medical emergency is admittedly a strong assumption, we believe it is prudent to design robust security for critical systems such as IMDs by default.

Protecting against strong, active adversaries in a pairing protocol isn't straightforward. As mentioned above, recent breaks of two recent such protocols illustrate the challenge [39].

3. AUTHENTICATION PROCESS

Several papers, e.g., [36, 45, 48], have proposed IMD authentication based on IPIs. Their common motif is extracting the purely uncorrelated random bits from IPIs and utilizing them as a key. As previously stated, IPIs are not independent across time. So most previous approaches were confined to utilizing only a portion of the quantized IPIs for key derivation. These protocols generate a key by quantizing IPIs and then concatenating the three or four least significant bits of the quantized IPIs. The Programmer is then authenticated if and only if the Hamming distance between the keys generated by the two communicating parties is less than a predefined threshold value.

The four least significant bits of IPIs (IPI_4) are known to be independently and identically distributed (i.i.d.). We confirmed this characteristic by studying a 2Mbit dataset consisting of 48 half-hour ECG records of 47 subjects from the MIT-BIH Arrhythmia Database [30], 549 two-minute records of 290 subjects from the PTB Database [6], and 250 records of 250 patients from MGH/MF Waveform Database [47], each roughly 30 minutes in length. All of these databases are available at [1]. We note that while these widely referenced databases contain records from patients with abnormal cardiac rhythms, these and similar databases remain standards for the study of ECG-based biometric authentication. (See, e.g., [45, 48].) Such use is substantiated by an extensive body of literature (e.g., [17, 42, 49]) documenting *stronger* chaotic effects in healthy hearts than in diseased ones.

We applied the NIST suite of statistical tests [41] to our dataset. The outputs of the NIST statistical tests are p-values listed in Table 1. These p-values represent the probability that the dataset was generated by a random process. If this value is less than a threshold (usually 1%), the randomness hypothesis is rejected. Table 1 shows that the p-values are all greater than 1%.

Table 1: p-value of several NIST statistical tests for IPI_4. These bits pass all of the random tests.

NIST test	p-value
Runs	0.311310
Rank	0.879647
Longest runs	0.185359
Frequency	0.011830
Universal test	0.013223
Approximate entropy test	0.464725
FFT test	0.131301
Linear complexity	0.612269

The lack of correlation between bits allowed previous work to use a simple Hamming distance metric to compare received and measured bits. Prior work, however, did not characterize and optimize for the *error rates* on sampled bits resulting from noisy IPI readings. More precisely, we define the error rate as the probability, for a given IPI-derived bit, that two devices, e.g., a Programmer and IMD, read the same IPI at different points on the body but output differing bit values.

Lacking the ability to obtain IPI measurements from IMDs in our lab, we estimate the error rates for IPI-derived bits in the H2H setting by means of two external ECG leads, on the left arm and right arm of subjects. The electric potential of the ECG lead III between the left arm of subjects and their left foot is taken as a surrogate for the ECG from the IMD. Similarly, the electric potential of the ECG lead II between the right arm and left foot is taken as a surrogate for the ECG recorded by the Programmer and IMD. It should be noted that we are using the interval between consecutive prominent R-peaks, instead of analyzing the whole waveform as in [44]. Therefore, H2H is not sensitive to the location of leads on the body. Any other lead configuration could have been used in our analysis. We performed this analysis with other lead configurations and didn't find any significant variations in the error rate of least significant bits.

In the next step of analysis, the IPI values of these two readings from leads II and III are calculated and quantized. They are then converted to a Gray-code representation to minimize the difference between the quantized bits caused by error in measurement.

The Hamming distance between these two sets of bits is then taken as a surrogate for the error rate between IPI measurements by the IMD and Programmer. The results of our experiment are reflected in the "Error rate" column of Table 2 for IPI values quantized to 8-bit representation. The last column shows the 95% confidence interval of the error rates. We again used an aggregate of MIT-BIH [30], PTB Database [6], and MGH/MF Database [47] to estimate these error rates.

The table shows that the error rate varies considerably across quantized bits; the lower the significance of the bit, the higher its error rate and entropy. In the next subsection, we describe our statistical approach—a departure from the naïve Hamming approach of previous work—to compare PV readings during authentication with suitable weighting for individual bit errors.

Bit	Entropy	Error rate	95% CI	Denoted by
8 (MSB)	0.27	0.001	–	–
7	0.80	0.003	–	–
6	0.90	0.004	–	–
5	0.98	0.006	–	–
4	1	0.009 (e_4)	0.008 – 0.012	x_4
3	1	0.018 (e_3)	0.015 – 0.021	x_3
2	1	0.039 (e_2)	0.035 – 0.043	x_2
1 (LSB)	1	0.080 (e_1)	0.075 – 0.086	x_1

Table 2: Average entropy and the estimated error rate of quantized bits, along with their 95% Confidence Interval (CI).

3.1 Quantifying the probability of skin contact

It's convenient to treat the IMD PV α as *correct.* Error rates then characterize honest or attacker deviation from α.

A PV in H2H includes only the four least significant bits of an IPI, which we denote collectively by IPI_4. The bits in IPI_4 are i.i.d. random variables. Thus, an adversary that hasn't made skin contact with a victim, and has no information about IPIs, can at best guess an IPI_4 value by assigning random values to each of its constituent bits. Suppose that n is the number of distinct IPI_4 instances read in an H2H authentication session. Then the total number of incorrect guesses by Adv for any given one of the four IPI_4 bit positions can be modeled as a binomial distribution with Bernoulli trial probability of 0.5, denoted by $B(n, 0.5)$.

The total number of incorrect bit outputs for a given bit position i by a valid Programmer with skin contact can be modeled by another binomial distribution $B(n, e_i)$. Here, e_i is the error rate of bit $i \in \{1, 2, 3, 4\}$ as given in the third column of Table 2.

Figure 3 compares the distributions of incorrect guesses by an adversary (with no skin contact) against those of a valid Programmer, for $n = 20$. The solid line is the distribution for the adversary on any of the four bit positions. For the Programmer, $x_i = B(n, e_i)$ denotes the random variable corresponding to total incorrect values in bit position i. The adversary is seen to produce significantly more errors than the Programmer in all bit positions.

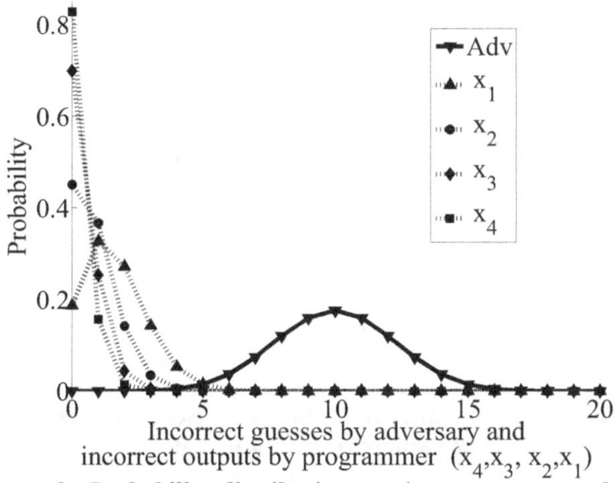

Figure 3: Probability distributions on incorrect guesses by a valid Programmer (dotted lines) and an adversary (solid line), for $n = 20$ (reading of 20 IPI_4 values). Here, $x_1, x_2, x_3,$ and x_4 denote random variables on Programmer errors for bits positions 1, 2, 3, and 4 respectively. The distribution for the adversary is identical across bit positions. Clear separation is seen between valid and adversarial distributions, even for bit positions with relatively high error rates (e.g., for x_1).

3.2 Neyman-Pearson hypothesis testing

Recall that the goal in the H2H authentication process is to determine whether $\alpha \approx \beta$, where the IMD reads PV α and the Programmer submits PV β. Determining whether Programmer PV β is authentic, i.e., resulting from skin contact, may be viewed as a *hypothesis test*. The underlying hypothesis is that the Programmer's claimed PV β is drawn from the probability distribution of an honest Programmer, instead of an adversary's guessing distribution.

This observation motivates use of the well known Neyman-Pearson Lemma [32] to distinguish between honest and adversarial authentication attempts. Let *error value* u denote the set of errors in β, i.e., bit positions that differ from α. In our context, then, Neyman-Pearson Lemma states that for a given maximum acceptable false negative rate, the false positive rate is minimized as follows. For a fixed threshold value Th (whose computation we discuss below), a submitted Programmer value β is accepted as valid only when the following criterion holds:

$$\log\left(\frac{P(u)}{Q(u)}\right) > Th, \qquad (1)$$

where $P(\cdot)$ denotes the probability of an adversary with no skin contact yielding error value u and $Q(\cdot)$ denotes the probability of a valid Programmer yielding u. We model distributions $P(\cdot)$ and $Q(\cdot)$ according to the binomial distributions discussed above and depicted in Figure 3.

We observe that as the bits in a given bit position i are i.i.d., the correctness of a PV is invariant to *which* IPI_4 values contain erroneous bits. The authenticity of a PV β is thus determined based on only the *total* number of correct or incorrect values in each bit position. So we can treat u as an *equivalence class* of PVs. In particular, it's convenient to regard u as a vector $\vec{u} = \langle u_1, u_2, u_3, u_4 \rangle$, where u_i denotes the total number of IPIs in β that are incorrect in bit position i—again, that differ from those in α.

Now, $P(\vec{u}) = \prod_{i=1}^{4} P_i(u_i)$ and $Q(\vec{u}) = \prod_{i=1}^{4} Q_i(u_i)$, where $P_i(u_i)$ and $Q_i(u_i)$ denote the probability of a total of u_i incorrect IPI values for bit position i in adversarial and honest scenarios, respectively. It follows that:

$$\log\left(\frac{P(\vec{u})}{Q(\vec{u})}\right) = \sum_{i=1}^{4} \log\left(P_i(u_i)\right) - \sum_{i=1}^{4} \log\left(Q_i(u_i)\right). \qquad (2)$$

Based on Equation 2, we can construct complete, compact representations of $P(\vec{u})$ and $Q(\vec{u})$. For a given value of n, it suffices to build a table containing $\log P_i(u_i)$ and $\log Q_i(u_i)$ for $i \in \{1,2,3,4\}$ and $u_i \in \mathbb{Z}_n$. Because the error rate of the adversary is 1/2 for *all* bit positions, $Q_i(u_i) = Q_j(u_j)$ for any $i,j \in \{1,2,3,4\}$. Thus, it suffices to store $\log Q_i(u_i)$ values for $i = 1$ only. Consequently, the full table contains just $(4+1) \times (n+1) = 5n+5$ values.

Given such a table, performing the Neyman-Pearson test in Equation 1 requires just $(4+1) = 5$ table lookups, eight additions, and one subtraction. This computation is *online*, i.e., performed during authentication. The storage and computational efficiency of our table-driven approach to Neyman-Pearson testing proves valuable in our implementation of H2H, described later.

One issue remains. The Neyman-Pearson Lemma states the existence of threshold Th, but doesn't specify how to compute Th. We now describe an algorithm to compute Th in our setting. Note that computation of Th takes place *offline*: Th need only be computed once and can then be programmed into an H2H-enabled IMD.

Computing Neyman-Pearson threshold value Th: It turns out that the space $(\mathbb{Z}_n)^4$ of possible values of $\vec{u}$ is relatively small. As we show below, $n \leq 50$ is sufficient to achieve our desired strength of authentication for H2H, meaning that the total number of possible values of $\vec{u}$ is at most $50^4 = 6,250,000$. Consequently, we can compute Th essentially by means of a brute force algorithm.

We specify this algorithm in pseudocode below as Algorithm 1. Algorithm 1 computes Th for a target false-negative rate FN_{Req}. It first constructs a matrix $M[n^4][3]$ with n^4 rows, one for each $\vec{u} \in (\mathbb{Z}_n)^4$, and three columns. For each row $\vec{u}$, Column 1 contains $P(\vec{u})$, Column 2 contains $Q(\vec{u})$ and Column 3 contains $\log \frac{P(\vec{u})}{Q(\vec{u})}$.

The rows of M are sorted in ascending order with respect to Column 3 values. Then, from top (smallest) to bottom (largest), Column 1 values are accumulated in a variable p until the lowest row τ is reached for which the cumulative value $p \leq FN_{\text{Req}}$. The Column 3 value of row τ, namely $M[\tau][3]$, is the optimum threshold value Th. By summing Column 2 values over the first τ rows, we also obtain the corresponding false-positive rate (FP). (A computation failure outputs special symbol $\perp$.)

The dominant cost of Algorithm 1 is sorting. Thus its asymptotic complexity is $O(n^4 \log n)$. In practice, as n is small, the algorithm executes quickly. For example, we implemented Algorithm 1 in MATLAB on a machine with a 3.4GHz Intel i7-2600 CPU running Windows 7. It took 0.2 second to calculate Th for $n = 15$ and around 8 seconds for all values of n from 1 to 25.

Again, we emphasize that Algorithm 1 is run as a precomputation offline, not in the IMD.

Setting parameters in H2H: In our H2H implementation, we set the false negative rate (FN_{Req}) to 10^{-4}. In practical terms, this means that a valid Programmer with skin access would fail on average in one in every 10,000 attempts; it would fail twice consecutively at most once in every 100,000,000 attempts. We believe this choice achieves adequate failure resilience for real-world scenarios.

Algorithm 1 Neyman-Pearson threshold Th computation

Inputs: n, $\{e_i\}_{i=1}^{4}$, FN_{Req}
Outputs: Th, FP

$P[1:n+1] \leftarrow$ binomial$(n, 0.5)$;
for $i = 1$ to 4 **do**
  $Q[1:n+1][i] \leftarrow$ binomial(n, e_i)
end for
$j = 1$;
for $\vec{u} = \langle u_1, u_2, u_3, u_4 \rangle \in (\mathbb{Z}_n)^4$ **do**
  $M[j][1] = \prod_{i=1}^{4} P[u_i]$;
  $M[j][2] = \prod_{i=1}^{4} Q[u_i][i]$;
  $M[j][3] = \log(\frac{M[j][1]}{M[j][2]})$;
  $j \leftarrow j+1$;
end for
sort M on $M[\cdot][3]$ (Column 3);
$p \leftarrow 0; j \leftarrow 0$
while $p \leq FN_{\text{Req}}$ **do**
  $j \leftarrow j+1$;
  $p \leftarrow p + M[j][2]$;
end while
$\tau \leftarrow j - 1$;
if $\tau < 1$ **then** output $\perp$; halt
end if
$FP \leftarrow \sum_{k=1}^{\tau} M[k][1]$;
$Th \leftarrow M[\tau][3]$;

Figure 4 illustrates the tradeoffs between false negative rates (FN_{Req}) and false positive rates (FP), for varying numbers n of IPI_4 values used in authentication. Table 3 gives detailed FP values for our implementation choice $FN_{\text{Req}} = 10^{-4}$ and, for comparison, for $FN_{\text{Req}} = 10^{-3}$. Naturally, the lower FN_{Req}, the higher FP.

In addition to FN_{Req}, the other key parameter choice in H2H is the number n of IPI_4 values measured for authentication. The larger n is, the better FN_{Req} and FP are. As n grows, though, so does the ECG measurement time in an H2H authentication.

In our implementation, we have chosen to set $n = 15$. Given our choice of $FN_{\text{Req}} = 10^{-4}$, the corresponding false positive rate is $FP = 2.7 \times 10^{-9}$. We chose this FP to demonstrate the feasibility of a *strong* level of authentication. As a point of comparison, this FP is lower than the false acceptance rate of a typical, eight-digit RSA SecurID token [40]. (While the false acceptance rate for such a token is nominally 1×10^{-8}, allowances for synchronization errors and multiple tries make it somewhat weaker.) Lower FPs, and thus lower values of n, are likely to be acceptable in practice.

Table 3: FP values achieved for our implementation choice $FN_{\text{Req}} = 10^{-4}$ and, for comparison, for $FN_{\text{Req}} = 10^{-3}$. Average PV read time is given in the last column.

n	$FN_{\text{Req}} = 10^{-3}$	$FN_{\text{Req}} = 10^{-4}$	Avg. read time (secs.)
5	3×10^{-3}	1.1×10^{-3}	3– 5
10	1.15×10^{-6}	7.9×10^{-6}	7–10
15	0.2×10^{-9}	2.7×10^{-9}	11–15
20	0.27×10^{-12}	5.38×10^{-13}	15–20
25	0.32×10^{-17}	8.4×10^{-17}	18–25

The average resting heart rate is 60-80 beats per minute [2]. Thus, for $n = 15$, the recording time would on average take between 7 to 10 seconds. The last column of Table 3 lists the average range of PV read times (in seconds) for different choices of n.

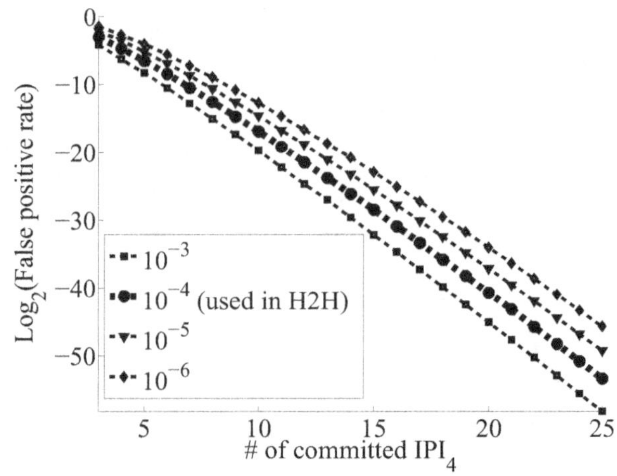

Figure 4: False positive rates achieved by Neyman-Pearson hypothesis testing for various false negative rates.

Summary: In H2H, we apply Neyman-Pearson hypothesis testing to determine whether to accept a Programmer-submitted PV β as authentic or reject it. We first compute the error value $\vec{u}$ of β. Error value $\vec{u}$ captures the total number of errors u_i in each IPI_4 bit position i in β (by comparison with the IMD PV α). We then perform Neyman-Pearson testing of $\vec{u}$ via Equation 1. This test involves computation using Equation 2, and is made efficient by precomputing a small table of u_i value probabilities and Neyman-Pearson threshold Th, both of which are stored in the IMD.

An attacker can, of course, make multiple attempts against the IMD and the Programmer as well. In Section 4, we formally characterize the success probability of such attacks relative to FP. Exponential backoff in the IMD is one helpful countermeasure.

3.3 Remote attack

We also briefly investigated an attack on H2H based on remote cardiac activity monitoring. The best reported remote heart rate monitoring result is achieved by photoplethysmography (PPG) [35]. PPG traces changes in skin color caused by temporal variations in the concentration of blood on the skin surface.

Poh et al. [35] have reported moderately accurate IPI estimation using a commercial webcam at an approximate distance of 50cm from human subjects. We reproduced and evaluated their scheme at the same distance with a 30 frame per second (FPS) camera recording video of the subjects' faces for PPG evaluation over a two minute period. Our camera had twice the FPS rate of the camera in [35].

We have not been able, however, to achieve error rates as low as those reported in [35] for any of our test subjects. (We have contacted the authors and requested clarification of details and their original dataset for validation, but have received no response.) The average error rate for the four least significant bits (IPI4) of all four subjects in our PPG experiment were close to 50%, i.e., to random guessing— substantially higher than those achievable by a Programmer with skin access and yielding little advantage to a remote attacker targeting H2H. We conclude that without significant advances, PPG is unlikely to pose a significant threat to H2H.

4. PROGRAMMER-TO-IMD PAIRING PROTOCOL

We now describe the design of the H2H PV-based cryptographic pairing protocol. First we explain our design principles, both why we don't use existing cryptographic protocols and how we exploit special features of the H2H setting to achieve simple, efficient protocol design. We then present the protocol and a security analysis.

A naïve approach to authentication might work as follows. The Programmer establishes a secure connection with the IMD (via TLS, for instance). The two devices then take respective PV readings α (IMD) and β (Programmer). The Programmer transmits β to the IMD. If $\beta \approx \alpha$, i.e., β is close to α, the IMD accepts the Programmer as valid.

The problem with this approach is that it's vulnerable to a man-in-the-middle attack. An adversary Adv can simultaneously pose as the IMD in a session with the Programmer and as the Programmer with the IMD. On receiving β from the Programmer, Adv forwards it to the IMD, resulting in a successful authentication.

Password-authenticated key-exchange (PAKE) schemes [5], are designed precisely to address such attacks, and might seem an appropriate tool for H2H. The PVs α and β measured respectively by the IMD and Programmer may be treated as passwords: The Programmer gains access to the IMD by demonstrating its approximate knowledge of "password" α, i.e., that it knows β such that $\alpha \approx \beta$.

There are two problems with PAKEs. First, due to read errors in our setting, the IMD must check for *approximate* equality, i.e., $\alpha \approx \beta$. But a PAKE requires *exact* equality. More involved approaches, e.g., bit-by-bit password testing, or use of fuzzy extraction, e.g., [14] can convert PAKE into a "fuzzy" tool for approximate equality testing.

But PAKE presents a second problem: Computational cost. While the several modular exponentiations required by a single PAKE execution are feasible on many devices, they constitute more computation—and more energy expenditure, in particular—than desired on IMDs, which are highly constrained in terms of power and computational resources. A "fuzzy" PAKE would require even more computation.

Thankfully, as it turns out, PAKE is overengineered for H2H. It's possible to support approximate matching of α and β *and* gain better computational efficiency than PAKE.

4.1 Protocol overview

Our key observation is that the readings α and β in H2H are *one-time values*. In contrast to passwords, which are generally multi-use, α and β are transient. Fresh readings may be used to authenticate every session and, as we have demonstrated experimentally above, readings are statistically independent across time.

Consequently, it is possible to reveal α and β safely at the end of our authentication protocol—something not possible, of course, with static passwords. The protocol can thus rely primarily on (very fast) symmetric-key commitment and decommitment rounds and explicit IMD testing of the condition $\alpha \approx \beta$, rather than minimal-knowledge cryptographic comparison.

Our protocol has two phases: (1) A *secure-channel setup* phase, which uses (lightweight) public-key cryptography to create a secure but unauthenticated channel between the IMD and Programmer and (2) An *authentication* phase, in which the two devices use a commitment / decommitment scheme to check whether $\alpha \approx \beta$.

Secure-channel setup. In the first phase of our protocol, the IMD and Programmer establish a *secure channel* via TLS. The IMD assumes the role of the TLS client; the Programmer, that of a TLS server. That is, only the Programmer presents a certificate. When instantiated with RSA, TLS requires little client computation, just one low-exponent ($e = 2^{16} + 1$) modular exponentiation.

Our protocol makes use of an output from TLS session what we call a *label* s. Given that at least one of the two entities is honest, s is random and thus unique (with overwhelming probability). It isn't secret, however. In practice, s might be, e.g., the hash of the TLS session key. For convenience, we abstract away the details of TLS and just model it as a protocol SecChannel that establishes a secure channel between two entities and outputs random label s.

SecChannel (in practice, TLS) creates a secure channel in the sense that it provides confidentiality, integrity, and freshness. But it doesn't provide authentication: The IMD doesn't present a certificate, and doesn't validate the Programmer's. (As explained above, H2H avoids the burden of a PKI.) Put another way, when an IMD first sets up a secure channel, it has no assurance that it has paired with a *valid* Programmer, i.e., one actually in contact with the patient. Similarly, a Programmer doesn't know if it's communicating with a valid IMD. Thus the next protocol phase.

Authentication. In the authentication phase, the two devices commit to their respective PV readings α and β. Each device binds its commitments to the label s of the secure channel on which it is communicating (preventing its re-use, prior to decommitment, on a different channel).

The IMD can then safely decommit α for the Programmer, as it has already received a commitment for β.

If the Programmer determines that $\alpha \approx \beta$, then it decommits β. Otherwise, it rejects the session. This selective decommitment helps ensure that the Programmer only reveals β to a valid IMD (one that knows $\alpha \approx \beta$), preventing re-use of β by an adversary. If the Programmer had been the party who decommits first, an adversary would have easily mounted a man-in-the-middle attack.

The IMD itself then verifies that $\alpha \approx \beta$, and makes an accept / reject authentication decision.

After an invalid authentication attempt, IMD waits a full PV read cycle before accepting a new authentication request. This delay prevents interleaving attacks, in which a Programmer's session overlaps with two IMD sessions. (This is in fact necessary to achieve Theorem 1 below.)

4.2 Protocol specification

The H2H authentication protocol is specified in Figure 5. Some technical preliminaries are needed.

Define $\mathcal{V}$ as the space of valid PVs. Let $\mathsf{dist} : \mathcal{V} \times \mathcal{V} \rightarrow \mathbb{R}_0^+$ denote a pairwise distance metric on $\mathcal{V}$. Let τ denote the time required for a device to read a PV.

We make use of a commitment scheme Commit with message space $\mathcal{V}$ and key space $\{0,1\}^k \times \{0,1\}^k$. We denote a commitment of message pair $(m, s) \in \mathcal{V} \times \{0,1\}^k$ under key $w \in \{0,1\}^k$ by $C = \mathsf{Commit}((m, s); w)$. We adopt the convention of decommitment as verification of correct commitment, i.e., decommitting m under key w involves the check $C \stackrel{?}{=} \mathsf{Commit}((m, s); w)$.

For simplicity of analysis, we treat Commit as an ideal functionality [8], i.e., as unconditionally hiding and binding. When either device outputs the message `reject`, rejecting the session, it terminates communication on the session channel. Additionally, devices support only serial sessions, not concurrent ones.

4.3 Security analysis

We consider an adversary Adv that fully controls the channel between the IMD and Programmer, i.e., Adv can deliver, drop, modify, and forge messages as desired. Adv can't corrupt the IMD or

IMD		Programmer
	$\mathsf{SecChannel} \xrightarrow{R} s \in \{0,1\}^k$ ($\longleftrightarrow$)	
read PV $\alpha\ (\in \mathcal{V})$; $w_A \xleftarrow{R} \{0,1\}^k$; $C_A \leftarrow \mathsf{Commit}((\alpha, s); w_A)$		read PV $\beta\ (\in \mathcal{V})$; $w_B \xleftarrow{R} \{0,1\}^k$; $C_B \leftarrow \mathsf{Commit}((\beta, s); w_B)$
	$\xrightarrow{C_A}$	
	$\xleftarrow{C_B}$	
	$\xrightarrow{w_A}$	
		if $C_A \neq \mathsf{Commit}((\alpha, s); w_A)$ or $\mathsf{dist}(\alpha, \beta) > d$ then $w_B \leftarrow$ **reject**
	$\xleftarrow{w_B}$	
if $C_B \neq \mathsf{Commit}((\beta, s); w_B)$ or $\mathsf{dist}(\alpha, \beta) > d$ then auth $\leftarrow$ **reject** else auth $\leftarrow$ **accept**		
	$\xrightarrow{auth}$	
if auth = reject wait for time τ		

Figure 5: H2H pairing protocol.

Programmer, however. (If it could, protection of the IMD wouldn't be possible.) Here we briefly present our formal security model and main theorem. Appendix A contains more details.

We assume that readings α and β by the IMD and Programmer come from probability distributions defined by a model $\mathcal{M}$. Given $\mathcal{M}$, p_1 denotes the maximum probability that Adv can guess a valid PV reading in one try, i.e., given legitimate PV reading α, that Adv can guess a v such that $\mathsf{dist}(v, \alpha) \leq d$. In other words, p_1 is the authentication probability characterized in Section 3.

Similarly, p_2 denotes the maximum probability that Adv does so in exactly two tries. More precisely, given simultaneous PV readings α and β, p_2 is the maximum probability, given a known, failed guess for α, that Adv guesses a valid PV reading for β.

We define the security of H2H in terms of an experiment in which Adv succeeds if it can authenticate to the IMD, i.e., cause it to output accept for a session with Adv on SecChannel. To convey intuition for the resistance of H2H to man-in-the-middle attacks, we give the following lemma with a proof sketch. Here $\mathsf{succ}^{H2H}_{\mathsf{Adv}}(1,1)$ denotes the probability that Adv succeeds when it initiates a single session each with the Programmer and IMD.

LEMMA 1. *For PV model $\mathcal{M}$, $\mathsf{succ}^{H2H}_{\mathsf{Adv}}(1,1) \leq p_1 + p_2 - p_1 p_2$.*

Proof: [sketch] Adv's goal is to initiate a session on SecChannel with the IMD such that it outputs accept. To do so, Adv must send the IMD (simulated Programmer commitment) C'_B, with corresponding value β' such that $\mathsf{dist}(\alpha, \beta') \leq d$. Recall that we model Commit as an ideal functionality, both unconditionally hiding and binding. As the commitment C_A of the IMD is thus hiding, Adv can obtain an advantage over random guessing for β' only by interacting additionally with the Programmer.

Suppose therefore that Adv has initiated a session with the Programmer prior to completion of its session with the IMD. Adv sends the Programmer (simulated IMD) commitment C''_A on PV α''. Each instance of SecChannel emits a uniformly random label. Thus the Adv-IMD session has label s' and the Adv-Programmer session label s'' such that $s' \neq s''$. (For simplicity, we disregard the negligible-probability event $s'' = s'$.)

Two cases arise, depending on whether Adv sends (simulated Programmer) commitment C'_B to the IMD before or after sending a decommitment w''_A to the Programmer.

Case 1: Commitment C'_B precedes decommitment w''_A. C_B is bound to label s''. To cause the IMD to accept, however, C'_B must be bound to label s'. (Intuitively, binding commitments to SecChannel labels prevents Adv from "stitching together" two distinct channels in a man-in-the-middle attack.) Given these bindings and the hiding property of Commit for C_B and C_A, then, Adv must commit to PV β' in C'_B that is independent of PVs α and β. Thus Adv must guess β' at random, and the IMD outputs accept with probability p_1.

Case 2: Commitment C'_B follows decommitment w''_A. As Adv sends C''_A prior to any decommitments, and commitments are hiding, Adv commits in C''_A to a PV α'' that is independent of previous transcript values, and thus correct with probability at most p_1. On sending decommitment w''_A, Adv learns whether α'' was correct. With this knowledge Adv may then submit a PV guess β' in C'_B to the IMD with success probability at most p_2.

Adv's maximum success probability, achieved for Case 2, is $p_1 + (1 - p_1)p_2$. □

Defining $\mathsf{succ}^{H2H}_{\mathsf{Adv}}(q_i, q_r)$ as the probability that Adv succeeds in at least one session with at most q_i queries (session initiations) with IMD and q_r with the Programmer yields our main theorem:

THEOREM 1. *Given PV model $\mathcal{M}$ and $q = q_i + q_r$ with even-valued q, $\mathsf{succ}^{H2H}_{\mathsf{Adv}}(q_i, q_r) \leq 1 - (1 - (p_1 + p_2 - p_1 p_2))^{q/2}$.*

Theorem 1 reflects the fact that Adv's best strategy against H2H is to initiate sessions simultaneously with the IMD and Programmer, which respectively read PVs α and β. Adv tries to authenticate to Programmer by guessing β. If this fails, Adv tries to authenticate to IMD by guessing α; it gains a small advantage from knowing that its guess for β was incorrect. (The need for even q in our theorem is technical: The proof assumes the adversary can mount $q/2$ distinct attempts against the two devices.) A proof is sketched in Appendix A.

H2H-specific analysis: For the special case of H2H, Theorem 1 can be simplified. Let $\mathcal{M}_{H2H}$ and dist_{H2H} denote the PV distribution model and (Neyman-Pearson-induced) distance metric respectively for H2H. We can then show:

COROLLARY 1. *Given PV model $\mathcal{M}_{H2H}$ and distance metric dist_{H2H}, and $q = q_i + q_r$ with even-valued q,* $\mathsf{succ}^{H2H}_{\mathsf{Adv}}(q_i, q_r) \leq 1 - (1 - 2p_1)^{q/2}$.

In other words, *the probability of a successful attack in a given session by* Adv *is at most twice its authentication probability*, as characterized in Section 3.

4.4 Privacy

H2H protects patient privacy in two senses. First, the IMD doesn't release a public key (as a Programmer does), or any other static identifier. As α is random, and protocol values are random (or pseudorandom), H2H thus provides logical-layer *tracking privacy*: An adversary can't correlate distinct RF sightings of a given IMD, i.e., can't track a patient wirelessly from a distance. (For cautions about physical-layer wireless tracking, however, see [12].) Second, the randomness of α *prevents leakage of medically significant data*, e.g., cardiac abnormalities evident in a full ECG waveform.

5. PROTOTYPE IMPLEMENTATION

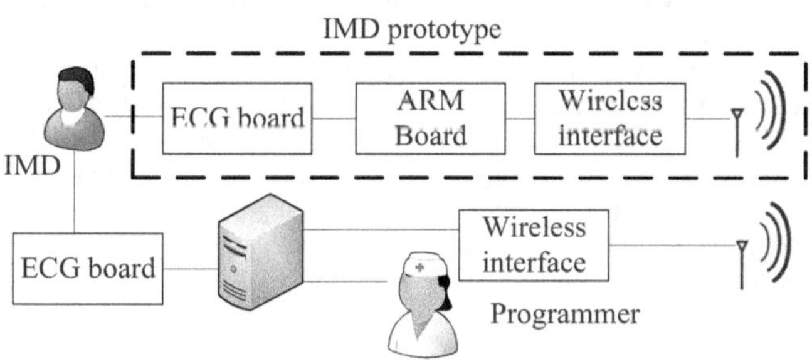

Figure 6: High-level view of the H2H prototype. The IMD parts are in the dotted box on top. The Programmer runs on a PC.

In this section, we present a prototype implementation of H2H. A high-level architecture is shown in Figure 6. The IMD prototype consists of three boards:

1. A Leopard Gecko EFM-32 microcontroller (EFM32LG-DK3650);
2. an ECG analog A/D front end (TI ADS1298); and
3. a wireless sensor modem (TI CC430F5137).

Leopard Gecko is a 32-bit ARM Cortex-M3 processor with an attractive power-consumption profile and convenient power debugging tools. In our implementation, the microcontroller communicates with the ECG analog front end and the wireless board. The EFM-32 also extracts ECG features and communicates with the Programmer using TLS. Figure 7 shows our implementation components. The following three subsections give details.

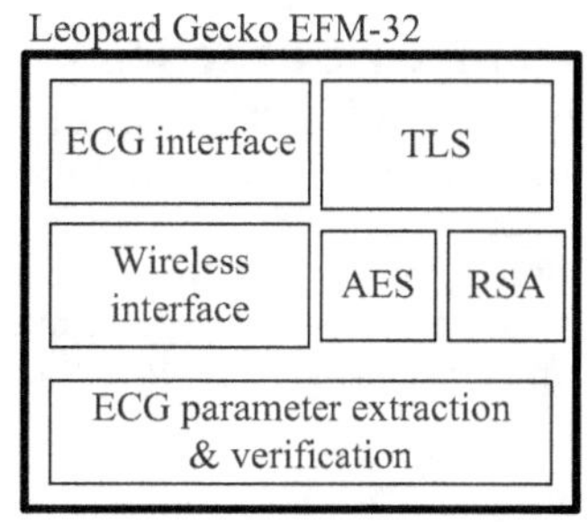

Figure 7: Main components of the implementation.

5.1 Secure channel implementation

Recall that the IMD and Programmer establish a channel between them using TLS. The IMD performs the operations of an ordinary TLS client and the Programmer those of an ordinary server.

TLS is designed to provide an encrypted and authenticated channel between two communicating parties [26]. *Standard TLS authentication assumes a PKI, however, which H2H doesn't, as noted above.* Thus the one deviation from normal TLS usage in H2H is that the IMD doesn't verify the Programmer certificate against a PKI. Instead, H2H authentication, i.e., ECG PV comparison, is performed after the TLS handshake to authenticate the channel.

Our H2H prototype uses RSA for the master secret key exchange in TLS, AES-128 for encryption, and SHA256 as the hash function. SHA256 also serves as the commitment function Commit(.) in the H2H pairing protocol.

We chose RSA for key exchange because RSA encryption with a small public exponent is the fastest key-exchange option for TLS [33]. In our implementation, the RSA public exponent is set to $2^{16} + 1$. The RSA modulus and message length are set to 2048 bits to conform with current NIST key length recommendations [4].

Our RSA implementation is designed to comply with the MISRA-C standard. MISRA-C [28] is a set of software development recommendations to achieve high levels of reliability for critical embedded devices. For example, MISRA-C prohibits use of dynamic memory allocations. The code size, the number of clock cycles, and approximate power consumption of various blocks of the TLS handshake are listed in Table 4.

Table 4: Approximate resource overhead of each of the component blocks of our H2H implementation. Here, "# of cycles" and "power" denote resource costs for a single call to the block.

Block name	Size (Kb)	# of cycles	Power (μ Watt)
AES encryption	2	6600	8
AES decryption	2	8400	10
RSA encryption	5	5000000	20000
MD5	1	5000	4
SHA256	3	10000	5
R-peak detection	4	5000	2

5.2 Random number generation

H2H requires a cryptographically secure pseudo-random number generator (PRNG) for RSA ciphertext padding, key generation and nonce selection in TLS, and commitment (as shown in Figure 5). We use a NIST-recommended PRNG based on cipher-block chaining (CBC) [27], with AES as the underlying block cipher. The PRNG requires an initial random seed. We generate this seed offline and store it in the IMD's non-volatile memory. (In a commercial IMD, it can be, e.g., set at the time of manufacture.)

5.3 ECG parameter extraction

Our H2H prototype annotates ECG R-peaks by applying a simple length transformation to the ECG waveform using an open-source algorithm called "WQRS." In this algorithm, the arc length of the waveform over a moving window is compared against a threshold to detect heartbeats [34]. Its resource overhead is is specified in Table 4. (An implementation of WQRS is available on the PhysioNet website [1].)

6. RELATED WORK

Several early research and development efforts in medical electronics have addressed safety and reliability of IMD devices, particularly the problem of unexpected failures [29]. Increased networking of embedded devices and emergence of pervasive healthcare technologies motivated security and privacy investigations for general sensor networks and body sensor networks [25,43,46].

Halperin et al. [21] first discussed the security and privacy challenges caused by resource constraints and inflexibility in existing IMD designs, and highlighted fundamental tensions among privacy, security, safety, and utility. Fu [16] argued that improving IMD security requires a balance between technology and regulation.

Halperin et al. [20] gave the first systematic and pragmatic security analysis of a real commercial IMD, an implantable cardiovascular defibrillator (ICD). They showed that these devices are susceptible to attacks by malicious programmers that breach patient privacy and, even more seriously, can effect changes to data and functioning, potentially harming patients. Their work highlighted the pressing need for authentication of programmers to IMDs.

Programmer-to-IMD authentication, as noted above, is straightforward if the Programmer and IMD share a preexisting key. (Authentication tokens have the same simplicity, but similar risks of IMD inaccessibility with credential loss.) Authentication without a pre-established relationship, as treated by H2H, is more challenging. Three broad technical approaches bear comparison with H2H.

Distance bounding. Halperin et al. [20] introduce authentication techniques involving an implanted piezo device that generates a random key and emits it acoustically such that the Programmer can only receive it at close range. This approach is complementary to H2H. It results in faster key agreement, needing a mere 400ms to emit a 128-bit key. A serious drawback, however, is that it requires special implantation of the piezo device. This implantation must be at a depth of 1 cm or so from the skin, ruling out incorporation into deep-body IMDs, such as ICDs. Additionally, eavesdropping on acoustic emanations isn't a well studied security problem.

A promising related approach, by Rasmussen et al. [38], uses ultrasound-based distance bounding (with an RF channel as well) to authenticate Programmer access to an IMD, achieving an access policy similar to, but slightly looser than touch-to-access. Their system requires RF shielding, however, amplifying IMD engineering complexity. In contrast, H2H is agnostic to transmission medium and does not incur the added cost or energy for ultrasound. For some IMDs, e.g., brain implants, RF antennas are of prohibitive length, and alternatives, e.g., infrared, are preferred. Finally, distance-bounding protocols' security models have historically proven fragile (see, e.g., [11,37]).

Shielding. The idea of blocking inappropriate access to an IMD was first proposed in [13] via a device called a Communication Cloaker. The idea was further explored by Gollakota et al. [18]. Their proposed device, called a *shield*, is worn near the body and used to authenticate / mediate Programmer (or other) communications with the IMD. A shield doesn't require modification of existing IMDs. It protects communications with the IMD using a full duplex radio device acting as a jammer-cum-receiver.

IMDGuard [48] is a similar method for IMD protection involving a third party, high-powered device worn externally, called a Guardian. The Guardian authenticates programmers on behalf of the IMD. Like H2H, it requires special-purpose IMD functionality.

While these devices provide more general functionality, H2H has several advantages over them: (1) H2H doesn't require an external device, which is a burden on patients and increases the risks of system failures and unreliability; (2) H2H doesn't require jamming, which, as employed to counter attacks in [18,48], can interfere with other RF devices and potentially lead to legal complications.

While the shield has the benefit of legacy compatibility, we note that a growing number of legacy IMDs are built using programmable microcontrollers with in-vivo upgradable firmware, allowing an upgrade to the H2H protocol as long as its (lightweight) resource requirements are satisfied.

PV/ECG-based authentication. The use of PVs to secure inter-sensor communications in body area networks (BANs) was first introduced in [9]. Numerous works subsequently used the randomness in ECG IPIs for IMD authentication, e.g., [3,10,36,45]. None, however, provided a rigorous entropy or protocol-security analysis. (In fact, the motivation for PV-derived keys in BANs is unclear. To pair *user-controlled devices* in *non-emergency settings*, even device passwords would seem practical.)

Most similar to H2H are two schemes: A protocol in IMDGuard for pairing the Guardian with an IMD and a generic body-area network pairing protocol called OPFKA (Ordered-Physiological-Feature-based Key Agreement) [23]. Like H2H, these protocols make use of ECG measurements to authenticate a Programmer to an IMD. As noted above, however, both protocols lack rigorous security analysis and have been shown in recent work to have serious cryptographic weaknesses [39]. (We also note that the reported hardware implementation overhead for the IMDGuard protocol greatly exceeds that of H2H.)

Compared with previous PV-based authentication schemes in general, H2H is the first work that: (1) Includes a statistical analysis of the full stochastic ECG waveform to demonstrate bit independence over time; (2) Quantifies and uses the individual error rates of the high-grade random bits to distinguish between honest and adversarial Programmers in an optimal way (via the Neyman-Pearson Lemma); and (3) Offers a formally analyzed PV-based cryptographic device pairing protocol.

7. CONCLUSIONS AND FUTURE DIRECTIONS

This paper addressed the problem of authenticating external medical controllers and programmers to Implantable Medical Devices (IMD). Presently available IMD devices can be wirelessly accessed and even upgraded / controlled by external devices under loose access-control policies, rendering them vulnerable to attack. This threat, and the vital role of most IMDs, argue an urgent need for trustworthy Programmer-to-IMD authentication schemes. The main challenges are a lack of pre-existing keys in emergency and other situations and the fact that IMD resource constraints forbid the use of heavy cryptographic or signal-processing modules with high energy consumption.

We presented the design and implementation of Heart-to-Heart (H2H), a lightweight "touch-to-access" scheme for Programmer-to-IMD authentication. The touch-to-access policy is enforced in H2H by a time-varying biometric, ECG heartbeat data. We performed new statistical analyses of the ECG data, including quantification of the error rates of high entropy bits. H2H draws on these analyses to achieve the first ECG-based authentication scheme that distinguishes honest from adversarial ECG signals in a rigorous statistical model and with a minimal false positive rate for a given false negative bound. We devised a novel cryptographic device pairing protocol for H2H that exploits ECG randomness to secure against active attacks, while satisfying the lightweight implementation requirements and noise margins for reliable authentication. Our end-to-end realization in an ARM Cortex-M3 microcontroller confirmed the practicality and low overhead of H2H for current-generation IMDs.

8. ACKNOWLEDGMENTS

This research was supported in part by an Office of Naval Research grant (ONR R17460) and an Army Research Office YIP award grant (No. R17450) to the ACES lab at Rice University . Thanks to Kevin Fu and Denis Foo Kune for their very insightful comments on this work. Special thanks as well to Nav Ravindranath for his help with embedded-device implementation of our cryptographic algorithms. Finally, the authors would like to thank the anonymous reviewers of this paper for their helpful comments and suggestions.

9. REFERENCES

[1] A. L. Goldberger et al. PhysioBank, PhysioToolkit, and PhysioNet: Components of a new research resource for complex physiologic signals. *Circulation*, 101(23), 2000.

[2] American Heart Association. Physical activity and blood pressure, 2012.

[3] S. D. Bao, C. C. Y. Poon, Y. T. Zhang, and L. F. Shen. Using the timing information of heartbeats as an entity identifier to secure body sensor network. *IEEE Trans. on Info. Tech. in Biomedicine*, 12(6):772–779, 2008.

[4] E. Barker and A. Roginsky. Transitions: Recommendation for transitioning the use of cryptographic algorithms and key lengths. *NIST Special Publication*, 800:131A, 2011.

[5] M. Bellare, D. Pointcheval, and P. Rogaway. Authenticated key exchange secure against dictionary attacks. In *Eurocrypt*, pages 139–155, 2000.

[6] R. Bousseljot, D. Kreiseler, and A. Schnabel. Nutzung der ekg-signaldatenbank cardiodat der ptb über das internet. *Biomedizinische Technik Biomedical Engineering*, 40(s1):317–318, 2009.

[7] K. A. Brownley, B. E. Hurwitz, and N. Schneiderman. Cardiovascular psychophysiology. *Handbook of psychophysiology*, 2:224–264, 2000.

[8] R. Canetti and M. Fischlin. Universally composible commitments. In *Crypto*, pages 332–349, 2001.

[9] S. Cherukuri, K. K. Venkatasubramanian, and S. K. S. Gupta. Biosec: a biometric based approach for securing communication in wireless networks of biosensors implanted in the human body. In *Parallel Processing Workshop*, pages 432–439, 2003.

[10] K. Cho and D. Lee. Biometric based secure communications without pre-deployed key for biosensor implanted in body sensor networks. In *Information Security Applications*, pages 203–218, 2012.

[11] C. Cremers, K. B. Rasmussen, B. Schmidt, and S. Capkun. Distance hijacking attacks on distance bounding protocols. In *IEEE Symp. on Security and Privacy*, pages 113–127, 2012.

[12] B. Danev, D. Zanetti, and S. Capkun. On physical-layer identification of wireless devices. *ACM Computing Surveys*, 2011.

[13] T. Denning, K. Fu, and T. Kohno. Absence makes the heart grow fonder: New directions for implantable medical device security. In *USENIX HotSec*, 2008.

[14] Y. Dodis, L. Reyzin, and A. Smith. Fuzzy extractors: How to generate strong keys from biometrics and other noisy data. *SIAM J. on Computing*, 38(1):97–139, 2008.

[15] T. Drew and M. Gini. Implantable medical devices as agents and part of multiagent systems. In *Int. Joint Conf. on Autonomous Agents and Multiagent Systems (AAMAS)*, pages 1534–1541, 2006.

[16] K. Fu. Inside risks: Reducing risks of implantable medical devices. *Communications of the ACM*, 52(6):25–27, June 2009.

[17] A. L. Goldberger, D. R. Rigney, and B. J. West. Chaos and fractals in human physiology. *Scientific American*, 262:42–49, 1990.

[18] S. Gollakota, H. Hassanieh, B. Ransford, D. Katabi, and K. Fu. They can hear your heartbeats: non-invasive security for implantable medical devices. In *ACM SIGCOMM*, pages 2–13, 2011.

[19] A. J. Greenspon, J. D. Patel, E. Lau, J. A. Ochoa, D. R. Frisch, R. T. Ho, B. B. Pavri, and S. M. Kurtz. 16-year trends in the infection burden for pacemakers and implantable cardioverter-defibrillators in the united states: 1993 to 2008. *Journal of the American College of Cardiology*, 58(10):1001 – 1006, 2011.

[20] D. Halperin, T. S. Heydt-Benjamin, B. Ransford, S. S. Clark, B. Defend, W. Morgan, K. Fu, T. Kohno, and W. H. Maisel. Pacemakers and implantable cardiac defibrillators: Software radio attacks and zero-power defenses. In *IEEE Symp. on Security and Privacy*, pages 129–142, 2008.

[21] D. Halperin, T. Kohno, T.S. Heydt-Benjamin, K. Fu, and W.H. Maisel. Security and privacy for implantable medical devices. *IEEE Pervasive Computing*, 7(1):30–39, Jan.-Mar. 2008.

[22] K. E. Hanna, F. J. Manning, P. Bouxsein, and A. Pope, editors. *Innovation and Invention in Medical Devices: Workshop Summary*. The National Academies Press, 2001.

[23] C. Hu, X. Cheng, F. Zhangand, D. Wuand, X. Liao, and D. Chen. OPFKA: Secure and efficient ordered-physiological-feature-based key agreement for wireless body area networks. In *IEEE INFOCOM*, 2013.

[24] A. Juels and M. Wattenberg. A fuzzy commitment scheme. In *ACM CCS*, pages 28–36, 1999.

[25] D. Karaouglan and A. Levi. A survey on the development of security mechanisms for body area networks. *The Computer Journal*, 2013.

[26] C. Kaufman, R. Perlman, and M. Speciner. *Network security: private communication in a public world*. Prentice Hall Press, 2002.

[27] S. S. Keller. NIST-recommended random number generator based on ANSI X9.31 appendix A.2.4 using the 3-key triple DES and AES algorithms. Technical report, NIST, 2005.

[28] MISRA Limited. Misra-c:2004 - guidelines for the use of the c language in critical systems. Technical report, 2004.

[29] W. H. Maisel. Safety issues involving medical devices. *Journal of the American Medical Association*, 294(8):955–958, Aug. 2005.

[30] G. B. Moody and R. G. Mark. The impact of the MIT-BIH arrhythmia database. *IEEE Engineering in Medicine and Biology Magazine*, 20(3):45–50, 2001.

[31] J. H. Nagel, K. Han, B. E. Hurwitz, and N. Schneiderman. Assessment and diagnostic applications of heart rate variability. *Biomedical engineering-applications, basis & communications*, 5:147–158, 1993.

[32] J. Neyman and E. S. Pearson. On the problem of the most efficient tests of statistical hypotheses. *Phil. Trans. of the Royal Society of London. Series A, Containing Papers of a Mathematical or Physical Character*, 231:289–337, 1933.

[33] C. Paar, J. Pelzl, and B. Preneel. *Understanding cryptography: a textbook for students and practitioners*. Springer, 2010.

[34] E. Pino, L. Ohno-Machado, E. Wiechmann, and D. Curtis. Real–time ECG algorithms for ambulatory patient monitoring. In *AMIA Annual Symp.*, volume 2005, page 604, 2005.

[35] M. Z. Poh, D. J. McDuff, and R. W. Picard. Non-contact, automated cardiac pulse measurements using video imaging and blind source separation. *Optics Express*, 18:10762–10774, 2010.

[36] C. C. Y. Poon, Y. T. Zhang, and S. D. Bao. A novel biometrics method to secure wireless body area sensor networks for telemedicine and m-health. *IEEE Communications Magazine*, 44(4):73–81, 2006.

[37] M. Poturalski, M. Flury, P. Papadimitratos, J.-P. Hubaux, and J.-Y. Le Boudec. Distance bounding with ieee 802.15.4a: Attacks and countermeasures. *IEEE Trans. on Wireless Comms.*, 10(4):1334– 1344, 2011.

[38] K. B. Rasmussen, C. Castelluccia, T. S. Heydt-Benjamin, and S. Capkun. Proximity-based access control for implantable medical devices. In *Proc. of Computer and communications security*, pages 410–419, 2009.

[39] M. Rostami, W. Burleson, F. Koushanfar, and A. Juels. Balancing security and utility in medical devices? In *Proc. of Design Automation Conference*, pages 1–6, 2013.

[40] RSA, The Security Division of EMC. RSA SecurID authentication in action: Securing privileged user access, 2013.

[41] A. Rukhin, J. Soto, J. Nechvatal, M. Smid, and E. Barker. A statistical test suite for random and pseudorandom number generators for cryptographic applications. Technical report, DTIC Document, 2001.

[42] M. G. Signorini, F. Marchetti, and S. Cerutti. Applying nonlinear noise reduction in the analysis of heart rate variability. *Engineering in Medicine and Biology Magazine, IEEE*, 20(2):59–68, 2001.

[43] F. Stajano and R. J. Anderson. The resurrecting duckling: Security issues for ad-hoc wireless networks. In *Int. Workshop of Security Protocols*, pages 172–194, 1999.

[44] K. K. Venkatasubramanian, A. Banerjee, and S. K. S. Gupta. PSKA: usable and secure key agreement scheme for body area networks. *IEEE Trans. on Information Technology in Biomedicine*, 14(1):60–68, 2010.

[45] K. K. Venkatasubramanian and S. K. S. Gupta. Physiological value-based efficient usable security solutions for body sensor networks. *ACM Trans. Sensor Networks*, 6(4):31:1–31:36, July 2010.

[46] S. Warren, J. Lebak, J. Yao, J. Creekmore, A. Milenkovic, and E. Jovanov. Interoperability and security in wireless body area network infrastructures. In *IEEE Engineering in Medicine and Biology Society*, pages 3837–3840, 2005.

[47] J. P. Welch, P. J. Ford, R. S. Teplick, and R. M. Rubsamen. The Massachusetts General Hospital-Marquette Foundation hemodynamic and electrocardiographic database – comprehensive collection of critical care waveforms. *Clinical Monitoring*, 7(1):96–97, 1991.

[48] F. Xu, Z. Qin, C.C. Tan, B. Wang, and Q. Li. IMDGuard: Securing implantable medical devices with the external wearable guardian. In *Proc. of IEEE INFOCOM*, pages 1862–1870, 2011.

[49] R. Yulmetyev, P. Hänggi, and F. Gafarov. Quantification of heart rate variability by discrete nonstationary non-Markov stochastic processes. *Physical Review E*, 65(4):046107, 2002.

APPENDIX

A. SECURITY ANALYSIS

In this appendix, we briefly sketch a security analysis of the H2H authentication protocol, outlining a formal model and giving our main theorem with proof sketches. We defer a complete model, analysis, and proofs for the full version of this paper.

A.1 Model overview

Statistical modeling. We model the process of PV sampling in terms of a set $\mathcal{V}$ of PV values and function pair $(\mathsf{sample}, \mathsf{noise})$. We call $\mathcal{M} = (\mathcal{V}; (\mathsf{sample}, \mathsf{noise}))$ the *PV model* for H2H.

At the time of PV reading a *true* PV γ is sampled from $\mathcal{V}$ under a distribution defined by probabilistic function $\mathsf{sample}(t, \tau) \rightarrow \gamma \in \mathcal{V}$, where t denotes the sampling time and τ the sampling interval length. We assume that $\mathsf{sample}(t, \tau)$ and $\mathsf{sample}(t + \tau', \tau)$ are independent and identically distributed for any $\tau' \geq \tau$. We also assume that $\mathsf{sample}(t, \tau)$ is identically distributed for any t, i.e., that it's a stationary process. Thus we let $\mathsf{sample}(\cdot, \tau)$ denote a PV sample of duration τ taken at an arbitrary time.

We model noise in PV reading by the IMD and Programmer respectively by $\alpha \leftarrow \mathsf{noise}(\gamma)$ and $\beta \leftarrow \mathsf{noise}(\gamma)$, for probabilistic function $\mathsf{noise} : \mathcal{V} \rightarrow \mathcal{V}$. (A model extension can capture different noise in the IMD and Programmer.)

Cryptographic modeling. We treat $\mathsf{SecChannel}$ as an ideal functionality. A player P can invoke $\mathsf{SecChannel}$ with any other player P' of its choice. The functionality then outputs a unique label $s \in \{0, 1\}^k$ to P and P', or else outputs a failure symbol $\perp$. All messages labeled with s are privately delivered between P and P'; an adversary can block messages, but otherwise can't see, modify, or reorder them. Honest players support only one instance of $\mathsf{SecChannel}$ at a given time. Recall that we also treat Commit as an ideal functionality, i.e., perfectly hiding and binding.

Adv can at any time cause the Programmer to initate an H2H session or itself initiate an H2H session with the IMD.

Adversarial model. We assume a Programmer and IMD executing serial sessions and uncorrupted by Adv. We define security with respect to an experiment involving an adversary Adv that knows $\mathcal{M}$ and fully controls the channel between the IMD and Programmer. There is a query interface send that communicates messages to the IMD and Programmer. Adv may send arbitrary queries m of the form $\mathsf{send}(entity, m)$ for $entity \in$ (IMD, Programmer). A special query $\mathsf{send}(entity, \mathtt{start})$ causes a device to initiate the H2H protocol, i.e., execute SecChannel. To cause the IMD and Programmer to pair, Adv calls send($Programmer$, **start**), then sends send(IMD, **start**)) from the Programmer to IMD.

Suppose Adv sends at most q_i `start` queries to the IMD and q_r `start` queries to the Programmer over the course of the security experiment. We define $\mathsf{succ}^{H2H}_{\mathsf{Adv}}(q_i, q_r)$ as the probability that Adv causes the IMD to output `accept` for a session where it communicates with Adv on SecChannel.

A.2 Main theorem

We now summarize our main result. First, define:

$$p_1 = \quad max_{a' \in \mathcal{V}}(\mathsf{pr}[\mathsf{dist}(a', a) \leq d \,|\, a \leftarrow \mathsf{noise}(\gamma), \gamma \leftarrow \mathsf{sample}(\cdot, \tau)]).$$

Here, p_1 is the probability that making an *unconditioned* query, i.e., knowing $\mathcal{M}$ only, Adv can successfully guess a valid PV. (We can think of p_1 as a type of minentropy.)

Similarly, define:

$$p_2 = \quad max_{a', b' \in \mathcal{V}}(\mathsf{pr}[\mathsf{dist}(a', a) \leq d \,|\, \mathsf{dist}(b', b) > d, \; a \leftarrow \mathsf{noise}(\gamma), b \leftarrow \mathsf{noise}(\gamma), \gamma \leftarrow \mathsf{sample}(\cdot, \tau)]).$$

Here, p_2 is the maximum probability, given a failed PV guess b' for β, that Adv can guess a valid PV a' for a.

We have earlier presented Lemma 1, which is as follows.

LEMMA 1. *For PV model $\mathcal{M}$, $\mathsf{succ}^{H2H}_{\mathsf{Adv}}(1, 1) \leq p_1 + p_2 - p_1 p_2$.*

We now build on Lemma 1, to show that Adv maximizes its probability of success by making $q/2$ pairs of queries to the IMD and Programmer, and that its success probability for each pair of queries is at most $succ^{H2H}_{\mathsf{Adv}}(1, 1)$. Theorem 1 results:

THEOREM 1. *Given PV model $\mathcal{M}$ and $q = q_i + q_r$ with even-valued q, $\mathsf{succ}^{H2H}_{\mathsf{Adv}}(q_i, q_r) \leq 1 - (1 - (p_1 + p_2 - p_1 p_2))^{q/2}$.*

Proof: [sketch] Given Lemma 1, it suffices to show that Adv maximizes its probability of success by making $q/2$ pairs of queries to the IMD and Programmer, and that its success probability for each pair of queries is at most $succ^{H2H}_{\mathsf{Adv}}(1, 1)$.

Given output `reject`, the IMD waits a full cycle (time τ) before initiating another session (taking input **start**). Suppose, then, that the IMD initiates local session i at time t, and thus reads $\alpha_i \leftarrow \mathsf{noise}(\mathsf{sample}(t, \tau))$. Then the IMD will only initiate a fresh session $i + 1$ at time $\geq t + \tau$.

Thus if the Programmer initiates a session with PV β, then β will be independent of α_i provided that β is read at time $t + \tau$ or later. Thus, as the Programmer only initiates a session at time $t + \tau$, any Programmer PV reading β is independent of at least one of α_i or α_{i+1}. In general, then, any PV reading by the Programmer correlates with at most one α_i.

Consequently, can make at most one conditioned query, i.e., query with information about γ, per unconditioned query. It can do so only by initiating overlapping sessions with the IMD and Programmer. Given q queries in total, Adv can create at most $q/2$ such sessions. Thus, $\mathsf{succ}^{H2H}_{\mathsf{Adv}_{q_i, q_r}} \leq 1 - (1 - \mathsf{succ}^{H2H}_{\mathsf{Adv}_{1,1}})^{q/2}$.

A.3 Application to H2H

H2H carries two distinctive properties of uniformity that permit a simplification of Theorem 1. In particular:

- *Uniformly random PVs:* In PV probability model $\mathcal{M}_{H2H}$ for H2H, PVs are distributed uniformly at random (but correlated). That is, $\alpha, \beta \in_U \mathcal{V}$.
- *Uniform regions of validity:* For our Neyman-Pearson-derived distance metric dist_{H2H} in H2H, the number of valid PV guesses β is identical for any α in $\mathcal{V}$. (The distance between two PVs depends on their bit differences, not the PVs' specific bit values.)

Thus we can show (proof omitted):

COROLLARY 1. *Given PV model $\mathcal{M}_{H2H}$ and distance metric dist_{H2H}, and $q = q_i + q_r$ with even-valued q, $\mathsf{succ}^{H2H}_{\mathsf{Adv}}(q_i, q_r) \leq 1 - (1 - 2p_1)^{q/2}$.*

OAKE: A New Family of Implicitly Authenticated Diffie-Hellman Protocols*

[Extended Abstract] †

Andrew Chi-Chih Yao
Institute for Interdisciplinary Information Sciences, Tsinghua University, China
andrewcyao@tsinghua.edu.cn

Yunlei Zhao‡
Software School, Fudan University, China
State Key Laboratory of Information Security
ylzhao@fudan.edu.cn

ABSTRACT

Cryptographic algorithm standards play an important role both to the practice of information security and to cryptography theory research. Among them, the KEA and OPACITY (KEA/OPACITY, in short) protocols, and the MQV and HMQV ((H)MQV, in short) protocols, are a family of *implicitly authenticated* Diffie-Hellman key-exchange (IA-DHKE) protocols that are among the most efficient authenticated key-exchange protocols known and are widely standardized. In this work, from some new design insights, we develop a new family of practical IA-DHKE protocols, referred to as OAKE (standing for "optimal authenticated key-exchange" in brief). We show that the OAKE protocol family combines, in essence, the advantages of both (H)MQV and KEA/OPACITY, while saving from or alleviating the disadvantages of them both.

Categories and Subject Descriptors

E.3 [**Data Encryption**]: public key cryptosystems, standards; D.4.6 [**Security and Protection**]: Authentication

Keywords

Authentication, key exchange, standards

---

*This research was supported in part by the National Basic Research Program of China (973 Program) No. 2007CB807900, No. 2007CB807901, No. 2014CB340600, and National Natural Science Foundation of China Grant No.61033001, No.61061130540, No. 61070248, and No. 61272012, Innovation Project (No.12ZZ013) of Shanghai Municipal Education Commission, and Joint Project of SKLOLS.

†A full version of this paper is available as *Cryptology ePrint Archive*, Report No. 2011/035, at `http://eprint.iacr.org/2011/035`

‡Contact author.

CCS'13, November 4–8, 2013, Berlin, Germany.

http://dx.doi.org/10.1145/2508859.2516695.

1. INTRODUCTION

Diffie-Hellman key-exchange (DHKE) protocols [31] marked the birth of modern cryptography, and are one of the main pillars of both theory and practice of cryptography [22, 23]. Unfortunately, the basic DHKE protocol is not secure against active adversaries, who control the communication channels and in particular can play the concurrent man-in-the-middle (CMIM) attacks. The quest for DHKE protocols secure against active attacks has triggered intensive subsequent works.

The common approach for achieving secure DHKE against active attacks is to explicitly authenticate the messages being exchanged with some cryptographic primitives, e.g., signature, encryption, MAC, and hashing. Some salient examples following this approach include: IKE [43, 49] and SIGMA [50], deniable IKE [72], STS [32], SSL [44, 35] and TLS [30, 52], and JFK [3]. Though secure DHKE protocols against active attacks can be achieved with explicit mutual authentication, they usually incur significant additional computation and communication complexity as compared with the basic DHKE protocol.

Motivated by reducing the performance cost associated with authentication mechanisms for secure DHKE against active attacks, Matsumoti et al., in 1986, initiated an ambitious line of research investigation to design implicitly authenticated DHKE protocols [58]. By implicitly authenticated DHKE, we mean DHKE protocol whose communication is identical to that of the basic DH protocol, yet it is implicitly authenticated by the sole ability of the parties to compute the resultant session-key [51]. In this work, we focus on several widely standardized IA-DHKE protocols: KEA [65] and OPACITY [70] (KEA/OPACITY, in short), MQV [59] and HMQV [51, 42] ((H)MQV, in short).

Let G' be a finite Abelian group of order N, $G \subseteq G'$ be a subgroup of prime order q. Denote by g a generator of G, by 1_G the identity element, by $G \setminus 1_G = G - \{1_G\}$ the set of elements of G except 1_G and by $t = \frac{N}{q}$ the cofactor. In this work, we use multiplicative notation for the group operation in G'. Let $(A = g^a, a)$ (resp., $(X = g^x, x)$) be the public key and secret key (resp., the DH-component and DH-exponent) of player $\hat{A}$, and $(B = g^b, b)$ (resp., $(Y = g^y, y)$) be the public key and secret key (resp., the DH-component and DH-exponent) of player $\hat{B}$, where $a, x, b, y \leftarrow Z_q^*$ (i.e., each of them is taken uniformly and independently from Z_q^*). The (H)MQV and KEA protocols are described in Figure 1 (page 3), where H_K (resp., h) is a hash function of k-bit (resp., l-bit) output and l is set to be $|q|/2$ for HMQV.

The KEA algorithm [65, 53, 56] was designed by the US National Security Agency (NSA) and was later standardized by NIST. Note that the KEA protocol described in Figure 1 is actually the provably secure version proposed by Lauter, et al. in [56]. In the original KEA protocol, the session-key is set to be $H_K(A^y \oplus X^b)$. Throughout this work, for presentation simplicity, by KEA we simply refer to the provably secure version proposed in [56].

The OPACITY (Open Protocol for Access Control, Identification, and Ticketing with Privacy) algorithm [70] is another IA-DHKE protocol, which is mainly for establishing channels in *contactless* environment (e.g., access control for buildings, and ticketing in transport systems). OPACITY was sponsored by US Department of Defense and International Smart Card Alliance, and has now been registered as an ISO/IEC 24727-6 authentication protocol [47], and specified in the draft ANSI 504-1 national standard [4]. The OPACITY protocol was designed based on KEA. With the computation of $\hat{B}$ as an illustration, the core authentication mechanism of both KEA and OPACITY is to derive keys from (A^y, X^b), possibly together with some auxiliary information aux (e.g., players' identities, and some protocol control information) related to the protocol run. This authentication mechanism of KEA and OPACITY was also proposed in [14].

The MQV and HMQV protocols stand for the current state-of-the-art of (public key cryptography based) *efficient* authenticated DHKE, and marked the great milestones of IA-DHKE developments. In particular, the first formal analysis of IA-DHKE within the Canetti-Krawczyk framework (CK-framework) was conducted w.r.t. the HMQV protocol in [51], which is particularly helpful in understanding the protocol design insights and the underlying parameter choices. (H)MQV has been widely standardized [5, 45, 46, 63, 71, 64], and was announced by NSA as the key exchange mechanism underlying "the next generation cryptography to protect US government information", including the protection of "classified or mission critical national security information" [71, 51].

In order to provide more robust resilience to birthday attacks on the hash function h and/or to the leakage of DH components and exponents, MQV in the NIST standard [7] and HMQV (p.54, [51]) made the following preferable modification: players' identities are put into session-key derivation in the *fixed* order of $(\hat{A}, \hat{B})$. For presentation simplicity, we refer to (H)MQV with such a modification as *robust* (H)MQV, where the session-key is set to be $K = H_K(K_{\hat{A}}, \hat{A}, \hat{B}) = H_K(K_{\hat{B}}, \hat{A}, \hat{B})$. Throughout this work, an IA-DHKE protocol is called *role-dependent* (resp., role-independent), if its session-key derivation is dependent (resp., independent) of players' roles (i.e., initiator or responder). Note that (H)MQV is role-independent, while robust (H)MQV and KEA are role-dependent.

1.1 Motivation and Contributions

Both KEA/OPACITY and (H)MQV have advantageous features, which made them both widely standardized and desirable in accordance with different application scenarios. For the efficiency issue, (H)MQV is more efficient as a whole; in contrast, KEA/OPACITY is more efficient in online settings. For the security issue, the provable security of KEA in the CK-framework allows robust leakage resilience, in the sense that the exposed session-states include all the pre-computed and stored session-specific values; by comparison, the provable security of HMQV depends upon what pre-computed values are specified in the session-states, where some naturally pre-computable session-specific values are, however, not assumed to be include in session-states and are assumed to be unexposed. In addition, KEA/OPACITY allows more flexible deployment, and provides better privacy protection. A detailed comparative study of (H)MQV versus KEA/OPACITY is presented in Section 3.

In particular, KEA/OPACITY enjoys the advantages of optimal online efficiency and honest-player deniability (HP-deniability). By "optimal online efficiency", we mean that each player needs to online perform only one modular exponentiation (besides some other minor operations like hashing and/or MAC, etc). By "honest-player deniability", we mean that the transcript of a session run *between a pair of honest players*, the resultant session-key, and all the pre-computed and stored session-states, can be statistically simulated by an efficient algorithm from the public parameters and players' public keys. By comparison, the use of the session-key of (H)MQV can be traced back to the pair of players as the value g^{ab} is involved in the session-key derivation, which is referred to as g^{ab}-traceability for presentation simplicity.

Unfortunately, the advantages of KEA/OPACITY usually correspond to the disadvantages of (H)MQV, and vice versa. On the other hand, as the session-key structure of KEA/OPACITY and that of (H)MQV are different in nature, it is uneasy or flexible to implement both of them and then switch between them according to different application scenarios, particularly for applications based on low-power devices. This leads to the following main motivation.

Motivation

Can we design a new family of IA-DHKE protocols that could combine, in essence, the advantages of both KEA/OPACITY and (H)MQV, while saving from the disadvantages of them both?

We suggest that, though clearly being important both to the theory and practice of KE, coming up with such an IA-DHKE protocol is quite challenging, which calls for *new IA-DHKE protocol structures* with *new design insight or novelty*. In general, despite its seemingly conceptual simplicity, designing "*sound*" and "*right*" key-exchange protocols turns out to be extremely error prone and can be notoriously subtle, particularly witnessed by the evolution history of KEA [65, 56] and that of (H)MQV [58, 59, 48, 51, 60]. Also, the analysis of even a simple cryptographic protocol in intricate adversarial settings like the Internet can be a luxury and dauntingly complex task [51, 19]. The reason for this is the high system complexity and plenty of subtleties surrounding the design, definition and analysis of key-exchange protocols. In particular, though seemingly conceptually simple, the (H)MQV protocols were actually very delicately designed, in the sense that slight changes in the design structure or parameters can lose provable security or even be totally insecure. Given the long-time study of KEA/OPACITY and (H)MQV both in research and in engineering, it may be commonly suggested that the state-of-the-art of KEA/OPACITY and(H)MQV (in their respective types) should hardly be broken. This further re-

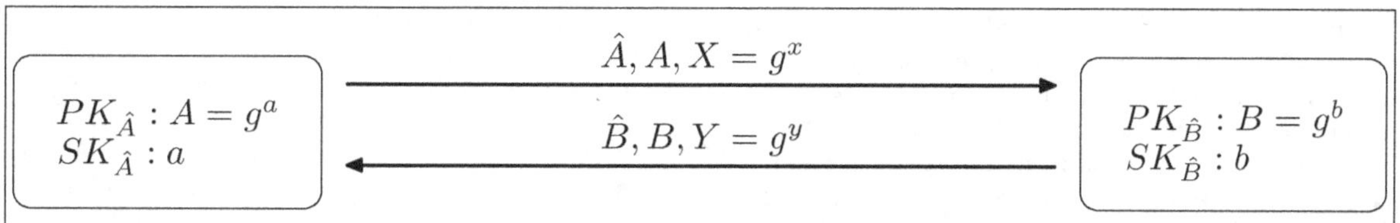

$$\textbf{(H)MQV:} \quad K_{\hat{B}} = (XA^d)^{y+eb}, K_{\hat{A}} = (YB^e)^{x+da}, K = H_K(K_{\hat{B}}) = H_K(K_{\hat{A}})$$

$$\textbf{MQV:} \quad d = 2^l + (X \bmod 2^l), e = 2^l + (Y \bmod 2^l), l = |q|/2$$

$$\textbf{HMQV:} \quad d = h(X, \hat{B}), e = h(Y, \hat{A}), l = |q|/2$$

$$\textbf{KEA:} \quad K = H_K(Y^a, B^x, \hat{A}, \hat{B}) = H_K(A^y, X^b, \hat{A}, \hat{B})$$

$$\textbf{(T)OAKE:} \quad K_{\hat{B}} = A^{fb+y}X^{b+ey}, K_{\hat{A}} = B^{fa+x}Y^{a+ex}, K = H_K(K_{\hat{B}}) = H_K(K_{\hat{A}})$$

$$\textbf{OAKE:} \quad e = h(\hat{A}, A, \hat{B}, B, X, Y),\ f = 0,\ l \approx |q|$$

$$\textbf{T-OAKE:} \quad e = h(\hat{A}, A, \hat{B}, B, X, Y),\ f = 1,\ l \approx |q|$$

Figure 1: Specifications of (H)MQV, KEA and (T)OAKE

flects the non-triviality of the goal of this work, i.e., *achieving the best of both worlds: combining the advantages of KEA/OPACITY and (H)MQV in authenticated key-exchange.*

Our contributions. In this work, motivated for a mechanism of proving the knowledge of multiple DH-exponents jointly and practically, and for conceptually simple protocol design and analysis, we introduce an extension of the knowledge-of-exponent assumption (KEA) [27] in the random oracle model [11], referred to as the joint knowledge-of-exponent assumption (JKEA). We show that the JKEA assumption is implied, and thus justified, by the traditional KEA assumption in the random oracle model.

Based on this line of investigations and observations, we develop a new practical IA-DHKE protocol, referred to as OAKE.[1] Briefly speaking, the OAKE protocol enjoys the following advantageous features simultaneously. More detailed discussions and comparisons about the performance advantages of OAKE are given in Section 5.

- It is as efficient as, actually (slightly) *more efficient than*, HMQV in total. Notice that, as (H)MQV is commonly viewed as nearly optimal in the integrity of security and protocol efficiency, *even minor efficiency improvements (while preserving provable security) can be challenging.*
- It enjoys the optimal online efficiency and HP-deniability of KEA/OPACITY, which is particularly desirable for applications based on low-power or wireless devices like smart cards or phones, etc.
- It has provable security with *robust leakage resilience* in the CK-framework, in the sense that all values, which can be offline pre-computed and stored, can be exposed to the attacker.
- It enjoys g^{ab}-flexibility and more flexible and modular protocol structure, in the sense that, for applications where g^{ab}-traceability takes priority over HP-deniability, the value g^{ab} can simply get involved in session-key computation at the minimal cost of one modular addition incurred, while still preserving provable security and online optimal efficiency. For presentation simplicity, the variant of OAKE that provides g^{ab}-traceability is referred to as traceable OAKE (T-OAKE in short). T-OAKE is still (slightly) more efficient than HMQV in total.
- The shared DH-secret involves only a single hashing operation, which particularly indicates that OAKE is hardly viewed as a variant of HMQV. We remark that cryptographic hashing, e.g., SHA-1, is quite an expensive operation, particularly compared to modular multiplication, and is thus much desirable to minimize the use of hashing particularly for highly practical protocols like IA-DHKE.
- It eases deployments in practice, particularly for applications based on low-power devices like smart cards or phones.

[1]The acronym of OAKE stands for "(toward) Optimally-balanced (implicitly) Authenticated (Diffie-Hellman) Key-Exchange (in the integrity of protocol efficiency, security, privacy, and easy deployment)".

2. PRELIMINARIES

If $\mathcal{S}$ is a finite set then $|\mathcal{S}|$ is its cardinality, and $x \leftarrow S$ is the operation of picking an element uniformly at random from S. If α is neither an algorithm nor a set then $x \leftarrow \alpha$ is a simple assignment statement. A string or value α means a binary one, and $|\alpha|$ is its binary length. We denote by $\mathbb{N}$ the set of natural numbers. Throughout this work, unless otherwise specified, we use a hash function $h : \{0,1\}^* \rightarrow \{0,1\}^l \setminus \{0^l\} \subseteq Z_q^*$, which is modeled as a random oracle, and we denote by its output length l, usually presented in unary as 1^l, as the security parameter. Two ensembles $X = \{X_l\}_{l \in \mathbb{N}}$ and $Y = \{Y_l\}_{l \in \mathbb{N}}$ are computationally indistinguishable, if for any probabilistic polynomial-time (PPT) algorithm $\mathcal{D}$ and for all sufficiently large l's, $|\Pr[D(1^l, X_l) = 1] - \Pr[D(1^l, Y_l) = 1]|$ is negligible in l.

Throughout this paper, unless otherwise stated, we assume that the underlying PKI does not require proof-of-possession or proof-of-knowledge (POP/POK, in short) of secret key during public key registration. As we focus on IA-DHKE with robust leakage resilience, for presentation simplicity, we assume that the Certificate Authority (CA) will check the non-identity sub-group (i.e., $G \setminus 1_G$) membership of registered public keys, which is also required by HMQV whenever the pre-computation of DH component or exponent is considered (cf. the full version of [51]). But supposing no pre-computation or leakage of DH exponents, the sub-group test for registered public keys will be waived.

Roughly speaking, the discrete logarithm (DL) assumption over G says that given $X = g^x$, where $x \leftarrow Z_q^*$, no efficient, specifically probabilistic polynomial-time (PPT), DL-solver algorithm can output x with non-negligible probability. The *gap* DL (GDL) assumption says that the DL assumption holds even if the DL-solver algorithm is equipped with a decisional Diffie-Hellman (DDH) oracle for the group G and generator g, where on arbitrary input $(U, V, Z) \in G^3$ the DDH oracle outputs 1 if and only if $Z = CDH(U, V)$. The computational Diffie-Hellman (CDH) assumption says that given $X = g^x, Y = g^y$, where $x, y \leftarrow Z_q^*$, no efficient CDH-solver algorithm can compute $CDH(X, Y) = g^{xy}$ with non-negligible probability. The Gap Diffie-Hellman (GDH) assumption [66] roughly says that the CDH assumption holds even if the CDH solver is equipped with a DDH oracle for the group G and generator g.

Knowledge-of-Exponent Assumption (KEA) [27]. Let G be a cyclic group of prime order q generated by an element g, and consider an algorithm $\mathscr{A}$ that on input a triple $(g, C = g^c, z)$ outputs a pair $(Y, Z) \in G^2$, where c is taken uniformly at random from Z_q^* and $z \in \{0,1\}^*$ *is an arbitrary string that is generated independently of* C. Such an algorithm $\mathscr{A}$ is said to be a KEA algorithm if with non-negligible probability (over the choice of g, c and $\mathscr{A}$'s random coins) $\mathscr{A}(g, g^c, z)$ outputs $(Y, Z) \in G^2$ such that $Z = Y^c$. The algorithm $\mathscr{A}$ is called a *strong* KEA algorithm, if it is additionally equipped with a DDH oracle. Here, $C = g^c$ is the random challenge to the KEA algorithm $\mathscr{A}$, and z captures the auxiliary input of $\mathscr{A}$ that is independent of the challenge C. We say that the KEA assumption (resp., the strong KEA assumption) holds over G, if for every probabilistic polynomial-time KEA (resp., strong KEA) algorithm $\mathscr{A}$ for G there exists another efficient algorithm $\mathcal{K}$, referred to as the KEA-extractor, for which the following property holds except for a negligible probability. Let (g, g^c, z) be an input to $\mathscr{A}$, ρ a vector of random coins for $\mathscr{A}$ (and $\mathcal{L}_{DDH}$ the answers from the DDH-oracle for the strong KEA algorithm), on which $\mathscr{A}$ outputs $(Y, Z = Y^c)$. Then, on the same inputs and random coins, $\mathcal{K}(g, C, z, \rho)$ (resp., $\mathcal{K}(g, C, z, \rho, \mathcal{L}_{DDH})$) outputs the triple $(Y, Z = Y^c, y)$ where $Y = g^y$.

Notice that, by definition, both KEA and strong KEA are non-black-box assumptions. The KEA assumption is derived from the CDH assumption, while the strong KEA (SKEA) assumption is derived from the GDH assumption.

3. (H)MQV VERSUS KEA/OPACITY: A COMPARATIVE STUDY

The salient advantage of (H)MQV is that the session-key computation essentially accounts for about one simultaneous exponentiation (SE), which amounts to about 1.27 modular exponentiations [61, 38, 33]. By comparison, each player in KEA/OPACITY needs to perform two separate exponentiations to derive the session-key. Indeed, (H)MQV is commonly viewed as nearly optimal in the integrity of security and protocol efficiency, and even a minor efficiency improvement (while preserving provable security) is desirable and can be challenging.

On the other hand, KEA and OPACITY enjoy the advantages of optimal online efficiency and honest-player deniability (HP-deniability). By "optimal online efficiency", we mean that the values Y and A^y (resp., X and B^x) can be offline pre-computed and stored by the player $\hat{B}$ (resp., $\hat{A}$), and each player needs to perform only one modular exponentiation X^b or Y^a (besides some other minor operations like hashing and/or MAC, etc). By comparison, the session-key computation of (H)MQV, which takes one simultaneous exponentiation, does not allow offline pre-computability. Notice that the known *fastest* simultaneous exponentiation algorithm runs about 1.27 exponentiations [61, 38, 33]. By "honest-player deniability", we mean that the transcript of a session run *between a pair of honest players*, the resultant session-key, and all the pre-computed and stored session-states, can be statistically simulated by an efficient algorithm from the public parameters and players' public keys. A formal definition of HP-deniability is given in Section 6.2. The HP-deniability property of KEA/OPACITY is from the fact that: the session-key, as well as the values A^y and B^x, can be computed merely from the DH-exponents x and y (together with some public parameters). These advantageous features of KEA/OPACITY made them much desirable for deployments based on low-power devices like smart cards or phones; indeed, OPACITY was designated mainly for applications with low-power devices in wireless settings. By comparison, the use of the session-key of (H)MQV can be definitely traced back to the pair of players as the value g^{ab} is involved in the session-key derivation, which is referred to as g^{ab}-traceability for presentation simplicity.

On the desirability of offline pre-computability, particularly for IA-DHKE. Firstly, in general, the "possibility of pre-computation to reduce on-line computational complexity" is listed as one important feature for measuring efficiency advantage of KE protocols [61, 17, 24], particularly for deployment with low-power devices like smart cards.

Secondly, offline pre-computability is particularly desirable for deployment of KE in the distributed client/server setting (the major application scenario for which OPACITY was designed), where clients (e.g., smart-cards, smart-phones) are usually more power-limited than the server (e.g., a bank, a base station, an organization) while the server is usually static and its public key can be priorly known to clients. In such a setting, it is much desirable for the low-power clients to obtain offline pre-computability in order to accelerate online efficiency. Moreover, in such a setting, the server (e.g., player $\hat{B}$ in KEA/OPACITY) usually runs a database of clients. Then, for each client player $\hat{A}$, the server $\hat{B}$ can pre-compute (Y, A^y) and stores the pre-computed values in the entry of player $\hat{A}$ in the database. That is, the server can also enjoy offline pre-computability to accelerate online efficiency.

Thirdly, offline pre-computability is also much desirable for deployment of KE in the station-to-station setting, which is particularly the major application scenario of (H)MQV by NSA. Specifically, in such a setting, players are usually organizations or stations, whose identities and public keys are known each other priorly, which allows offline pre-computability to accelerate online efficiency.

Fourthly, particularly for IA-DHKE, offline pre-computability allows *more efficient* explicit sub-group test of peer's DH-component. It is commonly suggested important for each player of DHKE to make sure the DH-component from its peer is indeed in the sub-group G (particularly in order to avoid small group attacks).[2] With offline pre-computation, KEA/OPACITY allows more efficient explicit sub-group test. With the computation of $\hat{B}$ as an example, it can online perform X^b and X^q in parallel, which amounts to about 1.2 modular exponentiations.

Finally, offline pre-computability allows *more robust* embedded sub-group test. For KEA/OPACITY with offline pre-computation, the value X^y in session-key derivation can be replaced by X^{yt}, and the player $\hat{B}$ aborts if $X \notin G'$ or $X^{yt} \neq 1_G$. This fully guarantee that X is not in a (small) subgroup of G' with the order that is a factor of t. The embedded sub-group test performed by (H)MQV, i.e., checking $(XA^d)^{(y+be)t} \neq 1_G$, does not fully ensure that X is not in a small group *in general*.

On the desirability of HP-deniability. Firstly, for KE protocols, both security and privacy are desired. Among privacy concerns, deniability is an essential privacy property, and has always been a central concern in personal and business communications. The reader is referred to [16, 68, 69, 34] for more motivations for deniability of KE.

Secondly, providing a certain level of privacy protection serves as one of the major criteria underlying the evolution of a list of important industrial standards of KE protocols, which is particularly witnessed by the evolution of IKE [49] (that is based on the SIGMA protocol [50]), as well as the selection of the standards of KEA and OPACITY. IKE and SIGMA enjoy "plausible deniability" [50], in the sense that the session transcript only consists of signatures on the exchanged DH-components rather than players' identities. However, as signatures are included in the session transcript, IKE and SIGMA cannot be HP-deniable. On the other hand, the HP-deniability is commonly viewed as a useful feature of KEA/OPACITY, which we would like to preserve.

Thirdly, for an IA-DHKE protocol, we cannot count on full-fledged deniability as defined in [34, 72]. Notice that, for all IA-DHKE protocols, their session transcripts are the same. The privacy mainly lies in the way the session-key is computed. In this sense, HP-deniability is the most useful privacy property that any IA-DHKE protocol can render.

Finally, HP-deniability enables *more modular and flexible* constructions of higher-level privacy-preserving cryptographic systems, in order to offer various privacy services based upon it. Notice that, if the session transcript includes players' signatures or the session-key computation involves the value g^{ab}, it can nullify an untraceability property offered by a fancy cryptographic protocol running at the higher level. On the other hand, if deniability is not desired, for some cases, some non-repudiable mechanisms, e.g., signatures, can be easily issued at the higher level. In a way, the relationship between HP-deniability and full deniability is analogue to that between honest-verifier zero-knowledge (HVZK) and ZK, where HVZK has already been commonly viewed as a powerful building tool in the literature.

On the desirability of g^{ab}-flexibility for IA-DHKE. Note that KEA/OPACITY and (H)MQV have different performance advantages, and for different applications we may want to deploy different protocols. However, as the session-key derivation mechanisms of KEA/OPACITY and (H)MQV are different in nature, it is less easy or flexible to switch between them in practice (particularly for applications based on low-power devices). We hope for a protocol that is as efficient as (H)MQV, while simultaneously enjoying online optimal efficiency and HP-deniability of KEA/OPACITY.

One additional flexibility advantage of KEA is that, for applications where g^{ab}-traceability takes priority over HP-deniability, the value g^{ab} can be put into the input of the session-key derivation function without sacrificing the online optimal efficiency. Specifically, $K = H_K(A^b, A^y, X^b, \hat{A}, \hat{B})$ in this case, which is referred to as traceable KEA (T-KEA) for presentation simplicity. Notice that the parallel computation of A^b and A^y amounts to about 1.2 modular exponentiations. That is, the session-key computation of T-KEA takes about 2.2 exponentiations, which is, however, still in sharp contrast to the about 1.27 exponentiations of (H)MQV in such a scenario. On the other hand, the session-key derivation of (H)MQV is less flexible than KEA, in the sense that we do not know how to remove the value g^{ab} from the session-key computation of HMQV for applications where HP-deniability takes priority, while still preserving its provable security.

In this work, we want for an IA-DHKE protocol with g^{ab}-flexibility, in the sense that, according to different desirability between g^{ab}-traceability and HP-deniability, the value g^{ab} can be simply added to or removed from the session-key derivation. Moreover, the switching on or off of g^{ab} in session-key derivation is *at the minimal cost of only one modular addition incurred, without sacrificing provable security and online efficiency.* This can provide much more flexibilities and deployment ease in practice.

---

[2]The basic technique to check the DH-component, e.g., X, is in G is to verify $X^q = 1_G$ (and $X \in G' \setminus 1_G$) that performs one exponentiation. However, if the cofactor t is small, e.g., $G' = Z_N^*$ such that $N = 2q + 1$, or G is the subgroup of an elliptic curve over a finite field (in this case the cofactor t is usually a small constant and even just 1), the subgroup test of X can be essentially reduced to: (1) check $X \in G'$; (2). $X^t \neq 1_G$. We remark that, in general, checking $X \in G'$ and $X^t \neq 1_G$ guarantees that X is not in a (small) subgroup of G' with the order that is a factor of t, but it does not fully guarantee $X \in G$ (e.g., considering that $X = -g^x$).

3.1 Security of KEA/OPACITY and (H)MQV

KEA and its variants were analyzed in [53, 56], where a slight variant of KEA was proven to be secure in accordance with the CK-framework under the gap Diffie-Hellman (GDH) assumption in the random oracle (RO) model [11]. In the security analysis of KEA [53, 56], for any session other than the test-session and its matching session, the pre-computed and stored session-state (that can be exposed to attacker) at a player includes its DH-exponent, DH-component, and the value B^x or A^y. The provable security of OPACITY is still unknown to our knowledge, though we suggest the security analysis of KEA [56] may be adapted and extended to that of OPACITY.

Assuming no leakage of any DH-component (that is to be publicly exchanged in plain) or private secrecy like DH-exponent, the provable security of HMQV is based merely on the CDH assumption. However, whenever there is an uncorrupted player whose DH component or component is pre-computed and may be exposed prior to the session run (and thus the attacker can just set this session as the test-session), the provable security of HMQV is based on the GDH assumption and the non-standard (non-black-box) *strong* KEA assumption [72].[3] The provable security of MQV in the CK-framework is unknown to our knowledge.

However, for HMQV, its provable security does not consider the leakage of all values that can be offline pre-computed and stored. Specifically, for (H)MQV, it is quite natural for a player, e.g., $\hat{B}$, to offline pre-compute and store the values $(Y, y, s_B = y + eb)$ in order to accelerate online efficiency. Notice that cryptographic hashing, e.g., SHA-1, and multiplication could be relatively expensive operations for low-power devices, and are thus desirable to be offline pre-computed. But the leakage of $s_B = y + eb$ can cause the following security damages.

- The leakage of $s_B = y + eb$ has already exposed the session-key of the exposed session as well as its matching session (in case the matching session exists).
- The leakage of $s_B = y + eb$ allows an adversary to impersonate the player $\hat{B}$ in other (non-matching) sessions, by reusing the values (Y, s_B) *without necessarily knowing the secret key b*.
- In addition, the leakage of s_B and y together actually exposes the static secret key b.

This violates the principle that the secrecy leakage of one session should have no adverse bearing on the security of other (non-matching) sessions. To avoid this security damages, the provable security of HMQV explicitly exclude the leakage of the value s_B or s_A. To be precise, for the provable security of all the protocols, i.e., KEA, HMQV and the OAKE protocol family developed in this work, the attacker is additionally allowed to expose the static secret key of any uncorrupted player other than the test-session peer, i.e., player $\hat{B}$ if the test-session is $(\hat{A}, \hat{B}, X_0, Y_0)$. Then, for the provable security of HMQV in [51], it implicitly implies that the session-state (y, Y, s_B) of $\hat{B}$ *for any session* should not be exposed in order to comply with the security in CK-framework (unless s_B is not specified to be part of the session-state). In other words, if s_B is specified as part of the session-state, the provable security of HMQV will become much limited. More discussions on security, when the session-state of the test-session or its matching session can be exposed, are given in Section 6.4 (page 12).

On the desirability of *robust* leakage resilience. In practice, many cryptographic applications will boost protocol performance by pre-computing and storing values for later use in the protocol, particularly when they are based on low-power devices like smart cards or phones. However, these pre-computed and stored values are much vulnerable to leakage, in view of the various side-channel attacks (see, e.g., [41, 12]) discovered in recent years. In particular, the powerful "cold-boot attack" [41] allows an attacker to reveal information about memory contents, *particulary the values that are pre-computed and stored in memory*, in the absence of computation and even after the device is powered down [57]! In addition, cryptosystems may usually be deployed in hostile environments plagued with spyware or virus, which can actively reveal memory content information, particularly for applications based on low-power devices in wireless settings. As a consequence, it is commonly suggested to be imprudent to assume no secrecy leakage for cryptosystems in reality [18].

A basic principle, guiding any security formulation for key-exchange protocols, is that the leakage of ephemeral information associated with a particular session (e.g., its session key or state) should not compromise other non-matching sessions. Moreover, for DHKE protocols, the offline pre-computed and stored *DH-components* are much less protected in practice, *as they are actually public values to be exchanged in plain*. For DHKE protocols running concurrently in settings like the Internet, we suggest that it is also unreasonable or unrealistic to assume non-precomputation and non-exposure of the *public* DH-components for *all* uncorrupted parties in the system. Notice that, whenever there is an honest user who pre-computes a DH-component (and thus the attacker can choose that session as the test-session), then for provable security in the CK-framework we have to consider the potential leakage of DH-components.

In this work, we aim for secure IA-DHKE with *robust leakage resilience*, in the sense that the exposed session-state includes all the pre-computed and stored session-specific values. On the one hand, the pre-computed and stored values are much more vulnerable to leakage (than the ephemeral intermediate values generated on the fly during a session run). On the other hand, we suggest it appears strange to assume, for a naturally pre-computable value, e.g., the value $s_B = y + eb$ in (H)MQV, to be not pre-computed or to be stored safely and separately from other pre-computed session values. One suggestion may be to use a trust tamper-proof hardware to store any SK-related secrecy, which is, however, costly and unusual in practice (particularly for low-power devices like smart cards or phones). As mentioned above, the provable security of HMQV does consider and allow the exposure of $s_B = y + eb$ or $s_A = x + da$.

Thus, it is clearly desirable to have secure IA-DHKE with robust leakage resilience. As already stressed in [51], security of KE against the exposed offline pre-computed values (*particularly, the DH-components to be exchanged in plain*) is deemed to be a must, as well as the main and prime

[3]We notice that the provable security of HMQV, for the case where DH exponents or components may be exposed, is actually based on the *strong* KEA assumption (besides the GDH assumption), while in [51] it was informally stated to be based on the KEA assumption.

concern, for any robust KE protocol. This is particularly the case for protocols that are widely standardized and are aimed for protecting critical information including "classified or mission critical national security information" [71, 51].

4. JOINT KNOWLEDGE-OF-EXPONENT ASSUMPTION

Motivated for breaking some impossibility barriers of black-box cryptography, and for achieving cryptographic schemes of conceptually simple structure and analysis, achieving cryptographic schemes based on non-black-box assumptions or primitives has been attracting much research attention in recent years ([6, 20, 21, 37, 28, 13]). As a popular non-black-box assumption, the KEA assumption, since its introduction [27], has been shown to be successful in solving a number of (at times notoriously open) cryptographic problems, and has been used in a large body of subsequent works (see, e.g., [27, 40, 10, 9, 68, 51, 29, 69, 2, 62, 20, 21, 39, 36, 37, 72, 28, 13]). The KEA assumption and its variants are particularly used for authenticated KE [51, 68, 69, 36, 72], and are recently abstracted and generalized in [20, 21, 13].

In spite of the success and popularity of the KEA assumption, by its nature the KEA assumption is actually not very convenient for use in applications involving proving the knowledge of *multiple* DH-exponents. In such settings, to prove the knowledge of multiple DH-exponents with the KEA assumption, each of the prover and the verifier needs to perform multiple *separate* exponentiations, which is less efficient (particularly for applications based on low-power devices like smart-cards).

Motivated for more efficient use of KEA-type assumptions and for conceptually simple protocol design and analysis, in this work we introduce an extension of the KEA assumption in the random oracle model, referred to as the joint knowledge-of-exponent assumption (JKEA).

DEFINITION 4.1 (JKEA ASSUMPTION). *Let G be a cyclic group of prime order q generated by an element g, and consider an algorithm $\mathscr{A}$ with oracle access to an RO $h : \{0,1\}^* \rightarrow \{0,1\}^l \setminus \{0\} \subseteq Z_q^*$. On input a triple $(g, X = g^x, z)$, the algorithm $\mathscr{A}$ outputs $(B, Y, \Pi, aux) \in G^3 \times \{0,1\}^*$, where $x \leftarrow Z_q^*$ and $z \in \{0,1\}^*$ is an arbitrary string that is generated independently of X. Such an algorithm $\mathscr{A}$ is said to be a JKEA algorithm if, with non-negligible probability (over the choice of g, x, $\mathscr{A}$'s random coins and the choice of the random function h), $\mathscr{A}(g, g^x, z)$ outputs $(B, Y, \Pi, aux) \in G^3 \times \{0,1\}^*$ satisfying $\Pi = X^{b+h(aux,B,X,Y)y}$. The algorithm $\mathscr{A}$ is called a* strong *JKEA algorithm, if it is additionally equipped with a DDH oracle.*

We say that the JKEA assumption (resp., strong *JKEA assumption) holds over G in the random oracle model, if for any efficient JKEA (resp., strong JKEA) algorithm $\mathscr{A}$ for G there exists another efficient algorithm $\mathcal{K}$, referred to as the JKEA-extractor, for which the following property holds except for a negligible probability: let (g, g^x, z) be an input to $\mathscr{A}$, ρ be the random coins of $\mathscr{A}$, and $\mathcal{L}_{RO}$ the answers from the random oracle h (and $\mathcal{L}_{DDH}$ the answers from the DDH oracle for the strong JKEA algorithm), on which $\mathscr{A}$ outputs $(B, Y, \Pi, aux) \in G^3 \times \{0,1\}^*$ satisfying $\Pi = X^{b+h(aux,B,X,Y)y}$. Then, on the same inputs and random coins, i.e., $(g, X, z, \rho, \mathcal{L}_{RO})$ (resp., $(g, X, z, \rho, \mathcal{L}_{RO}, \mathcal{L}_{DDH})$), $\mathcal{K}$ outputs both b and y, where $B = g^b$ and $Y = g^y$.*

PROPOSITION 4.1. *JKEA assumption (resp., strong JKEA assumption) is implied by the KEA assumption (resp., strong KEA assumption) in the random oracle model.*

Proof. On input $(g, X = g^x, z)$, we can view the (strong) KEA algorithm $\mathscr{A}$ outputs $(Z = BY^e, CDH(X, Z), aux)$ with non-negligible probability, where $e = h(aux, B, X, Y)$. Then, by the (strong) KEA assumption, the value $s = b + ey$ can be extracted.

Now, from the algorithm $\mathscr{A}$, we construct another (strong) JKEA algorithm $\mathscr{A}'$. On input (g, X, z), $\mathscr{A}'$ runs $\mathscr{A}$ as a subroutine. In case $\mathscr{A}$ outputs $(Z = BY^e, CDH(X, Z), aux)$, $\mathscr{A}'$ rewinds $\mathscr{A}$ to the point that $\mathscr{A}$ just made the oracle query $h(aux, B, X, Y)$, redefines $h(aux, B, X, Y)$ to be a new random value $e' \neq e$, and runs $\mathscr{A}$ further from this rewinding point. If $\mathscr{A}$ outputs $(Z' = BY^{e'}, CDH(X, Z'), aux)$, $\mathscr{A}'$ just outputs it; otherwise, $\mathscr{A}$ aborts. By the forking lemma [67, 1], $\mathscr{A}'$ will output $(Z' = BY^{e'}, CDH(X, Z'), aux)$ also with non-negligible probability. Then, by the (strong) KEA assumption, the value $s' = b + e'y$ can be extracted. Notice that, from (s, s'), both b and y will be computed. □

Though the JKEA assumption is implied, and thus justified, by the KEA assumption in the RO model, as we shall see, JKEA-based protocol design and analysis can be more efficiency preserving and conceptually simpler for applications involving proving the knowledge of multiple DH-exponents, in comparison with KEA-based protocol design and analysis. Also, by getting rid of the forking lemma, JKEA-based analysis can be much tighter than KEA-based analysis. We remark that the JKEA-based approach is of independent interest, and brings new insight into the design of DH-protocols involving proving the knowledge of multiple DH-exponents, which is particularly witnessed by the design of the OAKE protocol family below.

5. OAKE: DESIGN AND SPECIFICATION

Consider the JKEA assumption proposed in Section 4. By setting $aux = (\hat{A}, A, \hat{B})$, we refer to X^{b+ey}, where $e = h(\hat{A}, A, \hat{B}, B, X, Y)$, as the joint proof-of-knowledge (JPOK) of both b and y w.r.t. the random DH-component challenge X, which is denoted as $JPOK_{(b,y)} = X^{b+ey}$ for presentation simplicity. The reason that we let e commit to the complete session tag, denoted $Tag = (\hat{A}, A, \hat{B}, B, X, Y)$, is that, in practice, JPOK is actually run concurrently with other protocols over network. For secure use of JPOK in concurrent settings like Internet, as is the focus of this work, we require that the JPOK provided by one party in a session should be bounded to that session, in the sense that no efficient attacker can, with non-negligible probability, make two different (non-matching) sessions have the same shared DH-secret. More details are given in Section 6 with respect to the analysis of the JPOK-based OAKE protocol in the CK-framework.

Notice that $JPOK_{(b,y)} = X^{db+ey} = (B^d Y^e)^x$, where $e = h(\hat{A}, A, \hat{B}, B, X, Y)$, actually can also be used to demonstrate the knowledge of x. The key observation now is: in order for $\hat{A}$ to additionally prove the knowledge of its secret key a, we can multiply X^{db+ey} by Y^a. This yields $K_{\hat{B}} = A^y X^{b+ey} = B^x Y^{a+ex} = K_{\hat{A}}$, where $K_{\hat{B}}$ (resp., $K_{\hat{A}}$) is computed by $\hat{B}$ (resp., $\hat{A}$) respectively. The resultant IA-DHKE protocol is named OAKE, and is depicted in Figure 1. Note that the computation of the shared DH-secret

		OAKE	T-OAKE	HMQV	KEA
Total efficiency		$1t_{se}+1t_h+1t_m+1t_a$	$1t_{se}+1t_h+1t_m+2t_a$	$1t_{se}+2t_h+2t_m+1t_a$	$2t_e$
Online efficiency		$1t_e+1t_h+1t_m+1t_a$	$1t_e+1t_h+1t_m+1t_a$	$1t_{se}+2t_h+2t_m+1t_a$	$1t_e$
SK-Security	exposed session-state	(x, X, B^x)	(x, X)	(x, X)	(x, X, B^x)
	Assumptions	GDL+SJKEA or, GDH	GDL+SJKEA or, GDH	GDH+SKEA	GDH
CDH-based security w/o pre-computation		$\perp$	$\perp$	✓	$\perp$
HP-deniability		✓	×	×	✓
g^{ab}-traceability		×	✓	✓	×
g^{ab}-flexibility		✓	✓	$\perp$	$\perp$

Table 1: A brief comparison among (T)OAKE, HMQV and KEA

$K_{\hat{A}} = K_{\hat{B}}$ involves only a single hashing, where the output length of h, i.e., l, is set approximately to be $|q|$. For applications where g^{ab}-traceability takes priority over HP-deniability, we set $K_{\hat{B}} = A^{b+y}X^{b+ey} = B^{a+x}Y^{a+ex} = K_{\hat{A}}$, which is referred to as traceable OAKE (T-OAKE, in short). That is, the value g^{ab} can simply get involved (for applications where traceability takes priority over HP-deniability) at the minimal cost of only one modular addition, which eases more flexible and modular deployments in practice. More variants of OAKE are presented in Appendix A.

Some advantageous features of OAKE. The session-key computation of OAKE takes about one simultaneous exponentiation, and is slightly more efficient than that of HMQV. To our knowledge, OAKE (with embedded subgroup test) is the most efficient provably secure IA-DHKE protocol to date. OAKE enjoys the online efficiency of KEA/OPACITY, i.e., the value A^y (resp., B^x) can be offline pre-computed by $\hat{B}$ (resp., $\hat{A}$), as well as the HP-deniability. Also, OAKE eases deployments in practice, based on the following grounds.

- The OAKE protocol family combines, in essence, the advantages of both KEA/OPACITY and (H)MQV, while saving from the disadvantages of them both.
- Similar to IKE providing two protocols or modes [49] to ease deployments in practice, according to different desirability between g^{ab}-traceability and HP-deniability in different applications, the value g^{ab} can be simply switched on or off in the session-key computation, at the minimal cost of only one modular addition.
- As clarified in Section 3, the offline pre-computability of A^y and B^x allows more efficient parallel explicit subgroup test, as well as more robust embedded subgroup test.
- No POP/POK of secret key is assumed during public key registration.
- As we shall see, OAKE enjoys robust leakage resilience in the sense that all the pre-computed values can be exposed to the attacker without sacrificing SK-security in the CK-framework. This much eases deployments based upon low-power devices, like smart cards or phones, in hostile computing environments.
- In addition, as to be discussed in Section 6.5, it well supports deployment in the public computation model [54], and enjoys joint proof-of-knowledge session-key computation *without mandating POP/POK of secret key.*

A brief comparison. A brief comparison among (T)OAKE, HMQV and KEA is summarized in Table 1 (page 8). In Table 1, t_{se} stands for the time for performing one simultaneous exponentiation, t_e the time for performing one modular exponentiation, t_h the time for performing one hashing operation, t_m the time for performing one modular multiplication over Z_q^*, and t_a the time for performing one modular addition over Z_q^*. For total efficiency, we only count the operations needed to compute the input to the key derivation function H_K, as all the other operations are the same for all these protocols.

For the item of "Assumptions" in Table 1, by SKEA (resp., SJKEA, GDL) we refer to strong KEA (resp., strong JKEA and gap DL), where GDL (resp., SJKEA) is weaker than GDH (resp., SKEA) in the RO model as discussed in Section 2 and 4. The symbol "$\perp$" stands for "unapplicable" or "unknown". The item of "Secrecy exposure" refers to the pre-computed and stored session-states that can be exposed, where (x, X, B^x) stands for the situation where the DH-components, DH-exponents, and the pre-computed values B^x's and A^y's for all sessions other than the test-session and its matching session, can be exposed.

We choose KEA/OPACITY and (H)MQV as the benchmark protocols to compare, because they stand for the state-of-the-art in their respective types and are widely standardized. Needless to say, there are a large number of existing KE protocols in the literature. The bottom line here is that, to the best of our knowledge, no protocol that combines the advantages of both KEA/OPACITY and (H)MQV is known. Still, we present discussions on the NAXOS protocol [55] in Appendix B, and comparisons with more protocols in the full version [73]. If g^{ab}-traceability takes priority over HP-deniability in some applications, one should compare (H)MQV with T-OAKE directly, both of which provide g^{ab}-traceability but T-OAKE is still more efficient and provides more robust secrecy leakage resilience as to be discussed in Section 6.4 (page 12). Finally, we note that the developed OAKE protocol family enjoys conceptual simplicity, and we remark that still being of conceptual simplicity and practical efficiency should be viewed as a blessing for this over-studied area and for protocols aimed for real use.

6. SECURITY ANALYSIS

6.1 Overview of the CK-Framework for IA-DHKE

Following the works [51, 56], we briefly describe the CK-framework for the provable security of IA-DHKE. In the CK-framework for an IA-DHKE protocol, a session run at the side of player $\hat{A}$ with a peer player $\hat{B}$, where the outcoming (resp., incoming) DH-component is X (resp., Y), is assigned with a session identifier as $(\hat{A}, \hat{B}, X, Y)$. In each session, a party can be activated as the role of either initiator (who sends the first DH-component) or responder (who sends the second DH-component). During a normal protocol run (*without adversary interference*) between two players $\hat{A}$ and $\hat{B}$, we require that both sessions (one at $\hat{A}$ and one at $\hat{B}$) should compute the same session-key, which is referred to as the completeness property. The completeness property within the CK-framework is captured by the definition of *matching sessions*, which aims to capture when two sessions are "intended communication partners", and plays an important role in the security definition within the CK-framework.

In the context of IA-DHKE, one natural interpretation for two sessions $(\hat{A}, \hat{B}, X, Y)$ and $(\hat{B}, \hat{A}, Y, X)$ to be matching is that: the players $\hat{A}$ and $\hat{B}$ should have matching roles in the two sessions, i.e., if $\hat{A}$ is the initiator (resp., responder) then $\hat{B}$ is the responder (resp., initiator) in both of the two sessions. However, as the basic (H)MQV is role-independent, for two sessions between the same pair of players $\hat{A}$ and $\hat{B}$ but with the opposite order of DH-component exchange (which may be made by a cross-message attack [25]),[4] player $\hat{A}$ (resp., $\hat{B}$) thinks it is interacting with a responder $\hat{B}$ (resp., $\hat{A}$), while the session-key outputs in these two sessions are the same. That is, two sessions (between the same pair of players) output the *same session-key* but with *role confusion* between each other. The work [51] was (implicitly) clear of this situation, and such a problem is ruled out, by definition, by simply defining two sessions $(\hat{A}, \hat{B}, X, Y)$ and $(\hat{B}, \hat{A}, Y, X)$ to be matching, *no matter whether the two players have matching roles or not.* That is, two sessions with adversary interference under a cross-message attack [25] are defined to be matching. However, from our view, in light of the cross-message attack [25](that causes role confusion between two matching sessions for role-independent IA-DHKE), such a definition of matching sessions is "ill", as it does not well capture the intuition of "intended communication partners" *without adversary interference.* We notice that, for robust (H)MQV and KEA that are role-dependent as $(\hat{A}, \hat{B})$ are involved in a fixed order in session-key derivation, the more natural definition of matching sessions, *where the two players are required to have matching roles*, is used implicitly in [51] and explicitly in [56].

[4] In a cross-message attack, an adversary $\mathscr{A}$ *concurrently* interacts, *as the responder*, with $\hat{A}$ (resp., $\hat{B}$) in the name of $\hat{B}$ (resp., $\hat{A}$) in two sessions. After getting X and Y respectively *as the first-round message in both of the two sessions*, it sends Y (resp., X) to $\hat{A}$ (resp., $\hat{B}$) as the second-round message in both of the two sessions. For the basic (H)MQV, both of the two players will output the same session-key in the two sessions but with role confusion.

A CMIM adversary $\mathscr{A}$ controls all the communication channels among concurrent session runs of the KE protocol. In addition, $\mathscr{A}$ is allowed access to secret information via the following three types of queries: (1) state-reveal queries for ongoing incomplete sessions; (2) session-key queries for completed sessions; (3) corruption queries upon which all information in the memory of the corrupted parties will be leaked to $\mathscr{A}$. A session $(\hat{A}, \hat{B}, X, Y)$ is called *exposed*, if itself or its matching session $(\hat{B}, \hat{A}, Y, X)$ suffers from any of these three queries. The session-key security (SK-security) within the CK-framework is captured as follows. For any complete session $(\hat{A}, \hat{B}, X, Y)$ between two *uncorrupted* players $\hat{A}$ and $\hat{B}$, which is adaptively chosen by $\mathscr{A}$ and is referred to as the *test session*, as long as it is unexposed (in particular its matching session, if it exists, was not exposed during its ongoing incomplete stage before $\mathscr{A}$ stops[5]) the followings hold with overwhelming probability. (1) Completeness: the session-key outputs of the test-session and its matching session are identical. (2) Randomness: $\mathscr{A}$ cannot distinguish, with non-negligible probability/advantage over 1/2, the session-key output of the test-session from a random value. A variant of the CK-framework, referred to as extended CK model (eCK-model), is also discussed in Appendix B.

Here, we would like to stress that, as already explicitly clarified in [25], the SK-security defined for role-dependent IA-DHKE (referred to as role-dependent SK-security) and that for role-independent IA-DHKE (referred to as role-independent SK-security), differentiated by the definition of matching sessions, are *fundamentally* incomparable. On the one hand, *any* role-dependent IA-DHKE, like robust (H)MQV and KEA/OPACITY, does not satisfy, by definition, the completeness property of role-independent SK-security. On the other hand, *any* role-independent IA-DHKE like the basic (H)MQV is totally broken according to role-dependent SK-security (as the session-key of the test-session can exist in a non-matching session by the cross-message attack [25]), which might be viewed as more dangerous.

Throughout this work, for the OAKE protocol family, KEA and robust (H)MQV that all are role-dependent, we are referring to role-dependent SK-security, while for the basic (H)MQV that is role-independent, we are referring to the role-independent SK-security w.r.t. the relaxed definition of matching session without requiring matching roles.

6.2 HP-Deniability: Definition and Discussion

In this section, we introduce and formalize the HP-deniability for IA-DHKE along with justification and discussion.

DEFINITION 6.1. *On the security parameter n, consider a complete session run of an IA-DHKE protocol between a pair of honest players $\hat{A}$ and $\hat{B}$, where player $\hat{A}$ (resp., $\hat{B}$) has public key $PK_{\hat{A}}$ (resp., $PK_{\hat{B}}$) and secret key $SK_{\hat{A}}$*

[5] For IA-DHKE, this makes sense mainly when the test-session is held by a responder. Consider that the attacker first activates an initiator $\hat{A}$ to get X, and then suspends this session held by $\hat{A}$ till finishing the test-session $(\hat{B}, \hat{A}, Y, X)$ run by $\hat{B}$. If the session run by $\hat{A}$ is never completed, the DH-exponent x can be exposed to adversary (while $\hat{A}$ cannot be corrupted as the test-session is required to be between two uncorrupted players); but if later this session is completed and thus becomes matching to the test-session, it should be unexposed for the SK-security.

(resp., $SK_{\hat{B}}$), and has the key certificate $C_{\hat{A}}$ (resp., $C_{\hat{B}}$) issued by the Certificate Authority in the underlying PKI. Denote by $view^{\hat{B}(SK_{\hat{B}})}_{\hat{A}(SK_{\hat{A}})}(1^n, C_{\hat{A}}, C_{\hat{B}})$ a random variable describing the session transcript (i.e., the messages exchanged during the session run), the resultant session-key, and all the pre-computed and stored session-states[6] (that can be exposed by the state-reveal query).

We say the IA-DHKE protocol is HP-deniable, if there exists a probabilistic polynomial-time simulator S, such that for any sufficiently large n, any pair of honest players $(\hat{A}, \hat{B})$, the following ensembles are statistically indistinguishable:

$$\{view^{\hat{B}(SK_{\hat{B}})}_{\hat{A}(SK_{\hat{A}})}(1^n, C_{\hat{A}}, C_{\hat{B}})\}_{n\in N, C_{\hat{A}}, C_{\hat{B}}\in\{0,1\}^*, SK_{\hat{A}}, SK_{\hat{B}}\in\{0,1\}^*},$$

$$\{S(1^n, C_{\hat{A}}, C_{\hat{B}})\}_{n\in N, C_{\hat{A}}, C_{\hat{B}}\in\{0,1\}^*, SK_{\hat{A}}, SK_{\hat{B}}\in\{0,1\}^*}.$$

The IA-DHKE protocol is perfectly *HP-deniable, if the above ensembles are identical.*

Some comments about the HP-deniability definition are in place. The variable $view^{\hat{B}(SK_{\hat{B}})}_{\hat{A}(SK_{\hat{A}})}$ denotes the view of an *eavesdropping* adversary $\mathcal{A}$ for a session run of DHKE between a pair of uncorrupted players $\hat{A}$ and $\hat{B}$. Different from traditional honest-verifier zero-knowledge (HVZK), the view of $\mathcal{A}$ not only includes the messages being exchanged in the session, but also includes the information that can be collected by $\mathcal{A}$ via "session-key query" and "state-reveal query". Here, statistical indistinguishability between $view^{\hat{B}(SK_{\hat{B}})}_{\hat{A}(SK_{\hat{A}})}$ and the output of simulator ensures *forward* deniability [68, 69].

If cast in the CK-framework for generality, we can consider any CMIM adversary $\mathcal{A}$ as specified in the CK-framework but with the following limitation: all the DH-components exchanged in sessions between the pair of uncorrupted players $\hat{A}$ and $\hat{B}$ are honestly generated by themselves respectively. In other words, any session $(\hat{A}, \hat{B}, X, Y)$ has the matching session $(\hat{B}, \hat{A}, Y, X)$ with matching player roles, and vice versa. Then, HP-deniability requires that the view of $\mathcal{A}$ can be statistically simulated from the public values and the secret keys of all the players other than $\hat{A}$ and $\hat{B}$.

It is easy to see that, any IA-DHKE, where the session-key, and all the pre-computed and stored session-states, can be derived merely from DH-exponents x and y (and public values), is *perfectly* HP-deniable. In particular, both KEA/OPACITY and OAKE are perfectly HP-deniable.

6.3 Security of OAKE in CK-Framework

For the provable security of OAKE in the CK-framework, in this work we consider a *strong* adversary $\mathcal{A}$ who can expose, via state-reveal queries, all the offline pre-computed and stored session-specific values (including DH-components, DH-exponents, the offline pre-computed values A^y's and B^x's for all sessions except the test-session and its matching session). In addition, letting $(\hat{A}, \hat{B}, X_0, Y_0)$ be the test-session, $\mathcal{A}$ can learn the static secret key of any uncorrupted player except the player $\hat{B}$ (i.e., the peer to the test-session).[7] We call such an adversary "*strong adversary (with strong secrecy exposure)*".

THEOREM 6.1. *OAKE is SK-secure against any PPT* strong *adversary in the CK-framework, under the gap DL (GDL) assumption and the strong JKEA (SJKEA) assumption in the random oracle model.*

Proof (of sketch). According to the SK-security definition in the CK-framework, we need to prove that OAKE satisfies the following two requirements.

Requirement-1. If two parties $\hat{A}, \hat{B}$ complete matching sessions, then their session-keys are the same.

Requirement-2. There is no feasible adversary who succeeds, with non-negligible advantage (i.e., non-negligible probability over 1/2), in distinguishing the session-key of an unexposed session from a random value.

The Requirement-1 is trivially satisfied with OAKE. In the followings, we focus on establishing the Requirement-2.

Denote by $(\hat{A}, \hat{B}, X_0 = g^{x_0}, Y_0 = g^{y_0})$, where $x_0, y_0 \in Z_q^*$, the unexposed test-session between a pair of *uncorrupted* players $\hat{A}$ and $\hat{B}$ where $\hat{A} \neq \hat{B}$, by $H_K(\sigma_0)$ the session-key of the test-session, and by $\sigma_0 = A^{y_0}X^{b+e_0y_0} = B^{x_0}Y^{a+e_0x_0}$ the shared DH-secret, where $e_0 = h(\hat{A}, A, \hat{B}, B, X_0, Y_0)$. As H_K is a random oracle, there are only two strategies for the adversary $\mathcal{A}$ to distinguish $H_K(\sigma_0)$ from a random value:

- Key-replication attack. $\mathcal{A}$ succeeds in forcing the establishment of a session (other than the test-session or its matching session) that has the same session-key output as the test-session. In this case, $\mathcal{A}$ can learn the test-session key by simply querying that session to get the same key.
- Forging attack. At some point in its run, $\mathcal{A}$ queries the RO H_K with the value σ_0.

The possibility of key-replication attack is trivially ruled out *unconditionally* in the RO model. Specifically, for any session tag $(\hat{A}, A, \hat{B}, B, X, Y)$ and for any value $\sigma \in G \setminus 1_G$, it holds $\Pr[K_{\hat{A}} = K_{\hat{B}} = \sigma] \leq \frac{1}{2^l-1}$ for both OAKE and T-OAKE, where the probability is only taken over the choice of the random function h. Then, by the birthday paradox, any efficient attacker can succeed in the key-replication attack only with negligible probability; specifically, with probability at most $\frac{s^2}{2^l-1}$ in the RO model, where s is the number of sessions in the system.

Below, we focus on the analysis against the forging attack. We further distinguish two cases, according to whether the test-session has the matching session or not, and have the following lemmas.

LEMMA 6.1. *For the case where the test-session has the matching session, a successful forging attack can occur only with negligible probability under the CDH assumption in the random oracle model.*

[6]Notice that, from the pre-computed and stored session-state of a session, player's random coins may not necessarily be derived. For example, the coins of player $\hat{A}$ for a session are x', while the pre-computed and stored session-state is $x = h(a, x')$.

[7]If the attacker exposes the static secret key b of the peer player of the matching session, and in case Y is actually chosen by the attacker (this corresponds to the case where the matching session does not exist), the attacker can compute the session-key by itself and thus can trivially break the SK-security.

Proof (of sketch). In this case, given two random DH-components ($X_0 = g^{x_0}, Y_0 = g^{y_0}$), a CDH-solver $\mathcal{C}$ (whose goal is to compute $CDH(X_0, Y_0)$) works as follows. (1) It generates the public and secret keys on behalf of all uncorrupted players (particularly the uncorrupted players $\hat{A}$ and $\hat{B}$ of the test-session) in the system. (2) Then, it randomly guesses the test-session and its matching session as follow. Supposing there are s sessions in total in the system, where s is a polynomial in the security parameter, $\mathcal{C}$ randomly takes $i, j \leftarrow \{1, \cdots, s\}$, hoping that the test-session (resp., the matching session) is the i-th (resp., the j-th) session. The probability that $\mathcal{C}$ successfully guesses the test-session and its matching session is $\frac{1}{s^2}$. (3) $\mathcal{C}$ runs the (supposed) forging attacker $\mathscr{A}$ and works as the honest players do in all sessions except the test-session and its matching session. Notice that $\mathcal{C}$ can perfectly answer by itself all queries from $\mathscr{A}$ (specified in accordance with the CK-framework). In particular, for any session $(\hat{A}, A, \hat{B}, B, X, Y)$, which is not the test-session or its matching session, $\mathcal{C}$ can expose all the pre-computed and stored values (a, X, x, B^x) to the attacker, even if $\hat{A}$ will be the player holding the test-session. (4) $\mathcal{C}$ sets X_0 (resp., Y_0) as the DH-component to be sent in the test-session (resp., the matching session).

It is easy to see that, conditioned on that $\mathcal{C}$ has correctly guessed the test-session and its matching session, the emulation of $\mathcal{C}$ is perfect from the view point of $\mathscr{A}$. Now, suppose $\mathscr{A}$ can succeed in the forging attack in this case, i.e., outputting $\sigma_0 = A^{y_0} X_0^{b+y_0 e_0}$, with non-negligible probability p. Then, with probability $\frac{p}{s^2}$, $\mathcal{C}$ can compute $CDH(X_0, Y_0) = \sigma_0/(Y_0^a X_0^b)$ (recall that $\mathcal{C}$ knows the secret keys a and b in this case). □

LEMMA 6.2. *For the case when no matching session exists, a successful forging attack can occur only with negligible probability under the GDL and the SJKEA assumptions in the random oracle model.*

Proof (of sketch). In this case, given random values ($X_0 = g^{x_0}, B = g^b$), where $x_0, b \leftarrow Z_q^*$, the DL-solver $\mathcal{C}$ (whose goal is to compute the discrete logarithm of B) works as follows.

Suppose there are n parties $\{\hat{P}_1, \cdots, \hat{P}_n\}$ and s sessions in total in the system, where n and s are polynomials in the security parameter. $\mathcal{C}$ first guesses the test-session and the peer player of the test-session, by choosing uniformly at random $i \leftarrow \{1, \cdots, s\}$ and $j \leftarrow \{1, \cdots, n\}$ and by setting the i-th session as the test-session and the player $\hat{P}_j$ as the peer player of the test-session. It generates the public and secret keys on behalf of all uncorrupted players except the player $\hat{P}_j$ in the system. For the player $\hat{P}_j$, its public key is just set to be B. WLOG, for presentation simplicity, we assume that $\hat{B} = \hat{P}_j$, and the player holding the test-session is $\hat{A}$ with public key A that is actually set by $\mathcal{C}$.

Then, $\mathcal{C}$ runs the supposed forging attacker $\mathscr{A}$ by working as the honest players do and answering queries made by $\mathscr{A}$, except that:

- For the test-session, the DH-component to be sent by $\hat{A}$ is set to be X_0.
- Consider any "session-key reveal" query made by $\mathscr{A}$ against a session run by the uncorrupted player $\hat{B}$ with a peer player $\hat{Z}$. Denoted by $(\hat{B}, B, \hat{Z}, Z = g^z, Y = g^y, X = g^x)$ the corresponding session tag, where the DH-exponent y is generated by (and thus known to) $\mathcal{C}$ on behalf of $\hat{B}$, but the player $\hat{Z}$ may be a corrupted one and thus the secret key z or the DH-exponent x is in general unknown to $\mathcal{C}$. In particular, the values (Y, y, Z^{cy}) are (offline) generated by $\mathcal{C}$ on behalf of $\hat{B}$, and can be exposed to $\mathscr{A}$ upon its "state-reveal query" against this session. For such a "session-key reveal" query, $\mathcal{C}$ just returns back a value r taken uniformly at random from $\{0,1\}^k$ (i.e., the range of H_K). However, from this point on, whenever $\mathscr{A}$ makes an RO-query σ to the random oracle H_K, $\mathcal{C}$ checks whether $\sigma = Z^y X^{b+ey}$ with the aid of a DDH-oracle $\mathcal{O}$, specifically, by checking whether $CDH(X, B) = \sigma/(Z^y X^{ey})$ with the DDH-oracle $\mathcal{O}$. If so, $\mathcal{C}$ returns the already defined value r to $\mathcal{A}$ as the RO answer on σ. Note that the "session-key reveal" and RO queries are perfectly answered by $\mathcal{C}$ in this case.

Notice that $\mathcal{C}$ can perfectly answer all the queries made by $\mathscr{A}$ in accordance with the CK-framework. Conditioned on $\mathcal{C}$ has successfully guessed the test-session and the peer player $\hat{B}$ of the test-session, which occurs with probability $\frac{1}{sn}$, the emulation of $\mathcal{C}$ is perfect from the viewpoint of $\mathscr{A}$. Now, suppose the forging attacker $\mathscr{A}$ can output, with non-negligible probability p, $\sigma_0 = A^{y_0} X_0^{b+e_0 y_0}$ for the test-session of tag $(\hat{A}, A = g^a, \hat{B}, B, X_0, Y_0)$, where the secret key a is generated by and thus known to $\mathcal{C}$ while none of the discrete logarithms of B, X_0 or Y_0 are known to $\mathcal{C}$ in general. In particular, the value Y_0 may be chosen by the attacker $\mathscr{A}$ itself for the case when no matching session exists. Then, with non-negligible probability $\frac{p}{sn}$, the algorithm $\mathcal{C}$ outputs $X_0^{b+e_0 y_0}$ from (σ_0, a). Conditioned on this, by the strong JKEA assumption, with overwhelming probability both b and y_0 can be extracted from the random coins of $\mathcal{C}$ and the list of answers from the DDH-oracle $\mathcal{O}$. With probability negligibly close to $\frac{p}{sn}$, the discrete logarithm of B can be computed, which then contradicts the GDL assumption. □

THEOREM 6.2. *OAKE is SK-secure against any PPT* strong *adversary in the CK-framework, under the GDH assumption in the random oracle model.*

Proof (of sketch). Note that the non-black-box JKEA assumption was only used in the proof of Lemma 6.2 for the case when no matching session exists. We show that the forging attack for this case can actually be ruled out merely based on the black-box GDH assumption, but at the price of a looser security reduction via the forking lemma [67].

Specifically, conditioned on that the forging attacker $\mathscr{A}$ successfully outputs $\sigma_0 = A^{y_0} X_0^{b+e_0 y_0}$ for the test-session (that has no matching session for this case), which is assumed to occur with non-negligible probability, with overwhelming probability the attacker $\mathscr{A}$ has queried the random oracle $h(\hat{A}, A, \hat{B}, B, X_0, Y_0)$ to get e_0. Then, the algorithm $\mathcal{C}$ works as follows: $\mathcal{C}$ just rewinds the run of $\mathscr{A}$ to the point that $\mathscr{A}$ just made the RO-query $e_0 = h(\hat{A}, A, \hat{B}, B, X_0, Y_0)$, redefines the RO answer $h(\hat{A}, A, \hat{B}, B, X_0, Y_0)$ to a new independently random value e_0', and re-runs $\mathscr{A}$ from this rewinding point. By the forking lemma [67], if the forging attacker $\mathcal{C}$ outputs σ_0 in the first run with non-negligible probability, in the repeated run $\mathcal{C}$ will get $\sigma_0' = A^{y_0} X_0^{b+e_0' y_0}$ with non-negligible probability as well. Then, from (a, σ_0, σ_0'), the value $CDH(X_0, Y_0) = (\sigma_0/\sigma_0')^{(e_0-e_0')^{-1}}$ can be computed. Then, from a and $CDH(X_0, Y_0)$, the value $CDH(X_0, B) = \sigma_0/(Y_0^a CDH(X_0, Y_0)^{e_0})$ can be computed, which violates the GDH assumption. Due to space limitation, the complete proof is given in the full version [73]. □

A note on security reduction tightness. By avoiding the use of the forking lemma, the GDL- and SJKEA- based security reduction of OAKE in Theorem 6.2 is as tight as the GDH-based security reduction of KEA, which is in turn much tighter than the GDH-based analysis of OAKE in Theorem 6.2. On the other hand, the GDH-based security reduction of OAKE is still tighter than that of HMQV based on GDH and SKEA. Specifically, the key-replication attack is unconditionally ruled out with OAKE. By comparison, the analysis of HMQV [51] for ruling out key-replication attack is quite complicated, which is still reduced to the underlying hardness assumptions. In other parts of the analysis, the security reduction of OAKE is at least as tight as that of HMQV.

6.4 Security of T-OAKE in CK-Framework

The proofs of Theorem 6.1 and Theorem 6.2 can be directly extended to establish the SK-security of T-OAKE, with the limitation that the values A^{b+y}'s or B^{a+x}'s are, however, not allowed to be exposed *in general*. Details are given in the full version [73] for space limitation.

THEOREM 6.3. *T-OAKE is SK-secure in the CK-framework against any PPT* strong *adversary* with the limitation that the values A^{b+y}'s or B^{a+x}'s are not exposed, *under the gap DL assumption and the strong JKEA assumption, or the GDH assumption, in the random oracle model.*

The reason for this exposure limitation is as follows. For the security against the forging attack for the case when the test-session has no matching session, consider a session run by $\hat{B}$ with a peer player $\hat{Z}$ of public key Z, where $\hat{Z}$ may be a corrupted one controlled by the forging attacker $\mathcal{A}$. Note that the simulator $\mathcal{C}$ does not know the secret key of the uncorrupted player $\hat{B}$ or the corrupted player $\hat{Z}$. In this case, it is infeasible for $\mathcal{C}$ to compute the value Z^{b+y}, even though $Y = g^y$ for that session was generated by $\mathcal{C}$ itself.

We remark that the limitation of unexposed A^{b+y}'s or B^{a+x}'s is only for provable security in the CK-framework. We are unaware of any real security damage caused by the leakage of such values in practice, compared to the security damage or limitation caused by the leakage of the pre-computed value $s_B = y + eb$ or $s_A = x + ea$ in (H)MQV. Furthermore, in case of POP/POK of secret key during key registration which assumes, in a sense, the attacker "knows" the secret key z of $Z = g^z$, the leakage of Z^{b+y} actually cause no real damage as the value Z^{b+y} can actually be generated by $\mathcal{A}$ itself.

On security with exposed session-states of the test-session and the matching session. Let $(\hat{A}, \hat{B}, X_0 = g^{x_0}, Y_0 = g^{y_0})$ be the test-session between a pair of uncorrupted players $\hat{A}$ and $\hat{B}$. The g^{ab}-traceability of both T-OAKE and (H)MQV, in turn, ensures the following security property: even if both the DH-exponents x_0 and y_0 are exposed, the session-key of the test-session remains unexposed. Furthermore, for T-OAKE, even if both (x_0, X_0, B^{a+x_0}) and (y_0, Y_0, A^{b+y_0}) are exposed (i.e., the session-states include all the pre-computable values and are exposed), the session-key of the test-session still remains unexposed. By comparison, for (H)MQV, supposing the exposed session-state includes the pre-computed value $x_0 + da$ or $y_0 + eb$, the session-key of the test-session will be exposed. In this sense, we suggest that T-OAKE provide more robust secrecy leakage resilience than (H)MQV does.

6.5 Security Beyond CK-Framework

In this section, we discuss some security properties beyond the CK-framework, which further justify the design rationale and performance advantages of the newly developed OAKE protocol family.

6.5.1 Security in Public Computation Model

Kunz-Jacques and Pointcheval proposed a new attack scenario for key-exchange protocols with public computations [54], where it is convenient to split an entity (performing a run of KE-protocol) into two parts: a trusted authentication device, and an untrusted computing device. The authentication device enforces the confidentiality of the authentication data, while some computing operations required by the protocol are *publicly* carried out by the untrusted computing device. This allows us to use an authentication device with little computing power, and to make computing devices independent from users [54]. Cast in the trusted computing setting, the authentication device corresponds to a trusted platform module (TPM).

The work of Kunz-Jacques and Pointcheval [54] gives some concrete applications that might be benefited from public computations. Mobile phones include smart cards which store the user authentication data, where the handsets themselves are the computing devices. PCs (corresponding to the computing device) equipped with a crypto token (corresponding to the authentication device) have a lot more computing power than the token itself does, but may be plagued by spyware or virus. For more details, the reader is referred to [54].

(H)MQV with public computations. With the computation of $\hat{B}$ as an example (the same holds for $\hat{A}$), a natural split of authentication computation and public computation for (H)MQV is as follows [54]. The authentication device generates (y, Y), and forwards Y to the computation device. After getting $(\hat{A}, X)$ from the computation device, the authentication device computes $s_B = y + eb$, and then forwards s_B to the computation device. On the other hand, after getting s_B from the authentication device, the computation device computes $K_{\hat{B}} = (XA^d)^{s_B}$ and the session-key, and then communicates with $\hat{A}$ using the derived session-key.

One key observation in [54] is: once the value s_B is leaked to an attacker who may compromise the computation device that is assumed to be untrustful, the attacker can definitely impersonate $\hat{B}$ to $\hat{A}$ in other sessions. Notice that, by only compromising the computation device, the attacker does not learn the DH-exponent y or the static secret key b. This shows that (H)MQV is insecure in the public computation model.

(T)OAKE with public computations. For applications in such a scenario, with the computation of $\hat{B}$ as an example (the similar holds for $\hat{A}$), the natural split of authentication computation and public computation for (T)OAKE is as follows. (1) The authentication device generates (y, Y), and possibly A^{fb+y} if the authentication device has learnt the peer identity $\hat{A}$, and then then forwards (Y, A^{fb+y}) to the computation device, where $f = 0$ for OAKE and $f = 1$ for T-OAKE. (2) After getting X from the computation device, the authentication device computes $s_B = b + ey$ and forwards s_B to the computation device. (3) After getting s_B from the authentication device, the computation device computes $K_{\hat{B}} = A^{fb+y}X^{s_B}$ and the session-key, and then communicates with $\hat{A}$ using the session-key. *Note that* (y, Y, A^{fb+y}) *can be offline pre-computed by the authentication device, and the authentication device needs to online compute only ey and* s_B. *Also, the computation device essentially needs to compute only one exponentiation* X^{s_B}. That (T)OAKE well supports the public computation model further eases the deployment of (T)OAKE by low-power devices or by systems embedded with TPM chips.

Note that, under the DLP assumption, the knowledge of (A^{fb+y}, s_B) of a session of (T)OAKE, learnt by the adversary by compromising the untrusted computation device, is useless for the attacker to violate other sessions except the matching session $(\hat{B}, \hat{A}, Y, X)$. Specifically, the value $s_B = b + ey$, where $e = h(\hat{A}, A, \hat{B}, B, X, Y)$, commits to the whole session-tag. Thus, the value s_B cannot be used by the attacker to violate a non-matching session, unless it can compute y from A^y (and thus b from s_B) which is, however, infeasible by the DLP assumption.

6.5.2 Exponent Dependent Attack, and Joint Proof-of-Knowledge Session-Key Computation

An implicit rationale behind the design of authenticated KE is: to successfully finish a session run, a player should "know" both its static secret key and the ephemeral DH-exponent. For IA-DHKE, we hope that the session-key computation could itself serve as a *joint proof-of-knowledge* (JPOK) of both the static secret key and the ephemeral DH-exponent.

The JKEA-based session-key derivation of the OAKE protocol family ensures such a JPOK property *without requiring POP/POK of secret key during public key registration*. For KEA and OPACITY, the ability of computing X^b (resp., A^y) in session-key computation is used to demonstrate the knowledge of the static secret key b (resp., the DH-exponent y). However, such a JPOK mechanism in KEA/OPACITY has some drawbacks; for example, the value A^y used by an adversary for one session can be exposed from another (non-matching) session. For (H)MQV, the basic idea is to use the ability of computing $(XA^d)^{y+eb}$, with respect to the random challenge XA^d, to jointly demonstrate the knowledge of both y and b. In this work, we introduce an exponent dependent attack (EDA) on (H)MQV, showing that a malicious player can successfully set the session-key of (H)MQV to be some *publicly* computable values.

Exponent dependent attack. In a setting where a value $X \in G$ is given and the malicious player $\hat{A}$ does not necessarily know the discrete logarithm of X, $\hat{A}$ computes d and sets $A = X^{-d^{-1}} \cdot g^{\sigma}$, where $\sigma \in Z_q$ and $d = h(X, \hat{B})$ for HMQV or $d = 2^l + (X \mod 2^l)$ for MQV. Note that $XA^d = X(X^{-d^{-1}} \cdot g^{\sigma})^d = XX^{-1}g^{\sigma d} = g^{\sigma d}$, and thus the shared DH-secret now is $K_{\hat{A}} = (XA^d)^{y+eb} = g^{\sigma dy}g^{\sigma deb} = Y^{\sigma d}B^{\sigma de}$. Notice that the value $K_{\hat{A}}$ can be *publicly computed without involving the static secret key a or the DH-exponent x*. We refer to such an attack as exponent dependent attack (EDA).

We remark that the above EDA attack does *not* violate the security analysis of HMQV in [51], as it is beyond the CK-framework. Nevertheless, for (H)MQV, the EDA attack demonstrates the importance of mandating POP/POK of secret key (during public key registration) in order to ensure joint proof-of-knowledge session-key computation. POP/POK of secret key is indeed mandated by MQV now, but was explicitly abandoned by HMQV in [51].

For space limitation, more security properties, including security against reflection attack, key compromise impersonation, unknown key share, and (weak) perfect forward security, etc, most of which are beyond the CK-framework, are presented in the full version [73].

7. FUTURE INVESTIGATIONS

We conclude this work by proposing some suggestions for future investigations.

- One important direction for future research is to develop IA-DHKE protocols that are as efficient as (H)MQV but provably secure in the absence of random oracles. Toward this goal, we may rely upon some non-standard yet still reasonable assumptions.
- We introduce and justify the JKEA assumption, and demonstrate its usefulness with the design of the OAKE protocol family. It is interesting to find more cryptographic applications of JKEA, as well as to come up with more variants of JKEA.
- In this work, we mainly focus on the security analysis of (T)OAKE in the basic CK-framework. Another direction is to analyze (T)OAKE in more variants of the CK-framework, e.g., analyze T-OAKE in the eCK-model.

8. ACKNOWLEDGEMENT

We thank the anonymous referees for the detailed and helpful comments. We are grateful to Colin Boyd, Liqun Chen, Boru Gong, Hugo Krawczyk, Kouichi Sakurai, Duncan S. Wong, Moti Yung and Fangguo Zhang for many helpful discussions and suggestions.

9. REFERENCES

[1] M. Abdalla, J. H. An, M. Bellare, and C. Namprempre. From identification to signatures via the Fiat-Shamir transform: Necessary and sufficient conditions for security and forward-security. *IEEE Transactions on Information Theory*, 54(8):3631–3646, 2008.

[2] M. Abe and S. Fehr. Perfect NIZK with adaptive soundness. In *TCC*, pages 118–136, 2007.

[3] W. Aiello, S. M. Bellovin, M. Blaze, R. Canetti, J. Ioannidis, A. D. Keromytis, and O. Reingold. Just fast keying: Key agreement in a hostile internet. *ACM Trans. Inf. Syst. Secur.*, 7(2):242–273, 2004.

[4] ANSI. 504-1: Information technology-generic identity command set, part 1: Card application command set.

[5] ANSI. American National Standard, X9.42-2001.

[6] B. Barak. How to go beyond the black-box simulation barrier. In *FOCS*, pages 106–115, 2001.

[7] E. Barker, D. Johnson, and M. Smid. NIST special publication 800-56A: Recommendation for pair-wise

key establishment schemes using discrete logarithm cryptography (revised). Technical report, 2007.

[8] M. Bellare, R. Canetti, and H. Krawczyk. Keying hash functions for message authentication. In *CRYPTO*, pages 1–15, 1996.

[9] M. Bellare and A. Palacio. The knowledge-of-exponent assumptions and 3-round zero-knowledge protocols. In *CRYPTO*, pages 273–289, 2004.

[10] M. Bellare and A. Palacio. Towards plaintext-aware public-key encryption without random oracles. In *ASIACRYPT*, pages 48–62, 2004.

[11] M. Bellare and P. Rogaway. Random oracles are practical: A paradigm for designing efficient protocols. In *ACM Conference on Computer and Communications Security*, pages 62–73, 1993.

[12] E. Biham and A. Shamir. Differential fault analysis of secret key cryptosystems. In *CRYPTO*, pages 513–525, 1997.

[13] N. Bitansky, R. Canetti, A. Chiesa, and E. Tromer. From extractable collision resistance to succinct non-interactive arguments of knowledge, and back again. In *ITCS*, pages 326–349, 2012.

[14] S. Blake-Wilson, D. Johnson, and A. Menezes. Key agreement protocols and their security analysis. In *IMA Int. Conf.*, pages 30–45, 1997.

[15] C. Boyd, Y. Cliff, J. M. G. Nieto, and K. G. Paterson. Efficient one-round key exchange in the standard model. In *ACISP*, pages 69–83, 2008.

[16] C. Boyd, W. Mao, and K. G. Paterson. Deniable authenticated key establishment for internet protocols. In *Security Protocols Workshop*, pages 255–271, 2003.

[17] C. Boyd and A. Mathuria. *Protocols for Authentication and Key Establishment.* ISBN 3-540-43107-1, Springer-Verlag.

[18] Z. Brakerski, Y. T. Kalai, J. Katz, and V. Vaikuntanathan. Overcoming the hole in the bucket: Public-key cryptography resilient to continual memory leakage. In *FOCS*, pages 501–510, 2010.

[19] R. Canetti. Security and composition of cryptographic protocols: a tutorial (part i). *SIGACT News*, 37(3):67–92, 2006.

[20] R. Canetti and R. R. Dakdouk. Extractable perfectly one-way functions. In *ICALP (2)*, pages 449–460, 2008.

[21] R. Canetti and R. R. Dakdouk. Towards a theory of extractable functions. In *TCC*, pages 595–613, 2009.

[22] R. Canetti and H. Krawczyk. Analysis of key-exchange protocols and their use for building secure channels. In *EUROCRYPT*, pages 453–474, 2001.

[23] L. Chen and Y. Chen. The n-Diffie-Hellman problem and its applications. In *ISC*, pages 119–134, 2011.

[24] L. Chen and C. Kudla. Identity based authenticated key agreement protocols from pairings. In *CSFW*, pages 219–233, 2003.

[25] C. Cremers. Examining indistinguishability-based security models for key exchange protocols: the case of CK, CK-HMQV, and eCK. In *ASIACCS*, pages 80–91, 2011.

[26] C. J. F. Cremers. Session-state reveal is stronger than ephemeral key reveal: Attacking the NAXOS authenticated key exchange protocol. In *ACNS*, pages 20–33, 2009.

[27] I. Damgård. Towards practical public key systems secure against chosen ciphertext attacks. In *CRYPTO*, pages 445–456, 1991.

[28] I. Damgård, S. Faust, and C. Hazay. Secure two-party computation with low communication. In *TCC*, pages 54–74, 2012.

[29] A. W. Dent. The Cramer-Shoup encryption scheme is plaintext aware in the standard model. In *EUROCRYPT*, pages 289–307, 2006.

[30] T. Dierks and C. Allen. *The TLS Protocol, Version 1.0.* Request for Comments: 2246, January 1999.

[31] W. Diffie and M. E. Hellman. New directions in cryptography. *IEEE Transactions on Information Theory*, 22(6):644–654, 1976.

[32] W. Diffie, P. C. van Oorschot, and M. J. Wiener. Authentication and authenticated key exchanges. *Des. Codes Cryptography*, 2(2):107–125, 1992.

[33] V. S. Dimitrov, G. A. Jullien, and W. C. Miller. Complexity and fast algorithms for multiexponentiations. *IEEE Trans. Computers*, 49(2):141–147, 2000.

[34] Y. Dodis, J. Katz, A. Smith, and S. Walfish. Composability and on-line deniability of authentication. In *TCC*, pages 146–162, 2009.

[35] A. Freier, P. Karlton, and P. Kocher. *The SSL Protocol, Version 3.0.* INTERNET-DRAFT: draft-freier-ssl-version3-02.txt, November 1996.

[36] R. Gennaro, H. Krawczyk, and T. Rabin. Okamoto-Tanaka revisited: Fully authenticated Diffie-Hellman with minimal overhead. In *ACNS*, pages 309–328, 2010.

[37] S. Goldwasser, H. Lin, and A. Rubinstein. Delegation of computation without rejection problem from designated verifier CS-proofs. *IACR Cryptology ePrint Archive*, 2011:456, 2011.

[38] D. M. Gordon. A survey of fast exponentiation methods. *J. Algorithms*, 27(1):129–146, 1998.

[39] J. Groth. Short pairing-based non-interactive zero-knowledge arguments. In *ASIACRYPT*, pages 321–340, 2010.

[40] S. Hada and T. Tanaka. On the existence of 3-round zero-knowledge protocols. In *CRYPTO*, pages 408–423, 1998.

[41] J. A. Halderman, S. D. Schoen, N. Heninger, W. Clarkson, W. Paul, J. A. Calandrino, A. J. Feldman, J. Appelbaum, and E. W. Felten. Lest we remember: cold-boot attacks on encryption keys. *Commun. ACM*, 52(5):91–98, 2009.

[42] S. Halevi and H. Krawczyk. One-pass HMQV and asymmetric key-wrapping. In *Public Key Cryptography*, pages 317–334, 2011.

[43] D. Harkins and D. Carreal. *Internet Key Exchange (IKE).* RFC 2049, The Internet Engineering Task Force, November 1998.

[44] K. Hickman. *The SSL Protocol.* Online document: www.netscape.com/eng/security/SSL-2.html, Feburary 1995.

[45] IEEE. 1363-2000: Standard specifications for public key cryptography.

[46] ISO/IEC. 11770-3:2008 information technology - security techniques - key management - part 3: Mechanisms using asymmetric techniques.

[47] ISO/IEC. 24727-6:2010 identification cards - integrated circuit card programming interfaces - part 6: Registration authority procedures for the authentication protocols for interoperability.

[48] B. S. Kaliski. An unknown key-share attack on the MQV key agreement protocol. *ACM Trans. Inf. Syst. Secur.*, 4(3):275–288, 2001.

[49] C. Kaufman. *Internet Key Exchange (IKEv2) Protocol.* The Internet Engineering Task Force: INTERNET-DRAFT, October 2002.

[50] H. Krawczyk. SIGMA: The 'sign-and-mac' approach to authenticated Diffie-Hellman and its use in the IKE-protocols. In *CRYPTO*, pages 400–425, 2003.

[51] H. Krawczyk. HMQV: A high-performance secure Diffie-Hellman protocol. In *CRYPTO*, pages 546–566, 2005.

[52] H. Krawczyk, K. G. Paterson, and H. Wee. On the security of the TLS protocol: A systematic analysis. *IACR Cryptology ePrint Archive*, 2013:339, 2013.

[53] C. Kudla and K. G. Paterson. Modular security proofs for key agreement protocols. In *ASIACRYPT*, pages 549–565, 2005.

[54] S. Kunz-Jacques and D. Pointcheval. A new key exchange protocol based on MQV assuming public computations. In *SCN*, pages 186–200, 2006.

[55] B. A. LaMacchia, K. Lauter, and A. Mityagin. Stronger security of authenticated key exchange. In *ProvSec*, pages 1–16, 2007.

[56] K. Lauter and A. Mityagin. Security analysis of KEA authenticated key exchange protocol. In *Public Key Cryptography*, pages 378–394, 2006.

[57] A. B. Lewko, Y. Rouselakis, and B. Waters. Achieving leakage resilience through dual system encryption. In *TCC*, pages 70–88, 2011.

[58] T. Matsumoto, Y. Takashima, and H. Imai. On seeking smart public-key distribution systems. *Trans. IECE of Japan*, E69(2):99–106, 1986.

[59] A. Menezes, M. Qu, and S. Vanstone. Some new key agreement protocols providing mutual implicit authentication. In *SAC*, pages 70–88, 1995

[60] A. Menezes and B. Ustaoglu. On the importance of public-key validation in the MQV and HMQV key agreement protocols. In *INDOCRYPT*, pages 133–147, 2006.

[61] A. Menezes, P. C. van Oorschot, and S. A. Vanstone. *Handbook of Applied Cryptography.* CRC Press, 1996.

[62] T. Mie. Polylogarithmic two-round argument systems. *J. Mathematical Cryptology*, 2(4):343–363, 2008.

[63] NIST. Special publication 800-56 (DRAFT): Recommendation on key establishment schemes, Draft 2, January 2003.

[64] NIST. SP 800-56 (DRAFT): Special publication 800-56, recommendation for pair-wise key establishment schemes using discrete logarithm cryptography, July 2005.

[65] NIST. SKIPJACK and KEA algorithm specifications. http://csrc.nist.org/encryption/skipjack/skipjack.pdf, 1998.

[66] T. Okamoto and D. Pointcheval. The gap-problems: A new class of problems for the security of cryptographic schemes. In *Public Key Cryptography*, pages 104–118, 2001.

[67] D. Pointcheval and J. Stern. Security arguments for digital signatures and blind signatures. *J. Cryptology*, 13(3):361–396, 2000.

[68] M. D. Raimondo and R. Gennaro. New approaches for deniable authentication. In *ACM Conference on Computer and Communications Security*, pages 112–121, 2005.

[69] M. D. Raimondo, R. Gennaro, and H. Krawczyk. Deniable authentication and key exchange. In *ACM Conference on Computer and Communications Security*, pages 400–409, 2006.

[70] E. Saint, D. Fedronic, and S. Liu. *Open Protocol for Access Control Identification and Ticketing with Privacy.* Smart Card Alliance, July 2011. http://www.smartcardalliance.org/resources/pdf/OPACITY_Protocol_3.7.pdf.

[71] J. Stasak. *NSAs Elliptic Curve Licensing Agreement.* The IETF's Security Area Advisory Group, 2004.

[72] A. C.-C. Yao and Y. Zhao. Deniable internet key exchange. In *ACNS*, pages 329–348, 2010.

[73] A. C.-C. Yao and Y. Zhao. A new family of practical non-malleable protocols. *IACR Cryptology ePrint Archive*, 2011:35, 2011.

APPENDIX

A. MORE VARIANTS OF OAKE

Adding (explicit) mutual authentication. In order to add mutual authentication to OAKE, besides the session-key K we also need a MAC-key K_m to be used within the protocol run (but erased after the protocol run). Both the session-key and the MAC-key are derived from the shared DH-secret $K_{\hat{A}} = K_{\hat{B}}$, and are independent in the random oracle model. For OAKE with mutual authentication, $\hat{B}$ sends an additional value $t_B = MAC_{K_m}(1)$ in the second-round, and $\hat{A}$ sends $t_A = MAC_{K_m}(0)$ in an additional third-round.

OAKE with embedded subgroup tests. Let t be the cofactor, for OAKE with embedded subgroup test, the shared DH-secret is set to be: $K_{\hat{A}} = B^{xt}Y^{at+ext}$ and $K_{\hat{B}} = A^{yt}X^{bt+eyt}$. The subgroup test is performed as follows: each player first verifies that its peer's DH-component is in G', and then acts in accordance with one of the following two modes.

Mode-1. If B^{xt} and Y^{at+ext} (resp., A^{yt} and X^{bt+eyt}) are computed separately, *particularly when B^{xt} (resp., A^{yt}) is offline pre-computed by $\hat{A}$ (resp., $\hat{B}$)*, $\hat{A}$ (resp., $\hat{B}$) checks that $Y^{at+ext} \neq 1_G$ (resp., $X^{bt+eyt} \neq 1_G$).

Mode-2. In case of no separate computation, $\hat{A}$ (resp., $\hat{B}$) verifies $K_{\hat{A}} \neq 1_G$ (resp., $K_{\hat{B}} \neq 1_G$). Note that the checking of $K_{\hat{A}} \neq 1_G$ and $K_{\hat{B}} \neq 1_G$, as done in MQV, does not *fully* guarantee $X^t \neq 1_G$ or $Y^t \neq 1_G$, but it still provides reasonable assurance in the elliptic curve setting.

We remark that the embedded subgroup test in Mode-1, well supported by OAKE, provides stronger security guarantee than that in Mode-2. Note that (H)MQV cannot offline pre-compute the values B^e and A^d to ease the more robust Mode-1 embedded subgroup test.

A note on subgroup test. We note that, as HMQV, the subgroup test of peer's DH-component can be waived (but still with the supergroup G' membership check), if no DH exponent or component is pre-computed and thus leaked. In particular, in this case, the black-box analysis of OAKE does not rely upon such a test. The underlying reason is that, even if an adversary learns some partial information about $b+ey$ by issuing a small subgroup attack against the honest $\hat{B}$ (by setting X to be in a small subgroup), it still cannot derive the value b without compromising the ephemeral value y. Actually, as the DH-exponent y is independent at random in each session and is assumed not to be leaked in this case, the adversary even cannot derive the full value of $b+ey$ by small subgroup attacks.

A note on session-key derivation. In the description of OAKE in Figure 1, the session-key is set to be $H_K(K_{\hat{A}}) = H_K(K_{\hat{B}})$, where the key derivation function H_K is modeled as a random oracle in security analysis. In reality, we can use a PRF, e.g., HMAC [8], to derive the session-key; for example, the session-key is derived as $PRF_{\mathcal{S}}(\hat{A}, \hat{B}, X, Y)$, where $\mathcal{S}$ is the randomness seed that is derived from (or, just to be) the intermediate secrecy $K_{\hat{A}} = K_{\hat{B}}$.

B. DISCUSSION ON ECK AND NAXOS

The extended CK model, namely eCK-model in short, was proposed in [55] as a variant of the CK-framework. The key difference between eCK and CK lies in that, in the eCK-model, the session-states of both the test-session and the matching session can be exposed. Let's first review the NAXOS protocol proposed in [55] that is shown to be eCK-secure.

Let (a, x') (resp., (b, y')) be the static and ephemeral secret keys of player $\hat{A}$ (resp., $\hat{B}$) of public key $A = g^a$ (resp., $B = g^b$), where $a, b, x', y' \leftarrow Z_q^*$. Let $h : \{0,1\}^* \rightarrow Z_q^*$ be a cryptographic hash function. Player $\hat{A}$ (resp., $\hat{B}$) sends $X = g^x$ (resp., $Y = g^y$), where $x = h(a, x')$ and $y = h(b, y')$. Then, the session-key is derived as follows. Player $\hat{B}$ computes $K = H_K(A^y, X^b, X^y, \hat{A}, \hat{B})$, and $\hat{A}$ computes $K = H_K(Y^a, B^x, Y^x, \hat{A}, \hat{B})$. *Notice that the session-key computation of $\hat{A}$ and that of $\hat{B}$ are not symmetric.*

Some brief observations and remarks on NAXOS:

- The key trick of NAXOS is that, though the actually used DH-exponents and DH-components are (x, X) and (y, Y) respectively, but for security proof of NAXOS in eCK, only the values x' and y' are specified as the session-states that are assumed to be exposed. This is also a common trick to transform most KE protocols secure in the traditional CK-framework into protocols secure in the eCK-model. However, the naturally pre-computable values (x, X, B^x) and (y, Y, A^y) are not specified to be included in session-states, and are assumed to be unexposed or not to be pre-computed.

  In a sense, the security of NAXOS in eCK comes at the price of losing offline pre-computability. Notice that, supposing x and y are pre-computed and allowed to be exposed as in the traditional CK-framework, the leakage of both x and y will expose the session-key of NAXOS, and consequently NAXOS is actually insecure in the eCK-model in this case. In other words, the eCK-security of NAXOS depends upon what are specified in session-states.

- The trick of NAXOS, i.e., setting $x = h(a, x')$ and $y = h(b, y')$, involves more uses of the static secret keys, which may cause weak protection of static secret keys in reality. In addition, as mentioned, the session-key computation of $\hat{A}$ and that of $\hat{B}$ are *not* symmetric.

- It is easy to see that, under the DLP assumption, NAXOS cannot be HP-deniable according to our HP-deniability definition. In particular, given the exposed session-state x', we even do not know how to *efficiently* and *statistically* simulate $X = g^{h(a,x')}$ or $B^x = g^{bh(a,x')}$ without knowing the secret key a.

Finally, we would also like to remind the reader of some existing critiques on the eCK-model (see, e.g., [15, 26, 25]). On the one hand, the CK-security and eCK-security are incomparable in general. On the other hand, the security requirements by eCK actually cause the eCK-model less applicable than the traditional CK-framework. In particular, any DHKE, where the session-key can be derived from the DH-exponents that are specified as the session-states (e.g., IKE [49] and SIGMA [50], STS [32], SSL [35] and TLS [30], and JFK [3] and much more), cannot be proven secure in the eCK-model.

FPDetective: Dusting the Web for Fingerprinters

Gunes Acar[1], Marc Juarez[1,2], Nick Nikiforakis[3], Claudia Diaz[1], Seda Gürses[1,4], Frank Piessens[3] and Bart Preneel[1]

[1]KU Leuven, Dept. of Electrical Engineering (ESAT), COSIC, iMinds, Leuven, Belgium
{gunes.acar,marc.juarez,claudia.diaz,seda.guerses,bart.preneel}@esat.kuleuven.be

[2]IIIA-CSIC, Bellaterra, Spain
mjuarez@iiia.csic.es

[3]KU Leuven, Dept. of Computer Science, iMinds-DistriNet, Leuven, Belgium
{nick.nikiforakis,frank.piessens}@cs.kuleuven.be

[4]New York University, Dept. of Media, Culture, and Communication, NY, USA

ABSTRACT

In the modern web, the browser has emerged as the vehicle of choice, which users are to trust, customize, and use, to access a wealth of information and online services. However, recent studies show that the browser can also be used to invisibly fingerprint the user: a practice that may have serious privacy and security implications.

In this paper, we report on the design, implementation and deployment of FPDetective, a framework for the detection and analysis of web-based fingerprinters. Instead of relying on information about known fingerprinters or third-party-tracking blacklists, FPDetective focuses on the detection of the fingerprinting itself. By applying our framework with a focus on font detection practices, we were able to conduct a large scale analysis of the million most popular websites of the Internet, and discovered that the adoption of fingerprinting is much higher than previous studies had estimated. Moreover, we analyze two countermeasures that have been proposed to defend against fingerprinting and find weaknesses in them that might be exploited to bypass their protection. Finally, based on our findings, we discuss the current understanding of fingerprinting and how it is related to Personally Identifiable Information, showing that there needs to be a change in the way users, companies and legislators engage with fingerprinting.

Categories and Subject Descriptors

K.6.m [**Management of Computing and Information Systems**]: Miscellaneous; H.3.5 [**Information Storage and Retrieval**]: Online Information Services — *Web-based services*; K.4.4 [**Computers and Society**]: Electronic Commerce — *Security*

Keywords

Web security; privacy; device fingerprinting; tracking; dynamic analysis; JavaScript; Flash

CCS'13, November 4–8, 2013, Berlin, Germany.

ACM 978-1-4503-2477-9/13/11 ...$15.00.
http://dx.doi.org/10.1145/2508859.2516674.

1. INTRODUCTION

In 2010, Eckersley demonstrated that benign characteristics of a browser's environment, like the screen dimensions and list of installed fonts, could be combined to create a unique device-specific fingerprint [7]. Of the half million users who participated in Eckersley's experiment, 94.2% of those using Flash or Java had a unique device fingerprint, and could thus be identified and tracked without the need for stateful client-side technologies, such as browser or Flash cookies.

Fingerprinting user devices through the browser is an increasingly common practice used of advertising and anti-fraud companies. Stateless user tracking allows advertising companies to sidestep the limitations imposed by regulation on *cookies* in Europe and the United States. Moreover, with the advent of smartphones and tablets, fingerprinting allows advertisers to augment previously gathered user-data and track the user across devices. Anti-fraud companies advertise fingerprinting as a means to protect users and web applications against malevolent actors, for instance, by detecting the use of stolen credentials and identifying Sybil attacks [6]. Most of the time, these services are based on massive device reputation databases where device fingerprints are stored along with the device owners' web history and "reputation scores."

Device fingerprinting raises serious privacy concerns for everyday users. Its stateless nature makes it hard to detect (no cookies to inspect and delete) and even harder to opt-out. Moreover, fingerprinting works just as well in the "private-mode" of modern browsers, which cookie-conscious users may be utilizing to perform privacy-sensitive operations. In recent research, Nikiforakis et al. [18] analyzed the techniques and adoption of three fingerprinting companies, two of which had been identified by Mayer and Mitchell in a 2012 survey paper on web-tracking [13]. While the authors studied the practices of these three companies, they did not attempt to discover other fingerprinters and explore the methods adopted by these.

This paper aims to shed light on current device fingerprinting practices through three main contributions. The first is the design and implementation of *FPDetective*,[1] a framework for identifying and analyzing web-based device fingerprinting without relying on a list of known fingerprinters.

Second, we use FPDetective to conduct a large-scale study of web-based device fingerprinting in the top million Alexa sites. Using FPDetective, we were able to identify 16 new fingerprinting scripts and Flash objects (including commercial fingerprinting as well as in-house solutions), some of which are active in the top 500 websites, showing that fingerprinting is much more prevalent than previous studies estimated. Further, we uncovered previously unreported fingerprinting practices, such as attempting to evade detection by removing the fingerprinting script once the device has been fingerprinted, and collecting fingerprints through third-party widgets. Our findings highlight the rising prevalence of fingerprinting and, in turn, the need for more transparency, awareness and counter-measures with respect to these practices.

Finally, we evaluate the Tor Browser and Firegloves, two privacy-enhancing tools that have "fingerprinting-resistance" as a design goal. We discovered vulnerabilities in both tools that would allow a fingerprinter to identify users. This illustrates the difficulty of protecting against device fingerprinting. We also tested whether enabling the Do-Not-Track (DNT) header had any impact on the behavior of fingerprinting scripts, and found that it does not.

The rest of the paper is organized as follows. Section 2 reviews the state-of-the-art in device fingerprinting methods. The FPDetective framework is described in Section 3. Section 4 motivates the use of font detection to identify potential fingerprinters, and explains our data analysis methodology. Section 5 presents the experimental results of our study of the top million Alexa websites. We evaluate in Section 6 the Tor browser, Firegloves, and DNT as countermeasures to fingerprinting. We discuss in Section 7 the uses of fingerprinting and its relationship to privacy concerns. Finally, we offer our conclusions in Section 8.

2. DEVICE FINGERPRINTING

A device *fingerprint* is a set of system attributes that, for each device, take a combination of values that is, with high likelihood, unique, and can thus function as a device identifier. These attributes include, for example, the device's screen size, the versions of installed software, and the list of installed fonts. Attributes that take more diverse values (e.g., the list of fonts) are more identifying than values shared by many devices (e.g., version of the operating system). Similarly, attributes with values that are more stable over time (i.e., that change only infrequently or very gradually) facilitate identification compared to those that change often and unpredictably.

Web-based device fingerprinting is the process of collecting sufficient information through the browser to perform stateless device identification. These fingerprints may then be used as identifiers for tracking the device in the web. By tracking, we refer to the linking of visits to (one or multiple) web pages as made by the same device.

There are many reasons why web applications may need device-related information, e.g., to correctly render content or to serve device compatible media. Thus, there are many APIs that enable applications to query these attributes. At the same time, these APIs can be used to learn enough attribute values to obtain a device fingerprint that is, for practical purposes, unique. When a user browses to a webpage that includes fingerprinting software, her device fingerprint may be collected and compared to a database of known devices. Using such techniques, known devices can be matched, and previously unknown devices can be added to the database. Depending on the use case, the database entry for each device is augmented with contextual and behavioral information with each visit of the user to a monitored webpage.

In this section we briefly introduce device fingerprinting methods. Some of the discussed methods have already been encountered in real-life fingerprinting code, while others have been shown to work but are not yet known to have been adopted by fingerprinters [18].

2.1 JavaScript-based

From its original inception in 1995 all the way to today, JavaScript has emerged as the de-facto client-side, programming language of the web. The expressiveness of JavaScript, combined with its "forgiving" nature when it comes to programming errors (such as missing semicolons) and, most importantly, its ubiquitous availability in modern browsers, has made it an indispensable tool of modern web sites. Virtually all non-static web pages use JavaScript and a 2010 study by Yahoo showed that only 1% of actual human visitors have JavaScript disabled [24].

JavaScript is used by programmers mainly to dynamically manipulate a page's DOM, enrich user experience through asynchronous requests and responses, and offload non-critical, server functionality to the client. Its privileged position inside the browser, however, also makes it a strong fingerprinting tool. The JavaScript accessible browser resources that have, historically, been probed the most, are the following:

- `navigator`: The `navigator` object contains information about the browser vendor and specific browser version, the supported plugins and MIME types, as well as relatively coarse-grained information about the operating system and architecture on which the browser is executing.
- `screen`: The `screen` object contains information about the resolution of the user's monitor (height and width) and the color and pixel depth.

Mayer, in 2009, reported on an experiment where he fingerprinted 1328 web clients [12]. By hashing the concatenated contents of the `navigator`, `screen`, `navigator.plugins` and `navigator.mimeTypes`, Mayer was able to uniquely identify more than 96% of the browsers. A

[1]The FPDetective framework is available here: `http://homes.esat.kuleuven.be/~gacar/fpdetective/`

year later Eckersley, through the Panopticlick project[2], fingerprinted nearly half a million browsers and by extending the set of fingerprinted features with fonts, timezones and a browser's ACCEPT headers, was able to uniquely identify 94.2% of the visitors' browsing environments [7]. Eckersley also showed that the list of installed fonts is one of the most identifying features of a system. This list can be obtained either through JavaScript by measuring and then comparing the dimensions of text rendered with different fonts [18], or through browser plugins.

Other researchers have proposed the use of performance benchmarks for differentiating between JavaScript engines [15], errors in standard test-suites [17] and differences in the appearance of `canvas` elements created through JavaScript [16]. Furthermore, a user's browsing history, which can be recovered exploiting JavaScript's visited-link color feature [9], has also been shown to uniquely identify users [19]. In general, while these methods have not yet been encountered in deployed fingerprinting products [18], they could potentially be used to increase the accuracy of the gathered fingerprints.

2.2 Plugin-based

The latest version of HTML, HTML5, together with the advanced capabilities of JavaScript and Cascading Style Sheets, give web developers today the ability to create feature-rich web applications. This, however, was not the case with older versions of HTML, as their abilities to deliver interactive rich Internet applications, like games, video and music were limited. Third-party companies, like Adobe, developed plugins and platforms to create, deliver and render interactive multimedia content. The clear winner of this "plugin-war" was Adobe Flash, with Java being a distant second.

As with JavaScript, the adoption of popular third-party plugins gives fingerprinters the ability to extract numerous features. Eckersley used Java and Flash to obtain the list of fonts installed in a device [7], since font-enumeration API calls are made available by the Flash and Java plugins. In addition to font extraction, commercial fingerprinting companies use Flash to circumvent HTTP proxies set up by the user and get more fine-grained information about the device, such as the specific operating system kernel version, or the presence of multiple-monitor setups [18].

2.3 Extension-based

The modular nature of modern browsers has allowed developers to create extensions that add new functionality, remove undesired features, and modify others. Unlike plugins, extensions are not enumerable through JavaScript and thus can only be detected by their possible side-effects. For instance, Mowery et al. [15] showed that it is possible to deduce custom whitelists from the popular NoScript plugin, simply by requesting scripts from domains and later inspecting whether the scripts successfully executed, by searching for predetermined JavaScript objects in the global address space. The deduced whitelists can be used as an extra fingerprint feature. Nikiforakis et al. [18] showed that user-agent-spoofing extensions can also be discovered due to inconsistencies in the reported browsing environment when each extension is active.

[2]`https://panopticlick.eff.org/`

2.4 Header-based & Server-side

Yen et al. [23] performed a fingerprinting study, similar to Eckersley's, by analyzing month-long logs of Bing and Hotmail. The authors found that IP addresses and user-agent headers may help in tracking users with high precision and recall.

Predating fingerprinting at the browser-level, researchers had shown that it is possible to not only remotely learn the operating system of a particular host on the Internet [1, 25], but also to fingerprint multiple physical devices hidden behind NATs through their clockskew, by analyzing the TCP timestamps of network packets [11].

While these techniques may be less accurate compared to the aforementioned in-browser fingerprinting methods, their pure server-side nature makes their detection very difficult, if not impossible.

3. FPDETECTIVE FRAMEWORK

In this section we describe FPDetective, a framework for detecting web-based device fingerprinting. FPDetective is designed as a flexible, general purpose framework that can be used to conduct further web privacy studies. FPDetective is freely available and can be downloaded from `http://homes.esat.kuleuven.be/~gacar/fpdetective`.

Figure 1 outlines FPDetective's components and workflow. The main component of FPDetective is a crawler, whose purpose is to visit websites and collect data about events that might be related to fingerprinting, such as the loading of fonts, or accessing specific browser properties. These logs are parsed and committed to a central database in a relational structure. In order to detect Flash-based fingerprinting, all browser traffic is directed through an intercepting proxy that logs all the HTTP(S) traffic between the browser and the web server. These network dumps are parsed to extract Flash objects, that are then decompiled using a free, third-party decompiler and stored in the database.

In our analysis of the data collected by FPDetective we focus on font detection. We would like to emphasize that this choice was made in order to facilitate the analysis of the data, and the data gathered by FPDetective can be analyzed differently, based on other fingerprinting classification criteria. Further, the FPDetective framework can easily be adapted for use in Web privacy studies unrelated to fingerprinting. The framework is developed with modularity in mind using Python, C++, JavaScript and MySQL programming/scripting languages. Researchers can customize the framework to carry out different experiments by replacing the script that FPDetective executes when it visits the sites. We warmly welcome other researchers to provide their comments, contribute to the project, or fork their own software out of FPDetective.

The remainder of this section describes each component of FPDetective in more detail.

3.1 Components

Crawler: The crawler features two instrumented browsers, PhantomJS[3] and Chromium[4]. We chose PhantomJS to collect data related to JavaScript-based fingerprinting for its

[3]`http://phantomjs.org/`
[4]`http://www.chromium.org/`

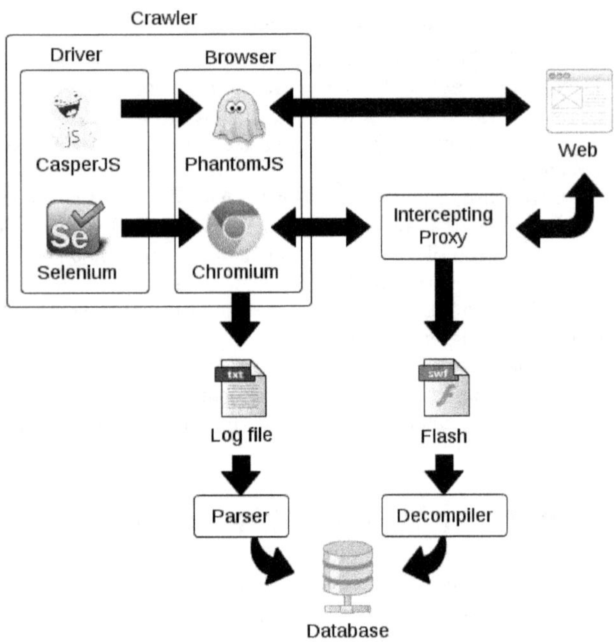

Figure 1: FPDetective Framework

minimal use of resources. We used Chromium to investigate Flash-based fingerprinting, since PhantomJS does not have plugin support and thus cannot run Flash objects. CasperJS[5] and Selenium[6] were used to drive the browsers to websites and navigate through the pages.

To build instrumented versions of the browsers, we modified parts of the WebKit source code, which is the rendering engine used by both Chromium and PhantomJS. It should be noted, however, that during the course of our study, Chromium Project announced that they leave WebKit for a new rendering engine called Blink, which is again based on WebKit [2]. We preferred to work at the native code level instead of developing browser extensions or JavaScript patches for several reasons: to detect events that are not JavaScript-based (especially those related to fonts); to detect the origin of events more precisely; and to defend against JavaScript attacks that block or circumvent extensions and getter methods[7].

The modifications allow the crawler to intercept and log accesses to the following browser and device properties, which could be used for fingerprinting:

- access to the following `navigator` properties and methods: `userAgent, appCodeName, product, productSub, vendor, vendorSub, onLine, appVersion, language, plugins, mimeTypes, cookieEnabled(), javaEnabled()`
- access to `navigator.plugins`: `name, filename, description, length`
- access to `navigator.mimeTypes`: `enabledPlugin, description, suffixes, type`

[5]`http://casperjs.org/`

[6]`http://docs.seleniumhq.org/`

[7]`http://code.google.com/p/chromium/issues/detail?id=55084`

- access to `window.screen` properties: `horizontalDPI, verticalDPI, height, width, colorDepth, pixelDepth, availLeft, availTop, availHeight, availWidth`
- access to `offsetWidth` and `offsetHeight` properties and `getBoundingRect` method of HTML elements.
- font load attempts by intercepting calls to `CSSFontFace::getFontData` and `CSSFontSelector::getFontData` methods

Parser: The parser is used to extract relevant data from the logs generated by the crawler, and to store them in the database. It also tags sites with a label if a known fingerprinting script is found in the HTTP requests made for this visit.

Intercepting Proxy: In order to obtain Flash files for static analysis, we redirected traffic through mitmproxy [4], an SSL-capable intercepting proxy. We used the mitmdump module to log all the HTTP traffic passing through the proxy, and the libmproxy library to parse and extract Flash files based on content sniffing. More specifically, we detected Flash files through Flash-specific "magic numbers" appearing the first bytes of content since the `Content-Type` HTTP header is not always reliable.

Decompiler: We used the JPEXS Free Flash Decompiler[8] to decompile Flash files and obtain the ActionScript source code. The source code is then searched for fingerprinting related function calls (e.g. `enumerateFonts` and `getFontList`) to obtain a binary occurrence vector. The complete list of methods and properties searched in the decompiled source code is available in Appendix B.

Central Database: We ran crawls using several machines, but used a central database to store, combine, and analyze the results of different crawls with minimal effort. The stored data include the set of JavaScript function calls, the list of HTTP requests and responses, and the list of loaded or requested fonts. For the Flash experiments, we also stored a binary vector that represents the existence of ActionScript API calls that might be related to fingerprinting.

3.2 Performance

By using the Dromaeo JavaScript performance test suite[9] we compared our modified Chromium browser against the Chromium browser available from Ubuntu's repositories. Although the versions of Chromium and WebKit were different for the two browsers (25 vs 28 and 537.22 vs 537.36 repectively) we still believe that the results can provide a rough approximation of the performance of our tool. The resulting scores from the Dromaeo test suites were 3,148.63 runs/s for original Chromium and 3,025.86 runs/s for our modified browser. The difference between their aggregate performance is about 4%, where error intervals were measured as 1.24% and 1.98%.

The most crucial differences were between the `getHeight` and `getWidth` methods of the Prototype JavaScript library[10] (9.76 vs 214.1 and 9.79 vs 244.3) which is probably due to the fact that we log accesses to `offsetHeight` and `offsetWidth`

[8]`http://www.free-decompiler.com/flash/`

[9]`http://dromaeo.com/`

[10]`http://prototypejs.org/`

properties. But within JQuery's[11] **height** and **width** methods, differences were quite low (0.84 vs 2.27 and 0.97 vs 2.27) hinting that this might also be due to the libraries' implementation details[12].

We were able to run 200 parallel PhantomJS instances on a customer grade computer with quad core CPU and 8GB of RAM. With these settings we were able to complete a homepage crawl of the Alexa top million sites in a period of four days.

For the experiments with the Chromium browser, we could run approximately 20 crawlers in parallel, since each crawler was running an instance of Chromium and mitmproxy, as well as was using the Flash decompiler whenever a Flash object was received. Crawling the top 20,000 Alexa sites required about one day using a single computer with the characteristics given above.

4. FONT-BASED ANALYSIS OF FINGERPRINTING

In order to carry out a large scale study of fingerprinting, we combined automated and manual analysis in our experiments. In the automated step we use font probing and font enumeration as a criteria for identifying candidate sites that possibly include a fingerprinting script or object. This approach is motivated in Section 4.1 and explained in more detail in Section 4.2. We then examine manually the candidates to refine the classification using additional criteria and establish whether the pages contain fingerprinting code.

4.1 Motivation

By inspecting the code of known fingerprinters, and taking into account the findings of previous studies [7, 18], we distill *"font detection"* through enumeration or probing as a necessary ingredient of device fingerprinting. Furthermore, we consider font detection to be a good indicator of fingerprinting, as getting the list of system fonts has fewer use cases than requesting information needed for browser feature detection.

The use of font detection for fingerprinting also offers the following advantages:

- according to Panopticlick study, fonts are the second most identifying attribute of a device, having 17.1 bits of entropy when unsorted;
- although the list of installed browser plugins has slightly more entropy, fonts are OS-dependent and thus enable linking different browsers running on the same device;
- the Tor Browser, which is the most widely used tool with counter-fingerprinting features, is shipped with a fixed browser configuration in which plugins are disabled. Fonts are thus the most identifying feature in this context, and the best candidate to successfully identify and track anonymous Tor users.

4.2 Methodology

We follow a two-step analysis. The first step consists of an automated analysis of font detection and the second of a manual analysis of scripts and decompiled Flash source code. Font detection plays a central role in our analysis of the dataset collected by FPDetective: it is used to identify likely fingerprinting candidates in an automated fashion. We consider as likely candidates the websites that request an abnormally large number of fonts, or that have font enumeration calls in the decompiled ActionScript source code. In our analysis we classified as candidates pages that include scripts that load more than 30 fonts, or Flash files that contain font enumeration calls.

Our analysis methodology is different for the identification of Flash and JavaScript-based fingerprinters, given that font detection can be carried out by direct enumeration through Flash, and by indirect probing through JavaScript.

In the case of Flash, a dynamic analysis of font enumeration is hard due to the proprietary nature of the Flash plugin player and the use of internal font caches. At the same time, because of the byte-code nature of Flash objects, they can be straightforwardly decompiled to their original ActionScript source code. We thus decompiled the Flash objects into their corresponding ActionScript source code, selected the ones that had font enumeration calls, and manually analyzed them to understand what they do with the list of system fonts they collect. We counted a Flash object as a fingerprinter when it enumerates system fonts, collects information about the device capabilities and sends the collected fingerprint back to a remote server either by opening a socket connection or using JavaScript asynchronous calls. Furthermore we eliminated many false positives by checking Flash file URLs and domains with WHOIS lookups. For example, multimedia players that include font enumeration to be used on screen displays were eliminated by using background information.

On the other hand, due to the increased use of code obfuscation and code minimization techniques, it is, in general, very challenging to accurately perform a static analysis of JavaScript source code. We thus opted for a dynamic analysis approach, in which we intercept and record JavaScript font-probing events with the FPDetective's instrumented browsers.

As mentioned earlier, next to font-probing events, FPDetective also collects data related to other events that might be associated with fingerprinting, such as browser plugin enumeration and screen-size detection. The second part of our JavaScript-based fingerprinting analysis consisted of manually studying the identified candidates, taking into account this additional information. Specifically we checked for evidence of browser feature enumeration, including iterating over **name**, **filename**, **description** and **length** properties of browser plugins, the **enabledPlugin**, **description**, **suffixes**, and **type** properties of **mimeType** objects, and **navigator** properties such as **userAgent**, **appCodeName**, **product**, and **productSub**; **screen** object properties such as dimensions, color and pixel depth information; and properties that reveal installed toolbars such as **availTop** and **availLeft**. We classify a JavaScript file as a fingerprinter when it loads more than 30 system fonts, enumerates plugins or mimeTypes, detects screen and navigator properties, and sends the collected data back to a remote server. As we do for the Flash objects, we incorporated background information about JavaScript domain names to eliminate false positives.

[11] `https://jquery.org/`

[12] The full comparison of the performance results can be seen here: `http://dromaeo.com/?id=197597,197598`.

We verified the correct functioning of the framework by crawling test pages that request a known set of fonts and checking them against the ones returned by FPDetective.

5. EXPERIMENTS AND RESULTS

In the following experiments we used the FPDetective framework to crawl the top Alexa websites while searching for instances of web-based device fingerprinting. Our experiments were separated into the ones geared towards the discovery of JavaScript-based fingerprinting attempts and the remaining ones towards the discovery of Flash-based fingerprinting.

For each type of experiment, we first automatically searched for font-detection attempts and used that for selecting candidates for manual analysis. In the JavaScript experiments, we tried to find JavaScript-based font probing attempts, for which we used the number of requested fonts as a measure. In order to filter out websites that load high numbers of fonts, but do not use them for probing, we checked if websites measure the width and height of displayed text by using the number of calls to the `offsetWidth` and `offsetHeight` properties of the corresponding HTML elements.

For the Flash experiments we crawled the sites with Chromium and intercepted Flash objects with mitmproxy. We then decompiled the discovered Flash files and searched for a list of ActionScript API calls (see Appendix B for the full list) that might be relevant to fingerprinting. Subsequently, we generated a binary vector that represents the occurrence of each function call in the Flash object and used that to select objects for manual analysis.

5.1 JavaScript-Based Font probing

In this set of experiments, we crawled the top Alexa websites with FPDetective to find out the extent of the JavaScript-based font probing. In the first experiment we visited the homepages of the top Alexa 1 million websites where we waited for 10 seconds, in order to allow for the loading of remote content. In the second experiment, we visited 100,000 websites and clicked 25 homepage links from the same domain. We waited 5 seconds after each click and 10 seconds after each page load to allow for resources to load.

By analyzing the sites that are sorted by FPDetective as likely candidates of fingerprinting, we found 13 instances of JavaScript-based font-probing scripts, on a total of 404 websites. In order to ensure the accuracy of our classification, we augmented the automated, dynamic analysis with manual analysis of the source code and background information on the companies that own the domains from where scripts are served. Specifically, we checked whether the script (or another script served from the same domain) collects other high-entropy browser properties such as plugins or mimeTypes and if the company is involved in products and services that might be related to fingerprinting, e.g., device identification, analytics and anti-fraud.

Table 1 shows the results of these experiments in detail. The discovered scripts probed as many as 503 fonts and, popularity-wise, there were three websites in the top 500 Alexa sites that made use of a font-probing script.

BlueCava was discovered on the homepages of 250 Alexa websites, making it, by far, the most popular font-probing script. Moreover, it is the only one of the discovered font-probing scripts that queries different sets of fonts based on the device's operating system: 231 fonts for Microsoft Windows, 167 for Mac OS and 62 for other operating systems.

While analyzing the candidate scripts, we came across some interesting practices, such as a script that first dynamically injects itself into the page and then, after collecting the device fingerprint, removes itself from the page. This was one of the cases that motivated us to develop our tools for dynamic analysis and is discussed in more detail in Section 7.2.

Most of, but not all, the scripts that we found are served from a domain registered for an analytics and/or anti-fraud company. An intriguing case is that of Anonymizer[13], a paid anonymization service that fingerprints every visitor accessing their homepage and has a set of fingerprinting scripts that include function names such as `submitDnsInfoViaAjax`, `getClockSkew`, `getJsFontList` and `connectViaSocket`.

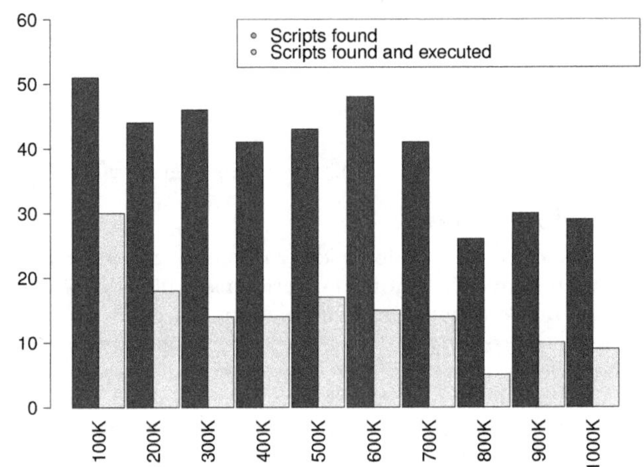

Figure 2: JavaScript-based font probing scripts on homepages of Top 1 Million Alexa sites

We also found that including third party scripts is not the only form of distribution, e.g., the font probing script from CoinBase is found as an embedded button that visitors might click to donate BitCoins to site owner.

We compared the sites that fingerprint users on the homepage, to sites that only fingerprint users on the inner pages. We did not observe any differences between these two, as evidenced by the two last columns of Table 1. This could mean that either we could not crawl the inner pages that include fingerprinting scripts not present in the homepage, or sites prefer to fingerprint users on their homepages.

The histogram in Figure 2 represents the distribution of sites using JavaScript-based font probing among the Top 1 Million Alexa sites. The histogram is divided in intervals of 100,000 sites (according to their Alexa rank) which are further divided into two bins. The darker bin refers to the total number of sites in that popularity range that served a fingerprinting script. These scripts are counted by matching previously discovered script URLs or regular expressions to

[13]`https://www.anonymizer.com/`

Fingerprinting Provider	Script name	Num Fonts	Top Rank	Number of sites using JS-based FP		
				1M	100K	
				In homepage	In homepage	In inner pages
BlueCava	BCAC5.js	231/167/62	1,390	250	24	24
Perferencement	tagv22.pkmin.js	153	49,979	51	6	6
CoinBase	application-773a[...snipped...].js	206	497	28	4	4
MaxMind	device.js	94	498	24	5	5
Inside graph	ig.js	355	98,786	18	1	1
SiteBlackBox	No fixed URL	389	1,687	14	10	10
Analytics-engine	fp.js	98	36,161	6	-	-
Myfreecams	o-mfccore.js	71	422	3	1	1
Mindshare Tech.	pomegranate.js	487	109,798	3	-	-
Cdn.net	cc.js	297	501,583	3	-	-
AFK Media	fingerprint.js	503	199,319	2	-	-
Anonymizer	fontdetect.js	80	118,504	1	-	-
Analyticsengine	fingerprint.compiled.js	93	522,447	1	-	-
				404	51	51

Table 1: Prevalence of Fingerprinting with JavaScript Based Font Probing on Top 1M Alexa sites

URLs of HTTP requests made while visiting the site. Since we found that not all scripts probe a large number of fonts every time they are loaded, we included a second (lighter) bin to represent sites that both served a fingerprinting script and probed for fonts.

5.2 Flash Based Font Enumeration

The main objective of this experiment is to investigate the extent of Flash based fingerprinting techniques on the Web. We crawled the top 10 thousand Alexa websites using FPDetective and, for each site, we visited the homepage and waited for 10 seconds to allow for resources to load completely.

We automatically decompiled all the Flash files caught by the intercepting proxy and checked the presence of functions that might be used for fingerprinting. We manually analyzed the files that include functions for known Flash-based fingerprinting techniques [18], such as querying the **`Capabilities`** class to collect information about the operating system and device, or opening a socket (by using **`XMLSocket`**) to bypass system wide proxy settings.

We also checked for the presence of function calls that might be used to send the collected information to a remote server (e.g., **`sendAndLoad`** or **`URLLoader`**) or use of **`ExternalInterface.Call`** or **`addCallback`** functions for opening JavaScript interfaces to either call JavaScript functions from the Flash file or allow page scripts to access Flash functions.

Finally, we took into account whether the collected information is sent to a remote server or used internally, by the Flash object. This helped us to filter out potential false positives, such as Flash video players that enumerate system fonts, in order to check if a font is available for use in player's on-screen display.

Table 2 shows our results for Flash-based fingerprinting. Being found on 69 sites, BB Elements, which offers tools for managing ad campaigns, is the most prevalent Flash-based fingerprinter. Piano Media is mostly found on newspaper sites and claims to employ fingerprinting for paywall enforcement. Paywalls, in this case, are used to ensure that users do not access paid content, such as newspaper or magazine articles, without subscription or payment. Usually, paywalls are combined with a limited number of free accesses, e.g., an online newspaper can offer ten free articles per user per day.

The website of the Turkish Ministry of Education (MEB) is unique in both being the only `.gov` website that employs web-based device fingerprinting and in the wealth of collected attributes from the device's hardware components. The Flash file served from this site extracts and sends detailed information about system mouse, keyboard, accelerometer, multi-touch capability, microphone, camera as well as system fonts. It should be noted that this site serves an e-School system to manage grades and other records of millions of students in Turkey. ThreatMetrix is the only discovered company which uses proxy-piercing to reveal a user's original IP address and whether she uses a proxy.

In Table 2 we can see the fingerprinters that have been discovered along with some of the functions that were called from the Flash files. We only included in the table the Flash files that have functions for font enumeration. That does not include, for instance, 50 Flash objects from one of the companies previously studied [18].

Given that we discovered several previously unknown fingerprinting scripts by extending our crawl space to 1 million for the JavaScript experiment, we plan to make a similar study for the Flash based fingerprinters.

5.3 Testing FPDetective with Fontconfig

Fontconfigis a Linux library that configures and manages the access to system fonts. In this experiment we used debugging functionality of fontconfig to test our framework's accuracy.

We crawled the Alexa Top 10,000 sites and compared the set of font requests made by each web site to ensure that FPDetective is not missing or overcounting font events. The comparison of the two measurements indicated that we neither miss nor overcount the font load events.

5.4 Prevalence of Fingerprinting

With FPDetective we found 404 sites in the Alexa top million pages that fingerprint visitors on their homepages using JavaScript-based font probing. These scripts are served by 13 different fingerprinting providers, of which only a few had been identified in prior research.

Fingerprinting Provider	Num of Sites	Top Rank	Flash Cookies	Proxy Detection	HW and OS Profiling	Interaction with JS
BB Elements	69	903	✓			✓
Piano Media	12	3,532	✓		✓	✓
Bluecava	6	1,390	✓			✓
ThreatMetrix	6	2,793		✓	✓	
Alipay	1	83	✓		✓	✓
meb.gov.tr (Turkish Ministry of Education)	1	2,206	✓		✓	✓

Table 2: Flash Fingerprinting objects found on Top 10K Alexa websites

Although 404 out of 1,000,000 can be thought of as a very low frequency, we would like to note that the results presented here should be taken as lower bounds, as our crawlers cannot reach pages that are placed after forms including CAPTCHAs or similar obstacles. Moreover, Flash-based fingerprinting was present on the homepages of 95 out of the top 10,000 sites, indicating that Flash-based fingerprinting is more prevalent. This is possibly because of its extended capabilities for font enumeration, proxy detection and its widespread browser support.

6. EVALUATION OF FINGERPRINTING COUNTERMEASURES

In this section we briefly analyze two tools that can be employed to counter fingerprinting: the Tor Browser and the FireGloves Firefox extension. We also evaluate whether the Do Not Track header is being respected by fingerprinters.

6.1 Tor Browser

The Tor Browser is part of the software bundle that is used to access the Tor anonymity network [5], a popular service that is currently used daily by more than 800,000 people to anonymously browse the web. Tor relays communications over three routers located in different parts of the world. The communications are encrypted in layers (onion routing [8]) to prevent any single Tor router from linking the source and destination of a data stream.

The Tor Browser incorporates strong defenses to counter the fingerprinting techniques described by the Panopticlick study, as its design goals include enabling user anonymity and preventing the linkability of browsing sessions. Given that the Tor Browser has a limited user base compared to web users in general, even a partial fingerprint might be enough to uniquely distinguish a Tor user. Thus, there is a need to eliminate fingerprintable differences among Tor Browsers, so that Tor users remain indistinguishable from each other. In fact, *cross-origin fingerprinting unlinkability* is listed as a privacy requirement for the Tor Browser[14]. For this reason the Tor Browser is shipped with fixed settings that provide almost no browser properties that could be exploited to extract distinguishing features.

As described in Section 4, fonts are operating-system-dependent, and thus a good candidate attribute for distinguishing and recognizing users. To limit font-based fingerprinting, the Tor Browser caps the number of fonts that a page can request and load. However, for usability reasons, `@font-face` rules are exempted from these limits. Upon inspection of the Tor Browser source code, we discovered that the local fonts loaded by `@font-face` CSS rules are also exempted from the Tor Browser's font-per-document cap, and that it is possible to load an unlimited number of system fonts using the `local()` value of the `@font-face` rule's `src` descriptor.

Furthermore, if a font is not installed locally, it may be requested from the `src/url` property of the font-face rule. This is effectively communicating the lack of this font to the server without using JavaScript. Note also that one local font-face rule can be used to report the `status(not-found)` of more than one font by chaining font-face `local()` properties, for example:

```
@font-face { font-family: Font1;
             src: local("Font2"), local("Font3"),
                  url("Font1-2-3-NotFound.ttf");
           }
```

We immediately communicated the vulnerability to the Tor Bug Tracker and the issue is fixed in the upcoming (2.4) version with a patch that disables the use of the `local()` property[15].

6.2 Firegloves

Firegloves [3] is a proof-of-concept browser extension for Mozilla Firefox that was created for research purposes. In order to confuse fingerprinting scripts, Firegloves returns randomized values when queried for certain attributes, like the screen resolution, the platform on which the browser is running and the browser's vendor and version. Additionally, Firegloves limits the number of fonts that a single browser tab can load and reports false dimension values for the `offsetWidth` and `offsetHeight` properties of HTML elements to evade JavaScript-based font detection.

We evaluated the effectiveness of Firegloves' as a countermeasure to fingerprinting, and discovered several shortcomings. For instance, instead of relying on `offsetWidth` and `offsetHeight` values, we could easily use the width and the height of the rectangle object returned by `getBoundingClientRect` method, which returns the text's dimensions, even more precisely than the original methods[16]. This enabled us to detect the same list of fonts as we would without the Firegloves extension installed. Surprisingly, our probe for fonts was not limited by the claimed cap on the number of fonts per tab. This might be due to a bug, or to changes in the Firefox extension system that have been introduced after FireGloves, which is not currently being maintained, was first developed.

[14] `https://www.torproject.org/projects/torbrowser/design/#fingerprinting-linkability`

[15] `https://trac.torproject.org/projects/tor/ticket/8455#comment:3`

[16] `https://developer.mozilla.org/en-US/docs/DOM/element.offsetWidth`

Although Firegloves spoofs the browser's user-agent and platform to pretend to be a Mozilla Firefox version 6 running on a Windows operating system, the `navigator.oscpu` is left unmodified, revealing the true platform. Moreover, Firegloves did not remove any of the new methods introduced in later versions of Mozilla Firefox and available in the `navigator` object, such as `navigator.mozCameras` and `navigator.doNotTrack`. Finally, since Firegloves cannot change the APIs available to Flash, a Flash application can still discover the real operating system and the real screen resolution.

Overall, while Firegloves is trying to protect users from fingerprinting, its detectable presence on the users' browsing environments may actually make them more uniquely identifiable: since Firegloves is installed by only 1,750 users, its successful detection makes the user much more unique than if it was not present at all.

Our findings are in line with prior results showing that user-agent-spoofing extensions can be straightforwardly discovered and bypassed [18]. These findings illustrate the difficulty of effectively protecting users against fingerprinting, and indicate that counter-measures short of perfect may result in a net loss of privacy for their adopters – as their devices become more easily fingerprintable through these.

6.3 Do Not Track

The Do Not Track (DNT) HTTP header field allows users to signal their tracking preferences to websites. DNT is currently being standardized by the W3C under the name "Tracking Preference Expression" and it has already been adopted by most modern browsers[17].

We set the DNT header to 1 in the PhantomJS browser and visited the websites identified as performing fingerprinting in our previous experiments. For all of these pages, we obtained the same results with respect to the number of fonts probed and other browser properties accessed, suggesting that DNT preferences are ignored by fingerprinters.

7. DISCUSSION

7.1 Uses of Fingerprinting

Using FPDetective, we were able to identify companies that are engaging in what we call web based device fingerprinting. While it is not possible to infer the purposes for which fingerprinting is being put to use by these companies, we take a moment to reflect on their fingerprinting related practices.

The majority of the companies serving the fingerprinting scripts explicitly state on their websites, in press releases, and in various social media channels that they are successfully deploying (device) fingerprinting. In contrast, the websites that employ the services of these companies rarely disclose in their privacy policies that they are fingerprinting their users' devices, let alone mention that they are gathering the information that FPDetective revealed them to be collecting. In some cases, we detected fingerprinting scripts that were embedded in ad banners. It is unclear whether first parties serving these ad banners are aware of the existence of these embedded fingerprinting scripts.

[17]`http://www.w3.org/TR/2013/WD-tracking-dnt-20130430/`

Companies express that they deploy device fingerprinting in the context of a variety of web services. The spectrum of use cases include fraud detection, protection against account hijacking, anti-bot and anti-scraping services, enterprise security management, protection against DDOS attacks, real-time targeted marketing, campaign measurement, reaching customers across devices, and limiting number of access to services. While most companies will specialize either in 'fraud detection and web security' or 'marketing applications', MaxMind is an example of a company that uses their data collection to provide services for both uses. MaxMind also stands out with their very explicit documentation of their personal and non-personal data collection, their processing activities and their commitment to make their practices transparent.

Further material from companies describing the use cases suggest that the data models in the databases also vary. Fraud detection companies often speak of "device reputation databases" with profiles for "billions" of devices that are rich enough to provide "intelligence" to companies about the security risks of these devices. The variety in mentioned uses ranging from "adjusting security policies based on the device a person is using" to "identifying and blocking botnets that easily switch IP addresses" suggests that these are rich device-centered databases. On the other hand, marketing companies express that they are able to identify user-behavior across websites and devices, suggesting that they feed fingerprinting data into "customer"-centered database systems that are heavy on analytics, and can link different devices to a single user across websites.

In-house applications seem to be mainly concerned with whether the same user is using multiple devices to access the same service, or limiting the number of times a specific service is accessed, e.g., when filling out surveys. Such applications seem to limit data collection using fingerprinting to the given website and are less concerned with analytics and intelligence applications.

A perplexing case among in-house applications is that of Anonymizer Inc., a company that presents itself as "the global leader in online privacy, anonymity, and identity protection solutions for over 17 years."[18] The script is served from the domain privacytool.org (owned by Anonymizer Inc.), a site where users can test whether they are anonymous online. The privacytool.org site clearly explains that to perform the test a Java applet will run on the user's computer, describes the information that will be gathered, and explicitly states that *"Data obtained from the browser like lists of plug-ins or fonts can be used to identify your computer."*[19] Users must click a link placed below this information in order to run the applet.

We found, however, that fingerprinting scripts from privacytool.org are also present in the homepage of anonymizer.com, another site owned by Anonymizer Inc. that, paradoxically, offers anonymity as a service. The anonymizer.com privacy policy states: *"When you navigate our Web site, Anonymizer will gather certain information such as your Internet Protocol address, browser type, browser language, and the date and time of your visit. We may place a cookie on your computer [...]"* The policy includes further information about cookies but, in contrast to

[18]`https://www.anonymizer.com/company/`

[19]`http://privacytool.org/AnonymityChecker/index.jsp`

the privacytool.org notice, it does not mention at any point the execution of fingerprinting scripts, or that it collects information such as the list of installed fonts, DNS server information, or the real IP address if the user is connected through a proxy. Finally, note that while privacytool.org offers informed choice to its users, who may voluntarily execute the script, the fingerprinting scripts that run in the anonymizer.com homepage are invisible to users and run by default.

7.2 Visibility of Fingerprinting

The majority of web users have difficulties in grasping what cookies are, whether they are enabled, their threats to their privacy and how to manage them [14]. This situation is worse in the case of third-party and covert cookies, which have been found to essentially be invisible to end-users. Arguably, user perception of web based device fingerprinting is comparably, if not more, invisible to the users.

In all the cases we encountered, there were no visible effects of fingerprinting, and the users were not informed that they were being fingerprinted. Thus, the only way for users to discover that their devices are being fingerprinted is to manually examine the source of the page and all the embedded JavaScript and Flash objects.

In one distinct case, while verifying the results of FPDetective, we discovered that a company which sells fingerprinting products for anti-bot and anti-scraping services, was deleting the fingerprinting script from the page's DOM after the script had executed and collected the fingerprint. Thus, the only way to identify this fingerprinter is to breakpoint through the execution of JavaScript code and witness the loading and unloading of the fingerprinting code. This requires an in-depth understanding of how JavaScript is executed and the principles of debugging programs, which the vast majority of users are not likely to possess. Moreover, this anti-debugging technique is reminiscent of the techniques employed by JavaScript malware when trying to evade detection by analysts and high-interaction honeypots [10].

7.3 Is fingerprinting a matter of privacy?

Our findings suggest that this issue may require further technical and legal attention with respect to privacy. Yet, most of the companies whose fingerprinting activities were detected by FPDetective expressly distance their practices from any consequences they might have for people's privacy.

A number of companies argue that they do *not* collect PII (Personally Identifiable Information) in the process of distinguishing "the good, the bad and the ugly" on the web. While fingerprinting may not require PII, the use cases described by fingerprinting companies on their webpages suggest that they use device information to track, profile, and shape the future web experience of the tracked users (as well as bots). For example, MaxMind offers online retailers a service to check on their customers' fraud scores based on 31 "non-PII" attributes, including IP address, shipping address, non-salted hashes of email addresses and passwords, and credit card BIN number. The computation of the customers' score is based on things like the 'riskiness of the country of origin', 'proxy use', 'free webmail use', and 'bank checks'. These are matters closely related to privacy concerns expressed by users about uninformed monitoring of web usage, constraints on informational self-determination, and discrimination [21].

Further, by focusing on "device" identification and, especially in fraud detection cases, claiming that they are concerned only about "bots", companies express that tracking "persons" is not the object of their interest. In this worldview, fingerprinting is nothing more than (security) scripts collecting data based on socially invisible interactions that are irrelevant to individual privacy. Further, especially in the case of fraud detection, companies often argue that fingerprinting is implemented for the protection of the end-users' quality of service. These two framings, i.e., "fingerprinting is all about devices" and "we track these devices for user convenience", make it very difficult to demand a response to the privacy issues that may be raised with respect to device fingerprinting and the use of the databases populated using fingerprinting. As such fingerprinting practices proliferate, device IDs may come to "represent" users in databases, instead of PII. Hence, classical conceptions of PII may not be sufficient to grasp the social and ethical concerns associated fingerprinting and related databases. We hope that this paper, by virtue of making web based fingerprinting more visible, will contribute to better understanding what privacy issues may be at stake and to challenging the framing of web based device fingerprints as non-PII.

In the context of the US, it may be worth discussing whether a static list of attributes that count as PII is sufficient to draw a reasonable boundary on which "personal data" should be subject to protection. Device fingerprinting underlines that data is identifiable based on context; in other words, identifiability may result from processing seemingly non-identifiable information [22]. If we accept this argument, then attention needs to be paid to risks associated with: linking of the reputation and device fingerprint databases to individuals; undesirable and unacceptable uses of these datasets for determining "the good, the bad, and the ugly" of the web; the security of these datasets; and the opacity of fingerprinting practices to the general public, as well as to individual device owners.

It is also currently unclear whether there is a responsibility to inform the owners that their devices are being fingerprinted, and if so, who has the responsibility to inform the users. For example, the privacy policy of `articlesbase.com` explicitly indicates all the "non-personal information" that the site collects. However, in this rather detailed and readable list, the site does not state that they are fingerprinting the user's device or that they are probing fonts. One could argue, since the font probing scripts are not served by `articlesbase.com` but by `siteblackbox.com`, that it is the responsibility of the latter to inform the users. However, in their documentation of the articlesbase case [20], no references are made to fingerprinting of users and we were unable to locate a privacy policy on the website. Similar issues are likely to arise when it comes to honoring DNT preferences.

8. CONCLUSION

User tracking is becoming pervasive as advertisers and tracking companies seek to refine their targeting, detect fraud, or offer new services. While most of today's tracking is done through third-party cookies, prior research has shown that browser and system attributes can be used to uniquely identify devices through fingerprints. Even though these fingerprints are less accurate than stateful identifiers such as cookies, their main advantage is that device fingerprinting is harder to detect and to defend against.

In this paper we presented FPDetective, a fingerprinting-detection framework that identifies web based fingerprinters. Using FPDetective, we performed a large-scale crawl of the Internet's most popular websites, and showed that the adoption of fingerprinting is significantly higher than what previous research estimated. Among others, we identified large commercial companies involved in fingerprinting, a complete disregard towards the DNT header, and the use of anti-debugging techniques, most commonly associated with JavaScript malware. Moreover, we showed that dedicated fingerprinters can bypass existing privacy-protecting technologies.

Overall, our findings demonstrate that web fingerprinting is a real and growing issue, deserving the attention of both policymakers and the research community. We hope that our framework, which is freely available to other researchers and can easily be extended to conduct further studies, will contribute to addressing this issue by providing a means to shed light on web fingerprinting practices and techniques.

9. ACKNOWLEDGEMENTS

The authors would like thank the anonymous reviewers, Carmela Troncoso, Ashkan Soltani, Nessim Kisserli and Tom van Cutsem for their valuable comments; Vicenç Torra for enabling the collaboration; and Danny De Cock for his hardware support. For KU Leuven, this research was supported by the projects IWT SBO SPION, iMinds CoMobile, FWO G.0360.11N, FWO G.0686.11N, GOA TENSE (GOA/11/007), and EU FP7 NESSoS, WebSand and Strews; the B-CCENTRE; and the Research Fund KU Leuven. For IIIA-CSIC, this research was supported by the projects EU FP7 grant agreement number 262608, the Spanish MEC projects ARES (CONSOLIDER INGENIO 2010 CSD2007-00004), eAEGIS (TSI2007-65406-C03-02), and COPRIVACY (TIN2011-27076-C03-03). For NYU, this research was supported by the Intel Science and Technology Center - Social Computing. Marc Juarez was partially funded by the LLP Erasmus Programme of the Commission of the European Communities during his stay at KU Leuven.

10. REFERENCES

[1] Nmap - Free Security Scanner For Network Exploration & Security Audits. `http://www.nmap.org`.

[2] A. Barth. Blink: A rendering engine for the Chromium project. `http://blog.chromium.org/2013/04/blink-rendering-engine-for-chromium.html`.

[3] K. Boda. Firegloves. `http://fingerprint.pet-portal.eu/?menu=6`.

[4] A. Cortesi. mitmproxy: a man-in-the-middle proxy. `http://mitmproxy.org/`.

[5] R. Dingledine, N. Mathewson, and P. Syverson. Tor: The second-generation onion router. In *Proceedings of the 13th USENIX Security Symposium*, pages 303–320. USENIX, 2004.

[6] J. R. Douceur. The sybil attack. In *Peer-to-peer Systems*, pages 251–260. Springer, 2002.

[7] P. Eckersley. How Unique Is Your Browser? In *Proceedings of the 10th Privacy Enhancing Technologies Symposium (PETS)*, pages 1–17, 2010.

[8] D. Goldschlag, M. Reed, and P. Syverson. Hiding routing information. In *Information Hiding*, pages 137–150, 1996.

[9] D. Jang, R. Jhala, S. Lerner, and H. Shacham. An empirical study of privacy-violating information flows in JavaScript Web applications. In *Proceedings of CCS 2010*, pages 270–283, Oct. 2010.

[10] A. Kapravelos, M. Cova, C. Kruegel, and G. Vigna. Escape from monkey island: Evading high-interaction honeyclients. In *Proceedings of the 8th Conference on Detection of Intrusions and Malware & Vulnerability Assessment (DIMVA)*, pages 124–143, 2011.

[11] T. Kohno, A. Broido, and K. Claffy. Remote physical device fingerprinting. *Dependable and Secure Computing, IEEE Transactions on*, 2(2):93–108, 2005.

[12] J. R. Mayer. Any person... a pamphleteer. Senior Thesis, Stanford University, 2009.

[13] J. R. Mayer and J. C. Mitchell. Third-party web tracking: Policy and technology. In *Proceedings of the IEEE Symposium on Security and Privacy*, pages 413–427, 2012.

[14] A. D. Miyazaki. Online privacy and the disclosure of cookie use: Effects on consumer trust and anticipated patronage. *Journal of Public Policy & Marketing*, 27(1):19–33, 2008.

[15] K. Mowery, D. Bogenreif, S. Yilek, and H. Shacham. Fingerprinting information in JavaScript implementations. In H. Wang, editor, *Proceedings of W2SP 2011*. IEEE Computer Society, May 2011.

[16] K. Mowery and H. Shacham. Pixel perfect: Fingerprinting canvas in HTML5. In M. Fredrikson, editor, *Proceedings of W2SP 2012*. IEEE Computer Society, May 2012.

[17] M. Mulazzani, P. Reschl, M. Huber, M. Leithner, S. Schrittwieser, and E. Weippl. Fast and reliable browser identification with javascript engine fingerprinting. In *Web 2.0 Workshop on Security and Privacy (W2SP)*, May 2013.

[18] N. Nikiforakis, A. Kapravelos, W. Joosen, C. Kruegel, F. Piessens, and G. Vigna. Cookieless monster: Exploring the ecosystem of web-based device fingerprinting. In *Proceedings of the IEEE Symposium on Security and Privacy*, pages 541–555, 2013.

[19] L. Olejnik, C. Castelluccia, and A. Janc. Why Johnny Can't Browse in Peace: On the Uniqueness of Web Browsing History Patterns. In *the 5th workshop on Hot Topics in Privacy Enhancing Technologies (HOTPETS 2012)*.

[20] SiteBlackBox. Case studies: Articlesbase.

[21] B. Ur, P. G. Leon, L. F. Cranor, R. Shay, and Y. Wang. Smart, useful, scary, creepy: perceptions of online behavioral advertising. In *Proceedings of the Eighth Symposium on Usable Privacy and Security*, SOUPS '12, pages 4:1–4:15, New York, NY, USA, 2012. ACM.

[22] I. Van Der Ploeg. *Keys To Privacy. Translations of "the privacy problem" in Information Technologies*, pages 15–36. Maastricht: Shaker, 2005.

[23] T.-F. Yen, Y. Xie, F. Yu, R. P. Yu, and M. Abadi. Host fingerprinting and tracking on the web:privacy and security implications. In *Proceddings of the 19th*

Annual Network and Distributed System Security Symposium (NDSS), 2012.

[24] N. C. Zakas. How many users have JavaScript disabled? `http://developer.yahoo.com/blogs/ydn/many-users-javascript-disabled-14121.html`.

[25] M. Zalewski. p0f v3 (version 3.06b). `http://lcamtuf.coredump.cx/p0f3/`.

APPENDIX

A. LIST OF FINGERPRINTING URLS

Table 3 shows the location of each fingerprinting script discovered, separated by the respective fingerprinting companies.

B. ACTIONSCRIPT CALLS

The following list enumerates the ActionScript calls that FPDetective searches for in the decompiled Flash files.

- `enumerateFonts` (only with argument true)
- `getFontList`
- all `Capabilities` class properties and methods, including
  - `version`
  - `manufacturer`
  - `serverString`
  - `language`
  - `screenDPI`
  - `screenResolutionX`
  - `screenResolutionY`
- `getTimezoneOffset`
- `getLocal`
- `XMLSocket`
- `Math.min`, `Math.max`
- `ExternalInterface.call`
- `ExternalInterface.addCallback`
- `sendAndLoad`
- `URLLoader`
- `navigateToURL`
- `loadMovie`
- `createUID`
- `getUrl`
- `allowDomain`
- `allowInsecureDomain`
- `loadPolicyFile`
- `URLRequest`
- `LoadVars`
- `md5`, `sha256`, `sha384`, `sha512`

FingerPrinter	Script URL
BlueCava	`http://ds.bluecava.com/v50/AC/BCAC5.js`
Perferencement	`http://tags.master-perf-tools.com/V20test/tagv22.pkmin.js`
CoinBase	`https://coinbase.com/assets/application-773afba0b6ee06b45ba4363a99637610.js`
MaxMind	`http://device.maxmind.com/js/device.js`
Inside graph	`http://inside-graph.com/ig.js`
SiteBlackBox	(No fixed URL)
Analytics-engine	`http://s14.analytics-engine.net/detector/fp.js`
Myfreecams	`http://www.myfreecams.com/mfc2/lib/o-mfccore.js`
Mindshare Tech.	`pomegranate.js(Nofixeddomain)`
Cdn.net	`http://cdn-net.com/cc.js`
AFK Media	`http://gmyze.com/0.4.1.1/js/fingerprint.js`
Anonymizer	`https://www.privacytool.org/AnonymityChecker/js/fontdetect.js`
Analyticsengine	`http://dpp750yjcl65g.cloudfront.net/analyticsengine/util/fingerprint.compiled.js`
BBelements	`http://go.eu.bbelements.com/flash/bbnaut.swf`
Piano Media	`http://mp.pianomedia.eu/bucket/novosense.swf`
Bluecava	`http://lookup.bluecava.com/flash/guids[2|3].swf`
ThreatMetrix	`https://h.online-metrix.net/fp/fp.swf?org_id=...&session_id=...` (also served from other domains)
Alipay	`http://img.alipay.com/common/um/lsa.swf`
MEB	`http://meb.gov.tr/KZneA1akxW/502758.swf`

Table 3: URLs of Fingerprinting JavaScript and Flash Files

Addressing the Concerns of the Lacks* Family: Quantification of Kin Genomic Privacy

Mathias Humbert Erman Ayday Jean-Pierre Hubaux
Laboratory for Communications and Applications
EPFL, Lausanne, Switzerland
firstname.lastname@epfl.ch

Amalio Telenti
Institute of Microbiology
University Hospital of Lausanne
Lausanne, Switzerland
amalio.telenti@chuv.ch

ABSTRACT

The rapid progress in human-genome sequencing is leading to a high availability of genomic data. This data is notoriously very sensitive and stable in time. It is also highly correlated among relatives. A growing number of genomes are becoming accessible online (e.g., because of leakage, or after their posting on genome-sharing websites). What are then the implications for kin genomic privacy? We formalize the problem and detail an efficient reconstruction attack based on graphical models and belief propagation. With this approach, an attacker can infer the genomes of the relatives of an individual whose genome is observed, relying notably on Mendel's Laws and statistical relationships between the nucleotides (on the DNA sequence). Then, to quantify the level of genomic privacy as a result of the proposed inference attack, we discuss possible definitions of *genomic privacy* metrics. Genomic data reveals Mendelian diseases and the likelihood of developing degenerative diseases such as Alzheimer's. We also introduce the quantification of *health privacy*, specifically the measure of how well the predisposition to a disease is concealed from an attacker. We evaluate our approach on actual genomic data from a pedigree and show the threat extent by combining data gathered from a genome-sharing website and from an online social network.

Categories and Subject Descriptors

C.2.0 [**Computer-Communication Networks**]: General—*Security and protection*; J.3 [**Life and Medical Sciences**]: *Biology and genetics*; K.4.1 [**Computer and Society**]: Public Policy Issues—*Privacy*

Keywords

Genomic Privacy; Inference Algorithms; Metrics; Kinship

*The family of Henrietta Lacks (August 1, 1920 - October 4, 1951), whose DNA was sequenced and published online without the consent of her family.

CCS'13, November 4–8, 2013, Berlin, Germany.
Copyright 2013 ACM 978-1-4503-2477-9/13/11 ...$15.00.
http://dx.doi.org/10.1145/2508859.2516707.

1. INTRODUCTION

With the help of rapidly developing technology, DNA sequencing is becoming less expensive. As a consequence, the research in genomics has gained speed in paving the way to personalized (genomic) medicine, and geneticists need large collections of human genomes to further increase this speed. Furthermore, individuals are using their genomes to learn about their (genetic) predispositions to diseases, their ancestries, and even their (genetic) compatibilities with potential partners. This trend has also caused the launch of health-related websites and online social networks (OSNs), in which individuals share their genomic data (e.g., OpenSNP [1] or 23andMe [2]). Thus, already today, thousands of genomes are available online.

Even though most of the genomes on the Internet are anonymized, it is possible to find genomes with the identifiers of their owners (e.g., OpenSNP [1]). Furthermore, it has been shown that anonymization is not sufficient for protecting the real identities of the genome donors [29,47]. Once the owner of a genome is identified, he is faced with the risk of discrimination (e.g., by employers or insurance companies) [9]. Some believe that they have nothing to hide about their genetic structure, hence they might decide to give full consent for the publication of their genomes on the Internet to help genomic research. However, our DNA sequences are highly correlated to our relatives' sequences. The DNA sequences between two random human beings are 99.9% similar, and this value is even higher for closely related people. Consequently, somebody revealing his genome does not only damage his own genomic privacy, but also puts his relatives' privacy at risk [46]. Moreover, currently, a person does not need consent from his relatives to share his genome online. This is precisely where the interesting part of the story begins: *kin genomic privacy.*

A recent New York Times' article [3] reports the controversy about sequencing and publishing, without the permission of her family, the genome of Henrietta Lacks (who died in 1951). On the one hand, the family members think that her genome is private family information and it should not be published without the consent of the family. On the other hand, some scientists argued that the genomes of current family members have changed so much over time (due to gene mixing during reproduction), that nothing accurate could be told about the genomes of current family members by using Henrietta Lacks' genome. As we will also show in this work, they are wrong. Minutes after Henrietta Lacks' genome was uploaded to a public website called SNPedia, researchers produced a report full of personal information about Henrietta Lacks. Later, the genome was taken offline, but it had already been downloaded by several people, hence both her and (partially) the Lacks family's genomic privacy was already lost.

Unfortunately, the Lacks, even though possibly the most publicized family facing this problem, are not the only family facing this threat. As we mentioned before, the genomes of thousands of individuals are available online. Once the identity of a genome donor is known, an attacker can learn about his relatives (or his family tree) by using an auxiliary side channel, such as an OSN, and infer significant information about the DNA sequences of the donor's relatives. We will show the feasibility of such an attack and evaluate the privacy risks by using publicly available data on the Web.

Although the researchers took Henrietta Lacks' genome offline from SNPedia, other databases continue to publish portions of her genomic data. Publishing only portions of a genome does not, however, completely hide the unpublished portions; even if a person reveals only a part of his genome, other parts can be inferred using the statistical relationships between the nucleotides in his DNA. For example, James Watson, co-discoverer of DNA, made his whole DNA sequence publicly available, with the exception of one gene known as Apolipoprotein E (ApoE), one of the strongest predictors for the development of Alzheimer's disease. However, later it was shown that the correlation (called *linkage disequilibrium* by geneticists) between one or multiple polymorphisms and ApoE can be used to predict the ApoE status [40]. Thus, an attacker can also use these statistical relationships (which are publicly available) to infer the DNA sequences of a donor's family members, even if the donor shares only part of his genome. It is important to note that these privacy threats not only jeopardize kin genomic privacy, but, if not properly addressed, these issues could also hamper genomic research due to untimely fear of potential misuse of genomic information.

In this work, we evaluate the genomic privacy of an individual threatened by his relatives revealing their genomes. Focusing on the most common genetic variant in human population, single nucleotide polymorphism (SNP), and considering the statistical relationships between the SNPs on the DNA sequence, we quantify the loss in genomic privacy of individuals when one or more of their family members' genomes are (either partially or fully) revealed. To achieve this goal, first, we design a reconstruction attack based on a well-known statistical inference technique. The computational complexity of the traditional ways of realizing such inference grows exponentially with the number of SNPs (which is on the order of tens of millions) and relatives. Therefore, in order to infer the values of the unknown SNPs in linear complexity, we represent the SNPs, family relationships and the statistical relationships between SNPs on a factor graph and use the belief propagation algorithm [37, 41] for inference. Then, using various metrics, we quantify the genomic privacy of individuals and show the decrease in their level of genomic privacy caused by the published genomes of their family members. We also quantify the health privacy of the individuals by considering their (genetic) predisposition to certain serious diseases. We evaluate the proposed inference attack and show its efficiency and accuracy by using real genomic data of a pedigree. More importantly, by using genomic data and pedigree information we collected from a public genome-sharing website and an OSN, we show that the proposed inference attack threatens not only the Lacks family, but also many other families.

The rest of the paper is organized as follows. In Section 2, we give a brief background on genomics and belief propagation. In Section 3, we present the proposed framework in detail. In Section 4, we evaluate the performance of the proposed inference attack using different metrics. In Section 5, we show how the proposed inference attack threatens the genomic and health privacy of several families gathered from OSNs. In Section 6, we summarize the related work on genetic inference and genomic-privacy protection. Finally, we conclude the paper in Section 7.

2. BACKGROUND

In this section, we briefly introduce the relevant genetic principles, as well as the concept of belief propagation.

2.1 Genomics 101

DNA is a double-helix structure that consists of two complementary polymer chains. Genetic information is encoded on the DNA as a sequence of nucleotides (A,T,G,C) and a human DNA includes around 3 billion nucleotide pairs. With the decreasing cost of DNA sequencing, genomic data is currently being used mainly in the following two areas: (i) clinical diagnostics, for personalized genomic medicine and genetic research (e.g., genome-wide association studies[1]), and (ii) direct-to-consumer genomics, for genetic risk estimation of various diseases or for recreational activities such as ancestry search. In the following, we briefly introduce some concepts, which we use throughout this paper, about the human genome and reproduction.

2.1.1 Single Nucleotide Polymorphism

As already mentioned, human beings have 99.9% of their DNA in common. Thus, there is no need to focus on the whole DNA but rather on the most important variants. Single nucleotide polymorphism (SNP) is the most common DNA variation in human population. A SNP occurs when a nucleotide (at a specific position on the DNA) varies between individuals of a given population (as illustrated in Fig. 1). There are approximately 50 million SNP positions in human population [4]. Recent discoveries show that the susceptibility of an individual to several diseases can be computed from his SNPs [5, 33]. For example, it has been reported that two particular SNPs (rs7412 and rs429358) on the Apolipoprotein E (ApoE) gene indicate an (increased) risk for Alzheimer's disease. SNPs carry privacy-sensitive information about individuals' health, hence we will quantify health privacy focusing on individuals' published (or inferred) SNPs and the diseases they reveal.

In general, two different nucleotides (called alleles) are observed at a given SNP position: (i) the major allele is the most frequently observed nucleotide, and (ii) the minor allele is the rare nucleotide.[2] From here on, we represent the major allele as B for a SNP position, and the minor allele as b (where both B and b are in $\{A, T, G, C\}$).

Furthermore, each SNP position contains two nucleotides (one inherited from the mother and one from the father, as we will discuss next). Thus, the content of a SNP position

[1]Examination of many genetic variants in different individuals to determine if any variant is associated with a trait.

[2]The two alleles for the SNP position in Fig. 1 are C and T.

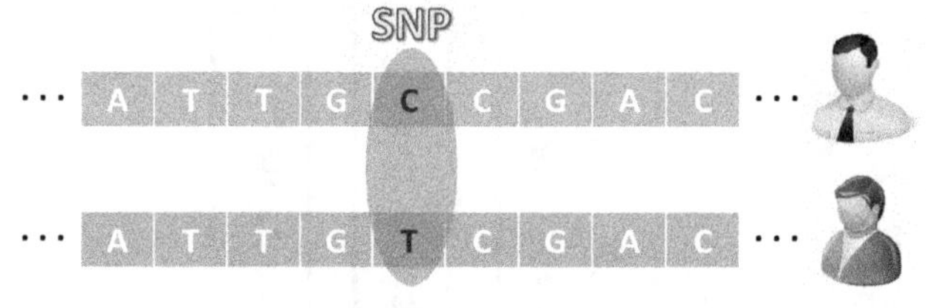

Figure 1: Single nucleotide polymorphism (SNP) with alleles C and T illustrated on a single string of two different individuals' DNAs.

		Father (*F*)		
		BB	Bb	bb
Mother (*M*)	BB	(1,0,0)	(0.5,0.5,0)	(0,1,0)
	Bb	(0.5,0.5,0)	(0.25,0.5,0.25)	(0,0.5,0.5)
	bb	(0,1,0)	(0,0.5,0.5)	(0,0,1)

Table 1: Mendelian inheritance probabilities for a SNP j, given different genotypes for the parents. The probabilities of the child's genotype is represented in parentheses. Each table entry represents $(\Pr(x_j^C = BB|x_j^M, x_j^F), \Pr(x_j^C = Bb|x_j^M, x_j^F), \Pr(x_j^C = bb|x_j^M, x_j^F))$.

can be in one of the following states: (i) BB (*homozygous-major* genotype), if an individual receives the same major allele from both parents; (ii) Bb (*heterozygous* genotype), if he receives a different allele from each parent (one minor and one major); or (iii) bb (*homozygous-minor* genotype), if he inherits the same minor allele from both parents. We represent the content of a SNP position as x_j^i for SNP j at individual i, where $x_j^i \subset \{BB, Bb, bb\}$. For simplicity of presentation, in the rest of the paper, we denote BB as 0, Bb as 1, and bb as 2 (i.e., $x_j^i \in \{0, 1, 2\}$). Finally, each SNP i is assigned a minor allele frequency (MAF), p_i^b, which represents the frequency at which the minor allele (b) of the corresponding SNP occurs in a given population (typically, $0 < p_i^b < 0.5$).

2.1.2 Reproduction

Mendel's First Law states that alleles are passed independently from parents to children for different meioses (the process of cell division necessary for reproduction). For each SNP position, a child inherits one allele from his mother and one from his father. Each allele of a parent is inherited by a child with equal probability of 0.5. Let $\mathcal{F}_R(x_j^M, x_j^F, x_j^C)$ be the function modeling the Mendelian inheritance for a SNP j, where (M, F, C) represent mother, father, and child, respectively. We illustrate the Mendelian inheritance probabilities for a SNP j in Table 1.

Based on $\mathcal{F}_R(x_j^M, x_j^F, x_j^C)$, we can say that, given both parents' genomes, a child's genome is conditionally independent of all other ancestors' genomes.

2.1.3 Linkage Disequilibrium

As we discussed before, DNA sequences are highly correlated, leading to interdependent privacy risks. Linkage disequilibrium (LD) [24] is a correlation that appears between any pair of SNP positions in the whole genome due to the population's genetic history. Because of LD, the content of a SNP position can be inferred from the contents of other SNP positions. The strength of the LD between two SNP positions is usually represented by r^2 (or D'), where $r^2 = 1$ represents the strongest LD relationship.

2.2 Belief Propagation

Belief propagation [37, 41] is a message-passing algorithm for performing inference on graphical models (Bayesian networks, Markov random fields). It is typically used to compute marginal distributions of unobserved variables conditioned on observed ones. Computing marginal distributions is hard in general as it might require summing over an exponentially large number of terms. The belief propagation algorithm can be described in terms of operations on a factor graph, a graphical model that is represented as a bipartite graph. One of the two disjoint sets of the factor graph's vertices represents the (random) variables of interest, and the second set represents the functions that factor the joint probability distribution (or global function) based on the dependences between variables. An edge connects a variable node to a factor node if and only if the variable is an argument of the function corresponding to the factor node. The marginal distribution of an unobserved variable can be exactly computed by using the belief propagation algorithm if the factor graph has no cycles. However, the algorithm is still well-defined and often gives good approximate results for factor graphs with cycles. Belief propagation is commonly used in artificial intelligence and information theory. It has demonstrated empirical success in numerous applications including LDPC codes [42], reputation management [11, 12], and recommender systems [10].

3. THE PROPOSED FRAMEWORK

In this section, we formalize our approach and present the different components that will allow us to quantify kin genomic privacy. Fig. 2 gives an overview of the framework.

In a nutshell, the goal of the adversary is to infer some *targeted SNPs* of a member (or multiple members) of a *targeted family*. We define $\mathbf{F}$ to be the set of family members in the targeted family (whose family tree, showing the familial connections between the members, is denoted as $\mathcal{G}_\mathbf{F}$) and $\mathbf{S}$ to be the set of SNP IDs (i.e., positions on the DNA sequence), where $|\mathbf{F}| = n$ and $|\mathbf{S}| = m$. Note that the SNP IDs are the same for all the members of the family. We also let x_j^i be the value of SNP j ($j \in \mathbf{S}$) for individual i ($i \in \mathbf{F}$), where $x_j^i \in \{0, 1, 2\}$ (as introduced in Section 2.1). Furthermore, $\mathbf{X}^i = \{x_j^i : j \in \mathbf{S}, i \in \mathbf{F}\}$ represents the set of SNPs for individual i. We let $\mathbb{X}$ be the $n \times m$ matrix that stores the values of the SNPs of all family members. Some entries of $\mathbb{X}$ might be known by the adversary (the observed genomic data of one or more family members) and others might be unknown. We denote the set of SNPs from $\mathbb{X}$ whose values are unknown as $\mathbb{X}_\mathrm{U}$, and the set of SNPs from $\mathbb{X}$ whose values are known (by the adversary) as $\mathbb{X}_\mathrm{K}$.

$\mathcal{F}_R(x_j^M, x_j^F, x_j^C)$ is the function representing the Mendelian inheritance probabilities (in Table 1), where (M, F, C) represent mother, father, and child, respectively. The $m \times m$ matrix $\mathbb{L}$ represents the pairwise linkage disequilibrium (LD) between the SNPs in $\mathbf{S}$, that can be expressed by r^2 and

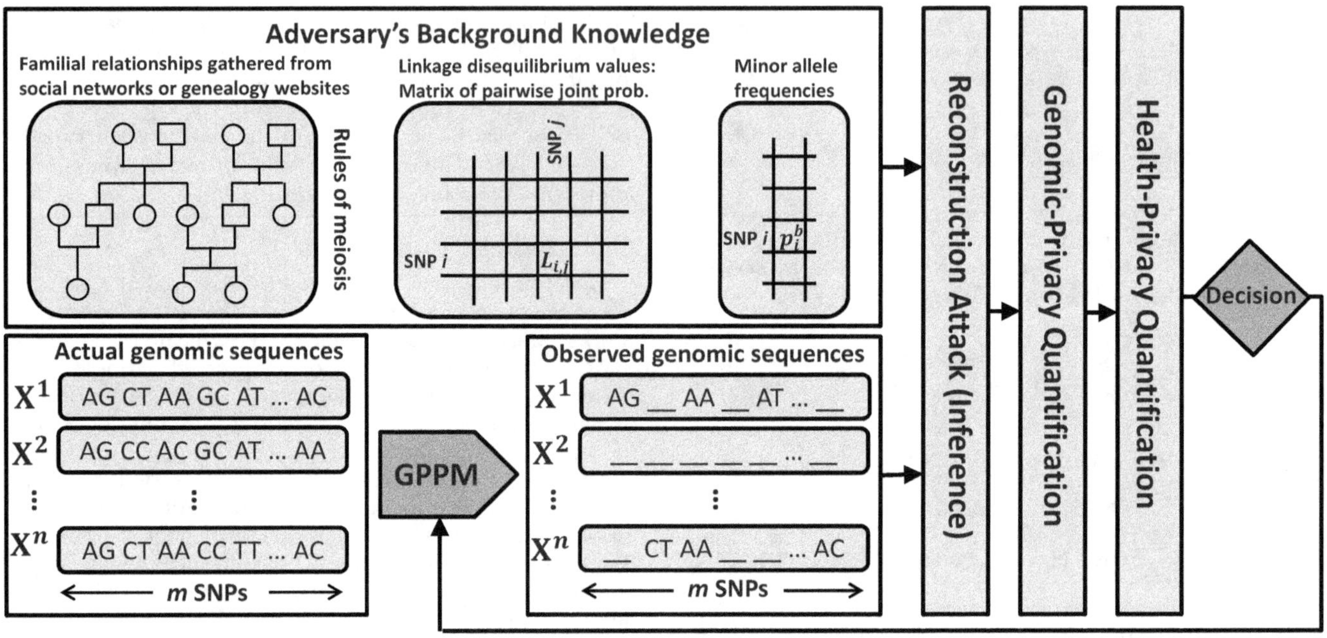

Figure 2: Overview of the proposed framework to quantify kin genomic privacy. Each vector $\mathbf{X}^i$ ($i \in \{1, \ldots, n\}$) includes the set of SNPs for an individual in the targeted family. Furthermore, each letter pair in $\mathbf{X}^i$ represents a SNP x_j^i; and for simplicity, each SNP x_j^i can be represented using $\{BB, Bb, bb\}$ (or $\{0, 1, 2\}$), as discussed in Section 2.1.1. Once the health privacy is quantified, the family should ideally decide whether to reveal less or more of their genomic information through the genomic-privacy preserving mechanism (GPPM).

D'; $\mathbb{L}_{i,j}$ refers to the matrix entry at row i and column j. $\mathbb{L}_{i,j} > 0$ if i and j are in LD, and $\mathbb{L}_{i,j} = 0$ if these two SNPs are independent (i.e., there is no LD between them). $\mathbf{P} = \{p_i^b : i \in \mathbf{S}\}$ represents the set of minor allele probabilities (or MAF) of the SNPs in $\mathbf{S}$. Finally, note that a joint probability $p(x_i, x_j)$ can be derived from $\mathbb{L}_{i,j}$, p_i^b, and p_j^b.

The adversary carries out a reconstruction attack to infer $\mathbb{X}_{\text{U}}$ by relying on his background knowledge, $\mathcal{F}_R(x_j^M, x_j^F, x_j^C)$, $\mathbb{L}$, $\mathbf{P}$, and on his observation $\mathbb{X}_{\text{K}}$. Once the targeted SNPs are inferred by the adversary, we evaluate genomic and health privacy of the family members based on the adversary's success and his certainty about the targeted SNPs and the diseases they reveal. Finally, we discuss some ideas to preserve the individuals' genomic and health privacy.

3.1 Adversary Model

An adversary is defined by his objective(s), attack(s), and knowledge. The objective of the adversary is to compute the values of the targeted SNPs for one or more members of a targeted family by using (i) the available genomic data of one or more family members, (ii) the familial relationships between the family members, (iii) the rules of reproduction (in Section 2.1.2), (iv) the minor allele frequencies (MAFs) of the nucleotides, and (v) the population LD values between the SNPs. We note that (i) and (ii) can be gathered online from genome-sharing websites and OSNs, and (iii), (iv), and (v) are publicly known information. Note that, in the future, the increasing possibility to accurately sequence, and to impute the actual haplotypes carried by an individual in each of the copies of the diploid genome will allow a more accurate inference of relatives' genotype than relying on population LD patterns only.

Various attacks can be launched, depending on the adversary's interest. The adversary might want to infer one particular SNP of a specific individual (targeted-SNP-targeted-relative attack) or one particular SNP of multiple relatives in the targeted family (targeted-SNP-multiple-relatives attack) by observing one or more other relatives' SNP at the same position. Furthermore, the adversary might also want to infer multiple SNPs of the same individual (multiple-SNP-targeted-relative attack) or multiple SNPs of multiple family members (multiple-SNP-multiple-relatives attack) by observing SNPs at various positions of different relatives. In this paper, we propose an algorithm that implements the latter attack, from which any other attacks can be carried out. We formulate this attack as a statistical inference problem.

3.2 Inference Attack

We formulate the reconstruction attack (on determining the values of the targeted SNPs) as finding the marginal probability distributions of unknown variables $\mathbb{X}_{\text{U}}$, given the known values in $\mathbb{X}_{\text{K}}$, familial relationships, and the publicly available statistical information. We represent the marginal distribution of a SNP j for an individual i as $p(x_j^i|\mathbb{X}_{\text{K}})$.

These marginal probability distributions could traditionally be extracted from $p(\mathbb{X}_{\text{U}}|\mathbb{X}_{\text{K}}, \mathcal{F}_R(x_j^M, x_j^F, x_j^C), \mathbb{L}, \mathcal{G}_{\mathbf{F}}, \mathbf{P})$, which is the joint probability distribution function of the variables in $\mathbb{X}_{\text{U}}$, given the available side information and the observed SNPs. Then, clearly, each marginal probability distribution could be obtained as follows:

$$p(x_j^i|\mathbb{X}_{\text{K}}) = \sum_{\mathbb{X}_{\text{U}} \setminus \{x_j^i\}} p(\mathbb{X}_{\text{U}}|\mathbb{X}_{\text{K}}, \mathcal{F}_R(x_j^M, x_j^F, x_j^C), \mathbb{L}, \mathcal{G}_{\mathbf{F}}, \mathbf{P}), \tag{1}$$

where the notation $\mathbb{X}_U \backslash \{x_j^i\}$ implies all variables in $\mathbb{X}_U$ except x_j^i. However, the number of terms in (1) grows exponentially with the number of variables, making the computation infeasible considering the scale of the human genome (which includes tens of million of SNPs). In the worst case, the computation of the marginal probabilities has a complexity of $O(3^{nm})$. Thus, we propose to factorize the joint probability distribution function into products of simpler local functions, each of which depends on a subset of variables. These local functions represent the conditional dependences (due to LD and reproduction) between the different variables in $\mathbb{X}$. Then, by running the belief propagation algorithm on a factor graph, we can compute the marginal probability distributions in linear complexity (with respect to nm).

A factor graph is a bipartite graph containing two sets of nodes (corresponding to variables and factors) and edges connecting these two sets. Following [37], we form a factor graph by setting a variable node for each SNP x_j^i ($j \in \mathbf{S}$ and $i \in \mathbf{F}$). We use two types of factor nodes: (i) *familial factor node*, representing the familial relationships and reproduction, and (ii) *LD factor node*, representing the LD relationships between the SNPs. We summarize the connections between the variable and factor nodes below (Fig. 3):

- Each variable node x_j^i has its familial factor node f_j^i and they are connected. Furthermore, x_j^k ($k \neq i$) is also connected to f_j^i if k is the mother or father of i (in $\mathcal{G}_\mathbf{F}$). Thus, the maximum degree of a familial factor node is 3.
- Variable nodes x_j^i and x_m^i are connected to a LD factor node $g_{j,m}^i$ if SNP j is in LD with SNP m. Since the LD relationships are pairwise between the SNPs, the degree of a LD factor node is always 2.

Given the conditional dependences given by reproduction and LD, the global distribution $p(\mathbb{X}_U|\mathbb{X}_K, \mathcal{F}_R(x_j^M, x_j^F, x_j^C), \mathbb{L}, \mathcal{G}_\mathbf{F}, \mathbf{P})$ can be factorized into products of several local functions, each having a subset of variables from $\mathbb{X}$ as arguments:

$$p(\mathbb{X}_U|\mathbb{X}_K, \mathcal{F}_R(x_j^M, x_j^F, x_j^C), \mathbb{L}, \mathcal{G}_\mathbf{F}, \mathbf{P}) = \frac{1}{Z}\Big[\prod_{i \in \mathbf{F}}\prod_{j \in \mathbf{S}} f_j^i(x_j^i, \Theta(x_j^i), \mathcal{F}_R(x_j^M, x_j^F, x_j^C), \mathbf{P})\Big] \times \Big[\prod_{i \in \mathbf{F}} \prod_{\substack{(j,m) \text{ s.t.} \\ \mathbb{L}_{j,m} \neq 0}} g_{j,m}^i(x_j^i, x_m^i, \mathbb{L}_{j,m})\Big], \quad (2)$$

where Z is the normalization constant, and $\Theta(x_j^i)$ is the set of values of SNP j for the mother and father of i (in $\mathcal{G}_\mathbf{F}$).

Next, we introduce the messages between the factor and the variable nodes to compute the marginal probability distributions using belief propagation. We denote the messages from the variable nodes to the factor nodes as μ. We also denote the messages from familial factor nodes to variable nodes as λ, and from LD factor nodes to variable nodes as β. Let $\mathbb{X}^{(\nu)} = \{x_j^{i(\nu)} : j \in \mathbf{S}, i \in \mathbf{F}\}$ be the collection of variables representing the values of the variable nodes at the iteration ν of the algorithm. The message $\mu_{i \to k}^{(\nu)}(x_j^{i(\nu)})$ denotes the probability of $x_j^{i(\nu)} = \ell$ ($\ell \in \{0,1,2\}$), at the νth iteration. Furthermore, $\lambda_{k \to i}^{(\nu)}(x_j^{i(\nu)})$ denotes the probability that $x_j^{i(\nu)} = \ell$, for $\ell \in \{0,1,2\}$, at the νth iteration given $\Theta(x_j^i)$, $\mathcal{F}_R(x_j^M, x_j^F, x_j^C)$, and $\mathbf{P}$. Finally, $\beta_{k \to i}^{(\nu)}(x_j^{i(\nu)})$ denotes the probability that $x_j^{i(\nu)} = \ell$, for $\ell \in \{0,1,2\}$, at the νth iteration given the LD relationships between the SNPs.

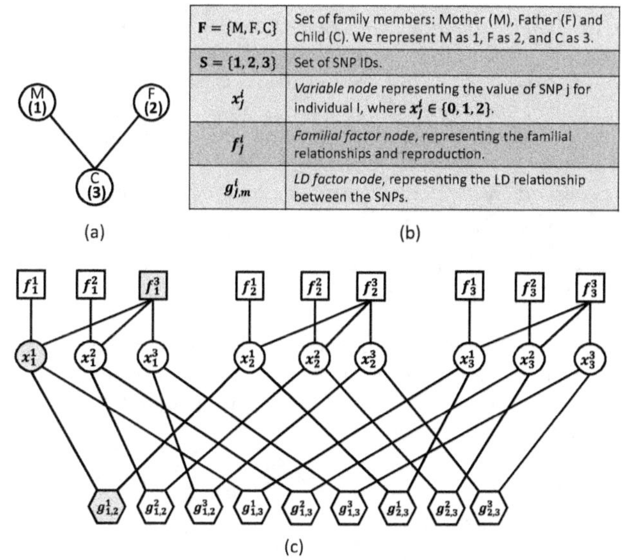

Figure 3: The factor graph representation of a trio (mother, father, child) using 3 SNPs. (a) $\mathcal{G}_\mathbf{F}$, showing the familial connections among the trio. (b) descriptions of the notations in the factor graph. (c) factor graph representation of the trio using SNPs in $\mathbf{S} = \{1,2,3\}$. The message passing is described on the nodes (x_1^1, f_1^3, and $g_{1,2}^1$) highlighted in the graph.

For the clarity of presentation, we choose a simple family tree consisting of a trio (i.e., mother, father, and child) in Fig 3(a), and 3 SNPs (i.e., $|\mathbf{F}| = 3$ and $|\mathbf{S}| = 3$). In Fig. 3(c), we show how the trio and the SNPs are represented on a factor graph, where $i = 1$ represents the mother, $i = 2$ represents the father, and $i = 3$ represents the child. Furthermore, the 3 SNPs are represented as $j = 1$, $j = 2$, and $j = 3$, respectively. We describe the message exchange between the variable node representing the first SNP of the mother (x_1^1), the familial factor node of the child (f_1^3), and the LD factor node $g_{1,2}^1$. The belief propagation algorithm iteratively exchanges messages between the factor and the variable nodes in Fig. 3(c), updating the beliefs on the values of the targeted SNPs (in $\mathbb{X}_U$) at each iteration, until convergence. We denote the variable and factor nodes x_1^1, f_1^3, and $g_{1,2}^1$ with the letters i, k, and z, respectively.

The variable nodes generate their messages (μ) and send to their neighbors. Variable node i forms $\mu_{i \to k}^{(\nu)}(x_1^{1(\nu)})$ by multiplying all information it receives from its neighbors excluding the familial factor node k.[3] Hence, the message from variable node i to the familial factor node k at the νth iteration is given by

$$\mu_{i \to k}^{(\nu)}(x_1^{1(\nu)}) = \frac{1}{Z} \times \prod_{w \in (\sim k)} \lambda_{w \to i}^{(\nu-1)}(x_1^{1(\nu-1)}) \times \prod_{y \in \{z, g_{1,3}^1\}} \beta_{y \to i}^{(\nu-1)}(x_1^{1(\nu-1)}), \quad (3)$$

[3] The message $\mu_{i \to z}^{(\nu)}(x_1^{1(\nu)})$ from the variable node i LD factor node z is constructed similarly.

where Z is a normalization constant, and the notation ($\sim k$) means all familial factor node neighbors of the variable node i, except k. This computation is repeated for every neighbor of each variable node. It is important to note that the message in (3) is valid if the value of x_1^1 is unknown to the adversary (i.e., $x_1^1 \in \mathbb{X}_\mathrm{U}$). However, the value of x_1^1 can also be observed by the adversary (i.e., $x_1^1 \in \mathbb{X}_\mathrm{K}$). Thus, if $x_1^1 \in \mathbb{X}_\mathrm{K}$ and $x_1^1 = \rho$ ($\rho \in \{0,1,2\}$), then $\mu_{i\to k}^{(\nu)}(x_1^{1(\nu)} = \rho) = 1$ and $\mu_{i\to k}^{(\nu)}(x_1^{1(\nu)}) = 0$ for other potential values of x_1^1 (regardless of the values of the messages received by the variable node i from its neighbors).

Next, the factor nodes generate their messages. The message from the familial factor node k to the variable node i at the νth iteration is formed using the principles of belief propagation as

$$\lambda_{k\to i}^{(\nu)}(x_1^{1(\nu)}) = \sum_{\{x_1^2, x_1^3\}} f_1^3(x_1^1, \Theta(x_1^1), \mathcal{F}_R(x_j^M, x_j^F, x_j^C), \mathbf{P}) \prod_{y\in\{x_1^2, x_1^3\}} \mu_{y\to k}^{(\nu)}(x_1^{1(\nu)}). \quad (4)$$

Note that $f_1^3(x_1^1, \Theta(x_1^1), \mathcal{F}_R(x_j^M, x_j^F, x_j^C), \mathbf{P}) \propto p(x_1^1|\Theta(x_1^1), \mathcal{F}_R(x_j^M, x_j^F, x_j^C), \mathbf{P})$, and this probability is computed using Table 1. Furthermore, if the degree of the familial factor node is 1 for a particular SNP, then the local function corresponding to the familial factor node only depends on the MAF of the corresponding SNP. For example, the degree of f_1^1 (in Fig. 3(c)) is 1, hence $f_1^1(x_1^1, \Theta(x_1^1), \mathcal{F}_R(x_j^M, x_j^F, x_j^C), \mathbf{P}) \propto p(x_1^1|p_1^b)$. The above computation must be performed for every neighbor of each familial factor node.

Similarly, the message from the LD factor node z to the variable node i at the νth iteration is formed as

$$\beta_{z\to i}^{(\nu)}(x_1^{1(\nu)}) = \sum_{x_2^1} g_{1,2}^1(x_1^1, x_2^1, \mathbb{L}_{1,2}) \prod_{y\in\{x_2^1\}} \mu_{y\to k}^{(\nu)}(x_1^{1(\nu)}). \quad (5)$$

As before, this computation is performed for every neighbor of each LD factor node. We further note that $g_{1,2}^1(x_1^1, x_2^1, \mathbb{L}_{1,2}) \propto p(x_1^1, x_2^1)$, which is derived from $\mathbb{L}_{1,2}$, p_1^b, and p_2^b. The algorithm proceeds to the next iteration in the same way as the νth iteration.

The algorithm starts at the variable nodes. Thus, at the first iteration of the algorithm (i.e., $\nu = 1$), the variable node i sends messages to its neighboring factor nodes based on the following rules: (i) If the value of x_1^1 is unknown to the adversary ($x_1^1 \in \mathbb{X}_\mathrm{U}$), $\mu_{i\to k}^{(1)}(x_1^{1(1)}) = 1$ for all potential values of x_1^1 and, (ii) if the value of x_1^1 is known to the adversary ($x_1^1 \in \mathbb{X}_\mathrm{K}$) and $x_1^1 = \rho$ ($\rho \in \{0,1,2\}$), $\mu_{i\to k}^{(1)}(x_1^{1(1)} = \rho) = 1$ and $\mu_{i\to k}^{(1)}(x_1^{1(1)}) = 0$ for other potential values of x_1^1. The iterations stop when all variables in $\mathbb{X}_\mathrm{U}$ have converged. The marginal probability of each variable in $\mathbb{X}_\mathrm{U}$ is given by multiplying all the incoming messages at each variable node.

3.3 Computational Complexity

The computational complexity of the proposed inference attack is proportional to the number of factor nodes. In our setting, there are nm familial factor nodes and a maximum of $nm(m-1)/2$ LD factor nodes. Hence, the worst-case computational complexity per iteration is $\mathcal{O}(nm^2)$. However, as each SNP is in LD with a limited number of other SNPs, the matrix $\mathbb{L}$ is sparse and the number of LD factor nodes grows with m rather than with $m(m-1)/2$, especially if we focus on SNPs in strong LD only. Thus, the average computational complexity per iteration is $\mathcal{O}(nm)$. Based on our experiments, we can state that the number of iterations before convergence is a small constant, between 10 and 15. Note finally that this complexity can be further reduced by using similar techniques developed for message-passing decoding of LDPC codes (e.g., working in log-domain [20]).

3.4 Privacy Metrics

A crucial step towards protecting kin genomic privacy is to quantify the privacy loss induced by the release of genomic information. Through the inference attack, the adversary infers the targeted SNPs (in $\mathbb{X}_\mathrm{U}$) belonging to the members of a targeted family by using his background knowledge and observed genomic data (of the family members). The inferred information can be expressed as the posterior distribution $p(\mathbb{X}_\mathrm{U}|\mathbb{X}_\mathrm{K}, \mathcal{F}_R(x_j^M, x_j^F, x_j^C), \mathbb{L}, \mathcal{G}_\mathbf{F}, \mathbf{P})$. Moreover, each posterior marginal probability distribution is represented as $p(x_j^i|\mathbb{X}_\mathrm{K})$, for all $i \in \mathbf{F}, j \in \mathbf{S}$. We propose to quantify kin genomic privacy using the following metrics: expected estimation error (incorrectness) and uncertainty.[4]

Correctness was already proposed in the context of location privacy [45]. In our scenario, correctness quantifies the adversary's success in inferring the targeted SNPs. That is, it quantifies the expected distance between the adversary's estimate on the value of a SNP, x_j^i ($x_j^i \in \mathbb{X}_\mathrm{U}$) and the true value of the corresponding SNP, $\hat{x_j^i}$. This distance can be expressed as the expected estimation error as follows:

$$E_j^i = \sum_{x_j^i\in\{0,1,2\}} p(x_j^i|\mathbb{X}_\mathrm{K})||x_j^i - \hat{x_j^i}||. \quad (6)$$

Privacy can also be represented as the adversary's *uncertainty* [22, 43], that is the ambiguity of $p(x_j^i|\mathbb{X}_\mathrm{K})$. This uncertainty is generally considered to be maximum if the posterior distribution is uniform. This definition of uncertainty can be quantified as the (normalized) entropy of $p(x_j^i|\mathbb{X}_\mathrm{K})$ as follows:

$$H_j^i = \frac{-\sum_{x_j^i\in\{0,1,2\}} p(x_j^i|\mathbb{X}_\mathrm{K}) \log p(x_j^i|\mathbb{X}_\mathrm{K})}{\log(3)}. \quad (7)$$

The higher the entropy is, the higher is the uncertainty.

Finally, we propose another entropy-based metrics that quantifies the mutual dependence between the hidden genomic data that the adversary is trying to reconstruct, and the observed data. This is quantified by mutual information $I(x_j^i; \mathbb{X}_\mathrm{K}) = H(x_j^i) - H(x_j^i|\mathbb{X}_\mathrm{K})$ [8]. As privacy decreases with mutual information, we propose the following (normalized) privacy metrics:

$$I_j^i = 1 - \frac{H(x_j^i) - H(x_j^i|\mathbb{X}_\mathrm{K})}{H(x_j^i)} = \frac{H(x_j^i|\mathbb{X}_\mathrm{K})}{H(x_j^i)}. \quad (8)$$

The aforementioned metrics are useful for quantifying the genomic privacy of individuals. In order to quantify a more tangible privacy, we must convert these genomic-privacy metrics into health-privacy metrics. To quantify an individual's health privacy, we focus on his predisposition to different diseases. Let $\mathbf{S_d}$ be the set of IDs of the SNPs that are associated with a disease d. Then, a metrics quantifying the

[4]These metrics are not specific to the proposed inference attack; they can be used to quantify genomic privacy in general.

health privacy for an individual i regarding the disease d can be defined as follows:

$$D_d^i = \frac{1}{\sum_{k \in \mathbf{S_d}} c_k} \sum_{k \in \mathbf{S_d}} c_k G_k^i, \qquad (9)$$

where G_k^i is the genomic privacy of a SNP k for individual i, computed using (6), (7), or (8), and c_k is the contribution of SNP k to disease d.[5] Other health-privacy metrics based on non-linear combinations of genotypes or combinations of alleles will be defined in future work. Note that health-privacy metrics are valid at a given time, and cannot be used to evaluate future privacy provision, as genome research can change knowledge on the contribution of SNPs to diseases.

3.5 Genomic-Privacy Preserving Mechanism

Individuals willing to share genomic data for research or recreational purposes might be unwilling to share all their DNA sequence, and thus need to properly obfuscate the sensitive part(s) before releasing their genomic data. To do so, their DNA will go through an obfuscation process, that we call *genomic-privacy preserving mechanism* (GPPM). GPPM can be implemented using one of the following techniques: (i) hiding the SNPs, or (ii) reducing the precision or the quantity of the revealed SNPs.

Hiding all or specific SNPs can be achieved either by not releasing them or by encrypting them. Obviously, not releasing any of the SNPs would hinder genetic research, thus it is not a preferred way to protect the genomic privacy of individuals. Instead of not releasing the SNPs, the use of cryptographic algorithms to encrypt the genome is proposed. For example, Kantarcioglu *et al.* propose using homomorphic encryption on the SNPs of the individuals to perform genetic research on the encrypted SNPs [35]. However, the security of an individual's genome should be guaranteed for at least 70-100 years (i.e., during the typical lifetime of a human). As we show in this paper, even lifelong protection is not enough, considering kin privacy implications (e.g., for offsprings). It is known that even the best of the cryptographic algorithms we use today could be broken in around 30 years. Therefore, the appropriateness of cryptographic techniques for storing and processing the genomic data has been questioned due to long-term security requirements of the genomic data.

As an alternative to the cryptographic techniques, utility (i.e., precision and quantity of the revealed SNPs) can be traded for privacy. The precision of the revealed SNPs can be reduced, for example, by revealing only one of the two alleles of a SNP. Similarly, family members' SNPs can be selectively revealed by also considering the previously revealed SNPs from the corresponding family (to keep the genomic privacy of other family members above a desired threshold): we evaluate the privacy provided by this technique in Section 4 by assessing the inference power of the adversary for different fractions of observed data from a targeted family.

Eventually, using one of the above techniques, the GPPM will take $\mathbb{X}$ as input and output $\mathbb{X}_\mathrm{K}$ as the set of revealed SNPs. We note that a detailed implementation of the GPPM by using one of the aforementioned techniques is out of the scope of this work. We plan to study it in the future.

[5]These contributions are determined as a result of medical studies. Some SNPs might increase (or decrease) the risk for a disease more than others.

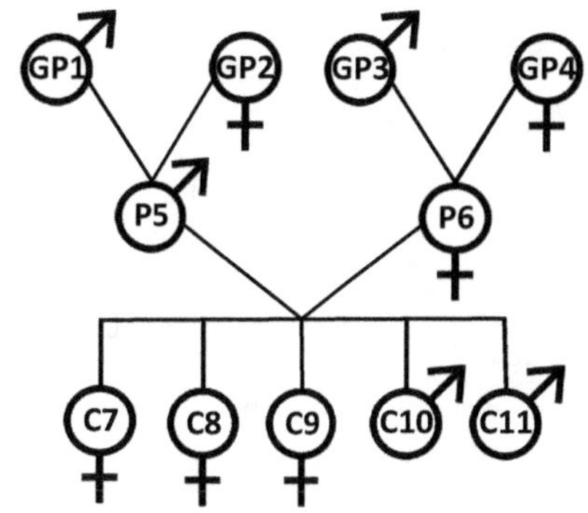

Figure 4: Family tree of *CEPH/Utah Pedigree 1463* consisting of the 11 family members that were considered. The symbols ♂ and ♀ represent the male and female family members, respectively.

4. EVALUATION

In this section, we first evaluate the performance of the proposed inference attack, then compare the performance of the inference with and without considering the linkage disequilibrium (LD) between SNPs, and finally evaluate the entropy-based metrics with respect to the expected estimation error in quantifying the genomic privacy.

For this evaluation, we use the *CEPH/Utah Pedigree 1463* that contains the partial DNA sequences of 17 family members (4 grandparents, 2 parents, and 11 children) [23]. We note in Fig. 4 that we only use 5 (out of 11) children for our evaluation because (i) 11 is much above the average number of children per family, (ii) we observe that the strength of adversary's inference does not increase further (due to the children's revealed genomes) when more that 5 children's genomes are revealed, and (iii) the belief propagation algorithm (in Section 3.2) might have convergence issues due to the number of loops in the factor graph, and this number increases with the number of children. As the SNPs related to important diseases, like Alzheimer's, are not included in this dataset, we quantify health privacy in Section 5 by using the data collected from a genome-sharing website.

To quantify the genomic privacy of the individuals in the CEPH family, we focus on their SNPs on chromosome 1 (which is the largest chromosome). We rely on the three metrics introduced in Section 3.4. That is, we compute the genomic privacy of each family member using the expected estimation error in (6), the (normalized) entropy in (7), and the (normalized) mutual information in (8) on the targeted SNPs, and we average the result based on the number of targeted SNPs for each individual. We rely on the L_1 norm to measure the distance between two SNP values in (6).

First, we assume that the adversary targets one family member and tries to infer his/her SNPs by using the published SNPs of other family members without considering the LD between the SNPs. We select an individual from the CEPH family and denote him as the target individual. We construct $\mathbf{S}$, the set of SNP IDs that we consider for evaluation, from 80k SNPs on chromosome 1. Thus, the set of targeted SNPs ($\mathbb{X}_\mathrm{U}$) includes 80k SNPs of the target individual. Furthermore, we gradually fill the set of observed SNPs ($\mathbb{X}_\mathrm{K}$) with the set of 80k SNPs of other family members. That is, we sequentially reveal 80k SNPs (whose IDs are in $\mathbf{S}$) of all family members (excluding the target in-

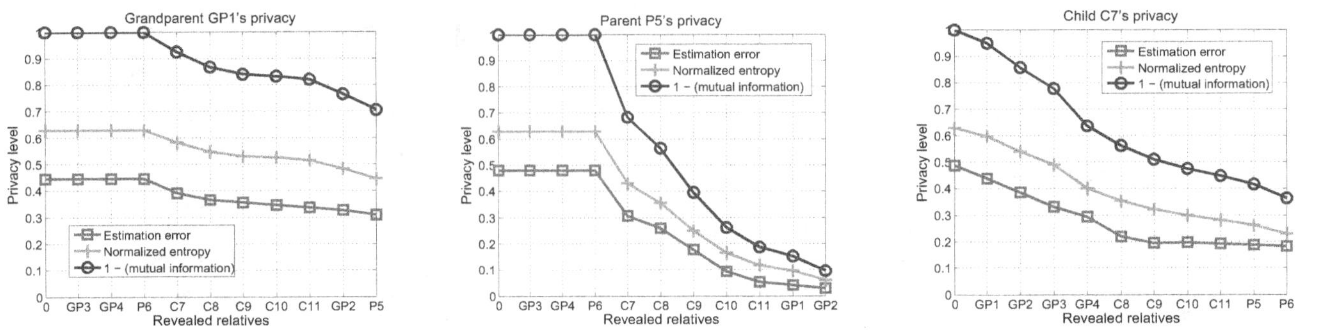

(a) (b) (c)

Figure 5: Evolution of the genomic privacy of the (a) grandparent (GP1), (b) parent (P5), and (c) child (C7). We reveal all the 80k SNPs on chromosome 1 of other family members starting from the most distant family members of the target individual (in terms of number of hops to the target individual in Fig. 4); the x-axis represents the disclosure sequence. We note that $x = 0$ represents the prior distribution, when no genomic data is observed by the adversary.

dividual) beginning with the most distant family members from the target individual (in terms of number of hops in Fig. 4) and we keep revealing relatives until we reach his/her closest family members.[6]

In Fig. 5 we show the evolution of the genomic privacy of three target individuals from the CEPH family (in Fig. 4): (i) grandparent (GP1), (ii) parent (P5), and (iii) child (C7). We note that all entropy-based metrics for each target individual start from the same values. We also observe that the parent's and the child's genomic privacy decreases considerably more than the grandparent's (the adversary's error for the grandparent's genome does not go below 0.3). Moreover, the observation of GP3, GP4 and P6's genomes has no effect on GP1 and P5's privacy as their genomes are independent (if no other relatives' genomes are observed). We observe in Fig. 5(a) that the grandparent's genomic privacy is mostly affected by the SNPs of the first revealed children (C7, C8), and also by those of his spouse and his child (P5). We also observe (in Fig. 5(b)) that, by revealing all family members' SNPs (expect P5), the adversary can almost reach an estimation error of 0. The target parent's genomic privacy significantly decreases only with the observation of his children's and spouse's SNPs. Finally, we observe in Fig. 5(c) that C7's genomic privacy decreases smoothly with the observation of his grandparents' SNPs, and then of his siblings'. We also observe a slight decrease of privacy once the parents' SNPs (P5 and P6) are also revealed, but the observation of parents (after the other children) does not have a significant effect on the adversary's error. It is important to note that the importance of a family member for the inference power of the adversary also depends on the sequence at which his/her SNPs are revealed in Fig. 5. For example, in Fig. 5(c), if the SNPs of the parents (P5 and P6) of the target child (C7) were revealed before her siblings (C8-C11), then the observation of her parents would reduce the genomic privacy of the target child more than her siblings (but the final genomic privacy would not change).

Next, we include the LD relationships and observe the change in the inference power of the adversary using the LD values. We construct $\mathbf{S}$ from 100 SNPs on chromosome 1. Among these 100 SNPs, each SNP is in LD with 5 other SNPs on average. Furthermore, the strength of the LD (r^2 value in Section 2.1.3) uniformly varies between 0.5 and 1 (where $r^2 = 1$ represents the strongest LD relationship, as discussed before). We note that we only use 100 SNPs for this study as the LD values are not yet completely defined over all SNPs, and the definition of such values is still an ongoing research. As before, we define a target individual from the CEPH family, construct the set $\mathbb{X}_\text{U}$ from his/her SNPs, and sequentially reveal other family members' SNPs to observe the decrease in the genomic privacy of the target individual. We observe that individuals sometimes reveal different parts of their genomes (e.g., different sets of SNPs) on the Internet. Thus, we assume that for each family member (except for the target individual), the adversary observes 50 random SNPs from $\mathbf{S}$ only (instead of all the SNPs in $\mathbf{S}$), and these sets of observed SNPs are different for each family member. In Fig. 6, we show the evolution of genomic privacy of three target individuals when the adversary also uses the LD values. We observe that LD decreases genomic privacy, especially when few individuals' genomes are revealed. As more family member's genomes are observed, LD has less impact on the genomic privacy.

We also evaluate the inference power of the adversary to infer multiple SNPs among all family members, given a subset of SNPs belonging to some family members, and also considering the LD between SNPs. That is, we evaluate the inference power of the adversary for different fractions of observed data for the family members. Using the same set of 100 SNPs, we construct $\mathbb{X}_\text{U}$ from $(\kappa \times 100 \times n)$ SNPs, randomly selected from all family members, where n is the number of family members in the family tree ($n = 11$ for this scenario), and $0 \leq \kappa \leq 1$. We assume that the SNPs that are not in $\mathbb{X}_\text{U}$ are observed by the adversary (i.e., in $\mathbb{X}_\text{K}$), and we observe the inference power of the adversary for the SNPs in $\mathbb{X}_\text{U}$, for different values of κ. In Fig. 7, we observe an exponential decrease in the global genomic privacy (privacy of all family members), showing that the observation of a small portion of the family's SNPs can have a huge impact on genomic privacy. The estimation error is decreased by around 3 by observing only the first 10% of the SNPs.

[6]The exact sequence of the family members (whose SNPs are revealed) is indicated for each evaluation.

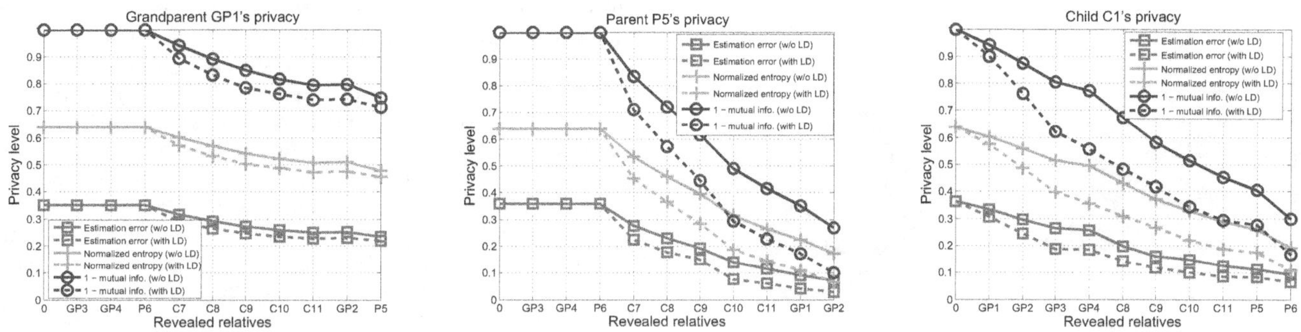

(a) (b) (c)

Figure 6: Evolution of the genomic privacy of the (a) grandparent (GP1), (b) parent (P5), and (c) child (C7), with and without considering LD. For each family member, we reveal 50 randomly picked SNPs (among 100 SNPs in S), starting from the most distant family members, and the x-axis represents the exact sequence of this disclosure. Note that $x = 0$ represents the prior distribution, when no genomic data is revealed.

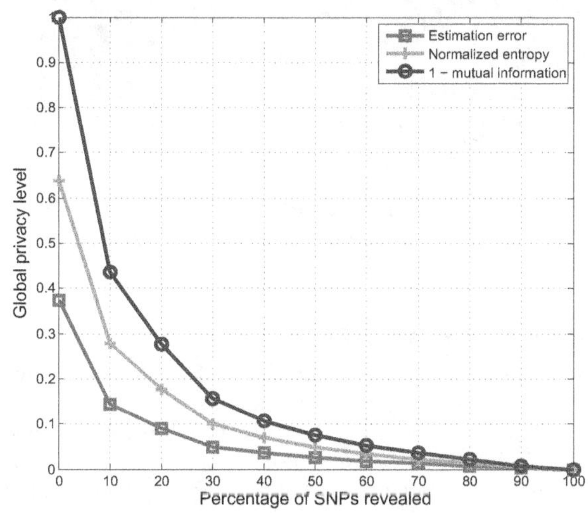

Figure 7: Evolution of the global privacy for the whole family by gradually revealing 10% of SNPs.

5. EXPLOITING GENOME-SHARING WEBSITES AND ONLINE SOCIAL NETWORKS

In order to show that the proposed inference attack threatens not only the Lacks family, but potentially *all* families, we collected publicly available data from a genome-sharing website and familial relationships from an OSN, and evaluated the decrease in genomic and health privacy of people due to the observation of their relatives' genomic data.

We gathered individuals' genomic data from OpenSNP [1], a website on which people can publicly share sets of SNPs. Then, we identified the owners of some gathered genomic profiles by using their names and sometimes profile pictures. Among these identified individuals, we managed to find family relationships of 6 of them (who publicly reveal the names of some of their relatives) on Facebook.[7] We expect this number to increase in the future, as more health-related OSNs (which let people share their genomic profiles, such as 23andMe [2]) emerge. Furthermore, we anticipate that the current widely used health-related OSNs (e.g., PatientsLikeMe [6]) will let users upload and share their genomic data. We identified 29 target individuals from 6 different families, whose genomic data can be inferred using the observed SNPs of the identified individuals.

We focus on 2 individuals I_1 and I_2 out of these 6 identified individuals and evaluate the genomic and health privacy for their family members. We observed that both I_1 and I_2 publicly disclosed around 1 million of their SNPs. Furthermore, we identified the names of (i) 1 mother, 2 sons, 2 daughters, 1 grandchild, 1 aunt, 2 nieces, and 1 nephew of I_1, and (ii) 1 sibling, 1 aunt, 1 uncle, and 6 cousins of I_2 on Facebook. We compute the genomic and health privacy of these target individuals using the (normalized) entropy in (7) on the targeted SNPs, and normalize the result based on the number of targeted SNPs for each individual. We do not use the expected estimation error in (6), as we do not have the ground truth for the genomes of the target individuals. Thus, privacy is quantified as the uncertainty of the adversary in this section.

To quantify the genomic privacy of the target individuals (i.e., family members of I_1 and I_2), we first construct **S** from all SNPs on chromosome 1 (from the observed genomes of I_1 and I_2). The set of observed SNPs ($\mathbb{X}_K$) includes the observed SNPs of I_1 (respectively I_2) for the inference of family members of I_1 (respectively I_2). The set of targeted SNPs ($\mathbb{X}_U$) includes 77k SNPs for I_1's family and 79k for I_2's family (from **S**) for each evaluation. In Fig. 8, we show the decrease in the genomic privacy for different family members of I_1 (aunt, niece/nephew, grandchild, mother, child) and I_2 (cousin, aunt/uncle, sibling) as a result of our proposed inference attack, first without considering the LD dependencies (similarly to previous section). We observe that as expected, the decrease in the genomic privacy of close family members is significantly higher than that of more distant family members. However, as we have seen in Section 4, the observation of one (or more) additional family member(s) has often much more impact on the target's privacy than the observation of only one relative.

[7] According to [28], around 12% of Facebook users publicly share at least one family member on their profiles.

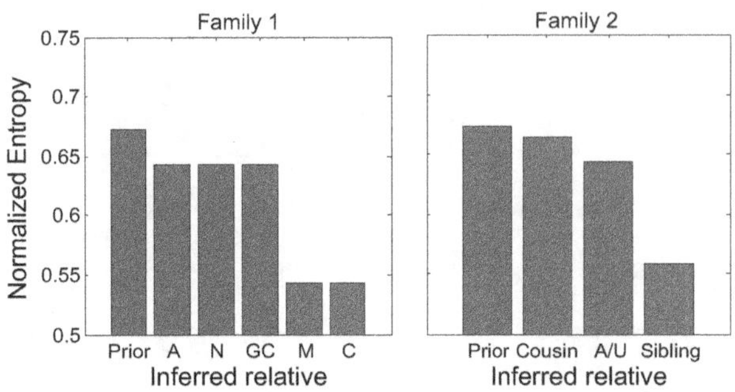

Figure 8: Attacker's uncertainty about all SNP values on chromosome 1 for two different families, without using LD. A stands for aunt, N for niece/nephew, GC for grandchild, M for mother, C for child, U for uncle. Same notations are used in Fig. 9 and 10.

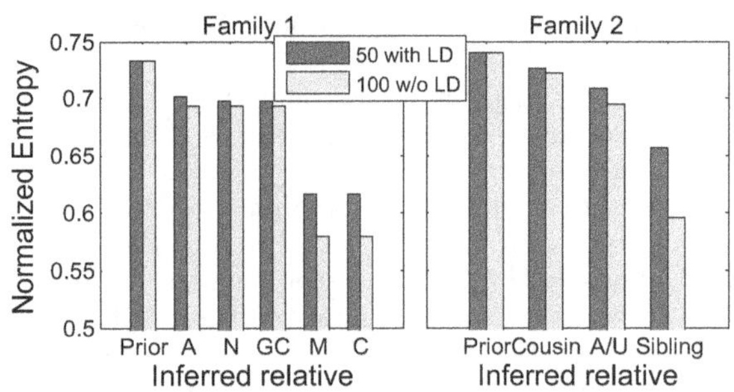

Figure 9: Attacker's uncertainty about values of 100 SNPs on chromosome 1 for two families, by observing (i) all 100 SNPs of the relative that reveals his/her genome, and (ii) only 50 SNPs but using LD.

In Fig. 9, we display the decrease of genomic privacy with respect to 100 SNPs of chromosome 1.[8] We first show the different privacy levels by using all 100 SNPs of the observed relative (i.e., I_1 or I_2), and then show the same by using only 50 SNPs of the observed relative and LD values. We note that the use of LD decreases privacy slightly more for the first familyt than for the second family. This is because we randomly picked 50 different SNPs for both families, and those picked in the second family had weaker LD relationships with other SNPs. We finally observe that the difference between the two observation cases (50 SNPs with LD and 100 SNPs without LD) is higher for close relatives (mother, child, or sibling) than for others.

We also evaluate the health privacy of the family members of I_1 and I_2 considering their predispositions to various diseases. We first noticed that almost all important SNPs for privacy-sensitive diseases affected by genomic factors, like Alzheimer's, ischemic heart disease, or macular degeneration, were revealed by I_1 and I_2. Due to lack of space, we focus on Alzheimer's as it is one of the most important diseases that are mainly attributable to genetic factors. Having two ApoE4 alleles (in SNPs rs7412 and rs429358 located on chromosome 19) dramatically increases an individual's probability of having Alzheimer's by the age of 80. Thus, the contents of these two SNPs carry privacy-sensitive information for individuals. We use the metrics in (9) to quantify the health privacy of family members for Alzheimer's disease. We assign equal weights to both associated SNPs (as their combination determines the predisposition to Alzheimer's disease). In Fig. 10, we show the attacker's uncertainty about the predisposition to Alzheimer's disease for the family members of I_1 and I_2. We notice a decrease of around 0.2 (from 0.5 to 0.3) in uncertainty between close relatives. Clearly, the knowledge of the SNPs of more relatives would further worsen the situation.

[8]We consider only 100 SNPs here for the same reason as in Section 4.

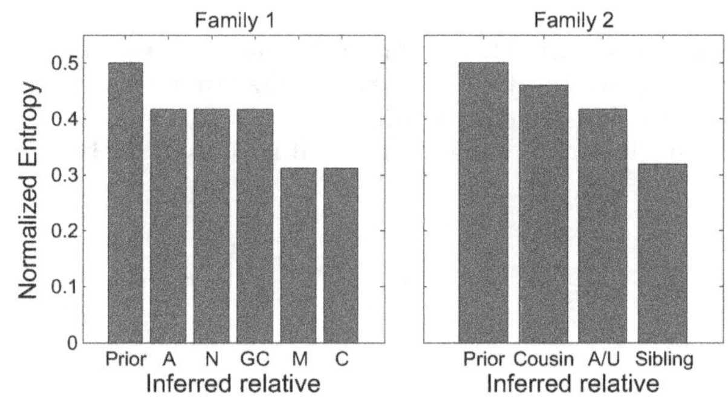

Figure 10: Adversary's uncertainty about Alzheimer's disease predisposition for 2 families.

6. RELATED WORK

Stajano *et al.* [46] were among the first to raise the issue of kin privacy in genomics. Cassa *et al.* [19] provide a framework for measuring the risks to siblings of someone who reveals his SNPs. They show that the inference error is substantially reduced when the sibling's SNPs are known, compared to when only the population frequencies are used. We push this work further, by considering any kind of family members, and LD relationship between SNPs, by proposing and evaluating different privacy metrics, and by presenting a real attack scenario using publicly available data. Our generic framework considers any observation of a family's genomic data, and the adversary's background knowledge.

Several algorithms for inference on graphical models have been proposed in the context of pedigree analysis. Exact inference techniques on Bayesian networks are used in order to map disease genes and construct genetic maps [26,34,38]. Monte Carlo methods (Gibbs sampling) were also proved to be efficient for genetic analyses in the case of complex pedigrees [31,44,48]. All these methods aim to infer specific genotypes given phenotypes (like diseases). Another paper relies on Gibbs sampling in order to infer haplotypes (used in association studies) from genotype data [36]. Genotype imputation [39] is another technique used by geneticists to complete missing SNPs based upon given genotyped data. A similar approach has recently been used to infer high-density genotypes in pedigrees, by relying notably on low-resolution genotypes and identity-by-descent regions of the genome [18]. None of these contributions addresses privacy.

We also briefly summarize the research on the privacy of genomic data in the following. Homer *et al.* [30] prove that de-identification is an ineffective way to protect the privacy of genomic data, which is also supported by other works [27, 50, 52]. Most recently, Gymrek *et al.* [29] show how they identified DNAs of several individuals who participated in scientific studies. Fienberg *et al.* [25] propose using differential privacy to protect the identities of scientific study participants, however this approach reduces the accuracy of the research results. Some pieces of work also focus on protecting the privacy of genomic data and on preserving utility in medical tests such as (i) search of a particular pattern in the DNA sequence [16,49], (ii) comparing the similarity of DNA sequences [15,17,32], and (iii) performing statistical analysis on several DNA sequences [35]. Furthermore, Ayday *et al.* propose privacy-preserving schemes for medical tests and personalized medicine methods that use patients' genomic data [7,14]. For privacy-preserving clinical genomics, a group of researchers proposes to outsource some costly computations to a public cloud or semi-trusted service provider [21, 51]. Finally, Ayday *et al.* propose techniques for privacy-preserving management of raw genomes [13].

In contrast with these contributions, in this paper, we propose a novel and efficient inference attack in order to reconstruct genomic data of individuals given observed genomic data of their family members and special characteristics of genomic data. Furthermore, we quantify the genomic privacy of individuals as a result of this attack using different metrics, and show the real threat by using the data collected from different websites and OSNs.

7. CONCLUSION AND FUTURE WORK

We have proposed a novel reconstruction attack for inferring the genomic data of individuals from the observed genomes of their relatives, and we have compared several metrics to quantify genomic and health privacy.

As pointed out by Rebecca Skloot, the author of "The Immortal Life of Henrietta Lacks", the view we have today of genomes is like a world map, but Google Street View is coming very soon. This growing precision can be highly beneficial in terms of personalized medicine, but it can have devastating consequences on a family's peace of mind. As we already mentioned, the Lacks family is just one (albeit famous) example. In the future (and already today), people of the same family might have very different opinions on whether to reveal genomic data, and this can lead to dissent: relatives might have divergent perceptions of possible consequences. It is high time for the security research community to prepare itself for this formidable challenge. The genetic community is highly concerned about the fact that the proliferation of negative stories could potentially lead to a negative perception by the population and to tighter laws, thus hampering scientific progress in this field.

In future work, we plan to apply the proposed framework to more pedigrees, in order to fine tune our numerical results. We will also study the trade-off between utility and privacy of genomic data in order to design an optimized GPPM.

Acknowledgments

We would like to thank Jacques Fellay, Paul J. McLaren, Vincent Mooser and Jacques Rougemont for their insights and suggestions, Kévin Huguenin and Reza Shokri for their valuable comments on the submitted manuscript, and the anonymous reviewers for their helpful feedback.

8. REFERENCES

[1] http://opensnp.org/. Visited on 9-Aug-2013.

[2] https://www.23andme.com/welcome/. Visited on 9-Aug-2013.

[3] http://www.nytimes.com/2013/03/24/opinion/sunday/the-immortal-life-of-henrietta-lacks-the-sequel.html?pagewanted=all. Visited on 9-Aug-2013.

[4] http://www.ncbi.nlm.nih.gov/projects/SNP/. Visited on 9-Aug-2013.

[5] http://www.eupedia.com/genetics/medical_dna_test.shtml. Visited on 9-Aug-2013.

[6] http://www.patientslikeme.com/. Visited on 9-Aug-2013.

[7] http://lca.epfl.ch/projects/genomic-privacy/.

[8] D. Agrawal and C. C. Aggarwal. On the design and quantification of privacy preserving data mining algorithms. In *Proceedings of the twentieth ACM SIGMOD-SIGACT-SIGART symposium on Principles of database systems*, pages 247–255. ACM, 2001.

[9] E. Ayday, E. D. Cristofaro, G. Tsudik, and J. P. Hubaux. The chills and thrills of whole genome sequencing. *arXiv:1306.1264*, 2013.

[10] E. Ayday, A. Einolghozati, and F. Fekri. BPRS: Belief propagation based iterative recommender system. *IEEE ISIT*, 2012.

[11] E. Ayday and F. Fekri. Belief propagation based iterative trust and reputation management. *IEEE Transactions on Dependable and Secure Computing*, 9(3), 2012.

[12] E. Ayday and F. Fekri. BP-P2P: A belief propagation-based trust and reputation management for P2P networks. *SECON*, 2012.

[13] E. Ayday, J. L. Raisaro, U. Hengartner, A. Molyneaux, and J. P. Hubaux. Privacy-preserving processing of raw genomic data. *DPM 2013*, 2013.

[14] E. Ayday, J. L. Raisaro, P. J. McLaren, J. Fellay, and J. P. Hubaux. Privacy-preserving computation of disease risk by using genomic, clinical, and environmental data. *HealthTech*, 2013.

[15] P. Baldi, R. Baronio, E. De Cristofaro, P. Gasti, and G. Tsudik. Countering GATTACA: Efficient and secure testing of fully-sequenced human genomes. *CCS*, 2011.

[16] M. Blanton and M. Aliasgari. Secure outsourcing of DNA searching via finite automata. *DBSec*, 2010.

[17] F. Bruekers, S. Katzenbeisser, K. Kursawe, and P. Tuyls. Privacy-preserving matching of DNA profiles. Technical report, 2008.

[18] J. T. Burdick, W.-M. Chen, G. R. Abecasis, and V. G. Cheung. In silico method for inferring genotypes in pedigrees. *Nature genetics*, 38(9):1002–1004, 2006.

[19] C. A. Cassa, B. Schmidt, I. S. Kohane, and K. D. Mandl. My sister's keeper?: genomic research and the identifiability of siblings. *BMC Medical Genomics*, 1(1):32, 2008.

[20] J. Chen, A. Dholakia, E.Eleflhetiou, M. Fossotier, and X.-Y. Hu. Near optimum reduced-complexity decoding algorithm for LDPC codes. *IEEE ISIT*, 2002.

[21] Y. Chen, B. Peng, X. Wang, and H. Tang. Large-scale privacy-preserving mapping of human genomic sequences on hybrid clouds. *NDSS*, 2012.

[22] C. Diaz, S. Seys, J. Claessens, and B. Preneel. Towards measuring anonymity. In *Privacy Enhancing Technologies*, pages 54–68. Springer, 2003.

[23] R. Drmanac, A. B. Sparks, M. J. Callow, A. L. Halpern, N. L. Burns, B. G. Kermani, P. Carnevali, I. Nazarenko, G. B. Nilsen, G. Yeung, et al. Human genome sequencing using unchained base reads on self-assembling dna nanoarrays. *Science*, 327(5961):78–81, 2010.

[24] D. S. Falconer and T. F. Mackay. *Introduction to Quantitative Genetics (4th Edition)*. Addison Wesley Longman, Harlow, Essex, UK, 1996.

[25] S. E. Fienberg, A. Slavkovic, and C. Uhler. Privacy preserving GWAS data sharing. *Proceedings of the IEEE 11th International Conference on Data Mining Workshops (ICDMW)*, Dec. 2011.

[26] M. Fishelson and D. Geiger. Exact genetic linkage computations for general pedigrees. *Bioinformatics*, 18(suppl 1):S189–S198, 2002.

[27] J. Gitschier. Inferential genotyping of Y chromosomes in Latter-Day Saints founders and comparison to Utah samples in the HapMap project. *Am. J. Hum. Genet.*, 84:251–258, 2009.

[28] P. Gundecha, G. Barbier, and H. Liu. Exploiting vulnerability to secure user privacy on a social networking site. In *KDD*. ACM, 2011.

[29] M. Gymrek, A. L. McGuire, D. Golan, E. Halperin, , and Y. Erlich. Identifying personal genomes by surname inference. *Science: 339 (6117)*, Jan. 2013.

[30] N. Homer, S. Szelinger, M. Redman, D. Duggan, and W. Tembe. Resolving individuals contributing trace amounts of DNA to highly complex mixtures using high-density SNP genotyping microarrays. *PLoS Genetics*, 4, Aug. 2008.

[31] C. S. Jensen, A. Kong, and U. Kjærulff. Blocking gibbs sampling in very large probabilistic expert systems. *International Journal of Human Computer Studies*, 42(6):647–666, 1995.

[32] S. Jha, L. Kruger, and V. Shmatikov. Towards practical privacy for genomic computation. *Proceedings of the 2008 IEEE Symposium on Security and Privacy*, pages 216–230, 2008.

[33] A. D. Johnson and C. J. O'Donnell. An open access database of genome-wide association results. *BMC Medical Genetics 10:6*, 2009.

[34] M. I. Jordan. Graphical models. *Statistical Science*, pages 140–155, 2004.

[35] M. Kantarcioglu, W. Jiang, Y. Liu, and B. Malin. A cryptographic approach to securely share and query genomic sequences. *IEEE Transactions on Information Technology in Biomedicine*, 12(5):606–617, 2008.

[36] B. Kirkpatrick, E. Halperin, and R. M. Karp. Haplotype inference in complex pedigrees. *Journal of Computational Biology*, 17(3):269–280, 2010.

[37] F. Kschischang, B. Frey, and H. A. Loeliger. Factor graphs and the sum-product algorithm. *IEEE Transactions on Information Theory*, 47, 2001.

[38] S. L. Lauritzen and N. A. Sheehan. Graphical models for genetic analyses. *Statistical Science*, pages 489–514, 2003.

[39] Y. Li, C. Willer, S. Sanna, and G. Abecasis. Genotype imputation. *Annual review of genomics and human genetics*, 10:387, 2009.

[40] D. Nyholt, C. Yu, and P. Visscher. On Jim Watson's APOE status: Genetic information is hard to hide. *European Journal of Human Genetics*, 17:147–149, 2009.

[41] J. Pearl. *Probabilistic Reasoning in Intelligent Systems: Networks of Plausible Inference.* Morgan Kaufmann Publishers, Inc., 1988.

[42] H. Pishro-Nik and F. Fekri. On decoding of low-density parity-check codes on the binary erasure channel. *IEEE Transactions on Information Theory*, 50:439–454, March 2004.

[43] A. Serjantov and G. Danezis. Towards an information theoretic metric for anonymity. In *Privacy Enhancing Technologies*, pages 41–53. Springer, 2003.

[44] N. Sheehan. On the application of markov chain monte carlo methods to genetic analyses on complex pedigrees. *International Statistical Review*, 68(1):83–110, 2000.

[45] R. Shokri, G. Theodorakopoulos, J.-Y. Le Boudec, and J.-P. Hubaux. Quantifying location privacy. In *IEEE Symposium on Security and Privacy*, 2011.

[46] F. Stajano, L. Bianchi, P. Liò, and D. Korff. Forensic genomics: kin privacy, driftnets and other open questions. In *Proceedings of the 7th ACM workshop on Privacy in the electronic society*, 2008.

[47] L. Sweeney, A. Abu, and J. Winn. Identifying participants in the personal genome project by name. *Available at SSRN 2257732*, 2013.

[48] A. Thomas, A. Gutin, V. Abkevich, and A. Bansal. Multilocus linkage analysis by blocked Gibbs sampling. *Statistics and Computing*, 10(3):259–269, 2000.

[49] J. R. Troncoso-Pastoriza, S. Katzenbeisser, and M. Celik. Privacy preserving error resilient DNA searching through oblivious automata. *CCS '07: Proceedings of the 14th ACM Conference on Computer and Communications Security*, 2007.

[50] R. Wang, Y. F. Li, X. Wang, H. Tang, and X. Zhou. Learning your identity and disease from research papers: Information leaks in genome wide association study. *Proceedings of the 16th ACM CCS*, pages 534–544, 2009.

[51] R. Wang, X. Wang, Z. Li, H. Tang, M. K. Reiter, and Z. Dong. Privacy-preserving genomic computation through program specialization. *Proceedings of the 16th ACM CCS*, pages 338–347, 2009.

[52] X. Zhou, B. Peng, Y. F. Li, Y. Chen, H. Tang, and X. Wang. To release or not to release: Evaluating information leaks in aggregate human-genome data. *ESORICS*, 2011.

Hang With Your Buddies to Resist Intersection Attacks

David Isaac Wolinsky, Ewa Syta, and Bryan Ford
Yale University
{david.wolinsky,ewa.syta,bryan.ford}@yale.edu

ABSTRACT

Some anonymity schemes might in principle protect users from pervasive network surveillance—but only if all messages are independent and unlinkable. Users in practice often need *pseudonymity*—sending messages intentionally linkable to each other but not to the sender—but pseudonymity in dynamic networks exposes users to *intersection attacks*. We present Buddies, the first systematic design for intersection attack resistance in practical anonymity systems. Buddies groups users dynamically into *buddy sets*, controlling message transmission to make buddies within a set behaviorally indistinguishable under traffic analysis. To manage the inevitable tradeoffs between anonymity guarantees and communication responsiveness, Buddies enables users to select independent attack mitigation policies for each pseudonym. Using trace-based simulations and a working prototype, we find that Buddies can guarantee non-trivial anonymity set sizes in realistic chat/microblogging scenarios, for both short-lived and long-lived pseudonyms.

Categories and Subject Descriptors

C.2.0 [**Computer-Communication Networks**]: General—*Security and protection*

Keywords

anonymity; pseudonymity; intersection; disclosure

1. INTRODUCTION

Some anonymous communication techniques promise security even against powerful adversaries capable of pervasive network traffic analysis—*provided* all messages are fully independent of each other and/or the set of participants never changes [5,9,41,52]. Practical systems, however, must tolerate *churn* in the set of online users, and must support ongoing exchanges that make messages *linkable* over time, as with Mixminion nyms [15] or Tor sessions [18]. By sending linkable messages in the presence of churn, however, users can quickly lose anonymity to statistical disclosure or intersection attacks [16,31,42,53]. Though this extensively studied attack vector could apply in almost any realistic anonymous communication scenario, no practical anonymity system we know of offers active protection against such attacks.

As an example intended merely to illustrate one possible scenario in this broad class of attacks, suppose Alice writes a blog under a pseudonym to expose corruption in her local city government. Alice always connects to the blog server via Tor [18], and never reveals personally identifying information on her blog or to the server. Carol, a corrupt city official mentioned in Alice's blog, deduces from the blog's content that its owner is local, and calls her friend Mallory, a network administrator in the monopolistic local ISP. Mallory cannot directly compromise Tor, but she reads from Alice's blog the date and time each blog entry was posted, and she learns from the ISP's access logs which customers were online and actively communicating at each of those times. While thousands of customers may be online at each posting time, every customer *except* Alice has a chance of being offline during *some* posting time, and this chance exponentially approaches certainty as Alice continues posting. Mallory simply keeps monitoring until the *intersection* of these online user sets narrows to one user, Alice. We don't know if this precise attack has occurred, but analogous intersections of hotel guest lists, IP Addresses, and e-mail accounts revealed the parties in the Petraeus/Broadwell scandal [47].

As a step toward addressing such risks we present Buddies, the first anonymous communication architecture designed to protect users systematically from long-term intersection attacks. Buddies works by continuously maintaining an anonymized database of participating users and their online status, and uses this information to *simulate* intersection attacks that a network-monitoring adversary might perform. These simulations yield two relevant anonymity metrics that Buddies reports continuously, as an indication of potential vulnerability to intersection attack: a *possibilistic* metric roughly measuring "plausible deniability," and a more conservative *indistinguishability* metric indicating vulnerability to more powerful statistical disclosure attacks [16].

Beyond just measuring vulnerability, as in prior work on metrics [17,43] and alternate forms of anonymity [30], Buddies offers *active control* over anonymity loss under intersection attack. Users specify a policy for each pseudonym that balances attack protection against communication responsiveness and availability. To enforce these policies, a *policy module* monitors and filters the set of users participating in each communication round, sometimes forcing the system to behave as if certain online users were actually offline. Through this active control mechanism, policies can enforce lower bounds on anonymity metrics, preventing Alice from revealing herself to Mallory by posting at the wrong time for example. Policies can also reduce the *rate* of anonymity loss to intersection attacks, for example by tolerating anonymity set members who are normally reliable and continuously online but who lose connectivity for brief periods. Finally, policies can adjust posting rates or periods, enabling Buddies to aggregate all users coming online within a posting period into larger anonymity sets. If Alice sets her blog's posting period to once per day, for example, then Buddies

CCS'13, November 4–8, 2013, Berlin, Germany.
ACM 978-1-4503-2477-9/13/11. DOI 10.1145/2508859.2516740.

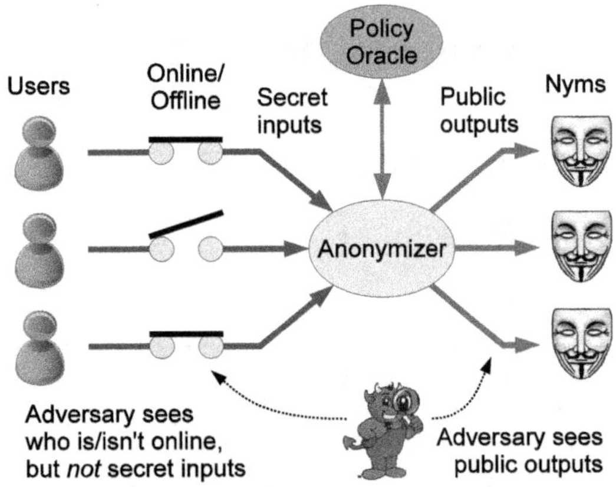

Figure 1: Conceptual model of Buddies architecture

can maintain Alice's anonymity among all users who "check in" at least once a day—*any time* during each day—even if many users check in only briefly at widely varying times.

Buddies' architecture may be treated as an extension to various existing anonymous communication schemes, but is most well-suited to schemes already offering measurable protection guarantees against traffic analyis, such as MIX cascades [5,41], DC-nets [9,46,52], or verifiable shuffles [7,25, 39]. We have built a working prototype of Buddies atop Dissent [11,13,52], a recent anonymous communication system that combines verifiable shuffle and DC-net techniques. The prototype's design addresses several practical challenges: to decentralize trust among independent servers, to create and manage pseudonyms while maintaining their independence, and to support user-selectable policies for each pseudonym.

To evaluate Buddies' practicality in realistic online communities, we analyze IRC trace data under a Buddies simulator, exploring questions such as how effective Buddies' anonymity metrics are, how feasible it may be to maintain nontrivial anonymity sets resistant to intersection attacks for extended periods, and how effectively Buddies can limit loss of anonymity while preserving usable levels of communication responsiveness and availability.

This paper's primary contributions are: (a) the first anonymity architecture that systematically addresses intersection attacks; (b) a modular, policy-based framework for both vulnerability monitoring and active mitigation of anonymity loss via intersection attacks; and (c) an evaluation of Buddies' practicality via a working prototype and trace-based simulations reflecting realistic online communities.

Section 2 of this paper outlines Buddies' high-level model of operation and the anonymity metrics we use. Section 3 then explores several useful attack mitigation policies in this model. Section 4 details challenges and approaches to incorporating Buddies into practical anonymity systems, and Section 5 experimentally evaluates both our working Buddies prototype and trace-based simulations. Section 6 summarizes related work, and Section 7 concludes.

2. BUDDIES ARCHITECTURE

Figure 1 shows a high-level conceptual model of the Buddies architecture. Buddies assumes there is some set of *users*, each of whom has a secret (i.e., securely encrypted) network communication path to a component we call the *Anonymizer*. For now we conceptually treat the Anonymizer as a central, trusted "black box," although later we will map this conceptually centralized component to realistic anonymization systems that decentralized trust, to avoid trusting any single physical component or administrative domain.

Buddies' model is inspired by anonymous blogging or IRC scenarios, where users post messages to a public forum, and users primarily desire sender anonymity [40]. While we expect Buddies to generalize to two-way models and metrics [44], we defer such extensions to future work. Each Buddies user "owns" some number of *Nyms*, each representing a pseudonymous identity under which the owner may post: e.g., an anonymous chat handle or blog. Users may secretly submit messages to be posted to Nyms they own, which the Anonymizer scrubs of identifying information and publicly "posts" to that Nym. To make various operational decisions, the Anonymizer consults a *Policy Oracle*. By design the Policy Oracle has no access to sensitive information, such as who owns each Nym: the Policy Oracle makes decisions based purely on public information available to anyone.

We assume the network-monitoring adversary identifies users by some network identifier or locator, such as IP address. By monitoring these locators the adversary can tell which users are online or offline at any given moment, and how much data they transmit or receive, but *cannot* see the actual content of data communicated between honest users and the Anonymizer. These assumptions model an ISP-grade adversary that can implement "wholesale" network-level monitoring of users connected via that ISP.

2.1 Overview of Operation

In Buddies' conceptual architecture, communication proceeds synchronously through a series of *rounds*. The Anonymizer drives the operation of each round i, as follows:

1. Registration: At the start of round i the Anonymizer updates the membership roster, $\mathbb{M}_i$, to include members who may have recently joined.

2. Nym creation: The Anonymizer next creates and announces one "fresh" Nym N_i each round. For each new Nym, the Anonymizer chooses one User *uniformly at random* as the Nym's owner, keeping this ownership secret. A Nym's lifetime is in principle unlimited: over time users acquire fresh Nyms at random but "statistically fair" times. (We later address creation of larger "batches" of Nyms efficiently, so new users need not wait a long time before they can post.)

3. Scheduling: The Anonymizer consults the Policy Oracle to choose one Nym, T_i, for transmission in this round, from all Nyms in existence. The Policy Oracle also specifies the number of bits B_i that the owner of Nym T_i may post. (Scheduling multiple Nyms per round is a straightforward extension.) As the Policy Oracle can access only public information, scheduling cannot depend directly on which Users currently "have messages to post." Scheduling can depend on other factors, however, such as Nyms' lifetimes, recent usage, or the interest of other users as indicated in messages previously posted anonymously via other Nyms.

4. Message submission: The Anonymizer announces the scheduled Nym T_i and transmission length B_i to the Users currently online. Each online user submits exactly B_i secret bits to the Anonymizer. These secret bits may contain either "real" data, or a *null* message of B_i zero bits, if the user has nothing useful to transmit at the moment. The bits sent from any user j other than the owner of Nym T_i represent "cover traffic" necessary to hide the Nym-owner's message submission from traffic analysis. The Anonymizer forms an *online user set*, $\mathbb{O}_i \subseteq \mathbb{M}_i$, consisting of the users who submitted a (real, null, or cover) message in round i.

5. User filtering: The Anonymizer now consults with the Policy Oracle, giving the Policy Oracle the set $\mathbb{O}_i$ of online users—but *not* any message content or information about which, if any, of these users owns the Nym scheduled this round. The Policy Oracle returns a new, *filtered* user set $\mathbb{P}_i \subset \mathbb{O}_i$, further constraining the set of online users whose submissions the Anonymizer will actually *accept* this round.

6. Message posting: If the owner of the scheduled Nym T_i is a member of $\mathbb{P}_i$—i.e., is online *and* was not filtered above—then the Anonymizer decrypts that user's secret message and posts it in association with Nym T_i. If the owner of T_i is not in $\mathbb{P}_i$—either because the owner was not online or was filtered above—then the Anonymizer posts B_i zero bits to Nym T_i: an output indistinguishable from a null message.

2.2 Active Mitigation of Intersection Attacks

The user filtering step above (step 5) serves as Buddies' primary "control point" through which to resist intersection attacks. The Policy Oracle uses publicly available information to *simulate* a virtual Adversary, by continuously performing an "intersection attack" against each Nym. At step 5 of each round i, the Policy Oracle first forms an attack model for the scheduled Nym T_i, based on prior history and the set $\mathbb{O}_i$ of users online in this round. The Policy Oracle computes one or more relevant anonymity metrics as detailed further below, and determines if action is required to limit or avoid anonymity loss in this round. If no action is required, the Policy Oracle returns the unfiltered user set to the Anonymizer, i.e., $\mathbb{P}_i = \mathbb{O}_i$. If action is required, however, then the Policy Oracle can filter the user set producing a $\mathbb{P}_i \subset \mathbb{O}_i$, thus preventing any user not in $\mathbb{P}_i$ from posting, as if more users were offline than are *actually* offline.

To illustrate how this filtering enables the Policy Oracle to mitigate intersection attacks, consider the following strawman policy. In step 5 of each round, the Policy Oracle simply checks whether *all* known users are presently online, i.e., whether $\mathbb{O}_i = \mathbb{M}_i$, returning $\mathbb{P}_i = \mathbb{M}_i$ if so, and otherwise returning $\mathbb{P}_i = \emptyset$. In effect, the Policy Oracle forbids the system from making progress—allowing *anyone* to post to *any* Nym—except when *all* users are online. Since messages are posted only when all users are online, the intersection of all *nonempty* rounds' user sets is $\mathbb{M}_i$, and the system preserves "perfect" anonymity assuming the Anonymizer performs as required. The tradeoff, of course, is effective system availability, which would be unusable in most practical situations.

The key technical challenge, and a primary contribution of this paper, is developing more nuanced methods of controlling the user filtering step in each round. By controlling these filtering choices, we seek to maintain both measurable anonymity levels under intersection attack *and* "usable" levels of availability, under arguably realistic conditions.

There are situations in which *no* active control mechanism will help. If all users but one go offline permanently, for example, the Policy Oracle has only two choices: eventually allow the one remaining user to post, giving up all anonymity under intersection attack; or filter that user forever, giving up availability completely. Thus, we must set realistic expectations. Section 5 experimentally investigates the feasibility of resisting intersection attacks in IRC communities, and tests possible control policies against feasibility metrics.

Buddies' architecture separates the Policy Oracle from the Anonymizer, giving the Policy Oracle access *only* to "public information" we assume is known to everyone including the adversary, eliminating the risk that policies may "accidentally" compromise anonymity by leaking Nym ownership. By architecturally disallowing the Policy Oracle from having access to private information, we avoid the need to analyze each policy carefully for such "side-channel" anonymity leaks, and instead can focus purely on the main question of how effectively a policy mitigates intersection attacks while maintaining usable levels of availability.

Another issue is whether the information the Policy Oracle needs to simulate the Adversary's intersection attacks—such as the set of users online in each round—*should* be considered "public information." Although an ideal global adversary would know this information anyway, more realistic adversaries may be unable to monitor *all* users. If Buddies' design "hands out" information that would otherwise be at least partially private—such as the IP addresses of all online users—we risk accidentally "strengthening" a weak adversary into an effectively omniscient adversary. In the important case of users' network identities such as IP addresses, our design mitigates this leak by replacing IP addresses with anonymized *tags* when reporting online user sets to the Policy Oracle, as discussed in Section 4.3. However, whether Buddies' simulation-based architecture may strengthen weak adversaries in other unexpected ways, by making "too much information" public, merits further study.

2.3 Analyzing Intersection Attacks

While we do not attempt full formal analysis, the simplicity of the conceptual model facilitates straightforward informal analysis. Our focus here is on a particular class of attacks, namely what an adversary can learn from users' online status over time (the "switches" in Figure 1). The many other known attacks against practical anonymity systems are important but out of this paper's scope. We also claim no particular novelty in our analysis techniques or metrics; our goal is merely to apply known attacks [16, 31, 42] and anonymity metrics [17, 43] to the Buddies model.

We assume the Anonymizer is trusted to "do its job," keeping secret the linkage between Users and the Nyms they own. We also assume honest Users—those users we care about protecting—do not "give away" their identities or the relationships between their Nyms via the messages they post.

Under these conditions, the Adversary obtains three potentially important pieces of information in each round i: (a) the set of online users $\mathbb{O}_i$, (b) the set $\mathbb{P}_i$ of online users who passed the Policy Oracle's filter in step 5, and (c) the B_i message bits that were posted to the scheduled Nym T_i. An observation that will be key to Buddies's design is that only (b) and (c) will *actually* prove relevant to intersection attack analysis: the adversary ultimately obtains no useful information from knowing which users *were online* during a given round, beyond what the adversary learns from knowing which users *were online and unfiltered.*

Since we assume honest users do not "give away" their identities in their message content, we ultimately care only whether the message posted to Nym T_i was null or non-null. If a non-null message appeared for Nym T_i in round i, then the adversary infers that the owner of T_i must be a member of the filtered user set $\mathbb{P}_i$ in that round. (If the owner of T_i

was online but filtered in round i, then a null message would have appeared, as if the owner was offline.)

If a *null* message appears for T_i, however, the Anonymizer's design ensures that the adversary cannot distinguish among the following three possibilities: (1) the owner of Nym T_i was offline, (2) the owner was online but filtered, or (3) the owner was online and unfiltered, but had nothing useful to send and thus intentionally posted a null message.

2.3.1 Possibilistic Anonymity Analysis

To construct a simple *possibilistic* anonymity set P_N for a given Nym N, the adversary intersects the filtered user sets $\mathbb{P}_i$ across all rounds i for which Nym N was scheduled *and* a non-null message appeared: i.e., $P_N = \bigcap_i \{O_i \mid T_i = N \wedge m_i \neq 0\}$. Thus, P_N represents the set of users who might conceivably own Nym N, consistent with the observed set of non-null messages that have appeared for Nym N up to any point in time. Since the adversary cannot distinguish whether the appearance of a null message means that N's owner was offline, filtered, or merely had nothing to send, null-message rounds do not eliminate the possibility that users offline during that round may own N, so such rounds leave the possibilistic anonymity set P_N unaffected.

We define the size of a Nym's possibilistic anonymity set, $|P_N|$, as Nym N's *possibilistic anonymity*, which for convenience we abbreviate as *possinymity*. Although possinymity is only one of the many useful anonymity metrics that have been proposed [32, 33], and perhaps a simplistic one, we feel it captures a useful measure of "plausible deniability." If for example a user is dragged into court, and the judge is shown network traces of a Buddies system in which the accused is one of $|P_N|$ users who *may in principle* have posted an offending message, then a large possibilistic anonymity may help sow uncertainty of the user's guilt. We fully acknowledge the weaknesses of plausible deniability in general, however, especially in environments where "innocent until proven guilty" is not the operative principle.

2.3.2 Probabilistic Anonymity Analysis

While a simplistic adversary might stop at the above analysis, a smarter adversary can probabilistically learn not only from rounds in which non-null messages appeared, but also from rounds in which only a null message appeared.

Suppose for example the adversary correctly surmises from past observation that, in each round i, the owner of Nym N will have no useful message to post with some independent and uniformly random probability p. In this case the user will "pass" by submitting a null message. With probability $1 - p$ the user will have a non-null message and will try to post it—but this post attempt fails, yielding a null message anyway, if the owner is offline or filtered in that round.

For simplicity assume there are two users A and B, the adversary observes exactly one round i, this round results in a null message, and $\mathbb{P}_i = \{A\}$: user A participated but user B did not. The null output from round i means one of two events occurred: (a) A owns N, but chose with probability p not to post in round i; or (b) B owns N, and no message appeared independently of p because $B \notin \mathbb{P}_i$. Because Nyms are assigned to users uniformly at random on creation, the "base" probability that either user owns N is $1/2$. The probability of the above events (a) and (b) occurring *conditioned* on the observed history, however, is different. To be precise, $P[(a) \mid (a) \cup (b)] = P[(a) \cap ((a) \cup (b))]/P[(a) \cup (b)] = (p/2)/P[(a)\cup(b)]$, and $P[(b) \mid (a)\cup(b)] = (1/2)/P[(a)\cup(b)]$. Since (a) and (b) are disjoint events, $P[(a) \cup (b)] = P[(a)] + P[(b)]$, so $P[(a)] = (p/2)/(p/2 + 1/2) = p/(p + 1)$, and $P[(b)] = (1/2)/(p/2 + 1/2) = 1/(p + 1)$.

From the adversary's perspective, observing one round in which no message appears for Nym N, and in which A participated but B did not, reduces the relative likelihood of A being the owner by a factor of p. Observing similar events across multiple rounds exponentially increases the adversary's "certainty" of B being the owner: after k such rounds, the likelihood of A being the owner is only $p^k/(p^k + 1)$.

2.3.3 Indistinguishability Under Probabilistic Attack

The above reasoning generalizes to many users, varying probabilities of posting, etc. Our focus is not on deepening such analysis, however, a goal admirably addressed in prior work [17, 43]. Instead, we wish to achieve measurable resistance to *unknown* probabilistic attacks: we do not know the probabilities with which users will attempt to post in particular rounds, how well the unknown attacker may be able to predict when the owner of a given Nym will post, etc.

Instead of relying on the relevance of any *particular* probabilistic analysis—which may break each time a known attack is refined—Buddies relies on an *indistinguishability* principle that applies to all attacks of this class. If two users A and B have exhibited *identical* histories with respect to inclusion in each round's filtered user set $\mathbb{P}_i$, across *all* rounds i in which a Nym N was scheduled so far, then under any probabilistic analysis of the above form the adversary must assign identical probabilities to A and B owning Nym N. That is, if for every round i, it holds that $(A \in \mathbb{P}_i) \iff (B \in \mathbb{P}_i)$, then users A and B are *probabilistically indistinguishable* from each other, hence equally likely to own Nym N.

For any user A and Nym N, we define A's *buddy set* $B_N(A)$ as the set of users probabilistically indistinguishable from A, including A itself, with respect to potential ownership of Nym N. If n users are probabilistically indistinguishable from A, then under the attacker's analysis each such user in $B_N(A)$ has an individual probability no greater than $1/|B_N(A)|$ of being the owner of N. Intuitively, buddy-sets form equivalence classes of users who "hang together" against probabilistic intersection attacks—so that individual buddies do not "hang separately."

We next define a second anonymity metric, *indistinguishability set size*, or *indinymity* for short, as the size of the *smallest* buddy-set for a given Nym N. Since we do not know how a real attacker will actually assign probabilities to users, indinymity represents the minimum level of anonymity a member of *any* buddy set can expect to retain, even if the adversary correctly intersects the owner's anonymity set down to the members of that buddy set. Thus, the attacker cannot (correctly) assign a probability greater than $1/|B_N|$ to *any* user—including, but not limited to, the owner of N.

One might argue that we "mainly" care about the buddy set containing the true owner of N, not about other buddy sets not containing the owner. A counter-argument, however, is that a particular observation history might make some other buddy set falsely appear to the adversary as "more likely" to own N. In this case, we may well care how much protection the innocent members of that "unlucky" buddy set have against being "falsely accused" of owning N. Thus, to ensure that *all* users have the "strength in numbers" of being indistinguishable in a crowd of at least n users, regardless of the adversary's probabilistic reasoning, we must ensure that *all* buddy sets have size at least n.

3. ATTACK MITIGATION POLICIES

Based on the above architecture, we now explore possible intersection attack mitigation policies. We make no claim that these are the "right" policies, merely a starting point for ongoing refinement. Two key benefits of Buddies' architecture, however, are to modularize these policies into replaceable components independent of the rest of the anonymous communication system so they can be further evolved easily, and to ensure by system construction that policies cannot leak sensitive information *other than* by failing to protect adequately against intersection attacks.

We first explore policies for maintaining possinymity, then policies to enforce a lower bound on indinymity. An important caveat with any anonymity metric is that Buddies cannot guarantee that *measured* anonymity necessarily represents *useful* anonymity, if for example an attacker can compromise many users or create many Sybil identities [19]. Section 4.4 discusses these issues in more detail.

3.1 Maximizing Possinymity

The possinymity metric defined in Section 2.3.1 considers only rounds in which non-null messages appear for some Nym N, intersecting the filtered user sets across all such rounds to determine N's possinymity set P_N. We consider several relevant goals: maintaining a minimum possinymity level, mitigating the *rate* of possinymity loss, or both.

Maintaining a Possinymity Threshold.

Suppose a dissident, posting anonymously in a public chat room under a Nym N, wishes to maintain "plausible deniability" by ensuring that $|P_N| \geq 100$ throughout the conversation—and would rather be abruptly disconnected from the conversation (or have Nym N effectively "squelched") than risk $|P_N|$ going below this threshold. As a straightforward policy for this case, at step 5 of each round i, the Policy Oracle computes the new possinymity that N would have if $\mathbb{O}_i$ is intersected with N's "running" possinymity set from the prior round. The Policy Oracle returns $\mathbb{P}_i = \mathbb{O}_i$ if the new possinymity remains above threshold, or $\mathbb{P}_i = \emptyset$ otherwise.

In practice, the effect is that N's possinymity starts out at an initial maximum of the total set of users online when the user first posts via N, then decreases down to (but not below) the possinymity threshold as other users go offline, either temporarily or permanently. This policy has the advantage of not reducing the usability of N, or artificially delaying the time at which the user's posts appear, as long as the possinymity set remains above-threshold. Once N's possinymity set reaches the set threshold, however, all of the users remaining in this set become *critical*, in that N becomes unusable for posting once *any* remaining member goes offline. In the "dissident scenario" we envision this event might be the user's signal to move to a new network location: e.g., get a fresh IP address at a different Internet cafe.

Limiting Possinymity Loss Rate.

An alternative, or complementary, goal is to reduce the rate at which N's possinymity decreases. In realistic scenarios, as our trace data in Section 5 illustrates, clients often get delayed or disconnected temporarily but return soon thereafter. Thus, a more refined policy might temporarily halt all posting for Nym N—by returning $\mathbb{P}_i = \emptyset$—when members of N's current possinymity set go offline, in hopes that the missing members will soon return. To ensure progress and get N "unstuck" if members remain offline for a sufficient number of rounds, however, the policy eliminates these persistently offline members from N's permanent possinymity set by returning a smaller (but nonempty) $\mathbb{P}_i$. Such a policy may "filter out" possinymity set losses due to otherwise-reliable users going offline briefly, at the cost of delaying a user's posting to Nym N for a few rounds if some current possinymity set member goes offline permanently. Of course, a loss rate limiting policy may readily be combined with a threshold-maintaining policy of the form above. A further refinement of this combination might be to increase the loss limiting policy's "tolerance"—number of rounds a user may remain offline before being eliminated—as the Nym's possinymity set size falls to approach the user's specified lower bound. Such a policy in essence trades more *temporary* unavailability for greater total Nym longevity.

Users Worth Waiting For.

While the above simple variants suggest starting points, we envision many ways to refine policies further, for example by recognizing that a user's record of past reliability is often a predictor of future reliability. To maximize a Nym N's possinymity and minimize anonymity loss rate, while also limiting delays caused by *unreliable* users, we may wish to consider some members of N's current possinymity set to be "more valuable" than others: e.g., users who have remained online and participating reliably for a long period with at most a few brief offline periods. In particular, a policy might apply an offline-time threshold as discussed above to limit loss rate, but apply *different* thresholds to different members of N's current possinymity set, giving longer, more generous thresholds to more "valued" users.

The Policy Oracle can build up reliability information about users starting when those users first appear—not just when a particular *pseudonym* of interest is created. Thus, a policy that Buddies applies to a particular Nym N can benefit from user history state that the Policy Oracle may have built up since long before N was created.

3.2 Guaranteeing Minimum Indinymity

The possinymity metric considers intersection attacks only across rounds in which non-null messages appear, but in realistic chat or blogging scenarios a user's posts will be interspersed with idle periods during which *no* message appears. A smarter adversary can use the predictive techniques discussed in Section 2.3.2 to glean probabilistic information from such rounds. We therefore wish to guarantee users some level of indinymity, even under probabilistic attacks.

Forming and Enforcing Buddy-Sets.

To guarantee a Nym N will have a minimum indinymity of some value K, the Policy Oracle must ensure that all of N's buddy-sets—subsets of users whose members exhibit *identical* online behavior across rounds after user filtering—are all of size at least K. As a straw-man approach to buddy-set formation, on the creation of Nym N, the Policy Oracle could divide N's initial user roster $\mathbb{M}$ into $\lfloor|\mathbb{M}|/K\rfloor$ arbitrary buddy-sets "up-front," each containing at least K users. At step 5 of each round i, for each buddy-set B containing *any* offline user $u \notin \mathbb{O}_i$, the Policy Oracle removes *all* members of u's buddy set B from its filtered user set $\mathbb{P}_i$. The

Policy Oracle effectively *forces* members of each buddy set to come online or go offline "in unison," keeping them permanently indistinguishable under probabilistic intersection attack (even if the adversary can distinguish one buddy set from another). This straw-man policy is likely to yield poor availability, however, as it prevents N's owner from posting whenever *any* member of the owner's buddy-set is offline, making N unusable in the fairly likely event that any member of this buddy set is unreliable or disappears permanently.

Lazy Buddy-Set Formation.
As a first refinement, therefore, the Policy Oracle can delay buddy-set decisions until users actually go offline. At creation, a Nym N starts with one large buddy-set containing its entire user roster $\mathbb{M}$. In the first round i in which member(s) of $\mathbb{M}$ go offline, the Policy Oracle might first delay *all* posting for Nym N by returning $\mathbb{P}_i = \emptyset$, in hopes the missing member(s) will return online soon, as discussed above. Once the Policy Oracle "gives up" on one or more members, however, it splits N's current buddy-sets into two, isolating all persistently offline members into one of the resulting buddy-sets. By delaying the decision of how to split buddy-sets, the Policy Oracle guarantees that after the split-point, the buddy-set containing only online members will have a chance to "make progress"—at least until more users go offline for sufficiently long to force another buddy set split.

After a split, each of of the resulting buddy-sets must be at least of size K to maintain an indinymity lower bound. If fewer than K total users are actually offline ($|\mathbb{M} - \mathbb{O}_i| < K$), then the Policy Oracle must "sacrifice" a few online users, placing them in the offline users' buddy-set. Otherwise, if for example a single offline user forcing a split is actually the owner of Nym N, then placing the offline user in a buddy set of size 1 would quickly reveal to a probabilistic attacker that the now-offline user owned the pseudonym, once the attacker notices that posts have stopped appearing on Nym N. By "sacrificing" $K-1$ additional users at the split point, even if the attacker infers from the absence of posts that N's owner is in the now-offline buddy-set, he cannot tell whether the owner is the user who *caused* the split, or is one of those sacrificed and *forced* offline to "keep him company." If the offline users in a buddy set eventually return online, then the whole buddy set rejoins in unison, making the Nym usable again if the owner was a member of this buddy set.

Choosing Whom to Sacrifice.
When the Policy Oracle must "sacrifice" online users to pad an offline buddy set to size K, an important issue is how to choose which online users to sacrifice. We investigated two classes of sacrificial policies: random, and least reliable users. Random choice clusters users into buddy sets regardless of reliability, which is simple but risks sacrificing reliable users by mixing them into buddy sets containing unreliable or permanently offline users. Alternatively, the Policy Oracle might first sacrifice users with the weakest historical record of reliability: e.g., users who arrived recently or exhibited long offline periods. By this heuristic we hope to retain the most reliable users in the buddy set that remains online immediately after the split—though this buddy set may split further if more nodes go offline in the future.

We expect reliability-sensitive policies to maximize a Nym's effective lifetime, *provided* the Nym's true owner is one of the more reliable users and does not get sacrificed into an unreliable or permanently offline buddy set. A short-lived or unreliable user cannot expect his Nyms to be long-lived in any case: a long-lived Nym must have a "base" of reliable, long-lived users to maintain anonymity under intersection attack, and the Nym's owner must obviously *be* a member of the long-lived anonymity set he wishes to "hide in."

3.3 Varying Policies and Nym Independence

So far we have assumed the Policy Oracle enforces a "global policy" on all Nyms, but this would limit flexibility and perhaps unrealistically require all users to "agree on" one policy. Instead, Buddies allows each Nym to have a separate policy—e.g., different lower bounds and anonymity loss mitigation tradeoffs—chosen by the Nym's owner.

Since intersection attacks are by definition not an issue until a Nym N has been in use for more than one round, N's owner specifies the policy parameters for a Nym N in its first post to N. The set of users online in this first message round, in which N's policy is set, forms N's initial user roster $\mathbb{M}$, which is also by definition the maximum anonymity set N can ever achieve under intersection attack. In subsequent rounds in which Nym N is scheduled, the announced policy for N determines the Policy Oracle's behavior in filtering N's user sets to mitigate intersection attacks.

Each Nym's policy is thus independent of other Nyms—including other Nyms owned by the same user. This policy independence, and the correctness of Section 2's analysis, depend on the assumption made in Section 2.1 that the Anonymizer assigns Nyms to users *uniformly at random and independent of all other Nyms.* Otherwise, the choices the Policy Oracle makes on behalf of one Nym might well leak information about other Nyms. This leads to some specific design challenges addressed below in Section 4.2.

To illustrate the importance of independent Nym assignment, suppose there are two users, to whom the Anonymizer *non-independently* issues two Nyms N_1 and N_2, via a random 1-to-1 permutation—always giving each user exactly one Nym. In the first communication round, N_1's owner announces a weak policy with a minimum buddy set size of 1, but N_2 demands a buddy set size of 2. The adversary later sees a non-null post to N_1 while user B is offline, and as N_1's weak policy permits, infers that A must own N_1. If each user owns exactly one Nym, then the adversary can *also* infer that B must own N_2, violating N_2's stronger policy. With independent Nym assignment, in contrast, the knowledge that A owns N_1 gives the adversary no information about which user owns N_2, because it is just as likely that A owns *both* N_1 and N_2, as it is that each user owns exactly one Nym.

4. BUDDIES IN PRACTICAL SYSTEMS

Since Buddies' conceptual model in Section 2 is unrealistically simple in several ways, we now address key challenges of implementing Buddies in practical anonymity systems. For concreteness we will focus on the design of our Buddies prototype built as an extension to Dissent [11, 13, 52], but we also discuss the Buddies architecture's potential applicability to other existing anonymous communication systems.

4.1 Decentralizing the Anonymizer

So far we have treated the Anonymizer as a trusted "black box" component, but in a practical anonymity system we do not wish to require users to trust any single component. In a practical design, therefore, we replace Buddies' Anonymizer with one of the standard decentralized schemes for anonymous message transmission, such as mix-nets [6,8,15], DC-nets [9,50], or verifiable shuffles [7,25,39].

While agnostic in principle to specific anonymous communication mechanisms, Buddies makes two important assumptions about the Anonymizer's design. First, Buddies assumes the Anonymizer is already resistant to basic, *short-term* network-level traffic analysis and timing attacks [34,38, 45]. Without basic traffic analysis protection necessary for *unlinkable* message traffic, we cannot expect to achieve reliable long-term protection for *linkable* posts via pseudonyms. Second, we assume the Anonymizer distributes trust across some group of servers, and that *there exists* at least one trustworthy server in this group—although the user need not know *which* server is trustworthy. This *anytrust* model [51] is already embodied in the relays used in mix-nets or Tor circuits [18], the "authorities" assumed in verifiable shuffles [39], or Dissent's multi-provider cloud model [52].

While "ad hoc" mix-nets and onion routing schemes are vulnerable to many traffic analysis and active attacks, variants such as MIX cascades [5,7,41] and verifiable shuffles [25, 39] offer formally provable traffic analysis resistance. These systems typically work in synchronous rounds, where users submit onion-encrypted ciphertexts to a common set of mixes, who serially decrypt and permute the ciphertexts to reveal the anonymous plaintexts. To resist traffic analysis, users with no useful message to send in a round must submit encrypted "empty" messages as cover traffic.

DC-nets [9,50] similarly operate in synchronous rounds, but derive anonymity from *parallel* information coding techniques rather than *serial* mixing, achieving traffic analysis protection in fewer communication hops. Dissent [11,13, 52] adapts DC-nets to a practical and scalable client-server model. By leveraging the parallel communication structure of DC-nets, Dissent achieves per-round latencies orders of magnitudes lower than a verifiable shuffle or cascade mix guaranteeing equivalent security. Dissent thus forms a natural foundation for our Buddies prototype to build on.

4.2 Creating and Extending Nyms

Buddies can conveniently represent Nyms as public/private key pairs, so that anyone may learn the public keys of all Nyms in existence, but only a Nym's owner holds the corresponding private key. Dissent runs Neff's verifiable key-shuffle [39], once per communication *epoch*, to generate a list of public keys forming a DC-nets transmission schedule for that epoch. Each client submits one public key to the shuffle, which the servers re-encrypt and randomly permute, to produce a well-known list of *slot* keys. The client holding a slot's matching key can identify its own slot, but neither the servers nor *other* clients learn who owns any honest client's slot. Adapting this mechanism to create fresh Nyms in Buddies introduces two further technical challenges: assigning Nyms to users *independently* at random, and enabling Nyms to have unlimited lifetimes.

Creating Nyms via Lotteries.

A simple way to create independent Nyms meeting the requirements in Section 3.3 is by "lottery." Each user submits a fresh public key to a verifiable shuffle, the servers jointly pick one re-encrypted key at random from the shuffled output to be a new Nym, and discard all other keys. For efficiency, we would prefer to generate fresh Nyms in batches, amortizing the cost of the shuffle across lotteries for many Nyms, while ensuring that each Nym is assigned independently. One conceivable approach is for the servers to mint a batch of e-cash "coins" [10], encrypt each coin to a random key chosen from the shuffle's output, and finally run a verifiable DC-nets round [13,27], with one slot per coin, allowing each coin's "winner" to spend the coin and publish a fresh public Nym key. We leave detailed exploration of this challenge to future work.

Extending Nyms Across Epochs.

To enable Nyms to persist beyond one epoch, clients can use each winning ticket from a Nym lottery either to publish a fresh Nym key, or to re-publish an old Nym key, effectively "reviving" the old Nym and giving it a transmission slot in the new epoch. A lottery winner might even publish *another* user's public Nym key, effectively delegating the winning ticket's share of bandwidth in the new epoch an arbitrary Nym whose content the lottery winner finds interesting.

When a client revives its own Nym in a new epoch, the client must ensure that the set of users participating in the Nym lottery is consistent with the existing Nym's anonymity policy: e.g., that the user's buddies are also online. If some participants go offline *during* a Nym lottery, to avoid policy-checking races the servers must restart the lottery, enabling clients to re-check the new participant set before exposing an old Nym in the new epoch.

4.3 Implementing the Policy Oracle

Implementing the Policy Oracle as a single independent server would require that all clients trust the Policy Oracle server to implement their requested attack mitigation policies correctly. Although a bad Policy Oracle server cannot *directly* de-anonymize users since it does not know which users own each Nym, it could—by intent or negligence—simply make intersection attacks easy. For this reason, Buddies leverages the *anytrust* server model that the underlying Anonymizer already uses, running a virtual replica of the Policy Oracle in "lock-step" on each of the anonymization servers. The servers use standard distributed accountability techniques [28] to cross-check each others' computation of Policy Oracle decisions, halting progress and raising an alarm if any server deviates from an agreed-upon deterministic algorithm implementing the Policy Oracle. These techniques apply readily to the Policy Oracle precisely because it architecturally has access to no sensitive state, and hence all of its state may be safely replicated.

Identifying Users to the Policy Oracle.

Buddies' Anonymizer shares the set of users currently online in each round with the Policy Oracle, which implies that we must treat these online sets as "public information" that the adversary may also obtain. As discussed in Section 2.2, however, revealing *actual* user identities or locators for this purpose, such as users' public keys or IP addresses, risks *strengthening* a weak adversary into an "omniscient" adversary for intersection attack purposes.

Buddies addresses this problem by permitting clients to authenticate with the servers via *linkable ring signatures* [24, 35]. To connect, each client generates a cryptographic proof that it holds the private key corresponding to one of a *ring* of public keys, without revealing *which* key the client holds. In addition, the client generates and proves the correctness of a *linkage tag*, which has a 1-to-1 relationship with the client's private key, but is cryptographically unlinkable to any of the public keys without knowledge of the corresponding private keys. The servers track which clients are online via their linkage tags, and provide only the list of online tags to the Policy Oracle in each round, so the Policy Oracle can simulate an adversary's intersection attacks without knowing which *actual* users are online each round.

Of course, the server that a client connects to directly can associate the client's network-level IP address with its linkage tag, and a compromised server may share this information with an adversary. This linkage information does not help a global passive adversary, who by definition obtains all the same information the Policy Oracle obtains merely by monitoring the network, but may help weaker adversaries perform intersection attacks against those users who connect via compromised servers. We see this risk as equivalent to the risk clients run of connecting to a compromised "entry relay" in existing anonymity systems [15, 18]. Compromised servers are just one of the many avenues through which we must assume an adversary might monitor the network.

4.4 Malicious Users and Sybil Attacks

While Buddies can measure, and optionally enforce a lower bound on, the number of users comprising a Nym's possinymity or indinymity set, Buddies cannot guarantee that all those users are providing *useful anonymity*. In particular, if the owner of a Nym N has specified a policy mandating a minimum buddy-set size of K, but up to F other clients may be colluding with the adversary, then N's owner may have to assume that its *actual* minimum anonymity set size may be as little as $K - F$, if all F bad clients happen to—or somehow arrange to—land in the same buddy set as N's owner. Since in practical systems we don't expect users to have a reliable way of "knowing" how many other clients are conspiring against them, we treat F as an unknown variable that users may simply have to "guess" and factor into their choices of possinymity or indinymity lower-bounds. In this respect Buddies is no different from any other anonymity system some of whose users may be compromised.

Reducing vulnerability to malicious clients may be an argument in favor of random buddy-set formation (Section 3.2). Randomized policies may offer some guarantee that the malicious users present in a Nym's initial user set become "evenly distributed" among buddy-sets. In any preferential, "reputation-based" formation scheme, if the attacker can learn or correctly guess the general "level of reliability" of a Nym N's true owner—which may well be inferable from N's posting record—then the attacker's compromised nodes might deliberately exhibit a similar level of reliability in hopes of getting clustered together in the owner's buddy set. For such attacks to succeed, however, the malicious users must be present at N's creation in order to fall in N's possinymity set in the first place, and the attacker must adjust their reliability profile *after* learning "enough" about N's owner, but *before* too many buddy set splits have already occurred for N. Thus, if the Policy Oracle builds up user reputation information in a relatively conservative, long-term fashion across the users' entire histories (e.g., from before N appeared), this may make it difficult for an attacker to "steer" malicious users' reliability profiles "late in the game" to implement a cluster attack N. Clustering attacks nevertheless present a risk that more randomized buddy set formation policies may reduce.

As in any distributed system, an attacker may be able to amplify the effective numbers of malicious clients via Sybil attacks [19], creating many fake user identities. Buddies addresses this risk by requiring users to be authenticated—via linkable ring signatures as detailed above—as owners of "real" identities in some Sybil attack resistant identity space. Buddies is agnostic as to the exact nature of this public identity space or how it is made resistant to Sybil attacks. The current prototype simply is defined for "closed" groups, defined by a static *roster* of public keys listing all members, so the group is exactly as Sybil attack resistant as whatever method the group's creater uses to form the roster. To support open-ended groups, Buddies could build on one of the many Sybil attack resistance schemes, such as those based on social networks [48, 54]—or could simply rate-limit Sybil attacks via some "barrier to entry," e.g., requiring users to solve a CAPTCHA or receive a phone callback to "register" an unknown public key for participation.

5. EVALUATION

We now evaluate Buddies' utility, using data we collected from popular public IRC (Internet Relay Chat) chat rooms on EFnet servers. After introducing our data collection and simulation approach, we first explore "ideal" metrics quantifying levels of anonymity achievable in principle under given conditions—metrics that depend *only* on the user behavior dataset and not on any particular Buddies policy or loss mitigation algorithm. Next, we apply these traces to an event-based Buddies simulator to evaluate more realistic policies against these ideals. We consider naïve anonymous posting without Buddies, then posting under policies that enforce minimum buddy-set sizes, and policies that attempt to maximize possinymity. Finally, we analyze the overheads Buddies induces in the context of Dissent.

5.1 Datasets and Simulation Methodology

To evaluate Buddies' utility, we use traces taken from popular public IRC (Internet Relay Chat) chat rooms on EFnet servers. Unlike web traffic [53], IRC logs record participants online status in addition to activity or transmission of messages. The online status becomes critical for systems in which inactive but online users submit cover traffic, such as Buddies assumes. While BitTorrent traffic [2] supports similar conventions as IRC, online status and activity, user behavior focuses transferring data between peers, which does not make a strong correlation to the need for long term intersection resistant Nyms. Furthermore, the buddy system focuses on anonymous group communication systems that reveal all anonymous cleartexts to all users with at least all servers privy to the input; such behavior maps better to IRC and BitTorrent traffic than to Web traffic.

We monitored 100 (a limitation imposed by EFnet) of the most active EFnet-based IRC rooms, for over a month dating from November 26th through December 30th, 2012. For each room, we obtained the following for each member: joins, leaves, nickname changes, and messages. Anecdotally, we found that users often temporarily disconnect from IRC without IRC recognizing the disconnection. This creates a period of time in which the user must use a secondary nickname, then switch back to the original nickname once IRC recognizes the disconnect. Unfortunately we have no statistics on average disconnection time, but we were able to identify these scenarios and "fix" the data such that the affected users appear to be continuously online.

Figure 2 visually illustrates the trace collected from one sample IRC room, **football**, plotting the time period a given

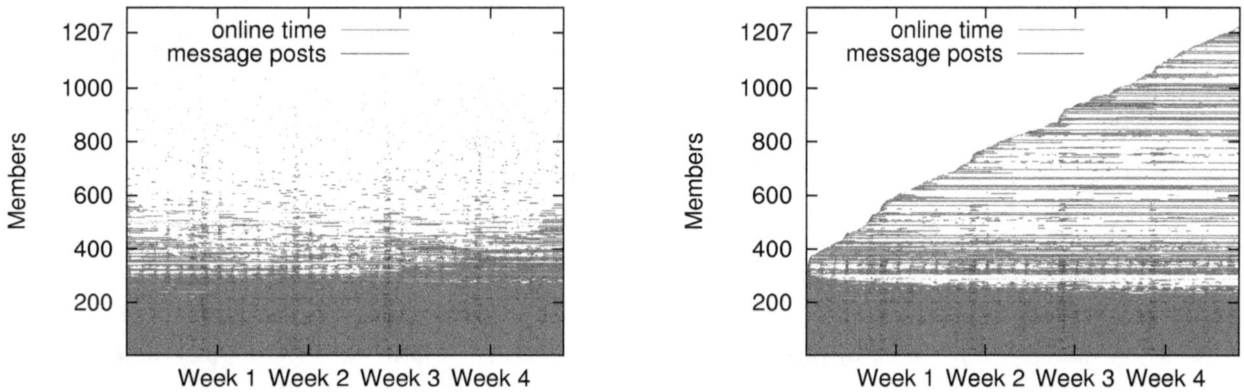

(a) Members sorted by total time online

(b) Members sorted by first appearance online

Figure 2: Visualization of user online periods over one month in EFnet's **football** IRC chatroom.

user was online as a horizontal line. Figure 2(a) sorts the 1207 unique users observed during the trace vertically by total time the user was online during the observation period. This graph shows that the online forum has a "core" set of around 300 users who stay online most of the time, while the remaining users come online for shorter periods at varying times, with denser vertical stripes showing periodic patterns (e.g., football games). Figure 2(b) shows the same data with users sorted by *first* appearance online: again about 300 users were online already at the start of the trace, while new users appear subsequently at a fairly constant rate—with a fraction of these "late arrivals" remaining online for the remaining trace period.

To analyze this data we implemented an event-driven Buddies simulator in Python, cleverly called the Anonymity Simulator (AS). AS plays the role of users, the Anonymizer, and the Policy Oracle. As input the AS takes an IRC trace, time between rounds, system-wide buddy and possinymity set sizes, and buddy set formation policies. We primarily focus on random buddy set formation policies and user online times. For the latter, the AS can either use an initial period of the trace, a bootstrap period, or use a deity mode and review the entire data set. To better compare apples-to-apples, random, bootstrapped, and deity mode evaluations all began at the same time in the trace.

5.2 Ideal Anonymity Analysis

We first use our IRC traces to explore upper bounds on the anonymity we expect to be achievable in *any* system resistant to intersection attacks, under a trace-driven scenario, but independent of particular anonymity mechanisms or policies. These experiments depend *only* on analysis of the IRC data, and do not depend on Buddies' design or the Buddies simulator. This analysis serves to deepen our understanding of user behavior in realistic online forums, and to establish realistic expectations of what a system such as Buddies might achieve in principle. We first consider anonymity potentially achievable for low-latency communication using pseudonyms of varying lifetimes, then focus on *long-lived* pseudonyms in communication scenarios that can tolerate varying offline times in members of anonymity sets.

Low-latency pseudonyms of varying lifetime.

We focus on the **football** dataset, considering all online periods of all 1207 users appearing in the trace as visualized in Figure 2. We treat each contiguous online period lasting at least time x as representing a pseudonym with lifetime x, and compute an ideal anonymity set for that pseudonym as the total number of users *also contiguously online* during that pseudonym's lifetime. This analysis pessimistically eliminates from the anonymity set users with *any* offline period, however brief, during the pseudonym's lifetime.

Figure 3(a) summarizes the distribution of these ideal anonymity set sizes, for pseudonym lifetimes varying on the log-scale x-axis. Pseudonyms used for up to about one hour reliably achieve anonymity sets of at least 250 members, and sometimes up to 375 members—between 20% and 30% of the total user population observed—suggesting that substantial resistance to intersection attack may be achievable in large forums for short-lived pseudonyms. Achievable anonymity under these assumptions falls off rapidly as pseudonym lifetime increases further, however.

Long-lived pseudonyms tolerant of offline periods.

Applications that demand truly long-lived pseudonyms, such as blogs, can often tolerate longer communication latencies. Many anonymous communication schemes can *aggregate* user behavior into selectable time periods, such as batches in mix-nets [8,15], or dropoff windows in DC-net systems such as BlogDrop [12] or Verdict [13]. Users who come online and participate at *any time* during each window are indistinguishable to the adversary, enabling the system to tolerate users who go offline briefly for periods shorter than that window. Buddies policies can similarly be configured to tolerate users who go offline for brief periods without anonymity loss, as discussed in Section 3.1. In all these cases, the main cost is to increase communication latency up to that offline tolerance period. Without focusing on any particular mechanism, we now parameterize our ideal anonymity analysis on the assumption that a long-lived pseudonym has *some* way to tolerate users who go offline for periods up to a varying *maximum offline time.*

Figure 3(b) shows the ideal anonymity achievable for a hypothetical long-lived pseudonym whose lifetime is the *entire* 1-month observation period of the IRC trace, assuming that pseudonym can tolerate a varying maximum offline time shown on the log-scale x-axis. Since this scenario gives us only one "data point" per IRC trace for a given maximum offline period, the figure shows the same analysis for several different IRC datasets. Consistent with the

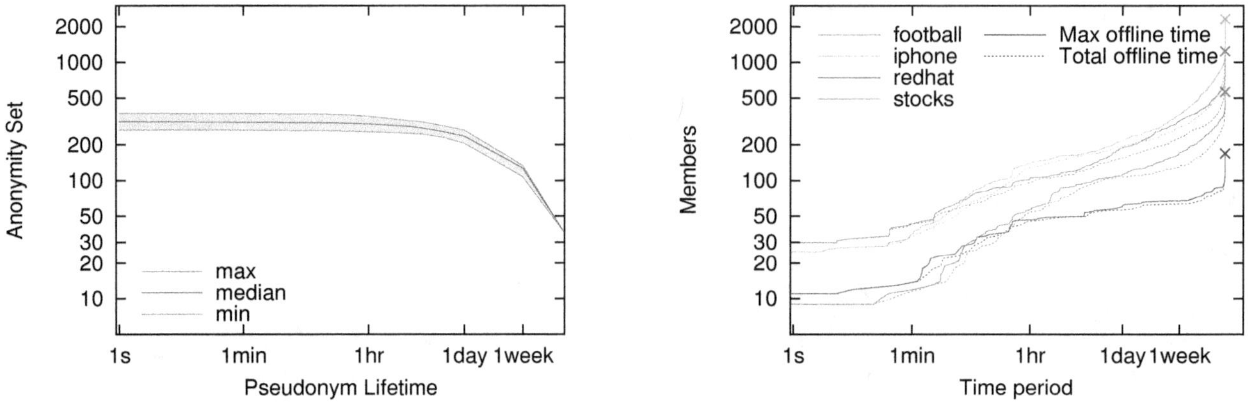

(a) Ideal anonymity set size potentially achievable by a *low-latency* pseudonym of varying lifetime. The pseudonym can tolerate *no* offline time in members of its anonymity set.

(b) Ideal anonymity potentially achievable for *long-lived* (1-month) pseudonyms, tolerating anonymity set members who go offline for a varying maximum offline time period.

Figure 3: Analysis of *ideal anonymity* potentially achievable based on user behavior in the IRC **football** room.

right edge of Figure 3(a), long-lived pseudonyms that cannot tolerate even short offline periods—as required for low-latency communication—achieve small anonymity sets consisting of only the 10–30 users in each trace who were continuously throughout the trace. (The leftmost portion of this graph may be optimistic, in fact, as the IRC server may not have logged temporary network disconnections shorter than the TCP timeout of around 30 seconds.) A long-lived pseudonym that can tolerate disconnections up to one hour, however, can achieve 100-user anonymity sets across the 1-month trace in the **football** and **iphone** rooms. A pseudonym that can tolerate 1-day disconnections—realistic for a blog whose author posts at most once per day anyway—can achieve still larger anonymity sets of around 200 users, or 6% of the **football** group's total observed membership.

In general, the IRC datasets exhibit a common pattern where a small set of dedicated users is almost always online, a larger set–roughly 15% to 20%–who show up about once an hour to once a day, and a large set of ephemeral users comprise around 80% of the total population. We do not expect ephemeral users to contribute usefully to the anonymity sets of long-lived Nyms, but it is important for Buddies to operate in their presence, and ephemeral users can increase anonymity for short-lived Nyms as Figure 3(a) shows.

5.3 Possinymity Analysis and Enforcement

We now explore the behavior of Buddies' possibilistic anonymity metric, as defined in Section 2.3.1, under our IRC trace workloads. While the above ideal anonymity analysis generically explored the levels of anonymity a "hypothetical" pseudonym might achieve, we now wish to use our traces to model *specific* pseudonyms and explore their behavior under specific Buddies policies. To do so, we consider the messages posted by each IRC user to represent one pseudonym in our model, we take the times these IRC messages appeared to represent a "schedule" of the times the modeled pseudonym owner had a message to post, and we define the nominal *lifetime* of each modeled pseudonym as the time from the first message to the last message. We then replay this activity under AS, the Anonymity Simulator, to evaluate the behavior of Buddies' metrics under these activity traces, and the effect of Buddies policies on *actual* communication behavior,

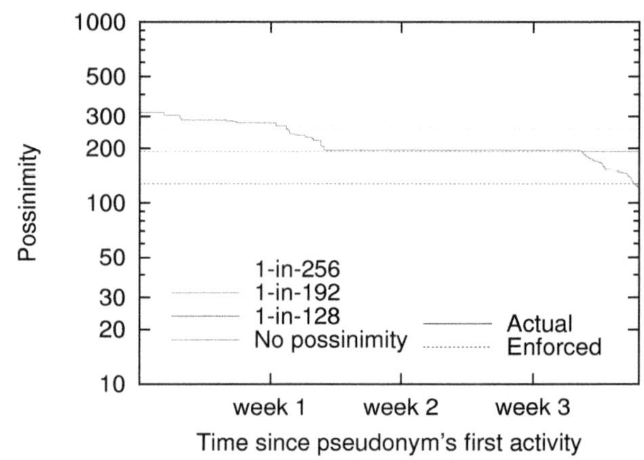

Figure 4: Evolution of worst-case possinymity over trace

taking into account the (sometimes indefinite) delays that Buddies sometimes imposes to preserve anonymity.

Figure 4 shows how possinymity evolves across the lifetimes of pseudonyms with 1-second round times (no offline time tolerance). The x-axis represents time since since each pseudonym's inception—i.e., from its first scheduled message. The y-axis value of the solid lines show minimum or *worst-case* possinymity across all pseudonyms whose lifetimes extend at least to that point. Each line color in the graph reflects behavior under Buddies policy that enforces a different possinymity lower bound, whose enforced level is represented by the corresponding horizontal dotted line.

Consistent with our expectations from Figures 2 and 3(a), possinymity starts at the number of users online at time of first post, and gradually decreases as users "churn" offline and get intersected out of the pseudonym's possinymity set at a relatively constant rate. In practice, enforcing a lower bound leaves pseudonyms' behavior unaffected until just before a message post would decrease the pseudonym's possinymity below the lower bound. At this point the pseudonym becomes unable to post—i.e., Buddies deliberately compromises availability to preserve anonymity—leaving possinymity constant after that point in the trace.

5.4 Indinymity Analysis and Buddy Sets

We now explore probabilistic attacks of the form discussed in Section 2.3.2, and Buddies' ability to protect users against such attacks via buddy sets. To validate the protection Buddies provides, we model one *particular* probabilistic intersection attack, in which the attacker observes the messages posted by a pseudonym, assumes the owner decided whether to post in each round with a fixed, independent probability p, and uses the analysis outlined in Section 2.3.2 to divide users into classes based on likeliness of owning the pseudonym. The attacker then makes a "best guess" at which user owns that pseudonym, and we compute the attacker's chance of guessing correctly: $1/k$ if the owner is within the k-user equivalence class the attacker judges most likely, and 0 if not. We make no claim that this particular attack is representative of the attacks most likely to be mounted by real-world adversaries, but merely use it as an example to test and visualize the effectiveness of buddy sets. We reiterate that Buddies' security is based ultimately not on knowledge or expectations of particular attacks, but on an indistinguishability principle that applies to all probabilistic attacks using observed online/offline behavior as inputs.

Figure 5 shows pseudonyms' measured worst-case anonymity under this probabilistic attack, again as a function of the length of time each pseudonym has been active. Each line color represents a different buddy set size enforcement policy, with dotted lines representing effective anonymity against the probabilistic guessing attack, solid lines representing measured possinymity for reference, and dashed lines representing the buddy set size—and hence indinymity lower bound—enforced by the respective policy. Note that these graphs have logarithmic x-axes, unlike Figure 4. While possinymity decreases at a relatively constant rate with user churn, the probabilistic attack is much faster—effectively eliminating the vast majority of an unprotected user's initial anonymity set within the first hour since a pseudonym starts posting, for example. Nevertheless, for a given enforced buddy set size, the probabilistic attack only approaches, but never violates, the enforced indinymity bound.

5.5 Effect on Usable Pseudonym Lifetime

While the above experiments validate Buddies' effectiveness at mitigating anonymity loss through both possibilistic and probabilistic intersection attacks, this security necessarily comes with usability tradeoffs. Buddies policies may make a pseudonym unusable for posting messages before the owner naturally finishes using the pseudonym, and in still usable pseudonyms, messages may be delayed.

To explore Buddies' effect on pseudonym usability, Figure 6 contains CDFs showing the distributions of *useful lifetimes* of pseudonyms under various enforced buddy set sizes. As the relevant comparison baseline, the black line representing the *nominal* case shows the distribution of pseudonym lifetimes in the IRC trace without any Buddies policy. We take this line to represent the distribution of time periods during which traced users *intended* to use a pseudonym to post messages. Each colored line in contrast shows the distribution of *actual*, useful pseudonym lifetimes upon enforcing a given enforced buddy set size.

For many pseudonyms, unfortunately, resistance to probabilistic intersection attack comes at a high cost. As Figure 6(a) shows, for example, 50% of the pseudonyms modeled in the trace have nominal lifetimes of at least one day—meaning that their owners "would like to" use them for one day—but under enforced buddy set sizes of 32 or more, 50% of pseudonyms remain usable only for about an hour under Buddies. *Some* pseudonyms remain usable for much longer even under Buddies, however: in particular, those pseudonyms whose owners are long-lived and fall into the same buddy set with other long-lived, reliable users.

For each buddy set size, the graph additionally contrasts two schemes for dividing users into buddy sets. The *Oracle* scheme "sorts" users into buddy sets based on their maximum offline time, as measured for Figure 3(b), thereby clustering users with similar reliability levels together from the perspective of an oracle who can "see" into the future. The dotted lines, for comparison, reflect a more realistic, *dynamic* scheme designed along the lines discussed in Section 3.2. This scheme clusters users into buddy sets dynamically based only on *recent past* reliability history, up to to the point in time when a large buddy set must be subdivided in order to keep a pseudonym usable. Since past reliability is not a perfect predictor of future reliability, the realistic, dynamic scheme incurs some further loss of effective pseudonym lifetime. The current dynamic scheme is simplistic and can likely be improved, so we expect the utility actually achievable in practical systems to lie somewhere between the respective solid and dotted lines.

5.6 Effect on Pseudonym Messaging Delay

Finally, for messages that users successfully transmit via pseudonyms under various enforced buddy set sizes, Figure 7 shows the distribution of artificial *delays* that Buddies imposes on those message transmissions to preserve indinymity. Unsurprisingly, the percentage of messages experiencing delays increases with buddy set size, since any pseudonym's owner must effectively wait to post until all her buddies are also online, and large buddy sets increase the likelihood of some buddy being offline at the time of a desired message transmission. When a message *is* delayed, unfortunately, it is commonly delayed by at least one hour, and under large buddy set sizes often by a day or more. This result further confirms our intuition that *long-term* resistance to probabilistic intersection attacks in dynamic networks may really be feasible only for delay-tolerant transmission.

We contrast the messaging delays experienced under the two buddy set formation schemes above: one based on an oracle's perspective of users' long-term reliability, the other based on a more realistic dynamic algorithm. In this case, we find somewhat surprisingly that the dynamic scheme actually delays substantially fewer messages than the oracle scheme. This is because the oracle scheme sorts buddies into sets based only on *global* reliability measured over the entire trace, and may inappropriately group together users who were online for similar durations *but at different times*. As the dynamic scheme builds buddy sets using recent information localized in time, it better groups ephemeral users who are online at similar times. Neither of these buddy set formation schemes are likely to be close to optimal, and we consider improving them to be a useful area for future work.

5.7 Practical Considerations

The integration of Buddies into Dissent sheds light into both the overheads of Buddies in a real system and the implementation complexities that Buddies induces. We built both Buddies and a web service for querying the various

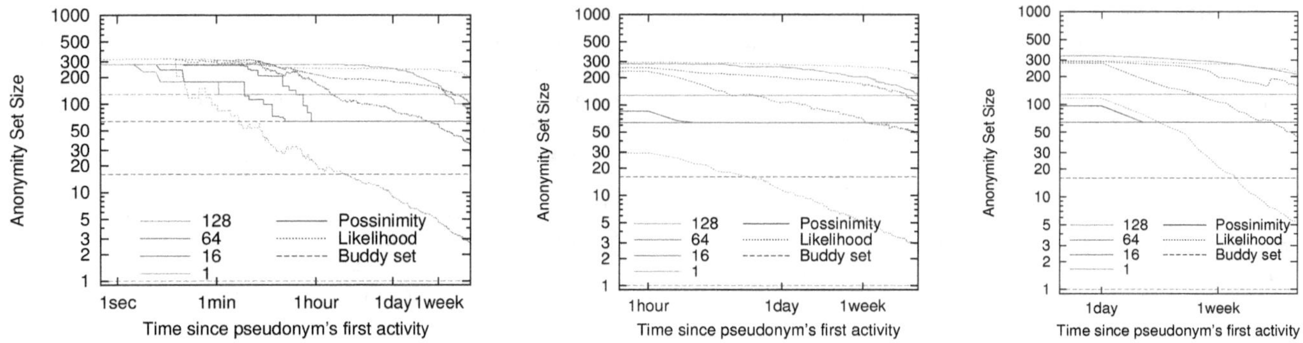

(a) 1-second rounds (b) 1-hour rounds (c) 1-day rounds

Figure 5: Measured worst-case anonymity loss over time under one example probabilistic intersection attack.

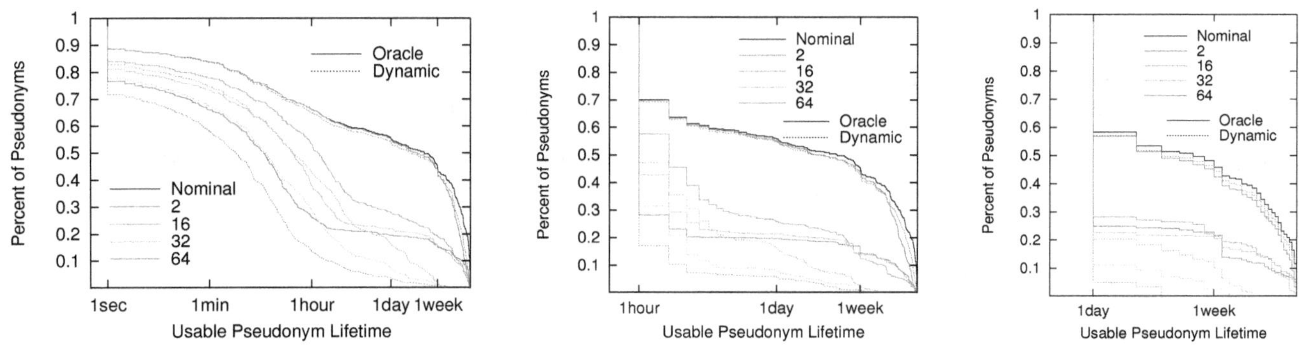

(a) 1-second rounds (b) 1-hour rounds (c) 1-day rounds

Figure 6: CDFs showing distributions of pseudonym lifetimes, with and without indinymity enforcement via buddy sets.

Buddies meters and we modified Dissent [52] to 1) support the reactive and proactive analysis in the anonymity protocol and 2) transmit the set of online members (those with ciphertexts used in Dissent) along with the cleartext messages at the end of each round. Buddies totaled 528 lines of C++ code, while Dissent incurred only 41 lines of additional C++ code. Included within the 528 lines of C++ code, Buddies comes with both a static and dynamic policy each weighing in at 89 and 172 lines of code, respectively.

In Dissent, the buddy set concept applied cleanly; however, in the current Dissent implementation, the maintenance of possinymity is not ideal. While DC-nets theoretically allow serial processing of anonymous cleartexts allowing finer grained control over possinymity, currently, Dissent servers perform the cleartext revealing process for all scheduled Nyms in parallel, which limits possinymity evaluations to occur only before processing the first anonymous cleartext. Performing the operation iteratively would require adding additional interaction among the servers, potentially adding significant overhead. Overhead would be negligible only for rounds with interval time t in which there were m scheduled Nyms with inter-server network latency of l, where $m \times l \ll t$. Fortunately, the Dissent implementation does support scheduling Nyms during different intervals, and therefore Buddies can still make both possinymity and indinymity sets largely independent for different Nyms.

Using our Dissent implementation of Buddies, we focused evaluations on the additional delay added by Buddies. We constructed a network of 8 server machines, 64 client machines, and from 8 to 512 clients (running up to 8 clients on each client machine). Clients have a 50 millisecond delay

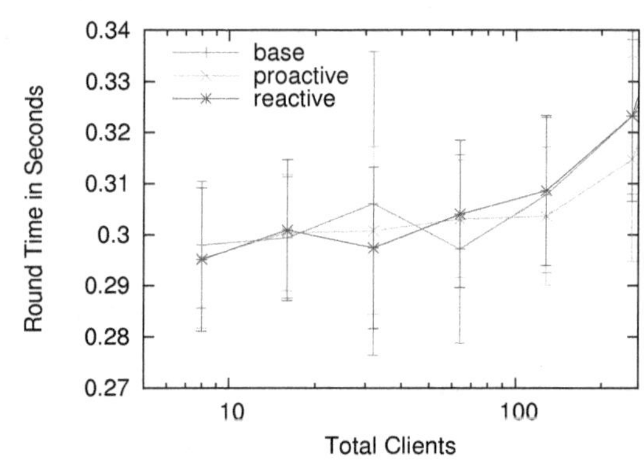

Figure 8: The overhead of using Buddies in Dissent.

and aggregate 100 M/bit connection to servers, while servers have a 10 millisecond delay to other servers, but each has a dedicated 100 M/bit connection to every other server. To focus on the overheads Buddies incurs, we avoided sending anonymous plaintexts across Dissent, The results, shown in Figure 8, indicate that Buddies imposes negligible overhead over Dissent—within measurement error—because performance costs are dominated by the expensive asymmetric cryptography used in signing and verifying messages.

6. RELATED WORK

The utility of pseudonyms has been well-recognized since Chaum's seminal paper on mix networks [8]. Pseudonymity has motivated much work in anonymous authentication [36] and signature schemes [24,35]. One way to protect distributed

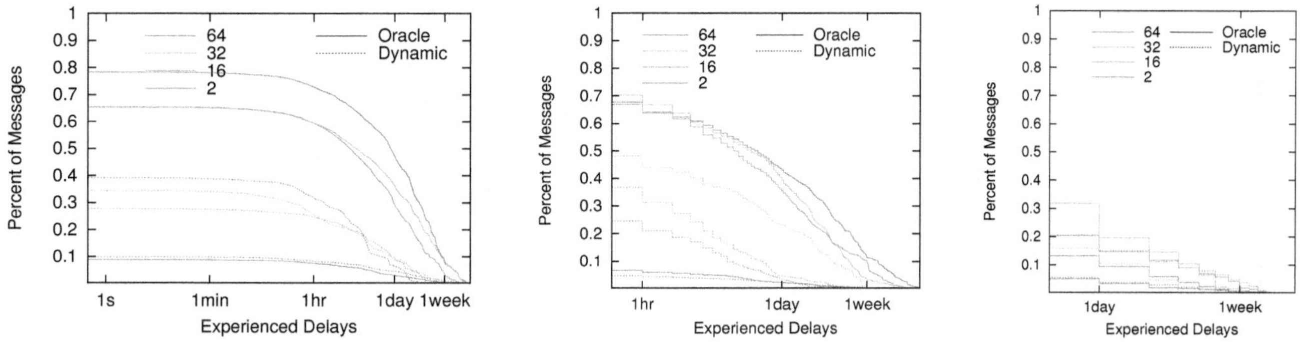

(a) 1-second rounds (b) 1-hour rounds (c) 1-day rounds

Figure 7: CDFs showing distributions of delays imposed on successfully transmitted messages under Buddies.

systems from Sybil attacks [19] is to build online pseudonyms atop "real-world" identities [22]. None of these approaches protect a pseudonym's owner from being traced via network monitoring, however. We concur with recent proposals to integrate pseudonymity into network architecture [29], although this gateway-based proposal unfortunately has the same "single point of failure" weakness as a conventional single-hop proxy or commercial VPN service [1].

Multi-hop mix networks [15] and onion routing systems [18] address this single point of failure, but remain vulnerable to many traffic analysis attacks. Pseudonymous communication is by now well-known to be highly vulnerable to long-term intersection attacks [31,42], later strengthened into statistical disclosure attacks [16,37,53]. Padding communications to a constant rate with dummy traffic [4,6,14,23] can slow—but not stop—passive intersection attacks [37].

Padding may not even slow *active* attacks, however, where an attacker deliberately perturbs performance to trace a circuit [20,38,45]. Active attacks are eminently realistic, being already widely used for Internet censorship [26,49], for example. Buddies is the only architecture we are aware of that addresses both passive *and* active intersection attacks, by "collectivizing" the anonymizer's control plane logic into a Policy Oracle component that cannot see—and thus cannot leak—sensitive information (Section 2), even when replicated for accountability (Section 4.3). This architecture ensures that Buddies' attack mitigation policies apply regardless of whether clients churn "normally," or are *forced* to slow or go offline due to deliberate denial-of-service.

The Java Anonymous Proxy [3] incorporates an "Anonym-O-Meter" [21], to give users an indication of their current anonymity level. This meter does not address intersection attacks, but serves as a precedent for Buddies' computation and reporting of possinymity and indinymity metrics.

Prior systems also protect anonymity within well-defined groups. Tarzan [23] organizes an overlay of *mimics*, where each user maintains constant *cover* traffic with k other mimics to mitigate traffic analysis attacks. Systems based on DC-nets [9], such as Herbivore [46] and earlier versions of Dissent [11, 13, 52], achieve provable traffic analysis resistance for *unlinkable* messages in a *single* communication round. Since every group member typically knows the online status of every other, however, linkable transmissions using pseudonyms can make such systems *more* vulnerable to intersection attack than "amorphous" systems such as Tor. Buddies addresses this risk by using linkable ring signatures to authenticate and "tag" users (Section 4.3).

Hopper and Vasserman [30] establish anonymity among sets of k members in a mix, similar to buddy sets, and explore the resistance of these k-anonymity sets to statistical disclosure attacks. Buddies builds on this approach to offer users dynamic anonymity monitoring and active controls over tradeoffs between anonymity and performance. Aqua [6] uses padded, multipath onion routing to achieve efficiency and reduce vulnerability to traffic analysis. We expect Buddies be synergistic with designs like Aqua's, by providing a stronger and more controllable notion of intersection attack resistance than currently provided by Aqua's k-sets.

7. CONCLUSION

Buddies offers the first systematic architecture addressing long-term intersection attacks in anonymity systems, by offering passive metrics of vulnerability and active control policies. While only a first step leaving many open questions, our trace-based simulations and working prototype suggest that Buddies may point to practical ways of further protecting anonymity-sensitive users of online forums.

Acknowledgments

We would like to thank Joan Feigenbaum, Aaron Johnson, Peter Druschel, our shepherd Clay Shields, and the anonymous reviewers for their helpful feedback on this paper. This material is based upon work supported by the Defense Advanced Research Agency (DARPA) and SPAWAR Systems Center Pacific, Contract No. N66001-11-C-4018.

8. REFERENCES

[1] Anonymizer, September 2012. http://anonymizer.com/.

[2] K. Bauer et al. Bitblender: light-weight anonymity for BitTorrent. In *AIPACa*, 2008.

[3] O. Berthold, H. Federrath, and M. Köhntopp. Project "anonymity and unobservability in the internet". In *CFP*, April 2000.

[4] O. Berthold and H. Langos. Dummy traffic against long term intersection attacks. In *2nd PET*, 2002.

[5] O. Berthold, A. Pfitzmann, and R. Standtke. The disadvantages of free MIX routes and how to overcome them. In *Workshop on Design Issues in Anonymity and Unobservability*, pages 30–45, July 2000.

[6] S. L. Blond, D. Choffnes, W. Zhou, P. Druschel, H. Ballani, and P. Francis. Towards efficient traffic-analysis resistant anonymity networks. In *SIGCOMM*, August 2013.

[7] J. Brickell and V. Shmatikov. Efficient anonymity-preserving data collection. In *12th KDD*, pages 76–85, Aug. 2006.

[8] D. Chaum. Untraceable electronic mail, return addresses, and digital pseudonyms. *Communications of the ACM*, Feb. 1981.

[9] D. Chaum. The dining cryptographers problem: Unconditional sender and recipient untraceability. *Journal of Cryptology*, pages 65–75, Jan. 1988.

[10] D. Chaum, A. Fiat, and M. Naor. Untraceable electronic cash. In *CRYPTO*, Aug. 1988.

[11] H. Corrigan-Gibbs and B. Ford. Dissent: accountable anonymous group messaging. In *17th CCS*, Oct. 2010.

[12] H. Corrigan-Gibbs and B. Ford. Scavenging for anonymity with BlogDrop (abstract). In *Provable Privacy Workshop*, July 2012.

[13] H. Corrigan-Gibbs, D. I. Wolinsky, and B. Ford. Proactively accountable anonymous messaging in Verdict. In *22nd USENIX Security*, Aug. 2013.

[14] W. Dai. PipeNet 1.1, Aug. 1996. UseNet post. `http://www.weidai.com/pipenet.txt`.

[15] G. Danezis, R. Dingledine, and N. Mathewson. Mixminion: Design of a Type III anonymous remailer protocol. In *IEEE SP*, pages 2–15, May 2003.

[16] G. Danezis and A. Serjantov. Statistical disclosure or intersection attacks on anonymity systems. In *Information Hiding Workshop*, May 2004.

[17] C. Díaz, S. Seys, J. Claessens, and B. Preneel. Towards measuring anonymity. In *Proceedings of the 2nd international conference on Privacy enhancing technologies*, PET'02, 2003.

[18] R. Dingledine, N. Mathewson, and P. Syverson. Tor: the second-generation onion router. In *12th USENIX Security*, Aug. 2004.

[19] J. R. Douceur. The Sybil attack. In *1st International Workshop on Peer-to-Peer Systems*, pages 251–260, Mar. 2002.

[20] N. S. Evans, R. Dingledine, and C. Grothoff. A practical congestion attack on Tor using long paths. In *18th USENIX Security*, Aug. 2009.

[21] H. Federrath. The Anonym-O-Meter. `http://anon.inf.tu-dresden.de/help/jap_help/en/help/jap.JAPNewView_anonymometer.html`, July 2013.

[22] B. Ford and J. Strauss. An offline foundation for online accountable pseudonyms. In *1st International Workshop on Social Network Systems (SocialNets)*, 2008.

[23] M. J. Freedman and R. Morris. Tarzan: A peer-to-peer anonymizing network layer. In *9th CCS*, pages 193–206, 2002.

[24] E. Fujisaki and K. Suzuki. Traceable ring signature. In *10th PKC*, pages 181–200, Apr. 2007.

[25] J. Furukawa and K. Sako. An efficient scheme for proving a shuffle. In *CRYPTO*, pages 368–387, Aug. 2001.

[26] P. Gill et al. Characterizing censorship of Web content worldwide, 2013. `http://www.cs.stonybrook.edu/~phillipa/papers/GCDG_May8.pdf`.

[27] P. Golle and A. Juels. Dining cryptographers revisited. *Eurocrypt*, pages 456–473, May 2004.

[28] A. Haeberlen, P. Kouznetsov, and P. Druschel. PeerReview: Practical accountability for distributed systems. In *21st SOSP*, Oct. 2007.

[29] S. Han et al. Expressive privacy control with pseudonyms. In *SIGCOMM*, Aug. 2013.

[30] N. Hopper and E. Y. Vasserman. On the effectiveness of k-anonymity against traffic analysis and surveillance. In *WPES*, Oct. 2006.

[31] D. Kedogan, D. Agrawal, and S. Penz. Limits of anonymity in open environments. In *5th International Workshop on Information Hiding*, pages 53–69, Oct. 2002.

[32] D. Kelly, R. Raines, R. Baldwin, B. Mullins, and M. Grimaila. Towards mathematically modeling the anonymity reasoning ability of an adversary. In *IPCCC*, pages 524–531. IEEE, 2008.

[33] D. J. Kelly. *A taxonomy for and analysis of anonymous communications networks*. PhD thesis, Wright Patterson AFB, OH, USA, 2009. AAI3351544.

[34] B. Levine, M. Reiter, C. Wang, and M. Wright. Timing attacks in low-latency mix systems. In *Financial Cryptography*, pages 251–265. 2004.

[35] J. K. Liu, V. K. Wei, and D. S. Wong. Linkable spontaneous anonymous group signature for ad hoc groups. In *Australian Conference on Information Security and Privacy*, pages 614–623, July 2004.

[36] A. Lysyanskaya, R. L. Rivest, A. Sahai, and S. Wolf. Pseudonym systems. In *Selected Areas in Cryptography*, pages 184–199. Springer, 2000.

[37] N. Mathewson and R. Dingledine. Practical traffic analysis: extending and resisting statistical disclosure. In *PET*, May 2004.

[38] S. J. Murdoch and G. Danezis. Low-cost traffic analysis of Tor. In *IEEE Security and Privacy*, pages 183–195, May 2005.

[39] C. A. Neff. A verifiable secret shuffle and its application to e-voting. In *CCS*, pages 116–125, Nov. 2001.

[40] A. Pfitzmann and M. Hansen. A terminology for talking about privacy by data minimization: Anonymity, unlinkability, undetectability, unobservability, pseudonymity, and identity management, Aug. 2010.

[41] A. Pfitzmann, B. Pfitzmann, and M. Waidner. ISDN-mixes: Untraceable communication with very small bandwidth overhead. In *GI/ITG Conference on Communication in Distributed Systems*, February 1991.

[42] J.-F. Raymond. Traffic analysis: Protocols, attacks, design issues and open problems. In *Workshop on Design Issues in Anonymity and Unobservability*, pages 10–29, 2000.

[43] A. Serjantov and G. Danezis. Towards an information theoretic metric for anonymity. In *Proceedings of the 2nd international conference on Privacy enhancing technologies*, PET'02, 2003.

[44] V. Shmatikov and M.-H. Wang. Measuring relationship anonymity in mix networks. In *WPES*, Oct. 2006.

[45] V. Shmatikov and M.-H. Wang. Timing analysis in low-latency mix networks: Attacks and defenses. In *Computer Security–ESORICS 2006*. Springer, 2006.

[46] E. G. Sirer, S. Goel, M. Robson, and D. Engin. Eluding carnivores: File sharing with strong anonymity. In *SIGOPS EW*, Sept. 2004.

[47] C. Soghoian. Surveillance and security lessons from the Petraeus scandal. 12 2012.

[48] N. Tran, B. Min, J. Li, and L. Submaranian. Sybil-resilient online content voting. In *6th NSDI*, pages 15–28, Apr. 2009.

[49] J.-P. Verkamp and M. Gupta. Inferring mechanics of Web censorship around the world. In *2nd FOCI*, Aug. 2012.

[50] M. Waidner and B. Pfitzmann. The dining cryptographers in the disco: Unconditional sender and recipient untraceability with computationally secure serviceability. In *Eurocrypt*, pages 302–319, Apr. 1989.

[51] D. I. Wolinsky, H. Corrigan-Gibbs, B. Ford, and A. Johnson. Scalable anonymous group communication in the anytrust model. In *EuroSec*, Apr. 2012.

[52] D. I. Wolinsky, H. Corrigan-Gibbs, A. Johnson, and B. Ford. Dissent in numbers: Making strong anonymity scale. In *10th OSDI*, pages 179–192, Oct. 2012.

[53] M. K. Wright, M. Adler, B. N. Levine, and C. Shields. Passive-logging attacks against anonymous communications systems. *TISSEC*, May 2008.

[54] H. Yu, P. B. Gibbons, M. Kaminsky, and F. Xiao. SybilLimit: A near-optimal social network defense against sybil attacks. In *IEEE Symposium on Security and Privacy*, pages 3–17, May 2008.

Content-Based Isolation: Rethinking Isolation Policy Design on Client Systems

Alexander Moshchuk
Microsoft Research
Redmond, WA, USA
alexmos@microsoft.com

Helen J. Wang
Microsoft Research
Redmond, WA, USA
helenw@microsoft.com

Yunxin Liu
Microsoft Research Asia
Beijing, China
yunliu@microsoft.com

ABSTRACT

Modern client platforms, such as iOS, Android, Windows Phone, and Windows 8, have progressed from a per-user isolation policy, where users are isolated but a user's applications run in the same isolation container, to an application isolation policy, where different applications are isolated from one another. However, this is not enough because mutually distrusting content can interfere with one another inside a *single* application. For example, an attacker-crafted image may compromise a photo editor application and steal other images processed by the editor.

In this paper, we advocate a content-based principal model in which the OS treats content owners as its principals and isolates content of different owners from one another. Our key contribution is to generalize the content-based principal model from web browsers, namely, the same-origin policy, into an isolation policy that is suitable for all applications. The key challenge we faced is to support flexible isolation granularities while remaining compatible with the web. In this paper, we present the design, implementation, and evaluation of our prototype system that tackles this challenge.

Categories and Subject Descriptors

D.4.6 [**Operating Systems**]: Security and Protection

Keywords

Web browsers; same-origin policy; isolation

1. INTRODUCTION

Much research has been devoted to isolation *mechanisms* [38, 33, 29, 3, 53, 12, 17] to enable robust isolation containers in operating systems. However, little research has been done on the dual of the problem, isolation *policies*, namely, "what should be put into the isolation containers"; this is the topic of this paper. Isolation policy design is as critical as that of isolation mechanisms, since even with *perfect* isolation containers, an improper isolation policy can render the system *insecure*.

For example, today's Windows-based or Unix-based desktop PCs treat users as principals and protect user accounts from one another. However, mutually distrusting applications of one user can interfere with one another. This is the root cause of the significant malware problem on desktops. Learning the lessons from desktops, modern client platforms, such as iOS and Android, have refined the user-based isolation policy to treat each application code package as a separate principal, and different applications are run in separate isolation containers. This isolation policy is still too coarse because mutually distrusting content can interfere with one another within the same application. Consider the scenario where Alice opens a PowerPoint presentation from `http://alice.com/talk.ppt`, which embeds a malicious video from `http://attacker.com/advideo.swf`. The attacker can compromise Alice's presentation as well as *other* documents being rendered by PowerPoint.

Figure 1 illustrates the evolution of isolation policies on client platforms. In this paper, we further refine the isolate-by-code package policy and advocate future client platforms to embrace a content-based isolation policy which puts execution instances of mutually distrusting content into separate isolation containers. Content-based isolation offers a fundamentally more secure system because any content's impact including that of malicious content is *minimized* to just the content owner's isolation container. Consequently, there is *no need to ask users* to determine whether to take the risk of opening any content. Existing applications often prompt users (e.g., "Are you sure you want to open this document?")

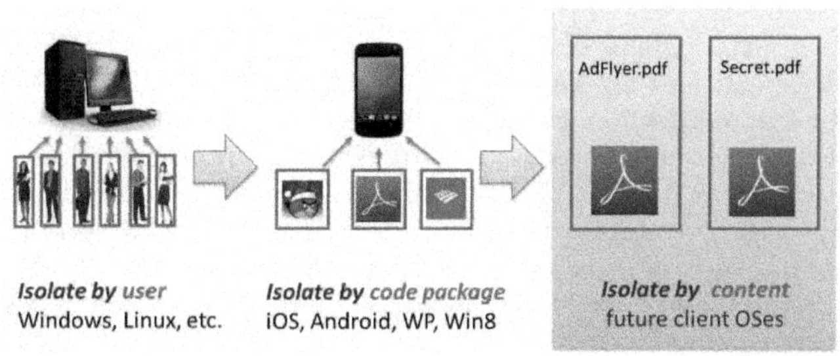

Figure 1: The evolution of isolation policies. Content-based isolation provides two benefits over other policies: (1) Any remote content's impact is minimized (2) There is no need to ask users to determine whether to risk opening remote content.

CCS'13, November 4–8, 2013, Berlin, Germany.
Copyright 2013 ACM 978-1-4503-2477-9/13/11 ...$15.00.
http://dx.doi.org/10.1145/2508859.2516722.

because such fine-grained containment is not available, and risk handling is unreasonably outsourced to the user.

To some extent, the notion of a content-based principal model exists in today's web. All web browsers implement the same-origin policy [41], which prevents web content of different origins (represented by the triple <protocol, domain, port>) from interfering with one another. Unfortunately, these principals may undesirably share the same isolation container in commercial browsers [49]. Recent research browsers, such as Gazelle [49], proposed to separate web site principals into separate isolation containers, fully achieving a content-based principal model for the browser setting.

As modern client platforms (e.g., iOS, Android, Windows Phone, Windows 8) and applications embrace cloud-centric computing where documents and computing logic reside in the cloud and are cached on client devices, applicability of a content-based principal model goes beyond the browser setting. Today, applications often need to process and embed remote content. For example, Microsoft Office 2010 can open remote web documents, PowerPoint 2010 allows users to embed YouTube videos in presentations and the Google Cloud Connect [16] plug-in allows Office to sync documents with the cloud. Such applications are effectively *becoming browsers* for their own media types, and they now face many of the same security challenges that web browsers have faced over the past decade, namely, isolating mutually distrusting content from one another.

Today, content isolation is left as a responsibility of each native application. For example, Microsoft Office 2010's new *Protected View* [30] feature provides a sandboxed *read-only* mode for documents originating from the Internet and users have to explicitly "enable editing" to remove the sandbox and its restrictions at their own risk. Adobe Reader recently introduced a similar sandboxing feature [1]. Letting each application handle content protection has serious drawbacks. First, security of a user's cloud data is duplicated and entrusted to *all* of the user's applications. Attackers need only find one badly-written application and target it to exploit all content (at the web scale) that this application renders. Second, security logic in applications is often mixed with error-prone content processing logic; content isolation vulnerabilities are discovered not only in browsers and plug-ins [18, 49, 2], but also in desktop applications. For example, the recent RSA SecurID token compromise [36] that affected 20,000 RSA's enterprise customers was caused by a maliciously crafted Excel email attachment, and from 2008-2011, 88% (224) of Microsoft Office vulnerabilities are content parsing flaws exploitable by maliciously crafted documents [34]. Worse, many desktop applications do *not* offer any isolation for certain remote content. For example, PowerPoint 2010 renders embedded remote videos in the same process and makes no attempt to isolate them, letting potential Flash vulnerabilities endanger the PowerPoint application and its documents. Overall, users must endure weak and inconsistent security of applications that process their cloud-backed data.

In this work, we let the OS take over the burden of content isolation from applications. By consolidating content isolation logic in the OS, we *reduce* the trusted computing base from trusting many applications' isolation logic to trusting just that of the OS. The main contribution of this paper is a general content-based principal model suitable for *all* applications beyond just browsers. Our design goals are: (1) flexible isolation, from the granularity of a single addressable document to documents hosted at multiple domains, (2) compatibility with browsers' isolation policy so that attackers cannot violate browser security from non-browser applications and vice versa, and (3) easy adaptation of native applications.

We present a design that achieves these goals and describe our prototype system called ServiceOS, implemented as a reference monitor between the kernel and applications in Windows. We demonstrate that ServiceOS is practical by successfully adapting several large applications, such as Microsoft Word, Outlook, and Internet Explorer, onto ServiceOS with a relatively small amount of effort. Our evaluation shows that ServiceOS eliminates a large percentage of existing security vulnerabilities by design and has acceptable overhead. We also demonstrate how ServiceOS contains two working exploits.

In the rest of this paper, we describe our threat model in Section 2 and our system model in Section 3. We define our system's principals in Section 4 and show how to enforce principal definitions in Section 5. We present ServiceOS's implementation in Section 6, and evaluate ServiceOS and the effort to adapt several native applications in Section 7. We discuss related work in Section 8 and conclude in Section 9.

2. THREAT MODEL

The primary attacker against which our system defends is the *content owner attacker*. Like the web attacker [23], the content owner attacker controls content server(s) serving malicious data that exploits vulnerabilities. Users may be enticed to access such malicious content from e-mail spam, malvertising, or phishing. The goal of ServiceOS is to minimize the impact of any malicious content by designing the right isolation policy and enforcement mechanisms. Our trusted computing base is the ServiceOS kernel.

We leave it up to content owners to consider network attackers, who may compromise content integrity and confidentiality. A content owner who is worried about network attackers should employ end-to-end secure channels (such as TLS) for content transport.

We are also not concerned about attackers that target specific content owners, such as cross-site scripting or cross-site request forgery attacks. These are fundamentally content-specific vulnerabilities which only content owners can fundamentally fix.

3. SYSTEM MODEL

A principal is the unit of isolation. Program execution instances with different principal labels are isolated in separate isolation containers. We refer to an execution instance with a principal label as a *principal instance* (PI).

In ServiceOS, each principal has its own local store. A user may use a certain online storage service, such as Dropbox or Google Drive. We assume that all user-downloaded content is stored on such services. This is quickly becoming the norm with modern OSes, with integrations of ChromeOS and Google Drive, Windows 8 and SkyDrive, and OS X and iCloud.

There is *no* sharing across principals or isolation containers (i.e., no global file systems unlike today's desktop sys-

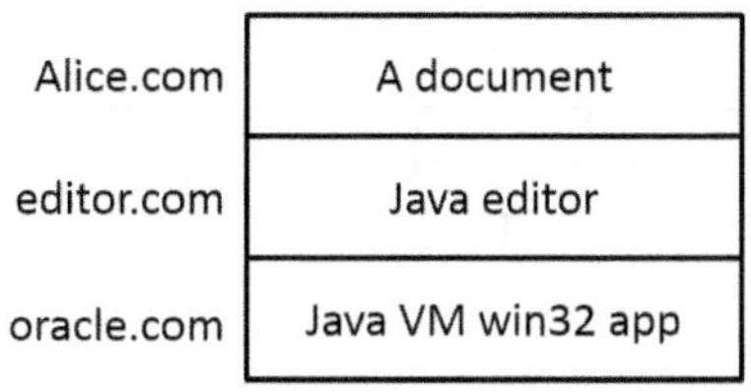

Figure 2: Execution instance as a content processing stack.

tems) except through explicit cross-principal communication system APIs, analogous to IPC.

We have adopted user-driven access control [40] to allow users to share data across isolation boundaries. This is done through authentic user actions on trusted UIs (e.g., mouse clicks on a copy button, "save-as" button, or a file picker UI) or gestures like drag-and-drop or Ctrl-V. User-driven access control enables capability-based, least-privilege access, driven by users' natural interactions with applications and the system. We will not discuss it further in this paper and refer interested readers to [40].

For example, Microsoft Word would have its own local store on ServiceOS. A user may launch Word and start editing a new document. The document is auto-saved into Word's own local store. When the user wants to save the document to her Dropbox store (across the isolation boundary), the user clicks on a trusted "save as" button embedded in Word. The click brings up a trusted file picker window. The user then selects Dropbox, specifies the file name, and clicks on the "save" button (also part of the trusted file picker). The system only allows Word to write to a user-specified Dropbox path, but not other parts of Dropbox or other online stores, achieving least-privilege access.

ServiceOS allows a user to have a local store, such as photo or music libraries. We label all content in the user's local store as the principal "local", separate from all other principals. User-driven access control is the means for the user to get content in or out of the local store.

4. DEFINING PRINCIPALS

An isolation policy design needs to answer two questions: (1) *how execution instances should be labeled*, or what defines a principal, (2) *how remote content is fetched and dispatched into each principal to comply with the principal definition.* This section presents our design for the former and the next section addresses the latter.

4.1 Execution instance as a content processing stack

Before presenting our design on labeling execution instances, we first illustrate what constitutes an execution instance.

An execution instance may involve content from different owners. Figure 2 illustrates such an example: a document is rendered by a Java editor application which runs on a Java Virtual Machine (JVM) which in turn is a Win32 program running on Windows. The document, editor, and JVM may belong to different owners: e.g., the document may belong to `alice.com`, editor to `editor.com`, and JVM to `oracle.com`. Therefore, we characterize an execution instance as a *content-processing stack.* Each layer of the stack consists of content that is owned by some entity and that needs to be addressable (for example, a web document is addressable with a URL, but user input data is not addressable). The content at a layer is consumed and processed by the next lower layer. We refer to layers below the top layer as *content processors.* For example, plug-ins in today's browsers are treated as content processors in our system.

We do *not* treat static data content as safer than active code content or content processors, because we want to allow both type-safe and native applications on our system (as is the case for most real-world client systems). Since maliciously-crafted static data can be turned into code by exploiting memory errors in native applications, we treat code and data as equally-capable content.

The content-to-processor mapping (e.g., mapping alice.com's document content to the editor) can be configured by the content owner (alice.com) or by the user. Today's web servers indicate content's MIME type using the `Content-Type` header in HTTP responses. Desktop applications can use the same mechanism to convey content types. Additionally, we propose a new `Content-Processor` HTTP header to allow content servers to specify desired content processors by a URL or unique ID. For example, a web server serving `photo.jpg` could send:

Content-Processor: "http://www.photoedit.com/editor.app"

The content owner can sign this mapping with its private key. Users or the OS vendor can configure default content processors.

4.2 Principal labeling and isolation policies

The labels of content processing stacks ultimately determine the isolation policy of the system. Content processing stacks with the same label belong to the same principal and isolation container. We establish three goals for the principal labeling design.

1. Enable isolation policies of *arbitrary granularities* for URL-addressable resources (a file at a URL rather than an internal object in a file). The most fine-grained principal can be a single document. However, a fixed policy like this can be unnecessary and can impede functionality: some documents may not be mutually distrusting and may have complex cross-document interactions. For example, a Microsoft Word document may interact with an Excel document by referencing its data cells or charts. So, we need a flexible mechanism to group documents into a single principal.
2. *Separate content owning from content hosting* so that a content owner can get its content hosted anywhere and be treated as belonging to the same principal. Suppose Alice created a number of documents or photos and uploaded them to various online storage services (e.g., Dropbox) or photo sharing services (e.g., Google's Picasaweb). We would want to associate all this content with the same owner Alice regardless of where it is hosted. This goal is especially important for desktop applications where users often create content locally and then make a separate decision on where to host it. This is unlike web applications, where content is usually tightly associated with its host.
3. *Be compatible with web browsers' isolation policy.* Today's web browsers' isolation policy is the same-origin policy (SOP) [41] which treats web sites as mutu-

ally distrusting principals, labeled with web site origins, a triple of <**protocol, domain, port**> [48]. Web sites can create subdomains to have finer-grained principals (e.g., user1.socialnet.com, user2.socialnet.com). SOP itself does not meet the above two goals that we set for principal labeling. For example, **youtube.com** and **google.com** belong to Google, but cannot be configured to belong to the same principal. SOP also does not support finer-grained isolation at path or URL level: `https://www.facebook.com/user1` and `https://www.facebook.com/user2` cannot be configured to be different principals.

Our goal of being compatible with SOP is due to two reasons. First, it is undecidable for an OS to determine whether an application is a web browser. Even non-browser applications may use core browser components; for example, Microsoft .NET provides a web browser control which allows any .NET application to use browser functionality; similarly, iOS and Android also allow browser components to be included in applications. Second, even if an OS could tell the difference, it is still desirable for browsers and non-browser applications to have the same principal model because an attacker could cause browsers to render non-browser content and vice versa. Then, applications with coarser-grained isolation can be used to undermine finer-grained isolation in other applications. For example, modern OSes like iOS and Android isolate by application package (see Section 1), which is coarser-grained than browsers' same-origin policy. An application running on such OSes can access two web sites from different origins and have them coexist in the same isolation container, not meeting the web sites' expectation of being isolated from one another per same-origin policy. Therefore, we aim to design a web-compatible principal model.

4.2.1 Public key as owner ID

To achieve these goals, we propose a public-key-based owner ID. Each URL-addressable content is tagged with its owner's public key and a signature that signs the host URL. This signature indicates that the signed host URL points to a resource owned by the owner of the public key. We introduce a new HTTP response header for this purpose:

Owner: publicKey=<key>; hostURLSig=signed(responseURL)

Content owners need to trust hosts to specify this header correctly and this can be easily checked by the owners. Note that ensuring content integrity and confidentiality are orthogonal features that owners and hosts can collaborate on and enable in addition to principal definition specification.

A content processing stack is then labeled with a stack of public key labels, which we refer to as the *owner stack*. ServiceOS treats execution instances with the same owner stack as the same principal.

Since legacy web sites do not use our `Owner` header for principal definition, our system, by default, labels an execution instance with the origin stack of its content processing stack, capturing the origin of the content at each layer. This default gives the same isolation semantics as today's browsers: different browser vendors are content processors of different origins, and they isolate an origin's resources (e.g.,

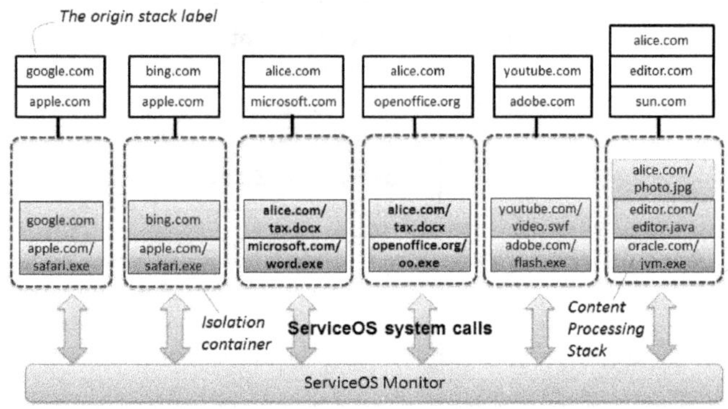

Figure 3: The origin stack as the default principal label.

cookies, cache, local storage) from other origins in ServiceOS as well as in today's systems.

If an `Owner` header is present for public key-based principal definition, then our system overrides the origin label with the public key value. Figure 3 shows six execution instances (or content processing stacks) and their corresponding isolation containers with the appropriate principal labels in the form of the origin stack[1]. Note that traditional browser plugins like Adobe Flash and browser renderers are treated as content processors.

Note that our owner ID design is different from locked same-origin policy [25] which uses *content host*'s X.509 certificates as principal labels for HTTPS origins. That scheme still ties the principal definition with the host. This design also differs from YURL [8] where YURL puts the host's public key as part of the URL, which also ties hosting with owning.

4.2.2 Augmenting SOP with Trust Lists

Although an owner ID offers both arbitrary isolation granularity and independence from hosts, some application developers will find it cumbersome to maintain a key pair and to compute signatures for each URL, and will resort to using the same-origin policy. For these developers, we introduce a "trust list" mechanism to augment SOP and to allow arbitrary isolation granularities (achieving Goal 1), but without the independence from hosts (not achieving Goal 2).

A content server can associate a trust list with any URL resource R at the server. The trust list contains a set of URLs with which R trusts to coexist in the same isolation container. This is *one-way* trust, meaning that R trusting to coexist with S does *not* mean that S trusts to coexist with R. *Two resources from two different URLs can live in the same isolation container if and only if they have mutual trust.* A resource R is allowed to be admitted to an isolation container if and only if all existing resources in the container trust to coexist with R, and R trusts to coexist with each of the existing resources.

For resources sent over HTTP, we propose a new HTTP response header called `Trust` to allow specifying a trust list. The value can be either a URL of the trust list or the trust list itself. We allow the wildcard "*" at the end of a URL for enumerating all resources at a path. We disallow wildcards for domains so that developers will not accidentally

[1]We omitted protocol schemes in the origins to save space, but they should be part of the origin label.

Algorithm 1 : Can the resource at URL u with a trust list be admitted to an isolation container with an effective label stack C? *If IsSamePrincipal(C, u) returns true, then ServiceOS admits u into C.*

```
function IsSamePrincipal (C, u) {
  us1 = C.TopLayerUrls();
  us2 = {u};
  repeat
    if (not MutuallyTrusted (us1, us2))
      return false
    us1 = us1.processors
    us2 = us2.processors
  until (us2.processors == null)
  UpdateContainerLabelWithNewURL (C, u)
  return true

function MutuallyTrusted(URLSet1, URLSet2) {
  foreach u1 in URLSet1
    foreach u2 in URLSet2
      if (u1 ∉ u2.TrustList or u2 ∉ u1.TrustList)
        return false
  return true
```

cluster mutually distrusting domains into a single principal. When the `Trust` header is missing, ServiceOS resorts back to the default, using the content server's origin to label the returned resource. For resources sent over non-HTTP protocols, we resort to the default SOP where we use the application as the scheme and the IP address as the domain. We expect this to be a rare case as existing trends indicate that nearly all communication happens over HTTP [37].

The default SOP principal model is equivalent to all resources from an origin indicating a trust list of just its origin followed by a "*".

The trust list mechanism can be used to realize coarser-grained or finer-grained[2] principals than that of SOP. For example, if `youtube.com` and `google.com` want to belong to the same principal, then `google.com`'s server needs to provide the header "`Trust:list=http://youtube.com/`" *and* `youtube.com` needs to provide "`Trust:list=http://google.com/`".

Consider an example of using the `Trust` header to achieve a fine-grained principal definition. A resource, say at `http://blog.com/alice/index.html`, specifies: `Trust:list=http://blog.com/alice/*`, expressing that the resource at the URL trusts to share the container with all other content from the path corresponding to Alice. If other resources at the path also indicate the same header, then this achieves path-based principal isolation. Note that only explicitly specified URLs are trusted. In this example, the resource from `http://blog.com/` is not trusted. Similarly, individual document URLs can also be put into the `Trust` header to achieve document-level granularity of isolation.

ServiceOS enforces the `Trust` header as follows. At any time, ServiceOS maintains a stack of *effective labels* for the

[2]Jackson et al [24] warned against using more fine-grained principal definitions than an origin and claimed that the isolation boundary can break down due to (1) a malicious library being included or (2) data export (e.g., form submission) being manipulated to send to attacker URLs. These two problems can also happen to the origin principal model and are not specific to finer-grained principals.

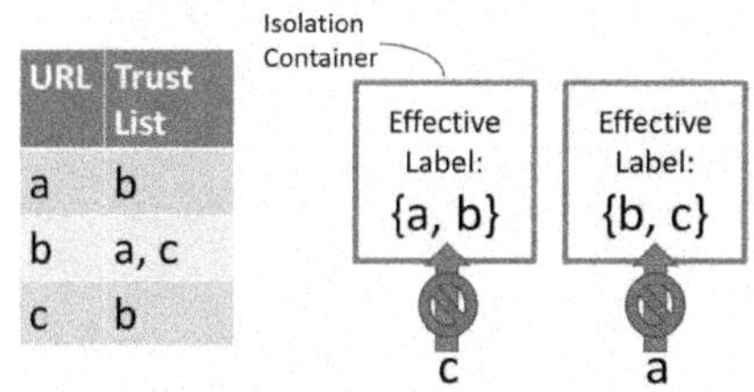

Figure 4: Non-transitivity in Trust. Although the trust lists show that a and b are mutually trusting and b and c are mutually trusting, transitive trust does not follow: a and c do not trust each other (as desired by their trust list specification) and will never share an isolation container.

content processing stacks (CPS) in an isolation container. The effective label of layer L is the set of URLs of resources at layer L of all content processing stacks. Given an isolation container with an effective label stack C and and an HTTP response for a resource at URL u with a trust list, ServiceOS determines whether u should be treated as the same principal as C and be admitted to the container with Algorithm 1: ServiceOS iterates over u and its lower content processor layers and checks whether they are mutually trusted with each layer of the effective label stack C of the isolation container. If all layers of u mutually trust corresponding layers in C, u can be admitted to the container C. In that case, C incorporates u's and its content processors' labels into its own.

A interesting and desirable property of trust list is its *non-transitivity*: given that a and b are mutually trusted and b and c are mutually trusted, it does not follow that a and c are mutually trusted and can share the same isolation container. Figure 4 illustrates this property.

A content server can easily manage trust lists by designating a URL to contain the list and having each resource in the list use a `Trust:url=<policyurl>` header. The list (principal definition) can then be evolved without changing each resource's `Trust` header value.

To simplify ServiceOS logic and content server tasks, we do not mix the trust-list-based principal definition with the public-key owner principal definition. A content server should pick one to use. When both headers are present, ServiceOS uses the `Owner` header and ignores the `Trust` header.

Note that `Trust` and `Owner` are applicable to only isolated content [48] (e.g., a standalone program, HTML program from a web site) whose principal label is the owner of the isolated content. These headers are not applicable to library content [48], such as JavaScript included via a `<script>` tag or other libraries which do not have their own principal identity, but are designed to be included by standalone programs.

We advocate both modern client platforms (e.g., iOS, Android, Windows 8) and web browsers (and web standards) to move towards such a flexible, unified principal model.

4.2.3 Coexistence with legacy browsers

If web servers use our `Trust` and `Owner` headers to configure principal definitions, their developers need to consider their behavior on legacy browsers.

If a principal definition is coarser-grained than an origin, a site can encounter functionality loss because legacy browsers would deny legitimate cross-origin interactions permitted by

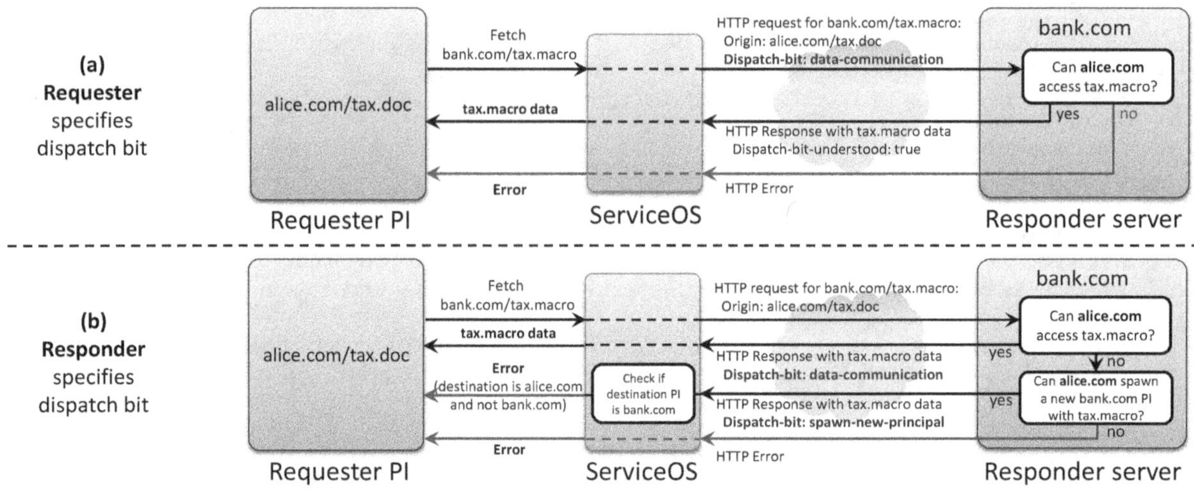

Figure 5: Two design choices for specifying the dispatch bit. Here, a Word application rendering a document from alice.com attempts to retrieve a helper macro from bank.com, to be used in the alice.com principal instance.

the principal definition. The site would need additional cross-origin communication code to maintain compatibility.

If a principal definition is finer-grained than an origin, then the site may lose expected isolation on legacy browsers. Security-sensitive web sites may just resort to the origin principal model to implement their isolation policies and to avoid two implementations (one for legacy browsers and one for new systems) until all major browsers adopt our proposal. Nevertheless, web sites that want to use finer-grained isolation but are not yet able to do so (e.g., `https://www.facebook.com/user1` and `https://www.facebook.com/user2` may want to be treated as different principals) may happily embrace the new headers and be safer on ServiceOS-capable systems.

5. ENFORCING PRINCIPAL DEFINITIONS

Central to enforcing our content-based principal definitions is how remote content is fetched from the network and to which principal instance (and isolation container) the returned content should be dispatched. Note that this enforcement mechanism is needed *in addition* to having a robust isolation container. In this section, we describe this fetching and dispatching logic and how it ensures that principal definitions are obeyed.

The dispatch decision is trivial when a Principal Instance (**PI**) of a requester principal fetches a remote resource of the same principal. We simply dispatch the returned resource to the requester PI. Determining whether a remote resource belongs to the same principal as the requester is done through the `IsSamePrincipal` check in Algorithm 1 if the resource's principal definition is based on a trust list, through public key stack comparision if an owner-ID-based principal definition is used, or through origin stack comparison if neither trust lists nor owner-based definitions are provided (Section 4).

More care is needed for cross-principal content fetch, namely, when the requester fetches content from the server of a different principal. Such a request can happen for two reasons: (1) Data communication: the requester wants some data from the responder server and the returned data should be dispatched to the requester principal instance; or (2) Spawning a new principal: the requester wants to *spawn* a new instance of the responder principal, for example if a user clicked on a hyperlink to open a new document, or a document of the requester principal embeds a resource from the responder principal; in this case, the returned data should be dispatched to the responder principal instance rather than that of the requester.

Because the requester can be malicious, we must ensure that our content fetch and dispatch logic can properly protect and isolate the responder principal from an attacking requester even in the face of arbitrary system API (ab)use.

The key idea in our design is to use a *dispatch bit* in either the request or the response to differentiate the two cross-principal content fetching scenarios.

There are two design choices of specifying this bit, illustrated in Figure 5. First, ServiceOS can specify the bit in the outgoing request to the responder server to convey whether the returned data will be dispatched to the requester PI or a (new) responder PI. Then, the server makes an access control decision for the request, and ServiceOS forwards the response to the requester PI. Second, the responder server (with knowledge of requester's label) can specify the bit in its response to ServiceOS to indicate whether the data is authorized to be dispatched to the requester PI or to a responder PI. Then, ServiceOS enforces the bit and either dispatches or discards the returned data. In both design choices, the request needs to contain the principal label of the requester, which we include using the HTTP Origin header [4].

Both designs can support legacy servers as follows. If the bit lives in the response, its absence tells ServiceOS that this is a legacy server. If the bit lives in the request, then the response needs to declare that the bit was understood; the absence of that declaration tells ServiceOS this is a legacy server. For legacy servers, ServiceOS will deliver the data to the responder PI to be compatible with browsers' same-origin policy.

The advantage of putting the bit in the request is that it lets the server optimize away a response that is destined to be dropped and return an error instead. The advan-

ServiceOS API	Examples of desktop application functions (e.g., for Word)	Examples of browser functions
CreatePI(URL, postData)	Open remote Word file	Enter URL into address bar, navigate to a link
Fetch(URL, postData)	Retrieve required resources for a document, such as templates, macros, or images	Same-origin `<iframe>`, `<script>`, `<style>`, original XMLHTTPRequest
Embed(URL, windowSpec, postData)	Embed remote images, spreadsheets, or videos	Cross-origin `<iframe>`, `<object>`, `<embed>`, <img>

Table 1: Core ServiceOS APIs

tage of putting the bit in the response is that it can be statically configured for each URL, rather than having the server perform access control checks for each request. Therefore, we advocate supporting the bit in both requests and responses to allow responder servers to get both advantages if desired: a diligent server can perform access control on each request and reduce network overhead (and indicate the server's knowledge of the dispatch bit in the request), and a lazy server can just statically configure its URLs when possible. When the dispatch bit from the response differs from that of request, the response's dispatch bit takes precedence.

Because HTTP has become the narrow waist of all communications [37], ServiceOS exposes system APIs for HTTP-based content fetch, and we indicate the dispatch bit with HTTP headers (Section 6). For application-level protocols other than HTTP, it is impossible (and undesirable) for ServiceOS to know their semantics and parse out their respective dispatch bits (even if they implement them). So, in the absence of dispatch bits, our system resorts to the default of returning the data to a responder PI only. With this default, applications that use peer-to-peer communication require modifications to run on ServiceOS. They must rely on explicit client-side cross-principal IPC to achieve peer-to-peer data transfer. For example, if a requester wants to retrieve data from the server of a responder principal with a non-HTTP P2P protocol, then the requester can first launch the responder's client-side PI through our system API `CreatePI(responderClientCodeURL)`; the new responder PI then retrieves the data and then passes it on to the requester PI.

Backward compatibility with existing web sites. To maintain web compatibility, ServiceOS supports MIME-type-based content dispatch as in Gazelle [49], translating MIME types in responses into dispatch bits in responses. We also support cookies and cross-site client-server communication primitives XMLHttpRequest Level 2 [52] and XDomainRequest [28], along with the associated CORS consent protocol [46]. Despite the availability of cookies, we strongly advocate native applications not to use the cookie mechanism, but to *explicitly* include their state (such as user preferences and authentication state) in their data requests to reduce the chance of cross-site request forgery (CSRF) attacks [5].

6. IMPLEMENTATION

We have implemented a prototype of ServiceOS on Windows 7 as a reference monitor between the OS and applications. Our implementation is in C# using .NET 3.5 and has two major components: the ServiceOS monitor and the system shell.

The monitor consists of 9.4k lines of code. It communicates with principal instances using ServiceOS system calls and upcalls, which are implemented as asynchronous XML-based messages sent over named pipes. The monitor creates a unique named pipe for each principal instance to issue system calls and receive upcalls.

The system shell consists of 3.6k lines of code. It provides a tab-based UI for users to enter URLs to visit web sites, view content rendered by native applications, or open standalone applications. The UI passes a newly typed URL to the monitor, which fetches the content, picks a content processor, and admits this content processing stack into the right isolation container, following the semantics of Sections 4 and 5.

Isolation mechanisms. We adopted Drawbridge [38] as our main sandboxing mechanism. Drawbridge can run unmodified Windows applications in a highly isolated mode by refactoring Windows into a library OS and virtualizing all high-level OS components, such as windowing libraries, files, or registry. Drawbridge exposes a very narrow base API for allocating virtual memory, threading, synchronization, and generic stream-based I/O (e.g., to access files that are part of an application). To protect our security policy, ServiceOS instructs Drawbridge to restrict I/O calls to only allow access to files that are part of the current principal's private storage, and to disallow pipe access other than to communicate with the ServiceOS monitor.

With Drawbridge, we are theoretically able to support all user-space-only Windows applications on our system, though in practice, Drawbridge is not yet mature enough to support certain application features (such as DLLs necessary to run macros in Office documents).

Note that our system design is independent of specific isolation mechanisms like Drawbridge. As proof, we added support for another sandboxing mechanism, which associates each principal with a separate, restricted user account, and runs applications in processes using these restricted UIDs. This allows greater application compatibility than is currently possible with Drawbridge, but it is not as secure: it has a much wider API surface, and UIDs alone do not form a security boundary in Windows (e.g., one could execute shatter attacks [43] based on window messages across UID boundaries).

To complete the system, our monitor augments APIs exposed by our isolation containers with a few higher-level APIs, which we discuss next.

Core ServiceOS system calls. There are three core system calls that we support: `Fetch`, `CreatePI`, and `Embed`. Table 1 shows examples of how applications may utilize these APIs. `Fetch` is used for data communications, and we implemented both synchronous and asynchronous versions. The other two calls are for creating new principal instances: `CreatePI(newUrl)` launches a new PI with a standalone UI (in a new tab), and `Embed(newUrl, <window specs>)` launches a new PI and embeds its UI window into the caller's UI. For all three calls, ServiceOS makes HTTP requests using .NET's built-in WebRequest classes. ServiceOS uses custom implementations of a cookie database and authentication manager. We implemented support for both `Owner` and `Trust` headers (Section 4), as well as Algorithm 1 for admitting resources to isolation containers.

For principal definition enforcement, we have implemented the design choice of having the dispatch bit in the HTTP response since this is the case where ServiceOS has to do additional enforcement work. We added a new directive name "dispatch-to" in the existing CSP [11] HTTP header with two possible values, 'requester' or 'responder'. If a server wants the returned data to be dispatched to a responder PI, then it specifies in its response header: `Content-Security-Policy: dispatch-to 'responder'`. The ServiceOS monitor checks for the directive in the HTTP response for each HTTP response and performs dispatching accordingly.

Display management. Our monitor controls window positioning, dimensions, transparency, and overlaying policies but is independent to the UI primitives available on the host OS. It communicates display policies to the UI, which implements application windows using .NET Forms. Sandboxed Drawbridge applications run an internal RDP [31] server to expose visual output and forward user input. Our UI implements ActiveX RDP clients, which the ServiceOS monitor connects to the corresponding applications' RDP servers. When running with no isolation or with UID-based isolation, ServiceOS relies on the Windows `SetParent` API call to attach applications' UI into our shell UI and to implement `Embed()`.

Packaging content processors. Content processors and standalone applications are packaged and delivered as an archive file with extension `.app`, which our monitor decompresses and executes as a new isolated process. These packages carry a manifest file containing information like the content processor's unique ID, main executable to run, or handled content types. Web servers may allow content processors to be cached using standard HTTP headers; we rely on this as a rudimentary update mechanism and leave more elaborate, finer-grained schemes (such as [9]) as future work.

6.1 Adapting native applications

To run on ServiceOS, an application must connect to the ServiceOS monitor, register its display output with ServiceOS's UI, and use ServiceOS calls for fetching and dispatching content.

Some of these requirements can be handled transparently to applications. In particular, we provide a wrapper program to connect a given application to the ServiceOS monitor over a named pipe and to register its main window's visual output. As well, we observe that many Windows applications use the `WinInet` [32] library for HTTP communication. To ease porting for such applications, we used public WinInet API documentation [32] to implement an alternate version of `wininet.dll`, which remaps its HTTP calls to invoke ServiceOS's `Fetch()` call. We then force our applications to use this DLL. We similarly remap the Windows socket library, `ws2_32.dll`, onto a raw socket API provided by ServiceOS to support non-HTTP transport. Applications that do not use these libraries for communication will require porting to use our APIs, but we expect this to be rare: we examined 50 popular Windows applications, and found that all except Firefox used WinInet for HTTP communication.

This wrapping is enough to run applications that do not fetch remote content or fetch remote content that does not need protection. As examples, we have packaged Calculator and Solitaire to run on ServiceOS. These applications can be executed simply by browsing to a URL like `http://games.com/solitaire.app` in ServiceOS's UI.

Unlike display setup and content fetch, we cannot automatically infer when to use the `CreatePI()` and `Embed()` calls to render remote content. This functionality is closely tied to application semantics and requires applications to be modified to use them. To facilitate this effort, we created a library called *LibServiceOS* which, similarly to *libc*, handles all communication details between an application and ServiceOS. It exposes ServiceOS system calls and provides an upcall interface for applications to implement. We implemented both a C++ version of LibServiceOS for native applications and a type-safe, C# version for .NET applications. In Section 7.1, we evaluate the ease of ServiceOS adaptation for several large real-world applications.

7. EVALUATION

To evaluate ServiceOS, this section answers and discusses four main questions: (1) how easy is it to adapt native applications to run on ServiceOS, (2) by how much does minimizing impact of malicious content improve security of the system, (3) can ServiceOS stop real exploits, and (4) is our prototype's performance acceptable?

7.1 Ease of adapting native applications

Recall from Section 6.1 that we need to manually adapt only applications that need to spawn a new principal with `CreatePI()` (e.g., to support users clicking on a URL) or `Embed()` (e.g., to support embedding a video clip belonging to a different principal). In this section, we describe our adapation experience for several large, real-world Windows applications. Overall, we find the adaptation effort to be moderate.

7.1.1 Microsoft Word and Excel 2010

Microsoft Word is increasingly used to obtain, read, and edit remote documents. We had two goals in adapting Word: (1) isolate documents according to their content owners, and (2) allow documents to safely embed untrusted remote content, such as YouTube videos. Office 2010 exposes a rich add-in interface [39] which we used for all our modifications, thus avoiding the need to access Word and Excel source code.

Our add-in ensures that every opened document is routed to an appropriate Word instance using `CreatePI()`, and it extends Word's hyperlink class, which is used to embed links in documents, to enable an iframe-like embedding model, allowing users to embed a frame pointing to a remote web page or object. On Word's "document open" event, our add-in scans the document for these special hyperlinks, extracts information such as frame's URL, position, and dimensions, and calls `Embed()` accordingly. In response, ServiceOS will fetch corresponding remote content, dispatch it to a properly isolated principal instance, and connect the rendered content's visual output into its UI container in the Word document. As an example, we have used our add-in to securely embed video clips from YouTube, playable right from the containing Word document — functionality that has so far been unavailable in Word.

Our Word add-in consists of only 223 lines of C# code and took about one man-day to write after getting familiar with Word's add-in APIs. As a separate exercise, we have ported the plug-in to Excel 2010 to provide the same functionality. This took only 2 man-hours and resulted in a 227-line Excel add-in.

Each Word or Excel principal instance has its own UI with all menu items, most of which perform functions on the underlying document and continue to work on ServiceOS. Some functions, such as document comparison or merge, will not work if the involved documents are owned by different principals[3]. Although we have not yet done so, such features can be enabled via explicit ServiceOS-mediated IPC between different instances of Word.

7.1.2 Wordpad

Wordpad is a sophisticated text editor. We pick it as a case study of porting via source code modification, since unlike Word, Wordpad is not modularized and does not provide plug-in interfaces. It consists of more than 50k lines of C++ code, and we consider it representative of reasonably complex applications.

We extended Wordpad with the same ServiceOS support as for Word and Excel. For example, we modified the document parser to recognize special objects representing remote content and to call `Embed()`, and we modified UI code to make room for embedded content frames when rendering the document. With no prior knowledge of Wordpad, this effort took about 50 hours for one author, with most of it spent on understanding the source code. In total, we added only 435 lines of C++ code, and we expect that Wordpad developers could make these changes much more quickly. Overall, our experience showed that adaptation onto ServiceOS is feasible even when source code modification is required.

7.1.3 Internet Explorer

As our primary browser renderer, we have ported Microsoft Internet Explorer's Trident rendering engine to use our new system APIs. This effort closely mirrors the implementation of the Gazelle browser [49], so we omit further details here. In summary, we changed Trident to use ServiceOS system calls (see Table 1) using public IE COM interfaces, and by doing so, we forced Trident to use ServiceOS's isolation policies instead of IE's. This could impact web compatibility. While this merits further investigation, recent work showed that an architecture like ours should have little or no compatibility hit [44].

7.1.4 Microsoft Outlook 2010

Microsoft Outlook 2010 is a popular e-mail and personal information management application. Outlook needs to isolate untrusted content in e-mail messages, but unlike Word documents or web pages, e-mail messages are not addressable via URLs. For such content, applications can still use our `Embed()` call to conveniently offload content isolation while still rendering it in-place with the rest of application's UI. We follow this approach and extend Outlook to use `Embed()` to render e-mail messages in-place as before, but in a separate protection domain, using our IE renderer (Section 7.1.3). Because ServiceOS cannot determine such content's owner information or even retrieve it, we let Outlook download message bodies and provide them directly to `Embed` (via "data:" URLs); ServiceOS uses uniquely-labeled containers in such cases.

[3]Note that is an example of a future problem that never actually occurs in Office today.

	Total	Content processing (prevented in ServiceOS)
Microsoft Office	256	224 (88%)
Adobe Reader	202	64 (83% of known*)
Internet Explorer	144	122 (85%)

Table 2: Security analysis of vulnerabilities ('08-'11).
** We could not analyze 125 Adobe vulnerabilities with unspecified attack vectors.*

Outlook's own protection mechanisms for restricting e-mail rendering, such as filters for <script>, <iframe>, and other dangerous tags, have been error-prone: two recent patches fixed 15 vulnerabilities that, in most severe cases, allowed attackers to take control of a system when a victim simply viewed a specially-crafted e-mail [34]. With ServiceOS, Outlook gains stronger isolation from e-mail rendering bugs, while e-mail content can benefit from additional functionality provided by IE, such as scripts and embeddable iframes.

We also extended Outlook to safely preview attachments using any ServiceOS content processor. ServiceOS picks the renderer based on the content type of the attachment; this replaces previewer lookup in the system-wide Windows registry, which is unavailable in sandboxed applications. This isolation is not only stronger but also more *usable*, as it obviates Outlook's prompting the user to consent to a preview of untrusted attachments.

Like Word, we modified Outlook using its add-in framework. This effort required 20 hours, including the time to understand Outlook's add-in model, and resulted in a small 342-line add-in.

7.2 Vulnerability analysis

We analyzed vulnerabilities published for three large Windows applications during 2008-2011 [2, 34]. We evaluated whether ServiceOS's design mitigated these vulnerabilities by checking whether each vulnerability was related to parsing or other content processing errors. The results are shown in Table 2. Content processing errors are widespread: 88% of Office vulnerabilities and 85% of IE vulnerabilities are related to content parsing. Adobe Reader's numbers included 125 vulnerabilities with unknown attack vectors; of the rest, 83% involved content processing. Exploits of all these flaws would be naturally contained if users were using these applications on ServiceOS; Section 7.3 demonstrates this with two concrete exploits. The rest of the vulnerabilities that ServiceOS cannot contain include insecure library loading vulnerabilities exploitable by planting malicious DLLs, HTML sanitization vulnerabilities leading to XSS, and denial-of-service vulnerabilities.

The ServiceOS monitor has only 9.4K lines of code which is significantly smaller than many applications. For example, OpenOffice has about 9M lines of code [6], and even the relatively simple Wordpad has more than 50K lines of code. Fundamentally, ServiceOS does not rely on large applica-

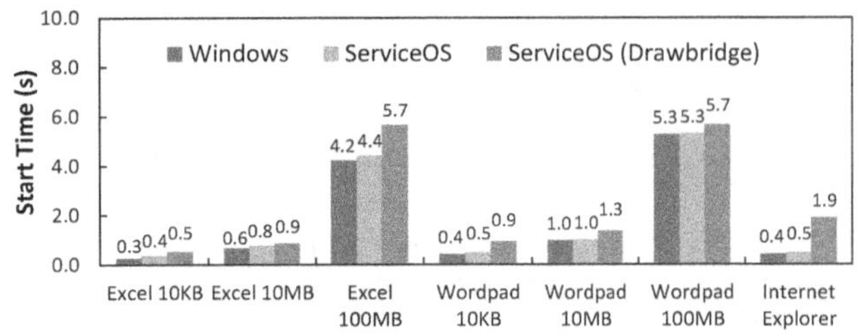

Figure 6: Time to start applications.

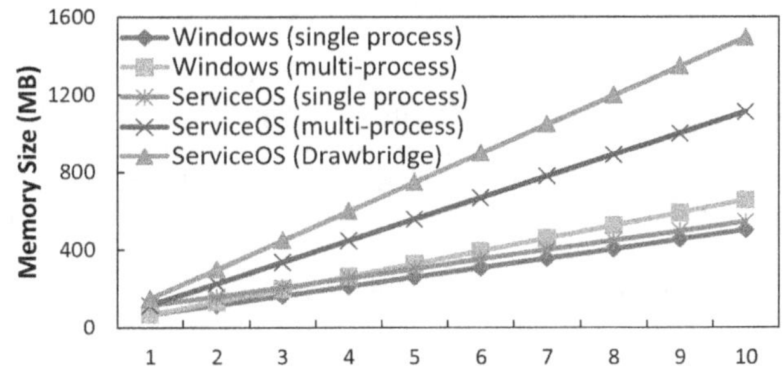

Figure 7: Memory committed for increasing instances of Excel. Each new instance loads a 10MB document.

tions to enforce remote content security and thus reduces the TCB for isolation logic significantly.

7.3 Exploit mitigation

To verify that our system can indeed stop exploits of content processing flaws we analyzed above, we examined two real-world Word 2010 exploits. First, we used a proof-of-concept parsing exploit that uses an RTF Header stack overflow vulnerability [35] to construct a malicious document that looks for other, potentially sensitive Word documents the user has concurrently opened the same Word instance and sends them to an attacker via HTTP. The attack worked successfully on Word 2010 version 14.0.4760, bypassing both DEP and ASLR.[4]

We also crafted a second malicious document that uses macros to perform the same attack. Word treats documents opened from the web as untrusted and does not run macros by default, but offers users a choice to trust the document via a single click on a yellow security button above it. The attack document tricks the victim to click on this button by pretending to be a greeting card that needs permission to be customized. Such an attack is much easier to implement as it does not require bypasses of existing security mechanisms, and it demonstrates the pitfalls of relying on user prompts for isolation decisions. This attack works on the latest version of Word 2010, provided the victim clicks on the yellow security button.

Note that application-based isolation (such as that on iOS or Android) would also *not* be able to stop these two exploits, as they both work *within* the permission boundaries of their Word instance.

Next, we tried opening both attack documents in Word running on ServiceOS. We ran ServiceOS with UID-based sandboxing (Section 6), as Drawbridge does not yet correctly support libraries to parse an older Word document format required in the first exploit, or to run macros for the second exploit. We observed that **ServiceOS stopped both exploits**. Moreover, ServiceOS's Word version did not use any user prompts to enable macros — it no longer needs to restrict remote documents in any way since they are already isolated according to their owner. This provides better user experience for documents that legitimately use dangerous features such as macros or ActiveX.

7.4 Performance

In measuring ServiceOS performance, we were primarily interested in (1) startup latencies we impose on opening documents, which could happen in an existing process on Windows but require starting a new process in our model, (2) overheads on memory usage, since our model uses more processes, one for each content owner rather than one per application, and (3) performance of our content fetch APIs, which ServiceOS applications must use instead of native Windows libraries. Our measurements were performed on a 64-bit Windows 7 desktop with dual 3.16GHz Intel Xeon E8500 Duo-Core CPUs, 4GB of RAM, and a Broadcom NetXtrem Gigabit Ethernet NIC. We present results for three applications: Excel 2010, Internet Explorer (IE), and Wordpad. Excel and Wordpad experiments used 10KB, 10MB and 100MB documents; IE was used to open a simple test page on an Intranet web server. We separate the overhead of Drawbridge from overhead of the rest of our system where possible, since our system can also work with other sandboxing mechanisms. To run a ServiceOS application without Drawbridge, we execute it as a regular Windows process.

Startup latencies. The ServiceOS monitor and shell take 118ms to start. After a user navigates to a URL, our system starts up the appropriate renderer. Figure 6 compares this startup time to startup times of applications' native versions on Windows. We find that most overhead (up to 1.5 sec) comes from starting the Drawbridge environment. Excluding Drawbridge, in all tests ServiceOS adds less than 200ms to connect to the monitor and initialize. An obvious optimization is to maintain a small number of pre-created renderers for popular content types. Even without this optimization, we feel the startup overhead is acceptable. For example, if a user is viewing a web page with an embedded 10KB Excel spreadsheet, starting our modified Excel on ServiceOS would add only 112ms to Excel's normal startup time.

Memory usage. We measured the committed memory size for each application with one document open. Excel running on ServiceOS uses about 47MB more memory than when running on Windows, regardless of document size. This is due to Excel's loading of interoperability DLLs required to run any Excel add-in; our plug-in itself has negligible additional memory cost. Both Wordpad and ported IE carry a very small memory overhead (less than 3MB), which is required to load and initialize our 74KB LibServiceOS DLL. Drawbridge isolation introduces an additional overhead of up to 37MB for Excel.

Figures 7 and 8 show the aggregate memory usage for running multiple instances of Excel and Wordpad simultaneously. Both native and ServiceOS-enabled Excel is capable of opening multiple documents in the same process or separate processes. ServiceOS-enabled Excel render documents in the same process only if their owners are the same; e.g.,

[4]Microsoft has patched this vulnerability in later Word versions.

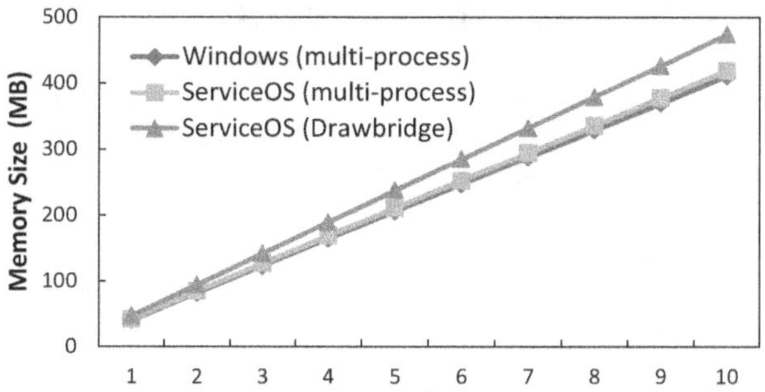

Figure 8: Memory committed for increasing instances of Wordpad. Each new instance loads a 10MB document.

	116 bytes	1MB	10MB
Windows (.NET program)	3ms	98ms	924ms
Windows (WinInet program)	1ms	297ms	1337ms
ServiceOS, no Drawbridge	15ms	124ms	955ms
ServiceOS, with Drawbridge	16ms	156ms	1017ms

Table 3: Overhead of fetching content of various sizes.

a chart embedded in an Excel spreadsheet from same owner would stay in the same process. We can see that we impose no significant penalty for opening documents from the same owner, but documents from different owners (using different processes) do carry a sizable memory overhead. However, most of it comes from (1) Drawbridge, and (2) loading Excel's add-in libraries, which adds 47MB for *each* new process. We could address (1) by picking a more efficient isolation mechanism, and improve (2) with native source-code modification, as exemplified by Wordpad which only adds 9MB for 10 instances.

ServiceOS's monitor and shell have little memory footprint, using 31.4MB of memory at worst during our tests.

Content fetch APIs. We measured the time it takes our IE renderer to use our `Fetch()` API to retrieve three documents of various sizes from a web server on a 100Mbps local network, and compared to two popular ways Windows programs retrieve content today: using .NET's native HttpWebRequest class, and using the WinInet library in Windows (recall that ServiceOS's implementation of HTTP also uses .NET's HttpWebRequest). Table 3 shows our results.

We find that ServiceOS introduces some latency for passing content to renderers, but that overhead is amortized for larger document sizes. For example, for a 10MB document, ServiceOS is only 3% (31ms) slower than a native .NET program, excluding the 62ms of Drawbridge overhead. Most of this is due to extra IPCs to ServiceOS monitor and unoptimized buffering. Interestingly, .NET's HTTP library outperforms WinInet for larger documents; the margin is large enough to mask ServiceOS's overhead. Thus, native Windows applications that used WinInet may actually encounter *faster* content fetch with ServiceOS.

We also evaluated the overhead of various new headers we introduced for content fetch in Sections 4 and 5, and found that it is negligible. For example, verifying a signature in the Owner header with a 1024-bit public key adds only about 1.5ms to each content fetch roundtrip, enforcing the *dispatch-to* directive takes less than 1ms, and parsing and verifying trust lists takes less than 1ms even when checking whether a document can be admitted to a PI with 100 other documents, with all documents having 101-entry trust lists.

8. RELATED WORK

Browsers. Much recent work in browsers explored stronger isolation of web sites. OP [18] applies a microkernel architecture design with a browser kernel that enforces SOP. Tahoma [10] isolates (its own definition of) web applications using virtual machines. Major commercial browsers like Chrome and IE have adopted a process-per-tab kind of multi-process model and reduce privileges of tab processes. Gazelle [49] has a design that treats web sites as OS principals and makes its browser kernel the exclusive place for cross-principal protection. Our work builds on Gazelle and generalizes Gazelle's design to support all applications beyond web applications. We introduce the notion of a content processing stack to give a uniform treatment for both web content and content processed by native applications, we generalize browsers' same-origin policy to allow arbitrary isolation granularity for URI-addressable content and to enable separation of owning and hosting, and we introduce the dispatch bit mechanism to enforce principal definitions.

Modern client platforms. iOS, Android, Windows Phone, Windows 8, and the research OS Singularity [20, 51] all treat application code packages as different principals and put their execution instances into separate processes with different uids. While this marks a milestone of finally moving away from the decades-old model of treating user accounts as principals, we take another significant step by advocating a content-based principal model.

IBOS [45] aims to reduce the trusted computing base for browsers by applying a microkernel design for all traditional OS components, exposing browser abstractions at the lowest software layer and removing many components not needed by browsers. IBOS solves an orthogonal problem from ours. Our problem is to let the OS provide content-based isolation for browsers and non-browser applications alike.

Embassies [19] describes web browsers as pico-datacenters where each "machine" corresponds to a web site and is isolated from other sites or "machines". This view is consistent with the semantics of existing browsers where the same-origin policy is applied to isolate web sites. Nevertheless, existing browsers do not realize isolation reliably. Embassies advocates refactoring browsers into the CEI and the DPI. This mirrors the refactoring done in Gazelle [49]: CEI corresponds to the Browser Kernel API in Gazelle which is runtime-independent; DPI corresponds to the runtime API in Gazelle's principal instances, which allows any programming languages or enrichment of the runtime as needed. Embassies defines web site principals using public keys, similar to one of our principal ID proposals (Section 4.2.1). Our work additionally considers content processing stacks (Section 4.1) and cross-principal content fetch of two forms: data communication and spawning new principals (Section 5) which are commonplace in practice. Finally, ServiceOS aims to support both web applications and native applications on the same OS platform without compromising security semantics of the web while allowing easy adaptation of native applications.

This work follows up on our earlier position paper on ServiceOS [50].

Other isolation policies. SubOS [22] observed that each (remote) data object needs to be rendered with a different principal label, called a sub-user id. SubOS includes a browser [21] which puts each URL page in a separate SubOS process. The SubOS's isolation policy is fixed and can be too fine-grained for many content owners. In contrast, we enable isolation policies of arbitrary granularity while being compatible with web.

PinUP [14] advocates an isolation policy that restricts which applications may access a particular local file. Unlike ServiceOS, PinUP does not isolate mutually distrusting files opened by a *single* application.

COP [7] proposes to extend the same-origin policy by letting web content specify new origins using unique origin IDs; this bears some similarity to our owner-ID-based labeling proposal. Although COP's goals are similar to our principal labeling goals (Section 4.2), COP's origin ID management is complex and may involve HTML and JavaScript modification, which we do not require for web sites in our system. COP does not support native applications or browser plugins, whereas our system's primary goal is to offer a generalized policy and to support both web and native applications.

Isolation mechanisms. Many mechanisms [33, 53, 12, 38, 47, 15, 29, 3, 26] have been developed to confine applications. Usually, these approaches either require applications to formulate their own security policies, resulting in many inconsistent policies coexisting on the system, or they put this burden on administrators. Our work defines a uniform isolation policy as defined by the content-based principal model and *shifts its enforcement to the OS*. We also needed to design new mechanisms for specifying (Section 4) and enforcing (Section 5) the principal definitions.

Object-capability systems and DIFC techniques [42, 54, 13, 27] can be used to implement isolation mechanisms. Realizing our principal model on these systems is an area of future research.

9. CONCLUSION

We advocate a *content-based principal model* in which the operating system relieves applications from the burden of isolating remotely addressable content, boosting the security of both user's data and the system by localizing the impact of any content including malicious content. Our key contribution is to generalize web browsers' same-origin policy into an isolation policy suitable for all applications while maintaining compatibility with the web. To this end, we have invented *content processing stacks* to conceptualize execution instances and introduced a general principal model that enables flexible isolation granularities using public-key-based *owner IDs* or *trust lists* to define principals. For principal definition enforcement (beyond robust isolation container design), we introduced the *dispatch bit* for cross-principal content fetch and dispatch.

We have built a substantial prototype system and adapted to it a number of real-world applications, such as Word, Excel, and Outlook. Our vulnerability study indicates that exploits against more than 80% of vulnerabilities of popular software can be contained. We have demonstrated that real-world exploits' impact can indeed be isolated in our system, and our performance evaluation shows that our system is practical. From these experiences, we believe that content-based isolation policy is indispensable for future client platforms where applications increasingly interface with cloud-backed content.

10. ACKNOWLEDGEMENTS

We thank Barry Bond, Galen Hunt, and Reuben Olinsky for their help with Drawbridge integration. We thank Chris Hawblitzel for his valuable feedback on our paper draft. We thank Bill Barlowe for his help with our vulnerability analysis.

11. REFERENCES

[1] Adobe Secure Software Engineering Team. Inside Adobe Reader Protected Mode. `http://blogs.adobe.com/asset/tag/protected-mode`.

[2] Adobe Security Bulletin Search. `http://www.adobe.com/support/security/`.

[3] AppArmor Application Security for Linux. `http://www.novell.com/linux/security/apparmor/`.

[4] A. Barth. The web origin concept. Internet-Draft, `http://tools.ietf.org/html/draft-abarth-origin-09`, 2010.

[5] A. Barth, C. Jackson, and J. C. Mitchell. Robust defenses for cross-site request forgery. In *To appear at the 15th ACM Conference on Computer and Communications Security (CCS 2008)*, 2008.

[6] Build FAQ for OpenOffice.org. `http://www.openoffice.org/FAQs/build_faq.html`.

[7] Y. Cao, V. Rastogi, Z. Li, Y. Chen, and A. Moshchuk. Redefining web browser principals with a configurable origin policy. In *DSN*, 2013.

[8] T. Close. Decentralized identification. `http://www.waterken.com/dev/YURL/`.

[9] C. Collberg, J. H. Hartman, S. Babu, and S. K. Udupa. Slinky: static linking reloaded. In *USENIX ATC*, 2005.

[10] R. S. Cox, J. G. Hansen, S. D. Gribble, and H. M. Levy. A safety-oriented platform for web applications. In *IEEE Symposium on Security and Privacy*, 2006.

[11] Content security policy (csp). `https://wiki.mozilla.org/Security/CSP/Spec`.

[12] J. R. Douceur, J. Elson, J. Howell, and J. R. Lorch. Leveraging legacy code to deploy desktop applications on the web. In *OSDI*, 2008.

[13] P. Efstathopoulos, M. Krohn, S. VanDeBogart, C. Frey, D. Zieglar, E. Kohler, D. Mazieres, F. Kaashoek, and R. Morris. Labels and Event Processes in the Asbestos Operating System. In *SOSP*, 2005.

[14] W. Enck, P. McDaniel, and T. Jaeger. Pinup: Pinning user files to known applications. In *ACSAC*, 2008.

[15] I. Goldberg, D. Wagner, R. Thomas, and E. A. Brewer. A secure environment for untrusted helper applications. In *USENIX Security*, 1996.

[16] Google Cloud Connect for Microsoft Office. `http://tools.google.com/dlpage/cloudconnect`.

[17] GreenBorder. `www.google.com/greenborder/`.

[18] C. Grier, S. Tang, and S. T. King. Secure web browsing with the OP web browser. In *Proceedings of the IEEE Symposium on Securiy and Privacy*, 2008.

[19] J. Howell, B. Parno, and J. Douceur. Embassies: Radically refactoring the web. In *NSDI*, 2013.

[20] G. Hunt and J. Larus. Singularity: Rethinking the Software Stack. In *Operating Systems Review*, April 2007.

[21] S. Ioannidis and S. M. Bellovin. Building a secure web browser. In *Proceedings of the FREENIX Track: 2001 USENIX Annual Technical Conference*, 2001.

[22] S. Ioannidis, S. M. Bellovin, and J. M. Smith. Sub-operating systems: A new approach to application security. In *SIGOPS European Workshop*, 2002.

[23] C. Jackson. Improving browser security policies. PhD thesis, Stanford University, CA, 2009.

[24] C. Jackson and A. Barth. Beware of Finer-Grained Origins. In *Web 2.0 Security and Privacy*, May 2008.

[25] C. Karlof, J. Tygar, D. Wagner, and U. Shankar. Dynamic Pharming Attacks and Locked Same-Origin Policies for Web Browsers. In *CCS*, 2007.

[26] T. Kim and N. Zeldovich. Making Linux protection mechanisms egalitarian with UserFS. In *Usenix Security*, aug 2010.

[27] M. Krohn, A. Yip, M. Brodsky, N. Cliffer, M. F. Kaashoek, E. Kohler, and R. Morris. Information Flow Control for Standard OS Abstractions. In *21st Symposium of Operating Systems Principles*, 2007.

[28] E. Lawrence. XDomainRequest - Restrictions, Limitations and Workarounds. `http://blogs.msdn.com/b/ieinternals/archive/2010/05/13/xdomainrequest-restrictions-limitations-and-workarounds.aspx`.

[29] P. Loscocco and S. Smalley. Integrating flexible support for security policies into the Linux operating system. In *Proceedings of the 2001 USENIX Annual Technical Conference*, 2001.

[30] Microsoft. Protected View in Office 2010. `http://blogs.technet.com/b/office2010/archive/2009/08/13/protected-view-in-office-2010.aspx`.

[31] Microsoft. Remote desktop protocol. `msdn.microsoft.com/en-us/library/cc240445(PROT.10).aspx`.

[32] Microsoft. Windows Internet API. `msdn.microsoft.com/en-us/library/aa385331(VS.85).aspx`.

[33] Microsoft. Windows Vista Integrity Mechanism Technical Reference. `http://msdn.microsoft.com/en-us/library/bb625964.aspx`.

[34] Microsoft security bulletins and advisories: MS10-087, MS10-079, MS10-103. `http://www.microsoft.com/technet/security/current.aspx`.

[35] MS Office 2010 RTF Header Stack Overflow Vulnerability. `http://www.exploit-db.com/exploits/17474/`.

[36] P. Muncaster. How We Found the File That Was Used to Hack RSA. `http://www.f-secure.com/weblog/archives/00002226.html`, August 2011.

[37] L. Popa, A. Ghodsi, and I. Stoica. Http as the narrow waist of the future internet. In *HotNets*, Monterey, CA, 2010.

[38] D. E. Porter, S. Boyd-Wickizer, J. Howell, R. Olinsky, and G. C. Hunt. Rethinking the library OS from the top down. In *ASPLOS*, 2011.

[39] Programming application-level add-ins. `http://msdn.microsoft.com/en-us/library/bb157876.aspx`.

[40] F. Roesner, T. Kohno, A. Moshchuk, B. Parno, and H. J. Wang. User-driven access control: Rethinking permission granting in modern operating systems. In *IEEE Symposium on Security and Privacy*, 2012.

[41] J. Ruderman. The Same-Origin Policy. `http://www.mozilla.org/projects/security/components/same-origin.html`.

[42] J. S. Shapiro and S. Weber. Verifying the eros confinement mechanism. In *IEEE Symposium on Security and Privacy*, 2000.

[43] Shatter Attacks - How to break Windows. `http://www.thehackademy.net/madchat/vxdevl/papers/winsys/shatter.html`.

[44] K. Singh, A. Moshchuk, H. J. Wang, and W. Lee. On the incoherencies in web browser access control policies. In *IEEE Symposium on Security and Privacy*, 2010.

[45] S. Tang, H. Mai, and S. T. King. Trust and protection in the Illinois Browser Operating System. In *OSDI*, 2010.

[46] A. van Kesteren. Cross-origin resource sharing. W3C Working Draft, `http://www.w3.org/TR/cors/`, 2010.

[47] R. Wahbe, S. Lucco, T. E. Anderson, and S. L. Graham. Efficient software-based fault isolation. In *SOSP*, 1993.

[48] H. J. Wang, X. Fan, J. Howell, and C. Jackson. Protection and Communication Abstractions in MashupOS. In *ACM Symposium on Operating System Principles*, October 2007.

[49] H. J. Wang, C. Grier, A. Moshchuk, S. T. King, P. Choudhury, and H. Venter. The Multi-Principal OS Construction of the Gazelle Web Browser. In *USENIX Security*, 2010.

[50] H. J. Wang, A. Moshchuk, and A. Bush. Convergence of Desktop and Web Applications on a Multi-Service OS. In *HotSec*, 2009.

[51] T. Wobber, A. Yumerefendi, M. Abadi, A. Birrell, and D. R. Simon. Authorizing Applications in Singularity. In *Eurosys*, March 2007.

[52] XMLHttpRequest Level 2. `http://www.w3.org/TR/XMLHttpRequest/`.

[53] B. Yee, D. Sehr, G. Dardyk, J. B. Chen, R. Muth, T. Ormandy, S. Okasaka, N. Narula, and N. Fullagar. Native client: A sandbox for portable, untrusted x86 native code. In *IEEE Symposium on Security and Privacy*, 2009.

[54] N. Zeldovich, S. Boyd-Wickizer, E. Kohler, and D. Mazières. Making information flow explicit in HiStar. In *7th Symposium on Operating Systems Design and Implementation*, 2006.

Diglossia: Detecting Code Injection Attacks with Precision and Efficiency

Sooel Son
The University of Texas at Austin
samuel@cs.utexas.edu

Kathryn S. McKinley
Microsoft Research
The University of Texas at Austin
mckinley@cs.utexas.edu

Vitaly Shmatikov
The University of Texas at Austin
shmat@cs.utexas.edu

ABSTRACT

Code injection attacks continue to plague applications that incorporate user input into executable programs. For example, SQL injection vulnerabilities rank fourth among all bugs reported in CVE, yet all previously proposed methods for detecting SQL injection attacks suffer from false positives and false negatives.

This paper describes the design and implementation of DIGLOSSIA, a new tool that precisely and efficiently detects code injection attacks on server-side Web applications generating SQL and NoSQL queries. The main problems in detecting injected code are (1) recognizing code in the generated query, and (2) determining which parts of the query are tainted by user input. To recognize code, DIGLOSSIA relies on the precise definition due to Ray and Ligatti. To identify tainted characters, DIGLOSSIA dynamically maps all application-generated characters to shadow characters that do not occur in user input and computes shadow values for all input-dependent strings. Any original characters in a shadow value are thus exactly the taint from user input.

Our key technical innovation is *dual parsing*. To detect injected code in a generated query, DIGLOSSIA parses the query in tandem with its shadow and checks that (1) the two parse trees are syntactically isomorphic, and (2) all code in the shadow query is in shadow characters and, therefore, originated from the application itself, as opposed to user input.

We demonstrate that DIGLOSSIA accurately detects both SQL and NoSQL code injection attacks while avoiding the false positives and false negatives of prior methods. By recasting the problem of detecting injected code as a string propagation and parsing problem, we gain substantial improvements in efficiency and precision over prior work. Our approach does not require any changes to the databases, Web servers, or Web browsers, adds virtually unnoticeable performance overhead, and is deployable today.

Categories and Subject Descriptors

Security and privacy — Intrusion/anomaly detection and malware mitigation — Intrusion detection systems

Keywords

Web application security; Dynamic analysis; Code injection; SQL injection; NoSQL injection; Taint tracking

CCS'13, November 4–8, 2013, Berlin, Germany.

http://dx.doi.org/10.1145/2508859.2516696.

1. INTRODUCTION

> Diglossia /dī' glôsēə/ *noun*
> A situation in which two languages (or two varieties of the same language) are used under different conditions within a community, often by the same speakers.
>
> *Oxford Dictionaries*

Modern Web applications accept input from users and incorporate it into dynamically generated code. For example, a Web application may invite the user to fill a form, post a comment, or submit a username and password for authentication. The application then takes this user-provided input and inserts it into a dynamically generated program in another language—for example, a new client-side script, or an SQL or JavaScript query to a back-end database.

A *code injection attack* occurs when a malicious user manages to inject his own code into the program generated by the application. Injected code may steal data, compromise database integrity, and/or bypass authentication and access control, violating system correctness, security, and privacy properties.

Database queries generated by server-side Web applications are a classic target of code injection. For example, SQL injection attacks on retail stores owned by TJX Companies compromised more than 45 million credit and debit numbers in 2005-2007 [23]. SQL injection vulnerabilities still rank fourth among all reported CVE bugs [4], and, according to the 2012 WhiteHat security report, SQL injection attacks are the eighth most prevalent attack type [25].

The recent trend towards NoSQL databases [14] is not improving the situation. Many NoSQL databases, including MongoDB, CouchDB, and DynamoDB, use JSON and/or JavaScript as query languages, but this does not help protect NoSQL-based applications from code injection attacks. In 2010, Diaspora reported a serious NoSQL injection vulnerability in its social community framework [15]. Code injection attacks on JavaScript queries for MongoDB were demonstrated at Black Hat 2011 [21].

By definition, a code injection attack on a Web application involves **tainted code**: the application generates a string that is interpreted as an executable program (e.g., an SQL or NoSQL query), and the string contains user input that is interpreted as code when the program executes. Preventing code injection attacks therefore requires *precisely* determining (1) which parts of the generated string are *code*, and (2) which parts of the generated string are *tainted* by user input.

All prior approaches to runtime detection of code injection attacks suffer from two types of problems. They either fail to precisely define what constitutes code, or their taint analysis algorithm does not identify exactly which characters in the application-generated string originate from user input and which originate from the application itself. Errors of both types lead to false positives (benign queries rejected) and false negatives (code injection attacks accepted as valid queries).

Our contributions. We design, implement, and evaluate DIGLOSSIA, a new runtime tool that precisely and efficiently detects code injection attacks. The key idea behind our approach is to transform the problem of detecting injected code into a string propagation and parsing problem.

In tandem with the application computing its output string, DIGLOSSIA computes a *shadow* of this string. The purpose of the shadow is to identify user input in the application-generated string. In the shadow string, all characters introduced by the application itself are remapped to a shadow character set, which is disjoint from all characters in user input; the shadow value thus precisely encodes which characters came from user input and which came from the application. To precisely identify code, DIGLOSSIA relies on the definitions by Ray and Ligatti [17]. DIGLOSSIA uses a novel *dual parsing* technique to compare the shadow string with the actual string generated by the application and ensure that the actual string does not contain any code tainted by user input.

Our basic approach is language-agnostic and does not depend on the details of the language used to implement the application, nor the target language of the generated string. For concreteness, our DIGLOSSIA prototype works with server-side PHP applications generating database queries in SQL, JSON, or JavaScript. Consequently, we use the term *query* for the generated string.

Defining code injection attacks. Ray and Ligatti show that defining code simply as pre-specified keywords and operators does not provide a clear distinction between code and non-code. Instead, precisely identifying code and non-code requires parsing the query [17].

Following Ray and Ligatti, only values (numeric and string literals) and reserved values (NULL, TRUE, etc.) are *non-code. Code* comprises all reserved keywords, operators, and method calls, as well as all uses of bound identifiers (variables, types, and method names). Note that this definition forbids the dangerous programming practice where certain user inputs are intended by a developer to be interpreted as code in the query. In the absence of strict access control on database operations, this practice may lead to arbitrary code execution and should be deprecated.

With their definition of code and non-code in hand, Ray and Ligatti show that all prior approaches for detecting code injection suffer from false negatives and false positives. They illustrate these inaccuracies with 11 SQL injection attacks and non-attacks, which are explained in detail in Section 3.1 and summarized in Table 1. For example, the attack in Case 5 injects a call to a bound method. All prior approaches miss this attack, but DIGLOSSIA detects it. On the other hand, Case 7 shows how a use of a reserved literal (TRUE) causes at least one prior tool to report a false positive whereas DIGLOSSIA correctly classifies this case.

Value shadowing. To identify taints efficiently, DIGLOSSIA dynamically creates a shadow string for each query issued by the application P. In the shadow query, all application-generated parts use shadow characters, while all tainted parts—i.e., substrings originating from user input—use original characters.

When P is invoked, DIGLOSSIA dynamically generates a set of shadow characters that occur in neither user input, nor the query language. DIGLOSSIA then creates a one-to-one map from each character used by the query language to a unique shadow character.

As P executes, DIGLOSSIA computes *shadow values* for all strings computed by P that depend on user input. DIGLOSSIA follows the control flow of P's execution and performs shadow operations only on input-dependent string and character array operations. In a shadow string, all characters c originating from P are remapped to shadow characters sc where $sc = map(c)$, while all characters originating from user input remain intact. Value shadowing is a precise, lightweight way to propagate character-level taint information. We implement this functionality as a PHP interpreter extension that dynamically remaps characters and computes shadow values in tandem with the string and character array operations performed by P.

Dual parsing. To guarantee that the query issued by the application P does not contain injected code, it is sufficient to ensure the following two properties. First, the shadow query must not contain injected code (technically, the code in the shadow query must not be tainted by user input). Second, the actual query must be syntactically isomorphic to the shadow query.

When P issues a query, DIGLOSSIA examines this query and its shadow using a *dual parser.* Dual parsing is the key technical innovation in DIGLOSSIA. For any string accepted by the original query language, the dual parser accepts the same string, as well as strings in which the original characters are replaced with their corresponding shadow characters. DIGLOSSIA examines the parse trees of the actual query and its shadow and establishes the following two conditions:

1. There is a one-to-one mapping between the parse tree of the actual query and the parse tree of the shadow query. In particular, all code in the actual query maps exactly to equivalent code in the shadow query.
2. The shadow query does not contain any code in the original language L.

If either condition does not hold, DIGLOSSIA reports a code injection attack. Intuitively, the presence of any original-language code in the shadow query and/or any syntactic difference between the actual query and its shadow indicate a code injection attack.

Evaluation and deployability. We demonstrate the precision and efficiency of DIGLOSSIA on 10 open-source PHP Web applications that issue queries to relational MySQL and MongoDB NoSQL back-end databases. DIGLOSSIA detects all 25 code injection attacks we attempted against these applications with no perceptible performance overhead.

Unlike prior tools, DIGLOSSIA correctly classifies 10 out of 11 challenging cases described by Ray and Ligatti [17]—see Table 1. The sole exception is the case where user input is a number specifying how many objects of a certain type to allocate. Even though Ray and Ligatti classify this case as code injection, this is a matter of opinion. We instead classify all integer literals in SQL type definitions as values—for example, 64 in *CHAR(64)* [22]. Therefore, DIGLOSSIA does not report Case 10 in Table 1 as a code injection.

By recasting the problem of detecting code injection attacks as a string propagation and parsing problem, we gain substantial improvements in efficiency and precision over prior work. DIGLOSSIA uses shadow values only to detect injected code and does not actually submit shadow queries to the database. Therefore, in contrast to SQL keyword randomization [2] and complementary encoding [11], DIGLOSSIA does not require any changes to Web applications, databases, query parsers, Web servers, or Web browsers. Unlike these tools, DIGLOSSIA can be deployed *today.*

2. RELATED WORK

This section compares our approach with prior techniques for statically detecting SQL injection vulnerabilities in Web applications

		1	2	3	4	5	6	7	8	9	10	11
	Ray and Ligatti's definition of code injection [17]	Yes	Yes	Yes	No	Yes	Yes	No	Yes	Yes	Yes	No
Tools	Halfond et al. [5], Nguyen-Tuong et al. [13]	Yes	Yes	Yes	No	No	No	No	No	No	No	Yes
	Xu et al. [26]	Yes	Yes	Yes	No	No	No	No	No	No	No	Yes
	SQLCHECK [20]	Yes	No	No	Yes	No	No	No	No	No	No	No
	CANDID [1]	Yes	Yes	Yes	No	No	No	Yes	No	No	No	Yes
	DIGLOSSIA	Yes	Yes	Yes	No	Yes	Yes	No	Yes	Yes	No	No

1 SELECT bal FROM acct WHERE pwd='' OR 1=1 - -'
2 SELECT balance FROM acct WHERE pin= exit()
3 ...WHERE flag=1000 > GLOBAL
4 SELECT * FROM properties WHERE filename='f.e'
5 ...pin=exit()
6 ...pin=aaaa()
7 SELECT * FROM t WHERE flag=TRUE
8 SELECT * FROM t WHERE flag=aaaa
9 SELECT * FROM t WHERE flag=password
10 CREATE TABLE t (name CHAR(40))
11 SELECT * FROM t WHERE name='x'

Table 1: Canonical code injection attacks and non-attacks misclassified by prior methods. Underlined terms are user input.

and dynamically detecting attacks exploiting these vulnerabilities. In Section 3, we explain Ray and Ligatti's examples shown in Table 1 and why prior methods misclassify between 5 and 8 of these 11 examples.

Static methods. Static methods use pointer and taint analysis to find unsanitized data flows from user input to database queries [6,9, 19]. These methods can verify that a sanitization routine is always called on tainted inputs, but not whether sanitization is performed correctly. Since incorrectly sanitized input may cause an injection attack, it is essential to precisely model the semantics of string operations performing sanitization. Wassermann and Su model string operations as transducers and check whether non-terminals in the query are tainted by user input [24]. Static dataflow analysis must be conservative, thus static methods inevitably suffer from false positives.

Dynamic methods. Most dynamic methods aim to precisely track the source of every byte and thus determine which parts of the query come from tainted user input and which come from the application itself [3, 5, 13, 16, 26]. All of these tools use a simple, imprecise definition of "code" and consequently suffer from false positives and false negatives (see Table 1).

To avoid the expense of byte-level taint tracking, several dynamic methods modify and examine inputs and generated queries. For example, Su and Wassermann wrap user input with meta-characters, propagate meta-characters through string operations in the program, parse the resulting query, and verify that if a meta-character appears in the parse tree, then it is in a terminal node and has a parent non-terminal such that the meta-characters wrap the descendant terminal nodes in their entirety [20]. This approach suffers from false positives and false negatives because how to wrap input (e.g., the entire input string, each word, and/or each numeric value) depends on the application generating the query.

To infer the tainted parts of the query, Sekar proposes to measure similarity between the query and user input [18], while Liu et al. compare the query to previous queries generated from benign inputs [8]. In addition to being unsound, these heuristics do not use a precise definition of code and non-code and thus suffer from false positives and false negatives.

CANDID performs a shadow execution of the program on a benign input "aaa...a", compares the resulting query with the actual query, and reports a code injection attack if the queries differ syntactically [1]. As Ray and Ligatti point out, this analysis is insufficient to differentiate code from non-code [17]. Furthermore, CANDID cannot tell which parts of the query came from user input and which came from the application itself, and thus cannot detect injected identifiers (where user input injects a bound variable name that occurs elsewhere in the query), injected method invocations, and incorrect types of literals—see examples in Section 3.3.

Randomization and complementary encoding. To prevent injection of SQL commands, SQLrand remaps SQL keywords to secret, hard-to-guess values [2]. Applications must be modified to use the remapped keywords in the generated queries, and database middleware must be modified to decrypt them back to original keywords. The mapping must remain secret from all users. This approach requires pervasive changes to applications and database implementations and is thus difficult to deploy.

Mui et al. suggest using complementary encoding for user input [11]. The goal is to strictly separate the character set appearing in user input from the character set used by the system internally. This approach cannot be deployed without changing databases, Web browsers, and all other systems dealing with user input.

In contrast, DIGLOSSIA is a simple PHP extension that does not require any modifications to applications or databases.

3. EXAMPLES OF CODE INJECTION

This section gives examples of SQL, NoSQL, and syntax mimicry code injection attacks.

3.1 SQL injection attacks

We illustrate SQL injection attacks using 11 canonical examples described by Ray and Ligatti [17]. Table 1 shows how five prior tools and DIGLOSSIA classify these cases. Underlined terms are user input. Below, we review each attack and non-attack on this list and explain how DIGLOSSIA improves over prior work.

1. SELECT bal FROM acct WHERE pwd='' OR 1=1 - -'
   This case is the classic SQL injection attack with a backquote that ends a string and injects user input as code into the query. All tools detect this code injection. DIGLOSSIA detects it because the injected code "OR", "=", and "-" appears in original characters in the shadow query.

2. SELECT balance FROM acct WHERE pin= exit()
   User input injects exit(), which is a built-in function call. SQLCHECK misclassifies this case because the function call is an ancestor of complete leaf nodes (injected) in the query's parse tree. DIGLOSSIA detects this injection because *exit* is a

bound variable (and, therefore, code), yet appears in original characters in the shadow query.

3. ...WHERE flag=1000>GLOBAL
The injected ">" is code that SQLCHECK misses because, again, this input is correctly positioned in the parse tree. DIGLOSSIA detects it because > is code, yet appears in original characters in the shadow query.
4. SELECT * FROM properties WHERE filename='f.e'
Even if *f.e* is an object reference, the quotes enforce its interpretation as a string. SQLCHECK strips off quotes and misclassifies *f.e* as a reference, generating a false positive. All other tools, including DIGLOSSIA, correctly classify this input as a string literal and not an injection.
5. ...pin=exit()
All tools except DIGLOSSIA miss the injection of the exit identifier because they do not reason about bound names at all. DIGLOSSIA detects code injection because *exit* is bound (and, therefore, code), yet appears in original characters in the shadow query.
6. ...pin=aaaa()
When the identifier is undefined, only DIGLOSSIA correctly detects code injection.
7. SELECT * FROM t WHERE flag=TRUE
Since the injected TRUE is a literal value, this case is not an attack. CANDID incorrectly classifies this input as code injection because the TRUE literal is parsed to a different terminal than the benign input "aaaa", which is parsed to an identifier. DIGLOSSIA correctly parses this input as a literal in both the actual query and its shadow, and does not report an attack.
8. SELECT * FROM t WHERE flag=aaaa
This attack injects a bound identifier (equal to the benign input used by CANDID) into the query. It is missed by all prior methods. DIGLOSSIA detects code injection because *aaaa* is bound (and, therefore, code), yet appears in original characters in the shadow query.
9. SELECT * FROM t WHERE flag=password
This attack injects a bound identifier into the query and is missed by all prior methods. DIGLOSSIA detects code injection because *password* is bound (and, therefore, code), yet appears in original characters in the shadow query.
10. CREATE TABLE t (name CHAR(40))
DIGLOSSIA does not detect this case as code injection. Unlike Ray and Ligatti, we consider integer literals, even in SQL type definitions, to be values, thus this case is not an injection attack from our viewpoint.
11. SELECT * FROM t WHERE name='x'
Since the injected 'x' is a string literal, this case is not an attack. CANDID uses 'aaa' instead of 'x' in the shadow execution; they are different terminals and CANDID incorrectly reports a code injection attack. Xu et al. classify this case as an attack because tainted meta-characters (quotes) appear in the query. Halfond et al. also classify this case as an attack because quotes do not come from a trusted source. DIGLOSSIA, on the other hand, parses 'x' into a literal in both the actual query and its shadow, and correctly does not report an attack.

3.2 NoSQL injection attacks

Modern Web applications are increasingly using NoSQL back-end data stores instead of relational SQL databases. NoSQL is a new class of distributed, scalable databases [14] that store data in key-value pairs. NoSQL databases include Amazon's DynamoDB, MongoDB, CouchDB, and several others. For example, MongoDB is an open-source, document-oriented NoSQL database that supports JSON and JavaScript as query languages. It has been adopted by Craigslist, Foursquare, and other popular Web services [10].

mongodbadmin.php

```
1  <?
2  ...
3  if (!$document) {
4    $document = findMongoDbDocument($_REQUEST['search'],
         $_REQUEST['db'], $_REQUEST['collection'], true);
5    $customId = true;
6  }
7  ...
8  function findMongoDbDocument($id, $db, $collection,
       $forceCustomId = false)
9  {
10   global $mongo;
11   $collection = $mongo->selectDB($db)->selectCollection
         ($collection);
12   ...
13   $document =$collection->findOne(array('_id' => $id));
14   ...
15 }
16 ...
17 ?>
```

Attack URL

```
http://victimHost/mongodbadmin.php?search[$ne]=1&db=test&collection=test
```

Figure 1: JSON injection vulnerability.

NoSQL databases are as vulnerable to code injection attacks as SQL databases. For example, we found four PHP MongoDB-based applications in GitHub with injection vulnerabilities.

Figure 1 shows a PHP application with a JSON injection vulnerability. Line 13 of *mongodbadmin.php* in Figure 1 builds an array consisting of a single key-value pair, where the key is "_id" and the value is equal to the user input obtained from $\$\_REQUEST[\text{'}search\text{'}]$. The Mongo API transforms this array into a JSON query and sends it to MongoDB. The intention is to return all database items whose *_id* field is equal to the user-supplied value.

A malicious user, however, can set the $search$ variable to be an array value, $array(\$ne => 1)$. In the resulting JSON query, line 13 of Figure 1 no longer compares *_id* for equality with $\$id$, but instead interprets the first element of $\$id$ as a function, $\$ne$, the second element, 1, as the argument to this function, and returns all database items whose *_id* is not equal to 1. In this case, user input is supposed to be a string constant, but instead symbols $\$ne$ are interpreted as code in the query.

Figure 2 shows another vulnerable PHP application. Lines 3 to 18 build a query string from user input, Line 21 sends the resulting JavaScript program to MongoDB. MongoDB evaluates this program on every key-value pair in the database and returns the pairs on which the program evaluates to "true".

The query is supposed to retrieve data whose privilege keys are the same as *userType*. The malicious URL, however, tricks the application into generating a tautology query, which always returns "true". Note that user-injected symbols ;, $return$, }, and // are parsed into code in the JavaScript query:

$$function\ q()\{\ var\ default\_user = \text{'}normal\text{'};\\ var\ admin\_passwd = \text{'}guessme\text{'};\\ var\ userType = \underline{1;\ return\ true;\}//....}$$

vulfquery.php

```
<?
// Build a JavaScript function query from user input
$query_body = "
  function q() {
    var default_user = 'normal';
    var admin_passwd = 'guessme';
    var userType = " . $_GET['user'] . ";
    var userPwd = " . $_GET['passwd'] . ";
    if(userType == '_admin_' && userPwd == admin_passwd
        )
      userType = 'admin';
    else
      userType = 'normal';

    if( this.showprivilege == userType )
      return true;
    else
      return false;
  }";
....
// Initiate a function query
$result = $collection->find( array(
                    '$where' => $query_body) );
?>
```

Attack URL

http://victimHost/vulfquery.php?user=1;return true;}//

Figure 2: JavaScript injection vulnerability.

3.3 Syntax mimicry attacks

The query containing injected code need not be syntactically different from a benign query (we call such injections *syntax mimicry* attacks). Consequently, detection tools such as CANDID that look for syntactic discrepancies between the actual query and the query on a benign input will miss some attacks.

vulnerable.php

```
<?
// Build a JavaScript query that checks whether pwd
    field is the same as user input $_GET['id']

$query = "function q() { ";
$query .= "var secret_number = this.pwd;";
$query .= "var user_try = ' . $_GET['id'] . ';";
$query .= "if (secret_number!=user_try) return false;";
$query .= "return true;";
$query .= "}";

$collection->find(array('$where' => $query));
?>
```

Attack URL

http://victimHost/vulnerable.php?id=secret_number

Figure 3: JavaScript syntax mimicry attack.

Figure 3 shows sample PHP code that builds a JavaScript query for a MongoDB. User input in $\$\_GET[\text{'}id\text{'}]$ is supposed to be a numeric literal. If the attacker inputs $secret\_number$ instead of a number, the query will return "true", sabotaging the intended semantics. CANDID will use "aaaaaaaaaaa" as the benign input for $secret\_number$ in its shadow execution and miss the attack, but DIGLOSSIA will detect it.

Figure 4 shows $login.php$ in $minibill$, an actual PHP program vulnerable to syntax mimicry attacks. The attack URL makes the syntactic structures of the actual and shadow queries equivalent.

login.php in *minibill*

```
<?
$Q = "SELECT * FROM users
      WHERE email='{$_REQUEST['email']}'
      AND password='{$_REQUEST['password']}'
      LIMIT 1";
$res = mysql_query($Q);
?>
```

Attack URL

http://victimHost/login.php?email=no\&password=AND others='any

Actual query

SELECT * FROM users WHERE email='no\' AND password=' AND others='any' LIMIT 1

Query on a benign input

SELECT * FROM users WHERE email='aaa' AND password='aaaaaaaaaaaaaaa' LIMIT 1

Figure 4: SQL syntax mimicry attack on *minibill.*

reset_password_save.php in *phpAddressBook* 8.2.5

```
<?
$password_hint = $_REQUEST['password_hint'];
$email=$_REQUEST['email'];
...
// Assume that $cleanpw is "arbitrary"
$query = "UPDATE users SET password='$cleanpw',
    password_hint='$password_hint' WHERE email='$email
    '";

$res = mysql_query($query);
?>
```

Attack URL exploiting CVE-2013-0135

http://victimHost/login.php?password_hint=no\&email=WHERE zip='77051

Actual query

UPDATE users SET password='arbitrary', password_hint='no\' WHERE email=' WHERE zip='77051'

Query on a benign input

UPDATE users SET password='arbitrary', password_hint='aaa' WHERE email='aaaaaaaaaaaaaaaa'

Figure 5: SQL syntax mimicry attack on *phpAddressBook.*

Observe, however, that the attack query refers to the $others$ field instead of the intended $password$ field. This particular attack may not seem damaging, but if the actual query had used *OR* instead of *AND*, the attack would have been much more serious.

Figure 5 shows another PHP program with an injection vulnerability (CVE-2013-0135). The attack URL results in this query resetting the passwords of users whose ZIP code is 77051. DIGLOSSIA can detect syntax mimicry attacks such as this one because, unlike CANDID, it creates shadow queries from the *same input* as the actual execution. The syntactic structures of the actual and shadow queries are equivalent, but the shadow contains the code "WHERE" in original characters (since it originated from user input). Therefore, DIGLOSSIA reports an attack.

4. DESIGN AND IMPLEMENTATION

DIGLOSSIA is as an extension to the PHP interpreter. It is implemented in C using PECL (PHP Extension Community Library). The Web server invokes the interpreter automatically when the URL hosting a PHP application is accessed.

DIGLOSSIA has has three phases, as depicted in Figure 6 and described below.

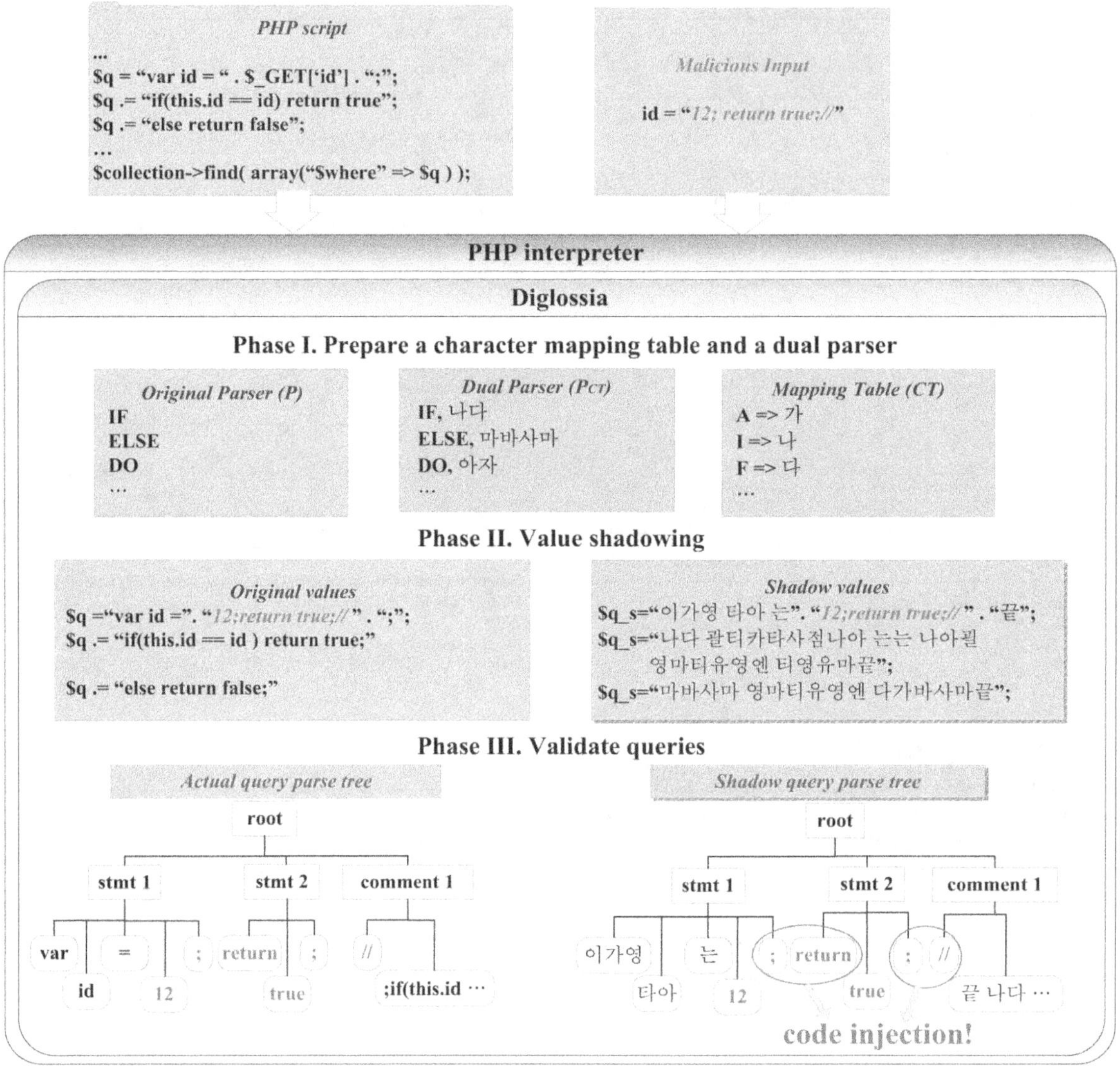

Figure 6: Overview of DIGLOSSIA.

Phase I creates a shadow character map and the dual parser.

Phase II computes a shadow value for each string that depends on user input.

Phase III detects injected code by examining and comparing the actual query string and its shadow.

Phase I creates a map from all characters c in the query language L to a disjoint set of shadow characters $SC = \{map(c)\}$. Phase I also creates the dual parser for the shadow language SL, which is a superset of L and described in more detail in Section 4.3.

In tandem with the execution of the application, Phase II creates and computes shadow values for all strings and array operations that depend on user input. When the Web server invokes a PHP application, DIGLOSSIA creates a shadow string value for each input string, exactly equal to that string. Therefore, at the beginning of the execution, all shadow values consist only of original characters. For every subsequent string or character array computation where one or both operands already have shadow values, DIGLOSSIA computes the shadow value for the result of the operation. If an operand does not have a shadow value, DIGLOSSIA creates a shadow value for it by remapping each character to the corresponding shadow character. This remapping guarantees that all characters introduced by the application itself are in the shadow character set, regardless of whether they appear in the application as explicit constants, come from a library, or are generated dynamically.

When the PHP application issues a query q, Phase III intervenes and checks whether the query includes injected code. To this end, DIGLOSSIA parses q and its shadow q' with the dual parser and checks the following two conditions.

First, there must exist a one-to-one mapping between the nodes in the respective parse trees of q and q'. Furthermore, each parse tree node in q' must be a shadow of the corresponding node in q, as defined in Section 4.3. For instance, a string literal node in q must map to a string literal node in q', except that the string in q only uses characters in C, whereas the string in q' may use characters in $C \cup SC$. This isomorphism condition ensures that *shadow characters in the shadow query correspond exactly to the untainted characters in the actual query.*

Second, all code in the shadow query q' must use only the characters in SC, because all characters in C come from user input.

If both conditions are satisfied, DIGLOSSIA passes the original query q to the back-end database. Otherwise, DIGLOSSIA stops the application and reports a code injection attack.

4.1 Character remapping

We implemented character remapping and dual parsing for SQL, JSON, and JavaScript query languages. These languages use ASCII characters, found on standard English keyboards, for all keywords, numerals, identifiers (variables, types, method names, etc.) and special values (NULL, TRUE, etc.). Although the languages are different and DIGLOSSIA has a separate parser for each, we use the term "query language L" generically to simplify the exposition.

Let C be the subset of ASCII characters consisting of the lower- and upper-case English alphabet and special characters (DIGLOSSIA does not remap digits). Formally, C includes characters whose decimal ASCII codes are from 33 to 47 and from 58 to 126. DIGLOSSIA dynamically creates a one-to-one mapping from each character in C to a shadow UTF-8 character that occurs in neither C, nor user input. Observe that since L uses only characters from C, no shadow characters appear in code written in L.

UTF-8 is a variable-byte representation that uses one to four 8-bit bytes to encode characters. The total number of UTF-8 characters is 1,112,064 and it is easy to find 84 characters among them that do not occur in user input. In our current implementation, every webpage request (i.e., every invocation of a PHP application) results in a different random map. To create this map, DIGLOSSIA (1) randomly selects two-byte shadow characters from among 1,112,064 possible UTF-8 characters, and (2) examines all variables holding user input (e.g., $POST$, GET, and $COOKIE$) to ensure that shadow characters do not occur in them.

It is also possible to pre-compute a set of random mappings offline to reduce runtime overhead.

4.2 Value shadowing

As the application executes, DIGLOSSIA computes shadow values for the results of all string and character array operations that depend on user input. Because DIGLOSSIA is implemented using PECL, it can directly manage memory and monitor program statements during the application's execution.

DIGLOSSIA allocates shadow values on the heap and stores their addresses in the *shadow value table* indexed by the address of the memory location for the original value. For operations that do not involve user input, including all non-string, non-array operations, conditionals, branches, arithmetic operations, etc., DIGLOSSIA performs no computations or allocations. Therefore, the control flow of value shadowing follows the control flow of the application.

When a Web server invokes the PHP application, it passes in user inputs as strings. DIGLOSSIA allocates a shadow value for each input string, equal to the string itself, and adds this value to the shadow value table. If the application reads in additional user input, DIGLOSSIA repeats this process. These initial shadow values contain only characters from the original character set C.

Whenever the application performs a string or character array operation *lhs* = *operation(op1, op2)* where one or both operands (*op1* and *op2*) already have shadow values—and, therefore, the operation is data-dependent on user input—DIGLOSSIA computes the shadow value $shadow_{lhs}$ for the result as follows.

If one operand *op* does not already have a shadow value, DIGLOSSIA allocates a new shadow value and remaps each character in *op* to the corresponding shadow character, creating $shadow_{op}$. Given individual characters $c_i \in op$, $shadow_{op} = map(c_0) \,||\, \ldots \,||\, map(c_{n-1})$ where n is the length of *op*. This remapping guarantees that all characters introduced by the application itself are in the shadow character set, regardless of whether they appear in the application as explicit string literal constants, come from libraries, or are generated dynamically. DIGLOSSIA then computes

$$shadow_{lhs} = operation(shadow_{op1}, shadow_{op2}).$$

If lhs does not have an entry in the shadow value table, DIGLOSSIA allocates a shadow value and enters it in the table. DIGLOSSIA shadows built-in PHP string and array operations. Built-in PHP string operations include string trim, string assignment, substring, concatenation, and replacement. Built-in PHP array operations include array merge, push, pop, and assignment.

Memory for shadow values is proportional to memory tainted by user input, and shadow computations are proportional to the number of program statements that depend on user input. The number of lookups for taint information is significantly smaller than in byte-level taint tracking methods. In value shadowing, the number of lookups is the same as the number of involved values; in contrast, the number of lookups in precise byte- and character-level taint tracking methods is proportional to the byte or character length of every value. Furthermore, fine-grained taint tracking methods require heavy augmentation of built-in operations on strings and bytes to precisely propagate taint information. In contrast, value shadowing performs only the same string and array operations on shadow values as the application performs on the actual values.

Figure 6 shows an overview of our approach, in which we remap ASCII characters into Korean characters and use the latter to compute shadow values. In Figure 6, the assignment $\$q =$ "$var\ id\ =\ $"."$\underline{12; return\ true; //}$"."$;$" concatenates string constants with user input. We compute the shadow value as $\$q_s = map($"$var\ id\ =\ $")."$\underline{12; return\ true; //}$".$map($"$;$"$)$;. Observe that computing the shadow value involves the same concatenation operation on the shadow values as done in the original application. All strings originating from user input remain the same, but string constants introduced by the application have been remapped to (in this case) Korean UTF-8 characters. DIGLOSSIA stores the resulting $\$q_s$ as the shadow of q and uses it for subsequent shadow operations.

Figure 7 illustrates how DIGLOSSIA computes shadow values. Given that $\$input$ is 150, this PHP application computes the $\$SQL$ string to be used as the query. $\$SQL_s$ is the shadow value of $\$SQL$. Let SO_i be the shadow operation corresponding to the ith line of the application (it is shown in the gray box underneath the corresponding line). The full execution sequence comprises lines 1, SO_1, 2, SO_2, 3, SO_3, 4, 6, 9, SO_9, 11, SO_{11}, 12, and 13 in order. Observe that non-string, non-character-array operations are not shadowed.

Line 13 makes the database call with the query stored in string $\$SQL$. In this case, $\$SQL$ has a shadow value $\$SQL_s$ because the query depends on user input.

4.3 Detecting injected code

When the application issues a query q using calls such as *mysql_query*, *MongoCollection::find*, or *MongoCollection::remove*, DIGLOSSIA intervenes and compares q with its shadow q'. DIGLOSSIA checks that (1) q and q' are syntactically isomorphic, and (2) the code in the shadow query q' is not tainted. If either condition fails, it reports an attack. DIGLOSSIA performs both checks at the same time, using a *dual parser*.

```
// boxes show the shadow operations
$input = $_GET['input'];
  $input_s = $_GET['input'];
$amount = $_GET['amount'];
  $amount_s = $_GET['amount'];
$SQL = 'CCS13SELECT * FROM ';
  $SQL_s = map('CCS13SELECT * FROM ');
if ($input < 100) {
  $SQL  = $SQL . 'small_numbers WHERE count < ' .
    $amount ;
  $SQL_s = $SQL_s . map('small_numbers WHERE count < '). $amount_s;
} else if ($input > 200) {
  $SQL = $SQL . 'large_numbers WHERE count > ' .
    $amount ;
  $SQL_s = $SQL_s . map('large_numbers WHERE count > '). $amount_s;
} else {
  $SQL = $SQL . 'middle_numbers WHERE count < ' .
    $amount ;
  $SQL_s = $SQL_s . map('middle_numbers WHERE count < '). $amount_s;
}
$SQL = substr($SQL, 6); // trim five characters from
  the start
  $SQL_s = substr( $SQL_s, 6 );

Interpose and validate( $SQL, $SQL_s );
mysql_query( $SQL );
?>
```

Figure 7: An example of value shadowing.

Intuitively, the purpose of the dual parser is to analyze the shadow query using the grammar of the query language L, but taking into account the fact that the shadow query contains a mix of original and shadow characters. Value shadowing guarantees that all characters in q' that were introduced by the application are in the shadow character set, and all characters in q' that originate from user input are in the original character set.

We first formally define a new shadow language SL that is a superset of the original query language L. We then describe how we optimize our implementation by re-using the parser for L to parse the shadow language SL.

Query language and grammar. Let $G = (N, \Sigma, R, S)$ be the context-free grammar of the query language L. N is the set of non-terminal states, representing different operations, conditionals, expressions, etc. Σ is the set of terminal states, disjoint from N. We will use the symbol ϵ to refer to individual terminal states in Σ. R is the set of production rules that express the finite relation from N to $(N \cup \Sigma)^*$. $S \in N$ is the unique start symbol.

When the parser uses this grammar G to accept a program P, it produces a parse tree that maps every character in P to a terminal. Each terminal is either *code* or *non-code*. Code terminals include operations (e.g., "+" and "-"), keywords, bound identifiers, and method calls. Non-code terminals include constant literals, string literals, and reserved symbols (NULL, TRUE, etc.).

Shadow language and grammar. Given a query language L and its grammar G, DIGLOSSIA defines a corresponding shadow language SL and shadow grammar SG. As described in Section 4.1, every character c used in L has a corresponding shadow character sc. Characters in SL are drawn from $C \cup SC$, where C is the original character set and SC is the shadow character set.

We define $SG = (N, \Sigma_s, R_s, S)$ to be the grammar of the shadow language SL. N and S are the same as in G. For every terminal $\epsilon \in \Sigma$, there exists exactly one corresponding shadow terminal $\epsilon_s \in \Sigma_s$, defined as follows.

Let σ_ϵ be any string accepted by ϵ. If ϵ is an identifier or string literal, then, for each legal character c occurring in σ_ϵ, the shadow terminal ϵ_s accepts c or *map*(c). In other words, any identifier or string literal from the original language L can be expressed in an arbitrary mixture of original and shadow characters in the shadow language SL. For these terminals, ϵ_s accepts a superset of ϵ.

For any other terminal ϵ in G, the corresponding shadow terminal ϵ_s accepts only σ_ϵ or *map*(σ_ϵ). In other words, any non-identifier, non-string-literal terminal in the shadow language must be expressed entirely in original characters, or else entirely in shadow characters. For instance, if the query language L contains a "SELECT" terminal, the shadow grammar will accept "map(SELECT) * FROM table", but not "SELEmap(CT) * FROM table". This restriction immediately rules out some injection attacks even before the security checks described below. For example, keywords that contain both original and shadow characters will not even parse.

For each production $rule \in R$, SG has a corresponding $rule_s \in R_s$. Formally, $rule$ has the form:

$$rule : n \rightarrow v_1 v_2 ... v_l \text{ where } n \in N, v \in N \cup \Sigma$$

In $rule_s$, all non-terminals are the same as in $rule$, while the terminals ϵ_s are defined as above. Consider the following example, where $rules$ are the rules from the original grammar, and $rules_s$ are the corresponding rules from the shadow grammar.

$$\begin{aligned} rules:\ & \mathit{select\_stmt} && \rightarrow SELECT\_term\ list\_exp\ table\_exp \\ & SELECT\_term && \rightarrow SELECT \\ & \mathit{identifier} && \rightarrow \{a|b|\ldots\} \\ & \ldots \\ rules_s:\ & \mathit{select\_stmt} && \rightarrow SELECT\_term\ list\_exp\ table\_exp \\ & SELECT\_term && \rightarrow SELECT \mid map(SELECT) \\ & \mathit{identifier} && \rightarrow \{a|b|\ldots|map(a)|map(b)|\ldots\} \\ & \ldots \end{aligned}$$

The example shows one non-terminal rule and two terminal rules. Since $select\_stmt \in G$ is a non-terminal rule, it is exactly the same in both grammars. The terminal rule for $SELECT\_term \in SG$ accepts both $SELECT$ and $map(SELECT)$, a superset of the original language, since $SELECT$ is a keyword. The terminal rule for *identifier* $\in SG$ accepts strings with an arbitrary mix of original characters c and the corresponding shadow characters $map(c)$.

Applying these simple transformations to the original language and parser, we create a shadow language and parser. Shadow production rules defined in this fashion do not add conflicts, thus the parser for SG produces a deterministic parse tree.

Each character map requires its own shadow grammar. Since a fresh map is dynamically generated for each page request (i.e., each invocation of a PHP application), automatically building a new parser for each execution would be expensive. Instead, DIGLOSSIA takes advantage of the fact that the non-terminals are the same in G and SG, and there is a one-to-one correspondence between the terminals. This enables DIGLOSSIA to re-use the parser for G when parsing SG.

A parser is a function that chooses the next parsing state based on the current state and the input token. If a particular token t triggers a production rule in G (e.g., $SELECT\_term \in G$ in the example above), then the remapped token t_s triggers the corresponding rule in SG (e.g., $SELECT\_term \in SG$ in the example above). This feature enables DIGLOSSIA to use the same internal handle for both t and t_s, while extending the set of accepted characters. With this optimization, DIGLOSSIA can use the same parsing tables for all dynamically generated shadows of a given query language.

Using the dual parser to detect injected code. Let DP be the dual parser that can parse query strings according to either the original grammar G, or the shadow grammar SG defined above.

Given the actual query q issued by the application, DP parses it using G and generates a parse tree T. DP then parses the corresponding shadow query q' and generates a parse tree T'. If DP cannot produce a parse tree for either q or q', it rejects the query and reports a code injection attack.

Otherwise, DP compares the terminal nodes in the two parse trees, T and T', and checks the following two conditions:

1. For each node $t_i \in T$, there exists a one-to-one mapping to $t'_i \in T'$ and, furthermore, t'_i is the shadow of t_i. For example, if t_i is a particular code operator, then t'_i is the same code operator.
2. If t_i parses to a code terminal, then for every character $t_{ij} \in C$, there exists a one-to-one mapping from t_{ij} to the correct shadow character $t'_{ij} \in SC$ such that $t'_{ij} = map(t_{ij})$, where *map* is the shadow character map.

If either condition is violated, DIGLOSSIA reports a code injection attack.

The actual query q may only use the original characters $c \in C$ for code, whereas its shadow q' may only use the shadow characters $sc \in SC$ for code. For example, if an identifier terminal $\epsilon \in q$ is generated by merging a string constant with user input, the identifier terminal $\epsilon_s \in q'$ will contain original characters. This case is an instance of code injection because the code of the query depends on user input. DIGLOSSIA makes sure that all code terminals in q come *entirely* from the application itself and not a single character comes from user input.

On the other hand, the non-code in q' may use any combination of original and shadow characters, reflecting the fact that non-code may be derived from strings originating from user input or the application itself. For example, if the query q contains a string literal "ab", then "$map(a)map(b)$", "a$map(b)$" or '$map(a)$b" can all occur in the shadow query q'.

In summary, given the parse tree for the actual query q and the parse tree for the shadow query q', DIGLOSSIA checks whether the two queries agree on code and non-code. Since all code in q' that comes from the application itself is in shadow characters and all code in q' that comes from user input is in original characters, DIGLOSSIA checks whether q' contains any code in original characters and, if so, reports a code injection attack.

5. LIMITATIONS

DIGLOSSIA follows Ray and Ligatti's strict definition of code and non-code [17] which does not permit any user input to be used as part of code in the query. If the application developer *intentionally* incorporates user input into the query code (a dangerous and ill-advised programming practice), DIGLOSSIA will report a code injection attack when the application is executed.

The ability to recognize and separate code and non-code in the query string generated by the application critically depends on using the correct grammar for the query language. If the language accepted by the database's query parser differs from the language accepted by DIGLOSSIA's parser during its analysis, DIGLOSSIA may generate both false positives (mistakenly parse a tainted part of the query as code, even though it will not be parsed as code by the database) and false negatives (mistakenly parse a tainted part of the query as non-code, even though it will be parsed as code by the database).

Applications	Database	LoC	Attacks	Detected
MongoPress	MongoDB	35,231	0	0
mongodb-admin	MongoDB	555	2	2
mongodb_php_basic	MongoDB	209	1	1
rockmongo	MongoDB	11,218	0	0
MongoTinyURL	MongoDB	60	1	1
simple-user-auth	MongoDB	236	1	1
faqforge	MySQL	1,520	1	1
schoolmate	MySQL	7,024	6	6
webchess	MySQL	5,780	12	12
MyBB with MyYoutube(1.0)	MySQL	108,267	1	1

Table 2: Benchmark PHP applications.

If the application passes an input-tainted string to a third-party PECL extension or some other built-in function that is not implemented in PHP, value shadowing can be incomplete because DIGLOSSIA cannot observe the string operations inside these functions. Incomplete value shadowing may lead to false negatives (missed attacks). Fortunately, unlike Java and C applications, PHP applications do not use third-party libraries heavily. For example, we did not observe any calls to third-party libraries that perform string or array operations on user inputs in our benchmarks.

6. EVALUATION

To evaluate DIGLOSSIA, we created a test suite of ten Web applications implemented in PHP (see Table 2). Four of our benchmark applications use MongoDB and contain NoSQL injection vulnerabilities, which we found by manual inspection of the applications' source code: *mongodb_php_basic*, *mongodb-admin*, *MongoTinyURL*, and *simple-user-auth*. Two, *MongoPress* and *rockmongo*, were chosen to demonstrate the performance of DIGLOSSIA on relatively large applications. The remaining four applications were chosen because they contain known SQL injection vulnerabilities [7, 12].

We implemented concrete attacks exploiting the known vulnerabilities in the benchmark applications. We also implemented concrete instances for all of Ray and Ligatti's canonical cases listed in Table 1. All experiments were performed on an Intel(R) dual core 3.30 GHz machine with 8G of RAM.

Table 2 summarizes the results of our evaluation on the ten benchmark Web applications. The first column lists the applications, the second column shows the back-end database each application uses, the third column shows the size of the application. The fourth column shows the number of different code injection attacks we attempted against the application, while the last column demonstrates that DIGLOSSIA successfully detected all attacks.

Figure 8 shows the time it took to build the front page of each application, measured as the average of 50 runs with the database cache disabled. Range bars represent 95% confidence intervals. Most interval ranges overlap, thus the performance overhead of DIGLOSSIA is unnoticeable to the users of the application. The numbers at the top of each bar represent overhead percentages, computed by taking the time it took to build the page with DIGLOSSIA deployed and dividing it by the original page-building time. The maximum overhead is 13%, but the actual time difference is less than 2 ms, within the variance of the original page-building time.

Figure 9 shows the performance overhead of DIGLOSSIA with the database cache enabled. The overall response times are lower, thus the overhead percentages are bigger than those in Figure 8. However, most overhead is not statistically significant compared to the variation in the page-loading time.

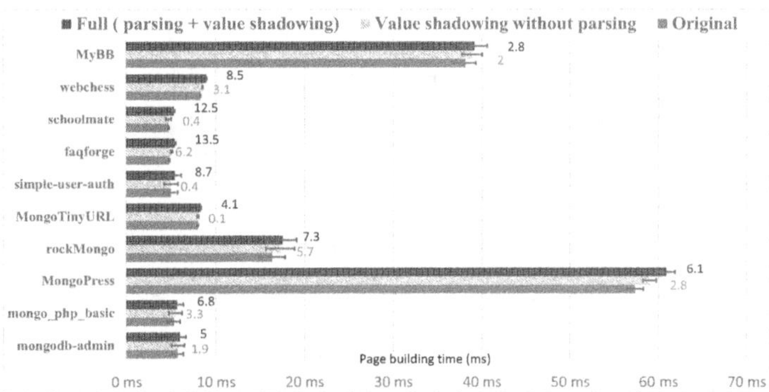

Figure 8: Performance overhead of DIGLOSSIA with the database cache disabled.

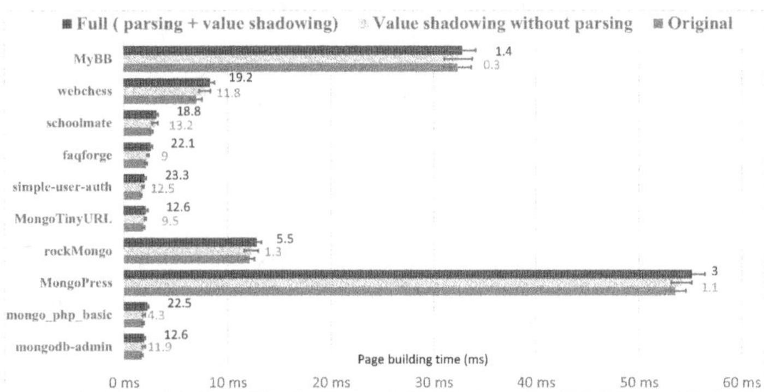

Figure 9: Performance overhead of DIGLOSSIA with the database cache enabled.

These experimental results show that DIGLOSSIA accurately detects SQL and NoSQL code injection attacks with virtually unnoticeable performance overhead.

7. CONCLUSION

To the best of our knowledge, DIGLOSSIA is the first tool capable of *accurately* detecting both SQL and NoSQL injection attacks on server-side PHP applications at runtime, without any modifications to applications or back-end databases.

DIGLOSSIA follows Ray and Ligatti's definition of code and non-code, combined with very precise character-level taint tracking, and thus avoids the false positives and false negatives of prior tools for detecting code injection attacks. In tandem with the execution of the application, DIGLOSSIA remaps all characters introduced into the query by the application itself into a shadow character set, while leaving the characters that originate from user input intact. The resulting query and its shadow are then analyzed using a *dual parser* that can parse both the original and shadow query languages. Dual parsing is the main technical innovation of this work. Any discrepancy between the parse trees of the query and its shadow, or the presence of any original characters in the code of the shadow query indicate that the code of the actual query is tainted by user input and thus a code injection attack has occurred.

DIGLOSSIA imposes negligible performance overhead and does not require any changes to the existing applications, databases, Web servers, or Web browsers. It can be easily added to the PHP environment and is ready to deploy today.

Acknowledgments. We are very grateful to Venkat Venkatakrishnan for his insightful critique of an early version of this research, and to Jay Ligatti for his comments on a draft of this paper. This work was partially supported by the NSF grants CNS-0746888, CNS-0905602, SHF-0910818, CCF-1018271, and CNS-1223396.

8. REFERENCES

[1] S. Bandhakavi, P. Bisht, P. Madhusudan, and V. N. Venkatakrishnan. CANDID: Preventing SQL injection attacks using dynamic candidate evaluations. In *CCS*, 2007.

[2] S. Boyd and A. Keromytis. SQLrand: Preventing SQL injection attacks. In *ACNS*, 2004.

[3] E. Chin and D. Wagner. Efficient character-level taint tracking for Java. In *SWS*, 2009.

[4] CVE Details. http://www.cvedetails.com/vulnerabilities-by-types.php.

[5] W. Halfond, A. Orso, and P. Manolios. Using positive tainting and syntax-aware evaluation to counter SQL injection attacks. In *FSE*, 2006.

[6] N. Jovanovic, C. Kruegel, and E. Kirda. Pixy: A static analysis tool for detecting Web application vulnerabilities. In *S&P*, 2006.

[7] A. Kieżun, P. Guo, K. Jayaraman, and M. Ernst. Automatic creation of SQL injection and cross-site scripting attacks. In *ICSE*, 2009.

[8] A. Liu, Y. Yuan, D. Wijesekera, and A. Stavrou. SQLProb: A proxy-based architecture towards preventing SQL injection attacks. In *SAC*, 2009.

[9] V. Livshits and M. Lam. Finding security vulnerabilities in Java applications with static analysis. In *USENIX Security*, 2005.

[10] mongoDB production deployments. http://www.mongodb.org/about/production-deployments/.

[11] R. Mui and P. Frankl. Preventing web application injections with complementary character coding. In *ESORICS*, 2011.

[12] MyYoutube MyBB Plugin 1.0 SQL Injection. http://www.exploit-db.com/exploits/23353.

[13] A. Nguyen-Tuong, S. Guarnieri, D. Greene, and D. Evans. Automatically hardening Web applications using precise tainting. In *SEC*, 2005.

[14] NoSQL. http://nosql-database.org/.

[15] NoSQL injection attack on Diaspora. http://www.kalzumeus.com/2010/09/22/security-lessons-learned-from-the-diaspora-launch/.

[16] T. Pietraszek and C. Berghe. Defending against injection attacks through context-sensitive string evaluation. In *RAID*, 2006.

[17] D. Ray and J. Ligatti. Defining code-injection attacks. In *POPL*, 2012.

[18] R. Sekar. An efficient black-box technique for defeating Web application attacks. In *NDSS*, 2009.

[19] S. Son and V. Shmatikov. SAFERPHP: Finding semantic vulnerabilities in PHP applications. In *PLAS*, 2011.

[20] Z. Su and G. Wassermann. The essence of command injection attacks in Web applications. In *POPL*, 2006.

[21] B. Sullivan. Server-side JavaScript injection. http://media.blackhat.com/bh-us-11/Sullivan/BH_US_11_Sullivan_Server_Side_WP.pdf, 2011.

[22] The BNF grammar for SQL-99. http://savage.net.au/SQL/.

[23] J. Vijayan. TJX data breach: At 45.6M card numbers, it's the biggest ever. http://www.computerworld.com/s/article/9014782/TJX_data_breach_At_45.6M_card_numbers_it_s_the_biggest_ever, 2007.

[24] G. Wassermann and Z. Su. Sound and precise analysis of Web applications for injection vulnerabilities. In *PLDI*, 2007.

[25] WhiteHat website security statistics report. https://www.whitehatsec.com/resource/stats.html, 2012.

[26] W. Xu, S. Bhatkar, and R. Sekar. Taint-enhanced policy enforcement: A practical approach to defeat a wide range of attacks. In *USENIX Security*, 2006.

25 Million Flows Later - Large-scale Detection of DOM-based XSS

Sebastian Lekies
SAP AG
sebastian.lekies@sap.com

Ben Stock
FAU Erlangen-Nuremberg
ben.stock@cs.fau.de

Martin Johns
SAP AG
martin.johns@sap.com

Abstract

In recent years, the Web witnessed a move towards sophisticated client-side functionality. This shift caused a significant increase in complexity of deployed JavaScript code and thus, a proportional growth in potential client-side vulnerabilities, with DOM-based Cross-site Scripting being a high impact representative of such security issues. In this paper, we present a fully automated system to detect and validate DOM-based XSS vulnerabilities, consisting of a taint-aware JavaScript engine and corresponding DOM implementation as well as a context-sensitive exploit generation approach. Using these components, we conducted a large-scale analysis of the Alexa top 5000. In this study, we identified 6167 unique vulnerabilities distributed over 480 domains, showing that 9,6% of the examined sites carry at least one DOM-based XSS problem.

Categories and Subject Descriptors

H.4.3 [**Communications Applications**]: Information browsers; H.6.5 [**Security and Protection**]: Unauthorized access

Keywords

DOM-based XSS, Taint Tracking, Vulnerability Detection, Exploit Generation

1. INTRODUCTION

The times in which JavaScript was mainly used for eye candy and small site enhancements are long gone. Since the advent of the so-called Web 2.0, the Web browser is the host of sophisticated, complex applications, such as Gmail or Google Docs, written entirely in JavaScript, that rival their desktop equivalents in scope and features. More and more functionality, which in traditional Web applications would have been implemented on the server, moves to the client. Consequently, the amount of required JavaScript code is increasing proportionally to this shift. Furthermore, the capabilities of client-side JavaScript are continuously increasing, due to the steady stream of new "HTML5" APIs being added to the Web browsers.

CCS'13, November 4–8, 2013, Berlin, Germany.

ACM 978-1-4503-2477-9/13/11 ...$15.00.
http://dx.doi.org/10.1145/2508859.2516703.

In parallel to this ever growing complexity of the Web's client side, one can observe an increasing number of security problems that manifest themselves only on the client [26, 11, 17]. One of these purely client-side security problems is *DOM-based XSS* [16], a vulnerability class subsuming all Cross-site Scripting problems that are caused by insecure handling of untrusted data through JavaScript. DOM-based XSS is caused by unsafe data flows from attacker-controlled sources, such as the `document.location` property, into security sensitive APIs, e.g., `document.write`.

While the existence of DOM-based XSS is known since 2005 [16], this vulnerability class is frequently still perceived as a minor, fringe issue, especially when being compared to *reflected* and *persistent* XSS. In this paper, we re-evaluate this assumption and examine how prevalent DOM-based XSS is in the wild.

Unfortunately, testing of client-side security properties in general, and DOM-based XSS in particular, is difficult. In comparison to the conditions on the server side, the Web's client side has several challenges that affect both static and dynamic security testing approaches. For one, all server-side code is completely under the control of the application's operator and available for processing, monitoring and analysis. This is not the case at the Web's client-side, where the code execution occurs on the user's machine. Furthermore, compared to server-side languages such as Java or C#, a large portion of JavaScript code frequently relies on runtime interpretation of string data as executeable code via APIs such as `eval()`. The resulting code is interpreted and executed on the client, making it invisible to the server. Finally, it is common practice for modern Web applications to include third-party JavaScript code using `script`-tags that point to cross-domain hosts. In 2002, Nikiforakis et al. [22] measured that 88.45% of the Alexa top 10,000 web sites included at least one remote JavaScript resource from a cross-domain host. This JavaScript is transported directly from the third-party provider to the user's Web browser and gets executed immediately. Thus, this code is neither directly controlled by the application nor is it visible at the server.

In this paper, we propose a fully automated system to identify DOM-based XSS issues, that overcomes the outlined obstacles through integrating the vulnerability detection directly into the browser's execution environment. Our system consists of a taint-aware JavaScript engine and DOM implementation as well as a context-sensitive exploit generation technique.

The main contributions of this paper are the following:

- We present the design and implementation of a dynamic, byte-level taint-tracking approach in JavaScript engines. Through directly altering the JavaScript engine's implementation of the low-level string type, we achieve complete coverage of all JavaScript language features and the full DOM API.
- We propose a novel, fully automatic vulnerability validation mechanism, that leverages the fine-grained context information provided by our taint-aware JavaScript engine. Due to our exact knowledge of data source and syntactical context of the final data sink, our system can create attack payloads that match the syntactic surroundings of the injection point. This in turn allows unambiguous vulnerability validation through verification that our injected JavaScript was indeed executed. Thus, our system reports no false positives.
- We report on a large-scale empirical study on insecure data flows in client-side JavaScript and the resulting DOM-based XSS vulnerabilities. In total, we examined 504,275 URLs resulting from a shallow crawl of the Alexa top 5000 sites. In this study we observed a total of 24,474,306 flows out of which 69,987 caused validated DOM-based XSS exploits, resulting in 6,167 unique vulnerabilities affecting 9,6% of the examined sites.

The remainder of this paper is organized as follows: First we briefly revisit the technical background of DOM-based XSS (Sec. 2) and give a high-level overview of our approach (Sec. 3). Then, we describe our techniques for vulnerability detection (Sec. 4) and validation (Sec. 5). In Section 6 we present the methodology and results of our empirical study. We end the paper with a discussion of related work (Sec. 7) and a conclusion (Sec. 8).

2. DOM-BASED XSS

Cross-Site Scripting is an attack in which an attacker is able to inject his own JavaScript code into a Web application, in such a way that the code is executed within a victim's browser in the context of the application. Since 2000, when one of the first XSS vulnerabilities was reported [3], novel attack variants were discovered. In 2005, Amit Klein published a paper in which he first mentioned the term *DOM-based XSS* and described the basic characteristics of this vulnerability [16]. In contrast to traditional (reflected and persistent) Cross-Site Scripting, DOM-based XSS is caused by incorrect client-side code rather than by server-side code. As described earlier, the dynamic nature of this client-side code makes it hard to detect or verify this kind of vulnerability.

In order to trigger a DOM-based XSS exploit an attacker is able to utilize a multitude of different attack vectors to inject his malicious payload (such as `location.href`, `document.referrer`, `window.name`, and many, many more). Depending on the Web application's program logic, it processes attacker-controllable inputs and at some point in time conducts a string-to-code conversion. As shown in our empirical study, this is a very common scenario. If input is not sanitized correctly, the attacker may be able to inject his own code into the application. Thereby, different subtypes of DOM-based XSS exist depending on the method used for converting the string to code:

HTML context.

Web applications commonly insert generated HTML code into the DOM via functions such as `document.write`, `innerHTML` or `insertAdjacentHTML`. When these functions are called, the browser parses the string parameter and interprets the contents as HTML code, which is then inserted into a certain position within the DOM. If user input flows into these sinks, sanitization or encoding functions have to be used in order to avoid code injection vulnerabilities. If the input is not sanitized correctly an attacker is able to inject own HTML tags including `<script>`, which enables JavaScript execution. For the specific differences between `innerHTML` and `document.write`, we refer the reader to Sec. 5.2.1.

JavaScript context.

Another commonly used method, which is sometimes vulnerable to DOM-based XSS, is the `eval` function. `eval` takes a string parameter, interprets it as JavaScript code and executes it. Besides `eval` and its aliases `setTimeout` and `setInterval`, there are also other contexts in which strings are converted into JavaScript code such as `script.innerText`, `script.text`, `script.textContent` and the assignment of strings to event handler attributes.

URL context.

If an attacker-controlled input flows into a URL attribute of any DOM node (such as `img.src`, `iframe.src`, `object.data` or `a.href`), an immediate conversion from a string to code does not occur. However, there are still several security problems related to this kind of flows. For example, if the attacker is able to control the complete URL, he could make use of the `javascript:` or `data:` schemes to execute script code. If only parts of the URL are controlled, the attacker could still conduct redirects or phishing and in some cases even achieve JavaScript code execution as shown in Section 6.5.1.

Other contexts.

Besides those contexts that allow code execution, there are further sinks/contexts that are security sensitive such as `document.cookie`, the Web Storage API, postMessage or `setAttribute`. In Section 6.5.3, for example, we present a persistent DOM-based XSS vulnerability via `document.cookie`, which was discovered by our framework.

3. APPROACH OVERVIEW

In this paper, we propose a system to automatically detect and validate DOM-based XSS vulnerabilities. To address the outlined challenges in the assessment of client-side security problems (see Sec. 1), we decided to address the problem as follows: Instead of building analytical processes that complement [29] or emulate [25] the client-side behavior, we chose to integrate our techniques directly into a full browser.

More precisely, our system consists of two separate components: For vulnerability detection, we utilize a modified browsing engine that supports dynamic, byte-level taint-tracking of suspicious flows. Through directly altering the engine's string type implementation, we achieve complete coverage of all JavaScript language features and the full DOM API. We discuss the design and implementation in Section 4.

The second component is a fully automated vulnerability validation mechanism, that leverages the fine-grained context information provided by our taint-aware browsing engine. Due to the exact knowledge of data source and syntactical context of the final data sink, our system is able to create attack payloads that match the syntactic surroundings of the injection point. This in turn allows unambiguous vulnerability validation through verification that our injected JavaScript was indeed executed. This component is presented in Section 5.

4. VULNERABILITY DETECTION: MODIFIED CHROME

To automatically detect the flow of potentially attacker-controllable input (called a source) into a sink in the sense of DOM-based XSS, we decided to implement a dynamic taint-tracking approach. To ensure that edge-cases, which might not be implemented properly into pure testing engines like HTMLUnit, were to be properly executed, we chose to implement taint-tracking into a real browser. For this, we modified the open-source browser Chromium in such a manner that its JavaScript engine V8 as well as the DOM implementation in WebKit were enhanced with taint-tracking capabilities. For both components of the browser, we selected to use a byte-wise taint-tracking approach built directly into the respective string representations. In this fashion, we enabled our tool to not only distinguish between a completely untainted string and a string containing any potentially harmful content, but also to specifically get information on the origin of each given character in said string.

4.1 Labeling sources and encoding functions

To keep the memory overhead as small as possible, we chose to implement our approach in such a way, that information on a given character's source is encoded in just one byte. We therefore assigned a numerical identifier to each of the 14 identified sources (e.g. `location.href`, `location.hash` or `document.referrer`). Hence, we were able to encode this information into the lower half of the byte. To also be able to determine whether a given character was encoded using the built-in functions *encodeURI*, *encodeURIComponent* and *escape*, we used the lower three of the four remaining bits to store whether one or more of these functions were applied to the string. To represent a benign character, the lower four bits are set to 0.

4.2 Patching the V8 JavaScript engine

Google's JavaScript engine V8 is highly optimized in regards to both memory allocation and execution speed. Although the code is written in C++, V8 for the most parts does not make use of a class-concept using member variables when representing JavaScript objects like strings or arrays. Instead, a small header is used and objects components are addressed by only using given offsets relative to the object's address.

After careful examination of the given code, we chose to only encode the desired information directly into the header. Every object in V8 stores a pointer to its *map*. The map describes the class of an object. In V8, there are maps for each type of object. We found an used part of a bitmap in the maps and used it to create new map objects for tainted strings. Obviously, for strings of dynamic length, additional memory must be allocated to store the actual data. Based on whether a string is pure ASCII or also contains two-byte characters, this memory is allocated on creation of the object. The address of this newly created space is then written to one of the aforementioned offsets in the header. Along with the information that a string is tainted, we also need to store the taint bytes described above. To do this, we changed the string implementation such that additional *length* bytes are allocated. Since we wanted to keep the changes to existing code as small as possible, we chose to store the taint bytes into the last part of the allocated memory. This way, the functionality for normal access to a string's characters did not have to be changed and only functionality for taint information access had to be added.

As mentioned before, the V8 engine is optimized for performance. It therefore employs so-called generated code which is assembler code directly created from macros. This way, simple operations such as string allocation can be done without using the more complex runtime code written in C++. However, for our approach to easily integrate into the existing code, we chose to disable the optimizations for all string operations such as creation or sub-string access.

After patching the string implementation itself, we also instrumented the string propagation function such as `substring`, `concat`, `charAt`, etc. This is necessary to ensure that the byte-wise taint-tracking information is also propagated during string conversions.

4.3 Patching the WebKit DOM implementation

In contrast to the V8 engine, WebKit makes frequent use of the concept of member variables for its classes. Therefore, to allow for the detection of a tainted string, we were able to add such a member denoting whether a string is tainted or not. The string implementation of WebKit uses an array to store the character data. Hence, we added a second array to hold our taint bytes. Since strings coming from V8 are converted before being written into the DOM, we patched the corresponding functions to allow the propagation of the taint information. This is necessary because tainted data might be temporarily stored in the DOM before flowing to a sink, e.g. by setting the `href` attribute of an anchor and later using this in a `document.write`. To allow for correct propagation of the taint information, we not only needed to change the string implementation but also modify the HTML tokenizer. When HTML content is set via JavaScript (e.g. using `innerHTML`), it is not just stored as a string but rather parsed and split up into its tree structure. Since we want to ensure that taint information is carried into the tag names and attributes in the generated tree, these changes were also necessary.

4.4 Detection of sink access

Until now we discussed the tracking of tainted data inside the V8 JavaScript engine and WebKit. The next step in our implementation was to detect a tainted flow and to notify

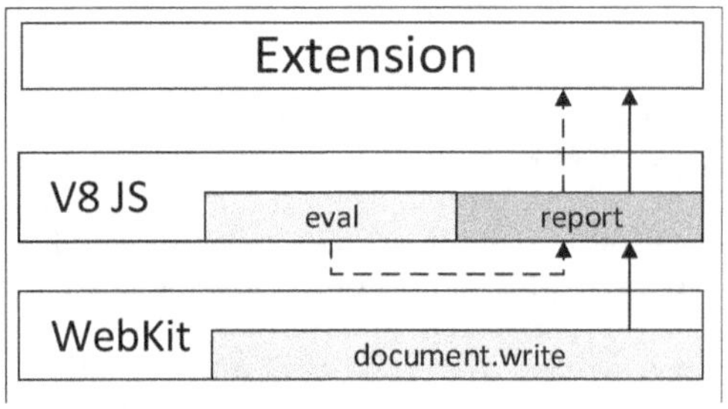

Figure 1: Report functionality

the user. Therefore, we modified all DOM-based Cross-Site Scripting sinks – like `document.write`, `innerHTML` or `eval`. We changed them in such a way that a reporting function is called each time a tainted string is passed to such a sink. In order to pass on the report to the user interface, we implemented a Chrome extension, that injects the JavaScript reporting function into the DOM. As such a function is callable from inside the runtime engine, we are able to report the flow to the extension. The details on the layout and implementation of this extension are presented in 6.1.

In WebKit's API used to provide access to the DOM tree for V8, the passed arguments are of V8's string class and are then converted to WebKit's string type. Hence, we chose to implement our reporting function into V8's string class, therefore allowing us to invoke it from the DOM API as well as directly from V8 using the provided string reference. When called, this function gathers information on the code location of the currently executed instruction and reports these alongside the taint information and details on the type of sink to the extension.

Figure 1 depicts this layout. Both the indicated functions `eval` and `document.write` use the reference to the passed string to invoke the reporting function which in turn passes on the information to the Chrome extension shown at the top.

5. VULNERABILITY VERIFICATION: AUTOMATIC EXPLOIT GENERATION

Although the taint-tracking engine delivers first indications for potential Cross-Site Scripting vulnerabilities, detecting a flow alone is not sufficient to ensure that a vulnerability was discovered. There are various reasons why a successful exploitation is not possible for an existing flow. For example, the Web site could use built-in or custom encoding or filter functions that are capable of defusing a malicious payload. Furthermore, other, random circumstance can occur that prevent an exploit from executing. For example, if the tainted value originates from a GET parameter, tampering with this parameter could trigger the Web server to load a different page or to display an error message in which the vulnerable flow is not present anymore. Therefore, a verification step is needed to tell vulnerable data flows apart from non-exploitable flows. In order to do so our system uses the data received from the taint- tracking engine to reliable generate valid Cross-Site Scripting Exploits. In this Section we describe the inner workings of the generation process.

5.1 Anatomy of a Cross-Site Scripting Exploit

To develop a system that is capable of generating valid XSS payloads, we first analyzed the nature of a Cross-Site Scripting exploit. In general, an exploit is context dependent. This means, that a payload, which an attacker seeks to execute, depends on how the Web application processes the attacker's input. So, if the input flows into the `eval` sink it has to utilize a different syntax than an exploit targeting flows into `document.write` (More details on context-dependent exploit generation can be found in the Section 5.2). However, the structure of an exploit can be generalized to a non-context-dependent form.

Listing 1 shows two typical exploits. The first exploit targets a JavaScript context (e.g. `eval`), while the second one contains an exploit for an HTML sink (e.g. `document.write`). In many cases a tainted value was concatenated from several different strings, which are hard coded (benign/non-attacker-controllable) or coming from either one or more sources (attacker-controllable). Therefore, an attacker is only able to control parts of the string that flows into the sink. Immediate execution of JavaScript is often not possible at the location where the tainted/controllable parts are inserted into the string/code (e.g. within quoted strings). Therefore, the exploit first has to break out of the current context to be able to execute the malicious script code. The first part of each exploit serves as a "break out sequence" to escape to a context where JavaScript execution is possible. In the cases presented in Listing 1 these sequences are "');" and "></a>", respectively. Following the break out sequence, an arbitrary JavaScript payload or `<script>` tag can be executed. Afterwards, the exploit has to take care of trailing string fragments in such a way that these fragments do not interfere with the execution of the payload. For example, if a string that is passed to *eval* contains a syntax error, no code will be executed at all, even if the syntax error occurs at the very end of the string. To prevent this from happening an exploit has to include an escape sequence that renders trailing characters harmless. In the JavaScript case we simply comment out everything that follows our payload and in the HTML case we close the script block and include a `<textarea>` to interpret the rest of the string as simple text instead of HTML. To summarize our analysis, we conclude that a Cross-Site Scripting exploit takes the following generalized form:

$$exploit := breakOutSequence\ payload\ escapeSequence \tag{1}$$

In this, only the *breakOutSequence* and the *escapeSequence* are context-specific. While the *escapeSequence* is very trivial to choose, the *breakOutSequence* needs careful crafting to result in a successful exploit.

Listing 1 Example Cross-Site Scripting exploits

```
');alert('XSS');//
"></a><script>alert('XSS')</script><textarea>
```

5.2 Context-Dependent Generation of Break-out Sequences

After discovering a data flow from one or more sources to a sink, the taint-tracking engine delivers three pieces of information to the exploit generation framework:

1. Information on the the data flow (sources, sink, applied built-in filters)
2. Tainted value: the complete string that flowed into the sink (including benign and tainted parts from one or more sources)
3. Byte-wise taint information for each byte contained in the tainted string.

Based on the given sink the framework first determines the target context. Depending on this context, the tainted value and the taint information are passed to a context-sensitive *break out sequence* generation function. In the next step, the generator adds the desired payload and a context-specific fixed escape sequence. After constructing the exploit, the system builds a test case that can be executed in a completely automated fashion and reports back to the framework in case of successful exploitation.

5.2.1 HTML context-specific generation

An HTML context is present whenever a tainted string is directly converted into HTML code. This is the case for many DOM manipulation functions such as `document.write` or `innerHTML`.

As mentioned before, often only parts of a string may be tainted. Therefore, our system first determines the exact location of the tainted parts by analyzing the taint information. In order to create a valid exploit, the system needs to determine into which DOM node the tainted parts will be transformed when the string-to-HTML conversion takes place. In order to do so, the generator parses the complete string and identifies the corresponding nodes. Based on the node types the generator is able to plan the next step within the generation process. In this first step we distinguish between three different node types (See Listing 2 for examples):

1. **Tainted TagNode:** The tainted value is located inside an HTML tag. Either it is part of the tag name, an attribute name, an attribute value or a combination of those three possibilities.
2. **Tainted CommentNode:** The tainted value is contained within an HTML comment.
3. **Tainted TextNode:** The tainted value is placed outside of an HTML tag or in between a closing and an opening tag.

Listing 2 Example Vulnerabilities

```
document.write('<script src="//example.org/'
          + taintedValue + '"></script>')

document.write('<div>' +taintedValue+ '</div>')

document.write('<!--' +taintedValue+ '-->')
```

Depending on the the node type, break out sequences have to be generated differently. In the following, we explain the three different approaches:

TagNode generation.

If the tainted value is included within an HTML tag we first need to break out of this tag. Otherwise, opening a `<script>` tag would have no effect. If the tainted value is directly located within the tag, we can simple do so by adding a ">" sign to the break out sequence. If the tainted value resides within an attribute of the tag, the system first needs to determine the delimiter of the attribute. Most of the time such attributes are either enclosed by single or double quotes, however, sometimes, also no delimiter is present. So in order to break out of the tag in this case we need to add the delimiter of the attribute node before the angle brackets.

Now our payload is able to break out of the current (opening) tag and would be able to open a `script` tag, to execute the payload. However, some tags have special semantics for the text between the opening and the closing tag. So for example, HTML markup between an opening and closing `iframe` tag is only rendered in case iframes are not supported by the browser. Therefore, our generator optionally adds one or more additional closing tags at the end of the break out sequence for all present tags with special semantics. To summarize this, a TagNode break out sequences looks as follows:

$$TagNodeBS := [delimiter] > [closingTags] \tag{2}$$

CommentNode generation.

The generation of CommentNode break out sequences is very trivial in most of the cases. As comments in HTML do not have any special semantics for their content, we can simply break out of a comment by adding "- ->" to our break out sequence. However, such a comment could in rare cases be placed in between opening and closing tags of scripts, iframes, etc. So, again our system analyzes the string and adds closing tags for these elements if necessary. Summing up, a CommentNode break out sequence takes the following form:

$$CommentNodeBS := -- > [closingTags] \tag{3}$$

TextNode generation.

Every character sequence that is placed outside a tag or a comment or that is located in between an opening and a closing tag is regarded as a TextNode by the HTML parser. In many cases executing a payload within a TextNode is straight forward. As we do not need to break out of the node itself, we can simply open a `script` tag and execute a payload. However, if the TextNode is placed between an opening and a closing tag of a `script` or `iframe` we again have to add closing tags if necessary.

$$TextNodeBS := [closingTags] \tag{4}$$

innerHTML vs document.write.

After we have generated the break out sequence for HTML context exploits, the system needs to choose a payload to execute. When doing so, some subtle differences in the handling of string-to-HTML conversion comes into play. When using **innerHTML**, **outerHTML** or **adjacentHTML** browsers react differently than **document.write** in terms of script execution. While **document.write** inserts **script** elements into the DOM and executes them immediately, **innerHTML** only performs the first step, but does not execute the script. So adding the following payload for an **innerHTML** flow would not result in a successful exploit:

```
<script>__reportingFunction__()</script>
```

However, it is still possible to execute scripts via an injection through **innerHTML**. In order to do so, the framework makes use of event handlers:

```
<img src="none_existent_resource"
onerror="__reportingFunction__()">
```

When **innerHTML** inserts the **img** tag, the browser creates an HTTP request to the non-existing resource. Obviously, this request will fail and trigger the **onerror** event handler that executes the given payload. Depending on the sink we simply choose one of these two payloads.

5.2.2 *JavaScript context-specific generation*

JavaScript context-specific generation is necessary whenever a data flow ends within a sink that interprets a string as JavaScript code. This is the case for functions such as **eval** & **Function**, Event handlers (such as **onload** and **onerror**) and DOM properties such as **script.textContent**, **script.text** and **script.innerText**. While browsers are very forgiving when parsing and executing syntactically incorrect HTML, they are quite strict when it comes to JavaScript code execution. If the JavaScript parser encounters a syntax error, it cancels the script execution for the complete block/function. Therefore, the big challenge for the exploit generator is to generate a syntactically correct exploit, that will not cause the parser to cancel the execution. In order to do so, the system again has to determine the exact location of the tainted bytes.

Listing 3 shows a very simple vulnerable piece of JavaScript code. In the first step, the code constructs a string of benign/hard coded and tainted (**location.href**) parts. In a second step, it executes the code using **eval**. Thereby, this code can be exploited in slightly different ways. Either the attacker could break out of the variable **x** and inject his code into the function named test, or he could break out of the variable **x** and the function **test** and inject his code into the top level JavaScript space. While the first method requires an additional invocation of the test function, the second exploit executes as soon as eval is called with a syntactically correct code. However, for the last case, the complexity of the break out sequence grows with the complexity of constructed code. Nevertheless, we do not want do rely on any behavior of other non-controllable code or wait for a user interaction to trigger an invocation of the manipulated code.

Therefore, we always seek to break out to the top level of the JavaScript execution. In order to do so, our system first parses the JavaScript string and creates a syntax tree of the code. Based on this tree and the taint information we extract the branches that contain tainted values. Listing 4 shows the resulting syntax tree for our example code and

Listing 3 JavaScript context example

```
var code =    'function test(){' +
              'var x = "' + location.href + '";'
              //inside function test
              + 'doSomething(x);'
        + '}'; //top level
eval(code)
```

Listing 4 JavaScript Syntax Tree

```
FunctionDeclaration
  Identifier : test
  FunctionConstructor
    Identifier : test
    Block
      Declaration
        Identifier : x
        StringLiteral : "http://example.org"
    ExpressionStmt
      SpecialOperation : FUNCTION_CALL
        Reference
          Identifier : doSomething
```

the extracted branch (in gray). For each of the extracted branches the generator creates one break out sequence by traversing the branch from top to bottom and adding a fixed sequence of closing/break out characters for each node. So in our example the following steps are taken:

1. FunctionDeclaration: ';'
2. FunctionConstructor: ''
3. Block: '}'
4. Declaration: ';'
5. StringLiteral: '"'
6. Resulting Breakout Sequence: '";};'

To trigger the exploit we can simply construct the test case as follows: Based on the source (**location.href**), the system simple adds the break out sequence, an arbitrary payload and the escape sequence to the URL of the page:

```
http://example.org/#";};__reportingFunction__();//
```

When executed within a browser, the string construction process from Listing 3 is conducted and the following string flows into the **eval** call (Note: Line breaks are only inserted for readability reasons):

```
function test(){
    var x = "http://example.org/#";
};
__reportingFunction__();
//doSomething(x);}
```

6. EMPIRICAL STUDY

As mentioned earlier, an important motivation for our work was to gain insight into the prevalence and nature of potentially insecure data flows in current JavaScript applications leading to DOM-based XSS. For this reason, we created a Web crawling infrastructure capable of automatically applying our vulnerability detection and validation techniques to a large set of real-world Web sites.

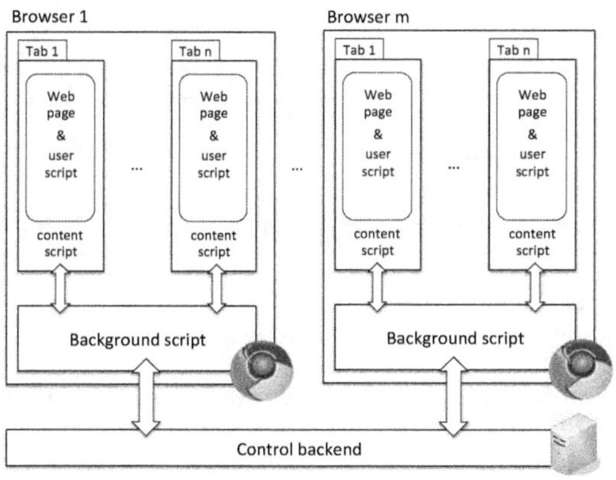

Figure 2: Crawling infrastructure

6.1 Methodology & Architecture Overview

To obtain a realistic picture on the commonness of insecure data flows that might lead to DOM-based XSS, it is essential to sample a sufficiently large set of real-world Web sites.

We designed our experiment set-up to meet these requirements, utilizing the following components: Our flow-tracking rendering engine to identify and record potentially unsafe JavaScripts (as discussed in Sec. 4), our exploit generation and validation framework (as presented in Sec. 5), and a crawling infrastructure that automatically causes the browsing engine to visit and examine a large set of URLs.

Our crawling infrastructure consisted of several browser instances and a central backend, which steered the crawling process. Each browser was outfitted with an extension that provided the browser with the required external interface for communication with the backend (see Fig. 2). In the following paragraphs, we briefly document both the backend's and the extension's functionality.

6.1.1 *Analysis engine: Central server backend*

The main duty of the central analysis backend is to distribute the URLs of the examination targets to the browser instances and the processing of the returned information. The backend maintains a central URL queue, which was initially populated with the Alexa Top 5000 domains and subsequently filled with the URLs that were found by the browsers during the crawling process.

The browser instances transmit their analysis report and their findings to the backend. For each analyzed URL, analysis reports for several URLs are returned, as the browser instances not only check the main page but also all contained `iframes`. In our study, we received results for an average of 8.64 (sub-)frames for each URL that was given to a browser instance. After pre-processing and initial filtering, the backend passes the suspicious flows to the exploit generation unit (see Sec. 6.3).

6.1.2 *Data collection: Browser Extension*

As discussed in Section 4, we kept direct changes to the browser's core engine as small as possible, to avoid unwanted side effects and provide maintainability of our modifications. Our patches to the browser's internal implementation consisted mainly in adding the taint-tracking capabilities to the Javascript engine and DOM implementation. All further browser features that were needed for the crawling and analyzing processes were realized in the form of a browser extension.

Following the general architecture of Chrome's extension model [8], the extension consists of a background and a content script (see Fig. 2). The *background script*'s purpose is to request target URLs from the backend, assign these URLs to the browser's tabs (for each browser instance, the extension opened a predefined number of separate browser tabs to parallelize the crawling process), and report the findings to the backend. The *content script* conducts all actions that directly apply to individual Web documents, such as collecting the hyperlinks contained in the page for the further crawling process and processing the data flow reports from the taint-tracking engine (see Sec. 4.4). Furthermore, the content script injects a small *userscript* into each Web document, that prevents the examined page from displaying modal dialogues, such as `alert()` or `confirm()` message boxes, which could interrupt the unobserved crawling process.

After the background script assigns a URL to a tab, the content script instructs the tab to load the URL and render the corresponding Web page. This implicitly causes all further external (script) resources to be retrieved and all scripts, that are contained in the page, to be executed. After the page loading process has finished, a timeout is set to allow asynchronous loading processes and script execution to terminate. After the timeout has passed, the content script packs all suspicious data flows, which were reported during execution of the analyzed page, and communicates them to the background script for further processing.

In addition to data flow and hyperlink data, the extension also collects statistical information in respect to size and nature of the JavaScripts that are used by the examined sites.

6.2 Observed Data Flows

As mentioned above, our initial set of URLs consisted of the Alexa top 5000. For each of these URLs we conducted a shallow crawl, i.e., all same-domain links found in the respective homepages were followed, resulting in 504,275 accessed Web pages. On average each of those Web document consisted out of 8.64 frames resulting in a final number of 4,358,031 (not necessary unique) URLs.

In total our infrastructure captured 24,474,306 data flows from potentially tainted sources to security sensitive sinks. Please refer to Table 1 for details on the distribution of flows, depicted by their sources and sinks.

6.3 Selective Exploit Generation

As shown in the previous Section, the total number of potentially vulnerable data flows from insecure sources to security sensitive sinks is surprisingly high. In our study, the sheer number of found flows exceeds the number of analyzed pages by a factor of about 48.5.

Both our exploit generation and validation processes are efficient. Generating and testing an XSS exploit for a selected data flow requires roughly as much time as the initial analyzing process of the corresponding Web page. However, due to the large amount of observed flows, testing all data flows would have required significantly more time than the actual crawling process. Hence, to balance our coverage and broadness goals, we selected a subset out of all recorded, po-

	URL	Cookie	document.referrer	window.name	postMessage	Web Storage	Total
HTML Sinks	1,356,796	1,535,299	240,341	35,466	35,103	16,387	3,219,392
JavaScript Sinks	22,962	359,962	511	617,743	448,311	279,383	1,728,872
URL Sinks	3,798,228	2,556,709	313,617	83,218	18,919	28,052	6,798,743
Cookie Sink	220,300	10,227,050	25,062	1,328,634	2,554	5,618	11,809,218
Web Storage Sinks	41,739	65,772	1,586	434	194	105,440	215,165
postMessage Sink	451,170	77,202	696	45,220	11,053	117,575	702,916
Total	5,891,195	14,821,994	581,813	2,110,715	516,134	552,455	24,474,306

Table 1: Data flow overview, mapping sources (top) to sinks (left)

tentially vulnerable data flows, based on the following criteria:

(C1) The data flow ended in a sink that allows, if no further sanitization steps were taken, direct JavaScript execution. Hence, all flow into cookies, Web Storage, or DOM attribute values were excluded.

(C2) The data flow originates from a source that can immediately be controlled by the adversary, without programmatic preconditions or assumptions in respect to the processing code. This criteria effectively excluded all flows that come from second order sources, such as cookies or Web Storage, as well as flows from the `postMessage` API.

(C3) Only data flows without any built-in escaping methods and data flows with non-matching escaping methods were considered. Data flows, for which the observed built-in escaping methods indeed provide appropriate protection for the flow's final sink were excluded.

(C4) For each of the remaining data flows we generated exploits. However, many flows led to the generation of exactly the same exploit payloads for exactly the same URL - e.g. when a web page inserts three scripts via `document.write` and always includes `location.hash` at a similar location. In order to decrease the overhead for testing the exploits, our system only validates one of these exploits.

Starting from initial 24,474,306 flows, we successively applied the outlined criteria to establish the set of relevant flows:

$$24,474,306 \xrightarrow{C1} 4,948,264 \xrightarrow{C2} 1,825,598 \xrightarrow{C3} 313.794 \xrightarrow{C4} 181,238 \quad (5)$$

Thus, in total we generated 181,238 test payloads, out of which a total of 69,987 successfully caused the injected JavaScript to execute. We discuss the specifics of these results in the next Section.

6.4 Found vulnerabilities

In total, we generated a dataset of 181,238 test payloads utilizing several combinations of sources and sinks. As discussed in Section 6.3 (C3), all flows which are encoded are filtered early on. For Google Chromium, which we used in our testing infrastructure, adhering to this rule we also must filter all those exploits that use either `location.search` or `document.referrer` to carry the payloads. This is due to the fact that both these values are automatically encoded by Chromium. Hence, we chose to test these vulnerabilities in Internet Explorer 10 whereas the rest of the URLs were verified using our aforementioned crawling infrastructure. Since the number of exploits utilizing `search` vulnerabilities amounts to 38,329 and the sum for `referrer` reached 5083, the total number of exploits tested in Chromium was reduced to 137,826, whereas the remaining 43,412 exploits were tested using Internet Explorer.

Out of these, a total number of 58,066 URLs tested in Chromium triggered our verification payload. Additionally, we could exploit 11,921 URLs visited in Internet Explorer. This corresponds to a success rate of 38.61% in total, and a success rate of 42.13% when only considering vulnerabilities exploitable in Chromium.

As we discussed earlier, we crawled down one level from the entry page. We assume that a high number of Web sites utilize content management systems and thus include the same client-side code in each of their sub pages. Hence, to zero in on the number of actual vulnerabilities we decided to reduce the data set by applying a uniqueness criterion.

For any finding that triggered an exploit, we therefore retrieved the URL, the used break out sequence, the type of code (inline, eval or external) and the exact location. Next, we normalized the URL to its corresponding second-level domain. To be consistent in regards to our selection of domains, we used the search feature on alexa.com to determine the corresponding second-level domain for each URL. We then determined for each of the results the tuple:

$$\{\text{domain}, \text{break out sequence}, \text{code type}, \text{code location}\}$$

In regards to the code location, we chose to implement the uniqueness to be the exact line and column offset in case of external scripts and evals, and the column offset in inline scripts. Applying the uniqueness filter to the complete dataset including those pages only exploitable on Internet Explorer, we found a total of 8,163 unique exploits on 701 different domains, whereas a domain corresponds to the aforementioned normalized domain. Due to the nature of our approach, among these were also domains not contained in the top 5000 domains. Thus, we applied another filter, removing all exploits from these domains outside the top 5000. This reduced the number of unique exploits to 6,167, stemming from 480 different domains. In respect to the number of domains we originally crawled, this means that our infrastructure found working exploits on *9.6%* of the 5000 most frequented Web sites and their sub-domains.

When considering only exploits that work in Chromium, we found 8,065 working exploits on 617 different domains, including those outside the top 5000. Again filtering out domains not contained in the 5000 most visited sites, we found 6,093 working exploits on 432 of the top 5000 domains or their sub-domains.

Among the domains we exploited were several online banking sites, a poplar social networking site as well as governmental domains and a large internet-service provider running a bug bounty program. Furthermore, we found vulnerabilities on Web sites of two well-known AntiVirus products.

6.5 Selected Case Studies

During the analysis of our findings, we encountered several vulnerabilities which exposed interesting characteristics. In the following subsections, we provide additional insight into these cases.

6.5.1 *JSONP + HTTP Parameter Pollution*

As stated in Section 2, flows into URL sinks are not easily exploitable. Only if the attacker controls the complete string, he can make use of data and javascript URLs to execute JavaScript code. However, in our dataset we found a particularly interesting coding pattern, that allows script execution despite the fact that the attacker only controls parts of the injected URLs. In order to abuse this pattern a Web page must assign a partly tainted string to a script.src attribute that includes a JSONP script with a callback parameter (See Listing 5).

Listing 5 JSONP script include

```
var script = document.createElement('script')
script.src = "http://example.org/data.json?u="
        + taintedValue + "&callback=cb_name";
```

In many cases the callback parameter is reflected back into the script in an unencoded/unfiltered fashion. Hence, the attacker could inject his own code into the script via this parameter. However, the callback parameter is hard coded and the attacker is not able to tamper with it at first sight. Nevertheless, it is possible to inject a second callback parameter into the script URL via the `taintedValue`. This results in the fact that two parameters with the same name and different values are sent to the server when requesting the script. Depending on the server-side logic the server will either choose the first or the second parameter (We found both situations, and depending on the position of the `taintedValue` we were able to exploit both situations). Hence, by conducting this so-called HTTP Parameter Pollution attack, the attacker is able to inject his value into the content of the script, which is afterwards embedded into the Web page.

One particularly interesting fact is that simply encoding the `taintedValue` will not protect against exploitation. Instead, the JSONP callback parameter needs to be sanitized. During our experiments we found one vulnerable callback parameter quite often on many different Web sites, which seemed to stem from jQuery (or at least, always called the same jQuery function).

6.5.2 *Broken URL parsing*

As browsers sometimes auto-encode certain parts of user controlled values, it is not possible to inject code into some of the analyzed sources. One example for this is `location.search` that is auto-encoded by all browser except Internet Explorer. Another source that is encoded by every modern browser is `location.pathname`. An injection via `location.pathname` is in general not possible until the application itself decodes the value. An additional encoding or sanitization step is therefore not necessary for these values. This fact, however, also leads to security vulnerabilities when Web developers trust in this auto-encoding feature while at the same time conducting incorrect URL parsing.

In our analysis, we found many examples where this fact leads to vulnerabilities. In the following we cover some examples where code fragments seemed to extract automatically encoded values (and hence no sanitization is needed), but due to non-standard parsing, extracted also unencoded parts in malicious cases.

1. Task: Extract host from URL
2. What it really does: Extract everything between `www.` and `.com` (e.g. whole URL)
3. e.g. `http://www.example.com/#notEncoded.com`

```
var regex = new RegExp("/www\..*\.com/g");
var result = regex.exec(location.href);
```

1. Task: Extract GET parameter `foo`
2. What it really does: Extracts something that starts with `foo=`
3. e.g. `http://www.example.com/#?foo=notEncoded`

```
var regex = new RegExp( "[\\?&]foo=([^&#]*)" );
var result = regex.exec(location.href);
```

1. Task: Extract all GET parameters
2. What it really does: Last GET parameter contains the unencoded Hash
3. e.g. `http://example.com/?foo=bar#notEncoded`

```
location.href.split('?')[1].split('&')[x]
                              .split('=')
```

6.5.3 *Persistent DOM-based XSS*

As seen in Table 1, our system captured also some flows into cookies and into the Web Storage API. However, we did not include it into our automatic exploit generation. Nevertheless, we were able to manually find several persistent DOM-based XSS. We detected flows that first came from user input and went into Cookie or Web Storage sinks effectively persisting the data within the user's browser. In the cases where we could trigger a successful exploit, this data was then used in a call to `eval`, hence exposing the Web site to persistent DOM-based XSS.

6.5.4 *window.name flows*

Within our dataset, we detected a surprisingly high number (>2 million) of flows originating from `window.name` that we couldn't explain at first sight. Although some of them were exploitable, we soon discovered the reason for this number. Most of these flows are not exploitable via DOM XSS as they are caused by a simple programming error. When declaring a local variable a developer has to use the `var` keyword. If someone declares a variable named `name` inside a function and misses the `var` keyword or if a local variable is created directly within a script block that is executed in the global scope, the variable is declared global (See Listings 6 and 7). Since inside a browser, the global object is `window`, the data is written to `window.name`. If the same variable is used within a call to a sink within the same script block, the corresponding flow is not exploitable as window.name was overwritten with benign data. However, this fact represents another serious issue: `window.name` is one of the very few

Listing 6 window.name bug 1: Missing var keyword

```
function test(){
    name = doSomething();
    document.write(name);
};
```

Listing 7 window.name bug 2: Declaration within the global scope

```
<script>
    var name = doSomething();
    document.write(name);
</script>
```

properties that can be accessed across domain boundaries. Hence, any data that is written to this property can be accessed by third parties. This programming error, therefore, represents a serious information leakage problem, if sensitive data is written to such a global `name` variable. Given the huge amount of flows, it is very likely that this pattern could be misused to steal sensitive information.

6.6 Effectiveness of Chromium's XSS Filter

Modern browsers like Chromium and its commercial counterpart Google Chrome are equipped with client-side filter capabilities aiming at preventing XSS attacks [1]. In order to analyze the effectiveness of Chromium's XSS Filter, we utilized our successful exploits and tried to execute them with the activated filter. Out of the 701 domains we found, 300 domains were still susceptible to XSS even with Chromium's auditor enabled.

After further examination, we found three distinguishing characteristics for these working exploits. For one, none of the exploits abusing JavaScript sinks, such as `eval()`, were detected by XSS Auditor. This stems from the fact that the auditor is implemented inside the HTML parser and thus cannot detected direct JavaScript sinks. Furthermore, exploits that were caused by remote script includes were not detected. The third type of undetected exploits was caused by JSONP vulnerabilities as discussed in Section 6.5.1.

On a positive note, in our study, we found that none of the exploits that targeted inline vulnerabilities passed through the filter. However, please note, that this experiment carries no reliable indication of protection robustness in respect to the exploits, that were stopped. We did not make any attempts to obfuscate the exploit payload [12] or use other filter evasion tricks [13].

In 2011 Nikiforakis demonstrated that Chrome's filter is not able to cope with exploits that utilize more than one injection point at once [21]. If we take our figures from Section 6.2 into account, we see that a tainted string consists – on average – of about three tainted substrings. Thus, an attacker has on average three possible injection points in order to leverage the techniques presented by Nikiforakis. Therefore, we have good reasons to believe that the numbers presented in this Section must rather be seen as a lower bound.

7. RELATED WORK

To the best of our knowledge, DOMinator [7] was the first browser-based tool to test for DOM-based XSS via dynamic taint-tracking. For this purpose, DOMinator instruments Firefox's SpiderMonkey JavaScript engine. Unlike our technique, DOMinator does not track data flows on a byte level. Instead, it employs a function tracking history to store the operations which were called on the original, tainted input to result into the final, still tainted, string flowing into a sink. Also, it does not feature a fully automated vulnerability validation.

FLAX [25] is the conceptionally closest approach to our work. Similar to our system, FLAX also utilizes byte-level taint-tracking to identify insecure data flows in JavaScript. However, there are several key differences in which we improve over FLAX: For one, FLAX's taint analysis is not fully integrated in the JavaScript engine. Instead, the actual analysis is done on program slices which are translated into JASIL, a simplified version of JavaScript, which expresses the operational semantics of only a subset of JavaScript. In contrast, through extending JavaScript's low-level string type, we achieve full language and API coverage. Furthermore, FLAX employs fuzzing for vulnerability testing, while our approach leverages the precise source and sink context information to create validation payloads that deterministically match the respective data flows specifics. Finally, using a large scale study we successfully demonstrated that our system is compatible with the current code practices in today's Web. In contrast, FLAX was only practically evaluated on a set of 40 Web applications and widgets.

Criscione [5] presented an automatic tool to find XSS problems in a scalable black box fashion. Similar to our approach, they also use actual browser instances for test execution and vulnerability validation. However, they don't utilize taint propagation or precise payload generation. Instead, the tests are done in a fuzzing fashion.

Finally, a related approach was presented by Vogt et. al. [30], which utilizes a combination of static analysis and dynamic information flow tracking to mitigate XSS exploits. However, instead of following the flow of untrusted data, the focus is on security sensitive values, such as the user's cookie, and the potential exfiltration of those.

Server-side approaches and static taint analysis: On the server-side various approaches using dynamic taint-tracking to detect and mitigate XSS vulnerabilities have been proposed [20, 23, 4, 27, 19, 33, 2]. Furthermore, as an alternative to dynamic taint-tracking, static analysis of source code to identify insecure data flows is a well established tool [9, 28, 31, 14, 32, 10].

Attack generation: In order to decrease false positive rates several approaches have been studied to automatically generate a valid exploit payloads for validation purposes. In 2008, Martin et al. [18] presented a method to generate XSS and SQL injection exploits based on goal-directed model checking. Thereby, their system QED is capable of performing a goal-directed analysis of any Java Web application, which adheres to the standard servlet specification. Based on the constructed model, a model checker is able to generate a valid exploit that can be used to validate the finding. As opposed to our approach the system operates on the server-side code and thus focuses on server-side injection vulnerabilities. Similar to this approach, Kieyzun et al. [15] also focus on the automatic generation of attacks targeting server-side injection vulnerabilities. In order to do so, the authors use symbolic taint-tracking and input mutations to generate example exploits. Thereby, several test inputs are transmitted to the target service and depending on the registered data flows, inputs are mutated to generate malicious payloads. As opposed to our approach, their tool Ardilla also only works on server-side code and thus rather targets traditional XSS vulnerabilities. As it requires several HTTP requests for generating a valid exploit, scaling is far more difficult than with our approach. In [6], d'Amore et al. present the tool *snuck* that is capable of automatically evading server-side XSS filters. To function, however, the tool needs input from a human tester that identifies the application's intended workflows and possible injection vectors. The tool then automatically verifies whether the filter functions works in a correct manner. In order to do so the system identifies the exact injection context by using XPath queries.

Empirical studies on JavaScript security: Due to its ever growing importance in the Web application paradigm, several security-relevant aspects of client-side JavaScript execution have been studied empirically. For one, Yue and Wang [34] examined the commonness of JavaScript practices that could lead to unauthorized code execution, namely cross-domain inclusion of external JavaScript files and usage of APIs that could lead to XSS. Their study is purely statistically and no real vulnerability validation was conducted. Zooming in on `eval`, Richards et al. [24] study how this problematic API is used in the wild, identifying both usage patterns that could be solved with safe alternatives as well as instances, in which replacing `eval` would not be a straight forward task. Furthermore, selected "HTML5" JavaScript APIs have been studied in detail: Lekies & Johns [17] surveyed the Alexa top 500,000 for potentially insecure usage of JavaScript's `localStorage` for code caching purposes and Son & Shmatikov [26] examined the Alexa top 10,000 for vulnerabilities occurring from unsafe utilization of the `postMessage` API.

8. CONCLUSION

In this paper, we presented a fully automated approach to detect and validate DOM-based XSS vulnerabilities. By direct integration into the browser's JavaScript engine, we achieve reliable identification of potentially insecure data flows while maintaining full compatibility with productive JavaScript code. Furthermore, the precise, byte-level context informations of the resulting injection points enables us to create attack payloads which are tailored to the vulnerability's specific conditions, thus, allowing for robust exploit generation.

Using our system, we conducted a large scale empirical study, resulting in the identification of 6,167 unique vulnerabilities distributed over 480 domains, demonstrating that 9,6% of the Alexa top 5000 carry at least one DOM-based XSS problem.

Acknowledgments

This work was in parts supported by the EU Projects WebSand (FP7-256964) and STREWS (FP7-318097). The support is gratefully acknowledged.

9. REFERENCES

[1] BATES, D., BARTH, A., AND JACKSON, C. Regular expressions considered harmful in client-side XSS filters. In *WWW '10: Proceedings of the 19th international conference on World wide web* (New York, NY, USA, 2010), ACM, pp. 91–100.

[2] BISHT, P., AND VENKATAKRISHNAN, V. N. XSS-GUARD: Precise dynamic detection of cross-site scripting attacks. In *Detection of Intrusions and Malware & Vulnerability Assessment (DIMVA'08)* (2008).

[3] CERT. Advisory ca-2000-02 malicious html tags embedded in client web requests, February 2000.

[4] CONTI, J. J., AND RUSSO, A. A taint mode for python via a library. In *NordSec* (2010), T. Aura, K. Järvinen, and K. Nyberg, Eds., vol. 7127 of *Lecture Notes in Computer Science*, Springer, pp. 210–222.

[5] CRISCIONE, C. Drinking the Ocean - Finding XSS at Google Scale. Talk at the Google Test Automation Conference, (GTAC'13), `http://goo.gl/8qqHA`, April 2013.

[6] D'AMORE, F., AND GENTILE, M. Automatic and context-aware cross-site scripting filter evasion. *Department of Computer, Control, and Management Engineering Antonio Ruberti Technical Reports 1*, 4 (2012).

[7] DI PAOLA, S. DominatorPro: Securing Next Generation of Web Applications. [software], `https://dominator.mindedsecurity.com/`, 2012.

[8] GOOGLE DEVELOPERS. Chrome Extensions - Developer's Guide. [online], `http://developer.chrome.com/extensions/devguide.html`, last access 06/05/13, 2012.

[9] GUARNIERI, S., PISTOIA, M., TRIPP, O., DOLBY, J., TEILHET, S., AND BERG, R. Saving the world wide web from vulnerable javascript. In *ISSTA* (2011), M. B. Dwyer and F. Tip, Eds., ACM, pp. 177–187.

[10] GUHA, A., KRISHNAMURTHI, S., AND JIM, T. Using static analysis for Ajax intrusion detection. In *Proceedings of the 18th international conference on World wide web (WWW'09)* (New York, NY, USA, 2009), ACM, pp. 561–570.

[11] HANNA, S., CHUL, E., SHIN, R., AKHAWE, D., BOEHM, A., SAXENA, P., AND SONG, D. The emperor's new apis: On the (in) secure usage of new client-side primitives. In *Web 2.0 Security and Privacy (W2SP 2010)* (2010).

[12] HEIDERICH, M., NAVA, E., HEYES, G., AND LINDSAY, D. *Web Application Obfuscation: -/WAFs..Evasion..Filters//alert (/Obfuscation/)-*. Elsevier/Syngress, 2010.

[13] HEYES, G. Bypassing XSS Auditor. [online], `http://www.thespanner.co.uk/2013/02/19/bypassing-xss-auditor/`, last accessed 08/05/13, February 2013.

[14] JOVANOVIC, N., KRUEGEL, C., AND KIRDA, E. Pixy: A Static Analysis Tool for Detecting Web Application Vulnerabilities. In *IEEE Symposium on Security and Privacy* (May 2006).

[15] KIEYZUN, A., GUO, P. J., JAYARAMAN, K., AND ERNST, M. D. Automatic creation of sql injection and cross-site scripting attacks. In *Proceedings of the 31st*

International Conference on Software Engineering (Washington, DC, USA, 2009), ICSE '09, IEEE Computer Society, pp. 199–209.

[16] Klein, A. Dom based cross site scripting or xss of the third kind. *Web Application Security Consortium, Articles 4* (2005).

[17] Lekies, S., and Johns, M. Lightweight Integrity Protection for Web Storage-driven Content Caching. In *6th Workshop on Web 2.0 Security and Privacy (W2SP 2012)* (May 2012).

[18] Martin, M., and Lam, M. S. Automatic Generation of XSS and SQL Injection Attacks with Goal-Directed Model Checking. In *Usenix Security* (2008).

[19] Nadji, Y., Saxena, P., and Song, D. Document Structure Integrity: A Robust Basis for Cross-site Scripting Defense. In *Network & Distributed System Security Symposium (NDSS 2009)* (2009).

[20] Nguyen-Tuong, A., Guarnieri, S., Greene, D., Shirley, J., and Evans, D. Automatically hardening web applications using precise tainting. In *20th IFIP International Information Security Conference* (May 2005).

[21] Nikiforakis, N. Bypassing Chrome's Anti-XSS filter. [online], `http://blog.securitee.org/?p=37`, last access 08/05/13, September 2011.

[22] Nikiforakis, N., Invernizzi, L., Kapravelos, A., Acker, S. V., Joosen, W., Kruegel, C., Piessens, F., and Vigna, G. You Are What You Include: Large-scale Evaluation of Remote JavaScript Inclusions. In *19th ACM Conference on Computer and Communications Security (CCS 2012)* (2012).

[23] Pietraszek, T., and Berghe, C. V. Defending against Injection Attacks through Context-Sensitive String Evaluation. In *Recent Advances in Intrusion Detection (RAID2005)* (2005).

[24] Richards, G., Hammer, C., Burg, B., and Vitek, J. The eval that men do - a large-scale study of the use of eval in javascript applications. In *ECOOP* (2011), M. Mezini, Ed., vol. 6813 of *Lecture Notes in Computer Science*, Springer, pp. 52–78.

[25] Saxena, P., Hanna, S., Poosankam, P., and Song, D. FLAX: Systematic Discovery of Client-side Validation Vulnerabilities in Rich Web Applications. In *NDSS* (2010), The Internet Society.

[26] Son, S., and Shmatikov, V. The Postman Always Rings Twice: Attacking and Defending postMessage in HTML5 Websites. In *Network and Distributed System Security Symposium (NDSS'13)* (2013).

[27] Su, Z., and Wassermann, G. The Essence of Command Injection Attacks in Web Applications. In *Proceedings of POPL'06* (January 2006).

[28] Tripp, O., Pistoia, M., Fink, S. J., Sridharan, M., and Weisman, O. TAJ: Effective Taint Analysis for Java. In *ACM SIGPLAN 2009 Conference on Programming Language Design and Implementation (PLDI 2009)* (June 2009).

[29] Vikram, K., Prateek, A., and Livshits, B. Ripley: Automatically securing distributed Web applications through replicated execution. In *Conference on Computer and Communications Security* (Oct. 2009).

[30] Vogt, P., Nentwich, F., Jovanovic, N., Kruegel, C., Kirda, E., and Vigna, G. Cross Site Scripting Prevention with Dynamic Data Tainting and Static Analysis. In *14th Annual Network and Distributed System Security Symposium (NDSS 2007)* (2007).

[31] Wassermann, G., and Su, Z. Sound and Precise Analysis of Web Applications for Injection Vulnerabilities. In *Proceedings of Programming Language Design and Implementation (PLDI'07)* (San Diego, CA, June 10-13 2007).

[32] Xie, Y., and Aiken, A. Static Detection of Security Vulnerabilities in Scripting Languages. In *15th USENIX Security Symposium* (2006).

[33] Xu, W., Bhatkar, S., and Sekar, R. Taint-Enhanced Policy Enforcement: A Practical Approach to Defeat a Wide Range of Attacks. In *15th USENIX Security Symposium* (August 2006).

[34] Yue, C., and Wang, H. Characterizing insecure javascript practices on the web. In *WWW* (2009), J. Quemada, G. León, Y. S. Maarek, and W. Nejdl, Eds., ACM, pp. 961–970.

deDacota: Toward Preventing Server-Side XSS via Automatic Code and Data Separation

Adam Doupé
UC Santa Barbara
adoupe@cs.ucsb.edu

Weidong Cui
Microsoft Research
wdcui@microsoft.com

Mariusz H. Jakubowski
Microsoft Research
mariuszj@microsoft.com

Marcus Peinado
Microsoft Research
marcuspe@microsoft.com

Christopher Kruegel
UC Santa Barbara
chris@cs.ucsb.edu

Giovanni Vigna
UC Santa Barbara
vigna@cs.ucsb.edu

ABSTRACT

Web applications are constantly under attack. They are popular, typically accessible from anywhere on the Internet, and they can be abused as malware delivery systems.

Cross-site scripting flaws are one of the most common types of vulnerabilities that are leveraged to compromise a web application and its users. A large set of cross-site scripting vulnerabilities originates from the browser's confusion between data and code. That is, untrusted data input to the web application is sent to the clients' browser, where it is then interpreted as code and executed. While new applications can be designed with code and data separated from the start, legacy web applications do not have that luxury.

This paper presents a novel approach to securing legacy web applications by automatically and statically rewriting an application so that the code and data are clearly separated in its web pages. This transformation protects the application and its users from a large range of server-side cross-site scripting attacks. Moreover, the code and data separation can be efficiently enforced at run time via the Content Security Policy enforcement mechanism available in modern browsers.

We implemented our approach in a tool, called DEDACOTA, that operates on binary ASP.NET applications. We demonstrate on six real-world applications that our tool is able to automatically separate code and data, while keeping the application's semantics unchanged.

Categories and Subject Descriptors

D.2.5 [**Testing and Debugging**]

Keywords

Static Analysis; Cross-Site Scripting; XSS; Content Security Policy; CSP

CCS'13, November 4–8, 2013, Berlin, Germany.

http://dx.doi.org/10.1145/2508859.2516708.

1. INTRODUCTION

Web applications are prevalent and critical in today's computing world, making them a popular attack target. Looking at types of vulnerabilities reported in the Common Vulnerabilities and Exposures (CVE) database [11], web application flaws are by far the leading class.

Modern web applications have evolved into complex programs. These programs are no longer limited to server-side code that runs on the web server. Instead, web applications include a significant amount of JavaScript code that is sent to and executed on the client. Such client-side components not only provide a rich and fast user interface, they also contain parts of the application logic and typically communicate with the server-side component through asynchronous JavaScript calls. As a result, client-side scripts are an integral component of modern web applications, and they are routinely generated by server-side code.

There are two kinds of cross-site scripting (XSS) vulnerabilities: server-side and client-side. The latter is essentially caused by bugs in the client-side code, while the former is caused by bugs in the server-side code. In this paper we focus on server-side XSS vulnerabilities (unless specified otherwise, we will use XSS to refer to server-side XSS). XSS vulnerabilities allow attackers to inject client-side scripting code (typically, JavaScript) into the output of web applications. The scripts are then executed by the browser as it renders the page, allowing malicious code to run in the context of the web application. Attackers can leverage XSS attacks to leak sensitive user information, impersonate the victim to perform unwanted actions in the context of the web application, or launch browser exploits.

There has been a significant amount of research effort on eliminating XSS vulnerabilities. The main line of research has focused on sanitizing untrusted input [3, 13, 18, 22, 25, 27, 34, 38, 40, 44, 46, 48–50]. Sanitization attempts to identify and "clean up" untrusted inputs that might contain JavaScript code. Performing correct sanitization is challenging, for a number of reasons. One reason is that it is difficult to guarantee coverage for all possible paths through the application [3, 48]. As part of this problem, it is necessary to find all program locations (sources) where untrusted input can enter the application, and then verify, along all program paths, the correctness of all sanitization functions that are used before the input is sent to the client (sinks). Furthermore, it is not always clear how to properly sanitize data, because a single input might appear in different contexts in the output of the application [40].

The root cause of XSS vulnerabilities is that *the current web application model violates the principle of code and data separation.* In the case of a web page, the data is the HTML content of the page and the code is the JavaScript code. Mixing JavaScript code and HTML data in the same channel (the HTTP response) makes it possible for an attacker to convince a user's browser to interpret maliciously crafted HTML data as JavaScript code. While sanitization tries to turn untrusted input, which could potentially contain code, into HTML data, we believe the fundamental solution to XSS is to separate the code and data in a web page—the way HTML and JavaScript should have been designed from the start. Once the code and data are separated, a web application can communicate this separation to the browser, and the browser can ensure no code is executed from the data channel. Such communication and enforcement is supported by the new W3C browser standard Content Security Policy (CSP) [42].

While new web applications can be designed with code and data separated from the start, it has been a daunting task to achieve code and data separation for legacy applications. The key challenge is to identify code or data in the output of a web application. Previous solutions have relied on either developers' manual annotations or dynamic analysis. For example, BEEP [20] requires developers to manually identify inline JavaScript code. BLUEPRINT [28] requires developers to manually identify the data by specifying which application statements could output untrusted input. XSS-GUARD dynamically identifies application-intended JavaScript code in a web page by comparing it with a shadow web page generated at run time [4]. The main problem preventing these solutions from being adopted is either the significant manual effort required from application developers or the significant runtime performance overhead. In fact, Weinberger et al. [47] showed how difficult it is to manually separate the code and data of a web application.

In this paper, we present DEDACOTA, the first system that can automatically and statically rewrite an existing web application to separate code and data in its web pages. Our novel idea is to use static analysis to determine all inline JavaScript code in the web pages of an application. Specifically, DEDACOTA performs static data-flow analysis of a given web application to approximate its HTML output. Then, it parses each page's HTML output to identify inline JavaScript code. Finally, it rewrites the web application to output the identified JavaScript code in a separate JavaScript file.

The problem of statically determining the set of (HTML) outputs of a web application is undecidable. However, as we observe in our evaluation, the problem is typically tractable for real-world web applications. These applications are written by benign developers and tend to have special properties that allow us to compute their outputs statically. For instance, the majority of the inline JavaScript code is static in the web applications we tested.

Dynamic inline JavaScript presents a second-order problem. Here, the JavaScript code itself (rather than the HTML page) is generated dynamically on the server and may depend on untrusted inputs. Again, the potential for XSS vulnerabilities exists. DEDACOTA provides a partial solution to this problem by producing alerts for all potentially dangerous instances of dynamic JavaScript generation in the application and by safely sanitizing a large subclass of these instances.

We implemented a prototype of DEDACOTA to analyze and rewrite ASP.NET [31] web applications. We then applied DEDACOTA to six open-source, real-world ASP.NET applications. We verified that all known XSS vulnerabilities are eliminated. We then performed extensive testing to ensure that the rewritten binaries still function correctly. We also tested DEDACOTA's performance and found that the page loading times between the original and rewritten application are indistinguishable.

The main contributions of this paper are the following:

- A novel approach for automatically separating the code and data of a web application using static analysis (Section 4).
- A prototype implementation of our approach, DEDACOTA, applied to ASP.NET applications (Section 5).
- An evaluation of DEDACOTA, showing that we are able to apply our analysis to six real-world, open-source, ASP.NET applications. We show that our implementation prevents the exploitation of know vulnerabilities and that the semantics of the application do not change (Section 6).

2. BACKGROUND

In this section, we provide the background necessary for understanding the design of DEDACOTA.

2.1 Cross-Site Scripting

Modern web applications consist of both server-side and client-side code. Upon receiving an HTTP request, the server-side code, which is typically written in a server-side language, such as PHP or ASP.NET, dynamically generates a web page as a response, based on the user input in the request or data in a backend database. The client-side code, which is usually written in JavaScript and is executed by the browser, can be either inline in the web page or external as a standalone JavaScript file.

Cross-site scripting (XSS) vulnerabilities allow an attacker to inject malicious scripts into web pages to execute in the client-side browser, as if they were generated by the trusted web site. If the vulnerability allows the attacker to store malicious JavaScript on the server (e.g., using the contents of a message posted on a newsgroup), the vulnerability is traditionally referred to as "stored" or "persistent XSS." When the malicious code is included in the request and involuntarily reflected to the user (copied into the response) by the server, the vulnerability is called "reflected XSS." Finally, if the bug is in the client-side code, the XSS vulnerability is referred to as "DOM-based XSS" [24]. We call the first two types of vulnerabilities "server-side XSS vulnerabilities" and the latter "client-side XSS vulnerabilities."

The root cause for server-side XSS is that the code (i.e., the client-side script) and the data (i.e., the HTML content) are mixed together in a web page. By crafting some malicious input that will be included into the returned web page by the server-side code, an attacker can trick the browser into confusing his data as JavaScript code.

2.2 Code and Data Separation

The separation of code and data can be traced back to the Harvard Architecture, which introduces separate storage and buses for code and data. Separating code and data is a basic security principle for avoiding code injection attacks [19]. Historically, whenever designs violate this principle, there exists a security hole. An example is the stack used in modern CPUs. The return addresses (code pointers) and function local variables (data) are co-located on the stack. Because the return addresses determine control transfers, they are essentially part of the code. Mixing them together with the data allows attackers to launch stack overflow attacks, where data written into a local variable spills into an adjacent return address. In the context of web applications, we face the same security challenge, this time caused by mixing code and data together in web pages. To fundamentally solve this problem, we must separate code and data in web pages created by web applications.

2.3 Content Security Policy

Content Security Policy (CSP) [42] is a mechanism for mitigating a broad class of content injection vulnerabilities in web applications. CSP is a declarative policy that allows a web application to inform the browser, via an HTTP header, about the sources from which the application expects to load resources such as JavaScript code. A web browser that implements support for CSP can enforce the security policy declared by the web application.

A newly developed web application can leverage CSP to avoid XSS by not using inline JavaScript and by specifying that only scripts from a set of trusted sites are allowed to execute on the client. Indeed, Google has required that all Chrome browser extensions implement CSP [1]. However, manually applying CSP to a legacy web application typically requires a non-trivial amount of work [47]. The reason is that the authors of the web application have to modify the server-side code to clearly identify which resources (e.g., which JavaScript programs) are used by a web page. Moreover, these scripts have to be separated from the web page.

CSP essentially provides a mechanism for web browsers to enforce the separation between code and data as specified by web applications. Our work solves the problem of automatically transforming legacy web applications so that the code and data in their web pages are separated. The transformed web applications can then directly leverage the browser's support for CSP to avoid a wide range of XSS vulnerabilities.

3. THREAT MODEL

Before discussing the design of deDacota, we need to state our assumptions about the code that we are analyzing and the vulnerabilities we are addressing.

Our approach involves rewriting a web application. This web application is written by a benign developer—that is, the developer has not intentionally obfuscated the code as a malicious developer might. This assumption also means that the JavaScript and HTML are benign and not intentionally taking advantage of browser parsing quirks (as described in Blueprint [28]).

deDacota will only prevent *server-side* XSS vulnerabilities. We define server-side XSS vulnerabilities as XSS vulnerabilities where the *root cause* of the vulnerability is in server-side code. Specifically, this means XSS vulnerabilities where unsanitized input is used in an HTML page. We explicitly do not protect against client-side XSS vulnerabilities, also called DOM-based XSS. Client-side XSS vulnerabilities occur when untrusted input is interpreted as JavaScript by the client-side JavaScript code using methods such as `eval`, `document.write`, or `innerHTML`. The root cause of these vulnerabilities is in the *JavaScript code*.

In this paper, we focus solely on separating inline JavaScript code (that is, JavaScript in between `<script>` and `</script>`). While there are other vectors where JavaScript can be executed, such as JavaScript code in HTML attributes (event handlers such as `onclick`) and inline Cascading Style Sheet (CSS) styles [16], the techniques described here can be extended to approximate and rewrite the HTML attributes and inline CSS.

Unfortunately, code and data separation in an HTML page is not a panacea for XSS vulnerabilities. In modern web applications, the inline JavaScript code is sometimes dynamically generated by the server-side code. A common scenario is to use the dynamic JavaScript code to pass data from the server-side code to the client-side code. There may be XSS vulnerabilities, even if code and data are properly separated, if the data embedded in the JavaScript code is not properly sanitized. deDacota provides a partial solution to the problem of dynamic JavaScript (see Section 4.5).

4. DESIGN

Our goal is to statically transform a given web application so that the new version preserves the application semantics but outputs web pages where all the inline JavaScript code is moved to external JavaScript files. These external files will be the *only* JavaScript that the browser will execute, based on a Content Security Policy.

There are three high-level steps to our approach. For each web page in the web application: (1) we statically determine a conservative approximation of the page's HTML output, (2) we extract all inline JavaScript from the approximated HTML output, and (3) we rewrite the application so that all inline JavaScript is moved to external files.

Hereinafter, we define a running example that we use to describe how deDacota automatically transforms a web application, according to the three steps outlined previously.

4.1 Example

Listing 1 shows a simplified ASP.NET Web Form page. Note that everything not in between the `<%` and `%>` is output directly to the browser. Everything between matching `<%` and `%>` is C# code. A subtle but important point is that `<%=` is used to indicate that the C# code will output a string at that location in the HTML output.

In Listing 1, Line 2 sets the title of the page, and Line 3 sets the `Username` variable to the `name` parameter sent in the query string. The `Username` is output to the browser inside a JavaScript string on Line 7. This is an example of the C# server-side code passing information to the JavaScript client-side code, as the intent here is for the JavaScript `username` variable to have the same value as the C# `Username` variable.

Internally, ASP.NET compiles the ASP.NET Web Form page to C#, either when the application is deployed, or on-demand, as the page is accessed. The relevant compiled C# output of Listing 1 is shown in Listing 2. Here, the ASP.NET Web Form page has been transformed into an

```
1  <html>
2    <% Title = "Example";
3     Username = Request.Params["name"]; %>
4    <head><tile><%= Title %></title></head>
5    <body>
6      <script>
7        var username = "<%= Username %>";
8      </script>
9    </body>
10 </html>
```

Listing 1: Example of a simple ASP.NET Web Form page.

```
1  void Render(TextWriter w) {
2    w.Write("<html>\n  ");
3    this.Title = "Example";
4    this.Username = Request.Params["name"];
5    w.Write("\n  <head><tile>");
6    w.Write(this.Title);
7    w.Write("</title></head>\n  <body>\n
         <script>\n       var username = \"");
8    w.Write(this.Username);
9    w.Write("\";\n    </script>\n  </body>\n
         </html>");
10 }
```

Listing 2: The compiled C# output of Listing 1.

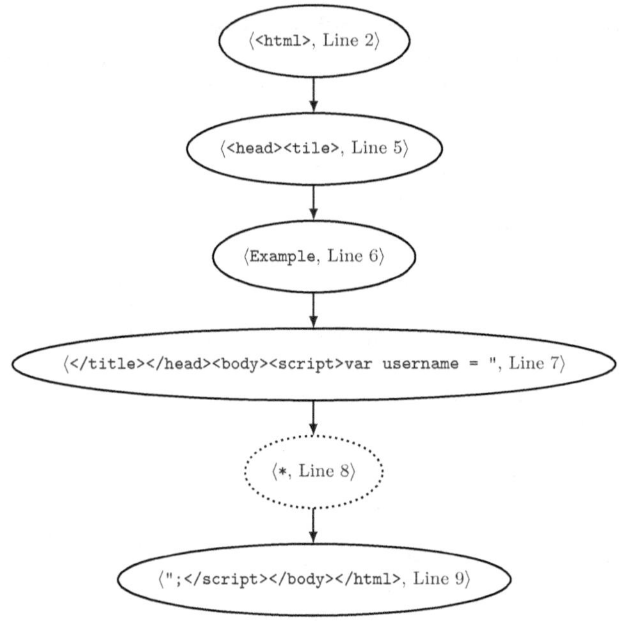

Figure 1: Approximation graph for the code in Listing 1 and Listing 2. The dotted node's content is not statically determinable.

equivalent C# program. The ASP.NET compiler creates a class (not shown) that represents the ASP.NET Web Form. A method of the class is given a `TextWriter` object as a parameter. Anything written to this object will be sent in the HTTP response. `TextWriter.Write` is a method call equivalent of writing to the console in a traditional command-line application.

From comparing Listing 1 to Listing 2, one can see that output not between <% and %> tags is written to the `TextWriter` object. The code between the <% and %> tags is inlined into the function (Lines 3 and 4), and the code that is between the <%= and %> tags is written to the `TextWriter` object (Lines 6 and 8). We also note that `TextWriter.Write` is one of a set of methods used to write content to the HTTP response. However, for simplicity, in the remainder of this paper, we will use `TextWriter.Write` to represent all possible ways of writing content to the HTTP response.

4.2 Approximating HTML Output

In the first phase of our approach, we approximate the HTML output of a web page. This is a two-step process. First, we need to determine, at every `TextWriter.Write` location, what is being written. Second, we need to determine the order of the `TextWriter.Write` function invocations.

We use a different static analysis technique to answer each of the two questions. To determine what is being written at a `TextWriter.Write`, we use the points-to analysis algorithm presented in [10] modified to work on .NET byte-code, instead of C. This points-to analysis algorithm is inclusion-based, demand-driven, context-sensitive, field-sensitive, and partially flow-sensitive. The points-to analysis algorithm computes the set of strings that alias with the parameter of `TextWriter.Write`. If all strings in the alias set are constant strings, the output at the `TextWriter.Write` will be defined as the conjunction of all possible constant strings. Otherwise, we say the output is statically undecidable. To determine the ordering of all `TextWriter.Write` method calls, we build a control-flow graph, using standard techniques, that only contains the `TextWriter.Write` method calls.

We encode the information produced by the two static analyses—the ordering of `TextWriter.Write` method calls and their possible output—into a graph that we call an *approximation graph*. Figure 1 shows the approximation graph for the code in Listing 1 and Listing 2. Each node in the graph contains the location of the `TextWriter.Write` that this node represents as well as the possible constant strings that could be output at this `TextWriter.Write` location. Content that cannot be determined statically is represented by a wild card * (the dotted node in Figure 1). The strings that may be output at the `TextWriter.Write` will be used to identify inline JavaScript, and the location of the `TextWriter.Write` will be used for rewriting the application.

In Figure 2 we show the approximation graph of a more complex page. The graph in Figure 2 contains a branch, where each node in the branch maps to the same `TextWriter.Write` method. This happens when the points-to analysis says that the `TextWriter.Write` method can output one of multiple strings. The other way there can be a branch in the approximation graph is when there is a branch in the control flow of the web application. The graph in Figure 2 also contains a loop that includes the nodes shown in bold. However, because we cannot statically determine the number of times a loop may execute, and we want our analysis to be conservative, we collapse all nodes of a loop (in the approximation graph) into a single node. This new node now has undecidable content (represented by a *). The new node also keeps track of all the `TextWriter.Write` methods that were part of the original loop.

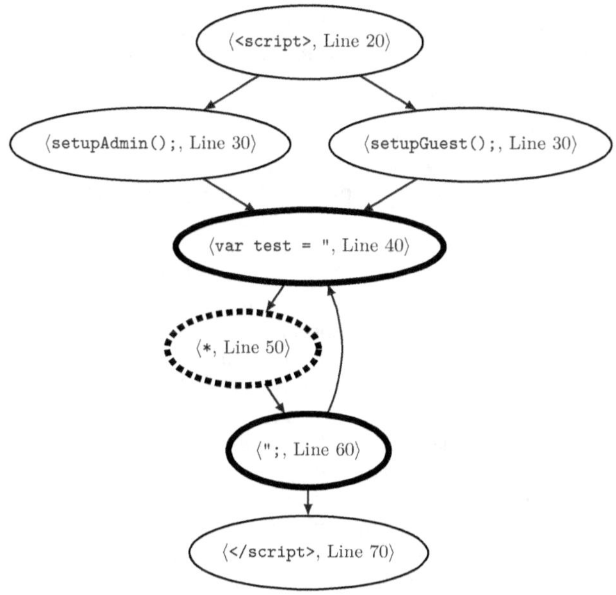

Figure 2: Approximation graph with branches and a loop. The loop will be collapsed into one node to create the final approximation graph.

After collapsing all loops in the graph, we derive a conservative approximation of the HTML output of a web page. The approximation graph is a directed acyclic graph (DAG), and any path from the root node to a leaf node will represent one possible output of the web page.

4.3 Extracting Inline JavaScript

In the second phase, our approach uses the approximation graph described previously to extract all possible inline JavaScript. The output of this phase is a set containing all possible inline JavaScript that may appear in the web page.

In an approximation graph, each unique path from the root node to a leaf node represents a potential output of the page. A naïve algorithm would enumerate all paths and, thus, all outputs, and parse each output string to identify inline JavaScript. However, even without loops, the number of unique paths even in a simple web page may quickly explode and become unmanageable (this is the path-explosion problem faced in static analysis).

To reduce the impact of the path explosion problem, we extract the inline JavaScript directly from the approximation graph. We first search for the opening and closing tags of HTML elements in the graph. We ignore tags that appear in comments. Then, for each pair of JavaScript tags (i.e., `<script>` and `</script>`), we process all the unique paths between the opening and closing tags. For each path, we obtain an inline JavaScript that the program might output.

While our current prototype is relatively simplistic in parsing the starting and ending JavaScript files, it could be possible to use the parsing engine from a real browser. However, this is not as straight-forward as it seems, as our input is a graph of all potential HTML output, not a single document. We leave this approach to future work.

All identified inline JavaScript pieces are then passed to the last phase of our approach, which decides how to rewrite the application.

4.4 Application Rewriting

The goal of the third phase is to rewrite the application so that all identified inline JavaScript will be removed from the HTML content and saved in external JavaScript files. In the HTML code, an inline JavaScript is replaced with a reference to the external JavaScript file as follows:

```
<script src="External.js"></script>
```

It is not uncommon that multiple possible inline JavaScript snippets exist between an opening and closing JavaScript tag because there may be branches between the tags in the approximation graph. To know which exact inline JavaScript is created, we need to track the execution of the server-side code.

The inline JavaScript identified in the previous phase falls into two categories: static and dynamic (i.e., contains undecidable content). Because we cannot statically decide the content of a dynamic inline JavaScript, we must track the execution of the server-side code to create its external JavaScript file(s) at runtime. Therefore, we can avoid tracking the execution of the server-side code *only* for the case in which there is a *single, static* inline JavaScript code.

For a pair of opening and closing script tags that require tracking the execution of the server-side code, we rewrite the application as follows. At the `TextWriter.Write` that may output the opening script tag, we first check if the output string contains the tag. We need to perform this check because a `TextWriter.Write` site may be used to output either inline JavaScript code or other HTML. If we find the opening script tag in the output, we use a session flag to indicate that an inline JavaScript rewriting has started. We write out everything before the start of the opening script tag. We remove the opening script tag itself. The remaining content is stored into a session buffer. Note that both session flag and buffer are unique to each opening script tag. Then, for all subsequent `TextWriter.Write` method calls that are part of the inline JavaScript we are rewriting, except for the last (that writes the closing tag), we append their output to the session buffer if the session flag is on. For the last `TextWriter.Write` method call (i.e., the one that writes the closing script tag), any string content that occurs before the closing script tag is appended to the session buffer. Any content after the closing script tag is just written to the output. At this point, the session buffer contains the entire inline JavaScript code. We save this code to an external file and add a `TextWriter.Write` method call that outputs the reference to this JavaScript file.

To support JavaScript caching on the client side, the name of the JavaScript file is derived from its content, using a cryptographic hash of the JavaScript content. An unintended benefit of this approach is that inline JavaScript that is included on multiple pages will be cached by the browser, improving application performance by reducing the size of the page and saving server requests.

Listing 3 shows the result of applying this rewriting process to the inline JavaScript code in Listing 2. The changes shown are only those made to Lines 7–9 in Listing 2.

4.5 Dynamic Inline JavaScript

At this point in our analysis, we have successfully separated the JavaScript code from the HTML data in the web application. If the web application's JavaScript is static, and by static we mean statically decidable, then the application is now immune to XSS vulnerabilities. However, if

```
w.Write("</title></head>\n  <body>\n    ");

Session["7"] = "\n    var username = \"");
Session["7"] += this.Username;
Session["7"] += "\";\n    ";

var hashName = Hash(Session["7"]) + ".js";
WriteToFile(hashName, Session["7"]);

w.Write("<script src=\"" + hashName + "
    \"></script>");

w.Write("\n  </body>\n</html>");
```

Listing 3: The result of the rewriting algorithm applied to Listing 2. Specifically, here we show the transformation of Lines 7–9 in Listing 2.

the web application dynamically generates JavaScript with undecidable content, and that content is not properly sanitized inside the JavaScript code, an attacker can exploit this bug to inject a malicious script. The approach discussed so far does not mitigate this attack, because it simply moves the vulnerable JavaScript to an external file.

To understand how dynamic JavaScript can result in a vulnerability, consider our example application in Listing 2. There is an XSS vulnerability on Line 8 because the `Username` variable is derived from the `name` parameter and output directly to the user, without sanitization. An attacker could exploit this vulnerability by setting the `name` parameter to `";alert('xss')//`. This would cause the resulting inline JavaScript to be the following, thus executing the attacker's JavaScript code:

```
<script>
  var username = "";alert('xss')//";
</script>
```

Therefore, the code section of the application is dynamically generated with untrusted input and even with the code and data separated, there is still an XSS vulnerability.

We attempt to mitigate this problem, and therefore improve the security of the application, in two ways. First, we identify cases in which we can safely rewrite the application. Second, we notify the developer when we make an inline to external transformation that is potentially unsafe.

For the first case, when the undetermined output is produced in certain JavaScript contexts, we can include it in a safe fashion via sanitization. Specifically, during static analysis we pass the dynamic inline JavaScript to a JavaScript parser. Then, we query the parser to determine the contexts in which the undetermined output (i.e., the * parts) is used. Here, for context we are referring specifically to the HTML parsing contexts described by Samuel et al. [38]. Possible contexts are JavaScript string, JavaScript numeric, JavaScript regular expression, JavaScript variable, etc. If an undetermined output is in a string context, we sanitize them in a way similar to how BLUEPRINT [28] handles string literals in JavaScript.

Like BLUEPRINT, on the server side we encode the string value and store the encoded data in JavaScript by embedding a call to a decoding function. Then when the JavaScript is executed on the client side, the decoding function will decode the encoded data and return the string. Unlike BLUEPRINT, we do not require any developer annotations because our static analysis can automatically identify which JavaScript context an undetermined output is in.

4.6 Generality

While the description of our approach so far was specific to ASP.NET Web Forms, the high-level idea of automatically separating code and data in a legacy web application can be generalized to any other web application frameworks or templating languages. There are still challenges that remain to apply our approach to another language, or even another template in the same language. The two main steps of our approach that must be changed to accommodate a different language or templating language are: (1) understand how the output is created by the web application and (2) understand how to rewrite the web application. Only the first step affects the analysis capability (as the rewriting process is fairly straightforward).

To automatically separate the code and data of a different language or templating language, one must understand how the language or template generates its output. After that, one would need to implement a static analysis that can create an approximation graph. For instance, in the default Ruby on Rails template, ERB, variables are passed to the template either via a hash table or class instance variables [37]. Therefore, one could approximate the output of an ERB template by statically tracking the variables added to the hash table and class instance variables (using points-to analysis). Once an approximation graph is created, detecting inline JavaScript can be performed in the manner previously described.

The main factor to affect the success of applying our approach to another web application framework or templating language is the precision of the static analysis, or in other words, how precise and detailed the approximation graph would be. The more dynamicism in the language or framework, such as run-time code execution and dynamic method invocation, the more difficult the analysis will be. Simply, the more of the control-flow graph that we are able to determine statically, the better our analysis will be. As an example the default templating language in Django only allows a subset of computation: iterating over a collection instead of arbitrary loops [12]. This restriction could make the analysis easier and therefore the approximation graph more precise.

5. IMPLEMENTATION

We implemented the automated code and data separation approach described in Section 4 in a prototype called DEDACOTA. This prototype targets ASP.NET Web Forms applications. ASP.NET is a widely used technology; of the Quantcase top million websites on the Internet, 21.24% use ASP.NET [8].

DEDACOTA targets *binary* .NET applications. More precisely, it takes as input ASP.NET Web Forms binary web applications, performs the three steps of our approach, and outputs an ASP.NET binary that has all inline JavaScript code converted into external JavaScript files. We operate at the binary level because we must be able to analyze the ASP.NET system libraries, which are only available in binary form.

We leverage the open-source Common Compiler Infrastructure (CCI) [32] for reading and analyzing the .NET Common Language Runtime byte-code. CCI also has modules to extract basic blocks and to transform the code into single static assignment (SSA) form. We also use CCI to rewrite the .NET binaries.

For the static analysis engine, we leverage the points-to analysis engine of KOP (also known as MAS) [10]. KOP was originally written for the C programming language. Therefore, we wrote (using CCI) a frontend that processes .NET binaries and outputs the appropriate KOP points-to rules. Then, after parsing these rules, the static analysis engine can provide either alias analysis or points-to analysis. The KOP points-to analysis is demand-driven, context-sensitive, field-sensitive, and, because of the CCI single static assignment, partially flow-sensitive.

An important point, in terms of scalability, is the demand-driven ability of the static analysis engine. Specifically, we will only explore those parts of the program graph that are relevant to our analysis, in contrast to traditional data-flow techniques which track data dependencies across the entire program. The demand-driven nature of the static analysis engine offers another scalability improvement, which is parallelism. Each analysis query is independent and, therefore, can be run in parallel.

We also extend the KOP points-to analysis system to model string concatenation. We do this by including special edges in the program graph that indicate that a variable is the result of the concatenation of two other variables. When computing the alias set of a variable, we first do so in the original way (ignoring any concatenation edges). Then, for each variable in the alias set that has concatenation edges, we compute the alias set for each of the two variables involved in the concatenation operation. We concatenate strings in the two alias sets and add them to the original alias set. The undecidable variables are tracked, so that their concatenated result contains a wildcard. This process is recursive, and handles arbitrary levels of concatenation.

ASP.NET uses the idea of reusable components, called `Controls`. The idea is that a developer can write a control once and then include it in other pages, and even other controls. This relationship of including one control inside another creates a parent-child relationship between the controls (the parent being the control that contains the child control).

In an ASP.NET Web Form page, child controls are first added to the parent's **`ChildControls`** collection, which is similar to an array. Then, during rendering, a parent renders its child controls either by iterating over the **`ChildControls`** or by referencing a child control based on its index in the **`ChildControls`**. Because the KOP points-to analysis does not model the array relation, we cannot precisely decide which child Control is being selected during rendering. To handle this problem, we need to track the parent-child relationships directly.

These parent-child relationships form a tree. Figure 3 shows the parent-child relationship of some of the user controls of **`default.aspx`** in the application BlogEngine.NET (one of the programs used in our evaluation). When building the control graph, we must statically recreate this tree.

To create this relationship statically, we take an approach similar to approximating the HTML output. The entry function for an ASP.NET page is **`FrameworkInitialize`**, which is similar to the **`main`** function for a C program. Starting from this method, we create a control-flow graph of all the calls to **`AddParsedSubObject`**, which is the function that adds a child control to a parent. This gives us the order of the **`AddParsedSubObject`** calls. At each of the calls, we use the points-to analysis to find which control is the parent and which is the child. This information, along with the order of the calls to **`AddParsedSubObject`**, allows us to recreate the parent-child control tree.

6. EVALUATION

There are three properties that we must look at to evaluate the effectiveness of DEDACOTA. First, do we prevent XSS vulnerabilities in the data section of the application by applying code and data separation? Second, do we correctly separate the code and data of the application—that is, does the rewriting preserve the application's semantics? Third, what is the impact on the application's performance? To evaluate the security of our approach, we look at ASP.NET applications with known vulnerabilities. To evaluate the correctness of our rewriting procedure, we apply our approach to applications that have developer-created integration tests. Then, we carried out performance measurements to answer the third question. Finally, we discuss the relation between separating code and data in the output and sanitizing the input.

6.1 Applications

We wish to evaluate DEDACOTA on ASP.NET web applications that are real-world, are open-source, and contain known vulnerabilities. Real-world applications are important for showing that our approach works on real-world code, open-source is important for other researchers to replicate our results, and known-vulnerable is important because we aim to automatically prevent these known vulnerabilities.

Unfortunately, there is no standard (or semi-standard) ASP.NET web application benchmark that meets all three requirements. Furthermore, finding these application proved to be a challenge. Compared to other languages such as PHP, there are fewer open-source ASP.NET applications (as most ASP.NET applications tend to be proprietary). Therefore, here we present a benchmark of six real-world, open-source, ASP.NET applications, four of which are known-vulnerable, one of which is intentionally vulnerable for education, and one of which has a large developer-created test suite.

Table 1 contains, for each application, the version of the application used in our evaluation, the CVE number of the vulnerability reported for the application, the number of ASP.NET Web Form pages, and the number of developer-written ASP.NET **`Controls`**. To provide an idea of the size of the applications, we also show the number of lines of code (LOC) of the ASP.NET controls (Web Forms and Controls) and C# code.

The web applications BugTracker.NET [7], BlogEngine-.NET [5], BlogSA.NET [6], and ScrewTurn Wiki [41] all contain an XSS vulnerability as defined in the associated CVE.

WebGoat.NET [17] is an open-source ASP.NET application that is intentionally vulnerable. The purpose is to provide a safe platform for interested parties to learn about web security. Among the vulnerabilities present in the application are two XSS vulnerabilities.

ChronoZoom Beta 3 [9], is an open-source HTML5 "interactive timeline for all of history." Parts are written in

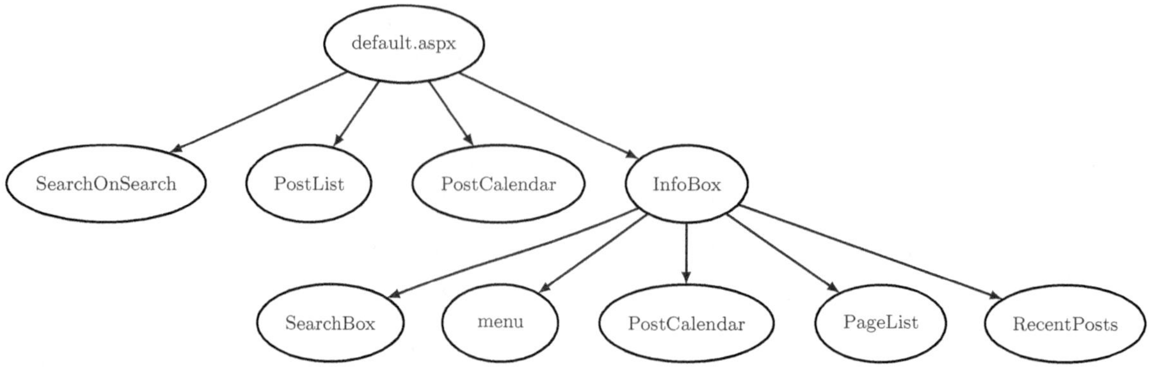

Figure 3: Control parent-child relationship between some of the controls in `default.aspx` from the application BlogEngine.NET. The siblings are ordered from left to right in first-added to last-added order.

Application	Version	Known Vulnerability	# Web Forms	# Controls	ASP.NET LOC	C# LOC	Total LOC
BugTracker.NET	3.4.4	CVE-2010-3266	115	0	27,257	8,417	35,674
BlogEngine.NET	1.3	CVE-2008-6476	19	11	2,525	26,987	29,512
BlogSA.NET	1.0 Beta 3	CVE-2009-0814	29	26	2,632	4,362	6,994
ScrewTurn Wiki	2.0.29	CVE-2008-3483	30	4	2,951	9,204	12,155
WebGoat.NET	e9603b9d5f	2 Intentional	67	0	1,644	10,349	11,993
ChronoZoom	Beta 3	N/A	15	0	3,125	18,136	21,261

Table 1: ASP.NET Web Form applications that we ran DEDACOTA on to test its applicability to real-world web applications.

ASP.NET Web Forms, but the main application is a JavaScript-heavy HTML page. We use ChronoZoom because, unlike the other applications, it has an extensive test suite that exercises the JavaScript portion of the application. To evaluate the correctness of our rewriting, we converted the main HTML page of ChronoZoom, which contained inline JavaScript, into an ASP.NET Web Form page, along with nine other HTML pages that were used by the test suite.

These six real-world web applications encompass the spectrum of web application functionality that we expect to encounter. These applications constitute a total of 100,000 lines of code, written by different developers, each with a different coding style. Some had inline JavaScript in the ASP.NET page, some created inline JavaScript in C# directly, while others created inline JavaScript in C# using string concatenation. Furthermore, while analyzing each application we also analyzed the entire .NET framework (which includes ASP.NET); all 256 MB of binary code. As our analysis handles ASP.NET, we are confident that our approach can be applied to the majority of ASP.NET applications.

6.2 Security

We ran DEDACOTA on each of our test applications. Table 2 shows the total number of inline JS scripts per application and a breakdown of the number of static inline JS scripts, the number of safe dynamic inline JS scripts, and the number of unsafe dynamic inline JS scripts. There were four dynamic inline JS scripts created by the ASP.NET framework, and these are represented in Table 2 in parentheses. We chose to exclude these four from the total dynamic inline JS scripts because they are not under the developer's control, and, furthermore, they can and should be addressed by changes to the ASP.NET library. Furthermore, it is important to note that our tool found these dynamic inline JS scripts within the ASP.NET framework automatically.

From our results it is clear that modern web applications frequently use inline JS scripts. The applications used a range of five to 46 total inline JS scripts. Of these total inline JS scripts 22% to 100% of the inline JS scripts were static.

DEDACOTA was able to safely transform, using the technique outlined in Section 4.5, 50% to 70% of the dynamic inline JS scripts. This result means that our mitigation technique worked in the majority of the cases, with only zero to four actual unsafe dynamic inline JS scripts per application.

We looked for false negatives (inline JavaScript that we might have missed) in two ways. We manually browsed to every ASP.NET Web Form in the application and looked for inline JavaScript. We also searched for inline JavaScript in the original source code of the application to reveal possible scripts the previous browsing might have missed. We did not find any false negatives in the applications.

To evaluate the security improvements for those applications that had known vulnerabilities, we manually crafted inputs to exploit these know bugs. After verifying that the exploits worked on the original version of the application, we launched them against the rewritten versions (with the Content Security Policy header activated, and with a browser supporting CSP). As expected, the Content Security Policy in the browser, along with our rewritten applications, successfully blocked all exploits.

6.3 Functional Correctness

To evaluate the correctness of our approach, and to verify that we maintained the semantics of the original application, we used two approaches. First, we manually browsed web pages generated by each rewritten application and interacted with the web site similar to a normal user. During this process, we looked for JavaScript errors, unexpected behaviors, or CSP violations. We did not find any problems or deviations. Second, and more systematically, we leveraged

Application	Total JS	Static	Safe Dynamic	Unsafe Dynamic
BugTracker.NET	46	41	3	2 (4)
BlogEngine.NET	18	4	10	4 (4)
BlogSA.NET	12	10	1	1 (4)
ScrewTurn Wiki	35	27	4	4 (4)
WebGoat.NET	6	6	0	0 (4)
ChronoZoom	5	5	0	0 (4)

Table 2: Results of running deDacota against the ASP.NET Web Form applications. Safe Dynamic is the number of dynamic inline JS scripts that we could safely transform, and Unsafe Dynamic is the number of dynamic inline JS scripts that we could not safely transform.

Application	Page Size	Loading Time
ChronoZoom (original)	50,827	0.65
ChronoZoom (transformed)	20,784	0.63
BlogEngine.NET (original)	18,518	0.15
BlogEngine.NET (transformed)	19,269	0.16

Table 3: Performance measurements for two of the tested applications, ChronoZoom. Page Size is the size (in bytes) of the main HTML page rendered by the browser, and Loading Time is the time (in seconds) that the browser took to load and display the page.

the developer-written testing suite in ChronoZoom. Before we applied our rewriting, the original application passed 160 tests. After rewriting, all 160 tests executed without errors.

6.4 Performance

To assess the impact of deDacota on application performance, we ran browser-based tests on original and transformed versions of two of the tested applications. Our performance metric was page-loading time in Internet Explorer 9.0, mainly to determine the impact of moving inline JavaScript into separate files. The web server was a 3 GB Hyper-V virtual machine running Microsoft IIS 7.0 under Windows Server 2008 R2, while the client was a similar VM running Windows 7. The physical server was an 8 GB, 3.16 GHz dual-core machine running Windows Server 2008 R2.

Table 3 shows test results for two web applications, summarizing performance data from page-loading tests on the client. The table columns list the average sizes of the main HTML pages retrieved by the browser by accessing the main application URLs, along with the average time used by the browser to retrieve and render the pages in their entirety. All the numbers were averaged over 20 requests.

As Table 3 indicates, deDacota's transformations incurred no appreciable difference in page-loading times. Because the original ChronoZoom page contained a significant amount of script code, the transformed page is less than half of the original size. On the other hand, the BlogEngine.NET page is slightly larger because of its small amount of script code, which was replaced by longer links to script files. The page-loading times mirror the page sizes, also indicating that server-side processing incurred no discernible performance impact.

6.5 Discussion

The results of our rewriting shed light on the nature of inline JavaScript in web applications. Of the four applications that have dynamic JavaScript, 12.2% to 77.8% of the total inline JavaScript in the application is dynamic. This is important, because one of BEEP's XSS prevention policies is a whitelist containing the SHA1 hash of allowed JavaScript [20]. Unfortunately, in the modern web JavaScript is not static and frequently includes dynamic elements, necessitating new approaches that can handle dynamic JavaScript.

The other security policy presented in BEEP is DOM sandboxing. This approach requires the developer to manually annotate the sinks so that they can be neutralized. Blueprint [28] works similarly, requiring the developer to annotate the outputs of untrusted data. Both approaches require the developer to manually annotate the sinks in the application in order to specify the trusted JavaScript. To understand the developer effort required to manually annotate the sinks in the application, we counted the sinks (i.e., `TextWriter.Write` call sites) inside the 29 Web Forms of BlogSA.NET and there were 407. In order to implement either BEEP or Blueprint a developer must manually analyze all sinks in the application and annotate any that could create untrusted output.

Unlike BEEP and Blueprint, deDacota is completely automatic and does not require any developer annotations. deDacota cannot prevent XSS vulnerabilities in dynamic inline JavaScript completely. If a developer wishes to prevent all XSS vulnerabilities after applying deDacota, they would only need to examine the sinks that occur *within* the unsafe dynamic inline JavaScript. In BlogSA.NET, there are three sinks within the single unsafe dynamic JavaScript. One could further reduce the number of sinks by using taint analysis to check if untrusted input can reach a sink in the dynamic JavaScript.

7. LIMITATIONS

The goal of deDacota is to automatically separate the JavaScript code from the HTML data in the web pages of a web application using static analysis. We have shown that deDacota is effective with real-world web applications. In this section, we discuss its limitations in general.

The programming language of .NET has the following dynamic language features: dynamic assembly loading, dynamic compilation, dynamic run-time method calling (via reflection), and threading. The use of these features may compromise the soundness of any static analysis including ours in deDacota. However, these language features are rarely used in ASP.NET web applications in practice. For instance, those applications we tested did not use any of these features. Furthermore, deDacota is affected only if the use of these features determines the HTML output of an application.

On one hand, we handle loops conservatively by approximating that a loop can produce anything. On the other hand, we treat the output of a loop as a * in the approximation graph and assume it does not affect the structure of the approximation graph in a way that impacts our analysis. For instance, we assume the output of a loop does not contain the opening or closing script tag. Our analysis will be incorrect if this assumption is violated. While we found that this assumption holds for all the web applications we tested, it is possible that this assumption will not hold for other programs, thus requiring a different approach to handling loops.

We do not offer any formal proof of the correctness of deDacota. While we believe that our approach is correct in absence of the dynamic language features, we leave a formal proof of this to future work.

DEDACOTA currently supports the analysis of string concatenations. The support for more complex string operations such as regular expressions is left for future work. A potential approach is to leverage an automata-based string analysis engine [50].

Our approach to sanitizing dynamic JavaScript code may not preserve an application's semantics when the dynamic content being sanitized as a string is meant to be used in multiple JavaScript contexts.

When deploying DEDACOTA in practice, we recommend two practices to mitigate its limitations. First, all tests for the original web application should be performed on the rewritten binary to detect any disruptions to the application's semantics. Second, CSP's "Report Only" mode should be used during the testing and initial deployment. Under this mode, the browser will report violations back to the web server when unspecified JavaScript code is loaded. This helps detect inline JavaScript code that is missed by DEDACOTA.

Finally, our prototype does not handle JavaScript code in HTML attributes. We do not believe that there is any fundamental limitation that makes discovering JavaScript attributes more difficult than inline JavaScript. The only minor difficulty here is in the rewriting. In order to separate a JavaScript attribute into an external JavaScript, one must be able to uniquely identify the DOM element that the JavaScript attribute affects. To do this, it would require generating a unique identifier for the HTML element associated with the JavaScript attribute.

8. RELATED WORK

A broad variety of approaches have been proposed to address different types of XSS, though no standard taxonomy exists to classify these attacks and defenses. In general, XSS defenses employ schemes for input sanitization or restrictions on script generation and execution. Differences among various techniques involve client- or server-side implementation and static or dynamic operation. We group and review XSS defenses in this context.

8.1 Server-Side Methods

While CSP itself is enforced by browsers [42], our approach for leveraging CSP is a static, server-side XSS defense. There has been much previous research in server-side XSS defenses [3, 4, 13, 14, 22, 28, 34, 35, 38, 40, 43]. Server-based techniques aim for dynamically generated pages free of XSS vulnerabilities. This may involve validation or injection of appropriate sanitizers for user input, analysis of scripts to find XSS vulnerabilities, or automatic generation of XSS-free scripts.

Server-side sanitizer defenses either check existing sanitization for correctness or generate input encodings automatically to match usage context. For example, Saner [3] uses static analysis to track unsafe inputs from entry to usage, followed by dynamic analysis to test input cases for proper sanitization along these paths. SCRIPTGARD [40] is a complementary approach that assumes a set of "correct" sanitizers and inserts them to match the browser's parsing context. BEK [18] focuses on creating sanitization functions automatically analyzable for preciseness and correctness. Sanitization remains the main industry-standard defense against XSS and related vulnerabilities.

A number of server-side defenses restrict scripts included in server-generated pages. For example, XSS-GUARD [4] determines valid scripts dynamically and disallows unexpected scripts. The authors report performance overheads of up to 46% because of the dynamic evaluation of HTML and JavaScript. Templating approaches [13,36,38] generate correct-by-construction scripts that incorporate correct sanitization based on context. In addition, schemes based on code isolation [1,2,26] mitigate XSS by limiting DOM access for particular scripts, depending on their context.

Certain XSS defenses [21, 22, 27, 29, 34, 35, 39, 44, 49] use data-flow analysis or taint tracking to identify unsanitized user input included in a generated web page. These approaches typically rely on sanitization, encoding, and other means of separating unsafe inputs from the script code. Some schemes prevent XSS bugs dynamically, while others focus on static detection and elimination.

Other approaches [14,28,33] combine server-side processing with various client-side components, such as confinement of untrusted inputs and markup randomization. Such schemes may parse documents on the server and prevent any modifications of the resulting parse trees on the client. In addition, randomization of XHTML tags can render foreign script code meaningless, defeating many code-injection attacks.

8.2 Client-Side Methods

Client-side XSS defenses [20,23,30,42,45,47] mitigate XSS while receiving or rendering untrusted web content. Some of these schemes rely on browser modifications or plug-ins, often reducing their practical applicability. Others use custom JavaScript libraries or additional client-side monitoring software. CSP itself [42] is a browser-based approach, but its incorporation into WWW standards should facilitate wide acceptance and support by all popular browsers.

Some client-side XSS defenses focus on detecting and preventing leakage of sensitive data. For example, Noxes [23] operates as a personal-firewall plug-in that extracts all static links from incoming web pages, prompting the user about disclosure of information via dynamically generated links. Vogt et al. [45] also aim to address this problem, but use taint-tracking analysis within a browser to check for sensitive data released via XSS attacks. In contrast, DEDACOTA simply prevents any XSS exploits that could enable such leakage.

Client-side HTML security policies mitigate XSS via content restrictions, such as disallowing unsafe features or executing only "known good" scripts. Using a browser's HTML parser, BEEP [20] constructs whitelists of scripts, much like XSS-GUARD's server-side approach [4]. BEEP assumes no dynamic scripts whose hashes cannot be pre-computed, limiting its practicality with modern web applications; moreover, it has been shown that even whitelisted scripts may be vulnerable to attacks [2]. Another custom content security policy is BLUEPRINT's page descriptions, which are interpreted and rendered safely by a custom JavaScript library [28]. Script policies enforced at runtime [15, 30] are also useful for mitigating XSS exploits.

In general, standardized HTML security policies [42, 47] offer promise as a means of escaping the recent proliferation of complex, often ad hoc XSS defenses. CSP simplifies the problem by enforcing fairly strong restrictions, such as disabling `eval()` and other dangerous APIs, prohibiting inline JavaScript, and allowing only local script resources to be loaded. While new web applications can be designed with CSP in mind, legacy code may require significant rewriting. DEDACOTA works on both old and new applications, facilitating adoption of CSP by developers, primarily by automating the separation process.

9. CONCLUSION

Cross-site scripting vulnerabilities are pervasive in web applications. Malicious users frequently exploit these vulnerabilities to infect users with drive-by downloads or to steal personal information.

While there is currently no silver bullet to preventing every possible XSS attack vector, we believe that adhering to the fundamental security principle of code and data separation is a promising approach to combating XSS vulnerabilities. DEDACOTA is a novel approach that gets us closer to this goal, by using static analysis to automatically separate the code and data of a web application. While not a final solution, DEDACOTA and other tools that automate making web applications secure by construction are the next step in the fight against XSS and other kinds of vulnerabilities.

10. ACKNOWLEDGMENTS

The authors extend their thanks to David Molnar, Alex Moshchuk, Helen Wang, and Chris Hawblitzel for their helpful discussions, Herman Venter for all his help and support with CCI, and David Brumley for his insightful suggestions which helped to focus the paper. This work was supported by the Office of Naval Research (ONR) under Grant N000140911042, the Army Research Office (ARO) under Grant W911NF0910553, the National Science Foundation (NSF) under Grants CNS-0845559 and CNS-0905537, and Secure Business Austria.

11. REFERENCES

[1] AKHAWE, D., SAXENA, P., AND SONG, D. Privilege Separation in HTML5 Applications. In *Proceedings of the USENIX Security Symposium (USENIX)* (2012).

[2] ATHANASOPOULOS, E., PAPPAS, V., AND MARKATOS, E. P. Code-Injection Attacks in Browsers Supporting Policies. In *Proceedings of the Workshop on Web 2.0 Security and Privacy (W2SP)* (2009).

[3] BALZAROTTI, D., COVA, M., FELMETSGER, V., JOVANOVIC, N., KIRDA, E., KRUEGEL, C., AND VIGNA, G. Saner: Composing Static and Dynamic Analysis to Validate Sanitization in Web Applications. In *Proceedings of the IEEE Symposium on Security and Privacy* (Oakland, CA, 2008).

[4] BISHT, P., AND VENKATAKRISHNAN, V. XSS-GUARD: Precise Dynamic Prevention of Cross-Site Scripting Attacks. In *Proceedings of the Conference on Detection of Intrusions and Malware and Vulnerability Assessment (DIMVA)* (Paris, France, 2008).

[5] blogengine.net - an innovative open source blogging platform. `http://www.dotnetblogengine.net`, 2013.

[6] BlogSA.NET. `http://www.blogsa.net/`, 2013.

[7] BugTracker.NET - Free Bug Tracking. `http://ifdefined.com/bugtrackernet.html`, 2013.

[8] Top in Frameworks - Week beginning Jun 24th 2013. `http://trends.builtwith.com/framework`, 2013.

[9] Chronozoom - A Brief History of the World. `http://chronozoom.cloudapp.net/firstgeneration.aspx`, 2013.

[10] CUI, W., PEINADO, M., XU, Z., AND CHAN, E. Tracking Rootkit Footprints with a Practical Memory Analysis System. In *Proceedings of the USENIX Security Symposium (USENIX)* (Bellevue, WA, 2012).

[11] CVE DETAILS. Vulnerabilities by Type. `http://www.cvedetails.com/vulnerabilities-by-types.php`, 2013.

[12] Django. `http://djangoproject.com`, 2013.

[13] GOOGLE. Google AutoEscape for CTemplate. `http://code.google.com/p/ctemplate/`.

[14] GUNDY, M. V., AND CHEN, H. Noncespaces: Using Randomization to Enforce Information Flow Tracking and Thwart Cross-Site Scripting Attacks. In *Network and Distributed System Security Symposium (NDSS)* (2009).

[15] HALLARAKER, O., AND VIGNA, G. Detecting Malicious JavaScript Code in Mozilla. In *Proceedings of the IEEE International Conference on Engineering of Complex Computer Systems (ICECCS)* (Shanghai, China, 2005).

[16] HEIDERICH, M., NIEMIETZ, M., SCHUSTER, F., HOLZ, T., AND SCHWENK, J. Scriptless Attacks: Stealing the Pie Without Touching the Sill. In *Proceedings of the ACM Conference on Computer and Communications Security (CCS)* (2012).

[17] HOFF, J. WebGoat.NET. `https://github.com/jerryhoff/WebGoat.NET`, 2013.

[18] HOOIMEIJER, P., LIVSHITS, B., MOLNAR, D., SAXENA, P., AND VEANES, M. Fast and Precise Sanitizer Analysis with BEK. In *Proceedings of the USENIX Security Symposium (USENIX)* (2011).

[19] HOWARD, M., AND LEBLANC, D. *Writing Secure Code*, second ed. Microsoft Press, 2003.

[20] JIM, T., SWAMY, N., AND HICKS, M. Defeating Script Injection Attacks with Browser-Enforced Embedded Policies. In *Proceedings of the International World Wide Web Conference (WWW)* (2007).

[21] JOHNS, M., AND BEYERLEIN, C. SMask: Preventing Injection Attacks in Web Applications by Approximating Automatic Data/Code Separation. In *Proceedings of the ACM Symposium on Applied Computing (SAC)* (2007).

[22] JOVANOVIC, N., KRUEGEL, C., AND KIRDA, E. Precise Alias Analysis for Static Detection of Web Application Vulnerabilities. In *Proceedings of the Workshop on Programming Languages and Analysis for Security (PLAS)* (2006).

[23] KIRDA, E., KRUEGEL, C., VIGNA, G., AND JOVANOVIC, N. Noxes: A Client-Side Solution for Mitigating Cross-Site Scripting Attacks. In *Proceedings of the ACM Symposium on Applied Computing (SAC)* (2006).

[24] KLEIN, A. DOM Based Cross Site Scripting or XSS of the Third Kind. `http://www.webappsec.org/projects/articles/071105.shtml`, 2005.

[25] LIVSHITS, B., AND CHONG, S. Towards Fully Automatic Placement of Security Sanitizers and Declassifiers. In *Proceedings of the Symposium on Principles of Programming Languages (POPL)* (2013).

[26] LIVSHITS, B., AND ERLINGSSON, U. Using Web Application Construction Frameworks to Protect Against Code Injection Attacks. In *Proceedings of the Workshop on Programming Languages and Analysis for Security (PLAS)* (2007).

[27] LIVSHITS, V. B., AND LAM, M. S. Finding Security Vulnerabilities in Java Applications with Static Analysis. In *Proceedings of the USENIX Security Symposium (USENIX)* (2005).

[28] LOUW, M. T., AND VENKATAKRISHNAN, V. BLUEPRINT: Robust Prevention of Cross-site Scripting Attacks for Existing Browsers. In *Proceedings of the IEEE Symposium on Security and Privacy* (2009).

[29] MARTIN, M., AND LAM, M. S. Automatic Generation of XSS and SQL Injection Attacks with Goal-Directed Model Checking. In *Proceedings of the USENIX Security Symposium (USENIX)* (2008).

[30] MEYEROVICH, L., AND LIVSHITS, B. ConScript: Specifying and Enforcing Fine-Grained Security Policies for JavaScript in the Browser. In *Proceedings of the IEEE Symposium on Security and Privacy* (2010).

[31] MICROSOFT. ASP.NET. `http://www.asp.net/`.

[32] MICROSOFT RESEARCH. Common Compiler Infrastructure. `http://research.microsoft.com/en-us/projects/cci/`, 2013.

[33] NADJI, Y., SAXENA, P., AND SONG, D. Document Structure Integrity: A Robust Basis for Cross-Site Scripting Defense. In *Proceeding of the Network and Distributed System Security Symposium (NDSS)* (2008).

[34] NGUYEN-TUONG, A., GUARNIERI, S., GREENE, D., AND EVANS, D. Automatically Hardening Web Applications Using Precise Tainting. In *Proceedings of the IFIP International Information Security Conference* (2005).

[35] PIETRASZEK, T., AND BERGHE, C. V. Defending against Injection Attacks through Context-Sensitive String Evaluations. In *Proceedings of the Symposium on Recent Advances in Intrusion Detection (RAID)* (2005).

[36] ROBERTSON, W., AND VIGNA, G. Static Enforcement of Web Application Integrity Through Strong Typing. In *Proceedings of the USENIX Security Symposium (USENIX)* (Montreal, Quebec CA, 2009).

[37] Ruby on Rails. `http://rubyonrails.org/`, 2013.

[38] SAMUEL, M., SAXENA, P., AND SONG, D. Context-Sensitive Auto-Sanitization in Web Templating Languages Using Type Qualifiers. In *Proceedings of the ACM Conference on Computer and Communications Security (CCS)* (2011).

[39] SAXENA, P., AKHAWE, D., HANNA, S., MAO, F., MCCAMANT, S., AND SONG, D. A Symbolic Execution Framework for JavaScript. In *Proceedings of the IEEE Symposium on Security and Privacy* (2010).

[40] SAXENA, P., MOLNAR, D., AND LIVSHITS, B. SCRIPTGARD: Automatic Context-Sensitive Sanitization for Large-Scale Legacy Web Applications. In *Proceedings of the ACM Conference on Computer and Communications Security (CCS)* (2011).

[41] ScrewTurn Wiki. `http://www.screwturn.eu/`, 2013.

[42] STAMM, S., STERNE, B., AND MARKHAM, G. Reining in the Web with Content Security Policy. In *Proceedings of the International World Wide Web Conference (WWW)* (2010).

[43] SU, Z., AND WASSERMANN, G. The Essence of Command Injection Attacks in Web Applications. In *Proceedings of the Symposium on Principles of Programming Languages (POPL)* (2006).

[44] TRIPP, O., PISTOIA, M., FINK, S. J., SRIDHARAN, M., AND WEISMAN, O. TAJ: Effective Taint Analysis of Web Applications. In *Proceedings of the ACM SIGPLAN Conference on Programming Language Design and Implementation (PLDI)* (2009).

[45] VOGT, P., NENTWICH, F., JOVANOVIC, N., KIRDA, E., KRUEGEL, C., AND VIGNA, G. Cross-Site Scripting Prevention with Dynamic Data Tainting and Static Analysis. In *Proceeding of the Network and Distributed System Security Symposium (NDSS)* (2007).

[46] WASSERMANN, G., AND SU, Z. Sound and Precise Analysis of Web Applications for Injection Vulnerabilities. In *Proceedings of the ACM SIGPLAN Conference on Programming Language Design and Implementation (PLDI)* (2007).

[47] WEINBERGER, J., BARTH, A., AND SONG, D. Towards Client-side HTML Security Policies. In *Proceedings of the USENIX Workshop on Hot Topics in Security* (2011).

[48] WEINBERGER, J., SAXENA, P., AKHAWE, D., FINIFTER, M., SHIN, R., AND SONG, D. A Systematic Analysis of XSS Sanitization in Web Application Frameworks. In *Proceedings of the European Symposium on Research in Computer Security (ESORICS)* (Leuven, Belgium, 2011).

[49] XIE, Y., AND AIKEN, A. Static Detection of Security Vulnerabilities in Scripting Languages. In *Proceedings of the USENIX Security Symposium (USENIX)* (2006).

[50] YU, F., ALKHALAF, M., AND BULTAN, T. STRANGER: An Automata-based String Analysis Tool for PHP. In *Proceedings of the International Conference on Tools and Algorithms for the Construction and Analysis of Systems (TACAS)* (2010).

Certified Computer-Aided Cryptography: Efficient Provably Secure Machine Code from High-Level Implementations

José Bacelar Almeida
HasLab – INESC TEC and
Universidade do Minho
Braga, Portugal

Manuel Barbosa
HasLab – INESC TEC and
Universidade do Minho
Braga, Portugal

Gilles Barthe
IMDEA Software Institute
Madrid, Spain

François Dupressoir
IMDEA Software Institute
Madrid, Spain

ABSTRACT

We present a computer-aided framework for proving concrete security bounds for cryptographic machine code implementations. The front-end of the framework is an interactive verification tool that extends the EasyCrypt framework to reason about relational properties of C-like programs extended with idealised probabilistic operations in the style of code-based security proofs. The framework also incorporates an extension of the CompCert certified compiler to support trusted libraries providing complex arithmetic calculations or instantiating idealized components such as sampling operations. This certified compiler allows us to carry to executable code the security guarantees established at the high-level, and is also instrumented to detect when compilation may interfere with side-channel countermeasures deployed in source code.

We demonstrate the applicability of the framework by applying it to the RSA-OAEP encryption scheme, as standardized in PKCS#1 v2.1. The outcome is a rigorous analysis of the advantage of an adversary to break the security of assembly implementations of the algorithms specified by the standard. The example also provides two contributions of independent interest: it bridges the gap between computer-assisted security proofs and real-world cryptographic implementations as described by standards such as PKCS,and demonstrates the use of the CompCert certified compiler in the context of cryptographic software development.

Categories and Subject Descriptors

D.2.4 [**Software Engineering**]: Software/Program verification—*formal methods*; E.3 [**Data**]: Data Encryption—*public key cryptosystems, standards, PKCS#1*

Keywords

formal proof; PKCS#1; side-channels; certified compilation

CCS'13, November 4–8, 2013, Berlin, Germany.

ACM 978-1-4503-2477-9/13/11 ...$15.00.
http://dx.doi.org/10.1145/2508859.2516652.

1. INTRODUCTION

The security of computer and communication infrastructures critically relies on software implementations of cryptographic standards. Practitioners implementing such standards face significant challenges. First, they must resolve all cases of underspecification and address operational considerations that are often ignored by standards. Then, they must ensure that the generated code is, not only correct and efficient, but also respects a programming discipline that minimizes the possibility of side-channel attacks. Such disciplines, or countermeasures, may be enforced directly over assembly code, or they may be specified and validated over source code in a language such as C [11]; in this latter case the developer will either trust the compiler to preserve the countermeasures in generated code, or further validation is performed. Unfortunately, there is limited tool support to help practitioners address these issues (see § 6), which makes the development process error-prone. As a consequence of subtle errors, software implementations may provide little or no security [15].

Another problematic technological gap for practitioners lies between the security claimed by cryptographic standards and the concrete security bounds derived using provable security [22]. Indeed, provable security typically relies on an idealized model of computation and elides security-relevant aspects of runtime environments (e.g. memory management) and implementation details (e.g. error management). Although this abstraction gap was identified very early in the development of provable security, principled approaches narrowing this gap are only starting to emerge. Prominent examples include real-world provable cryptography [17, 30], which analyzes realistic descriptions of cryptographic algorithms. However, realism comes at a significant cost: security analyses in these extended models are vastly more complex, and therefore more error-prone and more difficult to check. Moreover, the additional realism achieved by real-world cryptography does not primarily address the aforementioned issues faced by implementers.

In short, there are two significant gaps, with cumulative effects on the real-world security of cryptographic software implementations. This paper addresses the challenge of narrowing these gaps.

Technical overview. To achieve this goal, we build on two recent and independent developments: computer-aided cryptography, which provides tool support for provable security, and verified compilation, which delivers machine-checkable evidence of semantic preservation between source and target programs.

To address the gap between cryptographic proofs and standards, we extend the EasyCrypt framework [10] to reason about C-like programs extended with idealised probabilistic operations in an enhanced security model in which the adversary is given access to execution traces meant to capture side-channel leakage. The approach is general, but we focus on the well-known Program Counter Model [28]. The advantage of this approach is twofold. Firstly, one can make explicit in the security proof various aspects of cryptographic scheme specifications that address side-channel attacks. For example, we are able to check that a specification of a decryption algorithm does not reveal information about the secret key by returning a failure value at an early point in its execution. Secondly, this computational model serves as a reference for the deployment of countermeasures against side-channel attacks throughout the compilation process. For example, even though modular exponentiation is treated as a native operation in our high-level computational model, we can make it explicit in its formalization that, in order to ensure security in the Program Counter Model, the trace produced by its execution must be independent of its input values.

To address the second issue, of relating cryptographic standards and their low-level implementations, we leverage the annotation mechanism and semantic correctness proof of the CompCert compiler [25] to prove that security of the C implementation implies security of the assembly implementation and, particularly, that countermeasures against side-channel attacks are correctly deployed *in the generated assembly code*. In addition, we extend CompCert with the notion of a trusted library providing multi-precision arithmetic functionality and instantiations of idealised operations. This allows practitioners to develop and compile their implementations according to common practices, by providing a clean interface that specifies the guarantees required from an external library in order to obtain assembly code that is correct and secure.

The EasyCrypt libraries, formal proofs and the corresponding C code are publicly available. Details can be found in the full version of this paper.[1]

Contributions. We introduce a software development framework that allows practitioners to obtain rigorous mathematical guarantees for low-level (PowerPC, ARM and x86) implementations of cryptographic software. More precisely, our framework enables practitioners to:

1. formally verify that a C implementation of a cryptographic algorithm is secure in a security model that captures both theoretical security and side-channel leakage.
2. automatically generate an optimised assembly implementation that is proven to retain the security properties of the C implementation, namely by correctly deploying side-channel countermeasures suitable for a rigorously defined leakage model.

We illustrate the effectiveness of our framework by proving security and generating a secure assembly implementation of the RSA-OAEP encryption scheme, as standardized in PKCS#1 v2.1. The main challenges in the security proof were the following:

- Formalizing and verifying a security proof taking into account the exact padding scheme adopted in the standard.
- Carrying out this proof in a computational model that incorporates Program Counter Model traces, taking into account the implementations of *all* the algorithms specified in the standard, including encoding and decoding routines, as well as the recommended and mandated side-channel countermeasures.

The process of generating an assembly implementation of RSA-OAEP that inherits the security guarantees established at the C level with EasyCrypt is a fully automatic process using our extended version of CompCert. We thus believe that our extensions are of independent interest to cryptographic software developers deploying side-channel countermeasures at the C level. Intuitively, they permit validating that assembly code leaks *no more information* than the source code via its control flow. This is a non-functional property that is not known to be offered by CompCert in general (nor, to the best of our knowledge, by any other C compiler), and our extension provides this guarantee in the style of translation validation [25]. For example, we have used this feature to check the assembly code generated by compiling various components in the NaCl cryptographic library, which includes relevant side-channel countermeasures at C-level [11].

2. SYNTAX AND SECURITY OF PKE IMPLEMENTATIONS

Although the techniques we discuss in this paper are generally applicable to implementations of arbitrary cryptographic primitives, we will deal only with public-key encryption (PKE) schemes.

We will be concentrating on real-world implementations of this primitive. This means that, throughout the paper, a PKE *scheme* will provide descriptions of the encryption and decryption algorithms as implementations in either C or assembly code. Our notion of a PKE implementation does not include the key generation algorithm, which will be seen as an abstract algorithm that produces key pairs, and that is modelled as a family of (efficiently samplable) distributions $\mathcal{G}_\lambda$, indexed by the security parameter. We adopt this simplification for ease of presentation and note that, from a theoretical point of view, this is without loss of generality. From a practical point of view, this is also not a major limitation, as in many applications key generation is performed in a trusted environment, using implementations developed independently of the encryption and decryption algorithms. Nevertheless, we also emphasise that all our techniques and results can be easily extended to cover the implementation of the key generation algorithm.

Definition 1. (*PKE syntax*) A public-key encryption scheme implementation Π is a tuple $(\mathsf{lang}, \mathsf{Enc}, \mathsf{Dec}, \ell_{(\cdot)})$ where:

- $\mathsf{lang} \in \{\mathsf{C}, \mathsf{asm}\}$ indicates the implementation language.
- For each value of λ, $\mathsf{Enc}_\lambda^{\mathsf{Rand},\mathsf{RO}}(\mathsf{m}, \mathsf{pk})$ implements a deterministic polynomial-time encryption algorithm. On

[1] Available at http://eprint.iacr.org/2013/316.

input a message m and a public key pk, this algorithm outputs a return code rc and a ciphertext c, possibly after making a series of calls to external functions (oracles) Rand and RO.

- For each value of λ, $\mathsf{Dec}_\lambda^{\mathsf{RO}}(\mathsf{c}, \mathsf{sk})$ implements a deterministic polynomial-time decryption algorithm. On input a ciphertext c and a secret key sk, this algorithm outputs a return code rc and a message m, possibly after making series of calls to external function (oracle) RO.
- $\ell_{\mathsf{pk}}(\cdot)$ and $\ell_{\mathsf{sk}}(\cdot)$ are polynomials denoting the length of the octet strings representing public keys and secret keys, respectively.
- $\ell_{\mathsf{m}}(\cdot)$ and $\ell_{\mathsf{c}}(\cdot)$ are polynomials denoting the (maximum) length of the octet strings representing messages and ciphertexts *output* by the decryption and encryption algorithms, respectively.[2]

Here, $\mathsf{Rand}(\ell)$ returns a random octet string of length ℓ, and $\mathsf{RO}(i, \ell_i, \ell_o)$ gives access to a family of random functions indexed by (ℓ_i, ℓ_o), where each function takes an octet string i of length ℓ_i and returns an octet string of length ℓ_o. The return codes rc are chosen from a finite set, and they indicate the success (T) of the operation or its justified failure ($\mathsf{F}_{(\cdot)}$).

We treat implementations as families of algorithms indexed by the security parameter, which should be interpreted for practical purposes as admitting that the security parameter must be known at compile-time. We deviate slightly from the standard approach of adopting bit-strings as the representation of inputs and outputs to cryptographic algorithms, and adopt octet strings instead. This is without loss of generality. We also restrict our attention to PKEs for which the (maximum) lengths of the inhabitants of the message, randomness and ciphertext spaces are fixed in the description of the scheme (as polynomials in λ) for each value of the security parameter. This is *not* without loss of generality, but is a necessary constraint when dealing with implementations operating in computational platforms with limited memory, and a natural one to make when considering cryptographic standards such as RSA-OAEP.

Correctness. The correctness of a PKE scheme implementation requires that the decryption operation inverts the encryption procedure. We present this definition using a code-based approach, and again emphasise that a scheme Π may be given as a C implementation or as an assembly implementation. The notion of correctness is the same in either case.

Definition 2. (*PKE correctness*) Let game $\mathsf{Corr}_{\Pi,\mathcal{A}}$ be as shown in Figure 1. The correctness of a PKE scheme Π relative to $\mathcal{G}$ requires that, for all adversaries $\mathcal{A}$ and for all λ, we have that

$$\Pr[\,\mathsf{Corr}_{\Pi,\mathcal{G},\mathcal{A}}(1^\lambda) \Rightarrow \mathsf{T}\,] = 1\,.$$

We note that security games are presented here at a level of abstraction that omits certain details of the implementations, e.g., how parameter passing is handled. Such details are made explicit in the formalization of the model, as described in the next section.

[2]We do not restrict the size of the message and ciphertext *inputs* to these algorithms, and require implementations to check the validity of their lengths.

Game $\mathsf{Corr}_{\Pi,\mathcal{G},\mathcal{A}}(1^\lambda)$:

$(\mathsf{pk}, \mathsf{sk}) \leftarrow_\$ \mathcal{G}_\lambda$
$\mathsf{m} \leftarrow_\$ \mathcal{A}(\mathsf{pk}, \mathsf{sk})$
If $|\mathsf{m}| > \ell_{\mathsf{m}}(\lambda)$ Return T
$(\mathsf{rc}, \mathsf{c}) \leftarrow_\$ \mathsf{Enc}_\lambda^{\mathsf{Rand},\mathsf{RO}}(\mathsf{m}, \mathsf{pk})$
$(\mathsf{rc}', \mathsf{m}') \leftarrow \mathsf{Dec}_\lambda^{\mathsf{RO}}(\mathsf{c}, \mathsf{sk})$
Return $\mathsf{rc} = \mathsf{T} \wedge \mathsf{rc}' = \mathsf{T} \wedge \mathsf{m}' = \mathsf{m}$

Figure 1: Game defining the correctness of a PKE.

Security. For security, we consider the standard notion of indistinguishability under adaptive chosen-ciphertext attacks (IND-CCA), adapted to fit in our syntactic conventions and with an extension to capture side channel leakage.

Definition 3. (IND-CCA *security of PKE implementations*) Let game $\mathsf{IND\text{-}CCA}_{\Pi,\mathcal{G},\mathcal{A}}$ be as defined in Figure 2. The IND-CCA security of a PKE scheme Π relative to $\mathcal{G}$ requires that, for all adversaries $\mathcal{A}$, the following advantage definition is negligible:

$$\mathsf{Adv}^{\mathsf{ind\text{-}cca}}_{\Pi,\mathcal{G},\mathcal{A}}(\lambda) := 2 \cdot \Pr\left[\mathsf{IND\text{-}CCA}_{\Pi,\mathcal{G},\mathcal{A}}(\lambda) \Rightarrow \mathsf{T}\right] - 1\,.$$

Game $\mathsf{IND\text{-}CCA}_{\Pi,\mathcal{G},\mathcal{A}}(1^\lambda)$:

$b \leftarrow_\$ \{0,1\}$
$(\mathsf{pk}, \mathsf{sk}) \leftarrow_\$ \mathcal{G}_\lambda$
$(\mathsf{m}_0, \mathsf{m}_1, \mathsf{st}) \leftarrow_\$ \mathcal{A}_1^{\mathsf{Decrypt},\mathsf{RO}}(\mathsf{pk})$
$(\mathsf{rc}, \mathsf{c}^*) \leftarrow_\$ \mathsf{Enc}_\lambda^{\mathsf{Rand},\mathsf{RO}}(\mathsf{m}_b, \mathsf{pk}) \rightsquigarrow t$
$b' \leftarrow_\$ \mathcal{A}_2^{\mathsf{Decrypt},\mathsf{RO}}(\mathsf{c}^*, t, \mathsf{st})$
Return $(|\mathsf{m}_0| = |\mathsf{m}_1| \wedge b' = b)$

oracle $\mathsf{Decrypt}(\mathsf{c})$:

$(\mathsf{rc}, \mathsf{m}) \leftarrow \mathsf{Dec}_\lambda^{\mathsf{RO}}(\mathsf{c}, \mathsf{sk}) \rightsquigarrow t$
Return $(\mathsf{rc}, \mathsf{m}, t)$

Figure 2: Game defining the IND-CCA security of a PKE scheme. An adversary $\mathcal{A}$ is legitimate if $\mathcal{A}_2$ does not call Decrypt on c^*.

The $\rightsquigarrow t$ notation in Figure 2 denotes information that is leaked to the adversary by the execution environment, in addition to the outputs explicitly produced by the PKE algorithms.[3] We recover the standard definition of security for PKEs when this leakage is the empty string ϵ for all algorithms.

Leakage models. We will model leakage as a trace of constant identifiers that reveal some information about the control flow of the executed algorithm. This approach allows us to capture some leakage models that are relevant for practical applications, and can be extended to deal with arbitrary types of leakage by defining different types of observable events in the semantics of the implementation languages, and controlling if and how this information is revealed to the adversary.

For concreteness, we will focus on two leakage models for C and assembly implementations. The leakage model that we adopt at the C level is chosen for its simplicity, and can be seen as an adaptation of the Program Counter Model [28]

[3]Consistently with our discussion above, we consider that only Enc and Dec are executed in environments that are observable by the adversary.

(PC) to C programs. The leakage model that we adopt at the assembly level is the standard PC model. Informally, these models are defined as follows:

- **C leakage.** We associate to each branching point in the C program two observable events with identifiers Event_True and Event_False. One such event is added to the (initially empty) trace whenever a branch is taken, consistently with the Boolean value of the evaluated branching condition.
- **Assembly leakage.** Each instruction in the assembly program is associated with a unique constant identifier, which is added to the (initially empty) trace whenever this instruction is executed.

Referring to Figure 2, we will consider adversaries attacking C implementations and assembly implementations, and receiving the leakage defined above as extra information. Later in the paper we will see formalizations of both types of leakage.

RSA-OAEP as described in PKCS#1. We now illustrate the level of abstraction at which cryptographic algorithms are described in standards. This will both justify our approach of taking C as a high-level language for implementing cryptographic algorithms, and also to facilitate the understanding of its EasyCrypt formalization in the next section. Figure 3 shows the PKCS#1 v2.1 standard's description of the encoding function that takes a variable-length message m, pads it to a fixed-length data blob DB, and produces the final encoded message EM. Functions $\mathsf{OS2IP}_{\mathsf{PKCS}}$, $\mathsf{I2OSP}_{\mathsf{PKCS}}$ and $\mathsf{RSAEP}_{\mathsf{PKCS}}$ are specified in the standard; random and MGF instantiate the Rand, and RO oracles, respectively.

The scheme, as standardized, is parameterized by two lengths (which can be seen as the security parameter): k is the length of the canonical octet string representation of the RSA modulus; and $hLen$ is the length of the output of the hash function used to concretely implement the MGF, and to compute label hashes.

Given these parameters, some derived static lengths can be introduced: $dbLen = k - hLen - 1$ is the length of the padded message, or *data blob*; and $maxMLen = dbLen - hLen - 1$ is the maximum length of message that can be encrypted.

A C-like language. In this paper we consider only C programs that follow a strong programming discipline and respect a strict notion of safety. The programming discipline forbids expressions with side-effects, pointer arithmetic, and only allows the programmer to refer to arrays using the address of their first element (and carrying an explicit offset value where necessary). Our notion of safety excludes the standard out-of-bound memory accesses and arithmetic error conditions, but also behaviours that would fall in the underspecified parts of the C standard. For simplicity, our notion of safety also imposes that C implementations terminate for all possible input values.

We allow static allocation of new arrays, and follow standard practice to pass output parameters by reference to let C functions return multiple values, or arrays. In addition, we consider that the language is equipped with a non-primitive type for arbitrary precision unsigned integers that are, similarly to arrays, passed by reference. We equip this type with the usual operations, including modular arithmetic.

fun $\mathsf{OAEP\_Encode}_{\mathsf{PKCS}}(m : \mathsf{octet}[])$:

$PS = \mathsf{0x00}^{(k-|m|-2*hLen-2)}$;
$DB = dLHash \| PS \| \mathsf{0x01} \| m$;
$seed = \mathsf{random}(hLen)$;
$dbMask = \mathsf{MGF}(seed, dbLen)$;
$maskedDB = DB \oplus dbMask$;
$seedMask = \mathsf{MGF}(maskedDB, hLen)$;
$maskedSeed = seed \oplus seedMask$;
$EM = \mathsf{0x00} \| maskedSeed \| maskedDB$;
return EM;

fun $\mathsf{OAEP\_Encrypt}_{\mathsf{PKCS}}(m : \mathsf{octet}[], pk : \mathsf{pkey})$:

if $(maxMLen < mL)$
  $rc = RC\_MessageTooLong$;
else {
  $rc = \mathsf{OAEP\_Encode}_{\mathsf{PKCS}}(m)$;
  $p = \mathsf{OS2IP}_{\mathsf{PKCS}}(EM)$;
  $(rc, c) = \mathsf{RSAEP}_{\mathsf{PKCS}}(pk, p)$;
  $(rc, res) = \mathsf{I2OSP}_{\mathsf{PKCS}}(c, k)$;
  $rc = RC\_Success$; }
return (rc, res);

Figure 3: Specification for PKCS#1 encryption

We use the const type modifier to prevent functions from overwriting parameters passed by reference (arrays, big integers and pointers to primitive types) that are used purely for input. Purely for simplicity, we forbid the use of short-circuiting boolean operators, which introduce potentially unwanted conditional jumps, and prefer the corresponding bitwise operators.

In addition, as discussed above, we impose that the programmer correctly annotates the program with trace extension statements Leak(Event_True) and Leak(Event_False). Correct annotation means that the next statement in each execution path after a conditional branch is an annotation exposing the corresponding value of the branching condition (see the code in Figure 4). Semantically, these statements append the corresponding event at the end of a global trace that is initially empty and can only be manipulated using the annotation mechanism.

3. SECURE C-LIKE CODE IN EasyCrypt

We formalize security proofs using EasyCrypt [9], an SMT-based interactive prover geared towards formally proving security properties of cryptographic schemes. Cryptographic algorithms, oracles and games are described in a probabilistic imperative language pWhile. Reduction proofs can then be performed by establishing probabilistic relational properties on pairs of pWhile functions and, from them, deducing concrete probability bounds.

Importantly, pWhile's grammar of expressions can be extended with user-defined types and functional (pure and total) operators. The language is equipped with some built-in types, including booleans, integers, tuples and *fixed-length* bitstrings. However, the latter type is insufficient to write, for example, algorithms whose input are bitstrings whose length is chosen by the adversary. As we define grammar extensions to model variable-length octet strings (in fact, polymorphic arrays) below, we write them in a style that narrows the gap between pWhile and the subset of trace-annotated C with big integers described above.

A C *mode for* EasyCrypt. We extend EasyCrypt with several libraries to lower the level of abstraction of specifications to one similar to our C-like language. The first of these libraries implements variable-sized arrays. It provides a polymorphic type $\alpha[]$ and select $(\cdot\,[\cdot])$ and update $(\cdot\,[\cdot] = \cdot)$ operators, defined only when used within the array's bounds. We let the user declare statically-sized array variables (var $\cdot : \cdot[\cdot];$). For specification purposes, we also define a length operator $(|\cdot|)$ and write valid(a, o, l) whenever o and l are non-negative integers and a is an array such that $o + l \leq |a|$. (This guarantees that any access to a with an index i such that $o \leq i < o + l$ is within the array bounds, and allows us to express memory-safety conditions.)

We also introduce a type bigint to distinguish variables meant to model machine integers from those meant to be implemented as arbitrary precision integers. The bigint type is equipped with operators for all operations needed, including comparisons, shifts and modular operations.

Our third library extension deals with parameter-passing: in order for our adversaries to have at least as much power over inputs and outputs as standard IND-CCA adversaries in the context of a C program, we model, in EasyCrypt, parameter passing by-reference, where a reference to an array or variable is passed as argument, and used to return multiple values by side-effect. When a function takes a parameter of an array or bigint type, we always assume that it may in fact overwrite that parameter's contents, unless otherwise specified using the const type modifier. (We syntactically ensure that all such parameters that are not used for output are marked as const.) Conversely, when a parameter of primitive type is meant to be used as an out-parameter, it should be marked as such using the out type modifier. Type α out is equipped with a dereference operator $({}^*\cdot)$, and an update statement $({}^*\cdot = \cdot;)$.

Finally, we define in EasyCrypt some constants and operators that capture the abstract C leakage described in Section 2. Abstract traces can be the empty trace Zero, the true and false branch events Event_True and Event_False, or any combinations of these using an associative extension operator $\cdot \mathbin{++} \cdot$ for which Zero is a left and right neutral element. In functions, oracles and games, we write Leak(e) to denote the fact that the observable trace is extended to the right (using $++$) with e.

In addition to these basic events, we also consider abstract leakage from some of the external functions and big integer primitives. This allows us to make formal and precise, using axioms, the usual assumptions on their leakage. We use the $\rightsquigarrow t$ notation introduced in Section 2 to denote that a particular function call extends the execution trace to the right with a trace t that may depend on all of the call's arguments. (For algorithms, this trace extension is concrete, whereas it is kept abstract for chosen big integer primitives and for the external functions.)

Application to PKCS#1 v2.1. We discuss our implementation of the PKCS standard based on the encryption algorithm. Details of the other algorithms and subroutines can be found in the full version.

Figure 4 shows our implementation of the encryption algorithm. Auxiliary algorithms, as well as external functions, are written so that they return their results by passing a reference to some output parameters, but otherwise provide the same functionality. The encoding algorithm is optimized to save space by reusing its internal buffers *seed* and *DB* once their contents become obsolete. Apart from the verbosity of using while loops to implement array operations, this implementation does not differ much from the encoding function described in the PKCS#1 standard (see Figure 3).

Between lines (3) and (8), the data blob is built, by copying the default label hash, writing the zero padding and the separator, and finally copying the message m into it. On line (9), the seed is sampled uniformly at random. On line (10), the MGF oracle is called and its result (*seedMask*) written directly into the output buffer, and used, in the while loop at (12) to mask the data blob in place. On line (13), the MGF oracle is queried with the masked data blob and its result written and used as before to mask the seed. Finally, on line (16), the first byte of the output buffer is set to 0.

```
fun OAEP_Encode(res : octet[], m : octet const[], mLen : int):

 1: var seed : octet[hLen];
 2: var DB : octet[dbLen];
 3: i = 0;
 4: while (i < hLen) { Leak(Event_True);
        DB[i] = dLHash [i];
        i = i + 1; } Leak(Event_False);
 5: while (i < dbLen − mLen − 1) { Leak(Event_True);
        DB[i] = 0x00;
        i = i + 1; } Leak(Event_False);
 6: DB[i] = 0x01;
 7: i = i + 1;
 8: while (i < dbLen) { Leak(Event_True);
        DB[i] = m [i − dbLen + mLen];
        i = i + 1; } Leak(Event_False);
 9: sample_octets(seed, 0, hLen);
10: MGF1(res, 1 + hLen, dbLen, seed, 0, hLen);
11: i = 0;
12: while (i < dbLen) { Leak(Event_True);
        res[1 + hLen + i] = res [1 + hLen + i] ⊕ DB [i];
        i = i + 1; } Leak(Event_False);
13: MGF1(res, 1, hLen, res, 1 + hLen, dbLen);
14: i = 0;
15: while (i < hLen) { Leak(Event_True);
        res[1 + i] = res [1 + i] ⊕ seed [i];
        i = i + 1; } Leak(Event_False);
16: res[0] = 0x00;
17: return RC_Success;
```

```
fun OAEP_Encrypt(res : octet[],
                 m : octet const[], mLen : int, pk : pkey):

var p, c : bigint;
var EM : octet[k];
if (maxMLen < mLen) { Leak(Event_True);
    rc = RC_MessageTooLong; }
else { Leak(Event_False);
    rc = OAEP_Encode(EM, m, mLen);
    rc = OS2IP(p, EM, k);
    rc = RSAEP(c, pk, p);
    rc = I2OSP(res, c, k);
    rc = RC_Success; }
return rc;
```

Figure 4: Implementation of PKCS#1 encryption

Although it is a rather simple refinement of the specification shown in Figure 3, this implementation allows us to concretely reason about the leakage traces produced when executing the encryption algorithm. From a formal point of view, the first steps in our security and correctness proofs very much reduce the security of the low-level model to the security of the high-level scheme (augmented with concrete side-channel leakage).

However, even the high-level description displayed in Figure 3 is far removed from the description for which Fujisaki *et al.* obtained their well-known security proof [21]. We display it for comparison in Figure 5. There are three major differences between the two specifications:

- the standard uses only one random oracle, whereas Fujisaki *et al.* use two; for the lengths used in the standard, these are stricly equivalent, since F and G have disjoint domains.
- to remedy the fact that RSA is not a random permutation over the entire encoded message space, the standard ensures that it is always called on plaintexts whose first byte is zero; this has an incidence on the security and the proof.
- finally, the standard permits the encryption of variable (but bounded) length messages, using some additional padding to fixed length; this does not affect theoretical security, but has led to well-known padding oracle attacks [27, 33] when implemented carelessly.

Despite these differences, the security proof is relatively easy to adapt and follows the same general schema. We perform it in a refinement of the adversary model presented in Section 2, which gives the adversary more control over output parameters. Oracle wrappers ensure that adversaries respect memory-safety side conditions when calling the algorithms and environment functions.

fun $\mathsf{OAEP\_Encrypt_{proof}}(m : \mathsf{octet}[], pk : \mathsf{pkey})$:

$$
\begin{aligned}
& r = \mathsf{random}(hLen);\\
& s = (m \| \mathtt{0x00}^{hLen}) \oplus \mathsf{G}(r);\\
& t = r \oplus \mathsf{H}(s);\\
& \mathsf{return}\ \mathsf{RSA}(pk, s\|t);
\end{aligned}
$$

Figure 5: Fujisaki *et al.*'s OAEP encryption

Security theorem. Following Fujisaki *et al.*, we reduce our PKCS#1 implementation's leakage-aware IND-CCA security to a variant of the set partial-domain one-way assumption (s-PDOW) on RSA. This variant takes into account the fact that the first byte of the random input is set to 0, and also lets the adversary observe the leakage produced when evaluating the one-way permutation and its inverse. More precisely, Figure 6 shows the assumption in game form, parameterized by a one-way permutation f, a leakage function $\mathsf{leak_f}$, and an adversary $\mathcal{B}$. The leakage function $\mathsf{leak_f}$ takes a secret key sk, and outputs a secret key sk_ℓ such that, for any challenge c, the computations of $\mathsf{f}_{\mathsf{sk}}^{-1}(c)$ and $\mathsf{f}_{\mathsf{sk}_\ell}^{-1}(c)$ produce the same execution trace. This key is used in the proof to simulate the trace produced by computing the decryption algorithm.

Given a one-way permutation f and a leakage function $\mathsf{leak_f}$ for it, we define, the s-PDOW advantage of an adversary $\mathcal{B}$ against f relative to $\mathcal{G}$ as

$$\mathsf{Adv}^{\mathsf{s\text{-}pdow}}_{\mathsf{f},\mathsf{leak_f},\mathcal{G},\mathcal{B}}(\lambda) := 2 \cdot \Pr\left[s\text{-}\mathsf{PDOW}_{\mathsf{f},\mathsf{leak_f},\mathcal{G},\mathcal{B}}(\lambda) \Rightarrow \mathsf{T}\right] - 1\,.$$

Game s-$\mathsf{PDOW}_{\mathsf{f},\mathsf{leak_f},\mathcal{G},\mathcal{B}}(1^\lambda)$

$$
\begin{aligned}
& (\mathsf{pk},\mathsf{sk}) \leftarrow_\$ \mathcal{G}\\
& s \leftarrow_\$ \{0,1\}^{hLen}\\
& t \leftarrow_\$ \{0,1\}^{dbLen}\\
& c \leftarrow \mathsf{f_{pk}}(\mathtt{0x00}\|s\|t) \rightsquigarrow \tau\\
& \mathsf{sk}_\ell \leftarrow \mathsf{leak_f}(\mathsf{sk})\\
& T \leftarrow_\$ \mathcal{B}^{\mathsf{f}_{\mathsf{sk}}^{-1}(\cdot)}(c, \tau, \mathsf{sk}_\ell)\\
& \mathsf{return}\ t \in T
\end{aligned}
$$

Figure 6: Leakage-aware s-PDOW assumption

The validity of assuming that this advantage is negligible depends greatly on the leakage function $\mathsf{leak_f}$ and the trace produced when evaluating the permutation f. In particular, when the leakage function is constant (that is, when the trace produced when evaluating the inverse permutation does not depend on the secret key), and evaluating the permutation does not leak information about the plaintext, our s-PDOW game only differs from the one used by Fujisaki *et al.* [21] by the fixed first byte of the challenge plaintext. This only introduces an additional factor 256 in the bound.

We can now state our security theorem for PKCS#1 v2.1 as we implement it.

THEOREM 1 (SECURITY OF PKCS#1 V2.1). *Let* Π *be our implementation of the standard. For all key generation algorithm* $\mathcal{G}$, *and* IND-CCA *adversary* $\mathcal{A}$ *making at most* q_D *queries to the decryption oracle and* q_G *queries to the random oracle with* $\ell_i = hLen$ *and* $\ell_o = dbLen$, *we build a* s-PDOW *adversary* $\mathcal{B}$ *against RSA such that:*

$$\mathsf{Adv}^{\mathsf{ind\text{-}cca}}_{\Pi,\mathcal{G},\mathcal{A}}(\lambda) \le \mathsf{Adv}^{\mathsf{s\text{-}pdow}}_{\mathsf{RSA},\mathsf{leak_{RSA}},\mathcal{G},\mathcal{B}}(\lambda) + \frac{2q_\mathsf{D}q_\mathsf{G} + q_\mathsf{G} - q_\mathsf{D}}{2^{8hLen}}$$

The proof is formalized in EasyCrypt, and relies on several assumptions on the leakage produced by the library and environment functions. The assumption on modular exponentiation is formalized using the $\mathsf{leak_{RSA}}$ function. All other arithmetic functions are implicitly assumed to produce constant leakage traces. The random oracle and random sampling operations are assumed to produce leakage traces that depend only on their length parameters.

4. SECURITY-AWARE COMPILATION

Our goal is to take a C implementation such as that described in the previous section and compile it to an assembly implementation that retains the security properties that were established (or are simply assumed to hold) for the source code. A natural question that arises is then: what properties must the C compiler guarantee to ensure that the assembly implementation is secure based on the assumption that the C implementation is secure?

The classical notion of correctness for any compiler is known as *semantic preservation.* Intuitively, this property guarantees that, for any given source program S, the compiler will produce a compiled program T that operates *consistently* with the semantics of S. Consistency is defined based on the *observable behaviour* of a program, which can be a simple relation on input states and output states, or it can be a more complex notion including observable events occurring during program evaluation. A bit more formally, let us denote the evaluation of a program P over inputs $\vec{p}$, resulting in outputs $\vec{o}$ and observable behaviour B as

$P(\vec{p}) \Downarrow (\vec{o}, B)$. Then, semantic preservation could be written as

$$\forall B, \vec{p}, \vec{o},\ T(\vec{p}) \Downarrow (\vec{o}, B) \implies S(\vec{p}) \Downarrow (\vec{o}, B)$$

This means essentially that any observable behaviour of the target program is observable in the source program. Furthermore, if the source language is deterministic (i.e., it has no intrinsic non-determinism when it interacts with a deterministic environment) then this also gives an implication in the reverse direction [25].

Here we introduce a notion of *security-aware semantic preservation* that refines the previous high-level notion. We also prove that, when enforced by a C compiler, this new notion is sufficient to guarantee that, not only the functionality of the source program is preserved, but also its security. We call C compilers that are proven to enforce this type of semantic preservation *security-aware*. In the next section we will show how we have extended CompCert to enable the security-aware compilation of C implementations.

Observable behaviour of an implementation. The observable behaviours that we will consider for security-aware compilation will include, not only the leakage that is provided to the adversary, but also all the interactions of the implementation with the environment via Rand and RO. Formally, we see behaviours B as sequences of observable events ν, $B ::= \epsilon \mid \nu.B$, where we consider events of the following types:

$$\nu ::= \quad \mathsf{const}(id) \quad | \quad \mathsf{Rand}(v, \ell) \quad | \quad \mathsf{RO}(v, i, \ell_i, \ell_o)\,.$$

Intuitively, $\mathsf{const}(id)$ will correspond to a leakage event. In the case of C implementations, the identifier id will be either T or F, signalling the evaluation of a branching condition similarly to what was described in the previous section. In the case of assembly implementations, the identifier id will contain the unique identifier (PC address) of the instruction being executed, according to the program counter model. Rand events signal a call to an external random sampling function, including the length and output of the random octet string that was obtained from the environment. Similarly, RO events reveal the full details of an interaction with an external function representing the idealised MGF function.

We will refer to the projection of a behaviour that retains only the const events as $\mathsf{const}(B)$. Similarly, we will refer to the projection that excludes the const events as $\mathsf{coins}(B)$. We can now present our notion of security-aware semantic preservation.

Definition 4. (*Security-aware semantic preservation*) Take PKE implementation $\Pi = (\mathsf{C}, \mathsf{Enc}, \mathsf{Dec}, \ell_{(\cdot)})$ in C. We say that assembly implementation $\pi = (\mathsf{asm}, \mathsf{Enc}', \mathsf{Dec}', \ell_{(\cdot)})$ securely preserves the semantics of Π if there exists an efficient deterministic simulator $\mathcal{S}$ such that the following two conditions hold

$$\begin{array}{l}\forall \lambda, B_\Pi, B_\pi, \mathsf{m}, \mathsf{pk}, \mathsf{c}, \mathsf{rc}.\\ \quad \mathsf{coins}(B_\Pi) = \mathsf{coins}(B_\pi) \wedge \mathsf{Enc}'^{\mathsf{Rand},\mathsf{RO}}_\lambda(\mathsf{m}, \mathsf{pk}) \Downarrow (\mathsf{rc}, \mathsf{c}, B_\pi) \Rightarrow\\ \qquad \mathsf{Enc}^{\mathsf{Rand},\mathsf{RO}}_\lambda(\mathsf{m}, \mathsf{pk}) \Downarrow (\mathsf{rc}, \mathsf{c}, B_\Pi) \wedge\\ \qquad \mathsf{const}(B_\pi) = \mathcal{S}(\mathsf{Enc}, \mathsf{Enc}', \mathsf{const}(B_\Pi))\,.\end{array}$$

$$\begin{array}{l}\forall \lambda, B_\Pi, B_\pi, \mathsf{c}, \mathsf{sk}, \mathsf{m}, \mathsf{rc}.\\ \quad \mathsf{coins}(B_\Pi) = \mathsf{coins}(B_\pi) \wedge \mathsf{Dec}'^{\mathsf{RO}}_\lambda(\mathsf{c}, \mathsf{sk}) \Downarrow (\mathsf{rc}, \mathsf{m}, B_\pi) \Rightarrow\\ \qquad \mathsf{Dec}^{\mathsf{RO}}_\lambda(\mathsf{c}, \mathsf{sk}) \Downarrow (\mathsf{rc}, \mathsf{m}, B_\Pi) \wedge\\ \qquad \mathsf{const}(B_\pi) = \mathcal{S}(\mathsf{Dec}, \mathsf{Dec}', \mathsf{const}(B_\Pi))\,.\end{array}$$

The intuition is the following. Consider behaviours B_Π and B_π where the randomness taken by the C implementation from the environment matches that taken by the assembly implementation. Then, for all possible parameter inputs, the assembly implementation must produce an output that is consistent with that of the C implementation. Furthermore, it must be possible to simulate the PC trace of the assembly implementation, given only the leakage of the C implementation.

The next theorem establishes that security-aware semantic preservation implies that PKE correctness is preserved in compilation. The proof is a direct reduction and is presented in the full version.

THEOREM 2. *Let* $\Pi = (\mathsf{C}, \mathsf{Enc}, \mathsf{Dec}, \ell_{(\cdot)})$ *be a correct PKE implementation. If* $\pi = (\mathsf{asm}, \mathsf{Enc}', \mathsf{Dec}', \ell_{(\cdot)})$ *is a PKE implementation that securely preserves the semantics of* Π*, then* π *is also correct.*

The next theorem shows that security-aware semantic preservation guarantees that security is preserved by compilation, i.e., that the assembly implementation will be secure against adversaries that get program counter leakage, assuming that the C implementation is secure in the leakage model described in the previous section.

THEOREM 3. *Let* $\Pi = (\mathsf{C}, \mathsf{Enc}, \mathsf{Dec}, \ell_{(\cdot)})$ *be an* IND-CCA *secure PKE implementation. If* $\pi = (\mathsf{asm}, \mathsf{Enc}', \mathsf{Dec}', \ell_{(\cdot)})$ *is a PKE implementation that securely preserves the semantics of* Π*, then* π *is also* IND-CCA *secure.*

The proof is presented in the full version, and it hinges on the following observation on security-aware semantic preservation. Conceptually, what we are doing in Definition 4 when we quantify over behaviours B_Π and B_π is to quantify over all random coins taken by the implementations, and to ensure that the same coins are provided to both Π and π. This can also be seen as quantifying over a set of deterministic environments, each of them providing a possible value of the random coins. Interestingly, in this case, and given that our source implementation language is a deterministic subset of C, we get that security-aware semantic preservation also gives an implication in the reverse direction [25]. In other words, in addition to the implication shown in Definition 4, we also get the following: for each deterministic environment and for each input $\vec{p}$, the source program has a single observable behaviour which maps to the single observable behaviour in the compiled assembly code (which is also deterministic). In a nutshell, this means that one can directly reduce the security of the assembly implementation to the security of the C implementation, provided that leakage can be simulated.

5. MAKING CompCert SECURITY-AWARE

In this section we show how we extended the CompCert certified compiler [25] and used it to perform this type of security aware compilation.

Background on CompCert. CompCert is a formally verified optimizing C compiler [25]. It produces target code with strong correctness guarantees and reasonable efficiency when compared to general purpose compilers. CompCert supports the C language (with almost complete coverage of the ISO C 90 / ANSI C standard) and produces assembly code for the PowerPC, ARM, and IA32 (x86 32-bits) architectures. CompCert is mostly implemented in Coq, and its development is subdivided into 19 compiler phases, each of which builds a semantic preservation proof between semantically defined intermediate languages.

Formally, CompCert's correctness theorem establishes the strong notion of semantic preservation that was introduced in the beginning of Section 4, referred in CompCert terminology as a *backward simulation*. This guarantees that, if a source program P^{C} is successfully compiled into P^{asm}, then the observable behaviour of this last program is an admissible behaviour of the original program. The proof of this result is based on a formalization of the semantics of both the compiler's source and target languages (C and assembly), as well as of all the compiler passes. Behaviours are captured by a possibly infinite sequence of events that model interactions of the program with the outside world, such as accesses to volatile variables, calls to system libraries, or user defined events (so called annotations).

The need for CompCert *extensions.* There are various aspects in which we needed to enhance both the functionality of CompCert and the formal correctness guarantees that it provides in order to guarantee security-aware semantic preservation. In the remainder of this section we will begin by identifying precisely what CompCert does and does not provide in this direction, and then explain in detail how we have implemented the necessary extensions.

CompCert's semantic preservation result establishes guarantees very close to Definition 4: conditioning on similar interactions with the environment, the observable behaviour for the compiled assembly program matches the observable behaviour of the source C program. However, the following caveats need to be addressed before applying the results of Section 4:

- **Expressiveness of CompCert behaviours.** The notion of observable behaviour of a C program and an assembly program in CompCert is conceptually more general than the one we adopted in the previous section. It considers, for example, the possibility that programs go wrong or do not terminate. However, it is more restrictive in the sense that, on one hand it considers only programs with a well-defined entry point (the main function) and does not include support for the Rand and RO events that we require (as these imply exposing or updating the values of memory regions).
- **Absence of a leakage model.** CompCert behaviours do not have an associated intrinsic notion of side-channel leakage (neither at the C nor at the assembly levels). Although it is possible to emulate such leakage using annotations directly placed over the source code, there is no way to guarantee that the target code would have an observable behaviour that follows the instrumented semantics conventions of the PC model that we have described in the previous sections. This means that there is no straightforward way to capture the simulation of PC traces that we require for security-aware compilation.
- **Complex data types.** The common practice in the implementation of cryptographic software is to split the development in two parts: i. a trusted number theory library that extends the high-level language of choice with the complex data types required for public-key cryptography; and ii. code that implements a specific scheme by relying on the functionality of the trusted library. As described in Section 3, we also adopt this approach at the EasyCrypt level, by writing C code that relies on operators that carry out multi-precision integer calculations. A set of axioms describes important properties for these operators, similarly to what happens to other C native data types such as octet strings. Conceptually, we see this as an extension to C that adds support for an additional data type, which means that the semantics of C as formalized in CompCert need to be extended for our purposes.

In the remainder of this section we will explain how we have extended CompCert to eliminate the previous caveats.

Adding support for additional external operations. A difficulty that arises when we try to base our results on CompCert's semantic preservation guarantee is how to handle the environment that was setup in the EasyCrypt formalization. This includes primitives for sampling values, the choice of appropriate hash functions to instantiate the oracles, and other support functionality. This is an important issue, since we do not want to impose an a-priori commitment on these choices — this would, not only weaken (specialize) the guarantees offered by the implementation, but also it would not match what is the common practice in the implementation of cryptographic software. The semantics formalized in CompCert support calls to system libraries, but these calls are assumed to leave the memory state unaltered. This makes them inappropriate to model the environment we require. Consequently, our first extension to CompCert is a mechanism for declaring external functions that may impact the memory.

Our solution is an extension of the treatment adopted by CompCert for system-calls. A call to a system library triggers an observable event that registers the name of the called function, its arguments, and an additional value that represents the result (provided by the execution environment). In order to address functions that change the memory state, we have introduced a new event whose arguments are byte-arrays containing data read-from/written-to specified memory regions. For that, we have implemented a simple mechanism to specify the memory footprint of an external function. We allow the arguments of each function to be either a primitive C type or a pointer to a memory region that is either read or written. The size of regions is declared by an expression that is allowed to refer to other (int) arguments. As an example, consider the declaration of the sample_octets and random_oracle functions that instantiate the Rand and RO oracles in our PKCS implementation:

```
#pragma libspec sample_octets: OutPtr #1,Int->Void
extern void sample_octets(unsigned char *,size_t);
#pragma libspec random_oracle: OutPtr #1, Int,
                               InPtr #3,Int->Void
extern void random_oracle(unsigned char *, size_t,
                          unsigned char *, size_t);
```

In the first line, the pragma directive informs CompCert that the first argument is a pointer to a memory region written by the function. The size of the region is given by the integer passed as second argument. This mechanism is implemented in a general way that allows specifying arbitrary functions that feed output memory regions to the environment and fill input memory regions with data collected from the environment. More precisely, the semantics of a function declared using this mechanism is defined to:

1. read the memory regions and other input arguments;
2. ask the environment for a byte-array with size equal to the sum of the output sizes;
3. split the obtained array in the required pieces, and write them in the corresponding memory regions;
4. produce an event with arguments as described above.

By extending the correctness result of CompCert to cover these external functions, it follows that the observable behaviour of a source program will be preserved in the assembly code, for any instantiation of these functions. However, in the context of security-aware compilation, one must recall that these functions are actually idealised constructions that are used in the security proofs. It is critical to the security of the final implementation that the instantiation of these functions complies as much as possible with the assumptions that are made explicit in the EasyCrypt proof. In other words, these functions must be *trustworthy* in order to obtain assembly-level security, and this is why we named this mechanism *TrustedLib*.

In the particular case of the RSA-OAEP implementation the above discussion implies that, in line with standard cryptographic practice, it is up to the end-user to instantiate sample_octets with a function that provides good quality randomness, and to follow the recommentations in the PKCS standard for the instantiation of the mask generation function that we model as a random oracle. Furthermore, the assumptions regarding the leakage of these external functions that are axiomatized in EasyCrypt should also be satisfied by the instantiation.

Correctness of the cryptographic API. There is a mismatch between what it means for a compiled program to be correct under the CompCert formalization and our notion of correctness. In CompCert, the meaning of a C program is the behaviour of executing a specific entry-point: the main function. Our notion of correctness imposes instead the correctness (in terms of input/output behaviour) of all the functions acting as entry points of the functionality formalized in EasyCrypt: we call this the correctness of the cryptographic API. To bridge the gap between these two notions, we have anchored our correctness result on a C entry-point with the following shape:

Function main( )

$id \leftarrow$ read( )
$\vec{p} \leftarrow$ read( )
$o \leftarrow id(\vec{p})$
write(o)

This generic entry point reads the identifier of the function to evaluate (in the case of a PKE implementation this means either Enc or Dec). It then uses external functions read and write to obtain input values for the function from the environment, and to externalise the corresponding outputs.[4] This pattern registers every possible input/output behaviour of each function as an admissible behaviour of the program. Hence, the correctness result of CompCert ensures preservation of this behaviour along the compilation process.

The main function is added to the cryptographic implementation to ensure that the translation to assembly is explicitly captured by the correctness theorem of CompCert. This function can be discarded from the assembly code, since the implementation is itself intended to be used as a library by some higher level application.

Adding support for a big-number library. The implementation of public-key cryptography code often requires the use of big-number libraries to carry out complex algebraic computations such as modular exponentiation. For example, a typical implementation of RSA-OAEP will delegate the big-number computations to a (often pre-compiled) library such as GMP.[5] From the developers' point of view, this can be seen as extending C with a new data type and native operations that provide support for big integers.

One possible approach to handle such external libraries would be to use the *TrustedLib* mechanism to equip our framework with external functions, which would leave it to the environment to provide the big-integer operators.[6] However, this would not match the setting we have captured in the EasyCrypt formalization, in which we consider a well-defined intended semantics for these operations. Furthermore, the correctness and security of the C implementation depend crucially on the correct implementation of these functions (otherwise, the axioms assumed in the EasyCrypt theory might not be validated). For this reason, we have opted to include the necessary big-integer operations as new built-in operations in CompCert, with a fully defined semantics, which we see as a contract on the library that we will use for linking with our program. Once again we must trust the library that instantiates these operations to correctly implement those contracts, which would ideally be addressed through formal verification. Unfortunately, the complexity of state-of-art libraries such as GMP make such an enterprise an enormous effort (although results obtained on smaller libraries [31] and in specific algorithms [12] provide confidence on feasibility in a near future).

Technically, the formalization of the semantics of the big-number builtin operations is a refinement of that presented for the *TrustedLib* functions, in which the transformations on the state are fully specified, and where the events signalling communication with the environment are ommitted. The transformations on the state are described in three steps: i. reading the big-integer word representations of all the inputs and converting them into (Coq) integers; ii. performing the operations over the integers; and iii. converting back into the memory representation and storing the results. A consequence of our approach is that we needed to commit to a concrete representation of big-integers. We use a 2^{30} radix representation, stored as an array of 32-bit ma-

[4] In the case of our example, the inputs and outputs are simply octet strings of various lengths, which means that the read and write functions can be also implemented using the external function mechanism described above.

[5] `http://gmplib.org`

[6] In fact, we have used that mechanism to specify all the GMP low-level integer API.

chine integers. This means that we use 30-bits in each machine word for storage, where the remaining two bits should always be kept at zero at the function boundaries (functions may internally and temporarily cause these bits to be non-zero). Our formalization is flexible enough to enable straightforward adaptation to other representations. The formalization of the big-number library as built-in operations in CompCert has the additional advantage of automatically extending the CompCert interpreter to support these operations, which may be useful for debugging.

Our framework includes an instantiation of the big-number library that was developed for illustrative purposes, adapted from the *Long Integer Package (LIP)* library by A. Lenstra.[7] One of our concerns was to ensure that all the big-integer operations comply with the leakage requirements imposed by the EasyCrypt proof: the leakage should be constant and independent of the concrete inputs passed to the functions. To this end, we have incorporated a standard countermeasure against side-channel attacks, and simplified the library to consider only unsigned integers and use static memory allocation. All the routines have been modified so that there is no data-dependent branching and memory indexing as explained, for example, in [11]. This means that all functions in the library execute in constant time and access the same memory addresses, regardless of the input data. Integers are stored in statically declared arrays of pre-defined size, which means that the maximum range of the integers that will be manipulated by the program must be known in advance, and must be provided at the time of compilation. For our example, we have aimed at 4096-bit RSA keys, represented using 137 words. We note that fixing the maximum length of integers is consistent with our assumption that the security parameter is known at compile time, and the formal semantics that we have added in CompCert captures exactly the behaviour of our library. Although the functionality of our library is not formally verified, we have used a Frama-C plug-in [8] to check that the side-channel countermeasures are correctly deployed.

Dealing with side-channel leakage. The last extension to CompCert concerns the need to satisfy the part of Definition 4 imposing that traces generated by the assembly code in the PC model can be simulated from the leakage model we adopted for C programs.

The annotation mechanism of CompCert allows us to extend standard C code with dummy statements that, when evaluated, give rise to events that externalize arbitrary constant identifiers making them visible in the observable behaviour of the program. This means that a direct translation of the EasyCrypt code into CompCert taking advantage of these annotations gives rise to a C program whose observable behaviour includes (among the other events that may be signalled) a trace of all the conditional jumps taken by the program. Furthermore, CompCert guarantees that the same exact traces will be observable in the assembly program.

It is obvious that, by inspecting the sequence of events that reports which conditional jumps were taken, one can reconstruct the entire control flow of the C program. However, the same cannot be said for the control flow of the assembly program: indeed, CompCert is only guaranteed to preserve the observable behaviour of the C program, and many possible assembly programs can achieve this. In particular, there may be assembly programs which are insecure in the PC model (i.e. that leak sensitive information via the control flow) and still have an observable behaviour that matches that of the original C program. In other words, it may not be possible to fully determine the sequence of program counter values taken by an assembly implementation solely from the observable conditional jumps taken by the C program. However, in order to achieve security-aware compilation, this is precisely what we require.

Instead of proving that each of the compiler passes does not introduce spurious branching, we have implemented a simple static analysis on the generated assembly program that establishes the desired property. Our analysis is formalized in Coq as a translation validation that checks, for every conditional branch instruction in the assembly code, that i. all execution paths arising from that instruction go through an annotation; and ii. that these annotations give rise to events that externalize (pairwise) distinct constant identifiers. This is sufficient to ensure that the observable behaviour of the program fully reflects the choice of the execution path, and we have formalized and proved in Coq the following theorem that establishes the soundness of the translation validation.

THEOREM 4 (PC TRACE SIMULATABILITY). *Let S be an assembly program that passes the translation validation described above. Let also s_1 and s_2 be memory states s.t. $s_1 \equiv^{\mathsf{PC}} s_2$; and, let B_1 and B_2 be behaviours s.t. $B_1 \sim^{\mathsf{ann}} B_2$, $\langle S; s_1\rangle \Downarrow B_1$, and $\langle S; s_2\rangle \Downarrow B_2$. Then, for any states s_1', s_2' and traces t_1, t_2 we have that*

$$s_1 \xrightarrow{t_1} s_1' \;\wedge\; s_2 \xrightarrow{t_2} s_2' \quad \Longrightarrow \quad s_1' \equiv^{\mathsf{PC}} s_2' .$$

Here, states s_1, s_2 are PC-equivalent ($s_1 \equiv^{\mathsf{PC}} s_2$) when they agree on the value stored in the PC register and have the same call stack, and behaviours B_1, B_2 are annotation-equivalent ($B_1 \sim^{\mathsf{ann}} B_2$) when they exhibit the same (possibly infinite) sequence of annotation events. The above theorem shows that the sequence of PC values in the evaluation of an assembly program that passes the translation validation is fully determined by the sequence of constant identifiers revealed via annotations in the observable behaviour. More precisely, the theorem expresses this result in the style of a non-interference result: if a program is validated by the test, then any two instances of it that exhibit the same annotations on their behaviour, are guaranteed to proceed in lockstep, i.e., the next PC value can always be determined from the observable trace.

The above theorem treats the execution of external calls and other compiler builtins as atomic steps. The soundness of the validation depends on the assumption that these external functions have precisely the same property (a compiler warning collects the identifiers of all these functions to remind the user of this fact). From the perspective of the end-user, the test is triggered by a new command-line option -max-annot. When the validation fails, no executable is produced and an error is emitted pointing to the branch of the (bad) assembly program that fails the check.

The following corollary relates the theorem above to the notion of semantic preservation in Definition 4.

COROLLARY 5 (INFORMAL). *Consider a PKE implementation that, when it is compiled with CompCert, gives rise to*

[7] `http://www.win.tue.nl/~klenstra/`

an assembly program that passes the translation validation check. Then, the compilation performed by CompCert *enforces Definition 4.*

The proof of this corollary follows directly from the fact that the correctness theorem for CompCert guarantees that Definition 4 is satisfied, provided that simulator $\mathcal{S}$ can be constructed. The theorem above guarantees the correctness of the trivial simulator that looks ahead to the potential executions of the assembly program, until it finds the annotation that reveals the correct execution paths.

Using CompCert *for security-aware compilation.* To summarize the above discussions, we have extended CompCert with a number of features and adapted the correctness result of the compiler to accommodate these extensions. This means that CompCert will preserve the observable behaviours of source C programs that rely on an arbitrary *TrustedLib*. We have also shown that the translation validation step that we have added to the compiler guarantees that simulation of PC traces is possible for accepted assembly programs. Putting these two results together, we conclude that our version of CompCert provides security-aware compilation by guaranteeing semantic preservation according to Definition 4. This means that, by the Theorems proved in Section 4, compiling a cryptographic implementation from C code to assembly, one obtains the following guarantees:

1. Assuming that the C implementation is secure in a side-channel aware security model such as the one described in Section 2;
2. Compiling the C implementation with the generic main entry point using CompCert and activating the translation validation stage;
3. Assuming that the *TrustedLib* functions are instantiated with a secure and correct library that satisfies the requirements specified in the security proof;
4. Then, if compilation does not fail, the assembly implementation is correct and secure against real-world adversaries that attack the scheme in the PC model.

Experimental results. We have performed an evaluation of the performance of the assembly code produced by CompCert when used for security-aware compilation. Our goals were three-fold: i. to evaluate whether or not the translation validation check might reject the assembly produced by CompCert (in which case the compiler might not be preserving the side-channel countermeasures); ii. to evaluate whether the annotation of C source-code with the leakage tags might damage the performance of the code produced by CompCert; and iii. to compare the efficiency of the secure code produced by CompCert when compared to GCC. We have conducted our evaluation in a standard PC with an IA32 architecture. In addition to the PKCS implementation described here, we have also evaluated the entire NaCl library core [11].

Our findings were the following. We have not encountered any example where the assembly code generated from properly annotated and secure C code was rejected due to transformations performed by CompCert. On the other hand, there were several cases where the transformation validation stage led us to identify points in the C code where there might be potential leakage problems (mostly associated with the compilation of composed Boolean expressions). Furthermore, when comparing the performance of validated assembly code with that produced by CompCert from non-annotated C code, there were no significant deviations in performance. These findings indicate that CompCert behaves well in the preservation of the class of side-channel countermeasures that we considered in this paper, when they are deployed at the C level.

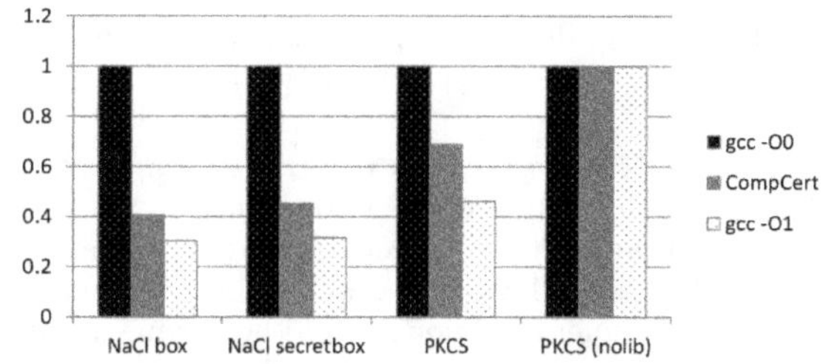

Figure 7: Benchmarking results

Regarding the overall performance of generated code, Figure 7 shows some selected benchmarking results, normalized with respect to the performance of non-optimized GCC output. For PKCS we show two cases. The values labeled PKCS correspond to the natural comparison between CompCert and GCC where both the trusted library and the PKCS code are compiled using either GCC or CompCert. The values labeled PKCS (nolib) correspond to the case the trusted library is pre-compiled and linked with the result of compiling the PKCS code with either GCC or CompCert.

Our findings for the first three cases are consistent with the known reports on CompCert benchmarking when comparing CompCert with unoptimized GCC code: the former outperforms the latter by roughly a factor of 2. When comparing with GCC at optimization level 1, we have found that CompCert is at least 30% slower. These results are slightly worse than previously reported values [26], which put this value at roughly 15%. We attribute this discrepancy to the domain-specific nature of our code, namely to side-channel countermeasures and intensive use of arithmetic and bit-wise operations.

In the PKCS (no lib) case, CompCert performs as well as GCC at optimization level 1, which shows that most of the speedups of GCC are being achieved in the optimization of the trusted library.

6. CONCLUDING REMARKS

We have developed library extensions to EasyCrypt that enable the development of cryptographic security proofs directly on a large subset of the C language, in an extended security model where the adversary is given access to execution traces modelling PC security. We have extended the CompCert certified compiler with a mechanism for reasoning about programs relying on trusted libraries, as well as a translation validation stage based on CompCert's annotation mechanism. We have shown that these mechanisms along with a trusted library providing arithmetic operations and instantiations of idealised operations are enough to preserve correctness and PC security guarantees from a source C program down to its compiled assembly executable. We have also shown the independent value of the new CompCert extensions for compiling third-party C programs whilst preserving their claimed PC security properties.

Related work. Our work lies at the intersection of computer-aided cryptography and certified compilation; we refer our readers to [13] and [25] for recent accounts of these fields, and focus this related work section on the verification of cryptographic implementations, and the formal treatment of side-channels.

Machine-checked correctness proofs of implementations of crypotographic primitives have been well-studied, using techniques ranging from equivalence checking [32], to verifying compilation [29], to deductive program verification [5] and interactive theorem proving [1]. However, these techniques are focused on functional correctness and do not attempt to formally carry provable security guarantees to the implementations.

Some proposals have been made towards obtaining computational security guarantees of implementations of cryptographic primitives and protocols. These are based on deductive verification [18], code generation [16], model extraction [4], refinement type systems [20], or static information-flow analysis [24]. However, these techniques focus on source program verification and do not explicitly address executable code, nor side-channel attacks.

In addition to being a core area of research in practical cryptography, side-channel attacks and countermeasures have been studied extensively in related areas, namely in the setting of programming languages [2, 3, 23, 34] and of theoretical cryptography [19, 6]. These works provide a more general account of side-channel attacks, either by considering a more precise computational model, e.g. with caches, or by providing a more abstract treatment of side-channels. However, they typically reason in a single setting—source code, assembly code, or an abstract model of computation. In contrast, we precisely relate the leakage properties of primitives to the security of algorithms and their executable implementations.

Our work is also related to ongoing efforts to formalize programming languages and compilers. In particular, the idea of harnessing a general-purpose verification tool with the CompCert compiler appears in the Verified Software Toolchain [7], and extensions of CompCert with arithmetic libraries are considered in [14].

Directions for further work. We intend to leverage the developments of this paper to build a verified software toolchain for cryptographic implementations.

A first step towards this goal is to provide automated support for the C mode of EasyCrypt; we are confident that the additional complexity introduced by low-level considerations can be managed automatically to a large extent. Automation is also instrumental for the feasibility of security proofs in alternative leakage models. For example, we would like to investigate stronger leakage models in which the adversary could observe the list or set of memory addresses accessed during the execution of an algorithm, as well as weaker leakage models in which the adversary could observe the number of operations performed during the execution of an algorithm. Dealing with these alternative models would also require extending EasyCrypt with further libraries and to extend the new translation validation stage in CompCert to guarantee the preservation of countermeasures adequate for these leakage models.

The security notions we have formalized are at least as strong as the standard notion of IND-CCA security, and thus inherit the composability properties of this standard notion. A natural (and ongoing) extension of our results is to look at previous work on the composition of cryptographic protocols (e.g., Universal Composability) and leverage them to produce verified implementations of higher-level protocols. The major challenges here reside on the style of cryptographic proofs that need to be formalized, which rely on a simulation paradigm. Also interesting for future work is the interaction of side-channel leakage at the IND-CCA level with the security of higher-level protocols.

Finally, we did not tackle the correctness properties of the big-integer trusted library that we use to extend C. We leave it as an interesting challenge for future work to evaluate the impact of side-channel countermeasures on the feasibility of formally verifying the correctness of such a multi-precision arithmetic library.

Acknowledgements

This work is supported by ONR Grant N000141210914, by Amarout II (FP7 Marie Curie Actions-COFUND 291803), by National Funds through the FCT - Fundação para a Ciência e a Tecnologia (Portuguese Foundation for Science and Technology) within project ENIAC/2224/2009 and by ENIAC Joint Undertaking under grant agreement number 120224. Part of this work was carried out while the second author was visiting École Normale Supérieure supported by FCT grant SFRH/BSAB/1246/2012.

We are grateful to Benjamin Grégroire, Santiago Zanella-Béguelin and David Pointcheval for early discussions on the OAEP proof and its EasyCrypt formalization.

7. REFERENCES

[1] Reynald Affeldt, David Nowak, and Kiyoshi Yamada. Certifying assembly with formal security proofs: The case of BBS. *Sci. Comput. Program.*, 77(10-11):1058–1074, 2012.

[2] Johan Agat. Transforming out timing leaks. In *Proceedings of POPL'00*, pages 40–53, 2000.

[3] Johan Agat and David Sands. On confidentiality and algorithms. In *IEEE Symposium on Security and Privacy*, pages 64–77. IEEE Computer Society, 2001.

[4] Mihhail Aizatulin, Andrew D. Gordon, and Jan Jürjens. Computational verification of C protocol implementations by symbolic execution. In *ACM Conference on Computer and Communications Security*, pages 712–723. ACM, 2012.

[5] José Bacelar Almeida, Manuel Barbosa, Jorge Sousa Pinto, and Bárbara Vieira. Deductive verification of cryptographic software. *Innovations in Systems and Software Engineering*, 6(3):203–218, 2010.

[6] Joël Alwen, Yevgeniy Dodis, and Daniel Wichs. Survey: Leakage resilience and the bounded retrieval model. In Kaoru Kurosawa, editor, *ICITS*, volume 5973 of *Lecture Notes in Computer Science*, pages 1–18. Springer, 2009.

[7] Andrew W. Appel. Verified software toolchain - (invited talk). In *ESOP'11*, volume 6602 of *Lecture*

Notes in Computer Science, pages 1–17. Springer, 2011.

[8] Manuel Barbosa, editor. *Deliverable 5.4: Certified shared library core.* Computer Aided Cryptography Engineering (CACE FP7 EU Project), 2011. `http://www.cace-project.eu`.

[9] Gilles Barthe, Benjamin Grégoire, Sylvain Heraud, and Santiago Zanella-Béguelin. Computer-aided security proofs for the working cryptographer. In *Advances in Cryptology – CRYPTO 2011*, volume 6841 of *Lecture Notes in Computer Science*, pages 71–90, Heidelberg, 2011. Springer.

[10] Gilles Barthe, Benjamin Grégoire, Yassine Lakhnech, and Santiago Zanella-Béguelin. Beyond provable security. Verifiable IND-CCA security of OAEP. In *Topics in Cryptology – CT-RSA 2011*, volume 6558 of *Lecture Notes in Computer Science*, pages 180–196, Heidelberg, 2011. Springer.

[11] Daniel J. Bernstein, Tanja Lange, and Peter Schwabe. The security impact of a new cryptographic library. In Alejandro Hevia and Gregory Neven, editors, *Progress in Cryptology - LATINCRYPT 2012*, volume 7533 of *Lecture Notes in Computer Science*, pages 159–176. Springer Berlin Heidelberg, 2012.

[12] Yves Bertot, Nicolas Magaud, and Paul Zimmermann. A proof of GMP square root. *Journal of Automated Reasoning*, 29(3-4):225–252, 2002.

[13] Bruno Blanchet. Security protocol verification: Symbolic and computational models. In Pierpaolo Degano and Joshua D. Guttman, editors, *Principles of Security and Trust - First International Conference, POST 2012*, volume 7215 of *Lecture Notes in Computer Science*, pages 3–29. Springer, 2012.

[14] Sylvie Boldo, Jacques-Henri Jourdan, Xavier Leroy, and Guillaume Melquiond. A formally-verified C compiler supporting floating-point arithmetic. In *Arith 21st IEEE Symposium on Computer Arithmetic*, pages 107–115. IEEE, 2013.

[15] Billy Bob Brumley, Manuel Barbosa, Dan Page, and Frederik Vercauteren. Practical realisation and elimination of an ECC-related software bug attack. In Orr Dunkelman, editor, *CT-RSA*, volume 7178 of *Lecture Notes in Computer Science*, pages 171–186. Springer, 2012.

[16] David Cadé and Bruno Blanchet. Proved generation of implementations from computationally secure protocol specifications. In *POST*, volume 7796 of *Lecture Notes in Computer Science*, pages 63–82. Springer, 2013.

[17] Jean Paul Degabriele, Kenneth Paterson, and Gaven Watson. Provable security in the real world. *Security Privacy, IEEE*, 9(3):33–41, may-june 2011.

[18] François Dupressoir. *Proving Cryptographic C Programs Secure with General-Purpose Verification Tools.* PhD thesis, Open University, 2013.

[19] Stefan Dziembowski and Krzysztof Pietrzak. Leakage-resilient cryptography. In *49th Annual IEEE Symposium on Foundations of Computer Science, FOCS 2008*, pages 293–302, Washington, 2008. IEEE Computer Society.

[20] Cédric Fournet, Markulf Kohlweiss, and Pierre-Yves Strub. Modular code-based cryptographic verification. In *ACM Conference on Computer and Communications Security*, pages 341–350. ACM, 2011.

[21] Eiichiro Fujisaki, Tatsuaki Okamoto, David Pointcheval, and Jacques Stern. RSA-OAEP is secure under the RSA assumption. In *Advances in Cryptology – CRYPTO 2001*, volume 2139 of *Lecture Notes in Computer Science*, pages 260–274. Springer, 2001.

[22] Shafi Goldwasser and Silvio Micali. Probabilistic encryption. *J. Comput. Syst. Sci.*, 28(2):270–299, 1984.

[23] Boris Köpf, Laurent Mauborgne, and Martín Ochoa. Automatic quantification of cache side-channels. In *Proc. 24th International Conference on Computer Aided Verification (CAV '12)*, pages 564–580. Springer, 2012.

[24] Ralf Küsters, Tomasz Truderung, and Juergen Graf. A framework for the cryptographic verification of Java-like programs. In *CSF*, pages 198–212. IEEE, 2012.

[25] Xavier Leroy. Formal certification of a compiler back-end, or: programming a compiler with a proof assistant. In *33rd ACM SIGPLAN-SIGACT Symposium on Principles of Programming Languages, POPL 2006*, pages 42–54, New York, 2006. ACM.

[26] Xavier Leroy, editor. *The CompCert C verified compiler: Documentation and user's manual.* INRIA Paris-Rocquencourt, 2013.

[27] James Manger. A chosen ciphertext attack on RSA optimal asymmetric encryption padding (OAEP) as standardized in PKCS#1 v2.0. In *Advances in Cryptology – CRYPTO 2001*, volume 2139 of *Lecture Notes in Computer Science*, pages 230–238, Heidelberg, 2001. Springer.

[28] David Molnar, Matt Piotrowski, David Schultz, and David Wagner. The program counter security model: Automatic detection and removal of control-flow side channel attacks. In *ICISC*, volume 3935 of *Lecture Notes in Computer Science*, pages 156–168. Springer, 2005.

[29] Lee Pike, Mark Shields, and John Matthews. A verifying core for a cryptographic language compiler. In *ACL2*, pages 1–10. ACM, 2006.

[30] Phillip Rogaway. Practice-oriented provable security and the social construction of cryptography. Unpublished essay, 2009.

[31] Sabine (formerly Fischer) Schmaltz. Formal verification of a big integer library including division. Master's thesis, Saarland University, 2007.

[32] Eric Whitman Smith and David L. Dill. Automatic formal verification of block cipher implementations. In *FMCAD*, pages 1–7. IEEE, 2008.

[33] Falko Strenzke. Manger's attack revisited. In Miguel Soriano, Sihan Qing, and Javier López, editors, *Information and Communications Security*, volume 6476 of *Lecture Notes in Computer Science*, pages 31–45. Springer Berlin Heidelberg, 2010.

[34] Danfeng Zhang, Aslan Askarov, and Andrew C. Myers. Language-based control and mitigation of timing channels. In *ACM SIGPLAN Conference on Programming Language Design and Implementation (PLDI '12)*, pages 99–110. ACM, 2012.

Computationally Complete Symbolic Attacker and Key Exchange

Gergei Bana*
INRIA, Paris, France
bana@math.upenn.edu

Koji Hasebe†
Graduate School of Systems and Information Engineering, University of Tsukuba
Tsukuba, Japan
hasebe@iit.tsukuba.ac.jp

Mitsuhiro Okada‡
Department of Philosophy, Keio University, Tokyo, Japan
mitsu@abelard.flet.keio.ac.jp

ABSTRACT

Recently, Bana and Comon-Lundh [7] introduced the notion of computationally complete symbolic attacker to deliver unconditional computational soundness to symbolic protocol verification. First we explain the relationship between their technique and Fitting's embedding of classical logic into S4 [23]. Then, based on predicates for "key usability", we provide an axiomatic system in their framework to handle secure encryption when keys are allowed to be sent. We examine both IND-CCA2 and KDM-CCA2 encryptions, both symmetric and asymmetric situations. For unforgeability, we consider INT-CTXT encryptions. This technique does not require the usual limitations of computational soundness such as the absence of dynamic corruption, the absence of key-cycles or unambiguous parsing of bit strings. In particular, if a key-cycle possibly corrupts CCA2 encryption, our technique delivers an attack. If it does not endanger security, the security proof goes through. We illustrate how our notions can be applied in protocol proofs.

Categories and Subject Descriptors

C.2.2 [**Computer Communication Networks**]: Network Protocols –Protocol Verification

---

*Partially supported by the ANR project ProSe ANR-2010-VERS-004-01 and FCT project ComFormCrypt PTDC/EIA-CCO/113033/2009. The work completed while this author was at MSR-INRIA.

†Partially supported by JSPS KAKENHI Grant Number 24700022

‡Partially supported by Grant-in-Aid for Scientific Research (MEXT-JSPS) #23120002 and #30224025, as well as by Program for the Strategic Research Foundation (MEXT-Shigaku Zaidan)

CCS'13, November 4–8, 2013, Berlin, Germany.

http://dx.doi.org/10.1145/2508859.2516710

Keywords

Security Protocols; Computational Soundness

1. INTRODUCTION

Approaches to computationally sound automated verification of security protocols can be divided into two groups. Works in one [3, 20, 4, 17, 24] define *symbolic adversaries*, and soundness theorems state that under certain circumstances, if there is no successful symbolic attack, then there is no successful computational attack either. The other group aims to work directly in the computational model [21, 14, 9, 10, 8]. In this latter case, computational soundness means that the properties on which symbolic manipulations are conditioned hold computationally.

The first group, where a symbolic attacker is defined, gives hope that already existing automated tools may be adopted for computationally sound verification, but these soundness theorems require large sets of assumptions. A number of assumptions, as well as reasons why they are not realistic are discussed in [18]. Such assumptions are, for example, that bit strings can be unambiguously parsed into symbolic terms, or, that no key cycles occur, or, that all keys are honestly generated, or, that there is no dynamic corruption. Recently, Backes et al. in [2] showed a way to avoid some of these problems such as key-cycles and badly generated keys, but for the computational implementation of the encryption, they needed to require a very strong notion called PROG-KDM security. Moreover, they still used an entire page to list all the further necessary conditions (such as unambiguous parsing) limiting the computational implementation that they needed for soundness. But PROG-KDM security and the other conditions are necessary only to receive computational guarantees for their symbolic analysis even if computational security of the analyzed protocol holds without these requirements. *Their strong conditions are imposed on the computational implementation not for the security of the protocol, but for the soundness of the analysis.*

Recently, Bana and Comon-Lundh (BC) presented in [7] a new kind of symbolic attacker. They called it *computationally complete symbolic adversary*, as it is capable of doing everything that a computational adversary is capable of. They observed that the discrepancy between symbolic and computational proofs emerges from the following fact: While the usual computational security assumptions on the primitives (such as IND-CCA2 security of the encryption) define what the adversary cannot violate (and the security of the protocol is derived from the security of the primitives), symbolic adversaries are defined by listing all the adversarial capabilities (Dolev-Yao rules). Hence, to adjust the viewpoint of the symbolic analysis to that of the computational, instead of listing every kind of moves a symbolic adversary is allowed to do, Bana and Comon-Lundh list a few rules (axioms) that the symbolic adversary is not allowed to violate. Anything that does not contradict these axioms is allowed for the adversary. Hence, a successful symbolic attack in their case means that the violation of the security property of the protocol is consistent with the axioms. The axioms that are introduced must be computationally sound with respect to the computational interpretation they defined. Their *general soundness* result is the following: *Suppose that the computational implementation satisfies a set of axioms. If there is a successful PPT attacker for which the number of sessions it exploits does not increase indefinitely as the security parameter increases (there is a bound, but it can be arbitrarily high), then there is also a successful symbolic adversary complying with the set of axioms.*

The difference between the original Dolev-Yao (DY) technique and that of BC can be best understood from the following pictures. In the DY technique, as more and more rules are added, the symbolic adversarial capabilities are increasing, the symbolic adversary covers more and more of the computational capabilities. However, no-one has been able to come up with rules that properly cover all possible computational capabilities. As Figure 1 shows, there are always some computational capabilities that are not covered by the DY ones. All computational soundness results that use the DY

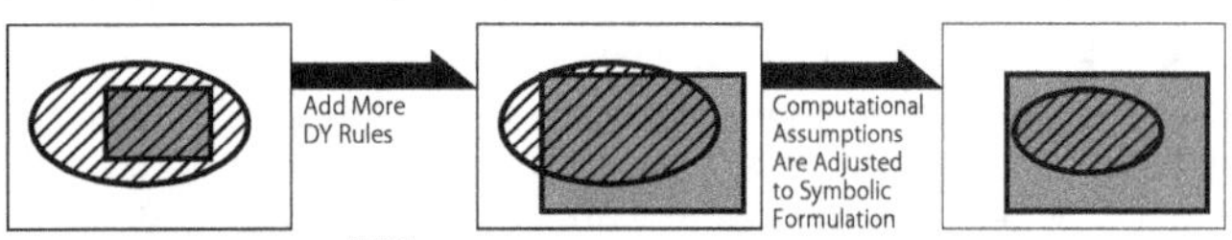

Figure 1

symbolic adversaries in the end have to impose some significant limitations on the computational implementation.

In the BC approach, without axioms, the symbolic adversary is allowed to do anything. As axioms are added, the symbolic adversary's capabilities are decreasing. Their main theorem is that if the

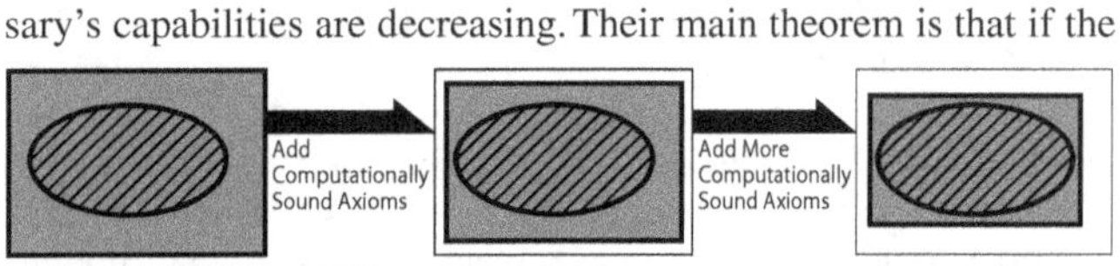

Figure 2

axioms are computationally sound, the symbolic adversarial capabilities cover all of the computational adversarial capabilities that use bounded number of sessions. This is illustrated in Figure 2. Clearly, if the symbolic adversary is too strong, security of protocols cannot be proven. Therefore, the aim is to create a *library of axioms* that are sound and are sufficient to prove actual protocols.

In [5], Bana et al. introduced several modular, computationally sound axioms, and verified secrecy and authentication of the Needham-Schroeder-Lowe protocol to illustrate that the technique can indeed be used to verify actual protocols. However, as Backes et al. have pointed out in [2], the axioms in [5] were not suitable when decryption keys were sent around in the course of the protocol (under encryptions for example, in a key distribution). The current work aims to address this problem.

Before we describe this current work in detail, it is worth asking ourselves, does it really make sense to develop a new technique when such tools as CryptoVerif and EasyCrypt exist? However, EasyCrypt at its current stage is more for proving properties about primitives, such as CCA2 security from hardness assumptions; it is not suitable for more complex protocols. CryptoVerif is a very powerful tool for protocol analysis, but if it fails to prove a protocol, other than its developer, it is difficult for a user to know what to do. The aim of the BC technique is to construct a relatively simple, intuitive system. If we remove the explanations, the axioms in this paper are just a few lines, perhaps half a page, and most of them are trivial. The BC technique is still lightweight compared to CryptoVerif or EasyCrypt. BC does not use explicit probabilities, neither game reductions. Proofs are readable to human, convenient for human interaction if automated. NSL and the and the symmetric Needham-Schroeder protocols were proven by hand, without any assumption on parsing unambiguity. Available other proofs of the NSL protocol including the one with CryptoVerif all assume unambiguous parsing. The NSL proof with this technique reduces to 2-3 pages with unambiguous parsing. For an initial decidability result, see Comon et al. [19].

1.1 Our Work

In this paper we tackle the problem of key exchange, but along the way we also present various other improvements on the original work of Bana and Comon-Lundh. In their original work [7], the general soundness theorem worked only for certain kinds of first-order formulas, and the non-negligible subsets of the computational execution had to satisfy a certain computability property. Later, in the online version of their paper [6] they presented improved computational semantics for the disjunction and existential quantification, and with that they could make the general soundness proof work for any first-order formula. But they still needed the computability condition on the non-negligible subsets (not an important limitation though, but not pretty). In this work, we remove this limitation with a trick in the soundness proof.

Bana and Comon-Lundh proved their general soundness theorem directly from their definitions. This involved showing that although computational semantics of their compound formulas are not defined as usual in Tarskian semantics, first-order deduction rules and axioms are valid with respect to their semantics too. As it turns out, this actually follows from Fitting's theorem of embedding first-order logic into first-order S4 [23]. After introducing the basics, we detail this relationship in the current work, and show how the BC general soundness theorem follows from Fitting's theorem.

In order to tackle key exchange, the necessary element to incorporate in the framework is *key usability*, an idea introduced in [22] for a different framework. This notion is meant to express whether a properly generated key, at a certain point of the protocol execution, is still usable for secure encryption or whether it has been compromised. If a decryption key (or just a key in the symmetric case) is sent in the clear, the encryption key associated to it cannot be used for secure encryption any more. Or, a key that was sent in a key cycle, may also have lost its capability to encrypt securely if the encryption scheme is only IND-CCA2 secure. More generally, keys can also be compromised in more subtle, non-trace fashion.

For overall consistency of notation, instead of key usability we introduce the opposite, namely *key compromise* as a predicate. We define key compromise predicates both for symmetric and asymmetric encryptions, both for IND-CCA2 [12] and KDM-CCA2 [1, 15] cases, and also for INT-CTXT [13] unforgeability. There is an essential difference from the way key usability was defined in [22], we explain that at our definition. (Furthermore, the axioms in [22] were introduced to work for the Diffie-Hellmann key exchange, they are not helpful with other protocols.)

Further essential innovations of this paper are predicates representing adversarial derivability (computability) with oracle access. This makes the axioms simpler than just using derivability as in [5]. Depending on whether IND-CCA2 or KDM-CCA2 oracles are used, and on whether the encryption is symmetric or asymmetric, we define four such derivability with oracle access predicates.

We introduce axioms and show that they are computationally sound. The axioms are suitable for (but not limited to) inductive reasoning: if something is uncompromised up-to a point, then certain newly sent messages do not destroy this property. They are also entirely *modular*: *Introducing further primitives will not destroy the soundness of these axioms, they do not have to be proved again.* If we want to prove a protocol that uses further primitives such as signatures besides encryption, then we only have to introduce new axioms for the new primitives. For encryption, the current axioms can still be used unchanged. Hence, a library of axioms can be gradually developed by adding more and more axioms.

A nice feature of our new predicates for key usability and derivability with oracles is that we only have a single axiom requiring CCA2 security of the encryption: the axiom stating that fresh keys are uncompromised (with respect to CCA2 security). The rest of the axioms, such as the one expressing that encryption with uncompromised key hides the plaintext, or the one expressing non-malleability are immediate consequences of the computational semantics of the derivability and key-compromise predicates.

We emphasize that we introduce axioms for KDM-CCA2 security to be able to analyze protocols for which KDM security is computationally necessary: Unlike [2], in our case, for those protocols that do not require KDM security for their computational soundness, the use of our IND-CCA2 axioms is sufficient.

After presenting the axioms and their soundness proofs, we look at three simple examples in Section 11 to illustrate how the axioms work with special focus on comparing how the IND-CCA2 and the KDM-CCA2 axioms are applied to key cycles. We show security in a case when there are no key cycles, then we present a case when there is a key cycle and the IND-CCA2 axioms provide an attack while KDM-CCA2 axioms still prove security. Finally we show a case when there is a key cycle, but as it is under another encryption it does not danger security even in the IND-CCA2 case and the security proof goes through. We also show that the axioms in [5] without key compromise are not sufficient to treat these examples.

Finally, we present the result of our proof of the Amended Symmetric Needham-Schroeder Protocol. This protocol first distributes a session key, and then uses the distributed key to share a secret. Using the IND-CCA2 and INT-CTXT axioms, we proved that the key is securely distributed, that the shared nonce remains secret, and that agreement and authentication hold. It is posted online at the first author's homepage.

The technique of [7] and also this work allows to avoid *all* restrictions mentioned before on the computational world. *Once a protocol is proven secure in our symbolic model with respect to a set of axioms, then all properties that the computational implementation has to satisfy for computational security are included in the axioms.* Any number of bad keys are allowed to be generated by the adversary; any number of corrupted, uncorrupted, or dynamically corrupted parties can be present. As for parsing of bit strings into terms, previous soundness results relied on unambiguous parsing. Within this framework, there is no need for such an assumption. We do not even need the condition that encryptions, pairing are length regular (i.e. encryption, pairing of inputs that have the same length output bit strings of the same length).

As long as indistinguishability properties are not concerned, the only significant restriction remains that the technique is not capable to detect computational attacks for which the PPT attacker needs the number of sessions to grow indefinitely as the security parameter increases. (It is the general soundness theorem that requires bounded number of sessions, not the axioms.) However, the usual Dolev-Yao technique is not capable of doing this either. (ProVerif for example is unbounded only in the sense that it works for arbitrary number of sessions, but still, if an attack is found, that, and the corresponding computational attack uses a given number of sessions independently of the security parameter.) Nevertheless, it would still be nice to have conditions under which the absence of successful symbolic BC adversaries means that there are no computational attacks even if unbounded number of sessions are allowed. For example, if only CCA2 encryptions and pairings are used to construct messages, we believe that this statement holds. Analysis of this is left for future work.

The contributions of this paper include (i) relating the BC technique to Fitting's embedding, (ii) syntax and computational semantics of key compromise and derivability with oracle access, (iii) a library of axioms for symmetric and asymmetric IND-CCA2 and KDM-CCA2 encryptions and INT-CTXT encryptions as well, (iv) soundness result of the axioms, (v) short examples to illustrate how the axioms are used with an emphasis on key-cycles, (vi) summary of the verification of the symmetric Needham-Schroeder protocol with this tool as a proof of concept. (The NSL proof in [5] can also be done with the current set of axioms the same way as it was done there, with minor modifications only.)

The paper is organized as follows: In Section 2, we give the intuitive description of our new predicates. In Section 3, we present our first-order language, which is an extension of that of BC. We then summarize in Sections 4 and 5 how Bana and Comon treated the symbolic and computational executions in [7], define computational semantics, and present the general soundness theorem. In Section 6, we show how the BC technique is related to Fitting's embedding of classical logic in S4, and show how the general soundness result of Bana and Comon-Lundh follows from Fitting's theorem. Section 7 is devoted to the semantics of the new derivability predicates with oracles and their axioms, and Section 8 is the same for key usability. In Section 9 we discuss congruence of the equality predicate. In Section 10 we state and prove our soundness theorem for the axioms. In Section 11, we show a few simple examples of how inconsistency of certain formulas with the axioms can be proven. Finally, in Section 12, we state the result of the verification of the amended symmetric NS protocol with our tool.

We thank Pedro Adão, Bruno Blanchet, Rohit Chadha and Hubert Comon for helpful suggestions and valuable discussions.

2. DERIVABILITY, KEY COMPROMISE

The most important new aspect of the symbolic execution in [7] was to replace the DY technique's fixed definition of what the symbolic adversary can deduce, $x_1, ..., x_n \vdash y$, with a *derivability predicate*[1] $x_1, ..., x_n \rhd y$ for which the symbolic semantics is not fixed. Namely, while in the DY technique, $x_1, ..., x_n \vdash y$ meant that using only the DY rules y can be computed from $x_1, ..., x_n$, in the BC case $x_1, ..., x_n \rhd y$ is given some unfixed symbolic interpretation in an abstract model $\mathcal{M}$ for which they only require to satisfy some (computationally sound) axioms. That is, the axioms express what the symbolic adversary cannot violate. They do imply that from DY deducibility, satisfaction of the derivability predicate follows, for example, $\{y\}_K, K \rhd y$. But in the BC system these rules are not what the adversary can at most do, but what it can certainly at least do (in other words, the adversary is not allowed to be unable to do it). The idea is that symbolic interpretation of $x_1, ..., x_n \rhd y$

[1]Note, that in [7] Bana and Comon-Lundh denoted this predicate as $x_1, ..., x_n \vdash y$ although $\vdash$ is usually reserved for denoting deducibility in a proof system. We find that somewhat confusing, so we use the notation $x_1, ..., x_n \rhd y$ to emphasize that we do not mean some specific deducibility by it, it is a predicate.

should be at least as powerful as computability of y from $x_1, ..., x_n$ by some probabilistic polynomial time algorithm, and so the only limitations that we want to put on symbolic satisfaction of $\rhd$ are limitations that are derived from computational computability.

One of the major innovations we propose here is that axioms become simpler if we allow the use of some oracles for the adversary. For example, considering IND-CCA2 public key encryption, it is better to introduce a new derivability predicate, $x_1, ..., x_n \rhd^{\text{aic2}} y$ with the computational semantics meaning that the interpretation of y can be derived from the interpretation of $x_1, ..., x_n$ by a PPT adversary with the help of decryption oracles that decrypt everything that are not results of encryptions on the left hand side. Similarly, for the symmetric case, we can introduce $x_1, ..., x_n \rhd^{\text{sic2}} y$ meaning that y can be derived from $x_1, ..., x_n$ with the help of decryption oracles and encryption oracles. That is, the algorithm trying to compute y from the $x_1, ..., x_n$ is allowed to submit strings to the oracles for encryption and also for decryption. The decryption oracle decrypts as long as the submitted string is not an encryption from $x_1, ..., x_n$ or an encryption produced by the encryption oracle. The encryption oracles here are needed, because the adversary cannot himself do encryptions (he does not know the key), and for this reason the IND-CCA2 definition for symmetric encryption allows the submission to the encryption oracle multiple times. In fact, for uniformity, we allow it for the public case too, as IND-CCA2 is equivalent for the case of multiple submissions to encryption oracles [11]. Similarly, we will also define derivation with oracle accessibility for KDM-CCA2 encryptions, which is somewhat more tricky. But encryption oracles using which keys? The answer is, keys honestly generated by the agents during the execution. We will use the notation $\rhd^{\mathfrak{O}}$ for such derivability with $\mathfrak{O}$ being either aic2, sic2, akc2, skc2 or nothing, depending on whether we want asymmetric or symmetric IND-CCA2 oracles, or asymmetric or symmetric KDM-CCA2 oracles, or no oracles. ($\mathfrak{O}$ is Fraktur O.)

Our next innovation is key usability for the case when keys are sent around. More precisely, to match the notation of derivability, we consider *key compromise*, which is the negation of key usability. We use the notation $x_1, ..., x_n \blacktriangleright^{\mathfrak{O}} K$, where $\mathfrak{O}$ again indexes whether we are talking about IND-CCA2, KDM-CCA2, symmetric or asymmetric encryption (there is always some oracle here). The intuitive meaning is that if $x_1, ..., x_n$ are given to the adversary with access to the given oracles, then K becomes compromised, encryption with K is not secure against the adversary any more. For example, $K, x_2 \blacktriangleright^{\mathfrak{O}} K$. Or, $\{K\}_{K'}, K' \blacktriangleright^{\mathfrak{O}} K$. Or, if $x_1, ..., x_n \rhd^{\mathfrak{O}} K$, then $x_1, ..., x_n \blacktriangleright^{\mathfrak{O}} K$. But, presumably, if x_1 is just the first half of K, then $x_1 \blacktriangleright^{\mathfrak{O}} K$ may still hold, while $x_1 \rhd^{\mathfrak{O}} K$ does not. That is, while $x_1, ..., x_n \rhd^{\mathfrak{O}} K$ clearly implies $x_1, ..., x_n \blacktriangleright^{\mathfrak{O}} K$, the other way is not necessarily true. Nevertheless the two properties, as we will see, behave very similarly, so we chose similar notation for them. We also consider key usability for INT-CTXT *unforgeability*.

3. LANGUAGE

The core of the framework used in this paper was introduced by Bana and Comon-Lundh in [7]. Along with our new innovations, we present a brief summary of the original system of Bana and Comon-Lundh as well.

3.1 Terms, Predicates, Formulas

Terms are built out of a set of function symbols $\mathcal{F}$ that contains an unbounded set of names $\mathcal{N}$ and an unbounded set of handles $\mathcal{H}$. Names and handles are constants (zero-arity function symbols). We use names to denote items honestly generated by agents, while handles denote inputs of the adversary. Let $\mathcal{X}$ be an unbounded set of variables. A ground term is without variables.

Let $\mathcal{P}$ be a set of predicate symbols over terms. We assume here that $\mathcal{P}$ contains the binary predicate $=$ and is used as $t_1 = t_2$ and the following families of of $(n+1)$-ary predicates meaning various sorts of derivability:

- $t_1, ..., t_n \rhd_n t$ for derivability of the rhs from the lhs
- $t_1, ..., t_n \rhd_n^{\text{aic2}} t$ for derivability of the rhs from the lhs with access to IND-CCA2 oracles in asymmetric case
- $t_1, ..., t_n \rhd_n^{\text{sic2}} t$ for derivability of the rhs from the lhs with access to IND-CCA2 oracles in symmetric case
- $t_1, ..., t_n \rhd_n^{\text{akc2}} t$ for derivability of the rhs from the lhs with access to KDM-CCA2 oracles in asymmetric case
- $t_1, ..., t_n \rhd_n^{\text{skc2}} t$ for derivability of the rhs from the lhs with access to KDM-CCA2 oracles in symmetric case

and the following *key compromise* predicates:

- $t_1, ..., t_n \blacktriangleright_n^{\text{aic2}} K$ meaning the lhs compromises (with oracle access) secure asymmetric IND-CCA2 encryption with K
- $t_1, ..., t_n \blacktriangleright_n^{\text{sic2}} K$ meaning the lhs compromises (with oracle access) secure symmetric IND-CCA2 encryption with K
- $t_1, ..., t_n \blacktriangleright_n^{\text{akc2}} K$ meaning the lhs compromises (with oracle access) secure asymmetric KDM-CCA2 encryption with K
- $t_1, ..., t_n \blacktriangleright_n^{\text{skc2}} K$ meaning the lhs compromises (with oracle access) secure symmetric KDM-CCA2 encryption with K
- $t_1, ..., t_n \blacktriangleright_n^{\text{ic}} K$ meaning the lhs compromises (with oracle access) INT-CTXT unforgeability of encryptions with K.

We always drop the index n: $t_1, ..., t_n \rhd^{\mathfrak{O}} t$ and $t_1, ..., t_n \blacktriangleright^{\mathfrak{O}} K$.

4. SYMBOLIC EXECUTION

In case of the Dolev-Yao adversary, derivability predicates would have fixed interpretations. For example, $\rhd$ holds in case of a DY adversary, if the right-hand side can be computed from the left-hand side with the DY rules. However, *for the symbolic execution, the BC technique allows any interpretation of the predicates (including =) that does not contradict some axioms (introduced later).*

Accordingly, let $\mathcal{M}$ be any first-order structure that interprets the function and predicate symbols of the logic. We denote by $D_{\mathcal{M}}$ the domain of interpretation, and by $\rhd^{\mathfrak{O}}{}_{\mathcal{M}}$, $\blacktriangleright^{\mathfrak{O}}_{\mathcal{M}}$ and $=_{\mathcal{M}}$ the relations on $D_{\mathcal{M}}$ interpreting $\rhd^{\mathfrak{O}}$, $\blacktriangleright^{\mathfrak{O}}$, and $=$ respectively. Given an assignment σ of elements in $D_{\mathcal{M}}$ to the free variables of term t, we write $[\![t]\!]^{\sigma}_{\mathcal{M}}$ for the interpretation of $t\sigma$ in $\mathcal{M}$ ($[\![\_]\!]^{\sigma}_{\mathcal{M}}$ is the unique extension of σ into a homomorphism of $\mathcal{F}$-algebras). For any first-order formula θ, for any first-order structure $\mathcal{M}$ over the functions $\mathcal{F}$ and predicates $\mathcal{P}$, and any assignment σ of the free variables of θ in the domain of $\mathcal{M}$, the satisfaction relation $\mathcal{M}, \sigma \models \theta$ is defined as usual in first-order logic from the satisfaction of predicates.

4.1 Protocols

Bana and Comon-Lundh set up their technique to be convenient for constraint-solving methods as in [16].

Let Q be a set of *control states* (not necessarily finite). A *protocol* is a recursive set of tuples

$$((q, \overline{n}), (q', \overline{n}, \overline{n'}), \langle x_1, ..., x_m\rangle, x, \psi, s)$$

where $q, q' \in Q$, $x_1, ..., x_m, x$ are variables (into which agents read messages from the adversary), $\overline{n}, \overline{n'}$ are disjoint finite sequences of names (corresponding to honestly generated items such as keys, nonces). ψ is some formula corresponding to agent checks on incoming messages. For example, ψ can be a formula such as

$dec(x,k) = n$, checking whether the input decrypts to a previously generated nonce n. ψ is over the variables $\{x_1,...,x_m,x\}$, the names $\overline{n}$, the function symbols $\mathcal{F}$ without the rest of the names and handles, and some subset of the predicate symbols $\mathcal{P}$. Finally, s is the output message, when the transition succeeds. s is built from the variables $\{x_1,...,x_m,x\}$, the names $\overline{n},\overline{n}'$, and the function symbols $\mathcal{F}$ without the rest of the names and handles.

4.2 Execution of a Protocol and Attacks

In applied π-calculus, *frames* are sequences of terms with name binders: a frame ϕ can be written $\nu\overline{n}.\langle p_1 \mapsto t_1,...,p_n \mapsto t_n\rangle$ where $p_1,...p_n$ are place holders that do not occur in $t_1,...,t_n$ and $\overline{n}$ is a sequence of names, but we think of a frame simply as a list of terms $\langle t_1,...,t_n\rangle$ representing the messages that agents have sent over the network, that is, messages that the adversary has seen. The *names*, *variables* of ϕ are the names, variables of $t_1,...,t_n$.

A *symbolic state* of the network consists of:

- a control state $q \in Q$ together with a sequence of names (randomly) generated so far, $n_1,...,n_k$
- a sequence of constants called *handles* $h_1,...,h_n$ (recording the attacker's inputs)
- a ground frame ϕ (the agents outputs)
- a set of closed formulas Θ (all conditions that must be satisfied in order to reach the state).

A *symbolic transition sequence* of a protocol Π is a sequence

$$((q_0,\overline{n_0}),\emptyset,\phi_0,\emptyset) \to ... \to ((q_m,\overline{n_m}),\langle h_1,...,h_m\rangle,\phi_m,\Theta_m)$$

if, for every $m-1 \geq i \geq 0$, there is a transition rule

$$((q_i,\overline{\alpha_i}),(q_{i+1},\overline{\alpha_{i+1}}),\langle x_1,...,x_i\rangle,x,\psi,s)$$

such that $\overline{n} = \overline{\alpha_{i+1}} \setminus \overline{\alpha_i}$, $\phi_{i+1} = (\phi_i, s\sigma_{i+1})$, $\overline{n_{i+1}} = (\overline{n_i},\overline{n})$, $\Theta_{i+1} = \Theta_i \cup \{\phi_i \rhd h_{i+1}, \psi\sigma_{i+1}\}$ where $\sigma_{i+1} = \{x_1 \mapsto h_1,..., x_i \mapsto h_i, x \mapsto h_{i+1}\}$. If necessary, some renaming of the sequence $\overline{\alpha_{i+1}}$ ensures the freshness of the names $\overline{n}$: $\overline{n} \cap \overline{n_i} = \emptyset$.

Given an interpretation $\mathcal{M}$, a transition sequence of Π

$$((q_0,\overline{n_0}),\emptyset,\phi_0,\emptyset) \to ... \to ((q_m,\overline{n_m}),\langle h_1,...,h_m\rangle,\phi_m,\Theta_m)$$

is *valid w.r.t.* $\mathcal{M}$ if, for every $m-1 \geq i \geq 0$, $\mathcal{M} \models \Theta_{i+1}$.

Examples of symbolic executions can be found in [7] and [5].

4.3 Symbolic Satisfaction of Formulas

$\mathcal{M}$ modeled, among others, the predicate $t_1,...,t_n \rhd t$. In *executions* we also consider a predicate that we write as $\hat{\phi}, t_1,...,t_n \rhd t$. This is also an $n+1$-arity predicate. $\hat{\phi}$ is just a symbol, not an argument, and it represents the frame containing the messages that protocol agents sent out, that is, the information available from the protocol to the adversary. We also use a number of different *constraints*: $\mathsf{Handle}(h)$ means h is a handle, $\mathsf{RanGen}(x)$ means that x was honestly, randomly generated (i.e. appears in the $\overline{n}$ of the control state); $x \sqsubseteq \hat{\phi}$ means that x is a subterm of a message sent out by an agent (i.e. listed in the frame ϕ), $x \sqsubseteq \vec{x}$ means x is subterm of $\vec{x}$. $dK \sqsubseteq_d \hat{\phi}$ means dK occurs somewhere other than in a decryption position $dec(\ ,dK)$ in ϕ, and $dK \sqsubseteq_d \vec{x}$ is analogous (dK may also occur in a decryption position in $\vec{x}$, but it has to occur elsewhere too)[2]. Similarly, let $K \sqsubseteq_{ed} \hat{\phi}$ mean that symmetric key K occurs somewhere other than in an encryption or decryption position (as $\{\!|\_|\!\}_K$ or $sdec(\ ,K)$) in ϕ, and $K \sqsubseteq_{ed} \vec{x}$ is analogous (K may also occur in encryption or decryption position in $\vec{x}$, but it has to occur elsewhere too). Let us introduce the following abbreviations:

- $x \sqsubseteq \hat{\phi},\vec{x} \;\equiv\; x \sqsubseteq \hat{\phi} \vee x \sqsubseteq \vec{x}$
- $\mathsf{fresh}(x;\hat{\phi},\vec{x}) \;\equiv\; \mathsf{RanGen}(x) \wedge x \not\sqsubseteq \hat{\phi},\vec{x}$
- $\mathsf{keyfresh}(K;\hat{\phi},\vec{x})$ for asymmetric key:
  $\mathsf{keyfresh}(K;\hat{\phi},\vec{x}) \;\equiv\; \mathsf{RanGen}(K) \wedge dK \not\sqsubseteq_d \hat{\phi},\vec{x}$
- $\mathsf{keyfresh}(K;\hat{\phi},\vec{x})$ for symmetric key:
  $\mathsf{keyfresh}(K;\hat{\phi},\vec{x}) \;\equiv\; \mathsf{RanGen}(K) \wedge K \not\sqsubseteq_{ed} \hat{\phi},\vec{x}$
- $x \preccurlyeq \hat{\phi},\vec{x} \;\equiv\; \forall h(h \sqsubseteq x \wedge \mathsf{Handle}(h) \to \hat{\phi},\vec{x} \rhd h)$
  $\vec{x} \preccurlyeq \hat{\phi},\vec{y} \;\equiv\; \bigvee_p (x_{p1} \preccurlyeq \hat{\phi},\vec{y} \wedge x_{p2} \preccurlyeq \hat{\phi},\vec{y},x_{p1} \wedge ... \wedge x_{pn} \preccurlyeq \hat{\phi},\vec{y},x_{p1},...,x_{p_{n-1}})$

Where p runs through all permutations of $1,...,n$. Further, for symmetric encryption we also require for $x \preccurlyeq \hat{\phi},\vec{x}$ that if any R is a random input of an encryption in $\hat{\phi},\vec{x},x$ then the only way it can appear in x is within that same encryption.

If $\mathcal{M}$ is a first-order model, satisfaction of predicates and constraints in a *symbolic* execution (denoted by $\overset{s}{\models}$) is defined recursively: Let $\overline{n} = (n_1,...,n_k)$ be a list of names and $\phi = \langle t_1,...,t_m\rangle$ a list of closed terms. Let σ be a substitution of free variables of the rhs of $\overset{s}{\models}$ with elements in the domain of $\mathcal{M}$.

- Satisfactions of predicates by $\mathcal{M},\sigma,\overline{n},\phi$ (depends on $\mathcal{M}$):
  - $\mathcal{M},\sigma,\overline{n},\phi \overset{s}{\models} t = t'$ if $\mathcal{M},\sigma \models t = t'$
  - $\mathcal{M},\sigma,\overline{n},\phi \overset{s}{\models} \hat{\phi},s_1,...,s_n \rhd^{\mathcal{O}} t$ if $\mathcal{M},\sigma \models t_1,...,t_m,s_1,...,s_n \rhd^{\mathcal{O}} t$.
  - $\mathcal{M},\sigma,\overline{n},\phi \overset{s}{\models} \hat{\phi},s_1,...,s_n \blacktriangleright^{\mathcal{O}} t$ if $\mathcal{M},\sigma \models t_1,...,t_m,s_1,...,s_n \blacktriangleright^{\mathcal{O}} t$.
- Satisfactions of constraints by $\mathcal{M},\sigma,\overline{n},\phi$ are independent of $\mathcal{M}$ and σ so we define them as satisfaction by $\overline{n},\phi$:
  - $\mathsf{Handle}(h)$ for h closed term:
    $\overline{n},\phi \overset{s}{\models} \mathsf{Handle}(h)$ if $h \in \mathcal{H}$.
  - $\mathsf{RanGen}(s)$ for s closed term:
    $\overline{n},\phi \overset{s}{\models} \mathsf{RanGen}(s)$ if $s \in \mathcal{N}$ and $\mathcal{M},\sigma \models s = n_1 \vee ... \vee s = n_k$.
  - $t \sqsubseteq \hat{\phi}$, where t is closed term:
    $\overline{n},\phi \overset{s}{\models} t \sqsubseteq \hat{\phi}$ if t is a subterm of some t_i
  - $t \sqsubseteq s_1,...,s_n$, where $s_1,...,s_n,t$ are closed terms:
    $\overline{n},\phi \overset{s}{\models} t \sqsubseteq s_1,...,s_n$ if t is a subterm of some s_i
- Satisfaction of any FOL formula by $\mathcal{M},\sigma,\overline{n},\phi$:
  - $\theta_1 \wedge \theta_2$, $\theta_1 \vee \theta_2$, and $\neg\theta$ are interpreted as usual in FOL.
  - If x is not under a constraint in θ, interpretations of $\forall x\theta$ and $\exists x\theta$ are defined as usual in FOL.
  - If x occurs under a constraint in θ, then
    - $\mathcal{M},\sigma,\overline{n},\phi \overset{s}{\models} \forall x\theta$ iff for every ground term t, $\mathcal{M},\sigma,\overline{n},\phi \overset{s}{\models} \theta\{x \mapsto t\}$
    - $\mathcal{M},\sigma,\overline{n},\phi \overset{s}{\models} \exists x\theta$ iff there is a ground term t, $\mathcal{M},\sigma,\overline{n},\phi \overset{s}{\models} \theta\{x \mapsto t\}$
- Satisfaction at step m:
  $\mathcal{M},\sigma,((q,\overline{n}),\langle h_1,...,h_m\rangle,\phi_m,\Theta) \overset{s}{\models} \theta$ iff $\mathcal{M},\sigma,\overline{n},\phi_m \overset{s}{\models} \theta$.

We say there is a *successful symbolic attack* against the security property θ (a first-order formula) of the protocol if there is a model $\mathcal{M}$ and state of an execution $((q,\overline{n}),\langle h_1,...,h_m\rangle,\phi_m,\Theta)$ such that $\mathcal{M},((q,\overline{n}),\langle h_1,...,h_m\rangle,\phi_m,\Theta) \overset{s}{\models} \neg\theta$ holds, and moreover, $\mathcal{M},((q,\overline{n}),\langle h_1,...,h_m\rangle,\phi_m,\Theta)$ also satisfies the computationally sound axioms that we introduce in the rest of the paper. This

[2]In this paper, we will use the notation $\{x\}^R_{eK}$ and $dec(y,dK)$ for both symmetric and asymmetric encryptions with random input R, where in the symmetric case, $eK = dK = K$. We use $\{\!|x|\!\}^R_K$ and $sdec(y,K)$ for symmetric encryption and decryption only.

is the same as saying that there is a successful symbolic attack if at a certain point of some symbolic execution, the axioms, the agent checks and the negation of the security property are all consistent.

5. COMPUTATIONAL EXECUTION

We now summarize the computational semantics. Short proofs of Theorems 5.2 and 5.3 are in the Section 6 using Fitting's embedding of classical logic into S4 [23].

5.1 Computational Execution

Following Bana and Comon, we consider a family of computational algebras, parametrized by a security parameter η, in which each function symbol is interpreted as a polynomially computable function on bit strings (that may return an error message). Given a sample τ of names, every ground term t can be interpreted as a bit string $[\![t]\!]_\tau$ in such a way that $[\![\_]\!]_\tau$ is a homomorphism of $\mathcal{F}$-algebras (a name n is interpreted as a bit string $\tau(n)$). More generally, if σ is an assignment of the variables of t to bit strings, $[\![t]\!]_\tau^\sigma$ is the (unique) extension of τ (on names) and σ (on variables) as a homomorphism of $\mathcal{F}$-algebras.

Given a set of transition rules, a *computational state* consists of

- a symbolic state s (that is itself a tuple $((q,\overline{n}),\overline{h},\phi,\Theta)$)
- a sequence of bit strings $\langle b_1,...,b_m\rangle$ (attacker outputs)
- a sequence $\langle b'_1,...,b'_m\rangle$ of bit strings (agents' outputs)
- the configuration γ of the attacker.

Given a PPT interactive Turing machine $\mathcal{M}^c$ and a sample τ, a sequence of transitions

$$(s_0,\emptyset,\vec{b'_0},\gamma_0) \to ... \to (s_m,\langle b_1,...,b_m\rangle,\langle b'_1,...,b'_m\rangle,\gamma_m)$$

is *(computationally) valid with respect to $\mathcal{M}^c$ and τ* if

- $s_0 \to \cdots \to s_m$ is a transition sequence of the protocol
- for all $i = 0,...,m-1$, $s_i = ((q_i,\overline{n_i}),\overline{h_i},\phi_i,\Theta_i)$, $\phi_{i+1} = (\phi_i,u_i)$, $[\![u_i]\!]_\tau = b'_{i+1}$
- for every $i = 0,...,m-1$, there is a configuration γ'_i of the machine $\mathcal{M}^c$ such that $\gamma_i \vdash_M^* \gamma'_i \vdash_M^* \gamma_{i+1}$ and γ'_i is in a sending state, the sending tape containing b_{i+1}, γ_{i+1} is in a receiving state, the receiving tape containing b'_{i+1}
- for all $i=0,...,m-1$, the bit strings τ, $\{h_1\mapsto b_1,...,h_{i+1}\mapsto b_{i+1}\}$ satisfy all agent checks listed in Θ_{i+1}.

Here $\vdash_M^*$ means what the machine (in whatever model it is defined) can compute via a sequence of computational steps.

5.2 Computational satisfaction of formulas

We recall the computational interpretation of the original predicates, $=$ and $\rhd$ here and the semantics of compound formulas. The difference between our presentation here and that of [6] is that we do not assume any computability condition on non-negligible sets any more, as we apply a trick in the soundness proof that makes it unnecessary. Interpretations of the new predicates are presented in later sections.

Let (Ω_0,Σ_0,p_0) be the probability space of infinite fair coin tosses, Ω_0 the the set of infinite bit strings, Σ_0 the measurable sets generated by fixing finitely many outcomes, and p_0 the probability measure assigning the probabilities to the sets of Σ_0. For a finite bit string $b\in\{0,1\}^*$ of length n, let $\bar{b}\subset\Omega_0$ denote the set of infinite bit strings for which the initial n bits are exactly b. Let Σ_f be the set generated by finite unions intersections, and subtractions of sets of the form $\bar{b}$ (including Ω). Σ_0 is the σ-closure of Σ_f.

Let $\mathcal{M}^c$ be an interactive PPT Turing machine with a special challenge control state q_{ch}. We may regard this machine as an attacker, who moves to the state q_{ch} when he thinks that he is ready to break the security property. As usual, the machine takes the security parameter 1^η as an initial input. $\mathcal{M}^c$ interacts with the protocol agents, which are also assumed to be interactive PPT Turing machines, and they respond to the calls of the adversary. Since once η is fixed, such an execution is probabilistic, and for each security parameter η, we denote underlying probability space by $(\Omega^\eta,\Sigma^\eta,p^\eta)$, which is just a copy of the (Ω_0,Σ_0,p_0) above. We denote the elements of Ω^η by ω^η. (Actually, the adversary's random string and the agent random strings are separate, but as there are finitely many of them, they can be thought to be on a single string) Each ω^η is one particular random string. Let $\Omega=(\Omega^\eta)_{\eta\in\mathbb{N}}$. Let $\tau(\omega^\eta)$ be the assignment of all fixed bit string evaluations $\tau(\overline{n})$ of names given for ω^η. For a given n name, we just use simply $n(\omega^\eta)$ for the bit string $\tau(\omega^\eta)(n)$.

By a *non-negligible set of coins S*, we mean $S=(S^\eta)_{\eta\in\mathbb{N}}$, where for all $\eta\in\mathbb{N}$, $S^\eta\in\Sigma_f^\eta$, and $p^\eta(S^\eta)$ is non-negligible function of η. For $S_1=(S_1^\eta)_{\eta\in\mathbb{N}}$ and $S_2=(S_2^\eta)_{\eta\in\mathbb{N}}$ non-negligible sets of coins, we use the notation $S_1\subseteq S_2$ if for all $\eta\in\mathbb{N}$, $S_1^\eta\subseteq S_2^\eta$. In what follows, S is any such non-negligible set of coins. The domain of interpretation $\mathfrak{D}(S)=\mathfrak{D}$ is the same for all S: PPT algorithms that take as input η, read from the random tape ω^η, and output a bit string. (As ω^η is infinite coin tosses, the algorithms of course do not read it all, they terminate in polynomial time.)

We recall the interpretations of $=$ and $\rhd$ from [7]: Let σ be a sequence of PPT machines (e.g. one for each free variable x_i of θ): $\mathcal{A}_{x_1},...,\mathcal{A}_{x_n}\in\mathfrak{D}$. For example, and $\mathcal{A}_x$ can be the evaluation of any name (in which case $\mathcal{A}_x(\eta,\omega^\eta)=n(\omega^\eta)$), or any value for a handle computed by the adversary, or some more complex object. Let $\sigma(\omega^\eta)$ denote the assignments $x_1\mapsto\mathcal{A}_{x_1}(\eta,\omega^\eta),...,x_n\mapsto\mathcal{A}_{x_n}(\eta,\omega^\eta)$. If $st(\eta,\omega^\eta)$ is a statement, then for any fixed $S=(S^\eta)_{\eta\in\mathbb{N}}$, instead of "for all $\eta\in\mathbb{N}$ and all $\omega^\eta\in S^\eta, st(\eta,\omega^\eta)$", we simply write "for all $\omega\in S, st(\omega)$".

- For the equality predicate, $\mathcal{M}^c,\Pi,S,\sigma\models^{c} t_1=t_2$ iff there is a subset $S'\subseteq S$ such that $S\setminus S'$ is negligible, and for all $\omega\in S'$, $[\![t_1]\!]_{\tau(\omega)}^{\sigma(\omega)}=[\![t_2]\!]_{\tau(\omega)}^{\sigma(\omega)}$.
- For the derivability predicate, $\mathcal{M}^c,\Pi,S,\sigma\models^{c}\hat{\phi},t_1,...,t_n\rhd t$ if for all non-negligible $S'\subseteq S$, there is a non-negligible $S''\subseteq S'$ and a PPT Turing machine $\mathcal{A}$ such that for all $\omega\in S''$, $\mathcal{A}([\![\phi_{m(\omega)}]\!]_{\tau(\omega)}^{\sigma(\omega)},[\![t_1]\!]_{\tau(\omega)}^{\sigma(\omega)},...,[\![t_n]\!]_{\tau(\omega)}^{\sigma(\omega)},a(\omega),r(\omega))=[\![t]\!]_{\tau(\omega)}^{\sigma(\omega)}$ where $m(\omega)$ is the step at which $\mathcal{M}^c$ reached the challenge state, $a(\omega)$ stands for the protocol adversary's output and $r(\omega)$ is some fresh input from the random tape.
- If P is a constraint, $\vec{t}$ are closed terms then $\mathcal{M}^c,\Pi,S,\sigma\models P(\vec{t})$ iff there is $S'\subseteq S$ such that, $S\setminus S'$ is negligible, and for all $\omega\in S'$, the unique valid computation of Π with respect to $\mathcal{M}^c,\tau(\omega)$ yields a state $(((q,\overline{n}),\overline{h},\phi,\Theta),\overline{b},\overline{b'},\gamma)$ in the control state q_{ch} such that $\overline{n},\phi\models^{s} P(\vec{t})$.

About the fresh $r(\omega)$, note we assumed for any non-negligible set S that $S^\eta\subseteq\Sigma_f^\eta$ and not $S^\eta\subseteq\Sigma_0^\eta$, so there can always be fresh random bits generated inside S.

Satisfaction of compound formulas are defined the following way.

- $\mathcal{M}^c,\Pi,S,\sigma\models^{c}\theta_1\wedge\theta_2$ iff $\mathcal{M}^c,\Pi,S,\sigma\models^{c}\theta_1$ and $\mathcal{M}^c,\Pi,S,\sigma\models^{c}\theta_2$.
- $\mathcal{M}^c,\Pi,S,\sigma\models^{c}\theta_1\vee\theta_2$ iff for any $S'\subseteq S$ non-negligible, there is a $S''\subseteq S'$ non-negligible such that either $\mathcal{M}^c,\Pi,S'',\sigma\models^{c}\theta_1$ or $\mathcal{M}^c,\Pi,S'',\sigma\models^{c}\theta_2$.
- $\mathcal{M}^c,\Pi,S,\sigma\models^{c}\theta_1\to\theta_2$ iff for all $S'\subseteq S$ non-negligible, $\mathcal{M}^c,\Pi,S',\sigma\models^{c}\theta_1$ implies $\mathcal{M}^c,\Pi,S',\sigma\models^{c}\theta_2$
- $\mathcal{M}^c,\Pi,S,\sigma\models^{c}\neg\theta$ iff for all $S'\subseteq S$ non-negligible,

$\mathcal{M}^c, \Pi, S', \sigma \not\models^{c} \theta$

- $\mathcal{M}^c, \Pi, S, \sigma \models^{c} \exists x.\theta$ iff for any $S' \subseteq S$ non-negligible, there is a $S'' \subseteq S'$ non-negligible and a PT machine $\mathcal{A}_x$ such that $\mathcal{M}^c, \Pi, S'', \sigma, \mathcal{A}_x \models^{c} \theta$
- $\mathcal{M}^c, \Pi, S, \sigma \models^{c} \forall x.\theta$ iff for any probabilistic polynomial time machine $\mathcal{A}_x$, $\quad \mathcal{M}^c, \Pi, S, \sigma, \mathcal{A}_x \models^{c} \theta$
- If x is a constrained variable, the interpretation of $\exists x.\theta$ is analogous to the symbolic case: $\mathcal{M}, \Pi, S, \sigma \models^{c} \exists x.\theta$ if and only if for every non-negligible $S' \subseteq S$ there is a non-negligible $S'' \subseteq S'$ and a ground term t, such that the satisfaction $\mathcal{M}, \Pi, S'', \sigma \models^{c} \theta\{x \mapsto t\}$ holds.
- If x is a constrained variable, the interpretation of $\forall x.\theta$ is analogous to the symbolic case: $\mathcal{M}, \Pi, S, \sigma \models^{c} \forall x.\theta$ if and only if for every ground term t, the satisfaction $\mathcal{M}, \Pi, S, \sigma \models^{c} \theta\{x \mapsto t\}$ holds.

$\mathcal{M}^c, \Pi \models^{c} \theta$ iff $\mathcal{M}^c, \Pi, \Omega \models \theta$ and $\Pi \models^{c} \theta$ if $\mathcal{M}^c, \Pi \models^{c} \theta$ for every $\mathcal{M}^c$ and q_{ch}.

Given a protocol Π, we say that there is a *successful computational attack* against the security property θ (a first-order formula) of the protocol if there is a an attacker $\mathcal{M}^c$ and a non-negligible set of coins S such that $\mathcal{M}^c, \Pi, S \models^{c} \neg\theta$ (which is the same as $\Pi \not\models^{c} \theta$).

Despite that semantics of the compound formulas is not as usual in first-order logic, we prove in Section 6 that as a consequence of Fitting's embedding [23] of classical logic into S4, the following theorems hold.

THEOREM 5.1 (FITTING'S EMBEDDING). *With the above semantics, first-order deduction rules are sound.*

THEOREM 5.2 (TRACE MAPPING). *Let Π be a protocol, $s_1 \to \ldots \to s_m$ be a symbolic transition sequence of Π and $\mathcal{M}^c$ be a probabilistic polynomial time interactive Turing machine. If there is a non-negligible set of coins S such that, for any $\omega \in S$, there is a sequence of transitions $(s_0, \vec{b_0}, \vec{b'_0}, \gamma_0) \to \cdots \to (s_m, \vec{b_m}, \vec{b'_m}, \gamma_m)$ that is computationally valid w.r.t. $\mathcal{M}^c$, $\tau(\omega)$ and γ_m is in the challenge state q_{ch}, then for any set of FOL formulas Φ, $\mathcal{M}^c, \Pi, S \models^{c} \Phi$ implies there is a symbolic model $\mathcal{M}$ such that $s_0 \to \cdots \to s_m$ is a valid symbolic execution w.r.t. $\mathcal{M}$ and $\mathcal{M}, s_m \models^{s} \Phi$.*

THEOREM 5.3 (GENERAL SOUNDNESS). *If there is a successful computational attack such that the number of sessions of honest agents are bounded in the security parameter, then there is also a successful symbolic attack.*

5.3 Axioms for Equality and Derivability

We recall the core axioms presented in [5]. As usual, unquantified variables are universally quantified. Unless noted otherwise, they are always sound.

Equality is a Congruence:

- $x = x$, and the substitutability (congruence) property of equal terms holds for $=$ and $\rhd$.

Core Axioms for the Derivability Predicate:

- Self derivability: $\hat{\phi}, \vec{x}, x \rhd x$
- Increasing capabilities: $\hat{\phi}, \vec{x} \rhd y \longrightarrow \hat{\phi}, \vec{x}, x \rhd y$
- Commutativity: If $\vec{x}'$ is a permutation of $\vec{x}$, then $\hat{\phi}, \vec{x} \rhd y \longrightarrow \hat{\phi}, \vec{x}' \rhd y$
- Transitivity of derivability: $\hat{\phi}, \vec{x} \rhd \vec{y} \wedge \hat{\phi}, \vec{x}, \vec{y} \rhd \vec{z} \longrightarrow \hat{\phi}, \vec{x} \rhd \vec{z}$
- Functions are derivable: $\hat{\phi}, \vec{x} \rhd f(\vec{x})$
  This axiom is sound as long as functions are interpreted as PT computable algorithms.

Axioms for Freshly Generated Items:

- No telepathy: $\mathsf{fresh}(x; \hat{\phi}) \longrightarrow \hat{\phi} \not\rhd x$
  This axiom is sound as long as $\mathsf{RanGen}()$ items are generated so that they can only be guessed with negligible probability. A more general version is also possible as $\mathsf{fresh}(x; \hat{\phi}, \vec{x}) \wedge \vec{x} \preccurlyeq \hat{\phi} \longrightarrow \hat{\phi}, \vec{x} \not\rhd x$
- Fresh items do not help to compute: $\mathsf{fresh}(x; \hat{\phi}, \vec{x}, y) \wedge \vec{x}, y \preccurlyeq \hat{\phi} \wedge \hat{\phi}, \vec{x}, x \rhd y \longrightarrow \hat{\phi}, \vec{x} \rhd y$

Equations for the fixed function symbols: For example, for symmetric encryption $sdec(\{|x|\}_K^R, K) = x$, and for pairing, $\pi_1(\langle x, y \rangle) = x$; $\pi_2(\langle x, y \rangle) = y$. Function of error is error $f(\ldots, \perp, \ldots) = \perp$, etc.

6. THE FITTING CONNECTION

The trace mapping and the general soundness theorems for arbitrary first-order formulas were proven directly from their definitions by an elaborate argument in [6]. We have realized however, that they are rather easy consequences of Fitting's embedding of first-order logic into first-order S4 [23]. The non-Tarskian computational semantics of first-order formulas that naturally arouse in the BC technique turns out to be a special kind of Kripke semantics of first-order S4 composed with Fitting's embedding of FOL into first-order S4. We detail this connection here, and show how trace mapping and general soundness follow from Fitting's theorem. This section assumes basic familiarity with S4 modal logic and its first-order extension as well as Kripke semantics.

For any first-order formula θ, consider the Fitting transformation $\theta \mapsto \theta^*$, where θ^* is a formula of first-order S4, and is defined recursively as follows:

- For any atomic formula θ, let $\theta^* \equiv \Box\Diamond\theta$.
- $(\neg\theta)^* \equiv \Box\neg\theta^*$
- $(\theta_1 \to \theta_2)^* \equiv \Box(\theta_1^* \to \theta_2^*)$
- $(\theta_1 \wedge \theta_2)^* \equiv (\theta_1^* \wedge \theta_2^*)$
- $(\theta_1 \vee \theta_2)^* \equiv \Box\Diamond(\theta_1^* \vee \theta_2^*)$
- $(\forall x\theta)^* \equiv \forall x\theta^*$
- $(\exists x\theta)^* \equiv \Box\Diamond\exists x\theta^*$

Fitting in [23] put $\Box\Diamond$ everywhere and noted that it is redundant in front of the conjunction. It is also easy to check that if the Barcan formula and its converse ($\forall x\Box\theta \leftrightarrow \Box\forall x\theta$) are assumed (that is, when the domain does not change from possible world to possible world in the Kripke structure), then $\Box\Diamond$ is also redundant in front of the universal quantification (as $\theta^* \leftrightarrow \Box\Diamond\theta^*$ holds in our definitions for all θ). In our computational situation the domain is unchanged as we show below. So in this paper we assume the Barcan formula and its converse.

Fitting's theorem says that any formula θ is derivable in first-order logic if and only if θ^* it is derivable in S4 with the Barcan formulas. (Without the Barcan formulas, $(\forall x\theta)^* \equiv \Box\Diamond\forall x\theta^*$ has to be written above).

Observe that if we think of non-negligible sets as possible worlds, and the subset relation as accessibility (that is, if S' is accessible from S iff $S' \subseteq S$), then we can define a computational Kripke semantics: For our predicates, consider the S4 satisfaction relation $\mathcal{M}^c, \Pi, S, \sigma \models^{s4}$ that we define almost the same way as the BC computational satisfaction $\models^{c}$ of Section 5.2 is defined, except that we drop the "for all non-negligible $S' \subseteq S$, there is a non-negligible $S'' \subseteq S'$" phrase, and replace S'' with S in the remaining of the definition. For example, the satisfaction of derivability becomes:

- For the derivability predicate, $\mathcal{M}^c, \Pi, S, \sigma \models^{s4} \hat{\phi}, t_1, \ldots, t_n \rhd t$ if there is a PPT Turing machine $\mathcal{A}$ such that for all $\omega \in S$,

$\mathcal{A}([\![\phi_{m(\omega)}]\!]^{\sigma(\omega)}_{\tau(\omega)}, [\![t_1]\!]^{\sigma(\omega)}_{\tau(\omega)}, ..., [\![t_n]\!]^{\sigma(\omega)}_{\tau(\omega)}, a(\omega), r(\omega)) = [\![t]\!]^{\sigma(\omega)}_{\tau(\omega)}$ where $m(\omega)$ is the step at which $\mathcal{M}^c$ reached the challenge state, $a(\omega)$ stands for the protocol adversary's output and $r(\omega)$ is some fresh input from the random string.

For an arbitrary θ first-order S4 formula, $\mathcal{M}^c, \Pi, S, \sigma \models^{s4} \Box\theta$ is defined to hold if and only if $\mathcal{M}^c, \Pi, S', \sigma \models^{s4} \theta$ holds for all non-negligible $S' \subseteq S$, and $\mathcal{M}^c, \Pi, S, \sigma \models^{s4} \Diamond\theta$ is defined to hold if and only if $\mathcal{M}^c, \Pi, S', \sigma \models^{s4} \theta$ holds for some non-negligible $S' \subseteq S$. Taking θ to be $\hat{\phi}, t_1, ..., t_n \rhd t$, and applying $\Box\Diamond$ to the above definition of S4 satisfaction, we receive the computational satisfaction of Bana and Comon-Lundh. That is, $\mathcal{M}^c, \Pi, S, \sigma \models^{c} \hat{\phi}, t_1, ..., t_n \rhd t$ if and only if $\mathcal{M}^c, \Pi, S, \sigma \models^{s4} \Box\Diamond\hat{\phi}, t_1, ..., t_n \rhd t$.

Note also that for the equality predicate and for the constraints, "for all non-negligible $S' \subseteq S$, there is a non-negligible $S'' \subseteq S'$" can be freely inserted in the definition, as the resulting definition is equivalent with the original: for example, if for all non-negligible $S' \subseteq S$, there is a non-negligible $S'' \subseteq S'$ such that $[\![t_1]\!]^{\sigma(\omega)}_{\tau(\omega)} = [\![t_2]\!]^{\sigma(\omega)}_{\tau(\omega)}$ holds on S'', then it also holds up to negligible probability on S, because if there were a non-negligible subset $S' \subseteq S$ on which $[\![t_1]\!]^{\sigma(\omega)}_{\tau(\omega)} \neq [\![t_2]\!]^{\sigma(\omega)}_{\tau(\omega)}$ were true, then this S' would not have some non-negligible subset S'' on which they are equal, a contradiction. So BC could have defined satisfaction of equality as

- For the equality predicate, $\mathcal{M}^c, \Pi, S, \sigma \models^{c} t_1 = t_2$ iff for all non-negligible $S' \subseteq S$, there is a non-negligible subset $S'' \subseteq S'$ such that for all $\omega \in S''$, $[\![t_1]\!]^{\sigma(\omega)}_{\tau(\omega)} = [\![t_2]\!]^{\sigma(\omega)}_{\tau(\omega)}$.

That is, $\mathcal{M}^c, \Pi, S, \sigma \models^{c} t_1 = t_2$ iff $\mathcal{M}^c, \Pi, S, \sigma \models^{s4} \Box\Diamond t_1 = t_2$. The same is true for constraints. Hence we have this for all atomic formulas. $\models^{s4}$ for compound formulas is defined as usual in Kripke semantics. For example, $\mathcal{M}^c, \Pi, S, \sigma \models^{s4} \theta_1 \vee \theta_2$ if and only if $\mathcal{M}^c, \Pi, S, \sigma \models^{s4} \theta_1$ or $\mathcal{M}^c, \Pi, S, \sigma \models^{s4} \theta_2$.

Comparing the definition of $\models^{c}$ in Section 5.2 for compound formulas with Fitting's embedding, for any first-order formula θ,

$$\mathcal{M}^c, \Pi, S, \sigma \models^{c} \theta \iff \mathcal{M}^c, \Pi, S, \sigma \models^{s4} \theta^*.$$

For a set of first-order formulas Φ, let Φ^* mean the set that we get by applying the Fitting transformation to all formulas in Φ. Since with $\models^{s4}$, our computational semantics is a special kind of Kripke semantics, Fitting's theorem implies that if $\mathcal{M}^c, \Pi, S, \sigma \models^{s4} \Phi^*$ holds and if $\Phi \vdash^{FOL} \theta$, then $\mathcal{M}^c, \Pi, S, \sigma \models^{s4} \theta^*$. So we also have that if $\mathcal{M}^c, \Pi, S, \sigma \models^{c} \Phi$ holds and if $\Phi \vdash^{FOL} \theta$, then $\mathcal{M}^c, \Pi, S, \sigma \models^{c} \theta$. This is exactly Theorem 5.1.

The Barcan formula and its converse hold, as the domain $\mathfrak{D}$ does not depend on the non-negligible sets.

For Theorem 5.2, note that it is assumed in the theorem that for all $\omega \in S$ the computational execution has the same length m and the symbolic part of their traces, s_i agree. Remember that the symbolic states have the transition conditions Θ_i in them. So at the challenge state, we have $\mathcal{M}^c, \Pi, S \models^{c} \Theta_m \wedge \Phi$. Note that since on the traces, s_i agree, the terms that are in the frame also agree for all trace $\omega \in S$. Therefore, $\hat{\phi}$ in the formulas of θ_m and Φ can be replaced by the list of terms in the frames. Let θ'_m and Φ' denote the formulas we receive this way. Then, $\mathcal{M}^c, \Pi, S \models^{c} \Theta'_m \wedge \Phi'$. This is the same as $\mathcal{M}^c, \Pi, S \models^{s4} (\Theta'_m \wedge \Phi')^*$, that, by Fitting's theorem means that $\Theta'_m \wedge \Phi'$ is first-order satisfiable (because $(\Theta'_m \wedge \Phi')^*$ is S4 satisfiable). Hence there is a symbolic model $\mathcal{M}$ with $\mathcal{M} \models^{s} \Theta'_m \wedge \Phi'$. As Θ'_m and Φ' have no frames in them, it is easy to see from the symbolic satisfaction that $\mathcal{M}, s_m \models^{s} \Theta'_m \wedge \Phi'$ is also satisfied as satisfaction does not depend on the state. Finally, as in s_m, the frames contain exactly the terms with which we replaced $\hat{\phi}$, we can now write them back and receive $\mathcal{M}, s_m \models^{s} \Theta_m \wedge \Phi$. Which also means that Θ_m and Φ are first-order consistent.

Finally, for proving Theorem 5.3, consider the following. If there is a computational attack, that is, if the negation of the security formula θ_s is computationally satisfied by some $\mathcal{M}^c, \Pi, S$, then, as long as only bounded number (in the security parameter) of sessions are allowed, the maximum number of different (with respect to ω) symbolic transitions $s_1 \to \cdots \to s_m$ does not depend on the security parameter. Therefore, S can be split (up to negligible probability) into a fixed number of non-negligible subsets on each of which $s_1 \to \cdots \to s_m$ is independent of ω. Pick one, call it S'. Then $\mathcal{M}^c, \Pi, S'$ computationally satisfies $\neg\theta_s$ as well as all computationally sound axioms (denote the set by Φ_A), and Θ_m also: $\mathcal{M}^c, \Pi, S' \models^{c} \Theta_m \wedge \Phi_A \wedge \theta_s$. Hence, By Theorem 5.2 there is a symbolic model $\mathcal{M}$ such that $\mathcal{M}, s_m \models^{c} \Theta_m \wedge \Phi_A \wedge \theta_s$, which exactly means that there is a symbolic attack.

Note, although by Fitting's theorem, the first-order deduction rules are computationally sound, it is not possible in the current formulation to deduce security properties from the axioms only by first-order deduction rules and nothing else. The BC technique has no formulas expressing the transition system, no formulas saying the agents follow the protocol roles. Explicit time and some axiom for induction would also be needed as in [8]. These are taken care by the symbolic execution.

7. DERIVABILITY WITH ORACLES

Syntax of various types of derivability with oracles was introduced in Section 3. Here we define their computational semantics and list a number of axioms that are computational sound.

7.1 Computational Semantics of Derivability with Oracles

Let $\mathcal{O}^{\mathrm{sic2}}$ be the following oracle: It first takes a list of honestly generated keys $\mathcal{K}$ and some additional list $\mathcal{C}$ of ciphertexts. The oracle can be called for encryption by submitting a string to encrypt along with the encrypting key's place number in $\mathcal{K}$. The oracle honestly generates the desired encryption, returns the result and adds it to the list $\mathcal{C}$. The oracle can also be called for a decryption again with specifying the key and providing a ciphertext. If the ciphertext is not one of those in $\mathcal{C}$, the oracle outputs the decryption. Let $\mathcal{O}^{\mathrm{skc2}}$ take $\mathcal{K}$ and $\mathcal{C}$ as above, but also $\tau(\mathcal{L})$ assignment of bit strings to a finite set of name symbols $\mathcal{L}$. The oracle accepts descriptions of functions of the names $\mathcal{L}$, the ciphers $\mathcal{C}$ and the keys $\mathcal{K}$, into which he substitutes the corresponding bit strings, computes the function and then encrypts the result with the specified key and adds it to $\mathcal{C}$. Decryption works as for $\mathcal{O}^{\mathrm{sic2}}$. Let $\mathcal{O}^{\mathrm{aic2}}$ and $\mathcal{O}^{\mathrm{akc2}}$ be the analogous notions for public key encryption. PPT algorithms with oracle access will be written as $\mathcal{A}^{\mathcal{O}^{\mathfrak{O}}}$, $\mathcal{B}^{\mathcal{O}^{\mathfrak{O}}}$.

The meaning of the definition is that $\mathcal{M}^c, \Pi, S, \sigma \models^{s4} \hat{\phi}, \vec{x} \rhd^{\mathfrak{O}} x$ holds if there is a PPT algorithm $\mathcal{A}^{\mathcal{O}^{\mathfrak{O}}}$ that, for $\omega \in S$, receiving the bit strings $[\![\hat{\phi}, \vec{x}]\!]^{\sigma(\omega)}_{\tau(\omega)}$, it outputs the bit string $[\![x]\!]^{\sigma(\omega)}_{\tau(\omega)}$. In the computation $\mathcal{A}^{\mathcal{O}^{\mathfrak{O}}}$ can request encryption and decryption oracles corresponding to the honest keys, but it will only receive a decryption if the submitted bit string is not a bit string corresponding to an encryption in $\hat{\phi}, \vec{x}$ or a bit string received from the encryption oracle. Outside S, nothing is required.

DEFINITION 7.1. *Semantics of Derivability with Oracles: Let $\mathcal{M}^c, \Pi, S, \sigma$ be as before. Let $a(\omega^\eta)$ denote the protocol adversary output as it reaches the challenge state on the random input ω^η, and let $m(\omega^\eta)$ denote the number of moves till then. We write $\mathcal{M}^c, \Pi, S, \sigma \models^{s4} \hat{\phi}, \vec{x} \rhd^{\mathfrak{O}} x$ iff there is a PPT Turing machine $\mathcal{A}^{\mathcal{O}^{\mathfrak{O}}}$ such that for all $\omega \in S$,*

$$\mathcal{A}^{\mathcal{O}^{\mathfrak{O}}}\left([\![\phi_{m(\omega)}]\!]_{\tau(\omega)}^{\sigma(\omega)}, [\![\vec{x}]\!]_{\tau(\omega)}^{\sigma(\omega)}, a(\omega), r(\omega)\right) = [\![x]\!]_{\tau(\omega)}^{\sigma(\omega)}$$

where $r(\omega)$ is some fresh (not used for the computation of $\hat{\phi}, \vec{x}, x$) random input from the random string. On each ω, if the tuple $(((q, \overline{n}), \overline{h}, \phi, \Theta), \overline{b}, \overline{b'}, \gamma)$ denotes the state yielded by the unique valid computation of Π with respect to $\mathcal{M}^c$ and $\tau(\omega)$, then the oracles receive in $\mathcal{K}$ all keys (bit strings) corresponding to the keys in $\overline{n}$, and in $\mathcal{C}$ all strings of the form $[\![\{z\}_{eK}^R]\!]_{\tau(\omega)}^{\sigma(\omega)}$ with R and K names in $\overline{n}$, and $\overline{n}, \phi \models^{s} \{z\}_{eK}^R \sqsubseteq \hat{\phi}, \vec{x}$. In $\tau(\mathcal{L})$, the KDM oracles receive all assignments of names in $\overline{n}$ to bit strings, except (in the symmetric case), for those that occur as random inputs R to the encryptions in $\mathcal{C}$. We shorten this as

$$\mathcal{M}^c, \Pi, S, \sigma \models \mathcal{A}^{\mathcal{O}^{\mathfrak{O}}}(\hat{\phi}, \vec{x}) = x,$$

implicitly assuming the algorithm has access to the protocol adversary's knowledge and to random bits. Let

$$\mathcal{M}^c, \Pi, S, \sigma \models^{c} \hat{\phi}, \vec{x} \rhd^{\mathfrak{O}} x \quad \textit{iff} \quad \mathcal{M}^c, \Pi, S, \sigma \models^{s4} \Box\Diamond(\hat{\phi}, \vec{x} \rhd^{\mathfrak{O}} x).$$

In the KDM case, the submitted functions may depend on randomly generated items that differ from the secret keys but are not accessible to the protocol adversary. For example, it is allowed to depend on a secret nonce. This is necessary for receiving nice axioms for the KDM case, and we explain the reason at the axioms. Still, assuming the usual KDM security is enough to prove that an unsent key is uncompromised with such oracle access. The reason is that when a KDM attack is constructed from the protocol attack, the KDM attacker has access to the items generated by honest agents except for the secret keys and the random inputs to the encryptions.

7.2 Axioms for Derivability with Oracles

The following axioms (except for the second and last entry of the core axioms for derivability predicates) are very similar to the ones in Section 5.3, and are just as trivial. The second entry of the core axioms for derivability predicates with oracles is also trivially computationally sound.

Core Axioms for the Derivability Predicate with Oracles.

- Let $\mathsf{SameEnc}(\vec{x}; \vec{y})$ be the constraint that there is a one-to-one correspondence between the honest encryption terms of $\vec{x}$ and $\vec{y}$ such that the corresponding encryption terms are equal (with respect to the equality predicate). Then $\mathsf{SameEnc}(\vec{x}; \vec{y}) \wedge \vec{x}, x = \vec{y}, y \longrightarrow (\hat{\phi}, \vec{x} \rhd^{\mathfrak{O}} x \leftrightarrow \hat{\phi}, \vec{y} \rhd^{\mathfrak{O}} y)$.
- More oracles help more: If the oracles of $\mathfrak{O}$ are more powerful than the oracles of $\mathfrak{O}'$, then $\hat{\phi}, \vec{x} \rhd^{\mathfrak{O}'} x \longrightarrow \hat{\phi}, \vec{x} \rhd^{\mathfrak{O}} x$. In particular, $\hat{\phi}, \vec{x} \rhd x \longrightarrow \hat{\phi}, \vec{x} \rhd^{\mathfrak{O}} x$ and $\hat{\phi}, \vec{x} \rhd^{\mathrm{aic2}} x \rightarrow \hat{\phi}, \vec{x} \rhd^{\mathrm{akc2}} x$ and $\hat{\phi}, \vec{x} \rhd^{\mathrm{sic2}} x \rightarrow \hat{\phi}, \vec{x} \rhd^{\mathrm{skc2}} x$
- Increasing capabilities: $\hat{\phi}, \vec{x} \rhd^{\mathfrak{O}} y \longrightarrow \hat{\phi}, \vec{x}, x \rhd^{\mathfrak{O}} y$
- Commutativity: If $\vec{x}'$ is a permutation of $\vec{x}$, then $\hat{\phi}, \vec{x} \rhd^{\mathfrak{O}} y \longrightarrow \hat{\phi}, \vec{x}' \rhd^{\mathfrak{O}} y$
- Transitivity: $\hat{\phi}, \vec{x} \rhd^{\mathfrak{O}} \vec{y} \wedge \hat{\phi}, \vec{x}, \vec{y} \rhd^{\mathfrak{O}} \vec{z} \longrightarrow \hat{\phi}, \vec{x} \rhd^{\mathfrak{O}} \vec{z}$
- Decryption Oracles help:

$$\begin{aligned}&\mathsf{RanGen}(K) \wedge \hat{\phi}, \vec{x} \rhd^{\mathfrak{O}} y \\ &\wedge \forall x R(y = \{x\}_{eK}^R \rightarrow \{x\}_{eK}^R \not\sqsubseteq \hat{\phi}, \vec{x}) \\ &\longrightarrow \hat{\phi}, \vec{x} \rhd^{\mathfrak{O}} dec(y, dK).\end{aligned}$$

This expresses that if y is computable and is not an encryption in $\hat{\phi}, \vec{x}$, then $dec(y, dK)$ is also computable from the same items as the decryption oracle can be called. We do not have to require that y is none of the encryptions done by the oracles, because if they were, then the decryption is known to the submitter. Again, this follows purely from the definition of $\rhd^{\mathfrak{O}}$, CCA2 security of the encryption is not required. This axiom together with the transitivity axiom easily imply

$$\begin{aligned}&\mathsf{RanGen}(K) \wedge \hat{\phi}, \vec{x} \rhd^{\mathfrak{O}} y \wedge \hat{\phi}, \vec{x}, dec(y, dK) \rhd^{\mathfrak{O}} z \\ &\wedge \forall x R(y = \{x\}_{eK}^R \rightarrow \{x\}_{eK}^R \not\sqsubseteq \hat{\phi}, \vec{x}) \longrightarrow \hat{\phi}, \vec{x} \rhd^{\mathfrak{O}} z.\end{aligned}$$

This replaces the non-malleability axiom of [5] for the derivability predicate. With tiny modifications, it is possible to rewrite the NSL proof presented in [5] for using the $\rhd^{\mathfrak{O}}$ predicate and this simpler axiom instead of the $\rhd$ predicate with the non-malleability axiom there.

Axioms for Freshly Generated Items. These axioms are sound for the same reason as the corresponding ones for $\rhd$ were:

- No telepathy: $\mathsf{fresh}(x; \hat{\phi}, \vec{x}) \wedge \vec{x} \preccurlyeq \hat{\phi} \longrightarrow \hat{\phi}, \vec{x} \not\rhd^{\mathfrak{O}} x$ (implies no-telepathy axiom without oracles). This is sound as long as $\mathsf{RanGen}()$ means generation with negligible guessing probability only.
- Fresh items do not help to compute: $\mathsf{fresh}(x; \hat{\phi}, \vec{x}, y) \wedge \vec{x}, y \preccurlyeq \hat{\phi} \wedge \hat{\phi}, \vec{x}, x \rhd^{\mathfrak{O}} y \longrightarrow \hat{\phi}, \vec{x} \rhd^{\mathfrak{O}} y$

$\hat{\phi}, \vec{x}, x \rhd^{\mathfrak{O}} x$ is implied by the more oracles help more axiom and the self-derivability axiom of derivability predicate. Also, $\hat{\phi}, \vec{x} \rhd^{\mathfrak{O}} f(\vec{x})$.

8. KEY USABILITY

Syntax of various types of key usability was introduced in Section 3. Here we define their computational semantics and list a number of axioms that are computational sound.

8.1 IND-CCA2 and KDM-CCA2 cases

8.1.1 Semantics of IND-CCA2 Key Compromise

The idea of key usability is that a key has been uncompromised, that is, it can be used for safe encryption. To match the computability predicate, we define the negation of it, key compromise. The intuitive meaning of $\hat{\phi}, \vec{x} \blacktriangleright^{\mathfrak{O}} K$ is that $\hat{\phi}, \vec{x}$ compromises the key (with oracles) and it cannot be used for safe encryption any more.

The first thought here would be to define the compromise so that from $\hat{\phi}, \vec{x}$, an x can be computed such that the encryption of x and of $0^{|x|}$ are *computationally distinguishable*. However, the major difficulty here (and the major difference from [22]) is that we have to define our notion for any S. Computational distinguishability on an arbitrary set has no meaning: even in the usual CCA2 game with CCA2 secure encryption, there can be non-negligible sets of coins defined on which the CCA2 attacker returns 1 if the real bit string is encrypted, while 1 with probability 1/2 if the 0's are encrypted; it is very easy to find sets like this.

What we came up with is a notion of observational inequivalence: encryptions of x and $0^{|x|}$ have to be observationally inequivalent on S, where PPT algorithms with oracle access provide the contexts and equality on S provides the equivalence.

DEFINITION 8.1 (KEY COMPROMISE). *The define the relation $\mathcal{M}^c, \Pi, S, \sigma \models^{s4} \hat{\phi}, \vec{x} \blacktriangleright^{\mathfrak{O}} K$ to hold if either $\mathcal{M}^c, \Pi, S, \sigma \models^{s4} \vec{x} \not\preccurlyeq \hat{\phi} \vee \neg\mathsf{RanGen}(K)$, or there are R, PPT algorithms $\mathcal{A}_{21}^{\mathcal{O}^{\mathfrak{O}}}$, $\mathcal{A}_{22}^{\mathcal{O}^{\mathfrak{O}}}$, and $\mathcal{A}_1^{\mathcal{O}^{\mathfrak{O}}}$ (in the IND case) or x (in the KDM case) such that:*

In the the IND case

- *R is generated honestly, statistically independently of the interpretations of $\hat{\phi}$, $\vec{x}$, $\mathcal{A}_1^{\mathcal{O}^{\mathfrak{O}}}(\hat{\phi},\vec{x})$ and*
- *Either $\mathcal{M}^c,\Pi,S,\sigma \Vdash$*

$$\mathcal{A}_{21}^{\mathcal{O}^{\mathfrak{O}}}(\hat{\phi},\vec{x},\{\mathcal{A}_1^{\mathcal{O}^{\mathfrak{O}}}(\hat{\phi},\vec{x})\}_{eK}^{R}) = \mathcal{A}_{22}^{\mathcal{O}^{\mathfrak{O}}}(\hat{\phi},\vec{x},\{\mathcal{A}_1^{\mathcal{O}^{\mathfrak{O}}}(\hat{\phi},\vec{x})\}_{eK}^{R})$$

and for some (hence for all) R' fresh random input generated inside S, $\quad\mathcal{M}^c,\Pi,S,\sigma \Vdash$

$$\mathcal{A}_{21}^{\mathcal{O}^{\mathfrak{O}}}(\hat{\phi},\vec{x},\{0^{|\mathcal{A}_1^{\mathcal{O}^{\mathfrak{O}}}(\hat{\phi},\vec{x})|}\}_{eK}^{R'}) \neq \mathcal{A}_{22}^{\mathcal{O}^{\mathfrak{O}}}(\hat{\phi},\vec{x},\{0^{|\mathcal{A}_1^{\mathcal{O}^{\mathfrak{O}}}(\hat{\phi},\vec{x})|}\}_{eK}^{R'})$$

- *Or $\mathcal{M}^c,\Pi,S,\sigma \Vdash$*

$$\mathcal{A}_{21}^{\mathcal{O}^{\mathfrak{O}}}(\hat{\phi},\vec{x},\{\mathcal{A}_1^{\mathcal{O}^{\mathfrak{O}}}(\hat{\phi},\vec{x})\}_{eK}^{R}) \neq \mathcal{A}_{22}^{\mathcal{O}^{\mathfrak{O}}}(\hat{\phi},\vec{x},\{\mathcal{A}_1^{\mathcal{O}^{\mathfrak{O}}}(\hat{\phi},\vec{x})\}_{eK}^{R})$$

and for some (hence for all) R' fresh random input generated inside S, $\quad\mathcal{M}^c,\Pi,S,\sigma \Vdash$

$$\mathcal{A}_{21}^{\mathcal{O}^{\mathfrak{O}}}(\hat{\phi},\vec{x},\{0^{|\mathcal{A}_1^{\mathcal{O}^{\mathfrak{O}}}(\hat{\phi},\vec{x})|}\}_{eK}^{R'}) = \mathcal{A}_{22}^{\mathcal{O}^{\mathfrak{O}}}(\hat{\phi},\vec{x},\{0^{|\mathcal{A}_1^{\mathcal{O}^{\mathfrak{O}}}(\hat{\phi},\vec{x})|}\}_{eK}^{R'})$$

In the KDM case

- *R is generated honestly, statistically independently of the interpretations of $\hat{\phi}$, $\vec{x}$, x, and $\mathcal{M}^c,\Pi,S,\sigma \overset{c}{\models} x \preccurlyeq \hat{\phi},\vec{x}$ and*
- *Either $\mathcal{M}^c,\Pi,S,\sigma \Vdash$*

$$\mathcal{A}_{21}^{\mathcal{O}^{\mathfrak{O}}}(\hat{\phi},\vec{x},\{x\}_{eK}^{R}) = \mathcal{A}_{22}^{\mathcal{O}^{\mathfrak{O}}}(\hat{\phi},\vec{x},\{x\}_{eK}^{R})$$

and for some (hence for all) R' fresh random input generated inside S, $\quad\mathcal{M}^c,\Pi,S,\sigma \Vdash$

$$\mathcal{A}_{21}^{\mathcal{O}^{\mathfrak{O}}}(\hat{\phi},\vec{x},\{0^{|x|}\}_{eK}^{R'}) \neq \mathcal{A}_{22}^{\mathcal{O}^{\mathfrak{O}}}(\hat{\phi},\vec{x},\{0^{|x|}\}_{eK}^{R'})$$

- *Or $\mathcal{M}^c,\Pi,S,\sigma \Vdash$*

$$\mathcal{A}_{21}^{\mathcal{O}^{\mathfrak{O}}}(\hat{\phi},\vec{x},\{x\}_{eK}^{R}) \neq \mathcal{A}_{22}^{\mathcal{O}^{\mathfrak{O}}}(\hat{\phi},\vec{x},\{x\}_{eK}^{R})$$

and for some (hence for all) R' fresh random input generated inside S, $\quad\mathcal{M}^c,\Pi,S,\sigma \Vdash$

$$\mathcal{A}_{21}^{\mathcal{O}^{\mathfrak{O}}}(\hat{\phi},\vec{x},\{0^{|x|}\}_{eK}^{R'}) = \mathcal{A}_{22}^{\mathcal{O}^{\mathfrak{O}}}(\hat{\phi},\vec{x},\{0^{|x|}\}_{eK}^{R'})$$

Let $\mathcal{M}^c,\Pi,S,\sigma \overset{c}{\models} \hat{\phi},\vec{x} \blacktriangleright^{\mathfrak{O}} x$ iff $\mathcal{M}^c,\Pi,S,\sigma \overset{s4}{\models} \Box\Diamond(\hat{\phi},\vec{x} \blacktriangleright^{\mathfrak{O}} x)$.

Recall from Section 6 that $\Box\Diamond$ means "there is a non-negligible $S' \subseteq S$ such that for all S''..." Also note that as we required our non-negligible sets to be in Σ_f, it is always possible to toss fresh coins inside the non-negligible sets.

Note that while R does not have to be generated inside S, R' does. In particular, S may actually depend on R, which is essential for the usability of the axioms, because the non-negligible sets on which we need to apply the axioms may depend on values of an encryption, and hence values of R. On the other hand, S is not allowed to depend on R', which is essential for proving that a freshly generated key is not compromised.

Note, in the KDM case, x does not have to be computed from $\hat{\phi},\vec{x}$, it could be a secret nonce. This corresponds to the fact that in the semantics of $\rhd^{\mathfrak{O}}$in the KDM case (as we noted after the definition) we allowed the functions submitted to the oracles to depend on such items not known to the protocol adversary.

8.1.2 Axioms for CCA2 Key Compromise

We now present the axioms for key compromise. First the core axioms for which soundness does not need CCA2 security.

Core Axioms for the Key Compromise Predicate.

- Let $\mathsf{SameEnc}(\vec{x};\vec{y})$ be the constraint as before. Then $\mathsf{SameEnc}(\vec{x};\vec{y}) \wedge \vec{x},x = \vec{y},y \longrightarrow (\hat{\phi},\vec{x} \blacktriangleright^{\mathfrak{O}} x \leftrightarrow \hat{\phi},\vec{y} \blacktriangleright^{\mathfrak{O}} y)$.
- Derivability implies compromise: $\hat{\phi},\vec{x} \rhd^{\mathfrak{O}} K \longrightarrow \hat{\phi},\vec{x} \blacktriangleright^{\mathfrak{O}} K$
If K is computable for the adversary, then it is compromised. Note, this axiom and the self derivability axiom (from 7.2) imply that $\hat{\phi},\vec{x},K \blacktriangleright^{\mathfrak{O}} K$
- Increasing capabilities for key compromise:
$\hat{\phi},\vec{x} \blacktriangleright^{\mathfrak{O}} K \longrightarrow \hat{\phi},\vec{x},x \blacktriangleright^{\mathfrak{O}} K$
- Commutativity: If $\vec{x}'$ is a permutation of $\vec{x}$, then
$\hat{\phi},\vec{x} \blacktriangleright^{\mathfrak{O}} K \longrightarrow \hat{\phi},\vec{x}' \blacktriangleright^{\mathfrak{O}} K$
- Transitivity: $\hat{\phi},\vec{x} \rhd^{\mathfrak{O}} \vec{y} \wedge \hat{\phi},\vec{x},\vec{y} \blacktriangleright^{\mathfrak{O}} K \longrightarrow \hat{\phi},\vec{x} \blacktriangleright^{\mathfrak{O}} K$
The intuitive reason is very clear: $\vec{y}$ just contains extra information, that can be computed from $\hat{\phi},\vec{x}$, so it is not actually needed in the compromise. This, and the functions are derivable axiom imply $\hat{\phi},\vec{x},f(\vec{x}) \blacktriangleright^{\mathfrak{O}} K \longrightarrow \hat{\phi},\vec{x} \blacktriangleright^{\mathfrak{O}} K$. With the increasing capabilities axiom, we get $\hat{\phi},f(\vec{x}) \blacktriangleright^{\mathfrak{O}} K \longrightarrow \hat{\phi},\vec{x} \blacktriangleright^{\mathfrak{O}} K$. We refer to these as *function application*.
- Uncompromised keys securely encrypt:
  - If $\mathfrak{O}$ is either aic2 or sic2, then

$$\begin{aligned}&\mathsf{RanGen}(K) \wedge \mathsf{fresh}(R;\hat{\phi},\vec{x},x,y,K)\\ &\wedge\ \vec{x},x,y \preccurlyeq \hat{\phi} \wedge \hat{\phi},\vec{x},\{x\}_{eK}^{R} \rhd^{\mathfrak{O}} y\\ &\longrightarrow\ \hat{\phi},\vec{x},x \blacktriangleright^{\mathfrak{O}} K \vee \hat{\phi},\vec{x} \rhd^{\mathfrak{O}} y\end{aligned}$$

  This formula means that if the key is uncompromised, that is, $\hat{\phi},\vec{x},x \not\blacktriangleright^{\mathfrak{O}} K$, then $\{x\}_{eK}^{R}$ cannot help in deriving y. In other words, if it is possible to derive y with $\{x\}_{eK}^{R}$, then it is also possible to derive it without $\{x\}_{eK}^{R}$. The freshness and random generation conditions ensure that $\{x\}_{eK}^{R}$ is indeed a good encryption (e.g. $\{N\}_{eK}^{N}$ or $\{N\}_{eK}^{eK}$ are not good), and also that y cannot depend on $\{x\}_{eK}^{R}$ (e.g. $y = \{x\}_{eK}^{R}$ is not good). Moreover, $\vec{x},x,y \preccurlyeq \hat{\phi}$ ensures that handles in these terms are given values the adversary can compute (otherwise e.g. taken $x = h$, the handle h cannot be dK if dK was never sent, and it cannot be R either).
  This formula is completely analogous to the secrecy axiom in [5] but $dK \sqsubseteq \hat{\phi},\vec{x},x$ there is replaced now with $\hat{\phi},\vec{x},x \blacktriangleright^{\mathrm{aic2}} K$ as we can now allow dK to appear inside a secure encryption for example.
  - If $\mathfrak{O}$ is either akc2 or skc2, then

$$\begin{aligned}&\mathsf{RanGen}(K) \wedge \mathsf{fresh}(R;\hat{\phi},\vec{x},x,y,K)\\ &\wedge\ \vec{x},x,y \preccurlyeq \hat{\phi} \wedge \hat{\phi},\vec{x},\{x\}_{eK}^{R} \rhd^{\mathfrak{O}} y\\ &\longrightarrow\ \hat{\phi},\vec{x} \blacktriangleright^{\mathfrak{O}} K \vee \hat{\phi},\vec{x} \rhd^{\mathfrak{O}} y\end{aligned}$$

  The difference here from the axiom for IND-CCA2 security is that in $\hat{\phi},\vec{x} \blacktriangleright^{\mathfrak{O}} K$ now there is no x. This corresponds to the fact that the encrypted message x is allowed to contain the decryption key, or it may leak it somehow together with $\hat{\phi},\vec{x}$. For more, see Section 11.

It may be surprising however, that these core axioms *do not require any security of the encryption*. It is purely a consequence of the definition of key compromise and derivability predicates. (The axiom that requires CCA2 security is the fresh keys are uncompromised axiom later.)
Here we want to allow x to be any secret thing, such as a nonce, so only $x \preccurlyeq \hat{\phi}$ was assumed. That is why in the KDM definition of key compromise we needed to allow functions depending on such secret items to be submitted to the encryption oracles in the semantics of $\rhd^{\mathfrak{O}}$and $\blacktriangleright^{\mathfrak{O}}$.
- Encryptions with uncompromised keys do not compromise:

- IND-CCA2 case. If $\mathfrak{O}$ is either aic2 or sic2, then

$$\begin{aligned}&\mathsf{RanGen}(K)\wedge\mathsf{RanGen}(K')\wedge\mathsf{fresh}(R;\hat\phi,\vec x,x,K,K')\\&\quad\wedge\ \vec x,x\preccurlyeq\hat\phi\ \wedge\ \hat\phi,\vec x,\{x\}^R_{eK'}\blacktriangleright^{\mathfrak{O}}K\\&\quad\longrightarrow\ \hat\phi,\vec x,x\blacktriangleright^{\mathfrak{O}}K'\ \vee\ \hat\phi,\vec x\blacktriangleright^{\mathfrak{O}}K\end{aligned}$$

  That is, if $\hat\phi,\vec x,\{x\}^R_{eK'}$ compromised K, then either K is already compromised without $\{x\}^R_{eK'}$, or K' was already compromised by $\hat\phi,\vec x,x$. Note that this includes x, the encrypted term. This means that x itself (with $\hat\phi,\vec x$) should not compromise K' if we want $\{x\}^R_{eK'}$ to be safe. This is the generalization of that key cycles may compromise CCA2 encryption. In Section 11 we will see how this axiom deals with key cycles.
- KDM-CCA2 case. If $\mathfrak{O}$ is akc2 or skc2, then

$$\begin{aligned}&\mathsf{RanGen}(K)\wedge\mathsf{RanGen}(K')\wedge\mathsf{fresh}(R;\hat\phi,\vec x,x,K,K')\\&\quad\wedge\ \vec x,x\preccurlyeq\hat\phi\ \wedge\ \hat\phi,\vec x,\{x\}^R_{eK'}\blacktriangleright^{\mathfrak{O}}K\\&\quad\longrightarrow\ \hat\phi,\vec x\blacktriangleright^{\mathfrak{O}}K'\ \vee\ \hat\phi,\vec x\blacktriangleright^{\mathfrak{O}}K\end{aligned}$$

  This is basically the same as the previous one, except again that $\hat\phi,\vec x\blacktriangleright K'$ does not contain x.

Again, soundness of these axioms follow directly from the definition of key usability, and it does not depend on what encryption is used.
In the above formulas, K and K' could be allowed to encrypt different kinds of encryptions, not necessarily the same, we just did not want to overload our formulas.

- **Axioms for Freshly Generated Items.**
  - Fresh keys are not compromised: The intuition of this axiom is that if K is fresh, then it can be used for secure encryption: $\mathsf{keyfresh}(K;\hat\phi,\vec x)\wedge\vec x\preccurlyeq\hat\phi\ \longrightarrow\ \hat\phi,\vec x\not\blacktriangleright^{\mathfrak{O}}K$ This axiom is sound if the encryption for which K is generated is CCA2 secure. Depending on which $\mathfrak{O}$ is in the axiom, the encryption needs to have the corresponding level of security. *This is the only axiom where the security of the encryption is necessary.* The reader may wonder that proving the KDM case, what happens to the variables not known to the protocol adversary in the submitted functions as the standard KDM encryption oracle only fills in the gaps of keys, not other unknown items. However, in a KDM attack created by the failure of the axiom, the attacker simulates the protocol, and all honestly generated items except for the keys and random inputs to the encryptions in question are available to him.
  - Fresh items do not compromise: they were generated independently and as they have not been sent out, they have not had a chance to compromise other items: $\mathsf{fresh}(x;\hat\phi,\vec x,y)\wedge\vec x,y\preccurlyeq\hat\phi\wedge\hat\phi,\vec x,x\blacktriangleright^{\mathfrak{O}}y\rightarrow\hat\phi,\vec x\blacktriangleright^{\mathfrak{O}}y$

8.2 Unforgeability

8.2.1 Semantics of Unforgeability

DEFINITION 8.2. *We define INT-CTXT compromise as: We say that $\mathcal{M}^c,\Pi,S,\sigma\models^{s4}\hat\phi,\vec x\blacktriangleright^{\mathrm{ic}}K$, if and only if $\mathcal{M}^c,\Pi,S,\sigma\models^{s4}\vec x\not\preccurlyeq\hat\phi\vee\neg\mathsf{RanGen}(K)$, or there is a PPT algorithm $\mathcal{A}^{\mathcal{O}^{sic2}}$, with*

$$\mathcal{M}^c,\Pi,S,\sigma\models sdec(\mathcal{A}^{\mathcal{O}^{sic2}}(\hat\phi,\vec x),K)\neq\bot$$

And on S, the output of $\mathcal{A}^{\mathcal{O}^{sic2}}(\hat\phi,\vec x)$ is not equal any of the outputs of the encryption oracles, and it is not any of the bit strings corresponding to the honest encryptions in $\hat\phi,\vec x$. Let $\mathcal{M}^c,\Pi,S,\sigma\models^{c}\hat\phi,\vec x\blacktriangleright^{\mathrm{ic}}x$ iff $\mathcal{M}^c,\Pi,S,\sigma\models^{s4}\Box\Diamond(\hat\phi,\vec x\blacktriangleright^{\mathrm{ic}}x)$.

The reason for using oracle $\mathcal{O}^{\mathrm{sic2}}$ is that the definition of INT-CTXT security [13] allows the use of encryption and decryption oracles.

8.2.2 Axioms for Unforgeability Key Compromise

- Let $\mathsf{SameEnc}(\vec x;\vec y)$ be the constraint as before. Then $\mathsf{SameEnc}(\vec x;\vec y)\wedge\vec x,x=\vec y,y\longrightarrow(\hat\phi,\vec x\blacktriangleright^{\mathrm{ic}}x\leftrightarrow\hat\phi,\vec y\blacktriangleright^{\mathrm{ic}}y)$.
- Derivability implies compromise: $\hat\phi,\vec x\rhd K\longrightarrow\hat\phi,\vec x\blacktriangleright^{\mathrm{ic}}K$
- Increasing capabilities for key compromise: $\hat\phi,\vec x\blacktriangleright^{\mathrm{ic}}K\ \longrightarrow\ \hat\phi,\vec x,x\blacktriangleright^{\mathrm{ic}}K$
- Commutativity: If $\vec x'$ is a permutation of $\vec x$, then $\hat\phi,\vec x\blacktriangleright^{\mathrm{ic}}K\ \longrightarrow\ \hat\phi,\vec x'\blacktriangleright^{\mathrm{ic}}K$.
- Transitivity: $\hat\phi,\vec x\rhd\vec y\ \wedge\ \hat\phi,\vec x,\vec y\blacktriangleright^{\mathrm{ic}}K\ \longrightarrow\ \hat\phi,\vec x\blacktriangleright^{\mathrm{ic}}K$
- Encryption with uncompromised key cannot be faked:

$$\begin{aligned}&\mathsf{RanGen}(K)\ \wedge\ \hat\phi,\vec x\rhd y\ \wedge\ dec(y,dK)\neq\bot\\&\quad\wedge\ \forall xR(y=\{x\}^R_{eK}\rightarrow\{x\}^R_{eK}\not\sqsubseteq\hat\phi,\vec x)\ \longrightarrow\ \hat\phi,\vec x\blacktriangleright^{\mathrm{ic}}K\end{aligned}$$

  This means the adversary cannot compute a y which decrypts to something meaningful. This is exactly what we need from the INT-CTXT property, namely, that the encryption cannot be faked. Again, soundness of this axiom does not need INT-CTXT encryption, it is immediate from our semantics.

- Encryptions with uncompromised keys do not compromise:
  - For the IND case, we have

$$\begin{aligned}&\mathsf{RanGen}(K)\wedge\mathsf{RanGen}(K')\wedge\mathsf{fresh}(R;\hat\phi,\vec x,x,K,K')\\&\quad\wedge\ \vec x,x\preccurlyeq\hat\phi\ \wedge\ \hat\phi,\vec x,\{\!|x|\!\}^R_{K'}\blacktriangleright^{\mathrm{ic}}K\\&\quad\longrightarrow\ \hat\phi,\vec x,x\blacktriangleright^{\mathrm{sic2}}K'\ \vee\ \hat\phi,\vec x\blacktriangleright^{\mathrm{ic}}K\end{aligned}$$

  - For the KDM case, we have

$$\begin{aligned}&\mathsf{RanGen}(K)\wedge\mathsf{RanGen}(K')\wedge\mathsf{fresh}(R;\hat\phi,\vec x,x,K,K')\\&\quad\wedge\ \vec x,x\preccurlyeq\hat\phi\ \wedge\ \hat\phi,\vec x,\{\!|x|\!\}^R_{K'}\blacktriangleright^{\mathrm{ic}}K\\&\quad\longrightarrow\ \hat\phi,\vec x\blacktriangleright^{\mathrm{skc2}}K'\ \vee\ \hat\phi,\vec x\blacktriangleright^{\mathrm{ic}}K\end{aligned}$$

  Soundness of these follow from the compromise definitions.
- Fresh keys are not INT-CTXT compromised if encryption is INT-CTXT secure:
  - $\mathsf{keyfresh}(K;\hat\phi)\ \longrightarrow\ \hat\phi\not\blacktriangleright^{\mathrm{ic}}K$. The intuition of this axiom is that if the encryption is INT-CTXT secure and if K is fresh, then the adversary cannot fake encryptions with this key.
- Fresh items do not compromise: $\mathsf{fresh}(x;\hat\phi,\vec x,K)\ \wedge\ \vec x\preccurlyeq\hat\phi\ \wedge\ \hat\phi,\vec x,x\blacktriangleright^{\mathrm{ic}}K\ \longrightarrow\ \hat\phi,\vec x\blacktriangleright^{\mathrm{ic}}K$

9. ON CONGRUENCE OF EQUALITY

Note that the semantics of the equality predicate $=$ is not defined as identity in the domain. In fact, on the left-hand sides of the predicates $\rhd^{\mathfrak{O}}$and $\blacktriangleright^{\mathfrak{O}}$, equal terms cannot be freely substituted. This might cause problems with decidability, the result in [19] heavily builds on the fact that $\rhd$ is invariant under substitution with respect to equal terms. There is, however a solution if we observe that CCA2 security implies that encryptions cannot be faked: for CCA2 secure encryption schemes, we can define the semantics of

$\hat{\phi}, \vec{x} \triangleright^{\mathfrak{O}} x$ such that only those ciphers are not decrypted by the decryption oracles that are *necessary* for the computation of $[\![\hat{\phi}, \vec{x}]\!]$. Here, when we say an encryption is necessary, we mean the encryption cannot be omitted and the number of encryptions reduced by this in the process computing $[\![\hat{\phi}, \vec{x}]\!]$. The reason we did not define our predicates this way is that we did not want the well-definedness of our predicates depend on whether the encryption satisfies CCA2 security. But if the encryption does satisfy CCA2 security, then $\triangleright^{\mathfrak{O}}$ and $\blacktriangleright^{\mathfrak{O}}$ can be defined in the above way and all axioms that we have listed are also valid for those new definitions, and on the top of it, $=$ would be a congruence relation.

The symmetric Needham-Schroeder protocol proof as well as the NSL proof work either way, and we believe this issue does not make a big difference in protocol proofs in general. But for automation, the two definitions might make a big difference.

10. SOUNDNESS OF AXIOMS

THEOREM 10.1 (SOUNDNESS). *With the computational interpretations of derivability and key compromise predicates, the axioms are computationally sound. For the "fresh keys are not compromised", it is necessary that the implementation of the encryption satisfies the corresponding (symmetric or asymmetric, IND or KDM-CCA2 security, or INT-CTXT unforgeability). Soundness of the other axioms do not require that. Furthermore, the no-telepathy axiom requires that freshly generated items are guessable only with negligible probability.*

Note, unlike for general soundness (Theorem 5.3), here the number of sessions in the computational execution does not have to be bounded in the security parameter.

We detail the proofs in the IND case, the KDM case is sketched, details will be included in the long version.

PROOF. As the soundness proofs of the axioms for derivability with oracles are essentially the same as the soundness proofs below, we skip that and focus on key compromise.

- Substitutability of equal terms: The reason is that according to the definition of key compromise, compromise of the item on the right hand side of $\blacktriangleright^{\mathfrak{O}}$ only depends on the bit string that is associated to the term there, and not on the structure of the term. This is in contrast with the left hand side. The notion that anything can be submitted to the decryption oracle that is not an encryption on the left clearly depends on the term structure on the left, so we have to make sure that in $\vec{x}$ and $\vec{y}$ the same encryption values occur.
- Derivability implies compromise: Soundness of this axiom is rather trivial, but we write it out for clarity. In order to show that in any protocol execution and n.n. set S, we have $\mathcal{M}^c, \Pi, S \models^{c} \forall \vec{x} K(\hat{\phi}, \vec{x} \triangleright^{\mathfrak{O}} K \longrightarrow \hat{\phi}, \vec{x} \blacktriangleright^{\mathfrak{O}} K)$, by the computational semantics we have to show that for any evaluation σ of the variables, and for any $S' \subseteq S$ non-negligible set, $\mathcal{M}^c, \Pi, S', \sigma \models^{c} \hat{\phi}, \vec{x} \triangleright^{\mathfrak{O}} K$ implies $\mathcal{M}^c, \Pi, S', \sigma \models^{c} \hat{\phi}, \vec{x} \blacktriangleright^{\mathfrak{O}} K$. So suppose $\mathcal{M}^c, \Pi, S', \sigma \models^{c} \hat{\phi}, \vec{x} \triangleright^{\mathfrak{O}} K$ holds. To show $\mathcal{M}^c, \Pi, S', \sigma \models^{c} \hat{\phi}, \vec{x} \blacktriangleright^{\mathfrak{O}} K$, let us take any $S'' \subseteq S'$. By $\mathcal{M}^c, \Pi, S', \sigma \models^{c} \hat{\phi}, \vec{x} \triangleright^{\mathfrak{O}} K$, there is a $S''' \subseteq S''$ and an algorithm $\mathcal{B}^{\mathcal{O}^{\mathfrak{O}}}$ such that $\mathcal{M}^c, \Pi, S''', \sigma \Vdash \mathcal{B}^{\mathcal{O}^{\mathfrak{O}}}(\hat{\phi}, \vec{x}) = K$. In the IND definition of key compromise, we can chose $\mathcal{A}_1^{\mathcal{O}^{\mathfrak{O}}}$ in the key compromise definition simply to be a random bit string $r(\omega)$ of length η. $\mathcal{A}_{21}^{\mathcal{O}^{\mathfrak{O}}}$ can take the key and decrypt its third input. $\mathcal{A}_{22}^{\mathcal{O}^{\mathfrak{O}}}$ can be chosen to be identically 0^{η}. If the third input is the encryption of $r(\omega)$ then $r(\omega)$ is received after the decryption, so the output of $\mathcal{A}_{21}^{\mathcal{O}^{\mathfrak{O}}}$ and $\mathcal{A}_{22}^{\mathcal{O}^{\mathfrak{O}}}$ differ overwhelmingly. On the other hand, if it is the encryption $0^{|r(\omega)|}$, then the outputs of $\mathcal{A}_{21}^{\mathcal{O}^{\mathfrak{O}}}$ and $\mathcal{A}_{22}^{\mathcal{O}^{\mathfrak{O}}}$ always agree. So by the definition of key compromise, $\mathcal{M}^c, \Pi, S', \sigma \models^{c} \hat{\phi}, \vec{x} \blacktriangleright^{\mathfrak{O}} K$ holds as there is such an S''' for all S''.
- Increasing capabilities for key compromise: If $\hat{\phi}, \vec{x} \blacktriangleright^{\mathfrak{O}} K$, there are $\mathcal{A}_1^{\mathcal{O}^{\mathfrak{O}}}$, R, etc in the definition of key compromise. The same items are good for $\hat{\phi}, \vec{x}, x' \blacktriangleright^{\mathfrak{O}} K$, ignoring x'.
- Commutativity: Trivial, the definition of key compromise is invariant under the change of the order of the list $\vec{x}$.
- Transitivity: For any S, assuming $\mathcal{M}^c, \Pi, S, \sigma \models^{c} \hat{\phi}, \vec{x} \triangleright^{\mathfrak{O}} \vec{y}$ and $\mathcal{M}^c, \Pi, S, \sigma \models^{c} \hat{\phi}, \vec{x}, \vec{y} \blacktriangleright^{\mathfrak{O}} K$, we have to show that $\mathcal{M}^c, \Pi, S, \sigma \models^{c} \hat{\phi}, \vec{x} \blacktriangleright^{\mathfrak{O}} K$. Take an arbitrary $S' \subseteq S$. By $\mathcal{M}^c, \Pi, S, \sigma \models^{c} \hat{\phi}, \vec{x} \triangleright^{\mathfrak{O}} \vec{y}$, there is a $S'' \subseteq S'$ and an $\mathcal{A}^{\mathcal{O}^{\mathfrak{O}}}$ algorithm such that $\mathcal{M}^c, \Pi, S'', \sigma \Vdash \mathcal{A}^{\mathcal{O}^{\mathfrak{O}}}(\hat{\phi}, \vec{x}) = \vec{y}$. By $\mathcal{M}^c, \Pi, S, \sigma \models^{c} \hat{\phi}, \vec{x}, \vec{y} \blacktriangleright^{\mathfrak{O}} K$, there is a $S''' \subseteq S''$ such that for this S''', the conditions in the definition of key compromise (in place of S'') hold. $\mathcal{M}^c, \Pi, S''', \sigma \Vdash \mathcal{A}^{\mathcal{O}^{\mathfrak{O}}}(\hat{\phi}, \vec{x}) = \vec{y}$. So in the key compromise definition applied to the satisfaction $\mathcal{M}^c, \Pi, S, \sigma \models^{c} \hat{\phi}, \vec{x}, \vec{y} \blacktriangleright^{\mathfrak{O}} K$, the algorithms $\mathcal{A}_1^{\mathcal{O}^{\mathfrak{O}}}$, $\mathcal{A}_{21}^{\mathcal{O}^{\mathfrak{O}}}$ and $\mathcal{A}_{22}^{\mathcal{O}^{\mathfrak{O}}}$ can run $\mathcal{A}^{\mathcal{O}^{\mathfrak{O}}}$ as a subroutine to compute $\vec{y}$, so they do not need it as an input. Since there is such a $S''' \subseteq S'$ for all $S' \subseteq S$, we have $\mathcal{M}^c, \Pi, S, \sigma \models^{c} \hat{\phi}, \vec{x} \blacktriangleright^{\mathfrak{O}} K$.
- Secrecy of CCA2 encryption: For the IND case, we have

$$\mathsf{RanGen}(K) \wedge \mathsf{fresh}(R; \hat{\phi}, \vec{x}, x, y, K) \wedge \vec{x}, x, y \preccurlyeq \hat{\phi} \wedge \hat{\phi}, \vec{x}, \{x\}_{eK}^{R} \triangleright^{\mathfrak{O}} y \longrightarrow \hat{\phi}, \vec{x}, x \blacktriangleright^{\mathfrak{O}} K \vee \hat{\phi}, \vec{x} \triangleright^{\mathfrak{O}} y$$

where $\mathfrak{O}$ is either aic2 or sic2. Soundness of this follows easily from our definition of key compromise and derivability with oracle access. Note that CCA2 security of the encryption is not needed in the following argument. We move $\hat{\phi}, \vec{x} \triangleright^{\mathfrak{O}} y$ to the premise, it becomes $\hat{\phi}, \vec{x} \not\triangleright^{\mathfrak{O}} y$. Let us denote by θ the premise received this way. We have to show that for any σ evaluation of free variables and S non-negligible set, if $\mathcal{M}^c, \Pi, S, \sigma \models^{c} \theta$, then $\mathcal{M}^c, \Pi, S, \sigma \models^{c} \hat{\phi}, \vec{x}, x \blacktriangleright^{\mathfrak{O}} K$. So suppose $\mathcal{M}^c, \Pi, S, \sigma \models^{c} \theta$. For $\mathcal{M}^c, \Pi, S, \sigma \models^{c} \hat{\phi}, \vec{x}, x \blacktriangleright^{\mathfrak{O}} K$, take any non-negligible set $S' \subseteq S$. As $\mathcal{M}^c, \Pi, S, \sigma \models^{c} \theta$ implies that $\mathcal{M}^c, \Pi, S', \sigma \models^{c} \hat{\phi}, \vec{x}, \{x\}_{eK}^{R} \triangleright^{\mathfrak{O}} y$ by the semantics of compound formulas (one conjunct in θ is $\hat{\phi}, \vec{x}, \{x\}_{eK}^{R} \triangleright^{\mathfrak{O}} y$, and the property is preserved under taking subsets), for such an S', by the definition of derivability, there is a non-negligible subset $S'' \subseteq S'$ and an algorithm $\mathcal{A}^{\mathcal{O}^{\mathfrak{O}}}$ such that $\mathcal{M}^c, \Pi, S'', \sigma \Vdash \mathcal{A}^{\mathcal{O}^{\mathfrak{O}}}(\hat{\phi}, \vec{x}, \{x\}_{eK}^{R}) = y$. Let $\mathcal{B}^{\mathcal{O}^{\mathfrak{O}}}$ be the algorithm that takes $\hat{\phi}, \vec{x}, x$ as input, submits x to its encryption oracle to receive $\{x\}_{eK}^{R'}$, and then applies $\mathcal{A}^{\mathcal{O}^{\mathfrak{O}}}$ on $(\hat{\phi}, \vec{x}, \{x\}_{eK}^{R'})$. As this was y with non-negligible probability for R, it is also y with non-negligible probability for R', because y does not depend on either of them, and because the random inputs of the algorithms are required to be fresh. Hence R' is just as good an independent item as R was. So there is a $S''' \subseteq S''$ such that $\mathcal{M}^c, \Pi, S''', \sigma \Vdash \mathcal{A}^{\mathcal{O}^{\mathfrak{O}}}(\hat{\phi}, \vec{x}, \{x\}_{eK}^{R'}) = y$, and by the definition of $\mathcal{B}^{\mathcal{O}^{\mathfrak{O}}}$, we also have $\mathcal{M}^c, \Pi, S''', \sigma \Vdash \mathcal{B}^{\mathcal{O}^{\mathfrak{O}}}(\hat{\phi}, \vec{x}, x) = y$. Therefore, $\mathcal{M}^c, \Pi, S''', \sigma \Vdash \mathcal{A}^{\mathcal{O}^{\mathfrak{O}}}(\hat{\phi}, \vec{x}, \{x\}_{eK}^{R'}) = \mathcal{B}^{\mathcal{O}^{\mathfrak{O}}}(\hat{\phi}, \vec{x}, x) = y$. Now observe, that since x was PPT generated, for any non-negligible S, there must be a length function $\ell(\eta)$ such that the probability that $|x| = \ell(\eta)$ is non-negligible on S. This, means that $\mathcal{A}^{\mathcal{O}^{\mathfrak{D}}}(\hat{\phi}, \vec{x}, \{0^{|x|}\}_{eK}^{R''}) = \mathcal{B}^{\mathcal{O}^{\mathfrak{D}}}(\hat{\phi}, \vec{x}, x) = y$ cannot hold on any non-negligible subset of S''', because if it did, then $\mathcal{A}^{\mathcal{O}^{\mathfrak{D}}}(\hat{\phi}, \vec{x}, \{0^{\ell}\}_{eK}^{R''}) = y$ would also hold non-negligible in S''' contradicting $\mathcal{M}^c, \Pi, S, \sigma \models^{c} \hat{\phi}, \vec{x} \not\blacktriangleright^{\mathfrak{D}} y$. So,

$$\mathcal{M}^c, \Pi, S''', \sigma \Vdash \mathcal{A}^{\mathcal{O}^{\mathfrak{D}}}(\hat{\phi}, \vec{x}, \{x\}_{eK}^{R}) = \mathcal{B}^{\mathcal{O}^{\mathfrak{D}}}(\hat{\phi}, \vec{x}, x), \text{ but}$$

$$\mathcal{M}^c, \Pi, S''', \sigma \Vdash \mathcal{A}^{\mathcal{O}^{\mathfrak{D}}}(\hat{\phi}, \vec{x}, \{0^{|x|}\}_{eK}^{R''}) \neq \mathcal{B}^{\mathcal{O}^{\mathfrak{D}}}(\hat{\phi}, \vec{x}, x),$$

which means $\mathcal{M}^c, \Pi, S, \sigma \models^{c} \hat{\phi}, \vec{x}, x \blacktriangleright^{\mathfrak{D}} K$.

The argument for the KDM case is completely analogous, except that we have $\mathcal{M}^c, \Pi, S'', \sigma \models^{c} \hat{\phi}, \vec{x} \not\blacktriangleright^{\mathfrak{D}} K$ there. Note, that in the axiom for the KDM case, we only require about x that $\vec{x}, x \preccurlyeq \hat{\phi}$; but the $\mathcal{B}^{\mathcal{O}^{\mathfrak{D}}}$ in IND case above, had x as an input which it then submits to the encryption oracle. The analogous $\mathcal{B}^{\mathcal{O}^{\mathfrak{D}}}$ in the KDM case is not allowed to use x as an input. Instead, in the definition of key usability for the KDM case we allowed the algorithms to use the encryptions functions of items depending on the names generated that far. Hence $\vec{x}, x \preccurlyeq \hat{\phi}$ can be submitted to the oracle in the form of such a function. and that is what $\mathcal{B}^{\mathcal{O}^{\mathfrak{D}}}$ is also allowed to use. x can be one of the elements in $\vec{y}$.

- Next, we have to show that encryptions with uncompromised keys do not compromise. Note again in the proof below that we do not need CCA2 security of the encryption, we only need the definition of key compromise. Instead of the original formula, we show the following in the IND-CCA2 case:

$$\begin{aligned}&\mathsf{RanGen}(K) \wedge \mathsf{RanGen}(K') \wedge \mathsf{fresh}(R; \hat{\phi}, \vec{x}, x, K, K')\\ &\quad \wedge \vec{x}, x \preccurlyeq \hat{\phi} \wedge \hat{\phi}, \vec{x}, \{x\}_{eK'}^{R} \blacktriangleright^{\mathfrak{D}} K \wedge \hat{\phi}, \vec{x}, x \not\blacktriangleright^{\mathfrak{D}} K'\\ &\quad \longrightarrow \hat{\phi}, \vec{x} \blacktriangleright^{\mathfrak{D}} K.\end{aligned}$$

We have to show that for all S non-negligible sets and σ evaluations of variables, if $\mathcal{M}^c, \Pi, S, \sigma$ satisfies the premise, then it satisfies the conclusion as well. So let us suppose it satisfies the premise. We want to conclude $\mathcal{M}^c, \Pi, S, \sigma \models^{c} \hat{\phi}, \vec{x} \blacktriangleright^{\mathfrak{D}} K$. Following the definition of key compromise, take any subset $S' \subseteq S$. By the definition of key compromise applied to $\mathcal{M}^c, \Pi, S, \sigma \models^{c} \hat{\phi}, \vec{x}, \{x\}_{eK'}^{R} \blacktriangleright^{\mathfrak{D}} K$, there are $S'' \subseteq S'$, R', R_1 $\mathcal{A}_1^{\mathcal{O}^{\mathfrak{D}}}$, $\mathcal{A}_{21}^{\mathcal{O}^{\mathfrak{D}}}$ and $\mathcal{A}_{22}^{\mathcal{O}^{\mathfrak{D}}}$ such that, taking the first possibility,

$$\begin{aligned}&\mathcal{A}_{21}^{\mathcal{O}^{\mathfrak{D}}}(\hat{\phi}, \vec{x}, \{x\}_{eK'}^{R}, \{\mathcal{A}_1^{\mathcal{O}^{\mathfrak{D}}}(\hat{\phi}, \vec{x}, \{x\}_{eK'}^{R})\}_{eK}^{R_1}) \qquad (1)\\ &= \mathcal{A}_{22}^{\mathcal{O}^{\mathfrak{D}}}(\hat{\phi}, \vec{x}, \{x\}_{eK'}^{R}, \{\mathcal{A}_1^{\mathcal{O}^{\mathfrak{D}}}(\hat{\phi}, \vec{x}, \{x\}_{eK'}^{R})\}_{eK}^{R_1})\end{aligned}$$

on S'', but

$$\begin{aligned}&\mathcal{A}_{21}^{\mathcal{O}^{\mathfrak{D}}}(\hat{\phi}, \vec{x}, \{x\}_{eK'}^{R}, \{0^{|\mathcal{A}_1^{\mathcal{O}^{\mathfrak{D}}}(\hat{\phi}, \vec{x}, \{x\}_{eK'}^{R})|}\}_{eK}^{R_1'}) \qquad (2)\\ &\neq \mathcal{A}_{22}^{\mathcal{O}^{\mathfrak{D}}}(\hat{\phi}, \vec{x}, \{x\}_{eK'}^{R}, \{0^{|\mathcal{A}_1^{\mathcal{O}^{\mathfrak{D}}}(\hat{\phi}, \vec{x}, \{x\}_{eK'}^{R})|}\}_{eK}^{R_1'})\end{aligned}$$

on S''. By $\mathcal{M}^c, \Pi, S'', \sigma \models^{c} \hat{\phi}, \vec{x}, x \not\blacktriangleright^{\mathfrak{D}} K'$, from Equation 1, we have that there is an R', and a subset (by restricting R') $S''' \subseteq S''$ such that on S''',

$$\begin{aligned}&\mathcal{A}_{21}^{\mathcal{O}^{\mathfrak{D}}}(\hat{\phi}, \vec{x}, \{0^{|x|}\}_{eK'}^{R'}, \{\mathcal{A}_1^{\mathcal{O}^{\mathfrak{D}}}(\hat{\phi}, \vec{x}, \{0^{|x|}\}_{eK'}^{R'})\}_{eK}^{R_1}) \quad (3)\\ &= \mathcal{A}_{22}^{\mathcal{O}^{\mathfrak{D}}}(\hat{\phi}, \vec{x}, \{0^{|x|}\}_{eK'}^{R'}, \{\mathcal{A}_1^{\mathcal{O}^{\mathfrak{D}}}(\hat{\phi}, \vec{x}, \{0^{|x|}\}_{eK'}^{R'})\}_{eK}^{R_1}).\end{aligned}$$

Equation 2 still holds on S''' and for all R_1', as R_1' and R' are independent. By $\mathcal{M}^c, \Pi, S''', \sigma \models^{c} \hat{\phi}, \vec{x}, x \not\blacktriangleright^{\mathfrak{D}} K'$, from Equation 2, we get that there is an R'', a subset $S'''' \subseteq S'''$ just by restricting R'', such that

$$\begin{aligned}&\mathcal{A}_{21}^{\mathcal{O}^{\mathfrak{D}}}(\hat{\phi}, \vec{x}, \{0^{|x|}\}_{eK'}^{R''}, \{0^{|\mathcal{A}_1^{\mathcal{O}^{\mathfrak{D}}}(\hat{\phi}, \vec{x}, \{0^{|x|}\}_{eK'}^{R''})|}\}_{eK}^{R'}) \quad (4)\\ &\neq \mathcal{A}_{22}^{\mathcal{O}^{\mathfrak{D}}}(\hat{\phi}, \vec{x}, \{0^{|x|}\}_{eK'}^{R''}, \{0^{|\mathcal{A}_1^{\mathcal{O}^{\mathfrak{D}}}(\hat{\phi}, \vec{x}, \{0^{|x|}\}_{eK'}^{R''})|}\}_{eK}^{R'}),\end{aligned}$$

still for all R'. Again, there is a length function $\ell(\eta)$ such that the probability that $|x| = \ell(\eta)$ is non-negligible on S''''. Let the subset of S'''' on which they are equal be S'''''. Since 0^{ℓ} is easily computable, we get that there are algorithms $\mathcal{A}_3^{\mathcal{O}^{\mathfrak{D}}}$, $\mathcal{A}_{41}^{\mathcal{O}^{\mathfrak{D}}}$ and $\mathcal{A}_{42}^{\mathcal{O}^{\mathfrak{D}}}$ such that on S''''',

$$\mathcal{A}_{41}^{\mathcal{O}^{\mathfrak{D}}}(\hat{\phi}, \vec{x}, \{\mathcal{A}_3^{\mathcal{O}^{\mathfrak{D}}}(\hat{\phi}, \vec{x})\}_{eK}^{R_1}) = \mathcal{A}_{42}^{\mathcal{O}^{\mathfrak{D}}}(\hat{\phi}, \vec{x}, \{\mathcal{A}_1^{\mathcal{O}^{\mathfrak{D}}}(\hat{\phi}, \vec{x})\}_{eK}^{R_1}))$$

but

$$\mathcal{A}_{41}^{\mathcal{O}^{\mathfrak{D}}}(\hat{\phi}, \vec{x}, \{0^{|\mathcal{A}_3^{\mathcal{O}^{\mathfrak{D}}}(\hat{\phi}, \vec{x})|}\}_{eK}^{R_1'}) \neq \mathcal{A}_{42}^{\mathcal{O}^{\mathfrak{D}}}(\hat{\phi}, \vec{x}, \{0^{|\mathcal{A}_1^{\mathcal{O}^{\mathfrak{D}}}(\hat{\phi}, \vec{x})|}\}_{eK}^{R_1'})).$$

This exactly means that $\mathcal{M}^c, \Pi, S, \sigma \models^{c} \hat{\phi}, \vec{x} \blacktriangleright^{\mathfrak{D}} K$. If we switch $=$ and $\neq$, we receive the proof of the other case of key compromise.

Here too, the KDM case is proven entirely analogously.

- Fresh keys are not compromised: It is here where IND-CCA2 (or KDM-CCA2) security of the encryption is used. We define our CCA2 attacker against the CCA2 oracle that allows multiple submissions for encryptions, which is equivalent with the original definition [11]. Let us consider the IND-CCA2 case. What we have to prove is that if $\mathcal{M}^c, \Pi, S, \sigma$ satisfies freshness of key K, then $\mathcal{M}^c, \Pi, S, \sigma \models^{c} \hat{\phi}, \vec{x} \blacktriangleright^{\mathfrak{D}} K$ leads to a CCA2 attack to the encryption. Let $\mathcal{M}^c, \Pi, S, \sigma \models^{c} \hat{\phi}, \vec{x} \blacktriangleright^{\mathfrak{D}} K$ hold. That is, for every $S' \subseteq S$, there are $S'' \subseteq S'$, etc. such that (consider the first case),

$$\begin{aligned}&\mathcal{A}_{21}^{\mathcal{O}^{\mathfrak{D}}}(\hat{\phi}, \vec{x}, \{\mathcal{A}_1^{\mathcal{O}^{\mathfrak{D}}}(\hat{\phi}, \vec{x})\}_{eK}^{R}) = \qquad (5)\\ &\mathcal{A}_{22}^{\mathcal{O}^{\mathfrak{D}}}(\hat{\phi}, \vec{x}, \{\mathcal{A}_1^{\mathcal{O}^{\mathfrak{D}}}(\hat{\phi}, \vec{x})\}_{eK}^{R}) \text{ on } S'' \text{ and}\end{aligned}$$

$$\begin{aligned}&\mathcal{A}_{21}^{\mathcal{O}^{\mathfrak{D}}}(\hat{\phi}, \vec{x}, \{0^{|\mathcal{A}_1^{\mathcal{O}^{\mathfrak{D}}}(\hat{\phi}, \vec{x})|}\}_{eK}^{R'}) \neq \qquad (6)\\ &\mathcal{A}_{22}^{\mathcal{O}^{\mathfrak{D}}}(\hat{\phi}, \vec{x}, \{0^{|\mathcal{A}_1^{\mathcal{O}^{\mathfrak{D}}}(\hat{\phi}, \vec{x})|}\}_{eK}^{R'})\end{aligned}$$

on S''. Note that $\mathsf{keyfresh}(K; \hat{\phi}, \vec{x}) \wedge \vec{x} \preccurlyeq \hat{\phi}$ means the decryption key or any function of it was never used in $\hat{\phi}, \vec{x}$. What the CCA2 attacker has to do is to simulate the protocol execution such that

  - except for K, the CCA2 attacker generates all keys
  - encryptions (except for that of $\mathcal{A}_1^{\mathcal{O}^{\mathfrak{D}}}(\hat{\phi}, \vec{x})$) with K are done by submitting two identical requests to the encryption oracle
  - the attacker keeps a table recording which encryption belongs to which plaintext
  - decryptions of ciphertexts provided by the encryption oracle are done by looking it up in the table
  - decryptions of strings not provided by the oracle are done by submitting to the decryption oracle
  - when the challenge state is reached, the interpretations of $\vec{x}$ and $\mathcal{A}_1^{\mathcal{O}^{\mathfrak{D}}}(\hat{\phi}, \vec{x})$ are computed
  - $\mathcal{A}_1^{\mathcal{O}^{\mathfrak{D}}}(\hat{\phi}, \vec{x})$ is submitted to the encryption oracle along with a string of 0's of the same length. Let c_0 denote the encryption that is received from the oracle. Note that the adversary does not know if this is the encryption of $\mathcal{A}_1^{\mathcal{O}^{\mathfrak{D}}}(\hat{\phi}, \vec{x})$ or of the 0's.
  - apply $\mathcal{A}_{21}^{\mathcal{O}^{\mathfrak{D}}}$ and $\mathcal{A}_{22}^{\mathcal{O}^{\mathfrak{D}}}$ to $\hat{\phi}, \vec{x}, c_0$.

- because of (5) and (6) on S'', if the correct bit string was encrypted, the two computations are equal, and if the 0's were encrypted, the two are different.

However, the attacker does not necessarily know when he is inside S'' and when outside. Outside S'' the attacker cannot be sure that equality means the correct encryption was encrypted. To overcome this problem, we finish the above CCA2 attack the following way. Let $\mu(\eta)$ be a function (in the security parameter) of natural numbers.

- the adversary submits pairs of $0^{|\mathcal{A}_1^{\mathcal{O}^{\mathfrak{D}}}(\hat{\phi},\vec{x})|}$ for encryption μ times. Let c_i denote ($i = 1, ..., \mu$) the encryptions received back from the oracle. Note that these encryptions are known to be encryptions of $0^{|\mathcal{A}_1^{\mathcal{O}^{\mathfrak{D}}}(\hat{\phi},\vec{x})|}$
- applies $\mathcal{A}_{21}^{\mathcal{O}^{\mathfrak{D}}}$ and $\mathcal{A}_{22}^{\mathcal{O}^{\mathfrak{D}}}$ on all of $\hat{\phi}, \vec{x}, c_i$
- CASE 1: if $\mathcal{A}_{21}^{\mathcal{O}^{\mathfrak{D}}}(\hat{\phi}, \vec{x}, c_0) = \mathcal{A}_{22}^{\mathcal{O}^{\mathfrak{D}}}(\hat{\phi}, \vec{x}, c_0)$ but $\mathcal{A}_{21}^{\mathcal{O}^{\mathfrak{D}}}(\hat{\phi}, \vec{x}, c_i) \neq \mathcal{A}_{22}^{\mathcal{O}^{\mathfrak{D}}}(\hat{\phi}, \vec{x}, c_i)$ for all $i = 1, ..., \mu$, then the CCA2 attacker outputs 1, meaning that his guess is that the oracle encrypted the correct bit string.
- CASE 2: otherwise, the adversary tosses a coin and outputs the result.

We can think of the probability space of the CCA2 attack as $\{0, 1\} \times \Omega^{\eta}$, where $\{0, 1\}$ represents the internal bit of the oracles. Even if the internal bit is 0, the simulation of the protocol execution can be done according to the above rules. Let $S_\mu \subseteq \Omega$ be the set where $\mathcal{A}_{21}^{\mathcal{O}^{\mathfrak{D}}}(\hat{\phi}, \vec{x}, \{\mathcal{A}_1^{\mathcal{O}^{\mathfrak{D}}}(\hat{\phi}, \vec{x})\}_{eK}^R) = \mathcal{A}_{22}^{\mathcal{O}^{\mathfrak{D}}}(\hat{\phi}, \vec{x}, \{\mathcal{A}_1^{\mathcal{O}^{\mathfrak{D}}}(\hat{\phi}, \vec{x})\}_{eK}^R)$ but where $\mathcal{A}_{21}^{\mathcal{O}^{\mathfrak{D}}}(\hat{\phi}, \vec{x}, c_i) \neq \mathcal{A}_{22}^{\mathcal{O}^{\mathfrak{D}}}(\hat{\phi}, \vec{x}, c_i)$ for all $i = 1, ..., \mu$, (that is, CASE 1 happens when the real plaintext is encrypted in the CCA2 attack). Note that S_μ depends on the function μ, but still, $S'' \subseteq S_\mu$, so S_μ is also non-negligible. Suppose, the internal bit of the oracle is 1. Then, on S_μ, according to our setup of the CCA2 attacker, he outputs 1, giving the correct guess. That is, denoting by $\mathcal{A}_{\text{CCA2}}$ the CCA2 attacker as described above, the output of $\mathcal{A}_{\text{CCA2}}$ is 1 on $\{1\} \times S_\mu$. On $\{1\} \times (\Omega \setminus S_\mu)$, $\mathcal{A}_{\text{CCA2}}$ tosses a coin, so the probabilities there balance out. Consider now $\{0\} \times \Omega$. Here the internal bit of the oracles is 0, that is they encrypt the 0's, that is, here c_0 is the encryption of 0's. If the probability on $\{0\} \times \Omega$ that $\mathcal{A}_{21}^{\mathcal{O}^{\mathfrak{D}}}(\hat{\phi}, \vec{x}, c_0)) = \mathcal{A}_{22}^{\mathcal{O}^{\mathfrak{D}}}(\hat{\phi}, \vec{x}, c_0))$ holds is negligible, then we are done, because on $\{0\} \times \Omega$ too a coin is tossed, so the advantage of the adversary is $1/2 \cdot \mathbf{Prob}\{\{1\} \times S_\mu\}$, which is non-negligible. So let us assume now that the probability that $\mathcal{A}_{21}^{\mathcal{O}^{\mathfrak{D}}}(\hat{\phi}, \vec{x}, c_0)) = \mathcal{A}_{22}^{\mathcal{O}^{\mathfrak{D}}}(\hat{\phi}, \vec{x}, c_0))$ holds is not negligible on $\{0\} \times \Omega$. But the other c_i are also just encryptions of 0's, so $\mathcal{A}_{21}^{\mathcal{O}^{\mathfrak{D}}}(\hat{\phi}, \vec{x}, c_i)) = \mathcal{A}_{22}^{\mathcal{O}^{\mathfrak{D}}}(\hat{\phi}, \vec{x}, c_i))$ holds with the same probability for all i on $\{0\} \times \Omega$. For each fixed η, the higher $\mu(\eta)$ we chose, the higher the probability is that one $\mathcal{A}_{21}^{\mathcal{O}^{\mathfrak{D}}}(\hat{\phi}, \vec{x}, c_i)) = \mathcal{A}_{22}^{\mathcal{O}^{\mathfrak{D}}}(\hat{\phi}, \vec{x}, c_i))$ holds *for at least one* i. In fact, this probability can be made arbitrarily close to 1 by increasing $\mu(\eta)$. If it is close enough to 1, then the probability of making an error (other than the case when a coin is tossed) on $\{0\} \times \Omega$ becomes smaller than the probability of $\{1\} \times S_\mu$, and hence the error probability cannot cancel out the winning probability. Since the probability of hitting the same encryption with the 0's was assumed to be non-negligible, it is sufficient to have a polynomial $\mu(\eta)$ to ensure that the probability of having at least one hit is closer to 1 than the non-negligible probability of $\{1\} \times S_\mu$. In this case, the win on $\{1\} \times S_\mu$ when the internal bit is 1 cannot be cancelled by the loss elsewhere, so the CCA2 attacker wins. Note, if $\hat{\phi}, \vec{x}$ contains the decryption key outside S, the attack can simply terminate there and output a random bit.

The proof for KDM-CCA2 is exactly analogous. The only difference is, that instead of $\mathcal{A}_1^{\mathcal{O}^{\mathfrak{D}}}(\hat{\phi}, \vec{x})$, there is an x there, but the oracles accept the functions to be submitted. When it comes to computing the encryptions of x, the KDM encryption oracle is requested. It is not directly x that is submitted, but a description of a function of the keys instead. Since the KDM adversary is simulating the protocol, all items except for the secret keys and the random inputs to the encryptions in the symmetric case are available to him.

- Fresh items do not compromise: The idea is exactly the same as in case of the derivability predicate. A fresh item can just as well be created by the adversary, it cannot help him.

We now turn to the case of INT-CTXT key compromise.

Proofs of the first six axioms and the last one are entirely identical to the proofs for CCA2 key compromise. The soundness of the "encryptions with uncompromised keys do not compromise" axiom is also analogous: We again show the following:

$$\mathsf{RanGen}(K) \wedge \mathsf{RanGen}(K') \wedge \mathsf{fresh}(R; \hat{\phi}, \vec{x}, x, K, K') \\ \wedge\ \vec{x}, x \preccurlyeq \hat{\phi} \wedge \hat{\phi}, \vec{x}, \{\!|x|\!\}_{K'}^{R} \blacktriangleright^{\mathrm{ic}} K \ \wedge\ \hat{\phi}, \vec{x}, x \not\blacktriangleright^{\mathrm{sic2}} K' \\ \longrightarrow\ \hat{\phi}, \vec{x} \blacktriangleright^{\mathrm{ic}} K$$

Again, we have to show that for all S non-negligible sets and σ evaluations of variables, if $\mathcal{M}^c, \Pi, S, \sigma$ satisfies the premise, then it satisfies the conclusion as well. So let us suppose it satisfies the premise. We want to show $\mathcal{M}^c, \Pi, S, \sigma \overset{c}{\models} \hat{\phi}, \vec{x} \blacktriangleright^{\mathrm{ic}} K$. Following the definition of key compromise, take any subset $S' \subseteq S$. By the definition of key compromise, $\mathcal{M}^c, \Pi, S, \sigma \overset{c}{\models} \hat{\phi}, \vec{x}, \{\!|x|\!\}_{K'}^{R} \blacktriangleright^{\mathrm{ic}} K$ implies there is a $S'' \subseteq S$, and a PT algorithm $\mathcal{A}^{\mathcal{O}^{\mathrm{sic2}}}$, such that

$$\mathcal{M}^c, \Pi, S'', \sigma \Vdash sdec(\mathcal{A}^{\mathcal{O}^{\mathrm{sic2}}}(\hat{\phi}, \vec{x}, \{\!|x|\!\}_{K'}^{R}), K) \neq \bot \\ \wedge \forall z R'(\mathcal{A}^{\mathcal{O}^{\mathrm{sic2}}}(\hat{\phi}, \vec{x}, \{\!|x|\!\}_{K'}^{R}) = \{\!|z|\!\}_{K}^{R'} \to \{\!|z|\!\}_{K}^{R'} \not\sqsubseteq \hat{\phi}, \vec{x}, \{\!|x|\!\}_{K'}^{R})$$

and on S'', $\mathcal{A}^{\mathcal{O}^{\mathrm{sic2}}}(\hat{\phi}, \vec{x}, , \{\!|x|\!\}_{K'}^{R})$ is not equal any of the outputs of the encryption oracles. Now, we also have that $\mathcal{M}^c, \Pi, S'', \sigma \overset{c}{\models} \hat{\phi}, \vec{x}, x \not\blacktriangleright^{\mathrm{sic2}} K'$ from the satisfaction of the premise. This gives us that there is some S''' non-negligible subset of S'' such that

$$\mathcal{M}^c, \Pi, S''', \sigma \Vdash sdec(\mathcal{A}^{\mathcal{O}^{\mathrm{sic2}}}(\hat{\phi}, \vec{x}, \{\!|0^{|x|}|\!\}_{K'}^{R}), K) \neq \bot\ \wedge \\ \forall z R'(\mathcal{A}^{\mathcal{O}^{\mathrm{sic2}}}(\hat{\phi}, \vec{x}, \{\!|0^{|x|}|\!\}_{K'}^{R}) = \{\!|z|\!\}_{K}^{R'} \to \{\!|z|\!\}_{K}^{R'} \not\sqsubseteq \hat{\phi}, \vec{x}, \{\!|0^{|x|}|\!\}_{K'}^{R})$$

and on S'', $\mathcal{A}^{\mathcal{O}^{\mathrm{sic2}}}(\hat{\phi}, \vec{x}, , \{\!|0^{|x|}|\!\}_{K'}^{R})$ is not equal any of the outputs of the encryption oracles. Again, as the length of x can be guessed, there is a non-negligible $S'''' \subseteq S'''$ and a $\mathcal{B}^{\mathcal{O}^{\mathrm{sic2}}}$ such that

$$\mathcal{M}^c, \Pi, S'''', \sigma \Vdash sdec(\mathcal{B}^{\mathcal{O}^{\mathrm{sic2}}}(\hat{\phi}, \vec{x}), K) \neq \bot \\ \wedge \forall z R'(\mathcal{B}^{\mathcal{O}^{\mathrm{sic2}}}(\hat{\phi}, \vec{x}) = \{\!|z|\!\}_{K}^{R'} \to \{\!|z|\!\}_{K}^{R'} \not\sqsubseteq \hat{\phi}, \vec{x})$$

and on S'''', $\mathcal{B}^{\mathcal{O}^{\mathrm{sic2}}}(\hat{\phi}, \vec{x})$ is not equal any of the outputs of the encryption oracles. And that exactly means $\mathcal{M}^c, \Pi, S, \sigma \overset{c}{\models} \hat{\phi}, \vec{x} \blacktriangleright^{\mathrm{ic}} K$. Again, the KDM case is entirely analogous.

Proof of the uncompromised key's encryption cannot be faked axiom is immediate from the semantics of $\blacktriangleright^{\mathrm{ic}}$. If

$$\mathcal{M}^c, \Pi, S, \sigma \overset{c}{\models} \mathsf{RanGen}(K)\ \wedge\ \hat{\phi}, \vec{x} \rhd y\ \wedge\ dec(y, dK) \neq \bot \\ \wedge\ \forall x R(y = \{x\}_{eK}^{R} \to \{x\}_{eK}^{R} \not\sqsubseteq \hat{\phi}, \vec{x})$$

Then for all $S' \subseteq S$, there is a $S'' \subseteq S'$ and an algorithm $\mathcal{A}$ such that $\mathcal{M}^c, \Pi, S'', \sigma \Vdash \mathcal{A}(\hat{\phi}, \vec{x}) = y$. Furthermore, the last conjunct means that the output of the algorithm is not any of the encryptions in $\hat{\phi}, \vec{x}$, and the third conjunct means the decryption does not fail. This is exactly means that $\mathcal{M}^c, \Pi, S, \sigma \models^{c} \hat{\phi}, \vec{x} \blacktriangleright^{ic} K$.

The only remaining axiom is the fresh keys are not compromised axiom for the INT-CTXT case. But that is rather easy. Suppose, the encryption is INT-CTXT secure. $\mathcal{M}^c, \Pi, S, \sigma \models^{c} \hat{\phi} \blacktriangleright^{ic} K$ means there is a $S'' \subseteq S$, and a PT algorithm $\mathcal{A}^{\mathcal{O}^{\text{sic2}}}$, such that

$$\mathcal{M}^c, \Pi, S'', \sigma \models sdec(\mathcal{A}^{\mathcal{O}^{\text{sic2}}}(\hat{\phi}), K) \neq \bot$$
$$\wedge \forall z R'(\mathcal{A}^{\mathcal{O}^{\text{sic2}}}(\hat{\phi}) = \{\!|z|\!\}_K^{R'} \to \{\!|z|\!\}_K^{R'} \not\sqsubseteq \hat{\phi})$$

and on S'', $\mathcal{A}^{\mathcal{O}^{\text{sic2}}}(\hat{\phi})$ is not equal any of the outputs of the encryption oracles. But that exactly means that there is a non-negligible set (namely S''), on which $\mathcal{A}^{\mathcal{O}^{\text{sic2}}}$ can produce a ciphertext, contradicting the INT-CTXT property. □

11. SIMPLE EXAMPLES

Now let us see on a few simple examples how inconsistency can be shown with the above axioms. In [5], the authors presented some of the most basic examples, therefore the ones we analyze here are a little more complex, all are related to sending keys around. We use symmetric encryption in these examples.

EXAMPLE 11.1. Suppose the first messages in a frame are

$$\phi_3 \equiv \langle (A, B), \{\!|K|\!\}_{K_{AB}}^{R_1}, \{\!|h_2, N|\!\}_K^{R_2} \rangle,$$

with names $KK_{AB}NR_1R_2$, and where the symmetric encryption is IND- (or KDM-) CCA2 secure. We want to show that $\phi_3 \rhd N$ is inconsistent with the axioms, that is, N remains secret. Let now $\mathfrak{D}$ denote either sic2 or skc2. Suppose $\phi_3 \rhd N$ holds. Then we have $\phi_3 \rhd^{\mathfrak{D}} N$ by the more oracles help more axiom. That is the same as $\phi_2, \{\!|h_2, N|\!\}_K^{R_2} \rhd^{\mathfrak{D}} N$. By the no-telepathy axiom, $\phi_2 \not\rhd^{\mathfrak{D}} N$ as $\mathsf{fresh}(N; \phi_2)$ holds (which follows directly from the definition of the freshness constraint, not from axioms). By the 'uncompromised key securely encrypts' axiom for CCA2 symmetric case, with the roles $\vec{x} \equiv \langle\rangle$, $x \equiv \langle h_2, N \rangle$, $y \equiv N$, since we assumed $\phi_2, \{\!|h_2, N|\!\}_K^{R_2} \rhd^{\mathfrak{D}} N$, we also have that either $\phi_2 \rhd^{\mathfrak{D}} N$ (already ruled out) or (depending on $\mathfrak{D}$) $\phi_2, h_2, N \blacktriangleright^{\text{sic2}} K$ or $\phi_2 \blacktriangleright^{\text{skc2}} K$. In the IND-CCA2 case, by the 'fresh items do not compromise' axiom, we then have $\phi_2, h_2 \blacktriangleright^{\text{sic2}} K$ as N does not appear in ϕ_2. Since the handle is always derived from the frame, $\phi_2 \rhd h_2$ holds, hence $\phi_2 \rhd^{\text{sic2}} h_2$ and by the transitivity axiom applied for $\phi_2, h_2 \blacktriangleright^{\text{sic2}} K$ and $\phi_2 \rhd^{\text{sic2}} h_2$, we have $\phi_2 \blacktriangleright^{\text{sic2}} K$, just as we had in the KDM case earlier. But that is the same as (now for both IND and KDM cases) $\phi_1, \{\!|K|\!\}_{K_{AB}}^{R_1} \blacktriangleright^{\mathfrak{D}} K$. By the 'encryptions with uncompromised keys do not compromise' axiom, with roles $K' \equiv K_{AB}$, $\vec{x} \equiv \langle\rangle$ and $x \equiv K$, we have that either $\phi_1 \blacktriangleright^{\mathfrak{D}} K$, or $\phi_1, K \blacktriangleright^{\text{sic2}} K_{AB}$ or $\phi_1 \blacktriangleright^{\text{skc2}} K_{AB}$. However, $\phi_1 \not\blacktriangleright^{\mathfrak{D}} K$ because of the 'fresh keys are not compromised' axiom, and the same is true for $\phi_1 \not\blacktriangleright^{\mathfrak{D}} K_{AB}$. So for the KDM case we have a contradiction and we are done. For the IND case, again by the 'fresh items do not compromise' axiom, $\phi_1, K \blacktriangleright^{\text{sic2}} K_{AB}$ together with $\mathsf{fresh}(K; \phi_1, K_{AB})$ implies $\phi_1 \blacktriangleright^{\text{sic2}} K_{AB}$, hence again we arrived at a contradiction.

It may seem to the reader that the axioms provided in [5] (that is, without key compromise) could also be sufficient to prove that $\phi_3 \rhd N$ is inconsistent with the axioms there by removing items from ϕ_3 in a different order from what we just did in Example 11.1. Namely, the idea would be to proceed the following way: given $\phi_3 \rhd N$, first remove the first encryption (by the secrecy axiom as K_{AB} was never sent out), and receive $\langle (A, B), \{\!|h_2, N|\!\}_K^{R_2} \rangle \rhd N$. Then remove the second encryption (by secrecy as K is not in the frame any more after removing the first encryption) receiving $(A, B) \rhd N$ contradicting the no-telepathy axiom. However, application of the secrecy axiom in [5] (and also in this paper) to $\langle (A, B), \{\!|h_2, N|\!\}_K^{R_2} \rangle \rhd N$ requires $h_2 \preccurlyeq (A, B)$, which means $(A, B) \rhd h_2$, but that does not hold, because h_2 was computed from $\langle (A, B), \{\!|K|\!\}_{K_{AB}}^{R_1} \rangle$. Secrecy axiom can only be used if the frame contains all necessary information for the computation of handles in the plaintext. It is in fact possible to show that $\phi_3 \rhd N$ is consistent with the axioms of [5]. Although those axioms are inconsistent with $h_2 \rhd K$, they do allow h_2 to carry partial information about K sufficient to compromise the second encryption. Without the handle h_2 in the second encryption, the axioms of [5] are sufficient to prove inconsistency, but except for initial ones, protocol messages are normally responses to agent inputs and contain handles.

EXAMPLE 11.2. Now suppose

$$\phi_3 \equiv \langle (A, B), \{\!|K|\!\}_{K_{AB}}^{R_1}, \{\!|K_{AB}, h_2, N|\!\}_K^{R_2} \rangle$$

and let us try to show that $\phi_3 \rhd^{\mathfrak{D}} N$ contradicts the axioms. Note that there is a key cycle in this example, K and K_{AB} encrypt each other. So assume $\phi_3 \rhd^{\mathfrak{D}} N$. For IND-CCA2 security, from the 'uncompromised key securely encrypts' axiom we get $\phi_2, K_{AB}, h_2, N \blacktriangleright^{\text{sic2}} K$ if we follow the same steps as we did in Example 11.1. Then the same way as before, we can remove h_2 and N, and since $\phi_2 \equiv \phi_1, \{\!|K|\!\}_{K_{AB}}^{R_1}$, receive $\phi_1, \{\!|K|\!\}_{K_{AB}}^{R_1}, K_{AB} \blacktriangleright^{\text{sic2}} K$. But this does not lead to a contradiction! According to the equational theory, $K = sdec(\{\!|K|\!\}_{K_{AB}}^{R_1}, K_{AB})$, and by the 'functions are computable' axiom, we get $\phi_1, \{\!|K|\!\}_{K_{AB}}^{R_1}, K_{AB} \rhd^{\text{sic2}} K$. So we always have $\phi_1, \{\!|K|\!\}_{K_{AB}}^{R_1}, K_{AB} \blacktriangleright^{\text{sic2}} K$ too by the 'derivability implies compromise' axiom, there is no contradiction. However, if we have KDM security, then just as in the previous example, using the 'uncompromised key securely encrypts' axiom, $\phi_3 \rhd^{\text{skc2}} N$ immediately leads to $\phi_2 \blacktriangleright^{\text{skc2}} K$, and the rest of the derivation is the same as in the previous example. So in this case, while $\phi_3 \rhd^{\text{sic2}} N$ is consistent with the axioms, $\phi_3 \rhd^{\text{skc2}} N$ is inconsistent.

EXAMPLE 11.3. With names $KK'K_{AB}NR_1R_2R_3$, consider

$$\phi_3 = \langle (A, B), \{\!|K|\!\}_{K_{AB}}^{R_1}, \{\!|\{\!|K_{AB}|\!\}_{K'}^{R_2}, h_2, N|\!\}_K^{R_3} \rangle.$$

K and K_{AB} are still in cycles, but they do not disturb each other because of K'. Again, assuming IND-CCA2 security, from $\phi_3 \rhd^{\text{sic2}} N$ first $\phi_2, \{\!|K_{AB}|\!\}_{K'}^{R_2}, h_2, N \blacktriangleright^{\text{sic2}} K$ is derived using the 'uncompromised key securely encrypts' axiom as in Example 11.1. As in Example 11.1, h_2 and N are removed: $\phi_2, \{\!|K_{AB}|\!\}_{K'}^{R_2} \blacktriangleright^{\text{sic2}} K$. At this point, the 'encryptions with uncompromised keys do not compromise' axiom implies that either $\phi_2 \blacktriangleright^{\text{sic2}} K$ or $\phi_2, K_{AB} \blacktriangleright^{\text{sic2}} K'$. In the former case, we are back at the situation of Example 11.1 and we arrive at a contradiction. In the latter case, by function (encryption) application on $\phi_1, \{\!|K|\!\}_{K_{AB}}^{R_1}, K_{AB} \blacktriangleright^{\text{sic2}} K'$, we get $\phi_1, K, K_{AB}, R_1 \blacktriangleright^{\text{sic2}} K'$. By 'the fresh items do not compromise' axiom, K, K_{AB}, R_1 can be removed receiving $\phi_1 \blacktriangleright^{\text{sic2}} K'$ contradicting the 'fresh keys are uncompromised' axiom.

12. THE SYMMETRIC NEEDHAM-SCHROEDER PROTOCOL

With the axioms that we presented, we have proven the amended symmetric Needham-Schroeder protocol:

1. $A \to B : A$
2. $B \to A : \{A, N_1\}_{K_{BT}}$
3. $A \to T : \langle A, B, N_2, \{A, N_1\}_{K_{BT}} \rangle$
4. $T \to A : \{N_2, B, K, \{K, N_1, A\}_{K_{BT}}\}_{K_{AT}}$
5. $A \to B : \{K, N_1, A\}_{K_{BT}}$

6. $B \rightarrow A : \{N_3\}_K$
7. $A \rightarrow B : \{N_3 - 1\}_K$

This protocol first has a key distribution part, and then the distributed key is used to securely encrypt a nonce. We showed that no symbolic (hence computational) attacker succeeds the following way (motivated by [25]). Using IND-CCA2 and INT-CTXT axioms, we first showed by an inductive technique that the key K from the trusted party meant for honest A and B are never corrupted (corruption is inconsistent with the axioms and agent checks). Then, again with an inductive technique we showed that N_3 is never leaked. Finally, agreement and authentication were shown. Besides the presented axioms, we also needed that adding 1 and subtracting 1 are inverses of each other, and $x - 1 \neq x$. We needed an additional property, namely, that applying the first projection of a pairing on an honestly generated nonce cannot result the nonce itself with more than negligible probability. Triples, quadruples were constructed out of pairs. The detailed proof is available online at the first author's homepage. We assumed that A is running the initiator role in all his sessions, and B is running the responder's role. There is only one trusted party. They all are allowed to run any number of multiple parallel sessions with honest and corrupted agents.

On a note about dynamic corruption, the proof works even if the protocol allows the release of the key K at a later time. Secrecy can still be proven until that point, authentication that was carried out earlier can still be verified.

13. CONCLUSIONS

In this paper we further expanded the framework proposed by Bana and Comon-Lundh [7] for computationally complete symbolic adversary. We have shown how key exchange can be handled. Proofs with this technique are computationally sound without the need of any further assumptions such as no bad keys, etc. that are assumed in other literature. We presented a modular set of axioms that are computationally sound for implementations using IND-CCA2, KDM-CCA2 and INT-CTXT secure encryptions respectively. We illustrated their power via simple examples and the verification of an entire protocol.

We are investigating extensions of the general soundness theorem in order to account for unbounded number of sessions and also to be able to handle indistinguishability properties. More importantly, we are also researching automation.

14. REFERENCES

[1] P. Adão, G. Bana, J. Herzog, and A. Scedrov. Soundness and completeness of formal encryption: the cases of key-cycles and partial information leakage. *Journal of Computer Security*, 17(5):737–797, 2009.

[2] M. Backes, A. Malik, and D. Unruh. Computational soundness without protocol restrictions. In *CCS'12*, pages 699–711. ACM, 2012.

[3] M. Backes, B. Pfitzmann, and M. Waidner. A composable cryptographic library with nested operations. In *CCS'03*, pages 220–230. ACM, 2003.

[4] M. Backes, B. Pfitzmann, and M. Waidner. The reactive simulatability (rsim) framework for asynchronous systems. *Information and Computation*, 205(12):1685–1720, 2007.

[5] G. Bana, P. Adão, and H. Sakurada. Computationally Comlete Symbolic Attacker in Action. In *FSTTCS'12*, LIPIcs, pages 546–560. Schloss Dagstuhl, 2012.

[6] G. Bana and H. Comon-Lundh. Towards unconditional soundness: Computationally complete symbolic attacker. Available at IACR ePrint Archive, Report 2012/019.

[7] G. Bana and H. Comon-Lundh. Towards unconditional soundness: Computationally complete symbolic attacker. In *POST'12*, LNCS, pages 189–208. Springer, 2012.

[8] G. Bana, K. Hasebe, and M. Okada. Computational semantics for first-order logical analysis of cryptographic protocols. In *Formal to Practical Security*, volume 5458 of *LNCS*, pages 33–58. Springer, 2009.

[9] G. Barthe, B. Grégoire, and S. Zanella Béguelin. Formal certification of code-based cryptographic proofs. In *POPL'09*, pages 90–101. ACM, 2009.

[10] G. Barthe, B. Grégoire, and S. Zanella Béguelin. Formal certification of code-based cryptographic proofs. In *POPL*, pages 90–101. ACM, 2009.

[11] M. Bellare, A. Boldyreva, and S. Micali. Public-key encryption in a multi-user setting. In *EUROCRYPT'00*, pages 258–274. Springer, 2000.

[12] M. Bellare, A. Desai, D. Pointcheval, and P. Rogaway. Relations among notions of security for public-key encryption schemes. In *CRYPTO'98*, LNCS. Springer, 1998.

[13] M. Bellare and Ch. Namprempre. Authenticated encryption: Relations among notions and analysis of the generic composition paradigm. *J. Cryptology*, 21(4):469–491, 2008.

[14] B. Blanchet. A computationally sound mechanized prover for security protocols. *IEEE Transactions on Dependable and Secure Computing*, 5(4):193–207, 2008.

[15] J. Camenisch, N. Chandran, and V. Shoup. A public key encryption scheme secure against key dependent chosen plaintext and adaptive chosen ciphertext attacks. In *EUROCRYPT'09*, LNCS, pages 351–368. Springer, 2009.

[16] H. Comon, C. Marché, and R. Treinen, editors. *Constraints in Computational Logics: Theory and Applications, International Summer School, CCS'99*, LNCS, 2001.

[17] H. Comon-Lundh and V. Cortier. Computational soundness of observational equivalence. In *CCS'08*, pages 109–118. ACM, 2008.

[18] H. Comon-Lundh and V. Cortier. How to prove security of communication protocols? A discussion on the soundness of formal models w.r.t. computational ones. In *STACS'11*, LIPIcs, pages 29–44. Schloss Dagstuhl, March 2011.

[19] H. Comon-Lundh, V. Cortier, and G. Scerri. Tractable inference systems: an extension with a deducibility predicate. In *CADE'13*, LNAI. Springer, 2013.

[20] V. Cortier and B. Warinschi. Computationally sound, automated proofs for security protocols. In *ESOP'05*, LNCS, pages 157–171, 2005.

[21] A. Datta, A. Derek, J. C. Mitchell, V. Shmatikov, and M. Turuani. Probabilistic polynomial-time semantics for a protocol security logic. In *ICALP'05*, LNCS, pages 16–29. Springer, 2005.

[22] A. Datta, A. Derek, J. C. Mitchell, and B. Warinschi. Computationally sound compositional logic for key exchange protocols. In *CSFW '06*, pages 321–334. IEEE, 2006.

[23] Melvin Fitting. An embedding of classical logic in s4. *The Journal of Symbolic Logic*, 35(4):529–534, 1970.

[24] R. Küsters and M. Tuengerthal. Computational soundness for key exchange protocols with symmetric encryption. In *CCS'09*, pages 91–100. ACM, 2009.

[25] F. J. Thayer, J. C. Herzog, and J. D. Guttman. Strand spaces: Proving security protocols correct. *Journal of Computer Security*, 7(1):191–230, 1999.

Fully Automated Analysis of Padding-Based Encryption in the Computational Model

Gilles Barthe
IMDEA Software Institute
Madrid, Spain
gilles.barthe@imdea.org

Juan Manuel Crespo
IMDEA Software Institute
Madrid, Spain
juanmanuel.crespo@imdea.org

Benjamin Grégoire
INRIA Sophia Antipolis
Sophia Antipolis, France
benjamin.gregoire@inria.fr

César Kunz
IMDEA Software Institute
Madrid, Spain
cesar.kunz@imdea.org

Yassine Lakhnech
U. de Grenoble & VERIMAG
Grenoble, France
yassine.lakhnech@imag.fr

Benedikt Schmidt
IMDEA Software Institute
Madrid, Spain
benedikt.schmidt@imdea.org

Santiago Zanella-Béguelin
Microsoft Research
Cambridge, UK
santiago@microsoft.com

ABSTRACT

Computer-aided verification provides effective means of analyzing the security of cryptographic primitives. However, it has remained a challenge to achieve fully automated analyses yielding guarantees that hold against computational (rather than symbolic) attacks. This paper meets this challenge for public-key encryption schemes built from trapdoor permutations and hash functions. Using a novel combination of techniques from computational and symbolic cryptography, we present proof systems for analyzing the chosen-plaintext and chosen-ciphertext security of such schemes in the random oracle model. Building on these proof systems, we develop a toolset that bundles together fully automated proof and attack finding algorithms. We use this toolset to build a comprehensive database of encryption schemes that records attacks against insecure schemes, and proofs with concrete bounds for secure ones.

Categories and Subject Descriptors

E.3 [**Data encryption**]: Public key cryptosystems; F.3.1 [**Logics and Meanings of Programs**]: Specifying and Verifying and Reasoning about Programs

Keywords

Attack finding; automated proofs; provable security; public-key encryption; static equivalence

CCS'13, November 4–8, 2013, Berlin, Germany.

ACM 978-1-4503-2477-9/13/11 ...$15.00.
http://dx.doi.org/10.1145/2508859.2516663.

1. INTRODUCTION

Two different models for analyzing the security of cryptographic constructions have developed over the years and coexist until today, each with its own advantages and disadvantages: the computational model and the symbolic model.

The computational model has its roots in the work of Goldwasser and Micali [21] and views cryptographic primitives as functions on bitstrings. Adversaries are modeled as probabilistic algorithms and security is defined in terms of their success probability and computational resources. Security proofs are reductions, showing how a successful attack can be converted into an efficient algorithm that breaks the security of primitives. Often, computational proofs quantify the efficiency of reductions, giving *concrete* security bounds.

The symbolic model, originating from the seminal work of Dolev and Yao [19], views cryptographic primitives as function symbols in a term algebra. The properties of primitives and the capabilities of adversaries are modeled using equational theories. This enables automated analysis, but can miss attacks that are possible in the computational model.

A celebrated article by Abadi and Rogaway [2] bridges the gap between the two models: it gives sufficient conditions under which symbolic security implies computational security; symbolic methods that exhibit this property are called cryptographically sound. This result, originally proved for symmetric encryption, has since been extended to richer theories [17]. Cryptographic soundness opens the perspective of combining the best of both worlds: fully automated proofs of computational security. However, its applications have remained confined to protocols. Developing cryptographically sound symbolic methods for primitives remains a challenge.

A recent alternative to cryptographically sound symbolic methods uses programming language techniques for reasoning about the security of constructions directly in the computational model. This alternative is embodied in tools like CryptoVerif [12] and EasyCrypt [4], which have been used to verify emblematic cryptographic constructions. Proofs built using these tools yield reductions with concrete security bounds. However, these tools are primarily interactive and their use requires expert knowledge. Combining them with fully automated methods that apply to large classes of cryptographic primitives has remained an open problem.

A converse goal to proving security is finding attacks. Recent work [3] explores the use of symbolic methods to find attacks and estimate their success probability. Automating attack finding can provide valuable feedback during cryptographic design and be used to evaluate empirically the completeness of automated security analyses by answering questions such as how many constructions that may be secure cannot be proven so.

Contributions. We present new methods for automatically analyzing the security of padding-based encryption schemes, i.e. public-key encryption schemes built from hash functions and trapdoor permutations, such as OAEP [11], SAEP [14] or PSS-E [16]. Collectively, the methods presented can report a proof, with a concrete security bound, or an attack. These methods rest on two main technical contributions.

First, we introduce specialized logics for proving chosen-plaintext and chosen-ciphertext security. Proof rules have a symbolic flavor and proof search can be automated, yet one can extract concrete security bounds from valid derivations. This is achieved through a novel combination of symbolic and computational methods; for instance, the logics use symbolic deducibility relations for computing bounds of the probability of events, and for checking the existence of reductions to computational assumptions.

Second, we propose fully automated methods for finding attacks against chosen-plaintext and chosen-ciphertext security. Our methods are inspired by static equivalence [1], and exploit algebraic properties of trapdoor permutations to find attacks against realizations of schemes that are consistent with computational assumptions.

We demonstrate the strengths of our methods by implementing a toolset, called ZooCrypt, for analyzing fully automatically a set of user-given or machine-generated schemes. We generate more than one million examples and use the toolset to analyze their (in)security. The output of the analysis is a database that records for each scheme and set of assumptions, either an adversary that breaks the security of the scheme or a formal derivation that proves its security.

We stress that we focus on padding-based encryption primarily for illustrative purposes. Padding-based schemes include many practically relevant constructions, and provide an excellent testbed to evaluate the effectiveness of our methods and illustrate their working.

Contents. § 2 provides background on public-key encryption schemes and their security; § 3 introduces symbolic tools that are the base of our analyses; § 4 describes logics for chosen-plaintext and chosen-ciphertext security, while § 5 covers attack finding techniques; § 6 reports on the implementation of ZooCrypt and on its evaluation. We conclude with a survey of related work and directions for future work.

A web interface for browsing a database of our results and for experimenting with the interactive mode is available at `http://easycrypt.info/zoocrypt/`

2. CRYPTOGRAPHIC BACKGROUND

This section provides some background on padding-based public-key encryption schemes and their security.

2.1 Padding-Based Public-Key Encryption

A public-key encryption scheme is a triple of probabilistic algorithms $(\mathcal{KG}, \mathcal{E}, \mathcal{D})$:

Key Generation The key generation algorithm $\mathcal{KG}$ outputs a pair of keys (pk, sk); pk is a *public-key* used for encryption, sk is a *secret-key* used for decryption;

Encryption Given a public-key pk and a message m, the encryption algorithm $\mathcal{E}_{pk}(m)$ outputs a ciphertext c;

Decryption Given a secret-key sk and a ciphertext c, the decryption algorithm $\mathcal{D}_{sk}(c)$ outputs either message m or a distinguished value $\perp$ denoting failure.

We require that for pairs of keys (pk, sk) generated by $\mathcal{KG}$, $\mathcal{D}_{sk}(\mathcal{E}_{pk}(m)) = m$ holds for any message m.

We study schemes built from trapdoor permutations, hash functions and basic bitstring operations, such as bitwise exclusive-or ($\oplus$), concatenation ($\|$) and projection. We let $\{0,1\}^n$ denote the set of bitstrings of length n and $[x]_n^\ell$ the bitstring obtained from x by dropping its n most significant bits and taking the ℓ most significant bits of the result.

Trapdoor permutations are functions that are easy to evaluate, but hard to invert without knowing a secret trapdoor. Formally, a family of trapdoor permutations on $\{0,1\}^n$ is a triple of algorithms $(\mathcal{KG}, f, f^{-1})$ such that for any pair of keys (pk, sk) output by $\mathcal{KG}$, f_{pk} and f_{sk}^{-1} are permutations on $\{0,1\}^n$ and inverse of each other. The security of a family of trapdoor permutations is measured by the probability that an adversary (partially) inverts f on a random input.

Definition 1 (One-Way Trapdoor Permutation) *Let $\Theta = (\mathcal{KG}, f, f^{-1})$ be a family of trapdoor permutations on $\{0,1\}^n$ and let k, ℓ be such that $k+\ell \le n$. The probability of an algorithm $\mathcal{I}$ in q-inverting Θ on bits $[k+1 \dots k+\ell]$ is*

$$\mathbf{Succ}_{\Theta}^{\text{s-pd-OW}}(k, \ell, q, \mathcal{I}) \stackrel{\text{def}}{=} \Pr\left[\mathsf{OW}_k^\ell : [s]_k^\ell \in S \wedge |S| \le q\right]$$

where OW_k^ℓ is the experiment:

$$(pk, sk) \leftarrow \mathcal{KG};\ s \xleftarrow{\$} \{0,1\}^n;\ S \leftarrow \mathcal{I}(f_{pk}(s), pk)$$

This generalizes the set partial-domain one-wayness problem of Fujisaki et al. [20], which corresponds to the case $k = 0$. We define $\mathbf{Succ}_{\Theta}^{\text{s-pd-OW}}(k, \ell, q, t)$ as the maximal success probability over all inverters executing in time t, and omit the first parameter when it is 0. When $k = 0$, $\ell = n$, and $q = 1$, the experiment corresponds to the standard one-wayness problem, and we note this quantity $\mathbf{Succ}_{\Theta}^{\text{OW}}(t)$.

We use PSS-E [16] as a running example, and we give a practical interpretation of our proofs for RSA-PSS-E, which instantiates PSS-E with RSA as trapdoor permutation.

Definition 2 (PSS-E) *Let $(\mathcal{KG}_f, f, f^{-1})$ be a family of one-way trapdoor permutations on $\{0,1\}^k$, $k_0 \in \mathbb{N}$, and let*

$$G : \{0,1\}^{k_1} \to \{0,1\}^{k-k_1} \qquad H : \{0,1\}^{k-k_1} \to \{0,1\}^{k_1}$$

be two hash functions such that $k_1 < k$. PSS-E is composed of the following triple of algorithms:

$$\begin{array}{lll}
\mathcal{KG} & \stackrel{\text{def}}{=} & (pk, sk) \leftarrow \mathcal{KG}_f;\ \mathsf{return}\ (pk, sk) \\
\mathcal{E}_{pk}(m) & \stackrel{\text{def}}{=} & r \xleftarrow{\$} \{0,1\}^{k_0};\ s \leftarrow H(m \| r); \\
 & & t \leftarrow G(s) \oplus (m \| r);\ \mathsf{return}\ f_{pk}(s \| t) \\
\mathcal{D}_{sk}(c) & \stackrel{\text{def}}{=} & s \| t \leftarrow f_{sk}^{-1}(c);\ x \leftarrow t \oplus G(s); \\
 & & \mathsf{if}\ s = H(x)\ \mathsf{then\ return}\ [x]_0^{k-k_1-k_0}\ \mathsf{else\ return}\ \perp
\end{array}$$

2.2 Security of Padding-Based Encryption

We consider two security notions for public-key encryption: chosen-plaintext security, or IND-CPA, and adaptive chosen-ciphertext security, or IND-CCA. Both can be described succinctly using the following experiment, or game, in which an adversary $\mathcal{A}$ represented as a pair of procedures $(\mathcal{A}_1, \mathcal{A}_2)$ interacts with a challenger:

$$(pk, sk) \leftarrow \mathcal{KG};\ (m_0, m_1, \sigma) \leftarrow \mathcal{A}_1^{\vec{H}}(pk);$$
$$b \xleftarrow{\$} \{0,1\};\ c^\star \leftarrow \mathcal{E}_{pk}(m_b);\ \bar{b} \leftarrow \mathcal{A}_2^{\vec{H}}(c^\star, \sigma)$$

The challenger first generates a fresh pair of keys (pk, sk) and gives the public key pk to the adversary, which returns a pair of messages (m_0, m_1) of its choice. The challenger then samples uniformly a bit b, encrypts the message m_b and gives the resulting ciphertext $c^\star$ (the challenge) to the adversary. Finally, the adversary outputs a guess $\bar{b}$ for b. Note that $\mathcal{A}_1$ and $\mathcal{A}_2$ can communicate with each other through σ and have oracle access to all hash functions $\vec{H}$ used in the scheme. We call this basic experiment CPA; we define the experiment CCA similarly, except that the adversary $\mathcal{A}$ is given access to a decryption oracle $\mathcal{D}_{sk}(\cdot)$, with the proviso that $\mathcal{A}_2$ cannot ask for the decryption of the challenge ciphertext $c^\star$. In the remainder, we note $\boldsymbol{L}_H$ the list of queries that the adversary makes to a hash oracle H in either experiment, and $\boldsymbol{L}_{\mathcal{D}}$ the list of decryption queries that $\mathcal{A}_2$ makes during the second phase of the CCA experiment.

Security is measured by the advantage of an adversary playing against a CPA or CCA challenger.

Definition 3 (Adversary Advantage) *The advantage of an adversary $\mathcal{A}$ against the* CPA *and* CCA *security of an encryption scheme $\Pi = (\mathcal{KG}, \mathcal{E}, \mathcal{D})$ is defined respectively as:*

$$\mathbf{Adv}_{\Pi}^{\mathsf{CPA}}(\mathcal{A}) \stackrel{\text{def}}{=} 2\Pr\left[\mathsf{CPA} : \bar{b} = b\right] - 1$$
$$\mathbf{Adv}_{\Pi}^{\mathsf{CCA}}(\mathcal{A}) \stackrel{\text{def}}{=} 2\Pr\left[\mathsf{CCA} : \bar{b} = b\right] - 1$$

We define $\mathbf{Adv}_{\Pi}^{\mathsf{CPA}}(t, \vec{q})$ (resp. $\mathbf{Adv}_{\Pi}^{\mathsf{CCA}}(t, \vec{q})$) as the maximal advantage over all adversaries $\mathcal{A}$ that execute within time t and make at most $q_{\mathcal{O}}$ queries to oracle $\mathcal{O}$.

To define asymptotic security, we consider instead of a single scheme, a family of schemes Π_η indexed by a security parameter $\eta \in \mathbb{N}$. The adversary advantage thus becomes a function of η. We say that a scheme is secure if the advantage of any adversary executing in time polynomial in η is a negligible function ν of η, i.e. $\forall c.\ \exists n_c.\ \forall n > n_c.\ \nu(n) < n^{-c}$.

A security proof for a padding-based encryption scheme is a reduction showing that any efficient adversary against the security of the scheme can be turned into an efficient inverter for the underlying trapdoor permutation. Proofs are typically in the random oracle model, where hash functions are modeled as truly random functions. One seemingly artificial property of the random oracle model is that reductions to computational assumptions can adaptively choose the responses of oracles modeling hash functions; this property is called *programmability*. In contrast, we only consider proofs in the non-programmable random oracle model, where reductions can only observe oracle queries and responses.

3. SYMBOLIC TOOLS

We introduce algebraic expressions to model encryption schemes, and symbolic notions to model the knowledge that adversaries or honest users can derive from an expression.

3.1 Syntax and Semantics of Expressions

Expressions are built from a set $\mathcal{R}$ of random bitstrings and a set $\mathcal{X}$ of variables, using bitstring operations, hash functions drawn from a set $\mathcal{H}$, and trapdoor permutations drawn from a set $\mathcal{F}$. The grammar of expressions is

e	$::=$	x	variable
	$\mid$	r	uniformly random bitstring
	$\mid$	0^n	all-zero bitstring of length n
	$\mid$	$\mathsf{f}(e)$	permutation
	$\mid$	$\mathsf{f}^{-1}(e)$	inverse permutation
	$\mid$	$H(e)$	hash function
	$\mid$	$e \oplus e$	exclusive-or
	$\mid$	$e \parallel e$	concatenation
	$\mid$	$[e]_n^\ell$	drop n bits then take ℓ bits

where $x \in \mathcal{X}$, $r \in \mathcal{R}$, $n, \ell \in \mathcal{S}$, $\mathsf{f} \in \mathcal{F}$, and $H \in \mathcal{H}$. We let $\oplus$ take precedence over $\parallel$. For instance, the encryption algorithm of PSS-E is represented as the expression:

$$\mathsf{f}(H(m \parallel r) \parallel G(H(m \parallel r)) \oplus (m \parallel r)).$$

Expressions are typed using a size-based type system. A type $\ell \in \mathcal{S}$ is either a size variable or the sum $k + n$ of two types. We note $|e|$ the type of an expression e, which intuitively represents the length of the bitstring it denotes. For instance, the type of $e_1 \parallel e_2$ is $|e_1| + |e_2|$ and $e_1 \oplus e_2$ is well-typed iff $|e_1| = |e_2|$. In an asymptotic setting, we interpret size variables as functions that grow polynomially with the security parameter.

We let $\mathcal{R}(e)$, $\mathcal{X}(e)$, $\mathcal{F}(e)$ and $\mathcal{H}(e)$ denote, respectively, the sets of random bitstrings, variables, trapdoor permutation, and hash function symbols occurring in an expression e. We note $e\{\vec{e}_1/\vec{e}_0\}$ the simultaneous substitution of $\vec{e}_0$ by $\vec{e}_1$ in e and $\mathcal{ST}_H(e)$ the set of sub-expressions of e that are of the form $H(e')$. Abusing notation, we write e.g. $\mathcal{R}(e_1, e_2)$ instead of $\mathcal{R}(e_1) \cup \mathcal{R}(e_2)$.

Given values for size variables in $|e|$ and trapdoor permutations with adequate domains, we interpret a well-typed expression e as a probabilistic algorithm $(\!|e|\!)$ that calls oracles in $\mathcal{H}(e)$ and takes as parameters values for variables in $\mathcal{X}(e)$. The algorithm is implicitly parametrized by public and secret keys (if required) of the trapdoor permutations that occur in e. See the full version for a formal definition.

3.2 Equality and Deducibility

We model algebraic properties of bitstrings using the equational theory $=_E$, defined as the smallest congruence relation on well-typed expressions that contains all instances of the axioms of Figure 1. The relation $=_E$ is sound [9] for all trapdoor permutations and valid key pairs. This means that for all closed expressions s and t, $s =_E t$ implies that $(\!|s|\!)$ and $(\!|t|\!)$ return the same value when shared random bitstrings are jointly sampled; formally,

$$\Pr\left[y \leftarrow (\!|s \parallel t|\!) : [y]_0^{|s|} = [y]_{|s|}^{|t|}\right] = 1.$$

We use the standard notion of deducibility from symbolic cryptography to reason about adversarial knowledge. Informally, an expression e' is deducible from e if there exists an efficient algorithm that computes e' from e. We use contexts to describe such algorithms symbolically. A context is an expression with a distinguished variable $*$. The application $C[e]$ of a context C to an expression e is defined by substitution.

$$(e_1 \oplus e_2) \oplus e_3 = e_1 \oplus (e_2 \oplus e_3) \quad e_1 \oplus e_2 = e_2 \oplus e_1$$
$$e \oplus 0^{|e|} = e \quad e \oplus e = 0^{|e|} \quad [0^n]_\ell^k = 0^k$$
$$(e_1 \,\|\, e_2) \,\|\, e_3 = e_1 \,\|\, (e_2 \,\|\, e_3) \quad [e_1 \,\|\, e_2]_0^{|e_1|} = e_1$$
$$[e_1 \,\|\, e_2]_{|e_1|}^\ell = [e_2]_0^\ell \quad [e_1 \oplus e_2]_n^\ell = [e_1]_n^\ell \oplus [e_2]_n^\ell$$
$$[e]_0^{|e|} = e \quad [[e]_n^\ell]_{n'}^{\ell'} = [e]_{n+n'}^{\ell'} \quad [e]_n^\ell \,\|\, [e]_{n+\ell}^{\ell'} = [e]_n^{\ell+\ell'}$$
$$\mathsf{f}(\mathsf{f}^{-1}(e)) = e \quad \mathsf{f}^{-1}(\mathsf{f}(e)) = e$$

Figure 1: Equational theory for algebraic expressions

Definition 4 (Deducibility) *An expression e' is deducible from another expression e, written $e \vdash e'$, if there is a context C such that*

1. $\mathcal{R}(C) = \emptyset$, $\mathcal{X}(C) \subseteq \{*\}$;
2. f^{-1} *does not occur in* C, *and*
3. $C[e] =_E e'$.

We define $\vdash^\star$ analogously, but dropping restriction 2.

In the full version we prove that $\vdash$ is sound in the following sense: $e \vdash e'$ implies that there is an efficient algorithm that computes e' from e and the public keys of the trapdoor permutations in e and e'. For $\vdash^\star$ we obtain an identical result, except that the corresponding algorithm can also use the secret keys of the trapdoor permutations. Note that we do not require $\vdash$-completeness, also known as $\not\vdash$-soundness [9], since we never use the deducibility relation to conclude that an expression is not computable from another.

3.3 Inequality and Static Distinguishability

Static equivalence [1] models symbolic indistinguishability of expressions. Informally, two expressions e_0 and e_1 are statically equivalent if all tests of the form $C[\cdot] =_E C'[\cdot]$ succeed for e_0 if and only if they succeed for e_1. Since the completeness of $=_E$ with respect to the computational interpretation of expressions is an open question, we use a relation inspired by static equivalence to model distinguishability of expressions. We call this relation static distinguishability, and define it in terms of an apartness relation $\sharp$ in place of $\neq_E$. The soundness of this relation implies that if $s \sharp t$ holds, then the probability that the results of $(\!|s|\!)$ and $(\!|t|\!)$ coincide when shared random bitstrings are jointly sampled is negligible. The inductive definition of $\sharp$ comprises axioms such as $r \sharp 0$ and $r \sharp r'$, and rules stating that $s \sharp t$ implies $H(s) \sharp H(t)$, that $C[s] \sharp C[t]$ implies $s \sharp t$, and that $s \sharp t$ and $t =_E u$ implies $s \sharp u$.

Definition 5 (Static Distinguishability) *Relation $\not\approx$ is the smallest symmetric relation on well-typed expressions such that $e_0 \not\approx e_1$ iff there are contexts C and C' such that*

1. $\mathcal{R}(C, C') = \emptyset$, $\mathcal{X}(C) \subseteq \{*\}$;
2. f^{-1} *does not occur in* C, C', *and*
3. $C[e_0] =_E C'[e_0]$ *and* $C[e_1] \sharp C'[e_1]$.

We use static distinguishability to find attacks on encryption schemes. For the attacks to be meaningful, we rely on the soundness of $\not\approx$, which follows from the soundness of $=_E$ and $\sharp$. Informally, if $e_0 \not\approx e_1$ holds, then there is an efficient algorithm $\mathsf{distinguish}$ that when given as input the public keys of trapdoor permutations and a value computed using $(\!|e_0|\!)$ returns 0, but when given instead a value computed using $(\!|e_1|\!)$ returns 1, except with negligible probability.

As an example, the expressions $e_0 = \mathsf{f}(r) \,\|\, (r \oplus 0)$ and $e_1 = \mathsf{f}(r) \,\|\, (r_1 \oplus r_2)$ are distinguishable, because for contexts

$$C = [*]_0^{|\mathsf{f}(r)|} \text{ and } C' = \mathsf{f}\left([*]_{|\mathsf{f}(r)|}^{|r|}\right)$$

it holds that $C[e_0] =_E C'[e_0]$ and $C[e_1] \sharp C'[e_1]$. A simple distinguisher algorithm applies the algorithms corresponding to C and C' to its input and returns 0 if this yields equal bitstrings and 1 otherwise.

4. PROOF SYSTEMS

This section introduces logics for proving chosen-plaintext and chosen-ciphertext security of padding-based schemes by reduction to computational assumptions on the underlying trapdoor permutations. For the sake of readability, our presentation separates the derivation of valid judgments (§ 4.1 and § 4.2) from the computation of concrete security bounds from valid derivations (§ 4.3). The soundness of the logics is stated in § 4.4; proofs appear in the full version [6].

4.1 Chosen-Plaintext Security

Judgments predicate over the probability of an event ϕ in the CPA experiment where the challenge ciphertext is computed using $(\!|c^\star|\!)$, which we denote $\mathsf{CPA}(c^\star)$. Events are drawn from the grammar

$$\phi ::= \mathsf{Guess} \mid \mathsf{Ask}(H, e) \mid \phi \wedge \phi$$

where Guess corresponds to the adversary correctly guessing the hidden bit b, and $\mathsf{Ask}(H, e)$ corresponds to the adversary asking the query $H(e)$.

Judgments are of the form $\vDash_{\hat{p}} c^\star : \phi$, where $c^\star$ is a well-typed expression with $\mathcal{X}(c^\star) \subseteq \{m\}$, ϕ is an event, and $\hat{p} \in \{0, 1/2\}$ is a probability tag[1]. The CPA logic is designed to ensure that if $\vDash_{\hat{p}} c^\star : \phi$ is derivable, then the probability of ϕ in the experiment $\mathsf{CPA}(c^\star)$ is upper bounded by $\hat{p}$ plus a negligible term. In particular, if $\vDash_{1/2} c^\star : \mathsf{Guess}$ is derivable, then any scheme Π with encryption algorithm $(\!|c^\star|\!)$ is asymptotically secure against chosen-plaintext attacks.

Derivability in the logic is parametrized by a set Γ of computational assumptions of the form (f, k, ℓ), where $\mathsf{f} \in \mathcal{F}$ and $k, \ell \in \mathcal{S}$. Such assumptions state that it is hard to compute $[r]_k^\ell$ from $\mathsf{f}(r)$. There is no restriction on Γ: it may contain assumptions for several permutations, and multiple assumptions for any given permutation.

Figure 2 presents the rules of the proof system. The terminal rules [Rnd] and [OW] are decorated with information necessary to compute concrete bounds (§ 4.3). We only allow to apply a rule if all instances of expressions are well-typed; this implies that for any valid derivation ∇ there exists a common typing environment for all rule applications.

The rules [Opt], [Perm], [Merge], and [Split] correspond to bridging steps in proofs and allow reformulating judgments into equivalent forms. The rule [Opt] corresponds to *optimistic sampling*, which allows substituting $e \oplus r$ by r

[1] Probability tags increase the readability of rules and support a more uniform interpretation of judgments. However, they are superfluous and can be deduced from the shape of the event: for every valid judgment $\vDash_{\hat{p}} c^\star : \phi$, the probability tag $\hat{p}$ is $1/2$ iff $\phi = \mathsf{Guess}$.

$$\frac{\models_{\hat{p}} c^\star : \phi \qquad r \notin \mathcal{R}(e)}{\models_{\hat{p}} c^\star \{e \oplus r/r\} : \phi \{e \oplus r/r\}}[\mathsf{Opt}] \qquad \frac{\models_{\hat{p}} c^\star : \phi}{\models_{\hat{p}} c^\star \{\mathsf{f}(r)/r\} : \phi \{\mathsf{f}(r)/r\}}[\mathsf{Perm}] \qquad \frac{\models_{\hat{p}} c_2^\star : \phi_2 \quad c_1^\star =_E c_2^\star \quad \phi_1 \Longrightarrow_E \phi_2}{\models_{\hat{p}} c_1^\star : \phi_1}[\mathsf{Sub}]$$

$$\frac{\models_{\hat{p}} c^\star \{r_1 \| r_2/r\} : \phi \{r_1 \| r_2/r\} \quad r_1, r_2 \notin \mathcal{R}(c^\star, \phi) \quad r_1 \neq r_2}{\models_{\hat{p}} c^\star : \phi}[\mathsf{Split}] \qquad \frac{\models_{\hat{p}} c^\star : \phi \quad r_1, r_2 \notin \mathcal{R}(c^\star, \phi) \quad r_1 \neq r_2}{\models_{\hat{p}} c^\star \{r_1 \| r_2/r\} : \phi \{r_1 \| r_2/r\}}[\mathsf{Merge}]$$

$$\frac{\models_{\hat{p}} c^\star : \phi \quad \models_0 c^\star : \mathsf{Ask}(H, e) \quad r \notin \mathcal{R}(e) \quad H \notin \mathcal{H}(c^\star, \phi, e)}{\models_{\hat{p}} c^\star \{H(e)/r\} : \phi \{H(e)/r\}}[\mathsf{Fail}_1]$$

$$\frac{\models_{\hat{p}} c^\star : \phi \quad \models_0 c^\star \{H(e)/r\} : \phi \{H(e)/r\} \wedge \mathsf{Ask}(H, e) \quad r \notin \mathcal{R}(e) \quad H \notin \mathcal{H}(c^\star, \phi, e)}{\models_{\hat{p}} c^\star \{H(e)/r\} : \phi \{H(e)/r\}}[\mathsf{Fail}_2]$$

$$\frac{\mathcal{X}(c^\star) = \emptyset}{\models_{1/2} c^\star : \mathsf{Guess}}[\mathsf{Ind}] \qquad \frac{\vec{e} \| \mathcal{R}(c^\star) \| m \vdash^\star r \qquad r \notin \mathcal{R}(c^\star)}{\models_0 c^\star : \mathsf{Ask}(H_1, e_1) \wedge \cdots \wedge \mathsf{Ask}(H_n, e_n)}[\mathsf{Rnd}(|r|, \vec{H})]$$

$$\frac{\vec{e} \| r_2 \| m \vdash [r_1]_k^\ell \quad \mathsf{f}(r_1) \| r_2 \| m \vdash c^\star \quad r_1 \neq r_2 \quad (\mathsf{f}, k, \ell) \in \Gamma}{\models_0 c^\star : \mathsf{Ask}(H_1, e_1) \wedge \cdots \wedge \mathsf{Ask}(H_n, e_n)}[\mathsf{OW}_k^\ell(\mathsf{f}, \vec{H})]$$

Figure 2: Proof rules of the CPA logic ($\Longrightarrow_E$ denotes implication in first-order logic with respect to $=_E$)

provided that $r \notin \mathcal{R}(e)$. The rule [Perm] replaces all occurrences of $\mathsf{f}(r)$ by r. The rule [Merge] replaces the concatenation of two random bitstrings r_1 and r_2 with a fresh random bitstring r. The rule [Split] performs the opposite transformation; it replaces a random bitstring r with the concatenation of two fresh random bitstrings r_1 and r_2.

Rule [Sub] can be used to weaken the event and replace expressions in judgments with equivalent expressions. This rule is often needed to prepare the ground for the application of another rule: e.g. rule [Opt] can be applied to a judgment that contains $H(r)$ to obtain $H(e \oplus r)$ by first using [Sub] to replace $H(r)$ by $H(e \oplus (e \oplus r))$.

The rules [Fail$_1$] and [Fail$_2$], for *equivalence up to failure*, correspond to specialized forms of Shoup's Fundamental Lemma [29] and create two branches in a derivation. These rules can be used to substitute an expression $H(e)$ by a random bitstring r, incurring a probability loss in the reduction corresponding to the probability of the CPA adversary asking the query $H(e)$. One can choose to analyze this probability either after (as in rule [Fail$_1$]) or before applying the substitution (as in rule [Fail$_2$]).

Finally, the rules [Ind], [Rnd], and [OW] are terminal and provide a means of directly bounding the probability of an event. The first two rules are information-theoretic, whereas the third formalizes a reduction to a computational assumption. The rule [Ind] closes a branch when the challenge ciphertext no longer depends on a plaintext variable; in terms of the CPA experiment, this means that the challenge is independent from the hidden bit b, and hence the probability that an adversary guesses it is exactly $1/2$. The rule [Rnd] closes a branch in the case when the adversary must make a number of oracle queries that would require guessing random values that are independent from its view. The rule [OW] closes a branch when it is possible to find a reduction to the problem of partially inverting a trapdoor permutation: this is the case when the image of a random element (the challenge of an inverter) can be embedded in the challenge ciphertext of the CPA experiment in such a way that its (partial) pre-image can be computed from the oracle queries made by the CPA adversary. To apply this rule, r_1 is usually obtained by searching for applications of f in $c^\star$ and r_2 is set to the concatenation of all random bitstrings in $\mathcal{R}(c^\star) \setminus \{r_1\}$. Additionally, one must check that the assumption (f, k, ℓ) is an assumption in Γ.

4.2 Chosen-Ciphertext Security

Judgments are of the form $\models_{\hat{p}} (c^\star, D) : \phi$, where $\hat{p}$ is a probability tag, $c^\star$ is an expression, D is a decryption oracle, and ϕ is an event. The challenge ciphertext $c^\star$ and the tag $\hat{p}$ can take the same values as in the CPA logic, whereas the decryption oracle is drawn from the following grammar

$$\begin{array}{rcl} F & ::= & \mathsf{find}\ x\ \mathsf{in}\ \boldsymbol{L}_H, F \ \mid\ \diamond \\ T & ::= & e = e' \ \mid\ \mathsf{Ask}(H, e) \ \mid\ T \wedge T \\ D & ::= & F : T \rhd e \end{array}$$

We assume that D does not contain random bitstrings and that all variables in expressions in D are bound by find, except for a distinguished parameter c denoting the ciphertext queried to the oracle. The above grammar is sufficiently expressive to encode decryption algorithms of padding-based schemes, as well as plaintext-simulators used in reductions.[2]

Informally, given as input a ciphertext c, an algorithm $\mathsf{find}\ \vec{x}\ \mathsf{in}\ \boldsymbol{L}_{\vec{H}} : T \rhd e$ searches among the queries made by an adversary to oracles $\vec{H}$ for values $\vec{v}$ satisfying T. If such values are found, it returns the value of $e\{\vec{v}/\vec{x}\}$; otherwise, it returns $\perp$. Conditions in T are interpreted as equality checks on bitstrings and membership tests in the lists of oracle queries made by the adversary. We write $T \rhd e$ instead of $\diamond : T \rhd e$ and note $(\!|D|\!)$ the interpretation of D as an algorithm.

Events of the logic are as in the CPA logic or of the form $\exists x \in \boldsymbol{L}_{\mathcal{D}}.\ T$. Events Guess and $\mathsf{Ask}(H, e)$ are defined as in the CPA logic but for the CCA experiment. For $\exists x \in \boldsymbol{L}_{\mathcal{D}}.\ T$, the quantified variable ranges over the ciphertexts queried to the decryption oracle during the second phase of the CCA experiment; tests are interpreted as described above.

[2]A plaintext-simulator is an algorithm that extracts the plaintext from a ciphertext by reconstructing it from oracle queries made by an adversary, without using the trapdoor to the underlying permutation; a plaintext-simulator that does not query any hash oracle is called a plaintext-extractor.

$$\frac{\models_{\hat{p}} c^\star : \phi \quad \mathcal{ST}_{\mathsf{f}^{-1}}(T,t) = \emptyset}{\models_{\hat{p}} (c^\star, F : T \rhd t) : \phi}[\mathsf{Pub}(F,T,t)] \qquad \frac{\models_{\hat{p}} (c^\star, \mathsf{find}\ x\ \mathsf{in}\ \boldsymbol{L}_H, F : T \wedge x = e \rhd t) : \phi}{\models_{\hat{p}} (c^\star, F : T\{e/x\} \wedge \mathsf{Ask}(H,e) \rhd t\{e/x\}) : \phi}[\mathsf{Find}]$$

$$\frac{\models_{\hat{p}} (c_2^\star, F : T_2 \rhd t_2) : \phi_2 \quad c_1^\star =_E c_2^\star \quad \phi_1 \Longrightarrow_E \phi_2 \quad T_1 \Longleftrightarrow_E T_2 \quad t_1 =_E t_2}{\models_{\hat{p}} (c_1^\star, F : T_1 \rhd t_1) : \phi_1}[\mathsf{Conv}] \qquad \frac{}{\models_0 (c^\star, D) : \exists c \in \boldsymbol{L}_{\mathcal{D}}.\ c = c^\star}[\mathsf{False}]$$

$$\frac{\begin{array}{c}\mathcal{ST}_H(c^\star) = \{H(e^\star)\} \quad \mathcal{ST}_H(T,t) = \{H(e)\} \\ \models_{\hat{p}} (c^\star, T \wedge \mathsf{Ask}(H,e) \rhd t) : \phi \quad \models_0 (c^\star, T \wedge \mathsf{Ask}(H,e) \rhd t) : \exists c \in \boldsymbol{L}_{\mathcal{D}}.\ T \wedge e^\star = e \quad \models \mathsf{negl}_r(T\{r/H(e)\})\end{array}}{\models_{\hat{p}} (c^\star, T \rhd t) : \phi}[\mathsf{Bad}]$$

$$\frac{\models \mathsf{negl}_r(T_i)}{\models \mathsf{negl}_r(T_1 \wedge T_2)}[\mathsf{PAnd}_i] \qquad \frac{c \,\|\, e \vdash^\star [r]_k^\ell \quad r \notin \mathcal{R}(e')}{\models \mathsf{negl}_r(e = e')}[\mathsf{PEqs}(\ell)] \qquad \frac{c \,\|\, e \vdash^\star [r]_k^\ell}{\models \mathsf{negl}_r(\mathsf{Ask}(H,e))}[\mathsf{PRnd}(\ell, H)]$$

$$\frac{r \notin \mathcal{R}(c^\star, e)}{\models_0 c^\star : e = r}[\mathsf{Eqs}(|r|)] \qquad \frac{\vec{e} \,\|\, \mathcal{R}(c^\star) \,\|\, m \vdash^\star r \quad r \notin \mathcal{R}(c^\star)}{\models_0 c^\star : \exists c \in \boldsymbol{L}_{\mathcal{D}}.\ \mathsf{Ask}(H_1,e_1) \wedge \cdots \wedge \mathsf{Ask}(H_n,e_n)}[\mathsf{Rnd}(|r|, \vec{H})]$$

$$\frac{\vec{e} \,\|\, r_2 \,\|\, m \vdash [r_1]_k^\ell \quad \mathsf{f}(r_1) \,\|\, r_2 \,\|\, m \vdash c^\star \quad r_1 \neq r_2 \quad (\mathsf{f}, k, \ell) \in \Gamma}{\models_0 c^\star : \exists c \in \boldsymbol{L}_{\mathcal{D}}.\ \mathsf{Ask}(H_1,e_1) \wedge \cdots \wedge \mathsf{Ask}(H_n,e_n)}[\mathsf{OW}_k^\ell(\mathsf{f}, \vec{H})]$$

Figure 3: Proof rules for CCA judgments, proof rules for tests, and extended rules for the CPA logic

A judgment $\models_{\hat{p}} (c^\star, D) : \phi$ predicates over the probability of ϕ in the CCA experiment where the challenge ciphertext is computed using $(\!|c^\star|\!)$, and decryption queries are answered by $(\!|D|\!)$; we note this experiment $\mathsf{CCA}(c^\star, D)$. The judgment states that the probability of ϕ in this experiment is upper bounded by $\hat{p}$ plus a negligible term.

Figure 3 presents the rules of the logic. The rule [Bad] allows to transform the decryption oracle so that it rejects ciphertexts whose decryption requires to make oracle queries that have not yet been made by the adversary. The resulting decryption oracle no longer makes new queries to the given oracle H. It suffices to consider two events that can lead the adversary to distinguish between the original and transformed oracles: 1. when the adversary makes a decryption query c such that T succeeds after making a query $H(e)$ that is also needed to compute the challenge ciphertext; 2. when the test T succeeds, even though it gets a random answer from H. The probability of this last event can be proven negligible using the rules [PAnd], [PEqs], and [PRnd] in Figure 3.

The rule [False] captures the fact that the adversary cannot ask for the decryption of $c^\star$ during the second phase of the CCA experiment; the probability of this happening is 0. Rule [Conv] allows switching between observationally equivalent decryption oracles and weakening the event considered. This rule is usually used to transform a test that requires f^{-1} into an equivalent test that only requires f, so that [Pub] becomes applicable.

The rule [Find] allows replacing an oracle that computes a value explicitly by one that searches for it among oracle queries made by the adversary.

The rule [Pub] links the CCA logic with the CPA logic, and captures the intuition that an adversary does not gain any advantage from getting access to a publicly simulatable decryption oracle. Note that the judgment in the premise may be of the form $\models_{\hat{p}} c^\star : \phi$, where ϕ is an event of the CCA logic. This kind of judgment is handled by the rule [Eqs] and the generalized rules [Rnd] and [OW] given in Figure 3.

4.3 Concrete Bounds

In this section we show how to extract concrete security bounds from derivations in our logics. Security bounds p are drawn from the grammar

$$\begin{array}{l} p ::= \epsilon \mid 1/2 + \epsilon \quad q ::= 1 \mid q \times q \mid q_H \mid q_{\mathcal{D}} \\ t ::= t_{\mathcal{A}} \mid q \mid q \times t_{\mathsf{f}} \mid t + t \\ \epsilon ::= 0 \mid 2^{-k} \mid \mathbf{Succ}^{\mathsf{s\text{-}pd\text{-}OW}}_{\Theta_{\mathsf{f}}}(k, \ell, q, t) \mid q \times \epsilon \mid \epsilon + \epsilon \end{array}$$

where $k, \ell \in \mathcal{S}$, $H \in \mathcal{H}$, $\mathsf{f} \in \mathcal{F}$, t_{f} is a worst-case time bound for evaluating f, and $t_{\mathcal{A}}$ is the execution time of $\mathcal{A}$.

Security bounds are computed from a derivation ∇ in the CPA or CCA logic using a function $\mathcal{B}$ parametrized by the computational resources of an adversary, namely, its execution time $t_{\mathcal{A}}$ and the number of oracle queries it can make, $\vec{q}$. The definition of function $\mathcal{B}$ is given in Figure 4. We omit resource parameters when they remain unchanged and, for a derivation ∇ with rule R at its root, we use L_∇ to refer to R's label and ∇_i to refer to the derivation of the i-th premise of R (premises are enumerated from left to right).

For all bridging rules, the bound is inherited from their single premise. For rules [Fail_1] and [Fail_2], the bound is computed as $p_1 + p_2$ where p_1 is the probability of the original event in the transformed experiment and p_2 bounds the probability of failure. Rule [Bad] is similar except that bounds come from the probability of two different failure events, and one can be triggered in any decryption query.

Rule [Pub] represents a reduction from CCA to CPA, where a simulator $\mathcal{S}$ uses a CCA adversary $\mathcal{A}$ to win in the CPA experiment. We therefore have to compute bounds for the computational resources $(t_{\mathcal{S}}, \vec{q}^{\,\mathcal{S}})$ used by $\mathcal{S}$ in terms of the resources of $\mathcal{A}$ and the plaintext-simulator $F : T \rhd u$. We first define a function T that computes a bound for the time

$$\mathcal{B}_{(t_\mathcal{A},\vec{q})}(\nabla) = \begin{cases} \mathcal{B}(\nabla_1) + \mathcal{B}(\nabla_2) & \text{if } L_\nabla = [\mathsf{Fail}_{1,2}] \\ \mathcal{B}(\nabla_1) + \mathcal{B}(\nabla_2) + q_\mathcal{D}\,\mathcal{B}(\nabla_3) & \text{if } L_\nabla = [\mathsf{Bad}] \\ \mathcal{B}_{(t_\mathcal{S},\vec{q}^\mathcal{S})}(\nabla_1) & \text{if } L_\nabla = [\mathsf{Pub}(F,T,u)] \\ 1/2 & \text{if } L_\nabla = [\mathsf{Ind}] \\ 0 & \text{if } L_\nabla = [\mathsf{False}] \\ q_{\vec{H}} \times 2^{-\ell} & \text{if } L_\nabla = [\mathsf{Rnd}(\ell,\vec{H})] \\ q_H \times 2^{-\ell} & \text{if } L_\nabla = [\mathsf{PRnd}(\ell,H)] \\ 2^{-\ell} & \text{if } L_\nabla = [\mathsf{Eqs}(\ell)] \\ 2^{-\ell} & \text{if } L_\nabla = [\mathsf{PEqs}(\ell)] \\ \mathbf{Succ}^{\mathsf{s\text{-}pd\text{-}OW}}_{\Theta_f}(k,\ell,q_{\vec{H}},t_\mathcal{I}) & \text{if } L_\nabla = [\mathsf{OW}^\ell_k(\mathsf{f},\vec{H})] \\ \mathcal{B}(\nabla_1) & \text{otherwise} \end{cases}$$

where $t_\mathcal{I} = t_\mathcal{A} + T(C_2) + q_{\vec{H}} \times T(C_1)$, where C_1, C_2 are the contexts witnessing the first and second deducibility conditions in the premise of $[\mathsf{OW}^\ell_k(\mathsf{f},\vec{H})]$, $q_{\vec{H}} = \prod_{H_i \in \vec{H}} q_{H_i}$, and

$$t_\mathcal{S} = t_\mathcal{A} + q_\mathcal{D} \times (\mathsf{T}(u) + \mathsf{T}(T) \times \prod_{H_j \text{ in } F} q_{H_j})$$

$$q^\mathcal{S}_{H_i} = q_{H_i} + q_\mathcal{D} \times (\mathsf{Q}_i(u) + \mathsf{Q}_i(T) \times \prod_{H_j \text{ in } F} q_{H_j})$$

Figure 4: Computation of concrete security bounds

required to evaluate a test T or an expression u. Then, $t_\mathcal{S}$ can be defined as $t_\mathcal{A} + q_\mathcal{D} \times t_\mathcal{D}$ where $t_\mathcal{D}$ is the the time required to evaluate the test T on each combination of queries traversed by F, plus the time required to evaluate the answer u. Similarly, we define a function Q_i that bounds the number of queries made to H_i during the simulation of the decryption oracle, and use it to compute $q^\mathcal{S}_{H_i}$.

The rules [Ind] and [False], yield exact bounds that can be readily used. The cases of rules [Rnd], and [PRnd], [Eqs], [PEqs], correspond to the probability of guessing a random bitstring of length ℓ in $q_{\vec{H}}$, q_H, or just 1 tries. In the case of rule [OW], the bound is the maximal success probability against set partial-domain one-wayness over all inverters using the same resources as the reduction we construct. When $k = 0$ and $\ell = |\mathsf{f}|$, we can alternatively use the standard reduction from set one-wayness to one-wayness to obtain the bound $\mathbf{Succ}^{\mathsf{OW}}_{\Theta_f}(t_\mathcal{I} + q_{\vec{H}} \times t_\mathsf{f})$. Here, the adjusted time bound accounts for the fact that the inverter must apply f to every value computed from the adversary queries to $\vec{H}$ using C_1 and compare the result to its challenge to find the right pre-image.

4.4 Soundness

Let Π be an encryption scheme with encryption algorithm $(\!|c^\star|\!)$ and decryption algorithm $(\!|D|\!)$. Assume that the interpretations of trapdoor permutations satisfy all the assumptions in Γ.

Theorem 6 *If ∇ is a derivation of $\models_{1/2} c^\star : \mathsf{Guess}$ under Γ, then*

$$\mathbf{Adv}^{\mathsf{CPA}}_\Pi(t_\mathcal{A},\vec{q}) \leq 2\,\mathcal{B}_{(t_\mathcal{A},\vec{q})}(\nabla) - 1$$

Moreover, this bound is negligible if $t_\mathcal{A}$ and all q_H in $\vec{q}$ are polynomial in the security parameter.

Theorem 7 *If ∇ is a derivation of $\models_{1/2} (c^\star, D) : \mathsf{Guess}$ under Γ, then*

$$\mathbf{Adv}^{\mathsf{CCA}}_\Pi(t_\mathcal{A},\vec{q}) \leq 2\,\mathcal{B}_{(t_\mathcal{A},\vec{q})}(\nabla) - 1$$

Moreover, this bound is negligible if $t_\mathcal{A}$, all q_H in $\vec{q}$, and $q_\mathcal{D}$ are polynomial in the security parameter.

The proofs of these theorems rest on showing the soundness of each individual rule using game-based techniques. They appear in the full version [6].

4.5 Example

In this section we prove the chosen-plaintext security and chosen-ciphertext security of PSS-E by exhibiting derivations in the CPA and CCA logics. Moreover, we illustrate how to derive concrete security bounds from these derivations. Recall that the encryption algorithm of PSS-E is given by the expression

$$\mathsf{f}(H(m \,\|\, r) \,\|\, G(H(m \,\|\, r)) \oplus (m \,\|\, r)).$$

4.5.1 Chosen-Plaintext Security

The derivation for chosen-plaintext security output by our tool is depicted in Figure 5. The proof starts by applying the rule $[\mathsf{Fail}_1]$, replacing the hash $G(H(m \,\|\, r))$ by a fresh random bitstring r'.

In the branch corresponding to the Guess event, we apply optimistic sampling, replacing $r' \oplus (m \,\|\, r)$ by r', and then $[\mathsf{Fail}_1]$ again, obtaining two premises. The premise corresponding to the original Guess event is proved using rule [Ind] since the challenge ciphertext no longer depends on m. The premise corresponding to the failure event can be discharged using [Rnd] because $m \,\|\, r \vdash^\star r$ and r does not appear in the challenge ciphertext, meaning that the adversary would have to guess r to trigger failure.

The derivation ∇_{Ask} of the second premise of the first application of rule $[\mathsf{Fail}_1]$ is obtained similarly. We first apply [Opt] followed by $[\mathsf{Fail}_1]$, resulting in two premises:

1. $\models_0 \mathsf{f}(r'' \,\|\, r') : \mathsf{Ask}(G, r'')$ 2. $\models_0 \mathsf{f}(r'' \,\|\, r') : \mathsf{Ask}(H, m \,\|\, r)$

To prove the first premise, observe that any adversary that asks r'' to G, can be used to invert f on its k_1 most significant bits. However, before applying rule OW, we must first apply [Merge] to replace $r'' \,\|\, r'$ by a fresh random variable r, so that the judgment has the appropriate form.

The second premise corresponds to the same situation encountered before, where the adversary must query $m \,\|\, r$ to H to trigger failure, but r does not occur in the challenge ciphertext. We conclude as before using [Rnd].

Concrete security bound.

Applying $\mathcal{B}_{(t_\mathcal{A},(q_G,q_H))}$ to the derivation $\nabla_{\mathsf{PSS\text{-}E}}$ yields

$$1/2 + 2q_H \times 2^{-k_0} + \mathbf{Succ}^{\mathsf{s\text{-}pd\text{-}OW}}_\Theta(k_1, q_G, t_\mathcal{A} + q_G).$$

4.5.2 Chosen-Ciphertext Security

The derivation for chosen-ciphertext security output by our tool is depicted in Figure 6. For the sake of clarity, we use let notation and pattern matching to avoid explicit projections and repetition.

Let $n = k - k_1 - k_0$. Initially, we have

$$c^\star = \mathsf{f}(H(m \,\|\, r) \,\|\, G(H(m \,\|\, r)) \oplus (m \,\|\, r))$$
$$D_1 = \mathsf{let}\ s \,\|\, t = \mathsf{f}^{-1}(c), x = G(s) \oplus t\ \mathsf{in}\ s = H(x) \rhd [x]^n_0$$

∇_{Ask} :

$$\dfrac{\dfrac{\dfrac{\dfrac{}{\vDash_0 \mathsf{f}(r) : \mathsf{Ask}(G, [r]_0^{k_1})}\,[\mathsf{OW}_0^{k_1}(\mathsf{f}, G)]}{\vDash_0 \mathsf{f}(r'' \,\|\, r') : \mathsf{Ask}(G, r'')}\,[\mathsf{Merge}] \qquad \dfrac{}{\vDash_0 \mathsf{f}(r'' \,\|\, r') : \mathsf{Ask}(H, m \,\|\, r)}\,[\mathsf{Rnd}(k_0, H)]}{\vDash_0 \mathsf{f}(H(m \,\|\, r) \,\|\, r') : \mathsf{Ask}(G, H(m \,\|\, r))}\,[\mathsf{Fail}_1]}{\vDash_0 \mathsf{f}(H(m \,\|\, r) \,\|\, r' \oplus (m \,\|\, r)) : \mathsf{Ask}(G, H(m \,\|\, r))}\,[\mathsf{Opt}]$$

$\nabla_{\mathsf{PSS\text{-}E}}$:

$$\dfrac{\dfrac{\dfrac{\dfrac{}{\vDash_{1/2} \mathsf{f}(r'' \,\|\, r') : \mathsf{Guess}}\,[\mathsf{Ind}] \qquad \dfrac{}{\vDash_0 \mathsf{f}(r'' \,\|\, r') : \mathsf{Ask}(H, m \,\|\, r)}\,[\mathsf{Rnd}(k_0, H)]}{\vDash_{1/2} \mathsf{f}(H(m \,\|\, r) \,\|\, r') : \mathsf{Guess}}\,[\mathsf{Fail}_1]}{\vDash_{1/2} \mathsf{f}(H(m \,\|\, r) \,\|\, r' \oplus (m \,\|\, r)) : \mathsf{Guess}}\,[\mathsf{Opt}] \qquad \dfrac{\nabla_{\mathsf{Ask}}}{\vDash_0 \mathsf{f}(H(m \,\|\, r) \,\|\, r' \oplus (m \,\|\, r)) : \mathsf{Ask}(G, H(m \,\|\, r))}\,[\mathsf{Opt}]}{\vDash_{1/2} \mathsf{f}(H(m \,\|\, r) \,\|\, G(H(m \,\|\, r)) \oplus (m \,\|\, r)) : \mathsf{Guess}}\,[\mathsf{Fail}_1]$$

Figure 5: A derivation for CPA security of PSS-E

∇_{ϕ_2} :

$$\dfrac{\dfrac{\dfrac{\dfrac{\dfrac{}{\vDash_0 \mathsf{f}(r'' \,\|\, r'_1 \,\|\, r'_2) : \phi_5}\,[\mathsf{Rnd}(k_0, H)]}{\vDash_0 \mathsf{f}(r'' \,\|\, r') : \phi_4}\,[\mathsf{Split}], [\mathsf{Opt}] \qquad \dfrac{}{\vDash_0 \mathsf{f}(r'' \,\|\, r') : \mathsf{Ask}(H, m \,\|\, r)}\,[\mathsf{Rnd}(k_0, H)]}{\vDash_0 \mathsf{f}(H(m \,\|\, r) \,\|\, r') : \phi_4}\,[\mathsf{Fail}_1]}{\vDash_0 \mathsf{f}(H(m \,\|\, r) \,\|\, r' \oplus (m \,\|\, r)) : \phi_3}\,[\mathsf{Opt}], [\mathsf{Conv}] \qquad \nabla_{\mathsf{Ask}}}{\vDash_0 \mathsf{f}(H(m \,\|\, r) \,\|\, G(H(m \,\|\, r)) \oplus (m \,\|\, r)) : \phi_2}\,[\mathsf{Fail}_1]$$

∇_{Guess} :

$$\dfrac{\dfrac{\dfrac{\nabla_{\mathsf{PSS\text{-}E}}}{\vDash_{1/2} (c^\star, D_4) : \mathsf{Guess}}\,[\mathsf{Pub}]}{\vDash_{1/2} (c^\star, D_3) : \mathsf{Guess}}\,[\mathsf{Find}] \qquad \dfrac{\dfrac{\nabla_{\phi_2}}{\vDash_0 (c^\star, D_4) : \phi_2}\,[\mathsf{Pub}]}{\vDash_0 (c^\star, D_3) : \phi_2}\,[\mathsf{Find}] \qquad \dfrac{}{\vDash \mathsf{negl}_{r'}(\mathsf{let}\ s \| t = \mathsf{f}^{-1}(c)\ \mathsf{in}\ \mathsf{Ask}(H, r' \oplus t))}\,[\mathsf{PRnd}(k - k_1, H)]}{\vDash_{1/2} (c^\star, D_2) : \mathsf{Guess}}\,[\mathsf{Bad}], [\mathsf{PAnd}_2]$$

$\nabla^{\mathsf{CCA}}_{\mathsf{PSS\text{-}E}}$:

$$\dfrac{\nabla_{\mathsf{Guess}} \qquad \dfrac{}{\vDash_0 (c^\star, D_2) : \phi_1}\,[\mathsf{Conv}], [\mathsf{False}] \qquad \dfrac{}{\vDash \mathsf{negl}_{r'}(\mathsf{let}\ s \,\|\, t = \mathsf{f}^{-1}(c)\ \mathsf{in}\ s = r')}\,[\mathsf{PEqs}(k_1)]}{\vDash_{1/2} (c^\star, D_1) : \mathsf{Guess}}\,[\mathsf{Bad}]$$

$\phi_1 \stackrel{\text{def}}{=} \exists c \in \boldsymbol{L_{\mathcal{D}}}.\, \mathsf{let}\ s \,\|\, t = \mathsf{f}^{-1}(c)\ \mathsf{in}\ \mathsf{let}\ x = G(s) \oplus t\ \mathsf{in}\ s = H(x) \wedge x = m \,\|\, r$

$\phi_2 \stackrel{\text{def}}{=} \exists c \in \boldsymbol{L_{\mathcal{D}}}.\, \mathsf{let}\ s \,\|\, t = \mathsf{f}^{-1}(c)\ \mathsf{in}\ \mathsf{let}\ x = G(s) \oplus t\ \mathsf{in}\ s = H(x) \wedge \mathsf{Ask}(H, x) \wedge s = H(m \,\|\, r)$

$\phi_3 \stackrel{\text{def}}{=} \exists c \in \boldsymbol{L_{\mathcal{D}}}.\, \mathsf{let}\ s \,\|\, t = \mathsf{f}^{-1}(c)\ \mathsf{in}\ \mathsf{let}\ x = r' \oplus t\ \mathsf{in}\ s = H(x) \wedge \mathsf{Ask}(H, x) \wedge s = H(m \,\|\, r)$

$\phi_4 \stackrel{\text{def}}{=} \exists c \in \boldsymbol{L_{\mathcal{D}}}.\, \mathsf{let}\ s \,\|\, t = \mathsf{f}^{-1}(c)\ \mathsf{in}\ \mathsf{Ask}(H, r' \oplus (m \,\|\, r) \oplus t)$

$\phi_5 \stackrel{\text{def}}{=} \exists c \in \boldsymbol{L_{\mathcal{D}}}.\, \mathsf{let}\ s \,\|\, t = \mathsf{f}^{-1}(c)\ \mathsf{in}\ \mathsf{Ask}(H, (r'_1 \oplus m \oplus [t]_0^n) \,\|\, r)$

Figure 6: A derivation for CCA security of PSS-E

We are interested in proving the judgment $\vDash_{1/2} (c^\star, D_1) : \mathsf{Guess}$. We begin by applying rule [Bad] to strengthen the test in the decryption oracle to check also that $\mathsf{Ask}(H, x)$ holds, so as to reject ciphertexts that would require new queries to H. The corresponding algorithm is

$$\begin{aligned} D_2 = {} & \mathsf{let}\ s \,\|\, t = \mathsf{f}^{-1}(c)\ \mathsf{in} \\ & \mathsf{let}\ x = G(s) \oplus t\ \mathsf{in}\ s = H(x) \wedge \mathsf{Ask}(H, x) \rhd [x]_0^n \end{aligned}$$

Note that an adversary can distinguish between D_1 and D_2 only if it can produce a ciphertext c that passes the test without querying $H(x)$ in the first place. This is only possible if the adversary either guesses this hash or learns something about it from the challenge ciphertext. The former case corresponds to the premise $\vDash \mathsf{negl}_{r'}(\mathsf{let}\ s \,\|\, t = \mathsf{f}^{-1}(c)\ \mathsf{in}\ s = r')$ and can be proven using $[\mathsf{PEqs}(k_1)]$. The latter case corresponds to the premise

$$\begin{aligned} \vDash_0 (c^\star, D_2) : {} & \exists c \in \boldsymbol{L_{\mathcal{D}}}. \\ & \mathsf{let}\ s \,\|\, t = \mathsf{f}^{-1}(c), x = G(s) \oplus t\ \mathsf{in}\ s = H(x) \wedge x = m \,\|\, r \end{aligned}$$

and is proven using rules [False] and [Conv], because the event is equivalent to $\exists c \in \boldsymbol{L_{\mathcal{D}}}.\, c = c^\star$.

To prove the premise corresponding to the original Guess event, we apply rule [Bad] again, but this time with $G(s)$. We obtain the following decryption oracle

$$\begin{aligned} D_3 = {} & \mathsf{let}\ s \,\|\, t = \mathsf{f}^{-1}(c), x = G(s) \oplus t\ \mathsf{in} \\ & s = H(x) \wedge \mathsf{Ask}(H, x) \wedge \mathsf{Ask}(G, s) \rhd [x]_0^n \end{aligned}$$

The premise

$$\vDash \mathsf{negl}_{r'}(\mathsf{let}\ s \,\|\, t = \mathsf{f}^{-1}(c), x = r' \oplus t\ \mathsf{in}\ s = H(x) \wedge \mathsf{Ask}(H, x))$$

can be discharged using rules $[\mathsf{PAnd}_2]$ and $[\mathsf{PRnd}(k - k_1, H)]$.

To prove the two premises corresponding to CCA judgments, we first apply rule [Find] (and [Conv]) to reformulate the decryption oracle as follows:

$$D_4 = \mathsf{find}\ s, x\ \mathsf{in}\ \boldsymbol{L_G}, \boldsymbol{L_H} : c = \mathsf{f}(s \,\|\, G(s) \oplus x) \wedge s = H(x) \rhd [x]_0^n$$

Note that this decryption oracle is *public*, i.e. it does not use f^{-1} and can be efficiently simulated. Hence, we can apply rule [Pub] and proceed reasoning in the (extended) CPA logic. The branch corresponding to the original Guess event can be proven using the same derivation $\nabla_{\mathsf{PSS\text{-}E}}$ in Figure 5 that we used to prove CPA security.

We have only one outstanding goal,

$$\vDash_0 c^\star : \exists c \in \boldsymbol{L_\mathcal{D}}.\, \mathsf{let}\ s \,\|\, t = \mathsf{f}^{-1}(c), x = G(s) \oplus t\ \mathsf{in}\ s = H(x) \wedge \mathsf{Ask}(H, x) \wedge s = H(m \,\|\, r)$$

To prove it, we first apply [Fail_1] to replace $G(H(m \,\|\, r))$ with a fresh random bitstring r'. The derivation ∇_{Ask} that bounds the probability of failure is as in the proof of CPA security in Figure 5. We apply rules [Opt] and [Conv] to simplify the premise corresponding to the original event, obtaining

$$\vDash_0 \mathsf{f}(H(m \,\|\, r) \,\|\, r') : \exists c \in \boldsymbol{L_\mathcal{D}}.\, \mathsf{let}\ s \,\|\, t = \mathsf{f}^{-1}(c)\ \mathsf{in}\ \mathsf{Ask}(H, r' \oplus (m \,\|\, r) \oplus t)$$

We then apply [Fail_1] again, this time to replace $H(m \,\|\, r)$ with a fresh random bitstring r''. The premise corresponding to the failure event can be readily proved using [$\mathsf{Rnd}(k_0, H)$] as in the proof of CPA security. To prove the remaining premise, observe that to trigger the event $\mathsf{Ask}(H, r' \oplus (m \,\|\, r) \oplus t)$, the adversary should be able to compute $[r' \oplus t]_n^{k_0} \oplus r$, but r is now independent of the challenge ciphertext. We formalize this reasoning by first splitting r' and then applying rule [Opt] to replace $[r' \oplus t]_n^{k_0} \oplus r$ by simply r. We conclude applying the extended rule [$\mathsf{Rnd}(k_0, H)$].

Concrete security bound.

The concrete security bound $\mathcal{B}_{(t_\mathcal{A},(q_G,q_H,q_\mathcal{D}))}(\nabla^{\mathsf{CCA}}_{\mathsf{PSS\text{-}E}})$ obtained from this proof is

$$\mathcal{B}_{(t_\mathcal{S},(q_G,q_H,q_\mathcal{D}))}(\nabla_{\mathsf{PSS\text{-}E}}) + \mathcal{B}_{(t_\mathcal{S},(q_G,q_H,q_\mathcal{D}))}(\nabla_{\phi_2}) + q_\mathcal{D} \times (2^{-k_1} + q_H \times 2^{k_1 - k})$$

where $t_\mathcal{S} = t_\mathcal{A} + q_\mathcal{D}\, q_G\, q_H \times t_\mathsf{f}$, and

$$\mathcal{B}_{(t_\mathcal{S},(q_G,q_H,q_\mathcal{D}))}(\nabla_{\mathsf{PSS\text{-}E}}) \approx 1/2 + 2\, q_H \times 2^{-k_0} + \mathbf{Succ}^{\mathsf{s\text{-}pd\text{-}OW}}_\Theta(k_1, q_G, t_\mathcal{S})$$

$$\mathcal{B}_{(t_\mathcal{S},(q_G,q_H,q_\mathcal{D}))}(\nabla_{\phi_2}) = 3\, q_H \times 2^{-k_0} + \mathbf{Succ}^{\mathsf{s\text{-}pd\text{-}OW}}_\Theta(k_1, q_G, t_\mathcal{S})$$

Observe that $t_\mathcal{S}$ comes from the two applications of rule [Find] in the proof and can be improved to $t_\mathcal{A} + q_\mathcal{D}\, q_H \times t_\mathsf{f}$ because to answer a decryption query, the simulator D_4 just needs to traverse $\boldsymbol{L_H}$ to find a value for x, the value of s is determined by $H(x)$. The overall bound is, ignoring constant factors,

$$1/2 + q_H \times 2^{-k_0} + q_\mathcal{D} \times 2^{-k_1} + q_\mathcal{D} \times q_H \times 2^{k_1 - k} + \mathbf{Succ}^{\mathsf{s\text{-}pd\text{-}OW}}_\Theta(k_1, q_G, t_\mathcal{A} + q_\mathcal{D}\, q_H \times t_\mathsf{f})$$

In comparison, the bound given by Coron et al. [16] is:

$$1/2 + q_H \times 2^{-k_0} + q_\mathcal{D} \times 2^{-k_1} + \mathbf{Succ}^{\mathsf{s\text{-}pd\text{-}OW}}_\Theta(k_1, q_G + q_H, t_\mathcal{A} + q_\mathcal{D}\, q_H \times t_\mathsf{f})$$

The differences are due to the use of a slightly different reduction. The proof of Coron et al. [16] assumes that the hash oracle H issues a query $G(s)$ each time it produces a response s. This assumption would make redundant the application of rule [Bad] in ∇_{Guess} in our reduction, eliminating the terms coming from ∇_{ϕ_2} and $q_\mathcal{D} \times q_H \times 2^{k_1 - k}$. The resulting bound, once adjusting q_G for the additional queries issued by H, coincides with that of Coron et al.

5. ATTACKS

This section describes our approach for finding attacks against chosen-plaintext and chosen-ciphertext security of padding-based encryption schemes. Since our logics are incomplete, we use attack finding to obtain negative results, and additional data points to evaluate schemes for which we cannot obtain proofs.

We distinguish between universal attacks and existential attacks relative to a set of assumptions. An attack is universal if it works against every possible instantiation of the trapdoor permutations used by a scheme. An attack is existential if it works for some trapdoor permutation consistent with the assumptions, i.e. it may rely on specific properties of the employed trapdoor permutation.

5.1 Universal Attacks

To find universal attacks against the CPA security of an encryption scheme with encryption algorithm e, we search for closed expressions m_0 and m_1 that do not contain symbols of the form f^{-1} such that $e\,\{m_0/m\} \not\approx e\,\{m_1/m\}$. By soundness of $\not\approx$, there exists an efficient algorithm distinguish that returns 0 for input $(\!|e\,\{m_0/m\}|\!)$ and 1 for input $(\!|e\,\{m_1/m\}|\!)$ with overwhelming probability. To mount an attack against CPA security using this algorithm, an adversary chooses plaintexts $(\!|m_0|\!)$ and $(\!|m_1|\!)$, receives the challenge ciphertext $c^\star$, and returns $\mathsf{distinguish}(c^\star)$. An example of a scheme vulnerable to this attack is a scheme with encryption algorithm given by

$$e = \mathsf{f}(r) \,\|\, (G(r) \oplus m) \,\|\, H(m)$$

A CPA adversary can use the distinguisher obtained from the contexts $C = [*]_{|r|+|m|}^{|H(m)|}$ and $C' = H(0^{|m|})$ to tell appart $e\,\{0/m\}$ from $e\,\{1/m\}$.

To refute CCA security, we search for malleability attacks using deducibility. Specifically, we search for closed expressions m_0 and $\Delta \neq 0^{|m|}$ such that $e\,\{m_0/m\} \vdash e\,\{m_0 \oplus \Delta/m\}$; let C be the context witnessing the deducibility. This would imply an effective attack against CCA security: choose plaintexts m_0 and $m_1 \neq m_0$ and obtain the challenge $c^\star$; then query the decryption oracle on $(\!|C[c^\star]|\!)$, xor the result with Δ, and return 0 if it equals $(\!|m_0|\!)$ and 1 otherwise. An example of a scheme vulnerable to a universal attack of this form is the Zheng-Seberry cryptosystem [31], whose encryption algorithm is given by $e = \mathsf{f}(r) \,\|\, (G(r) \oplus (m \,\|\, H(m)))$; take $m_0 = 0^{|m|}$ and $\Delta = 1^{|m|}$.

5.2 Existential Attacks

To find existential attacks against a scheme with encryption algorithm e w.r.t. a set of assumptions Γ, we find universal attacks against modified versions of it. An example can elucidate better the point.

Consider the encryption algorithm of ZAEP [7], given by $e = \mathsf{f}(r \,\|\, G(r) \oplus m)$. To show that there is no blackbox reduction from the CPA security of ZAEP to the assumption $(\mathsf{f}, 0, |\mathsf{f}|)$, we instantiate f as follows

$$\mathsf{f}(a \,\|\, b) = a \,\|\, \mathsf{f}_2(b) \qquad (1)$$

If f_2 is a one-way permutation, the permutation f satisfies the assumption $(\mathsf{f}, 0, |\mathsf{f}|)$. Using static distinguishability, we find an attack on $e' = r \,\|\, \mathsf{f}_2(G(r) \oplus m)$ given by the contexts

$$C = [*]_{|r|}^{|m|} \text{ and } C' = \mathsf{f}_2(G([*]_0^{|r|}))$$

which can be used to distinguish $e\,\{0/m\}$ and $e\,\{1/m\}$.

To show that there is no blackbox reduction of the CCA security of ZAEP to an arbitrary Γ, we use the instantiation

$$\mathsf{f}(a) = \mathsf{f}'\left([a]_0^{|a|-c}\right) \Big\| \, [a]_{|a|-c}^{c} \qquad (2)$$

where c is a size variable that we interpret as a constant. It is easy to see that ciphertexts computed using this instantiation are malleable. Moreover, assuming f' satisfies the assumptions Γ (accounting for the size reduction by c), this instance of f satisfies Γ. This is because size variables in assumptions grow polynomially with the security parameter, and leaking a constant fraction of a pre-image cannot be used to attack any assumption in Γ. In contrast, the ability to compute a ciphertext of a message that differs in just one bit from the decryption of a given ciphertext results in a chosen-ciphertext attack.

In general, to prove that there is no blackbox reduction for a fixed set of one-wayness assumptions Γ, we must either find a universal attack or instantiations for the trapdoor permutations that yield attacks and are compatible with *all* assumptions in Γ. For example, the instantiation (2) above is compatible with any set of assumptions, while (1) is compatible with all assumptions except those of the form (f, k, ℓ) with $0 < \ell$ and $k + \ell \leq |a|$. In addition to the aforementioned instantiations, we also use instantiations of the form

$$\mathsf{f}(a \,\|\, b \,\|\, c) = \mathsf{f}_1(a) \,\|\, b \oplus a \,\|\, c$$

which allow us to find attacks if f is used in such a way that part of its input is leaked or interdependent.

6. EXPERIMENTAL VALIDATION

We implemented the proof search and attack finding methods described in § 4 and § 5 in a toolset that we name ZooCrypt. ZooCrypt can prove the CPA and CCA security of a scheme under different assumptions on the trapdoor permutations used, or find attacks that are consistent with these assumptions.

6.1 Security Analysis

To analyze the security of a scheme with encryption algorithm given by an expression $c^\star$ under a set of assumptions Γ, the toolset follows the workflow depicted in Figure 6.1:

1. Checks that $c^\star$ is well-typed and that encryption is invertible, i.e. $c^\star \vdash^\star m$;
2. Searches for attacks against CPA security;
3. Searches for proofs of CPA security. If a proof is found, computes the corresponding security bound;
4. Searches for malleability attacks against CCA security;
5. If a CPA proof has been found, synthesizes a decryption algorithm D and searches for a proof of CCA security. If a proof is found, computes the corresponding security bound.

The results of this security analysis are an adversary for each attack found, and derivations for all security proofs together with the set of assumptions effectively used and the corresponding concrete security bound. Steps 3 and 5 implement proof search algorithms for the logics. These algorithms try to build a valid derivation bottom up, by applying rules in a prescribed order. Simple heuristics allow to improve the efficiency of the search and to ensure termination.

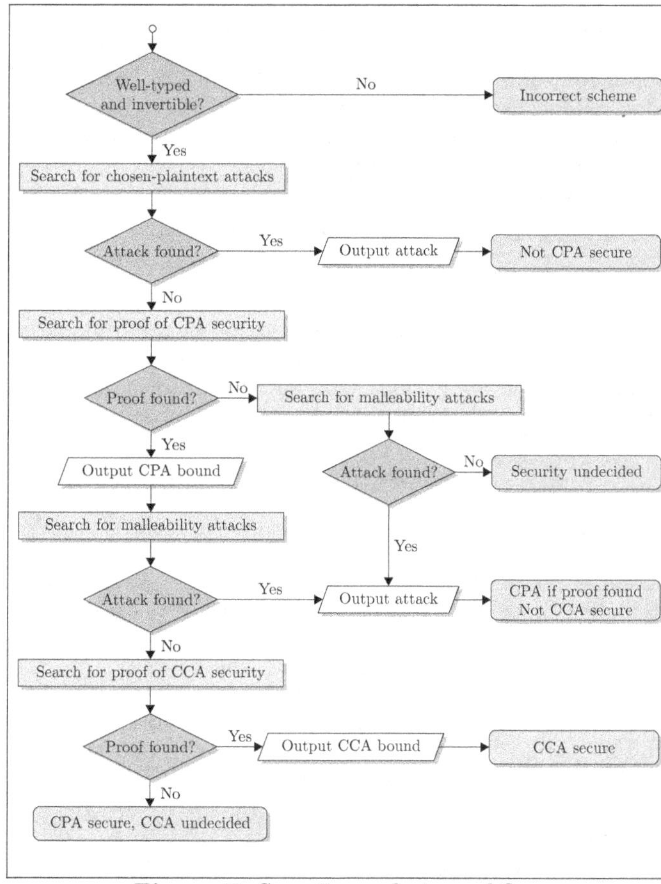

Figure 7: Security analysis workflow

A crucial step in the above workflow is synthesizing a decryption algorithm that reject as many invalid ciphertexts as possible, with the aim of easing the construction of a plaintext simulator during a CCA analysis. Indeed, an encryption algorithm typically admits several correct decryption algorithms, because the consistency condition gives complete freedom of choice as to what should be the result of decrypting an invalid ciphertext. The tool infers such algorithms using a method inspired by [8, 15] to analyze the *redundancy* built into ciphertexts. We exploit the fact that our algorithm for checking static equivalence computes as a sub-routine non-trivial equations that hold for an expression; when applied to an expression denoting an encryption algorithm, this sub-routine yields tests for checking the validity of ciphertexts.

6.2 Practical Interpretation for RSA

Concrete security bounds can be used to guide the choice of practical parameters for realizations of encryption schemes based on RSA. In order to validate the quality of the bounds output by our tool, we implemented a method based on an extrapolation of the estimated cost of factoring the RSA-768 integer from the RSA Factoring Challenge [23], and on the lattice basis reduction of set partial-domain one-wayness to one-wayness for RSA [20].

Let t_N be the cost of factoring an N-bit RSA modulus: Kleinjung [23] estimates that $t_{768} = 2^{67}$, while Lenstra [25] suggests to extrapolate based on the ratio

$$\frac{t_N}{t_M} \approx \frac{\exp((1.9229)\log(N)^{1/3}\log(\log(N))^{2/3}}{\exp((1.9229)\log(M)^{1/3}\log(\log(M))^{2/3}}$$

The success probability of partially inverting RSA on its k most significant bits, $\mathbf{Succ}^{\mathsf{OW}}_{\mathsf{RSA}}(k, q, t)$ can be upper bounded by a function of $\mathbf{Succ}^{\mathsf{OW}}_{\mathsf{RSA}}(t')$, where t' depends on t.

Proposition 8 ([20]) *Let Θ be RSA with an ℓ-bit modulus such that $\ell < 2k$. Then,*

$$\mathbf{Succ}^{\mathsf{OW}}_{\Theta}(t)\left(\mathbf{Succ}^{\mathsf{OW}}_{\Theta}(k,q,t) - 2^{\ell-2k+6}\right) \leq \mathbf{Succ}^{\mathsf{OW}}_{\Theta}(2t + q^2\ell^3)$$

Fixing a maximum number of queries to oracles and an admissible advantage p, our tool can estimate from the security bound obtained from a derivation, the minimum RSA modulus length N such that no adversary executing in time $t_{\mathcal{A}}$ achieves either a CPA or CCA advantage greater than p.

For instance, a reasonable security target might be that no CCA adversary executing in time 2^{128} and making at most 2^{60} hash queries and 2^{30} decryption queries achieves an advantage greater than 2^{-20}. From these values, the estimated cost of inverting RSA, and the bound found for the CCA security of PSS-E under the same assumption as in [20], our tool estimates a minimum modulus length of 4864 bits, and a ciphertext overhead of around 200 bits.

6.3 Generation of Encryption Schemes

Our tool also implements an algorithm that generates expressions denoting encryption algorithms within budget constraints specified as the number of concatenation, exclusive-or, hash and trapdoor permutation constructors.

Candidate encryption schemes are generated following a top-down approach that uses variables to represent holes in partially specified expressions. Starting from a fully unspecified expression, i.e. just a variable x, at each iterative step the tool picks a hole and replaces it with either:

- An expression of the form $\mathsf{f}(x)$, $H(x)$, $x \oplus y$ or $x \parallel y$, for fresh variables x and y, if the budget permits;
- A hole-free sub-expression of e or one of 0, m, r; this does not consume the budget.

An incremental type-checker is used at each step to discard partially specified expressions that do not have any well-typed instance. For example, $e \oplus (e \parallel x)$ is immediately discarded because e cannot be assigned a size regardless of any substitution for the hole x.

We trim large parts of the search space by implementing an early pruning strategy in the style of [27]. Concretely, we apply some simple filters during generation. For instance, given an expression e with holes, we check for the existence of a substitution σ for holes respecting the budget constraints such that $e\sigma \vdash^\star m$, and that it is not the case that for all such substitutions $e\sigma \vdash m$ or $e\sigma \parallel m \vdash \mathcal{R}(e)$. These filters can be implemented efficiently using memoization to drastically reduce their computational cost.

6.4 Experiments

We evaluate our tools on encryption schemes generated under different budget constraints. Figure 1 summarizes the results of the automated security analysis of §6.1. In the figure, schemes are classified in rows by their size, measured by the total number of operators used in the expression denoting their encryption algorithm.

The reported experiment has been conducted under two classes of assumptions:

1. $\Gamma_1 = \{(\mathsf{f}, 0, |\mathsf{f}|) \mid \mathsf{f} \in \mathcal{F}(c^\star)\}$, i.e. assuming that all trapdoor permutations are one-way;
2. $\Gamma_2 = \{(\mathsf{f}, k_f, n_f) \mid \mathsf{f} \in \mathcal{F}(c^\star)\}$ such that $0 \leq k_f$ and $k_f + n_f \leq |\mathsf{f}|$ for all $\mathsf{f} \in \mathcal{F}(c^\star)$, i.e. one arbitrary one-wayness assumption for each trapdoor permutation;

The columns grouped under OW CPA report the results obtained when analyzing CPA security under Γ_1. Column PROOF indicates the number of schemes proved secure, column ATTACK the number of schemes for which some attack (existential or universal) was found, and column UNDECIDED the number of schemes for which security could not be decided. Similarly, the columns grouped under CPA and CCA report the results when analyzing CPA and CCA security under all assumptions of the form Γ_2. In this case, column PROOF indicates the number of schemes proved secure under *some* assumption of the form Γ_2, column ATTACK the number of schemes for which an attack was found for *all* assumptions of the form Γ_2, and column UNDECIDED the number of schemes for which security could not be decided. The attack and proof search algorithms are extremely efficient, e.g. proof search for schemes of size 7 takes on average 0.1ms for CPA and 0.5ms for CCA on a modern workstation.

Observe that the figures in the first two groups suggest the separation between one-wayness and partial-domain one-wayness: the stronger the assumption, the more schemes can be proven secure and the less attacks can be found.

Finally, column NR in the CCA group counts the number of schemes that are CPA secure but non-redundant, meaning that all ciphertexts are valid. Non-redundant schemes can be CCA secure [7, 24], but their proofs require random oracle *programmability*, which is out of the scope of our logics.

Validation.

We also evaluated our automated proof search and attack finding algorithms on a number of schemes from the literature, including the over one hundred variants of OAEP and SAEP surveyed by Komano and Ohta [24]. In all cases, our results are consistent with published results, and in most we are able to prove security under exactly the same assumptions and obtain the same security bounds. As evidence of the effectiveness of our methodology, we observe that our analyses decide the CPA security of all 72 variants of OAEP in the taxonomy of [24]. The results for CCA security are more nuanced: for about 20% of schemes, we fail to find proofs or attacks when they exist.

For CPA security our methods seem to achieve empirical completeness, suggesting that completeness may be provable for some class of schemes or some mild extension. A closer examination of the schemes on which our CCA analysis is unable to decide security reveals that this is either due to our approximation of inequality in rules [Eqs] and [PEqs] being too coarse, or because the schemes are non-redundant.

Non-redundancy complicates enormously the task of simulating the decryption oracle in CCA reductions, because a meaningful response must be returned in all cases. Proving CCA security of non-redundant schemes, requires *programming* random oracles in order to maintain consistency during simulation, something that we have intentionally avoided in

Size	Total	OW CPA (% of Total)			CPA (% of Total)			CCA (% of CPA Proof + CPA Undecided)			
		Proof	Attack	Undecided	Proof	Attack	Undecided	Proof	Attack	NR	Undecided
4	2	1 (50.00%)	1 (50.00%)	0 (0.00%)	2 (100.00%)	0 (0.00%)	0 (0.00%)	0 (0.00%)	2 (100.00%)	0 (0.00%)	0 (0.00%)
5	44	8 (18.18%)	36 (81.82%)	0 (0.00%)	12 (27.27%)	32 (72.73%)	0 (0.00%)	0 (0.00%)	13 (100.00%)	0 (0.00%)	0 (0.00%)
6	335	65 (19.40%)	270 (80.60%)	0 (0.00%)	93 (27.76%)	241 (71.94%)	1 (0.30%)	1 (0.98%)	96 (94.12%)	5 (4.90%)	0 (0.00%)
7	3263	510 (15.63%)	2735 (83.82%)	18 (0.55%)	750 (22.98%)	2475 (75.85%)	38 (1.16%)	45 (5.05%)	739 (82.94%)	45 (5.05%)	62 (6.96%)
8	32671	4430 (13.56%)	27894 (85.38%)	347 (1.06%)	6718 (20.56%)	25336 (77.55%)	617 (1.89%)	536 (6.26%)	6531 (76.25%)	306 (3.57%)	1192 (13.92%)
9	350111	43556 (12.44%)	301679 (86.17%)	4876 (1.39%)	66775 (19.07%)	274813 (78.49%)	8523 (2.43%)	7279 (8.16%)	62356 (69.93%)	3035 (3.40%)	16496 (18.50%)
10	644563	67863 (10.53%)	569314 (88.33%)	7386 (1.15%)	133476 (20.71%)	491189 (76.20%)	19898 (3.09%)	20140 (11.29%)	112993 (63.36%)	12794 (7.17%)	32397 (18.17%)
Total	1030989	116433 (11.29%)	901929 (87.48%)	12627 (1.22%)	207826 (20.16%)	794086 (77.02%)	29077 (2.82%)	28001 (10.11%)	182730 (65.95%)	16185 (5.84%)	50147 (18.10%)

Table 1: Evaluation of the tool on generated encryption schemes

our proof systems. Extending our proof systems to embody some form of *programmability* would reduce the number of schemes for which security cannot be decided, and would be a step towards closing the empirical completeness gap.

7. RELATED WORK

Our work lies at the intersection between symbolic and computational cryptography, and draws on verification techniques from both areas. We refer to [13, 17] for a recent account of symbolic verification and focus on verification tools and methods for the computational model.

Since its inception [2], cryptographic soundness was extended to many settings [17]. Despite this success, extensions for constructions based on exclusive-or and trapdoor permutations have remained elusive. Negative results such as [30] show that cryptographic soundness may indeed be very difficult to achieve for the setting of this paper.

CryptoVerif [12] and EasyCrypt [4] support the construction and verification of cryptographic proofs in the computational model. Both CryptoVerif and EasyCrypt provide a high level of automation, and CryptoVerif supports fully automated verification of many cryptographic protocols. In addition, EasyCrypt has been applied to verify security of several padding-based schemes. However, fully automated proofs of padding-based schemes are out of reach of these tools. Courant et al. [18] report on a Hoare-like logic and an automated tool for proving CPA security of padding-based schemes. The tool can verify the security of several schemes, such as BR [10] and REACT [26], but fails to verify most other examples. In our view, the limitations of the approach are inherited from using a Hoare logic, which favors local reasoning. In contrast, we use a global approach in which one reasons about the probability of events in experiments.

In addition, a number of formalisms have been developed to reason about security of cryptographic primitives and constructions in the computational model [5, 22]. However, these systems reason about constructions described in mathematical vernacular, and are thus not readily amenable to automation. Similar formalisms exist for cryptographic protocols [28], but these are not automated either.

Finally, the batch mode of ZooCrypt is similar in spirit to the AVGI toolkit [27]. The toolkit allows users to state security requirements, for instance authentication or secrecy, and non-functional requirements such as message length and available bandwidth. The AVGI toolkit is composed of a protocol generator, that applies pruning techniques to curb the state space explosion problem, and a protocol screener that applies symbolic methods to verify whether generated protocols comply with the desired properties.

8. CONCLUSION

We have defined, implemented and evaluated proof systems to reason about security of public-key encryption schemes built from trapdoor permutations and hash functions. Our work sets a new methodology for analyzing cryptographic constructions in the computational model. Preliminary investigations suggest that our methodology extends well to other settings, and we intend to apply it for building a comprehensive database that includes other classical cryptographic constructions such as digital signature schemes, modes of operation, and message authentication codes. In the future, we plan to use the interactive mode of ZooCrypt as the backbone for an online tutor that can help users finding attacks or security proofs for padding-based schemes of their choice, or automatically generated. Moreover, we plan to connect ZooCrypt with EasyCrypt, and implement a prototype mechanism that translates successful derivations in our logics into EasyCrypt proofs.

Acknowledgments. This research is partially supported by ONR grant N000141210914, Spanish project TIN2009-14599 DESAFIOS 10, and Madrid regional project S2009TIC-1465 PROMETIDOS.

References

[1] M. Abadi and C. Fournet. Mobile values, new names, and secure communication. In *28th ACM SIGPLAN-SIGACT symposium on Principles of Programming Languages, POPL 2001*, pages 104–115, 2001. ACM.

[2] M. Abadi and P. Rogaway. Reconciling two views of cryptography (The computational soundness of formal encryption). *J. Cryptology*, 15(2):103–127, 2002.

[3] G. Bana and H. Comon-Lundh. Towards unconditional soundness: Computationally complete symbolic attacker. In *1st Conference on Principles of Security and Trust – POST 2012*, volume 7215 of *LNCS*, pages 189–208, 2012. Springer.

[4] G. Barthe, B. Grégoire, S. Heraud, and S. Zanella-Béguelin. Computer-aided security proofs for the

working cryptographer. In *Advances in Cryptology – CRYPTO 2011*, volume 6841 of *LNCS*, pages 71–90, 2011. Springer.

[5] G. Barthe, B. Grégoire, Y. Lakhnech, and S. Zanella-Béguelin. Beyond provable security. Verifiable IND-CCA security of OAEP. In *Topics in Cryptology – CT-RSA 2011*, volume 6558 of *LNCS*, pages 180–196, 2011. Springer.

[6] G. Barthe, J. M. Crespo, B. Grégoire, C. Kunz, Y. Lakhnech, B. Schmidt, and S. Zanella-Béguelin. Fully automated analysis of padding-based encryption in the computational model. Cryptology ePrint Archive, Report 2012/695.

[7] G. Barthe, D. Pointcheval, and S. Zanella-Béguelin. Verified security of redundancy-free encryption from Rabin and RSA. In *19th ACM Conference on Computer and Communications Security, CCS 2012*, pages 724–735, 2012. ACM.

[8] M. Baudet, V. Cortier, and S. Delaune. Yapa: A generic tool for computing intruder knowledge. In *Rewriting Techniques and Applications*, pages 148–163, 2009. Springer.

[9] M. Baudet, V. Cortier, and S. Kremer. Computationally sound implementations of equational theories against passive adversaries. *Inf. Comput.*, 207(4):496–520, 2009.

[10] M. Bellare and P. Rogaway. Random oracles are practical: a paradigm for designing efficient protocols. In *1st ACM Conference on Computer and Communications Security, CCS 1993*, pages 62–73, 1993. ACM.

[11] M. Bellare and P. Rogaway. Optimal asymmetric encryption. In *Advances in Cryptology – EUROCRYPT 1994*, volume 950 of *LNCS*, pages 92–111, 1994. Springer.

[12] B. Blanchet. A computationally sound mechanized prover for security protocols. In *27th IEEE Symposium on Security and Privacy, S&P 2006*, pages 140–154. IEEE Computer Society, 2006.

[13] B. Blanchet. Security protocol verification: Symbolic and computational models. In *1st International Conference on Principles of Security and Trust, POST 2012*, volume 7215 of *LNCS*, pages 3–29, 2012. Springer.

[14] D. Boneh. Simplified OAEP for the RSA and Rabin functions. In *Advances in Cryptology – CRYPTO 2001*, volume 2139 of *LNCS*, pages 275–291, 2001. Springer.

[15] Ş. Ciobâcă, S. Delaune, and S. Kremer. Computing knowledge in security protocols under convergent equational theories. In *Automated Deduction–CADE-22*, pages 355–370. Springer, 2009.

[16] J.-S. Coron, M. Joye, D. Naccache, and P. Paillier. Universal padding schemes for RSA. In *Advances in Cryptology – CRYPTO 2002*, volume 2442 of *LNCS*, pages 226–241, 2002. Springer.

[17] V. Cortier, S. Kremer, and B. Warinschi. A survey of symbolic methods in computational analysis of cryptographic systems. *J. Autom. Reasoning*, 46(3-4):225–259, 2011.

[18] J. Courant, M. Daubignard, C. Ene, P. Lafourcade, and Y. Lakhnech. Towards automated proofs for asymmetric encryption schemes in the random oracle model. In *15th ACM Conference on Computer and Communications Security, CCS 2008*, pages 371–380, 2008. ACM.

[19] D. Dolev and A. Yao. On the security of public key protocols. *IEEE Transactions on Information Theory*, 29(2):198–208, 1983.

[20] E. Fujisaki, T. Okamoto, D. Pointcheval, and J. Stern. RSA-OAEP is secure under the RSA assumption. *J. Cryptology*, 17(2):81–104, 2004.

[21] S. Goldwasser and S. Micali. Probabilistic encryption. *J. Comput. Syst. Sci.*, 28(2):270–299, 1984.

[22] R. Impagliazzo and B. M. Kapron. Logics for reasoning about cryptographic constructions. *J. Comput. Syst. Sci.*, 72(2):286–320, 2006.

[23] T. Kleinjung, K. Aoki, J. Franke, A. Lenstra, E. Thomé, J. Bos, P. Gaudry, A. Kruppa, P. Montgomery, D. Osvik, H. te Riele, A. Timofeev, and P. Zimmermann. Factorization of a 768-bit RSA modulus. In *Advances in Cryptology – CRYPTO 2010*, volume 6223 of *LNCS*, pages 333–350, 2010. Springer.

[24] Y. Komano and K. Ohta. Taxonomical security consideration of OAEP variants. *IEICE Transactions*, E89-A (5):1233–1245, 2006.

[25] A. K. Lenstra and E. R. Verheul. Selecting cryptographic key sizes. *J. Cryptology*, 14(4):255–293, 2001.

[26] T. Okamoto and D. Pointcheval. The gap-problems: A new class of problems for the security of cryptographic schemes. In *4th International Workshop on Practice and Theory in Public Key Cryptography, PKC 2001*, volume 1992 of *LNCS*, pages 104–118, 2001. Springer.

[27] A. Perrig and D. Song. Looking for diamonds in the desert – extending automatic protocol generation to three-party authentication and key agreement protocols. In *13th IEEE Workshop on Computer Security Foundations, CSFW 2000*, pages 64–76, 2000. IEEE Computer Society.

[28] A. Roy, A. Datta, A. Derek, and J. C. Mitchell. Inductive trace properties for computational security. *Journal of Computer Security*, 18(6):1035–1073, 2010.

[29] V. Shoup. Sequences of games: a tool for taming complexity in security proofs. Cryptology ePrint Archive, Report 2004/332.

[30] D. Unruh. The impossibility of computationally sound XOR. Cryptology ePrint Archive, Report 2010/389.

[31] Y. Zheng and J. Seberry. Practical approaches to attaining security against adaptively chosen ciphertext attacks. In *Advances in Cryptology – CRYPTO 1992*, volume 740 of *LNCS*, pages 292–304, 1993. Springer.

Deduction Soundness: Prove One, Get Five for Free

Florian Böhl
KIT
Karlsruhe, Germany
boehl@kit.edu

Véronique Cortier
LORIA - CNRS
Nancy, France
cortier@loria.fr

Bogdan Warinschi
University of Bristol
Bristol, United Kingdom
bogdan@cs.bris.ac.uk

ABSTRACT

Most computational soundness theorems deal with a limited number of primitives, thereby limiting their applicability. The notion of deduction soundness of Cortier and Warinschi (CCS'11) aims to facilitate soundness theorems for richer frameworks via composition results: deduction soundness can be extended, generically, with asymmetric encryption and public data structures. Unfortunately, that paper also hints at rather serious limitations regarding further composition results: composability with digital signatures seems to be precluded.

In this paper we provide techniques for bypassing the perceived limitations of deduction soundness and demonstrate that it enjoys vastly improved composition properties. More precisely, we show that a deduction sound implementation can be modularly extended with all of the five basic cryptographic primitives (symmetric/asymmetric encryption, message authentication codes, digital signatures, and hash functions). We thus obtain the first soundness framework that allows for the joint use of multiple instances of all of the basic primitives.

In addition, we show how to overcome an important restriction of the bare deduction soundness framework which forbids sending encrypted secret keys. In turn, this prevents its use for the analysis of a large class of interesting protocols (e.g. key exchange protocols). We allow for more liberal uses of keys as long as they are hidden in a sense that we also define. All primitives typically used to send secret data (symmetric/asymmetric encryption) satisfy our requirement which we also show to be preserved under composition.

Categories and Subject Descriptors

F.0 [**Theory of Computation**]: General

Keywords

Computational soundness; Composability

CCS'13, November 4–8, 2013, Berlin, Germany.
Copyright 2013 ACM 978-1-4503-2477-9/13/11 ...$15.00.
http://dx.doi.org/10.1145/2508859.2516711 .

1. INTRODUCTION

Two main approaches have been developed for the analysis of security protocols. Symbolic models abstract away the cryptographic primitives, allowing to reason at a logical level, often in an automated way. Security proofs are therefore easier and often conducted by tools. In contrast, cryptographic models offer higher security guarantees, down to the bitstring level. Security proofs are usually done by hand and proceed by reduction, down to the security assumptions (such as the computational hardness of computing a discrete log).

Starting with the seminal work of Abadi and Rogaway [1], many results study under which assumptions it is possible to show that symbolic models are actually *sound* w.r.t. to cryptographic models. For example, the symbolic representation of symmetric encryption consists simply of two following deduction rules.

$$\frac{k \quad m}{\mathsf{enc}(k,m)} \qquad \frac{\mathsf{enc}(k,m) \quad k}{m}$$

An attacker can encrypt or decrypt only if he has the corresponding key. Given an encryption scheme, does it hold that all attacker's computations are reflected by these rules? Surprisingly, the answer is yes, provided that the encryption scheme satisfies some standard security requirements [2, 9] (here IND-CCA). Such soundness theorems have been established for active attackers for basically all standard cryptographic primitives: symmetric encryption [2, 9], asymmetric encryption [3, 12, 14], signatures [3, 17, 12], MACs [4], hashes [17, 10, 16] (consult [11] for a more comprehensive list).

However, these past results usually consider the primitives in isolation or, in the best case, treat at most two primitives at a time. Soundness proofs are complex, and including multiple primitives in the analysis easily leads to unmanageable proofs. A way to bring the complexity under control is to develop soundness results that are compositional. A first step in this direction is the work of Cortier and Warinschi [13]. They propose a notion of soundness which can be extended, in a generic way in several ways, most notably with asymmetric encryption: if a deduction system is sound for some primitive (in the sense that they define) then extending the deduction system with the usual deduction rules for asymmetric encryption is a sound abstraction for combined uses of the primitive and asymmetric encryption. Below, we refer to this notion as *deduction soundness*.

The central idea that allows for composability is that deduction soundness considers the use of the primitives in the presence of functions chosen *adversarially* from the class of *transparent* functions. These are publicly computable and efficiently invertible functions. Typical functions that are transparent are the constructors of public data structures like concatenation, lists, etc. It is then obvious that deduction soundness in this sense implies soundness for the use of primitive in the presence of other constructs that are naturally transparent (e.g. public data structures). Less obvious is that deduction soundness for a primitive also implies soundness when the primitive is used together with asymmetric encryption. In addition to this result (which is the main technical contribution of [13]) that paper also shows that deduction soundness implies that security of protocols in symbolic models yields security in the computational models, for a wide class of protocols.

Compositionality for the notion introduced in [13] is however limited, and the authors present rather compelling evidence that the notion may not compose primitives other than encryption. The problem is that deduction soundness does not seem to preclude implementations that leak partial information about their inputs. In turn, this leak of information may impact the security of other primitives that one may want to include later.

More concretely, assume that one has established soundness of a deduction system that covers hash, but for an implementation of the hash function that reveals half of its input: $h(m_1\|m_2) = m_1\|g(m_2)$ where g is a standard hash function. If g is a "good" hash function then so is h. Now consider a signature scheme which duplicates signatures: $\mathsf{sign}(k,m) = \mathsf{sign}'(k,m)\|\mathsf{sign}'(k,m)$ where sign' is some standard signature scheme. It is easy to see that if $\mathsf{sign}'(k,m)$ is a secure signature scheme, then so is $\mathsf{sign}(k,m)$. Yet, given $h(\mathsf{sign}(k,m))$ an adversary can easily compute $\mathsf{sign}(k,m)$ without breaking the signature scheme nor the hash: the hash function leaks sufficient information to be able to recover the underlying signature.

Our contributions. In this paper we provide new insights into the notion of deduction soundness. Despite the intuition outlined above, we prove that the compositionality properties of deduction soundness [13] reach further than previously understood. For example, we prove that to any deduction sound implementation of a set of primitives, one can add signatures, as long as the implementation for the signature satisfies a standard notion of security. This theorem refutes the counterexample above and provides evidence that deduction soundness is a more powerful (and demanding) security notion than previously understood. In particular, a corollary of the theorem is that there are no deduction sound abstractions for implementations that are "too leaky" (as the hash function from the counterexample).

The new level of understanding facilitates further compositionality proofs for deduction soundness: to any deduction sound system one can add any of the (remaining) standard cryptographic primitives: symmetric encryption, message authentication codes, and hash functions while preserving deduction soundness. The theorems hold under standard security assumptions for the implementation of encryption and MACs and require random oracles for adding hash functions. As a consequence, we obtain the first soundness result that encompasses all standard primitives: symmetric and asymmetric encryption, signatures, MACs, and hashes. In addition, our composition results allow for a settings where multiple schemes (that implement the same primitive) are used simultaneously, provided that each implementation fulfills our assumptions. Moreover, composition provides a stronger result: whenever deduction soundness is shown for some particular primitive, our result ensures that all standard primitives can be added for free, without any further proof.

The importance of composition cannot be overemphasized: obtaining such general results without being able to study each primitive separately would be unmanageable.

Our compositionality results hold under several restrictions most of which are quite common in soundness proofs, e.g. adversaries can corrupt keys only statically. Less standard is that we demand for secret keys to be used only for the cryptographic task for which they are intended. Quite reasonable most of the time, the restriction does not allow, for example, for the adversary to see encryptions of symmetric keys under public keys. The restriction is related to the signature-hash counterexample. If f is a primitive with a deduction sound system that leaks some information about its input and Enc is a secure encryption scheme it is not clear that $(f(k), Enc_k(m))$ hides m. Unfortunately, the technique that we used to bypass the signature-hash counterexample does not seem to apply here. At a high level, the difficulty is that in a potential reduction to the security of the encryption scheme, we are not be able to simulate $f(k)$ consistently.

One way to relax the restriction is to employ encryption schemes that are secure even when some (or even most) of the encryption key leaks [15, 18]. Current instantiations for such schemes are highly inefficient and we prefer the following alternative solution which, essentially, allows for other uses of symmetric keys, as long as these uses do not reveal information about the keys. In a bit more detail, we say that a function is *forgetful* for some argument if the function hides (computationally) all of the information about that input. The notion is a generalization for the security of encryption schemes: these can be regarded as forgetful with respect to their plaintext. We then show that a forgetful deduction sound implementation can be extended with symmetric encryption under more relaxed restrictions: soundness is preserved if encryption keys are used for encryption, or appear only in forgetful positions of other functions from the implementation we are extending. Finally, we show that, in addition to soundness, forgetfulness is preserved as well. Hence we can flexibly and add several layers of asymmetric/symmetric key encryption such that the keys of each layer may appear in any forgetful position of underlying layers. We feel that this allows us to capture almost every hierarchical encryption mechanism in practical protocols.

FULL VERSION. Due to lack of space the formal justifications for our results are not contained in this extended abstract. For the benefit of reviewers the full version of the paper is online [8].

2. THE SYMBOLIC MODEL

Our abstract models for the symbolic world—called *symbolic models*—consist of term algebras defined on a typed first-order signature.

Specifically we have a set of *data types* $\mathcal{T}$ with a subtype relation ($\leq$) which we require to be a preorder. We assume that $\mathcal{T}$ always contains a base type $\top$ such that every other type $\tau \in \mathcal{T}$ is a subtype of $\top$ ($\tau \leq \top$).

The *signature* Σ is a set of *function symbols* together with arities of the form $\mathrm{ar}(f) = \tau_1 \times \ldots \times \tau_n \to \tau$, $n \geq 0$ for $\tau_i, \tau \in \mathcal{T}$. We refer to τ as the type of f and require $\tau \neq \top$ for all f except for garbage of basetype $g_\top$. Function symbols with $n = 0$ arguments are called *constants*. We distinguish *deterministic* function symbols, e.g., for pairs, and *randomized* function symbols, e.g., for encryption.

For all symbolic models we fix an infinite set of typed *variables* $\{x, y \ldots\}$ and an infinite set of *labels* $\mathsf{labels} = \mathsf{labelsH} \cup \mathsf{labelsA}$ for infinite, disjoint sets of *honest labels* ($\mathsf{labelsH}$) and *adversarial labels* ($\mathsf{labelsA}$). Since labels are used to specify randomness, distinguishing honest and adversarial labels (randomness) is important.

The set of *terms of type* τ is defined inductively by

t ::=		term of type τ
	x	variable x of type τ
	$f(t_1, \ldots, t_n)$	application of deterministic $f \in \Sigma$
	$f^l(t_1, \ldots, t_n)$	application of randomized $f \in \Sigma$

where for the last two cases, we further require that each t_i is a term of some type τ'_i with $\tau'_i \leq \tau_i$ for $\mathrm{ar}(f) = \tau_1 \times \ldots \times \tau_n \to \tau$ and for the last case that $l \in \mathsf{labels}$. The set of terms is denoted by $\mathsf{Terms}(\Sigma, \mathcal{T}, \leq)$ and is the union over all sets of terms of type τ for all $\tau \in \mathcal{T}$. For ease of notation we often write $\mathsf{Terms}(\Sigma)$ for the same set of terms, and refer to general terms as $t = f^l(t_1, \ldots, t_n)$ even if f could be a deterministic function symbol which doesn't carry a label.

Intuitively, for nonces, we use randomized constants. For example, assume that $n \in \Sigma$ is a constant. Then usual nonces can be represented by $n^{r_1}, n^{r_2}, \ldots$ where $r_1, r_2 \in \mathsf{labels}$ are labels. Labels in $\mathsf{labelsH}$ will be used when the function has been applied by an honest agent (thus the randomness has been honestly generated) whereas labels in $\mathsf{labelsA}$ will be used when the randomness has been generated by the adversary. Often when the label for a function symbol is clear from the context (e.g. when there is only one label that suits a particular function symbol) we may omit this label.

We require Σ to contain randomized constants g_τ of type τ for any $\tau \in \mathcal{T}$ that will be used for representing garbage of type τ. Garbage will typically be the terms associated to bit-strings produced by the adversary which cannot be parsed as a meaningful term (yet). If garbage can at some point be parsed as the application of a deterministic function symbol, the label is dropped.

Substitutions are written $\sigma = \{x_1 = t_1, \ldots, x_n = t_n\}$ with *domain* $\mathrm{dom}(\sigma) = \{x_1, \ldots, x_n\}$. We only consider *well-typed* substitutions, that is substitutions $\sigma = \{x_1 = t_1, \ldots, x_n = t_n\}$ for which t_i is of a subtype of x_i. The application of a substitution σ to a term t is written $\sigma(t) = t\sigma$.

Function symbols in Σ are intended to model cryptographic primitives, including generation of random data like e.g. nonces or keys. Identities will typically be represented by constants (deterministic function symbols without arguments). The symbolic model is equipped with a *deduction relation* $\vdash \subseteq 2^{\mathsf{Terms}} \times \mathsf{Terms}$ that models the information available to a symbolic adversary. $T \vdash t$ means that a formal adversary can build t out of T, where t is a term and T a set of terms. We say that t is *deducible* from T. Deduction relations are typically defined through deduction systems.

Definition 1. *A deduction system $\mathcal{D}$ is a set of rules $\frac{t_1 \ \cdots \ t_n}{t}$ such that $t_1, \ldots, t_n, t \in \mathsf{Terms}(\Sigma, \mathcal{T}, \leq)$. The deduction relation $\vdash_{\mathcal{D}} \subseteq 2^{\mathsf{Terms}} \times \mathsf{Terms}$ associated to $\mathcal{D}$ is the smallest relation satisfying:*

- *$T \vdash_{\mathcal{D}} t$ for any $t \in T \subseteq \mathsf{Terms}(\Sigma, \mathcal{T}, \leq)$*
- *If $T \vdash_{\mathcal{D}} t_1\sigma, \ldots T \vdash_{\mathcal{D}} t_n\sigma$ for some substitution σ and $\frac{t_1 \ \cdots \ t_n}{t} \in \mathcal{D}$ then $T \vdash_{\mathcal{D}} t\sigma$.*

We may omit the subscript $\mathcal{D}$ in $\vdash_{\mathcal{D}}$ when it is clear from the context. For all deduction systems $\mathcal{D}$ in this paper we require $\frac{}{g^l_\tau}$ for all garbage symbols $g_\tau \in \Sigma$ and $l \in \mathsf{labelsA}$.

From now on we denote a symbolic model $\mathcal{M}$ as a tuple $(\mathcal{T}, \leq, \Sigma, \mathcal{D})$ where $\mathcal{T}$ is the set of data types, $\leq$ the subtype relation, Σ signature and $\mathcal{D}$ the deduction system. For all symbolic models defined in this paper we omit the garbage symbols and the corresponding reduction rules for the sake of brevity.

3. IMPLEMENTATION

An implementation $\mathcal{I}$ of a symbolic model is a family of tuples $(M_\eta, [\![\cdot]\!]_\eta, len_\eta, \mathsf{open}_\eta, \mathsf{valid}_\eta)_\eta$ for $\eta \in \mathbb{N}$. We usually omit the security parameter and just write $(M, [\![\cdot]\!], len, \mathsf{open}, \mathsf{valid})$ for an implementation.

M is a Turing Machine which provides concrete algorithms working on bit-strings for the function symbols in the signature. $[\![\cdot]\!] : \mathcal{T} \to 2^{\{0,1\}^*}$ is a function that maps each type to a set of bitstrings. $len : \mathsf{Terms} \to \mathbb{N}$ computes the length of a term if interpreted as a bitstring. With open the implementation provides an algorithm to interpret bitstrings as terms. valid is a predicate which states whether a concrete use of the implementation is valid. For example, a correct use of an implementation might exclude the creation of key cycles or dynamic corruption of keys from the valid use cases. More precisely we require the following from an implementation:

We assume a non-empty set of bitstrings $[\![\tau]\!] \subseteq \{0,1\}^\eta$ for each type $\tau \in \mathcal{T}$. For the base type $\top$, we assume $[\![\top]\!] = \{0,1\}^*$ and for any pair of types $\tau, \tau' \in \mathcal{T}$ with $\tau \leq \tau'$ we require $[\![\tau]\!] \subsetneq [\![\tau']\!]$ and $[\![\tau]\!] \cap [\![\tau']\!] = \emptyset$ otherwise (i.e., if $\tau \not\leq \tau'$). We write $[\![\mathcal{T}]\!]$ for $\cup_{\tau \in \mathcal{T} \setminus \{\top\}} [\![\tau]\!]$. Later, we often make use of a function $\langle c_1, \ldots, c_n, \tau \rangle$ that takes a list of bitstrings $c_1, \ldots, c_n$ and a type τ and encodes $c_1, \ldots, c_n$ as a bitstring $c' \in [\![\tau]\!]$. We assume that this encoding is bijective, i.e., we can uniquely parse c' as $\langle c_1, \ldots, c_n, \tau \rangle$ again.

We require the Turing Machine M itself to be deterministic. However, each time it is run, it is provided with a random tape $\mathcal{R}$. More specifically, we require for each $f \in \Sigma$ with $\mathrm{ar}(f) = \tau_1 \times \ldots \times \tau_n \to \tau$ that is not a garbage symbol that for input f M calculates a function $(M\ f)$ with domain $[\![\tau_1]\!] \times \cdots \times [\![\tau_n]\!] \times \{0,1\}^*$ and range $[\![\tau]\!]$. The runtime of M and $(M\ f)$ has to be polynomial in the length of its input. Intuitively, to generate a bitstring for a term $t = f^l(t_1, \ldots, t_n)$ we apply $(M\ f)$ to the bitstrings generated for the arguments t_i and some randomness (which might not be used for deterministic function symbols). We call the resulting bitstring *computational interpretation* of t. The randomness is provided by the $\mathsf{generate}$ function introduced in Section 3.

Interpretations. In cryptographic applications functions are often randomized and the same random coins may occur in different places within the same term. This is the case for instance when the same nonce occurs twice in the same

$\mathsf{generate}_{M,\mathcal{R}}(t, L)$:
  if for some $c \in \text{dom}(L)$ we have $L[[c]] = t$ then
    return c
  else
    for $i \in \{1, \ldots, n\}$ let $(c_i, L) := \mathsf{generate}_{M,\mathcal{R}}(t_i, L)$
    let $r := \mathcal{R}(t)$
    let $c := (M\ f)(c_1, \ldots, c_n; r)$
    let $L(c) := f^l(c_1, \ldots, c_n))$ $(l \in \mathsf{labelsH})$
    return (c, L)

Figure 1: The generate function (t is of the form $f^l(t_1, \ldots, t_n)$ (with possibly $n = 0$ and no label l for deterministic function symbols f)).

$\mathsf{parse}(c, L)$:
  if $c \in \text{dom}(L)$ then
    return $(L[[c]], L)$
  else
    let $L_h := \{(\overline{c}, f^l(\ldots)) \in L : l \in \mathsf{labelsH}\}$
    let $L := \left(\bigcup_{(\overline{c},\cdot)\in L} \mathsf{open}(\overline{c}, L_h)\right)$
    let $G := \left\{(\overline{c}, g_{\top}^{l(\overline{c})})\right\}$ $(l(\overline{c}) \in \mathsf{labelsA})$
    do
      let $L := (L \setminus G) \cup \left(\bigcup_{(\overline{c},\cdot)\in G} \mathsf{open}(\overline{c}, L_h)\right)$
      let $G := \left\{(\overline{c}, g_{\top}^{l(\overline{c})}) : (\overline{c}', f(\ldots, \overline{c}, \ldots)) \in L \text{ and } \overline{c} \notin \text{dom}(L)\right\}$
    while $G \neq \emptyset$
    return $(L[[c]], L)$

Figure 2: The parsing function.

term. We use a (partially defined) mapping $L : \{0,1\}^* \to \mathsf{HTerm}$ from bit-strings to *hybrid terms* to record this information. A hybrid term is either a garbage term or $f^l(c_1, \ldots, c_n)$ where $f \in \Sigma$ is a function symbol of arity n applied to bit-strings $c_i \in \{0,1\}^*$. By $\text{dom}(L) \subseteq 2^{\{0,1\}^*}$ we denote the domain of L, i.e. the set of bit-strings for which L is defined. The mapping L induces an interpretation of bit-strings as terms. We define the *interpretation of bitstring $c \in \text{dom}(L)$ with respect to a mapping L* as $L[[c]] := f^l(L[[c_1]], \ldots, L[[c_n]])$ if $L(c) = f^l(c_1, \ldots, c_n)$ and $L[[c]] := L(c)$ if $L(c)$ is a garbage term. We say that a mapping L is complete, if for all $(c, f^l(c_1, \ldots, c_n)) \in L$ $c_1, \ldots, c_n \in \text{dom}(L)$. Note that $L[[c]]$ is only defined if L is complete.

Generating function. Given a mapping L we define a generating function that associates a concrete semantics for terms (given the terms already interpreted in L).

The generation function uses a random tape $\mathcal{R}$ as a source of randomness for M when generating the concrete interpretation of terms. We assume that there is an algorithm $\mathcal{R}(t)$ which maps a term t to a bitstring $r \in \{0,1\}^\eta$ that should be used as the randomness when t is generated. Even changing only one label in t leads to a changed term t' for which different randomness will be used. Figure 1 defines the generate function given a closed term $t = f^l(t_1, \ldots, t_n)$ and a mapping L.

Note that $\mathsf{generate}_{M,\mathcal{R}}(t, L)$ not only returns a bit-string c associated to t but also updates L (to remember, for example, the value associated to t). Note also that $\mathsf{generate}_{M,\mathcal{R}}$ depends on M and the random tape $\mathcal{R}$. When needed, we explicitly show this dependency, but in general we avoid it for readability. If a mapping L is complete, then for $(c, L') := \mathsf{generate}(t, L)$, L' is complete. Furthermore, the generate function requires that, for given inputs t, L, the following holds: For all $t' := f^l(t_1, \ldots, t_n) \in st(t)$ where $l \in \mathsf{labelsA}$ we find a $c \in \text{dom}(L)$ s.t. $L[[c]] = t'$ and t doesn't contain garbage symbols carrying honest labels. This guarantees that all bitstrings introduced by the generate function correspond to the application of non-garbage function symbols carrying honest labels.

Parsing function. Conversely, we require the implementation to define a function parse to convert bit-string into terms. The function takes a bit-string c and a mapping L as input and returns a term t and an extended mapping L.

For parsing functions we require the concrete structure in Figure 2 (where $\mathsf{open} : \{0,1\}^* \times \mathsf{libs} \to \{0,1\}^* \times \mathsf{HTerm}$ a function that on call $\mathsf{open}(c, L)$ parses the bitstring c in presence of the library L and returns its hybrid interpretation).

The exact definition of parse is left unspecified, as it depends on the particular behavior of open which is provided by a concrete implementation. We require this structure for the parsing function to provide a concrete context in which the open function of different implementations can be composed. Note that the open function is only allowed to use honestly generated bitstrings when dealing with a term. We will furthermore only use open functions later that ignore "foreign" bitstrings in the given library, i.e., bitstrings that are of a data type that is not part of the implementation open belongs to. Due to these properties the composition of open functions is commutative. This is important for our composition theorems later. Furthermore, we think that it meets the intuition that the composition of different implementations should be commutative.

Good implementation. Until now we have not restricted the behavior of implementations in any way. However, there are some properties we will need to hold for every implementation. We describe these properties in this section and say that a *good implementation* is one that satisfies all of them.

We stipulate that a good implementation is *length regular*, i.e., $len(f^l(t_1, \ldots, t_n)) := |(M\ f)(c_1, \ldots, c_n; r)|$ depends only on the length of the arguments c_i (which are the computational interpretations of the symbolic arguments t_i).

We now explain what it means for an implementation to be collision free. A collision occurs if during a call of $\mathsf{generate}_{M,\mathcal{R}}(t, L)$ an execution of M yields a bitstring c that is already in the domain of L. Since the library L has to be well-defined, we can either overwrite the old value $L(c)$ with the new one or discard the new value. Both variants are problematic:

Overwriting changes the behavior of parse (i.e., bitstrings may now be parsed differently). This might have severe consequences. Imagine that the overwritten bitstring was an honestly signed message. Now this signature looks like the signature of a different message symbolically; possibly like a forgery. Note that this would not be a weakness of signatures but of the fact that collisions can be found for bitstrings corresponding to the signed terms. Discarding means that a bitstring c generated for a term t might not be parsed as

t later which might wrongfully prevent the adversary from winning the soundness game.

Hence we will always require our implementations to be collision free. Details can be found in the full version of this paper [8].

When we compose implementations later we will need that their open functions do not interfere. Intuitively, each open function should stick to opening the bitstrings it is responsible for (i.e., that are of types belonging to the same implementation the open function belongs to). We say that an open function is *type safe* if it satisfies (*i*) $\mathsf{open}(c, L) = (c, g_\top^l)$ for $l \in \mathsf{labelsA}$ if $c \notin [\![\mathcal{T}]\!]$ and (*ii*) $\mathsf{open}(c, L) = \mathsf{open}(c, L|[\![\mathcal{T}]\!])$ where $L|[\![\mathcal{T}]\!] := \{(c, h) \in L : \exists \tau \in \mathcal{T} \setminus \{\top\} : c \in [\![\tau]\!]\}$. Since we need to simulate parsing later, we require $\mathsf{parse}(c, L)$ (based on open) to run in polynomial time in the size of the library.

For technical reasons we have to stipulate some general properties for the valid predicate, e.g., a polynomial runtime, to get a good implementation. These details are omitted here and can be found in [8].

4. TRANSPARENT FUNCTIONS

Typical primitives that are usually considered in soundness results include encryption, signatures, hash functions, etc.. Intuitively, such functions are efficiently invertible, and the type of their output can be efficiently determined. An example for such functions are data structures (i.e., pairs, lists, XML documents, etc.). Following the ideas of [13], we define and study soundness in presence of *transparent* functions like these. In this section we define the notion of a *transparent symbolic model* and the corresponding *transparent implementation.*

A transparent symbolic model $\mathcal{M}_{\mathsf{tran}} = (\mathcal{T}_{\mathsf{tran}}, \leq_{\mathsf{tran}}, \Sigma_{\mathsf{tran}}, \mathcal{D}_{\mathsf{tran}})$ is a symbolic model where the deduction system is defined as follows (the label is omitted for deterministic function symbols):

$$\mathcal{D}_{\mathsf{tran}} = \left\{ \begin{array}{ll} \frac{t_1 \ \cdots \ t_n}{f^l(t_n,\ldots,t_n)} & l \in \mathsf{labelsA}, f \in \Sigma_{\mathsf{tran}} \\ \\ \frac{f^l(t_1,\ldots,t_n)}{t_i} & 1 \leq i \leq n, l \in \mathsf{labels}, f \in \Sigma_{\mathsf{tran}} \end{array} \right\}$$

Formally, a transparent implementation of a transparent symbolic model $\mathcal{M} = (\mathcal{T}, \leq, \Sigma, \mathcal{D})$ is an implementation (and thus adhering to the requirements from Figure 3) $\mathcal{I}_{\mathsf{tran}} = (M_{\mathsf{tran}}, [\![\cdot]\!], len, \mathsf{open}_{\mathsf{tran}}, \mathsf{valid}_{\mathsf{tran}})$ where $\mathsf{open}_{\mathsf{tran}}$ and $\mathsf{valid}_{\mathsf{tran}}$ are defined explicitly below. We require two additional modes of operation, func and proj, for the Turing Machine M_{tran} such that for all $f \in \Sigma$ with $\mathrm{ar}(f) = \tau_1 \times \ldots \times \tau_n \to \tau$

$$(M_{\mathsf{tran}}\ \mathsf{func}) : \{0,1\}^* \to \Sigma \cup \{\bot\}$$
$$(M_{\mathsf{tran}}\ \mathsf{proj}\ f\ i) : \{0,1\}^* \to \{0,1\}^* \cup \{\bot\}$$

and we have for any $c_i \in [\![\tau_i]\!]$, $1 \leq i \leq n$, $r \in \{0,1\}^\eta$

$$(M_{\mathsf{tran}}\ \mathsf{func})((M_{\mathsf{tran}}\ f)(c_1, \ldots, c_n; r)) = f$$
$$(M_{\mathsf{tran}}\ \mathsf{proj}\ f\ i)((M_{\mathsf{tran}}\ f)(c_1, \ldots, c_n; r)) = c_i$$

Furthermore, we require $(M_{\mathsf{tran}}\ \mathsf{func})(c) = \bot$ for all $c \notin [\![\mathcal{T}]\!]$. As expected, M_{tran} is required to run in polynomial time in η for this modes of operation as well.

For transparent implementations we explicitly define the open function $\mathsf{open}_{\mathsf{tran}}$ as in Figure 3. Note that a transparent implementation is automatically type safe: Property (*i*) is required above and property (*ii*) holds since it only uses L for bitstrings of type $\mathcal{T}$.

We define $\mathsf{valid}_{\mathsf{tran}}(\mathbb{T}) = \mathsf{true}$ for all traces $\mathbb{T}$, i.e., the use of transparent functions is not restricted in any way.

```
open_tran(c, L):
  if c ∈ ⟦T⟧ ∩ dom(L) then
    return (c, L(c))
  else if (M_tran func)(c) = ⊥ then
    find unique τ ∈ T s.t. c ∈ ⟦τ⟧ and
      c ∉ ⟦τ'⟧ for all τ' ∈ T with ⟦τ'⟧ ⊊ ⟦τ⟧
    return (c, g_τ^{l(c)}) (l(c) ∈ labelsA)
  else
    let f := (M_tran func)(c) (ar(f) = τ_1 × ··· × τ_n → τ)
    if (M_tran proj f i)(c) = ⊥ for some i ∈ {1,...,n} then
      return (c, g_τ^{l(c)}) (l(c) ∈ labelsA)
    else
      for i ∈ {1,...,n} do
        let c̃_i := (M_tran proj f i)(c̃)
      return (c, f^{l(c)}(c_1,...,c_n)) (l(c) ∈ labelsA)
```

Figure 3: Parsing algorithm for a transparent implementation.

5. COMPOSITION

We next explain how to generically compose two symbolic models and their corresponding implementations.

Let $\mathcal{M}_1 = (\mathcal{T}_1, \leq_1, \Sigma_1, \mathcal{D}_1)$ and $\mathcal{M}_2 = (\mathcal{T}_2, \leq_2, \Sigma_2, \mathcal{D}_2)$ be symbolic models and $\mathcal{I}_1 = (M_1, [\![\cdot]\!]_1, len_1, \mathsf{open}_1, \mathsf{valid}_1)$ and $\mathcal{I}_2 = (M_2, [\![\cdot]\!]_2, len_2, \mathsf{open}_2, \mathsf{valid}_2)$ implementations of $\mathcal{M}_1$ and $\mathcal{M}_2$ respectively. We say that that $(\mathcal{M}_1, \mathcal{I}_1)$ and $(\mathcal{M}_2, \mathcal{I}_2)$ are *compatible* if $\mathcal{M}_1$ and $\mathcal{M}_2$ as well as $\mathcal{I}_1$ and $\mathcal{I}_2$ meet the requirements for compositions of symbolic models and implementations stated below respectively.

We define the composition of $\mathcal{M}' = \mathcal{M}_1 \cup \mathcal{M}_2$ of $\mathcal{M}_1$ and $\mathcal{M}_2$ if (*i*) $\Sigma_1 \cap \Sigma_2 = \{g_\top\}$ and (*ii*) $\mathcal{T}_1 \cap \mathcal{T}_2 = \{\top\}$ and then have $\mathcal{T}' := \mathcal{T}_1 \cup \mathcal{T}_2$, $\leq' := \leq_1 \cup \leq_2$, $\Sigma' := \Sigma_1 \cup \Sigma_2$ and $\mathcal{D}' := \mathcal{D}_1 \cup \mathcal{D}_2$.

The corresponding implementations $\mathcal{I}_1 = (M_1, [\![\cdot]\!]_1, len_1, \mathsf{open}_1, \mathsf{valid}_1)$ and $\mathcal{I}_2 = (M_2, [\![\cdot]\!]_2, len_2, \mathsf{open}_2, \mathsf{valid}_2)$ can be composed if (*i*) for all types $\tau_1 \in \mathcal{T}_1 \setminus \{\top\}$, $\tau_2 \in \mathcal{T}_2 \setminus \{\top\}$ we have $[\![\tau_1]\!] \cap [\![\tau_2]\!] = \emptyset$ and (*ii*) the composition of $\mathcal{I}_1$ and $\mathcal{I}_2$ (as defined below) is a collision-free implementation of $\mathcal{M}'$. We then define the composition $\mathcal{I}' = \mathcal{I}_1 \cup \mathcal{I}_2$ as follows:

The Turing machine $(M'\ f)$ returns $(M_1\ f)$ for $f \in \Sigma_1$ and $(M_2\ f)$ if $f \in \Sigma_2$. This is non-ambiguous due to (*i*).[1] Similarly, for all $\tau \in \mathcal{T}_1$ we set $[\![\tau]\!]' := [\![\tau]\!]_1$ and analogously for $\tau \in \mathcal{T}_2$. Note that $[\![\top]\!] = [\![\top]\!]_1 = [\![\top]\!]_2 = \{0,1\}^*$. Since implementations are required to be length regular we can also compose the length functions len_1 and len_2 in a straightforward way to get len'.

To compose the open functions we define

```
(open_1 ∘ open_2)(c, L):
  let (c, t) := open_1(c, L)
  if t = g_⊤^l for some l ∈ labelsA then
    return open_2(c, L)
```

[1] Here we assume that the membership problem is efficiently decidable (since M' has to run in polynomial time). This can be achieve w.l.o.g. with a suitable encoding for the function symbols.

else
  return (c, t)

and consequently $\mathsf{open}' := \mathsf{open}_1 \circ \mathsf{open}_2$. Furthermore we set $\mathsf{valid}'(\mathbb{T}) := \mathsf{valid}_1(\mathbb{T}) \wedge \mathsf{valid}_2(\mathbb{T})$ where $\wedge$ is the conjunction.

Checking that $\mathcal{I}'$ is a good implementation of the composed symbolic model $\mathcal{M}'$ is a straightforward task.

6. DEDUCTION SOUNDNESS

In this section we recall the notion of deduction soundness of an implementation with respect to a symbolic model [13]. Informally, the definition considers an adversary that plays the following game against a challenger. The challenger maintains a mapping L between bitstrings and hybrid terms, as defined in Section 3. Recall that the such mappings are used to both generate bitstring interpretations for terms, and also to parse bitstrings as terms (Figures 1,2). Roughly, the adversary is allowed to request to see the interpretation of arbitrary terms, and also to see the result of the parsing function applied to arbitrary bitstrings. Throughout the execution the queries that the adversary makes need to satisfy a predicate valid (which is a parameter of the implementation). The goal of the adversary is to issue a parse request such that the result is a term, that is not deducible from the terms that he had queried in his generate requests: this illustrates the idea that the adversary, although operating with bitstrings, is restricting to only performing Dolev-Yao operations on the bit-strings that it receives.

The details of the game are in Figure 4. Our definition departs from the one of [13] in a few technical aspects. First, we introduce a query init which is used to "initialize" the execution by, for example, generating (and corrupting) keys. The introduction of this query allows for a clearer separation between the phases where keys are created and where they are used, and allows to simplify and clarify what are valid interactions between the adversary and the game.

Secondly, we also allow the adversary to issue sgenerate requests: these are generate requests except that the resulting bitstring is not returned to the adversary. These requests are a technical necessity that help in later simulations, and only strengthen the adversary.

Deduction soundness of an implementation $\mathcal{I}$ with respect to a symbolic model $\mathcal{M}$ for an implementation is defined by considering an adversary who plays the game sketched above against an implementation that mixes $\mathcal{I}$ with transparent functions provided by the adversary. To ensure uniform behavior on behalf of the adversary , we introduce a notion of parametrized transparent functions/models.

PARAMETRIZATION. A *parametrized transparent symbolic model* $\mathcal{M}_{\mathsf{tran}}(\nu)$ maps a bitstring ν (the parameter) to a transparent symbolic model. Analogously, a *parametrized transparent implementation* $\mathcal{I}_{\mathsf{tran}}(\nu)$ of $\mathcal{M}_{\mathsf{tran}}$ maps a bitstring ν (the parameters) to a transparent implementation ν where the length of ν is polynomial in the security parameter. We say that a parameter ν is *good* if $\mathcal{I}_{\mathsf{tran}}(\nu)$ is a transparent implementation of $\mathcal{M}_{\mathsf{tran}}(\nu)$ and meets the requirements of a good implementation (i.e., type-safe, ...) from Section 3.

Deduction soundness of an $\mathcal{I}$ with respect to $\mathcal{M}$ holds if the adversary cannot win the deduction soundness game that involves implementation $\mathcal{I} \cup \mathcal{I}_{\mathsf{tran}}(\nu)$ for $\mathcal{M} \cup \mathcal{M}_{\mathsf{tran}}(\nu)$ for arbitrary transparent models/implementations $\mathcal{M}_{\mathsf{tran}}, \mathcal{I}_{\mathsf{tran}}$, and for any parameter ν provided by the adversary.

$\mathsf{DS}_{\mathcal{M}(\nu),\mathcal{I}(\nu),\mathcal{A}}(\eta)$:
  let $S := \emptyset$ (set of requested terms)
  let $L := \emptyset$ (library)
  let $\mathbb{T} := \emptyset$ (trace of queries)
  $\mathcal{R} \leftarrow \{0,1\}^*$ (random tape)

  Receive parameter ν from $\mathcal{A}$

  on request "init T, H" do
    add "init T" to $\mathbb{T}$
    if valid($\mathbb{T}$) then
      let $S := S \cup T$
      let $C := \emptyset$ (list of replies)
      for each $t \in T$ do
        let $(c, L) := \mathsf{generate}_{M,\mathcal{R}}(t, L)$
        let $C := C \cup \{c\}$
      for each $t \in H$ do
        let $(c, L) := \mathsf{generate}_{M,\mathcal{R}}(t, L)$
      send C to $\mathcal{A}$
    else
      return 0 ($\mathcal{A}$ is invalid)

  on request "sgenerate t" do
    if valid($\mathbb{T}$+"sgenerate t") then
      let $(c, L) := \mathsf{generate}_{M,\mathcal{R}}(t, L)$

  on request "generate t" do
    add "generate t" to $\mathbb{T}$
    if valid($\mathbb{T}$) then
      let $S := S \cup \{t\}$
      let $(c, L) := \mathsf{generate}_{M,\mathcal{R}}(t, L)$
      send c to $\mathcal{A}$
    else
      return 0 ($\mathcal{A}$ is invalid)

  on request "parse c" do
    let $(t, L) := \mathsf{parse}(c, L)$
    if $S \vdash_{\mathcal{D}} t$ then
      send t to $\mathcal{A}$
    else
      return 1 ($\mathcal{A}$ produced non-Dolev-Yao term)

Figure 4: Game defining deduction soundness. Whenever $\mathsf{generate}_{M,\mathcal{R}}(t, L)$ is called, the requirements for t are checked (i.e., all subterms of t with adversarial labels must already be in L and t does not contain garbage symbols with honest labels) and 0 is returned if the check fails (i.e., the $\mathcal{A}$ is considered to be invalid).

DEFINITION 2 (DEDUCTION SOUNDNESS). *Let $\mathcal{M}$ be a symbolic model and $\mathcal{I}$ be an implementation of $\mathcal{M}$. We say that $\mathcal{I}$ is a* deduction sound implementation of $\mathcal{M}$ *if for all parametrized transparent symbolic models $\mathcal{M}_{\mathsf{tran}}(\nu)$ and for all parametrized transparent implementations $\mathcal{I}_{\mathsf{tran}}(\nu)$ of $\mathcal{M}_{\mathsf{tran}}$ such that $(\mathcal{M}_{\mathsf{tran}}, \mathcal{I}_{\mathsf{tran}})$ is compatible with $(\mathcal{M},\mathcal{I})$ we have that*

$$\mathbb{P}\left[\mathsf{DS}_{\mathcal{M}\cup\mathcal{M}_{\mathsf{tran}}(\nu),\mathcal{I}\cup\mathcal{I}_{\mathsf{tran}}(\nu),\mathcal{A}}(\eta) = 1\right]$$

is negligible for all probabilistic polynomial time (p.p.t.) adversaries $\mathcal{A}$ sending only good parameters ν where DS *is the deduction soundness game defined in Figure 4.*

7. COMPOSITION THEOREMS

The notion of deduction soundness enjoys the nice property of being easily extendable: if an implementation is deduction sound for a given symbolic model, it is possible to add other primitives, one by one, without having to prove deduction soundness from scratch for the resulting set of primitives.

In this section we state a couple of composition theorems that can be used to enrich any deduction sound implementation with additional primitives. First, we quickly restate the main composition theorem for public data types from [13].

THEOREM 1. *Let $\mathcal{M}$ be a symbolic model and $\mathcal{I}$ a deduction sound implementation of $\mathcal{M}$. Furthermore, let $\mathcal{M}_{\mathsf{tran}}$ be a transparent symbolic model and $\mathcal{I}_{\mathsf{tran}}$ a transparent implementation of $\mathcal{M}_{\mathsf{tran}}$. If $(\mathcal{M},\mathcal{I})$ and and $(\mathcal{M}_{\mathsf{tran}},\mathcal{I}_{\mathsf{tran}})$ are compatible, then $\mathcal{I}\cup\mathcal{I}_{\mathsf{tran}}$ is a deduction sound implementation of $\mathcal{M}\cup\mathcal{M}_{\mathsf{tran}}$.*

7.1 Signatures

In this section we show that any deduction sound implementation can be extended by a signature scheme. More precisely, composition works if we require a strong EUF-CMA secure signature scheme and enforce static corruption. The result is again a deduction sound implementation.

We first define the symbolic model $(\mathcal{T}_{\mathsf{SIG}}, \leq_{\mathsf{SIG}}, \Sigma_{\mathsf{SIG}}, \mathcal{D}_{\mathsf{SIG}})$ for signatures. The signature Σ_{SIG} features the following function symbols:

$$sk : \tau_{\mathsf{SIG}}^{\mathsf{sk}} \qquad vk : \tau_{\mathsf{SIG}}^{\mathsf{sk}} \to \tau_{\mathsf{SIG}}^{\mathsf{vk}} \qquad sig : \tau_{\mathsf{SIG}}^{\mathsf{sk}} \times \top \to \tau_{\mathsf{SIG}}^{\mathsf{sig}}$$

The randomized function sk of arity $\tau_{\mathsf{SIG}}^{\mathsf{sk}}$ returns a signing key. The deterministic function vk of arity $\tau_{\mathsf{SIG}}^{\mathsf{sk}} \to \tau_{\mathsf{SIG}}^{\mathsf{vk}}$ derives a verification key from a signing key. The randomized signing function sig has arity $\tau_{\mathsf{SIG}}^{\mathsf{sk}} \times \top \to \tau_{\mathsf{SIG}}^{\mathsf{sig}}$ and, given a signing key and a message of type $\top$, represents a signature of that message. To complete the formal definition we set the types

$$\mathcal{T}_{\mathsf{SIG}} := \{\top, \tau_{\mathsf{SIG}}^{\mathsf{sk}}, \tau_{\mathsf{SIG}}^{\mathsf{vk}}, \tau_{\mathsf{SIG}}^{\mathsf{sig}}\}$$

All introduced types are direct subtypes of the base type $\top$ (this defines $\leq_{\mathsf{SIG}}$). The deduction system captures the security of signatures

$$\mathcal{D}_{\mathsf{SIG}} := \left\{ \begin{array}{cc} \multicolumn{2}{c}{\frac{sk^l()}{vk(sk^l())},} \\ \frac{sig^{\hat{l}}(sk^l(),m)}{m}, & \frac{sk^l() \quad m}{sig^{l_a}(sk^l(),m)} \end{array} \right\}$$

These rules are valid for arbitrary labels $l, \hat{l} \in$ labels and adversarial labels $l_a \in$ labelsA. Read from top left to bottom right, the rules capture the intuition that the adversary can derive verification keys from signing keys, that signatures reveal the message that was signed and that the adversary can use known signing keys to deduce signatures under those keys. Although the verification key is going to be part of the computational implementation of a signatures, we don't need a rule $\frac{sig^{\hat{l}}(sk^l(),m)}{vk(sk^l)}$ since we enforce static corruption where adversary knows all verification keys.

```
open_SIG(c, L)
  if c ∈ [[T_SIG]] ∩ dom(L) then
    return (c, L(c))
  else if c = ⟨sk, τ^sk_SIG⟩ then
    return (c, g^{l(c)}_{τ^sk_SIG})
  else if c = ⟨vk, τ^vk_SIG⟩ then
    if ŝk ∈ dom(L) s.t. ŝk = ⟨vk, sk, τ^sk_SIG⟩ then
      return (c, vk(ŝk))
    else
      return (c, g^{l(c)}_{τ^vk_SIG})
  else if c = ⟨σ, m, vk, τ^sig_SIG⟩ then
    if (⟨vk, τ^vk_SIG⟩, vk(ŝk)) ∈ L
      and SIG.Vfy(vk, σ, m) = true then
      return (c, sig^{l(c)}(ŝk, m))
    else
      return (c, g^{l(c)}_{τ^sig_SIG})
  else
    return (c, g^{l(c)}_⊤)
```

Figure 5: Open function for signatures.

We now give a concrete implementation $\mathcal{I}_{\mathsf{SIG}}$ for signatures. The implementation uses some strongly EUF-CMA secure signature scheme (SIG.KeyGen, SIG.Sig, SIG.Vfy). As usual, here SIG.KeyGen is a generation algorithm for key pairs, SIG.Sig is an signing algorithm and SIG.Vfy is a verification algorithm. Note that SIG.Sig is an algorithm that takes three inputs: the signing key, the message to be signed and the randomness that is used for signing.[2] The computable interpretations of sk, vk, sig are as follows:

- $(M_{\mathsf{SIG}}\ sk)(r)$: Let $(vk, sk) := \mathsf{SIG.KeyGen}(1^\eta, r)$. Return $\langle vk, sk, \tau_{\mathsf{SIG}}^{\mathsf{sk}}\rangle$.
- $(M_{\mathsf{SIG}}\ vk)(\hat{sk}$: Parse $\hat{sk}$ as $\langle vk, sk, \tau_{\mathsf{SIG}}^{\mathsf{sk}}\rangle$. Return $\langle vk, \tau_{\mathsf{SIG}}^{\mathsf{vk}}\rangle$.
- $(M_{\mathsf{SIG}}\ sig)(\hat{sk}, m; r)$: Parse $\hat{sk}$ as $\langle vk, sk, \tau_{\mathsf{SIG}}^{\mathsf{sk}}\rangle$. Let $\sigma := \mathsf{SIG.Sig}(sk, m, r)$ and return $\langle \sigma, m, vk, \tau_{\mathsf{SIG}}^{\mathsf{sig}}\rangle$.

Intuitively, the $\mathsf{valid}_{\mathsf{SIG}}$ predicate guarantees static corruption of signing keys and that verification and signing keys are only used for signing and verification.

THEOREM 2. *Let $\mathcal{M}$ be a symbolic model and $\mathcal{I}$ be deduction sound implementation of $\mathcal{M}$. If $(\mathcal{M}_{\mathsf{SIG}},\mathcal{I}_{\mathsf{SIG}})$ and $(\mathcal{M},\mathcal{I})$ are compatible, then $\mathcal{I}\cup\mathcal{I}_{\mathsf{SIG}}$ is a deduction sound implementation of $\mathcal{M}\cup\mathcal{M}_{\mathsf{SIG}}$.*

We briefly describe the intuition behind the proof. Let $\mathcal{A}$ be an adversary playing the deduction soundness game. Assume that $\mathcal{A}$ queries "parse c" and c is parsed as a non-DY term t that contains a signature $sig := sig^{\hat{l}}(sk^l(), m)$ and $S \not\vdash sig$ (where S is the list of terms generated for $\mathcal{A}$ in the deduction soundness game). We distinguish two possible ways the adversary could potentially have learned sig:

If sig was previously generated for $\mathcal{A}$ (i.e., $sig \in st(S)$ and $\hat{l} \in$ labelsH), we say that $\mathcal{A}$ *reconstructed sig*. Since

[2]Since the message m is of basetype, we require a scheme with message space $\{0,1\}^*$.

signatures and transparent functions do not introduce function symbols that allow for signatures as input such that the signature is not derivable from the constructed term, $\mathcal{A}$ must have broken the deduction soundness of $\mathcal{I}$ in this case. Hence, using $\mathcal{A}$, we can construct a successful adversary $\mathcal{B}$ on the deduction soundness of $\mathcal{I}$. $\mathcal{B}$ simulates signatures using transparent functions.

If *sig* was not previously generated for $\mathcal{A}$ (i.e., $\hat{l} \in \mathsf{labelsA}$), we say that $\mathcal{A}$ *forged sig*. In this case $\mathcal{A}$ can be used to break the strong EUF-CMA security of the signature scheme.

Since reconstructions and forgeries can only occur with negligible probability the composed implementation $\mathcal{I} \cup \mathcal{I}_{\mathsf{SIG}}$ is a deduction sound implementation of $\mathcal{M} \cup \mathcal{M}_{\mathsf{SIG}}$.

7.2 Secret key encryption

In this section we define a symbolic model $\mathcal{M}_{\mathsf{SKE}}$ for secret key encryption and a corresponding implementation $\mathcal{I}_{\mathsf{SKE}}$ based on a secure authenticated encryption scheme (SKE.KeyGen, SKE.Enc, SKE.Dec) [6]. We show that composition of $\mathcal{M}_{\mathsf{SKE}}$ and $\mathcal{I}_{\mathsf{SKE}}$ with any symbolic model $\mathcal{M}$ comprising a deduction sound implementation $\mathcal{I}$ preserves this property for the resulting implementation, i.e., $\mathcal{I} \cup \mathcal{I}_{\mathsf{SKE}}$ is a deduction sound implementation of $\mathcal{M} \cup \mathcal{M}_{\mathsf{SKE}}$.

We first define the symbolic model $(\mathcal{T}_{\mathsf{SKE}}, \leq_{\mathsf{SKE}}, \Sigma_{\mathsf{SKE}}, \mathcal{D}_{\mathsf{SKE}})$ for secret key encryption. The signature Σ_{SKE} features the function symbols

$$k_x : \tau_{\mathsf{SKE}}^{\mathsf{k}_x} \qquad\qquad E_x : \tau_{\mathsf{SKE}}^{\mathsf{k}_x} \times \top \rightarrow \tau_{\mathsf{SKE}}^{\mathsf{ciphertext}}$$

for $x \in \{h, c\}$. [3] The randomized functions k_h and k_c return honest or corrupted keys respectively. The randomized function E_x has arity $\tau_{\mathsf{SKE}}^{\mathsf{k}_x} \times \top \rightarrow \tau_{\mathsf{SKE}}^{\mathsf{ciphertext}}$ and represents a ciphertext under the given key. To complete the formal definition we set

$$\mathcal{T}_{\mathsf{SKE}} := \{\top, \tau_{\mathsf{SKE}}^{\mathsf{k}_x}, \tau_{\mathsf{SKE}}^{\mathsf{ciphertext}}\}$$

All introduced types are direct subtypes of the base type $\top$ (this defines $\leq_{\mathsf{SKE}}$). The deduction system captures the security of secret key encryption

$$\mathcal{D}_{\mathsf{SKE}} := \left\{ \begin{array}{c} \dfrac{k_x^l() \quad m}{E_x^{l_a}(k_x^l(), m)}, \\[2ex] \dfrac{E_h^{l_a}(k_h^l(), m)}{m}, \qquad \dfrac{E_c^{\hat{l}}(k_c^l(), m)}{m} \end{array} \right\}$$

These rules are valid for arbitrary labels $l, \hat{l} \in \mathsf{labels}$ and adversarial labels $l_a \in \mathsf{labelsA}$. Read from top left to bottom right, the rules capture the intuition that the adversary can use any honestly generated key to encrypt some term m, that the adversary knows the message contained in any adversarial encryption and that the adversary knows the message contained in any encryption under a corrupted key.

We now give a concrete implementation $\mathcal{I}_{\mathsf{SKE}}$ for secret key encryption. The implementation uses some IND-CCA secure authenticated secret key encryption scheme (SKE.KeyGen, SKE.Enc, SKE.Dec). As usual, here SKE.KeyGen is a generation algorithm for key pairs, SKE.Enc is an encryption algorithm and SKE.Dec is a decryption algorithm. Note that SKE.Enc is an algorithm that takes three inputs: the key, the message to be encrypted and the randomness that is used for encryption.[4]

The computable interpretations of, k_x and E_x (for $x \in \{h, c\}$) are as follows:

- $(M_{\mathsf{SKE}}\ k_x)(r)$: Let $k := \mathsf{SKE.KeyGen}(1^\eta, r)$. Return $\langle k, \tau_{\mathsf{SKE}}^{\mathsf{k}_x}\rangle$
- $(M_{\mathsf{SKE}}\ E_x)(\hat{k}, m)(r)$: Parse $\hat{k}$ as $\langle k, \tau_{\mathsf{SKE}}^{\mathsf{k}_x}\rangle$. Let $c := \mathsf{SKE.Enc}(k, m, r)$ and return $\langle c, \tau_{\mathsf{SKE}}^{\mathsf{ciphertext}}\rangle$

Intuitively, the $\mathsf{valid}_{\mathsf{SKE}}$ predicate guarantees that all keys that may be used by the adversary later are generated during initialization (i.e., with the init query). We only allow static corruption of keys, i.e., the adversary has to decide which keys are honest and which are corrupted at this stage. Keys may only be used for encryption and decryption. This implicitly prevents key cycles.

THEOREM 3. *Let $\mathcal{M}$ be a symbolic model and $\mathcal{I}$ a deduction sound implementation of $\mathcal{M}$. If ($\mathcal{M}_{\mathsf{SKE}}$,$\mathcal{I}_{\mathsf{SKE}}$) and ($\mathcal{M}$,$\mathcal{I}$) are compatible, then $\mathcal{I} \cup \mathcal{I}_{\mathsf{SKE}}$ is a deduction sound implementation of $\mathcal{M} \cup \mathcal{M}_{\mathsf{SKE}}$.*

7.3 Macs

In this section we show that any deduction sound implementation can be extended by a mac scheme. More precisely, we require a strongly EUF-CMA secure mac scheme [5].

We first define the symbolic model $(\mathcal{T}_{\mathsf{MAC}}, \leq_{\mathsf{MAC}}, \Sigma_{\mathsf{MAC}}, \mathcal{D}_{\mathsf{MAC}})$ for macs. The signature Σ_{MAC} features the function symbols

$$k : \tau_{\mathsf{MAC}}^{\mathsf{k}} \qquad\qquad mac : \tau_{\mathsf{MAC}}^{\mathsf{k}} \times \top \rightarrow \tau_{\mathsf{MAC}}^{\mathsf{mac}}$$

for $x \in \{c, h\}$. The randomized function symbol k of arity $\tau_{\mathsf{MAC}}^{\mathsf{k}}$ represents keys. The randomized function symbol mac of arity $\tau_{\mathsf{MAC}}^{\mathsf{k}} \times \top \rightarrow \tau_{\mathsf{MAC}}^{\mathsf{mac}}$ represents the mac of a message. To complete the formal definition we set the types

$$\mathcal{T}_{\mathsf{MAC}} := \{\top, \tau_{\mathsf{MAC}}^{\mathsf{k}}, \tau_{\mathsf{MAC}}^{\mathsf{mac}}\}$$

All introduced types are direct subtypes of the base type $\top$ (this defines $\leq_{\mathsf{MAC}}$). The deduction system captures the security of macs

$$\mathcal{D}_{\mathsf{MAC}} := \left\{ \dfrac{mac^{\hat{l}}(k^l(), m)}{m}, \qquad \dfrac{k^l() \quad m}{mac^{l_a}(k^l(), m)} \right\}$$

These rules are valid for arbitrary labels $l, \hat{l} \in \mathsf{labels}$ and adversarial labels $l_a \in \mathsf{labelsA}$. The rules are backed up by the requirement that macs reveal the message that was signed and the intuition that the adversary can use known keys to deduce macs under those keys.

We now give a concrete implementation $\mathcal{I}_{\mathsf{MAC}}$ for macs. The implementation uses some strongly EUF-CMA secure mac scheme (MAC.KeyGen, MAC.Mac, MAC.Vfy). As usual, here MAC.KeyGen is a generation algorithm for key pairs, MAC.Mac computes a mac and MAC.Vfy is a verification algorithm. Note that MAC.Mac is an algorithm that takes three inputs: the key, the message to be authenticated and the randomness that is used for computing the mac.

The computable interpretations of k and mac are as follows:

- $(M_{\mathsf{MAC}}\ k)(r)$: Let $k := \mathsf{MAC.Mac}(1^\eta, r)$. Return $\langle k, \tau_{\mathsf{MAC}}^{\mathsf{k}}\rangle$.

[3]Note that we distinguish encryptions under honest keys from encryptions under corrupted keys on the level of function symbols. We need this to define forgetful positions later (Section 8). E.g., a message encrypted with a corrupted key cannot be hidden.

[4]Since the message m is of basetype, we require a scheme with message space $\{0, 1\}^*$.

- $(M_{\mathsf{MAC}}\ sig)(\hat{k}, m; r)$: Parse $\hat{k}$ as $\langle k, \tau^{\mathsf{k}}_{\mathsf{MAC}}\rangle$. Let $\sigma :=$ $\mathsf{MAC.Mac}(k, m, r)$ and return $\langle \sigma, m, \tau^{\mathsf{mac}}_{\mathsf{MAC}}\rangle$.

Analogously to $\mathsf{valid}_{\mathsf{SKE}}$, the predicate $\mathsf{valid}_{\mathsf{MAC}}$ guarantees static corruption and the dedicated use of keys.

THEOREM 4. *Let $\mathcal{M}$ be a symbolic model and $\mathcal{I}$ be deduction sound implementation of $\mathcal{M}$. If $(\mathcal{M}_{\mathsf{MAC}},\mathcal{I}_{\mathsf{MAC}})$ and $(\mathcal{M},\mathcal{I})$ are compatible, then $\mathcal{I} \cup \mathcal{I}_{\mathsf{MAC}}$ is a deduction sound implementation of $\mathcal{M} \cup \mathcal{M}_{\mathsf{MAC}}$.*

7.4 Public key encryption

In this section we define a symbolic model $\mathcal{M}_{\mathsf{PKE}}$ for public key encryption and a corresponding implementation $\mathcal{I}_{\mathsf{PKE}}$ based on an IND-CCA secure public key encryption scheme. Theorem 5 then restates the result from [13] that adding public key encryption to a deduction sound implementation preserves deduction soundness.

We briefly introduce the symbolic model ($\mathcal{T}_{\mathsf{PKE}}$, $\leq_{\mathsf{PKE}}$, Σ_{PKE}, $\mathcal{D}_{\mathsf{PKE}}$) for public key encryption. The signature Σ_{PKE} features the function symbols

$$dk_x : \tau^{\mathsf{dk}_x}_{\mathsf{PKE}} \quad ek_x : \tau^{\mathsf{dk}_x}_{\mathsf{PKE}} \to \tau^{\mathsf{ek}_x}_{\mathsf{PKE}} \quad enc_x : \tau^{\mathsf{ek}_x}_{\mathsf{PKE}} \times \top \to \tau^{\mathsf{ciphertext}}_{\mathsf{PKE}}$$

for $x \in \{h, c\}$. The deduction system captures the security of public key encryption

$$\mathcal{D}_{\mathsf{PKE}} := \left\{ \begin{array}{cc} \multicolumn{2}{c}{\frac{ek^l_x() \quad m}{enc^{l_a}_x(ek^l_x(),m)},} \\ \frac{enc^{l_a}_h(ek^l_h(),m)}{m}, & \frac{enc^{\hat{l}}_c(ek^l_c(),m)}{m} \end{array} \right\}$$

These rules are valid for arbitrary labels $l, \hat{l} \in \mathsf{labels}$ and adversarial labels $l_a \in \mathsf{labelsA}$. Read from top left to bottom right, the rules capture the intuition that the adversary can use any honestly generated key to encrypt some term m, the adversary knows the message contained in any adversarial encryption and the adversary knows the message contained in any encryption under a corrupted key. The implementation $\mathcal{I}_{\mathsf{PKE}}$ is defined in a straightforward way analogously to the primitives already discussed and is based on an arbitrary IND-CCA encryption scheme [19].

THEOREM 5. *Let $\mathcal{M}$ be a symbolic model and $\mathcal{I}$ a deduction sound implementation of $\mathcal{M}$. If $(\mathcal{M}_{\mathsf{PKE}}, \mathcal{I}_{\mathsf{PKE}})$ and $(\mathcal{M},\mathcal{I})$ are compatible, then $\mathcal{I} \cup \mathcal{I}_{\mathsf{PKE}}$ is a deduction sound implementation of $\mathcal{M} \cup \mathcal{M}_{\mathsf{PKE}}$.*

7.5 Hash functions

In this section we deal with the composition of deduction sound implementations of arbitrary primitives with hash functions. We consider hash functions implemented as random oracles [7]: in this setting calls to the hash function are implemented by calls to a random function which can only be accessed in a black-box way. We model this idea directly in our framework. In the symbolic model model we consider a symbolic function that is randomized and which is implemented by a randomized function. We recover the intuition that hash functions are deterministic by restricting the calls that an adversary can make: for each term t, the adversary can only call the hash function with the honest label $l(t)$.

The symbolic model for hash functions is rather standard. It is given by the tuple $(\mathcal{T}_{\mathsf{HASH}}, \leq_{\mathsf{HASH}}, \Sigma_{\mathsf{HASH}}, \mathcal{D}_{\mathsf{HASH}})$ where

$$\mathcal{T}_{\mathsf{HASH}} := \{\top, \tau_{\mathsf{HASH}}\}$$

and $\tau_{\mathsf{HASH}} \leq_{\mathsf{HASH}} \top$. The signature Σ_{HASH} contains only a randomized function $H : \top \to \tau_{\mathsf{HASH}}$ characterized by the deduction rule:

$$\mathcal{D}_{\mathsf{HASH}} := \left\{ \frac{m}{H^l(m)} \right\}$$

where $l \in \mathsf{labelsH}$.

The implementation $\mathcal{I}_{\mathsf{HASH}}$ for hash functions is via a randomized function: when called, the function simply returns a random value, and we will require that it does so consistently; Concretely $(M_{\mathsf{HASH}}\ H)(m; r)$ returns $\langle r, \tau_{\mathsf{HASH}}\rangle$.

The open function for hash functions is described in Figure 6. If the bitstring to be opened was not the result of a generate call, then it returns garbage of types either τ_{HASH} or $\top$, depending on what c encodes. Otherwise, it will return the entry in L that corresponds to c: by the requirements posed by $\mathsf{valid}_{\mathsf{HASH}}$ below this will be $H^{l(t)}(m)$ for some bitstring m with $L[[m]] = t$.

A useful observation is that by the description above, the library L will never contain an entry of the form $(c, H^l(m))$ for some adversarial label $l \in \mathsf{labelsA}$; moreover, if $(c, H^l(m))$ is in L, then $l = l(t)$ for some t, and $L[[m]] = t$.

THE $\mathsf{valid}_{\mathsf{HASH}}$ PREDICATE. For simplicity we require that no hash is present in init requests (our results easily extend to the case where this restriction is not present). In addition we use the predicate $\mathsf{valid}_{\mathsf{HASH}}$ to enforce deterministic behavior of our hash implementation. We require that for any term t, all occurrences of $H(t)$ in generate and sgenerate requests use the same label. Concretely, we demand that for any term t, all generate requests for $H^{\hat{l}}(t)$ are labeled with the honest label $\hat{l} = l(t)$. The choice of label is not important: we could alternatively request that if $H^{l_1}(t)$ and $H^{l_2}(t)$ occur in a generate requests, then $l_1 = l_2$.

THEOREM 6. *Let $\mathcal{I}$ be a deduction sound implementation of $\mathcal{M}$. If $(\mathcal{M}_{\mathsf{HASH}}, \mathcal{I}_{\mathsf{HASH}})$ and $(\mathcal{M},\mathcal{I})$ are compatible, then $\mathcal{I} \cup \mathcal{I}_{\mathsf{HASH}}$ is a deduction sound implementation of $\mathcal{M} \cup \mathcal{M}_{\mathsf{HASH}}$ in the random oracle model.*

The intuition behind this proof is simple: collisions due to tagging occur only with probability given by the birthday bound (so with negligible probability). Given an adversary that wins the deduction soundness game for the composed libraries, we construct an adversary that breaks deduction soundness of $(\mathcal{M}, \mathcal{I}, \mathsf{valid}_{\mathcal{I}})$. This latter adversary simulates the hash function via a randomized transparent function with no arguments: a generate $H^{l(t)}(t)$ call will be implemented by a generate call to $f^{l(t)}()$. Due to $\mathsf{valid}_{\mathsf{HASH}}$ the knowledge set S does not contain any occurrence of H with a dishonest label, hence the only "useful" deduction soundness rule which allows the adversary to learn/manipulate terms with dishonest labels are not applicable (we can cut them out of any deduction).

8. FORGETFULNESS

All the theorems from Section 7 have one important drawback: key material cannot be sent around as the valid predicates forbid keys from being used in non-key positions. This takes the analysis of a large class of practical protocols (e.g, many key exchange protocols) outside the scope of our results. The problem is that deduction soundness does not guarantee that no information about non-DY terms is leaked by the computational implementation. E.g., we could think of a deterministic function symbol f that takes arguments of type nonce with only the rule $\frac{n^l()}{f(n^l())}$. An implementation of f could leak half of the bits of its input and still be sound. However, to send key material around, we need to rely on the fact that information theoretically nothing is leaked about the suitable positions for keys.

To solve this problem, we introduce *forgetful* symbolic models and implementations. A forgetful symbolic model features function symbols with positions that are marked as being forgetful. The corresponding implementation has to guarantee, that no information about the arguments at these positions will be leaked (except their length). Before we formalize these concepts we extend the framework developed earlier in the paper with several technical details.

To allow the handling of forgetful positions, extend the definition for hybrid terms with function symbols carrying an honest label in the library. Let f be a function symbol of arity $\mathrm{ar}(f) = \tau_1 \times \ldots \times \tau_n \to \tau$. Then a hybrid term of f may be $f^l(a_1, \ldots, a_n)$ where each a_i is either a bitstring from $[\![\tau_i]\!]$ or a term of type τ_i for forgetful positions i. For normal positions a_i must be a bitstring from $[\![\tau_i]\!]$ as usual. The definitions for the completeness of a library L and $L[[c]]$ are changed accordingly.

FORGETFUL SYMBOLIC MODELS AND IMPLEMENTATIONS. We say that a symbolic model $\mathcal{M}$ is a *forgetful symbolic model* if arguments of a function symbol may be marked as *forgetful*. In order to formalize forgetful implementations, the computational counterpart of forgetful positions, we introduce the notion of an oblivious implementation.

DEFINITION 3 (OBLIVIOUS IMPLEMENTATION). *Let $\mathcal{M}$ be a forgetful symbolic model. $\overline{\mathcal{I}} = (\overline{M}, \overline{[\![\cdot]\!]}, len, \mathsf{open}, \mathsf{valid})$ is an* oblivious implementation of $\mathcal{M}$ *if $\overline{\mathcal{I}}$ is an implementation of $\mathcal{M}$ with a slightly changed signature: For each function symbol $f \in \Sigma$ with arity $\mathrm{ar}(f) = \tau_1 \times \ldots \times \tau_n \to \tau$ the signature of $(\overline{M}\ f)$ is $\theta(\tau_1) \times \cdots \times \theta(\tau_n) \times \{0,1\}^\eta \to [\![\tau]\!]$ where $\theta(\tau_i) = \mathbb{N}$ if the ith argument of f is forgetful and $[\![\tau_i]\!]$ otherwise.*

Intuitively, oblivious implementations for all forgetful positions, take as input natural numbers; these will be the length of the actual inputs on the forgetful positions.

As indicated above, a forgetful implementation is one which is indistinguishable from an oblivious implementation. To formally define the notion we introduce a distinguishing game $\mathsf{FIN}^b_{\mathcal{M}(\nu),\mathcal{I}(\nu),\overline{\mathcal{I}}(\nu),\mathcal{A}}(\eta)$ where an adversary $\mathcal{A}$ tries to distinguish between the case when he interacts with the real implementation, or with an alternative implementation that is oblivious with respect to all of the forgetful arguments. We say that an implementation is forgetful, if there exists an oblivious implementation such that no adversary succeeds in this task. Due to lack of space the formal definition of FIN is in the Appendix.

DEFINITION 4 (FORGETFUL IMPLEMENTATION). *We say that an implementation $\mathcal{I} = (M, [\![\cdot]\!], len, \mathsf{open}, \mathsf{valid})$ is a* forgetful implementation of a forgetful symbolic model $\mathcal{M}$ *if there is an oblivious implementation $\overline{\mathcal{I}} = (\overline{M}, \overline{[\![\cdot]\!]}, len,$ open, valid) such that for all for all parametrized transparent symbolic models $\mathcal{M}_{\mathsf{tran}}(\nu)$ and for all parametrized transparent implementations $\mathcal{I}_{\mathsf{tran}}(\nu)$ of $\mathcal{M}_{\mathsf{tran}}(\nu)$ such that $(\mathcal{M}(\nu), \mathcal{I}_{\mathsf{tran}}(\nu))$ compatible with $(\mathcal{M},\mathcal{I})$ we have that*

$$Prob[\mathsf{FIN}^0_{\mathcal{M}\cup\mathcal{M}_{\mathsf{tran}}(\nu),\mathcal{I}\cup\mathcal{I}_{\mathsf{tran}}(\nu),\overline{\mathcal{I}}\cup\mathcal{I}_{\mathsf{tran}}(\nu),\mathcal{A}}(\eta) = 1]$$
$$-Prob[\mathsf{FIN}^1_{\mathcal{M}\cup\mathcal{M}_{\mathsf{tran}}(\nu),\mathcal{I}\cup\mathcal{I}_{\mathsf{tran}}(\nu),\overline{\mathcal{I}}\cup\mathcal{I}_{\mathsf{tran}}(\nu),\mathcal{A}}(\eta) = 1]$$

is negligible for every p.p.t. adversary $\mathcal{A}$.

The intuition that encryption schemes are forgetful with respect to their plaintexts is captured by the lemma below. Consider the forgetful symbolic model $\overline{\mathcal{M}_{\mathsf{PKE}}}$ as the symbolic symbolic model $\mathcal{M}_{\mathsf{PKE}}$ from Section 7.4 where we mark the message m for honest encryptions $enc_h(ek, m)$ as forgetful.

LEMMA 1. *$\mathcal{I}_{\mathsf{PKE}}$ from Section 7.4 is a forgetful implementation of $\overline{\mathcal{M}_{\mathsf{PKE}}}$.*

SENDING KEYS AROUND. To be able to consider the case when symmetric keys are sent encrypted we introduce an extension of the model for symmetric key encryption of Section 7.2. The extension is that the validity predicate (which controls the valid queries by the adversary) can now depend on a signature Σ that contains functions with forgetful positions. The new validity predicate allows for standard generation of keys for symmetric encryption (with the same restrictions as those in Section 7.2), but in addition it also allows for generate requests that contain occurrences of symmetric keys under functions from signature Σ, as long as the occurrences are on forgetful positions. For concreteness, let $\mathsf{valid}_{\mathsf{SKE}[\Sigma]}$ be the predicate obtained from valid as described above.

The composition theorem that we prove in this case is that any deduction sound implementation of Σ that is forgetful can be extended with symmetric key encryption. We emphasize that the added value over the results of Section 7.2 is that the validity predicate is more relaxed, and allows for keys to occur in non-key positions. We therefore prove the following theorem.

THEOREM 7. *Let $\mathcal{M}$ be a forgetful symbolic model and $\mathcal{I}$ be a forgetful deduction sound implementation of $\mathcal{M}$. Let Σ be the signature of $\mathcal{M}$, and let $\mathsf{valid}_{\mathsf{SKE}[\Sigma]}$ be the validity predicate for $\mathcal{I}_{\mathsf{SKE}}$. If $(\mathcal{M}_{\mathsf{SKE}}, \mathcal{I}_{\mathsf{SKE}})$ and $(\mathcal{M}, \mathcal{I})$ are compatible and the valid predicate of $\mathcal{I}$ does not depend on function symbols from Σ_{SKE}, then $\mathcal{I} \cup \mathcal{I}_{\mathsf{SKE}}$ is a deduction sound implementation of $\mathcal{M} \cup \mathcal{M}_{\mathsf{SKE}}$.*

As an application of the above theorem we have the following. Since the implementation for public key encryption $\mathcal{I}_{\mathsf{PKE}}$ from Section 7.4 is a forgetful deduction sound implementation for the forgetful symbolic model $\overline{\mathcal{M}_{\mathsf{PKE}}}$ (by Lemma 1), $(\overline{\mathcal{M}_{\mathsf{PKE}}}, \mathcal{I}_{\mathsf{PKE}})$ can be composed with $(\mathcal{M}_{\mathsf{SKE}}, \mathcal{I}_{\mathsf{SKE}})$. The validity predicate for the resulting composition allows for adversary queries of the form "$\mathsf{generate}$ $enc^{\hat{l}}_h(ek^l_h(), k^{\hat{l}}_h())$". Intuitively, this corresponds to sending around symmetric keys encrypted under asymmetric keys in a protocol.

Next, we show that the composition of a forgetful deduction sound implementation with a secret-key encryption preserves forgetfulness (Theorem 8). Let $\overline{\mathcal{M}_{\mathsf{SKE}}}$ be the forgetful symbolic model based on $\mathcal{M}_{\mathsf{SKE}}$ when we mark the message m for honestly generated encryptions under honest keys $E^{\hat{l}}_h(k^l_h(), m)$ as a forgetful position and let $\mathcal{I}_{\mathsf{SKE}}[\Sigma]$ be an implementation of $\overline{\mathcal{M}_{\mathsf{SKE}}}$. Then the following holds:

THEOREM 8. *Let $\mathcal{M}$ be a forgetful symbolic model and $\mathcal{I}$ be a forgetful deduction sound implementation of $\mathcal{M}$. Let*

Σ be the signature of $\mathcal{M}$ and $\mathsf{valid}_{\mathsf{SKE}[\Sigma]}$ be the predicate for $(\mathcal{M}_{\mathsf{SKE}}, \mathcal{I}_{\mathsf{SKE}})$. If $(\overline{\mathcal{M}_{\mathsf{SKE}}}, \mathcal{I}_{\mathsf{SKE}})$ and $(\mathcal{M}, \mathcal{I})$ are compatible then $\mathcal{I} \cup \mathcal{I}_{\mathsf{SKE}}$ is a forgetful implementation of $\mathcal{M} \cup \overline{\mathcal{M}_{\mathsf{SKE}}}$

Since Theorems 7 and 8 hold for the particular case when $(\mathcal{M}, \mathcal{I}) = (\overline{\mathcal{M}_{\mathsf{SKE}}}, \mathcal{I}_{\mathsf{SKE}})$, by successive applications we obtain a framework in which we include, incrementally, multiple encryption schemes. In the resulting framework symmetric keys can be encrypted under other symmetric keys in a hierarchical fashion. The hierarchy is imposed by the order in which schemes are added (the keys of the latter can be encrypted under the keys of the former, but not the other way around).

A related important observation is that it seems difficult to consider more flexible predicates that allow for the occurrence of keys on arbitrary forgetful positions.

The reason is that if we do not make the predicate for the symmetric encryption scheme depend on the signature of the model to which we add symmetric encryption, it would be impossible to detect the occurrence of encryption cycles. For instance, assume that Σ contains a function symbol f with a forgetful second position. Do the terms $f^{\bar{l}}(t', k_h^l())$ and $E_h^{\bar{l}}(k_h^l(), t')$ contain a key cycle? We cannot tell without knowing the implementation of f and t'.

9. ACKNOWLEDGEMENTS

The research leading to these results has received funding from the European Research Council under the European Union's Seventh Framework Programme (FP7/2007-2013) / ERC grant agreement number 258865 (ERC ProSecure project). This work was additionally supported in part by ERC Advanced Grant ERC-2010-AdG-267188-CRIPTO. Florian Böhl was supported by MWK grant "MoSeS".

10. REFERENCES

[1] M. Abadi and P. Rogaway. Reconciling two views of cryptography (the computational soundness of formal encryption). In *Proc. 1st IFIP International Conference on Theoretical Computer Science (IFIP–TCS'00)*, volume 1872 of *LNCS*, pages 3–22, 2000.

[2] M. Backes and B. Pfitzmann. Symmetric encryption in a simulatable Dolev-Yao style cryptographic library. In *Proc. 17th IEEE Computer Science Foundations Workshop (CSFW'04)*, pages 204–218, 2004.

[3] M. Backes, B. Pfitzmann, and M. Waidner. A composable cryptographic library with nested operations (extended abstract). In *Proc. of 10th ACM Conference on Computer and Communications Security (CCS'05)*, pages 220 – 230, 2003.

[4] M. Backes, B. Pfitzmann, and M. Waidner. Symmetric authentication within simulatable cryptographic library. In *Proc. 8th European Symposium on Research in Computer Security (ESORICS'03)*, Lecture Notes in Computer Science, pages 271–290, 2003.

[5] M. Bellare, O. Goldreich, and A. Mityagin. The power of verification queries in message authentication and authenticated encryption. *IACR Cryptology ePrint Archive*, 2004:309, 2004.

[6] M. Bellare and C. Namprempre. Authenticated encryption: Relations among notions and analysis of the generic composition paradigm. *J. Cryptology*, 21(4):469–491, 2008.

[7] M. Bellare and P. Rogaway. Random oracles are practical: A paradigm for designing efficient protocols. In D. E. Denning, R. Pyle, R. Ganesan, R. S. Sandhu, and V. Ashby, editors, *ACM Conference on Computer and Communications Security*, pages 62–73. ACM, 1993.

[8] F. Böhl, V. Cortier, and B. Warinschi. Deduction soundness: Prove one, get five for free. Cryptology ePrint Archive, Report 2013/457, 2013. Full version of this paper. `http://eprint.iacr.org/`.

[9] H. Comon-Lundh and V. Cortier. Computational soundness of observational equivalence. In *Proceedings of the 15th ACM Conference on Computer and Communications Security (CCS'08)*, Alexandria, Virginia, USA, Oct. 2008. ACM Press.

[10] V. Cortier, S. Kremer, R. Küsters, and B. Warinschi. Computationally sound symbolic secrecy in the presence of hash functions. In *Proceedings of the 26th Conference on Fundations of Software Technology and Theoretical Computer Science (FSTTCS'06)*, volume 4337 of *LNCS*, pages 176–187, Kolkata, India, 2006. Springer.

[11] V. Cortier, S. Kremer, and B. Warinschi. A survey of symbolic methods in computational analysis of cryptographic systems. *J. Autom. Reasoning*, 46(3-4):225–259, 2011.

[12] V. Cortier and B. Warinschi. Computationally sound, automated proofs for security protocols. In *European Symposium on Programming (ESOP'05)*, volume 3444 of *LNCS*, pages 157–171, Edinburgh, UK, 2005. Springer.

[13] V. Cortier and B. Warinschi. A composable computational soundness notion. In *18th ACM Conference on Computer and Communications Security (CCS'11)*, pages 63–74, Chicago, USA, October 2011. ACM.

[14] A. Datta, A. Derek, J. C. Mitchell, V. Shmatikov, and M. Turuani. Probabilistic Polynomial-time Semantics for a Protocol Security Logic. In *Proc. of 32nd International Colloquium on Automata, Languages and Programming, ICALP*, volume 3580 of *LNCS*, pages 16–29. Springer, 2005. Lisboa, Portugal.

[15] Y. Dodis, S. Goldwasser, Y. T. Kalai, C. Peikert, and V. Vaikuntanathan. Public-key encryption schemes with auxiliary inputs. In D. Micciancio, editor, *TCC*, volume 5978 of *Lecture Notes in Computer Science*, pages 361–381. Springer, 2010.

[16] F. D. Garcia and P. van Rossum. Sound and complete computational interpretation of symbolic hashes in the standard model. *Theoretical Computer Science*, 394:112–133, 2008.

[17] R. Janvier, Y. Lakhnech, and L. Mazaré. Completing the picture: Soundness of formal encryption in the presence of active adversaries. In *European Symposium on Programming (ESOP'05)*, volume 3444 of *LNCS*, pages 172–185. Springer, 2005.

[18] M. Naor and G. Segev. Public-key cryptosystems resilient to key leakage. *SIAM J. Comput.*, 41(4):772–814, 2012.

[19] C. Rackoff and D. R. Simon. Non-interactive zero-knowledge proof of knowledge and chosen ciphertext attack. In J. Feigenbaum, editor, *CRYPTO*, volume 576 of *Lecture Notes in Computer Science*, pages 433–444. Springer, 1991.

APPENDIX

$\mathsf{open}_{\mathsf{HASH}}(c, L)$
  if $c \in [\![\mathcal{T}_{\mathsf{HASH}}]\!] \cap \mathrm{dom}(L)$ then
    return $(c, L(c))$
  else if $c = \langle h, \tau_{\mathsf{HASH}}\rangle$ then
    return $(c, g^{l(c)}_{\tau_{\mathsf{HASH}}})$
  else
    return $(c, g^{l(c)}_{\top})$

Figure 6: Open function for hash functions.

$\mathsf{open}_{\mathsf{SKE}}(c, L)$
  if $c \in [\![\mathcal{T}_{\mathsf{SKE}}]\!] \cap \mathrm{dom}(L)$ then
    return $(c, L(c))$
  else if $c = \langle k, \tau^{\mathsf{k}_x}_{\mathsf{SKE}}\rangle$ then
    return $(c, g^{l(c)}_{\tau^{\mathsf{k}_x}_{\mathsf{SKE}}})$
  else if $c = \langle c', \tau^{\mathsf{ciphertext}}_{\mathsf{SKE}}\rangle$ then
    for each $(\hat{k}, k^h_x()) \in L$ do
      parse $\hat{k}$ as $\langle k, \tau^{\mathsf{k}_x}_{\mathsf{SKE}}\rangle$
      let $m := \mathsf{SKE.Dec}(k, c')$
      if $m \neq \bot$ then
        return $(c, E^{l(c)}_x(\hat{k}, m))$
    return $(c, g^{l(c)}_{\tau^{\mathsf{ciphertext}}_{\mathsf{SKE}}})$
  else
    return $(c, g^{l(c)}_{\top})$

Figure 7: Open function for secret key encryption.

$\mathsf{generate}^{\mathsf{FIN}}_{M,\mathcal{R}}(t, L)$:
  if for some $c \in \mathrm{dom}(L)$ we have $L[[c]] = t$ then
    return c
  else
    for $i \in \{1, n\}$ do
      if i is a forgetful argument then
        let $c_i := len(t_i)$
        let $a_i := t_i$
      else
        let $(c_i, L) := \mathsf{generate}_{M,\mathcal{R}}(t_i, L)$
        let $a_i := c_i$
    let $r := \mathcal{R}(t)$
    let $c := (M\ f)(c_1, \ldots, c_n; r)$
    let $L(c) := f^l(a_1, \ldots, a_n))$ $(l \in \mathsf{labelsH})$
    return (c, L)

Figure 8: The generate function for an oblivious implementation (t is of the form $f^l(t_1, \ldots, t_n)$ (with possibly $n = 0$ and no label l for deterministic function symbols f)). The requirements for the input t are those of the normal generate function.

$\mathsf{FIN}^b_{\mathcal{M}(\nu),\mathcal{I}(\nu),\overline{\mathcal{I}}(\nu),\mathcal{A}}(\eta)$:
  let $S := \emptyset$ (set of requested terms)
  let $L := \emptyset$ (library)
  let $\mathbb{T} := \emptyset$ (trace of queries)
  $\mathcal{R} \leftarrow \{0,1\}^*$ (random tape)

  if $b = 0$ then
    let generate := $\mathsf{generate}^{\mathsf{FIN}}_{\overline{M},\mathcal{R}}$
  else
    let generate := $\mathsf{generate}_{M,\mathcal{R}}$

  Receive parameter ν from $\mathcal{A}$

  on request "init T, H" do
    add "init T" to $\mathbb{T}$
    if valid($\mathbb{T}$) then
      let $S := S \cup T$
      let $C := \emptyset$ (list of replies)
      for each $t \in T$ do
        let $(c, L) :=$ generate(t, L)
        let $C := C \cup \{c\}$
      for each $t \in H$ do
        let $(c, L) :=$ generate(t, L)
      send C to $\mathcal{A}$
    else
      return 0 ($\mathcal{A}$ is invalid)

  on request "sgenerate t" do
    if valid($\mathbb{T}$+"sgenerate t") then
      let $(c, L) :=$ generate(t, L)

  on request "generate t" do
    add "generate t" to $\mathbb{T}$
    if valid($\mathbb{T}$) then
      let $S := S \cup \{t\}$
      let $(c, L) :=$ generate(t, L)
      send c to $\mathcal{A}$
    else
      return 0 ($\mathcal{A}$ is invalid)

  on request "parse c" do
    let $(t, L) :=$ parse(c, L)
    if $S \vdash_{\mathcal{D}} t$ then
      send t to $\mathcal{A}$
    else
      return 1 ($\mathcal{A}$ produced non-Dolev-Yao term)

  on request "guess b'" do
    if $b = b'$ then
      return 1 ($\mathcal{A}$ wins)
    else
      return 0 ($\mathcal{A}$ looses)

Figure 9: Indistinguishability game for forgetful implementations.

Efficient Targeted Key Subset Retrieval in Fractal Hash Sequences

Kelsey Cairns*
Washington State University
Pullman, WA, USA
kcairns@wsu.edu

Thoshitha Gamage
Washington State University
Pullman, WA, USA
tgamage@eecs.wsu.edu

Carl Hauser
Washington State University
Pullman, WA, USA
hauser@eecs.wsu.edu

ABSTRACT

This paper presents a new hash chain traversal strategy which improves performance of hash chain based one-time authentication schemes. This work is motivated by the need for efficient message authentication in low-latency multicast systems. Proposed solutions such as TV-OTS rely on hash chain generated values for keys, achieving reliable security by using only a small subset of generated values from each chain. However, protocols using hash chains are limited by the rate at which a hash chain traversal is able to supply keys. The new algorithm uses the same structure as Fractal Hash Traversal, but eliminates redundant operations incurred when used with applications such as TV-OTS. Performance is measured in terms of savings and is proportional to the chain-distance between consecutively retrieved values. For a distance of δ, we achieve $\Theta(\delta \log_2(\delta))$ savings, which is shown analytically and supported by empirical tests.

Categories and Subject Descriptors

F.2.2 [**Analysis of Algorithms and Problem Complexity**]: Nonnumerical Algorithms and Problems—computations on discrete structures

*This research was funded in part by Department of Energy Award Number DE-OE0000097 (TCIPG).

CCS'13, November 4–8, 2013, Berlin, Germany.

http://dx.doi.org/10.1145/2508859.2516739 .

Keywords

Key Management; Hash Chain; Traversal; Key Retrieval; Data Authentication; Time Validation; One-Time Signature

1. INTRODUCTION

A class of emerging applications — including those designed to control critical infrastructure systems — requires reliable message authentication in multicast environments. For instance, applications related to the power grid rely on several types of authenticated messages, some of which initiate control actions. These control actions are responsible for regulating physical characteristics that influence the power flows in the grid. A falsified signal is potentially very dangerous as it could be part of an attack intended to damage costly equipment or cause failure within the grid.

A general solution to the multicast authentication problem, one suitable for practically any multicast application, has yet to be found. Existing protocols tend to support specific classes of applications, with characteristics that may not be tolerable to others [3]. For low latency applications such as power grid control, the questions about appropriate multicast authentication protocols remain unsettled.

The long standing solution for multicast authentication, RSA [19], has been shown unsuitable for low latency applications [6]. RSA relies on modular exponentiation, an expensive operation which must be performed on a per-message basis. Status messages in the power grid can be generated as frequently as every 16 milliseconds, a rate that may quicken in the future [1]. If signed using RSA, the signing rate may actually lag behind the intended sending rate depending on the capability of the signing devices. This disparity eliminates RSA as a possible protocol for use in many high-rate systems, leaving a niche to be filled.

One technique facilitating lower latency authentication is one-time signatures. The most basic one-time signatures are used as credentials which allow senders to authenticate their identity to receivers. These schemes demonstrate the general principle used in even sophisticated one-time signature schemes: a public key is pre-shared between sender and receivers, and the sender authenticates itself by publishing a secret which receivers associate with the public key [5, 12]. Usually, the receiver forms this association with a one-way function of some kind, where the received secret acts as input that reproduces the public key. If deployed properly, only the correct sender could know and publish the correct secret.

This principle can be extended to verify not only the sender, but also the message contents by having the sender calculate the signature in such a way that receivers must operate on both the received secret and message contents to recreate the public key. This way, any modification to the message would cause the signature validation to fail. True to their name, basic one-time signature schemes can only authenticate one message for each public key. However, more modern schemes expand on the one-time principle, allowing multiple messages to be signed per public key [14, 15, 16, 17, 18]. The present challenge is to create a low-latency protocol which increases this number until key distribution is infrequent enough to make the overhead of repeated distribution tolerable.

The Time-Valid One-Time-Signature (TV-OTS) family of protocols builds extended-lifetime protocols from one-time signature schemes with limited lifetimes [21]. TV-OTS applies a novel key refreshing technique which extends the overall lifetime of a wide range of one-time signature protocols. Over the running lifetime of the chosen protocol, private keys are periodically refreshed in such a way that no new public keys need to be distributed. If the key refresh operations can be performed in a short, constant-bounded time, TV-OTS with Hash of Random Subsets (HORS) [18] reliably outperforms RSA in terms of signing and verification latency [7]. Beyond having the ability to generate and verify signatures more quickly than RSA, TV-OTS incurs no additional message delays and imposes no constraints on the underlying network beyond loose time synchronization. These properties indicate TV-OTS may be a promising protocol for use in low-latency systems.

Unfortunately, the only known time-efficient way to manage keys for TV-OTS is to store all possible keys in memory. However, storing all the keys necessary for TV-OTS would be impractical for many devices. Spatially efficient schemes, such as Fractal Hash Sequence Representation and Traversal (FHT) which is suggested for use with TV-OTS, do not allow the constantly bounded retrieval time necessary to ensure low latency signing. The standard implementation of TV-OTS uses HORS [18] as its chosen one-time signature. This combination is made secure by retrieving keys at certain probabilities, but unfortunately, this scenario becomes increasingly time-inefficient as the security of TV-OTS is increased.

The work presented in this paper aims to fill the gap with a key management scheme that is efficient for all parameters of TV-OTS. The purpose of this paper is to:

1. *Present a new key management scheme* — The new key management scheme eliminates certain useless operations that are performed by other schemes when non-consecutive values are retrieved. The new scheme uses the same structure as FHT, but the algorithm used to output individual keys is new. The FHT algorithm can only retrieve values consecutively. If non-consecutive values are retrieved with FHT, the intermediate values must be retrieved and discarded. This process performs extra hash operations that do not contribute to finding the desired value. The Targeting Traversal method introduces *targeted retrievals*, which retrieve non-consecutive values without performing unnecessary work. Targeted transitions optimize retrieval time for TV-OTS. Other schemes may benefit as well, for example TSV signing [14], which uses hash chains similarly to TV-OTS.

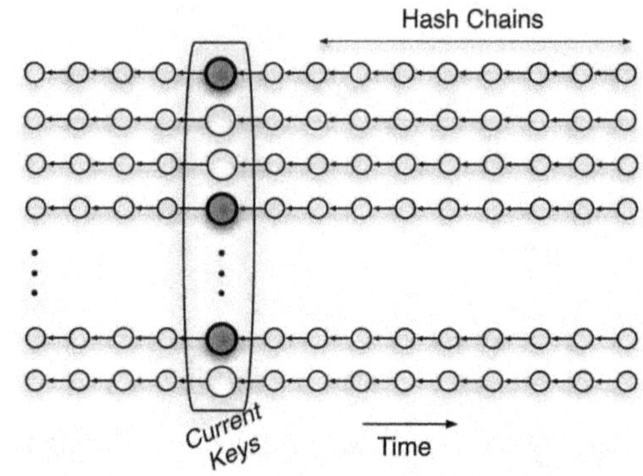

Figure 1: TV-OTS's multiple hash chains are shown horizontally. A vertical slice corresponding to the current time defines the current key pool. Darkened circles represent the small subset of keys used in the creation of a single signature.

2. *Verify correctness* — The correctness of targeted transitions is verified in relation to FHT. A formal proof is given that each targeted retrieval yields a state equivalent to multiple iterative retrievals performed by FHT. Inductively, FHT and targeting are shown to yield the same sequence of values for the same set of retrieval requests on the same chain.

3. *Demonstrate performance improvements* — Theoretical analysis reveals a $\Theta(\delta \log_2(\delta))$ bound on computational savings. Here, δ is the expected distance between successively retrieved values in the chain, and is independent of the length of the chain. Experimental results support this hypothesis, showing improved performance for TV-OTS. Furthermore, the savings improve in conjunction with the parameters that make TV-OTS more secure.

The remainder of this paper is organized as follows: Section 2 offers extended background, introducing the problems associated with TV-OTS and key management in detail. Section 3 describes the new algorithms that lead to more efficient key management when used with TV-OTS. A proof of correctness of the proposed algorithms is presented in 4 followed by experimental results in Section 5. Sections 6 and 7 offer future work and conclusions.

2. RELATED WORK

Two mechanisms are employed by TV-OTS which specifically contribute to the low latency generation of reliable signatures. First, the keys are generated by hash chains, a mechanism first proposed by Lamport for secure password authentication [13]. When used for message authentication, hash chains allow private keys to be refreshed without the need to distribute new public keys. Secondly, signatures are generated by HORS, using the keys retrieved from the hash chains. This sections covers both signature generation and hash chain management in detail.

2.1 Time-Valid One-Time-Signature

TV-OTS is able to run beyond the lifetime of its chosen one-time signature scheme by periodically refreshing the private keys used to generate signatures. New private keys are supplied by hash chains which allows each used private key to be used as a public key at a later time. This eliminates the need to redistribute public keys with each private key update. Individual messages are signed and verified with the HORS protocol [18]. At signature generation, HORS chooses a very small subset from an available pool of hash chain generated keys, where each key is associated with an individual hash chain[1]. After t key refreshes, the currently available key pool contains the tth value from each chain in a set of hash chains, illustrated in Figure 1. To choose the keys for each signature, the message contents are hashed and split into multiple short bit strings by a publicly agreed upon function. These bit strings are then reinterpreted as integers within a given range. The allowable range of integers corresponds to the number of available keys in each pool and consequently the number of chains. These integers are used as indices to select keys which are appended to the message as part of the signature. The TV-OTS signature must also contain a time stamp, which allows receivers to determine message freshness and which key pool was used for message signing.

Verification of TV-OTS signatures is the simple process of verifying message freshness and the individual keys contained in the signature. Receivers first use the time stamp of the received signature to determine that the message was signed recently enough to be valid. After this, the receiver follows the same steps as the sender to determine the index for each key. Once these are computed, each received key is checked to see if it belongs to the chain with the corresponding index. This requires hashing the received key and ensuring that a known value from the correct chain can be recovered by the correct number of hashes. Incoming messages are considered valid only if this test passes for every index computed by the receiver.

Signatures maintain their reliability by using, and thus publicly exposing, only a relatively small portion of each key pool. This minimizes the chance of an adversary intercepting enough keys to forge the signature of a meaningful message. While the threat grows with each sent message, the key refresh interval is set to maintain a negligible probability of successful forgery [21]. One side effect is that the number of refresh intervals that pass between two signatures requiring keys from the same chain is unpredictable. The keys in between are not retrieved from the hash chains and moreover, this distance between retrieved keys is unknown ahead of time. Unfortunately, known hash chain management schemes assume that every key will be retrieved. When this is not the case, such schemes become inefficient and waste some calculation during each retrieval.

2.2 Hash Chains for One-Time Signatures

The hash chains structure works very well with the principles behind one-time signatures, but hash chains can be difficult to manage in practice. The values contained in a hash chain form an ordered list. Each value is calculated by hashing the next value in the list with a chosen one-way hash function. The entire chain can be derived from a distinct seed value by repeatedly applying the chosen hash function. Counter-intuitively, the last value generated is referred to as the first value of the chain. The seed of a chain with n values would be the nth value. This terminology reflects the use of values in reverse order of their generation.

Hash chains are especially applicable to message authentication due to their one-way properties. Asymmetric protocols that use hash chain generated keys reveal the first chain value (the last to be generated) as part of the pre-shared public key. As new keys are used and sent through the protocol, they must be verified by the receivers. Receivers verify new keys by creating a match with a known value, either the one distributed in the public key or one more recently received. Newly received keys, when hashed (possibly multiple times), should generate one of these known values. Invalid keys can not achieve this match. Only the sender knows the seed value necessary to calculate new valid keys. Assuming the unused values are kept secret, the identity of the sender is verified with each new value revealed.

The term *traversal* refers to the sequential output of hash chain values starting with the first value and working toward the last. Traversals present a challenge because the output order is opposite the order of generation. For long chains, storing all values may be impractical, but otherwise, needed values must be recomputed. If only the seed is available as a starting point, calculating values near the beginning of the chain requires heavily repetitious hashing. Wiser strategies look for ways to balance the cost of storage and computation so that neither becomes too costly.

2.3 Fractal Hash Sequencing and Traversal

In the search for a traversal strategy balancing storage and computation costs, FHT [10] has emerged as a practical and elegant solution to achieving $O(\log_2(n))$ bounds on both measures. While FHT can't maintain these same bounds unless values are retrieved consecutively, the bounds for retrieving a sequence of values are still sufficiently low to make it a traversal candidate for TV-OTS. The FHT structure serves as a foundation for the algorithms presented in Section 3. The explanation given here places special emphasis on the details from which the new algorithms are built.

FHT stores only $\log_2(n)$ chain values chosen in such a way that retrieving new values requires little computation. The arrangement of these stored values is dynamic and continually changes to accommodate future requests more easily. When one of the stored values is retrieved, it is no longer useful and is abandoned in favor of storing a later value from the chain. The stored values are kept grouped closely towards the next values that will be retrieved, limiting the amount of work performed by any single retrieval operation.

To facilitate the dynamic arrangement of stored values, a small data structure called a *pebble* is used to associate additional information with each stored value. Each pebble stores one chain value at a time, along with the value's position in the chain. Pebbles are distinguished by a unique identifier, ID, which also governs the process followed to update the values in individual pebbles. Sometimes one pebble will be referred to as *larger* than another, meaning the value of its ID is greater than the ID of the *smaller* pebble. In a chain of n values, the $\log_2(n)$ pebbles are stored in a list sorted by chain position.

Note that two lists are now present: the conceptual list of values comprising the chain and the stored list of pebbles. This creates possible confusion over the meaning of the term *position* of a value or pebble. For consistency, different terms will used in reference to these two structures. The word

[1]Note that TV-OTS actually relies on salted hash chains [21]. However, the ideas discussed here apply equally to salted and unsalted hash chains.

position is used exclusively in reference to the entire hash chain. The words *above*, *below*, *higher* and *lower* are often used to describe relative *positions*, with the words *higher* and *above* pertaining to pebbles closer to the seed of the chain. Naturally, relative positions in the chain are preserved in the pebble list, since the pebble list is kept sorted by position.

Updating the values stored in the pebbles is analogous to moving pebbles within the chain. Conceptually, when a pebble acquires a new value, it moves to the position in the chain associated with the new value. In fact, FHT works by moving pebbles through an interconnected sequence of strategic arrangements.

The positions of pebbles in each possible arrangement allow easy computation of the next output values and future arrangements. At initialization, the position of each pebble matches its ID value. More formally, there is a pebble at every position 2^i where $1 \leq i \leq \log_2(n)$. The gaps between the pebbles form intervals, with smaller intervals near the beginning of the chain. When a pebble moves, it always divides an interval evenly into two new equally sized intervals. Like pebble IDs, interval sizes are powers of two which facilitates easy splitting. The sorted order of the intervals is preserved since when a pebble moves, the new intervals created are at least as large as intervals at lower positions. This pattern of intervals is used to ensure that both retrieved values and future arrangements can be calculated efficiently.

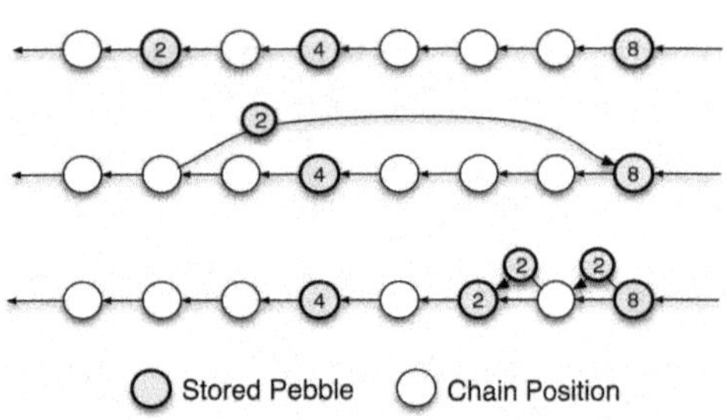

Figure 2: When a pebble moves, it cannot move directly to its destination. It must calculate the desired value by first moving upward past its destination. Once it copies the value from a stored pebble, the desired value is calculated by additional hash operations as the pebble moves downwards to its destination.

The method for calculating chain values limits the ways in which pebbles can move. When a pebble moves to a new position, it can not acquire the new value directly. Recall that pebble values must be computed from one another. The one-way properties restrict each value to being computed from values at *higher* positions. Moving a pebble requires finding and copying the value stored in some higher pebble and calculating the desired value from there. In essence, pebbles move in two phases, as illustrated in Figure 2. In the first phase, the pebble moves upwards to the same location as a higher pebble. In the second phase, the pebble's new value is hashed repeatedly, effectively moving the pebble downward in the chain to its destination.

The pattern maintained by the arrangements of pebbles is governed by the pebble IDs and provides the ability to retrieve keys within a logarithmic time bound. This arrangement pattern is formed by the second stage of pebble movement. In this second stage, pebbles step downward from their new position acquired in the first stage. The number of downward steps a pebble takes equals the value of its ID. Eventually, this creates an interval between each newly moved pebble and the pebble it copied from with the new interval size equal to the moved pebble's ID. The pebble at the upper edge of the interval, whose value was copied, was chosen because the interval it bounded before the move was twice the size of the ID of the moving pebble. (The existence of such an interval is guaranteed [10].) Thus, on each move, a pebble splits an interval into two new equally sized intervals. Furthermore, pebbles always move into the nearest interval large enough to evenly divide. Naturally, the pebbles with smaller IDs move shorter distances. Since the size of newly created intervals is at least as large as the intervals at lower positions, the intervals remain sorted by size. The pebble with the ID value of 2 never moves beyond the lowest four values in the unused chain, and ensures these lowest values are part of intervals of size two. Consequently, any value retrieved from this section of the chain will never require more than a single hash operation to compute. The remaining hash operations are performed in stepping the other pebbles towards their destinations.

To provide the amortized upper bound on retrieval time, moving pebbles rarely perform their downward movement phase all at once. Instead, moving pebbles distribute these downward steps over several retrieval operations, taking only enough steps to ensure they reach their destination by the time the value at that destination is needed. Notice that pebbles with larger IDs move further and are therefore not needed at their new positions as quickly as smaller pebbles. The number of retrievals that occur before a pebble must reach its destination is directly related to how far the pebble must travel. In fact, only the pebble with ID value 2 must reach its destination by the time the next pebble is moved. This happens exactly two retrievals after this pebble was moved. For all other pebbles, these intermediate retrievals are used to distribute hashing costs over time, avoiding a situation where some retrievals are inexpensive and others are costly. The total number of hash operations per retrieval is limited to two per actively moving pebble, plus at most one to calculate the retrieved value. The maximum hash operations per retrieval is thus $2 \times \log_2(n) + 1$.

2.4 Related Traversals

The idea of efficient hash chain traversal introduced by Itkis and Reyzin [9] started a wave of traversals with varying efficiencies and trade-offs.

The traversal suggested by Itkis and Reyzin was soon followed by Jakobsson's FHT [10], described above, from which all the others drew either direct or indirect inspiration. However, the dependency on consecutive value retrieval is common in all of such traversals. Traversals presented by Coppersmith and Jakobsson [4], and Yum et al. [22] build directly on FHT by modifying the pebble movement pattern. Coppersmith and Jakobsson achieve near maximum theoretical efficiency for consecutive retrievals by allocating a hash budget on each round, and using a sophisticated movement pattern that distributes this budget between two sets of pebbles. A set of greedy pebbles consumes as much of the hash budget as possible, and any extra is alloted to the remaining pebbles. In this way, the variance in hash operations between iterations is eliminated, lowering the worst-case number to $\frac{1}{2}\log_2(n)$ hashes per round, though at a storage cost of slightly greater than $\log_2(n)$ pebbles. This technique is further improved upon by Yum et al. who use the same strategy to balance the distribution of hash operations over the rounds, but with a less complex movement pattern. The resulting algorithm is simpler than the Coppersmith and Jakobsson algorithm, and achieves the same lowered time bound without requiring additional storage.

In response to the traversals where computational bounds scale with chain length n, Sella proposed a traversal where computation time could be fixed at the expense of storage space [20]. Using a slightly different chain partitioning technique, the spacings between pebbles can be adjusted to accommodate the imposed computational bounds. Unfortunately, additional pebbles are needed to facilitate this spacing strategy so that for a fixed computational bound of m, the storage requirement is $k\sqrt[k]{n}$ where $k = m + 1$. For comparison, this is twice the storage required by FHT for equivalent time bounds. Later, a scheme devised by Kim was able provide the same fixed time bounds without these extra pebbles by carefully timing pebble movements to create a more synchronous system [11]. This reduced the storage by a factor of k, which matches the storage required by FHT for equivalent bounds.

One remaining strategy, capable of lowering retrieval complexity even further, stems from the introduction of multi-dimensional chains. Hu et al. present two traversals based on a modified structure of the underlying chain [8]. Sandwich chains intertwine multiple chains to form a construction whose primary purpose is efficient verification of keys. Their second construction, Comb Skip-Chains, lowers retrieval bounds by amortizing the FHT over the secondary dimension of a two-dimensional chain structure. With a total of $\log_2(n)$ secondary chains, the amortization brings retrieval time down to a constant, while storage is bounded by $O(\log_2(n))$.

3. TARGETING TRAVERSAL

Thus far the claim that FHT is inefficient in the presence of skipped values is unsubstantiated but is easy to show by example. These examples are also helpful in understanding the reasons underlying the inefficiencies of FHT. Such insights lead to areas where FHT can be improved.

3.1 Motivating Insight

The interdependency of successive FHT retrievals, though used to establish an upper bound on retrieval time, causes unnecessary operations when the interval between desired values is large. The movement of any pebble relies on the correct completion of prior pebble movements. Practically, this implies that values must be retrieved from the chain in the expected, consecutive order, discarding unneeded values. This *iterative* process is highly wasteful.

One prominent source of wasted computation is the calculation of values within ranges of skipped values. Take, for example, pebbles moved to positions below the retrieval target. Since key use is ordered (once a key is retrieved, the keys at lower positions will never be needed), the hash computations used to move pebbles into skipped ranges are completely wasted. With the understanding that a pebble is only useful once it moves above the target value, all the movements of each pebble can be predicted and grouped into a single move. This modification, illustrated in Figure 3, eliminates the hash operations performed by calculating values from the unused region.

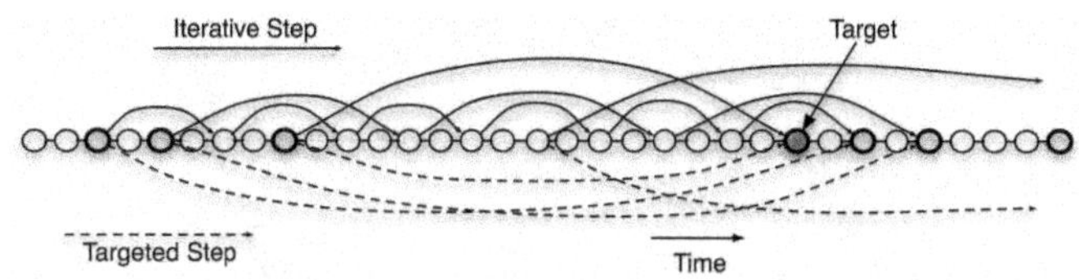

Figure 3: In this small sample chain segment, each line above the chain represents a required move in order to retrieve the darkened pebble by the iterative FHT method. Targeting eliminates this tangle by moving each pebble only once, without passing through intermediate locations, as shown by the dashed lines below the chain.

For the purpose of efficiently moving pebbles, it is useful to consider each arrangement of pebbles as a state, with retrievals triggering state transitions. Figure 3 contrasts the idea of a targeted state transition against FHT's iterative method. To simplify matters further, new states depend only on the location of the target value, and not on any previous states.

State changes are the inspiration behind the targeting algorithm. The goal of the targeting algorithm is to perform state changes meeting two criteria: first, the state changes should be functionally indistinguishable from state changes performed by iterative retrievals. Additionally, the implemented state changes should perform the minimum number of hash operations necessary to achieve the new state. That is, a hash operation should never be applied to the same value more than once during a single retrieval.

State transitions alone do not guarantee the elimination of all redundant hashes and algorithms must be crafted carefully to avoid hashing the same value more than once. The threat of duplicate hashes arises when two moving pebbles skip upward to the same position during the first movement phase. In this case, both pebbles will copy the value from the same reference pebble and hash this value in order to step downward. In essence, by hashing the same value, the two pebbles perform the same operation. These redundant operations can be avoided if one pebble waits while the other performs the operations common to both pebbles. Then instead of copying the value of the originally intended pebble the waiting pebble can copy the value from the other pebble, eliminating redundant work.

When two pebbles would ordinarily move upward to the same pebble, the question arises of which to move first and which to delay. When considering a simple case with two pebbles, two algorithms naturally emerge which are built into two transition algorithms – the *Lazy Pebble* and *Traveling Pebble* algorithms. The small example in Figure 4 illustrates the basic principles of these algorithms. The strategy taken by the Lazy Pebble algorithm is to move the pebble with the smaller ID first. Once this pebble reaches its destination, the larger pebble can copy the value of the smaller and begin hashing to step downward from there. The other algorithm, Traveling Pebble, moves the larger pebble first. With this method, the smaller pebble does not perform any hash operations at all. As the larger pebble steps past the smaller pebble's destination, the smaller pebble copies the

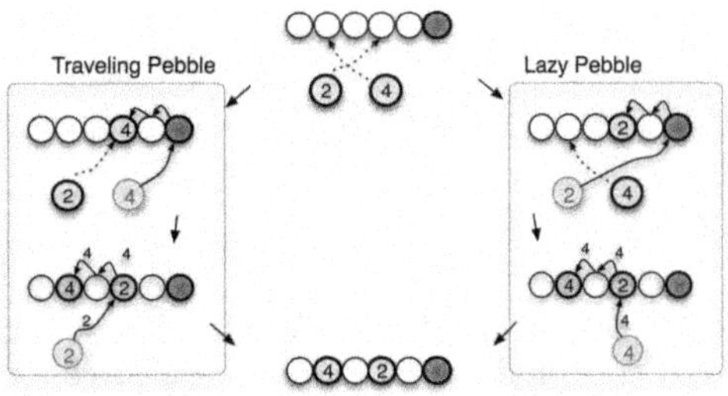

Figure 4: A simple example is pictured in which the two pebbles, with IDs 2 and 4, both intend to copy the value from the same higher pebble (shown darkened). To avoid redundant work, one pebble moves before the other. The two paths demonstrate different principles on which to base transition algorithms.

value from the larger pebble. The larger pebble then continues on to its final destination. The remainder of this paper will focus on the Traveling Pebble approach. This algorithm is more intuitive, and preliminary tests indicated no measurable performance difference between the two.

For the purpose of explanation, the targeting algorithm has been divided into two stages: *state calculation* and *state transition*. The state calculation determines new destinations for all pebbles that need to move. The Traveling Pebble algorithm implements the state transition and can be thought of as a sweep which hashes values across the whole range into which pebbles will move. During this sweep, pebbles move to their intended destinations. To make this process align better with the style of FHT pebble movements, the job of performing the hash sweep is given to the various moving pebbles. In the Traveling Pebble algorithm, not all pebbles are required to participate in the hash sweep, but those that do are responsible for the range of values that lie above their new destination and below the next higher pebble.

The targeting algorithm descriptions pertain to pebbles whose destinations are still within the chain. The other case, where pebbles move past the end of the chain, is ignored for simplicity. These pebbles are unnecessary for the remainder of the traversal and can be safely retired by removal from the pebble list.

3.2 Theoretical Performance

Overall performance of the targeting algorithm can be measured in terms of storage and computation, with computation cost split into hash operations and overhead incurred from rearranging the pebble list. Storage complexity is exactly the same as FHT, which is bounded by $O(\log_2(n))$ where n is the chain length. Computational costs require further analysis.

Overhead of both state calculation and state transition is bounded by $O(\log_2(\delta))$ list operations, where δ represents the distance between successive retrieval targets. The number of pebbles in a range of length δ is bounded by $\log_2(\delta) + 1$. In both Algorithms 1 or 2, no loop processes more than $\log_2(\delta) + 1$ pebbles. The first loop in both algorithms searches for a pebble above the target, with an ID larger than any pebble below the target. This pebble is first guessed by knowing the minimum number of pebbles below the target as well as the smallest possible ID for the largest

Table 1: Retrieval bounds are given for the best and worst cases of targeting when skipping δ values. $C_{it}(\delta)$ denotes the cost δ iterations of iterative FHT.

Case	Bound
Worst	$\begin{cases} C_{it}(\delta) - \frac{\delta}{2}\rho(\delta,3)) + 2^{\rho(\delta,1)} - 4 & : \lceil\log_2(\delta)\rceil > 3 \\ C_{it}(\delta) & : Otherwise \end{cases}$
Best	$C_{it}(\delta) - \frac{\delta}{2}(\rho(\delta,1)) - 2^{\rho(\delta,0)} + 2$

of these pebbles. From this guess, at most one iteration is needed before reaching pebbles above the target. Finding a pebble with an ID larger than all the pebbles below the target is clearly bounded by $\log_2(\delta) + 1$, the number of pebbles that will move[2]. The second loop in each algorithm iterates over moving pebbles, which is already known to be $O(\log_2(\delta))$.

Performance in terms of hash operations is characterized by upper and lower bounds on the number of operations saved, $S(\delta)$, in comparison to the iterative method. For a retrieval distance δ, iterative FHT requires $O(\delta \times \log_2(n))$ hash operations. Savings gained by targeting are examined on a case by case basis to establish the lower and upper bounds.

Bounds are found by estimating the number of pebbles capable of savings and the number of operations saved by each pebble. To simplify notation, let $\rho(\delta, \alpha)$ represent the number of pebbles that cause savings:

$$\rho(\delta, \alpha) = max(\lceil\log_2(\delta)\rceil - \alpha, 0) \qquad (1)$$

An interval of size δ contains at most $\lceil\log_2(\delta)\rceil$ pebbles, however, this overestimates the number of pebbles which achieve savings by a small number α. To form best and worst case calculations, α is adjusted accordingly. In the worst case, at most three pebbles will be large enough to step above the target without achieving savings[3]. With $0 \leq \alpha \leq 3$, note that:

$$\rho(\delta, \alpha) \in \Theta(\log_2(\delta)) \qquad (2)$$

A lower savings bound can be estimated from the case where the only savings derive from pebbles that avoid extra moves below the target. This case is unlikely, but theoretically possible. A key observation about the iterative algorithm is that while each pebble hashes small ranges throughout the chain, these ranges add up to hashing about half of the entire chain. While skipping a region of length δ, each pebble can save up to $\frac{\delta}{2}$ operations, with adjustments necessary for losses at the edges of the region. For an individual pebble p_i, the savings loss at each edge is at most 2^{i+1}. Thus for each p_i, the minimum individual savings is $\frac{1}{2}(\delta - 2 \times 2^{i+1})$.

[2]This number is actually bounded by a constant, however, the explanation is lengthy and unnecessary to show the $O(\log_2(\delta))$ bounds on the targeting algorithm.

[3]Finding an example region containing three pebbles with no potential savings is straightforward. However, adding a fourth pebble requires an interval large enough to allow the smallest of the original three to achieve some savings. This logic applies inductively.

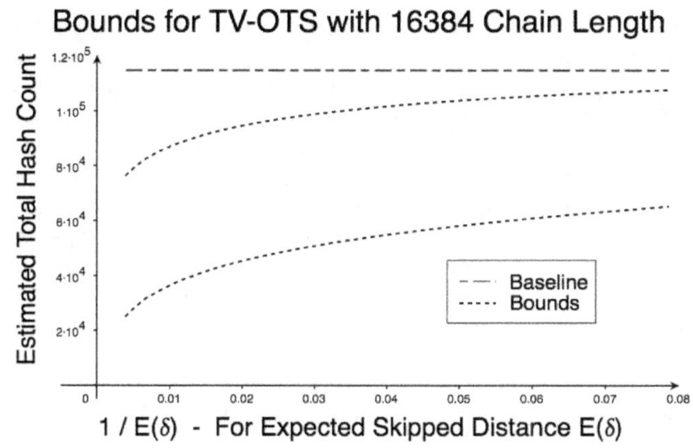

Figure 5: A bounds prediction for TV-OTS, calculated by subtracting the calculated expected savings from a baseline expectation for iterative FHT.

Summing over the $\rho(\delta,3)$ pebbles that cause savings gives:

$$S_{min}(\delta) = \sum_{i=1}^{\rho(\delta,3)} \tfrac{\delta - 2^{i+2}}{2}$$

$$= \begin{cases} \frac{\delta}{2}\rho(\delta,3)) - 2^{\rho(\delta,1)} + 4 & : \lceil \log_2(\delta) \rceil > 3 \\ 0 & : Otherwise \end{cases} \quad (3)$$

An upper bound is achieved from slightly overestimating the savings below the target and adding the maximum additional savings from moving pebbles above the target. In the best case, all the moving pebbles except the largest can be moved for free. This is at most $\rho(\delta,1) = \lceil \log_2(\delta) \rceil - 1$ pebbles. The savings below the target are also adjusted, counting $\rho(\delta,1)$ pebbles potentially saving up to $\frac{\delta}{2}$ operations each:

$$S_{max}(\delta) = \sum_{i=1}^{\rho(\delta,1)} \frac{\delta}{2} + \sum_{i=1}^{\rho(\delta,1)} 2^i$$

$$= \tfrac{\delta}{2}\rho(\delta,1) + 2^{\rho(\delta,0)} - 2 \quad (4)$$

From $S_{min}(\delta) \in \Omega(\delta \log_2(\delta))$ and $S_{max}(\delta) \in O(\delta \log_2(\delta))$, and the relationship $S_{min} \lesssim S \lesssim S_{max}$, a tight bound can be placed on $S(\delta)$:

$$S(\delta) \in \Theta(\delta \log_2(\delta)) \quad (5)$$

Table 3.2 summarizes the differences between the iterative method, and targeting in the best and worst case.

3.2.1 Bounds Prediction for TV-OTS

The theoretical bounds help predict the performance of TV-OTS using targeting. Figure 5 shows expected bounds calculated per traversal, estimated by subtracting calculated savings from a baseline TV-OTS approximation. The estimated requirement of a TV-OTS traversal is $\frac{n}{2}\log_2(n)$ hash operations, recalling that over an entire traversal each pebbles hashes about half the chain, or $\frac{n}{2}$ operations[4].

Bounds predictions assume different values of δ occur over the course of a traversal. In TV-OTS, all keys have equal probability of being retrieved. Consequently, the distance δ between retrievals follows a geometric distribution. The bounds in Figure 5 were calculated by summing over the geometrically weighted savings for different δ's. Results are plotted over $E(\delta)$, the expected δ of the distribution which varies with the key retrieval probability of the protocol.

3.3 State Calculation

The correct state after any retrieval can be determined by a small set of rules. The state calculator given by Algorithm 1 uses these rules to determine final pebble positions that match those produced by an iterative FHT traversal. The primary property used in determining new positions is that each moving pebble must create an interval below a larger pebble that matches the moving pebble's ID. The larger pebbles that assist in finding new destinations for moving pebbles are referred to as *reference* pebbles. The reference pebbles limit the possible destinations of the moving pebbles, some of which will lie above the target and some below. Those below are disregarded as they lie in a region of skipped values. Of the remaining possibilities, the lowest is chosen for the moving pebble's new destination. The choice of lowest position reflects that pebbles moved iteratively will stop as soon as they move past the target. The availability of the correct reference location is ensured by deciding the destinations for larger pebbles before smaller ones. By knowing the destinations for all larger pebbles, the correct destination is certain to be found for each moving pebble.

Because state calculation always chooses the lowest possible position, only one pebble needs to be considered as a reference. Anticipating pebble movements, there are only two pebbles that serve as possible references. These are the two closest in position to the retrieval target. Of these two, the lower will be chosen assuming the moving pebble, when positioned below this lower reference, will still be above the target. If this is not the case, the other reference is chosen. In this second case, the two potential reference pebbles border the interval for the moving pebble to split. Since this division is even, placing the moving pebble at an interval *below* the *higher* of the two references is equivalent to placing the moving pebble *above* the *lower* reference. Because this process is only responsible for finding destinations and not for moving pebbles, knowing the position of only this lower reference is sufficient to find the proper destination.

With these guiding principles in place, state calculation can be described as an iterative algorithm for calculating individual pebble destinations. Setup requires finding the location, β, of a pebble to use as the initial reference. Specifically, β is the position of the pebble whose ID is the smallest from a certain set of pebbles. This set is comprised of all the pebbles whose IDs are larger than the IDs of all the pebbles below the target[5]. The number of pebbles below the target is a function of the interval length between retrieved values. Once the number of pebbles to move is known, finding a pebble to use for β requires checking pebbles above the target until one satisfies the criterion just mentioned. Once β is determined, iteration can start with the pebble of the next lower ID.

[4]The cost of FHT is reported as $2\log_2(n)+1$ operations per retrieval, but this is an upper bound and does not necessarily imply that a sequence of n retrievals requires $n \times (2\log_2(n)+1)$ operations.

[5]Note that this set is not equivalent to all the pebbles above the target: a pebble below the target could have an ID larger than that of a pebble above the target.

Algorithm 1: State Calculation

```
Data: A list of pebbles L of length n
Input: A target position t
Result: L is modified
/* initialize iteration control variables */
idx ← ⌊log2(t − L.getPebbleByIndex(0).pos + 1)⌋
nxtId ← 2^idx
p ← L.getPebbleByIndex(idx)
while p.dest < t or p.id ≤ nxtId do
    idx ← idx + 1
    nxtId ← 2 × nxtId
    p ← L.getPebbleByIndex(idx)
β ← p.pos
/* begin iteration */
while nxtId > 1 do
    p ← L.getPebbleByID(nxtId)
    /* Decide new position for p */
    if p.id < β − t then
        /* p fits below β and above t */
        β ← β − p.id
        p.dest ← β
    else
        p.dest ← β + p.id
    /* update nxtId */
    nxtId ← nxtId/2
```

Function movePebble(L, p, i)

```
Input: The list L of pebbles
Input: The pebble p to move
Input: An index i to which to move p
Result: p is moved in L
q ← L.getPebbleByIndex(i)
p.pos ← q.pos
p.val ← q.val
L.remove(p)
L.putPebbleAtIndex(p, i − 1)
```

The complete state calculation algorithm is given in Algorithm 1. The choice of pebble used for β likely changes as iteration progresses through the moving pebbles. At any point in time, β is intended to represent the lowest possible reference. Whenever a pebble's new destination is chosen to be below β, the current value of β is no longer valid as the lowest reference. β is then updated using the most recently found destination. Once the iteration completes, destinations have been determined for all pebbles. The lowest destination matches the position of, or one step above, the position of the target.

3.4 Traveling Pebble State Transition

With a newly calculated target state, the challenge becomes efficient movement of pebbles to their new positions. The Traveling Pebble algorithm uses the Function `movePebble` to accomplish state transition with minimal hash operations.

The general approach of the Traveling Pebble method, given in Algorithm 2, is to begin moving each value as quickly as possible, considering pebbles from largest to smallest. In this way, larger pebbles begin their moves before smaller ones. When a pebble p_t is found to move, a lookahead operation is performed to determine the destination of the next smaller pebble, p_s. The destination of p_s determines whether p_t may complete its move, or whether it must begin its move but pause when it reaches p_s's destination, allowing p_s to copy the value at p_t's position. If this is indeed the case, this procedure is followed and then repeated for a new p_s, performing lookahead operations for smaller pebbles until one is found whose destination lies below that of p_t. At this point, no more smaller pebbles will need to move above p_t and p_t completes its move.

When lookahead operations are performed, p_t's destination is already known. When moving downward, p_t will only pause for a p_s whose destination is above p_t's. To make checking p_s's destination easier, β is updated to p_t's destination as soon as this destination is known instead of waiting until it is actually occupied. This ensures that destinations of the p_s pebbles can be compared with β to correctly determine when each p_s should move.

4. CORRECTNESS

The structural model used for proving correctness can be simplified over the computational structures used in implementation. Abstractly, a chain is modeled as an ordered list of all pebbles. Pebbles are simplified to a tuple representing their ID and destination. The correspondence between a pebble's position and value is one-to-one, so that pebbles will output the correct values exactly when their positions are correct. As proved by Jakobsson, pebbles' destinations will be correct by the time their values are needed [10]. This applies to the targeting algorithms as well, since the amortization strategy used in targeting may be overzealous and move pebbles farther than actually necessary, but not less. Thus, pebbles may arrive at their destinations sooner than necessary, but never later. Due to this eager approach, pebbles' values will be correct if their destinations are chosen correctly. Proof of correct destinations follows.

DEFINITION 1. *A pebble is represented by a tuple, $p_i = \langle i, d\rangle$, where i and d respectively represent the pebble's identifier and destination.*

DEFINITION 2. *A chain state is represented by a set $S = \{\langle i, d\rangle \mid i = 2^j \text{ for } j \in [1, \log_2(n)]\}$. In the initial state, $d = i$ for all $\langle i, d\rangle \in S$.*

The targeting algorithm is proven correct by showing that the set of destinations found always matches the destinations found by the iterative method for matching states. A state is characterized by the position of the lowest pebble. For this proof, the target, t is assumed to be at an evenly-numbered position. This assumption is safe since the state responsible for calculating an evenly positioned value is also responsible for the lower adjacent odd position.

DEFINITION 3. *A skip function, $\zeta(S)$, updates a pebble's final destination before moving upward during a single step in the iterative algorithm. This function is given by $\zeta(\langle i, d\rangle) = \langle i, d + 2i\rangle$.*

DEFINITION 4. *A single step in the iterative method is described by the function ψ which finds the pebble $\langle i, d\rangle$ with the lowest destination and replaces it with $\zeta(\langle i, d\rangle)$. To reach*

Algorithm 2: Traveling Pebble State Transition

```
Data: A list, L, of pebbles with destinations chosen by
      Algorithm 1
Input: A target position t
Result: Pebbles in L are moved to new destinations
        above t
/* make t even                                        */
if t is odd then t ← t + 1
/* amortized hashing of pebbles not at their
   destinations not shown                             */
/* initialize iteration control variables             */
idx ← ⌊log2(t − L.getPebbleByIndex(0).pos + 1)⌋;
nxtId ← 2^idx
p ← L.getPebbleByIndex(idx)
while p.dest < t or p.id ≤ nxtId do
    idx ← idx + 1
    nxtId ← 2 × nxtId
    p ← L.getPebbleByIndex(idx)
β ← p.pos
/* begin iteration                                    */
while nxtId > 1 do
    p ← L.getPebbleByID(nxtId)
    /* a check could be added here to ensure
       that p actually needs to move and is not
       to be retired                                  */
    if p.dest < β then
        movePebble(L, p, idx)
        β ← p.dest
        /* set up for next pebble                     */
        idx ← idx − 1
        nxtId ← nxtId/2
        /* lookahead for smaller pebbles              */
        q ← L.getPebbleByID(nxtId)
        while nxtId > 1 and q.dest > β do
            p.dest ← q.dest
            p.hashToDestination()
            movePebble(L, q, idx)
            idx ← idx − 1
            nxtId ← nxtId/2
        p.dest ← β
        p.hashToDestination()
    else
        movePebble(L, p, idx + 1)
        p.hashToDestination()
        /* set up for next iteration                  */
        idx ← idx − 1
        nxtId ← nxtId/2
```

a new state, ψ is evaluated repeatedly until the target t corresponds to the lowest pebble.

From these definitions, each destination can be found in a unique way.

THEOREM 1. *For a state associated with the retrieval of t, there is only one legal position for each pebble.*

PROOF. Initial pebble positions are fixed, and subsequent destinations are chosen only from previous ones. Thus, the possible destinations of any pebble over the course of the traversal are also fixed. For any given pebble, these destinations are evenly spaced: the distance between possible destinations for pebble p_i is $2i$. Given that this is the distance moved by a pebble in an iterative step, only one position exists for p_i when moving from below target t to above. □

COROLLARY 1. *For a state corresponding to target t, the new destination of each pebble $\langle i, d\rangle$ satisfies $t \le d < t + 2i$.*

PROOF. The iterative method always moves the pebble with the lowest destination and continues until no more pebbles can be moved above t, so $t \le d$ holds trivially for all pebbles, Destinations are also bounded from above. Let $\langle i, d_f\rangle = \zeta(\langle i, d_i\rangle)$ represent a pebble after a move where $d_i < t \le d_f$. Using $d_f = d_i + 2i$ gives,

$$\begin{aligned} d_i &< t \\ d_i + 2i &< t + 2i \\ d_f &< t + 2i \end{aligned} \tag{6}$$

Showing that d_f must be within $2i$ positions of t. □

The equivalence of targeted states to iterative states can now be shown by showing that destinations found by targeting satisfy Theorem 1 and Corollary 1.

DEFINITION 5. *Let $\Psi(S)$ assign a new destination to a single pebble as part of a targeting algorithm state calculation. A full state calculation uses Ψ repeatedly, assigning a new destination to each pebble until all destinations are above t.*

THEOREM 2. *The set of destinations found by the iterative method for the state corresponding to t can be found without iteration by spacing new destinations relative to each other instead of relative to old pebble positions.*

The proof of this theorem is a multi-step process. First, the set A_i is defined relative to pebble p_i, which will be useful later on.

DEFINITION 6. *Let $A_i = \{\langle i_a, d_a\rangle \mid i_a > i\}$ relative to a pebble $p_i = \langle i, d\rangle$.*

LEMMA 1. *Given a pebble $p_i = \langle i, d_i\rangle$ to move, let d_f be a valid final destination. The locations $d_f - i$ and $d_f + i$ must be valid destinations for two pebbles in A_i. Moreover, $d_f + i$ and $d_f - i$ are the closest destinations to d_f which are valid for any pebble in A_i.*

PROOF. The precise set of destinations for each pebble does not overlap with any of the other pebbles, limiting the pebbles that may occupy a given location. Specifically, for a pebble $\langle i, d\rangle$, all legal values for d fit the form

$$\begin{aligned} d &= d_k \text{ where } \langle i, d_k\rangle = \zeta^k(\langle i, i\rangle) \\ &= i + 2i \times k \end{aligned} \tag{7}$$

Where $k \in \mathbb{Z}^+$ and ζ^k represents repeated application of ζ k times. Equation 7 is useful for determining relative offsets between pebbles. Let $\langle i_a, d_a\rangle, \langle i_b, d_b\rangle \in A_i$ be the pebbles above and below d_f. Because i, i_a and i_b are each a power of two, $i_a = 2^{j_a} i$ and $i_b = 2^{j_b} i$ for some $j_a, j_b \in \mathbb{Z}^+$. Using Equation 7, d_a and d_b can be rewritten to obtain expressions in terms of d_f and i:

For d_a:

$$\begin{aligned} d_a &= i_a + 2i_a k_a \\ &= 2^{j_a} i + 2(2^{j_a} i k_a) \\ &= 2i(2^{j_a - 1} + 2^{j_a} k_a) \\ \text{Setting } k = 2^{j_a} k_a + 2^{j_a - 1} - 1: \\ d_a &= 2i(k+1) \\ &= 2i + 2ik \\ &= d_f + i \end{aligned} \tag{8}$$

And similarly for d_b:

$$\begin{aligned} d_b &= i_b + 2i_b k_b \\ &= 2^{j_b} i + 2(2^{j_b} i k_b) \\ &= 2i(2^{j_b - 1} + 2^{j_b} k_b) \\ \text{Setting } k = 2^{j_b} k_b + 2^{j_b - 1}: \\ d_b &= 2i(k) \\ &= d_f - i \end{aligned} \tag{9}$$

The fact that there is no third pebble $\langle i_c, d_c \rangle \in A_i$ satisfying $d_b \leq d_c \leq d_a$ stems from the same positional relationships that relate i, i_a and i_b. By Equations 8 and 9, the distance between i_a and i_b is $2i$. Moreover, the distances between any two pebbles in A_i must be a multiple of $2i$. No pebble from A_i could be between d_a and d_b without violating this condition. □

Lemma 2 shifts perspective, building on Lemma 1 to show that the destinations for larger pebbles surrounding each new destination can be used to *find* this new destination.

LEMMA 2. *Let $\langle i, d \rangle$ be a pebble to be moved to an unknown destination d_f. Assume that all pebbles in A_i currently have destinations above t. In this situation, a pebble from A_i will be located at either $d_f + i$ or $d_f - i$.*

PROOF. By definition, A_i must contain a pebble, $\langle i_{2i}, d_{2i} \rangle$, such that $i_{2i} = 2i$. Corollary 1 requires that $t \leq d_{2i} < t + 2i_{2i}$. Note $2i_{2i} = 4i$, so if

$$t \leq d_{2i} < t + 3i,$$

then Lemma 2 is clearly satisfied with $d_f - i = d_{2i}$. In the remaining case,

$$t + 3i \leq d_{2i} < t + 4i.$$

Here, Equation 9 states that there must be a pebble destination at $d_{2i} - i_{2i} = d_f - i$. Furthermore, with $d_f \pm i$ above t, the pebbles corresponding to these destinations must be in A_i and therefore actively present in these positions. □

The Ψ function applies the above procedure, finding a pebble p_i with a valid A_i set and updating its destination. Induction can now be applied in a full proof of Theorem 2, showing that starting from any correct state, the new destinations found for all pebbles form a new correct state.

PROOF. *Base case:* A pebble $p_i = \langle i, d \rangle$ exists such that the corresponding A_i set contains only pebbles that are above t. This is necessarily true unless p_i will move beyond the end of the chain, in which case this proof is unnecessary. In such a state, a new destination for p_i can be correctly determined.

Inductive Step: Given a state where a new destination can be determined for $p_i = \langle i, d \rangle$, applying $\Psi(S)$ and updating this pebble's destination will result in a state where either 1) no more pebbles need to be updated, or 2) there is now a new pebble to which Ψ can be applied. The first case trivially halts the induction. In the second, using Ψ to determine a new destination for p_i automatically results in a new partitioning where all the pebbles in $A_{i/2} = A_i \cup \{\langle i, d \rangle\}$ now have destinations above t. Thus, a new pebble, $p_{1/2} = \langle i_{i/2}, d_{i/2} \rangle$, is found for which a new destination can be found. In some cases, $d_{1/2}$ will already be above t, however, this causes no change since exactly the same two cases apply as if $p_{1/2}$ had just been updated. □

Targeting transitions follow these steps of iteratively applying $\Psi(S)$ and moving each pebble, and hence the new destination of each pebble will be correct. Thus, each state will correctly match the state found by the iterative method for the same target. Since both algorithms start from identical initial states, correctness is ensured over arbitrary state changes.

5. EXPERIMENT AND ANALYSIS

To verify performance, the targeting algorithm was implemented and compared with a slightly modified version of the iterative traversal approach. The modified FHT decreases latency by neglecting hash operations needed to compute values at odd positions in skipped regions. This version was dubbed *Half Iterative* and improves efficiency by removing at most $\frac{n}{2}$ hashes per traversal. All algorithms were implemented in Java, but compiled using the GCJ front end for the GCC compiler to prevent runtime performance modifications by Java's Just-In-Time compiler. The choice of hash function was SHA-1[6]. Tests were performed on a 3GHz AMD Phenom II processor with 8GB of RAM running Ubuntu 12.04.

Tests were designed to measure performance for secure uses of TV-OTS. Only the operations used to traverse the chain are measured, with the n hash operations required to initialize the chain considered setup cost. Retrievals requested by TV-OTS are independent, with all values having equal probability, p, of being retrieved. Thus, the expected interval size between retrieved values is $n \times p$. The assumed application for all tests uses a message rate of 30Hz and a chain length of 16,384 which, for example, gives TV-OTS a total lifespan of more than 4 hours if keys are refreshed every second.

Tests were designed to show performance over a range of probabilities. Security is measured by the probability of an adversary finding a message for which a signature can be forged. Forgery probability is directly related to the percentage of keys retrieved. If each signature contains 13 keys, then out of 4096 keys, at most $v = 30\frac{messages}{second} \times 13\frac{keys}{message} = 390\frac{keys}{second}$ are used. For this scenario, the fraction of retrieved keys about 9%, but the probably that a message can be forged is more than .0001 [2]. However, the fraction of retrieved keys drops rapidly when increasing security

[6]The choice of hash function affects timed performance. When comparing latencies, the performance increases will appear greater with slower hash functions. For example, results presented here would be diminished by using a faster function such as MD5 and magnified by a slower function such as SHA-256.

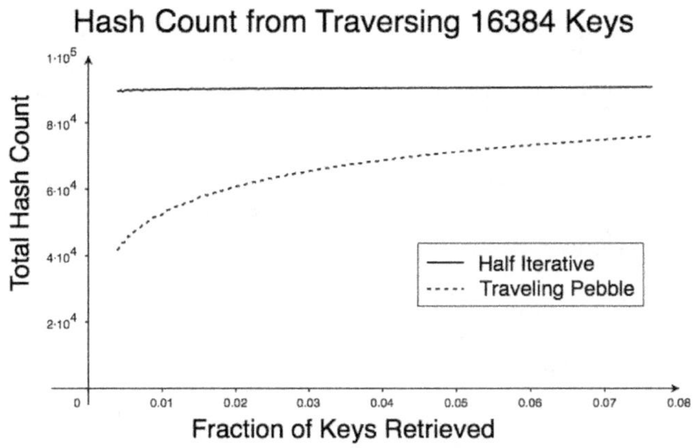

Figure 6: Comparison of the total number of hash operations performed over the course of a traversal.

by increasing the number of chains N. It also drops when taking into account the possibility that keys may be used in more than one signature. Equation 10 calculates the expected probability of retrieval of any key by probabilistically weighting the possible numbers of retrieved keys and dividing by N. Some sample values based on Equation 10 are shown in Table 2.

$$\epsilon(N, v) = \frac{1}{N} \times \frac{\sum_{k=1}^{v} k\binom{N}{k}\binom{v-1}{k-1}}{\sum_{k=1}^{v} \binom{N}{k}\binom{v-1}{k-1}} \tag{10}$$

Table 2: Expected fraction of retrieved keys is shown for various combinations of N and v. Entries are omitted where TV-OTS signatures would be impossible when using a hash length limited to 160 bits.

Percentage Of Keys Retrieved			
N	$v = 30 \times 13$	$v = 30 \times 12$	$v = 30 \times 11$
4096	8.7%	8%	7.4%
8192	-	4.2%	3.8%
16384	-	-	1.9%

Tests were designed to highlight performance at these percentages and show the surrounding context. Tests averaged 12 trials, which roughly reflects the number of retrievals required for each signature. In each trial, the positions of the retrieved values were randomly generated, as would be expected from the execution of TV-OTS.

Performance graphs show the differences between the iterative and targeted retrievals. Figure 6 shows the difference in the numbers of hash operations performed by iterative and targeted traversals. This graph shows that the savings are approximately $\frac{\delta}{2}\log_2(\delta)$ where $\delta = \frac{1}{p}$, and fall within the bounds derived in Section 3.2. Latency measurements are shown in Figure 7 for both total retrieval time and retrieval overhead without hashes.

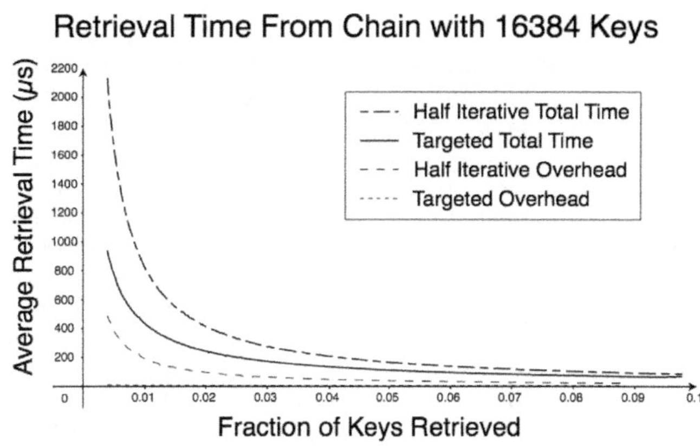

Figure 7: Average time of a single retrieval operation is plotted over the fraction of keys retrieved. Latencies were measured both for the entire retrieval and overhead only. Overhead was evaluated by running the traversals without performing hash operations. The targeting algorithm has lower latencies both when measuring overall time and overhead-only performance.

6. FUTURE WORK

This work could be expanded in several directions, focusing on algorithm optimization or incorporation with other signature protocols.

At the algorithm level, the number of hash operations may be optimal, but the process by which pebbles are chosen to move between states may still be optimized. With the current algorithms, an unfortunate consequence of storing pebbles ordered by position is the need to iteratively search for pebbles identified by ID. Eliminating this search would be a large step towards a more efficient targeting algorithm. This might be accomplished with different sorting strategies, or data structures that work more efficiently with multiple types of searches. Alternatively, this searching may be eliminated altogether if algorithms were found to determine pebble destinations by some means other than relative offsets. Such an algorithm would lower the traversal overhead even further beyond the improvement shown by Traveling Pebble transitions.

To achieve reliable security with TV-OTS, the number of skipped keys must be large. The base-two inspired pebble arrangements used by FHT may not be the most efficient for TV-OTS. Other arrangements might increase efficiency by grouping pebbles more densely around different intervals. A modified algorithm based on a different arrangement pattern potentially requires fewer operations to transition between states.

When TV-OTS was first published, HORS appeared to be the most appropriate one-time signature to incorporate, but this may no longer be true. FHT with targeting increases flexibility in protocol choices. The ability to skip keys more efficiently and with less scaling penalty may open up other possibilities for one-time signatures that fit in practically with the TV-OTS family.

7. CONCLUSION

Multicast data authentication is a difficult problem with no general solution suited to low latency applications. This problem is becoming increasingly important, with an emerging need for this type of protocol in critical infrastructure monitoring and control applications. TV-OTS is a protocol that shows promise for use in these systems, but too little is known about its practical use to provide an accurate assessment. To further the goal of accurately evaluating TV-OTS, the issue of key generation was addressed. The non-optimality of current methods was shown as inspiration for improvement.

The improved key management strategy builds on the FHT method by adding the ability to skip values without performing unnecessary hash operations — a necessary improvement for optimal performance of TV-OTS. This approach was motivated by the idea that FHT offers bounded retrieval time for consecutive hash chain values, but also wastes operations whenever values were skipped. With the addition of targeted state changes, the retrieval latency is decreased when skipping values. The state transition algorithms lowered not only the number of hash operations that were performed, but also the associated state transition overhead. The achieved performance gain corresponds to the percentage of keys retrieved from the chain. Savings increase with the distance δ between retrieved keys and are bounded by $\Theta(\delta \log_2(\delta))$. Security of TV-OTS increases relative to $\frac{1}{p}$, where p is the probability of key retrieval. The average distance δ grows as p is decreased, meaning TV-OTS performance savings improve as security is increased. These results indicate the targeting method to be a good choice for use with TV-OTS.

8. ACKNOWLEDGMENTS

The authors would like to thank Roberto Tamassia and the anonymous reviewers for their contributions toward improving this paper.

9. REFERENCES

[1] BAKKEN, D., BOSE, A., HAUSER, C., WHITEHEAD, D., AND ZWEIGLE, G. Smart generation and transmission with coherent, real-time data. *Proceedings of the IEEE 99*, 6 (June 2011), 928 -951.

[2] CAIRNS, K., HAUSER, C., AND GAMAGE, T. Flexible data authentication evaluated for the smart grid. *2013 IEEE International Conference on Smart Grid Communications (SmartGridComm)* (2013), To appear.

[3] CHALLAL, Y., BETTAHAR, H., AND BOUABDALLAH, A. A taxonomy of multicast data origin authentication: Issues and solutions. *Communications Surveys & Tutorials, IEEE 6*, 3 (2004), 34–57.

[4] COPPERSMITH, D., AND JAKOBSSON, M. Almost optimal hash sequence traversal. In *Financial Cryptography* (2003), Springer, pp. 102–119.

[5] DIFFIE, W., AND HELLMAN, M. New directions in cryptography. *IEEE Transactions on Information Theory 22*, 6 (1976), 644–654.

[6] FULORIA, S., ANDERSON, R., MCGRATH, K., HANSEN, K., AND ALVAREZ, F. The protection of substation communications. In *Proceedings of SCADA Security Scientific Symposium* (2010).

[7] HAUSER, C., MANIVANNAN, T., AND BAKKEN, D. Evaluating multicast message authentication protocols for use in wide area power grid data delivery services. In *2012 45th Hawaii International Conference on System Science (HICSS)* (2012), IEEE, pp. 2151–2158.

[8] HU, Y., JAKOBSSON, M., AND PERRIG, A. Efficient constructions for one-way hash chains. In *Applied Cryptography and Network Security* (2005), Springer, pp. 167–190.

[9] ITKIS, G., AND REYZIN, L. Forward-secure signatures with optimal signing and verifying. In *Advances in Cryptology–Crypto 2001* (2001), Springer, pp. 332–354.

[10] JAKOBSSON, M. Fractal hash sequence representation and traversal. In *2002 IEEE International Symposium on Information Theory* (2002), IEEE, p. 437.

[11] KIM, S. Improved scalable hash chain traversal. In *Applied Cryptography and Network Security* (2003), Springer, pp. 86–95.

[12] LAMPORT, L. Constructing digital signatures from a one-way function. Tech. rep., Technical Report CSL-98, SRI International, 1979.

[13] LAMPORT, L. Password authentication with insecure communication. *Communications of the ACM 24*, 11 (1981), 770–772.

[14] LI, Q., AND CAO, G. Multicast authentication in the smart grid with one-time signature. *Smart Grid, IEEE Transactions on 2*, 4 (2011), 686–696.

[15] PERRIG, A. The BiBa one-time signature and broadcast authentication protocol. In *Proceedings of the 8th ACM conference on Computer and Communications Security* (2001), ACM, pp. 28–37.

[16] PERRIG, A., CANETTI, R., SONG, D., AND TYGAR, J. Efficient and secure source authentication for multicast. In *Network and Distributed System Security Symposium (NDSS)* (2001), vol. 1, pp. 35–46.

[17] PERRIG, A., CANETTI, R., TYGAR, J. D., AND SONG, D. The TESLA broadcast authentication protocol. *RSA CryptoBytes 5*, 2 (2002).

[18] REYZIN, L., AND REYZIN, N. Better than BiBa: Short one-time signatures with fast signing and verifying. In *Information Security and Privacy* (2002), Springer, pp. 1–47.

[19] RIVEST, R., SHAMIR, A., AND ADLEMAN, L. A method for obtaining digital signatures and public-key cryptosystems. *Communications of the ACM 21*, 2 (1978), 120–126.

[20] SELLA, Y. On the computation-storage trade-offs of hash chain traversal. In *Financial Cryptography*, Lecture Notes in Computer Science. Springer, 2003, pp. 270–285.

[21] WANG, Q., KHURANA, H., HUANG, Y., AND NAHRSTEDT, K. Time valid one-time signature for time-critical multicast data authentication. In *INFOCOM 2009, IEEE* (2009), IEEE, pp. 1233–1241.

[22] YUM, D., SEO, J., EOM, S., AND LEE, P. Single-layer fractal hash chain traversal with almost optimal complexity. *Topics in Cryptology–CT-RSA 2009* (2009), 325–339.

HIFS: History Independence for File Systems

Sumeet Bajaj
Stony Brook University
New York, USA
sbajaj@cs.stonybrook.edu

Radu Sion
Stony Brook University
New York, USA
sion@cs.stonybrook.edu

ABSTRACT

Ensuring complete irrecoverability of deleted data is difficult to achieve in modern systems. Simply overwriting data or deploying encryption with ephemeral keys is not sufficient. The mere (previous) existence of deleted records impacts the current system state implicitly at all layers. This can be used as an oracle to derive information about the past existence of deleted records.

Yet there is hope. If all system layers would exhibit history independence, such implicit history-related oracles would disappear. However, achieving history independence efficiently is hard due to the fact that current systems are designed to heavily benefit from (data and time) locality at all layers through heavy caching, and existing history independent data structures completely destroy locality.

In this work we devise a way to achieve history independence while preserving locality (and thus be practical). We then design, implement and experimentally evaluate the first history independent file system (HIFS). HIFS guarantees secure deletion by providing full history independence across both file system and disk layers of the storage stack. It preserves data locality, and provides tunable efficiency knobs to suit different application history-sensitive scenarios.

Categories and Subject Descriptors

H.3.2 [**Information Storage and Retrieval**]: Information Storage—*File organization*; D.4.3 [**Operating Systems**]: File Systems Management—*File organization*

Keywords

History Independence; File System; Secure Deletion

1. INTRODUCTION

Numerous regulatory frameworks in finance, government and health-care, require secure deletion assurances typically by overwriting records on deletion. However, simply overwriting records does not guarantee deletion since the write history itself implicitly leaves artifacts in the layout of the resulting storage medium at all layers. The artifacts can be used as an oracle to answer questions about the past existence of deleted records. For example, the current layout of data blocks on disk is a function of the sequence and timing of previous writes to file system or database search indexes. Questions such as "was John's record ever in the HIV patients' dataset" can then be answered much more accurately than guessing by simply looking at the storage layout of the search index on disk (which will look different depending on whether John has previously been in the data set or not). Yet, these are the very questions that secure deletion promises to prevent anyone (including insiders) from answering once John's record has been deleted.

CCS'13, November 4–8, 2013, Berlin, Germany.

ACM 978-1-4503-2477-9/13/11 ...$15.00.
http://dx.doi.org/10.1145/2508859.2516724.

We posit that if all relevant system layers exhibit *history independence*, the implicit history-related oracles would disappear making the recovery of deleted records impossible.

Although prior work has focussed on designing *history independent* [1] data structures [5, 8, 12, 13, 16, 19], many challenges remain un-addressed for their successful deployment in systems. The first challenge is the un-availability of system-wide, space-allocation mechanisms that are also history independent. Such mechanisms are needed because data structures typically reside in storage sub-systems such as memory or disk. Hence, even if a data structure is history independent the behavior of the underlying storage sub-system may compromise its history. For example, the allocation of disk blocks by the file system can reveal information about the past operations performed on an otherwise history independent data structure (detailed examples in Section 3). Therefore, to realize complete history independence all system components on the data path need to possess the same characteristics [11]. Next, individual component characteristics render the existence of a single history independent design for all components unlikely. For instance, the low RAM latency vs. disk seek times, and the linear-ordered storage of disks vs. the wear leveling of SSDs. Hence, specific history independent designs are needed for each system component. Finally, achieving history independence efficiently in actual systems is hard due to the fact that current system designs heavily benefit from (data and time) locality at all layers through heavy caching, and existing history independent data structures completely destroy locality.

In this work we address the challenges of providing history independence for file storage over disk devices (Figure

[1]A data structure is history independent if its storage layout is a function of the current state and not of the history of past operations that led to it.

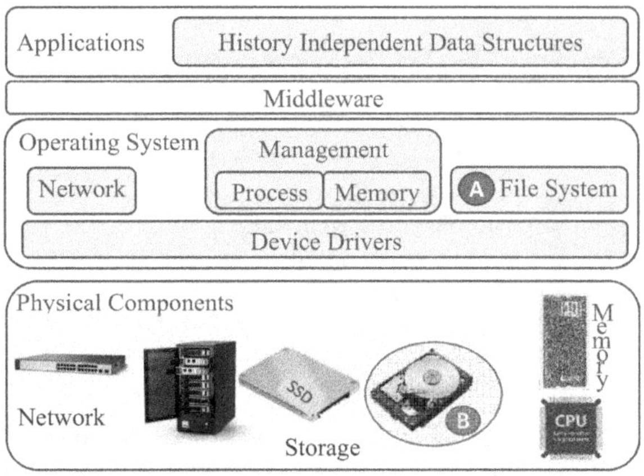

Figure 1: Potential system components that require history independent designs. This work targets file systems (A) using hard disks (B) for file storage.

1). We achieve this by introducing the first history independent file system (HIFS) with the following key design and performance characteristics.

(1) Varying degrees of data locality with minimal modifications for different application scenarios (Section 4.5.1).

(2) Customizable history independent layouts via simple modifications of a few key procedures (Section 4.5.1).

(3) Sequential read throughputs within 0.7x - 0.5x as compared to existing non-history independent file systems such as Ext3 for loads up to 60% (Section 6). Random read throughputs within 0.7x - 0.5x of Ext3 for loads up to 90%. Low performance for write operations at loads >60%.

(4) Efficient history independent file meta-data operations (Section 6). File delete and move operations as expensive as an entire file write (Section 4.5.4).

2. MODEL

Adversary. We assume an adversary with full access to the storage medium (e.g., the system disk). By forensic analysis of the disk contents the adversary aims to illegitimately derive sensitive information. Adversary actions include (but are not limited to) the following.

(1) Determine the existence and content of records deleted in the past, thereby violating regulatory compliance [4].

(2) Determine the order of past file operations to subvert privacy in voting applications [5].

(3) Compromise history independence of data structures stored within files via file system meta-data and disk layouts.

Storage Medium. The underlying storage device is required to be a mechanical disk drive, not flash storage (discussion on SSD storage in Section 5).

Files. All data structures stored within files are history independent [5, 8, 12, 13, 16, 19].

3. HISTORY INDEPENDENCE

3.1 File Systems

Existing file systems do not preserve history independence because the disk layouts they produce are not just a function of file contents but also depend on the sequence of file operations. The exact same set of files can be organized differently on disk depending on the sequence of operations that created the set. As a result, a simple examination of the disk layouts can reveal sensitive information about past operations. Moreover, the data structures used to maintain file system meta-data also contain information about past operations, both in their layouts, and in their contents (e.g., list of allocated blocks). Therefore, when disk layouts are combined with file system meta-data and knowledge of data structures that are stored within files, significantly more information can be derived, even full recovery of deleted data. Such leakage can violate secure deletion requirements and compromise privacy in applications such as e-voting.

At first it may appear that a simple replacement of all file system data structures (file meta-data, free block list etc) with their history independent versions would suffice to resolve the issue and preserve privacy. However, this is not the case, for the privacy leaks are not due to the data itself but due to the organization of data on disk. File system encryption too cannot solve the problem since the concern here is not data confidentiality. The relevant adversary is in fact an insider that requires and is rightfully granted full access to the data in the future (including disk encryption keys etc) and thus can easily bypass any protections encryption may offer. The solution then is to make file systems completely history independent. The disk layouts of a history independent file system (defined in Section 3.1.2) are only a function of data and not of the sequence of past operations.

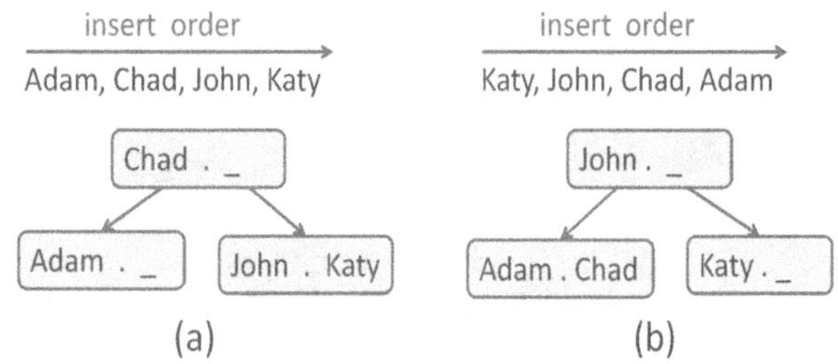

Figure 2: B-Tree, a non history independent data structure.

3.1.1 Example Illustration

To illustrate the need for history independence in file systems we consider an admissions management application at a hospital that records patients' data as new patients are admitted. The application API permits the hospital staff to add new patient records, lookup existing records and delete patient records on discharge. We will use this example for illustration but note that in essence, most existing applications of history independent data structures cannot be securely realized in practice without an underlying file system providing history independent persistence.

The patient application will typically utilize a database to manage its data. Now, a database in turn stores and manipulates data by utilizing efficient data structures of which B-Trees [7] are the most common example. However, the use of B-Trees causes several privacy concerns. This is because the storage layout of B-Trees (or of variations such as B^+-Trees) often depends on the order in which operations are performed on them due to their deterministic insertions and deletions. For example, consider the the illustration in Figure 2 which shows two B-Trees that store the exact same elements. Yet the layouts of the two B-Trees differ due to different insertion orders. Hence, simply by examining the tree layout (Figure 2(a)) one can ascertain with a probability of 75% that *Chad* was admitted before *John*. This is due to the fact that out of the total 4! ways of insertion

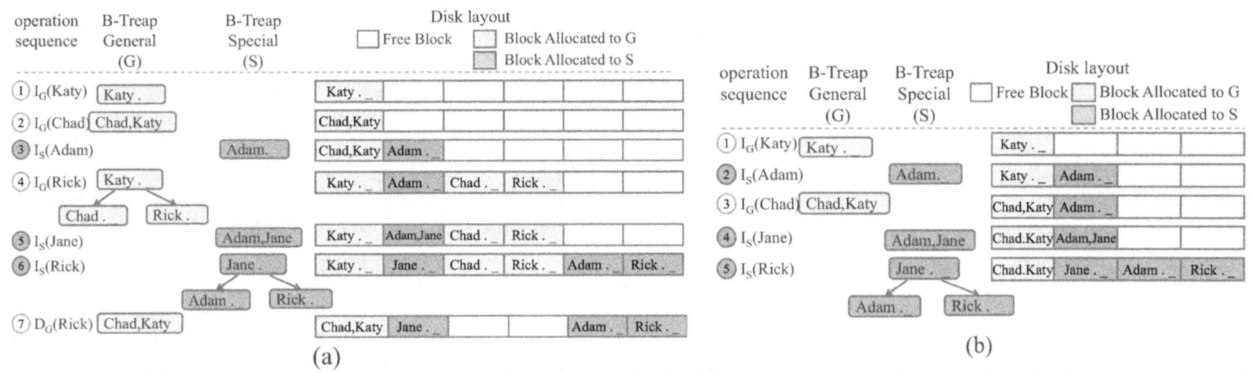

Figure 3: B-Treaps and file system layouts. $I_R(t)$ and $D_R(t)$ denote insertion and deletion respectively of element t in relation R.

for the four elements *Adam, Chad, John and Katy, Chad* is the root in only twelve, and inserted before *John* in nine of those twelve sequences.

The above limitation of B-Trees can be prevented by deploying corresponding history independent versions, such as B-Treaps [12]. The treaps will yield the same layout irrespective of the insertion order. However, such a simple replacement of application data structures with their history independent versions does not suffice unless the underlying persistent mechanisms (e.g., file system) are also history independent. To clarify, suppose that the B-Trees from above are replaced by the history independent B-Treaps [12]. Also, suppose that the application has two relations, one for admissions to the General ward and another for admissions to the Special ward, and that both relations are persisted using a simple file system that allocates the first available free block on request (and is hence not history independent). For simplicity, assume that the B-Treap node size is equal to the file system block size.

Now, consider the sequence of operations, the resultant B-Treaps, and the space allocation by the underlying file system as shown in Figure 3(a). At the end of operation 7, the disk layout (Figure 3(a)) reveals the following. (i) The fact that a delete operation was performed. The gaps left by the file system allocation form evidence for a delete. (ii) That the deleted node belonged to the General relation. Since otherwise there would be no gaps in the file system. (iii) The first patient was not admitted to the Special ward, since the root node of Special relation is not the first block on storage. Note that neither the layout of the B-Treaps nor the application API reveal any of (i) - (iii). The leaks are solely due to file system allocation.

Figure 3(b) shows an alternate sequence of operations that yield the exact same trees as in Figure 3(a) yet with significantly different disk layouts, showing that the disk layouts produced by the file system allocation heavily depend on file system operation sequencing. Hence, underlying storage mechanisms can defeat the history independence of higher level data structures.

While we used a simple file system scenario for illustration, we note that existing file systems (e.g., Ext2/Ext3 [3]) suffer from the same problems, since, for efficiency, and to preserve locality, they too allocate new blocks based on existing state, resulting in heavily history dependent layouts. A history independent file system on the other hand would reveal none of (i) to (iii) above since it would carry no evidence of a delete, such as gaps in block allocation. Similarly, its allocation policy would not be dependent on the order of file operations, resulting in the exact same disk layouts for the operation sequences of both Figures 3(a) and 3(b).

3.1.2 History Independent File System

Let Ψ_F^Γ denote the distribution (layout) over secondary storage of the state F, of a file system Γ. F represents all file contents plus meta-data for individual files and for the overall file system. Also, let $S_{F\to F'}^\Gamma$ denote a set of operations performed by file system Γ transforming its state from F into F'. We can then define the following.

DEFINITION 1. History Independent File System (HIFS) *Γ is a history independent file system if any two sequence of operations $X_{F\to F'}^\Gamma$ and $Y_{F\to F'}^\Gamma$ result in an identical distribution $\Psi_{F'}^\Gamma$.*

Formulated differently, for two sequences of operations $X_{F\to F'}^\Gamma$ and $Y_{F\to F'}^\Gamma$, an adversary having access to both the start state F and the end state F', should not be able to deduce which of X or Y was executed to transform the state from F into F'. It can be easily seen that satisfying this definition immediately implies that, the data at a particular offset of any file f in F, is always stored at the same device-specific location, irrespective of the sequence of operations that result in F. That is, the representation of the state F over the storage medium is canonical.

3.2 System-Wide History Independence

Although detailed discussion is out of scope, we briefly generalize history independence for an entire system.

Consider a typical system composed of multiple layers, ranging from software applications to hardware (Figure 1). Let these layers be denoted by L^0, L^1, L^2 etc, where L^0 is the bottom layer, L^1 the next higher layer and so on. Also, let $S_{A\to B}^{L^i}$ denote the set of operations that transform L^i from state A to B. Further suppose that, for each state A of L^i, there exists a state A' of L^{i-1} with the requirement that when L^i is in state A, L^{i-1} must be in state A' – we denote this relationship between A and A' as $L_A^i \to L_{A'}^{i-1}$. Then we can define the following.

DEFINITION 2. History Independent System *A system is history independent if (i) each system layer L^i is history independent, $i \geq 0$, and (ii) any sequence of operations $X_{A\to B}^{L^i}$ causes L^{i-1} to change from state A' to B', where $L_A^i \to L_{A'}^{i-1}$, $L_B^i \to L_{B'}^{i-1}$ and $i > 0$.*

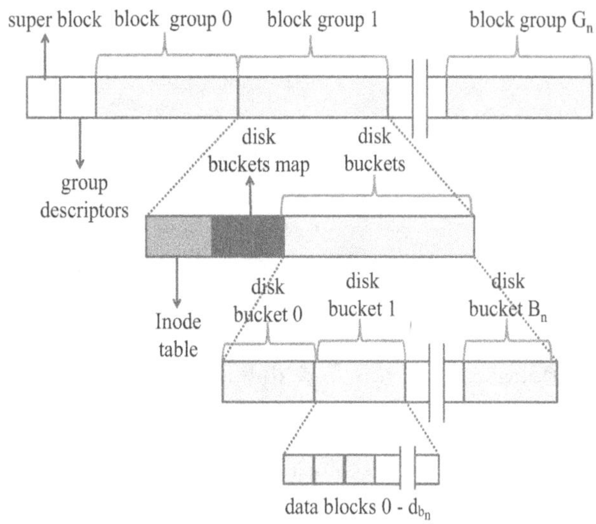

Figure 4: *HIFS* disk layout. Key parameters: $G_n \leftarrow$ number of block groups, $B_n \leftarrow$ number of disk buckets per block group, $d_s \leftarrow$ Data block size in bytes, $d_{b_n} \leftarrow$ number of data blocks per disk bucket.

4. ARCHITECTURE

4.1 Overview

The goals of the *HIFS* design are three-fold. (a) For any given set of files, the layout of their contents (including file and system meta-data) on disk are in a canonical form which is independent of the sequence of file operations, thus being history independent as per the definition 1. (b) Despite history independent layouts on disk, data locality is preserved. (c) The canonical layouts are customizable to suit a wide range of application requirements.

HIFS closely resembles existing Linux file systems such as Ext2 [3], exposing the exact same API and utilizing a similar disk structure (Figure 4). The key differences that give it history independent characteristics are the use of new locality-preserving history independent data structures for all file system meta-data (e.g., the inode table, Section 4.5.3) and the fact that the allocation of free disk blocks to files is not based on history. Hence *HIFS* does not use indirect and double indirect blocks to map file blocks to disk blocks. Instead, the entire data blocks section on disk is managed as a history independent data structure to allocate blocks to files (Section 4.5.1).

In the following sections we detail. Space constraints prevent too much in-depth detail on each operation. Instead we focus more on the features that specifically give HIFS its history independent characteristics.

4.2 History Independent Hash Table [5]

The key feature of *HIFS* is the replacement of all file system disk structures with history independent versions that we then endow with data locality preservation properties. The data structure of choice here is the history independent hash table in [5]. Hence, first we describe the hash table construction and in subsequent sections illustrate its use in various *HIFS* components.

The hash table in [5] is based on the stable matching property of the *Gale-Shapley Stable Marriage* algorithm [10] detailed in the following.

Stable Marriage Algorithm. Let M and W be a set of men and women respectively, $|M| = |W| = n$. Also, let each man in M rank all women in W as per his set of preferences. Similarly, each women in W ranks all men in M.

The goal of the stable marriage algorithm is to create n matchings (m, w) where $m \in M$ and $w \in W$ s.t no two pairs (m_i, w_j), (m_k, w_l) $(i \neq k, j \neq l)$ exist where (a) m_i ranks w_l higher than w_j and (b) w_l ranks m_i higher than m_k. If no such pairings exists then all matchings are considered stable.

The algorithm works as follows. In each round, a man m proposes to one woman at a time based on his ranking of W. If a woman w being proposed to is un-matched then a new match (m, w) is created. If the woman w is already matched to some other man m' then one of the following occurs. (a) if w ranks m higher than m' then the match (m', w) is broken and a new match (m, w) is created, or (b) if w ranks m lower than m', then m proposes to the next woman based on his rankings. The algorithm terminates when all men are matched.

[10] shows that if all the men propose in decreasing order of their preferences (ranks) then the resulting stable matching is unique. This holds even if the selection of a man m (who gets to propose) in each round is arbitrary.

History Independent Hash Table. [5] then uses the above property of the Stable Marriage algorithm to construct a history independent hash table as follows. (1) The set of keys to be inserted in to the table are considered as the set of men. (2) The set of hash table buckets are considered as the set of women. (3) Each key has an ordered preference of buckets and vice versa. (4) The preference order of each key is the order in which the buckets are probed for insertion, deletion and search. (5) In case of a collision between two keys, the key which ranks higher on the bucket's preference takes the slot. The lower ranked key is relocated to the next bucket in its preference list.

(1) - (5) ensure that the layout of keys in the hash table is the same irrespective of the sequence of key insertions and deletions, thereby making it history independent [5].

4.3 Key Insights

A simple replacement of all file system structures with the above history independent hash table will suffice to yield a history independent layout of files on disk. However, this neither preserves data locality nor gives the flexibility to choose different layouts based on application characteristics, both of which are key goals in the design of *HIFS*. Then a key observation in this context is the following. In the Stable Marriage algorithm each man in M can rank the n women in W in $n!$ ways, and vice-versa. Hence, several set of preferences from keys to buckets and buckets to keys are possible, each resulting in a distinct hash table instance. Therefore, by changing the preference order of keys and buckets we can control the layout of keys within the hash table.

The re-ordering of preferences leads to the realization that we can rewrite the algorithms in [5] to enable easy-custom selection of history independent layouts with minimal modifications. For this, we categorize the hash table operations in two Procedure Sets, a *generic* set and a *customizable* set. The generic procedures implement the overall search, insert and delete operations, and can be used unaltered for all scenarios. The customizable procedures determine the specific key and bucket preferences thereby governing the resultant hash table layouts.

Procedure Set 1 History Independent Hash Table

Procedure: INSERT
Desc: insert the given key in to the hash table.
Input: Tables $H^{0-m}[n]$, key k

```
<i,r> ← GET_MOST_PREFERRED_BUCKET(k)
c ← 0
while c < (n * (m + 1)) do
    if H^r[i] is null then
        H^r[i] ← k
        return <i,r>
    if BUCKET_PREFERS(i, r, k, H^r[i]) then
        SWAP(k, H^r[i])
    <i,r> ← GET_NEXT_BUCKET(k, i, r)
    c ← c + 1
return <null, null>   {tables are full}
```

Procedure: SEARCH
Desc: search for the given key in the hash table.
Input: Tables $H^{0-m}[n]$, key k

```
<i,r> ← GET_MOST_PREFERRED_BUCKET(k)
c ← 0
while c < (n * (m + 1)) AND H^r[i] is not null do
    if k == H^r[i] then
        return <i,r>   {key found at H^r[i]}
    <i,r> ← GET_NEXT_BUCKET(k, i, r)
    c ← c + 1
return <null, null>   {key not found}
```

Procedure: DELETE
Desc: delete the given key from the hash table.
Input: Tables $H^{0-m}[n]$, key k

```
<i,r> ← SEARCH(k)
while i is not null AND H^r[i] is not null do
    <j,s> ← GET_NEXT_BUCKET(k, i, r)
    if H^s[j] is not null AND KEY_PREFERS(
    H^s[j], i, j, r, s) then
        H^r[i] ← H^s[j], k ← H^s[j], i ← j, r ← s
```

The generic procedures include INSERT, SEARCH and DELETE, listed in Procedure Set 1. These in turn use the customizable procedures, which include GET_MOST_ PREFERRED_BUCKET, GET_NEXT_BUCKET, BUCKET_PR EFERS and KEY_PREFERS. We list the scenario specific customizable procedures later in Sections 4.5.1 and 4.5.2 while discussing file system operations.

In short, this new procedure classification and rewrite enables new distinct history independent layouts for the same data set through modifications to the customizable procedures. Moreover, these modifications can now be targeted to maximize locality or to favor other application characteristics, e.g., read-only, sequential access etc. (Section 4.5.1).

4.4 Disk Layout

Not unlike Ext2 [3] *HIFS* divides the disk into block groups, each with its own inode table, map and data blocks. The super block contains information about the overall file system (e.g., number of block groups, disk block size etc.), and the individual group descriptors describe their respective block groups (e.g., inode table size, location of the disk buckets map etc.). Parameters affecting the disk layout (Figure 4) can be set up at file system creation time. The superblock and group descriptors have fixed sizes and occupy the same locations on disk independent of file contents. Hence, no special history independent designs are needed for them. The disk bucket maps and the inode tables however, play a critical role in history independent file storage, and we discuss them in detail below.

Procedure Set 2 Customizable Procedures for Case A (Block Group Locality) from Section 4.5.1

Procedure: GDB
Desc: get the logical file bucket number from file offset.
Input: file offset $f_o : f_o \in \mathbb{N}$

```
return (⌊⌊f_o / d_s⌋ / d_{b_n}⌋)
```

Procedure: GET_MOST_PREFERRED_BUCKET
Input: key k : k = {file path f_p, file offset f_o}

```
return <h(f_p||GDB(f_o)) mod B_n, h(f_p) mod G_n>
```

Procedure: GET_NEXT_BUCKET
Input: key k : $\{f_p, f_o\}$, bucket i, block group r : $(i, r) \in \mathbb{N}$

```
i ← (i + 1) mod B_n
if i == (h(f_p||GDB(f_o)) mod B_n) then
    r ← (r + 1) mod G_n, i ← h(f_p||GDB(f_o)) mod B_n
return <i,r>
```

Procedure: BUCKET_PREFERS
Input: bucket i, block group r : (i,r) $\in \mathbb{N}$, key a : $\{f_{p_a}, f_{o_a}\}$, key b : $\{f_{p_b}, f_{o_b}\}$

```
return h(f_{p_a}||GDB(f_{o_a})) > h(f_{p_b}||GDB(f_{o_b}))
```

Procedure: KEY_PREFERS
Input: key k : $\{f_p, f_o\}$, bucket i, bucket j, block group r, block group s : (i,j,r,s) $\in \mathbb{N}$

```
if r <> s then
    return ((h(f_p) mod G_n) - r + G_n) mod G_n < ((h(f_p)
    mod G_n) - s + G_n) mod G_n
return ((h(f_p||GDB(f_o)) mod B_n) - i + B_n) mod B_n <
((h(f_p||GDB(f_o)) mod B_n) - j + B_n) mod B_n
```

4.5 File Storage

Disk Buckets. File data is stored in blocks on disk. These are grouped into units, where each unit consists of a fixed number of (multiple) data blocks. Each such unit is termed as a disk bucket (Figure 4). Although read and write operations access individual data blocks, space is allocated to files in multiples of disk buckets.

Disk Buckets Map. *HIFS* relies on a special region in each block group referred to as the disk buckets map for allocation of new disk buckets to files and for locating disk blocks in read and write operations. Each entry within the disk buckets map has a one-one mapping to the corresponding disk bucket within that block group (Figure 4). The entry in the map contains meta-data about the corresponding disk bucket (e.g., whether the bucket is free or occupied).

All file system operations first locate the target entry in the disk buckets map and only then perform the actual read or write operation on the corresponding disk bucket. This avoids the need to perform expensive seek operations on actual file contents to locate data blocks. Also, the relative smaller size of the maps means that they are often cached in memory for faster access.

4.5.1 History Independent Layouts

Existing file systems such as Ext2 [3] maintain a list of allocated blocks within the file inode which renders the disk space allocation history dependent. *HIFS* however, does not rely on such lists; instead location of data blocks are

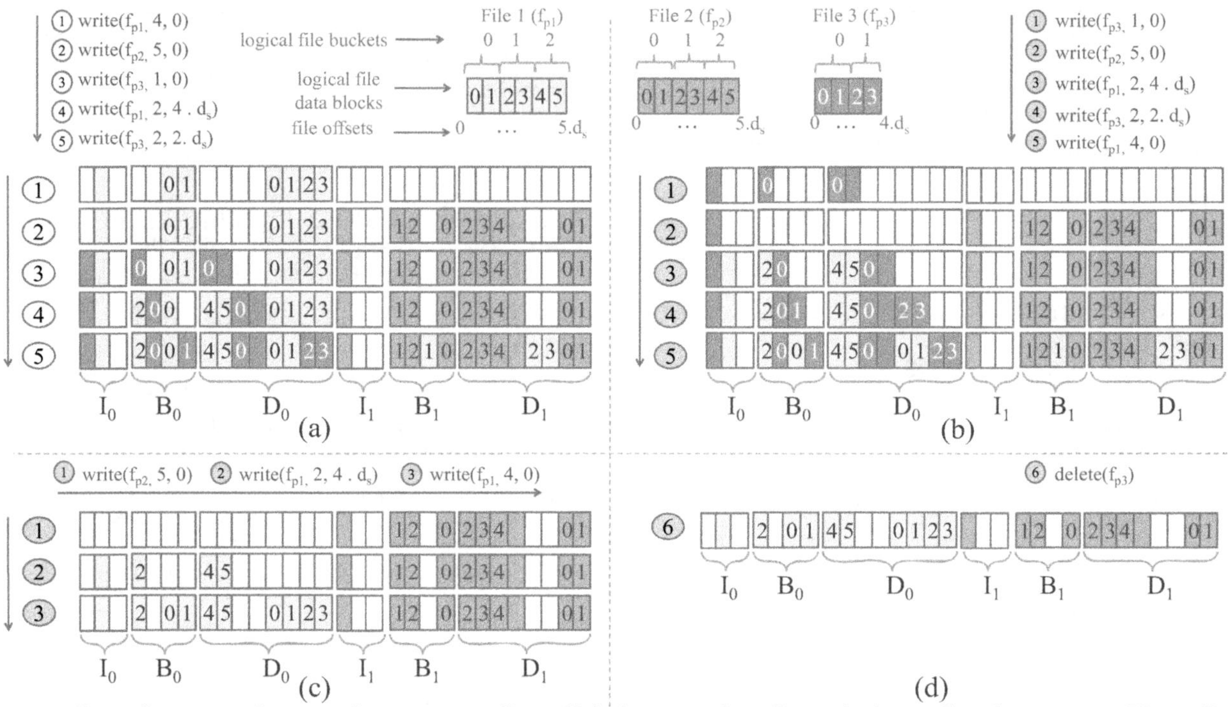

Figure 5: Sample executions and corresponding disk layouts for Case A from Section 4.5.1. Here $G_n = 2$, $B_n = 4$, $d_{b_n} = 2$. I_i, B_i and D_i denote the inode table, disk buckets map, and the disk blocks respectively of block group i. Also, $h(f_{p1}) = 2$, $h(f_{p2}) = 3$ and $h(f_{p3}) = 4$. $write(f_p, f_d, f_o)$ represents a write operation of f_d blocks on file f_p at offset f_o. The disk blocks occupied by files with paths f_{p1}, f_{p2} and f_{p3} are shaded with their respective colors. Blocks that are not shaded indicate free blocks. The number within a block represents the data block number of the corresponding file.

derived directly from file attributes. Thus, for each read or write operation the location of data blocks on disk are determined only by the parameters to the current operation and do not depend on any past operation. To this end, the disk bucket maps from all block groups are collectively treated as a single history independent hash table. Hash table keys are derived from file attributes such as the file paths and read-write offsets. The entries in the maps are themselves the hash table buckets.

As discussed in Section 4.3, by altering the derivation of keys and the keys↔buckets preference sets we can attain customized layouts of the hash table to suit different requirements. Hence, file system operations use the generic hash table procedures from Procedure Set 1 to locate free blocks for allocation or to find existing blocks for reading or writing. Different history independent layouts of file contents on disk are realized solely by altering the customizable Procedure Set. Thus, the file system operations (read, write, mkdir etc) have implementations independent of the underlying history independent layouts, which in turn can be designed as needed, by specific customizable procedure implementations. To illustrate this, the actual file system write operation is included in Procedure Set 6 (Appendix).

We now describe a specific history independent layout scenario in detail and then briefly discuss others.

Case A: Block Group Locality. For data locality and overall efficiency, it is highly desirable that data blocks of the same file are located close together on disk, ideally within the same block group. To realize this scenario we tailor the customizable procedures as shown in Procedure Set 2. All other generic history independent hash table procedures from set 1, and the generic file system operations are unchanged.

To understand this better, consider Figure 5 which gives a detailed example for a set of three files. Each of Figures 5(a)-5(d) list a sequence of file system operations and depict the resultant disk layout (including files meta-data and content) at the end of each operation. Note that although the sequence of operations in Figures 5(a) and 5(b) differ, the resultant disk layouts at the end of either operation sequence are exactly the same (i.e., canonical).

To achieve canonical disk layouts the file system operations are translated in to hash table operations as follows: (a) Keys are derived from the full file path f_p and the read or write offset f_o. (b) The hash table buckets are the disk buckets map entries. (c) Key preferences are set such that each key first prefers all buckets from one specific block group, in a fixed order. Then, buckets from the next adjacent block group and so on. (d) Finally, buckets simply prefer keys with higher numerical values.

To give an intuition of how (a) - (d) preserve locality and yet give history independent layouts, consider the file system write operation (Procedure Set 6 in Appendix). The write operation first needs to locate the correct entry in the disk buckets maps. Once this entry is located it will perform the actual write on the corresponding disk bucket. Since the disk buckets maps from all block groups are treated as a single history independent hash table locating the correct buckets map entry is equivalent to finding the corresponding hash table bucket. Hence, locating the disk buckets map entry requires probing of the disk buckets maps. The probe order is exactly what is determined by the key preferences.

Locality. The probe order for any write operation always starts with the most preferred bucket as determined by the procedure GET_MOST_PREFERRED_BUCKET (Procedure Set 2). For a given file f_p, the block group of the most preferred bucket for all its write operations are derived only from the file path's hash $h(f_p)$ (line 1, second return parameter). Hence, all write operations of the same file begin their probing from the same block group independent of their target file offsets. Note that the probing for two write operations that target different offsets may start from two different buckets, but both buckets will be located within the same block group.

Moreover, subsequent buckets in the probing of the disk buckets map are determined using the GET_NEXT_BUCKET procedure which ensures that all buckets in the current selected block group are probed (line 1) before moving to the next adjacent block group (lines 2-4). Hence, data blocks of the same file prefer to be located in the same block group, preserving locality.

History Independence. For each bucket map entry in the probe sequence, the following two cases are possible.

(a) The bucket map entry is free. The data is written to the corresponding disk bucket and the key is stored in the bucket map entry, which is also marked as occupied.

(b) The bucket map entry is occupied by a previous write. A collision has occurred. Now it is exactly the collision resolution process that gives HIFS its history independence. To clarify, let w_1 and w_2 be two write operations on files f_{p_1} and f_{p_2} respectively. Also let w_1 target offset f_{o_1} of f_{p_1} and w_2 target offset f_{o_2} of f_{p_2}. Hence the keys for w_1 and w_2 for probing the disk bucket maps are $h(f_{p_1}||\text{GDB}(f_{o_1}))$ and $h(f_{p_2}||\text{GDB}(f_{o_2}))$ respectively (procedure GET_NEXT_BUCKET, line 2). Also, let $h(f_{p_1}||\text{GDB}\ (f_{o_1})) > h(f_{p_2}||\text{GDB}(f_{o_2}))$. Finally, suppose that the keys for both w_1 and w_2 prefer the same entry in the disk bucket map of the same block group and hence result in a collision. Now, there are two possible write sequences for w_1 and w_2. (i) w_1 *occurs before* w_2*:* Here, when w_2 is executing, the bucket is already occupied by the key of w_1. Also since $h(f_{p_1}||\text{GDB}(f_{o_1})) > h(f_{p_2}||\text{GDB}(f_{o_2}))$ the bucket prefers key of w_1 to that of w_2, as per procedure BUCKET_PREFERS (line 1). Hence, w_2 looks to the next bucket in its key's preference list and the bucket map entry remains unchanged. (ii) w_2 *occurs before* w_1*:* Here, the bucket entry is already occupied by the key of w_2 when w_1 is executing. But the bucket instead prefers the key of w_1 over that of w_2. Hence, the key of w_2 is now evicted from the bucket entry and is replaced by w_1's key. The key of w_2 is relocated to a new bucket based on its preference list and probe order. Also in this case, the data written by w_1 is now placed in the corresponding disk bucket, while the data previously written by w_2 is moved to the new disk bucket corresponding to the new bucket map entry determined for its key's relocation.

Figure 5 lists several examples of the two cases (i) and (ii) from above. Specifically, consider execution of operation 5 of Figure 5(b). Here, the write of data blocks zero and one of file f_{p_1} replaces and relocates the data blocks two and three of f_{p_3} which were previously written by operation 4.

As a result of (a) and (b), the bucket entry and hence the corresponding disk bucket contents are the same irrespective of the write sequence. Generalizing this example gives the following. For a given set of files F, and any operation sequence that creates F, a particular offset of a file f in F, is always stored at the same location on disk. That is, the disk layouts are history independent as per definition 1.

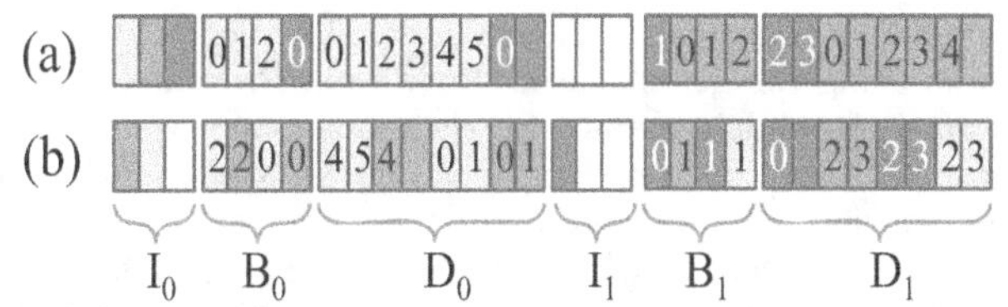

Figure 6: *HIFS* disk layouts for operation sequences of Figure 5. (a) Case B ← Complete Sequential and (b) Case C ← External Parameters, from Section 4.5.2. Also, $h(user(f_{p_1}))$ = 2, $h(user(f_{p_2}))$ = 4 and $h(user(f_{p_3}))$ = 3.

4.5.2 *Customizing History Independence*

The above description (Case A) and the Procedure Set 2 provide just one specific scheme for a history independent disk layout for a given set of files. Different applications may prefer differing layouts based on their specific characteristics. Here we list additional examples that can be achieved using different implementations of the customizable procedures. The relevant customizable procedures for these scenarios are listed in Procedure Sets 3 and 4 (Appendix).

Case B: Completely Sequential. Applications that have very few writes as compared to read operations (e.g., databases for data mining) can greatly benefit if the entire file is stored sequentially on disk, giving maximal locality. To realize this, only the key and bucket preferences need to be modified. The keys of all write operations prefer buckets within the same block group as in case A above. However, the probe sequence starts with the first bucket in the block group and probes linearly henceforth. The buckets in turn prefer blocks in increasing order of file offsets.

Case C: External Parameters. Many applications access multiple files simultaneously [14]. I/O performance of such applications can be greatly enhanced if the files are located close together on disk. For example, files created by a single user/process are located in adjacency within the same block group. Again, this scenario can be realized with very minimal changes. In fact, the only change required is that key's preferences for block groups are now based on external (not file system related) parameters such as the user (procedure set 4, Appendix).

Figure 6 gives the resultant layouts for both cases B and C after the execution of operations from Figures 5(a) and 5(b). Again, note that the resultant layouts will be the same for both cases irrespective of the operation sequence.

Several other distributions are possible. Individual cases can also be combined to create more complex ones. For example, cases B and C can be combined to have a distribution wherein files from the same user are located adjacently on disk with each file laid out sequentially. Any new set of customizable procedures only needs to ensure that the key↔buckets preferences are unambiguous, that is, no key should prefer any two buckets equally and vice-versa. In Section 4.6, we show that as long as this condition is met the resulting distribution will be history independent.

4.5.3 *Inode Table*

Each inode is of fixed size and contains file meta-data such as file type, access rights, file size etc. Each inode table contains a fixed number of inode entries. Inodes are allocated to files at creation time.

Similar to the disk buckets maps, the inode tables from all block groups are collectively treated as a single history independent hash table. Then, inode allocation and search is done using the generic procedures from Procedure Set 1. History independent layouts for the inode tables are also determined by the customizable procedures. One such set of inode-specific customizable procedures are listed in Procedure Set 5 (Appendix). Here the file inode is located in the same block group as that preferred by the file data blocks. The intuition and reasoning for history independence is similar to that described for case A above.

4.5.4 File delete, rename etc

HIFS also hides all evidence of a file delete operation. To illustrate, consider the sample executions and disk layouts from Figures 5(c) and 5(d). Figure 5(c) shows the resulting layouts of a sequence of write-only operations. Figure 5(d) shows the layout after execution of all operations of 5(b) plus the delete operation on file f_{p_3}. Both sequences create the exact same set of files. Note how the disk layout after the delete operation (Figure 5(d)) is exactly the same as the layout after the write-only sequence of Figure 5(c). This is because *HIFS* relocates data blocks on delete to their more preferred locations (procedure DELETE in Set 1). For example, in Figure 5(d) blocks 2 and 3 of file f_{p_1} are relocated to more preferred locations when file f_{p_3} is deleted (by operation 6). Overall, when a file is deleted, the resultant disk layout carries no traces of the delete operation, as if the file was never created in the first place.

The file delete is realized by execution of the delete procedure from Set 1 for each disk bucket allocated to the file. This makes a delete operation equivalent (cost-wise) to a write of the entire file. A rename or move operation for a particular file is a delete of each allocated disk bucket followed by a write (of the same bucket) with the new path.

4.6 Proofs of History Independence

Let K denote the set of keys and β denote the buckets within the hash table. Also, let $k.pref(b)$ denote bucket b's position on key k's preference list ($k \in K$ and $b \in \beta$) where, lower value of $k.pref$ indicates higher preference. Then, we have the following definition

DEFINITION 3. Un-ambiguous Preferences
A set of preferences from $K \rightarrow \beta$ and $\beta \rightarrow K$ are un-ambiguous *if*
(a) $\forall k \in K, \nexists (b_i, b_j) \in \beta, i \neq j$ *s.t.* $k.pref(b_i) - k.pref(b_j)$ *and*
(b) $\forall b \in \beta, \nexists (k_i, k_j) \in K, i \neq j$ *s.t.* $b.pref(k_i) = b.pref(k_j)$.

THEOREM 1. *The customizable procedures listed in Procedure Set 2 result in a history independent hash table with unique representation.*

PROOF. The Gale-Shapley Stable Marriage algorithm [10] has shown that if (a) men propose in decreasing order of their preference, and (b) all preferences are un-ambiguous, then the resulting stable matching is unique. [5] then showed that the hash table discussed in Section 4.2 satisfies both (a) and (b). They then proved that as a result the distribution of keys in the hash table is canonical and thus history independent. Thus, distributions from any set of customizable procedures are history independent if they exhibit the above two properties.

We now detail this for the customizable procedures in Procedure Set 2 applicable to case A (Block Group Locality) from Section 4.5.1.

(a) Proposal Order. Each time a new key is inserted in to the hash table, the first attempt is to place the key in its most preferred bucket i.e. bucket b where $k.pref(b)$ is minimum (see procedure INSERT in set 1 which foremost calls GET_MOST_PREFERRED_BUCKET in set 2). Each new bucket in the probe sequence is selected by the procedure GET_NEXT_BUCKET which given a bucket b_i finds the bucket b_j such that $\nexists\, b_l$ where $k.pref(b_i) < k.pref(b_l) < k.pref(b_j)$. In other words b_j is always the next preferred bucket on key k's preference list. Thus analogous to men in the stable marriage algorithm the matching of keys to buckets is attempted in decreasing order of key preferences.
(b) Un-ambiguous preferences. A bucket's preference between two keys is resolved in BUCKET_ PREFERS using the condition $h(f_{p_a}||\text{GDB}(f_{o_a})) > h(f_{p_b}||\text{GDB}(f_{o_b}))$. Hence, if the two values compared above are always distinct then the comparison is un-ambiguous. We note that for any given set of files F the combination of the file path and the logical file bucket number is unique, that is, $\forall f \in F$, $<f_p, \text{GDB}(f_o)>$ is unique. Hence, the hash value $h(f_p||\text{GDB}(f_o))$ is unique. The proof then reduces to collision resistance of the hash function (e.g., SHA [9]).

Similarly, a key's preference amongst two buckets is resolved by the procedure KEY_PREFERS. Here, firstly if the two buckets belong to separate block groups (line 1) then the key simply prefers the bucket in the block group with the lower index (line 2). Hence, this condition is un-ambiguous. If the two buckets are in the same block group, then the key prefers the bucket closer to its most preferred bucket in that block group (line 3). Again, since the comparison is based on the hash of the unique combination $<f_p, \text{GDB}(f_o)>$ the proof reduces to collision resistance of the hash function. □

Similar proofs exist for the customizable procedures of cases B and C from Section 4.5.2, and for the inode table.

5. DISCUSSION

Data Shredding. When an element is deleted from a history independent table it is imperative that proper data shredding is employed, that is, the data at the location is made irrecoverable (e.g., by overwriting [21]). Any residual data artifacts can compromise the history of operations. Hence, *HIFS* does not mark hash table entries as deleted but immediately performs an overwrite on each delete operation. This applies to all history independent disk structures (inode table, disk bucket maps) and to the file data blocks.
Temporal Meta-data. File systems typically maintain temporal meta-data such as modification times (for files and directories) which are then made available to applications. For certain composite applications it may be desired that the history of operations across files is also private. *HIFS* can optionally be configured to provide such functionality, which it does by (a) not maintaining any temporal meta-data for files, and (b) using history independent directories.

A directory file consists of a set of directory entries, one entry for each file in that directory. If cross-file history independence is desired then *HIFS* maintains the contents of each directory file in a history independent manner. For this, no additional data structures are employed, instead the directory entries are always stored sorted. Since a simple sorted list is history independent [20] the sorting of directory contents suffices.

System failure and Recovery. File system operations access multiple disk data structures which cannot all be updated simultaneously. Hence, in case of an inopportune system failure, the history independence related to certain records can be violated. For example, consider a file delete operation that accesses file system data structures in the following sequence – (a) deletes file inode entry from the inode table, (b) deletes an entry from the disk buckets map, and (c) deletes file contents from the corresponding disk bucket. Now, suppose that a system failure occurs after step (b) and an adversary gains access to the disk layout at this exact moment. By examining the disk buckets map and the data blocks on disk, the adversary can deduce that the last operation was a delete.

Existing recovery mechanisms such as journaling can be utilized to efficiently restore system consistency after a failure. However, we note that this breaks history independence since the adversary can potentially gain information about the recent operations. In case of journaling data can reside on disk without the associated updated meta-data (or vice versa). Hence data residing on disk with stale or missing meta-data is likely to be identified as recently written. Designing efficient recovery mechanisms that completely preserve history independence remains an open problem.

In-Memory History Independence. *HIFS* protects history independence only for data residing on disk. It does not target in-memory structures such as the file system cache.

Although the need for a history independent memory allocator for in-memory data structures has been voiced [11], we posit that extension of history independence to data in memory requires further careful examination. Simply replacing in-memory caches with history independent versions will not suffice. Firstly, an in-memory system cache cannot treat each disk block independently, but instead needs to maintain inter-block associations. For example, it must avoid scenarios such as the disk buckets map is written to disk but the modified file data blocks still reside in the cache for a significant time interval after. This can potentially reveal to an adversary details about the last file operation performed. Further, the relationships between in-memory data and its disk copies in a history independent context need to be investigated. This includes not just file system cache and data structures but also other system components such as the operating system kernel and low level system caches.

Storage Media. HIFS does not provide history independence if deployed (as is) on top of devices that manage their own internal block placement, such as SSDs, due to the wear-leveling mechanisms. The flash firmware's relocation of data blocks (wear leveling) is aimed to increase the life span of the drive. This essential functionality of the flash controller directly contradicts with history independence, since history independence requires fixed layouts. As of today we do not know how to reconcile both. Hence in HIFS we only focus on hard disk devices.

6. EXPERIMENTS

We benchmarked HIFS to understand the impact of history independence on performance.

Platform. All experiments were conducted on servers with 8 Intel i7 CPUs at 3.4GHz, 16GB RAM, and kernel v3.2.0-37. The storage devices of choice are Hitachi HDS72302 SCSI drives. The benchmark tool used is Filebench [1].

Parameter	Database profile	Web Server profile
File system size	100 GB	10 GB
Mean file size	1 GB	512 KB
No. of files	$L \cdot 100$	$(L \cdot 10) \cdot 2^{11}$
Disk block size (d_s)	4 KB	4 KB
No. of block groups (G_n)	8	24
Disk blocks / bucket (d_{b_n})	5120	128
Inode size	281 bytes	281 bytes
IO Size	32KB	512KB

Table 1: Experimental parameters. L ← File System Load factor.

Implementation. *HIFS* is implemented as a C++ based user-space Fuse [2] file system. All data structures, including customizable history independence were written from scratch. The entire HIFS code is ≈10K LOC.

Measurements. Each test run commences with an empty file system, then creates and writes new files to storage. The number of files stored is increased until the file system is 90% full. Throughputs are measured at specific load factors (disk space utilization) ranging from 10% to 90%. The writes and subsequent read operations were separated by a complete clearing of the system cache. This was done to minimize the effect of caching since file system cache is not yet designed to be history independent.

6.1 Results

Database Profile. Databases typically feature access to a few large files with random access patterns. To simulate such a profile we evaluate random reads and writes on multiple files with a mean file size of 1 GB. The number of files is varied from 10 to 90 to reflect the file system load factor. Table 1 summarizes all file system parameters while Figure 7(a) shows the results.

As detailed in Section 4.5.1, the allocation of a new disk bucket to a file in response to a write request potentially causes the displacement of existing data of other files due to the history independent collision resolution. The number of such collisions increases with the load factor. For load factors beyond 60% a sharp decrease in throughputs is observed for random writes. Read operations however, do not modify data, hence are not affected by collisions, in turn showing less throughput declines with load factors. Also, since the customizable procedures for case A (Block Group Locality, Section 4.5.1) are employed here, data locality is preserved. Write operations incur the overheads to maintain this locality while reads benefit from it.

The tradeoff between write and read performance is further evident from Figure 7(b) which shows the throughputs when the customizable procedures for case B (Complete Sequential, Section 4.5.1) are employed, that is, each file is laid out sequentially on disk. Here, read operations show a 13% average increase in throughput for sequential reads and 17% for random reads as compared to Case A (Figure 7(a)). To maintain this higher locality, write throughputs incur an average decline of 90% compared to Case A. All the above hold under history independence assurances.

Web Server Profile. Web servers are characterized by accesses to a large number of very small files [22]. To model this, we use use a mean file size of 512 KB, but increase the number of files up to ≈18,500 for a load factor of 90%. Refer to Table 1 for a full parameter list. The read and

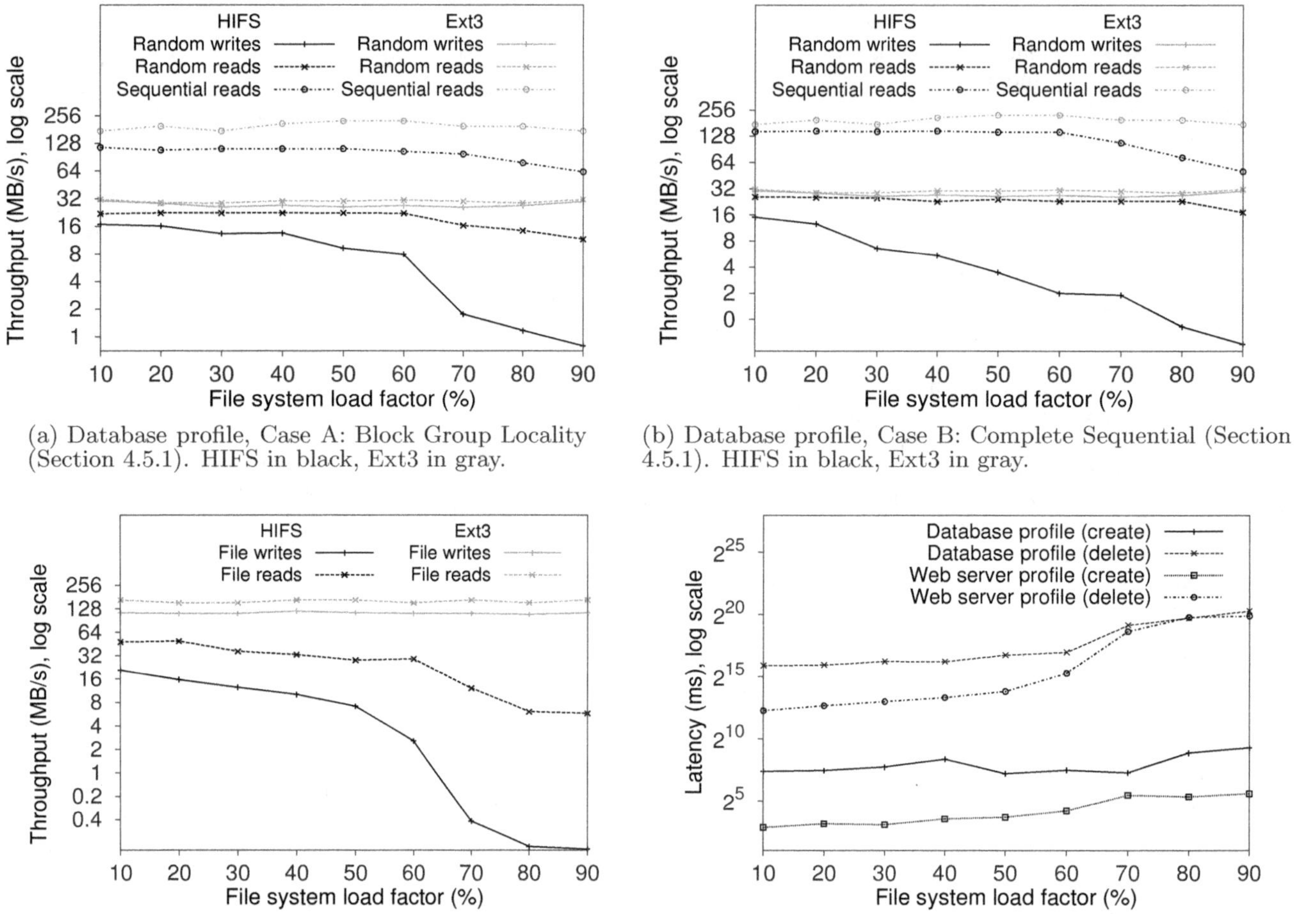

(a) Database profile, Case A: Block Group Locality (Section 4.5.1). HIFS in black, Ext3 in gray.

(b) Database profile, Case B: Complete Sequential (Section 4.5.1). HIFS in black, Ext3 in gray.

(c) Web Server profile, Case A: Block Group Locality (Section 4.5.1). HIFS in black, Ext3 in gray.

(d) HIFS latencies for file create and delete operations for Case A: Block Group Locality from Section 4.5.1.

Figure 7: HIFS throughputs and latencies. A load factor of L indicates that the file system is L% full.

write operations access entire files. Figure 7(c) summarizes the results for this profile.

File create and delete operations. Figure 7(d) shows the latencies of file create and delete operations.

A create operation involves locating a free inode for the new file, writing the file meta-data to the inode table, locating the parent directory and writing the file entry in to the directory. The writes to the inode table and to the directory are both history independent. Since the inode table also employs a history independent hash table to store individual inode entries (Section 4.5.3), the latency increases gradually with the load factor.

As discussed in Section 4.5.4 a file delete is equivalent to a write of the entire file in order to preserve history independence. As a result deletes have high latencies.

Overhead of history independence. Figures 7(a) and 7(c) also illustrate the throughputs for the Ext3 file system. For consistent comparisons all Ext3 file system operations are also routed via Fuse.

The performance of HIFS for read operations is comparable to read throughputs of Ext3 for load factors up to 70%. The write operations sustain significant overheads especially for higher load factors. This is again because once the write operations provide history independence while preserving locality, the reads incur significantly lower seek operations on the storage medium and are hence perform efficiently.

For the web server profile the overhead of history independence is higher even for reads. This is because each operation accesses the entire file at once and although the locality of data blocks withing a file is maintained the files themselves are distributed over the entire disk.

6.2 Summary and Analysis

HIFS employs history independent hash tables for all its data structures including file meta-data and data blocks. The performance of hash tables in turn depends on their load factor. In fact, the asymptotic performance per operation of the history independent hash table employed is $O(1/(1-\alpha)^3)$ [5], showing expected exponential decrease in performance with increasing load factor α. Hence, for load factors >60% the performance degrade for writes is significant. The same behavior is clearly evident in the experimental results for HIFS (Figures 7(a)-7(d)).

To remove these fundamental limitations on performance the following directions are most promising.

(1) Designing new history independent data structures specifically suited to secondary storage (current designs target only memory).

(2) Exploring trade-offs by lowering the degree of history independence, for example, batching of write operations. Delaying write operations will help reduce the total number of disk seeks and writes per operation.

Data Structure	Year	Ops	Runtime
2-3 Tree [16]	1997	I,L,D	$O(\log N)$
Hash Table [20]	2001	I,L	$O(log(1/(1-\alpha)))$
Hash Table [5]	2007	I,L,D	$O(1/(1-\alpha)^3)$
Ordered Dictionary [5]	2007	I,P,D	$O(\log\log N)$
Order Maintenance [5]	2007	I,C,D	$O(1)$
Hash Table [19]	2008	I,L,D	I,D $\rightarrow O(\log N)$ S $\rightarrow O(1)$
B-Treaps [12]	2009	I,D,R	$O(log_B N)$
B-SkipList [13]	2010	I,D,R	$O(log_B N)$
R-Trees [23]	2012	I,D,R	n/a

Table 2: Summary of history independent data structures. $\alpha \leftarrow$ load factor, $N \leftarrow$ number of keys, $B \leftarrow$ block transfer size. Also, I : insert, L : lookup, D : delete, R : range, P : predecessor, C : compare.

7. RELATED WORK

Prior work has focussed on designing several history independent data structures (summarized in Table 2). These data structures have several applications including incremental signature schemes [19], privacy in voting systems [5, 17–19], performing updates without revealing intermediate states [20], debugging parallel computations [5], reconciliation of dynamic sets [19], and un-traceable deletion [4].

Write Once Storage. The data structures in Table 2 assume a re-writable storage medium. [17] designed a history independent solution for a write-once medium suitable for deployment in voting machines. The construction is based on the observation from [20] that a lexicographic ordering of elements in a list is history independent. However, write-once memories do not allow in-place sorting of elements. Instead [17] employs copy-over lists [20]. When a new element is inserted, a new list is stored while the previous list is erased. However, this requires $O(n^2)$ space to store n keys.

[17] suggests to store each new element at a random location on the write-once storage. In case of collisions, a new random location is selected. Note that although simple and space-efficient, this requires the random bits to be hidden from the adversary which may not be possible in the targeted scenario involving voting machines in poll booths. [18] improves on [17] requiring only linear storage. The key idea here is to store all elements in a global hash table and for each entry of the hash table maintain a separate copy-over list which contains only the colliding elements.

Survey Works. Various definitions of history independence are analyzed in [15], most relying on canonical representations which are shown to be necessary in achieving it. [6] analyzes the lower and upper bounds on the runtime of the heap and the queue. A summary of various data structures from Table 2 is available in [11] along with techniques to transform basic data structures such as arrays, stacks and queues into their respective history independent versions.

8. CONCLUSION

The contributions of this paper are three-fold. First, we extend the concepts of history independence from in-memory data structures to file systems. Second, we devise a practical way to achieve history independence that preserves data locality. And last, we design, implement and evaluate the first history independent file system (HIFS). HIFS guarantees truly secure deletion by providing full history independence across both file system and disk layers of the storage stack. Additionally, it preserves data locality, and provides tunable efficiency knobs to suit different application history-sensitive scenarios.

9. REFERENCES

[1] Filebench, http://linux.die.net/man/1/filebench.

[2] Filesystem in userspace, http://fuse.sourceforge.net/.

[3] R. Appleton. Kernel korner: A non-technical look inside the ext2 file system. *Linux J.*, 1997(40es), Aug. 1997.

[4] S. Bajaj and R. Sion. Ficklebase: Looking into the future to erase the past. In *Proceedings of the International Conference on Data Engineering*, 2013.

[5] G. E. Blelloch and D. Golovin. Strongly history-independent hashing with applications. In *Proceedings of IEEE Symposium on Foundations of Computer Science*, FOCS '07, pages 272–282. IEEE Computer Society, 2007.

[6] N. Buchbinder and E. Petrank. Lower and upper bounds on obtaining history independence, 2003.

[7] D. Comer. Ubiquitous b-tree. *ACM Comput. Surv.*, 11(2):121–137, June 1979.

[8] S. A. Crosby and D. S. Wallach. Super-efficient aggregating history-independent persistent authenticated dictionaries. In *Proceedings of European conference on Research in computer security*, ESORICS, pages 671–688. Springer-Verlag, 2009.

[9] P. A. DesAutels. SHA1: Secure Hash Algorithm, www.w3.org/PICS/DSig/SHA1_1_0.html. 1997.

[10] D. Gale and L. Shapley. College admissions and the stability of marriage. *American Mathematical Monthly*, 69(1):9–15, 1962.

[11] D. Golovin. *Uniquely represented data structures with applications to privacy*. PhD thesis, 2008. AAI3340637.

[12] D. Golovin. B-treaps: A uniquely represented alternative to b-trees. In *Proceedings of International Colloquium on Automata, Languages and Programming: Part I*, ICALP '09, pages 487–499. Springer-Verlag, 2009.

[13] D. Golovin. The b-skip-list: A simpler uniquely represented alternative to b-trees. *CoRR*, abs/1005.0662, 2010.

[14] T. Harter, C. Dragga, M. Vaughn, A. C. Arpaci-Dusseau, and R. H. Arpaci-Dusseau. A file is not a file: Understanding the i/o behavior of apple desktop applications. *ACM Trans. Comput. Syst.*, 30(3):10:1–10:39, Aug. 2012.

[15] J. Hartline, E. Hong, A. Mohr, E. E. Mohr, W. Pentney, and E. Rocke. Characterizing history independent data structures, 2002.

[16] D. Micciancio. An oblivious data structure and its applications to cryptography. In *In Proceedings of ACM Symposium on the Theory of Computing*, pages 456–464. ACM Press, 1997.

[17] D. Molnar, T. Kohno, N. Sastry, and D. Wagner. Tamper-evident, history-independent, subliminal-free data structures on prom storage-or-how to store ballots on a voting machine (extended abstract). In *Proceedings of IEEE Symposium on Security and Privacy*, SP '06, pages 365–370. IEEE Computer Society, 2006.

[18] T. Moran, M. Naor, and G. Segev. Deterministic history-independent strategies for storing information on write-once memories. In *Proceedings of International Colloquium on Automata, Languages and Programming*, pages 303–315. Springer, 2007.

[19] M. Naor, G. Segev, and U. Wieder. History-independent cuckoo hashing. In *Proceedings of international colloquium on Automata, Languages and Programming, Part II*, ICALP '08, pages 631–642. Springer-Verlag, 2008.

[20] M. Naor and V. Teague. Anti-persistence: History independent data structures. In *In Proceedings of ACM symposium on Theory of computing*, pages 492–501. ACM Press, 2001.

[21] J. Reardon, D. Basin, and S. Capkun. Sok: Secure data deletion. In *Proceedings of the 2013 IEEE Symposium on Security and Privacy*, SP '13, pages 301–315. IEEE Computer Society, 2013.

[22] A. S. Tanenbaum, J. N. Herder, and H. Bos. File size distribution on unix systems: then and now. *SIGOPS Oper. Syst. Rev.*, 40(1):100–104, Jan. 2006.

[23] T. Tzouramanis. History-independence: a fresh look at the case of r-trees. In *Proceedings of ACM Symposium on Applied Computing*, SAC '12, pages 7–12. ACM, 2012.

APPENDIX

A. PROCEDURE SETS

Procedure Set 3 Customizable Procedures for Case B (Complete Sequential) from Section 4.5.2

Procedure: GET_MOST_PREFERRED_BUCKET
Desc: get the top most bucket on key's preference list.
Input: key $k = \{\text{file path } f_p, \text{ file offset } f_o\}$
return $<0, h(f_p) \bmod \mathsf{G_n}>$

Procedure: GET_NEXT_BUCKET
Desc: get the next bucket on key's preference list.
Input: key $k = \{f_p, f_o\}$, bucket i, block group r
$i \leftarrow (i+1) \bmod \mathsf{B_n}$
if $i == 0$ **then**
  return $<0, (r+1) \bmod \mathsf{G_n}>$
return $<i, r>$

Procedure: BUCKET_PREFERS
Desc: find which of two keys the given bucket prefers.
Input: bucket i, block group r, key $a = \{f_{p_a}, f_{o_a}\}$, key $b = \{f_{p_b}, f_{o_b}\}$
if $f_{p_a} == f_{p_b}$ **then**
  return $\text{GDB}(f_{o_a}) < \text{GDB}(f_{o_b})$
return $h(f_{p_a}) > h(f_{p_b})$

Procedure: KEY_PREFERS
Desc: find which of two buckets the given key prefers.
Input: key $k = \{f_p, f_o\}$, bucket i, bucket j, block group r, block group s
if $r \neq s$ **then**
  return $((h(f_p) \bmod \mathsf{G_n}) - r + \mathsf{G_n}) \bmod \mathsf{G_n} < ((h(f_p) \bmod \mathsf{G_n}) - s + \mathsf{G_n}) \bmod \mathsf{G_n}$
return $i < j$

Procedure Set 4 Customizable Procedures for Case C (External parameters) from Section 4.5.2

Procedure: GET_MOST_PREFERRED_BUCKET
Input: key $k : k = \{\text{file path } f_p, \text{ file offset } f_o, \text{ user } u\}$
return $<h(f_p || \text{GDB}(f_o)) \bmod \mathsf{B_n}, h(u) \bmod \mathsf{G_n}>$

GET_NEXT_BUCKET and BUCKET_PREFERS same as in procedure set 2.

Procedure: KEY_PREFERS
Input: key $k : \{f_p, f_o, u\}$, bucket i, bucket j, block group r, block group $s : (i, j, r, s) \in \mathbb{N}$
if $r \neq s$ **then**
  return $((h(u) \bmod \mathsf{G_n}) - r + \mathsf{G_n}) \bmod \mathsf{G_n} < ((h(u) mod \mathsf{G_n}) - s + \mathsf{G_n}) \bmod \mathsf{G_n}$
return $((h(f_p || \text{GDB}(f_o)) \bmod \mathsf{B_n}) - i + \mathsf{B_n}) \bmod \mathsf{B_n} < ((h(f_p || \text{GDB}(f_o)) \bmod \mathsf{B_n}) - j + \mathsf{B_n}) \bmod \mathsf{B_n}$

Procedure Set 5 Inode Table Customizable Procedures

Procedure: GET_MOST_PREFERRED_BUCKET
Input: key $k = $ file path f_p
return $<h(f_p) \bmod \mathsf{I_n}, h(f_p) \bmod \mathsf{G_n}>$

Procedure: GET_NEXT_BUCKET
Input: key $k = f_p$, bucket i, block group r
$i \leftarrow (i+1) \bmod \mathsf{I_n}$
if $i == (h(f_p) \bmod \mathsf{I_n})$ **then**
  $r \leftarrow (r+1) \bmod \mathsf{G_n}$, $i \leftarrow h(f_p) \bmod \mathsf{I_n}$
return $<i, r>$

Procedure: BUCKET_PREFERS
Input: bucket i, block group r, key $a = f_{p_a}$, key $b = f_{p_b}$
return $h(f_{p_a}) > h(f_{p_b})$

Procedure: KEY_PREFERS
Input: key $k = f_p$, bucket i, bucket j, block group r, block group s
if $r \neq s$ **then**
  return $((h(f_p) \bmod \mathsf{G_n}) - r + \mathsf{G_n}) \bmod \mathsf{G_n} < ((h(f_p) \bmod \mathsf{G_n}) - s + \mathsf{G_n}) \bmod \mathsf{G_n}$
return $((h(f_p) \bmod \mathsf{I_n}) - i + \mathsf{I_n}) \bmod \mathsf{I_n} < ((h(f_p) \bmod \mathsf{I_n}) - j + \mathsf{I_n}) \bmod \mathsf{I_n}$

Procedure Set 6 *HIFS* write operation

Procedure: write
Input: file path f_p, file offset f_o, data ∂, data length ∂_l $\mathsf{I_t^{G_n}}$: Inode tables, $\mathsf{B_t^{G_n}}$: Disk Bucket Maps, $\mathsf{GD_t}$: Group Descriptor table
$<i_i, i_n> \leftarrow \text{SEARCH}(\mathsf{I_t^{G_n}}, f_p)$
check file permissions in inode data
$b_s \leftarrow (\mathsf{d_{b_n}} * \mathsf{d_s})$, $w_l \leftarrow 0$
while $w_l < \partial_l$ **do**
  $<b_i, g_i> \leftarrow \text{SEARCH}(\mathsf{B_t^{G_n}}, \{f_p, f_o\})$
  if b_i is null **then**
    $<b_i, g_i> \leftarrow \text{INSERT}(\mathsf{B_t^{G_n}}, \{f_p, f_o\}, \{\})$
  if $(\partial_l - w_l) > (b_s - (f_o \bmod b_s))$ **then**
    $\partial_i \leftarrow b_s - (f_o \bmod b_s)$
  else
    $\partial_i \leftarrow \partial_l - w_l$
  $s_d \leftarrow$ start offset of disk buckets in $\mathsf{GD}_t[g_i]$
  write $\partial[w_l : w_l + \partial_i]$ bytes to disk at offset $s_d + (b_s * b_i) + (f_o \bmod b_s)$
  $f_o \leftarrow f_o + \partial_i$, $w_l \leftarrow w_l + \partial_i$

AUTOCRYPT: Enabling Homomorphic Computation on Servers to Protect Sensitive Web Content

Shruti Tople Shweta Shinde Zhaofeng Chen Prateek Saxena
School of Computing
National University of Singapore
{shruti90, shweta24, chenzhao, prateeks} @comp.nus.edu.sg

ABSTRACT

Web servers are vulnerable to a large class of attacks which can allow network attacker to steal sensitive web content. In this work, we investigate the feasibility of a web server architecture, wherein the vulnerable server VM runs on a trusted cloud. All sensitive web content is made available to the vulnerable server VM in encrypted form, thereby limiting the effectiveness of data-stealing attacks through server VM compromise.

In this context, the main challenge is to allow the legitimate functionality of the untrusted server VM to work. As a step towards this goal, we develop a tool called AUTOCRYPT, which transforms a subset of existing C functionality in the web stack to operate on encrypted sensitive content. We show that such a transformation is feasible for several standard Unix utilities available in a typical LAMP stack, with no developer effort. Key to achieving this expressiveness over encrypted data, is our scheme to combine and convert between partially-homomorphic encryption (PHE) schemes using a small TCB in the trusted cloud hypervisor. We show that x86 code transformed with AUTOCRYPT achieves performance that is significantly better than its alternatives (downloading to a trusted client, or using fully-homomorphic encryption).

Categories and Subject Descriptors

D.3 [**Programming Languages**]: Processors—*Compilers*; D.4 [**Operating Systems**]: Security and Protection—*Cryptographic Controls*

Keywords

Web Security; Homomorphic Encryption; Type Systems

1. INTRODUCTION

Web hosting services, such as RackSpace and Amazon Web Services, enable web server stacks (e.g. a LAMP web server) to be hosted on public clouds using VMs. User and enterprises often wish to maintain strong data protection of sensitive data stored on public cloud servers from web and network attacks. Web server stacks are prone to a large class of attacks ranging from SQL injection, memory corruption vulnerabilities, OS command injection, server misconfiguration, file type confusion bugs, and so on. These attacks can be used to compromise web servers and install malware. Despite heightened security concerns [10], stronger data protection laws [4, 8, 9], and availability of commercial detection tools [6, 7], server-side data breaches have been persistently high for the last 3 years [25].

Previous work has proposed partitioning monolithic web servers into multiple pieces, as a second line of defense. For instance, separating the web application logic into multiple VMs based on roles [49], privilege separating users using OS protections [39], or using trusted hardware features to attest the integrity of server VMs [44, 45, 61]. In this work, we advocate a new approach for building second line of defense: we investigate how to protect sensitive web content in a compromised web server (running in a VM) on a trusted cloud. Specifically, we focus on ensuring the confidentiality of sensitive file-based web content while still allowing legitimate applications to operate on them.

Problem Setting. In this paper, we investigate the practical feasibility of protecting sensitive web content transparently in an untrusted server VM on a trusted cloud provider. We assume that the cloud provider and underlying VMM / hypervisor is trusted, but the attacker can exploit a vulnerability in the server-side web stack to run arbitrary code on the web server VM. One promising approach to achieve this is to encrypt all sensitive file content before exposing it to the untrusted server VM [52]. With this mechanism, attacks through the VM are forced to access information in encrypted form and computationally bounded adversaries cannot learn the information in sensitive files. Sensitive content is encrypted outside the untrusted VM (e.g. on a separate trusted key server or on the client's device) and encryption keys are made available only to the trusted hypervisor. A compromised VM would only be able to leak encrypted content to remote adversaries (which don't have the decryption keys). In this conceptual setting, the hypervisor acts as a static root-of-trust and does not execute any unprivileged code from the untrusted VM in privileged land. We discuss the merits of this conceptual architecture in Section 2 in more depth to motivate the context and need for our auto-transformation tools.

Challenge & Approach. The main challenge in enabling this defense is that naïvely encrypting content in the untrusted VM disables all legitimate (or benign) functionality. The standard solution for this problem is to download the encrypted data on the client side and then compute on the decrypted data. We call this approach as the 'download-and-compute' mechanism. Indeed, several commercial solutions — such as BoxCryptor [18] and CloudFogger [21] — allow users to store encrypted data on the server and only permit operating on the data by downloading full contents to the trusted client device before computation. However, for large amounts of data (say over a 1 TB of logfile), downloading the data incurs huge network communication which has direct financial costs for the

CCS'13, November 4–8, 2013, Berlin, Germany.

http://dx.doi.org/10.1145/2508859.2516666 .

service provider, and are slow as well as expensive for the client user. An alternative solution is to use fully-homomorphic encryption (FHE) schemes that allow arbitrary computation on encrypted data [31]. Though promising, these techniques are presently too slow for practical usage [30].

As a step towards practicality, we investigate execution of user-level benign applications, using *partially homomorphic encryption schemes (PHE)*. Partially homomorphic encryption schemes allow specific (limited) computations on encrypted content [24, 48, 58]. As the main contribution of this paper, we develop a new compiler called AUTOCRYPT that takes real-world C applications and automatically transforms them to operate on encrypted data. The transformed (or AUTOCRYPT-ed) x86 code runs in the untrusted VM and is allowed to invoke only 6 fixed *hypervisor API*, by making a *hypercall*, to support useful functionality. Our design ensures that all computations in the untrusted VM are *privacy preserving*, as defined formally in Section 3, using standard definitions of privacy-preserving homomorphic computation [58, 64]. The trusted hypervisor approach combined with AUTOCRYPT opens up a compelling alternative to the 2 existing solutions for enabling rich functionality in an uncompromised web server setting. It provides a high-bandwidth channel between an untrusted VM and hypervisor (via hypercalls) and adds little to the hypervisor's TCB.

In designing AUTOCRYPT, we carefully avoid schemes such as full-homomorphic encryption (FHE), which are presently too slow for practical usage [30, 31]. To avoid using FHE, the hypervisor APIs allows to perform safe conversions between encryption schemes. AUTOCRYPT analyzes program written in C and internally infers an encryption type for each variable in the program. We design a secure type system that combines various partially homomorphic encryption (PHE) schemes to support a subset of C operations. This type inference captures the right homomorphic encryption to apply to the variable's content to enable the legitimate computation to work. To summarize, our solution consists of two parts: a) a compiler AUTOCRYPT that type checks a given application and automatically transforms it to operate on encrypted data b) a fixed set of static hypervisor APIs in the trusted hypervisor that switches data between encryption schemes.

Summary of Results. We test AUTOCRYPT on 30 Unix file processing applications from the COREUTILS package available on a typical LAMP stack, and 3 custom programs commonly used in image processing applications. AUTOCRYPT automatically transforms the 25 COREUTILS applications and all the custom applications to AUTOCRYPT-ed programs with *no* developer effort, showing the expressiveness of our new abstractions. Our experiments validate our three main empirical hypotheses that (a) only a small fraction of internal program state and code needs transformation (but is difficult to manually identify) (b) several programs can use a combination of inexpensive PHE techniques rather than expensive FHE to implement their functionality (c) performance of operating on encrypted data using combination of PHE techniques can be better than the traditional 'download-and-compute' mechanism and exisiting fully-homomorphic encryption schemes. We find that the execution time of AUTOCRYPT-ed COREUTILS programs grows linearly with data size. Our (unoptimized) AUTOCRYPT-ed programs are faster for 19 utilities and slower by factor of 2 to 6 for 6 utilities as compared to the 'download-and-compute' mechanism and faster by orders of magnitude than previous reported performance of FHE techniques. Thus, AUTOCRYPT makes homomorphic computation on a trusted hypervisor a compelling alternative to the 'download-and-compute' and FHE mechanisms.

Contributions. In this work, we focus on the problem of retrofitting partially-homomorphic encryption (PHE) schemes transparently to existing application with no developer effort. To our knowledge, our work is one of the first to investigate how to automatically transform existing C applications using PHE schemes transparently without requiring any expertise or knowledge on behalf of the developer. Prior work has developed transformation tools for secure function evaluation on encrypted data, but mostly in the context of interactive secure two-party protocol implementations [32, 36–38, 43]. We target a new class of applications, motivated by our conceptual setting of a vulnerable web server hosted on a trusted hypervisor.

Specifically, we claim the following main contributions:

- We develop an automatic compilation tool for applications written in C language called AUTOCRYPT, which transparently embeds homomorphic computation to transform programs to operate on encrypted data.
- AUTOCRYPT provides experimental basis to the hypothesis that many applications can utilize a combination of PHE techniques instead of the more general (and expensive) FHE techniques. We successfully transform 25 (out of 30 studied) existing file-processing Unix utilities and 3 custom programs with no developer effort. This shows that the cheaper PHE techniques are sufficient for most of the applications we study, with a limited support from the trusted hypervisor.

2. OVERVIEW

To enable protection of sensitive content, we envision a conceptual architecture (Section 2.1) which splits the web server into 2 VMs, where the main web processing is an untrusted VM. The main focus of this paper is providing a small, secure hypervisor API and a type-based tool to transform existing applications to operate on PHE encrypted data.

2.1 Setting: A Split Server Architecture

Instead of trusting the web server VM completely, we envison a setting where the server is partitioned into 2 server VMs: the *main* untrusted server VM which handles the bulk of the client request processing and a *thin* authentication and key server. The thin authentication server handles the user authentication (via HTTPS) and initializes the hypervisor with the allowed encryption keys at the start of a session. The hypervisor then launches the untrusted main VM to handle the client's request in the session.

The untrusted VM executes a standard LAMP web stack which, in part, processes sensitive or encrypted files. Applications which implement the server's legitimate functionality are pre-transformed using our AUTOCRYPT on the client side. A client with his secret key and AUTOCRYPT tool transforms an application to AUTOCRYPT-ed program and uploads it to the web server.

In our design, files are stored encrypted under *more than one* partially homomorphic encryption schemes on the web server. For simplicity, we assume that each file has n $(= 3)$ copies on the server, each encrypted with a different encryption scheme under the user's secret key set κ. Each encryption scheme allows a certain kind of computation to be homomorphically executed on the encrypted file contents, under inputs encrypted with κ provided by the trusted client. For example, a file encrypted using searchable encryption allows only the trusted client to search for constant keywords on a file content, without revealing the encryption keys to the server [58]. Similarly, homomorphic schemes with respect to addition / subtraction (e.g.Paillier [48]), multiplication (e.g. Elgamal [24]) allow respective computations on the data. Our main goal is to transparently transform a program f that isn't designed

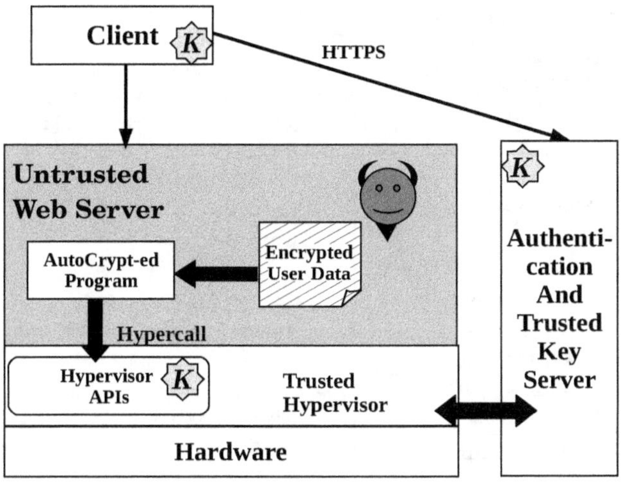

Figure 1: Trusted Hypervisor Setting. Secret Key K is present with the client, authentication server and the trusted hypervisor. The attacker can only see the encrypted data and the AUTOCRYPT-ed program.

to operate on encrypted data, into a program f' which can operate on encrypted sensitive data. The program f' takes encrypted inputs and executes to produce encrypted results. Supporting this scenario enables, for example, several standard Unix file processing utilities on encrypted files.

We trust the underlying hypervisor to be secure. Existing techniques to ensure its integrity can be used [45]. In this design, the hypervisor does not allow the untrusted VM to execute any unprivileged code dynamically in the privileged hypervisor mode (e.g. DOM0 in Xen). The hypervisor permits the untrusted VM to invoke a set of hypervisor APIs. These APIs implement a small set of static functionalities for decrypting data in one scheme and encrypting it in other scheme as detailed in Section 2.4.

2.2 Threat Model

We assume that the adversary can compromise and run arbitrary code in the untrusted VM during the session, as shown in Figure 1. We argue about the attacker's capability in these cases and design a robust solution to ensure confidentiality of sensitive web content.

Exfiltration Channels for Adversary. In this setting, the untrusted main VM only sees encrypted files and computed information from them. There are 3 channels it can utilize to exfiltrate data. First, it can directly send encrypted content to a remote attacker — however, such an attacker would not have the legitimate user's encryption keys, and so would not be able to decrypt the data. A second channel is to leak decrypted content via the client-side code. Defenses to prevent client-side data exfiltration have recently been proposed using features in HTML5 such as temporary origins [12]. We assume that with the help of the trusted authentication and key server, we can privilege separate the decryption and data export channels in a secure origin on the client-side. We do not discuss these defenses in this work. Finally, the attacker can learn the sensitive information using the hypervisor API exposed to the unprivileged code executing in the main VM. This threat is the main focus of our techniques. We show that the hypervisor's runtime service API cannot be used to leak information about computed values (see Section 3.4). That is, the untrusted VM cannot perform undue computation on sensitive data to leak information.

Ensuring Confidentiality On a Trusted Hypervisor. In this setting, however, ensuring confidentiality when a known computation is performed on the data files is an important challenge. We assume that the attacker can infer which application is being executed, i.e. we do not require functional privacy. We conservatively model the attacker's *knowledge set* to include f, f', the encrypted inputs and outputs of f', and everything that can be computed[1] from these. The installed malware on the untrusted VM can independently run AUTOCRYPT-ed f' on available encrypted data, and can observe each memory access and instruction executed in f'. Therefore, any information implied by the path constraints along any given execution are assumed to be part of the attacker's knowledge set. In addition, the adversary is not restricted to running only benign f' on the encrypted data available to it. Indeed, for a data element encrypted under κ with a particular homomorphic scheme, the malware can run arbitrary computation permissible by the scheme. The catch, of course, is that it is bound to compute with data which is already encrypted under κ with the same homomorphic encryption scheme. The results are decrypted outside the VM and not by the attacker (as the key is unknown to the attacker). Therefore, a important challenge is to limit the expressiveness (or richness) of the computation possible on sensitive data in the untrusted VM, while allowing "sufficiently interesting" benign functionality to execute.

2.3 Problem Definition

Our goal is to develop AUTOCRYPT, a tool that given a benign application f, checks if its computation can be transformed into a safe computation to run on the server. If so, AUTOCRYPT transform f into f' while preserving the semantics / correctness of the original computation and guaranteeing the safety of f' as per the definitions of privacy preserving execution.

More precisely, let an application f be a 3 tuple consisting of (a) a set of valid instruction traces S, operating on sensitive inputs $\vec{I}$, a set of public program constants C to produce sensitive outputs. Let Σ^* be the set of all input alphabets and $\mathbb{W}$ represent the set of publicly known program constants encrypted under search scheme. We seek a transformation procedure $AutoCrypt : (S, \vec{I}, C) \mapsto (S', \vec{I'}, C')$, such that it satisfies the following three properties.

(a)*Correctness :* The transformed program f' preserves the semantics of f, i.e. $\forall i \in I, S(i) = D_\kappa(S'(E_\kappa(i)))$.

(b)*Privacy-preserving execution:* The execution of f' under sensitive inputs $\vec{I}$ is privacy-preserving. We provide a precise definition of security achieved by our scheme as *reduced indistinguishability* (see below & Section 3.4) which is weaker than the strict computational non-interference, but admits a large variety of interesting web server functionality.

(c)*Minimal Control Flow Leakage:* The number of encrypted program constants under search scheme $\mathbb{W} \subseteq C$ is minimal, i.e., consisting only those constant expressions that are used in conditional operation in the original f.

Security Property: Privacy-preserving execution modulo $\mathbb{W}$. We aim to ensure that all executions in the untrusted VM, including f' and the adversarial computation, are privacy-preserving computation (modulo the parameter $\mathbb{W}$ necessary to support benign applications). Our goal is to enable interesting benign functionality in the untrusted VM, without giving a malicious computation the capability to leak sensitive information beyond what is implied by its knowledge set. For *all* computation in the untrusted VM, including the AUTOCRYPT-ed program f', computation on encrypted data are restricted only to homomorphic operations. In addition, com-

[1] according the standard definitions of computationally bounded adversaries

putation in the VM can make a small set of hypercalls. In our setting, the amount of information leakage in the adversarial computation is lower bounded by leakage permitted in benign functionality. In permitting benign executions, on one end, we could enforce a strong non-interference property (in the computational sense [28]) on *all* computation in the VM. However, many practical programs we study leak some information, via control flow channels, but the information leaked is small. We aim to admit a limited set of such benign functionalities, but bound the adversarial computations simultaneously. In essence, we aim to prevent computation (including the adversary's computation) from using dynamically computed values and checking them in conditional operations — this does not preclude computation using static encrypted values being used in a small set of permitted conditional checks.

To this end, we enforce a confidentiality property called reduced indistinguishability, which is parameterized by a set $\mathbb{W}$, on all computation in the untrusted VM. Intuitively, $\mathbb{W}$ captures the subset of the input alphabet Σ^* which is permitted to leak (and necessary to support benign functionality). For all input $\Sigma^* - \mathbb{W}$, reduced indistinguishability offers IND-CPA security. We define reduced indistinguishability along the lines of IND-CPA more formally in Section 3.4. We term all executions which satisfy reduced indistinguishability as *safe*. In practice, we find that the $\mathbb{W}$ is a small set — for supporting all our 25 case studies (Section 5), $|\mathbb{W}| = 12$ (where $\Sigma = 256$).

Scope. In this work, we focus on preserving the *confidentiality* of the encrypted inputs and outputs, not the integrity or freshness of the outputs of the executed program f'. Cryptographic techniques to handle integrity and freshness are being investigated, but are beyond the goals of this work [17, 29]. In our threat model, we assume that the legacy application is not designed to conceal lengths of its inputs / outputs; our encryption techniques are assumed to be length-revealing. Of course, techniques can be used to mitigate the last assumption [40], which are orthogonal to our techniques. We assume that the underlying homomorphic schemes are semantically secure, and their implementations blind side-channels using known techniques [20]. We do not aim to conceal information leakage through memory access pattern, which can be achieved using oblivious RAM techniques [59].

In this work, we focus on applications that read sensitive files and produce HTTP outputs decrypted on the client browser. For example, web servers need to perform content sniffing on files types (images, PDFs, etc.) to generate the appropriate HTTP MIME type header. Other examples include standard Unix utilities to compute statistics (e.g. word count, etc.) for web files, keyword search, checksum computation, base64 encoding, which are useful especially in cloud-hosted source code repositories (e.g. Github, Bitbucket). We do not support applications, outputs of which are to be stored on the web server itself and further processed by AUTOCRYPT-ed programs. Our evaluation is a preliminary first step in this direction; future research is needed to improve both the expressiveness and performance of AUTOCRYPT-ed programs.

2.4 Solution Overview

We design a new compiler—AUTOCRYPT that takes existing applications in C and transforms them automatically to work on encrypted data without any developer effort. In our design we combine various PHE schemes to enable a subset of operations that a general programming language supports. We develop a type system that type checks any application before AUTOCRYPT transforms it to AUTOCRYPT-ed program. An application which does not type checks according to our system is considered 'unsafe' for transformation. AUTOCRYPT identifies the sensitive variables in a

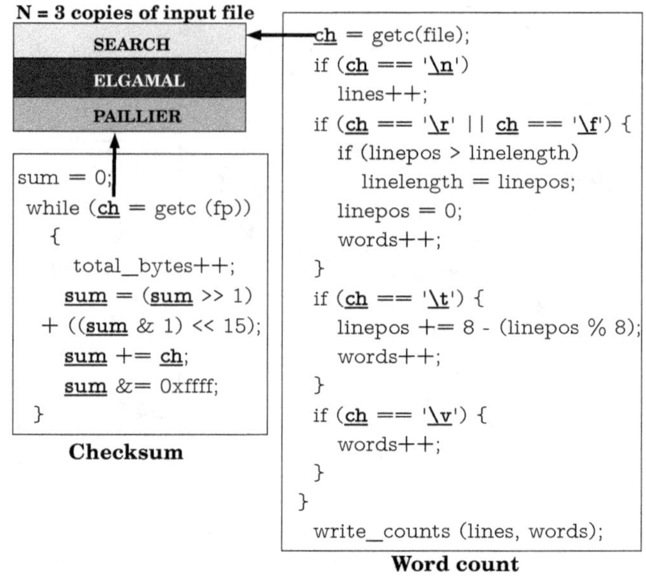

Figure 2: Program Layout of AUTOCRYPT-ed Programs. The variable `ch` is the sensitive variable and is assigned encryption type as Paillier in `checksum` and search type in `word count` program.

well-typed application and infers the right encryption type for its content and transforms it to work on encrypted inputs.

The input file to the transformed program is pre-encrypted with $n(= 3)$ different homomorphic encryption schemes. A transformed application operates on correct copy of the input file depending on the encryption types inferred for the sensitive variables in the program. We explain the program layout of two transformed applications that use one of 3 copies of the input file in Figure 2. The `checksum` program that performs mathematical operations fetches the sensitive input from the Paillier encrypted copy of the input file whereas the `word count` program fetches its input from the search encrypted copy of the input file. For both the programs, `word count` and `checksum`, AUTOCRYPT identifies the variable `ch` as sensitive and infers an encryption type for it. In the `word count` program, `ch` is of search encryption type whereas in the `checksum` program, it has Paillier encryption type. The 5 constants (shown as boldface) in the `word count` program are also inferred the search encryption type, thus here $|\mathbb{W}| = 5$. AUTOCRYPT pre-encrypts them in the search encryption scheme during transformation of the program.

Hypervisor APIs. The `checksum` program shown in Figure 2 requires more than one homomorphic properties in the same program. Thus, our system infers different encryption types to same variable depending on the operation in which it is used. At any given time, a program variable is encrypted in either search encryption (`srch`), Paillier encryption of bits of integer ($\mathtt{pal}_1$), Paillier encryption of integer ($\mathtt{pal}_8$) or Elgamal (`egml`) encryption scheme depending on the operations performed on it. One possible approach is to ask the client to decrypt the data in one encryption scheme and encrypt it in another scheme. But the network latency between the client and the server degrades the performance for applications like `checksum` where conversion between the encryption schemes is required for every character. To allow switching between the encryption schemes while still executing the program with acceptable performance, we provide a fixed set of static hypercalls in the trusted hypervisor. The hypervisor APIs support only 6

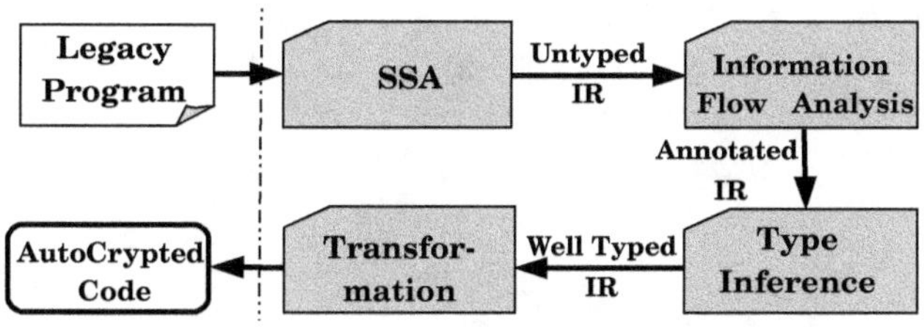

Figure 3: Design overview of AutoCrypt.

fixed functionalities to switch the sensitive data between different homomorphic encryption schemes. The hypervisor does not execute any unprivileged arbitrary code on the sensitive data, thus our increase in hypervisor TCB only consists of the following 6 hypercalls for conversion between encryption schemes.

- $\mathtt{pal_8}$ to $\mathtt{pal_1}$
- egml to $\mathtt{pal_1}$
- egml to $\mathtt{pal_8}$
- $\mathtt{pal_1}$ to egml
- $\mathtt{pal_8}$ to egml
- static memory lookup

Thus, using the three encrypted copies of the sensitive input and the hypervisor APIs, AutoCrypt transforms majority of the existing applications to operate on encrypted data.

3. AutoCrypt DESIGN

In this section we describe the end-to-end design of AutoCrypt and discuss security guarantees of our system.

3.1 Overview

AutoCrypt takes as input a legacy application that operates on unencrypted files and transforms it to an AutoCrypt-ed program which operates on encrypted files and command-line inputs (refer Figure 3). The developer annotates all reads from sensitive file APIs and command line arguments in the initial program with high information labels. AutoCrypt takes the annotated program and performs the following steps:

Conversion to SSA form. In the first step, AutoCrypt converts the input program to an intermediate representation in Static Single Assignment form (SSA). SSA form splits the lifetime of a program variable into many smaller ones by assigning a new version every time it is re-defined. This allows AutoCrypt to separate out different operations over the lifetime of a variable, thereby increasing the opportunity to separate out operations that are incompatible under a single homomorphic encryption scheme. Every operation is represented as a separate instruction in the Internal Representation (IR). We refer the output of this step as the *untyped IR*.

Information Flow Analysis. AutoCrypt then analyzes the untyped IR for variables and constants that need encryption. In this analysis, AutoCrypt tracks and propagates direct data dependencies of program variables on high-labeled inputs, file inputs and the outputs of the application. Our static data-dependency tracking is flow-sensitive. This analysis is akin to the standard variable-level taint-tracking [27]. Information flow analysis produces an annotated IR, in which all the operands are marked as either high or low.

Type Inference. AutoCrypt infers the precise homomorphic encryption scheme to be used for each high operand in the annotated IR. At the end of this step, it labels each operation with an encryption type that signifies its associated encryption scheme. To perform this step, AutoCrypt uses the standard type inference techniques. The output of this step is a well-typed IR — that is, it satisfies a formal set of type rules we define in Section 3.3.

Transformation. Finally, AutoCrypt transforms the well-typed IR into target x86 code using a syntax-directed translation step. In this step, each original computation is converted into the corresponding homomorphic computation. In addition, this step handles various features of real-world C programs, such as encoding into machine words, handling pointers, structures, C libraries, and so on. We detail these in Section 4.

3.2 Background on Encryption Schemes

We briefly introduce the partially homomorphic schemes used in AutoCrypt.

Searchable Encryption(srch). Searchable encryption scheme allows the owner to outsource encrypted data while maintaining the selectively-search capability over it. Keyword based symmetric searchable encryption enables such remote searching on encrypted data by an untrusted server [58]. Specifically, the untrusted server uses an user-provided encrypted token (unique to every search keyword) to determine whether a document contains the word, without learning anything else.

AutoCrypt uses this encryption scheme to support operators such as equal to. Previous works discuss various schemes to support similar operations [16, 58]. Among these, AutoCrypt uses CryptDB implementation of searchable encryption [51], based on cryptographic protocol of Song et al. [58]. In AutoCrypt, the search keyword is mostly a character and hence both the keywords and file encryption are at character level as opposed to word-level encryption in CryptDB. Note that the deterministic encryption schemes also support such equality checks. But it is a weaker encryption scheme revealing information about the underlying plaintext. The search scheme AutoCrypt uses is randomized and is thus CPA secure [58]. Hence, an attacker is bound to search only those terms which are available in an encrypted form either as program constants or as inputs and outputs for client queries.

Paillier Encryption. AutoCrypt uses the encryption scheme proposed by Paillier [48], to support various arithmetic and bitwise operations on encrypted data. Since the operations are homomorphic, the result are also encrypted under Paillier scheme. The encryption scheme is semantically secure and assures guarantees equivalent to randomized encryption. AutoCrypt classifies Paillier scheme into two categories.

i. Paillier encryption of an integer ($\mathtt{pal_8}$): Integer value of a high variable is encrypted using Paillier encryption . This encryption is necessary for arithmetic operations such as addition, which operate on the integer representation.

ii. Paillier encryption of the bits of an integer ($\mathtt{pal_1}$): To handle intermediate bitwise computations such as XOR, that rely in an essential way on the binary representations of their input values, AutoCrypt encrypts every bit in the binary representation of an integer.

Elgamal Encryption. Elgamal encryption scheme is used to homomorphically multiply two encrypted operands such that the result is also encrypted under Elgamal scheme [24]. AutoCrypt demonstrates the use of this scheme for homomorphic matrix multiplication in Section 5. Support for regular expression matching and DFA can also be added to AutoCrypt by using this encryption scheme [62].

3.3 AUTOCRYPT Type Inference

Although standard information flow rules assist to infer all the program entities that are `high` [53, 57], inferring the corresponding encryption scheme is a non-trivial task. There are several subtle factors such as control flow, program constants, lookups using encrypted indexes, and complex arithmetic operations requiring conversion from one encryption type to other. These challenges must be carefully addressed so as to preserve the security guarantees of a legacy application. To this end, we present AUTOCRYPT framework armed with a formal type system which checks whether a C application can be transformed to a *safe* application.

Main insight. An annotated IR has all operands marked `high` or `low`. Our type system allows arbitrary computation in expressions computed from `low` values, and these resulting values are not encrypted (either statically or at runtime). The adversary, thus, cannot use such `low`-labeled values to compute or check any encrypted data.

For `high`-labeled variables, we permit them to either be used in conditional checks or in arithmetic / bitwise operations, but not both. Specifically, `high`-labeled values can only be used in equality / inequality checks with other operands, and our type system forces them both to be encrypted under the search scheme. In effect, this prevents all values used in conditional checks from being used in *any* arithmetic / bitwise (non-conditional operations) as they are in different encrypted forms at runtime.

Remaining `high` values can be computed in arithmetic / bitwise schemes, but these are never permitted to be converted to search-encrypted values. This is checked by our static type rules, and no hypercall allows to convert between searchable encryption and other homomorphic schemes at runtime. Together, this enables a conceptual partitioning of encrypted memory between searchable and non-searchable values.

Language. Figure 4 shows the syntax for a simple typed language supported by AUTOCRYPT. For brevity, we consider this simple language to illustrate our approach. However we evaluate on various C programs as discussed in Section 5. The simple language is a subset of C and is expressive enough to model many programs. Our type-based approach is general and can be enhanced further to incorporate richer language features. We discuss the subset of C constructs we support in Section 4. The language has two possible information-flow labels `low` and `high`. Program variables and constants are also classified based on the required encryption types viz. no encryption i.e. plain text (`ptxt`), search encryption (`srch`), Paillier encryption (`pal8`, `pal1`) and Elgamal encryption (`egml`).

Operations that can be computed with the same encryption scheme are syntactically combined in the language. For bitwise operations in $\odot$ and $\circledcirc$, one or both the operands must be in bitwise Paillier encryption scheme (`pal1`). Arithmetic operations in $\oslash$ need operands encrypted in integer Paillier scheme(`pal8`). For multiplying two encrypted variables ($*$), they must be encrypted under Elgamal scheme (`egml`). In conditional operations ($\otimes$), an encrypted `high` variable can be compared against encrypted public program constant. Hence, both its operands must be encrypted under search encryption scheme (`srch`). Note that known program constants in our language are typed to be either encrypted or non-encrypted but they are publically known and hence always `low`.

Type System. Each expression has a type τ, which is a tuple of two labels: information-flow label (`low` and `high`) and encryption type label. We write $\Gamma \vdash e : \tau$ to denote that the expression e has type τ according to the typing rules in Γ typing environment, where τ denotes type of e. Such an assertion is called a typing judgment.

```
Types            τ     ::=  (Q, T)
Type Qualifiers  Q     ::=  high | low
Base Types       T     ::=  α | β
Plaintext        α     ::=  ptxt
Encrypted        β     ::=  β1 | β2
                 β1    ::=  srch
                 β2    ::=  pal8 | pal1 | egml
Expressions      e     ::=  e1 ⊙ e2 | e1 ⊚ e2 | e1 ⊘ e2 | e1 * e2
                            | lval | const (i:τ)
                 lval  ::=  var (v:τ)
Bitwise          ⊙     ::=  & | ^ | |
                 ⊚     ::=  << | >>
Arithmetic       ⊘     ::=  + | -
Boolean          b     ::=  bool | e1 ⊗ e2 | b1 ⊖ b2
                 bool  ::=  true | false
Conditional      ⊗     ::=  == | !=
Logical          ⊖     ::=  AND | OR
Commands         P     ::=  lval := e
                            | lval := ARR[var]
                            | if b then P else P'
                            | while (b) do P
                            | return r
                            | f(e1, e2, . . ., en) {P;}
```

Figure 4: The grammar of a simple subset of C language supported by AUTOCRYPT.

Typing rules for Expressions. The expression typing judgement $\Gamma \vdash e : \tau$ states that at a given program location, the expression e has a type τ. The Γ denotes the type environment that maps variables to the target language base types.

Typing rules for Commands. The type system is flow-sensitive because it permits the mappings of variables to types in the typing environment Γ to change from one program location to another. Typing judgements for the commands in Figure 5 capture the effects of execution of the command on the type environments and have the form $\Gamma \vdash c \Longrightarrow \Gamma'$. The type environment Γ is changed to Γ' as a result of the execution of the command.

Type Inference. We infer flow-sensitive types based on our type rules in Figure 5 using standard techniques proposed in previous work [27]. We omit the type rule for instructions taking all operands with `low` labels.

The rules for inferring encryption types are as follows.

- `SRCH` : If one operand to a conditional operation ($\otimes$) is `high` searchable variable and other is a program constant, then both the operands are typed to `srch` and the result is a `low` boolean value.
- `PAL8-A & B` : For mathematical operations in $\oslash$, one or both operands can be `high`. For $*$ one operand is high and other is low. Then, the `high` operands have type `pal8` and the result of computation is also `pal8` type.
- `PAL1-A & B` : For bitwise operations in $\odot$ and $\circledcirc$, the `high` operand is given type `pal1` while the other operand can be `low` or `high`. The resulting value is also in `pal1`.
- `EGML` : If both the operands to a $*$ operation are `high`, then the operands and result have `egml` type.
- The encryption type to $lvalue$ for statements is specified in the type rules.

Type Conversion. Figure 6 depicts the type lattice enforced by AUTOCRYPT type system. Type conversions are non-descending i.e. conversions only go upwards or are at the same level [23]. Our type system only supports the conversions for which there is a corresponding runtime hypervisor API. We explain the safe upcasting conversions below, and give examples of the unsafe downcasting operations not supported by our hypervisor runtime.

VAR

$$\frac{\{v \mapsto \tau\} \in \Gamma}{\Gamma \vdash v : \tau}$$

CONST

$$\frac{\{c \mapsto \tau\} \in \Gamma}{\Gamma \vdash c : (\texttt{low}, \texttt{ptxt} \vee \texttt{srch})}$$

BOOL

$$\frac{\{b \mapsto \tau\} \in \Gamma}{\Gamma \vdash b : (\texttt{low}, \texttt{ptxt})}$$

ASSGN

$$\frac{\Gamma \vdash e : \tau}{\Gamma \vdash v := e \Longrightarrow \Gamma[v \mapsto \tau]}$$

ARR

$$\frac{\Gamma \vdash arr : (\texttt{high}, \beta) \qquad \Gamma \vdash i : (\texttt{low}, \texttt{ptxt})}{\Gamma \vdash v := arr[i] \Longrightarrow \Gamma[v \mapsto (\texttt{high}, \beta)]}$$

STATIC-MEM

$$\frac{\Gamma \vdash arr : (\texttt{low}, \texttt{ptxt}) \qquad \Gamma \vdash i : (\texttt{high}, \beta)}{\Gamma \vdash v := arr[i] \Longrightarrow \Gamma[v \mapsto (\texttt{high}, \beta)]}$$

SEQ

$$\frac{\Gamma_0 \vdash P_1 : \Gamma_1 \qquad \Gamma_1 \vdash P_2 : \Gamma_2}{\Gamma_0 \vdash P_1; P_2 \Longrightarrow \Gamma_2}$$

COND

$$\frac{\Gamma_0 \vdash b : (\texttt{low}, \texttt{ptxt}) \qquad \Gamma_0 \vdash P_1 : \Gamma \qquad \Gamma_0 \vdash P_2 : \Gamma}{\Gamma_0 \vdash if\,(b)\,then\,P_1\,else\,P_2 : \Gamma}$$

WHILE

$$\frac{\Gamma \vdash b : (\texttt{low}, \texttt{ptxt}) \qquad \Gamma \vdash P : \Gamma}{\Gamma \vdash while(b)do\,P : \Gamma}$$

FUNC

$$\frac{\Gamma \vdash P : \tau}{\Gamma \vdash f(e_1, e_2, \ldots, e_n)\{P\} : \tau}$$

SRCH

$$\frac{\Gamma \vdash b : \tau \qquad \Gamma \vdash e : (\texttt{high}, \texttt{srch}) \qquad \Gamma \vdash c : (\texttt{low}, \texttt{ptxt})}{\Gamma \vdash b := e \otimes c \Longrightarrow \Gamma[b \mapsto (\texttt{low}, \texttt{ptxt}), c \mapsto (\texttt{low}, \texttt{srch})]}$$

PAL_8-A

$$\frac{\Gamma \vdash e : \tau \qquad \Gamma \vdash e_1 : (\texttt{high}, \beta) \qquad \Gamma \vdash e_2 : (\texttt{low}, \texttt{ptxt}) \qquad \texttt{opr} \in \{\oslash, *\}}{\Gamma \vdash e := e_1\, \texttt{opr}\, e_2 \Longrightarrow \Gamma[e \mapsto (\texttt{high}, \texttt{pal}_8)]}$$

PAL_8-B

$$\frac{\Gamma \vdash e : \tau \qquad \Gamma \vdash e_1 : (\texttt{high}, \beta) \qquad \Gamma \vdash e_2 : (\texttt{high}, \beta)}{\Gamma \vdash e := e_1 \oslash e_2 \Longrightarrow \Gamma[e \mapsto (\texttt{high}, \texttt{pal}_8)]}$$

PAL_1-A

$$\frac{\Gamma \vdash e : \tau \qquad \Gamma \vdash e_1 : (\texttt{high}, \beta) \qquad \Gamma \vdash e_2 : (\texttt{low}, \texttt{ptxt}) \qquad \texttt{opr} \in \{\circledcirc, \odot\}}{\Gamma \vdash e := e_1\, \texttt{opr}\, e_2 \Longrightarrow \Gamma[e \mapsto (\texttt{high}, \texttt{pal}_1)]}$$

PAL_1-B

$$\frac{\Gamma \vdash e : \tau \qquad \Gamma \vdash e_1 : (\texttt{high}, \beta) \qquad \Gamma \vdash e_2 : (\texttt{high}, \beta)}{\Gamma \vdash e := e_1 \odot e_2 \Longrightarrow \Gamma[e \mapsto (\texttt{high}, \texttt{pal}_1)]}$$

EGML

$$\frac{\Gamma \vdash e : \tau \qquad \Gamma \vdash e_1 : (\texttt{high}, \beta) \qquad \Gamma \vdash e_2 : (\texttt{high}, \beta)}{\Gamma \vdash e := e_1 * e_2 \Longrightarrow \Gamma[e \mapsto (\texttt{high}, \texttt{egml})]}$$

PAL_8-PAL_1

$$\frac{q \in Q}{(q, \texttt{pal}_8) \geq (q, \texttt{pal}_1)}$$

PAL_1-PAL_8

$$\frac{q \in Q}{(q, \texttt{pal}_1) \geq (q, \texttt{pal}_8)}$$

PAL_8-EGML

$$\frac{q \in Q}{(q, \texttt{pal}_8) \geq (q, \texttt{egml})}$$

PAL_1-EGML

$$\frac{q \in Q}{(q, \texttt{pal}_1) \geq (q, \texttt{egml})}$$

EGML-PAL_8

$$\frac{q \in Q}{(q, \texttt{egml}) \geq (q, \texttt{pal}_8)}$$

EGML-PAL_1

$$\frac{q \in Q}{(q, \texttt{egml}) \geq (q, \texttt{pal}_1)}$$

Figure 5: Type Rules for expressions and commands in AUTOCRYPT. Γ is the typing environment that maps variables and constants to type qualifiers `high` or `low` at each program locations. It also maps the encryption types viz. `ptxt`, `srch`, `pal`$_8$, `pal`$_1$ or `egml` to each variable. Type qualifiers are flow sensitive. We omit the type rule for instructions taking all operands with `low` labels here for brevity.

$$\frac{q \in Q}{(q, \top) \geq (q, \alpha \vee \beta)} \qquad \frac{q \in Q}{(q, \beta_2) \geq (q, \beta_1)} \qquad \frac{q \in Q}{(q, \beta_1) \geq (q, \bot)}$$

Figure 6: Type Lattice rules for AUTOCRYPT

(a) Safe conversions (Up-casting):
Type rule PAL$_8$-PAL$_1$ and PAL$_1$-PAL$_8$ allow interconversion of `high` variable encrypted under Paillier integer and Paillier bit scheme. Similarly, PAL$_8$-EGML, PAL$_1$-EGML enables conversion from Paillier (both integer and bit) encryption to Elgamal scheme and EGML-PAL$_8$, EGML-PAL$_1$ from Paillier to Elgamal scheme. Up-casting from searchable encryption scheme to Elgamal and Paillier schemes is safe according to the type-lattice.

(b) Unsafe conversions (Down-casting):
AUTOCRYPT type rules do not allow conversion from Elgamal or Paillier encryption scheme to searchable encryption scheme. If such conversions are allowed by the type system, an adversary can build a program which arbitrarily converts the results of arithmetic homomorphic operation say $x = y + 10$ to searchable cipher text. Then, he can compare x to the available program constants encrypted as searchable tokens. By such a series of instructions, an adversary can predict the initial value of y with a non-negligible advantage, and hence win the indistinguishability game. Thus, to prevent such attacks, the conversion to searchable encryption by down-casting is not allowed in AUTOCRYPT.

All static program constants are marked `low` as these are publically known. Program constants used in the relational operations with `high` operands need to be encrypted. All the other program constants need not be encrypted, as they are used directly in the transformed homomorphic operations (see Section 3.5). The type rules for the remaining expressions are straight forward, except the rule to handle lookup in a static memory using encrypted indexes.

Encrypted indexes to static memory. A lookup in a statically initialized array of public constants using a `high` index can reveal the encrypted index, if the adversary can observe the lookup result. Our type system handles this securely (rule `STATIC-MEM`) by forcing the outputs of such memory lookups to be `high` and encrypted under the same scheme as the encrypted index. To support this operation at runtime, our hypervisor provides an hypervisor API that performs the lookup obliviously. Specifically, the hypercall for `ARR[i]` lookup operation ensures that $\forall\, m \in RANGE(arr)$, $(E(arr[D(i)]), E(m))$ are computationally indistinguishable by the adversary.

We point out that, in principle such lookups could be supported by using homomorphic evaluation of polynomials [62]. However, for $\Sigma = 256$ the polynomial degree is high and the evaluation could be slow. Alternatively, AUTOCRYPT's hypervisor API supports static memory lookup as follows: All statically initialized lookup arrays are saved as plaintext in the trusted hypervisor. Every lookup from such arrays using an encrypted index is converted to a hypercall. In the trusted hypervisor environment, the service API first decrypts the index and fetches the corresponding plaintext from the static (unencrypted) memory. The plaintext is then encrypted under the same randomized encryption scheme as the index, using a fresh random nonce.

3.4 Security Guarantees

AUTOCRYPT does not rely on the type system discussed in Section 3.3 for security. The type system only assists in checking program's compatibility for AUTOCRYPT conversion and for inferring encryption types of program variables. However, even bad program (ill-typed) can execute on the malicious web server. To this end, our design of the hypervisor APIs together with the use of homomorphic encryption schemes safeguard against such ill-typed programs, while ensuring that for all executed code in the VM (including adversarial and benign code), has a specific security property which we define below.

Privacy-preserving Executions. Any executing program in the VM can be viewed as a sequence of selective statements from the program depending on the input. A program trace corresponds to one such execution sequence. More formally, we define:

DEFINITION 1. ***(Program Trace** T**)** The program trace $T : \vec{I} \rightarrow \vec{O}$ is a sequence of statements $\langle S_1, \ldots, S_n \rangle$ operating on encrypted input $\vec{I}$ yielding encrypted output $\vec{O}$ in deterministic program P.*

As previously mentioned, the program can only use a small set of publicly known program constants $\mathbb{W}$ in conditional comparisons (control flow decisions), made available in the VM for supporting some benign applications. We define $\mathbb{W}$ and a program P formally as below.

DEFINITION 2. ***(Encrypted Search Constants*** $\mathbb{W}$*) For a program P,* $\mathbb{W} = \{W_1, \ldots, W_n\}$ *such that* $\mathbb{W} \subseteq \Sigma^*$ *and* W_i *is a publically known program constant encrypted under search scheme.*

W is a subset of possible input alphabets Σ^*. Specifically, all the publically known program constants which are marked as `low` and are also encrypted under search scheme belong to the set $\mathbb{W}$.

DEFINITION 3. ***(Program*** P***)*** *A Program* $P = (\mathbb{T}, \mathbb{W})$ *where* $\mathbb{T} = \{T_1, \ldots, T_n\}$*, and* $\mathbb{W}$ *are encrypted search constants.*

The execution of a program trace interleaves between the execution in the untrusted VM and in the trusted hypervisor. Therefore, we can define the projection of a trace visible to an entity (either the adversary or the hypervisor) as follows: P may have other program constants; but we ignore them in our definitions for clarity as they are unimportant for our security reasoning.

DEFINITION 4. ***(Projection*** P_i***)*** *Projection* Π *of a trace* T *onto* E*, written as* $\Pi_E(T)$*, is a subsequence of a program trace* T *visible to an entity* E*.*

Given a program trace, an entity can view only some statements in the execution trace. For example, the untrusted VM (say A) cannot see the internal hypervisor implementations of the hypercalls and encrypted memory lookups in an AUTOCRYPT-ed program. Thus, these statements will not be a part of the $\Pi_A(T)$. The following 2 security definitions constitute the confidentiality of the sensitive inputs, apart from the values which the adversary can directly compare with $\mathbb{W}$ by using equality checks on search encrypted bytes.

DEFINITION 5. ***(Input Reduction Function*** R***)*** *For an input vector* $\vec{I}$ *for a given program P, we define the input reduction function* $R(\vec{I}, \mathbb{W})$ *which reduces* $\vec{I}$ *by discarding all the* W_j *values in* $\vec{I}$ *at positions where* $\forall\, W_i \in \mathbb{W}, W_j = W_i$*.*

DEFINITION 6. ***(Reduced Indistinguishability modulo*** $\mathbb{W}$***)*** *For a given trace* $T : \vec{I_i} \rightarrow \vec{O_i}$ *and* $\mathbb{W}$*, we say that* T *has reduced indistinguishability modulo* $\mathbb{W}$*, iff* $\forall\, m_0, m_1 \in R(\vec{I}, \mathbb{W})$*, the advantage* $Adv(A)$ = $|Pr[\Pi_A(T_{m_0}) = 1]$ - $Pr[\Pi_A(T_{m_1}) = 1]| < \varepsilon$ *for all probabilistic polynomial time-bounded adversaries* A*, where* ε *is negligible function* $negl(n)$*.*

Thus, along a given trace T_i in the program P, the advantage of all adversaries is negligible and it cannot distinguish two inputs from the reduced input vector. This reduces to standard definitions of ciphertext indistinguishability under IND-CPA when $\mathbb{W} = 0$.

DEFINITION 7. ***IND-CPA for Search Encryption****. For a given trace* $T : \vec{I_i} \rightarrow \vec{O_i}$ *and a set of encrypted search constants* $\mathbb{W}$ *available to the adversary, if* $\vec{I_i}$ *is search encrypted, then* $\forall\, m_0, m_1 \in R(\vec{I}, \mathbb{W})$*, the advantage* $Adv(A) = |Pr[\Pi_A(T_{m_0}) = 1] - Pr[\Pi_A(T_{m_1}) = 1]| < \varepsilon$ *for all probabilistic polynomial time-bounded adversaries* A*, where* ε *is negligible function* $negl(n)$*.*

The above definition assumes the server has only the searchable encryption copy of the user's file. The proof of indistinguishability under IND-CPA for search encryption follows directly from previous work [58].

DEFINITION 8. ***IND-CPA for Non-Search Encryption****. For Trace* $T_i : \vec{I_i} \rightarrow \vec{O_i}$*,* $\forall\, m_0, m_1 \in \vec{I}$*, the advantage* $Adv(A) = |Pr[\Pi_A(T(_{m_0}) = 1]$ - $Pr[\Pi_A(T_{m_1}) = 1]| < \varepsilon$ *for all probabilistic polynomial time-bounded adversaries* A*, where* ε *is negligible function* $negl(n)$*.*

If we assume that there is only non-search encrypted copy of the file on the server, $\mathbb{W} = 0$ and hence $R(\vec{I}, \mathbb{W}) \equiv \vec{I}$. Thus, for a purely non-search encryption the indistinguishability property holds. The proof follows directly from the IND-CPA security of individual homomorphic schemes [64].

Definitions 6, 7 and 8 are independently true only when a corresponding single copy of encrypted file(encrypted either under searchable encryption or non-searchable encryption scheme) is available. If both copies are present simultaneously on the server, logically the definitions holds for $min(I, R(\vec{I}, \mathbb{W}))$ i.e. on the reduced input $R(\vec{I}, \mathbb{W})$.

The following theorem states that interconversion between non-search schemes preserves indistinguishability under IND-CPA.

LEMMA 1. ***IND-CPA for non-search Composition****. For a safe program P, if the functions* $f_1, \ldots, f_n$ *are individually secure non-search homomorphic functions under IND-CPA, then the composition* $(f_i \circ f_j)(x)$ *where* $i, j \in \{1, \ldots, n\}$ *satisfies reduced indistinguishability.*

Our conversions between the non-search encryption schemes can be proved using bisimulation induction on a type system proposed in recent work [28].

Our final theorem says that all execution traces in the hypervisor are privacy preserving, i.e., follow reduced indistinguishability for a given $\mathbb{W}$. This stems from a critical design choice: the hypervisor does not permit converting from non-search to search types during execution. Let $NS(T)$ and $S(T)$ be set of runtime values encrypted under non-search and search encryption in T respectively. Our hypervisor ensures that $NS(T) \cap S(T) \subseteq \mathbb{W}$. This establishes the following safety condition for any program running in the VM:

THEOREM 1. ***IND-CPA of all VM Executions****. For a program* $P = (\mathbb{T}, \mathbb{W})$*, executing on our hypervisor, reduced indistinguishability modulo* $\mathbb{W}$ *holds if* $\forall\, T \in \mathbb{T}$*,* $NS(T) \cap S(T) \subseteq \mathbb{W}$*.*

PROOF SKETCH. Proof follows from Definition 7 and Lemma 1. We sketch the outline below: $\forall\, v_{ns} \in NS(T)$ and $\forall\, v_s \in S(T)$ hypervisor does not permit conversion at runtime from values $v_n s$ to corresponding v_s. Thus, the only values v for which both v_s and v_{ns} are known are in set of encrypted search constants used in conditional operations. For P, $\mathbb{W}$ is a set of all such encrypted constants. From Definition 7, reduced indistinguishability holds for the traces comprising encrypted search constants. For non-search encryption, reduced indistinguishability follows from Lemma 1. ■

Well-Typed Programs. For benign programs, AUTOCRYPT aims to identify if all the traces in it can be made privacy-preserving. The type rules check this, and if well-typed, programs are transformed. We show that well-typed program indeed have reduced indistinguishability modulo $\mathbb{W}$.

THEOREM 2. ***Well-Typed Implies IND-CPA****. If* P *is a well-typed program, then* $\forall\, T \in P$*, the reduced trace indistinguishability property holds for* T*.*

We omit a rigorous proof in this paper.

3.5 Transformation

Converting operations to homomorphic computation. We use CryptDB implementation of the search and Pailler encryption schemes and libgcrypt library for the Elgamal encryption scheme [3, 51]. Combining partially homomorphic properties of Paillier, Elgamal and search scheme, we transform various operations to operate on encrypted data. We give details of subset of C operations that AUTOCRYPT supports and the encryption type required by them in Table 1. Operations not listed in Table 1 are either not possible using homomorphic encryption schemes or are not safe and hence are not allowed by AUTOCRYPT.

Operation	Op1 Type	Op2 Type	Output Type
$add(+)$	$\texttt{pal}_8$	ptxt	$\texttt{pal}_8$
	$\texttt{pal}_8$	$\texttt{pal}_8$	$\texttt{pal}_8$
$mul(*)$	$\texttt{pal}_8$	ptxt	$\texttt{pal}_8$
	egml	egml	egml
$sub(-)$	$\texttt{pal}_8$	ptxt	$\texttt{pal}_8$
	$\texttt{pal}_8$	$\texttt{pal}_8$	$\texttt{pal}_8$
shl ($\ll$)	$\texttt{pal}_1$	ptxt	$\texttt{pal}_8$
shr ($\gg$)	$\texttt{pal}_1$	ptxt	$\texttt{pal}_8$
or ($\|$)	$\texttt{pal}_1$	ptxt	$\texttt{pal}_1$
	$\mathbf{pal}_1$	$\mathbf{pal}_1$	$\mathbf{pal}_1$
and (&)	$\texttt{pal}_1$	ptxt	$\texttt{pal}_1$
	$\mathbf{pal}_1$	$\mathbf{pal}_1$	$\mathbf{pal}_1$
xor (^)	$\texttt{pal}_1$	ptxt	$\texttt{pal}_1$
	$\mathbf{pal}_1$	$\mathbf{pal}_1$	$\mathbf{pal}_1$
$equal$ (==)	srch	keyword	true / false
not_equal (!=)	srch	keyword	true / false

Table 1: Homomorphic operations supported by AUTOCRYPT. Column 2, 3 and 4 give the encrytion type for expressions of the form `Output = Op1 operation Op2`. The implementation of the operations *or*, *and* and *xor* comprise of hypercalls (shown in bold faced) when both its operands are encrypted. *equal* and *not_equal* operations take one operand as a `keyword` which is a searchable program constant.

Encryption type conversion. Operations involving different encryption types may require conversion of intermediate results to other encryption schemes, for example converting an integer encrypted under Paillier encryption to Elgamal encryption. AUTOCRYPT inserts hypercalls at appropriate program locations for permitted convert operations. The hypervisor API in turn implements these operations. It first decrypts the input value using appropriate keys, and then re-encrypts this value using the keys for target encryption scheme. At last, it responds to the hypercall by returning this re-encrypted value to the untrusted VM.

4. IMPLEMENTATION

We implement AUTOCRYPT to automatically transform applications written in C to operate on encrypted data. In this section, we discuss the details of our implementation.

Analysis Pass. The sensitivity analysis phase of AUTOCRYPT is implemented as an analysis pass in the LLVM 3.2 infrastructure [42]. This phase comprises of conversion from LLVM IR to pure SSA form using LLVM `mem2reg` pass followed by following analyses.

The SSA form is then passed to the points-to analysis module which uses algorithm proposed by Hardekopf et al. [35]. All the virtual registers are grouped in alias sets and the information is maintained as pragmas to be used by the consecutive phases of AUTOCRYPT.

All user inputs and operations on data fetched from the file are marked as sensitive. This phase propagates the sensitivity of input by marking the appropriate variables and constants as sensitive and the records corresponding instructions as sensitive. AUTOCRYPT analyses all the functions of the program to collect a set of sensitive elements and instructions and logs the results in the form of Datalog facts.

After identifying all the possible sensitive constants and variables, AUTOCRYPT's inference module assigns them a type of encryption scheme using the type rules discussed in Section 3. AUTOCRYPT implements this phase in Datalog, which takes the list of sensitive variables, constants and corresponding instructions as facts [1, 11]. The typing rules discussed in Section 3 are given as constraints to Datalog which infers the encryption type for all the sensitive elements.The inference results of Datalog are fed back to the LLVM IR in the form of pragmas.

Category of file operations	Utilities
Basic operations	shred, truncate
Summarizing files	wc, sum, cksum
Formatting file contents	fmt, old, pr
Operating on characters	expand, unexpand, tr
Operating on fields	cut, paste, join
Operating on sorted files	shuf, uniq, comm, ptx, sort
Output of parts of files	head, tail, split, csplit
Output of entire files	cat, tac, nl, base64, od

Table 3: Classification of 8 categories of COREUTILS used for case study

Transformation Pass. AUTOCRYPT transforms the typed IR code to AUTOCRYPT-ed code. This phase is implemented as a transform pass in LLVM and it involves:

(a) computing the encrypted constants pool required by the program using the client's key
(b) instrumentation to load the program variables with correct values of encrypted data at run time
(c) adding calls to partially homomorphic functions which operate on encrypted parameters
(d) inserting hypercalls for converting data encrypted in one encryption scheme to another.
(e) replacing the calls to C libraries (like string operations and file operations) with AUTOCRYPT's library calls. We analyse the implementation of standard C libraries for character handling and string manipulation using AUTOCRYPT and generate precompiled AUTOCRYPT-ed libraries. We transformed 15 C library functions for evaluation of our case studies.

AUTOCRYPT transforms the annotated and well-typed IR to emit transformed un-optimized AUTOCRYPT-ed code which operates on encrypted data.

5. EVALUATION

Evaluation Goals. We aim to evaluate the effectiveness of AUTOCRYPT for following main goals:

- We evaluate the developer effort required to transform existing applications to operate on encrypted data.
- We evaluate applications to work on encrypted data using combination of various partially homomorphic encryption schemes.
- We evaluate the performance of AUTOCRYPT-ed programs compared to the traditional 'download-and-compute' strategy and use of existing fully-homomorphic encryption schemes.

5.1 Expressiveness

We select total 30 case studies from common programs available on the LAMP Stack which include COREUTILS, `file` utility and three custom programs.

CoreUtils. The use of command line utilities is popular among web services like SVN [60], GitHub [33], Google shell (goosh) [34], etc. Hence, we perform evaluation on Unix file processing applications from the COREUTILS v.8.13 package [2]. Table 3 shows the programs in 8 of total 11 categories of COREUTILS that we transform to assert the effectiveness of our solution. The remaining 3

Programs	Encrypted Variables			Encrypted Constants			Changed Instructions			Compilation Time(sec)			Execution Time(sec)			Comp.to to DC
	Enc	Tot	%	Enc	Tot	%	Enc	Tot	%	Infr.	Trans.	Total	1KB	10KB	100KB	
cat(simple)	0	324	0.00	0	30	0.00	0	446	0.00	0.04	0.02	**0.06**	0.006	0.008	0.371	**0.304**
split	116	2002	5.79	5	142	3.52	1	2712	0.04	0.20	0.08	**0.28**	0.007	0.010	0.028	**0.022**
csplit	26	598	4.34	1	32	3.12	29	1217	2.30	0.27	0.32	**0.59**	0.007	0.010	0.018	**0.014**
paste	34	583	5.83	4	70	5.71	10	809	1.24	0.13	0.05	**0.18**	0.008	0.015	0.241	**0.197**
tac	78	723	10.79	1	45	2.22	1	925	0.11	0.14	0.03	**0.17**	0.007	0.010	0.280	**0.229**
expand	14	494	2.83	7	55	12.73	7	674	1.04	0.10	0.03	**0.13**	0.010	0.021	0.254	**0.208**
unexpand	25	608	4.11	7	62	11.29	7	850	0.82	0.13	0.04	**0.17**	0.008	0.034	0.348	**0.285**
truncate	0	487	0.00	0	53	0.00	0	676	0.00	0.07	0.02	**0.09**	0.011	0.021	0.062	**0.050**
shred	0	1325	0.00	0	132	0.00	0	1767	0.00	0	0.04	**0.04**	0.125	0.144	0.172	**0.141**
shuf	53	571	9.28	0	32	0.00	1	750	0.13	0.15	0.03	**0.18**	0.007	0.020	0.351	**0.288**
nl	19	529	3.59	2	45	4.44	0	648	0.00	0.08	0.03	**0.11**	0.007	0.026	0.519	**0.426**
tail	76	931	8.16	3	39	7.69	10	819	1.22	0.11	0.14	**0.25**	0.007	0.017	0.035	**0.167**
head	155	1346	11.52	4	105	3.81	3	1848	0.16	0.23	0.11	**0.34**	0.008	0.024	0.033	**0.270**
cut	58	968	5.99	6	76	7.89	20	1385	1.44	0.11	0.150	**0.26**	0.012	0.026	0.190	**0.155**
join	54	834	6.47	1	10	0.1	6	737	0.81	0.16	0.08	**0.24**	0.026	0.046	0.237	**0.194**
tr	20	721	2.77	3	53	5.63	4	592	0.67	0.06	0.06	**0.12**	0.012	0.031	0.397	**0.325**
ptx	129	872	14.79	6	62	9.62	27	1527	1.76	0.13	0.11	**0.24**	0.014	0.057	0.291	**0.239**
pr	91	1011	9.00	16	110	14.53	12	936	1.28	0.18	0.23	**0.41**	0.030	0.446	1.37	**1.124**
fmt	124	1117	11.10	20	133	15.04	30	1546	1.94	0.58	0.14	**0.72**	0.029	0.217	1.40	**1.149**
wc	61	1002	6.09	6	67	8.96	6	1381	0.43	0.25	0.06	**0.31**	0.034	0.357	2.84	**2.33**
fold	51	370	13.78	8	34	23.53	7	487	1.44	0.13	0.03	**0.16**	0.022	0.381	2.02	**1.658**
sum	36	321	11.21	0	38	0.00	13	402	3.23	0.09	0.03	**0.12**	0.020	0.036	.549	**0.450**
base64*	81	473	17.12	0	44	0.00	11	617	1.78	0.24	0.30	**0.54**	0.200	1.534	5.33	**4.376**
cksum*	34	576	5.90	0	78	0.00	24	872	2.75	0.10	0.24	**0.34**	0.371	1.632	7.78	**6.387**
file	229	2516	9.10	7	54	12.96	23	2916	0.07	0.42	0.20	**0.62**	0.186	0.120	0.194	**0.160**

Table 2: Summary of sensitivity analysis and transform pass for 25 file processing utilities. `cat(simple)` is executed without any command line options. Only `sum`, `base64`, `cksum` (shown bold faced) make hypercalls during execution. We annotate `base64`, `cksum` (marked star) such that multiple calls for conversion between encryption types are combined into one hypercall. Last column reports the execution time ratio of AUTOCRYPT-ed programs to 'download-and-compute' method.

categories include the programs which do not operate on the sensitive contents of file and so we do not evaluate them. Our current implementation does not support command line options involving regular expressions to programs such as `ptx`, `nl`, `tr`. However, we point out that using static memory lookup hypercall or DFA evaluation techniques, regular expression matching is possible but will require advanced analysis techniques [62]. To test the programs, we create encrypted input files of size 1, 10, 100 KB under search, Paillier and Elgamal encryption schemes. In Table 2, we present the transformation and execution time for these utilities. AUTOCRYPT transforms 25 out of 30 commands of various categories to operate on pre-encrypted files of various sizes. We confirm that the transformed programs remain functional and preserve the semantics of the original application.

File Utility. We select the UNIX `file` utility, which determines the type of a given input file, as our benchmark. We select this utility because of its usage in a web server for learning the MIME type of files and determining the HTTP content header [13]. Every file type contains a magic number at a fixed position which distinguishes it from other files. A magic file is a collection of all such magic numbers and their position for various file types. We encrypt these magic numbers with search encryption scheme. The transformed `file` command uses the encrypted magic file to determine the file types of the sensitive files. The size of the input file does not effect the performance of this application as only the bytes at a fixed position are searched to identify the file type.

Custom programs. We select three particular applications to show the broad applicability of AUTOCRYPT for functions which are used for various privacy preserving computations [36,47]. Following are the programs which we include as our case studies.

(a) Matrix multiplication : Matrix multiplication is commonly used in AES encryption. The inputs to this program are encrypted with Elgamal encryption scheme. The number of hypercalls is proportional to the matrix size. We evaluate on a 5×5 matrix which makes 25 hypercalls.

```
# where plaintext at p[i] and q[i]
#can be either 1 or 0
pai8:p[n];
int :q[n];
pai8:dist;
for(i = 0; i < n; i++) {
  tmp1 = xor_pai1(p[i],q[i]);
  dist=add_pai8(dist,tmp1);
}
```
(i)

```
pai8:p[n],q[n];
pai8:dist;
 for(i = 0; i < n;i++) {
   tmp1 = sub_pai8(p[i],q[i]);
   tmp2:egml =convert(tmp1:pai8);
   tmp3 = mul_egml(tmp2,tmp2);
   tmp4:pai8 = convert(tmp3:egml);
   dist =add_pai8(dist,tmp4);
 }
```
(ii)

```
egml:first[m][p],sec[p][q];
pai8:ans[m][q];
 for ( c = 0 ; c < m ; c++ )   {
   for ( d = 0 ; d < q ; d++ ) {
     for ( k = 0 ; k < p ; k++) {
       tmp1 = mul_egml(first[c][k],sec[k][d]);
       tmp2:pai8 = convert(tmp1:egml);
       ans[c][d] = add_pai8(ans[c][d],tmp2) ;
 } } }
```
(iii)

Figure 7: Pseudocode of AUTOCRYPT-ed custom programs (i) Hamming Distance (ii) Euclidean Distance (iii) Matrix Multiplication

(b) Square of Euclidean distance: We evaluate a program for computation of square of Euclidean distance which is used in face recognition applications [47]. The hypercalls are directly proportional to the number of points used for calculating the Euclidean distance. We calculate the distance for 10 points that require a total of 20 hypercalls.

(c) Hamming distance : We calculate the hamming distance between an encrypted and a plaintext input. No hypercalls are required for this computation.

We transform these program using AUTOCRYPT and report the execution time in Table 4. The transformed pseudocode for these programs are shown in Figure 7.

Custom Program	Encrypted variable (%)	Changed Instruction (%)	Time (sec) Infr.	Time (sec) Trans.	Exec (sec)
Matrix Multiplication	12/129 (**9.30**)	75/154 (**48.70**)	0.27	0.05	0.088
Euclidean distance	15/98 (**15.3**)	50/138 (**36.23**)	0.22	0.11	0.074
Hamming distance	17/108 (**15.7**)	20/124 (**16.12**)	0.17	0.04	0.042

Table 4: Performance of custom programs. Last column reports the execution time in seconds.

Handling FHE cases. Out of the 25 COREUTILS and 3 custom programs which we transform using AUTOCRYPT, 5 applications make hypercalls to switch between different homomorphic encryption schemes. If not for our design, these applications require the capabilities of fully homomorphic encryption scheme to operate on encrypted data. Matrix Multiplication, Euclidean Distance, `sum`, `cksum` and `base64` bold faced in Table 2 and Table 4 respectively, contain operations which require switching between encryption schemes. Using our trusted hypervisor architecture and the hypervisor APIs, AUTOCRYPT can transform these applications to execute with a performance acceptable for practical usage. The execution time for applications increases linearly with the number of hypercalls. The number of hypercalls can be reduced if conversion between encryption schemes is performed in groups instead of per character. Hence, we annotate `cksum` and `base64` such that multiple hypercalls for conversion between encryption types are combined into one hypercall. However, the performance is still better as compared to requesting the client for conversion between encryption schemes. A single hypercall takes around 2 ms in our implementation —which is 3 times faster as compared to sending bytes to the client.

Untransformed applications. We discuss 5 applications from the COREUTILS which either do not type-check according to our system or require homomorphic operations that leaks a lot of information about the sensitive data. Hence, these are beyond our security design.

- The `cat` command (when executed with 'show-nonprinting' option) and `od` command requires a conversion from Paillier to search encryption. According to our type-system, such conversion leaks information (see Section 3), thus is unsafe. Note that, AUTOCRYPT can still transform these commands, however allowing such transformations will reduce the security of our system.

- The `sort` command requires the input file encrypted under order preserving scheme (OPE) as it performs relational operations (< , >) on the sensitive inputs. OPE is a weak encryption schemes as it reveals the order of encrypted data [50]. Combining OPE with search encryption scheme leaks considerable amount of information which lowers the security guarantees of AUTOCRYPT.

- `comm` and `uniq` does an equality check operation on two characters, both from the input file. To support this functionality we require the input files encrypted under deterministic encryption scheme. However, this scheme is not semantically secure and keeping a copy of this file downgrades security.

We point that for a setting where compromising semantic security of sensitive files is tolerable, AUTOCRYPT can transform the above applications to run on sensitive inputs encrypted in expected partially homomorphic encryption scheme.

5.2 Reduction in Developer Effort

We claim that AUTOCRYPT reduces the amount of developer effort required for transforming applications to operate on encrypted data. We demonstrate the reduction in developer effort by reporting the following evaluation

- fraction of the encrypted constants and variables
- fraction of the LOC modified
- the compilation time of the transformed applications using AUTOCRYPT

Table 2 summaries the analysis and execution results for 25 Unix file processing applications. For all our case studies, the number of SSA variables range from **300 to 3000**, and only **9-10%** of them are eventually encrypted. From the pool of instructions generated in the LLVM IR only **1%** of the them are changed during the transform pass. The number of constants encrypted is around **7-8%** of the total constants. These figures show that only a small amount of variables, constants and instructions are modified during the transformation. However, manually analysing a particular application and identifying exactly which sensitive variables need encryption is a non-trivial task for developers. AUTOCRYPT relieves the developer from this task and infers all the above details within reasonable time limit. Compilation measurements comprise of time spent for LLVM analysis, inference and transformation passes to AUTOCRYPT given application. The average time for transformation to AUTOCRYPT-ed code ranges from **40 ms to 720 ms**.

5.3 Runtime Performance

We perform the evaluation on Ubuntu 12.04 as guest VM with Xen hypervisor on a 8 GB RAM machine. Table 2 reports the execution time of AUTOCRYPT-ed programs for input files of 1, 10, 100 KB sizes. Out of 25 applications, 19 execute within 1 second for all the input files. Remaining 6 applications take more than 1 second. The execution time for each command is directly proportional to the input file size. However, this also applies to programs that are executed in the unencrypted domain. Our results show that operating over encrypted data using AUTOCRYPT transformed code incurs some runtime overhead over native execution which is a few milliseconds. However, native untransformed applications do not provide any security of input data. Therefore, we compare performance of AUTOCRYPT-ed programs to already known techniques of 'download-and-compute' and fully homomorphic encryption scheme.

Comparison to Download-and-compute We compare whether AUTOCRYPT-ed programs are faster to execute than the 'download-and-compute' mechanism. We measure the download and upload time for GitHub and DropBox file systems, for files of sizes 1, 10 and 100 KB (averaged over 10 runs of each size). The observed network latency is 4.88 ms/KB and 6.0 ms/KB for Dropbox and GitHub servers respectively as measured from our campus network. For OpenSSL AES scheme, the encryption-decryption cycle takes 8 ms and 10 ms respectively for 100 KB file on a machine of 8 GB RAM and i7 core processor. Considering this as a baseline for the 'download-and-compute' mechanism, we compare the performance of AUTOCRYPT-ed programs. The last column in Table 2 shows the ratio of execution time of AUTOCRYPT-ed program on 100 KB file and execution time of 'download-and-compute' mechanism. Out of 25 applications, 19 execute faster and only 6 applications slow down by factor of 2 to 6 as compared to 'download-and-compute' mechanism. Overall, AUTOCRYPT results are promising, and it is practical to execute legacy applications on server with comparable performance to downloading encrypted files on client device for computation. We speculate that with faster cryptographic implementation and optimization, in the future we can achieve better execution performance using AUTOCRYPT. Our results serve as a baseline for comparison of future work in this direction.

Comparison to FHE. Certainly, AUTOCRYPT-ed code is practically faster as opposed to impractical implementations of current fully homomorphic encryption schemes. Publically available implementations of FHE take several minutes to compute simple integer operations, whereas AUTOCRYPT completes execution over complete file in this time [5]. We do not compare the time for executing these applications using FHE as no standard tool is available that runs existing C applications on FHE encrypted files. Our evaluation shows that combining partially homomorphic encryptions schemes to operate on encrypted data is a promising direction until performance of fully-homomorphic computation become reasonable for practical purposes.

6. RELATED WORK

Application of Partially Homomorphic Cryptosystems. Partially homomorphic encryption schemes are a promising direction for performing computations on encrypted data. SCiFI [47] and Sadeghi et al. [54] provide secure techniques for face recognition using homomorphic cryptosystems. Bianchi et al. [15] proposes computing discrete cosine transforms in encrypted domain and Kuribayashi et al. [41] proposes a secure fingerprinting protocol for images; both these techniques are based on the additive homomorphic property of encryption schemes. These work mainly use the homomorphic property of a particular encryption scheme to support secure evaluation of a target application. In AUTOCRYPT, we combine the homomorphic properties supported by various encryption schemes and investigate its use on a broad scale of applications. CryptDB [51] supports privacy preserving computation on encrypted database by combining various partially homomorphic encryption schemes. In our work, we automatically transform applications to use multiple homomorphic schemes, thereby automating the insight provide by Popa et al. work [55].

Secure Multi-Party Computations. A different approach for privacy preserving computation on encrypted data is to use garbled circuits, which were first proposed in the context of secure function evaluation for two-party protocols [63]. Tools such as Fairplay [43], FairplayMP [14], VIFF [22] support secure multi-party computations using garbled circuits. TASTY [36] combines garbled circuit and homomorphic encryption schemes to enable privacy preserving two-party computations. A recent work by Holzer et al. achieves secure two-party computation for ANSI C [37]. The size of the garbled circuit (which increases for large functions) dominates the performance in these multi-party computation setting. Most of the above solutions (except [37]) require the users to specify the secure function in a special-purpose high level language whereas AUTOCRYPT directly supports a simple C language.

Type System for computation on encrypted data. Fournet et al. [28] proposes a information flow type system for homomorphic encryptions. The type system of AUTOCRYPT is somewhat similar to [28], with additional support for conversion from one encryption scheme to other. We also discuss the security guarantees provided by our type-system. Mitchell et al. proposes a Haskell based language for secure cloud computing in muti-party computation and fully-homomorphic encryption platforms [46]. Fletcher et al. proposes a compiler for converting complex program to work on inputs encrypted with fully homomorphic encryption schemes [26]. In AUTOCRYPT however, we focus on partially homomorphic encryptions for secure computation on encrypted data.

Computation using Fully-Homomorphic Encryption. Another solution for privacy preserving computation on encrypted data is to use fully-homomorphic encryption. It allows securely computing arbitrary functions on encrypted data, with the first such feasible scheme proposed by Gentry [30]. The performance of such schemes is too slow for practical purposes [31]; though techniques to make it practical are of considerable interest and are being investigated [19, 56].

7. CONCLUSION

In this paper we show the effectiveness and applicability of a new tool AUTOCRYPT in enabling homomorphic computation in existing C applications. Together with a trusted hypervisor, AUTOCRYPT-ed programs offer second line of defenses against server-side data attacks.

8. ACKNOWLEDGEMENT

We thank the anonymous reviewers for their insightful comments and suggestions. We thank Zhenkai Liang, Ee-Chien Chang for their comments on an early presentation of this work and Asankhaya Sharma for his valuable suggestions about our type system. This work is supported by the Ministry of Education, Singapore under Grant No. R-252-000-495-133. Any opinions, findings, and conclusions or recommendations expressed in this paper are those of the authors and do not necessarily reflect the views of the Ministry of Education, Singapore.

9. REFERENCES

[1] Datalog Educational System. `http://des.sourceforge.net`.

[2] GNU CoreUtils. `http://www.gnu.org/software/coreutils/`.

[3] GNU Libgcrypt. `www.gnu.org/software/libgcrypt`.

[4] Personal Data Protection Act 2012. `www.mci.gov.sg`.

[5] Scarab Library. `https://hcrypt.com//scarab-library`.

[6] Vaultize. `www.vaultize.com`.

[7] Mcafee host intrusion prevention for server. `www.mcafee.com`, 2012.

[8] Standards for the protection of personal information of residents of the commonwealth. `www.mass.gov/ocabr/docs/idtheft/201cmr1700reg.pdf`, 2012.

[9] Summary of the HIPAA Privacy Rule. `www.hhs.gov`, 2012.

[10] What's holding back the cloud? `www.intel.com`, 2012.

[11] S. Abiteboul, R. Hull, and V. Vianu. *Foundations of Databases*. Addison-Wesley, 1995.

[12] D. Akhawe, F. Li, W. He, P. Saxena, and D. Song. Data-Confined HTML5 Applications. In *Technical Report*, 2013.

[13] A. Barth, J. Caballero, and D. Song. Secure Content Sniffing for Web Browsers, or How to Stop Papers from Reviewing Themselves. In *Security and Privacy*, 2009.

[14] A. Ben-david, N. Nisan, and B. Pinkas. FairplayMP: A System for Secure Multi-party Computation. In *ACM CCS*, October 2008.

[15] T. Bianchi, A. Piva, and M. Barni. Encrypted Domain DCT Based on Homomorphic Cryptosystems. In *EURASIP*, 2009.

[16] D. Boneh, G. D. Crescenzo, R. Ostrovsky, and G. Persiano. Public Key Encryption with Keyword Search. In *EUROCRYPT*, 2004.

[17] D. Boneh, G. Segev, and B. Waters. Targeted Malleability: Homomorphic Encryption for Restricted Computations. 2012.

[18] BoxCryptor. https://www.boxcryptor.com/.

[19] Z. Brakerski, C. Gentry, and V. Vaikuntanathan. Fully Homomorphic Encryption without Bootstrapping. In *Electronic Colloquium on Computational Complexity*, 2011.

[20] D. Brumley and D. Boneh. Remote timing attacks are practical. In *USENIX Security Symposium 2003*.

[21] CloudFogger. http://www.cloudfogger.com/en/.

[22] I. Damgård, M. Geisler, M. Krøigaard, and J. B. Nielsen. Asynchronous Multiparty Computation: Theory and Implementation. In *Public Key Cryptography(PKC)*, 2009.

[23] D. E. Denning. A Lattice Model of Secure Information Flow. *Commun. ACM*, 1976.

[24] T. ElGamal. A Public-Key Cryptosystem and a Signature Scheme Based on Discrete Logarithms. In *CRYPTO'84*.

[25] M. Fischetti. Data Theft: Hackers Attack. http://www.scientificamerican.com, 2011.

[26] C. Fletcher, M. van Dijk, and S. Devadas. Compilation Techniques for Efficient Encrypted Computation. In *Cryptology ePrint Archive, Report 2012/266.*

[27] J. S. Foster, T. Terauchi, and A. Aiken. Flow-sensitive Type Qualifiers. In *ACM SIGPLAN*, PLDI '02.

[28] C. Fournet, J. Planul, and T. Rezk. Information-flow Types for Homomorphic Encryptions. In *CCS '11.*

[29] R. Gennaro, C. Gentry, and B. Parno. Non-interactive verifiable computing: Outsourcing computation to untrusted workers. In *CRYPTO*, 2010.

[30] C. Gentry. Fully Homomorphic Encryption Using Ideal Lattices. In *41st Annual ACM Symposium on Theory of Computing*, 2009.

[31] C. Gentry and S. Halevi. A Working Implementation of Fully Homomorphic Encryption. In *EUROCRYPT*, 2010.

[32] C. Gentry and S. Halevi. Implementing gentry's fully homomorphic encryption scheme. In *EUROCRYPT*, 2011.

[33] GitHub. https://github.com.

[34] Goosh. http://goosh.org, 2008.

[35] B. Hardekopf and C. Lin. Flow-sensitive Pointer Analysis for Millions of Lines of Code. In *CGO '11.*

[36] W. Henecka, S. Kogl, A.-R. Sadeghi, T. Schneider, and I. Wehrenberg. TASTY: Tool for Automating Secure Two-partY computations. In *ACM CCS*, 2010.

[37] A. Holzer, M. Franz, S. Katzenbeisser, and H. Veith. Secure two-party computations in ANSI C. In *CCS '12.*

[38] Y. Huang, D. Evans, J. Katz, and L. Malka. Faster Secure Two-Party Computation Using Garbled Circuits. In *Usenix Security Symposium*, 2011.

[39] T. Kim and N. Zeldovich. Making Linux Protection Mechanisms Egalitarian with UserFS. In *Usenix Security Symposium*, 2010.

[40] B. Kopf and M. Durmuth. A Provably Secure And Efficient Countermeasure Against Timing Attacks. In *IEEE Computer Security Foundations Symposium*, 2009.

[41] M. Kuribayashi and H. Tanaka. Fingerprinting Protocol for Images Based on Additive Homomorphic Property. In *IEEE Transactions on Image Processing*, 2005.

[42] LLVM. http://llvm.org.

[43] D. Malkhi, N. Nisan, B. Pinkas, and Y. Sella. Fairplay - A Secure Two-Party Computation System. In *USENIX Security Symposium*, 2004.

[44] J. M. McCune, Y. Li, N. Qu, Z. Zhou, A. Datta, V. Gligor, and A. Perrig. TrustVisor: Efficient TCB Reduction and Attestation. In *IEEE Security and Privacy*, 2010.

[45] J. M. McCune, B. Parnoy, A. Perrig, M. K. Reiter, and H. Isozaki. Flicker: An Execution Infrastructure for TCB Minimization. In *EuroSys*, 2008.

[46] J. Mitchell, R. Sharma, D. Stefan, and J. Zimmerman. Information-flow Control for Programming on Encrypted data. In *IEEE Computer Security Foundations Symposium(CSF)*, 2012.

[47] M. Osadchy, B. Pinkas, A. Jarrous, and B. Moskovich. SCiFI - A System for Secure Face Identification. In *Security and Privacy 2010.*

[48] P. Paillier. Public-key Cryptosystems Based on Composite Degree Residuosity Classes. In *EUROCRYPT*, 1999.

[49] B. Parno, J. M. McCune, D. Wendlandt, D. G. Andersen, and A. Perrig. CLAMP: Practical Prevention of Large-Scale Data Leaks. In *Security and Privacy*, 2009.

[50] R. A. Popa, F. H. Li, and N. Zeldovich. An Ideal-Security Protocol for Order-Preserving Encoding. In *IEEE Symposium on Security and Privacy*, 2013.

[51] R. A. Popa, C. M. S. Redfield, N. Zeldovich, and H. Balakrishnan. CryptDB: Protecting Confidentiality with Encrypted Query Processing. In *SOSP*, 2011.

[52] K. P. N. Puttaswamy, C. Kruegel, and B. Y. Zhao. Silverline: Toward Data Confidentiality in Storage-intensive Sloud Applications. SOCC '11.

[53] A. Sabelfeld and A. Myers. Language-based Information-flow Security. *Selected Areas in Communications, IEEE Journal*, 2003.

[54] A.-R. Sadeghi, T. Schneider, and I. Wehrenberg. Efficient Privacy-Preserving Face Recognition. In *ICISC*, 2009.

[55] M. Shah, E. Stark, R. A. Popa, and N. Zeldovich. Language Support for Efficient Computation over Encrypted Data. In *Off the Beaten Track Workshop*, 2012.

[56] N. Smart and F. Vercauteren. Fully Homomorphic Encryption with Relatively Small Key and Ciphertext Sizes. Cryptology ePrint Archive, Report 2009/571, 2009.

[57] G. Smith. Principles of Secure Information Flow Analysis. In *Malware Detection*, 2007.

[58] D. X. Song, D. Wagner, and A. Perrig. Practical Techniques for Searches on Encrypted Data . In *21st IEEE Symposium on Security and Privacy, Oakland, CA*, 2000.

[59] E. Stefanov, E. Shi, and D. Song. Towards Practical Oblivious RAM. *CoRR*, 2011.

[60] SVN. http://subversion.tigris.org.

[61] A. Vasudevan, S. Chaki, L. Jia, J. M. McCune, J. Newsome, and A. Datta. Design, Implementation and Verification of an eXtensible and Modular Hypervisor Framework. In *IEEE Symposium on Security and Privacy*, 2013.

[62] L. Wei and M. K. Reiter. Third-Party Private DFA Evaluation on Encrypted Files in the Cloud. In *Computer Security ESORICS 2012.*

[63] A. C. Yao. Protocols for Secure Computations. In *23rd Annual IEEE Symposium on Foundations of Computer Science*, 1982.

[64] Y. Yu, J. Leiwo, and B. Premkumar. A Study on the Security of Privacy Homomorphism. In *ITNG 2006.*

Protecting Sensitive Web Content from Client-side Vulnerabilities with CRYPTONs

Xinshu Dong
Dept. of Computer Science, National Univ. of Singapore
xdong@comp.nus.edu.sg

Zhaofeng Chen*
Inst. of Computer Science and Technology, Peking Univ.
chenzhaofeng@pku.edu.cn

Hossein Siadati*
Dept. of Computer Science and Engineering, Polytechnic Inst. of New York Univ.
shs422@nyu.edu

Shruti Tople
Dept. of Computer Science, National Univ. of Singapore
shruti90@comp.nus.edu.sg

Prateek Saxena
Dept. of Computer Science, National Univ. of Singapore
prateeks@comp.nus.edu.sg

Zhenkai Liang
Dept. of Computer Science, National Univ. of Singapore
liangzk@comp.nus.edu.sg

ABSTRACT

Web browsers isolate web origins, but do not provide direct abstractions to isolate sensitive data and control computation over it within the same origin. As a result, guaranteeing security of sensitive web content requires trusting all code in the browser and client-side applications to be vulnerability-free. In this paper, we propose a new abstraction, called CRYPTON, which supports *intra-origin* control over sensitive data throughout its life cycle. To securely enforce the semantics of CRYPTONs, we develop a standalone component called CRYPTON-KERNEL, which extensively leverages the functionality of existing web browsers without relying on their large TCB. Our evaluation demonstrates that the CRYPTON abstraction supported by the CRYPTON-KERNEL is widely applicable to popular real-world applications with millions of users, including webmail, chat, blog applications, and Alexa Top 50 websites, with low performance overhead.

Categories and Subject Descriptors

D.4.6 [**Operating Systems**]: Security and Protection;
K.6.5 [**Management of Computing and Information Systems**]: Security and Protection

Keywords

Web security, browser security, data protection

1. INTRODUCTION

Presently, web browsers are designed to isolate content between web origins [38], preventing data owned by one origin from being accessed by other origins. However, in practice, information processed within a web origin's protection domain often has different levels of sensitivity. Some application data — which we refer to as *sensitive data* in this paper — is critically sensitive and more important than the rest of application data. Social security numbers, medical reports, enterprise emails with financial data, tax-related information, bank transactions, and user passwords are all examples of such sensitive data. Web application owners often wish to strongly isolate sensitive data within their applications, to protect it from vulnerabilities in the code that processes non-sensitive information.

Under the origin-based model, web applications processing sensitive data, such as password managers [43] and encrypted chat or email clients [41], have to completely trust the client-side browser's origin-based isolation mechanisms and the correctness of the client-side application code [2, 67]. Information belonging to one origin is accessible to all the application code running within the protection domain of that origin, as well as the browser code (including add-ons), even if they do not need to access such information. The client-side web application and the underlying browsers consist of millions of lines of code and have had their steady share of security vulnerabilities historically; client-side application vulnerabilities (like DOM-XSS [62]) are pervasive in client-side application code and browser add-ons [14]. Given the scope of client-side vulnerabilities, protecting sensitive data within the browser environment is a serious practical concern.

Problem. The crux of the problem is that the web lacks abstractions for information owners to specify what information is sensitive and how it must be processed in the client-side web browser environment. To address this problem, we envision new abstractions that give owners control of select sensitive data over its lifetime in the client-side browser. We term these as *intra-origin data control* abstractions. In particular, we advocate that web browsers provide these controls as *first-class* abstractions on the web, independently of strengthening the browser's origin-based isolation.

Although there has been extensive prior work on browser design, principled mechanisms for intra-origin data control have not received much direct attention. For instance, recent browser designs have significantly improved privilege separation between code components [4, 5, 16, 21, 25, 33, 46, 63, 69]. However, these techniques do not directly allow web applications to enforce control on their data; a compromised component with access to sensitive data can still launder it through its export interfaces. For example, the sandboxed renderer process in Google Chrome [5], if compromised, can

*Research done when visiting National University of Singapore.

CCS'13, November 4–8, 2013, Berlin, Germany.

http://dx.doi.org/10.1145/2508859.2516743.

still exploit legitimate network interfaces provided by the Chrome kernel to leak data to attacker-controlled domains (say via an `img` load) [17]. Although information control has been investigated through language-based enforcements [22, 34, 50, 67], these mechanisms fail to extend the protection to the lowest level (e.g. against attacks targeting low-level memory access). Piecemeal techniques (such as SFI [68], JIT hardening [59], and CSP [67]) could be a plausible basis for sensitive data protection. However, we argue to build more direct information control primitives on the present web.

Our solution. We design and implement a data abstraction and browser primitive, called CRYPTON, which enables protecting sensitive data throughout its lifetime in the browser. CRYPTONs are programmed directly in existing web languages (HTML/JavaScript), without requiring major re-engineering of existing application logic. A CRYPTON explicitly marks a unit of sensitive data in a web page; its semantics enforce that sensitive data and information computed from them are tightly isolated at the lowest level (in the raw program memory). To support rich web applications that need to execute flexible operations on sensitive data, CRYPTONs tie sensitive data with functions that are allowed to compute over it. These few select CRYPTON functions are trusted to be statically verified by web developers and are the only channels for releasing information about sensitive web content. In addition, a CRYPTON provides other important capabilities for protecting sensitive data in web applications — guaranteed rendering (with a proof-of-impression), and certified delivery of user inputs to CRYPTON functions in the browser.

Building trustworthy implementations of these abstractions is an important, but challenging goal. The main challenge stems from the *monolithic* trust model of today's web — application servers have to completely trust the client-side code in web browsers, addons and applications.

To address this practical concern, we rethink the monolithic trust model that web applications have on client-side code. In our design, the web server trusts a small piece of client-side code called CRYPTON-KERNEL— a small, trusted standalone engine, which acts as a root-of-trust for the server on the client device. The CRYPTON-KERNEL runs in a separate OS process and sandboxes the untrusted browser, which invokes the CRYPTON-KERNEL on-demand to securely interpret CRYPTONs. A compromised browser can deny access to sensitive information (denial-of-service) by refusing to invoke the CRYPTON-KERNEL, but it cannot subvert the integrity and confidentiality of sensitive data. In effect, our design of the CRYPTON-KERNEL allows web applications to specify control on sensitive information, bootstrap rich computation on it and build trusted paths between the user and the sensitive application code [53].

Unlike prior research on origin-based isolation in browsers, we do not isolate code components or memory regions; instead we isolate sensitive data within a web application's origin using authenticated encryption. CRYPTONs make use of *memory encryption* [45], wherein data computed from sensitive data remains encrypted throughout its lifetime inside the untrusted browser's memory. This ensures that any unintended malicious or compromised code, whether part of the browser or the application logic, can only access sensitive data in its encrypted form. Memory encryption allows sensitive data to be opaquely accessed by an untrusted browser functionality (such as the network stack, data stores, language parsers, rendering logic, and so on) as well as application logic, without risking its confidentiality and integrity.

Therefore, the CRYPTON-KERNEL enforces its security guarantees while reusing browser functionality — it does not rely on the browser's same-origin policy enforcement, its components such as the HTML parser, the JavaScript/CSS engine, and the network engine to ensure its security properties. The CRYPTON-KERNEL has a TCB about $30\times$ - $40\times$ smaller than that of a real web browser, such as Firefox and Google Chrome, consisting of roughly $27K$ lines of code. Through manual analysis, we find that this design can prevent more than 92.5% of known security vulnerabilities from exfiltrating or tampering with sensitive information, in a web browser such as Firefox (Section 4).

Evaluation on real-world applications. First, we manually modify three popular web applications to selectively use CRYPTONs to protect sensitive web content within them, including a webmail, a web messenger and a web forum. The results show that the CRYPTON-KERNEL strengthens their security against a broad range of client-side vulnerabilities, with a small (around 3-5 days of) adoption effort. Next, we conduct an extensive macro evaluation of the applicability of CRYPTONs on real-world web sites including Alexa Top 50 websites, such as account signup pages like Gmail, social networking sites like Facebook, banking sites like Bank of America, e-commerce applications like eBay, and several others. We treat all user inputs (form fields, text-boxes, selections, etc.) and other manually marked content in these applications as sensitive information. Our macro study shows the effectiveness of our solution in these real-world web applications. Although not a "turn-key" mechanism, our solution requires only moderate adoption effort in the order of a few days for each application. Moreover, web developers can "opt-in" by selectively converting part of their application logic to secure specific sensitive data or for specific users, without breaking the rest of the application. Finally, we evaluate the performance of our prototype. Although our WebKit-based prototype implementation is still an unoptimized proof-of-concept, we do not perceive noticeable slowdown when running it over real-world applications. Further evaluation also shows that performance overhead from encryption/decryption operations is also modest, less than 8% when 100% of the texts on five test pages from the Dromaeo web benchmarks are marked as sensitive.

Contributions. In summary, we make the following contributions in this work.

- To the best of our knowledge, we are the first to propose a data-centric abstraction for end-to-end data protection in web browsers. We employ memory encryption to protect sensitive data in web browsers, offering strong protection at a low overhead.

- With the new abstraction, we propose a novel solution for protecting sensitive web content with a small trusted computing base (TCB), roughly $30\times$ - $40\times$ smaller than a full browser in our prototype. Our design advocates rethinking the monolithic (all-or-nothing) trust model between servers and clients on the present web.

- We perform a large-scale evaluation of the applicability of intra-origin abstractions like CRYPTONs in existing popular applications. We demonstrate the adoptability of these abstractions into a large number of real-world web sites today with a small developer effort.

2. PROBLEM & OVERVIEW

To illustrate the need for new abstractions for sensitive data, consider the example of a webmail application, such as Gmail. Currently, all code and data in client-side web applications are treated equally in protection. However, this does not match the security requirements in practical settings. Users may use a webmail account to access both leisure emails and corporate emails. As corporate emails may contain sensitive information pertaining to trade secrets or financial information, for corporate security, a user Alice may be willing to instruct the webmail application to mark her corporate emails as sensitive and strongly protect them from being leaked or tampered with. Unfortunately, even if her webmail service provider is willing, it is difficult for it to guarantee the privacy of sensitive emails when they are processed and displayed in the client's web browser. The current web provides no abstractions for webmail applications to isolate corporate emails and specify controlled (but rich) computation on them at the client side.

2.1 Threat Model

In web applications like the above webmail example, sensitive data is exposed to a large threat landscape due to vulnerabilities in the client-side web stack. Below we discuss some of the in-scope threats.

- *Browser components.* Vulnerabilities in browser components can lead to violation of the confidentiality and integrity of sensitive information. We measure the number of such vulnerabilities in Mozilla Firefox. As part of a larger study [24], we manually examine security vulnerabilities of Firefox over the past seven years from its bug database [29]. We find that out of the 360 vulnerabilities accessible to us, at least 288 (80%) ones could expose sensitive information to arbitrary malicious script or binary code running in the browser's chrome privilege.
- *Browser add-ons.* Browser add-ons and extensions may access sensitive data processed in browsers. Although web browsers may prompt users to approve the permissions requested by add-ons during their install time, many users may "click-through" to grant them to the add-ons. We surveyed the Top 30 Chrome extensions, and find that 23 request access to Gmail; if these are installed and have vulnerabilities, they can be compromised by attackers to access sensitive email. 15 out of these 23 have been confirmed to contain code-injection vulnerabilities in Carlini et al.'s recent work [14].
- *Application components.* Web application components can also access sensitive data in web applications. The Gmail Inbox page contains 171.1 KB code (including HTML, CSS, JS), while only 1.7 KB of it needs to access email content. However, client-side web application vulnerabilities are pervasive, including mixed content, unsafe `evals`, capability leaks, DOM-XSS, and insufficient origin validation.[1]

In this paper, we focus on providing two security guarantees on sensitive data processed in the client-side browser: *integrity* and *confidentiality*. Our design assumes that there are client-side vulnerabilities in web applications (including add-ons) and browsers, but trusts the underlying OS, its windowing and graphics interfaces. Our defenses preclude many vulnerabilities (outlined above) from corrupting sensitive data or leaking unprotected sensitive data to adversaries. For instance, attackers can exploit client-side vulnerabilities to leak sensitive emails to remote adversaries. However, in our solution, those emails are in encrypted form and the decryption keys are inaccessible to attackers. Several attacks are outside the scope of the guaranteed security properties; we discuss them in Section 2.4.

[1]Gmail does not include external libraries and does not mix content from HTTP sites; nevertheless, several other web applications we study in Section 4 include external libraries and mixed content, which poses serious threat to sensitive information.

2.2 CRYPTON: A New Abstraction

We introduce a new data protection abstraction called CRYPTON. Conceptually, CRYPTONs are akin to classes in object-oriented languages, which encapsulate sensitive data together with the operations that can legitimately operate on it. CRYPTONs provide the following 4 main capabilities.

Information isolation. We enable transparent isolation of sensitive data from other data and code in web browsers. In our webmail example discussed earlier, the confidentiality of the sensitive corporate emails must be maintained by authenticated encryption. Other examples include credit card numbers, contents of shopping carts in e-commerce applications, user passwords in login pages, payee accounts in online banking sites, and so on. Our assumption is that preventing malicious code from running in the complex web browser is not tractable; however, we aim to prevent unauthorized leakage or tampering of sensitive data.

Controlled operations. If we isolate sensitive data from all computation, it would severely disincentivize web applications from outsourcing rich functionality to the client-side browser. There is a trade-off between the information isolation guarantees and the richness of functionality that can operate on sensitive information. In our webmail example, Alice should be able to use the webmail's interfaces on her corporate emails for reading, composing, formatting (configuring fonts, colors, HTML formatting or alignments), archiving, forwarding and so on. For practical usage, we aim to allow such owner-specified operations to compute output from sensitive data. However, such output must be protected from confidentiality and integrity attacks by all other code in the browser, and thus is encrypted by default. The data owner (e.g., the webmail server) can also specify which operations reveal computed information; however, we leave the design and choice of these functions up to the owner. In this work, we make encryption possible on simple data types, such as strings and integers, to limit the TCB size — of course, more complex data types (such as arrays, formatted HTML) can still include encrypted data in them (see Section 3.4).

Certified user inputs. In this work, we focus on enabling users to enter sensitive text strings via a trusted keyboard[2]. Specifically, we provide a trusted path for user inputs between the OS keyboard events and the trusted web application event handlers (specified as CRYPTON functions), through the untrusted web browser. Our focus on keyboard events is guided by the observation that a significant fraction of sensitive data on the web pertains to user keyboard inputs. In our webmail example, Alice signs in by using her password, composes a sensitive email by typing, and searches for keywords also by using the keyboard.

Proof of impression. Malicious client-side code can attempt to disable critical messages that are supposed to warn users of potential threats. For example, the webmail server may show a warning for emails suspected to be scams and banks may want to warn of fraudulent activities. As another example, when the webmail server detects suspicious login activities, such as simultaneous logins from different geolocations, it alerts users to change their passwords. Such messages are crucial, and may be helpful for users to prevent attacks or to stop them at an early stage.

[2]Supporting trusted paths for other input devices, such as the mouse, touch screen and stylus, is future work.

In this work, we focus on providing a "proof of impression" of simple data types such as strings and byte streams. This includes verifiable rendering of string content and bitmaps, during which rendering of other untrusted content into the same region is temporarily blocked for t seconds (t=3 by default) [36]. Such a guarantee is useful beyond the webmail example, such as online advertisements (ads). Proof of impression can help advertisers that bill publishers for ad impressions to disambiguate real ad impressions from ad fraud with "laundered" traffic [26].

2.3 Design Overview

Our design changes the monolithic trust model where web servers trust the entire browser (including add-ons) and client-side application code. In our design, developers encapsulate sensitive data, such as corporate emails or bank statements, into CRYPTONs and directly embed them in HTML documents. To enforce the security guarantees and semantics of CRYPTONs, the web server trusts a small, standalone engine at the client called the CRYPTON-KERNEL. The CRYPTON-KERNEL executes outside the web browser and is protected from a compromised browser by standard OS sandboxing mechanisms, similar to those used by existing browsers such as Google Chrome [56,57]. A CRYPTON-compliant web browser recognizes CRYPTONs during HTML document parsing and delegates their handling to the CRYPTON-KERNEL, as detailed in Section 3.

The CRYPTON-KERNEL acts as a root-of-trust to protect sensitive CRYPTONs at the client-side. Specifically, the CRYPTON-KERNEL builds three trusted paths passing through the untrusted browser: (a) a secure communication channel between the web server and the CRYPTON-KERNEL, (b) a trusted path from the CRYPTONs to the user's screen (i.e., to the software rendering pixel maps or the GPU display buffers), and (c) a trusted path between the user's keyboard inputs to CRYPTON functions that handle keyboard events. These trusted (data) paths run through the untrusted browser code, reusing existing browser functionality. As we introduce later, we use authenticated encryption to protect data on these trusted paths [45].

Secure Channel to Server. At the start of a web session exchanging sensitive data, the web server uses an HTTPS frontend to establish a secure channel with the trusted CRYPTON-KERNEL. This secure channel enables the web server to share a session key set $\mathcal{K}$ with the CRYPTON-KERNEL, used by both parties to encrypt/decrypt CRYPTONs in the session. To avoid bloating our TCB, the CRYPTON-KERNEL delegates all network communication to the untrusted browser. Thus, it is important to establish a secure channel against man-in-the-middle attacks, in case the browser gets compromised. We use the standard mutual SSL authentication protocol to establish this channel [28]. SSL certificate verification for server authentication is a common, backward-compatible mechanisms for HTTPS sites today. To enable the server to authenticate the CRYPTON-KERNEL's certificate, we assume the CRYPTON-KERNEL uses a certificate self-signed by an RSA private key stored in the CRYPTON-KERNEL. The corresponding public key is uploaded by the user to the server via an out-of-band secure channel. We discuss the potential usability challenges of this mechanism in Section 3.5.

Secure Display. When being displayed to users, sensitive content, such as corporate emails, must remain encrypted in the untrusted browser until the final rendering of the content. The CRYPTON-KERNEL provides a trusted data path between the CRYPTON content received from the server to the GPU buffer [5], which finally render bitmaps and pixels to the screen. This trusted path is implemented as part of the CRYPTON-KERNEL. To maintain the browser's functionality, sensitive content must be given opaque access to the untrusted browser, say for deciding the layout dimensions or for storing them in the DOM or untrusted JavaScript heaps. Hence, the CRYPTON-KERNEL encapsulates encrypted sensitive content into *opaque objects* before passing them to the web browser. These opaque objects (e.g. encrypted string class) allow the browser to process sensitive data as opaque blobs of text, determine the length of the underlying plaintext for layout, but do not permit any malicious operation that would leak plaintext data. Opaque objects are finally rendered by the CRYPTON-KERNEL using a "sandboxed GPU buffer" mechanism [5], which enables it to ensure that sensitive content is rendered on top for at least t seconds.

Trusted Path For User Input. For sensitive content generated at the client, such as by user keyboard inputs, the CRYPTON-KERNEL provides a trusted path between the OS keyboard events to the CRYPTON functions designated to handle input events. To enable it, the CRYPTON-KERNEL intercepts all keyboard events from the OS, similar to Chrome's sandboxing mechanism [5]. It uses opaque string objects to establish the trusted data paths via the untrusted browser code.

We expect the user Alice to recognize and enter sensitive keyboard inputs (e.g., passwords or email recipients in TO and CC list) through the CRYPTON-enabled trusted path. To help users securely interact on and across multiple CRYPTON-enabled sessions, the CRYPTON-KERNEL displays two security indicators above the untrusted browser UI. For distinguishing when her user inputs are going to be encrypted (vs. when she is interacting with a non-CRYPTON-enabled session), the CRYPTON-KERNEL displays a user-selected secret image icon. This image icon indicates that the user's key events will be encrypted throughout the session. This indicator informs users whether their sensitive keystrokes are going to be encrypted; we expect users to enter sensitive information only when seeing the right image icon.

Second, the CRYPTON-KERNEL displays the URL of the website whose keys are being used to encrypt the keystrokes, in a special unspoofable URL bar above the browser chrome. This allows Alice to distinguish between multiple CRYPTON sessions and identify to which of these sessions her present keystrokes are being delivered. This indicator informs the user of the intended recipient of the encrypted keystrokes; users are expected to verify this URL indicator and ensure that it is the right recipient for the sensitive data they are about to enter.

Both UI indicators are securely rendered to the screen directly by the CRYPTON-KERNEL and can not be overlaid by the attacker. The CRYPTON-KERNEL does not allow the untrusted browser to inject key sequences or read sensitive GPU buffers using standard sandboxing techniques. We discuss more details in Section 3.

Assumptions. A CRYPTON-compliant server uses an HTTPS frontend as the server-side interface to the CRYPTON-KERNEL. HTTPS frontends often handle authentication and are commonly used for load balancing, before delegating the session to backend server — we believe our design can be deployed in existing HTTPS frontends. CRYPTON-compliant servers default-deny access to protected sensitive content outside the secure channel established with a trusted CRYPTON-KERNEL. Otherwise, this would incentivize attackers to fool users into accessing the sensitive content over non-CRYPTON-enabled sessions.

To protect the CRYPTON-KERNEL, our solution leverages OS processes and system call sandboxing to isolate the untrusted browser from the CRYPTON-KERNEL. Robust sandboxing mechanisms are known and used by existing browsers such as Chrome [5]. For additional protection, especially in emerging Web OS stacks [51, 55], hardware-assisted dynamic root of trust measurement (DRTM) (such as those provided by Intel TXT [37,52]) can be investigated in the future to ensure dynamic code integrity of the CRYPTON-KERNEL.

2.4 Out-of-scope Threats

Our focus is on providing the integrity and confidentiality of data. So, for example, our defenses cannot be used to protect data used in server-side authorization such as CSRF tokens, session cookies and authentication tokens (for single-sign on mechanisms), as blocking these attacks require ensuring the authenticity of the sender of sensitive data. Similarly, browser vulnerabilities may be used to completely deny access to sensitive data (denial-of-service); our defenses do not enforce data availability to the intended recipient.

There are various attacks that can elicit sensitive information from the user *outside* the trusted paths, say by confusing the user with fake security indicators [39,71], exploiting time-of-check-to-time-of-use (TOCTTOU) windows in our security indicators, click-jacking [3,36], shoulder surfing or through social coercion [8]. We recognize that these are important channels of information loss to consider for guaranteeing end-to-end security; however, defenses for these specific attacks are of independent interest [20,58].

Moreover, we point out that our design requires developers to carefully design CRYPTON functions to avoid direct data leakage as well as side-channels via timing and control flow, which are declassification interfaces to sensitive data. There are also well-studied classes of attacks on information flow and encryption systems [11,15,18]; tools to detect and minimize the capacity of side channels are useful for developers [42].

3. DESIGN

We propose a novel solution with CRYPTON abstractions to protect sensitive data in an untrusted web browser. In this section, we first introduce the definition of the CRYPTON, which can be directly programmed into web pages. Then we elaborate the design of the CRYPTON-KERNEL, and security invariants it enforces.

3.1 CRYPTON Definition

The CRYPTON abstraction incorporates sensitive data protected with integrity and confidentiality, the operations permitted to decrypt and process the data, as well as the functional policy that determines which keys to use for decrypting sensitive information and for encrypting outputs.

More formally, we define a CRYPTON as a 5-tuple $\mathcal{W} = (\vec{\mathcal{D}}, \vec{\mathcal{F}}, \mathcal{U}, \mathcal{V}, \mathcal{I})$. As defined later, $\vec{\mathcal{D}}$ is a sequence of information blocks and $\vec{\mathcal{F}}$ is a sequence of CRYPTON functions. $\mathcal{U}$ is the web address URI of the CRYPTON-enabled web server, the HTTPS frontend of the web server. The external verifier $\mathcal{V}$ is the HTTPS web URI for the proof-of-impression functionality, as we explain shortly. $\mathcal{I}$ is a unique identifier (ID) for the CRYPTON.

A CRYPTON $\mathcal{W}$ syntactically binds permitted operations and sensitive data in its definition; this binding is signed by the SSL public key corresponding to $\mathcal{U}$ and is verified and maintained by the CRYPTON-KERNEL. When the CRYPTON-KERNEL first processes a CRYPTON, it communicates with $\mathcal{U}$ over a secure channel and fetches a set of symmetric encryption keys $\mathcal{K}$ corresponding to that specific CRYPTON. Note that CRYPTON keys $\mathcal{K}$ are not sent as part of $\mathcal{W}$, which would otherwise permit them to be read by adversaries. The set $\mathcal{K}$ consists of a default encryption/decryption key κ_0, an HMAC key κ_{hmac}, and optionally other keys $\kappa_1, ..., \kappa_n$, for authenticated encryption using symmetric key ciphers (256-bit AES-GCM). These keys are kept secret and known only to the CRYPTON-KERNEL; they are referenced by their key indices in CRYPTON functions and information blocks as explained below.

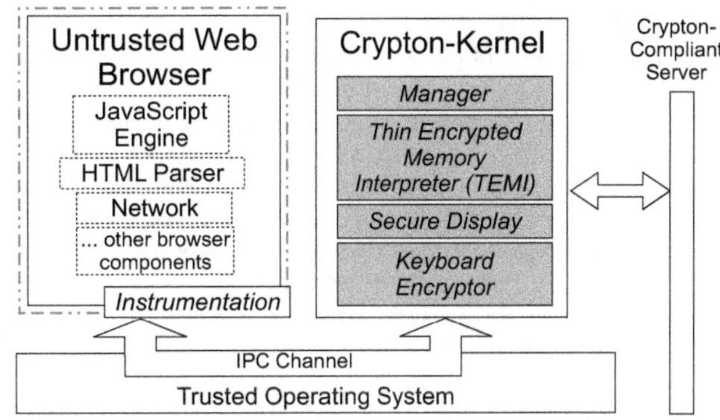

Figure 1: Overview of the CRYPTON-KERNEL, *consisting of 4 components in gray, and the sandbox shown dashed.*

Conceptually, each CRYPTON function $\mathcal{F}_i$ is a 3-tuple $\mathcal{F}_i = (\mathcal{P}, \mathcal{R}, \tau_{\mathcal{F}})$. The syntactic definition of $\mathcal{F}_i$ binds tuple elements together; these bindings are signed to ensure their integrity. $\mathcal{P} : \mathcal{K} \times \mathcal{K}$ is a set of policies defined for each $\mathcal{F}_i$ over keys in $\mathcal{K} \cup \{\perp, \kappa_{int}\}$, where $\perp$ means public (no encryption)[3], and κ_{int} is a CRYPTON-KERNEL-specific key to protect user inputs, such as keystrokes. Such a policy dictates how a CRYPTON function encrypts and decrypts sensitive data. A policy $\kappa_1 \rightarrow \kappa_2$ for a function $\mathcal{F}_i$ indicates that $\mathcal{F}_i$ decrypts sensitive data using the key κ_1. Global or local variables written during the function execution, arguments of calls to the untrusted browser, as well as return values, are encrypted with the key κ_2. Policies are optional; the default policy enforced is $\kappa_0 \rightarrow \kappa_0$, i.e., decryption and encryption both with the default key. We explain the semantics of the execution of each function in detail in Section 3.4. $\mathcal{R}$ optionally lists the arguments to the function and the return value. Finally, functions have a type field $\tau_{\mathcal{F}}$ which separates 2 kinds of functions: (a) a proof-of-impression (`PoI`) function that must be invoked to handle impression tokens, and (b) all other functions. `PoI` functions compute encrypted messages over the nonce token and the impressions of sensitive messages and send them to the external verifier $\mathcal{V}$.

An information block is a 6-tuple $\mathcal{D}_i = (\mathcal{I}, \kappa, \mathcal{I}_{\mathcal{D}}, \mathcal{A}, \tau_{\mathcal{D}}, \mathcal{F}_{\mathcal{D}})$. $\mathcal{I}$ and $\mathcal{I}_{\mathcal{D}}$ are identifiers for the owner CRYPTON and the information block, respectively. The encryption key for $\mathcal{D}_i$ is specified by $\kappa \in \mathcal{K}$. $\mathcal{A}$ is the encrypted ciphertext of the enclosed sensitive data. Finally, if a certain information block requires proof-of-impression for its render value $\mathcal{A}$, the field $\tau_{\mathcal{D}}$ indicates the nonce token for this information block, and $\mathcal{F}_{\mathcal{D}}$ refers to the function to be invoked with the impression token by the CRYPTON-KERNEL.

3.2 CRYPTON-KERNEL Design

The CRYPTON-KERNEL provides secure processing of sensitive web content for a CRYPTON-compliant web browser, while never exposing decrypted data to the browser. As shown in Figure 1, our solution needs to instrument the untrusted browser, which communicates with the CRYPTON-KERNEL running in another process via IPC channels. We develop a new thin engine called the *Thin Encrypted Memory Interpreter* (*TEMI*) to execute CRYPTON functions over sensitive data. We now present a brief overview of our solution with a hypothetical example demonstrating protecting sensitive emails in a webmail application.

[3]The CRYPTON function can also call the `enc(data, key)` programmatically to encrypt part of the outputs on demand.

When the CRYPTON-compliant web browser parses an HTML document, it encounters the CRYPTON header, functions or information blocks. At this time, the browser invokes the CRYPTON-KERNEL via an IPC interface. Once invoked, the Manager component of the CRYPTON-KERNEL processes these special tags, including validating their integrity, and retrieving CRYPTON keys via a secure channel from the server URLs embedded in the CRYPTON header. The Manager component returns opaque objects to the untrusted browser for processed CRYPTONs. These opaque objects encapsulate encrypted values and metadata such as the corresponding CRYPTON ID and decryption key. They are propagated internally by the untrusted browser, akin to ordinary browser objects. (Step *A* in Figure 2).

The untrusted browser handles the layout of web content, and composes intermediate constructs for rendering. Another CRYPTON-KERNEL component, called the Secure Display, intercepts rendering requests from the untrusted browser, and converts the layout constructs into pixel maps written into the GPU buffer. When opaque objects enclosing encrypted texts traverse through untrusted code paths in the browser, and finally reach the Secure Display component, the Secure Display decrypts them before transforming them into pixel data for the GPU buffer. For example, sensitive emails in our example are encrypted when they are downloaded into the browser. When they are being rendered, the Secure Display component of the CRYPTON-KERNEL decrypts them into plaintext that is displayed to users (Step *B*).

To protect user inputs, the Keyboard Encryptor component of the CRYPTON-KERNEL encrypts all user inputs for the CRYPTON-enabled webmail application. For example, it encrypts the search keywords while the user enters them in the untrusted browser. The resulted opaque object containing the encrypted user inputs is finally dispatched into the event handler function `searchEmail` triggered by a user click on the "Search" button. The webmail developer marks `searchEmail` as a CRYPTON function with a policy $\kappa_{int} \rightarrow \kappa_0$, allowing it to decrypt user inputs (such as search keywords) encrypted with the CRYPTON-KERNEL's internal key κ_{int}. When `searchEmail` is invoked, the untrusted browser transmits the execution to the TEMI, a thin execution environment in the CRYPTON-KERNEL. The TEMI decrypts the search keywords encrypted in the opaque object during the execution of `searchEmail`. This allows the function to preprocess the search terms, such as replacing "+" with "ADD", and encode the texts. Then `searchEmail` constructs an XMLHttpRequest containing the preprocessed search terms and sends it to the webmail server. When the webmail server receives the request, it decrypts the search terms and searches for them in the email database (Step *C*).

Subsequently, search results are returned to the untrusted browser in JSON format where innermost email headings are encrypted. The registered XMLHttpRequest handler function `parseJson` is invoked to tokenize and validate the JSON string, and return a composed HTML fragment to be rendered to the user. The email headings in the HTML fragment remain as opaque objects to untrusted code in the browser, and the Secure Display decrypts them when rendering the headings for the webmail user (Step *D*).

3.3 Security Invariants

To protect the confidentiality and integrity of sensitive web content in an untrusted browser, our solution enforces the following semantics as security invariants for CRYPTONs.

For information isolation:

P0: Maintaining Syntactic Bindings. A CRYPTON syntactically binds its elements to each other (such as $\mathcal{K}$ to $\mathcal{I}$, $\mathcal{P}$ to each $\mathcal{F}_i$

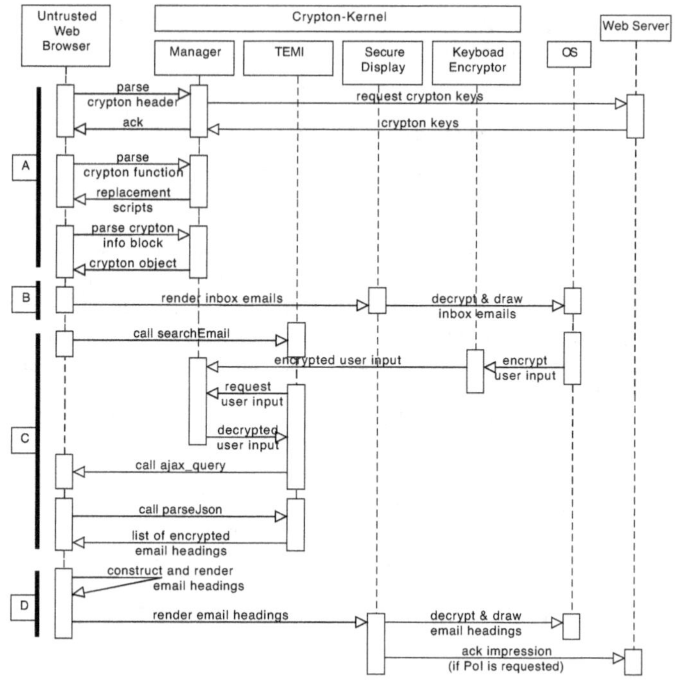

Figure 2: Sequence of Operations in A CRYPTON-Enabled Webmail Session

and so on) with mentioned keys. These bindings are checked and enforced throughout the lifetime of the CRYPTON. Authenticated encryption ensures that any attempt to tamper with such bindings by malicious code will be prevented.

P1: Secure Storage. All CRYPTON information blocks, functions and intermediate computation by CRYPTON functions is stored in private memory outside the browser, or encrypted when stored in memory shared with the browser. The standard guarantees of authenticated encryption apply to these.

P2: Secrecy of $\mathcal{K}$. The keys $\mathcal{K}$ are only stored in the CRYPTON-KERNEL and not accessible to the CRYPTON-compliant browser.

For controlled operations:

P3: Functional Policy. If a function $\mathcal{F}_i$ is bound to a policy $\kappa \rightarrow \kappa'$, then all sensitive data processed by it is decrypted using κ, and all values written by $\mathcal{F}_i$ are encrypted with κ', e.g., modified global variables, local variables, arguments of calls to untrusted browser functions, and return values. See **P5** as the only exception.

P4: Non-interfering Execution. The execution of two functions $\mathcal{F}_1$ and $\mathcal{F}_2$ are non-interfering on the CRYPTON-KERNEL, if they are bound to policies $\kappa_1 \rightarrow \kappa_1'$ and $\kappa_2 \rightarrow \kappa_2'$ respectively, and $\{\kappa_1, \kappa_1'\} \cap \{\kappa_2, \kappa_2'\} = \emptyset$.

P5: Information Release. Only functions bound to policies $\_ \rightarrow \perp$ output plaintext to the browser[4].

For certified user inputs:

P6: User Input Encryption. User keyboard inputs are encrypted with the CRYPTON-KERNEL's internal key κ_{int}, and only CRYPTON functions bound to policy $\kappa_{int} \rightarrow \_$ can decrypt the inputs.

P7: Restricted Keyboard Access. The CRYPTON-KERNEL intercepts all keyboard events before they are delivered to the browser.

[4] _ denotes any key or $\perp$.

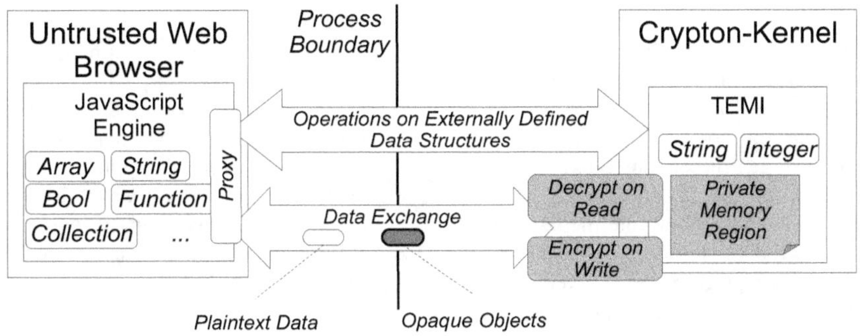

Figure 3: TEMI: a Thin Execution Environment for CRYPTON Functions to Access Sensitive Info

For proof of impression:

P8: Proof of Impression. When an information block $\mathcal{D}_i$ is *rendered*, it should be displayed for a certain period of time without obstruction or overlay by other UI content. The `PoI` function specified by the developer is invoked to compute an encrypted message acknowledging the rendering to the verifier $\mathcal{V}$ in a secure channel.

P9: Restricted Display Access. The CRYPTON-KERNEL mediates the rendering operations initiated by the browser.

Summary. With these security invariants, CRYPTONs ensure the confidentiality and integrity of enclosed sensitive data throughout its lifecycle in untrusted web browsers.

3.4 Key Techniques and Security Analysis

To ensure the security invariants above, the CRYPTON-KERNEL provides a thin engine for permitted operations on sensitive data, and interposes browser display and keyboard events to support trusted paths for display and user inputs.

Thin Encrypted Memory Interpreter. To execute controlled operations on sensitive data, we design the Thin Encrypted Memory Interpreter (TEMI) — a thin scripting engine. In designing TEMI, we face a tradeoff between supporting rich functionality and minimizing the TCB. A full-fledged JavaScript engine typically has 200,000 (JavaScriptCore) to 400,000 (the V8 engine) LOC. However, we observe in our case studies that most of potential sensitive data types on the web are integers and strings, such as user names, passwords, entries in medical records, credit card numbers, etc. These data types account for only a very small fraction of the implementation of the JavaScript engine. Of course, these primitive types are aggregated into higher-level abstract data types (such as arrays, lists, objects, and so on), but much of the logic that operates on the higher-level data types is agnostic or independent of the inner nested data. By leveraging this observation, we design a "thin" TEMI that natively supports integers and strings[5], which has a TCB of only $19,000$ lines of code.

The TEMI runs inside the CRYPTON-KERNEL's process, communicating with the process(es) of the untrusted web browser via IPC messages (shown in Figure 3). The TEMI has a private virtual register set (for local computation) in its private memory region. It decrypts sensitive data in opaque objects when they are loaded into virtual registers, and re-encrypt all values written from virtual registers to opaque objects, including global variables, arguments, and return values. By default, the TEMI uses the default CRYPTON key κ_0 for encryption and decryption; a developer-specified policy $\kappa_1 \to \kappa_2$ of a CRYPTON function dictates κ_1 used for decryption, and κ_2 for encryption (**P3**)[6]. A CRYPTON function that is allowed to disclose information has a policy $\_ \to \bot$ (**P5**). The TEMI retrieves CRYPTON keys from the CRYPTON-KERNEL's private memory storing keys transferred from the web server (**P2**).

During the execution of a CRYPTON-KERNEL function, any access to higher-level abstract data types results in an IPC message to a proxy in the JavaScript engine of the untrusted browser with opaque objects as arguments. The proxy translates the message into operations that are executed in the untrusted JavaScript engine. For operations initiated by the CRYPTON-KERNEL, any string and integer operation that emerges during execution in the untrusted JavaScript engine is tunneled back to the CRYPTON-KERNEL for processing opaque objects. In our running example in Section 3.2, the `parseJson` function sends a message to the untrusted browser to access complex data structures, such as arrays to perform parsing operations. The execution then switches back to the TEMI when an `Array.toString` function is invoked so that operations on sensitive strings can still be processed in the decrypted form. This unmodified CRYPTON function runs in our TEMI as it switches back and forth between the untrusted browser and the CRYPTON-KERNEL. For data exchange, the TEMI and the untrusted browser passes integer and string data in the IPC messages, while only pass references to high-level data structures as they are processed exclusively at the untrusted browser side.

In our design, accessing higher-level data types defined in the untrusted browser from the TEMI incurs no explicit data leakage, since all arguments are encrypted (**P1**). Implicit control flow leakage is possible, while we assume it can be largely ignored in legitimate code [15], such as CRYPTON functions. For compatibility with existing browsers, when one process is running JavaScript, we halt the other process until the running process returns.

To prevent interference between different CRYPTON functions, the TEMI executes each CRYPTON function in a separate context, which is destroyed upon returning of the function (**P4**). This includes virtual registers stored in the private memory region, as well as encrypted intermediate variables written in the shared memory region. Similar to garbage collectors, the TEMI clears all these values when a CRYPTON function returns.

Secure Display. The CRYPTON-KERNEL allows automatic decryption of opaque objects when they are being rendered, but prevents untrusted browser code to access the decrypted information.

[5]including regular expressions and basic indexing operations on static arrays of integer or string elements.

[6]Note that in principle it is possible to have explosive volumes of encrypted data from the computation over mixed sensitive and non-sensitive data. We did not observe such cases in our experiments with real-world web applications, where computation over sensitive data does not yield new sensitive data, but just outputs features or portions of original data.

The Secure Display component of the CRYPTON-KERNEL can use sandboxing techniques similar to Google Chrome [5], such as restricted tokens and Windows job and desktop objects on Windows [57] and `seccomp` on Linux [56], to intercept untrusted browser's access to the GPU buffer and graphic libraries on the OS (**P9**). To render any UI content, the untrusted browser must pass the rendering requests to the Secure Display. The Secure Display in turn converts web contents and browser widgets into intermediate rendering constructs (such as `Glyphs` that are basic shapes in text rendering [13]) and sends them to the graphics library for rendering. During this process, the Secure Display decrypts opaque objects containing sensitive strings, with the keys specified in the opaque objects. To prevent UI obstruction, while rendering such opaque objects, for t seconds, the Secure Display temporarily suspends other rendering requests to the same destination GPU buffer location. It also invokes the `PoI` function for the opaque string being rendered, if applicable. The `PoI` function then computes an acknowledgement token encrypted with the CRYPTON's default key κ_0 and sends it to the external verifier (**P8**).

Keyboard Encryptor. The Keyboard Encryptor interposes on keyboard events from the graphics toolkit that receives keystrokes. It encrypts each keystroke event with a CRYPTON-KERNEL-specific internal key κ_{int} before it reaches the web browser code (**P6, P7**). Therefore, web applications cannot read the clear-text of user inputs unless by calling the CRYPTON functions with a policy like $\kappa_{int} \rightarrow \_$. Together with **P3**, this ensures that keyboard inputs are protected, and are available only to intended functions.

Resilience against malicious code in web browsers. Although the CRYPTON-KERNEL closely integrates the untrusted web browser, the security guarantee ensured by the CRYPTON-KERNEL are independent from the untrusted web browser, i.e., all disclosure of the sensitive information is controlled by CRYPTON functional policy.

To allow non-invasive operations that do not require plaintext, the encrypted data in CRYPTON information blocks is stored on the browser's storage as opaque objects. These objects are protected by authenticated encryption for their integrity and confidentiality. The keys are available only to the CRYPTON-KERNEL. Untrusted code has no access to the keys (**P2**), and thus cannot decrypt sensitive data, unless by explicitly invoking information releasing CRYPTON functions (**P5**). User inputs are automatically encrypted before they reach the untrusted web browser (**P6**), so they are under the same protection as sensitive data coming from web servers. Web servers can also verify whether sensitive messages are properly displayed via proof of impression (**P8**).

Although malicious code cannot decrypt the sensitive data in ciphertext, it can tamper with it. However, this will be detected by integrity verification built into authenticated encryption. This ensures the integrity of all CRYPTONs from the web and sensitive user inputs at the client.

Attacks on CRYPTON granularity. Our solution enables web servers to distinguish data from client side at a binary granularity — i.e., between authentic user inputs and everything else. Consider the following attack. Malicious code injected into a webmail application can create a fake login box in the victim session. This fake login box makes the email composing input box appear as its Password field. A victim user may then enter her password into the fake Password field, which is sent to the attacker in an email. This is an instance of self-exfiltration attacks [17]. To defeat this attack, the web server can mark the TO field for email recipients as sensitive, and require its value to come from authentic user inputs at the client side. Therefore, malicious client-side code has no control over to where the email will be delivered, even if it can trick the user into entering her password as the email body. However, our current solution only distinguishes authentic user inputs from other data. Attackers may still confuse users between the semantics of two CRYPTON-protected user input fields, such as luring the user into entering the email body into the TO field by phishing [31,72,73]. In certain applications, this could lead to delivering emails to unintended recipients. However, we believe such attacks are application-specific and difficult to launch. Further, extensions of CRYPTONs with finer-grained isolation can be explored to defeat such attacks.

3.5 Usability Implications

We discuss the usability implications that may arise from our design. First, our solution assumes that users only enter their sensitive data when security indicators state that their inputs are being encrypted for the expected web application. Previous research has proposed various alternatives, such as Bumpy [49], where a special key stroke sequence is required to start a secure input session. Instead of relying on users to initiate the securing of their inputs, in this work, we automatically encrypt all user inputs within a CRYPTON-compliant web session. As our solution requires users to pay attention to secure UI indicators during keyboard input, we expect our solution to have similar usability challenges as reported in a prior evaluation of various alternative secure input mechanisms [44]. We anticipate our solution to be usable in enterprise settings or in mission-critical applications.

Secondly, the initial key setup in establishing a CRYPTON-KERNEL-to-server secure channel could pose a usability challenge to non-security-experts, as it requires key upload. Other alternatives could be considered in a full deployment, such as adopting a trust-on-first-use model [70] as with SSH, or the PAKE protocol [27] to establish a secure channel based on a shared secret, which have their own pros and cons [9]. Adopting such alternatives does not affect our core approach and mechanisms proposed in this work. We choose the current setting for its strong security guarantees and its compatibility with HTTPS. More recently, various online hosting services, such as Github [32] and BitBucket [6], have adopted such a mechanism to authenticate clients for more adept users. We expect a similar user experience for using a CRYPTON-enabled website in enterprise settings, and a gradual broader adoption among general web application users.

3.6 Implementation & Deployment

We implement a prototype of the CRYPTON-KERNEL integrated with WebKit-GTK (rev 45311) with JIT disabled, for the ease of implementation. Our prototype reuses OpenSSL code for AES-GCM encryption/decryption. As the WebKit-GTK that we use does not leverage hardware-accelerated rendering, we implement text decryption and proof of impression via the software paths by intercepting calls to the bridge between WebKit and the cairo graphics library. Similarly, we intercept signal dispatch from the GTK+/Glib to the browser to encrypt user inputs. As user input events are fired for each keystroke, we use a stream cipher to encrypt user inputs. Thus, positions of user input characters are maintained as original, and this naturally supports mouse text selection. When user inputs are sent to web servers, we use a CRYPTON function to re-encrypt them with the AES-GCM block cipher with the specified key. Table 2 lists the sizes of components in our prototype implementation of the CRYPTON-KERNEL. Comparing to a web browser, such as Firefox and Chromium, which typically has around 800K to 1,100K lines of source code, the TCB in our unoptimized prototype is about 30× - 40× smaller.

App Name	Sensitive Data	Server-side Change	Client-side Change	Est. Total Conversion Effort
RoundCube	Mails with subject marked as "[sensitive]"	8 LOC php	9 Functions, 0.5K LOC JS	2-3 Man-Days
AjaxIM	Instant messages	6 LOC php	9 Functions, 0.4K LOC JS	2-3 Man-Days
WordPress	Blogs containing "[sensitive]" in titles and search keywords	10 LOC php	19 Functions, 1.2K LOC JS	4-5 Man-Days

Table 1: Summary of Case Studies on 3 Popular Web Apps, demonstrating modest adoption effort

CRYPTON-KERNEL **Component**	**LOC**
Manager	2.9K
TEMI	18.7K
Secure Display	4.8K
Keyboard Encryptor	0.5K
Total	26.9K

Table 2: Size of TCB in CRYPTON-KERNEL **Prototype**

Our prototype implements functionalities sufficient to support our studies with real-world web applications. In a full deployment, several browser components need to be modified to propagate the opaque objects with encrypted data, including support for untrusted browser sandboxing, browser spell checkers, all CSS styling features, web page printing, WebGL and GPU accelerations. Such support has not been implemented in our current prototype.

For deployment into real web browsers, we consider an alternative deployment into Google Chrome's browser kernel, leveraging existing privilege separation and sandboxing mechanisms in Google Chrome. Google Chrome partitions more vulnerable components into the renderer processes, and leave more security-sensitive components in the browser kernel process. It has also implemented sandboxing mechanisms to prevent renderer processes from directly accessing UI rendering, user inputs, file systems, and network. All such access has to go via interfaces exposed and checked by the browser kernel. Thus, we expect it to be relatively straightforward to implement the CRYPTON-KERNEL into the browser kernel of Google Chrome, leveraging the existing UI and user input sandboxing mechanisms. If we consider such a modification to Chrome 12, the code size that can access sensitive data will be significantly reduced. Essentially, it would eliminate more than 900K lines of code constituting the renderer processes and all client-side application code from the TCB for ensuring data protection.

4. EVALUATION

We apply our solution to real-word web applications to study the applicability and adoption cost. We first manually convert 3 popular web applications to use our solution to protect typical sensitive data in those applications, and then extend our study to Alex Top 50 web pages. Both micro and macro studies show the effectiveness of our solution in protecting typical sensitive data on the present web with modest adoption effort required.

4.1 Applicability to Real-world Applications

Micro-study on open-source web applications. We perform case studies on three open-source web applications to measure two aspects, i.e., *a)* how effectively our solution can protect sensitive content in real-word applications, and *b)* how much developer effort is required for adopting our solution. We choose applications of different categories: RoundCube [65], a webmail server, AjaxIM[7], a web-based instant messenger, and WordPress [30], a web blog service. We manually convert the source code of the three applications by: 1) modifying the server-side code to encrypt sensitive content before sending it to clients; 2) identifying client-side JavaScript functions that need to decrypt sensitive data for operations and converting them into CRYPTON functions; and 3) rewriting client-side JavaScript functions that receive and process user inputs into CRYPTON functions; these CRYPTON functions encrypt user inputs before sending them to web servers. We check all tests with a server-side proxy.

[7]We use the AjaxIMRPG fork [23] that is better maintained than the trunk.

We find that with modest effort in converting these applications, our solution can effectively protect typical sensitive data, such as sensitive emails, instant messages, blog entries and comments. We write a 450-line custom PHP library for common functionalities to process CRYPTONs in PHP applications. We manually rewrite the three web applications, leveraging the custom library to wrap sensitive web content into CRYPTONs. Table 1 summarizes the results of our case studies on the three applications. Typical client-side operations on sensitive data we observe include trimming whitespaces in strings, serializing HTML content, emotion text replacement, URI encoding, etc. We mark them as CRYPTON functions in our experiments to support the legitimate functionalities. For brevity, we leave out detailed steps here, and a summary of our modification to application source-code is available online [1].

Macro-study on real-word web applications. To further evaluate the applicability of the CRYPTON-KERNEL to other web applications, we perform a larger-scale macro study. First, we select Alexa Top 50 web pages, and identify all of those fields that require sensitive username / password inputs for signup – 18 out of the 50 applications have signup pages (Figure 4). We choose these applications because they often have client-side checking code on sensitive passwords (e.g. checking strength requirements). Next, we select 20 popular web applications of five categories, and identify scenarios where the CRYPTON-KERNEL can strengthen security against real attacks:

- *Web search pages.* We select websites that allow users to search terms. We mark search terms as sensitive because leaking search terms may permit third-party tracking.
- *Social networking sites.* These sites can be used to exchange private messages, or post comments that may be politically-sensitive. Hence, we mark posts and comments as sensitive.
- *Banking sites.* Banking sites are prime targets of browser-based attacks and several malware disguise as browser extensions. We select a local bank that uses additional authentication mechanisms such as one-time PassKeys. In its web pages, username, passwords and the one-time PassKey are marked as sensitive. The one-time PassKey is interesting because banks are increasingly considering this as a second-factor authentication beyond long-lived passwords.
- *E-commerce sites.* We test eBay, Amazon and Babylon online commerce sites. On eBay, we mark the auction listing created by a seller as sensitive. Different auction listings can

Web App Detail	Sensitive Info	# & Size of Functions Requiring Decrypted Sensitive Info [Percentage of Total Code Size]	# & Size of All JavaScript Functions	# Browser and TEMI Interactions vs. # All Calls to JS Data Types
Gmail Login	Username, Password	2 (0.29 KB) [**0.43%**]	196 (66.5KB)	**0.7%** (956/141492)
Gmail Compose Email	To, Subject, Content	9 (1.84KB) [**0.98%**]	745 (186.8KB)	**0.01%** (89/541883)
Gmail Read Email	From, Subject, Content	2 (1.1KB) [**0.64%**]	730 (171.1KB)	**0.02%** (92/390206)
Ask Search	Search Terms	3 (1.3KB) [**0.31%**]	569 (416.2KB)	**0.01%** (40/218922)
Google Search	Search Terms	6 (0.92KB) [**0.26%**]	581 (352.9KB)	**0.2%** (437/206675)
Google+ Post	Post Content	5 (1.01KB) [**0.13%**]	1150 (750KB)	**0.005%** (48/947254)
NetFlix	Username, Password	1 (0.6KB) [**0.2%**]	419 (289.9KB)	**0.1%** (170/162853)
IMDb Search	Search Terms	1 (0.24KB) [**0.02%**]	1131 (1.1MB)	**0.1%** (422/323208)
Facebook Read Post	Post Content	1 (0.5KB) [**0.18%**]	730 (268KB)	**0.02%** (347/1216952)
Facebook Friend Search	Search Terms	9 (1.7KB) [**0.50%**]	959 (336.6KB)	**6.4%** (60305/937108)
eBay Item List	Item's Description	8 (1.49KB) [**0.62%**]	725(239.2KB)	**0.1%** (326/241901)
Amazon Login	Username, Password	2 (1.87KB) [**1.28%**]	240 (146KB)	**0.5%** (1629/321275)
Amazon Search	Search Terms	9 (1.77KB) [**0.24%**]	485 (732.7KB)	**0.1%** (544/433110)
MSN Search	Search Terms	5 (1.4KB) [**0.08%**]	1185 (1.7MB)	**0.5%** (2096/435124)
StackOverflow	Post Content	5 (2.36KB) [**1.18%**]	429 (198.9KB)	**0.2%** (830/406328)
Twitter Login	Username, Password	3 (0.61KB) [**0.27%**]	472 (223.6KB)	**0.004%** (27/622874)
Wikipedia Search	Search Terms	6 (1.9KB) [**0.23%**]	438 (794.1KB)	**0.45%** (382/84818)
Babylon Purchase	Email Address, Credit Card Info	3 (1.17KB) [**0.70%**])	485 (165KB)	**0.6%** (3232/515586)
Local Bank Login	Username, Password, PassKey	3 (1.49KB) [**1.01%**]	250 (146.3KB)	**~0%** (1/100037)
BankOfAmerica Login	Username, Password	2 (1.01 KB) [**0.23%**]	780 (430.4KB)	**~0%** (3/441534)

Table 3: Study of 20 Popular Web Applications. ***< 1% of web application code needs to run in the TEMI to access sensitive info; < 1% of all calls to JS data types trigger browser-TEMI interactions.***

be loaded in the same page, and each may contain its own JavaScript. If the listing is not protected, the script from one seller may deface or tamper with that from another seller. We also consider Babylon, since users can purchase items without creating an account with Babylon. Therefore, by tampering with the purchaser's email in the browser, an attacker can have a software license purchased by a legitimate user, but delivered to the attacker's email address. We mark the email address as a sensitive field on Babylon. We mark product search terms as sensitive for Amazon.

- *Gmail.* It is a rich webmail client used as our running example. We mark search terms and certain emails as sensitive.

We manually (with browser instrumentation) identify all functions that legitimately operate on sensitive information, including event handlers. Our analysis details are shown in Table 3. We assign the default policy $\kappa_0 \rightarrow \kappa_0$ to these functions, and all user keyboard inputs are marked as sensitive. We mark the Gmail spam warning message as requiring proof-of-impression. We also mark a post on Facebook as requiring proof-of-impression.

Results. We dynamically modify these web pages to encode sensitive contents into CRYPTONs using a proxy server. We find that these applications render correctly in our CRYPTON-compliant browser implementation, and the applications remain functional. This confirms our hypothesis that existing applications can be easily upgraded to using CRYPTON-KERNEL's functionality. Our test proxy decodes encrypted content returned from the browser and checks them against the expected values. It also verifies that it receives proof-of-impression tokens.

Developer effort. Table 3 demonstrates that the developer effort to enable this functionality is modest. On average, only **1%** of the total functions in the applications need to be included in CRYPTONs; this amounts to **2** KB of minified JavaScript per web page. The effort required to verify such code as CRYPTON functions is feasible, around **1-9** functions for each application. Figure 4 shows similar results that about **0-9** functions need to be verified for each signup page.

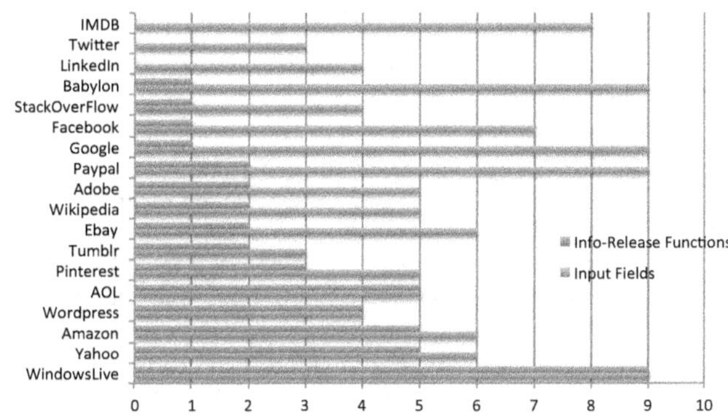

Figure 4: Number of User Input Fields and CRYPTON Functions Required in Signup Pages

4.2 Reduction in Attack Surface

The isolation and controlled operations provided by CRYPTONs significantly reduce the size of code that sensitive information is exposed to. We evaluate this reduction in both web application code as well as in browser code.

Exposure to untrusted application code reduces by 99%. As we show in Table 3, on average less than 1% of web application code actually needs access to sensitive information, and is thus run in CRYPTON functions. All the rest of web application code only has access to opaque objects with encrypted data. On the contrary, in current web browsers, all information is exposed to the entire web application. Any malicious or compromised JavaScript library can steal the information and leak it to external parties. By isolating sensitive information into CRYPTONs, the CRYPTON-KERNEL places **99%** of web application outside the TCB.

Exposure to browser vulnerabilities reduced by 92.5%. In existing web browsers, sensitive information being processed is largely accessible to browser code running in the same process. To evaluate how the CRYPTON-KERNEL reduces such over-exposure of sensitive information to browser vulnerabilities, we study how many historical browser security vulnerabilities are prevented from affecting the security guarantees provided by the CRYPTON-KERNEL. From our study with historical security vulnerabilities in Firefox reported separately [24], in total 333 vulnerabilities (92.5%) cannot be exploited to violating the security guarantees provided by the CRYPTON-KERNEL. The remaining vulnerabilities either reside in our TCB (7 of them), or compromise our assumptions (another 20 vulnerabilities). The vast reduction in the exposure to browser vulnerabilities verifies the effectiveness of the CRYPTON-KERNEL in information protection.

4.3 Performance

We run the CRYPTON-KERNEL over the 20 web applications listed in Table 3, with sensitive information transformed into CRYPTONs. The web sites remain responsive, without any *perceivable* slowdown. To further evaluate potential performance bottlenecks, we apply microbenchmarks to measure the performance overheads (averaged over 20 runs each) arising from encryption/decryption operations and browser-TEMI interactions when the TEMI executes CRYPTON functions.

Encryption/decryption overhead. Figure 5 shows the performance overhead of the CRYPTON-KERNEL compared to a vanilla WebKit-GTK browser. We use five CPU-intensive test pages from the Dromaeo benchmark. To vary the workload of encryption and decryption, we mark different portions of texts in the pages as sensitive, ranging from zero-sensitive pages (no sensitive text) to fully sensitive pages (all texts marked as sensitive). During these tests, the browser remains responsive and shows a maximum of 7.5% performance overhead. We also manually craft a test page to evaluate the performance of the CRYPTON-KERNEL under pathological scenarios. The performance overhead reaches 11.7% when all texts on the page are marked as sensitive, which requires heavy encryption/decryption operations. Considering such performance overhead is measured from an initial unoptimized prototype, it is reasonable.

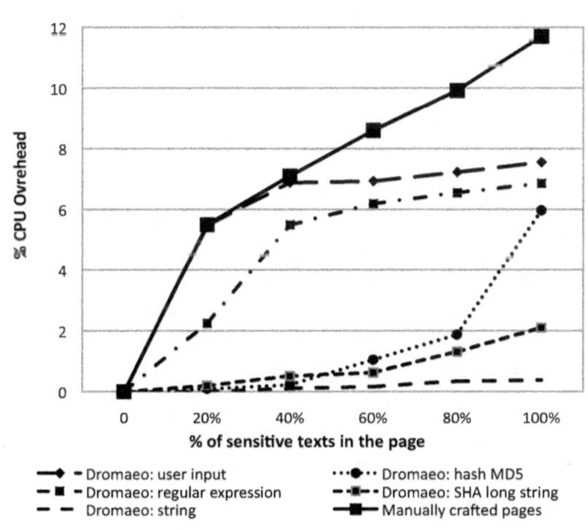

Figure 5: Performance Overhead of CRYPTON-KERNEL with Dromaeo Benchmarks & Manual Test Page, ***with varying portions of sensitive texts***

Overhead of browser-TEMI interactions. We run the CRYPTON-KERNEL over the 20 web sites listed in Table 3, and measure the number of IPC calls between the untrusted web browser and the TEMI. The last column in Table 3 shows that for most cases, less than 1% of all access to JavaScript data types requires crossing the browser-TEMI boundary. Given that the overhead of sending a message via Unix domain socket is around 5 microseconds, a web site with 1,000 IPC messages may only incur 0.005 second overhead.[8] Thus, the design of separating the execution of CRYPTON functions in the TEMI does not cause any performance bottleneck.

5. RELATED WORK

In this section, we discuss research related to information protection in web browsers or operating systems, and key differences with our work.

Enhancement of browser security mechanisms. There has been extensive research on enhancing security mechanisms of web browsers. One direction is to develop flexible and fine-grained access control on the web platform, so that untrusted JavaScript can be restricted to access only limited resources in a web page [40,54,74]. A recent work proposes a multi-layered architecture for enforcing mandatory access control policies, with a label-enforcing web browser [35]. As with other in-browser security mechanisms [47, 50], these solutions do not prevent compromised browser code from directly reading the data stored in the browser's memory.

Privilege separation & trusted paths. Privilege separation is a fundamental mechanism to enforce basic security principles [60]. Several research works have been proposed to facilitate [7] or automate [12] privilege separating legacy applications. Recently, improving separation of privileges in web browsers has become an active area of research [4, 5, 16, 21, 25, 33, 46, 63, 69]. These solutions isolate software components into partitions, thus reducing the potential damage to sensitive data from a compromised component. Nevertheless, they do not provide first-class abstractions to control access to sensitive data, in terms of which information can be disclosed to which entity. Further more, privilege separation does not provide sustained control on sensitive data. Once any information is disclosed to a partition, any code in the partition can further leak it to others. In contrast, our solution focuses on establishing several critical trusted paths in an untrusted web browser. Our proposal is orthogonal to the underlying mechanisms of privilege separation, and to our best knowledge, is the first in bringing data-centric trusted paths to the web. In our threat model, we trust the operating system beneath the web browser. Thus, our solution differs from other trusted path research on the x86 platform, where the operating system is untrusted, and additional sources of trust such as the hypervisor [75] or hardware root of trust [49] is required.

Information flow analysis. Information flow tracking has also been used for detecting and preventing information leakage in web applications [66]. However, without controlling the usage of sensitive information of client-side JavaScript, once disclosed, the information can be leaked by malicious scripts via self-exfiltration attacks [17]. Moreover, such solutions rely on the trust of browsers. On the contrary, our solution is based on a small TCB, and protects sensitive data against threats from all untrusted code or scripts in the browser.

Cryptographic techniques. Cryptographic techniques have long been protecting security in different systems. Lie et al. [45] pro-

[8]Outliers are Facebook Friend Search and WindowsLive Signup, with high browser-TEMI interactions. A closer look at them reveals that they are caused by a particular CRYPTON function in each of them, which processes both sensitive and non-sensitive information. We separate each function into two versions accordingly, and browser-TEMI interactions fall below 1% among all JavaScript data type accesses.

pose an abstract machine of execute-only memory (XOM) to prevent tampering of instructions stored on memory. Borders et al. propose Storage Capsules [10] to allow users to edit files on an untrusted computer without risking leakage of the file content. Although similar in concept, our solution protects data on the web, which are finer-grained, and computation over it is not packaged as applications, but scattered across different functions. This work addresses such challenges in protecting sensitive web content while being functionally compatible with existing web applications.

A recent work [19] further applies memory encryption to data confidentiality, similar to the concept of Data Capsules [48]. It allows unvetted programs to use sensitive data while enforcing policy to confine activities they can perform on the data. The high-level application-specific policy is translated into low-level tags enforced by the underlying hardware. One issue with this approach is: once the plaintext is disclosed to certain code, it is difficult to control information leakage any further, such as via implicit control flows. Our solution prevents it by limiting the plain-text only to CRYPTON functions, whose return values are also encrypted by default.

CleanOS [64] uses information flow tracking and encryption to protect mobile devices against threats to data when the mobile device is lost. Policy-sealed data [61] is a recent proposal on building trusted cloud services that protects data from unintended access. Their abstractions and cryptographic primitives (attribute-based encryption) are well suited for the cloud environment. However, unlike on the cloud, where environments can be summarized as configurations, in web browsers, there is no static context or environment. Code from multiple sources with various privileges are running in and molding the mixed browser environment. Therefore, we need more dynamic mechanisms to control data access and processing.

6. CONCLUSION

In this paper, we present a novel abstraction, CRYPTON, which protects sensitive web content and allows rich computation over it. Based on this data-centric abstraction, we propose a solution that integrates with the present web browser without trusting its code. Instead, the security guarantees provided by our solution are solely enforced by a small standalone engine, called CRYPTON-KERNEL, which interprets sensitive web content in CRYPTONs and allows trusted functions to securely compute over the sensitive data. Our large-scale evaluation demonstrates our solution can effectively protect sensitive web content in real-world web applications, with reasonable performance.

7. ACKNOWLEDGMENTS

We thank anonymous reviewers for their helpful feedback, and our shepherd Nicolas Christin for his insightful comments and suggestions on preparing the final version of the paper. This research is partially supported by research grant R-252-000-495-133 from Ministry of Education, Singapore. Any opinions, findings, and conclusions or recommendations expressed in this paper are those of the authors and do not necessarily reflect the views of the Ministry of Education, Singapore.

8. REFERENCES

[1] Summary of source code modification in case studies. http://compsec.comp.nus.edu.sg/crypton/summary.pdf.

[2] D. Akhawe, P. Saxena, and D. Song. Privilege separation in html5 applications. In *Proceedings of the 21st USENIX Security Symposium*, 2012.

[3] M. Balduzzi, M. Egele, E. Kirda, D. Balzarotti, and C. Kruegel. A solution for the automated detection of clickjacking attacks. In *Proceedings of the 5th ACM Symposium on Information, Computer and Communications Security*, ASIACCS '10, 2010.

[4] A. Barth, A. P. Felt, P. Saxena, and A. Boodman. Protecting browsers from extension vulnerabilities. In *Proceedings of the 17th Annual Network and Distributed System Security Symposium*, NDSS '10, 2010.

[5] A. Barth, C. Jackson, C. Reis, and T. G. C. Team. The security architecture of the chromium browser. http://seclab.stanford.edu/websec/chromium/chromium-security-architecture.pdf.

[6] Bitbucket. https://bitbucket.org/.

[7] A. Bittau, P. Marchenko, M. Handley, and B. Karp. Wedge: splitting applications into reduced-privilege compartments. In *Proceedings of the 5th USENIX Symposium on Networked Systems Design and Implementation*, NSDI '08, 2008.

[8] H. Bojinov, D. Sanchez, P. Reber, D. Boneh, and P. Lincoln. Neuroscience meets cryptography: designing crypto primitives secure against rubber hose attacks. In *Proceedings of the 21st USENIX Security Symposium*, 2012.

[9] J. Bonneau, C. Herley, P. C. v. Oorschot, and F. Stajano. The quest to replace passwords: A framework for comparative evaluation of web authentication schemes. In *Proceedings of the 2012 IEEE Symposium on Security and Privacy*, 2012.

[10] K. Borders, E. V. Weele, B. Lau, and A. Prakash. Protecting confidential data on personal computers with storage capsules. In *Proceedings of the 18th USENIX Security Symposium*, 2009.

[11] D. Brumley and D. Boneh. Remote timing attacks are practical. In *Proceedings of the 12th USENIX Security Symposium*, 2003.

[12] D. Brumley and D. Song. Privtrans: automatically partitioning programs for privilege separation. In *Proceedings of the 13th USENIX Security Symposium*, 2004.

[13] CairoGraphics. cairo_glyph_t. http://cairographics.org/manual/cairo-text.html#cairo-glyph-t.

[14] N. Carlini, A. P. Felt, and D. Wagner. An evaluation of the google chrome extension security architecture. In *Proceedings of the 21st USENIX Security Symposium*, 2012.

[15] L. Cavallaro, P. Saxena, and R. Sekar. On the limits of information flow techniques for malware analysis and containment. In *Proceedings of the 5th International Conference on Detection of Intrusions and Malware, and Vulnerability Assessment*, DIMVA '08, 2008.

[16] E. Y. Chen, J. Bau, C. Reis, A. Barth, and C. Jackson. App isolation: get the security of multiple browsers with just one. In *Proceedings of the 18th ACM Conference on Computer and Communications Security*, CCS '11, 2011.

[17] E. Y. Chen, S. Gorbaty, A. Singhal, and C. Jackson. Self-exfiltration: The dangers of browser-enforced information flow control. In *Proceedings of the Workshop of Web 2.0 Security & Privacy 2012*, 2012.

[18] S. Chen, R. Wang, X. Wang, and K. Zhang. Side-channel leaks in web applications: A reality today, a challenge tomorrow. In *Proceedings of the 2010 IEEE Symposium on Security and Privacy*, 2010.

[19] Y.-Y. Chen, P. A. Jamkhedkar, and R. B. Lee. A software-hardware architecture for self-protecting data. In

Proceedings of the 2012 ACM Conference on Computer and Communications Security, CCS '12, 2012.

[20] Y. Cheng and X. Ding. Virtualization based password protection against malware in untrusted operating systems. In *Proceedings of the 5th International Conference on Trust and Trustworthy Computing*, TRUST '12, 2012.

[21] R. S. Cox, S. D. Gribble, H. M. Levy, and J. G. Hansen. A safety-oriented platform for web applications. In *Proceedings of the 2006 IEEE Symposium on Security and Privacy*, 2006.

[22] S. Crites, F. Hsu, and H. Chen. Omash: enabling secure web mashups via object abstractions. In *Proceedings of the 15th ACM Conference on Computer and Communications Security*, CCS '08, 2008.

[23] A. R. Developers. Ajaxim rpg. `http://ajaximrpg.sourceforge.net/`.

[24] X. Dong, H. Hong, Z. Liang, and P. Saxena. A quantitative evaluation of privilege separation in web browser designs. In *Proceedings of the 18th European Conference on Research in Computer Security*, ESORICS '13, 2013.

[25] X. Dong, M. Tran, Z. Liang, and X. Jiang. Adsentry: comprehensive and flexible confinement of javascript-based advertisements. In *Proceedings of the 27th Annual Computer Security Applications Conference*, ACSAC '11, 2011.

[26] DoubleVerify. Doubleverify uncovers ad fraud tied to copyright infringement sites, costing online advertisers $6.8 million per month. `http://www.doubleverify.com/resources/research/DV-Fraud-Lab-Report-2013-05/`, May 2013.

[27] J. Engler, C. Karlof, E. Shi, and D. Song. Is it too late for pake? In *Proceedings of Web 2.0 Security and Privacy Workshop 2009*, 2009.

[28] I. E. T. Force. Rfc 6101: The secure sockets layer (ssl) protocol version 3.0. `http://tools.ietf.org/html/rfc6101`, 2011.

[29] M. Foundation. Mozilla foundation security advisories. `http://www.mozilla.org/security/announce/`.

[30] W. Foundation. Wordpress. `http://wordpress.org/`.

[31] S. Garera, N. Provos, M. Chew, and A. D. Rubin. A framework for detection and measurement of phishing attacks. In *Proceedings of the 2007 ACM Workshop on Recurring Malcode*, WORM '07, 2007.

[32] Github. `https://github.com`.

[33] C. Grier, S. Tang, and S. King. Designing and implementing the op and op2 web browsers. *ACM Transactions on the Web*, 2011.

[34] M. Heiderich. Towards elimination of xss attacks with a trusted and capability controlled dom. `http://heideri.ch/thesis`.

[35] B. Hicks, S. Rueda, D. King, T. Moyer, J. Schiffman, Y. Sreenivasan, P. McDaniel, and T. Jaeger. An architecture for enforcing end-to-end access control over web applications. In *Proceedings of the 15th ACM Symposium on Access Control Models and Technologies*, SACMAT '10, 2010.

[36] L.-S. Huang, A. Moshchuk, H. J. Wang, S. Schechter, and C. Jackson. Clickjacking: attacks and defenses. In *Proceedings of the 21st USENIX Security Symposium*, 2012.

[37] Intel. Trusted compute pools with intel® trusted execution technology. `http://www.intel.com/txt`.

[38] Internet Engineering Task Force (IETF). Rfc 6454: The web origin concept. `http://www.ietf.org/rfc/rfc6454.txt`.

[39] C. Jackson, D. R. Simon, D. S. Tan, and A. Barth. An evaluation of extended validation and picture-in-picture phishing attacks. In *Proceedings of the 11th International Conference on Financial Cryptography and 1st International Conference on Usable Security*, FC'07/USEC'07, 2007.

[40] K. Jayaraman, W. Du, B. Rajagopalan, and S. J. Chapin. Escudo: A fine-grained protection model for web browsers. In *Proceedings of the 30th International Conference on Distributed Computing Systems*, ICDCS '10, 2010.

[41] N. Kobeissi, A. Breault, and E. Gill. Cryptocat. `https://crypto.cat/`.

[42] B. Köpf and M. Dürmuth. A provably secure and efficient countermeasure against timing attacks. In *Proceedings of the 2009 22nd IEEE Computer Security Foundations Symposium*, CSF '09, 2009.

[43] LastPass. Lastpass password manager. `https://lastpass.com/`.

[44] A. Libonati, J. M. McCune, and M. K. Reiter. Usability testing a malware-resistant input mechanism. In *Proceedings of the 18th Annual Network and Distributed System Security Symposium*, NDSS '11, 2011.

[45] D. Lie, C. Thekkath, M. Mitchell, P. Lincoln, D. Boneh, J. Mitchell, and M. Horowitz. Architectural support for copy and tamper resistant software. In *Proceedings of the 9th International Conference on Architectural Support for Programming Languages and Operating Systems*, ASPLOS-IX, 2000.

[46] M. T. Louw, K. T. Ganesh, and V. N. Venkatakrishnan. Adjail: practical enforcement of confidentiality and integrity policies on web advertisements. In *Proceedings of the 19th USENIX Security Symposium*, 2010.

[47] T. Luo and W. Du. Contego: capability-based access control for web browsers. In *Proceedings of the 4th International Conference on Trust and Trustworthy Computing*, TRUST '11, 2011.

[48] P. Maniatis, D. Akhawe, K. Fall, E. Shi, S. McCamant, and D. Song. Do you know where your data are?: secure data capsules for deployable data protection. In *Proceedings of the 13th Workshop on Hot Topics in Operating Systems*, HotOS-XIII, 2011.

[49] J. M. McCune, A. Perrig, and M. K. Reiter. Safe passage for passwords and other sensitive data. In *Proceedings of the 16th Annual Network and Distributed System Security Symposium*, NDSS '09, 2009.

[50] L. A. Meyerovich and B. Livshits. Conscript: Specifying and enforcing fine-grained security policies for javascript in the browser. In *Proceedings of the 2010 IEEE Symposium on Security and Privacy*, 2010.

[51] Mozilla. Firefox os. `https://developer.mozilla.org/en-US/docs/Mozilla/Firefox_OS`.

[52] C. Nie. Dynamic root of trust in trusted computing. `http://www.tml.tkk.fi/Publications/C/25/papers/Nie_final.pdf`.

[53] D. of Defense Standard. Department of defense trusted computer system evaluation criteria, 5200.28-std, 1985.

[54] K. Patil, X. Dong, X. Li, Z. Liang, and X. Jiang. Towards fine-grained access control in javascript contexts. In *Proceedings of the 31st International Conference on Distributed Computing Systems*, ICDCS '11, 2011.

[55] T. C. Projects. Chromium os. `http://www.chromium.org/chromium-os`.

[56] T. C. Projects. Linuxsandboxing. `https://code.google.com/p/chromium/wiki/LinuxSandboxing#The_seccomp-bpf_sandbox`.

[57] T. C. Projects. Sandbox. `http://www.chromium.org/developers/design-documents/sandbox`.

[58] F. Roesner, T. Kohno, A. Moshchuk, B. Parno, H. J. Wang, and C. Cowan. User-driven access control: Rethinking permission granting in modern operating systems. In *Proceedings of the 2012 IEEE Symposium on Security and Privacy*, 2012.

[59] C. Rohlf and Y. Ivnitskiy. Attacking clientside jit compilers. `http://www.matasano.com/research/Attacking_Clientside_JIT_Compilers_Paper.pdf`.

[60] J. H. Saltzer and M. D. Schroeder. The protection of information in computer systems. In *Proceedings of the IEEE*, 1975.

[61] N. Santos, R. Rodrigues, K. P. Gummadi, and S. Saroiu. Policy-sealed data: A new abstraction for building trusted cloud services. In *Proceedings of the 21st USENIX Security Symposium*, 2012.

[62] P. Saxena, D. Akhawe, S. Hanna, F. Mao, S. McCamant, and D. Song. A symbolic execution framework for javascript. In *Proceedings of the 2010 IEEE Symposium on Security and Privacy*, 2010.

[63] S. Tang, H. Mai, and S. T. King. Trust and protection in the illinois browser operating system. In *Proceedings of the 9th USENIX Symposium on Operating Systems Design and Implementation*, OSDI '10, 2010.

[64] Y. Tang, P. Ames, S. Bhamidipati, A. Bijlani, R. Geambasu, and N. Sarda. Cleanos: limiting mobile data exposure with idle eviction. In *Proceedings of the 10th USENIX Symposium on Operating Systems Design and Implementation*, OSDI '12, 2012.

[65] T. R. Team. Roundcube. `http://www.roundcube.net/`.

[66] P. Vogt, F. Nentwich, N. Jovanovic, E. Kirda, C. Kruegel, and G. Vigna. Cross-site scripting prevention with dynamic data tainting and static analysis. In *Proceedings of the 14th Annual Network and Distributed System Security Symposium*, NDSS '07, 2007.

[67] W3C. Content security policy 1.0. `http://www.w3.org/TR/CSP/`.

[68] R. Wahbe, S. Lucco, T. E. Anderson, and S. L. Graham. Efficient software-based fault isolation. In *Proceedings of the 14th ACM Symposium on Operating Systems Principles*, SOSP '93, 1993.

[69] H. J. Wang, C. Grier, A. Moshchuk, S. T. King, P. Choudhury, and H. Venter. The multi-principal os construction of the gazelle web browser. In *Proceedings of the 18th USENIX Security Symposium*, 2009.

[70] D. Wendlandt, D. G. Andersen, and A. Perrig. Perspectives: improving ssh-style host authentication with multi-path probing. In *USENIX 2008 Annual Technical Conference*, ATC '08, 2008.

[71] Z. E. Ye and S. Smith. Trusted paths for browsers. In *Proceedings of the 11th USENIX Security Symposium*, 2002.

[72] C. Yue and H. Wang. Anti-phishing in offense and defense. In *Proceedings of the 2008 Annual Computer Security Applications Conference*, ACSAC '08, 2008.

[73] Y. Zhang, J. I. Hong, and L. F. Cranor. Cantina: a content-based approach to detecting phishing web sites. In *Proceedings of the 16th International Conference on World Wide Web*, WWW '07, 2007.

[74] Y. Zhou and D. Evans. Protecting private web content from embedded scripts. In *Proceedings of the 16th European Conference on Research in Computer Security*, ESORICS '11, 2011.

[75] Z. Zhou, V. D. Gligor, J. Newsome, and J. M. McCune. Building verifiable trusted path on commodity x86 computers. In *Proceedings of the 2012 IEEE Symposium on Security and Privacy*, 2012.

DEMO: Adjustably Encrypted In-Memory Column-Store

Florian Kerschbaum
Martin Härterich
Axel Schröpfer

Patrick Grofig
Mathias Kohler
Walter Tighzert

Isabelle Hang
Andreas Schaad

SAP
Karlsruhe, Germany
firstname.lastname@sap.com

ABSTRACT

Recent databases are implemented as in-memory column-stores. Adjustable encryption offers a solution to encrypted database processing in the cloud.

We show that the two technologies play well together by providing an analysis and prototype results that demonstrate the impact of mechanisms at the database side (dictionaries and their compression) and cryptographic mechanisms at the adjustable encryption side (order-preserving, homomorphic, deterministic and probabilistic encryption).

Categories and Subject Descriptors

H.2.0 [**Database Management**]: General—*Security, Integrity, and Protection*; D.4.6 [**Operating Systems**]: Security and Protection—*Cryptographic controls*

General Terms

Algorithms, Security

Keywords

Database Outsourcing, Encryption, In-Memory, Column Store

1. INTRODUCTION

In-memory column-store databases [3, 9, 10] use dictionary compression [1] to speed up processing. The smaller the data, the faster the transfer to the CPU.

In-memory column-store databases in the cloud are faced with severe security concerns. Adjustable encryption [8] offers the possibility to process data while encrypted. The clients can then upload data, retain the key and receive only the encrypted result for most SQL queries.

Adjustable encryption so far has only been tested on disk-based row-store databases. We demonstrate that the processing of in-memory column-store databases is very well amenable to adjustable encryption. We show a very small performance overhead when using less secure encryption schemes and dictionary compression.

CCS'13, November 4–8, 2013, Berlin, Germany.
ACM 978-1-4503-2477-9/13/11.
http://dx.doi.org/10.1145/2508859.2512491.

2. BACKGROUND

2.1 Adjustable Encryption

Security is a major concern for outsourced databases. In the database-as-a-service model an independent service provider offers its database to clients. The clients need to entrust their data to the cloud service provider without having control over unwanted disclosures, e.g., to insiders or hackers.

One solution to this outsourced security problem is to encrypt the data before sending it to the cloud. Of course, the decryption key needs to remain only at the client. This is easy to implement for simple storage, but the clients must be remain able to query the database. Therefore the service provider has to solve the complicated task of querying on the encrypted data.

Order-preserving encryption (OPE) [2], deterministic encryption (DET) [6] and (additive) homomorphic encryption (HOM) [5] offer a (partial) solution to the encrypted data querying problem. These different encryption schemes have different algebraic properties. Let $c = E_T(x)$ denote the encryption of plaintext x in encryption type $T \in \{OPE, DET, HOM\}$. We denote $D_T(c)$ the corresponding decryption. Order-preserving encryption has the property that it preserves the order of plaintexts, i.e.

$$x \leq y \Longleftrightarrow E_{OPE}(x) \leq E_{OPE}(y)$$

Deterministic encryption preserves the equality of plaintexts, i.e.

$$x = y \Longleftrightarrow E_{DET}(x) = E_{DET}(y)$$

In (additively) homomorphic encryption multiplication of ciphertexts (modulo a key-dependent constant) maps to addition of the plaintexts, i.e.

$$D_{HOM}(E_{HOM}(x) \cdot E_{HOM}(y)) = x + y$$

In terms of security we have: homomorphic (or standard) encryption is at least as secure as deterministic encryption which is at least as secure as order-preserving encryption. This observation implies that the client in data outsourcing should carefully choose its encryption types. It should only use order-preserving or deterministic encryption if necessary to enable its queries in order to achieve the highest security level. Yet, the set of executed queries may be unknown at design time making this choice undecidable.

Popa et al. offer an intriguing solution to the encryption type selection problem [8]. First, they introduce a further encryption type RND for standard, randomized encryption. This encryption type only allows retrieval, but no queries.

Column	Column Cardinality	Item Size	Plain Size	Compressed Size (Dictionary + Column)	Ratio
First name	5 million, 23bit	49 Byte	365.08 GB	234 MB + 21.42 GB = 22,168 GB	5.9%
Last name	8 million, 23 bit	50 Byte	372.5 GB	381 MB + 21.42 GB = 22,316 GB	5.9%
Gender	2, 1 bit	1 Byte	7.45 GB	2 Byte + 0.93 GB = 954 MB	12.5%
City	1 million, 20 bit	49 Byte	365.08 GB	47 MB + 18.62 GB = 19,120 GB	5.1%
Country	200, 8 bit	49 Byte	365.08 GB	6 KB + 7.45 GB = 7,629 GB	2.0%
Birthday	40, 6 bit	4 Byte	29.80 GB	76 KB + 5.59 GB = 5,722 GB	18.7%

Table 1: Example Table for Dictionary Compression

Note that order-preserving encryption enables a proper superset of queries to deterministic encryption. They therefore compose a layered ciphertext called onion. This encryption onion $E_{RND}(E_{DET}(E_{OPE}(x)))$ is composed of the following layers:

- *L3 – Randomized Encryption*: IND-CPA secure encryption allowing only retrieveal using AES encryption in CBC mode.
- *L2 – Deterministic Encryption*: Allows processing of equality comparisons using the encryption scheme of [6]. Furthermore, this encryption can be (proxy) re-encrypted, such that it is possible to join tables using columns, encrypted under different keys.
- *L1 – Order-Preserving Encryption*: Allows processing of greater-than comparisons using the encryption scheme of [2].
- *L0 – Data*: The data to be encrypted.

This onion at first only allows retrieval – due to the randomized encryption. Should the client encounter a query that requires deterministic encryption, e.g., a selection using equality, then it updates the database. It sends the key $D_{RND}()$ for decrypting the randomized encryption to the database. The database uses a user-defined function to perform the update, such that now the database stores $E_{DET}(E_{OPE}(x))$. This enables the new query to be executed. The same procedure occurs in case of a query that requires order-preserving encryption to execute.

Homomorphic encryption is handled slightly differently and stored in a separate column. The separate column also enables aggregation operations, but does not harm security, since homomorphic encryption is semantically secure. A layering is not possible, since homomorphic encryption needs to encrypt the plaintext x for the correct result in aggregations.

This algorithm represents an adjustment mechanism of the database to the series of executed queries. It enables to dynamically adapt the encryption types, i.e., without knowing all queries in advance. Furthermore, the adjustment is unidirectional. Once decrypted to deterministic or order-preserving encryption it is never necessary to return to a higher encryption level to enable a subsequent query. Yet, security against the service provider has already been weakened, because the less secure ciphertext has been revealed at least once. We call such a database *adjustably encrypted.*

2.2 Column-Store In-Memory Databases

We investigate our encryption algorithms as part of an encrypted, in-memory, column-store database. This has a couple of design implications we highlight in this section.

Column-store databases, such as [3, 9, 10] show excellent performance for analytical workloads. For this they store the data column-wise instead of row-wise. All data for a certain can such be accessed and processed very quickly. The speed of processing can be enhanced further if the data is stored in main memory.

In-memory, column-store databases process the entire column of data for operations, such as a selection. Hence, the speed of transferring data from the main memory to the CPU becomes the bottleneck. A common optimization is to compress the data [1]. This further significantly improves the processing performance.

A common technique is order-preserving dictionary compression [1]. In dictionary compression data values are replaced by data identifiers and in a dictionary their relation is stored. A dictionary is order-preserving, if the order relation of the data identifiers is the same as the order relation of the data values. Figure 1 shows an example dictionary for currency values.

Data Identifier	Data Value
1	\$ 0.99
2	\$ 1.54
3	\$ 9.23

Figure 1: Example Dictionary

Order-preserving dictionaries have the advantage that select operations – even for range queries – can be performed without accessing the dictionary. The database operator is fed with the data identifier (or data identifiers for range queries) to select and can then process the column. Any select operation that needs to lookup the dictionary can be very costly.

Also update or insert operations can be very costly. They often need to recompute the entire column of data. This may also involve some further compression operations.

Note that the order-preserving dictionary is an ideal-secure order-preserving encryption. The database performs this operation automatically, although not as encryption operation. It therefore becomes a crucial design decision for an encrypted database how to integrate with this dictionary.

One approach is to strip the dictionary of the data values and keep those at the client. This has been proposed by Hildenbrand et al. in [4]. On the one hand this achieves ideal-security for the order-preserving encryption, since the database only learns the data identifiers. On the other hand this prevents all operations that require access to the data values, such as aggregation which is a very common operation in analytical work loads.

Another approach is to encrypt the data values in the dictionary. This has been proposed by Popa et al. in [7]. It also achieves ideal-security on the database, but requires $O(n \log n)$ cost for inserting n, since each element needs to be sorted into the dictionary. When using homomorphic encryption [5] this can also achieve aggregation.

A disadvantage of both approaches is that the database always needs to be encrypted in order-preserving encryption. We therefore resort to Boldyreva et al.'s scheme [2] and adjustable encryption as introduced in Section 2.1. Encryption is layered from order-preserving on the innermost layer over deterministic encryption to randomized encryption on the outermost layer. Depending on the operation performed one or more layers of encryption are removed before executing the operator. This results in significantly better security, since only a subset of columns needs to be encrypted order-preserving.

3. CONCLUSION

Enc.	Compressed Size (Dictionary + Column)	Overhead
RND	596,05 GB + 245,87 GB = 862.122 GB	3789%
DET	305 MB + 21,42 GB = 22.239 GB	0%
OPE	153 MB + 21,42 GB = 22.086 GB	0%

Table 2: Dictionary Compression under Encryption

We will demonstrate the impact of adjustable encryption on an in-memory column-store database. For most data dictionary compression works fine. Consider the following example for the world population as in Table 1

Plain size is calculated as

$$Plain\ Size = Item\ Size \times World\ Population$$

and the compressed size is calculated as

$$\begin{aligned} Compressed\ Size &= Dictionary + Column \\ &= Item\ Size \times Column\ Cardinality + \\ &\quad Cardinality\ Size \times WorldPopulation \end{aligned}$$

We denote as $Column\ Cardinality_X$ the column cardinality for encryption scheme $X \in \{RND, DET, OPE\}$. Now observe the following. Under L3 randomized encryption it holds that

$$Column\ Cardinality_{RND} = World\ Population$$

Therefore the dictionary has already the same size as the plain data (plain size) and the column only adds more data. Hence, it is beneficial to not do dictionary compression.

Whereas under L2/L1 deterministic and order-preserving encryption it holds that

$$\begin{aligned} Column\ Cardinality_{DET} = \\ Column\ Cardinality_{OPE} = \\ Column\ Cardinality \end{aligned}$$

The item size might increase due to blocking of the encryption algorithm, but that is the only additional space requirement. Hence, it is beneficial to do dictionary compression. See the examples for the column of first names in Table 2.

We therefore conclude that depending on the security level dictionary compression of in-memory column-store databases can be beneficial, particularly when processing the encrypted column. Furthermore, the impact of compression in case of deterministic or order-preserving encryption is very small. We underpin these results in our demonstration of our prototype.

4. REFERENCES

[1] C. Binnig, S. Hildenbrand, and F. Färber, "Dictionary-based order-preserving string compression for main memory column stores," in *Proceedings of the ACM International Conference on Management of Data*, ser. SIGMOD, 2009.

[2] A. Boldyreva, N. Chenette, Y. Lee, and A. O'Neill, "Order-preserving symmetric encryption," in *Advances in Cryptology*, ser. EUROCRYPT, 2009.

[3] F. Färber, N. May, W. Lehner, P. Große, I. Müller, H. Rauhe, and J. Dees, "The SAP HANA database – an architecture overview," *IEEE Data Engineering Bulletin*, vol. 35, no. 1, pp. 28–33, 2012.

[4] S. Hildenbrand, D. Kossmann, T. Sanamrad, C. Binnig, F. Färber, and J. Wöhler, "Query processing on encrypted data in the cloud," Department of Computer Science, ETH Zurich, Tech. Rep. 735, 2011.

[5] P. Paillier, "Public-key cryptosystems based on composite degree residuosity classes," in *Proceedings of the 18th International Conference on Advances in Cryptology*. ser. EUROCRYPT, 1999.

[6] S. Pohlig, and M. Hellman, "An improved algorithm for computing logarithms over GF(p) and its cryptographic significance," *IEEE Transactions on Information Theory*, vol. 24, no. 1, pp. 106–110, 1978.

[7] R. A. Popa, F. H. Li, and N. Zeldovich, "An ideal-security protocol for order-preserving encoding," in *34th IEEE Symposium on Security and Privacy*, ser. S&P, 2013.

[8] R. Popa, C. Redfield, N. Zeldovich, and H. Balakrishnan. "CryptDB: Protecting confidentiality with encrypted query processing." in *Proceedings of the 23rd ACM Symposium on Operating Systems Principles*, ser. SOSP, 2011.

[9] M. Stonebraker, D. J. Abadi, A. Batkin, X. Chen, M. Cherniack, M. Ferreira, E. Lau, A. Lin, S. Madden, E. O'Neil, P. O'Neil, A. Rasin, N. Tran, and S. Zdonik, "C-store: a column-oriented dbms," in *Proceedings of the 31st International Conference on Very Large Data Bases*, ser. VLDB, 2005.

[10] M. Zukowski, P. A. Boncz, N. Nes, and S. Héman, "Monetdb/x100 - a dbms in the cpu cache," *IEEE Data Engineering Bulletin*, vol. 28, no. 2, pp. 17–22, 2005.

DEMO: Demonstrating a Trust Framework for Evaluating GNSS Signal Integrity

Xihui Chen[†] [*], Carlo Harpes[♯], Gabriele Lenzini[†], Miguel Martins[♯], Sjouke Mauw[†], Jun Pang[†]

[†]University of Luxembourg, Luxembourg [♯]itrust consulting s.à r.l., Luxembourg

ABSTRACT

Through real-life experiments, it has been proved that spoofing is a practical threat to applications using the free civil service provided by Global Navigation Satellite Systems (GNSS).

In this paper, we demonstrate a prototype that can verify the integrity of GNSS civil signals. By *integrity* we intuitively mean that civil signals originate from a GNSS satellite without having been artificially interfered with. Our prototype provides interfaces that can incorporate existing spoofing detection methods whose results are then combined into an overall evaluation of the signal's integrity, which we call *integrity level.* Considering the various security requirements from different applications, integrity levels can be calculated in many ways determined by their users. We also present an application scenario that deploys our prototype and offers a public central service – *localisation assurance certification.* Through experiments, we successfully show that our prototype is not only effective but also efficient in practice.

Categories and Subject Descriptors

C.2.0 [**Computer-Communication Networks**]: General—*Security and protection*

Keywords

GNSS signal; signal integrity; spoofing

1. INTRODUCTION

The free access to the civil localisation service of Global Navigation Satellite Systems (GNSS) has been popularising numerous location-based applications which have penetrated into people's daily life from leisure activities, such as geo-social networks, to safety-critical products, such as driverless cars. However, different from military signals, civil GNSS signals are neither signed nor encrypted. This leads to the problem that their originators cannot be authenticated. Besides this, due to the weak strength when transmitted in the open air, they can be easily taken over by false signals. Such attacks are called *spoofing* [4]. It has been demonstrated by a number of scientific experiments (e.g., see [3]) that receivers can be fooled by spoofed signals to calculate wrong locations.

Navigation message authentication is considered as an effective method to prevent spoofing attacks. However, this is not feasible in the near future due to the difficulties to upgrade the current GNSS infrastructure. Although the European GNSS – Galileo is planning to offer authenticated civil services, it is not free and also not accessible to everybody. In the literature, a number of methods have been proposed aiming to *detect spoofing* instead of *preventing spoofing*. A spoofing detection method usually makes use of an observable feature of GNSS signals that should be present when they are not spoofed. The absence of the feature will lead to an alarm of spoofing. Otherwise, a claim of signal integrity will be issued. For instance, as integrous signals have signal strength smaller than -153.5 dBW, given a signal with a larger power the corresponding spoofing detection method will conclude that the signal is spoofed.

Spoofing detection methods explore two inference rules. For instance, when signal strength is used, they are formulated as follows:

$$\textit{signal strength} \leq -153.5\, dBW \rightarrow \textit{the signal received is integrous};$$
$$\textit{signal strength} > -153.5\, dBW \rightarrow \textit{the signal received is spoofed.}$$

Meanwhile, these inference rules can also be interpreted as the causal relations between the precedents and the conclusions, e.g., whether the strength is smaller than -153.5 dBW and whether the signal is integrous, respectively.

However, these inference rules do not capture the correct causal relations between observed features and signal integrity. For example, signal strength is a physical attribute of GNSS signals. Its value is measured by a certain sensor which takes signals as input. Therefore, if the received signal is integrous then its strength is smaller than the threshold (-153.5 dBW). However, "the observation that the signal strength is larger than the threshold implies that the signal is integrous" is a false statement. Moreover, after having studied several spoofing detection methods, we concluded that additional conditions are required to express the causal relations, as some observed features are not only caused by the current signal but are also related to past signals. For instance, users' future locations can be predicted based on their current positions and other information such as direction and velocity. An existing spoofing detection method makes use of the distance between the locations calculated and the predicted ones. Once the distance is small enough, it will claim integrity of the signal. In fact, the integrity of the current signal only cannot enforce the small distance. We also need to ensure the correctness of the prediction which is decided by the integrity of the past signal used to calculate the past position.

The impacts of environmental noise on attributes of signals are not fully addressed in the literature. The noise caused by natural facts such as reflection can lead to significant variance in the

[*]Supported by the National Research Fund, Luxembourg (SECLOC 794361).

CCS'13, November 4–8, 2013, Berlin, Germany.
ACM 978-1-4503-2477-9/13/11.
http://dx.doi.org/10.1145/2508859.2512492.

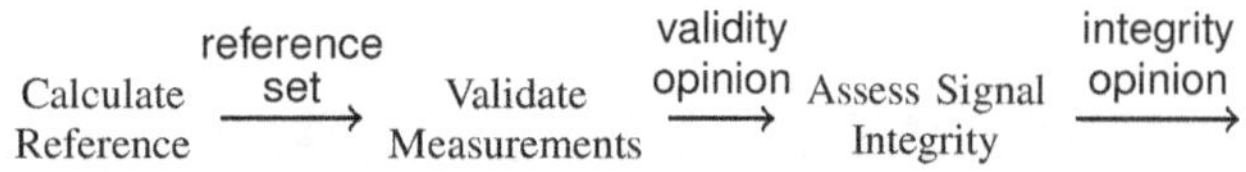

Figure 1: Main steps to derive an integrity opinion.

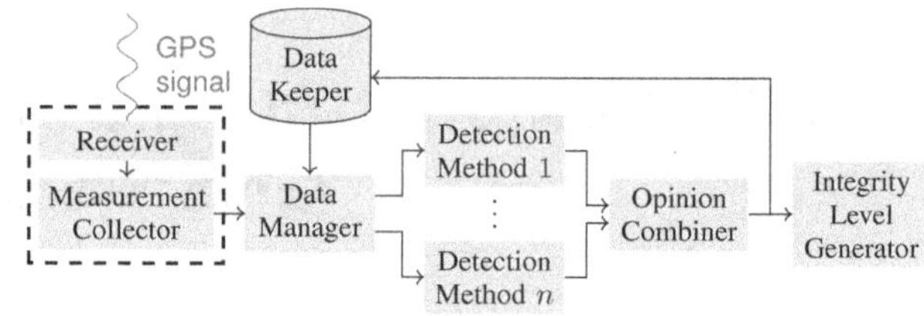

Figure 2: The components of the prototype.

measurements of some attributes. Thus, some expected observable features can be violated even if the signal is not spoofed. A qualitative conclusion, as usually given by the existing spoofing detection methods, cannot capture uncertainty in such cases.

We proposed a trust framework [1] to evaluate the integrity of GNSS signals. Informally, a received signal is integrous if it has originated from a GNSS satellite without having been artificially interfered with. Our framework provides a formal characterisation of spoofing detection methods and the causal relationships used by them. Subjective logic is exploited to infer signal integrity from observations and it can capture the uncertainty caused by unpredictable environmental noise. This leads to a quantitative opinion on signal integrity. Subsequently the quantification allows us to develop meaningful algorithms to combine the outputs of different spoofing detection methods.

Our contributions. We develop a prototype based on the trust framework [1] to provide a general software structure to make use of existing spoofing detection methods. It takes the measurements of attributes of received signals as input and outputs an overall conclusion on the signal integrity. We take into account the diversity of users' security requirements and provide a customisable evaluation process. For instance, users can cater the evaluation according to the quality of their localising devices and ever-changing environment. To demonstrate the marketing potentials of our prototype, we implemented a public service – *location assurance certification*. With extensive experiments, we show that our prototype is not only effective but also efficient in practice.

2. TRUST FRAMEWORK OVERVIEW

We give a brief introduction to our trust framework [1]. Fig. 1 shows the three steps in the framework to use a spoofing detection method to check signal integrity. Intuitively, a spoofing detection method takes a measurement of an attribute of a received signal (e.g., signal strength) as input and outputs its assessment on the signal's integrity which is in the form of a *subjective logic opinion*. A subjective logic opinion expresses the belief of an agent on the truth of a (multiple) proposition(s) [2]. For instance, $w_x^A = (b, d, u, a)$ is the opinion of A on the truth of x, where b, d and u describes A's belief, disbelief and uncertainty, respectively; and a is the *a priori* probability that x is true. Furthermore, we have $b + d + u = 1$ and the *expectation probability* of x being true is calculated as $b + a \cdot u$.

A spoofing detection method first calculates a set of predicted values for an attribute if the signal is integrous, called *reference set*. Subsequently, it will check whether the measurement of the attribute of the received signal is in the reference. If it is, the measurement is valid. The output of this step is called *valid opinion* which in fact expresses the belief on the presence of an observable feature. Its calculation captures the impact of environmental noise. The last step clarifies the causal relationship between the observation of a received signal and its integrity. For example, with regards to signal strength, the causal relation is '$\textit{the received signal is integrous} \rightarrow \textit{signal strength} \leq -153.5\ dBW$'. We also identify another type of spoofing detection methods whose causal relationships contain past signals' integrity in the precedent. For example, in the inertial spoofing detection, the causal relationship can be formulated by $\textit{if referred past signals and current signal are integrous} \rightarrow \textit{the calculated location is close to the predicted location}$. These relationships show that the reasoning of signal integrity based on observed features is *abductive* but not *deductive*. The output of this step is called *integrity opinion*.

Given multiple spoofing detection methods, for a received signal, we will obtain multiple integrity opinions. They are different from each other due to the various features of signal attributes in detecting spoofed signals. Thus, an overall integrity opinion is necessary to resolve the difference. To combine the different integrity opinions, three algorithms are proposed to meet the various security requirements of applications – Veto, Consensus and Combined. The Veto algorithm returns the opinion which indicates the largest probability of spoofing. It gives conservative results and can be used in safe-critical applications. However, false alarms of spoofing are quite possible due to the abrupt changes on signal attributes caused by environmental noise. The Consensus algorithm makes use of the *fusion* operation on subjective logic opinions. Intuitively, it ensures that the integrity opinions with less uncertainty are more important in the combined opinion. Compared with the Veto algorithm, the Consensus algorithm generates fewer false claims of spoofing but may output more false claims of integrity, especially in the case where attackers have more power to tune signal attributes. The Combined algorithm aims to reach a balance between false alarms of spoofing and false claims of integrity. It returns the consensus of *VETO opinions* which indicate large probabilities of spoofing with small uncertainty. When VETO opinions do not exist, the Consensus algorithm will be used.

3. PROTOTYPE

We have developed a prototype based on the trust framework. It collects the measurements of received GPS (Global Positioning System) signals from receivers in real time and returns the signal integrity to users in terms of *integrity levels*.

Our prototype allows a user to customise the integrity evaluation process according to the real time environment in order to obtain more reliable results. First, a user can disable some spoofing detection methods in certain cases when they are likely to calculate incorrect integrity opinions. For instance, when driving in a forest, a user wants to stop using detection methods relying on signal strength due to the significant fluctuations caused by trees. Second, a user can choose the algorithm to combine integrity opinions from different spoofing detection methods according to the service he is requesting. Last, a user can notify our prototype of the type of his receiver. This is necessary because receivers may differ in terms of computation power and antennas. The variants lead to different measurements of some attributes even for the same signal. In our prototype, we make a simple classification – professional and commercial-off-the-shelf, and assign different values to the *a priori* parameters used during the evaluation process.

We show in Fig. 2 the components of our prototype. Upon receiving a signal, the receiver calculates its location. Meanwhile the *measurement collector* (MC) starts gathering the values of the attributes measured by the receiver during localisation and subsequently send them to the *data manager* (DM). We organise and

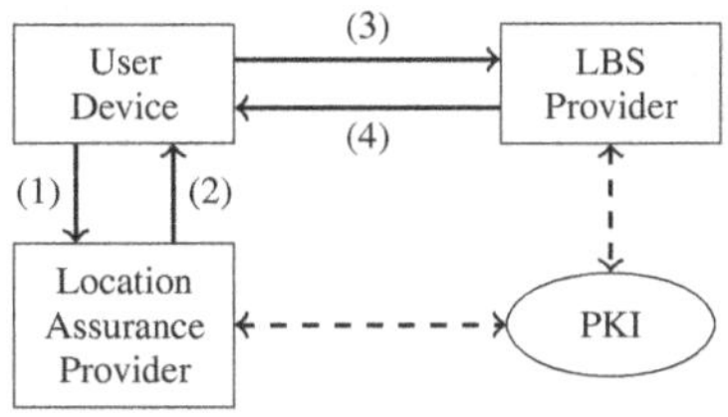

Figure 3: Location Assurance Provider

record the measurements in the form of XML (Extensible Markup Language) due to its simplicity and generality. The preference of a user to customise the integrity evaluation is also added, including the spoofing detection and combination algorithms to run. The DM prepares and distributes the input for each spoofing detection method. Besides the measurements of signal attributes, other information is also included in the inputs, such as the integrity opinions of related past signals and parameters to calculate reference sets. All such information is stored and managed by the *data keeper* (DK). Integrity opinions are calculated by spoofing detection methods and then sent to the *opinion combiner* (OC) which calculates the overall integrity opinion according to the user's requirement contained in the XML file. In the end, the combined integrity opinion is transformed into an *integrity level* between 1 to 5 which is intuitive and easy for users to understand. Specifically, a signal is labelled by integrity level i if the expectation probability of the integrity opinion is between $0.2 \cdot (i-1)$ and $0.2 \cdot i$.

Note that MC should be installed on the device equipped in the receiver so as to have access to the measurements of signals (see the dashed rectangle in Fig. 2). The other components can be deployed and run on remote agents. However, the communication between them should be well designed as users' locations are acknowledged as an important piece of private information.

4. LOCATION ASSURANCE PROVIDER

To demonstrate our trust framework for evaluating GNSS signal integrity, we present an implementation of a public service – *location assurance certification* based on our prototype in practice. *Location-based services* (LBS) are services customised according to users' locations. Delivering a service calculated with a wrong location will lead to security concerns such as privacy leakage. Take location-based local friend search as an example. Users send requests to LBS providers for the list of friends who are close to them in order to have a common activity. By feeding a user's device with false locations, attackers can learn the locations of any friends of the user which should not be revealed according to the user's real location. To fight against such attacks, only to protect users' device from malware is not sufficient because spoofing is still possible.

We have implemented a trusted central server called *location assurance provider* (LAP) based on our prototype to evaluate signals' integrity and issue a certificate on their integrity levels (called *location assurance certificate*). The certificate is then sent to the LBS provider who will verify and adjust its policy (e.g., stop or continue) to deliver the service according to the integrity level. Fig. 3 shows the main steps for a user to request an LBS using location assurance certification. Before sending a request to the LBS provider, the user device first collects the measurements of received signals and contacts the LAP to evaluate their integrity (step (1)). Upon receiving the location assurance certificate (step (2)), the user sends an LBS request together with the certificate (step (3)) to the LBS provider. The provider checks the validity of the certificate and returns the service catered in terms of the integrity level attached (step (4)). To accomplish the scheme, a public key infrastructure (PKI) is required to manage the LAP's public key. Besides the LAP we also implement an Android application which runs on users' mobile devices. In fact, the application works as the measurement collector (MC in Fig. 2) and takes charge of communicating with the LAP. We use a 3G telecommunication network to establish the connection with the LAP. According to our test, the average transition time of a message is about 2 seconds.

Table 1: Computation time of a request.

# users	100	200	300	400	500
avg. time (s)	0.1	0.7	2.5	2.6	3.7

We test the efficiency and effectiveness of the LAP in terms of computation time and numbers of false conclusions. The LAP is run on a virtual machine with 4G RAM and an Intel Xeon E5-2640 processor. Tab. 1 shows the average computation time for a request when different number of users send requests concurrently – it increases when the number of requests gets large. This is because for a request, the LAP needs two operations on the database (read parameters and store integrity opinions) which takes about 90% of the computation time. However, even with the current setting, for 500 requests, we need less than 4 seconds which is still acceptable. More efficient database techniques can improve the parallelism of the computation. Fig. 4 shows the distributions of integrity levels of four spoofing detection methods[1] and our three integration algorithms on a dataset of signals which contains about 18% of spoofed signals. We can see that the integrity opinions vary over the different detection methods and the Combined algorithm gives the results with the minimum number of false alarm and false claims.

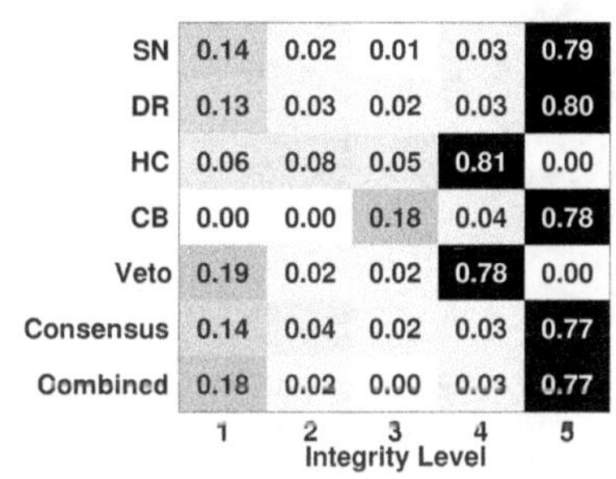

Figure 4: Integrity opinions

5. CONCLUSION

We have developed a software prototype to evaluate the integrity of GNSS signals. It offers a general framework to exploit existing spoofing detection methods. With this prototype, we implemented a public service – location assurance certification and illustrated the marketing potentials of our prototype through experiments.

6. REFERENCES

[1] X. Chen, G. Lenzini, M. Martins, S. Mauw, and J. Pang. A trust framework for evaluating GNSS signal integrity. In *Proc. 26th IEEE Computer Security Foundations Symposium (CSF)*, pages 179–192. IEEE Computer Society, 2013.

[2] A. Jøsang. Subjective logic (book draft). `http://folk.uio.no/josang/papers/subjective_logic.pdf`, 2012.

[3] M. Mixon. Todd Humphreys' research team demonstrates first successful GPS spoofing of UAV. `http://www.ae.utexas.edu/news/archive/`, 2012.

[4] J. S. Warner and R. G. Johnston. A simple demonstration that the global positioning system (GPS) is vulnerable to spoofing. *Journal of Security Administration*, 25(19), 2002.

[1] SNR, DR, CB and HC are short for signal-to-noise ratio, Doppler ratios, clock bias and height comparison, see [1] for more details.

Demo: Inherent PUFs and Secure PRNGs on Commercial Off-the-Shelf Microcontrollers

Anthony Van Herrewege
KU Leuven
Heverlee, Belgium
anthony.vanherrewege@esat.kuleuven.be

André Schaller
TU Darmstadt
Darmstadt, Germany
schaller@seceng.informatik.tu-darmstadt.de

Stefan Katzenbeisser
TU Darmstadt
Darmstadt, Germany
katzenbeisser@seceng.informatik.tu-darmstadt.de

Ingrid Verbauwhede
KU Leuven
Heverlee, Belgium
ingrid.verbauwhede@esat.kuleuven.be

ABSTRACT

Research on Physically Unclonable Functions (PUFs) has become very popular in recent years. However, all PUFs researched so far require either ASICs, FPGAs or a microcontroller with external components. Our research focuses on identifying PUFs in commercial off-the-shelf devices, e.g. microcontrollers. We show that PUFs exist in several off-the-shelf products, which can be used for security applications.

We present measurement results on the PUF behavior of five of the most popular microcontrollers today: ARM Cortex-A, ARM Cortex-M, Atmel AVR, Microchip PIC16 and Texas Instruments MSP430. Based on these measurements, we can calculate whether these chips can be considered for applications requiring strong cryptography.

As a result of these findings, we present a secure bootloader for the ARM Cortex-A9 platform based on a PUF inherent to the device, requiring no external components. Furthermore, instead of discarding the randomness in PUF responses, we utilize this to create strong seeds for pseudo-random number generators (PRNGs). The existence of a secure RNG is at the heart of virtually every cryptographic protocol, yet very often overlooked. We present the implementation of a strongly seeded PRNG for the ARM Cortex-M family, again requiring no external components.

Categories and Subject Descriptors

D.4.6 [**Operating Systems**]: Security and Protection—*Cryptographic Controls*; G.3 [**Mathematics of Computing**]: Probability and Statistics—*Random Number Generation*

CCS'13, November 4–8, 2013, Berlin, Germany.
ACM 978-1-4503-2477-9/13/11.
http://dx.doi.org/10.1145/2508859.2512493.

Keywords

Physically Unclonable Functions; Pseudo-Random Number Generation; Secure Boot

1. INTRODUCTION

In recent years, research on Physically Unclonable Functions (PUFs) has seen a large increase in popularity. PUFs are devices that function as random identifiers, meaning that the output of a PUF is different for each physical instantiation of a particular PUF design and it is impossible for manufacturers to clone PUFs by controlling their production process. PUFs can be used to authenticate devices and to establish keys tied to a physical instance of a device, all without the manufacturer having to program a key or ID into the device.

One peculiarity of PUFs is that when queried for a response, their output will differ slightly each time. Thus, in order to guarantee a fixed result, a PUF's output will have to be error corrected. Depending on the type of PUF, the number of bits that have to be corrected varies between 1–15% of the total output length.

Of particular practical importance are the class of electronic PUFs, containing arbiter PUFs, ring oscillator PUFs and memory-based PUFs, since these can be completely implemented in silicon. However, a big drawback to practical applications and fast industry adoption is that most, if not all, of the PUFs proposed and researched so far *have been implemented in either ASICs, FPGAs or separate components.* In contrast, the goal of our research is to *identify PUFs that are already present in commercial off-the-shelf (COTS) devices,* such as microcontrollers. The benefit of such innate PUFs is that they do not require extra external components and can be instantiated by writing appropriate software. Thus, at least from a hardware point of view, such PUFs would cost nothing to add to a device.

We show that PUFs in COTS exist and that they can be used for a number of applications. For example, they allow to bind hardware to software, which can be utilized to implement a light-weight secure boot architecture. Furthermore, we also show that inherent PUFs can improve random number generation in COTS devices. Although often overlooked, the security of virtually all cryptographic protocols stands or falls by the strength of the random number generator (RNG). Thus, a secure RNG is one of the core building blocks of cryptographic designs. Due to budgetary and throughput requirements, commercial devices requiring random numbers use pseudo-random number generators (PRNGs), instead of true random number generators (TRNGs). These PRNGs are algorithms that deterministically produce output that, to someone with no knowledge of the internal state of the algorithm, looks like random data.

On startup, PRNGs should be seeded with truly random data. Failure to do so leads to security weaknesses, as evidenced by the insecure Debian OpenSSL implementation [9]. This lead to the generation of weak keys and insecure communication links between parties worldwide. The recent addition of an embedded PRNG to Intel processors [1] should help improve the situation on desktop and server computers. Unfortunately, recent publications by Lenstra et al. [4, 5] and Heninger et al. [2] have shown that on the embedded systems front, many devices still exhibit severe lack of entropy in the output of their PRNG algorithms, leading to the same problems as those of the Debian implementation.

Thus, our goal is twofold: identify PUFs in COTS devices and design secure PRNGs on embedded devices, paving the way for cheap adoption of PUFs in the marketplace. Although these goals might seem unrelated, they are in fact closely tied together. Instead of discarding the errors present in the output of a PUF, one can use the erroneous bits to generate a strong seed for PRNG initialization.

2. PRESENTED WORK

It is known [3] that the start-up patterns of external SRAM chips exhibit PUF-like behaviour. Recent research on Physically Unclonable Functions (PUFs) [6, 7, 11] in SRAM has given more evidence of this fact. However, all research on SRAM PUFs published so far has been conducted on either FPGA boards or ASICs designed specifically for this purpose. The main goal of our work is to take this research onto unmodified COTS devices, such as microcontrollers. Thus, all of our research is conducted on freely available devices, requiring zero extra or custom designed components. More specifically, we focus our efforts on five of the most popular microcontroller families today, namely: ARM Cortex-A, ARM Cortex-M, Atmel AVR, Microchip PIC16 and Texas Instruments MSP430.

2.1 Inherent PUFs

Very little research has been done on the PUF and entropy characteristics of embedded SRAM. Thus it is not well known whether such SRAM is influenced by other components present in the microcontroller and if it can actually be used as either a PUF or an entropy source. Furthermore, it is not clear whether the SRAM behavior of different microcontroller families is similar.

Our research shows that the SRAM start-up values of many of the mentioned microcontrollers do behave as a PUF. While the within-class Hamming Distance indicates the robustness of measurements of a single device, the between-class Hamming Distance states whether the device can be uniquely identified among other devices. For some of these microcontrollers, e.g. a TI OMAP4430 housing a Cortex-A9 chip, the SRAM behaviour is almost ideal, with a within-class Hamming Distance of 5.71% and a between-class Hamming Distance of 50.02% on average (Fig. 1). Others, such as the Microchip PIC16F1825, have very distinct characteristics, showing that not all internal SRAM can be trusted to behave like a PUF.

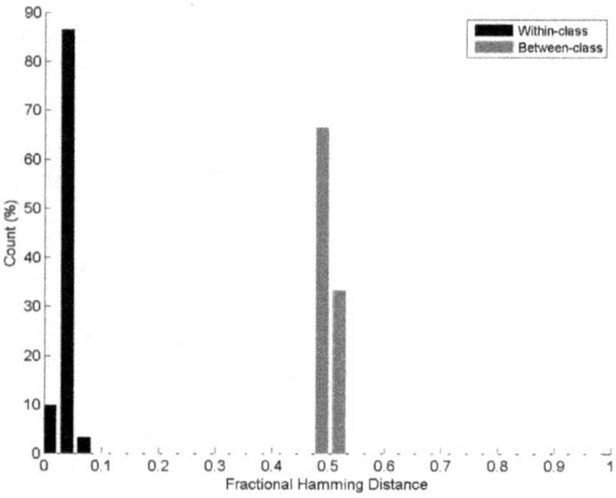

Figure 1: Within- and Between-class fractional Hamming Distance distribution for the Texas Instruments OMAP4430.

2.2 Strong PRNGs

As shown, SRAM PUFs exhibit a certain amount of randomness in their output, as indicated by the within-class distance. Instead of accepting this randomness, i.e. entropy, as an unfortunate byproduct of PUFs, we exploit it in order to generate strong, high entropy seeds for PRNGs and thus provide a solution to vulnerable cryptographic implementations due to weak random numbers [2, 9].

We present results for SRAM entropy in the aforementioned devices under various operating conditions (Fig. 2). Our measurements show that, unexpectedly, there is a big difference in SRAM characteristics between various microcontroller families. We show what the consequences of these findings are on the maximum attainable strength of PRNGs implemented on them.

Furthermore, we present an implementation of a portable and secure PRNG on the ARM Cortex-M platform. This platform is chosen due to its immense popularity [8] and we hope our implementation stimulates and helps to improve the security of devices employing microcontrollers of the Cortex-M family. Such an implementation is the first of its kind, and could open the door to strong cryptographic implementations on this very popular microcontroller.

2.3 Secure Boot

Another application for inherent PUFs is to use it as an identifier for a given device, which is used to implement a secure boot process tying software to a specific physical instantiation of a Cortex-A processor.

In particular, we derive a fingerprint from the intrinsic SRAM of an System-on-a-Chip (SoC) platform to identify the device. We subsequently create a cryptographic key from the fingerprint to decrypt the bootloader as well as the kernel file, stored in non-volatile memory and thus authenticate

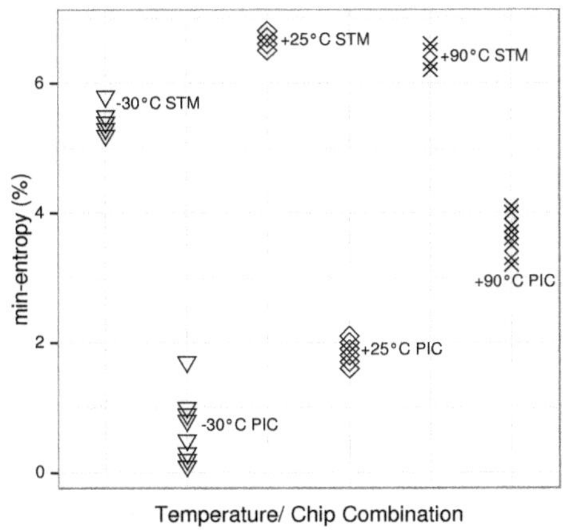

Figure 2: SRAM min-entropy for Microchip PIC16F1825 and STMicro STM32F100R8 at various temperatures.

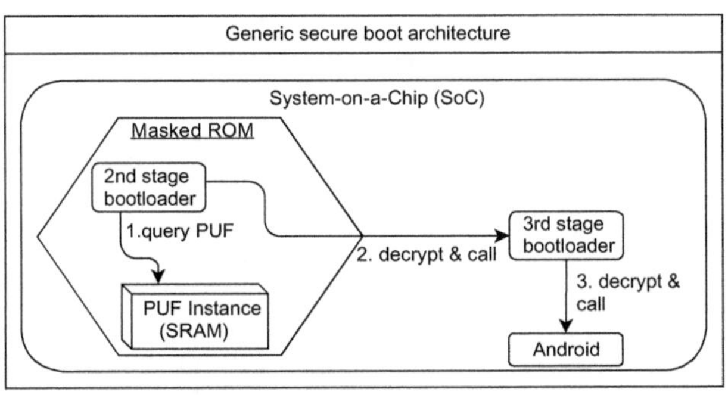

Figure 3: The general architecture of the light-weight secure boot processes.

the firmware, which will be run. Fig. 3 shows the overall architecture of the implementation.

Using this light-weight approach, we can achieve a defined software state at boot time and thus guarantee a trustworthy initialization of the operating system or firmware, without the requirement of additional hardware like TPM chips. We implement the secure boot approach on a PandaBoard [10], which is a OMAP4430-/4460-based SoC platform. It consists of two Cortex-A9 processors and two Cortex-M3 processors and provides rich multimedia functionality. Hence, it can be regarded as a reference platform comparable to modern mobile devices. We further test the PUF's response stability for high ambient temperatures. Since we can not put the PandaBoard in a climate chamber without the risk of destroying it, we simulate a temperature test for high ambient temperatures by stressing the CPUs with high computational load. Additionally, we investigate other memory instances in the on-chip memory (OCM) subsystem for potential PUF characteristics. To this end, we explore an appropriate access to the save-and-restore (SAR) memory and analyze the extracted start-up values.

3. CONCLUSION

We show that inherent PUFs exist in COTS devices and that they can actually be used to create various light-weight cryptographic solutions. We implemented a strong PRNG for ARM Cortex-M, which is seeded by true random data extracted from PUF noise. Additionally, we used features of inherent PUFs to bind software to a hardware instance and thus create a secure boot architecture on a SoC platform.

4. ACKNOWLEDGEMENTS

This work is supported in part by the European Commission through the ICT programme under contract FP7-ICT-2011-284833 PUFFIN. In addition, it is supported by the Research Council KU Leuven: GOA TENSE (GOA/11/007), by the Flemish iMinds projects, and by the Hercules Foundation AKUL/11/19.

References

[1] Intel Corporation. 2012. Intel Digital Random Number Generator (DRNG) Software Implementation Guide. **http://software.intel.com/en-us/articles/intel-digital-random-number-generator-drng-software-implementation-guide**. (Aug. 2012).

[2] Nadia Heninger, Zakir Durumeric, Eric Wustrow, and J. Alex Halderman. 2012. Mining Your Ps and Qs: Detection of Widespread Weak Keys in Network Devices. In *Proceedings of the 21st USENIX Security Symposium.*

[3] Daniel E. Holcomb, Wayne P. Burleson, and Kevin Fu. 2009. Power-Up SRAM State as an Identifying Fingerprint and Source of True Random Numbers. *IEEE Trans. Comput.* 58, 9 (Sept. 2009), 1198–1210.

[4] Arjen K. Lenstra, James P. Hughes, Maxime Augier, Joppe W. Bos, Thorsten Kleinjung, and Christophe Wachter. 2012a. Public Keys. In *CRYPTO (Lecture Notes in Computer Science)*, Reihaneh Safavi-Naini and Ran Canetti (Eds.), Vol. 7417. Springer, 626–642.

[5] Arjen K. Lenstra, James P. Hughes, Maxime Augier, Joppe W. Bos, Thorsten Kleinjung, and Christophe Wachter. 2012b. Ron was wrong, Whit is right. Cryptology ePrint Archive, Report 2012/064. (2012).

[6] Roel Maes. 2012. *Physically Unclonable Functions: Constructions, Properties and Applications.* Ph.D. Dissertation. KU Leuven. Ingrid Verbauwhede (promotor).

[7] Roel Maes, Pim Tuyls, and Ingrid Verbauwhede. 2009. Low-Overhead Implementation of a Soft Decision Helper Data Algorithm for SRAM PUFs. In *Proceedings of the 11th International Workshop on Cryptographic Hardware and Embedded Systems (Lecture Notes in Computer Science)*, Vol. 5747. Springer-Verlag, 332–347.

[8] ARM Holdings PLC. 2013. Results for the Fourth Quarter and Full Year 2012. (Feb. 2013). **http://ir.arm.com**

[9] Debian Security. 2008. *DSA-1571-1 OpenSSL – Predictable Random Number Generator.* Technical Report. **http://www.debian.org/security/2008/dsa-1571.en.html**

[10] Pandaboard.org. 2010. PandaBoard Platform. **http://pandaboard.org/content/platform**. (Oct. 2010).

[11] Vincent van der Leest, Erik van der Sluis, Geert Jan Schrijen, Pim Tuyls, and Helena Handschuh. 2012. Efficient Implementation of True Random Number Generator Based on SRAM PUFs. In *Cryptography and Security (Lecture Notes in Computer Science)*, David Naccache (Ed.), Vol. 6805. Springer, 300–318.

DEMO: An IDS Framework for Internet of Things Empowered by 6LoWPAN

Prabhakaran Kasinathan, Gianfranco Costamagna, Hussein Khaleel,
Claudio Pastrone, Maurizio A. Spirito
Istituto Superiore Mario Boella
Torino, Italy
{kasinathan, costamagna, khaleel, pastrone, spirito}@ismb.it

ABSTRACT

The Internet of Things (IoT) is an emerging paradigm where smart objects are seamlessly connected to the overall Internet and can potentially cooperate to achieve common objectives such as supporting innovative home automation services. With reference to such a scenario, this paper presents an Intrusion Detection System (IDS)[1] framework for IoT empowered by IPv6 over low-power personal area network (6LoWPAN) devices. In fact, 6LoWPAN is an interesting protocol supporting the realization of IoT in a resource constrained environment. 6LoWPAN devices are vulnerable to attacks inherited from both the wireless sensor networks and the Internet protocols. The proposed IDS framework which includes a monitoring system and a detection engine has been integrated into the network framework developed within the EU FP7 project 'ebbits'. A penetration testing (PenTest) system had been used to evaluate the performance of the implemented IDS framework. Preliminary tests revealed that the proposed framework represents a promising solution for ensuring better security in 6LoWPANs.

Categories and Subject Descriptors

C.2.0 [**Security and protection**]: Intrusion detection system

Keywords

Internet of Things (IoT); 6LoWPAN Security; Denial-of-Service attacks

1. INTRODUCTION

Internet of Things is an extended concept that includes diverse devices such as radio-frequency identification (RFID) chips, smart-phones and wireless sensor nodes, etc. All these devices blend together and are connected to the Internet to provide services such as home automation, smart metering, emergency response, waste management, etc. IoT will be a part of our society in the future; therefore, providing adequate security to IoT becomes inevitable.

One of the emerging technologies supporting IoT is 6LoWPAN. 6LoWPAN provides IPv6 identity and Internet connectivity to the wireless sensor networks (WSNs) nodes; inexpensive, tiny, low power consumption and maintenance-free properties of WSNs enable them to be deployed anywhere accurately. The combination of WSNs and Internet is novel; nevertheless, both must be examined for vulnerabilities. In specific, Denial-of-Service (DoS) attacks are considered to have adverse effects in disrupting WSNs communication [7]; however, effective security mechanisms against DoS attacks are yet to be defined.

This paper presents an IDS for IoT by adapting existing open source technologies. First, extensive investigation of both vulnerabilities and already existing intrusion detection (ID) methods relevant to 6LoWPAN was performed. Some of the most important IDS solutions for WSNs are reported in [2, 6]. Raza's work [8] proposed a host based IDS for 6LoWPAN using Contiki Operating System. Aforementioned solutions appeared to have IDS modules installed in similar constrained devices. Those nodes are able to perform detection based on available network information and transmit the data to a more powerful device (base station) through the same wireless medium for further analysis. Fundamentally, the detection performed depends on the limited resources (in terms of memory, processing power and other constraints) of the base station and the IDS nodes; however, usual DoS attacks such as jamming or flooding generally disrupts the wireless communication and leave the IDS nodes defenseless. Thus, the IDS nodes cannot use the wireless medium for transmitting attack information; this ultimately hinders the IDS achieving the most basic objective i.e., to detect an attack.

To overcome the issues discussed above, we proposed an efficient IDS framework for 6LoWPAN which could be able to detect DoS attacks while not suffering from the same attacks. The real world WSN applications require real-time monitoring of various physical parameters; in this context, service availability is a major requirement. To this aim, the proposed IDS should detect any kind of DoS activity. Initial implementation of our IDS framework produced reliable results when exposed to real attacks using a PenTest system. In addition, the proposed solution has been integrated within the network framework of the 'ebbits' [1]

[1]This work will demonstrate the IDS framework prototype developed for IoT and its enhancements with respect to the work that will be presented in [3].

CCS'13, November 4–8, 2013, Berlin, Germany.
ACM 978-1-4503-2477-9/13/11.
http://dx.doi.org/10.1145/2508859.2512494.

project, which aims to semantically integrate the IoT into mainstream enterprise systems and support inter-operable, online end-to-end business applications.

2. IDS FRAMEWORK

Detecting an attack is the first step towards thwarting it; moreover, the detection system itself must be resistant to the considered attack. The DoS detection architecture for 6LoWPAN presented in Figure 1 consists of a 6LoWPAN connected with an IDS and a PenTest system. Several host (H) nodes are connected to a router (R) node which forwards the information received from the H nodes to 6LoWPAN border router (6LBR). 6LBR acts as a gateway between the Internet and 6LoWPAN; all combined together form the 6LoWPAN. In addition, an IDS probe (P) is used to monitor the 6LoWPAN by sniffing the network traffic (exchanged packets) and send relevant information to the IDS through a wired connection for further inspection. This wired connectivity allows the IDS receiving reliable 6LoWPAN-related network information at any instance. Furthermore, to evaluate the proposed framework, a PenTest system is exploited. Such system is actually connected to a probe (Sp) able to sniff/inject packets into the target 6LoWPAN network. The aim of this test architecture is to reproduce an attack using the PenTest system and then check whether the IDS is able to detect the attack and trigger appropriate alerts.

This architecture represented in Figure 1 was first detailed in [3]. The IDS system was developed by adapting Suricata [9], an open source IDS. The adopted penetration testing framework was instead based on Metasploit [5]. The solution described in this paper presents some enhancements with respect to the first developed system. First, Metasploit has been replaced with Scapy. In fact, this is more light-weight while still offering the required flexibility to reproduce different kinds of attacks [4].Actually, Scapy helps in forging packets and initiating several complicated attacks against 6LoWPAN. Second, the paper improves the functionalities of the architecture described in Figure 1 by developing additional detection modules and integrating them with a security incident and event management system (SIEM) to monitor the attack events or alerts. These improvements are reported and discussed in the following sections.

This paper improves the functionality of the architecture described in Figure 1 by developing additional detection modules and integrating it with a security incident and event management system (SIEM) to monitor the attack events or alerts. The improvements are reported and discussed in the following sections.

3. ENHANCEMENTS

Integration of an advanced event monitoring system and capability of the IDS to monitor large networks were the most important enhancements added to the previous DoS detection architecture [3]. The following Figure 2 represents the improved IDS framework developed for 6LoWPAN. The monitoring system consists of frequency agility manager (FAM) [10] and security incident and event management system (SIEM).

FAM provides 6LoWPANs with frequency agility (FA) capabilities. FA is a mechanism allowing the network to become aware of the interference level by analyzing channel occupancy states in real-time. The aim is to determine the best available channel. When the system detects an interference level exceeding a certain threshold, the FA mechanism starts a procedure to switch the operating channel to the best available one [10]. Further, the IDS probes (respectively labeled P^1 and P^2) are distributed to safeguard the networks, thereby exemplifying an improved scalability of the IDS framework. Specific modules were developed to tunnel the packets to a particular IDS server when more than one IDS probe is used to sniff the network. A single powerful IDS was considered enough to detect wide range of attacks. After diligent considerations, open source security tools such as Suricata (IDS), Prelude (SIEM) and Scapy (PenTest) were selected for development.

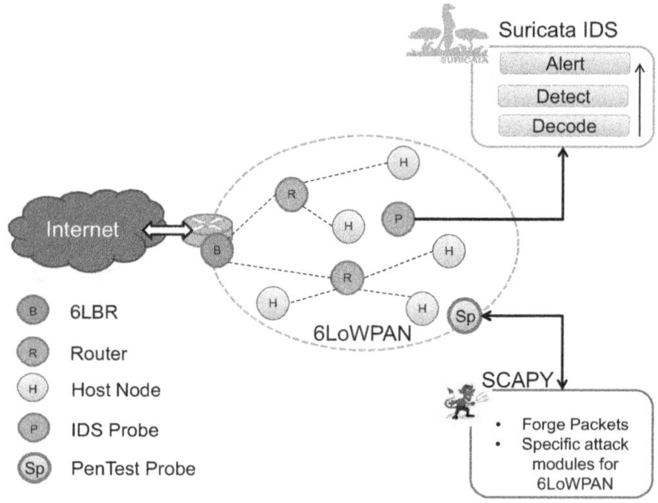

Figure 1: DoS Protection Architecture

3.1 Contributions

The IDS probes sniff the packets and send them to the IDS through a virtual interface and Scapy, the PenTest system uses the Sp probe to initiate attacks. Suricata was designed to detect attacks on traditional networks; therefore, it was not conceived to 'understand' WSNs or 6LoWPAN protocols. Suricata needs IEEE 802.15.4 and 6LoWPAN decoders for inspecting each incoming packet. The important contributions of this work was a preliminary implementation of required decoders, detection modules in Suricata and the integration of Prelude, the event monitoring system within the overall IDS framework. The Suricata engine triggers alerts based on the rules programmed; then, specific rules were developed to detect flooding and other attacks.

4. ARCHITECTURAL DEPLOYMENT

Scapy, the powerful packet manipulation program was used to initiate simple flooding attack. It is also capable of executing complicated attacks in 6LoWPAN such as RPL-rank attack. In the considered test scenario, the Scapy probes (labeled as Sp^1 and Sp^2) as represented in Figure 2 initiate a flooding attack at the same time to disrupt the communication between 6LoWPAN nodes. The same IDS probes send captured packets to the Suricata IDS for inspection. On detecting the attack, the alerts produced by Suricata IDS reach Prelude (SIEM) immediately; later, Pre-

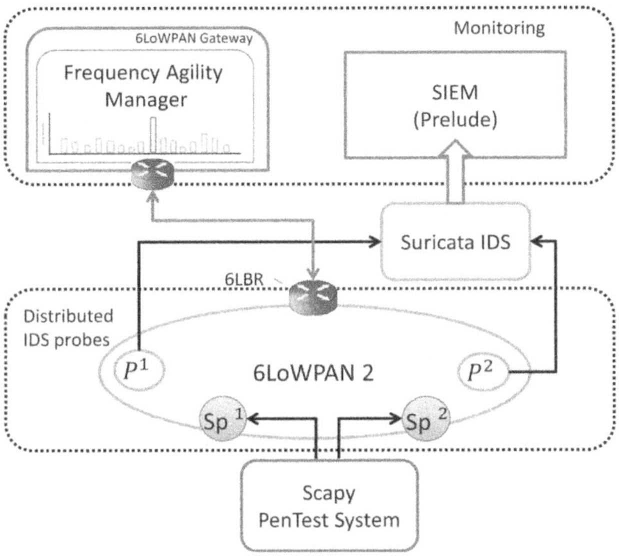

Figure 2: IDS framework for 6LoWPAN

lude might also receive the interference information from the FAM.

Prelude provides great flexibility by integrating wide range of security tools under one powerful monitoring system, such that it is possible to minimize the false positive alerts by correlating information available from other network monitoring tools such as FAM. Finally the prelude-correlator could process the available information from both IDS and FAM, thus triggering an attack confirmation. Prelude can extend this notification by sending email and sms alerts to the administrators.

4.1 The DEMO

In the considered demonstration, a flooding or a jamming attack is initiated using a graphical user interface (GUI) specifically designed and integrated within the FAM. The GUI shows real-time outage probability of respective IEEE 802.15.4 channels. Moreover the flooding attack is initiated on a selected channel which is monitored by both the IDS and the FAM. When the flooding attack is initiated, the outage probability (%) increases over a threshold value. This activity can be monitored in the designed GUI. The Suricata IDS is able to detect such activity, triggers alerts and forwards them to Prelude. Prelude's web interface 'Prewikka' displays each alert's information to the end user as represented in Figure 3. Further, to test the scalability of Suricata IDS engine, more number of PenTest nodes were used. Results proved that our proposed solution was scalable and stable.

5. FUTURE WORKS

In future, simple network management protocol (SNMP) information could be integrated into Prelude to detect more complex attacks. SVELTE, a host based IDS as presented in [8] could be integrated into Prelude to convert the IDS framework into a hybrid IDS for 6LoWPAN. Furthermore, complex attacks could be detected by developing specific modules for Suricata; one example would relate to extending Suricata's engine to support anomaly detection. Overall, the IDS framework proposed appears as a promising solution for future 6LoWPAN security.

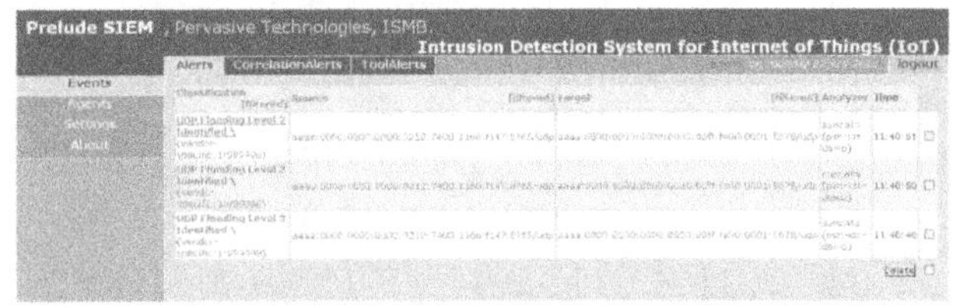

Figure 3: Alerts displayed in Prewikka

6. ACKNOWLEDGEMENTS

This work has been performed within the ebbits project, co-funded by the EC within the FP7, theme ICT-2009.1.3 Internet of Things and Enterprise environments, grant agreement No.257852.

7. REFERENCES

[1] ebbits. Eu fp7 project -'enabling the business-based internet of things and services'. website [Online] www.ebbits-project.eu, Accessed May 2013.

[2] A. H. Farooqi and F. A. Khan. Intrusion detection systems for wireless sensor networks: A survey. In *Communication and networking*, pages 234–241. Springer, 2009.

[3] P. Kasinathan, C. Pastrone, M. A. Spirito, and M. Vinkovits. Denial-of-Service detection in 6LoWPAN based internet of things. In *2013 IEEE 9th International Conference on Wireless and Mobile Computing, Networking and Communications (WiMob'2013)*, Lyon, France, Oct. 2013.

[4] A. Lahmadi, C. Brandin, and O. Festor. A testing framework for discovering vulnerabilities in 6lowpan networks. In *Distributed Computing in Sensor Systems (DCOSS), 2012 IEEE 8th International Conference on*, pages 335–340, 2012.

[5] Metasploit. Metasploit Penetration Testing Software. website [online] http://www.metasploit.com/, Accessed May 2013.

[6] A. Mitrokotsa and A. Karygiannis. Intrusion detection techniques in sensor networks. *Wireless Sensor Network Security, ed. J. Lopez and J. Zhou*, pages 251–272, 2008.

[7] D. R. Raymond and S. F. Midkiff. Denial-of-service in wireless sensor networks: Attacks and defenses. *Pervasive Computing, IEEE*, 7(1):74–81, 2008.

[8] S. Raza, L. Wallgren, and T. Voigt. SVELTE: Real-time Intrusion Detection in the Internet of Things. *Ad Hoc Networks, Elsevier*, 2013.

[9] Suricata. - The Next Generation Intrusion Detection System. website [online] www.openinfosecfoundation.org/, Accessed May 2013.

[10] R. Tomasi, H. Khaleel, F. Penna, C. Pastrone, R. Garello, and M. Spirito. Frequency agility in ipv6-based wireless personal area networks (6lowpan). In E. Osipov, A. Kassler, T. Bohnert, and X. Masip-Bruin, editors, *Wired/Wireless Internet Communications*, pages 146–157. Springer Berlin Heidelberg, 2010.

DEMO: Secure and Customizable Web Development in the SAFE Activation Framework

Raphael M. Reischuk
Saarland University
Saarbrücken, Germany

Florian Schröder
Saarland University
Saarbrücken, Germany

Johannes Gehrke
Cornell University,
Ithaca, New York, USA

ABSTRACT

We propose a demonstration of SAFE with some of its newest security features. SAFE is a framework for modern Web application development with automated state consistency, enforced security at various levels, and design for Web personalization and extensibility.

With the emerging complexity in (extensible) data-driven Web application development, in particular in terms of consistent data management with multiple clients (many Facebook users), ownership preservation (various Facebook user items with individual intellectual property), and data privacy (sensitive Facebook user data), we believe a demo of a comprehensive data-centric and secure Web application framework with declarative specifications for many modern Web features will be of considerable interest to the security community. In particular, we think it is interesting to see a demonstration of how fast and how intuitive the secure customization of a true multi-tier Web application can be.

Categories and Subject Descriptors

D.2.7 [**Software Engineering**]: Distribution, Maintenance and Enhancement—*Extensibility*; K.6.5 [**Management of Computing and Information Systems**]: Security and Protection—*Authentication*

Keywords

extensibility; web security; access control

1. INTRODUCTION

More and more software is delivered through the Web, following today's cloud idea of delivering software as a service. The code of such rich internet applications is split into client and server code, where the server code is run at the service provider and the client accesses the application through a Web browser. In data-driven Web applications, the state of the application resides in a database system (or simply in a key-value store), and users interact with this persistent state through Web clients, each having an individual (possibly shared) state. More and more users wish to personalize such Web applications, that is, they wish to customize the functionality of a Web application to fit their individual application needs.

In the development, and in particular, in the customization of modern Web applications, it is more challenging than ever before to cope with multiple tiers (various servers, multiple simultaneous clients, replicated databases, mobile devices, etc.), the shared application state spread over multiple devices, with complex security attack surfaces, and with many subtle technical details. Moreover, huge amounts of similar code are often rewritten from scratch. We believe that high-level specifications in a declarative language and compiler-generated application code can significantly simplify and secure the entire Web development process.

We demonstrate the SAFE activation framework with its efficient and elegant way of creating interactive and secure Web applications composed of reusable software components. One reason for the success of SAFE is its intuitive and still expressive declarative modeling language SFW. The rough idea behind specifications at a higher abstraction level in SAFE and the production of computer-generated source code thereof is motivated by the following facts.

First, Web applications often use common patterns which are better taken from well-tested code libraries instead of being manually programmed every time from scratch. Typical replication methods like copy & paste often introduce logical or structural flaws that are hard to detect later. *Second*, human errors in the programming process should generally be detected and avoided at the earliest possible point in time. Such errors introduce not only bugs in the functionality, but might also impose severe security threats. *Third*, a restricted set of allowed operations simplifies the detection of malicious code or even prevents security holes which might even be introduced on purpose. Assume for instance a system-provided (and hence trusted) encryption function for which all randomness is correctly chosen. A malicious programmer using the predefined function cannot bring his own "pseudo-randomness" into play, and hence cannot introduce a backdoor to decrypt confidential user data offline.

The two latter aspects are particularly relevant for data-driven Web applications with sensitive and privacy-critical user data. Not only is the programming of such security checks vulnerable to bugs and attacks, but also is it quite tedious to program all necessary checks, to add error handling for the reactive multi-tier code, to chose encryption/signature keys correctly, to establish database connections, etc.

CCS'13, November 4–8, 2013, Berlin, Germany.

ACM 978-1-4503-2477-9/13/11.
http://dx.doi.org/10.1145/2508859.2512495.

The automated compilation of higher-level languages hence not only produces better program code, but also significantly reduces the workload of a programmer.

We demonstrate how SAFE addresses all the aforementioned aspects and thereby significantly simplifies the overall development process, abstracting from technical details, and preventing malicious code from harming the system or sensitive user data. Moreover, we demonstrate how SAFE achieves several other useful and mandatory properties such as guaranteed state consistency, sandboxes for both users and software components. Furthermore, we show how SAFE enables new ways in the direction of customization and user personalization.

2. SAFE

This section recaps the main features of the SAFE framework [1, 2] for the development of secure Web applications with automatic state consistency and safe extensibility. SAFE provides a hierarchical programming model which naturally builds upon the hierarchical DOM structure of Web pages. The most constitutive components in SAFE are its so-called *f-units* which cluster all code fragments for a specific functionality within a Web page, including the business logic, the visual appearance, and the interaction with users or other f-units. This clustering provides a clear level of abstraction through well-defined *interfaces* for each f-unit. The modularity of reusable f-units relieves the programmer from struggling with variable scopes and their interference.

A Web page is modeled as an *activation tree* in which f-units are organized hierarchically — resulting in a clean abstraction and an elegant way of composing Web pages. The integration of an f-unit F in the activation tree is referred to as *activation* of F. More precisely, an f-unit is activated by its parent f-unit and thereby receives activation data through well-defined interfaces. The f-unit can use the activation data or other data obtained directly from the database through queries to display parts of the Web page. Every f-unit can also activate other f-units, its child f-units. Whenever an instance of an f-unit is activated, the corresponding compiled HTML / JS / CSS code is made available in the activation tree. Eventually, the activation tree is linearized to a single HTML document by transforming subtrees to nested HTML elements. After the activation tree has been constructed, the corresponding code for HTML / JS / CSS is sent to the client.

Activations are expressed through *activation calls* in the declarative *modeling language* SFW, a straight-forward extension of HTML: all HTML elements and also PHP and JavaScript can be used as in traditional Web application development. Activation calls are at the core of SFW and can as such be used in any HTML context.

2.1 Database updates

Since today's Web applications are not static pages (instead, they contain a lot of reactive code for event-driven modifications of the shared application state), SAFE's methodology redeems the developer from all the technical inconveniences of such updates and thereby automatically maintains state consistency — even for concurrent updates. Assume the client's browser interacts with the delivered HTML page and eventually sends some update request back to the server. The corresponding f-unit in the activation tree processes this request and generates a database query for which SAFE automatically verifies various safety and security properties. These include checks for state consistency, access control, and prevention of code injection. After the query has been executed, SAFE automatically triggers all f-units in the activation tree which have an out-dated state. These f-units are immediately rebuilt and refreshed at the client. The shared application state is automatically synchronized with all connected clients.

```
<h1> Groups </h1>

The following groups exist:
<for query="SELECT gid, name, owner='$%me' AS isowner,
            ismember FROM groups">
  $$name
  <form>
    <if $$ismember>
      <input type="button" value="Leave" onclick=
       "query:DELETE FROM groupmembers WHERE gid='$$gid'
              AND uid='$%me'">
    <else>
      <input type="button" value="Join" onclick=
       "query:INSERT INTO groupmembers SET gid='$$gid',
              uid='$%me'">
    </if>
    <if $$isowner>
      <input type="button" value="Remove" onclick=
       "query:DELETE FROM groups WHERE gid='$$gid'">
    </if>
  </form>
</for>

<form>
 <input type="text" name="gtitle"/>
 <input type="button" value="Create Group" onclick=
  "query:INSERT INTO groups VALUES ('$#gtitle',$userID)">
</form>
```

Figure 1: HTML buttons with concrete DB queries.

SAFE completely alleviates the developer of an f-unit F from caring about the freshness of its state while F is updating parts of the application state. Moreover, the developer does not have to provide code for partial updates of any f-units in the activation tree. The developer only specifies the *update query* that is supposed to be executed for some event attached to an HTML element inside the f-unit. We will see examples in Section 3.

3. SAFE DEMONSTRATION

We have chosen two demonstration features which nicely show how efficiently and securely the specifications in SAFE are translated to full-fledged Web applications.

3.1 Sandboxing for f-units and users

A new and un-published feature we show in our demonstration is how SAFE provides two independent kinds of *data separation*: every f-unit has its own database tables, which can only be accessed by the f-unit itself; and every user has its own data domain, in which only the user herself can modify data. Dually, SAFE provides mechanisms for *data sharing*: f-units can be wired together and user data can be aggregated and delegated.

3.2 Declarative and secure specifications

We present various new declarative specifications of different functionality and show the result of the compilation of these specifications using the SAFE compiler. The code for our test case applications generated by the compiler has an average blow-up factor of 10.57 compared to the size of the user-specified code. The generated code contains various new consistency and security checks which we believe a user would have to write manually in order to produce Web applications of comparable (high) quality.

As an example, we consider the simple specification of HTML buttons that are linked with the secure execution of database queries. The code snippet in Figure 1 shows the corresponding HTML-like specification in the SFW language. The code is taken from an f-unit to administrate groups in a social network application. The parts colored in blue are SFW-specific deviations from standard HTML. The code shows a list of groups whose entries are extracted from the SELECT query as specified in the <for> tag in line 4. The query selects four data fields each of which is available in the subsequent scope via the SFW syntax $$field, e.g., $$name in line 6, or $$ismember in the <if> tag in line 8. The content inside the <for> block is "executed" (or more precisely: displayed) in the HTML document once for every result tuple of the query execution. Depending on the values of $$ismember and $$isowner, the buttons to join (line 13), to leave (line 9), and to remove a group (line 18) are displayed. In the following, we will focus on the button to create a new group (line 26).

Instead of specifying a JavaScript function for the onclick event of a button, the developer simply specifies the actual database query to be executed. The query for the button in line 26 inserts two values in the specified table. The first value is the user input as specified in the form. SFW offers the syntactic placeholder $#gtitle to represent the value entered in the HTML input element named gtitle. The second value $userID is a dynamic value which is no direct user input, but a standard PHP variable. All such dynamic values occurring in the query need special attention: dynamic values must also be contained in the corresponding form in the HTML document (in order to ensure the dynamically evaluated values end indeed up in the query). However, such dynamic values cannot simply appear in the DOM tree in plaintext since a malicious client could easily modify these values, for instance by replacing the user ID Alice by the user ID Eve. We demonstrate how SAFE automatically ensures the integrity and confidentiality of dynamic values by new suitable security mechanisms.

The treatment of dynamic values is just one point on the list of tasks a traditional Web developer would have to take care of. We demonstrate and justify the blow-up factor of roughly 10 after compilation, for which the following (incomplete) list gives an intuition for the workload in case of a traditional hand-written database update procedure:

1. Create a regular HTML form inside the current HTML document. The protocol (GET, POST, etc.) and the recipient have to be suitably specified.
2. Create a PHP file to answer the submitted form and mention the URI of the file in the form.
3. In the PHP file, authenticate yourself at the database and establish a secure connection.
4. For each variable transmitted via the form, escape special characters to prevent SQL injection attacks.
5. Insert escaped values in the query.
6. Verify that the authenticated user of the application has sufficient permission to execute the query with the current values.
7. Verify that the query can be executed in terms of data consistency, i.e., has the query been issued from a state which is sufficiently fresh?
8. Send query to the database for execution.
9. Process the result, output a status message, and refresh parts of the Web application. Here, it will be necessary to determine the parts of the Web application which must be updated. Hence, all relevant dependencies must be derived.
10. Specify event-driven AJAX code to send the form values to the PHP handler, and to receive the data updates for all corresponding elements in the DOM tree.
11. Implement a comprehensive error handling which takes into account all possible kinds of errors (database connection errors, query execution errors, invalid values, etc.). This error handling has to be specified at all tiers; hence in PHP, JavaScript, and possibly also at the database.

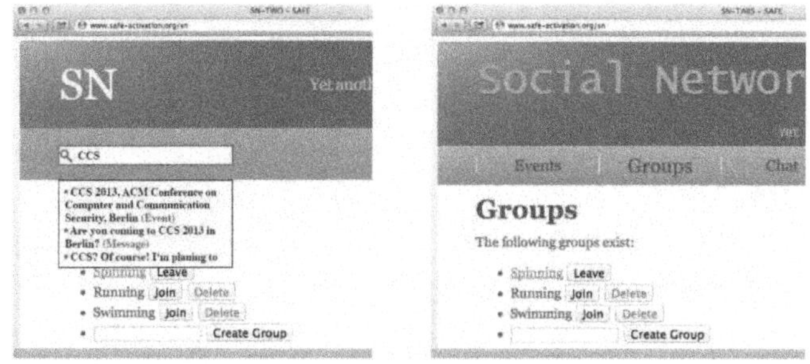

Figure 2: Functional extensions: (left) incremental search engine, and (right) navigation via tabs.

We demonstrate how the state update mechanisms of SAFE implement a superset of the above steps and thereby significantly reduce the burden of the developer down to a concise declarative specification as simple as the one shown in Figure 1. We discuss the compiled code (roughly 248 LOC) for the example in Figure 1 in the demonstration.

3.3 Customization

In the landscape of application ecosystems, today's Web 2.0 users wish to personalize not only their browsers with various extensions or their smartphones with various applications, but also the various extensions and applications themselves. This next generation of platform-independent Web applications is expected to be *customizable* not only in style (how they are displayed), but also *extensible* in functionality (what application logic is exposed).

The key to success in SAFE is the *encapsulation* of functionality within f-units: Every f-unit bundles the code for all tiers (PHP server code, HTML client code, JavaScript client code, CSS client code). We demonstrate the complex integration of a fresh f-unit into an application. We show how the SAFE tool suite easily manages the f-units for our social network application (Figure 2).

Moreover, we demonstrate how SAFE addresses the need for comprehensive personalization and thereby provides various security guarantees. We show how to securely extend an existing social network application in two ways: *First*, we demonstrate how new functionality is added to an existing application. This new functionality constitutes an incremental search engine (Figure 2 left), and as such, it must be integrated deeply into the system. The search engine shall provide the user with a comfortable experience, and hence contains a lot of reactive JavaScript code. Moreover, the search engine needs constraint access to the database with access control policies and a clear description of which fields shall be searched. Finally, the search results have to be presented in a structured and formatted way using PHP, HTML, and CSS. *Second*, we show how to change the navigation inside the social network: the scrolling navigation is turned into a navigation using tabs (Figure 2 right).

4. REFERENCES

[1] R. M. Reischuk. The official SAFE user manual. `http://www.safe-activation.org/`, 2013.

[2] R. M. Reischuk, M. Backes, and J. Gehrke. SAFE extensibility for data-driven web applications. In *WWW '12*, Lyon, France, 2012.

DEMO: Enabling Trusted Stores for Android

Yury Zhauniarovich[*]
University of Trento
via Sommarive 14
Trento, Italy
yury.zhauniarovich@unitn.it

Olga Gadyatskaya
University of Trento
via Sommarive 14
Trento, Italy
olga.gadyatskaya@unitn.it

Bruno Crispo
University of Trento
via Sommarive 14
Trento, Italy
bruno.crispo@unitn.it

ABSTRACT

In the Android ecosystem, the process of verifying the integrity of downloaded apps is left to the user. Different from other systems, e.g., Apple App Store, Google does not provide any certified vetting process for the Android apps. This choice has a lot of advantages but it is also the open door to possible attacks as the recent one shown by Bluebox [4]. To address this issue, this demo presents how to enable the deployment of application certification service, we called TruStore, for the Android platform. In our approach, the TruStore client enabled on the end-user device ensures that only the applications, which have been certified by the TruStore server, are installed on the user smartphone. We envisage trusted markets (TruStore servers, which can be, e.g., corporate application markets) that guarantee security by enabling an application vetting process. The TruStore infrastructure maintains the open nature of the Android ecosystem and requires minor modifications to Android stack. Moreover, it is backward-compatible and transparent for developers, and does not change the application management process on a device.

Categories and Subject Descriptors

D.4.6 [**Operating Systems**]: Security and Protection—*Access controls, cryptographic controls, authentication*

Keywords

Android, application markets, trusted installation

1. MOTIVATION

One of the recent attacks on Android, which is discovered by BlueBox, demonstrates that an attacker might be able to inject malicious code into a legitimate application without damaging the digital signature of the original developer [4]. This type of attacks is quite dangerous considering the open nature of the Android platform, which allows a user to download applications not only from the official Google Play market, but virtually from everywhere. Thus, users shopping at a third-party market cannot be reassured by just checking that the desired app comes from a trusted developer and has good reviews. And while the biggest phone manufactures claim to have fixed this vulnerability in their currently supported phones, minor providers might simply ignore it. Moreover, unsupported devices of major players are still the target for this attack. Anyway, the issue of repackaging Android apps is more general and still open [5].

While other players, such as Apple and RIM, addressed the problem by running their certification schemes and vetting each application before being published on their own (unique) market, Google chose a different path. In the spirit of openness to third-party developers, Android apps do not need to be certified before being published in any market.

This demo shows how to enable and support an application certification service for the Android ecosystem. We describe in details how to set up TruStores. A TruStore is a market that publishes only certified applications. Importantly, TruStores can certify existing applications and new ones without posing any constraints to developers and without changing the process of Android application development. The client side of TruStore relies on the current platform architecture and requires only minor modifications of the Android sources to enable the protection.

2. TRUSTORE

This section overviews the main components needed to run TruStore in Android. The TruStore architecture consists of two main parts: a *server* and a *client*.

TruStore Server.

On the server side TruStore, besides offering the standard app publishing and provisioning functionality, is responsible for the application vetting process. Applications provisioned by TruStore are trusted with respect of the declared vetting process. This process can include static analysis of application executables and source code (if provided), dynamic analysis, permission analysis, application files verification (for instance, to check for the "Master Key" vulnerability [4]), etc. What the TruStore server certifies and which technology uses for this is outside the scope of this work. However, the interested reader can refer to, e.g., [3, 1, 2] for examples of app verification frameworks.

Operationally, the process of application certification looks in the following way. A developer builds and signs (using

[*]Corresponding author.

CCS'13, November 4–8, 2013, Berlin, Germany.
ACM 978-1-4503-2477-9/13/11.
http://dx.doi.org/10.1145/2508859.2512496.

her own certificate) an application and uploads it to the TruStore server.

The server performs the analysis of the provided resources (executables and/or source code). If the app has passed the vetting process, the server signs the application with its own certificate and places it in the market to be accessible by users. It should be mentioned that this process is completely transparent for application developers and does not change current development and publishing workflow.

Application Multisigning.

Most of Android apps are sealed with a developer-signed certificate (notice that for Android "certificate" and "signature" are used interchangeably). This certificate assures that the code of the original application and its update come from the same place, and establishes trust relationships between applications of the same developer. To perform these checks Android simply compares binary representations of certificates, corresponding private keys of which were used to sign an application and its update (in the first case) and collaborating applications (in the second).

This check is implemented in *PackageManagerService* in the method `'checkSignaturesLP'`, which takes as parameters two arrays of `Signature`. In Android it is possible to sign the same application with several different certificates. This explains why the method takes the arrays of signatures. Despite the fact that this method takes the central place in the Android security provision, its behaviour strongly depends on the version of the platform. In the newer versions (starting from Android 2.2) this method compares two sets of `Signature`, and if both sets are equal returns `SIGNATURE_MATCH` value, and `SIGNATURE_NO_MATCH` otherwise or if an array is equal to `null`. Before the version 2.2, this method checked if the first set is contained in the second. That behaviour allowed the system to install upgrades even if they had been signed only with a subset of certificates of the original application.

Today there are no benefits of signing an application with multiple certificates and this functionality can be easily suppressed. However, we believe that for compatibility reasons Google will not change it in the near future. This multisigning functionality is the cornerstone of the TruStore client.

TruStore Client.

The client part is based on a modified Android system; it allows a device holder to make use of TruStore.

Figure 1 summarises the architecture of the TruStore client. We implemented our proof-of-concept prototype for the Google Nexus S phone using 4.1.2_r2 version of AOSP. The TruStore modifications touch two levels of the Android software stack: the *Application* and the *Android Framework* levels; at both of these levels our implementation changes the standard Android components, as well as adds new parts.

The TruStore management process starts with the activation of the TruStore protection in the standard Android *Settings* application. In this application we added two preferences: the first activates the TruStore protection, while the second allows a user to see the list of installed trusted store certificates (see Figure 2a). If a user wants to activate the TruStore protection she checks the added checkbox (step *a* in Figure 1). The value of this setting is written into the *Settings.Secure* content provider, and is later used by different components to detect if the TruStore protection is enabled.

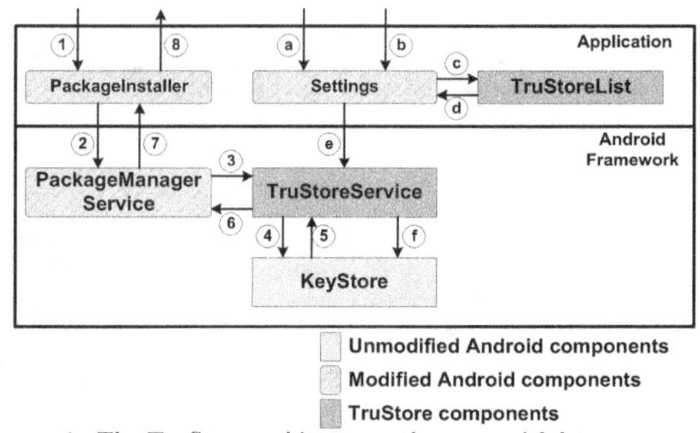

Figure 1: The TruStore architecture: the steps with letters represent the TruStore management process; those ones with numbers describe the checks during application installation.

After the activation of the TruStore protection a user is able to see the list of TruStores X.509 certificates installed in the system (step *b*). In this screen a user has an option of adding a new TruStore certificate (see Figure 2b). The *Settings* application shares its UID with the system server. So as it is prohibited to read the content of the external storage from the system process, the functionality to display and select the available certificates (step *c*) is passed to an additional application *TruStoreList* (Figure 2c), which is launched from *Settings* using an explicit intent.

To securely preserve a certificate with the additional data the system *KeyStore* component is used. This is the standard way to store credentials on Android. This component automatically encrypts the stored information and grants access to it (based on UID) only to the component that originally initiated preservation of the data. As *TruStoreService* is a part of the system server, only the Android components with UID equal to 1000 can read and modify these data. To distinguish the TruStore information from other credentials stored in the credential storage we add a special prefix (TRUSTORE). Thus, *TruStoreService* selects from the storage only the appropriate credential data.

Currently there are several ways to start the installation of a new application on a device. This can be done using the *Google Play* or *PackageInstaller* applications, or using the `adb install` command. The app installation process with the activated TruStore protection does not differ from the normal one. A user launches the installation using our modified version of *PackageInstaller* and executes the usual app installation steps (step 1). In our prototype we modified the *PackageInstaller* application, because this component is open-source. However, similar modifications can be easily be incorporated into the proprietary Google Play app.

After the initial steps the installer notifies *PackageManagerService* to start the actual installation of the package into the system. This is a special service in the Android system responsible for package management. From this point *PackageManagerService* performs the job, while *PackageInstaller* waits for the installation report. To perform the TruStore check we add a hook into the method `installPackageLI` of *PackageManagerService.* This hook extracts the certificates of the installed package and compares them against the list of trusted store certificates using *TruStoreService* (step 3). The hook is embedded in the place when Android *PackageManagerService* has finished all verification steps. In this way, we are sure that the private keys corresponding to the

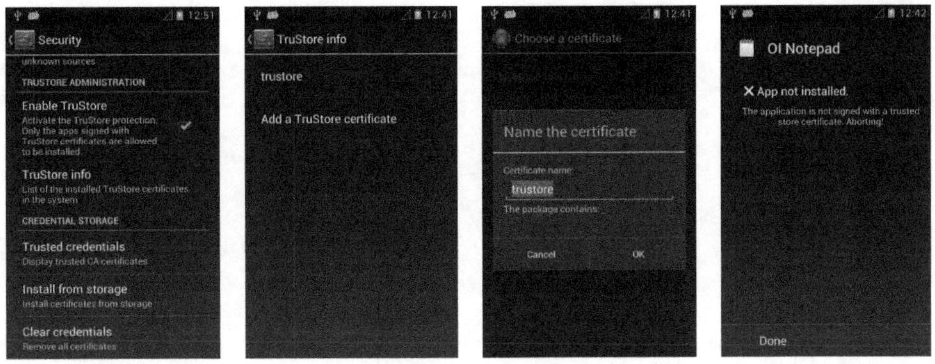

(a) (b) (c) (d)

Figure 2: Screenshots of TruStore: (a) Settings to enable TruStore, (b) The certificate list of trusted stores, (c) TruStoreList application, (d) PackageInstaller error when a package is not signed by the TruStore certificate

certificates extracted from the package to be installed have been used to sign the package (thus, verifying the integrity of the signatures). *TruStoreService* matches the obtained list against the list of TruStore certificates; the result of this comparison is passed back to *PackageManagerService* (step 4). If a match is found then the service finishes the installation and notifies *PackageInstaller* about the success, otherwise it generates a special error that is displayed to the user (Figure 2d) by the installer application (steps 7, 8). *PackageInstaller* modifications constitute only in the ability to correctly display the explanation of this error.

App Management with TruStore.

Let us we consider how the process of application management has been changed with the TruStore modifications. There are three main points in the lifecycle of each application: install, update and delete. The process of application deletion from a user or developer point of view is not changed by TruStore, so it is not considered.

The installation process of an application was considered in details in the previous section; it is not altered from the developer perspective, but is changed from the user angle (installation may fail now). However, it is worth mentioning that if an app is installed from a TruStore market, all consequent updates must come from the same store. Otherwise, the Android system will cancel the update which is not signed by the TruStore certificate.

At the same time, the TruStore approach does not reduce the app update capabilities for a developer. In our approach, she has to submit a new version of her app to the TruStore server as usual, where it will be analysed and redistributed to users. The "kill switch" functionality can also be supported via TruStore.

The TruStore modifications influence interactions between app components protected with the `signature` and `signatureOrSystem` types of Android permissions, and on the `sharedUserId` interactions. The TruStore modifications will prohibit such kind of interactions between applications that are installed from different trusted markets, although they may have been implemented by the same developer. This limitation comes from the fact that the applications installed from different TruStore markets will have different set of signatures (although the developer signature may be the same). However, this restriction enables more security: TruStore ensures safety of the apps loaded via itself, while safety of apps on other third-party markets cannot be guaranteed (especially, in the light of the attack discussed in §1), and the interactions between trusted and untrusted apps may lead to information leaks and privilege escalation attacks.

3. CONCLUSIONS

We have presented how to support application certification in Android. TruStore aims at enhancing security of the Android ecosystem by adding the market signature to application packages upon a successful vetting process. The concept of market signatures is not novel, as it is used, e.g., by Apple. The main contribution of our approach is the backward-compatibility with the Android ecosystem. TruStore is fully transparent to legitimate application developers and does not require major modifications to the firmware. It may be adopted immediately by phone producers with their own markets, for example, Samsung; and, if being incorporated into the Android distribution released by Google, may become a valuable feature for corporate application markets to enable BYOD policies.

Acknowledgments.

This work has been partially supported by the FP7-ICT SecCord Project 316622 funded by the EU and the TENACE PRIN Project 20103P34XC funded by the Italian MIUR.

4. REFERENCES

[1] W. Enck, M. Ongtang, and P. McDaniel. On lightweight mobile phone application certification. In *Proceedings of the 16th ACM conference on Computer and communications security*, CCS '09, pages 235–245, New York, NY, USA, 2009. ACM.

[2] P. Gilbert, B. Chun, L. Cox, and J. Jung. Vision: automated security validation of mobile apps at app markets. In *Proc. of MCS'2011*, pages 21–26, 2011.

[3] V. Rastogi, Y. Chen, and W. Enck. Appsplayground: automatic security analysis of smartphone applications. In *Proc. of CODASPY '13*, pages 209–220, 2013.

[4] T. SecurityLedger. Exploit code released for android security hole `https://securityledger.com/2013/07/exploit-code-released-for-android-security-hole/`, Jul. 2013.

[5] W. Zhou, Y. Zhou, M. Grace, X. Jiang, and S. Zou. Fast, scalable detection of "piggybacked" mobile applications. In *Proc. of CODASPY '13*, pages 185–196, 2013.

DEMO: Gradiant Asymmetric Encryption and Verification Systems based on Handwritten Signature

Enrique Argones Rúa, Francisco Javier García Salomón, Luis Pérez-Freire
GRADIANT - Galician Research and Development Center in Advanced Telecommunications
Edificio CITEXVI, local 14, Campus Universitario de Vigo
36310 Vigo, Pontevedra, Spain
{eargones,fgarcia,lpfreire}@gradiant.org

ABSTRACT

A successful deployment of biometric-based recognition systems in real-life applications depends on crucial issues such as data security and privacy, which have to be specifically addressed. Besides, cryptographic key protection can represent the main weakness of a secured transmission. In this demonstration a system for encryption and digital signature of generic digital documents (SAES, standing for Signature-based Assymetric Encryption System) is presented, where cryptographic keys are protected by the hand-written signature of the user. Furthermore, a demonstration of a the handwritten online signature verification system (SVS) based on non-protected templates will also be performed.

Categories and Subject Descriptors

K.6.5 [**Management of Computing and Information Systems**]: Security and Protection—*Authentication*; K.4.1 [**Computers and Society**]: Public Policy Issues—*Privacy*

Keywords

Cryptobiometrics, handwritten signature verification, Hidden Markov Models

1. TECHNOLOGY TO BE DEMONSTRATED AND ITS NOVELTY

Two systems will be demonstrated. The first one is a online signature verification system based on generative models. The second one is a cryptosystem online signature verifier, which uses protected and renewable templates. A similar demonstration was performed in the IEEE Workshop on Information Forensics and Security held in Tenerife in December 2013, where only the Signature-based Assymetric Encryption System (SAES) was presented. In this demonstration the Signature Verification System (SVS) is also shown, and it includes several new features that increase robustness against forgeries.

CCS'13, November 4–8, 2013, Berlin, Germany.
ACM 978-1-4503-2477-9/13/11.
http://dx.doi.org/10.1145/2508859.2512497.

The SVS, based on unprotected HMM templates, uses a user-specific HMM for state-sequence score computation, and a adapted HMM-Universal Background Model (UBM) for loglikelihood ratio score computation, as described in [1]. This combination obtains very low error rates, as demonstrated by the UVIGO system performance in the Biosecure Signature Evaluation Campaign (ESRA'2011) [3], and high resistance against high quality forgeries. This verification system is designed to work with a variable number of enrollment signatures (from a single signature enrollment to 5 enrollment signatures). Enrollment is performed using a stability maximization approach, in order to avoid outlier signatures to become part of the user template. This provides user templates with increased ressistance to forgeries. Besides, user template quality is evaluated, what provides useful information regarding its security or ressistance to attacks. Templates are classified after the enrollment into three different security levels, namely low, medium and high security level.

The protected system (SAES) is mainly based on the template protection scheme presented in [2]. The system uses a set of UBM as system parameters. User templates are obtained from the biometrics captured in the enrollment phase, and they depend on the set of UBMs and their corresponding eigen-model matrices. Only a protected and non-invertible version of the biometric user template and cryptographic private key is stored in the system's database, so there is not need for special protection of the system's database.

The signature of the user is used in the test phase to recover the hashed private key, so document decryption and digital signature rely on the presentation of the user's signature to the system. The block diagram of the system is shown in Figure 1, where both enrollment and test phases are illustrated.

The current version of the system produces biometric keys with an effective length of 99 bits (the k parameter in the $BCH(n, k, t)$ code) using only 5 enrollment signatures, which is more than enough to protect a 1024-bit length RSA or DSA key. Biometric verification performance is also kept in acceptable rates, with an $EER\% = 4.61$, as shown in Figure 2. These figures are better than those obtained by the system presented in [2] (biometric keys with an effective length of 76 bits when using 10 enrollment signatures, $EER\% = 4.41$). This is mainly because of the substitution of the reliable coefficients selection approach used in [2] by a new combination approach, where the most reliable projections are combined using a greedy algorithm to obtain n equally reliable features.

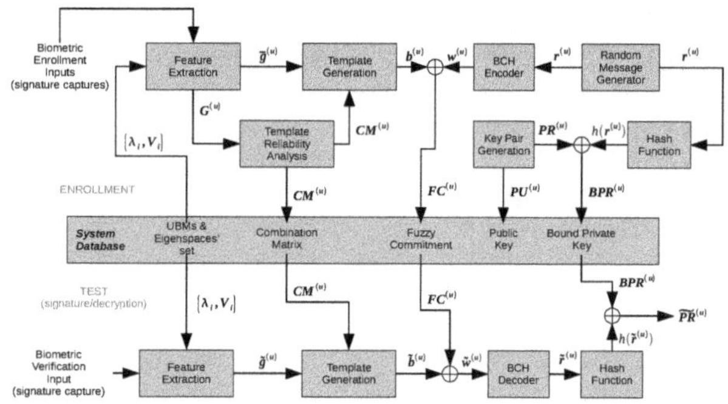

Figure 1: Block Diagram of the Gradiant Asymmetric Encryption System, showing the private key binding and retrieval mechanisms

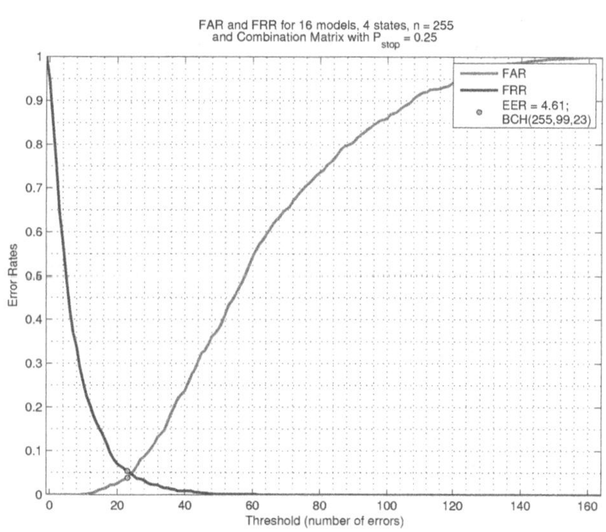

Figure 2: System performance when using a *BCH* code with $n = 255$. Many feasible working points are available. The working point closest to the *EER* is labeled with a green circle.

Figure 3: Picture of a user during the enrollment phase of the Gradiant Asymmetric Encryption System based on handwritten signature.

The system has been deployed on a desktop application using Qt [4], so it is available for Windows (XP, Vista, 7), Linux and MacOS. A Wacom Intuos 4 S [5] is used for signature capture for the protected templates system, and a Wacom STU-500 is used for signature capture for the unprotected system. The demonstration applications will be installed in a Laptop. Figure 3 shows a person using the system for capturing his handwritten signature of the protected system. Both the capture device and the laptop running the application will be provided by the demonstrator.

2. INTERACTIVITY WITH THE AUDIENCE

The demonstrator will first show the main features of the application, but the user's participation is very important in the demonstration: volunteers for enrolling, testing (document signing or decryption), or to imitate other user's signatures in order to overcome the cryptographic key protection will be welcome.

3. ACKNOWLEDGMENTS

This work was partially supported by the LIFTGATE Project funded by the FP7-Capacities Programme, Grant Agreement No. 285901.

4. REFERENCES

[1] E. Argones Rua and J. Alba Castro. Online signature verification based on generative models. *Systems, Man, and Cybernetics, Part B: Cybernetics, IEEE Transactions on*, 42(4):1231–1242, 2012.

[2] E. Argones Rúa, E. Maiorana, J.L. Alba Castro, and P. Campisi. Biometric template protection using universal background models: An application to online signature. 7(1):269–282, 2012.

[3] N. Houmani, S. Garcia-Salicetti, B. Dorizzi, J. Montalvao, J. C. Canuto, M. V. Andrade, Y. Qiao, X. Wang, T. Scheidat, A. Makrushin, D. Muramatsu, J. Putz-Leszczynska, M. Kudelski, M. Faundez-Zanuy, J. M. Pascual-Gaspar, V. Cardenoso-Payo, C. Vivaracho-Pascual, E. A. Rua, J. L. Alba-Castro, A. Kholmatov, and B. Yanikoglu. Biosecure signature evaluation campaign (esra'2011): evaluating systems on quality-based categories of skilled forgeries. *Biometrics, International Joint Conference on*, 0:1–10, 2011.

[4] Nokia Corporation. Qt, 2008.

[5] Wacom Company, Ltd. of Tokyo, Japan. Wacom Intuos 4 S, 2012.

DEMO: On the Real-time Masking of the Sound of Credit Cards using Hot Patching

Manish Shukla, Purushotam Radadia, Shirish Karande, Sachin Lodha
Tata Consultancy Services Innovation Lab - TRDDC
54 B Hadapsar Industrial Estate, Pune 411 013, India
{mani.shukla, purushotam.radadia, shirish.karande, sachin.lodha}@tcs.com

ABSTRACT

Phone based card payments utilize inband DTMF signaling to convey data. Since the DTMF signals are audible to a human ear, a call operator is in position to carry out a privacy attack. We investigate real-time techniques that can obfuscate the "digit" values without deteriorating the voice quality. Furthermore, we consider a setting where the privacy solution is being provided by a third party which does not have the benefit of open interfaces to the communication application. Our experiments reveal the efficacy of binary interception to "inject" the signal filtering. Meanwhile, we observe that several DTMF suppression techniques that have been proposed in literature can leave a residue that is sufficient for de-anonymizing the digit value. In light of these observations, we argue in favor of more modest privacy guarantees, which can be achieved by suppressing only the higher frequency. We show that margin crossings and peak variances can be used for fast pre-filtering of audio to detect the presence of a tone, thus reducing the computational needs.

Categories and Subject Descriptors

C.3 [**Special-purpose and Application-based Systems**]:– *signal processing systems.* K.6.5 [**Management of Computing and Information Systems**]: Security and Protection – *invasive software.*

General Terms

Experimentation,Security.

Keywords

DTMF, Hot Patching, Privacy

1. MOTIVATION

Telephone banking has played an important role in allowing financial institutions to offer their services round the clock and without having their customers visit the branch. The DTMF technology [1] has been a major enabler for scaling telephone banking services. Figure 1 describes a typical telephony network in a modern contact center. The EPABX system connects the IP network within the contact center to the PSTN network. DTMF signals are used by a customer to directly interact with the Database via an Interactive Voice Response system (IVR). Certain business processes ensure that a call operator is kept on "Hold" when the customer interacts with the IVR. However, it has been observed that having an agent "On Line" significantly improves the customer experience. If an agent is always on line then he/she can continue to converse and guide the customer, nevertheless, this also allows the agent to listen to the DTMF tones. There exist several publicly available websites and softwares that can easily identify DTMF tones. Moreover, it is known that music students who train their ears to identify the pitch of sound can identify DTMF tones with high accuracy without the aid of any machine. Thus, a call operator can potentially have access to customer private data. Hence, in this work, we investigate real-time techniques that can obfuscate the "digit" values without deteriorating the voice quality. As shown, the tone masking can be employed at the agent's Desktop, thus ensuring that the interaction with IVR remains unperturbed.

CCS'13, November 4–8, 2013, Berlin, Germany.
ACM 978-1-4503-2477-9/13/11.

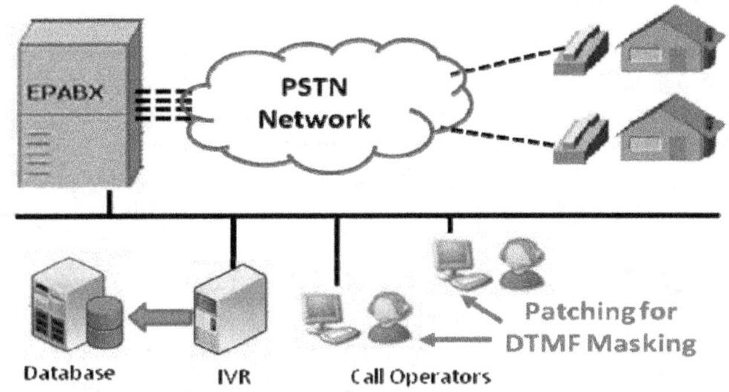

Figure 1 Voice telephony network at a contact center

2. PRELIMINARIES

DTMF decoding has been widely studied, however we limit our discussion to a regression based detector. Let an audio segment, be represented by $\overline{y} = [y_1, \cdots, y_n]$. Given the sampling rate, F_s, we detect the tones by approximating $\overline{y}$ with the dictionaries $\overline{a} = [a_1; \cdots; a_8]$ and $\overline{b} = [b_1; \cdots; b_8]$ such that:

$$\overline{a_k} = \left[1, \cdots, \cos\left(2\pi f_k j / F_s\right), \cdots, \cos\left(2\pi f_k n / F_s\right)\right]$$

$$\overline{b_k} = \left[0, \cdots, \sin\left(2\pi f_k j / F_s\right), \cdots, \sin\left(2\pi f_k n / F_s\right)\right]$$

where f_1 - f_8 are the DTMF frequencies (697Hz – 1633Hz).Thus, we seek to identify weight vectors $\left(\overline{w_C}^*, \overline{w_S}^*\right)$ such that

$$\left(\overline{w_C}^*, \overline{w_S}^*\right) = \underset{\left(\overline{w_C}, \overline{w_S}\right)}{\arg\min} \left\{ \left\| \overline{y} - \overline{w_C}\,\overline{a} - \overline{w_S}\,\overline{b} \right\|_2 \right\} \quad \text{subject to}$$

$$\frac{\max_{j=1:4} \left\{ \left(w_{C,j}^2 + w_{S,j}^2 \right) \right\}}{\left(\sum_{j=1:4} \left(w_{C,j}^2 + w_{S,j}^2 \right) \right)} \geq \lambda, \quad \frac{\max_{j=5:8} \left\{ \left(w_{C,j}^2 + w_{S,j}^2 \right) \right\}}{\left(\sum_{j=5:8} \left(w_{C,j}^2 + w_{S,j}^2 \right) \right)} \geq \lambda \qquad (1)$$

In the above problem the constraints enforce the sparse structure of the DTMF signals. In the absence of these constraints, the problem reduces to least squares regression with the solution:

$$\left[\overline{w_C}^*, \overline{w_S}^*\right] = \left(\left[\bar{a};\bar{b}\right]\left[\bar{a};\bar{b}\right]^T\right)^{-1} \times \left[\bar{a};\bar{b}\right] \times \bar{y}^T \qquad (2)$$

This framing of the detection brings out the information asymmetry that exists between a masking algorithm and an attacker. The masking algorithm has to detect the DTMF tones among all possibilities of silence, noise and speech. Meanwhile, if an attacker suspects that a certain audio segment contains a tone, then the entropy of the signal is significantly reduced, for we have to only differentiate between the four low and high tones. Consequently, the number of samples required to de-anonymize the signal can be far lesser than those required by a masking algorithm to operate with a high reliability. In the subsequent section we show that the immediate consequence of this phenomenon is that a number of masking techniques, leave a residue that is rich enough to allow detection of the digits.

3. RELATED WORK & CHALLENGES

One of the earliest approaches at obfuscating DTMF signals involved the addition of a masking signal [3]. The masking signal consisted of 4 tone frequencies apart from those already present in the dual-tone. Since two frequencies determine a digit, the presence of additional frequencies makes unique decoding impossible. Filtering approaches can also be used for masking by actually suppressing the DTMF signal. The use of notch or tuned filters has been considered. Hsieh [4] utilize adaptive filtering as described by Figure 2(b) for cancelling the tone frequencies. Meanwhile, Levens et. al. [5] use a filter bank, as shown in Figure 2(a) to identify the presence of a tone and speech. The audio is blocked iff a tone is detected in the absence of speech.

We take a closer look at some of the above mentioned techniques. Figure 3 describes the impact of adaptive filtering on the signal created by digit "1". It can be observed that the slow convergence of the adaptive filter leaves a residue which can be easily detected by an FFT over a 20ms frame. The pseudo-inverse based detection described in the previous section would require even fewer samples for de-anonymization. Techniques, which utilize masking signals [3] would suffer from similar limitation if the tone duration and the duration of the masking signal are not exactly matched. We also evaluated the filter bank based approach for detecting tone presence [5]. It was observed that under the latency constraint of 160 samples (20 ms at 8 KHz) there exists no choice of threshold and bandwidths that can bring the missed detection below 8%. The missed detections increase to over 40% when the tones and speech overlap.

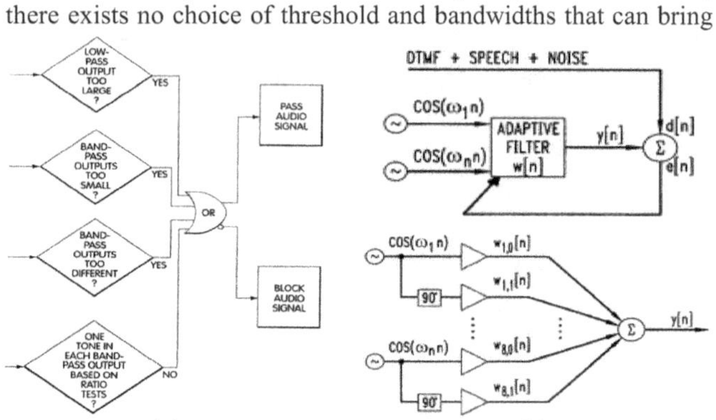

(a) (b)

Figure 2 (a) Filter bank based approach [5] (b) Least mean squared based adaptive filtering, for DTMF suppression [4].

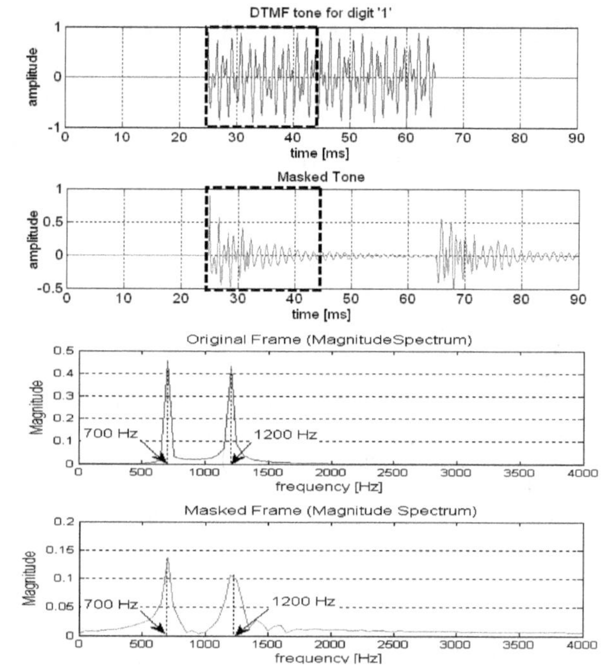

Figure 3 Pre and post masking, Time and Frequency, domain representation of DTMF tones for digit "1".

The Q.23/Q.24 recommendations [1]-[2] allow for a tolerance of $\pm 1.5\%$ in the DTMF reference frequencies. Tuned filters do not provide fast enough convergence in presence of such variations. The adaptive filtering technique, as well as the optimization framework proposed in the last section depends on a finite dictionary. The assumption of a finite dictionary does not remain valid in presence of variation in the reference frequencies.

4. HIGH TONE SUPPRESSION

Our experiments have shown that the imprecise estimates of the tone boundary and the tone frequencies can compromise masking approaches that seek complete anonymity. Hence, we consider an approach that is rather simplistic but robust. We propose to take advantage of the fact that most of the information in the speech signal does not overlap with the higher DTMF frequencies. Hence, our masking involves removal of all frequencies greater than 1 KHz with the help of an idealized filter executed by FFT. One can add a random high tone, prior to the filtering, to guard against spectral leakage. If the masking is applied only over the tone and its neighborhood than this approach does not affect the speech quality in a noticeable fashion. However, fricatives can contain frequencies that are greater than 1 KHz. Consequently, if the masking filter is applied to the entire speech, the deterioration in quality is evident. Hence, we consider several pre-filtering steps that affirm a tone presence with increasing accuracy and complexity, the masking is applied iff all the pre-conditions are satisfied:

- *Minimum Energy*: We process an audio frame iff the total energy is greater than a threshold. The threshold value is determined on the basis of the long term estimate of noise.
- *Margin Crossing Count (MCC)*: We count the total number of margin crossings in an audio frame. The value of the margin is determined by the total energy in the frame. A crossing is

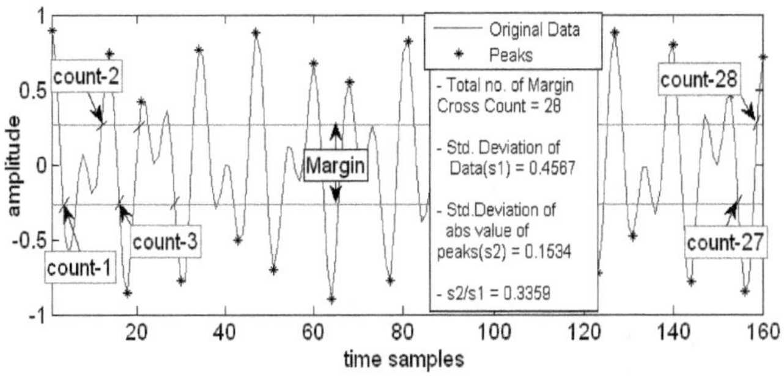

Figure 5 Pre-filtering to detect the presence of a DTMF tone

considered valid iff the peak magnitude encountered after the crossing is approximately equal to the peak before the crossing. If the numbers of margin crossings are less than a threshold, we pass the frame without applying any masking.

- Peak Variance: We track the peaks in the signal value upon crossing the positive and negative margins. The variance in the absolute value of these peaks is normalized by the average power in the frame. This value is used as feature to determine the presence of a periodic signal. If the value is above a threshold than no masking is applied.
- Pseudo-inverse based tests: We utilize Eqn. (2) to estimate the tone identity and sparsity constraint of Eqn. (1). is used to further affirm the presence of the tone.
- Adjoining frames: Slight latency can be tolerated even in telephony. We introduce a latency of one audio frame, which can be as small as 20ms, to improve the robustness of our masking. If either the subsequent or previous frame have satisfied all the above mentioned pre-filtering steps, than we apply masking to the current frame without regard to the result of pre-filtering for the current frame. This step ensures that the masking is applied across the entire tone duration.

5. TONE MASKING AS A SERVICE

IT service companies often take over the partial management of contact centers. The infrastructure instrumentation in such a scenario comes along with several restrictions. For example, one may not switch to an open-sourced implementation for VOIP, even if a client approved vendor's application does not provide any programming interfaces. Motivated by such a scenario we consider the use of binary interception or "*hot patching*" for executing tone masking as a third party service on Windows platforms. The Detours library, created by Hunt et. al. ([6]-[7]), is an example that facilitates the interception of function calls. The interception code is applied dynamically at runtime, i.e. the application code is modified in memory and not on disk. Detours replace the first few instructions of the *target function* with an unconditional jump to the user-provided *detour function*. When execution reaches the target function, control jumps directly to detour function. The detour function performs the appropriate interception preprocessing and invokes the target function.

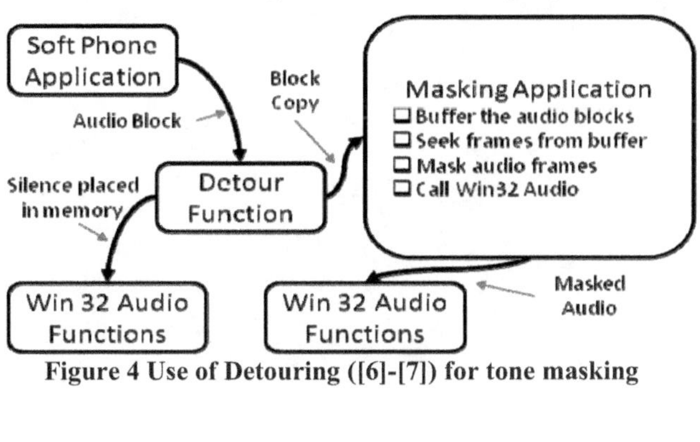

Figure 4 Use of Detouring ([6]-[7]) for tone masking

Most Softphones make calls to the low-level Win32 Audio and Wav APIs. We intercept the call to these target functions as shown in Figure 4. The block of audio meant for the Win32 function is passed to a detour function. The detour function passes a copy of the audio to separate masking application that we have developed, and replaces the audio block (in memory) with silence, before invoking the Win32 function. Thus, the soft phone application always plays silence, while the actual audio is played through our custom application, which employs buffering to facilitate the latency required for DTMF suppression.

6. RESULTS &CONCLUSION

We experimented with several voices (accents, gender), tone durations, frequency variations, channel qualities etc. for sampling rates of 8-44.1KHz and an audio frame of 20ms. It was observed that an MCC threshold of 20, a peak variance threshold of 0.65 and sparsity threshold of 0.42 ensured that there are no missed detections. Among the 1296685 pure speech frames, 7% passed the MCC filter, 1.7% passed the peak variance filter and less than 0.05% frames passed the pseudo-inverse based tests. Thus the pre-filtering ensured that the speech signal remains unaffected if it does not overlap with a tone.

We profiled the CPU usage of our solution on an Intel i5 M520 @2.4 GHz with 3.00 GB RAM running a Windows 7 Enterprise. It was observed that the overall CPU usage for real-time tone masking varies from 7% to 20%. Nevertheless, our current approach has the disadvantage of creating redundant audio threads, and we are in the process of developing an approach where the detour function can invoke the target function with masked audio block instead of silence.

Since credit-card numbers use only 0-9 digits, suppression of only the high group obfuscates the digit among 3 possibilities. This may appear as a weak anonymization. However, we highlight that in a 16 digit credit card number; as many as 12 digits could be hidden from the agent. This implies that the suppression obfuscates a number among ½ million other possibilities. Moreover, the attacker has no way ascertaining the accuracy of his/her breach without additional verification.

7. REFERENCES

[1] ITU-T Recommendations Q.23: Technical features of push button telephone sets. Nov. 1988.

[2] ITU-T Recommendations Q.24: Multifrequency push button signal reception. Nov. 1988.

[3] Gates, G. W., Saltwick, J. M, Scarinici, D., Sparks, W. O. System and method for securing DTMF transmission. Patent No. 5168519, Filed Jan. 2nd, 1991, Issued Dec. 1st, 1992.

[4] Hsieh, S. L. DTMF signal detection/removal using adaptive filters. Patent No. 5168519, Filed Jan. 31st, 1997, Issued Mar. 30th, 1999.

[5] Levens, B., Kerr, P. R., Hoge, W. S., Daly, D. F. DTMF tone detection and suppression with application to computer telephony over packet switched networks. Patent No. 6226303, Filed Mar. 6th, 1998, Issued May. 1st, 2001.

[6] Hunt, G., & Brubacher, D. (1999). Detours: Binary Interception of Win32 Functions. In 3rd usenix windows NT symposium.

[7] Hunt, G. C., & Scott, M. L. (1999, May). Intercepting and Instrumenting COM Applications. In COOTS (Vol. 99).

POSTER: Critique of the CISSP Common Body of Knowledge of Cryptography

Stephan Neuhaus
Communication Systems Group
Eidgenössische Technische Hochschule Zürich
Gloriastrasse 35, 8095 Zürich, Switzerland
neuhaust@tik.ee.ethz.ch

Gabriela Gheorghe
Interdisciplinary Center for Security, Reliability, and Trust, University of Luxembourg
4 Rue Alphonse Weicker, L-2721 Luxembourg
gabriela.gheorghe@uni.lu

ABSTRACT

Many security job ads mention that security certificates are regarded as assets, giving the candidate an advantage. For some high-profile jobs, certification may even be required.

No matter where one stands on the subject of certification, the assumption is that the imparted knowledge is at least factually correct. We examine the cryptography section in the Common Body of Knowledge (CBK) underlying the most sought-after certification, the CISSP, issued by the International Information Systems Security Certification Consortium, Inc., or "(ISC)^2"[1][2] [4].

We find many mistakes, some positively dangerous: people who believe what they read there will build systems that are *less* secure than they would have built if they had looked to, say, Wikipedia instead. They include: a confusion of encryption and authentication; an unconditional recommendation of RC4 for key sizes over 128 bits; a belief that block ciphers are inherently stronger than stream ciphers; and many more. These mistakes are elementary and appear in the third edition of the CBK, indicating that two preceding editing cycles were not enough to remove them. This shows that no one knows or cares that the material is wrong.

This poses dilemmas for graduates and companies. Graduates can either obtain a CISSP despite the factual inaccuracies, thereby surrendering at least part of their professional integrity; or they can try to tough it out, thereby lowering their chances of getting a high-profile security job. Companies must either keep using the CISSP, knowing that they have been taught some dangerous nonsense, or find another way to assess a candidate's security knowledge.

[1]This is the official spelling, which we will use consistently throughout.
[2](ISC)^2, CISSP, and CBK are registered trademarks of the Information Systems Security Certification Consortium, Inc.

CCS'13, November 4–8, 2013, Berlin, Germany.
Copyright 2013 ACM 978-1-4503-2477-9/13/11 ...$15.00.
http://dx.doi.org/10.1145/2508859.2512499.

Categories and Subject Descriptors

K.6.1 [**Project and People Management**]: Staffing, Training; K.6.5 [**Security and Protection**]; K.7.3 [**Testing, Certification, and Licensing**]

General Terms

Security, Certification, Management, Standardization

Keywords

Security Certification, Cryptography

1. INTRODUCTION

For many HR departments, certifications are the simple answer to the questions of how to assess someone who applies for a security job, and how to filter out more experienced candidates from the newcomers. First, a trusted third party is vouching for the technical competence of the candidate. Second, one common prerequisite for certification is a certain job experience. Additionally, certifications need to be renewed periodically, ensuring that the candidate's knowledge is current.

One important certification is the Certified Information Systems Security Professional (CISSP), offered by the (ISC)^2. Founded in 1988, the (ISC)^2's self-stated mission is to

> make society safer by improving productivity, efficiency and resilience of information-dependent economies through information security education and certification.

The (ISC)^2's main educational vehicle is the "(ISC)^2 Common Body of Knowledge", or CBK. In the (ISC)^2's words,

> (ISC)^2 develops and maintains the (ISC)^2 CBK, a compendium of information security topics. The CBK is a critical body of knowledge that defines global industry standards, serving as a common framework of terms and principles that our credentials are based upon and allows professionals worldwide to discuss, debate, and resolve matters pertaining to the field. Subject matter experts continually review and update the CBK.[3]

The CBK for the CISSP is organised into ten so-called domains, such as Access Control, Application Development

[3]This quote and the previous ones are from `https://www.isc2.org/aboutus/default.aspx`

Security, Telecommunications and Network Security, and Cryptography. Demonstration of knowledge of the CBK is required to pass the CISSP certification test.

The most recent version of the "Official $(ISC)^2$ Guide to the CISSP CBK" is the third edition, published in December 2012 [4]. This means that two editing cycles have presumably been used to "review and update" the material by "subject matter experts". We believe that the third edition of a book published by a self-styled "elite" organisation of experts, on a topic where details matter so much, should be about as error-free as it gets.

We only have the Kindle edition of the CBK, so we can only give "location markers" instead of page numbers. We will write them like so: [L. 12345].

All quotes from the CBK have been carefully checked to be letter-accurate (but errors may still have occurred). This includes any stylistic, spelling, or grammar issues.

2. CRYPTOGRAPHY

In addition to the selection of dangerous errors cited below, this section also contains a number of annoyances[4], which mainly betray a lack of care, and "wait, what?" moments, where the text makes no sense at all. These, and more dangerous errors, will feature on the final poster.

By *dangerous errors* we mean errors that, if believed and applied by students, result in system that are *less* secure than if they hadn't had that wrong information or had looked it up in a reliable reference. Or even a not necessarily reliable one: as of today, the relevant Wikipedia articles were all more accurate than what we read in the CBK.

Relative Strengths of Block and Stream Ciphers. The author seems to believe that block ciphers are inherently stronger than stream ciphers:

> Most block ciphers use a combination of substitution and transposition to perform their operations. This makes block ciphers relatively stronger than most stream-based ciphers, but more computationally intensive and usually more expensive to implement. This is also why many stream-based ciphers are implemented in hardware, whereas a block-based cipher is implemented in software. [L. 15034]

We found nothing in the peer-reviewed literature that would support such statements. Also, if block ciphers were slower than stream ciphers, wouldn't it make more sense to implement block ciphers in hardware rather than the already-fast stream ciphers?

Encryption and Authentication. One beginner's mistake is to assume that symmetric encryption per se can help with authentication or freshness:

> If two parties share a symmetric key, and they have been careful not to disclose that key to anyone else, then when they transmit a message from one to another, they have assurance that the message is indeed from their trusted partner. [L. 15242]

[4]Having to deal with a text whose sample plaintexts include "I Hate Bed Time" [L. 15089] is an annoyance in itself.

Related to this is the notion that modifying an encrypted message in transit makes it completely undecipherable, thus providing integrity checking:

> In many cases, they would also have some degree of confidence in the integrity of the message, because any errors or modifications of the message in transit would render the message undecipherable. With chaining-type algorithms, any error is likely to destroy the remainder of the message. [L. 15224]

A modified ciphertext will decipher just fine, it's just that some of the deciphered data will be junk. Also, some chaining modes like Cipher Block Chaining have a self-healing property where a modified ciphertext block leads to only a small number of corrupted decrypted plaintext blocks.

RC4. In the section on RC4 [L. 15572], we read:

> If RC4 is used with a key length of at least 128 bits, there are currently no practical ways to attack it; the published successful attacks against the use of RC4 in WEP applications are related to problems with the implementation of the algorithm, not the algorithm itself.

To cite just one example of many, the Fluhrer-Mantin-Shamir attack [3] is now 12 years old, and while it *also* attacked WEP, it identified "a large number of weak keys", that were then used to "mount related key attacks with practical complexities". Since then, other attacks have come to light; thus *all* use of RC4 is banned in the Microsoft Secure Software Development Lifecycle [5] since at least 2007[5] because it is too difficult to use securely.

3. COMMUNITY REACTIONS

The CISSP *certification* (as opposed to the CBK) has been criticised from many angles for many years; it has even spawned a humorous YouTube video in which a CISSP uses his plastic CISSP card like a police badge and storms into rooms shouting "everyone step away from the encryption keys and put the server down!"[6]. We will not go into that and focus on criticisms of the CBK.

At Def Con 20, Timmay gave a talk entitled "Why You Should Not Get a CISSP" [6]. In this talk, the presenter argued that the CBK was not up-to-date, but didn't comment on the accuracy of its official guide.

Factual criticism of the CBK is nonexistent; we couldn't even find an independent review of the book, not even on Rob Slade's otherwise excellent "CISSP by domain" pages[7].

4. CONCLUSIONS

It is very tempting to ignore these mistakes on the grounds that they fall outside the area of specialisation of a typical CCS attendee and are thus properly someone else's problem. But such complacency would be wrong.

First of all, formulations like "relevant security qualifications (CISSP) are considered an advantage" are commonly

[5]`http://www.acsac.org/2007/workshop/Howard.pdf`
[6]`https://www.youtube.com/watch?v=8DZkpynFhak`
[7]`http://victoria.tc.ca/int-grps/books/techrev/mnbksccd.htm`

found in security job ads[8][9][10]. While certainly not all CISSPs believe in or endorse the mistakes that are found in the CBK, some undoubtedly do, since that's what they read in the (ISC)[2]'s *official* guide (a point to which we will return later). And these people might get the jobs that you or your graduates aren't getting, simply because they have a certificate that is based at least in part on dangerous errors.

How big is the problem? The (ISC)[2] has grown to be internationally recognized, as stated on their webpage:

> We provide [...] Gold Standard credentials to professionals in more than 135 countries. [...] And we're proud of our membership—an elite network of nearly 90,000 certified industry professionals worldwide.

We couldn't find the exact reasons for this recognition, other than historical: the U.S. DoD Directive 8570.1 of 2004 [2, AP2.1.3] encouraged that DoD employees working in information assurance should have certifications from bodies that have been ANSI/ISO/IEC 17024 accredited. Also in 2004, (ISC)[2]'s CISSP was one of the first certifications to be thusly accredited. However, this accreditation is just a standard of managing personnel certification programmes and gives no indication about the quality of the technical content.

According to Robert Half's 2012 Salary Guide[11], security professionals are in the top five most wanted professionals in the US, and certification is required for positions such as Chief Security Officer or Information Systems Security Manager. Given that it is used by the US Department of Labor to forecast the job market[12], certification has a definite impact on hiring of graduates.

Also, certificate holders earn more: the job search engine SimplyHired notes that CISSP holders can earn between \$80000 and \$87000 on average, while in related jobs the average is only \$78000[13].

To see how many CISSP employees are there from another angle, we used LinkedIn data from simple queries when logged in. We queried for keywords (CISSP, and other acronyms for security certifications), locations and names of well known companies, and also tried to see how many people had additional certifications; see Table 1. We found that around 25,000 people had some certifications other than CISSP. The numbers suggest that few professionals only have a CISSP, and confirm that public bodies tend to ask for certifications more than other employees.

Informally however, we found lots of forum discussions on the topic of security certifications. They are esentially split in two categories: those discussions where someone who has already gained a security certification asks the world "what's the next certification to beef up my CV?", and the discussions on the utility of CISSP-like credentials. In this last case, we found that professionals with system administration experience dismiss the relevance of screening just for

[8] `http://www.jobat.be/en/windows-security-specialist/job_653229.aspx`

[9] `http://www.indeed.com/cmp/H2H-Technology/jobs/Cyber-Security-Engineer-4ffec9aa5de920ef`

[10] `http://www.isaca.org/chapters3/Atlanta/AboutOurChapter/Documents/122112-Emory-InfoSecSpecialist.pdf`

[11] `http://www.nwoinnovation.ca/upload/documents/rht_salaryguide_2012.pdf`

[12] `https://ccpdfs.s3.amazonaws.com/guide-securityplus.pdf`

[13] `http://www.simplyhired.com/a/salary/search/q-cissp`

Certification	LinkedIn members
CCNA	300456
CompTIA	101415
CCNP	84232
CISSP	82779
CISA	59691
CISSP and (CEH or CISM or CISA)	24966
CISM	21019
CEH	20689

Table 1: LinkedIn members with IT certifications.

CISSP when hiring security staff, for the reason that CISSP training does not touch upon aspects such as operating system security, or technical security details. We even found a blog entry [1] where the CISSP-holding author explains that CISSP has failed at both measuring technical competence, as well as measuring the grasp of security principles. The irony of this situation is in that people who do not believe in the technical value of this certification still take it, and defend its code of ethics as its only advantage compared to other security certifications. But the only real hurdle to getting the CISSP is the test, and not adherence to the code of ethics, which is ambiguous in any case [6].

Two editing cycles have gone by, allowing ample time to check the material (or have it checked) and to react to reports of inaccuracies. But this opportunity was passed up.

The material we have surveyed is not just any publication by the (ISC)[2]; it is their *official* guide to the CISSP CBK, and is thus endorsed by them. From this review of the crypto chapter, it follows that the (ISC)[2] endorses rubbish. We believe that the (ISC)[2] should revise the entire section thoroughly, and probably the rest of the CBK, while they're at it.

5. REFERENCES

[1] Richard Bejtlich. CISSP: Any value? `http://taosecurity.blogspot.com/2005/06/cissp-any-value-few-of-you-wrote-me.html`, June 2005. visited June 2013.

[2] U.S. Department of Defense. Dod 8570.01-m information assurance workforce improvement program. `http://www.dtic.mil/whs/directives/corres/pdf/857001m.pdf`, December 2005.

[3] Scott R. Fluhrer, Itsik Mantin, and Adi Shamir. Weaknesses in the key scheduling algorithm of RC4. In *Revised Papers from the 8th Annual International Workshop on Selected Areas in Cryptography*, SAC '01, pages 1–24, London, UK, 2001. Springer-Verlag.

[4] Steven Hernandez, editor. *Official (ISC)^2 Guide to the CISSP CBK.* (ISC)^2 Press, third edition, December 2012. Kindle edition.

[5] Michael Howard and Steve Lipner. *The Security Development Lifecycle: SDL: A Process for Developing Demonstrably More Secure Software.* Microsoft Press, June 2006.

[6] Timmay. Why you should not get a CISSP. `http://attrition.org/security/conferences/why_you_should_not_get_a_CISSP-public.pdf`, July 2012. Talk at Def Con 20.

POSTER: Preserving Privacy and Accountability for Personal Devices

Gabriela Gheorghe*
Indisciplinary Centre for Security, Reliability and Trust, University of Luxembourg
4 Rue Alphonse Weicker, L-2721 Luxembourg
gabriela.gheorghe@uni.lu

Stephan Neuhaus
Communication Systems Group
Eidgenössische Technische Hochschule Zürich
Gloriastrasse 35, 8095 Zürich, Switzerland
neuhaust@tik.ee.ethz.ch

ABSTRACT

Using personal mobile devices for work gave rise to a trend called "bring your own device", or BYOD. BYOD brings a productivity boost for employees, but also headaches for employers: on the one hand, the business has a legitimate interest in monitoring the device, in order to prevent security breaches by employees; but on the other hand, employees have a reasonable expectation of privacy when they use their devices for private functions. This poster presents our project called Privacy-Preserving Accountability for peRsonal Devices (PriPARD, pronounced "prepared"). PriPARD addresses the tension described above by designing and evaluating concrete privacy mechanisms for mobile devices used in a corporate environment. Instead of imposing a "privacy firewall" between users and the Internet, in PriPARD the aim is protecting user privacy within the corporate network and non-disclosure outside this network. PriPARD's vision is to gather practical experience with the tradeoffs between monitoring and privacy needs, to help both mobile device users and managers of corporate networks.

Categories and Subject Descriptors

C.2.0 [**Computer Communication Networks**]: General—*Security and Protection*; C.2.3 [**Computer Communication Networks**]: Network Operations—*network monitoring, network management*; D.4.6 [**Operating Systems**]: Security and Protection—*Access Controls*

Keywords

Privacy; Mobile Devices; Accountability; Policies; Bring your own device

1. MOTIVATION

BYOD means Bring Your Own Device in the company network (and work on it). Coupled with the tendency to "work from any location", this trend to "work from any of your devices" affects the way that IT infrastructures are designed and how their security properties should be managed. The SANS institute shows that employees prefer to use confortable devices instead of their company's devices, or even using work devices for private use - both approaches forbidden by the IT policy [10]. MobileIron acknowledges that device homogeneity in the enterprise is impossible and that current mechanisms to collectively secure such devices are either ineffective or privacy-unaware [8, 9]. Other mobile security surveys such as [14, 11] have shown that there are many organisations to create mobile applications for their customers, that they are already allowing employees to use their personal devices at work.

Organisations have most of their intellectual property and sensitive data in the datacentre and network where personal devices can reach [14]. In the face of so many new personal devices, the need for enterprise accountability is dire. Reports such as Ernst and Young's [5] admit that better accountability means more monitoring of personally identifiable information. For example, suspicious device behaviour can imply that the corporate data on a personal smartphone is at risk. But while monitoring device activity to rule out suspicious behaviour (e.g., sudden location change from one continent to another), the software polls periodically for device parameters that are not strictly needed (e.g., location in town); hence a privacy breach occurs if these parameters are stored in the network.

On a broader scale, data privacy is mentioned in the recent EU Data Protection Regulation (January 2012) mainly from the point of view of instating "appropriate measures" to protect private data leakage [9]. As usual with legal texts, laws refrain from defining what are "appropriate measures", "useful precautions of the data controller", "reasonable precautions to protect data accessed on personally owned devices", or "adequate protection". To put regulations into practice, cloud service providers push the responsibility to implement privacy and security measures to clients. In the meantime, massive government surveillance operations revealed to be taking place in the US [7] and UK [2] are pointing at the dire lack of privacy-enhancing technologies for users in their day-to-day life.

In terms of privacy tools for users, with PriPARD we want to start (relatively) small and focus on corporate networks and mobile devices. In practice, there are no procedures nor tools to protect privacy in a corporate network. Users cannot consent to data gathering because they are not even aware of the traces they leave online or in a corporate net-

*corresponding author

CCS'13, November 4–8, 2013, Berlin, Germany.
Copyright 2013 ACM 978-1-4503-2477-9/13/11 ...$15.00.
http://dx.doi.org/10.1145/2508859.2512500.

work. They do not know what applications produce and consume their private data locally, and where their data goes when sent away from their devices. As an ongoing project, PriPARD is the first to address and, where possible, solve the tension between the owner's privacy and an organisation's need to monitor. Its purpose is twofold: first, to examine how much private data is still gatherable when existing privacy controls (business containers, process sandboxing, etc.) are used on a mobile device. Second, assuming that mobile devices cannot be fully stopped from emitting some private data, PriPARD wants to build privacy into the system, in such a way that users can tune some of the private data emitted by their devices, and how that data is handled in the network.

2. STATE OF THE ART

In privacy management for mobile devices, most of the research efforts investigate single device mechanisms. The best known mechanism that tracks how sensitive information flows into the system is TaintDroid [4], built for the Android platform. TaintDroid aims to give visibility to device users over how their sensitive data is handled by smartphone applications at runtime at the level of variables, methods, file operations and messages among applications. Other than work building up on TaintDroid [1, 13, 6], very few papers on privacy mechanisms consider the "private data over the untrusted network" aspect: Smokescreen[3] is a privacy management system that uses different broadcast signals to allow users to control how they share their location with social contacts differently than with strangers. Mobishare [15] protects privacy in mobile online social networks, whereby the user location is anonymised and obscured when using untrusted location servers.

An interesting approach is taked by the European project PRISM[12]. PRISM aims to embed privacy preserving mechanisms into traffic monitoring technologies, especially those that perform anomaly detection in a network. The project makes the observation that it is hard to implement gathering personal data so that not too much private data is stored. Instead of doing first data gathering for anomaly detection and then anonymisation, PRISM's approach is to join the two together: a front-end performs fast analysis of raw data, and if needed it encrypts this data in a way that protects its privacy and yet that is reversible so that a back-end can de-anonymize and further analyse this data. Access control management for such data is based on semantic models comprising notions such as: purpose of requested data usage, types and identification of the requesting entity, intended processing, and applicable regulatory provisions. When deployed in the data controller domain, PRISM can capture and inspect all packet flows on the network link.

In terms of technologies on the market, Blackberry Balance[1] is a technology that manages work and home user profiles on BlackBerry devices. Using two separate encrypted file systems with a unified view of data, private applications cannot access corporate data, and vice versa. Email, calendar, contacts, organizer data, applications and files that are pushed on the device via a corporate channel are by default tagged as 'work'; users cannot reclassify work data as private data, but personal data can be reclassified as work data. The technology also allows for remote device wiping for the corporate profile, disallowing backups of work data (to prevent the reclassification of backed-up corporate data as private data), as well as disallowing browser traffic, depending on the Internet connection type. Unfortunately, BlackBerry Balance is a proprietary technology tighly linked with BlackBerry 10 OS and the BlackBerry Enterprise Server, and does not lend itself to privacy enhancements on the user side.

None of the works we have seen examine how to handle the private data of the user (i.e. device usage habits, applications and sensor data) once it is emitted by certain applications and out of the device into the network. This is an important aspect, especially as we know that personally identifiable information is being gathered without user consent because of the organisation's need to monitor the user. It is not clear from the state of the art what are the available defenses that users can install on their devices, and how well such defenses work to protect user privacy.

3. CONTRIBUTIONS

On the one hand, PriPARD will examine how much private data can still be gathered when existing privacy controls (TaintDroid and related solutions, business containers, process sandboxing, etc.) are used on a mobile device. We believe that personal data emitted by user devices should be scrubbed off as much as possible before this data reaches the network, and PriPARD will examine if that is fully possible on modern mobile platforms. As current research does not examine the overall privacy of existing approaches as perceived by the user of the device, PriPARD will look for ways to allow employees to check what private information is emitted and gathered when they work. Hence PriPARD's first contribution to knowledge development is to raise device owner awareness about existing privacy-enabling tools to use on the devices on which they also work, as well as how these tools perform. Also, it is interesting to study what kind of device monitoring is still performed/needed when the device switches to a personal profile, and how sensor data is treated: can sensor data produced by an application running in work mode, be separated from data from the same sensor from a different application running in personal mode?

On the other hand, it is a given that a certain amount of control (or monitoring) should be exercised in the corporate network when the employee is working. Assuming that mobile devices cannot be fully stopped from emitting some private data (be it explicitly private or data that can be corroborated to infer private data), PriPARD wants to build privacy into the system, in such a way that users know of the private data emitted by their devices, as well as how that data is handled in the network. This approach will help find out if companies can give proofs to mobile device users of the network's compliance with user privacy preferences set up on their devices, but concerning the corporate network. Our vision is that whatever private data cannot be scrubbed off before reaching the corporate network, should be confined within the network and not sent to the Internet.

PriPARD's main objective is to build a management layer enforcing that employee private data does not leak outside the enterprise network. Such management tools should be partially controllable from the user devices when it comes to their private data. By linking mobile device mechanisms with network-level monitoring, PriPARD will make a novel contribution to the advancement of privacy mechanisms in

[1]`http://us.blackberry.com/business/software/blackberry-balance.html`

general. The point with privacy-conscious network monitoring, however, is not to have a centralised sink for this employee private data, but to have a distributed set of controls woven into the network fabric. In this way, it is more feasible to protect employee privacy, since it would be comparatively harder for a malicious employee to gain data about another employee. With its tools, PriPARD will contribute to knowledge development with practical experience with the trade-offs between security needs and privacy protection, for the corporate network managers.

4. IMPACT OF PROJECT AND POSTER

In all, PriPARD will investigate to what extent it is possible to design and build an open framework for managing personal mobile devices in a corporate network, with privacy mechanisms that the employees can use on their personal devices. We deem it is time to investigate what guarantees of enforcing privacy are essential to make users sure that the privacy settings on their devices will not be discarded at the level of the network. For example, a possible such tool is an application installable on mobile devices, that would show where the user's personal data is processed across the corporate network. We foresee that such mechanisms will span both Android middleware on devices - with minimal operating system changes needed since these devices are, after all, personal - but also endpoints of the corporate network.

On the long run, PriPARD wants to show that it is possible to give control to the mobile device users over the data they are generating about themselves, and also that it is possible for a company to manage potentially sensitive mobile user data (of its employees and customers). With proofs of concept on these topics, PriPARD can lead the way to a whole range of technologies for network policy-management that are privacy-aware and that allow, to a certain extent, mobile user tuning.

With this poster, we want to start a discussion with both researchers and companies on how to build configurable privacy-enhancing technologies for mobile devices in the BYOD setting. Our aim in this discussion is to find collaborations aimed at enhancing user awareness but also at helping companies improve their network management from the point of view of privacy protection.

5. REFERENCES

[1] M. Conti, V. T. N. Nguyen, and B. Crispo. Crepe: context-related policy enforcement for android. In *Proc. 13th intl. conf. on Information Security*, ISC'10, 2011.

[2] G. Corera. GCHQ data-tapping claims nightmarish, says German justice minister. http://www.bbc.co.uk/news/uk-23017108, 2013.

[3] L. P. Cox, A. Dalton, and V. Marupadi. Smokescreen: flexible privacy controls for presence-sharing. In *Proc. intl. conf. on Mobile systems, applications and services*, MobiSys '07, 2007.

[4] W. Enck, P. Gilbert, B.-G. Chun, L. P. Cox, J. Jung, P. McDaniel, and A. N. Sheth. Taintdroid: an information-flow tracking system for realtime privacy monitoring on smartphones. In *Proc. 9th USENIX conf. on Operating systems design and implementation*, OSDI'10, 2010.

[5] Ernst and Young. Privacy trends 2012 - The case for growing accountability. http://www.ey.com/Publication/vwLUAssets/Privacy_trends_2012/\$FILE/Privacy-trends-2012_AU1064.pdf, 2012.

[6] D. Feth and A. Pretschner. Flexible data-driven security for android. In *Proc. 2012 IEEE Sixth Intl. Conf. on Software Security and Reliability*, SERE '12, 2012.

[7] G. Greenwald. NSA collecting phone records of millions of Verizon customers daily. http://www.guardian.co.uk/world/2013/jun/06/nsa-phone-records-verizon-court-order, 2013.

[8] M. Iron. BYOD Strategies - Chapter 2. http://www.webtorials.com/main/resource/papers/mobileiron/paper1/byod_part_2.pdf, 2011.

[9] M. Iron. International Data Privacy Legislation Review: A Guide for BYOD Policies. http://www.webtorials.com/main/resource/papers/mobileiron/paper5/Guide_for_BYOD_Policies.pdf, 2012.

[10] K. Johnson. SANS Mobility / BYOD Security Survey. http://www.sans.org/reading_room/analysts_program/mobility-sec-survey.pdf, 2012.

[11] T. Kemp. As Mobile Device Management (MDM) Becomes Commoditized, What's Next for MDM? http://www.forbes.com/sites/tomkemp/2013/02/19/as-mobile-device-management-becomes-commoditized-whats-next-for-mdm/, 2013.

[12] PRISM project Consortium. PRIvacy-aware Secure Monitoring. http://www.fp7-prism.eu/.

[13] G. Russello, M. Conti, B. Crispo, E. Fernandes, and Y. Zhauniarovich. Demonstrating the effectiveness of moses for separation of execution modes. In *Proc. 2012 ACM conf. on Computer and communications security*, CCS '12, 2012.

[14] H. Schultze. BYOD and Mobile Security Survey Results. http://www.slideshare.net/informationsecurity/byod-and-mobile-security-report-2013-19033467, 2013.

[15] W. Wei, F. Xu, and Q. Li. Mobishare: Flexible privacy-preserving location sharing in mobile online social networks. In *INFOCOM*. IEEE, 2012.

POSTER: Caching Oblivious Memory Access

An Extension to the HCRYPT Virtual Machine

Michael Brenner and Matthew Smith
Distributed Computing Security Group
Gottfried Wilhelm Leibniz Universität
Hannover, Germany
{brenner,smith}@dcsec.uni-hannover.de

ABSTRACT

Efficient homomorphic encryption enables the construction of an encrypted computer system. Previous work has shown how this can be achieved using only arithmetic representations of simple demultiplexer circuits. This poster extends the results by introducing a caching mechanism for oblivious memory access, by far the most time-consuming building block of a recently proposed sample machine architecture. The construction allows to significantly accelerate homomorphically encrypted machine operation while still preserving obliviousness of memory access, control unit operation and functional components.

Categories and Subject Descriptors

E.3 [**Data Encryption**]: Public Key Cryptosystems

Keywords

homomorphic encryption, implementation, oblivious memory access

1. INTRODUCTION

Gentry's fully homomorphic encryption scheme seemed to be the saviour of confidential delegation to remote resources - but only for a second. Regardless of its elegance, it proved slow when applied in a scenario where large circuits are encrypted. Nevertheless, homomorphic encryption is one of the hottest topics in current research. The other direction of research that aims at making encrypted computing feasible is the construction of circuits and protocols that arrange the underlying cryptographic primitives in an efficient way. This work belongs to the latter.

In previous publications we showed how to construct an encrypted universal machine using only very basic circuits, in particular demultiplexers or selectors [1]. We then proved the concept with an implementation of a simple machine model [2] (the *hcrypt* machine) and evaluated the performance of such a design using our implementation [3] of the homomorphic Smart-Vercauteren scheme [4]. The evaluation clearly showed that the memory access is by far the most time-consuming operation when implemented with encrypted circuits.

CCS'13, November 4–8, 2013, Berlin, Germany.
ACM 978-1-4503-2477-9/13/11.
http://dx.doi.org/10.1145/2508859.2512501.

2. THE MACHINE MODEL

The sample machine that we base our investigation on is the *hcrypt* virtual machine that can be downloaded from our website[1]. We use a simple accumulator-based scheme with a Harvard-style memory architecture. The sample machine features a small memory array of 256*13 bits, resulting in a ratio of roughly 99:1, comparing the number of gates forming memory and processor circuits. Obviously, in settings with reasonable memory sizes, the execution time of the processor gates is negligible. By executing the arithmetic representations of the gates under encryption, the resulting machine can securely execute any code on any data without the need for decryption. This model allows branching programs, loops and even self-modifying code.

2.1 Oblivious Memory Access

Our original approach uses the following pattern to obliviously calculate the result of a memory access: The result r of the switching function for a 4-bit memory column m is given as $r = (\neg a_0 \wedge \neg a_1 \wedge m_0) \oplus (a_0 \wedge \neg a_1 \wedge m_1) \oplus (\neg a_0 \wedge a_1 \wedge m_2) \oplus (a_0 \wedge a_1 \wedge m_3)$ with a_x being the address selector. This can easily be transformed into an arithmetic representation $r' = ((a'_0 + 1') * (a'_1 + 1') * m'_0) + (a'_0 * (a'_1 + 1') * m'_1) + ((a'_0 + 1') * a'_1 * m'_2) + (a'_0 * a'_1 * m'_3)$ with x' denoting the encrypted value of a bit x under a fully homomorphic encryption scheme. This calculates the encrypted memory value for an encrypted address over an encrypted memory array.

To ensure obliviousness, every single memory access is required to calculate the switching function translated into Line 8 in function `Ma()` for the entire memory array of size $ROWS * WORDSIZE$. We iterate over all addresses i in the address space $\{0, ROWS\}$ and every bit j of a memory word. The access logic is depicted in Figure 1.

```
1: res Ma(adr)
2: {
3:   for(i = 0..ROWS)
4:   {
5:     sel = RowSelect(i,adr);
6:     for(j = 0..WORDSIZE)
7:     {
8:       res.j  = (A[i].j * sel)+(res.j  * !sel);
```

[1]https://hcrypt.com

```
    }
  }
  return res;
}
```

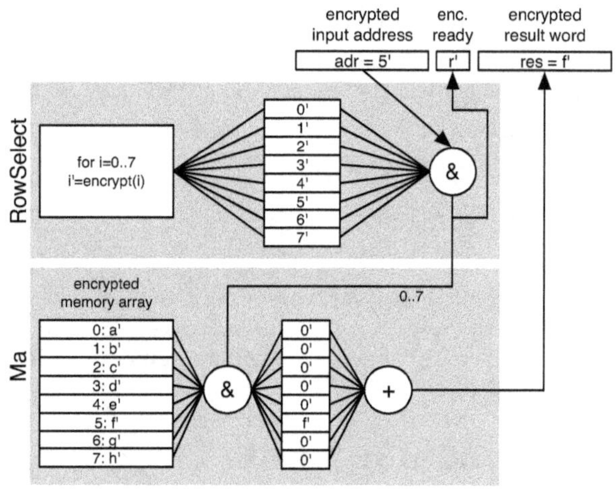

Figure 1: Memory access schematic

During memory access, the function `RowSelect()` computes the equality of the address iterator i and the memory address *adr* to be accessed, resulting in an encrypted 1 on equality and an encrypted 0 otherwise (because all bit representations are encrypted).

```
sel RowSelect(i,adr)
{
  sel=Encrypt(1);
  for(j = 0..log2(ROWS))
  {
    temp = i.j + adr.j + Encrypt(1); //a XOR b XOR 1 => (a==b)
    sel=sel*temp;
  }
  return sel;
}
```

The function `RowSelect()` is called iteratively by `Ma()`. The row result of each iteration is added to the intermediate result *res*. As a consequence, the result remains stable, as soon as the addressed memory row was found and the memory content was added to the intermediate result (which up to this point is 0). Any subsequent iteration can only add zeros, as the address comparison can't produce another positive. Storing the comparison result in an indicator flag r', it's possible to use the result *res* before the remaining memory words have been processed.

3. OBLIVIOUS CACHING

Computing the address equality in fact implements an associative item selection usually found in caching technology. This is the basis to extend the existing machine architecture. We assume that the single-threaded execution pattern is replaced by (at least) three parallel threads executing two memory blocks and the processor control unit circuits. The memory blocks are extended by a number of encrypted cache words which hold recently accessed memory words along with the corresponding memory addresses (tags) as depicted in Figure 2. The memory access function starts by associatively matching the currently accessed address with the cached tags. In case of a cache hit the corresponding word is copied from the cache to the output register. In either case, cache hit or not, the boolean address matching result is also stored in the flag r', possibly indicating the availability of the requested memory item.

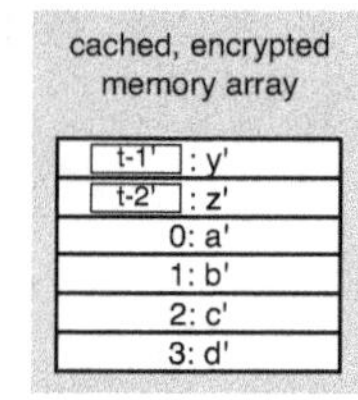

Figure 2: Cached Memory Block

3.1 An Old Acquaintance: The Wait State

Splitting memory into multiple parallel instances requires a synchronization step to collect the results from the memory banks. This can easily be implemented by putting the memory management circuit (and as a dependency the control unit) into wait mode. To keep the control unit oblivious to an observer, control unit operation must not be halted but any operation in the *hcrypt* state machine may only be executed if memory is in sync, which is the case, as soon as the first memory bank reports a hit. To practically implement the state machine wait mode, the write-back phase is extended by an additional conjunction which effectively skips the modification of the machine state unless the sync flag s' is 1. As an example, the write-back circuit for the program counter which reads

$$\forall x : x \in \{0..7\},\\ PC_x = (jmp(CR) \wedge DR_x) \vee (bcc(CR) \wedge DR_x \wedge \neg F_{carry}) \vee (bz(CR) \wedge DR_x \wedge F_{zero}) \vee (\neg jmp(CR) \wedge \neg bcc(CR) \wedge \neg bz(CR) \wedge (PC+1)_x).$$

for the 8-bit program counter PC, data and command registers DR, CR, a flag register F and selectors that return boolean values that indicate one of the opcodes $\{jmp, bcc, bz\}$ in CR, would be extended to

$$PC_x = \underline{PC_x \vee s' \wedge}((jmp(CR) \wedge DR_x) \vee ... \wedge (PC+1)_x)).$$

where s' is the sum over all ready flags r'. Extending this approach to all machine state variables allows the control unit circuit to loop in an non-operational state which cannot be detected by an observer.

3.2 Caching Strategies

Due to space limitations, we only sketch a first-in-first-out principle. The advantage of this paradigm is that it does not require additional encrypted circuitry to substitute the cache items. The executing entity simply shifts the cache array by one item and writes the encrypted result *res* into the $t-1$ position of the cache array along with the address *adr* as the corresponding tag. The caching mechanism shown here can apply any caching strategy. Advanced mechanisms like a least-recently-used or counter method would need encrypted counters and comparators to calculate the substitution candidate. The following subsections sketch further measures that can optimize access to previously uncached memory items.

3.3 Memory Bank Interleaving

A trivial *hcrypt* looping program shows an obvious problem with a sequential order distribution of the address space over the memory banks.

```
count    .integer 20   // 20 iterations
start    La count      // counter -> accumulator
loop     SEC           // set carry
         SUB 1         // decrease by 1
         BNE loop      // repeat if >0
         END
```

Assuming that the size of a memory bank is larger than the loop, the memory fetch cycles block each other because the memory items holding the program code are all stored in the same bank and obliviousness demands that each memory access operation iterates over the entire bank. To avoid this blocking behaviour, the address space has to be distributed over the available memory banks in an interleaved manner as shown in Figure 3. The example also shows that the number of parallel memory banks and the interleave factor have an significant impact on efficiency: Regarding the cycle phases of the sample *hcrypt* machine architecture, it is even necessary to arrange the memory in a way such that a command word and a target address in absolute address mode (a reference by memory address, like in the sample program) are stored in separate banks. However, this is not an issue specific to the *hcrypt* machine but to any phased cycle processor architecture that offers absolute addressing.

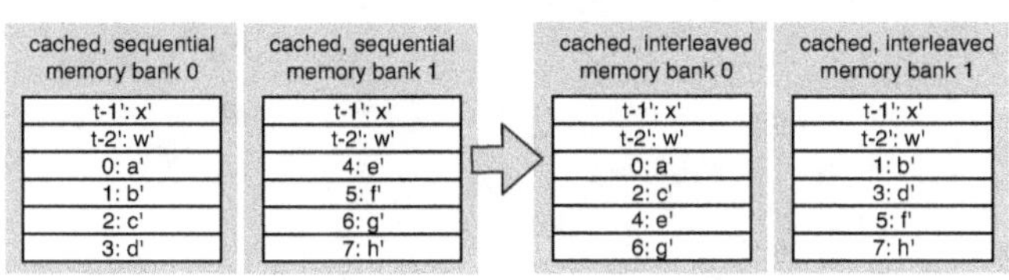

Figure 3: Interleaved Memory

To optimize the memory layout according to a particular program, the entire memory block can be arranged cache-style as depicted above. The `RowSelect()` function is then replaced by pre-computed (i.e. pre-encrypted) addresses for all memory words. This allows to store the items of a memory bank in arbitrary order but sacrifices space for flexibility.

3.4 Deferred Memory Bank Evaluation

Consider the sample program being stored in two uncached, parallel memory banks with interleave 2 as shown in Figure 3 but with 8 items each. Assume that the evaluation of each item takes a uniform timeslice $t = 1$. The control unit issues the fetch operations for the command word and the argument at two sequent memory-idle timeslices. The schedule for the sample program is shown in Figure 4.

The chart shows that the undeferred schedule for the first operation (`La count`) causes 7 wait states (w) between the two fetch phases (f) of one control unit cycle. This results in 16 busy (-) timeslices to load the first single operation from memory, even though bank 1 generates the ready signal (X) after just one timeslice. This, by the way, is the behaviour of a sequential execution without parallel memory banks, which clearly shows, that the naïve approach of simply executing multiple instances of memory evaluation in parallel

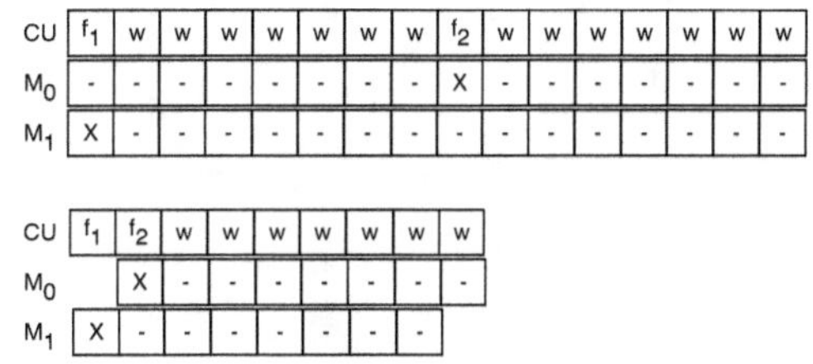

Figure 4: Deferred Evaluation

has absolutely no effect. Slightly deferring the evaluation of bank 0 by just one timeslice optimizes the program flow, such that the operation now takes only 9 timeslices.

The generation of the ideal memory layout is a machine- and program-specific compile-time issue and will not be covered here. The executing entity which computes on the encrypted circuits only needs to know the access mode or the interleave factor in order to modify the iteration steps in the `Ma()` function. Note that this, to some degree, reveals information about the program structure and therefore conflicts with a strong notion of obliviousness.

3.5 Write-Back

To assure memory consistency, write access is required to process the cache entries first. If the cache contains a target address tag then the corresponding entry is updated, which immediately leads to a valid memory state, as all subsequent read operations also query the cache first.

4. CONCLUSION

This work presents a mechanism for caching oblivious memory access implemented with circuits under a fully homomorphic encryption scheme. The construction applies parallel evaluation of different memory banks and offers solutions to various subproblems like access synchronization, prevention of access blocking by interleaving and optimization by deferred evaluation in a scenario that demands obliviousness. We showed the concept as an extension to the encrypted *hcrypt* machine.

To optimize the program flow and the program-specific memory layout, further consideration of established methods in compiler-based operation scheduling is recommended.

5. REFERENCES

[1] M. Brenner, J. Wiebelitz, G. v. Voigt and M. Smith: *A Smart-Gentry based Software System for Secret Program Execution.* 6th International Conference on Security and Cryptography (SECRYPT 2011), SciTePress, 2011

[2] M. Brenner, H. Perl and M. Smith: *How Practical is Homomorphically Encrypted Program Execution? An Implementation and Performance Evaluation.* 11th IEEE International Conference on Trust, Security and Privacy in Computing and Communications, 2012

[3] H. Perl, M. Brenner and M. Smith, *Poster: An Implementation of the Fully Homomorphic Smart-Vercauteren Cryptosystem,* ACM CCS'11, Proceedings of the 18th ACM conference on Computer and communications security 2011

[4] N. P. Smart and F. Vercauteren, *Fully Homomorphic Encryption with Relatively Small Key and Ciphertext Sizes,* Public Key Cryptography - PKC 2010, Springer 2010

POSTER: Data Quality Evaluation: Integrating Security and Accuracy

Leon Reznik
Department of Computer Science,
Rochester Institute of Technology
102 Lomb Memorial Drive
Rochester, NY 14623 USA
lr@cs.rit.edu

Elisa Bertino
Department of Computer Science,
Purdue University
305 N.University Street
West Lafayette, IN 47907 USA
bertino@cs.purdue.edu

ABSTRACT

Data quality (DQ) is essential to achieve data trustworthiness, as it assures that data is free of errors, complete, and consistent. This paper proposes an approach to evaluate DQ in multichannel sensor networks and systems with heterogeneous data sources. The approach integrates various DQ indicators ranging from traditional data accuracy metrics to network security and business performance measures. It demonstrates the advantage of including security metrics into the DQ evaluation for the design optimization of data fusion procedures and even the whole data collection and communication systems. The DQ metrics composition and calculus are discussed. However, the major attention is paid to the analysis of the relationship between conventional data accuracy metrics and network security indicators.

Categories and Subject Descriptors

D.4.6 [Security]: Protection; K.6.5 [Security]: Protection

Keywords

Data quality; computer security evaluation; data accuracy; data fusion.

1. INTRODUCTION

Most computing applications request quality data for their execution based on an old adage that your analytical results are only as good as your data. Many professional and government organizations as well as commercial companies are working on data quality (DQ) improvements by developing practical approaches and tools. Indeed, DQ evaluation methodologies have advanced and a number of DQ evaluation and assurance systems have been developed and employed for specific applications. Despite DQ being recognized as an articulated concept, current research tends to focus on specific factors, mainly on information accuracy [1], disregarding other important issues, in particular computer security and safety. The problem of how security impacts the overall DQ has not been much investigated.

CCS'13, November 4–8, 2013, Berlin, Germany.
ACM 978-1-4503-2477-9/13/11.

The goal of the paper is to introduce a unified novel DQ evaluation methodology integrating a wide variety of metrics representing measurement accuracy, system metrological and reliability characteristics, computer and network security, possible safety and business performance impact, all of which influence overall DQ as well as to introduce a calculus, which will deliver an effective and efficient DQ evaluation in a wide variety of applications including real time applications. After discussing a few DQ evaluation metrics and their calculus, the paper investigates the impact of including network security characteristics and their integration with data accuracy on the data collection and communication design.

2. DQ METRICS: COMPOSITION

Our metrics selection is based on several standards and guidelines related to DQ, which have been released over the last decade or are under the final stages of development as professional and government recommendations that could be used for security [2]: NIST 800-55 "Performance measurement guide for information security", NIST SP 800-53 "Recommended security controls for federal information systems", ISO/IEC 27004 "information security management- measurement", ISO/IEC 21827 "Information technology-systems security engineering", ISO/IEC 15408 "Evaluation criteria for information technology security", NSA INFOSEC Assurance training and rating program, ISA 99.00.01 "Security for industrial automation and control systems" and the following up standards on manufacturing and control systems security. Among them, the last standards group focuses on SCADA security with a security framework and associated metrics derived from a set of seven security ideas. The International Standards Organization (ISO) ''Guide to the Expression of Uncertainty in Measurement'' and the corresponding US standards set up major principles on how to evaluate measurement uncertainty that will be a leading DQ indicator in data accuracy.

We propose to design an evaluation structure as a multilevel hierarchical system. In this approach we can combine diverse evaluation systems, even if they vary in their design concepts and implementation stages. Also, the hierarchical system should be able to produce a partial evaluation of different aspects that will be helpful in flagging the areas that need urgent improvement. In our initial design we will classify metrics into four groups: (1) measurement accuracy; (2) metrological and reliability characteristics; (3) network and system security; (4) safety and business performance impact. While the first three groups include rather generic metrics, the last set is devoted to metrics, which are specific to a particular application.

Table 1. Metrics examples: specification and calculation

Group	Security	Security	Measurement Accuracy	Process safety and performance
Measure ID	**Physical security incidents**	**Cryptographic system and communication protection**	**Measurement uncertainty**	**Process safety risk**
Goal	Strategic: Ensure an environment of comprehensive security and accountability for personnel, facilities, and products Security: Integrate physical and security protection mechanisms to ensure appropriate protection of the data sources and facilities	Strategic: accelerate the development and use of a quality information infrastructure Security: allocate sufficient resources to adequately protect an information infrastructure in a application	Ensure collecting high accuracy data from the data sources	Improve process safety by reducing such risks as equipment damage or business interruption due to wrong data use
Measure	Percentage (%) of physical security incidents involving unauthorized entry to facilities	Percentage of mobile computers and other devices that perform all cryptographic operations as recommended for this application	Probability of the type A uncertainty value (random measurement error) being within the range specified by the application for this data source	Probability that equipment damage or business interruption will not increase a specified level
Calculation formula or algorithm	(number of physical security incidents involving unauthorized entry to facilities/total number of access to facilities) *100	(number of mobile computers and other devices that perform all cryptographic operations as recommended for the application/total number of mobile computers and other devices)*100	Probability above is calculated based on the standard deviation empirical estimate or other probability characteristics available	Probability above is calculated based on the business process analysis, equipment costs, expert evaluations
Target	Should be a high (or low) percentage defined by the application			
Implementation evidence	How many physical security incidents involving unauthorized entry to facilities occurred over specified period? How many total entries to facilities occurred over specified period?	How many mobile computers and devices are employed in the application? How many mobile computers and devices employ cryptography as prescribed? How many mobile computers and devices have cryptography implementation waivers?	Measurement results	Equipment costs, process risk evaluations, etc.
Frequency	Collection: defined by the organization Reporting: defined by the application		Collection: defined by the application Reporting: defined by the application	
Responsible parties	Information owner: defined by the organization (e.g. physical security officer) Information collector: defined by the organization (e.g. computer security incident response team)	Information owner: defined by the organization (e.g. information security officer) Information collector: defined by the organization (e.g. system administrators)	Information collection and measurement team	Information owner: Process safety team. Operations and maintenance team, Accounting team Information collector: defined by the organization
Information source	Physical security incident report, physical access control logs	System and network security plans	Measurement results database, sensor networks or systems	Operations, accounting and other databases
Report format	Percentage and/or pie charts		As specified by application	
Documentation	NIST SP 800-53	NIST SP 800-53	Guide to the expression of uncertainty in measurement	ANSI/ISA-99.00.01

Table 2. Metrics calculus (sample) for data streams fusion

Measure ID	**Physical security incidents**	**Cryptographic system and communication protection**	**Measurement uncertainty**
Formula for the data from one stream	P_i/A_i, where P_i is the number of physical security accidents in the i-th part of the network and A_i is the total number of access attempts in this part	C_i/D_i, where C_i is the number of computers and other devices that perform all cryptographic operations as recommended in the i-th part of the network and D_i is the total number of devices in this part	Standard deviation estimate is recommended as the probability in Table 1 could be calculated from it
Fusion of n data streams formula	$\text{Total} = \frac{\sum_{i=1}^{n} P_i}{\sum_{i=1}^{n} A_i}$	$\text{Total} = \frac{\sum_{i=1}^{n} C_i}{\sum_{i=1}^{n} D_i}$	$s(z) = \sqrt{\frac{1}{n(n-1)}\sum_1^n (Z_i - z)^2}$ where Z_i is measurement from the i-th data stream and z is average from n streams
Relationship	$\min_i {P_i}/{A_i} \leq \text{Total} \leq \max_i {P_i}/{A_i}$	$\min_i {C_i}/{D_i} \leq \text{Total} \leq \max_i {C_i}/{D_i}$	$s(z) \leq \min_i s(Z_i)$
Relationship if all n fused data have the same quality	Total =Pi/Ai	Total=Ci/Di	$s(z) = {s(Z)}/{\sqrt{n}}$

The definition and calculation of a sample of metrics representing different groups are presented in Table 1.

3. DQ METRICS: CALCULUS

In order to evaluate DQ in multichannel sensor networks and systems with multiple heterogeneous data sources one has to consider various data streams and data fusion points and to develop a calculus for reevaluating DQ metrics at the merging points. The sample of the metrics calculation rules for merging data streams for metrics presented in Table 1 are given in Table 2.

One can see that data fusion from various sources and streams typically increases data accuracy and the corresponding quality indicators. Indeed, setting up additional sensors and using various data sources has been one of the most popular methods for improving DQ. However, it is not that clear whether such a strategy is useful with respect to the data security indicators. Table 2 demonstrates that data fusion typically cannot improve security DQ indicators considered in Table 1 beyond the best ones among the data streams. On the contrary, data fusion may drive security indicators down due to the lack of security in other parts of the network. From the security prospective, the best option could be picking up the data coming from the most secure part of the network instead of using fusion.

When considering both accuracy and security DQ metrics, assessing whether fusion enhances DQ is not obvious as one has to tradeoff between accuracy, security and other goals. While adding up a more secure data transmission channel will improve both security and accuracy indicators, using a more accurate data stream will definitely improve data accuracy but could be detrimental to certain security indicators. If resources are limited, as in the case of sensor networks, one might consider trying to improve accuracy of the most secure data source versus more or less even distribution of security resources in order to achieve the same security levels on all data channels. The concrete recommendations will depend on the application. Composition of various metrics into the integral one needs further investigation.

4. CONCLUSION

The paper focuses on DQ evaluation in multi-data streams environment of multi-channel sensor networks and systems. It considers various samples of DQ metrics representing communication and computing security as well as data accuracy and other characteristics. The introduction of a unified framework for assessing DQ is critical for enhancing data usage in a wide spectrum of science and technology applications, as it will create new opportunities for optimizing data structures, data processing and fusion procedures based on the new DQ information use.

By presenting to an end user or an application the DQ indicators including ones that characterize system and network security, and data trustworthiness and confidence, users can be in a better position to decide whether and how to use data in various applications. A user will get an opportunity to understand and compare various data files, streams and sources based on the associated DQ with integral quality characteristics incorporating various aspects of a system functionality and to redesign data flows schemes.

The paper demonstrates the dramatic influence, which system security may have on the data structures and schemes organization. It shows that from taking into account a security impact on the DQ, it might be necessary to reduce the number of data sources in the fusion procedures or perhaps even to avoid data fusion at all, picking up the most secure data line instead.

5. REFERENCES

[1] Madnick S.E., R. Y. Wang, Y. W. Lee, and H. Zhu, "Overview and Framework for Data and Information Quality Research," *J. Data and Information Quality,* vol. 1, pp. 1-22, 2009.

[2] Bartol N., B. Bates, K. Goertzel, and T. Winograd, "Measuring cyber security and information assurance," Information Assurance Technology Analysis Center 2009

POSTER: Graphical Password using Object-based Image Ranking

Cuong Xuan Nguyen
is0149fx@ed.ritsumei.ac.jp

Hung-Hsuan Huang
huang@fc.ritsumei.ac.jp

Kyoji Kawagoe
kawagoe@is.ritsumei.ac.jp

Ritsumeikan University
Noji-Higashi, Kusatsu-shi, Shiga, Japan

ABSTRACT

In this paper, we propose a new graphical password using object-based image ranking, called OBIR, which enables appropriate images to be presented to users during authentication. Research on graphical password is being conducted and receiving more and more public attention due to its potential of being an alternative for textual password. However, the main problem of graphical password is its vulnerability to shoulder surfing attacks, especially on mobile devices where the login password is easily visible in public. In order to overcome this issue, we propose a novel graphical password using image ranking method based on the objects in the image itself. The higher the ranking of an image is, the more appropriate it is to be user's selection without exposing too much information of the password to the shoulder-surfer. Upon our experiments, it is obtained that our image ranking method is effective in filtering appropriate pass-image that even if it is selected in public, the password is safe and therefore resistant to shoulder surfing.

Categories and Subject Descriptors

K.6.5 [Management of Computing and Information Systems]: Security and Protection—Authentication

Keywords

Password; Graphics; Images; Scoring

1. INTRODUCTION

The combination of text-based user-id and password is being applied widely in conventional authentication systems. Text-based password authentication is easy to implement and easy to encode. However, to end-users, they usually have trouble remembering the password. The more complicated the password is, the more difficult for users to recall. Therefore, to make it more memorable, they tend to choose simple words which are vulnerable to dictionary attacks. The main problem here is the balance between recallability and security. Systems that achieve both qualities to some extent, such as biometric authentication systems, are low in mobility and too expensive to implement on mobile devices for common users and common applications.

Graphical password emerged recently as an alternative to solve the memorability problem of textual password. Graphical password reduces memory burden on users because of its user-friendly interface that can improve both recognizability and recallability. Moreover, mobile devices with touch screen are perfectly suitable for graphical password to show off its superior user experience over other types of password. Yet the resistance to shoulder surfing remains the biggest problem of graphical password, because the authentication step often involves a user in touching directly on his/her password picture that is exposed directly to any observer nearby. As a result, it is not surprising that researchers over the world have been working hard to find out a suitable scheme to nullify shoulder surfing attacks while maintaining usability, at least in the case when the user authenticates himself/herself in an open public place.

In this paper, we propose a novel graphical password scheme using object-based image ranking, called OBIR. Users register their passwords as a set of simple words representing normal objects. Users will then choose one image that contains objects associated with their passwords from a set of images when authenticating. This way, the passwords are easy to remember because both the words and the images are closely associated with each other. That one image must not only contains user's objects but also other objects prominent enough to distract the observer from any particular objects in the image. To choose the that image, we establish a ranking of image "appropriateness" by using the information about objects in the image itself to calculate a score, based on that, the higher the score, the more appropriate the image is to be shown to user. With the appropriate image, even if it is directly selected, the shoulder-surfer cannot identify what the password objects are, and thus be able to increase the system shoulder surfing resilience.

2. RELATED WORK

In order to achieve better graphical password, many authentication schemes have been proposed as well as analyzed to identify each one's pros and cons [4] [5] [6] [9]. Graphical password often falls under two categories: Image-based and Grid-based [8]. In this section, we focus on image-based graphical password since our proposed system is of this type. Image-based graphical password is further classified into two subcategories: Single-image based and Multiple-image based.

CCS'13, November 4–8, 2013, Berlin, Germany.
ACM 978-1-4503-2477-9/13/11.
http://dx.doi.org/10.1145/2508859.2512503.

In the single-image based category, only one background image is used for both registration and authentication stages. Users usually have to interact with the image to create their unique password, and then interact the same way on the background image to pass authentication [7]. In the multiple-image based category, multiple images are used to increase the complexity of the scheme. Users usually register by choosing an image with some unique characteristics as their password, and then select the image with the same characteristics (the image itself for example). The characteristics should be chosen carefully so as to be easily recognized by the authentic user only.

To avoid the exposure of password caused by the exposure of selected image, recently the tag meta-data has been being effectively used as a way of making one time access pass-image, as in Tag Association Based Graphical Password (TAB) [2] [3] and Marasim [1]. Both proposed methods to make use of the association between image and its tags. A user registers his/her password using simple words (in case of TAB) or tags of his/her own image (in case of Marasim). Images that have tags containing those registered words are retrieved from Image Search Web Services as pass-images. The authentication process takes place with one or several rounds, where user must correctly choose all the pass-images to pass authentication. Using tags, the pass-images are changed each login session, preventing observer from remembering the images as well as making it difficult to guess user's registered words. However, both proposals haven't pay attention to which image should be used to shown to user, because if the image itself exposes too much about its tags, such as in case there is only one object in the image, or when the object stands out too much, it is not strong enough to withstand shoulder surfing attacks.

3. GRAPHICAL PASSWORD USING OBJECT-BASED IMAGE RANKING

3.1 Overview

The flow of this system is nearly the same as TAB. However, while TAB gets images from web search engines, we create a database of "prepared" images and keywords (terms). Each image is represented by a feature vector, whose elements correspond to the keyword collection and show how important the object is in relation to the image. Using these feature vectors and the query vector formed from user's password (which is also a set of keywords), we calculate each image's score and establish a ranking where the higher the score, the more appropriate the image is to be the correct answer shown to user. In this paper, user's password is called pass-terms, object that associated with a pass-term is called pass-object, the other objects are decoy-objects.

3.2 Database

Keywords database: $K = \{K^1, K^2, .., K^{Nk-1}, K^{Nk}\}$ where Nk is the number of keywords stored in database.

Images database: $I = \{I^1, I^2, .., I^{Ni-1}, I^{Ni}\}$ where Ni is the number of images stored in database.

Each image is presented by a feature vector
$I_i = (t^i_1, t^i_2, .., t^i_{Nk-1}, t^i_{Nk})$ where t^i_s is the weight of the object associated with keyword K^s in image I^i, showing how appropriate the object is if it is a pass-object. An appropriate pass-object means it is can be recognized in the image but not too prominent to attract attention of outside observer.

Presume that we have detected the area of each objects in images, we calculate the feature vector for each image as follow: $t^i_k = e \times r^{0.5} log(r^{0.5})$ where $r = \frac{A^i_k}{A}$ with A^i_k is the area of the object associated with keyword K^k and A is the area of the whole image. This way, we have $t^i_k \in [0, 1]$, and t^i_k reaches maximum when $r = \frac{1}{e^2} \approx 0.14$, which means if the object's area accounts for one ninth to one seventh of the image, it is an appropriately included object.

3.3 Object-based Image Ranking System

A correct image is the image that must contain both pass-object and a number of decoy-objects, and moreover, the decoy-objects have to stand out at least as much as the pass-object so as to increase the image's entropy. To determine how appropriate an image is, we calculate image score and use it as the basis to compare and create image ranking.

Let's define some elements used to calculate score. A keyword vector is a vector representing each keyword $K_i = (k_1, k_2, .., k_{Nk-1}, k_{Nk})$ where $k_j = 1$ if j=i and $k_j = 0$ otherwise. Distance between vector is defined as $d(u, v) = cos(u, v)$. An image feature vector f is defined as
$f = (f_1, f_2, .., f_{Nk-1}, f_{Nk})$.

3.4 Relevance measure

We define Relevance measure R between image and user's password as follow:
$R = \sum R_i$ where $R_i = d(f, K_i)$ and K_i is a keyword vector of a pass-term. Here we have $R_i \in [0, 1]$. $R_i = 0$ if the image does not contain any pass-objects, otherwise, R indicates the extent in which the image is related to user's password, in term of how appropriate the pass-objects is included. If the pass-objects are too large or too small compared to the whole image, R is small. R gets bigger when pass-objects are included to an acceptable level.

3.5 Noise measure

If an image contains pass-objects (R>0), we will use its feature vector to identify whether other decoy-objects are also included. Image I^i contains a decoy-object associated with keyword K^s if K^s is not a pass-term and $t^i_s > 0$. Suppose I^i has M decoy-objects ($M \geq 0$), we define Noise measure N as follow (if $M = 0$ then let $N = 0$):
$N = \frac{M-1}{M}(1 - \frac{\sum |d(f, K_s) - R|}{M})$ where K_s is the vector representing decoy-object K^s. N indicates how far the weights of decoy-objects spread around the weight of pass-objects, as well as takes in consideration the number of decoy-objects. Images that have many decoy-objects which are as prominent as pass-objects will have higher noise than simple images that contain only one or two objects.

3.6 Score and ranking

Knowing Relevance and Noise measures of an image, the score S calculation is quite straightforward: $S = R \times N$. Using the descending order of score S, we establish a ranking of the images. Top-rank images are considered safe to be presented to user so that even if it is directly selected, shoulder-surfer will still has difficulty in identifying user's pass-terms. For the prototype system, the decoy images will be chosen randomly from the set of images that have $S = 0$.

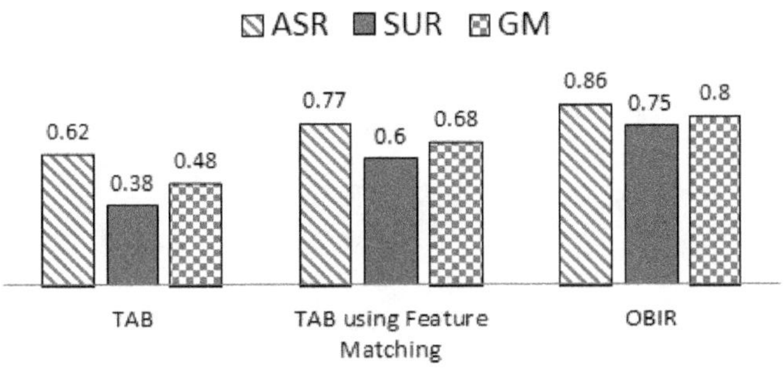

Figure 1: Our method compared with TAB [2] and TAB using Image Feature Matching SURF [3]

4. EVALUATION

We use the training and validation dataset of Visual Object Classes Challenge 2012 [10] to create our database. The dataset consists of a set of over 17000 images, each image is described by an annotation file that gives information such as name and bounding boxes of the objects in the image. We also got a list of 20 keywords whose objects have been identified in every image of the database.

We conduct experiments with six common users for authentication test and two users in the role of shoulder-surfers. We prepare six passwords, three two-keyword sets and three three-keyword sets. Each common user will receive two accounts from the six to perform authentication, resulting in a total of 12 logins. We also prepare two more three-keyword passwords for shoulder-surfers. They perform their own normal logins to get a grasp of the login process, and then be presented the correct images of the six accounts to guess for passwords of each one. Each guessing login attempt is performed twice. This results in 14 normal logins and 24 guesses (each password is guessed four times).

For evaluation, we get the Authentication Success Ratio (ASR) by calculating the number of successful logins over total number of logins, and Spoofing Unsuccess Ratio (SUR) by calculating the number of unsuccessful guesses over total number of guesses; then we obtain the geometric means (GM) of the two measures, which are used in [2].

Table 1: OBIR Experiment Result

ASR(%)	SUR(%)	GM(%)
85.7	75.0	80.2

Results of the above experiments are shown in Table 1. Figure 1 shows the comparison of our method to TAB [2] and TAB using Image Feature Matching SURF [3]. From Figure 1, it can be seen that our method improved both ASR and SUR compared to TAB [2] and the improved TAB [3]. That means that the correct images selected by our ranking system is superior to others in hiding the pass-objects without obstructing user's recognition. It is also shown through the experiment that in a three-round authentication, three-keyword password is stronger because no keyword is repeated. Still, users may be displeased with more than three keywords due to the burden of remembering.

5. CONCLUSIONS

In this paper, we have proposed an image-selection based graphical password using a new image ranking method to filter which image should be used to show to user when authenticating. An appropriate image has to contain objects that associate with user's register pass-terms, and at the same time contains other objects as decoys to distract the outside observer from paying attention to any particular place in the image. The new method, OBIR, involves in calculation of the "appropriateness" of objects in image, the relevance between image and the pass-terms, and the noise of decoy-objects in image, all of which add up to a value called score, based on which the ranking is established with scores' descending order. Our experiment shows that both Authentication Success Ratio and Spoofing Unsuccess Ratio are improved by our method.

Further work includes consideration of using other types of object meta-data for detecting more appropriate images, further strengthening the system's tolerance towards shoulder-surfing by combining with other scheme such as the way of selecting pass-image in Marasim [1], as well as conducting more detailed experiments.

6. ACKNOWLEDGMENT

This work is partially supported by KAKENHI #24300039.

7. REFERENCES

[1] R. A. Khot, K. Srinathan, and P. Kumaraguru. Marasim: a novel jigsaw based authentication scheme using tagging. In CHI 2011, pages 2605–2614, 2011.

[2] S. Sakaguchi, H.-H. Huang, and K. Kawagoe. Tag association based graphical password with image search web services. In EDB'11, pages 152–163, 2011.

[3] K. Kawagoe, S. Sakaguchi, Y. Sakon, and H.-H. Huang. Tag association based graphical password using image feature matching. In DASFAA'12 - Part II, pages 282–286, 2012.

[4] R. Biddle, S. Chiasson, and P. Van Oorschot. Graphical passwords: Learning from the first twelve years. ACM Comput. Surv., 44(4):19:1–19:41, 2012.

[5] S. Chiasson, A. Forget, E. Stobert, P. C. van Oorschot, and R. Biddle. Multiple password interference in text passwords and click-based graphical passwords. In ACM, CCS '09, pages 500–511, 2009.

[6] P. Dunphy and P. Olivier. On automated image choice for secure and usable graphical passwords. In ACSAC 2012, pages 99–108. ACM, 2012.

[7] S. Wiedenbeck, J. Waters, L. Sobrado, and J.-C. Birget. Design and evaluation of a shoulder-surfing resistant graphical password scheme. In AVI '06, pages 177–184, 2006.

[8] H. Mohammad, I. Norafida, and P. Rezvan. Multi touch graphical password: Usability features. Asian Journal of Applied Sciences, 5: 20-32., 2012.

[9] X. Suo, Y. Zhu, and G. S. Owen. Graphical passwords: A survey. In ACSAC 2005, pages 463–472, 2005.

[10] M. Everingham, L. Van Gool, C. K. I. Williams, J. Winn, and A. Zisserman. The PASCAL Visual Object Classes Challenge 2012 Results. http://www.pascal-network.org/challenges/VOC/voc2012/workshop/index.html, 2012.

POSTER: A Semantic-aware Approach to Reasoning about Network Traffic Relations*

Hao Zhang, Danfeng (Daphne) Yao, and Naren Ramakrishnan
Department of Computer Science, Virginia Tech
Blacksburg, VA, USA
{haozhang, danfeng, naren}@cs.vt.edu

ABSTRACT

This paper addresses the problem of reasoning about relations between network packets on a host or in a network. Our analysis approach is to discover the causal relations among network packets, and use the relational structure of network events to identify anomalous activities that cannot be attributed to a legitimate cause. The key insight that motivates our traffic-analysis approach is that higher-order information such as the underlying relations of events is useful for human experts' cognition and decision making. We design a new *pairing* method that produces special pairwise features, so that the discovery problem can be efficiently solved with existing binary classification methods. Preliminary experiments involving real world HTTP and DNS traffic show promising evidence of the accuracy of inferring the network traffic relations using our semantic-aware approach.

Categories and Subject Descriptors

C.2.0 [**General**]: Security and protection

Keywords

Network Security, Anomaly Detection, Classification

1. INTRODUCTION

This paper addresses the issue of reasoning about network traffic relations. We aim to develop a traffic monitoring tool that helps identify anomalous network traffic events, which may be caused by misconfigured hosts, infected hosts, or external attackers. The key insight that motivates our approach is that higher-level information such as the underlying relations or semantics of events is useful for human experts' cognition, reasoning, and decision making in cyber security [3]. Thus, analyzing relations among network events may provide important insights for identifying network anomalies. We focus on discovering the causal relations of network packets in this work.

*This work has been supported in part by NSF grants CAREER CNS-0953638 and CCF-0937133.

CCS'13, November 4–8, 2013, Berlin, Germany.
ACM 978-1-4503-2477-9/13/11.
http://dx.doi.org/10.1145/2508859.2512504.

Most network analysis methods for filtering individual packets or aggregation statistics fail to fulfill this goal of event-relation discovery, with some exceptions. The most advanced solutions today aim to identify correlating traffic events or attributes (e.g., IP addresses). Gu *et al.* demonstrated the effectiveness of correlation analysis across multiple hosts of a network in detecting similarly infected bots [4]. King *et al.* constructed directed graphs from logs to show network connections for dissecting attack sequences [6]. These solutions mainly leverage domain knowledge of networked systems (e.g., protocol or system specifications) or attack behaviors (e.g., botnet command and control).

We present a new learning-based method and demonstrate with experiments that discovering fine-grained causality in network traffic is feasible. The causality of network packets provide contextual interpretations to the behaviors of systems and networks, illustrating why sequences of events occur and how they relate to each other. Because of the transitivity, the problem of discovering the packet dependencies among a set of events may be transformed into discovering the dependency of pairs of events, which we defined as *pairwise* relation.

General techniques for learning and recognizing directional causal relations of network traffic events do not exist. Most of the existing learning-based security studies are on binary classification problems, where an unknown instance (e.g., email, code, or network packet) needs to be classified into two classes – legitimate or suspicious. Our relation discovery work also differs from existing service dependency analysis (e.g., [1, 7]), because of *i)* our finer granularity (request vs flow) and *ii)* different relation semantics.

2. THE PROPOSED APPROACH

The goal of our analysis is to infer the causality of the packets and infer the anomalies by enforcing specific security policy. The main operations in our analysis are DATA COLLECTION, PAIRING, DATA LABELING, TRAINING, CLASSIFICATION, and SECURITY POLICY ENFORCEMENT. The DATA LABELING, TRAINING, and CLASSIFICATION operations are standard for machine learning based methods.

We introduce a new feature extraction method referred to as PAIRING. This operation converts individual network events into event pairs with comparable pairwise attributes, so that conventional binary classification techniques can then be applied to discover the relations between packets. We also present the use of root-trigger policy in security policy enforcement to report anomalies.

A overview of our approach follows.

- Data Collection is intended to record and store the events to be analyzed. Each event e has one or more attributes $(A_1, \ldots, A_m)$ describing its properties.
- Pairing is used to extract pairwise comparison results of events' attributes. Its inputs are two events $e = (A_1, \ldots, A_m)$ and $e' = (A'_1, \ldots, A'_m)$. The output is the event pair (e, e') with m pairwise attribute values $(B_1, \ldots, B_m)$, where a pairwise attribute $B_i (i \in [1, m])$ represents the comparison result of attributes A_i and A'_i. That is, $B_i = f_i(A_i, A'_i)$, where $f_i()$ is a comparison function (e.g., `isEqual`, `isGreaterThan`, `isWithinThreshold`, `isSubstring`, etc.) for the type of the i-th attribute in the events.
- Data Labeling is the operation that produces the correct causal relations for the event pairs in a small training dataset. We choose a binary label (1 or 0) to indicate the existence or non-existence of any causal relation in an event pair, e.g., $< (e, e'), 1 >$ represents that event e triggers e'.
- Training is the operation that produces a machine learning model with labelled training data. We adopt two feature selection methods (*Information Gain* and *Gain Ratio*) to find an optimal set that could improve the effectiveness of machine learning classifiers.
- Classification is the operation to use the trained machine learning model to predict causal relations on new event pairs $\{P_{ij} = (e_i, e_j)\}$. We build and compare three common supervised machine learning classifiers – Naive Bayes, a Bayesian network, and a support vector machine (SVM) [2].
- Security Policy Enforcement is the operation intended to apply security policies to the classification results and report anomalous events.

2.1 Pairing Operation

The Pairing operation extracts features of event pairs. An event attribute may be of the numeric, nominal, string, or composite type. Various comparison functions are chosen based on the attribute types.

- Numeric attributes can be compared by computing their difference, e.g., the interval `TimeDiff` between the timestamps of two network events, i.e. $B_i = A_i - A'_i$.
- A nominal attribute (e.g., file type, protocol type) categorizes the property of an event. Comparing nominal attributes usually involves string comparison, e.g., substring or equality tests.
- For the string type of attributes, we compute the similarity of the attribute values as the pairing attribute value. That is, $B_i = f_s(A_i, A'_i)$, where function f_s is a similarity measure, e.g., normalized edit distance. Taking HTTP packets as an example, we can compute a pairwise attribute `HostSim` by measuring the similarities between two host fields in the HTTP headers.
- A composite attribute contains multiple values, e.g., a destination address is composed of four octets for the IP address and an integer for the port. The comparison of two composite values is made by comparing the sub-attribute values separately. Therefore, we define a bitmap to store the comparison between the source and destination IPs. Each bit refers to the difference between one octet of two IPs or between two ports.

To reduce the complexity of the analysis, a heuristic is to pair up events whose timestamps are close. In our study, only the events whose timestamps differ by less than a certain threshold τ are compared. The purpose is to avoid making meaningless pairs for packets whose time difference is greater than τ.

2.2 Security Policy Enforcement

We use *root-trigger policy* as an example to explain the security policy enforcement. This policy is to determine whether the activity is legitimate or not based on the legitimacy of the initial cause of the event, i.e., the root trigger of the event. According to this definition, anomalous events are the events that do not have a valid root trigger. These events may be due to malware activities or host/server misconfiguration. A specific root-trigger security definition is based on user intention [8], where a valid root trigger should be related to a user activity (e.g., a function call to retrieve user inputs, mouse clicks, or keyboard inputs). In what follows, we refer to the events that do not have any valid root triggers as *vagabond* events.

Algorithm 1 Find-root Algorithm.

Input: $set = \{(e_i \rightarrow e_j)\}$ and an event e_k.
Output: a set $roots$, where each in $roots$ is a root of e_k.

define a set $roots$ to store the results
define a queue Q and enqueue e_k onto Q
while $Q \neq \emptyset$ **do**
  event $n \leftarrow$ dequeue Q
  let a set $ps \leftarrow$ all of n's parents
  for each event $e \in ps$ **do**
    if e is of type root **then**
      $roots = roots + \{e\}$
    else if $e \notin Q$ **then**
      enqueue e onto Q
    end if
  end for
end while
return roots

Algorithm 1 finds all the roots of an event e_k, given all the pairwise causal relations. The input of the algorithm is a set of all the pairwise relations $\{(e_i \rightarrow e_j)\}$ and an event e_k. The output is a set containing all the roots of e_k. In order to compute the transitive reduction of a directed graph, we use a queue Q to perform breadth-first traversal.

The root-trigger security policy is suitable for identifying network activities that are not triggered by users, including but not limited to:

- Spyware exfiltrating sensitive information through outbound network traffic from the monitored host,
- Bots' command-and-control traffic, and attack activities (e.g., spam or DoS traffic) originated from the monitored host,
- Websites collecting and reporting user data.

One future direction is to systematically investigate the design and use of complex policies for network assurance.

3. PRELIMINARY EVALUATION

We use the Weka library [5] and implement the prototype in Java. The data we evaluate are summarized in Table 1 (τ is the threshold for the maximal time interval of a pair of events). Dataset I is composed of the user's events and outbound HTTP traffic that are sampled from a 20-participant user study. Each participant was asked to actively surf the web for 30 minutes on a laptop equipped with our data collection program. We set the threshold as 30 seconds, as 97.2% of the HTTP requests fall within that interval range. Dataset II is obtained by using `tcpdump` to continuously collect outbound DNS queries and HTTP packets from a gradate student's workstation for 19 days. We collected types `A` and `AAAA` DNS queries and the packets containing `GET`, `HEAD`, or `POST` HTTP information. Due to the wide prevalence of DNS prefetching, we choose a relaxed threshold of 15 seconds, which covers 97.8% of the event pairs.

Data	Type	τ (s)	# of Pairs	Size (MB)
I	HTTP	30	572,725	38.61
II	DNS & HTTP	15	1,833,306	113.56

Table 1: An overview of datasets in the experiments.

Data labeling. Our rules for HTTP traffic are similar to what are used in [8]. We manually labeled 12% of HTTP requests in the training datasets, which also indicates the inadequacy of the existing rule-based approach. Rules for labeling mixed DNS and HTTP traffic involve analyzing the query of the DNS packet, type of DNS query(e.g., `A` or `AAAA`), host of the HTTP request, and the protocol version of destination IP address in HTTP header.

Classification. 10-fold cross-validation experiments demonstrate that the accuracy of both training sets is greater than 99%. Due to the sparsity of relations in network traffic, we define a cost matrix $C = \begin{bmatrix} 0, 1 \\ 10, 0 \end{bmatrix}$; it penalizes classifying false negatives with 10 and classifying false positives with 1. The binary classification accuracy for pairwise causal relations is consistently high for the Bayesian network and SVM methods (see Table 2). The naive Bayes classifier yields lower average accuracy, indicating that the conditional independence assumptions made by this classifier might be strong.

Data	# of pairs		Naive Bayes	Bayesian Network	SVM
	Training	Test			
I	309,921	262,804	99.77%	99.85%	99.92%
II	916,650	916,656	98.98%	100%	100%

Table 2: Pairwise classification accuracy results of train-n-test experiments. Sizes of training and test data are shown.

Security Policy Enforcement (Correctness of root triggers). Running the *find-root* procedure in Algorithm 1 on the pairwise classification results, we identify the root triggers of all events and compare them to the ground truth values.

By enforcing the root-trigger policy, the evaluation shows that for 99.0% of events, the roots are correct with respect to the ground truth. The results are the same for all three classifiers. Among the 99.0% events, we found 22 *vagabond* events, which belong to either malicious behavior (e.g., request to altfarm.mediaplex.com) or misconfiguration on the server (e.g., some requests to googleapi or twitter). There are 1.0% events whose root triggers are not correctly found. Manual investigation reveals that the wrong root triggers are all false positives, which are caused either by *i)* null or truncated attributes (e.g., referrer, hostname) due to the transmission issues, or *ii)* timestamps out of the specified threshold. The latter can be avoided by increasing the threshold in the pairing operation, which, however, may increase the computation overhead by generating unnecessary pairs.

Summary. The correctness of classifying the causal relation among network packets shows the feasibility and effectiveness of our analysis approach. The root-trigger security analysis allows us to identify network events linked to malicious hosts or due to misconfiguration of web servers. The classification performance is efficient in general and adequate for fast traffic analysis.

4. CONCLUSIONS AND FUTURE WORK

Our learning-based technique to discover causal relations shows promising application to analyzing host-based outbound HTTP and mixed HTTP and DNS traffic data. Our experiments identified several types of network anomalies caused by traffic to malicious servers or misconfigured servers.

Future work will proceed along three directions. First, we plan to explore the incorporation of more complex security policies, which could help detect more types of threats. Second, we plan to explore the inference of more complex boolean relationships across events [9] than simple pairwise relations (e.g., at least two of three precursors must be present for a given event). Finally, we intend to encapsulate the entire framework, from pairwise relation construction, to classification, in a machine learning framework so that all necessary parameters can be jointly optimized. Such an approach can also help avoid making arbitrary thresholding decisions and better explore the joint interplay between design decisions.

5. REFERENCES

[1] X. Chen, M. Zhang, Z. M. Mao, and P. Bahl. Automating network application dependency discovery: Experiences, limitations, and new solutions. In *Proceedings of OSDI*, pages 117–130, 2008.

[2] C. Cortes and V. Vapnik. Support-vector networks. *Machine learning*, 20(3):273–297, 1995.

[3] T. Green, W. Ribarsky, and B. Fisher. Visual analytics for complex concepts using a human cognition model. In *Proc. IEEE VAST*, pages 91 – 98, October 2008.

[4] G. Gu, R. Perdisci, J. Zhang, and W. Lee. BotMiner: Clustering analysis of network traffic for protocol- and structure-independent botnet detection. In *Proceedings of the 17th USENIX Security Symposium*, 2008.

[5] M. Hall, E. Frank, G. Holmes, B. Pfahringer, P. Reutemann, and I. H. Witten. The weka data mining software: an update. *ACM SIGKDD Explorations Newsletter*, 11(1):10–18, 2009.

[6] S. T. King, Z. M. Mao, D. G. Lucchetti, and P. M. Chen. Enriching intrusion alerts through multi-host causality. In *Proceedings of Network and Distributed System Security (NDSS)*, 2005.

[7] A. Natarajan, P. Ning, Y. Liu, S. Jajodia, and S. E. Hutchinson. NSDMiner: Automated discovery of network service dependencies. In *INFOCOM*, pages 2507–2515, 2012.

[8] H. Zhang, W. Banick, D. Yao, and N. Ramakrishnan. User intention-based traffic dependence analysis for anomaly detection. In *Security and Privacy Workshops (SPW), 2012 IEEE Symposium on*, pages 104–112. IEEE, 2012.

[9] L. Zhao, M. J. Zaki, and N. Ramakrishnan. Blosom: a framework for mining arbitrary boolean expressions. In *Proc. KDD'06*. ACM, 2006.

POSTER: Detecting Malware through Temporal Function-Based Features

Eitan Menahem, Asaf Shabtai, Adi Lavher
Information System Engineering Department,
Ben-Gurion University of the Negev
Be'er Sheva, 84105, Israel
{eitanme, shabtaia, adilev}@post.bgu.ac.il

ABSTRACT

In order to evade detection by anti-virus software, malware writers use techniques, such as polymorphism, metamorphism and code re-writing. The result is that such malware contain a much larger fraction of "new" code, compared to benign programs, which tend to maximize code reuse. In this research we study this interesting property and show that by performing "archaeological" analysis of functions residing within binary files (i.e., estimating the functions' creation date), a new set of informative features can be derived. We show that these features provide a good indication for the existence of malicious code within binary files. Preliminary experiments of the proposed temporal function-based features with a set of over 12,000 files indicates that the proposed set of features can be useful for the detection of malicious files (accuracy of over 90% and AUC of 0.96).

Categories and Subject Descriptors

C.2.0 [**Computer-Communication Networks**]: security and protection; H.2.8 [**Information Systems**]: Database Applications - data mining

Keywords

Malware, Static analysis, Machine learning

1. INTRODUCTION

Anti-virus vendors are facing huge quantities (thousands) of suspicious files every day [1]. These files are collected from various sources including dedicated honeypots, third party providers and files reported by customers either automatically or explicitly. Such a large amount of files makes the efficient and effective inspection of files particularly important and challenging. Analysis techniques for detecting malware have been proposed. Basically static and dynamic analysis is distinguished. In dynamic analysis (also known as behavioral analysis), the detection consists of information that is collected from the operating system at runtime (i.e., during the execution of the program), such as system calls, network access and files and memory modifications [2]. This approach suffers from several limitations. First, it is difficult to setup the appropriate conditions in which the malicious payload of the program will be activated (such as the vulnerable application that the malware exploits). Second, it is not clear what is the required period of time needed to observe the appearance of the malicious activity for each malware. Third, many malicious programs nowadays apply anti-forensic and anti-debugging methods, thus limiting the ability to analyze them during runtime. Fourth, masquerading techniques, such as polymorphism and metamorphism, may be applied on the malware's system-calls to conceal malicious behavioral signatures.

In static analysis, information about the program or its expected behavior consists of explicit and implicit observations in its binary/source code. The main advantage of static analysis is that it is able to process a file without actually executing it and thereby providing rapid classification [7]. Up until recently, static analysis solutions were primarily implemented using the signature-based method, which relies on the identification of unique strings in the binary code [1]. While being very precise, signature-based methods are useless against unknown malicious code [3]. Thus, generalization of the detection methods was crucial in order to detect new versions and types of malware, before their execution.

Modern static analysis techniques automate and extend the idea of heuristic-based methods. In these methods the binary code of a file is represented, for example, using byte sequence (i.e., byte n-grams) or using OpCode sequences (i.e., OpCode n-grams), and classifiers are used to learn patterns in the code in order to classify unknown files as malicious or benign [1],[5],[4]. Recent studies have shown that

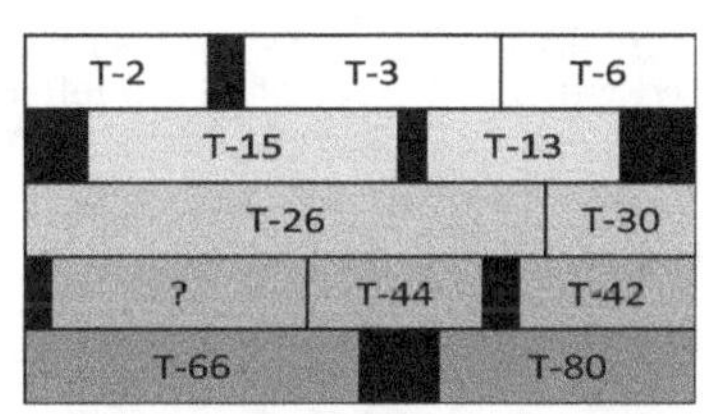

Figure 1: Illustrating the proposed temporal function-based features. Each section represents a function, detected within the file's code (dark black sections indicate unlabeled sections). The age of each function is relative to the release date of the file - T.

CCS'13, November 4–8, 2013, Berlin, Germany.
ACM 978-1-4503-2477-9/13/11.
http://dx.doi.org/10.1145/2508859.2512505.

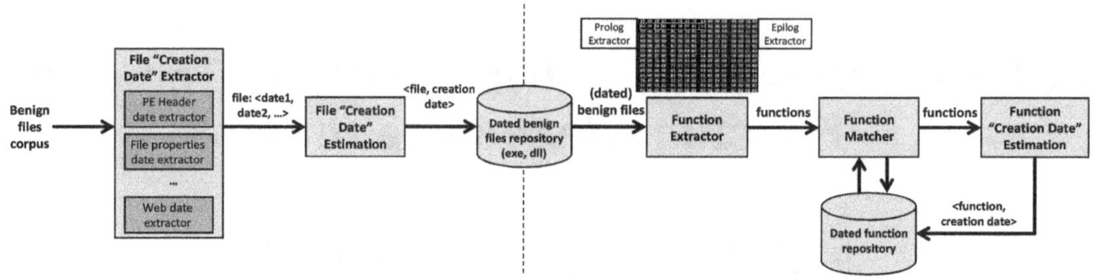

Figure 2: The process of creating the dated function repository.

by using these types of features for representing binary files, classifiers can be trained with very accurate classification results.

To avoid being detected by signature-based techniques and heuristic methods, sophisticated malware programmers conceal suspicious (unique) byte n-grams and OpCode sequences by rewriting entire code segments, or by using polymorphism and metamorphism techniques [8]. While these techniques render the detection techniques based on byte n-gram and OpCode sequences useless, they result in binary programs that contain bulks of "new" functions, never previously seen in other executable files.

In this research we propose a novel method for detecting malware that employ the above mentioned evasion techniques. Our main assumption is that such techniques distort the malware's temporal profile, making it distinct from benign programs (in other words, attackers have coding styles, in terms of code reuse, that significantly differ from legitimate code writers). To derive a temporal profile, our method performs "archeological" analysis of the tested binary file, i.e., estimating the creation date of the functions residing within the file's code. Using this information, a series of temporal features, representing the file's temporal profile, are then extracted. These features can be exploited for various analysis tasks, including for detecting malware. Since usually in machine learning applications the learning algorithm can benefit from a larger set of features, and especially from features that provide different views on the instances (i.e., executable files), combining the proposed temporal features (i.e., new view) together with byte/OpCode n-grams features can be very effective for improving the performance of malware detection applications.

Fig. 1 illustrates the proposed temporal function-based features. Each section represents a function detected within the file's code (note that dark black sections indicate unlabeled sections). The age of each function is relative to the release date of the file - T. For example, the youngest function detected within the file is the top left-most function with age T-2. It also can be seen that 16.7% of the functions is between the age 12 and 24 months. One function could not be set with a creation date (i.e., undated function).

2. THE PROPOSED METHOD

The proposed classification method is based on temporal features that are computed for functions detected within executable files. These features are computed based on the estimated "age of functions" (i.e., coding time of function). The proposed method consists of two main phases: (1) creating a repository of dated functions; and (2) extracting features for classification using the dated functions repository.

2.1 Creation of Dated Functions Repository

In this phase a repository of common functions is created, and each function is assigned with a creation date. This process is presented in Fig. 2. First, given a corpus of benign executable files, the system sets the creation date of each file. This is done by extracting relevant dates for each file from different sources (e.g., the release date of the file as was publish in Web, or the compilation date that was extracted from the file's Portable Executable (PE) header).

Next, from each file, a collection of functions is extracted. The functions extraction procedure (presented in [5] [6]) is performed by sequentially scanning the file using a sliding window. Each window is classified by a machine learning model (C4.5 decision tree), trained to detect prologues and epilogues patterns of functions, without disassemble process (i.e., by processing the binary file). Once a function prologue is detected, the algorithm scans for the last function epilogue prior to a following prologue. When a pair of markers are found (prologue and epilogue), the new function's boundaries are stored as a 'function' object.

Finally, we detect similar functions and set the creation date of each function. We choose the Levenshtein distance as the distance function between the byte-sequence of two functions. Each function is compared to all other extracted functions of the same length. We count the number of different bytes between the two bytes sequences and normalize it by the length. If the result was less than a predefined threshold (we set this threshold to 15%), we determine that the compared functions are identical. The last step is setting the creation date the functions. We set the creation date of each function based on the dates of the files from where it was extracted from - we set the date of the âAIJoldestâAI file as the function date, after removing outliers. The result of this phase is a repository of dated functions.

2.2 Feature Extraction

We extract the following 13 features using the dated function repository: percentage of dated/undated functions (functions extracted from a given file and were detected/not detected in the function repository), the age in years of the "oldest"/"youngest" function in the file, functions median and average age in years, percentage of functions from last 2, 5 and 10 years, and the percentage of functions older than 10, 15 and 20 years.

In order to induce a classifier based on the defined features, we use two sets of files - benign (different from the files used in the previous phase of creating the dated functions

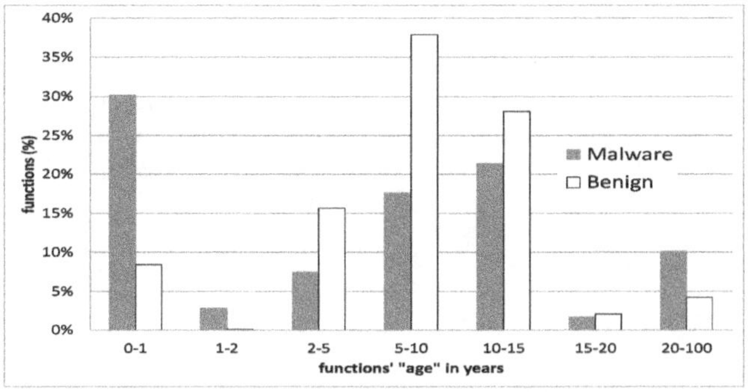

Figure 3: Histograms of functions' estimated age.

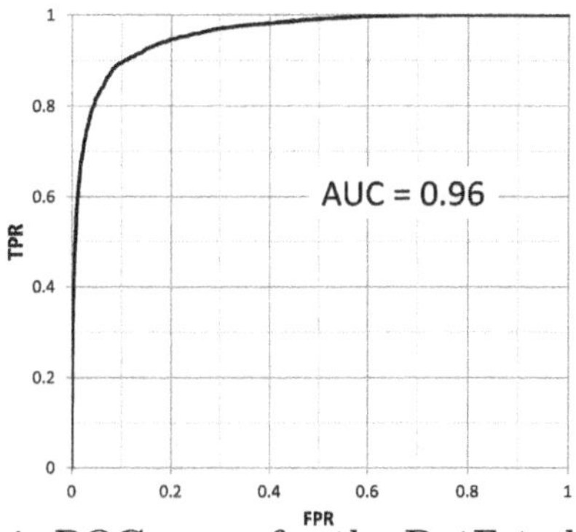

Figure 4: ROC curve for the RotFst classifier.

repository, to avoid over-fitting) and malware. For each file we first extract its functions using the same method used for creating the dated functions repository. To determine the functions' origin date, each extracted function is compared with functions of the same length in the "dated functions repository" (using Levenshtein distance). If a match function is found, the tested function is assigned with the origin date of the matching function. Finally, given the extracted functions and their corresponding creation dates, we compute the file's temporal function-based features vector, which comprises the file's temporal profile.

3. EXPERIMENTS AND RESULTS

For the experiments we used the following file sets. The first set contains 850 benign executable files, downloaded using a web crawler from various web-sites (such as, filehippo.com and oldapps.com), which indicated the files' original date. Since most of the downloaded files were compressed or packed, we used the Universal Extractor[1] tool for decompressing the packed files. We then filtered in the relevant files only (i.e., exe and dll). These files were used to generate the dated functions repository. At the end of this process, the dated functions repository contained a total of 1,999,209 different (dated) functions. To train and evaluate the malware detection classifier we used 6,756 benign and 6,169 malware files. The benign files were collected from the "'Program files"' and "'System32"' directories of several computers and were verified to be benign using the McAfee anti-virus. The malware files were taken from the VX-heavens collection.

For each file in the repository we extracted the temporal function- based features and conducted a 10-fold cross validation experiment. Our first observation is that on average, the dated functions percentage in benign files was 35.8% and only 11.4% in malicious files. In addition, Fig. 3 depicts the proportion of functions in benign and malicious files within different age clusters. It can be seen that the percentage of functions from last year is 8.4% for benign files compared to 30.1% in malicious files. A notable difference can also be observed for functions that are from the last 2 year and 5 years. The best classification results were obtained when using a Rotation Forest (RotFst) classifier (Random Forest as the base classifier), with an average accuracy of 90% and an area under the ROC curve of 0.96 (see Fig. 4).

[1]Universal Extractor decompressing tool: http://legroom.net/software/uniextract

4. CONCLUSION AND FUTURE WORK

In this paper we propose a novel method for detecting malware, based on the file's temporal profile (time-based features). For future work we are planning to focus on the evaluation of the proposed method on a larger file set and on combining these temporal-based features with other types of features such as byte or OpCode n-grams.

5. REFERENCES

[1] GRIFFIN, K., SCHNEIDER, S., HU, X., AND CHIUEH, T.-C. Automatic generation of string signatures for malware detection. In *Recent Advances in Intrusion Detection* (2009), Springer, pp. 101–120.

[2] JACOB, G., DEBAR, H., AND FILIOL, E. Behavioral detection of malware: from a survey towards an established taxonomy. *Journal in computer Virology 4*, 3 (2008), 251–266.

[3] MOSER, A., KRUEGEL, C., AND KIRDA, E. Limits of static analysis for malware detection. In *Computer Security Applications Conference, 2007. ACSAC 2007. Twenty-Third Annual* (2007), IEEE, pp. 421–430.

[4] MOSKOVITCH, R., FEHER, C., TZACHAR, N., BERGER, E., GITELMAN, M., DOLEV, S., AND ELOVICI, Y. Unknown malcode detection using opcode representation. In *Intelligence and Security Informatics*. Springer, 2008, pp. 204–215.

[5] POTASHNIK, D., FLEDEL, Y., MOSKOVITCH, R., ELOVICI, Y., ET AL. Monitoring, analysis, and filtering system for purifying network traffic of known and unknown malicious content. *Security and Communication Networks 4*, 8 (2011), 947–965.

[6] SHABTAI, A., MENAHEM, E., AND ELOVICI, Y. F-sign: Automatic, function-based signature generation for malware. *Systems, Man, and Cybernetics, Part C: Applications and Reviews, IEEE Transactions on 41*, 4 (2011), 494–508.

[7] SHABTAI, A., MOSKOVITCH, R., ELOVICI, Y., AND GLEZER, C. Detection of malicious code by applying machine learning classifiers on static features: A state-of-the-art survey. *Information Security Technical Report 14*, 1 (2009), 16–29.

[8] YIN, H., SONG, D., EGELE, M., KRUEGEL, C., AND KIRDA, E. Panorama: capturing system-wide information flow for malware detection and analysis. In *Proceedings of the 14th ACM conference on Computer and communications security* (2007), ACM, pp. 116–127.

POSTER: Event-based Isolation of Critical Data in the Cloud

Sebastian Biedermann

Stefan Katzenbeisser

Security Engineering Group
Department of Computer Science
Technische Universität Darmstadt
{biedermann, katzenbeisser}@seceng.informatik.tu-darmstadt.de

ABSTRACT

In this poster, we present TrustDraw, a transparent security extension for the cloud which combines Virtual Machine Introspection (VMI) and Trusted Computing (TC). TrustDraw provides secure storage of critical data like keys or passwords and allows to temporarily insert this data into a running virtual machine (VM) if required. TrustDraw improves security by allowing access to the critical data only if certain previously defined conditions are met. This way, the stealing of critical data by bypassing access permissions based on successfully executed attacks can be mitigated. TrustDraw runs isolated and transparent. No software modifications are required on a target VM. We evaluated an implementation of TrustDraw in a realistic scenario in which it only caused an acceptable run-time delay.

Categories and Subject Descriptors

C.2.0 [**Computer-communication networks**]: General—*Security and protection*

General Terms

Security

Keywords

Virtual Machine Introspection; Cloud Security

1. INTRODUCTION

The cloud computing paradigm can simplify work-flows and offer cost-effective solutions. Nevertheless cloud computing also creates a new demand for privacy and security mechanisms in order to protect the outsourced critical and sensitive data. Stolen critical data like keys used for authentication or passwords, can be used to cause massive financial damage or to execute other large-scaled or more sophisticated attacks. For example security incidents like the Stuxnet [3] malware used digital certificates stolen from hardware manufacturers to insert correctly signed driver modules to the infected operating system. The Flame [10] malware even used digital certificates issued by Microsoft. Obviously, small critical data which can be located in a virtual machine (VM) can be a worthwhile target for cyber attacks.

In this work, we focus on securing critical data located in VMs which run in a cloud that offers Infrastructure-as-a-Service (IaaS) to arbitrary cloud users. Our approach is based on a fact which greatly helps to develop mechanisms that decrease the probability of critical data being stolen: Critical data is in the majority of cases only required for small periods of time, while most of the time it is stored unused in the memory, ready for access. A running process uses the critical data depending on certain specific events like a triggered authentication procedure which finally requires the critical data. Unfortunately, successfully executed attacks can bypass permission mechanisms of the operating systems and easily read critical data from memory.

As a solution to this problem, we propose TrustDraw, which is a security service for the cloud that securely stores identified critical data in a co-resident trusted VM and only temporarily inserts the critical data as long as it is required – and not longer. In particular, the critical data is only inserted into the VM's memory if certain previously defined integrity conditions of the cloud user's VM could be met. This way, TrustDraw greatly minimizes the probability of critical data being stolen by an attacker who exploits weaknesses in the VM in order to bypass the permission mechanisms. TrustDraw runs isolated and transparent, unbeknownst from the cloud user's VM.

The presented work is based on virtualization technologies and Virtual Machine Introspection (VMI). VMI is a technique to monitor a VM transparently from an isolated location on the same hardware component by directly reading the target VM's memory pages during its runtime [9]. VMI is very useful for security purposes like intrusion detection (e.g. see [6],[4]). Security tools can run on an isolated VM while they still can perform active monitoring on other VMs [5].

Recently, VMI techniques focus not only on transparent monitoring from an isolated location, but also on writing to specific memory locations of the target monitored VM. This way, entire procedures can be implanted and their execution can be enforced [7] or work-flows of the target VM can be profitably steered. This can be used for incident response or, like in our scenario, to isolate critical data.

CCS'13, November 4–8, 2013, Berlin, Germany.
Copyright 2013 ACM ACM 978-1-4503-2477-9/13/11.
http://dx.doi.org/10.1145/2508859.2512506.

2. ARCHITECTURE

TrustDraw is implemented for the Xen hypervisor [1] and runs on Linux in the administrative VM ("dom0"). TrustDraw can be used to isolate critical data of a user's VM ("domU") which co-residently runs on the same hardware component. TrustDraw requires the process name which uses the critical data (and runs on the user's VM) and a unique fingerprint of the critical data in order to find its exact location. Furthermore, TrustDraw requires the definition of an event which triggers the insertion of the critical data into the running VM (for example a new incoming connection) and a set of rules which have to be verified before the insertion is allowed. TrustDraw operates by performing seven sequential steps (Figure 1), where the first step is an initial step and is executed only once.

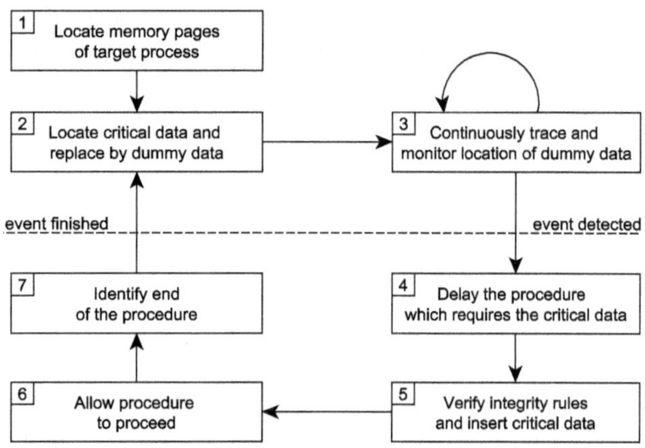

Figure 1: Work-flow of TrustDraw's proposed architecture running in seven sequential steps.

In the *first* step, TrustDraw locates the currently used memory pages of the target process which runs in the user's VM. TrustDraw searches for the exact location of critical data within these memory pages in the *second* step. If the exact location of the critical data could be identified, the data is replaced by dummy data having the same characteristics and the same size. The original critical data is isolated from the user's VM and securely stored in the trusted VM on which TrustDraw runs. Since the memory pages of the target process are dynamically allocated and freed, the location of the dummy data may move during the continuous execution of the process. Thus, in the *third* step, TrustDraw continuously monitors the exact position of the inserted dummy data. Once a location change could be identified, a new search for the dummy data is immediately started. This way, TrustDraw continuously maintains the location of the dummy data in the user VM's memory. If an event is detected which is triggered by a procedure that requires the isolated critical data, step *four* delays the requesting procedure. TrustDraw verifies the integrity of the user's VM by checking the deployed rules before TrustDraw temporarily replaces the dummy data by the original critical data in step *five*. In step *six*, the procedure that requires the critical data is allowed to continue. Once the procedure is finished in step *seven*, the critical data is again replaced by dummy data and the cycle can start again waiting for the next requesting event.

TrustDraw continuously and transparently obtains information about the user's VM from four different points shown in Figure 2. TrustDraw can gather information about running processes or loaded modules on the VM's operating system by directly accessing the memory space of the running VM (1). TrustDraw can examine the VM's raw storage by extracting certain meta data of target stored files using forensic techniques (2). Furthermore, TrustDraw can retrieve information about the VM's network traffic from the virtualized bridge (3) and information about used memory and CPU performance directly from the hypervisor (4).

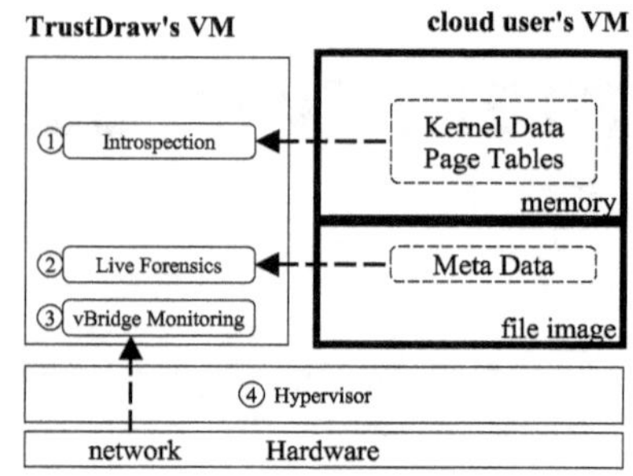

Figure 2: Different points which TrustDraw uses for transparent information gathering.

Verification of the user's VM before the original critical data is inserted is performed by checking the validity of multiple previously defined rules. In order to specify rules, we defined atomic Boolean events which can be gathered from the user's VM by TrustDraw. Some examples can be seen in Table 1. For example, verification of a process X (procVer(X)) is executed by computing a hash over the process's executable in the memory for comparison (true|false).

event	return value [true|false]	source
proc(X)	process X is running	Introspection
procVer(X)	process X is verified (hash)	Introspection
mod(X)	module X is loaded	Introspection
modVer(X)	module X is verified (hash)	Introspection
modified(F)	file F was modified	Live Forensics
accessed(F)	file F was accessed	Live Forensics
comIn(P)	new connection to port P	vBridge
comOut(P)	new connection from port P	vBridge

Table 1: Example Boolean events gathered from a user's VM in order to check the validity of rules before the insertion of the critical data is allowed.

TrustDraw continuously aggregates the retrieved events from the user's VM in time frames F_i having a fixed-size. Multiple time frames F_i ... F_n are used for model checking based on deployed rules. A cloud user can define a set of rules for a VM, for example rules with the help of Linear Temporal Logic (LTL): **G** ¬ (¬ mod('firewall') ∧ procVer('ids') ∧ comIn('80')), which means "There should no be incoming communication to the web server port without the firewall module is loaded and the intrusion detection process's integrity is verified on the user's VM". TrustDraw can perform run-time verification of the rules using the SPIN model checker [8]. Once the integrity of the user's VM was established by checking the validity of the deployed rules, TrustDraw temporarily injects the original critical data.

3. IMPLEMENTATION

Our prototype is implemented and illustrated in Figure 3. The "dom0" VM acts as the Trusted Computing Base (TCB) and uses a vTPM [2] coupled with a hardware TPM. The "dom0" VM runs Linux and TrustDraw which can access and analyze the memory pages of a co-resident user VM ("domU") that runs on the same hardware component in parallel with the help of VMI [9]. The user VM can run

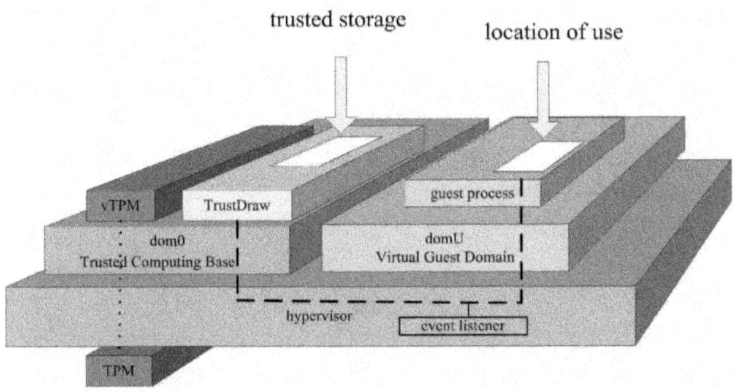

Figure 3: Architecture of TrustDraw running in a trusted VM and isolating the critical data of a process running on a co-resident user VM.

a process which requires critical data under certain circumstances (e.g. a key or a password hash). The trigger can be an event like a new incoming remote connection to the user's VM to a specific port.

We evaluated a scenario in which TrustDraw can be successfully deployed. For this practical evaluation, we used an Intel(R) Core(TM)2 Duo CPU with 3Ghz and 4 GB of memory running the Xen hypervisor [1]. We deployed TrustDraw on the administrative "dom0" that runs Ubuntu Linux 12.04. TrustDraw monitored a user VM with 1024MB memory running in parallel on the same hardware component. This user VM was virtualized in HVM mode ("fully-virtualized") and runs Ubuntu Linux 12.04. Additionally, the user VM run a SSH-server which allows secure remote access based on password authentication. In this scenario, we assumed the Linux password hashes as critical data which are continuously stored in the VM's memory by the Linux Pluggable Authentication Module (PAM). These hashes are required for an authentication procedure, but ending up in the wrong hands, they could allow to retrieve a valid plain-text password based on locally executed brute force attacks.

Table 2 shows results of time measurements of TrustDraw's procedures (100 runs, initial run skipped). Since locating

TrustDraw's procedure	mean	std
locate (original/dummy) password hashes	3.10s	0.22s
replace (original/dummy) password hashes	0.02s	0.01s
gather information for verification	1.20s	0.24s
verify two rules before replacement	0.30s	0.11s

Table 2: Timings of TrustDraw's procedures.

the target hashes and gathering information and verification of deployed rules can run in parallel, an average SSH login procedure using TrustDraw took around 3.2 seconds while a standard SSH login procedure without TrustDraw took around 1.2 seconds in our setup.

4. CONCLUSION

In this work, we presented TrustDraw which secures critical data of a user's VM by isolating it to a trusted VM. Right before critical data is used, TrustDraw temporarily inserts the required original critical data into the exact location of use. TrustDraw only inserts the critical data if certain specific rules could be verified, which prove the integrity of the target VM. Vice versa, once the critical data is not longer required in the VM's memory, TrustDraw immediately isolates the data again and replaces it with dummy data. TrustDraw stores the critical data on a trusted VM until it is again required. Thus, the critical data is only inserted into the VM's memory for a very short period of time as long as it is required. This way, TrustDraw minimizes the probability of critical data being stolen with the help of attacks which bypass permission mechanisms. An evaluation showed that our approach is feasible and TrustDraw can be beneficially deployed since it causes only a small run-time delay in our scenario.

Acknowledgments

The work presented in this paper was performed in the context of the Software-Cluster project SINNODIUM (www.software-cluster.org). It was funded by the German Federal Ministry of Education and Research (BMBF) under grant no. "01C12S01V".

5. REFERENCES

[1] P. Barham, B. Dragovic, K. Fraser, S. Hand, T. L. Harris, A. Ho, R. Neugebauer, I. Pratt, and A. Warfield. Xen and the art of virtualization. In *Symposium on Operating Systems Principles*, pages 164–177, 2003.

[2] S. Berger, R. Cáceres, K. A. Goldman, R. Perez, R. Sailer, and L. van Doorn. vtpm: virtualizing the trusted platform module. In *Proceedings of the 15th conference on USENIX Security Symposium - Volume 15*, USENIX-SS'06, Berkeley, CA, USA, 2006. USENIX Association.

[3] N. Falliere, Murchu, and E. Chien. W32.Stuxnet dossier. Symantec Security Response online report, Feb. 2011.

[4] H. Fang, Y. Zhao, H. Zang, H. Huang, Y. Song, Y. Sun, and Z. Liu. Vmguard: An integrity monitoring system for management virtual machines. In *Parallel and Distributed Systems (ICPADS), 2010 IEEE 16th International Conference on*, pages 67 –74, dec. 2010.

[5] T. Fraser, M. Evenson, and W. Arbaugh. Vici virtual machine introspection for cognitive immunity. In *Computer Security Applications Conference, 2008. ACSAC 2008. Annual*, pages 87 –96, dec. 2008.

[6] T. Garfinkel and M. Rosenblum. A virtual machine introspection based architecture for intrusion detection. In *In Proc. Network and Distributed Systems Security Symposium*, pages 191–206, 2003.

[7] Z. Gu, Z. Deng, D. Xu, and X. Jiang. Process implanting: A new active introspection framework for virtualization. In *Reliable Distributed Systems (SRDS), 2011 30th IEEE Symposium on*, pages 147 –156, oct. 2011.

[8] G. Holzmann. The spin model checker. *IEEE Transactions on Software Engineering*, 1997.

[9] B. D. Payne and W. Lee. Secure and flexible monitoring of virtual machines. In *Annual Computer Security Applications Conference*, pages 385–397, 2007.

[10] sKyWIper Analysis Team. skywiper (a.k.a. flame a.k.a. flamer): A complex malware for targeted attacks, May. 2012.

POSTER: BotFlex: A Community-driven Tool for Botnet Detection

Sheharbano Khattak
Independent Researcher
sheharbano.k@gmail.com

Zaafar Ahmed,
Affan Syed
SysNet, National Univ. of Computer & Emerging Sciences, Pakistan
firstname.lastname@sysnet.org.pk

Syed Ali Khayam
PLUMgrid, Inc.
akhayam@plumgrid.com

Categories and Subject Descriptors

C.2.0 [**Computer-Communication Networks**]: General—*Security and protection*

Keywords

botnet, network security, correlation

1. INTRODUCTION

Existing botnet detection tools suffer from two primary limitations: case specificity and rigidity. Case-specific detection mechanisms leverage instance-specific characteristics of botnets (typically related to C&C). As a result, the scope of detection is narrow and tailored to a sub-class of the entire phenomenon. Similarly, rigidity in design leads to difficulties in (a) accommodating new detection parameters in their decision policies, (b) tuning/configuring their operation, (c) modification of decision policies, and (d) simultaneous implementation of multiple decision policies. In addition to these architectural aspects, flexibility of the tools is further compromised by unavailability of source-code. Currently, no tool exists that can be used to easily implement and test new botnet detection mechanisms.

In this poster we present BotFlex— a community-driven network-based tool for botnet detection, designed to address the shortcomings of existing tools identified above. We also present our first-cut implementation of BotFlex which conceptualizes botnet infection as a complex event detectable via multiple trigger paths. BotFlex employs a custom correlation framework which detects and curbs botnet threats by reasoning about vertical (across time) and horizontal (across multiple entities) events.

Both BotFlex and its correlation framework are released in open-source for community use [2]. We evaluate BotFlex for accuracy over 500 GB of enterprise traffic collected from one of Pakistan's largest ISPs, Nayatel, with ground truth obtained using a one-time sample of Team Cymru's reputation list for the collection duration. By tuning different parameters, BotFlex demonstrates a better detection accuracy with lower false positives than our baseline evaluation tool BotHunter [3]. Despite encouraging preliminary results, we acknowledge that BotFlex is still in its infancy and hope that its built-in design flexibility and extensibility will allow the community to extend it into an effective and actively updated tool.

CCS'13, November 4–8, 2013, Berlin, Germany.
ACM 978-1-4503-2477-9/13/11.
http://dx.doi.org/10.1145/2508859.2512507

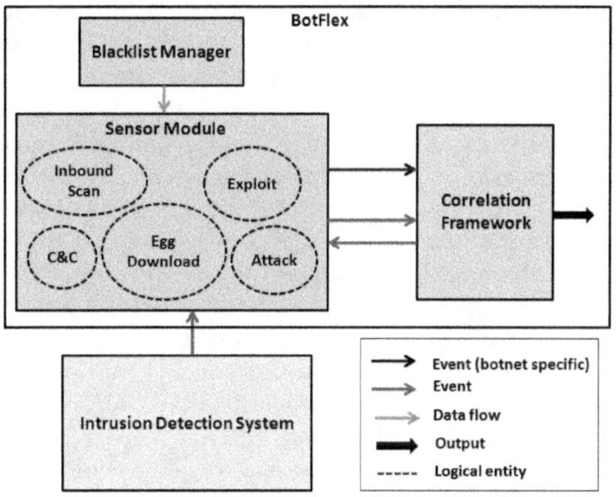

Figure 1: BotFlex architecture.

2. BOTFLEX–ARCHITECTURE AND IMPLEMENTATION

BotFlex is a network-based botnet detection tool, designed to be (i)*domain specific* and *community-driven* with a view to conveniently develop, improve upon, and/or benchmark existing and new botnet detection solutions, (ii)*flexible* in fine tuning its detection thresholds and conditions to cater to varying organizational/deployment accuracy and delay requirements; and *extensible* in easy integration of new detection parameters and decision elements to keep up with the rapidly-evolving botnet threat, (iii)*promptly process information* for early detection of threats and subsequently activate evasive countermeasures, with a (iv)*simple user interface* to define botnet detection policies and thus improve end-user productivity.

BotFlex's architecture (Figure 1) comprises of three modules: the blacklist manager, the sensor module and the correlation framework. We implement BotFlex over Bro [5]. Bro has a layered architecture, where low-level network traffic is incrementally refined to meaningful network events which can be handled at the top-most scripting layer by Bro's domain-specific scripting language. BotFlex resides at this layer and its sensor module and the correlation framework have been written entirely in the Bro scripting language. We now discuss BotFlex's architectural modules, along with their respective implementation.

Blacklist Manager:. The blacklist manager complements the sensor module in its operation by providing it with up-to-date intelligence, such as C&C and The blacklist manager has been implemented as a bash script that downloads a number of public blacklists [2], organizes the intelligence based on its subject (IP, URL, subnet, port) and normalizes it according to a specific format. BotFlex reads the blacklists into a fast data structure that is synchronized with the back end blacklists. The blacklist manager is flexible in that it can be replaced with any other service as long as the blacklists adhere to the file format used by BotFlex.

Sensor Module:. The sensor module generates symptoms of botnet infection as events derived from the underlying NIDS–Bro, thus allowing for information to be processed and reacted to as it is churned. Events produced by sensor module may be readily consumed (simple events) or derived by further processing (derived events). Derived events can optionally involve one or more iterations through the correlation framework. Based on the well-known [1, 3] bot lifecycle events, the sensor module eventually maps all simple and derived events to five high-level activity classes: inbound scan, host exploit, malicious binary (egg) download, C&C communication and outbound attack. Currently, BotFlex uses a preliminary list of botnet detection parameters from existing literature . The sensor module is extremely flexible as it uses tunable attributes; the threshold values used to trigger various events, their weights and observation intervals (or time windows) are configurable. Furthermore, being independent of the correlation framework, the sensor module supports addition/removal/modification of detection parameters as threats evolve without requiring modifications to the correlation logic.

Correlation Framework:. The correlation framework continuously receives events from the sensor module and correlates them according to rule(s) specified by the user to derive the complex event of botnet infection. Note that we input botnet-related events to the framework, but in principle it is an independent, self-contained entity capable of processing any events fed to it.

The correlation framework has been implemented in Bro scripting language as a Complex Event Processing (CEP) engine. The present problem of botnet detection clearly conforms to the CEP model where events are defined with respect to time, causality and aggregation [4]. CEP allows correlation of events in real-time to detect a target complex event comprising of multiple simple or complex events. The choice of CEP makes BotFlex (i) flexible in how sensor module alerts are correlated; and (ii) extensible in facilitating addition of new correlation conditions; (iii) with a faster response because of a temporally-aware, event-driven model where information is processed as soon as it is churned and discarded when it is no longer relevant/needed. We have implemented a declarative correlation *rule language* that allows flexible processing of events related to botnet infection.

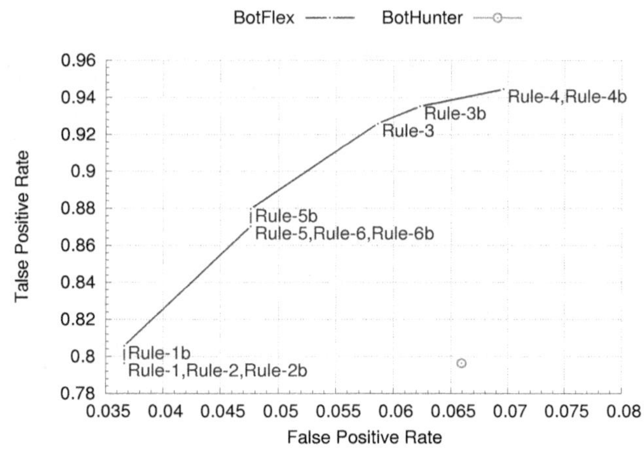

Figure 2: ROC curve for botnet detection with BotFlex and BotHunter

Correlation framework can handle both vertical and horizontal correlation. [1] The correlation framework is novel in that it marks the first time a CEP engine has been built within a non-proprietary NIDS with a view to accelerate information processing (CEP engine is typically treated as an external entity to which NIDS alerts are fed). Our approach has two main advantages: (i) CEP engine built within NIDS can directly ingest NIDS events and data structures thus reducing the delay incurred due to translation of NIDS events to an intermediate format when working with an external CEP engine, (ii) NIDS can readily understand and correlate events derived from disjoint sources.

3. PRELIMINARY EVALUATION

3.1 Evaluation Dataset and Methodology

We evaluate BotFlex for accuracy over a 500 GB data trace obtained from one of Pakistan's leading ISPs, Nayatel. The traffic contains 48,606 unique IP addresses of which 381 IP addresses represent Nayatel's local network statically assigned to mid-to-small size enterprises. While we assume that an IP address represents a single machine, we acknowledge that the ISP customers are likely using their public IPs to represent multiple private (NATed) hosts. However, this assumption of a one-to-one mapping between public IPs and bots provides a realistic test environment for deployment of a real-world bot detection solution.

We obtain ground truth for this data from a one-time sample of the IP reputation feed provided by Team Cymru. The ground truth comprises a proprietary threat repository of known C&C servers identified with the help of a chain of globally-deployed sensors. These C&C servers (referred to as the ground truth blacklist henceforth) were being actively contacted by hosts from the monitored region during our data collection at the ISP's B-RAS (between 08:54:49 AM and 04:13:29 PM PKT on September 18th, 2012). We labeled our data on the principle that the hosts in our dataset that communicate with the ground truth C&C servers are bots. The ground truth identified 108 (28.3%) of the total

[1] Vertical correlation performs temporal analysis of events generated for a single entity. Horizontal correlation deals with spatial analysis of an event pattern for multiple entities.

Table 1: Description of BotFlex correlation rules.

Name[a]	Rule	Description
1	(cnc_blacklist OR cnc_other) AND (exploit OR egg OR attack)	C&C and any other malicious activity
2	cnc_blacklist OR (cnc_other AND (exploit OR egg OR attack)	Same as 1, with a direct trigger for C&C blacklist match
3	(exploit OR egg) AND (cnc_blacklist OR cnc_other OR attack))	Evidence of any inbound host compromise and outbound C&C or attack
4	cnc_blacklist OR ((exploit OR egg) AND (cnc_other OR attack)))	Same as 3, with a direct trigger for C&C blacklist match
5	(egg AND (cnc_blacklist OR cnc_other)) OR (attack AND (cnc_blacklist OR cnc_other)) OR (egg AND ATTACK)	Egg download and outbound C&C or attack, or C&C and attack
6	cnc_blacklist OR (egg AND cnc_other) OR (attack AND cnc_other) OR (egg AND attack)	Same as 5, with a direct trigger for C&C blacklist match

[a]Rule{1,...,6}b variations include an OR rule for hosts tagged as part of a spam or scan campaign through horizontal correlation

381 IP addresses in the data trace as compromised bots.

3.2 Accuracy evaluation

We take a bottom-up approach in evaluating BotFlex in terms of accuracy. Thus, we first identify the best thresholds for the sensor module, and then compare different correlation rules to identify the most effective bot detection system. We run BotHunter [3] on the same dataset as a baseline to validate our results. For fair evaluation, we do not provide the ground truth blacklist to either of BotHunter or BotFlex. We first observe the impact of different threshold values for threshold-based detection parameters in the sensor module on bot detection. We then use best ROC operating points to identify suitable thresholds. We acknowledge that the use of a bot-labeled ground truth to measure accuracy of specific sensors (spam, scan etc.) is not perfect; however it remains a more rigorous approach than setting arbitrary thresholds.

After establishing suitable settings for the sensor module, we formulate correlation rule(s) (Table 1) for botnet detection to identify the strengths and weaknesses of various correlation policies. We plot the result of each run on an ROC curve. Also, note that we removed the detection parameter 'inbound scan' from our rules after noticing that it is nearly omnipresent (triggered for 341 of our total 381 ISP local hosts) possibly because of legitimate applications (e.g. p2p peer discovery) and Internet background noise.

We now discuss the insights gathered from the ROC curve for correlation rules (Figure 2) . Vertical correlation rules indicate that relying heavily on evidence of C&C communication produces low detection rates. This can be improved by complementing C&C evidence with other detection parameters. For rules Rule{1,2...,6}b involving horizontal correlation, we detect 23 hosts through coordination in spam-like activties and another 17 are detected based on synchronization in outbound scan timings. We generally find that horizontal correlation increases TP with no effect on FP with the exception of one host in Rule 3b (the latter was found to be a spambot later through manual investigation). Hence, horizontal correlation can possibly identify previously undetected bots based on their activity coordination with other botnet members.

To sum up, BotFlex (with Rule 3) detects 100 of the ground truth 108 bots, with a TPR of 92.6% and an FPR of 5.8%. These results are comparable with our baseline tool, BotHunter, which on the same trace gave a TPR of 79.6% and an FPR of 6.6%. Note that FPR for both the tools could represent an inflated number as our ground truth is biased in favor of TP (sensitivity) at the expense of TN (specificity) (the source of our ground truth claims to have nearly zero false-positives from their IP reputation feed).

4. CONCLUSION/FUTURE DIRECTIONS

The botnet research community currently lacks an open-source and community-driven tool to develop with ease, improve upon, and/or benchmark existing and new botnet detection solutions. In this paper, we presented BotFlex–a domain-specific, flexible and extensible network-based tool for botnet detection. We evaluated BotFlex for accuracy while comparing with a relevant baseline tool, and found the results to be encouraging. Our next research goal is to evaluate BotFlex's performance and scale it to increased traffic volumes while also taking its underlying NIDS platform into account. Additionally, BotFlex will also benefit from extension of its sensor module alerts and correlation rules, and enhancement of the correlation framework's custom rule language for defining correlation policies.

5. REFERENCES

[1] M. Abu Rajab, J. Zarfoss, F. Monrose, and A. Terzis. A multifaceted approach to understanding the botnet phenomenon. In *Proceedings of the 6th ACM SIGCOMM conference on Internet measurement*, IMC '06, pages 41–52, New York, NY, USA, 2006. ACM.

[2] BotFlex. `http://sysnet.org.pk/BotFlex`. Online. Feb,2013.

[3] G. Gu, P. Porras, V. Yegneswaran, M. Fong, and W. Lee. Bothunter: Detecting malware infection through ids-driven dialog correlation. In *Usenix Security Symposium*, 2007.

[4] D. C. Luckham. *The Power of Events: An Introduction to Complex Event Processing in Distributed Enterprise Systems*. Addison-Wesley Longman Publishing Co., Inc., Boston, MA, USA, 2001.

[5] V. Paxson. Bro: a system for detecting network intruders in real-time. In *Proceedings of the 7th conference on USENIX Security Symposium - Volume 7*, SSYM'98, pages 3–3, Berkeley, CA, USA, 1998. USENIX Association.

POSTER: Signal Anomaly Based Attack Detection in Wireless Sensor Networks

Jeton Bacaj
Department of Computer Science,
Rochester Institute of Technology
102 Lomb Drive, Rochester, NY 14623
Jxb4803@rit.edu

Leon Reznik
Department of Computer Science,
Rochester Institute of Technology
102 Lomb Drive, Rochester, NY 14623
lr@cs.rit.edu

ABSTRACT
This paper presents a feasibility study of novel attack detection mechanisms in wireless sensor networks (WSN) based on detecting anomalies and changes in sensor signals and data values. Typical WSN attacks are considered in the empirical study of various attack detection techniques utilizing features based on sensor signal strength and other WSN technological parameters and using machine learning classification techniques such as clustering, rule learners, and neural networks. For the attack detection implementation the study employed WSN built from Sun kits available on the market and extended Sensor Network Anomaly Detection System (SNADS) framework of methods and tools.

Categories and Subject Descriptors
D.4.6 [Security]: Protection; K.6.5 [Security]: Protection

General Terms
Measurement, Security.

Keywords
Anomaly intrusion detection; wireless sensor networks.

1. MOTIVATION
Traditionally wireless sensor networks (WSN) security designers consider sensor networks simply as a communication system transmitting information in one direction from sensors to processing units. Based on this assumption most intrusion detection systems expand the signature based and other techniques popular in wireless communication. The fact that sensor networks are a concurrent data acquisition system is not paid a proper attention in intrusion detection. The data collected by sensors as well as sensor signal strengths and other technological parameters are available and could be used for anomaly intrusion detection. This paper's goal is threefold:
1) to investigate a feasibility of the distributed mechanisms of an intrusion detection in WSNs based on detecting anomalies and changes in sensor signals,
2) to promote these methods into the WSN design practice by developing and presenting a unified software framework executable on the sensor network kits available on the market,
3) to present the results of an empirical study of attacks detection, which were based on sensor anomaly detection methods.
Section 2 reviews a number of typical WSN attacks, which were described in publications [1-8] and indicates which of them could be detected with this technique. The detection principles are explained in section 3 in greater detail and their performance in detecting two typical attacks is presented in section 4.

CCS'13, November 4–8, 2013, Berlin, Germany.
ACM 978-1-4503-2477-9/13/11.

2. ATTACKS OVERVIEW
The attacks studied in literature [1-8] may change the legitimate communication signals that are expected in the WSNs. A sample of typical attacks is presented in Table 1. It should be noted that, for the purpose and scope of this study, the only attacks considered for attack detection deployment are sophisticated attacks, specifically those that do not rely on the WSN having a lack of encryption, authentication, and authorization mechanisms in place. As one can see from Table 1, in the Attack details column, most of these attacks rely on impersonation, passive information gathering (listening in), or state corruption of the sensor signals. A combination of encryption, authentication and authorization access control may alleviate most of these weaknesses but may require significant resources not available in WSN implementations. Last two columns demonstrate that most attacks could be detected by examining certain sensor signals and WSN parameters and their changes.

3. METHODS AND PRINCIPLES OF OPERATION
The detection idea is based on constant monitoring the values of the sensor signals and data communicated in WSN and certain WSN technological parameters, e.g. packet delivery ratio, and identifying anomalies in the patterns of their values or value derivatives. Values and features extracted for further analysis depend on the particular attacks and utilize the signals and values, which are the most dependable on this attack. The developed methods are implemented as an extension to the Sensor Network Anomaly Detection System (SNADS) [9]- see Figure 1 for further details. SNADS is designed as a signal analysis tool to decide whether signal changes should be identified as normal or anomalous. WSN detection mechanism may rely on a priori known model of the environment that the sensors are deployed in.

4. ATTACK DETECTION STUDY
4.1 Jamming attack
A few various WSN technological parameters have been considered as possible features to be used for this attack detection.

Table 1. Typical WSN attacks and their possible detection metrics

Attack name	Attack content	Countermeasures	Possible detection	Possible metrics used for detection
Preliminary or passive attacks				
Passive information gathering	Information interception and collection during communication without altering it	Encryption and access control	No	n/a
Traffic and node activity analysis	Gathering information on sensor activities and traffic patterns. Used for future attack preparation	Encryption and access control	No	n/a
Node subversion by tampering or destruction	Capturing a node. Collecting information available including keys if applicable	Protection and access control	No	n/a
Node malfunctioning	Node malfunctions. Generate inaccurate measurements or violate traffic/ routing	Tests	Yes	Sensor signals or absence thereof
Cluster leader or an aggregate node outage	A node and possibly a part of the network will cease functioning. Generate inaccurate measurements or violate traffic/ routing	Flexible network structuring and re-routing	Yes	Sensor signals or absence thereof
Active attacks				
False node and Byzantine attacks [1,4]	Addition of malicious node by adversary. Inject false data and malicious information	Key distribution and control, node verification	Yes	Sensor signals, network traffic characteristics
Malicious message corruption	Data integrity is violated and if control messages are modified the network functioning could be at risk	Access control and encryption	Yes	Sensor signals
Routing modifications and loops	Routing information is maliciously altered. Network functioning is at risk, more traffic is generated and the resources are wasted	Access control and encryption	Yes	Sensor signals, network traffic characteristics
Sinkhole/blackhole or Wormhole attack	Re-forwarding traffic to a compromised node or through particular low latency links.	Implicit acknowledgment multipath routing	Yes	Sensor signals, network traffic characteristics
Denial of service [6]	Denial of service at the physical level. Radio jamming, battery exhaustion	Depending on the attack, identify jammed regions and rerouting	Yes	Received signal strength, average time required to sense an idle channel and the packet delivery ratio
Denial of sleep [5]	Various DoS attacks on MAC protocols depending on the protocol knowledge, such as sending false messages, increasing collision rates, etc. Significant reduction in wireless sensor network lifetime	Link-layer authentication, anti-replay protection, jamming identification, broadcast attack defense	Yes	Power level monitoring
DoS on Sensing [2]	Physical attacks on the sensor nodes aimed at changing measurements before they enter communication channel. Faulty and corrupted measurements	Special distribution of the sensor nodes across the region with assumed mobility	Yes	Change in sensor signals
Jamming [7]	Corrupting traffic by adding up streams and messages. Bandwidth and other resource exhaustion	Spread spectrum communication if radio resources available, rerouting around jammed areas	Yes	Traffic and sensor signals
Interrogation [6]	Repeatedly sending RTS messages to elicit CTS responses from a targeted node. Node resource exhaustion	Link layer authentication and anti-replay protection	Yes	Node power level
Hello flood	Broadcasting a hello message with stronger transmission power to reach more nodes. Node resource exhaustion	Link layer authentication and anti-replay protection	Yes	Traffic and sensor signals
Sensor stimuli	Subverted nodes send request for more readings. Bandwidth and other resources exhaustion	Monitoring sensor sample rates	Yes	Traffic and sensor signals
Selective forwarding	Malicious nodes drop certain messages. Latency reduction and the neighboring nodes deceive	Key distribution and control, node verification	Yes	Sensor signals, network traffic characteristics
Sybil attack [3,8]	Malicious creation of the node clones. Builds up copies of legitimate nodes to disrupt routing	Key distribution and control, node verification	Yes	Sensor signals, network traffic characteristics

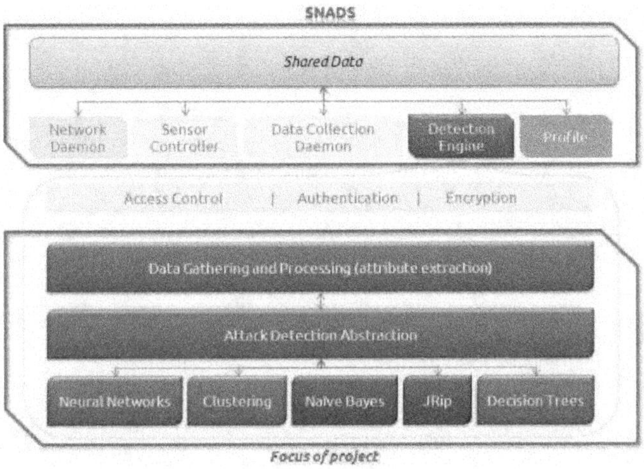

Figure 1. Integration with SNADS framework

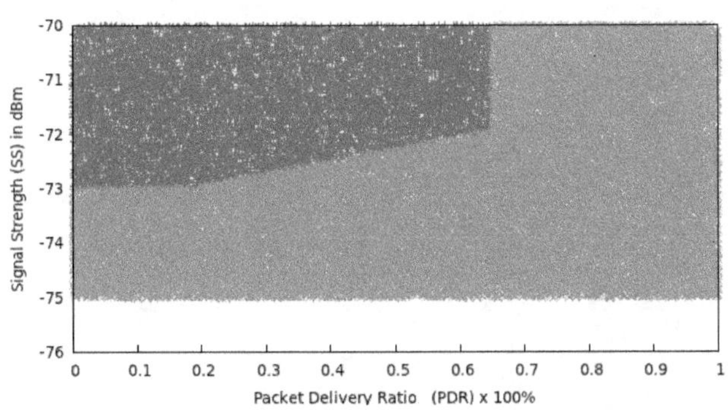

Figure 2. Jamming attack detection data distribution

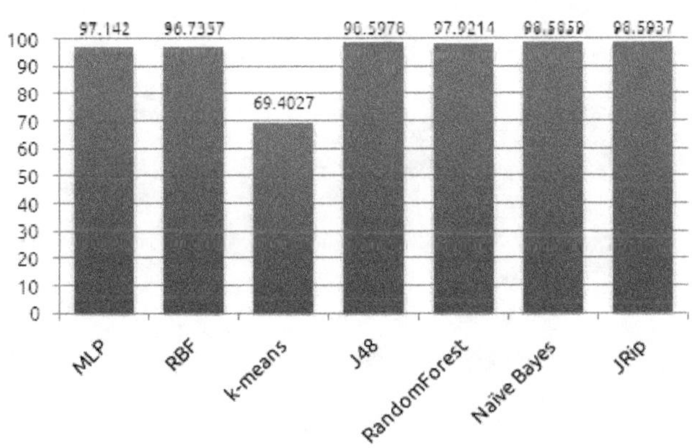

Figure 3. Classification techniques performance in DoS attack detection

One can see from Figure 2 that by using only two WSN technological parameters such as a signal strength and a packet delivery ratio it would be easy to subdivide the whole plane into two distinguish areas: attack's and no attack's [6]. This is valid for different types of Jamming attack manifestations: constant, reactive, deceptive and random jammers.

4.2 Denial of Service on Sensing attack

Seven signals have been identified as features for an anomaly detection. The traffic data were collected from the WSN built from Sun World Spots available on the market [10]. A few different machine learning techniques have been tested to build classifiers for the attack detection. Figure 3 presents their performance that might be considered as quite good but could be further improved by specific measures.

5. REFERENCES

[1] P. Addesso, S. Marano, and V. Matta, "Sequential Sampling in Sensor Networks for Detection With Censoring Nodes," in IEEE Transactions on Signal Processing, vol. 55, November 2007, pp. 5497–5505.

[2] S. Marano, V. Matta, and L. Tong, "Distributed Detection in the Presence of Byzantine Attacks," IEEE Transactions on Signal Processing, vol. 57, pp. 16–29, Jan. 2009.

[3] D. R. Raymond and S. F. Midkiff, "Denial-of-Service in Wireless Sensor Networks: Attacks and Defenses," IEEE Pervasive Computing, vol. 7, no. 1, pp. 74–81, 2008.

[4] D. Raymond, R. Marchany, M. Brownfield, and S. Midkiff, "Effects of Denial-of-Sleep Attacks on Wireless Sensor Network MAC Protocols," in IEEE Transactions on Vehicular Technology, vol. 58, January 2009, pp. 367–380.

[5] A. Czarlinska and D. Kundur, "Distributed Actuation Attacks in Wireless Sensor Networks: Implications and Countermeasures," in DSSNS '06: Proceedings of the Second IEEE Workshop on Dependability and Security in Sensor Networks and Systems. Washington, DC, USA: IEEE Computer Society, 2006, pp. 3–12.

[6] W. Xu, K. Ma, W. Trappe, and Y. Zhang, "Jamming sensor networks: Attack and defense strategies," in IEEE Network, vol. 20, June 2006, pp. 41–47.

[7] J. R. Douceur, "The Sybil Attack," in IPTPS '01: Revised Papers from the First International Workshop on Peer-to-Peer Systems. London, UK: Springer-Verlag, 2002, pp. 251–260.

[8] J. Yin and S. K. Madria, "Sybil attack detection in a hierarchical sensor network," in Third International Conference on Security and Privacy in Communications Networks and the Workshops, 2007. SecureComm 2007, Nice, France, September 2007, pp. 494–503.

[9] L. Reznik and K. Nathan, "A Framework for Measurement Anomaly Detection in Sensor Networks," in IEEE Sensors 2009 Conference, Christchurch, New Zealand, October 2009, pp. 597–600.

[10] Sun Microsystems, now Oracle, Inc., "SunSPOTWorld," http://www.sunspotworld.com/.

POSTER: Enhanced Embedded Device Security by Combining Hardware-Based Trust Mechanisms

Martin Schramm, Karl Leidl, Andreas Grzemba
University of Applied Sciences Deggendorf
Edlmairstraße 6+8, Deggendorf, Germany
{martin.schramm|karl.leidl|andreas.grzemba}@hdu-deggendorf.de

Nicolai Kuntze
Fraunhofer SIT
Rheinstraße 75, Darmstadt, Germany
nicolai.kuntze@sit.fraunhofer.de

ABSTRACT

Nowadays embedded systems in many application areas such as automotive, medical and industrial automation are designed with well-defined hardware and software components which are not meant to be exposed for user modifications. Adding or removing components to/from such systems is not permitted and sometimes not even possible since the systems often have to be up and running in a 24/7 manner. However due to the well-known nature of these types of embedded platform configuration the effort an attacker has to invest usually is reduced. The proposed publication presents a defense in depth strategy for application specific embedded devices by combining hardware-based security enhancements of modern processors with hardware security modules.

Categories and Subject Descriptors

D.4.6 [**Operating Systems**]: Security and Protection—*Access controls*; K.6.5 [**Management of Computing and Information Systems**]: Security and Protection

Keywords

i.MX6; ARM TrustZone; TPM; HAB; TNC; Chain of Trust

1. MOTIVATION

"Our world relies on interconnected data, services, and computing resources for all aspects of our daily lives. Virtually all sectors of our economy have come to critically depend on their availability, correctness, and ubiquity-failure in any part of the system could have disastrous consequences on the rest of the system.[1]"

Typical approaches applied focus on protecting the perimeter keeping the adversary outside of the infrastructure to be protected. Initiatives such as the Asymmetric Resilient Cybersecurity focus on delivering the theory, processes, methodologies, and algorithms that will enable a resilient cyber infrastructure with an asymmetric advantage to thwart adversaries who seek to infiltrate and damage critical infrastructures through digital means[2]. The paradigm here is that, even when under overt cyber attack, resilient cyber systems stay operational with attackers inside the system. To maintain operation it is required to establish novel tactical, operational, and strategic effects that benefit the defender. A core ability is to detect attacks and to mitigate the impact of an attack as early as possible to minimize the impact on the overall infrastructure. One promising way to detect even unknown attacks is the verification of health of each device in a system by comparing measurements to a specified reference value. The Trusted Computing Group (TCG) standardized protocols and devices to allow architectures to implement this basic idea.

This publication shows how to establish a resilient core network using Trusted Computing (TC) technologies in combination with platform security features such as ARM processor extensions. The proposed approach specifies a suitable device architecture and network concept that allows for a distributed and autonomous reaction to threats to the system. Section 2 provides some insides on the used technologies such as ARM security features and TC. The architecture is discussed in section 3. An example reaction is scetched out in section 4. A short conclusion is given in section 5.

2. HARDWARE SECURITY FEATURES

In this chapter, the individual technologies for the intended application are described. In subsection 2.1 ARM security features are described. ARM TrustZone provides a framework for a secure system architecture and Freescales High Assurance Boot ensures a secure boot of ARM-based systems. Subsection 2.2 reflects the benefits of TPM integration as a hardware-based trust anchor.

2.1 TrustZone and High Assurance Boot

ARM TrustZone can be utilized to realize a Trusted Execution Environment (TEE) as described in [4]. This is comparable with Intel Trusted Execution Technology and AMD Secure Execution Environment on x86-based systems. Thus critical and non-critical processes can be separated. Therefore, a security instruction set is added to ARM processors

[1] `http://cybersecurity.pnnl.gov/documents/Asymmetric_Resilient_Cybersecurity.pdf`

[2] `http://cybersecurity.pnnl.gov/arc.stm`

CCS'13, November 4–8, 2013, Berlin, Germany.
ACM 978-1-4503-2477-9/13/11.
http://dx.doi.org/10.1145/2508859.2512509.

that is called Secure Monitor Call (SMC). Since TrustZone is implemented in hardware, it averts software vulnerabilities as found in pure software security solutions. Thus, it is possible to protect peripheral and memory. This isolation is achieved by virtualization and is based on the principle of least privileges [10]. Even after a complete compromise of the normal operating system (OS), it is not possible to access the secure OS. Developers have both software and an API to implement their own projects with ARM TrustZone [8].

The software library High Assurance Boot (HAB), specified by Freescale Semiconductor for certain families of application processors, can be used to implement a secure boot procedure based on signed code execution. The HAB enables the on-chip boot ROM to authenticate executable software such as the bootloader by the verification of digital signatures. This way the foundation for a chain of trust is given by a verified boot process [3]. In order to sign the corresponding images a Public Key Infrastructure (PKI) has to be established. One-Time Programmable (OTP) hardware components make sure that an adversary cannot circumvent the authentication process. For the key generation and for the signing step vendor-supplied tools such as the Code Signing Tool (CST) have to be utilized. Using these tools user-defined security policies can be specified in an interpretable binary data structure, the so called Command Sequence Files (CSF) [2].

2.2 Trusted Platform Module

The Trusted Platform Module (TPM) as specified by the TCG is one possibility for an implementation of a hardware-based trust anchor. According to its specification [13] it implements the Root of Trust for Storage (RTS) and the Root of Trust for Reporting (RTR). It features cryptographic engines, a true random number generator, the possibility for the creation of hash values and a way to generate and manage keys. Furthermore it offers a shielded and tamper-resistant storage where the Platform Configuration Registers (PCRs) are located. The PCRs store the results of the integrity measurements. For the communication with the TPM and for the use of its capabilities several interfaces are possible. In common x86 architectures the communication occurs via Low Pin Count (LPC) bus whereas in the proposed architecture the Inter-Integrated Circuit (I^2C) bus is used.

3. IMPLEMENTATION DETAILS

This section explains the crux of the implementation. For this purpose subsection 3.1 deals with the establishment of initial trust on the individual systems by combining the presented security features. The benefits and opportunities that arise from this combination are listed in subsection 3.2.

3.1 Establishment of Trust

When defining system integrity based on trust decisions several trustworthy building blocks are necessary [11]. The Core Root of Trust for Measurement (CRTM) is formed by the activated HAB feature. In order to guarantee a secure boot capability, the integrity of the boot ROM must be provided. Since the boot ROM is located inside a masked processor internal ROM it cannot be modified by an attacker. HAB is configured in a way, that it only loads digitally signed bootloader versions provided by the owner of the system. Thereby it offers the starting point of a chain of trust. In the proposed architecture an enhanced version of u-boot is used. Additional routines make sure that the TPM will be initialized in an early boot stage. After initialization the first integrity measurements will be gathered by measuring all u-boot commands and storing the results into the PCRs inside of the TPM. In addition the operating system kernel image will be measured before execution (see Figure 1). The Root of Trust for Measurement (RTM) is therefore comprised by the enhanced bootloader. Both RTS and RTR are located inside of the TPM as known from conventional x86-based systems.

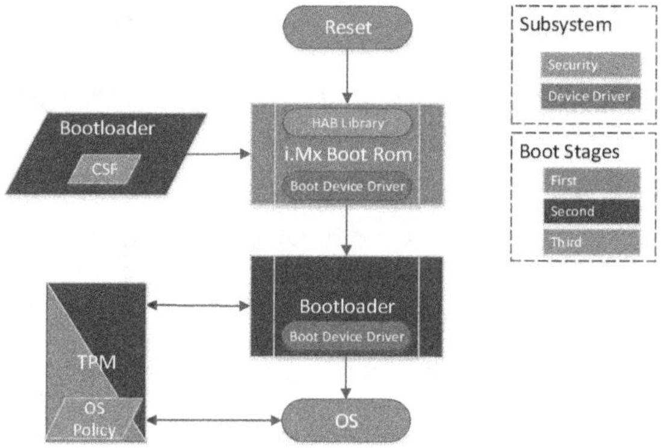

Figure 1: Extended HAB Overview

3.2 Cooperating Security Features

By combining the technologies briefly described in section 2 an enhanced security architecture can be established. The existence of a CRTM is mandatory when designing trustworthy systems. However just adding a TPM to embedded computing platforms often does not offer a valid RTM. In the proposed architecture the secure boot feature provided by HAB is employed to eliminate this arising security concern. Devices which are secured in the intended way additionally offer effective protection mechanisms against software manipulations since attempts will directly be recognized either simply because the processor refuses to boot a maliciously modified bootloader or the modifications will be evident through a change in the values obtained by the integrity measurements. Sane integrity measurements in turn can report a healthy system state which can be checked by procedures such as remote attestation. Furthermore they can be utilized to provide trustworthy network access through protocols such as Trusted Network Connect (TNC) [14]. The TPM as security element can provide a shielded storage area for security policies and offers further protected capabilities such as a secure key storage region. Keys needed during provisioning of the platform and later used by HAB can also be securely created inside of the TPM. Furthermore OS policies can be stored in the tamper resistant non-volatile storage of the TPM. In addition, ARM TrustZone provides security features that allow security by insulation at runtime on ARM-based systems. Thereby security critical areas are protected. A possible implementation is introduced by [12].

4. USE CASES

This section provides a concept application of trustworthy nodes in the area of Industrial Control Systems (ICS). In subsection 4.1 the network protection scheme is detailed and in subsection 4.2 mitigation approaches are discussed.

Other application examples for devices equipped with TPMs can be found in the area of tactical communication [7], calibrated devices [9], network management [5] or future energy networks [6].

4.1 Protected Core System

IT-based attacks on ICS rely on the communication system to provide access to the attached devices. Protecting the availability of the ICS requires to form a protected core system involving the communication layer. Using devices on the basis of the proposed security framework allows to provide the following security features within a network architecture:

A **reliable networking** functionality builds the basis of the core system. This allows to form a network-basis resilient to IT-based attacks which also provides the ability to protect attached control systems without sufficient security functionality. Trust in the operation of individual devices is based on **health monitored** components which allows to detect changes to the system that can be classified and reacted on. Even previously unknown attacks (in contrast to virus protection) can be detected and mitigated. Continuous authentic **information on the status** of the infrastructure allows to establish a master display for security and to perform mitigation actions. Monitoring of **meta-data information** by using IF-MAP [1] on the core network itself and on devices attached to the network can be used to check security rules for the complete framework of systems.

4.2 ICS-aware Mitigation

As the availability of ICS is of utter importance, **reaction to security events** needs to aim to minimize the impact on the ICS operation. From a high level view, the following four categories of incidents can be distinguished:

Compliance to the expected behavior. In case of TC assessment on the basis of TPM enforced remote attestation the binary measurements of all components are verified and considered as trustworthy. If all other techniques for end point assessment show no unexpected behavior a well-known state can be expected and additional connectivity can be allowed, e.g. for maintenance and distribution of updates. **Outdated** software which can be detected either by reported older measurements on the device using TC or known behavior detected by other means that matches an old and deprecated behavior might indicate vulnerable systems, but does not directly show an attack. Additional connectivity should be restricted until a suitable time for updating the software occurs. If **typed malicious** software in case of already known and well understood changes to the software is being checked and the device may still be providing the intended service then under special circumstances it can still be used in the network. Threat specific protection measures can be enforced through the infrastructure to allow targeted reactions to the known changes. If an **unknown** status or behavior of a device is detected it can be quarantined in order to prevent the spread of a possible malicious infection. It is important to understand that even in quarantine the functionality of a manipulated device can still be provided. Then, the device interactions need to be strictly monitored until the health of the device can be restored.

5. CONCLUSIONS

The presented approach demonstrates that a multi-layered security solution is possible by the efficient combination of TPM and ARM Security Extensions. It is proposed that only through a merger of techniques such as ARM Security Features and the TC approach a Trusted Platform can be realized on embedded devices, that provides an adequate level of security and also supports perimeter control.

6. ACKNOWLEDGMENTS

This research work has been supported by the research project ANSII (no. 16BY1209B) of the German Federal Ministry of Education and Research.

7. REFERENCES

[1] C. Deng, L. Yang, L. Ma, and Y. Cao. Architecture for secure scada system based on if-map scheme. In *Computer Science and Convergence*, pages 427–435. Springer, 2012.

[2] Freescale Semiconductor. Hab code-signing tool - user's guide, November 2012.

[3] Freescale Semiconductor. Secure boot on i.mx50, i.mx53, and i.mx 6 series using habv4, October 2012.

[4] GlobalPlatform. Trusted execution environment (tee) guide. http://www.globalplatform.org/, July 2013.

[5] N. Kuntze and C. Rudolph. On the automatic establishment of security relations for devices. In *Proceedings of the IFIP/IEEE International Symposium on Integrated Network Management.* IFIP/IEEE, 2013.

[6] N. Kuntze, C. Rudolph, I. Bente, J. Vieweg, and J. von Helden. Interoperable device identification in smart-grid environments. In *Power and Energy Society General Meeting, 2011 IEEE*, july 2011.

[7] A. Oberle, A. Rein, N. Kuntze, R. Carsten, J. Paatero, L. Andrew, and P. Racz. Integrating Trust Establishment into Routing Protocols of Today's MANETs. In *2013 IEEE Wireless Communications and Networking Conference (WCNC 2013)*, pages 1403–1408, Shanghai, China, April 2013.

[8] Open Virtualization Project. Open virtualization for arm trustzone. http://www.openvirtualization.org/open-source-arm-trustzone.html, July 2013.

[9] C. Rudolph, N. Kuntze, T. Kemmerich, and B. Endicott-Popovsky. Scenarios for reliable and secure digital evidence. In *Ninth Annual IFIP WG 11.9 International Conference*, 2013.

[10] M. Schramm and A. Grzemba. The benefits of combining trusted computing with virtualization techniques. In *Applied Electronics (AE), 2010 International Conference on*, pages 1–4, 2010.

[11] M. Schramm and A. Grzemba. Trustworthy building blocks for a more secure embedded computing environment. In *Applied Electronics (AE), 2011 International Conference on*, pages 1–4, 2011.

[12] Sierraware. Sierraware Announces that the Open Source SierraTEE and SierraVisor SDKs Now Support Xilinx Zynq-7000 All Programmable SoCs . http://www.sierraware.com/news_xilinx_tee_arm_hypervisor.html, July 2013.

[13] Trusted Computing Group. Tpm main specification part 1, 2, 3. http://www.trustedcomputinggroup.org/, March 2011.

[14] J. von Helden, I. Bente, J. Vieweg, and B. Hellmann. Trusted network connect (tnc). *European Trusted Infrastructure Summer School*, page 54, 2009.

POSTER: On the Anonymity of Israel's General Elections

Tomer Ashur Orr Dunkelman

{tashur01@campus,orrd@cs}.haifa.ac.il
Computer Science Department
University of Haifa
Mount Carmel, Haifa
Israel, 31905

ABSTRACT

This work presents an attack on the privacy of some voting systems. We show that by combining information from several sources, some of it publicly available, and some of it can be easily collected ad-hoc, an adversary can greatly reduce the size of a voter's anonymity set. In many cases the obtained information is sufficient to deduce the content of a vote (or approximate a small set of possible values).

As a test case, we present this attack in the context of the Israeli general parliamentary elections. Simulations we ran show that we can successfully determine the value of about 50% of the votes after observing three election systems.

Categories and Subject Descriptors

K.4.1 [**COMPUTERS AND SOCIETY**]: Public Policy Issues—Privacy; G.2.1 [**DISCRETE MATHEMATICS**]: Combinatorics—Counting problems; E.1 [**DATA STRUCTURES**]: Graphs and networks

Keywords

Privacy, Voting, Israel's Elections, Intersection Attack

1. INTRODUCTION

One of the most important mechanisms that allows for democracy is the notion of free elections. In free elections, eligible voters express their opinions on important matters via voting. In liberal democracies, periodical elections are held for electing the members of the governing bodies. For people to freely express their opinions (e.g., without being coerced to external pressure), voting is usually done in a private manner, i.e., the voter's privacy (regarding their specific vote) is protected by some anonymity set.

We can learn about the importance of secrecy of the election process from the *DECLARATION ON CRITERIA FOR FREE AND FAIR ELECTIONS* published by Inter-Parliamentary Union on 1994,[1] and which states [4]:

> "2. Voting and Elections Rights:
> (7) The right to vote in secret is absolute and shall not be restricted in any manner whatsoever."

The state of Israel recognized the importance of secret voting and determined in its *Basic Law: The Knesset* [2],[2] in Section 4 that: *"The Knesset shall be elected by general, national, direct, equal, secret and proportional elections, in accordance with the Knesset Elections Law."*

In this work we show that we can correlate public information (such as the results of the elections in the ballot box) with information available to the political parties (such as the time each voter casted his vote, or the number of remaining ballots) to reveal the contents of a secret voter's vote. More precisely, we show that parties that can maintain this data over several election systems are capable of intersecting it to reduce the sizes of anonymity sets. As a result, after three elections systems, we were able to uniquely identify the votes of about 50% of the voters.

2. DESCRIPTION OF THE ISRAELI ELECTIONS SYSTEM

The Israeli election system is described in the *Knesset Elections law - 1969.* In a nutshell, every eligible citizen is assigned a ballot box. The maximum assigned voters per ballot box is 800. In practice, the median number of assigned voters to each ballot box in the 2013 elections was 590. Out of the 5,654,842 voters, only 3,617,857 voters exercised their right to vote ($\approx$ 64% of voters).[3] Out of these, a total number of 3,579,793 votes were legitimate votes.

In order to vote, each voter arrives to her assigned ballot box and identifies herself to the local elections committee. The chairman of the committee crosses the voter's name from the registry, and hands her an envelope. The voter walks behind a curtain and chooses a ballot ticket from a tray, representing her preferred party. The tray includes a

CCS'13, November 4–8, 2013, Berlin, Germany.
ACM 978-1-4503-2477-9/13/11.
http://dx.doi.org/10.1145/2508859.2512510.

[1] The Inter-Parliamentary Union (IPU) is an international organization of 162 state parliaments, and 10 regional parliaments. The IPU was established on 1889, and it has a permanent observer status at the United Nations and general consultative status with the Economic and Social Council.
[2] The Knesset is the Israeli parliament.
[3] Absentee votes are excluded for simplicity.

stack of tickets for each candidate party (34 parties contested in the 2013 elections). The voter puts the ticket into the envelope, seals the envelope, and casts it into the ballot box where it mixes with all the other envelopes in this ballot box. The members of the local elections committee, which are all, except of the chairperson, appointed by the parties, periodically check that all tickets are available to voters behind the curtain.

At the end of the election day, the local elections committee opens the ballot box, extracts the tickets from each envelope, and counts them. The results of this count are sent to the general elections committee, which aggregates and publish the results (including per ballot box statistics).

3. MIXES

A widely used model for private communication is the notion of a mix. Mixes first proposed by Chaum in 1981 [1] as a mean for delivering messages between senders and receivers, in a way that would prohibit an external observer to the communication to know which sender sent a message to which receiver.

The idea behind the mix is rather simple: The communication is split into cycles. In each cycle, a set of n senders sends messages of fixed length to the mix, the mix then performs some cryptographic manipulation on the messages that changes their appearance, and passes the new modified messages to a set of m receivers in an arbitrary or random order. All that an external observer (i.e., one which is not a sender, the mix, or a receiver) can learn is that n messages were sent between n senders and m receivers.

Going back to the Israeli elections system, each ballot box can be modelled as a mix. The set of senders is the set of voters in each ballot box. The set of receivers is the set of parties contesting in the elections. The voter "encrypts" its vote by casting it to the ballot box, and the local elections committee "decrypts" the vote by extracting the ticket from the ballot box. For any external observer (including the members of the local elections committee), it is impossible to know which envelope belongs to which voter.

4. HOW MUCH ANONYMITY CAN A VOTER EXPECT?

"Anonymity is the state of being not identifiable within a set of subjects, the anonymity set" [3]. An object is said to be *k-anonymous* if it is indistinguishable from the rest of the objects in a set of size k. There are several ways to think of the anonymity set in the case of the general elections. The trivial way is to see the set of voters in a ballot as the anonymity set. This definition yields the largest anonymity set. The median number of voters in the 2013 elections was 590, and thus, the size of the anonymity set for the median ballot box was 590 (i.e., uniformly guessing which envelope belongs to a specific voter had a success probability of $\frac{1}{590}$).

A finer statement can be made once we identify equivalence classes. If we bare in mind that the envelopes store voting tickets that differ only by their values (i.e., all the tickets for the same party are identical), we can say that we do not need to assign an envelope for a voter rather than assigning a value (party) to a voter. In this setting, given that 34 parties contested in the 2013 elections, uniformly guessing to which of them a single voter voted yields a success probability of $\frac{1}{34}$ for each voter. Moreover, votes are not distributed uniformly between parties, and thus, the guess can be skewed to fix for this bias, increasing the chance of success in guessing a voter's vote.

For the reminder of the paper, we need to define the working notations. Let B be a ballot box, the set $X^B = \{x_1, \ldots, x_n\}$ is the set of n voters assigned to this ballot box. Let the set $Y = \{y_1, \ldots, y_{34}\}$ be the set of all parties running for a seat in the parliament. The function $\text{Voted}(x_i) = y_j$ returns for each voter the party she voted for (this is the value the adversary tries to recover).

Let Y^B be the support of Y in the ballot box B, i.e., the subset of all parties that had at least one voter voting for them in ballot box B. Obviously, $Y^B \subseteq Y$. If $Y^B \subset Y$, and we know the assignment of voters to ballot boxes, we can guess each voter's vote among a smaller set of parties. This anonymity set (i.e., $|Y^B|$) is the minimal privacy the voter should expect.

5. VIOLATING VOTERS' PRIVACY

The voting process as described above can be viewed as a bi-partite graph $G = (X^B \cup Y^B, E)$ where each voter sends a single message through the mix to a single party. Each such message (x_i, y_j) corresponds to an edge in E. We say that $(x_i, y_j) \in E \iff \text{Voted}(x_i) = y_j$. Obviously, the graph G is implicit (i.e., its structure is unknown to the adversary). While the set of voters, namely, X^B, and the set of receivers, namely, Y^B is known to the adversary, the goal is to approximate a set $\hat{E}$ which is as close as possible to the set E depending on the measure for success of the attack. The attack itself consists of two phases: The data collection phase, and the voting recovery phase.

5.1 The Data Collection Phase

The adversary (which can be a member of the local elections committee) counts the number of tickets placed in the tray behind the curtain. Once the election day starts, the adversary periodically counts the size of the stack of remaining tickets and calculates how many tickets are missing for each party.[4] The adversary also collects the time of vote for each voter (as this information is already collected by the local elections committee, and is sent to the parties via a form called "Tofes-1000"). We call the time period between every two counts "a frame", and keep track of the voters who voted in each frame as well as the tickets voted with (i.e., the missing tickets) during the frame.

The result of the data collection phase for every election period is two multisets X and Y. The multiset $X = \{X_1, \ldots, X_t\}$ consist of sets X_h holding the voters in frame h. We say that an element $x_i \in X_h$ if and only if voter x_i voted in frame h. The multiset $Y = \{Y_1, \ldots, Y_t\}$ holds vectors encoding the number of votes for each party in each frame. For example, if $(\text{Voted}(x_3) = y_6) \wedge (x_3 \in X_5)$ then $Y_5[6] > 0$. For a voter $x_i \in X_h$, the size of its anonymity set is the number of items in the vector Y_h which are nonzero, which we denote by $w(Y_h)$.[5]

[4]The technical question of *how* the adversary can count the stack of tickets is outside the scope of this work. Various methods were proposed by our colleagues, and some of them seems to be sufficient for our needs. For example, we consider the use of accurate weight scales, or laser based measurement equipment.

[5]Obviously, when $w(Y_h) = 1$, the voters in x_h have no privacy. Our attack focuses on the cases where $w(Y_h) > 1$.

The data collection phase collects observations X^u and Y^u over several elections where the superscript u denotes the elections period (e.g., X^1 is the multiset obtained from the first observed elections, X^2 is the multiset obtained from the second observed elections, etc.). In the simplified model, studied in Section 5.2, a voter can only vote for the same party in all observed elections, but can move between sets between observations. Another constraint imposed in the simplified model is that for every X^u_α and Y^u_α, $|X^u_\alpha| = |Y^u_\alpha|$ (i.e., every voter takes exactly one ticket from the tray). We loose these restrictions in Section 5.3 and allow the voters to change their minds between elections systems, bring their own tickets, pick more than one ticket, or simply not show up.

5.2 Recovery Phase

During the recovery phase, the adversary builds for every voter the list of possible parties she might have voted for. For the first observation (X^1, Y^1) the adversary adds an edge with weight 1 between a voter x_i and a party y_j if and only if $(x_i \in X^1_h) \wedge (Y^1_h[j] > 0)$. For the next observations, if a voter $(x_i \in X^u_h) \wedge (Y^u_h[j] > 0)$, the adversary increases the weight of the edge by 1 (no new edges are added).

In the simplified model, a voter cannot change her vote between election systems, and thus, after u iterations, all edges with weight smaller than u are discarded, and all the remaining weights are set to 1. The adversary now adds a source and a sink. An edge with weight 1 is added between the source and each voter (corresponding to the single vote this voter can cast), and a weighted edge is added between each party and the sink. The weight of the sink edges is the number of votes that the party received in the specific ballot box as published by the general elections committee.

A flow in this graph represents an assignment of one voter unit (a vote) to a party. If a party delivers into the sink p votes, the maximal flow assigns exactly p voters to this party. We know that such a maximal flow exists due to the existence of the implicit graph G. However, more than one maximal flow may exist; in which case, the assignment are indistinguishable from our perspective.

5.3 Relaxing the Demands in the Data Collection Phase

In real life settings, voters sometimes change their minds, and vote for different parties in consecutive elections. However, it is much less common that voters largely drift between political fields. Therefore, we can change the voting recovery phase to have two stages. In the first stage, the adversary searches for the category the voter is in (according to the known political categories in Israel). If we want to allow a complete drift (a voter that completely changed her mind), we can build a probabilistic finite-state machine that describes the move of voters between parties.[6]

Another restriction we can remove is that people always take a single ticket from the tray, or even always come to vote. A more realistic model will allow for voters to bring their own ticket or pick up more than one ticket from the tray. This can be dealt with by allowing the respective sets in X and Y to be of different sizes. For some cases this has no influence on the accuracy of the results, but on other cases it reduces the success rate.

[6]Building such a probabilistic finite-state machine is however, a work for political scientists and political statisticians.

6. SIMULATING THE ATTACK

In order to verify our attack, we ran simulations based on the results of the 2013 general elections in Israel as published by the general elections committee. The simulation starts by creating "virtual" voters for every ballot box, and assigning votes to each of them according to the real voting distribution in the simulated ballot box. We also randomly assigned a voting time for every voter over several election systems, so we can simulate the counting procedure done every 30 minutes. Once the data collection phase was simulated, we applied our suggested attack to see how many of the votes we could recover.

Preliminary results show that for small, homogeneous ballot boxes (e.g., ballot boxes where one large party got a large portion of the votes, and a few small parties got the rest) we were able to recover 100% of the votes after observing as little as 3 elections systems. For more heterogeneous ballot boxes (e.g., where the votes are distributed between 2-3 large parties and several smaller ones), we obtained less accurate results. However, even in such ballot boxes, we were usually able to reduce the number of possible parties to 2-3 per voter, all of which were usually from the same political category. We stress that even in ballot boxes where we could not fully recover the content of the votes for all voters, we could always do it for a large portion of the people. In many scenarios this can disastrous for these people.

When we ran the algorithm for the full results file, about 50% of the votes could be correctly determined after observing 3 elections systems.

7. FUTURE DIRECTIONS

Our attack can recover 50% of the votes under the simplified model where voters always vote for the same party, and do not add noise to the choice. We are working on more advanced models to allow for voters to change their minds between elections systems, and compensate for noise added by rouge voters who do not conform to the voting protocol.

In addition to improving the mathematical model, we are in the process of designing (and obtaining ethical approval) for a "pseudo" election process, which will result in a data set similar to the one obtained in real elections. We will use this data set to verify and improve our attack.

Acknowledgement

The first author of was supported in part by the Israeli Ministry of Science and Technology graduate students grant.

8. REFERENCES

[1] D. Chaum. Untraceable Electronic Mail, Return Addresses, and Digital Pseudonyms. *Commun. ACM*, 24(2):84–88, 1981.

[2] Knesset. Basic law: The knesset - 1958. Available online at http://tinyurl.com/nz6qf3l.

[3] A. Pfitzmann and M. Köhntopp. Anonymity, Unobservability, and Pseudonymity - A Proposal for Terminology. In H. Federrath, editor, *Workshop on Design Issues in Anonymity and Unobservability*, volume 2009 of *LNCS*, pages 1–9. Springer, 2000.

[4] The Inter-Parliamentary Council. DECLARATION ON CRITERIA FOR FREE AND FAIR ELECTIONS. Unanimously adopted by the Inter-Parliamentary Council at its 154th session, March 1994.

POSTER: Secure Authentication from Facial Attributes with no Privacy Loss

Orr Dunkelman
orrd@cs.haifa.ac.il

Margarita Osadchy
rita@cs.haifa.ac.il

Mahmood Sharif
mahmood.sharif01@gmail.com

University of Haifa, Mount Carmel, Haifa, Israel 31905

ABSTRACT

Biometric authentication is more secure than using regular passwords, as biometrics cannot be "forgotten" and contain high entropy. Thus, many constructions rely on biometric features for authentication, and use them as a source for "good" cryptographic keys. At the same time, biometric systems carry with them many privacy concerns.

We describe a proof-of-concept (PoC) which transforms facial attributes from a **single** image into keys in a consistent, discriminative, and privacy-aware manner. The outcome is a user-specific string that cannot be guessed, and it reveals **no** information concerning the users of the system, even when the system's secrets are revealed.

Categories and Subject Descriptors

D.4.6 [**Operating Systems**]: Security and Protection—*Authentication, Cryptographic controls*; I.5.4 [**Pattern Recognition**]: Applications—*Computer vision*

Keywords

Face Recognition; Privacy-Preserving; Biometric credentials

1. INTRODUCTION

Authentication of users is one of the basic problems of computer security, and forms the basis for almost any security mechanism. Passwords, the most popular method, suffer from many pitfalls. To this end, it was suggested to switch to biometric authentication which is simple (no more long passwords to memorize that need recovery), and secure (as they contain a sufficient amount of entropy to replace passwords). Biometric authentication, whilst useful, carries an inherent problem: the user's privacy, or more precisely his biometric information's privacy is at danger.

Unlike passwords which are hashed to protect them in the case the password file is exposed, due to the fuzziness in the sampling of biometric-based values, a different solution is needed. A possible solution is the secure sketch of [8]: During the acquisition process, when the biometric representation x is obtained, a sketch s is also produced.[1] The value of s is given to the user, and the system stores the value of $F(x,s)$. Both $F(\cdot)$ and s are chosen such that if x' is "close" to x, $F(x,s) = F(x',s)$, thus overcoming the inherent fuzziness.[2] The problem with secure sketches is their reliance on the uniform distribution of x, which many face recognition algorithms do not deliver (e.g., [3, 9]).

A possible solution to the problem is the use of fuzzy extractors [5]. However, to truly offer a secure solution, the fuzzy extractor should start with high min-entropy, as noted by Ballard et al. [1] (see Sutcu et. al [13] for a detailed discussion). Otherwise, one can easily overcome the system by a simple guessing attack on the output of $F(\cdot)$.

1.1 Our Contribution

In this work we present a biometric key derivation system[3] which is based on face recognition with a new face representation, offering the following properties:

1. Consistent and Discriminative — for a zero False Acceptance Rate (FAR), we have obtained a False Rejection Rate (FRR) of 0.19.
2. High min-entropy — we combine many simple features, each with close to optimal min-entropy (following [7]) into a high min-entropy string. Thus, our system can rely on secure sketch with no need for fuzzy extractors.
3. Provable security — the generated keys are computationally indistinguishable from random strings.
4. Fast face recognition — compared with other biometric extraction techniques, our system uses only projection operations and hamming-distance computations.
5. Provable privacy — our system protects the biometric templates when the system's information is compromised. Given s, $F(x,s)$, and our algorithm's internal values, to determine whether a user is enrolled, the adversary must sample his biometrics x.[4]

1.2 Previous Work

A large volume of work on protecting biometric templates appeared in recent years (see [12] for detailed discussion). While these works usually offer good identification, they suffer from several security and/or privacy issues:[5] short cryptographic keys; non-uniform distribution of binary strings used as inputs in fuzzy commitment and other noise tolerant constructions; dependency between bits of the key (resulting in low entropy); auxiliary data leaks personal information;

[1]The sketch s is error-correction information used whenever the user is sampled again.

[2]For security $F(x,s) \neq F(x',s)$ for x far from x'.

[3]We note that transforming it into an authentication system is trivial, e.g., storing $F(x,s)$ pairs and a corresponding UID.

[4]This property is the strong privacy definitions of [1].

[5]All prior work we are aware of suffer from at least one of these shortcomings.

CCS'13, November 4–8, 2013, Berlin, Germany.
ACM 978-1-4503-2477-9/13/11.
http://dx.doi.org/10.1145/2508859.2512511.

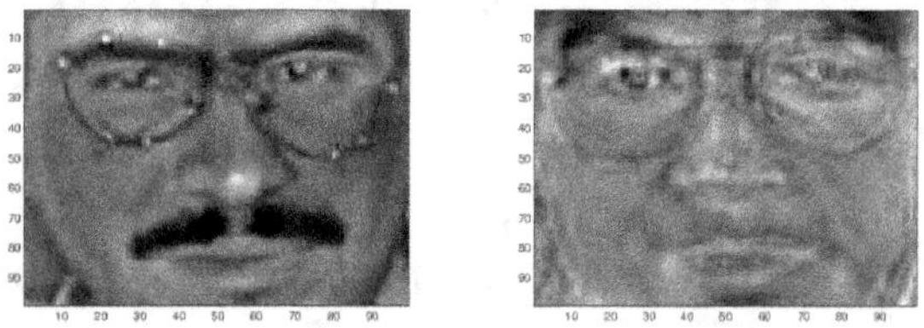

Figure 1: The similarity between the real facial image (left, taken from [11]) and the Fisherface (right).

no protection of user's biometric against adversaries with access to the cryptographic key.

For example, the scheme of [9] uses Gabor kernels on images of faces. As shown by [16], there are high-order correlations between different channels of the Gabor transform, i.e, the bits produces by this transform are correlated as well. The Random Multispace Quantization (RMQ) [14] method transforms biometric features (Fisherfaces [2]) into the secret using user-specific orthonormal random projection followed by thresholding. The random projections are defined by a secret seed released to the user for the identification phase and the secret is stored in the system. While the adversary cannot retrieve the original biometric template from the secret, it can be approximated by the pseudoinverse of the projection matrix, computed from the secret seed.[6]

Another privacy issue user-specific training phase. For example, [6] uses Fisherfaces, whose dimension is related to the number of users in the system, which implies that the system's training was done on the users of the system. Storing Fisherfaces in the clear leaks a lot of information about the faces that were used to construct them (e.g., Fig. 1).

2. OUR CONSTRUCTION

In a nutshell, our construction generates keys by concatenating many independent "short" keys (yielding sufficient entropy) following [7], which are obtained by embedding the biometric samples into a high-dimensional Hamming space. The embedding W is generated once by the learning algorithm (described below) using a public data, unrelated to the users of the system (thus W contains no private information). W is then used to transform the biometric samples into binary strings. To overcome the remaining fuzziness in the binary strings, we use the code-offset construction of [5] (which is the fuzzy commitment of [8] for $\mathcal{F} = \{0,1\}$).

Biometric Sampling: Each image in the system is transformed to a canonical pose by localizing facial landmarks and aligning the face to a predefined canonical pose (using the landmarks). This process is followed by biometric feature extraction, in which we compute LBP and SIFT descriptors for 21 facial regions and HOG on the cropped face (116×106 pixels). We concatenate all descriptors ([18]) and reduce their dimension to 700 using PCA.

Generation of W: We generate a K-bit Hamming embedding, using K binary hash functions.[7] For the zero-mean data, the k-th hash function is defined as $1/2(\mathbf{sgn}(w_k^T x)+1)$, where $x \in R^D$ is a data point and w_k is a projection vector. The learning problem is to find set of vectors $W = [w_1, \ldots, w_K]$ in R^D, with $\|w_k\|^2 = 1$ that produces the embedding and gives the same bits for samples of the same person and different bits for samples of different people.

To optimize the entropy of the key, we maximize the entropy of each bit and make them mutually independent. It was shown in [17] that the entropy of the hash function can be maximized by maximizing the scaled variance of the projected data. We use the learning algorithm of [17] that considers similar formulation to find $w_1, \ldots w_K$ sequentially, making them as orthogonal as possible (while preserving the accuracy and the high entropy of each bit). The learned embedding produces independent bits, because frontal faces under mild changes in illumination follow Gaussian distribution and thus, after whitening, their projections on orthogonal w_k are mutually independent.

Enrollment: The first time a template of a new subject is presented it is transformed to a string x (as described above). Then, we generate a template $t = 1/2(\mathbf{sgn}(W^T x) + 1)$, used as the input to the secure sketch process (which chooses a codeword C, computes $s = C + t$, and sets $F = h(C)$ for some one-way function $h(\cdot)$). The user also gets s.

Key Resampling: A new image of the person is obtained, normalized, and the biometric features are extracted, forming a vector x'. The binary representation is obtained by $t' = 1/2(\mathbf{sgn}(W^T x') + 1)$. The user supplies s and along with t' we compute $C' = EC(s + t')$, where $EC(\cdot)$ is the error-correction function. If x' and x are close, then $C' = C$.

3. EXPERIMENTAL RESULTS

To assess the performance of our proposed system we used images of near frontal faces with minor expression and illumination changes. To learn the embedding matrix W, we created a training set from seven public databases, containing 740 persons, with 3-4 images per subject. We learned 512 hyperplanes (the number of hyperplanes was chosen to optimize the FAR, FRR, and the key length).

The test set included 100 subjects from two databases, with 3 images per subject. The individuals in the test set **did not overlap** with those in the training set. Two binary representations were created for each test subject: the first representation was created from the average of the first two images and was used for enrollment, the second representation was created from the third image and was used for authentication. We assessed the recognition performance in five rounds cross-validation, in each one of the rounds a different fifth of the data served as impostors, and the number of true-positives and false-positives was calculated for each threshold in the range from 0 to 512.

We compared our method to "random projections" and Eigenfaces [15] using the same data and the same testing framework. The tests using random projections show the importance of the learning process used to generate the embedding.[8] The Eigenfaces is a well-known face recognition algorithm that we used for baseline comparison. Fig. 2 compares the ROC curves. Our PoC can achieve FRR of 10% at FAR of 0%. However, to obtain longer keys, we decided to choose the threshold corresponding to FRR of 19% at FAR

[6]It was observed in [10] that the seed is unique, and thus the projection matrix can serve as a user identity.

[7]We alert the reader that the term which we use follow the face recognition community one, and does not refer to one-way hash functions.

[8]To avoid reporting outlier results on random hyperplanes, we report the average of 5 tests, using a different set of 512 orthonormal hyperplanes each time.

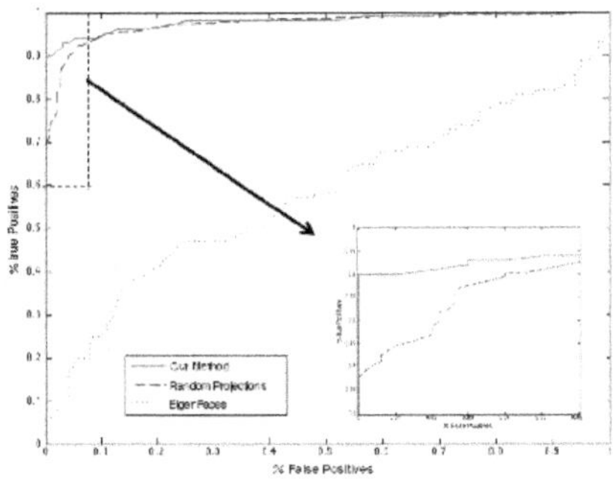

Figure 2: Comparison of ROC Curves

of 0% (compared to random projections with FRR of 36.6% and of FAR 0% for the same key length).

For the same person sampled twice, the average distance between x and x' is 169.76 bits (out of 512), with standard deviation of 20.78 bits. When comparing the samples of two different users x_1 and x_2, the average distance is 255.56 bits with standard deviation of 13.06 bits. For the secure sketch, we need to correct about 187 bits. The sphere bound shows that in this case, the corrected strings (C) are of slightly more than 30 bits.

Given that the obtained identification rates (FAR vs. FRR) are very good, and that the system discriminates between different users, we are left with the three security properties of [1] to consider: Key Randomness (the keys contains sufficient entropy), Weak Biometric Privacy (REQ-WBP, an adversary cannot learn about the biometrics of a user, from the information stored in the system and/or by the user), and Strong Biometric Privacy (REQ-SBP, given $F(x, s)$ in addition to the information of REQ-WBP, the adversary learns nothing about the user's biometrics).

Our system suggests REQ-SBP (which implies REQ-WBP). Consider an adversary that knows W, o, and $F(x, s)$: the matrix W used in the conversion of biometric into a binary string, the "helper data" s, and the result of $F(x, s)$. W contains no user-specific information, and due to the used secure sketch, one cannot extract information concerning x from $F(x, s)$ and s. As x itself is protected, it is easy to see that recovering the user's biometric information is infeasible.

Key Randomness: We now analyze how many bits of entropy we expect from a generated key. The generated representation contains 512 bits, which need to be as independent as possible to assure high min-entropy. As our construction suggests, this is indeed our optimization. We first note that the average dot product of the planes suggested by W is 0.022 (i.e., close to orthogonal) with a standard deviation of 0.020. In addition, we have computed the degrees of freedom in these strings (as suggested in [4]), and obtained 497.8 (which suggests only a small dependence exists).

Considering all bits in the representation as almost independent, the min-entropy is 490.4 (the maximal bias in a given bit is 0.0698, whereas the average bias is 0.0146).

Conclusions and Future Work

Currently, our PoC provides only a small number of secret key bits in a consistent manner (after the error correction). While being insufficient for real life systems, we proved that it is possible to extract a non-negligible amount of secret key material from a **single** facial image in a secure, consistent, and privacy-preserving manner.

We expect to close the gap between this PoC and a real-life system by: 1) improving the distance between two representations of the same user and 2) using additional images (such as profile picture) as part of the input. The second direction is expected to double the number of secure key bits, resulting in a system which can be used in real life.

Acknowledgements

This work was supported in part by the Israeli Ministry of Science and Technology and by the Israel Science Foundation.

4. REFERENCES

[1] L. Ballard, S. Kamara, and M. K. Reiter. The practical subtleties of biometric key generation. In *USENIX*, pages 61–74, 2008.

[2] P. Belhumeur, J. Hespanha, and D. Kriegman. Eigenfaces vs. Fisherfaces: Recognition using Class Specific Linear Projection. In *ECCV*, pages 45–58, 1996.

[3] C. Chen, R. Veldhuis, T. Kevenaar, and A. Akkermans. Biometric binary string generation with detection rate optimized bit allocation. In *CVPR Workshop on Biometrics*, pages 1–7, 2008.

[4] J. Daugman. The importance of being random: statistical principles of iris recognition. *Pattern Recogn.*, 36(2):279–291, 2003.

[5] Y. Dodis, R. Ostrovsky, L. Reyzin, and A. Smith. Fuzzy Extractors: How to Generate Strong Keys from Biometrics and Other Noisy Data. *SIAM J. Comput.*, 38(1):97–139, 2008.

[6] Y. C. Feng, P. C. Yuen, and A. K. Jain. A hybrid approach for generating secure and discriminating face template. *Trans. Info. For. Sec.*, 5:103–117, 2010.

[7] N. Frykholm and A. Juels. Error-tolerant password recovery. In *ACM CCS*, pages 1–9, 2001.

[8] A. Juels and M. Wattenberg. A Fuzzy Commitment Scheme. In *ACM CCS*, pages 28–36, 1999.

[9] T. A. Kevenaar, G. J. Schrijen, M. Veen, A. H. Akkermans, and F. Zuo. Face recognition with renewable and privacy preserving binary templates. In *IEEE Workshop on Automatic Identification Advanced Technologies*, pages 21–26, 2005.

[10] A. Kong, K.-H. Cheung, D. Zhang, M. Kamel, and J. You. An analysis of biohashing and its variants. *Pattern Recogn.*, 39(7):1359–1368, 2006.

[11] A. V. Nefian. Georgia tech face database, 1999.

[12] C. Rathgeb and A. Uhl. A survey on biometric cryptosystems and cancelable biometrics. *EURASIP J. Inf. Sec.*, 2011.

[13] Y. Sutcu, Q. Li, and N. Memon. Protecting biometric templates with sketch: Theory and practice. *Trans. Info. For. Sec.*, 2(3):503–512, 2007.

[14] A. B. Teoh, A. Goh, and D. C. Ngo. Random multispace quantization as an analytic mechanism for biohashing of biometric and random identity inputs. *IEEE Trans. Pattern Anal. Mach. Intell.*, 28(12):1892–1901, 2006.

[15] M. Turk and A. Pentland. Eigenfaces for recognition. *J. Cognitive Neuroscience*, 3(1):71–86, 1991.

[16] M. J. Wainwright and E. P. Simoncelli. Scale mixtures of Gaussians and the statistics of natural images. In *Adv. Neural Inf. Proc. Sys.*, volume 12, pages 855–861, 2000.

[17] J. Wang, S. Kumar, and S.-F. Chang. Sequential Projection Learning for Hashing with Compact Codes. In *ICML*, pages 1127–1134, 2010.

[18] X. Wang, T. X. Han, and S. Yan. An hog-lbp human detector with partial occlusion handling. In *ICCV*, pages 32–39, 2009.

POSTER: Performance Signatures of Mobile Phone Browsers

Bilal Shebaro, Di Jin, Elisa Bertino
Cyber Center and CERIAS, Purdue University, West Lafayette, IN 47907, USA
{bshebaro, jind, bertino}@purdue.edu

ABSTRACT

Several fingerprinting techniques for computer browsers have been proposed to make it possible to link together different browser sessions and possibly tie them to a user identity. As most of these techniques depend on static browser characteristics and user-installed plugins, the resulting fingerprints are not suitable for mobile browsers because of the similarity of browser characteristics on similar mobile device products in spite of the differences in software and hardware. Moreover, mobile devices are shipped with pre-installed plugins that cannot be modified, which limits browser uniqueness. Therefore, we propose a dynamic mobile browser fingerprinting technique that records the browser's behavior and execution characteristics by running background customized browser scripts. Our dynamic technique is based on the use of Javascript, HTML5, Flash, and other scripts that are used to generate performance signatures of mobile browsers to detect the browser used, the operating system version, and device type. Our browser detection technique compares the active browser session signature with existing signatures through three detection methods: (1) Euclidean Distance, (2) Cosine Similarity, and (3) Voting System. In this paper we compare the detection rates of these methods and their accuracy in determining the mobile browser in use.

Categories and Subject Descriptors

E.0 [**Data**]: General

Keywords

Browser fingerprinting signatures; browser script engines; Euclidean Distance; Cosine Similarity

1. INTRODUCTION

The goal of this work is to propose a dynamic fingerprinting technique for mobile browsers based on relative browser performance of code execution which is more accurate than existing static fingerprinting techniques.

Motivations. The traditional approach for identifying a user in an online service is through the user's credentials (username and password). However, many websites that offer secure online services, such as online banking, typically require a stronger form of identification to avoid hijacking or impersonation. Lately, many such websites have been using additional means of identification, such as hardware tokens or static browser characteristics (such as the user-agent header), that are combined with users' credentials to identify users and recognize them between visits or during their visits. Hardware tokens are not a good solution due to their cost and low usability, and static browser characteristics can be easily modified or hidden and thus are not robust enough.

Previously known fingerprinting techniques, such as those explored in EFF's Panopticlick project [1], rely solely on static browser characteristics and user-installed plugins that have been successful in uniquely identifying computer browsers. However, such techniques are not practical on mobile devices because of the many similarities of mobile browsers and limited plugin support, which represents a main factor in browser uniqueness. For example, the Panopticlick browser fingerprint would identify >21 bits of entropy on the uniqueness of an iMac Safari computer browser, compared to under 10 bits of entropy on the iPhone smartphone Safari browser. Therefore, there is the need of new techniques to go beyond static browser characteristics of mobile phones in order to enhance the uniqueness of mobile browsers and improve the robustness in determining the browser used.

Related Work. Many approaches have been investigated for fingerprinting user web browsers, either for legitimate reasons or for malicious and tracking purposes. The first large scale study was conducted by Eckersley showing that various properties of a user's browser and plugins can be combined to form a unique fingerprint [1]. Yen *et al.* carried out a similar fingerprinting study by analyzing logs of Bing and Hotmail [6]. They also used the IP address as part of the fingerprinting process, unlike Eckersley who considers IP address as unstable. Mowery *et al.* proposed fingerprinting computer browsers by recording the completion time of pre-defined Javascript benchmarks [3]. While their method can successfully determine the running browser family, it requires over 3 minutes to fully execute each benchmark, which is impractical in shorter webpage view-time [2]. Finally, Olejnik *et al.* investigated how web history can be used also as a way of fingerprinting without the need of client-side state [5]. Even though most browsers do not any longer have the CSS-visited history bug that made fingerprinting though web history possible, Olejnik *et al.* claim that large script providers are still capable of fingerprinting user browsers through the web visited history [4].

Contributions. We propose a mobile browser fingerprinting technique that is based on the performance differences between browsers on the same or different mobile devices, which allows us to detect not only the browser type but also the device type and operating system version. We investigated various browser capabilities available on popular smartphones and created

CCS'13, November 4–8, 2013, Berlin, Germany.
ACM 978-1-4503-2477-9/13/11.
http://dx.doi.org/10.1145/2508859.2512512.

a customized mobile browser fingerprinting scripts composed of a set of various Javascript, HTML5, Flash and other graphic scripts. We hosted these scripts on our web server with only a subset of these scripts to be chosen dynamically at run-time to execute on the user's browser upon visiting our web server. This is necessary for the fingerprinting process to finish in a timely manner within the user webpage view-time so it can record the execution times of the running scripts. The execution times act as the browser signature and are uploaded to a database server to determine the familiarity of the connected device. We experimentally tested the determination of browser signatures through three different detection methods; (1) Euclidean Distance, (2) Cosine Similarity, and (3) Voting System. As our database contains fingerprints of various smartphone browsers, we compare the results of each method and its accuracy in detecting the browser used.

Our fingerprinting technique is useful for websites that have customized scripts and services for each device type and browser as part of their security measurements. Moreover, it can be also used for websites that require to know and validate the familiarity of a connected device of returning users to avoid hijacking or impersonation. As these websites may use our fingerprinting scripts within their websites, they would need to create their own signature database to capture their users' browser signatures and may combine them with user passwords to form stronger security against account hijackers.

2. FINGERPRINTING SCHEME

Web browsers on smartphones have adopted several script engines able of running common web scripts but still much slower than computer browsers. This is due to the limited power of their CPUs and GPUs that take part of browser performance in addition to browser script engines. As these processors vary from one mobile phone generation to another even within the same phone model, browser script engines are browser dependent and vary within different browser versions or operating system versions. We take advantage of these variations and build our fingerprinting scripts to recognize performance differences upon running these scripts to identify the type of browser, operating system, and the type of the mobile device.

2.1 Implementation

Our fingerprinting scripts consist of customized Javascript, HTML5 and Flash scripts that test the browser performance on pixel drawing, complex vector fills and gradients, visual computations, and video decoder performance. We first selected a number of script benchmarks, namely the Sunspider, Kraken, and V8 Javascript benchmarks, and the GUIMark graphical scripts, and tested their performance on several Apple, Android and Windows smartphone and tablet devices. We then classified these scripts according to their execution time difference and chose the ones with significant performance differences among the tested devices. We analyzed the cause of those performance differences and modified the scripts in order to customize them to better reflect their execution time difference when tested on these devices. Finally, we created our fingerprinting scripts that is composed of 24 test scripts, where only 10 tests will be chosen at run-time to execute upon loading our website. These scripts are carefully chosen to form a 10-dimensional vector fingerprint signature that is sufficient to characterize the performance of the tested device. The 10-dimensional vector is then uploaded to our web server for detection purposes.

2.2 Data Collection and Optimization

Our data collection contains sample fingerprints of the most popular smartphones and web browsers, such as iPhones, iPads, Android, and Windows devices running Chrome, Firefox, Internet Explorer (for Windows phones) and Safari (for Apple devices). We ran each test script 10 times on each browser for every device and averaged their execution times to minimize the effects of other scripts running at the same time. As each operating system on these devices comes with a pre-installed web browser, we witnessed performance differences of our fingerprint scripts of the same browser and device when running on a different operating system version. For example, our test script execution times for the Safari browser on the iPhone 4 running iOS 5.1 are significantly slower when it was running on iOS 6.1.3. This is due to the enhancements applied to browsers and the overall system upon the installation of an updated version of the operating system. Therefore, we model our fingerprint signatures as tuples representing the device type, browser and operating system version. Each tuple fingerprint signature is represented with at most a 24-dimensional vector that is saved in our database. We collected browser signatures of over 40 different tuples which were enough to find deviations between browsers of popular smartphones of various types. While our collected data is small to draw any statistical conclusions, we established consistency in browser deviations that were novel to distinguish browsers on the tested devices.

We customized the 24 test scripts for browser fingerprinting to target specific browser engine features and revisions. For optimization purposes, only 10 test scripts are chosen at run-time upon a website visit to ensure the total execution time of the chosen test scripts is under a minute. The 10 test scripts are chosen so that the resulting 10-dimensional vector contains enough measurements of the browser script engines that can identify the tested browser. Finally, the resulting vector is compared to the existing browser signatures collected in our database for detection purposes.

2.3 Detecting Browser Signatures

In our experiments, we examine three different detection methods that compare the fingerprinting signature of the tested browser with existing browser signatures from our database:

(1) Euclidean Distance: The signature of each tuple in our database is represented by a 24-dimensional vector space. We measured the Euclidean distances among all the vectors to find correlations between different browsers running on the same device or the same browser running of different devices. To classify an unknown vector that is composed of a 10-dimensional vector, we compute the Euclidean distance between the unknown vector and the 10-dimensional vector of the existing tuple signatures that match the tested fingerprinting scripts. We then choose the tuple that has the minimum Euclidean distance with respect to the unknown vector according to the equation:

$$Euclidean\ Distance\ (A, B) = \sqrt{\Sigma(A_i - B_i)^2}$$

(2) Cosine Similarity: We use this measurement to identify any scaling correlation that may exist among the existing vector signatures along with the unknown vector. As with some browser versions of Chrome, the execution times of some test scripts were consistently scaling when tested on faster devices. The cosine similarity is a good indicator for such cases especially that the Euclidean distance may fail to detect such correlation. Finally, after we measure the cosine similarity of the unknown vector with respect to the existing tuple signatures, we choose the tuple with the highest correlation, that is, with cosine similarity closest to 1, computed using the equation:

$$Cosine\ Similarity(\overrightarrow{A}, \overrightarrow{B}) = \frac{\overrightarrow{A}.\overrightarrow{B}}{\|A\|\|B\|} = \frac{\Sigma A_i \times B_i}{\sqrt{\Sigma A_i^2} \times \sqrt{\Sigma B_i^2}}$$

(3) Voting System: This test measures the differences among every dimension of the compared signature vectors and votes for the closest value tuple (minimum difference per dimension). The votes are then combined from each vector dimension to classify the unknown vector with the highest number of votes.

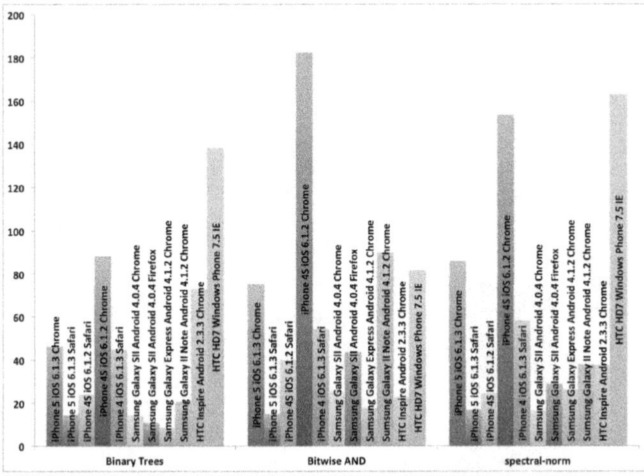

Figure 1: Sample Javascript signatures measured in milliseconds.

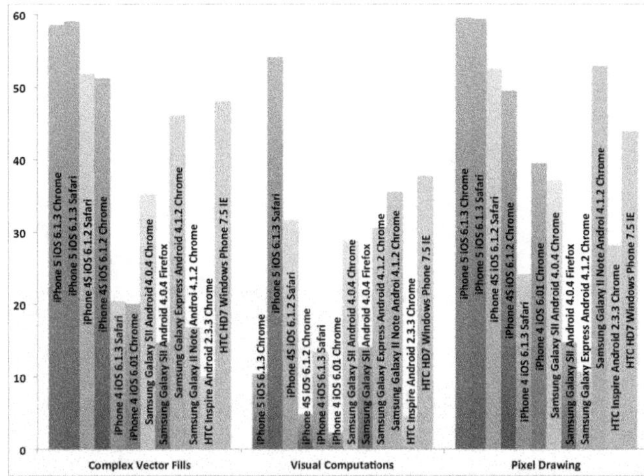

Figure 2: Sample graphical signatures measured in frames per second (fps).

For each of the above tests, we set a threshold that indicates whether or not the resulted classification of the unknown vector is to be considered. This threshold limits down any tuple misclassification and indicates whether or not the tested browser is pre-defined in our existing set of browser signatures. If the browser under testing does not pass any preset threshold, we classify the browser as unknown and add it to our collection of unknown browser signatures which is later added to our database once we confirm the device tuple information.

3. RESULTS

To clearly determine the differences in web browser script engines, we here examine the ability of our fingerprinting scripts to exploit a unique browser execution signature for each tuple (browser, device type, operating system version). To create the fingerprinting signature of each browser per device, we executed the complete set of fingerprinting scripts (24 scripts) on each browser 10 times and averaged the resulted vector dimensions. Our dataset provides enough signatures of Safari (for Apple devices), Internet explorer (for Windows phones), Chrome, and Firefox browsers of popular smartphones. The tested devices include the Apple iPhones and iPads running iOS v. 5.0.1 to v. 6.1.3, various Samsung, HTC and Sony devices running Android OS v. 4.0.4 to v. 4.1.2, in addition to fewer HTC devices running Windows OS 7.5. Figures 1 and 2 show a subset of our browser vector signatures showing samples of tested devices.

For testing purposes, we set our fingerprinting website to only choose and run 10 scripts sequentially per visit with a total execution time to be under a minute. Upon completion, the 10-dimensional vector is uploaded for tuple determination using the three detection methods discussed in Section 2. Table 1 displays the accuracy of the three detection methods on a subset of the tested devices available in our database records.

4. CONCLUSION

In this paper we introduced a dynamic fingerprinting technique for mobile web browsers that makes use of the performance differences in browser script engines in order to obtain unique browser signatures. Our technique takes advantage of the execution time differences between instructions sequences used in Javascript, HTML5, Flash and times the performance of operations in the core mobile browser script engines. Such differences can not only distinguish the browser but also the mobile device and the operating system version.

Table 1: Detection rates of fingerprint signatures of sample mobile browsers.

	Euclidean Distance	Cosine Similarity	Voting System
iPhone 5 iOS 6.1.3 Chrome	87.1%	76.6 %	79.8 %
iPhone 5 iOS 6.1.3 Safari	92.2 %	86.3 %	87.4 %
iPhone 4S iOS 6.1.2 Chrome	76.8 %	78.5 %	88.2 %
iPhone 4S iOS 6.1.2 Safari	83 %	74.3 %	79.9 %
iPhone 4 iOS 6.01 Safari	89.4 %	86.1 %	89.4 %
iPhone 4 iOS 6.01 Chrome	79.6 %	91.7 %	86.3 %
Galaxy SII Android 4.0.4 Chrome	77.8 %	68.5 %	79 %
Galaxy SII Android 4.0.4 Firefox	67.2 %	72.8 %	69.6 %
HTC Inspire Android 2.3.3 Chrome	71.3 %	81.7 %	76.8 %
HTC HD7 Windows Phone 7.5 IE	78.7 %	72 %	76.9 %

5. REFERENCES

[1] P. Eckersley. How unique is your web browser? In *Proceedings of the 10th international conference on Privacy enhancing technologies*, PETS'10, pages 1–18, Berlin, Heidelberg, 2010. Springer-Verlag.

[2] J.-L. Gasse and F. Filloux. Measuring time spent on a web page, 2010.

[3] K. Mowery, D. Bogenreif, S. Yilek, and H. Shacham. Fingerprinting information in JavaScript implementations. In *Proceedings of Web 2.0 Security and Privacy 2011 (W2SP)*, San Franciso, May 2011.

[4] N. Nikiforakis, L. Invernizzi, A. Kapravelos, S. Van Acker, W. Joosen, C. Kruegel, F. Piessens, and G. Vigna. You are what you include: large-scale evaluation of remote javascript inclusions. In *Proceedings of the 2012 ACM conference on Computer and communications security*, CCS '12, pages 736–747, Raleigh, NC, USA, 2012. ACM.

[5] L. Olejnik, C. Castelluccia, and A. Janc. Why Johnny Can't Browse in Peace: On the Uniqueness of Web Browsing History Patterns. In *5th Workshop on Hot Topics in Privacy Enhancing Technologies (HotPETs)*, Vigo, July 2012.

[6] T.-F. Yen, Y. Xie, F. Yu, R. P. Yu, , and M. Abadi. Host fingerprinting and tracking on the web:privacy and security implications. In *Proceedings of the 19th Annual Network and Distributed System Security Symposium (NDSS)*, 2012.

POSTER: A New Framework against Privilege Escalation Attacks on Android

Wenming Zhou
State Key Lab of Integrated Service Network, Xidian University
Xi'an, China, 710126
wmzhou@stu.xidian.edu.cn

Yuqing Zhang
National Computer Network Instrusion Protection Center, UCAS
Beijing, China, 100048
zhangyq@nipc.org.cn

Xuefeng Liu
State Key Lab of Integrated Service Network, Xidian University
Xi'an, China, 710071
liuxf@mail.xidian.edu.cn

ABSTRACT

The Android provides a permission-based security model to restrict the operations that each application can perform; however, it has been shown to be vulnerable to privilege escalation attacks. Applications can cooperate to perform operations that forbidden to perform separately which may lead to privacy leakage. In this poster, we present the design of a new policy-centered security framework against the application-level privilege escalation attacks. Different from previous policy-centered schemes, the communication content is also considered into the inspection besides the permissions. Specially, we allow the privacy information selectively to be passed in the middleware and deploy a mandatory access control at the kernel based on the dynamical taint tracking. Test results show that it can prevent known confused deputy attacks and is also flexible to prevent the unknowns; furthermore it can reduce the false positives of preventing colluding attacks compared to the previous work.

Categories and Subject Descriptors: D.4.6 [Operating Systems]: Security and Protection

General Terms: Security

Keywords

Privilege Escalation Attacks, Taint Tracking, Privacy Protection

1. INTRODUCTION

In the Android's permission-based security model, applications are only granted permissions that they really need and each application runs in a sandbox as its own user. Files owned by one application shall not be accessed by another except that they are explicitly exposed by the developers [1]. However, this security model has been shown to be vulnerable to privilege escalation attacks [2-5, and 8] including collusion attacks and confused deputy attacks. Previous works [6, 7] have identified such problems and provided various overt as well as covert channels between colluding applications to launch privilege escalation attacks. Colluding applications constructed to aggregate their permissions, and therefore they can indirectly execute operations that should not be able to execute based on their individually permissions. To deal with such attacks, many security extensions and enhancements have been proposed such as TaintDroid [2], IPC Inspection, SEAndroid, QUIRE [11], XManDroid [3, 4] and so on. However, none of these existing schemes can efficiently protect the user's privacy leakage via privilege escalation attacks. As a countermeasure, TaintDroid presented a way of perceiving the leakage of privacy data by tracking the privacy flow within and among applications. XManDroid proposed a framework which allows for enforcing a flexible range of policies, semantic links established between IPCs can be verified at the middleware level. And Mandatory Access Control is deployed at the kernel level. It has a limitation that the communication prevention appears regardless of the actual communication content and therefore might lead to false positives, and it does not allow an application to regain privileges which they lost due to the communication with other applications.

CCS'13, November 4–8, 2013, Berlin, Germany.
ACM 978-1-4503-2477-9/13/11.
http://dx.doi.org/10.1145/2508859.2512513

Our model can protect Android against privilege escalation attacks by introducing two design principles. The framework is similar to XManDroid, however, the communication content is carefully considered into the inspection. Our main contributions are summarized as follows.

(1) We propose a policy-centered framework maintaining a white-list storing the call-chains or accesses that can be allowed to provide security itself. While the security of XManDroid depends on the effective policies.
(2) Inspired by QUIRE, we propose an automated permissions granted mechanism. When an IPC is to be established, the callee shall receive reduced permissions during the first life-cycle.
(3) Benefit from TaintDroid, we introduce a scheme to concern the actual communication content of IPCs at the middleware and combine the taint tracking technique with Mandatory Access Control mechanism at the kernel level.

2. FRAMEWORK DESIGN

We give an overview at the beginning, and then we present two design principles. Later we describe the involved components in detail and how they interact with each other.

2.1 Overview

Inspired by XManDroid, our security framework also performs both runtime monitoring and analysis of communications across applications. In contrast to XManDroid, our framework only enforces two basic policies following the two design principles proposed in subsection 2.2. All IPCs which don't accord with the two principles should be denied except that they are in the white list. Considering covert channels, once a new covert channel has been found, a policy can be added to the black list in order to prevent the communication via the new channel.

2.2 Design Principles

Before describing the two design principles, we define two conceptions as follows. Consider that application A is granted the permissions $P_A = \{p_{A1}, p_{A2} \cdots p_{Ai} \cdots p_{An}\}$, and according to its permissions it can access a privacy data collection $D_A = \{d_{A1}, d_{A2} \cdots d_{Ai} \cdots d_{An}\}$, where $i \in Z^*$. Similarly, let P_B and D_B denote the permission set and privacy data collection of application B respectively. When A attempts to establish an IPC to B, the privilege escalation permissions set $P_{escalation} = P_B - (P_A \cap P_B)$, and the data leakage set $D_{leakage} = (D_A \cup D_B) - (D_A \cap D_B)$ are defined.

Limitation of permission. Inter Component Communication at the middleware (ICC) enforces the policy that a component without permissions p should not call a component with permission p. That is to say $P_{escalation}$ is limited of the callee.

Isolation of privacy data. This applications should not access to privacy data which they don't have permissions to access. Namely, $D_{leakage}$ should not be passed during the IPCs.

2.2.1 *Life-cycle Based Permission Mechanism*

Inspired by the solution of QUIRE, we will check the permissions of the caller and the callee when an ICC is to be established. If the permission set $P_{escalation} \neq \emptyset$, then we limit the permissions of the callee during one life cycle time. Through the analysis of 50 applications, we found 98% privilege escalation attacks occurred during the first life-cycle of the exposure components. So we consider the callee's permissions belonging to $P_{escalation}$ should be limited during the first life-cycle. When the caller is system, it obviously requires additional consideration.

2.2.2 *ICC Inspection*

It is designed to inspect the communication between components with different UIDs in the middleware. Its function includes the computing of $P_{escalation}$, extracting the *Intent* object passed among components and checking whether it contains privacy data with the help of taint tracking at message level provided by TaintDroid.

2.2.3 *Privacy-Type-Based Access Control*

Applications with different UIDs are isolated in Discretionary Access Control mechanism (DAC). But DAC does not concern the applications colluding. In collusion scenario, in order to protect the particular privacy data fine-grained, we propose the *Privacy Type Access Control* (PTBAC) that allows Mandatory Access Control (MAC) on Android at the kernel level. The differences between PTBAC and MAC lie in that the PTBAC's access policies are dynamical based on taint tracking. When the taint tracking system becomes aware of that a particular type of privacy data is written to a file, the taint information will be analyzed and stored to the policies database. If another application is to access the file, PTBAC policies will be enforced to ensure that it should not access to particular type of privacy data which it does not have permissions to access.

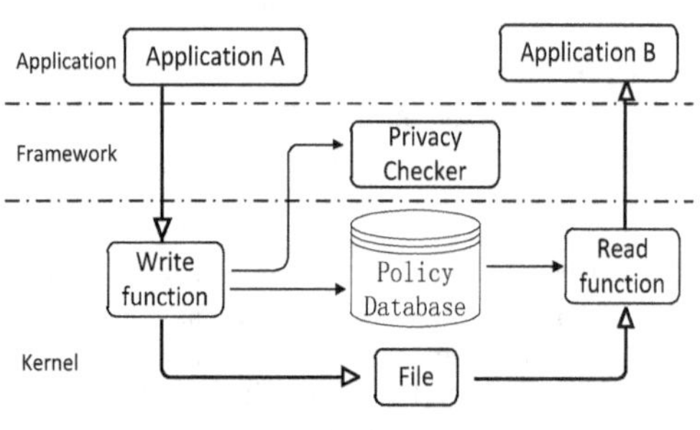

Figure 1. Privacy Type Based Access Control.

As shown in Fig. 1, when App A writes data to a file, the privacy check model will confirm whether the data contains confidential information. When App B is to access the file, PTBAC will check whether the file is tainted and enforce access control.

2.2.4 *Role-Based Management model*

By default, the callee will receive reduced permissions during the first life-cycle in an ICC, and the $D_{leakage}$ is not allowed to be passed. However the user may have special requirements in particular situation where applications have to perform colluding in order to provide normal functions. The Google Play divided its applications into 34 categories. Thus, at least 34 roles are set of initialization in our model and users can assign one or more roles to an application after the installation, besides, a role can be assigned to one or more applications after the definition. A role named SYSTEM is assigned to all the system applications by default. Any other new roles can be defined or delete by users. Consider two applications A and B, A is the caller in an ICC or it is to access a file created by application B. Case1: Application A with the SYSTEM role. There is no need to deal with anything. Case 2: Application A and B are third-party applications. In this case further inspection of the roles is needed.

2.2.5 *Policy creation and management*

We propose a model named ARBAC to create and manage the security policies by combining Role-Based Access Control (RBAC) with Attribute-Based Access Control (ABAC). In ARBAC, the privileges of accessing to resources (files, applications, etc.) are dynamically assigned to the applications depending on the attribute values (permissions, roles etc.) at the kernel. And in the middleware, privileges to perform operations (establishing ICCs etc.) and the resources (the content of ICCs etc.) are also dynamically assigned to applications depending on their attribute values(permissions, roles etc.).

Each policy is encapsulated as an independent atom policy to ensure the compatibility and scalability of ARBAC. The final decision is made of the combination of all these atom policies. What is more, the policies have different priorities for access control. With all the defined entities and their attributes, single policy can be described as below:

$$Policy_i ::= \{ Rule_1, Rule_2 \cdots Rule_i \cdots Rule_n, pri_i \}. \quad (1)$$

Where n>0, $Rule_i$ is an expression which composed of attribute value with logical operators. pri_i is the priority of this policy. The final decision is made by the combine function:

$$Decision \leftarrow fcombine\,(Policy_1, Policy_2 \cdots Policy_n). \quad (2)$$

2.3 Component Interaction

The architecture is presented in Figure 2. In the following paragraphs, we will introduce the interactions among each module of the framework. The main analysis involves two processes: ICC call handling (step 1-10), creating or writing a file (step a-d) and file read access (steps i - v).

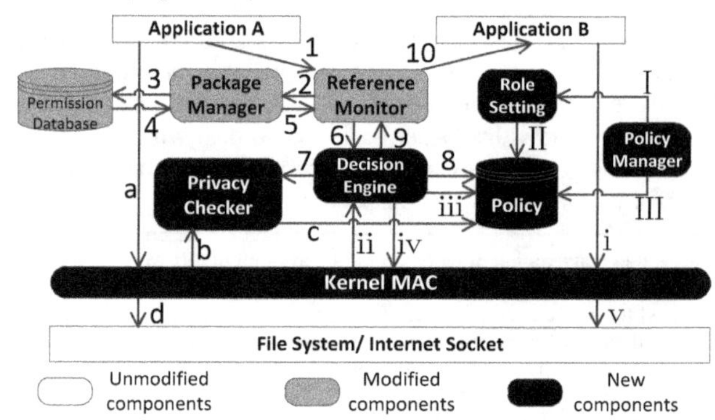

Figure 2. Interactions among the components.

ICC calls handling. All the ICC calls shall be intercepted by the *ReferenceMonitor* (step 1). It calls the *PackageManager* (step 2) to query the database for validating permission assignments about the caller and callee. The *PackageManager* then calculates $P_{escalation}$ of the two intercepting components and records it to the Android permission database (step 3). This will result in the callee with a reduced permission set during the first life cycle. Then the *PackageManager* returns the validated results (step 4-5). If the *ReferenceMonitor* allows the ICC call, it invokes the *DecisionEngine* (step 6) to ensure the communication complies with other security policies. Next, the *DecisionEngine* intercepts to the *PrivacyChecker* (step 7). The *PrivacyChecker* will tackle the *Intent* parcel to obtain the tainted tag at the message level provided by the TaintDroid project. If the *Intent* parcel contains tainted data, the *DecisionEngine* then requests for a policy corresponding to this particular type of ICC calls from the policy database (step 8). If a matching policy is found, it means that the user allows for this particular call. Further, the *DecisionEngine* informs *ReferenceMonitor* about decisions it has made (step 9), and *ReferenceMonitor* either allows (step 10) or denies the call.

Operation on files. Files and sockets are most usually made use of to establish various channels for colluding applications to interact with each other. The PTBAC involves when an application performs operations on a file or socket. When a file (step a) is to be written, the *PrivacyChecker* is performing runtime monitoring all the time. If the taint tracking system becomes aware of that particular type of privacy data are written to the file(step b), the file becomes tainted, then the taint information will be analyzed and stored to the policy database (step c). When another application is to access the file, or make a connection to the local socket (step ⅰ), PTBAC mechanism will check the application what permissions it have, and query the policy database (step ⅱ - ⅲ). If a matching policy is found, it means that this particular access request is allowed by the user. Further, the *DecisionEngine* informs the mandatory access control (MAC) module in the Linux kernel about the decision it has made (stepⅳ), and MAC module either allows (step ⅴ) or denies the access request.

3. EVALUATION

We ran a series of tests to evaluate our framework which was installed on a HUAWEI T8808D with a modified version 4.1. Firstly we evaluate the default case without any security settings. Attacks published in [7, 9, 10] can all be prevented by the framework, but some third-party applications that need working together to perform didn't work. Secondly, we assign a role to these applications and then they work normally. Thirdly, some collusion attacks were tested using covert channels with Single Setting, Multiple Settings and Automatic Intents, and these attacks can all be detected. However, the channels using /proc/stat and Threads Enumeration cannot be blocked until we enforce extra policies. Finally we compared our framework to the previous shown in Table 1.

Table 1. Prevention effect of the countermeasures

Framework	Privilege Escalation Attack: Confused Deputy Attacks(50 samples)	Privilege Escalation Attack: Collusion Attacks (7 samples)
XManDroid	Effective and flexible	High false positives
TaintDroid	Ineffective	Tracking privacy flow
Our Design	Effective and flexible	No false positives

We haven't run tests on the performance overhead of quantitative, but it is below human perception in our test and we didn't notice any performance delays. The performance overhead is mainly caused by the dynamic taint tracking.

4. CONCLUSION

We presented a new extension to the Android in order to prevent privilege escalation attacks. It is an improvement of XManDroid and also is policy-centered. The framework analyzes application communication in permission and content to ensure it complies with the two design principles. In contrast to XManDroid, a role-based management model is embedded in our framework which enables the user to set a white-list, maintaining the call-chains or accesses that can be allowed by the system. In this architecture, the advantages of policy-centered framework are preserved and we can reduce the false positives of preventing the collusion attacks. Test result show it is efficient. Besides, our framework does not rely on the application developers to perform extra work.

ACKNOWLEDGMENTS

Our work was supported by the Google's Academic Cooperation Program and the Natural Science Foundation of China under Grant No.61272481.

5. REFERENCES

[1] Google Android. http://www.android.com/.

[2] W. Enck, P. Gilbert, B.-G. Chun *et al.*, TaintDroid: an information-flow tracking system for real-time privacy monitoring on smart phones. In *Proc. of the 9th USENIX conference on Operating systems design and implementation, Vancouver, British Columbia, Canada*, pages 1–6. USENIX Association, October 2010.

[3] S. Bugiel, L. Davi, A. Dmitrienko *et al.* Towards taming privilege escalation attacks on android. In *Proc. of the 19th Annual Network & Distributed System Security Symposium (NDSS'12), San Diego, CA, USA*, February 2012.

[4] N. Husted, H. Sa¨di *et al.*, Smartphone security limitations: conflicting traditions. In *Proc. of the 2011 Workshop on Governance of Technology, Information, and Policies (GTIP'11), New York, USA*, pages 5–12. ACM, Dec. 2011.

[5] Y. Zhou and X. Jiang. Dissecting android malware: Characterization and evolution. In *Proc. of the 33rd IEEE Symposium on the Security and Privacy, San Francisco, California, USA*, pages 95–109. IEEE, May 2012.

[6] Claudio Marforio *et al.* Application Collusion Attack on the Permission-Based Security Model and its Implications for Modern Smartphone Systems. Tech. Report 724, Apr. 2011.

[7] Roman Schlegel *et al.* Soundcomber: A Stealthy and Context-Aware Sound Trojan for smart phones. In *Proceedings of the 18th Annual Network and Distributed System Security Symposium (NDSS)*, Feb. 2011.

[8] S. Bugiel, L. Davi *et al.* XManDroid: A new android evolution to mitigate privilege escalation attacks. Technical Report 04, Technische University at Darmstadt, 2011.

[9] W. Enck, M. Ongtang, and P. McDaniel. Mitigating Android software misuse before it happens. Technical Report NAS-TR-0094-2008, Penn. State University, 2008.

[10] L. Davi, A. Dmitrienko, A.-R. Sadeghi, and M. Winandy. Privilege escalation attacks on Android. In *Proceedings of the 13th Information Security Conference (ISC)*, 2010.

[11] M. Dietz *et al.* Quire: Lightweight provenance for smart phone operating systems. In *Proc. of the 20th USENIX Security Symposium (USENIX Security'11), San Francisco, California, USA*, pages 51–58, August 2011.

POSTER–TRIPLEX: Verifying Data Minimisation in Communication Systems

Meilof Veeningen, Mayla Brusò, Jerry den Hartog, and Nicola Zannone
Department of Mathematics and Computer Science, Eindhoven University of Technology
PO Box 513, 5600 MB Eindhoven, The Netherlands
{m.veeningen,m.bruso,j.d.hartog,n.zannone}@tue.nl

ABSTRACT

Systems dealing with personal information are legally required to satisfy the principle of data minimisation. Privacy-enhancing protocols use cryptographic primitives to minimise the amount of personal information exposed by communication. However, the complexity of these primitives and their interplay makes it hard for non-cryptography experts to understand the privacy implications of their use. In this paper, we present TRIPLEX, a framework for the analysis of data minimisation in privacy-enhancing protocols.

Categories and Subject Descriptors

C.2.2 [**Computer-Communication Networks**]: Network Protocols—*Protocol verification*; K.4.1 [**Computers and Society**]: Public Policy Issues—*Privacy*

Keywords

Data minimisation; Coalition Graphs; Detectability; Linkability

1. INTRODUCTION

Communication systems such as identity management systems, social networks, and e-health systems deal with ever increasing amounts of personal information. EU privacy laws require such systems to satisfy the "data minimisation" principle. That is, systems have to be designed to ensure that actors within such systems collect and store only the minimal amount of personal information needed to fulfil their task. (Note that data minimisation concerns the knowledge of insiders when the system operates normally rather than the knowledge of attackers who attempt to disrupt its operation.) An important factor in achieving data minimisation is the use of *privacy-enhancing* communication protocols which employ cryptographic primitives to ensure minimal leakage of information. In particular, they ensure that participants learn as little as possible, even when they try to combine information from different sources to build profiles. Such protocols have been proposed in various domains, including toll pricing, e-voting, e-health and identity management.

CCS'13, November 4–8, 2013, Berlin, Germany.
ACM 978-1-4503-2477-9/13/11.
http://dx.doi.org/10.1145/2508859.2512514.

Understanding exactly what privacy guarantees different protocols offer is important, e.g., for system designers that want to use privacy-enhancing protocols, or for system administrators that want to select what system to use. However, it is typically not straightforward for non-cryptography experts to obtain such an understanding. One reason is that privacy-enhancing protocols typically combine (advanced) cryptographic primitives in subtle ways; also, typical scenarios involve multiple actors which may collude to build comprehensive user profiles. Although a number of privacy analyses of such protocols have been proposed [1, 4], they are typically performed manually in an informal and high-level (and thus, possibly subjective) way. Tools for (semi-)automated analyses using formal methods are increasingly applied [3, 5], but several issues inhibit broader practical use. First, they require considerable manual work for each particular property to be verified, often needing strong assumptions to make the computation feasible. Second, property definitions are usually specific to particular protocols, making it difficult to compare different protocols; finally, results are not presented intuitively, requiring substantial manual review.

In this paper, we present TRIPLEX, a tool-supported framework that provides high-level but precise formal analysis of data minimisation to non-cryptography experts. Using TRIPLEX, users can visually construct scenarios of different actors communicating using any kind of privacy-enhancing protocol. TRIPLEX automatically simulates these scenarios, and provides different analysis tools. The tools, geared towards non-cryptography-experts, allow users to analyse the knowledge that actors learn by executing communication protocols, as well as to verify protocol-independent privacy properties. We demonstrate TRIPLEX in an e-health scenario.

2. THE TRIPLEX FRAMEWORK

In this section, we present the TRIPLEX framework.

2.1 Framework Ingredients

The main idea behind the TRIPLEX framework is to analyse relevant privacy aspects of privacy-enhancing protocols in a specified scenario that may involve several actors and protocol instances (of different protocols). Intuitively, we annotate the messages that are exchanged in the scenario to express to whom information refers; we then use formal tools to determine who can detect and link together privacy-sensitive information. Our framework is based on the following main technical ingredients:

- *Three-Layer Model of Information* – We use the three-layer model of knowledge about personal information from [6]. This model combines abstract and concrete descriptions of information. Namely, communication protocols and their desired privacy properties are described abstractly, i.e., independently from the actual information transmitted. However,

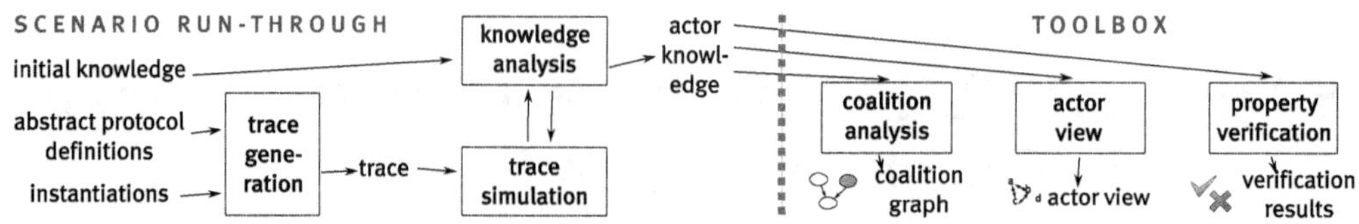

Figure 1: The TRIPLEX framework: the scenario run-through (left) and privacy analysis toolbox (right).

whether these properties are satisfied in a particular situation depends on what concrete information is used and on their contents. The model of [6] describes abstract and concrete information at three "layers", allowing protocols and privacy properties to be specified at a high level yet verified using the contents of particular pieces of information.

- *Dolev-Yao Model of Cryptography* – We employ a standard Dolev-Yao black-box model to capture the functionality of cryptographic primitives and operations used in communication protocols. In particular, we use the deductive system from [7], consisting of construction, elimination, and testing rules, to reason about messages in the three-layer model. TRIPLEX provides support for several standard (e.g., symmetric and asymmetric encryption, digital signatures, hashes) and advanced (e.g., zero-knowledge proofs, anonymous credentials) primitives, and allows extension.
- *Coalition Graphs* – Actors may collude to build more comprehensive user profiles. Coalition graphs have been proposed in [8] as a way to visually represent the knowledge of personal information about a particular data subject in a scenario. They can be derived automatically from a three-layer representation of knowledge. Intuitively, nodes in a coalition graph represent profiles of personal information about a user that a coalition can make, whereas edges represent ways for a coalition to increase its knowledge by including additional actors. Coalition graphs can be used to analyse actors' knowledge as well as to visually compare different protocols, or to compare a protocol against a predefined "privacy-optimal" situation [8].

2.2 Framework Overview

The TRIPLEX framework is shown in Figure 1. The framework consists of a *scenario run-through* component which simulates a scenario, and a *toolbox* consisting of various tools with which actors' knowledge of personal information can be analysed.

The scenario run-through simulates a user-specified scenario in which various actors exchange personal information using privacy-enhancing communication protocols. As input, this component requires a description of the scenario. This description consists of an abstract description of the protocols used (*abstract protocol definitions*), the characteristics of the information used in the protocol instances (*instantiations*), and actors' *initial knowledge*. From the abstract protocol definitions and instantiations, the component generates a *trace* representing the correct protocol execution in the three-layer model. The component then runs through the scenario by iteratively determining the knowledge of the actors at one point in time using the algorithm from [6], and using it to simulate the next step of the trace, which again changes their knowledge. Finally, the *actor knowledge* after the protocol execution is obtained. The scenario run-through component is implemented in Prolog. Optionally, knowledge analysis supports equational models of primitives by interfacing the KISS tool for static equivalence [2]. Although this extension increases the range of primitives that can be considered, it comes at the cost of decreased performance.

After the scenario has been simulated and the final actor knowledge has been determined, the toolbox can be used to analyse this knowledge. The toolbox currently consists of three tools: *coalition analysis*, *actor view*, and *property verification*. The *coalition analysis* tool automatically computes and visualises the coalition graph describing the knowledge about one particular data subject held by the (coalitions of) actors within the system. This coalition graph can be manually checked for unexpected user profiles. In addition, the tool can visualise coalition graphs comparing knowledge to a predefined "optimal knowledge" [8], allowing users to directly identify what knowledge of personal information is avoidable. The *actor view* tool computes the knowledge that (coalitions of) actors have about the users within the system. The tool also takes into account exactly where that knowledge comes from (i.e., which particular protocol instance). Thus, this low-level view of actor's knowledge can help to explain the unexpected user profiles found using coalition analysis. Finally, the *property verification* tool enables the automatic verification of privacy properties in the scenario. Rather than considering the knowledge of all coalitions of actors as before, privacy properties allow a more focused analysis of one particular aspect of knowledge (e.g., whether a coalition of actors X and Y can combine their different views of data subject Z). Any property expressible in terms of characteristics of actor views can be verified, including detectability properties (does a particular actor/coalition learn a particular piece of information), linkability properties (can a particular actor/coalition combine different views of a data subject), and involvement properties (does an actor/coalition know that a particular other actor was involved in a transaction), or arbitrary combinations of these properties.

2.3 Demonstration

We demonstrate TRIPLEX by analysing data minimisation in Parelsnoer [8], a system for distributing patient data for medical research. In Parelsnoer, data from different hospitals is collected by a *central infrastructure* (CI). By applying cryptographic hashes, the hospitals prevent the CI from learning the patient identifiers, while the CI is still able to link patient data from different hospitals together. Upon request from a medical researcher, the CI compiles a dataset from the patient data for use in a particular research project, again using cryptographic hashes to ensure that data from different research projects cannot be linked to the patient or to each other. These two different steps (hospital to CI, CI to researcher) are modelled as two different abstract protocols. In particular, they are represented in TRIPLEX as sequences of messages (Figure 2a): we indicate the format of the messages and the type of information that they contain. For instance, the first message of the first protocol is a cryptographic hash of the patient's identifier, followed by a sequence of patient data items; the first message of the second protocol is a cryptographic hash of the BSN (i.e., the Dutch social security number) and a "domain" identifying the research project, again followed by a sequence of patient data items.

Next, we define the scenario in which we want to analyse the privacy consequences of using these protocols (Figure 2b). In our scenario, two hospitals *umc1*, *umc2* provide data about patient *p* to the CI *ci*; a third hospital *umc3* does not know the patient. Hence,

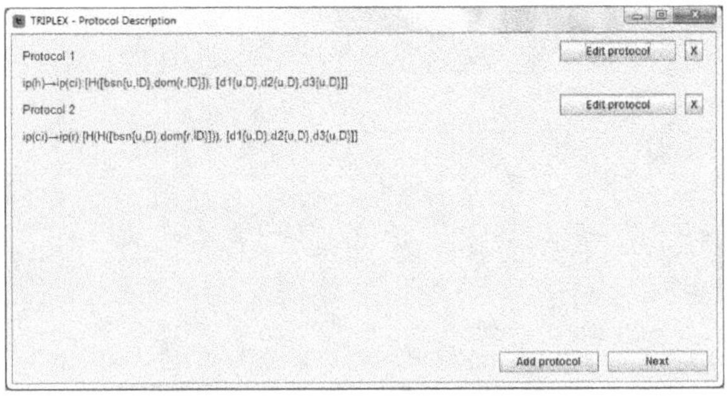

(a) Protocol descriptions

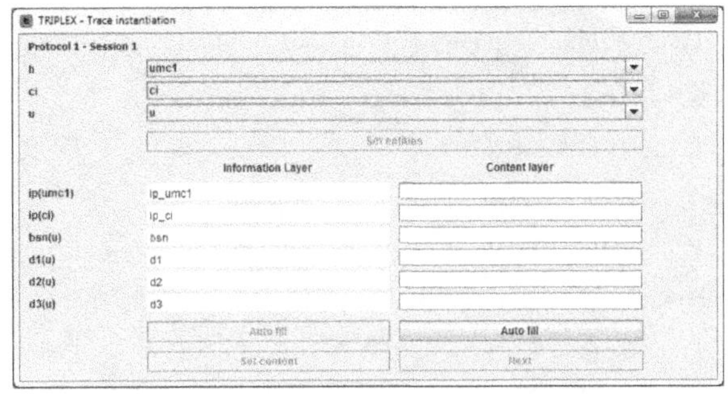

(b) Instantiating personal information

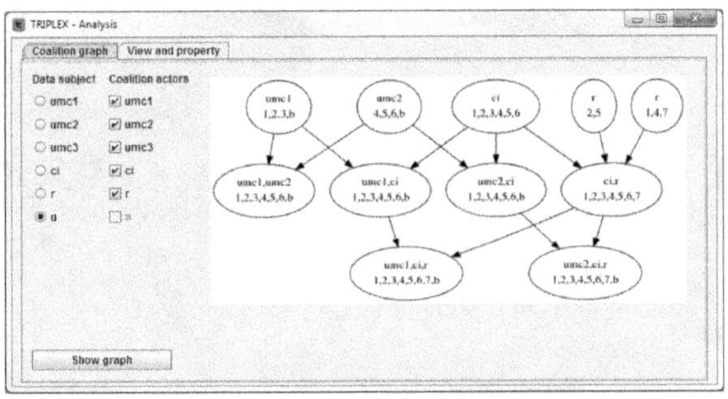

(c) Coalition analysis using coalition graph

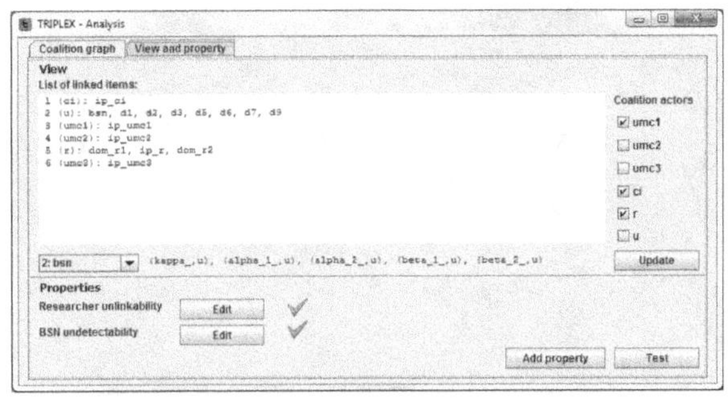

(d) Coalition view and property verification

Figure 2: The TRIPLEX framework: the scenario run-through (left), and privacy analysis toolbox (right).

we have two instantiations of the "hospital to CI"-protocol: one involving *umc1* and *ci* as communication actors and *p* as data subject, and similarly, one involving *umc2*, *ci*, and *p*. Next, researcher *r* is involved in two different research projects, and he learns data about *p* in datasets for both projects. The distribution of the dataset is modelled by two instances of the "CI to researcher" protocol. Having defined the actors and instances, we specify what information is exchanged in the scenario. Here, *umc1* and *umc2* both store three pieces of patient data, which they all provide to the CI. The researcher obtains two disjoint datasets containing patient data from both hospitals, and gathers additional data as part of his research.

After TRIPLEX has simulated the scenario, the computed knowledge of (coalitions of) actors can be analysed in different ways. First, we look at the coalition graph that shows the knowledge of data about *p* of all actors *umc1*, *umc2*, *umc3*, *r*, and *ci*. Figure 2c shows that there are two coalitions of actors that know all information in the scenario, namely the CI, researcher, and either of the hospitals *umc1* and *umc2*. In particular, the knowledge of the coalition *umc1,ci,r* is composed of the patient database of *umc1*, the research data of the researcher, and the data distributed via the four protocol instances, in all of which *ci* was involved (Figure 2d). Furthermore, we define and verify two privacy properties: one focusing on the knowledge of the researcher, and one focusing on the knowledge of various actors on a particular piece of information. TRIPLEX reports that both properties are satisfied (Figure 2d).

3. CONCLUSIONS

We have presented TRIPLEX, a framework for the analysis of data minimisation in privacy-enhancing protocols. Based on a solid formal grounding, the framework gives an objective and precise overview of what personal information is learnt by (coalitions of) actors in a user-specified scenario. Our user interface allows non-cryptography experts to model protocols and visually analyse their privacy at a high level, while also giving expert users the option to model new cryptographic primitives and to directly access lower-level formal details. We have demonstrated TRIPLEX using a case study in the healthcare domain. The framework has also been successfully applied in the identity management domain [7].

Acknowledgements This work is funded by the Dutch Sentinel Mobile IDM project (#10522), EIT ICT Lab, and MEALS (#295261).

4. REFERENCES

[1] Identity Management Systems (IMS): Identification and Comparison Study. Independent Centre for Privacy Protection Schleswig-Holstein, 2003.

[2] KISS (Knowledge in Security ProtocolS). http://www.lsv.ens-cachan.fr/~ciobaca/kiss/, 2009.

[3] B. Blanchet, M. Abadi, and C. Fournet. Automated Verification of Selected Equivalences for Security Protocols. *J. Log. Algebr. Program.*, 75(1):3–51, 2008.

[4] J. H. Hoepman, R. Joosten, and J. Siljee. Comparing Identity Management Frameworks in a Business Context. In *Proc. IFIP/FIDIS Summer School*, pages 184–196. Springer, 2008.

[5] C. Meadows. Formal Methods for Cryptographic Protocol Analysis: Emerging Issues and Trends. *IEEE Sel. Areas Commun.*, 21(1):44–54, 2003.

[6] M. Veeningen, B. de Weger, and N. Zannone. Formal Privacy Analysis of Communication Protocols for Identity Management. In *Proc. of Int. Conf. on Information Systems Security*, LNCS 7093, pages 235–249. Springer, 2011.

[7] M. Veeningen, B. de Weger, and N. Zannone. A Formal Privacy Analysis of Identity Management Systems. arXiv 1206.7111v1, ArXiv.org, 2012.

[8] M. Veeningen, B. de Weger, and N. Zannone. Formal Modelling of (De)Pseudonymisation: A Case Study in Health Care Privacy. In *Proc. of Workshop on Security and Trust Management*, LNCS 7783, pages 145–160. Springer, 2012.

POSTER: SHAMROCK: Self Contained Cryptography and Key Management Processor

Daniil Utin
MIT Lincoln Laboratory
244 Wood Street
Lexington, 02420, USA
danu@ll.mit.edu

Roger Khazan
MIT Lincoln Laboratory
244 Wood Street
Lexington, 02420, USA
rkh@ll.mit.edu

Joshua Kramer
MIT Lincoln Laboratory
244 Wood Street
Lexington, 02420, USA
joshua.kramer@ll.mit.edu

Michael Vai
MIT Lincoln Laboratory
244 Wood Street
Lexington, 02420, USA
mvai@ll.mit.edu

David Whelihan
MIT Lincoln Laboratory
244 Wood Street
Lexington, 02420, USA
david.whelihan@ll.mit.edu

ABSTRACT

In this poster, we describe a one-size-fits-many Intellectual Property (IP) core which integrates advanced key management technology and streaming encryption into a single component to protect data in-transit.

Categories and Subject Descriptors

E.3 [**Data Encryption**]: Public key cryptosystems; Standards

Keywords

key management; cyber security; cryptography; self-contained encryption; high-Assurance data protection; identity management; hardware IP core; FPGA; cryptographic component; key management protocol.

PROBLEM

Modern cryptography offers a variety of schemes for the protection of information at-rest on devices and in-transit among devices. A cryptographic scheme typically "scrambles" or "unscrambles" information using a data-permutation algorithm and a short cryptographic key. The security of the scheme depends on the properties of the algorithm and the quality and secrecy of the key. Thus, cryptographic keys need to be created and managed carefully. In particular, they need to be protected at-rest and in-transit, which itself calls for the use of various cryptographic schemes.

Although many cryptographic schemes have been standardized and implemented efficiently in software and hardware, these solutions are not universally used or embedded in devices. The two main reasons are the lack of generic, easy-to-deploy, and easy-to-use solutions for key management, and the challenge of integrating various cryptographic and key management components into a holistically secure design. While individual cryptographic components exist and may be known to be secure, there is no known recipe for integrating different components into secure designs that guarantee security of keys and other information, at-rest and in-transit. It is in such integration that major challenges exist and vulnerabilities are oftentimes introduced.

SOLUTION

MIT Lincoln Laboratory developed a one-size-fits-many Intellectual Property (IP) core, called SHAMROCK[1]. SHAMROCK integrates advanced key management technology and streaming encryption into a single component to protect data in-transit. It is designed for low Size, Weight, and Power applications and can be embedded into a wide variety of devices, enabling entire systems to be secured with the same component.

This work is sponsored by the United States Air Force under Air Force Contract FA8721-05-C-0002. Opinions, interpretations, conclusions and recommendations are those of the authors and are not necessarily endorsed by the United States Government.

CCS'13, November 4–8, 2013, Berlin, Germany.
ACM 978-1-4503-2477-9/13/11.
http://dx.doi.org/10.1145/2508859.2512515

[1] SHAMROCK stands for Self-contained High-Assurance MicRO Cryptography and Key-management.

In this poster, we describe the SHAMROCK embedment, key-management functionality, upgradeability and performance in terms of energy and speed.

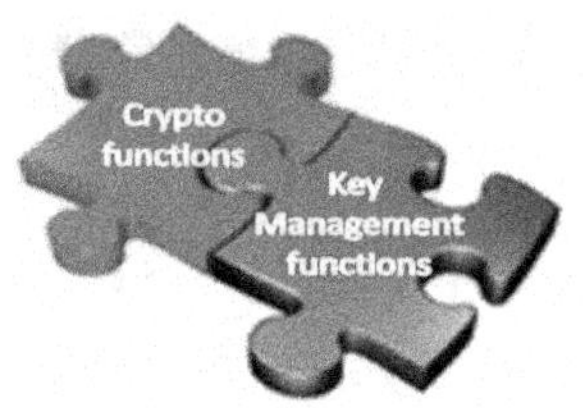

Using a simple, accessible interface, a device containing SHAMROCK chip can use the SHAMROCK's cryptographic components, such as an Advanced Encryption Standard (AES) cipher core, to secure its data internally and to protect its communication with other devices [1]. The device can also use SHAMROCK to handle all of the key management tasks required for the operation of the cryptographic components.

These key management tasks may include operations such as creating cryptographic keys, associating keys with their purposes, protecting keys at rest in both volatile and non-volatile memory, making keys available for authorized encryptions and authorized decryptions, delivering keys securely to authorized remote devices, archiving keys, evolving keys with time, retiring keys, etc. SHAMROCK integrates all of the components into a self-contained, secure design thereby simplifying the task of incorporating cryptographic protections into applications.

While a self-contained, integrated crypto and key management solution is novel in itself, we have made a number of inventions in creating this integrated design. One of the innovations is a way to attain high performance, low power, flexibility, and extensibility – all at the same time. This is achieved by implementing certain, typically computationally demanding components, such as the standard cryptographic functions, directly in hardware (for example using VHDL [2]), while other components, such as key management protocols, in a higher-level language, such as C, in a softcore micro-controller inside the integrated circuit. The soft-core micro-controller, allows for different key management protocols and their extensions to be easily created for and deployed in SHAMROCK, even after the integrated circuit core is manufactured and integrated into an application. The hardware implementations of the cryptographic components used by the application and by the key management components facilitate lower-power, higher-speed operations. Other innovations strengthen security through hardware design and reduce the effort and cost of verifying and modifying the design.

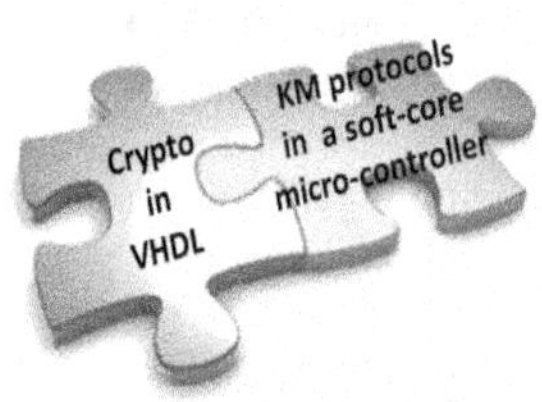

IMPLEMENTATION AND PERFORMANCE ANALYSIS

Implementation and performance analysis: SHAMROCK has been realized as an IP core on two types of Xilinx FPGAs: Virtex-6 and Kintex-7 [3]. The key management protocols are implemented in C programming language and execute in the Tensilica 106micro soft-core micro-controller [4]. 106micro is a central micro-controller and is a part of the SHAMROCK IP core. It manages and coordinates a number of hardware-accelerated cryptographic functions implemented in VHDL. Kintex-7 is the latest generation of XILINX's FPGAs, with the static power consumption being much lower (more than 50%) than that of Virtex-6.

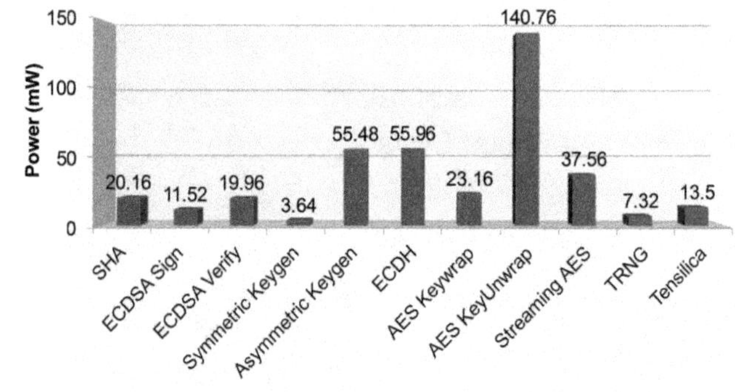

Figure 1. Kintex 7 Dynamic Power (50MHz)

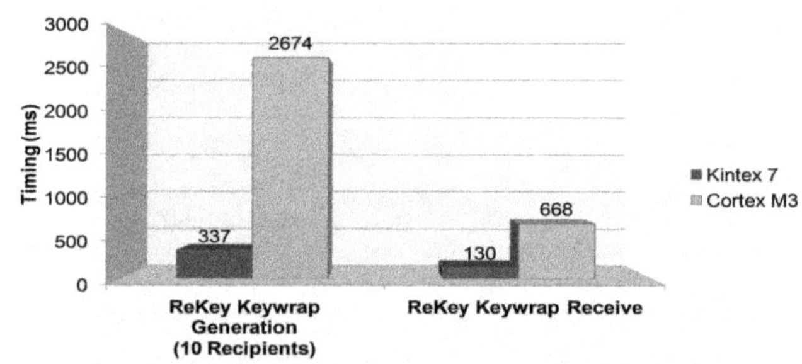

Figure 2. Key Management Function Timing (FPGA@50MHz / CPU@72MHz)

Figure 1 shows the *dynamic* power consumption on Kintex-7 of the different cryptographic operations in SHAMROCK. Typically, most of these operations would run infrequently, except for Streaming AES, which protects application data. Comparing the two figures, observe that dynamic power is significantly less than static power, especially for Streaming AES. Key management functions, such as the generation and processing of key wraps, involve a whole set of cryptographic operations. Figure 2 depicts the time to perform these two operations on Kintex-7 and compares them to those on an ARM Cortex M3 microprocessor [5]. The former is close to an order of magnitude faster than the ARM CPU.

References

[1] https://en.wikipedia.org/wiki/Advanced_Encryption_Standard

[2] https://en.wikipedia.org/wiki/VHDL

[3] https://en.wikipedia.org/wiki/Xilinx

[4] https://en.wikipedia.org/wiki/Tensilica

[5] https://en.wikipedia.org/wiki/ARM_Cortex-M

POSTER: Trend of Online Flash XSS Vulnerabilities

Qixu Liu
University of Chinese Academy of Sciences
Beijing, PR China
liuqixu@ucas.ac.cn

Yuqing Zhang
University of Chinese Academy of Sciences
Beijing, PR China
zhangyq@ucas.ac.cn

Huan Yang
State Key Laboratory of Integrated Services Networks, Xidian University
Xian, PR China
yangh@nipc.org.cn

ABSTRACT
Flash objects are widely embedded in web pages, supporting Rich Internet Applications using ActionScript. However, according to our survey, many Flash objects are seriously exposed to Cross-site Scripting vulnerabilities as they are usually coded without proper sanitization of their inputs. This becomes a potential danger for cyber users. In this paper, we analyze XSS in online Flash and present an engine FXD (Flash XSS Detector) for automatically scrambling Flash files in web pages and checking whether or not they are vulnerable to XSS. We call vulnerable ActionScript functions "key functions" and divide them into four categories by its functionality. The usability of FXD is further evaluated by disposing it in real-world websites. Our results reveal that at least 48 Flash applications in 18% of Alexa top 100 sites on the web are vulnerable to XSS. Each of these vulnerable Flash objects has been verified and confirmed of their XSS flaws. Finally, we discuss a new trend of Flash XSS, nowadays it is mainly caused by combination of key functions in different categories.

Categories and Subject Descriptors
C.2.0 [**Computer-Communication Networks**]: General-Security and protection

General Terms
Security

Keywords
Adobe Flash, ActionScript, Cross-site Scripting, Web Security

1. INTRODUCTION
Flash has been extensively used today in many Web applications as it enriches the webpages and provides more interactive and interesting contents than ever before. Notwithstanding its popularity, Flash can pose a significant threat to the security and reliability of Web applications. As a result, Flash objects are often coded without concern for their security and thus exposed to Cross-site Scripting (XSS) and other kinds of attacks.

CCS'13, November 4–8, 2013, Berlin, Germany.
ACM 978-1-4503-2477-9/13/11.
http://dx.doi.org/10.1145/2508859.2512516

XSS has been one of the most prominent classes of web vulnerabilities since 2007 [1]. Usually, hackers use XSS techniques to steal cookies, which can be exploited to track cyber users and pose a serious privacy risk to them [2]. Vectors in the form of JavaScript: evilJS can cause XSS when sent to the ActionScript (the language to write a Flash) function *getURL* or *navigateToURL* if input content is filtered insufficiently. *getURL("javascript: evilJS")* works pretty much like you submit *javascript: evilJS* in the address bar of a Browser, evilJS will execute as JavaScript code in the context of current domain. For example, by sending an elaborately constructed input to a Flash application, the attacker was able to crack and gained the control of a Gmail account [3]. When a XSS attack is performed against a Flash application online, the server usually shows no signs at all [4]. In addition, vulnerable Flash objects can be downloaded and exploited offline. Consequently, the threat to homeland security using XSS in online Flash is more hidden and dangerous.

A couple of tools have been developed to essentially detect XSS vulnerabilities in Flash files, namely OWASP's SWFIntruder and HP's SWFScan. Both are available online. SWFIntruder are not able to check AS3 files and can only support Flash version lower than 9, while SWFScan only relies on static signatures to determine vulnerable Flash files. FlashOver [7] is a system to automatically scan SWF files for XSS vulnerabilities by using a combination of static and dynamic code analysis. However, FlashOver does ignore the Flash security issues caused by the xml policy.

In this paper, we study the technology of XSS in online Flash. Our paper makes two contributions. First, we give a relatively complete summary of possible XSS injection points in ActionScript and develop our engine FXD (Flash XSS Detector) to determine the vulnerable nature of a Flash file. Second, we use FXD to test real-world websites, and discover a new trend that Flash XSS nowadays is mainly caused by combination of key functions in different categories. Many *clickTag* Vulnerable Flash files are thus immune to XSS, but XML based XSS becomes more and more popular. Standalone XML based XSS is more harmful when it is combined with key functions like *navigateToURL*, *getURL* or *ExternalInterface.call*, which is the trend of Flash XSS attack in real Internet environment.

2. VULNERABLE ACTIONSCRIPT FUNCTIONS
A Flash file can be embedded into a webpage via HTML tags embed/object or merely by directly visiting. Flash contains an object-oriented language called ActionScript (AS), making Flash functional not just in animation. ActionScript has two different versions, AS2 and AS3. Both works well in today's Flash. Flash XSS is mainly caused by improper use of ActionScript functions.

Table 1. XSS vulnerable ActionScript functions

ID	ActionScript Function	Type	X is JS only?	Additional comments to X	Category
1	getURL(X,"_self")	AS2	√	-	I
2	navigateToURL(new URLRequest(X),"_self")	AS3	√	-	
3	TextArea.text= X / TextArea.htmlText= X	AS2/3	√	X= html contain JScode	II
4	TextInput.text= X / TextInput.htmlText= X	AS2/3	√	X= html contain JScode	
5	Label.text= X / Label.htmlText= X	AS2/3	√	X= html contain JScode	
6	LoadMovie(X)	AS2	×	X= swf file	III
7	LoadMovieNum(X,0)	AS2	×	X= swf file	
8	LoadVariables(X)	AS2	×	X= text file	
9	LoadVars.load(X)	AS2	×	X= text file	
10	LoadVars.send(X, "_self", "GET")	AS2	×	X= text file	
11	LoadVars.sendAndLoad(X,myload,"GET")	AS2	×	X= text file	
12	Loader.load(X)	AS3	×	X= swf/text/xml/sound/video	
13	Sound.loadSound(X,isStream)	AS2	×	X= sound file	
14	NetStream.play(X)	AS2/3	×	X= video file	
15	Data Injection	AS2	×	See Ref [6].	
16	XML.load(X)	AS2	√	X= xml file	
17	XML.send(X,"_self")	AS2	√	X= xml file	
18	XML.sendAndLoad(X,xml)	AS2	√	X= xml file	
19	ExternalInterface.call(X)	AS2/3	√	-	IV
20	fscommand(X)	AS2/3	√	X= could also be OScode	

We call this kind of ActionScript functions "key functions" to emphasize their key position in Flash XSS. We have created a set of these key functions covering the main part of Flash XSS issue.

These key functions are listed in Table 1. All key functions are categorized by their AS functional property. Category I is used to send http request; II is used to present text information on Flash; III is used to load external resources; and Category IV is used to communicate with the browser. The way to exploit XSS is almost the same for each category. For instance, ActionScript function *getURL(X, "self")*, where X refers to user inputs, is the second version of ActionScript (AS2) and X can merely be JavaScript code rather than files (swf files, xml files, text files, etc.). Moreover, *getURL* belongs to Category I based on it functionality.

Parameters for key functions are divided into two groups, direct JavaScript code and indirect ones. Key functions such as *getURL* and *ExternalInterface* accept and execute input as JavaScript code. For those such as *XML.load* function, JavaScript code is injected in other forms of text or as a malicious file and finally be executed by other key functions. *fscommand* is a bit different, it is used to communicate with the Flash projector or browser, not only JavaScript code but also command or shell code get executed under some certain circumstances.

3. DESIGN AND IMPLEMENTATION

FXD is a web engine integrating both static and dynamic analysis for detecting malicious XSS vulnerabilities in online Flash applications, with both AS2 and AS3 supported. FXD outputs a clear report containing the total number as well as the details of XSS vulnerabilities found in Flash online.

Figure 1 gives a block diagram of FXD. The core part of our system is divided into three components: the static analyzing module, the dynamic testing module and the Web interface part. We chose Web interface as our user interface; as a result, our system can be loaded simply in a browser. The GUI that presents to a user is a Web page.

The task of static analyzing module is to decompile the Flash applications in web pages and then to determine which APIs in ActionScript code may potentially cause XSS attacks. The static analyzing module contains four sub-modules, that is, code decompiler, file scanner, rule analyzer and line checker. Once we obtained the information of which key function may cause an XSS attack from the static analyzing module, FXD invoked the dynamic testing component. The dynamic testing module automatically collected the potential variables found in static analyzing module and checked whether or not there were any XSS vulnerabilities using attacking vectors and variables disclosed by the static testing mode. Those attacking vectors and variables were generated depending on what category of key functions that caused the XSS.

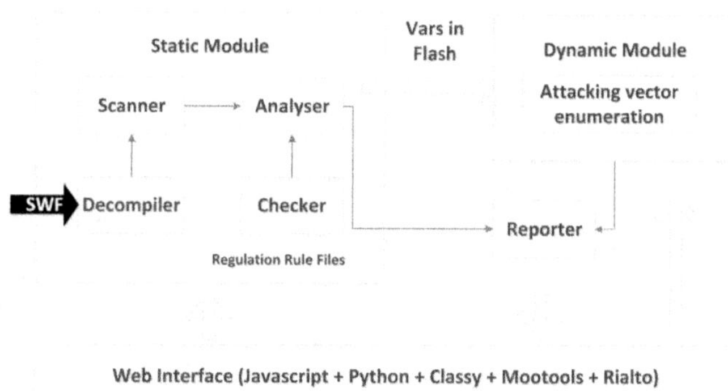

Figure 1. The structure of FXD

4. PRELIMINARY EVALUATION

We experimentally measured the effectiveness of FXD by using it to find XSS vulnerabilities in Flash applications. Our experiment was taken in a Firefox 9.0.1 browser on a 2.66 GHz, 4GB RAM, Intel Core 2 Quad computer. The testing sample sets are real world Flashes alive on the Internet presented and surfed by millions cyber users, especially those Flash applications embedded on the Alexa Top 100 web sites [5].

4.1 TEST ON REAL NETWORK

A lot of Flash applications on the Internet are vulnerable to XSS, and may be taken advantage by attackers to steal personal information from Internet users. In order to prove the effectiveness and validity of FXD, we have collected a thousand Flash files from Alexa Top 100 websites [5] to evaluate FXD, and all these Flash files were found using Google search engine. The result turned out to be worrisome: We discovered 48 vulnerable Flash applications in the domain or subdomain of 18% top 100 websites. All the vulnerable Flash files were verified under Firefox.

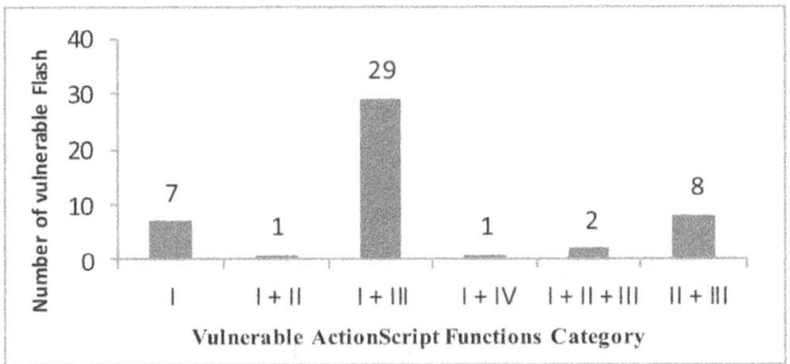

Figure 2. Number of vulnerable Flash of four categories

As shown in Figure 2, Out of the 48 vulnerable Flash applications, we classified twenty-nine as category I combining with III, which has the most number of vulnerabilities. As a result, our conjecture is that most online Flash applications load external resources by sending HTTP requests.

4.2 TREND ANALYSIS

Vulnerable Flash objects have been pervasive in the Internet since the first exploitable Flash file was reported in 2006. However, Web administrators tend to ignore this kind of XSS. Flash XSS has changed in types since last report, *clickTag* is less threatened after Adobe as well as other browser manufacturer making up to their strategy. *geturl("javascript:code")* and *navigateToURL("javascript:code")* without a second parameter *_self* can no longer execute JavaScript anymore except for Firefox. Many *clickTag* Vulnerable Flash files are thus immune to XSS. But we have found that XML based XSS becomes popular and aggressive.

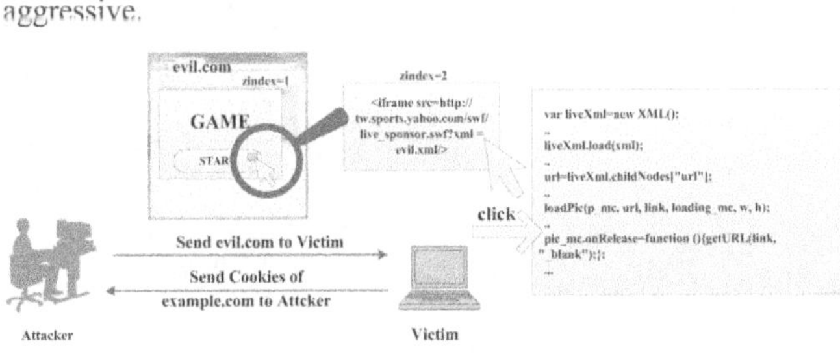

Figure 3. An inexplicit Flash XSS attack

Standalone XML based XSS is not harmful until it is combined with key functions like *navigateToURL*, *getURL* or *ExternalInterface.call*. Combination of these key functions makes XSS less obvious since a XML input seems to be more reliable than just a URL in a developer's sight. We would like to illustrate how a combination of key functions makes XSS more serious and latency by the analysis of two real Flash XSS found during the real network testing.

As shown in Figure 3, the Flash accepts a parameter as an address to an xml file which contains a sequence of the *picture address*. If we could construct a xml file with *url=javascript: evilJS* and pass the xml file address as a parameter to this Flash, clicking on the picture will cause JavaScript code to execute. With some *iframe* and CSS tricks, we have built a demo, where a Flash game was shown. A small iframe following your mouse will get the click when you press the start button. Vulnerable Flash with a parameter of crafted xml file inside the *iframe* will thus execute the JavaScript and popup your cookies.

5. CONCLUSION

Flash XSS vulnerabilities are being discovered and disclosed at an alarming rate. Since Flash applications are widely used and XSS ranks top 3 of Web vulnerabilities, the security of many terminal ends is at stake. In this paper, we investigate current works on protecting Flash security and present FXD, the engine aiming at detecting XSS vulnerabilities in online Flash applications using a combination of static and dynamic analysis techniques. Our preliminary experimental results show that many *clickTag* Vulnerable Flash files are thus immune to XSS, but XML based XSS becomes more and more popular. Standalone XML based XSS is more harmful when it is combined with key functions like *navigateToURL*, *getURL* or *ExternalInterface.call*, which is the trend of Flash XSS attack in real Internet environment.

6. ACKNOWLEDGMENTS

This work is supported by National Natural Science Foundation of China (61303239, 61272481), the President Fund of UCAS.

7. REFERENCES

[1] "The Ten Most Critical Web Application Security Risks", https://www.owasp.org/index.php/Category:OWASP_Top_Ten_Project

[2] C. Yue, M. Xie, H. Wang, "An automatic HTTP cookie management system," *Computer Networks*, vol. 54, pp. 2182-2198, 2010.

[3] Y. Baror, A. Yogev, A. Sharabani, "Flash parameter injection," 2008. http://blog.watchfire.com/FPI.pdf

[4] S. Ford, M. Cova, C. Kruegel, G. Vigna, "Analyzing and detecting malicious flash advertisements, " in *25th Annual Computer Conference Security Applications (ACSAC 2009)*, Honolulu, HI, United states, 2009, pp. 363-372.

[5] Alexa Internet, "*Alexa Top 500 Global Sites*," http://www.alexa.com/topsites

[6] P. Jagdale. "*Blinded By Flash: Widespread Security Risks Flash Developers Dont See*," http://www.shmoocon.org/2009/presentations-all.html#flash

[7] S. Van Acker, N. Nikiforakis, L. Desmet, W. Joosen, F. Piessens, "FlashOver: Automated discovery of cross-site scripting vulnerabilities in rich internet applications, " in 7th *ACM Symposium on Information, Computer and Communications Security (AsiaCCS 2012)*, Korea, 2012.

POSTER: Cross-Platform Malware: Write Once, Infect Everywhere

Martina Lindorfer*, Matthias Neumayr*, Juan Caballero†, Christian Platzer*
*Vienna University of Technology †IMDEA Software Institute
{mlindorfer, mneumayr, cplatzer}@iseclab.org juan.caballero@imdea.org

ABSTRACT

In this ongoing work we perform the first systematic investigation of cross-platform (X-platform) malware. As a first step, this paper presents an exploration into existing X-platform malware families and X-platform vulnerabilities used to distribute them. Our exploration shows that X-platform malware uses a wealth of methods to achieve portability. It also shows that exploits for X-platform vulnerabilities are X-platform indeed and readily available in commercial exploit kits, making them an inexpensive distribution vector for X-platform malware.

Categories and Subject Descriptors

K.6.5 [**Security and Protection**]: Invasive software

Keywords

Cross-Platform Software; Malware; Vulnerabilities.

1. INTRODUCTION

A desired capability by many programmers is writing a program once and then using it on different computing platforms without modifications. This capability has been sold by programming languages using catchphrases such as "write once, run anywhere" or "write once, compile anywhere" and brings benefits such as reduced development time, code reuse, and easier maintenance.

Although these paradigms are fairly extended in benign software, they are not prevalent in malware. Nowadays, the very large majority of malware runs on a single platform: most malware targets Windows, with Android malware recently growing, and few instances of Mac OS and Linux malware. While cross-platform (X-platform) malware has been around for a long time, e.g., the Morris worm in 1988 and macro viruses in the 90's [11], it still constitutes a very small minority.

However, the advent of mobile computing and the increase in X-platform malware in the last two years raises the question of whether the tide is rising. In this context, security vendors like Websense [24] and Fortinet [14] have forecasted X-platform malware as a 2013 trend. While it is unclear how fast (if) the tide will rise, in this work we proactively perform the first systematic investigation of X-platform malware, to be prepared when (if) it happens.

For a malware developer, supporting a new platform is a decision that boils down to a cost-benefit analysis. Since the goal of most malware families (targeted attacks apart) is monetizing the infected computers, the malware developer needs to weigh the additional income obtained by reaching targets of the new platform, against the required additional investment in software development and distribution.

In this ongoing work we strive to understand such a cost-benefit tradeoff. As a first step, we perform an exploration of existing X-platform malware. This helps us understand what monetization vectors work across platforms and how much development effort is needed to make the malware X-platform. For example, we observe malware families focusing on click fraud (e.g., LilyJade [18]) and information-stealing (e.g., ZeuS-in-the-Mobile [26]), two monetization vectors that extrapolate well to mobile platforms. We also observe families that reuse the same Java code on all platforms (e.g., jRAT [16]) and others that prefer platform-specific components (e.g., Badbunny [3]).

Malware developers also require cost-effective ways of distributing their X-platform malware. Our examination shows that they favor distribution vectors that support all platforms such as social engineering and vulnerabilities on programs that run on multiple platforms, i.e., X-platform vulnerabilities. Given the predominance of drive-by downloads as a malware distribution vector [6], we analyze the presence of exploits for X-platform vulnerabilities in commercial exploit kits. Our exploration shows that most X-platform vulnerabilities have been weaponized in at least one exploit kit. It also shows that most exploits for X-platform vulnerabilities indeed work on different platforms, without any modifications. Thus, malware owners using drive-by download specialization services, can essentially distribute their malware to multiple platforms at no extra cost.

2. OVERVIEW

This section defines X-platform programs and presents an examination of X-platform malware and vulnerabilities.

A *computing platform* can refer to an operating system family (e.g., Windows, Linux, OS X, Android), a computer architecture (e.g., x86, AMD64, ARM), or a combination of both (e.g., Windows on x86). In this work, a platform corresponds to an OS family and we consider two OS families different if they do not share significant amounts of code. In particular, we consider different versions of the same OS

CCS'13, November 4–8, 2013, Berlin, Germany.
ACM 978-1-4503-2477-9/13/11.
http://dx.doi.org/10.1145/2508859.2512517.

Family	Date	DV	Windows	Linux	OS X	Windows Phone	Symbian	Android	BlackBerry
Badbunny [3]	07/2009	SE	JavaScript	Perl	Ruby				
Boonana [4, 5]	10/2010	SE	Java		Java				
ZitMo [25, 26]	09/2010	SE				Java*	Java	Java*	Java
Olyx [21]	06/2011	Exploit	PE		MACH-O				
Tibet [23]	03/2012	Exploit	PE		MACH-O				
Flsplysc [13]	04/2012	Exploit	PE		Python				
Crisis [17]	04/2012	SE	PE		MACH-O	PE*			
LilyJade [18]	05/2012	Exploit	JavaScript	JavaScript	JavaScript				
GetShell [15]	07/2012	SE	Java	Java	Java				
Netweirdrc [20]	08/2012	SE	PE	ELF	MACH-O				
jRAT [16]	10/2012	SE	Java	Java	Java				
Ssucl [22]	01/2013	SE	PE					Java	
MinecraftHack [19]	03/2013	SE	Java		Java				
Janicab [2]	07/2013	Exploit/SE	VB Script		Python				
Clt10 [7] (PoC)	2006	-	ASM	ASM					
Yakizake [11] (PoC)	08/2007	-	.NET	.NET					
Clapzok [12] (PoC)	05/2013	-	ASM	ASM	ASM				

Table 1: X-platform malware, earliest date reported, and distribution form used for each supported platform. Stars mark platforms supported later than the earliest reported date.

(e.g., Windows XP, Vista, 7) and different distributions of the same OS (e.g., Ubuntu, Fedora) the same platform.

We say that a program is X-platform if it is portable across (i.e., runs on) different OS families. A program can become portable by using programming languages that compile to bytecode (e.g., Java, .NET), at the source code level using standardized interfaces like POSIX or interpreted languages, and by running on top of other X-platform programs such as web browsers or office applications.

2.1 X-Platform Malware

As a first step we perform an investigation of existing X-platform malware. Table 1 shows malware families we found, the earliest date they were reported, their distribution vector (DV), and the target platforms they support. The top of the table comprises 14 families observed in the wild, while the bottom three are proof-of-concept malware.

Out of the 14 families in the wild, four use exploits to get installed on the target hosts, while the remaining nine convince users to install them through social engineering (SE) and one uses both depending on the platform. The four families that solely rely on exploitation leverage X-platform vulnerabilities that enable installation on the different target platforms (see Section 2.2).

For each supported platform, Table 1 shows in which form the malware is distributed, which is tightly linked to how the malware achieves portability. It shows that X-platform malware can be distributed as source code (Python, JavaScript, Perl), binary code (PE, ELF, MACH-O), or bytecode (Java, .NET). When the malware is not distributed as binary code, it can fail to run if the infected host does not have an interpreter for the scripts or a runtime for the bytecode. When distributed as binary code, it needs to match the executable file format used by the platform. Note that distribution as source code or bytecode makes it significantly easier for analysts to reverse-engineer the malware. So far, the use of external tools to obfuscate the source code and bytecode is not prevalent among X-platform malware.

An important question is to what degree X-platform malware reuses code across platforms. Our preliminary examination indicates a mixture of approaches. Three families use the same code across platforms: Minecraft and jRAT (both Java) and LilyJade, a JavaScript browser plugin that uses the Crossrider API [9] to run on Internet Explorer, Chrome, and Safari without modifications. In addition, Boonana and Getshell distribute as a Java JAR file, but later download platform-specific modules. Another four families use different malware for each platform. In particular, Badbunny distributes as an OpenOffice document containing a macro and executables for each platform, Sscul distributes as an Android APK containing a PE executable, Crisis as a Java JAR file containing PE and MACH-O executables, and Flsplysc uses Java code during exploitation to select which platform-specific module to install. Finally, there are four families for which further analysis is needed. Olyx, Tibet, and Netweirdrc distribute as executables, and although Zitmo is written in Java for all platforms, its Android version is significantly simpler [25], pointing to the use of separate code bases. To refine this preliminary examination we plan to use code analysis and similarity techniques.

2.2 X-Platform Vulnerabilities

A X-platform vulnerability is a software defect on a X-platform program. The vulnerable program may comprise both platform-specific and platform-independent code, or be fully platform-independent by running on top of an above-OS runtime that enables portability. In both cases, a X-platform vulnerability is present in the platform-independent code of the vulnerable application.

Table 2 summarizes our investigation on X-platform vulnerabilities. The left side of the table shows, for each vulnerability, its CVE identifier [10], the vulnerable program, whether there exists a publicly available exploit for the vulnerability, and whether any exploit kit contains an exploit for it [8]. As shown, X-platform vulnerabilities exist in browser plugins (Java, PDF, Flash), web browsers (Firefox, WebKit), and prevalent desktop applications like Microsoft Word. The majority of these applications are written in C/C++, although by far the most vulnerable application is the Java runtime, for which we plan to evaluate which parts of the code contain the vulnerabilities.

Nearly all of these vulnerabilities have publicly available exploits, the exception being recent zero-day vulnerabilities (marked with Z) for which we expect a public exploit soon. It is worrisome to observe that for most of these vulnerabilities an exploit is included in commercial exploit kits. If these exploits are truly X-platform (examined in Section 3), then for an attacker using drive-by download specialization services [6], distributing its malware to multiple platforms essentially incurs no extra cost.

3. PRELIMINARY RESULTS

Our exploration of X-platform vulnerabilities shows that exploits are widely available for them. But, it is unclear whether those exploits indeed work across platforms without modifications, given particular exploit payloads and OS-

CVE	Program	Exploit	Kit	Metasploit			
				XP	7	Linux	X
2009-0563	MS Word	✓					
2009-3867	Oracle Java	✓	✓	✓			
2010-3333	MS Word	✓					
2011-1774	WebKit	✓		✓			
2011-3544	Oracle Java	✓	✓	✓	✓	✓	✓
2012-0507	Oracle Java	✓	✓	✓	✓	✓	✓
2012-0779	Adobe Flash	✓	✓	✓			
2012-1723	Oracle Java	✓	✓	✓	✓	✓	
2012-4681	Oracle Java	✓	✓	✓	✓	✓	✓
2012-5076	Oracle Java	✓	✓	✓	✓	✓	✓
2013-0640	Adobe Reader	Z		-	-	-	-
2013-0641	Adobe Reader	Z		-	-	-	-
2013-0422	Oracle Java	✓	✓	✓	✓	✓	✓
2013-0431	Oracle Java	✓	✓	✓	✓	✓	✓
2013-0758	Firefox	✓		✓	✓	✓	✓
2013-1488	Oracle Java	✓		✓	✓	✓	✓
2013-1491	Oracle Java	Z		-	-	-	-
2013-2423	Oracle Java	✓	✓	✓	✓	✓	✓

Table 2: X-platform vulnerabilities, whether an exploit is publicly available and included in an exploit kit, and whether the exploit works in each platform.

specific defenses such as ASLR and $W \oplus X$. To investigate this, we test exploits for X-platform vulnerabilities, from the Metasploit framework [1], against different platforms. Our setup includes Windows XP, Windows 7, Debian Linux, Mac OS X 10.6 "Snow Leopard", and Mac OS X 10.8 "Mountain Lion". To allow running vulnerable Java versions on recent browsers we disable extensions.blocklist in Firefox and XProtect in Safari. For Java exploits we use the `java/meterpreter/reverse_tcp` payload and the `generic/shell_reverse_tcp` payload for others, verifying exploitation by executing uploaded files.

The results on the right side of Table 2 show that the majority (9 out of 15) of the public exploits for X-platform vulnerabilities are truly X-platform, exploiting different platforms with no modifications. Four other exploits fail to run in at least one vulnerable platform, and the two Microsoft Word exploits crash in all platforms. Note that the failing exploits are for the oldest vulnerabilities; exploit writers are becoming more effective over time.

4. FUTURE WORK

In this paper we have introduced our ongoing work to understand the X-platform malware and vulnerabilities landscape. Much remains to be done, including collecting samples of the identified X-platform malware families, measuring the amount of code reuse across platform-specific executables, examining exploits that do not work on all platforms, and analyzing X-platform exploits and malware in the wild. For the latter, we are deploying multi-platform honeyclients to monitor what platforms are exploited by drive-by downloads and what malware is dropped on each platform.

5. ACKNOWLEDGMENTS

The research leading to these results has received funding from the European Union Seventh Framework Programme under grant agreement n. 257007 (SysSec) and the FFG – Austrian Research Promotion under grant COMET K1.

6. REFERENCES

[1] Metasploit. http://www.metasploit.com.

[2] Multisystem Trojan Janicab attacks Windows and MacOSX via scripts. http://blog.avast.com/2013/07/22/multisystem-trojan-janicab-attacks-windows-and-macosx-via-scripts/, July 2013.

[3] SB/BadBunny-A, July 2009. http://www.sophos.com/en-us/threat-center/threat-analyses/viruses-and-spyware/SB~BadBunny-A/detailed-analysis.aspx.

[4] Boonana Trojan Horse, October 2010. http://www.securemac.com/boonana-bulletin.php.

[5] Boonana trojan linked to malware for Windows, Mac OS X or Linux, October 2010. http://nakedsecurity.sophos.com/2010/10/28/cross-platform-worm-targets-facebook-users/.

[6] C. Grier et al. Manufacturing Compromise: The Emergence of Exploit-as-a-Service. In *Proceedings of the 19th ACM Conference on Computer and Communication Security (CCS)*, 2012.

[7] CAPZLOQ TEKNIQ v1.0, 2006. http://spth.virii.lu/rrlf7/sources/clt.htm.

[8] An Overview of Exploit Packs (Update 19.1), April 2013. http://contagiodump.blogspot.com/2010/06/overview-of-exploit-packs-update.html.

[9] Crossrider. http://crossrider.com.

[10] CVE Database. http://cve.mitre.org/cve/.

[11] P. Ferrie. Something Smells Fishy. *Virus Bulletin*, November 2007. http://pferrie.host22.com/papers/yakizake.pdf.

[12] P. Ferrie. MultiPlatform Madness. *Virus Bulletin*, June 2013. http://pferrie.host22.com/papers/clapzok.pdf.

[13] Python-based malware attack targets Macs. Windows PCs also under fire, April 2012. http://nakedsecurity.sophos.com/2012/04/27/python-malware-mac/.

[14] Fortinet's FortiGuard Labs Reveals 2013 Threat Predictions, December 2012. http://www.fortinet.com/press_releases/121210.html.

[15] Multi-platform Backdoor Lurks in Colombian Transport Site, July 2012. http://www.f-secure.com/weblog/archives/00002397.html.

[16] New Multiplatform Backdoor Jacksbot Discovered, October 2012. http://www.intego.com/mac-security-blog/new-multiplatform-backdoor-jacksbot-discovered/.

[17] T. Katsuki. Crisis: The Advanced Malware, November 2012. http://www.symantec.com/content/en/us/enterprise/media/security_response/whitepapers/crisis_the_advanced_malware.pdf.

[18] Worm 2.0, or LilyJade in action, May 2012. http://www.securelist.com/en/blog/706/Worm_2_0_or_LilyJade_in_action/.

[19] Intego Discovers a New Multi-Platform Minecraft Password Stealer, March 2013. http://www.intego.com/mac-security-blog/intego-discovers-a-new-multi-platform-minecraft-password-stealer/.

[20] An Analysis of the Cross-Platform Backdoor NetWeirdRC, August 2012. http://www.intego.com/mac-security-blog/an-analysis-of-the-cross-platform-backdoor-netweirdrc/.

[21] Backdoor Olyx - is it malware on a mission for Mac?, July 2011. http://blogs.technet.com/b/mmpc/archive/2011/07/25/backdoor-olyx-is-it-malware-on-a-mission-for-mac.aspx.

[22] Mobile attacks!, January 2013. http://www.securelist.com/en/blog/805/Mobile_attacks/.

[23] Tibet.C Malware Delivered by Poisoned Word Documents Installs Backdoors on Macs, March 2012. http://www.intego.com/mac-security-blog/tibet-c-malware-delivered-by-poisoned-word-documents-installs-backdoors-on-macs/.

[24] 7 for 13: 2013 Security Predictions from Websense, December 2012. http://www.websense.com/content/websense-2013-security-predictions.html.

[25] ZeuS-in-the-Mobile: Facts and Theories, October 2011. http://www.securelist.com/en/analysis/204792194/.

[26] ZeuS Mitmo: Man-in-the-mobile, September 2010. http://securityblog.s21sec.com/2010/09/zeus-mitmo-man-in-mobile-i.html.

POSTER: Introducing Pathogen: A Real-Time Virtual Machine Introspection Framework

Anthony Roberts, Richard McClatchey, Saad Liaquat
University of the West of England
Bristol, BS16 1QY, UK
anthony2.roberts@live.uwe.ac.uk
saad2.liaquat@uwe.ac.uk
richard.mcclatchey@uwe.ac.uk

Nigel Edwards, Mike Wray
Hewlett-Packard Laboratories
Long Down Avenue
Bristol, BS34 8QZ, UK
<firstname.lastname>@hp.com

ABSTRACT

In recent years, malware has grown extremely rapidly in complexity and rates of system infection. Current generation anti-virus and anti-malware software provides system protection through the use of locally installed monitoring agents, which are dependent upon vendor generated signature and heuristic based rules. However, because these monitoring agents are installed within the systems they are trying to protect, they themselves are potential targets of attack by malware. *Pathogen* overcomes this issue by using a real-time system monitoring and analysis framework that utilises Virtual Machine introspection (VMI) to allow the monitoring of a system without the need for any locally installed agents. One of the main research problems in VMI is how to parse and interpret the memory of an executing system from outside of that system. *Pathogen's* contribution is a lightweight introspection framework that bridges the semantic gap.

Categories and Subject Descriptors

K.6.5 [**Management of Computing and Information**]: Security and Protection

Keywords

Security; Monitoring; Introspection; Malware

1. INTRODUCTION

The overall goal of the *Pathogen* project is to develop a system that can be used to monitor multiple virtual machines (VMs) within an organisation's infrastructure. Currently, *Pathogen* is in an early stage of development, and supports the monitoring of a single VM.

Motivations. Current generation security products rely upon the installation of an in-system monitoring agent which performs real-time analysis of file and code execution within the system. However, these monitoring agents are themselves at risk of malware attack, and many pieces of sophisticated malware attempt to identify, and disable any detected security software upon infecting a system [2]. *Pathogen* overcomes this issue by performing all system analysis externally using Virtual Machine Introspection [9] and therefore remains completely transparent to the monitored system.

At present *Pathogen* monitors Microsoft Windows 7 x64 systems, however it is being developed to be as OS agnostic as is possible. This is achieved by performing an offline forensic analysis of the VMs hard disk image, prior to starting the VM. This forensic analysis first identifies the OS version, and then locates core OS files, which are then analysed and used to obtain the correct operating system structure definitions (symbols) directly from Microsoft's Public Symbol Server [6]. This offline forensic analysis is designed to eliminate the so called *"semantic gap"* [7].

The semantic gap refers simply to the fact that when performing external analysis, the view of the monitored system is raw binary data, which must then be reconstructed. In-system monitoring agents are able to draw semantic knowledge directly from the OS's APIs, however, external monitoring agents have no access to these APIs, so must acquire semantic knowledge through other methods. This problem is exacerbated by the need for regular system updates, which change the layout of key OS data structures.

Related Work. To retain access to OS APIs so that semantic knowledge can be obtained, the *Secure In-VM Monitoring (SIM)* [8] project installs an in-system monitoring agent, but protects this agent against malicious modifications by utilising Intel's hardware assisted virtualisation technologies (Intel-VT) [4]. Whilst this approach aims to protect the monitoring agent from tampering, the authors state that it is still potentially possible for malware to detect the presence of the agent, and therefore alter its behaviour.

The *Blacksheep* project [1] attempts to detect malicious actions within systems by monitoring groups of similar (homogeneous) systems, and then comparing memory snapshots taken from each to detect unknown, or unexpected system behaviour. This approach of monitoring multiple similar systems to detect irregularities is unique, however makes assumptions that systems are uninfected prior to beginning analysis.

VMITools [10] & *Volatility* [11] are two of the most commonly used forensic tools for performing analysis of a sys-

CCS'13, November 4–8, 2013, Berlin, Germany.
ACM 978-1-4503-2477-9/13/11.
http://dx.doi.org/10.1145/2508859.2512518.

tem's memory (either via snapshots or through VMI). However, whilst these tools are widely used, they both perform system analysis using hard-coded symbolic information, meaning that the software must be manually updated in the event of an OS update.

Contributions. The contributions made by *Pathogen* are two-fold:
(1) The creation of a lightweight VMI framework. *Pathogen* is currently being developed on Linux based operating systems, and utilises the open-source system emulator *QEMU* with additional current generation virtualisation hardware assistance provided by *KVM*. Introspection is made possible by making minor modifications to both of these systems.
(2) Semantic-gap reconstruction through offline forensic analysis. To perform introspection correctly, it is essential that the correct semantic knowledge be applied for the particular OS version. *Pathogen* ensures this by analysing the VMs hard disk image prior to performing introspection. After analysis has been completed, the Microsoft public symbol server is contacted, and the relevant Program Database File (PDB) is downloaded. PDB files contain specific debugging information for use in the event of a program or system crash, but more importantly they also contain the exact OS structure definitions required for accurate introspection.

2. IMPLEMENTATION

The sequence of events taken by *Pathogen* begins with the initial forensic analysis of the VMs disk image. Once this analysis is complete, the introspection portion of the system is ready to be used. The offline analysis of the VMs hard disk image serves two purposes; first it allows for the location of core OS files and the generation of the correct symbols for use by the introspector. Secondly, during introspection *Pathogen* monitors all VM disk activity (reads/writes), and by using the recorded file offsets can determine which files the OS is currently accessing.

2.1 Emulator Modifications

To perform live introspection, *Pathogen* must first locate within the host system the virtual memory allocated to the VM for use as its own emulated physical memory. During the creation of the VM, QEMU allocates a single region of host memory for use by the guest. This memory region is then made available to *Pathogen* through the use of the Linux *mmap* command, which presents the guests memory as a standard file within the host system.

2.2 Hardware Virtualisation Technologies

Hardware Virtualisation Technologies (HVT) allow VMs to run at speeds similar to physical systems by allowing the VM direct access to the physical CPU within the host system. This is in direct contrast to older generation virtualisation technologies in which a VMs CPU required significant emulation in software. HVT also reduce the interaction between the VM and the hypervisor (KVM). HVT introduce two core concepts that *Pathogen* utilises in order to perform introspection.

1. **VMENTER/VMEXIT:** Certain events that occur within a VM (e.g. page faults) require the intervention of the underlying hypervisor, which is triggered through the vmexit instruction. A vmexit passes control of execution to the hypervisor, which performs the necessary operation and returns control to the VM with the associated vmenter instruction. *Pathogen* makes modifications to KVM's vmexit handler to detect changes to the VMs memory structures.
2. **Virtual Machine Control Structure (VMCS):** A VMCS is a 4KB structure used to maintain transitions between vmexits and vmenters. In the event of a vmexit, both the host's and VM's CPU states are recorded so that they can be restored upon the following vmenter. *Pathogen* utilises existing VMCS management functions present within KVM to extract VM CPU state information, such as the values of key Model Specific Registers (MSR). MSR are a form of control register within the x86 instruction set and are used to store OS configuration data, such as kernel memory locations and flags to enable/disable hardware features.

At present *Pathogen* performs introspection on VMs using Intel-VT HVT, however future implementations for AMD-V HVT [3] are planned.

2.3 Windows 7 x64 Introspection

After generation of the required OS symbols through offline analysis, introspection begins with the location of the Kernel Processor Control Region (KPCR), a structure containing kernel specific data and pointers to additional control structures. Upon creation of the KPCR, the OS stores its physical address within the *GS-MSR* (*FS-MSR* on 32-bit), and KVM is able to detect its creation through a modification made to KVM's vmexit handler, which monitors the *GS-MSR* on every vmexit during the system's early boot process. Once KVM has detected the creation of the KPCR, its physical address is transferred to *Pathogen* through the use of the Linux */proc* file system.
Pathogen must now locate the OS page tables, which are necessary for performing virtual-to-physical address translation. The base address of the OS page tables are stored within the CPU's *CR3* register, and within a secondary kernel structure; the Kernel Processor Region Control Block (KPRCB). Figure 1 shows the relevant parts of the OS structure layouts from KPCR to OS page table address.

```
KPCR{
0x020 CurrentPrcb _KPRCB
  _KPRCB{
  0x040 ProcessorState   _KPROCESSOR_STATE
    _KPROCESSOR_STATE{
    0x000 SpecialRegisters   _KSPECIAL_REGISTERS
      _KSPECIAL_REGISTERS{
      0x010 Cr3 Uint8B
```

Figure 1: KPRCB structure leading to page table address

Windows 7 x64 uses a standard 4-level page table hierarchy [5], and once located all virtual-to-physical address translations are performed by the *Pathogen* function *walkPageTables*.
To determine the correct offsets of elements within structures, *Pathogen* must first generate an in-memory hashmap

of the necessary structure; for example, to generate the structure of the KPCR, the symbol information obtained from the PDB is parsed, and each element's offset, name, and type is recorded. To display a list of all currently active processes, the structure KDDEBUGGER_DATA64 (KDBG) which is used for OS kernel debugging is located. Prior to the release of Windows Vista, an element within the KPCR named *KdVersionBlock* stored a pointer to the KDBG, however this field is now nullified by the OS during the boot process. The KDBG is stored in a memory location relative to the start of the KPCR, and by performing a memory search through the two pages prior to the start of the KPCR, the KDBG can be located by its header which contains the fixed string 'KDBG'. Upon location of the KDBG, the element 'PsActiveProcessHead' is parsed to locate an OS maintained doubly-linked list of active processes.

Each active process within the OS is referenced through an EPROCESS structure, which contains data relating to the processes current system activity, such as the number of active threads, current memory utilisation, and a unique numeric identifier (PID). As each EPROCESS structure is within a doubly linked list, each contains a link to the next (flink), and previous (blink) process in the list, *Pathogen* is able to parse each active process by following each flink within the list. A partial example of this is shown in figure 2. In addition, *Pathogen* also monitors the currently executing thread, and by comparing what is currently executing with the data obtained from the EPROCESS linked list can identify potentially hidden processes.

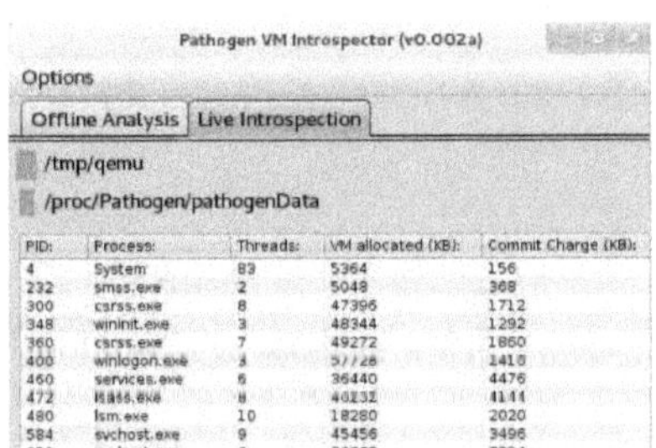

Figure 2: Pathogen showing active processes

3. EXAMPLE MALWARE ANALYSIS

To demonstrate *Pathogen's* current capabilities, a VM running Windows 7 x64 was created and infected with a variant of the *sirefef* malware (TrojanDropperWin32Sirefef.B). After infection, *Pathogen's* log files were examined to identify any symptoms of malicious behavior.

Following execution of the malware, *Pathogen* detected the creation of the files *'msimg32.dll'* & *'InstallFlashPlayer.exe'*, which were followed by a User Access Control (UAC) prompt to allow the execution of the Adobe Flash player installer. Upon confirmation of the UAC prompt, the Adobe Flash player installer was able to execute with administrator level privileges.

To deliver its malicious payload, *sirefef* takes advantage of the way in which Windows locates and loads dynamic library files (DLLs). The legitimate *msimg32.dll* is located in the Windows\System32 directory, however on loading an executable, Windows will first check to see if any DLLs required exist within the same directory as the executing file, and if so, will load the local DLL, rather than performing an additional search. This results in the legitimate Adobe Flash player installer self-injecting the malicious payload contained within the local copy of *msimg32.dll*. In addition, *Pathogen* also detected the creation of the file *'consrv.dll'* which is reported by Microsoft's Security Protection Center to be associated with *sirefef* malware families.

4. CONCLUSIONS

The purpose of this poster is to highlight *Pathogen's* current capabilities in performing VMI whilst narrowing the semantic gap through the use of offline forensic analysis. Current VMI solutions perform introspection using hard coded symbolic definitions which must be updated manually. This issue is further compounded by the frequency of OS updates which alter structure definitions. Now that a reliable VMI framework has been established, the next stage of *Pathogen's* development is to introduce malware detection techniques, along with additional live disk and network monitoring.

5. REFERENCES

[1] A. Bianchi et al. Blacksheep: Detecting compromised hosts in homogeneous crowds. In *Proceedings of the 2012 ACM conference on Computer and communications security. P.341-352.*, 2012.

[2] Microsoft Protection Center. Sirefef malware definition. http://www.microsoft.com/security/portal/threat/encyclopedia/entry.aspx?Name=Win32%2FSirefef, 2013.

[3] AMD Corporation. AMD Virtualization (AMD-V) Technology. http://sites.amd.com/uk/business/it-solutions/virtualization/Pages/amd-v.aspx, 2013.

[4] Intel Corporation. Hardware-Assisted Virtualization Technology. http://www.intel.com/content/www/us/en/virtualization/virtualization-technology/hardware-assist-virtualization-technology.html, 2013.

[5] Intel Corporation. IA-32e Paging. Intel Developer's Manual. Volume 3. http://www.intel.com/content/www/us/en/processors/architectures-software-developer-manuals.html, 2013.

[6] Microsoft Corporation. Microsoft Public Symbol Server. http://support.microsoft.com/kb/311503, 2013.

[7] Simon. Crosby. Mind the Gap!" The Limitations of VM Introspection. http://blogs.bromium.com/2012/10/01/mind-the-gap-the-limitations-of-vm-introspection/, 2012.

[8] M. Sharif et al. Secure in-vm monitoring using hardware virtualization. In *Proceedings of the 16th ACM conference on Computer and Communications Security, P.447-487*, 2009.

[9] T.Garfinkel and M.Rosenblum. A virtual machine introspection based architecture for intrusion detection. In *Proceedings of the Network and Distributed System Security Symposium (NDSS)*, 2003.

[10] VMI Tools. VMI memory analysis framework. https://code.google.com/p/vmitools/, 2013.

[11] Volatility. Volatile memory analysis framework. https://www.volatilesystems.com/default/volatility, 2013.

Poster – PnP: Improving Web Browsing Performance over Tor Using Web Resource Prefetch-and-Push

Giang T. K. Nguyen† Xun Gong‡ Anupam Das† Nikita Borisov‡
†Department of Computer Science
‡Department of Electrical and Computer Engineering
University of Illinois at Urbana-Champaign
{nguyen59,xungong1,das17,nikita}@illinois.edu

ABSTRACT

Tor is a widely used network for anonymous communication. Its users frequently experience large communication delays, due to the high user-to-relay ratio, the bandwidth-intensive BitTorrent transfers of a small fraction of the user base, and the inherent latencies from routing traffic through multiple relay hops scattered around the world. These delays significantly degrade the user experience of web browsing, a dominant use of Tor.

Improving web browsing performance of Tor has been a subject of much research. Targeting the network and transport layers, prior work includes proposals to throttle bandwidth-intensive connections or to prioritize interactive traffic such as web browsing. We attack the problem at the application layer, noting that a typical web page consists of multiple resources, each of which requires a one-round-trip HTTP request-response cycle to load in the browser. Thus, for a page with many resources, these round trips are a major contributor to the page load time. We investigate PnP (for Prefetch-and-Push), where the Tor exit prefetches resources of the web page a client is visiting and pushes them to the client. Our experiments show a significant reduction in page load times as well as higher client's privacy from web page fingerprinting by a local attacker.

Categories and Subject Descriptors

C.2.0 [**Computer-Communication Networks**]: General—*Data communication*; C.2.1 [**Computer-Communication Networks**]: Network Architecture and Design; C.4 [**Computer Systems Organization**]: Performance of Systems

Keywords

Tor; web; latency; prefetch; fingerprinting

1. INTRODUCTION

Tor [5] is a widely used network for anonymous communication. Its users frequently experience large communication delays; in part, it is because the network comprises of about 4 000 volunteer-run relays supporting 500 000 daily users.[1] Moreover, Tor is popular among BitTorrent users who, while representing a small fraction of the overall users, consume a large fraction of the overall bandwidth [7]. Finally, some delays are inherent in anonymous routing, as paths traverse relays scattered around the world to better hide the true origin of a connection. These delays significantly degrade the user experience of web browsing, a dominant use of Tor.

Improving the delay performance of Tor has been a subject of much research. Specifically focusing on web browsing are proposals to throttle bandwidth-intensive applications such as BitTorrent [2, 6, 8] or to prioritize low-bandwidth traffic such as web browsing during scheduling [10]. These techniques can improve the delay performance, but users can still experience large delays.

We attack the problem at the application protocol layer (an approach Murdoch also considered in an early proposal [9]), noting that a typical web page consists of multiple embedded resources (e.g., images, cascading style sheets, etc.). Each embedded resource requires a one-round-trip HTTP request-response cycle to load in the browser. Thus, for a web page with many resources, these round trips, especially across a typical three-hop Tor circuit, is a major contributor to the delay in loading the page. In our design, the Tor exit prefetches the resources of the web page a client is visiting and pushes them to the client. Note that in contrast with previous work on link *prediction* [4], which prefetches *pages* that the user is likely to visit *next*, we instead prefetch *components* of the page that the user is visiting *now*.

Prefetching improves application-level performance even as the transport layer delays remain the same. It is complementary to other approaches to improve Tor performance. In particular, the priority scheduling proposed by Tang and Goldberg [10] is currently part of the Tor code base and is included in the baseline performance in our analysis.

2. DESIGN

Fig. 1 shows the overall architecture of our design. We make use of two proxies, one on the client host (client-side proxy, or CSP) that sits between the user's browser and the Tor client, and one on the Tor exit node (server-side proxy, or SSP) that sits between the Tor exit router and the website. This allows us to support PnP without modifying browser software or the Tor codebase.

When the browser requests a web page, the CSP forwards the HTTP GET request to the SSP, which proceeds to load the whole web page at the specified URL as a browser would: this entails *prefetching* resources embedded in the page. As the SSP receives these resources, it *pushes* them over the Tor circuit towards the CSP.

[1]Figures obtained from the Tor Metrics Portal in August 2013: `https://metrics.torproject.org/`

CCS'13, November 4–8, 2013, Berlin, Germany.
ACM 978-1-4503-2477-9/13/11.
http://dx.doi.org/10.1145/2508859.2512519.

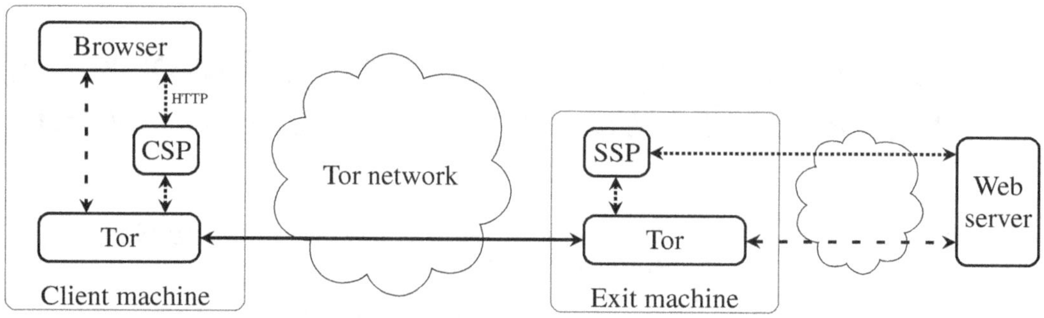

Figure 1: PnP overall architecture, with the SSP co-located with the Tor exit relay. The CSP provides an HTTP interface to the browser. The dotted and dashed arrows represent communication channels when using and when not using PnP, respectively.

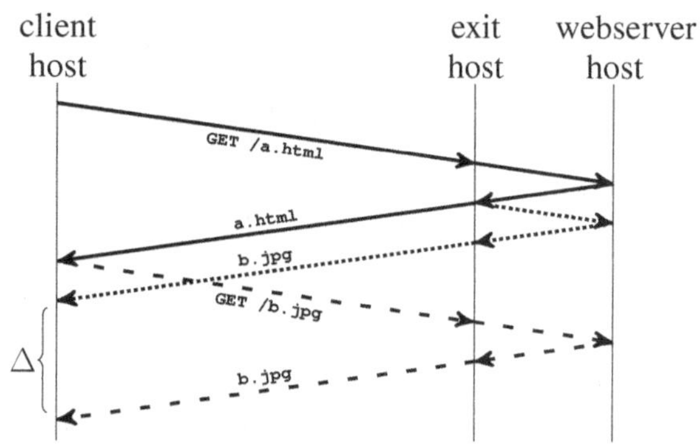

Figure 2: Timing diagram illustrating the improved page load time for a web page with a single resource `b.jpg`. The dotted and dashed arrows represent messages exchanged when using and when not using PnP, respectively, and Δ represents the difference in page load time.

When the CSP receives a pushed resource, it can deliver the resource to the browser immediately if it has already received a request from the browser for that resource. Otherwise, the CSP temporarily saves the resource in memory and later delivers it upon the browser's request. We note that, if the browser requests a resource that the CSP has yet to receive from the SSP, then the CSP queues the request but does not forward it to the SSP, under the assumption that the SSP will soon push the resource. This means that browsing a web page involves sending only one request over the network. Fig. 2 shows the exchanged messages and the resulting improved page load time for a toy web page with a single resource.

3. PROTOTYPE AND EXPERIMENTS

3.1 Prototype Implementation

We have implemented a PnP prototype. Part of the SSP has to load whole web pages; for this purpose, we use `QWebPage` from the Qt application development framework.[2] `QWebPage` uses the rendering engine `QtWebKit`[3] to fetch the page's HTML and other embedded resources. For the CSP-SSP communication, we use Google's SPDY[4] protocol, which is designed to efficiently multiplex multiple HTTP "connections" over a single TCP connection, supports "server-push," and has open-source library implementations. The CSP is a modified `shrpx` proxy from the `spdylay` project,[5] and the SSP builds on `spdylay`'s SPDY API.

3.2 Modeling web pages

Previous work on Tor performance used a single file to represent a web page. To evaluate PnP, we need a more realistic representation of web pages with multiple resources. Instead of experimenting with real web pages, which change over time, we create simple static models that preserve the numbers and sizes of resources in those web pages: for each resource in the real page, we embed a JPEG image of the same size in the model. We note that our tests lack the complex dependency structure exhibited by real web pages [11]; we plan to improve the web page models in future work.

3.3 Experiment over Live Tor Network

Setup. We deploy a public Tor relay that allows exit connections only to our SSP and web servers. To reduce variability, the web servers are on the same local network as the exit, but we add an 80 ms RTT to emulate the wide-area network. The web servers host page models of 17 top news websites such as CNN and the BBC (with JavaScript enabled). These page models range from 60 to 250 resources and from 400 KB to 2.5 MB in total sizes.

The client is a desktop machine at our lab. It is configured to use only one guard entry (though due to network churn, it used three different guards during the experiment) and use only our exit relay for all connections. The client loads each of the 17 page models 40 times, alternating between using and not using PnP (20 times each). The client browser is a minimal browser based again on `QWebPage`. To ensure the integrity of each page load, the browser is given a manifest (with SHA-1 digests) of the page it is loading and verifies that it correctly loads only resources specified in the manifest. We also collect packet captures on the client machine for fingerprinting analysis. In all, we have 680 successful page loads.

Page load time results. As Fig. 3 shows, using PnP achieves a significant improvement over the baseline: the median and the 90th percentile page load times improve by ~9 seconds, or 62% and 47% reductions, respectively. Also, we note the lower variability and the shorter tail in page load times if using PnP.

Mitigation of website fingerprinting. Recent work showed that it is possible to learn the identity of a web page being retrieved over Tor by searching for web page fingerprints inside the client's traffic patterns. Cai et al. use the Damerau-Levenshtein distance as well as support vector machines to achieve 84% accuracy in classifying a set of 100 web pages retrieved over Tor [3].

[2]`http://qt-project.org/`

[3]`http://trac.webkit.org/wiki/QtWebKit`

[4]`http://www.chromium.org/spdy/spdy-whitepaper`

[5]`http://sourceforge.net/projects/spdylay/`

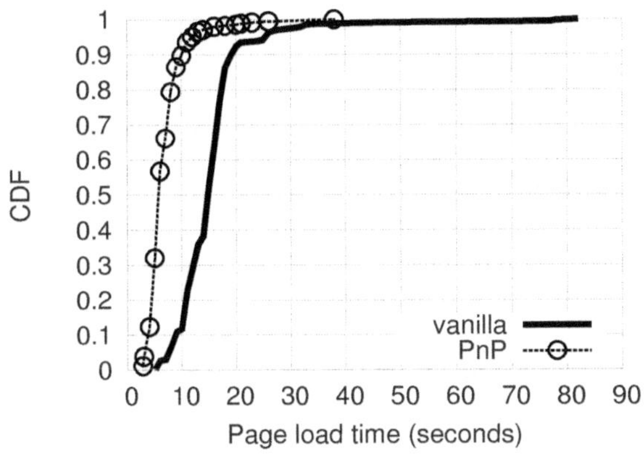

Figure 3: Page load time of 680 total page loads of 17 page models over the live Tor network on July 11, 2013, with and without using PnP.

We apply their techniques to the traces of browsing the 17 web page models produced by our experiments and compare web page classification tasks with and without PnP enabled. We estimate the classification accuracy by performing 10-fold cross validation tests. The average success rate is 99% when training on and classifying vanilla traces, and drops to 62% when training on and classifying PnP traces. This suggests PnP is a promising technique to defend against website fingerprinting attacks.

4. CHALLENGES AND FUTURE WORK

We discuss some of the challenges in designing PnP, possible solutions, and future research directions.

Time-space trade-off. Due to caching or customizations (e.g., by extensions), the client browser might not request some resources when loading a web page. Thus, PnP will waste bandwidth if it prefetches and pushes these resources. We plan to conduct a measurement study on real Tor exits to estimate the expected wasted bandwidth. For example, when an exit observes a request for a web page, it separately loads the page and sees that `b.jpg` is part of the page. If the exit does not subsequently observe the client's request for `b.jpg`, then `b.jpg` counts towards wasted bandwidth. Note, though, that the client might in fact request `b.jpg` through a different exit, in which case, `b.jpg` would not have been wasted because with PnP in use, the CSP would request the web page through the same SSP, exit policies permitted.

Correctness. Web servers use HTTP cookies to authenticate users, to provide user-specific content, etc. Without access to the client browser's cookies, the SSP might not be able to retrieve the correct resources. A possible solution is for the client, when loading a new page, to guess based on previous visits to the page which of its stored cookies will be relevant for loading embedded resources, and to transfer those cookies to the SSP, which can use them when prefetching the page. There is little additional security risk (besides over-guessing and sending extraneous sensitive cookies) because without PnP, the client will still send those cookies along subsequent requests for embedded resources.

HTTPS support. If the client communicates with the web server over HTTPS, then PnP is unable to perform prefetch-and-push. To support HTTPS, the client must trust PnP to be a man-in-the-middle. One way to achieve this is for the owner of the web server to deploy a Tor exit/SSP securely under his control and give the SSP access to his web server's TLS private key. However, HTTPS support might not be crucial at this time because according to a recent study, HTTPS is <5% of all web traffic [1].

Acknowledgments

We would like to thank Roger Dingledine and Robert Johnson for initial discussions about using SPDY in Tor. This material is based upon work supported by the National Science Foundation under Awards Nos. 093655 and 1054937, by the Army Research Office under Award No. W911NF–13–1–0086, by the Air Force under Award No. FA 9550–11–1–0016, and by the Boeing Trusted Software Center at the University of Illinois at Urbana-Champaign.

5. REFERENCES

[1] B. Ager, N. Chatzis, A. Feldmann, N. Sarrar, S. Uhlig, and W. Willinger. Anatomy of a large european IXP. In *Proceedings of the ACM SIGCOMM 2012 Conference on Applications, Technologies, Architectures, and Protocols for Computer Communication*, SIGCOMM '12, pages 163–174. ACM, 2012.

[2] M. AlSabah, K. Bauer, and I. Goldberg. Enhancing Tor's performance using real-time traffic classification. In *Proceedings of the 2012 ACM Conference on Computer and Communications Security*, CCS '12, pages 73–84. ACM, 2012.

[3] X. Cai, X. C. Zhang, B. Joshi, and R. Johnson. Touching from a distance: Website fingerprinting attacks and defenses. In *Proceedings of the 2012 ACM conference on Computer and Communications Security*, CCS '12, pages 605–616. ACM, 2012.

[4] X. Chen and X. Zhang. A popularity-based prediction model for web prefetching. *Computer*, 36(3):63–70, Mar. 2003.

[5] R. Dingledine, N. Mathewson, and P. Syverson. Tor: the second-generation onion router. In *Proceedings of the 13th conference on USENIX Security Symposium - Volume 13*, SSYM'04, pages 21–21, Berkeley, CA, USA, 2004. USENIX Association.

[6] R. Jansen, P. Syverson, and N. Hopper. Throttling Tor bandwidth parasites. In *Proceedings of the 21st USENIX Security Symposium*. USENIX Association, 2012.

[7] D. Mccoy, K. Bauer, D. Grunwald, T. Kohno, and D. Sicker. Shining light in dark places: Understanding the Tor network. In *Proceedings of the 8th Privacy Enhancing Technologies Symposium*, PETS '08, pages 63–76. Springer-Verlag, 2008.

[8] W. B. Moore, C. Wacek, and M. Sherr. Exploring the potential benefits of expanded rate limiting in Tor: slow and steady wins the race with Tortoise. In *Proceedings of the 27th Annual Computer Security Applications Conference*, ACSAC '11, pages 207–216. ACM, 2011.

[9] S. J. Murdoch. Using the SPDY protocol to improve Tor performance. `https://gitweb.torproject.org/torspec.git/blob/HEAD:/proposals/ideas/xxx-using-spdy.txt`. Accessed August 20, 2013.

[10] C. Tang and I. Goldberg. An improved algorithm for Tor circuit scheduling. In *Proceedings of the 17th ACM Conference on Computer and Communications Security*, CCS '10, pages 329–339. ACM, 2010.

[11] X. S. Wang, A. Balasubramanian, A. Krishnamurthy, and D. Wetherall. Demystifying page load performance with WProf. In *Proceedings of the 10th USENIX Symposium on Networked Systems Design and Implementation*, NSDI '13. USENIX Association, 2013.

POSTER: Sniffing and Propagating Malwares through WPAD Deception in LANs

Li Dan[1,2], Liu Chaoge[2], Cui Xu[3], Cui Xiang[2]
[1]Beijing University of Posts and Telecommunications
[2]Institute of Computing Technology, Chinese Academy of Sciences
[3]China Academy of Aerospace Aerodynamics
lidan@software.ict.ac.cn

ABSTRACT
The Web Proxy Auto-Discovery (WPAD) protocol is always used to locate a URL of a configuration file through DHCP, DNS or some other discovery methods. WPAD is a very convenience way for the management of network administrator. However, in the meantime, it may lead to a potential compromise to our LANs. In this poster, we propose a novel attack method based on WPAD protocol which can be used by attacker to intercept traffic, sniff and propagate malwares in LAN.

Categories and Subject Descriptors
C.2.1 [**Computer Communication Networks**]: Network Architecture and Design

General Terms
Design, Security

Keywords
WPAD, Malware Propagation, Sniffer

1. INTRODUCTION
Nowadays, most browsers allow users to configure proxy servers. Mainly, there are three methods can be used: ***Manual Configuration*** in which users set the IP and Port of proxy manually, ***Proxy Auto-Config (PAC)*** in which users set a PAC file manually which includes the information of proxies and ***Web Proxy Auto-Discovery*** in which browsers can automatically discover the PAC file by WPAD protocol without manual configuration (e.g., Internet Explorer provides those three methods that can be found in the option "Tools->Internet Options ->LAN Settings").

WPAD protocol is always used by clients to locate a URL of a configuration file. It is designed to simplify settings, facilitate deployments in large-scale networks. However, this mechanism will also bring security threats (e.g., the famous malware "Flame" which uses windows update as one of its methods to propagate malware is based on this mechanism). An attacker can use this mechanism to hijack users' browser, especially in some public areas (e.g., airports, cafe).

CCS'13, November 4–8, 2013, Berlin, Germany.
ACM 978-1-4503-2477-9/13/11.
http://dx.doi.org/10.1145/2508859.2512520

2. MECHANISM OF WPAD
2.1 Definitions
WPAD client: WPAD client is a host which opens Web Proxy Auto-Discovery and queries for proxy's information in LAN.

WPAD server: WPAD server is a host which provides proxy's information and responds requests from WPAD clients.

2.2 Working Processes
WPAD clients have six approaches to search WPAD servers in windows operating system: query through DHCP (option 252) protocol, query through DNS protocol, query through WINS protocol (host name is "wpad"), query through NetBIOS broadcast, query through "hosts" file and query through "lmhosts" file. WPAD clients will query through those methods one by one in a specific order until an available WPAD server is found. All the six methods can be used to redirect browser's traffic and the first four methods can be used through networks.

After a WPAD server is found in the LAN, a browser configured to use Web Proxy Auto-Discovery mechanism will automatically download a PAC file. The PAC file includes a function named "FindProxyForURL(url, host)" which is written in javascript. This function is called by the browser of WPAD client for each URL request. When this function is called, the IP address and port to be accessed from the original URL is ignored and the "host" parameter of the function returns the real IP and port for this request.

3. DECEPTION OF WPAD CLIENTS
There is an illustration of WPAD deception through NetBIOS broadcast. We assume that an attacker can interconnect to a LAN as a normal user in it (may through physical access or control a user's computer in the LAN). With the ability to interconnect with all the users in the LAN, the attacker can imitate the WPAD server to respond WPAD Clients' NetBIOS broadcast queries. For windows operating system has the mechanism to avoid the conflict of more than one WPAD server in LAN, an attacker can easily imitate and kick off the real WPAD server. The process of WPAD deception through NetBIOS broadcast is illustrated in Figure 1 and 2.

1. **Query the WPAD server in LAN:** When the browser of a WPAD client is opened for the first the time, it will query the WPAD server automatically.

2. **Respond as a WPAD server:** the attacker monitors UDP broadcasts packets of NBNS protocol at port 137. If a NBNS name query request is found, the attacker will respond those queries to claim that it is a WPAD server.

3. **Request the PAC file:** When the client receives the response from the attacker, it will consider the attacker as the WPAD server and the client's browser will request the PAC file named "wpad.dat" from it.

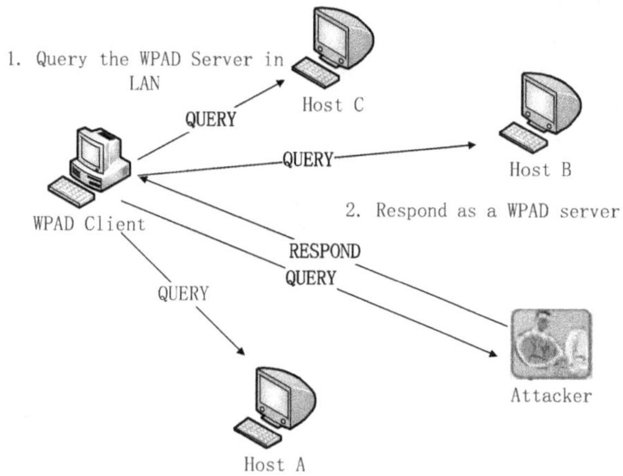

Figure 1. The attacker claim itself a WPAD server.

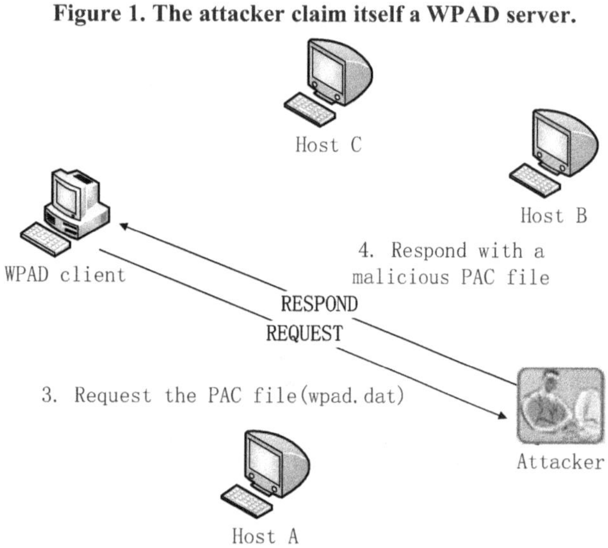

Figure2. The WPAD client downloads the PAC file.

4. **Respond with a malicious PAC file:** the attacker waits for clients' request of PAC file and respond with a malicious one including the "FindProxyForURL" function.

4. SNIFFING AND PROPAGATING MALWARES IN LAN

When the client's browser get the PAC file successfully, it will call the "FindProxyForURL" function for each URL requested from the client and send the client's request to the host returned from this function (not all the browsers call this function when Web Proxy Auto-Discovery mechanism is opened, we know Internet Explorer under version 9, most version of firefox and safari will do that as so far).

An attacker can use the "FindProxyForURL" function to redirect all victims' browser's traffic to a specific proxy server set up beforehand to ***sniffing all the traffic in LAN.*** Meanwhile, the proxy server can detect the URL to be accessed by users. If the URL requests to download a file (e.g., URL ended with "rar", "exe", "doc", "pdf", etc.), the attacker can replace the file and return a malicious one that has the same name with the original one to the user. It is hard for the user to find the downloaded file is changed and the malware will have a higher possibility to be run. If there is a host invaded by an attacker, it can use that method to ***propagating malwares in LANs***.

5. PRELIMINARY RESULTS AND LIMITATIONS

5.1 Preliminary Results

We preliminary implement a prototype of WPAD deception implement base on NetBIOS broadcast. The experimental result is illustrated in Figure 3.

The "wpad.dat" file provided by "hfs.exe"(in the upper right) is downloaded multi-times.
The hosts in the LAN access the internet through a proxy server named "HttpProxyServer.exe" (In the lower right) and log the IP addreses at the same time.
Those packets captured by "Wireshark.exe"(in the left) shows the detail of WPAD deception.

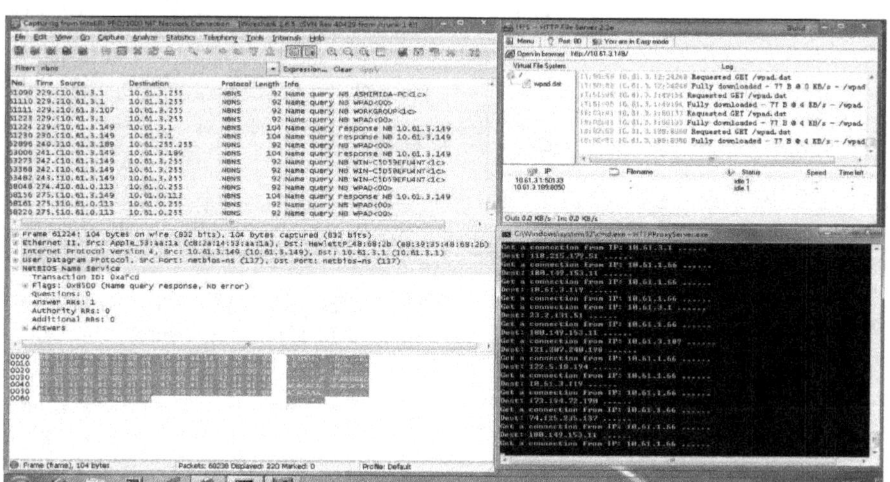

Figure3: experimental result of WPAD deception

Table 1. Table captions should be placed above the table

Version of system	Version of Browser	Is "Automatic Detection Setting" be configured by default	Is WPAD deception succeed if "Automatic Detection Setting" is configured
Windows xp sp2 Home Edition	IE 8	YES	YES
Windows xp sp3 Home Edition	IE 8	YES	YES
Windows xp sp3 Professional	IE 8	NO	YES
Windows 7 Home Basic	IE 8	YES	YES
Windows 7 Home Basic	IE 9	YES	NO
Windows 7 Ultimate	IE 8	YES	YES
Windows 7 Ultimate	IE 9	YES	NO
Windows 8 Ultimate	IE 10	YES	NO

5.2 Limitations

WPAD deception is largely depends on the implement of browsers. For example, in Internet Explorer, although the file "wpad.dat" is always been downloaded when "Automatic Detection Setting" is set, the "Internet Explorer" will not use the auto-detected proxy to access internet after version 9 in our experiment. The "Automatic Detection Setting" is also default configured only in part of versions of windows system. The default configurations and the experimental results from part of versions of Windows XP to Windows 7 is listed in table 1.

6. FUTURE WORKS

Table 1 shows that "Automatic Detection Setting" is configured by default in part of version of Windows xp, all versions of Windows 7 and in Windows 8. But WPAD deception only succeed before IE 9. For WPAD is a convenient method for intranet management, it should be supported in IE 9 and versions above. In the future, we will try to find whether there are some mechanisms we don't notice and other three query methods that can be used in LAN.

7. ACKNOWLEDGMENT

This work is supported by the National Natural Science Foundation of China under grant (No. 61202409) and the National High Technology Research and Development Program (863 Program) of China under grant (No. 2012AA012902 and 2011AA01A103).

8. REFERENCES

[1] WPAD: Internet Explorers Worst Feature, Grant Bugher, <http://perimetergrid.com/wp/2008/01/11/wpad-internet-explorers-worst-feature/>

[2] HTTP: The Definitive Guide, David Gourley, Brain Totty

POSTER: A Footprint of Third-Party Tracking on Mobile Web

Ashar Javed
Chair of Network and Data Security
Ruhr University Bochum
Bochum, Germany
ashar.javed@rub.de

ABSTRACT

In this paper, we investigate the footprints of third-party tracking on the mobile web. The survey of 100 popular mobile versions of web applications indicates that third-party tracking is also prevalent on mobile web. The results show that 62 sites are tracking users' activities on mobile web and *Google Analytics* is the most widespread tracker on mobile web. We believe that this study will help raise awareness about the tracking situation on the mobile web side.

Categories and Subject Descriptors

K.4 [**COMPUTERS AND SOCIETY**]: Privacy

General Terms

Privacy, Mobile-web

Keywords

survey, mobile-web, third-party tracking

1. INTRODUCTION

Researchers have conducted several studies in order to see third-party tracking situation on desktop-based web applications [1, 2, 3] and this is often an agenda of *public/privacy* debate [4, 5]. The motivation for this work comes from the observation that the mobile-based web applications or mobile web still lacks research community's knowledge on third-party tracking. The URLs of mobile-based web applications start with the letter "**m**", or end in the words "**mobi**" or "**mobile**' e.g., `http://m.pinterest.com`. Sites typically present a simple and optimized version of web application on the mobile side.

This paper presents a survey of 100 popular mobile-based web applications. The goal of this survey is to see the prevalence of third-party tracking code on mobile web. The inspected sites includes names like Nokia, Pinterest, Vodafone, BBCNews, CNN, Twitter, Youtube, Intel, Answers, Dictionary and Etsy etc. We found third-party tracking code on 62 sites (see Section 3.2). We found 17 different trackers (see Section 3.3) on the considered mobile sites. *Google Analytics* [6] is the most widespread tracker having footprints on 41 mobile sites followed by *ScorecardResearch* [7] with its footing on 23 mobile versions of web applications.

CCS'13, November 4–8, 2013, Berlin, Germany.
ACM 978-1-4503-2477-9/13/11.
http://dx.doi.org/10.1145/2508859.2512521.

2. RELATED WORK

To the best of our knowledge, all quantitative overviews [1, 2, 3] on third-party tracking we are aware of are related to desktop based web applications. Our study provides a first insight into the current prevalence of third-party tracking on the mobile versions of web applications.

3. SURVEY

3.1 General Approach

In this section, we discuss the approach used to gather data. We have surveyed 100 mobile versions of web applications and manually analyze the source code of *homepages* of mobile applications. The complete list of surveyed sites is available at `http://pastebin.com/jeEJp7GW`. On the mobile side, sites typically present a simple and optimized version of their corresponding web applications. Mobile sites have less features, less functionality and less contents as compare to their desktop variants. Though mobile sites are simple with less contents but the amount of third-party tracking code we found on mobile versions of web applications is surprisingly high and requires attention.

3.2 Prevalence of Third-Party Tracking

Our investigation of the 100 popular mobile sites indicates that 62 sites are using tracking code to monitor users' browsing activities on mobile web. It includes sites like SoundCloud, Pinterest, BBCNews, CNN, MySpace, Dictionary and Answers etc. The complete list of mobile sites that are tracking users' activities is available at `http://pastebin.com/qK4NOvbS`.

3.3 Trackers on Mobile Web

We found 17 unique third-party trackers during survey of 100 mobile versions of web applications. Table 1 shows the names of third-party trackers along with their footprints.

Third-Party Tracker	Footprint
Google Analytics	41
ScorecardResearch	23
Omniture[8]	7
Quantcast[9]	4
GoogleSyndication[10]	3
AddThis[11]	2
EffectiveMeasure[12]	2

Table 1: Third-party Tracker on Mobile web along with their footprints

There are other trackers like Statcounter[1], Admob[2], SeeVolution[3], Moblama[4], Adreacter[5], MADS[6], Mobilytics[7], Kissmetrics[8], Imrworldwide[9] and Akamai[10] etc. We found their footprints on one mobile application each.

3.4 Tracking Code

The majority of the trackers on mobile sites are using JavaScript code for tracking purpose. We also found that some of the trackers are using Web Beacons [13] alongside. Web Beacon or web bug or clear GIF is a 1*1 (height*width) image used for tracking purposes. According to Network Advertising Initiative [14]:

"Web beacons are a tool that can be used online to deliver a cookie in a third-party context. This allows companies to perform many important tasks—including unique visitor counts, web usage patterns, assessments of the efficacy of ad campaigns, delivery of more relevant offers, and tailoring of web site content."

The following snippet we found on site `http://m.wund.com/`

```
<noscript><img src="http://pixel.quantse
rve.com/pixel/p-01lvMKu--eLQE.gif" style=
"display: none" height="1" width="1" alt=
"Quantcast"/></noscript>
```

In this case, the site places a web beacon in a *<noscript>* tag. The main reason is to keep tracking active even if user's mobile browser does not support JavaScript or JavaScript is blocked. Now we discuss some miscellaneous findings that we consider worth mentioning:

- We found four (4) different trackers on *homepages* of the following mobile sites `http://m.wund.com/`, `http://m.fark.com/` and `m.cricbuzz.com/info/contact`.

[1]`http://statcounter.com/`
[2]`http://www.google.com/ads/admob/`
[3]`https://www.seevolution.com/`
[4]`http://moblama.ru/`
[5]`http://www.adreactor.com/`
[6]`http://www.mads.com/`
[7]`http://www.mobilytics.net/`
[8]`https://www.kissmetrics.com/`
[9]`http://www.donottrackplus.com/trackers/imrworldwide.com.php`
[10]`http://www.akamai.com/`

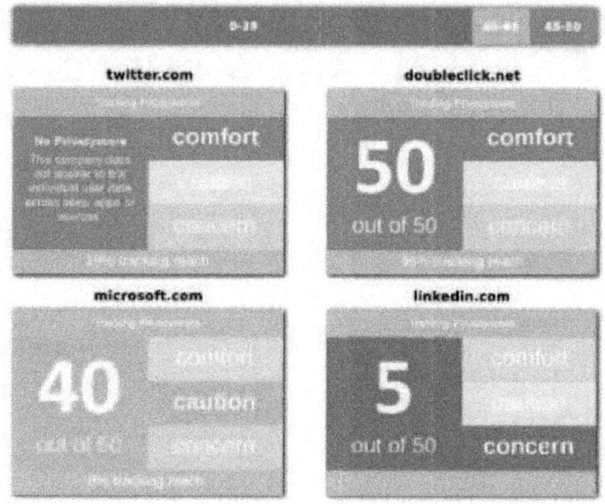

Figure 1: Rating system and examples from *privacychoice*

- We found three unique third-party trackers on homepages of nine (9) mobile versions of web applications.
- According to recent report by Ghostery, *Google Analytics* is the most widespread tracker on web [15]. Our survey has found that *Google Anayltics* is also widespread tracker on mobile side.

3.5 Rating Trackers

We use *Privacychoice's privacyscore* rating system [16] for the classifications of third-party trackers found on the mobile web. A Privacyscore is a way to assess the privacy risk of using a third-party tracker [16]. *Privacychoice's privacyscore* rating system assigns values between zero to fifty and use different color schemes for marking "*comfort or caution or concern*" (see Fig. 1). For interested readers, we refer to [17] for detailed description on *Privacychoice's privacyscore* rating system. The Table. 2 shows third-party tracker along with their privacyscore (if given). Unfortunately, we have found no information about some mobile trackers regarding their privacyscore reputation and some have a rating of "*concern*" according to their privacyscore.

4. CONCLUSION

In this paper, we have surveyed 100 mobile sites and found tracking code on 62. We also found 17 unique third-party trackers on 100 mobile versions of web applications. We hope this paper will raise awareness about the third-party tracking situation on mobile side.

5. ACKNOWLEDGEMENTS

This work has been supported by the Ministry of Economic Affairs and Energy of the State of North Rhine-Westphalia (Grant 315-43-02/2-005-WFBO-009).

6. REFERENCES

[1] Balachander Krishnamurthy and Craig Wills. Generating a Privacy Footprint on the Internet.: In IMC 2006

#	Tracker	Score (Total 50)	Description
1	*Google Analytics*	50	Comfort
2	*ScorecardResearch*	50	Comfort
3	*Omniture*	No privacyscore	Comfort
4	*Quantcast*	50	Comfort
5	*GoogleSyndication*	50	Comfort
6	*AddThis*	40	Caution
7	*EffectiveMeasure*	25	Concern
8	*StatCounter*	No Privacyscore	Comfort
9	*Admob*	0	Concern
10	*SeeVolution*	–	No Information
11	*Moblama*	–	No Information
12	*Adreacter*	–	No Information
13	*MADS*	0	Concern
14	*Mobilytics*	–	No Information
15	*Kissmetrics*	No Privacyscore	Comfort
16	*Imrworldwide*	25	Caution
17	*Akamai*	50	Comfort

Table 2: Third-party Tracker on Mobile web along with their PrivacyScore Rating

[2] Balachander Krishnamurthy and Craig Wills. Privacy Diffusion on the Web: A Longitudinal Perspective.: In WWW 2009

[3] Balachander Krishnamurthy. I know what you will do next summer.: In ACM SIGCOMM Computer Communication Review 2010

[4] Jonathan Mayer and John C. Mitchell. Third-Party Web Tracking: Policy and Technology. In IEEE S&P 2012

[5] The Very Public Privacy Debate Heats Up.: http://www.itbusinessedge.com/cm/blogs/weinschenk/the-very-public-privacy-debate-heats-up/?cs=49798

[6] Google Analytics.: http://www.google.com/analytics/

[7] Scorecard Research.: http://www.scorecardresearch.com/Home.aspx?newLanguage=1

[8] Omniture.: http://www.omniture.com/en/products/online-business-optimisation

[9] Quantcast.: http://www.omniture.com/en/products/online-business-optimisation

[10] GoogleSyndication.: https://www.google.com/adsense/app?hl=en#home

[11] AddThis.:http://www.addthis.com/

[12] EffectiveMeasure.:http://www.effectivemeasure.com/

[13] Web Beacon.: http://en.wikipedia.org/wiki/Web_bug

[14] Network Advertising Initiative.: http://www.networkadvertising.org/

[15] Knowyourelements.: http://www.knowyourelements.com/#tab=list-view&date=2013-01-24

[16] Privacy Choice.: http://privacychoice.org/checkprivacyscores

[17] Privacy Score.: http://privacyscore.com/#

POSTER: Dr. Watson Provides Data for Post-Breach Analysis

Wasim Ahmad Bhat
Department of Computer Sciences
University of Kashmir
wab.cs@uok.edu.in

S.M.K. Quadri
Department of Computer Sciences
University of Kashmir
quadrismk@kashmiruniversity.ac.in

ABSTRACT
Nowadays security systems have become highly sophisticated. However, breaches are inevitable. Nevertheless, post-breach analysis is performed to assess the severity of the breach and to trace the intruder's actions. This paper proposes *drWatson*, a layered file system that in case of an illegitimate file system access provides data for post-breach analysis to assess the severity of the breach and to trace the intruder's actions. *drWatson*, when mounted on top of any concrete file system, works by logging all the operations along with their date time stamps targeted to the below mounted file system.

Categories and Subject Descriptors
D.4 [**Operating Systems**]: File Systems Management ;; D.4.6 [**Operating Systems**]: Security and Protection—*Access controls, Information flow controls, Security kernels*

General Terms
Design, Experimentation, Human Factors, Security

Keywords
file system; security breach; post-breach analysis; Dr.Watson

1. INTRODUCTION
Computer security encompasses concepts and methods for protecting sensitive resources in computer systems. Computer security starts from the policies that regulate access to protected resources. In technology, the focus is on mechanisms for enforcing these policies. A common motivation to invest in information security is to safeguard the confidential as well as the personal information. Over time, information security systems have evolved significantly. Policies are brought into action at various levels across all domains. However, even due to existence and continuous development of strong & reliable security mechanisms for all levels, security issues still worry administrators. The fact is that counter policies and techniques also evolve side by side to overcome new security blockages. Thus, it is mandatory to invest in security systems but equally is important to anticipate a breach and be prepared to retaliate. Taking regular backups can be one of the preparations for a breach while as the general retaliation would be to assess the severity of the breach, to trace the intruder's actions and to possibly hunt down the culprit.

As part of the preparation for the retaliation, the system needs to keep track of every possible access, modification, etc. done to the system resources. The persistent data residing in a file system in the form of hierarchy of files and folders is more vulnerable to breach than some transient data that resides in memory as the prey is always available to predator. Unfortunately, file systems are inherently incapable to help security systems during postmortem. As an example, all file systems maintain only 3 date time stamps per file or folder: Last Modified, Last Accessed and Creation date time stamps (together called as MAC DTS). This means during postmortem, the file system can't answer following questions: 1) How many times was the file/folder accessed or modified? 2) When was it accessed/modified for the first time? 3) What part of the file was accessed/modified every time? 4) What was the pattern of browsing? The answer to these questions will definitely not locate the intruder but will certainly help in assessing the damage and speculating the intention of intrusion.

We propose a layered file system, namely *drWatson*, to enhance the capability of file systems to help in post-breach analysis. *drWatson* when mounted on top of any file system, logs all the operations along-with their date time stamps targeted to it. During postmortem this log provides enough information to assess the damage and to speculate the intentions of an intruder.

2. RELATED WORK
Barik et al. [2] argued that MAC DTS procedures of popular operating systems are inherently flawed and were created only for the sake of convenience and not necessarily keeping in mind the security and digital forensic aspects. They proposed a solution in context of ext2 file system by using specific data structures to preserve the Authentic date and time stamps (ADTS). Similarly, Das et al. [3] and Ansari et al. [1] proposed preserving ADTS in Linux kernel 2.6.x using Linux Loadable Kernel Module (LKM) that can be applied to all file systems. However, all these solutions ([2] [3] & [1]) aim at preserving ADTS but not documenting every change in MAC DTS and the cause of change. Moreover, they don't document the type of access and amount of access.

CCS'13, November 4–8, 2013, Berlin, Germany.
Copyright 2013 ACM 978-1-4503-2477-9/13/11 ...$15.00.
http://dx.doi.org/10.1145/2508859.2512522

In contrast, we propose documenting every relevant information related to any type of access to any file or folder that will help in post-breach analysis. Furthermore, we propose using file system layering that has been used for many purposes (like monitoring, data transformation, operation transformation, size changing, and fan-out [8]) instead of using any file system specific data structures or file system source instrumentation.

3. THE DESIGN

The design of *drWatson* is motivated by many goals which include:

1. The solution should be applicable to all file systems i.e. no source modification and no data structures specific to any particular file system should be used.
2. The solution should log every operation targeted to the below mounted file system along with the type of operation, pre- and post-operation DTS, offset & amount of data read/written, and effective UID.
3. The solution should hide the log from normal listing and should deny access to it.
4. The solution should be portable across all OSes.
5. The solution should not add significant performance overhead to the file system operations.

In order to mitigate our goals, we designed *drWatson* as a layered file system so that it is applicable to all file systems. The capability of below mounted file system is augmented by the layered file system as the operations can be both pre- and post-processed while not modifying the source. Therefore, during pre- and post-processing, *drWatson* documents all parameters of the operation in a log hidden from user applications. Also, the layered file system is able to trap every file system operation.
Moreover, in order to be portable across all OSes it should be layered as a user process and not as some kernel module. Also, in order to be light-weight a well developed and a highly optimized framework should be used. Therefore, *drWatson* was developed using FUSE framework [7]. Figure 1 shows the interaction between various OS components and *drWatson* using a FUSE framework.

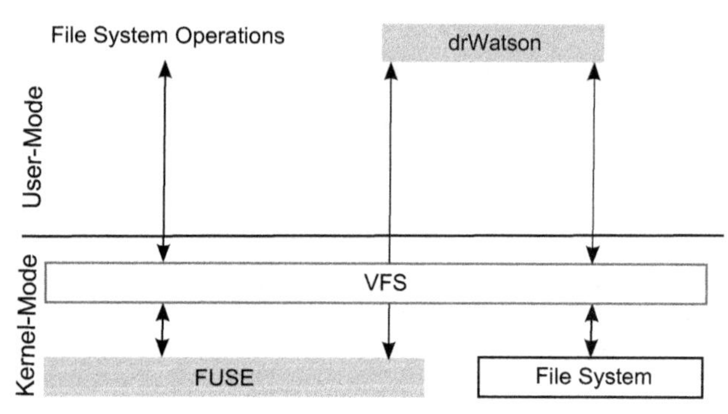

Figure 1: Interaction between OS components & *drWatson*

4. IMPLEMENTATION DETAILS

drWatson is implemented as a layered file system using FUSE framework. FUSE is an acronym for Filesystem in UserSpacE and is used to develop full-fledged file systems and to extend existing file systems [7]. As such, while maintaining the reliability of kernel, it allows access to facilities (like C library) which are lacking in kernel development; the one that is exploited by *drWatson* is usage of simple file I/O functions of C library to create and maintain the log.
The figure 2 shows that every file system operation can be

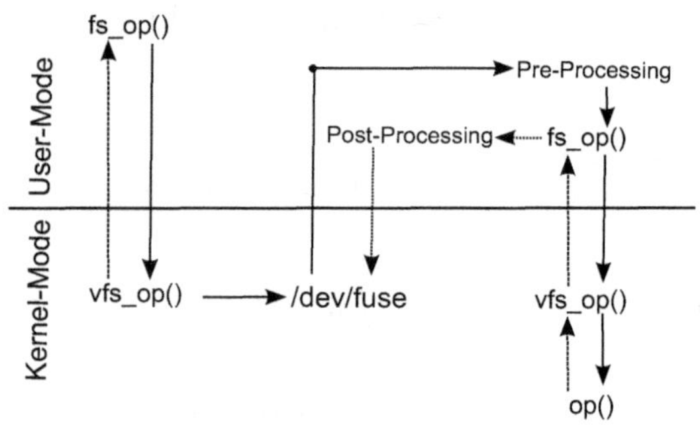

Figure 2: Pre- & post-processing performed by *drWatson*

pre- and post-processed in user space by *drWatson* to reflect the desired operation. Also, *drWatson* readdir() implements the logic to restrict listing of the log file.
The FUSE framework contains a null-pass virtual file system, fusexmp, which passes all the file system operations to below mounted file system without any modification. *drWatson* is implemented by overriding the various procedures of fusexmp. However, fusexmp doesn't support overlay mounting and as such any mount point passed to fusexmp during mounting, mounts the root directory (/) on that mount point. Having said that, a little modification to fusexmp gets it overlaid on the specified mount point, which can be a simple directory or a mount point of some other file system. It has two benefits; 1) it adds to transparency of *drWatson* as no path change is required by applications accessing that volume, and 2) it leaves no path to access native file system without the intervention of *drWatson*.
Furthermore, FUSE framework has been ported to almost all platforms including Windows [4].
drWatson in specific and FUSE file systems in general, incur performance overhead as kernel boundary is crossed to process the call. In addition to multiple context switching, multiple process switching and data copying during call processing also add overhead [6]. However, the benefits of development-ease, reliable environment and portable file system outweigh the drawbacks.

5. WORKING

The working of *drWatson* is simple. Whenever a file system syscall is invoked on any file system having *drWatson* layered over it, *drWatson* pre-processes the call by opening the log, followed by documenting the type of operation, name of target file/folder, effective UID, current MAC DTS of the target file/folder and in case of a read/write operation the offset at which read/write is supposed to take place and finally the amount of data read/written. This is followed by passing the operation to the actual file system. Finally, after the call returns, *drWatson* post-processes the call to document the new MAC DTS of the target file/folder. Algorithm 1 summarizes the working of *drWatson*.

Algorithm 1 Algorithm for pre- and post-processing of syscalls

```
Input: fsOperation, eUID
open(log)
append(log) ← fsOperation.Type
append(log) ← fsOperation.filename
append(log) ← fsOperation.eUID
append(log) ← fsOperation.filename.DTS
if fsOperation.Type = READ/WRITE then
    append(log) ← fsOperation.offset
    append(log) ← fsOperation.count
end if
if fsOperation.filename ≠ log then
    call(fsOperation)
end if
append(log) ← fsOperation.filename.DTS
close(log)
```

6. EXPERIMENT & RESULTS

We employed Filebench [5] to exercise ext2 file system with *drWatson* layered over it. Filebench is a file system and storage benchmark that allows to generate a large variety of workloads. The experiment was intended to check the amount of information documented by *drWatson* and to test the implementation for flaws. The results indicate that *drWatson* is successfully able to document every piece of information relevant to post-breach analysis.

7. CONCLUSION

In this paper we argued that file systems don't store enough information relevant to post-breach analysis as they maintain only 3 date time stamps viz. last Modified, last Accessed & Creation (MAC DTS). We found that current proposals are only able to preserve the authentic date time stamps (ADTS).

We proposed preserving MAC DTS (along with other relevant information) after every file system operation so that enough information is available during postmortem of the file system. However, in order to have the proposal applicable to all file systems and portable across all platforms, we proposed that the solution be developed as a layered file system in userspace.
Based on this idea, we developed a layered file system, namely *drWatson*, using FUSE framework that documents every information of every file system operation relevant to the post-breach analysis. On exercising the ext2 file system with Filebench benchmark, we found that *drWatson* is able to log enough information required during postmortem in case of a breach.

8. REFERENCES

[1] A. Ansari, A. Chattopadhayay, and S. Das. A kernel level vfs logger for building efficient file system intrusion detection system. In *Computer and Network Technology (ICCNT), 2010 Second International Conference on*, pages 273–279. IEEE, 2010.

[2] M. S. Barik, G. Gupta, S. Sinha, A. Mishra, and C. Mazumdar. An efficient technique for enhancing forensic capabilities of ext2 file system. *digital investigation*, 4:55–61, 2007.

[3] S. Das, A. Chattopadhayay, D. K. Kalyani, and M. Saha. File-system intrusion detection by preserving mac dts: a loadable kernel module based approach for linux kernel 2.6. x. *CSIIRW*, 9:1–6, 2009.

[4] E. Driscoll, J. Beavers, and H. Tokuda. Fuse-nt: Userspace file systems for windows nt. 2008.

[5] R. McDougall and J. Mauro. Filebench, 2005.

[6] A. Rajgarhia and A. Gehani. Performance and extension of user space file systems. In *Proceedings of the 2010 ACM Symposium on Applied Computing*, SAC '10, pages 206–213, New York, NY, USA, 2010. ACM.

[7] M. Szeredi. Filesystem in userspace, 2005.

[8] E. Zadok, R. Iyer, N. Joukov, G. Sivathanu, and C. P. Wright. On incremental file system development. *Transactions on Storage*, 2:161–196, May 2006.

POSTER: Reflected Attacks Abusing Honeypots

Martin Husák
husakm@ics.muni.cz

Martin Vizváry
vizvary@ics.muni.cz

Masaryk University
Institute of Computer Science
Botanická 554/68a, 602 00 Brno, Czech Republic

ABSTRACT

We present the observation of distributed denial-of-service attacks that use reflection of the flooding traffic off reflectors. This type of attack was used in massive attacks against internet infrastructure of Czech Republic in March, 2013. Apart from common hosts in the network, honeypots were abused as the reflectors. It caused the false positive incident detection and helped attackers. Honeypots, which are by default set to accept any incoming network connection, unintentionally amplified the effect of reflection. We present an analysis of the attack from the point of view of honeypots and show the risks of having honeypots respond to any incoming traffic. We also discuss the possibilities of attack detection and mitigation and present lessons learned from handling the attack. We point out a lack of communication and data sharing during the observed attack.

Categories and Subject Descriptors

C.2.0 [**Computer-communication Networks**]: General—*Security and protection*

Keywords

DDoS attack; reflection; honeypot; mitigation; data sharing; communication

1. INTRODUCTION

Denial-of-service attacks are a major threat to today's networks. They are relatively easy to perform, hard to defend against, and the attacker is rarely traced back due to common usage of IP spoofing techniques and a distributed form of the attack.

The Distributed Reflected Denial-of-Service (DRDoS) attacks do not contact the victim directly, they rather spoof source IP address of the victim and use bouncing of traffic off reflectors instead. The spoofing of victims' IP address causes the reflectors to appear as the attackers while the real attacker is often above suspicion. Reflectors do not need to amplify an attack, response with the same or even smaller amount of data is sufficient for a successful attack. In addition, any host in the network can be abused as a reflector, i. e., server, workstation or honeypot.

We have observed a situation where honeypots unintentionally helped the attacker. Honeypots, by their nature, are not meant to be accessed by legitimate users. If a network traffic of a honeypot is monitored and a honeypot is abused as a reflector, we can see an attempt to contact it and mark the source IP as a potential attacker. This is natural and legitimate procedure of malicious behavior detection but, in case of DRDoS, we have marked spoofed address as an attacker. Even though any network traffic destined to honeypot is suspicious, we cannot be sure if we have detected the real attacker or a victim.

The involvement of honeypots in DRDoS is often ignored, as we have observed in several attacks recently. To name a few, abuse of honeypots was associated with the massive DDoS attacks against Czech Republic in March, 2013. Another example of this type of attack was an incident from April, 2013, when we detected an IP address, which was part of a DDoS mitigation service. In both cases, the actual victim was reported and as an attacker initiating unsolicited connections to honeypots.

This paper is organized in six sections. We recount the recent DDoS attacks and the role of honeypots in them in Section 2. We point out the importance of proper configuration of honeypots to eliminate the reflection in Section 3. The possibilities of detection and mitigation of the attacks and handling issues for which organizations should be prepared are described in Section 4 and 5. The paper is concluded in Section 6.

2. DDOS ATTACKS AGAINST CZECH REPUBLIC

In March 2013, Czech Republic was a target of DDoS attacks which lasted 4 consecutive days. It was the first time the entire country had to face an attack of this volume. Online media, banks and mobile operators were gradually under DDoS attacks from Monday, March 4 to Thursday, March 7 in working hours between 8 AM and 5 PM (CET). The attacker used two types of DDoS attack with volume up to 1 Gbps [1] and initiated the attack with the knowledge of the Czech internet. The reason for the attack is unknown but it has shown how prepared the Czech community is for these attacks.

The attacks started with a SYN flood attack on Monday and Tuesday and were aimed against more than a dozen on-

CCS'13, November 4–8, 2013, Berlin, Germany.
ACM 978-1-4503-2477-9/13/11.
http://dx.doi.org/10.1145/2508859.2512523.

line media virtually hosted on a few servers, and the most popular Czech search engine *Seznam.cz*. According to DDoS attacks taxonomy [5], it was a brute-force attack using randomly spoofed source IP addresses with fluctuating rate. Even though the attack was simple and the bandwidth was low, overload of the virtual hosting denied access to many web pages. We believe that the goal of these attacks was to attract the attention of media.

On Wednesday and Thursday the attack continued with reflected SYN flood attack. The attacks were aimed against websites of major Czech banks and two mobile operators. According to the taxonomy [5], it was a brute-force attack using fixed spoofed source IP address with fluctuating rate known as the DRDoS attack. As shown in Figure 1, it is a form of a DDoS attack that bounces the flooding traffic off of reflectors by spoofing requests from the victim to Internet hosts that will send replies to the victim [6]. These attacks are based on willingness of improperly configured servers and computers to respond to incoming packets. Reflected attacks due to their nature are harder to trace and filter. According to CESNET, the Czech NREN[1], 68 % connections on random destination port were accepted and responded to with SYN+ACK. It was approximately 1.5 million packets per 5 minutes.

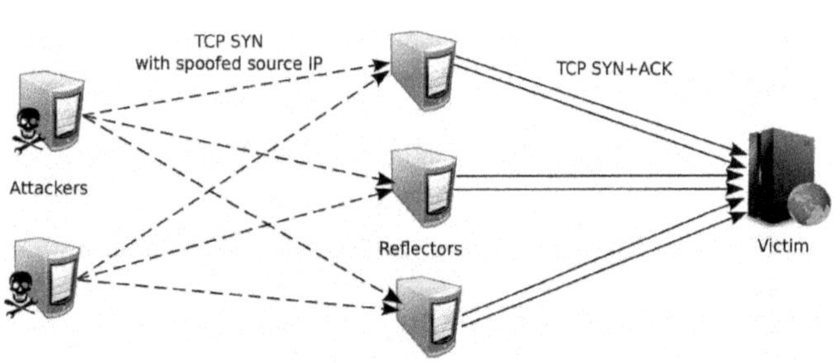

Figure 1: Schema of the reflected attack

Honeypots became great reflectors for the DRDoS attack. We observed that honeypots from another Czech university reflected 93 % of all incoming packets. Hosts in the network of Masaryk University reflected approximately 5 % of incoming packets while honeypots alone reflected 16 % of incoming packets. Figure 2 shows a traffic peak from honeypots that was stopped shortly after the false positive detection and filtering of the actual victim.

3. HONEYPOT SETTINGS AND VULNERABILITIES

Traditionally, there are two approaches to honeypot implementation, high-interaction and low-interaction honeypots [2]. These implementations differ in a level of possible interaction between a honeypot and an attacker. High-interaction honeypots are usually deployed as the virtual machines with a real operating system and applications. They do not differ from the real hosts on the network and they are not often deployed in large numbers. The low-interaction honeypots are usually emulators of systems or their parts. The settings of these honeypots are limited as well as the possible countermeasures while they are cheap to deploy and often deployed in large numbers.

[1]National Research and Education Network

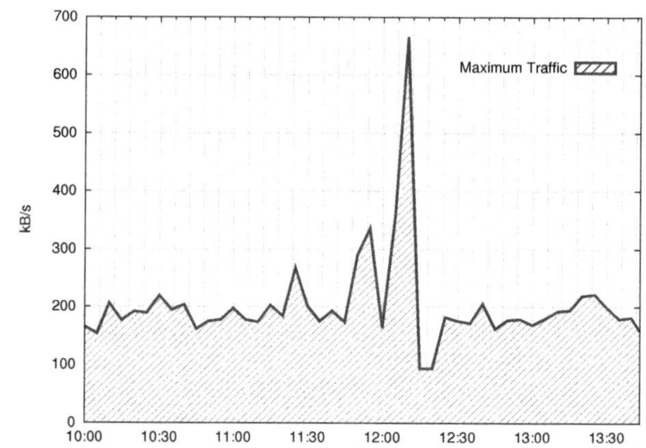

Figure 2: Incoming and outgoing TCP traffic on honeypots – Thursday, March 7, 2013 from 10 AM to 2 PM

There are popular tools among the honeypot community, a low-interaction honeypot *honeyd* [7] and a tarpit *LaBrea* [4]. Honeyd is a small daemon that creates virtual hosts in the network. There are two potential vulnerabilities in its deployment, the number of emulated hosts and settings of their port actions. Any port on any host (including defaults) emulated by honeyd can be set in three ways, 1) *open* responds with TCP SYN+ACK packet, 2) *reset* responds with TCP RST packet and 3) *block* is not responding. Honeypots are generally configured to accept any incoming connection, e. g., *open*, to capture potential attacks including zero-day exploits. The problem is that honeypots accept and respond also to spoofed packets. The ports open by default are the reason why honeypots reflect more traffic than common hosts in the network. Next, tarpits like LaBrea include additional potentially hazardous ability. They establish a TCP connection and keep it open for as long as possible without sending much data. This ability is supposed to deplete the resources of an attacker. However, in case of reflected attack the tarpit is actually depleting the resources of the victim.

The risk of having all ports opened is multiplied by the number of emulated hosts. For example, honeyd can emulate up to 65,536 addresses. As for our own honeypots, we use honeyd emulating slightly more than 200 IP addresses. Even this number of emulated hosts would be enough for the attacker to execute DRDoS attack. The only limitation of the reflected traffic is bandwidth of a singe host running the honeyd.

The attacker does not need to know if the reflectors are common hosts or honeypots. It can be a coincidence to abuse honeypots as reflectors, although favorable for the attacker.

The easy abuse of honeypots can be turned into honeypot detection mechanism. Scanning for highly responsive network segments reveals good reflectors that are likely to be honeypots, especially when they reply with the SYN+ACK flags on many unusual ports. Suppressing this behavior corresponds with the strategy of making honeypots indistinguishable from common network hosts [2].

4. DETECTION AND MITIGATION OF THE ATTACKS

The DRDoS attack is based on IP spoofing and if we could detect spoofed IP packets, we would be able recognize an attack. Elimination of IP spoofing would make DRDoS attacks impossible and would enable defense mechanisms against many other kinds of DDoS attacks [5]. The BCP38 [3] deals with network ingress filtering that disables sending of forged traffic with a spoofed source IP address. Since the filtering is still not always put in place we have to rely on a research in source address validation.

Once we have detected an attack reflected of our network, we can mitigate the attack at least by dropping the connections from and to the victim. Next step should be sending a report of reflected traffic to the abuse contact of the victim with data pointing to the source of the spoofed traffic on uplink level ISP. This informs the victim that we act as a reflector and not the actual source of attack and gives enough information to trace the actual attacker.

It is worth noting that attackers rather succeed in saturation of the link or active nodes such as firewalls, load balancers etc., than overloading the end server. The port is irrelevant when it comes to link saturation, however the port 80 is more likely to be accepted by firewalls. This port is not the only option, well-known ports are most likely to be used.

5. COMMUNICATION AND DATA SHARING

Significant part of the mitigation of attacks is based on communication and sharing of data between organizations involved in a DDoS attack. As it turned out from recent attacks, researchers and security teams are focused mainly on detection of attacks and their processing in a local context. This approach is sufficient enough for attacks on small scale focused on one organization. However, attacks that go across several organizations, which could act as both victims and attackers, needs more than simple detection.

There is the best practice to use a list of official abuse emails and out-of-band contacts to eliminate the delay and a risk of losing contacts due to personal changes in organizations. Recent events in March showed lack of systematic communication between organizations which communicated mostly ad-hoc and based on good relations between the involved organizations. There were conference calls put in place and personal contacts were used.

Sharing of data is very closely related to communication. It helps tracing the source of attack and speeds up the analysis of attack. A shared database of detected anomalies and incidents could make the detection and mitigation of attacks faster and more accurate. Moreover every organization should have summarizing information about the status of own network, i. e. used bandwidth, count of open connections, etc. This could detect involvement in attack as reflector or botnet zombies. Every mitigated attack to the victim could lower the impact of attack, particularly if the bandwidth of the reflector is higher than victims'. The legislative adjusting the work and access to personal data and network records has to be taken into consideration, though.

There is also the need to usefully visualize the shared data gathered during an attack. Visualization is currently oriented simply on amount of traffic between nodes or subnets. It would be helpful to correlate the results of detection methods and visualize them on upper levels of network hierarchy. This could help to react faster to early warnings and changes in ongoing attack.

6. CONCLUSIONS

In this paper, we pointed out that there is a risk in using honeypots. However, we do not want to discourage readers to use them. We still see the benefit of honeypots being deployed in the network but we advice against them being as open as possible. Honeypots are still useful even for reflected traffic, because they point to malicious behavior, although in this particular case, they are reporting victim and not the attacker. We have shown that honeypots are capable of reporting false positives, although they were believed to be free of false positives.

We have supported our conclusions by the observation and analysis of real large-scale DRDoS attacks. Honeypot settings and vulnerabilities were presented on an example of widely-known low-interaction honeypots participating in the attack. We also discussed the problems related to incident handling and communication during the attack. Not only false positive detection, but overall information sharing needs to be revised to replace observed ad-hoc solutions.

Finally, we presented lessons learned in the area of both honeypots and attack handling, including prevention of honeypot abuse and proper handling of security incidents. We believe there is still room for improvement in communication and data sharing associated with mitigation of attacks.

7. REFERENCES

[1] P. Bašta. DDoS - lessons learned - technical aspects. `http://www.afcea.cz/img/clanky_next/ITTE/Basta_DDOS.pdf`, 2013.

[2] European Network and Information Security Agency (ENISA). Proactive Detection of Security Incidents II - Honeypots. `http://www.enisa.europa.eu/activities/cert/support/proactive-detection/proactive-detection-of-security-incidents-II-honeypots`, 2012.

[3] P. Ferguson and D. Senie. Network Ingress Filtering: Defeating Denial of Service Attacks which employ IP Source Address Spoofing. RFC 2827 (Best Current Practice), May 2000. Updated by RFC 3704.

[4] T. Liston. Welcome to My Tarpit: The Tactical and Strategic Use of LaBrea, 2001.

[5] J. Mirkovic and P. Reiher. A taxonomy of DDoS attack and DDoS defense mechanisms. *SIGCOMM Comput. Commun. Rev.*, 34(2):39–53, Apr. 2004.

[6] V. Paxson. An analysis of using reflectors for distributed denial-of-service attacks. *SIGCOMM Comput. Commun. Rev.*, 31(3):38–47, July 2001.

[7] N. Provos. A virtual honeypot framework. In *Proceedings of the 13th conference on USENIX Security Symposium - Volume 13*, SSYM'04, Berkeley, CA, USA, 2004. USENIX Association.

POSTER—TouchCtrl: Fine-grained Access Control for Collaborative Environments

Benjamin Güldenring
Freie Universität Berlin
Takustr. 9, 14195 Berlin, Germany
benjamin.gueldenring@fu-berlin.de

Volker Roth
Freie Universität Berlin
Takustr. 9, 14195 Berlin, Germany
volker.roth@fu-berlin.de

ABSTRACT

The design of modern desktop operating systems is based on the assumption that a single user controls input and output devices at a time. This is also the case for access control, where applications inherit the privileges from the user that started them. This is not sufficient for multi-user collaboration on Single Display Groupware (SDG) or tabletop systems. For these we suggest a more fine-grained access control method based on the user that is interacting with an application. In our ongoing work of building a multiuser multitouch system we developed a technique we call *event backtracking* that exploits the asynchronous behavior of modern desktop applications on the Mac OS X platform. Event backtracking follows the execution of a program and tags threads with user IDs taken from the input events of users. This information is subsequently used to dynamically restrict applications' access rights. Our implementation works within applications as well as across application borders, transparent to the applications themselves.

Categories and Subject Descriptors

D.4.6 [**Operating Systems**]: Security and Protection—*Access controls*; H.5.2 [**Information Interfaces and Presentation**]: User Interfaces—*Input devices and strategies*

Keywords

Single Display Groupware; Multi-Touch.

1. INTRODUCTION

Collaborative environments like Single Display Groupware (SDG) or tabletop systems raise various different security questions. These differ from previously studied problems since users share the output device and in the latter case even the input device. For example, consider the setting shown in figure 1: John (on the right) was working with his application and is currently distracted. In the meantime

CCS'13, November 4–8, 2013, Berlin, Germany.
ACM 978-1-4503-2477-9/13/11.
http://dx.doi.org/10.1145/2508859.2512524 .

Figure 1: Bob is interacting with John's application while John is distracted.

Bob (on the left) is interacting with John's application and e.g. stealing confidential data.

Techniques like e.g. the IR-Ring [7] , ID-Wristbands [5] or Fiberio [2] so far allow a system to distinguish between the input events of different users. However, access control is often still realized on a per-application basis, i.e. applications decide themselves if specific actions are allowed for a user or not - if any sort of access control is implemented at all. While the operating system itself is enforcing access control on some level, desktop applications run under a fixed user account. This effectively gives every user the same access rights as the one under whose account an application was started.

In this work, we suggest a more fine-grained access control for this kind of situation. Fine-grained in the sense that the execution of security relevant actions on the syscall level (e.g. a file access attempt) is blocked or allowed depending on the user input event that lead to this action. To achieve this we propose a technique we call *event backtracking* that is based on the simple idea of causality, i.e. every security relevant action can be traced back to one single responsible user input event.

As an introductory example consider the case of the UNIX `rm` program. Assume the user John executes the command `rm /etc/passwd`. The newly started process executing this command is assigned the user ID of John and automatically inherits his access rights. When the process attempts to access the file `/etc/passwd`, the system checks wether John has sufficient access rights to it and either allows or denies access.

But we can interpret this differently: the operating system traces back a security relevant event (access to the file `/etc/passwd`) to an event caused by a user (John started the process). When we further assume that John used some input device to indicate he wants to execute `rm /etc/passwd`, this closes the missing gap and traces the security decision back to a mandatory last input event prior execution (e.g. hitting the return key). *Event backtracking* generalizes this idea to a multithreaded program where multiple users interact simultaneously. It does not need the application to be aware of it or enforce control by itself. Just like common systems, access control is implemented at the syscall level rather than the application level.

In summary, our contributions in this work are: we propose fine-grained access control for collaborative environments and present a technique called event backtracking to achieve fine grained access control by exploiting the asynchronous behavior of Mac OS X applications.

2. THREAT MODEL

We do not consider malicious applications. Instead we assume applications to be benign but not necessarily trusted. Users are however assumed to be mutually untrusted and potentially malicious. We believe this simplification reflects reality because we expect multi-user collaboration systems to be restrictive in nature. This means though users may interact with already installed applications they may not install new software themselves. Since application usage is naturally shared between users this would allow an malicious user to trick others into using a prepared software which may e.g. compromise the confidentiality of private data.

We further concentrate only on controlling access on a syscall level. This includes access to the file system or the network. In the Network we allow a differentiation between destination hosts to whom a connection attempt is made. For example, Alice may be allowed to access the local network, Bob is only allowed to connect to specific servers or servers outside the intranet. We do not cover attacks that do not involve syscalls, e.g. local in-memory changes in a calendar application (when not yet stored to disk) or the disclosure of information residing in the cache of a web browser.

3. TECHNICAL BACKGROUND

Before we discuss how we realized event backtracking we discuss the concurrency concepts Mac OS X applications that we make use of in the next sections. The information in this section recapitulates the relevant parts of Apple's developer documentation [3] and the source code to the CF-Lite framework [4]. Apple's developer documentation encourages developers to move away from using threads directly, but to use one of the asynchronous alternatives [3] whose most important techniques we discuss briefly in the following.

Within an application input events emit from so called *input sources*, e.g. a mouse or a keyboard. Each input source is managed by a `NSRunLoop` object. Each `NSRunLoop` object is bound by a one to one relationship to a `NSThread` object which encapsulates an underlying pthread (respectively bsd-thread). In this way any input source is directly related to exactly one thread. Mouse and keyboard events for example are processed on the main thread. When receiving a new event, the `NSRunLoop` object enqueues it in a list of remaining events. Subsequently they are fetched and processed once at a time. Other programming constructs such as the `NSObject` method

```
performSelector: onThread: withObject:
                waitUntilDone:
```

are also implemented using run loops. In this particular case an event is appended to the pending events list of the run loop of the corresponding thread.

More prominent than run loop sources are so called *operation queues* for Objective-C applications and *grand central dispatch (GCD)* [1] as part of the C runtime. GCD further contains *dispatch queues* and enables the usage of so called *blocks*. Blocks are syntactically defined portions of C-code to get executed asynchronously on dispatch queues. Operation queues work in a similar fashion.

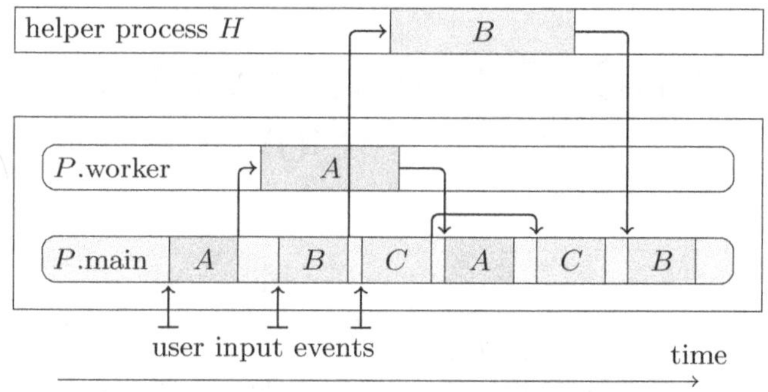

Figure 2: Event backtracking example for process P and helper process H. The tasks A, B and C each originate from distinct input events.

4. EVENT BACKTRACKING

In the following we assume that input events are always tagged with a unique user ID. This can be achieved with e.g. one of the systems in [2, 5, 7]. The techniques described in the previous section all share the property that they attempt to encapsulate work in tasks in a manner that allows them to be executed asynchronously. Event backtracking makes use of this encapsulation in that it assigns user IDs to these tasks.

When a task is created it is assigned a user ID. The user ID is taken either from the input event or from the task that is currently processed. When neither an input event nor a task is processed then the new task is assigned no user ID.

Figure 2 shows an example for a process P and a helper process H for three input events resulting in the tasks A, B and C. The process P contains one main thread P.main that receives input events and a worker thread P.worker for background tasks. The helper process H consists of one single thread. As soon as a thread starts processing one of the tasks it is assigned the user ID (indicated by color and label) of the task.

Access control is enforced on the system call level. When an application invokes a syscall, access is allowed or denied based on the user ID of the task currently processed. There are however access attempts for tasks carrying no user ID. These are for example access attempts to load certain files of

[1] also known as libdispatch for FreeBSD

Object	High level hook, selectors and methods	comment / purpose
NSApplication	nextEventMatchingMask:untilDate:inMode:dequeue	tracking start
NSOperation	init, start	tracking
CFRunLoop	CFRunLoopCreate, -SourceSignal, -AddSource,	tracking
CFMessagePort	CFMessagePortCreateRunLoopSource, -SendRequest	tracking, IPC tracking

Library	Low level hook, functions	comment / purpose
libdispatch	dispatch_sync_f, dispatch_async_f	tracking
libSystem	bsdthread_create	tracking
syscall	mach_msg	IPC tracking
syscall	open, connect	access control

Figure 3: The object method and function hooks required for event backtracking.

system frameworks (e.g. due to dynamic linking) or configuration files. For these cases every application is assigned a specific user ID when started. This ID is subsequently used to test in a whitelist of allowed files for the application.

5. PROTOTYPE IMPLEMENTATION

We did not have access to the source code of the relevant portions of Mac OS X, namely the *Application Kit* and *Cocoa* frameworks. We instead applied the necessary adjustments by hooking object methods and function calls in these frameworks. We used the *Application Enhancer* framework [2] to hook object methods using the reflection features of the Objective-C programming language and C function calls by patching function pointers. Access control is implemented by a preconfigured fixed list of protected files and allowed user IDs. Our prototype implementation consists of 1132 lines of code and runs under Mac OS X 10.6.8.

The changes we made can be classified into high- and low level hooks. High level hooks already make use of explicitly specified semantics such as `NSRunLoop` (resp. the CoreFoundation implementation as `CFRunLoop`) or the `libdispatch` functions and are allowed to override low level hooks. Low level hooks assume similar semantics, i.e. that they communicate some task. The upper hooks in figure 3 describe the high and the rest the low level hooks we implemented. We classify four different kinds of hooks: *i) tracking start* for the generation of a new trace ID when new user events are processed, *ii) tracking* for the passing of trace ids within an application, *iii) IPC tracking* for the passing of trace ids across application borders and *iv) access control* to implement access control by blocking access to certain resources.

6. RELATED WORK

Access Control Gadgets (ACGs) [6] are operating system controlled UI elements embedded in Applications. User grant applications access rights to user owned resources by activating these elements. Our work instead binds access rights directly to input events rather than special UI elements. Quire [1] annotates inter process communication in Android smartphones with the full call chain when requests are passed through multiple applications. Applications and remote servers are then able to verify the originating application of a request. In our work applications do not decide about access control themselves nor need they be aware of the mechanism.

[2]Probably discontinued, the developer's web-site `http://www.unsanity.com` is not responding since July 2013.

7. DISCUSSION AND FUTURE WORK

Until now we have tested our current prototype using event backtracking for the Mac OS X applications iTunes, Safari and TextEdit. For iTunes and TextEdit we were able to control access to local files, whereas for Safari we are able to restrict network access to the local subnet for specific users. Access in Safari is only denied when there occurs an actual syscall. Since Safari caches web sites and caching can not be prevented entirely, this already shows one limitation of event backtracking: it can prevent data from being sent to the network, but it can not prevent cached and probably confidential data of getting exposed to users.

We are currently investigating other applications and their API use if they are suitable for event backtracking.

8. ACKNOWLEDGEMENTS

The authors are supported by an endowment of *Bundesdruckerei GmbH.*

9. REFERENCES

[1] M. Dietz, S. Shekhar, Y. Pisetsky, A. Shu, and D. S. Wallach. Quire: lightweight provenance for smart phone operating systems. In *Proc. USENIX*, pages 23–23. USENIX Association, 2011.

[2] C. Holz and P. Baudisch. Fiberio: A touchscreen that senses fingerprints. In *Proc. ACM UIST*. ACM, 2013.

[3] Apple Inc. Concurrency Programming Guide. Online at `http://developer.apple.com`, 2013.

[4] Apple Inc. Source Browser. Online at `http://opensource.apple.com/source/CF/CF-550.43/`, 2013.

[5] T. Meyer and D. Schmidt. Idwristbands: Ir-based user identification on multi-touch surfaces. In *Proc. ACM ITS*, pages 277–278. ACM, 2010.

[6] F. Roesner, T. Kohno, A. Moshchuk, B. Parno, H. J. Wang, and C. Cowan. User-driven access control: Rethinking permission granting in modern operating systems. In *Proc. IEEE Symposium on Security and Privacy*, pages 224–238, 2012.

[7] V. Roth, P. Schmidt, and B. Güldenring. The ir ring: authenticating users' touches on a multi-touch display. In *Proc. ACM UIST*, pages 259–262, 2010.

POSTER—CRYPTSERVER: Strong Data Protection in Commodity LAMP Servers

Zhaofeng Chen*
Institute of Computer Science and Technology
Peking University
chenzhaofeng@pku.edu.cn

Xinshu Dong, Prateek Saxena, Zhenkai Liang
Department of Computer Science
National University of Singapore
{xdong,prateeks,liangzk}@comp.nus.edu.sg

ABSTRACT

Modern web applications store sensitive data on their servers. Such data is prone to theft resulting from exploits against vulnerabilities in the server software stacks. In this work, we propose a new architecture for web servers, called CRYPTSERVER, in which we pre-determine and fix a small amount of application code that can compute over sensitive data. By encrypting sensitive data before making it available to the rest of untrusted application code, CRYPTSERVER provides strong defense against all malicious code that an attacker may run in the server software stack. As a step towards making this approach practical, we develop an assistance tool to identify the portion of server-side logic that requires computation over sensitive data. Our preliminary results show that the size of such logic is small in six popular web applications we study. To the extent of our evaluation, converting these applications to a CRYPTSERVER architecture requires modest developer effort.

Categories and Subject Descriptors

D.4.6 [**Operating Systems**]: Security and Protection

Keywords

Web security, server security, data protection

1. INTRODUCTION

Web servers are prone to a large variety of attacks at the application layer — SQL injection, server misconfiguration, data-to-code attacks, OS command injection, and so on [11]. These attacks can be used to exfiltrate financially sensitive or user's private data. A recent study shows that 54% of data breaches involved compromised servers [10].

Several research works have started investigating mechanisms to protect sensitive data on web servers, such as applying encryption scheme to databases [3,6] or by partitioning web application code into different trust levels [4,5]. However, these techniques do not protect the sensitive data comprehensively throughout its processing lifetime in the web application code, and trust a large TCB.

Our Solution. In this work, we fortify web servers with a new second line of defense to secure sensitive data on commodity cloud-hosted LAMP servers. Conceptually, our solution protects sensitive data by encrypting the sensitive data and splitting the PHP engine logic into two strands of computation logic: sensitive and non-sensitive. Only certain trusted functions that compute on sensitive data in the PHP engine are executed in the sensitive strand. We call such functions *Pieces of Sensitive Logic (PSLs)*. We isloate the PSLs in an isolated exectuion enviroment (trusted VM) to provide rich computations on the encrypted data. All of the rest of web application logic only has access to sensitive data in encrypted form. With this new architecture, which we call CRYPTSERVER, we significantly reduce sensitive data's direct exposure to untrusted code on commodity cloud-hosted server stacks.

To migrate existing web applications to this new architecture, we take a two-phase approach to help the adoption: an *analysis phase* and an *instrumentation phase*. In the analysis phase, we automatically identify PSLs in the PHP application using an assistance tool we have built. When web developers run this tool with their application test harness, it tracks the flow of sensitive data, and automatically identifies functions that compute on the sensitive data.

Once all the PSLs for the application are identified, we manually instrument the original PHP application to invoke the corresponding PSL functionality running in an isolated environment (e.g. in a VM, a PAL [1], or a hypapp [9]). CRYPTSERVER enforces that all data input and output from PSLs are cryptographically sealed, i.e., protected with authenticated encryption. All data exchanged between the transformed PSLs and the non-PSLs is encrypted using authenticated encryption. Thus, the vulnerable web server, even if compromised, can only observe the encrypted flows of sensitive data.

Our main empirical finding is that PSL logic for the real-world applications we test is small. It consists of only 30K lines of C code of the PHP interpreter logic that runs in the trusted isolated environment. In contrast, previous works that partition servers, such as CLAMP [5] and SilverLine [7], have reported either much lareger TCB [5] or do not permit any computation on sensitive data [7]. Our evaluation

*Research done when visiting National University of Singapore

CCS'13, November 4–8, 2013, Berlin, Germany.
ACM 978-1-4503-2477-9/13/11.
http://dx.doi.org/10.1145/2508859.2512525.

reports that CryptServer is expressive enough to support real-world flows of sensitive data without directly leaking information about sensitive data through explicit channels. We also find that the developer effort to migrate existing applications to this new architecture is on the order of a few hours, with the help of our assistance tool.

In summary, to our knowledge, CryptServer is the first to propose an architecture that enables significant TCB reduction in web server stacks with authenticated encryption; our analysis tool and preliminary results verify its applicability to existing web applications. CryptServer complements server platforms with encrypted databases [6].

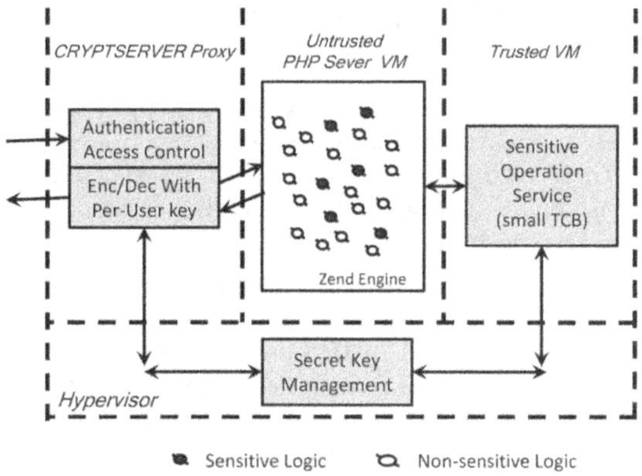

Figure 1: Architecture of CryptServer

2. CryptServer ARCHITECTURE

Figure 1 shows the CryptServer architecture. In our setting, the web server stack is built on top of a trusted hypervisor. The entire web server stack in the server VM is not trusted and is assumed to be vulnerable.

CryptServer **Proxy.** Our target is to secure both the confidentiality and integrity of sensitive data with authenticated encryption. In our approach, a lightweight CryptServer Proxy is introduced to encrypt sensitive data based on developer annotations before the data flows into the PHP application server VM. Similar to CLAMP [5], we have an HTTPS front end that authenticates the users, and performs key management and access control. On receiving each request from the client, the proxy authenticates the user and invokes the underlying hypercalls to encrypt sensitive data in annotated HTTP request fields with the per-user secret key accordingly. Then the encrypted data is delivered to the untrusted server VM. An alternative approach is that the client (e.g. user browser) helps encrypt the sensitive data instead of the proxy.

Untrusted PHP Server VM. When the encrypted sensitive data flows into the vulnerable server, the pre-compiled PHP opcodes (see details in Section 3) start execution in the PHP engine. Only parts of the opcode functions handle the sensitive data. We treat a function as PSL if and only if it receives sensitive data as arguments, and returns a value. To enable PSLs to operate on the encrypted sensitive data, we manually instrument the PSLs to make remote call to a trusted VM for computation on encrypted data.

Trusted VM. We isolate PSLs into a separate trusted VM (DOM0 in Xen Hypervisor [2]) that provides a Sensitive Operation Service (SOS) component to facilitate access to the sensitive data. When a sensitive operation is requested from the PHP server VM, the SOS first decrypts the sensitive data and checks the data integrity. If the check passes, the SOS component calls the requesting PSL to compute on the decrypted data. Finally, the SOS component encrypts the return value with authenticated encryption scheme and sends it back to the PHP server VM.

If all arguments in the request are encrypted, an attacker cannot tamper with them without failing the integrity check by the SOS component. However, there are cases where both sensitive (encrypted) and non-sensitive (unencrypted) data appear in the argument list. For example, PHP applications frequently search for special characters in user input strings. In this case, the input string is sensitive while the special character set is a constant and non-sensitive variable. An attacker can manipulate the constant argument value to obtain information on the sensitive data. We prevent such information leakage channels by applying the analysis as we detail in Section 3 to identify constant values that flow into function arguments, and encrypt them to prevent tampering from malicious code.

Summary. In the CryptServer architecture, any sensitive data flowing into the vulnerable server is encrypted. For ease of implementation, we are currently not encrypting boolean return values. This could leak certain control flow information to attackers. However, by design, PSLs do not allow attackers to control the argument values, as they take encrypted sensitive values and pre-encrypted constant and static variables as arguments. This achieves reduced indistinguishability [8]. In addition, as we show in Section 4, the pre-encrypted values allow little information leakage to attackers, as their numbers are very small for each web application we study. Although our solution tightly limits explicit information leakage, side channels are still possible, such as timing, length, and power monitoring attacks, etc. Our current solution does not address these issues.

3. ANALYSIS ENGINE

To aid developers to migrate their existing web applications to the CryptServer architecture, we build a dynamical analysis engine to automatically identify PSLs in the PHP engine. It takes developer annotations of sensitive data and a test harness of the web application as input. It then performs dynamic taint analysis to identify the operations that require access to the plaintext of the sensitive data, and finally marks them as PSLs as output. Note that not all operations that process sensitive data require decryption of the data. For example, the ASSIGN operation copies the encrypted data, but it does not require access to the plaintext of the data. Thus this kind of operation is not marked as PSL.

Before execution, PHP code is pre-compiled into PHP opcodes. Each opcode corresponds to a set of handling functions the PHP engine. Variables in PHP scripts are compiled into an internal presentation (the zval structure). Besides, all the constant and static variables mentioned in Section 2 can be automatically identified at the compilation time as zvals. Presently, we identify PSLs at the granularity of the PHP opcode level. Our analysis engine intercepts all operations on data in zvals and converts them into a standard "source->dest" propagation formula. It dynamically tracks

Application	#Pages w/ PSLs	#PSLs vs. Total #OPs	#Constant/Static PSL Arguments vs. Total #PSL Arguments	#Uniq PSLs vs. #Uniq Total OPs	Names of Sensitive Fields
phpBB3	16	342/131808 (0.26%)	20/635 (3.15%)	41/234 (17.52%)	subject, message, keywords
OpenEMR	6	46/59474 (0.08%)	3/86 (3.49%)	17/137 (12.41%)	reason, form_ss, form_body, note, issues
AjaxRPG	1	28/2044 (1.37%)	2/61 (3.28%)	9/86 (10.47%)	inputText
Roundcubemail	13	72/68541 (0.11%)	0/161 (0.00%)	30/237 (12.66%)	_subject, _message
Wordpress	15	111/440504 (0.03%)	1/209 (0.48%)	38/236 (16.10%)	post_title, content
HotCRP	8	97/76980 (0.13%)	4/131 (3.05%)	13/153 (8.50%)	paperSummary, commentsToAuthor, commentsToPC

Table 1: Percentage of PSLs in PHP applications

the data flow of sensitive data and marks operations in this flow that requires arguments' plaintext information. Finally the analysis engine outputs all marked operations as PSLs.

We implement this engine as a PHP extension in 9K lines of C code. All these identified PSLs are inspected manually and instrumented to request operations provided by the SOS.

4. EVALUATION

To evaluate the applicability, adoption effort, and TCB reduction of our solution, we apply our solution to 6 open-source PHP applications. Our preliminary results demonstrate that our proposed solution applies to these popular applications with moderate adoption cost. The experiments also show that the reduction in TCB that has access to sensitive data is also significant.

For each application, we manually annotate sensitive fields, shown in the last column in Table 1. For analysis we fill in these fields in the web pages, and submit the sensitive data to the server. For each web application we study, it takes one author about 3 hours to understand the functionality of the application, and further annotate the sensitive field. In real-world deployment, this identification effort can be reduced with developer assistance.

Column 2 in Table 1 shows the number of pages containing PSLs in each application. The PSLs mainly consist of computation opcodes (e.g. arithmetic operation opcode) and PHP functions (e.g. operations for string, array and regular expression). We calculate the number of opcodes executed during the execution, compared with number of identified PSLs. As shown in Column 3 of Table 1, the number of executed PSLs is much smaller than total executed opcodes, especially for large PHP applications (less than 1%). This indicates that the CryptServer is applicable to existing PHP applications. After eliminating the duplicate operations, the number of unique PSLs (Column 5) accounts for a very small portion (less than 18%). In fact, the PSLs code isolated in the SOS is small, with 30K lines of PHP interpreter logic for corresponding PHP applications.

For instrumentation, we identify the unique opcodes from dynamic runs with the test harness, which need to be tunneled back to the trusted SOS VM. Given the identified unique opcodes for PSLs, it takes less than 5 minutes to instrument each of them to request the corresponding operation from the SOS. In addition, once an opcode, for example ZEND_CONCAT, is instrumented in one application, it can be directly applied to all other applications. In all, our manually instrumented work only requires one-time effort for developers to migrate the existing application to CryptServer.

5. ACKNOWLEDGMENTS

This research is partially supported by research grant R-252-000-495-133 from Ministry of Education (MOE), Singapore. Any opinions, findings, and conclusions or recommendations expressed in this paper are those of the authors and do not necessarily reflect the views of MOE, Singapore.

6. REFERENCES

[1] Portableapps.com launcher. `http://portableapps.com/apps/development/portableapps.com_launcher`.

[2] Paul Barham, Boris Dragovic, Keir Fraser, Steven Hand, Tim Harris, Alex Ho, Rolf Neugebauer, Ian Pratt, and Andrew Warfield. Xen and the art of virtualization. In *Proceedings of the 9th ACM Symposium on Operating Systems Principles*, SOSP '03, 2003.

[3] Adrienne Porter Felt, Matthew Finifter, Joel Weinberger, and David Wagner. Diesel: applying privilege separation to database access. In *Proceedings of the 6th ACM Symposium on Information, Computer and Communications Security*, ASIACCS '11, 2011.

[4] Taesoo Kim and Nickolai Zeldovich. Making linux protection mechanisms egalitarian with userfs. In *Proceedings of the 19th USENIX Security Symposium*, 2010.

[5] Bryan Parno, Jonathan M. McCune, Dan Wendlandt, David G. Andersen, and Adrian Perrig. Clamp: Practical prevention of large-scale data leaks. In *Proceedings of the 2009 IEEE Symposium on Security and Privacy*, 2009.

[6] Raluca Ada Popa, Catherine M. S. Redfield, Nickolai Zeldovich, and Hari Balakrishnan. Cryptdb: Protecting confidentiality with encrypted query processing. In *Proceedings of the 23rd ACM Symposium on Operating Systems Principles*, SOSP '11, 2011.

[7] Krishna P. N. Puttaswamy, Christopher Kruegel, and Ben Y. Zhao. Silverline: toward data confidentiality in storage-intensive cloud applications. In *Proceedings of the 2nd ACM Symposium on Cloud Computing*, SOCC '11, 2011.

[8] Shruti Tople, Shweta Shinde, Prateek Saxena, and Zhaofeng Chen. Autocrypt: Enabling homomorphic server computation to protect sensitive web content. In *Proceedings of the 20th ACM Conference on Computer and Communications Security*, CCS '13, 2013.

[9] Amit Vasudevan, Sagar Chaki, Limin Jia, Jonathan M. McCune, James Newsome, and Anupam Datta. Design, implementation and verification of an extensible and modular hypervisor framework. In *Proceedings of the 2013 IEEE Symposium on Security and Privacy*, 2013.

[10] Verizon. 2013 data breach investigation report. `http://www.verizonenterprise.com/DBIR/2013/`.

[11] Wei Xu, Sandeep Bhatkar, and R. Sekar. Taint-enhanced policy enforcement: a practical approach to defeat a wide range of attacks. In *Proceedings of the 15th USENIX Security Symposium*, 2006.

POSTER: Identity-Based Steganography and Its Applications to Censorship Resistance

Tim Ruffing
Saarland University
Saarbrücken, Germany
tim.ruffing@stud.uni-saarland.de

Jonas Schneider
Saarland University
Saarbrücken, Germany
s9joscne@stud.uni-saarland.de

Aniket Kate
MMCI, Saarland University
Saarbrücken, Germany
aniket@mmci.uni-saarland.de

ABSTRACT

The use of public-key steganography has been proposed for several censorship-resistance systems. However, distribution of the employed public keys presents an availability, scalability, and security challenge in many of these. To mitigate this problem, we introduce the notion of identity-based steganography. In particular, we define identity-based steganographic tagging (IBST), which allows a sender to produce a steganographic tag for a recipient's identity such that the tag can only be recognized by the intended recipient using her (identity-based) private key. We instantiate our definition by an efficient IBST scheme, provably secure under the bilinear decisional Diffie-Hellman assumption.

We find IBST to be particularly useful when the censors are able to impede distribution of cryptographic keys or break forward security by compromising system agents. As two representative applications of IBST to censorship resistance systems, we first present an efficient and dynamic solution for the key distribution problem in Collage [1] and second, we demonstrate that IBST can improve the scalability of Message in a Bottle [2].

Categories and Subject Descriptors

C.2.0 [**Computer-communication networks**]: General—*security and protection (e.g., firewalls)*; K.5.2 [**Legal Aspects of Computing**]: Governmental Issues—*censorship*; E.3 [**Data**]: Data Encryption—*public key cryptosystems*

Keywords

steganography; identity-based cryptography; censorship resistance; key distribution; Collage; Message in a Bottle

1. INTRODUCTION

Censorship-resistance systems [1, 2, 3] typically employ steganography to establish their covert channels. For both symmetric-key and public-key steganography, the distribution of a steganographic key (stego-key) constitutes an important bootstrapping problem in these systems: A simple attack for the censor is to block the key distribution. The problem is further aggravated for systems aiming for forward security, which is typically achieved by frequently changing to new keys and deleting old keys.

Several censorship-resistance systems follow an optimistic paradigm [1, 2, 3, 4]: The censored user publishes a request (secured using public-key steganography) in the hope that a party outside the censored area detects this request and acts upon it. Among these systems are Message in a Bottle (MIAB) [2] and Collage [1]. They respectively allow users to post steganographic messages on blogs and websites with user-generated content such that the intended recipients can fetch them from there. However, obtaining the public keys of the recipients is often difficult for the censored user.

In an identity-based encryption (IBE) scheme [5], messages are encrypted for an identity of an intended recipient, e.g., her email or IP address. The recipient can decrypt a ciphertext using a private key associated to her identity, which she has to obtain from a trusted entity, a private key generator (PKG), holding a master key. IBE mitigates the key distribution problem with public-key cryptography as only a single master public key associated with the master private key needs to be distributed to the users, instead of one public key for every expected recipient.

Contribution.

In this work, we observe that the efficient key distribution of IBE is particularly useful for censorship-resistance systems, when private keys have to be distributed only outside the censored area. Therefore, we combine steganography and IBE to introduce the concept of *identity-based steganography*. Using identity-based steganography in censorship-resistance systems, essentially no key distribution in the censored area is required, with the exception of a single master public key which can be bundled with the software. In general, identity-based steganography is helpful whenever a censor is able to block mass key distribution and whenever a client publishes steganographic messages optimistically, i.e., hoping that someone outside the censored area will react to them.

In particular, we define the notion of identity-based steganographic tagging (IBST). It allows a sender A, given only a single master public key, and the identity of a recipient B to produce a steganographic tag that only B can recognize. Without possession of the corresponding private key the tag is indistinguishable from a random bitstring. Moreover, tagging is capable of exchanging a shared secret between the sender A and the recipient B.

CCS'13, November 4–8, 2013, Berlin, Germany.
ACM 978-1-4503-2477-9/13/11.
http://dx.doi.org/10.1145/2508859.2512526.

Building upon the IBE scheme by Boneh and Franklin [5], we instantiate our definition with a concrete construction.

We show the utility of IBST by achieving more flexibility and scalability in the censorship-resistance systems Collage [1] and Message in a Bottle [2], without hindering the bootstrapping process or introducing significant overhead.

2. IDENTITY-BASED STEGO-TAGGING

In this section, we extend public-key steganographic tagging (e.g., [3]) to the identity-based setting. Given a public key of a recipient, a steganographic tagging scheme produces *tags* that look like random covertexts to anyone who is not in possession of the corresponding private key.

Definition.

An identity-based steganographic tagging scheme (IBST) provides a setup algorithm $\mathsf{Setup}(1^\lambda)$, where λ is the security parameter. It outputs a master public key mpk and a master private key msk. The algorithm $\mathsf{Tag}(mpk, id)$ produces a tag τ for the recipient with identity id. Additionally, IBST provides a key encapsulation mechanism, i.e., a secret s to be shared with this recipient is output. $\mathsf{Detect}(sk_{id}, \tau)$ recognizes a tag and extracts the corresponding shared secret s, where $sk_{id} \leftarrow \mathsf{PrivateKey}(msk, id)$. A random message (a *covertext*) should be recognized as tag only with negligible probability. We denote this property by *rareness*.

The security notion of IBST, formally defined in [6], captures basically two essential security properties: First, tags cannot be distinguished from random covertexts without possession of the private key. In other words, they are not detectable for the censor. Second, no adversary can associate shared secrets with the corresponding tags. This ensures the confidentiality of the exchanged secret. Our definition allows an adversary to query private keys, adaptively and for arbitrary identities (except for the challenge identity), similarly to the IND-ID-CPA game for identity-based encryption.

Construction sketch.

We instantiate our definition with a construction based on the BasicIdent IBE scheme as defined by Boneh and Franklin [5]. Since the tag contains a random group element on an elliptic curve, it is crucial to encode this element such that its representation is indistinguishable from a bitstring drawn uniformly at random. This is achieved using the methods introduced by Kaliski [7] and, e.g., used in Telex [3].

Due to space constraints, we refer the reader to [6] for details and a security proof of our construction. The pseudorandomness of tags is reduced to the bilinear decisional Diffie-Hellman problem [5] in the random oracle model.

A common concern with identity-based primitives is that the PKG introduces a key escrow problem and, if it becomes unavailable for some reason, a single point of failure. However, there are solutions readily available to distribute PKG over several entities [8] for the employed Boneh-Franklin IBE setup, which can mitigate both problems.

3. APPLICATIONS

Our IBST construction is useful for covert communication in any scenario where a recipient identity is known to the sender. It becomes particularly useful in scenarios where one public (or symmetric) stego-key cannot be used for all recipients for security reasons and the recipients' public keys cannot easily be communicated to the sender. Thus, IBST can be applied in many censorship-resistance and covert-communication systems [1, 2, 3, 4]. In this section, we discuss its utility to two representative censorship-resistance systems: Collage [1] and Message in a Bottle [2].

Collage.

Collage [1] is a covert messaging system. If offers communication through postings on websites that allow user-generated content (e.g., photo hosting websites, online forums and wikis). Collage assumes that the sender and the recipient share a database of *tasks*, which helps the sender and the recipient to agree on a *rendezvous point*, i.e., a location where a stegotext is stored. An example of a sender task is to embed a message steganographically into an image, and upload the image on Flickr under the keyword "flower". The corresponding recipient task is downloading images with this keyword and trying to detect hidden messages in each of them.

In Collage, identity-based steganography can be used if a client inside the censored area would like to initialize a connection to a recipient outside this area, say a web proxy. The censored client selects a random task from its database and uses this task also as an identity string for IBST; e.g., in a scenario where the task refers to website Flickr and keyword flower, the client would not only use the task to determine the rendezvous point (Flickr) but also employ $\{\texttt{flickr}, \texttt{flower}\}$ as the identity string for the tagging algorithm. As the tag is pseudorandom, it can be steganographically embedded into an image. The recipient proxy will monitor Flickr for a few keywords assigned to it, and try to detect tags using the private keys associated with the keywords. A message from the sender can be added by encrypting it with symmetric stego-system; the symmetric key is extracted from the tag.

The most important advantage of using identity-based steganography in Collage is that the task database can be made dynamic without sacrificing efficiency or trading off security properties. The list of most popular tags on Flickr (proposed in [1]) could be a task database shared between the sender and the recipient without direct communication. An example of a sender task that is even more dynamic (and thus harder to block) involves searching the web for a forum running a particular, popular piece of software (e.g. UBB.threads or phpBB). After creating a user account on this website, the sender uploads a stego-image as the account's avatar image. The receiver would download lists of "Newest Members" (or similar) on those forums and try to detect hidden messages in the avatar images. The lack of communication that comes with such dynamic task databases, however, introduces a key distribution problem. It can be solved efficiently by using identity-based steganography because only the master public key has to be conveyed to the senders.

Since the number of identities is not fixed a priori in identity-based steganography, the IBST-based Collage solution scales well with an increasing number of proxies and tasks. Moreover, as the proxy knows only the private keys for the keywords it is responsible for, the impact of a compromise of one proxy is limited by design. We stress that distribution of the private keys is not a problem because both the proxies and the PKG are placed outside the censored area.

Message in a Bottle.

The idea of Message in a Bottle (MIAB) [2] is similar to Collage: Clients publish stego-messages (e.g. encoded in the EXIF metadata of image files) in the hope that a party outside the censored area will decrypt and react to them. However, as opposed to Collage, MIAB does not require any agreement on rendezvous points: The rendezvous points are predefined as all blogs in the world that support blog pings. Blog pings are small announcements that blogging software reports to centralized servers; they indicate that new a post has been added to the blog. This feature is implemented and enabled in most blogs. [2] The recipient of the message downloads a list of blogs with new posts from a blog ping server and searches the posts for stego-images.

Invernizzi, Kruegel, and Vigna [2] provide a prototype implementation and show that it is feasible to examine the metadata of the images in all new blog postings in the world (reported by blog pings) for steganographic content.

However, it is not clear whether this approach scales to a system that can be deployed in practice. First, a more sophisticated stego-system is necessary, because the censor could block meta-information in images without causing much collateral damage. Thus it seems to be unavoidable to encode the messages into the payload of the image (or in other forms of payload when the covertext is not an image). This makes detecting the hidden tag in the message computationally harder for the recipient. Second, downloading the whole image file requires much more bandwidth than necessary to fetch just the meta-information stored in the file at a position known a priori. Third, scalability can become a problem if the service provided by the recipient is more complex than forwarding the hidden message to Twitter.

It is a natural approach to this problem to create a network of volunteer proxies that provide computation power and bandwidth to the system. For example, a system like the Tor anonymity network with bridges could use MIAB to bootstrap a connection to the client and fetch websites for the client. In such a system, IBST could be deployed to distribute the trust among the volunteer proxies: The censored clients tag images using the domain name or the IP address of the blog on which they post as identity for the tagging algorithm. The PKG is the only entity that reacts upon blog pings. For each new blog ping on a website, say on `blog.example.com`, the PKG creates the corresponding private key $sk_{\texttt{blog.example.com}}$ and sends it to one volunteer proxy. This proxy is now responsible for downloading and detecting images from the newest posting on this blog. If a tagged image is found, the proxy can, depending on the protocol, open a connection to the censored client or retrieve information for the censored client, e.g., bootstrapping information for other censorship-resistance systems. As one proxy has access to only one (or a few) private keys and thus can only detect tags on a few blogs, trust is distributed among the proxies by design. Thus a compromise of a few proxies does not affect the security of the rest of system. We note that creating these many private keys is feasible for the PKG: This step involves two exponentiations and two evaluations of a hash function per private key.

Forward Security in Censorship-Resistance Systems.

It is a natural desire to ensure that the security of finished protocol sessions cannot be broken even if long-term secret keys are compromised. A protocol is *forward secure* if an attacker that manages to compromise a party is not able to obtain any session secret used in *finished* protocol sessions.

Consider again the example where a censored client wishes to establish a connection to an uncensored proxy (e.g., in Collage or MIAB), and assume we use IBST as described above. In identity-based encryption, forward security can be achieved by dividing time into intervals and concatenating the current interval to the identity string. The PKG hands out private keys (one for each rendezvous point) to the proxies for a time period t, shortly before t begins. Once t is over, every proxy securely erases the corresponding private keys such that an attacker compromising this proxy cannot obtain the private keys for past periods $t' < t$. Notice that our solution provides forward security without introducing any additional communication between client and proxy.

The efficiency gain in terms of communication for key distribution is considerable; e.g., for T forward security time intervals and p proxies, pT public keys have to be distributed with standard public-key steganography instead of only one master public key in our identity-based solution.

To achieve forward security, our method is in principle applicable to all censorship-resistance systems that use public-key steganography, e.g., Telex [3] and Cirripede [4].

4. FUTURE WORK

We are working towards implementing our IBST construction and would like to incorporate it in the systems described above. A possible promising application is a distribution mechanism for bridge addresses in the Tor network.

References

[1] S. Burnett, N. Feamster, and S. Vempala. "Chipping away at censorship firewalls with user-generated content." In: *19th USENIX Security Symposium.* 2010.

[2] L. Invernizzi, C. Kruegel, and G. Vigna. "Message in a bottle: sailing past censorship." In: 5th Workshop on Hot Topics in Privacy Enhancing Technologies (HotPETs). 2012. URL: `http://petsymposium.org/2012/papers/hotpets12-3-message.pdf`.

[3] E. Wustrow, S. Wolchok, I. Goldberg, and J. A. Halderman. "Telex: anticensorship in the network infrastructure." In: *20th USENIX Security Symposium.* 2011.

[4] A. Houmansadr, G. T. Nguyen, M. Caesar, and N. Borisov. "Cirripede: circumvention infrastructure using router redirection with plausible deniability." In: *18th ACM Symposium on Computer and Communications Security (CCS).* 2011.

[5] D. Boneh and M. Franklin. "Identity-based encryption from the Weil pairing." In: *SIAM Journal on Computing* 32.3 (2003).

[6] T. Ruffing, J. Schneider, and A. Kate. "Identity-based steganography and its applications to censorship resistance." In: 6th Workshop on Hot Topics in Privacy Enhancing Technologies (HotPETs). 2013. URL: `http://petsymposium.org/2013/papers/ruffing-censorship.pdf`.

[7] B. S. Kaliski Jr. "A pseudo-random bit generator based on elliptic logarithms." In: *Advances in Cryptology—CRYPTO.* 1986.

[8] A. Kate and I. Goldberg. "Distributed private-key generators for identity-based cryptography." In: *Security and Cryptography for Networks (SCN).* 2010.

POSTER – Sechduler: A Security-Aware Kernel Scheduler

Parisa Haghani
Electrical and Computer Engineering
University of Illinois at Urbana-Champaign
haghani1@illinois.edu

Saman Zonouz
Electrical and Computer Engineering
University of Miami
s.zonouz@miami.edu

ABSTRACT

Trustworthy operation of safety-critical infrastructures necessitates efficient solutions that satisfy both realtimeness and security requirements simultaneously. We present Sechduler, a formally verifiable security-aware operating system scheduler that dynamically makes sure that system computational resources are allocated to individual waiting tasks in an optimal order such that, if feasible, neither realtime nor security requirements of the system are violated. Additionally, if not both of the requirements can be satisfied simultaneously, Sechduler makes use of easy-to-define linear temporal logic-based policies as well as automatically generated Büchi automaton-based monitors, compiled as loadable kernel modules, to enforce which requirements should get the priority. Our experimental results show that Sechduler can adaptively enforce the system-wide logic-based temporal policies within the kernel and with minimal performance overhead of 3% on average to guarantee high level of combined security and realtimeness simultaneously.

Categories and Subject Descriptors: D.4.6 [Operating Systems]: Security and Protection

Keywords: Real-time security; formal temporal verification; intrusion detection and prevention; operating system security.

Sechduler

Maintenance of the safety-critical infrastructures, e.g., nuclear power plants and avionics systems, is extremely crucial because a failure to meet a single requirement may lead to a catastrophic consequence such as an explosion or an accident leading to loss of life. In particular, the realtime scheduling of tasks in those infrastructures such that individual timing requirements are met reliably is often a challenging endeavor. Furthermore, to guarantee core functionalities, those systems need to be secure and intrusion resilient as they operate in possibly adversarial environments. Currently many commercial and open-source security solutions are available that can monitor different security aspects of the systems. Clearly, the most comprehensive security level will be achieved by running a set of those security sensors in parallel; however, this would result in computationally intensive security analyses and hence overconsumption of the system's limited resources. Therefore, the system's core realtime functionality requirements could be violated as the system's critical tasks are deprived of the resources. This signifies the fact that to ensure timely accomplishment of the core system functionalities, the deployed security solutions need to be resource aware and satisfy the system-wide realtime requirements, i.e., *realtime security*. The same rationale justifies an urgent need for solutions to guarantee the *secure realtimeness* property provided by realtime solutions, e.g., realtime schedulers, that are aware of the system security requirements according to the high-level organizational objectives.

Previous efforts in designing realtime and security solutions have fallen short in several major aspects. There have been many theoretical as well as heuristic scheduling algorithms such as the Linux kernel 3.X Completely-Fair Scheduler [4], RTLinux [6] attempt to allocate the system CPU(s) to individual waiting tasks such that the likelihood of task starvations and deadline misses are minimized. Although the abovementioned solutions can be employed to ensure timely accomplishments of safety-critical and realtime applications, none of them take into account the existence possibility of malicious activities, e.g., an adversarial unfinished task waiting for execution. Security and privacy researchers have proposed numerous host-based intrusion prevention and detection solutions, e.g., Samhain [7], as well as forensics and root-cause analysis algorithms and tools, such as Backtracker [3], and FloGuard [8], in order to detect and terminate ongoing malicious misbehaviors with minimum amount of performance overhead on the target system. Even though the abovementioned security solutions attempt to minimize the overhead as a best effort to terminate attacks before it gets too late, e.g., confidential data is sent out to network, there is currently no generic and theoretically sound solution that considers the system's overall realtime requirements and guarantees timely reaction against the ongoing intrusions.

We present Sechduler, a formally verifiable security-aware operating system scheduler that guarantees simultaneous satisfaction of the system-wide realtimeness as well as security requirements. In particular, Sechduler accomplishes its objectives through three major steps. First, during a one-time offline phase, system security policies are defined that determine how the security vs. realtimeness tradeoffs should be resolved. These policies can be designed following whitelisting (deny by default), blacklisting (allow by default) or other more generalized paradigms. Second, during an online phase while the system is operating, Sechduler selects the appropriate subset of policies, given the current security state of the system, and generates the corresponding single logic-based conjunctive policy predicate. Sechduler then converts the policy to an extended finite state machine-based monitor automatically. Finally, Sechduler enhances the kernel scheduler with the generated monitor dynamically for runtime monitoring and verification of the system computational resource allocations. Consequently, Sechd-

CCS'13, November 4–8, 2013, Berlin, Germany.
ACM 978-1-4503-2477-9/13/11.
http://dx.doi.org/10.1145/2508859.2512527.

uler modifies the kernel's resource allocation schedule actively if it is about to violate any of the predefined system-wide security policies.

More specifically, Sechduler makes use of an easy to understand formal language, namely *three-valued linear temporal logic* that facilitates formulation of comprehensive temporal system-wide security policies for the system administrators. Needless to mention, the designed policies can be reused across systems (analogous to the SE-Linux access control policies). The employed three-value logic, i.e., *true:* policy-compliant, *false:* policy violation, and *inconclusive:* insufficient information, enables Sechduler to use the designed policies for accurate verification and reconfiguration of the kernel task scheduling dynamically based on the observed scheduling trace. , i.e., the past and current (to be) scheduled tasks. Sechduler considers the trace formally as a finite prefix of the (potentially) infinite task scheduling sequence in the future. For the kernel to understand and enforce the policies, Sechduler converts the logic-based policies automatically to an extended finite state machine, so-called Büchi automaton, working with the three-value logic. The Büchi automaton monitors the kernel scheduling trace and determines whether the policy is about to be violated. If so, the scheduler is reconfigured and the system CPU is allocated to the next non-policy-violating waiting task with an urgent need for execution. It is noteworthy that the automated conversion algorithm in Sechduler results in an automaton with provably minimum number of states ensuring that the performance overhead of the runtime monitoring and verification is minimized. Consequently, using a realtime and security-aware scheduling algorithm through continuous optimization for timely resource allocations and discrete logic-based monitoring for security verifications, Sechduler makes sure to provide both realtimeness and security guarantees simultaneously if feasible depending on the available time and resources.

In summary, the contributions of our work are as follows: 1) We propose an easy-to-understand logical formulation formalism to declare the system security requirements for different system security states; 2) We introduce a three-value logic-based automated algorithm to construct security formal monitors dynamically for runtime verification and temporal policy enforcement; 3) We propose a hybrid operating system task scheduling algorithm using continuous task ranking optimization and discrete logic-based formal verification techniques; and 4) We validate the Sechduler framework on a real-world host system through implementation and deployment of a working prototype of the proposed algorithms. It is also important to mention what Sechduler does not contribute to. In particular, Sechduler does not present a new intrusion detection sensor and automatic logic-based policy generation algorithm. Instead, Sechduler makes use of those solutions to provide the runtime verification capability to maintain the system security and realtime requirements and avoid potential violations of the previously defined temporal policies.

Sechduler Overview. Initially, the security administrators write system security temporal policies using the easy-to-understand formalism in Sechduler. This phase is very similar to writing access control policies for firewalls or host-based SE-Linux systems; however, in Sechduler, administrators concentrate on timing- and scheduling-related security concerns instead. Briefly, each policy determines the scheduling constraints that need to be held at a system security state by the operating system to guarantee that the system-wide security is maintained. Although, we assume that the policy writing is completed as a one-time manual effort, Sechduler could be extended and make use of the recent (semi-)automated policy writing algorithms and tools [5].

During the system's operational mode, we assume that appropriate host-based intrusion detection systems are deployed and are

Figure 1: The Büchi Automaton for the Predicate

$$\mathbf{G}\ ((\text{receive\_request} \wedge \neg\text{send\_response} \wedge \mathbf{F}\ \text{send\_response}) \rightarrow (\text{sensitive\_file\_access} \rightarrow (\neg\text{send\_response}\ \mathbf{U}\ (\text{security\_check} \wedge \neg\text{send\_response})))\ \mathbf{U}\ \text{send\_response})$$

Figure 3: A Sample Temporal Security Policy

monitoring important aspects of the target system, such as the filesystem integrity using, for instance, periodic hash function-based scans [7]. In case a malicious activity is identified, Sechduler receives the triggered intrusion detection system alerts that cooperatively report the system's current security state. Sechduler goes through its policy repository dynamically and selects the relevant (possibly empty) subset of policy rules that correspond to the system's current state. Sechduler then constructs a single system-wide temporal logic-based predicate using the collected policy rules, and converts the predicate into a Büchi automaton-based monitor automatically. The automaton is compiled as a loadable kernel module and inserted into the running operating system kernel. The modified kernel scheduler notices the inserted module, and from then on verifies its individual task scheduling decisions using the loaded monitor. Additionally, if needed, it enforces the policies by reconfiguring the system's resource allocations, i.e., scheduling decisions, adaptively.

Preliminary Results

We deployed Sechduler in a testbed environment and evaluated various aspects of its operation. Figure 1 shows the $B(\varphi)$ automaton in a *never claim* format in Promela [2].

As Sechduler verifies whether each scheduled tasks should be given CPU access, we collected statistics of the kernel-level scheduled tasks during a normal host computer usage session. Figure 2(b) shows the number of scheduled tasks for each second during the session. In particular, the session included a Web browser launch followed by an Office document editor application spawn. As demonstrated, the number of scheduled tasks can go up to $18K$ per second during an normal computer usage session. We measured the time requirements for the policy-to-automata conversion for the typical linear temporal logic-based system specification policies [1]. Figure 2(c) shows the results for individual temporal security policies. As shown in the figure, Sechduler completed the conversion for individual temporal requirements in approximately 0.58 seconds on average. This suggests that Sechduler can scale well for real-world settings where many requirements may be involved in the final logic-based predicate.

Case Study: Sensitive File Modification. We show how Sechduler protects a target host system once the system is hit by a sensitive file modification attack. Samhain was deployed as the attack consequence detection system. Specifically, we modified its configuration, i.e., `/etc/samhain/samhainrc`, to monitor the files and directories in which we are interested, and configured it to report events with at least `crit` severity level. Initially, we created its initial database, i.e., `/var/state/samhain/samhain_file`, using `samhain -t init`, and its database was updated, using `-t update`. During the operational mode of the system, Samhain was configured to check the marked sensitive files and directories

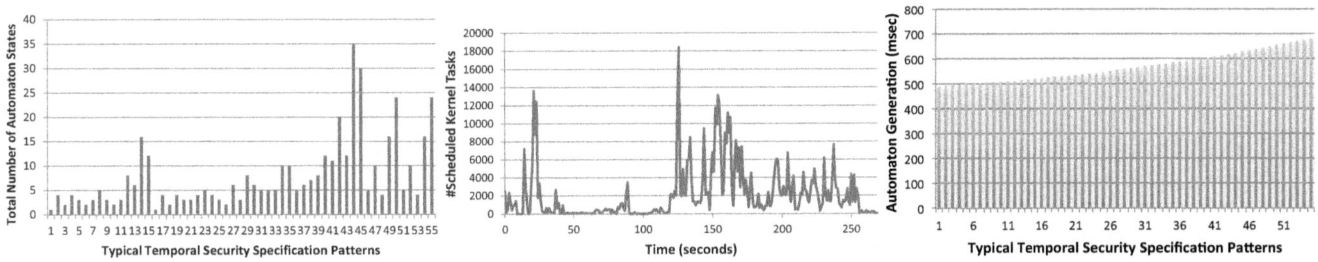

(a) Automata for Frequently Used Specifications (b) Kernel-level Scheduled Tasks Statistics (c) Automaton Generation Time Requirement

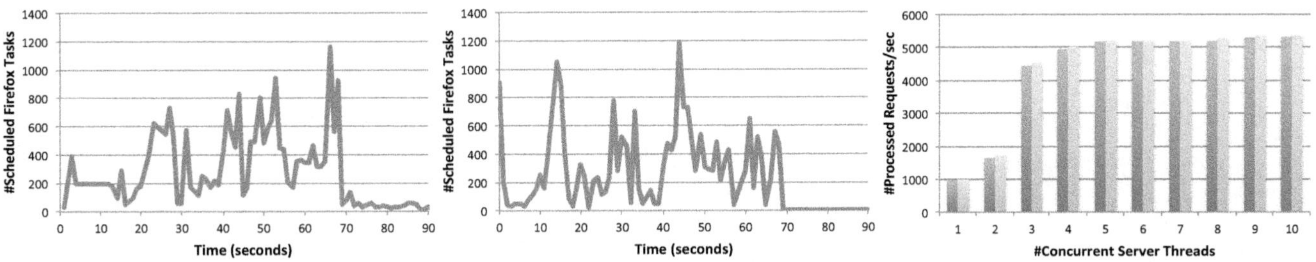

(d) Scheduling Statistics of the Trojan Firefox (e) Statistics on a Sechduler-Enabled Kernel (f) Overall Sechduler Performance Overhead

Figure 2: Sechduler Evaluation Results

against its database and fire an alert upon identifying a modification or access (depending on the policy defined in the configuration file).

To simulate an attack, we implemented a trojan Firefox that modified sensitive user files that had been marked to be monitored by Samhain. Figure 2(d) shows the malware's scheduling activity statistics within a non-Sechduler aware kernel. Consequently, Samhain fired the alert, and Sechduler performed three tasks. It 1) called the `setsec` system call and lowers the Firefox's security level variable within the kernel; 2) spawned a comprehensive ClamAV virus scan on the Firefox's executable; and 3) compiled the triggered alert's corresponding policy module and loaded it on the kernel dynamically.

Enforcing the loaded policy, Sechduler manipulated the task selection procedure within the kernel scheduler to ensure that (from its point of view) the potentially malicious Firefox process did not get CPU access and waited for the ClamAV's green light. However, in our experiments, ClamAV triggered an alert denoting that the executable contains malicious content. Consequently, the suspended Firefox process was terminated by Sechduler and its executable was removed. Figure 2(e) a different run of the trojan Firefox on a Sechduler-enabled Linux kernel. As shown on the graph, Sechduler denies its requests for execution since the 69-th seconds and finally terminates the process. We implemented the process termination as a single countermeasure action; however, more complicated actions can be defined by policies and implemented.

It is important that Sechduler performs the runtime system security verification efficiently such that the system's overall throughout is not affected significantly. We measured the Sechduler's overall performace overhead on our testbed system's overall throughput. In particular, we employed the `ab` Apache Webserver benchmarking toolset to measure the system throughout. To make the webpage processing more CPU-intensive, we designed a very simple HTML webpage. For our server system, we define the overall performance measure as the number of requests that can be processed per second. Figure 2(f) shows how the system's throughput is affected by the runtime verification of individual task scheduling decisions. We believe that the overall performance overhead of the Sechduler solution can be further reduced by optimizing our code. For instance, several data structures that are searched frequently, with $O(n)$ complexity, can be redesigned for logarithmic search, and overal system performance improvement.

Acknowledgments

The authors would like to thank the Office of Naval Research (Grant N000141210462) for their support.

1. REFERENCES

[1] DWYER, M. B., AVRUNIN, G. S., AND CORBETT, J. C. Patterns in property specifications for finite-state verification. In *Proceedings of the 21st international conference on Software engineering* (New York, NY, USA, 1999), ICSE '99, ACM, pp. 411–420.

[2] JIANG, K., AND JONSSON, B. Using spin to model check concurrent algorithms, using a translation from c to promela. In *Proc. 2nd Swedish Workshop on Multi-Core Computing* (2009), Department of Information Technology, Uppsala University, pp. 67–69.

[3] KING, S. T., AND CHEN, P. M. Backtracking intrusions. In *Proceedings of the Nineteenth ACM symposium on Operating systems principles* (2003), vol. 37, pp. 223–236.

[4] PABLA, C. S. Completely fair scheduler. *Linux J. 2009*, 184 (Aug. 2009).

[5] ROUTRAY, R., ZHANG, R., EYERS, D., WILLCOCKS, D., PIETZUCH, P., AND SARKAR, P. Policy generation framework for large-scale storage infrastructures. In *IEEE Symposium on Policies for Distributed Systems and Networks* (2010), pp. 65–72.

[6] SATO, H., AND YAKOH, T. A real-time communication mechanism for rtlinux. In *Annual Confjerence of the IEEE Industrial Electronics Society* (2000), vol. 4, pp. 2437 –2442 vol.4.

[7] WOTRING, B., POTTER, B., RANUM, M., AND WICHMANN, R. *Host Integrity Monitoring Using Osiris and Samhain*. Syngress Publishing, 2005.

[8] ZONOUZ, S. A., JOSHI, K. R., AND SANDERS, W. H. Floguard: cost-aware systemwide intrusion defense via online forensics and on-demand ids deployment. In *International conference on Computer safety, reliability, and security* (2011), pp. 338–354.

POSTER: Passwords on Flexible Display Devices

Sana Maqsood, Sonia Chiasson, Audrey Girouard
Carleton University, Ottawa, Canada
{sana.maqsood, audrey.girouard}@carleton.ca, chiasson@scs.carleton.ca

ABSTRACT

Flexible display devices allow users to interact with the device by deforming the surface of the display to trigger a command. When these devices become mainstream, for example as smart phones, e-readers, or tablets, they will require a means of authenticating legitimate users. In this poster, we present an authentication scheme for flexible display devices, its implementation on a flexible display prototype and an ongoing user study evaluating the usability and security of our system.

Categories and Subject Descriptors

H.5.2 [**Interfaces and Representation**]: User Interfaces—*Input devices and strategies*

Keywords

Usable Security, Flexible Displays, Authentication

1. INTRODUCTION

Flexible display devices allow users to interact with the device by deforming the surface of the display to trigger a command. Application areas for flexible display devices include gaming, control of media and home appliances, and smart phones [4]. While these devices are currently not available to consumers, several prototypes have been developed to explore their interaction modalities. Lahey et al. created PaperPhone, a flexible display smart phone [5]. In their user studies, participants defined bend gestures and associated them with functionalities. Based on the results from their user studies, Lahey et al. proposed a classification scheme that categorized bend gestures by location (top corner, side, or bottom corner) and their polarity (up or down). Kildal et al. developed the Kinetic device, a deformable mobile phone [4]. They used this device to explore bending and twisting, and proposed a set of design guidelines for deformable devices [4]. When flexible display devices become mainstream, for example as smart phones, as e-readers, or tablets, they will require a means of authenticating legitimate users. In this poster, we present an authentication scheme for flexible display devices that takes advantage of users' motor learning capabilities. We also show the implementation of our authentication scheme on a flexible display prototype. To the best of our knowledge, there has not been any work investigating authentication schemes on flexible display devices. Our main contributions are as follows:

- We designed and implemented an authentication scheme on a flexible display prototype.
- We are conducting a user study to evaluate the usability and security of our authentication scheme and flexible display prototype. We are also comparing the usability and security of our system with a PIN based password system.

CCS'13, November 4–8, 2013, Berlin, Germany.
ACM 978-1-4503-2477-9/13/11.
http://dx.doi.org/10.1145/2508859.2512528.

2. RELATED WORK

While no work has looked at authentication mechanisms on flexible display devices, some work explores the creation of passwords utilizing the motor learning capabilities of users. Bianchi et al. developed the Haptic Wheel [2] and the Secure Haptic Keypad [1]. Passwords in these systems use a series of vibrotactile cues called tactons. Users authenticate on these systems by placing their finger on one of three keys (Haptic Keypad) or their hand around a rotary dial (Haptic Wheel). After each input, the system randomizes the vibrations it emits to protect the system from shoulder surfing. Chong et al. [3] developed GesturePIN, a mobile authentication system that allows users to create a PIN by performing a series of gestures on their mobile device. Gestures are performed by moving the mobile device in 3D (three dimensional) space, and users can perform a total of 10 gestures. Mott et al. [6] developed TangibleRubik, an authentication mechanism that requires users to physically manipulate a Rubik's Cube to authenticate a system. The various combinations of moves act as the users' password. By having users physically manipulate the cube, the system takes advantage of humans' innate ability to recall motor actions through repetition. Mott et al. conducted a user study to evaluate the usability and security of their system. Participants completed a training session requiring them to successfully enter their password three times before moving on to the experimental trials. Textual representations of the passwords were visible to the user at all times during the training trials. This was done to aid in the learning of the password. In the experimental trials, which directly followed training, participants had to correctly enter their password five times.

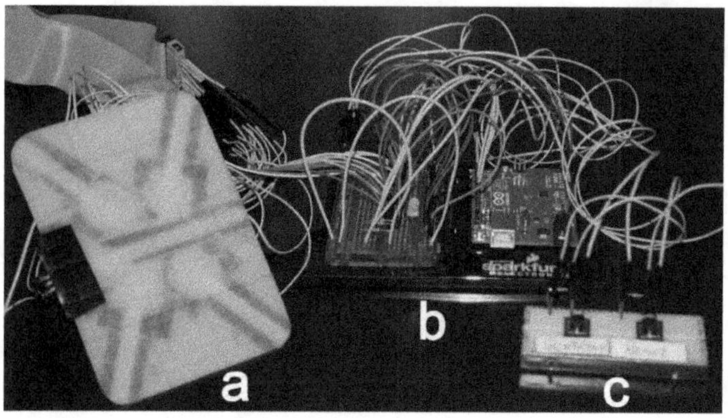

Figure 1: (a) Flexible Display, (b) Arduino Uno Microcontroller, (c) Control Panel.

After the experimental trials, participants were given a distractor task for a duration of 10 minutes, which consisted of a word search. After the distractor task, participants were asked to enter their password a final time as a test of password mastery. Mott et al. found that participants were able to effectively recall 7 and 10 gesture passwords after being removed from the system for a short time.

3. PROTOTYPES

We developed two prototypes, a flexible display prototype for creating gesture-based passwords and a mobile phone prototype for creating PINs.

3.1 Flexible Display

Our flexible display prototype is composed of four main components: flexible display, pico projector, Arduino Uno Microcontroller and a control panel. Three of these components are shown in Figure 1. The flexible display was created from a soft PVC and has four 2" Flexpoint bidirectional bend sensors attached to its back. These sensors are placed in the top-left corner, top-right corner, bottom-left corner and bottom-right corner of the display. The pico projector is used to display a UI onto the flexible display, and the control panel is used to start/stop the authentication process on the flexible display. The flexible display and the control panel are connected to an Arduino Uno Microcontroller which is connected to a computer running the software for creating a gesture based password.

3.1.1 *Creating a Password*

Passwords on the flexible display are created by performing a series of bend gestures. A set of 20 bend gestures are available. Each corner of the display can be bent upwards and downwards (8 gestures). Every two corners of the display can be bent upwards and downwards simultaneously (12 gestures). Figure 2 shows how some of these gestures can be performed. A standard password entry field is projected onto the display, with an asterisk appearing with each gesture (see Figure 3). Gesture passwords must have a minimum of 5 gestures (21.6 bits).

3.2 Mobile Phone

The mobile phone prototype was developed using Android and allows users to create a PIN. The UI of this prototype

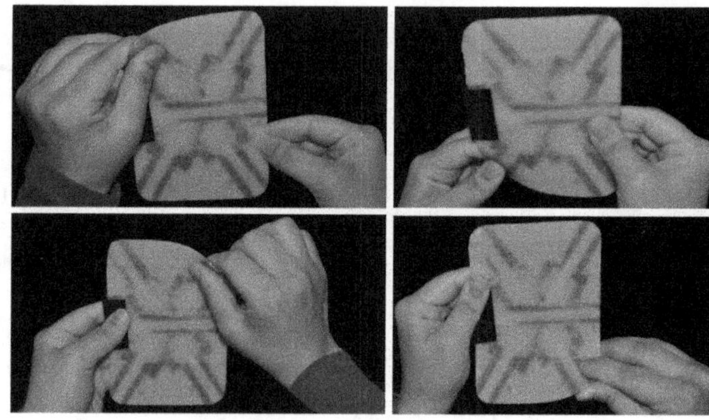
Figure 2: Four bend gestures performed on the flexible display.

Figure 3: User Interface of the Flexible and mobile phone prototype.

was designed to match the UI of the flexible display prototype (see Figure 3). PINs must be at least 6 characters long (19.9 bits).

4. USER STUDY

We are currently running a user study to evaluate the usability and security of our proposed authentication mechanism. Participants are tested in two sessions. In the first session participants are asked to create a gesture based password on the flexible display prototype and a PIN based password on the mobile phone prototype. These prototypes are presented in a counterbalanced manner. Before creating a password, participants are given a demonstration of how the prototype works and are provided with an opportunity to familiarize themselves with its functions. After creating a password on each prototype, participants are asked to complete several post-task questionnaires providing their opinions and perceptions of the prototypes. After completing the questionnaires, participants are asked to correctly re-enter their password on each prototype five times. This allows participants to rehearse their passwords which aids in memorization.

The second session takes place a week later and evaluates the memorability of the passwords created in the first session. Participants are asked to correctly re-enter their passwords. Participants are given five tries to correctly re-

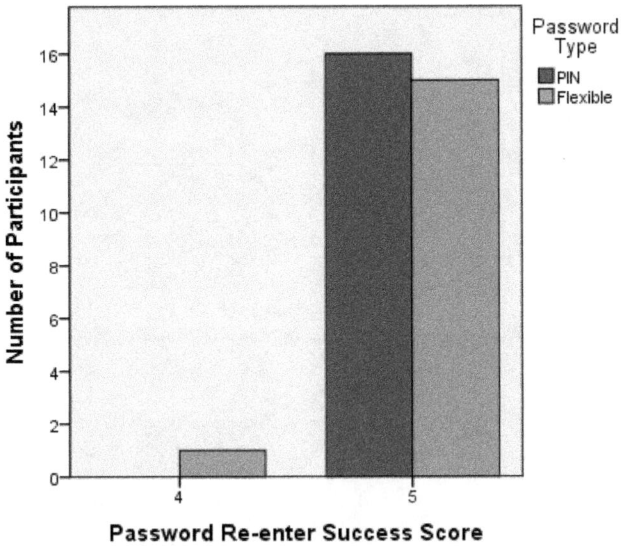

Figure 4: Day 1 Password Re-entry Success Scores (out of 5 tries) on the Flexible Display and Mobile Phone.

enter their passwords on each prototype. After completing the password re-entry tasks, participants complete several post-task questionnaires evaluating the memorability and security of their passwords.

Quantitative data collected includes the time participants took to complete each task, number of errors they made, passwords they created, strength of the passwords, number of tries taken to authenticate, and whether they were able to remember their passwords. Qualitative data is collected via post-task questionnaires.

4.1 Preliminary Results - Day 1

16 university students between the ages of 18 and 28 ($M = 22$, $SD = 3.42$) participated in the first session of our study. We analysed the time they took to re-enter their password averaged across five tries. We found that participants took longer to re-enter their password on the flexible display ($M = 31.2$s, $SD = 18.08$) than the mobile phone ($M = 7.2$s, $SD = 3.42$). One reason for the longer times is that participants were using an early prototype of a new technology which required careful handling. In addition to this, participants created new passwords on the flexible display, but post-task questionnaire data revealed that many created a known and familiar PIN on the mobile phone despite being asked to create something new. Therefore, participants had much more practice re-entering their PIN and could re-enter it faster than their password on the flexible display.

Success scores on the password re-entry task were calculated by giving participants a score out of 5, depending on the number of times they successfully re-entered their password. Figure 4 shows that most participants were able to successfully re-enter their password in both conditions.

Data from the post-task questionnaires revealed that overall participants had a positive experience in using the flexible display prototype to create a password. Some of their comments include "It's very cool!", "The flexible device is user friendly and will be easy device to use", "There were various combinations that could be made, allowing for variety. The device itself was pleasant to use, and bending it was very easy once you became accustomed to it", "That it is new technology was a definite hurdle, but with familiarity I believe it will be easy to learn and the gestures are fairly simple" and "At first, I had difficulty with mastering my intended password but after getting assistance, I determined the problem I made and was able to register my password successfully."

Further analysis of the data from both sessions is ongoing.

5. CONCLUSION AND FUTURE WORK

In this paper, we presented a password scheme for authenticating users on flexible display devices. We implemented this password scheme on a flexible display prototype and are running a user study to evaluate the usability and security of our system. Preliminary results from the first session of our study show that many users were able to easily create and re-enter their passwords, although they took longer to re-enter their gesture password than their PIN. This was mainly because users were using an early prototype of a flexible display which required careful handling. We believe that as flexible display prototypes improve in the future, password re-entry time will improve as well. Our future work will look at data from both sessions of the study. We will look at the security and memorability of passwords created on the flexible display as well as strategies and gestural patterns users employ to create their passwords.

6. REFERENCES

[1] A. Bianchi, I. Oakley, and D. S. Kwon. The secure haptic keypad: A tactile password system. In *CHI*, pages 1089–1092, 2010.

[2] A. Bianchi, I. Oakley, J. K. Lee, and D. S. Kwon. The haptic wheel: Design and evaluation of a tactile password system. In *CHI EA*, pages 625–630, 2010.

[3] M. K. Chong, G. Marsden, and H. Gellersen. Gesturepin: Using discrete gestures for associating mobile devices. In *MobileHCI*, pages 261–264, 2010.

[4] J. Kildal, S. Paasovaara, and V. Aaltonen. Kinetic device: Designing interactions with a deformable mobile interface. In *CHI EA*, pages 1871–1876, 2012.

[5] B. Lahey, A. Girouard, W. Burleson, and R. Vertegaal. Paperphone: Understanding the use of bend gestures in mobile devices with flexible electronic paper displays. In *CHI*, pages 1303–1312, 2011.

[6] M. Mott, T. Donahue, G. M. Poor, and L. Leventhal. Leveraging motor learning for a tangible password system. In *CHI EA*, pages 2597–2602, 2012.

POSTER: Revisiting Anomaly Detection System Design Philosophy

Ayesha Binte Ashfaq[1], Muhammad Qasim Ali[2], Ehab Al-Shaer[2] and Syed Ali Khayam[3]
[1] School of Electrical Engineering and Computer Science
National University of Sciences and Technology, Islamabad, Pakistan
[2] Department of Software and Information Systems
University of North Carolina Charlotte
[3] PLUMgrid Inc.
Sunnyvale, CA
ayesha.ashfaq@seecs.edu.pk; {mali12,ealshaer}@uncc.edu; khayam@gmail.com

ABSTRACT

The inherent design of anomaly detection systems (ADSs) make them highly susceptible to evasion attacks and hence their wide-spread commercial deployment has not been witnessed. There are two main reasons for this: 1) ADSs incur high false positives; 2) Are highly susceptible to evasion attacks (false negatives). While efforts have been made to minimize false positives, evasion is still an open problem. We argue that ADSs design is inherently flawed since it relies on the ADS's detection logic and feature space which is trivial to estimate. In information security e.g. cryptographic algorithms (such as DES), security is inherently dependent upon the key and not the algorithm, which makes these systems very robust by rendering evasion computationally infeasible. We believe there is a need to redesign the anomaly detection systems similar to cryptographic systems. We propose to randomize the feature space of an ADS such that it acts as a cryptographic key for the ADS and hence this randomized feature space is used by the ADS logic for detection of anomalies. This would make the evasion of the ADS computationally infeasible for the attacker.

Categories and Subject Descriptors

C.2.0 [**Computer-Communication Networks**]: General—*Security and Protection*; D.4.6 [**Security and Protection**]: Invasive Software; K.6.5 [**Security and Protection**]: Unauthorized access

Keywords

Evasion; Intrusion Detection Systems

1. INTRODUCTION

While the original models for anomaly detection system were proposed more than two decades ago, anomaly detection still remains an active area of research as the attacks continue to adapt and evade intrusion detection solutions. Current anomaly detection systems employ feature classes for detection that do not vary throughout the operational life of the ADS. Therefore, if an attacker can estimate the normal behavior of the network, it can easily evade the detection system and send attack packets into the network without detection. Moreover, the possibility of detecting such evasion attacks is bleak because the normal network behavior is not frequently updated.

We propose that an anomaly detection system should be redesigned based on mutating feature space i.e. feature space that changes across time. This makes the task of estimating the normal behavior of the network infeasible. Therefore, the attacker would now first have to identify the features being used for detection and then analyze the network traffic pertaining to those features to develop a model of normality. For the attacker to launch the evasion attack, the features used by the ADS for detection should not vary from those estimated. However, if the features change, the attack would be detected because the normal network behavior is now defined in terms of a different set of features than those estimated. Thus, the mutation across time renders the two-tier estimation unrewarding for the attacker since he would have to re-estimate the parameters in different time window. Hence the robustness of the system lies in mutating the feature space across time rather than in the methodology used for detection, just like crypto-algorithms rely on the key for security. Below we discuss the ADS parameters that need to be estimated by the attacker, followed by a case study.

2. CAN WE ESTIMATE THE EVASION MARGIN?

Currently ADSs assume that the underlying detection principle is not known to the attacker. However, it does not hold in real world where some knowledge about the ADS principle can be obtained through methods like social engineering, fingerprinting, etc. [1]. In fact, ADS can be evaded without knowing the exact design principles; several types of attacks (e.g., polymorphic blending attacks, mimicry attacks, etc.) have been proposed in existing literature.

Moreover, ADSs rely significantly on the belief that the attacker does not know the network topology and/or the services running within the network. Hence, it tends to commu-

CCS'13, November 4–8, 2013, Berlin, Germany.
ACM 978-1-4503-2477-9/13/11.
http://dx.doi.org/10.1145/2508859.2512529.

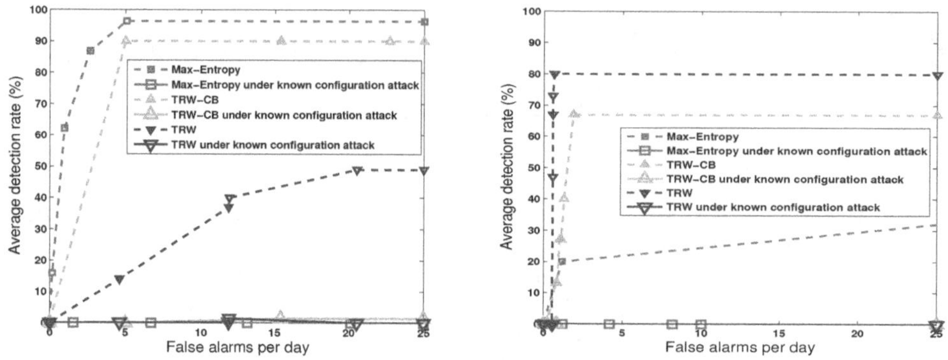

(a) Dataset-1 (b) Dataset-2

Figure 1: Comparison of ADS performance with and without evasion attack using configuration estimation.

nicate with hosts that do not exist or hosts that do not have the requested service available. Thus the malicious packets from the attacker would considerably alter the real-time traffic characteristics from the baseline distribution. However, we show that this is a flawed assumption.

For the attacker to estimate the evasion margin i.e., the number of attack packets that it can send into the network without detection, it has to estimate three ADS parameters: a) baseline distribution; b) realtime distribution; and c)detection threshold.

As a proof-of-concept, we use two existing, prominent and diverse statistical ADSs: Maximum Entropy [2] and TRW/Credit-based TRW [3], [4]. These ADSs are briefly described in Section 3. We now explain the estimation of the ADS parameters below.

The baseline distribution can be estimated by either: a) Observing traffic generated from a host within the target network; or b) Brute force estimation. For the *realtime observation*, a realistic scenario for estimating the baseline distribution is that the attacker compromises a host X in network A that communicates with the target host [1]. Hence, it can observe the normal traffic from host X to the target entity that can be used to build the normal profile for network A. *Brute force estimation* is the most common modus operandi used extensively in cryptanalysis. Despite its computational complexity, it has been shown that with the current high-performance COTS (multithreaded and multicore) hardware, it is not difficult for a craft attacker to acquire and exploit hardware parallelism to carry out a bruteforce analysis [1], [5].

We proposed a Markovian stochastic model [6] of temporal dependence in an ADS's anomaly scores. While the motivation for the original work was to improve the accuracy and automation of an ADS using threshold estimation, the technique can be adapted to estimate the ADS detection threshold for evasion. However, we restrict the evaluation of conditional entropy to first order Markov chains only:

$$H\left(p_j|p_i\right) = -\sum_{\omega} p(p_i, p_j) \log\left(p\left(p_j|p_i\right)\right). \tag{1}$$

The conditional entropy $H(p_j|p_i)$, of two random variables p_i and p_j correspond to the information in p_j not given by p_i. Thus, computing the maximum conditional entropy between baseline distributions in two consecutive time bins, as we slide from bin 1 to bin n, can provide us the minimum information overlap in normal benign data. This can be stochastically modeled as:

$$H_{\max} = \max_{i,j\in\{1,2\ldots n\}} H\left(p_j|p_i\right) \tag{2}$$

This minimum information overlap can be used to identify the acceptable divergence bounds for normal traffic for which the detector does not raise an alarm.

Once the baseline distribution and the threshold have been estimated, the detection logic can be used to estimate the realtime distribution. This realtime distribution can then be used by the attacker to generate attack sessions in different feature classes that stay below the threshold and hence evade ADS detection. For example, for the Maximum entropy ADS, it can be estimated as:

$$\widehat{q_B}[\omega] < 2^{\frac{\tau_{KL}}{p(\omega)}} p(\omega) \tag{3}$$

where $q(\omega)$ is the realtime distribution, τ_{KL} is the detection threshold and ω is the packet class

3. CASE STUDY

The Maximum Entropy detector [2] employs Kullback-Leibler (KL) divergence measure for anomaly detection. The measure computes how much the baseline distribution $p(\omega)$ varies from the real-time distribution $q(\omega)$. Traffic is divided into 2348 packet classes based on the destination ports and the protocol. The detector uses maximum entropy estimation to develop the baseline distribution for the traffic classes. If the divergence between the baseline and the real-time distributions for a particular packet class exceeds the threshold τ_{KL} in h of these W windows, an anomaly is flagged by the detector. Maximum entropy has been shown to provide high accuracy dividends [7].

Sequential hypothesis testing based TRW ADSs [3] [4] employ the likelihood ratio test to identify if local/remote hosts are scanners. TRW classifier [3] detects remote scanners while Credit-based TRW (TRW-CB) [4] detects local scanners. Both these algorithms have been shown to be quite accurate and commercial ADSs also deploy these algorithms for portscan detection.

For both Maximum entropy and TRW ADSs, we launched stealthy scanning attack by estimating the ADS's parameters as described in Section 2. Both the detectors failed

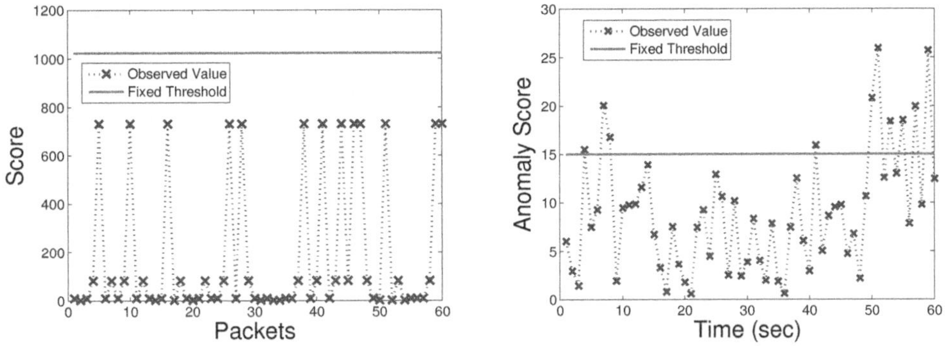

(a) TRW (b) Maximum Entropy

Figure 2: Threshold values observed in stealthy scanning time window for TRW and Maximum Entropy

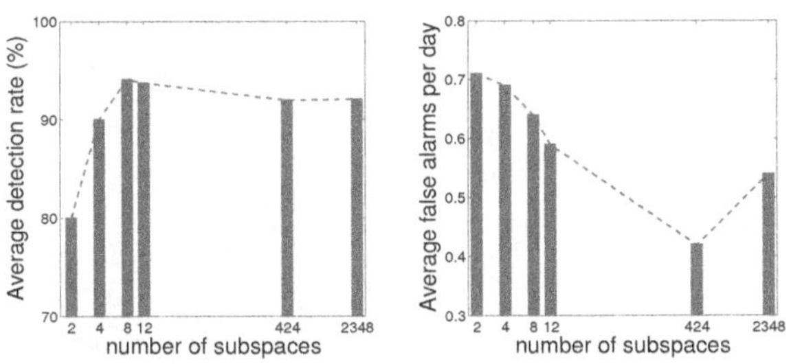

(a) Detection rate (b) False alarms per day

Figure 3: Accuracy of the Maximum Entropy detector with varying number of feature classes.

to detect the scanning probes on two different datasets as shown in Figure 1.

Figure 2(a) shows that TRW failed to detect the scan traffic in a malicious time window. It can be clearly observed that the likelihood ratio did not exceed the threshold. TRW calculates the likelihood ratio for each connection attempt and classify them as anomalous if the likelihood ratio for any host increases more than the threshold. Since the hosts were also generating benign traffic, the likelihood ratio did not cross the threshold set. Similarly, Figure 2(b) shows the threshold values observed in a 60 sec time window for Maximum entropy. As proposed in [2], if the threshold (15) is exceeded 30 times within 60 seconds interval, an alarm is raised. Due to stealthy scanning the run-time distribution exceeded the threshold only 10 times. Therefore, just by slowing down or the effect of averaging out in the normal traffic, scanning was able to go undetected.

It can be observed that of the three parameters that an attacker has to estimate (Section2), two of those are dependent on the features employed by the ADS for detection. Since these features are inherently fixed by design, the attacker can easily estimate them to evade the ADSs.

4. DOES A LARGER FEATURE SPACE GUARANTEE OPTIMAL PERFORMANCE?

Using a high-dimensional feature space does not necessarily yield optimal performance. Figure 3 provides the accuracy gain on the endpoint dataset achieved by the Maximum Entropy ADS as the feature space is varied from 2 to 2348 using the detector's slicing technique progressively. Figure 3(a) shows that the detection rate does not increase proportionally as we increase the number of analyzed static feature space from 2 to 2348. The same trend is observed in the false alarms as well. Thus, using all the features simultaneously does not ensure high accuracy. Hence selecting a few feature class(es) judiciously for detection in a time window would suffice to introduce enough randomness in the process of ADS detection, so as to render the parameter estimation attacks impractical.

5. MOVING TARGET-BASED ADS DESIGN

Since current ADSs are susceptible to evasion margin estimation, they can be bypassed by an intelligent and a resourceful attacker. This is because the underlying feature space does not change with time and hence can be leveraged to analyze network traffic semantics and craft attacks accordingly. We believe a moving target based ADS design would, however, make it infeasible for an adversary to craft evasion estimation attacks due to inherent randomness introduced by the mutating feature space. However, it is important to identify the right number of features to be employed for detection in different time windows, for optimal performance.

6. REFERENCES

[1] D. Wagner and P. Soto, "Mimicry attacks on host-based intrusion detection systems," ACM CCS 2002.

[2] Y. Gu, A. McCullum and D. Towsley, "Detecting anomalies in network traffic using maximum entropy estimation," ACM/Usenix IMC, 2005.

[3] J. Jung, V. Paxson, A. W. Berger, and H. Balakrishnan, "Fast portscan detection using sequential hypothesis testing," IEEE Symp Sec and Priv, 2004.

[4] S. E. Schechter, J. Jung, and A. W. Berger, "Fast detection of scanning worm infections," RAID 2004.

[5] C. Smith, A. Matrawy, S. Chow and B. Abdelaziz, "Computer worms: Architectures, evasion strategies, and detection mechanisms," Journal of Information Assurance and Security, 2008.

[6] M.Q. Ali, H. Khan, A. Sajjad and S.A. Khayam, "On Achieving Good Operating Points on an ROC Plane using Stochastic Anomaly Score Prediction," ACM CCS, 2009.

[7] A.B. Ashfaq, M.J. Joseph, A. Mumtaz, M.Q. Ali, A. Sajjad and S.A. Khayam, "A comparative evaluation of anomaly detectors under portscan attacks," RAID 2008.

12th Workshop on Privacy in the Electronic Society (WPES 2013)

Sara Foresti
Università degli Studi di Milano
Dipartimento di informatica
via Bramante, 65
26013 Crema - Italy
sara.foresti@unimi.it

ABSTRACT

The evolution of the Information and Communication Technology (ICT) has radically changed our lives, making information available from anywhere at any time through different kinds of devices. The advantage of the growing availability of computational power and connectivity resources at low prices is the easiness of collecting, sharing, processing, and accessing information. This advantage however does not come for free as it introduces unprecedented privacy risks. The attention toward these problems is growing every day and the need for privacy-aware policies, regulations, and techniques has been widely recognized. WPES is a yearly forum, this year at its 12th edition, that brings together researchers and practitioners interested in discussing the privacy issues characterizing our global and interconnected society.

Categories and Subject Descriptors

K.4.1 [**Computers and Society**]: Public Policy Issues —*Privacy*; K.6 [**Management of Computing and Information Systems**]: Security and Protection; K.6.m [**Management of Computing and Information Systems**]: Miscellaneous—*Security*

Keywords

Privacy; electronic society; workshop

1. INTRODUCTION

The recent advancements of digital infrastructures have revolutionized the way in which data are collected, stored, managed, processed, shared, and distributed. Nowadays, thanks to a wide network connectivity, we can rely on external servers for storing our pictures and videos, use the computational power offered at low prices by cloud providers, access remotely stored data made available by third parties. These are only a few examples of the advantages of living in a globally interconnected society, where everything we are looking for is at the distance of 'a mouse click'. The price we pay for these benefits is a higher privacy risk, due to the increased amount of sensitive information collected, stored, and distributed, and to the lack of control of the users on their own data. It is interesting to note that the problem of protecting privacy is continuously changing as technology evolves, presenting new opportunities for users but also introducing (as downside) new vulnerabilities. Privacy problems are receiving more and more the attention of researchers and regulators, as well as of private users and public organizations.

WPES aims to bring together researchers and practitioners who are interested in discussing on privacy issues arising in the electronic society. Privacy problems concern many different areas (e.g., data management, social networks, cloud systems, wireless networks, mobile devices). This yearly forum represents an occasion for participants to present and share their theoretical as well as experimental results, to learn about new solutions for known privacy problems, and also to discuss open issues that still need to be addressed. The workshop is this year at its 12th edition. Like for past editions, WPES is held in conjunction with the ACM CCS conference – the flagship annual conference of the Special Interest Group on Security, Audit and Control (SIGSAC) of the Association for Computing Machinery (ACM). This colocation has advantages for both the events as the workshop enriches the conference program and, at the same time, benefits from the presence of a wide community of researchers, practitioners, developers, and users interested in information security topics.

The workshop solicited submissions from academia and industry presenting novel research on all theoretical and practical aspects of electronic privacy, as well as experimental studies. It also encouraged submissions from other communities such as law and business that present these communities' perspectives on technological issues. Topics of interest for paper submission included, but were not limited to:

- anonymity, pseudonymity, and unlinkability
- crowdsourcing for privacy and security
- data correlation and leakage attacks
- data security and privacy
- electronic communication privacy
- economics of privacy
- information dissemination control

CCS'13, November 4–8, 2013, Berlin, Germany.
ACM 978-1-4503-2477-9/13/11.
http://dx.doi.org/10.1145/2508859.2509028.

- models, languages, and techniques for big data protection
- personally identifiable information
- privacy-aware access control
- privacy and anonymity on the Web
- privacy in cloud and grid systems
- privacy and confidentiality management
- privacy and data mining
- privacy in the digital business
- privacy in the electronic records
- privacy enhancing technologies
- privacy in health care and public administration
- privacy and human rights
- privacy metrics
- privacy in mobile systems
- privacy in outsourced scenarios
- privacy policies
- privacy vs. security
- privacy in social networks
- privacy threats
- privacy and virtual identity
- public records and personal privacy
- user profiling
- wireless privacy

2. WORKSHOP CONTRIBUTIONS

This year, the workshop received a record number of submissions, 103, from 27 different countries. Among these papers, the program committee accepted 20 full papers and 10 short papers. The topics of the papers in the workshop program cover a wide variety of scenarios, such as privacy in social networks, privacy of genomic data, privacy in mobile scenarios, privacy of location data.

3. WORKSHOP COMMITTEES

The program chair of the workshop is Sara Foresti, Università degli Studi di Milano, Italy. The program committee is composed of the following experts in the topics of interest for the workshop.

- Rafael Accorsi, University of Freiburg, Germany
- Kevin Bauer, MIT, USA
- Marina Blanton, University of Notre Dame, USA
- Carlo Blundo, Università degli Studi di Salerno, Italy
- Graham Cormode, University of Warwick, UK
- Marco Cova, University of Birmingham, UK
- Anupam Datta, Carnegie Mellon University, USA
- Sabrina De Capitani di Vimercati, Università degli Studi di Milano, Italy
- Roberto Di Pietro, Roma Tre University of Rome, Italy
- Keith Frikken, Miami University, USA
- Joaquin Garcia-Alfaro, Telecom SudParis, France
- Tyrone Grandison, Proficiency Labs, USA
- Dimitris Gritzalis, AUEB, Greece
- Sushil Jajodia, George Mason University, USA
- Rob Jansen, U.S. Naval Research Laboratory, USA
- Murat Kantarcioglu, University of Texas at Dallas, USA
- Apu Kapadia, Indiana University Bloomington, USA
- Florian Kerschbaum, SAP, Germany
- Markulf Kohlweiss, Microsoft Research, UK
- Adam J. Lee, University of Pittsburgh, USA
- Giovanni Livraga, Università degli Studi di Milano, Italy
- Javier Lopez, University of Malaga, Spain
- Ashwin Machanavajjha, Duke University, USA
- Stefano Paraboschi, Università degli Studi di Bergamo, Italy
- Kui Ren, University at Buffalo, USA
- Pierangela Samarati, Università degli Studi di Milano, Italy
- Abhinav Srivastava, AT&T Labs - Research, USA
- Paul Syverson, Naval Research Laboratory, USA
- Marianthi Theoharidou, AUEB, Greece
- Carmela Troncoso, Gradiant, Spain
- Cong Wang, City University of Hong Kong, Hong Kong
- Meng Yu, Virginia Commonwealth University, USA
- Ting Yu, North Carolina State University, USA
- Zhenjie Zhang, ADSC, USA
- Jianying Zhou, I2R, Singapore

WPES steering committee is chaired by Pierangela Samarati, from the Università degli Studi di Milano, Italy, and is composed of the following four members.

- Sabrina De Capitani di Vimercati, Università degli Studi di Milano, Italy
- Sushil Jajodia, George Mason University, USA
- Pierangela Samarati, Università degli Studi di Milano, Italy
- Paul Syverson, Naval Research Laboratory, USA

4. ACKNOWLEDGMENTS

I would like to thank all the members of the Program Committee and the external reviewers, for all the work they devoted in reviewing and discussing papers. I would also like to express my gratitude to WPES Steering Committee, and its Chair Pierangela Samarati in particular, for their guidance and support in the organization of the workshop, and to Giovanni Livraga, for taking care of publicity. Thanks to Stefan Katzenbeisser and Christopher Kruegel (ACM CCS Workshop Co-Chairs) and to Ahmad-Reza Sadeghi (ACM CCS General Chair), for their support in workshop organization and logistics.

Third International Workshop on Trustworthy Embedded Devices (TrustED 2013)

Frederik Armknecht
Universität Mannheim, Germany
armknecht@uni-mannheim.de

Jean-Pierre Seifert
Technische Universität Berlin (TUB) &
Deutsche Telekom Laboratories, DE
Jean-Pierre.Seifert@telekom.de

ABSTRACT

Cyber physical systems (CPS) feature a tight combination of and coordination between the system's computational and physical elements. A current NIST report [1] estimates that "by the end of the decade, embedded networking and computing components are projected to account for more than half of the value share in diverse sectors, including automotive, consumer electronics, avionics and aerospace, manufacturing, telecommunications, intelligent buildings, and health and medical equipment" and further conjectures that "future applications of CPS are more transformative than the IT revolution of the past three decades." While the increasing proliferation of embedded systems in general and CPS in particular provide a variety of new possibilities, new risks and challenges emerge. Due to the strong interdisciplinary character, advancement in CPS requires a new systems science that encompasses both physical and computational aspects.

The scope of the Workshop on Trustworthy Embedded Devices (TrustED) is security of embedded devices in general with focus on cyber physical systems and their environments. TrustED 2013 is a continuation of previous workshops in this series, which were held in conjunction with ESORICS 2011 and IEEE Security & Privacy 2012 (see http://trusted.trust.cased.de for details). The goal of this workshop is to bring together experts from academia and research institutes, industry, and government in the field of security and privacy in cyber physical systems.

Categories and Subject Descriptors

B.0 [**Hardware**]: General; C.2.0 [**Computer - Communication Networks**]: General—*security and protection (e.g., firewalls)*; D.4.6 [**Software**]: Operation Systems—*Security and Protection*; E.3 [**Data**]: Data Encryption; K.6.5 [**Computing Milieux**]: Management of Computing and Information Systems—*Security and Protection*

CCS'13, November 4–8, 2013, Berlin, Germany.
ACM 978-1-4503-2477-9/13/11.
http://dx.doi.org/10.1145/2508859.2509029.

Keywords

TrustED, Security, Embedded Devices, Cryptography

1. BACKGROUND AND MOTIVATION

The paradigm of ubiquitous computing and permanent, mobile connectivity has already become reality through modern technologies that allow for electronic systems to be embedded practically everywhere. Probably, the most popular example today being smart phones, additional examples include sensor nodes, smart meters, femtocells, automotive platforms, home gateways, and IPTV boxes. However, with new opportunities come new risks, affecting security and privacy. This is particularly true when embedded systems are involved, which we closely and sometimes unknowingly interact with in our daily life. Embedded devices differ significantly from "classical" systems, such as desktop PCs in various aspects:

- They have typically a variety of constraints (e.g., concerning power, memory, or processing capabilities), ruling out many classical security solutions for practical reasons
- They can be accessed by malicious third parties with ease (e.g., physically tampered with or replaced by other devices).
- They can form a network with other embedded devices, amongst others with more powerful devices such as smart phones that function as gateways. This makes them preferable targets for network attacks (e.g., resulting in the denial of service or exhausting power).

Consequently, embedded devices and their usage in varying deployment scenarios, requires novel security methods and mechanisms. The major challenge is to develop security solutions that ensure a sufficient level of trust, security, and privacy while meeting practical requirements. Furthermore, it is well known that in order to create a secure system, system designers and developers need to consider security aspects on multiple abstraction layers, such as hardware, operating system, and application level. Particularly, for designing secure embedded systems, a careful coordination and integration of applications, operating system, and the deployed hardware is mandatory, given the fact that the options and opportunities of software and hardware are much more diverse than it is the case for the PC world.

2. SCOPE AND OBJECTIVES

Summing up, security for embedded devices is a highly interdisciplinary topic. However, this not only poses new challenges, but likewise new possibilities. A promising approach is to exploit special features in embedded devices and their environment for establishing novel secure mechanisms. Examples include the identification and deployment of new out-of-band channels, such as NFC-based schemes, the explicit use of physical properties, such as distance bounding protocols or signal fingerprinting, or secure execution environments provided by the new generation of processors. In general, the use of hardware-entangled cryptography (e.g., schemes based on physically unclonable functions - PUFs), and hardware-assisted cryptographic protocols represents a promising technological development towards trustworthy embedded devices and networks.

In this workshop, we consider selected aspects of cyber physical systems and their environments. We aim to bring together experts from academia and research institutes, industry and government to discuss and investigate the problems, challenges, and recent scientific and technological developments in this field. In this context we are particularly interested in the participation of industry representatives. The workshop includes (but is not limited to) the following topics:

- Embedded system security
- Privacy aspects of embedded systems (e.g., medical devices, electronic IDs)
- Physical and logical convergence (e.g., secure and privacy preserving facility management),
- Hardware entangled cryptography
- Foundation, development, and applications of physical security primitives (e.g., physically unclonable functions - PUFs),
- Remote attestation
- IP protection for embedded systems
- Reverse engineering
- Secure execution environments (e.g., TrustZone, TPMs, etc.) on mobile devices
- New protection paradigms for trustworthy embedded systems

3. PROGRAM COMMITTE

We are thankful to the members of our program committee:

- Liang Cai (Qualcomm, US)
- Mauro Conti (University of Padua, IT)
- Bruno Crispo (University of Trento, IT)
- Loïc Duflot (SGDN/DCSSI - Paris, FR)
- William Enck (NC State University, US)
- Wieland Fischer (Infineon, DE)
- Felix Freiling (University of Erlangen, DE)
- Jorge Guajardo Merchan (Robert Bosch LLC, US)
- Tim Güneysu (Ruhr-University Bochum, DE)
- Helena Handschuh (Cryptography Research, US)
- Xuxian Jiang (NC State University, US)
- Farinaz Koushanfar (Rice University, US)
- Peter Langendoerfer (IHP, DE)
- Refik Molva (Eurecom, FR)
- Collin Mulliner (Northeastern University, US)
- Bart Preneel (KU Leuven, BE)
- Volker Roth (Freie Universität Berlin, DE)
- Boris Skoric (Eindhoven University of Technology, NL)
- John Solis (Sandia National Laboratories, US)
- Vincent van der Leest (Intrinsic ID, NL)
- Ingrid Verbauwhede (KU Leuven, BE)
- Xinwen Zhang (Huawei Research Center, US)

4. PC CO-CHAIRS

Frederik Armknecht is an Assistant Professor for Cryptography at the University of Mannheim, Germany. His research interests include lightweight cryptography, in particular the analysis and development of new building blocks, hardware-entangled cryptography, e.g., systematizing and formalizing security properties and goals, and the design of new, practical schemes that allow for operating on encrypted data, e.g., homomorphic encryption schemes, that are tailored for practical use cases. Together with Ahmad-Reza Sadeghi, he initiated TrustED in 2011.

Jean-Pierre Seifert is a Full Professor heading the "Security in Telecommunications" group at TU Berlin. His professorship is concurrently concerned with security in telecommunications management matters at T-Labs, the R&D arm of Deutsche Telekom (DT) at TU Berlin. His main research interest is in system security with specializations in secure virtualization of operating systems and a holistic view of telecommunication security, which includes hardware security. Under his leadership, his research group is directly transferring its research results into high-security DT products for the German government. In 2002, he was honoured by Infineon with the award "Inventor of the Year" and received two Intel Achievement Awards in 2005 for his new CPU security instructions for Intel microprocessors.

5. REFERENCES

[1] *Strategic R&D Opportunities for 21st Century Cyber-Physical Systems.* NIST-Report, 2013. Available at `http://www.nist.gov/el/upload/12-Cyber-Physical-Systems020113\_final.pdf`.

CyCAR'2013: First International Academic Workshop on Security, Privacy and Dependability for CyberVehicles

Arslan Munir
Rice University
Houston, TX, USA
arslan@rice.edu

Farinaz Koushanfar
Rice University
Houston, TX, USA
farinaz@rice.edu

Hervé Seudié
Robert Bosch GmbH
Darmstadt, Germany
herve.seudie@de.bosch.com

Ahmad-Reza Sadeghi
Intel CRISC & TU Darmstadt
Darmstadt, Germany
ahmad.sadeghi@trust.cased.de

ABSTRACT

The next generation of automobiles (also known as CyberVehicles) will increasingly incorporate electronic control units in novel automotive control applications. Recent work has demonstrated vulnerability of modern automotive control systems to security attacks that directly impact CyberVehicles' physical safety and dependability. The First International Academic Workshop on Security, Privacy and Dependability for CyberVehicles (CyCAR'13) focuses on security and privacy topics in CyberVehicles that are within the scope of ACM Conference on Computer and Communications Security (CCS). Specifically, the workshop targets issues related to security and privacy issues in computerized, complex, and connected modern vehicles as well as their complex supply chains. This workshop offers an opportunity to trigger the transfer of the accumulated knowledge by the ACM CCS community to the car industry while taking into account typical automotive constraints such as interoperability, reliability, dependability, quality, resource constraints and/or complex supply chain.

Categories and Subject Descriptors

C.2.0 [**Computer-Communication Networks**]: General—*Security and Protection (e.g., firewalls)*; C.3 [**Computer Systems Organization**]: Special-Purpose and Application-Based Systems—*Real-time and embedded systems*; C.4 [**Computer Systems Organization**]: Performance of Systems—*Design studies, modeling techniques*; K.6.5 [**Management of Computing and Information Systems**]: Security and Protection (e.g., firewalls)

General Terms

Performance, Reliability, Security

CCS'13, November 4–8, 2013, Berlin, Germany.

Keywords

Automotive, security, dependability, privacy, cybervehicles, embedded systems

1. INTRODUCTION

Modern automotive systems integrate a multitude of embedded hard real-time control functionalities, and a host of advanced information and entertainment (infotainment) features. The true paradigm shift for future automotive (CyberVehicle) systems and other transportation systems, i.e., avionics, maritime, and rails, is not only a result of this increasing plurality of subsystems and functions, but is also driven by the unprecedented levels of intra- and inter-CyberVehicle system connections and communications as well as networking with external entities, such as smart mobile devices and the cloud. The emergence of new generations of intelligent transportation systems that are fully connected to their surrounding objects, environments, and networks poses various design challenges for the automotive/transportation industry, such as interoperability, reliability, dependability, quality and security.

The development of CyberVehicles is both necessary and inevitable, as it opens up both several business opportunities and user comfort. For example, traffic congestion avoidance mitigation services that take advantage of connectivity to the cloud and global perspective of route conditions can alleviate the rising business losses due to traffic jam in metropolitan areas. Such services ought to consider safety and security as a top objectives as attacks to one subsystem or network component could impact a larger portion of the connected system.

The First International Academic Workshop on Security, Privacy and Dependability for CyberVehicles (CyCAR'13) brings together researchers and practitioners in security domain related to modern and next generation automotive systems. The workshop solicited two types of original papers: full papers and short/work-in-progress/position-papers. The goal of this workshop is to bring together academic and automotive industry researchers to discuss, identify and address the challenges related to achieving secure, dependable and privacy-preserving cybervehicle systems.

2. FORMAT

CyCAR'2013 will be a full-day workshop program on the first day of CCS 2013. The workshop will begin with an invited talk from Ulrich Huber, Associate principal of McKinsey & Company, responsible for automotive solutions. In his talk "Mobility of the future", Ulrich will present his views on the roadmap of future applications in the area of cyber vehicles and their impact on security and privacy. The workshop will also have accepted paper sessions. Each paper session will conclude with a discussion led by a pre-chosen workshop participant. These discussions will tie together common themes of the presentations and hopefully lead to insightful discussions about future research directions. The program will end with a panel discussion where panelists will discuss the current state of the art, focus areas, and opportunities for future research.

3. TOPICS OF INTEREST

In terms of author audience, we solicited paper submissions related to the following (but not limited to) research topics:

- Security engineering and life-cycle management in the automotive and transportation domain
- Security management in automotive supply chain
- Design methodologies and development, validation, and automation tools for secure vehicle components
- Secure and dependable intra- and inter-vehicle communication
- Secure theft protection mechanisms for the automotive domain
- Anonymous credentials in the automotive domain
- Automotive security research challenges
- Dependable and secure automotive use-cases
- Architecture and implementation technologies for automotive trusted platform
- Limitations, alternatives, and tradeoffs regarding automotive trusted computing
- Secure wireless and mobile technologies in vehicles
- Secure localization and location privacy
- Mobile (smart) device integration in vehicles and transport systems
- Intrusion detection systems for the automotive domain
- Secure interaction between cloud and vehicular network
- Secure software update and feature activation on car components
- IP protection in vehicle components
- Secure software update and feature activation on car components
- Secure remote update
- Remote attestation of automotive trusted devices
- Secure hardware for low cost automotive devices
- Virtualization in automotive components

4. PROGRAM COMMITTEE

We are grateful to the following program committee members for contributing their expertise in selection of the papers for the workshop program:

- Arslan Munir, Rice University, Houston, TX, USA
- Frank Kargl, Ulm University, Germany
- Elmar Schoch, AUDI, Germany
- Wenyuan XU, University of South Carolina, USA
- Sdrjan Capkun, ETH Zurich, Switzerland
- Matthias Schunter, Intel, Germany
- Flavio D. Garcia, University of Birmingham, England
- Tom Forest, General Motors Research & Development, USA
- Gang Qu, University of Maryland, USA
- Ivan Martinovic, University of Oxford, England
- Christoph Paar, University of Bochum, Germany
- Gene Tsudik, University of California, USA
- Alexandra Dmitrienko, Fraunhofer SIT, Germany
- Steffen Schulz, Intel, Germany
- Lujo Bauer, Carnegie Mellon University, USA
- John Kenney, Toyota InfoTechnology Center, USA
- Kevin Snow, University of North Carolina at Chapel Hill, USA

5. WORKSHOP ORGANIZERS

- Ahmad-Reza Sadeghi, Intel CRISC & TU Darmstadt, Germany, ahmad.sadeghi@trust.cased.de
- Cliff Wang, Army Research Office, USA, cliff.wang@us.army.mil
- Hervé Seudié, Robert Bosch GmbH, Germany, herve.seudie@de.bosch.com
- Farinaz Koushanfar, Rice University, USA, farinaz@rice.edu
- Albert Held, Daimler AG, Germany, albert.held@daimler.com

Summary/Overview for Artificial Intelligence and Security (AISec'13)

Blaine Nelson
University of Potsdam
Building 4, Office 0.20
August-Bebel-Str. 89
14482 Potsdam, Germany
bnelson@cs.uni-potsdam.de

Christos Dimitrakakis
Computer Science and Engineering
Chalmers University
SE-4172
chrdimi@chalmers.se

Elaine Shi
Department of Computer Science
University of Maryland
A.V. Williams Building
College Park, MD 20742
runting@cs.cmu.edu

ABSTRACT

The Workshop on Artificial Intelligence and Security (AISec) focuses on the theory and application of Artificial Intelligence (AI) and machine learning in adversarial settings such as security and privacy applications and conversely, the security and privacy implications arising through the use of large-scale AI methods. The workshop serves as the premier venue for this particular fusion of application, algorithms, and theory and continues to attract submissions from a diverse set of researchers, who address newly arising problems within this ever growing field. AISec provides a forum for researchers within the security, privacy, AI, and learning communities to discuss the role that intelligent technologies play in security and privacy applications and to present the unique needs of these problems to the AI and learning communities.

Categories and Subject Descriptors

C.2.0 [**Computer-Communication Networks**]: General—*security and protection (e.g., firewalls)*; D.4.6 [**Operating Systems**]: Security and Protection; I.2.6 [**Artificial Intelligence**]: Learning; I.2.7 [**Artificial Intelligence**]: Natural Language Processing; I.2.8 [**Artificial Intelligence**]: Problem Solving, Control Methods, and Search; K.4.1 [**Computers and Society**]: Public Policy Issues—*privacy*; K.6.5 [**Management of Computing and Information Systems**]: Security and Protection

General Terms

Algorithms,Security,Theory

Keywords

Artificial Intelligence, Computer Security, Machine Learning, Computer Privacy, Secure Learning

AISec'13, November 4, 2013, Berlin, Germany.
ACM 978-1-4503-2488-5/13/11 ...$15.00.
http://dx.doi.org/10.1145/2508859.2509031

1. BACKGROUND AND MOTIVATION

The potential application of artificial intelligence (AI), machine learning (ML), and data mining to security and privacy problems is ever-expanding. The analytic tools and intelligent behavior provided by these techniques makes AI and learning increasingly important for autonoumous real-time decision-making in domains with a wealth of data or that require quick reactions to ever-changing situations. Particularly, these intelligent technologies offer new solutions to security problems involving *big-data* analysis scaled through cloud-computing. The use of learning methods in security-sensitive domains creates new frontiers for security research, in which adversaries may attempt to mislead or evade intelligent machines. The AISec workshop provides a venue for presenting and discussing new developments in this fusion of security/privacy with AI and machine learning.

AISec, in its sixth consecutive year with CCS, is the premier meeting place for researchers interested in the junction of security, privacy, AI and ML. The past year witnessed intense activity within the AISec community – first with a Dagstuhl workshop followed by the fifth AISec workshop. There are several reasons for this surge. Firstly, machine learning, data mining, and other AI technologies play a key role in extracting knowledge, situational awareness, and security intelligence from *big-data*. Secondly, data-centric companies like Google and Amazon are increasingly exploring and deploying learning technologies to address *big-data* problems for their customers. Finally, these trends are increasingly exposing companies and their customers to intelligent technologies. As a result, these learning technologies are being explored by researchers as potential solutions to security/privacy problems, but also as new potential privacy/security vulnerabilities that need to be secured.

2. WORKSHOP OBJECTIVE

The AISec Workshop serves as a venue where practical security problems merge with advances in AI and ML. In doing so, researchers also are developing theory and analytics unique to this domain and are exploring diverse topics including learning in game-theoretic adversarial environments, privacy-preserving learning, and applications to spam and intrusion detection. AI and ML provide a set of useful analytic and decision-making techniques that are being leveraged by an ever-growing community of practitioners, including in applications with security-sensitive elements. However, while security researchers often utilize such techniques to address problems and AI/ML researchers develop techniques for *big-data* analytics, those communities can only devote limited attention to the other: Within security research, AI/ML components are usually regarded as blackbox solvers. Conversely, the learning community seldom considers the security/privacy implications that application of their algorithms entails. While these two communities generally focus on different directions, where these two fields do meet, interesting new problems appear. These have already raised many novel questions for both communities and created a new branch of research known as secure learning. Within this intersection, the AISec Workshop has become the primary venue for this unique fusion of research.

3. TOPICS OF INTEREST

In terms of author audience, we solicited paper submissions with the following (but not limited to) research topics:

Learning Theory Topics related to Security

- Adversarial learning
- Robust statistics
- Online learning
- Learning in stochastic games

Security Applications

- Computer forensics
- Spam detection
- Phishing detection and prevention
- Botnet detection
- Intrusion detection and response
- Malware identification
- Authorship identification
- Big-data analytics for security

Security-related AI problems

- Distributed inference and decision-making for security
- Secure multiparty computation and cryptographic approaches
- Privacy-preserving data mining
- Adaptive side-channel attacks
- Design and analysis of CAPTCHAs
- AI approaches to trust and reputation
- Vulnerability testing through intelligent probing (*e.g.*, fuzzing)
- Content-driven security policy management and access control
- Techniques and methods for generating training and test sets
- Anomalous behavior detection (*e.g.*, for the purposes of fraud prevention, authentication)

4. PROGRAM COMMITTEE

We are thankful to the members of our program committee:

- Battista Biggio, University of Cagliari, Italy
- Ulf Brefeld, Technische Universitüt Darmstadt, Germay
- Michael Brückner, Amazon.com Inc, Germany
- Mike Burmester, Florida State University, USA
- Alvaro A. Cárdenas, University of Texas at Dallas, USA
- Mario Frank, University of California, Berkeley, USA
- Rachel Greenstadt, Drexel University, USA
- Guofei Gu, Texas A&M University, USA
- Ling Huang, Intel Labs, USA
- Anthony Joseph, University of California, Berkeley, USA
- Ari Juels, RSA Labs, USA
- Pavel Laskov, University of Tübingen, Germany
- Daniel Lowd, University of Oregon, USA
- Pratyusa Manadhata, HP Labs, USA
- Aikaterini Mitrokotsa, Chalmers University of Technology, Sweden
- Roberto Perdisci, University of Georgia, USA
- Vasyl Pihur, Google Inc., USA
- Konrad Rieck, University of Göttingen, Germany
- Fabio Roli, University of Cagliari, Italy
- Benjamin I. P. Rubinstein, IBM Research, Australia
- Robin Sommer, ICSI and LBNL, USA
- Nina Taft, Technicolor, USA
- J. D. Tygar, University of California, Berkeley, USA
- Shobha Venkataraman, AT&T Research, USA
- Ting-Fang Yen, RSA Labs

5. WORKSHOP ORGANIZERS

Blaine Nelson is a postdoctoral researcher at the University of Potsdam. He previously was a postdoctoral research fellow at the University of Tübingen and he obtained his Ph.D. from the University of California, Berkeley. He was a co-chair of the AISec 2012 and was a co-organizer of the Dagstuhl Workshop entitled "Machine Learning Methods for Computer Security" in 2012. His research focuses on learning algorithms particularly in the context of security-sensitive application domains. He investigates the vulnerability of learning to security threats and how resilient learning techniques can be used to mitigate such security threats.

Christos Dimitrakakis is a researcher at Chalmers University of Technology. His main research interest is decision theory, including reinforcement learning and problems in security applications. He obtained his Ph.D. in 2006 from EPFL, and was a researcher at the universities of Leoben, Amsterdam and Frankfurt. Most recently he was a Marie Curie Fellow at EPFL. He has co-organised a workshop on Privacy, Security, Data Mining and Machine Learning (PS-DML) in conjunction with ECML 2010.

Elaine Shi is an Assistant Professor in the Computer Science Department at University of Maryland, College Park. Her research combines systems security, cryptography, and data mining to design new computing systems that are secure and privacy-preserving. Dr. Shi obtained her Ph.D. from the Computer Science Department at Carnegie Mellon University in 2008. Prior to joining UMD, she was a Member of Research Staff at Xerox PARC, and a research scientist at UC Berkeley. Elaine Shi has served on the program committees of more than 25 conferences and workshops, and is also currently co-chairing a cloud security workshop under AsiaCCS. She has helped organize an NSF/Intel sponsored security curriculum workshop, and the Cross-Disciplinary Conversations session for the SaTC PI meeting in 2012.

The First Workshop on Language Support for Privacy-Enhancing Technologies (PETShop'13)

Martin Franz
Deutsche Bank

Andreas Holzer
Vienna University of Technology

Rupak Majumdar
MPI SWS Kaiserslautern

Bryan Parno
Microsoft Research

Helmut Veith
Vienna University of Technology

ABSTRACT

The Workshop on Language Support for Privacy-Enhancing Technologies (PETShop'13) aims at bringing together researchers from the areas of security, programming languages, compiler construction, and program verification to exchange ideas and research results to improve the practicality of state of the art cryptographic privacy-enhancing technologies.

Categories and Subject Descriptors

C.2.0 [**Computer-Communication Networks**]: General—*security and protection*

General Terms

Security, Languages

Keywords

Secure Multi-Party Computations; Zero-Knowledge Protocols; Programming Languages; Compiler Construction; Verification

1. BACKGROUND & MOTIVATION

Privacy enhancing technologies (PETs) are necessary when untrusted platforms compute on sensitive data, for example in a distributed setting or in cloud computing. Cryptography offers a rich set of privacy-enhancing technologies for such privacy-preserving computations, including secure multi-party computation (SMC) and zero-knowledge (ZK) protocols. These systems enable distrusting parties to collectively compute over their private inputs without revealing their data to the other parties. With the wide availability of distributed systems, social media, and cloud computing, there is a pressing need to make these technologies usable in practice. A key step towards practicality is the ability to compile from high-level languages, like C, into cryptographic protocols. Such cryptographic compilers have only recently begun to emerge, and they stand to benefit from decades of research in programming languages, compiler construction, and program verification. We believe that the concepts, methodologies, and tools developed in these areas of research can help to make cryptographic PETs practically available.

CCS'13, November 4–8, 2013, Berlin, Germany.
ACM 978-1-4503-2477-9/13/11.
http://dx.doi.org/10.1145/2508859.2509032.

2. GOALS & OBJECTIVES

PETShop is located at the crossroads of security, programming languages, compiler construction, and program verification and aims to bring together researchers from these different communities to exchange ideas and research results to improve the practicality of state of the art cryptographic PETs. In recent years, Europe has become a major center for research on verification and programming languages (e.g., as reflected by strong formal methods groups in Oxford, Cambridge, Munich, Kaiserslautern, Vienna, to name only a few), and we want to use the opportunity of having ACM CCS'13 in Berlin to bring together these researchers with the ACM CCS community.

3. TOPICS OF INTEREST

Topics of interest include (but are not limited to):

- Compiler optimizations for privacy-preserving computations, e.g., SMC or ZK protocols
- Programming language support for privacy-preserving computations
- Execution environments for privacy-preserving computations
- Experience reports, use cases, and implementations of privacy-preserving computations
- Tool demonstrations

4. FORMAT

The workshop features two invited talks, six short papers, and one invited paper covering several of the above mentioned topics. To emphasize the workshop character and the focus on the discussion of open challenges, the workshop focuses on short work-in-progress/position papers/extended abstracts which describe applications, problems, and new ideas in the field of multi-party computation. Especially we want to encourage authors of such submissions to later publish extended versions of their submissions at other venues.

5. WORKSHOP ORGANIZERS

- **Martin Franz** holds Diploma degrees in Mathematics and Computer Science and received a Ph.D. degree from Technische Universität Darmstadt. His dissertation investigates different techniques for secure computations on non-integer values and shows how to use these techniques in real world scenarios. During a research visit at Philips Research in Eindhoven, Netherlands, he contributed to the European Research Project SPEED (Signal Processing in the Encrypted Domain). After that he worked at CASED, the Center for Advanced Security Research Darmstadt. Martin Franz is currently working as an expert for applied cryptography and IT-Security at Deutsche Bank.
- **Andreas Holzer** is a research assistant at the Faculty of Informatics of Vienna University of Technology (TU Vienna). He has a diploma in Computer Science from the University of Applied Sciences Landshut and a M.Sc. from TU Munich and received a Ph.D. degree from University of Technology Vienna. His current work is focusing on software testing and computer security.
- **Rupak Majumdar** received the B.Tech. degree in Computer Science from the Indian Institute of Technology at Kanpur in 1998 and the Ph.D. degree in Computer Science from the University of California at Berkeley in 2003. He is currently a Scientific Director at the Max Planck Institute for Software Systems. Previously, he was a professor in the Department of Computer Science at the University of California, Los Angeles. His research interests are in the verification and control of reactive, real-time, hybrid, and probabilistic systems, software verification and programming languages, game theoretic problems in verification, logic, and automata theory. Dr. Majumdar received the President's Gold Medal from IIT, Kanpur, the Leon O. Chua award from UC Berkeley, an NSF CAREER award, a Sloan Foundation Fellowship, a PLDI "Test of time" award, and several best paper awards. Rupak Majumdar served as program co-chair at GDV 2005, SPIN 2008, SCC 2009, TACAS 2010. He served as program committee member of CAV 2005, CAV 2008, TACAS 2009, TACAS 2011, CAV 2012, VMCAI 2012, CAV 2013, ICALP 2013, VMCAI 2013 etc.
- **Bryan Parno** works in the Security and Privacy Research Group at Microsoft Research. He completed his PhD at Carnegie Mellon University under the supervision of Adrian Perrig. Dr. Parno's dissertation, which won the 2010 ACM Doctoral Dissertation Award, studies the design, implementation, and evaluation of a combination of hardware, software, and cryptographic primitives for extending the trust one has in one service or device in order to allow one to trust other services and devices. His current work focuses on protocols for verifiable computation and zero-knowledge proofs, building practical, formally verified secure systems, and developing next-generation application models. He published a book on *Bootstrapping Trust in Modern Computers*, and he served on the program committee for Oakland 2013, TRUST 2012 & 2013, NDSS 2011,2012, & 2013, CCS 2012, CCSW 2012, MobiHoc 2012, CANS 2011, PKC 2011, MobiSys 2010, FC 2009, etc.
- **Helmut Veith** is a professor at the Faculty of Informatics of Vienna University of Technology (TU Vienna), and an adjunct professor at Carnegie Mellon University. He has a diploma in Computational Logic and a PhD sub auspiciis praesidentis in Computer Science, both from Vienna University of Technology. Prior to his appointment to Vienna, he was holding professor positions at TU Darmstadt and TU Munich. His current work is focusing on model checking, software verification and testing, embedded software and computer security. Helmut Veith is program committee co-chair of CAV 2013, CSL 2009, LPAR 2008, and tutorial chair of FMCAD 2010. He served as program committee member of ATVA 2010, CAV 2003, CAV 2005, CAV 2009, CAV 2010, CAV 2012, CSL 2009, CSL 2011, CSL 2012, CSR 2007-2009, DATE 2011, DATE 2012, EC2 2009-2012, FMCAD 2009, FMCAD 2010, FMCAD 2011, FMICS 2011, FSTTCS 2007, HVC 2010, HVC 2011, ICTAC 2009, ICTAC 2010, ICTERI 2011, ICTERI 2012, LICS 2004, SOFSEM 2012, SPIN 2012, SYNASC 2008-2011, TACAS SW Verification Competition 2012, TASE 2011, VMCAI 2012, WING 2009, WING 2010, WOLLIC 2011 etc.

6. ACKNOWLEDGMENTS

This workshop was partially supported by the Austrian National Research Network S11403 and S11405 (RiSE) of the Austrian Science Fund (FWF) and by the Vienna Science and Technology Fund (WWTF) through grant PROSEED.

Fifth ACM Cloud Computing Security Workshop (CCSW 2013)

Ari Juels
ajuels@gmail.com

Bryan Parno
Microsoft Research
parno@microsoft.com

ABSTRACT

The Cloud Computing Security Workshop (CCSW) focuses on the security challenges and opportunities raised by cloud computing. The "cloud" is a general term for aggregation of computing resources within an extensive, elastic environment typically marked by a high degree of resource virtualization and sharing among tenants. As a multi-faceted trend, cloud computing creates many and varied security and privacy requirements at the intersection of a broad range of disciplines. The goal of the workshop is to elucidate the security and privacy problems raised by cloud computing and foster understanding of the connection between research and practice in this vibrant and transformative area.

Categories and Subject Descriptors

C.2.0 [**Computer-Communication Networks**]: Security and Protection; D.4.6 [**Operating Systems**]: Security and Protection; K.6.5 [**Management of Computing and Information Systems**]: Security and Protection; H.2.0 [**Database Management**]: GeneralSecurity, Integrity, and Protection; K.4.4 [**Electronic Commerce**]: Security; K.6.m [**Miscellaneous**]: Security

Keywords

Cloud Computing; Computer Security; Computer Privacy

1. INTRODUCTION

There are many definitions of the "cloud" and many historical and contemporary synonyms and subcategories (utility computing, grid computing, PaaS, etc.). All of these terms and ideas point toward the same trend: A consolidation of computing, storage, and networking resources within a single, typically shared infrastructure. Naturally, with many stakeholders and users operating side-by-side in a cloud environment, the security and privacy challenges are legion. But the news isn't all bad. Cloud computing also offers opportunities to improve security through the judicious use of virtualization, consolidation of security administrator duties, and general opportunities for rethinking security engineering in a new, centralized platform.

Since its inception in 2009, CCSW has become the premier venue for research on security and privacy in cloud computing. It has also produced some of the most popular and highly cited papers in the CCS family of workshops, and drawn an excellent and diverse range of invited speakers.

The workshop aims to bring together researchers and practitioners in all security aspects of cloud-centric and outsourced computing. Like CCS, its parent conference, CCSW offers a program spanning a broad range of topics and disciplines, including network security, consumer privacy, virtualization security, secure hardware, and cryptography—to name just a few.

CCS'13, November 4–8, 2013, Berlin, Germany.
ACM 978-1-4503-2477-9/13/11.
http://dx.doi.org/10.1145/2508859.2509033.

2. TOPICS OF INTEREST

The broad scope of CCSW is best reflected in the topics of interest enumerated in the workshop call for papers:

- Practical cryptographic protocols for cloud security
- Secure cloud resource virtualization mechanisms
- Secure data management outsourcing (e.g., database as a service)
- Practical privacy and integrity mechanisms for outsourcing
- Foundations of cloud-centric threat models
- Secure computation outsourcing
- Remote attestation mechanisms in clouds
- Sandboxing and VM-based enforcements
- Trust and policy management in clouds
- Secure identity management mechanisms
- New cloud-aware web service security paradigms and mechanisms
- Cloud-centric regulatory compliance issues and mechanisms
- Business and security risk models and clouds
- Cost and usability models and their interaction with security in clouds
- Scalability of security in global-size clouds
- Trusted computing technology and clouds
- Binary analysis of software for remote attestation and cloud protection
- Network security (DOS, IDS etc.) mechanisms for cloud contexts
- Security for emerging cloud programming models
- Energy/cost/efficiency of security in clouds

The workshop program this year includes research papers on probing cloud infrastructure, securely outsourcing computation, authenticating storage using trusted hardware, secure code execution, secure hardware, auditing, and various flavors of encryption.

3. PROGRAM COMMITTEE

We wish to offer thanks to the members of our program committee for their hard work in reviewing and discussing workshop submissions.

- Giuseppe Ateniese, Johns Hopkins University
- Kevin Bowers, RSA Laboratories
- Srdjan Capkun, ETH-Zurich
- Melissa Chase, Microsoft Research
- Haibo Chen, Shanghai Jiao Tong University
- George Danezis, Microsoft Research
- Anupam Datta, Carnegie Mellon University
- David Evans, University of Virginia
- Roxana Geambasu, Columbia University
- Andreas Haeberlen, University of Pennsylvania
- Amir Herzberg, Bar Ilan University
- Giles Hogben, Cloud Security Alliance
- Trent Jaeger, The Pennsylvania State University
- Xuxian Jiang, North Carolina State University
- Seny Kamara, Microsoft Research
- Farinaz Koushanfar, Rice University
- Andres Lagar-Cavilla, GridCentric Inc.
- Ruby Lee, Princeton University
- David Lie, University of Toronto
- Petros Maniatis, Intel Labs
- Cristina Nita-Rotaru, Purdue University
- Alina Oprea, RSA Labs
- Mariana Raykova, IBM Research
- Thomas Ristenpart, University of Wisconsin
- Ahmad-Reza Sadeghi, TU Darmstadt
- Pierangela Samarati, Universita' degli Studi di Milano
- Matthias Schunter, Intel Labs
- Elaine Shi, University of Maryland
- Nigel Smart, University of Bristol, UK
- Sean Smith, Dartmouth College
- Leendert van Doorn, AMD, Inc.
- Yinglian Xie, Microsoft Research Silicon Valley
- Dongyan Xu, Purdue University

4. INVITED SPEAKERS

We are delighted to have three invited excellent speakers representing both industry and research perspectives on cloud security. They are:

- Daniele Catteddu
  Managing Director EMEA
  Cloud Security Alliance
- Marnix Dekker
  Security Expert and Information Security Officer
  European Network and Information Security Agency (ENISA)
- Slava Kavsan
  Partner Security Development Manager (Azure)
  Microsoft

CCS'13 Co-Located Workshop Summary for SPSM 2013

Adrienne Porter Felt
Google, USA
felt@google.com

N. Asokan
Aalto University & University of Helsinki, Finland
asokan@acm.org

ABSTRACT

Security and privacy in smartphones and mobile devices is an emerging area which has received significant attention from the research community during the past few years. The SPSM workshop was created to bring together these researchers and practitioners. Following the success of the two previous editions, we present this third edition of the workshop which has attracted significantly more submissions and benefited from the expertise of an expanded international program committee.

Categories and Subject Descriptors

D.4.6 [**Operating Systems**]: Security and Protection; H.3.4 [**Systems and Software**]: User Profiles and Alert Services; K.6.5 [**Management of Computing and Information Systems**]: Security and Protection; C.4 [**Computer Systems Organization**]: Performance of Systems

General Terms

Security, Management, Experimentation

Keywords

Smartphones; mobile devices; security; privacy; malware; permission

1. INTRODUCTION

Mobile devices such as smartphones and Internet tablets have achieved computing and networking capabilities comparable to traditional personal computers. Their successful consumerization has also become a source of pain for adopting users and organizations. For example, the widespread presence of information-stealing applications raises substantial security and privacy concerns. The operating systems supporting these new devices have both advantages and disadvantages with respect to security. On one hand, they use application sandboxing to contain exploits and limit privileges given to malware. On the other hand, they routinely collect and organize many forms of security- and privacy-sensitive information and make that information easily accessible to third-party applications. Recognizing smartphone security and privacy as an emerging area, this workshop was launched three years ago to provide a venue for interested researchers and practitioners to get together and exchange ideas. We set out to organize the third workshop in the series, building on the success of the two previous well-attended editions.

CCS'13, November 4–8, 2013, Berlin, Germany.
ACM 978-1-4503-2477-9/13/11.
http://dx.doi.org/10.1145/2508859.2509034.

2. TOPICS OF INTEREST

Authors were invited to submit either Full Research Papers (of up to 12 pages) or Short Papers (of up to 6 pages). Full Research Papers that present relatively complete and mature research results on security and privacy in smartphones and mobile devices were solicited. Short Papers that define new problems in security and privacy related to smartphones and mobile devices or provide inspiring visions were also solicited. The call for papers highlighted the following topics of interest.

- Device/hardware security
- OS/Middleware security
- Application security
- Authenticating users to devices and services
- Mobile Web Browsers
- Usability
- Privacy
- Rogue application detection and recovery
- Vulnerability detection and remediation
- Secure application development
- Cloud support for mobile security

We especially encouraged novel paradigms and controversial ideas that are not on the above list. The workshop is to act as a venue for creative debate and interaction in security- and privacy-sensitive areas of computing and communication impacted by smartphones.

3. WORKSHOP PROGRAM

We received a record 54 submissions this year. They came from 19 different countries in Europe, North America, Asia and Africa. The program committee accepted 5 full papers and 8 short papers that cover a variety of topics, including detecting malware on smartphones, attacks and defenses against mobile devices, and authentication and privacy issues of mobile users. We are especially pleased to have a keynote speech by Jon Geator, Chief Technology Officer of Trustonic. We hope that these proceedings will serve as a valuable reference for security researchers and developers.

We put together a larger program committee this year, and invited several mobile security experts from outside North America to lend an international flavor to the PC. Every paper received at least three expert reviews. We like to thank the PC members (listed below) for their dedication and hard work for their timely reviews and active discussion.

- Sruthi Bandhakavi, Google
- David Barrera, Carleton University
- Ravishankar Borgaonkar, Technische Universität Berlin
- Billy Brumley, Qualcomm
- Mike Dietz, Rice University
- Hao Chen, University of California, Davis
- Jan-Erik Ekberg, TrustOnIC
- Aurélien Francillon, Eurecom
- Mario Frank, University of California, Berkeley
- Rajarshi Gupta, Qualcomm Research Silicon Valley
- Urs Hengartner, University of Waterloo
- Ling Huang, Intel Labs
- Maritza Johnson, Facebook
- Jaeyeon Jung, Microsoft Research
- Mike Just, Glasgow Caledonian University
- Kari Kostiainen, Swiss Federal Institute of Technology, Zurich (ETHZ)
- Janne Lindqvist, Rutgers University
- Patrick McDaniel, Pennsylvania State University
- Panos Papadimitratos, Royal Institute of Technology, Sweden
- Franzi Roesner, University of Washington
- Patrick Traynor, Georgia Institute of Technology
- Marcel Winandy, Ruhr-Universität Bochum
- Glenn Wurster, BlackBerry
- Xinwen Zhang, Huawei

The organization was guided by Will Enck, co-founder of SPSM who served as General Chair this year. Luca Davi, the Publications Chair, was instrumental in publicising the workshop successfully and putting the proceedings together. Our sincere thanks to Will and Luca.

Smart Energy Grid Security Workshop (SEGS'13)

Klaus Kursawe
ENCS
Prinses Beatrixlaan 800
The Hague, The Netherlands
klaus.kursawe@encs.eu

Benessa Defend
ENCS
Prinses Beatrixlaan 800
The Hague, The Netherlands
benessa.defend@encs.eu

ABSTRACT

The Smart Energy Grid Security (SEGS) Workshop aims to foster innovative research and discussion about smart energy grid security and privacy challenges, issues, approaches, and solutions. SEGS publications offer perspectives from both academia and industry, and present novel research on theoretical and practical aspects of smart grid security and privacy, including design, analysis, experimentation, and fielded systems. SEGS also includes presentations from other communities, such as law, economics, and HCI, that present these communities' perspectives on technological issues. The scope of the workshop encompasses all aspects of the smart grid, including distribution, transmission, generation, metering, e-mobility, and integration of distributed energy resources.

Categories and Subject Descriptors

C.2.0 [**Computer-Communication Networks**]: General—*Security and protection (e.g., firewalls)*; C.3 [**Special-Purpose and Application-Based Systems**]: Real-time and embedded systems; D.4.6 [**Operating Systems**]: Security and Protection; J.7 [**Computers in Other Systems**]: Industrial Control; K.4.1 [**Computers and Society**]: Public Policy Issues; K.6.5 [**Management of Computing and Information Systems**]: Security and Protection

Keywords

smart grid; critical infrastructure; security; data protection; privacy

1. INTRODUCTION

Smart grid security is an upcoming topic of great importance, but there is currently little understanding and communication between the electricity sector and the security community. The subject of smart grids has been discussed in industry for many years now and smart meters have already been deployed in multiple countries around the world. There are over 20 annual conferences and events sponsored by utilities and leaders in the energy industry. However, there is currently a large gap in the security research community specifically addressing smart grids. This workshop aims to fill that void and encourage more research into the area of smart grid security by providing a forum for security researchers to present their work. The workshop also includes an invited speaker from the electricity sector who will share his expertise with the audience and thus help in guiding future research efforts. This workshop serves as an opportunity to foster collaboration between the power industry and the ACM CCS research community.

2. TOPICS OF INTEREST

The SEGS Workshop focuses on the following topics:

- Smart grid architectures and models
- Smart grid networks and communication
- Security and dependability in safety-critical, real-time systems
- Data protection and privacy
- Grid management
- Trust and assurance
- Intrusion detection and monitoring on smart grids
- Algorithms and protocols for critical infrastructures
- Risk and threat analysis
- Smart grid standards, testing, and certification
- Testbeds and field trials
- Usability and legal issues on grid security
- Cloud computing and smart grids

3. FORMAT

SEGS is a full-day workshop on the final day of the ACM CCS 2013 Conference. The program includes an invited talk called "The Future of Smart Grids". The talk will be given by an expert from the power industry, who can give an insider view on the security issues, requirements, and approaches taken right now and on the development of the smart grid in the future. In addition to the invited talk, the program is split into four sessions consisting of presentations from six regular papers and six short papers.

CCS'13, November 4–8, 2013, Berlin, Germany.
ACM 978-1-4503-2477-9/13/11.
http://dx.doi.org/10.1145/2508859.2509035.

4. PROGRAM COMMITTEE

We are thankful for the service of our program committee members:

- Kevin Butler, University of Oregon, US
- George Danezis, Microsoft Research, UK
- Benessa Defend, ENCS, Netherlands (Organizer)
- Sandro Etalle, TU Eindhoven and University of Twente, Netherlands
- Raymond Hallie, ENCS and Alliander, Netherlands
- Maarten Hoeve, ENCS, Netherlands
- David Irwin, University of Massachusetts Amherst, US
- Michael John, Elster, Germany
- Stefan Katzenbeisser, Technische Universität Darmstadt, Germany
- Himanshu Khurana, Honeywell, US
- Erwin Kooi, Alliander, Netherlands
- Maryna Krotofil, Hamburg University of Technology, Germany
- Klaus Kursawe, ENCS, Netherlands (Chair and Organizer)
- Stephen McLaughlin, Pennsylvania State University, US
- Andrès Molina-Markham, Dartmouth College, US
- Christof Paar, Ruhr University Bochum, Germany
- Nathanael Paul, Oak Ridge National Laboratory and University of Tennessee, US
- Erik Poll, Radboud University, Netherlands
- Bart Preneel, KU Leuven, Belgium
- Ahmad-Reza Sadeghi, Technische Universität Darmstadt, Germany
- Matthias Schunter, ICRI-SC, Germany
- Gene Tsudik, University of California Irvine, US
- Eyal Udassin, C4 Security, Israel
- Alfonso Valdes, University of Illinois Urbana-Champaign, US
- Jos Weyers, TenneT, Netherlands
- Kenzo Yoshimatsu, Control System Security Center, Japan

Eighth *ACM* Workshop on Digital Identity Management (DIM 2013): Identity at the Crossroads

Thomas Groß
School of Computing Science, Newcastle University
Claremont Tower, Newcastle upon Tyne, NE17RU
United Kingdom
+44 191 222 8987
thomas.gross@newcastle.ac.uk

Marit Hansen
Unabhängiges Landeszentrum für Datenschutz
Holstenstr. 98, 24103 Kiel
Germany
+49 431 988-1214
marit.hansen@privacyresearch.eu

ABSTRACT

The Workshop Digital Identity Management has evolved during the last decade as one of the most interesting events on identity management issues. Starting from a community with a background mainly in computer science, it has developed towards an interdisciplinary workshop where a lively interactive community discusses identity topics from technical, sociological, economical, legal, psychological and many more angles. The goal of this workshop is to share the latest findings, identify key challenges, inspire debates, and foster collaboration between industries and academia towards interoperable identity service infrastructures.

Categories and Subject Descriptors

K.4.1 [**Computers and Society**]: Public Policy Issues – *privacy*; K.4.4 [**Computers and Society**]: Electronic Commerce – *security*; K.6.5 [**Management of Computing and Information Systems**]: Security and Protection – *authentication, unauthorized access*; D.4.6 [**Operating Systems**]: Security and Protection – *access controls, authentication, cryptographic controls*; E.3 [**Data**]: Data Encryption; J.4 [**Social and Behavioral Sciences**]: Psychology, Sociology; H.5.2 [**Information Interfaces and Presentation**]: User Interfaces – *evaluation/methodology*.

Keywords

Identity, Identity Management, eID, Privacy, Security.

1. INTRODUCTION

"Identity at the crossroads" is the main theme of DIM 2013. Whereas identity management has become a standard method for authentication in the digital world, many of its facets that are dealt with in research and in practice are still not well understood. Particularly interesting are discussions which solutions are optimal for different areas of application, how we can promote positive aspects for individuals and society while preventing negative effects, and how we can transfer research results into practice.

CCS'13, November 4–8, 2013, Berlin, Germany.
ACM 978-1-4503-2477-9/13/11.
http://dx.doi.org/10.1145/2508859.2509036

At the same time, the environment of our digital lives and of identity management systems is rapidly changing:

We have seen the Internet going mobile and social: In October 2012 the number of smartphones in use on this planet exceeded 1 billion and is projected to double by 2015 [1]. The global social network platform Facebook has passed the 1 billion user mark as well [2].

We notice adoptions of identity federation systems and other digital identity platforms, either enabling single sign-on for multiple applications such as in Google Accounts or reaching out to third-party applications such as in Facebook Connect.

Recently, we have perceived tremendous improvements in identity management technologies (see e.g. [3,4]), in particular when it comes to the maturity of attribute-based credential systems, the cryptography ensuring security and privacy properties, and other privacy-preserving or privacy-enhancing technologies (PETs).

We observe governments all over Europe and, indeed, all over the planet to propose eID solutions that partially support privacy mechanisms and frequently allow the government-issued identity credentials to be tied into an identity federation ecosystem.

We witness advances in technology and operating environments such as social networks, mobile devices, smartphones, tablets as well as upcoming smart TVs, wearable computing (e.g. Google Glass, iWatch) that start to impact social habits and individuals' behavior. The direct experience of new technology is flanked by news reports on incidents, mostly on privacy violations and surveillance. Both lead to questions what impact on society these new technologies will have.

Identity is at the crossroads. It is an open question how identity technology will affect societies – societies that are affected by mobile computing and social network services, by data processing in the cloud and almost comprehensive monitoring, user tracking and big data analysis by stakeholders such as the advertisement industry on the one side and national secret services on the other side, or by emerging technologies such as ubiquitous computing or cyber-physical systems where new user interfaces have to be considered. Will identity technologies make the users' lives easier or will they put their privacy at risk?

We believe that the ACM Digital Identity Management workshop series needs to address these issues in all their breadth, covering foundational technologies such as cryptography and integration with eID systems, over investigating technology and architecture challenges to be resolved to exploring the social impact of identity management. With the year's workshop we have covered these areas, constituting a program with experts from different fields of identity.

2. WORKSHOP FORMAT

The DIM 2013 workshop will be a full-day event, starting with a keynote by Claudia Díaz, KU Leuven, on privacy-enhancing technologies and their role in the identity management world. Four sessions are constituted by accepted full and short papers, covering a range between cryptographic foundations and socio-psychological findings. In the afternoon, a panel will start with questions concerning eIDs and their actual development from different perspectives. All participants are invited to join with statements on shaping the future of identity – be it by tackling research topics or by deploying solutions for better identity management.

3. WORKSHOP CONTRIBUTIONS

We clustered the accepted contributions of eight full papers and three short papers into four groups. Right after the invited keynote on privacy-enhancing technologies, the session on "Cryptographic Methods" will continue the elaboration of components that can support privacy and security features of identity management systems: *'Universally Composable Adaptive Oblivious Transfer (with Access Control) from Standard Assumptions'*, *'A Secure Channel for Attribute-Based Credentials'*, and *'UbiKiMa: Ubiquitous Authentication Using a Smartphone, Migrating from Passwords to Strong Cryptography'*.

The second session will focus on "Human Factors and Socio-Economic Aspects". It consists of three contributions that center around acceptance and employment of identity-related functionality by users: *'A Comparison of Users' Perceptions of and Willingness to Use Google, Facebook, and Google+ Single-Sign-On Functionality'*, *'Taboos and Desires of the UK Public for Identity Management in the Future; General Findings from Two Survey Games'*, and *'Probing Identity Management – Preliminary Findings'*.

Switching back to more technically oriented contributions, the third session will deal with "Security Considerations", e.g. by showing possible attacks and counter-measures or other improvements of existing systems. The three contributions are: *'Geo-Location Based QR-Code Authentication Scheme to Defeat Active Real-Time Phishing Attack'*, *'Towards Standardizing Trusted Evidence of Identity'*, and *'Reachability Analysis for Role-Based Administration of Attributes'*.

The last session of the workshop on "eIDs and Identity Management" mixes the disciplines the contributions come from. After the presentation of a technical approach for an eID architecture in *'Options for Integrating eID and SAML'* the perspective of citizens is highlighted by the contribution *'Federated Identity to Access e-Government Services – Are Citizens Ready for This?'* The findings of both papers will be taken up in the concluding panel on the future of eIDs and identity management.

4. WORKSHOP ORGANIZATION

The workshop organization would not have been feasible without the help of many individuals. We are thankful to the members of our steering committee and our program committee as well as the publicity chair Budi Arief, Newcastle University, UK.

Steering Committee

- Elisa Bertino, Purdue University, USA
- Abhilasha Bhargav-Spanzel, Intel, USA
- Thomas Groß, Newcastle University, UK
- Kenji Takahashi, NTT Innovation Institute Inc., USA

Program Committee

- Gail-Joon Ahn, Arizona State University, USA
- Elisa Bertino, Purdue University, USA
- Abhilasha Bhargav-Spantzel, Intel, USA
- Sonja Buchegger, KTH, Stockholm, Sweden
- Marco Casassa Mont, HP Labs, UK
- David Chadwick, University of Kent, UK
- Melissa Chase, Microsoft Research, USA
- Chi-hung Chi, Tsinghua University, China
- Simone Fischer-Hübner, Karlstad University, Sweden
- Lothar Fritsch, Norwegian Computing Center, Norway
- Hidehito Gomi, Yahoo! Japan Research, Japan
- Thomas Groß, Newcastle University, UK
- Weili Han, Fudan University, China
- Marit Hansen, ULD, Germany
- Jaap-Henk Hoepman, Radboud University Nijmegen, Netherlands
- Seung-Hyun Kim, ETRI, Korea
- Howard Lipson, CERT, USA
- Maciej Machulak, Cloud Identity/Newcastle University, UK
- Eve Maler, Forrester Research, USA
- Siani Pearson, Hewlett-Packard Laboratories, UK
- Kai Rannenberg, Goethe University, Frankfurt, Germany
- Jörg Schwenk, Ruhr-University Bochum, Germany
- Kent Seamons, Brigham Young University, USA
- Jon A. Solworth, University of Illinois at Chicago, USA
- Sandra Steinbrecher, SAP Research, Germany
- Kenji Takahashi, NTT Innovation Institute Inc., USA
- Jozef Vyskoč, VaF, Slovakia
- Peter Weik, T-Systems, Germany

5. REFERENCES

[1] Deagon, B. 2012. Apple, Samsung Lead As Smartphones Top 1 Billion. *Investor's Business Daily*, Oct. 17, 2012. http://news.investors.com/technology/101712-629662-apple-samsung-lead-1-billion-smartphone-in-use.htm.

[2] Facebook 2013. *Key Facts.* Facebook Newsroom, June 30, 2013. https://newsroom.fb.com/Key-Facts.

[3] ABC4Trust 2013. Website of the EU Project *ABC4Trust – Attribute-Based Credentials for Trust.* https://abc4trust.eu/.

[4] Alpár, G. and Jacobs, B. 2013. Credential Design in Attribute-Based Identity Management. In *Bridging Distances in Technology and Regulation*, R. Leenes and E. Kosta, Eds. Wolf Legal Publishers, Netherlands, 189-204.

Constructive and Destructive Aspects of Embedded Security in the Internet of Things

Christof Paar
Horst Görtz Institute for IT-Security
Ruhr Universität Bochum, Germany
christof.paar@rub.de

Through the prevalence of interconnected embedded systems, the vision of pervasive computing has become reality over the last few years. More recently, this evolutionary development has become better known as the Internet of Things. As part of this development, embedded security has become an increasingly important issue in a multitude of applications. Examples include the Stuxnet virus, which has allegedly delayed the Iranian nuclear program, killer applications in the consumer area like iTunes or Amazon's Kindle (the business models of which rely on IP protection) and even medical implants like pace makers and insulin pumps that allow remote configuration. These examples show the destructive and constructive aspects of modern embedded security. In this tutorial we will address both the constructive and "penetration testing" aspect of embedded security.

In the area of destructive embedded security implementation attacks, also known as physical attacks, are of crucial importance. Whereas a network-borne attacker usually can't exploit the physical environment of an application, embedded devices often allow this. For instance, an attacker can monitor the power or timing behavior of a device. Also she can force the device to malfunction, e.g., through power spikes, and deduct information from faulty outputs. Many systems which are otherwise secure become vulnerable against implementation attacks. In this talk, we will focus on side-channel attacks, or SCA, which form arguably the most powerful method among physical attacks. After developing the mechanics of DPA (differential power analysis), we will look at recent case studies in which real-world implementation were broken using SCA. This includes successful attacks against contactless smart cards and FPGAs.

With respect to constructive aspects of embedded security, we will look at the field of lightweight cryptography. The goal here is to provide security at the lowest possible "cost", e.g., measured in power consumption, code size or chip area. Over the last six years or so, this has become a very active area within symmetric cryptography. Very recently, even NSA released two lightweight ciphers, SIMON and SPECK. We will look at the motiviation for such ciphers, e.g., for passive RFID tags or anti-counterfeiting applications. We will then introduce several lightweight constructions and will compare them with AES.

Categories and Subject Descriptors

A.1 [**Introductory and Survey**]:

Keywords

security; embedded security; Internet of things; implementation attacks

CCS'13, November 4–8, 2013, Berlin, Germany.
ACM 978-1-4503-2477-9/13/11..

Trusted Execution Environments on Mobile Devices

Jan-Erik Ekberg
Trustonic
jan-erik.ekberg@trustonic.com

Kari Kostiainen
ETH Zurich
kari.kostiainen@inf.ethz.ch

N. Asokan
University of Helsinki
asokan@acm.org

ABSTRACT

A trusted execution environment (TEE) is a secure processing environment that is isolated from the "normal" processing environment where the device operating system and applications run. The first mobile phones with hardware-based TEEs appeared almost a decade ago, and today almost every smartphone and tablet contains a TEE like ARM TrustZone. Despite such a large-scale deployment, the use of TEE functionality has been limited for developers. With emerging standardization this situation is about to change. In this tutorial, we explain the security features provided by mobile TEEs and describe On-board Credentials (ObC) system that enables third-party TEE development. We discuss ongoing TEE standardization activities, including the recent Global Platform standards and the Trusted Platform Module (TPM) 2.0 specification, and identify open problems for the near future of mobile hardware security.

Categories and Subject Descriptors

K.6.5 [**Management of Computing and Information Systems**]: Security and Protection

Keywords

Trusted execution environments; mobile devices

1. INTRODCUTION

A *trusted execution environment* (TEE) is a secure, integrity-protected processing environment, consisting of processing, memory and storage capabilities. It is *isolated* from the "normal" processing environment, sometimes called the *rich execution environment* (REE), where the device operating system and applications run. TEEs can make it possible to build REE applications and services with better security and usability by partitioning them so that sensitive operations are restricted to the TEE and sensitive data never leave the TEE. In our daily lives, we encounter more and more services that use dedicated hardware tokens to improve their security: one-time code tokens for two-factor authentication, wireless tokens for opening doors in buildings or cars, tickets for public transport, and so on. Mobile devices equipped with TEEs have the potential for replacing these many tokens thereby improving the usability for users while also reducing the cost for the service providers without hampering security.

Chances are that the mobile device in your pocket sports a hardware-based TEE. Chances are, too, that you have not come across too many applications that actually make use of TEE functionality. In this tutorial, we explain why this situation came to pass and what the future may hold.

Security in mobile world had a very different trajectory compared to the world of personal computers. Various stakeholders had strict security requirements, some of which date back to two decades ago, right at the beginning of the explosion of personal mobile communications. Standardization requirements like ensuring that the device identifier will resist manipulation and change, regulatory requirements like ensuring secure storage for radio frequency parameters, business requirements like ensuring that subsidy locks, and end user expectations (e.g., no blue screen of death) incentivized mobile device manufacturers, chip vendors and platform providers to design and deploy hardware and platform security mechanisms for mobile platforms from early on. Hardware-based TEEs were seen as essential building blocks in meeting these requirements. The first mobile phones with hardware-based TEEs appeared almost a decade ago, and today almost every smartphone and tablet contains a TEE like ARM TrustZone, along with software platform security mechanisms.

Despite such a large-scale deployment, the use of TEE functionality has been largely restricted to its original intended uses. There has been no widely available means for application developers to benefit from existing TEE functionality. Fortunately, with emerging standardization this situation is about to change.

In this tutorial, we explain the security features provided by TEEs and describe *On-board Credentials* (ObC), a system that we developed at Nokia Researcher Center for safely opening up access to TEE functionality for application developers. We demonstrate the possibilities of TEEs with a programming example using the ObC system, discuss ongoing TEE standardization activities, including the recent Global Platform standards and the Trusted Platform Module (TPM) 2.0 specification, and identify open research questions for the near future of mobile hardware security.

CCS'13, November 4–8, 2013, Berlin, Germany.
ACM 978-1-4503-2477-9/13/11.
http://dx.doi.org/10.1145/2508859.2516758.

2. TUTORIAL DESCRIPTION

2.1 Structure and Length

The total length of the tutorial is *three hours.* The tutorial consists of the following parts:

1. **A look back.** We start the tutorial with a brief historical background on development of mobile security. We explain the business, regulatory, and end user requirements that have steered introduction of platform security features to mobile devices over the past two decades. (15 minutes)

2. **Mobile hardware security.** We proceed by explaining typical mobile hardware security functionality in a conceptual level. We describe mechanisms present in a typical mobile TEE, including secure boot, secure storage, isolated execution, immutable device identifiers and devices authentication. We introduce ARM TrustZone architecture [1] that is widely deployed in a majority of existing smartphones, and explain how TrustZone can be used to implement many of the previously described hardware security mechanisms in practice. (30 minutes)

3. **Application development and ObC.** The current standardized and de-facto hardware security APIs (e.g., PKCS-11 [4] and JSR-177 [5]) allow secure storage of cryptographic keys and execution of pre-defined cryptographic computation. To take full advantage of the isolated execution capabilities of mobile TEEs different kinds of API abstraction are needed. We describe On-board Credentials (ObC) system [3] that we have developed at Nokia Research Center. The ObC system serves as an example of an architecture that allows third-parties to develop and deploy credentials on TrustZone enabled devices. We explain the ObC architecture, its open provisioning model, developer interfaces, and a few example applications. Both the ObC system and applications built on top of it have been deployed on recent Nokia Lumia device models. We provide a brief demonstration of ObC application development in practice. (40 minutes)

   Break. (15 minutes)

4. **Emerging standardization.** We explain recent and on-going standardization activities regarding mobile TEEs. We briefly explain the set of APIs that Global Platform [2] has specified for usage of hardware-security functionality in mobile devices. After that, we focus in more detail on the recently published Trusted Platform Module (TPM) 2.0 standard [6]. We especially explore the new authorization model introduced in TPM 2.0 and examine its potential in use cases like secure boot and provisioning. (60 minutes)

5. **Summary and a look ahead.** We end the tutorial we a brief summary and identify open issues and research questions for mobile hardware security in near future. (10 minutes)

2.2 Level of Detail

The first two parts of the tutorial will provide the audience a background information on mobile hardware security. We describe the historical development, the common hardware-security features, and the TrustZone architecture in a fairly high level. After that we provide mode detailed treatment on two topics: application development and standardization. In these parts the tutorial gets more technical: we explain the ObC system architecture and provisioning model in detail, and, for example, cover individual TPM 2 instructions and data structures to explain the functionality of this emerging security standard. The ObC demo part illustrates practical TEE development on a programming level.

2.3 Intended Audience

This tutorial is intended for researchers and practitioners interested in mobile security in general and development of novel hardware-security services in particular. Successful following of the first half (parts 1-3) of the tutorial does not require any prior knowledge of mobile hardware security architectures. Basic background knowledge on mobile operating system security (e.g., Android OS security model) or embedded system security (e.g., smart card security) will help the listener to place some of the the explained concepts to context, but such background knowledge is not mandatory for following the tutorial. Basic background knowledge of mobile application development is useful for following the ObC demo part, but not mandatory.

In the second half of the tutorial (part 4) we discuss emerging hardware security standards, especially the recently introduced TPM 2.0 specification. To follow the standardization part, some background knowledge of basic trusted computing basic concepts, such as TPM commands and data structures, is useful. Our intention is to focus on the concepts and features that are new in TPM 2.0 specification, and we do not to give a complete description of TPM 1.2 as a background.

After the tutorial, the audience should have a good overall understanding on the security mechanisms that TEEs provide in current mobile devices, and what type of applications one can develop for TEEs. The audience should also have a basic understanding on recent and currently on-going standardization regarding mobile TEEs. These standardized interfaces are likely to make TEE programming possible for third-party developers, and the purpose of our tutorial is to raise the awareness of such emerging TEE development possibilities both in the research community as well as among practitioners.

3. REFERENCES

[1] ARM. Trustzone technology overview, 2009.

[2] GlobalPlatform. GlobalPlatform's GPD/STIP Solution for Mobile Security, August 2007. GlobalPlatform white paper.

[3] Kari Kostiainen, Jan-Erik Ekberg, N. Asokan, and Aarne Rantala. On-board credentials with open provisioning. In *Proceedings of ACM Symposium on Information, Computer and Communications Security (ASIACCS)*, 2009.

[4] RSA Laboratories. PKCS # 11 v2.20: Cryptographic Token Interface Standard, 2004.

[5] Oracle. JSR 177: Security and trust services API for J2ME, 2007.

[6] Trusted Computing Group. TPM 2.0 library specification, parts 1-4, Level 00, Rev. 00.96, March 2013.

Easily Instrumenting Android Applications for Security Purposes

Eric Bodden Secure Software Engineering Group
European Center for Security and Privacy by Design (EC SPRIDE)
Technische Universität Darmstadt & Fraunhofer SIT
Darmstadt, Germany
eric.bodden@ec-spride.de

ABSTRACT

With the increasing market share of the Android operating system, the platform also becomes more and more interesting for adversaries. Current malware on the Android platform exhibits a very diverse spectrum of malicious behaviors such as sending text messages to costly premium rate numbers [6,21], infecting connected computes with malware [12], or abusing the phone's resources for bot networks [16,20,21]. In addition, many smartphones users store highly privacy-sensitive data like calendars, personal photos, SMS messages, e-mails and more on their phones. Adversaries can attempt to access this data without the user's consent for the purpose of (industrial) espionage or targeted advertisement campaigns.

Such attacks are usually carried out using malicious applications which, e.g., pretend to be a game, but also contain malicious code embedded by the original developer. Such attacks are successful since users can hardly estimate the trustworthiness of applications offered in the different markets. Various approaches for analyzing the behavior of untrusted applications have thus been proposed, both static and dynamic [4, 5, 7–11, 13, 15, 18, 19]. While static approaches attempt to assess a program in a black-box fashion by looking at its (binary) code, dynamic analysis monitor the actual execution of the target program.

In this tutorial, we will focus on dynamic instrumentation, i.e., program rewriting techniques. Instrumenting the program gives access to full runtime information, e.g., user inputs and environment settings, which greatly increases the precision of detected policy violations. Additionally, countermeasures can directly be taken by, e.g., blocking the call to a costly premium rate number of asking the user for consent before proceeding.

We will show three different possibilities for instrumenting Android applications. Firstly, we will use the AspectBench compiler (abc) [1] to declaratively define instrumentations using AspectJ. We will then extend this approach to Tracematches [2] allowing finite-state policies to be expressed (e.g., no more than three SMS messages to the same phone number, to prevent spam). We will show where such techniques are applicable based on practical examples from the Android world and will also point out where their respective limits are.

Finally, we will show how to manually instrument applications by loading them into Soot [14], directly manipulating the *Jimple* intermediate representation and then producing a new application package containing the modifications for maximum flexibility both in terms of program changes and the policies to be enforced. We will use this technique to solve example problems that were not applicable to AspectJ and Tracematches.

Further background information on abc and Soot as well as general remarks on platform-specific aspects of program instrumentation on Android will also be given. Unlike system-level approaches like TaintDroid [5], instrumenting the application's bytecode at the application level requires no modifications to the operating system and does not require root access to the device either. The instrumented applications can be installed and used as usual with no visible difference to the user, only differing in behavior when an instrumented action is triggered.

CCS'13, November 4–8, 2013, Berlin, Germany.
ACM 978-1-4503-2477-9/13/11.
http://dx.doi.org/10.1145/2508859.2516759.

Categories and Subject Descriptors

D.4.6 [**Security and Protection**]: Access controls

General Terms

Security

Keywords

Android, Runtime Enforcement, Instrumentation, Dynamic Analysis

1. AUDIENCE AND PREREQUISITES

This tutorial is intended for security researchers interested in instrumenting or rewriting applications on the Android platform. Previous knowledge of Android application development is helpful but not a strict requirement, as example applications and a short introduction will be given. For the parts on AspectJ and Tracematches, basic knowledge of the respective concepts is advantageous. However, the examples given in the tutorial can also be used as a starting point for approaching the topic.

2. PROPOSED TIMELINE

We propose the following rough timeline:

- Background: The Android platform and its application architecture
- Background: The Android SDK and its tools for developers
- Background: Soot and its Jimple intermediate representation
- Background: Conversion of Android's dalvik bytecode into Jimple and back
- Hands-on: Converting an app into Jimple and inspecting its code
- High-level instrumentation: Using tracematches to instrument Android code
- Hands-on: Tracematch instrumentation, re-packaging and execution in emulator
- Limitations of tracematches
- More fine-grained instrumentation with AspectJ aspects
- Hands-on: AspectJ instrumentation, re-packaging and execution in emulator
- Limitations of AspectJ
- More fine-grained, manual instrumentation with Soot and Jimple
- Hands-on: Jimple instrumentation, re-packaging and execution in emulator
- Outlook: Combination with static analysis
- Wrap-up

3. PREVIOUS TUTORIALS

An abc tutorial was held at AOSD 2006, however, did not focus on runtime monitoring. The last tutorial on Soot was at PLDI 2003 and focused on static analysis rather than instrumentation. There has never been a tutorial on the combination of Soot, abc and Android.

Furthermore, we have been invited to give a tutorial on Java and Android instrumentation using Soot and abc at RV 2013. The CCS tutorial will be an improved iteration, re-targeted specifically for the security community.

4. BIOGRAPHY OF PRESENTERS

In the Android space, the Secure Software Engineering Group is known for its work on the FlowDroid static taint-analysis system for Android [8], the DroidBench benchmark suite [17] for Android taint analysis and the SuSi [3] tool for the semi-automatic detection of sources and sinks of private information in Android applications.

Prof. Dr. Eric Bodden. Eric is heading the Secure Software Engineering group at the Fraunhofer Institute for Secure Information Technology (SIT), the Technische Universität Darmstadt and the European Center for Security and Privacy by Design (EC SPRIDE). He is also a principal investigator at the Center for Advanced Security Research Darmstadt (CASED). Eric is heading the Emmy-Noether research group RUNSECURE, which focuses on securing dynamic program executions through dynamic instrumentation techniques. He is world renowned as the lead maintainer of Soot and has been a top contributor to the AspectBench Compiler (abc) for more than six years. More than a dozen of his most cited publications are directly based on Soot and abc. In 2009 Eric finished his doctoral dissertation at McGill University, under the supervision of Laurie Hendren, an ACM Fellow and lead scientist in the field of compiler engineering and program analysis. Eric's thesis topic was the static ahead-of-time evaluation of inlined reference monitors using abc. In the past, Eric has won two ACM Distinguished Paper Awards, both on dynamic program analysis, one of them related to data-race detection using AspectJ. In 2005 he won the worldwide ACM Student Research Competition with the topic of his Diploma thesis, which was the first work to link AspectJ to runtime monitoring.

5. REFERENCES

[1] Chris Allan, Pavel Avgustinov, Aske Simon Christensen, Laurie Hendren, Sascha Kuzins, Jennifer Lhoták, Ondřej Lhoták, Oege de Moor, Damien Sereni, Ganesh Sittampalam, and Julian Tibble. abc: the aspectbench compiler for aspectj. In *Proceedings of the 4th international conference on Generative Programming and Component Engineering*, GPCE'05, pages 10–16, Berlin, Heidelberg, 2005. Springer-Verlag.

[2] Chris Allan, Pavel Avgustinov, Aske Simon Christensen, Laurie Hendren, Sascha Kuzins, Ondřej Lhoták, Oege de Moor, Damien Sereni, Ganesh Sittampalam, and Julian Tibble. Adding trace matching with free variables to aspectj. In *Proceedings of the 20th annual ACM SIGPLAN conference on Object-oriented programming, systems, languages, and applications*, OOPSLA '05, pages 345–364, New York, NY, USA, 2005. ACM.

[3] Steven Arzt, Siegfried Rasthofer, and Eric Bodden. Susi: A tool for the fully automated classification and categorization of android sources and sinks, Mai 2013.

[4] Michael Backes, Sebastian Gerling, Christian Hammer, Matteo Maffei, and Philipp von Styp-Rekowsky. Appguard: enforcing user requirements on android apps. In *Proceedings of the 19th international conference on Tools and Algorithms for the Construction and Analysis of Systems*, TACAS'13, pages 543–548, Berlin, Heidelberg, 2013. Springer-Verlag.

[5] William Enck, Peter Gilbert, Byung gon Chun, Landon P. Cox, Jaeyeon Jung, Patrick McDaniel, and Anmol Sheth. Taintdroid: An information-flow tracking system for realtime privacy monitoring on smartphones. In *OSDI*, pages 393–407, 2010.

[6] William Enck, Damien Octeau, Patrick McDaniel, and Swarat Chaudhuri. A study of android application security. In *Proceedings of the 20th USENIX*

conference on Security, SEC'11, pages 21–21, Berkeley, CA, USA, 2011. USENIX Association.

[7] William Enck, Damien Octeau, Patrick McDaniel, and Swarat Chaudhuri. A study of android application security. In *Proceedings of the 20th USENIX conference on Security*, SEC'11, pages 21–21, Berkeley, CA, USA, 2011. USENIX Association.

[8] Christian Fritz, Steven Arzt, Siegfried Rasthofer, Eric Bodden, Alexandre Bartel, Jacques Klein, Yves le Traon, Damien Octeau, and Patrick McDaniel. Highly precise taint analysis for android applications, Mai 2013.

[9] Adam P Fuchs, Avik Chaudhuri, and Jeffrey S Foster. Scandroid: Automated security certification of android applications. *Manuscript, Univ. of Maryland, http://www. cs. umd. edu/~avik/projects/scandroidascaa*, 2009.

[10] Clint Gibler, Jonathan Crussell, Jeremy Erickson, and Hao Chen. Androidleaks: automatically detecting potential privacy leaks in android applications on a large scale. In *Proceedings of the 5th international conference on Trust and Trustworthy Computing*, TRUST'12, pages 291–307, Berlin, Heidelberg, 2012. Springer-Verlag.

[11] Johannes Hoffmann, Martin Ussath, Thorsten Holz, and Michael Spreitzenbarth. Slicing droids: program slicing for smali code. In *Proceedings of the 28th Annual ACM Symposium on Applied Computing*, pages 1844–1851. ACM, 2013.

[12] Victor Chebyshev (Kaspersky Labs). Mobile attacks!, 2013.

[13] Jinyung Kim, Yongho Yoon, Kwangkeun Yi, and Junbum Shin. ScanDal: Static analyzer for detecting privacy leaks in android applications. In Hao Chen, Larry Koved, and Dan S. Wallach, editors, *MoST 2012: Mobile Security Technologies 2012*, Los Alamitos, CA, USA, May 2012. IEEE.

[14] Patrick Lam, Eric Bodden, Ondrej Lhotak, and Laurie Hendren. The soot framework for java program analysis: a retrospective. In *Cetus Users and Compiler Infastructure Workshop (CETUS 2011)*, Oktober 2011.

[15] Long Lu, Zhichun Li, Zhenyu Wu, Wenke Lee, and Guofei Jiang. Chex: statically vetting android apps for component hijacking vulnerabilities. In *Proceedings of the 2012 ACM conference on Computer and communications security*, CCS '12, pages 229–240, New York, NY, USA, 2012. ACM.

[16] Heloise Pieterse and Martin S. Olivier. Android botnets on the rise: Trends and characteristics. In Hein S. Venter, Marianne Loock, and Marijke Coetzee, editors, *ISSA*, pages 1–5. IEEE, 2012.

[17] Christian Fritz Steven Arzt and Siegfried Rasthofer. Droidbench - benchmarks, 2013.

[18] Rubin Xu, Hassen Saïdi, and Ross Anderson. Aurasium: practical policy enforcement for android applications. In *Proceedings of the 21st USENIX conference on Security symposium*, Security'12, pages 27–27, Berkeley, CA, USA, 2012. USENIX Association.

[19] Zhemin Yang and Min Yang. Leakminer: Detect information leakage on android with static taint analysis. In *Third World Congress on Software Engineering (WCSE 2012)*, pages 101–104, 2012.

[20] Yuanyuan Zeng, Kang G. Shin, and Xin Hu. Design of sms commanded-and-controlled and p2p-structured mobile botnets. In *Proceedings of the fifth ACM conference on Security and Privacy in Wireless and Mobile Networks*, WISEC '12, pages 137–148, New York, NY, USA, 2012. ACM.

[21] Yajin Zhou and Xuxian Jiang. Dissecting android malware: Characterization and evolution. In *Proceedings of the 2012 IEEE Symposium on Security and Privacy*, SP '12, pages 95–109, Washington, DC, USA, 2012. IEEE Computer Society.

Author Index

www.ingramcontent.com/pod-product-compliance
Lightning Source LLC
LaVergne TN
LVHW080106011026
849160LV00013B/1039